A NOTE ON THE COVER

Photograph of Walter De Maria's *Lightning Field*

Lightning Field—we are talking about the real thing, not the photograph of it—is located in southern New Mexico in a semi-arid basin surrounded by mountains, thirty-three miles from Quemado, and two hundred miles southwest of Albuquerque. In an area one mile by one kilometer (5,280 feet by 3,300 feet), De Maria's crew embedded four hundred stainless steel poles four feet deep in the earth, 220 feet apart, in sixteen rows, 25 poles to a row. The tops of the poles, each sharpened to a point, are aligned on a single plane; but because the ground undulates, the poles vary in height from about fifteen feet to almost twenty-seven feet.

Lightning Field is an example of Land-Art or Earthwork, an artwork that exists not in a frame or on a pedestal in an art gallery or museum, but rather as a vast part of nature, usually in a relatively remote place. The creators of Land-Art believe that people who wish to experience such a work must be deeply motivated, and must be seeking an almost mystical experience by witnessing the union of art and nature. One might think that four hundred pointed steel poles would appear to violate nature, but some visitors claim that the poles somehow beautifully transform both nature and the viewer. When the sun is high the poles are barely noticeable, but at dawn and at dusk the slant-ing rays of light reflect off the poles and give *Lightning Field* a magical appearance. Passing clouds, and moonlight, too, transform it. And in late July and August, when lightning sometimes strikes, the few visitors who are there find the sight awe-inspiring. We say "few visitors" because only a handful make the effort to visit this remote place, and because the small cabin near the field can house only eight guests overnight. Even if large numbers wished to visit the site, they would not be permitted by the Dia Foundation, which maintains the place.

Earlier centuries would describe the effect as *sublime*, a term that especially in the eigh-teenth century was contrasted with "the picturesque". A farmhouse with hollyhocks nearby and a few cows browsing or drinking from a stream was picturesque, but mountains, torrents, volcanoes, and views of the ocean or of turbulent skies were sublime. The sublime was vast, unknowable, tran-scendent, and it evoked awe. Certainly lightning was sublime: Fire from heaven was both death-dealing and (because it accompanied rain) life-giving. In the Hebrew Bible, lightning often accompa-nies God's earthly visitations in Exodus 19.16–18, when lightning announces to Moses the presence of God on Mount Sinai. Further, blinding light is said to force viewers to close their eyes, allowing "the inner light" to work, i.e. allowing them to meditate.

Lightning Field is meant to create a profound experience for the visitor, which is why we chose a photograph of it for the cover of *Introduction to Literature*. We don't want to press this point too hard—we don't expect most readers to be knocked out, bowled over, or shocked into new expe-riences—but we do hope that all of our readers will find the works in this book stimulating, and we hope that at least some readers will find some works transforming. Visitors to *Lightning Field* (if they go in the right season and are lucky) may encounter the bolts of lightning whose beauty and whose power provide them with unforgettable moments on which they may meditate for the rest of their lives. Readers of the stories, poems, and plays in *Introduction to Literature* will encounter "bolts of melody" (we are quoting Emily Dickinson) that may similarly remain with them—and that may even transform them.

Manuscript of Emily Dickinson's "I heard a Fly buzz—when I died" (see page 875).

FOURTEENTH EDITION

An Introduction to Literature

Fiction, Poetry, and Drama

SYLVAN BARNET
Tufts University

WILLIAM BURTO
University of Lowell

WILLIAM E. CAIN
Wellesley College

PEARSON
Longman

New York   San Francisco   Boston
London   Toronto   Sydney   Tokyo   Singapore   Madrid
Mexico City   Munich   Paris   Cape Town   Hong Kong   Montreal

Editor-in-Chief: Joseph Terry
Development Editor: Katharine Glynn
Executive Marketing Manager: Ann Stypuloski
Senior Supplements Editor: Donna Campion
Media Supplements Editor: Jenna Egan
Production Manager: Eric Jorgensen
Project Coordination, Text Design, and Electronic Page Makeup: Pre-Press Company, Inc.
Cover Design Manager: John Callahan
Cover Photo: "Lightning Field," 1971–1977, Walter De Maria. Collection Dia Art Foundation.
Photo Researcher: Vivette Porges
Senior Manufacturing Manager: Dennis J. Para
Printer and Binder: Quebecor World, Taunton
Cover Printer: Phoenix Color Corporation

For permission to use copyrighted material, grateful acknowledgment is made to the copyright holders on pp. 1825–1836, which are hereby made part of this copyright page.

Library of Congress Cataloging-in-Publication Data

Barnet, Sylvan.
    An introduction to literature: fiction, poetry, drama / Sylvan Barnet, William Burto, William E. Cain.
      p. cm.
    Includes index.
    ISBN 0-321-35601-2
      1. Literature—Collections. I. Burto, William. II. Cain, William E., (date)-III. Title.

PN6014.I498 2006
808—dc22

2005048668

Visit us at www.ablongman.com/barnet

ISBN 0-321-35601-2

2 3 4 5 6 7 8 9 10—QWT—08 07 06

PART IV

Drama   1025

PART V

Critical Perspectives   1739

APPENDIXES

PART II

Fiction   59

3   Approaching Fiction: Responding in Writing   61

4   Stories and Meanings: Plot, Character, Theme   72

5   Narrative Point of View   97

9   Law and Disorder: Narratives from Biblical Times to the Present   273

10   American Voices: Fiction for a Diverse Nation   297

11   A Collection of Short Fiction   371

PART III

Poetry   661

PART V

Critical Perspectives 1739

An Introduction to Literature, Fourteenth Edition, begins with two introductory chapters concerning reading, thinking, and writing (drawing on stories and poems ranging from The Parable of the Prodigal Son to works by W. B. Yeats, Katherine Mansfield, Grace Paley, Lorna Dee Cervantes, José Armas, and Jamaica Kincaid); the book then offers an anthology of literature arranged by genre (fiction, poetry, and drama). This genre anthology, like the introductory chapters, includes ample material to help students become active readers and careful, engaged writers.

NEW TO THIS EDITION

- **New primary texts.** We have added thirteen stories, twenty-five poems, and three plays (we now include *Othello* as well as *Hamlet* and *A Midsummer Night's Dream,* and we have also added two plays by women). The unit on poetry now includes an amplified study of poetic forms (including shaped poetry) and a new chapter on narrative poetry.
- **American voices.** The popular unit consisting of poems concerned with the diversity of the nation is now complemented with *American Voices: Stories for a Diverse Nation* and *American Voices: Drama for a Diverse Nation.* Diversity is broadly interpreted to include not only representations of ethnic minorities but also of gay populations and of the mentally retarded.
- **Increased emphasis on argument.** The apparatus emphasizes that most of the writing that students will be doing should have an argumentative edge. The text includes material devoted to such topics as "Why We Write Arguments about Literature," "Explication as Argument," "Writing Arguments about Fiction," "Writing Arguments about Poetry," and "Writing Arguments about Drama."
- **Additional author given in depth.** In the unit on fiction we now include (in addition to substantial representations of Kate Chopin, Flannery O'Connor, and Raymond Carver), two stories and an essay by Alice Munro as well as an interview with her.
- **Revised unit on translating poetry.** We have reorganized the material, and given greater prominence to a writing assignment in which students familiar with a language other than English discuss the difficulties of translation.
- **Increased attention to drama on the stage, and increased representation of women.** For most plays, we have added to our Topics for Critical Thinking and Writing issues that are specifically concerned with

the play on the stage. Further, in addition to the casebook on *Hamlet* there is now a portfolio of images of Othello, raising the issue of whether he is represented as a Moor or as a sub-Saharan African. We have also added two plays by women, Eve Merriam's *Out of Our Father's House,* and Jane Martin's important one-act play, *Rodeo.* Finally, we have shifted the position of Clare Boothe Luce's *Slam the Door Softly,* so that readers can immediately see its intimate connection with Ibsen's *A Doll's House.*

ABOUT THE LITERATURE

- **Canonical works.** The book contains 71 stories, 1 short novel, 296 poems, and 15 plays. About a third of the selections are canonical works that for many decades—in some cases even centuries—have given readers great pleasure. Writers such as Sophocles, Shakespeare, Walt Whitman, and Emily Dickinson have stood the test of time, including the test of today's students enrolled in introductory courses in literature and composition. No editor and no instructor need apologize for asking students to read, think, and write about these authors. In "Tradition and the Individual Talent," T. S. Eliot makes the point well: "Someone said, 'The dead writers are remote from us because we know so much more than they did.' Precisely, and they are that which we know."

- **A new canon.** The remaining two-thirds of the selections are contemporary material, some of it by writers who established their reputations several decades ago (for instance, John Updike and Alice Walker), but much of it by writers who are still young (for instance, Amy Tan and Lorrie Moore). We have tried to read widely in today's writing, and we think we have found important new stories, poems, and plays worth the time of busy students and busy instructors. Again, no editor and no instructor need apologize for asking students to study and take pleasure in these authors and to see how they often return us to the authors of the past, the authors whose place in the canon is established and secure.

- **Strong representation of women and minority authors.** We have made a special effort to include excellent work by women and writers of color. For example, we reprint 29 stories by women, 9 of which are by minority authors. In the poetry section, 57 poems are by multicultural authors, including a rich, diverse section by Langston Hughes (12 poems and 2 essays). And in Drama we have 4 plays by women as well as 2 plays by multicultural playwrights.

- **In-depth representation and critical perspectives.** We represent in depth four fiction writers—Flannery O'Connor (two stories and observations on literature), Raymond Carver (three stories, an interview, and comments on writing), Alice Munro (two stories, an essay, and an interview), and Kate Chopin (three stories and a novel, *The Awakening*). Among the poets, we represent in depth Emily Dickinson (poems and letters), Robert Frost (poems and comments on poetry), and Langston Hughes (poems and comments on poetry). Of the dramatists, we give two plays by Sophocles and three by Shakespeare; we also include relevant comments by playwrights on their work—for instance, Arthur Miller on tragedy. We think these features of the book are especially valuable and that the kinds of writing assignments we have developed—assignments that have emerged from our experiences in the classroom—will interest students and be productive for them.

- **Plays in contexts.** Most of the plays are accompanied by stimulating comments by their authors, giving students a look behind the scenes.

WRITING ABOUT LITERATURE

Instructors know that one of the best ways to become an active reader is to read with a pencil in hand—that is, to annotate a text, to make jottings in a journal, and ultimately to draft and revise essays. We think that students, too, will find themselves saying of their experiences with literature what the philosopher Arthur C. Danto said about his experience with works of art:

> I get a lot more out of art, now that I am writing about it, than I ever did before. I think what is true of me must be true of everyone, that until one tries to write about it, the work of art remains a sort of aesthetic blur. . . . I think in a way everyone might benefit from becoming a critic in his or her own right. After seeing the work, write about it. You cannot be satisfied for very long in simply putting down what you felt. You have to go further.
>
> —*Embodied Meanings* (1994)

To this end, we have included the following:

- **Samples of annotated pages, entries in journals, and 9 essays by students.** To prompt students to respond to the works of literature in this book and then to think and write critically about their responses, we include not only a chapter devoted to the concepts of getting ideas and revising them by means of writing (Chapter 2), but also examples of annotated pages, entries in journals, and nine essays by students (some with the students' preliminary journal entries).
- **Explorative questions.** About a third of the selections in the book are equipped with questions intended to help draw attention to matters that deserve careful thinking. Most of these questions are in effect invitations to write argumentative essays, not mere paragraphs or descriptions.
- **Material about argument.** In addition to furnishing "Topics for Critical Thinking and Writing" that raise issues for argument, our apparatus emphasizes that students, in their essays, must advance a thesis and support it with evidence, rather than merely provide reports of their responses.
- **Critical perspectives.** A chapter on "Critical Approaches," sketching such approaches as reader-response criticism and the New Historicism, will help students develop a repertoire of points of view.
- **Glossary.** Literary terms, defined and discussed throughout the text, are concisely defined in a convenient glossary at the end of the book, with page references to fuller discussions.
- **Manuscript form.** An appendix includes pages on the format of an essay—for example, margins, capitalization in a title, and so on.
- **Research and Internet resources.** Three appendixes give information on doing research and presenting findings in a documented essay (MLA

style). These appendixes include material about writing with a word processor, the uses and misuses of a photocopier, and researching and using the Internet and electronic sources effectively.

RESOURCES FOR STUDENTS AND INSTRUCTORS

For qualified adopters:

Writing About Literature: Craft of Argument CD-ROM   This CD-ROM allows students to learn the skills of writing and argumentation interactively through writing activities and assignments. Paintings, photographs, and audio and film clips spark student interest in the literacy selections. All media are supported with apparatus and assignments. This CD-ROM is available free when value-packed with *An Introduction to Literature,* Fourteenth Edition. ISBN 0-321-10763-2.

MyLiteratureLab.com   is a Web-based, state-of-the-art, interactive learning system designed to enhance introductory literature courses. It adds a whole new dimension to the study of literature with *Longman Lectures*—evocative, richly illustrated audio readings along with advice on how to read, interpret, and write about literary works from our own roster of Longman authors. This powerful program also features Diagnostic Tests, Interactive Readings with clickable prompts, student sample papers, Literature Timelines, Avoiding Plagiarism and Research Navigator research tools, and "Exchange," an electronic instructor/ peer feedback tool. MyLiteratureLab.com can be delivered within Course Compass, Web CT, or Blackboard course management systems enabling instructors to administer their entire course online.

Instructor's Manual   An instructor's manual with detailed comments and suggestions for teaching each selection is available. This important resource also contains references to critical articles and books that we have found to be most useful. ISBN 0-321-36490-2.

Video Program   For qualified adopters, an impressive selection of videotapes is available to enrich students' experience of literature. Contact your sales representative to learn how to qualify.

Responding to Literature: A Writer's Journal   This journal provides students with their own personal space for writing. Helpful prompts for responding to fiction, poetry, and drama are also included. Available free when value-packed with *An Introduction to Literature,* Fourteenth Edition. ISBN 0-321-09542-1.

Evaluating a Performance   Perfect for the student assigned to review a local production, this supplement offers students a convenient place to record their evaluation. Useful tips and suggestions of things to consider when evaluating a production are included. Available free when value-packed with *An Introduction to Literature,* Fourteenth Edition. ISBN 0-321-09541-3.

Take Note!   A complete information management tool for students who are working on research papers or other projects that require the use of outside sources. This cross-platform CD-ROM integrates note taking, outlining, and bibliography management into one easy-to-use package. Available at a discount when value-packed with *An Introduction to Literature,* Fourteenth Edition. ISBN 0-321-13608-X.

Merriam-Webster's Reader's Handbook: Your Complete Guide to Literary Terms   Includes nearly 2,000 entries, including Greek and Latin terminology, and descriptions for every major genre, style, and era of writing. Assured authority from the combined resources of Merriam-Webster and Encyclopedia Britannica. Available at a significant discount when value-packed with *An Introduction to Literature,* Fourteenth Edition. ISBN 0-321-10541-9.

Penguin Discount Novel Program   In cooperation with Penguin Putnam, Inc., one of our sibling companies, Longman is proud to offer a variety of Penguin paperbacks at a significant discount when packaged with any Longman title. The available titles include works by authors as diverse as Toni Morrison, Julia Alvarez, Mary Shelley, and Shakespeare. To review the complete list of titles available, visit the Longman-Penguin-Putnam Website *<http://www.ablongman.com/penguin>*. Discounted prices of individual Penguin novels are available on the Website.

ACKNOWLEDGMENTS

We wish to thank the people who helped us write this book. For the preparation of the fourteenth edition, we are indebted to Joe Terry, Katharine Glynn, Eric Jorgensen, John Callahan of Longman, and Katy Faria at Pre-Press Company, Inc. The book in many ways reflects their guidance. For expert assistance in obtaining permission to reprint copyrighted material, we are indebted to Virginia Creeden. We also wish to thank Katherine Snead for expert copyediting, which is to say that she was sharp-eyed but never sharp-tongued, exactly the sort of reader that a writer hopes for.

We are grateful to the reviewers of the fourteenth edition: Michael Anzelone, Nassau Community College; Christine Caver, The University of Texas at San Antonio; Philip Collington, Niagara University; Andrea Kaston Tange, Eastern Michigan University; Donald Kummings, University of Wisconsin—Parkside; Walter S. Minot, Spring Hill College; Lyle W. Morgan, Pittsburg State University; Stacy Mulder, Davenport University; Lee Newton, Bradley University; Patricia Sheehy Colella, Bunker Hill Community College; Andrew Silver, Mercer University; JoAnna Stephens Mink, Minnesota State University; Tony Procell, El Paso Community College; and David Thomson, Henderson State University.

The following instructors read the manuscript for previous editions and offered invaluable advice: Michael de Benedictis, Miami-Dade Community College; Bill Dynes, University of Indianapolis; Gabriel Fagan, La Salle University; Ruth Harrison, Arkansas Tech University; Beverly A. McCabe, John A. Logan College; Christie Rubio, American River College; Kathleen Shumate, Grossmant College; Barbara L. Stafford, City College of San Francisco; Darlene Sybert, University of Missouri–Columbia; and Catherine G. Thwing, Pima Community College; Olga Abella, Eastern Illinois University; Dr. Karen Aubrey, Augusta State University;

Lillie Bailey, Virginia State University; Arnold J. Bradford, Northern Virginia Community College; Bob Brien, Madison Area Technical College; Carol Ann Britt, San Antonio College; Mark J. Bruhn, Regis University; Sandra Bryzek, Moraine Valley Community College; Vilma Chemers, California State University, Long Beach; Mickie Christensen, San Francisco State University; Nancy Cox, Arkansas Tech University; Corla Dawson, Missouri Western State College; Mindy Faines, Gateway Community College; Bart Friedberg, Nassau Community College; Carolyn Smith Geyer, Augustana College; Wendy Greenstein, Long Beach City College; George V. Griffith, Chadron State College; Styron Harris, East Tennessee State University; Mary Hickerson, Southwest State University; Susan Hines, LaSalle University; Lois Leveen, University of California at Los Angeles; Elaine Lomber, Community College of the Finger Lakes; Linda J. McPherson, Indiana University of Pennsylvania; Carlene Murphy, University of Toledo; Philip F. O'Mara, Bridgewater College; Leland S. Person, University of Alabama at Birmingham; Caroline Poor, Wharton County Junior College; Elaine Razzano, Lyndon State College; Marcia E. Tannebaum, Nichols College; William Wilson, San Jose State University; Ann Woodlief, Virginia Commonwealth University; Xiao-Ming Yang, Ocean County College; and Sue Ziefler, DeAnza College. Our debt to those whom we have named is deep, but we are still not done with acknowledging our indebtedness. We owe much to the instructors and friends who advised us when we were preparing earlier editions: Judith Leet, Janet Frick, Ken Anderson, Floyd College; Alfred Arteaga, University of California, Berkeley; Rance Baker, San Antonio College; Lois Birky, Illinois Central College; Carol Boyd, Black Hawk College; Lois Bragg, Galludet University; Conrad Carroll, Northern Kentucky University; Robert Coltrane, Lock Haven University; Charles Darling, Greater Hartford Community College; Richard Dietrich, University of South Florida; Gail Duffy, Dean Junior College; Marilyn Edelstein, Santa Clara University; Toni Empringham, El Camino College; Craig Etchison, Glenville State College; Robert Farrell, Housatonic Community College; Elaine Fitzpatrick, Massasoit College; James E. Ford, University of Nebraska—Lincoln; Donna Galati, University of South Dakota; Marvin P. Garrett, University of Cincinnati; Francis B. Hanify, Luzerne County Community College; Blair Hemstock, Keyano College (Canada); Paul Hester, Indian Hills Community College; James L. Johnson, California State University, Fresno; Edwina Jordan, Illinois Central College; Kate Kiefer, Colorado State University; Sandra Lakey, Pennsylvania College of Technology; Wayne P. Lindquist, University of Wisconsin—Eau Claire; Cecilia G. Martyn, Montclair State College; Paul McVeign, Northern Virginia Community College, Elizabeth Metzger, University of South Florida; William S. Nicholson, Eastern Shore Community College; Stephen O'Neill, Bucks County Community College; Richard Pepp, Massasoit Community College; Betty Jo Hicks Peters, Morehead State University; Frank Perkins, Quincy College; Barbara Pokdowka, Commonwealth College; John C. Presley, Central Virginia Community College; Patricia R. Rochester, University of Southwestern Louisiana; Betty Rhodes, Faulkner State College; Martha Saunders, West Georgia College; Allison Shumsky, Northwestern Michigan College; Isabel B. Stanley, East Tennessee State University; LaVonne Swanson, National College; Beverly Taylor, University of North Carolina, Chapel Hill; Merle Thompson, North Virginia Community College; Cyrilla Vessey, North Virginia Community College; Mildred White, Oholone College; Margaret Whitt, University of Denver; Betty J. Williams, East Tennessee State University; Donald R. Williams, North Shore Community College; and Donnie Yeilding, Central Texas College.

Our thanks also the many users of the earlier editions who gave us advice on how and where to make improvements: Linda Bamber, David Cavitch, Robert Cyr, Arthur Friedman, Nancy Grayson, Martha Hicks-Courant, Billie Ingram, Martha Lappen, Judy Maas, Deirdre McDonald, Patricia Meier, Ronald E. Pepin, William Roberts, Claire Seng-Niemoeller, Virginia Shine, and Charles L. Walker.

We are especially grateful for the comments and suggestions offered by the following scholars: Priscilla B. Bellair, Carroll Britch, Don Brunn, Malcolm B. Clark, Terence A. Dalrymple, Franz Douskey, Gerald Duchovnay, Peter Dumanis, Estelle Easterly, Adam Fischer, Martha Flint, Robert H. Fossum, Gerald Hasham, Richard Henze, Catherine M. Hoff, Grace S. Kehrer, Nancy E. Kensicki, Linda Kraus, Juanita Laing, Vincent J. Liesenfeld, Martha McGowan, John H. Meagher III, Stuart Millner, Edward Anthony Nagel, Peter L. Neff, Robert F. Panara, Ronald E. Pepin, Jane Pierce, Robert M. Post, Kris Rapp, Mark Reynolds, John Richardson, Donald H. Sanborn, Marlene Sebeck, Frank E. Sexton, Peggy Skaggs, David Stuchler, James E. Tamer, Carol Teaff, C. Uejio, Hugh Witemeyer, Manfred Wolf, Joseph Zaitchik.

Finally, we are also grateful for valuable suggestions made by Barbara Harman, X. J. Kennedy, Carolyn Potts, Marcia Stubbs, Helen Vendler, and Ann Chalmers Watts.

SYLVAN BARNET
WILLIAM BURTO
WILLIAM E. CAIN

We hope that you already enjoy reading literature and that *An Introduction to Literature* will help you enjoy it even more. But as you begin your course this semester with our book, we want to say a little more about why we wrote it, how we believe it can help you, and in what ways we think it can deepen and enrich your pleasure in studying literature.

Throughout the process of writing and rewriting *An Introduction to Literature,* we saw ourselves as teachers, offering the kinds of suggestions and strategies that, over many years, we have offered to our students.

As you can tell from a glance at the Contents, *An Introduction to Literature* includes practical advice about reading and responding to literature and writing analytical papers, advice that comes directly from our experience not only as readers and writers but also as teachers. This experience derives from classrooms, from conferences with students, and from assignments we have given, read, responded to, and graded. We have learned from our experiences and have done our best to give you the tools that will help you make yourself a more perceptive reader and a more careful, cogent writer.

Speaking of making and remaking, we are reminded of a short poem by William Butler Yeats, who was a persistent reviser of his work. (You can find three versions of his poem "Leda and the Swan" on page 840.)

> The friends that have it I do wrong
> Whenever I remake a song,
> Should know what issue is at stake:
> It is myself that I remake.

Like Yeats, you will develop throughout your life: you will find you have new things to say, and you may even come to find that the tools you acquired in college—and that suited you for a while—are not fully adequate to the new self that you have become. We can't claim to equip you for the rest of your life—though some of these works of literature surely will remain in your mind for years—but we do claim that, with your instructor, we are helping you develop skills that are important for your mental progress. We have in mind skills useful not merely in the course in which you are now enrolled, or other literature courses, or even courses in the humanities in general that you may take. We go further. We think that these skills in reading and writing are important for your development as an educated adult. Becoming an alert reader and an effective writer should be among the central goals of your education, and they are goals that *An Introduction to Literature* is designed to help you reach.

The skills we stress in *An Introduction to Literature* will enable you to gain confidence as a reader of literary works so that you will increase your understanding of what literature offers. You need not enjoy all authors equally. You'll have your favorites—and also some authors whom you do not like much at all. There's nothing wrong with that; reading literature is very much a personal encounter. But at the same time, the skills we highlight in *An Introduction to Literature* can help you know and explain why one author means much to you and another does not. In this respect, reading and studying literature is more than personal; as we share our responses and try to express them effectively in writing, the work that we perform becomes cooperative and communal, a type of cultural conversation among fellow students, teachers, and friends.

As you proceed through *An Introduction to Literature* and gain further experience as a reader and writer, you will start to see features of poems, stories, and plays that you had not noticed before, or that you had noticed but not really understood, or that you had understood but not, so to speak, fully experienced. You may even find yourself enjoying an author you thought you disliked and would never be able to understand. The study of literature calls for concentration, commitment, and discipline. It's work—sometimes hard, challenging work. But it is rewarding work, and we believe that it will lead you to find literature more engaging and more pleasurable.

We hope that *An Introduction to Literature* will have this effect for you. Feel free to contact us with your comments and suggestions. We are eager to know what in this book has served you well, and what we might do better. You can write to us in care of Literature Editor, Longman Publishers, 1185 Avenue of the Americas, New York, NY 10036.

SYLVAN BARNET
WILLIAM BURTO
WILLIAM E. CAIN

An Introduction to Literature

PART

I

Reading, Thinking, and Writing Critically about Literature

Writers of literature (as opposed to other writers, such as journalists, authors of do-it-yourself manuals, and authors of textbooks) specialize in recording their responses to life and in imagining the responses of others. They tell us how it feels to live the life they live, or the lives they know about or imagine, and by some sort of magic they set forth their responses so effectively that our own lives are expanded. Their reports, for at least a moment, become ours and cause our own pulses to beat faster. As Ezra Pound put it, "Literature is news that *stays* news." In the first chapter of this book you will read a very short story that is almost two thousand years old (The Parable of the Prodigal Son) as well as half a dozen works—stories and poems—that were written in the last fifty or so years, some by men, some by women. One of the stories, only about a page long, is by Jamaica Kincaid, whose name at birth was Elaine Potter Richardson.

Kincaid was born in 1949 in Antigua, then a British colony. At seventeen she came (or was sent by her mother) to work in New York as an au pair—i.e., someone who does domestic work in exchange for not much more than room and board and a chance to experience a different society. After leaving the New York family she did some photography, then studied at Franconia College in New Hampshire, and, then, back in New York, she began to write fiction. In 1973 she changed her name because her family disapproved of her writing. (When you read the story we reprint you may understand why her family disapproved.) She has written a book about

Antigua called *A Small Place* (1988) and also other nonfiction, including books about gardening, but she is best known for her fiction—short stories and novels, though she insists that in these works she has not "created" characters but has drawn upon the people who have entered into her life.

In various interviews Kincaid has mentioned her "insistence on truth," even if—especially if—the truth is painful. Thus, in an interview published in *Mother Jones* (Sept./Oct. 1997) she said, "I feel it's my duty to make everyone a little less happy." This may seem to be an odd goal for a writer, but it is not unusual for writers to insist that in their fictions they present truths, they tell it as it is, they wake us up, make us take off our rose-colored glasses, and make us see and feel reality. Joseph Conrad, for example, said:

> My task . . . is by the power of the written word to make you hear, to make you feel—it is, before all, to make you *see*.

And here is Franz Kafka on the role of the writer:

> A book must be the ax that breaks the frozen sea within us.

The truth that a writer makes us see is the "news that stays news" that Ezra Pound spoke of. Kincaid's story, like most of her other fiction, deals with a vexed family relationship. It's our hunch that the story will ring true to you and that you will also find it highly entertaining—two qualities we hope you find in all of the works in this book.

1

Reading and Responding to Literature

WHAT IS LITERATURE?

Large books have been written on this subject, and large books will continue to be written on it. But we can offer a few brief generalizations that may be useful.

First, the word "literature" can be used to refer to anything written. The Department of Agriculture will, upon request, send an applicant "literature on canning tomatoes." People who ask for such material expect it to be clear and informative, but they do not expect it to be interesting in itself. They do not read it for the experience of reading it; they read it only if they are thinking about canning tomatoes.

There is, however, a sort of literature that people *do* read without expecting a practical payoff. They read the sort of writing that is in *An Introduction to Literature,* because they expect it to hold their interest and to provide pleasure. They may vaguely feel that it will be good for them, but they don't read it *because* it will be good for them, any more than they dance because dancing provides healthful exercise. Dancing may indeed be healthful, but that's not why people dance. They dance because dancing affords a special kind of pleasure. For similar reasons people watch athletic contests and go to concerts or to the theater. We participate in activities such as these not because we expect some sort of later reward but because we know that the experience of participating is in itself rewarding. Perhaps the best explanation is that the experiences are absorbing—which is to say they take us out of ourselves for a while—and that (especially in the case of concerts, dance performances, and athletic contests) they allow us to appreciate excellence, to admire achievement. Most of us can swim or toss a ball and maybe even hit a ball, but when we go to a swimming meet or to a ball game we see a level of performance that evokes our admiration.

Looking at an Example: Robert Frost's "Immigrants"

Let's begin, then, by thinking of literature as (to quote Robert Frost) "a performance in words." And let's begin with a very short poem by Frost (1874–1963), probably America's best-known poet. Frost wrote these lines for a pageant at

Plymouth, Massachusetts, celebrating the three-hundredth anniversary of the arrival of the *Mayflower* from England.

Immigrants   [1920]

No ship of all that under sail or steam
Have gathered people to us more and more
But Pilgrim-manned the Mayflower in a dream
Has been her anxious convoy in to shore.

To find this poem—this performance in words—of any interest, a reader probably has to know that the *Mayflower* brought the Pilgrims to America. Second, a reader has to grasp a slightly unfamiliar construction: "No ship . . . but . . . has . . . ," which means, in effect, "every ship has." (Compare: "No human being but is born of woman," which means "Every human being is born of woman.")

If, then, we *paraphrase* the poem—translate it into other words in the same language—we get something roughly along these lines:

Every ship of all the ships (whether sailing vessels or steamships) that have collected people in increasing numbers and brought them to this country has had the *Mayflower,* with its Pilgrims, as its eager (or worried?) escort to the coast.

We have tried to make this paraphrase as accurate and as concise as possible, but for reasons that we'll explain in a moment, we have omitted giving an equivalent for Frost's "in a dream." Why, one might ask, is our paraphrase so much less interesting than the original?

Performance

First, the poem is metrical. With only a few exceptions, every second syllable is accented more than the preceding syllable. Take the first line. Although "No" probably receives at least as much stress as the word that follows it, "ship," in the rest of the line the pattern is clear:

Nó shíp   ŏf all   thăt un   dĕr sáil   ŏr steám

(Of course not all of the stresses are equally heavy. When you read the line aloud you will probably put less emphasis on the first syllable of "under," for instance, than you put on "sail" or "steam.")

The language, then, is highly patterned, and you doubtless have experienced the force of patterned language—of rhythmic thought—whether from other poems or songs ("We shall overcome,/We shall overcome") or football chants ("Block that kick! Block that kick!"). Take a moment to reread the first line, without heavily emphasizing the stressed syllables but with some awareness of them. (Don't read the line mechanically; read it for sense, not for fixed pattern—but you'll *feel* a pattern.)

No ship of all that under sail or steam . . . .

Further, repetition is not limited to the pattern of stresses in the lines. We get the same number of syllables (ten) in each line. (There may be a few variations. For instance, in the third line if we pronounce "Mayflower" with three syllables, the line has eleven syllables. Probably we should pronounce it with two syllables: "Mayflow'r," maybe something like "Mayflar.") And we also get repetitions of sounds at the ends of the lines: "steam" rhymes with "dream," and "more" with "shore."

Probably, too, the repetition of *s* in "sail or steam" catches the ear. The two words are somewhat alike in that they are both monosyllables, they both begin with the same sound, and they both evoke images of ships. Compare "sail or steam" with "sail or gas" or "sail or engine" and you will probably agree that the original is more pleasing and more interesting.

One can see what Frost meant when he said that a poem is a performance in words: four lines, each with the same basic pattern of stresses, each ending with a word that rhymes, and all this in a single grammatical sentence. The thing looks easy enough, but we know that it took great skill to make the words behave properly—that is, to get the right words in the right order. Frost went into the lions' cage, did his act, and came out unharmed.

Significance

We've been talking about Frost's skill in handling words, but we haven't said anything (except in our clumsy paraphrase) about *what* Frost is saying in "Immigrants." One of the things that literature does is to make us see—hear, feel, love—what the author thinks is a valuable part of the experience of living. A thousand years ago a Japanese writer, Lady Murasaki, made this point when she had one of the characters in her book talk about what motivates an author:

> Again and again something in one's own life or in that around one will
> seem so important that one cannot bear to let it pass into oblivion.
> There must never come a time, the writer feels, when people do not
> know about this.

We can probably agree with Lady Murasaki that writers of literature try to get at something important in their experiences, emotions, or visions, and try to make the reader feel the importance. And so writers show us what it is like (for instance) to be in love (plenty of room for comedy as well as tragedy here), or what forgiveness is like, or what is at the heart of immigration to America.

We can't be certain about what Frost really thought of the Pilgrims and of the *Mayflower,* but we do have the poem, and that's what we are concerned with. It celebrates the anniversary, of course, but it also celebrates at least two other things: the continuing arrival of new immigrants and the close connection between the early and the later immigrants.

Persons whose ancestors came over on the *Mayflower* have a reputation for being rather sniffy about later arrivals, but Frost reminds his Yankee audience that their ancestors, the *Mayflower* passengers, were themselves immigrants. However greatly the histories and the experiences of the early immigrants differed from those of later immigrants, the experience of emigration and the hopes for a better life link the *Mayflower* passengers with more recent arrivals.

The poem says, if our paraphrase is roughly accurate, that the *Mayflower* and its passengers accompany all later immigrants. Now, what does this mean? Literally, of course, it is nonsense. The *Mayflower* and its passengers disappeared centuries ago.

▧ TOPICS FOR CRITICAL THINKING AND WRITING

1. In our paraphrase, in an effort to avoid complexities, we did not give
   any equivalent for "in a dream." The time has now come to face this
   puzzle in line 3: "But Pilgrim-manned the Mayflower in a dream." Some
   readers take Frost to be saying that the long-deceased passengers of the

Mayflower still dream of others following them. Other readers, however, interpret the line as saying that later immigrants dream of the *Mayflower*. Now, this paraphrase, even if accurate, makes an assertion that is not strictly true, since many later immigrants probably had never even heard of the *Mayflower*. But in a larger sense the statement is true. The later immigrants—with the terrible exception of involuntary immigrants from Africa who were brought here in chains—dreamed of a better life, just as the *Mayflower* passengers did. Some hoped for religious freedom, some hoped to escape political oppression or starvation, but again, all were seeking a better life. What do you make of line 3?

2. In our paraphrase we mentioned that "anxious" might be paraphrased either as "eager" or as "worried." (Contrast, for instance, "She was anxious to serve the community" and "She was anxious about the exam.") Is Frost's "anxious convoy" *eagerly* accompanying the ships with immigrants, or is it *nervously* accompanying them, perhaps worried that these new arrivals may not be the right sort of people, or worried that the new arrivals may not be able to get on in the new country? Or does the word "anxious," which seems to modify "convoy" (here, Mayflower), really refer to the new immigrants, who are worried that they may not succeed? Or perhaps they are worried that America may not in fact correspond to their hopes.

   Read the poem aloud two or three times, and then think about which of these meanings—or some other meanings that you come up with—you find most rewarding. You might consider, too, whether more than one meaning can be present. Frost himself in a letter wrote that he liked to puzzle his readers a bit—to baffle them and yet (or thereby) propel them forward:

   > My poems—I should suppose everybody's poems—are all set to trip the reader head foremost into the boundless. Ever since infancy I have had the habit of leaving my blocks carts chairs and such like ordinaries where people would be pretty sure to fall forward over them in the dark. Forward, you understand, *and* in the dark.

   What we have been saying is this: a reader of a work of literature finds meanings in the work, but also (even when the meaning is uncertain) takes delight in the details, takes delight in the way that the work has been constructed, takes delight in (again) the performance. When we have got at what we think may be the "meaning" of a work, we do not value or hold on to the meaning only and turn away from the work itself; rather, we value even more the craftsmanship that the work displays. And we come to see that the meaning is inseparable from all of the details that go to make up the work.

3. "Pilgrim-manned" may disturb some readers. Conscious of sexist language, today we try to avoid saying things like "This shows the greatness of man" or "Man is a rational animal" when we are speaking not about males but about all people. Does Frost's "Pilgrim-manned" strike you as slighting women? If not, why not?

4. We have already mentioned that Frost's poem cannot possibly be thought to describe involuntary immigrants. Is this a weakness in the poem? If so, how serious a weakness?

5. Frost's poem celebrates immigration and does not consider its effect on the Native American population. The poem does not, so to speak, tell the whole truth; but no statement, however long, could tell the "whole truth" about such a complex topic. Do you agree that if the poem doesn't give us the whole truth, perhaps we get enough if the poem reminds us of *a* truth?

Looking at a Second Example: Pat Mora's "Immigrants"

Pat Mora, after graduating from Texas Western College, earned a master's degree at the University of Texas at El Paso. She is best known for her poems, but she has also published essays on Chicano culture.

Immigrants
[1986]

wrap their babies in the American flag,
feed them mashed hot dogs and apple pie,
name them Bill and Daisy,
buy them blonde dolls that blink blue
eyes or a football and tiny cleats   5
before the baby can even walk,
speak to them in thick English, hallo, babee, hallo,
whisper in Spanish or Polish
when the babies sleep, whisper
in a dark parent bed, that dark   10
parent fear, "Will they like
our boy, our girl, our fine american
boy, our fine american girl?"

Pat Mora's experience—that of a Mexican-American woman in the United States—obviously must be very different from that of Frost, an Anglo-Saxon male and almost the official poet of the country. Further, Mora is writing in our own time, not three-quarters of a century ago. A reader expects, and finds, a very different sort of poem. We won't discuss this poem at length, but we will say that in our view she too gets at something important. Among the many things in this verbal performance that give us pleasure are these:

1. The wit of making the title part of the first sentence. A reader expects the title to be relevant to the poem but does not expect it to be grammatically the first word of the poem. We like the fresh way in which the title is used.
2. We also like the aptness with which Mora has caught the immigrants' eager yet worried attempt to make their children "100% American."

3. We like the mimicry of the immigrants talking to their children: "hallo, babee, hallo." If this mimicry came from an outsider it would be condescending and offensive, but since it is written by someone known for her concern with Mexican-American culture, it probably is not offensive. It is almost affectionate.

TOPICS FOR CRITICAL THINKING AND WRITING

1. The last comment may be right, so far as it goes, but isn't it too simple? Reread the poem—preferably aloud—and then try to decide exactly what Mora's attitude is toward the immigrants. Do you think that she fully approves of their hopes? On what do you base your answer?
2. What does it mean to say that someone—a politician, for instance— "wraps himself in the American flag"? What does Mora mean when she says that immigrants "wrap their babies in the American flag"? How would you paraphrase the line?
3. After reading the poem aloud two or three times, what elements of "verbal performance"—we might say of skillful play—do you notice? Mora does not use rhyme, but she does engage in some verbal play. What examples can you point to?
4. What is your own attitude toward the efforts of some immigrants to assimilate themselves to an Anglo-American model? How does your attitude affect your reading of the poem?

GROUNDS FOR ARGUMENT:
THE PARABLE OF THE PRODIGAL SON

Good prose narratives, too, like good poems, are carefully constructed. Let's look at a story, one told by Jesus, and reported in the fifteenth chapter of the Gospel according to St. Luke. Jesus here tells a **parable,** a short story from which a lesson is to be drawn. Luke reports that just before Jesus told the story, the Pharisees and scribes—persons whom the Gospels depict as opposed to Jesus because he sometimes found their traditions and teachings inadequate— complained that Jesus was a man of loose morals, one who "receives sinners and eats with them." According to Luke, Jesus responded thus:

And he said, "A certain man had two sons: and the younger of them said to his father, 'Father, give me the portion of goods that falleth to me.' And he divided unto them his living. And not many days after, the younger son gathered all together, and took his journey into a far country, and there wasted his substance with riotous living.

"And when he had spent all, there arose a mighty famine in that land, and he began to be in want. And he went and joined himself to a citizen of that country, and he sent him into his fields to feed swine. And he would fain have filled his belly with the husks that the swine did eat: and no man gave unto him.

"And when he came to himself he said, 'How many hired servants of my father's have bread enough and to spare, and I perish with hunger? I will arise and go to my father, and will say unto him, 'Father,

I have sinned against heaven, and before thee. And am no more worthy to be called thy son: make me as one of thy hired servants.'

"And he arose, and came to his father. But when he was yet a great way off, his father saw him, and had compassion, and ran, and fell on his neck, and kissed him. And the son said unto him, 'Father, I have sinned against heaven, and in thy sight, and am no more worthy to be called thy son.' But the father said to his servants, 'Bring forth the best robe, and put it on him, and put a ring on his hand, and shoes on his feet. And bring hither the fatted calf and kill it, and let us eat, and be merry. For this my son was dead, and is alive again; he was lost, and is found.' And they began to be merry.

"Now his elder son was in the field, and as he came and drew nigh to the house, he heard music and dancing. And he called one of the servants, and asked what these things meant. And he said unto him, 'Thy brother is come, and thy father hath killed the fatted calf, because he hath received him safe and sound.' And he was angry, and would not go in: therefore came his father out, and entreated him. And he answering said to his father, 'Lo, these many years do I serve thee, neither transgressed I at any time thy commandment, and yet thou never gavest me a kid, that I might make merry with my friends: but as soon as this thy son was come, which hath devoured thy living with harlots, thou has killed for him the fatted calf.' And he said unto him, 'Son, thou art ever with me, and all that I have is thine. It was meet that we should make merry, and be glad: for this thy brother was dead, and is alive again: and was lost, and is found.'" (Luke 15:11–32, King James Version)

Now, to begin with a small point, it is not likely that any but strictly observant Jews, or Muslims (who, like these Jews, do not eat pork), can feel the disgust that Jesus' audience must have felt at the thought that the son was reduced to feeding swine and that he even envied the food that swine ate. Further, some of us may be vegetarians; if so, we are not at all delighted at the thought that the father kills the fatted calf (probably the wretched beast has been force-fed) in order to celebrate the son's return.

And, of course, some of us do not believe in God, and hence are not prepared to take the story, as many people take it, as a story whose message is that we, like God (the father in this parable is usually taken to stand for God), ought to rejoice in the restoration of the sinner. Probably, then, for all sorts of obvious reasons none of us can put ourselves back into the first century CE and hear the story exactly as Jesus' audience heard it.

Still, most of us can probably agree on what we take to be the gist of the story, and, second, we can enjoy the skillful way in which it is told. This skill will become apparent, however, only after several readings. What are some examples of superb storytelling here, and what can a reader gain from a thoughtful reading? We can begin by noting a few points:

1. Although the story is customarily called "The Parable of the Prodigal Son" or "The Parable of the Lost Son," it tells of two sons, not of one. When we reread the story, we increasingly see that these brothers are compared and contrasted: the prodigal leaves his father's house for a different way of life—he thus seems lost to the father—but then he repents and returns to the father, whereas the older son, who physically remains with the father, is spiritually remote from the father, or is lost in a different way. By virtue of his self-centeredness the older son is remote from the father in feeling or spirit.

2. Again, reading and rereading reveal small but telling details. For instance, when the prodigal plans to return home, he thinks of what he will say to his father. He has come to his senses and repudiated his folly, but he still does not understand his father, for we will see in a moment that the prodigal has no need of this speech. Jesus tells us that as soon as the father saw the prodigal returning, he "had compassion, and ran, and fell on his neck, and kissed him." And (another very human touch) the prodigal—although already forgiven—nevertheless cannot refrain from uttering his heartfelt but, under the circumstances, unnecessary speech of repentance.

3. The elder son, learning that the merrymaking is for the returning prodigal, "was angry, and would not go in." This character is sketched only briefly, but a reader immediately recognizes the type: self-centered, unforgiving, and petulant. The older son does not realize it, but he is as distant from his father as the younger son had been. What is the father's response to this son, who is so different from the forgiving father?

> Therefore came his father out, and entreated him.

The father goes out to the dutiful son, just as he had gone out to the prodigal son. (What the father *does* is as important as what he *says*.) Notice, too, speaking of sons, that the older son, talking to his father, somewhat distances himself from his brother, disdainfully referring to the prodigal as "this thy son." And what is the father's response? To the elder son's "this thy son," the father replies, "this thy brother."

No matter how closely we look, however, we will not be able to find certain pieces of information; certain **blanks** or **gaps** will remain. For instance, we are not given information about the relationship of the brothers before the story begins. Nor are we told if the older son learns a lesson, and repents of his nasty behavior. We can offer guesses based on our understanding of others and based on our own nature, but the story is not explicit about these matters, and other readers may offer different guesses. We may even, perhaps, deny that the stay-at-home's behavior *is* nasty, and we may say that the father was sentimental and foolish to forgive the prodigal so easily.

There may also be **indeterminacies** in a story, passages that remain unclear even to careful readers of the story. Thus, the father says to the older son, "All that I have is thine," but is this true? After all, he has just killed the fatted calf, and has never offered even "a kid" (young goat) to the older son. And—a very large issue—readers may even question the historical accuracy of the picture of the Pharisees and scribes, for sources other than the Gospels depict them more sympathetically.

Such thoughts may come to mind because, again, we inevitably bring ourselves to all that we experience (and reading is an experience). It may turn out that, finally, we will (so to speak) go against the grain of the story and give it a **counter-reading**, a reading that argues against or replaces the more obvious meaning we might at first give it. Just as a reader of Frost's "Immigrants" might argue that it gives a white New Englander's view of immigration and overlooks the disastrous effects of colonization on Native Americans and on black slaves, so a reader may feel that The Parable of the Prodigal Son obscures another story and that the son should show his repentance in more than words. Or a reader may interpret the story from a psychoanalytic perspective as a story of sibling rivalry. We may come to feel that this whole story of a father and his two sons is an example of the sort of male-dominated or patriarchal thinking that (one might argue) gives little or no value to women; these sons seem to have no mother, and the only women mentioned are harlots.

Thoughtful, plausible responses of this sort, based on a close reading, can be valuable, and it is useful to set them forth in writing so that we share them with our colleagues. If, however, we let the work of literature merely trigger our stock responses rather than try to let it induce new, deeper responses, we may be the losers. We may, to put it bluntly, simply retain our prejudices and miss the experience of encountering something more important, more substantial.

▓ TOPIC FOR CRITICAL THINKING AND WRITING

> This story is traditionally called The Parable of the Prodigal Son. Can a case be made for the view that it ought to be called The Parable of the Prodigal Father? Forget, if you can, the traditional title, and ask yourself if the story tells of a father who is prodigal with his property and who at the end is prodigal with his love. Explain why you accept or reject this interpretation.

STORIES TRUE AND FALSE

The word "story" comes from "history"—the stories that historians, biographers, and journalists narrate are supposed to be true accounts of what happened. The stories of novelists and short-story writers, however, are admittedly untrue; they are "fiction," things made up, imagined, manufactured. As readers, we come to a supposedly true story with expectations different from those we bring to fiction.

Consider the difference between reading a narrative in a newspaper and one in a book of short stories. If, while reading a newspaper, we come across a story of, say, a subway accident, we assume that the account is true, and we read it for the information about a relatively unusual event. Anyone hurt? What sort of people? In our neighborhood? Whose fault? When we read a book of fiction, however, we do not expect to encounter literal truths; we read novels and short stories not for facts but for pleasure and for some insight or for a sense of what an aspect of life means to the writer. Consider the following short story by Grace Paley.

GRACE PALEY

Born in 1922 in New York City, Grace Paley attended Hunter College and New York University, but left without a degree. While raising two children she wrote poetry and then, in the 1950s, turned to writing fiction.

Paley's chief subject is the life of little people struggling in the Big City. Of life she has said, "How daily life is lived is a mystery to me. You write about what's mysterious to you. What is it like? Why do people do this?" Of the short story she has said, "It can be just telling a little tale, or writing a complicated philosophical story. It can be a song, almost."

Samuel   [1968]

Some boys are very tough. They're afraid of nothing. They are the ones who
climb a wall and take a bow at the top. Not only are they brave on the roof,
but they make a lot of noise in the darkest part of the cellar where even the
super hates to go. They also jiggle and hop on the platform between the
locked doors of the subway cars.

Four boys are jiggling on the swaying platform. Their names are Alfred,
Calvin, Samuel, and Tom. The men and the women in the cars on either side
watch them. They don't like them to jiggle or jump but don't want to interfere. Of course some of the men in the cars were once brave boys like these.
One of them had ridden the tail of a speeding truck from New York to Rockaway Beach without getting off, without his sore fingers losing hold. Nothing
happened to him then or later. He had made a compact with other boys who
preferred to watch: Starting at Eighth Avenue and Fifteenth Street, he would
get to some specified place, maybe Twenty-third and the river, by hopping the
tops of the moving trucks. This was hard to do when one truck turned a corner in the wrong direction and the nearest truck was a couple of feet too high.
He made three or four starts before succeeding. He had gotten his idea from a
film at school called *The Romance of Logging.* He had finished high school,
married a good friend, was in a responsible job and going to night school.

These two men and others looked at the four boys jumping and jiggling
on the platform and thought, It must be fun to ride that way, especially now
the weather is nice and we're out of the tunnel and way high over the
Bronx. Then they thought, These kids do seem to be acting sort of stupid.
They *are* little. Then they thought of some of the brave things they had
done when they were boys and jiggling didn't seem so risky.

The ladies in the car became very angry when they looked at the four
boys. Most of them brought their brows together and hoped the boys could
see their extreme disapproval. One of the ladies wanted to get up and say,
Be careful you dumb kids, get off that platform or I'll call a cop. But three of
the boys were Negroes and the fourth was something else she couldn't tell
for sure. She was afraid they'd be fresh and laugh at her and embarrass her.
She wasn't afraid they'd hit her, but she was afraid of embarrassment. Another lady thought, Their mothers never know where they are. It wasn't
true in this particular case. Their mothers all knew that they had gone to see
the missile exhibit on Fourteenth Street.

5   Out on the platform, whenever the train accelerated, the boys would
raise their hands and point them up to the sky to act like rockets going off,
then they rat-tat-tatted the shatterproof glass pane like machine guns, although no machine guns had been exhibited.

For some reason known only to the motorman, the train began a sudden
slowdown. The lady who was afraid of embarrassment saw the boys jerk forward and backward and grab the swinging guard chains. She had her own
boy at home. She stood up with determination and went to the door. She slid
it open and said, "You boys will be hurt. You'll be killed. I'm going to call the
conductor if you don't just go into the next car and sit down and be quiet."

Two of the boys said, "Yes'm," and acted as though they were about to
go. Two of them blinked their eyes a couple of times and pressed their lips
together. The train resumed its speed. The door slid shut, parting the lady
and the boys. She leaned against the side door because she had to get off at
the next stop.

The boys opened their eyes wide at each other and laughed. The lady blushed. The boys looked at her and laughed harder. They began to pound each other's back. Samuel laughed the hardest and pounded Alfred's back until Alfred coughed and the tears came. Alfred held tight to the chain hook. Samuel pounded him even harder when he saw the tears. He said, "Why you bawling? You a baby, huh?" and laughed. One of the men whose boyhood had been more watchful than brave became angry. He stood up straight and looked at the boys for a couple of seconds. Then he walked in a citizenly way to the end of the car, where he pulled the emergency cord. Almost at once, with a terrible hiss, the pressure of air abandoned the brakes and the wheels were caught and held.

People standing in the most secure places fell forward, then backward. Samuel had let go of his hold on the chain so he could pound Tom as well as Alfred. All the passengers in the cars whipped back and forth, but he pitched only forward and fell head first to be crushed and killed between the cars.

10   The train had stopped hard, halfway into the station, and the conductor called at once for the trainmen who knew about this kind of death and how to take the body from the wheels and brakes. There was silence except for passengers from other cars who asked, What happened! What happened! The ladies waited around wondering if he might be an only child. The men recalled other afternoons with very bad endings. The little boys stayed close to each other, leaning and touching shoulders and arms and legs.

When the policeman knocked at the door and told her about it, Samuel's mother began to scream. She screamed all day and moaned all night, though the doctors tried to quiet her with pills.

Oh, oh, she hopelessly cried. She did not know how she could ever find another boy like that one. However, she was a young woman and she became pregnant. Then for a few months she was hopeful. The child born to her was a boy. They brought him to be seen and nursed. She smiled. But immediately she saw that this baby wasn't Samuel. She and her husband together have had other children, but never again will a boy exactly like Samuel be known.

You might think about the ways in which "Samuel" differs from a newspaper story of an accident in a subway. (You might even want to write a newspaper version of the happening.) In some ways, Paley's story faintly resembles an account that might appear in a newspaper. Journalists are taught to give information about Who, What, When, Where, and Why, and Paley does provide this. Thus, the *characters* (Samuel and others) are the journalist's Who; the *plot* (the boys were jiggling on the platform, and when a man pulled the emergency cord one of them was killed) is the What; the *setting* (the subway, presumably in modern times) is the When and the Where; the *motivation* (the irritation of the man who pulls the emergency cord) is the Why.

Ask yourself questions about each of these elements, and think about how they work in Paley's story. You might also think about responses to the following questions. Your responses will teach you a good deal about what literature is and about some of the ways in which it works.

✲ TOPICS FOR CRITICAL THINKING AND WRITING

1. Paley wrote the story, but an unspecified person *tells* it. Describe the voice of this narrator in the first paragraph. Is the voice neutral and objective, or do you hear some sort of attitude, a point of view? If you do hear an attitude, what words or phrases in the story indicate it?

2. What do you know about the setting of "Samuel"? What can you infer about the neighborhood?

3. In the fourth paragraph we are told that "three of the boys were Negroes and the fourth was something else." Is race important in this story? Is Samuel "Negro" or "something else"? Does it matter?

4. Exactly *why* did a man walk "in a citizenly way to the end of the car, where he pulled the emergency cord"? Do you think the author blames him? What evidence can you offer to support your view? Do *you* blame him? Or do you blame the boys? Or anyone? Explain.

5. The story is called "Samuel," and it is, surely, about him. But what happens after Samuel dies? (You might want to list the events.) What else is the story about? (You might want to comment on why you believe the items in your list are important.)

6. Can you generalize about what the men think of the jigglers and about what the women think? Is Paley saying something about the sexes? About the attitudes of onlookers in a big city?

WHAT'S PAST IS PROLOGUE

The two poems and two stories that you have just read cannot, of course, stand for all works of literature. For one thing, although Mora's "Immigrants" and the two prose stories include some dialogue, none of these works is in dramatic form, designed for presentation on a stage. Still, these four examples, as well as works of literature that you are already familiar with, will provide something of a background against which you can read the other works in this book. For instance, if you read a story that, like The Parable of the Prodigal Son, seems strongly to imply a moral, think about how the moral is controlled by what the characters *do* as well as by what they *say,* and how one character is defined by being set against another. If you read a poem that, like Mora's "Immigrants," seems to play one tone of voice against another (for instance, the voice of the speaker of the poem against a voice quoted within the poem), think about how the voices relate to each other and how they perhaps harmonize to create a complex vision.

In short, a work of literature is not a nut to be cracked open so that a kernel of meaning can be extracted and devoured, and the rest thrown away; the whole—a performance in words—is something to be experienced and enjoyed.

We end this chapter with three short stories and two short poems.

KATHERINE MANSFIELD

Katherine Mansfield (1888–1923), née Kathleen Mansfield Beauchamp, was born in New Zealand. In 1902 she went to London for schooling; in 1906 she returned to New Zealand, but dissatisfied with its provincialism, in 1908 she returned to London to become a writer. After a disastrous marriage and a love affair, she went to Germany, where she wrote stories; in 1910 she returned to London, published a book of stories in 1911, and in 1912 met and began living with the writer John Middleton Murry. In 1918, after her first husband at last divorced her, she married Murry. She died of tuberculosis in 1923, a few months after her thirty-fourth birthday.

Mansfield published about seventy stories, and left some others unpublished. An early admirer of Chekhov, she read his works in German translations before they were translated into English.

Miss Brill

[1920]

Although it was so brilliantly fine—the blue sky powdered with gold and great spots of light like white wine splashed over the Jardins Publiques[1]— Miss Brill was glad that she had decided on her fur. The air was motionless, but when you opened your mouth there was just a faint chill, like a chill from a glass of iced water before you sip, and now and again a leaf came drifting—from nowhere, from the sky. Miss Brill put up her hand and touched her fur. Dear little thing! It was nice to feel it again. She had taken it out of its box that afternoon, shaken out the moth-powder, given it a good brush, and rubbed the life back into the dim little eyes. "What has been happening to me?" said the sad little eyes. Oh, how sweet it was to see them snap at her again from the red eiderdown! . . . But the nose, which was of some black composition, wasn't at all firm. It must have had a knock, somehow. Never mind—a little dab of black sealing-wax when the time came— when it was absolutely necessary. . . . Little rogue! Yes, she really felt like that about it. Little rogue biting its tail just by her left ear. She could have taken it off and laid it on her lap and stroked it. She felt a tingling in her hands and arms, but that came from walking, she supposed. And when she breathed, something light and sad—no, not sad, exactly—something gentle seemed to move in her bosom.

There were a number of people out this afternoon, far more than last Sunday. And the band sounded louder and gayer. That was because the Season had begun. For although the band played all year round on Sundays, out of season it was never the same. It was like some one playing with only the family to listen; it didn't care how it played if there weren't any strangers present. Wasn't the conductor wearing a new coat, too? She was sure it was new. He scraped with his foot and flapped his arms like a rooster about to crow, and the bandsmen sitting in the green rotunda blew out their cheeks and glared at the music. Now there came a little "flutey" bit—very pretty!— a little chain of bright drops. She was sure it would be repeated. It was; she lifted her head and smiled.

Only two people shared her "special" seat: a fine old man in a velvet coat, his hands clasped over a huge carved walking-stick, and a big old woman, sitting upright, with a roll of knitting on her embroidered apron. They did not speak. This was disappointing, for Miss Brill always looked forward to the conversation. She had become really quite expert, she thought, at listening as though she didn't listen, at sitting in other people's lives just for a minute while they talked round her.

She glanced, sideways, at the old couple. Perhaps they would go soon. Last Sunday, too, hadn't been as interesting as usual. An Englishman and his wife, he wearing a dreadful Panama hat and she button boots. And she'd gone on the whole time about how she ought to wear spectacles; she knew she needed them; but that it was no good getting any; they'd be sure to

---

[1] **Jardins Publiques** Public Gardens (French).

break and they'd never keep on. And he'd been so patient. He'd suggested everything—gold rims, the kind that curved round your ears, little pads inside the bridge. No, nothing would please her. "They'll always be sliding down my nose!" Miss Brill had wanted to shake her.

5   The old people sat on the bench, still as statues. Never mind, there was always the crowd to watch. To and fro, in front of the flower-beds and the band rotunda, the couples and groups paraded, stopped to talk, to greet, to buy a handful of flowers from the old beggar who had his tray fixed to the railings. Little children ran among them, swooping and laughing; little boys with big white silk bows under their chins, little girls, little French dolls, dressed up in velvet and lace. And sometimes a tiny staggerer came suddenly rocking into the open from under the trees, stopped, stared, as suddenly sat down "flop," until its small high-stepping mother, like a young hen, rushed scolding to its rescue. Other people sat on the benches and green chairs, but they were nearly always the same, Sunday after Sunday, and—Miss Brill had often noticed—there was something funny about nearly all of them. They were odd, silent, nearly all old, and from the way they stared they looked as though they'd just come from dark little rooms or even—even cupboards!

Behind the rotunda the slender trees with yellow leaves down drooping, and through them just a line of sea, and beyond the blue sky with gold-veined clouds.

Tum-tum-tum tiddle-um! tiddle-um! tum tiddley-um tum ta! blew the band.

Two young girls in red came by and two young soldiers in blue met them, and they laughed and paired and went off arm-in-arm. Two peasant women with funny straw hats passed, gravely, leading beautiful smoke-colored donkeys. A cold, pale nun hurried by. A beautiful woman came along and dropped her bunch of violets, and a little boy ran after to hand them to her, and she took them and threw them away as if they'd been poisoned. Dear me! Miss Brill didn't know whether to admire that or not! And now an ermine toque[2] and a gentleman in grey met just in front of her. He was tall, stiff, dignified, and she was wearing the ermine toque she'd bought when her hair was yellow. Now everything, her hair, her face, even her eyes, was the same color as the shabby ermine, and her hand, in its cleaned glove, lifted to dab her lips, was a tiny yellowish paw. Oh, she was so pleased to see him—delighted! She rather thought they were going to meet that afternoon. She described where she'd been—everywhere, here, there, along by the sea. The day was so charming—didn't he agree? And wouldn't he, perhaps? . . . But he shook his head, lighted a cigarette, slowly breathed a great deep puff into her face, and, even while she was still talking and laughing, flicked the match away and walked on. The ermine toque was alone; she smiled more brightly than ever. But even the band seemed to know what she was feeling and played more softly, played tenderly, and the drum beat, "The Brute! The Brute!" over and over. What would she do? What was going to happen now? But as Miss Brill wondered, the ermine toque turned, raised her hand as though she'd seen some one else, much nicer, just over there, and pattered away. And the band changed again and played more quickly, more gaily than ever, and the old couple on Miss Brill's seat got up and marched away, and

---

[2]**toque** a brimless, close-fitting woman's hat.

such a funny old man with long whiskers hobbled along in time to the music and was nearly knocked over by four girls walking abreast.

Oh, how fascinating it was! How she enjoyed it! How she loved sitting here, watching it all! It was like a play. It was exactly like a play. Who could believe the sky at the back wasn't painted? But it wasn't till a little brown dog trotted on solemn and then slowly trotted off, like a little "theatre" dog, a little dog that had been drugged, that Miss Brill discovered what it was that made it so exciting. They were all on the stage. They weren't only the audience, not only looking on; they were acting. Even she had a part and came every Sunday. No doubt somebody would have noticed if she hadn't been there; she was part of the performance after all. How strange she'd never thought of it like that before! And yet it explained why she made such a point of starting from home at just the same time each week—so as not to be late for the performance—and it also explained why she had quite a queer, shy feeling at telling her English pupils how she spent her Sunday afternoons. No wonder! Miss Brill nearly laughed out loud. She was on the stage. She thought of the old invalid gentleman to whom she read the newspaper four afternoons a week while he slept in the garden. She had got quite used to the frail head on the cotton pillow, the hollowed eyes, the open mouth and the high pinched nose. If he'd been dead she mightn't have noticed for weeks; she wouldn't have minded. But suddenly he knew he was having the paper read to him by an actress! "An actress!" The old head lifted; two points of light quivered in the old eyes. "An actress—are ye?" And Miss Brill smoothed the newspaper as though it were the manuscript of her part and said gently: "Yes, I have been an actress for a long time."

10   The band had been having a rest. Now they started again. And what they played was warm, sunny, yet there was just a faint chill—a something, what was it?—not sadness—no, not sadness—a something that made you want to sing. The tune lifted, lifted, the light shone; and it seemed to Miss Brill that in another moment all of them, all the whole company, would begin singing. The young ones, the laughing ones who were moving together, they would begin, and the men's voices, very resolute and brave, would join them. And then she too, she too, and the others on the benches—they would come in with a kind of accompaniment—something low, that scarcely rose or fell, something so beautiful—moving. . . . And Miss Brill's eyes filled with tears and she looked smiling at all the other members of the company. Yes, we understand, we understand, she thought—though what they understood she didn't know.

Just at that moment a boy and a girl came and sat down where the old couple had been. They were beautifully dressed; they were in love. The hero and heroine, of course, just arrived from his father's yacht. And still soundlessly singing, still with that trembling smile, Miss Brill prepared to listen.

"No, not now," said the girl. "Not here, I can't."

"But why? Because of that stupid old thing at the end there?" asked the boy. "Why does she come here at all—who wants her? Why doesn't she keep her silly old mug at home?"

"It's her fu-fur which is so funny," giggled the girl. "It's exactly like a fried whiting."[3]

---

[3]**whiting** a kind of fish.

15   "Ah, be off with you!" said the boy in an angry whisper. Then: "Tell me, my petite chère[4]—"

"No, not here," said the girl. "Not *yet.*"

On her way home she usually bought a slice of honey-cake at the baker's. It was her Sunday treat. Sometimes there was an almond in her slice, sometimes not. It made a great difference. If there was an almond it was like carrying home a tiny present—a surprise—something that might very well not have been there. She hurried on the almond Sundays and struck the match for the kettle in quite a dashing way.

But today she passed the baker's by, climbed the stairs, went into the little dark room—her room like a cupboard—and sat down on the red ei-derdown. She sat there for a long time. The box that the fur came out of was on the bed. She unclasped the necklet quickly; quickly, without look-ing, laid it inside. But when she put the lid on she thought she heard some-thing crying.

---

[4]*petite chère* darling.

 ## TOPICS FOR CRITICAL THINKING AND WRITING

1. Why do you think Mansfield did not give Miss Brill a first name?
2. What would be lost (or gained?) if the first paragraph were omitted?
3. Suppose someone said that the story is about a woman who is justly punished for her pride. What might be your response?

JAMAICA KINCAID

Jamaica Kincaid (b. 1949) was born in St. John's, Antigua, in the West Indies. She was educated at the Princess Margaret School in Antigua, and, briefly, at Westchester Community College and Franconia College. Since 1974 she has been a contributor to The New Yorker.

Kincaid is the author of several books, among them At the Bottom of the River *(1983, a collection of short pieces, including "Girl"),* Annie John *(1985, a second book recording a girl's growth, including "Columbus in Chains"),* A Small Place *(1988, a passionate essay about the destructive effects of colonialism) and* Lucy *(1990, a short novel about a young black woman who comes to the United States from the West Indies).*

Girl   [1978]

Wash the white clothes on Monday and put them on the stone heap; wash the color clothes in Tuesday and put them on the clothesline to dry; don't walk barehead in the hot sun; cook pumpkin fritters in very hot sweet oil; soak your little clothes right after you take them off; when buying cotton to make yourself a nice blouse, be sure that it doesn't have gum on it, because that way it won't hold up well after a wash; soak salt fish overnight before you cook it; is it true that you sing benna[1] in Sunday School? always eat your food in such a way that it won't turn someone else's stomach; on Sundays try to walk like a lady and not like the slut you are so bent on becoming; don't sing benna in Sunday School; you musn't speak to wharf-rat boys, not even to give directions; don't eat fruits on the street—flies will follow you; *but I don't sing benna on Sundays at all and never in Sunday school;* this is how to sew on a button; this is how to make a buttonhole for the button you have just sewed on; this is how to hem a dress when you see the hem coming down and so to prevent yourself from looking like the slut I know you are so bent on becoming; this i show you iron your father's khaki shirt so that it doesn't have a crease; this is how you iron your father's khaki pants so that they don't have a crease; this is how you grow okra—far from the house, because okra tree harbors red ants; when you are growing dasheen, make sure it gets plenty of water or else it makes your throat itch when you are eating it; this is how you sweep a corner; this is how you sweep a whole house; this is how you sweep a yard; this is how you smile to someone you don't like too much; this is how you set a table for dinner with an important guest; this is how you smile to some you don't like at all; this is how you smile to someone you like completely; this is how you set a table for tea; this is how you set a table for dinner; this is how you set a table for lunch; this is how you set a table for breakfast; this i show to be- have in the presence of men who don't know you very well, and this way they won't recognize immediately the slut I have warned you against be- coming; be sure to wash every day, even if it is with your own spit; don't squat down to play marbles—you are not a boy, you know; don't pick peo- ple's flowers—you might catch something; don't throw stones at black- birds, because it might not be a blackbird at all; this is how to make a bread pudding; this is how to make duokona;[2] this is how to make a pepper pot; this is how to make a good medicine for a cold; this is how to make a good medicine to throw away a child before it even becomes a child; this is how to catch a fish; this is how to throw back a fish you don't like, and that way something bad won't fall on you; this is who to bully a man; this is how a man bullies you; this is how ot love a man, and if this doesn't work there are other ways, and if they don't work don't feel too bad about giving up; this is how to spit up in the air if you feel like it, and this is how to move quick so that it doesn't fall on you; this is how to make ends meet; always squeeze bread to make sure it's fresh; *but what if the baker won't let me feel the bread?;* you mean to say that after all you are really going to be the kind of woman who the baker won't let near the bread?

---

[1]**benna** Calypso music.   [2]**duokona** a spicy pudding made of plaintains.

▓ TOPICS FOR CRITICAL THINKING AND WRITING

1. In a paragraph, identify the two characters whose voices we hear in this story. Explain what we know about them (their circumstances and their relationship). Cite specific evidence from the text. For example, what is the effect of the frequent repetition of "this is how"? Are there other words or phrases frequently repeated?

2. Try reading a section of "Girl" out loud in a rhythmical pattern, giving the principal and the second voices. Then reread the story, trying to incorporate this rhythm mentally into your reading. How does this rhythm contribute to the overall effect of the story? How does it compare to or contrast with speech rhythms that are familiar to you?

TOBIAS WOLFF

Tobias Wolff was born in Alabama in 1945, but he grew up in the state of Washington. He left high school before graduating, served as an apprentice seaman and as a weight-guesser in a carnival, and then joined the army, where he served four years as a paratrooper. After his discharge from the army, he hired private tutors to enable him to pass the entrance examination to Oxford University. At Oxford he did spectacularly well, graduating with First Class Honors in English. Wolff has written stories, novels, and an autobiography (This Boy's Life); *he now teaches in the Creative Writing Program at Stanford.*

Powder
[1992]

Just before Christmas my father took me skiing at Mount Baker. He'd had to fight for the privilege of my company, because my mother was still angry with him for sneaking me into a nightclub during his last visit, to see Thelonius Monk.

He wouldn't give up. He promised, hand on heart, to take good care of me and have me home for dinner on Christmas Eve, and she relented. But as we were checking out of the lodge that morning it began to snow, and in this snow he observed some quality that made it necessary for us to get in one last run. We got in several last runs. He was indifferent to my fretting. Snow whirled around us in bitter, blinding squalls, hissing like sand, and still we skied. As the lift bore us to the peak yet again, my father looked at his watch and said: "Criminey. This'll have to be a fast one."

By now I couldn't see the trail. There was no point in trying. I stuck to him like white on rice and did what he did and somehow made it to the bottom without sailing off a cliff. We returned our skis and my father put chains on the Austin-Healy while I swayed from foot to foot, clapping my mittens and wishing I were home. I could see everything. The green tablecloth, the plates with the holly pattern, the red candles waiting to be lit.

We passed a diner on our way out. "You want some soup?" my father asked. I shook my head. "Buck up," he said. "I'll get you there. Right, doctor?"

5   I was supposed to say, "Right, doctor," but I didn't say anything.

A state trooper waved us down outside the resort. A pair of sawhorses were blocking the road. The trooper came up to our car and bent down to my father's window. His face was bleached by the cold. Snowflakes clung to his eyebrows and to the fur trim of his jacket and cap.

"Don't tell me," my father said.

The trooper told him. The road was closed. It might get cleared, it might not. Storm took everyone by surprise. So much, so fast. Hard to get people moving. Christmas Eve. What can you do?

My father said: "Look. We're talking about four, five inches. I've taken this car through worse than that."

10   The trooper straightened up, boots creaking. His face was out of sight but I could hear him. "The road is closed."

My father sat with both hands on the wheel, rubbing the wood with his thumbs. He looked at the barricade for a long time. He seemed to be trying to master the idea of it. Then he thanked the trooper, and with a weird, old-maidy show of caution turned the car around. "Your mother will never forgive me for this," he said.

"We should have left before," I said. "Doctor."

He didn't speak to me again until we were both in a booth at the diner, waiting for our burgers. "She won't forgive me," he said. "Do you understand? Never."

"I guess," I said, but no guesswork was required; she wouldn't forgive him.

15   "I can't let that happen." He bent toward me. "I'll tell you what I want. I want us to be all together again. Is that what you want?"

"Yes, sir."

He bumped my chin with his knuckles. "That's all I needed to hear."

When we finished eating he went to the pay phone in the back of the diner, then joined me in the booth again. I figured he'd called my mother, but he didn't give a report. He sipped at his coffee and stared out the window at the empty road. "Come on, come on," he said. A little while later he said, "Come on!" When the trooper's car went past, lights flashing, he got up and dropped some money on the check. "O.K. Vámonos."

The wind had died. The snow was falling straight down, less of it now; lighter. We drove away from the resort, right up to the barricade. "Move it," my father told me. When I looked at him he said, "What are you waiting for?" I got out and dragged one of the sawhorses aside, then put it back after he drove through. He pushed the door open for me. "Now you're an accomplice," he said. "We go down together." He put the car into gear and gave me a look. "Joke, doctor."

20   "Funny, doctor."

Down the first long stretch I watched the road behind us, to see if the trooper was on our tail. The barricade vanished. Then there was nothing but snow: snow on the road, snow kicking up from the chains, snow on the trees, snow in the sky; and our trail in the snow. I faced around and had a shock. The lie of the road behind us had been marked by our own tracks, but there were no tracks ahead of us. My father was breaking virgin snow between a line of tall trees. He was humming "Stars Fell on Alabama." I felt snow brush along the floorboards under my feet. To keep my hands from shaking, I clamped them between my knees.

My father grunted in a thoughtful way and said, "Don't ever try this yourself."

"I won't."

"That's what you say now, but someday you'll get your license and then you'll think you can do anything. Only you won't be able to do this. You need, I don't know—a certain instinct."

25   "Maybe I have it."

"You don't. You have your strong points, but not . . . this. I only mention it, because I don't want you to get the idea this is something just anybody can do. I'm a great driver. That's not a virtue, O.K.? It's just a fact, and one you should be aware of. Of course you have to give the old heap some credit, too—there aren't many cars I'd try this with. Listen!"

I listened. I heard the slap of the chains, the stiff, jerky rasps of the wipers, the purr of the engine. It really did purr. The car was almost new. My father couldn't afford it, and kept promising to sell it, but here it was.

I said, "Where do you think that policeman went to?"

"Are you warm enough?" He reached over and cranked up the blower. Then he turned off the wipers. We didn't need them. The clouds had brightened. A few sparse, feathery flakes drifted into our slipstream and were swept away. We left the trees and entered a broad field of snow that ran level for a while and then tilted sharply downward. Orange stakes had been planted at intervals in two parallel lines and my father steered a course between them, though they were far enough apart to leave considerable doubt in my mind as to where exactly the road lay. He was humming again, doing little scat riffs around the melody.

30   "O.K. then. What are my strong points?"

"Don't get me started," he said. "It'd take all day."

"Oh, right. Name one."

"Easy. You always think ahead."

True. I always thought ahead. I was a boy who kept his clothes on numbered hangers to insure proper rotation. I bothered my teachers for homework assignments far ahead of their due dates so I could make up schedules. I thought ahead, and that was why I knew that there would be other troopers waiting for us at the end of our ride, if we got there. What I did not know was that my father would wheedle and plead his way past them—he didn't sing "O Tannenbaum" but just about—and get me home for dinner, buying a little more time before my mother decided to make the split final. I knew we'd get caught; I was resigned to it. And maybe for this reason I stopped moping and began to enjoy myself.

35   Why not? This was one for the books. Like being in a speedboat, but better. You can't go downhill in a boat. And it was all ours. And it kept coming, the laden trees, the unbroken surface of snow, the sudden white vistas. Here and there I saw hints of the road, ditches, fences, stakes, but not so many that I could have found my way. But then I didn't have to. My father was driving. My father in his 48th year, rumpled, kind, bankrupt of honor, flushed with certainty. He was a great driver. All persuasion, no coercion. Such subtlety at the wheel, such tactful pedalwork. I actually trusted him. And the best was yet to come—the switchbacks and hairpins. Impossible to describe. Except maybe to say this: If you haven't driven fresh powder, you haven't driven.

JAMES MERRILL

James Merrill (1926–1995) published his first book of poems in 1950, three years after graduating from college. (His manuscript was chosen by W. H. Auden for the Yale Younger Poets series.) Merrill was extremely inventive in his forms, and admirably successful in combining an engaging or even a playful tone with serious topics.

Christmas Tree

[1997]

                    To be
              Brought down at last
          From the cold sighing mountain
              Where I and the others
          Had been fed, looked after, kept still,   5
          Meant, I knew—of course I knew—
          That it would be only a matter of weeks,
          That there was nothing more to do.
          Warmly they took me in, made much of me,
          The point from the start was to keep my spirits up.   10
          I could assent to that. For honestly,
          It did help to be wound in jewels, to send
          Their colors flashing forth from vents in the deep
          Fragrant sables that cloaked me head to foot.
          Over me they wove a spell of shining—   15
          Purple and silver chains, eavesdripping tinsel,
          Amulets, milagros: software of silver,
          A heart, a little girl, a Model T,
          Two staring eyes. Then angels, trumpets, BUD and BEA
          (The children's names) in clownlike capitals,   20
          Somewhere a music box whose tiny song
          Played and replayed I ended before long
          By loving. And in shadow behind me, a primitive IV
          To keep the show going. Yes, yes, what lay ahead
          Was clear: the stripping, the cold street, my chemicals   25
          Plowed back into the Earth for lives to come—
          No doubt a blessing, a harvest, but one that doesn't bear,
          Now or ever, dwelling upon. To have grown so thin.
          Needles and bone. The little boy's hands meeting
          About my spine. The mother's voice: *Holding up wonderfully!* 30
          No dread. No bitterness. The end beginning. Today's
                    Dusk room aglow
                    For the last time
                    With candlelight.
                    Faces love-lit,   35
                    Gifts underfoot.
          Still to be so poised, so
          Receptive. Still to recall, to praise.

❊ TOPICS FOR CRITICAL THINKING AND WRITING

1. How would you characterize the tone of the first sentence (lines 1–8)? That is, what do you take to be the speaker's attitude(s)?
2. Beginning with the last line of the lowest branches ("No dread"), and continuing to the end of the poem, how would you characterize the tone(s)? Does this ending satisfy you? Why, or why not? (In your

response to this question about the ending, you will of course take into consideration everything that precedes the ending.)

3. About two-thirds of the way through the poem, the tree speaks of "a primitive IV / To keep the show going." What is an IV literally, and what is it in this poem?

4. If you find some lines that strike you as especially witty, point them out. And do you find some lines especially moving? If so, which ones, and why?

5. If someone asked you what the poem is about, what would you say?

6. When did you become aware of the shape that this poem makes on the page? Does this shaping of the poem make it more or less effective? Explain your position.

W. F. BOLTON

W. F. Bolton, a graduate of Northeastern University and Boston University, is a retired technical writer. John Coltrane (1926–1967), mentioned after the title, was an African-American saxophonist, composer, and bandleader.

Might We Too?   [1998]

After listening to John Coltrane

We who have lived for song
Yet never ourselves sung,
Never mastered the string, the horn.
Made a living apart from the voice
Within us.   5
We who have sat in hopeless admiration,
As lookers-on,
Stood at the high office window
Watching the hobo cross his tracks,
Sling himself into a passing boxcar   10
With the agility of the acrobat
Or disappear among the underslung shadows,
Riding the rails into dangerous night.

Is it talent or persistence?
Might we too have done that?   15
Rolled the miles off, over ties—bars
And riffs of gorgeous flight?

▨ TOPICS FOR CRITICAL THINKING AND WRITING

1. The poem asks questions, essentially (1) Is the strength of an artist (defined so that "artist" includes the hobo who agilely "slings himself into a passing boxcar") "talent or persistence"? and (2) "Might we too have done that"? If you are familiar with Coltrane's music, what are your answers to the questions, with reference to Coltrane? Or take

some other performer—perhaps a musician but perhaps an athlete, a dancer, a juggler, an actor, or a writer—and answer the question.

2. How would you distinguish between *talent* (line 14) and *skill?* Between *talent* and *genius?*

3. Have you ever met someone whom you would describe as a genius? (Do not limit the word to someone with highly exceptional intellectual ability. One can be a genius with the violin or perhaps with a basketball team, or, for that matter, with a basketball. At the root of *genius* is a Roman word for a guardian deity assigned to a person at birth.) Explain why *genius* strikes you as the right word for this person.

John Coltrane.

2

Writing about Literature:
From Idea to Essay

WHY WRITE ARGUMENTS
ABOUT LITERATURE?

If you have ever put exclamation points or questions marks or brief annotations ("this is ridiculous," or "great!") in the margins of your books, you are aware of the *pleasure* one gets from putting responses into writing. But people also write about literature—not only in margins of books but, let's say, in notebooks or journals and ultimately in essays—in order to clarify and account for their responses to works that interest or excite or frustrate them.

In putting words on paper you will have to take a second and a third look at what is in front of you and what is within you. Writing, then, is not only a way of expressing pleasure but also a way of *learning*. The last word about complex thoughts and feelings is never said, but when we write we hope to make at least a little progress in the difficult but rewarding job of talking about our responses. We learn, and then we hope to interest our readers because we are communicating to them our responses to something that for one reason or another is worth talking about.

This communication is, in effect, teaching. You may think that you are writing for the teacher, but that is a misconception; when you write, *you* are the teacher, offering an argument. An essay on literature is an attempt to help someone see the work as you see it. If this chapter had to be boiled down to a single sentence, that sentence would be: Because you are teaching, your essay should embody those qualities that you value in teachers—intelligence, open-mindedness, effort, a desire to offer what help one can.

GETTING IDEAS: PRE-WRITING

"All there is to writing," Robert Frost said, "is having ideas. To learn to write is to learn to have ideas." But how does one "learn to have ideas"? Among the methods are these: reading with a pen or pencil in hand, so that you can annotate the text; keeping a journal, in which you jot down reflections about your reading; talking with others (including your instructor) about the reading. Let's look at the first of these, annotating.

Annotating a Text

In reading, if you own a book don't hesitate to mark it up, indicating (by high-lighting or underlining or by making marginal notes) what puzzles you, what pleases or interests you, and what displeases or bores you. Later, of course, you'll want to think further about these responses, asking yourself, on rereading, if you still feel that way, and if not, why not, but these first responses will get you started.

One kind of annotation is a question mark in the margin, jotted down in order to indicate your uncertainty about the meaning of a word. It's a good idea to keep a **dictionary** nearby while you are reading. Of course you won't look up every word that you are unsure about—this might spoil the fun of reading—but sometimes you will sense that you need to know the precise meanings and implications of the writer's words in order to feel and appreciate the effects he or she is trying to create. And the more you become aware of how richly meaning-ful the words can be in a literary text, the more sensitive and self-aware you will be about the words you use in your own prose.

We have already looked at Pat Mora's short poem "Immigrants" (page 7), but here it is again, with a student's first annotations.

unusual to use title as first word?

Immigrants

wrap their babies in the American flag,   *so what's wrong with hot dogs and apple pie?*
feed them mashed hot dogs and apple pie,
name them Bill and Daisy,
buy them (blonde) dolls that blink (blue)
eyes or a football and tiny cleats   *Anglo types—not Asian American or Latino types*   5

Is Mora making fun of immigrants?
before the baby can even walk,
speak to them in thick English,
(hallo, babee, hallo,)
whisper in Spanish or Polish

do only immigrants show a "parent fear"? Don't all parents fear for their children?
when the babies sleep, whisper   10
in a dark parent bed, that dark
(parent fear,) "Will they like
our boy, our girl, our fine (a)merican   *why not a capital letter?*
boy, our fine (a)merican girl?"

Notice that most of these annotations are questions that the student is asking herself. Asking questions is an excellent way to get yourself thinking. We will return to this method shortly.

Brainstorming for Ideas for Writing

Unlike annotating, which consists of making brief notes and small marks on the printed page, "brainstorming"—the free jotting down of ideas—asks that you jot down at length whatever comes to mind, without inhibition. But before we talk further about brainstorming, read the following short story.

KATE CHOPIN

Kate Chopin (1851-1904)—the name is pronounced in the French way, somewhat like "show pan"—was born in St. Louis, with the name Katherine O'Flaherty. Her father was an immigrant from Ireland, and her mother was descended from an old Creole family. (In the United States, a Creole is a person descended from the original French settlers in Louisiana or the original Spanish settlers in the Gulf States.) At the age of nineteen she married Oscar Chopin, a cotton broker in New Orleans. They had six children, and though Kate Chopin had contemplated a literary career, she did not turn seriously to writing until after her husband's death in 1883. Most of her fiction concerns the lives of the descendants of the French who had settled in Louisiana.

The Story of an Hour

[1894]

Knowing that Mrs. Mallard was afflicted with a heart trouble, great care was taken to break to her as gently as possible the news of her husband's death.

It was her sister Josephine who told her, in broken sentences, veiled hints that revealed in half concealing. Her husband's friend Richards was there, too, near her. It was he who had been in the newspaper office when intelligence of the railroad disaster was received, with Brently Mallard's name leading the list of "killed." He had only taken the time to assure himself of its truth by a second telegram, and had hastened to forestall any less careful, less tender friend in bearing the sad message.

She did not hear the story as many women have heard the same, with a paralyzed inability to accept its significance. She wept at once, with sudden, wild abandonment, in her sister's arms. When the storm of grief had spent itself she went away to her room alone. She would have no one follow her.

There stood, facing the open window, a comfortable, roomy armchair. Into this she sank, pressed down by a physical exhaustion that haunted her body and seemed to reach into her soul.

5   She could see in the open square before her house the tops of trees that were all aquiver with the new spring life. The delicious breath of rain was in the air. In the street below a peddler was crying his wares. The notes of a distant song which some one was singing reached her faintly, and countless sparrows were twittering in the eaves.

There were patches of blue sky showing here and there through the clouds that had met and piled one above the other in the west facing her window. She sat with her head thrown back upon the cushion of the chair quite motionless, except when a sob came up into her throat and shook her, as a child who has cried itself to sleep continues to sob in its dreams.

She was young, with a fair, calm face, whose lines bespoke repression and even a certain strength. But now there was a dull stare in her eyes, whose gaze was fixed away off yonder on one of those patches of blue sky. It was not a glance of reflection, but rather indicated a suspension of intelligent thought.

There was something coming to her and she was waiting for it, fearfully. What was it? She did not know; it was too subtle and elusive to name. But she felt it, creeping out of the sky, reaching toward her through the sounds, the scents, the color that filled the air.

Now her bosom rose and fell tumultuously. She was beginning to recognize this thing that was approaching to possess her, and she was striving to beat it back with her will—as powerless as her two white slender hands would have been.

10   When she abandoned herself a little whispered word escaped her slightly parted lips. She said it over and over under her breath: "Free, free, free!" The vacant stare and the look of terror that had followed it went from her eyes. They stayed keen and bright. Her pulses beat fast, and the coursing blood warmed and relaxed every inch of her body.

She did not stop to ask if it were not a monstrous joy that held her. A clear and exalted perception enabled her to dismiss the suggestion as trivial.

She knew that she would weep again when she saw the kind, tender hands folded in death; the face that had never looked save with love upon her, fixed and gray and dead. But she saw beyond that bitter moment a long procession of years to come that would belong to her absolutely. And she opened and spread her arms out to them in welcome.

There would be no one to live for her during those coming years; she would live for herself. There would be no powerful will bending her in that blind persistence with which men and women believe they have a right to impose a private will upon a fellow creature. A kind intention or a cruel intention made the act seem no less a crime as she looked upon it in that brief moment of illumination.

And yet she had loved him—sometimes. Often she had not. What did it matter! What could love, the unsolved mystery, count for in face of this possession of self-assertion which she suddenly recognized as the strongest impulse of her being.

15   "Free! Body and soul free!" she kept whispering.

Josephine was kneeling before the closed door with her lips to the keyhole, imploring for admission. "Louise, open the door! I beg; open the door—you will make yourself ill. What are you doing, Louise? For heaven's sake open the door."

"Go away. I am not making myself ill." No; she was drinking in a very elixir of life through that open window.

Her fancy was running riot along those days ahead of her. Spring days, and summer days, and all sorts of days that would be her own. She breathed a quick prayer that life might be long. It was only yesterday she had thought with a shudder that life might be long.

She arose at length and opened the door to her sister's importunities. There was a feverish triumph in her eyes, and she carried herself unwittingly like a goddess of Victory. She clasped her sister's waist, and together they descended the stairs. Richards stood waiting for them at the bottom.

20   Some one was opening the front door with a latchkey. It was Brently Mallard who entered, a little travel-stained, composedly carrying his gripsack and umbrella. He had been far from the scene of accident, and did not even know there had been one. He stood amazed at Josephine's piercing cry; at Richards' quick motion to screen him from the view of his wife.

But Richards was too late.

When the doctors came they said she had died of heart disease—of joy that kills.

In brainstorming, don't worry about spelling, about writing complete sentences, or about unifying your thoughts; just let one thought lead to another. Later you can review your jottings, deleting some, connecting with arrows others that are related, expanding still others, but for now you want to get going, and so there is no reason to look back. Thus you might jot down something about the title.

```
Title speaks of an hour, and story covers an hour,
but maybe takes five minutes to read
```

And then, perhaps prompted by "an hour," you might happen to add something to this effect:

```
Doubt that a woman who got news of the death of her
husband could move from grief to joy within an hour
```

Your next jotting might have little or nothing to do with this issue; it might simply say:

```
Enjoyed "Hour" especially because "Hour" is so shocking
```

And then you might ask yourself:

```
By shocking, do I mean "improbable," or what? Come to
think of it, maybe it's not so improbable. A lot de-
pends on what the marriage was like.
```

Focused Free Writing

Focused, or directed, free writing is a method related to brainstorming that some writers use to uncover ideas they may want to write about. Concentrating on one issue—for instance, a question that strikes them as worth puzzling over (What kind of person is Mrs. Mallard?)—they write at length, nonstop, for perhaps 5 or 10 minutes.

Writers who find free writing helpful put down everything they can think of that has bearing on the one issue or question they are examining. They do not stop at this stage to evaluate the results, and they do not worry about niceties of sentence structure or of spelling. They just pour out their ideas in a steady stream of writing, drawing on whatever associations come to mind. If they pause in their writing, it is only to refer to the text, to search for more detail— perhaps a quotation—that will help them answer their question.

After the free-writing session, these writers usually go back and reread what they have written, highlighting or underlining what seems to be of value. Of course they find much that is of little or no use, but they also usually find that some strong ideas have surfaced and have received some development. At this point the writers are often able to make a scratch outline and then begin a draft.

Here is an example of one student's focused free writing, again on Chopin's "The Story of an Hour."

```
    What do I know about Mrs. Mallard? Let me put
everything down here I know about her or can figure out
from what Kate Chopin tells me. When she finds herself
alone after the death of her husband, she says,
"Free. Body and soul free" and before that she said,
```

"Free, free, free." Three times. So she has suddenly
perceived that she has not been free: she has been
under the influence of a "powerful will." In this case
it has been her husband, but she says no one, man nor
woman, should impose their will on anyone else. So
it's not a feminist issue--it's a power issue. No one
should push anyone else around is what I guess Chopin
means, force someone to do what the other person
wants. I used to have a friend that did that to me
all the time; he had to run everything. They say that
fathers--before the women's movement--used to run
things, with the father in charge of all the decisions, so maybe this is an honest reaction to having
been pushed around by a husband. I think Mrs. Mallard
is a believable character, even if the plot is not
all that believable--all those things happening in
such quick succession.

Listing and Clustering

In your preliminary thinking you may find it useful to make lists or to jot down
clusters of your ideas, insights, comments, questions. For "The Story of an Hour"
you might list Mrs. Mallard's traits, or you might list the stages of her development. (Such a list is not the same as a summary of a plot. The list helps the writer
to see the sequence of psychological changes, and it will help assist her to offer
a coherent argument about what happens.)

weeps (when she gets the news)

goes to room, alone

"pressed down by a physical exhaustion"

"dull stare"

"something coming to her"

strives to beat back "this thing"

"Free, free, free!" The "vacant stare went from her
    eyes"

"A clear and exalted perception"

rejects Josephine

"she was drinking in a very elixir of life"

gets up, opens door, "a feverish triumph in her eyes"

sees B, and dies

Unlike brainstorming and annotating, which let you go in all directions, listing
requires that you first make a decision about what you will be listing—traits of
character, images, puns, or whatever. Once you make the decision, you can

then construct the list, and, with a list in front of you, you will probably see patterns that you were not fully conscious of earlier.

On the other hand, don't be unduly concerned if something does not seem to fit into a list or cluster. You can return to it, and give it more thought—maybe it will come to fit later. But you might also realize that this point needs to be placed to the side. As far as you can tell, it doesn't appear to belong in one of your lists or to link well to other points you have begun to make, and in this way you may come to realize that it is not relevant to your development of possible topics for your essay.

Developing an Awareness of the Writer's Use of Language

In the first line of the story, Chopin notes that "Mrs. Mallard was afflicted with a heart trouble." You might want to look up "afflicted" in your dictionary. Why do you think that Chopin chose this word, as opposed to other words she might have chosen? How would the effect of the opening line be different if, for example, Chopin had written "Mrs. Mallard had a heart problem" or "Mrs. Mallard's heart was weak"?

Earlier we recommended that you keep a dictionary at hand when you read. It will help you, especially if you get into the habit of asking questions about the writer's choice of language. And this brings us to our next point.

Asking Questions

If you feel stuck, ask yourself questions. We suggest questions for fiction on pages 177–180, for poetry on pages 822–823, and for drama on pages 1544–1546. If, for instance, you are thinking about a work of fiction, you might ask yourself questions about the plot and the characters—are they believable, are they interesting, and what does it all add up to? What does the story mean *to you?* One student found it helpful to jot down the following questions:

```
Plot
    Ending false? unconvincing? or prepared for?
Character?
    Mrs. M. unfeeling? Immoral?
    Mrs. M. unbelievable character?
        What might her marriage have been like? Many
            gaps. (Can we tell what her husband was like?)
            "And yet she loved him--sometimes." Fickle?
            Realistic?
    What is "this thing that was approaching to
        possess her"?
Symbolism
    Set on spring day = symbolic of new life?
```

But, again, you don't have to be as tidy as this student was. You can begin by jotting down notes and queries about what you like or dislike and about what puzzles or amuses you. Here are the jottings of another student. They are, obviously, in no particular order—the student is brainstorming, putting down whatever occurs to her—though it is equally obvious that one note sometimes led to the next:

```
Title nothing special. What might be better title?
Could a woman who loved her husband be so heartless?
Is she heartless? Did she love him?
What are (were) Louise's feelings about her husband?
Did she want too much? What did she want?
Could this story happen today? Feminist interpretation?
Sister (Josephine)--a busybody?
Tricky ending--but maybe it could be true
"And yet she loved him--sometimes. Often she had not."
Why does one love someone "sometimes"?
Irony: plot has reversal. Are characters ironic too?
```

These jottings will help the reader-writer to think about the story, to find a special point of interest and to develop a thoughtful argument about it.

Keeping a Journal

A journal is not a diary, a record of what the writer did each day ("today I read Chopin's 'Hour'"); rather, a journal is a place to store some of the thoughts that you may have inscribed on a scrap of paper or in the margin of the text—for instance, your initial response to the title of a work or to the ending. It's also a place to jot down some further reflections. These reflections may include thoughts about what the work means to you or what was said in the classroom about writing in general or about specific works. You may, for instance, want to reflect on why your opinion is so different from that of another student, or you may want to apply a concept such as "character" or "irony" or "plausibility" to a story that later you may write an essay about.

You might even make an entry in the form of a letter to the author or in the form of a letter from one character to another. Similarly, you might write a dialogue between characters in two works or between two authors, or you might record an experience of your own that is comparable to something in the work.

A student who wrote about "The Story of an Hour" began with the following entry in his journal. In reading this entry, notice that one idea stimulates another. The student was, quite rightly, concerned with getting and exploring ideas, not with writing a unified paragraph.

```
Apparently a "well-made" story, but seems clever
rather than moving or real. Doesn't seem plausible.
Mrs. M's change comes out of the blue--maybe some
women might respond like this, but probably not most.
    Does literature deal with unusual people, or with
usual (typical?) people? Shouldn't it deal with
typical? Maybe not. (Anyway, how can I know?) Is
```

```
"typical" same as "plausible"? Come to think of it,
prob. not.
       Anyway, whether Mrs. M. is typical or not, is her
change plausible, believable?
       Why did she change? Her husband dominated her
life and controlled her action; he did "impose a pri-
vate will upon a fellow creature." She calls this a
crime. Why? Why not?
```

Arguing a Thesis

Having raised some questions, a reader goes back to the story, hoping to read it now with increased awareness. Some of the jottings will be dead ends, but some will lead to further ideas that can be arranged in lists. What the **thesis** of the essay will be—the idea that will be asserted and supported—is still in doubt, but there is no doubt about one thing: A good essay will have a thesis, a point, an argument. You ought to be able to state your point in a **thesis sentence.**

Consider these candidates as possible thesis sentences, as assertions that can be supported in an argument:

```
1. Mrs. Mallard dies soon after hearing that her hus-
   band had died.
```

True, but scarcely a point that can be argued, or even developed. About the most the essayist can do with this sentence is to amplify it by summarizing the plot of the story, a task not worth doing. An analysis may include a sentence or two of summary, to give readers their bearings, but a summary is not an essay.

```
2. The story is a libel on women.
```

In contrast to the first statement, this one can be developed into an argument. Probably the writer will try to demonstrate that Mrs. Mallard's behavior is despicable. Whether this point can be convincingly argued is another matter; the thesis may be untenable, but it is a thesis. A second problem, however, is this: Even if the writer demonstrates that Mrs. Mallard's behavior is despicable, he or she will have to go on to demonstrate that the presentation of one despicable woman constitutes a libel on women in general. That's a pretty big order.

```
3. The story is clever but superficial because it is
   based on an unreal character.
```

Here, too, is a thesis, a point of view that can be argued. Whether or not this thesis is true is another matter. The writer's job will be to support it by presenting evidence. Probably the writer will have no difficulty in finding evidence that the story is "clever"; the difficulty probably will be in establishing a case that the characterization of Mrs. Mallard is "unreal." The writer will have to set forth some ideas about what makes a character real and then will have to show that Mrs. Mallard is an "unreal" (unbelievable) figure.

4. The irony of the ending is believable partly because it is consistent with earlier ironies in the story.

It happens that the student who wrote the essay printed on page 40 began by drafting an essay based on the third of these thesis topics, but as she worked on a draft she found that she couldn't support her assertion that the character was unconvincing. In fact, she came to believe that although Mrs. Mallard's joy was the reverse of what a reader might expect, several early reversals in the story helped to make Mrs. Mallard's shift from grief to joy acceptable.

WRITING A DRAFT

After jotting down notes and then adding more notes stimulated by rereading and further thinking, you'll probably be able to formulate a tentative thesis. At this point most writers find it useful to clear the air by glancing over their preliminary notes and by jotting down the thesis and a few especially promising notes—brief statements of what they think their key points may be. These notes may include some brief key quotations that the writer thinks will help to support the thesis.

Here are the notes (not the original brainstorming notes, but a later selection from them, with additions) and a draft (following) that makes use of them. The final version of the essay—the product produced by the process—is given on page 40.

```
title: Ironies in an Hour (?) An Hour of Irony (?)
    Kate Chopin's Irony (?)

thesis: irony at the end is prepared for by earlier
    ironies

chief irony: Mrs. M. dies just as she is beginning to
    enjoy life

smaller ironies: 1. "sad message" brings her joy
                 2. Richards is "too late" at end
                 3. Richards is too early at start
```

Sample Draft of an Essay on Kate Chopin's "The Story of an Hour"

Now for the student's draft—not the first version, but a revised draft with some of the irrelevancies of the first draft omitted and some evidence added.

The digits within the parentheses refer to the page numbers from which the quotations are drawn, though with so short a work as "The Story of an Hour," page references are hardly necessary. Unless instructed otherwise, always provide page numbers for your quotations. This will enable your readers to quickly locate the passages to which you refer. (Detailed information about how to document a paper is given on pages 1776–1788.)

Crowe 1

Lynn Crowe
Professor O'Brian
English 102
1 November 2005

Ironies in an Hour

After we know how the story turns out, if we reread it we find irony at the very start, as is true of many other stories. Mrs. Mallard's friends assume, mistakenly, that Mrs. Mallard was deeply in love with her husband, Brently Mallard. They take great care to tell her gently of his death. The friends mean well, and in fact they do well. They bring her an hour of life, an hour of freedom. They think their news is sad. Mrs. Mallard at first expresses grief when she hears the news, but soon she finds joy in it. So Richards's "sad message" (28), though sad in Richards's eyes, is in fact a happy message.

Among the ironic details is the statement that when Mallard entered the house, Richards tried to conceal him from Mrs. Mallard, but "Richards was too late" (29). This is ironic because earlier Richards "hastened" (28) to bring his sad message; if he had at the start been "too late" (29), Brently Mallard would have arrived at home first, and Mrs. Mallard's life would not have ended an hour later but would simply have gone on as it had before. Yet another irony at the end of the story is the diagnosis of the doctors. The doctors say she died of "heart disease--of joy that kills" (29). In one sense the doctors are right: Mrs. Mallard has experienced a great joy. But of course the doctors totally misunderstood the joy that kills her.

The central irony resides not in the well-intentioned but ironic actions of Richards, nor

Crowe 2

in the unconsciously ironic words of the
doctors, but in her own life. In a way she has
been dead. She "sometimes" (29) loved her
husband, but in a way she has been dead. Now,
his apparent death brings her new life. This new
life comes to her at the season of the year when
"the tops of trees . . . were all aquiver with
the new spring life" (28). But, ironically, her
new life will last only an hour. She looks
forward to "summer days" (29) but she will not
see even the end of this spring day. Her years
of marriage were ironic. They brought her a sort
of living death instead of joy. Her new life is
ironic too. It grows out of her moment of grief
for her supposedly dead husband, and her vision
of a new life is cut short.

[New page]

Crowe 3

Work Cited

Chopin, Kate. "The Story of an Hour." An
    Introduction to Literature. Ed. Sylvan Barnet
    et al. 14th ed. New York: Longman, 2006.
    28-29.

Revising a Draft

The draft, although thoughtful and clear, is not yet a finished essay. The student
went on to improve it in many small but important ways.

First, the draft needs a good introductory paragraph, a paragraph that will
let readers know where the writer will be taking them. Doubtless you know
from your own experience as a reader that readers can follow an argument more
easily—and with more pleasure—if early in the discussion the writer alerts them

to the gist of the argument. (The title, too, can strongly suggest the thesis.) Second, some of the paragraphs could be clearer.

In revising paragraphs—or, for that matter, in revising an entire draft—writers unify, organize, clarify, and polish. Let's look at the nouns implicit in these verbs.

1. **Unity** is achieved partly by eliminating irrelevancies. Notice that in the final version, printed on pages 40–41, the writer has deleted "as is true of many other stories" from the first sentence of the draft.
2. **Organization** is largely a matter of arranging material into a sequence that will assist the reader to grasp the point.
3. **Clarity** is achieved largely by providing concrete details and quotations to support generalizations and by providing helpful transitions ("for instance," "furthermore," "on the other hand," "however").
4. **Polish** is small-scale revision. For instance, one deletes unnecessary repetitions. In the second paragraph of the draft, the phrase "the doctors" appears three times, but it appears only once in the final version of the paragraph. Similarly, in polishing, a writer combines choppy sentences into longer sentences, and breaks overly long sentences into shorter sentences.

Later, after producing a draft that seems close to a finished essay, writers engage in yet another activity.

5. **Editing** concerns such things as checking the accuracy of quotations by comparing them with the original, checking a dictionary for the spelling of doubtful words, checking a handbook for doubtful punctuation—for instance, whether a comma or a semicolon is needed in a particular sentence.

Peer Review

Your instructor may encourage (or even require) you to discuss your draft with another student or with a small group of students. That is, you may be asked to get a review from your peers. Such a procedure is helpful in several ways. First, it gives the writer a real audience, readers who can point to what pleases or puzzles them, who make suggestions, who may often disagree (with the writer or with each other), and who frequently, though not intentionally, *misread.* Though writers don't necessarily like everything they hear (they seldom hear "This is perfect. Don't change a word!"), reading and discussing their work with others almost always gives them a fresh perspective on their work, and a fresh perspective may stimulate thoughtful revision. (Having your intentions *misread* because your writing isn't clear enough can be particularly stimulating.)

The writer whose work is being reviewed is not the sole beneficiary. When students regularly serve as readers for each other, they become better readers of their own work and consequently better revisers.

When you produce a draft of your paper for peer review, it will not be in final form; the draft is an important step toward shaping the paper and bringing it to final form. But aim to do the best job possible on your draft; let your classmates respond to the best work you can do at this stage of the process.

```
QUESTIONS FOR PEER REVIEW                    ENGLISH 125A
Read each draft once, quickly. Then read it again,
with the following questions in mind.
1. What is the essay's topic? Is it one of the as-
   signed topics, or a variation from it? Does the
   draft show promise of fulfilling the assignment?
2. Looking at the essay as a whole, what thesis
   (main idea) is stated or implied? If implied, try
   to state it in your own words.
3. Is the thesis plausible? How might the argument
   be strengthened?
4. Looking at each paragraph separately:
     a. What is the basic point? (If it isn't clear to
        you, ask for clarification.)
     b. How does the paragraph relate to the essay's
        main idea or to the previous paragraph?
     c. Should some paragraphs be deleted? Be divided
        into two or more paragraphs? Be combined?
        Be put elsewhere? (If you outline the
        essay by jotting down the gist of each para-
        graph, you will get help in answering these
        questions.)
     d. Is each sentence clearly related to the sen-
        tence that precedes and to the sentence that
        follows?
     e. Is each paragraph adequately developed?
     f. Are there sufficient details, perhaps brief
        supporting quotations from the text?
5. What are the paper's chief strengths?
6. Make at least two specific suggestions that you
   think will assist the author to improve the paper.
```

You will have more work to do on this paper—you know that. But you don't want your classmates to be pointing out mistakes that you know are in the draft and that you could have fixed yourself.

If peer review is a part of the writing process in your course, the instructor may distribute a sheet with some suggestions and questions. An example of such a sheet is shown here.

THE FINAL VERSION

Here is the final version of the student's essay. The essay that was submitted to her instructor had been retyped, but here, so that you can easily see how the draft has been revised, we print the draft with the final changes written in by hand.

Crowe 1

Lynn Crowe

Professor O'Brian

English 102

1 November 2005

~~Ironies in an Hour~~ *Ironies of Life in Kate Chopin's "The Story of an Hour"*

Despite its title, Kate Chopin's "The Story of an Hour" ironically takes only a few minutes to read. In addition, the story turns out to have an ironic ending, but on rereading it one sees that the irony is not concentrated only in the outcome of the plot—Mrs. Mallard dies just when she is beginning to live—but is also present in many details.

After we know how the story turns out, if we reread it we find irony at the very start. /~~as is true of many other stories~~. *Because* ∧Mrs. Mallard's friends ∧ *and her sister* assume, mistakenly, that ~~Mrs. Mallard~~ *she* was deeply in love with her husband, Brently Mallard. *They* They take great care to tell her gently of his death. ~~The friends~~ *They* mean well, and in fact they do well. ∧ ~~They~~ bring *ing* ∧ her an hour of life, an hour of ∧ *joyous* freedom. ∧ *but it is ironic that* They think their news is sad. ∧ *True,* Mrs. Mallard at first expresses grief when she hears the news, but soon ∧ *(unknown to her friends)* she finds joy in it. So Richards's "sad message" (28), though sad in Richards's eyes, is in fact a happy message.

Among the ∧ *small but significant* ironic details is the statement ∧ *near the end of the story* that when Mallard entered the house, Richards tried to conceal him from Mrs. Mallard, but "Richards was too late" (29). This is ironic because ∧ ~~earlier~~ *almost at the start of the story, in the second paragraph,* Richards "hastened" (28) to bring his sad message; if he had at the start been "too late" (29), Brently Mallard would have arrived at home first, and Mrs. Mallard's

life would not have ended an hour later but would
simply have gone on as it had before. Yet another
irony at the end of the story is the diagnosis of the
doctors. ~~The doctors~~ They say she died of "heart disease--
of joy that kills" (29). In one sense ~~the doctors~~ they are
right: Mrs. Mallard for the last hour experienced a great joy. But of
course the doctors totally misunderstand the joy that
kills her. It is not joy at seeing her husband alive, but her realization
that the great joy she experienced during the last hour is over.

All of these ironic details add richness to the story, but
The central irony resides not in the well-
intentioned but ironic actions of Richards, nor in the
unconsciously ironic words of the doctors, but in ~~her~~ Mrs. Mallard's
own life. ~~In a way she has been dead.~~ She "sometimes"
(29) loved her husband, but in a way she has been
dead, a body subjected to her husband's will. Now, his apparent death brings her new life.
This new life comes to her at the season of the year
when "the tops of trees . . . were all aquiver with
the new spring life" (28). But, ironically, her new
life will last only an hour. She is "free, free, free"—but only until her husband walks through
She looks forward to the doorway.
"summer days" (29) but she will not see even the end
of this spring day. If Her years of marriage were
ironic, ~~They brought~~ bringing her a sort of living death
instead of joy, Her new life is ironic too, not only because It grows
out of her moment of grief for her supposedly dead
husband, but also because her vision of "a long progression of years"
and her vision of a new life is cut short
within an hour on a spring day.

[New page]

Work Cited

Chopin, Kate. "The Story of an Hour." <u>An Introduction</u>
<u>to Literature</u>. Ed. Sylvan Barnet et al. 14th ed.
New York: Longman, 2006. 28-29.

A Brief Overview of the Final Version

Finally, as a quick review, let's look at several principles illustrated by this essay.

1. The **title of the essay** is not merely the title of the work discussed; rather, it gives the readers a clue, a small idea of the essayist's topic.
2. The **opening** or **introductory paragraph** does not begin by saying "In this story . . . ." Rather, by naming the author and the title, it lets the reader know exactly what story is being discussed. It also develops the writer's thesis so readers know where they will be going.
3. The **organization** is effective. The smaller ironies are discussed in the second and third paragraphs, the central (chief) irony in the last paragraph. That is, the essay does not dwindle or become anticlimactic; rather, it builds up from the least important to the most important point.
4. Some **brief quotations** are used, both to provide evidence and to let the reader hear—even if only fleetingly—Kate Chopin's writing.
5. The essay is chiefly devoted to **analysis** (how the parts relate to each other), not to summary (a brief restatement of the happenings). The writer, properly assuming that the reader has read the work, does not tell the plot in great detail. But, aware that the reader has not memorized the story, the writer gives helpful reminders.
6. The **present tense** is used in narrating the action: "Mrs. Mallard dies"; "Mrs. Mallard's friends and her sister assume."
7. Although a **concluding paragraph** is often useful—if it does more than merely summarize what has already been clearly said—it is not essential in a short analysis. In this essay, the last sentence explains the chief irony and therefore makes an acceptable ending.

EXPLICATION

A line-by-line commentary on what is going on in a text is an explication (literally, unfolding, or spreading out). Although your explication will for the most part move steadily from the beginning to the end of the selection, try to avoid writing along these lines (or, one might say, along this one line): "In line one. . . . In the second line. . . . In the third line. . . ." That is, don't hesitate to write such things as

> The poem begins. . . . In the next line. . . . The
> speaker immediately adds. . . . He then introduces. . . .
> The next stanza begins by saying. . . .

And of course you can discuss the second line before the first if that seems the best way of handling the passage.

An explication is not concerned with the writer's life or times, and it is not a paraphrase (a rewording)—though it may include paraphrase if a passage in the original seems unclear, perhaps because of an unusual word or an unfamiliar expression. On the whole, however, an explication goes beyond paraphrase, seeking to make explicit what the reader perceives as implicit in the work. To this end it calls attention, as it proceeds, to the implications of words (for instance, to their tone), the function of rhymes (for instance, how they may connect ideas, as in "throne" and "alone"), the development of contrasts, and any other contributions to the meaning.

Obviously you will have ideas about the merit and the meaning of a poem, and your paper will implicitly have a *thesis*—an argument, for instance this poem is very difficult, or this poem begins effectively but quickly goes downhill, or this poem is excessively sentimental. Your essay, however, is largely devoted not to making assertions of this sort but to explaining how the details make the meaning.

A good way to stimulate responses to the poem is to ask some of the questions given on pages 822–823.

Many students find that by copying the poem (by hand, or on a computer) they gain an understanding of the uses of language in a literary work. *Don't* photocopy the poem; the act of writing or typing it will help you to get into the piece, word by word, comma by comma. Double-space, so that you have ample room for annotations.

If you use a word processing program, you can highlight key words, lines, stanzas. You can also rearrange lines and stanzas, and perhaps substitute different words for the words that the poet has selected. Some students like to make multiple printouts for contrast and comparison—the poem as the poet wrote it, the poem as the student has marked it up by using the highlighting feature of the computer program, the poem as it stands after the student has somewhat rearranged it.

A computer cannot interpret a poem or story for you. But you can employ it as a tool to deepen your own sense of how a poem is structured—why this or that word or image is crucial at this juncture, why this or that stanza or passage belongs here and could not be placed elsewhere, and so on. Your goal is to gain insight into how writers of literary texts use their artistic medium, and often a computer can be a good complement to the dictionary that you always keep nearby.

A Sample Explication

Read this short poem (published in 1917) by the Irish poet William Butler Yeats (1865–1939). The "balloon" in the poem is a dirigible, a blimp.

WILLIAM BUTLER YEATS

The Balloon of the Mind   [1917]

Hands, do what you're bid:
Bring the balloon of the mind
That bellies and drags in the wind
Into its narrow shed.

A student began thinking about the poem by copying it, double-spaced. Then she jotted down her first thoughts.

sounds abrupt

Hands, do what you're bid:

(B)ring the (b)alloon of the mind

That (b)ellies and drags in the wind

Into its narrow shed.

—balloon imagined by the mind? Or a mind like a balloon?

no real rhymes?

line seems to drag— it's so long!

Later she wrote some notes in a journal.

I'm still puzzled about the meaning of the words, "The balloon of the mind." Does "balloon of the mind" mean a balloon that belongs to the mind, sort of like "a disease of the heart"? If so, it means a balloon that the mind has, a balloon that the mind possesses, I guess by imagining it. Or does it mean that the mind is like a balloon, as when you say "he's a pig of a man," meaning he is like a pig, he is a pig? Can it mean both? What's a balloon that the mind imagines? Something like dreams of fame, wealth? Castles in Spain.

Is Yeats saying that the "hands" have to work hard to make dreams a reality? Maybe. But maybe the idea really is that the mind is like a balloon--hard to keep under control, floating around. Very hard to keep the mind on the job. If the mind is like a balloon, it's hard to get it into the hangar (shed).

"Bellies." Is there such a verb? In this poem it seems to mean something like "puffs out" or "flops around in the wind." Just checked The American Heritage Dictionary, and it says "belly" can be a verb, "to swell out," "to bulge." Well, you learn something every day.

A later entry:

OK; I think the poem is about a writer trying to keep his balloon-like mind from floating around, trying to keep the mind under control, trying to keep it working at the job of writing something, maybe writing something with the "clarity, unity, and coherence" I keep hearing about in this course.

Here is the student's final version of the explication.

Yeats's "Balloon of the Mind" is about writing poetry, specifically about the difficulty of getting one's floating thoughts down in lines on the page. The first line, a short, stern, heavily stressed command to the speaker's hands, perhaps implies by its severe or impatient tone that these hands will be disobedient or inept or careless if not watched closely: the poor bumbling body so often fails to achieve the goals of the mind. The bluntness of the command in the first line is emphasized by the fact that all the subsequent lines have more syllables. Furthermore, the first line is a grammatically complete sentence, whereas the thought of line 2 spills over into the next lines, implying the difficulty of fitting ideas into confining spaces, that is, of getting one's thoughts into order, especially into a coherent poem.

Lines 2 and 3 amplify the metaphor already stated in the title (the product of the mind is an airy but unwieldy balloon), and they also contain a second command, "Bring." Alliteration ties this command, "Bring," to the earlier "bid"; it also ties both of these verbs to their object, "balloon," and to the verb that most effectively describes the balloon, "bellies." In comparison with the abrupt first line of the poem, lines 2 and 3 themselves seem almost swollen, bellying and dragging, an effect aided by using adjacent unstressed syllables ("of the," "[bell]ies and," "in the") and by using an eye rhyme ("mind" and "wind") rather than an exact rhyme. And then comes the short last line: almost before we could expect it, the cumbersome balloon--here, the idea that is to be packed into the stanza--is successfully lodged in its "narrow shed."

Aside from the relatively colorless "into," the only words of more than one syllable in the poem are "balloon," "bellies," and "narrow," and all three emphasize the difficulty of the task. But after "narrow"--the word itself almost looks long and

narrow, in this context like a hangar--we get the
simplicity of the monosyllable "shed." The difficult
job is done, the thought is safely packed away, the
poem is completed--but again with an off rhyme ("bid"
and "shed"), for neatness can go only so far when
hands and mind and a balloon are involved.

Note: The reader of an explication needs to see the text, and because the explicated text is usually short, it is advisable to quote it all. (Remember, your imagined audience probably consists of your classmates; even if they have already read the work you are explicating, they have not memorized it, and so you helpfully remind them of the work by quoting it.) You can quote the entire text at the outset, or you can quote the first unit (for example, a stanza), then explicate that unit, and then quote the next unit, and so on. And if the poem or passage of prose is longer than, say, six lines, it is advisable to number every fifth line at the right for easy reference, or every fourth line if the poem is written in four-line stanzas.

EXPLICATION AS ARGUMENT

An explication unfolds or interprets a work; it is partly an exposition but it is also an *argument,* offering assertions that are supported by *reasons.* Re-read the explication of "The Balloon of the Mind," and notice that the first sentence makes a claim—the poem is "about" such-and-such—and notice, too, that the subsequent assertions are supported by evidence. For instance, when the writer says that lines 2 and 3 seem to drag, she goes on to support the claim by calling attention to "adjacent unstressed syllables." She does not merely assert; she argues.

COMPARISON AND CONTRAST: A WAY OF ARGUING

Something should be said about an essay organized around a comparison or a contrast, say, of the settings in two short stories, of two characters in a novel, or of the symbolism in two poems. (A comparison emphasizes resemblances whereas a contrast emphasizes differences, but we can use the word "comparison" to cover both kinds of writing.) Probably the student's first thought, after making some jottings, is to discuss one-half of the comparison and then go on to the second half. Instructors and textbooks (though not this one) usually condemn such an organization, arguing that the essay breaks into two parts and that the second part involves a good deal of repetition of categories set up in the first part. Usually they recommend that students organize their thoughts differently, making point-by-point comparisons. For example, in comparing *Huckleberry Finn* with *The Catcher in the Rye,* you might organize the material like this:

1. First similarity: the narrator and his quest
    a. Huck
    b. Holden

2. Second similarity: the corrupt world surrounding the narrator
    a. society in *Huckleberry Finn*
    b. society in *Catcher*
3. First difference: degree to which the narrator fulfills his quest and escapes from society
    a. Huck's plan to "light out" to the frontier
    b. Holden's breakdown

Here is another way of organizing a comparison and contrast:

1. First point: the narrator and his quest
    a. similarities between Huck and Holden
    b. differences between Huck and Holden
2. Second point: the corrupt world
    a. similarities between the worlds in *Huck* and *Catcher*
    b. differences between the worlds in *Huck* and *Catcher*
3. Third point: degree of success
    a. similarities between Huck and Holden
    b. differences between Huck and Holden

But a comparison need not employ either of these structures. There is even the danger that an essay employing either of them may not come into focus until the essayist stands back from the seven-layer cake and announces, in the concluding paragraph, that the odd layers taste better. In your preparatory thinking, you may want to make comparisons in pairs, but you must come to some conclusions about what these add up to before writing the final version. This final version should not duplicate the thought processes; rather, it should be organized to make the point clearly and effectively. You are making a list; you are arguing a case.

The point of the essay presumably is not to list pairs of similarities or differences, but to illuminate a work or works by making thoughtful comparisons. Although in a long essay the writer cannot postpone until page 30 a discussion of the second half of the comparison, in an essay of, say, fewer than ten pages nothing is wrong with setting forth one-half of the comparison and then, in light of it, the second half. The essay will break into two unrelated parts if the second half makes no use of the first or if it fails to modify the first half, but not if the second half looks back to the first half and calls attention to differences that the new material reveals. Learning how to write an essay with interwoven comparisons is worthwhile, but be aware that there is another, simpler and clearer way to write a comparison.

REVIEW: HOW TO WRITE AN EFFECTIVE ESSAY

Everyone must work out his or her own writing procedures and rituals (Hemingway liked to sharpen pencils; Robert Frost liked to do farm work before writing). The following suggestions may provide some help.

1. **Read the work carefully.**
2. **Choose a worthwhile and compassable subject,** something that interests you and is not so big that your handling of it must be superficial. As

you work, shape and narrow your topic—for example, from "The Character of Hester Prynne" to "The Effects of Alienation on Hester Prynne."

3. **Reread the work, jotting down notes** of all relevant matters. As you
   read, reflect on your reading and record your reflections. If you have a feeling or an idea, jot it down; don't assume that you will remember it when
   you get around to writing your essay. The margins of the book are a good
   place for initial jottings, but many people find that in the long run it is
   easiest to transfer these notes to 3×5 cards, writing on one side only, or to
   a file in a word processor.

4. **Sort out your cards into some kind of reasonable divisions,** and reject
   cards irrelevant to your topic. If you are writing an explication, the order
   probably is essentially the order of the lines or of the episodes, but if you are
   writing an analysis you almost surely will want to rearrange your notes. If you
   took notes on a word processor, print them and—well, here the authors of
   this text differ. One author recommends that you make jottings on the print-
   out ("put this with X," "put this at the end of file; probably not useful") so
   that you can, by block movements, rearrange the sequence in your file and
   thus have something fairly well organized to scan and think about on-screen.
   Another author, aiming for the same end result, recommends that you scissor
   the jottings apart, reorganize them just as you would reorganize index cards,
   and then, after much fiddling, rearrange the sequence in your file.

   Whichever method you use, get the notes into order. For instance, you
   may wish to organize your essay from the lesser material to the greater (to
   avoid anticlimax) or from the simple to the complex (to ensure intelligibil-
   ity). If, for instance, you are discussing the roles of three characters in a
   story, it may be best to build up to the one of the three that you think the
   most important. If you are comparing two characters it may be best to
   move from the most obvious contrasts to the least obvious. When you
   have arranged your notes into a meaningful sequence of packets, you have
   approximately divided your material into paragraphs, though of course
   two or three notes may be combined into one paragraph, or one packed
   note may turn into two or more paragraphs.

5. **Get it down on paper.** Most essayists find it useful to jot down some sort
   of outline, indicating the main idea of each paragraph and, under each
   main idea, supporting details that give it substance. An outline—not necessarily anything highly formal with capital and lowercase letters and roman
   and arabic numerals, but merely key phrases in some sort of order—will
   help you to overcome the paralysis called "writer's block" that commonly
   afflicts professionals as well as students. A page of paper with ideas in some
   sort of sequence, however rough, ought to encourage you to realize that
   you do have something to say. And so, despite the temptation to sharpen
   another pencil or put a new ribbon into the printer or check your e-mail,
   the best thing to do at this point is to sit down and start writing.

   If you don't feel that you can work from note cards and a rough outline,
   try another method: get something down on paper (or on a disk) by writing
   freely, sloppily, automatically, or whatever, but allowing your ideas about
   what the work means to you and how it conveys its meaning—rough as your
   ideas may be—to begin to take visible form. If you are like most people, you
   can't do much precise thinking until you have committed to paper at least a
   rough sketch of your initial ideas. Later you can push and polish your ideas
   into shape, perhaps even deleting all of them and starting over, but it's a lot
   easier to improve your ideas once you see them in front of you than it is to

do the job in your head. On paper or on the screen of a word processor one word leads to another; in your head one word often blocks another.

Just keep going; you may realize, as you near the end of a sentence, that you no longer believe it. OK, be glad that your first idea led you to a better one, and pick up your better one and keep going with it. What you are doing is, in a sense, by trial and error pushing your way not only toward clear expression but also toward sharper ideas and richer responses.

6. If there is time, **reread the work,** looking for additional material that strengthens or weakens your main point; take account of it in your outline or draft.

7. **By now your thesis (your argument) should be clear to you,** and you ought to be able to give your essay an informative title—*not* simply the title of the story, poem, or play, but something that lets your reader know where you will be going.

   With a thesis and title clearly in mind, improve your draft, checking your notes for fuller details, such as supporting quotations. If, as you work, you find that some of the points in your earlier jottings are no longer relevant, eliminate them, but make sure that the argument flows from one point to the next. As you write, your ideas will doubtless become clearer; some may prove to be poor ideas. (We rarely know exactly what our ideas are until we have them set down on paper. As the little girl said, replying to the suggestion that she should think before she spoke, "How do I know what I think until I say it?") Not until you have written a draft do you really have a strong sense of what your ideas are and how good your essay may be.

8. After a suitable interval, preferably a few days, **read the draft with a view toward revising it,** not with a view toward congratulating yourself. A revision, after all, is a re-vision, a second (and presumably sharper) view. When you revise, you will be in the company of Picasso, who said that in painting he advanced by a series of destructions. A revision—say, the substitution of a precise word for an imprecise one—is not a matter of prettifying but of thinking. As you read, correct things that disturb you (for example, awkward repetitions that bore, inflated utterances that grate), add supporting detail where the argument is undeveloped (a paragraph of only one or two sentences is usually an undeveloped paragraph), and ruthlessly delete irrelevancies however well written they may be. But remember that a deletion probably requires some adjustment in the preceding and subsequent material.

   Make sure that the argument, aided by **transitions,** runs smoothly. The **details** should be relevant, the organization reasonable, the argument clear. **Check all quotations** for accuracy. Quotations are evidence, usually intended to support your assertions, and it is not nice to alter the evidence, even unintentionally. If there is time (there almost never is), put the revision aside, reread it in a day or two, and revise it again, especially with a view toward deleting wordiness and, on the other hand, supporting generalizations with evidence.

9. **Type, write, or print a clean copy,** following the principles concerning margins, pagination, footnotes, and so on set forth on pages 1764–1765. If you have borrowed any ideas, be sure to give credit, usually in footnotes, to your sources. Remember that plagiarism is not limited to the unacknowledged borrowing of words; a borrowed idea, even when put into your own words, requires acknowledgment.

10. **Proofread and make corrections** as explained on pages 1765–1766. Remember that writing is a form of self-representation. Fairly or unfairly, readers will make judgments about you based on how you present yourself to them in your writing. With this in mind, proofread your work carefully, making sure that there are no misspellings, misquotations, and the like. The trick, of course, is not to feel so good about the paper that you find yourself skimming and congratulating yourself on your ideas, rather than reading word by word, with an eye for small errors.

ADDITIONAL READINGS

KATE CHOPIN

For a biographical sketch, see page 28.

Ripe Figs

[1893]

Maman-Nainaine said that when the figs were ripe Babette might go to visit her cousins down on the Bayou-Lafourche where the sugar cane grows. Not that the ripening of figs had the least thing to do with it, but that is the way Maman-Nainaine was.

It seemed to Babette a very long time to wait; for the leaves upon the trees were tender yet, and the figs were like little hard, green marbles.

But warm rains came along and plenty of strong sunshine, and though Maman-Nainaine was as patient as the statue of la Madone, and Babette as restless as a humming-bird, the first thing they both knew it was hot summertime. Every day Babette danced out to where the fig-trees were in a long line against the fence. She walked slowly beneath them, carefully peering between the gnarled, spreading branches. But each time she came disconsolate away again. What she saw there finally was something that made her sing and dance the whole long day.

When Maman-Nainaine sat down in her stately way to breakfast, the following morning, her muslin cap standing like an aureole about her white, placid face, Babette approached. She bore a dainty porcelain platter, which she set down before her godmother. It contained a dozen purple figs, fringed around with their rich, green leaves.

"Ah," said Maman-Nainaine arching her eyebrows, "how early the figs have ripened this year!"

"Oh," said Babette. "I think they have ripened very late."

"Babette," continued Maman-Nainaine, as she peeled the very plumpest figs with her pointed silver fruit-knife, "you will carry my love to them all down on Bayou-Lafourche. And tell your Tante Frosine I shall look for her at Toussaint—when the chrysanthemums are in bloom."

▨ TOPICS FOR CRITICAL THINKING AND WRITING

1. Compare and contrast Maman-Nainaine and Babette.
2. Two questions here: What, if anything, "happens" in "Ripe Figs"? And what, in your opinion, is the story about?

3. What, if anything, would be lost if the last line were omitted? (If you can think of a better final line, write it, and explain why your version is preferable.)

WILLIAM STAFFORD

William Stafford (1914–1993) was born in Hutchinson, Kansas, and was educated at the University of Kansas and the State University of Iowa. A conscientious objector during World War II, he worked for the Brethren Service and the Church World Service. After the war he taught at several universities and then settled at Lewis and Clark College in Portland, Oregon. In addition to writing several books of poems, Stafford wrote Down in My Heart *(1947), an account of his experiences as a conscientious objector.*

Traveling Through the Dark   [1960]

Traveling through the dark I found a deer
dead on the edge of the Wilson River road.
It is usually best to roll them into the canyon:
the road is narrow; to swerve might make more dead.   4

By glow of the tail-light I stumbled back of the car
and stood by the heap, a doe, a recent killing;
she had stiffened already, almost cold.
I dragged her off; she was large in the belly.   8

My fingers touching her side brought me the reason—
her side was warm; her fawn lay there waiting,
alive, still, never to be born.
Beside that mountain road I hesitated.   12

The car aimed ahead its lowered parking lights;
under the hood purred the steady engine.
I stood in the glare of the warm exhaust turning red;
around our group I could hear the wilderness listen.   16

I thought hard for us all—my only swerving—
Then pushed her over the edge into the river.

TOPICS FOR CRITICAL THINKING AND WRITING

1. Look at the first sentence (the first two lines) and try to recall what your impression of the speaker was, based only on these two lines, or pretend that you have not read the entire poem, and characterize him merely on these two lines. Then take the entire poem into consideration and characterize him.
2. What do you make of the title? Do you think it is a good title for this poem? Explain.

LORNA DEE CERVANTES

Lorna Dee Cervantes, born in San Francisco in 1954, founded a press and a poetry magazine, Mango, *chiefly devoted to Chicano literature. In 1978 she received a fellowship from the National Endowment for the Arts, and in 1981 she published her first book of poems. "Refugee Ship," originally written in 1974, was revised for the book. We print the revised version.*

Refugee Ship   [1981]

Like wet cornstarch, I slide
past my grandmother's eyes. Bible
at her side, she removes her glasses.
The pudding thickens.

Mama raised me without language.   5
I'm orphaned from my Spanish name.
The words are foreign, stumbling
on my tongue. I see in the mirror
my reflection: bronzed skin, black hair.

I feel I am a captive   10
aboard the refugee ship.
The ship that will never dock.
El barco que nunca atraca.°

---

13 *El barco que nunca atraca* The ship that never docks.

▨ TOPICS FOR CRITICAL THINKING AND WRITING

1. What do you think the speaker means by the comparison with "wet cornstarch" in line 1? And what do you take her to mean in line 6 when she says, "I'm orphaned from my Spanish name"?
2. Judging from the poem as a whole, why does the speaker feel she is "a captive / aboard the refugee ship"? How would you characterize such feelings?
3. In an earlier version of the poem, instead of "my grandmother's eyes" Cervantes wrote "*mi abuelita's* eyes"; that is, she used the Spanish words for "my grandmother." In line 5 instead of "Mama" she wrote "*mamá*" (again, the Spanish equivalent), and in line 9 she wrote "brown skin" instead of "bronzed skin." The final line of her original version was not in Spanish but in English, a repetition of the preceding line, which ran thus: "A ship that will never dock." How does each of these changes strike you?

JOSÉ ARMAS

Born in 1944, José Armas has been a teacher (at the University of New Mexico and at the University of Albuquerque), publisher, critic, and community organizer. His interest in community affairs won him a fellowship, which in 1974–1975 brought him into association with the Urban Planning Department at the Massachusetts Institute of Technology. In 1980 he was awarded a writing fellowship by the National Endowment for the Arts, and he now writes a column on Hispanic affairs for De Colores.

El Tonto del Barrio[1]

Romeo Estrado was called "El Cotorro"[2] because he was always whistling and singing. He made nice music even though his songs were spontaneous compositions made up of words with sounds that he liked but which seldom made any sense. But that didn't seem to bother either Romero or anyone else in the Golden Heights Centro where he lived. Not even the kids made fun of him. It just was not permitted.

Romero had a ritual that he followed almost every day. After breakfast he would get his broom and go up and down the main street of the Golden Heights Centro whistling and singing and sweeping the sidewalks for all the businesses. He would sweep in front of the Tortillería America,[3] the XXX Liquor Store, the Tres Milpas[4] Bar run by Tino Gabaldon, Barelas' Barber Shop, the used furniture store owned by Goldstein, El Centro Market of the Avila family, the Model Cities Office, and Lourdes Printing Store. Then, in the afternoons, he would come back and sit in Barelas' Barber Shop and spend the day looking at magazines and watching and waving to the passing people as he sang and composed his songs without a care in the world.

When business was slow, Barelas would let him sit in the barber's chair. Romero loved it. It was a routine that Romero kept every day except Sundays and Mondays when Barelas' Barber Shop was closed. After a period of years, people in the barrio got used to seeing Romero do his little task of sweeping the sidewalks and sitting in Barelas' Barber Shop. If he didn't show up one day someone assumed the responsibility to go to his house to see if he was ill. People would stop to say hello to Romero on the street and although he never initiated a conversation while he was sober, he always smiled and responded cheerfully to everyone. People passing the barber shop in the afternoons made it a point to wave even though they couldn't see him; they knew he was in there and was expecting some salutation.

When he was feeling real good, Romero would sweep in front of the houses on both sides of the block also. He took his job seriously and took great care to sweep cleanly, between the cracks and even between the sides of buildings. The dirt and small scraps went into the gutter. The bottles and

[1]**El Tonto del Barrio** the barrio dummy (in the United States, a *barrio* is a Spanish-speaking community). All notes are by the editors. [2]**El Cotorro** The Parrot. [3]**Tortillería America** America Tortilla Factory. [4]**Tres Milpas** Three Cornfields.

bigger pieces of litter were put carefully in cardboard boxes, ready for the garbage man.

5   If he did it the way he wanted, the work took him the whole morning. And always cheerful—always with some song.

Only once did someone call attention to his work. Frank Avila told him in jest that Romero had forgotten to pick up an empty bottle of wine from his door. Romero was so offended and made such a commotion that it got around very quickly that no one should criticize his work. There was, in fact, no reason to.

Although it had been long acknowledged that Romero was a little "touched," he fit very well into the community. He was a respected citizen.

He could be found at the Tres Milpas Bar drinking his occasional beer in the evenings. Romero had a rivalry going with the Ranchera songs on the jukebox. He would try to outsing the songs using the same melody but inserting his own selection of random words. Sometimes, like all people, he would "bust out" and get drunk.

One could always tell when Romero was getting drunk because he would begin telling everyone that he loved them.

10   "I looov youuu," he would sing to someone and offer to compose them a song.

"Ta bueno, Romero. Ta bueno, ya bete,"[5] they would tell him.

Sometimes when he got too drunk he would crap in his pants and then Tino would make him go home.

Romero received some money from Social Security but it wasn't much. None of the merchants gave him any credit because he would always forget to pay his bills. He didn't do it on purpose, he just forgot and spent his money on something else. So instead, the businessmen preferred to do little things for him occasionally. Barelas would trim his hair when things were slow. The Tortillería America would give him menudo[6] and fresh-made tortillas at noon when he was finished with his sweeping. El Centro Market would give him the overripe fruit and broken boxes of food that no one else would buy. Although it was unspoken and unwritten, there was an agreement that existed between Romero and the Golden Heights Centro. Romero kept the sidewalks clean and the barrio looked after him. It was a contract that worked well for a long time.

Then, when Seferino, Barelas' oldest son, graduated from high school he went to work in the barber shop for the summer. Seferino was a conscientious and sensitive young man and it wasn't long before he took notice of Romero and came to feel sorry for him.

15   One day when Romero was in the shop Seferino decided to act.

"Mira, Romero. Yo te doy 50 centavos por cada día que me barres la banqueta. Fifty cents for every day you sweep the sidewalk for us. Qué te parece?"[7]

Romero thought about it carefully.

"Hecho! Done!" he exclaimed. He started for home right away to get his broom.

"Why did you do that for, m'ijo?"[8] asked Barelas.

---

[5]**Ta bueno, ya bete** OK, now go away. [6]**menudo** tripe soup. [7]**Qué te parece?** How does that strike you? [8]**m'ijo** (mi hijo) my son.

20   "It don't seem right, Dad. The man works and no one pays him for his work. Everyone should get paid for what they do."

"He don't need no pay. Romero has everything he needs."

"It's not the same, Dad. How would you like to do what he does and be treated the same way? It's degrading the way he has to go around getting scraps and handouts."

"I'm not Romero. Besides you don't know about these things, m'ijo. Romero would be unhappy if his schedule was upset. Right now everyone likes him and takes care of him. He sweeps the sidewalks because he wants something to do, not because he wants money."

"I'll pay him out of my money, don't worry about it then."

25   "The money is not the point. The point is that money will not help Romero. Don't you understand that?"

"Look, Dad. Just put yourself in his place. Would you do it? Would you cut hair for nothing?"

Barelas just knew his son was putting something over on him but he didn't know how to answer. It seemed to make sense the way Seferino explained it. But it still went against his "instinct." On the other hand, Seferino had gone and finished high school. He must know something. There were few kids who had finished high school in the barrio, and fewer who had gone to college. Barelas knew them all. He noted (with some pride) that Seferino was going to be enrolled at Harvard University this year. That must count for something, he thought. Barelas himself had never gone to school. So maybe his son had something there. On the other hand . . . it upset Barelas that he wasn't able to get Seferino to see the issue. How can we be so far apart on something so simple, he thought. But he decided not to say anything else about it.

Romero came back right away and swept the front of Barelas' shop again and put what little dirt he found into the curb. He swept up the gutter, put the trash in a shoe box and threw it in a garbage can.

Seferino watched with pride as Romero went about his job and when he was finished he went outside and shook Romero's hand. Seferino told him he had done a good job. Romero beamed.

30   Manolo was coming into the shop to get his hair cut as Seferino was giving Romero his wages. He noticed Romero with his broom.

"What's going on?" He asked. Barelas shrugged his shoulders. "Qué tiene Romero?[9] Is he sick or something?"

"No, he's not sick," explained Seferino, who had now come inside. He told Manolo the story.

"We're going to make Romero a businessman," said Seferino. "Do you realize how much money Romero would make if everyone paid him just fifty cents a day? Like my dad says, 'Everyone should be able to keep his dignity, no matter how poor.' And he does a job, you know."

"Well, it makes sense," said Manolo.

35   "Hey, Maybe I'll ask people to do that," said Seferino. "That way the poor old man could make a decent wage. Do you want to help, Manolo? You can go with me to ask people to pay him."

"Well," said Manolo as he glanced at Barelas, "I'm not too good at asking people for money."

---

[9]**Qué tiene Romero?** What's with Romero?

This did not discourage Seferino. He went out and contacted all the businesses on his own, but no one else wanted to contribute. This didn't discourage Seferino either. He went on giving Romero fifty cents a day.

After a while, Seferino heard that Romero had asked for credit at the grocery store. "See, Dad. What did I tell you? Things are getting better for him already. He's becoming his own man. And look. It's only been a couple of weeks." Barelas did not reply.

But then the next week Romero did not show up to sweep any sidewalks. He was around but he didn't do any work for anybody the entire week. He walked around Golden Heights Centro in his best gray work pants and his slouch hat, looking important and making it a point to walk right past the barber shop every little while.

40   Of course, the people in the Golden Heights Centro noticed the change immediately, and since they saw Romero in the street, they knew he wasn't ill. But the change was clearly disturbing the community. They discussed him in the Tortillería America where people got together for coffee, and at the Tres Milpas Bar. Everywhere the topic of conversation was the great change that had come over Romero. Only Barelas did not talk about it.

The following week Romero came into the barber shop and asked to talk with Seferino in private. Barelas knew immediately something was wrong. Romero never initiated a conversation unless he was drunk.

They went into the back room where Barelas could not hear and then Romero informed Seferino, "I want a raise."

"What? What do you mean, a raise? You haven't been around for a week. You only worked a few weeks and now you want a raise?" Seferino was clearly angry but Romero was calm and insistent.

Romero correctly pointed out that he had been sweeping the sidewalks for a long time. Even before Seferino finished high school.

45   "I deserve a raise," he repeated after an eloquent presentation.

Seferino looked coldly at Romero. It was clearly a stand-off.

Then Seferino said, "Look, maybe we should forget the whole thing. I was just trying to help you out and look at what you do."

Romero held his ground. "I helped you out too. No one told me to do it and I did it anyway. I helped you many years."

"Well, let's forget about the whole thing then," said Seferino.

50   "I quit then," said Romero.

"Quit?" exclaimed Seferino as he laughed at Romero.

"Quit! I quit!" said Romero as he walked out the front of the shop past Barelas, who was cutting a customer's hair.

Seferino came out shaking his head and laughing.

"Can you imagine that old guy?"

55   Barelas did not seem too amused. He felt he could have predicted that something bad like this would happen.

Romero began sweeping the sidewalks again the next day with the exception that when he came to the barber shop he would go around it and continue sweeping the rest of the sidewalks. He did this for the rest of the week. And the following Tuesday he began sweeping the sidewalk all the way up to the shop and then pushing the trash to the sidewalk in front of the barber shop. Romero then stopped coming to the barber shop in the afternoon.

The barrio buzzed with fact and rumor about Romero. Tino commented that Romero was not singing anymore. Even if someone offered to buy him a beer he wouldn't sing. Frank Avila said the neighbors were complaining because he was leaving his TV on loud the whole day and night. He still greeted people but seldom smiled. He had run up a big bill at the liquor store and when the manager stopped his credit, he caught Romero stealing bottles of whiskey. He was also getting careless about his dress. He didn't shave and clean like he used to. Women complained that he walked around in soiled pants, that he smelled bad. Even one of the little kids complained that Romero had kicked his puppy, but that seemed hard to believe.

Barelas felt terrible. He felt responsible. But he couldn't convince Seferino that what he had done was wrong. Barelas himself stopped going to the Tres Milpas Bar after work to avoid hearing about Romero. Once he came across Romero on the street and Barelas said hello but with a sense of guilt. Romero responded, avoiding Barelas' eyes and moving past him awkwardly and quickly. Romero's behavior continued to get erratic and some people started talking about having Romero committed.

"You can't do that," said Barelas when he was presented with a petition.

60   "He's flipped," said Tino, who made up part of the delegation circulating the petition. "No one likes Romero more than I do, you know that Barelas."

"But he's really crazy," said Frank Avila.

"He was crazy before. No one noticed," pleaded Barelas.

"But it was a crazy we could depend on. Now he just wants to sit on the curb and pull up the women's skirts. It's terrible. The women are going crazy. He's also running into the street stopping the traffic. You see how he is. What choice do we have?"

"It's for his own good," put in one of the workers from the Model Cities Office. Barelas dismissed them as outsiders. Seferino was there and wanted to say something but a look from Barelas stopped him.

65   "We just can't do that," insisted Barelas. "Let's wait. Maybe he's just going through a cycle. Look. We've had a full moon recently, qué no?[10] That must be it. You know how the moon affects people in his condition."

"I don't know," said Tino. "What if he hurts. . . ."

"He's not going to hurt anyone," cut in Barelas.

"No, Barelas. I was going to say, what if he hurts himself. He has no one at home. I'd say, let him come home with me for a while but you know how stubborn he is. You can't even talk to him any more."

"He gives everyone the finger when they try to pull him out of the traffic," said Frank Avila. "The cops have missed him, but it won't be long before they see him doing some of his antics and arrest him. Then what? Then the poor guy is in real trouble."

70   "Well, look," said Barelas. "How many names you got on the list?"

Tino responded slowly, "Well, we sort of wanted you to start off the list."

"Let's wait a while longer," said Barelas. "I just know that Romero will come around. Let's wait just a while, okay?"

No one had the heart to fight the issue and so they postponed the petition.

---

[10]**qué no?** right?

There was no dramatic change in Romero even though the full moon had completed its cycle. Still, no one initiated the petition again and then in the middle of August Seferino left for Cambridge to look for housing and to register early for school. Suddenly everything began to change again. One day Romero began sweeping the entire sidewalk again. His spirits began to pick up and his strange antics began to disappear.

75   At the Tortillería America the original committee met for coffee and the talk turned to Romero.

"He's going to be all right now," said a jubilant Barelas. "I guarantee it."

"Well, don't hold your breath yet," said Tino. "The full moon is coming up again."

"Yeah," said Frank Avila dejectedly.

When the next full moon was in force the group was together again drinking coffee and Tino asked, "Well, how's Romero doing?"

80   Barelas smiled and said, "Well. Singing songs like crazy."

▓ TOPICS FOR CRITICAL THINKING AND WRITING

1. What sort of man do you think Barelas is? In your response take account of the fact that the townspeople "sort of want" Barelas "to start off the list" of petitioners seeking to commit Romero.
2. The narrator, introducing the reader to Seferino, tells us that "Seferino was a conscientious and sensitive young man." Do you agree? Why, or why not?
3. What do you make of the last line of the story?
4. Do you think this story could take place in almost any community? If you did not grow up in a barrio, could it take place in your community?

II

Fiction

Gish Jen, born Lillian Jen in 1956, is the daughter of Chinese immigrants. She graduated from Harvard University with a major in English, studied briefly at the business school at Stanford University, and then decided to become a writer. One of the first things she did as a writer was take a pen name, Gish, derived from the name of the silent screen star Lillian Gish. But to be a writer one must do more than adopt a pen name; one must have the desire to write, and the ability to write, and one must write. Gish Jen has the desire and the ability and she put them to work. One of her stories was selected by John Updike to be included in *Best American Short Stories of the Century,* a collection that includes work by Hemingway, Faulkner, and Flannery O'Connor.

Jen writes, not surprisingly, about the experiences of Chinese-Americans, but she also writes about the experiences of others—for instance, Irish-Americans and Jewish-Americans. As she put it in an interview,

> Of course, I'm interested in the Asian-American experience. But I'm also interested in architecture; I'm interested in religion. I'm very interested in the different realities, not just in my own ethnic group. . . . One of the greatest challenges, as a writer, that I set for myself [is] to see that through effort and imagination, you could penetrate another people's experience.

In another interview, when asked if her work is autobiographical, she said:

> It is and it isn't. A fellow writer described my situation when he said that making fiction is like making soup. There's lots of different ingredients: Some of the ingredients come from your life, some come from things you've read, or from other people's lives; many, many things you've just made up.

Gish Jen's comment about the origins of a story can be connected to Lady Murasaki's statement about a writer's motivation, made more than a thousand years ago:

> Again and again something in one's own life or in that around one will seem so important that one cannot bear to let it pass into oblivion. There must never come a time, the writer feels, when people do not know about this.

All good writers draw on the life around them as well as on their own inner lives, and all good writers develop a distinctive style and vision. No one else can write a good Jen story, just as no one else can write a good Chekhov story, or Chopin story, or Faulkner story, or Flannery O'Connor story. The writers whom we value, the writers whose work we want to read and reread, draw on the worlds around them, telling us of their responses to highly local conditions (one of Jen's novels concerns a Chinese who wants to convert to Judaism). Yet these writers make their readers value what might be thought to be remote experiences. We care about their reports of their worlds, and they help us to see our own worlds (and especially ourselves) freshly.

3

Approaching Fiction:
Responding in Writing

The next four chapters will look at specific elements, one by one, in fiction—
plot, character, symbolism, and so on—but first let's read a brief story by Ernest
Hemingway and then talk about it (and see how one student talked about it)
with little or no technical language.

ERNEST HEMINGWAY

*Ernest Hemingway (1899-1961) was born in Oak Park,
Illinois. After graduating from high school in 1917 he
worked on the Kansas City Star, but left to serve as a
volunteer ambulance driver in Italy, where he was
wounded in action. He returned home, married, and
then served as European correspondent for the Toronto
Star, but he soon gave up journalism for fiction. In 1922
he settled in Paris, where he moved in a circle of American expatriates that included Ezra Pound, Gertrude
Stein, and F. Scott Fitzgerald. It was in Paris that he wrote
stories and novels about what Gertrude Stein called a
"lost generation" of rootless Americans in Europe. (For Hemingway's reminiscences of the Paris years, see his posthumously published* A Moveable Feast.*)
He served as a journalist during the Spanish Civil War and during the Second
World War, but he was also something of a private soldier.*

*After the Second World War his reputation sank, though he was still active
as a writer (for instance, he wrote* The Old Man and the Sea *in 1952). In 1954
Hemingway was awarded the Nobel Prize in Literature, but in 1961, depressed
by a sense of failing power, he took his own life.*

Cat in the Rain
[1925]

There were only two Americans stopping at the hotel. They did not know
any of the people they passed on the stairs on their way to and from their
room. Their room was on the second floor facing the sea. It also faced the
public garden and the war monument. There were big palms and green

benches in the public garden. In the good weather there was always an artist with his easel. Artists liked the way the palms grew and the bright colors of the hotels facing the gardens and the sea. Italians came from a long way off to look up at the war monument. It was made of bronze and glistened in the rain. It was raining. The rain dripped from the palm trees. Water stood in pools on the gravel paths. The sea broke in a long line in the rain and slipped back down the beach to come up and break again in a long line in the rain. The motor cars were gone from the square by the war monument. Across the square in the doorway of the café a waiter stood looking out at the empty square.

The American wife stood at the window looking out. Outside right under their window a cat was crouched under one of the dripping green tables. The cat was trying to make herself so compact that she would not be dripped on.

"I'm going down and get that kitty," the American wife said.

"I'll do it," her husband offered from the bed.

5   "No, I'll get it. The poor kitty out trying to keep dry under a table."

The husband went on reading, lying propped up with the two pillows at the foot of the bed.

"Don't get wet," he said.

The wife went downstairs and the hotel owner stood up and bowed to her as she passed the office. His desk was at the far end of the office. He was an old man and very tall.

"Il piove,"[1] the wife said. She liked the hotel-keeper.

10   "Si, si, Signora, brutto tempo. It is very bad weather."

He stood behind his desk in the far end of the dim room. The wife liked him. She liked the deadly serious way he received any complaints. She liked his dignity. She liked the way he wanted to serve her. She liked the way he felt about being a hotel-keeper. She liked his old, heavy face and big hands.

Liking him she opened the door and looked out. It was raining harder. A man in a rubber cape was crossing the empty square to the café. The cat would be around to the right. Perhaps she could go along under the eaves. As she stood in the doorway an umbrella opened behind her. It was the maid who looked after their room.

"You must not get wet," she smiled, speaking Italian. Of course, the hotel-keeper had sent her.

With the maid holding the umbrella over her, she walked along the gravel path until she was under their window. The table was there, washed bright green in the rain, but the cat was gone. She was suddenly disappointed. The maid looked up at her.

15   "Ha perduto qualque coas, Signora?[2]

"There was a cat," said the American girl.

"A cat?"

"Si, il gatto."

"A cat?" the maid laughed. "A cat in the rain?"

20   "Yes," she said, "under the table." Then. "Oh, I wanted it so much. I wanted a kitty."

When she talked English the maid's face tightened.

---

[1]**Il piove** It's raining (Italian).   [2]**Ha . . . Signora** Have you lost something, Madam?

"Come, Signora," she said. "We must get back inside. You will be wet."

"I suppose so," said the American girl.

They went back along the gravel path and passed in the door. The maid stayed outside to close the umbrella. As the American girl passed the office, the padrone bowed from his desk. Something felt very small and tight inside the girl. The padrone made her feel very small and at the same time really important. She had a momentary feeling of being of supreme importance. She went on up the stairs. She opened the door of the room. George was on the bed, reading.

25   "Did you get the cat?" he asked, putting the book down.

"It was gone."

"Wonder where it went to," he said, resting his eyes from reading.

She sat down on the bed.

"I wanted it so much," she said. "I don't know why I wanted it so much. I wanted that poor kitty. It isn't any fun to be a poor kitty out in the rain."

30   George was reading again.

She went over and sat in front of the mirror of the dressing table looking at herself with the hand glass. She studied her profile, first one side and then the other. Then she studied the back of her head and her neck.

"Don't you think it would be a good idea if I let my hair grow out?" she asked, looking at her profile again.

George looked up and saw the back of her neck, clipped close like a boy's.

"I like it the way it is."

35   "I get so tired of it," she said. "I get so tired of looking like a boy."

George shifted his position in the bed. He hadn't looked away from her since she started to speak.

"You look pretty darn nice," he said.

She laid the mirror down on the dresser and went over to the window and looked out. It was getting dark.

"I want to pull my hair back tight and smooth and make a big knot at the back that I can feel," she said. "I want to have a kitty to sit on my lap and purr when I stroke her."

40   "Yeah?" George said from the bed.

"And I want to eat at a table with my own silver and I want candles. And I want it to be spring and I want to brush my hair out in front of a mirror and I want a kitty and I want some new clothes."

"Oh, shut up and get something to read," George said. He was reading again.

His wife was looking out of the window. It was quite dark now and still raining in the palm trees.

"Anyway, I want a cat," she said, "I want a cat. I want a cat now. If I can't have long hair or any fun, I can have a cat."

45   George was not listening. He was reading his book. His wife looked out of the window where the light had come on in the square.

Someone knocked at the door.

"Avanti,"[3] George said. He looked up from his book.

---

[3]**Avanti** Come in.

In the doorway stood the maid. She held a big tortoise-shell cat pressed tight against her and swung down against her body.

"Excuse me," she said, "the padrone asked me to bring this for the Signora."

RESPONSES: ANNOTATIONS AND JOURNAL ENTRIES

When you read a story—or, perhaps more accurately, when you reread a story before discussing it or writing about it—you'll find it helpful to jot an occasional note (for instance, a brief response or a question) in the margins and to underline or highlight passages that strike you as especially interesting. Here is part of the story, with a student's annotations.

The cat was trying to make herself so compact that she would not be dripped on.

"I'm going down and get that kitty," the American wife said.

"I'll do it," her husband offered from the bed. — *He doesn't make a move*

"No, I'll get it. The poor kitty out trying to keep dry under a table."

The husband went on reading, lying propped up with the two pillows at the foot of the bed. — *still doesn't move!*

"Don't get wet," he said. ← *Is he making a joke? Or maybe he just isn't even thinking about what he is saying?*

contrast with the husband — The wife went downstairs and the hotel owner stood up and bowed to her as she passed the office. His desk was at the far end of the office. He was an old man and very tall.

"Il piove," the wife said. She liked the hotel-keeper.

"Si, si, Signora, brutto tempo. It is very bad weather."

He stood behind his desk in the far end of the dim room. The wife liked him. She liked the deadly serious way he received any complaints. She liked his dignity. *She respects him and she is pleased by the attention he shows* She liked the way he wanted to serve her. She liked the way he felt about being a hotel-keeper. She liked his old, heavy face and big hands.

to emphasize the bad weather?? Liking him she opened the door and looked out. It was raining harder. A man in a rubber cape was crossing the empty square to the café. The cat would be around to the right.

Everything in a story presumably is important, but having read the story once, probably something has especially interested (or puzzled) you, such as the relationship between two people, or the way the end of the story is connected to the beginning. On rereading, then, pen in hand, you'll find yourself noticing things that you missed or didn't find especially significant on your first reading. Now that you know the end of the story, you will read the beginning in a different way.

And of course if your instructor asks you to think about certain questions, you'll keep these in mind while you reread, and you will find ideas coming to you. In "Cat in the Rain," suppose you are asked (or you ask yourself) if the story might just as well be about a dog in the rain. Would anything be lost?

Here are a few questions that you can ask of almost any story. After scanning the questions, you will want to reread the story, pen in hand, and then jot down your responses on a sheet of paper. As you write, doubtless you will go back and reread the story or at least parts of it.

1. *What happens?* In two or three sentences—say 25-50 words—summarize the gist of what happens in the story.
2. *What sorts of people are the chief characters?* In "Cat in the Rain" the chief characters are George, George's wife, and the innkeeper (the padrone). Jot down the traits that each seems to possess, and next to each trait briefly give some supporting evidence.
3. *What especially pleased or displeased you in the story?* Devote at least a sentence or two to the end of the story. Do you find the end satisfying? Why or why not? What evidence can you offer to support an argument with someone whose response differs from yours?
4. *Have you any thoughts about the title?* If so, what are they? If the story did not have a title, what would you call it?

After you have made your own jottings, compare them with these responses by a student. No two readers will respond in exactly the same way, but all readers can examine their responses and try to account for them, at least in part. If your responses are substantially different, how do you account for the differences?

1. A summary. A young wife, stopping with her husband
    at an Italian hotel, from her room sees a cat in the
    rain. She goes to get it, but it is gone, and so she
    returns empty-handed. A moment later the maid knocks
    at the door, holding a tortoise-shell cat.
2. The characters: The woman.
    kind-hearted (pities cat in rain)
    appreciates innkeeper's courtesy ("liked the way
       he wanted to serve her") and admires him ("She
       liked his dignity")
    unhappy (wants a cat, wants to change her hair,
       wants to eat at a table with her own silver)
    The husband, George.
    not willing to put himself out (says he'll go to
       garden to get cat but doesn't move)
    doesn't seem very interested in wife (hardly talks
       to her--he's reading; tells her to "shut up")
    but he does say he finds her attractive ("You look
       pretty darn nice")

The innkeeper.

serious, dignified ("She liked the deadly serious
 way he received any complaints. She liked his
 dignity")
courteous, helpful (sends maid with umbrella; at
 end sends maid with cat)

3. Dislikes and likes. "Dislikes" is too strong, but
 I was disappointed that more didn't happen at the
 end. What is the husband's reaction to the cat? Or
 his final reaction to his wife? I mean, what did he
 think about his wife when the maid brings the cat?
 And, for that matter, what is the wife's reaction?
 Is she satisfied? Or does she realize that the cat
 can't really make her happy? Now for the likes.
 (1) I guess I did like the way it turned out; it's
 sort of a happy ending, I think, since she wants
 the cat and gets it. (2) I also especially like
 the innkeeper. Maybe I like him partly because the
 wife likes him, and if she likes him he must be
 nice. And he is nice--very helpful. And I also
 like the way Hemingway shows the husband. I don't
 mean that I like the man himself, but I like the
 way Hemingway shows he is such a bastard--not getting off the bed to get the cat, telling his wife
 to shut up and read.

 Another thing about him is that the one time he
 says something nice about her, it's about her
 hair, and she isn't keen on the way her hair is.
 She says it makes her look "like a boy," and she
 is "tired" of looking like a boy. There's something wrong with this marriage. George hardly pays
 attention to his wife, but he wants her to look
 like a boy. Maybe the idea is that this macho guy
 wants to keep her looking like an inferior (immature) version of himself. Anyway, he certainly
 doesn't seem interested in letting her fulfill herself as a woman.

 I think my feelings add up to this: I like the
 way Hemingway shows us the relation between the
 husband and wife (even though the relation is

pretty bad), and I like the innkeeper. Even if the relation with the couple ends unhappily, the story has a sort of happy ending, so far as it goes, since the innkeeper does what he can to please his guest: he sends the maid, with the cat. There's really nothing more that he can do.

   More about the ending. The more I think about it, the more I feel that the ending is as happy as it can be. George is awful. When his wife says "I want a cat and I want a cat now," Hemingway tells us "George was not listening." And then, a moment later, almost like a good fairy the maid appears and grants the wife's wish.

4. The title. I don't suppose that I would have called it "Cat in the Rain," but I don't know what I would have called it. Maybe "An American Couple in Italy." Or maybe "The Innkeeper." I really do think that the innkeeper is very important, even though he only has a few lines. He's very impressive--not only to the girl, but to me (and maybe to all read-ers), since at the end of the story we see how car-ing the innkeeper is.

   But the more I think about Hemingway's title, the more I think that maybe it also refers to the girl. Like the "poor kitty" in the rain, the wife is in a pretty bad situation. "It isn't any fun to be a poor kitty out in the rain." Of course, the woman is indoors, but her husband generates lots of unpleasant weather. She may as well be out in the rain. She says "I want to have a kitty to sit on my lap and purr when I stroke her." This shows that she wants to be af-fectionate and that she also wants to have some-one respond to her affection. She is like a cat in the rain.

   Oh, I just noticed that the wife at first calls the cat "her" rather than "it." ("The cat was try-ing to make herself compact. . . .") Later she says "it," but at first she thinks of the cat as female--because (I think) she identifies with the cat.

The responses of this student probably include statements that you want to take issue with. Or perhaps you feel that the student did not even mention some things that you think are important. You may want to jot down some notes and raise some questions in class.

A SAMPLE ESSAY BY A STUDENT

The responses that we have quoted were written by Bill Yanagi, who later wrote an essay developing one of them. Here is the essay.

Yanagi 1

Bill Yanagi
Professor Lange
English 10B
20 October 2005

Hemingway's American Wife

My title alludes not to any of the four women to whom Hemingway was married, but to "the American wife" who is twice called by this term in his short story, "Cat in the Rain." We first meet her in the first sentence of the story ("There were only two Americans stopping at the hotel"), and the next time she is mentioned (apart from a reference to the wife and her husband as "they") it is as "the American wife," at the beginning of the second paragraph of the story. The term is used again at the end of the third paragraph.

She is, then, at least in the early part of this story, just an American or an American wife--someone identified only by her nationality and her marital status, but not at all by her personality, her individuality, her inner self. She first becomes something of an individual when she separates herself from her husband by leaving the hotel room and going to look for a cat that she has seen in the garden, in the rain. This act of separation, however, has not the slightest effect on her husband, who "went on reading" (62).

When she returns, without the cat, he puts down his book and speaks to her, but it is obvious that he has no interest in her, beyond as a physical object ("You look pretty darn nice"). This comment is produced when she says she is thinking of letting her hair grow out, because she is "so tired of looking like a boy" (63). Why, a reader wonders, does her husband, who has paid almost no attention to her up to now, assure her that she looks "pretty darn nice"? I think it is reasonable to conclude that he <u>wants</u> her to look like someone who is not truly a woman, in particular someone who is immature. That she does not feel she has much identity is evident when she continues to talk about letting her hair grow, and she says "I want to pull my hair back tight and smooth and make a big knot at the back that I can feel" (63). Long hair is, or at least was, the traditional sign of a woman; she wants long hair, and at the same time she wants to keep it under her control by tying it in a "big knot," a knot that she can feel, a knot whose presence reminds her, because she can feel it, of her feminine nature.

She goes on to say that she wants to brush her hair "in front of a mirror." That is, she wants to <u>see</u> and to feel her femininity, since her husband apparently--so far as we can see in the story, at least--scarcely recognizes it or her. Perhaps her desire for the cat ("I want a cat") is a veiled way of saying that she wants to express her animal nature, and not be simply a neglected woman who is made by her husband to

Yanagi 3

look like a boy. Hemingway tells us, however, that when she looked for the cat in the garden she could not find it, a sign, I think, of her failure to break from the man. At the end of the story the maid brings her the cat, but a woman cannot just be handed a new nature and accept it, just like that. She has to find it herself, and in herself, so I think the story ends with "the American wife" still nothing more than an American wife.

[New page]

Yanagi 4

Work Cited

Hemingway, Ernest. "Cat in the Rain." An
    Introduction to Literature. Ed. Sylvan Barnet
    et al. 14th ed. New York: Longman, 2006.
    61-64.

A few comments and questions may be useful.

- Do you find the essay interesting? Explain your response.
- Do you find the essay well written? Explain.
- Do you find the essay convincing? Can you suggest ways of strengthening it, or do you think its argument is mistaken? Carefully reread "Cat in the Rain," taking note of passages that give further support to this student's argument, or that seem to challenge or qualify it.
- We often say that a good critical essay sends us back to the literary work with a fresh point of view. Our rereading differs from our earlier reading. Does this essay change your reading of Hemingway's story?

▨ TOPICS FOR CRITICAL THINKING AND WRITING

1. Can we be certain that the cat at the end of the story is the cat that the woman saw in the rain? (When we first hear about the cat in the rain we

are not told anything about its color, and at end of the story we are not told that the tortoiseshell cat is wet.) Does it matter if there are two cats?

2. One student argued that the cat represents the child that the girl wants to have. Do you think there is something to this idea? How might you support or refute it?

3. Consider the following passage:

> As the American girl passed the office, the padrone bowed from his desk. Something felt very small and tight inside the girl. The padrone made her feel very small and at the same time really important. She had a momentary feeling of being of supreme importance.

Do you think there is anything sexual here? And if so, that the passage tells us something about her relations with her husband? Support your view.

4. What do you suppose Hemingway's attitude was toward each of the three chief characters? How might you support your hunch?

5. Hemingway wrote the story in Italy, when his wife Hadley was pregnant. In a letter to F. Scott Fitzgerald he said,

> Cat in the Rain wasn't about Hadley. . . . When I wrote that we were at Rapallo but Hadley was 4 months pregnant with Bumby. The Inn Keeper was the one at Cortina D'Ampezzo. . . . Hadley never made a speech in her life about wanting a baby because she had been told various things by her doctor and I'd—no use going into all that. (*Letters*, p. 180)

According to some biographers, the story shows that Hemingway knew his marriage was going on the rocks (Hemingway and Hadley divorced). Does knowing that Hemingway's marriage turned out unhappily help you to understand the story? Does it make the story more interesting? And do you think that the story tells a biographer something about Hemingway's life?

6. It is sometimes said that a good short story does two things at once: It provides a believable picture of the surface of life, and it also illuminates some moral or psychological complexity that we feel is part of the essence of human life. This dual claim may not be true, but for the moment accept it. Do you think that Hemingway's story fulfills either or both of these specifications? Support your view.

Later chapters will offer some technical vocabulary and will examine specific elements of fiction, but familiarity with technical vocabulary will not itself ensure that you will understand and enjoy fiction. There is no substitute for reading carefully, thinking about your responses, and (pen in hand) rereading the text, looking for evidence that accounts for your responses or that will lead you to different and perhaps richer responses. The essays that you will submit to your instructor are, finally, rooted in the annotations that you make in your text and the notes in which you record and explore your responses.

4

Stories and Meanings: Plot, Character, Theme

People tell stories for many reasons, including the sheer delight of talking, but probably most of the best storytelling proceeds from one of two more commendable desires: a desire to entertain or a desire to instruct. Among the most famous of the stories designed to instruct are the parables that Jesus told, including The Parable of the Prodigal Son, which we discussed in Chapter 1. (*Parable* comes from the Greek word meaning to "throw beside"—that is, "to compare." We are to compare these little stories with our own behavior.) We can say that the parable is told for the sake of the point; we also can say that it is told for our sake, because we are implicitly invited to see ourselves in the story, and to live our lives in accordance with it. This simple but powerful story, with its memorable characters—though nameless and briefly sketched—makes us feel the point in our hearts.

Even older than Jesus' parables are the **fables** attributed to Aesop, some of which go back to the seventh century before Jesus. These stories also teach lessons by recounting brief incidents from which homely morals may easily be drawn, even though the stories are utterly fanciful. Among famous examples are the stories of the hare and the tortoise, the boy who cried "Wolf," the ant and the grasshopper, and a good many others that stick in the mind because of the sharply contrasted characters in sharply imagined situations. The fables just mentioned take only four or five sentences apiece, but brief as they are, Aesop told some briefer ones. Here is the briefest of all, about a female fox and a lioness.

AESOP

Aesop, a semi-legendary Greek storyteller, was said to have lived in the sixth century BCE, but some of the stories he told are found in Egypt, in texts that are hundreds of years older.

The Vixen and the Lioness

A vixen sneered at a lioness because she never bore more than one cub. "Only one," the lioness replied, "but a lion."

Just that: a situation with a **conflict** (the mere confrontation of a fox and a lion brings together the ignoble and the noble) and a resolution (*something must come out of such a confrontation*). There is no setting (we are not told that "one day in June a vixen, walking down a road, met a lioness"), but none is needed here. What there is—however briefly set forth—is characterization. The fox's baseness is effectively communicated through the verb "sneered" and through her taunt, and the lioness's nobility is even more effectively communicated through the brevity and decisiveness of her reply. This reply at first seems to agree with the fox ("Only one") and then, after a suspenseful delay provided by the words "the lioness replied," the reply is tersely and powerfully completed ("but a lion"), placing the matter firmly in a new light. Granted that the story is not much of a story, still, it is finely told, and more potent—more memorable, more lively, we might even say more real, despite its talking animals—than the mere moral: "Small-minded people confuse quantity with quality."

The fable is frankly imaginative, made-up; no one believes that foxes and lions discuss their offspring, or, for that matter, that tortoises and hares engage in races. Here is another fable, this one not about animals but still quite evidently not to be taken as history.

W. SOMERSET MAUGHAM

W(illiam) Somerset Maugham (1874-1965), born in Paris but of English origin, grew up in England, where he was trained as a physician, but he never practiced medicine. Rather, he preferred to make his living as a novelist, playwright, and writer of short stories. The following story is in fact a speech uttered by a character in one of Maugham's plays, Sheppey *(1933).*

The Appointment in Samarra   [1933]

Death speaks: There was a merchant in Bagdad who sent his servant to market to buy provisions and in a little while the servant came back, white and trembling, and said, Master, just now when I was in the marketplace I was jostled by a woman in the crowd and when I turned I saw it was Death that jostled me. She looked at me and made a threatening gesture, now, lend me your horse, and I will ride away from the city and avoid my fate. I will go to Samarra and there Death will not find me. The merchant lent him his horse, and the servant mounted it, and he dug his spurs in its flanks and as fast as the horse could gallop he went. Then the merchant went down to the marketplace and he saw me standing in the crowd and he came to me and said, Why did you make a threatening gesture to my servant when you saw him this morning? That was not a threatening gesture, I said, it was only a start of surprise. I was astonished to see him in Bagdad, for I had an appointment with him tonight in Samarra.

The moral is not stated explicitly, and perhaps we might quibble a little about how we might word the moral, but the gist surely is clear: We cannot elude death; it comes to us at an appointed time. Man proposes, God disposes.

This is the sort of story that Maugham was especially fond of, the story with a decisive ending, and with relatively little interest in the personalities involved.

The emphasis is on *plot* (what happens), not on *character* (what kinds of people these are). Another sort of very short story, however, the **anecdote,** is likely to emphasize character as well as plot. An anecdote is a short narrative that is supposed to be true, such as the story of George Washington and the cherry tree. The six-year-old Washington, given a hatchet, tried it out on a cherry tree on his father's farm. When the father asked if the boy had chopped down the tree, George supposedly answered. "I cannot tell a lie; you know I cannot tell a lie. I cut it with my hatchet." In fact the story is an invention of Parson Weems, who told it in his *Life of Washington* (1800). Of course one can easily moralize an anecdote ("You should be honest, just as George Washington was"), but the emphasis in an anecdote usually is on the person involved, not the moral. (Think of numerous anecdotes that essentially show how unpretentious Abraham Lincoln was, or how witty Winston Churchill was.)

Here is a nineteenth-century Japanese anecdote of anonymous authorship. It is said to be literally true, but whether it really occurred or not is scarcely of any importance. It is the story, not the history, that counts.

Muddy Road

Two monks, Tanzan and Ekido, were once traveling together down a muddy road. A heavy rain was still falling.

Coming around a bend, they met a lovely girl in a silk kimono and sash, unable to cross the intersection.

"Come on, girl," said Tanzan at once. Lifting her in his arms, he carried her over the mud.

Ekido did not speak again until that night when they reached a lodging temple. Then he no longer could restrain himself. "We monks don't go near females," he told Tanzan, "especially not young and lovely ones. It is dangerous. Why did you do that?"

"I left the girl there," said Tanzan. "Are you still carrying her?"

A superb story: The opening paragraph, though simple and matter-of-fact, holds our attention as we sense that something interesting is going to happen during this journey along a muddy road on a rainy day. Perhaps we even sense, somehow, by virtue of the references to the mud and the rain, that the journey itself rather than the travelers' destination will be the heart of the story: getting there will be more than half the fun. And then, after the introduction of the two **characters** and the **setting,** we quickly get the **complication,** the encounter with the girl. Still there is apparently no **conflict,** though in "Ekido did not speak again until that night" we sense an unspoken conflict, an action (or, in this case, an inaction) that must be explained, an imbalance that must be righted before we are finished. At last Ekido, no longer able to contain his thoughts, lets his indignation burst out: "We monks don't go near females, especially not young and lovely ones. It is dangerous. Why did you do that?" His statement and his question reveal not only his moral principles, but also his insecurity and the anger that grows from it. And now, when the conflict is out in the open, comes the brief reply that reveals Tanzan's very different character as clearly as the outburst revealed Ekido's. This reply—though we could not have predicted it—strikes us as exactly right, bringing the story to a perfect end, that is to a point (like the ends of Jesus' parable and Aesop's fable) at which there is no more to be said. It provides the **dénouement** (literally, "unknotting"), or **resolution.**

Let's look now at another short piece, though this one is somewhat longer than the stories we have just read, and it is less concerned than they are with teaching a lesson.

ANTON CHEKHOV

Anton Chekhov (1860–1904) was born in Russia, the son of a shopkeeper. While a medical student at Moscow University, Chekhov wrote stories, sketches, and reviews to help support his family and to finance his education. In 1884 he received his medical degree, began to practice medicine, published his first book of stories, and suffered the first of a series of hemorrhages from tuberculosis. In his remaining twenty years, in addition to writing several hundred stories, he wrote plays, half a dozen of which have established themselves as classics. He died from tuberculosis at the age of forty-four.

Misery [1886]

Translated by Constance Garnett

"To Whom Shall I Tell My Grief?"

The twilight of evening. Big flakes of wet snow are whirling lazily about the street lamps, which have just been lighted, and lying in a thin soft layer on roofs, horses' backs, shoulders, caps. Iona Potapov, the sledgedriver, is all white like a ghost. He sits on the box without stirring, bent as double as the living body can be bent. If a regular snowdrift fell on him it seems as though even then he would not think it necessary to shake it off. . . . His little mare is white and motionless too. Her stillness, the angularity of her lines, and the stick-like straightness of her legs make her look like a halfpenny gingerbread horse. She is probably lost in thought. Anyone who has been torn away from the plough, from the familiar gray landscapes, and cast into this slough, full of monstrous lights, of unceasing uproar and hurrying people, is bound to think.

It is a long time since Iona and his nag have budged. They came out of the yard before dinner-time and not a single fare yet. But now the shades of evening are falling on the town. The pale light of the street lamps changes to a vivid color, and the bustle of the street grows noisier.

"Sledge to Vyborgskaya!" Iona hears. "Sledge!"

Iona starts, and through his snow-plastered eyelashes sees an officer in a military overcoat with a hood over his head.

5   "To Vyborgskaya," repeats the officer. "Are you asleep? To Vyborgskaya!"

In token of assent Iona gives a tug at the reins which sends cakes of snow flying from the horse's back and shoulders. The officer gets into the sledge. The sledge-driver clicks to the horse, cranes his neck like a swan, rises in his seat, and more from habit than necessity brandishes his whip. The mare cranes her neck, too, crooks her stick-like legs, and hesitatingly sets off. . . .

"Where are you shoving, you devil?" Iona immediately hears shouts from the dark mass shifting to and fro before him. "Where the devil are you going? Keep to the r-right!"

"You don't know how to drive! Keep to the right," says the officer angrily.

A coachman driving a carriage swears at him; a pedestrian crossing the road and brushing the horse's nose with his shoulder looks at him angrily and shakes the snow off his sleeve. Iona fidgets on the box as though he were sitting on thorns, jerks his elbows, and turns his eyes about like one possessed, as though he did not know where he was or why he was there.

10   "What rascals they all are!" says the officer jocosely. "They are simply doing their best to run up against you or fall under the horse's feet. They must be doing it on purpose."

Iona looks at his fare and moves his lips. . . . Apparently he means to say something, but nothing comes out but a sniff.

"What?" inquires the officer.

Iona gives a wry smile, and straining his throat, brings out huskily: "My son . . . , er . . . my son died this week, sir."

"H'm! What did he die of?"

15   Iona turns his whole body round to his fare, and says:

"Who can tell! It must have been from fever. . . . He lay three days in the hospital and then he died. . . . God's will."

"Turn round, you devil!" comes out of the darkness. "Have you gone cracked, you old dog? Look where you are going!"

"Drive on! drive on! . . . " says the officer. "We shan't get there till tomorrow going on like this. Hurry up!"

The sledge-driver cranes his neck again, rises in his seat, and with heavy grace swings his whip. Several times he looks round at the officer, but the latter keeps his eyes shut and is apparently disinclined to listen. Putting his fare down at Vyborgskaya, Iona stops by a restaurant, and again sits huddled up on the box. . . . Again the wet snow paints him and his horse white. One hour passes, and then another. . . .

20   Three young men, two tall and thin, one short and hunchbacked, come up, railing at each other and loudly stamping on the pavement with their galoshes.

"Cabby, to the Police Bridge!" the hunchback cries in a cracked voice. "The three of us, . . . twenty kopecks!"

Iona tugs at the reins and clicks to his horse. Twenty kopecks is not a fair price, but he has no thoughts for that. Whether it is a rouble or whether it is five kopecks does not matter to him now so long as he has a fare. . . . The three young men, shoving each other and using bad language, go up to the sledge, and all three try to sit down at once. The question remains to be settled: Which are to sit down and which one is to stand? After a long altercation, ill-temper, and abuse, they come to the conclusion that the hunchback must stand because he is the shortest.

"Well, drive on," says the hunchback in his cracked voice, settling himself and breathing down Iona's neck. "Cut along! What a cap you've got, my friend! You wouldn't find a worse one in all Petersburg. . . ."

"He-he! . . . he-he! . . . " laughs Iona. "It's nothing to boast of!"

25   "Well, then, nothing to boast of, drive on! Are you going to drive like this all the way? Eh? Shall I give you one in the neck?"

"My head aches," says one of the tall ones. "At the Dukmasovs' yesterday Vaska and I drank four bottles of brandy between us."

"I can't make out why you talk such stuff," says the other tall one angrily. "You lie like a brute."

"Strike me dead, it's the truth! . . . ."

"It's about as true as that a louse coughs."

30   "He-he!" grins Iona. "Me-er-ry gentlemen!"

"Tfoo! the devil take you!" cries the hunchback indignantly. "Will you get on, you old plague, or won't you? Is that the way to drive? Give her one with the whip. Hang it all, give it her well."

Iona feels behind his back the jolting person and quivering voice of the hunchback. He hears abuse addressed to him, he sees people, and the feeling of loneliness begins little by little to be less heavy on his heart. The hunchback swears at him, till he chokes over some elaborately whimsical string of epithets and is overpowered by his cough. His tall companions begin talking of a certain Nadyezhda Petrovna. Iona looks round at them. Waiting till there is a brief pause, he looks round once more and says:

"This week . . . er . . . my . . . er . . . son died!"

"We shall all die, . . . " says the hunchback with a sigh, wiping his lips after coughing. "Come, drive on! drive on! My friends, I simply cannot stand crawling like this! When will he get us there?"

35   "Well, you give him a little encouragement . . . one in the neck!"

"Do you hear, you old plague? I'll make you smart. If one stands on ceremony with fellows like you one may as well walk. Do you hear, you old dragon? Or don't you care a hang what we say?"

And Iona hears rather than feels a slap on the back of his neck.

"He-he! . . . " he laughs. "Merry gentlemen . . . God give you health!"

"Cabman, are you married?" asks one of the tall ones.

40   "I? He-he! Me-er-ry gentlemen. The only wife for me now is the damp earth. . . . He-ho-ho! . . . The grave that is! . . . Here my son's dead and I am alive. . . . It's a strange thing, death has come in at the wrong door. . . . Instead of coming for me it went for my son. . . ."

And Iona turns round to tell them how his son died, but at that point the hunchback gives a faint sigh and announces that, thank God! they have arrived at last. After taking his twenty kopecks, Iona gazes for a long while after the revelers, who disappear into a dark entry. Again he is alone and again there is silence for him. . . . The misery which has been for a brief space eased comes back again and tears his heart more cruelly than ever. With a look of anxiety and suffering Iona's eyes stray restlessly among the crowds moving to and fro on both sides of the street: can he not find among those thousands someone who will listen to him? But the crowds flit by heedless of him and his misery. . . . His misery is immense, beyond all bounds. If Iona's heart were to burst and his misery to flow out, it would flood the whole world, it seems, but yet it is not seen. It has found a hiding-place in such an insignificant shell that one would not have found it with a candle by daylight. . . .

Iona sees a house-porter with a parcel and makes up his mind to address him.

"What time will it be, friend?" he asks.

"Going on for ten. . . . Why have you stopped here? Drive on!"

45   Iona drives a few paces away, bends himself double, and gives himself up to his misery. He feels it is no good to appeal to people. But before five minutes have passed he draws himself up, shakes his head as though he feels a sharp pain, and tugs at the reins. . . . He can bear it no longer.

"Back to the yard!" he thinks. "To the yard!"

And his little mare, as though she knew his thoughts, falls to trotting. An hour and a half later Iona is sitting by a big dirty stove. On the stove, on the floor, and on the benches are people snoring. The air is full of smells and stuffiness. Iona looks at the sleeping figures, scratches himself, and regrets that he has come home so early. . . .

"I have not earned enough to pay for the oats, even," he thinks. "That's why I am so miserable. A man who knows how to do his work, . . . who has had enough to eat, and whose horse has had enough to eat, is always at ease. . . ."

In one of the corners a young cabman gets up, clears his throat sleepily, and makes for the waterbucket.

50   "Want a drink?" Iona asks him.

"Seems so."

"May it do you good. . . . But my son is dead, mate. . . . Do you hear? This week in the hospital. . . . It's queer business. . . ."

Iona looks to see the effect produced by his words, but he sees nothing. The young man has covered his head over and is already asleep. The old man sighs and scratches himself. . . . Just as the young man had been thirsty for water, he thirsts for speech. His son will soon have been dead a week, and he has not really talked to anybody yet. . . . He wants to talk of it properly, with deliberation. . . . He wants to tell how his son was taken ill, how he suffered, what he said before he died, how he died. . . . He wants to describe the funeral, and how he went to the hospital to get his son's clothes. He still has his daughter Anisya in the country. . . . And he wants to talk about her too. . . . Yes, he has plenty to talk about now. His listener ought to sigh and exclaim and lament. . . . It would be even better to talk to women. Though they are silly creatures, they blubber at the first word.

"Let's go out and have a look at the mare," Iona thinks. "There is always time for sleep. . . . You'll have sleep enough, no fear. . . ."

55   He puts on his coat and goes into the stables where his mare is standing. He thinks about oats, about hay, about the weather. . . . He cannot think about his son when he is alone. . . . To talk about him with someone is possible, but to think of him and picture him is insufferable anguish. . . .

"Are you munching?" Iona asks his mare, seeing her shining eyes. "There, munch away, munch away. . . . Since we have not earned enough for oats, we will eat hay. . . . Yes, . . . I have grown too old to drive. . . . My son ought to be driving, not I. . . . He was a real coachman. . . . He ought to have lived. . . ."

Iona is silent for a while, and then he goes on:

"That's how it is, old girl. . . . Kuzma Ionitch is gone. . . . He said goodby to me. . . . He went and died for no reason. . . . Now, suppose you had a little colt, and you were mother to that little colt. . . . And all at once that same little colt went and died. . . . You'd be sorry, wouldn't you? . . . "

The little mare munches, listens, and breathes on her master's hands. Iona is carried away and tells her all about it.

Let's look at Chekhov's "Misery" as a piece of craftsmanship. The happenings (here, a cabman seeks to tell his grief to several people, but is rebuffed and finally tells it to his horse) are the **plot;** the participants (cabman, officer, drunks, etc.) are the **characters;** the locale, time, and social circumstances (a snowy city in Russia, in the late nineteenth century) are the **setting;** and (though, as we will urge later, this word should be used with special caution) the meaning or point is the **theme**.

The traditional plot has this structure:

1. **Exposition** (setting forth of the initial situation)
2. **Conflict** (a complication that moves to a climax)
3. **Dénouement** (the outcome of the conflict; the resolution)

Chekhov's first paragraph, devoted to **exposition,** begins by introducing a situation that seems to be static: It briefly describes a motionless cabdriver, who "is all white like a ghost," and the cabdriver's mare, whose immobility and angularity "make her look like a halfpenny gingerbread horse." A reader probably anticipates that something will intrude into this apparently static situation; some sort of conflict will be established, and then in all probability will be (in one way or another) resolved. In fact, the inertia described at the very beginning is disturbed even before the paragraph ends, when Chekhov rather surprisingly takes us into the mind not of the cabdriver but of the horse, telling us that if we were in such a situation as the horse finds itself, we too would find it difficult not to think.

By the middle of the first paragraph, we have been given a brief but entirely adequate view of the **setting:** a Russian city in the days of horse-drawn sleighs, that is, in Chekhov's lifetime. Strictly speaking, the paragraph does not specify Russia or the period, but the author is a Russian writing in the late nineteenth century, the character has a Russian name, and there is lots of snow so one concludes that the story is set in Russia. (A reader somewhat familiar with Chekhov does not even have to read the first paragraph of this story to know the setting, since all of Chekhov's work is set in the Russia of his day.)

One might almost say that by the end of the first paragraph we have met all the chief **characters**—though we can't know this until we finish the story. In later paragraphs we will meet additional figures, but the chief characters—the characters whose fates we are concerned with—are simply the cabdriver and the horse. It's odd to call the horse a character; but as we noticed, even in the first paragraph Chekhov takes us into the mind of the horse. Notice, too, how Chekhov establishes connections between the man and the horse; for instance, when the first fare gets into the sleigh, the driver "cranes his neck" and "then the mare cranes her neck, too." By the end of the story, the horse seems almost a part of Iona. Perhaps the horse will be the best possible listener, since perhaps grief of Iona's sort can be told only to the self.

Before talking further about the characters, we should point out that the word "character" has two chief meanings:

1. A figure in a literary work (thus Iona is a character, the officer who hires the cab is another character, and the drunks are additional characters).
2. Personality, as when we say that Iona's character is described only briefly, or that Hamlet's character is complex, or that So-and-So's character is unpleasant.

Usually the context makes clear the sense in which the word is used, but in your own writing, make sure that there is no confusion.

It is sometimes said that figures in literature are either **flat characters** (one-dimensional figures, figures with simple personalities) or **round characters** (complex figures). The usual implication is that good writers give us round characters, believable figures who are more than cardboard cutouts holding up signs saying "jealous lover," "cruel landlord," "kind mother," and so forth. But a short story scarcely has space to show the complexity or roundness of several characters, and in fact, many good stories do not give even their central characters much complexity. In "Misery," for instance, Iona is shown chiefly as a grieving father aching to speak of the death of his son. We don't know what sort of food he likes, whether he ever gets drunk, what he thinks of the Czar, or whether he belongs to the church. But it is hard to imagine that knowing any of these things would be relevant and would increase our interest in him. Similarly, the other characters in the story are drawn with a few simple lines. The officer who first hires the cab is arrogant ("Sledge to Vyborgskaya! . . . Are you asleep? To Vyborgskaya!"), and though he at first makes a little joke that leads Iona to think the officer will listen to his story, the officer quickly changes the subject. We know of him only that he wants to get to Vyborg. The three noisy drunks whom Iona next picks up can be fairly characterized as just that—three noisy drunks. Again, we can hardly imagine that the story would be better if we knew much more about these drunks.

On the other hand, Iona is not quite so flat as we have perhaps implied. A careful reader notices, for instance, that Iona reveals other things about himself in addition to his need to express his grief. For instance, he treats his horse as kindly as possible. When the officer gets into the cab, Iona "more from habit than necessity brandishes his whip"—but he gets the horse moving by making a clicking sound, and he actually whips the horse only when the officer tells him to hurry. Later the hunchback will say of the mare, "Give her one with the whip. Hang it all, give it her well," but we feel that Iona uses his horse as gently as is possible.

It should be noted, however, that the drunks, though they are not much more than drunks, are not less than drunks either. They are quarrelsome and they even display touches of cruelty, but we cannot call them villains. In some degree, the fact that they are drunk excuses their "bad language," their "ill-tempers," and even their displays of cruelty. If these characters are fairly flat, they nevertheless are thoroughly believable, and we know as much about them as we need to know for the purposes of the story. Furthermore, the characters in a story help to characterize other characters, by their resemblances or their differences. How Iona might behave if he were an officer, or if he were drunk, we do not know, but he is in some degree contrasted with the other characters and thus gains some complexity, to the extent that we can at least say that he is *not* drunk, arrogant, or quarrelsome.

We need hardly ask if there is **motivation** (compelling grounds, external and also within one's personality) for Iona's final action. He has tried to express his grief to the officer, and then to the drunks. Next, his eyes search the crowds to "find someone who will listen to him." After speaking to the house-porter, Iona sees, Chekhov tells us, that "it is no good to appeal to people." When we read this line, we probably do not think, or at least do not think consciously, that he will turn from people to the mare, but when at the end of the story he does turn to the mare, the action seems entirely natural, inevitable.

In some stories, we are chiefly interested in plot (the arrangement of happenings or doings), in others we are chiefly interested in character (the personalities of the doers), but on the whole the two are so intertwined that interest in one involves interest in the other. Happenings occur (people cross paths), and personalities respond, engendering further happenings. As Henry James rhetorically asked, "What is character but the determination of incident? What is incident but the illustration of character?" Commonly, as a good story proceeds and we become increasingly familiar with the characters, we get intimations of what they may do in the future. We may not know precisely how they will act, but we have a fairly good idea, and when we see their subsequent actions, we usually recognize the appropriateness. Sometimes there are hints of what is to come, and because of this **foreshadowing,** we are not shocked by what happens later, but rather we experience suspense as we wait for the expected to come about. Coleridge had Shakespeare's use of foreshadowing in mind when he praised him for giving us not surprise, but expectation—the active reader participates in the work by reading it responsively—and then the fulfillment of expectation. E. M. Forster, in *Aspects of the Novel,* has a shrewd comment on the importance of both fulfilling expectation and offering a slight surprise: "Shock, followed by the feeling, 'Oh, that's all right,' is a sign that all is well with plot: characters, to be real, ought to run smoothly, but a plot ought to cause surprise."

Finally, a few words about **theme.** Usually we feel that a story is about something, it has a point—a theme. (What happens is the plot; what the happenings add up to is the theme.) But a word of caution is needed here. What is the theme of "Misery"? One student formulated the theme thus:

Human beings must utter their grief, even if only to an animal.

Another student formulated it thus:

Human beings are indifferent to the sufferings of others.

Still another student offered this:

Deep suffering is incommunicable, but the sufferer must try to find an outlet.

Many other formulations are possible. Probably there is no "right" statement of the theme of "Misery" or of any other good story: a story is not simply an illustration of an abstract statement of theme. A story has a complex variety of details that modify any summary statement we may offer when we try to say what it is about. And what lives in our memory is not an abstract statement—certainly not a thesis, that is, a proposition offered and argued, such as "We should pay attention to the suffering of others." What lives is an image that by every word in the story has convinced us that it is a representation, if not of "reality," of at least an aspect of reality.

Still, the writer is guided by a theme in the choice of details; of many possible details, Chekhov decided to present only a few. The musical sense of the word "theme" can help us to understand what a theme in literature is: "a melody constituting the basis of variation, development, or the like." The variations and the development cannot be random, but must have a basis. (We have already suggested that the episodes in "Misery"—the movement from the officer to the drunks and then to the house-porter and the other cabman—are not random, but somehow seem exactly "right," just as the remarks about the man and the horse both stretching their necks seem "right.") What is it, Robert Frost asks, that prevents the writer from jumping "from one chance suggestion to another in all directions as of a hot afternoon in the life of a grasshopper?" Frost's answer: "Theme alone can steady us down."

We can, then, talk about the theme—again, what the story adds up to—as long as we do not think a statement of the theme is equivalent to or is a substitute for the whole story. As Flannery O'Connor said, "Some people have the notion that you can read the story and then climb out of it into the meaning, but for the fiction writer himself the whole story is the meaning." A theme, she said, is not like a string tying a sack of chicken feed, to be pulled out so that the feed can be got at. "A story is a way to say something that can't be said any other way." That "something"—which can't be said in any other way—is the theme. (On theme, see also page 179.)

▦ TOPICS FOR CRITICAL THINKING AND WRITING

1. What do you admire or not admire about Chekhov's story? Why?
2. Try to examine in detail your response to the ending. Do you think the ending is, in a way, a happy ending? Would you prefer a different ending? For instance, should the story end when the young cabman falls asleep? Or when Iona sets out for the stable? Or can you imagine a better ending? If so, what?
3. A literary critic has said of "Misery": "For the story it tells, its length is perfect." Do you agree? Do you think that the story could be made even shorter? If so, where would you seek to cut or condense it? Could this story be made longer? If so, which features of it would you expand and develop further?
4. From working on the previous topic, what have you learned about Chekhov as a writer? What have you learned about the craft involved in the writing of a short story?
5. Which do you think is more challenging: writing a short story about a sad experience or about a happy one? Please be as specific as you can about the nature of the challenge and how you, as the writer of such a story, would attempt to deal with it. What would you do to make the story effective?

KATE CHOPIN   [1892]

For a biographical note, see page 28.

Désirée's Baby

As the day was pleasant, Madame Valmondé drove over to L'Abri to see Désirée and the baby.

It made her laugh to think of Désirée with a baby. Why, it seemed but yesterday that Désirée was little more than a baby herself; when Monsieur in riding through the gateway of Valmondé had found her lying asleep in the shadow of the big stone pillar.

The little one awoke in his arms and began to cry for "Dada." That was as much as she could do or say. Some people thought she might have strayed there of her own accord, for she was of the toddling age. The prevailing belief was that she had been purposely left by a party of Texans, whose canvas-covered wagon, late in the day, had crossed the ferry that Coton Maïs kept, just below the plantation. In time Madame Valmondé abandoned every speculation but the one that Désirée had been sent to her by a beneficent Providence to be the child of her affection, seeing that she was without child of the flesh. For the girl grew to be beautiful and gentle, affectionate and sincere,—the idol of Valmondé.

It was no wonder, when she stood one day against the stone pillar in whose shadow she had lain asleep, eighteen years before, that Armand Aubigny riding by and seeing her there, had fallen in love with her. That was the way all the Aubignys fell in love, as if struck by a pistol shot. The wonder was that he had not loved her before; for he had known her since his father brought him home from Paris, a boy of eight, after his mother died there. The passion that awoke in him that day, when he saw her at the gate, swept along like an avalanche, or like a prairie fire, or like anything that drives headlong over all obstacles.

5   Monsieur Valmondé grew practical and wanted things well considered: that is, the girl's obscure origin. Armand looked into her eyes and did not care. He was reminded that she was nameless. What did it matter about a name when he could give her one of the oldest and proudest in Louisiana? He ordered the *corbeille*[1] from Paris, and contained himself with what patience he could until it arrived; then they were married.

Madame Valmondé had not seen Désirée and the baby for four weeks. When she reached L'Abri she shuddered at the first sight of it, as she always did. It was a sad looking place, which for many years had not known the gentle presence of a mistress, old Monsieur Aubigny having married and buried his wife in France, and she having loved her own land too well ever to leave it. The roof came down steep and black like a cowl, reaching out beyond the wide galleries that encircled the yellow stuccoed house. Big, solemn oaks grew close to it, and their thick-leaved, far-reaching branches shadowed it like a pall. Young Aubigny's rule was a strict one, too, and under it his negroes had forgotten how to be gay, as they had been during the old master's easy-going and indulgent lifetime.

The young mother was recovering slowly, and lay full length, in her soft white muslins and laces, upon a couch. The baby was beside her, upon her arm, where he had fallen asleep, at her breast. The yellow nurse woman sat beside a window fanning herself.

Madame Valmondé bent her portly figure over Désirée and kissed her, holding her an instant tenderly in her arms. Then she turned to the child.

"This is not the baby!" she exclaimed, in startled tones. French was the language spoken at Valmondé in those days.

10   "I knew you would be astonished," laughed Désirée, "at the way he has grown. The little *cochon de lait!*[2] Look at his legs, mamma, and his hands and fingernails,—real fingernails. Zandrine had to cut them this morning. Isn't it true, Zandrine?"

The woman bowed her turbaned head majestically, "Mais si,[3] Madame."

"And the way he cries," went on Désirée, "is deafening. Armand heard him the other day as far away as La Blanche's cabin."

Madame Valmondé had never removed her eyes from the child. She lifted it and walked with it over to the window that was lightest. She scanned the baby narrowly, then looked as searchingly at Zandrine, whose face was turned to gaze across the fields.

"Yes, the child has grown, has changed," said Madame Valmondé, slowly, as she replaced it beside its mother. "What does Armand say?"

15   Désirée's face became suffused with a glow that was happiness itself.

"Oh, Armand is the proudest father in the parish, I believe, chiefly because it is a boy, to bear his name; though he says not—that he would have loved a girl as well. But I know it isn't true. I know he says that to please me. And mamma," she added, drawing Madame Valmondé's head down to her, and speaking in a whisper, "he hasn't punished one of them— not one of them—since baby is born. Even Négrillon, who pretended to

---

[1] *corbeille* wedding gifts from the groom to the bride.   [2] *cochon de lait* suckling pig (French).   [3] **Mais si** certainly (French).

have burnt his leg that he might rest from work—he only laughed, and said Négrillon was a great scamp. Oh, mamma, I'm so happy; it frightens me."

What Désirée said was true. Marriage, and later the birth of his son had softened Armand Aubigny's imperious and exacting nature greatly. This was what made the gentle Désirée so happy, for she loved him desperately. When he frowned she trembled, but loved him. When he smiled, she asked no greater blessing of God. But Armand's dark, handsome face had not often been disfigured by frowns since the day he fell in love with her.

When the baby was about three months old, Désirée awoke one day to the conviction that there was something in the air menacing her peace. It was at first too subtle to grasp. It had only been a disquieting suggestion; an air of mystery among the blacks; unexpected visits from far-off neighbors who could hardly account for their coming. Then a strange, an awful change in her husband's manner, which she dared not ask him to explain. When he spoke to her, it was with averted eyes, from which the old love-light seemed to have gone out. He absented himself from home; and when there, avoided her presence and that of her child, without excuse. And the very spirit of Satan seemed suddenly to take hold of him in his dealings with the slaves. Désirée was miserable enough to die.

She sat in her room, one hot afternoon, in her *peignoir,* listlessly drawing through her fingers the strands of her long, silky brown hair that hung about her shoulders. The baby, half naked, lay asleep upon her own great mahogany bed, that was like a sumptuous throne, with its satin-lined half-canopy. One of La Blanche's little quadroon boys—half naked too—stood fanning the child slowly with a fan of peacock feathers. Désirée's eyes had been fixed absently and sadly upon the baby, while she was striving to penetrate the threatening mist that she felt closing about her. She looked from her child to the boy who stood beside him, and back again; over and over. "Ah!" It was a cry that she could not help; which she was not conscious of having uttered. The blood turned like ice in her veins, and a clammy moisture gathered upon her face.

20   She tried to speak to the little quadroon boy; but no sound would come, at first. When he heard his name uttered, he looked up, and his mistress was pointing to the door. He laid aside the great, soft fan, and obediently stole away, over the polished floor, on his bare tiptoes.

She stayed motionless, with gaze riveted upon her child, and her face the picture of fright.

Presently her husband entered the room, and without noticing her, went to a table and began to search among some papers which covered it.

"Armand," she called to him, in a voice which must have stabbed him, if he was human. But he did not notice. "Armand," she said again. Then she rose and tottered towards him. "Armand," she panted once more, clutching his arm, "look at our child. What does it mean? tell me."

He coldly but gently loosened her fingers from about his arm and thrust the hand away from him. "Tell me what it means!" she cried despairingly.

25   "It means," he answered lightly, "that the child is not white; it means that you are not white."

A quick conception of all that this accusation meant for her nerved her with unwonted courage to deny it. "It is a lie; it is not true, I am white! Look at my hair, it is brown; and my eyes are gray, Armand, you know they are gray. And my skin is fair," seizing his wrist. "Look at my hand; whiter than yours, Armand," she laughed hysterically.

"As white as La Blanche's," he returned cruelly; and went away leaving her alone with their child.

When she could hold a pen in her hand, she sent a despairing letter to Madame Valmondé.

"My mother, they tell me I am not white. Armand has told me I am not white. For God's sake tell them it is not true. You must know it is not true. I shall die. I must die. I cannot be so unhappy, and live."

30 The answer that came was as brief:

"My own Désirée: Come home to Valmondé; back to your mother who loves you. Come with your child."

When the letter reached Désirée she went with it to her husband's study, and laid it open upon the desk before which he sat. She was like a stone image: silent, white, motionless after she placed it there.

In silence he ran his cold eyes over the written words. He said nothing. "Shall I go, Armand?" she asked in tones sharp with agonized suspense.

"Yes, go."

35 "Do you want me to go?"

"Yes, I want you to go."

He thought Almighty God had dealt cruelly and unjustly with him; and felt, somehow, that he was paying Him back in kind when he stabbed thus into his wife's soul. Moreover he no longer loved her, because of the unconscious injury she had brought upon his home and his name.

She turned away like one stunned by a blow, and walked slowly towards the door, hoping he would call her back.

"Good-by, Armand," she moaned.

40 He did not answer her. That was his last blow at fate.

Désirée went in search of her child. Zandrine was pacing the sombre gallery with it. She took the little one from the nurse's arms with no word of explanation, and descending the steps, walked away, under the live-oak branches.

It was an October afternoon; the sun was just sinking. Out in the still fields the negroes were picking cotton.

Désirée had not changed the thin white garment nor the slippers which she wore. Her hair was uncovered and the sun's rays brought a golden gleam from its brown meshes. She did not take the broad, beaten road which led to the far-off plantation of Valmondé. She walked across a deserted field, where the stubble bruised her tender feet, so delicately shod, and tore her thin gown to shreds.

She disappeared among the reeds and willows that grew thick along the banks of the deep, sluggish bayou; and she did not come back again.

45 Some weeks later there was a curious scene enacted at L'Abri. In the centre of the smoothly swept back yard was a great bonfire. Armand Aubigny sat in the wide hallway that commanded a view of the spectacle; and it was he who dealt out to a half dozen negroes the material which kept this fire ablaze.

A graceful cradle of willow, with all its dainty furbishings, was laid upon the pyre, which had already been fed with the richness of a priceless *layette.* Then there were silk gowns, and velvet and satin ones added to these; laces, too, and embroideries; bonnets and gloves; for the *corbeille* had been of rare quality.

The last thing to go was a tiny bundle of letters; innocent little scribblings that Désirée had sent to him during the days of their espousal. There was the remnant of one back in the drawer from which he took them. But it was not Désirée's; it was part of an old letter from his mother to his father. He read it. She was thanking God for the blessing of her husband's love:—

"But, above all," she wrote, "night and day, I thank the good God for having so arranged our lives that our dear Armand will never know that his mother, who adores him, belongs to the race that is cursed with the brand of slavery."

TOPICS FOR CRITICAL THINKING AND WRITING

1. Let's start with the ending. Readers find the ending powerful, but they differ in their interpretations of it. Do you think that when Armand reads the letter he learns something he had never suspected or, instead, something that he had sensed about himself all along? Find evidence in the text to support your view.
2. Describe Désirée's feelings toward Armand. Do you agree with the student who told us, "She makes him into a God"?
3. Chopin writes economically: each word counts, each phrase and sentence is significant. What is she revealing about Armand (and perhaps about the discovery he has made) when she writes, "And the very spirit of Satan seemed suddenly to take hold of him in his dealings with the slaves"?
4. Is this story primarily a character study, or is Chopin seeking to make larger points in it about race, slavery, and gender?

ALICE WALKER

Alice Walker was born in 1944 in Eatonton, Georgia, where her parents eked out a living as sharecroppers and dairy farmers; her mother also worked as a domestic. (In a collection of essays, In Search of Our Mothers' Gardens *[1984], Walker celebrates women who, like her mother, passed on a "respect for the possibilities [of life]—and the will to grasp them.") Walker attended Spelman College in Atlanta, and in 1965 she finished her undergraduate work at Sarah Lawrence College near New York City. She then became active in the welfare rights movement in New York and in the voter registration movement in Georgia. Later she taught writing and literature in Mississippi, at Jackson State College and Tougaloo College, and at Wellesley College, the University of Massachusetts, and Yale University.*

Walker has written essays, poetry, and fiction. Her best-known novel, The Color Purple *(1982), won a Pulitzer Prize and the National Book Award. She has said that her chief concern is "exploring the oppressions, the insanities, the loyalties, and the triumphs of black women."*

Everyday Use

[1973]

For your grandmama

I will wait for her in the yard that Maggie and I made so clean and wavy yesterday afternoon. A yard like this is more comfortable than most people know. It is not just a yard. It is like an extended living room. When the hard clay is swept clean as a floor and the fine sand around the edges lined with tiny, irregular grooves, anyone can come and sit and look up into the elm tree and wait for the breezes that never come inside the house.

Maggie will be nervous until after her sister goes: she will stand hopelessly in corners homely and ashamed of the burn scars down her arms and legs, eyeing her sister with a mixture of envy and awe. She thinks her sister has held life always in the palm of one hand, that "no" is a word the world never learned to say to her.

You've no doubt seen those TV shows where the child who has "made it" is confronted, as a surprise, by her own mother and father, tottering in weakly from backstage. (A pleasant surprise, of course: What would they do if parent and child came on the show only to curse out and insult each other?) On TV mother and child embrace and smile into each other's faces. Sometimes the mother and father weep, the child wraps them in her arms and leans across the table to tell how she would not have made it without their help. I have seen these programs.

Sometimes I dream a dream in which Dee and I are suddenly brought together on a TV program of this sort. Out of a dark and soft-seated limousine I am ushered into a bright room filled with many people. There I meet a smiling, gray, sporty man like Johnny Carson who shakes my hand and tells me what a fine girl I have. Then we are on the stage and Dee is embracing me with tears in her eyes. She pins on my dress a large orchid, even though she has told me once that she thinks orchids are tacky flowers.

5   In real life I am a large, big-boned woman with rough, man-working hands. In the winter I wear flannel nightgowns to bed and overalls during the day. I can kill and clean a hog as mercilessly as a man. My fat keeps me hot in zero weather. I can work outside all day, breaking ice to get water for washing. I can eat pork liver cooked over the open fire minutes after it comes steaming from the hog. One winter I knocked a bull calf straight in the brain between the eyes with a sledge hammer and had the meat hung up to chill before nightfall. But of course all this does not show on television. I am the way my daughter would want me to be: a hundred pounds lighter, my skin like an uncooked barley pancake. My hair glistens in the hot bright lights. Johnny Carson has much to do to keep up with my quick and witty tongue.

But that is a mistake. I know even before I wake up. Who ever knew a Johnson with a quick tongue? Who can even imagine me looking a strange white man in the eye? It seems to me I have talked to them always with one foot raised in flight, with my head turned in whichever way is farthest from them. Dee, though. She would always look anyone in the eye. Hesitation was no part of her nature.

"How do I look, Mama?" Maggie says, showing just enough of her thin body enveloped in pink skirt and red blouse for me to know she's there, almost hidden by the door.

"Come out into the yard," I say.

Have you ever seen a lame animal, perhaps a dog run over by some careless person rich enough to own a car, sidle up to someone who is ignorant enough to be kind to him? That is the way my Maggie walks. She has been like this, chin on chest, eyes on ground, feet in shuffle, ever since the fire that burned the other house to the ground.

10   Dee is lighter than Maggie, with nicer hair and a fuller figure. She's a woman now, though sometimes I forget. How long ago was it that the other house burned? Ten, twelve years? Sometimes I can still hear the flames and feel Maggie's arms sticking to me, her hair smoking and her dress falling off her in little black papery flakes. Her eyes seemed stretched open, blazed open by the flames reflected in them. And Dee. I see her standing off under the sweet gum tree she used to dig gum out of; a look of concentration on her face as she watched the last dingy gray board of the house fall in toward the red-hot brick chimney. Why don't you do a dance around the ashes? I'd wanted to ask her. She had hated the house that much.

I used to think she hated Maggie, too. But that was before we raised the money, the church and me, to send her to Augusta to school. She used to read to us without pity; forcing words, lies, other folks' habits, whole lives upon us two, sitting trapped and ignorant underneath her voice. She washed us in a river of make-believe, burned us with a lot of knowledge we didn't necessarily need to know. Pressed us to her with the serious way she read, to shove us away at just the moment, like dimwits, we seemed about to understand.

Dee wanted nice things. A yellow organdy dress to wear to her graduation from high school; black pumps to match a green suit she'd made from an old suit somebody gave me. She was determined to stare down any disaster in her efforts. Her eyelids would not flicker for minutes at a time. Often I fought off the temptation to shake her. At sixteen she had a style of her own: and knew what style was.

I never had an education myself. After second grade the school was closed down. Don't ask me why: in 1927 colored asked fewer questions than they do now. Sometimes Maggie reads to me. She stumbles along good-naturedly but can't see well. She knows she is not bright. Like good looks and money, quickness passed her by. She will marry John Thomas (who has mossy teeth in an earnest face) and then I'll be free to sit here and I guess just sing church songs to myself. Although I never was a good singer. Never could carry a tune. I was always better at a man's job. I used to love to milk till I was hoofed in the side in '49. Cows are soothing and slow and don't bother you, unless you try to milk them the wrong way.

I have deliberately turned my back on the house. It is three rooms, just like the one that burned, except the roof is tin; they don't make shingle roofs any more. There are no real windows, just some holes cut in the sides, like the portholes in a ship, but not round and not square, with rawhide holding the shutters up on the outside. This house is in a pasture, too, like the other one. No doubt when Dee sees it she will want to tear it down. She wrote me once that no matter where we "choose" to live, she will manage to come see us. But she will never bring her friends. Maggie and I thought about this and Maggie asked me, "Mama, when did Dee ever *have* any friends?"

15   She had a few. Furtive boys in pink shirts hanging about on washday after school. Nervous girls who never laughed. Impressed with her they worshiped the well-turned phrase, the cute shape, the scalding humor that erupted like bubbles in lye. She read to them.

When she was courting Jimmy T she didn't have much time to pay to us, but turned all her faultfinding power on him. He *flew* to marry a cheap gal from a family of ignorant flashy people. She hardly had time to recompose herself.

When she comes I will meet—but there they are!

Maggie attempts to make a dash for the house, in her shuffling way, but I stay her with my hand. "Come back here," I say. And she stops and tries to dig a well in the sand with her toe.

It is hard to see them clearly through the strong sun. But even the first glimpse of leg out of the car tells me it is Dee. Her feet were always neat-looking, as if God himself had shaped them with a certain style. From the other side of the car comes a short, stocky man. Hair is all over his head a foot long and hanging from his chin like a kinky mule tail. I hear Maggie suck in her breath. "Uhnnnh," is what it sounds like. Like when you see the wriggling end of a snake just in front of your foot on the road. "Uhnnnh."

20   Dee next. A dress down to the ground, in this hot weather. A dress so loud it hurts my eyes. There are yellows and oranges enough to throw back the light of the sun. I feel my whole face warming from the heat waves it throws out. Earrings, too, gold and hanging down to her shoulders. Bracelets dangling and making noises when she moves her arm up to shake the folds of the dress out of her armpits. The dress is loose and flows, and as she walks closer, I like it. I hear Maggie go "Uhnnnh" again. It is her sister's hair. It stands straight up like the wool on a sheep. It is black as night and around the edges are two long pigtails that rope about like small lizards disappearing behind her ears.

"Wa-su-zo-Tean-o!" she says, coming on in that gliding way the dress makes her move. The short stocky fellow with the hair to his navel is all grinning and he follows up with "Asalamalakim, my mother and sister!" He moves to hug Maggie but she falls back, right up against the back of my chair. I feel her trembling there and when I look up I see the perspiration falling off her chin.

"Don't get up," says Dee. Since I am stout it takes something of a push. You can see me trying to move a second or two before I make it. She turns, showing white heels through her sandals, and goes back to the car. Out she peeks next with a Polaroid. She stoops down quickly and lines up picture after picture of me sitting there in front of the house with Maggie cowering behind me. She never takes a shot without making sure the house is included. When a cow comes nibbling around the edge of the yard she snaps it and me and Maggie *and* the house. Then she puts the Polaroid in the back seat of the car, and comes up and kisses me on the forehead.

Meanwhile Asalamalakim is going through the motions with Maggie's hand. Maggie's hand is as limp as a fish, and probably as cold, despite the sweat, and she keeps trying to pull it back. It looks like Asalamalakim wants to shake hands but wants to do it fancy. Or maybe he don't know how people shake hands. Anyhow, he soon gives up on Maggie.

"Well," I say. "Dee."

25   "No, Mama," she says. "Not 'Dee,' Wangero Leewanika Kemanjo!"

"What happened to 'Dee'?" I wanted to know.

"She's dead," Wangero said. "I couldn't bear it any longer being named after the people who oppress me."

"You know as well as me you was named after your aunt Dicie," I said. Dicie is my sister. She named Dee. We called her "Big Dee" after Dee was born.

"But who was *she* named after?" asked Wangero.

30   "I guess after Grandma Dee," I said.

"And who was she named after?" asked Wangero.

"Her mother," I said, and saw Wangero was getting tired. "That's about as far back as I can trace it," I said. Though, in fact, I probably could have carried it back beyond the Civil War through the branches.

"Well," said Asalamalakim, "there you are."

"Uhnnnh," I heard Maggie say.

35   "There I was not," I said, "before 'Dicie' cropped up in our family, so why should I try to trace it that far back?"

He just stood there grinning, looking down on me like somebody inspecting a Model A car. Every once in a while he and Wangero sent eye signals over my head.

"How do you pronounce this name?" I asked.

"You don't have to call me by it if you don't want to," said Wangero.

"Why shouldn't I?" I asked. "If that's what you want us to call you, we'll call you."

40   "I know it might sound awkward at first," said Wangero.

"I'll get used to it," I said. "Ream it out again."

Well, soon we got the name out of the way. Asalamalakim had a name twice as long and three times as hard. After I tripped over it two or three times he told me to just call him Hakim-a-barber. I wanted to ask him was he a barber, but I didn't really think he was, so I didn't ask.

"You must belong to those beef-cattle peoples down the road," I said. They said "Asalamalakim" when they met you, too, but they didn't shake hands. Always too busy: feeding the cattle, fixing the fences, putting up saltlick shelters, throwing down hay. When the white folks poisoned some of the herd the men stayed up all night with rifles in their hands. I walked a mile and a half just to see the sight.

Hakim-a-barber said, "I accept some of their doctrines, but farming and raising cattle is not my style." (They didn't tell me, and I didn't ask, whether Wangero [Dee] had really gone and married him.)

45   We sat down to eat and right away he said he didn't eat collards and pork was unclean. Wangero, though, went on through the chitlins and corn bread, the greens and everything else. She talked a blue streak over the sweet potatoes. Everything delighted her. Even the fact that we still used the benches her daddy made for the table when we couldn't afford to buy chairs.

"Oh, Mama!" she cried. Then turned to Hakim-a-barber. "I never knew how lovely these benches are. You can feel the rump prints," she said, running her hands underneath her and along the bench. Then she gave a sigh and her hand closed over Grandma Dee's butter dish. "That's it!" she said. "I knew there was something I wanted to ask you if I could have." She jumped up from the table and went over in the corner where the churn stood, the milk in it clabber by now. She looked at the churn and looked at it.

"This churn top is what I need," she said. "Didn't Uncle Buddy whittle it out of a tree you all used to have?"

"Yes," I said.

"Uh huh," she said happily. "And I want the dasher, too."

50   "Uncle Buddy whittle that, too?" asked the barber.

Dee (Wangero) looked up at me.

"Aunt Dee's first husband whittled the dash," said Maggie so low you almost couldn't hear her. "His name was Henry, but they called him Stash."

"Maggie's brain is like an elephant's," Wangero said, laughing. "I can use the churn top as a centerpiece for the alcove table," she said, sliding a plate over the churn, "and I'll think of something artistic to do with the dasher."

When she finished wrapping the dasher the handle stuck out. I took it for a moment in my hands. You didn't even have to look close to see where hands pushing the dasher up and down to make butter had left a kind of sink in the wood. In fact, there were a lot of small sinks; you could see where thumbs and fingers had sunk into the wood. It was beautiful light yellow wood, from a tree that grew in the yard where Big Dee and Stash had lived.

55   After dinner Dee (Wangero) went to the trunk at the foot of my bed and started rifling through it. Maggie hung back in the kitchen over the dishpan. Out came Wangero with two quilts. They had been pieced by Grandma Dee and then Big Dee and me had hung them on the quilt frames on the front porch and quilted them. One was in the Lone Star pattern. The other was Walk Around the Mountain. In both of them were scraps of dresses Grandma Dee had worn fifty and more years ago. Bits and pieces of Grandpa Jarrell's paisley shirts. And one teeny faded blue piece, about the piece of a penny matchbox, that was from Great Grandpa Ezra's uniform that he wore in the Civil War.

"Mama," Wangero said sweet as a bird. "Can I have these old quilts?"

I heard something fall in the kitchen, and a minute later the kitchen door slammed.

"Why don't you take one or two of the others?" I asked. "These old things was just done by me and Big Dee from some tops your grandma pieced before she died."

"No," said Wangero. "I don't want those. They are stitched around the borders by machine."

60   "That'll make them last better," I said.

"That's not the point," said Wangero. "These are all pieces of dresses Grandma used to wear. She did all this stitching by hand. Imagine!" She held the quilts securely in her arms, stroking them.

"Some of the pieces, like those lavender ones, come from old clothes her mother handed down to her," I said, moving up to touch the quilts. Dee (Wangero) moved back just enough so that I couldn't reach the quilts. They already belonged to her.

"Imagine!" she breathed again, clutching them closely to her bosom.

"The truth is," I said, "I promised to give them quilts to Maggie, for when she marries John Thomas."

65   She gasped like a bee had stung her.

Quilt made by a slave in Mississippi about 1855–1858. (Courtesy of Michigan State University Museum.)

The crafting of a family heirloom.

"Maggie can't appreciate these quilts!" she said. "She'd probably be backward enough to put them to everyday use."

"I reckon she would," I said. "God knows I been saving 'em for long enough with nobody using 'em. I hope she will!" I didn't want to bring up how I had offered Dee (Wangero) a quilt when she went away to college. Then she had told me they were old-fashioned, out of style.

"But they're *priceless!*" she was saying now, furiously; for she has a temper. "Maggie would put them on the bed and in five years they'd be in rags. Less than that!"

"She can always make some more," I said. "Maggie knows how to quilt."

70   Dee (Wangero) looked at me with hatred. "You just will not understand. The point is these quilts, *these* quilts!"

"Well," I said, stumped. "What would *you* do with them?"

"Hang them," she said. As if that was the only thing you *could* do with quilts.

Maggie by now was standing in the door. I could almost hear the sound her feet made as they scraped over each other.

"She can have them, Mama," she said, like somebody used to never winning anything, or having anything reserved for her. "I can 'member Grandma Dee without the quilts."

75   I looked at her hard. She had filled her bottom lip with checkerberry snuff and it gave her face a kind of dopey, hangdog look. It was Grandma Dee and Big Dee who taught her how to quilt herself. She stood there with her scarred hands hidden in the folds of her skirt. She looked at her sister with something like fear but she wasn't mad at her. This was Maggie's portion. This was the way she knew God to work.

When I looked at her like that something hit me in the top of my head and ran down to the soles of my feet. Just like when I'm in church and the spirit of God touches me and I get happy and shout. I did something I never had done before: hugged Maggie to me, then dragged her on into the room, snatched the quilts out of Miss Wangero's hands and dumped them into Maggie's lap. Maggie just sat there on my bed with her mouth open.

"Take one or two of the others," I said to Dee.

But she turned without a word and went out to Hakim-a-barber.

"You just don't understand," she said, as Maggie and I came out to the car.

80   "What don't I understand?" I wanted to know.

"Your heritage," she said. And then she turned to Maggie, kissed her, and said, "You ought to try to make something of yourself, too, Maggie. It's really a new day for us. But from the way you and Mama still live you'd never know it."

She put on some sunglasses that hid everything above the tip of her nose and her chin.

Maggie smiled; maybe at the sunglasses. But a real smile, not scared. After we watched the car dust settle I asked Maggie to bring me a dip of snuff. And then the two of us sat there just enjoying, until it was time to go in the house and go to bed.

TOPICS FOR CRITICAL THINKING AND WRITING

1. Alice Walker wrote the story, but the story is narrated by one of the characters, Mama. How would you characterize Mama?
2. At the end of the story, Dee tells Maggie, "It's really a new day for us. But from the way you and Mama still live you'd never know it." What does Dee mean? And how do Maggie and Mama respond?"
3. In paragraph 76 the narrator says, speaking of Maggie, "When I looked at her like that something hit me in the top of my head and ran down to the soles of my feet." What "hit" Mama? That is, what does she understand at this moment that she had not understood before?
4. In "Everyday Use" why does the family conflict focus on who will possess the quilts? Why are the quilts important? What do they symbolize?

MARGARET ATWOOD

Born in 1939 in Ottawa, Canada, the poet, critic, novelist, and short-story writer Margaret Atwood now lives in Toronto. Her novels include The Edible Woman *(1969),* Surfacing *(1972), and* The Handmaid's Tale *(1985).*

Happy Endings

John and Mary meet.
What happens next?
If you want a happy ending, try A.

A

John and Mary fall in love and get married. They both have worthwhile and remunerative jobs which they find stimulating and challenging. They buy a charming house. Real estate values go up. Eventually, when they can afford live-in help, they have two children, to whom they are devoted. The children turn out well. John and Mary have a stimulating and challenging sex life and worthwhile friends. They go on fun vacations together. They retire. They both have hobbies which they find stimulating and challenging. Eventually they die. This is the end of the story.

B

Mary falls in love with John but John doesn't fall in love with Mary. He merely uses her body for selfish pleasure and ego gratification of a tepid kind. He comes to her apartment twice a week and she cooks him dinner, you'll notice that he doesn't even consider her worth the price of a dinner out, and after he's eaten the dinner he fucks her and after that he falls asleep, while she does the dishes so he won't think she's untidy, having all those dirty dishes lying around, and puts on fresh lipstick so she'll look good when he wakes up, but when he wakes up he doesn't even notice, he puts on his socks and his shorts and his pants and his shirt and his tie and his shoes, the reverse order from the one in which he took them off. He doesn't take off Mary's clothes, she takes them off herself, she acts as if she's dying for it every time, not because she likes sex exactly, she doesn't, but she wants John to think she does because if they do it often enough surely he'll get used to her, he'll come to depend on her and they will get married, but John goes out the door with hardly so much as a good-night and three days later he turns up at six o'clock and they do the whole thing over again.

Mary gets run-down. Crying is bad for your face, everyone knows that and so does Mary but she can't stop. People at work notice. Her friends tell her John is a rat, a pig, a dog, he isn't good enough for her, but she can't believe it. Inside John, she thinks, is another John who is much nicer. This other John will emerge like a butterfly from a cocoon, a Jack from a box, a pit from a prune, if the first John is only squeezed enough.

One evening John complains about the food. He has never complained about the food before. Mary is hurt.

Her friends tell her they've seen him in a restaurant with another woman, whose name is Madge. It's not even Madge that finally gets to Mary: it's the restaurant. John has never taken Mary to a restaurant. Mary collects all the sleeping pills and aspirins she can find, and takes them and half a bottle of sherry. You can see what kind of a woman she is by the fact that it's not even whiskey. She leaves a note for John. She hopes he'll discover her and get her to the hospital in time and repent and then they can get married, but this fails to happen and she dies.

John marries Madge and everything continues as in A.

C

John, who is an older man, falls in love with Mary, and Mary, who is only twenty-two, feels sorry for him because he's worried about his hair falling out. She sleeps with him even though she's not in love with him. She met him at work. She's in love with someone called James, who is twenty-two also and not yet ready to settle down.

John on the contrary settled down long ago: this is what is bothering him. John has a steady, respectable job and is getting ahead in his field, but Mary isn't impressed by him, she's impressed by James, who has a motorcycle and a fabulous record collection. But James is often away on his motorcycle, being free. Freedom isn't the same for girls, so in the meantime Mary spends Thursday evenings with John. Thursdays are the only days John can get away.

John is married to a woman called Madge and they have two children, a charming house which they bought just before the real estate values went up, and hobbies which they find stimulating and challenging, when they have the time. John tells Mary how important she is to him, but of course he can't leave his wife because a commitment is a commitment. He goes on about this more than is necessary and Mary finds it boring, but older men can keep it up longer so on the whole she has a fairly good time.

One day James breezes in on his motorcycle with some top-grade California hybrid and James and Mary get higher than you'd believe possible and they climb into bed. Everything becomes very underwater, but along comes John, who has a key to Mary's apartment. He finds them stoned and entwined. He's hardly in any position to be jealous, considering Madge, but nevertheless he's overcome with despair. Finally he's middle-aged, in two years he'll be bald as an egg and he can't stand it. He purchases a handgun, saying he needs it for target practice—this is the thin part of the plot, but it can be dealt with later—and shoots the two of them and himself.

Madge, after a suitable period of mourning, marries an understanding man called Fred and everything continues as in A, but under different names.

D

Fred and Madge have no problems. They get along exceptionally well and are good at working out any little difficulties that may arise. But their charming house is by the seashore and one day a giant tidal wave approaches. Real estate values go down. The rest of the story is about what caused the tidal wave and how they escape from it. They do, though thousands drown, but Fred and Madge are virtuous and lucky. Finally on high ground they clasp each other, wet and dripping and grateful, and continue as in A.

E

Yes, but Fred has a bad heart. The rest of the story is about how kind and understanding they both are until Fred dies. then madge devotes herself to charity work until the end of A. If you like, it can be "Madge," "cancer," "guilty and confused," and "bird watching."

F

If you think this is all too bourgeois, make John a revolutionary and Mary a counterespionage agent and see how far that gets you. Remember, this is Canada. You'll still end up with A, though in between you may get a lustful brawling saga of passionate involvement, a chronicle of our times, sort of.

You'll have to face it, the endings are the same however you slice it. Don't be deluded by any other endings, they're all fake, either deliberately fake, with malicious intent to deceive, or just motivated by excessive optimism if not by downright sentimentality.

The only authentic ending is the one provided here:
John and Mary die. John and Mary die. John and Mary die.

So much for endings. Beginnings are always more fun. True connoisseurs, however, are known to favor the stretch in between, since it's the hardest to do anything with.

That's about all that can be said for plots, which anyway are just one thing after another, a what and a what and a what.

Now try How and Why.

▨ TOPICS FOR CRITICAL THINKING AND WRITING

1. Did the form of Atwood's story surprise you?
2. Does this story have a plot? Does it present and develop characters?"
3. Describe your response to the final paragraphs, which focus on endings and beginnings. Which, in your view, is harder for a short-story writer, the beginning or the ending?
4. Some short stories are extremely short, while others are quite long. What do you think is the right length for a short story? Why do you say that? What kinds of arguments can you use to support your claim?
5. Please compose a part G for "Happy Endings."

5

Narrative Point of View

Every story is told by someone. Mark Twain wrote *Adventures of Huckleberry Finn,* but he does not tell the story; Huck tells the story, and he begins thus:

> You don't know about me without you have read a book by the name of *The Adventures of Tom Sawyer,* but that ain't no matter. That book was made by Mr. Mark Twain, and he told the truth, mainly. There was things which he stretched, but mainly he told the truth.

Similarly, Edgar Allan Poe wrote "The Cask of Amontillado," but the story is told by a man whose name, we learn later, is Montresor. Here is the opening:

> The thousand injuries of Fortunato I had borne as I best could, but when he ventured upon insult, I vowed revenge.

Each of these passages gives a reader a very strong sense of the narrator, that is, of the invented person who tells the story, and it turns out that the works are chiefly about the speakers. Compare those opening passages, however, with two others, which sound far more objective. The first comes from Chekhov's "Misery" (page 75):

> The twilight of evening. Big flakes of wet snow are whirling lazily about the street lamps, which have just been lighted, and lying in a thin soft layer on roofs, horses' backs, shoulders, caps. Iona Potapov, the sledge-driver, is all white like a ghost. He sits on the box without stirring, bent as double as the living body can be bent.

And another example, this one from Hawthorne's "Young Goodman Brown" (page 147):

> Young Goodman Brown came forth, at sunset, into the street at Salem village; but put his head back, after crossing the threshold, to exchange a parting kiss with his young wife. And Faith, as the wife was aptly named, thrust her own pretty head into the street, letting the wind play with the pink ribbons of her cap while she called to Goodman Brown.

In each of these two passages, a reader is scarcely aware of the personality of the narrator; our interest is almost entirely in the scene that each speaker reveals, not in the speaker's response to the scene.

The narrators of *Huckleberry Finn* and of "The Cask of Amontillado" immediately impress us with their distinctive personalities. We realize that whatever happenings they report will be colored by the special ways in which such personalities see things. But what can we say about the narrators of "Misery" and of "Young Goodman Brown"? A reader hardly notices them, at least in comparison with Huck and Montresor. We look, so to speak, not *at* these narrators, but at others (the cabman and Goodman Brown and Faith).

Of course, it is true that as we read "Misery" and "Young Goodman Brown" we are looking through the eyes of the narrators, but these narrators seem (unlike Huck and Montresor) to have 20/20 vision. This is not to say, however, that these apparently colorless narrators really are colorless or invisible. The narrator of "Misery" seems, at least if we judge from the opening sentences, to want to evoke an atmosphere. He describes the setting in some detail, whereas the narrator of "Young Goodman Brown" seems chiefly concerned with reporting the actions of people whom he sees. Moreover, if we listen carefully to Hawthorne's narrator, perhaps we can say that when he mentions that Faith was "aptly" named, he makes a judgment. Still, it is clear that the narrative voices we hear in "Misery" and "Young Goodman Brown" are relatively impartial and inconspicuous; when we hear them, we feel, for the most part, that they are talking about something objective, about something "out there." These narrative voices will produce stories very different from the narrative voices used by Twain and Poe. The voice that the writer chooses, then, will in large measure shape the story; different voices, different stories.

The narrative point of view of *Huckleberry Finn* and of "The Cask of Amontillado" (and of any other story in which a character in the story tells the story) is a **participant** (or **first-person**) point of view. The point of view of "Young Goodman Brown" (and of any other story in which a nearly invisible outsider tells the story) is a **nonparticipant** (or **third-person**) point of view.

PARTICIPANT (OR FIRST-PERSON) POINTS OF VIEW

In John Updike's "A & P" on page 101 the narrator is, like Mark Twain's Huck and Poe's Montresor, a major character. Updike has invented an adolescent boy who undergoes certain experiences and who has certain perceptions. Since the story is narrated by one of its characters, we can say that the author uses a first-person (or participant) point of view.

It happens that in Updike's "A & P" the narrator is the central character, the character whose actions—whose life, we might say—most interests the reader. But sometimes a first-person narrator tells a story that focuses on another character; the narrator still says "I" (thus the point of view is first person), but the reader feels that the story is not chiefly about this "I" but is about some other figure. For instance, the narrator may be a witness to a story about Jones, and our interest is in what happens to Jones, though we get the story of Jones filtered through, say, the eyes of Jones's friend, or brother, or cat.

When any of us tells a story (for instance, why we quit a job), our hearers may do well to take what we say with a grain of salt. After all, we are giving *our* side, our version of what happened. And so it is with first-person narrators of fiction. They may be reliable, in which case the reader can pretty much accept what they say, or they may be **unreliable narrators,** perhaps because they have an ax to grind, perhaps because they are not perceptive enough to grasp the full implications of what they report, or perhaps because they are mentally impaired, even insane. Poe's Montresor, in "The Cask of Amontillado," is so obsessed that we cannot be certain that Fortunato really did inflict a "thousand injuries" on him.

One special kind of unreliable first-person narrator (whether major or minor) is the **innocent eye:** the narrator is naive (usually a child, or a not-too-bright adult), telling what he or she sees and feels; the contrast between what the narrator perceives and what the reader understands produces an ironic effect. Such a story, in which the reader understands more than the teller himself does, is Ring Lardner's "Haircut," a story told by a garrulous barber who does not perceive that the "accident" he is describing is in fact a murder.

NONPARTICIPANT (OR THIRD-PERSON) POINTS OF VIEW

In a story told from a nonparticipant (third-person) point of view, the teller of the tale is not a character in the tale. The narrator has receded from the story. If the point of view is **omniscient,** the narrator relates what he or she wishes about the thoughts as well as the deeds of the characters. The omniscient teller can at any time enter the mind of any or all of the characters; whereas the first-person narrator can only say, "I was angry," or "Jones seemed angry to me," the omniscient narrator can say, "Jones was inwardly angry but gave no sign; Smith continued chatting, but he sensed Jones's anger."

Furthermore, a distinction can be made between **neutral omniscience** (the narrator recounts deeds and thoughts, but does not judge) and **editorial omniscience** (the narrator not only recounts, but also judges). The narrator in Hawthorne's "Young Goodman Brown" knows what goes on in the mind of Brown, and he comments approvingly or disapprovingly: "With this excellent resolve for the future, Goodman Brown felt himself justified in making more haste on his present evil purpose."

Because a short story can scarcely hope to effectively develop a picture of several minds, an author may prefer to limit his or her omniscience to the minds of only a few of the characters, or even to that of one of the characters; that is, the author may use **selective omniscience** as the point of view. Selective omniscience provides a focus, especially if it is limited to a single character. When thus limited, the author hovers over the shoulder of one character, seeing him or her from outside and from inside and seeing other characters only from the outside and from the impact they make on the mind of this selected receptor. In "Young Goodman Brown" the reader sees things mostly as they make their impact on the protagonist's mind.

> He could have well nigh sworn that the shape of his own dead father beckoned him to advance, looking downward from a smoke wreath, while a woman, with dim features of despair, threw out her hand to warn him back. Was it his mother? But he had no power to retreat one step, nor to resist, even in thought, when the minister and good old Deacon Gookin seized his arms and led him to the blazing rock.

When selective omniscience attempts to record mental activity ranging from consciousness to the unconscious, from clear perceptions to confused longings, it is sometimes labeled the **stream-of-consciousness** point of view. In an effort to reproduce the unending activity of the mind, some authors who use the stream-of-consciousness point of view dispense with conventional word order, punctuation, and logical transitions. The last forty-six pages in James Joyce's *Ulysses* are an unpunctuated flow of one character's thoughts.

Finally, sometimes a third-person narrator does not enter even a single mind, but records only what crosses a dispassionate eye and ear. Such a point of view is **objective** (sometimes called **the camera** or **fly-on-the-wall narrator**). The absence of editorializing and of dissection of the mind often produces the effect of a play; we see and hear the characters in action. Much of Hemingway's "Cat in the Rain" (page 61) is objective, consisting of bits of dialogue that make the story look like a play:

> "I'm going down and get that kitty," the American wife said.
> "I'll do it," her husband offered from the bed.
> "No, I'll get it. The poor kitty out trying to keep dry under a table."
> The husband went on reading, lying propped up with the two pil-
> lows at the foot of the bed.
> "Don't get wet," he said.   (62)

The absence of comment on the happenings forces readers to make their own evaluations of the happenings. In the passage just quoted, when Hemingway writes "'Don't get wet,' he said," readers probably are forced to think (and to sense that Hemingway is guiding them to think) that the husband is indifferent to his wife. After all, how can she go out into the rain and not get wet? A writer can use an objective point of view, then, and still control the feelings of the reader.

THE POINT OF A POINT OF VIEW

Generalizations about the effect of a point of view are risky, but two have already been made: that the innocent eye can achieve an ironic effect otherwise unattainable, and that an objective point of view (because we hear dialogue but get little or no comment about it) is dramatic. Three other generalizations are often made: (1) that a first-person point of view lends a sense of immediacy or reality, (2) that an omniscient point of view suggests human littleness, and (3) that the point of view must be consistent.

To take the first of these: it is true that when Poe begins a story "The thousand injuries of Fortunato I had borne as I best could, but when he ventured upon insult, I vowed revenge," we feel that the author has gripped us by the lapels; but, on the other hand, we know that we are only reading a piece of fiction, and we do not really believe in the existence of the "I" or of Fortunato; and furthermore, when we pick up a story that begins with *any* point of view, we agree (by picking up the book) to pretend to believe the fictions we are being told. That is, all fiction—whether in the first person or not—is known to be literally false but is read with the pretense that it is true (probably because we hope to get some sort of insight, or truth). The writer must hold our attention, and make us feel that the fiction is meaningful, but the use of the first-person pronoun does not of itself confer reality.

The second generalization, that an omniscient point of view can make puppets of its characters, is equally misleading; this point of view also can reveal in them a depth and complexity quite foreign to the idea of human littleness.

The third generalization, that the narrator's point of view must be consistent lest the illusion of reality be shattered, has been much preached by the followers of Henry James. But E. M. Forster has suggested, in *Aspects of the Novel,* that what is important is not consistency but "the power of the writer to bounce the reader into accepting what he says." Forster notes that in *Bleak House* Dickens uses in Chapter I an omniscient point of view, in Chapter II a selective omniscient point of view, and in Chapter III a first-person point of view. "Logically," Forster says, "*Bleak House* is all to pieces, but Dickens bounces us, so that we do not mind the shiftings of the viewpoint."

Perhaps the only sound generalizations possible are these:

1. Because point of view is one of the things that give form to a story, a good author chooses the point (or points) of view that he or she feels best for the particular story.
2. The use of any other point or points of view would turn the story into a different story.

JOHN UPDIKE

John Updike (b. 1932) grew up in Shillington, Pennsylvania, where his father was a teacher and his mother a writer. After receiving a B.A. degree in 1954 from Harvard, where he edited the Harvard Lampoon *(for which he both wrote and drew), he studied drawing at Oxford for a year, but an offer from* The New Yorker *brought him back to the United States. He was hired as a reporter for the magazine but soon began contributing poetry, essays, and fiction. In 1957 he left* The New Yorker *in order to write independently full time, though his stories and book reviews still appear regularly in it.*

In 1959 Updike published his first book of stories (The Same Door) *as well as his first novel* (The Poorhouse Fair); *the next year he published* Rabbit, Run, *a highly successful novel whose protagonist, "Rabbit" Angstrom, has reappeared in three later novels,* Rabbit Redux *(1971),* Rabbit Is Rich *(1981), and* Rabbit at Rest *(1990). The first and the last Rabbit books each won a Pulitzer Prize.*

A & P   [1962]

In walks these three girls in nothing but bathing suits. I'm in the third checkout slot, with my back to the door, so I don't see them until they're over by the bread. The one that caught my eye first was the one in the plaid green two-piece. She was a chunky kid, with a good tan and a sweet broad soft-looking can with those two crescents of white just under it, where the sun never seems to hit, at the top of the backs of her legs. I stood there with my hand on a box of HiHo crackers trying to remember if I rang it up or not. I ring it up again and the customer starts giving me hell. She's one of these cash-register-watchers, a witch about fifty with rouge on her cheekbones and no eyebrows, and I know it made her day to trip me up. She'd been watching cash registers for fifty years and probably never seen a mistake before.

By the time I got her feathers smoothed and her goodies into a bag—she gives me a little snort in passing, if she'd been born at the right time they would have burned her over in Salem—by the time I get her on her way the girls had circled around the bread and were coming back, without a pushcart, back my way along the counters, in the aisle between the checkouts and the Special bins. They didn't even have shoes on. There was this chunky one, with the two-piece—it was bright green and the seams on the bra were still sharp and her belly was still pretty pale so I guessed she just got it (the suit)—there was this one, with one of those chubby berry-faces, the lips all bunched together under her nose, this one, and a tall one, with black hair that hadn't quite frizzed right, and one of these sunburns right across under the eyes, and a chin that was too long—you know, the kind of girl other girls think is very "striking" and "attractive" but never quite makes it, as they very well know, which is why they like her so much—and then the third one, that wasn't quite so tall. She was the queen. She kind of led them, the other two peeking around and making their shoulders round. She didn't look around, not this queen, she just walked straight on slowly, on these long white prima-donna legs. She came down a little hard on her heels, as if she didn't walk in her bare feet that much, putting down her heels and then letting the weight move along to her toes as if she was testing the floor with every step, putting a little deliberate extra action into it. You never know for sure how girls' minds work (do you really think it's a mind in there or just a little buzz like a bee in a glass jar?) but you got the idea she had talked the other two into coming in here with her, and now she was showing them how to do it, walk slow and hold yourself straight.

She had on a kind of dirty pink—beige maybe, I don't know—bathing suit with a little nubble all over it and, what got me, the straps were down. They were off her shoulders looped loose around the cool tops of her arms, and I guess as a result the suit had slipped on her, so all around the top of the cloth there was this shining rim. If it hadn't been there you wouldn't have known there could have been anything whiter than those shoulders. With the straps pushed off, there was nothing between the top of the suit and the top of her head except just *her,* this clean bare plane of the top of her chest down from the shoulder bones like a dented sheet of metal tilted in the light. I mean, it was more than pretty.

She had sort of oaky hair that the sun and salt had bleached, done up in a bun that was unravelling, and a kind of prim face. Walking into the A & P with your straps down, I suppose it's the only kind of face you *can* have. She held her head so high her neck, coming up out of those white shoulders, looked kind of stretched, but I didn't mind. The longer her neck was, the more of her there was.

5   She must have felt in the corner of her eye me and over my shoulder Stokesie in the second slot watching, but she didn't tip. Not this queen. She kept her eyes moving across the racks, and stopped, and turned so slow it made my stomach rub the inside of my apron, and buzzed to the other two, who kind of huddled against her for relief, and then they all three of them went up the cat and dog food-breakfast cereal-macaroni-rice-raisins-seasonings-spreads-spaghetti-soft drinks-crackers-and-cookies aisle. From the third slot I look straight up this aisle to the meat counter, and I

watched them all the way. The fat one with the tan sort of fumbled with the cookies, but on second thought she put the package back. The sheep pushing their carts down the aisle—the girls were walking against the usual traffic (not that we have one-way signs or anything)—were pretty hilarious. You could see them, when Queenie's white shoulders dawned on them, kind of jerk, or hop, or hiccup, but their eyes snapped back to their own baskets and on they pushed. I bet you could set off dynamite in the A & P and the people would by and large keep reaching and checking oatmeal off their lists and muttering "Let me see, there was a third thing, began with A, asparagus, no, ah, yes, applesauce!" or whatever it is they do mutter. But there was no doubt, this jiggled them. A few house slaves in pin curlers even look around after pushing their carts past to make sure what they had seen was correct.

You know, it's one thing to have a girl in a bathing suit down on the beach, where what with the glare nobody can look at each other much anyway, and another thing in the cool of the A & P, under the fluorescent lights, against all those stacked packages, with her feet paddling along naked over our checker-board green-and-cream rubber-tile floor.

"Oh, Daddy," Stokesie said beside me. "I feel so faint."

"Darling," I said. "Hold me tight." Stokesie's married, with two babies chalked up on his fuselage already, but as far as I can tell that's the only difference. He's twenty-two, and I was nineteen this April.

"Is it done?" he asks, the responsible married man finding his voice. I forgot to say he thinks he's going to be a manager some sunny day, maybe in 1990 when it's called the Great Alexandrov and Petrooshki Tea Company or something.

10   What he meant was, our town is five miles from a beach, with a big summer colony out on the Point, but we're right in the middle of town, and the women generally put on a shirt or shorts or something before they get out of the car into the street. And anyway these are usually women with six children and varicose veins mapping their legs and nobody, including them, could care less. As I say, we're right in the middle of town, and if you stand at our front doors you can see two banks and the Congregational church and the newspaper store and three real estate offices and about twenty-seven old freeloaders tearing up Central Street because the sewer broke again. It's not as if we're on the Cape; we're north of Boston and there's people in this town haven't seen the ocean for twenty years.

The girls had reached the meat counter and were asking McMahon something. He pointed, they pointed, and they shuffled out of sight behind a pyramid of Diet Delight peaches. All that was left for us to see was old McMahon patting his mouth and looking after them sizing up their joints. Poor kids, I began to feel sorry for them, they couldn't help it.

Now here comes the sad part of the story, at least my family says it's sad, but I don't think it's so sad myself. The store's pretty empty, it being Thursday afternoon, so there was nothing much to do except lean on the register and wait for the girls to show up again. The whole store was like a pinball machine and I didn't know which tunnel they'd come out of. After a while they come around out of the far aisle, around the light bulbs, records at discount of the Caribbean Six or Tony Martin Sings or some such gunk you wonder they waste the wax on, six-packs of candy bars, and plastic toys done up in cellophane that fall apart when a kid looks at them anyway. Around they come, Queenie still leading the way, and holding a little gray jar in her hand. Slots Three through Seven are unmanned and I could see her wondering between Stokes and me, but Stokesie with his usual luck draws an old party in baggy gray pants who stumbles up with four giant cans of pineapple juice (what do these bums *do* with all that pineapple juice? I've often asked myself) so the girls come to me. Queenie puts down the jar and I take it into my fingers icy cold. Kingfish Fancy Herring Snacks in Pure Sour Cream: 49¢. Now her hands are empty, not a ring or a bracelet, bare as God made them, and I wonder where the money's coming from. Still with the prim look she lifts a folded dollar bill out of the hollow at the center of her nubbled pink top. The jar went heavy in my hand. Really, I thought that was so cute.

Then everybody's luck begins to run out. Lengel comes in from haggling with a truck full of cabbages on the lot and is about to scuttle into the door marked MANAGER behind which he hides all day when the girls touch his eye. Lengel's pretty dreary, teaches Sunday school and the rest, but he doesn't miss that much. He comes over and says, "Girls, this isn't the beach."

Queenie blushes, though maybe it's just a brush of sunburn I was noticing for the first time, now that she was so close. "My mother asked me to pick up a jar of herring snacks." Her voice kind of startled me, the way voices do when you see the people first, coming out so flat and dumb yet kind of tony, too, the way it ticked over "pick up" and "snacks." All of a sudden I slid right down her voice into her living room. Her father and the other men were standing around in ice-cream coats and bow ties and the women were in sandals picking up herring snacks on toothpicks off a big glass plate and they were all holding drinks the color of water with olives and sprigs of mint in them. When my parents have somebody over they get lemonade and if it's a real racy affair Schlitz in tall glasses with "They'll Do It Every Time" cartoons stencilled on.

15   "That's all right," Lengel said. "But this isn't the beach." His repeating this struck me as funny, as if it had just occurred to him, and he had been thinking all these years the A & P was a great big dune and he was the head lifeguard. He didn't like my smiling—as I say he doesn't miss much—but he concentrates on giving the girls that sad Sunday-school-superintendent stare.

Queenie's blush is no sunburn now, and the plump one in plaid, that I liked better from the back—a really sweet can—pipes up, "We weren't doing any shopping. We just came in for the one thing."

"That makes no difference," Lengel tells her, and I could see from the way his eyes went that he hadn't noticed she was wearing a two-piece before. "We want you decently dressed when you come in here."

"We *are* decent," Queenie says suddenly, her lower lip pushing, getting sore now that she remembers her place, a place from which the crowd that runs the A & P must look pretty crummy. Fancy Herring Snacks flashed in her very blue eyes.

"Girls, I don't want to argue with you. After this come in here with your shoulders covered. It's our policy." He turns his back. That's policy for you. Policy is what the kingpins want. What the others want is juvenile delinquency.

20   All this while, the customers had been showing up with their carts but, you know, sheep, seeing a scene, they had all bunched up on Stokesie, who shook open a paper bag as gently as peeling a peach, not wanting to miss a

word. I could feel in the silence everybody getting nervous, most of all Lengel, who asks me, "Sammy, have you rung up this purchase?"

I thought and said "No" but it wasn't about that I was thinking. I go through the punches, 4, 9, GROC, TOT—it's more complicated than you think and after you do it often enough, it begins to make a little song, that you hear words to, in my case "Hello (*bing*) there, you (*gung*) hap-py *peepul* (*splat*)!"—the *splat* being the drawer flying out. I uncrease the bill, tenderly as you may imagine, it just having come from between the two smoothest scoops of vanilla I had ever known were there, and pass a half and a penny into her narrow pink palm and nestle the herrings in a bag and twist its neck and hand it over, all the time thinking.

The girls, and who'd blame them, are in a hurry to get out, so I say "I quit" to Lengel quick enough for them to hear, hoping they'll stop and watch me, their unsuspected hero. They keep right on going, into the electric eye; the door flies open and they flicker across the lot to their car, Queenie and Plaid and Big Tall Goony-Goony (not that as raw material she was so bad), leaving me with Lengel and a kink in his eyebrow.

"Did you say something, Sammy?"

"I said I quit."

25   "I thought you did."

"You didn't have to embarrass them."

"It was they who were embarrassing us."

I started to say something that came out "Fiddle-de-doo." It's a saying of my grandmother's, and I know she would have been pleased.

"I don't think you know what you're saying," Lengel said.

30   "I know you don't," I said. "But I do." I pull the bow at the back of my apron and start shrugging it off my shoulders. A couple customers that had been heading for my slot begin to knock against each other, like scared pigs in a chute.

Lengel sighs and begins to look very patient and old and gray. He's been a friend of my parents for years. "Sammy, you don't want to do this to your Mom and Dad," he tells me. It's true, I don't. But it seems to me that once you begin a gesture it's fatal not to go through with it. I fold the apron, "Sammy" stitched in red on the pocket, and put it on the counter, and drop the bow tie on top of it. The bow tie is theirs, if you've ever wondered. "You'll feel this for the rest of your life," Lengel says, and I know that's true, too, but remembering how he made that pretty girl blush makes me so scrunchy inside I punch the No Sale tab and the machine whirs "pee-pul" and the drawer splats out. One advantage to this scene taking place in summer, I can follow this up with a clean exit, there's no fumbling around getting your coat and galoshes, I just saunter into the electric eye in my white shirt that my mother ironed the night before, and the door heaves itself open, and outside the sunshine is skating around on the asphalt.

I look around for my girls, but they're gone, of course. There wasn't anybody but some young married screaming with her children about some candy they didn't get by the door of a powder-blue Falcon station wagon. Looking back in the big windows, over the bags of peat moss and aluminum lawn furniture stacked on the pavement, I could see Lengel in my place in the slot, checking the sheep through. His face was dark gray and his back stiff, as if he'd just had an injection of iron, and my stomach kind of fell as I felt how hard the world was going to be to me hereafter.

▓ TOPICS FOR CRITICAL THINKING AND WRITING

1. In what sort of community is this A & P located? To what extent does this community resemble yours?
2. Do you think Sammy is a male chauvinist pig? Why, or why not? And if you think he is, do you find the story offensive? Again, why or why not?
3. In the last line of the story Sammy says, "I felt how hard the world was going to be to me hereafter." Do you think the world is going to be hard to Sammy? Why, or why not? And if it is hard to him, is this because of a virtue or a weakness in Sammy?
4. Write Lengel's version of the story (500–1000 words) as he might narrate it to his wife during dinner. Or write the story from Queenie's point of view.
5. In speaking of contemporary fiction Updike said:

   I want stories to startle and engage me within the first few sentences, and in their middle to widen or deepen or sharpen my knowledge of human activity, and to end by giving me a sensation of completed statement.

   Let's assume that you share Updike's view of what a story should do. To what extent do you think "A & P" fulfills these demands? (You may want to put your response in the form of a letter to Updike.)
6. During the course of an interview published in the *Southern Review* (Spring 2002), Updike said that the original ending of "A & P" differed from the present ending. In the original, after Sammy resigns he "goes down to the beach to try to see these three girls on whose behalf he's made this sacrifice of respectability, on whose behalf he's broken with the bourgeois norm and let his parents down and Mr. Lengel down. And he doesn't see the girls, and the story ended somewhere there." Updike's editor at *The New Yorker* persuaded him that the story "ended with the resignation." Your view?

JACK LONDON

Jack London (1876–1916) was born in San Francisco and educated at Oakland High School and the University of California, Berkeley, but his formal education was intermittent. At thirteen or fourteen he was a pirate raiding oyster beds in San Francisco Bay; a little later he worked in a cannery, and at seventeen he joined a sealing expedition to Japan and Siberia. Back in the United States he worked at odd jobs, became a socialist, finished high school (1895), spent one semester at the University of California, and then was off to the Klondike (at the age of twenty-one) looking—unsuccessfully, it turned out—for gold. He published his first story in 1899, his first collection of stories (The Son of the Wolf) in 1900, and his first novel (The Call of the Wild) in 1903. The novel was an immediate hit. London continued to write, both fiction and journalism, earning over a million dollars from his writing—at that time an astounding amount, and almost unthinkable for a writer.

To Build a Fire

[1908]

Day had broken cold and gray, exceedingly cold and gray, when the man turned aside from the main Yukon trail and climbed the high earth-bank, where a dim and little traveled trail led eastward through the fat spruce timberland. It was a steep bank, and he paused for breath at the top, excusing the act to himself by looking at his watch. It was nine o'clock. There was no sun nor hint of sun, though there was not a cloud in the sky. It was a clear day, and yet there seemed an intangible pall over the face of things, a subtle gloom that made the day dark, and that was due to the absence of sun. This fact did not worry the man. He was used to the lack of sun. It had been days since he had seen the sun, and he knew that a few more days must pass before that cheerful orb, due south, should just peep above the sky line and dip immediately from view.

The man flung a look back along the way he had come. The Yukon lay a mile wide and hidden under three feet of ice. On top of this ice were as many feet of snow. It was all pure white, rolling in gentle undulations where the ice jams of the freeze-up had formed. North and south, as far as his eye could see, it was unbroken white, save for a dark hairline that curved and twisted away into the north, where it disappeared behind another spruce-covered island. This dark hairline was the trail—the main trail—that led south five hundred miles to the Chilcoot Pass, Dyea, and salt water; and that led north seventy miles to Dawson, and still on to the north a thousand miles to Nulato, and finally to St. Michael, on Bering Sea, a thousand miles and half a thousand more.

But all this—the mysterious, far-reaching hairline trail, the absence of sun from the sky, the tremendous cold, and the strangeness and weirdness of it all—made no impression on the man. It was not because he was long used to it. He was a newcomer in the land, a *chechaquo,* and this was his first winter. The trouble with him was that he was without imagination. He was quick and alert in the things of life, but only in the things, and not in the significances. Fifty degrees below zero meant eighty-odd degrees of frost. Such fact impressed him as being cold and uncomfortable, and that was all. It did not lead him to meditate upon his frailty as a creature of temperature, and upon man's frailty in general, able only to live within certain narrow limits of heat and cold; and from there on it did not lead him to the conjectural field of immortality and man's place in the universe. Fifty degrees below zero stood for a bite of frost that hurt and that must be guarded against by the use of mittens, ear flaps, warm moccasins, and thick socks. Fifty degrees below zero was to him just precisely fifty degrees below zero. That there should be anything more to it than that was a thought that never entered his head.

As he turned to go on, he spat speculatively. There was a sharp, explosive crackle that startled him. He spat again. And again, in the air, before it could fall to the snow, the spittle crackled. He knew that at fifty below spittle crackled on the snow, but this spittle had crackled in the air. Undoubtedly it was colder than fifty below—how much colder he did not know. But the temperature did not matter. He was bound for the old claim on the left fork of Henderson Creek, where the boys were already. They had come over across the divide from the Indian Creek country, while he had come the roundabout way to take a look at the possibilities of getting out logs in the spring from the islands in the Yukon. He would be in to camp by six o'clock; a bit after dark, it was true, but the boys would be there, a fire would be going, and a hot supper would be ready. As for lunch, he pressed his hand against the protruding bundle under his jacket. It was also under his shirt, wrapped up in a handkerchief and lying against the naked skin. It was the only was to keep the biscuits from freezing, He smiled agreeably to himself as he thought of those biscuits, each cut open and sopped in bacon grease, and each enclosing a generous slice of fried bacon.

5   He plunged in among the big spruce trees. The trail was faint. A foot of snow had fallen since the last sled had passed over, and he was glad he was without a sled traveling light. In fact, he carried nothing but the lunch wrapped in the handkerchief. He was surprised, however, at the cold. It certainly was cold, he concluded, as he rubbed his numb nose and cheekbones with his mittened hand. He was a warm-whiskered man, but the hair on his face did not protect the high cheekbones and the eager nose that thrust itself aggressively into the frosty air.

At the man's heels trotted a dog, a big native husky, the proper wolf dog, gray-coated and without any visible or temperamental difference from its brother, the wild wolf. The animal was depressed by the tremendous cold. It knew that it was no time for traveling. Its instinct told it a truer tale than was told to the man by the man's judgment. In reality, it was not merely colder than fifty below zero; it was colder than sixty below, than seventy below. It was seventy-five below zero. Since the freezing point is thirty-two above zero, it meant that one hundred and seven degrees of frost obtained. The dog did not know anything about thermometers. Possibly in its brain there was no sharp consciousness of a condition of very cold such as was in the man's brain. But the brute had its instinct. It experienced a vague but menacing apprehension that subdued it and made it slink along at the man's heels, and that made it question eagerly every unwonted movement of the man as if expecting him to go into camp or to seek shelter somewhere and build a fire. The dog had learned fire, and it wanted fire, or else to burrow under the snow and cuddle its warmth away from the air.

The frozen moisture of its breathing had settled on its fur in a fine powder of frost, and especially were its jowls, muzzle, and eyelashes whitened by its crystalled breath. The man's red beard and mustache were likewise frosted, but more solidly, the deposit taking the form of ice and increasing with every warm, moist breath he exhaled. Also, the man was chewing tobacco, and the muzzle of ice held his lips so rigidly that he was unable to clear his chin when he expelled the juice. The result was that a crystal beard of the color and solidity of amber was increasing its length on his chin. If he fell down it would shatter itself, like glass, into brittle fragments. But he did not mind the appendage. It was the penalty all tobacco chewers paid in that country, and he had been out before in two cold snaps. They had not been so cold as this, he knew, but by the spirit thermometer at Sixty Mile he knew they had been registered at fifty below and at fifty-five.

He held on through the level stretch of woods for several miles, crossed a wide flat of nigger heads,[1] and dropped down a bank to the frozen bed of a small stream. This was Henderson Creek, and he knew he was ten miles from the forks. He looked at his watch. It was ten o'clock. He

---

[1]**nigger heads** exposed rocks.

was making four miles an hour, and he calculated that he would arrive at the forks at half-past twelve. He decided to celebrate that event by eating his lunch there.

The dog dropped in again at his heels, with a tail drooping discouragement, as the man swung along the creek bed. The furrow of the old sled trail was plainly visible, but a dozen inches of snow covered the marks of the last runners. In a month no man had come up or down that silent creek. The man held steadily on. He was not much given to thinking, and just then particularly he had nothing to think about save that he would eat lunch at the forks and that at six o'clock he would be in camp with the boys. There was nobody to talk to; and, had there been, speech would have been impossible because of the ice muzzle on his mouth. So he continued monotonously to chew tobacco and to increase the length of his amber beard.

10   Once in a while the thought reiterated itself that it was very cold and that he had never experienced such cold. As he walked along he rubbed his cheekbones and nose with the back of his mittened hand. He did this automatically, now and again changing hands. But, rub as he would, the instant he stopped his cheekbones were numb, and the following instant the end of his nose went numb. He was sure to frost his cheeks; he knew that, and experienced a pang of regret that he had not devised a nose strap of the sort Bud wore in cold snaps. Such a strap passed across the cheeks, as well, and saved them. But it didn't matter much, after all. What were frosted cheeks? A bit painful, that was all; they were never serious.

Empty as the man's mind was of thoughts, he was keenly observant, and he noticed the changes in the creek, the curves and bends and timber jams, and always he sharply noted where he placed his feet. Once, coming around a bend, he shied abruptly, like a startled horse, curved away from the place where he had been walking, and retreated several paces back along the trail. The creek he knew was frozen clear to the bottom—no creek could contain water in that arctic winter—but he knew also that there were springs that bubbled out from the hillsides and ran along under the snow and on top of the ice of the creek. He knew that the coldest snaps never froze these springs, and he knew likewise their danger. They were traps. They hid pools of water under the snow that might be three inches deep, or three feet. Sometimes a skin of ice half an inch thick covered them, and in turn was covered by the snow. Sometimes there were alternate layers of water and ice skin, so that when one broke through he kept on breaking through for a while, sometimes wetting himself to the waist.

That was why he had shied in such panic. He had felt the give under his feet and heard the crackle of a snow-hidden ice skin. And to get his feet wet in such a temperature meant trouble and danger. At the very least it meant delay, for he would be forced to stop and build a fire, and under its protection to bare his feet while he dried his socks and moccasins. He stood and studied the creek bed and its banks, and decided that the flow of water came from the right. He reflected awhile, rubbing his nose and cheeks, then skirted to the left, stepping gingerly and testing the footing for each step. Once clear of the danger, he took a fresh chew of tobacco and swung along at his four-mile gait.

In the course of the next two hours he came upon several similar traps. Usually the snow above the hidden pools had a sunken, candied appearance that advertised the danger. Once again, however, he had a close call; and once, suspecting danger, he compelled the dog to go in front. The dog did not want to go. It hung back until the man shoved it forward, and then it went quickly across the white, unbroken surface. Suddenly it broke through, floundered to one side, and got away to firmer footing. It had wet its forefeet and legs, and almost immediately the water that clung to it turned to ice. It made quick efforts to lick the ice off its legs, then dropped down in the snow and began to bite out the ice that had formed between the toes. This was a matter of instinct. To permit the ice to remain would mean sore feet. It did not know this. It merely obeyed the mysterious prompting that arose from the deep crypts of its being. But the man knew, having achieved a judgment on the subject, and removed the mitten from his right hand and helped tear out the ice particles. He did not expose his fingers more than a minute, and was astonished at the swift numbness that smote them. It certainly was cold. He pulled on the mitten hastily, and beat the hand savagely across his chest.

At twelve o'clock the day was at its brightest. Yet the sun was too far south on its winter journey to clear the horizon. The bulge of the earth intervened between it and Henderson Creek, where the man walked under a clear sky at noon and cast no shadow. At half-past twelve, to the minute, he arrived at the forks of the creek. He was pleased at the speed he had made. If he kept it up, he would certainly be with the boys by six. He unbuttoned his jacket and shirt and drew forth his lunch. The action consumed no more than a quarter of a minute, yet in that brief moment the numbness laid hold of the exposed fingers. He did not put the mitten on, but, instead, struck the fingers a dozen sharp smashes against his leg. Then he sat down on a snow-covered log to eat. The sting that followed upon the striking of his fingers against his leg ceased so quickly that he was startled. He had had no chance to take a bite of biscuit. He struck the fingers repeatedly and returned them to the mitten, baring the other hand for the purpose of eating. He tried to take a mouthful, but the ice muzzle prevented. He had forgotten to build a fire and thaw out. He chuckled at his foolishness, and as he chuckled he noted the numbness creeping into the exposed fingers. Also, he noted that the stinging which had first come to his toes when he sat down was already passing away. He wondered whether the toes were warm or numb. He moved them inside the moccasins and decided that they were numb.

15   He pulled the mitten on hurriedly and stood up. He was a bit frightened. He stamped up and down until the stinging returned to the feet. It certainly was cold, was his thought. That man from Sulphur Creek had spoken the truth when telling how cold it sometimes got in the country. And he had laughed at him at the time! That showed one must not be too sure of things. There was no mistake about it, it *was* cold. He strode up and down, stamping his feet and threshing his arms, until reassured by the returning warmth. Then he got out matches and proceeded to make a fire. From the undergrowth, where high water of the previous spring had lodged a supply of seasoned twigs, he got his firewood. Working carefully from a small beginning, he soon had a roaring fire, over which he thawed the ice from his face and in the protection of which he ate his biscuits. For the moment the cold of space was outwitted. The dog took satisfaction in the fire, stretching out close enough for warmth and far enough away to escape being singed.

When the man had finished, he filled his pipe and took his comfortable time over a smoke. Then he pulled on his mittens, settled the ear flaps of his cap firmly about his ears, and took the creek trail up the left fork. The dog was disappointed and yearned back toward the fire. This man did not know cold. Possibly all the generations of his ancestry had been ignorant of cold, of real cold, of cold one hundred and seven degrees below freezing point. But the dog knew; all its ancestry knew, and it had inherited the knowledge. And it knew that it was not good to walk abroad in such fearful cold. It was the time to lie snug in a hole in the snow and wait for a curtain of cloud to be drawn across the face of outer space whence this cold came. On the other hand, there was no keen intimacy between the dog and the man. The one was the toil slave of the other, and the only caresses it had ever received were the caresses of the whip lash and of harsh and menacing throat sounds that threatened the whip lash. So the dog made no effort to communicate its apprehension to the man. It was not concerned in the welfare of the man; it was for its own sake that it yearned back toward the fire. But the man whistled, and spoke to it with the sound of whip lashes, and the dog swung in at the man's heels and followed after.

The man took a chew of tobacco and proceeded to start a new amber beard. Also, his moist breath quickly powdered with white his mustache, eyebrows, and lashes. There did not seem to be so many springs on the left fork of the Henderson, and for half and hour the man saw no signs of any. And then it happened. At a place where there were no signs, where the soft, unbroken snow seemed to advertise solidity beneath, the man broke through. It was not deep. He wet himself halfway to the knees before he floundered out to the firm crust.

He was angry, and cursed his luck aloud. He had hoped to get into camp with the boys at six o'clock, and this would delay him an hour, for he would have to build a fire and dry out his footgear. This was imperative at that low temperature—he knew that much; and he turned aside to the bank, which he climbed. On top, tangled in the underbrush about the trunks of several small spruce trees, was a high-water deposit of dry firewood—sticks and twigs, principally, but also larger portions of seasoned branches and fine, dry last year's grasses. He threw down several large pieces on top of the snow. This served for a foundation and prevented the young flame from drowning itself in the snow it otherwise would melt. The flame he got by touching a match to a small shred of birch bark that he took from his pocket. This burned even more readily than paper. Placing it on the foundation, he fed the young flame with wisps of dry grass and with the tiniest dry twigs.

He worked slowly and carefully, keenly aware of his danger. Gradually, as the flame grew stronger, he increased the size of the twigs with which he fed it. He squatted in the snow, pulling the twigs out from their entanglement in the brush and feeding directly to the flame. He knew there must be no failure. When it is seventy-five below zero, a man must not fail in his first attempt to build a fire—that is, if his feet are wet. If his feet are dry, and he fails, he can run along the trail for half a mile and restore his circulation. But the circulation of wet and freezing feet cannot be restored by running when it is seventy-five below. No matter how fast he runs, the wet feet will freeze the harder.

20   All this man knew. The old-timer on Sulphur Creek had told him about it the previous fall, and now he was appreciating the advice. Already all sensation had gone out of his feet. To build the fire he had been forced to remove his mittens, and the fingers had quickly gone numb. His pace of four miles an hour had kept his heart pumping blood to the surface of his body and to all the extremities. But the instant he stopped, the action of the pump eased down. The cold of space smote the unprotected tip of the planet, and he, being on that unprotected tip, received the full force of the blow. The blood of his body recoiled before it. The blood was alive, like the dog, and like the dog it wanted to hide away and cover itself up from the fearful cold. So long as he walked four miles an hour, he pumped that blood, willy-nilly, to the surface; but now it ebbed away and sank down into the recesses of his body. The extremities were the first to feel its absence. His wet feet froze the faster, and his exposed fingers numbed the faster, though they had not yet begun to freeze. Nose and cheeks were already freezing, while the skin of all his body chilled as it lost its blood.

        But he was safe. Toes and nose and cheeks would be only touched by the frost, for the fire was beginning to burn with strength. He was feeding it with twigs the size of his finger. In another minute he would be able to feed it with branches the size of his wrist, and then he could remove his wet footgear, and, while it dried, he could keep his naked feet warm by the fire, rubbing them at first, of course, with snow. The fire was a success. He was safe. He remembered the advice of the old-timer on Sulphur Creek, and smiled. The old-timer had been very serious in laying down the law that no man must travel alone in the Klondike after fifty below. Well, here he was; he had had the accident; he was alone; and he had saved himself. Those old-timers were rather womanish, some of them, he thought. All a man had to do was to keep his head, and he was all right. Any man who was a man could travel alone. But it was surprising, the rapidity with which his cheeks and nose were freezing. And he had not thought his fingers could go lifeless in so short a time. Lifeless they were, for he could scarcely make them move together to grip a twig, and they seemed remote from his body and from him. When he touched a twig, he had to look and see whether or not he had hold of it. The wires were pretty well down between him and his finger ends.

        All of which counted for little. There was the fire, snapping and crackling and promising life with every dancing flame. He started to untie his moccasins. They were coated with ice; thick German socks were like sheaths of iron halfway to the knees; and the moccasin strings were like rods of steel all twisted and knotted as by some conflagration. For a moment he tugged with his numb fingers, then, realizing the folly of it, he drew his sheath knife.

        But before he could cut the strings, it happened. It was his own fault or, rather, his mistake. He should have not built the fire under the spruce tree. He should have built it in the open. But it had been easier to pull the twigs from the brush and drop them directly on the fire. Now the tree under which he had done this carried a weight of snow on its boughs. No wind had blown for weeks, and each bough was fully freighted. Each time he had pulled a twig he had communicated a slight agitation to the tree—an imperceptible agitation, so far as he was concerned, but an agitation sufficient to bring about the disaster. High up in the tree one bough capsized its load of snow. This fell on the boughs beneath, capsizing them. The process continued, spreading out and involving the whole tree. It grew like an avalanche, and it descended without warning upon the man and the fire, and the fire was blotted out! Where it had burned was a mantle of fresh and disordered snow.

The man was shocked. It was as though he had just heard his own sentence of death. For a moment he sat and stared at the spot where the fire had been. Then he grew very calm. Perhaps the old-timer on Sulphur Creek was right. If he had only had a trail mate he would have been in no danger now. The trail mate could have built the fire. Well, it was up to him to build the fire over again, and this second time there must be no failure. Even if he succeeded, he would most likely lose some toes. His feet must be badly frozen by now, and there would be some time before the second fire was ready.

25   Such were his thoughts, but he did not sit and think them. He was busy all the time they were passing though his mind. He made a new foundation for a fire, this time in the open, where no treacherous tree could blot it out. Next he gathered dry grasses and tiny twigs from the high-water flotsam. He could not bring his fingers together to pull them out, but he was able to gather them by the handful. In this way he got many rotten twigs and bits of green moss that were undesirable, but it was the best he could do. He worked methodically, even collecting an armful of the larger branches to be used later when the fire gathered strength. And all the while the dog sat and watched him, a certain yearning wistfulness in its eye, for it looked upon him as the fire provider, and the fire was slow in coming.

When all was ready, the man reached in his pocket for a second piece of birch bark. He knew the bark was there, and, though he could not feel it with his fingers, he could hear its crisp rustling as he fumbled for it. Try as he would, he could not clutch hold of it. And all the time, in his consciousness, was the knowledge that each instant his feet were freezing. This thought tended to put him in a panic, but he fought against it and kept calm. He pulled on his mittens with his teeth, and threshed his arms back and forth, beating his hands with all his might against his sides. He did this sitting down, and he stood up to do it; and all the while the dog sat in the snow, its wolf brush of a tail curled around warmly over its forefeet, its sharp wolf ears pricked forward intently as it watched the man. And the man, as he beat and threshed with his arms and hands, felt a great surge of envy as he regarded the creature that was warm and secure in its natural covering.

After a time he was aware of the first faraway signals of sensation in his beaten fingers. The faint tingling grew stronger till it evolved into a stinging ache that was excruciating, but which the man hailed with satisfaction. He stripped down the mitten from his right hand and fetched forth the birch bark. The exposed fingers were quickly going numb again. Next he brought out his bunch of sulphur matches. But the tremendous cold had already driven the life out of his fingers. In his effort to separate one match from the others, the whole bunch fell in the snow. He tried to pick it out of the snow, but failed. The dead fingers could neither touch nor clutch. He was very careful. He drove the thought of his freezing feet, and nose, and cheeks, out of his mind, devoting his whole soul to the matches. He watched, using the sense of vision in place of that of touch, and when he saw his fingers on each side the bunch, he closed them—that is, he willed to close them, for the wires were down, and the fingers did not obey. He pulled the mitten on the right hand, and beat it fiercely against his knee.

Then, with both mittened hands, he scooped the bunch of matches, along with much snow, into his lap. Yet he was not better off.

After some manipulation he managed to get the bunch between the heels of his mittened hands. In this fashion he carried it to his mouth. The ice crackled and snapped when by a violent effort he opened his mouth. He drew the lower jaw in, curled the upper lip out of the way, and scraped the bunch with his upper teeth in order to separate a match. He succeeded in getting one, which he dropped on his lap. He was no better off. He could not pick it up. Then he devised a way. He picked it up in his teeth and scratched it on his leg. Twenty times he scratched before he succeeded in lighting it. As it flamed he held it with his teeth to the birch bark. But the burning brimstone went up his nostrils and into his lungs causing him to cough spasmodically. The match fell into the snow and went out.

The old-timer on Sulphur Creek was right, he thought in the moment of controlled despair that ensued: after fifty below, a man should travel with a partner. He beat his hands, but failed in exciting any sensation. Suddenly he bared both hands, removing the mittens with his teeth. He caught the whole bunch between the heels of his hands. His arm muscles not being frozen enabled him to press the hand heels tightly against the matches. Then he scratched the bunch along his leg. It flared into flame, seventy sulphur matches at once! There was no wind to blow them out. He kept his head to one side to escape the strangling fumes, and held the blazing bunch to the birch bark. As he so held it, he became aware of sensation in his hand. His flesh was burning. He could smell it. Deep down below the surface he could feel it. The sensation developed into pain that grew acute. And still he endured it, holding the flame of the matches clumsily to the bark that would not light readily because his own burning hands were in the way, absorbing most of the flame.

30   At last, when he could endure no more, he jerked his hands apart. The blazing matches fell sizzling into the snow, but the birch bark was alight. He began laying dry grasses and the tiniest twigs on the flame. He could not pick and choose, for he had to lift the fuel between the heels of his hands. Small pieces of rotten wood and green moss clung to the twigs, and he bit them off as well as he could with his teeth. He cherished the flame carefully and awkwardly. It meant life, and it must not perish. The withdrawal of blood from the surface of his body now made him begin to shiver, and he grew more awkward. A large piece of green moss fell squarely on the little fire. He tried to poke it out with his fingers, but his shivering frame made him poke too far, and he disrupted the nucleus of the little fire, the burning grasses and little twigs separating and scattering. He tried to poke them together again, but in spite of the tenseness of the effort, his shivering got away from him, and the twigs were hopelessly scattered. Each twig gushed a puff of smoke and went out. The fire provider had failed. As he looked apathetically about him, his eyes chanced on the dog, sitting across the ruins of the fire from him, in the snow, making restless, hunching movements, slightly lifting one forefoot and then the other, shifting its weight back and forth on them with wistful eagerness.

The sight of the dog put a wild idea into his head. He remembered the tale of the man, caught in the blizzard, who killed a steer and crawled inside the carcass, and so was saved. He would kill the dog and bury his hands in the warm body until the numbness went out of them. Then he could build another fire. He spoke to the dog, calling it to him; but in his voice was a strange note of fear that frightened the animal, who had never known the man to speak in such a way before. Something was the matter, and its suspicious nature sensed danger—it knew not what danger, but somewhere, somehow, in its brain arose an apprehension of the man. It flattened its ears down at the sound of the man's voice, and its restless, hunching movements and the liftings and shiftings of its forefeet became more pronounced; but it would not come to the man. He got on his hands and knees and crawled toward the dog. This unusual posture again excited suspicion, and the animal sidled mincingly away.

The man sat up in the snow for a moment and struggled for calmness. Then he pulled on his mittens, by means of his teeth, and got upon his feet. He glanced down at first in order to assure himself that he was really standing up, for the absence of sensation in his feet left him unrelated to the earth. His erect position in itself started to drive the webs of suspicion from the dog's mind; and when he spoke peremptorily, with the sound of whip lashes in his voice, the dog rendered its customary allegiance and came to him. As it came within reaching distance, the man lost his control. His arms flashed out to the dog, and he experienced genuine surprise when he discovered that his hands could not clutch, that there was neither bend nor feeling in the fingers. He had forgotten for the moment that they were frozen and that they were freezing more and more. All this happened quickly, and before the animal could get away, he encircled his body with his arms. He sat down in the snow, and in this fashion held the dog, while it snarled and whined and struggled.

But it was all he could do, hold its body encircled in his arms and sit there. He realized that he could not kill the dog. There was no way to do it. With his helpless hands he could neither draw nor hold his sheath knife nor throttle the animal. He released it, and it plunged wildly away, with tail between its legs, and still snarling. It halted forty feet away and surveyed him curiously, with ears sharply pricked forward.

The man looked down at his hands in order to locate them, and found them hanging on the ends of his arms. It struck him as curious that one should have to use his eyes in order to find out where his hands were. He began threshing his arms back and forth, beating the mittened hands against his sides. He did this for five minutes, violently, and his heart pumped enough blood up to the surface to put a stop to his shivering. But no sensation was aroused in his hands. He had an impression that they hung like weights on the ends of his arms, but when he tried to run the impression down, he could not find it.

35   A certain fear of death, dull and oppressive, came to him. This fear quickly became poignant as he realized that it was no longer a mere matter of freezing his fingers and toes, or losing his hands and feet, but that it was a matter of life and death with the chances against him. This threw him into a panic, and he turned and ran up the creek bed along the old, dim trail. The dog joined in behind and kept up with him. He ran blindly, without intention, in fear such as he had never known in his life. Slowly, as he plowed and floundered through the snow, he began to see things again—the banks of the creek, the old timber jams, the leafless aspens, and the sky. The running made him feel better. He did not shiver. Maybe, if he ran on, his feet would thaw out; and, anyway, if he ran far enough, he would reach camp

and the boys. Without doubt he would lose some fingers and toes and some of his face; but the boys would take care of him, and save the rest of him when he got there. And at the same time there was another thought in his mind that said he would never get to the camp and the boys; that it was too many miles away, that the freezing had too great a start on him, and that he would soon be stiff and dead. This thought he kept in the background and refused to consider. Sometimes it pushed itself forward and demanded to be heard, but he thrust it back and strove to think of other things.

It struck him as curious that he could run at all on feet so frozen that he could not feel them when they struck the earth and took the weight of his body. He seemed to himself to skim along above the surface, and to have no connection with the earth. Somewhere he had once seen a winged Mercury,[2] and he wondered if Mercury felt as he felt when skimming over the earth.

His theory of running until he reached the camp and the boys had one flaw in it; he lacked the endurance. Several times he stumbled, and finally he tottered, crumpled up, and fell. When he tried to rise, he failed. He must sit and rest, he decided, and next time he would merely walk and keep on going. As he sat and regained his breath, he noted that he was feeling quite warm and comfortable. He was not shivering, and it even seemed that a warm glow had come to his chest and trunk. And yet, when he touched his nose and cheeks, there was no sensation. Running would not thaw them out. Nor would it thaw out his hands and feet. Then the thought came to him that the frozen portions of his body must be extending. He tried to keep this thought down, to forget it, to think of something else; he was aware of the panicky feeling that it caused, and he was afraid of the panic. But the thought asserted itself, and persisted, until it produced a vision of his body totally frozen. This was too much, and he made another wild run along the trail. Once he slowed down to a walk, but the thought of the freezing extending itself made him run again.

And all the time the dog ran with him, at his heels. When he fell down a second time, it curled its tail over its forefeet and sat in front of him, facing him, curiously eager and intent. The warmth and security of the animal angered him, and he cursed it till it flattened down its ears appeasingly. This time the shivering came more quickly upon the man. He was losing his battle with the frost. It was creeping into his body from all sides. The thought of it drove him on, but he ran no more than a hundred feet, when he staggered and pitched headlong. It was his last panic. When he had recovered his breath and control, he sat up and entertained in his mind the conception of meeting death with dignity. However, the conception did not come to him in such terms. His idea of it was that he had been making a fool of himself, running around like a chicken with its head cut off—such was the simile that occurred to him. Well, he was bound to freeze anyway, and he might as well take it decently. With this new-found peace of mind came the first glimmerings of drowsiness. A good idea, he thought, to sleep off to death. It was like taking an anesthetic. Freezing was not so bad as people thought. There were lots worse ways to die.

He pictured the boys finding his body the next day. Suddenly he found himself with them, coming along the trail and looking for himself. And, still

---

[2]**Mercury** Roman messenger god.

with them, he came around a turn in the trail and found himself lying in the snow. He did not belong with himself any more, for even then he was out of himself, standing with the boys and looking at himself in the snow. It certainly was cold, was his thought. When he got back to the States he could tell the folks what real cold was. He drifted on from this to a vision of the old-timer on Sulphur Creek. He could see him quite clearly, warm and comfortable, and smoking a pipe.

40   "You were right, old hoss; you were right," the man mumbled to the old-timer on Sulphur Creek.

Then the man drowsed off into what seemed to him the most comfortable and satisfying sleep he had ever known. The dog sat facing him and waiting. The brief day drew to a close in a long, slow twilight. There were no signs of a fire to be made, and besides, never in the dog's experience had it known a man to sit like that in the snow and make no fire. As the twilight drew on, its eager yearning for the fire mastered it, and with a great lifting and shifting of forefeet, it whined softly, then flattened its ears down in anticipation of being chidden by the man. But the man remained silent. Later the dog whined loudly. And still later it crept close to the man and caught the scent of death. This made the animal bristle and back away. A little longer it delayed, howling under the stars that leaped and danced and shone brightly in the cold sky. Then it turned and trotted up the trail in the direction of the camp it knew, where were the other food providers and fire providers.

 TOPICS FOR CRITICAL THINKING AND WRITING

1. Explain the significance of the sentence, "The trouble with him was that he was without imagination" (paragraph 3).
2. Did the ending of this story surprise you? Was there a point in your reading of the story when you knew how it would end?
3. Does London's story lose some of its power on a second reading, or does it become even more powerful? What does it mean to say that a story is powerful in its effect?
4. Why did London choose to include the dog? What would be missing in our experience of the story and its meanings if the dog were not part of it?
5. What does "To Build a Fire" tell us about London's attitude toward nature? Please locate passages to explain your response.
6. In a letter to a young writer, London said: "Don't you tell the reader. . . . But HAVE YOUR CHARACTERS TELL IT BY THEIR DEEDS, ACTIONS, TALKS, ETC. . . . The reader. . . doesn't want your dissertations on the subject, . . . your ideas—BUT PUT ALL THOSE THINGS WHICH ARE YOURS INTO THE STORIES." Good advice for a storyteller. Judging from this story, what do you suppose London's "ideas" were?
7. Have you ever been in a situation of extreme cold or heat? Were you frightened? Were you alone? What happened?
8. Do you think that the personal situation you just described would make for a good story? Or would your experiences be more interesting and engaging to a reader in the form of an essay?

ALICE ELLIOTT DARK

Alice Elliott Dark received a B.A. in Oriental studies from the University of Pennsylvania, and an M.F.A. in creative writing from Antioch University. She has published two books of stories, Naked to the Waist *(1991) and* In the Gloaming: Stories *(2000), as well as a novel,* Think of England *(2002), and she teaches at The Writer's Voice, in New York City.*

In the Gloaming   [1993]

Her son wanted to talk again, suddenly. During the days, he still brooded, scowling at the swimming pool from the vantage point of his wheelchair, where he sat covered with blankets despite the summer heat. In the evenings, though, Laird became more like his old self—his *old* self, really. He became sweeter, the way he'd been as a child, before he began to cloak himself with layers of irony and clever remarks. He spoke with an openness that astonished her. No one she knew talked that way—no man, at least. After he was asleep, Janet would run through the conversations in her mind, and realize what it was she wished she had said. She knew she was generally considered sincere, but that had more to do with her being a good listener than with how she expressed herself. She found it hard work to keep up with him, but it was the work she had pined for all her life.

A month earlier, after a particularly long and grueling visit with a friend who'd come up on the train from New York, Laird had declared a new policy: no visitors, no telephone calls. She didn't blame him. People who hadn't seen him for a while were often shocked to tears by his appearance, and, rather than having them cheer him up, he felt obliged to comfort them. She'd overheard bits of some of those conversations. The final one was no worse than the others, but he was fed up. He had said more than once that he wasn't cut out to be the brave one, the one who would inspire everybody to walk away from a visit with him feeling uplifted, shaking their heads in wonder. He had liked being the most handsome and missed it very much: he was not a good victim. When he had had enough he went into a self-imposed retreat, complete with a wall of silence and other ascetic practices that kept him busy for several weeks.

Then he softened. Not only did he want to talk again; he wanted to talk to *her.*

It began the night they ate outside on the terrace for the first time all summer. Afterward, Martin—Laird's father—got up to make a telephone call, but Janet stayed in her wicker chair, resting before clearing the table. It was one of those moments when she felt nostalgic for cigarettes. On nights like this, when the air was completely still, she used to blow her famous smoke rings for the children, dutifully obeying their commands to blow one through another or three in a row, or to make big, ropy circles that expanded as they floated up to the heavens. She did exactly what they wanted, for as long as they wanted, sometimes going through a quarter of a pack before they allowed her to stop. Incredibly, neither Anne nor Laird became smokers. Just the opposite; they nagged at her to quit, and were pleased when she finally did. She wished they had been just a little bit sorry; it was part of their childhood coming to an end, after all.

5   Out of habit, she took note of the first lightning bug, the first star. The lawn darkened, and the flowers that had sulked in the heat all day suddenly released their perfumes. She laid her head back on the rim of the chair and closed her eyes. Soon she was following Laird's breathing, and found herself picking up the vital rhythms, breathing along. It was so peaceful, being near him like this. How many mothers spend so much time with their thirty-three-year-old sons? she thought. She had as much of him now as she had had when he was an infant; more, in a way, because she had the memory of the intervening years as well, to round out her thoughts about him. When they sat quietly together she felt as close to him as she ever had. It was still him in there, inside the failing shell. *She still enjoyed him.*

"The gloaming," he said, suddenly.

She nodded dreamily, automatically, then sat up. She turned to him. "What?" Although she had heard.

"I remember when I was little you took me over to the picture window and told me that in Scotland this time of day was called the 'gloaming.'"

Her skin tingled. She cleared her throat, quietly, taking care not to make too much of an event of his talking again. "You thought I said 'gloomy.'"

10   He gave a smile, then looked at her searchingly. "I always thought it hurt you somehow that the day was over, but you said it was a beautiful time because for a few moments the purple light made the whole world look like the Scottish Highlands on a summer night."

"Yes. As if all the earth were covered with heather."

"I'm sorry I never saw Scotland," he said.

"You're a Scottish lad nonetheless," she said. "At least on my side." She remembered offering to take him to Scotland once, but Laird hadn't been interested. By then, he was in college and already sure of his own destinations, which had diverged so thoroughly from hers. "I'm amazed you remember that conversation. You couldn't have been more than seven."

"I've been remembering a lot lately."

15   "Have you?"

"Mostly about when I was very small. I suppose it comes from having you take care of me again. Sometimes, when I wake up and see your face, I feel I can remember you looking in on me when I was in my crib. I remember your dresses."

"Oh, no!" She laughed lightly.

"You always had the loveliest expressions," he said.

She was astonished, caught off guard. Then, she had a memory, too—of her leaning over Laird's crib and suddenly having a picture of looking up at her own mother. "I know what you mean," she said.

20   "You do, don't you?"

He looked at her in a close, intimate way that made her self-conscious. She caught herself swinging her leg nervously, like a pendulum, and stopped.

"Mom," he said. "There are still a few things I need to do. I have to write a will, for one thing."

Her heart went flat. In his presence she had always maintained that he would get well. She wasn't sure she could discuss the other possibility.

"Thank you," he said.

25   "For what?"

"For not saying that there's plenty of time for that, or some similar sentiment."

"The only reason I didn't say it was to avoid the cliché, not because I don't believe it."

"You believe there is plenty of time?"

She hesitated; he noticed, and leaned forward slightly. "I believe there is time," she said.

30   "Even if I were healthy, it would be a good idea."

"I suppose."

"I don't want to leave it until it's too late. You wouldn't want me to suddenly leave everything to the nurses, would you?"

She laughed, pleased to hear him joking again. "All right, all right, I'll call the lawyer."

"That would be great." There was a pause. "Is this still your favorite time of day, Mom?"

35   "Yes, I suppose it is," she said, "although I don't think in terms of favorites anymore."

"Never mind favorites, then. What else do you like?"

"What do you mean?" she asked.

"I mean exactly that."

"I don't know. I care about all the ordinary things. You know what I like."

40   "Name one thing."

"I feel silly."

"Please?"

"All right. I like my patch of lilies of the valley under the trees over there. Now can we change the subject?"

"Name one more thing."

45   "Why?"

"I want to get to know you."

"Oh, Laird, there's nothing to know."

"I don't believe that for a minute."

"But it's true. I'm average. The only extraordinary thing about me is my children."

50   "All right," he said. "Then let's talk about how you feel about me."

"Do you flirt with your nurses like this when I'm not around?"

"I don't dare. They've got me where they want me." He looked at her. "You're changing the subject."

She smoothed her skirt. "I know how you feel about church, but if you need to talk I'm sure the minister would be glad to come over. Or if you would rather have a doctor . . . ."

He laughed.

55   "What?"

"That you still call psychiatrists 'doctors.'"

She shrugged.

"I don't need a professional, Ma." He laced his hands and pulled at them as he struggled for words.

"What can I do?" she asked.

60   He met her gaze. "You're where I come from. I need to know about you."

    That night she lay awake, trying to think of how she could help, of what, aside from her time, she had to offer. She couldn't imagine.

    She was anxious the next day when he was sullen again, but the next night, and on each succeeding night, the dusk worked its spell. She set dinner on the table outside, and afterward, when Martin had vanished into the maw of his study, she and Laird began to speak. The air around them seemed to crackle with the energy they were creating in their effort to know and be known. Were other people so close, she wondered. She never had been, not to anybody. Certainly she and Martin had never really connected, not soul to soul, and with her friends, no matter how loyal and reliable, she always had a sense of what she could do that would alienate them. Of course, her friends had the option of cutting her off, and Martin could always ask for a divorce, whereas Laird was a captive audience. Parents and children were all captive audiences to each other; in view of this, it was amazing how little comprehension there was of one another's stories. Everyone stopped paying attention so early on, thinking they had figured it all out. She recognized that she was as guilty of this as anyone. She was still surprised whenever she went over to her daughter's house and saw how neat she was; in her mind, Anne was still a sloppy teenager who threw sweaters into the corner of her closet and candy wrappers under her bed. It still surprised her that Laird wasn't interested in girls. He had been, hadn't he? She remembered lying awake listening for him to come home, hoping that he was smart enough to apply what he knew about the facts of life, to take precautions.

    Now she had the chance to let go of those old notions. It wasn't that she liked everything about Laird—there was much that remained foreign to her—but she wanted to know about all of it. As she came to her senses every morning in the moment or two after she awoke, she found herself aching with love and gratitude; as if he were a small, perfect creature again and she could look forward to a day of watching him grow. Quickly, she became greedy for their evenings. She replaced her half-facetious, half-hopeful reading of the horoscope in the daily newspaper with a new habit of tracking the time the sun would set, and drew satisfaction from seeing it come earlier as the summer waned; it meant she didn't have to wait as long. She took to sleeping late, shortening the day even more. It was ridiculous, she knew. She was behaving like a girl with a crush, behaving absurdly. It was a feeling she had thought she'd never have again, and now here it was. She immersed herself in it, living her life for the twilight moment when his eyes would begin to glow, the signal that he was stirring into consciousness. Then her real day would begin.

    "Dad ran off quickly," he said one night. She had been wondering when he would mention it.

65   "He had a phone call to make," she said automatically.

    Laird looked directly into her eyes, his expression one of gentle reproach. He was letting her know he had caught her in the central lie of her life, which was that she understood Martin's obsession with his work. She averted his gaze. The truth was that she had never understood. Why couldn't he sit with her for half an hour after dinner, or, if not with her, why not with his dying son?

She turned sharply to look at Laird. The word "dying" had sounded so loudly in her mind that she wondered if she had spoken it, but he showed no reaction. She wished she hadn't even thought it. She tried to stick to good thoughts in his presence. When she couldn't, and he had a bad night afterward, she blamed herself, as her efficient memory dredged up all the books and magazine articles she had read emphasizing the effect of psychological factors on the course of the disease. She didn't entirely believe it, but she felt compelled to give the benefit of the doubt to every theory that might help. It couldn't do any harm to think positively. And if it gave him a few more months . . .

"I don't think Dad can stand to be around me."

"That's not true." It was true.

70   "Poor Dad. He's always been such a hypochondriac—we have that in common. He must hate this."

"He just wants you to get well."

"If that's what he wants, I'm afraid I'm going to have to disappoint him again. At least this will be the last time I let him down."

He said this merrily, with the old, familiar light darting from his eyes. She allowed herself to be amused. He had always been fond of teasing, and held no subject sacred. As the de facto authority figure in the house—Martin hadn't been home enough to be the real disciplinarian—she had often been forced to reprimand Laird, but, in truth, she shared his sense of humor. She responded to it now by leaning over to cuff him on the arm. It was an automatic response, prompted by a burst of high spirits that took no notice of the circumstances. It was a mistake. Even through the thickness of his terrycloth robe, her knuckles knocked on bone. There was nothing left of him.

"It's his loss," she said, the shock of Laird's thinness making her serious again. It was the furthest she would go in criticizing Martin. She had always felt it her duty to maintain a benign image of him for the children. He had become a character of her invention, with a whole range of postulated emotions whereby he missed them when he was away on a business trip and thought of them every few minutes when he had to work late. Some years earlier, when she was secretly seeing a doctor—a psychiatrist—she had finally admitted to herself that Martin was never going to be the lover she had dreamed of. He was an ambitious, competitive, self-absorbed man who probably should never have got married. It was such a relief to be able to face it that she wanted to share the news with her children, only to discover that they were dependent on the myth. They could hate his work, but they could not bring themselves to believe he had any choice in the matter. She had dropped the subject.

75   "Thank you, Ma. It's his loss in your case, too."

A throbbing began behind her eyes, angering her. The last thing she wanted to do was cry. There would be plenty of time for that. "It's not all his fault," she said when she had regained some measure of control. "I'm not very good at talking about myself. I was brought up not to."

"So was I," he said.

"Yes, I suppose you were."

"Luckily, I didn't pay any attention." He grinned.

80   "I hope not," she said, and meant it. "Can I get you anything?"

"A new immune system?"

She rolled her eyes, trying to disguise the way his joke had touched on her prayers. "Very funny. I was thinking more along the lines of an iced tea or an extra blanket."

"I'm fine. I'm getting tired, actually."

Her entire body went on the alert, and she searched his face anxiously for signs of deterioration. Her nerves darted and pricked whenever he wanted anything; her adrenaline rushed. The fight-or-flight response, she supposed. She had often wanted to flee, but had forced herself to stay, to fight with what few weapons she had. She responded to his needs, making sure there was a fresh, clean set of sheets ready when he was tired, food when he was hungry. It was what she could do.

85   "Shall I get a nurse?" She pushed her chair back from the table.

"O.K.," Laird said weakly. He stretched out his hand to her, and the incipient moonlight illuminated his skin so it shone like alabaster. His face had turned ashy. It was a sight that made her stomach drop. She ran for Maggie, and by the time they returned Laird's eyes were closed, his head lolling to one side. Automatically, Janet looked for a stirring in his chest. There it was: his shoulders expanded; he still breathed. Always, in the second before she saw movement, she became cold and clinical as she braced herself for the possibility of discovering that he was dead.

Maggie had her fingers on his wrist and was counting his pulse against the second hand of her watch, her lips moving. She laid his limp hand back on his lap. "Fast," she pronounced.

"I'm not surprised," Janet said, masking her fear with authority. "We had a long talk."

Maggie frowned. "Now I'll have to wake him up again for his meds."

90   "Yes, I suppose that's true. I forgot about that."

Janet wheeled him into his makeshift room downstairs and helped Maggie lift him into the rented hospital bed. Although he weighed almost nothing, it was really a job for two; his weight was dead weight. In front of Maggie, she was all brusque efficiency, except for the moment when her fingers strayed to touch Laird's pale cheek and she prayed she hadn't done any harm.

"Who's your favorite author?" he asked one night.

"Oh, there are so many," she said.

"Your real favorite."

95   She thought. "The truth is there are certain subjects I find attractive more than certain authors. I seem to read in cycles, to fulfill an emotional yearning."

"Such as?"

"Books about people who go off to live in Africa or Australia or the South Seas."

He laughed. "That's fairly self-explanatory. What else?"

"When I really hate life I enjoy books about real murders. 'True crime,' I think they're called now. They're very punishing."

100   "Is that what's so compelling about them? I could never figure it out. I just know that at certain times I loved the gore, even though I felt absolutely disgusted with myself for being interested in it."

"You need to think about when those times were. That will tell you a lot." She paused. "I don't like reading about sex."

"Big surprise!"

"No, no," she said. "It's not for the reason you think, or not only for that reason. You see me as a prude, I know, but remember, it's part of a mother's job to come across that way. Although perhaps I went a bit far . . ."

He shrugged amiably. "Water under the bridge. But go on about sex."

105   "I think it should be private. I always feel as though these writers are showing off when they describe a sex scene. They're not really trying to describe sex, but to demonstrate that they're not afraid to write about it. As if they're thumbing their noses at their mothers."

He made a moue.

Janet went on. "You don't think there's an element of that? I *do* question their motives, because I don't think sex can ever actually be portrayed—the sensations and the emotions are . . . beyond language. If you only describe the mechanics, the effect is either clinical or pornographic, and if you try to describe intimacy instead, you wind up with abstractions. The only sex you could describe fairly well is bad sex—and who wants to read about that, for God's sake, when everyone is having bad sex of their own?"

"Mother!" He was laughing helplessly, his arms hanging limply over the sides of his chair.

"I mean it. To me it's like reading about someone using the bathroom."

110   "Good grief!"

"Now who's the prude?"

"I never said I wasn't," he said. "Maybe we should change the subject."

She looked out across the land. The lights were on in other people's houses, giving the evening the look of early fall. The leaves were different, too, becoming droopy. The grass was dry, even with all the watering and tending from the gardener. The summer was nearly over.

"Maybe we shouldn't," she said. "I've been wondering. Was that side of life satisfying for you?"

115   "Ma, tell me you're not asking me about my sex life."

She took her napkin and folded it carefully, lining up the edges and running her fingers along the hems. She felt very calm, very pulled together and all of a piece, as if she'd finally got the knack of being a dignified woman. She threaded her fingers and laid her hands in her lap. "I'm asking about your love life," she said. "Did you love, and were you loved in return?"

"Yes."

"I'm glad."

"That was easy," he said.

120   "Oh, I've gotten very easy, in my old age."

"Does Dad know about this?" His eyes were twinkling wickedly.

"Don't be fresh," she said.

"You started it."

"Then I'm stopping it. Now."

125   He made a funny face, and then another, until she could no longer keep from smiling. His routine carried her back to memories of his childhood efforts to charm her: watercolors of her favorite vistas (unrecognizable without the captions), bouquets of violets self-consciously flung into her lap, chores performed without prompting. He had always gone too far, then backtracked to regain even footing. She had always allowed herself to be wooed.

Suddenly she realized: Laird had been the love of her life.

One night it rained hard. Janet decided to serve the meal in the kitchen, since Martin was out. They ate in silence; she was freed from the compulsion to keep up the steady stream of chatter that she used to affect when Laird hadn't talked at all; now she knew she could save her words for afterward. He ate nothing but comfort foods lately: mashed potatoes, vanilla ice cream, rice pudding. The days of his strict macrobiotic regime, and all the cooking classes she had taken in order to help him along with it, were past. His body was essentially a thing of the past, too; when he ate, he was feeding what was left of his mind. He seemed to want to recapture the cosseted feeling he'd had when he'd been sick as a child and she would serve him flat ginger ale, and toast soaked in cream, and play endless card games with him, using his blanket-covered legs as a table. In those days, too, there'd been a general sense of giving way to illness: then, he let himself go completely because he knew he would soon be better and active and have a million things expected of him again. Now he let himself go because he had fought long enough.

Finally, he pushed his bowl toward the middle of the table, signaling that he was finished. (His table manners had gone to pieces. Who cared?) She felt a light, jittery excitement, the same jazzy feeling she got when she was in a plane that was picking up speed on the runway. She arranged her fork and knife on the rim of her plate and pulled her chair in closer. "I had an odd dream last night," she said.

His eyes remained dull.

130   She waited uncertainly, thinking that perhaps she had started to talk too soon. "Would you like something else to eat?"

He shook his head. There was no will in his expression: his refusal was purely physical, a gesture coming from the satiation in his stomach. An animal walking away from its bowl, she thought.

To pass the time, she carried the dishes to the sink, gave them a good hot rinse, and put them in the dishwasher. She carried the ice cream to the counter, pulled a spoon from the drawer and scraped off a mouthful of the thick, creamy residue that stuck to the inside of the lid. She ate it without thinking, so the sudden sweetness caught her by surprise. All the while she kept track of Laird, but every time she thought she noticed signs of his readiness to talk and hurried back to the table, she found his face still blank.

She went to the window. The lawn had become a floodplain and was filled with broad pools; the branches of the evergreens sagged, and the sky was the same uniform grayish yellow it had been since morning. She saw him focus his gaze on the line where the treetops touched the heavens, and she understood. There was no lovely interlude on this rainy night, no heathered dusk. The gray landscape had taken the light out of him.

"I'm sorry," she said aloud, as if it were her fault.

135   He gave a tiny, helpless shrug.

She hovered for a few moments, hoping, but his face was slack, and she gave up. She felt utterly forsaken, too disappointed and agitated to sit with him and watch the rain. "It's all right," she said. "It's a good night to watch television."

She wheeled him to the den and left him with Maggie, then did not know what to do with herself. She had no contingency plan for this time. It was usually the one period of the day when she did not need the anesthesia of tennis games, bridge lessons, volunteer work, errands. She had not considered the present possibility. For some time, she hadn't given any thought to what Martin would call "the big picture." Her conversations with Laird had lulled her into inventing a parallel big picture of her own. She realized that a part of her had worked out a whole scenario: the summer evenings would blend into fall; then, gradually, the winter would arrive, heralding chats by the fire, Laird resting his feet on the pigskin ottoman in the den while she dutifully knitted her yearly Christmas sweaters for Anne's children.

She had allowed herself to imagine a future. That had been her mistake. This silent, endless evening was her punishment, a reminder of how things really were.

She did not know where to go in her own house, and ended up wandering through the rooms, propelled by a vague, hunted feeling. Several times, she turned around, expecting someone to be there, but, of course, no one ever was. She was quite alone. Eventually, she realized that she was imagining a person in order to give material properties to the source of her wounds. She was inventing a villain. There should be a villain, shouldn't there? There should be an enemy, a devil, an evil force that could be driven out. Her imagination had provided it with aspects of a corporeal presence so she could pretend, for a moment, that there was a real enemy hovering around her, someone she could have the police come and take away. But the enemy was part of Laird, and neither he nor she nor any of the doctors or experts or ministers could separate the two.

140   She went upstairs and took a shower. She barely paid attention to her own body anymore, and only noticed abstractly that the water was too hot, her skin turning pink. Afterward, she sat on the chaise lounge in her bedroom and tried to read. She heard something; she leaned forward and cocked her head toward the sound. Was that Laird's voice? Suddenly she believed that he had begun to talk after all—she believed he was talking to Maggie. She dressed and went downstairs. He was alone in the den, alone with the television. He didn't hear or see her. She watched him take a drink from a cup, his hand shaking badly. It was a plastic cup with a straw poking through the lid, the kind used by small children while they are learning to drink. It was supposed to prevent accidents, but it couldn't stop his hands from trembling. He managed to spill the juice anyway.

Laird had always coveted the decadent pile of cashmere lap blankets she had collected over the years in the duty-free shops of the various British airports. Now he wore one around his shoulders, one over his knees. She remembered similar balmy nights when he would arrive home from soccer practice after dark, a towel slung around his neck.

"I suppose it has to be in the church," he said.

"I think it should," she said, "but it's up to you."

"I guess it's not the most timely moment to make a statement about my personal disbeliefs. But I'd like you to keep it from being too lugubrious. No lilies, for instance."

145   "God forbid."

"And have some decent music."

"Such as?"

"I had an idea, but now I can't remember."

He pressed his hands to his eyes. His fingers were so transparent that they looked as if he were holding them over a flashlight.

150   "Please buy a smashing dress, something mournful yet elegant."
       "All right."
       "And don't wait until the last minute."
       She didn't reply.

       Janet gave up on the idea of a rapprochement between Martin and
       Laird; she felt freer when she stopped hoping for it. Martin rarely came
       home for dinner anymore. Perhaps he was having an affair? It was a thought
       she'd never allowed herself to have before, but it didn't threaten her now.
       Good for him, she even decided, in her strongest, most magnanimous mo-
       ments. Good for him if he's actually feeling bad and trying to do something
       to make himself feel better.
155   Anne was brave and chipper during her visits, yet when she walked
       back out to her car, she would wrap her arms around her ribs and shudder.
       "I don't know how you do it, Mom. Are you really all right?" she always
       asked, with genuine concern.
       "Anne's become such a hopeless matron," Laird always said, with fond
       exasperation, when he and his mother were alone again later. Once, Janet
       began to tease him for finally coming to friendly terms with his sister, but
       she cut it short when she saw that he was blinking furiously.
       They were exactly the children she had hoped to have: a companion-
       able girl, a mischievous boy. It gave her great pleasure to see them together.
       She did not try to listen to their conversations but watched from a distance,
       usually from the kitchen as she prepared them a snack reminiscent of their
       childhood, like watermelon boats or lemonade. Then she would walk Anne
       to the car, their similar good shoes clacking across the gravel. They hugged,
       pressing each other's arms, and their brief embraces buoyed them up—
       forbearance and grace passing back and forth between them like a piece of
       shared clothing, designated for use by whoever needed it most. It was the
       kind of parting toward which she had aimed her whole life, a graceful, se-
       cure parting at the close of a peaceful afternoon. After Anne left, Janet al-
       ways had a tranquil moment or two as she walked back to the house
       through the humid September air. Everything was so still. Occasionally
       there were the hums and clicks of a lawnmower or the shrieks of a band of
       children heading home from school. There were the insects and the birds.
       It was a straightforward, simple life she had chosen. She had tried never to
       ask for too much, and to be of use. Simplicity had been her hedge against
       bad luck. It had worked for so long. For a brief moment, as she stepped
       lightly up the single slate stair and through the door, her legs still harboring
       all their former vitality, she could pretend her luck was still holding.
       Then she would glance out the window and there would be the heart-
       catching sight of Laird, who would never again drop by for a casual visit.
       Her chest would ache and flutter, a cave full of bats.
       Perhaps she had asked for too much, after all.

160   "What did you want to be when you grew up?" Laird asked.
       "I was expected to be a wife and mother. I accepted that. I wasn't a
       rebel."
       "There must have been something else."
       "No," she said. "Oh, I guess I had all the usual fantasies of the day, of be-
       ing the next Amelia Earhart or Margaret Mead, but that was all they were—

fantasies. I wasn't even close to being brave enough. Can you imagine me flying across the ocean on my own?" She laughed and looked over for his laughter, but he had fallen asleep.

A friend of Laird's had somehow got the mistaken information that Laird had died, so she and Martin received a condolence letter. There was a story about a time a few years back when the friend was with Laird on a bus in New York. They had been sitting behind two older women, waitresses who began to discuss their income taxes, trying to decide how much of their tip income to declare to sound realistic so they wouldn't attract an audit. Each woman offered up bits of folk wisdom on the subject, describing in detail her particular situation. During a lull in the conversation, Laird stood up.

165   "Excuse me, I couldn't help overhearing," he said, leaning over them. "May I have your names and addresses, please? I work for the IRS."

The entire bus fell silent as everyone watched to see what would happen next. Laird took a small notebook and pen from the inside pocket of his jacket. He faced his captive audience. "I'm part of a new IRS outreach program," he told the group. "For the next ten minutes I'll be taking confessions. Does anyone have anything he or she wants to tell me?"

Smiles. Soon the whole bus was talking, comparing notes—when they'd first realized he was kidding, and how scared they had been before they caught on. It was difficult to believe these were the same New Yorkers who were supposed to be so gruff and isolated.

"Laird was the most vital, funniest person I ever met," his friend wrote.

Now, in his wheelchair, he faced off against slow-moving flies, waving them away.

170   "The gloaming," Laird said.

Janet looked up from her knitting, startled. It was midafternoon, and the living room was filled with bright October sun. "Soon," she said.

He furrowed his brow. A little flash of confusion passed through his eyes, and she realized that for him it was already dark.

He tried to straighten his shawl, his hands shaking. She jumped up to help; then, when he pointed to the fireplace, she quickly laid the logs as she wondered what was wrong. Was he dehydrated? She thought she recalled that a dimming of vision was a sign of dehydration. She tried to remember what else she had read or heard, but even as she grasped for information, facts, her instincts kept interrupting with a deeper, more dreadful thought that vibrated through her, rattling her and making her gasp as she often did when remembering her mistakes, things she wished she hadn't said or done, wished she had the chance to do over. She knew what was wrong, and yet she kept turning away from the truth, her mind spinning in every other possible direction as she worked on the fire, only vaguely noticing how wildly she made the sparks fly as she pumped the old bellows.

Her work was mechanical—she had made hundreds of fires—and soon there was nothing left to do. She put the screen up and pushed him close, then leaned over to pull his flannel pajamas down to meet his socks, protecting his bare shins. The sun streamed in around him, making him appear trapped between bars of light. She resumed her knitting, with mechanical hands.

175   "The gloaming," he said again. It did sound somewhat like "gloomy," because his speech was slurred.

"When all the world is purple," she said, hearing herself sound falsely bright. She wasn't sure whether he wanted her to talk. It was some time since he had talked—not long, really in other people's lives, perhaps two weeks—but she had gone on with their conversations, gradually expanding into the silence until she was telling him stories and he was listening. Sometimes, when his eyes closed, she trailed off and began to drift. There would be a pause that she didn't always realize she was making, but if it went on too long he would call out "Mom?" with an edge of panic in his voice, as if he were waking from a nightmare. Then she would resume, trying to create a seamless bridge between what she had been thinking and where she had left off.

"It was really your grandfather who gave me my love for the gloaming," she said. "Do you remember him talking about it?" She looked up politely, expectantly, as if Laird might offer her a conversational reply. He seemed to like hearing the sound of her voice, so she went on, her needles clicking. Afterward, she could never remember for sure at what point she had stopped talking and had floated off into a jumble of her own thoughts, afraid to move, afraid to look up, afraid to know at which exact moment she became alone. All she knew was that at a certain point the fire was in danger of dying out entirely, and when she got up to stir the embers she glanced at him in spite of herself and saw that his fingers were making knitting motions over his chest, the way people did as they were dying. She knew that if she went to get the nurse, Laird would be gone by the time she returned, so she went and stood behind him, leaning over to press her face against his, sliding her hands down his busy arms, helping him along with his fretful stitches until he finished this last piece of work.

Later, after the most pressing calls had been made and Laird's body had been taken away, Janet went up to his old room and lay down on one of the twin beds. She had changed the room into a guest room when he went off to college, replacing his things with guest room decor, thoughtful touches such as luggage racks at the foot of each bed, a writing desk stocked with paper and pens, heavy wooden hangers and shoe trees. She made an effort to remember the room as it had been when he was a little boy: she had chosen a train motif, then had to redecorate when Laird decided trains were silly. He had wanted it to look like a jungle, so she had hired an art student to paint a jungle mural on the walls. When he decided *that* was silly, he hadn't bothered her to do anything about it, but had simply marked time until he could move on.

Anne came over, offered to stay, but was relieved to be sent home to her children.

180   Presently, Martin came in. Janet was watching the trees turn to mere silhouettes against the darkening sky, fighting the urge to pick up a true-crime book, a debased urge. He lay down on the other bed.

"I'm sorry," he said.

"It's so wrong," she said angrily. She hadn't felt angry until that moment; she had saved it up for him. "A child shouldn't die before his parents. A young man shouldn't spend his early thirties wasting away talking to his mother. He should be out in the world. He shouldn't be thinking about me, or what I care about, or my opinions. He shouldn't have had to return my love to me—it was his to squander. Now I have it all back and I don't know what I'm supposed to do with it," she said.

She could hear Martin weeping in the darkness. He sobbed, and her anger veered away.

They were quiet for some time.

185   "Is there going to be a funeral?" Martin asked finally.

"Yes. We should start making the arrangements."

"I suppose he told you what he wanted."

"In general. He couldn't decide about the music."

She heard Martin roll onto his side, so that he was facing her across the narrow chasm between the beds. He was still in his office clothes. "I remember being very moved by the bagpipes at your father's funeral."

190   It was an awkward offering, to be sure, awkward and late, and seemed to come from someone on the periphery of her life who knew her only slightly. It didn't matter, it was perfectly right. Her heart rushed toward it.

"I think Laird would have liked that idea very much," she said.

It was the last moment of the gloaming, the last moment of the day her son died. In a breath, it would be night; the moon hovered behind the trees, already rising to claim the sky, and she told herself she might as well get on with it. She sat up and was running her toes across the bare floor, searching for her shoes, when Martin spoke again, in a tone she used to hear on those long-ago nights when he rarely got home until after the children were in bed and he relied on her to fill him in on what they'd done that day. It was the same curious, shy, deferential tone that had always made her feel as though all the frustrations and boredom and mistakes and rushes of feeling in her days as a mother did indeed add up to something of importance, and she decided that the next round of telephone calls could wait while she answered the question he asked her: "Please tell me—what else did my boy like?"

✴ TOPICS FOR CRITICAL THINKING AND WRITING

1. Dark presents her story in the third person, from Janet's point of view. How does this choice of point of view shape and influence our response to Janet, to her son Laird, and to her husband Martin?

2. How would our response to the story change if it were told in the first person, with Janet herself as the narrator?

3. Reread the first pages of the story, taking special note of the places where Dark makes us aware that we are seeing the other characters and understanding their thoughts and feelings, from Janet's point of view. Reread them again, but now imagine how the story might be rewritten from the point of view of Laird himself. Perform this experiment still another time, imagining Martin's point of view. Describe the strengths and limits that each of these points of view offers.

4. Do you think that Dark wants us to judge Martin harshly? Is he a bad father and husband? Does our response to him change at the end?

5. Have you known anyone like Laird? What was your response to the person and to the effects of his or her serious illness? Did your point of view—your thoughts and feelings—toward this person change over time as the illness took its toll?

V. S. NAIPAUL

V[idiadhar] S[urajprasad] Naipaul was born in 1932 in Trinidad. After completing his early education in Trinidad he emigrated to England and graduated from Oxford in 1954. A prolific novelist and a far traveler, he writes about the United States, Africa, India—where his grandfather was born— and, especially, about the Caribbean. Naipaul was awarded the Nobel Prize for Literature in 2001.

The Night Watchman's Occurrence Book   [1967]

November 21. 10.30 p.m. C. A. Cavander take over duty at C—— Hotel all corrected. *Cesar Alwyn Cavander*

7 a.m. C. A. Cavander hand over duty to Mr Vignales at C—— Hotel no report. *Cesar Alwyn Cavander*

November 22. 10.30 p.m. C. A. Cavander take over duty at C—— Hotel no report. *Cesar Alwyn Cavander*

7 a.m. C. A. Cavander hand over duty to Mr Vignales at C—— Hotel all corrected. *Cesar Alwyn Cavander*

This is the third occasion on which I have found C. A. Cavander, Night Watchman, asleep on duty. Last night, at 12.45 a.m., I found him sound asleep in a rocking chair in the hotel lounge. Night Watchman Cavander has therefore been dismissed. Night Watchman Hillyard: This book is to be known in future as "The Night Watchman's Occurrence Book." In it I shall expect to find a detailed account of everything that happens in the hotel tonight. Be warned by the example of ex-Night Watchman Cavander, *W. A. G. Inskip, Manager*

Mr Manager, remarks noted. You have no worry where I am concern sir. *Charles Ethelbert Hillyard, Night Watchman*

5   *November 23.* 11 p.m. Night Watchman Hillyard take over duty at C—— Hotel with one torch light 2 fridge keys and room keys 1, 3, 6, 10 and 13. Also 25 cartoons Carib Beer and 7 cartoons Heineken[1] and 2 cartoons American cigarettes. Beer cartoons intact Bar intact all corrected no report. *Charles Ethelbert Hillyard*

7 a.m. Night Watchman Hillyard hand over duty to Mr Vignales at C—— Hotel with one torch light 2 fridge keys and room keys, 1, 3, 6, 10 and 13, 32 cartoons beer. Bar intact all corrected no report. *Charles Ethelbert Hillyard*

Night Watchman Hillyard: Mr Wills complained bitterly to me this morning that last night he was denied entry to the bar by you. I wonder if you know exactly what the purpose of this hotel is. In future all hotel guests are to be allowed entry to the bar at whatever time they choose. It is your duty simply to note what they

---

[1]**Heineken** a Dutch beer.

take. This is one reason why the hotel provides a certain number of beer cartons (please note the spelling of this word). *W. A. G. Inskip*

Mr Manager, remarks noted. I sorry I didn't get the chance to take some education sir. *Chas. Ethelbert Hillyard*

November 24. 11 p.m. N. W. Hillyard take over duty with one Torch, 1 Bar Key, 2 Fridge Keys, 32 cartoons Beer, all intact. 12 Midnight Bar close and Barman left leaving Mr Wills and others in Bar, and they left at 1 a.m. Mr Wills took 16 Carib Beer, Mr Wilson 8, Mr Percy 8. At 2 a.m. Mr Wills come back in the bar and take 4 Carib and some bread, he cut his hand trying to cut the bread, so please dont worry about the stains on the carpet sir. At 6 a.m. Mr Wills come back for some soda water. It didn't have any so he take a ginger beer instead. Sir you see it is my intention to do this job good sir, I cant see how Night Watchman Cavander could fall asleep on this job sir. *Chas. Ethelbert Hillyard*

You always seem sure of the time, and guests appear to be in the habit of entering the bar on the hour. You will kindly note the exact time. The clock from the kitchen is left on the window near the switches. You can use this clock but you MUST replace it every morning before you go off duty. *W. A. G. Inskip*

Noted. *Chas. Ethelbert Hillyard*

November 25. Midnight Bar close and 12.23 a.m. Barman left leaving Mr Wills and others in Bar. Mr Owen take 5 bottles Carib, Mr Wilson 6 bottles Heineken, Mr Wills 18 Carib and they left at 2.52 a.m. Nothing unusual. Mr Wills was helpless, I don't see how anybody could drink so much, eighteen one man alone, this work enough to turn anybody Seventh Day Adventist, and another man come in the bar, I dont know his name, I hear they call him Paul, he assist me because the others couldn't do much, and we take Mr Wills up to his room and take off his boots and slack his other clothes and then we left. Don't know sir if they did take more while I was away, nothing was mark on the Pepsi Cola board, but they was drinking still, it looks as if they come back and take some more, but with Mr Wills I want some extra assistance sir.

Mr Manager, the clock break I find it break when I come back from Mr Wills room sir. It stop 3.19 sir. *Chas. E. Hillyard*

More than 2 lbs of veal were removed from the Fridge last night, and a cake that was left in the press was cut. It is your duty, Night Watchman Hillyard, to keep an eye on these things. I ought to warn you that I have also asked the Police to check on all employees leaving the hotel, to prevent such occurrences in the future. *W. A. G. Inskip*

Mr Manager, I don't know why people so anxious to blame servants sir. About the cake, the press lock at night and I dont have the key sir, everything safe where I am concern sir. *Chas. Hillyard*

November 26. Midnight Bar close and Barman left. Mr Wills didn't come, I hear he at the American base tonight, all quiet, nothing unusual.

Mr Manager, I request one thing. Please inform the Barman to let me know sir when there is a female guest in the hotel sir. *C. E. Hillyard*

This morning I received a report from a guest that there were screams in the hotel during the night. You wrote All Quiet. Kindly explain in writing. *W. A. G. Inskip* Write Explanation here:

EXPLANATION. Not long after midnight the telephone ring and a woman ask for Mr Jimminez. I try to tell her where he was but she say she cant hear properly. Fifteen minutes later she came in a car, she was looking vex and sleepy, and I went up to call him. The door was not lock, I went in and touch his foot and call him very soft, and he jump up and begin to shout. When he come to himself he said he had Night Mere, and then he come down and went away with the woman, was not necessary to mention.

Mr Manager, I request you again, please inform the Barman to let me know sir when there is a female guest in the Hotel. *C. Hillyard*

November 27. 1 a.m. Bar close, Mr Wills and a American 19 Carib and 2.30 a.m. a Police come and ask for Mr Wills, he say the American report that he was robbed of $200.00¢, he was last drinking at the C—— with Mr Wills and others. Mr Wills and the Police ask to open the Bar to search it, I told them I cannot open the Bar for you like that, the Police must come with the Manager. Then the American say it was only joke he was joking, and they try to get the Police to laugh, but the Police looking the way I feeling. Then laughing Mr Wills left in a garage car as he couldn't drive himself and the American was waiting outside and they both fall down as they was getting in the car, and Mr Wills saying any time you want a over-draft you just come to my bank kiddo. The Police left walking by himself. *C. Hillyard*

Night Watchman Hillyard: "Was not necessary to mention"!! You are not to decide what is necessary to mention in this night watch-man's occurrence book. Since when have you become sole owner of the hotel as to determine what is necessary to mention? If the guest did not mention it I would never have known that there were screams in the hotel during the night. Also will you kindly tell me who Mr Jimminez is? And what rooms he occupied or occu-pies? And by what right? You have been told by me personally that the names of all hotel guests are on the slate next to the light switches. If you find Mr Jimminez's name on this slate, or could give me some information about him, I will be most warmly obliged to you. The lady you ask about is Mrs Roscoe, Room 12, as you very well know. It is your duty to see that guests are not pestered by unauthorized callers. You should give no information about guests to such people, and I would be glad if in future you could direct such callers straight to me. *W. A. G. Inskip*

Sir was what I ask you two times, I dont know what sort of work I take up, I always believe that nightwatchman work is a quiet work and I dont like meddling in white people business, but the gentleman occupy Room 12 also, was there that I went up to call him, I didn't think it necessary to men-tion because was none of my business sir. *C.E.H.*

10   *November 28.* 12 Midnight Bar close and Barman left at 12.20 a.m. leav-ing Mr Wills and others, and they all left at 1.25 a.m. Mr Wills 8 Carib, Mr Wilson 12, Mr Percy 8, and the man they call Paul 12. Mrs Roscoe join the gentlemen at 12.33 a.m., four gins, everybody calling her Minnie from

Trinidad, and then they start singing that song, and some others. Nothing unusual. Afterwards there were mild singing and guitar music in Room 12. A man come in and ask to use the phone at 2.17 a.m. and while he was using it about 7 men come in and wanted to beat him up, so he put down the phone and they all ran away. At 3 a.m. I notice the padlock not on the press, I look inside, no cake, but the padlock was not put on in the first place sir. Mr Wills come down again at 6 a.m. to look for his sweet, he look in the Fridge and did not see any. He took a piece of pineapple. A plate was covered in the Fridge, but it didn't have anything in it. Mr Wills put it out, the cat jump on it and it fall down and break. The garage bulb not burning. *C.E.H.*

> You will please sign your name at the bottom of your report. You are in the habit of writing Nothing Unusual. Please take note and think before making such a statement. I want to know what is meant by nothing unusual. I gather, not from you, needless to say, that the police have fallen into the habit of visiting the hotel at night. I would be most grateful to you if you could find the time to note the times of these visits. *W. A. G. Inskip*

Sir, nothing unusual means everything usual. I dont know, nothing I writing you liking. I dont know what sort of work this night watchman work getting to be, since when people have to start getting Cambridge certificate to get night watchman job, I ain't educated and because of this everybody think they could insult me. *Charles Ethelbert Hillyard*

> *November 29.* Midnight Bar close and 12.15 Barman left leaving Mr Wills and Mrs Roscoe and others in the Bar. Mr Wills and Mrs Roscoe left at 12.30 a.m. leaving Mr Wilson and the man they call Paul, and they all left at 1.00 a.m. Twenty minutes to 2 Mr Wills and party return and left again at 5 to 3. At 3.45 Mr Wills return and take break and milk and olives and cherries, he ask for nutmeg too, I said we had none, he drink 2 Carib, and left ten minutes later. He also collect Mrs Roscoe bag. All the drinks, except the 2 Carib, was taken by the man they call Paul. I don't know sir I don't like this sort of work, you better hire a night barman. At 5.30 Mrs Roscoe and the man they call Paul come back to the bar, they was having a quarrel, Mr Paul saying you make me sick, Mrs Roscoe saying I feel sick, and then she vomit all over the floor, shouting I didn't want that damned milk. I was cleaning up when Mr Wills come down to ask for soda water, we got to lay in more soda for Mr Wills, but I need extra assistance with Mr Wills Paul and party sir.
>
> The police come at 2, 3.48 and 4.52. They sit down in the bar a long time. Firearms discharge 2 times in the back yard. Detective making inquiries. I dont know sir, I thinking it would be better for me to go back to some other sort of job. At 3 I hear somebody shout Thief, and I see a man running out of the back, and Mr London, Room 9, say he miss 80 cents and a pack of cigarettes which was on his dressing case. I don't know when the people in this place does sleep. *Chas. Ethelbert Hillyard*

> Night Watchman Hillyard: A lot more than 80 cents was stolen. Several rooms were in fact entered during the night, including my own. You are employed to prevent such things occurring. Your interest in the morals of our guests seems to be distracting your at-

tention from your duties. Save your preaching for your roadside prayer meetings. Mr Pick, Room 7, reports that in spite of the most pressing and repeated requests, you did not awaken him at 5. He has missed his plane to British Guiana as a result. No newspapers were delivered to the rooms this morning. I am again notifying you that papers must be handed personally to Doorman Vignales. And the messenger's bicycle, which I must remind you is the property of the hotel, has been damaged. What do you *do* at nights? *W. A. G. Inskip*

Please don't ask me sir.

Relating to the damaged bicycle: I left the bicycle the same place where I meet it, nothing took place so as to damage it. I always take care of all property sir. I don't know how you could think I have time to go out for bicycle rides. About the papers, sir, the police and them read it and leave them in such a state that I didn't think it would be nice to give them to guests. I wake up Mr Pick, room 7, at 4.50 a.m. 5 a.m. 5.15 a.m. and 5.30. He told me to keep off, he would not get up, and one time he pelt a box of matches at me, matches scatter all over the place. I always do everything to the best of my ability sir but God is my Witness I never find a night watchman work like this, so much writing I dont have time to do anything else, I dont have four hands and six eyes and I want this extra assistance with Mr Wills and party sir. I am a poor man and you could abuse me, but you must not abuse my religion sir because the good Lord sees All and will have His revenge sir, I don't know what sort of work and trouble I land myself in, all I want is a little quiet night work and all I getting is abuse. *Chas. E. Hillyard*

November 30. 12.25 a.m. Bar close and Barman left 1.00 a.m. leaving Mr Wills and party in Bar. Mr Wills take 12 Carib, Mr Wilson 6, Mr Percy 14. Mrs Roscoe five gins. At 1.30 a.m. Mrs Roscoe left and there were a little singing and mild guitar playing in Room 12. Nothing unusual. The police came at 1.35 and sit down in the bar for a time, not drinking, not talking, not doing anything except watching. At 1.45 the man they call Paul come in with Mr McPherson of the SS Naparoni, they was both falling down and laughing whenever anything break and the man they call Paul say Fireworks about to begin tell Minnie Malcolm coming the ship just dock. Mr Wills and party scatter leaving one or two bottles half empty and then the man they call Paul tell me to go up to Room 12 and tell Minnie Roscoe that Malcolm coming. I don't know how people could behave so the thing enough to make anybody turn priest. I notice the padlock on the bar door break off it hanging on only by a little piece of wood. And when I went up to Room 12 and tell Mrs Roscoe that Malcolm coming the ship just dock the woman get sober straight away like she dont want to hear no more guitar music and she asking me where to hide where to go. I dont know, I feel the day of reckoning is at hand, but she not listening to what I saying, she busy straightening up the room one minute packing the next, and then she run out into the corridor and before I could stop she she run straight down the back stairs to the annexe. And then 5 past 2, still in the corridor, I see a big red man running up to me and he sober as a judge and he mad as a drunkard and he asking me where she is where she is. I ask whether he is a authorized caller, he say you don't give me any of that crap now, where she is, where she is. So remembering about the last time Mr Jimminez I direct him to the manager office in the annexe. He hear a little scuffling inside Mr Inskip room and I make out Mr Inskip sleepy voice and Mrs Roscoe voice and the red man run inside and all I hearing for the next five minutes is bam bam bodow bodow bow and this woman screaming. I dont know what sort of work this night watchman getting I want something quiet like the police. In time things quiet down and the red man drag Mrs Roscoe out of the annexe and they take a taxi, and the Police sitting down quiet in the bar. Then Mr Percy and the others come back one by one to the bar and they talking quiet and they not drinking and they left 3 a.m. 3.15 Mr Wills return and take one whisky and 2 Carib. He asked for pineapple or some sweet fruit but it had nothing.

6 a.m. Mr Wills come in the bar looking for soda but it aint have none. We have to get some soda for Mr Wills sir.

6.30 a.m. the papers come and I deliver them to Doorman Vignales at 7 a.m. *Chas. Hillyard*

Mr Hillyard: In view of the unfortunate illness of Mr. Inskip, I am temporarily in charge of the hotel. I trust you will continue to make your nightly reports, but I would be glad if you could keep your entries as brief as possible. *Robt. Magnus, Acting Manager*

December 1. 10.30 p.m. C. E. Hillyard take over duty at C—— Hotel all corrected 12 Midnight Bar close 2 a.m. Mr Wills 2 Carib, 1 bread 6 a.m. Mr Wills 1 soda 7 a.m. Night Watchman Hillyard hand over duty to Mr Vignales with one torch light 2 Fridge keys and Room Keys 1, 3, 6 and 12. Bar intact all corrected no report. *C.E.H.*

❈ TOPICS FOR CRITICAL THINKING AND WRITING

1. How many people tell this story? How would you characterize each?
2. Do you assume that race—or, let's say, the color of the characters—is significant? Explain.
3. Did you enjoy reading this story? Please explain.
4. Is there a feature of Naipaul's story that you think is especially effective? Be as precise as possible, and cite evidence from the text to explain and support your response.
5. How does this story begin? How does it end? What is the relationship between the beginning and the ending?
6. If you were enrolled in a creative-writing course and were given the assignment, "Please write a story like 'The Night Watchman's Occurrence Book,'" what would be your response? Do you think you could write such a story? What would be the challenges of this assignment? What insights into the process of story-writing do you think your instructor might be trying to convey through such an assignment?

KATHERINE ANNE PORTER

Katherine Anne Porter (1890–1980) had the curious habit of inventing details in her life, but it is true that she was born in a log cabin in Indian Creek, Texas, that she was originally named Callie Russell Porter, that her mother died when she was two years old, and that Callie was brought up by her maternal grandmother in Kyle, Texas. Apparently the family was conscious of former wealth and position in Louisiana and Kentucky. She was sent to convent schools, where, in her words, she received "a strangely useless and ornamental education." At sixteen she left school, married (and soon divorced), and worked as a reporter, first in Texas and later in Denver and Chicago. She moved around a good deal, both within the United States and abroad; she lived in Mexico, Belgium, Switzerland, France, and Germany.

Even as a child Porter was interested in writing, but she did not publish her first story until she was thirty-three. She wrote essays and one novel (Ship of Fools), but she is best known for her stories. Porter's Collected Stories *won the Pulitzer Prize and the National Book Award in 1965.*

The Jilting of Granny Weatherall

[1929]

She flicked her wrist neatly out of Doctor Harry's pudgy careful fingers and pulled the sheet up to her chin. The brat ought to be in knee breeches. Doctoring around the country with spectacles on his nose! "Get along now, take your schoolbooks and go. There's nothing wrong with me."

Doctor Harry spread a warm paw like a cushion on her forehead where the forked green vein danced and made her eyelids twitch. "Now, now, be a good girl, and we'll have you up in no time."

"That's no way to speak to a woman nearly eighty years old just because she's down. I'd have you respect your elders, young man."

"Well, Missy, excuse me." Doctor Harry patted her cheek. "But I've got to warn you, haven't I? You're a marvel, but you must be careful or you're going to be good and sorry."

5   "Don't tell me what I'm going to be. I'm on my feet now, morally speaking. It's Cornelia. I had to go to bed to get rid of her."

Her bones felt loose, and floated around in her skin, and Doctor Harry floated like a balloon around the foot of the bed. He floated and pulled down his waistcoat and swung his glasses on a cord. "Well, stay where you are, it certainly can't hurt you."

"Get along and doctor your sick," said Granny Weatherall. "Leave a well woman alone. I'll call for you when I want you. . . . Where were you forty years ago when I pulled through milk leg and double pneumonia? You weren't even born. Don't let Cornelia lead you on," she shouted, because Doctor Harry appeared to float up to the ceiling and out. "I pay my own bills, and I don't throw my money away on nonsense!"

She meant to wave good-by, but it was too much trouble. Her eyes closed of themselves, it was like a dark curtain drawn around the bed. The pillow rose and floated under her, pleasant as a hammock in a light wind. She listened to the leaves rustling outside the window. No, somebody was swishing newspapers: no, Cornelia and Doctor Harry were whispering together. She leaped broad awake, thinking they whispered in her ear.

"She was never like this, *never* like this! "Well, what can we expect?" "Yes, eighty years old. . . ."

10   Well, and what if she was? She still had ears. It was like Cornelia to whisper around doors. She always kept things secret in such a public way. She was always being tactful and kind. Cornelia was dutiful; that was the trouble with her. Dutiful and good: "So good and dutiful," said Granny, "and I'd like to spank her." She saw herself spanking Cornelia and making a fine job of it.

"What'd you say, Mother?"

Granny felt her face tying up in hard knots.

"Can't a body think, I'd like to know?"

"I thought you might want something."

15   "I do. I want a lot of things. First off, go away and don't whisper."

She lay and drowsed, hoping in her sleep that the children would keep out and let her rest a minute. It had been a long day. Not that she was tired. It was always pleasant to snatch a minute now and then. There was always so much to be done, let me see: tomorrow.

Tomorrow was far away and there was nothing to trouble about. Things were finished somehow when the time came; thank God there was always a little margin over for peace: then a person could spread out the plan of life and tuck in the edges orderly. It was good to have everything clean and folded away, with the hair brushes and tonic bottles sitting straight on the white embroidered linen: the day started without fuss and the pantry shelves laid out with rows of jelly glasses and brown jugs and white stone-china jars with blue whirligigs and words painted on them: coffee, tea, sugar, ginger, cinnamon, allspice: and the bronze clock with the lion on top nicely dusted off. The dust that lion could collect in twenty-four hours! The box in the attic with all those letters tied up, she'd have to go through that tomorrow. All those letters—George's letters and John's letters and her letters to them both—lying around for the children to find afterwards made her uneasy. Yes, that would be tomorrow's business. No use to let them know how silly she had been once.

While she was rummaging around she found death in her mind and it felt clammy and unfamiliar. She had spent so much time preparing for death there was no need for bringing it up again. Let it take care of itself now. When she was sixty she had felt very old, finished, and went around making farewell trips to see her children and grandchildren, with a secret in her mind: This is the very last of your mother, children! Then she made her will and came down with a long fever. That was all just a notion like a lot of other things, but it was lucky too, for she had once for all got over the idea of dying for a long time. Now she couldn't be worried. She hoped she had better sense now. Her father had lived to be one hundred and two years old and had drunk a noggin of strong hot toddy on his last birthday. He told the reporters it was his daily habit, and he owed his long life to that. He had made quite a scandal and was very pleased about it. She believed she'd just plague Cornelia a little.

"Cornelia! Cornelia!" No footsteps, but a sudden hand on her cheek. "Bless you, where have you been?"

20   "Here, Mother."

"Well, Cornelia, I want a noggin of hot toddy."

"Are you cold, darling?"

"I'm chilly, Cornelia. Lying in bed stops the circulation. I must have told you that a thousand times."

Well, she could just hear Cornelia tell her husband that her Mother was getting a little childish and they'd have to humor her. The thing that most annoyed her was that Cornelia thought she was deaf, dumb, and blind. Little hasty glances and tiny gestures tossed around her and over her head saying, "Don't cross her, let her have her way, she's eighty years old," and she sitting there as if she lived in a thin glass cage. Sometimes Granny almost made up her mind to pack up and move back to her own house where nobody could remind her every minute that she was old. Wait, wait, Cornelia, till your own children whisper behind your back!

25   In her day she had kept a better house and had got more work done. She wasn't too old yet for Lydia to be driving eighty miles for advice when one of the children jumped the track, and Jimmy still dropped in and talked things over: "Now, Mammy, you've a good business head, I want to know what you think of this? . . ." Old. Cornelia couldn't change the furniture around without asking. Little things, little things! They had been so sweet when they were little. Granny wished the old days were back again with the children young and everything to be done over. It had been a hard pull, but not too much for her. When she thought of all the food she had cooked, and all the clothes she had cut and sewed, and all the gardens she had made—well, the children showed it. There they were, made out of her, and they couldn't get away from that. Sometimes she wanted to see John again and point to them and say, Well, I didn't do so badly, did I? But that would have to wait. That was for tomorrow. She used to think of him as a man, but now all the children were older than their father, and he would be a child beside her if she saw him now. It seemed strange and there was something wrong in the idea. Why he couldn't possibly recognize her. She had fenced in a hundred acres once, digging the post holes herself and clamping the wires with just a negro boy to help. That changed a woman. John would be looking for a young woman with the peaked Spanish comb in her hair and the painted fan. Digging post holes changed a woman. Riding country roads in the winter when women had their babies was another thing: sitting up nights with sick horses and sick negroes and sick children and hardly ever losing one. John, I hardly ever lost one of them! John would see that in a minute, that would be something he could understand, she wouldn't have to explain anything!

It made her feel like rolling up her sleeves and putting the whole place to rights again. No matter if Cornelia was determined to be everywhere at once, there were a great many things left undone on this place. She would start tomorrow and do them. It was good to be strong enough for everything, even if all you made melted and changed and slipped under your hands, so that by the time you finished you almost forgot what you were working for. What was it I set out to do? she asked herself intently, but she could not remember. A fog rose over the valley, she saw it marching across the creek swallowing the trees and moving up the hill like an army of ghosts. Soon it would be at the near edge of the orchard, and then it was time to go in and light the lamps. Come in, children, don't stay out in the night air.

Lighting the lamps had been beautiful. The children huddled up to her and breathed like little calves waiting at the bars in the twilight. Their eyes followed the match and watched the flame rise and settle in a blue curve, then they moved away from her. The lamp was lit, they didn't have to be scared and hang on to mother any more. Never, never, never more. God, for all my life I thank Thee. Without Thee, my God, I could never have done it. Hail, Mary, full of grace.

I want you to pick all the fruit this year and see that nothing is wasted. There's always someone who can use it. Don't let good things rot for want of using. You waste life when you waste good food. Don't let things get lost. It's bitter to lose things. Now, don't let me get to thinking, not when I am tired and taking a little nap before supper. . . .

The pillow rose about her shoulders and pressed against her heart and the memory was being squeezed out of it: oh, push down the pillow, some-body: it would smother her if she tried to hold it. Such a fresh breeze blow-ing and such a green day with no threats in it. But he had not come, just the same. What does a woman do when she has put on the white veil and set out the white cake for a man and he doesn't come? She tried to remember. No, I swear he never harmed me but in that. He never harmed me but in that . . . and what if he did? There was the day, the day, but a whirl of dark smoke rose and covered it, crept up and over into the bright field where everything was planted so carefully in orderly rows. That was hell, she knew hell when she saw it. For sixty years she had prayed against remembering him and against losing her soul in the deep pit of hell, and now the two things were mingled in one and the thought of him was a smoky cloud from hell that moved and crept in her head when she had just got rid of Doctor Harry and was trying to rest a minute. Wounded vanity, Ellen, said a sharp voice in the top of her mind. Don't let your wounded vanity get the upper hand of you. Plenty of girls get jilted. You were jilted, weren't you? Then stand up to it. Her eyelids wavered and let in streamers of blue-gray light like tissue paper over her eyes. She must get up and pull the shades down or she'd never sleep. She was in bed again and the shades were not down. How could that happen? Better turn over, hide from the light, sleeping in the light gave you nightmares. "Mother, how do you feel now?" and a stinging wetness on her forehead. But I don't like having my face washed in cold water!

30   Hapsy? George? Lydia? Jimmy? No, Cornelia, and her features were swollen and full of little puddles. "They're coming, darling, they'll all be here soon." Go wash your face, child, you look funny.

Instead of obeying, Cornelia knelt down and put her head on the pil-low. She seemed to be talking but there was no sound. "Well, are you tongue-tied? Whose birthday is it? Are you going to give a party?"

Cornelia's mouth moved urgently in strange shapes. "Don't do that, you bother me, daughter."

"Oh, no, Mother. Oh, no. . . ."

Nonsense. It was strange about children. They disputed your every word. "No what, Cornelia?"

35   "Here's Doctor Harry."

"I won't see that boy again. He just left five minutes ago."

"That was this morning, Mother. It's night now. Here's the nurse."

"This is Doctor Harry, Mrs. Weatherall. I never saw you look so young and happy!"

"Ah, I'll never be young again—but I'd be happy if they'd let me lie in peace and get rested."

40   She thought she spoke up loudly, but no one answered. A warm weight on her forehead, a warm bracelet on her wrist, and a breeze went on whispering, trying to tell her something. A shuffle of leaves in the everlasting hand of God. He blew on them and they danced and rattled. "Mother, don't mind, we're going to give you a little hypodermic." Look here, daughter, how do ants get in this bed? I saw sugar ants yesterday." Did you send for Hapsy too?

It was Hapsy she really wanted. She had to go a long way back through a great many rooms to find Hapsy standing with a baby on her arm. She seemed to herself to be Hapsy also, and the baby on Hapsy's arm was Hapsy and himself and herself, all at once, and there was no surprise in the meeting. Then Hapsy melted from within and turned flimsy as gray gauze and the baby was a gauzy shadow, and Hapsy came up close and said, "I thought you'd never come," and looked at her very searchingly and said, "You haven't changed a bit!" They leaned forward to kiss, when Cornelia began whispering from a long way off, "Oh, is there anything you want to tell me? Is there anything I can do for you?"

Yes, she had changed her mind after sixty years and she would like to see George. I want you to find George. Find him and be sure to tell him I forgot him. I want him to know I had my husband just the same and my children and my house like any other woman. A good house too and a good husband that I loved and fine children out of him. Better than I hoped for even. Tell him I was given back everything he took away and more. Oh, no, oh, God, no, there was something else besides the house and the man and the children, Oh, surely they were not all? What was it? Something not given back. . . . Her breath crowded down under her ribs and grew into a monstrous frightening shape with cutting edges; it bored up into her head, and the agony was unbelievable: Yes, John, get the doctor now, no more talk, my time has come.

When this one was born it should be the last. The last. It should have been born first, for it was the one she had truly wanted. Everything came in good time. Nothing left out, left over. She was strong, in three days she would be as well as ever. Better. A woman needed milk in her to have her full health.

"Mother, do you hear me?"

45   "I've been telling you—"

"Mother, Father Connolly's here."

"I went to Holy Communion only once last week. Tell him I'm not so sinful as all that."

"Father just wants to speak to you."

He could speak as much as he pleased. It was like him to drop in and inquire about her soul as if it were a teething baby, and then stay on for a cup of tea and a round of cards and gossip. He always had a funny story of some sort, usually about an Irishman who made his little mistakes and confessed them, and the point lay in some absurd thing he would blurt out in the confessional showing his struggles between native piety and original sin. Granny felt easy about her soul. Cornelia, where are your manners? Give Father Connolly a chair. She had her secret comfortable understanding with a few favorite saints who cleared a straight road to God for her. All as surely signed and sealed as the papers for the new Forty Acres. Forever . . . heirs and assigns forever. Since the day the wedding cake was not cut, but thrown out and wasted. The whole bottom dropped out of the world, and there she was blind and sweating with nothing under her feet and walls falling away. His hand had caught her under the breast, she had not fallen, there was the freshly polished floor with the green rug on it, just as before. He had cursed like a sailor's parrot and said, "I'll kill him for you." Don't lay a hand on him, for my sake leave something to God. "Now, Ellen, you must believe what I tell you. . . ."

50   So there was nothing, nothing to worry about any more, except sometimes in the night one of the children screamed in a nightmare, and they both hustled out shaking and hunting for the matches and calling, "There, wait a minute, here we are!" John, get the doctor now, Hapsy's time has come. But there was Hapsy standing by the bed in a white cap. "Cornelia, tell Hapsy to take off her cap. I can't see her plain."

    Her eyes opened very wide and the room stood out like a picture she had seem somewhere. Dark colors with the shadows rising towards the ceiling in long angles. The tall black dresser gleamed with nothing on it but John's picture, enlarged from a little one, with John's eyes very black when they should have been blue. You never saw him, so how do you know how he looked? But the man insisted the copy was perfect, it was very rich and handsome. For a picture, yes, but it's not my husband. The table by the bed had a linen cover and a candle and a crucifix. The light was blue from Cornelia's silk lampshade. No sort of light at all, just frippery. You had to live forty years with kerosene lamps to appreciate honest electricity. She felt very strong and saw Doctor Harry with a rosy nimbus around him. "You look like a saint, Doctor Harry, and I vow that's as near as you'll ever come to it."

    "She's saying something."

    "I heard you, Cornelia. What's all this carrying on?"

55   "Father Connolly's saying—"

    Cornelia's voice staggered and bumped like a cart in a bad road. It rounded corners and turned back again and arrived nowhere. Granny stepped up in the cart very lightly and reached for the reins, but a man sat beside her and she knew him by his hands, driving the cart. She did not look in his face, for she knew without seeing, but looked instead down the road where the trees leaned over and bowed to each other and a thousand birds were singing a Mass. She felt like singing too, but she put her hand in the bosom of her dress and pulled out a rosary, and Father Connolly murmured Latin in a very solemn voice and tickled her feet. My God, will you stop that nonsense? I'm a married woman. What if he did run away and leave me to face the priest by myself? I found another a whole world better. I wouldn't have exchanged my husband for anybody except St. Michael himself, and you may tell him that for me with a thank you in the bargain.

    Light flashed on her closed eyelids, and a deep roaring shook her. Cornelia, is that lightning? I hear thunder. There's going to be a storm. Close all the windows. Call all the children in. . . . "Mother, here we are, all of us." "Is that you, Hapsy?" "Oh, no, I'm Lydia. We drove as fast as we could." Their faces drifted above her, drifted away. The rosary fell out of her hands and Lydia put it back. Jimmy tried to help, their hands fumbled together, and Granny closed two fingers around Jimmy's thumb. Beads wouldn't do, it must be something alive. She was so amazed her thoughts ran round and round. So, my dear Lord, this is my death and I wasn't even thinking about it. My children have come to see me die. But I can't, it's not time. Oh, I always hated surprises. I wanted to give Cornelia the amethyst set—Cornelia, you're to have the amethyst set, but Hapsy's to wear it when she wants, and, Doctor Harry, do shut up. Nobody sent for you. Oh, my dear Lord, do wait a minute. I meant to do something about the Forty Acres, Jimmy doesn't need it and Lydia will later on, with that worthless husband of hers. I meant to finish the altar cloth and send six bottles of wine to Sister Borgia for her dyspepsia. I want to send six bottles of wine to Sister Borgia, Father Connolly, now don't let me forget.

Cornelia's voice made short turns and tilted over and crashed, "Oh, Mother, oh, Mother, oh, Mother. . . ."

"I'm not going, Cornelia. I'm taken by surprise. I can't go."

60   You'll see Hapsy again. What about her? "I thought you'd never come." Granny made a long journey outward, looking for Hapsy. What if I don't find her? What then? Her heart sank down and down, there was no bottom to death, she couldn't come to the end of it. The blue light from Cornelia's lampshade drew into a tiny point in the center of her brain, it flickered and winked like an eye, quietly it fluttered and dwindled. Granny lay curled down within herself, amazed and watchful, staring at the point of light that was herself; her body was now only a deeper mass of shadow in an endless darkness and this darkness would curl around the light and swallow it up. God, give a sign!

For the second time there was no sign. Again no bridegroom and the priest in the house. She could not remember any other sorrow because this grief wiped them all away. Oh, no, there's nothing more cruel than this—I'll never forgive it. She stretched her self with a deep breath and blew out the light.

☒ TOPICS FOR CRITICAL THINKING AND WRITING

1. How would you describe Granny Weatherall? In what ways does her name suit her?

2. The final paragraph begins: "For the second time there was no sign." What happened the first time? What is happening now? How are the two events linked? (The paragraph alludes to Christ's parable of the bridegroom, in Matthew 25.1–13. If you are unfamiliar with the parable, read it in the Gospel according to St. Matthew.)

3. What do you think happens in the last line of the story?

6

Allegory and Symbolism

In Chapter 4 we looked at some fables, short fictions that were meant to teach us: the characters clearly stood for principles of behavior, and the fictions as a whole evidently taught lessons. If you think of a fable such as "The Ant and the Grasshopper" (the ant wisely collects food during the summer in order to provide for the winter, whereas the grasshopper foolishly sings all summer and goes hungry in the winter), you can easily see that the characters may stand for something other than themselves. The ant, let's say, is the careful, foresighted person, and the grasshopper is the person who lives for the moment. Similarly, in the fable of the tortoise and the hare, the tortoise represents the person who is slow but steady, the rabbit the person who is talented but overly confident and, in the end, foolish.

A story in which each character is understood to have an equivalent is an **allegory.** Further, in an allegory, not only characters but also things (roads, forests, houses) have fairly clear equivalents. Thus, in John Bunyan's *The Pilgrim's Progress,* we meet a character named Christian, who, on the road to the Celestial City, meets Giant Despair, Mr. Worldly Wiseman, and Faithful, and passes through the City of Destruction and Vanity Fair. What all of these are equivalent to is clear from their names. It is also clear that Christian's journey stands for the trials of the soul in this world. There is, so to speak, a one-to-one relationship: A = B =, and so on. If, for example, we are asked what the road represents in *The Pilgrim's Progress,* we can confidently say that it stands for the journey of life. Thus, *The Pilgrim's Progress* tells two stories, the surface story of a man making a trip, during which he meets various figures and visits various places, and a second story, understood through the first, of the trials that afflict the soul during its quest for salvation.

Modern short stories rarely have the allegory's clear system of equivalents, but we may nevertheless feel that certain characters and certain things in the story stand for more than themselves, or hint at larger meanings. We feel, that is, that they are **symbolic.** But here we must be careful. How does one know that this or that figure or place is symbolic? In Hemingway's "Cat in the Rain" (page 61), is the cat symbolic? Is the innkeeper? Is the rain? Reasonable people may differ in their answers. Again, in Chopin's "The Story of an Hour" (page 28), is the railroad accident a symbol? Is Josephine a symbol? Is the season (springtime) a symbol? And again, reasonable people may differ in their responses.

Let's assume for the moment, however, that if writers use symbols, they want readers to perceive—at least faintly—that certain characters or places or seasons or happenings have rich implications, stand for something more than what they are on the surface. How do writers help us to perceive these things? By emphasizing them—for instance, by describing them at some length, or by introducing them at times when they might not seem strictly necessary, or by calling attention to them repeatedly.

Consider, for example, Chopin's treatment of the season in which "The Story of an Hour" takes place. The story has to take place at *some* time, but Chopin does not simply say, "On a spring day," or an autumn day, and let things go at that. Rather, she tells us about the sky, the trees, the rain, the twittering sparrows—and all of this in an extremely short story where we might think there is no time for talk about the setting. After all, none of this material is strictly necessary to a story about a woman who has heard that her husband was killed in an accident, who grieves, then recovers, and then dies when he suddenly reappears.

Why, then, does Chopin give such emphasis to the season? Because, we think, she is using the season symbolically. In this story, the spring is not just a bit of detail added for realism. It is rich with suggestions of renewal, of the new life that Louise achieves for a moment. But here, a caution. We think that the spring in this story is symbolic, but this is not to say that whenever spring appears in a story, it always stands for renewal, any more than whenever winter appears it always symbolizes death. Nor does it mean that since spring recurs, Louise will be reborn. In short, in *this* story Chopin uses the season to convey specific implications.

Is the railroad accident also a symbol? Our answer is no—though we don't expect all readers to agree with us. We think that the railroad accident in "The Story of an Hour" is just a railroad accident. It's our sense that Chopin is *not* using this event to say something about (for instance) modern travel, or about industrialism. The steam-propelled railroad train could of course be used, symbolically, to say something about industrialism displacing an agrarian economy, but does Chopin give her train any such suggestion? We don't think so. Had she wished to do so, she would probably have talked about the enormous power of the train, the shriek of its whistle, the smoke pouring out of the smokestack, the intense fire burning in the engine, its indifference as it charged through the countryside, and so forth. Had she done so, the story would be a different story. Or she might have made the train a symbol of fate overriding human desires. But, again in our opinion, Chopin does not endow her train with such suggestions. She gives virtually no emphasis to the train, and so we believe it has virtually no significance for the reader.

What of Chopin's "Ripe Figs" (page 50)? Maman-Nainaine tells Babette that when the figs are ripe Babette can visit her cousins. Maman may merely be setting an arbitrary date, but as we read the story we probably feel—because of the emphasis on the *ripening* of the figs, which occurs in the spring or early summer—that the ripening of the figs in some way suggests the maturing of Babette. If we do get such ideas, we will in effect be saying that the story is not simply an anecdote about an old woman whose behavior is odd. True, the narrator of the story, after telling us of Maman-Nainaine's promise, adds, "Not that the ripening of figs had the least thing to do with it, but that is the way Maman-Nainaine was." The narrator sees nothing special—merely Maman-Nainaine's eccentricity—in the connection between the ripening of the figs and Babette's visit to her cousins. Readers, however, may see more than the narrator sees or says. They may see in Babette a young girl maturing; they may see in Maman-Nainaine an older woman who, almost collaborating with nature, helps Babette to mature.

And here, as we talk about symbolism we are getting into the theme of the story. An apparently inconsequential and even puzzling action, such as is set forth in "Ripe Figs," may cast a long shadow. As Robert Frost once said,

> There is no story written that has any value at all, however straightforward it looks and free from doubleness, double entendre, that you'd value at all if it didn't have intimations of something more than itself.

The stranger, the more mysterious the story, the more likely we are to suspect some sort of significance, but even realistic stories such as Chopin's "The Storm" and "The Story of an Hour" may be rich in suggestions. This is not to say, however, that the suggestions (rather than the details of the surface) are what count. A reader does not discard the richly detailed, highly specific narrative (Mrs. Mallard learned that her husband was dead and reacted in such-and-such a way) in favor of some supposedly universal message or theme that it implies. We do not throw away the specific narrative—the memorable characters, or the interesting things that happen in the story—and move on to some "higher truth." Robert Frost went on to say, "The anecdote, the parable, the surface meaning has got to be good and got to be sufficient in itself."

Between these two extremes—on the one hand, writing that is almost all a richly detailed surface and, on the other hand, writing that has a surface so thin that we are immediately taken up with the implications or meanings—are stories in which we strongly feel both the surface happenings and their implications. In *Place in Fiction,* Eudora Welty uses an image of a china lamp to explain literature that presents an interesting surface texture filled with rich significance. When unlit, the lamp showed London; when lit, it showed the Great Fire of London. Like a painted porcelain lamp that, when illuminated, reveals an inner picture shining through the outer, the physical details in a work are illuminated from within by the author's imaginative vision. The outer painting (the literal details) presents "a continuous, shapely, pleasing, and finished surface to the eye," but this surface is not the whole. Welty happens to be talking about the novel, but her words apply equally to the short story:

> The lamp alight is the combination of internal and external, glowing at the imagination as one; and so is the good novel. . . . The good novel should be steadily alight, revealing.

Details that glow, that are themselves and are also something more than themselves, are symbols. Readers may disagree about whether in any particular story something is or is not symbolic—let's say the figs and chrysanthemums in Chopin's "Ripe Figs," or the season in "The Story of an Hour." And an ingenious reader may overcomplicate or overemphasize the symbolism of a work or may distort it by omitting some of the details and by unduly focusing on others. In many works the details glow, but the glow is so gentle and subtle that even to talk about the details is to overstate them and to understate other equally important aspects of the work.

Yet if it is false to overstate the significance of a detail, it is also false to understate a significant detail. The let's-have-no-nonsense literal reader who holds that "the figure of a man" whom Brown meets in the forest in Hawthorne's "Young Goodman Brown" is simply a man—rather than the Devil—impoverishes the story by neglecting the rich implications just as much as the symbol-hunter impoverishes "The Story of an Hour" by losing sight of Mrs. Mallard in an interpretation of the story as a symbolic comment on industrialism. To take only a single piece of evidence: the man whom Brown encounters holds a staff, "which bore the likeness of a great black snake, so curiously wrought that it might almost be seen to twist and wriggle itself like a living serpent." If we are familiar with the story of Adam and Eve, in which Satan took the form of a serpent, it is hard not to think that Hawthorne is here implying that Brown's new acquaintance is Satan. And, to speak more broadly, when reading the story one can hardly not set up opposing meanings (or at least suggestions) for the village (from which Brown sets out) and the forest (into which he enters). The village is associated with daylight, faith, and goodness; the forest with darkness, loss of faith, and evil. This is not to say that the story sets up neat categories. If you read the story, you will find that Hawthorne is careful to be ambiguous. Even in the passage quoted, about the serpent-staff, you'll notice that he does not say it twisted and wriggled, but that it "might almost be seen to twist and wriggle."

A NOTE ON SETTING

The **setting** of a story—not only the physical locale but also the time of day or the year or the century—may or may not be symbolic. Sometimes the setting is lightly sketched, presented only because the story has to take place somewhere and at some time. Often, however, the setting is more important, giving us the feel of the people who move through it. But if scenery is drawn in detail, yet adds up to nothing, we share the impatience Robert Louis Stevenson expressed in a letter: "'Roland approached the house; it had green doors and window blinds; and there was a scraper on the upper step.' To hell with Roland and the scraper."

Yes, of course, but if the green doors and the scraper were to tell us something about the tenant, they could be important. As the novelist Elizabeth Bowen said, "Nothing can happen nowhere. The locale of the happening always colors the happening, and often, to a degree, shapes it." And as Henry James neatly said, in fiction "landscape is character." But don't believe it simply because Bowen and James say it. Read the stories, and test the view for yourself.

NATHANIEL HAWTHORNE

Nathaniel Hawthorne (1804–1864) was born in Salem, Massachusetts, the son of a sea captain. Two of his ancestors were judges; one had persecuted Quakers, and another had served at the Salem witch trials. In his stories and novels Hawthorne keeps returning to the Puritan past, studying guilt, sin, and isolation. "Young Goodman Brown" was published in 1835, the same year as "The Maypole of Merry Mount."

Young Goodman Brown   [1835]

Young Goodman[1] Brown came forth, at sunset, into the street at Salem village; but put his head back, after crossing the threshold, to exchange a parting kiss with his young wife. And Faith, as the wife was aptly named, thrust

---

[1] **Goodman** polite term of address for a man of humble standing. (All notes are by editors.)

her own pretty head into the street, letting the wind play with the pink ribbons of her cap while she called to Goodman Brown.

"Dearest heart," whispered she, softly and rather sadly, when her lips were close to his ear, "prithee put off your journey until sunrise and sleep in your own bed to-night. A lone woman is troubled with such dreams and such thoughts that she's afeared of herself sometimes. Pray tarry with me this night, dear husband, of all nights in the year."

"My love and my Faith," replied young Goodman Brown, "of all nights in the year, this one night must I tarry away from thee. My journey, as thou callest it, forth and back again, must needs be done 'twixt now and sunrise. What, my sweet, pretty wife, dost thou doubt me already, and we but three months married?"

"Then God bless you!" said Faith, with the pink ribbons; "and may you find all well when you come back."

5   "Amen!" cried Goodman Brown. "Say thy prayers, dear Faith, and go to bed at dusk, and no harm will come to thee."

So they parted; and the young man pursued his way until, being about to turn the corner by the meeting-house, he looked back and saw the head of Faith still peeping after him with a melancholy air, in spite of her pink ribbons.

"Poor little Faith!" thought he, for his heart smote him. "What a wretch am I to leave her on such an errand! She talks of dreams, too. Methought as she spoke there was trouble in her face, as if a dream had warned her what work is to be done to-night. But no, no; 'twould kill her to think it. Well, she's a blessed angel on earth; and after this one night, I'll cling to her skirts and follow her to heaven."

With this excellent resolve for the future, Goodman Brown felt himself justified in making more haste on his present evil purpose. He had taken a dreary road, darkened by all the gloomiest trees of the forest, which barely stood aside to let the narrow path creep through, and closed immediately behind. It was all as lonely as could be; and there is this peculiarity in such a solitude, that the traveler knows not who may be concealed by the innumerable trunks and the thick boughs overhead; so that with lonely footsteps he may yet be passing through an unseen multitude.

"There may be a devilish Indian behind every tree," said Goodman Brown, to himself and he glanced fearfully behind him as he added, "What if the devil himself should be at my very elbow!"

10   His head being turned back, he passed a crook of the road, and, looking forward again, beheld the figure of a man, in grave and decent attire, seated at the foot of an old tree. He arose at Goodman Brown's approach and walked onward side by side with him.

"You are late, Goodman Brown," said he. "The clock of the Old South was striking as I came through Boston, and that is full fifteen minutes agone."

"Faith kept me back a while," replied the young man, with a tremor in his voice, caused by the sudden appearance of his companion, though not wholly unexpected.

It was now deep dusk in the forest, and deepest in that part of it where these two were journeying. As nearly as could be discerned, the second traveler was about fifty years old, apparently in the same rank of life as Goodman Brown, and bearing a considerable resemblance to him, though perhaps more in expression than features. Still they might have been taken for father and son. And yet, though the elder person was as simply clad as the younger, and as simple in manner too, he had an indescribable air of one who knew the world, and who would not have felt abashed at the governor's dinner table or in King William's court, were it possible that his affairs should call him thither. But the only thing about him that could be fixed upon as remarkable was his staff, which bore the likeness of a great black snake, so curiously wrought that it might almost be seen to twist and wriggle itself like a living serpent. This, of course, must have been an ocular deception, assisted by the uncertain light.

"Come, Goodman Brown," cried his fellow-traveler, "this is a dull pace for the beginning of a journey. Take my staff, if you are so soon weary."

15   "Friend," said the other, exchanging his slow pace for a full stop, "having kept covenant by meeting thee here, it is my purpose now to return whence I came. I have scruples touching the matter thou wot'st[2] of."

"Sayest thou so?" replied he of the serpent, smiling apart. "Let us walk on, nevertheless, reasoning as we go; and if I convince thee not thou shalt turn back. We are but a little way in the forest yet."

"Too far! too far!" exclaimed the goodman, unconsciously resuming his walk. "My father never went into the woods on such an errand, nor his father before him. We have been a race of honest men and good Christians since the days of the martyrs; and shall I be the first of the name of Brown that ever took this path and kept—"

"Such company, thou wouldst say," observed the elder person, interpreting his pause. "Well said, Goodman Brown! I have been as well acquainted with your family as with ever a one among the Puritans; and that's no trifle to say. I helped your grandfather, the constable, when he lashed the Quaker woman so smartly through the streets of Salem; and it was I that brought your father a pitch-pine knot, kindled at my own hearth, to set fire to an Indian village, in King Philip's war.[3] They were my good friends, both; and many a pleasant walk have we had along this path, and returned merrily after midnight. I would fain be friends with you for their sake."

"If it be as thou sayest," replied Goodman Brown, "I marvel they never spoke of these matters; or, verily, I marvel not, seeing that the least rumor of the sort would have driven them from New England. We are a people of prayer, and good works to boot, and abide no such wickedness."

20   "Wickedness or not," said the traveler with the twisted staff, "I have a very general acquaintance here in New England. The deacons of many a church have drunk the communion wine with me; the selectmen of divers towns make me their chairman; and a majority of the Great and General Court are firm supporters of my interest. The governor and I, too—But these are state secrets."

"Can this be so?" cried Goodman Brown, with a stare of amazement at his undisturbed companion. "Howbeit, I have nothing to do with the governor and council; they have their own ways, and are no rule for a simple husbandman[4] like me. But, were I to go on with thee, how should I meet the eye of that good old man, our minister, at Salem village? Oh, his voice would make me tremble both Sabbath day and lecture day."

---

[2]**wot'st** knowest.   [3]**King Philip's war** war waged by the Colonists (1675–1676) against the Wampanoag Indian leader Metcom, known as "King Philip."   [4]**husbandman** farmer, or, more generally, any man of humble standing.

Thus far the elder traveler had listened with due gravity; but now burst into a fit of irrepressible mirth, shaking himself so violently that his snake-like staff actually seemed to wriggle in sympathy.

"Ha! ha! ha!" shouted he again and again; then composing himself, "Well, go on, Goodman Brown, go on; but, prithee, don't kill me with laughing."

"Well, then, to end the matter at once," said Goodman Brown, considerably nettled, "there is my wife, Faith. It would break her dear little heart; and I'd rather break my own."

25   "Nay, if that be the case," answered the other, "e'en go thy ways, Goodman Brown. I would not for twenty old women like the one hobbling before us that Faith should come to any harm."

As he spoke he pointed his staff at a female figure on the path, in whom Goodman Brown recognized a very pious and exemplary dame, who had taught him his catechism in youth, and was still his moral and spiritual adviser, jointly with the minister and Deacon Gookin.

"A marvel, truly, that Goody[5] Cloyse should be so far in the wilderness at nightfall," said he. "But with your leave, friend, I shall take a cut through the woods until we have left this Christian woman behind. Being a stranger to you, she might ask whom I was consorting with and whither I was going."

"Be it so," said his fellow-traveler. "Betake you to the woods, and let me keep the path."

Accordingly the young man turned aside, but took care to watch his companion, who advanced softly along the road until he had come within a staff's length of the old dame. She, meanwhile, was making the best of her way, with singular speed for so aged a woman, and mumbling some indistinct words—a prayer, doubtless—as she went. The traveler put forth his staff and touched her withered neck with what seemed the serpent's tail.

30   "The devil!" screamed the pious old lady.

"Then Goody Cloyse knows her old friend?" observed the traveler, confronting her and leaning on his writhing stick.

"Ah, forsooth, and is it your worship indeed?" cried the good dame. "Yea, truly is it, and in the very image of my old gossip, Goodman Brown, the grandfather of the silly fellow that now is. But—would your worship believe it?—my broomstick hath strangely disappeared, stolen, as I suspect, by that unhanged witch, Goody Cory, and that, too, when I was all anointed with the juice of smallage and cinquefoil, and wolf's bane—"

"Mingled with fine wheat and the fat of a new-born babe," said the shape of old Goodman Brown.

"Ah, your worship knows the recipe," cried the old lady, cackling aloud. "So, as I was saying, being all ready for the meeting, and no horse to ride on, I made up my mind to foot it; for they tell me there is a nice young man to be taken into communion to-night. But now your good worship will lend me your arm, and we shall be there in a twinkling."

35   "That can hardly be," answered her friend. "I may not spare you my arm, Goody Cloyse; but here is my staff, if you will."

So saying, he threw it down at her feet, where, perhaps, it assumed life, being one of the rods which its owner had formerly lent to the Egyptian magi. Of this fact, however, Goodman Brown could not take cognizance.

---

[5]**Goody** contraction of Goodwife, a polite term of address for a married woman of humble standing.

He had cast up his eyes in astonishment, and, looking down again, beheld neither Goody Cloyse nor the serpentine staff but his fellow-traveler alone, who waited for him as calmly as if nothing had happened.

"That old woman taught me my catechism," said the young man; and there was a world of meaning in this simple comment.

They continued to walk onward, while the elder traveler exhorted his companion to make good speed and persevere in the path, discoursing so aptly that his arguments seemed rather to spring up in the bosom of his auditor than to be suggested by himself. As they went, he plucked a branch of maple to serve for a walking stick, and began to strip it of the twigs and little boughs, which were wet with evening dew. The moment his fingers touched them they became strangely withered and dried up as with a week's sunshine. Thus the pair proceeded, at a good free pace, until suddenly, in a gloomy hollow of the road, Goodman Brown sat himself down on the stump of a tree and refused to go any farther.

"Friend," said he, stubbornly, "my mind is made up. Not another step will I budge on this errand. What if a wretched old woman do choose to go to the devil when I thought she was going to heaven: is that any reason why I should quit my dear Faith and go after her?"

40 "You will think better of this by and by," said his acquaintance, composedly. "Sit here and rest yourself a while; and when you feel like moving again, there is my staff to help you along."

Without more words, he threw his companion the maple stick, and was as speedily out of sight as if he had vanished into the deepening gloom. The young man sat a few moments by the roadside, applauding himself greatly, and thinking with how clear a conscience he should meet the minister in his morning walk, nor shrink from the eye of good old Deacon Gookin. And what calm sleep would be his that very night, which was to have been spent so wickedly, but so purely and sweetly now, in the arms of Faith! Amidst these pleasant and praiseworthy meditations, Goodman Brown heard the tramp of horses along the road, and deemed it advisable to conceal himself within the verge of the forest, conscious of the guilty purpose that had brought him thither, though now so happily turned from it.

On came the hoof-tramps and the voices of the riders, two grave old voices, conversing soberly as they drew near. These mingled sounds appeared to pass along the road, within a few yards of the young man's hiding-place; but, owing doubtless to the depth of the gloom at that particular spot, neither the travelers nor their steeds were visible. Though their figures brushed the small boughs by the wayside, it could not be seen that they intercepted, even for a moment, the faint gleam from the strip of bright sky athwart which they must have passed. Goodman Brown alternately crouched and stood on tiptoe, pulling aside the branches and thrusting forth his head as far as he durst without discerning so much as a shadow. It vexed him the more, because he could have sworn, were such a thing possible, that he recognized the voices of the minister and Deacon Gookin, jogging along quietly, as they were wont to do, when bound to some ordination or ecclesiastical council. While yet within hearing, one of the riders stopped to pluck a switch.

"Of the two, reverend sir," said the voice like the deacon's, "I had rather miss an ordination dinner than to-night's meeting. They tell me that some of our community are to be here from Falmouth and beyond, and others from

Connecticut and Rhode Island, besides several of the Indian powwows, who, after their fashion, know almost as much deviltry as the best of us. Moreover, there is a goodly young woman to be taken into communion."

"Mighty well, Deacon Gookin!" replied the solemn old tones of the minister. "Spur up, or we shall be late. Nothing can be done, you know, until I get on the ground."

45   The hoofs clattered again; and the voices, talking so strangely in the empty air, passed on through the forest, where no church had ever been gathered or solitary Christian prayed. Whither, then, could these holy men be journeying so deep into the heathen wilderness? Young Goodman Brown caught hold of a tree for support, being ready to sink down on the ground, faint and overburdened with the heavy sickness of his heart. He looked up to the sky, doubting whether there really was a heaven above him. Yet there was the blue arch, and the stars brightening in it.

"With heaven above and Faith below, I will yet stand firm against the devil!" cried Goodman Brown.

While he still gazed upward into the deep arch of the firmament and had lifted his hands to pray, a cloud, though no wind was stirring, hurried across the zenith and hid the brightening stars. The blue sky was still visible, except directly overhead, where this black mass of cloud was sweeping swiftly northward. Aloft in the air, as if from the depths of the cloud, came a confused and doubtful sound of voices. Once the listener fancied that he could distinguish the accents of towns-people of his own, men and women, both pious and ungodly, many of whom he had met at the communion table, and had seen others rioting at the tavern. The next moment, so indistinct were the sounds, he doubted whether he had heard aught but the murmur of the old forest, whispering without a wind. Then came a stronger swell of those familiar tones, heard daily in the sunshine at Salem village, but never until now from a cloud of night. There was one voice, of a young woman, uttering lamentations, yet with an uncertain sorrow, and entreating for some favor, which, perhaps, it would grieve her to obtain; and all the unseen multitude, both saints and sinners, seemed to encourage her onward.

"Faith!" shouted Goodman Brown, in a voice of agony and desperation; and the echoes of the forest mocked him, crying, "Faith! Faith!" as if bewildered wretches were seeking her all through the wilderness.

The cry of grief, rage, and terror was yet piercing the night, when the unhappy husband held his breath for a response. There was a scream, drowned immediately in a louder murmur of voices, fading into far-off laughter, as the dark cloud swept away, leaving the clear and silent sky above Goodman Brown. But something fluttered lightly down through the air and caught on the branch of a tree. The young man seized it, and beheld a pink ribbon.

50   "My Faith is gone!" cried he, after one stupefied moment. "There is no good on earth; and sin is but a name. Come, devil; for to thee is this world given."

And, maddened with despair, so that he laughed loud and long, did Goodman Brown grasp his staff and set forth again, at such a rate that he seemed to fly along the forest path rather than to walk or run. The road grew wilder and drearier and more faintly traced, and vanished at length, leaving him in the heart of the dark wilderness, still rushing onward with the instinct that guides mortal man to evil. The whole forest was peopled with frightful sounds—the creaking of the trees, the howling of wild beasts, and the yell of Indians; while sometimes the wind tolled like a distant church bell, and sometimes gave a broad roar around the traveler, as if all Nature were laughing him to scorn. But he was himself the chief horror of the scene, and shrank not from its other horrors.

"Ha! ha! ha!" roared Goodman Brown when the wind laughed at him. "Let us hear which will laugh loudest. Think not to frighten me with your deviltry. Come witch, come lizard, come Indian powwow, come devil himself, and here comes Goodman Brown. You may as well fear him as he fear you!"

In truth, all through the haunted forest there could be nothing more frightful than the figure of Goodman Brown. On he flew among the black pines, brandishing his staff with frenzied gestures, now giving vent to an inspiration of horrid blasphemy, and now shouting forth such laughter as set all the echoes of the forest laughing like demons around him. The fiend in his own shape is less hideous than when he rages in the breast of man. Thus sped the demoniac on his course, until, quivering among the trees, he saw a red light before him, as when the felled trunks and branches of a clearing have been set on fire, and throw up their lurid blaze against the sky, at the hour of midnight. He paused, in a lull of the tempest that had driven him onward, and heard the swell of what seemed a hymn, rolling solemnly from a distance with the weight of many voices. He knew the tune; it was a familiar one in the choir of the village meeting-house. The verse died heavily away, and was lengthened by a chorus, not of human voices, but of all the sounds of the benighted wilderness pealing in awful harmony together. Goodman Brown cried out; and his cry was lost to his own ear by its unison with the cry of the desert.

In the interval of silence he stole forward until the light glared full upon his eyes. At one extremity of an open space, hemmed in by the dark wall of the forest, arose a rock, bearing some rude, natural resemblance either to an altar or a pulpit, and surrounded by four blazing pines, their tops aflame, their stems untouched, like candles at an evening meeting. The mass of foliage that had overgrown the summit of the rock was all on fire, blazing high into the night and fitfully illuminating the whole field. Each pendent twig and leafy festoon was in a blaze. As the red light arose and fell, a numerous congregation alternately shone forth, then disappeared in shadow, and again grew, as it were, out of the darkness, peopling the heart of the solitary woods at once.

55   "A grave and dark-clad company," quoth Goodman Brown.

In truth they were such. Among them, quivering to-and-fro between gloom and splendor, appeared faces that would be seen next day at the council board of the province, and others which, Sabbath after Sabbath, looked devoutly heavenward, and benignantly over the crowded pews, from the holiest pulpits in the land. Some affirm that the lady of the governor was there. At least three were high dames well known to her, and wives of honored husbands, and widows, a great multitude, and ancient maidens, all of excellent repute, and fair young girls, who trembled lest their mothers should espy them. Either the sudden gleams of light flashing over the obscure field bedazzled Goodman Brown, or he recognized a score of the church-members of Salem village famous for their especial sanctity. Good old Deacon Gookin had arrived, and waited at the skirts of that venerable saint, his revered pastor. But, irreverently consorting with these grave, reputable, and pious people, these elders of the church, these chaste dames and dewy virgins, there were men of dissolute lives and women of spotted fame, wretches given over to all mean and filthy vice, and suspected even of horrid crimes. It was strange to see that the good shrank not from the wicked, nor were the sinners abashed by the saints. Scattered also among their pale-faced enemies were the Indian priests, or powwows, who had often scared their native forest with more hideous incantations than any known to English witchcraft.

"But, where is Faith?" thought Goodman Brown; and, as hope came into his heart, he trembled.

Another verse of the hymn arose, a slow and mournful strain, such as the pious love, but joined to words which expressed all that our nature can conceive of sin, and darkly hinted at far more. Unfathomable to mere mortals is the lore of fiends. Verse after verse was sung; and still the chorus of the desert swelled between, like the deepest tone of a mighty organ; and with the final peal of that dreadful anthem there came a sound, as if the roaring wind, the rushing streams, the howling beasts, and every other voice of the unconcerted wilderness were mingling and according with the voice of guilty man in homage to the prince of all. The four blazing pines threw up a loftier flame, and obscurely discovered shapes and visages of horror on the smoke wreaths above the impious assembly. At the same moment the fire on the rock shot redly forth and formed a glowing arch above its base, where now appeared a figure. With reverence be it spoken, the figure bore no slight similitude, both in garb and manner, to some grave divine of the New England churches.

"Bring forth the converts!" cried a voice that echoed through the field and rolled into the forest.

60   At the word, Goodman Brown stepped forth from the shadow of the trees and approached the congregation, with whom he felt a loathful brotherhood by the sympathy of all that was wicked in his heart. He could have wellnigh sworn that the shape of his own dead father beckoned him to advance, looking downward from a smoke wreath, while a woman, with dim features of despair, threw out her hand to warn him back. Was it his mother? But he had no power to retreat one step, nor to resist, even in thought, when the minister and good old Deacon Gookin seized his arms and led him to the blazing rock. Thither came also the slender form of a veiled female, led between Goody Cloyse, that pious teacher of the catechism, and Martha Carrier, who had received the devil's promise to be queen of hell. A rampant hag was she. And there stood the proselytes beneath the canopy of fire.

"Welcome, my children," said the dark figure, "to the communion of your race. Ye have found thus young your nature and your destiny. My children, look behind you!"

They turned; and flashing forth, as it were, in a sheet of flame, the fiend worshippers were seen; the smile of welcome gleamed darkly on every visage.

"There," resumed the sable form, "are all whom ye have reverenced from youth. Ye deemed them holier than yourselves, and shrank from your own sin, contrasting it with their lives of righteousness and prayerful aspirations heavenward. Yet here are they all in my worshipping assembly. This night it shall be granted you to know their secret deeds: how hoary-bearded elders of the church have whispered wanton words to the young maids of their households; how many a woman, eager for widows' weeds, has given her husband a drink at bedtime and let him sleep his last sleep in her bosom; how beardless youths have made haste to inherit their fathers' wealth; and how fair damsels—blush not, sweet ones—have dug little graves in the garden, and bidden me, the sole guest, to an infant's funeral. By the sympathy of your human hearts for sin ye shall scent out all the places—whether in church, bedchamber, street, field, or forest—where crime has been committed, and shall exult to behold the whole earth one stain of guilt, one mighty blood spot. Far more than this. It shall be yours to penetrate, in every bosom, the deep mystery of sin, the fountain of all wicked arts, and which inexhaustibly supplies more evil impulses than human power—than my power at its utmost—can make manifest in deeds. And now, my children, look upon each other."

They did so; and, by the blaze of the hell-kindled torches, the wretched man beheld his Faith, and the wife her husband, trembling before that unhallowed altar.

65   "Lo, there ye stand, my children," said the figure, in a deep and solemn tone, almost sad with its despairing awfulness, as if his once angelic nature could yet mourn for our miserable race. "Depending upon one another's hearts, ye had still hoped that virtue were not all a dream. Now are ye undeceived. Evil is the nature of mankind. Evil must be your only happiness. Welcome, again, my children, to the communion of your race."

"Welcome," repeated the fiend worshippers, in one cry of despair and triumph.

And there they stood, the only pair, as it seemed, who were yet hesitating on the verge of wickedness in this dark world. A basin was hollowed, naturally, in the rock. Did it contain water, reddened by the lurid light? or was it blood? or, perchance, a liquid flame? Herein did the shape of evil dip his hand and prepare to lay the mark of baptism upon their foreheads, that they might be partakers of the mystery of sin, more conscious of the secret guilt of others, both in deed and thought, than they could now be of their own. The husband cast one look at his pale wife, and Faith at him. What polluted wretches would the next glance show them to each other, shuddering alike at what they disclosed and what they saw!

"Faith! Faith!" cried the husband, "look up to heaven, and resist the wicked one."

Whether Faith obeyed he knew not. Hardly had he spoken when he found himself amid calm night and solitude, listening to a roar of the wind which died heavily away through the forest. He staggered against the rock, and felt it chill and damp; while a hanging twig, that had been all on fire, besprinkled his cheek with the coldest dew.

70   The next morning young Goodman Brown came slowly into the street of Salem village, staring around him like a bewildered man. The good old minister was taking a walk along the graveyard to get an appetite for breakfast and meditate his sermon, and bestowed a blessing, as he passed, on Goodman Brown. He shrank from the venerable saint as if to avoid an anathema. Old Deacon Gookin was at domestic worship, and the holy words of his prayer were heard through the open window. "What God doth the wizard pray to?" quoth Goodman Brown. Goody Cloyse, that excellent old

Christian, stood in the early sunshine at her own lattice, catechizing a little girl who had brought her a pint of morning's milk. Goodman Brown snatched away the child as from the grasp of the fiend himself. Turning the corner by the meeting-house, he spied the head of Faith, with the pink ribbons, gazing anxiously forth, and bursting into such joy at sight of him that she skipped along the street and almost kissed her husband before the whole village. But Goodman Brown looked sternly and sadly into her face, and passed on without a greeting.

Had Goodman Brown fallen asleep in the forest and only dreamed a wild dream of a witch-meeting?

Be it so, if you will; but alas! it was a dream of evil omen for young Goodman Brown. A stern, a sad, a darkly meditative, a distrustful, if not a desperate man did he become from the night of that fearful dream. On the Sabbath day, when the congregation were singing a holy psalm, he could not listen because an anthem of sin rushed loudly upon his ear and drowned all the blessed strain. When the minister spoke from the pulpit with power and fervid eloquence, and, with his hand on the open Bible, of the sacred truths of our religion, and of saint-like lives and triumphant deaths, and of future bliss or misery unutterable, then did Goodman Brown turn pale, dreading lest the roof should thunder down upon the gray blasphemer and his hearers. Often, awaking suddenly at midnight, he shrank from the bosom of Faith; and at morning or eventide, when the family knelt down at prayer, he scowled and muttered to himself, and gazed sternly at his wife, and turned away. And when he had lived long, and was borne to his grave a hoary corpse, followed by Faith, an aged woman, and children and grandchildren, a goodly procession, besides neighbors not a few, they carved no hopeful verse upon his tombstone, for his dying hour was gloom.

❖ TOPICS FOR CRITICAL THINKING AND WRITING

1. Do you take Faith to stand only for religious faith, or can she here also stand for one's faith in one's fellow human beings? Explain.

2. Hawthorne describes the second traveler as "about fifty years old, apparently in the same rank as Goodman Brown, and bearing a considerable resemblance to him." Further, "they might have been taken for father and son." What do you think Hawthorne is getting at here?

3. In the forest Brown sees (or thinks he sees) Goody Cloyse, the minister, Deacon Gookin, and others. Does he in fact meet them, or does he dream of them? Or does he encounter "figures" and "forms" (rather than real people) whom the devil conjures up in order to deceive Brown?

4. Evaluate the view that when Brown enters the dark forest he is really entering his own evil mind.

5. A Hawthorne scholar we know says that he finds this story "terrifying." Do you agree? Or would you characterize your response to it differently? Explain, making reference to passages in the text.

6. Does a person have to be a Christian in order to understand "Young Goodman Brown"? Would a Christian reader find this story reassuring or disturbing? Can a non-Christian reader understand and appreciate the story? What might he or she learn from reading it?

7. Having read and studied "Young Goodman Brown," do you find you want to read more of Hawthorne's stories? Are you very eager, a little eager, or not really? Please explain.
8. "Young Goodman Brown" is often included in anthologies of American literature and in collections of short stories. In your view, why is this the case? Do you agree with this decision, or does it puzzle you?

JOHN STEINBECK

John Steinbeck (1902–1968) was born in Salinas, California, and much of his fiction concerns this landscape and its people. As a young man he worked on ranches, farms, and road gangs, and sometimes attended Stanford University—he never graduated—but he wrote whenever he could find the time. His early efforts at writing, however, were uniformly rejected by publishers. Even when he did break into print, he did not achieve much notice for several years: a novel in 1929, a book of stories in 1932, and another novel in 1933 attracted little attention. But the publication of Tortilla Flat *(1935), a novel about Mexican-Americans, changed all that. It was followed by other successful novels—*In Dubious Battle *(1936) and* Of Mice and Men *(1937)—and by* The Long Valley *(1938), a collection of stories that included "The Chrysanthemums." His next book,* The Grapes of Wrath *(1939), about dispossessed sharecropper migrants from the Oklahoma dustbowl, was also immensely popular and won a Pulitzer Prize. During the Second World War Steinbeck sent reports from battlefields in Italy and Africa. In 1962 he was awarded the Nobel Prize in Literature.*

The Chrysanthemums   [1937]

The high grey-flannel fog of winter closed off the Salinas Valley[1] from the sky and from all the rest of the world. On every side it sat like a lid on the mountains and made of the great valley a closed pot. On the broad, level land floor the gang plows bit deep and left the black earth shining like metal where the shares had cut. On the foothill ranches across the Salinas River, the yellow stubble fields seemed to be bathed in pale cold sunshine, but there was no sunshine in the valley now in December. The thick willow scrub along the river flamed with sharp and positive yellow leaves.

It was quiet and of waiting. The air was cold and tender. A light wind blew up from the southwest so that the farmers were mildly hopeful of a good rain before long; but fog and rain do not go together.

Across the river, on Henry Allen's foothill ranch there was little work to be done, for the hay was cut and stored and the orchards were plowed up to receive the rain deeply when it should come. The cattle on the higher slopes were becoming shaggy and rough-coated.

Elisa Allen, working in her flower garden, looked down across the yard and saw Henry, her husband, talking to two men in business suits. The three of them stood by the tractor shed, each man with one foot on the side

---

[1]**the Salinas Valley** a fertile area in central California.

of the little Fordson.[2] They smoked cigarettes and studied the machine as they talked.

5   Elisa watched them for a moment and then went back to her work. She was thirty-five. Her face was lean and strong and her eyes were as clear as water. Her figure looked blocked and heavy in her gardening costume, a man's black hat pulled low down over her eyes, clod-hopper shoes, a figured print dress almost completely covered by a big corduroy apron with four big pockets to hold the snips, the trowel and scratcher, the seeds and the knife she worked with. She wore heavy leather gloves to protect her hands while she worked.

She was cutting down the old year's chrysanthemum stalks with a pair of short and powerful scissors. She looked down toward the tractor shed now and then. Her face was eager and mature and handsome; even her work with the scissors was over-eager, over-powerful. The chrysanthemum stems seemed too small and easy for her energy.

She brushed a cloud of hair out of her eyes with the back of her glove, and left a smudge of earth on her cheek in doing it. Behind her stood the neat white farm house with red geraniums close-banked around it as high as the windows. It was a hard-swept looking little house with hard-polished windows, and a clean mud-mat on the front steps.

Elisa cast another glance toward the tractor shed. The strangers were getting into their Ford coupe. She took off a glove and put her strong fingers down into the forest of new green chrysanthemum sprouts that were growing around the old roots. She spread the leaves and looked down among the close-growing stems. No aphids were there, no sowbugs or snails or cutworms. Her terrier fingers destroyed such pests before they could get started.

Elisa started at the sound of her husband's voice. He had come near quietly, and he leaned over the wire fence that protected her flower garden from the cattle and dogs and chickens.

10   "At it again," he said. "You've got a strong new crop coming."

Elisa straightened her back and pulled on the gardening glove again. "Yes, they'll be strong this coming year." In her tone and on her face there was a little smugness.

"You've got a gift with things," Henry observed. "Some of those yellow chrysanthemums you had this year were ten inches across. I wish you'd work out in the orchard and raise some apples that big."

Her eyes sharpened. "Maybe I could do it, too. I've a gift with things, all right. My mother had it. She could stick anything in the ground and make it grow. She said it was having planters' hands that knew how to do it."

"Well, it sure works with flowers," he said.

15   "Henry, who were those men you were talking to?"

"Why, sure, that's what I came to tell you. They were from the Western Meat Company. I sold those thirty head of three-year-old steers. Got nearly my own price, too."

"Good," she thought. "Good for you."

"And I thought," he continued, "I thought how it's Saturday afternoon, and we might go into Salinas for dinner at a restaurant, and then to a picture show—to celebrate, you see."

"Good," she repeated. "Oh, yes. That will be good."

---

[2]**Fordson** a two-door Ford car.

20   Henry put on his joking tone. "There's fights tonight. How'd you like to go to the fights?"

"Oh, no," she said breathlessly. "No, I wouldn't like the fights."

"Just fooling, Elisa. We'll go to a movie. Let's see. It's two now. I'm going to take Scotty and bring down those steers from the hill. It'll take us maybe two hours. We'll go in town about five and have dinner at the Cominos Hotel. Like that?"

"Of course I'll like it. It's good to eat away from home."

"All right, then. I'll go get up a couple of horses."

25   She said, "I'll have plenty of time to transplant some of these sets, I guess."

She heard her husband calling Scotty down by the barn. And a little later she saw the two men ride up the pale yellow hillside in search of the steers.

There was a little square sandy bed kept for rooting the chrysanthemums. With her trowel she turned the soil over and over, and smoothed it and patted it firm. Then she dug ten parallel trenches to receive the sets. Back at the chrysanthemum bed she pulled out the little crisp shoots, trimmed off the leaves of each one with her scissors and laid it on a small orderly pile.

A squeak of wheels and plod of hoofs, came from the road. Elisa looked up. The country road ran along the dense bank of willows and cottonwoods that bordered the river, and up this road came a curious vehicle, curiously drawn. It was an old springwagon, with a round canvas top on it like the cover of a prairie schooner. It was drawn by an old bay horse and a little grey-and-white burro. A big stubble-bearded man sat between the cover flaps and drove the crawling team. Underneath the wagon, between the hind wheels, a lean and rangy mongrel dog walked sedately. Words were painted on the canvas, in clumsy, crooked letters. "Pots, pans, knives, sisors, lawn mores, Fixed." Two rows of articles, and the triumphantly definitive "Fixed" below. The black paint had run down in little sharp points beneath each letter.

Elisa, squatting on the ground, watched to see the crazy, loose-jointed wagon pass by. But it didn't pass. It turned into the farm road in front of her house, crooked old wheels skirling and squeaking. The rangy dog darted from between the wheels and ran ahead. Instantly the two ranch shepherds flew out at him. Then all three stopped, and with stiff and quivering tails, with taut straight legs, with ambassadorial dignity, they slowly circled, sniffing daintily. The caravan pulled up to Elisa's wire fence and stopped. Now the newcomer dog, feeling out-numbered, lowered his tail and retired under the wagon with raised hackles and bared teeth.

30   The man on the wagon called out, "That's a bad dog in a fight when he gets started."

Elisa laughed. "I see he is. How soon does he generally get started?"

The man caught up her laughter and echoed it heartily. "Sometimes not for weeks and weeks," he said. He climbed stiffly down, over the wheel. The horse and donkey drooped like unwatered flowers.

Elisa saw that he was a very big man. Although his hair and beard were greying, he did not look old. His worn black suit was wrinkled and spotted with grease. The laughter had disappeared from his face and eyes the moment his laughing voice ceased. His eyes were dark, and they were full of the brooding that gets in the eyes of teamsters and sailors. The calloused hands he rested on the wire fence were cracked, and every crack was a black line. He took off his battered hat.

"I'm off my general road, ma'am," he said. "Does this dirt road cut over across the river to the Los Angeles highway?"

35   Elisa stood up and shoved the thick scissors in her apron pocket. "Well, yes, it does, but it winds around and then fords the river. I don't think your team could pull it through the sand."

He replied with some asperity. "It might surprise you what them beasts can pull through."

"When they get started?" She asked.

He smiled for a second. "Yes. When they get started."

"Well," said Elisa, "I think you'll save time if you go back to the Salinas road and pick up the highway there."

40   He drew a big finger around the chicken wire and made it sing. "I ain't in any hurry, ma'am. I go from Seattle to San Diego and back every year. Takes all my time. About six months each way. I aim to follow nice weather."

Elisa took off her gloves and stuffed them in the apron pocket with the scissors. She touched under the edge of her man's hat, searching for fugitive hairs. "That sounds like a nice kind of a way to live," she said.

He leaned confidentially over the fence. "Maybe you noticed the writing on my wagon. I mend pots and sharpen knives and scissors. You got any of them things to do?"

"Oh, no," she said quickly. "Nothing like that." Her eyes hardened with resistance.

"Scissors is the worst thing," he explained. "Most people just ruin scissors trying to sharpen 'em, but I know how. I got a special tool. It's a little bobbit kind of thing, and patented. But it sure does the trick."

45   "No, My scissors are all sharp."

"All right, then. Take a pot," he continued earnestly, "a bent pot, or a pot with a hole. I can make it like new so you don't have to buy no new ones. That's a saving for you."

"No," she said shortly. "I tell you I have nothing like that for you to do."

His face fell to an exaggerated sadness. His voice took on a whining undertone. "I ain't had a thing to do today. Maybe I won't have no supper tonight. You see I'm off my regular road. I know folks on the highway clear from Seattle to San Diego. They save their things for me to sharpen up because they know I do it so good and save them money."

"I'm sorry," Elisa said irritably. "I haven't anything for you to do."

50   His eyes left her face and fell to searching the ground. They roamed about until they came to the chrysanthemum bed where she had been working. "What's them plants, ma'am?"

The irritation and resistance melted from Elisa's face. "Oh, those are chrysanthemums, giant whites and yellows. I raise them every year, bigger than anybody around here."

"Kind of a long-stemmed flower? Looks like a quick puff of colored smoke?" he asked.

"That's it. What a nice way to describe them."

"They smell kind of nasty till you get used to them," he said.

55   It's a good bitter smell," she retorted, "not nasty at all."

He changed his tone quickly. "I like the smell myself."

"I had ten-inch blooms this year," she said.

The man leaned farther over the fence. "Look. I know a lady down the road a piece, has got the nicest garden you ever seen. Got nearly every kind of flower but no chrysanthemums. Last time I was mending a copper-bottom wash-tub for her (that's a hard job but I do it good), she said to me, 'If you ever run acrost some nice chrysanthemums I wish you'd try to get me a few seeds.' That's what she told me."

Elisa's eyes grew alert and eager. "She couldn't have known much about chrysanthemums. You *can* raise them from seed, but it's much easier to root the little sprouts you see here."

60   "Oh," he said. "I s'pose I can't take none to her then."

"Why yes you can," Elisa cried. "I can put some in damp sand, and you can carry them right along with you. They'll take root in the pot if you keep them damp. And then transplant them."

"She'd sure like to have some, ma'am. You say they're nice ones?"

"Beautiful," she said. "Oh, beautiful." Her eyes shone. She tore off the battered hat and shook out her dark pretty hair. "I'll put them in a flower pot, and you can take them right with you. Come into the yard."

While them man came through the picket gate Elisa ran excitedly along the geranium-bordered path to the back of the house. And she returned carrying a big red flower pot. The gloves were forgotten now. She kneeled on the ground by the starting bed and dug up the sandy soil with her fingers and scooped it into the bright new flower pot. Then she picked up the little pile of shoots she had just prepared. With her strong fingers she pressed them into the sand and tamped around them with her knuckles. The man stood over her. "I'll tell you what to do," she said. "You remember so you can tell the lady."

65   "Yes, I'll try to remember."

"Well, look. These will take root in about a month. Then she must set them out, about a foot apart in good rich earth like this, see?" She lifted a handful of dark soil for him to look at. "They'll grow fast and tall. Now remember this: In July tell her to cut them down, about eight inches from the ground."

"Before they bloom?" he asked.

"Yes, before they bloom." Her face was tight with eagerness. "They'll grow right up again. About the last of September the buds will start."

She stopped and seemed perplexed. "It's the budding that takes the most care," she said hesitantly. "I don't know how to tell you." She looked deep into his eyes, searchingly. Her mouth opened a little, and she seemed to be listening. "I'll try to tell you," she said. "Did you ever hear of planting hands?"

70   "Can't say I have, ma'am."

"Well, I can only tell you what it feels like. It's when you're picking off the buds you don't want. Everything goes right down into your fingertips. You watch your fingers work. They do it themselves. You can feel how it is. They pick and pick the buds. They never make a mistake. They're with the plant. Do you see? Your fingers and the plant. You can feel that, right up your arm. They know. They never make a mistake. You can feel it. When you're like that you can't do anything wrong. Do you see that? Can you understand that?"

She was kneeling on the ground looking up at him. Her breast swelled passionately.

The man's eyes narrowed. He looked away self-consciously. "Maybe I know," he said. "Sometimes in the night in the wagon there—"

Elisa's voice grew husky. She broke in on him, "I've never lived as you do, but I know what you mean. When the night is dark—why, the stars are sharp-pointed, and there's quiet. Why, you rise up and up! Every pointed star gets driven into your body. It's like that. Hot and sharp and—lovely."

75   Kneeling there, her hand went out toward his legs in the greasy black trousers. Her hesitant fingers almost touched the cloth. Then her hand dropped to the ground. She crouched low like a fawning dog.

He said, "It's nice, just like you say. Only when you don't have no dinner, it ain't."

She stood up then, very straight, and her face was ashamed. She held the flower pot out to him and placed it gently in his arms. "Here. Put it in your wagon, on the seat, where you can watch it. Maybe I can find something for you to do."

At the back of the house she dug in the can pile and found two old and battered aluminum saucepans. She carried them back and gave them to him. "Here, maybe you can fix these."

His manner changed. He became professional. "Good as new I can fix them." At the back of his wagon he set a little anvil, and out of an oily tool box dug a small machine hammer. Elisa came through the gate to watch him while he pounded out the dents in the kettles. His mouth grew sure and knowing. At a difficult part of the work he sucked his under-lip,

80   "You sleep right in the wagon?" Elisa asked.

"Right in the wagon, ma'am. Rain or shine I'm dry as a cow in there."

"It must be nice," she said. "It must be very nice. I wish women could do such things."

"It ain't the right kind of life for a woman."

Her upper lip raised a little, showing her teeth. "How do you know? How can you tell?" she said.

85   "I don't know, ma'am," he protested. "Of course I don't know. Now here's your kettles done. You don't have to buy no new ones."

"How much?"

"Oh, fifty cents'll do. I keep my prices down and my work good. That's why I have all them satisfied customers up and down the highway."

Elisa brought him a fifty-cent piece from the house and dropped it in his hand. "You might be surprised to have a rival some time. I can sharpen scissors, too. And I can beat the dents out of little pots. I could show you what a woman might do."

He put his hammer back in the oily box and shoved the little anvil out of sight. "It would be a lonely life for a woman, ma'am, and a scarey life, too, with animals creeping under the wagon all night." He climbed over the singletree, steadying himself with a hand on the burro's white rump. He settled himself in the seat, picked up the lines. "Thank you kindly, ma'am," he said. "I'll do like you told me; I'll go back and catch the Salinas road."

90   "Mind," she called, "if you're long in getting there, keep the sand damp."

"Sand, ma'am? . . . Sand? Oh, sure. You mean around the chrysanthemums. Sure I will." He clucked his tongue. The beasts leaned luxuriously into their collars. The mongrel dog took his place between the back wheels. The wagon turned and crawled out the entrance road and back the way it had come, along the river.

Elisa stood in front of her wire fence watching the slow progress of the caravan. Her shoulders were straight, and her head thrown back, her eyes half-closed, so that the scene came vaguely into them. Her lips moved silently, forming the words "Good-bye—good-bye." Then she whispered, "That's a bright direction. There's a glowing there." The sound of her whisper startled her. She shook herself free and looked about to see whether anyone had been listening. Only the dogs had heard. They lifted their heads toward her from their sleeping in the dust, and then stretched out their chins and settled asleep again. Elisa turned and ran hurriedly into the house.

In the kitchen she reached behind the stove and felt the water tank. It was full of hot water from the noonday cooking. In the bathroom she tore off her soiled clothes and flung them into the corner. And then she scrubbed herself with a little block of pumice, legs and thighs, loins and chest and arms, until her skin was scratched and red. When she had dried herself she stood in front of a mirror in her bedroom and looked at her body. She tightened her stomach and threw out her chest. She turned and looked over her shoulder at her back.

After a while she began to dress, slowly. She put on her newest underclothing and her nicest stockings and the dress which was the symbol of her prettiness. She worked carefully on her hair, penciled her eyebrows and rouged her lips.

95   Before she was finished she heard the little thunder of hoofs and the shouts of Henry and his helper as they drove the red steers into the corral. She heard the gate bang shut and set herself for Henry's arrival.

His step sounded on the porch. He entered the house calling, "Elisa, where are you?"

"In my room, dressing. I'm not ready. There's hot water for your bath. Hurry up. It's getting late."

When she heard him splashing in the tub, Elisa laid his dark suit on the bed, and shirt and socks and tie beside it. She stood his polished shoes on the floor beside the bed. Then she went to the porch and sat primly and stiffly down. She looked toward the river road where the willow-line was still yellow with frosted leaves so that under the high grey fog they seemed a thin band of sunshine. This was the only color in the grey afternoon. She sat unmoving for a long time. Her eyes blinked rarely.

Henry came banging out of the door shoving his tie inside his vest as he came. Elisa stiffened and her face grew tight. Henry stopped short and looked at her. "Why—why, Elisa. You look so nice!"

100   "Nice? You think I look nice? What do you mean by 'nice'?"

Henry blundered on. "I don't know. I mean you look different, strong and happy."

"I am strong? Yes, strong. What do you mean by 'strong'?"

He looked bewildered. "You're playing some kind of a game," he said helplessly. "It's a kind of a play. You look strong enough to break a calf over your knee, happy enough to eat it like a watermelon."

For a second she lost her rigidity. "Henry! Don't talk like that. You didn't know what you said." She grew complete again. "I'm strong," she boasted. "I never knew before how strong."

105   Henry looked down toward the tractor shed, and when he brought his eyes back to her, they were his own again. "I'll get out the car. You can put on your coat while I'm starting."

Elisa went into the house. She heard him drive to the gate and idle down his motor, and then she took a long time to put on her hat. She pulled it here and pressed it there. When Henry turned the motor off she slipped into her coat and went out.

The little roadster bounced along on the dirt road by the river, raising the birds and driving the rabbit into the brush. Two cranes flapped heavily over the willow-line and dropped into the river-bed.

Far ahead on the road Elisa saw a dark speck. She knew.

She tried not to look as they passed it, but her eyes would not obey. She whispered to herself sadly, "He might have thrown them off the road. That wouldn't have been much trouble, not very much. But he kept the pot," she explained. "He had to keep the pot. That's why he couldn't get them off the road."

110   The roadster turned a bend and she saw the caravan ahead. She swung full around toward her husband so she could not see the little covered wagon and the mismatched team as the car passed them.

In a moment it was over. The thing was done. She did not look back.

She said loudly, to be heard above the motor, "It will be good, tonight, a good dinner."

"Now you're changed again," Henry complained. He took one hand from the wheel and patted her knee. "I ought to take you in to dinner oftener. It would be good for both of us. We get so heavy out on the ranch."

"Henry," she asked, "could we have wine at dinner?"

115   "Sure we could. Say! That will be fine."

She was silent for a while; then she said, "Henry, at those prize fights, do the men hurt each other very much?"

"Sometimes a little, not often. Why?"

"Well, I've read how they break noses, and blood runs down their chests. I've read how the fighting gloves get heavy and soggy with blood."

He looked around at her. "What's the matter, Elisa? I didn't know you read things like that." He brought the car to a stop, then turned to the right over the Salinas River bridge.

120   "Do any women ever go to the fights?" she asked.

"Oh, sure, some. What's the matter, Elisa? Do you want to go? I don't think you'd like it, but I'll take you if you really want to go."

She relaxed limply in the seat. "Oh, no. No. I don't want to go. I'm sure I don't." Her face was turned away from him. "It will be enough if we can have wine. It will be plenty." She turned up her coat collar so he could not see that she was crying weakly—like an old woman.

❊ TOPICS FOR CRITICAL THINKING AND WRITING

1. In the first paragraph of the story, the valley, shut off by fog, is said to be "a closed pot." Is this setting significant? Would any other setting do equally well? Why, or why not?

2. What does Elisa's clothing tell us about her? By the way, do you believe that all clothing says something about the wearers? Please explain.

3. Should we make anything special out of Elisa's interest in gardening? If so, what?
4. Describe Elisa's and Henry's marriage.
5. Evaluate the view that Elisa is responsible for her troubles.

EUDORA WELTY

Eudora Welty (1909-2001) was born in Jackson, Mississippi. Although she earned a bachelor's degree at the University of Wisconsin, and she spent a year studying advertising in New York City at the Columbia University Graduate School of Business, she lived almost all of her life in Jackson.
In the preface to her Collected Stories *she says:*

I have been told, both in approval and in accusation, that I seem to love all my characters. What I do in writing of any character is to try to enter into the mind, heart and skin of a human being who is not myself. Whether this happens to be a man or a woman, old or young, with skin black or white, the primary challenge lies in making the jump itself. It is the act of a writer's imagination that I set most high.

In addition to writing stories and novels, Welty has written a book about fiction, The Eye of the Story *(1977), and a memoir,* One Writer's Beginnings *(1984).*

A Worn Path   [1941]

It was December—a bright frozen day in the early morning. Far out in the country there was an old Negro woman with her head tied in a red rag, coming along a path through the pinewoods. Her name was Phoenix Jackson. She was very old and small and she walked slowly in the dark pine shadows, moving a little from side to side in her steps, with the balanced heaviness and lightness of a pendulum in a grandfather clock. She carried a thin, small cane made from an umbrella, and with this she kept tapping the frozen earth in front of her. This made a grave and persistent noise in the still air, that seemed meditative like the chirping of a solitary little bird.

She wore a dark striped dress reaching down to her shoe tops, and an equally long apron of bleached sugar sacks, with a full pocket: all neat and tidy, but every time she took a step she might have fallen over her shoelaces, which dragged from her unlaced shoes. She looked straight ahead. Her eyes were blue with age. Her skin had a pattern all its own of numberless branching wrinkles and as though a whole little tree stood in the middle of her forehead, but a golden color ran underneath, and the two knobs of her cheeks were illuminated by a yellow burning under the dark. Under the red rag her hair came down on her neck in the frailest of ringlets, still black, and with an odor like copper.

Now and then there was a quivering in the thicket. Old Phoenix said, "Out of my way, all you foxes, owls, beetles, jack rabbits, coons, and wild

animals! . . . Keep out from under these feet, little bob-whites. . . . Keep the
big wild hogs out of my path. Don't let none of those come running my direction. I got a long way." Under her small black-freckled hand her cane, limber as
a buggy whip, would switch at the brush as if to rouse up any hiding things.

On she went. The woods were deep and still. The sun made the pine
needles almost too bright to look at, up where the wind rocked. The cones
dropped as light as feathers. Down in the hollow was the mourning dove—
it was not too late for him.

5   The path ran up a hill. "Seem like there is chains about my feet, time I
get this far," she said, in the voice of argument old people keep to use with
themselves. "Something always take a hold of me on this hill—pleads I
should stay."

After she got to the top she turned and gave a full, severe look behind
her where she had come. "Up through pines," she said at length. "Now
down through oaks."

Her eyes opened their widest, and she started down gently. But before
she got to the bottom of the hill a bush caught her dress.

Her fingers were busy and intent, but her skirts were full and long, so
that before she could pull them free in one place they were caught in
another. It was not possible to allow the dress to tear. "I in the thorny
bush," she said. "Thorns, you doing your appointed work. Never want to let
folks pass—no sir. Old eyes thought you was a pretty little *green* bush."

Finally, trembling all over, she stood free, and after a moment dared to
stoop for her cane.

10   "Sun so high!" she cried, leaning back and looking, while the thick
tears went over her eyes. "The time getting all gone here."

At the foot of this hill was a place where a log was laid across the creek.

"Now comes the trial," said Phoenix.

Putting her right foot out, she mounted the log and shut her eyes. Lifting her skirt, levelling her cane fiercely before her, like a festival figure in
some parade, she began to march across. Then she opened her eyes and she
was safe on the other side.

"I wasn't as old as I thought," she said.

15   But she sat down to rest. She spread her skirts on the bank around her
and folded her hands over her knees. Up above her was a tree in a pearly
cloud of mistletoe. She did not dare to close her eyes, and when a little boy
brought her a little plate with a slice of marble-cake on it she spoke to him.
"That would be acceptable," she said. But when she went to take it there
was just her own hand in the air.

So she left that tree, and had to go through a barbed-wire fence. There
she had to creep and crawl, spreading her knees and stretching her fingers
like a baby trying to climb the steps. But she talked loudly to herself: she
could not let her dress be torn now, so late in the day, and she could
not pay for having her arm or leg sawed off if she got caught fast where
she was.

At last she was safe through the fence and risen up out in the clearing.
Big dead trees, like black men with one arm, were standing in the purple
stalks of the withered cotton field. There sat a buzzard.

"Who you watching?"

In the furrow she made her way along.

20   "Glad this not the season for bulls," she said, looking sideways, "and
the good Lord made his snakes to curl up and sleep in the winter. A plea-

sure I don't see no two-headed snake coming around that tree, where it come once. It took a while to get by him, back in the summer."

She passed through the old cotton and went into a field of dead corn. It whispered and shook and was taller than her head. "Through the maze now," she said, for there was no path.

Then there was something tall, black, and skinny there, moving before her.

At first she took it for a man. It could have been a man dancing in the field. But she stood still and listened, and it did not make a sound. It was as silent as a ghost.

"Ghost," she said sharply, "who be you the ghost of? For I have heard of nary death close by."

25   But there was no answer—only the ragged dancing in the wind.

She shut her eyes, reached out her hand, and touched a sleeve. She found a coat and inside that an emptiness, cold as ice.

"You scarecrow," she said. Her face lighted. "I ought to be shut up for good," she said with laughter. "My senses is gone, I too old. I the oldest people I ever know. Dance, old scarecrow," she said, "while I dancing with you."

She kicked her foot over the furrow, and with mouth drawn down, shook her head once or twice in a little strutting way. Some husks blew down and whirled in streamers about her skirts.

Then she went on, parting her way from side to side with the cane, through the whispering field. At last she came to the end, to a wagon track where the silver grass blew between the red ruts. The quail were walking around like pullets, seeming all dainty and unseen.

30   "Walk pretty," she said. "This the easy place. This the easy going."

She followed the track, swaying through the quiet bare fields, through the little strings of trees silver in their dead leaves, past cabins silver from weather, with the doors and windows boarded shut, all like old women under a spell sitting there. "I walking in their sleep," she said, nodding her head vigorously.

In a ravine she went where a spring was silently flowing through a hollow log. Old Phoenix bent and drank. "Sweet-gum makes the water sweet," she said, and drank more. "Nobody know who made this well, for it was here when I was born."

The track crossed a swampy part where the moss hung as white as lace from every limb. "Sleep on, alligators, and blow your bubbles." Then the track went into the road.

Deep, deep the road went down between the high green-colored banks. Overhead the live-oaks met, and it was as dark as a cave.

35   A black dog with a lolling tongue came up out of the weeds by the ditch. She was meditating, and not ready, and when he came at her she only hit him a little with her cane. Over she went in the ditch, like a little puff of milk-weed.

Down there, her senses drifted away. A dream visited her, and she reached her hand up, but nothing reached down and gave her a pull. So she lay there and presently went to talking. "Old woman," she said to herself, "that black dog come up out of the weeds to stall you off, and now there he sitting on his fine tail, smiling at you."

A white man finally came along and found her—a hunter, a young man, with his dog on a chain.

"Well, Granny!" he laughed. "what are you doing there?"

"Lying on my back like a June-bug waiting to be turned over, mister," she said, reaching up her hand.

40   He lifted her up, gave her a swing in the air, and set her down. "Anything broken, Granny?"

"No sir, them old dead weeds is springy enough," said Phoenix, when she had got her breath. "I thank you for your trouble."

"Where do you live, Granny?" he asked, while the two dogs were growling at each other.

"Away back yonder, sir, behind the ridge. You can't even see it from here."

"On your way home?"

45   "No, sir, I going to town."

"Why, that's too far! That's as far as I walk when I come out myself, and I get something for my trouble." He patted the stuffed bag he carried, and there hung down a little closed claw. It was one of the bob-whites, with its beak hooked bitterly to show it was dead. "Now you go on home, Granny!"

"I bound to go to town, mister," said Phoenix. "The time come around."

He gave another laugh, filling the whole landscape. "I know you old colored people! Wouldn't miss going to town to see Santa Claus!"

But something held Old Phoenix very still. The deep lines in her face went into a fierce and different radiation. Without warning, she had seen with her own eyes a flashing nickel fall out of the man's pocket onto the ground.

50   "How old are you, Granny?" he was saying.

"There is no telling, mister," she said, "no telling."

Then she gave a little cry and clapped her hands and said, "Git on away from here, dog! Look! Look at that dog!" She laughed as if in admiration. "He ain't scared of nobody. He a big black dog." She whispered, "Sic him!"

"Watch me get rid of that cur," said the man. "Sic him, Pete! Sic him!"

Phoenix heard the dogs fighting, and heard the man running and throwing sticks. She even heard a gunshot. But she was slowly bending forward by that time, further and further forward, the lids stretched down over her eyes, as if she were doing this in her sleep. Her chin was lowered almost to her knees. The yellow palm of her hand came out from the fold of her apron. Her fingers slid down and along the ground under the piece of money with the grace and care they would have in lifting an egg from under a sitting hen. Then she slowly straightened up, she stood erect, and the nickel was in her apron pocket. A bird flew by. Her lips moved. "God watching me the whole time. I come to stealing."

55   The man came back, and his own dog panted about them. "Well, I scared him off that time," he said, and then he laughed and lifted his gun and pointed it at Phoenix.

She stood straight and faced him.

"Doesn't the gun scare you?" he said, still pointing it.

"No, sir, I seen plenty go off closer by, in my day, and for less than what I done," she said, holding utterly still.

He smiled, and shouldered the gun. "Well, Granny," he said, "you must be a hundred years old, and scared of nothing. I'd give you a dime if I had any money with me. But you take my advice and stay home, and nothing will happen to you."

60   "I bound to go on my way, mister," said Phoenix. She inclined her head in the red rag. Then they went in different directions, but she could hear the gun shooting again and again over the hill.

     She walked on. The shadows hung from the oak trees to the road like curtains. Then she smelled wood-smoke, and smelled the river, and she saw a steeple and the cabins on their steep steps. Dozens of little black children whirled around her. There ahead was Natchez shining. Bells were ringing. She walked on.

     In the paved city it was Christmas time. There were red and green electric lights strung and crisscrossed everywhere, and all turned on in the daytime. Old Phoenix would have been lost if she had not distrusted her eyesight and depended on her feet to know where to take her.

     She paused quietly on the sidewalk where people were passing by. A lady came along in the crowd, carrying an armful of red-, green-, and silver-wrapped presents; she gave off perfume like the red roses in hot summer, and Phoenix stopped her.

     "Please, missy, will you lace up my shoe?" She held up her foot.

65   "What do you want, Grandma?"

     "See my shoe," said Phoenix. "Do all right for out in the country, but wouldn't look right to go in a big building."

     "Stand still then, Grandma," said the lady. She put her packages down on the sidewalk beside her and laced and tied both shoes tightly.

     "Can't lace 'em with a cane," said Phoenix. "Thank you, missy. I doesn't mind asking a nice lady to tie up my shoe, when I gets out on the street."

     Moving slowly and from side to side, she went into the big building and into a tower of steps, where she walked up and around and around until her feet knew to stop.

70   She entered a door, and there she saw nailed up on the wall the document that had been stamped with the gold seal and framed in the gold frame, which matched the dream that was hung up in her head.

     "Here I be," she said. There was a fixed and ceremonial stiffness over her body.

     "A charity case, I suppose," said an attendant who sat at the desk before her.

     But Phoenix only looked above her head. There was sweat on her face, the wrinkles in her skin shone like a bright net.

     "Speak up, Grandma," the woman said. "What's your name? We must have your history, you know. Have you been here before? What seems to be the trouble with you?"

75   Old Phoenix only gave a twitch to her face as if a fly were bothering her.

     "Are you deaf?" cried the attendant.

     But then the nurse came in.

     "Oh, that's just old Aunt Phoenix," she said. "She doesn't come for herself—she has a little grandson. She makes these trips just as regular as clockwork. She lives away back off the old Natchez Trace." She bent down. "Well, Aunt Phoenix, why don't you just take a seat? We won't keep you standing after your long trip." She pointed.

     The old woman sat down, bolt upright in the chair.

80   "Now, how is the boy?" asked the nurse.

     Old Phoenix did not speak.

     "I said, how is the boy?"

But Phoenix only waited and stared straight ahead, her face very solemn and withdrawn into rigidity.

"Is his throat any better?" asked the nurse. "Aunt Phoenix, don't you hear me? Is your grandson's throat any better since the last time you came for the medicine?"

85   With her hands on her knees, the old woman waited, silent, erect and motionless, just as if she were in armor.

"You mustn't take up our time this way, Aunt Phoenix," the nurse said. "Tell us quickly about your grandson, and get it over. He isn't dead, is he?"

At last there came a flicker and then a flame of comprehension across her face, and she spoke.

"My grandson. It was my memory had left me. There I sat and forgot why I made my long trip."

"Forgot?" The nurse frowned. "After you came so far?"

90   Then Phoenix was like an old woman begging a dignified forgiveness for waking up frightened in the night. "I never did go to school, I was too old at the Surrender," she said in a soft voice. "I'm an old woman without an education. It was my memory fail me. My little grandson, he is just the same, and I forgot it in the coming."

"Throat never heals, does it?" said the nurse, speaking in a loud, sure voice to Old Phoenix. By now she had a card with something written on it, a little list. "Yes. Swallowed lye. When was it—January—two-three years ago—"

Phoenix spoke unasked now. "No, missy, he not dead, he just the same. Every little while his throat begin to close up again, and he not able to swallow. He not get his breath. He not able to help himself. So the time come around, and I go on another trip for the soothing medicine."

"All right. The doctor said as long as you came to get it, you could have it," said the nurse. "But it's an obstinate case."

"My little grandson, he sit up there in the house all wrapped up, waiting by himself," Phoenix went on. "We is the only two left in the world. He suffer and it don't seem to put him back at all. He got a sweet look. He going to last. He wear a little patch quilt and peep out holding his mouth open like a little bird. I remembers so plain now. I not going to forget him again, no, the whole enduring time. I could tell him from all the others in creation."

95   "All right." The nurse was trying to hush her now. She brought her a bottle of medicine. "Charity," she said, making a check mark in a book.

Old Phoenix held the bottle close to her eyes and then carefully put it into her pocket.

"I thank you," she said.

"It's Christmas time, Grandma," said the attendant. "Could I give you a few pennies out of my purse?"

"Five pennies is a nickel," said Phoenix stiffly.

100   "Here's a nickel," said the attendant.

Phoenix rose carefully and held out her hand. She received the nickel and then fished the other nickel out of her pocket and laid it beside the new one. She stared at her palm closely, with her head on one side.

Then she gave a tap with her cane on the floor.

"This is what come to me to do," she said. "I going to the store and buy my child a little windmill they sells, made out of paper. He going to find it hard to believe there such a thing in the world. I'll march myself back where he waiting, holding it straight up in his hand."

She lifted her free hand, gave a little nod, turned round, and walked out of the doctor's office. Then her slow step began on the stairs, going down.

▦ TOPICS FOR CRITICAL THINKING AND WRITING

1. If you do not know the legend of the Phoenix, look it up in a dictionary or, even better, in an encyclopedia. Then carefully reread *A Worn Path*, to learn whether the story in any way connects with the legend.
2. What do you think of the hunter?
3. What would be lost if the episode (with all of its dialogue) of Phoenix falling into the ditch and being helped out of it by the hunter were omitted?
4. Is Christmas a particularly appropriate time in which to set the story? Why or why not?
5. What do you make of the title?
6. "A Worn Path" treats race relations as one of its themes. Is this theme primary, or would you say instead that it is secondary? How would the story be different in its effect if everything stayed the same except for Phoenix's race?
7. Have you ever made a difficult trip by foot? Was there a point when you were tempted to turn back? What kept you going? Do you think that your experience could be made the basis for a short story? How would you structure such a story—its beginning, middle, and end?

GABRIEL GARCÍA MÁRQUEZ

Gabriel García Márquez (b. 1928) was born in Aracataca, a small village in Colombia. After being educated in Bogota, where he studied journalism and law, he worked as a journalist in Latin America, Europe, and the United States. He began writing fiction when he was in Paris, and at twenty-seven he published his first novel, La hojarasca (Leaf Storm, *1955). During most of the 1960s he lived in Mexico, where he wrote film scripts and the novel that made him famous:* Cien años de soledad *(1967, translated in 1970 as* A Hundred Years of Solitude*). In 1982 Márquez was awarded the Nobel Prize in Literature.*

In addition to writing stories and novels—often set in Macondo, a town modeled on Aracataca—Márquez has written screenplays. A socialist, he now lives in Mexico because his presence is not welcome in Colombia.

A Very Old Man with Enormous Wings   [1968]

A Tale for Children

Translated by Gregory Rabassa

On the third day of rain they had killed so many crabs inside the house that Pelayo had to cross his drenched courtyard and throw them into the sea, because the newborn child had a temperature all night and they thought it was due to the stench. The world had been sad since Tuesday. Sea and sky were a single ash-gray thing and the sands of the beach, which on March nights glimmered like powdered light, had become a stew of mud and rotten shellfish. The light was so weak at noon that when Pelayo was coming back to the house after throwing away the crabs, it was hard for him to see what it was that was moving and groaning in the rear of the courtyard. He had to go very close to see that it was an old man, a very old man, lying face down in the mud, who, in spite of his tremendous efforts, couldn't get up, impeded by his enormous wings.

Frightened by that nightmare, Pelayo ran to get Elisenda, his wife, who was putting compresses on the sick child, and he took her to the rear of the courtyard. They both looked at the fallen body with mute stupor. He was dressed like a rag-picker. There were only a few faded hairs left on his bald skull and very few teeth in his mouth, and his pitiful condition of a drenched great-grandfather had taken away any sense of grandeur he might have had. His huge buzzard wings, dirty and half-plucked, were forever entangled in the mud. They looked at him so long and so closely that Pelayo and Elisenda very soon overcame their surprise and in the end found him familiar. Then they dared speak to him, and he answered in an incomprehensible dialect with a strong sailor's voice. That was how they skipped over the inconvenience of the wings and quite intelligently concluded that he was a lonely castaway from some foreign ship wrecked by the storm. And yet, they called in a neighbor woman who knew everything about life and death to see him, and all she needed was one look to show them their mistake.

"He's an angel," she told them. "He must have been coming for the child, but the poor fellow is so old that the rain knocked him down."

On the following day everyone knew that a flesh-and-blood angel was held captive in Pelayo's house. Against the judgment of the wise neighbor woman, for whom angels in those times were the fugitive survivors of a celestial conspiracy, they did not have the heart to club him to death. Pelayo watched over him all afternoon from the kitchen, armed with his bailiff's club, and before going to bed he dragged him out of the mud and locked him up with the hens in the wire chicken coop. In the middle of the night, when the rain stopped, Pelayo and Elisenda were still killing crabs. A short time afterward the child woke up without a fever and with a desire to eat. Then they felt magnanimous and decided to put the angel on a raft with fresh water and provisions for three days and leave him to his fate on the high seas. But when they went out into the courtyard with the first light of dawn, they found the whole neighborhood in front of the chicken coop having fun with the angel, without the slightest reverence, tossing him things to eat through the openings in the wire as if he weren't a supernatural creature but a circus animal.

5   Father Gonzaga arrived before seven o'clock, alarmed at the strange news. By that time onlookers less frivolous than those at dawn had already arrived and they were making all kinds of conjectures concerning the captive's future. The simplest among them thought that he should be named mayor of the world. Others of sterner mind felt that he should be promoted to the rank of five-star general in order to win all wars. Some visionaries hoped that he could be put to stud in order to implant on earth a race of winged wise men who could take charge of the universe. But Father Gon-

zaga, before becoming a priest, had been a robust woodcutter. Standing by the wire, he reviewed his catechism in an instant and asked them to open the door so that he could take a close look at that pitiful man who looked more like a huge decrepit hen among the fascinated chickens. He was lying in a corner drying his open wings in the sunlight among the fruit peels and breakfast leftovers that the early risers had thrown him. Alien to the impertinences of the world, he only lifted his antiquarian eyes and murmured something in his dialect when Father Gonzaga went into the chicken coop and said good morning to him in Latin. The parish priest had his first suspicion of an impostor when he saw that he did not understand the language of God or know how to greet His ministers. Then he noticed that seen close up he was much too human: he had an unbearable smell of the outdoors, the back side of his wings were strewn with parasites and his main feathers had been mistreated by terrestrial winds, and nothing about him measured up to the proud dignity of angels. Then he came out of the chicken coop and in a brief sermon warned the curious against the risks of being ingenuous. He reminded them that the devil had the bad habit of making use of carnival tricks in order to confuse the unwary. He argued that if wings were not the essential element in determining the difference between a hawk and an airplane, they were even less so in the recognition of angels. Nevertheless, he promised to write a letter to his bishop so that the latter would write to his primate so that the latter would write to the Supreme Pontiff in order to get the final verdict from the highest courts.

His prudence fell on sterile hearts. The news of the captive angel spread with such rapidity that after a few hours the courtyard had the bustle of a marketplace and they had to call in troops with fixed bayonets to disperse the mob that was about to knock the house down. Elisenda, her spine all twisted from sweeping up so much marketplace trash, then got the idea of fencing in the yard and charging five cents admission to see the angel.

The curious came from far away. A traveling carnival arrived with a flying acrobat who buzzed over the crowd several times, but no one paid any attention to him because his wings were not those of an angel but, rather, those of a sidereal bat. The most unfortunate invalids on earth came in search of health: a poor woman who since childhood had been counting her heartbeats and had run out of numbers; a Portuguese man who couldn't sleep because the noise of the stars disturbed him: a sleepwalker who got up at night to undo the things he had done while awake; and many others with less serious ailments. In the midst of that shipwreck disorder that made the earth tremble, Pelayo and Elisenda were happy with fatigue, for in less than a week they had crammed their rooms with money and the line of pilgrims waiting their turn to enter still reached beyond the horizon.

The angel was the only one who took no part in his own act. He spent his time trying to get comfortable in his borrowed nest, befuddled by the hellish heat of the oil lamps and sacramental candles that had been placed along the wire. At first they tried to make him eat some mothballs, which, according to the wisdom of the wise neighbor woman, were the food prescribed for angels. But he turned them down, just as he turned down the papal lunches that the penitents brought him, and they never found out whether it was because he was an angel or because he was an old man that in the end ate nothing but eggplant mush. His only supernatural virtue seemed to be patience. Especially during the first days, when the hens pecked at him, searching for the stellar parasites that proliferated in his wings, and the cripples pulled out feathers to touch their defective parts with, and even the most merciful threw stones at him, trying to get him to rise so they could see him standing. The only time they succeeded in arousing him was when they burned his side with an iron for branding steers, for he had been motionless for so many hours that they thought he was dead. He awoke with a start, ranting in his hermetic language and with tears in his eyes, and he flapped his wings a couple of times, which brought on a whirlwind of chicken dung and lunar dust and a gale of panic that did not seem to be of this world. Although many thought that his reaction had been one not of rage but of pain, from then on they were careful not to annoy him, because the majority understood that his passivity was not that of a hero taking his ease but that of a cataclysm in repose.

Father Gonzaga held back the crowd's frivolity with formulas of maidservant inspiration while awaiting the arrival of a final judgment on the nature of the captive. But the mail from Rome showed no sense of urgency. They spent their time finding out if the prisoner had a navel, if his dialect had any connection with Aramaic, how many times he could fit on the head of a pin, or whether he wasn't just a Norwegian with wings. Those meager letters might have come and gone until the end of time if a providential event had not put an end to the priest's tribulations.

10   It so happened that during those days, among so many other carnival attractions, there arrived in town the traveling show of the woman who had been changed into a spider for having disobeyed her parents. The admission to see her was not only less than the admission to see the angel, but people were permitted to ask her all manner of questions about her absurd state and to examine her up and down so that no one would ever doubt the truth of her horror. She was a frightful tarantula the size of a ram and with the head of a sad maiden. What was most heart-rending, however, was not her outlandish shape but the sincere affliction with which she recounted the details of her misfortune. While still practically a child she had sneaked out of her parents' house to go to a dance, and while she was coming back through the woods after having danced all night without permission, a fearful thunderclap rent the sky in two and through the crack came the lightning bolt of brimstone that changed her into a spider. Her only nourishment came from the meatballs that charitable souls chose to toss into her mouth. A spectacle like that, full of so much human truth and with such a fearful lesson, was bound to defeat without even trying that of a haughty angel who scarcely deigned to look at mortals. Besides, the few miracles attributed to the angel showed a certain mental disorder, like the blind man who didn't recover his sight but grew three new teeth, or the paralytic who didn't get to walk but almost won the lottery, and the leper whose sores sprouted sunflowers. Those consolation miracles, which were more like mocking fun, had already ruined the angel's reputation when the woman who had been changed into a spider finally crushed him completely. That was how Father Gonzaga was cured forever of his insomnia and Pelayo's courtyard went back to being as empty as during the time it had rained for three days and crabs walked through the bedrooms.

The owners of the house had no reason to lament. With the money they saved they built a two-story mansion with balconies and gardens and high netting so that crabs wouldn't get in during the winter, and with iron bars on the windows so that angels couldn't get in. Pelayo also set up a rabbit warren close to town and gave up his job as bailiff for good, and Elisenda bought some satin pumps with high heels and many dresses of iridescent silk, the kind worn on Sunday by the most desirable women in those times. The chicken coop was the only thing that didn't receive any attention. If they washed it down with creolin and burned tears of myrrh inside it every so often, it was not in homage to the angel but to drive away the dungheap stench that still hung everywhere like a ghost and was turning the new house into an old one. At first, when the child learned to walk, they were careful that he not get too close to the chicken coop. But then they began to lose their fears and got used to the smell, and before the child got his second teeth he'd gone inside the chicken coop to play, where the wires were falling apart. The angel was no less stand-offish with him than with other mortals, but he tolerated the most ingenious infamies with the patience of a dog who had no illusions. They both came down with chicken pox at the same time. The doctor who took care of the child couldn't resist the temptation to listen to the angel's heart, and he found so much whistling in the heart and so many sounds in his kidneys that it seemed impossible for him to be alive. What surprised him most, however, was the logic of his wings. They seemed so natural on that completely human organism that he couldn't understand why other men didn't have them too.

When the child began school it had been some time since the sun and rain had caused the collapse of the chicken coop. The angel went dragging himself about here and there like a stray dying man. They would drive him out of the bedroom with a broom and a moment later find him in the kitchen. He seemed to be in so many places at the same time that they grew to think that he'd been duplicated, that he was reproducing himself all through the house, and the exasperated and unhinged Elisenda shouted that it was awful living in that hell full of angels. He could scarcely eat and his antiquarian eyes had also become so foggy that he went about bumping into posts. All he had left were the bare cannulae of his last feathers. Pelayo threw a blanket over him and extended him the charity of letting him sleep in the shed, and only then did they notice that he had a temperature at night, and was delirious with the tongue twisters of an old Norwegian. That was one of the few times they became alarmed, for they thought he was going to die and not even the wise neighbor woman had been able to tell them what to do with dead angels.

And yet he not only survived his worst winter, but seemed improved with the first sunny days. He remained motionless for several days in the farthest corner of the courtyard, where no one would see him, and at the beginning of December some large, stiff feathers began to grow on his wings, the feathers of a scarecrow, which looked more like another misfortune of decrepitude. But he must have known the reason for those changes, for he was quite careful that no one should notice them, that no one should hear the sea chanteys that he sometimes sang under the stars. One morning Elisenda was cutting some bunches of onions for lunch when a wind that seemed to come from the high seas blew into the kitchen. Then she went to the window and caught the angel in his first attempts at flight. They were so clumsy that his fingernails opened a furrow in the vegetable patch and he was on the point of knocking the shed down with the ungainly flapping that slipped on the light and couldn't get a grip on the air.

But he did manage to gain altitude. Elisenda let out a sigh of relief, for herself and for him, when she saw him pass over the last houses, holding himself up in some way with the risky flapping of a senile vulture. She kept watching him even when she was through cutting the onions and she kept on watching until it was no longer possible for her to see him, because then he was no longer an annoyance in her life but an imaginary dot on the horizon of the sea.

▓ ❀ TOPICS FOR CRITICAL THINKING AND WRITING

1. The subtitle is "A Tale for Children." Do you think that the story is more suited to children than to adults? What in the story do you think children would especially like, or dislike?
2. Is the story chiefly about the inability of adults to perceive and respect the miraculous world?
3. Characterize the narrator of the story.
4. Characterize Pelayo, Elisenda, their son, and the man with wings.
5. What does it mean to say that a story is "realistic"? Could a story deal with magical events and supernatural experiences and still, somehow, be realistic? Please explain.
6. Do you enjoy stories that include elements of fantasy and magic? Are there examples that come to mind? Or do you prefer stories that are based only on the possible? Again, please give examples and reasons.

7

In Brief: Writing Arguments About Fiction

The following questions will help to stimulate ideas about stories. Not every question is, of course, relevant to every story, but if after reading a story and thinking about it, you then run your eye over these pages, you will find some questions that will help you to think further about the story—in short, that will help you to get ideas, to develop a thesis that can effectively be supported with evidence.

It's best to do your thinking with a pen or pencil in hand. If some of the following questions seem to you to be especially relevant to the story you will be writing about, jot down—freely, without worrying about spelling—your initial responses, interrupting your writing only to glance again at the story when you feel the need to check the evidence you are offering in support of your thesis.

PLOT

1. Does the plot grow out of the characters, or does it depend on chance or coincidence? Did something at first strike you as irrelevant that later you perceived as relevant? Do some parts continue to strike you as irrelevant?
2. Does surprise play an important role, or does foreshadowing? If surprise is very important, can the story be read a second time with any interest? If so, what gives it this further interest?
3. What conflicts does the story include? Conflicts of one character against another? Of one character against the setting, or against society? Conflicts within a single character?
4. Are certain episodes narrated out of chronological order? If so, were you puzzled? Annoyed? On reflection, does the arrangement of episodes seem effective? Why or why not? Are certain situations repeated? If so, what do you make out of the repetitions?

CHARACTER

1. Which character chiefly engages your interest? Why?
2. What purposes do minor characters serve? Do you find some who by their similarities and differences help to define each other or help to define the

major character? How else is a particular character defined—by his or her words, actions (including thoughts and emotions), dress, setting, narrative point of view? Do certain characters act differently in the same, or in a similar, situation?

3. How does the author reveal character? By explicit authorial (editorial) comment, for instance, or, on the other hand, by revelation through dialogue? Through depicted action? Through the actions of other characters? How are the author's methods especially suited to the whole of the story?

4. Is the behavior plausible—that is, are the characters well motivated?

5. If a character changes, why and how does he or she change? (You may want to jot down each event that influences a change.) Or did you change your attitude toward a character not because the character changes but because you came to know the character better?

6. Are the characters round or flat? Are they complex, or, on the other hand, highly typical (for instance, one-dimensional representatives of a social class or age)? Are you chiefly interested in a character's psychology, or does the character strike you as standing for something, such as honesty or the arrogance of power?

7. How has the author caused you to sympathize with certain characters? How does your response—your sympathy or lack of sympathy—contribute to your judgment of the conflict?

POINT OF VIEW

1. Who tells the story? How much does the narrator know? Does the narrator strike you as reliable? What effect is gained by using this narrator?

2. How does the point of view help shape the theme? After all, the basic story of "Little Red Riding Hood"—what happens—remains unchanged whether told from the wolf's point of view or the girl's, but if we hear the story from the wolf's point of view we may feel that the story is about terrifying yet pathetic compulsive behavior; if from the girl's point of view, about terrified innocence and male violence.

3. Does the narrator's language help you to construct a picture of the narrator's character, class, attitude, strengths, and limitations? (Jot down some evidence, such as colloquial or—on the other hand—formal expressions, ironic comments, figures of speech.) How far can you trust the narrator? Why?

SETTING

1. Do you have a strong sense of the time and place? Is the story very much about, say, New England Puritanism, or race relations in the South in the late nineteenth century, or midwestern urban versus small-town life? If time and place are important, how and at what points in the story has the author conveyed this sense? If you do not strongly feel the setting, do you think the author should have made it more evident?

2. What is the relation of the setting to the plot and the characters? (For instance, do houses or rooms or their furnishings say something about their

casks and puncheons intermingling, into the inmost recesses of the catacombs. I paused again, and this time I made bold to seize Fortunato by an
arm above the elbow.

"The nitre!" I said; "see, it increases. It hangs like moss upon the vaults.
We are below the river's bed. The drops of moisture trickle among the
bones. Come, we will go back ere it is too late. Your cough—"

"It is nothing," he said; "let us go on. But first, another draught of the
Medoc."

I broke and reached him a flagon of De Grâve. He emptied it at a
breath. His eyes flashed with a fierce light. He laughed and threw the bottle
upwards with a gesticulation I did not understand.

55   I looked at him in surprise. He repeated the movement—a grotesque
one.

"You do not comprehend?" he said.

"Not I," I replied.

"Then you are not of the brotherhood."

"How?"

60   "You are not of the masons."

"Yes, yes," I said, "yes, yes."

"You? Impossible! A mason?"

"A mason," I replied.

"A sign," he said.

65   "It is this," I answered, producing a trowel from beneath the folds of
my *roquelaure*.

"You jest," he exclaimed, recoiling a few paces. "But let us proceed to
the Amontillado."

"Be it so," I said, replacing the tool beneath the cloak, and again offering him my arm. He leaned upon it heavily. We continued our route in
search of the Amontillado. We passed through a range of low arches, descended, passed on, and descending again, arrived at a deep crypt, in which
the foulness of the air caused our flambeaux rather to glow than flame.

At the most remote end of the crypt there appeared another less spacious. Its walls had been lined with human remains piled to the vault overhead, in the fashion of the great catacombs of Paris. Three sides of this interior crypt were still ornamented in this manner. From the fourth the bones
had been thrown down, and lay promiscuously upon the earth, forming at
one point a mound of some size. Within the wall thus exposed by the displacing of the bones, we perceived a still interior recess, in depth about
four feet, in width three, in height six or seven. It seemed to have been constructed for no especial use within itself, but formed merely the interval between two of the colossal supports of the roof of the catacombs, and was
backed by one of their circumscribing walls of solid granite.

It was in vain that Fortunato, uplifting his dull torch, endeavored to pry
into the depths of the recess. Its termination the feeble light did not enable
us to see.

70   "Proceed," I said; "herein is the Amontillado. As for Luchesi—"

"He is an ignoramus," interrupted my friend, as he stepped unsteadily
forward, while I followed immediately at his heels. In an instant he had
reached the extremity of the niche, and finding his progress arrested by the
rock, stood stupidly bewildered. A moment more and I had fettered him to
the granite. In its surface were two iron staples, distant from each other

about two feet, horizontally. From one of these depended a short chain, from the other a padlock. Throwing the links about his waist, it was but the work of a few seconds to secure it. He was too much astounded to resist. Withdrawing the key I stepped back from the recess.

"Pass your hand," I said, "over the wall; you cannot help feeling the nitre. Indeed it is *very* damp. Once more let me *implore* you to return. No? Then I must positively leave you. But I must first render you all the little attentions in my power."

"The Amontillado!" ejaculated my friend, not yet recovered from his astonishment.

"True," I replied; "the Amontillado."

75   As I said these words I busied myself among the pile of bones of which I have before spoken. Throwing them aside, I soon uncovered a quantity of building-stone and mortar. With these materials and with the aid of my trowel, I began vigorously to wall up the entrance of the niche.

I had scarcely laid the first tier of masonry when I discovered that the intoxication of Fortunato had in a great measure worn off. The earliest indication I had of this was a low moaning cry from the depth of the recess. It was *not* the cry of a drunken man. There was then a long and obstinate silence. I laid the second tier, and the third, and the fourth; and then I heard the furious vibrations of the chain. The noise lasted for several minutes, during which, that I might hearken to it with the more satisfaction, I ceased my labors and sat down upon the bones. When at last the clanking subsided, I resumed the trowel, and finished without interruption the fifth, the sixth, and the seventh tier. The wall was now nearly upon a level with my breast. I again paused, and holding the flambeaux over the masonwork, threw a few feeble rays upon the figure within.

A succession of loud and shrill screams, bursting suddenly from the throat of the chained form, seemed to thrust me violently back. For a brief moment I hesitated—I trembled. Unsheathing my rapier, I began to grope with it about the recess; but the thought of an instant reassured me. I placed my hand upon the solid fabric of the catacombs, and felt satisfied. I reapproached the wall. I replied to the yells of him who clamored. I re-echoed—I aided—I surpassed them in volume and in strength. I did this, and the clamorer grew still.

It was now midnight, and my task was drawing to a close. I had completed the eighth, the ninth, and the tenth tier. I had finished a portion of the last and the eleventh; there remained but a single stone to be fitted and plastered in. I struggled with its weight; I placed it partially in its destined position. But now there came from out the niche a low laugh that erected the hairs upon my head. It was succeeded by a sad voice, which I had difficulty in recognizing as that of the noble Fortunato. The voice said—

"Ha! ha! ha!—he! he! he!—a very good joke indeed—an excellent jest. We will have many a rich laugh about it at the palazzo—he! he! he!—over our wine—he! he! he!"

80   "The Amontillado!" I said.

"He! he! he!—he! he! he!—yes, the Amontillado. But is it not getting late? Will not they be awaiting us at the palazzo, the Lady Fortunato and the rest? Let us be gone."

"Yes," I said, "let us be gone."

"For the love of God, Montresor!"

"Yes," I said, "for the love of God!"

85   But to these words I hearkened in vain for a reply. I grew impatient. I called aloud:

"Fortunato!"

No answer. I called again;

"Fortunato!"

No answer still. I thrust a torch through the remaining aperture and let it fall within. There came forth in return only a jingling of the bells. My heart grew sick—on account of the dampness of the catacombs. I hastened to make an end of my labor. I forced the last stone into its position; I plastered it up. Against the new masonry I reerected the old rampart of bones. For the half of a century no mortal has disturbed them. *In pace requiescat!*[4]

---

[4]*In pace requiescat!* May he rest in peace!

A STUDENT'S WRITTEN RESPONSE TO A STORY

Notes

If your instructor assigns a topic in advance—such as "Irony in 'The Cask of Amontillado'" or "Is Montresor Insane?"—even on your first reading of the story you will be thinking in a specific direction, looking for relevant evidence. But if a topic is not assigned, it will be up to you to find something that you think is worth talking about to your classmates. (All writers must imagine a fairly specific audience, such as the readers of *Ms.,* or the readers of *Playboy*—these audiences are quite different—or the readers of the high school newspaper, or the readers of a highly technical professional journal, and so on. It's a good idea to imagine your classmates as your audience.)

You may want to begin by asking yourself (and responding in your journal) what you like or dislike in the story; or you may want to think about some of the questions mentioned, at the beginning of this chapter, on plot, character, point of view, setting, symbolism, style, and theme. Or you may have annotated some passage that puzzled you, and, on rereading, you may feel that *this* passage is what you want to talk about. In any case, after several readings of the story you will settle not only on a *topic* (for instance, symbolism) but also on a *thesis,* an argument, a point (for instance, the symbolism is for the most part effective but in two places is annoyingly obscure).

It happens that the student whose essay we reprint decided to write about the narrator. The following notes are not her earliest jottings but are the jottings she recorded after she had tentatively chosen her topic.

```
Two characters: narrator (Montresor) and his enemy,
    Fortunato
1st person narrator, so we know Fort. only through
    what M. tells us
```

Fortunato
  has wronged Montresor ("thousand injuries"; but is
    M. telling the truth?)
  drinks a lot ("he had been drinking much")
  vain (Fort. insists he knows much more than
    Luchesi)
  courteous (in the vaults, drinks to M's buried
    relatives)
  foolish (?? hard to be sure about this)
Montresor
  first parag. tells us he seeks vengeance ("I vowed
    revenge") for "the thousand injuries" he suffered
    from Fort. ("I would be avenged")

of high birth
  1) he comes from a family with a motto: <u>Nemo</u> <u>me</u>
    <u>impune</u> <u>lacessit</u> (no one dare attack me with
    impunity)
  2) has coat of arms (human foot crushing serpent
    whose fangs are in heel). But what's the connec-
    tion? Is the idea that he and his noble family
    are like the <u>foot</u> crushing a serpent that has
    bitten them, or on the other hand is the idea
    that he and family are like the <u>serpent</u>--if
    stepped on (attacked, insulted), they will fight
    back? Maybe we are supposed to think that <u>he</u>
    thinks he is like the human foot, but <u>we</u> see
    that he is like the serpent.
highly educated? At least he uses hard words
  ("unredressed," "the thought of his immolation").
  (Check "<u>immolation</u>")   *Dictionary says*
                                              it is a sacrifice,
cunning: knows how to work on Fortunato   *a ritual killing*
  (implies that Luchesi is more highly regarded than F)
rich: lives in a "palazzo," and has servants crazy:
  1) murders for vengeance
  2) enjoys hearing the sound of Fort. shaking chains
    ("that I might hearken to it with the more sat-
    isfaction, I ceased my labors")
  3) when he hears the screams of F., <u>he</u> screams ("I
    surpassed them in volume and in strength")

Can we possibly sympathize with him? Can he possibly be acting fairly? Do we judge him? Do we judge (condemn) ourselves for liking the story? Why do I find the story interesting instead of repulsive? Because (thesis here) his motive is good, he thinks he is upholding family honor (in his eyes the killing is a family duty, a sacrifice; "immolation")

A Sample Response Essay

Here is the final version of the essay that grew out of the notes.

Geraghty 1

Ann Geraghty

Professor Duff

English 102

1 December 2005

Revenge, Noble and Ignoble

Because Poe's "The Cask of Amontillado"[1] is told by a first person narrator, a man named Montresor, we cannot be sure that what the narrator tells us is true. There are some things in the story, however, that we can scarcely believe. For instance, we can accept the fact that there is a character (even though we never see him) named Luchesi, because the narrator mentions him and the other character in the story--Fortunato--also talks about him. But how sure can we be that Fortunato is the sort of man that the narrator says Fortunato is?

[1]Reprinted in Sylvan Barnet et al., eds., _An Introduction to Literature_, 14th ed. (New York: Longman, 2006), 180-185. Page references to the story will be given parenthetically within the body of the essay.

Geraghty 2

In the first paragraph, Montresor says that
Fortunato has done him a "thousand injuries"
(180). He is never specific about these, and
Fortunato never says anything that we can
interpret as evidence that he has injured
Montresor. Further, Fortunato is courteous when
he meets Montresor, which seems to suggest that
he is not aware that he has injured Montresor.
It seems fair to conclude, then, that Fortunato
has not really injured Montresor, and that
Montresor has insanely imagined that Fortunato
has injured him.

What evidence is there that Montresor is
insane? First, we should notice the intensity
with which Montresor speaks, especially in the
first paragraph. He tells us that he "vowed
revenge" (180) and that he "would be avenged"
(180) and that he would "punish with impunity"
(180). He also tells us, all in the first
paragraph, that he himself must not get punished
for his act of vengeance ("A wrong is
unredressed when retribution overtakes its
redresser"), and, second, that "It is equally
unredressed when the avenger fails to make
himself felt as such to him who has done the
wrong." There is a common saying, "Don't get
mad, get even," but Montresor is going way
beyond getting even, and anyway it's not certain
that he was injured in the first place. He _is_
getting "mad," not in the sense of "angry" but
in the sense of "crazy."

If we agree that Montresor is insane, we can
ask ourselves two questions about this story.
First, is "The Cask of Amontillado" just a story
about a mysterious madman, a story that begins
and ends with a madman and does not even try to

explain his madness? Second, why have people
read this story for almost a hundred and fifty
years? If we can answer the first question
negatively, we may be able to answer the second.

I think that Montresor is insane, but his
insanity is understandable, and it is even based
on a concept of honor. He comes from a noble
family, a family with a coat of arms (a foot is
crushing a serpent that is biting the heel) and
a motto (<u>Nemo</u> <u>me</u> <u>impune</u> <u>lacessit</u>, which means
"No one dare attack me with impunity").
Fortunato may not have really injured him, but
for some reason Montresor thinks he has been
injured. As a nobleman who must uphold the honor
of his family, Montresor acts with a degree of
energy that is understandable for someone in
his high position. That is, he must live up
to his coat of arms, which shows a gold foot
(symbolizing a nobleman) crushing a serpent. The
motto in effect means that Montresor <u>must</u> take
vengeance if he is to uphold his family honor.
In fact, the unusual word "immolation" (180)
in the second paragraph tells us a good deal
about Montresor's action. To "immolate" is to
"sacrifice," to perform a ritual killing. Since
Montresor says his vengeance will be the
"immolation" of Fortunato, we can assume that
Montresor thinks that he has a duty, imposed by
his noble family, to kill Fortunato. He sees
himself as a priest performing a solemn
sacrifice.

Interestingly, however, the <u>reader</u> can
interpret the motto in a different way. The
reader may see Montresor as the serpent,
viciously stinging an enemy, and Fortunato
is an almost innocent victim who has somehow

Geraghty 4

accidentally offended (stepped on) Montresor. In reading the story we take pleasure in hearing, and seeing, a passionate nobleman performing what he thinks is a duty imposed on him by his rank. We also take pleasure in judging him accurately, that is, in seeing that his action is not really noble but is serpent-like, or base. We can thus eat our cake and have it too; we see a wicked action, a clever murder (and we enjoy seeing it), and, on the other hand, we can sit back and judge it as wicked (we see Montresor as a serpent) and therefore we can feel that we are highly moral.

TOPICS FOR CRITICAL THINKING AND WRITING

In reading this essay, you may wish to ask yourself the following questions (with an eye toward applying them also to your own writing):

1. Is the title appropriate and at least moderately interesting?
2. Does the essay have a thesis? If so, what is it?
3. Is the thesis (if there is one) adequately supported by evidence?
4. Is the organization satisfactory? Does one paragraph lead easily into the next, and is the argument presented in reasonable sequence?

8

Three Fiction Writers in Depth: Flannery O'Connor, Raymond Carver, and Alice Munro

We read stories by authors we are unfamiliar with, just as we try new foods or play new games or listen to the music of new groups, because we want to extend our experience. But we also sometimes stay with the familiar, for pretty much the same reason, oddly. We want, so to speak, to taste more fully, to experience not something utterly unfamiliar but a variation on a favorite theme. Having read, say, one story by Poe or by Alice Walker, we want to read another, and another, because we like the sort of thing that this author does, and we find that with each succeeding story we get deeper into an interesting mind talking about experiences that interest us.

This chapter includes

1. Two stories by Flannery O'Connor, along with some of her comments on her own work
2. Two stories by Alice Munro, an essay, and an interview
3. Three stories by Raymond Carver, and comments by him

We believe you'll find that each story takes on a richer significance when thought of along with other stories and comments by the same writer.

FLANNERY O'CONNOR: TWO STORIES AND COMMENTS ABOUT WRITING

FLANNERY O'CONNOR

Flannery O'Connor (1925-1964)—her first name was Mary but she did not use it—was born in Savannah, Georgia, but spent most of her life in Milledgeville, Georgia, where her family moved when she was 12. She was educated in parochial schools and at the local college and then went to the School for Writers at the University of Iowa, where she earned an M.F.A. in 1946. For a few months she lived at a writers' colony in Saratoga Springs,

New York, and then for a few weeks she lived in New York City, but most of her life was spent back in Milledgeville, where she tended her peacocks and wrote stories, novels, essays (posthumously published as Mystery and Manners [1970]), and letters (posthumously published under the title The Habit of Being [1979]).

In 1951, when she was 25, Flannery O'Connor discovered that she was a victim of lupus erythematosus, an incurable autoimmune disease that had crippled and then killed her father ten years before. She died at the age of 39. O'Connor faced her illness with stoic courage, Christian fortitude—and tough humor. Here is a glimpse, from one of her letters, of how she dealt with those who pitied her:

An old lady got on the elevator behind me and as soon as I turned around she fixed me with a moist gleaming eye and said in a loud voice, "Bless you, darling!" I felt exactly like The Misfit [in "A Good Man Is Hard to Find"] and I gave her a weakly lethal look, whereupon greatly encouraged she grabbed my arm and whispered (very loud) in my ear, "Remember what they said to John at the gate, darling!" It was not my floor but I got off and I suppose the old lady was astounded at how quick I could get away on crutches. I have a one-legged friend and I asked her what they said to John at the gate. She said she reckoned they said, "The lame shall enter first." This may be because the lame will be able to knock everybody else aside with their crutches.

A devout Catholic, O'Connor forthrightly summarized the relation between her belief and her writing:

I see from the standpoint of Christian orthodoxy. This means that for me the meaning of life is centered in our Redemption by Christ and what I see in the world I see in its relation to that.

A Good Man Is Hard to Find   [1953]

The grandmother didn't want to go to Florida. She wanted to visit some of her connections in east Tennessee and she was seizing every chance to change Bailey's mind. Bailey was the son she lived with, her only boy. He was sitting on the edge of his chair at the table, bent over the orange sports section of the *Journal.* "Now look here, Bailey," she said, "see here, read this," and she stood with one hand on her thin hip and the other rattling the newspaper at his bald head. "Here this fellow that calls himself The Misfit is aloose from the Federal Pen and headed toward Florida and you read here what it says he did to these people. Just you read it. I wouldn't take my children in any direction with a criminal like that aloose in it. I couldn't answer to my conscience if I did."

Bailey didn't look up from his reading so she wheeled around then and faced the children's mother, a young woman in slacks, whose face was as broad and innocent as a cabbage and was tied around with a green headkerchief that had two points on the top like rabbit's ears. She was sitting on the sofa, feeding the baby his apricots out of a jar. "The children have been to Florida before," the old lady said. "You all ought to take them somewhere else for a change so they would see different parts of the world and be broad. They never have been to east Tennessee."

The children's mother didn't seem to hear her, but the eight-year-old boy, John Wesley, a stocky child with glasses, said, "If you don't want to go to Florida, why dontcha stay at home?" He and the little girl, June Star, were reading the funny papers on the floor.

"She wouldn't stay at home to be queen for a day," June Star said without raising her yellow head.

5   "Yes, and what would you do if this fellow, The Misfit, caught you?" the grandmother said.

"I'd smack his face," John Wesley said.

"She wouldn't stay at home for a million bucks," June Star said. "Afraid she'd miss something. She has to go everywhere we go."

"All right, Miss," the grandmother said. "Just remember that the next time you want me to curl your hair."

June Star said her hair was naturally curly.

10   The next morning the grandmother was the first one in the car, ready to go. She had her big black valise that looked like the head of a hippopotamus in one corner, and underneath it she was hiding a basket with Pitty Sing, the cat, in it. She didn't intend for the cat to be left alone in the house for three days because he would miss her too much and she was afraid he might brush against one of the gas burners and accidentally asphyxiate himself. Her son, Bailey, didn't like to arrive at a motel with a cat.

She sat in the middle of the back seat with John Wesley and June Star on either side of her. Bailey and the children's mother and the baby sat in front and they left Atlanta at eight forty-five with the mileage on the car at 55890. The grandmother wrote this down because she thought it would be interesting to say how many miles they had been when they got back. It took them twenty minutes to reach the outskirts of the city.

The old lady settled herself comfortably, removing her white cotton gloves and putting them up with her purse on the shelf in front of the back window. The children's mother still had on slacks and still had her head tied up in a green kerchief, but the grandmother had on a navy blue straw sailor hat with a bunch of white violets on the brim and a navy blue dress with a small white dot in the print. Her collars and cuffs were white organdy trimmed with lace and at her neckline she had pinned a purple spray of cloth violets containing a sachet. In case of an accident, anyone seeing her dead on the highway would know at once that she was a lady.

She said she thought it was going to be a good day for driving, neither too hot nor too cold, and she cautioned Bailey that the speed limit was fifty-five miles an hour and that the patrolmen hid themselves behind billboards and small clumps of trees and sped out after you before you had a chance to slow down. She pointed out interesting details of the scenery: Stone Mountain; the blue granite that in some places came up to both sides of the highway; the brilliant red clay banks slightly streaked with purple; and the various crops that made rows of green lace-work on the ground. The trees were full of silver-white sunlight and the meanest of them sparkled. The children were reading comic magazines and their mother had gone back to sleep.

2

the grandmother

~~Of course she~~ was the first one ready to load up the next morning at six
o'clock. She had Baby Brother's bucking bronco ~~that~~ and ~~harrxaxixa~~ what she
called her "~~xileo~~" and Pitty Sing, the cat, ~~in there~~ packed in the car before
Boatwrite had a chance to ~~gxtxanythingxzxsaxixy~~ *get the* ~~come out of the door with the~~
rest of the luggage.out of the hall. They got off at seven-thirty, Boatwrite
and ~~Emby~~ the children's mother in the front and Granny, John Wesley, Baby Brother,
Little Sister Mary Ann, Pitty Sing, and the bucking bronco in the back.

"Why the hell did you bring that goddam rocking horse?" Boatwrite asked
because as soon as ~~the car began to move,~~ *they were out of the city + on the smooth highway* Baby Brother began to squall to get
on the bucking bronco. "He can't get on that thing in this car and that's final,"
his father who was a stern man said.

"Can we open the lunch now?" Little Sister ~~Maryxxxx~~ asked. "It'll shut
Baby Brother up. Mamma, can we open up the lunch?"

"No," their grandmother said. *It's only eight-thirty*

Their mother was ~~xxxxx~~ reading.SCREEN MOTHERS AND THEIR CHILDREN. "Yeah,
sure," she said.without looking up. She was all dressed up today. She had on
a purple silk dress and a hat and ~~xixxxxxxxx~~ a choker of pink beads and a new
pocket book, *her red* and high heel pumps.

"Let's go through Georgia quick so we won't have to look at it much," John
Wesley said. "~~I seen enough of it myxxx~~"

"You should see Tennessee," his grandmother said. "Now there is a *beautiful* state."

"Like hell," John Wesley said. "That's just a hillbilly dumping ground."

"Ha," *now* his mother said, and nudged Boatwrite. "Didjer hear that?" *She was* *from Arkansas.*
They ate their lunch and got along fine ~~after that~~ for a while until Pitty
Sing who had been asleep jumped into the front of the car and caused Boatwrite
to swerve to the right into a ditch. Pitty Sing was a large grey-striped cat
with a yellow hind leg and a ~~x~~ *big* ~~soe~~ soiled white face. Granny thought that she
was the only person in the world that he really loved but he had never ~~really~~ *the truth was*
looked ~~axxfaxzapxaxzkaxzfxxx~~ *up* ~~up~~ farther *up* than her middle and he didn't even
like other cats. He jumped snarling into the front seat and Boatwrite's shoulders

Manuscript page from Flannery O'Connor's "A Good Man Is Hard to Find."

"Let's go through Georgia fast so we won't have to look at it much,"
John Wesley said.

15   "If I were a little boy," said the grandmother, "I wouldn't talk about my
native state that way. Tennessee has the mountains and Georgia has the hills."

"Tennessee is just a hillbilly dumping ground," John Wesley said, "and
Georgia is a lousy state too."

"You said it," June Star said.

"In my time," said the grandmother, folding her thin veined fingers,
"children were more respectful of their native states and their parents and
everything else. People did right then. Oh look at the cute little pick-
aninny!" she said and pointed to a Negro child standing in the door of a

shack. "Wouldn't that make a picture, now?" she asked and they all turned and looked at the little Negro out of the back window. He waved.

"He didn't have any britches on," June Star said.

20   "He probably didn't have any," the grandmother explained. "Little niggers in the country don't have things like we do. If I could paint, I'd paint that picture," she said.

The children exchanged comic books.

The grandmother offered to hold the baby and the children's mother passed him over the front seat to her. She set him on her knee and bounced him and told him about the things they were passing. She rolled her eyes and screwed up her mouth and stuck her leathery thin face into his smooth bland one. Occasionally he gave her a faraway smile. They passed a large cotton field with five or six graves fenced in the middle of it, like a small island. "Look at the graveyard!" the grandmother said, pointing it out. "That was the old family burying ground. That belonged to the plantation."

"Where's the plantation?" John Wesley asked.

"Gone With the Wind," said the grandmother. "Ha. Ha."

25   When the children finished all the comic books they had brought, they opened the lunch and ate it. The grandmother ate a peanut butter sandwich and an olive and would not let the children throw the box and the paper napkins out the window. When there was nothing else to do they played a game by choosing a cloud and making the other two guess what shape it suggested. John Wesley took one the shape of a cow and June Star guessed a cow and John Wesley said, no, an automobile, and June Star said he didn't play fair, and they began to slap each other over the grandmother.

The grandmother said she would tell them a story if they would keep quiet. When she told a story, she rolled her eyes and waved her head and was very dramatic. She said once when she was a maiden lady she had been courted by a Mr. Edgar Atkins Teagarden from Jasper, Georgia. She said he was a very good-looking man and a gentleman and that he brought her a watermelon every Saturday afternoon with his initials cut in it, E. A. T. Well, one Saturday, she said, Mr. Teagarden brought the watermelon and there was nobody at home and he left it on the front porch and returned in his buggy to Jasper, but she never got the watermelon, she said, because a nigger boy ate when he saw the initials, E. A. T.! This story tickled John Wesley's funny bone and he giggled and giggled but June Star didn't think it was any good. She said she wouldn't marry a man that just brought her a watermelon on Saturday. The grandmother said she would have done well to marry Mr. Teagarden because he was a gentleman and had bought Coca-Cola stock when it first came out and that he had died only a few years ago, a very wealthy man.

They stopped at The Tower for barbecued sandwiches. The Tower was a part stucco and part wood filling station and dance hall set in a clearing outside of Timothy. A fat man named Red Sammy Butts ran it and there were signs stuck here and there on the building and for miles up and down the highway saying, TRY RED SAMMY'S FAMOUS BARBECUE. NONE LIKE FAMOUS RED SAMMY'S! RED SAM! THE FAT BOY WITH THE HAPPY LAUGH. A VETERAN! RED SAMMY'S YOUR MAN!

Red Sammy was lying on the bare ground outside The Tower with his head under a truck while a gray monkey about a foot high, chained to a small chinaberry tree, chattered nearby. The monkey sprang back into the tree and got on the highest limb as soon as he saw the children jump out of the car and run toward him.

Inside, The Tower was a long dark room with a counter at one end and tables at the other and dancing space in the middle. They all sat down at a broad table next to the nickelodeon and Red Sam's wife, a tall burnt-brown woman with hair and eyes lighter than her skin, came and took their order. The children's mother put a dime in the machine and played "The Tennessee Waltz," and the grandmother said that tune always made her want to dance. She asked Bailey if he would like to dance but he only glared at her. He didn't have a naturally sunny disposition like she did and trips made him nervous. The grandmother's brown eyes were very bright. She swayed her head from side to side and pretended she was dancing in her chair. June Star said play something she could tap to so the children's mother put in another dime and played a fast number and June Star stepped out onto the dance floor and did her tap routine.

30   "Ain't she cute?" Red Sam's wife said, leaning over the counter. "Would you like to come be my little girl?"

"No, I certainly wouldn't," June Star said. "I wouldn't live in a broken-down place like this for a million bucks!" and she ran back to the table.

"Ain't she cute?" the woman repeated, stretching her mouth politely.

"Aren't you ashamed?" hissed the grandmother.

Red Sam came in and told his wife to quit lounging on the counter and hurry with these people's order. His khaki trousers reached just to his hip bones and his stomach hung over them like a sack of meal swaying under his shirt. He came over and sat down at a table nearby and let out a combination sigh and yodel. "You can't win," he said, "You can't win," and he wiped his sweating red face off with a gray handkerchief. "These days you don't know who to trust," he said. "Ain't that the truth?"

35   "People are certainly not nice like they used to be," said the grandmother.

"Two fellers come in here last week," Red Sammy said, "driving a Chrysler. It was an old beat-up car but it was a good one and these boys looked all right to me. Said they worked at the mill and you know I let them fellers charge the gas they bought? Now why did I do that?"

"Because you're a good man!" the grandmother said at once.

"Yes'm, I suppose so," Red Sam said as if he were struck with this answer.

His wife brought the orders, carrying the five plates all at once without a tray, two in each hand and one balanced on her arm. "It isn't a soul in this green world of God's that you can trust," she said. "And I don't count nobody out of that, not nobody," she repeated, looking at Red Sammy.

40   "Did you read about that criminal, The Misfit, that's escaped?" asked the grandmother.

"I wouldn't be a bit surprised if he didn't attack this place right here," said the woman. "If he hears about it being here, I wouldn't be none surprised to see him. If he hears it's two cent in the cash register, I wouldn't be a tall surprised if he . . . ."

"That'll do," Red Sam said. "Go bring these people their Co'Colas," and the woman went off to get the rest of the order.

"A good man is hard to find," Red Sammy said. "Everything is getting terrible. I remember the day you could go off and leave your screen door unlatched. Not no more."

He and the grandmother discussed better times. The old lady said that in her opinion Europe was entirely to blame for the way things were now. She said the way Europe acted you would think we were made of money and Red Sam said it was no use talking about it, she was exactly right. The children ran outside into the white sunlight and looked at the monkey in the lacy chinaberry tree. He was busy catching fleas on himself and biting each one carefully between his teeth as if it were a delicacy.

45   They drove off again into the hot afternoon. The grandmother took cat naps and woke up every five minutes with her own snoring. Outside of Toombsboro she woke up and recalled an old plantation that she had visited in this neighborhood once when she was a young lady. She said the house had six white columns across the front and that there was an avenue of oaks leading up to it and two little wooden trellis arbors on either side in front where you sat down with your suitor after a stroll in the garden. She recalled exactly which road to turn off to get to it. She knew that Bailey would not be willing to lose any time looking at an old house, but the more she talked about it, the more she wanted to see it once again and find out if the little twin arbors were still standing. "There was a secret panel in this house," she said craftily, not telling the truth but wishing that she were, "and the story went that all the family silver was hidden in it when Sherman came through but it was never found . . ."

"Hey!" John Wesley said. "Let's go see it! We'll find it! We'll poke all the woodwork and find it! Who lives there? Where do you turn off at? Hey, Pop, can't we turn off there?"

"We never have seen a house with a secret panel!" June Star shrieked. "Let's go to the house with the secret panel! Hey, Pop, can't we go see the house with the secret panel!"

"It's not far from here, I know," the grandmother said. "It wouldn't take over twenty minutes."

Bailey was looking straight ahead. His jaw was as rigid as a horseshoe. "No," he said.

50   The children began to yell and scream that they wanted to see the house with the secret panel. John Wesley kicked the back of the front seat and June Star hung over her mother's shoulder and whined desperately into her ear that they never had any fun even on their vacation, that they could never do what THEY wanted to do. The baby began to scream and John Wesley kicked the back of the seat so hard that his father could feel the blows in his kidney.

"All right!" he shouted and drew the car to a stop at the side of the road. "Will you all shut up? Will you all just shut up for one second? If you don't shut up, we won't go anywhere."

"It would be very educational for them," the grandmother murmured.

"All right," Bailey said, "but get this. This is the only time we're going to stop for anything like this. This is the one and only time."

"The dirt road that you have to turn down is about a mile back," the grandmother directed. "I marked it when we passed."

55   "A dirt road," Bailey groaned.

After they had turned around and were headed toward the dirt road, the grandmother recalled other points about the house, the beautiful glass over the front doorway and the candle lamp in the hall. John Wesley said that the secret panel was probably in the fireplace.

"You can't go inside this house," Bailey said. "You don't know who lives there."

"While you all talk to the people in front, I'll run around behind and get in a window," John Wesley suggested.

"We'll all stay in the car," his mother said.

60   They turned onto the dirt road and the car raced roughly along in a swirl of pink dust. The grandmother recalled the times when there were no paved roads and thirty miles was a day's journey. The dirt road was hilly and there were sudden washes in it and sharp curves on dangerous embankments. All at once they would be on a hill, looking down over the blue tops of trees for miles around, then the next minute, they would be in a red depression with the dust-coated trees looking down on them.

"This place had better turn up in a minute," Bailey said, "or I'm going to turn around."

The road looked as if no one had traveled on it in months.

"It's not much farther," the grandmother said and just as she said it, a horrible thought came to her. The thought was so embarrassing that she turned red in the face and her eyes dilated and her feet jumped up, upsetting her valise in the corner. The instant the valise moved, the newspaper top she had over the basket under it rose with a snarl and Pitty Sing, the cat, sprang onto Bailey's shoulder.

The children were thrown to the floor and their mother, clutching the baby, was thrown out the door onto the ground; the old lady was thrown into the front seat. The car turned over once and landed right side up in a gulch on the side of the road. Bailey remained in the driver's seat with the cat—gray-striped with a broad white face and an orange nose—clinging to his neck like a caterpillar.

65   As soon as the children saw they could move their arms and legs, they scrambled out of the car, shouting, "We've had an ACCIDENT!" The grandmother was curled up under the dashboard, hoping she was injured so that Bailey's wrath would not come down on her all at once. The horrible thought she had had before the accident was that the house she had remembered so vividly was not in Georgia but in Tennessee.

Bailey removed the cat from his neck with both hands and flung it out the window against the side of a pine tree. Then he got out of the car and started looking for the children's mother. She was sitting against the side of the red gutted ditch, holding the screaming baby, but she only had a cut down her face and a broken shoulder. "We've had an ACCIDENT!" the children screamed in a frenzy of delight.

"But nobody's killed," June Star said with disappointment as the grandmother limped out of the car, her hat still pinned to her head but the broken front brim standing up at a jaunty angle and the violet spray hanging off the side. They all sat down in the ditch, except the children, to recover from the shock. They were all shaking.

"Maybe a car will come along," said the children's mother hoarsely.

"I believe I have injured an organ," said the grandmother, pressing her side, but no one answered her. Bailey's teeth were clattering. He had on a yellow sport shirt with bright blue parrots designed in it and his face was as yellow as the shirt. The grandmother decided that she would not mention that the house was in Tennessee.

70   The road was about ten feet above and they could see only the tops of the trees on the other side of it. Behind the ditch they were sitting in there were more woods, tall and dark and deep. In a few minutes they saw a car some distance away on top of a hill, coming slowly as if the occupants were

watching them. The grandmother stood up and waved both arms dramatically to attract their attention. The car continued to come on slowly, disappeared around a bend and appeared again, moving even slower on top of the hill they had gone over. It was a big black battered hearse-like automobile. There were three men in it.

It came to a stop just over them and for some minutes, the driver looked down with a steady expressionless gaze to where they were sitting, and didn't speak. Then he turned his head and muttered something to the other two and they got out. One was a fat boy in black trousers and a red sweat shirt with a silver stallion embossed on the front of it. He moved around on the right side of them and stood staring, his mouth partly open in a kind of loose grin. The other had on khaki pants and a blue striped coat and a gray hat pulled down very low, hiding most of his face. He came around slowly on the left side. Neither spoke.

The driver got out of the car and stood by the side of it, looking down at them. He was an older man than the other two. His hair was just beginning to gray and he wore silver-rimmed spectacles that gave him a scholarly look. He had a long creased face and didn't have on any shirt or undershirt. He had on blue jeans that were too tight for him and was holding a black hat and a gun. The two boys also had guns.

"We've had an ACCIDENT!" the children screamed.

The grandmother had the peculiar feeling that the bespectacled man was someone she knew. His face was as familiar to her as if she had known him all her life but she could not recall who he was. He moved away from the car and began to come down the embankment, placing his feet carefully so that he wouldn't slip. He had on tan and white shoes and no socks, and his ankles were red and thin. "Good afternoon," he said. "I see you all had you a little spill."

75   "We turned over twice!" said the grandmother.

"Oncet," he corrected. "We seen it happen. Try their car and see will it run, Hiram," he said quietly to the boy with the gray hat.

"What you got that gun for?" John Wesley asked. "Whatcha gonna do with that gun?"

"Lady," the man said to the children's mother, "would you mind calling them children to sit down by you? Children make me nervous. I want all you to sit down right together there where you're at."

"What are you telling us what to do for?" June Star asked.

80   Behind them the line of woods gaped like a dark open mouth. "Come here," said their mother.

"Look here now," Bailey began suddenly, "we're in a predicament! We're in . . . ."

The grandmother shrieked. She scrambled to her feet and stood staring. "You're The Misfit!" she said. "I recognized you at once!"

"Yes'm," the man said, smiling slightly as if he were pleased in spite of himself to be known, "but it would have been better for all of you, lady, if you hadn't of reckernized me."

Bailey turned his head sharply and said something to his mother that shocked even the children. The old lady began to cry and The Misfit reddened.

85   "Lady," he said, "don't get upset. Sometimes a man says things he don't mean. I don't reckon he meant to talk to you thataway."

"You wouldn't shoot a lady, would you?" the grandmother said and removed a clean handkerchief from her cuff and began to slap at her eyes with it.

The Misfit pointed the toe of his shoe into the ground and made a little hole and then covered it up again. "I would hate to have to," he said.

"Listen," the grandmother almost screamed, "I know you're a good man. You don't look a bit like you have common blood. I know you must come from nice people!"

"Yes ma'm," he said, "finest people in the world." When he smiled he showed a row of strong white teeth. "God never made a finer woman than my mother and my daddy's heart was pure gold," he said. The boy with the red sweat shirt had come around behind them and was standing with his gun at his hip. The Misfit squatted down on the ground. "Watch them children, Bobby Lee," he said. "You know they make me nervous." He looked at the six of them huddled together in front of him and he seemed to be embarrassed as if he couldn't think of anything to say. "Ain't a cloud in the sky," he remarked, looking up at it. "Don't see no sun but don't see no cloud neither."

90   "Yes, it's a beautiful day," said the grandmother. "Listen," she said, "you shouldn't call yourself The Misfit because I know you're a good man at heart. I can just look at you and tell."

"Hush!" Bailey yelled, "Hush! Everybody shut up and let me handle this!" He was squatting in the position of a runner about to sprint forward but he didn't move.

"I pre-chate that, lady," The Misfit said and drew a little circle in the ground with the butt of his gun.

"It'll take a half a hour to fix this here car," Hiram called, looking over the raised hood of it.

"Well, first you and Bobby Lee get him and that little boy to step over yonder with you," The Misfit said, pointing to Bailey and John Wesley. "The boys want to ask you something," he said to Bailey. "Would you mind stepping back in them woods there with them?"

95   "Listen," Bailey began, "we're in a terrible predicament! Nobody realizes what this is," and his voice cracked. His eyes were as blue and intense as the parrots in his shirt and he remained perfectly still.

The grandmother reached up to adjust her hat brim as if she were going to the woods with him but it came off in her hand. She stood staring at it and after a second she let it fall on the ground. Hiram pulled Bailey up by the arm as if he were assisting an old man. John Wesley caught hold of his father's hand and Bobby Lee followed. They went off toward the woods and just as they reached the dark edge, Bailey turned and supporting himself against a gray naked pine trunk, he shouted, "I'll be back in a minute, Mamma, wait on me!"

"Come back this instant!" his mother shrilled but they all disappeared into the woods.

"Bailey Boy!" the grandmother called in a tragic voice but she found she was looking at The Misfit squatting on the ground in front of her. "I just know you're a good man," she said desperately. "You're not a bit common!"

"Nome, I ain't a good man," The Misfit said after a second as if he had considered her statement carefully, "but I ain't the worst in the world either. My daddy said I was a different breed of dog from my brothers and sisters. 'You know,' Daddy said, 'It's some that can live their whole life without asking about it and it's others has to know why it is, and this boy is one of the latters. He's going to be into everything!'" He put on his black hat and looked up suddenly and then away deep into the woods as if he were embarrassed again. "I'm sorry I don't have on a shirt before you ladies," he said, hunching his shoulders slightly. "We buried our clothes that we had on when we escaped and we're just making do until we can get better. We borrowed these from some folks we met," he explained.

100   "That's perfectly all right," the grandmother said. "Maybe Bailey has an extra shirt in his suitcase."

"I'll look and see terrectly," The Misfit said.

"Where are they taking him?" the children's mother screamed.

"Daddy was a card himself," The Misfit said. "You couldn't put anything over on him. He never got in trouble with the Authorities though. Just had the knack of handling them."

"You could be honest too if you'd only try," said the grandmother. "Think how wonderful it would be to settle down and live a comfortable life and not have to think about somebody chasing you all the time."

105   The Misfit kept scratching in the ground with the butt of his gun as if he were thinking about it. "Yes'm, somebody is always after you," he murmured.

The grandmother noticed how thin his shoulder blades were just behind his hat because she was standing up looking down on him. "Do you ever pray?" she asked.

He shook his head. All she saw was the black hat wiggle between his shoulder blades. "Nome," he said.

There was a pistol shot from the woods, followed closely by another. Then silence. The old lady's head jerked around. She could hear the wind move through the tree tops like a long satisfied insuck of breath. "Bailey Boy!" she called.

"I was a gospel singer for a while," The Misfit said. "I been most everything. Been in the arm service, both land and sea, at home and abroad, been twict married, been an undertaker, been with the railroads, plowed Mother Earth, been in a tornado, seen a man burnt alive oncet," and he looked up at the children's mother and the little girl who were sitting close together, their faces white and their eyes glassy; "I even seen a woman flogged," he said.

110   "Pray, pray," the grandmother began, "pray, pray. . . ."

"I never was a bad boy that I remember of," The Misfit said in an almost dreamy voice, "but somewheres along the line I done something wrong and got sent to the penitentiary. I was buried alive," and he looked up and held her attention to him by a steady stare.

"That's when you should have started to pray," she said. "What did you do to get sent up to the penitentiary that first time?"

"Turn to the right, it was a wall," The Misfit said, looking up again at the cloudless sky. "Turn to the left, it was a wall. Look up it was a ceiling, look down it was a floor. I forget what I done, lady. I set there and set there, trying to remember what it was I done and I ain't recalled it to this day. Oncet in a while, I would think it was coming to me, but it never come."

"Maybe they put you in by mistake," the old lady said vaguely.

115   "Nome," he said. "It wasn't no mistake. They had the papers on me."

"You must have stolen something," she said.

The Misfit sneered slightly. "Nobody had nothing I wanted," he said. "It was a head-doctor at the penitentiary said what I had done was kill my daddy but I known that for a lie. My daddy died in nineteen ought nineteen of the epidemic flu and I never had a thing to do with it. He was buried in the Mount Hopewell Baptist churchyard and you can go there and see for yourself."

"If you would pray," the old lady said, "Jesus would help you."

"That's right," The Misfit said.

120   "Well then, why don't you pray?" she asked trembling with delight suddenly.

"I don't want no hep," he said. "I'm doing all right by myself."

Bobby Lee and Hiram came ambling back from the woods. Bobby Lee was dragging a yellow shirt with bright blue parrots in it.

"Throw me that shirt, Bobby Lee," The Misfit said. The shirt came flying at him and landed on his shoulder and he put it on. The grandmother couldn't name what the shirt reminded her of. "No, lady," The Misfit said while he was buttoning it up, "I found out the crime don't matter. You can do one thing or you can do another, kill a man or take a tire off his car, because sooner or later you're going to forget what it was you done and just be punished for it."

The children's mother had begun to make heaving noises as if she couldn't get her breath. "Lady," he asked, "would you and that little girl like to step off yonder with Bobby Lee and Hiram and join your husband?"

125   "Yes, thank you," the mother said faintly. Her left arm dangled helplessly and she was holding the baby, who had gone to sleep, in the other. "Hep that lady up, Hiram," The Misfit said as she struggled to climb out of the ditch, "and Bobby Lee, you hold onto that little girl's hand."

"I don't want to hold hands with him," June Star said. "He reminds me of a pig."

The fat boy blushed and laughed and caught her by the arm and pulled her off into the woods after Hiram and her mother.

Alone with The Misfit, the grandmother found that she had lost her voice. There was not a cloud in the sky nor any sun. There was nothing around her but woods. She wanted to tell him that he must pray. She opened and closed her mouth several times before anything came out. Finally she found herself saying, "Jesus, Jesus," meaning, Jesus will help you, but the way she was saying it, it sounded as if she might be cursing.

"Yes'm," The Misfit said as if he agreed. "Jesus thown everything off balance. It was the same case with Him as with me except He hadn't committed any crime and they could prove I had committed one because they had the papers on me. Of course," he said, "they never shown me my papers. That's why I sign myself now. I said long ago, you get you a signature and sign everything you do and keep a copy of it. Then you'll know what you done and you can hold up the crime to the punishment and see do they match and in the end you'll have something to prove you ain't been treated right. I call myself The Misfit," he said, "because I can't make what all I done wrong fit what all I gone through in punishment."

130   There was a piercing scream from the woods, followed closely by a pistol report. "Does it seem right to you, lady, that one is punished a heap and another ain't punished at all?"

"Jesus!" the old lady cried. "You've got good blood! I know you wouldn't shoot a lady! I know you come from nice people! Pray! Jesus, you ought not to shoot a lady. I'll give you all the money I've got!"

"Lady," The Misfit said, looking beyond her far into the woods, "there never was a body that give the undertaker a tip."

There were two more pistol reports and the grandmother raised her head like a parched old turkey hen crying for water and called, "Bailey Boy, Bailey Boy!" as if her heart would break.

"Jesus was the only One that ever raised the dead," The Misfit continued, "and He shouldn't have done it. He thown everything off balance. If He did what He said, then it's nothing for you to do but thow away everything and follow Him, and if He didn't, then it's nothing for you to do but enjoy the few minutes you got left the best way you can—by killing somebody or burning down his house or doing some other meanness to him. No pleasure but meanness," he said and his voice had become almost a snarl.

135   "Maybe He didn't raise the dead," the old lady mumbled, not knowing what she was saying and feeling so dizzy that she sank down in the ditch with her legs twisted under her.

"I wasn't there so I can't say He didn't," The Misfit said. "I wisht I had of been there," he said, hitting the ground with his fist. "It ain't right I wasn't there because if I had of been there I would of known. Listen lady," he said in a high voice, "if I had of been there I would of known and I wouldn't be like I am now." His voice seemed about to crack and the grandmother's head cleared for an instant. She saw the man's face twisted close to her own as if he were going to cry and she murmured, "Why you're one of my babies. You're one of my own children!" She reached out and touched him on the shoulder. The Misfit sprang back as if a snake had bitten him and shot her three times through the chest. Then he put his gun down on the ground and took off his glasses and began to clean them.

Hiram and Bobby Lee returned from the woods and stood over the ditch, looking down at the grandmother who half sat and half lay in a puddle of blood with her legs crossed under her like a child's and her face smiling up at the cloudless sky.

Without his glasses, The Misfit's eyes were red-rimmed and pale and defenseless-looking. "Take her off and thow her where you thown the others," he said, picking up the cat that was rubbing itself against his leg.

"She was a talker, wasn't she?" Bobby Lee said, sliding down the ditch with a yodel.

140   "She would of been a good woman," The Misfit said, "if it had been somebody there to shoot her every minute of her life."

"Some fun!" Bobby Lee said.

"Shut up, Bobby Lee," The Misfit said. "It's no real pleasure in life."

▨ TOPICS FOR CRITICAL THINKING AND WRITING

1. Explain the significance of the title.
2. Interpret and evaluate The Misfit's comment on the grandmother: "She would of been a good woman if it had been somebody there to shoot her every minute of her life."
3. O'Connor reported that once, when she read aloud "A Good Man Is Hard to Find," one of her hearers said that "it was a shame someone with so much talent should look upon life as a horror show." Two questions: What evidence of O'Connor's "talent" do you see in the story, and does the story suggest that O'Connor looked on life as a horror show?

4. What are the values of the members of the family?
5. Flannery O'Connor, a Roman Catholic, wrote, "I see from the standpoint of Christian orthodoxy. This means that for me the meaning of life is centered in our Redemption by Christ and what I see in the world I see in relation to that." In the light of this statement, and drawing on "A Good Man Is Hard to Find," explain what O'Connor saw in the world.

Revelation   [1964]

The doctor's waiting room, which was very small, was almost full when the Turpins entered and Mrs. Turpin, who was very large, made it look even smaller by her presence. She stood looming at the head of the magazine table set in the center of it, a living demonstration that the room was inadequate and ridiculous. Her little bright black eyes took in all the patients as she sized up the seating situation. There was one vacant chair and a place on a sofa occupied by a blond child in a dirty blue romper who should have been told to move over and make room for the lady. He was five or six, but Mrs. Turpin saw at once that no one was going to tell him to move over. He was slumped down in the seat, his arms idle at his sides and his eyes idle in his head; his nose ran unchecked.

Mrs. Turpin put a firm hand on Claud's shoulder and said in a voice that included anyone who wanted to listen, "Claud, you sit in that chair there," and gave him a push down into the vacant one. Claud was florid and bald and sturdy, somewhat shorter than Mrs. Turpin, but he sat down as if he were accustomed to doing what she told him to.

Mrs. Turpin remained standing. The only man in the room besides Claud was a lean stringy old fellow with a rusty hand spread out on each knee, whose eyes were closed as if he were asleep or dead or pretending to be so as not to get up and offer her his seat. Her gaze settled agreeably on a well-dressed grey-haired lady whose eyes met hers and whose expression said: If that child belonged to me, he would have some manners and move over—there's plenty of room there for you and him too.

Claud looked up with a sigh and made as if to rise.

5   "Sit down," Mrs. Turpin said. "You know you're not supposed to stand on that leg. He has an ulcer on his leg," she explained.

Claud lifted his foot onto the magazine table and rolled his trouser leg up to reveal a purple swelling on a plump marble-white calf.

"My!" the pleasant lady said. "How did you do that?"

"A cow kicked him," Mrs. Turpin said.

"Goodness!" said the lady.

10   Claud rolled his trouser leg down.

"Maybe the little boy would move over," the lady suggested, but the child did not stir.

"Somebody will be leaving in a minute," Mrs. Turpin said. She could not understand why a doctor—with as much money as they made charging five dollars a day to just stick their head in the hospital door and look at you—couldn't afford a decent-sized waiting room. This one was hardly bigger than a garage. The table was cluttered with limp-looking magazines and at one end of it there was a big green glass ash tray full of cigaret butts and cotton wads with little blood spots on them. If she had had anything to do

with the running of the place, that would have been emptied every so often. There were no chairs against the wall at the head of the room. It had a
rectangular-shaped panel in it that permitted a view of the office where the
nurse came and went and the secretary listened to the radio. A plastic fern
in a gold pot sat in the opening and trailed its fronds down almost to the
floor. The radio was softly playing gospel music.

Just then the inner door opened and a nurse with the highest stack of
yellow hair Mrs. Turpin had ever seen put her face in the crack and called
for the next patient. The woman sitting beside Claud grasped the two arms
of her chair and hoisted herself up; she pulled her dress free from her legs
and lumbered through the door where the nurse had disappeared.

Mrs. Turpin eased into the vacant chair, which held her tight as a
corset. "I wish I could reduce," she said, and rolled her eyes and gave a
comic sigh.

15   "Oh, *you* aren't fat," the stylish lady said.

"Ooooo I am too," Mrs. Turpin said. "Claud he eats all he wants to and
never weighs over one hundred and seventy-five pounds, but me I just look
at something good to eat and I gain some weight," and her stomach and
shoulders shook with laughter. "You can eat all you want to, can't you,
Claud?" she asked, turning to him.

Claud only grinned.

"Well, as long as you have such a good disposition," the stylish lady
said, "I don't think it makes a bit of difference what size you are. You just
can't beat a good disposition."

Next to her was a fat girl of eighteen or nineteen, scowling into a thick
blue book which Mrs. Turpin saw was entitled *Human Development*. The
girl raised her head and directed her scowl at Mrs. Turpin as if she did not
like her looks. She appeared annoyed that anyone should speak while she
tried to read. The poor girl's face was blue with acne and Mrs. Turpin
thought how pitiful it was to have a face like that at that age. She gave the
girl a friendly smile but the girl only scowled the harder. Mrs. Turpin herself
was fat but she had always had good skin, and, though she was forty-seven
years old, there was not a wrinkle in her face except around her eyes from
laughing too much.

20   Next to the ugly girl was the child, still in exactly the same position,
and next to him was a thin leathery old woman in a cotton print dress. She
and Claud had three sacks of chicken feed in their pump house that was in
the same print. She had seen from the first that the child belonged with the
old woman. She could tell by the way they sat—kind of vacant and white-
trashy, as if they would sit there until Doomsday if nobody called and told
them to get up. And at right angles but next to the well-dressed pleasant
lady was a lank-faced woman who was certainly the child's mother. She had
on a yellow sweat shirt and wine-colored slacks, both gritty-looking, and the
rims of her lips were stained with snuff. Her dirty yellow hair was tied behind with a little piece of red paper ribbon. Worse than niggers any day,
Mrs. Turpin thought.

The gospel hymn playing was, "When I looked up and He looked
down," and Mrs. Turpin, who knew it, supplied the last line mentally, "And
wona these days I know I'll we-era crown."

Without appearing to, Mrs. Turpin always noticed people's feet. The
well-dressed lady had on red and grey suede shoes to match her dress. Mrs.

Turpin had on her good black patent leather pumps. The ugly girl had on Girl Scout shoes and heavy socks. The old woman had on tennis shoes and the white-trashy mother had on what appeared to be bedroom slippers, black straw with gold braid threaded through them—exactly what you would have expected her to have on.

Sometimes at night when she couldn't go to sleep, Mrs. Turpin would occupy herself with the question of who she would have chosen to be if she couldn't have been herself. If Jesus had said to her before he made her, "There's only two places available for you. You can either be a nigger or white-trash," what would she have said? "Please, Jesus, please," she would have said, "just let me wait until there's another place available," and he would have said, "No, you have to go right now and I have only those two places so make up your mind." She would have wiggled and squirmed and begged and pleaded but it would have been no use and finally she would have said, "All right, make me a nigger then—but that don't mean a trashy one." And he would have made her a neat clean respectable Negro-woman, herself but black.

Next to the child's mother was a red-headed youngish woman, reading one of the magazines and working a piece of chewing gum, hell for leather, as Claud would say. Mrs. Turpin could not see the woman's feet. She was not white-trash, just common. Sometimes Mrs. Turpin occupied herself at night naming the classes of people. On the bottom of the heap were most colored people, not the kind she would have been if she had been one, but most of them; then next to them—not above, just away from—were the white-trash; then above them were the homeowners, and above them the home-and-land owners, to which she and Claud belonged. Above she and Claud were people with a lot of money and much bigger houses and much more land. But here the complexity of it would begin to bear in on her, for some of the people with a lot of money were common and ought to be below she and Claud and some of the people who had good blood had lost their money and had to rent and then there were colored people who owned their homes and land as well. There was a colored dentist in town who had two red Lincolns and a swimming pool and a farm with registered white-face cattle on it. Usually by the time she had fallen asleep all the classes of people were moiling and roiling around in her head, and she would dream they were all crammed in together in a box car, being ridden off to be put in a gas oven.

25   "That's a beautiful clock," she said and nodded to her right. It was a big wall clock, the face encased in a brass sunburst.

"Yes, it's very pretty," the stylish lady said agreeably. "And right on the dot too," she added, glancing at her watch.

The ugly girl beside her cast an eye upward at the clock, smirked, then looked directly at Mrs. Turpin and smirked again. Then she returned her eyes to her book. She was obviously the lady's daughter because, although they didn't look anything alike as to disposition, they both had the same shape of face and the same blue eyes. On the lady they sparkled pleasantly but in the girl's seared face they appeared alternately to smolder and to blaze.

What if Jesus had said, "All right, you can be white-trash or a nigger or ugly"!

Mrs. Turpin felt an awful pity for the girl, though she thought it was one thing to be ugly and another to act ugly.

30   The woman with the snuff-stained lips turned around in her chair and looked up at the clock. Then she turned back and appeared to look a little to the side of Mrs. Turpin. There was a cast in one of her eyes. "You want to know wher you can get one of themther clocks?" she asked in a loud voice.

"No, I already have a nice clock," Mrs. Turpin said. Once somebody like her got a leg in the conversation, she would be all over it.

"You can get you one with green stamps," the woman said. "That's most likely wher he got hisn. Save you up enough, you can get you most anything. I got me some joo'ry."

Ought to have got you a wash rag and some soap, Mrs. Turpin thought.

"I get contour sheets with mine," the pleasant lady said.

35   The daughter slammed her book shut. She looked straight in front of her, directly through Mrs. Turpin and on through the yellow curtain and the plate glass window which made the wall behind her. The girl's eyes seemed lit all of a sudden with a peculiar light, an unnatural light like night road signs give. Mrs. Turpin turned her head to see if there was anything going on outside that she should see, but she could not see anything. Figures passing cast only a pale shadow through the curtain. There was no reason the girl should single her out for her ugly looks.

"Miss Finley," the nurse said, cracking the door. The gum chewing woman got up and passed in front of her and Claud and went into the office. She had on red high-heeled shoes.

Directly across the table, the ugly girl's eyes were fixed on Mrs. Turpin as if she had some very special reason for disliking her.

"This is wonderful weather, isn't it?" the girl's mother said.

"It's good weather for cotton if you can get the niggers to pick it," Mrs. Turpin said, "but niggers don't want to pick cotton any more. You can't get the white folks to pick it and now you can't get the niggers—because they got to be right up there with the white folks."

40   "They gonna *try* anyways," the white-trash woman said, leaning forward.

"Do you have one of those cotton-picking machines?" the pleasant lady asked.

"No," Mrs. Turpin said, "they leave half the cotton in the field. We don't have much cotton anyway. If you want to make it farming now, you have to have a little of everything. We got a couple of acres of cotton and a few hogs and chickens and just enough white-face that Claud can look after them himself."

"One thang I don't want," the white-trash woman said, wiping her mouth with the back of her hand. "Hogs. Nasty stinking things, a-gruntin and a-rootin all over the place."

Mrs. Turpin gave her the merest edge of her attention. "Our hogs are not dirty and they don't stink," she said. "They're cleaner than some children I've seen. Their feet never touch the ground. We have a pig-parlor—that's where you raise them on concrete," she explained to the pleasant lady, "and Claud scoots them down with the hose every afternoon and washes off the floor." Cleaner by far than that child right there, she thought. Poor nasty little thing. He had not moved except to put the thumb of his dirty hand into his mouth.

45   The woman turned her face away from Mrs. Turpin. "I know I wouldn't scoot down no hog with no hose," she said to the wall.

You wouldn't have no hog to scoot down, Mrs. Turpin said to herself.

"A-gruntin and a-rootin and a-groanin," the woman muttered.

"We got a little of everything," Mrs. Turpin said to the pleasant lady. "It's no use in having more than you can handle yourself with help like it is. We found enough niggers to pick our cotton this year but Claud he has to go after them and take them home again in the evening. They can't walk that half a mile. No they can't. I tell you," she said and laughed merrily, "I sure am tired of buttering up niggers, but you got to love em if you want em to work for you. When they come in the morning, I run out and I say, 'Hi yawl this morning?' and when Claud drives them off to the field I just wave to beat the band and they just wave back." And she waved her hand rapidly to illustrate.

"Like you read out of the same book," the lady said, showing she understood perfectly.

50   "Child, yes," Mrs. Turpin said. "And when they come in from the field, I run out with a bucket of icewater. That's the way it's going to be from now on," she said. "You may as well face it."

"One thang I know," the white-trash woman said. "Two thangs I ain't going to do: love no niggers or scoot down no hog with no hose." And she let out a bark of contempt.

The look that Mrs. Turpin and the pleasant lady exchanged indicated they both understood that you had to *have* certain things before you could *know* certain things. But every time Mrs. Turpin exchanged a look with the lady, she was aware that the ugly girl's peculiar eyes were still on her, and she had trouble bringing her attention back to the conversation.

"When you got something," she said, "you got to look after it." And when you ain't got a thing but breath and britches, she added to herself, you can afford to come to town every morning and just sit on the Court House coping and spit.

A grotesque revolving shadow passed across the curtain behind her and was thrown palely on the opposite wall. Then a bicycle clattered down against the outside of the building. The door opened and a colored boy glided in with a tray from the drug store. It had two large red and white paper cups on it with tops on them. He was a tall, very black boy in discolored white pants and a green nylon shirt. He was chewing gum slowly, as if to music. He set the tray down in the office opening next to the fern and stuck his head through to look for the secretary. She was not in there. He rested his arms on the ledge and waited, his narrow bottom stuck out, swaying slowly to the left and right. He raised a hand over his head and scratched the base of his skull.

55   "You see that button there, boy?" Mrs. Turpin said. "You can punch that and she'll come. She's probably in the back somewhere."

"Is that right?" the boy said agreeably, as if he had never seen the button before. He leaned to the right and put his finger on it. "She sometime out," he said and twisted around to face his audience, his elbows behind him on the counter. The nurse appeared and he twisted back again. She handed him a dollar and he rooted in his pocket and made the change and counted it out to her. She gave him fifteen cents for a tip and he went out with the empty tray. The heavy door swung to slowly and closed at length with the sound of suction. For a moment no one spoke.

"They ought to send all them niggers back to Africa," the white-trash woman said. "That's wher they come from in the first place."

"Oh, I couldn't do without my good colored friends," the pleasant lady said.

"There's a heap of things worse than a nigger," Mrs. Turpin agreed. "It's all kinds of them just like it's all kinds of us."

60   "Yes, and it takes all kinds to make the world go round," the lady said in her musical voice.

As she said it, the raw-complexioned girl snapped her teeth together. Her lower lip turned downwards and inside out, revealing the pale pink inside of her mouth. After a second it rolled back up. It was the ugliest face Mrs. Turpin had ever seen anyone make and for a moment she was certain that the girl had made it at her. She was looking at her as if she had known and disliked her all her life—all of Mrs. Turpin's life, it seemed too, not just all the girl's life. Why, girl, I don't even know you, Mrs. Turpin said silently.

She forced her attention back to the discussion. "It wouldn't be practical to send them back to Africa," she said. "They wouldn't want to go. They got it too good here."

"Wouldn't be what they wanted—if I had anythang to do with it," the woman said.

"It wouldn't be a way in the world you could get all the niggers back over there," Mrs. Turpin said. "They'd be hiding out and lying down and turning sick on you and wailing and hollering and raring and pitching. It wouldn't be a way in the world to get them over there."

65   "They got over here," the trashy woman said. "Get back like they got over."

"It wasn't so many of them then," Mrs. Turpin explained.

The woman looked at Mrs. Turpin as if here was an idiot indeed but Mrs. Turpin was not bothered by the look, considering where it came from.

"Nooo," she said, "they're going to stay here where they can go to New York and marry white folks and improve their color. That's what they all want to do, every one of them, improve their color."

"You know what comes of that, don't you?" Claud asked.

70   "No, Claud, what?" Mrs. Turpin said.

Claud's eyes twinkled. "White-faced niggers," he said with never a smile.

Everybody in the office laughed except the white-trash and the ugly girl. The girl gripped the book in her lap with white fingers. The trashy woman looked around her from face to face as if she thought they were all idiots. The old woman in the feed sack dress continued to gaze expressionless across the floor at the high-top shoes of the man opposite her, the one who had been pretending to be asleep when the Turpins came in. He was laughing heartily, his hands still spread out on his knees. The child had fallen to the side and was lying now almost face down in the old woman's lap.

While they recovered from their laughter, the nasal chorus on the radio kept the room from silence.

You go to blank blank
And I'll go to mine
But we'll all blank along
To-geth-ther,
And all along the blank
We'll hep each other out
Smile-ling in any kind of
Weath-ther!

Mrs. Turpin didn't catch every word but she caught enough to agree with the spirit of the song and it turned her thoughts sober. To help anybody out that needed it was her philosophy of life. She never spared herself when she found somebody in need, whether they were white or black, trash or decent. And of all she had to be thankful for, she was most thankful that this was so. If Jesus had said, "You can be high society and have all the money you want and be thin and svelte-like, but you can't be a good woman with it," she would have had to say, "Well don't make me that then. Make me a good woman and it don't matter what else, how fat or how ugly or how poor!" Her heart rose. He had not made her a nigger or white-trash or ugly! He had made her herself and given her a little of everything. Jesus, thank you! she said. Thank you thank you thank you! Whenever she counted her blessings she felt as buoyant as if she weighed one hundred and twenty-five pounds instead of one hundred and eighty.

75   "What's wrong with your little boy?" the pleasant lady asked the white-trashy woman.

"He has a ulcer," the woman said proudly. "He ain't give me a minute's peace since he was born. Him and her are just alike," she said, nodding at the old woman, who was running her leathery fingers through the child's pale hair. "Look like I can't get nothing down them two but Co'Cola and candy."

That's all you try to get down em, Mrs. Turpin said to herself. Too lazy to light the fire. There was nothing you could tell her about people like them that she didn't know already. And it was not just that they didn't have anything. Because if you gave them everything, in two weeks it would all be broken or filthy or they would have chopped it up for lightwood. She knew all this from her own experience. Help them you must, but help them you couldn't.

All at once the ugly girl turned her lips inside out again. Her eyes were fixed like two drills on Mrs. Turpin. This time there was no mistaking that there was something urgent behind them.

Girl, Mrs. Turpin exclaimed silently, I haven't done a thing to you! The girl might be confusing her with somebody else. There was no need to sit by and let herself be intimidated. "You must be in college," she said boldly, looking directly at the girl. "I see you reading a book there."

80   The girl continued to stare and pointedly did not answer.

Her mother blushed at this rudeness. "The lady asked you a question, Mary Grace," she said under her breath.

"I have ears," Mary Grace said.

The poor mother blushed again. "Mary Grace goes to Wellesley College," she explained. She twisted one of the buttons on her dress. "In Massachusetts," she added with a grimace. "And in the summer she just keeps right on studying. Just reads all the time, a real book worm. She's done real well at Wellesley; she's taking English and Math and History and Psychology and Social Studies," she rattled on, "and I think it's too much. I think she ought to get out and have fun."

The girl looked as if she would like to hurl them all through the plate glass window.

85   "Way up north," Mrs. Turpin murmured and thought, well, it hasn't done much for her manners.

"I'd almost rather to have him sick," the white-trash woman said, wrenching the attention back to herself. "He's so mean when he ain't. Look like some children just take natural to meanness. It's some gets bad when they get sick but he was the opposite. Took sick and turned good. He don't give me no trouble now. It's me waitin to see the doctor," she said.

If I was going to send anybody back to Africa, Mrs. Turpin thought, it would be your kind, woman. "Yes, indeed," she said aloud, but looking up at the ceiling, "it's a heap of things worse than a nigger." And dirtier than a hog, she added to herself.

"I think people with bad dispositions are more to be pitied than anyone on earth," the pleasant lady said in a voice that was decidedly thin.

"I thank the Lord he has blessed me with a good one," Mrs. Turpin said. "The day has never dawned that I couldn't find something to laugh at."

90   "Not since she married me anyways," Claud said with a comical straight face.

Everybody laughed except the girl and the white-trash.

Mrs. Turpin's stomach shook. "He's such a caution," she said, "that I can't help but laugh at him."

The girl made a loud ugly noise through her teeth.

Her mother's mouth grew thin and tight. "I think the worst thing in the world," she said, "is an ungrateful person. To have everything and not appreciate it. I know a girl," she said, "who has parents who would give her anything, a little brother who loves her dearly, who is getting a good education, who wears the best clothes, but who can never say a kind word to anyone, who never smiles, who just criticizes and complains all day long."

95   "Is she too old to paddle?" Claud asked.

The girl's face was almost purple.

"Yes," the lady said. "I'm afraid there's nothing to do but leave her to her folly. Some day she'll wake up and it'll be too late."

"It never hurt anyone to smile," Mrs. Turpin said. "It just makes you feel better all over."

"Of course," the lady said sadly, "but there are just some people you can't tell anything to. They can't take criticism."

100   "If it's one thing I am," Mrs. Turpin said with feeling, "it's grateful. When I think who all I could have been besides myself and what all I got, a little of everything, and a good disposition besides, I just feel like shouting, 'Thank you, Jesus, for making everything the way it is!' It could have been different!" For one thing, somebody else could have got Claud. At the thought of this, she was flooded with gratitude and a terrible pang of joy ran through her. "Oh thank you, Jesus, Jesus, thank you!" she cried aloud.

The book struck her directly over her left eye. It struck almost at the same instant that she realized the girl was about to hurl it. Before she could utter a sound, the raw face came crashing across the table toward her, howling. The girl's fingers sank like clamps into the soft flesh of her neck. She heard the mother cry and Claud shout, "Whoa!" There was an instant when she was certain that she was about to be in an earthquake.

All at once her vision narrowed and she saw everything as if it were happening in a small room far away, or as if she were looking at it through the wrong end of a telescope. Claud's face crumpled and fell out of sight. The nurse ran in, then out, then in again. Then the gangling figure of the doctor rushed out of the inner door. Magazines flew this way and that as the table turned over. The girl fell with a thud and Mrs. Turpin's vision suddenly reversed itself and she saw everything large instead of small. The eyes of the white-trashy woman were staring hugely at the floor. There the girl, held down on one side by the nurse and on the other by her mother, was wrenching and turning in their grasp. The doctor was kneeling astride her, trying to hold her arm down. He managed after a second to sink a long needle into it.

Mrs. Turpin felt entirely hollow except for her heart which swung from side to side as if it were agitated in a great empty drum of flesh.

"Somebody that's not busy call for the ambulance," the doctor said in the off-hand voice young doctors adopt for terrible occasions.

105   Mrs. Turpin could not have moved a finger. The old man who had been sitting next to her skipped nimble into the office and made the call, for the secretary still seemed to be gone.

"Claud!" Mrs. Turpin called.

He was not in his chair. She knew she must jump up and find him but she felt like someone trying to catch a train in a dream, when everything moves in slow motion and the faster you try to run the slower you go.

"Here I am," a suffocated voice, very unlike Claud's, said.

He was doubled up in the corner on the floor, pale as paper, holding his leg. She wanted to get up and go to him but she could not move. Instead, her gaze was drawn slowly downward to the churning face on the floor, which she could see over the doctor's shoulder.

110   The girl's eyes stopped rolling and focused on her. They seemed a much lighter blue than before, as if a door that had been tightly closed behind them was now open to admit light and air.

Mrs. Turpin's head cleared and her power of motion returned. She leaned forward until she was looking directly into the fierce brilliant eyes. There was no doubt in her mind that the girl did know her, knew her in some intense and personal way, beyond time and condition. "What you got to say to me?" she asked hoarsely and held her breath, waiting, as for a revelation.

The girl raised her head. Her gaze locked with Mrs. Turpin's. "Go back to hell where you came from, you old wart hog," she whispered. Her voice was low but clear. Her eyes burned for a moment as if she saw with pleasure that her message had struck its target.

Mrs. Turpin sank back in her chair.

After a moment the girl's eyes closed and she turned her head wearily to the side.

115   The doctor rose and handed the nurse the empty syringe. He leaned over and put both hands for a moment on the mother's shoulders, which were shaking. She was sitting on the floor, her lips pressed together, holding Mary Grace's hand in her lap. The girl's fingers were gripped like a baby's around her thumb. "Go on to the hospital," he said. "I'll call and make the arrangements."

"Now let's see that neck," he said in a jovial voice to Mrs. Turpin. He began to inspect her neck with his first two fingers. Two little moonshaped lines like pink fish bones were indented over her windpipe. There was the beginning of an angry red swelling above her eye. His fingers passed over this also.

"Lea' me be," she said thickly and shook him off. "See about Claud. She kicked him."

"I'll see about him in a minute," he said and felt her pulse. He was a thin gray-haired man, given to pleasantries. "Go home and have yourself a vacation the rest of the day," he said and patted her on the shoulder.

Quit your pattin me, Mrs. Turpin growled to herself.

120   "And put an ice pack over that eye," he said. Then he went and squatted down beside Claud and looked at his leg. After a moment he pulled him up and Claud limped after him into the office.

Until the ambulance came, the only sounds in the room were the tremulous moans of the girl's mother, who continued to sit on the floor. The white-trash woman did not take her eyes off the girl. Mrs. Turpin looked straight ahead at nothing. Presently the ambulance drew up, a long dark shadow, behind the curtain. The attendants came in and set the stretcher down beside the girl and lifted her expertly onto it and carried her out. The nurse helped the mother gather up her things. The shadow of the ambulance moved silently away and the nurse came back in the office.

"That ther girl is going to be a lunatic, ain't she?" the white-trash woman asked the nurse, but the nurse kept on to the back and never answered her.

"Yes, she's going to be a lunatic," the white-trash woman said to the rest of them.

"Po' critter," the old woman murmured. The child's face was still in her lap. His eyes looked idly out over her knees. He had not moved during the disturbance except to draw one leg up under him.

125   "I thank Gawd," the white-trash woman said fervently, "I ain't a lunatic."

Claud came limping out and the Turpins went home.

As their pick-up truck turned into their own dirt road and made the crest of the hill, Mrs. Turpin gripped the window ledge and looked out suspiciously. The land sloped gracefully down through a field dotted with lavender weeds and at the start of the rise their small yellow frame house, with its little flower beds spread out around it like a fancy apron, sat primly in its accustomed place between two giant hickory trees. She would not have been startled to see a burnt wound between two blackened chimneys.

Neither of them felt like eating so they put on their house clothes and lowered the shade in the bedroom and lay down, Claud with his leg on a pillow and herself with a damp washcloth over her eye. The instant she was flat on her back, the image of a razor-backed hog with warts on its face and horns coming out behind its ears snorted into her head. She moaned, a low quiet moan.

"I am not," she said tearfully, "a wart hog. From hell." But the denial had no force. The girl's eyes and her words, even the tone of her voice, low but clear, directed only to her, brooked no repudiation. She had been singled out for the message, though there was trash in the room to whom it might justly have been applied. The full force of this fact struck her only now. There was a woman there who was neglecting her own child but she had been overlooked. The message had been given to Ruby Turpin, a respectable, hard-working, church-going woman. The tears dried. Her eyes began to burn instead with wrath.

130   She rose on her elbow and the washcloth fell into her hand. Claud was lying on his back, snoring. She wanted to tell him what the girl had said. At the same time she did not wish to put the image of herself as a wart hog from hell into his mind.

"Hey, Claud," she muttered and pushed his shoulder.

Claud opened one pale baby blue eye.

She looked into it warily. He did not think about anything. He just went his way.

"Wha, whasit?" he said and closed his eye again.

135   "Nothing," she said. "Does your leg pain you?"

"Hurts like hell," Claud said.

"It'll quit terreckly," she said and lay back down. In a moment Claud was snoring again. For the rest of the afternoon they lay there. Claud slept. She scowled at the ceiling. Occasionally she raised her fist and made a small stabbing motion over her chest as if she was defending her innocence to invisible guests who were the comforters of Job, reasonable-seeming but wrong.

About five-thirty Claud stirred. "Got to go after those niggers," he sighed, not moving.

She was looking straight up as if there were unintelligible handwriting on the ceiling. The protuberance over her eye had turned a greenish-blue. "Listen here," she said.

140   "What?"

"Kiss me."

Claud leaned over and kissed her loudly on the mouth. He pinched her side and their hands interlocked. Her expression of ferocious concentration did not change. Claud got up, groaning and growling, and limped off. She continued to study the ceiling.

She did not get up until she heard the pick-up truck coming back with the Negroes. Then she rose and thrust her feet in her brown oxfords, which she did not bother to lace, and stumped out onto the back porch and got her red plastic bucket. She emptied a tray of ice cubes into it and filled it half full of water and went out into the back yard. Every afternoon after Claud brought the hands in, one of the boys helped him put out hay and the rest waited in the back of the truck until he was ready to take them home. The truck was parked in the shade under one of the hickory trees.

"Hi yawl this evening?" Mrs. Turpin asked grimly, appearing with the bucket and the dipper. There were three women and a boy in the truck.

145   "Us doin nicely," the oldest woman said. "Hi you doin?" and her gaze stuck immediately on the dark lump on Mrs. Turpin's forehead. "You done fell down, ain't you?" she asked in a solicitous voice. The old woman was dark and almost toothless. She had on an old felt hat of Claud's set back on her head. The other two women were younger and lighter and they both had new bright green sun hats. One of them had hers on her head; the other had taken hers off and the boy was grinning beneath it.

Mrs. Turpin set the bucket down on the floor of the truck. "Yawl help yourselves," she said. She looked around to make sure Claud had gone. "No, I didn't fall down," she said. "It was something worse than that."

"Ain't nothing bad happen to you!" the old woman said. She said it as if they all knew Mrs. Turpin was protected in some special way by Divine Providence. "You just had you a little fall."

"We were in town at the doctor's office for where the cow kicked Mr. Turpin," Mrs. Turpin said in a flat tone that indicated they could leave off their foolishness. "And there was this girl there. A big fat girl with her face all broke out. I could look at that girl and tell she was peculiar but I couldn't tell how. And me and her mama were just talking and going along and all of a sudden WHAM! She throws this big book she reading at me and . . ."

"Naw!" the old woman cried out.

150 "And then she jumps over the table and commences to choke me."

"Naw!" they all exclaimed, "naw!"

"Hi come she do that?" the old woman asked. "What ail her?"

Mrs. Turpin only glared in front of her.

"Somethin ail her," the old woman said.

155 "They carried her off in an ambulance," Mrs. Turpin continued, "but before she went she was rolling on the floor and they were trying to hold her down to give her a shot and she said something to me." She paused. "You know what she said to me?"

"What she say?" they asked.

"She said," Mrs. Turpin began, and stopped, her face very dark and heavy. The sun was getting whiter and whiter, blanching the sky overhead so that the leaves of the hickory tree were black in the face of it. She could not bring forth the words. "Something real ugly," she muttered.

"She sho shouldn't said nothin ugly to you," the old woman said. "You so sweet. You're the sweetest lady I know."

"She pretty too," the one with the hat on said.

160 "And stout," the other one said. "I never knowed no sweeter white lady."

"That's the truth befo' Jesus," the old woman said. "Amen! You des as sweet and pretty as you can be."

Mrs. Turpin knew just exactly how much Negro flattery was worth and it added to her rage. "She said," she began again and finished this time with a fierce rush of breath, "that I was an old wart hog from hell."

There was an astounded silence.

"Where she at?" the youngest woman cried in a piercing voice.

165 "Lemme see her. I'll kill her!"

"I'll kill her with you!" the other one cried.

"She b'long in the sylum," the old woman said emphatically. "You the sweetest white lady I know."

"She pretty too," the other two said. "Stout as she can be and sweet. Jesus satisfied with her!"

"Deed he is," the old woman declared.

170 Idiots! Mrs. Turpin growled to herself. You could never say anything intelligent to a nigger. You could talk at them but not with them. "Yawl ain't drunk your water," she said shortly. "Leave the bucket in the truck when you're finished with it. I got more to do than just stand around and pass the time of day," and she moved off and into the house.

She stood for a moment in the middle of the kitchen. The dark protuberance over her eye looked like a miniature tornado cloud which might any moment sweep across the horizon of her brow. Her lower lip protruded dangerously. She squared her massive shoulders. Then she marched into the front of the house and out the side door and started down the road to the pig parlor. She had the look of a woman going single-handed, weaponless, into battle.

The sun was a deep yellow now like a harvest moon and was riding westward very fast over the far tree line as if it meant to reach the hogs before she did. The road was rutted and she kicked several good-sized stones out of her path as she strode along. The pig parlor was on a little knoll at the end of a lane that ran off from the side of the barn. It was a square of concrete as large as a small room, with a board fence about four feet high around it. The concrete floor sloped slightly so that the hog wash could drain off into a trench where it was carried to the field for fertilizer. Claud was standing on the outside, on the edge of the concrete, hanging onto the top board, hosing down the floor inside. The hose was connected to the faucet of a water trough nearby.

Mrs. Turpin climbed up beside him and glowered down at the hogs inside. There were seven long-snouted bristly shoats in it—tan with liver-colored spots—and an old sow a few weeks off from farrowing. She was lying on her side grunting. The shoats were running about shaking themselves like idiot children, their little slit pig eyes searching the floor for anything left. She had read that pigs were the most intelligent animal. She doubted it. They were supposed to be smarter than dogs. There had even been a pig astronaut. He had performed his assignment perfectly but died of a heart attack afterwards because they left him in his electric suit, sitting upright throughout his examination when naturally a hog should be on all fours.

A-gruntin and a-rootin and a-groanin.

175   "Gimme that hose," she said, yanking it away from Claud. "Go on and carry them niggers home and then get off that leg."

"You look like you might have swallowed a mad dog," Claud observed, but he got down and limped off. He paid no attention to her humors.

Until he was out of earshot, Mrs. Turpin stood on the side of the pen, holding the hose and pointing the stream of water at the hind quarter of any shoat that looked as if it might try to lie down. When he had had time to get over the hill, she turned her head slightly and her wrathful eyes scanned the path. He was nowhere in sight. She turned back again and seemed to gather herself up. Her shoulders rose and she drew in her breath.

"What do you send me a message like that for?" she said in a low fierce voice, barely above a whisper but with the force of a shout in its concentrated fury. "How am I a hog and me both? How am I saved and from hell too?" Her free fist was knotted and with the other she gripped the hose, blindly pointing the stream of water in and out of the eye of the old sow whose outraged squeal she did not hear.

The pig parlor commanded a view of the back pasture where their twenty beef cows were gathered around the hay-bales Claud and the boy had put out. The freshly cut pasture sloped down to the highway. Across it was their cotton field and beyond that a dark green dusty wood which they owned as well. The sun was behind the wood, very red, looking over the paling of trees like a farmer inspecting his own hogs.

180   "Why me?" she rumbled. "It's no trash around here, black or white, that I haven't given to. And break my back to the bone every day working. And do for the church."

She appeared to be the right size woman to command the arena before her. "How am I a hog?" she demanded. "Exactly how am I like them?" and she jabbed the stream of water at the shoats. "There was plenty of trash there. It didn't have to be me."

"If you like trash better, go get yourself some trash then," she railed. "You could have made me trash. Or a nigger. If trash is what you wanted why didn't you make me trash?" She shook her fist with the hose in it and a watery snake appeared momentarily in the air. "I could quit working and take it easy and be filthy," she growled. "Lounge about the sidewalks all day drinking root beer. Dip snuff and spit in every puddle and have it all over my face. I could be nasty."

"Or you could have made me a nigger. It's too late for me to be a nigger," she said with deep sarcasm, "but I could act like one. Lay down in the middle of the road and stop traffic. Roll on the ground."

In the deepening light everything was taking on a mysterious hue. The pasture was growing a peculiar glassy green and the streak of highway had turned lavender. She braced herself for a final assault and this time her voice rolled out over the pasture. "Go on," she yelled, "call me a hog! Call me a hog again. From hell. Call me a wart hog from hell. Put that bottom rail on top. There'll still be a top and bottom!"

185   A garbled echo returned to her.

A final surge of fury shook her and she roared, "Who do you think you are?"

The color of everything, field and crimson sky, burned for a moment with a transparent intensity. The question carried over the pasture and across the highway and the cotton field and returned to her clearly like an answer from beyond the wood.

She opened her mouth but no sound came out of it.

A tiny truck, Claud's, appeared on the highway, heading rapidly out of sight. Its gears scraped thinly. It looked like a child's toy. At any moment a bigger truck might smash into it and scatter Claud's and the niggers' brains all over the road.

190   Mrs. Turpin stood there, her gaze fixed on the highway, all her muscles rigid, until in five or six minutes the truck reappeared, returning. She waited until it had had time to turn into their own road. Then like a monumental statue coming to life, she bent her head slowly and gazed, as if through the very heart of the mystery, down into the pig parlor at the hogs. They had settled all in one corner around the old sow who was grunting softly. A red glow suffused them. They appeared to pant with a secret life.

Until the sun slipped finally behind the tree line, Mrs. Turpin remained there with her gaze bent to them as if she were absorbing some abysmal life-giving knowledge. At last she lifted her head. There was only a purple streak in the sky, cutting through a field of crimson and leading, like an extension of the highway, into the descending dusk. She raised her hands from the side of the pen in a gesture hieratic and profound. A visionary light settled in her eyes. She saw the streak as a vast swinging bridge extending upward from the earth through a field of living fire. Upon it a vast horde of souls were rumbling toward heaven. There were whole companies of white-trash, clean for the first time in their lives, and bands of black niggers in white robes, and battalions of freaks and lunatics shouting and clapping and leaping like frogs. And bringing up the end of the procession was a tribe of people whom she recognized at once as those who, like herself and Claud, had always had a little of everything and the God-given wit to use it right. She leaned forward to observe them closer. They were marching behind the others with great dignity, accountable as they had always been for good order and common sense and respectable behavior. They alone were on key. Yet she could see by their shocked and altered faces that even their virtues were being burned away. She lowered her hands and gripped the rail of the hog pen, her eyes small but fixed unblinkingly on what lay ahead. In a moment the vision faded but she remained where she was, immobile.

At length she got down and turned off the faucet and made her slow way on the darkening path to the house. In the woods around her the invisible cricket choruses had struck up, but what she heard were the voices of the souls climbing upward into the starry field and shouting hallelujah.

▩ TOPICS FOR CRITICAL THINKING AND WRITING

1. Why does Mary Grace attack Mrs. Turpin?
2. Characterize Mrs. Turpin before her revelation. Did your attitude toward her change at the end of the story?
3. The two chief settings are a doctor's waiting room and a "pig parlor." Can these settings reasonably be called "symbolic"? If so, symbolic of what?
4. When Mrs. Turpin goes toward the pig parlor, she has "the look of a woman going single-handed, weaponless, into battle." Once there, she dismisses Claud, uses the hose as a weapon against the pigs, and talks to herself "in a low fierce voice." What is she battling, besides the pigs?

ON FICTION: REMARKS FROM ESSAYS AND LETTERS

From "The Fiction Writer and His Country"

In the greatest fiction, the writer's moral sense coincides with his dramatic sense, and I see no way for it to do this unless his moral judgment is part of the very act of seeing, and he is free to use it. I have heard it said that belief in Christian dogma is a hindrance to the writer, but I myself have found nothing further from the truth. Actually, it frees the storyteller to observe. It is not a set of rules which fixes what he sees in the world. It affects his writing primarily by guaranteeing his respect for mystery. . . .

When I look at stories I have written I find that they are, for the most part, about people who are poor, who are afflicted in both mind and body, who have little—or at best a distorted—sense of spiritual purpose, and whose actions do not apparently give the reader a great assurance of the joy of life.

Yet how is this? For I am no disbeliever in spiritual purpose and no vague believer. I see from the standpoint of Christian orthodoxy. This means that for me the meaning of life is centered in our Redemption by Christ and what I see in the world I see in its relation to that. . . .

The novelist with Christian concerns will find in modern life distortions which are repugnant to him, and his problem will be to make these appear as distortions to an audience which is used to seeing them as natural; and he may well be forced to take ever more violent means to get his vision across to this hostile audience. When you can assume that your audience holds the same beliefs you do, you can relax a little and use more normal means of talking to it; when you have to assume that it does not, then you have to make your vision apparent by shock—to the hard of hearing you shout, and for the almost-blind you draw large and startling figures.

From "Some Aspects of the Grotesque in Southern Fiction"

If the writer believes that our life is and will remain essentially mysterious, if he looks upon us as beings existing in a created order to whose laws we freely respond, then what he sees on the surface will be of interest to him only as he can go through it into an experience of mystery itself. His kind of fiction will always be pushing its own limits outward toward the limits of mystery, because for this kind of writer, the meaning of a story does not begin except at a depth where adequate motivation and adequate psychology and the various determinations have been exhausted. Such a writer will be interested in what we don't understand rather than in what we do. He will be interested in possibility rather than in probability. He will be interested in characters who are forced out to meet evil and grace and who act on a trust beyond themselves—whether they know very clearly what it is they act upon or not. To the modern mind, this kind of character, and his creator, are typical Don Quixotes, tilting at what is not there.

From "The Nature and Aim of Fiction"

The novel works by a slower accumulation of detail than the short story does. The short story requires more drastic procedures than the novel because more has to be accomplished in less space. The details have to carry more immediate weight. In good fiction, certain of the details will tend to accumulate meaning from the story itself, and when this happens, they become symbolic in their action.

Now the word *symbol* scares a good many people off, just as the word *art* does. They seem to feel that a symbol is some mysterious thing put in arbitrarily by the writer to frighten the common reader—sort of a literary Masonic grip that is only for the initiated. They seem to think that it is a way of saying something that you aren't actually saying, and so if they can be got to read a reputedly symbolic work at all, they approach it as if it were a problem in algebra. Find x. And when they do find or think they find this abstraction, x, then they go off with an elaborate sense of satisfaction and the notion that they have "understood" the story. Many students confuse the *process* of understanding a thing with understanding it.

I think that for the fiction writer himself, symbols are something he uses simply as a matter of course. You might say that these are details that, while having their essential place in the literal level of the story, operate in depth as well as on the surface, increasing the story in every direction. . . .

People have a habit of saying, "What is the theme of your story?" and they expect you to give them a statement: "The theme of my story is the economic pressure of the machine on the middle class"—or some such absurdity. And when they've got a statement like that, they go off happy and feel it is no longer necessary to read the story.

Some people have the notion that you read the story and then climb out of it into the meaning, but for the fiction writer himself the whole story is the meaning, because it is an experience, not an abstraction.

From "Writing Short Stories"

Being short does not mean being slight. A short story should be long in depth and should give us an experience of meaning. . . .

Meaning is what keeps the short story from being short. I prefer to talk about the meaning in a story rather than the theme of a story. People talk about the theme of a story as if the theme were like the string that a sack of chicken feed is tied with. They think that if you can pick out the theme, the way you pick the right thread in the chicken-feed sack, you can rip the story open and feed the chickens. But this is not the way meaning works in fiction.

When you can state the theme of a story, when you can separate it from the story itself, then you can be sure the story is not a very good one. The meaning of a story has to be embodied in it, has to be made concrete in it. A story is a way to say something that can't be said any other way, and it takes every word in the story to say what the meaning is. You tell a story because a statement would be inadequate. When anybody asks what a story is about, the only proper thing is to tell him to read the story. The meaning of fiction is not abstract meaning but experienced meaning, and the purpose of making statements about the meaning of a story is only to help you to experience that meaning more fully.

"A Reasonable Use of the Unreasonable"   [1957]

Last fall I received a letter from a student who said she would be "graciously appreciative" if I would tell her "just what enlightenment" I expected her to get from each of my stories. I suspect she had a paper to write. I wrote her back to forget about the enlightenment and just try to enjoy them. I knew that was the most unsatisfactory answer I could have given because, of course, she didn't want to enjoy them, she just wanted to figure them out.

In most English classes the short story has become a kind of literary specimen to be dissected. Every time a story of mine appears in a Freshman anthology, I have a vision of it, with its little organs laid open, like a frog in a bottle.

I realize that a certain amount of this what-is-the-significance has to go on, but I think something has gone wrong in the process when, for so many students, the story becomes simply a problem to be solved, something which you evaporate to get Instant Enlightenment.

A story really isn't any good unless it successfully resists paraphrase, unless it hangs on and expands in the mind. Properly, you analyze to enjoy, but it's equally true that to analyze with any discrimination, you have to have enjoyed already, and I think that the best reason to hear a story read is that it should stimulate that primary enjoyment.

I don't have any pretensions to being an Aeschylus or Sophocles and providing you in this story with a cathartic experience out of your mythic background, though this story I'm going to read certainly calls up a good deal of the South's mythic background, and it should elicit from you a degree of pity and terror, even though its way of being serious is a comic one. I do think, though, that like the Greeks you should know what is going to happen in this story so that any element of suspense in it will be transferred from its surface to its interior.

I would be most happy if you have already read it, happier still if you knew it well, but since experience has taught me to keep my expectations along these lines modest, I'll tell you that this is the story of a family of six which, on its way driving to Florida, gets wiped out by an escaped convict who calls himself The Misfit. The family is made up of the Grandmother and her son, Bailey, and his children, John Wesley and June Star and the baby, and there is also the cat and the children's mother. The cat is named Pitty Sing, and the Grandmother is taking him with them, hidden in a basket.

Now I think it behooves me to try to establish with you the basis on which reason operates in this story. Much of my fiction takes its character from a reasonable use of the unreasonable, though the reasonableness of my use of it may not always be apparent. The assumptions that underlie this use of it, however, are those of the central Christian mysteries. These are assumptions to which a large part of the modern audience takes exception. About this I can only say that there are perhaps other ways than my own in which this story could be read, but none other by which it could have been written. Belief, in my own case anyway, is the engine that makes perception operate.

The heroine of this story, the Grandmother, is in the most significant position life offers the Christian. She is facing death. And to all appearances she, like the rest of us, is not too well prepared for it. She would like to see the event postponed. Indefinitely.

I've talked to a number of teachers who use this story in class and who tell their students that the Grandmother is evil, that in fact, she's a witch, even down to the cat. One of these teachers told me that his students, and particularly his Southern students, resisted this interpretation with a certain bemused vigor, and he didn't understand why. I had to tell him that they resisted it because they all had grandmothers or great-aunts just like her at home, and they knew, from personal experience, that the old lady lacked comprehension, but that she had a good heart. The Southerner is usually tolerant of those weaknesses that proceed from innocence, and he knows that a taste for self-preservation can be readily combined with the missionary spirit.

This same teacher was telling his students that morally The Misfit was several cuts above the Grandmother. He had a really sentimental attachment to The Misfit. But then a prophet gone wrong is almost always more interesting than your grandmother, and you have to let people take their pleasures where they find them.

It is true that the old lady is a hypocritical old soul; her wits are no match for The Misfit's, nor is her capacity for grace equal to his; yet I think the unprejudiced reader will feel that the Grandmother has a special kind of triumph in the story which instinctively we do not allow to someone altogether bad.

I often ask myself what makes a story work, and what makes it hold up as a story, and I have decided that it is probably some action, some gesture of a character that is unlike any other in the story, one which indicates where the real heart of the story lies. This would have to be an action or a gesture which was both totally right and totally unexpected; it would have to be one that was both in character and beyond character; it would have to suggest both the world and eternity. The action or gesture I'm talking about would have to be on the anagogical level, that is, the level which has to do with the Divine life and our participation in it. It would be a gesture that transcended any neat allegory that might have been intended or any pat moral categories a reader could make. It would be a gesture which somehow made contact with mystery.

There is a point in this story where such a gesture occurs. The Grandmother is at last alone, facing The Misfit. Her head clears for an instant and she realizes, even in her limited way, that she is responsible for the man before her and joined to him by ties of kinship which have their roots deep in the mystery she has been merely prattling about so far. And at this point, she does the right thing, she makes the right gesture.

I find that students are often puzzled by what she says and does here, but I think myself that if I took out this gesture and what she says with it, I would have no story. What was left would not be worth your attention. Our age not only does not have a very sharp eye for the almost imperceptible intrusions of grace, it no longer has much feeling for the nature of the violences which precede and follow them. The devil's greatest wile, Baudelaire has said, is to convince us that he does not exist.

I suppose the reasons for the use of so much violence in modern fiction will differ with each writer who uses it, but in my own stories I have found that violence is strangely capable of returning my characters to reality and preparing them to accept their moment of grace. Their heads are so hard that almost nothing else will do the work. This idea, that reality is something to which we must be returned at considerable cost, is one which is seldom understood by the casual reader, but it is one which is implicit in the Christian view of the world.

I don't want to equate The Misfit with the devil. I prefer to think that, however unlikely this may seem, the old lady's gesture, like the mustard-seed, will grow to be a great crow-filled tree in The Misfit's heart, and will be enough of a pain to him there to turn him into the prophet he was meant to become. But that's another story.

This story has been called grotesque, but I prefer to call it literal. A good story is literal in the same sense that a child's drawing is literal. When a child draws, he doesn't intend to distort but to set down exactly what he sees, and as his gaze is direct, he sees the lines that create motion. Now the lines of motion that interest the writer are usually invisible. They are lines of spiritual motion. And in this story you should be on the lookout for such things as the action of grace in the Grandmother's soul, and not for the dead bodies.

We hear many complaints about the prevalence of violence in modern fiction, and it is always assumed that this violence is a bad thing and meant to be an end in itself. With the serious writer, violence is never an end in itself. It is the extreme situation that best reveals what we are essentially, and I believe these are times when writers are more interested in what we are essentially than in the tenor of our daily lives. Violence is a form which can be used for good or evil, and among other things taken by it is the kingdom of heaven. But regardless of what can be taken by it, the man in the violent situation reveals those qualities least dispensable in his personality, those qualities which are all he will have to take into eternity with him; and since the characters in this story are all on the verge of eternity, it is appropriate to think of what they take with them. In any case, I hope that if you consider these points in connection with the story, you will come to see it as something more than an account of a family murdered on the way to Florida.

ON INTERPRETING "A GOOD MAN IS HARD TO FIND"

A professor of English had sent Flannery the following letter: "I am writing as spokesman for three members of our department and some ninety university students in three classes who for a week now have been discussing your story 'A Good Man Is Hard to Find.' We have debated at length several possible interpretations, none of which fully satisfies us. In general we believe that the appearance of The Misfit is not 'real' in the same sense that the incidents of the first half of the story are real. Bailey, we believe, imagines the appearance of The Misfit, whose activities have been called to his attention on the night before the trip and again during the stopover at the roadside restaurant. Bailey, we further believe, identifies himself with The Misfit and so plays two roles in the imaginary last half of the story. But we cannot, after great effort, determine the point at which reality fades into illusion or reverie. Does the accident literally occur, or is it a part of Bailey's dream? Please believe me when I say we are not seeking an easy way out of our difficulty. We admire your story and have examined it with great care, but we are convinced that we are missing something important which you intended for us to grasp. We will all be very grateful if you comment on the interpretation which I have outlined above and if you will give us further comments about your intention in writing 'A Good Man Is Hard to Find.'"

She replied:

28 March 61

To a Professor of English

The interpretation of your ninety students and three teachers is fantastic and about as far from my intentions as it could get to be. If it were a legitimate interpretation, the story would be little more than a trick and its interest would be simply for abnormal psychology. I am not interested in abnormal psychology.

There is a change of tension from the first part of the story to the second where The Misfit enters, but this is no lessening of reality. This story is, of course, not meant to be realistic in the sense that it portrays the everyday doings of people in Georgia. It is stylized and its conventions are comic even though its meaning is serious.

Bailey's only importance is as the Grandmother's boy and the driver of the car. It is the Grandmother who first recognizes The Misfit and who is most concerned with him throughout. The story is a duel of sorts between the Grandmother and her superficial beliefs and The Misfit's more profoundly felt involvement with Christ's action which set the world off balance for him.

The meaning of a story should go on expanding for the reader the more he thinks about it, but meaning cannot be captured in an interpretation. If teachers are in the habit of approaching a story as if it were a research problem for which any answer is believable so long as it is not obvious, then I think students will never learn to enjoy fiction. Too much interpretation is certainly worse than too little and where feeling for a story is absent, theory will not supply it.

My tone is not meant to be obnoxious. I am in a state of shock.

RAYMOND CARVER: THREE STORIES, AN INTERVIEW, AND COMMENTS ABOUT WRITING

RAYMOND CARVER

Raymond Carver (1938–1988) was born in Clatskanie, a logging town in Oregon. In 1963 he graduated from Humboldt State College in northern California and then did further study at the University of Iowa.

His early years were not easy—he married while still in college, divorced a little later, and sometimes suffered from alcoholism. In his last years he found domestic happiness, but he died of cancer at the age of fifty.

As a young man he wrote poetry while working at odd jobs (janitor, deliveryman, etc.); later he turned to fiction, though he continued to write poetry. Most of his fiction is of a sort called "minimalist," narrating in a spare, understated style stories about bewildered and sometimes exhausted men and women.

Below is the early version (the left-hand column) and a later version (the right-hand column) of a story. The first version, "Mine," was published in 1977, and the revised version in 1981, when Carver called it "Popular Mechanics." In 1986 he published the 1981 version again, but this time he retitled it as "Little Things." After reading the two versions carefully, you may want to evaluate the changes, including the change in title.

Mine [1977]	*Little Things* [1981]
During the day the sun had come out and the snow melted into dirty water. Streaks of water ran down from the little, shoulder-high window that faced the back yard. Cars slushed by on the street outside. It was getting dark, outside and inside.	Early that day the weather turned and the snow was melting into dirty water. Streaks of it ran down from the little shoulder-high window that faced the backyard. Cars slushed by on the street outside, where it was getting dark. But it was getting dark on the inside too.

He was in the bedroom pushing clothes into a suitcase when
she came to the door.

I'm glad you're leaving, I'm
glad you're leaving! she said. Do
you hear?

He kept on putting his things
into the suitcase and didn't look
up.

5   Sonofabitch! I'm so glad
you're leaving! She began to cry.
You can't even look me in the
face, can you? Then she noticed
the baby's picture on the bed and
picked it up.

He looked at her and she
wiped her eyes and stared at him
before turning and going back to
the living room.

Bring that back.

Just get your things and get
out, she said.

He did not answer. He fastened the suitcase, put on his
coat, and looked at the bedroom before turning off the light.
Then he went out to the living
room. She stood in the doorway
of the little kitchen, holding the
baby.

10   I want the baby, he said.

Are you crazy?

No, but I want the baby. I'll
get someone to come by for his
things.

You can go to hell! You're
not touching this baby.

The baby had begun to cry
and she uncovered the blanket
from around its head.

15   Oh, oh, she said, looking at
the baby.

He moved towards her.

For God's sake! she said. She
took a step back into the kitchen.

I want the baby.

Get out of here!

20   She turned and tried to hold
the baby over in a corner behind
the stove as he came up.

He was in the bedroom pushing clothes into a suitcase when
she came to the door.

I'm glad you're leaving! I'm
glad you're leaving! she said. Do
you hear?

He kept on putting his things
into the suitcase.

5   Son of a bitch! I'm so glad
you're leaving! She began to cry.
You can't even look me in the
face, can you?

Then she noticed the baby's
picture on the bed and picked it
up.

He looked at her and she
wiped her eyes and stared at him
before turning and going back to
the living room.

Bring that back, he said.

Just get your things and get
out, she said.

10   He did not answer. He fastened the suitcase, put on his
coat, looked around the bedroom before turning off the light.
Then he went out to the living
room.

She stood in the doorway of
the little kitchen, holding the baby.

I want the baby, he said.

Are you crazy?

No, but I want the baby. I'll
get someone to come by for his
things.

15   You're not touching this
baby, she said.

The baby had begun to cry
and she uncovered the blanket
from around his head.

Oh, oh, she said, looking at
the baby.

He moved toward her.

For God's sake! she said. She
took a step back into the kitchen.

20   I want the baby.

Get out of here!

She turned and tried to hold
the baby over in a corner behind
the stove.

He reached across the stove and tightened his hands on the baby.

Let go of him, he said.

Get away, get away! she cried.

The baby was red-faced and screaming. In the scuffle they knocked down a little flower pot that hung behind the stove.

25   He crowded her into the wall then, trying to break her grip, holding onto the baby and pushing his weight against her arm.

Let go of him, he said.

Don't, she said, you're hurting him!

He didn't talk again. The kitchen window gave no light. In the near dark he worked on her fisted fingers with one hand and with the other hand he gripped the screaming baby up under an arm near the shoulder.

She felt her fingers being forced open and the baby going from her. No, she said, just as her hands came loose. She would have it, this baby whose chubby face gazed up at them from the picture on the table. She grabbed for the baby's other arm. She caught the baby around the wrist and leaned back.

30   He would not give. He felt the baby going out of his hands and he pulled back hard. He pulled back very hard.

In this manner they decided the issue.

But he came up. He reached across the stove and tightened his hands on the baby.

Let go of him, he said.

25   Get away, get away! she cried.

The baby was red-faced and screaming. In the scuffle they knocked down a flowerpot that hung behind the stove.

He crowded her into the wall then, trying to break her grip. He held on to the baby and pushed with all his weight.

Let go of him, he said.

Don't, she said. You're hurting the baby, she said.

30   I'm not hurting the baby, he said.

The kitchen window gave no light. In the near-dark he worked on her fisted fingers with one hand and with the other hand he gripped the screaming baby up under an arm near the shoulder.

She felt her fingers being forced open. She felt the baby going from her.

No! she screamed just as her hands came loose.

She would have it, this baby. She grabbed for the baby's other arm. She caught the baby around the wrist and leaned back.

35   But he would not let go. He felt the baby slipping out of his hands and he pulled back very hard.

In this manner, the issue was decided.

Carver regarded this story as a breakthrough.

Cathedral   [1983]

This blind man, an old friend of my wife's, he was on his way to spend the night. His wife had died. So he was visiting the dead wife's relatives in Connecticut. He called my wife from his in-laws'. Arrangements were made. He would come by train, a five-hour trip, and my wife would meet him at the station. She hadn't seen him since she worked for him one summer in Seattle ten years ago. But she and the blind man had kept in touch. They made tapes and mailed them back and forth. I wasn't enthusiastic about his visit. He was no one I knew. And his being blind bothered me. My idea of blindness came from the movies. In the movies, the blind moved slowly and never laughed. Sometimes they were led by seeing-eye dogs. A blind man in my house was not something I looked forward to.

That summer in Seattle she had needed a job. She didn't have any money. The man she was going to marry at the end of the summer was in officers' training school. He didn't have any money, either. But she was in love with the guy, and he was in love with her, etc. She'd seen something in the paper: HELP WANTED—*Reading to Blind Man,* and a telephone number. She phoned and went over, was hired on the spot. She'd worked with this blind man all summer. She read stuff to him, case studies, reports, that sort of thing. She helped him organize his little office in the county social-service department. They'd become good friends, my wife and the blind man. How do I know these things? She told me. And she told me something else. On her last day in the office, the blind man asked if he could touch her face. She agreed to this. She told me he touched his fingers to every part of her face, her nose—even her neck! She never forgot it. She even tried to write a poem about it. She was always trying to write a poem. She wrote a poem or two every year, usually after something really important had happened to her.

When we first started going out together, she showed me the poem. In the poem, she recalled his fingers and the way they had moved around over her face. In the poem, she talked about what she had felt at the time, about what went through her mind when the blind man touched her nose and lips. I can remember I didn't think much of the poem. Of course, I didn't tell her that. Maybe I just don't understand poetry. I admit it's not the first thing I reach for when I pick up something to read.

Anyway, this man who'd first enjoyed her favors, the officer-to-be, he'd been her childhood sweetheart. So okay. I'm saying that at the end of the summer she let the blind man run his hands over her face, said goodbye to him, married her childhood etc., who was now a commissioned officer, and she moved away from Seattle. But they'd kept in touch, she and the blind man. She made the first contact after a year or so. She called him up one night from an Air Force base in Alabama. She wanted to talk. They talked. He asked her to send a tape and tell him about her life. She did this. She sent the tape. On the tape, she told the blind man about her husband and about their life together in the military. She told the blind man she loved her husband but she didn't like it where they lived and she didn't like it that he was part of the military-industrial thing. She told the blind man she'd written a poem and he was in it. She told him that she was writing a poem about what it was like to be an Air Force officer's wife. The poem wasn't finished yet. She was still writing it. The blind man made a tape. He sent her the tape. She made a tape. This went on for years. My wife's officer was posted to one base and then another. She sent tapes from Moody AFB, McGuire, McConnell, and finally Travis, near Sacramento, where one night she got to feeling lonely and cut off from people she kept losing in that moving-around life. She got to feeling she couldn't go it another step. She went in and swallowed all the pills and capsules in the medicine chest and washed them down with a bottle of gin. Then she got into a hot bath and passed out.

5   But instead of dying, she got sick. She threw up. Her officer—why should he have a name? he was the childhood sweetheart, and what more does he want?—came home from somewhere, found her, and called the ambulance. In time, she put it all on a tape and sent the tape to the blind man. Over the years, she put all kinds of stuff on tapes and sent the tapes off lickety-split. Next to writing a poem every year, I think it was her chief means of recreation. On one tape, she told the blind man she'd decided to live away from her officer for a time. On another tape, she told him about her divorce. She and I began going out, and of course she told her blind man about it. She told him everything, or so it seemed to me. Once she asked me if I'd like to hear the latest tape from the blind man. This was a year ago. I was on the tape, she said. So I said okay, I'd listen to it. I got us drinks and we settled down in the living room. We made ready to listen. First she inserted the tape into the player and adjusted a couple of dials. Then she pushed a lever. The tape squeaked and someone began to talk in this loud voice. She lowered the volume. After a few minutes of harmless chitchat, I heard my own name in the mouth of this stranger, this blind man I didn't even know! And then this: "From all you've said about him, I can only conclude—" But we were interrupted, a knock at the door, something, and we didn't ever get back to the tape. Maybe it was just as well. I'd heard all I wanted to.

Now this same blind man was coming to sleep in my house.

"Maybe I could take him bowling," I said to my wife. She was at the draining board doing scalloped potatoes. She put down the knife she was using and turned around.

"If you love me," she said, "you can do this for me. If you don't love me, okay. But if you had a friend, any friend, and the friend came to visit, I'd make him feel comfortable." She wiped her hands with the dish towel.

"I don't have any blind friends," I said.

10   "You don't have *any* friends," she said. "Period. Besides," she said, "god-damn it, his wife's just died! Don't you understand that? The man's lost his wife!"

I didn't answer. She'd told me a little about the blind man's wife. Her name was Beulah. Beulah! That's a name for a colored woman.

"Was his wife a Negro?" I asked.

"Are you crazy?" my wife said. "Have you just flipped or something?" She picked up a potato. I saw it hit the floor, then roll under the stove. "What's wrong with you?" she said. "Are you drunk?"

"I'm just asking," I said.

15   Right then my wife filled me in with more detail than I cared to know. I made a drink and sat at the kitchen table to listen. Pieces of the story began to fall into place.

Beulah had gone to work for the blind man the summer after my wife had stopped working for him. Pretty soon Beulah and the blind man had themselves a church wedding. It was a little wedding—who'd want to go to such a wedding in the first place?—just the two of them, plus the minister and the minister's wife. But it was a church wedding just the same. It was what Beulah had wanted, he'd said. But even then Beulah must have been carrying the cancer in her glands. After they had been inseparable for eight years—my wife's word, *inseparable*—Beulah's health went into a rapid decline. She died in a Seattle hospital room, the blind man sitting beside the bed and holding on to her hand. They'd married, lived and worked together, slept together—had sex, sure—and then the blind man had to bury her. All this without his having ever seen what the goddamned woman looked like. It was beyond my understanding. Hearing this, I felt sorry for the blind man for a little bit. And then I found myself thinking what a pitiful life this woman must have led. Imagine a woman who could never see herself as she was seen in the eyes of her loved one. A woman who could go on day after day and never receive the smallest compliment from her beloved. A woman whose husband could never read the expression on her face, be it misery or something better. Someone who could wear makeup or not—what difference to him? She could, if she wanted, wear green eye-shadow around one eye, a straight pin in her nostril, yellow slacks, and purple shoes, no matter. And then to slip off into death, the blind man's hand on her hand, his blind eyes streaming tears—I'm imagining now—her last thought maybe this: that he never even knew what she looked like, and she on an express to the grave. Robert was left with a small insurance policy and a half of a twenty-peso Mexican coin. The other half of the coin went into the box with her. Pathetic.

So when the time rolled around, my wife went to the depot to pick him up. With nothing to do but wait—sure, I blamed him for that—I was having a drink and watching the TV when I heard the car pull into the drive. I got up from the sofa with my drink and went to the window to have a look.

I saw my wife laughing as she parked the car. I saw her get out of the car and shut the door. She was still wearing a smile. Just amazing. She went around to the other side of the car to where the blind man was already starting to get out. This blind man, feature this, he was wearing a full beard! A beard on a blind man! Too much, I say. The blind man reached into the back seat and dragged out a suitcase. My wife took his arm, shut the car door, and, talking all the way, moved him down the drive and then up the steps to the front porch. I turned off the TV. I finished my drink, rinsed the glass, dried my hands. Then I went to the door.

My wife said, "I want you to meet Robert. Robert, this is my husband. I've told you all about him." She was beaming. She had this blind man by his coat sleeve.

20   The blind man let go of his suitcase and up came his hand. I took it. He squeezed hard, held my hand, and then he let it go.

"I feel like we've already met," he boomed.

"Likewise," I said. I didn't know what else to say. Then I said, "Welcome. I've heard a lot about you." We began to move then, a little group, from the porch into the living room, my wife guiding him by the arm. The blind man was carrying his suitcase in his other hand. My wife said things like, "To your left here, Robert. That's right. Now watch it, there's a chair. That's it. Sit down right here. This is the sofa. We just bought this sofa two weeks ago."

I started to say something about the old sofa. I'd liked that old sofa. But I didn't say anything. Then I wanted to say something else, small-talk, about the scenic ride along the Hudson. How going *to* New York, you should sit on the right-hand side of the train, and coming *from* New York, the left-hand side.

"Did you have a good train ride?" I said. "Which side of the train did you sit on, by the way?"

25   "What a question, which side!" my wife said. "What's it matter which side?" she said.

"I just asked," I said.

"Right side," the blind man said. "I hadn't been on a train in nearly forty years. Not since I was a kid. With my folks. That's been a long time. I'd nearly forgotten the sensation. I have winter in my beard now," he said. "So I've been told, anyway. Do I look distinguished, my dear?" the blind man said to my wife.

"You look distinguished, Robert," she said. "Robert," she said. "Robert, it's just so good to see you."

My wife finally took her eyes off the blind man and looked at me. I had the feeling she didn't like what she saw. I shrugged.

30   I've never met, or personally known, anyone who was blind. This blind man was late forties, a heavy-set, balding man with stooped shoulders, as if he carried a great weight there. He wore brown slacks, brown shoes, a light-brown shirt, a tie, a sports coat. Spiffy. He also had this full beard. But he didn't use a cane and he didn't wear dark glasses. I'd always thought dark glasses were a must for the blind. Fact was, I wished he had a pair. At first glance, his eyes looked like anyone else's eyes. But if you looked close, there was something different about them. Too much white in the iris, for one thing, and the pupils seemed to move around in the sockets without his knowing it or being able to stop it. Creepy. As I stared at his face, I saw the left pupil turn in toward his nose while the other made an effort to keep in one place. But it was only an effort, for that eye was on the roam without his knowing it or wanting it to be.

I said, "Let me get you a drink. What's your pleasure? We have a little of everything. It's one of our pastimes."

"Bub, I'm a Scotch man myself," he said fast enough in this big voice.

"Right," I said. Bub! "Sure you are. I knew it."

He let his fingers touch his suitcase, which was sitting alongside the sofa. He was taking his bearings. I didn't blame him for that.

35   "I'll move that up to your room," my wife said.

"No, that's fine," the blind man said loudly. "It can go up when I go up."

"A little water with the Scotch?" I said.

"Very little," he said.

"I knew it," I said.

40   He said, "Just a tad. The Irish actor, Barry Fitzgerald? I'm like that fellow. When I drink water, Fitzgerald said, I drink water. When I drink whiskey, I drink whiskey." My wife laughed. The blind man brought his hand up under his beard. He lifted his beard slowly and let it drop.

I did the drinks, three big glasses of Scotch with a splash of water in each. Then we made ourselves comfortable and talked about Robert's travels. First the long flight from the West Coast to Connecticut, we covered that. Then from Connecticut up here by train. We had another drink concerning that leg of the trip.

I remembered having read somewhere that the blind didn't smoke because, as speculation had it, they couldn't see the smoke they exhaled. I thought I knew that much and that much only about blind people. But this blind man smoked his cigarette down to the nubbin and then lit another one. This blind man filled his ashtray and my wife emptied it.

When we sat down at the table for dinner, we had another drink. My wife heaped Robert's plate with cube steak, scalloped potatoes, green beans. I buttered him up two slices of bread. I said, "Here's bread and butter for you." I swallowed some of my drink. "Now let us pray," I said, and the blind man lowered his head. My wife looked at me, her mouth agape. "Pray the phone won't ring and the food doesn't get cold," I said.

We dug in. We ate everything there was to eat on the table. We ate like there was no tomorrow. We didn't talk. We ate. We scarfed. We grazed that table. We were into serious eating. The blind man had right away located his foods, he knew just where everything was on his plate. I watched with admiration as he used his knife and fork on the meat. He'd cut two pieces of meat, fork the meat into his mouth, and then go all out for the scalloped potatoes, the beans next, and then he'd tear off a hunk of buttered bread and eat that. He'd follow this up with a big drink of milk. It didn't seem to bother him to use his fingers once in a while, either.

45   We finished everything, including half a strawberry pie. For a few moments, we sat as if stunned. Sweat beaded on our faces. Finally, we got up from the table and left the dirty places. We didn't look back. We took ourselves into the living room and sank into our places again. Robert and my wife sat on the sofa. I took the big chair. We had us two or three more drinks while they talked about the major things that had come to pass for them in the past ten years. For the most part, I just listened. Now and then I joined in. I didn't want him to think I'd left the room, and I didn't want her to think I was feeling left out. They talked of things that had happened to them—to them!—these past ten years. I waited in vain to hear my name on my wife's sweet lips: "And then my dear husband came into my life"— something like that. But I heard nothing of the sort. More talk of Robert. Robert had done a little of everything, it seemed, a regular blind jack-of-all-trades. But most recently he and his wife had had an Amway distributorship, from which, I gathered, they'd earned their living, such as it was. The blind man was also a ham radio operator. He talked in his loud voice about conversations he'd had with fellow operators in Guam, in the Philippines, in Alaska, and even in Tahiti. He said he'd have a lot of friends there if he ever wanted to go visit those places. From time to time, he'd turn his blind face toward me, put his hand under his beard, ask me something. How long had I been in my present position? (Three years.) Did I like my work? (I didn't.) Was I going to stay with it? (What were the options?) Finally, when I thought he was beginning to run down, I got up and turned on the TV.

My wife looked at me with irritation. She was heading toward a boil. Then she looked at the blind man and said, "Robert, do you have a TV?"

The blind man said, "My dear, I have two TVs. I have a color set and a black-and-white thing, an old relic. It's funny, but if I turn the TV on, and I'm always turning it on, I turn on the color set. It's funny, don't you think?"

I didn't know what to say to that. I had absolutely nothing to say to that. No opinion. So I watched the news program and tried to listen to what the announcer was saying.

"This is a color TV," the blind man said. "Don't ask me how, but I can tell."

50   "We traded up a while ago," I said.

The blind man had another taste of his drink. He lifted his beard, sniffed it, and let it fall. He leaned forward on the sofa. He positioned his ashtray on the coffee table, then put the lighter to his cigarette. He leaned back on the sofa and crossed his legs at the ankles.

My wife covered her mouth, and then she yawned. She stretched. She said, "I think I'll go upstairs and put on my robe. I think I'll change into something else. Robert, you make yourself comfortable," she said.

"I'm comfortable," the blind man said.

"I want you to feel comfortable in this house," she said.

55   "I am comfortable," the blind man said.

After she'd left the room, he and I listened to the weather report and then to the sports roundup. By that time, she'd been gone so long I didn't know if she was going to come back. I thought she might have gone to bed. I wished she'd come back downstairs. I didn't want to be left alone with a blind man. I asked him if he wanted another drink, and he said sure. Then I asked if he wanted to smoke some dope with me. I said I'd just rolled a number. I hadn't, but I planned to do so in about two shakes.

"I'll try some with you," he said.

"Damn right," I said. "That's the stuff."

I got our drinks and sat down on the sofa with him. Then I rolled us two fat numbers. I lit one and passed it. I brought it to his fingers. He took it and inhaled.

60   "Hold it as long as you can," I said. I could tell he didn't know the first thing.

My wife came back downstairs wearing her pink robe and her pink slippers.

"What do I smell?" she said.

"We thought we'd have us some cannabis," I said.

My wife gave me a savage look. Then she looked at the blind man and said, "Robert, I didn't know you smoked."

65   He said, "I do now, my dear. There's a first time for everything. But I don't feel anything yet."

"This stuff is pretty mellow," I said. "This stuff is mild. It's dope you can reason with," I said. "It doesn't mess you up."

"Not much it doesn't, bub," he said, and laughed.

My wife sat on the sofa between the blind man and me. I passed her the number. She took it and toked and then passed it back to me. "Which way is this going?" she said. Then she said, "I shouldn't be smoking this. I can hardly keep my eyes open as it is. That dinner did me in. I shouldn't have eaten so much."

"It was the strawberry pie," the blind man said. "That's what did it," he said, and he laughed his big laugh. Then he shook his head.

70   "There's more strawberry pie," I said.

"Do you want some more, Robert?" my wife said.

"Maybe in a little while," he said.

We gave our attention to the TV. My wife yawned again. She said, "Your bed is made up when you feel like going to bed, Robert. I know you must have had a long day. When you're ready to go to bed, say so." She pulled his arm. "Robert?"

He came to and said, "I've had a real nice time. This beats tapes, doesn't it?"

75   I said, "Coming at you," and I put the number between his fingers. He inhaled, held the smoke, and then let it go. It was like he'd been doing it since he was nine years old.

"Thanks, bub," he said. "But I think this is all for me. I think I'm beginning to feel it," he said. He held the burning roach out for my wife.

"Same here," she said. "Ditto. Me, too." She took the roach and passed
it to me. "I may just sit here for a while between you two guys with my eyes
closed. But don't let me bother you, okay? Either one of you. If it bothers
you, say so. Otherwise, I may just sit here with my eyes closed until you're
ready to go to bed," she said. "Your bed's made up, Robert, when you're
ready. It's right next to our room at the top of the stairs. We'll show you up
when you're ready. You wake me up now, you guys, if I fall asleep." She
said that and then she closed her eyes and went to sleep.

The news program ended. I got up and changed the channel. I sat back
down on the sofa. I wished my wife hadn't pooped out. Her head lay across
the back of the sofa, her mouth open. She'd turned so that her robe slipped
away from her legs, exposing a juicy thigh. I reached to draw her robe back
over her, and it was then that I glanced at the blind man. What the hell! I
flipped the robe open again.

"You say when you want some strawberry pie," I said.

80   "I will," he said.

I said, "Are you tired? Do you want me to take you up to your bed? Are
you ready to hit the hay?"

"Not yet," he said. "No, I'll stay up with you, bub. If that's all right. I'll
stay up until you're ready to turn in. We haven't had a chance to talk. Know
what I mean? I feel like me and her monopolized the evening." He lifted his
beard and he let it fall. He picked up his cigarettes and his lighter.

"That's all right," I said. Then I said, "I'm glad for the company."

And I guess I was. Every night I smoked dope and stayed up as long as I
could before I fell asleep. My wife and I hardly ever went to bed at the same
time. When I did go to sleep, I had these dreams. Sometimes I'd wake up
from one of them, my heart going crazy.

85   Something about the church and the Middle Ages was on the TV. Not
your run-of-the-mill TV fare. I wanted to watch something else. I turned to
the other channels. But there was nothing on them, either. So I turned back
to the first channel and apologized.

"Bub, it's all right," the blind man said. "It's fine with me. Whatever you
want to watch is okay. I'm always learning something. Learning never ends.
It won't hurt me to learn something tonight. I got ears," he said.

We didn't say anything for a time. He was leaning forward with his
head turned at me, his right ear aimed in the direction of the set. Very dis-
concerting. Now and then his eyelids drooped and then they snapped open
again. Now and then he put his fingers into his beard and tugged, like he
was thinking about something he was hearing on the television.

On the screen, a group of men wearing cowls was being set upon and
tormented by men dressed in skeleton costumes and men dressed as devils.
The men dressed as devils wore devil masks, horns, and long tails. This
pageant was part of a procession. The Englishman who was narrating the
thing said it took place in Spain once a year. I tried to explain to the blind
man what was happening.

"Skeletons," he said. "I know about skeletons," he said, and he nodded.

90   The TV showed this one cathedral. Then there was a long, slow look at
another one. Finally, the picture switched to the famous one in Paris, with

its flying buttresses and its spires reaching up to the clouds. The camera pulled away to show the whole of the cathedral rising above the skyline.

There were times when the Englishman who was telling the thing would shut up, would simply let the camera move around the cathedrals. Or else the camera would tour the countryside, men in fields walking behind oxen. I waited as long as I could. Then I felt I had to say something. I said, "They're showing the outside of this cathedral now. Gargoyles. Little statues carved to look like monsters. Now I guess they're in Italy. Yeah, they're in Italy. There's paintings on the walls of this one church."

"Are those fresco paintings, bub?" he asked, and he sipped from his drink.

I reached for my glass. But it was empty. I tried to remember what I could remember. "You're asking me are those frescoes?" I said. "That's a good question. I don't know."

The camera moved to a cathedral outside Lisbon. The differences in the Portuguese cathedral compared with the French and Italian were not that great. But they were there. Mostly the interior stuff. Then something occurred to me, and I said, "Something has occurred to me. Do you have any idea what a cathedral is? What they look like, that is? Do you follow me? If somebody says cathedral to you, do you have any notion what they're talking about? Do you know the difference between that and a Baptist church, say?"

95   He let the smoke dribble from his mouth. "I know they took hundreds of workers fifty or a hundred years to build," he said. "I just heard the man say that, of course. I know generations of the same families worked on a cathedral. I heard him say that, too. The men who began their life's work on them, they never lived to see the completion of their work. In that wise, bub, they're no different from the rest of us, right?" He laughed. Then his eyelids drooped again. His head nodded. He seemed to be snoozing. Maybe he was imagining himself in Portugal. The TV was showing another cathedral now. This one was in Germany. The Englishman's voice droned on. "Cathedrals," the blind man said. He sat up and rolled his head back and forth. "If you want the truth, bub, that's about all I know. What I just said. What I heard him say. But maybe you could describe one to me? I wish you'd do it. I'd like that. If you want to know, I really don't have a good idea."

I stared hard at the shot of the cathedral on the TV. How could I even begin to describe it? But say my life depended on it. Say my life was being threatened by an insane guy who said I had to do it or else.

I stared some more at the cathedral before the picture flipped off into the countryside. There was no use. I turned to the blind man and said, "To begin with, they're very tall." I was looking around the room for clues. "They reach way up. Up and up. Toward the sky. They're so big, some of them, they have to have these supports. To help hold them up, so to speak. These supports are called buttresses. They remind me of viaducts, for some reason. But maybe you don't know viaducts, either? Sometimes the cathedrals have devils and such carved into the front. Sometimes lords and ladies. Don't ask me why this is," I said.

He was nodding. The whole upper part of his body seemed to be moving back and forth.

"I'm not doing so good, am I?" I said.

100   He stopped nodding and leaned forward on the edge of the sofa. As he listened to me, he was running his fingers through his beard. I wasn't getting through to him, I could see that. But he waited for me to go on just the same. He nodded, like he was trying to encourage me. I tried to think what else to say. "They're really big," I said. "They're massive. They're built of stone. Marble, too, sometimes. In those olden days, when they built cathedrals, men wanted to be close to God. In those olden days, God was an important part of everyone's life. You could tell this from their cathedral-building. I'm sorry," I said, "but it looks like that's the best I can do for you. I'm just no good at it."

"That's all right, bub," the blind man said. "Hey, listen. I hope you don't mind my asking you. Can I ask you something? Let me ask you a simple question, yes or no. I'm just curious and there's no offense. You're my host. But let me ask if you are in any way religious? You don't mind my asking?"

I shook my head. He couldn't see that, though. A wink is the same as a nod to a blind man. "I guess I don't believe in it. In anything. Sometimes it's hard. You know what I'm saying?"

"Sure, I do," he said.

"Right," I said.

105   The Englishman was still holding forth. My wife sighed in her sleep. She drew a long breath and went on with her sleeping.

"You'll have to forgive me," I said. "But I can't tell you what a cathedral looks like. It just isn't in me to do it. I can't do any more than I've done."

The blind man sat very still, his head down, as he listened to me.

I said, "The truth is, cathedrals don't mean anything special to me. Nothing. Cathedrals. They're something to look at on late-night TV. That's all they are."

It was then that the blind man cleared his throat. He brought something up. He took a handkerchief from his back pocket. Then he said, "I get it, bub. It's okay. It happens. Don't worry about it," he said. "Hey, listen to me. Will you do me a favor? I got an idea. Why don't you find us some heavy paper? And a pen. We'll do something. We'll draw one together. Get us a pen and some heavy paper. Go on, bub, get the stuff," he said.

110   So I went upstairs. My legs felt like they didn't have any strength in them. They felt like they did after I'd done some running. In my wife's room, I looked around. I found some ballpoints in a little basket on her table. And then I tried to think where to look for the kind of paper he was talking about.

Downstairs, in the kitchen, I found a shopping bag with onion skins in the bottom of the bag. I emptied the bag and shook it. I brought it into the living room and sat down with it near his legs. I moved some things, smoothed the wrinkles from the bag, spread it out on the coffee table.

The blind man got down from the sofa and sat next to me on the carpet.

He ran his fingers over the paper. He went up and down the sides of the paper. The edges, even the edges. He fingered the corners.

"All right," he said. "All right, let's do her."

115   He found my hand, the hand with the pen. He closed his hand over my hand. "Go ahead, bub, draw," he said. "Draw. You'll see. I'll follow along with you. It'll be okay. Just begin now like I'm telling you. You'll see. Draw," the blind man said.

So I began. First I drew a box that looked like a house. It could have been the house I lived in. Then I put a roof on it. At either end of the roof, I drew spires. Crazy.

"Swell," he said. "Terrific. You're doing fine," he said. "Never thought anything like this could happen in your lifetime, did you, bub? Well, it's a strange life, we all know that. Go on now. Keep it up."

I put in windows with arches. I drew flying buttresses. I hung great doors. I couldn't stop. The TV station went off the air. I put down the pen and closed and opened my fingers. The blind man felt around over the paper. He moved the tips of his fingers over the paper, all over what I had drawn, and he nodded.

"Doing fine," the blind man said.

120   I took up the pen again, and he found my hand. I kept at it. I'm no artist. But I kept drawing just the same.

My wife opened up her eyes and gazed at us. She sat up on the sofa, her robe hanging open. She said, "What are you doing? Tell me, I want to know."

I didn't answer her.

The blind man said, "We're drawing a cathedral. Me and him are working on it. Press hard," he said to me. "That's right. That's good," he said. "Sure. You got it, bub, I can tell. You didn't think you could. But you can, can't you? You're cooking with gas now. You know what I'm saying? We're going to really have us something here in a minute. How's the old arm?" he said. "Put some people in there now. What's a cathedral without people?"

My wife said, "What's going on? Robert, what are you doing? What's going on?"

125   "It's all right," he said to her. "Close your eyes now," the blind man said to me.

I did it. I closed them just like he said.

"Are they closed?" he said. "Don't fudge."

"They're closed," I said.

"Keep them that way," he said. He said, "Don't stop now. Draw."

130   So we kept on with it. His fingers rode my fingers as my hand went over the paper. It was like nothing else in my life up to now.

Then he said, "I think that's it. I think you got it," he said. "Take a look. What do you think?"

But I had my eyes closed. I thought I'd keep them that way for a little longer. I thought it was something I ought to do.

"Well?" he said. "Are you looking?"

My eyes were still closed. I was in my house. I knew that. But I didn't feel like I was inside anything.

135   "It's really something," I said.

TOPICS FOR CRITICAL THINKING AND WRITING

1. Describe your response to the narrator in the opening paragraphs of the story. What is his tone of voice? What is his attitude toward himself and toward his wife and the blind man?

2. Does the narrator know who he is, or is he hiding from who he is?

3. The narrator has a lot to say, much of it unpleasant, about his wife. Write a page or two in the wife's voice, expressing her view of him.

4. Why does Carver want a blind man in this story? Wouldn't the story have worked just as effectively if the character had some other disability or affliction?
5. The narrator and the blind man make an important connection at the end, but what kind of connection is it? Is Carver suggesting that the narrator is now on the path to becoming a better person? Do you find this change convincing, or not?

TALKING ABOUT STORIES

Larry McCaffery and Sinda Gregory have interviewed many contemporary authors and have published some of the interviews in a collection entitled Alive and Writing *(1987). In the following selections from a long interview, Carver talks about his life and work.*

SINDA GREGORY. Many of your stories either open with the ordinary being slightly disturbed by this sense of menace you've just mentioned, or they develop in that direction. Is this tendency the result of your conviction that the world *is* menacing for most people? Or does it have more to do with an aesthetic choice—that menace contains more interesting possibilities for storytelling?

RAYMOND CARVER. The world is a menacing place for many of the people in my stories, yes. The people I've chosen to write about *do* feel menace, and I think, many, if not most, people feel the world is a menacing place. Probably not so many people who will see this interview feel menace in the sense I'm talking about. Most of our friends and acquaintances, yours and mine, don't feel this way. But try living on the other side of the tracks for a while. Menace is there, and it's palpable. As to the second part of your question, that's true, too. Menace does contain, for me at least, more interesting possibilities to explore. . . .

SINDA GREGORY. A reader is immediately struck with the "pared down" quality of your work, especially your work before *Cathedral.* Was this style something that evolved, or had it been with you from the beginning?

RAYMOND CARVER. From the very beginning I loved the rewriting process as much as the initial execution. I've always loved taking sentences and playing with them, rewriting them, paring them down to where they seem solid somehow. This may have resulted from being John Gardner's student, because he told me something I immediately responded to: If you can say it in fifteen words rather than twenty or thirty words, then say it in fifteen words. That struck me with the force of revelation. There I was, groping to find my own way, and here someone was telling me something that somehow conjoined with what I already wanted to do. It was the most natural thing in the world for me to go back and refine what was happening on the page and eliminate the padding. The last few days I've been reading Flaubert's letters, and he says some things that seem relevant to my own aesthetic. At one point when Flaubert was writing *Madame Bovary,* he would knock off at midnight or one in the morning and write letters to his mistress, Louise Colet, about the construction of the book and his general notion of aesthetics. One passage he wrote her that really struck me was when he said, "The artist in his work must be like God in his creation—invisible and all powerful; he must be everywhere felt but nowhere seen." I like the last part of that especially. There's another interesting remark when Flaubert is writing to his editors at the magazine that published the book in installments. They were just getting ready to serialize *Madame Bovary* and were going to make a lot of cuts in the text because they were afraid they were going to be closed down by the government if they published it just as Flaubert wrote it, so Flaubert tells them that if they make the cuts they can't publish the book, but they'll still be friends. The last line of this letter is: "I know how to distinguish between literature and literary business"—another insight I respond to. Even in these letters his prose is astonishing: "Prose must stand upright from one end to the other, like a wall whose ornamentation continues down to its very base." "Prose is architecture." "Everything must be done coldly, with poise." "Last week I spent five days writing one page." One of the interesting things about the Flaubert book is the way it demonstrates how self-consciously he was setting out to do something very special and different with prose. He consciously tried to make prose an art form. If you look at what else was being published in Europe in 1855, when *Madame Bovary* was published, you realize what an achievement the book really is. . . .

LARRY MCCAFFERY. Another distinctive feature of your work is that you usually present characters that most writers don't deal with—that is, people who are basically inarticulate, who can't verbalize their plights, who often don't seem to really grasp what is happening to them.

RAYMOND CARVER. I don't think of this as being especially "distinctive" or nontraditional because I feel perfectly comfortable with these people while I'm working. I've known people like this all my life. Essentially, I *am* one of those confused, befuddled people, I come from people like that, those are the people I've worked with and earned my living beside for years. That's why I've never had any interest whatsoever in writing a story or a poem that has anything to do with the academic life, with teachers or students and so forth. I'm just not that interested. The things that have made an indelible impression on me are the things I saw in lives I witnessed being lived around me, and in the life I myself lived. These were lives where people really *were* scared when someone knocked on their door, day or night, or when the telephone rang; they didn't know how they were going to pay the rent or what they could do if their refrigerator went out. Anatole Broyard tries to criticize my story "Preservation" by saying, "So the refrigerator breaks—why don't they just call a repairman and get it fixed?" That kind of remark is dumb. You bring a repairman out to fix your refrigerator and it's sixty bucks to *fix* it; and who knows how much if the thing is completely broken? Well, Broyard may not be aware of it, but some people can't afford to bring in a repairman if it's going to cost them sixty bucks, just like they don't get a doctor if they don't have insurance, and their teeth go bad because they can't afford to go to a dentist when they need one. That kind of situation doesn't seem unrealistic or artificial to me. It also doesn't seem that, in focusing on this group of people, I have really been doing anything all that different from other writers. Chekhov was writing about a submerged population a hundred years ago. Short story writers have always been doing that. Not all of Chekhov's stories are about people who are down and out, but a significant number of them deal with that submerged population I'm talking about. He wrote about doctors and businessmen and teachers sometimes, but he also gave voice to people who were not so articulate. He found a means of letting those people have their say as well. So in writing about people who aren't so articulate and who are confused and scared, I'm not doing anything radically different.

LARRY MCCAFFERY. Aren't there formal problems in writing about this group of people? I mean, you can't have them sit around in drawing rooms endlessly analyzing their situations, the way James does, or, in a different sense, the way Bellow does. I suppose setting the scene, composing it, must be especially important from a technical standpoint.

RAYMOND CARVER. If you mean literally just setting the scene, that's the least of my worries. The scene is easy to set: I just open the door and see what's inside. I pay a lot of attention to trying to make the people talk the right way. By this I don't mean just *what* they say, but *how* they say it, and *why*. I guess *tone* is what I'm talking about, partly. There's never any chit-chat in my stories. Everything said is for a reason and adds, I want to think, to the overall impression of the story.

SINDA GREGORY. People usually emphasize the realistic aspects of your work, but I feel there's a quality about your fiction that is *not* basically realistic. It's as if something is happening almost off the page, a dreamy sense of irrationality, almost like Kafka's fiction.

RAYMOND CARVER. Presumably my fiction is in the realistic tradition (as opposed to the really far-out side), but just telling it like it is bores me. It really does. People couldn't possibly read pages of description about the way people *really* talk, about what *really* happens in their lives. They'd just snore away, of course. If you look carefully at my stories, I don't think you'll find people talking the way people do in real life. People always say that Hemingway had a great ear for dialogue, and he did. But no one ever talked in real life like they do in Hemingway's fiction. At least not until after they've *read* Hemingway.

ON REWRITING

The following paragraph comes from Carver's afterword to Fires *(1983).*

I like to mess around with my stories. I'd rather tinker with a story after writing it, and then tinker some more, changing this, changing that, than have to write the story in the first place. That initial writing just seems to me the hard place I have to get to in order to go on and have fun with the story. Rewriting for me is not a chore—it's something I like to do. I think by nature I'm more deliberate and careful than I am spontaneous, and maybe that explains something. Maybe not. Maybe there's no connection except the one I'm making. But I do know that revising the work once it's done is something that comes naturally to me and is something I take pleasure in doing. Maybe I revise because it gradually takes me into the heart of what the story is *about*. I have to keep trying to see if I can find that out. It's a process more than a fixed position.

ON "CATHEDRAL"

This paragraph comes from an interview conducted by Kay Bonetti, published in Saturday Review, *September–October 1983.*

There was a period of several months when I didn't write anything. And then the first story that I wrote was "Cathedral," which is unlike anything I have ever done before. All the stories in this book [the book, like this story, is called *Cathedral*] are fuller and more interesting, somehow. They are more generous. They're not quite so pared down. I went as far in the other direction as I wanted to go. My life's changed to a degree since I started giving my work to a woman in Syracuse who has a word processor. She is able to type up the story and give me the fair copy, and I can mark it up and change it to my heart's content and give it back to her, and a few hours later I can have fair copy back again. I've never been able to work that way before, and I'm sure that that accounts to a degree for the fact that I was able to do, for me, so many stories in a fairly short period of time. But the rewriting and revising is something very dear to my heart and something close to the hearts of many writers of my acquaintance. Looking at the first drafts of great writers is very heartening and very instructive because there are so many changes. Tolstoy made so many changes in his proof that quite often the entire material would have to be set again, because he was revising right down to the time of publication. John Gardner worked that way. Any number of writers. I'm never quite finished with the work.

ALICE MUNRO: TWO STORIES, AN ESSAY, AND AN INTERVIEW

ALICE MUNRO

Alice Munro was born in 1931 in Wingham, Ontario, Canada, a relatively rural community and the sort of place in which she sets much of her fiction. She began publishing stories when she was an undergraduate at the University of Western Ontario. She left Western after two years, worked in a library and in a bookstore, then married, moved to Victoria, British Columbia, and founded a bookstore there. She continued to write while raising three children. She divorced and remarried; much of her fiction concerns marriage or divorce, which is to say it concerns shifting relationships in a baffling world.
We print two stories, an essay, and an interview.

Boys and Girls

[1968]

My father was a fox farmer. That is, he raised silver foxes, in pens; and in the fall and early winter, when their fur was prime, he killed them and skinned them and sold their pelts to the Hudson's Bay Company or the Montreal Fur Traders. These companies supplied us with heroic calendars to hang, one on each side of the kitchen door. Against a background of cold blue sky and black pine forests and treacherous northern rivers, plumed adventurers planted the flags of England or of France; magnificent savages bent their backs to the portage.

For several weeks before Christmas, my father worked after supper in the cellar of our house. The cellar was whitewashed, and lit by a hundred-watt bulb over the worktable. My brother Laird and I sat on the top step and watched. My father removed the pelt inside-out from the body of the fox, which looked surprisingly small, mean and rat-like, deprived of its arrogant weight of fur. The naked, slippery bodies were collected in a sack and buried at the dump. One time the hired man, Henry Bailey, had taken a swipe at me with this sack, saying, "Christmas present!" My mother thought that was not funny. In fact she disliked the whole pelting operation—that was what the killing, skinning, and preparation of the furs was called—and wished it did not have to take place in the house. There was the smell. After the pelt had been stretched inside-out on a long board my father scraped away delicately, removing the little clotted webs of blood vessels, the bubbles of fat; the smell of blood and animal fat, with the strong primitive odor of the fox itself, penetrated all parts of the house. I found it reassuringly seasonal, like the smell of oranges and pine needles.

Henry Bailey suffered from bronchial troubles. He would cough and cough until his narrow face turned scarlet, and his light blue, derisive eyes filled up with tears; then he took the lid off the stove, and, standing well back, shot out a great clot of phlegm—hsss—straight into the heart of the flames. We admired him for this performance and for his ability to make his stomach growl at will, and for his laughter, which was full of high whistlings and gurglings and involved the whole faulty machinery of his chest. It was sometimes hard to tell what he was laughing at, and always possible that it might be us.

After we had been sent to bed we could still smell fox and still hear Henry's laugh, but these things, reminders of the warm, safe, brightly lit downstairs world, seemed lost and diminished, floating on the stale cold air upstairs. We were afraid at night in the winter. We were not afraid of *outside* though this was the time of year when snowdrifts curled around our house like sleeping whales and the wind harassed us all night, coming up from the buried fields, the frozen swamp, with its old bugbear chorus of threats and misery. We were afraid of *inside,* the room where we slept. At this time the upstairs of our house was not finished. A brick chimney went up one wall. In the middle of the floor was a square hole, with a wooden railing around it; that was where the stairs came up. On the other side of the stairwell were the things that nobody had any use for anymore—a soldiery roll of linoleum, standing on end, a wicker baby carriage, a fern basket, china jugs and basins with cracks in them, a picture of the Battle of Balaclava, very sad to look at. I had told Laird, as soon as he was old enough to understand such things, that bats and skeletons lived over there; whenever a man escaped from the country jail, twenty miles away, I imagined that he had somehow let himself in the window and was hiding behind the linoleum. But we had rules to keep us safe. When the light was on, we were safe as long as we did not step off the square of worn carpet which defined our bedroom-space; when the light was off no place was safe but the beds themselves. I had to turn out the light kneeling on the end of my bed, and stretching as far as I could to reach the cord.

5   In the dark we lay on our beds, our narrow life rafts, and fixed our eyes on the faint light coming up the stairwell, and sang songs. Laird sang "Jingle Bells," which he would sing any time, whether it was Christmas or not, and I sang "Danny Boy." I loved the sound of my own voice, frail and supplicating, rising in the dark. We could make out the tall frosted shapes of the windows now, gloomy and white. When I came to the part, *When I am dead, as dead I well may be*—a fit of shivering caused not by the cold sheets but by pleasurable emotion almost silenced me. *You'll kneel and say, an Ave there above me*—What was an Ave? Every day I forgot to find out.

Laird went straight from singing to sleep. I could hear his long, satisfied, bubbly breaths. Now for the time that remained to me, the most perfectly private and perhaps the best time of the whole day, I arranged myself tightly under the covers and went on with one of the stories I was telling myself from night to night. These stories were about myself, when I had grown a little older; they took place in a world that was recognizably mine, yet one that presented opportunities for courage, boldness and self-sacrifice, as mine never did. I rescued people from a bombed building (it discouraged me that the real war had gone on so far away from Jubilee). I shot two rabid wolves who were menacing the schoolyard (the teachers cowered terrified at my back). I rode a fine horse spiritedly down the main street of Jubilee, acknowledging the townspeople's gratitude for some yet-to-be-worked-out piece of heroism (nobody ever rode a horse there, except King Billy in the Orangemen's Day[1] parade). There was always riding and shooting in these stories, though I had only been on a horse twice—bareback because we did not own a saddle—and the second time I had slid right around and dropped under the horse's feet; it had stepped placidly over me. I really was learning to shoot, but I could not hit anything yet, not even tin cans on fence posts.

Alive, the foxes inhabited a world my father made for them. It was surrounded by a high guard fence, like a medieval town, with a gate that was padlocked at night. Along the streets of this town were ranged large, sturdy pens. Each of them had a real door that a man could go through, a wooden ramp along the wire, for the foxes to run up and down on, and a kennel—something like a clothes chest with airholes—where they slept and stayed in winter and had their young. There were feeding and watering dishes attached to the wire in such a way that they could be emptied and cleaned from the outside. The dishes were made of old tin cans, and the ramps and kennels of odds and ends of old lumber. Everything was tidy and ingenious;

---

[1]**Orangemen's Day** The Orange Society is named for William of Orange, who, as King William III of England, defeated James II of England at the Battle of the Boyne on 12 July 1609. It sponsors an annual procession on 12 July.

my father was tirelessly inventive and his favorite book in the world was Robinson Crusoe. He had fitted a tin drum on a wheelbarrow, for bringing water to the pens. This was my job in summer, when the foxes had to have water twice a day. Between nine and ten o'clock in the morning, and again after supper, I filled the drum at the pump and trundled it down through the barnyard to the pens, where I parked it, and filled my watering can and went along the streets. Laird came too, with his little cream and green gardening can, filled too full and knocking against his legs and slopping water on his canvas shoes. I had the real watering can, my father's, though I could only carry it three-quarters full.

The foxes all had names, which were printed on a tin plate and hung beside their doors. They were not named when they were born, but when they survived the first year's pelting and were added to the breeding stock. Those my father had named were called names like Prince, Bob, Wally and Betty. Those I had named were called Star or Turk, or Maureen or Diana. Laird named one Maud after a hired girl we had when he was little, one Harold after a boy at school, and one Mexico, he did not say why.

Naming them did not make pets out of them, or anything like it. Nobody but my father ever went into the pens, and he had twice had blood-poisoning from bites. When I was bringing them their water they prowled up and down on the paths they had made inside their pens, barking seldom—they saved that for nighttime, when they might get up a chorus of community frenzy—but always watching me, their eyes burning, clear gold, in their pointed, malevolent faces. They were beautiful for their delicate legs and heavy, aristocratic tails and the bright fur sprinkled on dark down their backs—which gave them their name—but especially for their faces, drawn exquisitely sharp in pure hostility, and their golden eyes.

10   Besides carrying water I helped my father when he cut the long grass, and the lamb's quarter and flowering money-musk, that grew between the pens. He cut with the scythe and I raked into piles. Then he took a pitchfork and threw fresh-cut grass all over the top of the pens to keep the foxes cooler and shade their coats, which were browned by too much sun. My father did not talk to me unless it was about the job we were doing. In this he was quite different from my mother, who, if she was feeling cheerful, would tell me all sorts of things—the name of a dog she had when she was a little girl, the names of boys she had gone out with later on when she was grown up, and what certain dresses of hers had looked like—she could not imagine now what had become of them. Whatever thoughts and stories my father had were private, and I was shy of him and would never ask him questions. Nevertheless I worked willingly under his eyes, and with a feeling of pride. One time a feed salesman came down into the pens to talk to him and my father said, "Like to have you meet my new hired man." I turned away and raked furiously, red in the face with pleasure.

"Could of fooled me," said the salesman. "I thought it was only a girl."

After the grass was cut, it seemed suddenly much later in the year. I walked on stubble in the earlier evening, aware of the reddening skies, the entering silences, of fall. When I wheeled the tank out of the gate and put the padlock on, it was almost dark. One night at this time I saw my mother and father standing on the little rise of ground we called the gangway, in front of the barn. My father had just come from the meathouse; he had his stiff bloody apron on, and a pail of cut-up meat in his hand.

It was an odd thing to see my mother down at the barn. She did not often come out of the house unless it was to do something—hang out the wash or dig potatoes in the garden. She looked out of place, with her bare lumpy legs, not touched by the sun, her apron still on and damp across the stomach from the supper dishes. Her hair was tied up in a kerchief, wisps of it falling out. She would tie her hair up like this in the morning, saying she did not have time to do it properly, and it would stay tied up all day. It was true, too; she really did not have time. These days our back porch was piled with baskets of peaches and grapes and pears, bought in town, and onions and tomatoes and cucumbers grown at home, all waiting to be made into jelly and jam and preserves, pickles and chili sauce. In the kitchen there was a fire in the stove all day, jars clinked in boiling water, sometimes a cheesecloth bag was strung on a pole between two chairs straining blue-black grape pulp for jelly. I was given jobs to do and I would sit at the table peeling peaches that had been soaked in the hot water, or cutting up onions, my eyes smarting and streaming. As soon as I was done I ran out of the house, trying to get out of earshot before my mother thought of what she wanted me to do next. I hated the hot dark kitchen in summer, the green blinds and the flypapers, the same old oilcloth table and wavy mirror and bumpy linoleum. My mother was too tired and preoccupied to talk to me, she had no heart to tell about the Normal School Graduation Dance; sweat trickled over her face and she was always counting under her breath, pointing at jars, dumping cups of sugar. It seemed to me that work in the house was endless, dreary and peculiarly depressing; work done out of doors, and in my father's service, was ritualistically important.

I wheeled the tank up to the barn, where it was kept, and I heard my mother saying, "Wait till Laird gets a little bigger, then you'll have a real help."

15   What my father said I did not hear. I was pleased by the way he stood listening, politely as he would to a salesman or a stranger, but with an air of wanting to get on with his real work. I felt my mother had no business down here and I wanted him to feel the same way. What did she mean about Laird? He was no help to anybody. Where was he now? Swinging himself sick on the swing, going around in circles, or trying to catch caterpillars. He never once stayed with me till I was finished.

"And then I can use her more in the house," I heard my mother say. She had a dead-quiet, regretful way of talking about me that always made me uneasy. "I just get my back turned and she runs off. It's not like I had a girl in the family at all."

I went and sat on a feed bag in the corner of the barn, not wanting to appear when this conversation was going on. My mother, I felt, was not to be trusted. She was kinder than my father and more easily fooled, but you could not depend on her, and the real reasons for the things she said and did were not to be known. She loved me, and she sat up late at night making a dress of the difficult style I wanted, for me to wear when school started, but she was also my enemy. She was always plotting. She was plotting now to get me to stay in the house more, although she knew I hated it (*because* she knew I hated it) and keep me from working for my father. It seemed to me she would do this simply out of perversity, and to try her power. It did not occur to me that she could be lonely, or jealous. No grown-up could be; they were too fortunate. I sat and kicked my heels monotonously against a feed bag, raising dust, and did not come out till she was gone.

At any rate, I did not expect my father to pay any attention to what she said. Who could imagine Laird doing my work—Laird remembering the padlock and cleaning out the watering dishes with a leaf on the end of a stick, or even wheeling the tank without it tumbling over? It showed how little my mother knew about the way things really were.

I have forgotten to say what the foxes were fed. My father's bloody apron reminded me. They were fed horsemeat. At this time most farmers still kept horses, and when a horse got too old to work, or broke a leg or got down and would not get up, as they sometimes did, the owner would call my father, and he and Henry went out to the farm in the truck. Usually they shot and butchered the horse there, paying the farmer from five to twelve dollars. If they had already too much meat on hand, they would bring the horse back alive, and keep it for a few days or weeks in our stable, until the meat was needed. After the war the farmers were buying tractors and gradually getting rid of horses altogether, so it sometimes happened that we got a good healthy horse, that there was just no use for any more. If this happened in the winter we might keep the horse in our stable till spring, for we had plenty of hay and if there was a lot of snow—and the plow did not always get our road cleared—it was convenient to be able to go to town with a horse and cutter.[2]

20   The winter I was eleven years old we had two horses in the stable. We did not know what names they had had before, so we called them Mack and Flora. Mack was an old black workhorse, sooty and indifferent. Flora was a sorrel mare, a driver. We took them both out in the cutter. Mack was slow and easy to handle. Flora was given to fits of violent alarm, veering at cars and even at other horses, but we loved her speed and high-stepping, her general air of gallantry and abandon. On Saturdays we went down to the stable and as soon as we opened the door on its cosy, animal-smelling darkness Flora threw up her head, rolled her eyes, whinnied despairingly and pulled herself through a crisis of nerves on the spot. It was not safe to go into her stall; she would kick.

This winter also I began to hear a great deal more on the theme my mother had sounded when she had been talking in front of the barn. I no longer felt safe. It seemed that in the minds of the people around me there was a steady undercurrent of thought, not to be deflected, on this one subject. The word *girl* had formerly seemed to me innocent and unburdened, like the word *child;* now it appeared that it was no such thing. A girl was not, as I had supposed, simply what I was; it was what I had to become. It was a definition, always touched with emphasis, with reproach and disappointment. Also it was a joke on me. Once Laird and I were fighting, and for the first time ever I had to use all my strength against him; even so, he caught and pinned my arm for a moment, really hurting me. Henry saw this, and laughed, saying, "Oh, that there Laird's gonna show you, one of these days!" Laird was getting a lot bigger. But I was getting bigger too.

My grandmother came to stay with us for a few weeks and I heard other things. "Girls don't slam doors like that." "Girls keep their knees together when they sit down." And worse still, when I asked some questions, "That's none of girls' business." I continued to slam the doors and sit as awkwardly as possible, thinking by such measures I kept myself free.

---

[2]**cutter** a small sleigh.

When spring came, the horses were let out in the barnyard. Mack stood against the barn wall trying to scratch his neck and haunches, but Flora trotted up and down and reared at the fences, clattering her hooves against the rails. Snow drifts dwindled quickly, revealing the hard gray and brown earth, the familiar rise and fall of the ground, plain and bare after the fantastic landscape of winter. There was a great feeling of opening-out, of release. We just wore rubbers now, over our shoes; our feet felt ridiculously light. One Saturday we went to the stable and found all the doors open, letting in the unaccustomed sunlight and fresh air. Henry was there, just idling around looking at his collection of calendars which were tacked up behind the stalls in a part of the stable my mother had probably never seen.

"Come to say goodbye to your old friend Mack?" Henry said. "Here you give him a taste of oats." He poured some oats in Laird's cupped hands and Laird went to feed Mack. Mack's teeth were in bad shape. He ate very slowly, patiently shifting the oats around in his mouth, trying to find a stump of a molar to grind it on. "Poor old Mack," said Henry mournfully. "When a horse's teeth's gone, he's gone. That's about the way."

25   "Are you going to shoot him today?" I said. Mack and Flora had been in the stable so long I had almost forgotten they were going to be shot.

Henry didn't answer me. Instead he started to sing in a high, trembly, mocking-sorrowful voice. *Oh, there's no more work, for poor Uncle Ned, he's gone where the good darkies go.* Mack's thick, blackish tongue worked diligently at Laird's hand. I went out before the song was ended and sat down on the gangway.

I had never seen them shoot a horse, but I knew where it was done. Last summer Laird and I had come upon a horse's entrails before they were buried. We had thought it was a big black snake, coiled up in the sun. That was around in the field that ran up beside the barn. I thought that if we went inside the barn, and found a wide crack or a knothole to look through, we would be able to see them do it. It was not something I wanted to see; just the same, if a thing really happened, it was better to see, and know.

My father came down from the house, carrying the gun.

"What are you doing here?" he said.

30   "Nothing."

"Go on up and play around the house."

He sent Laird out of the stable. I said to Laird. "Do you want to see them shoot Mack?" and without waiting for an answer led him around to the front door of the barn, opened it carefully, and went in. "Be quiet or they'll hear us," I said. We could hear Henry and my father talking in the stable; then the heavy, shuffling steps of Mack being backed out of his stall.

In the loft it was cold and dark. Thin crisscrossed beams of sunlight fell through the cracks. The hay was low. It was a rolling country, hills and hollows, slipping under our feet. About four feet up was a beam going around the walls. We piled hay up in one corner and I boosted Laird up and hoisted myself. The beam was not very wide; we crept along it with our hands flat on the barn walls. There were plenty of knotholes, and I found one that gave me the view I wanted—a corner of the barnyard, the gate, part of the field. Laird did not have a knothole and began to complain.

I showed him a widened crack between two boards. "Be quiet and wait. If they hear you you'll get us in trouble."

35   My father came in sight carrying the gun. Henry was leading Mack by
the halter. He dropped it and took out his cigarette papers and tobacco; he
rolled cigarettes for my father and himself. While this was going on Mack
nosed around in the old, dead grass along the fence. Then my father opened
the gate and they took Mack through. Henry led Mack away from the path
to a patch of ground and they talked together, not loud enough for us to
hear. Mack again began searching for a mouthful of fresh grass, which was
not to be found. My father walked away in a straight line, and stopped short
a distance which seemed to suit him. Henry was walking away from Mack
too, but sideways, still negligently holding on to the halter. My father raised
the gun and Mack looked up as if he had noticed something and my father
shot him.

        Mack did not collapse at once but swayed, lurched sideways and fell,
first on his side; then he rolled over on his back and, amazingly, kicked his
legs for a few seconds in the air. At this Henry laughed, as if Mack had done
a trick for him. Laird, who had drawn a long, groaning breath of surprise
when the shot was fired, said out loud, "He's not dead." And it seemed to
me it might be true. But his legs stopped, he rolled on his side again, his
muscles quivered and sank. The two men walked over and looked at him in
a businesslike way; they bent down and examined his forehead where the
bullet had gone in, and now I saw his blood on the brown grass.

        "Now they just skin him and cut him up," I said. "Let's go." My legs
were a little shaky and I jumped gratefully down into the hay. "Now you've
seen how they shoot a horse," I said in a congratulatory way, as if I had seen
it many times before. "Let's see if any barn cat's had kittens in the hay."
Laird jumped. He seemed young and obedient again. Suddenly I remembered how, when he was little, I had brought him into the barn and told him
to climb the ladder to the top beam. That was in the spring, too, when the
hay was low. I had done it out of a need for excitement, a desire for something to happen so that I could tell about it. He was wearing a little bulky
brown and white checked coat, made down from one of mine. He went all
the way up just as I told him, and sat down on the top beam with the hay far
below him on one side, and the barn floor and some old machinery on the
other. Then I ran screaming to my father. "Laird's up on the top beam!" My
father came, my mother came, my father went up the ladder talking very
quietly and brought Laird down under his arm, at which my mother leaned
against the ladder and began to cry. They said to me, "Why weren't you
watching him?" but nobody ever knew the truth. Laird did not know
enough to tell. But whenever I saw the brown and white checked coat
hanging in the closet, or at the bottom of the rag bag, which was where it
ended up, I felt a weight in my stomach, the sadness of unexorcised guilt.

        I looked at Laird, who did not even remember this, and I did not like
the look on his thin, winter-paled face. His expression was not frightened or
upset, but remote, concentrating. "Listen," I said, in an unusually bright and
friendly voice, "you aren't going to tell, are you?"

        "No," he said absently.

40   "Promise."

        "Promise," he said. I grabbed the hand behind his back to make sure he
was not crossing his fingers. Even so, he might have a nightmare; it might
come out that way. I decided I had better work hard to get all thoughts of

what he had seen out of his mind—which, it seemed to me, could not hold very many things at a time. I got some money I had saved and that afternoon we went into Jubilee and saw a show, with Judy Canova,[3] at which we both laughed a great deal. After that I thought it would be all right.

Two weeks later I knew they were going to shoot Flora. I knew from the night before, when I heard my mother ask if the hay was holding out all right, and my father said. "Well, after tomorrow there'll just be the cow, and we should be able to put her out to grass in another week." So I knew it was Flora's turn in the morning.

This time I didn't think of watching it. That was something to see just one time. I had not thought about it very often since, but sometimes when I was busy working at school, or standing in front of the mirror combing my hair and wondering if I would be pretty when I grew up, the whole scene would flash into my mind: I would see the easy, practiced way my father raised the gun, and hear Henry laughing when Mack kicked his legs in the air. I did not have any great feeling of horror and opposition, such as a city child might have had; I was too used to seeing the death of animals as a necessity by which we lived. Yet I felt a little ashamed, and there was a new wariness, a sense of holding-off, in my attitude to my father and his work.

It was a fine day, and we were going around the yard picking up tree branches that had been torn off in winter storms. This was something we had been told to do, and also we wanted to use them to make a teepee. We heard Flora whinny, and then my father's voice and Henry's shouting, and we ran down to the barnyard to see what was going on.

45   The stable door was open. Henry had just brought Flora out, and she had broken away from him. She was running free in the barnyard, from one end to the other. We climbed up on the fence. It was exciting to see her running, whinnying, going up on her hind legs, prancing and threatening like a horse in a Western movie, an unbroken ranch horse, though she was just an old driver, an old sorrel mare. My father and Henry ran after her and tried to grab the dangling halter. They tried to work her into a corner, and they had almost succeeded when she made a run between them, wild-eyed, and disappeared around the corner of the barn. We heard the rail clatter down as she got over the fence, and Henry yelled. "She's into the field now!"

That meant she was in the long L-shaped field that ran up by the house. If she got around the center, heading toward the lane, the gate was open; the truck had been driven in the field this morning. My father shouted to me, because I was on the other side of the fence, nearest the lane. "Go shut the gate!"

I could run very fast. I ran across the garden, past the tree where our swing was hung, and jumped across a ditch into the lane. There was the open gate. She had not got out, I could not see her up the road; she must have run to the other end of the field. The gate was heavy, I lifted it out of the gravel and carried it across the roadway. I had it halfway across when she came in sight, galloping straight toward me. There was just time to get the chain on. Laird came scrambling through the ditch to help me.

Instead of shutting the gate, I opened it as wide as I could. I did not make any decision to do this, it was just what I did. Flora never slowed

---

[3]**Judy Canova** American comedian, popular in films in the 1940s.

down; she galloped straight past me, and Laird jumped up and down, yelling "Shut it, shut it!" even after it was too late. My father and Henry appeared in the field a moment too late to see what I had done. They only saw Flora heading for the township road. They would think I had not got there in time.

They did not waste any time asking about it. They went back to the barn and got the gun and the knives they used, and put these in the truck; then they turned the truck around and came bouncing up the field toward us. Laird called to them. "Let me go too, let me go too!" and Henry stopped the truck and they took him in. I shut the gate after they were all gone.

50   I supposed Laird would tell. I wondered what would happen to me. I had never disobeyed my father before, and I could not understand why I had done it. Flora would not really get away. They would catch up with her in the truck. Or if they did not catch her this morning somebody would see her and telephone us this afternoon or tomorrow. There was no wild country here for her to run to, only farms. What was more, my father had paid for her, we needed the meat to feed the foxes, we needed the foxes to make our living. All I had done was make more work for my father who worked hard enough already. And when my father found out about it he was not going to trust me any more; he would know that I was not entirely on his side. I was on Flora's side, and that made me no use to anybody, not even to her. Just the same, I did not regret it; when she came running at me and I held the gate open, that was the only thing I could do.

I went back to the house, and my mother said. "What's all the commotion?" I told her that Flora had kicked down the fence and got away. "Your poor father," she said, "now he'll have to go chasing over the countryside. Well, there isn't any use planning dinner before one." She put up the ironing board. I wanted to tell her, but thought better of it and went upstairs, and sat on my bed.

Lately I had been trying to make my part of the room fancy, spreading the bed with old lace curtains, and fixing myself a dressing table with some leftovers of cretonne for a skirt. I planned to put up some kind of barricade between my bed and Laird's, to keep my section separate from his. In the sunlight, the lace curtains were just dusty rags. We did not sing at night any more. One night when I was singing Laird said, "You sound silly," and I went right on but the next night I did not start. There was not so much need to anyway, we were no longer afraid. We knew it was just old furniture over there, old jumble and confusion. We did not keep to the rules. I still stayed awake after Laird was asleep and told myself stories, but even in these stories something different was happening, mysterious alterations took place. A story might start off in the old way, with a spectacular danger, a fire or wild animals, and for a while I might rescue people; then things would change around, and instead, somebody would be rescuing me. It might be a boy from our class at school, or even Mr. Campbell, our teacher, who tickled girls under the arms. And at this point the story concerned itself at great length with what I looked like—how long my hair was, and what kind of dress I had on; by the time I had these details worked out the real excitement of the story was lost.

It was later than one o'clock when the truck came back. The tarpaulin was over the back, which meant there was meat in it. My mother had to heat dinner up all over again. Henry and my father had changed from their bloody overalls into ordinary working overalls in the barn, and they washed their arms and necks and faces at the sink, and splashed water on their hair and combed it. Laird lifted his arm to show off a streak of blood. "We shot old Flora," he said, "and cut her up in fifty pieces."

"Well I don't want to hear about it," my mother said. "And don't come to my table like that."

55   My father made him go and wash the blood off.

We sat down and my father said grace and Henry pasted his chewing gum on the end of his fork, the way he always did; when he took it off he would have us admire the pattern. We began to pass the bowls of steaming, overcooked vegetables. Laird looked across the table at me and said proudly, distinctly. "Anyway it was her fault Flora got away."

"What?" my father said.

"She could of shut the gate and she didn't. She just open' it up and Flora run out."

"Is that right?" my father said.

60   Everybody at the table was looking at me. I nodded, swallowing food with great difficulty. To my shame, tears flooded my eyes.

My father made a curt sound of disgust. "What did you do that for?"

I did not answer. I put down my fork and waited to be sent from the table, still not looking up.

But this did not happen. For some time nobody said anything, then Laird said matter-of-factly, "She's crying."

"Never mind," my father said. He spoke with resignation, even good humor, the words which absolved and dismissed me for good. "She's only a girl," he said.

65   I didn't protest that, even in my heart. Maybe it was true.

▓ TOPICS FOR CRITICAL THINKING AND WRITING

1. What does the narrator mean when she says, "The word *girl* had formerly seemed to me innocent and unburdened, like the word *child*; now it appeared that it was no such thing. A girl was not, as I had supposed, simply what I was; it was what I had to become"?

2. The narrator says that she "could not understand" why she disobeyed her father and allowed the horse to escape. Can you explain her action to her? If so, do so.

3. Characterize the mother.

The Children Stay   [1997]

Thirty years ago, a family was spending a holiday together on the east coast of Vancouver Island. A young father and mother, their two small daughters, and an older couple, the husband's parents.

What perfect weather. Every morning, every morning it's like this, the first pure sunlight falling through the high branches, burning away the mist over the still water of Georgia Strait.

If it weren't for the tide, it would be hard to remember that this is the sea. You look across the water to the mountains on the mainland, the ranges that are the western wall of the continent of North America. These humps and peaks coming clear now through the mist are of interest to the grandfather and to his son, Brian. The two men are continually trying to decide which of these shapes are actual continental mountains and which are improbable heights of the islands that ride in front of the shore.

There is a map, set up under the glass, between the cottages and the beach. You can stand there looking at the map, then looking at what's in front of you and back at the map again, until you get things sorted out. The grandfather and Brian usually get into an argument—though you'd think there would not be much room for disagreement with the map right there.

5   Brian's mother won't look at the map. She says it boggles her mind. Her concern is always about whether anybody is hungry yet, or thirsty, whether the children have their sun hats on and have been rubbed with protective lotion. She makes her husband wear a floppy cotton hat and thinks that Brian should wear one, too—she reminds him of how sick he got from the sun that summer they went to the Okanagan, when he was a child. Sometimes Brian says to her. "Oh, dry up, Mother." His tone is mostly affectionate, but his father may ask him if that's the way he thinks he can talk to his mother nowadays.

"She doesn't mind," says Brian.

"How do you know?" says his father.

"Oh, for Pete's sake," says his mother.

Pauline, the young mother, slides out of bed as soon as she's awake every morning, slides out of reach of Brian's long, sleepily searching arms and legs. What wakes her is the first squeaks and mutters of the baby, Mara, in the children's room, then the creak of the crib as Mara—sixteen months old now, getting to the end of babyhood—pulls herself up to stand hanging on to the railing. She continues her soft amiable talk as Pauline lifts her out—Caitlin, nearly five, shifting about but not waking, in her nearby bed— and as she is carried into the kitchen to be changed, on the floor. Then she is settled into her stroller, with a biscuit and a bottle of apple juice, while Pauline gets into her sundress and sandals, goes to the bathroom, combs out her hair—all as quickly and quietly as possible. They leave the cottage and head for the bumpy unpaved road that runs behind the cottages, a mile or so north till it stops at the bank of the little river that runs into the sea. The road is still mostly in deep morning shadow, the floor of a tunnel under fir and cedar trees.

10   The grandfather, also an early riser, sees them from the porch of his cottage, and Pauline sees him. But all that is necessary is a wave. He and Pauline never have much to say to each other (though sometimes there's an affinity they feel, in the midst of some long-drawn out antics of Brian's or some apologetic but insistent fuss made by the grandmother, there's an awareness of not looking at each other, lest their look reveal a bleakness that would discredit others).

On this holiday Pauline steals time to be by herself—being with Mara is still almost the same thing as being by herself. Early morning walks, the late morning hour when she washes and hangs out the diapers. She could have had another hour or so in the afternoons, while Mara is napping. But Brian has fixed up a shelter on the beach, and he carries the playpen down every day, so that Mara can nap there and Pauline won't have to absent herself. He says his parents might be offended if she's always sneaking off. He agrees, though, that she does need some time to go over her lines for the play she's going to be in, back in Victoria, this September.

Pauline is not an actress. This is an amateur production, and she didn't even try out for the role. She was asked if she would like to be in this play by a man she met at a barbecue, in June. The people there were mostly teachers, and their wives or husbands—it was held at the house of the principal of the high school where Brian taught. The woman who taught French was a widow—she had brought her grown son, who was staying for the summer with her and working as a night clerk in a downtown hotel. She told everybody that he had got a job teaching college in western Washington State and would be going there in the fall.

Jeffrey Toom was his name. "Without the 'b,'" he said, as if the staleness of the joke wounded him.

What was he going to teach?

15   "Dram-ah," he said, drawing the word out in a mocking way.

He spoke of his present job disparagingly as well.

"It's a pretty sordid place," he said. "Maybe you heard—a hooker was killed there last February. And then we get the usual losers checking in to O.D. or bump themselves off."

People did not quite know what to make of this way of talking and drifted away from him. Except for Pauline.

"I'm thinking about putting on a play," he said. He asked her if she had ever heard of "Eurydice."

20   Pauline said, "You mean Anouilh's?" and he was unflatteringly surprised. He immediately said he didn't know if it would ever work out. "I just thought it might be interesting to see if you could do something different here in the land of Noël Coward."

Pauline did not remember when there had been a play by Noël Coward put on in Victoria, though she supposed there had been several. She said, "We saw 'The Duchess of Malfi' last winter at the college."

"Yeah. Well," he said, flushing. She had thought he was older than she was, at least as old as Brian—who was thirty, though people were apt to say he didn't act it—but as soon as he started talking to her, in this offhand, dismissive way, never quite meeting her eyes, she suspected that he was younger than he'd like to appear. Now, with that flush, she was sure of it.

As it turned out, he was a year younger than she was. Twenty-five.

She said that she couldn't be Eurydice—she couldn't act. But Brian came over to see what the conversation was about and said at once that she must try it.

25   "She just needs a kick in the behind," Brian said to Jeffrey. "She's like a little mule—it's hard to get her started. No, seriously, she's too self-effacing. I tell her that all the time. She's very smart. She's actually a lot smarter than I am."

At that Jeffrey did look directly into Pauline's eyes—impertinently and searchingly—and she was the one who was flushing.

He had chosen her immediately as his Eurydice because of the way she looked. But it was not because she was beautiful. "I'd never put a beautiful girl in that part," he said. "I don't know if I'd ever put a beautiful girl onstage in anything. It's distracting."

So what did he mean about the way she looked? He said it was her hair, which was long and dark and rather bushy (not in style at that time), and her pale skin ("Stay out of the sun this summer") and, most of all, her eyebrows.

"I never liked them," said Pauline, not quite sincerely. Her eyebrows were level, dark, luxuriant. They dominated her face. Like her hair, they were not in style. But if she had really disliked them, wouldn't she have plucked them?

30   Jeffrey seemed not to have heard her. "They give you a sulky look and that's disturbing," he said. "Also your jaw's a little heavy and that's sort of Greek. It would be better in a movie, where I could get you close up. The routine thing for Eurydice would be a girl who looked ethereal. I don't want ethereal."

As she walked Mara along the road, Pauline did work at the lines. There was a long speech at the end that was giving her trouble. She bumped the stroller along and repeated to herself, "You are terrible, you know, you are terrible like the angels. You think everybody's going forward, as brave and bright as you are—oh, don't look at me, please, darling, don't look at me—Perhaps I'm not what you wish I was, but I'm here, and I'm warm, I'm kind and I love you. I'll give you all the happiness I can. Don't look at me. Don't look. Let me live."

She had left something out. "Perhaps I'm not what you wish I was, but you feel me here, don't you? I'm warm and I'm kind—"

She had told Jeffrey that she thought the play was beautiful.

He said, "Really?" What she'd said didn't please or surprise him—he seemed to feel it was predictable, and superfluous. He would never describe a play in that way. He spoke of it more as a hurdle to be got over. Also a challenge to be flung at various enemies. At the academic snots, as he called them, who had done "The Duchess of Malfi." And at the social twits, as he called them, in the little theatre. He saw himself as an outsider heaving his weight against these people, putting on his play—he called it his—in the teeth of their contempt and opposition. In the beginning Pauline thought that this must be all in his imagination. Then something would happen that could be, but might not be, a coincidence—repairs to be done on the church hall where the play was to be performed, making it unobtainable, and unexpected increase in the cost of printing advertising posters—and she found herself seeing it his way. If you were going to be around him much, you almost had to see it his way—arguing was dangerous and exhausting.

35   "Son's of bitches," said Jeffrey between his teeth, but with some satisfaction. "I'm not surprised. I'm going to get to the bottom of this."

The rehearsals were help upstairs in an old building on Fisgard Street. Sunday afternoon was the only time that everybody could get there, though there were fragmentary rehearsals during the week. Pauline had to depend on sometimes undependable high-school babysitters—for the first six weeks of the summer Brian was busy teaching summer school. And Jeffrey himself had to be at his hotel job by eight o'clock in the evening. But on Sunday afternoons they were all there, laboring in the dusty high-ceilinged room on Fisgard Street. The windows were rounded at the top as in some plain and dignified church, and propped open in the heat with whatever objects could be found—ledger books from the nineteen-twenties, belonging to the hat shop that had once operated downstairs, pieces of wood left over from picture frames made by the artist whose canvases were now stacked against one wall and apparently abandoned. The glass was grimy, but outside the sunlight bounced off the sidewalks, the empty gravelled parking lots, the low stuccoed buildings, with what seemed a special Sunday brightness. Hardly anybody moved through these downtown streets. Nothing was open except the occasional hole-in-the-wall coffee shop or lackadaisical, flyspecked convenience store.

Pauline was the one who went out at the break to get soft drinks and coffee. She was the one who had the least to say about the play and the way it was going—even though she was the only one who had read it before—because she alone had never done any acting. So it seemed proper for her to volunteer. She enjoyed her short walk in the empty streets—she felt as if she had become an urban person, someone detached and solitary, who lived in the glare of an important dream. Sometimes she thought of Brian at home, working in the garden and keeping an eye on the children. Or perhaps he had taken them to Dallas Road—she recalled a promise—to sail boats on the pond. That life seemed ragged and tedious compared to what went on in the rehearsal room—the hours of effort, the concentration, the sharp exchanges, the sweating and tension. Even the taste of coffee, its scalding bitterness, and the fact that it was chosen by nearly everybody in preference to a fresher-tasting and maybe more healful drink out of the cooler, seemed satisfying to her.

When she said that she had to go away for the two-week holiday, Jeffrey looked thunderstruck, as if he had never imagined that things like holidays could come into her life. Then he turned grim and slightly satirical, as if this were just another blow that he might have expected. Pauline explained that she would miss only the one Sunday—the one in the middle of the two weeks—because she and Brian were driving up the Island on a Monday and coming back on a Sunday morning. She promised to get back in time for rehearsal. Privately she wondered how she would do this—it always took so much longer than you expected to pack up and get away. She wondered if she could possibly come back by herself, on the morning bus. That would probably be too much to ask for. She didn't mention it.

She couldn't ask him if it was only the play he was thinking about, only her absence from a rehearsal that caused the thundercloud. At the moment, it very likely was. When he spoke to her at rehearsals there was never any suggestion that he ever spoke to her in any other way. The only difference in his treatment of her was that perhaps he expected less of her, of her acting, than he did of the others. And that would be understandable to anybody. She was the only one chosen out of the blue, for the was she looked—the others had all shown up at the audition he had advertised on signs put up in cafes and bookstores around town.

40   Yet she thought they all knew what was going on, in spite of Jeffrey's offhand and abrupt and none too civil ways. They knew that after every one of them had straggled off home he would walk across the room and bolt the staircase door. (At first Pauline had pretended to leave with the rest and had even got into her car and circled the block, but later such a trick had come to seem insulting, not just to herself and Jeffrey but to the others, whom she was sure would never betray her, bound as they all were under the temporary but potent spell of the play.)

Jeffrey crossed the room and bolted the door. Every time, this was like a new decision that he had to make. Until it was done, she wouldn't look at him. The sound of the bolt being pushed into place, the ominous or fatalistic sound of metal hitting metal, gave her a localized shock of capitulation. But she didn't make a move, she waited for him to come back to her with the whole story of the afternoon's labor draining out of his face, the expression of matter-of-fact and customary disappointment cleared away, replaced by the live energy she always found surprising.

"So. Tell us what this play of yours is about," Brian's father said. "Is it one of those ones where they take their clothes off on the stage?"

"Now, don't tease her," said Brian's mother.

Brian and Pauline had put the children to bed and walked over to his parents' cottage for an evening drink. The sunset was behind them, behind the forests of Vancouver Island, but the mountains in front of them, all clear now and hard cut against the sky, shone in its pink light. Some high inland mountains were capped with pink summer snow.

45 "The story of Orpheus and Eurydice is that Eurydice died," Pauline said. "And Orpheus goes down to the underworld to try to get her back. And his wish is granted, but only if he promises not to look at her. Not to look back at her. She's walking behind him—"

"Twelve paces," said Brian. "As is only right."

"It's a Greek story, but it's set in modern times," said Pauline. "At least this version is. More or less modern. Orpheus is a musician traveling around with his father—they're both musicians—and Eurydice is an actress. This is in France."

"Translated?" Brian's father said.

"No," said Brian. "But don't worry, it's not in French. It was written in Transylvanian."

50 "It's so hard to make sense of anything," Brian's mother said with a worried laugh. "It's so hard, with Brian around."

"It's in English," Pauline said.

"And you're what's-her-name?"

She said, "I'm Eurydice."

"He get you back O.K.?"

55 "No," she said. "He looks back at me and then I have to stay dead."

"Oh, an unhappy ending," Brian's mother said.

"You're so gorgeous?" said Brian's father skeptically. "He can't stop himself from looking back?"

"It's not that," said Pauline. But at this point she felt that something had been achieved by her father-in-law, he had done what he meant to do, which was the same thing that he nearly always meant to do, in any conversation she had with him. And that was to break through the careful structure of some explanation he had asked her for, and she had unwillingly but patiently given, and with a seemingly negligent kick knock it into rubble. He had been dangerous to her for a long time in this way, though he wasn't particularly so tonight.

But Brian did not know that. Brain was still figuring out how to come to her rescue.

60 "Pauline is gorgeous," Brian said.

"Yes indeed," said his mother.

"Maybe if she'd go to the hairdresser," his father said. But Pauline's long hair was such an old objection of his that it had become a family joke. Even Pauline laughed. She said, "I can't afford to till we get the veranda roof fixed." And Brian laughed boisterously, full of relief that she was able to take all this as a joke. It was what he had always told her to do.

"Just kid him back. It's the only way to handle him."

"Yeah, well, if you'd got yourselves a decent house," said his father. But this, like Pauline's hair, was such a familiar sore point that it couldn't rouse anybody. Brian and Pauline had bought a handsome house in bad repair on a street in Victoria where old mansions were being turned into ill-used apartment buildings. The house, the street, the messy old Garry oaks, the fact that no basement had been blasted out under the house, was all a horror to Brian's father. So what he said now about a decent house might be some kind of peace signal. Or could be taken so.

65   Brian was an only son. He was a math teacher. His father was a civil engineer, and part owner of a contracting company. If he had hoped that he would have a son who was an engineer and might come into the company, there was never any mention of it. Pauline had asked Brian whether he thought the carping about their house, and her hair, and the books she read, might be a cover for this larger disappointment, but Brian had said, "Nope. In our family we complain about just whatever we want to complain about. We ain't subtle, Ma'am."

Pauline still wondered, when she head his mother talking about how teachers ought to be the most honored people in the world and they did not get half the credit they deserved and that she didn't know how Brian managed it, day after day. Then his father might say, "That's right," or "I sure wouldn't want to do it, I can tell you that. They couldn't pay me to do it."

And Brian would turn that into a joke, as he turned nearly everything into a joke.

"Don't worry, Dad. They don't pay you much."

Brian in his everyday life was a much more dramatic person than Jeffrey. He dominated his classes by keeping up a parade of jokes and antics, extending the role that he had always played, Pauline believed, with his mother and father. He acted dumb, he bounced back from pretended humiliations, he traded insults. He was a bully in a good cause—a chivying, cheerful, indestructible bully.

70   "You boy has certainly made his mark with us," the principal said to Pauline. "He has not just survived, which is something in itself. He has made his mark."

Your boy.

He called his students boneheads. His tone was affectionate, fatalistic. He said that his father was the King of the Philistines, a pure and natural barbarian. And that his mother was a dishrag, good-natured and worn out. But however he dismissed such people, he could not be long without them. He took his students on camping trips. And he could not imagine a summer without this shared holiday. He was mortally afraid, every year, that Pauline would refuse to go along. Or that, having agreed to go, she was going to be miserable, take offense at something his father said, complain about how much time she had to spend with his mother, sulk because there was no way they could do anything by themselves. She might decide to spend all day in their own cottage, reading, and pretending to have a sunburn.

All those things had happened, on previous holidays. But this year she was easing up. He told her he could see that, and he was grateful to her.

"I know it's an effort," he said. "It's different for me. They're my parents and I'm used to not taking them seriously."

75   Pauline came from a family that took things so seriously that her parents had got a divorce. Her mother was now dead. She had a distant, though cordial, relationship with her father and her two much older sisters. She said that they had nothing in common. She knew Brian could not understand how that could be a reason. She saw that comfort it gave him, this year, to see things going so well. She had thought it was laziness or cowardice that kept him from breaking the arrangement, but now she saw that it was something far more positive. He needed to have his wife and his parents and his children bound together like this, he needed to involve Pauline in his life with his parents and to bring his parents to some recognition of her—though the recognition, from his father, would always be muffled and contrary, and from his mother too profuse, too easily come by, to mean much. Also he wanted Pauline to be connected—and the children, too—to his own childhood. He wanted these holidays to be linked to the holidays of his youth with their lucky or unlucky weather, car troubles, boating scares, bee stings, marathon Monopoly games, to all the things that he told his mother he was bored to death hearing about. He wanted pictures from this summer to be taken, and fitted into his mother's album, a continuation of all the other pictures that he groaned at the mention of.

The only time they could talk to each other was in bed, late at night. But they did talk then, more than was usual with them at home, where Brian was so tired that often he fell immediately asleep. And in ordinary daylight it was hard to talk to him because of his jokes. She could see the joke brightening his eyes. (His coloring was very like hers—dark hair and pale skin and gray eyes—but her eyes were cloudy and his were light, like clear water over stones.) She could see it pulling at the corners of his mouth as he foraged among your words to catch a pun or the start of a rhyme—anything that could take the conversation away, into absurdity. His whole body, tall and loosely joined together and still almost as skinny as a teenager's, twitched with comic propensity, Before she married him, Pauline had a friend named Gracie, a rather grumpy-looking girl, subversive about men. Brian had thought her a girl whose spirits needed a boost, and so he made even more than the usual effort. And Gracie said to Pauline, "How can you stand the non-stop show?"

"That's not the real Brian," Pauline had said. "He's different when we're alone." But, looking back, she wondered how true that had ever been. Had she said it simply to defend her choice, as you did when you had made up your mind to get married?

Even in the cottage, with the window open on the unfamiliar darkness and stillness of the night, he teased a little. He had to speak to Jeffrey as Monsieur le Directeur, which made the play, or the fact that it was a French play, slightly ridiculous. Or perhaps it was Jeffrey himself, Jeffrey's seriousness about the play, that had to be called into question.

Pauline didn't care. It was such a pleasure and a relief to her to mention Jeffrey's name.

80   Though most of the time she didn't mention him, she circled around that pleasure. She described all the others instead. The hairdresser and the harbor pilot and the busboy and the old man who claimed to have once acted on the radio. He played Orphée's father, and gave Jeffrey the most trouble, because he had the stubbornest notions of his own about acting.

The middle-aged impresario, M. Dulac, was played by a twenty-four-year-old travel agent. And Mathias, who was Eurydice's former boyfriend, presumably around her own age, was played by the manager of a shoe store, who was married and a father.

"Why didn't Monsieur le Directeur cast those two the other way round?" said Brian.

"That's the way he does things," Pauline said. "What he sees in us is something different from the obvious."

For instance, she said the busboy was a difficult Orphée.

85   "He's only nineteen, he's terribly shy, but he's determined to be an actor. Even if it's like making love to his grandmother. Jeffrey has to keep at him. 'Keep your arms around her a little longer, stroke her a little—'"

"He might get to like it," Brian said. "Maybe I should come around and keep an eye on him."

At this Pauline snorted. When she had started to quote Jeffrey she had felt a giving-way in her womb or the bottom of her stomach, a shock that had traveled oddly upward and hit her vocal cords. She had to cover up this quaking by growling in a way that was supposed to be an imitation (though Jeffrey never growled or ranted or carried on in any theatrical way at all).

Stroke her a little.

"But there's a point about him being so innocent," she said hurriedly. "Being not so physical. Being awkward." She began to talk about Orphée in the play, not the busboy—Orphée's problems with love and reality. Orphée will not put up with anything less than perfection. He wants a love that is outside of ordinary life. He wants a perfect Eurydice.

90   "Eurydice is more realistic. She's carried on with Mathias and with M. Dulac. She's been around her mother and her mother's lover. She knows what people are like. But she loves Orphée. She loves him better, in a way, than he loves her. She loves him better because she's not such a fool. She loves him like a human person."

"She's slept with those other guys?"

"Well, with M. Dulac she had to, she couldn't get out of it. She didn't want to, but probably after a while she enjoyed it, because after a certain point she couldn't help enjoying it. Just because she's slept with those men doesn't mean she's corrupt," Pauline said. "She wasn't in love then. She hadn't met Orphée. There's one speech where he tells her that everything she's done is sticking to her, and it's disgusting. Lies she's told him. The other men. It's all sticking to her forever. And then of course M. Henri plays up to that. He tells Orphée that he'll be just as bad and that one day he'll walk down the street with Eurydice and he'll look like a man with a dog he's trying to lose."

Brian laughed. He said, "That could be true."

"But not inevitably," said Pauline. "That's what's silly. It's not inevitable at all."

95   So Orphée is at fault, Pauline said decidedly. He looks back at Eurydice on purpose to kill her and get rid of her because she isn't perfect. Because of him she has to die a second time.

Brian, on his back and with his eyes wide open (she knew that because of the tone of his voice), said, "But doesn't he die, too?"

"Yes. He chooses to."

"So then they're together?"

"Yes. Like Romeo and Juliet. Orphée is with Eurydice at last. That's what M. Henri says. That's the last line of the play. That's the end." Pauline rolled over onto her side and touched her cheek to Brian's shoulder—not to start anything but to emphasize what she said next. "It's a beautiful play in one way but in another it's so silly. And it isn't really like 'Romeo and Juliet,' because it isn't bad luck or circumstances. It's on purpose. So they don't have to go on with life and get married and have kids and buy an old house and fix it up and—"

100 "And have affairs," said Brian. "After all, they're French."

Then he said, "And be like my parents."

Pauline laughed. "Do they have affairs? I can't imagine."

"Oh, sure," said Brian. "I meant their life."

"Oh."

105 "Logically I can see killing yourself so you won't turn into your parents. I just don't believe anybody would do it."

They went on speculating, and comfortably arguing, in a way that was not usual, but not altogether unfamiliar to them. They had done this before, at long intervals in their married life—talked half the night about God or fear of death or how children should be educated or whether money was important. At last they admitted to being too tired to make sense any longer, and arranged themselves in a comradely cuddle and went to sleep.

Finally a rainy day. Brian and his parents were driving into Campbell River to get groceries, and gin, and to take Brian's father's car to a garage. Brian had to go along, with his car, just in case the other car had to be left in the garage overnight. Pauline said that she had to stay home because of Mara's nap.

She persuaded Caitlin to lie down, too—allowing her to take her music box to bed with her if she played it under the covers. Then Pauline spread the script on the kitchen table, and drank coffee and went over the scene in which Orphée says that it's intolerable, at last, to stay in two skins, two envelopes with their own blood and oxygen sealed up in their solitude, and Eurydice tells him to be quiet.

"Don't talk. Don't think. Just let your hand wander, let it be happy on its own."

110 Your hand is my happiness, says Eurydice. Accept that. Accept your happiness.

Of course he says he cannot.

Caitlin called out frequently to ask what time it was, and Pauline could hear the music box. She hurried to the bedroom door and hissed at her to turn it off, not to wake Mara.

"If you play it like that again I'll take it away from you. O.K.?"

But Mara was already rustling around in her crib and in the next few minutes there were sounds of soft, encouraging conversation from Caitlin, designed to get her sister wide awake. Then of Mara rattling the crib railing, pulling herself up, throwing her bottle out onto the floor, and starting the bird cries that would grow more and more desolate until they brought her mother.

115   "I didn't wake her," Caitlin said. "She was awake all by herself. It's not raining anymore. Can we go down to the beach?"

She was right. It wasn't raining. Pauline changed Mara, told Caitlin to get her bathing suit on and find her sand pail. She got into her own bathing suit and put on her shorts on top of it, in case the rest of the family arrived home while she was down there. ("Dad doesn't like the way some women just go right out of their cottages in their bathing suits," Brian's mother had said to her. "I guess he and I just grew up in other times.") She picked up the script to take it along, then laid it down. She was afraid that she would get too absorbed in it and take her eye off the children for a moment too long.

The thoughts that came to her, of Jeffrey, were not really thoughts at all—they were more like alterations in her body. This could happen when she was sitting on the beach (trying to stay in the half shade of a bush and so preserve her pallor, as Jeffrey had ordered). Or when she was wringing out diapers, or when she and Brian were visiting his parents. In the middle of Monopoly games, Scrabble games, card games. She went right on talking, listening, working, keeping track of the children, while some memory of her secret life disturbed her like a radiant explosion. Then a warm weight settled, reassurance filling up all her hollows. But it didn't last, this comfort leaked away, and she was like a miser whose windfall has vanished and who is convinced such luck can never strike again. Longing buckled her up and drove her to the discipline of counting days. Sometimes she even cut the days into fractions to figure out more exactly how much time had gone.

She thought of going in to Campbell River, making some excuse, so that she could get to a phone booth and call him. The cottages had no phones—the only public phone was in the hall of the Lodge, across from the entrance to the dining room. But she did not have the number of the hotel where Jeffrey worked. And, besides that, she could never get away to Campbell River in the evening. She was afraid that if she called him at home in the daytime his mother the French teacher might answer. He said she hardly ever left the house in the summer. Just once, she had taken the ferry to Vancouver for the day. Jeffrey had phoned Pauline to ask her to come over. Brian was teaching and Caitlin was at her play group.

Pauline said, "I can't. I have Mara."

120   "Couldn't you bring her along?" he asked.

She said no.

"Why not? Couldn't you bring some things for her to play with?"

No, said Pauline. "I couldn't," she said. "I just couldn't." It seemed too dangerous to her, to trundle her baby along on such a guilty expedition. To a house where cleaning fluids would not be bestowed on high shelves and all pills and cough syrups and cigarettes and buttons put safely out of reach. And even if she escaped poisoning or choking, Mara might be storing up time bombs—memories of a strange house where she was strangely disregarded, of a closed door, noises on the other side of it.

"I just wanted you," Jeffrey said, "I just wanted you in my bed."

125   She said again, weakly, "No."

Those words of his kept coming back to her. I wanted you in my bed. A half-joking urgency in his voice but also a determination, a practicality, as if "in my bed" meant something more, the bed he spoke of taking on large, less material dimensions.

Had she made a great mistake, with that refusal? With that reminder of how fenced in she was, in what anybody would call her real life?

The beach was nearly empty—people had got used to its being a rainy day. The sand was too heavy for Caitlin to make a castle or dig an irrigation system—projects she would undertake only with her father, anyway, because she sensed that his interest in them was wholehearted, and Pauline's was not. She wandered a bit forlornly at the edge of the water, missing the presence of other children, the nameless instant friends and occasional stone-throwing, water-kicking enemies, the shrieking and splashing and falling about. A boy a little bigger than she was and apparently all by himself stood knee deep in the water farther down the beach. If these two could get together it might be all right, the whole beach experience might be retrieved. Pauline couldn't tell if Caitlin was now making those little splashy runs into the water for his benefit, or whether he was watching her with interest or scorn.

Mara didn't need company, at least for now. She stumbled toward the water, felt it touch her feet and changed her mind, stopped, looked around, and spotted Pauline. "Paw. Paw," she said, in happy recognition. "Paw" was what she said for "Pauline," instead of "Mother" or "Mommy." Looking around overbalanced her; she sat down half on the sand and half in the water, made a squawk of surprise which turned into an announcement, and then, by some determined ungraceful maneuvers that involved putting her weight on her hands, rose to her feet, wavering and triumphant. She had been walking for half a year, but getting around on the sand was still a challenge. Now she came back toward Pauline, making some reasonable casual remarks in her own language.

130   "Sand," said Pauline, holding up a clot of it. "Look. Mara. Sand."

Mara corrected her, calling it something else—it sounded like "whap." Her thick diaper under her plastic pants and her terry-cloth playsuit gave her a fat bottom, and that, along with her plump cheeks and shoulders and her sidelong important expression, made her look like a roguish matron.

Pauline became aware of someone calling her name. It had been called two or three times, but because the voice was unfamiliar she had not recognized it. She stood up and waved. It was the woman who worked in the store at the Lodge. She was leaning over the porch rail calling, "Mrs. Keating. Mrs. Keating? Telephone, Mrs. Keating."

Pauline hoisted Mara onto her hip and summoned Caitlin. She and the little boy were aware of each other now: they were both picking up stones from the bottom and flinging them out into the water. At first she didn't hear Pauline, or pretended not to hear.

"Store," called Pauline. "Caitlin. Store." When she was sure Caitlin would follow—it was the word "store" that had done it, the reminder of the tiny store in the Lodge where you could buy ice cream and candy—she began the trek across the sand and up the flight of wooden steps. Halfway up she stopped, said, "Mara, you weigh a ton," and shifted the baby to her other hip. Caitlin followed, banging a stick against the railing.

135   "Can I have a Fudgsicle? Mother? Can I?"

"We'll see."

The public phone was beside a bulletin board on the other side of the main hall and across from the door to the dining room. A bingo game had been set up in there, because of the rain.

"Hope he's still hanging on," the woman who worked in the store called out. She was unseen now behind her counter.

Pauline, still holding Mara, picked up the dangling receiver and said breathlessly, "Hello?" She was expecting to hear Brian telling her about some delay in Campbell River or asking her what it was she had wanted him to get at the drugstore. It was just the one thing—calamine lotion—so he had not written it down.

140   "Pauline," said Jeffrey. "It's me."

Mara was bumping and scrambling along Pauline's side, eager to get down. Caitlin came along the hall and went into the store, leaving wet sandy footprints. Pauline said, "Just a minute, just a minute." She let Mara slide down and hurried to close the door that led to the steps. She did not remember telling Jeffrey the name of this place, though she had told him roughly where it was. She heard the woman in the store speaking to Caitlin in a sharper voice than she would use to children whose parents were beside them.

"Did you forget to put your feet under that tap?"

"I'm here," said Jeffrey. "I didn't get along so well without you. I didn't get along at all."

Mara made for the dining room, as if the male voice calling out "Under the N" were a direct invitation to her.

145   "Here. Where?" said Pauline.

She read the signs that were tacked up on the bulletin board beside the phone:

> No Person Under Fourteen Years of Age Not Accompanied by
> Adult Allowed in Boats or Canoes.
> Fishing Derby.
> Bake and Craft Sale, St. Bartholomew's Church.
> You life is in your hands. Palms and Cards read. Reasonable and
> Accurate. Call Claire.

"In a motel. In Campbell River."

Pauline knows where she is before she opens her eyes. Nothing surprises her. She has slept, but not deeply enough to let go of anything.

She had waited for Brian in the parking area of the Lodge, with the children in tow, and then she had asked for the keys. She told him in front of his parents that there was something else she needed, from Campbell River. He asked what was it? And did she have any money?

"Just something," she said, so he would think that it was tampons or birth-control supplies, something that she didn't want to mention.

150   "Sure. O.K., but you'll have to put some gas in," he said.

Later she had to speak to him on the phone. Jeffrey said she had to do it.

"Because he won't take it from me. He'll think I kidnapped you or something. He won't believe it."

But the strangest thing of all the things that day was that Brian did seem, immediately, to believe it. Standing where she had stood not so long before, in the public hallway of the Lodge—the bingo game over now, but people going past, she could hear them, people on their way out of the dining room after dinner—Brian had said, "Oh. Oh. Oh. O.K.," in a voice that would have to be quickly controlled but that seemed to draw on a supply of fatalism or foreknowledge that went far beyond that necessity.

"O.K.," he said. "What about the car?"

155   He said something else, something impossible, and then hung up, and she came out of the phone booth beside a row of gas pumps in Campbell River.

"That was quick," Jeffrey said. "Easier than you expected?"

Pauline said, "I don't know."

"He may have known it subconsciously. People do know."

She shook her head, to tell him not to say any more, and he said, "Sorry." They walked along the street not touching or talking.

160   Now, looking around at leisure—the first real leisure or freedom she's had since she came into that room—Pauline sees that there isn't much of anything in it. Just a junky dresser, the bed without a headboard, an armless upholstered chair. On the window a Venetian blind with a broken slat. Also a noisy air-conditioner—Jeffrey turned it off in the night and left the door open on the chain, since the window was sealed. The door is shut now. He must have got up in the night and shut it.

This is all she has. Her connection with the cottage where Brian lies now asleep or not asleep is broken. Also her connection with the house that has been an expression of her life with Brian, of the way they wanted to live. She has cut herself off from all the large solid acquisitions, like the washer and dryer and the oak table and the refinished wardrobe and the chandelier that is a copy of the one in a painting by Vermeer. And just as much from those things that were particularly hers—the pressed-glass tumblers that she had been collecting and the prayer rug that was probably not authentic, but beautiful. Especially from those things. The skirt and blouse and sandals she put on for the trip to Campbell River might as well be all she has now to her name. She would never go back to lay claim to anything. If Brian got in touch with her to ask what was to be done with things, she would tell him to do what he liked—throw everything into garbage bags and take it to the dump, if that was what he liked. (In fact she knows that he will probably pack up a trunk, which he does, sending on, scrupulously, not only her winter coat and boots but things like the waist cincher she wore at her wedding and never since, with the prayer rug draped on top of everything like a final statement of his generosity, either natural or calculated.)

She believes that she will never again care about what sort of rooms she lives in or what sort of clothes she puts on. She will not be looking for that sort of help to give anybody an idea of who she is, what she is like. Not even to give herself an idea. What she has done will be enough, it will be the whole thing.

What she has done will be what she has heard about and read about. It will be what Anna Karenina did and what Mme. Bovary wanted to do. And what a teacher at Brian's school did, with the school secretary. He ran off with her. That was what it was called. Running off with. Taking off with. It was spoken of disparagingly, humorously, enviously. It was adultery taken one step further. The people who did had almost certainly been having an affair already, committing adultery for quite some time before they became desperate or courageous enough to take this step. Once in a long while a couple might claim their love was unconsummated and technically pure, but these people would be thought of—if anybody believed them—as being not only very serious and high-minded but almost devastatingly foolish, almost in a class with those who gave up everything to go and work in some poor and dangerous country.

The others, the adulterers, were seen as irresponsible, immature, self-ish, or even cruel. Also lucky. They were lucky because the sex they had been having in parked cars or the long grass or in each other's sullied marriage beds or most likely in motels like this one must surely have been splendid. Otherwise they would never have got such a yearning for each other's company at all costs or such a faith that their shared future would be altogether better and different in kind from what they had in the past.

165   Different in kind. That is what Pauline must believe now—that there is this major difference in lives or in marriages or unions between people. That some of them have a necessity, a fatefulness about them, which others do not have. Of course she would have said the same thing a year ago. People did say that, they seemed to believe that, and to believe that their own cases were all of the first, the special kind, even when anybody could see that they were not.

It is too warm in the room. Jeffrey's body is too warm. Conviction and contentiousness seem to radiate from it, even in sleep. His torso is thicker than Brian's, he is pudgier around the waist. More flesh on the bones, yet not so slack to the touch. Not so good-looking in general—she is sure most people would say that. And not so fastidious. Brian in bed smells of nothing. Jeffrey's skin, every time she's been with him, has had a baked-in, slightly oily or nutty smell. He didn't wash last night—but, then, neither did she. There wasn't time. Did he even have a toothbrush with him? She didn't, but she had not known she was staying.

When she met Jeffrey here it was still in the back of her mind that she had to concoct some colossal lie to serve her when she got home. And she—they—had to hurry. When Jeffrey said to her that he had decided that they must stay together, that she would come with him to Washington State, that they would have to drop the play because things would be too difficult for them in Victoria, she had looked at him just in the blank way you'd look at somebody the moment that an earthquake started. She was ready to tell him all the reasons why this was not possible, she still thought she was going to tell him that, but her life was coming adrift in that moment. To go back would be like tying a sack over her head.

All she said was "Are you sure?"

He said, "Sure." He said sincerely, "I'll never leave you."

170   That did not seem the sort of thing that he would say. Then she realized he was quoting—maybe ironically—from the play. It was what Orphée says to Eurydice within a few moments of their first meeting in the station buffet.

So her life was falling forward, she was becoming one of those people who ran away. A woman who shockingly and incomprehensibly gave everything up. For love, observers would say wryly. Meaning, for sex. None of this would happen if it weren't for sex.

And yet what's the great difference there? It's not such a variable procedure, in spite of what you're told. Skins, motions, contact, results. Pauline isn't a woman from whom it's difficult to get results. Brian got them. Probably anybody would, who wasn't wildly inept or morally disgusting.

But nothing's the same, really. With Brian—especially, with Brian, to whom she has dedicated a selfish sort of good will, with whom she's lived in married complicity—there can never be this stripping away, the inevitable flight, the feelings she doesn't have to strive for but only to give in to like breathing or dying. That she believes can only come when the skin is on Jeffrey, the motions made by Jeffrey, and the weight that bears down on her has Jeffrey's heart in it, also his habits, thoughts, peculiarities, his ambition and loneliness (that for all she knows may have mostly to do with his youth).

For all she knows. There's a lot she doesn't know. She hardly knows anything about what he likes to eat or what music he likes to listen to or what role his mother plays in his life (no doubt a mysterious but important one, like the role of Brian's parents). One thing she's pretty sure of: whatever preferences or prohibitions he has will be definite. Plates in his armor.

175 She slides out from under Jeffrey's hand and from under the top sheet, which has a harsh smell of bleach, slips down to the floor where the bedspread is lying and wraps herself quickly in that rag of greenish-yellow chenille. She doesn't want him to open his eyes and see her from behind and note the droop of her buttocks. He's seen her naked before, but generally in a more forgiving moment.

She rinses her mouth and washes herself, using the bar of soap that is about the size of two thin squares of chocolate and firm as stone. She's hard used between the legs, swollen and stinking. Urinating takes an effort and it seems she's constipated. Last night when they went out and got hamburgers she found she could not eat. Presumably she'll learn to do all these things again, they'll resume their natural importance in her life. At the moment it's as if she can't quite spare the attention.

She has some money in her purse. She has to go out and buy a toothbrush, toothpaste, deodorant, shampoo. Also vaginal jelly. Last night they used condoms the first two times but nothing the third time.

She didn't bring her watch and Jeffrey doesn't wear one. There's no clock in the room, of course. She thinks it's early—there's still an early look to the light in spite of the heat. The stores probably won't be open, but there'll be someplace where she can get coffee.

Jeffrey has turned onto his other side. She must have wakened him, just for a moment.

180 They'll have a bedroom. A kitchen, an address. He'll go to work. She'll go to the laundromat. Maybe she'll go to work, too. Selling things, waiting on tables, tutoring students. She knows French and Latin—do they teach French and Latin in American high schools? Can you get a job if you're not and American? Jeffrey isn't.

She leaves him the key. She'll have to wake him to get back in. There's nothing to write a note with, or on.

It is early. The motel is on the highway at the north end of town, beside the bridge. There's no traffic yet. She scuffs back and forth under the cottonwood trees at the edge of the lot for quite a while before a vehicle of any kind rumbles over the bridge—though the traffic on it shook their bed regularly late into the night.

Something is coming now. A truck. But not just a truck—there's a large bleak fact coming at her. And it has not arrived out of nowhere—it's been waiting, cruelly nudging at her ever since she woke up or even all night.

Caitlin and Mara.

185 Last night on the phone, after speaking in such a flat and controlled and almost agreeable voice—as if he prided himself on not being shocked, not

objecting or pleading—Brian cracked open. He said with contempt and fury and no concern for whoever might hear him, "Well, then—what about the kids?"

The receiver began to shake against Pauline's ear.

She said, "We'll talk—" but he did not seem to hear her.

"The children," he said, in this same shivering and vindictive voice. Changing the word "kids" to "children" was like slamming a board down on her—a heavy, formal, righteous threat.

"The children stay," Brian said. "Pauline. Did you hear me?"

190   "No," said Pauline. "Yes. I heard you, but—"

"All right. You heard me. Remember. The children stay."

It was all he could do. To make her see what she was doing, what she was ending, and to punish her if she did so. Nobody would blame him. There might be finagling, there might be bargaining, there would certainly be humbling of herself, but there it was, like a round cold stone in her gullet, like a cannonball. And it would remain there unless she changed her mind entirely. The children stay.

Their car—hers and Brian's—is still sitting in the motel parking lot. Brian will have to ask his father or his mother to drive him up here today to get it. She has the keys in her purse. There are spare keys—he will surely bring them. She unlocks the car door and throws her keys on the seat, then locks the door from the inside and shuts it.

Now she can't go back. She can't get into the car and drive back and say that she'd been insane. If she did that he would forgive her but he'd never get over it and neither would she. They'd go on, though, as people did.

195   She walks out of the parking lot, she walks along the sidewalk, into town.

The weight of Mara on her hip yesterday. The sight of Caitlin's footprints on the floor.

Paw. Paw.

She doesn't need the keys to get back to them, she doesn't need the car. She could beg a ride on the highway. Give in, give in, get back to them any way at all—how can she not do that?

A sack over her head.

200   This is acute pain. It will become chronic. Chronic means that it will be permanent but perhaps not constant. It may also mean that you won't die of it. You won't get free of it but you won't die of it. You won't feel it every minute but you won't spend many days without it, either. And you'll learn some tricks to dull it or banish it or else you'll end up destroying what you've got. What you incurred this pain to get. It isn't his fault. He's still an innocent or a savage, who doesn't know there's a pain so durable in the world. Say to yourself, You lose them anyway. They grow up. For a mother there's always waiting this private, slightly ridiculous desolation. They'll forget this time, in one way or another they'll disown you. Or hang around till you don't know what to do about them, the way Brian has.

And, still, what pain. To carry along and get used to until it's only the past you're grieving for and no longer any possible present.

Her children have grown up. They don't hate her. For going away or staying away. They don't forgive her, either. Perhaps they wouldn't have forgiven her anyway, but it would have been about something different.

Caitlin remembers a little about the summer at the Lodge, Mara nothing. Caitlin calls it "that place Grandma and Grandpa stayed at."
    "The place we were at when you went away," she says. "Only we
didn't know you went away with the man who was Orphée."
205   Pauline has told them about the play.
    Pauline says, "It wasn't Orphée."
    "It wasn't Orphée? Oh, well. I thought it was."
    "No."
    "Who was it, then?"
210   "Just a man connected," says Pauline. "It wasn't him."

✳ TOPICS FOR CRITICAL THINKING AND WRITING

1. Pauline is interested in having an affair. Does Munro give any hints that
   something is missing from Pauline's life? Another way of putting this
   question: If an author says that a character is interested in having an affair, is the author obligated to suggest in what ways the character's life
   is unsatisfactory?
2. Characterize Brian. Why do you suppose Pauline married him?
3. Is it your guess that men differ from women in their responses to this
   story? Please explain your view.

*This essay originated as a lecture that was revised for publication in John
Metcalf's* Making It New: Contemporary Canadian Stories *(1982).*

What Is Real?   [1982]

Whenever people get an opportunity to ask me questions about my writing,
I can be sure that some of the questions asked will be these:
    "Do you write about real people?"
    "Did those things really happen?"
    "When you write about a small town are you really writing about Wing-
ham?" (Wingham is the small town in Ontario where I was born and grew
up, and it has often been assumed, by people who should know better, that
I have simply "fictionalized" this place in my work. Indeed, the local newspaper has taken me to task for making it the "butt of a soured and cruel
introspection.")
5   The usual thing, for writers, is to regard these either as very naive questions, asked by people who really don't understand the difference between
autobiography and fiction, who can't recognize the device of the first-
person narrator, or else as catch-you-out questions posed by journalists who
hope to stir up exactly the sort of dreary (and to outsiders, slightly comic)
indignation voiced by my home-town paper. Writers answer such questions
patiently or crossly according to temperament and the mood they're in.
They say, no, you must understand, my characters are composites; no, those
things didn't happen the way I wrote about them; no, of course not, that
isn't Wingham (or whatever other place it may be that has had the queer
unsought-after distinction of hatching a writer). Or the writer may, riskily,

ask the questioners what is real, anyway? None of this seems to be very satisfactory. People go on asking these same questions because the subject really does interest and bewilder them. It would seem to be quite true that they don't know what fiction is.

And how could they know, when what it is, is changing all the time, and we differ among ourselves, and we don't really try to explain because it is too difficult?

What I would like to do here is what I can't do in two or three sentences at the end of a reading. I won't try to explain what fiction is, and what short stories are (assuming, which we can't, that there is any fixed thing that it is and they are), but what short stories are to me, and how I write them, and how I use things that are "real." I will start by explaining how I read stories written by other people. For one thing, I can start reading them anywhere; from beginning to end, from end to beginning, from any point in between in either direction. So obviously I don't take up a story and follow it as if it were a road, taking me somewhere, with views and neat diversions along the way. I go into it, and move back and forth and settle here and there, and stay in it for a while. It's more like a house. Everybody knows what a house does, how it encloses space and makes connections between one enclosed space and another and presents what is outside in a new way. This is the nearest I can come to explaining what a story does for me, and what I want my stories to do for other people.

So when I write a story I want to make a certain kind of structure, and I know the feeling I want to get from being inside that structure. This is the hard part of the explanation, where I have to use a word like "feeling," which is not very precise, because if I attempt to be more intellectually respectable I will have to be dishonest. "Feeling" will have to do.

There is no blueprint for the structure. It's not a question of, "I'll make this kind of house because if I do it right it will have this effect." I've got to make, I've got to build up, a house, a story, to fit around the indescribable "feeling" that is like the soul of the story, and which I must insist upon in a dogged, embarrassed way, as being no more definable than that. And I don't know where it comes from. It seems to be already there, and some unlikely clue, such as a shop window or a bit of conversation, makes me aware of it. Then I start accumulating the material and putting it together. Some of the material I may have lying around already, in memories and observations, and some I invent, and some I have to go diligently looking for (factual details), while some is dumped in my lap (anecdotes, bits of speech). I see how this material might go together to make the shape I need, and I try it. I keep trying and seeing where I went wrong and trying again.

10   I suppose this is the place where I should talk about technical problems and how I solve them. The main reason I can't is that I'm never sure I do solve anything. Even when I say that I see where I went wrong, I'm being misleading. I never figure out how I'm going to change things, I never say to myself, "That page is heavy going, that paragraph's clumsy, I need some dialogue and shorter sentences." I feel a part that's wrong, like a soggy weight; then I pay attention to the story, as if it were really happening somewhere, not just in my head, and in its own way, not mine. As a result, the sentences may indeed get shorter, there may be more dialogue, and so on. But though I've tried to pay attention to the story, I may not have got it right; those shorter sentences may be an evasion, a mistake. Every final

draft, every published story, is still only an attempt, an approach, to the story.

I did promise to talk about using reality. "Why, if Jubliee isn't Wingham, has it got Shuter Street in it?" people want to know. Why have I described somebody's real ceramic elephant sitting on the mantelpiece? I could say I get momentum from doing things like this. The fictional room, town, world, needs a bit of starter dough from the real world. It's a device to help the writer—at least it helps me—but it arouses a certain baulked fury in the people who really do live on Shuter Street and the lady who owns the ceramic elephant. "Why do you put in something true and then go on and tell lies?" they say, and anybody who has been on the receiving end of this kind of thing knows how they feel.

"I do it for the sake of my art and to make this structure which encloses the soul of my story, that I've been telling you about," says the writer. "That is more important than anything."

Not to everybody, it isn't.

So I can see there might be a case, once you've written the story and got the momentum, for going back and changing the elephant to a camel (though there's always a chance the lady might complain that you made a nasty camel out of a beautiful elephant), and changing Shuter Street to Blank Street. But what about the big chunks of reality, without which your story can't exist? In the story *Royal Beatings,* I use a big chunk of reality: the story of the butcher, and of the young men who may have been egged on to "get" him. This is a story out of an old newspaper; it really did happen in a town I know. There is no legal difficulty about using it because it has been printed in a newspaper, and besides, the people who figure in it are all long dead. But there is a difficulty about offending people in that town who would feel that use of this story is a deliberate exposure, taunt and insult. Other people who have no connection with the real happening would say, "Why write about anything so hideous?" And lest you think that such an objection could only be raised by simple folk who read nothing but Harlequin Romances, let me tell you that one of the questions most frequently asked at universities is, "Why do you write about things that are so depressing?" People can accept almost any amount of ugliness if it is contained in a familiar formula, as it is on television, but when they come closer to their own place, their own lives, they are much offended by a lack of editing.

15   There are ways I can defend myself against such objections. I can say, "I do it in the interests of historical reality. That is what the old days were really like." Or, "I do it to show the dark side of human nature, the beast let loose, the evil we can run up against in communities and families." In certain countries I could say, "I do it to show how bad things were under the old system when there were prosperous butchers and young fellows hanging around livery stables and nobody thought about building a new society." But the fact is, the minute I say *to show* I am telling a lie. I don't do it to show anything. I put this story at the heart of my story because I need it there and it belongs there. It is the black room at the center of the house with all other rooms leading to and away from it. That is all. A strange defense. Who told me to write this story? Who feels any need of it before it is written? I do. I do, so that I might grab off this piece of horrid reality and install it where I see fit, even if Hat Nettleton and his friends were still around to make me sorry.

The answer seems to be as confusing as ever. Lots of true answers are. Yes and no. Yes, I use bits of what is real, in the sense of being really there and really happening, in the world, as most people see it, and I transform it into something that is really there and really happening, in my story. No, I am not concerned with using what is real to make any sort of record or prove any sort of point, and I am not concerned with any methods of selection but my own, which I can't fully explain. This is quite presumptuous, and if writers are not allowed to be so—and quite often, in many places, they are not—I see no point in the writing of fiction.

John Metcalf interviewed Alice Munro and published the interview in the Journal of Canadian Fiction *1:4 (Fall, 1972): 54-62. We reprint a passage that is especially concerned with differences between men and women as writers.*

A Conversation   [1972]

METCALF   How has being a woman affected the acceptance of your work or the rate of work produced by you?

MUNRO   I don't think it's affected the acceptance at all but I suppose it's affected the rate, you know, my productivity because of my life as a child-rearing person but on the other hand I have not had to be a wage-earning person so I always wonder about this . . . if I have any right to claim that I've had a tougher time. Though I think it's possible if you are a man to get a Canada Council Grant and say this is the year I'm going to write and usually one has a co-operative wife who keeps the kids away. This is my, perhaps, my . . . quite unreal vision of a man's life in that he goes into his room and locks the door and he writes. Well, a woman never does this.

METCALF   Would you describe yourself as a feminist?

MUNRO   I'm not really sure what a feminist is. You've got to define that further.

METCALF   O.K. Have you had any formal relationship with the Women's Liberation movement?

MUNRO   Yes I'm in general, sympathetic.

METCALF   But not particularly active in any political sort of . . . ?

MUNRO   But not active because I'm not a political person. Maybe this is a cop out. Maybe I should be active but I don't have enough energy to stand off in any other direction.

METCALF   Do you think it's really possible for a woman to combine being married in a conventional, traditional sense of what being married has meant and being a writer?

MUNRO   It's very hard . . . um . . . it's not just hard in the question of when do I get time to write or will my writing affect my husband's ego or, you know, all these sort of surface problems you can deal with. But I think it's hard to be a married woman and a writer because I feel that in traditional marriage, as it's been up to now, as it is with most women in my generation . . . a woman abdicates, in a way, . . . she . . . This is turning out to be hard to say . . . she is no longer a completely unbiased observer. She has something to defend. There may be truths that she sees that she would prefer not to see; that she can't see if she wants to maintain her situation and a writer, of course, has to be free of shackles of this sort. I don't know if the same might apply to a married man but I have noticed that men have . . . always seem freer to tell the truth. They tell the truth about their marriages and about themselves, about their bodies. Men write these novels in which they tell about how . . . they feel physically and about how hellish they look when they look in the mirror . . . and all this sort of crap. Women have been bound by quite a different set of conventions. It's much more difficult to explore your life honestly and if you're married it is just that much more difficult because you live within a certain framework that is pretty hard to question because if you start questioning it too far you may be in big trouble. Or your marriage may be in trouble.

METCALF   Does it frighten you that many successful women writers have led very a-typical lives?

MUNRO   Yes. It does frighten me because I'm a fairly security-demanding person. I don't think I'm in any danger of ever leading a bizarre life. I tend to be a person of rather dull habits just because I want to work so much. I don't endanger this by having an exciting life.

METCALF   Do you feel that it's purely and *simply* the traditional social set up and the traditional roles which are played by men and women which have driven women writers in the past into rather strange lifestyles? Is it *merely* the conflict between "a woman's place" and . . .

MUNRO   No. I think it's a conflict for all writers. Really, isn't it, for men *and* women? Don't almost as many men writers lead fairly a-typical lives?

METCALF   Well, in terms of the work-a-day world, yes. Writers are usually extremely egotistical people. When you come across a woman who has said I am this and I am creating this and I am doing this a traditional male reaction to this is to say this woman is insane or . . . voracious, or destructive or . . .

MUNRO   Yeah. So if you are a woman who is like this, you either become blatantly so and say to hell with them or you develop disguises which is the way I've managed so far. But there is probably a contradiction in many women writers in the woman *herself* . . . Between the woman who is ambitious and the woman who is there who is also . . . well, what, was called traditionally feminine, who is passive, who wants to be dominated, who wants to have someone between her and the world. And I know *I'm* like this. I have the two women. So . . .

METCALF   Various people, not in the academic world, but people who have read *Lives of Girls and Women* with delight and interest have remarked to me that they were surprised by the way in which the brother and the father seemed to disappear somehow . . . or were shunted off to the fox farm. They don't seem to figure very largely. Now I don't really know if I'm asking an autobiographical question here or a question which is concerned with the artistic purpose of the book. Could you comment on that?

MUNRO   Well, I'm not sure what the answer is either. In the book, I found, I didn't really intend to do this at the beginning, but I found that my emphasis, my interest was shifting so much to the mother that I had to be able to deal with her alone. I couldn't deal with both parents. I have a fairly narrow focus or something so the father tended to, sort of, fade away. But I think there is . . . well, you can see this in "Boys and Girls" too, the father picks the brother and their life is separated.

METCALF   He trains the son into the model that he is to become.

MUNRO   This is certainly what happened in my family and what happens in most traditional, say, farm families.

METCALF   I heard a tape that you made some time ago that was on the C.B.C. where I believe you said that women cannot create men characters as well as men can create women characters.

MUNRO   Hell! Did I say *that!* Well, I must have been crazy because I don't think men can create women characters either. I must have been worn down when I said that . . . because when people come up to me and say, as people have, you know at cocktail parties and things and say . . . well there aren't any real men in that book . . . I say, well, show me the real woman in a man's book. Not very many writers, the great ones *can* create characters of both sexes. But it doesn't often happen, I think.

METCALF   What do you think of D.H. Lawrence's women? I've always found them the most bizarre and peculiar creatures.

MUNRO   Oh. They're impossible. But there again, I suppose they're personifications of ideas. Except for the mother in *Sons and Lovers,* I find a real character. She is the only one I can think of. Can you think of any very good and convincing female characters created by men?

9

Law and Disorder: Narratives from Biblical Times to the Present

The law is the law and literature is literature, but they do have something in common other than both beginning with the same letter. Archibald MacLeish, a poet (see page 997) and a lawyer, wrote in an essay called "Art and Law":

> The business of the law is to make sense of the confusion of what we call human life—to reduce it to order but at the same time to give it possibility, scope, even dignity. (*Riders on Earth* [1978], p. 85)

MacLeish's idea that law attempts to make sense of confusion can be compared to a famous comment by Robert Frost, to the effect that every poem

> runs a course of lucky events, and ends in a clarification of life—not necessarily a great clarification, such as sects and cults are founded on, but in a momentary stay against confusion. (*Collected Poems, Prose, and Plays* [1994], p. 777)

Obviously literary forms—tragedy, comedy, the sonnet, the short story—impose a pattern on the chaos of experience, depicting a life as, say, a tragedy, or a comedy, or seeing an episode (real or invented) in the shape of a sonnet—with a beginning, a middle, and an end. Equally obviously, the law, as MacLeish says, seeks to find patterns: In the particular case of *X*, with all its specific details (some of which may be irrelevant), the law tries to fit the case into a set of known principles, and in fact the law may deliberately use fictions in order to clarify the reality. That is, in an effort to show that a particular highly detailed case conforms to a basic principle or pattern, a lawyer may say, "Consider the case of John Doe, who finds a wallet in the street," or "Let us assume that a woman, seeing a man slip on a banana peel, helps him to his feet, whereupon he slips again, this time doing great damage to his back. . . ."

In the process of making sense of what MacLeish calls "the confusion of . . . life," and what Frost calls "a course of lucky events," the reader of literature or the spectator in a courtroom is confronted with conflict, conflict that the author and the judge or jury ultimately resolve, presumably to general satisfaction. As we will try to show in our chapters on poetry, even a brief lyric poem

273

contains a sort of plot with a conflict, for instance (in a song called "Careless Love") a lover lamenting the loss of a partner. But some works of literature are explicitly based on a courtroom conflict, for instance Franz Kafka's *The Trial*, Shakespeare's *The Merchant of Venice*, and Melville's *Billy Budd*. This chapter includes several short literary works in which trials are central.

ANONYMOUS

The following story about King Solomon, customarily called "The Judgment of Solomon," appears in the Hebrew Bible, in the latter part of the third chapter of the book called 1 Kings or First Kings, probably written in the mid-sixth century BCE. *The translation is from the King James Version of the Bible (1611). Two expressions in the story need clarification: (1) The woman who "overlaid" her child in her sleep rolled over on the child and suffocated it; and (2) it is said of a woman that her "bowels yearned upon her son"—that is, her heart longed for her son. (In Hebrew psychology, the bowels were thought to be the seat of emotion.)*

The Judgment of Solomon

Then came there two women, that were harlots, unto the king, and stood before him. And the one woman said, "O my lord, I and this woman dwell in one house, and I was delivered of a child with her in the house. And it came to pass the third day after that I was delivered, that this woman was delivered also: and we were together; there was no stranger in the house, save we two in the house. And this woman's child died in the night; because she overlaid it. And she arose at midnight, and took my son from beside me, while thine handmaid slept, and laid it in her bosom, and laid her dead child in my bosom. And when I rose in the morning to give my child suck, behold, it was dead: but when I considered it in the morning, behold, it was not my son, which I did bear."

And the other woman said, "Nay; but the living is my son, and the dead is thy son." And this said, "No; but the dead is thy son, and the living is my son." Thus they spake before the king.

Then said the king, "The one saith, 'This is my son that liveth, and thy son is dead': and the other saith, 'Nay; but thy son is the dead, and my son is the living.'" And the king said, "Bring me a sword." And they brought a sword before the king. And the king said, "Divide the living child in two, and give half to the one, and half to the other."

Then spake the woman whose the living child was unto the king, for her bowels yearned upon her son, and she said, "O my lord, give her the living child, and in no wise slay it." But the other said, "Let it be neither mine nor thine, but divide it."

Then the king answered and said, "Give her the living child, and in no wise slay it: she is the mother thereof."

And all Israel heard of the judgment which the king had judged; and they feared the king, for they saw that the wisdom of God was in him to do judgment.

TOPICS FOR CRITICAL THINKING AND WRITING

1. In what ways is this story like a detective story?
2. Solomon was known for his wisdom. How would you characterize his wisdom?

JOHN

The following story, The Woman Taken in Adultery, appears in several places in various early manuscripts of the New Testament, for instance in the Gospel according to Luke, after 21.38, and in the Gospel according to John, after 7.36 and, in other manuscripts of John, after 7.53. The most famous English translation of the Bible, the King James Version (1611), gives it at John 8.1–11, and so it is commonly regarded as belonging to John. But most Biblical scholars agree that the language of this short story differs notably from the language of the rest of this Gospel, and that it is not in any manuscript of John before the sixth century is further evidence that it was not originally part of this Gospel.

The Gospel according to John was apparently compiled in the late first century. John 21.20–24 says the author, or "the disciple which testifieth of these things," is "the disciple whom Jesus loved, . . . which also leaned on his breast at supper, and said, Lord, which is he that betrayeth thee?" Since the second century the book has traditionally been ascribed to John, one of the inner circle of twelve disciples.

The Woman Taken in Adultery

Jesus went unto the mount of Olives. And early in the morning he came again into the temple, and all the people came unto him; and he sat down, and taught them.

And the scribes and Pharisees[1] brought unto him a woman taken in adultery; and when they had set her in the midst, they say unto him, "Master, this woman was taken in adultery, in the very act. Now Moses in the law commanded us that such should be stoned: but what sayest thou?" This they said, tempting him, that they might have to accuse him. But Jesus stooped down, and with his finger wrote on the ground, as though he heard them not. So when they continued asking him, he lifted up himself, and said unto them, "He that is without sin among you, let him first cast a stone at her." And again he stooped down, and wrote on the ground. And they which heard it, being convicted by their own conscience, went out one by one, beginning at the eldest, even unto the last: and Jesus was left alone, and the woman standing in the midst.

---

[1]**scribes and Pharisees** the scribes were specialists who copied and interpreted the Hebrew law; the Pharisees were members of a sect that emphasized strict adherence to the Mosaic law.

When Jesus had lifted up himself, and saw none but the woman, he said unto her, "Woman, where are those thine accusers? Hath no man condemned thee?" She said, "No man, Lord." And Jesus said unto her, "Neither do I condemn thee; go, and sin no more."

▨ TOPICS FOR CRITICAL THINKING AND WRITING

1. Do you interpret the episode of the Woman Taken in Adultery to say that crime should go unpunished? Or that adultery is not a crime? Or that a judge cannot punish a crime if he himself is guilty of it? Or what?
2. We read that Jesus wrote with his finger on the ground, but we are not told what Jesus wrote. How relevant to the story do you find this action by Jesus? Explain.
3. This story is widely quoted and alluded to. Why, in your opinion, does the story have such broad appeal?

FRANZ KAFKA

Frank Kafka (1883–1924) was born in Prague, Austria-Hungary, the son of German-speaking middle-class Jewish parents. Trained in law, he worked from 1907 to 1922 in an insurance company sponsored by the government. In 1923 he moved to Berlin to concentrate on becoming a writer, but he suffered from poor health, and during his brief literary career he published only a few stories, including "The Metamorphosis" (1915), which depicts the transformation of its main character into a gigantic insect.

Through the agency of his friend Max Brod, a number of works by Kafka were published posthumously, including The Trial *(1925; trans. 1937),* The Castle *(1926; trans. 1937), and* Amerika *(1927; trans. 1938). Among twentieth-century authors, Kafka's accounts of alienation and anxiety, of bewildered, isolated individuals trapped by law and bureaucracy, are unparalleled in their power and pain. In the words of the poet-critic W. H. Auden, writing in the late 1950s, "Had one to name the author who comes nearest to bearing the same kind of relation to our age as Dante, Shakespeare, and Goethe bore to theirs, Kafka is the first one would think of." "Before the Law" (1914) is among the stories that Kafka published during his lifetime.*

Before the Law   [1914]

Translated by Willa and Edwin Muir

Before the Law stands a doorkeeper. To this doorkeeper there comes a man from the country and prays for admittance to the Law. But the doorkeeper says that he cannot grant admittance at the moment. The man thinks it over and then asks if he will be allowed in later. "It is possible," says the doorkeeper, "but not at the moment." Since the gate stands open, as usual, and the doorkeeper steps to one side, the man stoops to peer through the gateway into the interior. Observing that, the doorkeeper laughs and says: "If you are so drawn to it, just try to go in despite my veto. But take note: I am powerful. And I am only the least of the doorkeepers. From hall to hall there is one doorkeeper after another, each more powerful than the last. The third doorkeeper is already so terrible that even I cannot bear to look at him." These are difficulties the man from the country has not expected; the Law, he thinks, should surely be accessible at all times and to everyone, but as he now takes a closer look at the doorkeeper in his fur coat, with his big sharp nose and long, thin, black Tartar beard, he decides that it is better to wait until he gets permission to enter. The doorkeeper gives him a stool and lets him sit down at one side of the door. There he sits for days and years. He makes many attempts to be admitted, and wearies the doorkeeper by his importunity. The doorkeeper frequently has little interviews with him, asking him questions about his home and many other things, but the questions are put indifferently, as great lords put them, and always finished with the statement that he cannot be let in yet. The man, who has furnished himself with many things for his journey, sacrifices all he has, however valuable, to bribe the doorkeeper. The doorkeeper accepts everything, but always with the remark: "I am only taking it to keep you from thinking you have omitted anything." During these many years the man fixes his attention almost continuously on the doorkeeper. He forgets the other doorkeepers, and this first one seems to him the sole obstacle preventing access to the Law. He curses his bad luck, in his early years boldly and loudly; later, as he grows old, he only grumbles to himself. He becomes childish, and since in his yearlong contemplation of the doorkeeper he has come to know even the fleas on his fur coat, he begs the fleas as well to help him and to change the doorkeeper's mind. At length his eyesight begins to fail, and he does not know whether the world is really darker or whether his eyes are only deceiving him. Yet in his darkness he is now aware of a radiance that streams inextinguishable from the gateway of the Law. Now he has not very long to live. Before he dies, all his experiences in these long years gather themselves in his head to one point, a question he has not yet asked the doorkeeper. He waves him nearer, since he can no longer raise his stiffening body. The doorkeeper has to bend low towards him, much to the man's disadvantage. "What do you want to know now?" asks the doorkeeper; "you are insatiable." "Everyone strives to reach the Law," says the man, "so how does it happen that for all these many years no one but myself has ever begged for admittance?" The doorkeeper recognizes that the man has reached his end, and, to let his failing senses catch the words, roars in his ears: "No one else could ever be admitted here, since this gate was made only for you. I am now going to shut it."

❈ TOPICS FOR CRITICAL THINKING AND WRITING

1. At a glance, we can see that this story consists of a single paragraph. Why would a writer want to do this? Won't such a story inevitably be too short?
2. Why is the first sentence so effective?
3. What is the significance of the man's failing eyesight? Of the imagery of darkness and radiance?
4. At the end of the story, as the man nears death, what at last does he learn? What is it that Kafka wants us as readers to learn?

5. Henry David Thoreau wrote in his *Journal* (1851) that "the man for whom law exists—the man of forms, the conservative—is a tame man." From your reading of "Before the Law," what do you think would be Kafka's response to this claim?

ELIZABETH BISHOP

Elizabeth Bishop (1911-1979) is chiefly known as a poet, and we include a poem (as well as a brief biography) later in this book. Here, however, we give a prose piece. In a letter (February 3, 1937) Bishop mentions the act that served as the immediate trigger for the piece, but of course far more experience of life is in the work than the trivial act she specifies: "I once hung [my cat's] artificial mouse on a string to a chairback, without thinking what I had done—it looked very sad."

The Hanging of the Mouse   [1937]

Early, early in the morning, even before five o'clock, the mouse was brought out, but already there were large crowds. Some of the animals had not gone to bed the night before, but had stayed up later and later; at first because of a vague feeling of celebration, and then, after deciding several times that they might as well wander about the town for an hour more, to conclude the night by arriving at the square in time for the hanging became only sensible. These animals hiccupped a little and had an air of cynical lassitude. Those who had got up out of bed to come also appeared weary and silent, but not so bored.

The mouse was led in by two enormous brown beetles in the traditional picturesque armor of an earlier day. They came on to the square through the small black door and marched between the lines of soldiers standing at attention: straight ahead, to the right, around two sides of the hollow square, to the left, and out into the middle where the gallows stood. Before each turn the beetle on the right glanced quickly at the beetle on the left; their traditional long, long antennae swerved sharply in the direction they were to turn and they did it to perfection. The mouse, of course, who had had no military training and who, at the moment, was crying so hard he could scarcely see where he was going, rather spoiled the precision and snap of the beetles. At each corner he fell slightly forward, and when he was jerked in the right direction his feet became tangled together. The beetles, however, without even looking at him, each time lifted him quickly into the air for a second until his feet were untangled.

At that hour in the morning the mouse's gray clothes were almost indistinguishable from the light. But his whimpering could be heard, and the end of his nose was rose-red from crying so much. The crowd of small animals tipped back their heads and sniffed with pleasure.

A raccoon, wearing the traditional black mask, was the executioner. He was very fastidious and did everything just so. One of his young sons, also

wearing a black mask, waited on him with a small basin and a pitcher of water. First he washed his hands and rinsed them carefully; then he washed
the rope and rinsed it. At the last minute he again washed his hands and
drew on a pair of elegant black kid gloves.

5   A large praying mantis was in charge of the religious end of the ceremonies. He hurried up on the stage after the mouse and his escorts, but
once there a fit of nerves seemed to seize him. He glided to the left a few
steps, to the right a few steps, lifted his arms gracefully, but could not seem
to begin; and it was quite apparent that he would have liked nothing better
than to have jumped quickly down and left the whole affair. When his arms
were stretched to Heaven his large eyes flashed toward the crowd, and
when he looked up, his body was twitching and he moved about in a really
pathetic way. He seemed to feel ill at ease with the low characters around
him: the beetles, the hangmen, and the criminal mouse. At last he made a
great effort to pull himself together and, approaching the mouse, said a few
words in a high, incomprehensible voice. The mouse jumped from nervousness, and cried harder than ever.

At this point the spectators would all undoubtedly have burst out
laughing, but just then the King's messenger appeared on the balcony
above the small black door the mouse and his guards had lately come
through. He was a very large, overweight bullfrog, also dressed in the traditional costume and carrying the traditional long scroll that dragged for several feet on the ground and had the real speech, on a little slip of paper,
pasted inside it. The scroll and the white plume on his hat made him look
comically like something in a nursery tale, but his voice was impressive
enough to awe the crowd into polite attention. It was a deep bass: "Glug!
Glug! Berrr-up!" No one could understand a word of the mouse's death
sentence.

With the help of some pushes and pinches from the beetles, the executioner got the mouse into position. The rope was tied exquisitely behind
one of his little round ears. The mouse raised a hand and wiped his nose
with it, and most of the crowd interpreted this gesture as a farewell wave
and spoke of it for weeks afterwards. The hangman's young son, at a signal
from his father, sprang the trap.

"Squee-eek! Squee-eek!" went the mouse.

His whiskers rowed hopelessly round and round in the air a few times
and his feet flew up and curled into little balls like young fern-plants.

10   The praying mantis, with an hysterical fling of his long limbs, had disappeared in the crowd. It was all so touching that a cat, who had brought her
child in her mouth, shed several large tears. They rolled down on to the
child's back and he began to squirm and shriek, so that the mother thought
that the sight of the hanging had perhaps been too much for him, but an excellent moral lesson, nevertheless.

🏵 TOPICS FOR CRITICAL THINKING AND WRITING

1. We have several times quoted Robert Frost's observation that a poem
   (he could have said any work of literature) is "a performance in words."
   Reread Bishop's first paragraph, and discuss it in terms of "perfor-

mance." Why, for instance, do you think she repeats the word "early" in the first sentence? In this paragraph notice that Bishop says the animals decided "several times that they might as well wander about the town for an hour more." What do you make of deciding "several times"? And then Bishop says that the idea of concluding the night by "arriving at the square in time for the hanging became only sensible." What do you make of "sensible," especially in the context that immediately follows it: "These animals hiccupped a little and had an air of cynical lassitude." What does "cynical lassitude" mean? How has Bishop juggled her words so as to convey what you assume is her attitude toward the animals?

2. Would you agree that there are humorous touches in the piece? If so, point them out. If you don't think there is anything humorous in it, point to something that someone might conceivably find amusing, and explain why you do not find it so.

3. Describe your response to the sentence, "The rope was tied exquisitely behind one of his little round ears."

4. In the final paragraph Bishop tells us that the cat believed "the sight of the hanging [provided] . . . an excellent moral lesson. . . ." Do you assume that Bishop agrees? By the way, executions used to be public, partly because it was felt that they served to educate the general public. As the proverb puts it, "Who hangs one corrects a thousand." Do you think Bishop would agree or disagree? Why?

JAMES ALAN McPHERSON

Born in a black district in Savannah, Georgia, in 1943, James Alan McPherson attended segrated schools, and then he attended a historically black college in Atlanta, Morris Brown College, from which he received a B.A. in 1965. McPherson next went to Harvard Law School, where he received his law degree in 1968. His first book was a collection of stories, Hue and Cry *(1969), which was followed by* Elbow Room *(1978), a book that was awarded the Pulitzer Prize in fiction. He has taught creative writing and African American literature at the University of Iowa, the University of Santa Cruz, Morgan State University, and the University of Virginia. He has edited special issues of the literary journals* Iowa Review *and* Ploughshares *and has published short stories, book reviews, and essays in other magazines and journals.*

In "On Becoming an American Writer," in the December 1978 issue of The Atlantic, *McPherson describes his goals as a writer and an American in these terms: "I believe that if one can experience diversity, touch a variety of its people, laugh at its craziness, distill wisdom from its tragedies, and attempt to synthesize all this inside oneself without going crazy, one will have earned the right to call oneself a citizen of the United States."*

An Act of Prostitution   [1969]

When he saw the woman the lawyer put down his pencil and legal pad and took out his pipe.

"Well," he said. "How do you want to play it?"

"I wanna get outta here," the whore said. "Just get me outta here."

"Now get some sense," said the lawyer, puffing on the pipe to draw in the flame from the long wooden match he had taken from his vest pocket. "You ain't got a snowball's chance in hell."

5   "I just want out," she said.

"You'll catch hell in there," he said, pointing with the stem of his pipe to the door which separated them from the main courtroom. "Why don't you just get some sense and take a few days on the city."

"I can't go up there again," she said. "Those dike matrons in Parkville hate my guts because I'm wise to them. They told me last time they'd really give it to me if I came back. I can't do no time up there again."

"Listen," said the lawyer, pointing the stem of his pipe at her this time, "you ain't got a choice. Either you cop a plea or I don't take the case."

"*You* listen, you two-bit Jew shyster." The whore raised her voice, pointing her very chubby finger at the lawyer. "*You* ain't got no choice. The judge told you to be my lawyer and you got to do it. I ain't no dummy, you know that?"

10   "Yeah," said the lawyer. "You're a real smarty. That's why you're out on the streets in all that snow and ice. You're a real smarty all right."

"You chickenshit," she said. "I don't want you on my case anyway, but I ain't got no choice. If you was any good, you wouldn't be working the sweatboxes in this court. I ain't no dummy."

"You're a real smarty," said the lawyer. He looked her up and down: a huge woman, pathetically blonde, big-boned and absurd in a skirt sloppily crafted to be mini. Her knees were ruddy and the flesh below them was thick and white and flabby. There was no indication of age about her. Like most whores, she looked at the same time young but then old, possibly as old as her profession. Sometimes they were very old but seemed to have stopped aging at a certain point so that ranking them chronologically, as the lawyer was trying to do, came hard. He put his pipe on the table, on top of the police affidavit, and stared at her. She sat across the room, near the door in a straight chair, her flesh oozing over its sides. He watched her pull her miniskirt down over the upper part of her thigh, modestly, but with the same hard, cold look she had when she came in the room. "You're a real smarty," he commented, drawing on his pipe and exhaling the smoke into the room.

The fat woman in her miniskirt still glared at him. "Screw you, Yid!" she said through her teeth. "Screw your fat mama and your chubby sister with hair under her arms. Screw your brother and your father and I hope they should go crazy playing with themselves in pay toilets."

The lawyer was about to reply when the door to the consultation room opened and another man came into the small place. "Hell, Jimmy," he said to the lawyer, pretending to ignore the woman, "I got a problem here."

15   "Yeah?" said Jimmy.

The other man walked over to the brown desk, leaned closer to Jimmy so that the woman could not hear and lowered his voice. "I got this kid," he said. "A nice I-talian boy that grabbed this Cadillac outta a parking lot. Now he only done it twice before and I think the Judge might go easy if he got in a good mood before the kid goes on, this being Monday morning and all."

"So?" said Jimmy.

"So I was thinking," the other lawyer said, again lowering his voice and leaning much closer and making a sly motion with his head to indicate the whore on the chair across the room. "So I was thinking. The Judge knows Philomena over there. She's here almost every month and she's always good for a laugh. So I was thinking, this being Monday morning and all and with a cage-load of nigger drunks out there, why not put her on first, give the old man a good laugh and then put my I-talian boy on. I know he'd get a better deal that way."

"What's in it for me?" said Jimmy, rapping the ashes from his pipe into an ashtray.

20   "Look, I done *you* favors before. Remember that Chinaman? Remember the tip I gave you?"

Jimmy considered while he stuffed tobacco from a can into his pipe. He lit the pipe with several matches from his vest pocket and considered some more. "I don't mind, Ralph," he said. "But if she goes first the Judge'll get a good laugh and then he'll throw the book at her."

"What the hell, Jimmy?" said Ralph. He glanced over at the whore who was eying them hatefully. "Look, buddy," he went on, "you know who that is? Fatso Philomena Brown. She's up here almost every month. Old Bloom knows her. I tell you, she's good for a laugh. That's all. Besides, she's married to a nigger anyway."

"Well," said Jimmy. "So far she ain't done herself much good with me. She's a real smarty. She thinks I'm a Jew."

"There you go," said Ralph. "Come on, Jimmy. I ain't got much time before the Clerk calls my kid up. What you say?"

25   Jimmy looked over at his client, the many pounds of her rolled in great logs of meat under her knees and around her belly. She was still sneering. "O.K." He turned his head back to Ralph. "O.K., I'll do it."

"Now look," said Ralph, "this is how we'll do. When they call me up I'll tell the Clerk I need more time with my kid for consultation. And since you follow me on the docket you'll get on pretty soon, at least before I will. Then after everybody's had a good laugh, I'll bring my I-talian on."

"Isn't *she* Italian?" asked Jimmy, indicating the whore with a slight movement of his pipe.

"Yeah. But she's married to a nigger."

"O.K.," said Jimmy, "we'll do it."

30   "What's that?" said the whore, who had been trying to listen all this time. "What are you two kikes whispering about anyway? What the hell's going on?"

"Shut up," said Jimmy, the stem of his pipe clamped far back in his mouth so that he could not say it as loud as he wanted. Ralph winked at him and left the room. "Now listen," he said to Philomena Brown, getting up from his desk and walking over to where she still sat against the wall. "If you got a story, you better tell me quick because we're going out there soon and I want you to know I ain't telling no lies for you."

"I don't want you on my case anyway, kike," said Philomena Brown.

"It ain't what *you* want. It's what the old man out there says you gotta do. Now if you got a story let's have it *now.*"

"I'm a file clerk. I was just looking for work."

35   "Like *hell!* Don't give *me* that shit. When was the last time you had your shots?"

"I ain't never had none," said Mrs. Brown.

Now they could hear the Clerk, beyond the door, calling the Italian boy into court. They would have to go out in a few minutes. "Forget the story," he told her. "Just pull your dress down some and wipe some of that shit off your eyes. You look like hell."

"I don't want you on the case, Moses," said Mrs. Brown.

"Well you got me," said Jimmy. "You got me whether you want me or not." Jimmy paused, put his pipe in his coat pocket, and then said: "And my name is *Mr. Mulligan!*"

40   The woman did not say anything more. She settled her weight in the chair and made it creak.

"Now let's get in there," said Jimmy.

The Judge was in his Monday morning mood. He was very ready to be angry at almost anyone. He glared at the Court Clerk as the bald, seemingly consumptive man called out the names of six defendants who had defaulted. He glared at the group of drunks and addicts who huddled against the steel net of the prisoners' cage, gazing toward the open courtroom as if expecting mercy from the rows of concerned parties and spectators who sat in the hot place. Judge Bloom looked as though he wanted very badly to spit. There would be no mercy this Monday morning and the prisoners all knew it.

"Willie Smith! Willie Smith! Come into Court!" the Clerk barked.

Willie Smith slowly shuffled out of the prisoners' cage and up to the dirty stone wall, which kept all but his head and neck and shoulders concealed from the people in the musty courtroom.

45   From the bench the Judge looked down at the hungover Smith.

"You know, I ain't never seen him sitting down in that chair," Jimmy said to one of the old men who came to court to see the daily procession, filling up the second row of benches, directly behind those reserved for court-appointed lawyers. There were at least twelve of these old men, looking almost semi-professional in faded gray or blue or black suits with shiny knees and elbows. They liked to come and watch the fun. "Watch old Bloom give it to this nigger," the same old man leaned over and said into Jimmy Mulligan's ear. Jimmy nodded without looking back at him. And after a few seconds he wiped his ear with his hand, also without looking back.

The Clerk read the charges: Drunkenness, Loitering, Disorderly Conduct.

"You want a lawyer, Willie?" the Judge asked him. Judge Bloom was now walking back and forth behind his bench, his arms gravely folded behind his back, his belly very close to pregnancy beneath his black robe. "The Supreme Court says I have to give you a lawyer. You want one?"

"No sir," the hung-over Smith said, very obsequiously.

50   "Well, what's your trouble?"

"Nothing."

"You haven't missed a Monday here in months."

"Yes sir."

"All that money you spend on booze, how do you take care of your family?"

55   Smith moved his head and shoulders behind the wall in a gesture that might have been a shuffle.

"When was the last time you gave something to your wife?"

"Last Friday."

"You're a liar. Your wife's been on the City for years."

"I help," said Smith, quickly.

60   "You help, all right. You help her raise her belly and her income every year."

The old men in the second row snickered and the Judge eyed them in a threatening way. They began to stifle their chuckles. Willie Smith smiled.

"If she has one more kid she'll be making more than me," the Judge observed. But he was not saying it to Smith. He was looking at the old men.

Then he looked down at the now bashful, smiling Willie Smith. "You want some time to sleep it off or you want to pay?"

"I'll take the time."

65   "How much you want, Willie?"

"I don't care."

"You want to be out for the weekend, I guess."

Smith smiled again.

"Give him five days," the Judge said to the Clerk. The Clerk wrote in his papers and then said in a hurried voice: "Defendant Willie Smith, you have been found guilty by this court of being drunk in a public place, of loitering while in this condition, and of disorderly conduct. This court sentences you to five days in the House of Correction at Bridgeview and one month's suspended sentence. You have, however, the right to appeal in which case the suspended sentence will not be allowed and the sentence will then be thirty-five days in the House of Correction."

70   "You want to appeal, Willie?"

"Naw sir."

"See you next week," said the Judge.

"Thank you," said Willie Smith.

A black fellow in a very neatly pressed Army uniform came on next. He stood immaculate and proud and clean-shaven with his cap tucked under his left arm while the charges were read. The prosecutor was a hard-faced black police detective, tieless, very long-haired in a short-sleeved white shirt with wet armpits. The detective was tough but very nervous. He looked at his notes while the Clerk read the charges. The Judge, bald and wrinkled and drooping in the face, still paced behind his bench, his nose twitching from time to time, his arms locked behind the back. The soldier was charged with assault and battery with a dangerous weapon on a police officer; he remained standing erect and silent, looking off into the space behind the Judge until his lawyer, a plump, greasy black man in his late fifties, had heard the charge and motioned for him to sit. Then he placed himself beside his lawyer and put his cap squarely in front of him on the table.

75   The big-bellied black detective managed to get the police officer's name, rank and duties from him, occasionally glancing over at the table where the defendant and his lawyer sat, both hard-faced and cold. He shuf-

fled through his notes, paused, looked up at the Judge, and then said to the white officer: "Now, Officer Bergin, would you tell the Court in your own words what happened?"

The white policeman put his hands together in a prayer-like gesture on the stand. He looked at the defendant whose face was set and whose eyes were fixed on the officer's hands. "We was on duty on the night of July twenty-seventh driving around the Lafayette Street area when we got a call to proceed to the Lafayette Street subway station because there was a crowd gathering there and they thought it might be a riot. We proceeded there, Officer Biglow and me, and when we got there sure enough there was a crowd of colored people running up and down the street and making noise and carrying on. We didn't pull our guns because they been telling us all summer not to do that. We got out of the car and proceeded to join the other officers there in forming a line so's to disperse the crowd. Then we spotted that fellow in the crowd."

"Who do you mean?"

"That fellow over there." Officer Bergin pointed to the defendant at the table. "That soldier, Irving Williams."

"Go on," said the black detective, not turning to look at the defendant.

80   "Well, he had on this red costume and a cape, and he was wearing this big red turban. He was also carrying a big black shield right outta Tarzan and he had that big long cane waving it around in the air."

"Where is that cane now?"

"We took it off him later. That's it over there."

The black detective moved over to his own table and picked up a long brown leather cane. He pressed a small button beneath its handle and then drew out from the interior of the cane a thin, silver-white rapier, three feet long.

"Is this the same cane?"

85   "Yes sir," the white officer said.

"Go on, Officer."

"Well, he was waving it around in the air and he had a whole lot of these colored people behind him and it looked to me that he was gonna charge the police line. So me and Tommy left the line and went in to grab him before he could start something big. That crowd was getting mean. They looked like they was gonna try something big pretty soon."

"Never mind," said the Judge. He had stopped walking now and stood at the edge of his elevated platform, just over the shoulder of the officer in the witness box. "Never mind what you thought, just get on with it."

"Yes sir." The officer pressed his hands together much tighter. "Well, Tommy and me, we tried to grab him and he swung the cane at me. Caught me right in the face here." He pointed his finger to a large red and black mark under his left eye. "So then we hadda use force to subdue him."

90   "What did you do, Officer?" the black detective asked.

"We hadda use the sticks. I hit him over the head once or twice, but not hard. I don't remember. Then Tommy grabbed his arms and we hustled him over to the car before these other colored people with him tried to grab us."

"Did he resist arrest?"

"Yeah. He kicked and fought us and called us lewd and lascivious names. We hadda handcuff him in the car. Then we took him down to the station and booked him for assault and battery."

"Your witness," said the black detective without turning around to face the other lawyer. He sat down at his own table and wiped his forehead and hands with a crumpled white handkerchief. He still looked very nervous but not as tough.

95 "May it please the Court," the defendant's black lawyer said slowly, standing and facing the pacing Judge. "I move . . ." And then he stopped because he saw that the Judge's small eyes were looking over his head, toward the back of the courtroom. The lawyer turned around and looked, and saw that everyone else in the room had also turned their heads to the back of the room. Standing against the back walls and along the left side of the room were twenty-five or so stern-faced, cold-eyed black men, all in African dashikies, all wearing brightly colored hats, and all staring at the Judge and the black detective. Philomena Brown and Jimmy Mulligan, sitting on the first bench, turned to look too, and the whore smiled but the lawyer said, "Oh hell," aloud. The men, all big, all bearded and tight-lipped, now locked hands and formed a solid wall of flesh around almost three-quarters of the courtroom. The Judge looked at the defendant and saw that he was smiling. Then he looked at the defendant's lawyer, who still stood before the Judge's bench, his head down, his shoulders pulled up towards his head. The Judge began to pace again. The courtroom was very quiet. The old men filling the second rows on both sides of the room leaned forward and exchanged glances with each other up and down the row. "Oh hell," Jimmy Mulligan said again.

Then the Judge stopped walking. "Get on with it," he told the defendant's lawyer. "There's justice to be done here."

The lawyer, whose face was now very greasy and wet, looked up at the officer, still standing in the witness box, but with one hand now at his right side, next to his gun.

"Officer Bergin," said the black lawyer. "I'm not clear about something. Did the defendant strike you *before* you asked him for the cane or *after* you attempted to take it from him?"

"Before. It was before. Yes sir."

100 "You *did* ask him for the cane, then?"

"Yes sir. I asked him to turn it over."

"And what did he do?"

"He hit me."

"But if he hit you before you asked for the cane, then it must be true that you asked him for the cane *after* he had hit you. Is that right?"

105 "Yes sir."

"In other words, after he had struck you in the face you were still polite enough to keep your hands off him and ask for the weapon."

"Yes sir. That's what I did."

"In other words, he hit you twice. Once, *before* you requested the cane and once *after* you requested it."

The officer paused. "No sir," he said quickly. "He only hit me once."

110 "And when was that again?"

"I thought it was before I asked for the cane but I don't know now."

"But you did ask for the cane before he hit you?"

"Yeah." The officer's hands were in prayer again.

"Now, Officer Bergin, did he hit you *because* you asked for the cane or did he hit you in the process of giving it to you?"

115 "He just hauled off and hit me with it."

"He made no effort to hand it over?"

"No, no sir. He hit me."

"In other words, he struck you the moment you got close enough for him to swing. He did not hit you as you were taking the cane from him?"

The officer paused again. Then he said: "No sir," He touched his face again, then put his right hand down to the area near his gun again. "I asked him for the cane and he hauled off and hit me in the face."

120   "Officer, are you telling this court that you did not get hit until you tried to take the cane away from this soldier, this Vietnam veteran, or that he saw you coming and immediately began to swing the cane?"

"He swung on me."

"Officer Bergin, did he swing on you, or did the cane accidentally hit you while you were trying to take it from him?"

"All I know is that he *hit me.*" The officer was sweating now.

"Then you don't know just when he hit you, before or after you tried to take the cane from him, do you?"

125   The black detective got up and said in a very soft voice: "I object."

The black lawyer for the defendant looked over at him contemptuously. The black detective dropped his eyes and tightened his belt, and sat down again.

"That's all right," the oily lawyer said. Then he looked at the officer again. "One other thing," he said. "Was the knife still inside the cane or drawn when he hit you?"

"We didn't know about the knife till later at the station."

"Do you think that a blow from the cane by itself could kill you?"

130   "Object!" said the detective. But again his voice was low.

"*Jivetime Uncle Tom motherfucker!*" someone said from the back of the room. "Shave that Afro off your head!"

The Judge's eyes moved quickly over the men in the rear, surveying their faces and catching what was in all their eyes. But he did not say anything.

"The prosecution rests," the black detective said. He sounded very tired.

"The defense calls the defendant, Irving Williams," said the black lawyer.

135   Williams took the stand and waited, head high, eyes cool, mouth tight, militarily, for the Clerk to swear him in. He looked always toward the back of the room.

"Now Mr. Williams," his lawyer began, "tell this court in your own words the events of the night of July twenty-seventh of this year."

"I had been to a costume party." Williams's voice was slow and deliberate and resonant. The entire courtroom was tense and quiet. The old men stared, stiff and erect, at Irving Williams from their second-row benches. Philomena Brown settled her flesh down next to her lawyer, who tried to edge away from touching her fat arm with his own. The tight-lipped Judge Bloom had reassumed the pacing behind his bench.

"I was on leave from the base," Williams went on, "and I was coming from the party when I saw this group of kids throwing rocks. Being in the military and being just out of Vietnam, I tried to stop them. One of the kids had that cane and I took it from him. The shield belongs to me. I got it in Taiwan last year on R and R. I was trying to break up the crowd with my shield when this honkie cop begins to beat me over the head with his club. Police brutality. I tried to tell . . . ."

"That's enough," the Judge said. "That's all I want to hear." He eyed the black men in the back of the room. "This case isn't for my court. Take it upstairs."

140   "If Your Honor pleases," the black lawyer began.

"I don't," said the Judge. "I've heard enough. Mr. Clerk, make out the papers. Send it upstairs to Cabot."

"This court has jurisdiction to hear this case," the lawyer said. He was very close to being angry. "This man is in the service. He has to ship out in a few weeks. We want a hearing today."

"Not in my court you don't get it. Upstairs, and that's *it!*"

Now the blacks in the back of the room began to berate the detective. "Jivetime cat! Handkerchief-head flunky! Uncle Tom motherfucker!" they called. "We'll get *you,* baby!"

145   "Get them out of here," the Judge told the policeman named Bergin. "Get them the hell out!" Bergin did not move. "Get them the hell out!"

At that moment Irving Williams, with his lawyer behind him, walked out of the courtroom. And the twenty-five bearded black men followed them. The black detective remained sitting at the counsel table until the Clerk asked him to make way for counsel on the next case. The detective got up slowly, gathered his few papers, tightened his belt again and moved over, his head held down, to a seat on the right side of the courtroom.

"Philomena Brown!" the Clerk called. "Philomena Brown! Come into Court!"

The fat whore got up from beside Jimmy Mulligan and walked heavily over to the counsel table and lowered herself into one of the chairs. Her lawyer was talking to Ralph, the Italian boy's counsel.

"Do a good job, Jimmy, please," Ralph said. "Old Bloom is gonna be awful mean now."

150   "Yeah," said Jimmy. "I got to really work on him."

One of the old men on the second row leaned over the back of the bench and said to Jimmy: "Ain't that the one that's married to a nigger?"

"That's her," said Jimmy.

"She's gonna catch hell. Make sure they give her hell."

"Yeah," said Jimmy. "I don't see how I'm gonna be able to try this with a straight face."

155   "Do a good job for me, please, Jimmy," said Ralph. "The kid's name is Angelico. Ain't that a beautiful name? He ain't a bad kid."

"Don't you worry, I'll do it." Then Jimmy moved over to the table next to his client.

The defendant and the arresting officer were sworn in. The arresting officer acted for the state as prosecutor and its only witness. He had to refer to his notes from time to time while the Judge paced behind his bench, his head down, ponderous and impatient. Then Philomena Brown got in the witness box and rested her great weight against its sides. She glared at the Judge, at the Clerk, at the officer in the box on the other side, at Jimmy Mulligan, at the old men smiling up and down the second row, and at everyone in the courtroom. Then she rested her eyes on the officer.

"Well," the officer read from his notes. "It was around one-thirty A.M. on the night of July twenty-eight. I was working the night duty around the combat zone. I come across the defendant there soliciting cars. I had seen the defendant there soliciting cars on previous occasions in the same vicinity. I had then on previous occasions warned the defendant there about such activities. But she kept on doing it. On that night I come across the defendant soliciting a car full of colored gentlemen. She was standing on the curb with her arm leaning up against the door of the car and talking with these two colored gentlemen. As I came up they drove off. I then arrested her, after informing her of her rights, for being a common streetwalker and a public nuisance. And that's all I got to say."

Counsel for the whore waived cross-examination of the officer and proceeded to examine her.

160   "What's your name?"

"Mrs. Philomena Brown."

"Speak louder so the Court can hear you, Mrs. Brown."

She narrowed her eyes at the lawyer.

"What is your religion, Mrs. Brown?"

165   "I am a Roman Catholic. Roman Catholic born."

"Are you presently married?"

"Yeah."

"What is your husband's name?"

"Rudolph Leroy Brown, Jr."

170   The old men in the second row were beginning to snicker and the Judge lowered his eyes to them. Jimmy Mulligan smiled.

"Does your husband support you?"

"Yeah. We get along all right."

"Do *you* work, Mrs. Brown?"

"Yeah. That's how I make my living."

175   "What do you do for a living?"

"I'm a file clerk."

"Are you working now?"

"No. I lost my job last month on account of a bad leg I got. I couldn't move outta bed."

The men in the second row were grinning and others in the audience joined them in muffled guffaws and snickerings.

180   "What were you doing on Beaver Avenue on the night of July twenty-eighth?"

"I was looking for a job."

Now the entire court was laughing and the Judge glared out at them from behind his bench as he paced, his arms clasped behind his back.

"Will you please tell this court, Mrs. Brown, how you intended to find a job at that hour?"

"These two guys in a car told me they knew where I could find some work."

185   "As a file clerk?"

"Yeah. What the hell else do you think?"

There was here a roar of laughter from the court, and when the Judge visibly twitched the corners of his usually severe mouth, Philomena Brown saw it and began to laugh too.

"Order! Order!" the Clerk shouted above the roar. But he was laughing.

Jimmy Mulligan bit his lip. "Now, Mrs. Brown, I want you to tell me the truth. Have you ever been arrested before for prostitution?"

190   "Hell no!" she fired back. "They had me in here a coupla times but it was all a fluke. They never got nothing on me. I was framed, right from the start."

"How old are you, Mrs. Brown?"

"Nineteen."

Now the Judge stopped pacing and stood next to his chair. His face was dubious: very close and very far away from smiling. The old men in the second row saw this and stopped laughing, awaiting a cue from him.

"That's enough of this," said the Judge. "I know you. You've been up here seven times already this year and it's still summer. I'm going to throw the book at you." He moved over to the left end of the platform and leaned down to where a husky, muscular woman Probation Officer was standing. She had very short hair and looked grim. She had not laughed with the others. "Let me see her record," said the Judge. The manly Probation Officer handed it up to him and then they talked together in whispers for a few minutes.

195   "All right, *Mrs. Brown,*" said the Judge, moving over to the right side of the platform near the defendant's box and pointing his finger at her. "You're still on probation from the last time you were up here. I'm tired of this."

"I don't wanna go back up there, Your Honor," the whore said. "They hate me up there."

"You're going back. That's it! You got six months on the State. Maybe while you're there you can learn how to be a file clerk so you can look for work during the day."

Now everyone laughed again.

"Plus you get a one-year suspended sentence on probation."

200   The woman hung her head with the gravity of this punishment.

"Maybe you can even learn a *good* profession while you're up there. Who knows? Maybe you could be a ballerina dancer."

The courtroom roared with laughter. The Judge could not control himself now.

"And another thing," he said. "When you get out, keep off the streets. You're obstructing traffic."

Such was the spontaneity of laughter from the entire courtroom after the remark that the lawyer Jimmy Mulligan had to wipe the tears from his eyes with his finger and the short-haired Probation Officer smiled, and even Philomena Brown had to laugh at this, her final moment of glory. The Judge's teeth showed through his own broad grin, and Ralph, sitting beside his Italian, a very pretty boy with clean, blue eyes, patted him on the back enthusiastically between uncontrollable bursts of laughter.

205   For five minutes after the smiling Probation Officer led the fat whore in a miniskirt out of the courtroom, there was the sound of muffled laughter and occasional sniffles and movements in the seats. Then they settled down again and the Judge resumed his pacings and the Court Clerk, very slyly wiping his eyes with his sleeve, said in a very loud voice: "Angelico Carbone! Angelico Carbone! Come into Court!"

※ TOPICS FOR CRITICAL THINKING AND WRITING

1. Now that you have read the story, explain the meaning and significance of the title.

2. When you began reading the story, did you find the language (the racial and ethnic epithets, for example) offensive? Why is McPherson using language that will offend some readers?

3. What is the function of the scene involving Irving Williams? Would the story be more effective if it focused entirely on Philomena Brown?
4. Is McPherson making a point about the legal system? Explain, and refer to specific passages to support your view.
5. Did you enjoy this story? What did you learn from it?

SHERMAN ALEXIE

The short-story writer, essayist, poet, and film director Sherman J. Alexie Jr. was born in October 1966 and was raised on the Spokane Indian Reservation in Wellpinit, Washington, located fifty miles northwest of Spokane. He went to high school off reservation in Reardan, Washington, where he was an excellent student and played on the basketball team. He attended Gonzaga University in Spokane for two years and then transferred to Washington State University in Pullman, where he began writing poetry, graduating with a degree in American Studies. His books include The Business of Fancydancing: Stories and Poems *(1992),* The Lone Ranger and Tonto Fistfight in Heaven *(1994), and* Reservation Blues *(1995).*

The Trial of Thomas Builds-the-Fire   [1993]

Someone must have been telling lies about Joseph K., for without having done anything wrong he was arrested one fine morning.

—Franz Kafka

Thomas Builds-the-Fire waited alone in the Spokane tribal holding cell while BIA[1] officials discussed his future, the immediate present, and of course, his past.

"Builds-the-Fire has a history of this kind of behavior," a man in a BIA suit said to the others. "A storytelling fetish accompanied by an extreme need to tell the truth. Dangerous."

Thomas was in the holding cell because he had once held the reservation postmaster hostage for eight hours with the idea of a gun and had also threatened to make significant changes in the tribal vision. But that crisis was resolved years ago as Thomas surrendered voluntarily and agreed to remain silent. In fact, Thomas had not spoken in nearly twenty years. All his stories remained internal; he would not even send letters or Christmas cards.

But recently Thomas had begun to make small noises, form syllables that contained more emotion and meaning than entire sentences constructed by the BIA. A noise that sounded something like *rain* had given Esther courage enough to leave her husband, tribal chairman David WalksAlong, who had been tribal police chief at the time of Thomas Builds-the-Fire's original crime. WalksAlong walked along with BIA policy so willingly that he took to calling

---

[1]**BIA** Bureau of Indian Affairs.

his wife *a savage in polyester pants.* She packed her bags the day after she listened to Thomas speak; Thomas was arrested the day after Esther left.

5   Now Thomas sat quietly in his cell, counting cockroaches and silverfish. He couldn't sleep, he didn't feel like eating. Often he closed his eyes and stories came to him quickly, but he would not speak. He nodded and laughed if the story was funny; cried a little when the stories were sad; pounded his fists against his mattress when the stories angered him.

"Well, the traveling judge is coming in tomorrow," one guy in a BIA suit said to the others. "What charges should we bring him up on?"

"Inciting a riot? Kidnapping? Extortion? Maybe murder?" another guy in a BIA suit asked, and the others laughed.

"Well," they all agreed. "It has to be a felony charge. We don't need his kind around here anymore."

Later that night, Thomas lay awake and counted stars through the bars in his window. He was guilty, he knew that. All that was variable on any reservation was how the convicted would be punished.

10   *The following report is adapted from the original court transcript.*
"Mr. Builds-the-Fire," the judge said to Thomas. "Before we begin this trial, the court must be certain that you understand the charges against you."

Thomas, who wore his best ribbon shirt and decided to represent himself, stood and spoke a complete sentence for the first time in two decades.

"Your Honor," he said. "I don't believe that the exact nature of any charges against me have been revealed, let alone detailed."

There was a hush in the crowd, followed by exclamations of joy, sadness, etc. Eve Ford, the former reservation postmaster held hostage by Thomas years earlier, sat quietly in the back row and thought to herself, *He hasn't done anything wrong.*

15   "Well, Mr. Builds-the-Fire," the judge said. "I can only infer by your sudden willingness to communicate that you do in fact understand the purpose of this trial."

"That's not true."

"Are you accusing this court of dishonesty, Mr. Builds-the-Fire?"

Thomas sat down, to regain his silence for a few moments.

"Well, Mr. Builds-the-Fire, we're going to dispense with opening remarks and proceed to testimony. Are you ready to call your first witness?"

20   "Yes, I am, Your Honor. I call myself as first and only witness to all the crimes I'm accused of and, additionally, to bring attention to all the mitigating circumstances."

"Whatever," the judge said. "Raise your right hand and promise me you'll tell the whole truth and nothing but the truth."

"Honesty is all I have left," Thomas said.

Thomas Builds-the-Fire sat in the witness stand, closed his eyes, and spoke this story aloud:

"It all started on September 8, 1858. I was a young pony, strong and quick in every movement. I remember this. Still, there was so much to fear on that day when Colonel George Wright took me and 799 of my brothers captive. Imagine, 800 beautiful ponies stolen at once. It was the worst kind of war crime. But Colonel Wright thought we were too many to transport, that we were all dangerous. In fact, I still carry his letter of that day which justified the coming slaughter:

25   Dear Sir:

As I reported in my communication of yesterday the capture of 800 horses on the 8th instant, I have now to add that this large band of horses composed the entire wealth of the Spokane chief Til-co-ax. This man has ever been hostile; for the last two years he has been constantly sending his young men into the Walla Walla valley, and stealing horses and cattle from the settlers and from the government. He boldly acknowledged these facts when he met Colonel Steptoe, in May last. Retributive justice has now overtaken him; the blow has been severe but well merited. I found myself embarrassed with these 800 horses. I could not hazard the experiment of moving with such a number of animals (many of them very wild) along with my large train; should a stampede take place, we might not only lose our captured animals, but many of our own. Under those circumstances, I determined to kill them all, save a few in service in the quartermaster's department and to replace broken-down animals. I deeply regretted killing these poor creatures, but a dire necessity drove me to it. This work of slaughter has been going on since 10 o'clock of yesterday, and will not be completed before this evening, and I shall march for the Coeur d'Alene Mission tomorrow.

Very respectfully, your obedient servant,

G. WRIGHT, Colonel 9th Infantry, Commanding.

"Somehow I was lucky enough to be spared while hundreds of my brothers and sisters fell together. It was a nightmare to witness. They were rounded into a corral and then lassoed, one by one, and dragged out to be shot in the head. This lasted for hours, and all that dark night mothers cried for their dead children. The next day, the survivors were rounded into a single mass and slaughtered by continuous rifle fire."

Thomas opened his eyes and found that most of the Indians in the courtroom wept and wanted to admit defeat. He then closed his eyes and continued the story:

"But I was not going to submit without a struggle. I would continue the war. At first I was passive, let one man saddle me and ride for a while. He laughed at the illusion of my weakness. But I suddenly rose up and bucked him off and broke his arm. Another man tried to ride me, but I threw him and so many others, until I was lathered with sweat and blood from their spurs and rifle butts. It was glorious. Finally they gave up, quit, and led me to the back of the train. They could not break me. Some may have wanted to kill me for my arrogance, but others respected my anger, my refusal to admit defeat. I lived that day, even escaped Colonel Wright, and galloped into other histories."

Thomas opened his eyes and saw that the Indians in the courtroom sat up straight, combed their braids gracefully, smiled with Indian abandon.

30   "Mr. Builds-the-Fire," the judge asked. "Is that the extent of your testimony?"

"Your Honor, if I may continue, there is much more I need to say. There are so many more stories to tell."

The judge looked at Thomas Builds-the-Fire for an instant, decided to let him continue. Thomas closed his eyes, and a new story was raised from the ash of older stories:

"My name was Qualchan and I had been fighting for our people, for our land. It was horrendous, hiding in the dirt at the very mouth of the Spokane River where my fellow warrior, Moses, found me after he escaped from Colonel Wright's camp. *Qualchan,* he said to me. *You must stay away from Wright's camp. He means to hang you.* But Wright had taken my father hostage and threatened to hang him if I did not come in. Wright promised he would treat me fairly. I believed him and went to the colonel's camp and was immediately placed in chains. It was then I saw the hangman's noose and made the fight to escape. My wife also fought beside me with a knife and wounded many soldiers before she was subdued. After I was beaten down, they dragged me to the noose and I was hanged with six other Indians, including Epseal, who had never raised a hand in anger to any white or Indian."

Thomas opened his eyes and swallowed air hard. He could barely breathe and the courtroom grew distant and vague.

35   "Mr. Builds-the-Fire," judge asked and brought Thomas back to attention. "What point are you trying to make with this story?"

"Well," Thomas said. "The City of Spokane is now building a golf course named after me, Qualchan, located in that valley where I was hanged."

The courtroom burst into motion and emotion. The judge hammered his gavel against his bench. The bailiff had to restrain Eve Ford, who had made a sudden leap of faith across the room toward Thomas.

"Thomas," she yelled. "We're all listening."

The bailiff had his hands full as Eve slugged him twice and then pushed him to the ground. Eve stomped on the bailiff's big belly until two tribal policemen tackled her, handcuffed her, and led her away.

40   "Thomas," she yelled. "We hear you."

The judge was red-faced with anger; he almost looked Indian. He pounded his gavel until it broke.

"Order in the court," he shouted. "Order in the fucking court."

The tribal policemen grew in number. Many were Indians that the others had never seen before. The policemen swelled in size and forced the others out of the courtroom. After the court was cleared and order restored, the judge pulled his replacement gavel from beneath his robe and continued the trial.

"Now," the judge said. "We can go about the administration of justice."

45   "Is that real justice or the idea of justice?" Thomas asked him, and the judge flew back into anger.

"Defense testimony is over," he said. "Mr. Builds-the-Fire, you will now be cross-examined."

Thomas watched the prosecuting attorney approach the witness stand.

"Mr. Builds-the-Fire," he said. "Where were you on May 16, 1858?"

"I was in the vicinity of Rosalia, Washington, along with 799 other warriors, ready to battle with Colonel Steptoe and his soldiers."

50   "And could you explain exactly what happened there that day?"

Thomas closed his eyes and told this story:

"My name was Wild Coyote and I was just sixteen years old and was frightened because this was to be my first battle. But we were confident because Steptoe's soldiers were so small and weak. They tried to negotiate a peace, but our war chiefs would not settle for anything short of blood. You must understand these were days of violence and continual lies from the white man. Steptoe said he wanted peace between whites and Indians, but he had cannons and had lied before, so we refused to believe him this time. Instead, we attacked at dawn and killed many of their soldiers and lost only a few warriors. The soldiers made a stand on a hilltop and we surrounded them, amazed at their tears and cries. But you must understand they were also very brave. The soldiers fought well, but there were too many Indians for them on that day. Night fell and we retreated a little as we always do during dark. Somehow the surviving soldiers escaped during the night, and many of us were happy for them. They had fought so well that they deserved to live another day."

Thomas opened his eyes and found the prosecuting attorney's long nose just inches from his own.

"Mr. Builds-the-Fire, how many soldiers did you kill that day?"

55   Thomas closed his eyes and told another story:

"I killed one soldier right out with an arrow to the chest. He fell off his horse and didn't move again. I shot another soldier and he fell off his horse, too, and I ran over to him to take his scalp but he pulled his revolver and shot me through the shoulder. I still have the scar. It hurt so much that I left the soldier and went away to die. I really thought I was going to die, and I suppose the soldier probably died later. So I went and lay down in this tall grass and watched the sky. It was beautiful and I was ready to die. It had been a good fight. I lay there for part of the day and most of the night until one of my friends picked me up and said the soldiers had escaped. My friend tied himself to me and we rode away with the others. That is what happened."

Thomas opened his eyes and faced the prosecuting attorney.

"Mr. Builds-the-Fire, you do admit, willingly, that you murdered two soldiers in cold blood and with premeditation?"

"Yes, I killed those soldiers, but they were good men. I did it with sad heart and hand. There was no way I could ever smile or laugh again. I'm not sorry we had to fight, but I am sorry those men had to die."

60   "Mr. Builds-the-Fire, please answer the question. Did you or did you not murder those two soldiers in cold blood and with premeditation?"

"I did."

Article from the Spokesman-Review, *October 7, 19—.*

Builds-the-Fire to Smolder in Prison

WELLPINIT, WASHINGTON—Thomas Builds-the-Fire, the self-proclaimed visionary of the Spokane Tribe, was sentenced today to two concurrent life terms in the Walla Walla State Penitentiary. His many supporters battled with police for over eight hours following the verdict.

U.S. District Judge James Wright asked, "Do you have anything you want to say now, Mr. Builds-the-Fire?" Builds-the-Fire simply shook his head no and was led away by prison officials.

Wright told Builds-the-Fire that the new federal sentencing guidelines "require the imposition of a life sentence for racially motivated murder." There is no possibility for parole, said U.S. Prosecuting Attorney, Adolph D. Jim, an enrolled member of the Yakima Indian Nation.

65   "The only appeal I have is for justice," Builds-the-Fire reportedly
said as he was transported away from this story and into the next.

Thomas Builds-the-Fire sat quietly as the bus traveled down the highway toward Walla Walla State Penitentiary. There were six other prisoners:
four African men, one Chicano, and a white man from the smallest town in
the state.
        "I know who you are," the Chicano said to Thomas. "You're that Indian
guy did all the talking."
        "Yeah," one of the African men said. "You're that story-teller. Tell us
some stories, chief, give us the scoop."
        Thomas looked at these five men who shared his skin color, at the
white man who shared this bus which was going to deliver them into a new
kind of reservation, barrio, ghetto, logging-town tin shack. He then looked
out the window, through the steel grates on the windows, at the freedom
just outside the glass. He saw wheat fields, bodies of water, and bodies of
dark-skinned workers pulling fruit from trees and sweat from thin air.
70   Thomas closed his eyes and told this story.

▓ TOPICS FOR CRITICAL THINKING AND WRITING

1. The story includes an epigraph from the Austrian writer Franz Kafka's
   unfinished novel *The Trial* (published in 1925, translated into English
   in 1935), about a bank assessor named Joseph K., who is mysteriously
   accused of an unnamed crime and who is then baffled by a legal system
   he cannot understand or communicate with. What does the epigraph
   contribute to Alexie's story? Would the story have a different effect
   without the epigraph?
2. Explain the phrase about Thomas in the third paragraph: "All his stories
   remained internal."
3. What is the response of the BIA (Bureau of Indian Affairs) to Thomas?
   What is the response of the legal system to him?
4. Focus on each of the stories that Thomas tells. What is he saying
   through each of them, and what is their meaning as a group?
5. What is the function of the final scene, and, in particular, the significance of the final sentence?
6. One critic has stated that Alexie's story is "too polemical, too political."
   Do you agree or disagree with this assessment?

10

American Voices: Fiction for a Diverse Nation

Almost a century ago the American writer Willa Cather, in her novel *O Pioneers* (1913), shrewdly observed:

> There are only two or three human stories, and they go on repeating themselves as if they had never happened before.

Among these is the story that essentially ends, "And they lived happily ever after." Not that *everyone* in the story need live happily ever after: Fiction often reassures us that the bad end badly, essentially showing us stories that support the Biblical assertion that "Whoso diggeth a pit shall fall therein, and he that rolleth a stone, it will return upon him" (Proverbs 26.27). There are, of course, countless variations on this theme—and we never tire of reading stories about it. Perhaps people keep writing about it, and reading about it, because it is true. Or perhaps, on the other hand, we read and write about it because life is such a mess, such a chaotic welter, that we are trying to impose order, trying to convince ourselves that indeed this pattern exists.

For all the sameness of many stories, there are countless local variations, especially variations taking account of different cultures, and especially in America—proverbially a nation of immigrants—fiction shows us distinctive kinds of behavior, behavior rooted in customs not shared by the population as a whole. In this chapter we offer stories about persons who belong to one or another of a range of minority groups: Native Americans, gays and lesbians, Asian-Americans, African-Americans, and Hispanic-Americans. We also include a story of a different, but we think related, kind that focuses on a retarded person; this story (by Katherine Anne Porter) reminds us that diversity and difference take multiple forms, and not all of them are sexual, religious, racial, or ethnic. We believe, however, that *all* of these stories speak to *all* readers, and we call your attention to the fact that other chapters also contain stories about members of some of these groups.

Somewhat comparable chapters appear later in the book, with poems and with plays about diverse cultures.

LESLIE MARMON SILKO

Leslie Marmon Silko was born in 1948 in Albuquerque, New Mexico, and grew up on the Laguna Pueblo Reservation some fifty miles to the west. Of her family she says,

We are mixed blood—Laguna, Mexican, white. . . . All those lan-
guages, all those ways of living are combined, and we live some-
where on the fringes of all three. But I don't apologize for this any
more—not to whites, not to full bloods—our origin is unlike any
other. My poetry, my storytelling rise out of this source.

After graduating from the University of New Mexico in 1969, Silko en-
tered law school but soon left to become a writer. She taught for two years at
Navajo Community College at Many Farms, Arizona, and then went to Alaska
for two years where she studied Eskimo-Aleut culture and worked on a novel,
Ceremony. *After returning to the Southwest, she taught at the University of*
Arizona and then at the University of New Mexico.

In addition to writing stories, a novel, and poems, Silko has written the
screenplay for Marlon Brando's film, Black Elk. *In 1981 she was awarded one*
of the so-called genius grants from the MacArthur Foundation, which sup-
ports "exceptionally talented individuals."

The Man to Send Rain Clouds   [1969]

One

They found him under a big cottonwood tree. His Levi jacket and pants
were faded light-blue so that he had been easy to find. The big cottonwood
tree stood apart from a small grove of winterbare cottonwoods which grew
in the wide, sandy arroyo. He had been dead for a day or more, and the
sheep had wandered and scattered up and down the arroyo. Leon and his
brother-in-law, Ken, gathered the sheep and left them in the pen at the sheep
camp before they returned to the cottonwood tree. Leon waited under the
tree while Ken drove the truck through the deep sand to the edge of the arroyo. He squinted up at the sun and unzipped his jacket—it sure was hot for
this time of year. But high and northwest the blue mountains were still deep
in snow. Ken came sliding down the low, crumbling bank about fifty yards
down, and he was bringing the red blanket.

Before they wrapped the old man, Leon took a piece of string out of his
pocket and tied a small gray feather in the old man's long white hair. Ken
gave him the paint. Across the brown wrinkled forehead he drew a streak of
white and along the high cheekbones he drew a strip of blue paint. He
paused and watched Ken throw pinches of corn meal and pollen into the
wind that fluttered the small gray feather. Then Leon painted with yellow
under the old man's broad nose, and finally, when he had painted green
across the chin, he smiled.

"Send us rain clouds, Grandfather." They laid the bundle in the back of
the pickup and covered it with a heavy tarp before they started back to the
pueblo.

They turned off the highway onto the sandy pueblo road. Not long after
they passed the store and post office they saw Father Paul's car coming toward them. When he recognized their faces he slowed his car and waved for
them to stop. The young priest rolled down the car window.

5   "Did you find old Teofilo?" he asked loudly.

Leon stopped the truck. "Good morning, Father. We were just out to the sheep camp. Everything is O.K. now."

"Thank God for that. Teofilo is a very old man. You really shouldn't allow him to stay at the sheep camp alone."

"No, he won't do that any more now."

"Well, I'm glad you understand. I hope I'll be seeing you at Mass this week—we missed you last Sunday. See if you can get old Teofilo to come with you." The priest smiled and waved at them as they drove away.

Two

10   Louise and Teresa were waiting. The table was set for lunch, and the coffee was boiling on the black iron stove. Leon looked at Louise and then at Teresa.

"We found him under a cottonwood tree in the big arroyo near sheep camp. I guess he sat down to rest in the shade and never got up again." Leon walked toward the old man's head. The red plaid shawl had been shaken and spread carefully over the bed, and a new brown flannel shirt and pair of stiff new Levis were arranged neatly beside the pillow. Louise held the screen door open while Leon and Ken carried in the red blanket. He looked small and shriveled, and after they dressed him in the new shirt and pants he seemed more shrunken.

It was noontime now because the church bells rang the Angelus.[1] They ate the beans with hot bread, and nobody said anything until after Teresa poured the coffee.

Ken stood up and put on his jacket. "I'll see about the gravediggers. Only the top layer of soil is frozen. I think it can be ready before dark."

Leon nodded his head and finished his coffee. After Ken had been gone for a while, the neighbors and clanspeople came quietly to embrace Teofilo's family and to leave food on the table because the gravediggers would come to eat when they were finished.

Three

15   The sky in the west was full of pale-yellow light. Louise stood outside with her hands in the pockets of Leon's green army jacket that was too big for her. The funeral was over, and the old men had taken their candles and medicine bags and were gone. She waited until the body was laid into the pickup before she said anything to Leon. She touched his arm, and he noticed that her hands were still dusty from the corn meal that she had sprinkled around the old man. When she spoke, Leon could not hear her.

"What did you say? I didn't hear you."

"I said that I had been thinking about something."

"About what?"

"About the priest sprinkling holy water for Grandpa. So he won't be thirsty."

---

[1] **Angelus** a devotional prayer commemorating the Annunciation (the angel Gabriel's announcement of the Incarnation of God in the human form of Jesus).

20   Leon stared at the new moccasins that Teofilo had made for the ceremonial dances in the summer. They were nearly hidden by the red blanket. It was getting colder, and the wind pushed gray dust down the narrow pueblo road. The sun was approaching the long mesa where it disappeared during the winter. Louise stood there shivering and watching his face. Then he zipped up his jacket and opened the truck door. "I'll see if he's there."

Ken stopped the pickup at the church, and Leon got out; and then Ken drove down the hill to the graveyard where people were waiting. Leon knocked at the old carved door with its symbols of the Lamb. While he waited he looked up at the twin bells from the king of Spain with the last sunlight pouring around them in their tower.

The priest opened the door and smiled when he saw who it was. "Come in! What brings you here this evening?"

The priest walked toward the kitchen, and Leon stood with his cap in his hand, playing with the earflaps and examining the living room—the brown sofa, the green armchair, and the brass lamp that hung down from the ceiling by links of chain. The priest dragged a chair out of the kitchen and offered it to Leon.

"No thank you, Father. I only came to ask you if you would bring your holy water to the graveyard."

25   The priest turned away from Leon and looked out the window at the patio full of shadows and the dining-room windows of the nuns' cloister across the patio. The curtains were heavy, and the light from within faintly penetrated; it was impossible to see the nuns inside eating supper. "Why didn't you tell me he was dead? I could have brought the Last Rites anyway."

Leon smiled. "It wasn't necessary, Father."

The priest stared down at his scuffed brown loafers and the worn hem of his cassock. "For a Christian burial it was necessary."

His voice was distant, and Leon thought that his blue eyes looked tired.

"It's O.K., Father, we just want him to have plenty of water."

30   The priest sank down in the green chair and picked up a glossy missionary magazine. He turned the colored pages full of lepers and pagans without looking at them.

"You know I can't do that, Leon. There should have been the Last Rites and a funeral Mass at the very least."

Leon put on his green cap and pulled the flaps down over his ears. "It's getting late, Father. I've got to go."

When Leon opened the door Father Paul stood up and said, "Wait." He left the room and came back wearing a long brown overcoat. He followed Leon out the door and across the dim churchyard to the adobe steps in front of the church. They both stooped to fit through the low adobe entrance. And when they started down the hill to the graveyard only half of the sun was visible above the mesa.

The priest approached the grave slowly, wondering how they had managed to dig into the frozen ground and then he remembered that this was New Mexico, and saw the pile of cold loose sand beside the hole. The people stood close to each other with little clouds of steam puffing from their faces. The priest looked at them and saw a pile of jackets, gloves, and scarves in the yellow, dry tumbleweeds that grew in the graveyard. He looked at the red blanket, not sure that Teofilo was so small, wondering if it wasn't some perverse Indian trick—something they did in March to ensure a good harvest—wondering if maybe old Teofilo was actually at sheep camp corraling the sheep for the night. But there he was, facing into a cold dry wind and squinting at the last sunlight, ready to bury a red wool blanket while the faces of the parishioners were in shadow with the last warmth of the sun on their backs.

35   His fingers were stiff, and it took them a long time to twist the lid off the holy water. Drops of water fell on the red blanket and soaked into dark icy spots. He sprinkled the grave and the water disappeared almost before it touched the dim, cold sand; it reminded him of something—he tried to remember what it was, because he thought if he could remember he might understand this. He sprinkled more water; he shook the container until it was empty, and the water fell through the light from sundown like August rain that fell while the sun was still shining, almost evaporating before it touched the wilted squash flowers.

The wind pulled at the priest's brown Franciscan robe and swirled away the corn meal and pollen that had been sprinkled on the blanket. They lowered the bundle into the ground, and they didn't bother to untie the stiff pieces of new rope that were tied around the ends of the blanket. The sun was gone, and over on the highway the eastbound lane was full of headlights. The priest walked away slowly. Leon watched him climb the hill, and when he had disappeared within the tall, thick walls, Leon turned to look up at the high blue mountains in the deep snow that reflected a faint red light from the west. He felt good because it was finished, and he was happy about the sprinkling of the holy water, now the old man could send them big thunderclouds for sure.

✳ TOPICS FOR CRITICAL THINKING AND WRITING

1. How would you describe the response of Leon, Ken, Louise, and Teresa to Teofilo's death? To what degree does it resemble or differ from responses to death that you are familiar with?
2. How do the funeral rites resemble or differ from those of your community?
3. How well does Leon understand the priest? How well does the priest understand Leon?
4. At the end of the story we are told that Leon "felt good." Do you assume that the priest also felt good? Why, or why not?
5. From what point of view is the story told? Mark the passages where the narrator enters a character's mind, and then explain what, in your opinion, Silko gains (or loses) by doing so.

JACK FORBES

Jack Forbes was born in California in 1934 of Powhattan and Delaware background. He teaches anthropology and Native American studies at the University of California, Davis, and is the author of fiction and nonfiction, including Columbus and Other Cannibals *(1992) and* African and Native Americans *(1993), a study of Red-Black peoples.*

Only Approved Indians Can Play: Made in USA   [1983]

The All-Indian Basketball Tournament was in its second day. Excitement was pretty high, because a lot of the teams were very good or at least eager and hungry to win. Quite a few people had come to watch, mostly Indians. Many were relatives or friends of the players. A lot of people were betting money and tension was pretty great.

A team from the Tucson Inter-Tribal House was set to play against a group from the Great Lakes region. The Tucson players were mostly very dark young men with long black hair. A few had little goatee beards or mustaches though, and one of the Great Lakes fans had started a rumor that they were really Chicanos. This was a big issue since the Indian Sports League had a rule that all players had to be of one-quarter or more Indian blood and that they had to have their BIA[1] roll numbers available if challenged.

And so a big argument started. One of the biggest, darkest Indians on the Tucson team had been singled out as a Chicano, and the crowd wanted him thrown out. The Great Lakes players, most of whom were pretty light, refused to start. They all had their BIA identification cards, encased in plastic. This proved that they were all real Indians, even a blonde-haired guy. He was really only about one-sixteenth but the BIA rolls had been changed for his tribe so legally he was one-fourth. There was no question about the Great Lakes team. They were all land-based, federally-recognized Indians, although living in a big midwestern city, and they had their cards to prove it.

Anyway, the big, dark Tucson Indian turned out to be a Papago. He didn't have a BIA card but he could talk Papago so they let him alone for the time being. Then they turned towards a lean, very Indian-looking guy who had a pretty big goatee. He seemed to have a Spanish accent, so they demanded to see his card.

5   Well, he didn't have one either. He said he was a full-blood Tarahumara Indian and he could also speak his language. None of the Great Lakes Indians could talk their languages so they said that was no proof of anything, that you had to have a BIA roll number.

The Tarahumara man was getting pretty angry by then. He said his father and uncle had been killed by the whites in Mexico and that he did not expect to be treated with prejudice by other Indians.

But all that did no good. Someone demanded to know if he had a reservation and if his tribe was recognized. He replied that his people lived high up in the mountains and that they were still resisting the Mexicanos, that the government was trying to steal their land.

"What state do your people live in," they wanted to know. When he said that his people lived free, outside of control of any state, they only shook their fists at him. "You're not an official Indian. All official Indians are under the whiteman's rule now. We all have a number given to us, to show that we are recognized."

Well, it all came to an end when someone shouted that "Tarahumaras don't exist. They're not listed in the BIA dictionary." Another fan yelled, "He's a Mexican. He can't play. This tournament is only for Indians."

10   The officials of the tournament had been huddling together. One blew his whistle and an announcement was made. "The Tucson team is disqualified. One of its member is a Yaqui. One is a Tarahumara. The rest are Papagos.

---

[1]**BIA** Bureau of Indian Affairs.

None of them have BIA enrollment cards. They are not Indians within the meaning of the laws of the government of the United States. The Great Lakes team is declared the winner by default."

A tremendous roar of applause swept through the stands. A white BIA official wiped the tears from his eyes and said to a companion, "God Bless America. I think we've won."

▨ TOPICS FOR CRITICAL THINKING AND WRITING

1. What expectations did the title, with its reference to "Approved Indians" and "Made in USA," suggest to you?
2. How would you describe the narrator's tone?

JOHN UPDIKE

John Updike (b. 1932) grew up in Shillington, Pennsylvania, where his father was a teacher and his mother a writer. After receiving a B.A. degree in 1954 from Harvard, where he edited the Harvard Lampoon *(for which he both wrote and drew), he studied drawing at Oxford for a year, but an offer from* The New Yorker *brought him back to the United States. He was hired as a reporter for the magazine but soon began contributing poetry, essays, and fiction. In 1957 he left* The New Yorker *in order to write independently full time, though his stories and book reviews appear regularly in it.*

In 1959 Updike published his first book of stories (The Same Door) *and also his first novel* (The Poorhouse Fair); *the next year he published* Rabbit, Run, *a highly successful novel whose protagonist, "Rabbit" Angstrom, has reappeared in three later novels,* Rabbit Redux *(1971),* Rabbit Is Rich *(1981), and* Rabbit at Rest *(1990). The first and last Rabbit books each won a Pulitzer Prize.*

The Rumor

[1990]

Frank and Sharon Whittier had come from the Cincinnati area and, with an inheritance of hers and a sum borrowed from his father, had opened a small art gallery on the fourth floor of a narrow building on West Fifty-seventh Street. They had known each other as children; their families had been in the same country-club set. They had married in 1971, when Frank was freshly graduated from Oberlin and Vietnam-vulnerable and Sharon was only nineteen, a sophomore at Antioch majoring in dance. By the time, six years later, they arrived in New York, they had two small children; the birth of a third led them to give up their apartment and the city struggle and move to a house in Hastings, a low stucco house with a wide-eaved Wright-style roof and a view, through massive beeches at the bottom of the yard, of the leaden, ongliding Hudson. They were happy, surely. They had dry midwestern taste, and by sticking to representational painters and abstract sculptors they managed to survive the uglier Eighties styles—faux graffiti, neo–German expressionism, cathode-ray prole play, ecological-protest trash art—and bring their quiet, chaste string of fourth-floor rooms into the calm lagoon of Nineties eclectic revivalism and subdued recession chic. They prospered; their youngest child turned twelve, their oldest was filling out college applications.

When Sharon first heard the rumor that Frank had left her for a young homosexual with whom he was having an affair, she had to laugh, for, far from having left her, there he was, right in the lamplit study with her, ripping pages out of *ARTnews*.

"I don't think so, Avis," she said to the graphic artist on the other end of the line. "He's right here with me. Would you like to say hello?" The easy refutation was made additionally sweet by the fact that, some years before, there had been a brief (Sharon thought) romantic flare-up between her husband and this caller, an overanimated redhead with protuberant cheeks and chin. Avis was a second-wave appropriationist who made color Xeroxes of masterpiece out of art books and then signed them in an ink mixed of her own blood and urine. How could she, who had actually slept with Frank, be imaging this grotesque thing?

The voice on the phone gushed as if relieved and pleased. "I know, it's wildly absurd, but I heard it from two sources with absolutely solemn assurance."

5   "Who were these sources?"

"I'm not sure they'd like you to know. But it was Ed Jaffrey and then that boy who's been living with Walton Forney, what does he call himself, one of those single names like Madonna—Jojo!"

"Well, then," Sharon began.

"But I've heard it from still others," Avis insisted. "All over town—it's in the air. Couldn't you and Frank *do* something about it, if it's not true?"

"If," Sharon protested, and her thrust of impatience carried, when she put down the receiver, into her conversation with Frank. "Avis says you're supposed to have run off with your homosexual lover."

10   "I don't have a homosexual lover," Frank said, too calmly, ripping an auction ad out of the magazine.

"She says all New York says you do."

"Well, what are you going to believe, all New York or your own experience? Here I sit, faithful to a fault, straight as a die, whatever that means. We made love just two nights ago."

It seemed possibly revealing to her that he so distinctly remembered, as if heterosexual performance were a duty he checked off. He was—had always been, for over twenty years—a slim blond man several inches under six feet tall, with a narrow head he liked to keep trim, even during those years when long hair was in fashion, milky-blue eyes set at a slight tilt, such as you see on certain taut Slavic or Norwegian faces, and a small, precise mouth he kept pursed over teeth a shade too prominent and yellow. He was reluctant to smile, as if giving something away, and was vain of his flat belly and lithe collegiate condition. He weighed himself every morning on the bathroom scale, and if he weighed a pound more than yesterday, he skipped lunch. In this, and in his general attention to his own person, he was as quietly fanatic as—it for the first time occurred to her—a woman.

"You know I've never liked the queer side of this business," he went on. "I've just gotten used to it. I don't even think anymore, who's gay and who isn't."

15   "Avis was *ju*bilant," Sharon said. "How could she think it?"

It took him a moment to focus on the question and realize that his answer was important to her. He became nettled. "Ask *her* how," he said. "Our brief and regrettable relationship, if that's what interests you, seemed satisfactory to me at least. What troubles and amazes me, if I may say so, is how *you* can be taking this ridiculous rumor so seriously."

"I'm *not,* Frank," she insisted, then backtracked. "But why would such a rumor come out of thin air? Doesn't there have to be *something?* Since we moved up here, we're not together so much, naturally, some days when I can't come into town you're gone sixteen hours. . . ."

"But *Shar*on," he said, like a teacher restoring discipline, removing his reading glasses from his almond-shaped eyes, with their stubby fair lashes. "Don't you *know* me? Ever since after that dance when you were sixteen, that time by the lake? . . ."

She didn't want to reminisce. Their early sex had been difficult for her; she had submitted to his advances out of a larger, more social, rather idealistic attraction. She knew that together they would have the strength to get out of Cincinnati and, singly or married to others, they would stay. "Well," she said, enjoying this sensation, despite the chill the rumor had awakened in her, of descending to a deeper level of intimacy than usual, "how well do you know even your own spouse? People are fooled all the time. Peggy Jacobson, for instance, when Henry ran off with that physical therapist, couldn't believe, even when the evidence was right there in front of her—"

20   "I'm *deeply* insulted," Frank interrupted, his mouth tense in that way he had when making a joke but not wanting to show his teeth. "My masculinity is insulted." But he couldn't deny himself a downward glance into his magazine; his tidy white hand jerked, as if wanting to tear out yet another item that might be useful to their business. Intimacy had always made him nervous. She kept at it, rather hopelessly. "Avis said two separate people had solemnly assured her."

"Who, exactly?"

When she told him, he said, exactly as she had done, "Well, then." He added, "You know how gays are. Malicious. Mischievous. They have all that time and money on their hands."

"You sound jealous." Something about the way he was arguing with her strengthened Sharon's suspicion that, outrageous as the rumor was—indeed, *because* it was outrageous—it was true.

In the days that followed, now that she was alert to the rumor's vaporous presence, she imagined it everywhere—on the poised young faces of their staff, in the delicate negotiatory accents of their artists' agents, in the heartier tones of their repeat customers, even in the gruff, self-occupied ramblings of the artists themselves. People seemed startled when she and Frank entered a room together: The desk receptionist and the security guard in their gallery halted their daily morning banter, and the waiters in their pet restaurant, over on Fifty-ninth, appeared especially effusive and attentive. Handshakes lasted a second too long, women embraced her with an extra squeeze, she felt herself ensnared in a soft net of unspoken pity.

25   Frank sensed her discomfort and took a certain malicious pleasure in it, enacting all the while his perfect innocence. He composed himself to appear, from her angle, aloof above the rumor. Dealing professionally in so much absurdity—the art world's frantic attention-getting, studied grotesqueries—he merely intensified the fastidious dryness that had sustained their gallery through wave after wave of changing-fashion, and that had, like a rocket's heat-resistant skin, insulated their launch, their escape from the comfortable

riverine smugness of this metropolis of dreadful freedom. The rumor amused him, and it amused him, too, to notice how she helplessly watched to see if in the metropolitan throngs his eyes now followed young men as once they had noticed and followed young women. She observed his gestures—always a bit excessively graceful and precise—distrustfully, and listened for the buttery, reedy tone of voice that might signal an invisible sex change.

That even in some small fraction of her she was willing to believe the rumor justified a certain maliciousness on his part. He couldn't help teasing her—glancing over at her, say, when an especially magnetic young waiter served them, or at home, in their bedroom, pushing more brusquely than was his style at her increasing sexual unwillingness. More than once, at last away from the countless knowing eyes of their New York milieu, in the privacy of their Hastings upstairs, beneath the wide midwestern eaves, she burst into tears and struck out at him, his infuriating, impervious, apparent blamelessness. He was like one of those photo-realist nudes, merciless in every detail and yet subtly, defiantly, not there, not human. "You're distant," she accused him, "You've always been."

"I don't mean to be. You didn't used to mind my manner. You thought it was quietly masterful."

"I was a teenage girl. I deferred to you."

"It worked out," he pointed out, lifting his hands in an effete, disclaiming way from his sides, to take in their room, their expensive house, their joint career. "What is it that bothers you, Sharon? The idea of losing me? Or the insult to your female pride? The people who started this ridiculous rumor don't even *see* women. Women to them are just background noise."

30   "It's *not* ridiculous—if it were, why does it keep on and on, even though we're seen together all the time?"

For, ostensibly to quiet her and to quench the rumor, he had all but ceased to go to the city alone, and took her with him even though it meant some neglect of the house and their sons.

Frank asked, "Who *says* it keeps on all the time? I've *never* heard it, never once, except from you. Who's mentioned it lately?"

"Nobody."

"Well, then." He smiled, his lips not quite parting on his curved teeth, tawny like a beaver's.

35   "You bastard!" Sharon burst out. "You have some stinking little secret!"

"I don't," he serenely half-lied.

The rumor had no factual basis. But was there, Frank asked himself, some truth to it after all? Not circumstantial truth, but some higher, inner truth? As a young man, slight of build, with artistic interests, had he not been fearful of being mistaken for a homosexual? Had he not responded to homosexual overtures as they arose, in bars and locker rooms, with a disproportionate terror and repugnance? Had not his early marriage, and then, ten years later, his flurry of adulterous womanizing, been an escape of sorts, into safe, socially approved terrain? When he fantasized, or saw a pornographic movie, was not the male organ the hero of the occasion for him, at the center of every scene? Were not those slavish, lapping starlets his robotlike delegates, with glazed eyes and undisturbed coiffures venturing where he did not dare? Did he not, perhaps, envy women their privilege of worshiping the phallus? But, Frank asked himself, in fairness, arguing both sides of the case, can homosexual strands be entirely disentangled from heterosexual in that pink muck of carnal excitement, of dream made flesh, of return to the presexual womb?

More broadly, had he not felt more comfortable with his father than with his mother? Was not this in itself a sinister reversal of the usual biology? His father had been a genteel Fourth Street lawyer, of no particular effectuality save that most of his clients were from the same social class, with the same accents and comfortably narrowed aspirations, here on this plateau by the swelling Ohio. Darker and taller than Frank, with the same long teeth and primly set mouth, his father had had the lawyer's gift of silence, of judicious withholding, and in his son's scattered memories of times together—a trip downtown on the trolley to buy Frank his first suit, each summer's one or two excursions to see the Reds play at old Crosley Field—the man said little. This prim reserve, letting so much go unstated and unacknowledged, was a relief after the daily shower of words and affection and advice Frank received from his mother. As an adult he was attracted, he had noticed, to stoical men, taller than he and nursing an unexpressed sadness; his favorite college roommate had been of this saturnine type, and his pet tennis partner in Hastings, and artists he especially favored and encouraged—dour, weathered landscapists and virtually illiterate sculptors, welded solid into their crafts and stubborn obsessions. With these men he became a catering, wifely, subtly agitated presence that Sharon would scarcely recognize.

Frank's mother, once a fluffy belle from Louisville, had been gaudy, strident, sardonic, volatile, needy, demanding, loving; from her he had inherited his "artistic" side, as well as his pretty blondness, but he was not especially grateful. Less—as was proposed by a famous formula he didn't know as a boy—would have been more. His mother had given him an impression of women as complex, brightly-colored traps, attractive but treacherous, their petals apt to harden in an instant into knives. A certain wistful pallor, indeed, a limp helplessness, had drawn him to Sharon and, after the initial dazzlement of the Avises of the world faded and fizzled, always drew him back. Other women asked more than he could provide; he was aware of other, bigger, warmer men they had had. But with Sharon he had been a rescuing knight, slaying the dragon of the winding Ohio. Yet what more devastatingly, and less forgivably, confirmed the rumor's essential truth than her willingness, she who knew him best and owed him most, to entertain it? Her instinct had been to believe Avis even though, far from run off, he was sitting there right in front of her eyes.

40   He was unreal to her, he could not help but conclude: all those years of uxorious cohabitation, those nights of lovemaking and days of homemaking ungratefully absorbed and now suddenly dismissed because of an apparition, a shadow of gossip. On the other hand, now that the rumor existed, Frank had become more real in the eyes of José, the younger, daintier of the two security guards, whose daily greetings had edged beyond the perfunctory; a certain mischievous dance in the boy's sable eyes animated their employer–employee courtesies. And Jennifer, too, the severely beautiful receptionist, with her rather Sixties-reminiscent bangs and shawls and serapes, now treated him more relaxedly, even offhandedly, as if he had somehow dropped out of her calculations. She assumed with him a comradely slanginess—"The boss was in earlier but she went out to exchange something at Berdorf's"—as if both he and she were in roughly parallel ironic bondage to "the boss." Frank's heart felt a reflex loyalty to Sharon, a single sharp beat, but then he too relaxed, as if his phantom male lover and the weightless, scandal-veiled life that lived with him

in some glowing apartment had bestowed at last what the city had withheld from the overworked, child-burdened married couple who had arrived fourteen years ago—a halo of glamour, of debonair uncaring.

In Hastings, when he and his wife attended a suburban party, the effect was less flattering. The other couples, he imagined, were slightly unsettled by the Whittiers stubbornly appearing together and became disjointed in their presence, the men drifting off in distaste, the women turning supernormal and laying up a chinkless wall of conversation about children's college applications, local zoning, and Wall Street layoffs. The women, it seemed to Frank, edged, with an instinctive animal movement, a few inches closer to Sharon and touched her with a deft, protective flicking on the shoulder or forearm, to express solidarity and sympathy.

Wes Robertson, Frank's favorite tennis partner, came over to him and grunted. "How's it going?"

"Fine," Frank said, staring up at Wes with what he hoped weren't unduly starry eyes. Wes, who had recently turned fifty, had an old motorcycle-accident scar on one side of his chin, a small pale rose of discoloration that seemed to concentrate on the man's self-careless manliness. Frank gave him more of an answer than he might have wanted: "In the art game we're feeling the slowdown like everybody else, but the Japanese are keeping the roof from caving in. The trouble with the Japanese, though, is, from the standpoint of a marginal gallery like ours, they aren't adventurous—they want blue chips, they want guaranteed value, they can't grasp that in art, value has to be subjective to an extent. Look at their own stuff—it's all standardized. Who the hell can tell a Hiroshige from a Hokusai?[1] When you think about it, their whole society, their whole success, really, is based on everybody being alike, everybody agreeing. The notion of art as a struggle, a gamble, as the dynamic embodiment of an existential problem, they just don't get it." He was talking too much, he knew, but he couldn't help it; Wes's scowling presence, his melancholy scarred face, and his stringy alcoholic body, which nevertheless could still whip a backhand right across the forecourt, perversely excited Frank, made him want to flirt.

Wes grimaced and contemplated Frank glumly. "Be around for a game Sunday?" Meaning, had he really run off?

45   "Of course. Why wouldn't I be?" This was teasing the issue, and Frank tried to sober up, to rein in. He felt a flush on his face and a stammer coming on. He asked, "The usual time? Ten forty-five, more or less?"

Wes nodded. "Sure."

Frank chattered on: "Let's try to get court 5 this time. Those brats having their lessons on court 2 drove me crazy last time. We spent all our time retrieving their damn balls. And listening to their moronic chatter."

Wes didn't grant this attempt at evocation of past liaisons even a word, just continued his melancholy, stoical nodding. This was one of the things, it occurred to Frank, that he liked about men: their relational minimalism, their gender-based realization that the cupboard of life, emotionally speaking, was pretty near bare. There wasn't that tireless, irksome, bright-eyed *hope* women kept fluttering at you.

Once, years ago, on a stag golfing trip to Bermuda, he and Wes had shared a room with two single beds, and Wes had fallen asleep within a minute and started snoring, keeping Frank awake for much of the night. Con-

---

[1]**Hiroshige . . . Hokusai** Ando Hiroshige (1797–1858) and Katsushika Hokusai (1760–1849) are chiefly known as designers of landscape prints.

templating the unconscious male body on its moonlit bed, Frank had been struck by the tragic dignity of this supine form, like a stone knight eroding on a tomb—the snoring profile in motionless gray silhouette, the massive, sacred warrior weight helpless as Wes's breathing struggled from phase to phase of the sleep cycle, from deep to REM to a near-wakefulness that brought a few merciful minutes of silence. The next morning, Wes said Frank should have reached over and poked him in the side; that's what his wife did. But he wasn't his wife, Frank thought, though in the course of that night's ordeal, he had felt his heart make many curious motions, among them the heaving, all-but-impossible effort women's hearts make in overcoming men's heavy grayness and achieving—a rainbow born of drizzle—love.

50   At the opening of Ned Forschheimer's show—Forschheimer, a shy, rude, stubborn, and now elderly painter of tea-colored, wintry Connecticut landscapes, was one of Frank's pets, unfashionable yet sneakily salable—none other than Walton Forney came up to Frank, his round face lit by white wine and odd, unquenchable self-delight, and said, "Say, Frank, old boy. Methinks I owe you an apology. It was Charlie Whit*field* that used to run that framing shop down on Eighth Street, who left his wife suddenly, with some little Guatemalan boy he was putting through CCNY on the side. They took off for Mexico and left the missus sitting with the shop mortgaged up to its attic and about a hundred prints of wild ducks left unframed. The thing that must have confused me, Charlie came from Ohio, too—Columbus or Cleveland, one of those. It was—what do they call it—a Freudian slip, an understandable confusion. Avis Wasserman told me Sharon wasn't all that thrilled to get the word a while ago, and you must have wondered yourself what the hell was up."

"We ignored it," Frank said, in a voice firmer and less catering than his usual one. "We rose above it." Walton was a number of inches shorter than Frank, with yet a bigger head; his gleaming, thin-skinned face, bearing smooth jowls that had climbed into his sideburns, was shadowed blue here and there, like the moon. His bruised and powdered look somehow went with his small, spaced teeth and the horizontal red tracks his glasses had left in the fat in front of his ears.

The man gazed at Frank with a gleaming, sagging lower lip, his near-sighted little eyes trying to assess the damage, the depth of the grudge. "Well, mea culpa, mea culpa, I guess, though I *didn't* tell Jojo and that *poisonous* Ed Jaffrey to go blabbing it all over town."

"Well, thanks for telling me, Wally, I guess." Depending on which man he was standing with, Frank felt large and straight and sonorous or, as with Wes, gracile and flighty. Sharon, scenting blood amid the vacuous burble of the party, pushed herself through the crowd and joined the two men. To deny Walton the pleasure, Frank quickly told her, "Wally just confessed to me he started the rumor because Charlie Whitfield downtown, who did run off with somebody, came from Ohio, too. Toledo, as I remember."

"Oh, that rumor," Sharon said, blinking once, as if her party mascara were sticking. "I'd forgotten it. Who could believe it, of Frank?"

55   "Everybody, evidently," Frank said. It was possible, given the strange, willful ways of women, that she had forgotten it, even while Frank had been brooding over its possible justice. If the rumor were truly dispersed—and Walton would undoubtedly tell the story of his Freudian slip around town as a self-promoting joke on himself—Frank would feel diminished. He would lose that small sadistic power to make her watch him watching waiters

in restaurants, and to bring her into town as his chaperon. He would feel emasculated if she no longer thought he had a secret. Yet that night, at the party, Walton Forney's Jojo had come up to him. He had seemed, despite an earring the size of a faucet washer and a stripe of bleach in the center of his hair, unexpectedly intelligent and low-key, offering, not in so many words, a kind of apology, and praising the tea-colored landscapes being offered for sale. "I've been thinking, in my own work, of going, you know, more traditional. You get this feeling of, like, a dead end with abstraction." The boy had a bony, rueful face, with a silvery line of a scar under one eye, and seemed uncertain in manner, hesitantly murmurous, as if at a point in life where he needed direction. The fat fool Forney could certainly not provide that, and it pleased Frank to imagine that Jojo was beginning to realize it.

The car as he and Sharon drove home together along the Hudson felt close; the heater fan blew oppressively, parchingly. "*You* were willing to believe it at first," he reminded her.

"Well, Avis seemed so definite. But you convinced me."

"How?"

She placed her hand high on his thigh and dug her fingers in, annoyingly, infuriatingly. "You know," she said, in a lower register, meant to be sexy, but almost inaudible with the noise of the heater fan.

60   "That could be mere performance," he warned her. "Women are fooled that way all the time."

"Who says?"

"Everybody. Books. Proust.[2] People aren't that simple."

"They're simple enough," Sharon said, in a neutral, defensive tone, removing her presumptuous hand.

"If you say so," he said, somewhat stoically, his mind drifting. That silvery line of a scar under Jojo's left eye . . . lean long muscles snugly wrapped in white skin . . . lofts . . . Hellenic fellowship,[3] exercise machines . . . direct negotiations, a simple transaction among equals. The rumor might be dead in the world, but in him it had come alive.

---

[2]**Proust** Marcel Proust (1871–1922), French homosexual novelist.   [3]**Hellenic fellowship** Greek friendship, with the implication of erotic love between a mature man and a youth.

▨ TOPICS FOR CRITICAL THINKING AND WRITING

1. What point of view is used in the first paragraph of the story?
2. Consider the following line from the story:

   "I don't have a homosexual lover," Frank said, too calmly, ripping an auction ad out of the catalog.

   What is the point of view?
3. How would you characterize the point of view in the following passage, from near the end of the story?

   She placed her hand high on his thigh and dug her fingers in, annoyingly, infuriatingly. "You know," she said in a lower register, meant to be sexy, but almost inaudible with the noise of the heater fan.

4. Do you think Frank is homosexual? Please explain.

5. Frank says, "You know how gays are. Malicious. Mischievous." To the best of your knowledge, is this a widespread stereotype of gays, or is the idea new to you? Might the characterization be applied to Frank himself?

GLORIA NAYLOR

Gloria Naylor (b. 1950), a native of New York City, holds a bachelor's degree from Brooklyn College and a master's degree in Afro-American Studies from Yale University. "The Two" comes from The Women of Brewster Place *(1982), a book that won the American Book Award for First Fiction. Naylor has subsequently published four novels and* Centennial *(1986), a work of nonfiction.*

The Two

[1982]

At first they seemed like such nice girls. No one could remember exactly when they had moved into Brewster. It was earlier in the year before Ben[1] was killed—of course, it had to be before Ben's death. But no one remembered if it was in the winter or spring of that year that the two had come. People often came and went on Brewster Place like a restless night's dream, moving in and out in the dark to avoid eviction notices or neighborhood bulletins about the dilapidated condition of their furnishings. So it wasn't until the two were clocked leaving in the mornings and returning in the evenings at regular intervals that it was quietly absorbed that they now claimed Brewster as home. And Brewster waited, cautiously prepared to claim them, because you never knew about young women, and obviously single at that. But when no wild music or drunken friends careened out of the corner building on weekends, and especially, when no slightly eager husbands were encouraged to linger around that first-floor apartment and run errands for them, a suspended sigh of relief floated around the two when they dumped their garbage, did their shopping, and headed for the morning bus.

The women of Brewster had readily accepted the lighter, skinny one. There wasn't much threat in her timid mincing walk and the slightly protruding teeth she seemed so eager to show everyone in her bell-like good mornings and evenings. Breaths were held a little longer in the direction of the short dark one—too pretty, and too much behind. And she insisted on wearing those thin Qiana dresses that the summer breeze molded against the maddening rhythm of the twenty pounds of rounded flesh that she swung steadily down the street. Through slitted eyes, the women watched their men watching her pass, knowing the bastards were praying for a wind. But since she seemed oblivious to whether these supplications went answered, their sighs settled around her shoulders too. Nice girls.

And so no one even cared to remember exactly when they had moved into Brewster Place, until the rumor started. It had first spread through the block like a sour odor that's only faintly perceptible and easily ignored until it starts growing in strength from the dozen mouths it had been lying in,

---

[1]**Ben** the custodian of Brewster Place.

among clammy gums and scum-coated teeth. And then it was everywhere—lining the mouths and whitening the lips of everyone as they wrinkled up their noses at its pervading smell, unable to pinpoint the source or time of its initial arrival. Sophie could—she had been there.

It wasn't that the rumor had actually begun with Sophie. A rumor needs no true parent. It only needs a willing carrier, and it found one in Sophie. She had been there—on one of those August evenings when the sun's absence is a mockery because the heat leaves the air so heavy it presses the naked skin down on your body, to the point that a sheet becomes unbearable and sleep impossible. So most of Brewster was outside that night when the two had come in together, probably from one of those air-conditioned movies downtown, and had greeted the ones who were loitering around their building. And they had started up the steps when the skinny one tripped over a child's ball and the darker one had grabbed her by the arm and around the waist to break her fall. "Careful, don't wanna lose you now." And the two of them had laughed into each other's eyes and went into the building.

5   The smell had begun there. It outlined the image of the stumbling woman and the one who had broken her fall. Sophie and a few other women sniffed at the spot and then, perplexed, silently looked at each other. Where had they seen that before? They had often laughed and touched each other—held each other in joy or its dark twin—but where had they seen *that* before? It came to them as the scent drifted down the steps and entered their nostrils on the way to their inner mouths. They had seen that—done that—with their men. That shared moment of invisible communion reserved for two and hidden from the rest of the world behind laughter or tears or a touch. In the days before babies, miscarriages, and other broken dreams, after stolen caresses in barn stalls and cotton houses, after intimate walks from church and secret kisses with boys who were now long forgotten or permanently fixed in their lives—that was where. They could almost feel the odor moving about in their mouths, and they slowly knitted themselves together and let it out into the air like a yellow mist that began to cling to the bricks on Brewster.

So it got around that the two in 312 were *that* way. And they had seemed like such nice girls. Their regular exits and entrances to the block were viewed with a jaundiced eye. The quiet that rested around their door on the weekends hinted of all sorts of secret rituals, and their friendly indifference to the men on the street was an insult to the women as a brazen flaunting of unnatural ways.

Since Sophie's apartment windows faced theirs from across the air shaft, she became the official watchman for the block, and her opinions were deferred to whenever the two came up in conversation. Sophie took her position seriously and was constantly alert for any telltale signs that might creep out around their drawn shades, across from which she kept a religious vigil. An entire week of drawn shades was evidence enough to send her flying around with reports that as soon as it got dark they pulled their shades down and put on the lights. Heads nodded in knowing unison—a definite sign. If doubt was voiced with a "But I pull my shades down at night too," a whispered "Yeah, but you're not *that* way" was argument enough to win them over.

Sophie watched the lighter one dumping their garbage, and she went outside and opened the lid. Her eyes darted over the crushed tin cans, vegetable peelings, and empty chocolate chip cookie boxes. What do they do with all them chocolate chip cookies? It was surely a sign, but it would take some time to figure that one out. She saw Ben go into their apartment, and she waited and blocked his path as he came out, carrying his toolbox.

"What ya see?" She grabbed his arm and whispered wetly in his face.

10   Ben stared at her squinted eyes and drooping lips and shook his head slowly. "Uh, uh, uh, it was terrible."

"Yeah?" She moved in a little closer.

"Worst busted faucet I seen in my whole life." He shook her hand off his arm and left her standing in the middle of the block.

"You old sop bucket," she muttered, as she went back up on her stoop. A broken faucet, huh? Why did they need to use so much water?

Sophie had plenty to report that day. Ben had said it was terrible in there. No, she didn't know exactly what he had seen, but you can imagine—and they did. Confronted with the difference that had been thrust into their predictable world, they reached into their imaginations and, using an ancient pattern, weaved themselves a reason for its existence. Out of necessity they stitched all of their secret fears and lingering childhood nightmares into this existence, because even though it was deceptive enough to try and look as they looked, talk as they talked, and do as they did, it had to have some hidden stain to invalidate it—it was impossible for them both to be right. So they leaned back, supported by the sheer weight of their numbers and comforted by the woven barrier that kept them protected from the yellow mist that enshrouded the two as they came and went on Brewster Place.

15   Lorraine was the first to notice the change in the people on Brewster Place. She was a shy but naturally friendly woman who got up early, and had read the morning paper and done fifty sit-ups before it was time to leave for work. She came out of her apartment eager to start her day by greeting any of her neighbors who were outside. But she noticed that some of the people who had spoken to her before made a point of having something else to do with their eyes when she passed, although she could almost feel them staring at her back as she moved on. The ones who still spoke only did so after an uncomfortable pause, in which they seemed to be peering through her before they begrudged her a good morning or evening. She wondered if it was all in her mind and she thought about mentioning it to Theresa, but she didn't want to be accused of being too sensitive again. And how would Tee even notice anything like that anyway? She had a lousy attitude and hardly ever spoke to people. She stayed in that bed until the last moment and rushed out of the house fogged-up and grumpy, and she was used to being stared at—by men at least—because of her body.

Lorraine thought about these things as she came up the block from work, carrying a large paper bag. The group of women on her stoop parted silently and let her pass.

"Good evening," she said, as she climbed the steps.

Sophie was standing on the top step and tried to peek into the bag. "You been shopping, huh? What ya buy?" It was almost an accusation.

"Groceries." Lorraine shielded the top of the bag from view and squeezed past her with a confused frown. She saw Sophie throw a knowing glance to the others at the bottom of the stoop. What was wrong with this old woman? Was she crazy or something?

20   Lorraine went into her apartment. Theresa was sitting by the window, reading a copy of *Mademoiselle.* She glanced up from her magazine. "Did you get my chocolate chip cookies?"

"Why good evening to you, too, Tee. And how was my day? Just wonderful." She sat the bag down on the couch. "The little Baxter boy brought in a puppy for show-and-tell, and the damn thing pissed all over the floor and then proceeded to chew the heel off my shoe, but, yes, I managed to hobble to the store and bring you your chocolate chip cookies."

Oh, Jesus, Theresa thought, she's got a bug up her ass tonight.

"Well, you should speak to Mrs. Baxter. She ought to train her kid better than that." She didn't wait for Lorraine to stop laughing before she tried to stretch her good mood. "Here, I'll put those things away. Want me to make dinner so you can rest? I only worked half a day, and the most tragic thing that went down was a broken fingernail and that got caught in my typewriter."

Lorraine followed Theresa into the kitchen. "No, I'm not really tired, and fair's fair, you cooked last night. I didn't mean to tick off like that; it's just that . . . well, Tee, have you noticed that people aren't as nice as they used to be?"

25   Theresa stiffened. Oh, God, here she goes again. "What people, Lorraine? Nice in what way?"

"Well, the people in this building and on the street. No one hardly speaks anymore. I mean, I'll come in and say good evening—and just silence. It wasn't like that when we first moved in. I don't know, it just makes you wonder; that's all. What are they thinking?"

"I personally don't give a shit what they're thinking. And their good evenings don't put any bread on my table."

"Yeah, but you didn't see the way that woman looked at me out there. They must feel something or know something. They probably—"

"They, they, they!" Theresa exploded. "You know, I'm not starting up with this again, Lorraine. Who in the hell are they? And where in the hell are we? Living in some dump of a building in this God-forsaken part of town around a bunch of ignorant niggers with the cotton still under their fingernails because of you and your theys. They knew something in Linden Hills, so I gave up an apartment for you that I'd been in for the last four years. And then they knew in Park Heights, and you made me so miserable there we had to leave. Now these mysterious theys are on Brewster Place. Well, look out that window, kid. There's a big wall down that block, and this is the end of the line for me. I'm not moving anymore, so if that's what you're working yourself up to—save it!"

30   When Theresa became angry she was like a lump of smoldering coal, and her fierce bursts of temper always unsettled Lorraine.

"You see, that's why I didn't want to mention it." Lorraine began to pull at her fingers nervously. "You're always flying up and jumping to conclusions—no one said anything about moving. And I didn't know your life has been so miserable since you met me. I'm sorry about that," she finished tearfully.

Theresa looked at Lorraine, standing in the kitchen door like a wilted leaf, and she wanted to throw something at her. Why didn't she ever fight back? The very softness that had first attracted her to Lorraine was now a frequent cause for irritation. Smoked honey. That's what Lorraine had reminded her of, sitting in her office clutching that application. Dry autumn days in Georgia woods, thick bloated smoke under a beehive, and the first glimpse of amber honey just faintly darkened about the edges by the burning twigs. She had flowed just that heavily into Theresa's mind and had stuck there with a persistent sweetness.

But Theresa hadn't known then that this softness filled Lorraine up to the very middle and that she would bend at the slightest pressure, would be constantly seeking to surround herself with the comfort of everyone's good-will, and would shrivel up at the least touch of disapproval. It was becoming a drain to be continually called upon for this nurturing and support that she just didn't understand. She had supplied it at first out of love for Lorraine, hoping that she would harden eventually, even as honey does when exposed to the cold. Theresa was growing tired of being clung to—of being the one who was leaned on. She didn't want a child—she wanted someone who could stand toe to toe with her and be willing to slug it out at times. If they practiced that way with each other, then they could turn back to back and beat the hell out of the world for trying to invade their territory. But she had found no such sparring partner in Lorraine, and the strain of fighting alone was beginning to show on her.

"Well, if it was that miserable, I would have been gone a long time ago," she said, watching her words refresh Lorraine like a gentle shower.

35   "I guess you think I'm some sort of sick paranoid, but I can't afford to have people calling my job or writing letters to my principal. You know I've already lost a position like that in Detroit. And teaching is my whole life, Tee."

"I know," she sighed, not really knowing at all. There was no danger of that ever happening on Brewster Place. Lorraine taught too far from this neighborhood for anyone here to recognize her in that school. No, it wasn't her job she feared losing this time, but their approval. She wanted to stand out there and chat and trade makeup secrets and cake recipes. She wanted to be secretary of their block association and be asked to mind their kids while they ran to the store. And none of that was going to happen if they couldn't even bring themselves to accept her good evenings.

Theresa silently finished unpacking the groceries. "Why did you buy cottage cheese? Who eats that stuff?"

"Well, I thought we should go on a diet."

"If *we* go on a diet, then you'll disappear. You've got nothing to lose but your hair."

40   "Oh, I don't know. I thought that we might want to try and reduce our hips or something." Lorraine shrugged playfully.

"No, thank you. We are very happy with our hips the way they are," Theresa said, as she shoved the cottage cheese to the back of the refrigerator. "And even when I lose weight, it never comes off there. My chest and arms just get smaller, and I start looking like a bottle of salad dressing."

The two women laughed, and Theresa sat down to watch Lorraine fix dinner. "You know, this behind has always been my downfall. When I was coming up in Georgia with my grandmother, the boys used to promise me penny candy if I would let them pat my behind. And I used to love those jawbreakers—you know, the kind that lasted all day and kept changing colors in your mouth. So I was glad to oblige them, because in one afternoon I could collect a whole week's worth of jawbreakers."

"Really. That's funny to you? Having some boy feeling all over you."

Theresa sucked her teeth. "We were only kids, Lorraine. You know, you remind me of my grandmother. That was one straight-laced old lady. She had a fit when my brother told her what I was doing. She called me into the smokehouse and told me in this real scary whisper that I could get pregnant from letting little boys pat my butt and that I'd end up like my cousin Willa.

But Willa and I had been thick as fleas, and she had already given me a step-by-step summary of how she'd gotten into her predicament. But I sneaked around to her house that night just to double-check her story, since that old lady had seemed so earnest. 'Willa, are you sure?' I whispered through her bedroom window. 'I'm tellin' ya, Tee,' she said. 'Just keep both feet on the ground and you home free.' Much later I learned that advice wasn't too biologically sound, but it worked in Georgia because those country boys didn't have much imagination."

45   Theresa's laughter bounced off of Lorraine's silent, rigid back and died in her throat. She angrily tore open a pack of the chocolate chip cookies. "Yeah," she said, staring at Lorraine's back and biting down hard into the cookie, "it wasn't until I came up north to college that I found out there's a whole lot of things that a dude with a little imagination can do to you even with both feet on the ground. You see, Willa forgot to tell me not to bend over or squat or—"

"Must you!" Lorraine turned around from the stove with her teeth clenched tightly together.

"Must I what, Lorraine? Must I talk about things that are as much a part of life as eating or breathing or growing old? Why are you always so uptight about sex or men?"

"I'm not uptight about anything. I just think it's disgusting when you go on and on about—"

"There's nothing disgusting about it, Lorraine. You've never been with a man, but I've been with quite a few—some better than others. There were a couple who I still hope to this day will die a slow, painful death, but then there were some who were good to me—in and out of bed."

50   "If they were so great, then why are you with me?" Lorraine's lips were trembling.

"Because—" Theresa looked steadily into her eyes and then down at the cookie she was twirling on the table. "Because," she continued slowly, "you can take a chocolate chip cookie and put holes in it and attach it to your ears and call it an earring, or hang it around your neck on a silver chain and pretend it's a necklace—but it's still a cookie. See—you can toss it in the air and call it a Frisbee or even a flying saucer, if the mood hits you, and it's still just a cookie. Send it spinning on a table—like this—until it's a wonderful blur of amber and brown light that you can imagine to be a topaz or rusted gold or old crystal, but the law of gravity has got to come into play, sometime, and it's got to come to rest—sometime. Then all the spinning and pretending and hoopla is over with. And you know what you got?"

"A chocolate chip cookie," Lorraine said.

"Uh-huh." Theresa put the cookie in her mouth and winked. "A lesbian." She got up from the table. "Call me when dinner's ready, I'm going back to read." She stopped at the kitchen door. "Now, why are you putting gravy on that chicken, Lorraine? You know it's fattening."

▓ TOPICS FOR CRITICAL THINKING AND WRITING

1. The first sentence says, "At first they seemed like such nice girls." What do we know about the person who says it? What does it tell us (and imply) about the "nice girls"?

2. What is Sophie's role in the story?
3. In the second part of the story, who is the narrator? Does she or he know Theresa's thoughts, or Lorraine's, or both?
4. How does the story end? What do you think will happen between Lorraine and Theresa?
5. Try writing a page or less that is the *end* of a story about two people (men, women, children—but *people*) whose relationship is going to end soon, or is going to survive, because of, or despite, its difficulties.

DIANA CHANG

Diana Chang, author of several novels and books of poems, teaches creative writing at Barnard College. She identifies herself as an American writer whose background is mostly Chinese.

The Oriental Contingent   [1989]

Connie couldn't remember whose party it was, whose house. She had an impression of kerosene lamps on brown wicker tables, of shapes talking in doorways. It was summer, almost the only time Connie has run into her since, too, and someone was saying, "You must know Lisa Mallory."

"I don't think so."

"She's here. You must know her."

Later in the evening, it was someone else who introduced her to a figure perched on the balustrade of the steps leading to the lawn where more shapes milled. In stretching out a hand to shake Connie's, the figure almost fell off sideways. Connie had pushed her back upright onto her perch and, peering, took in the fact that Lisa Mallory had a Chinese face. For a long instant, she felt nonplussed, and was rendered speechless.

5   But Lisa Mallory was filling the silence. "Well, now, Connie Sung," she said, not enthusiastically but with a kind of sophisticated interest, "I'm not in music myself, but Paul Wu's my cousin. Guilt by association!" She laughed. "No-tone music, I call his. He studied with John Cage, Varese, and so forth."

Surprised that Lisa knew she was a violinist, Connie murmured something friendly, wondering if she should simply ask outright, "I'm sure I should know, but what do you do?" but she hesitated, taking in her appearance instead, while Lisa went on with, "It's world class composing. Nothing's wrong with the level. But it's hard going for the layman, believe me."

Lisa Mallory wore a one-of-a-kind kimono dress, but it didn't make her look Japanese at all, and her hair was drawn back tightly in a braid which stood out from close to the top of her head horizontally. You could probably lift her off her feet by grasping it, like the handle of a pot.

"You should give a concert here, Connie," she said, using her first name right away, Connie noticed, like any American. "Lots of culturati around." Even when she wasn't actually speaking, she pursued her own line of thought actively and seemed to find herself mildly amusing.

"I'm new to the area," Connie said, deprecatingly. "I've just been a weekend guest, actually, till a month ago.

10   "It's easy to be part of it. Nothing to it. I should know. You'll see."

"I wish it weren't so dark," Connie found herself saying, waving her hand in front of her eyes as if the night were a veil to brush aside. She recognized in herself that intense need to see, to see into fellow Orientals, to fathom them. So far, Lisa Mallory had not given her enough clues, and the darkness itself seemed to be interfering.

Lisa dropped off her perch. "It's important to be true to oneself," she said. "Keep the modern stuff out of your repertory. Be romantic. Don't look like that! You're best at the romantics. Anyhow, take it from me. I know. And *I* like what I like."

Released by her outspokenness, Connie laughed and asked, "I'm sure I should know, but what is it that you do?" She was certain Lisa would say something like, "I'm with a public relations firm." "I'm in city services."

But she replied, "What do all Chinese excel at?" Not as if she'd asked a rhetorical question, she waited, then answered herself. "Well, aren't we all physicists, musicians, architects, or in software?"

15   At that point a voice broke in, followed by a large body which put his arms around both women, "The Oriental contingent! I've got to break this up."

Turning, Lisa kissed him roundly, and said over her shoulder to Connie, "I'll take him away before he tells us we look alike!"

They melted into the steps below, and Connie, feeling put off balance and somehow slow-witted, was left to think over her new acquaintance.

"Hello, Lisa Mallory," Connie Sung always said on the infrequent occasions when they ran into one another. She always said "Hello, Lisa Mallory," with a shyness she did not understand in herself. It was strange, but they had no mutual friends except for Paul Wu, and Connie had not seen him in ages. Connie had no one of whom to ask her questions. But sometime soon, she'd be told Lisa's maiden name. Sometime she'd simply call her Lisa. Sometime what Lisa did with her life would be answered.

Three, four years passed, with their running into one another at receptions and openings, and still Lisa Mallory remained an enigma. Mildly amused herself, Connie wondered if other people, as well, found her inscrutable. But none of her American friends (though, of course, Lisa and she were Americans, too, she had to remind herself), none of the Caucasian friends seemed curious about backgrounds. In their accepting way, they did not wonder about Lisa's background, or about Connie's or Paul Wu's. Perhaps they assumed they were all cut from the same cloth. But to Connie, the Orientals she met were unread books, books she never had the right occasion or time to fully pursue.

20   She didn't even see the humor in her situation—it was such an issue with her. The fact was she felt less, much less, sure of herself when she was with real Chinese.

As she was realizing this, the truth suddenly dawned on her. Lisa Mallory never referred to her own background because it was more Chinese than Connie's, and therefore a higher order. She was tact incarnate. All along, she had been going out of her way not to embarrass Connie. Yes, yes. Her assurance was definitely uppercrust (perhaps her father had been in the diplomatic service), and her offhand didacticness, her lack of self-doubt, was indeed characteristically Chinese-Chinese. Connie was not only impressed by these traits, but also put on the defensive because of them.

Connie let out a sigh—a sigh that follows the solution to a nagging problem . . . Lisa's mysteriousness. But now Connie knew only too clearly that her own background made her decidedly inferior. Her father was a second-generation gynecologist who spoke hardly any Chinese. Yes, inferior and totally without recourse.

Of course, at one of the gatherings, Connie met Bill Mallory, too. He was simply American, maybe Catholic, possibly lapsed. She was not put off balance by him at all. But most of the time he was away on business, and Lisa cropped up at functions as single as Connie.

Then one day, Lisa had a man in tow—wiry and tall, he looked Chinese from the Shantung area, or perhaps from Beijing, and his styled hair made him appear vaguely artistic.

25   "Connie," I'd like you to meet Eric Li. He got out at the beginning of the *détente,* went to Berkeley, and is assimilating a mile-a-minute," Lisa said, with her usual irony. "Bill found him and is grooming him, though he came with his own charisma."

Eric waved her remark aside. "Lisa has missed her calling. She was born to be in PR," he said, with an accent.

"Is that what she does?" Connie put in at once, looking only at him. "Is that her profession?"

"You don't know?" he asked, with surprise.

Though she was greeting someone else, Lisa turned and answered, "I'm a fabrics tycoon, I think I can say without immodesty." She moved away and continued her conversation with the other friend.

30   Behind his hand, he said, playfully, as though letting Connie in on a secret, "Factories in Hongkong and Taipei, and now he's—Bill, that is—is exploring them on the mainland."

"With her fabulous contacts over there!" Connie exclaimed, now seeing it all. "Of course, what a wonderful business combination they must make."

Eric was about to utter something, but stopped, and said flatly, "I have all the mainland contacts, even though I was only twenty when I left, but my parents . . ."

"How interesting," Connie murmured lamely. "I see," preoccupied as she was with trying to put two and two together.

Lisa was back and said without an introduction, continuing her line of thought, "You two look good together, if I have to say so myself. Why don't you ask him to one of your concerts? And you, Eric, you're in America now, so don't stand on ceremony, or you'll be out in left field." She walked away with someone for another drink.

35   Looking uncomfortable, but recovering himself with a smile, Eric said, "Lisa makes me feel more Chinese than I am becoming—it is her directness, I suspect. In China, we'd say she is too much like a man."

At which Connie found herself saying, "She makes me feel *less* Chinese."

"Less!"

"Less Chinese than she is."

"That is not possible," Eric said, with a shade of contempt—for whom? Lisa or Connie? He barely suppressed a laugh, cold as Chinese laughter could be.

40   Connie blurted out, "I'm a failed Chinese. Yes, and it's to you that I need to say it." She paused and repeated emphatically, "I am a failed Chinese." Her hear was beating quicker, but she was glad to have got that out, a confession and a definition that might begin to free her. "Do you know you make me feel that, too? You've been here only about ten years, right?"

"Right, and I'm thirty-one."

"You know what I think? I think it's harder for a Chinese to do two things."

At that moment, an American moved in closer, looking pleased somehow to be with them.

She continued, "It's harder for us to become American than, say, for a German, and it's also harder not to remain residually Chinese, even if you are third generation."

45   Eric said blandly, "Don't take yourself so seriously. You can't help being an American product.

Trying to be comforting, the American interjected with, "The young lady is not a product, an object. She is a human being, and there is no difference among peoples that I can see."

"I judge myself both as a Chinese and as an American," Connie said.

"You worry too much," Eric said, impatiently. Then he looked around and though she wasn't in sight, he lowered his voice. "She is what she is. I know what she is. But she avoids going to Hongkong. She avoids it."

Connie felt turned around. "Avoids it?"

50   "Bill's in Beijing right now. She's here. How come?"

"I don't know," Connie replied, as though an answer had been required of her.

"She makes up many excuses, reasons. Ask her. Ask her yourself," he said, pointedly.

"Oh, I couldn't do that. By the way, I'm going on a concert tour next year in three cities—Shanghai, Beijing and Nanking," Connie said. "It'll be my first time in China."

"Really! You must be very talented to be touring at your age," he said, genuinely interested for the first time. Because she was going to China, or because she now came across as an over-achiever, even though Chinese American?

55   "I'm just about your age," she said, realizing then that maybe Lisa Mallory had left them alone purposely.

"You could both pass as teenagers!" the American exclaimed.

Two months later, she ran into Lisa again. As usual, Lisa began in the middle of her own thought. "Did he call?"

"Who? Oh. No, no."

"Well, it's true he's been in China the last three weeks with Bill. They'll be back this weekend."

60   Connie saw her opportunity. "Are you planning to go to China yourself?"

For the first time, Lisa seemed at a loss for words. She raised her shoulders, then let them drop. Too airily, she said, "You know, there's always Paris. I can't bear not to go to Paris, if I'm to take a trip."

"But you're Chinese. You *have* been to China, you came from China originally, didn't you?"

"I could go to Paris twice a year, I love it so," Lisa said. "And then there's London, Florence, Venice."

"But—but your business contacts?"

65   "*My* contacts? Bill, he's the businessman who makes the contacts. Always has. I take care of the New York office, which is a considerable job. We have a staff of eighty-five."

Connie said, "I told Eric I'll be giving a tour in China. I'm taking Chinese lessons right now."

Lisa Mallory laughed, "Save your time. They'll still be disdainful over there. See, *they* don't care," and she waved her hand at the crowd. "Some of them have been born in Buffalo, too! It's the Chinese you can't fool. They know you're not the genuine article—you and I."

Her face was suddenly heightened in color, and she was breathing as if ready to flee from something. "Yes, you heard right. I was born in Buffalo."

"You were!" Connie exclaimed before she could control her amazement.

70   "Well, what about you?" Lisa retorted. She was actually shaking and trying to hide it by making sudden gestures.

"Westchester."

"But your parents at least were Chinese."

"Well, so were, so are, yours!"

"I was adopted by Americans. My full name is Lisa Warren Mallory."

75   Incredulous, Connie said, "I'm more Chinese than you!"

"Who isn't?" She laughed, unhappily. "Having Chinese parents makes all the difference. We're worlds apart."

"And all the time I thought . . . never mind what I thought."

"You have it over me. It's written all over you. I could tell even in the dark that night."

"Oh, Lisa," Connie said to comfort her, "none of this matters to anybody except us. Really and truly. They're too busy with their own problems."

80   "The only time I feel Chinese is when I'm embarrassed. I'm not more Chinese—which is a totally Chinese reflex I'd give anything to be rid of!"

"I know what you mean."

"And as for Eric looking down his nose at me, he's knocking himself out to be so American, *but as a secure Chinese!* What's so genuine about that article?"

Both of them struck their heads laughing, but their eyes were not merry.

"Say it again," Connie asked of her, "say it again that my being more Chinese is written all over me."

85   "Consider it said," Lisa said. "My natural mother happened to be there at the time—I can't help being born in Buffalo."

"I know, I know," Connie said with feeling. "If only you had had some say in the matter."

"It's only Orientals who haunt me!" Lisa stamped her foot. "Only them!"

"I'm so sorry," Connie Sung said, for all of them. "It's all so turned around."

"So I'm made in America, so there!" Lisa Mallory declared, making a sniffing sound, and seemed to be recovering her sangfroid.

90   Connie felt tired—as if she'd traveled—but a lot had been settled on the way.

▨ TOPICS FOR CRITICAL THINKING AND WRITING

1. In the first paragraph, a person (whose name we don't know) says, "You must know Lisa Mallory." Why does she make that assumption?

2. During their first meeting Connie thinks "she recognized in herself that intense need to see, to see into fellow Orientals, to fathom them" and she waves "her hand in front of her eyes." Does she know what she is looking for?

3. What does Eric do in the story? What is his function? And what about "the American" (paragraph 43)?
4. In paragraph 88 we read, "'I'm so sorry,' Connie Sung said, for all of them. 'It's all so turned around.'" What does the writer mean by "for all of them"? And what does Connie mean by "It's all so turned around"?

KATHERINE MIN

Katherine Min has published stories in several magazines notable for their excellent fiction, including Tri-Quarterly *and* Ploughshares. *She has received grants from the National Endowment for the Arts and from the New Hampshire State Arts Council, and she has four times been a fellow at the MacDowell Colony.*

Courting a Monk   [1996]

When I first saw my husband he was sitting cross-legged under a tree on the quad, his hair as short as peach fuzz, large blue eyes staring upward, the smile on his face so wide and undirected as to seem moronic. I went flying by him every minute or two, guarding man-to-man, or chasing down a pass, and out of the corner of my eye I would see him watching and smiling. What I noticed about him most was his tremendous capacity for stillness. His hands were like still-life objects resting on his knees; his posture was impeccable. He looked so rooted there, like some cheerful, exotic mushroom, that I began to feel awkward in my exertion. Sweat funneled into the valley of my back, cooling and sticking when I stopped, hands on knees, to regain my breath. I tried to stop my gape-mouthed panting, refashioned my ponytail, and wiped my hands on the soft front of my sweatpants.

He was still there two plays later when my team was down by one. Sully stole a pass and flipped to Graham. Graham threw me a long bomb that sailed wide and I leapt for it, sailing with the Frisbee for a moment in a parallel line—floating, flying, reaching—before coming down whap! against the ground. I groaned. I'd taken a tree root in the solar plexus. The wind was knocked out of me. I lay there, the taste of dry leaves in my mouth.

"Sorry, Gina. Lousy pass," Graham said, coming over. "You O.K.?"

"Fine," I gasped, fingering my ribs. "Just let me sit out for a while."

5   I sat down in the leaves, breathing carefully as I watched them play. The day was growing dark and the Frisbee was hard to see. Everyone was tired and played in a sloppy rhythm of errant throws and dropped passes.

Beside me on the grass crept the guy from under the tree. I had forgotten about him. He crouched shyly next to me, leaves cracking under his feet, and, when I looked up, he whispered, "You were magnificent," and walked away smiling.

I spotted him the next day in the vegetarian dining hall. I was passing through with my plate of veal cordon bleu when I saw him sitting by himself next to the window. He took a pair of wooden chopsticks out of the breast pocket of his shirt and poked halfheartedly at his tofu and wilted mung beans. I sat down across from him and demanded his life story.

It turned out he wanted to be a monk. Not the Chaucerian kind, bald-pated and stout, with a hooded robe, ribald humor and penchant for wine. Something even more baffling—a Buddhist. He had just returned from a semester in Nepal, studying in a monastery in the Himalayas. His hair was coming back in soft spikes across his head and he had a watchful manner—not cautious but receptive, waiting.

He was from King of Prussia, off the Philadelphia Main Line, and this made me mistrust the depth of his beliefs. I have discovered that a fascination for the East is often a prelude to a pass, a romantic overture set in motion by an "I think Oriental girls are so beautiful," and a vise-like grip on the upper thigh. But Micah was different. He understood I was not impressed by his belief, and he did not aim to impress.

10   "My father was raised Buddhist," I told him. "But he's a scientist now."

"Oh," said Micah. "So, he's not spiritual."

"Spirit's insubstantial," I said. "He doesn't hold with intangibility."

"Well, you can't hold atoms in your hand," Micah pointed out.

"Ah," I said, smiling, "But you can count them."

* * *

15 I told Micah my father was a man of science, and this was true. He was a man, also, of silence. Unlike Micah, whose reticence seemed calming, so undisturbed, like a pool of light on still water, my father's silence was like the lid on a pot, sealing off some steaming, inner pressure.

Words were not my father's medium. "Language," my father liked to say, "is an imprecise instrument." (For though he said little, when he hit upon a phrase he liked, he said it many times.) He was fond of Greek letters and numerals set together in intricate equations, symbolizing a certain physical law or experimental hypothesis. He filled yellow legal pads in a strong vertical hand, writing these beauties down in black, indelible felt-tip pen. I think it was a source of tremendous irritation to him that he could not communicate with other people in so ordered a fashion, that he could not simply draw an equals sign after something he'd said, have them solve for x or y.

That my father's English was not fluent was only part of it. He was not a garrulous man, even in Korean, among visiting relatives, or alone with my mother. And with me, his only child—who could speak neither of his preferred languages, Korean or science—my father had conspicuously little to say. "Pick up this mess," he would tell me, returning from work in the evening. "Homework finished?" he would inquire, raising an eyebrow over his rice bowl as I excused myself to go watch television.

He limited himself to the imperative mood, the realm of injunction and command; the kinds of statements that required no answer, that left no opening for discussion or rejoinder. These communications were my father's verbal equivalent to his neat numerical equations. They were hermetically sealed.

When I went away to college, my father's parting words constituted one of the longest speeches I'd heard him make. Surrounded by station wagons packed with suitcases, crates of books and study lamps, amid the excited chattering and calling out of students, among the adults with their nervous parental surveillance of the scene, my father leaned awkwardly forward with his hands in his pockets, looking at me intently. He said, "Study hard. Go to bed early: Do not goof off. And do not let the American boys take advantages."

20   This was the same campus my father had set foot on twenty years before, when he was a young veteran of the Korean War, with fifty dollars in his
pocket and about that many words of English. Stories of his college years constituted family legend and, growing up, I had heard them so often they were
as vivid and dream-like as my own memories. My father in the dorm bathroom over Christmas, vainly trying to hard-boil an egg in a sock by running it
under hot water; his triumph in the physics lab where his ability with the
new language did not impede him, and where his maturity and keen scientific mind garnered him highest marks and the top physics prize in his senior
year—these were events I felt I'd witnessed, like some obscure, envious
ghost.

In the shadow of my father's achievements then, on the same campus
where he had first bowed his head to a microscope, lost in a chalk-dust
mathematical dream, I pursued words. English words. I committed myself to
expertise. I studied Shakespeare and Eliot, Hardy and Conrad, Joyce and
Lawrence and Hemingway and Fitzgerald. It was important to get it right,
every word, every nuance, to fill in my father's immigrant silences, the gaps
he had left for me.

Other gaps he'd left. Staying up late and studying little, I did things my father would have been too shocked to merely disapprove. As for American
boys, I heeded my father's advice and did not let them take advantage. Instead I took advantage of them, of their proximity, their good looks, and the
amiable way they would fall into bed with you if you gave them the slightest encouragement. I liked the way they moved in proud possession of
their bodies, the rough feel of their unshaven cheeks, their shoulders and
smooth, hairless chests, the curve of their backs like burnished wood. I liked
the way I could look up at them, or down, feeling their shuddering climax
like a distant earthquake; I could make it happen, moving in undulant circles
from above or below, watching them, holding them, making them happy. I
collected boys like baubles, like objects not particularly valued, which you
stash away in the back of some drawer. It was the pleasant interchangeability
of their bodies I liked. They were all white boys.

Micah refused to have sex with me. It became a matter of intellectual
disagreement with us. "Sex saps the will," he said.

"Not necessarily," I argued. "Just reroutes it."

25   "There are higher forms of union," he said.

"Not with your clothes off," I replied.

"Gina," he said, looking at me with kindness, a concern that made me
flush with anger. "What need do you have that sex must fill?"

"Fuck you, Micah," I said. "Be a monk, not a psychologist."

He laughed. His laughter was always a surprise to me, like a small disturbance to the universe. I wanted to seduce him, this was true. I considered Micah the only real challenge among an easy field. But more than se-
duction, I wanted to rattle him, to get under that sense of peace, that
inward contentment. No one my age, I reasoned, had the right to such self-
possession.

30   We went for walks in the bird sanctuary, rustling along the paths slowly
discussing Emily Dickinson or maple syrup-making, but always I brought the
subject around.

"What a waste of life," I said once. "Such indulgence. All that monkly de-votion and quest for inner peace. Big deal. It's selfish. Not only is it selfish, it's a cop-out. An escape from this world and its messes."

Micah listened, a narrow smile on his lips, shaking his head regretfully. "You're so wonderfully passionate, Gina, so alive and in the world. I can't make you see. Maybe it is a cop-out as you say, but Buddhism makes no dis-tinction between the world outside or the world within the monastery. And historically, monks have been in the middle of political protest and persecu-tion. Look at Tibet."

"I was thinking about, ahem, something more basic," I said.

Micah laughed. "Of course," he said. "You don't seem to understand, Gina, Buddhism is all about the renunciation of desire."

35   I sniffed. "What's wrong with desire? Without desire, you might as well not be alive."

The truth was that I was fascinated by this idea, the renunciation of de-sire. My life was fueled by longing, by vast and clamorous desires; a striving toward things I did not have and, perhaps, had no hope of having. I could vaguely imagine an end, some point past desiring, of satiety, but I could not fathom the laying down of desire, walking away in full appetite.

"The desire to renounce desire," I said now, "is still desire, isn't it?"

Micah sunk his hands into his pockets and smiled. "It's not," he said, walking ahead of me. "It's a conscious choice."

We came to a pond, sun-dappled in a clearing, bordered by white birch and maples with the bright leaves of mid-autumn. A fluttering of leaves blew from the trees, landing on the water as gently as if they'd been placed. The color of the pond was a deep canvas green; glints of light snapped like sparks above the surface. There was the lyric coo of a mourning dove, the chitter-chitter of late-season insects. Micah's capacity for appreciation was vast. Whether this had anything to do with Buddhism, I didn't know, but watching him stand on the edge of the pond, his head thrown back, his eyes eagerly taking in the light, I felt his peace and also his sense of wonder. He stood motionless for a long time.

40   I pulled at ferns, weaved their narrow leaves in irregular samplers, braided tendrils together, while Micah sat on a large rock and, taking his chopsticks from his breast pocket, began to tap them lightly against one an-other in a solemn rhythm.

"Every morning in the monastery," he said, "we woke to the prayer drum. Four o'clock and the sky would be dark and you'd hear the hollow wooden sound—plock, plock, plock—summoning you to meditation." He smiled dreamily. The chopsticks made a somewhat less effectual sound, a sort of ta ta ta. I imagined sunrise across a Himalayan valley—the wisps of pink-tinged cloud on a cold spring morning, the austerity of a monk's chamber.

Micah had his eyes closed, face to the sun. He continued to tap the chopsticks together slowly. He looked singular and new, sitting on that rock, like an advance scout for some new tribe, with his crest of hair and calm, and the attentiveness of his body to his surroundings.

I think it was then I fell in love with him, or, it was in that moment that my longing for him became so great that it was no longer a matter of simple gratification. I needed his response. I understood what desire was then, the disturbance of a perfect moment in anticipation of another.

"Wake-up call," I said. I peeled off my turtleneck and sweater in one clever motion and tossed them at Micah's feet. Micah opened his eyes. I pulled my pants off and my underwear and stood naked. "Plock, plock, who's there?"

45   Micah did not turn away. He looked at me, his chopsticks poised in the air. He raised one toward me and held it, as though he were an artist with a paintbrush raised for a proportion, or a conductor ready to lead an orchestra. He held the chopstick suspended in the space between us, and it was as though I couldn't move for as long as he held it. His eyes were fathomless blue. My nipples constricted with the cold. Around us leaves fell in shimmering lights to the water, making a soft rustling sound like the rub of stiff fabric. He brought his hand down and I was released. I turned and leapt into the water.

A few nights later I bought a bottle of cheap wine and goaded Micah into drinking it with me. We started out on the steps of the library after it had closed for the night, taking sloppy swigs from a brown paper bag. The lights of the Holyoke range blinked in the distance, across the velvet black of the freshman quad. From there we wandered the campus, sprawling on the tennis courts, bracing a stiff wind from the terrace of the science center, sedately rolling down Memorial Hill like a pair of tumbleweeds.

"J'a know what a koan is?" he asked me, when we were perched at the top of the bleachers behind home plate. We unsteadily contemplated the steep drop off the back side.

"You mean like ice cream?" I said.

"No, a ko-an. In Buddhism."

50   "Nope."

"It's a question that has no answer, sort of like a riddle. You know, like 'What is the sound of one hand clapping?' Or 'What was your face before you were born?'"

"'What was my face before it was born?' That makes no sense."

"Exactly. You're supposed to contemplate the koan until you achieve a greater awareness."

"Of what?"

55   "Of life, of meaning."

"Oh, O.K.," I said, "I've got it." I was facing backwards, the bag with the bottle in both my hands. "How 'bout, 'What's the sound of one cheek farting?'"

He laughed for a long time, then retched off the side of the bleachers. I got him home and put him to bed; his forehead was feverish, his eyes glassy with sickness.

"Sorry," I said. "I'm a bad influence." I kissed him. His lips were hot and slack.

"Don't mind," he murmured, half-asleep.

60   The next night we slept in the same bed together for the first time. He kept his underwear on and his hands pressed firmly to his sides, like Gandhi among his young virgins. I was determined to make it difficult for him. I kept brushing my naked body against him, draping a leg across his waist, stroking his narrow chest with my fingertips. He wiggled and pushed away, feigning sleep. When I woke in the morning, he was gone and the *Ode to Joy* was blasting from my stereo.

Graham said he missed me. We'd slept together a few times before I met Micah, enjoying the warm, healthful feeling we got from running or playing Ultimate, taking a quick sauna and falling into bed. He was good-looking, dark and broad, with sinewy arms and a tight chest. He made love to a woman like he was lifting Nautilus, all grim purpose and timing. It was hard to believe that had ever been appealing. I told him I was seeing someone else.

"Not the guy with the crew cut?" he said. "The one who looks like a baby seal?"

I shrugged.

Graham looked at me skeptically. "He doesn't seem like your type," he said.

65   "No," I agreed. "But at least he's not yours."

Meanwhile I stepped up my attack. I asked endless questions about Buddhist teaching. Micah talked about *dukkha;*[1] the four noble truths; the five aggregates of attachment; the noble eightfold path to enlightenment. I listened dutifully, willing to acknowledge that it all sounded nice, that the goal of perfect awareness and peace seemed worth attaining. While he talked, I stretched my feet out until my toes touched his thigh; I slid my hand along his back; or leaned way over so he could see down my loose, barely-buttoned blouse.

"Too bad you aren't Tantric," I said. I'd been doing research.

Micah scoffed. "Hollywood Buddhism," he said. "Heavy breathing and theatrics."

"They believe in physical desire," I said. "They have sex."

70   "Buddha believes in physical desire," Micah said. "It's impermanent, that's all. Something to get beyond."

"To get beyond it," I said petulantly, "you have to do it."

Micah sighed. "Gina," he said, "you are beautiful, but I can't. There are a lot of guys who will."

"A lot of them do."

He smiled a bit sadly. "Well, then . . ."

75   I leaned down to undo his shoelaces. I tied them together in double knots. "But I want you," I said.

My parents lived thirty miles from campus and my mother frequently asked me to come home for dinner. I went only once that year, and that was with Micah. My parents were not the kind of people who enjoyed the company of strangers. They were insular people who did not like to socialize much or go out—or anyway, my father was that way, and my mother accommodated herself to his preferences.

My mother had set the table in the dining room with blue linen. There were crystal wine glasses and silver utensils in floral patterns. She had made some dry baked chicken with overcooked peas and carrots—the meal she reserved for when Americans came to dinner. When it came to Korean cooking, my mother was a master. She made fabulous marinated short ribs and sautéed transparent bean noodles with vegetables and beef, pork dumplings and

---

[1]**dukkha** a Pali word meaning "suffering," particularly the suffering that is caused by desire.

batter-fried shrimp, and cucumber and turnip kimchis[2] which she made herself and fermented in brown earthenware jars. But American cuisine eluded her; it bored her. I think she thought it was meant to be tasteless.

"Just make Korean," I had urged her on the phone. "He'll like that."

My mother was skeptical. "Too spicy," she said. "I know what Americans like."

80 "Not the chicken dish," I pleaded. "He's a vegetarian."

"We'll see," said my mother, conceding nothing.

Micah stared down at his plate. My mother smiled serenely. Micah nodded. He ate a forkful of vegetables, took a bite of bread. His Adam's apple seemed to be doing a lot of work. My father, too, was busy chewing, his Adam's apple moving up and down his throat like the ratchets of a tire jack. No one had said a thing since my father had uncorked the Chardonnay and read to us the description from his well-creased paperback edition of *The New York Times Guide to Wine*.

The sound of silverware scraping on ceramic plates seemed amplified. I was aware of my own prolonged chewing. My father cleared his throat. My mother looked at him expectantly. He coughed.

"Micah studied Buddhism in Nepal," I offered into the silence.

85 "Oh!" my mother exclaimed. She giggled.

My father kept eating. He swallowed exaggeratedly and looked up. "That so?" he said, sounding almost interested.

Micah nodded. "I was only there four months," he said, "Gina tells me you were brought up Buddhist."

My father grunted. "Well, of course," he said, "in Korea in those days, our families were all Buddhist. I do not consider myself a Buddhist now."

Micah and I exchanged a look.

90 "It's become quite fashionable, I understand," my father went on. "With you American college kids. Buddhism has become fad."

I saw Micah wince.

"I think it is wonderful, Hi Joon," my mother interceded, "for Americans to learn about Asian religion and philosophy. I was a philosophy major in college, Micah. I studied Whitehead,[3] American pragmatism."

My father leaned back in his chair and watched, frowning, while my mother and Micah talked. It was like he was trying to analyze Micah, not as a psychiatrist analyzes—my father held a dim view of psychology—but as a chemist would, breaking him down to his basic elements, the simple chemical formula that would define his makeup.

Micah was talking about the aggregates of matter, sensation, perception, mental formations, and consciousness that comprise being in Buddhist teaching. "It's a different sense of self than in Christian religions," he explained, looking at my mother.

95 "Nonsense," my father interrupted. "There is no self in Buddhist doctrine. . . ."

My mother and I watched helplessly as they launched into discussion. I was surprised that my father seemed to know so much about it, and by how much he was carrying forth. I was surprised also by Micah's deference. He seemed to have lost all his sureness, the walls of his conviction. He kept nod-

---

[2]**kimchis** pickles.   [3]**Whitehead** Alfred North Whitehead (1861–1947), British mathematician and philosopher.

ding and conceding to my father certain points that he had rigorously de-fended to me before. "I guess I don't know as much about it," he said more than once, and "Yes, I see what you mean" several times, with a sickening air of humility.

I turned from my father's glinting, pitiless intelligence, to Micah's re-spectfulness, his timid manner, and felt a rising irritation I could not place, anger at my father's belligerence, at Micah's backing down, at my own strange motives for having brought them together. Had I really expected them to get along? And yet, my father was concentrating on Micah with such an inten-sity—almost as though he were a rival—in a way in which he never focused on me.

When the dialogue lapsed, and after we had consumed as much of the food as we deemed polite, my mother took the dishes away and brought in a bowl of rice with kimchi for my father. Micah's eyes lit up. "May I have some of that, too, Mrs. Kim?"

My mother looked doubtful. "Too spicy," she said.

100   "Oh, I love spicy food," Micah assured her. My mother went to get him a bowl.

"You can use chopsticks?" my mother said, as Micah began eating with them.

"Mom, it's no big deal," I said.

My father looked up from his bowl. Together, my parents watched while Micah ate a large piece of cabbage kimchi.

"Hah!" my father said, suddenly smiling, "Gina doesn't like kimchi," he said. He looked at me. "Gina." he said, "This boy more Korean than you."

105   "Doesn't take much," I said.

My father ignored me. "Gina always want to be American," he told Micah. "Since she was little girl, she want blue eyes, yellow hair." He stabbed a chopstick toward Micah's face. "Like yours."

"If I had hair," said Micah, grinning, rubbing a hand across his head.

My father stared into his bowl. "She doesn't want to be Korean girl. She thinks she can be 100 percent American, but she cannot. She has Korean blood—100 percent. Doesn't matter where you grow up—blood is most im-portant. What is in the blood." He gave Micah a severe look. "You think you can become Buddhist. Same way. But it is not in your blood. You cannot know real Buddha's teaching. You should study Bible."

"God, Dad!" I said. "You sound like a Nazi!"

110   "Gina!" my mother warned.

"You're embarrassing me," I said. "Being rude to my guest. Discussing me as if I wasn't here. You can say what you want, Dad, I'm American whether you like it or not. Blood's got nothing to do with it. It's what's up here." I tapped my finger to my temple.

"It's not Nazi," my father said. "Is fact! What you have here," he pointed to his forehead, "is all from blood, from genetics. You got from me!"

"Heaven help me," I said.

"Gina!" my mother implored.

115   "Mr. Kim—" Micah began.

"You just like American girl in one thing," my father shouted. "You have no respect for father. In Korea, daughters do not talk back to their parents, is big shame!"

"In Korea, girls are supposed to be submissive doormats for fathers to wipe their feet on!" I shouted back.

"What do you know about Korea? You went there only once when you were six years old."

"It's in my blood," I said. I stood up. "I'm not going to stay here for this. Come on, Micah."

120   Micah looked at me uncertainly, then turned to my father.

My father was eating again, slowly levering rice to his mouth with his chopsticks. He paused. "She was always this way," he said, seeming to address the table. "So angry. Even as a little girl."

"Mr. Kim," Micah said, "Um, thank you very much. We're . . . I think we're heading out now."

My father chewed ruminatively. "I should never have left Korea," he said quietly, with utter conviction.

"Gina," my mother said. "Sit down. Hi Joon, please!"

125   "Micah," I said. "You coming?"

We left my father alone at the dining-room table.

"I should have sent you to live with Auntie Soo!" he called after me.

My mother followed us out to the driveway with a Tupperware container of chicken Micah hadn't eaten.

On the way home we stopped for ice cream. Koans, I told Micah. "What is the sound of Swiss chocolate almond melting?" I asked him. "What was the vanilla before it was born?"

130   Inside the ice-cream parlor the light was too strong, a ticking fluorescence bleaching everything bone-white. Micah leaned down to survey the cardboard barrels of ice cream in their plastic cases. He looked shrunken, subdued. He ordered a scoop of mint chocolate chip and one of black cherry on a sugar cone and ate it with the long, regretful licks of a child who'd spent the last nickel of his allowance. There was a ruefulness to his movements, a sense of apology. He had lost his monk-like stillness and seemed suddenly adrift.

The cold of the ice cream gave me a headache, all the blood vessels in my temples seemed strung out and tight. I shivered and the cold was like fury, spreading through me with the chill.

Micah rubbed my back.

"You're hard on your father," he said. "He's not a bad guy."

"Forget it," I said. "Let's go."

135   We walked from the dorm parking lot in silence. There were lights going on across the quad and music spilling from the windows out into the cool air. What few stars there were seemed too distant to wage a constant light.

Back in my room, I put on the Rolling Stones at full blast. Mick Jagger's voice was taunting and cruel. I turned out the lights and lit a red candle.

"O.K., this is going to stop," I said. I felt myself trembling. I pushed Micah back on the bed. I was furious. He had ruined it for me, the lightness, the skimming quality of my life. It had seemed easy, with the boys, the glib words and feelings, the simple heat and surface pleasures. It was like the sensation of flying, leaping for the Frisbee and sailing through the air. For a moment you lose a feeling for gravity, for the consciousness of your own skin or species. For a moment you are free.

I started to dance, fast, swinging and swaying in front of the bed. I closed my eyes and twirled wildly, bouncing off the walls like a pinball, stumbling on my own stockings. I danced so hard the stereo skipped, Jagger forced to stutter in throaty monosyllables, gulping repetitions. I whirled and circled, threw my head from side to side until I could feel the baffled blood, brought my hair up off my neck and held it with both hands.

Micah watched me dance. His body made an inverted-S upon my bed, his head propped by the pillar of his own arm. The expression on his face was the same as he'd had talking with my father, that look of deference, of fawn-eyed yielding. But I could see there was something hidden.

140   With white-knuckled fingers, I undid the buttons of my sweater and ripped my shirt lifting it off my head. I danced out of my skirt and underthings, kicking them into the corner, danced until the song was over, until I was soaked with sweat and burning—and then I jumped him.

It was like the taste of food after a day's starvation—unexpectedly strong and substantial. Micah responded to my fury, met it with his own mysterious passion; it was like a brawl, a fight, with something at stake that neither of us wanted to lose. Afterward we sat up in bed and listened to *Ode to Joy* while Micah, who had a surplus supply of chopsticks lying around the room, did his Leonard Bernstein impersonation. Later, we went out for a late-night snack to All-Star Dairy and Micah admitted to me that he was in love.

* * *

My father refused to attend the wedding. He liked Micah, but he did not want me to marry a Caucasian. It became a joke I would tell people. Korean custom, I said, to give the bride away four months before the ceremony.

Micah became a high-school biology teacher. I am an associate dean of students at the local college. We have two children. When Micah tells the story of our courtship, he tells it with great self-deprecation and humor. He makes it sound as though he were crazy to ever consider becoming a monk. "Think of it," he tells our kids. "Your dad."

Lately I've taken to reading books about Buddhism. Siddhartha Gotama was thirty-five years old when he sat under the Bodhi-tree on the bank of the river Neranjara and gained Enlightenment. Sometimes, when I see my husband looking at me across the breakfast table, or walking toward me from the other side of the room, I catch a look of distress on his face, a blinking confusion, as though he cannot remember who I am. I have happened on him a few times, on a Sunday when he has disappeared from the house, sitting on a bench with the newspaper in his lap staring across the town common, so immersed in his thoughts that he is not roused by my calling of his name.

145   I remember the first time I saw him, the tremendous stillness he carried, the contentment in his face. I remember how he looked on the rocks by that pond, like a pioneer in a new land, and I wonder if he regrets, as I do, the loss of his implausible faith. Does he miss the sound of the prayer drum, the call to an inner life without the configuration of desire? I think of my father, running a sock under heated water thousands of miles from home, as yet unaware of the daughter he will raise with the same hopeful, determined, and ultimately futile, effort. I remember the way I used to play around with koans, and I wonder, "What is the sound of a life not lived?"

▨ TOPICS FOR CRITICAL THINKING AND WRITING

1. Halfway through the story, in paragraph 43, the narrator says, "I think it was then I fell in love with him. . . ." Why does she fall in love with Micah at this moment? And how does she describe the feeling of love?

2. When we return to the beginning of the story—first, the Frisbee game, and, second, the scene at the dining hall—what signs do we see of the kind of relationship that will develop between the narrator and Micah? What do we learn about each of these persons and about what might draw them to one another?

3. What is your response to the narrator's father? Why do you think that Min chose to make him a scientist? Is our response to the father meant to be critical? Highly critical? Or, a lot or a little sympathetic?

4. Do you agree with Min's decision to include the brief scene with the narrator's former boyfriend, Graham, paragraphs 61–65? Is this scene important for the meaning of the story as a whole, or would you recommend that it be omitted?

5. Describe what happens during the love-making scene, beginning with paragraph 135. What is the narrator trying to do through her dance, and why? What leads Micah at last to respond to her?

6. Do sexual scenes in literature make you uncomfortable? Is there a right and a wrong way, in your view, to present such scenes?

GISH JEN

Gish Jen, born in 1955 in Yonkers, New York, and the daughter of Chinese immigrants, was named Lillian Jen by her parents. She disliked the name Lillian, and her school friends created a new name for her, derived from the name of a famous actress of the silent screen—Lillian Gish. Jen graduated from Harvard and then, in accordance with her parents' wishes, went to Stanford Business School (M.B.A., 1980). Then, following her own wishes, Jen went to the University of Iowa, where in 1983 she earned an M.F.A. in the writing program. She has published three novels and a book of short stories, Who's Irish? *We reprint the title story.*

Who's Irish?   [1998]

In China, people say mixed children are supposed to be smart, and definitely my granddaughter Sophie is smart. But Sophie is wild, Sophie is not like my daughter Natalie, or like me. I am work hard my whole life, and fierce besides. My husband always used to say he is afraid of me, and in our restaurant, busboys and cooks all afraid of me too. Even the gang members come for protection money, they try to talk to my husband. When I am there, they stay away. If they come by mistake, they pretend they are come to eat. They hide behind the menu, they order a lot of food. They talk about their mothers. Oh, my mother have some arthritis, need to take herbal medicine, they say. Oh, my mother getting old, her hair all white now.

I say, Your mother's hair used to be white, but since she dye it, it become black again. Why don't you go home once in a while and take a look? I tell them, Confucius[1] say a filial son knows what color his mother's hair is.

My daughter is fierce too, she is vice president in the bank now. Her new house is big enough for everybody to have their own room, including me. But Sophie take after Natalie's husband's family, their name is Shea. Irish. I always thought Irish people are like Chinese people, work so hard on the railroad, but now I know why the Chinese beat the Irish. Of course, not all Irish are like the Shea family, of course not. My daughter tell me I should not say Irish this, Irish that.

How do you like it when people say the Chinese this, the Chinese that, she say.

5   You know, the British call the Irish heathen, just like they call the Chinese, she say.

You think the Opium War[2] was bad, how would you like to live right next door to the British, she say.

And that is that. My daughter have a funny habit when she win an argument, she take a sip of something and look away, so the other person is not embarrassed. So I am not embarrassed. I do not call anybody anything either. I just happen to mention about the Shea family, an interesting fact: four brothers in the family, and not one of them work. The mother, Bess, have a job before she got sick, she was executive secretary in a big company. She is handle everything for a big shot, you would be surprised how complicated her job is, not just type this, type that. Now she is a nice woman with a clean house. But her boys, every one of them is on welfare, or so-called severance pay, or so-called disability pay. Something. They say they cannot find work, this is not the economy of the fifties, but I say, Even the black people doing better these days, some of them live so fancy, you'd be surprised. Why the Shea family have so much trouble? They are white people, they speak English. When I come to this country, I have no money and do not speak English. But my husband and I own our restaurant before he die. Free and clear, no mortgage. Of course, I understand I am just lucky, come from a country where the food is popular all over the world. I understand it is not the Shea family's fault they come from a country where everything is boiled. Still, I say.

She's right, we should broaden our horizons, say one brother, Jim, at Thanksgiving. Forget about the car business. Think about egg rolls.

Pad thai, say another brother, Mike. I'm going to make my fortune in pad thai. It's going to be the new pizza.

10   I say, You people too picky about what you sell. Selling egg rolls not good enough for you, but at least my husband and I can say, We made it. What can you say? Tell me. What can you say?

Everybody chew their tough turkey.

I especially cannot understand my daughter's husband John, who has no job but cannot take care of Sophie either. Because he is a man, he say, and that's the end of the sentence.

Plain boiled food, plain boiled thinking. Even his name is plain boiled: John. Maybe because I grew up with black bean sauce and hoisin sauce and garlic sauce, I always feel something is missing when my son-in-law talk.

---

[1]**Confucius** Chinese religious leader and philosopher (551–479 BCE).   [2]**Opium War** conflicts, 1839–1842 and 1856–1860, between China and Great Britain involving the opium trade.

But, okay: so my son-in-law can be man, I am baby-sitter. Six hours a day, same as the old sitter, crazy Amy, who quit. This is not so easy, now that I am sixty-eight, Chinese age almost seventy. Still, I try. In China, daughter take care of mother. Here it is the other way around. Mother help daughter, mother ask, Anything else I can do? Otherwise daughter complain mother is not supportive. I tell daughter, We do not have this word in Chinese, *supportive*. But my daughter too busy to listen, she has to go to meeting, she has to write memo while her husband go to the gym to be a man. My daughter say otherwise he will be depressed. Seems like all his life he has this trouble, depression.

15   No one wants to hire someone who is depressed, she say. It is important for him to keep his spirits up.

Beautiful wife, beautiful daughter, beautiful house, oven can clean itself automatically. No money left over, because only one income, but lucky enough, got the baby-sitter for free. If John lived in China, he would be very happy. But he is not happy. Even at the gym things go wrong. One day, he pull a muscle. Another day, weight room too crowded. Always something.

Until finally, hooray, he has a job. Then he feel pressure.

I need to concentrate, he say. I need to focus.

He is going to work for insurance company. Salesman job. A paycheck, he say, and at least he will wear clothes instead of gym shorts. My daughter buy him some special candy bars from the health-food store. They say THINK! on them, and are supposed to help John think.

20   John is a good-looking boy, you have to say that, especially now that he shave so you can see his face.

I am an old man in a young man's game, say John.

I will need a new suit, say John.

This time I am not going to shoot myself in the foot, say John.

Good, I say.

25   She means to be supportive, my daughter say. Don't start the send her back to China thing, because we can't.

Sophie is three years old American age, but already I see her nice Chinese side swallowed up by her wild Shea side. She looks like mostly Chinese. Beautiful black hair, beautiful black eyes. Nose perfect size, not so flat looks like something fell down, not so large looks like some big deal got stuck in wrong face. Everything just right, only her skin is a brown surprise to John's family. So brown, they say. Even John say it. She never goes in the sun, still she is that color, he say. Brown. They say, Nothing the matter with brown. They are just surprised. So brown. Nattie is not that brown, they say. They say, It seems like Sophie should be a color in between Nattie and John. Seems funny, a girl named Sophie Shea be brown. But she is brown, maybe her name should be Sophie Brown. She never go in the sun, still she is that color, they say. Nothing the matter with brown. They are just surprised.

The Shea family talk is like this sometimes, going around and around like a Christmas-tree train.

Maybe John is not her father, I say one day, to stop the train. And sure enough, train wreck. None of the brothers ever say the word *brown* to me again.

Instead, John's mother, Bess, say, I hope you are not offended.

30   She say, I did my best on those boys. But raising four boys with no father is no picnic.

You have a beautiful family, I say.

I'm getting old, she say.

You deserve a rest, I say. Too many boys make you old.

I never had a daughter, she say. You have a daughter.

35   I have a daughter, I say. Chinese people don't think a daughter is so great, but you're right. I have a daughter.

I was never against the marriage, you know, she say. I never thought John was marrying down. I always thought Nattie was just as good as white.

I was never against the marriage either, I say. I just wonder if they look at the whole problem.

Of course you pointed out the problem, you are a mother, she say. And now we both have a granddaughter. A little brown granddaughter, she is so precious to me.

I laugh. A little brown granddaughter, I say. To tell you the truth, I don't know how she came out so brown.

40   We laugh some more. These days Bess need a walker to walk. She take so many pills, she need two glasses of water to get them all down. Her favorite TV show is about bloopers, and she love her bird feeder. All day long, she can watch that bird feeder, like a cat.

I can't wait for her to grow up, Bess say. I could use some female company.

Too many boys, I say.

Boys are fine, she say. But they do surround you after a while.

You should take a break, come live with us, I say. Lots of girls at our house.

45   Be careful what you offer, say Bess with a wink. Where I come from, people mean for you to move in when they say a thing like that.

Nothing the matter with Sophie's outside, that's the truth. It is inside that she is like not any Chinese girl I ever see. We go to the park, and this is what she does. She stand up in the stroller. She take off all her clothes and throw them in the fountain.

Sophie! I say. Stop!

But she just laugh like a crazy person. Before I take over as baby-sitter, Sophie has that crazy-person sitter, Amy the guitar player. My daughter thought this Amy very creative—another word we do not talk about in China. In China, we talk about whether we have difficulty or no difficulty. We talk about whether life is bitter or not bitter. In America, all day long, people talk about creative. Never mind that I cannot even look at this Amy, with her shirt so short that her belly button showing. This Amy think Sophie should love her body. So when Sophie take off her diaper, Amy laugh. When Sophie run around naked, Amy say she wouldn't want to wear a diaper either. When Sophie go *shu-shu* in her lap, Amy laugh and say there are no germs in pee. When Sophie take off her shoes, Amy say bare feet is best, even the pediatrician say so. That is why Sophie now walk around with no shoes like a beggar child. Also why Sophie love to take off her clothes.

Turn around! say the boys in the park. Let's see that ass!

50   Of course, Sophie does not understand. Sophie clap her hands, I am the only one to say, No! This is not a game.

It has nothing to do with John's family, my daughter say. Amy was too permissive, that's all.

But I think if Sophie was not wild inside, she would not take off her shoes and clothes to begin with.

You never take off your clothes when you were little, I say. All my Chinese friends had babies, I never saw one of them act wild like that.

Look, my daughter say. I have a big presentation tomorrow.

55   John and my daughter agree Sophie is a problem, but they don't know what to do.

You spank her, she'll stop, I say another day.

But they say, Oh no.

In America, parents not supposed to spank the child.

It gives them low self-esteem, my daughter say. And that leads to problems later, as I happen to know.

60   My daughter never have big presentation the next day when the subject of spanking come up.

I don't want you to touch Sophie, she say. No spanking, period.

Don't tell me what to do, I say.

I'm not telling you what to do, say my daughter. I'm telling you how I feel.

I am not your servant, I say. Don't you dare talk to me like that.

65   My daughter have another funny habit when she lose an argument. She spread out all her fingers and look at them, as if she like to make sure they are still there.

My daughter is fierce like me, but she and John think it is better to explain to Sophie that clothes are a good idea. This is not so hard in the cold weather. In the warm weather, it is very hard.

Use your words, my daughter say. That's what we tell Sophie. How about if you set a good example.

As if good example mean anything to Sophie. I am so fierce, the gang members who used to come to the restaurant all afraid of me, but Sophie is not afraid.

I say, Sophie, if you take off your clothes, no snack.

70   I say, Sophie, if you take off your clothes, no lunch.

I say, Sophie, if you take off your clothes, no park.

Pretty soon we are stay home all day, and by the end of six hours she still did not have one thing to eat. You never saw a child stubborn like that.

I'm hungry! she cry when my daughter come home.

What's the matter, doesn't your grandmother feed you? My daughter laugh.

75   No! Sophie say. She doesn't feed me anything!

My daughter laugh again. Here you go, she say.

She say to John, Sophie must be growing.

Growing like a weed, I say.

Still Sophie take off her clothes, until one day I spank her. Not too hard, but she cry and cry, and when I tell her if she doesn't put her clothes back on I'll spank her again, she put her clothes back on. Then I tell her she is good girl, and give her some food to eat. The next day we go to the park and, like a nice Chinese girl, she does not take off her clothes.

80   She stop taking off her clothes, I report. Finally!

How did you do it? my daughter ask.

After twenty-eight years experience with you, I guess I learn something, I say.

It must have been a phase, John say, and his voice is suddenly like an expert.

His voice is like an expert about everything these days, now that he carry a leather briefcase, and wear shiny shoes, and can go shopping for a new car. On the company, he say. The company will pay for it, but he will be able to drive it whenever he want.

85   A free car, he say. How do you like that.

It's good to see you in the saddle again, my daughter say. Some of your family patterns are scary.

At least I don't drink, he say. He say, And I'm not the only one with scary family patterns.

That's for sure, say my daughter.

Everyone is happy. Even I am happy, because there is more trouble with Sophie, but now I think I can help her Chinese side fight against her wild side. I teach her to eat food with fork or spoon or chopsticks, she cannot just grab into the middle of a bowl of noodles. I teach her not to play with garbage cans. Sometimes I spank her, but not too often, and not too hard.

90   Still, there are problems. Sophie like to climb everything. If there is a railing, she is never next to it. Always she is on top of it. Also, Sophie like to hit the mommies of her friends. She learn this from her playground best friend, Sinbad, who is four. Sinbad wear army clothes every day and like to ambush his mommy. He is the one who dug a big hole under the play structure, a foxhole he call it, all by himself. Very hardworking. Now he wait in the foxhole with a shovel full of wet sand. When his mommy come, he throw it right at her.

Oh, it's all right, his mommy say. You can't get rid of war games, it's part of their imaginative play. All the boys go through it.

Also, he like to kick his mommy, and one day he tell Sophie to kick his mommy too.

I wish this story is not true.

Kick her, kick her! Sinbad say.

95   Sophie kick her. A little kick, as if she just so happened was swinging her little leg and didn't realize that big mommy leg was in the way. Still I spank Sophie and make Sophie say sorry, and what does the mommy say?

Really, it's all right, she say. It didn't hurt.

After that, Sophie learn she can attack mommies in the playground, and some will say, Stop, but others will say, Oh, she didn't mean it, especially if they realize Sophie will be punished.

This is how, one day, bigger trouble come. The bigger trouble start when Sophie hide in the foxhole with that shovel full of sand. She wait, and when I come look for her, she throw it at me. All over my nice clean clothes.

Did you ever see a Chinese girl act this way?

100   Sophie! I say. Come out of there, say you're sorry.

But she does not come out. Instead, she laugh. Naaah, naah-na, naaa-naaa, she say.

I am not exaggerate: millions of children in China, not one act like this.

Sophie! I say. Now! Come out now!

But she know she is in big trouble. She know if she come out, what will happen next. So she does not come out. I am sixty-eight, Chinese age almost seventy, how can I crawl under there to catch her? Impossible. So I yell, yell, yell, and what happen? Nothing. A Chinese mother would help, but American mothers, they look at you, they shake their head, they go home. And, of course, a Chinese child would give up, but not Sophie.

105   I hate you! she yell. I hate you, Meanie!

Meanie is my new name these days.

Long time this goes on, long long time. The foxhole is deep, you cannot see too much, you don't know where is the bottom. You cannot hear too much either. If she does not yell, you cannot even know she is still there or not. After a while, getting cold out, getting dark out. No one left in the playground, only us.

Sophie, I say. How did you become stubborn like this? I am go home without you now.

I try to use a stick, chase her out of there, and once or twice I hit her, but still she does not come out. So finally I leave. I go outside the gate.

110   Bye-bye! I say. I'm go home now.

But still she does not come out and does not come out. Now it is dinnertime, the sky is black. I think I should maybe go get help, but how can I leave a little girl by herself in the playground? A bad man could come. A rat could come. I go back in to see what is happen to Sophie. What if she have a shovel and is making a tunnel to escape?

Sophie! I say.

No answer.

Sophie!

115   I don't know if she is alive. I don't know if she is fall asleep down there. If she is crying, I cannot hear her.

So I take the stick and poke.

Sophie! I say. I promise I no hit you. If you come out, I give you a lollipop.

No answer. By now I worried. What to do, what to do, what to do? I poke some more, even harder, so that I am poking and poking when my daughter and John suddenly appear.

What are you doing? What is going on? say my daughter.

120   Put down that stick! say my daughter.

You are crazy! say my daughter.

John wiggle under the structure, into the foxhole, to rescue Sophie.

She fell asleep, say John the expert. She's okay. That is one big hole.

Now Sophie is crying and crying.

125   Sophie, my daughter say, hugging her. Are you okay, peanut? Are you okay?

She's just scared, say John.

Are you okay? I say too. I don't know what happen, I say.

She's okay, say John. He is not like my daughter, full of questions. He is full of answers until we get home and can see by the lamplight.

Will you look at her? he yell then. What the hell happened?

130   Bruises all over her brown skin, and a swollen-up eye.

You are crazy! say my daughter. Look at what you did! You are crazy!

I try very hard, I say.

How could you use a stick? I told you to use your words!

She is hard to handle, I say.

135   She's three years old! You cannot use a stick! say my daughter.

She is not like any Chinese girl I ever saw, I say.

I brush some sand off my clothes. Sophie's clothes are dirty too, but at least she has her clothes on.

Has she done this before? ask my daughter. Has she hit you before?

She hits me all the time, Sophie say, eating ice cream.

140   Your family, say John.

Believe me, say my daughter.

A daughter I have, a beautiful daughter. I took care of her when she could not hold her head up. I took care of her before she could argue with me, when she was a little girl with two pigtails, one of them always crooked. I took care of her when we have to escape from China, I took care of her when suddenly we live in a country with cars everywhere, if you are not careful your little girl get run over. When my husband die, I promise him I will keep the family together, even though it was just two of us, hardly a family at all.

But now my daughter take me around to look at apartments. After all, I can cook, I can clean, there's no reason I cannot live by myself, all I need is a telephone. Of course, she is sorry. Sometimes she cry, I am the one to say everything will be okay. She say she have no choice, she doesn't want to end up divorced. I say divorce is terrible, I don't know who invented this terrible idea. Instead of live with a telephone, though, surprise, I come to live with Bess. Imagine that. Bess make an offer and, sure enough, where she come from, people mean for you to move in when they say things like that. A crazy idea, go to live with someone else's family, but she like to have some female company, not like my daughter, who does not believe in company. These days when my daughter visit, she does not bring Sophie. Bess say we should give Nattie time, we will see Sophie again soon. But seems like my daughter have more presentation than ever before, every time she come she have to leave.

I have a family to support, she say, and her voice is heavy, as if soaking wet. I have a young daughter and a depressed husband and no one to turn to.

145   When she say no one to turn to, she mean me.

These days my beautiful daughter is so tired she can just sit there in a chair and fall asleep. John lost his job again, already, but still they rather hire a baby-sitter than ask me to help, even they can't afford it. Of course, the new baby-sitter is much younger, can run around. I don't know if Sophie these days is wild or not wild. She call me Meanie, but she like to kiss me too, sometimes. I remember that every time I see a child on TV. Sophie like to grab my hair, a fistful in each hand, and then kiss me smack on the nose. I never see any other child kiss that way.

The satellite TV has so many channels, more channels than I can count, including a Chinese channel from the Mainland and a Chinese channel from Taiwan, but most of the time I watch bloopers with Bess. Also, I watch the bird feeder—so many, many kinds of birds come. The Shea sons hang around all the time, asking when will I go home, but Bess tell them, Get lost.

She's a permanent resident, say Bess. She isn't going anywhere.

Then she wink at me, and switch the channel with the remote control.

150   Of course, I shouldn't say Irish this, Irish that, especially now I am become honorary Irish myself, according to Bess. Me! Who's Irish? I say, and she laugh. All the same, if I could mention one thing about some of the Irish, not all of them of course, I like to mention this: Their talk just stick. I don't know how Bess Shea learn to use her words, but sometimes I hear what she say a long time later. *Permanent resident. Not going anywhere.* Over and over I hear it, the voice of Bess.

TOPICS FOR CRITICAL THINKING AND WRITING

1. The word "fierce" is used several times in "Who's Irish?" Please look up the definition of "fierce" in a good dictionary, and explain its significance for your understanding of the story.
2. Does the narrator change as a result of the experiences she describes?
3. Imagine that you have been assigned to teach "Who's Irish?" in a course on creative writing. What are the features of its style and structure that you would highlight for your students?
4. Now that you have read and studied "Who's Irish?," what is your response to Jen's choice of title? If the author asked you to suggest an alternate title, what would it be? Explain in detail why you feel that your title would be a good one.
5. Does this story help you to perceive something new about "diversity"? Do you think that "diversity" is an overused term? Why or why not?
6. How would you describe the differences between the generations as these are expressed in Jen's story? Do you think in general that there are significant differences between members of older and younger generations, or would you say that these are exaggerated?
7. Do you believe that sometimes these are good reasons for classifying people by race and ethnicity? What are these reasons? Do you find them convincing? How should we classify "mixed race" persons?

TONI CADE BAMBARA

Toni Cade Bambara (1939–1995), an African-American writer, was born in New York City and grew up in black districts of the city. After studying at the University of Florence and at City College in New York, where she received a master's degree, she worked for a while as a case investigator for the New York State Welfare Department. Later she directed a recreation program for hospital patients. Once her literary reputation was established, she spent most of her time writing, though she also served as writer in residence at Spelman College in Atlanta.

The Lesson   [1972]

Back in the days when everyone was old and stupid or young and foolish and me and Sugar were the only ones just right, this lady moved on our block with nappy hair and proper speech and no makeup. And quite naturally we laughed at her, laughed the way we did at the junk man who went about his business like he was some big-time president and his sorry-ass horse his secretary. And we kinda hated her too, hated the way we did the winos who cluttered up our parks and pissed on our handball walls and stank up our hallways and stairs so you couldn't halfway play hide-and-seek without a goddam gas mask. Miss Moore was her name. The only woman on the block with no first name. And she was black as hell, cept for her feet, which were fish-white and spooky. And she was always planning these boring-ass things for us to do, us being my cousin, mostly, who lived on the block cause we all moved North the same time and to the same apartment then spread out gradual to breathe. And our parents would yank our heads into some kinda shape and crisp up our clothes so we'd be presentable for travel with Miss Moore, who always looked like she was going to church, though she never did. Which is just one of the things the grownups talked about when they talked behind her back like a dog. But when she came calling with some sachet she'd sewed up or some gingerbread she'd made or some book, why then they'd all be too embarrassed to turn her down and we'd get handed over all spruced up. She'd been to college and said it was only right that she should take responsibility for the young ones' education, and she not even related by marriage or blood. So they'd go for it. Specially Aunt Gretchen. She was the main gofer in the family. You got some old dumb shit foolishness you want somebody to go for, you send for Aunt Gretchen. She been screwed into the go-along for so long, it's a blood-deep natural thing with her. Which is how she got saddled with me and Sugar and Junior in the first place while our mothers were in la-de-da apartment up the block having a good ole time.

So this one day Miss Moore rounds us all up at the mailbox and it's puredee hot and she's knockin herself out about arithmetic. And school suppose to let up in summer I heard, but she don't never let up. And the starch in my pinafore scratching the shit outta me and I'm really hating this nappy-head bitch and her goddam college degree. I'd much rather go to the pool or to the show where it's cool. So me and Sugar leaning on the mailbox being surly, which is a Miss Moore word. And Flyboy checking out what everybody brought for lunch. And Fat Butt already wasting his peanut-butter-and-jelly sandwich like the pig he is. And Junebug punchin on Q.T.'s arm for potato chips. And Rosie Giraffe shifting from one hip to the other waiting for somebody to step on her foot or ask her if she from Georgia so she can kick ass, preferably Mercedes'. And Miss Moore asking us do we know what money is, like we a bunch of retards. I mean real money, she say, like it's only poker chips or monopoly papers we lay on the grocer. So right away I'm tired of this and say so. And would much rather snatch Sugar and go to the Sunset and terrorize the West Indian kids and take their hair ribbons and their money too. And Miss Moore files that remark away for next week's lesson on brotherhood, I can tell. And finally I say we oughta get to the subway cause it's cooler and besides we might meet some cute boys. Sugar done swiped her mama's lipstick, so we ready.

So we heading down the street and she's boring us silly about what things cost and what our parents make and how much goes for rent and how money ain't divided up right in this country. And then she gets to the part about we all poor and live in the slums, which I don't feature. And I'm ready to speak on that, but she steps out in the street and hails two cabs just like that. Then she hustles half the crew in with her and hands me a five-dollar bill and tells me to calculate 10 percent tip for the driver. And we're off. Me and Sugar and Junebug and Flyboy hangin out the window and hollering to everybody, putting lipstick on each other cause Flyboy a faggot anyway, and making farts with our sweaty armpits. But I'm mostly trying to figure how to spend this money. But they all fascinated with the meter ticking and Junebug starts laying bets as to how much it'll read when Flyboy can't hold his breath no more. Then Sugar lays bets as to how much it'll be when we get there. So I'm stuck. Don't nobody want to go for my plan, which is to jump out at the next light and run off to the first bar-b-que we can find. Then the driver tells us to get the hell out cause we there already. And the meter reads eighty-five cents. And I'm stalling to figure out the tip and Sugar

say give him a dime. And I decide he don't need it bad as I do, so later for
him. But then he tries to take off with Junebug foot still in the door so we
talk about his mama something ferocious. Then we check out that we on
Fifth Avenue and everybody dressed up in stockings. One lady in a fur coat,
hot as it is. White folks crazy.

"This is the place," Miss Moore say, presenting it to us in the voice she
uses at the museum. "Let's look in the windows before we go in."

5   "Can we steal?" Sugar asks very serious like she's getting the ground
rules squared away before she plays. "I beg your pardon," say Miss Moore,
and we fall out. So she leads us around the windows of the toy store and me
and Sugar screamin, "This is mine, that's mine. I gotta have that, that was
made for me. I was born for that," till Big Butt drowns us out.

"Hey, I'm going to buy that there."

"That there? You don't even know what it is, stupid."

"I do so," he say punchin on Rosie Giraffe. "It's a microscope."

"Whatcha gonna do with a microscope, fool?"

10   "Look at things."

"Like what, Ronald?" ask Miss Moore. And Big Butt ain't got the first notion. So here go Miss Moore gabbing about the thousands of bacteria in a
drop of water and the somethinorother in a speck of blood and the million
and one living things in the air around us is invisible to the naked eye. And
what she say that for? Junebug go to town on that "naked" and we rolling.
Then Miss Moore ask what it cost. So we all jam into the window smudgin
it up and the price tag say $300. So then she ask how long'd take for Big
Butt and Junebug to save up their allowances. "Too long," I say. "Yeh," adds
Sugar, "outgrown it by that time." And Miss Moore say no, you never out-
grow learning instruments. "Why, even medical students and interns and,"
blah, blah, blah. And we ready to choke Big Butt for bringing it up in the
first damn place.

"This here cost four hundred eighty dollars," say Rosie Giraffe. So we
pile up all over her to see what she pointin out. My eyes tell me it's a chunk
of glass cracked with something heavy, and different-color inks dripped into
the spits, then the whole thing put into a oven or something. But for $480 it
don't make sense.

"That's a paperweight made of semi-precious stones fused together under tremendous pressure," she explains slowly, with her hands doing the
mining and all the factory work.

"So what's a paperweight?" asks Rosie Giraffe.

15   "To weight paper with, dumbbell," say Flyboy, the wise man from the East.

"Not exactly," say Miss Moore, which is what she say when you warm or
way off too. "It's to weigh paper down so it won't scatter and make your
desk untidy." So right away me and Sugar curtsy to each other and then to
Mercedes who is more the tidy type.

"We don't keep paper on top of the desk in my class," say Junebug, figuring Miss Moore crazy or lyin one.

"At home, then," she say. "Don't you have a calendar and a pencil case
and a blotter and a letter-opener on your desk at home where you do your
homework?" And she know damn well what our homes look like cause she
nosys around in them every chance she gets.

"I don't even have a desk," say Junebug. "Do we?"

20   "No. And I don't get no homework neither," says Big Butt.

"And I don't even have a home," say Flyboy, like he do at school to keep the white folks off his back and sorry for him. Send this poor kid to camp posters, is his specialty.

"I do," says Mercedes. "I have a box of stationery on my desk and a picture of my cat. My godmother bought the stationery and the desk. There's a big rose on each sheet and the envelopes smell like roses."

"Who wants to know about your smelly-ass stationery," say Rosie Giraffe fore I can get my two cents in.

"It's important to have a work area all your own so that . . ."

25   "Will you look at this sailboat, please," say Flyboy, cuttin her off and pointin to the thing like it was his. So once again we tumble all over each other to gaze at this magnificent thing in the toy store which is just big enough to maybe sail two kittens across the pond if you strap them to the posts tight. We all start reciting the price tag like we in assembly. "Handcrafted sailboat of fiberglass at one thousand one hundred ninety-five dollars."

"Unbelievable," I hear myself say and am really stunned. I read it again for myself just in case the group recitation put me in a trance. Same thing. For some reason this pisses me off. We look at Miss Moore and she lookin at us, waiting for I dunno what.

"Who'd pay all that when you can buy a sailboat set for a quarter at Pop's, a tube of glue for a dime, and a ball of string for eight cents? It must have a motor and a whole lot else besides," I say. "My sailboat cost me about fifty cents."

"But will it take water?" say Mercedes with her smart ass.

"Took mine to Alley Pond Park once," say Flyboy. "String broke. Lost it. Pity."

30   "Sailed mine in Central Park and it keeled over and sank. Had to ask my father for another dollar."

"And you got the strap," laugh Big Butt. "The jerk didn't even have a string on it. My old man wailed on his behind."

Little Q.T. was staring hard at the sailboat and you could see he wanted it bad. But he too little and somebody'd just take it from him. So what the hell. "This boat for kids, Miss Moore?"

"Parents silly to buy something like that just to get all broke up," say Rosie Giraffe.

"That much money it should last forever," I figure.

35   My father'd buy it for me if I wanted it."

"Your father, my ass," say Rosie Giraffe getting a chance to finally push Mercedes.

"Must be rich people shop here," say Q.T.

"You are a very bright boy," say Flyboy. "What was your first clue?" And he rap him on the head with the back of his knuckles, since Q.T. the only one he could get away with. Though Q.T. liable to come up behind you years later and get his licks in when you half expect it.

"What I want to know is," I says to Miss Moore though I never talk to her, I wouldn't give the bitch that satisfaction, "is how much a real boat costs? I figure a thousand'd get you a yacht any day."

40   "Why don't you check that out," she says, "and report back to the group?" Which really pains my ass. If you gonna mess up a perfectly good swim day least you could do is have some answers. "Let's go in," she say like she got something up her sleeve. Only she don't lead the way. So me and Sugar turn the corner to where the entrance is, but when we get there I

kinda hang back. Not that I'm scared, what's there to be afraid of, just a toy store. But I feel funny, shame. But what I got to be shamed about? Got as much right to go in as anybody. But somehow I can't seem to get hold of the door, so I step away for Sugar to lead. But she hangs back too. And I look at her and she looks at me and this is ridiculous. I mean, damn, I have never ever been shy about doing nothing or going nowhere. But then Mercedes steps up and then Rosie Giraffe and Big Butt crowd in behind and shove, and next thing we all stuffed into the doorway with only Mercedes squeezing past us, smoothing out her jumper and walking right down the aisle. Then the rest of us tumble in like a glued-together jigsaw done all wrong. And people lookin at us. And it's like the time me and Sugar crashed into the Catholic church on a dare. But once we got in there and everything so hushed and holy and the candles and the bowin and the handkerchiefs on all the drooping heads, I just couldn't go through with the plan. Which was for me to run up to the altar and do a tap dance while Sugar played the nose flute and messed around in the holy water. And Sugar kept giving me the elbow. Then later teased me so bad I tied her up in the shower and turned it on and locked her in. And she'd be there till this day if Aunt Gretchen hadn't finally figured I was lying about the boarder takin a shower.

Same thing in the store. We all walkin on tiptoe and hardly touchin the games and puzzles and things. And I watched Miss Moore who is steady watchin us like she waiting for a sign. Like Mama Drewery watches the sky and sniffs the air and takes note of just how much slant is in the bird formation. Then me and Sugar bump smack into each other, so busy gazing at the toys, 'specially the sailboat. But we don't laugh and go into our fat-lady bump-stomach routine. We just stare at that price tag. Then Sugar run a finger over the whole boat. And I'm jealous and want to hit her. Maybe not her, but I sure want to punch somebody in the mouth.

"Watcha bring us here for, Miss Moore?"

"You sound angry, Sylvia. Are you mad about something?" Givin me one of them grins like she tellin a grown-up joke that never turns out to be funny. And she's looking very closely at me like maybe she plannin to do my portrait from memory. I'm mad, but I won't give her the satisfaction. So I slouch around the store being very bored and say, "Let's go."

Me and Sugar at the back of the train watchin the tracks whizzin by large then small then gettin gobbled up in the dark. I'm thinkin about this tricky toy I saw in the store. A clown that somersaults on a bar then does chin-ups just cause you yank lightly at his leg. Cost $35. I could see me askin my mother for a $35 birthday clown. "You wanna who that costs what?" she'd say, cocking her head to the side to get a better view of the hole in my head. Thirty-five dollars could buy new bunk beds for Junior and Gretchen's boy. Thirty-five dollars and the whole household could go visit Granddaddy Nelson in the country. Thirty-five dollars would pay for the rent and the piano bill too. Who are these people that spend that much for performing clowns and $1000 for toy sailboats? What kinda work they do and how they live and how come we ain't in on it? Where we are is who we are, Miss Moore always pointin out. But it don't necessarily have to be that way, she always adds then waits for somebody to say that poor people have to wake up and demand their share of the pie and don't none of us know what kind of pie she talkin about in the first damn place. But she ain't so smart cause I still got her four dollars from the taxi and she sure ain't getting it. Messin up my day with this shit. Sugar nudges me in my pocket and winks.

45   Miss Moore lines us up in front of the mailbox where we started from,
        seem like years ago, and I got a headache for thinkin so hard. And we lean all
        over each other so we can hold up under the draggy-ass lecture she always
        finishes off with at the end before we thank her for borin us to tears. But she
        just looks at us like she readin tea leaves. Finally she say, "Well, what did you
        think of F. A. O Schwarz?"
            Rosie Giraffe mumbles, "White folks crazy."
            "I'd like to go there again when I get my birthday money," says Mer-
        cedes, and we shove her out the pack so she has to lean on the mailbox by
        herself.
            "I'd like a shower. Tiring day," say Flyboy.
            Then Sugar surprises me by saying, "You know, Miss Moore, I don't think
        all of us put together eat in a year what that sailboat costs." And Miss
        Moore lights up like somebody goosed her. "And?" she say, urging Sugar on.
        Only I'm standin on her foot so she don't continue.
50   "Imagine for a minute what kind of society it is in which some people
        can spend on a toy what it would cost to feed a family of six or seven. What
        do you think?"
            "I think," say Sugar pushing me off her feet like she never done before,
        cause I whip her ass in a minute, "that this is not much of a democracy if you
        ask me. Equal chance to pursue happiness means an equal crack at the
        dough, don't it?" Miss Moore is beside herself and I am disgusted with
        Sugar's treachery. So I stand on her foot one more time to see if she'll shove
        me. She shuts up, and Miss Moore looks at me, sorrowfully I'm thinkin. And
        somethin weird is goin on, I can feel it in my chest.
            "Anybody else learn anything today?" lookin dead at me. I walk away
        and Sugar has to run to catch up and don't even seem to notice when I
        shrug her arm off my shoulder.
            "Well, we got four dollars anyway," she says.
            "Uh hunh."
55   "We could go to Hascombs and get half a chocolate layer and then go
        to the Sunset and still have plenty of money for potato chips and ice cream
        sodas."
            "Un hunh."
            "Race you to Hascombs," she say.
            We start down the block and she gets ahead which is O.K. by me cause
        I'm going to the West End and then over to the Drive to think this day
        through. She can run if she want to and even run faster. But ain't nobody
        gonna beat me at nuthin.

▓ TOPICS FOR CRITICAL THINKING AND WRITING

1. What is "the lesson" that Miss Moore is trying to teach the children?
   How much, if any, of this lesson does Sylvia learn? Point to specific passages to support your answers.
2. Since Miss Moore intends the lesson for the children's own good, why is
   Sylvia so resistant to it, so impatient and exasperated?
3. Toward the end of the story, Sylvia says that she is "disgusted with
   Sugar's treachery." Describe their relationship. What would be missing from the story if Bambara had not included Sugar among its
   characters?

KATHERINE ANNE PORTER

Katherine Anne Porter (1890–1980) had the curious habit of inventing details in her life, but it is true that she was born in a log cabin in Indian Creek, Texas, that she was originally named Callie Russell Porter, that her mother died when she was two years old, and that Callie was brought up by her maternal grandmother in Kyle, Texas. Apparently the family was conscious of former wealth and position in Louisiana and Kentucky. She was sent to convent schools, where, in her words, she received "a strangely useless and ornamental education." At sixteen she left school, married (and soon divorced), and worked as a reporter, first in Texas and later in Denver and Chicago. She moved around a good deal, both within the United States and abroad; she lived in Mexico, Belgium, Switzerland, France, and Germany.

Even as a child Porter was interested in writing, but she did not publish her first story until she was thirty-three. She wrote essays and one novel (Ship of Fools), but she is best known for her stories. Porter's Collected Stories won the Pulitzer Prize and the National Book Award in 1965.

He   [1927]

Life was very hard for the Whipples. It was hard to feed all the hungry mouths, it was hard to keep the children in flannels during the winter, short as it was: "God knows what would become of us if we lived north," they would say: keeping them decently clean was hard. "It looks like our luck won't never let up on us," said Mr. Whipple, but Mrs. Whipple was all for taking what was sent and calling it good, anyhow when the neighbors were in earshot. "Don't ever let a soul hear us complain," she kept saying to her husband. She couldn't stand to be pitied. "No, not if it comes to it that we have to live in a wagon and pick cotton around the country," she said, "nobody's going to get a chance to look down on us."

Mrs. Whipple loved her second son, the simple-minded one, better than she loved the other two children put together. She was forever saying so, and when she talked with certain of her neighbors, she would even throw in her husband and her mother for good measure.

"You needn't keep saying it around," said Mr. Whipple, "you'll make people think nobody else has any feeling about Him but you."

"It's natural for a mother," Mrs. Whipple would remind him. "You know yourself it's more natural for a mother to be that way. People don't expect so much of fathers, some way."

5   This didn't keep the neighbors from talking plainly among themselves. "A Lord's pure mercy if He should die," they sad. "It's the sins of the fathers," they agreed among themselves. "There's bad blood and bad doings somewhere, you can bet on that." This behind the Whipples' backs. To their faces everybody said, "He's not so bad off. He'll be all right yet. Look how He grows!"

Mrs. Whipple hated to talk about it, she tried to keep her mind off it, but every time anybody set foot in the house, the subject always came up, and she had to talk about Him first, before she could get on to anything else. It seemed to ease her mind. "I wouldn't have anything happen to Him for all the world, but it just looks like I can't keep Him out of mischief. He's so strong and active, He's always into everything; He was like that since He could walk. It's actually funny sometimes; the way He can do anything; it's laughable to see Him up to His tricks, Emly has more accidents; I'm forever tying up her bruises, and Adna can't fall a foot without cracking a bone. But He can do anything and not get a scratch. The preacher said such a nice thing once when he was here. He said, and I'll remember it to my dying day, 'The innocent walk with God—that's why He don't get hurt.'" Whenever Mrs. Whipple repeated these words, she always felt a warm pool spread in her breast, and the tears would fill her eyes, and then she could talk about something else.

He did grow and He never got hurt. A plank blew off the chicken house and struck Him on the head and He never seemed to know it. He had learned a few words, and after this He forgot them. He didn't whine for food as the other children did, but waited until it was given Him; He ate squatting in the corner, smacking and mumbling. Rolls of fat covered Him like an overcoat, and He could carry twice as much wood and water as Adna. Emly had a cold in the head most of the time—"she takes that after me," said Mrs. Whipple—so in bad weather they gave her the extra blanket off His cot. He never seemed to mind the cold.

Just the same, Mrs. Whipple's life was a torment for fear something might happen to Him. He climbed the peach trees much better than Adna and went a skittering along the branches like a monkey, just a regular monkey. "Oh, Mrs. Whipple, you hadn't ought to let Him do that. He'll lose His balance sometime. He can't rightly know what He's doing."

Mrs. Whipple almost screamed out at the neighbor. "He *does* know what He's doing! He's as able as any other child! Come down out of there, you!" When He finally reached the ground she could hardly keep her hands off Him for acting like that before people, a grin all over His face and her worried sick about Him all the time.

10   "It's the neighbors," said Mrs. Whipple to her husband. "Oh, I do mortally wish they would keep out of our business. I can't afford to let Him do anything for fear they'll come nosing around about it. Look at the bees, now. Adna can't handle them, they sting him up so; I haven't got time to do everything, and now I don't dare let Him. But if He gets a sting He don't really mind."

"It's just because He ain't got sense enough to be scared of anything," said Mr. Whipple.

"You ought to be ashamed of yourself," said Mrs. Whipple, "talking that way about your own child. Who's to take up for Him if we don't, I'd like to know? He sees a lot that goes on, He listens to things all the time. And anything I tell Him to do He does it. Don't never let anybody hear you say such things. They'd think you favored the other children over Him."

"Well, now I don't, and you know it, and what's the use of getting all worked up about it? You always think the worst of everything. Just let Him alone, He'll get along somehow. He gets plenty to eat and wear, don't He?" Mr. Whipple suddenly felt tired out. "Anyhow, it can't be helped now."

Mrs. Whipple felt tired too, she complained in a tired voice. "What's done can't never be undone, I know that good as anybody; but He's my child, and I'm not going to have people say anything. I get sick of people coming around saying things all the time."

15   In the early fall Mrs. Whipple got a letter from her brother saying he and his wife and two children were coming over for a little visit next Sunday week. "Put the big pot in the little one," he wrote at the end. Mrs. Whipple

read this part out loud twice, she was so pleased. Her brother was a great one for saying funny things. "We'll just show him that's no joke," she said, "we'll just butcher one of the sucking pigs."

"It's a waste and I don't hold with waste the way we are now," said Mr. Whipple. "That pig'll be worth money by Christmas."

"It's a shame and a pity we can't have a decent meal's vittles once in a while when my own family comes to see us," said Mrs. Whipple. "I'd hate for his wife to go back and say there wasn't a thing in the house to eat. My God, it's better than buying up a great chance of meat in town. There's where you'd spend the money!"

"All right, do it yourself then," said Mr. Whipple. "Christamighty, no wonder we can't get ahead!"

The question was how to get the little pig away from his ma, a great fighter, worse than a Jersey cow. Adna wouldn't try it: "That sow'd rip my insides out all over the pen." "All right, old fraidy," said Mrs. Whipple, *"He's* not scared. Watch *Him* do it." And she laughed as though it was all a good joke and gave Him a little push towards the pen. He sneaked up and snatched the pig right away from the teat and galloped back and was over the fence with the sow raging at His heels. The little black squirming thing was screeching like a baby in a tantrum, stiffening its back and stretching its mouth to the ears. Mrs. Whipple took the pig with her face stiff and sliced its throat with one stroke. When He saw the blood He gave a great jolting breath and ran away. "But He'll forget and eat plenty, just the same," thought Mrs. Whipple. Whenever she was thinking, her lips moved making words. "He'd eat it all if I didn't stop Him. He'd eat up every mouthful from the other two if I'd let Him."

20   She felt badly about it. He was ten years old now and a third again as large as Adna, who was going on fourteen. "It's a shame, a shame," she kept saying under her breath, "and Adna with so much brains!"

She kept on feeling badly about all sorts of things. In the first place it was the man's work to butcher; the sight of the pig scraped pink and naked made her sick. He was too fat and soft and pitiful-looking. It was simply a shame the way things had to happen. By the time she had finished it up, she almost wished her brother would stay at home.

Early Sunday morning Mrs. Whipple dropped everything to get Him all cleaned up. In an hour He was dirty again, with crawling under fences after a possum, and straddling along the rafters of the barn looking for eggs in the hayloft. "My Lord, look at you now after all my trying! And here's Adna and Emily staying so quiet. I get tired trying to keep you decent. Get off that shirt and put on another, people will say I don't half dress you!" And she boxed Him on the ears, hard. He blinked and blinked and rubbed His head, and His face hurt Mrs. Whipple's feelings. Her knees began to tremble, she had to sit down while she buttoned His shirt. "I'm just all gone before the day starts."

The brother came with his plump healthy wife and two great roaring hungry boys. They had a grand dinner, with the pig roasted to a crackling in the middle of the table, full of dressing, a pickled peach in his mouth and plenty of gravy for the sweet potatoes.

"This looks like prosperity all right," said the brother; "you're going to have to roll me home like I was a barrel when I'm done."

25   Everybody laughed out loud; it was fine to hear them laughing all at once around the table. Mrs. Whipple felt warm and good about it. "Oh, we've

got six more of these; I say it's as little as we can do when you come to see us so seldom."

He wouldn't come into the dining room, and Mrs. Whipple passed it off very well. "He's timider than my other two," she said. "He'll just have to get used to you. There isn't everybody He'll make up with, you know how it is with some children, even cousins." Nobody said anything out of the way.

"Just like my Alfy here," said the brother's wife. "I sometimes got to lick him to make him shake hands with his own grand-mammy."

So that was over, and Mrs. Whipple loaded up a big plate for Him first, before everybody. "I always say He ain't to be slighted, no matter who else goes without," she said, and carried it to Him herself.

"He can chin Himself on the top of the door," said Emly, helping along.

30   "That's fine, He's getting along fine," said the brother.

They went away after supper. Mrs. Whipple rounded up the dishes, and sent the children to bed and sat down and unlaced her shoes. "You see!" she said to Mr. Whipple. "That's the way my whole family is. Nice and consider-ate about everything. No out-of-the-way remarks—they *have* got refine-ment. I get awfully sick of people's remarks. Wasn't that pig good?"

Mr. Whipple said, "Yes, we're out three hundred pounds of pork, that's all. It's easy to be polite when you come to eat. Who knows what they had in their minds all along?"

"Yes, that's like you," said Mrs. Whipple. "I don't expect anything else from you. You'll be telling me next that my own brother will be saying around that we made Him eat in the kitchen! Oh, my God!" She rocked her head in her hands, a hard pain started in the very middle of her forehead. "Now it's all spoiled, and everything was so nice and easy. All right, you don't like them and you never did—all right, they'll not come here again soon, never you mind! But they *can't* say He wasn't dressed every lick as good as Adna—oh, honest, sometimes I wish I was dead!"

"I wish you'd let up," said Mr. Whipple. "It's bad enough as it is."

35   It was a hard winter. It seemed to Mrs. Whipple that they hadn't ever known anything but hard times, and now to cap it all a winter like this. The crops were about half of what they had a right to expect; after the cotton was in it didn't do much more than cover the grocery bill. They swapped off one of the plow horses, and got cheated, for the new one died of the heaves. Mrs. Whipple kept thinking all the time it was terrible to have a man you couldn't depend on not to get cheated. They cut down on everything, but Mrs. Whipple kept saying there are things you can't cut down on, and they cost money. It took a lot of warm clothes for Adna and Emly, who walked four miles to school during the three-months session. "He sets around the fire a lot, He won't need so much," said Mr. Whipple. "That's so," said Mrs. Whipple, "and when He does the outdoor chores He can wear your tarpau-lin coat. I can't do no better, that's all."

In February He was taken sick, and lay curled up under His blanket looking very blue in the face and acting as if He would choke. Mr. and Mrs. Whipple did everything they could for Him for two days, and then they were scared and sent for the doctor. The doctor told them they must keep Him warm and give Him plenty of milk and eggs. "He isn't as stout as He looks, I'm afraid," said the doctor. "You've got to watch them when they're like that. You must put more cover onto Him, too."

"I just took off His big blanket to wash," said Mrs. Whipple, ashamed. "I can't stand dirt."

"Well, you'd better put it back on the minute it's dry," said the doctor, "or He'll have pneumonia."

Mr. and Mrs. Whipple took a blanket off their own bed and put His cot in by the fire. "They can't say we didn't do everything for Him," she said, "even to sleeping cold ourselves on His account."

40   When the winter broke He seemed to be well again, but He walked as if His feet hurt him. He was able to run a cotton planter during the season.

"I got it all fixed up with Jim Ferguson about breeding the cow next time," said Mr. Whipple. "I'll pasture the bull this summer and give Jim some fodder in the fall. That's better than paying out money when you haven't got it."

"I hope you didn't say such a thing before Jim Ferguson," said Mrs. Whipple. "You oughtn't to let him know we're so down as all that."

"Godamighty, that ain't saying we're down. A man is got to look ahead sometimes. *He* can lead the bull over today. I need Adna on the place."

At first Mrs. Whipple felt easy in her mind about sending Him for the bull. Adna was too jumpy and couldn't be trusted. You've got to be steady around animals. After He was gone she started thinking, and after a while she could hardly bear it any longer. She stood in the lane and watched for Him. It was nearly three miles to go and a hot day, but He oughtn't to be so long about it. She shaded her eyes and stared until colored bubbles floated in her eyeballs. It was just like everything else in life, she must always worry and never know a moment's peace about anything. After a long time she saw Him turn into the side lane, limping. He came on very slowly, leading the big hulk of an animal by a ring in the nose, twirling a little stick in His hand, never looking back or sideways, but coming on like a sleepwalker with His eyes half shut.

45   Mrs. Whipple was scared sick of bulls; she had heard awful stories about how they followed on quietly enough, and then suddenly pitched on with a bellow and pawed and gored a body to pieces. Any second now that black monster would come down on Him, my God, He'd never have sense enough to run.

She mustn't make a sound nor a move; she mustn't get the bull started. The bull heaved his head aside and horned the air at a fly. Her voice burst out of her in a shriek, and she screamed at Him to come on, for God's sake. He didn't seem to hear her clamor, but kept on twirling His switch and limping on, and the bull lumbered along behind him as gently as a calf. Mrs. Whipple stopped calling and ran towards the house, praying under her breath: Lord, don't let anything happen to Him. Lord, you *know* people will say we oughtn't to have sent Him. You *know* they'll say we didn't take care of Him. Oh, get Him home, safe home, and I'll look out for Him better! Amen."

She watched from the window while He led the beast in, and tied him up in the barn. It was no use trying to keep up, Mrs. Whipple couldn't bear another thing. She sat down and rocked and cried with her apron over her head.

From year to year the Whipples were growing poorer and poorer. The place just seemed to run down of itself, no matter how hard they worked. "We're losing our hold," said Mrs. Whipple. "Why can't we do like other people and watch for our best chances? They'll be calling us poor white trash next."

"When I get to be sixteen I'm going to leave," said Adna. "I'm going to get a job in Powell's grocery store. There's money in that. No more farm for me."

50 "I'm going to be a schoolteacher," said Emly. "But I've got to finish the eighth grade, anyhow. Then I can live in town. I don't see any chances here."

"Emly takes after my family," said Mrs. Whipple. "Ambitious every last one of them, and they don't take second place for anybody."

When fall came Emly got a chance to wait on table in the railroad eating-house in the town near by, and it seemed such a shame not to take it when the wages were good and she could get her food too, that Mrs. Whipple decided to let her take it, and not bother with school until the next session. "You've got plenty of time," she said. "You're young and smart as a whip."

With Adna gone too, Mr. Whipple tried to run the farm with just Him to help. He seemed to get along fine, doing His work and part of Adna's without noticing it. They did well enough until Christmas time, when one morning He slipped on the ice coming up from the barn. Instead of getting up He thrashed round and round, and when Mr. Whipple got to Him, He was having some sort of fit.

They brought Him inside and tried to make Him sit up, but He blubbered and rolled, so they put Him to bed and Mr. Whipple rode to town for the doctor. All the way there and back he worried about where the money was to come from: it sure did look like he had about all the troubles he could carry.

55 From then on He stayed in bed. His legs swelled up double their size, and the fits kept coming back. After four months, the doctor said, "It's no use, I think you'd better put Him in the County Home for treatment right away. I'll see about it for you. He'll have good care there and be off your hands."

"We don't begrudge Him any care, and I won't let Him out of my sight," said Mrs. Whipple. "I won't have it said I sent my sick child off among strangers."

"I know how you feel," said the doctor. "You can't tell me anything about that, Mrs. Whipple. I've got a boy of my own. But you'd better listen to me. I can't do anything more for him, that's the truth."

Mr. and Mrs. Whipple talked it over a long time that night after they went to bed. "It's just charity," said Mrs. Whipple, "that's what we've come to, charity! I certainly never looked for this."

"We pay taxes to help support the place just like everybody else," said Mr. Whipple, "and I don't call that taking charity. I think it would be fine to have Him where He'd get the best of everything . . . and besides, I can't keep up with these doctor bills any longer."

60 "Maybe that's why the doctor wants us to send Him—he's scared he won't get his money," said Mrs. Whipple.

"Don't talk like that," said Mr. Whipple, feeling pretty sick, "or we won't be able to send Him."

"Oh, but we won't keep Him there long," said Mrs. Whipple. "Soon's he's better, we'll bring Him right back home."

"The doctor has told you and told you time and again He can't ever get better, and you might as well stop talking," said Mr. Whipple.

"Doctor's don't know everything," said Mrs. Whipple, feeling almost happy. "But anyhow, in the summer Emly can come home for vacation, and

Adna can get down for Sundays: we'll all work together and get on our feet again, and the children will feel they've got a place to come to."

65   All at once she saw it full summer again, with the garden going fine, and new white roller shades up all over the house, and Adna and Emly home, so full of life, all of them happy together. Oh, it could happen, things would ease up on them.

They didn't talk before Him much, but they never knew just how much He understood. Finally the doctor set the day and a neighbor who owned a double-seated carryall offered to drive them over. The hospital would have sent an ambulance, but Mrs. Whipple couldn't stand to see Him going away looking so sick as all that. They wrapped Him in blankets, and the neighbor and Mr. Whipple lifted Him into the back seat of the carryall beside Mrs. Whipple, who had on her black shirtwaist. She couldn't stand to go looking like charity.

"You'll be all right, I guess I'll stay behind," said Mr. Whipple. "It don't look like everybody ought to leave the place at once."

"Besides, it ain't as if He was going to stay forever," said Mrs. Whipple to the neighbor. "This is only for a little while."

They started away, Mrs. Whipple holding to the edges of the blankets to keep Him from sagging sideways. He sat there blinking and blinking. He worked His hands out and began rubbing His nose with His knuckles, and then with the end of the blanket. Mrs. Whipple couldn't believe what she saw; He was scrubbing away big tears that rolled out of the corners of His eyes. He sniveled and made a gulping noise. Mrs. Whipple kept saying, "Oh, honey, you don't feel so bad, do you? You don't feel so bad, do you?" for He seemed to be accusing her of something. Maybe He remembered that time she boxed His ears, maybe He had been scared that day with the bull, maybe He had slept cold and couldn't tell her about it; maybe He knew they were sending Him away for good and all because they were too poor to keep Him. Whatever it was, Mrs. Whipple couldn't bear to think of it. She began to cry, frightfully, and wrapped her arms tight around Him. His head rolled on her shoulder; she had loved Him as much as she possibly could, there were Adna and Emly who had to be thought of too, there was nothing she could do to make up to Him for His life. Oh, what a mortal pity He was ever born.

70   They came in sight of the hospital, with the neighbor driving very fast, not daring to look behind him.

▨ TOPICS FOR CRITICAL THINKING AND WRITING

1. Consider the narrator's voice. The narrator tells us, for instance, that Mrs. Whipple was "forever saying" that she loves Him "better than . . . the other two children put together," and (according to the narrator) she would "even throw in her husband and her mother for good measure." What does the narrator seem to think of Mrs. Whipple?

2. How do you view Mrs. Whipple? With compassion? With anger? With a mixture, or what? (By the way, do you think that she unconsciously hates Him?)

3. What function does Mr. Whipple serve in the story? Is he a voice of truth, in contrast to Mrs. Whipple?

4. Why do you think He cries at the end of the story?

BERNARD MALAMUD

Bernard Malamud (1914–1986) was born in Brooklyn of Russian-Jewish immigrant parents who ran a mom-and-pop grocery store. He was educated in the public school system, and then received a bachelor's degree from the City University of New York and a master's degree from Columbia University. For nine years he taught English in high school at night, and then found a job as an instructor in English at Oregon State University, where he taught from 1949 until 1961. During the years at Oregon, he published two novels, The Natural *(1952) and* The Assistant *(1957), and a collection of stories,* The Magic Barrel *(1958), and all of which were well received (*The Magic Barrel *won a National Book Award). In 1961 he began teaching at Bennington, and in that year he published* A New Life, *a satiric novel drawing on his years at Oregon State. Another novel—he wrote eight novels—*The Fixer *(1966), won a Pulitzer Prize.*

Black Is My Favorite Color   [1963]

Charity Quietness sits in the toilet eating her two hard-boiled eggs while I'm having my ham sandwich and coffee in the kitchen. That's how it goes, only don't get the idea of ghettoes. If there's a ghetto I'm the one that's in it. She's my cleaning woman from Father Divine[1] and comes in once a week to my small three-room apartment on my day off from the liquor store. "Peace," she says to me, "Father reached on down and took me right up in Heaven." She's a small person with a flat body, frizzy hair, and a quiet face that the light shines out of, and Mama had such eyes before she died. The first time Charity Quietness came in to clean, a little more than a year and a half, I made the mistake to ask her to sit down at the kitchen table with me and eat her lunch. I was still feeling not so hot after Ornita left, but I'm the kind of man—Nat Lime, forty-four, a bachelor with a daily growing bald spot on the back of my head, and I could lose frankly fifteen pounds—who enjoys company so long as he has it. So she cooked up her two hard-boiled eggs and sat down and took a small bite out of one of them. But after a minute she stopped chewing and she got up and carried the eggs in a cup to the bathroom, and since then she eats there. I said to her more than once, "Okay, Charity Quietness, so have it your way, eat the eggs in the kitchen by yourself and I'll eat when you're done," but she smiles absentminded, and eats in the toilet. It's my fate with colored people.

Although black is still my favorite color you wouldn't know it from my luck except in short quantities, even though I do all right in the liquor store business in Harlem, on Eighth Avenue between 110th and 111th. I speak with respect. A large part of my life I've had dealings with Negro people, most on a business basis but sometimes for friendly reasons with genuine feeling on both sides. I'm drawn to them. At this time of my life I should have one or two good colored friends, but the fault isn't necessarily mine. If they knew what was in my heart toward them, but how can you tell that to

---

[1] **Father Divine** Father Divine, whose name at birth was George Baker (1877–1965), was a popular religious leader in Harlem during the 1930s. He established the Peace Mission Movement, which provided food, clothing, and work opportunities for its followers.

anybody nowadays? I've tried more than once but the language of the heart either is a dead language or else nobody understands it the way you speak it. Very few. What I'm saying is, personally for me there's only one human color and that's the color of blood. I like a black person if not because he's black, then because I'm white. It comes to the same thing. If I wasn't white my first choice would be black. I'm satisfied to be white because I have no other choice. Anyway, I got an eye for color. I appreciate. Who wants everybody to be the same? Maybe it's like some kind of a talent. Nat Lime might be a liquor dealer in Harlem, but once in the jungle in New Guinea in the Second World War, I got the idea, when I shot at a running Jap and missed him, that I had some kind of a talent, though maybe it's the kind where you have a good idea now and then, but in the end what do they come to? After all, it's a strange world.

Where Charity Quietness eats her eggs makes me think about Buster Wilson when we were both boys in the Williamsburg section of Brooklyn. There was this long block of run-down dirty frame houses in the middle of a not-so-hot white neighborhood full of pushcarts. The Negro houses looked to me like they had been born and died there, dead not long after the beginning of the world. I lived on the next street. My father was a cutter with arthritis in both hands, big red knuckles and fingers so swollen he didn't cut, and my mother was the one who went to work. She sold paper bags from a secondhand pushcart on Ellery Street. We didn't starve but nobody ate chicken unless we were sick, or the chicken was. This was my first acquaintance with a lot of black people and I used to poke around on their poor block. I think I thought, brother, if there can be like this, what can't there be? I mean I caught an early idea what life was about. Anyway, I met Buster Wilson there. He used to play marbles by himself. I sat on the curb across the street, watching him shoot one marble lefty and the other one righty. The hand that won picked up the marbles. It wasn't so much of a game but he didn't ask me to come over. My idea was to be friendly, only he never encouraged, he discouraged. Why did I pick him out for a friend? Maybe because I had no others then, we were new in the neighborhood, from Manhattan. Also I liked his type. Buster did everything alone. He was a skinny kid and his brothers' clothes hung on him like worn-out potato sacks. He was a beanpole boy, about twelve, and I was then ten. His arms and legs were burnt-out matchsticks. He always wore a brown wool sweater, one arm half unraveled, the other went down to the wrist. His long and narrow head had a white part cut straight in the short woolly hair, maybe with a ruler there, by his father, a barber but too drunk to stay a barber. In those days though I had little myself I was old enough to know who was better off, and the whole block of colored houses made me feel bad in the daylight. But I went there as much as I could because the street was full of life. In the night it looked different, it's hard to tell a cripple in the dark. Sometimes I was afraid to walk by the houses when they were dark and quiet. I was afraid there were people looking at me that I couldn't see. I liked it better when they had parties at night and everybody had a good time. The musicians played their banjos and saxophones and the houses shook with the music and laughing. The young girls, with their pretty dresses and ribbons in their hair, caught me in my throat when I saw them through the windows.

But with the parties cam drinking and fights. Sundays were bad days after the Saturday night parties. I remember once that Buster's father, also long and loose, always wearing a dirty gray Homburg hat,[2] chased another black man in the street with a half-inch chisel. The other one, maybe five feet high, lost his shoe and when they wrestled on the ground he was already bleeding through his suit, a thick red blood smearing the sidewalk. I was frightened by the blood and wanted to pour it back in the man who was bleeding from the chisel. On another time Buster's father was playing in a crap game with two big bouncy red dice, in the back of an alley between two middle houses. Then about six men started fist-fighting there, and they ran out of the alley and hit each other in the street. The neighbors, including children, came out and watched, everybody afraid but nobody moving to do anything. I saw the same thing near my store in Harlem, years later, a big crowd watching two men in the street, their breaths hanging in the air on a winter night, murdering each other with switch knives, but nobody moved to call a cop. I didn't either. Anyway, I was just a young kid but I still remember how the cops drove up in a police paddy wagon and broke up the fight by hitting everybody they could hit with big nightsticks. This was in the days before La Guardia.[3] Most of the fighters were knocked out cold, only one or two got away. Buster's father started to run back in his house but a cop ran after him and cracked him on his Homburg hat with a club, right on the front porch. Then the Negro men were lifted up by the cops, one at the arms and the other at the feet, and they heaved them in the paddy wagon. Buster's father hit the back of the wagon and fell, with his nose spouting very red blood, on top of three other men. I personally couldn't stand it, I was scared of the human race so I ran home, but I remember Buster watching without expression in his eyes. I stole an extra fifteen cents from my mother's pocketbook and I ran back and asked Buster if he wanted to go to the movies, I would pay. He said yes. This was the first time he talked to me.

5   So we went more than once to the movies. But we never got to be friends. Maybe because it was a one-way proposition—from me to him. Which includes my invitations to go with me, my (poor mother's) movie money, Hershey chocolate bars, watermelon slices, even my best Nick Carter and Merriwell books[4] that I spent hours picking up in the junk shops, and that he never gave me back. Once, he let me go in his house to get a match so we could smoke some butts we found, but it smelled so heavy, so impossible, I died till I got out of there. What I saw in the way of furniture I won't mention—the best was falling apart in pieces. Maybe we went to the movies all together five or six matinees that spring and in the summertime, but when the shows were over he usually walked home by himself.

"Why don't you wait for me, Buster?" I said. "We're both going in the same direction."

But he was walking ahead and didn't hear me. Anyway he didn't answer.

---

[2]**Homburg Hat** a type of a man's hat, which takes its name from the town in Germany where such hats were made.   [3]**La Guardia** Fiorello Henry La Guardia (1842–1947) was the colorful, progressive mayor of New York City from 1934 to 1945.   [4]**Nick Carter and Merriwell books** Nick Carter, the name of a fictional detective in a widely read series of books published from the 1890s to the 1950s; Frank Merriwell, the name of a literary character, a star athlete at Yale, in a series of books for boys published from 1900 to 1933.

One day when I wasn't expecting it he hit me in the teeth. I felt like crying but not because of the pain. I spit blood and said, "What did you hit me for? What did I do to you?"

"Because you a Jew bastard. Take your Jew movies and your Jew candy and shove them up your Jew ass."

10   And he ran away.

I thought to myself how was I to know he didn't like the movies. When I was a man I thought, you can't force it.

Years later, in the prime of my life, I met Mrs. Ornita Harris. She was standing by herself under an open umbrella at the bus stop, crosstown on 110th, and I picked up her green glove that she had dropped on the wet sidewalk. It was in the end of November. Before I could ask her was it hers, she grabbed the glove out of my hand, closed her umbrella, and stepped in the bus. I got on right after her. I was annoyed so I said, "If you'll pardon me, Miss, there's no law that you have to say thanks, but at least don't make a criminal out of me."

"Well, I'm sorry," she said, "but I don't like white men trying to do me favors."

I tipped my hat and that was that. In ten minutes I got off the bus but she was already gone.

15   Who expected to see her again, but I did. She came into my store about a week later for a bottle of Scotch.

"I would offer you a discount," I told her, "but I know you don't like a certain kind of a favor and I'm not looking for a slap in the face."

Then she recognized me and got a little embarrassed.

"I'm sorry I misunderstood you that day."

"So mistakes happen."

20   The result was she took the discount. I gave her a dollar off.

She used to come in every two weeks for a fifth of Haig & Haig.[5] Sometimes I waited on her, sometimes my helpers, Jimmy or Mason, also colored, but I said to give the discount. They both looked at me but I had nothing to be ashamed. In the spring when she came in we used to talk once in a while. She was a slim woman, dark, but not the most dark, about thirty years I would say, also well built, with a combination nice legs and a good-size bosom that I like. Her face was pretty, with big eyes and high cheekbones, but lips a little thick and nose a little broad. Sometimes she didn't feel like talking, she paid for the bottle, less discount, and walked out. Her eyes were tired and she didn't look to me like a happy woman.

I found out her husband was once a window cleaner on the big buildings, but one day his safety belt broke and he fell fifteen stories. After the funeral she got a job as a manicurist in a Times Square barber shop. I told her I was a bachelor and lived with my mother in a small three-room apartment on West Eighty-third near Broadway. My mother had cancer, and Ornita said she was sorry.

One night in July we went out together. How that happened I'm still not so sure. I guess I asked her and she didn't say no. Where do you go out with a Negro woman? We went to the Village. We had a good dinner and walked in Washington Square Park. It was a hot night. Nobody was surprised when they saw us, nobody looked at us like we were against the law. If they

---

[5]**Haig & Haig** a fine Scotch whisky.

looked maybe they saw my new lightweight suit that I bought yesterday and my shiny bald spot when we walked under a lamp, also how pretty she was for a man my type. We went in a movie on West Eighth Street. I didn't want to go in but she said she had heard about the picture. We went in like strangers and we came out like strangers. I wondered what was in her mind and I thought to myself, whatever is in there it's not a certain white man that I know. All night long we went together like we were chained. After the movie she wouldn't let me take her back to Harlem. When I put her in a taxi she asked me, "Why did we bother?"

For the steak, I thought of saying. Instead I said, "You're worth the bother."

25   "Thanks anyway."

Kiddo, I thought to myself after the taxi left, you just found out what's what, now the best thing is forget her.

It's easy to say. In August we went out the second time. That was the night she wore a purple dress and I thought to myself, my God, what colors. Who paints that picture paints a masterpiece. Everybody looked at us but I had pleasure. That night when she took off her dress it was in a furnished room I had the sense to rent a few days before. With my sick mother, I couldn't ask her to come to my apartment, and she didn't want me to go home with her where she lived with her brother's family on West 115th near Lenox Avenue. Under her purple dress she wore a black slip, and when she took that off she had white underwear. When she took off the white underwear she was black again. But I know where the next white was, if you want to call it white. And that was the night I think I fell in love with her, the first time in my life, though I have liked one or two nice girls I used to go with when I was a boy. It was a serious proposition. I'm the kind of a man when I think of love I'm thinking of marriage. I guess that's why I am a bachelor.

That same week I had a holdup in my place, two big men—both black—with revolvers. One got excited when I rang open the cash register so he could take the money, and he hit me over the ear with his gun. I stayed in the hospital a couple of weeks. Otherwise I was insured. Ornita came to see me. She sat on a chair without talking much. Finally I saw she was uncomfortable so I suggested she ought to go home.

"I'm sorry it happened," she said.

30   "Don't talk like it's your fault."

When I got out of the hospital my mother was dead. She was a wonderful person. My father died when I was thirteen and all by herself she kept the family alive and together. I sat shiva for a week and remembered how she sold paper bags on her pushcart. I remembered her life and what she tried to teach me. Nathan, she said, if you ever forget you are a Jew a goy[6] will remind you. Mama, I said, rest in peace on this subject. But if I do something you don't like, remember, on earth it's harder than where you are. Then when my week of mourning was finished, one night I said, "Ornita, let's get married. We're both honest people and if you love me like I love you it won't be such a bad time. If you don't like New York I'll sell out here and we'll move someplace else. Maybe to San Francisco where nobody knows

---

[6]**goy** Yiddish term (often used disparagingly) for gentile.

us. I was there for a week in the Second War and I saw white and colored
living together."

"Nat," she answered me, "I like you but I'd be afraid. My husband woulda
killed me."

"Your husband is dead."

"Not in my memory."

35   "In that case I'll wait."

"Do you know what it'd be like—I mean the life we could expect?"

"Ornita," I said, "I'm the kind of man, if he picks his own way of life he's
satisfied."

"What about children? Were you looking forward to half-Jewish polka
dots?"

"I was looking forward to children."

40   "I can't," she said.

Can't is can't. I saw she was afraid and the best thing was not to push.
Sometimes when we met she was so nervous that whatever we did she
couldn't enjoy it. At the same time I still thought I had a chance. We were together more and more. I got rid of my furnished room and she came to my
apartment—I gave away Mama's bed and bought a new one. She stayed with
me all day on Sundays. When she wasn't so nervous she was affectionate,
and if I know what love is, I had it. We went out a couple of times a week,
and the same way—usually I met her in Times Square and sent her home in
a taxi, but I talked more about marriage and she talked less against it. One
night she told me she was still trying to convince herself but she was almost
convinced. I took an inventory of my liquor stock so I could put the store up
for sale.

Ornita knew what I was doing. One day she quit her job, the next she
took it back. She also went away a week to visit her sister in Philadelphia
for a little rest. She came back tired but said maybe. Maybe is maybe so I'll
wait. The way she said it, it was closer to yes. That was the winter two years
ago. When she was in Philadelphia I called up a friend of mine from the
army, now a CPA,[7] and told him I would appreciate an invitation for an
evening. He knew why. His wife said yes right away. When Ornita came
back we went there. The wife made a fine dinner. It wasn't a bad time and
they told us to come again. Ornita had a few drinks. She looked relaxed,
wonderful. Later, because of a twenty-four-hour taxi strike I had to take her
home on the subway. When we got to the 116th Street station she told me
to go back on the train, and she would walk the couple of blocks to her
house. I didn't like a woman walking alone on the streets at that time of the
night. She said she never had any trouble but I insisted nothing doing. I said
I would walk to her stoop with her and when she went upstairs I would go
to the subway.

On the way there, on 115th in the middle of the block before Lenox, we
were stopped by three men—maybe they were boys. One had a black hat
with a half-inch brim, one a green cloth hat, and the third wore a black
leather cap. The green hat was wearing a short coat and the other two had
long ones. It was under a streetlight but the leather cap snapped a six-inch
switchblade open in the light.

---

[7]**CPA** Certified Public Accountant.

"What you doin' with this white son of a bitch?" he said to Ornita.

45   "I'm minding my own business," she answered him, "and I wish you would too."

"Boys," I said, "we're all brothers. I'm a reliable merchant in the neighborhood. This young lady in my dear friend. We don't want any trouble. Please let us pass."

"You talk like a Jew landlord," said the green hat. "Fifty a week for a single room."

"Nor charge fo' the rats," said the half-inch brim.

"Believe me, I'm no landlord. My store is Nathan's Liquors between Hundred Tenth and Eleventh. I also have two colored clerks, Mason and Jimmy, and they will tell you I pay good wages as well as I give discounts to certain customers."

50   "Shut your mouth, Jewboy," said the leather cap, and he moved the knife back and forth in front of my coat button. "No more black pussy for you."

"Speak with respect about this lady, please."

I got slapped on my mouth.

"That ain't no lady," said the long face in the half-inch brim, "that's black pussy. She deserve to have evvy bit of her hair shave off. How you like to have evvy bit of your hair shave off, black pussy?"

"Please leave me and this gentleman alone or I'm gonna scream long and loud. That's my house three doors down."

55   They slapped her. I never heard such a scream. Like her husband was falling fifteen stories.

I hit the one that slapped her and the next I knew I was laying in the gutter with a pain in my head. I thought, goodbye, Nat, they'll stab me for sure, but all they did was take my wallet and run in three directions.

Ornita walked back with me to the subway and she wouldn't let me go home with her again.

"Just get home safely."

She looked terrible. Her face was gray and I still remembered her scream. It was a terrible winter night, very cold February, and it took me an hour and ten minutes to get home. I felt bad for leaving her but what could I do?

60   We had a date downtown the next night but she didn't show up, the first time.

In the morning I called her in her place of business.

"For God's sake, Ornita, if we got married and moved away we wouldn't have the kind of trouble that we had. We wouldn't come in that neighborhood any more."

"Yes, we would. I have family there and don't want to move anyplace else. The truth of it is I can't marry you, Nat. I got troubles enough of my own."

"I coulda sworn you love me."

65   "Maybe I do but I can't marry you."

"For God's sake, why?"

"I got enough trouble of my own."

I went that night in a cab to her brother's house to see her. He was a quiet man with a thin mustache. "She gone," he said, "left for a long visit to some close relatives in the South. She said to tell you she appreciate your intentions but didn't think it will work out."

"Thank you kindly," I said.

70   Don't ask me how I got home.

Once, on Eighth Avenue, a couple of blocks from my store, I saw a blind man with a white cane tapping on the sidewalk. I figured we were going in the same direction so I took his arm.

"I can tell you're white," he said.

A heavy colored woman with a full shopping bag rushed after us.

"Never mind," she said, "I know where he live."

75   She pushed me with her shoulder and I hurt my leg on the fire hydrant. That's how it is. I give my heart and they kick me in my teeth.

"Charity Quietness—you hear me?—come out of that goddamn toilet!"

▩ TOPICS FOR CRITICAL THINKING AND WRITING

1. Do you like Nat Lime? What in particular do you like about him? What is Malamud's attitude toward Nat?

2. What does the narrator mean when he says at the end of the first paragraph, "It's my fate with colored people"?

3. In the second paragraph, what does the narrator mean when he says, "I've tried more than once but the language of the heart is either a dead language or else nobody understands it the way you speak it"? Does the story as a whole support this view? Please explain, citing evidence in the text.

4. Is Nat foolish to imagine that he and Ornita could marry? Is the confrontation on the street with the three men intended to show Nat and Ornita should *not* marry—that there is too much hostility between many whites (especially, in this instance, Jews) and African-Americans? Or do you interpret this episode differently?

5. Why does Malamud begin and end the story with scenes involving Charity Quietness?

6. One scholar has stated that Malamud's point in this story is that efforts at integration are "hopeless." Do you agree? Do you think that Malamud's story is dated (it was first published in 1963), or does it remain relevant to our understanding of relationships among ethnic and racial groups?

OSCAR CASARES

Oscar Casares, born and raised in Brownsville, Texas, and now a resident of San Antonio, is a graduate of the Iowa Writers' Workshop. He has published widely and received numerous prizes, including the James Michener Award. We reprint a story from his collection, Brownsville Stories *(2003).*

Yolanda   [2003]

When I can't sleep at night I think of Yolanda Castro. She was a woman who lived next door to us one summer when I was growing up. I've never told Maggie about her because it's not something she'd appreciate knowing.

Trust me. Tonight, like most nights, she fell asleep before I was even done brushing my teeth. And now all I can hear are little snores. Sometimes she even talks to herself, shouts out other people's names, and then in the morning says she can't remember any of it. Either way, I let her go on sleeping. She's over on her side of the bed. It's right where she ought to be. This thing with Yolanda doesn't really concern her.

I was only twelve years old when Frank and Yolanda Castro moved into the beige house with green trim. Frank pulled up on our street in a U-Haul he'd driven all the way from California to Texas. I remember it being a different neighborhood back then. Everybody knew everybody, and people left their doors unlocked at night. You didn't worry about people stealing shit you didn't lock up. I'm talking about more than twenty years ago now. I'm talking about before some drunk spent all afternoon in one of the cantinas on Fourteenth Street, then drove his car straight into the Rivas front yard and ran over the Baby Jesus that was still lying in the manger because Lonny Rivas was too flojo[1] to put it away a month after Christmas, and then the guy tried to run, but fell down, asleep, in our yard, and when the cops were handcuffing him all he could say was *ma-ri-juan-a*, which even then, at the age of fifteen, I knew wasn't a good thing to say when you were being arrested. This was before Pete Zuniga was riding his brand-new ten-speed from Western Auto and, next to the Friendship Garden, saw a white dude who'd been knifed a couple of dozen times and was floating in the green water of the resaca.[2] Before some crazy woman hired a curandera[3] to put a spell on her daughter's ex-boyfriend, which really meant hiring a couple of hit men from Matamoros to do a drive-by. Before the cops ever had to show up at El Disco de Oro Tortillería. Like holding up a 7-Eleven was getting old, right? You know, when you could sit at the Brownsville Coffee Shop #1 and not worry about getting it in the back while you ate your menudo.[4] When you didn't have to put an alarm *and* the Club on your car so it wouldn't end up in Reynosa. Before my father had to put iron bars on the windows and doors because some future convict from the junior high was always breaking into the house. And before my father had to put a fence in the front because, in his words, I'm sick and tired of all those damn dogs making poo in my yard. I guess what I'm trying to say is, things were different back then.

Frank Castro was an older man, in his fifties by that point, and Yolanda couldn't have been more than thirty, if that. My mother got along with Yolanda okay and even helped her get a job at the HEB store where she had worked since before I was born. You could say that was where the problems started, because Frank Castro didn't want his wife working at HEB, or any other place for that matter. You have no business being in that grocery store, I heard him yell one night when I was trying to fall asleep. I could hear almost everything Frank yelled that summer. Our houses were only a few yards apart, and my window was the closest to the action. My father's bougainvilleas were the dividing line between the two properties. I heard Yolanda beg Frank to please let her take the job. I heard Frank yell something in Spanish about how no woman in his family had ever worked behind a cosmetics counter, selling lipstick. I heard her promise she'd only work part-time, and she'd quit if they ever scheduled her on nights or weekends. I

---

[1]**flojo** weak-willed.   [2]**resaca** dry streambed.   [3]**curandera** mid-wife.   [4]**menudo** tripe soup.

heard her tell him how much she loved him and how she'd never take a job that would keep them apart. Francisco, tú eres mi vida,[5] she said to him. I heard him get real quiet. Then I heard Frank and Yolanda Castro making love. I didn't know what making love sounded like back then, but I can tell you now that's what it was.

If you saw what Yolanda looked like, you might not have blamed Frank for not wanting her to leave the house. It also wouldn't have been a big mystery to you how she went into the store applying for a job in the meat department and ended up getting one in cosmetics. The only girl I'd ever seen that even came close to being as beautiful as Yolanda was in a *Playboy* I found under my parents' bed the summer before. The girl in the magazine had the same long black hair, light brown skin, and green eyes that Yolanda did, only she was sitting bareback on an Appaloosa.

5   The thing I remember most about Frank was his huge forearms. They were like Popeye's, except with a lot more black and gray hair mixed in. But the hair on his arms was just the beginning. There wasn't a time I saw the guy that he didn't look like he could've used a good shave. And it didn't help that his thick eyebrows were connected into one long eyebrow that stretched across the bottom of his forehead like a piece of electrical tape. He was average size, but he looked short and squatty when he stood next to Yolanda. Frank was a mechanic at the airport and, according to my father, probably made good money. I was with my father the first time he met Frank. He always made it a point to meet any new neighbors and then come back to the house and give a full report to my mother, who would later meet the neighbors herself and say he was exaggerating about how shifty so-and-so's eyes were or how rich he thought another neighbor might be because he had one of those new foreign cars in the driveway, un carro extranjero,[6] a Toyota or a Honda. Frank was beginning to mow his front yard when we walked up. My father introduced me as his boy, and I shook our neighbor's sweaty hand. I've lived thirty-six years on this earth and never shaken hands with a bear, but I have a good idea that it wouldn't be much different from shaking Frank Castro's hand. Even his fingers needed a haircut. Frank stood there answering a couple of my father's questions about whether he liked the neighborhood (he liked it) and how long he had lived in California before moving back to Texas (ten years—he held up both hands to show us exactly how many). Suddenly, my father nodded and said we had to go. He turned around and walked off, then looked over his shoulder and yelled at me to hurry up. This whole time, Frank had not shut off his mower. My father was forced to stand there and shout over the sound of the engine. The report on Frank wasn't pretty when we got back to the house. From that point on, my father would only refer to him as El Burro.

It wasn't just my father. Nobody liked Frank. He had this thing about his yard where he didn't want anybody getting near it. We found this out one day when Lonny and I were throwing the football around in the street. Lonny was showing off and he threw the ball over my head, way over, and it landed in Frank's yard. When I was getting the ball, Frank opened the front door and yelled something about it being private property. Then he went over, turned on the hose, and started watering his yard and half the street in

---

[5]**tú . . . vida** you are my life.   [6]**carro extranjero** foreign car.

front of his yard. He did this every afternoon from that day on. The hose with a spray gun in his right hand, and a Schlitz tallboy in his left. Lonny thought we should steal the hose when Frank wasn't home, or maybe poke a few holes in it, just to teach the fucker a lesson. One Saturday morning we even saw him turn the hose on some Jehovahs who were walking up the street towards his house. A skinny man wearing a tie and short-sleeve shirt kept trying to give him a pamphlet, but Frank wasn't listening.

My mother gave Yolanda a ride to work every day. In the afternoons, Yolanda got off work early enough to be waiting for Frank to pull up in his car and drive her back to the house. My mother told us at home that Yolanda had asked Frank to teach her how to drive when they first got married but that Frank had said she was his princesa now and any place she needed to go, he'd take her. One morning, when both my mother and Yolanda had the day off, my mother asked her if she wanted to learn how to drive. They drove out by the port, and my mother pulled over so Yolanda could take the wheel. I was hanging out at the Jiffy-Mart, down the street, when I saw Yolanda driving my mother's car. Yolanda honked the horn, and they both waved at me as they turned the corner.

    That night—like a lot of nights that summer—I listened to Frank and Yolanda Castro. What they said went something like this:

    "I can show you."

10   "I don't wanna see."

    "Why not?"

    "Because you have *no* business driving a car around town."

    "But this way you don't have to pick me up every day. You can come straight home, and I'll be here already, waiting."

    "I don't care. I'm talking about you learning to drive."

15   "Frank, it's nothing."

    "You don't even have a car. What do you want with a license?"

    "I can buy one."

    "With what?"

    "I've been getting bonuses. The companies gives us a little extra if we sell more of their makeup."

20   "Is that right?"

    "It isn't that much, Frank."

    "And then?"

    "Well, maybe I can buy a used one."

    "It's because of that store."

25   "What's wrong with the store?"

    "It's putting ideas in your head."

    "Frank, what ideas?"

    "Ideas! Is there some place I haven't taken you?"

    "No."

30   "Well, then?"

    "Francisco."

    "Don't 'Francisco' me."

    "Baby . . ."

    "¡Qué no!"[7]

---

[7] **¡Qué no!** Why not?

35   They were beginning to remind me of one of my mother's novellas, which she was probably watching in the living room at that very moment. Things like that usually made me want to laugh—and I did a little, into my pillow, but it was only because I couldn't believe I was actually hearing it, and I could see Frank Castro pounding me into the ground with his big forearms if he ever found out.

"No! I said."

"I'm not Trini."

"I never said . . ."

"Then stop treating me like her. ¿No sabes qué tanto te quiero, Francisco?"[8]

40   It got quiet for a while after that. Then there was the sound of something hitting the floor, the sound of two bodies dropping on a bed with springs that had seen better days (and nights), the sound of Yolanda saying, *Ay, Diosito,*[9] over and over and over again—just like my tía[10] Hilda did the day her son, my cousin Rudy, almost drowned in the swimming pool at the Civic Center—then the sound of the bed springs making their own crazy music, and the sound of what I imagine a bear is like when he's trying to make little bears.

Yolanda kept getting a ride to work with my mother, and Frank kept bringing her home in the afternoons. My mother had offered to drive Yolanda to the DPS office and let her borrow our car for the driving part of the test, but Yolanda said she'd changed her mind and didn't want to talk about it. I heard my mother telling my father what she'd said, and they agreed it probably had something to do with Frank. El Burro, my father let out when they didn't have anything else to say.

It was the Fourth of July when I got sick that summer. I remember my mother wouldn't let me go outside with Lonny. He kept yelling at me from the street that night to stop being a baby and come out of the house so I could pop some firecrackers. We'd been talking all week about shooting some bottle rockets in the direction of Frank's house. It didn't feel like anything at first, just a fever, but the next morning we knew it was the chicken pox. My mother had to miss a few days of work, staying home with me until I got over the worst part. After that, Yolanda volunteered to come look in on me when she wasn't working. But I told my mother I didn't want her coming over when I still looked like those dead people in that *Night of the Living Dead* movie. My mother said Yolanda would understand I was sick, and if she didn't, that's what I'd get for watching those kinds of movies. So for about a week she came over in the mornings and we watched *The Price Is Right* together. Yolanda was great at guessing the prices of things, and she said it was from working in a grocery store and having a good memory. I told her I thought she should go on the show. She laughed and said she probably wouldn't win anything, since she'd be too nervous. What I meant to say was that she should go on the show and be one of the girls who stands next to the car, smiling. She was prettier than any of them, but I never told her that, because I got embarrassed whenever I thought about saying it.

---

[8]**¿No . . . Francisco?** Don't you know how much I love you, Francisco?   [9]**Ay, Diosito** Oh, God.   [10]**tía** aunt.

If Yolanda came over in the afternoon, we'd watch *General Hospital* together. She said she'd been watching it for years. There wasn't anything else on at that hour, so I didn't really care. Once, she brought over some lime sherbert, and we played Chinese checkers in my room until she had to get home to Frank Castro. Each time she left she'd reach down and give me a little kiss on the cheek, and each time her hair smelled like a different fruit. Sometimes like a pear, sometimes like a strawberry, sometimes like an apple. The strawberry was my favorite.

This was about the time when Frank said that from now on, he would take Yolanda to work in the morning—no matter how out of the way it was for him, or the fact that he and my mother were always pulling out of the driveway at the same time. A week or two went by, and then my mother told my father that Frank had started showing up at the store in the middle of the day, usually during his lunch hour, but sometimes also at two or three in the afternoon. He wouldn't talk to Yolanda, but instead just hung out by the magazine rack, pretending to read a wrestling magazine. Yolanda tried to ignore him. My mother said she had talked to her in the break room, but Yolanda kept saying it was nothing, that Frank's hours had changed at the airport.

45   There was one Saturday when he was off from work, and as usual, he spent it in his front yard, sitting in a green lawn chair, drinking tallboys. He had turned on the sprinkler and was watching his grass and half the street get a good watering. Lonny and I were throwing the football around. Frank sat in that stupid chair all afternoon. He only went in to grab another beer and, I guess, take a piss. Each time he got up and turned around, we shot him the finger.

That night, I heard Frank's voice loud and clear. He wanted answers. Something about a phone number. Something about a customer he'd seen Yolanda talking to a couple of days earlier. Did she think he was blind? What the hell was so funny when the two of them were talking? How many times? he wanted to know. ¡Desgraciado![11] Where? Goddammit! he wanted to know. What game show? ¡El sanavabiche! Something shattered against the wall and then a few seconds later Yolanda screamed. I sat up. I didn't know if I could form words if I had to. What the hell were you doing listening anyway? they would ask me. There was another scream and then the sound of the back door slamming. I looked out my window and saw Frank Castro chase Yolanda into their backyard. She was wearing a nightgown that came down to her knees. Frank had on the same khakis and muscle shirt he'd worn that afternoon. He only ran a few feet down from the back steps before his head hit the clothesline, and he fell to the ground, hard. Yolanda didn't turn to look back and ran around the right side of their house. I thought she'd gone back inside to call the police. Then I heard footsteps and a tapping on my window. It was Yolanda whispering, Open it, open it.

I didn't say anything for a long time. Yolanda had climbed in and let down the blinds. We were lying on the bed, facing the window. She was behind me, holding me tight. I finally asked her is she wanted a glass of water or some Kool-Aid. I made it myself, I told her. It's the orange kind, I said. I

---

[11]**Desgraciado** disgraceful.

didn't know what else to talk about. She said no, and then she told me to be quiet. I kept thinking, This has to be a dream and any minute now my mother's going to walk in and tell me the barbacoa[12] is sitting on the table and to come eat because we're going to eleven o'clock mass and don't even think about putting on those blue jeans with the patches in the knees ¿me entiendes?[13] But that wasn't happening, and something told me then that no matter what happened after tonight, this was something I'd never forget. There would always be a time *before* Yolanda crawled into my bed and a time *after*. As she held me, I could feel her heart beating. Then I felt her chiches[14] pressed against my back. And even though I couldn't see them, I knew they were perfect like the rest of her. I knew that they'd fit right in the palms of my hands, if only I had enough guts to turn around. Just turn around, that's all I had to do. I thought back to when she was tapping on the window, and I was sure she wasn't wearing a bra. I was sure there was nothing but Yolanda underneath her nightgown. I could have sworn I'd seen even more. I'd been close to a woman's body before. But this wasn't like when my tía Gloria came into town and couldn't believe how much I'd grown, and then she squeezed me so hard my head got lost in her huge and heavily perfumed chiches. And it wasn't anything like the Sears catalog where the girls had a tiny rose at the top of their panties. No, this was Yolanda and she was in my bed, pressed up against my back, like it was the only place in the world for us to be.

I could go on and tell you the rest of the details—how I never turned around and always regretted it, how we stayed there and listened to Frank crying in his backyard, how Lonny's dad finally called the cops on his ass, how Yolanda had a cousin pick her up the next morning, how she ended up leaving Frank for a man who worked for one of the shampoo companies, how it didn't matter because she'd also been seeing an assistant manager and would be having his baby soon enough, and how it really didn't matter because the assistant manager was already married and wasn't about to leave his wife and kids, and how, actually, none of it mattered because she'd been taking money out of the register and was about to be caught—but that's not the part of the story I like to remember.

In that bed of mine, the one with the Dallas Cowboy pillows and covers, Yolanda and I were safe. We were safe from Frank Castro and safe from anybody else that might try to hurt us. And it was safe for me to fall asleep in Yolanda's arms, with her warm, beautiful body pressed against mine, and dream that we were riding off to some faraway place on an Appaloosa.

---

[12]**barbacoa** baked lamb or goat.   [13]**me entiendes** do you understand me?
[14]**chiches** breasts.

✖ TOPICS FOR CRITICAL THINKING AND WRITING

1. Characterize the narrator. Characterize Frank.
2. In the next-to-last paragraph we learn that Yolanda has been "taking money out of the register." Did this statement surprise you? Why do you think the author included it?
3. Do you think that the narrator is or was in love with Yolanda? Explain.

MICHELE SERROS

Michele Serros, born in Oxnard, California, in 1966, published her first book of poems and stories, Chicana Falsa and Other Stories of Death, Identity and Oxnard, *while she was still a student at Santa Monica City College. We reprint a story from her second book,* How to Be a Chicana Role Model *(2000), which achieved national attention.*

Senior Picture Day

Sometimes I put two different earrings in the same ear. And that's on a day I'm feeling preppy, not really new wave or anything. One time, during a track meet over at Camarillo High, I discovered way too late that I'd forgot to put on deodorant and that was the worst 'cause everyone knows how snooty those girls at Camarillo can be. Hmmm. Actually the worst thing I've ever forgotten to do was take my pill. That happened three mornings in a row and you can bet I was praying for weeks after that.

So many things to remember when you're seventeen years old and your days start at six A.M. and sometimes don't end until five in the afternoon. But today of all days there's one thing I have to remember to do and that's to squeeze my nose. I've been doing it since the seventh grade. Every morning with my thumb and forefinger I squeeze the sides of it, firmly pressing my nostrils as close as they possibly can get near the base. Sometimes while I'm waiting for the tortilla to heat up, or just when I'm brushing my teeth, I squeeze. Nobody ever notices. Nobody ever asks. With all the other shit seniors in high school go through, squeezing my nose is nothing. It's just like some regular early-morning routine, like yawning or wiping the egg from my eyes. Okay, so you might think it's just a total waste of time, but to tell you the truth, I do see the difference. Just last week I lined up all my class pictures and could definitely see the progress. My nose has actually become smaller, narrower. It looks less Indian. *I* look less Indian and you can bet that's the main goal here. Today, when I take my graduation pictures, my nose will look just like Terri's and then I'll have the best picture in the yearbook. I think about this as Mrs. Milne's Duster comes honking in the driveway to take me to school.

Terri was my best friend in seventh grade. She came from Washington to Rio Del Valle Junior high halfway through October. She was the first girl I knew who had contact lenses and *four* pairs of Chemin de Fers. Can you believe that? She told everyone that her daddy was gonna build 'em a swimming pool for the summer. She told me that I could go over to swim anytime I wanted. But until then, she told me, I could go over and we could play on her dad's CB.[1]

"You dad's really got a CB?" I asked her.

5   "Oh, yeah," she answered, jiggling her locker door. "You can come over and we can make up handles for ourselves and meet lots of guys. Cute ones."

Whaddaya mean, handles?" I asked.

---

[1]**CB** Citizens Band (a radio frequency used by the general public to talk to one another over a short distance).

"Like names, little nicknames. I never use my real name. I'm 'G.G.' when I get on. That stands for Golden Girl. Oh, and you gotta make sure you end every sentence with 'over.' You're like a total nerd if you don't finish with 'over.' I never talk to anyone who doesn't say 'over.' They're the worst."

Nobody's really into citizen band radios anymore. I now see 'em all lined up in pawnshops over on Oxnard Boulevard. But back in the seventh grade, everyone was getting them. They were way better than using a phone 'cause, first of all, there was no phone bill to bust you for talking to boys who lived past The Grade and second, you didn't have your stupid sister yelling at you for tying up the phone line. Most people had CBs in their cars, but Terri's dad had his in the den.

When I showed up at Terri's to check out the CB, her mama was in the front yard planting some purple flowers.

10   "Go on in already." She waved me in. "She's in her father's den."

I found Terri just like her mama said. She was already on the CB, looking flustered and sorta excited.

"Hey," I called out to her, and plopped my tote bag on her dad's desk.

She didn't answer but rather motioned to me with her hands to hurry up. Her mouth formed an exaggerated, "Oh, *my* God!" She held out a glass bowl of Pringles and pointed to a glass of Dr Pepper on the desk.

It turned out Terri had found a boy on the CB. An older *interested* one. He was fifteen, a skateboarder, and his handle was Lightning Bolt.

15   "Lightning Bolt," he bragged to Terri. "Like, you know, powerful and fast. That's the way I skate. So," he continued, "where you guys live? Over."

"We live near Malibu." Terri answered. "Between Malibu and Santa Barbara. Over."

"Oh, excuse me, fan-ceee. Over."

"That's right." Terri giggled. "Over."

We actually lived in Oxnard. Really, in El Rio, a flat patch of houses, churches, and schools surrounded by lots of strawberry fields and some new snooty stucco homes surrounded by chainlink. But man, did Terri have this way of making things sound better. I mean, it *was* the truth, geographically, and besides it sounded way more glamorous.

20   I took some Pringles from the bowl and thought we were gonna have this wonderful afternoon of talking and flirting with Lightning Bolt until Terri's dad happened to come home early and found us gabbing in his den.

"What the . . . !" he yelled as soon as he walked in and saw us hunched over his CB. "What do you think this is? Party Central? Get off that thing!" He grabbed the receiver from Terri's hand. "This isn't a toy! It's a tool. A tool for communication, you don't use it just to meet boys!"

"Damn, Dad," Terri complained as she slid off her father's desk. "Don't have a cow." She took my hand and led me to her room. "Come on, let's pick you out a handle."

When we were in her room, I told her I had decided on Cali Girl as my handle.

"You mean, like California?" she asked.

25   "Yeah, sorta."

"But you're Mexican."

"So?"

"So, you look like you're more from Mexico than California."

"What do you mean?"

30   "I mean, California is like, blond girls, you know."

"Yeah, but I *am* Californian. I mean, real Californian. Even my great-grandma was born here."

"It's just that you don't look like you're from California."

"And you're not exactly golden," I snapped.

We decided to talk to Lightning Bolt the next day, Friday, right after school. Terri's dad always came home real late on Fridays, sometimes even early the next Saturday morning. It would be perfect. When I got to her house the garage door was wide open and I went in through the side door. I almost bumped into Terri's mama. She was spraying the house with Pine Scent and offered me some Hi-C.

35   "Help yourself to a Pudding Pop, too," she said before heading into the living room through a mist of aerosol. "They're in the freezer."

Man, Terri's mama made their whole life like an afternoon commercial. Hi-C, Pringles in a bowl, the whole house smelling like a pine forest. Was Terri lucky or what? I grabbed a Pudding Pop out of the freezer and was about to join her when I picked up on her laugh. She was already talking to Lightning Bolt. Dang, she didn't waste time!

"Well, maybe we don't ever want to meet you," I heard Terri flirt with Lightning Bolt. "How do you know we don't already have boyfriends? Over."

"Well, you both sound like foxes. So, uh, what *do* you look like? Over."

"I'm about five-four and have green eyes and ginger-colored hair. Over."

40   Green? Ginger? I always took Terri for having brown eyes and brown hair.

"What about your friend? Over."

"What about her? Over."

Oh, this was about me! I *had* to hear this. Terri knew how to pump up things good.

"I mean, what does she look like?" Lightning Bolt asked. "She sounds cute. Over."

45   "Well . . ." I overheard Terri hesitate. "Well, she's real skinny and, uh . . ."

"I like skinny girls!"

"You didn't let me finish!" Terri interrupted. "And you didn't say 'over.' Over."

"Sorry," Lightning Bolt said. "Go ahead and finish. Over."

I tore the wrapper off the Pudding Pop and continued to listen.

50   "Well," Terri continued. "She's also sorta flat-chested, I guess. Over."

What? How could Terri say that?

"Flat-chested? Oh yeah? Over." Lightning Bolt answered.

"Yeah. Over."

Terri paused uncomfortably. It was as if she knew what she was saying was wrong and bad and she should've stopped but couldn't. She was saying things about a friend, things a real friend shouldn't be saying about another friend, but now there was a boy involved and he was interested in that other friend, in me, and her side was losing momentum. She would have to continue to stay ahead.

55   "Yeah, and she also has this, this nose, a nose like . . . like an *Indian.* Over."

"An, Indian?" Lightning Bolt asked. "What do ya mean an Indian? Over."

"You know, *Indian.* Like powwow Indian."

"Really?" Lightning Bolt laughed on the other end. "Like Woo-Woo-Woo Indian?" He clapped his palm over his mouth and wailed. A sound I knew all too well.

"Yeah, just like that!" Terri laughed. "In fact, I think she's gonna pick 'Li'l Squaw' as her handle!"

60   I shut the refrigerator door quietly. I touched the ridge of my nose. I felt the bump my mother had promised me would be less noticeable once my face "filled out." The base of my nose was far from feminine and was broad, like, well, like Uncle Rudy's nose, Grandpa Rudy's nose, and yeah, a little bit of Uncle Vincente's nose, too. Men in my family who looked like Indians and here their Indian noses were lumped together on me, on my face. My nose made me look like I didn't belong, made me look less Californian than my blond counterparts. After hearing Terri and Lightning Bolt laugh, more than anything I hated the men in my family who had given me such a hideous nose.

I grabbed my tote bag and started to leave out through the garage door when Terri's mama called out from the living room. "You're leaving already?" she asked. "I know Terri would love to have you for dinner. Her daddy's working late again."

I didn't answer and I didn't turn around. I just walked out and went home.

And so that's how the squeezing began. I eventually stopped hanging out with Terri and never got a chance to use my handle on her dad's CB. I know it's been almost four years since she said all that stuff about me, about my nose, but man, it still stings.

65   During freshman year I heard that Terri's dad met some lady on the CB and left her mama for this other woman. Can you believe that? Who'd wanna leave a house that smelled like a pine forest and always had Pudding Pops in the freezer?

As Mrs. Milne honks from the driveway impatiently, I grab my books and run down the driveway, squeezing my nose just a little bit more. I do it because today is Senior Picture Day and because I do notice the difference. I might be too skinny. My chest might be too flat. But God forbid I look too Indian.

▨ TOPICS FOR CRITICAL THINKING AND WRITING

1. How would you characterize the narrator? Do you regard her with amusement, pity, contempt, sympathy—or all of the above, or none? Please explain.

2. Briefly recounted within this story about the narrator is another story about Terri's parents. Why do you suppose Serros included this story?

3. In your library find a book about the Maya, with illustrations of Mayan sculpture. In an essay of 250 words, describe the noses of the figures and summarize—giving credit to your source—any comments that the book makes about Mayan ideas of beauty.

11

A Collection of Short Fiction

The stories of Cain and Abel, Ruth, Samson, and Joseph in the Hebrew Bible and the parables of Jesus in the New Testament are sufficient evidence that brief narratives existed in ancient times. The short tales in Boccaccio's *Decameron* and Chaucer's *Canterbury Tales* (the latter an amazing variety of narrative poems ranging from bawdy stories to legends of saints) are medieval examples of the ancient form. But, speaking generally, short narratives before the nineteenth century were either didactic pieces, with the narrative existing for the sake of a moral point, or they were "curious and striking" tales (to use Somerset Maugham's words for his favorite kind of story) recounted in order to entertain.

The contemporary short story is rather different from both of these genres, which can be called the parable and the anecdote. Like the parable, the contemporary short story has a point, a meaning; but unlike the parable, it has a richness of surface as well as depth, so that it is interesting whether or not the reader goes on to ponder "the meaning." Like the anecdote, the short story relates a happening, but whereas the happening in the anecdote is curious and is the center of interest, the happening in the contemporary story often is less interesting in itself than as a manifestation of a character's state of mind. A good short story usually has a psychological interest that an anecdote lacks.

The anecdotal story is what "story" means for most readers. It is an interesting happening or series of happenings, usually with a somewhat surprising ending. The anecdotal story, however, is quite different from most of the contemporary short stories in this book. The anecdote is good entertainment, and good entertainment should not be lightly dismissed. But it has two elements within it that prevent it (unless it is something in addition to an anecdote) from taking a high place among the world's literature. First, it cannot be reread with increasing or even continued pleasure. Even when it is well told, once we know the happening we may lose patience with the telling. Second, effective anecdotes are often highly implausible. Now, implausible anecdotes alleged to be true have a special impact by virtue of their alleged truth: they make us say to ourselves, "Truth is stranger than fiction." But the invented anecdote lacks this power; its unlikely coincidence, its unconvincing ironic situation, its surprise ending, are both untrue and unbelievable. It is entertaining but it is usually not especially meaningful.

The short story of the last hundred and fifty years is not an anecdote and is not an abbreviated novel. If it were the latter, *Reader's Digest* condensations of novels would be short stories. But they aren't; they are only eviscerated novels. Novelists usually cover a long period of time, presenting not only a few individuals but also something of a society. They often tell of the development of several many-sided figures. In contrast, short-story writers, having only a few pages, usually focus on a single figure in a single episode, revealing a character rather than recording its development.

Whereas the novel is narrative, the contemporary short story often seems less narrative than lyric or dramatic: in the short story we have a sense of a present mood or personality revealed, rather than the sense of a history reported. The revelation in a story is presented through incidents, of course, but the interest commonly resides in the character revealed through the incidents, rather than in the incidents themselves. Little "happens," in the sense that there is little rushing from place to place. What does "happen" is usually a mental reaction to an experience, and the mental reaction, rather than the external experience, is the heart of the story. In older narratives the plot usually involves a conflict that is resolved, bringing about a change in the protagonist's condition; in contemporary stories the plot usually is designed to reveal a protagonist's state of mind. This de-emphasis of overt actions results in a kinship with the lyric and the drama.

One way of looking at the matter is to distinguish between literature of *resolution* and literature of *revelation,* that is, between (1) literature that resolves a plot (literature that stimulates us to ask, "And what happened next?" and that finally leaves us with a settled state of affairs), and (2) literature that reveals a condition (literature that causes us to say, "Ah, now I understand how these people feel"). Two great writers of the later nineteenth century can be taken as representatives of the two kinds: Guy de Maupassant (1850–1893) usually put the emphasis on resolution, Anton Chekhov (1860–1904) usually on revelation. Maupassant's tightly plotted stories move to a decisive end, ordinarily marked by a great change in fortune (usually to the characters' disadvantage). Chekhov's stories, on the other hand, seem loosely plotted and may end with the characters pretty much in the condition they were in at the start, but *we* see them more clearly, even if *they* have not achieved any self-knowledge.

A slightly different way of putting the matter is this: much of the best short fiction from Chekhov onward is less concerned with *what happens* than it is with how a character (often the narrator) *feels* about the happenings. Thus the emphasis is not on external action but on inner action, feeling. Perhaps one can say that the reader is left with a mood rather than with an awareness of a decisive happening.

The distinction between a story of resolution and a story of revelation will probably be clear enough if you are familiar with stories by Maupassant and Chekhov, but of course the distinction should not be overemphasized. These are poles; most stories exist somewhere in between, closer to one pole or the other, but not utterly apart from the more remote pole. Consider again The Parable of the Prodigal Son, in Chapter 1. Insofar as the story stimulates responses such as "The son left, *and then what happened? Did he prosper?*" it is a story of resolution. Insofar as it makes increasingly evident the unchanging love of the father, it is a story of revelation.

The de-emphasis on narrative in the contemporary short story is not an invention of the twentieth-century mind. It goes back at least to three important American writers of the early nineteenth century—Washington Irving, Nathaniel Hawthorne, and Edgar Allan Poe. In 1824 Irving wrote:

> I fancy much of what I value myself upon in writing, escapes the observation of the great mass of my readers: who are intent more upon the story than the way in which it is told. For my part I consider a story

merely as a frame on which to stretch my materials. It is the play of thought, and sentiments and language; the weaving in of characters, lightly yet expressively delineated; the familiar and faithful exhibition of scenes in common life; and the half-concealed vein of humor that is often playing through the whole—these are among what I aim at, and upon which I felicitate myself in proportion as I think I succeed.

Hawthorne and Poe may seem stranger than Irving as forebears of the contemporary short story: both are known for their fantastic narratives (and, in addition, Poe is known as the inventor of the detective story, a genre in which there is strong interest in curious happenings). But because Hawthorne's fantastic narratives are, as he said, highly allegorical, the reader's interest is pushed beyond the narrative to the moral significance. Poe's "arabesques," as he called his fanciful tales (in distinction from his detective tales of "ratiocination"), are aimed at revealing and arousing unusual mental states. The weird happenings and personages are symbolic representations of the mind or soul. In "The Cask of Amontillado," for instance, perhaps the chief interest is not in what happens but rather in the representation of an almost universal fear of being buried alive. But, it must be noted, in both Hawthorne and Poe we usually get what is commonly called the tale rather than the short story: We get short prose fiction dealing with the strange rather than the usual. (The distinction between the wondrous and the ordinary is discussed at some length in Chapter 12, "The Novel.")

A paragraph from Poe's review (1842) of Hawthorne's *Twice Told Tales,* though more useful in revealing Poe's theory of fiction than Hawthorne's, illuminates something of the kinship between the contemporary short story and the best short fictions of the earlier nineteenth century. In the review Poe has been explaining that because "unity of effect or impression" is essential, a tale (Poe doubtless uses "tale" to mean short fiction in general, rather than the special type just discussed) that can be read at a single sitting has an advantage over the novel.

> A skillful artist has constructed a tale. He has not fashioned his thoughts to accommodate his incidents, but having deliberately conceived a certain single effect to be wrought, he then invents such incidents, he then combines such events, and discusses them in such tone as may best serve him in establishing this preconceived effect. If his very first sentence tends not to be outbringing of this effect, then in his very first step has he committed a blunder. In the whole composition there should be no word written of which the tendency, direct or indirect, is not to the one pre-established design. And by such means, with such care and skill a picture is at length painted which leaves in the mind of him who contemplates it with a kindred art, a sense of the fullest satisfaction. The idea of the tale, its thesis, has been presented unblemished, because undisturbed—an end absolutely demanded, yet, in the novel, altogether unattainable.

Nothing that we have said should be construed as suggesting that short fiction from the mid-nineteenth century to the present is necessarily better than older short narratives. The object of these comments has been less to evaluate than to call attention to the characteristics dominating short fiction of the last century and a half. Not that all of this fiction is of a piece; the stories in this book demonstrate something of its variety. Readers who do not like one story need not despair; they need only (in the words of an early writer of great short fiction) "turne over the leef and chese another tale."

LEO TOLSTOY

Leo Tolstoy (1828-1910) was born into a noble family on his parents' estate near Tula, Russia. Orphaned early, he was brought up by aunts and privately tutored. For a while he studied law at the University of Kazan, but he left without a degree and returned to his estate, where he made some unsuccessful efforts at educating the serfs. He then went to St. Petersburg and later to Moscow, where for a while he lived the life of a rake. While serving in the army (1851-1855) he wrote his first book, an autobiographical work called Childhood *(1852). After leaving the military Tolstoy shuttled between St. Petersburg and the family estate. His diary records his unhappiness with the loose life he was living. He then set up a school for peasants, which was unsuccessful. In 1862 he married, but his abundant infidelities made the marriage unhappy. During this period he wrote* War and Peace *(1869)—a prose epic on Napoleon's 1812 invasion of Russia—and* Anna Karenina *(1877), a novel about a woman tragically destroyed by her faith in romantic love.*

About 1876 Tolstoy began a reexamination of his life, which led to a conversion to the Christian doctrine of love and to a doctrine of nonresistance to evil. Obsessed with trying to live a simple and saintly life, he decided to leave his family, intending to enter a monastery. His journey ended in the waiting room of a nearby railway station where he was fatally stricken. According to one report, as Tolstoy lay dying on the station master's couch, he whispered these last words to his son: "I love Truth . . . very much. . . . I love Truth." Another version of his last words: "I wonder how a peasant would die."

Yet another quotation, this one setting forth his view of the qualities of a writer, is of special interest. Tolstoy said that his brother Nicholas

> *was a wonderful boy, and later a wonderful man. Turgenev used to say of him, very truly, that he lacked only certain faults to be a great writer. He lacked the chief fault necessary for authorship—vanity— and was not at all interested in what people thought of him. The qualities of a writer that he possessed were, first of all, a fine artistic sense, an extremely developed sense of proportion, a good-natured, gay sense of humor, an extraordinary, inexhaustible imagination, and a truthful and highly moral view of life.*

The Death of Ivan Ilych   [1886]

Translated by Louise and Aylmer Maude

I

During an interval in the Melvinski trial in the large building of the Law Courts, the members and public prosecutor met in Ivan Egorovich Shebek's private room, where the conversation turned on the celebrated Krasovski case. Fëdor Vasilievich warmly maintained that it was not subject to their jurisdiction, Ivan Egorovich maintained the contrary, while Peter Ivanovich, not having entered into the discussion at the start, took no part in it but looked through the *Gazette* which had just been handed in.

"Gentlemen," he said, "Ivan Ilych has died!"

"You don't say so!"

"Here, read it yourself," replied Peter Ivanovich, handing Fëdor Vasilievich the paper still damp from the press. Surrounded by a black border were the words: "Praskovya Fëdorovna Golovina, with profound sorrow, informs relatives and friends of the demise of her beloved husband Ivan Ilych Golovin, Member of the Court of Justice, which occurred on February the 4th of this year 1882. The funeral will take place on Friday at one o'clock in the afternoon."

5   Ivan Ilych had been a colleague of the gentlemen present and was liked by them all. He had been ill for some weeks with an illness said to be incurable. His post had been kept open for him, but there had been conjectures that in case of his death Alexeev might receive his appointment, and that either Vinnikov or Shtabel would succeed Alexeev. So on receiving the news of Ivan Ilych's death the first thought of each of the gentlemen in that private room was of the changes and promotions it might occasion among themselves or their acquaintances.

"I shall be sure to get Shtabel's place or Vinnikov's," thought Fëdor Vasilievich. "I was promised that long ago, and the promotion means an extra eight hundred rubles a year for me besides the allowance."

"Now I must apply for my brother-in-law's transfer from Kaluga," thought Peter Ivanovich. "My wife will be very glad, and then she won't be able to say that I never do anything for her relations."

"I thought he would never leave his bed again," said Peter Ivanovich aloud. "It's very sad."

"But what really was the matter with him?"

10   "The doctors couldn't say—at least they could, but each of them said something different. When last I saw him I thought he was getting better."

"And I haven't been to see him since the holidays. I always meant to go."

"Had he any property?"

"I think his wife had a little—but something quite trifling."

"We shall have to go to see her, but they live so terribly far away."

15   "Far away from you, you mean. Everything's far away from your place."

"You see, he never can forgive my living on the other side of the river," said Peter Ivanovich, smiling at Shebek. Then, still talking of the distances between different parts of the city, they returned to the Court.

Besides considerations as to the possible transfers and promotions likely to result from Ivan Ilych's death, the mere fact of the death of a near acquaintance aroused, as usual, in all who heard of it the complacent feeling that "it is he who is dead and not I."

Each one thought or felt, "Well, he's dead but I'm alive!" But the more intimate of Ivan Ilych's acquaintances, his so-called friends, could not help thinking also that they would now have to fulfill the very tiresome demands of propriety by attending the funeral service and paying a visit of condolence to the widow.

Fëdor Vasilievich and Peter Ivanovich had been his nearest acquaintances. Peter Ivanovich had studied law with Ivan Ilych and had considered himself to be under obligations to him.

20   Having told his wife at dinner-time of Ivan Ilych's death and of his conjecture that it might be possible to get her brother transferred to their circuit, Peter Ivanovich sacrificed his usual nap, put on his evening clothes, and drove to Ivan Ilych's house.

At the entrance stood a carriage and two cabs. Leaning against the wall in the hall downstairs near the cloak-stand was a coffin-lid covered with cloth of gold, ornamented with gold cord and tassels, that had been polished up with metal powder. Two ladies in black were taking off their fur cloaks. Peter Ivanovich recognized one of them as Ivan Ilych's sister, but the other was a stranger to him. His colleague Schwartz was just coming downstairs, but on seeing Peter Ivanovich enter he stopped and winked at him, as if to say: "Ivan Ilych has made a mess of things—not like you and me."

Schwartz's face with his Piccadilly whiskers[1] and his slim figure in evening dress, had as usual an air of elegant solemnity which contrasted with the playfulness of his character and had a special piquancy here, or so it seemed to Peter Ivanovich.

Peter Ivanovich allowed the ladies to precede him and slowly followed them upstairs. Schwartz did not come down but remained where he was, and Peter Ivanovich understood that he wanted to arrange where they should play bridge that evening. The ladies went upstairs to the widow's room, and Schwartz with seriously compressed lips but a playful look in his eyes, indicated by a twist of his eyebrows the room to the right where the body lay.

Peter Ivanovich, like everyone else on such occasions, entered feeling uncertain what he would have to do. All he knew was that at such times it is always safe to cross oneself. But he was not quite sure whether one should make obeisances while doing so. He therefore adopted a middle course. On entering the room he began crossing himself and made a slight movement resembling a bow. At the same time, as far as the motion of his head and arm allowed, he surveyed the room. Two young men—apparently nephews, one of whom was a high-school pupil—were leaving the room, crossing themselves as they did so. An old woman was standing motionless, and a lady with strangely arched eyebrows was saying something to her in a whisper. A vigorous, resolute Church Reader, in a frock-coat, was reading something in a loud voice with an expression that precluded any contradiction. The butler's assistant, Gerasim, stepping lightly in front of Peter Ivanovich, was strewing something on the floor. Noticing this, Peter Ivanovich was immediately aware of a faint odor of a decomposing body.

25   The last time he had called on Ivan Ilych, Peter Ivanovich had seen Gerasim in the study. Ivan Ilych had been particularly fond of him and he was performing the duty of a sick nurse.

Peter Ivanovich continued to make the sign of the cross, slightly inclining his head in an intermediate direction between the coffin, the Reader, and the icons[2] on the table in a corner of the room. Afterwards, when it seemed to him that this movement of his arm in crossing himself had gone on too long, he stopped and began to look at the corpse.

The dead man lay, as dead men always lie, in a specially heavy way, his rigid limbs sunk in the soft cushions of the coffin, with the head forever bowed on the pillow. His yellow waxen brow with bald patches over his sunken temples was thrust up in the way peculiar to the dead, the protruding nose seeming to press on the upper lip. He was much changed and had

---

[1]**Piccadilly whiskers** English-style sideburns.   [2]**icons** religious images, usually painted on small wooden panels.

grown even thinner since Peter Ivanovich had last seen him, but, as is always the case with the dead, his face was handsomer and above all more dignified than when he was alive. The expression on his face said that what was necessary had been accomplished, and accomplished rightly. Besides this there was in that expression a reproach and a warning to the living. This warning seemed to Peter Ivanovich out of place, or at least not applicable to him. He felt a certain discomfort and so he hurriedly crossed himself once more and turned and went out the door—too hurriedly and too regardless of propriety, as he himself was aware.

Schwartz was waiting for him in the adjoining room with legs spread wide apart and both hands toying with his top-hat behind his back. The mere sight of that playful, well-groomed, and elegant figure refreshed Peter Ivanovich. He felt that Schwartz was above all these happenings and would not surrender to any depressing influences. His very look said that this incident of a church service for Ivan Ilych could not be a sufficient reason for infringing the order of the session—in other words, that it would certainly not prevent his unwrapping a new pack of cards and shuffling them that evening while a footman placed four fresh candles on the table: in fact, that there was no reason for supposing that this incident would hinder their spending the evening agreeably. Indeed he said this in a whisper as Peter Ivanovich passed him, proposing that they should meet for a game at Fëdor Vasilievich's. But apparently Peter Ivanovich was not destined to play bridge that evening. Praskovya Fëdorovna (a short, fat woman who despite all efforts to the contrary had continued to broaden steadily from her shoulders downwards and who had the same extraordinarily arched eyebrows as the lady who had been standing by the coffin), dressed all in black, her head covered with lace, came out of her own room with some other ladies, conducted them to the room where the dead body lay, and said: "The service will begin immediately. Please go in."

Schwartz, making an indefinite bow, stood still, evidently neither accepting nor declining this invitation. Praskovya Fëdorovna, recognizing Peter Ivanovich, sighed, went close up to him, took his hand, and said: "I know you were a true friend of Ivan Ilych . . ." and looked at him awaiting some suitable response. And Peter Ivanovich knew that, just as it had been the right thing to cross himself in that room, so what he had to do here was to press her hand, sigh, and say, "Believe me. . . ." So he did all this and as he did it felt that the desired result had been achieved: that both he and she were touched.

30   "Come with me. I want to speak to you before it begins," said the widow. "Give me your arm."

Peter Ivanovich gave her his arm and they went to the inner rooms, passing Schwartz, who winked at Peter Ivanovich compassionately.

"That does for our bridge! Don't object if we find another player. Perhaps you can cut in when you do escape," said his playful look.

Peter Ivanovich sighed still more deeply and despondently, and Praskovya Fëdorovna pressed his arm gratefully. When they reached the drawing-room, upholstered in pink cretonne and lighted by a dim lamp, they sat down at the table—she on a sofa and Peter Ivanovich on a low pouffe, the springs of which yielded spasmodically under his weight. Praskovya Fëdorovna had been on the point of warning him to take another seat, but felt that such a warning was out of keeping with her present condition and so changed her mind. As he sat down on the pouffe Peter

Ivanovich recalled how Ivan Ilych had arranged this room and had consulted him regarding this pink cretonne with green leaves. The whole room was full of furniture and knick-knacks, and on her way to the sofa the lace of the widow's black shawl caught on the carved edge of the table. Peter Ivanovich rose to detach it, and the springs of the pouffe, relieved of his weight, rose also and gave him a push. The widow began detaching her shawl herself, and Peter Ivanovich again sat down, suppressing the rebellious springs of the pouffe under him. But the widow had not quite freed herself and Peter Ivanovich got up again, and again the pouffe rebelled and even creaked. When this was all over she took out a clean cambric handkerchief and began to weep. The episode with the shawl and the struggle with the pouffe had cooled Peter Ivanovich's emotions and he sat there with a sullen look on his face. This awkward situation was interrupted by Sokolov, Ivan Ilych's butler, who came to report that the plot in the cemetery that Praskovya Fëdorovna had chosen would cost two hundred rubles. She stopped weeping and, looking at Peter Ivanovich with the air of a victim, remarked in French that it was very hard for her. Peter Ivanovich made a silent gesture signifying his full conviction that it must indeed be so.

"Please smoke," she said in a magnanimous yet crushed voice, and turned to discuss with Sokolov the price of the plot for the grave.

35   Peter Ivanovich while lighting his cigarette heard her inquiring very circumstantially into the price of different plots in the cemetery and finally decided which she would take. When that was done she gave instructions about engaging the choir. Sokolov then left the room.

"I look after everything myself," she told Peter Ivanovich, shifting the albums that lay on the table; and noticing that the table was endangered by his cigarette-ash, she immediately passed him an ashtray, saying as she did so: "I consider it an affectation to say that my grief prevents my attending to practical affairs. On the contrary, if anything can—I won't say console me, but—distract me, it is seeing to everything concerning him." She again took out her handkerchief as if preparing to cry, but suddenly, as if mastering her feeling, she shook herself and began to speak calmly. "But there is something I want to talk to you about."

Peter Ivanovich bowed, keeping control of the springs of the pouffe, which immediately began quivering under him.

"He suffered terribly the last few days."

"Did he?" said Peter Ivanovich.

40   "Oh, terribly! He screamed unceasingly, not for minutes but for hours. For the last three days he screamed incessantly. It was unendurable. I cannot understand how I bore it; you could hear him three rooms off. Oh, what I have suffered!"

"Is it possible that he was conscious all that time?" asked Peter Ivanovich.

"Yes," she whispered. "To the last moment. He took leave of us a quarter of an hour before he died, and asked us to take Vasya away."

The thought of the sufferings of this man he had known so intimately, first as a merry little boy, then as a school-mate, and later as a grown-up colleague, suddenly struck Peter Ivanovich with horror, despite an unpleasant consciousness of his own and this woman's dissimulation. He again saw that brow, and that nose pressing down on the lip, and felt afraid for himself.

"Three days of frightful suffering and then death! Why, that might suddenly, at any time, happen to me," he thought, and for a moment felt terrified.

But—he did not himself know how—the customary reflection at once occurred to him that this had happened to Ivan Ilych and not to him, and that it
should not and could not happen to him, and that to think that it could would
be yielding to depression which he ought not to do, as Schwartz's expression
plainly showed. After which reflection Peter Ivanovich felt reassured, and began to ask with interest about the details of Ivan Ilych's death, as though
death was an accident natural to Ivan Ilych but certainly not to himself.

45   After many details of the really dreadful physical sufferings Ivan Ilych
had endured (which details he learnt only from the effect those sufferings
had produced on Praskovya Fëdorovna's nerves) the widow apparently
found it necessary to get to business.

"Oh, Peter Ivanovich, how hard it is! How terribly, terribly hard!" and
she again began to weep.

Peter Ivanovich sighed and waited for her to finish blowing her nose.
When she had done so he said, "Believe me . . ." and she again began talking and brought out what was evidently her chief concern with him—
namely, to question him as to how she could obtain a grant of money from
the government on the occasion of her husband's death. She made it appear
that she was asking Peter Ivanovich's advice about her pension, but he soon
saw that she already knew about that to the minutest detail, more even
than he did himself. She knew how much could be got out of the government in consequence of her husband's death, but wanted to find out
whether she could not possibly extract something more. Peter Ivanovich
tried to think of some means of doing so, but after reflecting for a while and,
out of propriety, condemning the government for its niggardliness, he said
he thought that nothing more could be got. Then she sighed and evidently
began to devise means of getting rid of her visitor. Noticing this, he put out
his cigarette, rose, pressed her hand, and went out into the anteroom.

In the dining-room where the clock stood that Ivan Ilych had liked so
much and had bought at an antique shop, Peter Ivanovich met a priest and
a few acquaintances who had come to attend the service, and he recognized Ivan Ilych's daughter, a handsome young woman. She was in black
and her slim figure appeared slimmer than ever. She had a gloomy, determined, almost angry expression, and bowed to Peter Ivanovich as though
he were in some way to blame. Behind her, with the same offended look,
stood a wealthy young man, an examining magistrate, whom Peter
Ivanovich also knew and who was her fiancé, as he had heard. He bowed
mournfully to them and was about to pass into the death-chamber, when
from under the stairs appeared the figure of Ivan Ilych's schoolboy son,
who was extremely like his father. He seemed a little Ivan Ilych, such as
Peter Ivanovich remembered when they studied law together. His tear-
stained eyes had in them the look that is seen in the eyes of boys of thirteen or fourteen who are not pure-minded. When he saw Peter Ivanovich
he scowled morosely and shamefacedly. Peter Ivanovich nodded to him
and entered the death-chamber. The service began: candles, groans, incense, tears, and sobs. Peter Ivanovich stood looking gloomily down at his
feet. He did not look once at the dead man, did not yield to any depressing
influence, and was one of the first to leave the room. There was no one in
the anteroom, but Gerasim darted out of the dead man's room, rummaged
with his strong hands among the fur coats to find Peter Ivanovich's, and
helped him on with it.

"Well, friend Gerasim," said Peter Ivanovich, so as to say something. "It's a sad affair, isn't it?"

50   "It's God's will. We shall all come to it some day," said Gerasim, displaying his teeth—the even, white teeth of a healthy peasant—and, like a man in the thick of urgent work, he briskly opened the front door, called the coachman, helped Peter Ivanovich into the sledge, and sprang back to the porch as if in readiness for what he had to do next.

Peter Ivanovich found the fresh air particularly pleasant after the smell of incense, the dead body, and carbolic acid.

"Where to, sir?" asked the coachman.

"It's not too late even now . . . . I'll call round on Fëdor Vasilievich."

He accordingly drove there and found them just finishing the first rubber, so that it was quite convenient for him to cut in.

II

55   Ivan Ilych's life had been most simple and most ordinary and therefore most terrible.

He had been a member of the Court of Justice, and died at the age of forty-five. His father had been an official who after serving in various ministries and departments in Petersburg[3] had made the sort of career which brings men to positions from which by reason of their long service they cannot be dismissed, though they are obviously unfit to hold any responsible position, and for whom therefore posts are specially created, which though fictitious carry salaries of from six to ten thousand rubles that are not fictitious, and in receipt of which they live on to a great age.

Such was the Privy Councillor and superfluous member of various superfluous institutions, Ilya Epimovich Golovin.

He had three sons, of whom Ivan Ilych was the second. The eldest son was following in his father's footsteps only in another department, and was already approaching that stage in the service at which a similar sinecure would be reached. The third son was a failure. He had ruined his prospects in a number of positions and was now serving in the railway department. His father and brothers, and still more their wives, not merely disliked meeting him, but avoided remembering his existence unless compelled to do so. His sister had married Baron Greff, a Petersburg official of her father's type. Ivan Ilych was *le phénix de la famille*[4] as people said. He was neither as cold and formal as his elder brother nor as wild as the younger, but was a happy mean between them—an intelligent, polished, lively, and agreeable man. He had studied with his younger brother at the School of Law, but the latter had failed to complete the course and was expelled when he was in the fifth class. Ivan Ilych finished the course well. Even when he was at the School of Law he was just what he remained for the rest of his life: a capable, cheerful, good-natured, and sociable man, though strict in the fulfillment of what he considered to be his duty, and he considered his duty, to be what was so considered by those in authority. Neither as a boy nor as a

[3]**Petersburg** the capital of Russia and its social and intellectual center from the eighteenth century until 1918. It was named for Peter the Great, who built it.   [4]*le phénix de la famille* French (members of the upper class often spoke French, a sign of their sophistication), literally meaning "the phoenix of the family" (i.e., the prodigy of the family).

man was he a toady, but from early youth was by nature attracted to people of high station as a fly is drawn to the light, assimilating their ways and views of life and establishing friendly relations with them. All the enthusiasms of childhood and youth passed without leaving much trace on him; he succumbed to sensuality, to vanity, and latterly among the highest classes to liberalism, but always within limits which his instinct unfailingly indicated to him as correct.

At school he had done things which had formerly seemed to him very horrid and made him feel disgusted with himself when he did them; but when later on he saw that such actions were done by people of good position and that they did not regard them as wrong, he was able not exactly to regard them as right, but to forget about them entirely or not be at all troubled at remembering them.

60   Having graduated from the School of Law and qualified for the tenth rank of the civil service, and having received money from his father for his equipment, Ivan Ilych ordered himself clothes at Scharmer's, the fashionable tailor, hung a medallion inscribed *respice finem*[5] on his watch-chain, took leave of his professor and the prince who was patron of the school, had a farewell dinner with his comrades at Donon's first-class restaurant, and with his new and fashionable portmanteau, linen, clothes, shaving and other toilet appliances, and a traveling rug, all purchased at the best shops, he set off for one of the provinces where, through his father's influence, he had been attached to the Governor as an official for special service.

In the province Ivan Ilych soon arranged as easy and agreeable a position for himself as he had had at the School of Law. He performed his official tasks, made his career, and at the same time amused himself pleasantly and decorously. Occasionally he paid official visits to country districts, where he behaved with dignity both to his superiors and inferiors, and performed the duties entrusted to him, which related chiefly to the sectarians,[6] with an exactness and incorruptible honesty of which he could not but feel proud.

In official matters, despite his youth and taste for frivolous gaiety, he was exceedingly reserved, punctilious, and even severe; but in society he was often amusing and witty, and always good-natured, correct in his manner, and *bon enfant*,[7] as the governor and his wife—with whom he was like one of the family—used to say of him.

In the province he had an affair with a lady who made advances to the elegant young lawyer, and there was also a milliner; and there were carousals with aides-de-camp who visited the district, and after-supper visits to a certain outlying street of doubtful reputation; and there was too some obsequiousness to his chief and even to his chief's wife, but all this was done with such a tone of good breeding that no hard names could be applied to it. It all came under the heading of the French saying: *"Il faut que jeunesse se passe."*[8] It was all done with clean hands, in clean linen, with French phrases, and above all among people of the best society and consequently with the approval of people of rank.

---

[5]*respice finem* Latin, "Consider the end" (i.e., keep death in mind).   [6]**sectarians** Old Believers, a sect that in the seventeenth century had broken with the Orthodox Church.   [7]*bon enfant* French, literally "good child," here "well-behaved."   [8]*Il faut que jeunesse se passe* French, "Youth will have its fling."

So Ivan Ilych served for five years and then came a change in his official life. The new and reformed judicial institutions were introduced, and new men were needed. Ivan Ilych became such a new man. He was offered the post of examining magistrate, and he accepted it though the post was in another province and obliged him to give up the connections he had formed and to make new ones. His friends met to give him a send-off; they had a group-photograph taken and presented him with a silver cigarette-case, and he set off to his new post.

65   As examining magistrate Ivan Ilych was just as *comme il faut*⁹ and decorous a man, inspiring general respect and capable of separating his official duties from his private life, as he had been when acting as an official on special service. His duties now as examining magistrate were far more interesting and attractive than before. In his former position it had been pleasant to wear an undress uniform made by Scharmer, and to pass through the crowd of petitioners and officials who were timorously awaiting an audience with the governor, and who envied him as with free and easy gait he went straight into his chief's private room to have a cup of tea and a cigarette with him. But not many people had been directly dependent on him—only police officials and the sectarians when he went on special missions—and he liked to treat them politely, almost as comrades, as if he were letting them feel that he who had the power to crush them was treating them in this simple, friendly way. There were then but few such people. But now, as an examining magistrate, Ivan Ilych felt that everyone without exception, even the most important and self-satisfied, was in his power, and that he need only write a few words on a sheet of paper with a certain heading, and this or that important, self-satisfied person would be brought before him in the role of an accused person or a witness, and if he did not choose to allow him to sit down, would have to stand before him and answer his questions. Ivan Ilych never abused his power; he tried on the contrary to soften its expression, but the consciousness of it and of the possibility of softening its effect, supplied the chief interest and attraction of his office. In his work itself, especially in his examinations, he very soon acquired a method of eliminating all considerations irrelevant to the legal aspect of the case, and reducing even the most complicated case to a form in which it would be presented on paper only in its externals, completely excluding his personal opinion of the matter, while above all observing every prescribed formality. The work was new and Ivan Ilych was one of the first men to apply the new Code of 1864.¹⁰

On taking up the post of examining magistrate in a new town, he made new acquaintances and connections, placed himself on a new footing, and assumed a somewhat different tone. He took up an attitude of rather dignified aloofness towards the provincial authorities, but picked out the best circle of legal gentlemen and wealthy gentry living in the town and assumed a tone of slight dissatisfaction with the government, of moderate liberalism, and of enlightened citizenship. At the same time, without at all altering the elegance of his toilet, he ceased shaving his chin and allowed his beard to grow as it pleased.

Ivan Ilych settled down very pleasantly in this new town. The society there, which inclined towards opposition to the governor, was friendly, his

---

⁹*comme il faut* French, "proper."   ¹⁰**Code of 1864** body of statutes governing judicial processes.

salary was larger, and he began to play *vint*,[11] which he found added not a little to the pleasure of life, for he had a capacity for cards, played good-humoredly, and calculated rapidly and astutely, so that he usually won.

After living there for two years he met his future wife, Praskovya Fëdorovna Mikhel, who was the most attractive, clever, and brilliant girl of the set in which he moved, and among other amusements and relaxations from his labors as examining magistrate, Ivan Ilych established light and playful relations with her.

While he had been an official on special service he had been accustomed to dance, but now as an examining magistrate it was exceptional for him to do so. If he danced now, he did it as if to show that though he served under the reformed order of things, and had reached the fifth official rank, yet when it came to dancing he could do it better than most people. So at the end of an evening he sometimes danced with Praskovya Fëdorovna, and it was chiefly during these dances that he captivated her. She fell in love with him. Ivan Ilych had at first no definite intention of marrying, but when the girl fell in love with him he said to himself: "Really, why shouldn't I marry?"

70   Praskovya Fëdorovna came of a good family, was not bad-looking, and had some little property. Ivan Ilych might have aspired to a more brilliant match, but even this was good. He had his salary, and she, he hoped, would have an equal income. She was well connected, and was a sweet, pretty, and thoroughly correct young woman. To say that Ivan Ilych married because he fell in love with Praskovya Fëdorovna and found that she sympathized with his views of life would be as incorrect as to say that he married because his social circle approved of the match. He was swayed by both these considerations: the marriage gave him personal satisfaction, and at the same time it was considered the right thing by the most highly placed of his associates.

So Ivan Ilych got married.

The preparations for marriage and the beginning of married life, with its conjugal caresses, the new furniture, new crockery, and new linen, were very pleasant until his wife became pregnant—so that Ivan Ilych had begun to think that marriage would not impair the easy, agreeable, gay, and always decorous character of his life, approved of by society and regarded by himself as natural, but would even improve it. But from the first months of his wife's pregnancy, something new, unpleasant, depressing, and unseemly, and from which there was no way of escape, unexpectedly showed itself.

His wife, without any reason—*de gaieté de coeur*[12] as Ivan Ilych expressed it to himself—began to disturb the pleasure and propriety of their life. She began to be jealous without any cause, expected him to devote his whole attention to her, found fault with everything, and made coarse and ill-mannered scenes.

At first Ivan Ilych hoped to escape from the unpleasantness of this state of affairs by the same easy and decorous relation to life that had served him heretofore: he tried to ignore his wife's disagreeable moods, continued to live in his usual easy and pleasant way, invited friends to his house for a game of cards, and also tried going out to his club or spending his evenings with friends. But one day his wife began upbraiding him so vigorously, using such coarse words, and continued to abuse him every time he did not

___
[11]*vint* a card game similar to bridge.   [12]*de gaieté de coeur* French, "from sheer whim."

fulfill her demands, so resolutely and with such evident determination not to give way till he submitted—that is, till he stayed at home and was bored just as she was—that he became alarmed. He now realized that matrimony—at any rate with Praskovya Fëdorovna—was not always conducive to the pleasures and amenities of life, but on the contrary often infringed both comfort and propriety, and that he must therefore entrench himself against such infringement. And Ivan Ilych began to seek for means of doing so. His official duties were the one thing that imposed upon Praskovya Fëdorovna, and by means of his official work and the duties attached to it he began struggling with his wife to secure his own independence.

75   With the birth of their child, the attempts to feed it and the various failures in doing so, and with the real and imaginary illnesses of mother and child, in which Ivan Ilych's sympathy was demanded but about which he understood nothing, the need of securing for himself an existence outside his family life became still more imperative.

As his wife grew more irritable and exacting and Ivan Ilych transferred the center of gravity of his life more and more to his official work so did he grow to like his work better and became more ambitious than before.

Very soon, within a year of his wedding, Ivan Ilych had realized that marriage, though it may add some comforts to life, is in fact a very intricate and difficult affair towards which in order to perform one's duty, that is, to lead a decorous life approved of by society, one must adopt a definite attitude just as towards one's official duties.

And Ivan Ilych evolved such an attitude towards married life. He only required of it those conveniences—dinner at home, housewife, and bed—which it could give him, and above all that propriety of external forms required by public opinion. For the rest he looked for light-hearted pleasure and propriety, and was very thankful when he found them, but if he met with antagonism and querulousness he at once retired into his separate fenced-off world of official duties, where he found satisfaction.

Ivan Ilych was esteemed a good official, and after three years was made Assistant Public Prosecutor. His new duties, their importance, the possibility of indicting and imprisoning anyone he chose, the publicity his speeches received, and the success he had in all these things made his work still more attractive.

80   More children came. His wife became more and more querulous and ill-tempered, but the attitude Ivan Ilych had adopted towards his home life rendered him almost impervious to her grumbling.

After seven years' service in that town he was transferred to another province as Public Prosecutor. They moved, but were short of money and his wife did not like the place they moved to. Though the salary was higher the cost of living was greater, besides which two of their children died and family life became still more unpleasant for him.

Praskovya Fëdorovna blamed her husband for every inconvenience they encountered in their new home. Most of the conversations between husband and wife, especially as to the children's education, led to topics which recalled former disputes, and those disputes were apt to flare up again at any moment. There remained only those rare periods of amorousness which still came to them at times but did not last long. These were islets at which they anchored for a while and then again set out upon that ocean of veiled hostility which showed itself in their aloofness from one another. This aloofness might have grieved Ivan Ilych had he considered that it ought not to exist, but he now regarded the position as normal, and even made it the goal at which he aimed in family life. His aim was to free himself more and more from those unpleasantnesses and to give them a semblance of harmlessness and propriety. He attained this by spending less and less time with his family, and when obliged to be at home he tried to safeguard his position by the presence of outsiders. The chief thing however was that he had his official duties. The whole interest of his life now centered in the official world and that interest absorbed him. The consciousness of his power, being able to ruin anybody he wished to ruin, the importance, even the external dignity of his entry into court, or meetings with his subordinates, his success with superiors and inferiors, and above all his masterly handling of cases, of which he was conscious—all this gave him pleasure and filled his life, together with chats with his colleagues, dinners, and bridge. So that on the whole Ivan Ilych's life continued to flow as he considered it should do—pleasantly and properly.

So things continued for another seven years. His eldest daughter was already sixteen, another child had died, and only one son was left, a schoolboy and a subject of dissension. Ivan Ilych wanted to put him in the School of Law, but to spite him Praskovya Fëdorovna entered him at the High School. The daughter had been educated at home and had turned out well: the boy did not learn badly either.

III

So Ivan Ilych lived for seventeen years after his marriage. He was already a Public Prosecutor of long standing, and had declined several proposed transfers while awaiting a more desirable post, when an unanticipated and unpleasant occurrence quite upset the peaceful course of his life. He was expecting to be offered the post of presiding judge in a University town, but Happe somehow came to the front and obtained the appointment instead. Ivan Ilych became irritable, reproached Happe, and quarreled both with him and with his immediate superiors—who became colder to him and again passed him over when other appointments were made.

85   This was in 1880, the hardest year of Ivan Ilych's life. It was then that it became evident on the one hand that his salary was insufficient for them to live on, and on the other that he had been forgotten, and not only this, but that what was for him the greatest and most cruel injustice appeared to others a quite ordinary occurrence. Even his father did not consider it his duty to help him. Ivan Ilych felt himself abandoned by everyone, and that they regarded his position with a salary of 3,500 rubles as quite normal and even fortunate. He alone knew that with the consciousness of the injustices done him, with his wife's incessant nagging, and with the debts he had contracted by living beyond his means, his position was far from normal.

In order to save money that summer he obtained leave of absence and went with his wife to live in the country at her brother's place.

In the country, without his work, he experienced *ennui* for the first time in his life, and not only *ennui* but intolerable depression, and he decided that it was impossible to go on living like that, and that it was necessary to take energetic measures.

Having passed a sleepless night pacing up and down the veranda, he decided to go to Petersburg and bestir himself, in order to punish those who had failed to appreciate him and to get transferred to another ministry.

Next day, despite many protests from his wife and her brother, he started for Petersburg with the sole object of obtaining a post with a salary of five thousand rubles a year. He was no longer bent on any particular department, or tendency, or kind of activity. All he now wanted was an appointment to another post with a salary of five thousand rubles, either in the administration, in the banks, with the railways, in one of the Empress Marya's Institutions, or even in the customs—but it had to carry with it a salary of 5,000 rubles and be in a ministry other than that in which they had failed to appreciate him.

90 And this quest of Ivan Ilych's was crowned with remarkable and unexpected success. At Kursk an acquaintance of his, F. I. Ilyin, got into the first-class carriage, sat down beside Ivan Ilych, and told him of a telegram just received by the Governor of Kursk announcing that a change was about to take place in the ministry: Peter Ivanovich was to be superseded by Ivan Semënovich.

The proposed change, apart from its significance for Russia, had a special significance for Ivan Ilych, because by bringing forward a new man, Peter Petrovich, and consequently his friend Zachar Ivanovich, it was highly favorable for Ivan Ilych, since Zachar Ivanovich was a friend and colleague of his.

In Moscow this news was confirmed, and on reaching Petersburg Ivan Ilych found Zachar Ivanovich and received a definite promise of an appointment in his former department of Justice.

A week later he telegraphed to his wife: "Zachar in Miller's place. I shall receive appointment on presentation of report."

Thanks to this change of personnel, Ivan Ilych had unexpectedly obtained an appointment in his former ministry which placed him two stages above his former colleagues besides giving him five thousand rubles salary and three thousand five hundred rubles for expenses connected with his removal. All his ill humor towards his former enemies and the whole department vanished, and Ivan Ilych was completely happy.

95 He returned to the country more cheerful and contented than he had been for a long time. Praskovya Fëdorovna also cheered up and a truce was arranged between them. Ivan Ilych told of how he had been fêted by everybody in Petersburg, how all those who had been his enemies were put to shame and now fawned on him, how envious they were of his appointment, and how much everybody in Petersburg had liked him.

Praskovya Fëdorovna listened to all this and appeared to believe it. She did not contradict anything, but only made plans for their life in the town to which they were going. Ivan Ilych saw with delight that these plans were his plans, that he and his wife agreed, and that, after a stumble, his life was regaining its due and natural character of pleasant lightheartedness and decorum.

Ivan Ilych had come back for a short time only, for he had to take up his new duties on the 10th of September. Moreover, he needed time to settle into the new place, to move all his belongings from the province, and to buy and order many additional things: in a word, to make such arrangements as he had resolved on, which were almost exactly what Praskovya Fëdorovna too had decided on.

Now that everything had happened so fortunately, and that he and his wife were at one in their aims and moreover saw so little of one another, they got on together better than they had done since the first years of marriage. Ivan Ilych had thought of taking his family away with him at once, but the insistence of his wife's brother and her sister-in-law, who had suddenly become particularly amiable and friendly to him and his family, induced him to depart alone.

So he departed, and the cheerful state of mind induced by his success and by the harmony between his wife and himself, the one intensifying the other, did not leave him. He found a delightful house, just the thing both he and his wife had dreamt of. Spacious, lofty reception rooms in the old style, a convenient and dignified study, rooms for his wife and daughter, a study for his son—it might have been specially built for them. Ivan Ilych himself superintended the arrangements, chose the wallpapers, supplemented the furniture (preferably with antiques which he considered particularly *comme il faut*), and supervised the upholstering. Everything progressed and progressed and approached the ideal he had set himself: even when things were only half completed they exceeded his expectations. He saw what a refined and elegant character, free from vulgarity, it would all have when it was ready. On falling asleep he pictured to himself how the reception-room would look. Looking at the yet unfinished drawing-room he could see the fireplace, the screen, the what-not, the little chairs dotted here and there, the dishes and plates on the walls, and the bronzes, as they would be when everything was in place. He was pleased by the thought of how his wife and daughter, who shared his taste in this matter, would be impressed by it. They were certainly not expecting as much. He had been particularly successful in finding, and buying cheaply, antiques which gave a particularly aristocratic character to the whole place. But in his letters he intentionally understated everything in order to be able to surprise them. All this so absorbed him that his new duties—though he liked his official work—interested him less than he had expected. Sometimes he even had moments of absent-mindedness during the Court Sessions, and would consider whether he should have straight or curved cornices for his curtains. He was so interested in it all that he often did things himself, rearranging the furniture, or rehanging the curtains. Once when mounting a step-ladder to show the upholsterer, who did not understand, how he wanted the hangings draped, he made a false step and slipped, but being a strong and agile man he clung on and only knocked his side against the knob of the window frame. The bruised place was painful but the pain soon passed, and he felt particularly bright and well just then. He wrote: "I feel fifteen years younger." He thought he would have everything ready by September, but it dragged on till mid-October. But the result was charming not only in his eyes but to everyone who saw it.

100   In reality it was just what is usually seen in the houses of people of moderate means who want to appear rich, and therefore succeed only in resembling others like themselves: there were damasks, dark wood, plants, rugs, and dull and polished bronzes—all the things people of a certain class have in order to resemble other people of that class. His house was so like

the others that it would never have been noticed, but to him it all seemed to be quite exceptional. He was very happy when he met his family at the station and brought them to the newly furnished house all lit up, where a footman in a white tie opened the door into the hall decorated with plants, and when they went on into the drawing-room and the study uttering exclamations of delight. He conducted them everywhere, drank in their praises eagerly, and beamed with pleasure. At tea that evening, when Praskovya Fëdorovna among other things asked him about his fall, he laughed and showed them how he had gone flying and had frightened the upholsterer.

"It's a good thing I'm a bit of an athlete. Another man might have been killed, but I merely knocked myself, just here; it hurts when it's touched, but it's passing off already—it's only a bruise."

So they began living in their new home—in which, as always happens, when they got thoroughly settled in they found they were just one room short—and with the increased income, which as always was just a little (some five hundred rubles) too little, but it was all very nice.

Things went particularly well at first, before everything was finally arranged and while something had still to be done: this thing bought, that thing ordered, another thing moved, and something else adjusted. Though there were some disputes between husband and wife, they were both so well satisfied and had so much to do that it all passed off without any serious quarrels. When nothing was left to arrange it became rather dull and something seemed to be lacking, but they were then making acquaintances, forming habits, and life was growing fuller.

Ivan Ilych spent his mornings at the law court and came home to dinner, and at first he was generally in a good humor, though he occasionally became irritable just on account of his house. (Every spot on the tablecloth or the upholstery, and every broken windowblind string, irritated him. He had devoted so much trouble to arranging it all that every disturbance of it distressed him.) But on the whole his life ran its course as he believed life should do: easily, pleasantly, and decorously.

105   He got up at nine, drank his coffee, read the paper, and then put on his undress uniform and went to the law courts. There the harness in which he worked had already been stretched to fit him and he donned it without a hitch: petitioners, inquiries at the chancery, the chancery itself, and the sittings public and administrative. In all this the thing was to exclude everything fresh and vital, which always disturbs the regular course of official business, and to admit only official relations with people, and then only on official grounds. A man would come, for instance, wanting some information. Ivan Ilych, as one in whose sphere the matter did not lie, would have nothing to do with him: but if the man had some business with him in his official capacity, something that could be expressed on officially stamped paper, he would do everything, positively everything he could within the limits of such relations, and in doing so would maintain the semblance of friendly human relations, that is, would observe the courtesies of life. As soon as the official relations ended, so did everything else. Ivan Ilych possessed this capacity to separate his real life from the official side of affairs and not mix the two, in the highest degree, and by long practice and natural aptitude had brought it to such a pitch that sometimes, in the manner of a virtuoso, he would even allow himself to let the human and official relations mingle. He let himself do this just because he felt that

he could at any time he chose resume the strictly official attitude again and drop the human relation. And he did it all easily, pleasantly, correctly, and even artistically. In the intervals between the sessions he smoked, drank tea, chatted a little about politics, a little about general topics, a little about cards, but most of all about official appointments. Tired, but with the feelings of a virtuoso—one of the first violins who has played his part in an orchestra with precision—he would return home to find that his wife and daughter had been out paying calls, or had a visitor, and that his son had been to school, had done his homework with his tutor, and was duly learning what is taught at High Schools. Everything was as it should be. After dinner, if they had no visitors, Ivan Ilych sometimes read a book that was being much discussed at the time, and in the evening settled down to work, that is, read official papers, compared the depositions of witnesses, and noted paragraphs of the Code applying to them. This was neither dull nor amusing. It was dull when he might have been playing bridge, but if no bridge was available it was at any rate better than doing nothing or sitting with his wife. Ivan Ilych's chief pleasure was giving little dinners to which he invited men and women of good social position, and just as his drawing-room resembled all other drawing-rooms so did his enjoyable little parties resemble all other such parties.

Once they even gave a dance. Ivan Ilych enjoyed it and everything went off well, except that it led to a violent quarrel with his wife about the cakes and sweets. Praskovya Fëdorovna had made her own plans, but Ivan Ilych insisted on getting everything from an expensive confectioner and ordered too many cakes, and the quarrel occurred because some of those cakes were left over and the confectioner's bill came to forty-five rubles. It was a great and disagreeable quarrel. Praskovya Fëdorovna called him "a fool and an imbecile," and he clutched at his head and made angry allusions to divorce.

But the dance itself had been enjoyable. The best people were there, and Ivan Ilych had danced with Princess Trufonova, a sister of the distinguished founder of the Society "Bear My Burden."

The pleasures connected with his work were pleasures of ambition; his social pleasures were those of vanity; but Ivan Ilych's greatest pleasure was playing bridge. He acknowledged that whatever disagreeable incident happened in his life, the pleasure that beamed like a ray of light above everything else was to sit down to bridge with good players, not noisy partners, and of course to four-handed bridge (with five players it was annoying to have to stand out, though one pretended not to mind), to play a clever and serious game (when the cards allowed it), and then to have supper and drink a glass of wine. After a game of bridge, especially if he had won a little (to win a large sum was unpleasant), Ivan Ilych went to bed in specially good humor.

So they lived. They formed a circle of acquaintances among the best people and were visited by people of importance and by young folk. In their views as to their acquaintances, husband, wife, and daughter were entirely agreed, and tacitly and unanimously kept at arm's length and shook off the various shabby friends and relations who, with much show of affection, gushed into the drawing-room with its Japanese plates on the walls. Soon these shabby friends ceased to obtrude themselves and only the best people remained in the Golovins' set.

110   Young men made up to Lisa, and Petrischev, an examining magistrate
and Dmitri Ivanovich Petrischev's son and sole heir, began to be so attentive to her that Ivan Ilych had already spoken to Praskovya Fëdorovna about
it, and considered whether they should not arrange a party for them, or get
up some private theatricals.
        So they lived, and all went well, without change, and life flowed
pleasantly.

IV

They were all in good health. It could not be called ill health if Ivan Ilych
sometimes said that he had a queer taste in his mouth and felt some discomfort in his left side.
        But this discomfort increased and, though not exactly painful, grew
into a sense of pressure in his side accompanied by ill humor. And his irri-
tability became worse and worse and began to mar the agreeable, easy, and
correct life that had established itself in the Golovin family. Quarrels between husband and wife became more and more frequent, and soon the
ease and amenity disappeared and even the decorum was barely maintained. Scenes again became frequent, and very few of those islets remained
on which husband and wife could meet without an explosion. Praskovya
Fëdorovna now had good reason to say that her husband's temper was trying. With characteristic exaggeration she said he had always had a dreadful
temper, and that it had needed all her good nature to put up with it for
twenty years. It was true that now the quarrels were started by him. His
bursts of temper always came just before dinner, often just as he began to
eat his soup. Sometimes he noticed that a plate or dish was chipped, or the
food was not right, or his son put his elbow on the table, or his daughter's
hair was not done as he liked it, and for all this he blamed Praskovya
Fëdorovna. At first she retorted and said disagreeable things to him, but
once or twice he fell into such a rage at the beginning of dinner that she realized it was due to some physical derangement brought on by taking food,
and so she restrained herself and did not answer, but only hurried to get the
dinner over. She regarded this self-restraint as highly praiseworthy. Having
come to the conclusion that her husband had a dreadful temper and made
her life miserable, she began to feel sorry for herself, and the more she
pitied herself the more she hated her husband. She began to wish he would
die; yet she did not want him to die because then his salary would cease.
And this irritated her against him still more. She considered herself dreadfully unhappy just because not even his death could save her, and though
she concealed her exasperation, that hidden exasperation of hers increased
his irritation also.
        After one scene in which Ivan Ilych had been particularly unfair and af-
ter which he had said in explanation that he certainly was irritable but that
it was due to his not being well, she said that if he was ill it should be attended to, and insisted on his going to see a celebrated doctor.
115   He went. Everything took place as he had expected and as it always
does. There was the usual waiting and the important air assumed by the
doctor, with which he was so familiar (resembling that which he himself assumed in court), and the sounding and listening, and the questions which

called for answers that were foregone conclusions and were evidently unnecessary, and the look of importance which implied that "if only you put yourself in our hands we will arrange everything—we know indubitably how it has to be done, always in the same way for everybody alike." It was all just as it was in the law courts. The doctor put on just the same air towards him as he himself put on towards an accused person.

The doctor said that so-and-so indicated that there was so-and-so inside the patient, but if the investigation of so-and-so did not confirm this, then he must assume that and that. If he assumed that and that, then . . . . and so on. To Ivan Ilych only one question was important: was his case serious or not? But the doctor ignored that inappropriate question. From his point of view it was not the one under consideration, the real question was to decide between a floating kidney, chronic catarrh, or appendicitis. It was not a question of Ivan Ilych's life or death, but one between a floating kidney and appendicitis. And that question the doctor solved brilliantly, as it seemed to Ivan Ilych, in favor of the appendix, with the reservation that should an examination of the urine give fresh indications the matter would be reconsidered. All this was just what Ivan Ilych had himself brilliantly accomplished a thousand times in dealing with men on trial. The doctor summed up just as brilliantly, looking over his spectacles triumphantly and even gaily at the accused. From the doctor's summing up Ivan Ilych concluded that things were bad, but that for the doctor, and perhaps for everybody else, it was a matter of indifference, though for him it was bad. And this conclusion struck him painfully, arousing in him a great feeling of pity for himself and of bitterness towards the doctor's indifference to a matter of such importance.

He said nothing of this, but rose, placed the doctor's fee on the table, and remarked with a sigh: "We sick people probably often put inappropriate questions. But tell me, in general, is this complaint dangerous, or not? . . ."

The doctor looked at him sternly over his spectacles with one eye, as if to say: "Prisoner, if you will not keep to the questions put to you, I shall be obliged to have you removed from the court."

"I have already told you what I consider necessary and proper. The analysis may show something more." And the doctor bowed.

120   Ivan Ilych went out slowly, seated himself disconsolately in his sledge, and drove home. All the way home he was going over what the doctor had said, trying to translate those complicated, obscure, scientific phrases into plain language and find in them an answer to the question: "Is my condition bad? Is it very bad? Or is there as yet nothing much wrong?" And it seemed to him that the meaning of what the doctor had said was that it was very bad. Everything in the streets seemed depressing. The cabmen, the houses, the passers-by, and the shops, were dismal. His ache, this dull gnawing ache that never ceased for a moment, seemed to have acquired a new and more serious significance from the doctor's dubious remarks. Ivan Ilych now watched it with a new and oppressive feeling.

He reached home and began to tell his wife about it. She listened, but in the middle of his account his daughter came in with her hat on, ready to go out with her mother. She sat down reluctantly to listen to this tedious story, but could not stand it long, and her mother too did not hear him to the end.

"Well, I am very glad," she said. "Mind now to take your medicine regularly. Give me the prescription and I'll send Gerasim to the chemist's."[13] And she went to get ready to go out.

While she was in the room Ivan Ilych had hardly taken time to breathe, but he sighed deeply when she left it.

"Well," he thought, "perhaps it isn't so bad after all."

125   He began taking his medicine and following the doctor's directions, which had been altered after the examination of the urine. But then it happened that there was a contradiction between the indications drawn from the examination of the urine and the symptoms that showed themselves. It turned out that what was happening differed from what the doctor had told him, and that he had either forgotten, or blundered, or hidden something from him. He could not, however, be blamed for that, and Ivan Ilych still obeyed his orders implicitly and at first derived some comfort from doing so.

From the time of his visit to the doctor, Ivan Ilych's chief occupation was the exact fulfillment of the doctor's instructions regarding hygiene and the taking of medicine, and the observation of his pain and his excretions. His chief interests came to be people's ailments and people's health. When sickness, deaths, or recoveries were mentioned in his presence, especially when the illness resembled his own, he listened with agitation which he tried to hide, asked questions, and applied what he heard to his own case.

The pain did not grow less, but Ivan Ilych made efforts to force himself to think that he was better. And he could do this so long as nothing agitated him. But as soon as he had any unpleasantness with his wife, any lack of success in his official work, or held bad cards at bridge, he was at once acutely sensible of his disease. He had formerly borne such mischances, hoping soon to adjust what was wrong, to master it and attain success, or make a grand slam. But now every mischance upset him and plunged him into despair. He would say to himself: "There now, just as I was beginning to get better and the medicine had begun to take effect, comes this accursed misfortune, or unpleasantness. . . ." And he was furious with the mishap, or with the people who were causing the unpleasantness and killing him, for he felt that this fury was killing him but could not restrain it. One would have thought that it should have been clear to him that this exasperation with circumstances and people aggravated his illness, and that he ought therefore to ignore unpleasant occurrences. But he drew the very opposite conclusion: he said that he needed peace, and he watched for everything that might disturb it and became irritable at the slightest infringement of it. His condition was rendered worse by the fact that he read medical books and consulted doctors. The progress of his disease was so gradual that he could deceive himself when comparing one day with another—the difference was so slight. But when he consulted the doctors it seemed to him that he was getting worse, and even very rapidly. Yet despite this he was continually consulting them.

That month he went to see another celebrity, who told him almost the same as the first had done but put his questions rather differently, and the interview with this celebrity only increased Ivan Ilych's doubts and fears. A friend of a friend of his, a very good doctor, diagnosed his illness again quite

---

[13]**chemist's** pharmacist's.

differently from the others, and though he predicted recovery, his questions and suppositions bewildered Ivan Ilych still more and increased his doubts. A homeopathist diagnosed the disease in yet another way, and prescribed medicine which Ivan Ilych took secretly for a week. But after a week, not feeling any improvement and having lost confidence both in the former doctor's treatment and in this one's, he became still more despondent. One day a lady acquaintance mentioned a cure effected by a wonder-working icon. Ivan Ilych caught himself listening attentively and beginning to believe that it had occurred. This incident alarmed him. "Has my mind really weakened to such an extent?" he asked himself. "Nonsense! It's all rubbish. I mustn't give way to nervous fears but having chosen a doctor must keep strictly to his treatment. That is what I will do. Now it's all settled. I won't think about it, but will follow the treatment seriously till summer, and then we shall see. From now there must be no more of this wavering!" This was easy to say but impossible to carry out. The pain in his side oppressed him and seemed to grow worse and more incessant, while the taste in his mouth grew stranger and stranger. It seemed to him that his breath had a disgusting smell, and he was conscious of a loss of appetite and strength. There was no deceiving himself: something terrible, new, and more important than anything before in his life, was taking place within him of which he alone was aware. Those about him did not understand or would not understand it, but thought everything in the world was going on as usual. That tormented Ivan Ilych more than anything. He saw that his household, especially his wife and daughter who were in a perfect whirl of visiting, did not understand anything of it and were annoyed that he was so depressed and so exacting, as if he were to blame for it. Though they tried to disguise it he saw that he was an obstacle in their path, and that his wife had adopted a definite line in regard to his illness and kept to it regardless of anything he said or did. Her attitude was this: "You know," she would say to her friends, "Ivan Ilych can't do as other people do, and keep to the treatment prescribed for him. One day he'll take his drops and keep strictly to his diet and go to bed in good time, but the next day unless I watch him he'll suddenly forget his medicine, eat sturgeon—which is forbidden—and sit up playing cards till one o'clock in the morning."

"Oh, come, when was that?" Ivan Ilych would ask in vexation. "Only once at Peter Ivanovich's."

"And yesterday with Shebek."

"Well, even if I hadn't stayed up, this pain would have kept me awake."

"Be that as it may you'll never get well like that, but will always make us wretched."

Praskovya Fëdorovna's attitude to Ivan Ilych's illness, as she expressed it both to others and to him, was that it was his own fault and was another of the annoyances he caused her. Ivan Ilych felt that this opinion escaped her involuntarily—but that did not make it easier for him.

At the law courts too, Ivan Ilych noticed, or thought he noticed, a strange attitude towards himself. It sometimes seemed to him that people were watching him inquisitively as a man whose place might soon be vacant. Then again, his friends would suddenly begin to chaff him in a friendly way about his low spirits, as if the awful, horrible, and unheard-of thing that was going on within him, incessantly gnawing at him and irresistibly drawing him away, was a very agreeable subject for jests. Schwartz in particular irritated him by his jocularity, vivacity, and *savoir-faire,* which reminded him of what he himself had been ten years ago.

135   Friends came to make up a set and they sat down to cards. They dealt, bending the new cards to soften them, and he sorted the diamonds in his hand and found he had seven. His partner said "No trumps" and supported him with two diamonds. What more could be wished for? It ought to be jolly and lively. They would make a grand slam. But suddenly Ivan Ilych was conscious of that gnawing pain, that taste in his mouth, and it seemed ridiculous that in such circumstances he should be pleased to make a grand slam.

He looked at his partner Mikhail Mikhaylovich, who rapped the table with his strong hand and instead of snatching up the tricks pushed the cards courteously and indulgently towards Ivan Ilych that he might have the pleasure of gathering them up without the trouble of stretching out his hand for them. "Does he think I am too weak to stretch out my arm?" thought Ivan Ilych, and forgetting what he was doing he over-trumped his partner, missing the grand slam by three tricks. And what was most awful of all was that he saw how upset Mikhail Mikhaylovich was about it but did not himself care. And it was dreadful to realize why he did not care.

They all saw that he was suffering, and said: "We can stop if you are tired. Take a rest." Lie down? No, he was not at all tired, and he finished the rubber. All were gloomy and silent. Ivan Ilych felt that he had diffused this gloom over them and could not dispel it. They had supper and went away, and Ivan Ilych was left alone with the consciousness that his life was poisoned and was poisoning the lives of others, and that this poison did not weaken but penetrated more and more deeply into his whole being.

With this consciousness, and with physical pain besides the terror, he must go to bed, often to lie awake the greater part of the night. Next morning he had to get up again, dress, go to the law courts, speak, and write; or if he did not go out, spend at home those twenty-four hours a day each of which was a torture. And he had to live thus all alone on the brink of an abyss, with no one who understood or pitied him.

V

So one month passed and then another. Just before the New Year his brother-in-law came to town and stayed at their house. Ivan Ilych was at the law courts and Praskovya Fëdorovna had gone shopping. When Ivan Ilych came home and entered his study he found his brother-in-law there—a healthy, florid man—unpacking his portmanteau himself. He raised his head on hearing Ivan Ilych's footsteps and looked up at him for a moment without a word. That stare told Ivan Ilych everything. His brother-in-law opened his mouth to utter an exclamation of surprise but checked himself, and that action confirmed it all.

140   "I have changed, eh?"

"Yes, there is a change."

And after that, try as he would to get his brother-in-law to return to the subject of his looks, the latter would say nothing about it. Praskovya Fëdorovna came home and her brother went out to her. Ivan Ilych locked the door and began to examine himself in the glass, first full face, then in profile. He took up a portrait of himself taken with his wife, and compared it with what he saw in the glass. The change in him was immense. Then he bared his arms to tihe elbow, looked at them, drew the sleeves down again, sat down on an ottoman, and grew blacker than night.

"No, no, this won't do!" he said to himself, and jumped up, went to the table, took up some law papers, and began to read them, but could not continue. He unlocked the door and went into the reception-room. The door leading to the drawing-room was shut. He approached it on tiptoe and listened.

"No, you are exaggerating!" Praskovya Fëdorovna was saying.

145   "Exaggerating! Don't you see it? Why, he's a dead man! Look at his eyes—there's no light in them. But what is it that is wrong with him?"

"No one knows. Nikolaevich said something, but I don't know what. And Leshchetitsky said quite the contrary. . . ."

Ivan Ilych walked away, went to his own room, lay down, and began musing: "The kidney, a floating kidney." He recalled all the doctors had told him of how it detached itself and swayed about. And by an effort of imagination he tried to catch that kidney and arrest it and support it. So little was needed for this, it seemed to him. "No, I'll go to see Peter Ivanovich again." He rang, ordered the carriage, and got ready to go.

"Where are you going, Jean?"[14] asked his wife, with a specially sad and exceptionally kind look.

This exceptionally kind look irritated him. He looked morosely at her.

150   "I must go to see Peter Ivanovich."

He went to see Peter Ivanovich, and together they went to see his friend, the doctor. He was in, and Ivan Ilych had a long talk with him.

Reviewing the anatomical and physiological details of what in the doctor's opinion was going on inside him, he understood it all.

There was something, a small thing, in the vermiform appendix. It might all come right. Only stimulate the energy of one organ and check the activity of another, then absorption would take place and everything would come right. He got home rather late for dinner, ate his dinner, and conversed cheerfully, but could not for a long time bring himself to go back to work in his room. At last, however, he went to his study and did what was necessary, but the consciousness that he had put something aside—an important, intimate matter which he would revert to when his work was done—never left him. When he had finished his work he remembered that this intimate matter was the thought of his vermiform appendix. But he did not give himself up to it, and went to the drawing-room for tea. There were callers there, including the examining magistrate who was a desirable match for his daughter, and they were conversing, playing the piano, and singing. Ivan Ilych, as Praskovya Fëdorovna remarked, spent that evening more cheerfully than usual, but he never for a moment forgot that he had postponed the important matter of the appendix. At eleven o'clock he said good-night and went to his bedroom. Since his illness he had slept alone in a small room next to his study. He undressed and took up a novel by Zola,[15] but instead of reading it he fell into thought, and in his imagination that desired improvement in the vermiform appendix occurred. There were the absorption and evacuation and the re-establishment of normal activity. "Yes, that's it!" he said to

---

[14]**Jean** French form of Ivan.   [15]**Émile Zola** French novelist and social critic.

himself. "One need only assist nature, that's all." He remembered his medicine, rose, took it, and lay down on his back watching for the beneficent action of the medicine and for it to lessen the pain. "I need only take it regularly and avoid all injurious influences. I am already feeling better, much better." He began touching his side: it was not painful to the touch. "There, I really don't feel it. It's much better already." He put out the light and turned on his side. . . . "The appendix is getting better, absorption is occurring." Suddenly he felt the old, familiar, dull, gnawing pain, stubborn and serious. There was the same familiar loathsome taste in his mouth. His heart sank and he felt dazed. "My God! My God!" he muttered. "Again, again! and it will never cease." And suddenly the matter presented itself in a quite different aspect. "Vermiform appendix! Kidney!" he said to himself. "It's not a question of appendix or kidney, but of life and . . . death. Yes, life was there and now it is going, going and I cannot stop it. Yes. Why deceive myself? Isn't it obvious to everyone but me that I'm dying, and that it's only a question of weeks, days . . . it may happen this moment. There was light and now there is darkness. I was here and now I'm going there! Where?" A chill came over him, his breathing ceased, and he felt only the throbbing of his heart.

"When I am not, what will there be? There will be nothing. Then where shall I be when I am no more? Can this be dying? No, I don't want to!" He jumped up and tried to light the candle, felt for it with trembling hands, dropped candle and candlestick on the floor, and fell back on his pillow.

155 "What's the use? It makes no difference," he said to himself, staring with wide-open eyes into the darkness. "Death. Yes, death. And none of them know or wish to know it, and they have no pity for me. Now they are playing." (He heard through the door the distant sound of a song and its accompaniment.) "It's all the same to them, but they will die too! Fools! I first, and they later, but it will be the same for them. And now they are merry . . . the beasts!"

Anger choked him and he was agonizingly, unbearably miserable. "It is impossible that all men have been doomed to suffer this awful horror!" He raised himself.

"Something must be wrong. I must calm myself—must think it all over from the beginning." And he again began thinking. "Yes, the beginning of my illness: I knocked my side, but I was still quite well that day and the next. It hurt a little, then rather more. I saw the doctors, then followed despondency and anguish, more doctors, and I drew nearer to the abyss. My strength grew less and I kept coming nearer and nearer, and now I have wasted away and there is no light in my eyes. I think of the appendix—but this is death! I think of mending the appendix, and all the while here is death! Can it really be death?" Again terror seized him and he gasped for breath. He leant down and began feeling for the matches, pressing with his elbow on the stand beside the bed. It was in his way and hurt him, he grew furious with it, pressed on it still harder, and upset it. Breathless and in despair he fell on his back, expecting death to come immediately.

Meanwhile the visitors were leaving. Praskovya Fëdorovna was seeing them off. She heard something fall and came in.

"What has happened?"

160 "Nothing. I knocked it over accidentally."

She went out and returned with a candle. He lay there panting heavily, like a man who has run a thousand yards, and stared upwards at her with a fixed look.

"What is it, Jean?"

"No . . . no . . . thing. I upset it." ("Why speak of it? She won't understand," he thought.)

And in truth she did not understand. She picked up the stand, lit his candle, and hurried away to see another visitor off. When she came back he still lay on his back, looking upwards.

165 "What is it? Do you feel worse?"

"Yes."

She shook her head and sat down.

"Do you know, Jean, I think we must ask Leshchetitsky to come and see you here."

This meant calling in the famous specialist, regardless of expense. He smiled malignantly and said "No." She remained a little longer and then went up to him and kissed his forehead.

170 While she was kissing him he hated her from the bottom of his soul and with difficulty refrained from pushing her away.

"Good-night. Please God you'll sleep."

"Yes."

VI

Ivan Ilych saw that he was dying, and he was in continual despair.

In the depth of his heart he knew he was dying, but not only was he not accustomed to the thought, he simply did not and could not grasp it.

175 The syllogism he had learnt from Kiezewetter's Logic:[16] "Caius is a man, men are mortal, therefore Caius is mortal," had always seemed to him correct as applied to Caius, but certainly not as applied to himself. That Caius—man in the abstract—was mortal, was perfectly correct, but he was not Caius, not an abstract man, but a creature quite, quite separate from all others. He had been little Vanya,[17] with a mama and a papa, with Mitya and Volodya, with the toys, a coachman and a nurse, afterwards with Katenka and with all the joys, griefs, and delights of childhood, boyhood, and youth. What did Caius know of the smell of that striped leather ball Vanya had been so fond of? Had Caius kissed his mother's hand like that, and did the silk of her dress rustle so for Caius? Had he rioted like that at school when the pastry was bad? Had Caius been in love like that? Could Caius preside at a session as he did? "Caius really was mortal, and it was right for him to die; but for me, little Vanya, Ivan Ilych, with all my thoughts and emotions, it's altogether a different matter. It cannot be that I ought to die. That would be too terrible."

Such was his feeling.

"If I had to die like Caius I should have known it was so. An inner voice would have told me so, but there was nothing of the sort in me and I and all

---

[16]**Kiezewetter's Logic** *The Outline of Logic According to Kantian Principles,* a widely used text in Russia, written by Klaus Kiezewetter and based on the philosophy of Immanuel Kant (1722-1804).   [17]**Vanya** diminutive of Ivan.

my friends felt that our case was quite different from that of Caius. And now here it is!" he said to himself. "It can't be. It's impossible! But here it is. How is this? How is one to understand it?"

He could not understand it, and tried to drive this false, incorrect, morbid thought away and to replace it by other proper and healthy thoughts. But that thought, and not the thought only but the reality itself, seemed to come and confront him.

And to replace that thought he called up a succession of others, hoping to find in them some support. He tried to get back into the former current of thoughts that had once screened the thought of death from him. But strange to say, all that had formerly shut off, hidden, and destroyed his consciousness of death, no longer had that effect. Ivan Ilych now spent most of his time in attempting to re-establish that old current. He would say to himself: "I will take up my duties again—after all I used to live by them." And banishing all doubts he would go to the law courts, enter into conversation with his colleagues, and sit carelessly as was his wont, scanning the crowd with a thoughtful look and leaning both his emaciated arms on the arms of his oak chair; bending over as usual to a colleague and drawing his papers nearer he would interchange whispers with him, and then suddenly raising his eyes and sitting erect would pronounce certain words and open the proceedings. But suddenly in the midst of those proceedings the pain in his side, regardless of the stage the proceedings had reached, would begin its own gnawing work. Ivan Ilych would turn his attention to it and try to drive the thought of it away, but without success. *It* would come and stand before him and look at him, and he would be petrified and the light would die out of his eyes, and he would again begin asking himself whether *It* alone was true. And his colleagues and subordinates would see with surprise and distress that he, the brilliant and subtle judge, was becoming confused and making mistakes. He would shake himself, try to pull himself together, manage somehow to bring the sitting to a close, and return home with the sorrowful consciousness that his judicial labors could not as formerly hide from him what he wanted them to hide, and could not deliver him from *It*. And what was worst of all was that *It* drew his attention to itself not in order to make him take some action but only that he should look at *It*, look it straight in the face: look at it and, without doing anything, suffer inexpressibly.

180   And to save himself from this condition Ivan Ilych looked for consolation—new screens—and new screens were found and for a while seemed to save him, but then they immediately fell to pieces or rather became transparent, as if *It* penetrated them and nothing could veil *It*.

In these latter days he would go into the drawing-room he had arranged—that drawing-room where he had fallen and for the sake of which (how bitterly ridiculous it seemed) he had sacrificed his life—for he knew that his illness originated with that knock. He would enter and see that something had scratched the polished table. He would look for the cause of this and find that it was the bronze ornamentation of an album, that had got bent. He would take up the expensive album which he had lovingly arranged, and feel vexed with his daughter and her friends for their untidiness—for the album was torn here and there and some of the photographs turned upside down. He would put it carefully in order and bend the ornamentation back into position. Then it would occur to him to place all those things in another corner of the room, near the plants. He could call the footman, but his daughter or wife would come to help him. They would not agree, and his wife would contradict him, and he would dispute and grow angry. But that was all right, for then he did not think about *It*. *It* was invisible.

But then, when he was moving something himself, his wife would say: "Let the servants do it. You will hurt yourself again." And suddenly *It* would flash through the screen and he would see it. It was just a flash, and he hoped it would disappear, but he would involuntarily pay attention to his side. "It sits there as before, gnawing just the same!" And he could no longer forget *It*, but could distinctly see it looking at him from behind the flowers. "What is it all for?"

"It really is so! I lost my life over that curtain as I might have done when storming a fort. Is that possible? How terrible and how stupid. It can't be true! It can't, but it is."

He would go to his study, lie down, and again be alone with *It*: face to face with *It*. And nothing could be done with *It* except to look at it and shudder.

VII

185   How it happened it is impossible to say because it came about step by step, unnoticed, but in the third month of Ivan Ilych's illness, his wife, his daughter, his son, his acquaintances, the doctors, the servants, and above all he himself, were aware that the whole interest he had for other people was whether he would soon vacate his place, and at last release the living from the discomfort caused by his presence and be himself released from his sufferings.

He slept less and less. He was given opium and hypodermic injections of morphine, but this did not relieve him. The dull depression he experienced in a somnolent condition at first gave him a little relief, but only as something new, afterwards it became as distressing as the pain itself or even more so.

Special foods were prepared for him by the doctors' orders, but all those foods became increasingly distasteful and disgusting to him.

For his excretions also special arrangements had to be made, and this was a torment to him every time—a torment from the uncleanliness, the unseemliness, and the smell, and from knowing that another person had to take part in it.

But just through this most unpleasant matter, Ivan Ilych obtained comfort. Gerasim, the butler's young assistant, always came in to carry the things out. Gerasim was a clean, fresh peasant lad, grown stout on town food and always cheerful and bright. At first the sight of him, in his clean Russian peasant costume, engaged on that disgusting task embarrassed Ivan Ilych.

190   Once when he got up from the commode too weak to draw up his trousers, he dropped into a soft armchair and looked with horror at his bare, enfeebled thighs with the muscles so sharply marked on them.

Gerasim with a firm light tread, his heavy boots emitting a pleasant smell of tar and fresh winter air, came in wearing a clean Hessian apron, the sleeves of his print shirt tucked up over his strong bare young arms; and refraining from looking at his sick master out of consideration for his feelings, and restraining the joy of life that beamed from his face, he went up to the commode.

"Gerasim!" said Ivan Ilych in a weak voice.

Gerasim started, evidently afraid he might have committed some blunder, and with a rapid movement turned his fresh, kind, simple young face which just showed the first downy signs of a beard.

"Yes, sir?"

195   "That must be very unpleasant for you. You must forgive me. I am helpless."

"Oh, why, sir," and Gerasim's eyes beamed and he showed his glistening white teeth, "what's a little trouble? It's a case of illness with you, sir."

And his deft strong hands did their accustomed task, and he went out of the room stepping lightly. Five minutes later he as lightly returned.

Ivan Ilych was still sitting in the same position in the armchair.

"Gerasim," he said when the latter had replaced the freshly-washed utensil. "Please come here and help me." Gerasim went up to him. "Lift me up. It is hard for me to get up, and I have sent Dmitri away."

200   Gerasim went up to him, grasped his master with his strong arms deftly but gently, in the same way that he stepped—lifted him, supported him with one hand, and with the other drew up his trousers and would have set him down again, but Ivan Ilych asked to be led to the sofa. Gerasim, without an effort and without apparent pressure, led him, almost lifting him, to the sofa, and placed him on it.

"Thank you. How easily and well you do it all!"

Gerasim smiled again and turned to leave the room. But Ivan Ilych felt his presence such a comfort that he did not want to let him go.

"One thing more, please move up that chair. No, the other one—under my feet. It is easier for me when my feet are raised."

Gerasim brought the chair, set it down gently in place, and raised Ivan Ilych's legs on to it. It seemed to Ivan Ilych that he felt better while Gerasim was holding up his legs.

205   "It's better when my legs are higher," he said. "Place that cushion under them."

Gerasim did so. He again lifted the legs and placed them, and again Ivan Ilych felt better while Gerasim held his legs. When he set them down Ivan Ilych fancied he felt worse.

"Gerasim," he said. "Are you busy now?"

"Not at all, sir," said Gerasim, who had learnt from the townsfolk how to speak to gentlefolk.

"What have you still to do?"

210   "What have I to do? I've done everything except chopping the logs for tomorrow."

"Then hold my legs up a bit higher, can you?"

"Of course I can. Why not?" And Gerasim raised his master's legs higher and Ivan Ilych thought that in that position he did not feel any pain at all.

"And how about the logs?"

"Don't trouble about that, sir. There's plenty of time."

215   Ivan Ilych told Gerasim to sit down and hold his legs, and began to talk to him. And strange to say it seemed to him that he felt better while Gerasim held his legs up.

After that Ivan Ilych would sometimes call Gerasim and get him to hold his legs on his shoulders, and he liked talking to him. Gerasim did it all easily, willingly, simply, and with a good nature that touched Ivan Ilych. Health, strength, and vitality in other people were offensive to him, but Gerasim's strength and vitality did not mortify but soothed him.

What tormented Ivan Ilych most was the deception, the lie, which for some reason they all accepted, that he was not dying but was simply ill, and that he only need keep quiet and undergo a treatment and then something very good would result. He however knew that do what they would nothing would come of it, only still more agonizing suffering and death. This deception tortured him—their not wishing to admit what they all knew and what he knew, but wanting to lie to him concerning his terrible condition, and wishing and forcing him to participate in that lie. Those lies—lies enacted over him on the eve of his death and destined to degrade this awful, solemn act to the level of their visitings, their curtains, their sturgeon for dinner—were a terrible agony for Ivan Ilych. And strangely enough, many times when they were going through their antics over him he had been within a hairbreadth of calling out to them: "Stop lying! You know and I know that I am dying. Then at least stop lying about it!" But he had never had the spirit to do it. The awful, terrible act of his dying was, he could see, reduced by those about him to the level of a casual, unpleasant, and almost indecorous incident (as if someone entered a drawing-room diffusing an unpleasant odor) and this was done by that very decorum which he had served all his life long. He saw that no one felt for him, because no one even wished to grasp his position. Only Gerasim recognized it and pitied him. And so Ivan Ilych felt at ease only with him. He felt comforted when Gerasim supported his legs (sometimes all night long) and refused to go to bed, saying: "Don't you worry, Ivan Ilych. I'll get sleep enough later on," or when he suddenly became familiar and exclaimed: "If you weren't sick it would be another matter, but as it is, why should I grudge a little trouble?" Gerasim alone did not lie; everything showed that he alone understood the facts of the case and did not consider it necessary to disguise them, but simply felt sorry for his emaciated and enfeebled master. Once when Ivan Ilych was sending him away he even said straight out: "We shall all of us die, so why should I grudge a little trouble?"—expressing the fact that he did not think his work burdensome, because he was doing it for a dying man and hoped someone would do the same for him when his time came.

Apart from this lying, or because of it, what most tormented Ivan Ilych was that no one pitied him as he wished to be pitied. At certain moments after prolonged suffering he wished most of all (though he would have been ashamed to confess it) for someone to pity him as a sick child is pitied. He longed to be petted and comforted. He knew he was an important functionary, that he had a beard turning grey, and that therefore what he longed for was impossible, but still he longed for it. And in Gerasim's attitude towards him there was something akin to what he wished for, and so that attitude comforted him. Ivan Ilych wanted to weep, wanted to be petted and cried over, and then his colleague Shebek would come, and instead of weeping and being petted, Ivan Ilych would assume a serious, severe, and profound air, and by force of habit would express his opinion on a decision of the Court of

Cassation and would stubbornly insist on that view. This falsity around him and within him did more than anything else to poison his last days.

VIII

It was morning. He knew it was morning because Gerasim had gone, and Peter the footman had come and put out the candles, drawn back one of the curtains, and begun quietly to tidy up. Whether it was morning or evening, Friday or Sunday, made no difference, it was all just the same: the gnawing, unmitigated, agonizing pain, never ceasing for an instant, the consciousness of life inexorably waning but not yet extinguished, the approach of that ever dreaded and hateful Death which was the only reality, and always the same falsity. What were days, weeks, hours, in such a case?

220   "Will you have some tea, sir?"

"He wants things to be regular, and wishes the gentlefolk to drink tea in the morning," thought Ivan Ilych, and only said "No."

"Wouldn't you like to move onto the sofa, sir?"

"He wants to tidy up the room, and I'm in the way. I am uncleanliness and disorder," he thought, and said only:

"No, leave me alone."

225   The man went on bustling about. Ivan Ilych stretched out his hand. Peter came up, ready to help.

"What is it, sir?"

"My watch."

Peter took the watch which was close at hand and gave it to his master. "Half-past eight. Are they up?"

230   "No, sir, except Vasily Ivanich" (the son) "who has gone to school. Praskovya Fëdorovna ordered me to wake her if you asked for her. Shall I do so?"

"No, there's no need to." "Perhaps I'd better have some tea," he thought, and added aloud: "Yes, bring me some tea."

Peter went to the door, but Ivan Ilych dreaded being left alone. "How can I keep him here? Oh yes, my medicine." "Peter, give me my medicine. Why not? Perhaps it may still do me some good." He took a spoonful and swallowed it. "No, it won't help. It's all tomfoolery, all deception," he decided as soon as he became aware of the familiar, sickly, hopeless taste. "No, I can't believe in it any longer. But the pain, why this pain? If it would only cease just for a moment!" And he moaned. Peter turned towards him. "It's all right. Go and fetch me some tea."

Peter went out. Left alone Ivan Ilych groaned not so much with pain, terrible though that was, as from mental anguish. Always and for ever the same, always these endless days and nights. If only it would come quicker! If only what would come quicker? Death, darkness? . . . No, no! Anything rather than death!

When Peter returned with the tea on a tray, Ivan Ilych stared at him for a time in perplexity, not realizing who and what he was. Peter was disconcerted by that look and his embarrassment brought Ivan Ilych to himself.

235   "Oh, tea! All right, put it down. Only help me to wash and put on a clean shirt."

And Ivan Ilych began to wash. With pauses for rest, he washed his hands and then his face, cleaned his teeth, brushed his hair, and looked in the glass. He was terrified by what he saw, especially by the limp way in which his hair clung to his pallid forehead.

While his shirt was being changed he knew that he would be still more frightened at the sight of his body, so he avoided looking at it. Finally he was ready. He drew on a dressing-gown, wrapped himself in a plaid, and sat down in the armchair to take his tea. For a moment he felt refreshed, but soon as he began to drink the tea he was again aware of the same taste, and the pain also returned. He finished it with an effort, and then lay down stretching out his legs, and dismissed Peter.

Always the same. Now a spark of hope flashes up, then a sea of despair rages, and always pain; always pain, always despair, and always the same. When alone he had a dreadful and distressing desire to call someone, but he knew beforehand that with others present it would be still worse. "Another dose of morphine—to lose consciousness. I will tell him, the doctor, that he must think of something else. It's impossible, impossible, to go on like this."

An hour and another pass like that. But now there is a ring at the door bell. Perhaps it's the doctor? It is. He comes in fresh, hearty, plump, and cheerful, with that look on his face that seems to say: "There now, you're in a panic about something, but we'll arrange it all for you directly!" The doctor knows this expression is out of place here, but he has put it on once for all and can't take it off—like a man who has put on a frock-coat in the morning to pay a round of calls.

240   The doctor rubs his hands vigorously and reassuringly.

"Brr! How cold it is! There's such a sharp frost; just let me warm myself!" he says, as if it were only a matter of waiting till he was warm, and then he would put everything right.

"Well now, how are you?"

Ivan Ilych feels that the doctor would like to say: "Well, how are our affairs?" but that even he feels that this would not do, and says instead: "What sort of a night have you had?"

Ivan Ilych looks at him as much as to say: "Are you really never ashamed of lying?" But the doctor does not wish to understand this question, and Ivan Ilych says: "Just as terrible as ever. The pain never leaves me and never subsides. If only something . . . ."

245   "Yes, you sick people are always like that. . . . There, now I think I am warm enough. Even Praskovya Fëdorovna, who is so particular, could find no fault with my temperature. Well, now I can say good-morning," and the doctor presses his patient's hand.

Then, dropping his former playfulness, he begins with a most serious face to examine the patient, feeling his pulse and taking his temperature, and then begins the sounding and auscultation.[18]

Ivan Ilych knows quite well and definitely that all this is nonsense and pure deception, but when the doctor, getting down on his knee, leans over him, putting his ear first higher then lower, and performs various gymnastic movements over him with a significant expression on his face, Ivan Ilych submits to it all as he used to submit to the speeches of the lawyers, though he knew very well that they were all lying and why they were lying.

---

[18]**auscultation** diagnosing the sounds made by internal organs.

The doctor, kneeling on the sofa, is still sounding him when Praskovya Fëdorovna's silk dress rustles at the door and she is heard scolding Peter for not having let her know of the doctor's arrival.

She comes in, kisses her husband, and at once proceeds to prove that she has been up a long time already, and only owing to a misunderstanding failed to be there when the doctor arrived.

250   Ivan Ilych looks at her, scans her all over, sets against her the whiteness and plumpness and cleanness of her hands and neck, the gloss of her hair, and the sparkle of her vivacious eyes. He hates her with his whole soul. And the thrill of hatred he feels for her makes him suffer from her touch.

Her attitude towards him and his disease is still the same. Just as the doctor had adopted a certain relation to his patient which he could not abandon, so had she formed one towards him—that he was not doing something he ought to do and was himself to blame, and that she reproached him lovingly for this—and she could not now change that attitude.

"You see he doesn't listen to me and doesn't take his medicine at the proper time. And above all he lies in a position that is no doubt bad for him—with his legs up."

She described how he made Gerasim hold his legs up.

The doctor smiled with a contemptuous affability that said: "What's to be done? These sick people do have foolish fancies of that kind, but we must forgive them."

255   When the examination was over the doctor looked at his watch, and then Praskovya Fëdorovna announced to Ivan Ilych that it was of course as he pleased, but she had sent today for a celebrated specialist who would examine him and have a consultation with Michael Danilovich (their regular doctor).

"Please don't raise any objections. I am doing this for my own sake," she said ironically, letting it be felt that she was doing it all for his sake and only said this to leave him no right to refuse. He remained silent, knitting his brows. He felt that he was so surrounded and involved in a mesh of falsity that it was hard to unravel anything.

Everything she did for him was entirely for her own sake, and she told him she was doing for herself what she actually was doing for herself, as if that was so incredible that he must understand the opposite.

At half-past eleven the celebrated specialist arrived. Again the sounding began and the significant conversations in his presence and in another room, about the kidneys and the appendix, and the questions and answers, with such an air of importance that again, instead of the real question of life and death which now alone confronted him, the question arose of the kidney and appendix which were not behaving as they ought to and would now be attacked by Michael Danilovich and the specialist and forced to amend their ways.

The celebrated specialist took leave of him with a serious though not hopeless look, and in reply to the timid question Ivan Ilych, with eyes glistening with fear and hope, put to him as to whether there was a chance of recovery, said that he could not vouch for it but there was a possibility. The look of hope with which Ivan Ilych watched the doctor out was so pathetic that Praskovya Fëdorovna, seeing it, even wept as she left the room to hand the doctor his fee.

260   The gleam of hope kindled by the doctor's encouragement did not last long. The same room, the same pictures, curtains, wallpaper, medicine bottles, were all there, and the same aching suffering body, and Ivan Ilych began to moan. They gave him a subcutaneous injection and he sank into oblivion.

It was twilight when he came to. They brought him his dinner and he swallowed some beef tea with difficulty, and then everything was the same again and night was coming on.

After dinner, at seven o'clock, Praskovya Fëdorovna came into the room in evening dress, her full bosom pushed up by her corset, and with traces of powder on her face. She had reminded him in the morning that they were going to the theater. Sarah Bernhardt was visiting the town and they had a box, which he had insisted on their taking. Now he had forgotten about it and her toilet offended him, but he concealed his vexation when he remembered that he had himself insisted on their securing a box and going because it would be an instructive and aesthetic pleasure for the children.

Praskovya Fëdorovna came in, self-satisfied but yet with a rather guilty air. She sat down and asked how he was, but, as he saw, only for the sake of asking and not in order to learn about it, knowing that there was nothing to learn—and then went on to what she really wanted to say: that she would not on any account have gone but that the box had been taken and Helen and their daughter were going, as well as Petrishchev (the examining magistrate, their daughter's fiancé), and that it was out of the question to let them go alone; but that she would have much preferred to sit with him for a while; and he must be sure to follow the doctor's orders while she was away.

"Oh, and Fëdor Petrovich" (the fiancé) "would like to come in. May he? And Lisa?"

265   "All right."

Their daughter came in in full evening dress, her fresh young flesh exposed (making a show of that very flesh which in his own case caused so much suffering), strong, healthy, evidently in love, and impatient with illness, suffering, and death, because they interfered with her happiness.

Fëdor Petrovich came in too, in evening dress, his hair curled *á la Capoul*,[19] a tight stiff collar round his long sinewy neck, an enormous white shirt-front, and narrow black trousers tightly stretched over his strong thighs. He had one white glove tightly drawn on, and was holding his opera hat in his hand.

Following him the schoolboy crept in unnoticed, in a new uniform, poor little fellow, and wearing gloves. Terribly dark shadows showed under his eyes, the meaning of which Ivan Ilych knew well.

His son had always seemed pathetic to him, and now it was dreadful to see the boy's frightened look of pity. It seemed to Ivan Ilych that Vasya was the only one besides Gerasim who understood and pitied him.

270   They all sat down and again asked how he was. A silence followed. Lisa asked her mother about the opera-glasses, and there was an altercation be-

---

[19]**hair curled *á la Capoul*** an elaborate hairstyle for men, named after a French singer.

tween mother and daughter as to who had taken them and where they had been put. This occasioned some unpleasantness.

Fëdor Petrovich inquired of Ivan Ilych whether he had ever seen Sarah Bernhardt. Ivan Ilych did not at first catch the question, but then replied: "No, have you seen her before?"

"Yes, in *Adrienne Lecouvreur*."[20]

Praskovya Fëdorovna mentioned some rôles in which Sarah Bernhardt was particularly good. Her daughter disagreed. Conversation sprang up as to the elegance and realism of her acting—the sort of conversation that is always repeated and is always the same.

In the midst of the conversation Fëdor Petrovich glanced at Ivan Ilych and became silent. The others also looked at him and grew silent. Ivan Ilych was staring with glittering eyes straight before him, evidently indignant with them. This had to be rectified, but it was impossible to do so. The silence had to be broken, but for a time no one dared to break it and they all became afraid that the conventional deception would suddenly become obvious and the truth become plain to all. Lisa was the first to pluck up courage and break that silence, but by trying to hide what everybody was feeling, she betrayed it.

275   "Well, if we are going it's time to start," she said, looking at her watch, a present from her father, and with a faint and significant smile at Fëdor Petrovich relating to something known only to them. She got up with a rustle of her dress.

They all rose, said good-night, and went away.

When they had gone it seemed to Ivan Ilych that he felt better; the falsity had gone with them. But the pain remained—that same pain and that same fear that made everything monotonously alike, nothing harder and nothing easier. Everything was worse.

Again minute followed minute and hour followed hour. Everything remained the same and there was no cessation. And the inevitable end of it all became more and more terrible.

"Yes, send Gerasim here," he replied to a question Peter asked.

IX

280   His wife returned late at night. She came in on tiptoe, but he heard her, opened his eyes, and made haste to close them again. She wished to send Gerasim away and to sit with him herself, but he opened his eyes and said: "No, go away."

"Are you in great pain?"

"Always the same."

"Take some opium."

He agreed and took some. She went away.

285   Till about three in the morning he was in a state of stupefied misery. It seemed to him that he and his pain were being thrust into a narrow, deep black sack, but though they were pushed further and further in they could not be pushed to the bottom. And this, terrible enough in itself, was accompanied by suffering. He was frightened yet wanted to fall through the sack, he struggled but yet cooperated. And suddenly he broke through, fell, and

---

[20]***Adrienne Lecouvreur*** tragedy (1849) by the French dramatist Eugéne Scribe.

regained consciousness. Gerasim was sitting at the foot of the bed dozing quietly and patiently, while he himself lay with his emaciated stockinged legs resting on Gerasim's shoulders; the same shaded candle was there and the same unceasing pain.

"Go away, Gerasim," he whispered.

"It's all right, sir. I'll stay a while."

"No. Go away."

He removed his legs from Gerasim's shoulders, turned sideways onto his arm, and felt sorry for himself. He only waited till Gerasim had gone into the next room and then restrained himself no longer but wept like a child. He wept on account of his helplessness, his terrible loneliness, the cruelty of man, the cruelty of God, and the absence of God.

290   "Why hast Thou done all this? Why hast Thou brought me here? Why, why dost Thou torment me so terribly?"

He did not expect an answer and yet wept because there was no answer and could be none. The pain grew more acute, but he did not stir and did not call. He said to himself: "Go on! Strike me! But what is it for? What have I done to Thee? What is it for?"

Then he grew quiet and not only ceased weeping but even held his breath and became all attention. It was as though he was listening not to an audible voice but to the voice of his soul, to the current of thoughts arising within him.

"What is it you want?" was the first clear conception capable of expression in words, that he heard.

"What do you want? What do you want?" he repeated to himself.

295   "What do I want? To live and not to suffer," he answered.

And again he listened with such concentrated attention that even his pain did not distract him.

"To live? How?" asked his inner voice.

"Why, to live as I used to—well and pleasantly."

"As you lived before, well and pleasantly?" the voice repeated.

300   And in imagination he began to recall the best moments of his pleasant life. But strange to say none of those best moments of his pleasant life now seemed at all what they had then seemed—none of them except the first recollections of childhood. There, in childhood, there had been something really pleasant with which it would be possible to live if it could return. But the child who had experienced that happiness existed no longer, it was like a reminiscence of somebody else.

As soon as the period began which had produced the present Ivan Ilych, all that had then seemed joys now melted before his sight and turned into something trivial and often nasty.

And the further he departed from childhood and the nearer he came to the present the more worthless and doubtful were the joys. This began with the School of Law. A little that was really good was still found there—there was lightheartedness, friendship, and hope. But in the upper classes there had already been fewer of such good moments. Then during the first years of his official career, when he was in the service of the Governor, some pleasant moments again occurred: they were the memories of love for a woman. Then all became confused and there was still less of what was good; later on again there was still less that was good, and the further he went the less there was. His marriage, a mere accident, then the disenchantment that followed it, his wife's bad breath and the sensuality and hypocrisy; then the deadly official life and those preoccupations about money, a year of it, and two, and ten, and twenty, and always the same thing. And the longer it lasted the more deadly it became. "It is as if I had been going downhill while I imagined I was going up. And that is really what it was. I was going up in public opinion, but to the same extent life was ebbing away from me. And now it is all done and there is only death."

"Then what does it mean? Why? It can't be that life is so senseless and horrible. But if it really has been so horrible and senseless, why must I die and die in agony? There is something wrong!"

"Maybe I did not live as I ought to have done," it suddenly occurred to him. "But how could that be, when I did everything properly?" he replied, and immediately dismissed from his mind this, the sole solution of all the riddles of life and death, as something quite impossible.

305   "Then what do you want now? To live? Live how? Live as you lived in the law courts when the usher proclaimed 'The judge is coming!' The judge is coming, the judge!" he repeated to himself. "Here he is, the judge. But I am not guilty!" he exclaimed angrily. "What is it for?" And he ceased crying, but turning his face to the wall continued to ponder on the same question: Why, and for what purpose, is there all this horror? But however much he pondered he found no answer. And whenever the thought occurred to him, as it often did, that it all resulted from his not having lived as he ought to have done, he at once recalled the correctness of his whole life and dismissed so strange an idea.

X

Another fortnight passed. Ivan Ilych now no longer left his sofa. He would not lie in bed but lay on the sofa, facing the wall nearly all the time. He suffered ever the same unceasing agonies and in his loneliness pondered always on the same insoluble question: "What is this? Can it be that it is Death?" And the inner voice answered: "Yes, it is Death."

"Why these sufferings?" And the voice answered, "For no reason—they just are so." Beyond and besides this there was nothing.

From the very beginning of his illness, ever since he had first been to see the doctor, Ivan Ilych's life had been divided between two contrary and alternating moods: now it was despair and the expectation of this uncomprehended and terrible death, and now hope and an intently interested observation of the functioning of his organs. Now before his eyes there was only a kidney or an intestine that temporarily evaded its duty, and now only that incomprehensible and dreadful death from which it was impossible to escape.

These two states of mind had alternated from the very beginning of his illness, but the further it progressed the more doubtful and fantastic became the conception of the kidney, and the more real the sense of impending death.

310   He had but to call to mind what he had been three months before and what he was now, to call to mind with what regularity he had been going downhill, for every possibility of hope to be shattered.

Latterly during that loneliness in which he found himself as he lay facing the back of the sofa, a loneliness in the midst of a populous town and surrounded by numerous acquaintances and relations but that yet could not have been more complete anywhere—either at the bottom of the sea or under the earth—during that terrible loneliness Ivan Ilych had lived only in memories of the past. Pictures of his past rose before him one after another. They always began with what was nearest in time and then went back to what was most remote—to his childhood—and rested there. If he thought of the stewed prunes that had been offered him that day, his mind went back to the raw shrivelled French plums of his childhood, their peculiar flavor and the flow of saliva when he sucked their stones, and along with the memory of that taste came a whole series of memories of those days: his nurse, his brother, and their toys. "No, I mustn't think of that. . . . It is too painful," Ivan Ilych said to himself, and brought himself back to the present—to the button on the back of the sofa and the creases in its morocco.[21] "Morocco is expensive, but it does not wear well: there had been a quarrel about it. It was a different kind of quarrel and a different kind of morocco that time when we tore father's portfolio and were punished, and mama brought us some tarts. . . ." And again his thoughts dwelt on his childhood, and again it was painful and he tried to banish them and fix his mind on something else.

Then again together with that chain of memories another series passed through his mind—of how his illness had progressed and grown worse. There also the further back he looked the more life there had been. There had been more of what was good in life and more of life itself. The two merged together. "Just as the pain went on getting worse and worse, so my life grew worse and worse," he thought. "There is one bright spot there at the back, at the beginning of life, and afterwards all becomes blacker and blacker and proceeds more and more rapidly—in inverse ratio to the square of the distance from death," thought Ivan Ilych. And the example of a stone falling downwards with increasing velocity entered his mind. Life, a series of increasing sufferings, flies further and further towards its end—the most terrible suffering. "I am flying. . . ." He shuddered, shifted himself, and tried to resist, but was already aware that resistance was impossible, and again, with eyes weary of gazing but unable to cease seeing what was before them, he stared at the back of the sofa and waited—awaiting that dreadful fall and shock and destruction.

"Resistance is impossible!" he said to himself. "If I could only understand what it is all for! But that too is impossible. An explanation would be possible if it could be said that I have not lived as I ought to. But it is impossible to say that," and he remembered all the legality, correctitude, and propriety of his life. "That at any rate can certainly not be admitted," he thought, and his lips smiled ironically as if someone could see that smile and be taken in by it. "There is no explanation! Agony, death. . . . What for?"

XI

Another two weeks went by in this way and during that fortnight an event occurred that Ivan Ilych and his wife had desired. Petrishchev formally proposed. It happened in the evening. The next day Praskovya Fëdorovna came into her husband's room considering how best to inform him of it, but that very night there had been a fresh change for the worse in his condition. She found him still lying on the sofa but in a different position. He lay on his back, groaning and staring fixedly straight in front of him.

---

[21]**morocco** soft, fine leather made of goatskin.

315   She began to remind him of his medicines, but he turned his eyes towards her with such a look that she did not finish what she was saying; so great an animosity, to her in particular, did that look express.

"For Christ's sake let me die in peace!" he said.

She would have gone away, but just then their daughter came in and went up to say good morning. He looked at her as he had done at his wife, and in reply to her inquiry about his health said dryly that he would soon free them all of himself. They were both silent and after sitting with him for a while went away.

"Is it our fault?" Lisa said to her mother. "It's as if we were to blame! I am sorry for papa, but why should we be tortured?"

The doctor came at his usual time. Ivan Ilych answered "Yes" and "No," never taking his angry eyes from him, and at last said: "You know you can do nothing for me, so leave me alone."

320   "We can ease your sufferings."

"You can't even do that. Let me be."

The doctor went into the drawing-room and told Praskovya Fëdorovna that the case was very serious and that the only resource left was opium to allay her husband's sufferings, which must be terrible.

It was true, as the doctor said, that Ivan Ilych's physical sufferings were terrible, but worse than the physical sufferings were his mental sufferings, which were his chief torture.

His mental sufferings were due to the fact that one night, as he looked at Gerasim's sleepy, good-natured face with its prominent cheekbones, the question suddenly occurred to him: "What if my whole life has really been wrong?"

325   It occurred to him that what had appeared perfectly impossible before, namely that he had not spent his life as he should have done, might after all be true. It occurred to him that his scarcely perceptible attempts to struggle against what was considered good by the most highly placed people, those scarcely noticeable impulses which he had immediately suppressed, might have been the real thing, and all the rest false. And his professional duties and the whole arrangement of his life and of his family, and all his social and official interests, might all have been false. He tried to defend all those things to himself and suddenly felt the weakness of what he was defending. There was nothing to defend.

"But if that is so," he said to himself, "and I am leaving this life with the consciousness that I have lost all that was given me and it is impossible to rectify it—what then?"

He lay on his back and began to pass his life in review in quite a new way. In the morning when he saw first his footman, then his wife, then his daughter, and then the doctor, their every word and movement confirmed to him the awful truth that had been revealed to him during the night. In them he saw himself—all that for which he had lived—and saw clearly that it was not real at all, but a terrible and huge deception which had hidden both life and death. This consciousness intensified his physical suffering tenfold. He groaned and tossed about, and pulled at his clothing which choked and stifled him. And he hated them on that account.

He was given a large dose of opium and became unconscious, but at noon his sufferings began again. He drove everybody away and tossed from side to side.

His wife came to him and said:

330   "Jean, my dear, do this for me. It can't do any harm and often helps. Healthy people often do it."

He opened his eyes wide.

"What? Take communion? Why? It's unnecessary! However. . . ."

She began to cry.

"Yes, do, my dear. I'll send for our priest. He is such a nice man."

335   "All right. Very well," he muttered.

When the priest came and heard his confession, Ivan Ilych was softened and seemed to feel a relief from his doubts and consequently from his sufferings, and for a moment there came a ray of hope. He again began to think of the vermiform appendix and the possibility of correcting it. He received the sacrament with tears in his eyes.

When they laid him down again afterwards he felt a moment's ease, and the hope that he might live awoke in him again. He began to think of the operation that had been suggested to him. "To live! I want to live!" he said to himself.

His wife came in to congratulate him after his communion, and when uttering the usual conventional words she added:

"You feel better, don't you?"

340   Without looking at her he said "Yes."

Her dress, her figure, the expression of her face, the tone of her voice, all revealed the same thing. "This is wrong, it is not as it should be. All you have lived for and still live for is falsehood and deception, hiding life and death from you." And as soon as he admitted that thought, his hatred and his agonizing physical suffering again sprang up, and with that suffering a consciousness of the unavoidable, approaching end. And to this was added a new sensation of grinding shooting pain and a feeling of suffocation.

The expression of his face when he uttered that "yes" was dreadful. Having uttered it, he looked her straight in the eyes, turned on his face with a rapidity extraordinary in his weak state and shouted:

"Go away! Go away and leave me alone!"

XII

From that moment the screaming began that continued for three days, and was so terrible that one could not hear it through two closed doors without horror. At the moment he answered his wife he realized that he was lost, that there was no return, that the end had come, the very end, and his doubts were still unsolved and remained doubts.

345   "Oh! Oh! Oh!" he cried in various intonations. He had begun by screaming "I won't!" and continued screaming on the letter O.

For three whole days, during which time did not exist for him, he struggled in that black sack into which he was being thrust by an invisible, resistless force. He struggled as a man condemned to death struggles in the hands of the executioner, knowing that he cannot save himself. And every moment he felt that despite all his efforts he was drawing nearer and nearer to what terrified him. He felt that his agony was due to his being thrust into that black hole and still more to his not being able to get right into it. He was hindered from getting into it by his conviction that his life had been a good one. That very justification of his life held him fast and prevented his moving forward, and it caused him most torment of all.

Suddenly some force struck him in the chest and side, making it still harder to breathe, and he fell through the hole and there at the bottom was a light. What had happened to him was like the sensation one sometimes experiences in a railway carriage when one thinks one is going backwards while one is really going forwards and suddenly becomes aware of the real direction.

"Yes, it was all not the right thing," he said to himself, "but that's no matter. It can be done. But what *is* the right thing?" he asked himself, and suddenly grew quiet.

This occurred at the end of the third day, two hours before his death. Just then his schoolboy son had crept softly in and gone up to the bedside. The dying man was still screaming desperately and waving his arms. His hand fell on the boy's head, and the boy caught it, pressed it to his lips, and began to cry.

350   At that very moment Ivan Ilych fell through and caught sight of the light, and it was revealed to him that though his life had not been what it should have been, this could still be rectified. He asked himself, "What *is* the right thing?" and grew still, listening. Then he felt that someone was kissing his hand. He opened his eyes, looked at his son, and felt sorry for him. His wife came up to him and he glanced at her. She was gazing at him open-mouthed, with undried tears on her nose and cheek and a despairing look on her face. He felt sorry for her too.

"Yes, I am making them wretched," he thought. "They are sorry, but it will be better for them when I die." He wished to say this but had not the strength to utter it. "Besides, why speak? I must act," he thought. With a look at his wife he indicated his son and said: "Take him away . . . sorry for him . . . sorry for you too. . . ." He tried to add, "forgive me," but said "forgo" and waved his hand, knowing that He whose understanding mattered would understand.

And suddenly it grew clear to him that what had been oppressing him and would not leave him was all dropping away at once from two sides, from ten sides, and from all sides. He was sorry for them, he must act so as not to hurt them: release them and free himself from these sufferings. "How good and how simple!" he thought. "And the pain?" he asked himself. "What has become of it? Where are you, pain?"

He turned his attention to it.

"Yes, here it is. Well, what of it? Let the pain be."

355   "And death . . . where is it?"

He sought his former accustomed fear of death and did not find it. "Where is it? What death?" There was no fear because there was no death.

In place of death there was light.

"So that's what it is!" he suddenly exclaimed aloud. "What joy!"

To him all this happened in a single instant, and the meaning of that instant did not change. For those present his agony continued for another two hours. Something rattled in his throat, his emaciated body twitched, then the gasping and rattle became less and less frequent.

360   "It is finished!" said someone near him.

He heard these words and repeated them in his soul.

"Death is finished," he said to himself. "It is no more!"

He drew in a breath, stopped in the midst of a sigh, stretched out, and died.

GUY DE MAUPASSANT

Born and raised in Normandy, the French novelist and short-story writer Guy de Maupassant (1850–1893) studied law in Paris, then served in the Franco-Prussian War. Afterward he worked for a time as a clerk for the government until, with the support of the novelist Gustave Flaubert (a friend of Maupassant's mother) and later Émile Zola, he decided to pursue a career as a writer. Ironic and pointed, detached yet compassionate, Maupassant explores human folly and its both grim and comic consequences. His first great success came in April 1880, with the publication of the story "Boule de Suif" ("Ball of Fat"), about a prostitute traveling by coach, with a number of bourgeois companions, through Prussian-occupied France during wartime. Maupassant published six novels, including Bel-Ami *(1885) and* Pierre et Jean *(1888), and a number of collections of stories, before his untimely death from the effects of syphilis, a month short of his forty-third birthday. Like many of his stories, "The Necklace" uses realistic observation and keenly chosen detail to tell its story of a misunderstanding and the years of hard labor that follow from it.*

The Necklace   [1885]

Translated by Marjorie Laurie

She was one of those pretty and charming girls who are sometimes, as if by a mistake of destiny, born in a family of clerks. She had no dowry, no expectations, no means of being known, understood, loved, wedded by any rich and distinguished man; and she let herself be married to a little clerk at the Ministry of Public Instruction.

She dressed plainly because she could not dress well, but she was as unhappy as though she had really fallen from her proper station, since with women there is neither caste nor rank: and beauty, grace and charm act instead of family and birth. Natural fineness, instinct for what is elegant, suppleness of wit, are the sole hierarchy, and make from women of the people the equals of the very greatest ladies.

She suffered ceaselessly, feeling herself born for all the delicacies and all the luxuries. She suffered from the poverty of her dwelling, from the wretched look of the walls, from the worn-out chairs, from the ugliness of the curtains. All those things, of which another woman of her rank would never even have been conscious, tortured her and made her angry. The sight of the little Breton peasant who did her humble housework aroused in her regrets which were despairing, and distracted dreams. She thought of the silent antechambers hung with Oriental tapestry, lit by tall bronze candelabra, and of the two great footmen in knee breeches who sleep in the big armchairs, made drowsy by the heavy warmth of the hot-air stove. She thought of the long *salons*[1] fitted up with ancient silk, of the delicate furniture carrying priceless curiosities, and of the coquettish perfumed boudoirs made for talks at five o'clock with intimate friends, with men famous and sought after, whom all women envy and whose attention they all desire.

---

[1] *salons* drawing rooms.

When she sat down to dinner, before the round table covered with a table-cloth three days old, opposite her husband, who uncovered the soup tureen and declared with an enchanted air, "Ah, the good *pot-au-feu!*[2] I don't know anything better than that," she thought of dainty dinners, of shining silverware, of tapestry which peopled the walls with ancient personages and with strange birds flying in the midst of a fairy forest; and she thought of delicious dishes served on marvelous plates, and of the whispered gallantries which you listen to with a sphinxlike smile, while you are eating the pink flesh of a trout or the wings of a quail.

5   She had no dresses, no jewels, nothing. And she loved nothing but that; she felt made for that. She would so have liked to please, to be envied, to be charming, to be sought after.

She had a friend, a former schoolmate at the convent, who was rich, and whom she did not like to go and see any more, because she suffered so much when she came back.

But one evening, her husband returned home with a triumphant air, and holding a large envelope in his hand.

"There," said he. "Here is something for you."

She tore the paper sharply, and drew out a printed card which bore these words:

10   "The Minister of Public Instruction and Mme. Georges Ramponneau request the honor of M. and Mme. Loisel's company at the palace of the Ministry on Monday evening, January eighteenth."

Instead of being delighted, as her husband hoped, she threw the invitation on the table with disdain, murmuring:

"What do you want me to do with that?"

"But, my dear, I thought you would be glad. You never go out, and this is such a fine opportunity. I had awful trouble to get it. Everyone wants to go; it is very select, and they are not giving many invitations to clerks. The whole official world will be there."

She looked at him with an irritated glance, and said, impatiently:

15   "And what do you want me to put on my back?"

He had not thought of that; he stammered:

"Why, the dress you go to the theater in. It looks very well, to me."

He stopped, distracted, seeing his wife was crying. Two great tears descended slowly from the corners of her eyes toward the corners of her mouth. He stuttered:

"What's the matter? What's the matter?"

20   But, by violent effort, she had conquered her grief, and she replied, with a calm voice, while she wiped her wet cheeks:

"Nothing. Only I have no dress and therefore I can't go to this ball. Give your card to some colleague whose wife is better equipped than I."

He was in despair. He resumed:

"Come, let us see, Mathilde. How much would it cost, a suitable dress, which you could use on other occasions, something very simple?"

She reflected several seconds, making her calculations and wondering also what sum she could ask without drawing on herself an immediate refusal and a frightened exclamation from the economical clerk.

---

[2]*pot-au-feu* stew.

25   Finally, she replied, hesitatingly:

"I don't know exactly, but I think I could manage it with four hundred francs."

He had grown a little pale, because he was laying aside just that amount to buy a gun and treat himself to a little shooting next summer on the plain of Nanterre, with several friends who went to shoot larks down there, of a Sunday.

But he said:

"All right. I will give you four hundred francs. And try to have a pretty dress."

30   The day of the ball drew near, and Mme. Loisel seemed sad, uneasy, anxious. Her dress was ready, however. Her husband said to her one evening:

"What is the matter? Come, you've been so queer these last three days."

And she answered:

"It annoys me not to have a single jewel, not a single stone, nothing to put on. I shall look like distress. I should almost rather not go at all."

He resumed:

35   "You might wear natural flowers. It's very stylish at this time of the year. For ten francs you can get two or three magnificent roses."

She was not convinced.

"No; there's nothing more humiliating than to look poor among other women who are rich."

But her husband cried:

"How stupid you are! Go look up your friend Mme. Forestier, and ask her to lend you some jewels. You're quite thick enough with her to do that."

40   She uttered a cry of joy:

"It's true. I never thought of it."

The next day she went to her friend and told of her distress.

Mme. Forestier went to a wardrobe with a glass door, took out a large jewel-box, brought it back, opened it, and said to Mme. Loisel:

"Choose, my dear."

45   She saw first of all some bracelets, then a pearl necklace, then a Venetian cross, gold and precious stones of admirable workmanship. She tried on the ornaments before the glass, hesitated, could not make up her mind to part with them, to give them back. She kept asking:

"Haven't you any more?"

"Why, yes. Look. I don't know what you like."

All of a sudden she discovered, in a black satin box, a superb necklace of diamonds, and her heart began to beat with an immoderate desire. Her hands trembled as she took it. She fastened it around her throat, outside her high-necked dress, and remained lost in ecstasy at the sight of herself.

Then she asked, hesitating, filled with anguish:

50   "Can you lend me that, only that?"

"Why, yes, certainly."

She sprang upon the neck of her friend, kissed her passionately, then fled with her treasure.

The day of the ball arrived. Mme. Loisel made a great success. She was prettier than them all, elegant, gracious, smiling, and crazy with joy. All the men looked at her, asked her name, endeavored to be introduced. All the attachés of the Cabinet wanted to waltz with her. She was remarked by the minister himself.

She danced with intoxication, with passion, made drunk by pleasure, forgetting all, in the triumph of her beauty, in the glory of her success, in a sort of cloud of happiness composed of all this homage, of all this admiration, of all these awakened desires, and of that sense of complete victory which is so sweet to a woman's heart.

55   She went away about four o'clock in the morning. Her husband had been sleeping since midnight, in a little deserted anteroom, with three other gentlemen whose wives were having a very good time. He threw over her shoulders the wraps which he had brought, modest wraps of common life, whose poverty contrasted with the elegance of the ball dress. She felt this, and wanted to escape so as not to be remarked by the other women, who were enveloping themselves in costly furs.

Loisel held her back.

"Wait a bit. You will catch cold outside. I will go and call a cab."

But she did not listen to him, and rapidly descended the stairs. When they were in the street they did not find a carriage; and they began to look for one, shouting after the cabmen whom they saw passing by at a distance.

They went down toward the Seine, in despair, shivering with cold. At last they found on the quay one of those ancient noctambulant coupés which, exactly as if they were ashamed to show their misery during the day, are never seen round Paris until after nightfall.

60   It took them to their door in the Rue des Martyrs, and once more, sadly, they climbed up homeward. All was ended, for her. And as to him, he reflected that he must be at the Ministry at ten o'clock.

She removed the wraps which covered her shoulders, before the glass, so as once more to see herself in all her glory. But suddenly she uttered a cry. She no longer had the necklace around her neck!

Her husband, already half undressed, demanded:

"What is the matter with you?"

She turned madly toward him:

65   "I have—I have—I've lost Mme. Forestier's necklace."

He stood up, distracted.

"What!—how?—impossible!"

And they looked in the folds of her dress, in the folds of her cloak, in her pockets, everywhere. They did not find it.

He asked:

70   "You're sure you had it on when you left the ball?"

"Yes, I felt it in the vestibule of the palace."

"But if you had lost it in the street we should have heard it fall. It must be in the cab."

"Yes. Probably. Did you take his number?"

"No. And you, didn't you notice it?"

75   "No."

They looked, thunderstruck, at one another. At last Loisel put on his clothes.

"I shall go back on foot," said he, "over the whole route which we have taken to see if I can find it."

And he went out. She sat waiting on a chair in her ball dress, without strength to go to bed, overwhelmed, without fire, without a thought.

Her husband came back about seven o'clock. He had found nothing.

80　　　He went to Police Headquarters, to the newspaper offices, to offer a reward: he went to the cab companies—everywhere, in fact, whither he was urged by the least suspicion of hope.

She waited all day, in the same condition of mad fear before this terrible calamity.

Loisel returned at night with a hollow, pale face; he had discovered nothing.

"You must write to your friend," said he, "that you have broken the clasp of her necklace and that you are having it mended. That will give us time to turn round."

She wrote at his dictation.

85　　　At the end of a week they had lost all hope.

And Loisel, who had aged five years, declared:

"We must consider how to replace that ornament."

The next day they took the box which had contained it, and they went to the jeweler whose name was found within. He consulted his books.

"It was not I, madame, who sold that necklace; I must simply have furnished the case."

90　　　Then they went from jeweler to jeweler, searching for a necklace like the other, consulting their memories, sick both of them with chagrin and anguish.

They found, in a shop at the Palais Royal, a string of diamonds which seemed to them exactly like the one they looked for. It was worth forty thousand francs. They could have it for thirty-six.

So they begged the jeweler not to sell it for three days yet. And they made a bargain that he should buy it back for thirty-four thousand francs, in case they found the other one before the end of February.

Loisel possessed eighteen thousand francs which his father had left him. He would borrow the rest.

He did borrow, asking a thousand francs of one, five hundred of another, five louis here, three louis[3] there. He gave notes, took up ruinous obligations, dealt with usurers and all the race of lenders. He compromised all the rest of his life, risked his signature without even knowing if he could meet it; and, frightened by the pains yet to come, by the black misery which was about to fall upon him, by the prospect of all the physical privation and of all the moral tortures which he was to suffer, he went to get the new necklace, putting down upon the merchant's counter thirty-six thousand francs.

95　　　When Mme. Loisel took back the necklace, Mme. Forestier said to her, with a chilly manner:

"You should have returned it sooner; I might have needed it."

She did not open the case, as her friend had so much feared. If she had detected the substitution, what would she have thought, what would she have said? Would she not have taken Mme. Loisel for a thief?

Mme. Loisel now knew the horrible existence of the needy. She took her part, moreover, all of a sudden, with heroism. That dreadful debt must be paid. She would pay it. They dismissed their servant; they changed their lodgings; they rented a garret under the roof.

---

[3]**louis** a gold coin worth 20 francs.

She came to know what heavy housework meant and the odious cares of the kitchen. She washed the dishes, using her rosy nails on the greasy pots and pans. She washed the dirty linen, the shirts, and the dishcloths, which she dried upon a line; she carried the slops down to the street every morning, and carried up the water, stopping for breath at every landing. And, dressed like a woman of the people, she went to the fruiterer, the grocer, the butcher, her basket on her arm, bargaining, insulted, defending her miserable money sou by sou.

100   Each month they had to meet some notes, renew others, obtain more time.

Her husband worked in the evening making a fair copy of some tradesman's accounts, and late at night he often copied manuscript for five sous a page.

And this life lasted for ten years.

At the end of ten years, they had paid everything, everything, with the rates of usury, and the accumulations of the compound interest.

Mme. Loisel looked old now. She had become the woman of impoverished households—strong and hard and rough. With frowsy hair, skirts askew, and red hands, she talked loud while washing the floor with great swishes of water. But sometimes, when her husband was at the office, she sat down near the window, and she thought of that gay evening of long ago, of the ball where she had been so beautiful and so fêted.

105   What would have happened if she had not lost that necklace? Who knows? Who knows? How life is strange and changeful! How little a thing is needed for us to be lost or to be saved!

But, one Sunday, having gone to take a walk in the Champs Elysées to refresh herself from the labor of the week, she suddenly perceived a woman who was leading a child. It was Mme. Forestier, still young, still beautiful, still charming.

Mme. Loisel felt moved. Was she going to speak to her? Yes, certainly. And now that she had paid, she was going to tell her all about it. Why not?

She went up.

"Good day, Jeanne."

110   The other, astonished to be familiarly addressed by this plain goodwife, did not recognize her at all, and stammered:

"But—madam!—I do not know—You must be mistaken."

"No. I am Mathilde Loisel."

Her friend uttered a cry.

"Oh, my poor Mathilde! How you are changed!"

115   "Yes, I have had days hard enough, since I have seen you, days wretched enough—and that because of you!"

"Of me! How so?"

"Do you remember that diamond necklace which you lent me to wear at the ministerial ball?"

"Yes. Well?"

"Well, I lost it."

120   "What do you mean? You brought it back."

"I brought you back another just like it. And for this we have been ten years paying. You can understand that it was not easy for us, us who had nothing. At last it is ended, and I am very glad."

Mme. Forestier had stopped.

"You say that you bought a necklace of diamonds to replace mine?"

"Yes. You never noticed it, then! They were very like."

125   And she smiled with a joy which was proud and naïve at once.

Mme. Forestier, strongly moved, took her two hands.

"Oh, my poor Mathilde! Why, my necklace was paste. It was worth at most five hundred francs!"

CHARLOTTE PERKINS GILMAN

Charlotte Perkins Gilman (1860–1935), née Charlotte Perkins, was born in Hartford, Connecticut. Her father deserted the family soon after Charlotte's birth; she was brought up by her mother, who found it difficult to make ends meet. For a while Charlotte worked as an artist and teacher of art, and in 1884, when she was twenty-four, she married an artist. In 1885 she had a daughter, but soon after the birth of the girl Charlotte had a nervous breakdown. At her husband's urging she spent a month in the sanitarium of Dr. S. Weir Mitchell, a physician who specialized in treating women with nervous disorders. (Mitchell is specifically named in "The Yellow Wallpaper.") Because the treatment—isolation and total rest—nearly drove her to insanity, she fled Mitchell and her husband. In California she began a career as a lecturer and writer on feminist topics. (She also supported herself by teaching school and by keeping a boardinghouse.) Among her books are Women and Economics *(1899) and* The Man-Made World *(1911), which have been revived by the feminist movement. In 1900 she married a cousin, George Gilman. From all available evidence, the marriage was successful. Certainly it did not restrict her activities as a feminist. In 1935, suffering from inoperable cancer, she took her own life.*

"The Yellow Wallpaper," written in 1892—that is, written after she had been treated by S. Weir Mitchell for her nervous breakdown—was at first interpreted either as a ghost story or as a Poe-like study of insanity. Only in recent years has it been seen as a feminist story. (One might ask oneself if these interpretations are mutually exclusive.)

The Yellow Wallpaper   [1892]

It is very seldom that mere ordinary people like John and myself secure ancestral halls for the summer.

A colonial mansion, a hereditary estate. I would say a haunted house, and reach the height of romantic felicity—but that would be asking too much of fate!

Still I will proudly declare that there is something queer about it.

Else, why should it be let so cheaply? And why have stood so long untenanted?

5   John laughs at me, of course, but one expects that in marriage.

John is practical in the extreme. He has no patience with faith, an intense horror of superstition, and he scoffs openly at any talk of things not to be felt and seen and put down in figures.

John is a physician, and *perhaps*—(I would not say it to a living soul, of course, but this is dead paper and a great relief to my mind)—*perhaps* that is one reason I do not get well faster.

You see he does not believe I am sick!

And what can one do?

10   If a physician of high standing, and one's own husband, assures friends and relatives that there is really nothing the matter with one but temporary nervous depression—a slight hysterical tendency—what is one to do?

My brother is also a physician, and also of high standing, and he says the same thing.

So I take phosphates or phosphites—whichever it is, and tonics, and journeys, and air, and exercise, and am absolutely forbidden to "work" until I am well again.

Personally, I disagree with their ideas.

Personally, I believe that congenial work, with excitement and change, would do me good.

15   But what is one to do?

I did write for a while in spite of them; but it *does* exhaust me a good deal—having to be so sly about it, or else meet with heavy opposition.

I sometimes fancy that in my condition if I had less opposition and more society and stimulus—but John says the very worst thing I can do is to think about my condition, and I confess it always makes me feel bad.

So I will let it alone and talk about the house.

The most beautiful place! It is quite alone, standing well back from the road, quite three miles from the village. It makes me think of English places that you read about, for there are hedges and walls and gates that lock, and lots of separate little houses for the gardeners and people.

20   There is a *delicious* garden! I never saw such a garden—large and shady, full of box-bordered paths, and lined with long grape-covered arbors with seats under them.

There were greenhouses, too, but they are all broken now. There was some legal trouble, I believe, something about the heirs and coheirs; anyhow, the place has been empty for years.

That spoils my ghostliness, I am afraid, but I don't care—there is something strange about the house—I can feel it.

I even said so to John one moonlight evening, but he said what I felt was a *draught,* and shut the window.

I get unreasonably angry with John sometimes. I'm sure I never used to be so sensitive. I think it is due to this nervous condition.

25   But John says if I feel so, I shall neglect proper self-control; so I take pains to control myself—before him, at least, and that makes me very tired.

I don't like our room a bit. I wanted one downstairs that opened on the piazza and had roses all over the window, and such pretty old-fashioned chintz hangings! but John would not hear of it.

He said there was only one window and not room for two beds, and no near room for him if he took another.

He is very careful and loving, and hardly lets me stir without special direction.

I have a schedule prescription for each hour in the day; he takes all care from me, and so I feel basely ungrateful not to value it more.

30   He said we came here solely on my account, that I was to have perfect rest and all the air I could get. "Your exercise depends on your strength, my dear," said he, "and your food somewhat on your appetite; but air you can absorb all the time." So we took the nursery at the top of the house.

It is a big, airy room, the whole floor nearly, with windows that look all ways, and air and sunshine galore. It was nursery first and then playroom and gymnasium, I should judge; for the windows are barred for little children, and there are rings and things in the walls.

The paint and paper look as if a boys' school had used it. It is stripped off—the paper—in great patches all around the head of my bed, about as far as I can reach, and in a great place on the other side of the room low down. I never saw a worse paper in my life.

One of those sprawling flamboyant patterns committing every artistic sin.

It is dull enough to confuse the eye in following, pronounced enough to constantly irritate and provoke study, and when you follow the lame uncertain curves for a little distance they suddenly commit suicide—plunge off at outrageous angles, destroy themselves in unheard of contradictions.

35   The color is repellent, almost revolting; a smouldering unclean yellow, strangely faded by the slow-turning sunlight.

It is a dull yet lurid orange in some places, a sickly sulphur tint in others.

No wonder the children hated it! I should hate it myself if I had to live in this room long.

There comes John, and I must put this away,—he hates to have me write a word.

We have been here two weeks, and I haven't felt like writing before, since that first day.

40   I am sitting by the window now, up in this atrocious nursery, and there is nothing to hinder my writing as much as I please, save lack of strength.

John is away all day, and even some nights when his cases are serious.

I am glad my case is not serious!

But these nervous troubles are dreadfully depressing.

John does not know how much I really suffer. He knows there is no *reason* to suffer, and that satisfies him.

45   Of course it is only nervousness. It does weigh on me so not to do my duty in any way!

I meant to be such a help to John, such a real rest and comfort, and here I am a comparative burden already!

Nobody would believe what an effort it is to do what little I am able,—to dress and entertain, and order things.

It is fortunate Mary is so good with the baby. Such a dear baby!

And yet I *cannot* be with him, it makes me so nervous.

50   I suppose John never was nervous in his life. He laughs at me so about this wallpaper!

At first he meant to repaper the room, but afterwards he said that I was letting it get the better of me, and that nothing was worse for a nervous patient than to give way to such fancies.

He said that after the wallpaper was changed it would be the heavy bedstead, and then the barred windows, and then that gate at the head of the stairs, and so on.

"You know the place is doing you good," he said, "and really, dear, I don't care to renovate the house just for a three months' rental."

"Then do let us go downstairs." I said, "there are such pretty rooms there."

55   Then he took me in his arms and called me a blessed little goose, and said he would go down to the cellar, if I wished, and have it whitewashed into the bargain.

But he is right enough about the beds and windows and things.

It is an airy and comfortable room as any one need wish, and, of course, I would not be so silly as to make him uncomfortable just for a whim.

I'm really getting quite fond of the big room, all but that horrid paper.

Out of one window I can see the garden, those mysterious deep-shaded arbors, the riotous old-fashioned flowers, and bushes and gnarly trees.

60   Out of another I get a lovely view of the bay and a little private wharf belonging to the estate. There is a beautiful shaded lane that runs down there from the house. I always fancy I see people walking in these numerous paths and arbors, but John has cautioned me not to give way to fancy in the least. He says that with my imaginative power and habit of story-making, a nervous weakness like mine is sure to lead to all manner of excited fancies, and that I ought to use my will and good sense to check the tendency. So I try.

I think sometimes that if I were only well enough to write a little it would relieve the press of ideas and rest me.

But I find I get pretty tired when I try.

It is so discouraging not to have any advice and companionship about my work. When I get really well, John says we will ask Cousin Henry and Julia down for a long visit; but he says he would as soon put fireworks in my pillow-case as to let me have those stimulating people about now.

I wish I could get well faster.

65   But I must not think about that. This paper looks to me as if it *knew* what a vicious influence it had!

There is a recurrent spot where the pattern lolls like a broken neck and two bulbous eyes stare at you upside down.

I get positively angry with the impertinence of it and the everlastingness. Up and down and sideways they crawl, and those absurd, unblinking eyes are everywhere. There is one place where two breadths didn't match, and the eyes go all up and down the line, one a little higher than the other.

I never saw so much expression in an inanimate thing before, and we all know how much expression they have! I used to lie awake as a child and get more entertainment and terror out of blank walls and plain furniture than most children could find in a toystore.

I remember what a kindly wink the knobs of our big, old bureau used to have, and there was one chair that always seemed like a strong friend.

70   I used to feel that if any of the other things looked too fierce I could always hop into that chair and be safe.

The furniture in this room is no worse than inharmonious, however, for we had to bring it all from downstairs. I suppose when this was used as a playroom they had to take the nursery things out, and no wonder! I never saw such ravages as the children have made here.

The wallpaper, as I said before, is torn off in spots, and it sticketh closer than a brother—they must have had perseverance as well as hatred.

Then the floor is scratched and gouged and splintered, the plaster itself is dug out here and there, and this great heavy bed which is all we found in the room, looks as if it had been through the wars.

But I don't mind it a bit—only the paper.

75   There comes John's sister. Such a dear girl as she is, and so careful of me! I must not let her find me writing.

She is a perfect and enthusiastic housekeeper, and hopes for no better profession. I verily believe she thinks it is the writing which made me sick!

But I can write when she is out, and see her a long way off from these windows.

There is one that commands the road, a lovely shaded winding road, and one that just looks off over the country. A lovely country, too, full of great elms and velvet meadows.

This wallpaper has a kind of sub-pattern in a different shade, a particularly irritating one, for you can only see it in certain lights, and not clearly then.

80   But in the places where it isn't faded and where the sun is just so—I can see a strange, provoking, formless sort of figure, that seems to skulk about behind that silly and conspicuous front design.

There's sister on the stairs!

Well, the Fourth of July is over! The people are all gone and I am tired out. John thought it might do me good to see a little company, so we just had mother and Nellie and the children down for a week.

Of course I didn't do a thing. Jennie sees to everything now. But it tired me all the same.

John says if I don't pick up faster he shall send me to Weir Mitchell in the fall.

85   But I don't want to go there at all. I had a friend who was in his hands once, and she says he is just like John and my brother, only more so!

Besides, it is such an undertaking to go so far.

I don't feel as if it was worth while to turn my hand over for anything, and I'm getting dreadfully fretful and querulous.

I cry at nothing, and cry most of the time.

Of course I don't when John is here, or anybody else, but when I am alone.

90   And I am alone a good deal just now. John is kept in town very often by serious cases, and Jennie is good and lets me alone when I want her to.

So I walk a little in the garden or down that lovely lane, sit on the porch under the roses, and lie down up here a good deal.

I'm getting really fond of the room in spite of the wallpaper. Perhaps *because* of the wallpaper.

It dwells in my mind so!

I lie here on this great immovable bed—it is nailed down, I believe— and follow that pattern about by the hour. It is as good as gymnastics, I assure you. I start, we'll say, at the bottom, down in the corner over there where it has not been touched, and I determine for the thousandth time that I *will* follow that pointless pattern to some sort of a conclusion.

95   I know a little of the principle of design, and I know this thing was not arranged on any laws of radiation, or alternation, or repetition, or symmetry, or anything else that I ever heard of.

It is repeated, of course, by the breadths, but not otherwise.

Looked at in one way each breadth stands alone, the bloated curves and flourishes—a kind of "debased Romanesque" with *delirium tremens*—go waddling up and down in isolated columns of fatuity.

But, on the other hand, they connect diagonally, and the sprawling outlines run off in great slanting waves of optic horror, like a lot of wallowing seaweeds in full chase.

The whole thing goes horizontally, too, at least it seems so, and I exhaust myself in trying to distinguish the order of its going in that direction.

100 They have used a horizontal breadth for a frieze, and that adds wonderfully to the confusion.

There is one end of the room where it is almost intact, and there, when the crosslights fade and the low sun shines directly upon it, I can almost fancy radiation after all,—the interminable grotesques seem to form around a common center and rush off in headlong plunges of equal distraction.

It makes me tired to follow it. I will take a nap I guess.

I don't know why I should write this.

I don't want to.

105 I don't feel able.

And I know John would think it absurd. But I *must* say what I feel and think in some way—it is such a relief.

But the effort is getting to be greater than the relief!

Half the time now I am awfully lazy, and lie down ever so much.

John says I mustn't lose my strength, and has me take cod liver oil and lots of tonics and things, to say nothing of ale and wine and rare meat.

110 Dear John! He loves me very dearly, and hates to have me sick. I tried to have a real earnest reasonable talk with him the other day, and tell him how I wish he would let me go and make a visit to Cousin Henry and Julia.

But he said I wasn't able to go, nor able to stand it after I got there; and I did not make out a very good case for myself, for I was crying before I had finished.

It is getting to be a great effort for me to think straight. Just this nervous weakness I suppose.

And dear John gathered me up in his arms, and just carried me upstairs and laid me on the bed, and sat by me and read to me till it tired my head.

He said I was his darling and his comfort and all he had, and that I must take care of myself for his sake, and keep well.

115 He says no one but myself can help me out of it, that I must use my will and self-control and not let any silly fancies run away with me.

There's one comfort, the baby is well and happy, and does not have to occupy this nursery with the horrid wallpaper.

If we had not used it, that blessed child would have! What a fortunate escape! Why, I wouldn't have a child of mine, an impressionable little thing, live in such a room for worlds.

I never thought of it before, but it is lucky that John kept me here after all. I can stand it so much easier than a baby, you see.

Of course I never mention it to them any more—I am too wise,—but I keep watch of it all the same.

120 There are things in that paper that nobody knows but me, or ever will.

Behind that outside pattern the dim shapes get clearer every day.

It is always the same shape, only very numerous.

And it is like a woman stooping down and creeping about behind that pattern. I don't like it a bit. I wonder—I begin to think—I wish John would take me away from here!

It is so hard to talk to John about my case, because he is so wise, and because he loves me so.

125   But I tried last night.

It was moonlight. The moon shines in all around just as the sun does.

I hate to see it sometimes, it creeps so slowly, and always comes in by one window or another.

John was asleep and I hated to waken him, so I kept still and watched the moonlight on that undulating wallpaper till I felt creepy.

The faint figure behind seemed to shake the pattern, just as if she wanted to get out.

130   I got up softly and went to feel and see if the paper *did* move, and when I came back John was awake.

"What is it, little girl?" he said. "Don't go walking about like that—you'll get cold."

I thought it was a good time to talk, so I told him that I really was not gaining here, and that I wished he would take me away.

"Why darling!" said he, "our lease will be up in three weeks, and I can't see how to leave before.

"The repairs are not done at home, and I cannot possibly leave town just now. Of course if you were in any danger, I could and would, but you really are better, dear, whether you can see it or not. I am a doctor, dear, and I know. You are gaining flesh and color, your appetite is better, I feel really much easier about you."

135   "I don't weigh a bit more," said I, "nor as much; and my appetite may be better in the evening when you are here, but it is worse in the morning when you are away!"

"Bless her little heart!" said he with a big hug, "she shall be as sick as she pleases! But now let's improve the shining hours by going to sleep, and talk about it in the morning!"

"And you won't go away?" I asked gloomily.

"Why, how can I, dear? It is only three weeks more and then we will take a nice little trip of a few days while Jennie is getting the house ready. Really dear you are better!"

"Better in body perhaps—" I began, and stopped short, for he sat up straight and looked at me with such a stern, reproachful look that I could not say another word.

140   "My darling," said he, "I beg of you, for my sake and for our child's sake, as well as for your own, that you will never for one instant let that idea enter your mind! There is nothing so dangerous, so fascinating, to a temperament like yours. It is a false and foolish fancy. Can you trust me as a physician when I tell you so?"

So of course I said no more on that score, and we went to sleep before long. He thought I was asleep first, but I wasn't and lay there for hours trying to decide whether that front pattern and the back pattern really did move together or separately.

On a pattern like this, by daylight, there is a lack of sequence, a defiance of law, that is a constant irritant to a normal mind.

The color is hideous enough, and unreliable enough, and infuriating enough, but the pattern is torturing.

You think you have mastered it, but just as you get well underway in following, it turns a back-somersault and there you are. It slaps you in the face, knocks you down, and tramples upon you. It is like a bad dream.

145   The outside pattern is a florid arabesque, reminding one of a fungus. If you can imagine a toadstool in joints, an interminable string of toadstools, budding and sprouting in endless convolutions—why, that is something like it.

That is, sometimes!

There is one marked peculiarity about this paper, a thing nobody seems to notice but myself, and that is that it changes as the light changes.

When the sun shoots in through the east window—I always watch for that first long, straight ray—it changes so quickly that I never can quite believe it.

That is why I watch it always.

150   By moonlight—the moon shines in all night when there is a moon—I wouldn't know it was the same paper.

At night in any kind of light, in twilight, candle light, lamplight, and worst of all by moonlight, it becomes bars! The outside pattern I mean, and the woman behind it as plain as can be.

I didn't realize for a long time what the thing was that showed behind, that dim sub-pattern, but now I am quite sure it is a woman.

By daylight she is subdued, quiet. I fancy it is the pattern that keeps her so still. It is so puzzling. It keeps me quiet by the hour.

I lie down ever so much now. John says it is good for me, and to sleep all I can.

155   Indeed he started the habit by making me lie down for an hour after each meal.

It is a very bad habit I am convinced, for you see I don't sleep.

And that cultivates deceit, for I don't tell them I'm awake—O no!

The fact is I am getting a little afraid of John.

He seems very queer sometimes, and even Jennie has an inexplicable look.

160   It strikes me occasionally, just as a scientific hypothesis,—that perhaps it is the paper!

I have watched John when he did not know I was looking, and come into the room suddenly on the most innocent excuses, and I've caught him several times *looking at the paper!* And Jennie too. I caught Jennie with her hand on it once.

She didn't know I was in the room, and when I asked her in a quiet, a very quiet voice, with the most restrained manner possible, what she was doing with the paper—she turned around as if she had been caught stealing, and looked quite angry—asked me why I should frighten her so!

Then she said that the paper stained everything it touched, that she had found yellow smooches on all my clothes and John's, and she wished we would be more careful!

Did not that sound innocent? But I know she was studying that pattern, and I am determined that nobody shall find it out but myself!

165   Life is very much more exciting now than it used to be. You see I have something more to expect, to look forward to, to watch. I really do eat better, and am more quiet than I was.

John is so pleased to see me improve! He laughed a little the other day, and said I seemed to be flourishing in spite of my wallpaper.

I turned it off with a laugh. I had no intention of telling him it was *because* of the wallpaper—he would make fun of me. He might even want to take me away.

I don't want to leave now until I have found it out. There is a week more, and I think that will be enough.

I'm feeling ever so much better! I don't sleep much at night, for it is so interesting to watch developments; but I sleep a good deal in the daytime.

170   In the daytime it is tiresome and perplexing.

There are always new shoots on the fungus, and new shades of yellow all over it. I cannot keep count of them, though I have tried conscientiously.

It is the strangest yellow, that wallpaper! It makes me think of all the yellow things I ever saw—not beautiful ones like buttercups, but old foul, bad yellow things.

But there is something else about that paper—the smell! I noticed it the moment we came into the room, but with so much air and sun it was not bad. Now we have had a week of fog and rain, and whether the windows are open or not, the smell is here.

It creeps all over the house.

175   I find it hovering in the dining-room, skulking in the parlor, hiding in the hall, lying in wait for me on the stairs.

It gets into my hair.

Even when I go to ride, if I turn my head suddenly and surprise it—there is that smell!

Such a peculiar odor, too! I have spent hours in trying to analyze it, to find what it smelled like.

It is not bad—at first, and very gentle, but quite the subtlest, most enduring odor I ever met.

180   In this damp weather it is awful, I wake up in the night and find it hanging over me.

It used to disturb me at first. I thought seriously of burning the house—to reach the smell.

But now I am used to it. The only thing I can think of that it is like is the *color* of the paper! A yellow smell.

There is a very funny mark on this wall, low down, near the mopboard. A streak that runs round the room. It goes behind every piece of furniture, except the bed, a long, straight, even *smooch,* as if it had been rubbed over and over.

I wonder how it was done and who did it, and what they did it for. Round and round and round—round and round and round—it makes me dizzy!

185   I really have discovered something at last.

Through watching so much at night, when it changes so, I have finally found out.

The front pattern *does* move—and no wonder! The woman behind shakes it!

Sometimes I think there are a great many women behind, and sometimes only one, and she crawls around fast, and her crawling shakes it all over.

Then in the very bright spots she keeps still, and in the very shady spots she just takes hold of the bars and shakes them hard.

190   And she is all the time trying to climb through. But nobody could climb through that pattern—it strangles so; I think that is why it has so many heads.

They get through, and then the pattern strangles them off and turns them upside down, and makes their eyes white!

If those heads were covered or taken off it would not be half so bad.

I think that woman gets out in the daytime!

And I'll tell you why—privately—I've seen her!

195   I can see her out of every one of my windows!

It is the same woman, I know, for she is always creeping, and most women do not creep by daylight.

I see her on that long road under the trees, creeping along, and when a carriage comes she hides under the blackberry vines.

I don't blame her a bit. It must be very humiliating to be caught creeping by daylight!

I always lock the door when I creep by daylight. I can't do it at night, for I know John would suspect something at once.

200   And John is so queer now, that I don't want to irritate him. I wish he would take another room! Besides, I don't want anybody to get that woman out at night but myself.

I often wonder if I could see her out of all the windows at once.

But, turn as fast as I can, I can only see out of one at one time. And though I always see her, she *may* be able to creep faster than I can turn!

I have watched her sometimes away off in the open country, creeping as fast as a cloud shadow in a high wind.

If only that top pattern could be gotten off from the under one! I mean to try it, little by little.

205   I have found out another funny thing, but I shan't tell at this time! It does not do to trust people too much.

There are only two more days to get this paper off, and I believe John is beginning to notice. I don't like the look in his eyes.

And I heard him ask Jennie a lot of professional questions about me. She had a very good report to give.

She said I slept a good deal in the daytime.

John knows I don't sleep very well at night, for all I'm so quiet!

210   He asked me all sorts of questions, too, and pretended to be very loving and kind.

As if I couldn't see through him!

Still, I don't wonder he acts so, sleeping under this paper for three months.

It only interests me, but I feel sure John and Jennie are secretly affected by it.

Hurrah! This is the last day, but it is enough. John is to stay in town over night, and won't be out until this evening.

215   Jennie wanted to sleep with me—the sly thing! But I told her I should undoubtedly rest better for a night all alone.

That was clever, for really I wasn't alone a bit! As soon as it was moonlight and that poor thing began to crawl and shake the pattern, I got up and ran to help her.

I pulled and she shook, I shook and she pulled, and before morning we had peeled off yards of that paper.

A strip about as high as my head and half round the room. And then when the sun came and that awful pattern began to laugh at me, I declared I would finish it to-day!

We go away to-morrow, and they are moving all the furniture down again to leave things as they were before.

220   Jennie looked at the wall in amazement, but I told her merrily that I did it out of pure spite at the vicious thing.

She laughed and said she wouldn't mind doing it herself, but I must not get tired.

How she betrayed herself that time!

But I am here, and no person touches this paper but me—not *alive!*

She tried to get me out of the room—it was too patent! But I said it was so quiet and empty and clean now that I believed I would lie down again and sleep all I could, and not to wake me even for dinner—I would call when I woke.

225   So now she is gone, and the servants are gone, and the things are gone, and there is nothing left but that great bedstead nailed down, with the canvas mattress we found on it.

We shall sleep downstairs to-night, and take the boat home to-morrow.

I quite enjoy the room, now it is bare again.

How those children did tear about here!

This bedstead is fairly gnawed!

230   But I must get to work.

I have locked the door and thrown the key down into the front path.

I don't want to go out, and I don't want to have anybody come in, till John comes.

I want to astonish him.

I've got a rope up here that even Jennie did not find. If that woman does get out, and tries to get away, I can tie her!

235   But I forgot I could not reach far without anything to stand on! This bed will *not* move!

I tried to lift and push it until I was lame, and then I got so angry I bit off a little piece at one corner—but it hurt my teeth.

Then I peeled off all the paper I could reach standing on the floor. It sticks horribly and the pattern just enjoys it! All those strangled heads and bulbous eyes and waddling fungus growths just shriek with derision!

I am getting angry enough to do something desperate. To jump out of the window would be admirable exercise, but the bars are too strong even to try.

Besides I wouldn't do it. Of course not, I know well enough that a step like that is improper and might be misconstrued.

240   I don't like to *look* out of the windows even—there are so many of those creeping women, and they creep so fast.

I wonder if they all come out of that wallpaper as I did?

But I am securely fastened now by my well-hidden rope—you don't get *me* out in the road there!

I suppose I shall have to get back behind the pattern when it comes night, and that is hard!

It is so pleasant to be out in this great room and creep around as I please!

245   I don't want to go outside. I won't, even if Jennie asks me to.

For outside you have to creep on the ground, and everything is green instead of yellow.

But here I can creep smoothly on the floor, and my shoulder just fits in that long smooch around the wall, so I cannot lose my way.

Why there's John at the door!

It is no use, young man, you can't open it!

250   How he does call and pound!

Now he's crying for an axe.

It would be a shame to break down that beautiful door!

"John dear!" said I in the gentlest voice, "the key is down by the front steps, under a plantain leaf!"

That silenced him for a few moments.

255   Then he said—very quietly indeed, "Open the door, my darling!"

"I can't," said I. "The key is down by the front door under a plantain leaf!"

And then I said it again, several times, very gently and slowly, and said it so often that he had to go and see, and he got it of course, and came in. He stopped short by the door.

"What is the matter?" he cried. "For God's sake, what are you doing!"

I kept on creeping just the same, but I looked at him over my shoulder.

260   "I've got out at last," said I, "in spite of you and Jane. And I've pulled off most of the paper, so you can't put me back!"

Now why should that man have fainted? But he did, and right across my path by the wall, so that I had to creep over him every time!

WILLA CATHER

Willa Cather (1873-1947) was born in Winchester, Virginia, but at the age of nine she moved with her family to the Nebraska prairie town of Red Cloud, which she later used and adapted for the settings, characters, and events of many of her novels and short stories.

After graduating from the University of Nebraska in 1985 Cather worked as a journalist and high school teacher in Pittsburgh, and betinning in 1904 as a member of the editorial staff of McLure's Magazine *in New York City. Her novels include* O Pioneers *(1913),* The Song of the Lark *(1915), and* Death Comes for the Archbishop *(1927).*

Paul's Case   [1905]

A Study in Temperament

It was Paul's afternoon to appear before the faculty of the Pittsburgh High School to account for his various misdemeanors. He had been suspended a week ago, and his father had called at the Principal's office and confessed his perplexity about his son. Paul entered the faculty room suave and smiling. His clothes were a trifle outgrown and the tan velvet on the collar of his open overcoat was frayed and worn; but for all that there was something of the dandy about him, and he wore an opal pin in his neatly knotted black four-in-hand, and a red carnation in his buttonhole. This latter adornment the faculty somehow felt was not properly significant of the contrite spirit befitting a boy under the ban of suspension.

Paul was tall for his age and very thin, with high, cramped shoulders and a narrow chest. His eyes were remarkable for a certain hysterical brilliancy, and he continually used them in a conscious, theatrical sort of way, peculiarly offensive in a boy. The pupils were abnormally large, as though he were addicted to belladonna, but there was a glassy glitter about them which that drug does not produce.

When questioned by the Principal as to why he was there, Paul stated, politely enough, that he wanted to come back to school. This was a lie, but Paul was quite accustomed to lying; found it, indeed, indispensable for overcoming friction. His teachers were asked to state their respective charges against him, which they did with such a rancor and aggrievedness as evinced that this was not a usual case. Disorder and impertinence were among the offenses named, yet each of his instructors felt that it was scarcely possible to put into words the real cause of the trouble, which lay in a sort of hysterically defiant manner of the boy's; in the contempt which they all knew he felt for them, and which he seemingly made not the least effort to conceal. Once, when he had been making a synopsis of a paragraph at the blackboard, his English teacher had stepped to his side and attempted to guide his hand. Paul had started back with a shudder and thrust his hands violently behind him. The astonished woman could scarcely have been more hurt and embarrassed had he struck at her. The insult was so involuntary and definitely personal as to be unforgettable. In one way and another, he had made all his teachers, men and women alike, conscious of the same feeling of physical aversion. In one class he habitually sat with his hand shading his eyes; in another he always looked out of the window during the recitation; in another he made a running commentary on the lecture, with humorous intention.

His teachers felt this afternoon that his whole attitude was symbolized by his shrug and his flippantly red carnation flower, and they fell upon him without mercy, his English teacher leading the pack. He stood through it smiling, his pale lips parted over his white teeth. (His lips were continually twitching, and he had a habit of raising his eyebrows that was contemptuous and irritating to the last degree.) Older boys than Paul had broken down and shed tears under that baptism of fire, but his set smile did not once desert him, and his only sign of discomfort was the nervous trembling of the fingers that toyed with the buttons of his overcoat, and an occasional jerking of the other hand that held his hat. Paul was always smiling, always glancing about him, seeming to feel that people might be watching him and trying to detect something. This conscious expression, since it was as far as possible from boyish mirthfulness, was usually attributed to insolence or "smartness."

5   As the inquisition proceeded, one of his instructors repeated an impertinent remark of the boy's, and the Principal asked him whether he thought that a courteous speech to have made a woman. Paul shrugged his shoulders slightly and his eyebrows twitched.

"I don't know," he replied. "I didn't mean to be polite or impolite, either. I guess it's a sort of way I have of saying things regardless."

The Principal, who was a sympathetic man, asked him whether he didn't think that a way it would be well to get rid of. Paul grinned and said he guessed so. When he was told that he could go, he bowed gracefully and went out. His bow was but a repetition of the scandalous red carnation.

His teachers were in despair, and his drawing master voiced the feeling of them all when he declared there was something about the boy which none of them understood. He added: "I don't really believe that smile of his comes altogether from insolence; there's something sort of haunted about it. The boy is not strong, for one thing. I happen to know that he was born in Colorado, only a few months before his mother died out there of a long illness. There is something wrong about the fellow."

The drawing master had come to realize that, in looking at Paul, one saw only his white teeth and the forced animation of his eyes. One warm afternoon the boy had gone to sleep at his drawing-board, and his master had noted with amazement what a white, blue-veined face it was; drawn and wrinkled like an old man's about the eyes, the lips twitching even in his sleep, and stiff with a nervous tension that drew them back from his teeth.

10   His teachers left the building dissatisfied and unhappy; humiliated to have felt so vindictive toward a mere boy, to have uttered this feeling in cutting terms, and to have set each other on, as it were, in the gruesome game of intemperate reproach. Some of them remembered having seen a miserable street cat set at bay by a ring of tormentors.

As for Paul, he ran down the hill whistling the Soldiers' Chorus from *Faust* looking wildly behind him now and then to see whether some of his teachers were not there to writhe under his light-heartedness. As it was now late in the afternoon and Paul was on duty that evening as usher at Carnegie Hall, he decided that he would not go home to supper. When he reached the concert hall the doors were not yet open and, as it was chilly outside, he decided to go up into the picture gallery—always deserted at this hour—where there were some of Raffaelli's gay studies of Paris streets and an airy blue Venetian scene or two that always exhilarated him. He was delighted to find no one in the gallery but the old guard, who sat in one corner, a newspaper on his knee, a black patch over one eye and the other closed. Paul possessed himself of the place and walked confidently up and down, whistling under his breath. After a while he sat down before a blue Rico and lost himself. When he bethought him to look at his watch, it was after seven o'clock, and he rose with a start and ran downstairs, making a face at Augustus, peering out from the cast-room, and an evil gesture at the Venus of Milo as he passed her on the stairway.

When Paul reached the ushers' dressing-room half-a-dozen boys were there already, and he began excitedly to tumble into his uniform. It was one of the few that at all approached fitting, and Paul thought it very becoming—though he knew that the tight, straight coat accentuated his narrow chest, about which he was exceedingly sensitive. He was always considerably excited while he dressed, twanging all over to the tuning of the strings and the preliminary flourishes of the horns in the music-room; but to-night he seemed quite beside himself, and he teased and plagued the boys until, telling him that he was crazy, they put him down on the floor and sat on him.

Somewhat calmed by his suppression, Paul dashed out to the front of the house to seat the early comers. He was a model usher; gracious and smiling he ran up and down the aisles; nothing was too much trouble for him; he carried messages and brought programmes as though it were his greatest pleasure in life, and all the people in his section thought him a charming boy, feeling that he remembered and admired them. As the house filled, he grew more and more vivacious and animated, and the color came to his cheeks and lips. It was very much as though this were a great reception and Paul were the host. Just as the musicians came out to take their places, his English teacher arrived with checks for the seats which a prominent manufacturer had taken for the season. She betrayed some embarrassment when she handed Paul the tickets, and a *hauteur* which subsequently made her feel very foolish. Paul was startled for a moment, and had the feeling of wanting to put her out; what business had she here among all these fine people and gay colors? He looked her over and decided that she was not appropriately dressed and must be a fool to sit downstairs in such togs. The tickets had probably been sent her out of kindness, he reflected as he put down a seat for her, and she had about as much right to sit there as he had.

When the symphony began Paul sank into one of the rear seats with a long sigh of relief, and lost himself as he had done before the Rico. It was not that symphonies, as such, meant anything in particular to Paul, but the first sigh of the instruments seemed to free some hilarious and potent spirit within him; something that struggled there like the Genius in the bottle found by the Arab fisherman. He felt a sudden zest of life; the lights danced before his eyes and the concert hall blazed into unimaginable splendor. When the soprano soloist came on, Paul forgot even the nastiness of his teacher's being there and gave himself up to the peculiar stimulus such personages always had for him. The soloist chanced to be a German woman, by no means in her first youth, and the mother of many children; but she wore an elaborate gown and a tiara, and above all she had that indefinable air of achievement, that world-shine upon her, which, in Paul's eyes, made her a veritable queen of Romance.

15   After a concert was over Paul was always irritable and wretched until he got to sleep, and to-night he was even more than usually restless. He had the feeling of not being able to let down, of its being impossible to give up this delicious excitement which was the only thing that could be called living at all. During the last number he withdrew and, after hastily changing his clothes in the dressing-room, slipped out to the side door where the soprano's carriage stood. Here he began pacing rapidly up and down the walk, waiting to see her come out.

Over yonder the Schenley, in its vacant stretch, loomed big and square through the fine rain, the windows of its twelve stories glowing like those of a lighted card-board house under a Christmas tree. All the actors and singers of the better class stayed there when they were in the city, and a number of the big manufacturers of the place lived there in the winter. Paul had often hung about the hotel, watching the people go in and out, longing to enter and leave school-masters and dull care behind him forever.

At last the singer came out, accompanied by the conductor, who helped her into her carriage and closed the door with a cordial *auf wiedersehen,* which set Paul to wondering whether she were not an old sweetheart of his. Paul followed the carriage over to the hotel, walking so rapidly as not to be far from the entrance when the singer alighted and disappeared behind the swinging glass doors that were opened by a negro in a tall hat and a long coat. In the moment that the door was ajar, it seemed to Paul that he, too, entered. He seemed to feel himself go after her up the steps, into the warm, lighted building, into an exotic, a tropical world of shiny, glistening surfaces and basking ease. He reflected upon the mysterious dishes that were brought into the dining-room, the green bottles in buckets of ice, as he had seen them in the supper party pictures of the *Sunday World* supplement. A quick gust of wind brought the rain down with sudden vehemence, and Paul was startled to find that he was still outside in the slush of the gravel driveway; that his boots were letting in the water and his scanty overcoat was clinging wet about him; that the lights in front of the concert hall were out, and that the rain was driving in sheets between him and the orange glow of the windows above him. There it was, what he wanted— tangibly before him, like the fairy world of a Christmas pantomime, but mocking spirits stood guard at the doors, and, as the rain beat in his face, Paul wondered whether he were destined always to shiver in the black night outside, looking up at it.

He turned and walked reluctantly toward the car tracks. The end had to come sometime; his father in his night-clothes at the top of the stairs, explanations that did not explain, hastily improvised fictions that were forever tripping him up, his upstairs room and its horrible yellow wall-paper; the creaking bureau with the greasy plush collar-box, and over his painted wooden bed the pictures of George Washington and John Calvin, and the framed motto, "Feed my Lambs," which had been worked in red worsted by his mother.

Half an hour later, Paul alighted from his car and went slowly down one of the side streets off the main thoroughfare. It was a highly respectable street, where all the houses were exactly alike, and where business men of moderate means begot and reared large families of children, all of whom went to Sabbath-school and learned the shorter catechism, and were interested in arithmetic; all of whom were as exactly alike as their homes, and of a piece with the monotony in which they lived. Paul never went up Cordelia Street without a shudder of loathing. His home was next the house of the Cumberland minister. He approached it to-night with the nerveless sense of defeat, the hopeless feeling of sinking back forever into ugliness and commonness that he had always had when he came home. The moment he turned into Cordelia Street he felt the waters close above his head. After each of these orgies of living, he experienced all the physical depression which follows a debauch; the loathing of respectable beds, of common food, of a house permeated by kitchen odors; a shuddering repulsion for the flavourless, colourless mass of everyday existence; a morbid desire for cool things and soft lights and fresh flowers.

20   The nearer he approached the house, the more absolutely unequal Paul felt to the sight of it all; his ugly sleeping chamber; the cold bathroom with the grimy zinc tub, the cracked mirror, the dripping spiggots; his father, at the top of the stairs, his hairy legs sticking out from his night-shirt, his feet thrust into carpet slippers. He was so much later than usual that there would certainly be inquiries and reproaches. Paul stopped short before the door. He felt that he could not be accosted by his father to-night;

that he could not toss again on that miserable bed. He would not go in. He would tell his father that he had no car fare, and it was raining so hard he had gone home with one of the boys and stayed all night.

Meanwhile, he was wet and cold. He went around to the back of the house and tried one of the basement windows, found it open, raised it cautiously, and scrambled down the cellar wall to the floor. There he stood, holding his breath, terrified by the noise he had made, but the floor above him was silent, and there was no creak on the stairs. He found a soap-box, and carried it over to the soft ring of light that streamed from the furnace door, and sat down. He was horribly afraid of rats, so he did not try to sleep, but sat looking distrustfully at the dark, still terrified lest he might have awakened his father. In such reactions, after one of the experiences which made days and nights out of the dreary blanks of the calendar, when his senses were deadened, Paul's head was always singularly clear. Suppose his father had heard him getting in at the window and had come down and shot him for a burglar? Then, again, suppose his father had come down, pistol in hand, and he had cried out in time to save himself, and his father had been horrified to think how nearly he had killed him? Then, again, suppose a day should come when his father would remember that night, and wish there had been no warning cry to stay his hand? With this last supposition Paul entertained himself until daybreak.

The following Sunday was fine; the sodden November chill was broken by the last flash of autumnal summer. In the morning Paul had to go to church and Sabbath-school, as always. On seasonable Sunday afternoons the burghers of Cordelia Street always sat out on their front "stoops," and talked to their neighbors on the next stoop, or called to those across the street in neighbourly fashion. The men usually sat on gay cushions placed upon the steps that led down to the sidewalk, while the women, in their Sunday "waists," sat in rockers on the cramped porches, pretending to be greatly at their ease. The children played in the streets; there were so many of them that the place resembled the recreation grounds of a kindergarten. The men on the steps—all in their shirt sleeves, their vests unbuttoned—sat with their legs well apart, their stomachs comfortably protruding, and talked of the prices of things, or told anecdotes of the sagacity of their various chiefs and overlords. They occasionally looked over the multitude of squabbling children, listened affectionately to their high-pitched, nasal voices, smiling to see their own proclivities reproduced in their offspring, and interspersed their legends of the iron kings with remarks about their sons' progress at school, their grades in arithmetic, and the amounts they had saved in their toy banks.

On this last Sunday of November, Paul sat all the afternoon on the lowest step of his "stoop," staring into the street, while his sisters, in their rockers, were talking to the minister's daughters next door about how many shirt-waists they had made in the last week, and how many waffles some one had eaten at the last church supper. When the weather was warm, and his father was in a particularly jovial frame of mind, the girls made lemonade, which was always brought out in a red-glass pitcher, ornamented with forget-me-nots in blue enamel. This the girls thought very fine, and the neighbors always joked about the suspicious colour of the pitcher.

Today Paul's father sat on the top step, talking to a young man who shifted a restless baby from knee to knee. He happened to be the young man who was daily held up to Paul as a model, and after whom it was his father's dearest hope that he would pattern. This young man was of a ruddy complexion, with a compressed, red mouth, and faded, near-sighted eyes, over which he wore thick spectacles, with gold bows that curved about his ears. He was clerk to one of the magnates of a great steel corporation, and was looked upon in Cordelia Street as a young man with a future. There was a story that, some five years ago—he was now barely twenty-six—he had been a trifle dissipated, but in order to curb his appetites and save the loss of time and strength that a sowing of wild oats might have entailed, he had taken his chief's advice, oft reiterated to his employees, and at twenty-one had married the first woman whom he could persuade to share his fortunes. She happened to be an angular school-mistress, much older than he, who also wore thick glasses, and who had now borne him four children, all near-sighted, like herself.

25   The young man was relating how his chief, now cruising in the Mediterranean, kept in touch with all the details of the business, arranging his office hours on his yacht just as though he were at home, and "knocking off work enough to keep two stenographers busy." His father told, in turn, the plan his corporation was considering, of putting in an electric railway plant at Cairo. Paul snapped his teeth; he had an awful apprehension that they might spoil it all before he got there. Yet he rather liked to hear these legends of the iron kings, that were told and retold on Sundays and holidays; these stories of palaces in Venice, yachts on the Mediterranean, and high play at Monte Carlo appealed to his fancy, and he was interested in the triumphs of these cash boys who had become famous, though he had no mind for the cash-boy stage.

After supper was over, and he had helped to dry the dishes, Paul nervously asked his father whether he could go to George's to get some help in his geometry, and still more nervously asked for car fare. This latter request he had to repeat, as his father on principle, did not like to hear requests for money, whether much or little. He asked Paul whether he could not go to some boy who lived nearer, and told him that he ought not to leave his school work until Sunday; but he gave him the dime. He was not a poor man, but he had a worthy ambition to come up in the world. His only reason for allowing Paul to usher was, that he thought a boy ought to be earning a little.

Paul bounded upstairs, scrubbed the greasy odor of the dish-water from his hands with the ill-smelling soap he hated, and then shook over his fingers a few drops of violet water from the bottle he kept hidden in his drawer. He left the house with his geometry conspicuously under his arm, and the moment he got out of Cordelia Street and boarded a downtown car, he shook off the lethargy of two deadening days, and began to live again.

The leading juvenile of the permanent stock company which played at one of the downtown theatres was an acquaintance of Paul's and the boy had been invited to drop in at the Sunday-night rehearsals whenever he could. For more than a year Paul had spent every available moment loitering about Charley Edwards's dressing-room. He had won a place among Edwards's following not only because the young actor, who could not afford to employ a dresser, often found him useful, but because he recognized in Paul something akin to what churchmen term "vocation."

It was at the theatre and at Carnegie Hall that Paul really lived; the rest was but a sleep and a forgetting. This was Paul's fairy tale, and it had for him all the allurement of a secret love. The moment he inhaled the gassy, painty, dusty odour behind the scenes, he breathed like a prisoner set free, and felt within him the possibility of doing or saying splendid, brilliant, poetic things. The moment the cracked orchestra beat out the overture from *Martha,* or jerked at the serenade from *Rigoletto,* all stupid and ugly things slid from him, and his senses were deliciously, yet delicately fired.

30   Perhaps it was because, in Paul's world, the natural nearly always wore the guise of ugliness, that a certain element of artificiality seemed to him necessary in beauty. Perhaps it was because his experience of life else-where was so full of Sabbath-school picnics, petty economies, wholesome advice as to how to succeed in life, and the unescapable odors of cooking, that he found this existence so alluring, these smartly-clad men and women so attractive, that he was so moved by these starry apple orchards that bloomed perennially under the limelight.

It would be difficult to put it strongly enough how convincingly the stage entrance of that theatre was for Paul the actual portal of Romance. Certainly none of the company ever suspected it, least of all Charley Edwards. It was very like the old stories that used to float about London of fabulously rich Jews, who had subterranean halls there, with palms, and fountains, and soft lamps and richly apparelled women who never saw the disenchanting light of London day. So, in the midst of that smoke-palled city, enamored of figures and grimy toil, Paul had his secret temple, his wishing carpet, his bit of blue-and-white Mediterranean shore bathed in perpetual sunshine.

Several of Paul's teachers had a theory that his imagination had been perverted by garish fiction, but the truth was that he scarcely ever read at all. The books at home were not such as would either tempt or corrupt a youthful mind, and as for reading the novels that some of his friends urged upon him—well, he got what he wanted much more quickly from music; any sort of music, from an orchestra to a barrel organ. He needed only the spark, the indescribable thrill that made his imagination master of his senses, and he could make plots and pictures enough of his own. It was equally true that he was not stage-struck—not, at any rate, in the usual acceptation of that expression. He had no desire to become an actor, any more than he had to become a musician. He felt no necessity to do any of these things; what he wanted was to see, to be in the atmosphere, float on the wave of it, to be carried out, blue league after blue league, away from everything.

After a night behind the scenes, Paul found the school-room more than ever repulsive; the bare floors and naked walls; the prosy men who never wore frock coats, or violets in their buttonholes; the women with their dull gowns, shrill voices, and pitiful seriousness about prepositions that govern the dative. He could not bear to have the other pupils think, for a moment, that he took these people seriously; he must convey to them that he considered it all trivial, and was there only by way of a jest, anyway. He had autograph pictures of all the members of the stock company which he showed his classmates, telling them the most incredible stories of his familiarity with these people, of his acquaintance with the soloists who came to Carnegie Hall, his suppers with them and the flowers he sent them. When these stories lost their effect, and his audience grew listless, he became desperate and would bid all the boys good-bye, announcing that he was going to travel for awhile; going to Naples, to Venice, to Egypt. Then, next Monday, he would slip back, conscious and nervously smiling; his sister was ill, and he should have to defer his voyage until spring.

Matters went steadily worse with Paul at school. In the itch to let his instructors know how heartily he despised them and their homilies, and how thoroughly he was appreciated elsewhere, he mentioned once or twice that he had no time to fool with theorems; adding—with a twitch of the eyebrows and a touch of that nervous bravado which so perplexed them—that he was helping the people down at the stock company; they were old friends of his.

35   The upshot of the matter was, that the Principal went to Paul's father, and Paul was taken out of school and put to work. The manager at Carnegie Hall was told to get another usher in his stead; the doorkeeper at the theatre was warned not to admit him to the house; and Charley Edwards remorsefully promised the boy's father not to see him again.

The members of the stock company were vastly amused when some of Paul's stories reached them—especially the women. They were hardworking women, most of them supporting indigent husbands or brothers, and they laughed rather bitterly at having stirred the boy to such fervid and florid inventions. They agreed with the faculty and with his father that Paul's was a bad case.

The east-bound train was ploughing through a January snow-storm; the dull dawn was beginning to show grey when the engine whistled a mile out of Newark. Paul started up from the seat where he had lain curled in uneasy slumber, rubbed the breath-misted window glass with his hand, and peered out. The snow was whirling in curling eddies above the white bottom lands, and the drifts lay already deep in the fields and along the fences, while here and there the long dead grass and dried weed stalks protruded black above it. Lights shone from the scattered houses, and a gang of labourers who stood beside the track waved their lanterns.

Paul had slept very little, and he felt grimy and uncomfortable. He had made the all-night journey in a day coach, partly because he was ashamed, dressed as he was, to go into a Pullman, and partly because he was afraid of being seen there by some Pittsburgh business man, who might have noticed him in Denny & Carson's office. When the whistle awoke him, he clutched quickly at his breast pocket, glancing about him with an uncertain smile. But the little, clay-bespattered Italians were still sleeping, the slatternly women across the aisle were in open-mouthed oblivion, and even the crumby, crying babies were for the nonce stilled. Paul settled back to struggle with his impatience as best he could.

When he arrived at the Jersey City station, he hurried through his breakfast, manifestly ill at ease and keeping a sharp eye about him. After he reached the Twenty-third Street station, he consulted a cabman, and had himself driven to a men's furnishing establishment that was just opening for the day. He spent upward of two hours there, buying with endless reconsidering and great care. His new street suit he put on in the fitting-room; the frock coat and dress clothes he had bundled into the cab with his linen. Then he drove to a hatter's and a shoe house. His next errand was at Tiffany's, where he selected his silver and a new scarf-pin. He would not wait to have his silver marked, he said. Lastly, he stopped at a trunk shop on Broadway, and had his purchases packed into various traveling bags.

40   It was a little after one o'clock when he drove up to the Waldorf, and after settling with the cabman, went into the office. He registered from

Washington; said his mother and father had been abroad, and that he had come down to await the arrival of their steamer. He told his story plausibly and had no trouble, since he volunteered to pay for them in advance, in engaging his rooms; a sleeping-room, sitting-room and bath.

Not once, but a hundred times Paul had planned this entry into New York. He had gone over every detail of it with Charley Edwards, and in his scrap book at home there were pages of description about New York hotels, cut from the Sunday papers. When he was shown to his sitting-room on the eighth floor, he saw at a glance that everything was as it should be; there was but one detail in his mental picture that the place did not realize, so he rang for the bell boy and sent him down for flowers. He moved about nervously until the boy returned, putting away his new linen and fingering it delightedly as he did so. When the flowers came, he put them hastily into water, and then tumbled into a hot bath. Presently he came out of his white bathroom, resplendent in his new silk underwear, and playing with the tassels of his red robe. The snow was whirling so fiercely outside his windows that he could scarcely see across the street, but within the air was deliciously soft and fragrant. He put the violets and jonquils on the taboret beside the couch, and threw himself down, with a long sigh, covering himself with a Roman blanket. He was thoroughly tired; he had been in such haste, he had stood up to such a strain, covered so much ground in the last twenty-four hours, that he wanted to think how it had all come about. Lulled by the sound of the wind, the warm air, and the cool fragrance of the flowers, he sank into deep, drowsy retrospection.

It had been wonderfully simple; when they had shut him out of the theatre and concert hall, when they had taken away his bone, the whole thing was virtually determined. The rest was a mere matter of opportunity. The only thing that at all surprised him was his own courage—for he realized well enough that he had always been tormented by fear, a sort of apprehensive dread that, of late years, as the meshes of the lies he had told closed about him, had been pulling the muscles of his body tighter and tighter. Until now, he could not remember the time when he had not been dreading something. Even when he was a little boy, it was always there— behind him, or before, or on either side. There had always been the shadowed corner, the dark place into which he dared not look, but from which something seemed always to be watching him—and Paul had done things that were not pretty to watch, he knew.

But now he had a curious sense of relief, as though he had at last thrown down the gauntlet to the thing in the corner.

Yet it was but a day since he had been sulking in the traces; but yesterday afternoon that he had been sent to the bank with Denny & Carson's deposit, as usual—but this time he was instructed to leave the book to be balanced. There was above two thousand dollars in checks, and nearly a thousand in the bank notes which he had taken from the book and quietly transferred to his pocket. At the bank he had made out a new deposit slip. His nerves had been steady enough to permit of his returning to the office, where he had finished his work and asked for a full day's holiday to-morrow, Saturday, giving a perfectly reasonable pretext. The bank book, he knew, would not be returned before Monday or Tuesday, and his father would be out of town for the next week. From the time he slipped the bank notes into his pocket until he boarded the night train for New York, he had not known

a moment's hesitation. It was not the first time Paul had steered through
treacherous waters.

45   How astonishingly easy it had all been; here he was, the thing done; and
this time there would be no awakening, no figure at the top of the stairs. He
watched the snow flakes whirling by his window until he fell asleep.

When he awoke, it was three o'clock in the afternoon. He bounded up
with a start; half of one of his precious days gone already! He spent more
than an hour in dressing, watching every stage of his toilet carefully in the
mirror. Everything was quite perfect; he was exactly the kind of boy he had
always wanted to be.

When he went downstairs, Paul took a carriage and drove up Fifth
Avenue toward the Park. The snow had somewhat abated; carriages and
tradesmen's wagons were hurrying soundlessly to and fro in the winter twilight; boys in woolen mufflers were shovelling off the doorsteps; the avenue
stages made fine spots of colour against the white street. Here and there on
the corners were stands, with whole flower gardens blooming under glass
cases, against the sides of which the snow flakes stuck and melted; violets,
roses, carnations, lilies of the valley—somehow vastly more lovely and alluring that they blossomed thus unnaturally in the snow. The Park itself was a
wonderful stage winter-piece.

When he returned, the pause of the twilight had ceased, and the tune of
the streets had changed. The snow was falling faster, lights streamed from
the hotels that reared their dozen stories fearlessly up into the storm, defy-
ing the raging Atlantic winds. A long, black stream of carriages poured down
the avenue, intersected here and there by other streams, tending horizontally. There were a score of cabs about the entrance of his hotel, and his driver
had to wait. Boys in livery were running in and out of the awning stretched
across the sidewalk, up and down the red velvet carpet laid from the door to
the street. Above, about, within it all was the rumble and roar, the hurry and
toss of thousands of human beings as hot for pleasure as himself, and on every
side of him towered the glaring affirmation of the omnipotence of wealth.

The boy set his teeth and drew his shoulders together in a spasm of
realization; the plot of all dramas, the text of all romances, the nerve-stuff of
all sensations was whirling about him like the snow flakes. He burnt like a
faggot in a tempest.

50   When Paul went down to dinner, the music of the orchestra came floating up the elevator shaft to greet him. His head whirled as he stepped into
the thronged corridor, and he sank back into one of the chairs against the
wall to get his breath. The lights, the chatter, the perfumes, the bewildering
medley of colour—he had, for a moment, the feeling of not being able to
stand it. But only for a moment; these were his own people, he told himself.
He went slowly about the corridors, through the writing-rooms, smoking-
rooms, reception-rooms, as though he were exploring the chambers of an
enchanted palace, built and peopled for him alone.

When he reached the dining-room he sat down at a table near a window. The flowers, the white linen, the many-colored wine glasses, the gay
toilettes of the women, the low popping of corks, the undulating repetitions
of the *Blue Danube* from the orchestra, all flooded Paul's dream with bewildering radiance. When the roseate tinge of his champagne was added—that
cold, precious bubbling stuff that creamed and foamed in his glass—Paul
wondered that there were honest men in the world at all. This was what all

the world was fighting for, he reflected; this was what all the struggle was about. He doubted the reality of his past. Had he ever known a place called Cordelia Street, a place where fagged-looking business men got on the early car; mere rivets in a machine they seemed to Paul—sickening men, with combings of children's hair always hanging to their coats, and the smell of cooking in their clothes. Cordelia Street—Ah! that belonged to another time and country; had he not always been thus, had he not sat here night after night, from as far back as he could remember, looking pensively over just such shimmering textures, and slowly twirling the stem of a glass like this one between his thumb and middle finger? He rather thought he had.

He was not in the least abashed or lonely. He had no especial desire to meet or to know any of these people; all he demanded was the right to look on and conjecture, to watch the pageant. The mere stage properties were all he contended for. Nor was he lonely later in the evening, in his loge at the Metropolitan. He was now entirely rid of his nervous misgivings, of his forced aggressiveness, of the imperative desire to show himself different from his surroundings. He felt now that his surroundings explained him. Nobody questioned the purple; he had only to wear it passively. He had only to glance down at his attire to reassure himself that here it would be impossible for any one to humiliate him.

He found it hard to leave his beautiful sitting-room to go to bed that night, and sat long watching the raging storm from his turret window. When he went to sleep, it was with the lights turned on in his bedroom; partly because of his old timidity, and partly so that, if he should wake in the night, there would be no wretched moment of doubt, no horrible suspicion of yellow wall-paper, or of Washington and Calvin above his bed.

Sunday morning the city was practically snow-bound. Paul breakfasted late, and in the afternoon he fell in with a wild San Francisco boy, a freshman at Yale, who said he had run down for a "little flyer" over Sunday. The young man offered to show Paul the night side of the town, and the two boys went out together after dinner, not returning to the hotel until seven o'clock the next morning. They had started out in the confiding warmth of a champagne friendship, but their parting in the elevator was singularly cool. The freshman pulled himself together to make his train, and Paul went to bed. He awoke at two o'clock in the afternoon, very thirsty and dizzy, and rang for ice-water, coffee, and the Pittsburgh papers.

55   On the part of the hotel management, Paul excited no suspicion. There was this to be said for him, that he wore his spoils with dignity and in no way made himself conspicuous. Even under the glow of his wine he was never boisterous, though he found the stuff like a magician's wand for wonder-building. His chief greediness lay in his ears and eyes, and his excesses were not offensive ones. His dearest pleasures were the grey winter twilights in his sitting-room; his quiet enjoyment of his flowers, his clothes, his wide divan, his cigarette and his sense of power. He could not remember a time when he had felt so at peace with himself. The mere release from the necessity of petty lying, lying every day and every day, restored his self-respect. He had never lied for pleasure, even at school; but to be noticed and admired, to assert his difference from other Cordelia Street boys; and he felt a good deal more manly, more honest, even, now that he had no need for boastful pretensions, now that he could, as his actor friends used to say, "dress the part." It was characteristic that remorse did not occur to

him. His golden days went by without a shadow, and he made each as perfect as he could.

On the eighth day after his arrival in New York, he found the whole affair exploited in the Pittsburgh papers, exploited with a wealth of detail which indicated that local news of a sensational nature was at a low ebb. The firm of Denny & Carson announced that the boy's father had refunded the full amount of the theft, and that they had no intention of prosecuting. The Cumberland minister had been interviewed, and expressed his hope of yet reclaiming the motherless lad, and his Sabbath-school teacher declared that she would spare no effort to that end. The rumor had reached Pittsburgh that the boy had been seen in a New York hotel, and his father had gone East to find him and bring him home.

Paul had just come in to dress for dinner; he sank into a chair, weak to the knees, and clasped his head in his hands. It was to be worse than jail, even; the tepid waters of Cordelia Street were to close over him finally and forever. The grey monotony stretched before him in hopeless, unrelieved years; Sabbath-school, Young People's Meeting, the yellow-papered room, the damp dish-towels; it all rushed back upon him with a sickening vividness. He had the old feeling that the orchestra had suddenly stopped, the sinking sensation that the play was over. The sweat broke out on his face, and he sprang to his feet, looked about him with his white, conscious smile, and winked at himself in the mirror. With something of the old childish belief in miracles with which he had so often gone to class, all his lessons unlearned, Paul dressed and dashed whistling down the corridor to the elevator.

He had no sooner entered the dining-room and caught the measure of the music than his remembrance was lightened by his old elastic power of claiming the moment, mounting with it, and finding it all sufficient. The glare and glitter about him, the mere scenic accessories had again, and for the last time, their old potency. He would show himself that he was game, he would finish the thing splendidly. He doubted, more than ever, the existence of Cordelia Street, and for the first time he drank his wine recklessly. Was he not, after all, one of those fortunate beings born to the purple, was he not still himself and in his own place? He drummed a nervous accompaniment to the Pagliacci music and looked about him, telling himself over and over that it had paid.

He reflected drowsily, to the swell of the music and the chill sweetness of his wine, that he might have done it more wisely. He might have caught an outbound steamer and been well out of their clutches before now. But the other side of the world had seemed too far away and too uncertain then; he could not have waited for it; his need had been too sharp. If he had to choose over again, he would do the same thing tomorrow. He looked affectionately about the dining-room, now gilded with a soft mist. Ah, it had paid indeed!

60   Paul was awakened next morning by a painful throbbing in his head and feet. He had thrown himself across the bed without undressing, and had slept with his shoes on. His limbs and hands were lead heavy, and his tongue and throat were parched and burnt. There came upon him one of those fateful attacks of clear-headedness that never occurred except when he was physically exhausted and his nerves hung loose. He lay still and closed his eyes and let the tide of things wash over him.

His father was in New York; "stopping at some joint or other," he told himself. The memory of successive summers on the front stoop fell upon him like a weight of black water. He had not a hundred dollars left; and he knew now, more than ever, that money was everything, the wall that stood between all he loathed and all he wanted. The thing was winding itself up; he had thought of that on his first glorious day in New York, and had even provided a way to snap the thread. It lay on his dressing-table now; he had got it out last night when he came blindly up from dinner, but the shiny metal hurt his eyes, and he disliked the looks of it.

He rose and moved about with a painful effort, succumbing now and again to attacks of nausea. It was the old depression exaggerated; all the world had become Cordelia Street. Yet somehow he was not afraid of anything, was absolutely calm; perhaps because he had looked into the dark corner at last and knew. It was bad enough, what he saw there, but somehow not so bad as his long fear of it had been. He saw everything clearly now. He had a feeling that he had made the best of it, that he had lived the sort of life he was meant to live, and for half an hour he sat staring at the revolver. But he told himself that was not the way, so he went downstairs and took a cab to the ferry.

When Paul arrived at Newark, he got off the train and took another cab, directing the driver to follow the Pennsylvania tracks out of the town. The snow lay heavy on the roadways and had drifted deep in the open fields. Only here and there the dead grass or dried weed stalks projected, singularly black, above it. Once well into the country, Paul dismissed the carriage and walked, floundering along the tracks, his mind a medley of irrelevant things. He seemed to hold in his brain an actual picture of everything he had seen that morning. He remembered every feature of both his drivers, of the toothless old woman from whom he had bought the red flowers in his coat, the agent from whom he had got his ticket, and all of his fellow-passengers on the ferry. His mind, unable to cope with vital matters near at hand, worked feverishly and deftly at sorting and grouping these images. They made for him a part of the ugliness of the world, of the ache in his head, and the bitter burning on his tongue. He stooped and put a handful of snow into his mouth as he walked, but that, too, seemed hot. When he reached a little hillside, where the tracks ran through a cut some twenty feet below him, he stopped and sat down.

The carnations in his coat were drooping with the cold, he noticed; their red glory all over. It occurred to him that all the flowers he had seen in the glass cases that first night must have gone the same way, long before this. It was only one splendid breath they had, in spite of their brave mockery at the winter outside the glass; and it was a losing game in the end, it seemed, this revolt against the homilies by which the world is run. Paul took one of the blossoms carefully from his coat and scooped a little hole in the snow, where he covered it up. Then he dozed a while, from his weak condition, seeming insensible to the cold.

65   The sound of an approaching train awoke him, and he started to his feet, remembering only his resolution, and afraid lest he should be too late. He stood watching the approaching locomotive, his teeth chattering, his lips drawn away from them in a frightened smile; once or twice he glanced nervously sidewise, as though he were being watched. When the right moment came, he jumped. As he fell, the folly of his haste occurred to him with merciless clearness, the vastness of what he had left undone. There flashed through his brain, clearer than ever before, the blue of Adriatic water, the yellow of Algerian sands.

He felt something strike his chest, and that his body was being thrown swiftly through the air, on and on, immeasurably far and fast, while his limbs were gently relaxed. Then, because the picture making mechanism was crushed, the disturbing visions flashed into black, and Paul dropped back into the immense design of things.

THE END

JAMES JOYCE

James Joyce (1882–1941) was born into a middle-class family in Dublin, Ireland. His father drank, became increasingly irresponsible and unemployable, and the family sank in the social order. Still, Joyce received a strong classical education at excellent Jesuit schools and at University College, Dublin, where he studied modern languages. In 1902, at the age of twenty, he left Ireland so that he might spend the rest of his life writing about life in Ireland. ("The shortest way to Tara," he said, "is via Holyhead," i.e., the shortest way to the heart of Ireland is to take ship away.) In Trieste, Zurich, and Paris he supported his family in a variety of ways, sometimes teaching English in a Berlitz language school. His fifteen stories, collected under the title of Dubliners, *were written between 1904 and 1907, but he could not get them published until 1914. Next came a highly autobiographical novel,* A Portrait of the Artist as a Young Man *(1916).* Ulysses *(1922), a large novel covering eighteen hours in Dublin, was for some years banned by the United States Post Office, though few if any readers today find it offensive. Joyce spent most of his remaining years working on* Finnegans Wake *(1939).*

Nine years before he succeeded in getting Dubliners *published, Joyce described the manuscript in these terms:*

> *My intention was to write a chapter of the moral history of my country and I chose Dublin for the scene because that city seemed to me the centre of paralysis. . . . I have written it for the most part in a style of scrupulous meanness and with the conviction that he is a very bold man who dares to alter in the presentment, still more to deform, whatever he has seen and heard.*

Araby [1905]

North Richmond Street, being blind,[1] was a quiet street except at the hour when the Christian Brothers' School set the boys free. An uninhabited house of two stories stood at the blind end, detached from its neighbors in a square ground. The other houses of the street, conscious of decent lives within them, gazed at one another with brown imperturbable faces.

The former tenant of our house, a priest, had died in the back drawing-room. Air, musty from having long been enclosed, hung in all the rooms, and the waste room behind the kitchen was littered with old useless papers. Among these I found a few papercovered books, the pages of which were

---

[1] **blind** a dead-end street.

curled and damp: *The Abbot,* by Walter Scott, *The Devout Communicant* and *The Memoirs of Vidocq.*[2] I liked the last best because its leaves were yellow. The wild garden behind the house contained a central apple-tree and a few straggling bushes under one of which I found the late tenant's rusty bicycle-pump. He had been a very charitable priest; in his will he had left all his money to institutions and the furniture of his house to his sister.

When the short days of winter came dusk fell before we had well eaten our dinners. When we met in the street the houses had grown sombre. The space of sky above us was the colour of everchanging violet and towards it the lamps of the street lifted their feeble lanterns. The cold air stung us and we played till our bodies glowed. Our shouts echoed in the silent street. The career of our play brought us through the dark muddy lanes behind the houses where we ran the gauntlet of the rough tribes from the cottages, to the back doors of the dark dripping gardens where odours arose from the ashpits, to the dark odorous stables where a coachman smoothed and combed the horse or shook music from the buckled harness. When we returned to the street light from the kitchen windows had filled the area. If my uncle was seen turning the corner we hid in the shadow until we had seen him safely housed. Or if Mangan's sister came out on the doorstep to call her brother in to his tea we watched her from our shadow peer up and down the street. We waited to see whether she would remain or go in and, if she remained, we left our shadow and walked up to Mangan's steps resignedly. She was waiting for us, her figure defined by the light from the half-opened door. Her brother always teased her before he obeyed and I stood by the railings looking at her. Her dress swung as she moved her body and the soft rope of her hair tossed from side to side.

Every morning I lay on the floor in the front parlour watching her door. The blind was pulled down to within an inch of the sash so that I could not be seen. When she came out on the doorstep my heart leaped. I ran to the hall, seized my books and followed her. I kept her brown figure always in my eye and, when we came near the point at which our ways diverged, I quickened my pace and passed her. This happened morning after morning. I had never spoken to her, except for a few casual words, and yet her name was like a summons to all my foolish blood.

5   Her image accompanied me even in places the most hostile to romance. On Saturday evenings when my aunt went marketing I had to go to carry some of the parcels. We walked through the flaring streets, jostled by drunken men and bargaining women, amid the curses of labourers, the shrill litanies of shop-boys who stood on guard by the barrels of pigs' cheeks, the nasal chanting of street-singers, who sang a *come-all-you* about O'Donovan Rossa,[3] or a ballad about the troubles in our native land. These noises converged in a single sensation of life for me: I imagined that I bore my chalice safely through a throng of foes. Her name sprang to my lips at moments in strange prayers and praises which I myself did not understand. My eyes were often full of tears (I

---

[2]*The Abbot* was one of Scott's popular historical romances; *The Devout Communicant* was a Catholic religious manual; *The Memoirs of Vidocq* were the memoirs of the chief of the French detective force.   [3]**Jeremiah O'Donovan** (1831–1915), a popular Irish leader who was jailed by the British for advocating violent rebellion. A **come-all-you** was a topical song that began "Come all you gallant Irishmen."

could not tell why) and at times a flood from my heart seemed to pour itself out into my bosom. I thought little of the future. I did not know whether I would ever speak to her or not or, if I spoke to her, how I could tell her of my confused adoration. But my body was like a harp and her words and gestures were like fingers running upon the wires.

One evening I went into the back drawing-room in which the priest had died. It was a dark rainy evening and there was no sound in the house. Through one of the broken panes I heard the rain impinge upon the earth, the fine incessant needles of water playing in the sodden beds. Some distant lamp or lighted window gleamed below me. I was thankful that I could see so little. All my senses seemed to desire to veil themselves and, feeling that I was about to slip from them, I pressed the palms of my hands together until they trembled, murmuring: *O love! O love!* many times.

At last she spoke to me. When she addressed the first words to me I was so confused that I did not know what to answer. She asked me was I going to Araby.

I forget whether I answered yes or no. It would be a splendid bazaar, she said; she would love to go.

—And why can't you? I asked.

10   While she spoke she turned a silver bracelet round and round her wrist. She could not go, she said, because there would be a retreat that week in her convent. Her brother and two other boys were fighting for their caps and I was alone at the railings. She held one of the spikes, bowing her head towards me. The light from the lamp opposite our door caught the white curve of her neck, lit up her hair that rested there and, falling, lit up the hand upon the railing. It fell over one side of her dress and caught the white border of a petticoat, just visible as she stood at ease.

—It's well for you, she said.

—If I go, I said, I will bring you something.

What innumerable follies laid waste my waking and sleeping thoughts after that evening! I wished to annihilate the tedious intervening days. I chafed against the work of school. At night in my bedroom and by day in the classroom her image came between me and the page I strove to read. The syllables of the word *Araby* were called to me through the silence in which my soul luxuriated and cast an Eastern enchantment over me. I asked for leave to go to the bazaar on Saturday night. My aunt was surprised and hoped it was not some Freemason[4] affair. I answered a few questions in class, I watched my master's face pass from amiability to sternness; he hoped I was not beginning to idle. I could not call my wandering thoughts together. I had hardly any patience with the serious work of life which, now that it stood between me and my desire, seemed to me child's play, ugly monotonous child's play.

On Saturday morning I reminded my uncle that I wished to go to the bazaar in the evening. He was fussing at the hallstand, looking for the hat-brush, and answered me curtly:

15   —Yes, boy, I know.

As he was in the hall I could not go into the front parlour and lie at the window. I left the house in bad humour and walked slowly towards the school. The air was pitilessly raw and already my heart misgave me.

---

[4]Irish Catholics viewed the Masons as their Protestant enemies.

When I came home to dinner my uncle had not yet been home. Still it was early. I sat staring at the clock for some time and, when its ticking began to irritate me, I left the room. I mounted the staircase and gained the upper part of the house. The high cold empty gloomy rooms liberated me and I went from room to room singing. From the front window I saw my companions playing below in the street. Their cries reached me weakened and indistinct and, leaning my forehead against the cool glass, I looked over at the dark house where she lived. I may have stood there for an hour, seeing nothing but the brown-clad figure cast by my imagination, touched discreetly by the lamplight at the curved neck, at the hand upon the railings and at the border below the dress.

When I came downstairs again I found Mrs. Mercer sitting at the fire. She was an old garrulous woman, a pawnbroker's widow, who collected used stamps for some pious purpose. I had to endure the gossip of the tea-table. The meal was prolonged beyond an hour and still my uncle did not come. Mrs. Mercer stood up to go: she was sorry she couldn't wait any longer, but it was after eight o'clock and she did not like to be out late, as the night air was bad for her. When she had gone I began to walk up and down the room, clenching my fists. My aunt said:

—I'm afraid you may put off your bazaar for this night of Our Lord.

20 At nine o'clock I heard my uncle's latchkey in the halldoor. I heard him talking to himself and heard the hallstand rocking when it had received the weight of his overcoat. I could interpret these signs. When he was midway through his dinner I asked him to give me the money to go to the bazaar. He had forgotten.

—The people are in bed and after their first sleep now, he said.

I did not smile. My aunt said to him energetically:

—Can't you give him the money and let him go? You've kept him late enough as it is.

My uncle said he was very sorry he had forgotten. He said he believed in the old saying: *All work and no play makes Jack a dull boy.* He asked me where I was going and, when I had told him a second time he asked me did I know *The Arab's Farewell to His Steed.*[5] When I left the kitchen he was about to recite the opening lines of the piece to my aunt.

25 I held a florin tightly in my hand as I strode down Buckingham Street towards the station. The sight of the streets thronged with buyers and glaring with gas recalled to me the purpose of my journey. I took my seat in a third-class carriage of a deserted train. After an intolerable delay the train moved out of the station slowly. It crept onward among ruinous houses and over the twinkling river. At Westland Row Station a crowd of people pressed to the carriage doors; but the porters moved them back, saying that it was a special train for the bazaar. I remained alone in the bare carriage. In a few minutes the train drew up beside an improvised wooden platform. I passed out on to the road and saw by the lighted dial of a clock that it was ten minutes to ten. In front of me was a large building which displayed the magical name.

I could not find any sixpenny entrance and, fearing that the bazaar would be closed, I passed in quickly through a turnstile, handing a shilling to a weary-looking man. I found myself in a big hall girdled at half its height

---

[5]"The Arab to His Favorite Steed" was a popular sentimental poem by Caroline Norton (1808–1877).

by a gallery. Nearly all the stalls were closed and the greater part of the hall was in darkness. I recognised a silence like that which pervades a church after a service. I walked into the center of the bazaar timidly. A few people were gathered about the stalls which were still open. Before a curtain, over which the words *Café Chantant* were written in coloured lamps, two men were counting money on a salver. I listened to the fall of the coins.

Remembering with difficulty why I had come I went over to one of the stalls and examined porcelain vases and flowered tea-sets. At the door of the stall a young lady was talking and laughing with two young gentlemen. I remarked their English accents and listened vaguely to their conversation.

—O, I never said such a thing!

—O, but you did!

30   —O, but I didn't!

—Didn't she say that?

—Yes! I heard her.

—O, there's a . . . fib!

Observing me the young lady came over and asked me did I wish to buy anything. The tone of her voice was not encouraging; she seemed to have spoken to me out of a sense of duty. I looked humbly at the great jars that stood like eastern guards at either side of the dark entrance to the stall and murmured:

35   —No, thank you.

The young lady changed the position of one of the vases and went back to the two young men. They began to talk of the same subject. Once or twice the young lady glanced at me over her shoulder.

I lingered before her stall, though I knew my stay was useless, to make my interest in her wares seem the more real. Then I turned away slowly and walked down the middle of the bazaar. I allowed the two pennies to fall against the sixpence in my pocket. I heard a voice call from one end of the gallery that the light was out. The upper part of the hall was now completely dark.

Gazing up into the darkness I saw myself as a creature driven and derided by vanity; and my eyes burned with anguish and anger.

WILLIAM FAULKNER

William Faulkner (1897–1962) was brought up in Oxford, Mississippi. His great-grandfather had been a Civil War hero, and his father was treasurer of the University of Mississippi in Oxford; the family was no longer rich, but it was still respected. In 1918 he enrolled in the Royal Canadian Air Force, though he never saw overseas service. After the war he returned to Mississippi and went to the university for two years. He then moved to New Orleans, where he became friendly with Sherwood Anderson, who was already an established writer. In New Orleans Faulkner worked for the Times-Picayune; *still later, even after he had established himself as a major novelist with* The Sound and the Fury *(1929), he had to do some work in Hollywood in order to make ends meet. In 1950 he was awarded the Nobel Prize in Literature.*

Almost all of Faulkner's writing is concerned with the people of Yoknapatawpha, an imaginary county in Mississippi. "I discovered," he said, "that

*my own little postage stamp of native soil was worth writing about and that
I would never live long enough to exhaust it." Though he lived for brief periods in Canada, New Orleans, New York, Hollywood, and Virginia (where he
died), he spent most of his life in his native Mississippi.*

A Rose for Emily

[1930]

I

When Miss Emily Grierson died, our whole town went to her funeral:
the men through a sort of respectful affection for a fallen monument, the
women mostly out of curiosity to see the inside of her house, which no one
save an old manservant—a combined gardener and cook—had seen in at
least ten years.

It was a big, squarish frame house that had once been white, decorated
with cupolas and spires and scrolled balconies in the heavily lightsome style
of the seventies, set on what had once been our most select street. But
garages and cotton gins had encroached and obliterated even the august
names of that neighborhood; only Miss Emily's house was left, lifting its
stubborn and coquettish decay above the cotton wagons and the gasoline
pumps—an eyesore among eyesores. And now Miss Emily had gone to
join the representatives of those august names where they lay in the cedar-
bemused cemetery among the ranked and anonymous graves of Union
and Confederate soldiers who fell at the battle of Jefferson.

Alive, Miss Emily had been a tradition, a duty, and a care; a sort of
hereditary obligation upon the town, dating from that day in 1894 when
Colonel Sartoris, the mayor—he who fathered the edict that no Negro
woman should appear on the streets without an apron—remitted her taxes,
the dispensation dating from the death of her father on into perpetuity. Not
that Miss Emily would have accepted charity. Colonel Sartoris invented an
involved tale to the effect that Miss Emily's father had loaned money to the
town, which the town, as a matter of business, preferred this way of repay-
ing. Only a man of Colonel Sartoris' generation and thought could have invented it, and only a woman could have believed it.

When the next generation, with its more modern ideas, became mayors
and aldermen, this arrangement created some little dissatisfaction. On the
first of the year they mailed her a tax notice. February came, and there was
no reply. They wrote her a formal letter, asking her to call at the sheriff's
office at her convenience. A week later the mayor wrote her himself, offering
to call or to send his car for her, and received in reply a note on paper of an
archaic shape, in a thin, flowing calligraphy in faded ink, to the effect that
she no longer went out at all. The tax notice was also enclosed, without
comment.

5   They called a special meeting of the Board of Aldermen. A deputation
waited upon her, knocked at the door through which no visitor had passed
since she ceased giving china-painting lessons eight or ten years earlier.
They were admitted by the old Negro into a dim hall from which a staircase
mounted into still more shadow. It smelled of dust and disuse—a close,
dank smell. The Negro led them into the parlor. It was furnished in heavy,

leather-covered furniture. When the Negro opened the blinds of one window they could see that the leather was cracked; and when they sat down,
a faint dust rose sluggishly about their thighs, spinning with slow motes in
the single sunray. On a tarnished gilt easel before the fireplace stood a
crayon portrait of Miss Emily's father.

They rose when she entered—a small, fat woman in black, with a thin
gold chain descending to her waist and vanishing into her belt, leaning on
an ebony cane with a tarnished gold head. Her skeleton was small and
spare; perhaps that was why what would have been merely plumpness in
another was obesity in her. She looked bloated, like a body long submerged
in motionless water, and of that pallid hue. Her eyes, lost in the fatty ridges
of her face, looked like two small pieces of coal pressed into a lump of
dough as they moved from one face to another while the visitors stated
their errand.

She did not ask them to sit. She just stood in the door and listened quietly until the spokesman came to a stumbling halt. Then they could hear the
invisible watch ticking at the end of the gold chain.

Her voice was dry and cold. "I have no taxes in Jefferson. Colonel Sartoris explained it to me. Perhaps one of you can gain access to the city
records and satisfy yourselves."

"But we have. We are the city authorities, Miss Emily. Didn't you get a
notice from the sheriff, signed by him?"

10   "I received a paper, yes," Miss Emily said. "Perhaps he considers himself the sheriff. . . . I have no taxes in Jefferson."

"But there is nothing on the books to show that, you see. We must go
by the—"

"See Colonel Sartoris. I have no taxes in Jefferson."

"But, Miss Emily—"

"See Colonel Sartoris." (Colonel Sartoris had been dead almost ten
years.) "I have no taxes in Jefferson. Tobe!" The Negro appeared. "Show
these gentlemen out."

II

15   So she vanquished them, horse and foot, just as she had vanquished their
fathers thirty years before about the smell. That was two years after her father's death and a short time after her sweetheart—the one we believed
would marry her—had deserted her. After her father's death she went out
very little; after her sweetheart went away, people hardly saw her at all. A
few of the ladies had the temerity to call, but were not received, and the
only sign of life about the place was the Negro man—a young man then—
going in and out with a market basket.

"Just as if a man—any man—could keep a kitchen properly," the ladies
said; so they were not surprised when the smell developed. It was another
link between the gross, teeming world and the high and mighty Griersons.

A neighbor, a woman, complained to the mayor, Judge Stevens, eighty
years old.

"But what will you have me do about it, madam?" he said.

"Why, send her word to stop it," the woman said. "Isn't there a law?"

20   "I'm sure that won't be necessary," Judge Stevens said. "It's probably
just a snake or a rat that nigger of hers killed in the yard. I'll speak to him
about it."

The next day he received two more complaints, one from a man who came in diffident deprecation. "We really must do something about it, Judge, I'd be the last one in the world to bother Miss Emily, but we've got to do something." That night the Board of Aldermen met—three gray-beards and one younger man, a member of the rising generation.

"It's simple enough," he said. "Send her word to have her place cleaned up. Given her a certain time to do it in, and if she don't . . ."

"Dammit, sir," Judge Stevens said, "will you accuse a lady to her face of smelling bad?"

So the next night, after midnight, four men crossed Miss Emily's lawn and slunk about the house like burglars, sniffing along the base of the brick-work and at the cellar openings while one of them performed a regular sow-ing motion with his hand out of a sack slung from his shoulder. They broke open the cellar door and sprinkled lime there, and in all the out-buildings. As they recrossed the lawn, a window that had been dark was lighted and Miss Emily sat in it, the light behind her, and her upright torso motionless as that of an idol. They crept quietly across the lawn and into the shadow of the locusts that lined the street. After a week or two the smell went away.

25   That was when people had begun to feel really sorry for her. People in our town remembering how old lady Wyatt, her great-aunt, had gone com-pletely crazy at last, believed that the Griersons held themselves a little too high for what they really were. None of the young men were quite good enough for Miss Emily and such. We had long thought of them as a tableau; Miss Emily a slender figure in white in the background, her father a sprad-dled silhouette in the foreground, his back to her and clutching a horse-whip, the two of them framed by the back-flung front door. So when she got to be thirty and was still single, we were not pleased exactly, but vindi-cated; even with insanity in the family she wouldn't have turned down all of her chances if they had really materialized.

When her father died, it got about that the house was all that was left to her; and in a way, people were glad. At last they could pity Miss Emily. Being left alone, and a pauper, she had become humanized. Now she too would know the old thrill and the old despair of a penny more or less.

The day after his death all the ladies prepared to call at the house and offer condolence and aid, as is our custom. Miss Emily met them at the door, dressed as usual and with no trace of grief on her face. She told them that her father was not dead. She did that for three days, with the ministers calling on her, and the doctors, trying to persuade her to let them dispose of the body. Just as they were about to resort to law and force, she broke down, and they buried her father quickly.

We did not say she was crazy then. We believed she had to do that. We remembered all the young men her father had driven away, and we knew that with nothing left, she would have to cling to that which had robbed her, as people will.

III

She was sick for a long time. When we saw her again, her hair was cut short, making her look like a girl, with a vague resemblance to those angels in colored church windows—sort of tragic and serene.

30   The town had just let the contracts for paving the sidewalks, and in the summer after her father's death they began to work. The construction com-

pany came with niggers and mules and machinery, and a foreman named Homer Barron, a Yankee—a big, dark, ready man, with a big voice and eyes lighter than his face. The little boys would follow in groups to hear him cuss the niggers, and the niggers singing in time to the rise and fall of picks. Pretty soon he knew everybody in town. Whenever you heard a lot of laughing anywhere about the square, Homer Barron would be in the center of the group. Presently we began to see him and Miss Emily on Sunday afternoons driving in the yellow-wheeled buggy and the matched team of bays from the livery stable.

At first we were glad that Miss Emily would have an interest, because the ladies all said. "Of course a Grierson would not think seriously of a Northerner, a day laborer." But there were still others, older people, who said that even grief could not cause a real lady to forget *noblesse oblige*—without calling it *noblesse oblige*. They just said, "Poor Emily. Her kinsfolk should come to her." She had some kin in Alabama; but years ago her father had fallen out with them over the estate of old lady Wyatt, the crazy woman, and there was no communication between the two families. They had not even been represented at the funeral.

And as soon as the old people said, "Poor Emily," the whispering began. "Do you suppose it's really so?" they said to one another. "Of course it is. . . ." This behind their hands; rustling of craned silk and satin behind jalousies closed upon the sun of Sunday afternoon as the thin, swift clop-clop-clop of the matched team passed: "Poor Emily."

She carried her head high enough—even when we believed that she was fallen. It was as if she demanded more than ever the recognition of her dignity as the last Grierson; as if it had wanted that touch of earthiness to reaffirm her imperviousness. Like when she bought the rat poison, the arsenic. That was over a year after they had begun to say "Poor Emily," and while the two female cousins were visiting her.

"I want some poison," she said to the druggist. She was over thirty then, still a slight woman, though thinner than usual, with cold, haughty black eyes in a face the flesh of which was strained across the temples and about the eyesockets as you imagine a lighthouse-keeper's face ought to look. "I want some poison," she said.

35　　"Yes, Miss Emily. What kind? For rats and such? I'd recom—"

"I want the best you have. I don't care what kind."

The druggist named several. "They'll kill anything up to an elephant. But what you want is—"

"Arsenic." Miss Emily said. "Is that a good one?"

"Is . . . arsenic? Yes ma'am. But what you want—"

40　　"I want arsenic."

The druggist looked down at her. She looked back at him, erect, her face like a strained flag. "Why, of course," the druggist said. "If that's what you want. But the law requires you to tell what you are going to use it for."

Miss Emily just stared at him, her head tilted back in order to look him eye for eye, until he looked away and went and got the arsenic and wrapped it up. The Negro delivery boy brought her the package; the druggist didn't come back. When she opened the package at home there was written on the box, under the skull and bones: "For rats."

IV

So the next day we all said, "She will kill herself"; and we said it would be the best thing. When she had first begun to be seen with Homer Barron, we had said, "She will marry him." Then we said, "She will persuade him yet," because Homer himself had remarked—he liked men, and it was known that he drank with the younger men in the Elks' Club—that he was not a marrying man. Later we said, "Poor Emily," behind the jalousies as they passed on Sunday afternoon in the glittering buggy, Miss Emily with her head high and Homer Barron with his hat cocked and a cigar in his teeth, reins and whip in a yellow glove.

Then some of the ladies began to say that it was a disgrace to the town and a bad example to the young people. The men did not want to interfere, but at last the ladies forced the Baptist minister—Miss Emily's people were Episcopal—to call upon her. He would never divulge what happened during that interview, but he refused to go back again. The next Sunday they again drove about the streets, and the following day the minister's wife wrote to Miss Emily's relations in Alabama.

45   So she had blood-kin under her roof again and we sat back to watch developments. At first nothing happened. Then we were sure that they were to be married. We learned that Miss Emily had been to the jeweler's and ordered a man's toilet set in silver, with the letters H.B. on each piece. Two days later we learned that she had bought a complete outfit of men's clothing, including a nightshirt, and we said, "They are married." We were really glad. We were glad because the two female cousins were even more Grierson than Miss Emily had ever been.

So we were surprised when Homer Barron—the streets had been finished some time since—was gone. We were a little disappointed that there was not a public blowing-off but we believed that he had gone on to prepare for Miss Emily's coming, or to give a chance to get rid of the cousins. (By that time it was a cabal, and we were all Miss Emily's allies to help circumvent the cousins.) Sure enough, after another week they departed. And, as we had expected all along, within three days Homer Barron was back in town. A neighbor saw the Negro man admit him at the kitchen door at dusk one evening.

And that was the last we saw of Homer Barron. And of Miss Emily for some time. The Negro man went in and out with the market basket, but the front door remained closed. Now and then we would see her at a window for a moment, as the men did that night when they sprinkled the lime, but for almost six months she did not appear on the streets. Then we knew that this was to be expected too; as if that quality of her father which had thwarted her woman's life so many times had been too virulent and too furious to die.

When we next saw Miss Emily, she had grown fat and her hair was turning gray. During the next few years it grew grayer and grayer until it attained an even pepper-and-salt iron-gray, when it ceased turning. Up to the day of her death at seventy-four it was still that vigorous iron-gray, like the hair of an active man.

From that time on her front door remained closed, save for a period of six or seven years, when she was about forty, during which she gave lessons in china-painting. She fitted up a studio in one of the downstairs rooms, where the daughters and granddaughters of Colonel Sartoris' contemporaries were sent to her with the same regularity and in the same spirit that they were sent on Sundays with a twenty-five cent piece for the collection plate. Meanwhile her taxes had been remitted.

50   Then the newer generation became the backbone and the spirit of the town, and the painting pupils grew up and fell away and did not send their children to her with boxes of color and tedious brushes and pictures cut from the ladies' magazines. The front door closed upon the last one and remained closed for good. When the town got free postal delivery Miss Emily alone refused to let them fasten the metal numbers above her door and attach a mailbox to it. She would not listen to them.

Daily, monthly, yearly we watched the Negro grow grayer and more stooped, going in and out with the market basket. Each December we sent her a tax notice, which would be returned by the post office a week later, unclaimed. Now and then we could see her in one of the downstairs windows—she had evidently shut up the top floor of the house—like the carven torso of an idol in a niche, looking or not looking at us, we could never tell which. Thus she passed from generation to generation—dear, inescapable, impervious, tranquil, and perverse.

And so she died. Fell ill in the house filled with dust and shadows, with only a doddering Negro man to wait on her. We did not even know she was sick; we had long since given up trying to get any information from the Negro. He talked to no one, probably not even to her, for his voice had grown harsh and rusty, as if from disuse.

She died in one of the downstairs rooms, in a heavy walnut bed with a curtain, her gray head propped on a pillow yellow and moldy with age and lack of sunlight.

V

The Negro met the first of the ladies at the front door and let them in, with their hushed, sibilant voices and their quick, curious glances, and then he disappeared. He walked right through the house and out the back and was not seen again.

55   The two female cousins came at once. They held the funeral on the second day, with the town coming to look at Miss Emily beneath a mass of bought flowers, with the crayon face of her father musing profoundly above the bier and the ladies sibilant and macabre; and the very old men—some in their brushed Confederate uniforms—on the porch and the lawn, talking of Miss Emily as if she had been a contemporary of theirs, believing that they had danced with her and courted her perhaps, confusing time with its mathematical progression, as the old do, to whom all the past is not a diminishing road, but, instead, a huge meadow which no winter ever quite touches, divided from them now by the narrow bottleneck of the most recent decade of years.

Already we knew that there was one room in that region above stairs which no one had seen in forty years, and which would have to be forced. They waited until Miss Emily was decently in the ground before they opened it.

dust and shadows, with only a doddering negro man to wait on
her. e did not even know she was sick; we had long since given up
trying to get any information from the negro. He talked to no
one, probably not even to her, for his voice had grown ⊘⊘⊘⊘
harsh and ⊘⊘⊘ rusty, as though with disuse; the sparse words
which he did speak sounded as though he had learned them that
morning by rote---just enough of them to carry him through
the day.

She died in one of the downstairs rooms, in a heavy
walnut bed with a curtain, her gray head propped on a pillow
yellow and moldy with age and lack of sunlight, her voice
cold and strong to the last.

"But not till I'm gone," she said. "Dont you let a
soul in until I'm gone, do you hear?" Standing beside the bed,
his head in the dim light nimbused by a faint halo of napped,
perfectly white hair, the negro made a brief gesture with his
hand. iss Emily lay with her eyes open, gazing into the opposite shadows of the room. Upon the coverlet her hands lay on
her breast, gnarled, blue with age, motionless. "Hah," she said.
"Then they can. et 'em go up there and see what's in that
room. ⊘⊘⊘/⊘⊘⊘/⊘⊘⊘⊘/⊘⊘/⊘⊘⊘/⊘⊘⊘⊘/⊘⊘⊘⊘/⊘⊘⊘⊘⊘ Fools. ⊘⊘⊘ Let
'em. ⊘⊘⊘/⊘⊘⊘/⊘⊘⊘⊘/⊘⊘/⊘⊘⊘/⊘⊘⊘⊘/⊘⊘⊘ Satisfy their minds that
I am crazy. Do you think I am?" The negro made no reply, no
movement. He stood above the bed, ⊘⊘⊘⊘⊘⊘⊘/⊘⊘⊘⊘⊘/⊘⊘⊘⊘/⊘⊘/⊘⊘⊘/
⊘⊘⊘/ motionless, musing: a secret and unfathomable soul behind
the death-mask of an ape and haloed like an angel. "Let 'em
go up there and open that door. And you wont be the last one,

13.

The printed version of Faulkner's "A Rose for Emily" omitted several passages of dialogue,
shown here in the typed manuscript of pages 13 to 15, between Miss Emily and her long-time
manservant. (*continued*)

either. Will you?"

"I wont have to," the negro said. "I know what's in that room. I dont have to see."

"Hah," Miss Emily said. "You do, do you. How long have you known?" Again he made that brief sign with his hand. Miss Emily had not turned her head. She stared into the shadows where the high ceiling was lost. "You should be glad. Now you can go to Chicago, like you've been talking about for thirty years. And with what you'll get for the house and furniture.... Colonel Sartoris has the will. He'll see they dont rob you."

"I dont want any house," the negro said.

"You cant help yourself. It's signed and sealed thirty-five years ago. Wasn't that our agreement when I found I couldn't pay you any wages? that you were to have everything that was left if you outlived me, and I was to bury you ~~with~~ in a coffin with your name on a gold plate if I outlived you?" He said nothing. "Wasn't it?" Miss Emily said.

"I was young then. Wanted to be rich. But now I dont want any house."

"Not when you have wanted to go to Chicago for thirty years?" Their breathing was alike: each that harsh, rasping breath of the old, the short inhalations that do not reach the bottom of the lungs: tireless, precarious, on the verge of cessation for all time, as if anything might suffice: a word, a look. "What are you going to do, then?"

"Going to the poorhouse."

"The poorhouse? When I'm trying to fix you so you'll

14.

have neither to worry nor lift your hand as long as you live"

"I dont want nothing," the negro said. "I'm going t
the poorhouse. I already told them."

"Well," Miss Emily said. She had not moved her head,
not moved at all. "Do you mind telling me why you want to go
to the poorhouse?"

Again he mused. The room was still save for their brea
ing: it was as though they had both quitted all living and all
dying; all the travail of mortality and of breath. "So I can
set on that hill in the sun all day and watch them trains pass.
See them at night too, with the engine puffing and lights in
all the windows.

"Oh," Miss Emily said. Motionless, her knotted hands
lying on the yellowed coverlet beneath her chin and her chin
resting upon her breast, she appeared to muse intently, as
though she were listening to dissolution setting up within her.
"Hah," she said.

Then she died, and the negro met the first of the ladies at the front door and let them in, with their hushed sibilant voices and their quick curious glances, and he went on
to the back and disappeared. He walked right through the house
and out the back and was not seen again.

The two female cousins came at once. They held the
funeral on the second day, with the town coming to look at
Miss Emily beneath a mass of bought flowers, with the crayon
face of her father musing profoundly above the bier and the la-

15.

grin cemented into what had once been a pillow by a substance like hardened sealing-wax. One side of the covers was flung back, as though he were preparing to rise; we lifted the covers completely away, liberating still another sluggish cloud of infinitesimal dust, invisible and tainted. The body had apparently once lain in the attitude of an embrace, but now the long sleep that out-lasts love, that conquers even the grimace of love, had cuckolded him: what was left of him lay beneath what was left of the nightshirt, become inextricable with the bed in which he lay, and upon him and upon the pillow beside him lay that even coat-ing of the patient and biding dust. /p/ Then we noticed that in the second pillow was the indentation of a head; one of us lifted something from it, and leaning forward, that faint and invisible dust lean and acrid in the nostrils, we saw a long strand of iron-gray hair.

The final paragraph of the typed manuscript was reworded and made into two paragraphs in the published version.

The violence of breaking down the door seemed to fill this room with pervading dust. A thin, acrid pall as of the tomb seemed to lie everywhere upon this room decked and furnished as for a bridal: upon the valance curtains of faded rose color, upon the rose-shaded lights, upon the dressing table, upon the delicate array of crystal and the man's toilet things backed with tarnished silver, silver so tarnished that the monogram was obscured. Among them lay a collar and tie, as if they had just been removed, which, lifted, left upon the surface a pale crescent in the dust. Upon a chair hung the suit, carefully folded; beneath it the two mute shoes and the discarded socks.

The man himself lay in the bed.

For a long while we just stood there, looking down at the profound and fleshless grin. The body had apparently once lain in the attitude of an embrace, but now the long sleep that outlasts love, that conquers even the grimace of love, had cuckolded him. What was left of him, rotted beneath what was left of the nightshirt, had become inextricable from the bed in which he lay; and upon him and upon the pillow beside him lay that even coating of the patient and biding dust.

60   Then we noticed that in the second pillow was the indentation of a head. One of us lifted something from it, and leaning forward, that faint and invisible dust dry and acrid in the nostrils, we saw a long strand of iron-gray hair.

Barn Burning

[1939]

The store in which the Justice of the Peace's court was sitting smelled of cheese. The boy, crouched on his nail keg at the back of the crowded room, knew he smelled cheese, and more: from where he sat he could see the ranked shelves close-packed with the solid, squat, dynamic shapes of tin cans whose labels his stomach read, not from the lettering which mean nothing to his mind but from the scarlet devils and the silver curve of fish— this, the cheese which he knew he smelled and the hermetic meat which his intestines believed he smelled coming in intermittent gusts momentary and brief between the other constant one, the smell and sense just a little of fear because mostly of despair and grief, the old fierce pull of blood. He could not see the table where the Justice sat and before which his father and his father's enemy (*our enemy* he thought in that despair; *ourn! mine and hisn both! He's my father!*) stood, but he could hear them, the two of them that is, because his father had said no word yet:

"But what proof have you, Mr. Harris?"

"I told you. The hog got into my corn. I caught it up and sent it back to him. He had no fence that would hold it. I told him so, warned him. The next time I put the hog in my pen. When he came to get it I gave him enough wire to patch up his pen. The next time I put the hog up and kept it. I rode down to his house and saw the wire I gave him still rolled on to the spool in his yard. I told him he could have the hog when he paid me a dollar pound fee. That evening a nigger came with the dollar and got the hog. He was a strange nigger. He said, 'He say to tell you wood and hay kin burn.' I said, 'What?' 'That whut he say to tell you,' the nigger said. 'Wood and hay kin burn.' That night my barn burned. I got the stock out but I lost the barn."

"Where is the nigger? Have you got him?"

5   "He was a strange nigger, I tell you. I don't know what became of him."

"But that's not proof. Don't you see that's not proof?"

"Get that boy up here. He knows." For a moment the boy thought too that the man meant his older brother until Harris said, "Not him. The little one. The boy," and, crouching, small for his age, small and wiry like his father, in patched and faded jeans even too small for him, with straight, uncombed, brown hair and eyes gray and wild as storm scud, he saw the men between himself and the table part and become a lane of grim faces, at the end of which he saw the Justice, a shabby, collarless, graying man in spectacles, beckoning him. He felt no floor under his bare feet; he seemed to walk beneath the palpable weight of the grim turning faces. His father, stiff in his black Sunday coat donned not for the trial but for the moving, did not even look at him. *He aims for me to lie*, he thought, again with that frantic grief and despair. *And I will have to do hit.*

"What's your name, boy?" the Justice said.

"Colonel Sartoris Snopes," the boy whispered.

10   "Hey?" the Justice said. "Talk louder. Colonel Sartoris? I reckon anybody named for Colonel Sartoris in this country can't help but tell the truth, can they?" The boy said nothing. *Enemy! Enemy!* he thought; for a moment he could not even see, could not see that the Justice's face was kindly nor discern that his voice was troubled when he spoke to the man named Harris: "Do you want me to question this boy?" But he could hear, and during those subsequent long seconds while there was absolutely no sound in the crowded little room save that of quiet and intent breathing it was as if he had swung outward at the end of a grape vine, over a ravine, and at the top of the swing had been caught in a prolonged instant of mesmerized gravity, weightless in time.

"No!" Harris said violently, explosively. "Damnation! Send him out of here!" Now time, the fluid world, rushed beneath him again, the voices coming to him again through the smell of cheese and sealed meat, the fear and despair and the old grief of blood:

"This case is closed. I can't find against you, Snopes, but I can give you advice. Leave this country and don't come back to it."

His father spoke for the first time, his voice cold and harsh, level, without emphasis: "I aim to. I don't figure to stay in a country among people who . . ." he said something unprintable and vile, addressed to no one.

"That'll do," the Justice said. "Take your wagon and get out of this country before dark. Case dismissed."

15   His father turned, and he followed the stiff black coat, the wiry figure walking a little stiffly from where a Confederate provost's man's musket ball had taken him in the heel on a stolen horse thirty years ago, followed the two backs now, since his older brother had appeared from somewhere in the crowd, no taller than the father but thicker, chewing tobacco steadily, between the two lines of grim-faced men and out of the store and across the worn gallery and down the sagging steps and among the dogs and half-grown boys in the mild May dust, where as he passed a voice hissed:

"Barn burner!"

Again he could not see, whirling; there was a face in a red haze, moon-like, bigger than the full moon, the owner of it half again his size, he leaping in the red haze toward the face, feeling no blow, feeling no shock when his head struck the earth, scrabbling up and leaping again, feeling no blow this time either and tasting no blood, scrabbling up to see the other boy in full flight and himself already leaping into pursuit as his father's hand jerked him back, the harsh, cold voice speaking above him: "Go get in the wagon."

It stood in a grove of locusts and mulberries across the road. His two hulking sisters in their Sunday dresses and his mother and her sister in calico and sunbonnets were already in it, sitting on and among the sorry residue of the dozen and more movings which even the boy could remember—the battered stove, the broken beds and chairs, the clock inlaid with mother-of-pearl, which would not run, stopped at some fourteen minutes past two o'clock of a dead and forgotten day and time, which had been his mother's dowry. She was crying, though when she saw him she drew her sleeve across her face and began to descend from the wagon. "Get back," the father said.

"He's hurt. I got to get some water and wash his . . ."

20   "Get back in the wagon," his father said. He got in too, over the tail-gate. His father mounted to the seat where the older brother already sat and struck the gaunt mules two savage blows with the peeled willow, but without heat. It was not even sadistic; it was exactly that same quality which in later years would cause his descendants to over-run the engine before putting a motor car into motion, striking and reining back in the same movement. The wagon went on, the store with its quiet crowd of grimly watching men dropped behind; a curve in the road hid it. *Forever* he thought. *Maybe he's done satisfied now, now that he has* . . . stopping himself, not to say it aloud even to himself. His mother's hand touched his shoulder.

"Does hit hurt?" she said.

"Naw," he said. "Hit don't hurt. Lemme be."

"Can't you wipe some of the blood off before hit dries?"

"I'll wash to-night," he said. "Lemme be, I tell you."

25   The wagon went on. He did not know where they were going. None of them ever did or ever asked, because it was always somewhere, always a house of sorts waiting for them a day or two days or even three days away. Likely his father had already arranged to make a crop on another farm before he . . . Again he had to stop himself. He (the father) always did. There was something about his wolflike independence and even courage when the advantage was at least neutral which impressed strangers, as if they got from his latent ravening ferocity not so much a sense of dependability as a feeling that his ferocious conviction in the rightness of his own actions would be of advantage to all whose interest lay with his.

That night they camped, in a grove of oaks and beeches where a spring ran. The nights were still cool and they had a fire against it, of a rail lifted from a nearby fence and cut into lengths—a small fire, neat, niggard almost, a shrewd fire; such fires were his father's habit and custom always, even in freezing weather. Older, the boy might have remarked this and wondered why not a big one; why should not a man who had not only seen the waste and extravagance of war, but who had in his blood an inherent voracious prodigality with material not his own, have burned everything in sight? Then he might have gone a step farther and thought that that was the reason: that niggard blaze was the living fruit of nights passed during those four years in the woods hiding from all men, blue or gray, with his strings of horses (captured horses, he called them). And older still, he might have divined the true reason: that the element of fire spoke to some deep mainspring of his father's being, as the element of steel or of powder spoke to other men, as the one weapon for the preservation of integrity, else breath were not worth the breathing, and hence to be regarded with respect and used with discretion.

But he did not think this now and he had seen those same niggard blazes all his life. He merely ate his supper beside it and was already half asleep over his iron plate when his father called him, and once more he followed the stiff back, the stiff and ruthless limp, up the slope and on to the starlit road where, turning, he could see his father against the stars but without face or depth—a shape black, flat, and bloodless as though cut from tin in the iron folds of the frockcoat which had not been made for him, the voice harsh like tin and without heat like tin:

"You were fixing to tell them. You would have told him." He didn't answer. His father struck him with the flat of his hand on the side of the head, hard but without heat, exactly as he had struck the two mules at the store, exactly as he would strike either of them with any stick in order to kill a horse fly, his voice still without heat or anger: "You're getting to be a man. You got to learn. You got to learn to stick to your own blood or you ain't going to have any blood to stick to you. Do you think either of them, any man there this morning, would? Don't you know all they wanted was a chance to get at me because they knew I had them beat? Eh?" Later, twenty years later, he was to tell himself, "If I had said they wanted only truth, justice, he would have hit me again." But now he said nothing. He was not crying. He just stood there. "Answer me," his father said.

"Yes," he whispered. His father turned.

30   "Get on to bed. We'll be there to-morrow."

To-morrow they were there. In the early afternoon the wagon stopped before a paintless two-room house identical almost with the dozen others it had stopped before even in the boy's ten years, and again, as on the other dozen occasions, his mother and aunt got down and began to unload the wagon, although his two sisters and his father and brother had not moved.

"Likely hit ain't fitten for hawgs," one of the sisters said.

"Nevertheless, fit it will and you'll hog it and like it," his father said. "Get out of them chairs and help your Ma unload."

The two sisters got down, big, bovine, in a flutter of cheap ribbons; one of them drew from the jumbled wagon bed a battered lantern, the other a worn broom. His father handed the reins to the older son and began to climb stiffly over the wheel. "When they get unloaded, take the team to the barn and feed them." Then he said, and at first the boy thought he was still speaking to his brother: "Come with me."

35   "Me?" he said.

"Yes," his father said. "You."

"Abner," his mother said. His father paused and looked back—the harsh level stare beneath the shaggy, graying, irascible brows.

"I reckon I'll have a word with the man that aims to begin to-morrow owning me body and soul for the next eight months."

They went back up the road. A week ago—or before last night, that is—he would have asked where they were going, but not now. His father had struck him before last night but never before had he paused afterward to explain why; it was as if the blow and the following calm, outrageous voice still rang, repercussed, divulging nothing to him save the terrible handicap of being young, the light weight of his few years, just heavy enough to prevent his soaring free of the world as it seemed to be ordered but not heavy enough to keep him footed solid in it, to resist it and try to change the course of its events.

40   Presently he could see the grove of oaks and cedars and the other flowering trees and shrubs where the house would be, though not the house yet. They walked beside a fence massed with honeysuckle and Cherokee roses and came to a gate swinging open between two brick pillars, and now, beyond a sweep of drive, he saw the house for the first time and at that instant he forgot his father and the terror and despair both, and even when he remembered his father again (who had not stopped) the terror and despair did not return. Because, for all the twelve movings, they had sojourned until now in a poor country, a land of small farms and fields and houses, and he had never seen a house like this before. *Hit's big as a courthouse* he thought quietly, with a surge of peace and joy whose reason he could not have thought into words, being too young for that: *They are safe from him. People whose lives are a part of this peace and dignity are beyond his touch, he no more to them than a buzzing wasp: capable of stinging for a little moment but that's all; the spell of this peace and dignity rendering even the barns and stable and cribs which belong to it impervious to the puny flames he might contrive . . .* this, the peace and joy, ebbing for an instant as he looked again at the stiff black back, the stiff and implacable limp of the figure which was not dwarfed by the house, for the reason that it had never looked big anywhere and which now, against the serene columned backdrop, had more than ever that impervious quality of something cut ruthlessly from tin, depthless, as though, sidewise to the sun, it would cast no shadow. Watching him, the boy remarked the absolutely undeviating course which his father held and saw the stiff foot come squarely down in a pile of fresh droppings where a horse had stood in the drive and which his father could have avoided by a simple change of stride. But it ebbed only for a moment, though he could not have thought this into words either, walking on in the spell of the house, which he could even want but without envy, without sorrow, certainly never with that ravening and jealous rage which unknown to him walked in the ironlike black coat before him: *Maybe he will feel it too. Maybe it will even change him now from what maybe he couldn't help but be.*

They crossed the portico. Now he could hear his father's stiff foot as it came down on the boards with clocklike finality, a sound out of all proportion to the displacement of the body it bore and which was not dwarfed either by the white door before it, as though it had attained to a sort of vicious and ravening minimum not to be dwarfed by anything—the flat, wide, black hat, the formal coat of broadcloth which had once been black but which had now that friction-glazed greenish cast of the bodies of old house flies, the lifted sleeve which was too large, the lifted hand like a curled claw. The door opened so promptly that the boy knew the Negro must have been watching them all the time, an old man with neat grizzled hair, in a linen jacket, who stood barring the door with his body, saying, "Wipe yo foots, white man, fo you come in here. Major ain't home nohow."

"Get out of my way, nigger," his father said, without heat too, flinging the door back and the Negro also and entering, his hat still on his head. And now the boy saw the prints of the stiff foot on the doorjamb and saw them appear on the pale rug behind the machinelike deliberation of the foot which seemed to bear (or transmit) twice the weight which the body compassed. The Negro was shouting "Miss Lula! Miss Lula!" somewhere behind them, then the boy, deluged as though by a warm wave by a suave turn of carpeted stair and a pendant glitter of chandeliers and a mute gleam of gold frames, heard the swift feet and saw her too, a lady—perhaps he had never seen her like before either—in a gray, smooth gown with lace at the throat and an apron tied at the waist and the sleeves turned back, wiping cake or biscuit dough from her hands with a towel as she came up the hall, looking not at his father at all but at the tracks on the blond rug with an expression of incredulous amazement.

"I tried," the Negro cried. "I tole him to . . ."

"Will you please go away?" she said in a shaking voice. "Major de Spain is not at home. Will you please go away?"

45   His father had not spoken again. He did not speak again. He did not even look at her. He just stood stiff in the center of the rug, in his hat, the shaggy iron-gray brows twitching slightly above the pebble-colored eyes as he appeared to examine the house with brief deliberation. Then with the same deliberation he turned; the boy watched him pivot on the good leg and saw the stiff foot drag round the arc of the turning, leaving a final long and fading smear. His father never looked at it, he never once looked down at the rug. The Negro held the door. It closed behind them, upon the hysteric and indistinguishable woman-wail. His father stopped at the top of the steps and scraped his boot clean on the edge of it. At the gate he stopped again. He stood for a moment, planted stiffly on the stiff foot, looking back at the house. "Pretty and white, ain't it?" he said. "That's sweat. Nigger sweat. Maybe it ain't white enough yet to suit him. Maybe he wants to mix some white sweat with it."

Two hours later the boy was chopping wood behind the house within which his mother and aunt and the two sisters (the mother and aunt, not the two girls, he knew that; even at this distance and muffled by walls the flat loud voices of the two girls emanated an incorrigible idle inertia) were setting up the stove to prepare a meal, when he heard the hooves and saw the linen-clad man on a fine sorrel mare, whom he recognized even before he saw the rolled rug in front of the Negro youth following on a fat bay carriage horse—a suffused, angry face vanishing, still at full gallop, behind the corner of the house where his father and brother were sitting in the two tilted chairs; and a moment later, almost before he could have put the axe down, he heard the hooves again and watched the sorrel mare go back out of the yard, already galloping again. Then his father began to shout one of the sisters' names, who presently emerged backward from the kitchen door dragging the rolled rug along the ground by one end while the other sister walked behind it.

"If you ain't going to tote, go on and set up the wash pot," the first said.

"You, Sarty!" the second shouted. "Set up the wash pot!" His father appeared at the door, framed against that shabbiness, as he had been against that other bland perfection, impervious to either, the mother's anxious face at his shoulder.

"Go on," the father said. "Pick it up." The two sisters stooped, broad, lethargic; stooping, they presented an incredible expanse of pale cloth and a flutter of tawdry ribbons.

50   "If I thought enough of a rug to have to git hit all the way from France I wouldn't keep hit where folks coming in would have to tromp on hit," the first said. They raised the rug.

"Abner," the mother said. "Let me do it."

"You go back and git dinner," his father said. "I'll tend to this."

From the woodpile through the rest of the afternoon the boy watched them, the rug spread flat in the dust beside the bubbling wash-pot, the two sisters stooping over it with that profound and lethargic reluctance, while the father stood over them in turn, implacable and grim, driving them though never raising his voice again. He could smell the harsh homemade lye they were using; he saw his mother come to the door once and look toward them with an expression not anxious now but very like despair; he saw his father turn, and he fell to with the axe and saw from the corner of his eye his father raise from the ground a flattish fragment of field stone and examine it and return to the pot, and this time his mother actually spoke: "Abner. Abner. Please don't. Please, Abner."

Then he was done too. It was dusk; the whippoorwills had already begun. He could smell coffee from the room where they would presently eat the cold food remaining from the midafternoon meal, though when he entered the house he realized they were having coffee again probably because there was a fire on the hearth, before which the rug now lay spread over the backs of the two chairs. The tracks of his father's foot were gone. Where they had been were now long, water-cloudy scoriations resembling the sporadic course of a liliputian mowing machine.

55   It still hung there while they ate the cold food and then went to bed, scattered without order or claim up and down the two rooms, his mother in one bed, where his father would later lie, the older brother in the other, himself, the aunt, and the two sisters on pallets on the floor. But his father was not in bed yet. The last thing the boy remembered was the depthless, harsh silhouette of the hat and coat bending over the rug and it seemed to him that he had not even closed his eyes when the silhouette was standing over him, the fire almost dead behind it, the stiff foot prodding him awake. "Catch up the mule," his father said.

When he returned with the mule his father was standing in the black door, the rolled rug over his shoulder. "Ain't you going to ride?" he said.

"No. Give me your foot."

He bent his knee into his father's hand, the wiry, surprising power flowed smoothly, rising, he rising with it, on to the mule's bare back (they had owned a saddle once; the boy could remember it though not when or where) and with the same effortlessness his father swung the rug up in front of him. Now in the starlight they retraced the afternoon's path, up the dusty road rife with honeysuckle, through the gate and up the black tunnel of the drive to the lightless house, where he sat on the mule and felt the rough warp of the rug drag across his thighs and vanish.

"Don't you want me to help?" he whispered. His father did not answer and now he heard again that stiff foot striking the hollow portico with that wooden and clocklike deliberation, that outrageous overstatement of the weight it carried. The rug, hunched, not flung (the boy could tell that even in the darkness) from his father's shoulder struck the angle of wall and floor with a sound unbelievably loud, thunderous, then the foot again, unhurried and enormous; a light came on in the house and the boy sat, tense, breathing steadily and quietly and just a little fast, though the foot itself did not increase its beat at all, descending the steps now; now the boy could see him.

60   "Don't you want to ride now?" he whispered. "We kin both ride now," the light within the house altering now, flaring up and sinking. *He's coming down the stairs now*, he thought. He had already ridden the mule up beside the horse block; presently his father was up behind him and he doubled the reins over and slashed the mule across the neck, but before the animal could begin to trot the hard, thin arm came round him, the hard, knotted hand jerking the mule back to a walk.

In the first red rays of the sun they were in the lot, putting plow gear on the mules. This time the sorrel mare was in the lot before he heard it at all, the rider collarless and even bareheaded, trembling, speaking in a shaking voice as the woman in the house had done. His father merely looking up once before stooping again to the hame he was buckling, so that the man on the mare spoke to his stooping back:

"You must realize you have ruined that rug. Wasn't there anybody here, any of your women . . ." he ceased, shaking, the boy watching him, the older brother leaning now in the stable door, chewing, blinking slowly and steadily at nothing apparently. "It cost a hundred dollars. But you never had a hundred dollars. You never will. So I'm going to charge you twenty bushels of corn against your crop. I'll add it in your contract and when you come to the commissary you can sign it. That won't keep Mrs. de Spain quiet but maybe it will teach you to wipe your feet off before you enter her house again."

Then he was gone. The boy looked at his father, who still had not spoken or even looked up again, who was now adjusting the loggerhead in the hame.

"Pap," he said. His father looked at him—the inscrutable face, the shaggy brows beneath which the gray eyes glinted coldly. Suddenly the boy went toward him, fast, stopping as suddenly. "You done the best you could!" he cried. "If he wanted hit done different why didn't he wait and tell you how? He won't git no twenty bushels! He won't git none! We'll gether hit and hide hit! I kin watch . . ."

65   "Did you put the cutter back in that straight stock like I told you?"

"No, sir," he said.

"Then go do it."

That was Wednesday. During the rest of that week he worked steadily, at what was within his scope and some which was beyond it, with an industry that did not need to be driven nor even commanded twice; he had this from his mother, with the difference that some at least of what he did he liked to do, such as splitting wood with the half-size axe which his mother and aunt had earned, or saved money somehow, to present him with at Christmas. In company with the two older women (and on one afternoon, even one of the sisters), he built pens for the shoat and the cow which were a part of his father's contract with the landlord, and one afternoon, his father being absent, gone somewhere on one of the mules, he went to the field.

They were running a middle buster now, his brother holding the plow straight while he handled the reins, and walking beside the straining mule, the rick black soil shearing cool and damp against his bare ankles, he thought *Maybe this is the end of it. Maybe even that twenty bushels that seems hard to have to pay for just a rug will be a cheap price for him to stop forever and always from being what he used to be;* thinking, dreaming now, so that his brother had to speak sharply to him to mind the mule: *Maybe he even won't collect the twenty bushels. Maybe it will all add up and balance and vanish—corn, rug, fire; the terror and grief, the being pulled two ways like between two teams of horses—gone, done with for ever and ever.*

70   Then it was Saturday; he looked up from beneath the mule he was harnessing and saw his father in the black coat and hat. "Not that," his father said. "The wagon gear." And then, two hours later, sitting in the wagon bed behind his father and brother on the seat, the wagon accomplished a final curve, and he saw the weathered paintless store with its tattered tobacco- and patent-medicine posters and the tethered wagons and saddle animals below the gallery. He mounted the gnawed steps behind his father and brother, and there again was the lane of quiet, watching faces for the three of them to walk through. He saw the man in spectacles sitting at the plank table and he did not need to be told this was a Justice of the Peace; he sent one glare of fierce, exultant, partisan defiance at the man in collar and cravat now, whom he had seen but twice before in his life, and that on a galloping horse, who now wore on his face an expression not of rage but of amazed unbelief which the boy could not have known was at the incredible circumstance of being sued by one of his own tenants, and came and stood against his father and cried at the Justice: "He ain't done it! He ain't burnt . . ."

"Go back to the wagon," his father said.

"Burnt?" the Justice said. "Do I understand this rug was burned too?"

"Does anybody here claim it was?" his father said. "Go back to the wagon." But he did not, he merely retreated to the rear of the room, crowded as that other had been, but not to sit down this time, instead, to stand pressing among the motionless bodies, listening to the voices:

"And you claim twenty bushels of corn is too high for the damage you did to the rug?"

75   "He brought the rug to me and said he wanted the tracks washed out of it. I washed the tracks out and took the rug back to him."

"But you didn't carry the rug back to him in the same condition it was in before you made the tracks on it."

His father did not answer, and now for perhaps half a minute there was no sound at all save that of breathing, the faint, steady suspiration of complete and intent listening.

"You decline to answer that, Mr. Snopes?" Again his father did not answer. "I'm going to find against you, Mr. Snopes. I'm going to find that you were responsible for the injury to Major de Spain's rug and hold you liable for it. But twenty bushels of corn seems a little high for a man in your circumstances to have to pay. Major de Spain claims it costs a hundred dollars. October corn will be worth about fifty cents. I figure that if Major de Spain can stand a ninety-five-dollar loss on something he paid cash for, you can stand a five-dollar loss you haven't earned yet. I hold you in damages to Major de Spain to the amount of ten bushels of corn over and above your contract with him, to be paid to him out of your crop at gathering time. Court adjourned."

It had taken no time hardly, the morning was but half begun. He thought they would return home and perhaps back to the field, since they

were late, far behind all other farmers. But instead his father passed on behind the wagon, merely indicating with his hand for the older brother to follow with it, and crossed the road toward the blacksmith shop opposite,
pressing on after his father, overtaking him, speaking, whispering up at the
harsh, calm face beneath the weathered hat: "He won't git no ten bushels
neither. He won't git one. We'll . . ." until his father glanced for an instant
down at him, the face absolutely calm, the grizzled eyebrows tangled above
the cold eyes, the voice almost pleasant, almost gentle:

80   "You think so? Well, we'll wait till October anyway."

The matter of the wagon—the setting of a spoke or two and the tightening of the tires—did not take long either, the business of the tires accomplished by driving the wagon into the spring branch behind the shop and
letting it stand there, the mules nuzzling into the water from time to time,
and the boy on the seat with the idle reins, looking up the slope and
through the sooty tunnel of the shed where the slow hammer rang and
where his father sat on an upended cypress bolt, easily, either talking or listening, still sitting there when the boy brought the dripping wagon up out
of the branch and halted it before the door.

"Take them on to the shade and hitch," his father said. He did so and returned. His father and the smith and a third man squatting on his heels inside the door were talking, about crops and animals; the boy, squatting too
in the ammoniac dust and hoof-parings and scales of rust, heard his father
tell a long and unhurried story out of the time before the birth of the older
brother even when he had been a professional horsetrader. And then his father came up beside him where he stood before a tattered last year's circus
poster on the other side of the store, gazing rapt and quiet at the scarlet
horses, the incredible poisings and convolutions of tulle and tights and the
painted leers of comedians, and said, "It's time to eat."

But not at home. Squatting beside his brother against the front wall, he
watched his father emerge from the store and produce from a paper sack a
segment of cheese and divide it carefully and deliberately into three with
his pocket knife and produce crackers from the same sack. They all three
squatted on the gallery and ate, slowly, without talking; then in the store
again, they drank from a tin dipper tepid water smelling of the cedar bucket
and of living beech trees. And still they did not go home. It was a horse lot
this time, a tall rail fence upon and along which men stood and sat and out
of which one by one horses were led, to be talked and trotted and then can-
tered back and forth along the road while the slow swapping and buying
went on and the sun began to slant westward, they—the three of them—
watching and listening, the older brother with his muddy eyes and his
steady, inevitable tobacco, the father commenting now and then on certain
of the animals, to no one in particular.

It was after sundown when they reached home. They ate supper by
lamplight, then, sitting on the doorstep, the boy watched the night fully accomplish, listening to the whippoorwills and the frogs, when he heard his
mother's voice: "Abner! No! No! Oh, God. Oh, God. Abner!" and he rose,
whirled, and saw the altered light through the door where a candle stub
now burned in a bottle neck on the table and his father, still in the hat and
coat, at once formal and burlesque as though dressed carefully for some
shabby and ceremonial violence, emptying the reservoir of the lamp back
into the five-gallon kerosene can from which it had been filled, while the

mother tugged at his arm until he shifted the lamp to the other hand and flung her back, not savagely or viciously, just hard, into the wall, her hands flung out against the wall for balance, her mouth open and in her face the same quality of hopeless despair as had been in her voice. Then his father saw him standing in the door.

85   "Go to the barn and get that can of oil we were oiling the wagon with," he said. The boy did not move. Then he could speak.

"What . . ." he cried. "What are you . . ."

"Go get that oil," his father said. "Go."

Then he was moving, running, outside the house, toward the stable: this the old habit, the old blood which he had not been permitted to choose for himself, which had been bequeathed him willy nilly and which had run for so long (and who knew where, battening on what of outrage and savagery and lust) before it came to him. *I could keep on,* he thought. *I could run on and on and never look back, never need to see his face again. Only I can't. I can't,* the rusted can in his hand now, the liquid sploshing in it as he ran back to the house and into it, into the sound of his mother's weeping in the next room, and handed the can to his father.

"Ain't you going to even send a nigger?" he cried. "At least you sent a nigger before!"

90   This time his father didn't strike him. The hand came even faster than the blow had, the same hand which had set the can on the table with almost excruciating care flashing from the can to ward him too quick for him to follow it, gripping him by the back of his shirt and on to tiptoe before he had seen it quit the can, the face stooping at him in breathless and frozen ferocity, the cold, dead voice speaking over him to the older brother who leaned against the table, chewing with that steady, curious, sidewise motion of cows:

"Empty the can into the big one and go on. I'll catch up with you."

"Better tie him up to the bedpost," the brother said.

"Do like I told you," the father said. Then the boy was moving, his bunched shirt and the hard, bony hand between his shoulderblades, his toes just touching the floor, across the room and into the other one, past the sisters sitting with spread heavy thighs in the two chairs over the cold hearth, and to where his mother and aunt sat side by side on the bed, the aunt's arms about his mother's shoulders.

"Hold him," the father said. The aunt made a startled movement. "Not you," the father said. "Lennie. Take hold of him. I want to see you do it." His mother took him by the wrist. "You'll hold him better than that. If he gets loose don't you know what he is going to do? He will go up yonder." He jerked his head toward the road. "Maybe I'd better tie him."

95   "I'll hold him," his mother whispered.

"See you do then." Then his father was gone, the stiff foot heavy and measured upon the boards, ceasing at last.

Then he began to struggle. His mother caught him in both arms, he jerking and wrenching at them. He would be stronger in the end, he knew that. But he had no time to wait for it. "Lemme go!" he cried. "I don't want to have to hit you!"

"Let him go!" the aunt said. "If he don't go, before God, I am going up there myself!"

"Don't you see I can't?" his mother cried. "Sarty! Sarty! No! No! Help me, Lizzie!"

100   Then he was free. His aunt grasped at him but it was too late. He whirled, running, his mother stumbled forward on to her knees behind him, crying to the nearer sister: "Catch him, Net! Catch him!" But that was too late too, the sister (the sisters were twins, born at the same time, yet either of them now gave the impression of being, encompassing as much living meat and volume and weight as any other two of the family) not yet having begun to rise from the chair, her head, face, alone merely turned, presenting to him in the flying instant an astonishing expanse of young female features untroubled by any surprise even, wearing only an expression of bovine interest. Then he was out of the room, out of the house, in the mild dust of the starlit road and the heavy rifeness of honeysuckle, the pale ribbon unspooling with terrific slowness under his running feet, reaching the gate at last and turning in, running, his heart and lungs drumming, on up the drive toward the lighted house, the lighted door. He did not knock, he burst in, sobbing for breath, incapable for the moment of speech; he saw the astonished face of the Negro in the linen jacket without knowing when the Negro had appeared.

"De Spain!" he cried, panted. "Where's . . ." then he saw the white man too emerging from a white door down the hall. "Barn!" he cried. "Barn!"

"What?" the white man said. "Barn?"

"Yes!" the boy cried. "Barn!"

105   "Catch him!" the white man shouted.

But it was too late this time too. The Negro grasped his shirt, but the entire sleeve, rotten with washing, carried away, and he was out that door too and in the drive again, and had actually never ceased to run even while he was screaming into the white man's face.

Behind him the white man was shouting, "My horse! Fetch my horse!" and he thought for an instant of cutting across the park and climbing the fence into the road, but he did not know the park nor how high the vine-massed fence might be and he dared not risk it. So he ran on down the drive, blood and breath roaring; presently he was in the road again though he could not see it. He could not hear either: the galloping mare was almost upon him before he heard her, and even then he held his course, as if the very urgency of his wild grief and need must in a moment more find him wings, waiting until the ultimate instant to hurl himself aside and into the weed-choked road-side ditch as the horse thundered past and on, for an instant in furious silhouette against the stars, the tranquil early summer night sky which, even before the shape of the horse and rider vanished, strained abruptly and violently upward: a long, swirling roar incredible and soundless, blotting the stars, and he springing up and into the road again, running again, knowing it was too late yet still running even after he heard the shot and, an instant later, two shots, pausing now without knowing he had ceased to run, crying "Pap! Pap!," running again before he knew he had begun to run, stumbling, tripping over something and scrabbling up again without ceasing to run, looking backward over his shoulder at the glares as he got up, running on among the invisible trees, panting, sobbing, "Father! Father!"

At midnight he was sitting on the crest of a hill. He did not know it was midnight and he did not know how far he had come. But there was no glare behind him now and he sat now, his back toward what he had called home for four days anyhow, his face toward the dark woods which he would enter when breath was strong again, small, shaking steadily in the chill darkness, hugging himself into the remainder of his thin, rotten shirt, the grief and despair now no longer terror and fear but just grief and despair. *Father. My father,* he thought. "He was brave!" He cried suddenly, aloud but not loud, no more than a whisper: "He was! He was in the war! He was in Colonel Sartoris' cav'ry!" not knowing that his father had gone to that war a private in the fine old European sense, wearing no uniform, admitting the authority of and giving fidelity to no man or army or flag, going to war as Malbrouck himself did: for booty—it meant nothing and less than nothing to him if it were enemy booty or his own.

The slow constellations wheeled on. It would be dawn and then sun-up after a while and he would be hungry. But that would be to-morrow and now he was only cold, and walking would cure that. His breathing was easier now and he decided to get up and go on, and then he found that he had been asleep because he knew it was almost dawn, the night almost over. He could tell that from the whippoorwills. They were everywhere now among the dark trees below him, constant and inflectioned and ceaseless, so that, as the instant for giving over to the day birds drew nearer and nearer, there was no interval at all between them. He got up. He was a little stiff, but walking would cure that too as it would the cold, and soon there would be the sun. He went on down the hill, toward the dark woods within which the liquid silver voices of the birds called unceasing—the rapid and urgent beating of the urgent and quiring heart of the late spring night. He did not look back.

JORGE LUIS BORGES

Jorge Luis Borges (1899–1986), one of the first writers in Spanish to achieve an international reputation, was born in Buenos Aires. His paternal grandfather was English, and Borges learned English before he learned Spanish. When his family went to Geneva before the First World War, he became fluent in German and French. After the war the family spent two years in Spain, in 1921 Borges returned to Argentina, and in 1925 he published his first book, a collection of poems. In 1938 he accepted a post as a municipal librarian in Buenos Aires, but in 1946—by which time Borges's fiction had won him an international reputation—the dictator Juan Perón removed him from the post. In 1955, after Perón was deposed, Borges—already blind from a congenital disease—was made the director of the National Library of Buenos Aires, and in 1956 he was appointed Professor of English at the University of Buenos Aires.

Borges, widely regarded as the greatest contemporary writer in Spanish, is known for his poetry, literary criticism, and especially his highly innovative and immensely influential short fiction. For him, stories are not representations of the surface of life but are re-creations of the cultural myths that human beings have devised.

The Gospel According to Mark   [1970]

These events took place at La Colorada ranch, in the southern part of the township of Junín, during the last days of March, 1928. The protagonist was a medical student named Baltasar Espinosa. We may describe him, for now, as one of the common run of young men from Buenos Aires, with nothing more noteworthy about him than an almost unlimited kindness and a capacity for public speaking that had earned him several prizes at the English school in Ramos Mejía. He did not like arguing, and preferred having his listener rather than himself in the right. Although he was fascinated by the probabilities of chance in any game he played, he was a bad player because it gave him no pleasure to win. His wide intelligence was undirected; at the age of thirty-three, he still lacked credit for graduation, by one course— the course to which he was most drawn. His father, who was a freethinker (like all the gentlemen of his day), had introduced him to the lessons of Herbert Spencer,[1] but his mother, before leaving on a trip for Montevideo, once asked him to say the Lord's Prayer[2] and make the sign of the cross every night. Through the years, he had never gone back on that promise.

Espinosa was not lacking in spirit; one day, with more indifference than anger, he had exchanged two or three punches with a group of fellow-students who were trying to force him to take part in a university demonstration. Owing to an acquiescent nature, he was full of opinions, or habits of mind, that were questionable: Argentina mattered less to him than a fear that in other parts of the world people might think of us as Indians; he worshiped France but despised the French; he thought little of Americans but approved the fact that there were tall buildings, like theirs, in Buenos Aires; he believed the gauchos of the plains to be better riders than those of hill or mountain country. When his cousin Daniel invited him to spend the summer months out at La Colorada, he said yes at once—not because he was really fond of the country, but more out of his natural complacency and also because it was easier to say yes than to dream up reasons for saying no.

The ranch's main house was big and slightly run-down; the quarters of the foreman, whose name was Gutre, were close by. The Gutres were three: the father, an unusually uncouth son, and a daughter of uncertain paternity. They were tall, strong, and bony, and had hair that was on the reddish side and faces that showed traces of Indian blood. They were barely articulate. The foreman's wife had died years before.

There in the country, Espinosa began learning things he never knew, or even suspected—for example, that you do not gallop a horse when approaching settlements, and that you never go out riding except for some special purpose. In time, he was to come to tell the birds apart by their calls.

5   After a few days, Daniel had to leave for Buenos Aires to close a deal on some cattle. At most, this bit of business might take him a week. Espinosa, who was already somewhat weary of hearing about his cousin's incessant luck with women and his tireless interest in the minute details of men's fashion, preferred staying on at the ranch with his textbooks. But the heat was unbearable, and even the night brought no relief. One morning at daybreak, thunder woke him. Outside, the wind was rocking the Australian pines. Listening to the first heavy drops of rain, Espinosa thanked God. All at once, cold air rolled in. That afternoon, the Salado overflowed its banks.

---

[1]**Herbert Spencer** British philosopher and sociologist (1820-1903).   [2]**the Lord's Prayer** the prayer Jesus taught to his disciples (Matthew 6.9-13).

The next day, looking out over the flooded fields from the gallery of the main house, Baltasar Espinosa thought that the stock metaphor comparing the pampa to the sea was not altogether false—at least, not that morning—though W. H. Hudson[3] had remarked that the sea seems wider because we view it from a ship's deck and not from a horse or from eye level.

The rain did not let up. The Gutres, helped or hindered by Espinosa, the town dweller, rescued a good part of the livestock, but many animals were drowned. There were four roads leading to La Colorada; all of them were under water. On the third day, when a leak threatened the foreman's house, Espinosa gave the Gutres a room near the tool shed, at the back of the main house. This drew them all closer; they ate together in the big dining room. Conversation turned out to be difficult. The Gutres, who knew so much about country things, were hard put to it to explain them.

One night, Espinosa asked them if people still remembered the Indian raids from back when the frontier command was located there in Junín. They told him yes, but they would have given the same answer to a question about the beheading of Charles I. Espinosa recalled his father's saying that almost every case of longevity that was cited in the country was really a case of bad memory or of a dim notion of dates. Gauchos are apt to be ignorant of the year of their birth or of the name of the man who begot them.

In the whole house, there was apparently no other reading matter than a set of the *Farm Journal,* a handbook of veterinary medicine, a deluxe edition of the Uruguayan epic *Tabaré,* a *History of Shorthorn Cattle in Argentina,* a number of erotic or detective stories, and a recent novel called *Don Segundo Sombra.* Espinosa, trying in some way to bridge the inevitable after-dinner gap, read a couple of chapters of this novel to the Gutres, none of whom could read or write. Unfortunately, the foreman had been a cattle drover, and the doings of the hero, another cattle drover, failed to whet his interest. He said that the work was light, that drovers always traveled with a packhorse that carried everything they needed, and that, had he not been a drover, he would never have seen such far-flung places as the Laguna de Gómez, the town of Bragado, and the spread of the Núñez family in Chacabuco. There was a guitar in the kitchen; the ranch hands, before the time of the events I am describing, used to sit around in a circle. Someone would tune the instrument without ever getting around to playing it. This was known as a guitarfest.

10   Espinosa, who had grown a beard, began dallying in front of the mirror to study his new face, and he smiled to think how, back in Buenos Aires, he would bore his friends by telling them the story of the Salado flood. Strangely enough, he missed places he never frequented and never would: a corner of Cabrera Street on which there was a mailbox; one of the cement lions of a gateway on Jujuy Street, a few blocks from the Plaza del Once; an old barroom with a tiled floor, whose exact whereabouts he was unsure of. As for his brothers and his father, they would already have learned from

---

[3]**W. H. Hudson** William Henry Hudson (1841–1920), born of American parents in Argentina, went to England in 1869 and spent most of the rest of his life there. Several of his books are about Argentina.

Daniel that he was isolated—etymologically, the word was perfect—by the floodwaters.

Exploring the house, still hemmed in by the watery waste, Espinosa came across an English Bible. Among the blank pages at the end, the Guthries—such was their original name—had left a handwritten record of their lineage. They were natives of Inverness;[4] had reached the New World, no doubt as common laborers, in the early part of the nineteenth century; and had intermarried with Indians. The chronicle broke off sometime during the eighteen-seventies, when they no longer knew how to write. After a few generations, they had forgotten English; their Spanish, at the time Espinosa knew them, gave them trouble. They lacked any religious faith, but there survived in their blood, like faint tracks, the rigid fanaticism of the Calvinist and the superstitions of the pampa Indian. Espinosa later told them of his find, but they barely took notice.

Leafing through the volume, his fingers opened it at the beginning of the Gospel according to St. Mark. As an exercise in translation, and maybe to find out whether the Gutres understood any of it, Espinosa decided to begin reading them that text after their evening meal. It surprised him that they listened attentively, absorbed. Maybe the gold letters on the cover lent the book authority. It's still there in their blood, Espinosa thought. It also occurred to him that the generations of men, throughout recorded time, have always told and retold two stories—that of a lost ship which searches the Mediterranean seas for a dearly loved island, and that of a god who is crucified on Golgotha.[5] Remembering his lessons in elocution from his school-days in Ramos Mejía, Espinosa got to his feet when he came to the parables.

The Gutres took to bolting their barbecued meat and their sardines so as not to delay the Gospel. A pet lamb that the girl adorned with a small blue ribbon had injured itself on a strand of barbed wire. To stop the bleeding, the three had wanted to apply a cobweb to the wound, but Espinosa treated the animal with some pills. The gratitude that this treatment awakened in them took him aback. (Not trusting the Gutres at first, he'd hidden away in one of his books the two hundred and forty pesos he had brought with him.) Now, the owner of the place away, Espinosa took over and gave timid orders, which were immediately obeyed. The Gutres, as if lost without him, liked following him from room to room and along the gallery that ran around the house. While he read to them, he noticed that they were secretly stealing the crumbs he had dropped on the table. One evening, he caught them unawares, talking about him respectfully, in very few words.

Having finished the Gospel according to St. Mark, he wanted to read another of the three Gospels that remained, but the father asked him to repeat the one he had just read, so that they could understand it better. Espinosa felt that they were like children, to whom repetition is more pleasing than

---

[4]**Inverness** a county in northwest Scotland.   [5]**two stories . . . Golgotha** the first story is Homer's *Odyssey*, in which Homer tells of the wanderings of Odysseus; the second story is of Jesus' crucifixion at Golgotha, "Place of the Skull" (the Semitic name for Calvary).

variations or novelty. That night—this is not to be wondered at—he dreamed of the Flood; the hammer blows of the building of the Ark woke him up, and he thought that perhaps they were thunder. In fact, the rain, which had let up, started again. The cold was bitter. The Gutres had told him that the storm had damaged the roof of the tool shed, and that they would show it to him when the beams were fixed. No longer a stranger now, he was treated by them with special attention, almost to the point of spoiling him. None of them liked coffee, but for him there was always a small cup into which they heaped sugar.

15   The new storm had broken out on a Tuesday. Thursday night, Espinosa was awakened by a soft knock at his door, which—just in case—he always kept locked. He got out of bed and opened it; there was the girl. In the dark he could hardly make her out, but by her footsteps he could tell she was barefoot, and moments later, in bed, that she must have come all the way from the other end of the house naked. She did not embrace him or speak a single word; she lay beside him, trembling. It was the first time she had known a man. When she left, she did not kiss him; Espinosa realized that he didn't even know her name. For some reason that he did not want to pry into, he made up his mind that upon returning to Buenos Aires he would tell no one about what had taken place.

The next day began like the previous ones, except that the father spoke to Espinosa and asked him if Christ had let Himself be killed so as to save all other men on earth. Espinosa, who was a freethinker but who felt committed to what he had read to the Gutres, answered, "Yes, to save everyone from Hell."

Gutre then asked, "What's Hell?"

"A place under the ground where souls burn and burn."

"And the Roman soldiers who hammered in the nails—were they saved, too?"

20   "Yes," said Espinosa, whose theology was rather dim.

All along, he was afraid that the foreman might ask him about what had gone on the night before with his daughter. After lunch, they asked him to read the last chapters over again.

Espinosa slept a long nap that afternoon. It was a light sleep, disturbed by persistent hammering and by vague premonitions. Toward evening, he got up and went out onto the gallery. He said, as if thinking aloud, "The waters have dropped. It won't be long now."

"It won't be long now," Gutre repeated, like an echo.

The three had been following him. Bowing their knees to the stone pavement, they asked his blessing. Then they mocked at him, spat on him, and shoved him toward the back part of the house. The girl wept. Espinosa understood what awaited him on the other side of the door. When they opened it, he saw a patch of sky. A bird sang out. A goldfinch,[6] he thought. The shed was without a roof; they had pulled down the beams to make the cross.

---

[6]**goldfinch** in art the infant Jesus is often shown holding a goldfinch. Legend says that at Calvary a goldfinch drew a thorn from Christ's brow.

LANGSTON HUGHES

Langston Hughes (1902–1967), an African-American writer, was born in Joplin, Missouri, lived part of his youth in Mexico, spent a year at Columbia University, served as a merchant seaman, and worked in a Paris nightclub, where he showed some of his poems to Dr. Alain Locke, a strong advocate of African-American literature. Encouraged by Locke, when Hughes returned to the United States he continued to write, publishing fiction, plays, essays, and biographies; he also founded theaters, gave public readings, and was, in short, a highly visible presence.

One Friday Morning   [1941]

The thrilling news did not come directly to Nancy Lee, but it came in little indirections that finally added themselves up to one tremendous fact: she had won the prize! But being a calm and quiet young lady, she did not say anything, although the whole high school buzzed with rumors, guesses, reportedly authentic announcements on the part of students who had no right to be making announcements at all—since no student really knew yet who had won this year's art scholarship.

But Nancy Lee's drawing was so good, her lines so sure, her colors so bright and harmonious, that certainly no other student in the senior art class at George Washington High was thought to have very much of a chance. Yet you never could tell. Last year nobody had expected Joe Williams to win the Artist Club scholarship with that funny modernistic water color he had done of the high-level bridge. In fact, it was hard to make out there was a bridge until you had looked at the picture a long time. Still, Joe Williams got the prize, was feted by the community's leading painters, club women, and society folks at a big banquet at the Park-Rose Hotel, and was now an award student at the Art School—the city's only art school.

Nancy Lee Johnson was a colored girl, a few years out of the South. But seldom did her high-school classmates think of her as colored. She was smart, pretty, and brown, and fitted in well with the life of the school. She stood high in scholarship, played a swell game of basketball, had taken part in the senior musical in a soft, velvety voice, and had never seemed to intrude or stand out, except in pleasant ways, so it was seldom even mentioned—her color.

Nancy Lee sometimes forgot she was colored herself. She liked her classmates and her school. Particularly she liked her art teacher, Miss Dietrich, the tall red-haired woman who taught her law and order in doing things; and the beauty of working step by step until a job is done; a picture finished; a design created; or a block print carved out of nothing but an idea and a smooth square of linoleum, inked, proofs made, and finally put down on paper—clean, sharp, beautiful, individual, unlike any other in the world, thus making the paper have a meaning nobody else could give it except Nancy Lee. That was the wonderful thing about true creation. You made something nobody else on earth could make—but you.

5   Miss Dietrich was the kind of teacher who brought out the best in her students—but their own best, not anybody else's copied best. For anybody else's best, great though it might be, even Michelangelo's, wasn't enough to please Miss Dietrich, dealing with the creative impulses of young men and women living in an American city in the Middle West, and being American.

Nancy Lee was proud of being American, a Negro American with blood out of Africa a long time ago, too many generations back to count. But her parents had taught her the beauties of Africa, its strength, its song, its mighty rivers, its early smelting of iron, its building of the pyramids, and its ancient and important civilizations. And Miss Dietrich had discovered for her the sharp and humorous lines of African sculpture, Benin, Congo, Makonde. Nancy Lee's father was a mail carrier, her mother a social worker in a city settlement house. Both parents had been to Negro colleges in the South. And her mother had gotten a further degree in social work from a Northern university. Her parents were, like most Americans, simple, ordinary people who had worked hard and steadily for their education. Now they were trying to make it easier for Nancy Lee to achieve learning than it had been for them. They would be very happy when they heard of the award to their daughter—yet Nancy did not tell them. To surprise them would be better. Besides, there had been a promise.

Casually, one day, Miss Dietrich asked Nancy Lee what color frame she thought would be best on her picture. That had been the first inkling.

"Blue," Nancy Lee said. Although the picture had been entered in the Artist Club contest a month ago, Nancy Lee did not hesitate in her choice of a color for the possible frame, since she could still see her picture clearly in her mind's eye—for that picture waiting for the blue frame had come out of her soul, her own life, and had bloomed into miraculous being with Miss Dietrich's help. It was, she knew, the best water color she had painted in her four years as a high-school art student, and she was glad she had made something Miss Dietrich liked well enough to permit her to enter in the contest before she graduated.

It was not a modernistic picture in the sense that you had to look at it a long time to understand what it meant. It was just a simple scene in the city park on a spring day, with the trees still leaflessly lacy against the sky, the new grass fresh and green, a flag on a tall pole in the center, children playing, and an old Negro woman sitting on a bench with her head turned. A lot for one picture, to be sure, but it was not there in heavy and final detail like a calendar. Its charm was that everything was light and airy, happy like spring, with a lot of blue sky; paper-white clouds, and air showing through. You could tell that the old Negro woman was looking at the flag, and that the flag was proud in the spring breeze, and that the breeze helped to make the children's dresses billow as they played.

10   Miss Dietrich had taught Nancy Lee how to paint spring, people, and a breeze on what was only a plain white piece of paper from the supply closet. But Miss Dietrich had not said make it like any other spring-people-breeze ever seen before. She let it remain Nancy Lee's own. That is how the old Negro woman happened to be there looking at the flag—for in her mind the flag, the spring, and the woman formed a kind of triangle holding a dream Nancy Lee wanted to express. White stars on a blue field, spring, children, ever-growing life, and an old woman. Would the judges at the Artist Club like it?

One wet, rainy April afternoon Miss O'Shay, the girls' vice-principal, sent for Nancy Lee to stop by her office as school closed. Pupils without umbrellas or raincoats were clustered in doorways, hoping to make it home between showers. Outside the skies were gray. Nancy Lee's thoughts were suddenly gray, too.

She did not think she had done anything wrong, yet that tight little knot came in her throat just the same as she approached Miss O'Shay's door. Perhaps she had banged her locker too often and too hard. Perhaps the note in French she had written to Sallie halfway across the study hall just for fun had never gotten to Sallie but into Miss O'Shay's hands instead. Or maybe she was failing in some subject and wouldn't be allowed to graduate. Chemistry! A pang went through the pit of her stomach.

She knocked on Miss O'Shay's door. That familiarly solid and competent voice said, "Come in."

Miss O'Shay had a way of making you feel welcome, even if you came to be expelled.

15   "Sit down, Nancy Lee Johnson," said Miss O'Shay. "I have something to tell you." Nancy Lee sat down. "But I must ask you to promise not to tell anyone yet."

"I won't, Miss O'Shay," Nancy Lee said, wondering what on earth the principal had to say to her.

"You are about to graduate," Miss O'Shay ° said. "And we shall miss you. You have been an excellent student, Nancy, and you will not be without honors on the senior list, as I am sure you know."

At that point there was a light knock on the door. Miss O'Shay called out, "Come in," and Miss Dietrich entered. "May I be a part of this, too?" she asked, tall and smiling.

"Of course," Miss O'Shay said. "I was just telling Nancy Lee what we thought of her. But I hadn't gotten around to giving her the news. Perhaps, Miss Dietrich, you'd like to tell her yourself."

20   Miss Dietrich was always direct. "Nancy Lee," she said, "your picture has won the Artist Club scholarship."

The slender brown girl's eyes widened, her heart jumped, then her throat tightened again. She tried to smile, but instead tears came to her eyes.

"Dear Nancy Lee," Miss O'Shay said, "we are so happy for you." The elderly white woman took her hand and shook it warmly while Miss Dietrich beamed with pride.

Nancy Lee must have danced all the way home. She never remembered quite how she got there through the rain. She hoped she had been dignified. But certainly she hadn't stopped to tell anybody her secret on the way. Raindrops, smiles, and tears mingled on her brown cheeks. She hoped her mother hadn't yet gotten home and that the house was empty. She wanted to have time to calm down and look natural before she had to see anyone. She didn't want to be bursting with excitement—having a secret to contain.

Miss O'Shay's calling her to the office had been in the nature of a preparation and a warning. The kind, elderly vice-principal said she did not believe in catching young ladies unawares, even with honors, so she wished her to know about the coming award. In making acceptance speeches she wanted her to be calm, prepared, not nervous, overcome, and frightened. So Nancy Lee was asked to think what she would say when the scholarship was conferred upon her a few days hence, both at the Friday morning high-school assembly hour, when the announcement would be made, and at the evening banquet of the Artist Club. Nancy Lee promised the vice-principal to think calmly about what she would say.

25   Miss Dietrich had then asked for some facts about her parents, her background, and her life, since such material would probably be desired for the papers. Nancy Lee had told her how, six years before, they had come up from the Deep South, her father having been successful in achieving a trans-

fer from the one post office to another, a thing he had long sought in order to give Nancy Lee a chance to go to school in the North. Now they lived in a modest Negro neighborhood, went to see the best plays when they came to town, and had been saving to send Nancy Lee to art school, in case she were permitted to enter. But the scholarship would help a great deal, for they were not rich people.

"Now Mother can have a new coat next winter," Nancy Lee thought, "because my tuition will all be covered for the first year. And once in art school, there are other scholarships I can win."

Dreams began to dance through her head, plans and ambitions, beauties she would create for herself, her parents, and the Negro people—for Nancy Lee possessed a deep and reverent race pride. She could see the old woman in her picture (really her grandmother in the South) lifting her head to the bright stars on the flag in the distance. A Negro in America! Often hurt, discriminated against, sometimes lynched—but always there were the stars on the blue body of the flag. Was there any other flag in the world that had so many stars? Nancy Lee thought deeply, but she could remember none in all the encyclopedias or geographies she had ever looked into.

"Hitch your wagon to a star," Nancy Lee thought, dancing home in the rain. "Who were our flag-makers?"

Friday morning came, the morning when the world would know—her high-school world, the newspaper world, her mother and dad. Dad could not be there at the assembly to hear the announcement, nor see her prize picture displayed on the stage, nor to listen to Nancy Lee's little speech of acceptance, but Mother would be able to come, although Mother was much puzzled as to why Nancy Lee was so insistent she be at school on that particular Friday morning.

30   When something is happening, something new and fine, something that will change your very life, it is hard to go to sleep at night for thinking about it, and hard to keep your heart from pounding, or a strange little knot of joy from gathering in your throat. Nancy Lee had taken her bath, brushed her hair until it glowed, and had gone to bed thinking about the next day, the big day, when before three thousand students, she would be the one student honored, her painting the one painting to be acclaimed as the best of the year from all the art classes of the city. Her short speech of gratitude was ready. She went over it in her mind, not word for word (because she didn't want it to sound as if she had learned it by heart), but she let the thoughts flow simply and sincerely through her consciousness many times.

When the president of the Artist Club presented her with the medal and scroll of the scholarship award, she would say:

"Judges and members of the Artist Club. I want to thank you for this award that means so much to me personally and through me to my people, the colored people of this city, who, sometimes, are discouraged and bewildered, thinking that color and poverty are against them. I accept this award with gratitude and pride, not for myself alone, but for my race that believes in American opportunity and American fairness—and the bright stars in our flag. I thank Miss Dietrich and the teachers who made it possible for me to have the knowledge and training that lie behind this honor you have conferred upon my painting. When I came here from the South a few years ago, I was not sure how you would receive me. You received me well. You have given me a chance and helped me along the road I wanted to follow. I suppose the judges know that every week here at assembly the students of this school pledge allegiance to the flag. I shall try to be worthy of that pledge, and of the help and friendship and understanding of my fellow citizens of whatever race or creed, and of our American dream of 'Liberty and justice for all!'"

That would be her response before the students in the morning. How proud and happy the Negro pupils would be, perhaps almost as proud as they were of the one colored star on the football team. Her mother would probably cry with happiness. Thus Nancy Lee went to sleep dreaming of a wonderful tomorrow.

The bright sunlight of an April morning woke her. There was breakfast with her parents—their half-amused and puzzled faces across the table, wondering what could be this secret that made her eyes so bright. The swift walk to school; the clock in the tower almost nine; hundreds of pupils streaming into the long, rambling old building that was the city's largest high school; the sudden quiet of the homeroom after the bell rang; then the teacher opening her record book to call the roll. But just before she began, she looked across the room until her eyes located Nancy Lee.

35   "Nancy," she said, "Miss O'Shay would like to see you in her office, please."

Nancy Lee rose and went out while the names were being called and the word *present* added its period to each name. Perhaps, Nancy Lee thought, the reporters from the papers had already come. Maybe they wanted to take her picture before assembly, which wasn't until ten o'clock. (Last year they had had the photograph of the winner of the award in the morning papers as soon as the announcement had been made.)

Nancy Lee knocked at Miss O'Shay's door.

"Come in."

The vice-principal stood at her desk. There was no one else in the room. It was very quiet.

40   "Sit down, Nancy Lee," she said. Miss O'Shay did not smile. There was a long pause. The seconds went by slowly. "I do not know how to tell you what I have to say," the elderly woman began, her eyes on the papers on her desk. "I am indignant and ashamed for myself and for this city." Then she lifted her eyes and looked at Nancy Lee in the neat blue dress, sitting there before her. "You are not to receive the scholarship this morning."

Outside in the hall the electric bells announcing the first period rang, loud and interminably long. Miss O'Shay remained silent. To the brown girl there in the chair, the room, grew suddenly smaller, smaller, smaller, and there was no air. She could not speak.

Miss O'Shay said, "When the committee learned that you were colored, they changed their plans."

Still Nancy Lee said nothing, for there was no air to give breath to her lungs.

"Here is the letter from the committee, Nancy Lee." Miss O'Shay picked it up and read the final paragraph to her.

45   "'It seems to us wiser to arbitrarily rotate the award among the various high schools of the city from now on. And especially in this case since the student chosen happens to be colored, a circumstance which unfortunately, had we known, might have prevented this embarrassment. But there have never been any Negro students in the local art school, and the presence of one there might create difficulties for all concerned. We have high

regard for the quality of Nancy Lee Johnson's talent, but we do not feel it would be fair to honor it with the Artist Club award.'" Miss O'Shay paused. She put the letter down.

"Nancy Lee, I am very sorry to have to give you this message."

"But my speech," Nancy Lee said, "was about. . . ." The words stuck in her throat. ". . . about America. . . ."

Miss O'Shay had risen; she turned her back and stood looking out the window at the spring tulips in the school yard.

"I thought, since the award would be made at assembly right after our oath of allegiance," the words tumbled almost hysterically from Nancy Lee's throat now, "I would put part of the flag salute in my speech. You know, Miss O'Shay, that part about 'liberty and justice for all.'"

50 "I know," said Miss O'Shay, slowly facing the room again. "But America is only what we who believe in it make it. I am Irish. You may not know, Nancy Lee, but years ago we were called the dirty Irish, and mobs rioted against us in the big cities, and we were invited to go back where we came from. But we didn't go. And we didn't give up, because we believed in the American dream, and in our power to make that dream come true. Difficulties, yes. Mountains to climb, yes. Discouragements to face, yes. Democracy to make, yes. That is it, Nancy Lee! We still have in this world of ours democracy to *make*. You and I, Nancy Lee. But the premise and the base are here, the lines of the Declaration of Independence and the words of Lincoln are here, and the stars in our flag. Those who deny you this scholarship do not know the meaning of those stars, but it's up to us to make them know. As a teacher in the public schools of this city, I myself will go before the school board and ask them to remove from our system the offer of any prizes or awards denied to any student because of race or color."

Suddenly Miss O'Shay stopped speaking. Her clear, clear blue eyes looked like those of the girl before her. The woman's eyes were full of strength and courage. "Lift up your head, Nancy Lee, and smile at me."

Miss O'Shay stood against the open window with the green lawn and the tulips beyond, the sunlight tangled in her gray hair, her voice an electric flow of strength to the hurt spirit of Nancy Lee. The Abolitionists who believed in freedom when there was slavery must have been like that. The first white teachers who went into the Deep South to teach the freed slaves must have been like that. All those who stand against ignorance, narrowness, hate, and mud on stars must be like that.

Nancy Lee lifted her head and smiled. The bell for assembly rang. She went through the long hall filled with students, toward the auditorium.

"There will be other awards," Nancy Lee thought. "There're schools in other cities. This won't keep me down. But when I'm a woman, I'll fight to see that these things don't happen to other girls as this has happened to me. And men and women like Miss O'Shay will help me."

55 She took her seat among the seniors. The doors of the auditorium closed. As the principal came onto the platform, the students rose and turned their eyes to the flag on the stage.

One hand went to the heart, the other outstretched toward the flag. Three thousand voices spoke. Among them was the voice of a dark girl whose cheeks were suddenly wet with tears, ". . . one nation indivisible, with liberty and justice for all."

"That is the land we must make," she thought.

RALPH ELLISON

Ralph Ellison (1913–1994—though the year of birth is often mistakenly given as 1914) was born in Oklahoma City. His father died when Ellison was three, and his mother supported herself and her child by working as a domestic. A trumpeter since boyhood, after graduating from high school Ellison went to study music at Tuskegee Institute, a black college in Alabama founded by Booker T. Washington. In 1936 he dropped out of Tuskegee and went to Harlem to study music composition and the visual arts; there he met Langston Hughes and Richard Wright, who encouraged him to turn to fiction. Ellison published stories and essays, and in 1942 became the managing editor of Negro Quarterly. *During the Second World War he served in the Merchant Marines. After the war he returned to writing and later taught in universities.*

"Battle Royal" was first published in 1947 and slightly revised (a transitional paragraph was added at the end of the story) for the opening chapter of Ellison's novel, Invisible Man *(1952), a book cited by* Book-Week *as "the most significant work of fiction written by an American" in the years between 1945 and 1965. In addition to publishing stories and one novel, Ellison published critical essays, which are brought together in* The Collected Essays of Ralph Ellison *(1995).*

Battle Royal
[1947]

It goes a long way back, some twenty years. All my life I had been looking for something, and everywhere I turned someone tried to tell me what it was. I accepted their answers too, though they were often in contradiction and even self-contradictory. I was naïve. I was looking for myself and asking everyone except myself questions which I, and only I, could answer. It took me a long time and much painful boomeranging of my expectations to achieve a realization everyone else appears to have been born with: That I am nobody but myself. But first I had to discover that I am an invisible man!

And yet I am no freak of nature, nor of history. I was in the cards, other things having been equal (or unequal) eighty-five years ago. I am not ashamed of my grandparents for having been slaves. I am only ashamed of myself for having at one time been ashamed. About eighty-five years ago they were told that they were free, united with others of our country in everything pertaining to the common good, and, in everything social, separate like the fingers of the hand. And they believed it. They exulted in it. They stayed in their place, worked hard, and brought up my father to do the same. But my grandfather is the one. He was an odd old guy, my grandfather, and I am told I take after him. It was he who caused the trouble. On his deathbed he called my father to him and said, "Son, after I'm gone I want you to keep up the good fight. I never told you, but our life is a war and I have been a traitor all my born days, a spy in the enemy's country ever since I give up my gun back in the Reconstruction. Live with your head in the lion's mouth. I want you to overcome 'em with yeses, undermine 'em with grins, agree 'em to death and destruction, let 'em swoller you till they vomit or bust wide open." They thought the old man had gone out of his mind. He had been the meekest of men. The younger children were rushed from the room, the shades drawn and the flame of the lamp turned so low that it sput-

Gordon Parks, *Ralph Ellison*. Parks, an African-American photographer with an international reputation, has published many books of photographs, including *Camera Portraits,* where this picture appears.

tered on the wick like the old man's breathing. "Learn it to the younguns," he whispered fiercely; then he died.

But my folks were more alarmed over his last words than over his dying. It was as though he had not died at all, his words caused so much anxiety. I was warned emphatically to forget what he had said and, indeed, this is the first time it has been mentioned outside the family circle. It had a tremendous effect upon me, however. I could never be sure of what he meant. Grandfather had been a quiet old man who never made any trouble, yet on his deathbed he had called himself a traitor and a spy, and he had spoken of his meekness as a dangerous activity. It became a constant puzzle which lay unanswered in the back of my mind. And whenever things went well for me I remembered my grandfather and felt guilty and uncomfortable. It was as though I was carrying out his advice in spite of myself. And to make it worse, everyone loved me for it. I was praised by the most lily-white men of the town. I was considered an example of desirable conduct—just as my grandfather had been. And what puzzled me was that the old man had defined it as *treachery.* When I was praised for my conduct I felt a guilt that in some way I was doing something that was really against the wishes of the white folks, that if they had understood they would have desired me to act just the opposite, that I should have been sulky and mean, and that that really would have been what they wanted, even though they were fooled and thought they wanted me to act as I did. It made me afraid that some day they would look upon me as a traitor and I would be lost. Still I was more afraid to act any other way because they didn't like that at all. The old man's words were like a curse. On my graduation day I delivered an oration in which I showed that humility was the secret, indeed, the very essence of progress. (Not that I believed this—how could I, remembering my grandfather?—I

only believed that it worked.) It was a great success. Everyone praised me
and I was invited to give the speech at a gathering of the town's leading
white citizens. It was a triumph for our whole community.

It was in the main ballroom of the leading hotel. When I got there I discovered that it was on the occasion of a smoker, and I was told that since I
was to be there anyway I might as well take part in the battle royal to be
fought by some of my schoolmates as part of the entertainment. The battle
royal came first.

5   All of the town's big shots were there in their tuxedoes, wolfing down
the buffet foods, drinking beer and whiskey and smoking black cigars. It was
a large room with a high ceiling. Chairs were arranged in neat rows around
three sides of a portable boxing ring. The fourth side was clear, revealing a
gleaming space of polished floor. I had some misgivings over the battle
royal, by the way. Not from a distaste for fighting, but because I didn't care
too much for the other fellows who were to take part. They were tough
guys who seemed to have no grandfather's curse worrying their minds. No
one could mistake their toughness. And besides, I suspected that fighting a
battle royal might detract from the dignity of my speech. In those pre-invisi-
ble days I visualized myself as a potential Booker T. Washington. But the
other fellows didn't care too much for me either, and there were nine of
them. I felt superior to them in my way, and I didn't like the manner in
which we were all crowded together into the servants' elevator. Nor did
they like my being there. In fact, as the warmly lighted floors flashed past
the elevator we had words over the fact that I, by taking part in the fight,
had knocked one of their friends out of a night's work.

We were led out of the elevator through a rococo hall into an anteroom
and told to get into our fighting togs. Each of us was issued a pair of boxing
gloves and ushered out into the big mirrored hall, which we entered looking
cautiously about us and whispering, lest we might accidentally be heard
above the noise of the room. It was foggy with cigar smoke. And already the
whiskey was taking effect. I was shocked to see some of the most important
men of the town quite tipsy. They were all there—bankers, lawyers, judges,
doctors, fire chiefs, teachers, merchants. Even one of the more fashionable
pastors. Something we could not see was going on up front. A clarinet was
vibrating sensuously and the men were standing up and moving eagerly forward. We were a small tight group, clustered together, our bare upper bodies
touching and shining with anticipatory sweat; while up front the big shots
were becoming increasingly excited over something we still could not see.
Suddenly I heard the school superintendent, who had told me to come, yell.
"Bring up the shines, gentlemen! Bring up the little shines!"

We were rushed up to the front of the ballroom, where it smelled even
more strongly of tobacco and whiskey. Then we were pushed into place. I
almost wet my pants. A set of faces, some hostile, some amused, ringed
around us, and in the center, facing us, stood a magnificent blond—stark
naked. There was dead silence. I felt a blast of cold air chill me. I tried to
back away, but they were behind me and around me. Some of the boys stood
with lowered heads, trembling. I felt a wave of irrational guilt and fear. My
teeth chattered, my skin turned to goose flesh, my knees knocked. Yet I was
strongly attracted and looked in spite of myself. Had the price of looking
been blindness, I would have looked. The hair was yellow like that of a circus kewpie doll, the face heavily powdered and rouged, as though to form

an abstract mask, the eyes hollow and smeared a cool blue, the color of a baboon's butt. I felt a desire to spit upon her as my eyes brushed slowly over
her body. Her breasts were firm and round as the domes of East Indian temples, and I stood so close as to see the fine skin texture and beads of pearly
perspiration glistening like dew around the pink and erected buds of her
nipples. I wanted at one and the same time to run from the room, to sink
through the floor, or go to her and cover her from my eyes and the eyes of
the others with my body; to feel the soft thighs, to caress her and destroy
her, to love her and murder her, to hide from her, and yet to stroke where below the small American flag tattooed upon her belly her thighs formed a
capital V. I had a notion that of all in the room she saw only me with her impersonal eyes.

And then she began to dance, a slow sensuous movement; the smoke of
a hundred cigars clinging to her like the thinnest of veils. She seemed like a
fair bird-girl girdled in veils calling to me from the angry surface of some gray
and threatening sea. I was transported. Then I became aware of the clarinet
playing and the big shots yelling at us. Some threatened us if we looked and
others if we did not. On my right I saw one boy faint. And now a man
grabbed a silver pitcher from a table and stepped close as he dashed ice water upon him and stood him up and forced two of us to support him as his
head hung and moans issued from his thick bluish lips. Another boy began to
plead to go home. He was the largest of the group, wearing dark red fighting
trunks much too small to conceal the erection which projected from him as
though in answer to the insinuating low-registered moans of the clarinet. He
tried to hide himself with his boxing gloves.

And all the while the blonde continued dancing, smiling faintly at the
big shots who watched her with fascination, and faintly smiling at our fear. I
noticed a certain merchant who followed her hungrily, his lips loose and
drooling. He was a large man who wore diamond studs in a shirtfront which
swelled with the ample paunch underneath, and each time the blonde
swayed her undulating hips he ran his hand through the thin hair of his bald
head and, with his arms upheld, his posture clumsy like that of an intoxicated panda, wound his belly in a slow and obscene grind. This creature was
completely hypnotized. The music had quickened. As the dancer flung herself about with a detached expression on her face, the men began reaching
out to touch her. I could see their beefy fingers sink into her soft flesh. Some
of the others tried to stop them and she began to move around the floor in
graceful circles, as they gave chase, slipping and sliding over the polished
floor. It was mad. Chairs went crashing, drinks were spilt, as they ran laughing and howling after her. They caught her just as she reached a door, raised
her from the floor, and tossed her as college boys are tossed at a hazing, and
above her red, fixed-smiling lips I saw the terror and disgust in her eyes, almost like my own terror and that which I saw in some of the other boys. As
I watched, they tossed her twice and her soft breasts seemed to flatten
against the air and her legs flung wildly as she spun. Some of the more sober
ones helped her to escape. And I started off the floor, heading for the anteroom with the rest of the boys.

10   Some were still crying and in hysteria. But as we tried to leave we were
stopped and ordered to get into the ring. There was nothing to do but what
we were told. All ten of us climbed under the ropes and allowed ourselves
to be blindfolded with broad bands of white cloth. One of the men seemed

to feel a bit sympathetic and tried to cheer us up as we stood with our backs against the ropes. Some of us tried to grin. "See that boy over there?" one of the men said. "I want you to run across at the bell and give it to him right in the belly. If you don't get him, I'm going to get you. I don't like his looks." Each of us was told the same. The blindfolds were put on. Yet even then I had been going over my speech. In my mind each word was as bright as flame. I felt the cloth pressed into place, and frowned so that it would be loosened when I relaxed.

But now I felt a sudden fit of blind terror. I was unused to darkness. It was as though I had suddenly found myself in a dark room filled with poisonous cottonmouths. I could hear the bleary voices yelling insistently for the battle royal to begin.

"Get going in there!"

"Let me at that big nigger!"

I strained to pick up the school superintendent's voice, as though to squeeze some security out of that slightly more familiar sound.

15   "Let me at those black sonsabitches!" someone yelled.

"No, Jackson, no!" another voice yelled. "Here, somebody, help me hold Jack."

"I want to get at that ginger-colored nigger. Tear him limb from limb," the first voice yelled.

I stood against the ropes trembling. For in those days I was what they called ginger-colored, and he sounded as though he might crunch me between his teeth like a crisp ginger cookie.

Quite a struggle was going on. Chairs were being kicked about and I could hear voices grunting as with a terrific effort. I wanted to see, to see more desperately than ever before. But the blindfold was as tight as a thick skin-puckering scab and when I raised my gloved hands to push the layers of white aside a voice yelled, "Oh, no, you don't, black bastard! Leave that alone!"

20   "Ring the bell before Jackson kills him a coon!" someone boomed in the sudden silence. And I heard the bell clang and the sound of the feet scuffling forward.

A glove smacked against my head. I pivoted, striking out stiffly as someone went past, and felt the jar ripple along the length of my arm to my shoulder. Then it seemed as though all nine of the boys had turned upon me at once. Blows pounded me from all sides while I struck out as best I could. So many blows landed upon me that I wondered if I were not the only blindfolded fighter in the ring, or if the man called Jackson hadn't succeeded in getting me after all.

Blindfolded, I could no longer control my motions. I had no dignity. I stumbled about like a baby or a drunken man. The smoke had become thicker and with each new blow it seemed to sear and further restrict my lungs. My saliva became like hot bitter glue. A glove connected with my head, filling my mouth with warm blood. It was everywhere. I could not tell if the moisture I felt upon my body was sweat or blood. A blow landed hard against the nape of my neck. I felt myself going over, my head hitting the floor. Streaks of blue light filled the black world behind the blindfold. I lay prone, pretending that I was knocked out, but felt myself seized by hands and yanked to my feet. "Get going, black boy! Mix it up!" My arms were like lead, my head smarting from blows. I managed to feel my way to the ropes and held on, trying to catch my breath. A glove landed in my mid-section and

I went over again, feeling as though the smoke had become a knife jabbed into my guts. Pushed this way and that by the legs milling around me, I finally pulled erect and discovered that I could see the black, sweat-washed forms weaving in the smoky-blue atmosphere like drunken dancers weaving to the rapid drum-like thuds of blows.

Everyone fought hysterically. It was complete anarchy. Everybody fought everybody else. No group fought together for long. Two, three, four, fought one, then turned to fight each other, were themselves attacked. Blows landed below the belt and in the kidney, with the gloves open as well as closed, and with my eye partly opened now there was not so much terror. I moved carefully, avoiding blows, although not too many to attract attention, fighting from group to group. The boys groped about like blind, cautious crabs crouching to protect their mid-sections, their heads pulled in short against their shoulders, their arms stretched nervously before them, with their fists testing the smoke-filled air like the knobbed feelers of hypersensitive snails. In one corner I glimpsed a boy violently punching the air and heard him scream in pain as he smashed his hand against a ring post. For a second I saw him bent over holding his hand, then going down as a blow caught his unprotected head. I played one group against the other, slipping and throwing a punch then stepping out of range while pushing the others into the melee to take the blows blindly aimed at me. The smoke was agonizing and there were no rounds, no bells at three minute intervals to relieve our exhaustion. The room spun round me, a swirl of lights, smoke, sweating bodies surrounded by tense white faces. I bled from both nose and mouth, the blood spattering upon my chest.

The men kept yelling, "Slug him, black boy! Knock his guts out!"

25 "Uppercut him! Kill him! Kill that big boy!"

Taking a fake fall, I saw a boy going down heavily beside me as though we were felled by a single blow, saw a sneaker-clad foot shoot into his groin as the two who had knocked him down stumbled upon him. I rolled out of range, feeling a twinge of nausea.

The harder we fought the more threatening the men became. And yet, I had begun to worry about my speech again. How would it go? Would they recognize my ability? What would they give me?

I was fighting automatically and suddenly I noticed that one after another of the boys was leaving the ring. I was surprised, filled with panic, as though I had been left alone with an unknown danger. Then I understood. The boys had arranged it among themselves. It was the custom for the two men left in the ring to slug it out for the winner's prize. I discovered this too late. When the bell sounded two men in tuxedoes leaped into the ring and removed the blindfold. I found myself facing Tatlock, the biggest of the gang. I felt sick at my stomach. Hardly had the bell stopped ringing in my ears than it clanged again and I saw him moving swiftly toward me. Thinking of nothing else to do I hit him smash on the nose. He kept coming, bringing the rank sharp violence of stale sweat. His face was a black bank of a face, only his eyes alive—with hate of me and aglow with a feverish terror from what had happened to us all. I became anxious. I wanted to deliver my speech and he came at me as though he meant to beat it out of me. I smashed him again and again, taking his blows as they came. Then on a sudden impulse I struck him lightly as we clinched, I whispered, "Fake like I knocked you out, you can have the prize."

"I'll break your behind," he whispered hoarsely.

30   "For *them?*"

        "For *me,* sonofabitch!"

They were yelling for us to break it up and Tatlock spun me half around with a blow, and as a joggled camera sweeps in a reeling scene, I saw the howling red faces crouching tense beneath the cloud of blue-gray smoke. For a moment the world wavered, unraveled, flowed, then my head cleared and Tatlock bounced before me. That fluttering shadow before my eyes was his jabbing left hand. Then falling forward, my head against his damp shoulder, I whispered,

        "I'll make it five dollars more."

        "Go to hell!"

35   But his muscles relaxed a trifle beneath my pressure and I breathed, "Seven!"

        "Give it to your ma," he said, ripping me beneath the heart.

And while I still held him I butted him and moved away. I felt myself bombarded with punches. I fought back with hopeless desperation. I wanted to deliver my speech more than anything else in the world, because I felt that only these men could judge truly my ability, and now this stupid clown was ruining my chances. I began fighting carefully now, moving in to punch him and out again with my greater speed. A lucky blow to his chin and I had him going too—until I heard a loud voice yell, "I got my money on the big boy."

Hearing this, I almost dropped my guard. I was confused: Should I try to win against the voice out there? Would not this go against my speech, and was not this a moment for humility, for nonresistance? A blow to my head as I danced about sent my right eye popping like a jack-in-the-box and settled my dilemma. The room went red as I fell. It was a dream fall, my body languid and fastidious as to where to land, until the floor became impatient and smashed up to meet me. A moment later I came to. An hypnotic voice said FIVE emphatically. And I lay there, hazily watching a dark red spot of my own blood shaping itself into a butterfly, glistening and soaking into the soiled gray world of the canvas.

When the voice drawled TEN I was lifted up and dragged to a chair. I sat dazed. My eye pained and swelled with each throb of my pounding heart and I wondered if now I would be allowed to speak. I was wringing wet, my mouth still bleeding. We were grouped along the wall now. The other boys ignored me as they congratulated Tatlock and speculated as to how much they would be paid. One boy whimpered over his smashed hand. Looking up front, I saw attendants in white jackets rolling the portable ring away and placing a small square rug in the vacant space surrounded by chairs. Perhaps, I thought, I will stand on the rug to deliver my speech.

40   Then the M.C. called to us, "Come on up here boys and get your money."

We ran forward to where the men laughed and talked in their chairs, waiting. Everyone seemed friendly now.

        "There it is on the rug," the man said. I saw the rug covered with coins of all dimensions and a few crumpled bills. But what excited me, scattered here and there, were the gold pieces.

        "Boys, it's all yours," the man said. "You get all you grab."

        "That's right, Sambo," a blond man said, winking at me confidentially.

45   I trembled with excitement, forgetting my pain. I would get the gold and the bills, I thought. I would use both hands. I would throw my body against the boys nearest me to block them from the gold.

"Get down around the rug now," the man commanded, "and don't anyone touch it until I give the signal."

"This ought to be good," I heard.

As told, we got around the square rug on our knees. Slowly the man raised his freckled hand as we followed it upward with our eyes.

I heard, "These niggers look like they're about to pray!"

50   Then, "Ready," the man said. "Go!"

I lunged for a yellow coin lying on the blue design of the carpet, touching it and sending a surprised shriek to join those rising around me. I tried frantically to remove my hand but could not let go. A hot, violent force tore through my body, shaking me like a wet rat. The rug was electrified. The hair bristled up on my head as I shook myself free. My muscles jumped, my nerves jangled, writhed. But I saw that this was not stopping the other boys. Laughing in fear and embarrassment, some were holding back and scooping up the coins knocked off by the painful contortions of the others. The men roared above us as we struggled.

"Pick it up, goddamnit, pick it up!" someone called like a bass-voiced parrot. "Go on, get it!"

I crawled rapidly around the floor, picking up the coins, trying to avoid the coppers and to get greenbacks and the gold. Ignoring the shock by laughing, as I brushed the coins off quickly, I discovered that I could contain the electricity—a contradiction, but it works. Then the men began to push us onto the rug. Laughing embarrassedly, we struggled out of their hands and kept after the coins. We were all wet and slippery and hard to hold. Suddenly I saw a boy lifted into the air, glistening with sweat like a circus seal, and dropped, his wet back landing flush upon the charged rug, heard him yell and saw him literally dance upon his back, his elbows beating a frenzied tatoo upon the floor, his muscles twitching like the flesh of a horse stung by many flies. When he finally rolled off, his face was gray and no one stopped him when he ran from the floor amid booming laughter.

"Get the money," the M.C. called. "That's good hard American cash!"

55   And we snatched and grabbed, snatched and grabbed. I was careful not to come too close to the rug now, and when I felt the hot whiskey breath descend upon me like a cloud of foul air I reached out and grabbed the leg of a chair. It was occupied and I held on desperately.

"Leggo, nigger! Leggo!"

The huge face wavered down to mine as the tried to push me free. But my body was slippery and he was too drunk. It was Mr. Colcord, who owned a chain of movie houses and "entertainment palaces." Each time he grabbed me I slipped out of his hands. It became a real struggle. I feared the rug more than I did the drunk, so I held on, surprising myself for a moment by trying to topple *him* upon the rug. It was such an enormous idea that I found myself actually carrying it out. I tried not to be obvious, yet when I grabbed his leg, trying to tumble him out of the chair, he raised up roaring with laughter, and, looking at me with soberness dead in the eye, kicked me viciously in the chest. The chair leg flew out of my hand. I felt myself going and rolled. It was as though I had rolled through a bed of hot coals. It seemed a whole century would pass before I would roll free, a century in which I was seared through the deepest levels of my body to the fearful breath within me and the breath seared and heated to the point of explosion. It'll all be over in a flash, I thought as I rolled clear. It'll all be over in a flash.

But not yet, the men on the other side were waiting, red faces swollen as though from apoplexy as they bent forward in their chairs. Seeing their fingers coming toward me I rolled away as a fumbled football rolls off the receiver's fingertips, back into the coals. That time I luckily sent the rug sliding out of place and heard the coins ringing against the floor and the boys scuffling to pick them up and the M.C. calling, "All right, boys, that's all. Go get dressed and get your money."

I was limp as a dish rag. My back felt as though it had been beaten with wires.

60   When we had dressed the M.C. came in and gave us each five dollars, except Tatlock, who got ten for being the last in the ring. Then he told us to leave. I was not to get a chance to deliver my speech, I thought. I was going out into the dim alley in despair when I was stopped and told to go back. I returned to the ballroom, where the men were pushing back their chairs and gathering in groups to talk.

The M.C. knocked on a table for quiet. "Gentlemen," he said, "we almost forgot an important part of the program. A most serious part, gentlemen. This boy was brought here to deliver a speech which he made at his graduation yesterday. . . ."

"Bravo!"

"I'm told that he is the smartest boy we've got out there in Greenwood. I'm told that he knows more big words than a pocket-sized dictionary."

Much applause and laughter.

65   "So now, gentlemen, I want you to give him your attention."

There was still laughter as I faced them, my mouth dry, my eye throbbing. I began slowly, but evidently my throat was tense, because they began shouting, "Louder! Louder!"

"We of the younger generation extol the wisdom of that great leader and educator," I shouted, "who first spoke these flaming words of wisdom: 'A ship lost at sea for many days suddenly sighted a friendly vessel. From the mast of the unfortunate vessel was seen a signal: "Water, water; we die of thirst!" The answer from the friendly vessel came back: "Cast down your bucket where you are." The captain of the distressed vessel, at last heeding the injunction, cast down his bucket, and it came up full of fresh sparkling water from the mouth of the Amazon River.' And like him I say, and in his words, 'To those of my race who depend upon bettering their condition in a foreign land, or who underestimate the importance of cultivating friendly relations with the Southern white man, who is his next-door neighbor, I would say: "Cast down your bucket where you are"—cast it down in making friends in every manly way of the people of all races by whom we are surrounded. . . .'"

I spoke automatically and with such fervor that I did not realize that the men were still talking and laughing until my dry mouth, filling up with blood from the cut, almost strangled me. I coughed, wanting to stop and go to one of the tall brass, sand-filled spittoons to relieve myself, but a few of the men, especially the superintendent, were listening and I was afraid. So I gulped it down, blood, saliva and all, and continued. (What powers of endurance I had during those days! What enthusiasm! What a belief in the rightness of things!) I spoke even louder in spite of the pain. But still they talked and still they laughed, as though deaf with cotton in dirty ears. So I spoke with greater emotional emphasis. I closed my ears and swallowed blood until I was nauseated. The speech seemed a hundred times as long as before, but I could not leave out a single word. All had to be said, each memorized nuance considered, rendered. Nor was that all. Whenever I uttered a word of three or more syllables a group of voices would yell for me to repeat it. I used the phrase "social responsibility" and they yelled:

"What's the word you say, boy?"

70   "Social responsibility," I said.

"What?"

"Social . . ."

"Louder."

". . . responsibility."

75   "More!"

"Respon—"

"Repeat!"

"—sibility."

The room filled with the uproar of laughter until, no doubt, distracted by having to gulp down my blood, I made a mistake and yelled a phrase I had often seen denounced in newspaper editorials, heard debated in private.

80   "Social . . ."

"What?" they yelled.

". . . equality—"

The laughter hung smokelike in the sudden stillness. I opened my eyes, puzzled. Sounds of displeasure filled the room. The M.C. rushed forward. They shouted hostile phrases at me. But I did not understand.

A small dry mustached man in the front row blared out, "Say that slowly, son!"

85   "What sir?"

"What you just said!"

"Social responsibility, sir," I said.

"You weren't being smart, were you, boy?" he said, not unkindly.

"No, sir!"

90   "You sure that about 'equality' was a mistake?"

"Oh, yes, sir," I said. "I was swallowing blood."

"Well, you had better speak more slowly so we can understand. We mean to do right by you, but you've got to know your place at all times. All right now, go on with your speech."

I was afraid. I wanted to leave but I wanted also to speak and I was afraid they'd snatch me down.

"Thank you, sir," I said, beginning where I had left off, and having them ignore me as before.

95   Yet when I finished there was a thunderous applause. I was surprised to see the superintendent come forth with a package wrapped in white tissue paper, and gesturing for quiet, address the men.

"Gentlemen you see that I did not overpraise this boy. He makes a good speech and some day he'll lead his people in the proper paths. And I don't have to tell you that that is important in these days and times. This is a good, smart boy, and so to encourage him in the right direction, in the name of the Board of Education I wish to present him a prize in the form of this . . ."

He paused, removing the tissue paper and revealing a gleaming calfskin brief case.

". . . in the form of this first-class article from Shad Whitmore's shop."

"Boy," he said, addressing me, "take this prize and keep it well. Consider it a badge of office. Prize it. Keep developing as you are and some day it will be filled with important papers that will help shape the destiny of your people."

100   I was so moved that I could hardly express my thanks. A rope of bloody saliva forming a shape like an undiscovered continent drooled upon the leather and I wiped it quickly away. I felt an importance that I had never dreamed.

"Open it and see what's inside," I was told.

My fingers a-tremble I complied, smelling the fresh leather and finding an official-looking document inside. It was a scholarship to the state college for Negroes. My eyes filled with tears and I ran awkwardly off the floor.

I was overjoyed; I did not even mind when I discovered that the gold pieces I had scrambled for were brass pocket tokens advertising a certain make of automobile.

When I reached home everyone was excited. Next day the neighbors came to congratulate me. I even felt safe from grandfather, whose deathbed curse usually spoiled my triumphs. I stood beneath his photograph with my brief case in hand and smiled triumphantly into his stolid black peasant's face. It was a face that fascinated me. The eyes seemed to follow everywhere I went.

105   That night I dreamed I was at a circus with him and that he refused to laugh at the clowns no matter what they did. Then later he told me to open my brief case and read what was inside and I did, finding an official envelope stamped with the state seal; and inside the envelope I found another and another, endlessly, and I thought I would fall of weariness. "Them's years," he said. "Now open that one." And I did and in it I found an engraved document containing a short message in letters of gold. "Read it," my grandfather said. "Out loud."

"To Whom It May Concern," I intoned, "Keep This Nigger-Boy Running."

I awoke with the old man's laughter ringing in my ears.

(It was a dream I was to remember and dream again for many years after. But at the time I had no insight into its meaning. First I had to attend college.)

CONTEMPORARY VOICES

JOHN UPDIKE

John Updike (b. 1932) grew up in Shillington, Pennsylvania, where his father was a teacher and his mother a writer. After receiving a B.A. degree in 1954 from Harvard, where he edited the Harvard Lampoon *(for which he both wrote and drew), he studied drawing at Oxford for a year, but an offer from* The New Yorker *brought him back to the United States. He was hired as a reporter for the magazine but soon began contributing poetry, essays, and fiction. In 1957 he left* The New Yorker *to write independently full time, though his stories and book reviews appear regularly in it.*

In 1959 Updike published his first book of stories (The Same Door) *and also his first novel* (The Poorhouse Fair); *the next year he published* Rabbit, Run, *a highly successful novel whose protagonist, "Rabbit" Angstrom, has reappeared in three later novels,* Rabbit Redux *(1971),* Rabbit Is Rich *(1981), and* Rabbit at Rest *(1990). The first and the last Rabbit books each won a Pulitzer Prize.*

Separating

[1979]

The day was fair. Brilliant. All that June the weather had mocked the Maples' internal misery with solid sunlight—golden shafts and cascades of green in which their conversations had wormed unseeing, their sad murmuring selves the only stain in Nature. Usually by this time of the year they had acquired tans; but when they met their elder daughter's plane on her return from a year in England they were almost as pale as she, though Judith was too dazzled by the sunny opulent jumble of her native land to notice. They did not spoil her homecoming by telling her immediately. Wait a few days, let her recover from jet lag, had been one of their formulations, in that string of gray dialogues—over coffee, over cocktails, over Cointreau—that had shaped the strategy of their dissolution, while the earth performed its annual stunt of renewal unnoticed beyond their closed windows. Richard had thought to leave at Easter; Joan had insisted they wait until the four children were at last assembled, with all exams passed and ceremonies attended, and the bauble of summer to console them. So he had drudged away, in love, in dread, repairing screens, getting the mowers sharpened, rolling and patching their new tennis court.

The court, clay, had come through its first winter pitted and wind-swept bare of redcoat. Years ago the Maples had observed how often, among their friends, divorce followed a dramatic home improvement, as if the marriage were making one last effort to live; their own worst crisis had come amid the plaster dust and exposed plumbing of a kitchen renovation. Yet, a summer ago, as canary-yellow bulldozers gaily churned a grassy, daisy-dotted knoll into a muddy plateau, and a crew of pigtailed young men raked and tamped clay into a plane, this transformation did not strike them as ominous, but festive in its impudence; their marriage could rend the earth for fun. The next spring, waking each day at dawn to a sliding sensation as if the bed were being tipped, Richard found the barren tennis court—its net and tapes still rolled in the barn—an environment congruous with his mood of purposeful desolation, and the crumbling of handfuls of clay into cracks and holes (dogs had frolicked on the court in a thaw; rivulets had eroded trenches) an activity suitably elemental and interminable. In his sealed heart he hoped the day would never come.

Now it was here. A Friday. Judith was re-acclimated; all four children were assembled, before jobs and camps and visits again scattered them. Joan thought they should be told one by one. Richard was for making an announcement at the table. She said, "I think just making an announcement is a cop-out. They'll start quarrelling and playing to each other instead of focusing. They're each individuals, you know, not just some corporate obstacle to your freedom."

"O.K., O.K. I agree." Joan's plan was exact. That evening, they were giving Judith a belated welcome-home dinner, of lobster and champagne. Then, the party over, they, the two of them, who nineteen years before would push her in a baby carriage along Fifth Avenue to Washington Square, were to walk her out of the house, to the bridge across the salt creek, and tell her, swearing her to secrecy. Then Richard Jr., who was going directly from work to a rock concert in Boston, would be told, either late when he returned on the train or early Saturday morning before he went off to his job; he was seventeen and employed as one of a golf-course maintenance crew. Then the two younger children, John and Margaret, could, as the morning wore on, be informed.

5   "Mopped up, as it were," Richard said.

"Do you have any better plan? That leaves you the rest of Saturday to answer any questions, pack, and make your wonderful departure."

"No," he said, meaning he had no better plan, and agreed to hers, though to him it showed an edge of false order, a hidden plea for control, like Joan's long chore lists and financial accountings and, in the days when he first knew her, her too-copious lecture notes. Her plan turned one hurdle for him into four—four knife-sharp walls, each with a sheer blind drop on the other side.

All spring he had moved through a world of insides and outsides, of barriers and partitions. He and Joan stood as a thin barrier between the children and the truth. Each moment was a partition, with the past on one side and the future on the other, a future containing this unthinkable *now*. Beyond four knifelike walls a new life for him waited vaguely. His skull cupped a secret, a white face, a face both frightened and soothing, both strange and known, that he wanted to shield from tears, which he felt all around him, solid as the sunlight. So haunted, he had become obsessed with battening down the house against his absence, replacing screens and sash cords, hinges and latches—a Houdini making things snug before his escape.

The lock. He had still to replace a lock on one of the doors of the screened porch. The task, like most such, proved more difficult than he had imagined. The old lock, aluminum frozen by corrosion, had been deliberately rendered obsolete by manufacturers. Three hardware stores had nothing that even approximately matched the mortised hole its removal (surprisingly easy) left. Another hole had to be gouged, with bits too small and saws too big, and the old hole fitted with a block of wood—the chisels dull, the saw rusty, his fingers thick with lack of sleep. The sun poured down, beyond the porch, on a world of neglect. The bushes already needed pruning, the windward side of the house was shedding flakes of paint, rain would get in and when he was gone, insects, rot, death. His family, all those he would lose, filtered through the edges of his awareness as he struggled with screw holes, splinters, opaque instructions, minutiae of metal.

10   Judith sat on the porch, a princess returned from exile. She regaled them with stories of fuel shortages, of bomb scares in the Underground, of Pakistani workmen loudly lusting after her as she walked past on her way to dance school. Joan came and went, in and out of the house, calmer than she should have been, praising his struggles with the lock as if this were one more and not the last of their long succession of shared chores. The younger of his sons for a few minutes held the rickety screen door while his father clumsily hammered and chiseled, each blow a kind of sob in Richard's ears. His younger daughter, having been at a slumber party, slept on the porch hammock through all the noise—heavy and pink, trusting and forsaken. Time, like the sunlight, continued relentlessly; the sunlight slowly slanted. Today was one of the longest days. The lock clicked, worked. He was through. He had a drink; he drank it on the porch, listening to his daughter. "It was so sweet," she was saying, "during the worst of it, how all the butchers and bakery shops kept open by candlelight. They're all so plucky and cute. From the papers, things sounded so much worse here—people shooting people in gas lines, and everybody freezing."

Richard asked her, "Do you still want to live in England forever?" *Forever:* the concept, now a reality upon him, pressed and scratched at the back of his throat.

"No," Judith confessed, turning her oval face to him, its eyes still childishly far apart, but the lips set as over something succulent and satisfactory. "I was anxious to come home. I'm an American." She was a woman. They had raised her; he and Joan had endured together to raise her, alone of the four. The others had still some raising left in them. Yet it was the thought of telling Judith—the image of her, their first baby, walking between them arm in arm to the bridge—that broke him. The partition between his face and the tears broke. Richard sat down to the celebratory meal with the back of his throat aching; the champagne, the lobster seemed phases of sunshine; he saw them and tasted them through tears. He blinked, swallowed, croakily joked about hay fever. The tears would not stop leaking through; they came not through a hole that could be plugged but through a permeable spot in a membrane, steadily, purely, endlessly, fruitfully. They became, his tears, a shield for himself against these others—their faces, the fact of their assembly, a last time as innocents, at a table where he sat the last time as head. Tears dropped from his nose as he broke the lobster's back; salt flavored his champagne as he sipped it; the raw clench at the back of his throat was delicious. He could not help himself.

His children tried to ignore his tears. Judith, on his right, lit a cigarette, gazed upward in the direction of her too energetic, too sophisticated exhalation; on her other side, John earnestly bent his face to the extraction of the last morsels—legs, tail segments—from the scarlet corpse. Joan, at the opposite end of the table, glanced at him surprised, her reproach displaced by a quick grimace, of forgiveness, or of salute to his superior gift of strategy. Between them, Margaret, no longer called Bean, thirteen and large for her age, gazed from the other side of his pane of tears as if into a shopwindow or something she coveted—at her father, a crystalline heap of splinters and memories. It was not she, however, but John who, in the kitchen, as they cleared the plates and carapaces away, asked Joan the question, *"Why is Daddy crying?"*

Richard heard the question but not the murmured answer. Then he heard Bean cry, "Oh, no-oh"—the faintly dramatized exclamation of one who had long expected it.

15 John returned to the table carrying a bowl of salad. He nodded tersely at his father and his lips shaped the conspiratorial words "She told."

"Told what?" Richard asked aloud, insanely.

The boy sat down as if to rebuke his father's distraction with the example of his own good manners. He said quietly, "The separation."

Joan and Margaret returned; the child, in Richard's twisted vision, seemed diminished in size, and relieved, relieved to have had the bogieman at last proved real. He called out to her—the distances at the table had grown immense—"You knew, you always knew," but the clenching at the back of his throat prevented him from making sense of it. From afar he heard Joan talking, levelly, sensibly, reciting what they had prepared: it was a separation for the summer, an experiment. She and Daddy both agreed it would be good for them; they needed space and time to think; they liked each other but did not make each other happy enough, somehow.

Judith, imitating her mother's factual tone, but in her youth off-key, too cool, said, "I think it's silly. You should either live together or get divorced."

20   Richard's crying, like a wave that has crested and crashed, had become tumultuous; but it was overtopped by another tumult, for John, who had been so reserved, now grew larger and larger at the table. Perhaps his younger sister's being credited with knowing set him off. "Why didn't you *tell* us?" he asked, in a large round voice quite unlike his own. "You should have *told* us you weren't getting along."

Richard was startled into attempting to force words through his tears. "We *do* get along, that's the trouble, so it doesn't show even to us—" *That we do not love each other* was the rest of the sentence; he couldn't finish it.

Joan finished for him, in her style. "And we've always, *especially,* loved our children."

John was not mollified. "What do you care about *us?*" he boomed. "We're just little things you *had.*" His sisters' laughing forced a laugh from him, which he turned hard and parodistic: "Ha ha *ha.*" Richard and Joan realized simultaneously that the child was drunk, on Judith's homecoming champagne. Feeling bound to keep the center of the stage, John took a cigarette from Judith's pack, poked it into his mouth, let it hang from his lower lip, and squinted like a gangster.

"You're not little things we had," Richard called to him. "You're the whole point. But you're grown. Or almost."

25   The boy was lighting matches. Instead of holding them to his cigarette (for they had never seen him smoke; being "good" had been his way of setting himself apart), he held them to his mother's face, closer and closer, for her to blow out. Then he lit the whole folder—a hiss and then a torch, held against his mother's face. Prismed by tears, the flame filled Richard's vision; he didn't know how it was extinguished. He heard Margaret say, "Oh stop showing off," and saw John, in response, break the cigarette in two and put the halves entirely into his mouth and chew, sticking out his tongue to display the shreds to his sister.

Joan talked to him, reasoning—a fountain of reason, unintelligible. "Talked about it for years . . . our children must help us . . . Daddy and I both want . . ." As the boy listened, he carefully wadded a paper napkin into the leaves of his salad, fashioned a ball of paper and lettuce, and popped it into his mouth, looking around the table for the expected laughter. None came. Judith said, "Be mature," and dismissed a plume of smoke.

Richard got up from this stifling table and led the boy outside. Though the house was in twilight, the outdoors still brimmed with light, the lovely waste light of high summer. Both laughing, he supervised John's spitting out the lettuce and paper and tobacco into the pachysandra. He took him by the hand—a square gritty hand, but for its softness a man's. Yet, it held on. They ran together up into the field, past the tennis court. The raw banking left by the bulldozers was dotted with daisies. Past the court and a flat stretch where they used to play family baseball stood a soft green rise glorious in the sun, each weed and species of grass distinct as illumination on parchment. "I'm sorry, so sorry," Richard cried. "You were the only one who tried to help me with all the goddam jobs around this place."

Sobbing, safe within his tears and champagne, John explained, "It's not just the separation, it's the whole crummy year, I *hate* that school, you can't make any friends, the history teacher's a scud."

They sat on the crest of the rise, shaking and warm from their tears but easier in their voices, and Richard tried to focus on the child's sad year—

the weekdays long with homework, the weekend spent in his room with model airplanes, while his parents murmured down below, nursing their separation. How selfish, how blind, Richard thought; his eyes felt scoured. He told his son, "We'll think about getting you transferred. Life's too short to be miserable."

30   They had said what they could, but did not want the moment to heal, and talked on, about the school, about the tennis court, whether it would ever again be as good as it had been that first summer. They walked to inspect it and pressed a few more tapes more firmly down. A little stiltedly, perhaps trying now to make too much of the moment, Richard led the boy to the spot in the field where the view was best, of the metallic blue river, the emerald marsh, the scattered islands velvety with shadow in the low light, the white bits of beach far away. "See," he said. "It goes on being beautiful. It'll be here tomorrow."

"I know," John answered, impatiently. The moment had closed.

Back in the house, the others had opened some white wine, the champagne being drunk, and still sat at the table, the three females, gossiping. Where Joan sat had become the head. She turned, showing him a tearless face, and asked, "All right?"

"We're fine," he said, resenting it, though relieved, that the party went on without him.

In bed she explained, "I couldn't cry I guess because I cried so much all spring. It really wasn't fair. It's your idea, and you made it look as though I was kicking you out."

35   "I'm sorry," he said. "I couldn't stop. I wanted to but couldn't."

"You *didn't* want to. You loved it. You were having your way, making a general announcement."

"I love having it over," he admitted. "God, those kids were great. So brave and funny." John, returned to the house, had settled to a model airplane in his room, and kept shouting down to them, "I'm O.K. No sweat." "And the way," Richard went on, cozy in his relief, "they never questioned the reasons we gave. No thought of a third person. Not even Judith."

"That *was* touching," Joan said.

He gave her a hug. "You were great too. Very reassuring to everybody. Thank you." Guiltily, he realized he did not feel separated.

40   "You still have Dickie to do," she told him. These words set before him a black mountain in the darkness; its cold breath, its near weight affected his chest. Of the four children, his elder son was most nearly his conscience. Joan did not need to add, "That's one piece of your dirty work I won't do for you."

"I know. I'll do it. You go to sleep."

Within minutes, her breathing slowed, became oblivious and deep. It was quarter to midnight. Dickie's train from the concert would come in at one-fourteen. Richard set the alarm for one. He had slept atrociously for weeks. But whenever he closed his lids some glimpse of the last hours scorched them—Judith exhaling toward the ceiling in a kind of aversion, Bean's mute staring, the sunstruck growth in the field where he and John had rested. The mountain before him moved closer, moved within him; he was huge, momentous. The ache at the back of his throat felt stale. His wife slept as if slain beside him. When, exasperated by his hot lids, his crowded heart, he rose from bed and dressed, she awoke enough to turn over. He told her then, "Joan, if I could undo it all, I would."

"Where would you begin?" she asked. There was no place. Giving him courage, she was always giving him courage. He put on shoes without socks in the dark. The children were breathing in their rooms, the downstairs was hollow. In their confusion they had left lights burning. He turned off all but one, the kitchen overhead. The car started. He had hoped it wouldn't. He met only moonlight on the road; it seemed a diaphanous companion, flickering in the leaves along the roadside, haunting his rearview mirror like a pursuer, melting under his headlights. The center of town, not quite deserted, was eerie at this hour. A young cop in uniform kept company with a gang of T-shirted kids on the steps of the bank. Across from the railroad station, several bars kept open. Customers, mostly young, passed in and out of the warm night, savoring summer's novelty. Voices shouted from cars as they passed; an immense conversation seemed in progress. Richard parked and in his weariness put his head on the passenger seat, out of the commotion and wheeling lights. It was as when, in the movies, an assassin grimly carries his mission through the jostle of a carnival—except the movies cannot show the precipitous, palpable slope you cling to within. You cannot climb back down; you can only fall. The synthetic fabric of the car seat, warmed by his cheek, confided to him an ancient, distant scent of vanilla.

A train whistle caused him to lift his head. It was on time; he had hoped it would be late. The slender draw-gates descended. The bell of approach tingled happily. The great metal body, horizontally fluted, rocked to a stop, and sleepy teen-agers disembarked, his son among them. Dickie did not show surprise that his father was meeting him at this terrible hour. He sauntered to the car with two friends, both taller than he. He said "Hi" to his father and took the passenger's seat with an exhausted promptness that expressed gratitude. The friends got in the back, and Richard was grateful; a few more minutes' postponement would be won by driving them home.

45   He asked, "How was the concert?"

"Groovy," one boy said from the back seat.

"It bit," the other said.

"It was O.K.," Dickie said, moderate by nature, so reasonable that in his childhood the unreason of the world had given him headaches, stomach aches, nausea. When the second friend had been dropped off at his dark house, the boy blurted, "Dad, my eyes are killing me with hay fever! I'm out there cutting that mothering grass all day!"

"Do we still have those drops?"

50   "They didn't do any good last summer."

"They might this." Richard swung a U-turn on the empty street. The drive home took a few minutes. The mountain was here, in his throat. "Richard," he said, and felt the boy, slumped and rubbing his eyes, go tense at his tone, "I didn't come to meet you just to make your life easier. I came because your mother and I have some news for you, and you're a hard man to get ahold of these days. It's sad news."

"That's O.K." The reassurance came out soft, but quick, as if released from the tip of a spring.

Richard had feared that his tears would return and choke him, but the boy's manliness set an example, and his voice issued forth steady and dry. "It's sad news, but it needn't be tragic news, at least for you. It should have no practical effect on your life, though it's bound to have an emotional effect. You'll work at your job, and go back to school in September. Your mother and I are really proud of what you're making of your life; we don't want that to change at all."

"Yeah," the boy said lightly, on the intake of his breath, holding himself up. They turned the corner; the church they went to loomed like a gutted fort. The home of the woman Richard hoped to marry stood across the green. Her bedroom light burned.

55   "Your mother and I," he said, "have decided to separate. For the summer. Nothing legal, no divorce yet. We want to see how it feels. For some years now, we haven't been doing enough for each other, making each other as happy as we should be. Have you sensed that?"

"No," the boy said. It was an honest, unemotional answer: true or false in a quiz.

Glad for the factual basis, Richard pursued, even garrulously, the details. His apartment across town, his utter accessibility, the split vacation arrangements, the advantages to the children, the added mobility and variety of the summer. Dickie listened, absorbing. "Do the others know?"

"Yes."

"How did they take it?"

60   "The girls pretty calmly. John flipped out; he shouted and ate a cigarette and made a salad out of his napkin and told us how much he hated school."

His brother chuckled. "He did?"

"Yeah. The school issue was more upsetting for him than Mom and me. He seemed to feel better for having exploded."

"He did?" The repetition was the first sign that he was stunned.

"Yes. Dickie, I want to tell you something. This last hour, waiting for your train to get in, has been about the worst of my life. I hate this. *Hate* it. My father would have died before doing it to me." He felt immensely lighter, saying this. He had dumped the mountain on the boy. They were home. Moving swiftly as a shadow, Dickie was out of the car, through the bright kitchen. Richard called after him, "Want a glass of milk or anything?"

65   "No thanks."

"Want us to call the course tomorrow and say you're too sick to work?"

"No, that's all right." The answer was faint, delivered at the door to his room; Richard listened for the slam that went with a tantrum. The door closed normally, gently. The sound was sickening.

Joan had sunk into that first deep trough of sleep and was slow to awake. Richard had to repeat, "I told him."

"What did he say?"

70   "Nothing much. Could you go say goodnight to him? Please." She left their room, without putting on a bathrobe. He sluggishly changed back into his pajamas and walked down the hall. Dickie was already in bed, Joan was sitting beside him, and the boy's bedside clock radio was murmuring music. When she stood, an inexplicable light—the moon?—outlined her body through the nightie. Richard sat on the warm place she had indented on the child's narrow mattress. He asked him, "Do you want the radio on like that?"

"It always is."

"Doesn't it keep you awake? It would me."

"No."

"Are you sleepy?"

75   "Yeah."

"Good. Sure you want to get up and go to work? You've had a big night."

"I want to."

Away at school this winter he had learned for the first time that you can go short of sleep and live. As an infant he had slept with an immobile, sweating intensity that had alarmed his babysitters. In adolescence he had often been the first of the four children to go to bed. Even now, he would go slack in the middle of a television show, his sprawled legs hairy and brown. "O.K. Good boy. Dickie, listen. I love you so much, I never knew how much until now. No matter how this works out, I'll always be with you. Really."

Richard bent to kiss an averted face but his son, sinewy, turned and with wet cheeks embraced him and gave him a kiss, on the lips, passionate as a woman's. In his father's ear he moaned one word, the crucial, intelligent word: "*Why?*"

80   *Why.* It was a whistle of wind in a crack, a knife thrust, a window thrown open on emptiness. The white face was gone, the darkness was featureless. Richard had forgotten why.

JOYCE CAROL OATES

Joyce Carol Oates was born in 1938 in Millerport, New York. She won a scholarship to Syracuse University, from which she graduated (Phi Beta Kappa and valedictorian) in 1960. She then did graduate work in English, first at the University of Wisconsin and then at Rice University, but she withdrew from Rice to devote more time to writing. Her first collection of stories, By the North Gate, *was published in 1963; since then she has published at least forty books— stories, poems, essays, and (in twenty-five years) twenty-two novels. She has received many awards, has been elected to the American Academy and Institute of Arts and Letters, and now teaches creative writing at Princeton University.*

Where Are You Going, Where Have You Been?   [1966]

To Bob Dylan

Her name was Connie. She was fifteen and she had a quick nervous giggling habit of craning her neck to glance into mirrors or checking other people's faces to make sure her own was all right. Her mother, who noticed everything and knew everything and who hadn't much reason any longer to look at her own face, always scolded Connie about it. "Stop gawking at yourself, who are you? You think you're so pretty?" she would say. Connie would raise her eyebrows at these familiar complaints and look right through her mother, into a shadowy vision of herself as she was right at that moment: she knew she was pretty and that was everything. Her mother had been pretty once too, if you could believe those old snapshots in the album, but now her looks were gone and that was why she was always after Connie.

"Why don't you keep your room clean like your sister? How've you got your hair fixed—what the hell stinks? Hair spray? You don't see your sister using that junk."

Her sister June was twenty-four and still lived at home. She was a secretary in the high school Connie attended, and if that wasn't bad enough—with her in the same building—she was so plain and chunky and steady that Connie had to hear her praised all the time by her mother and her mother's sisters. June did this, June did that, she saved money and helped clean the house and cooked and Connie couldn't do a thing, her mind was all filled with trashy daydreams. Their father was away at work most of the time and when he came home he wanted supper and he read the newspaper at supper and after supper he went to bed. He didn't bother talking much to them, but around his bent head Connie's mother kept picking at her until Connie wished her mother was dead and she herself was dead and it was all over. "She makes me want to throw up sometimes," she complained to her friends. She had a high, breathless, amused voice which made everything she said sound a little forced, whether it was sincere or not.

There was one good thing: June went places with girlfriends of hers, girls who were just as plain and steady as she, and so when Connie wanted to do that her mother had no objections. The father of Connie's best girlfriend drove the girls the three miles to town and left them off at a shopping plaza, so that they could walk through the stores or go to a movie, and when he came to pick them up again at eleven he never bothered to ask what they had done.

5   They must have been familiar sights, walking around that shopping plaza in their shorts and flat ballerina slippers that always scuffed the sidewalk, with charm bracelets jingling on their thin wrists; they would lean together to whisper and laugh secretly if someone passed by who amused or interested them. Connie had long dark blond hair that drew anyone's eye to it, and she wore part of it pulled up on her head and puffed out and the rest of it she let fall down her back. She wore a pull-over jersey blouse that looked one way when she was at home and another way when she was away from home. Everything about her had two sides to it, one for home and one for anywhere that was not home: her walk that could be childlike and bobbing, or languid enough to make anyone think she was hearing music in her head, her mouth which was pale and smirking most of the time, but bright and pink on these evenings out, her laugh which was cynical and drawling at home—"Ha, ha, very funny"—but high-pitched and nervous anywhere else, like the jingling of the charms on her bracelet.

Sometimes they did go shopping or to a movie, but sometimes they went across the highway, ducking fast across the busy road, to a drive-in restaurant where older kids hung out. The restaurant was shaped like a big bottle, though squatter than a real bottle, and on its cap was a revolving figure of a grinning boy who held a hamburger aloft. One night in midsummer they ran across, breathless with daring, and right away someone leaned out a car window and invited them over, but it was just a boy from high school they didn't like. It made them feel good to be able to ignore him. They went up through the maze of parked and cruising cars to the bright-lit, fly-infested restaurant, their faces pleased and expectant as if they were entering a sacred building that loomed out of the night to give them what haven and what blessing they yearned for. They sat at the counter and crossed their legs at the ankles, their thin shoulders rigid with excitement, and listened to the music that made everything so good: the music was always in the background like music at a church service, it was something to depend upon.

A boy named Eddie came in to talk with them. He sat backward on his stool, turning himself jerkily around in semicircles and then stopping and turning again, and after a while he asked Connie if she would like something to eat. She said she did and so she tapped her friend's arm on her way out— her friend pulled her face up into a brave droll look—and Connie said she would meet her at eleven, across the way. "I just hate to leave her like that," Connie said earnestly, but the boy said that she wouldn't be alone for long. So they went out to his car and on the way Connie couldn't help but let her eyes wander over the windshields and faces all around her, her face gleaming with a joy that had nothing to do with Eddie or even this place; it might have been the music. She drew her shoulders up and sucked in her breath with the pure pleasure of being alive, and just at that moment she happened to glance at a face just a few feet from hers. It was a boy with shaggy black hair, in a convertible jalopy painted gold. He stared at her and then his lips widened into a grin. Connie slit her eyes at him and turned away, but she couldn't help glancing back and there he was still watching her. He wagged a finger and laughed and said, "Gonna get you, baby," and Connie turned away again without Eddie noticing anything.

She spent three hours with him, at the restaurant where they ate hamburgers and drank Cokes in wax cups that were always sweating, and then down an alley a mile or so away, and when he left her off at five to eleven only the movie house was still open at the plaza. Her girlfriend was there, talking with a boy. When Connie came up the two girls smiled at each other and Connie said, "How was the movie?" and the girl said, "*You* should know." They rode off with the girl's father, sleepy and pleased, and Connie couldn't help but look at the darkened shopping plaza with its big empty parking lot and its signs that were faded and ghostly now, and over at the drive-in restaurant where cars were still circling tirelessly. She couldn't hear the music at this distance.

Next morning June asked her how the movie was and Connie said, "So-so."

10   She and that girl and occasionally another girl went out several times a week that way, and the rest of the time Connie spent around the house—it was summer vacation—getting in her mother's way and thinking, dreaming, about the boys she met. But all the boys fell back and dissolved into a single face that was not even a face, but an idea, a feeling, mixed up with the urgent insistent pounding of the music and the humid night air of July. Connie's mother kept dragging her back to the daylight by finding things for her to do or saying, suddenly, "What's this about the Pettinger girl?"

And Connie would say nervously, "Oh, her. That dope." She always drew thick clear lines between herself and such girls, and her mother was simple and kindly enough to believe her. Her mother was so simple, Connie thought, that it was maybe cruel to fool her so much. Her mother went scuffling around the house in old bedroom slippers and complained over the telephone to one sister about the other, then the other called up and the two of them complained about the third one. If June's name was mentioned her mother's tone was approving, and if Connie's name was mentioned it was disapproving. This did not really mean she disliked Connie and actually Connie thought that her mother preferred her to June because she was prettier, but the two of them kept up a pretense of exasperation, a sense that they were tugging and struggling over something of little value to either of them.

Sometimes, over coffee, they were almost friends, but something would come up—some vexation that was like a fly buzzing suddenly around their heads—and their faces went hard with contempt.

One Sunday Connie got up at eleven—none of them bothered with church—and washed her hair so that it could dry all day long, in the sun. Her parents and sister were going to a barbecue at an aunt's house and Connie said no, she wasn't interested, rolling her eyes to let her mother know just what she thought of it. "Stay home alone then," her mother said sharply. Connie sat out back in a lawn chair and watched them drive away, her father quiet and bald, hunched around so that he could back the car out, her mother with a look that was still angry and not at all softened through the windshield, and in the back seat poor old June all dressed up as if she didn't know what a barbecue was, with all the running yelling kids and the flies. Connie sat with her eyes closed in the sun, dreaming and dazed with the warmth about her as if this were a kind of love, the caresses of love, and her mind slipped over onto thoughts of the boy she had been with the night before and how nice he had been, how sweet it always was, not the way someone like June would suppose but sweet, gentle, the way it was in movies and promised in songs; and when she opened her eyes she hardly knew where she was, the back yard ran off into weeds and a fence line of trees and behind it the sky was perfectly blue and still. The asbestos "ranch house" that was now three years old startled her—it looked small. She shook her head as if to get awake.

It was too hot. She went inside the house and turned on the radio to drown out the quiet. She sat on the edge of her bed, barefoot, and listened for an hour and a half to a program called XYZ Sunday Jamboree, record after record of hard, fast, shrieking songs she sang along with, interspersed by exclamations from "Bobby King": "An' look here you girls at Napoleon's—Son and Charley want you to pay real close attention to this song coming up!"

And Connie paid close attention herself, bathed in a glow of slow-pulsed joy that seemed to rise mysteriously out of the music itself and lay languidly about the airless little room, breathed in and breathed out with each gentle rise and fall of her chest.

15   After a while she heard a car coming up the drive. She sat up at once, startled, because it couldn't be her father so soon. The gravel kept crunching all the way in from the road—the driveway was long—and Connie ran to the window. It was a car she didn't know. It was an open jalopy, painted a bright gold that caught the sunlight opaquely. Her heart began to pound and her fingers snatched at her hair, checking it, and she whispered "Christ, Christ," wondering how bad she looked. The car came to a stop at the side door and the horn sounded four short taps as if this were a signal Connie knew.

She went into the kitchen and approached the door slowly, then hung out the screen door, her bare toes curling down off the step. There were two boys in the car and now she recognized the driver: he had shaggy, shabby black hair that looked crazy as a wig and he was grinning at her.

"I ain't late, am I?" he said.

"Who the hell do you think you are?" Connie said.

"Toldja I'd be out, didn't I?"

20   "I don't even know who you are."

She spoke sullenly, careful to show no interest or pleasure, and he spoke in a fast bright monotone. Connie looked past him to the other boy, taking her time. He had fair brown hair, with a lock that fell onto his forehead. His sideburns gave him a fierce, embarrassed look, but so far he hadn't even bothered to glance at her. Both boys wore sunglasses. The driver's glasses were metallic and mirrored everything in miniature.

"You wanta come for a ride?" he said.

Connie smirked and let her hair fall loose over one shoulder.

"Don'tcha like my car? New paint job," he said. "Hey."

25   "What?"

"You're cute."

She pretended to fidget, chasing flies away from the door.

"Don'tcha believe me, or what?" he said.

"Look, I don't even know who you are," Connie said in disgust.

30   "Hey, Ellie's got a radio, see. Mine's broke down." He lifted his friend's arm and showed her the little transistor the boy was holding, and now Connie began to hear the music. It was the same program that was playing inside the house.

"Bobby King?" she said.

"I listen to him all the time. I think he's great."

"He's kind of great." Connie said reluctantly.

"Listen, that guy's *great*. He knows where the action is."

35   Connie blushed a little, because the glasses made it impossible for her to see just what this boy was looking at. She couldn't decide if she liked him or if he was just a jerk, and so she dawdled in the doorway and wouldn't come down or go back inside. She said, "What's all that stuff painted on your car?"

"Can'tcha read it?" He opened the door very carefully, as if he was afraid it might fall off. He slid out just as carefully, planting his feet firmly on the ground, the tiny metallic world in his glasses slowing down like gelatine hardening and in the midst of it Connie's bright green blouse. "This here is my name, to begin with," he said. ARNOLD FRIEND was written in tarlike black letters on the side, with a drawing of a round grinning face that reminded Connie of a pumpkin, except it wore sunglasses. "I wanta introduce myself, I'm Arnold Friend and that's my real name and I'm gonna be your friend, honey, and inside the car's Ellie Oscar, he's kinda shy." Ellie brought his transistor radio up to his shoulder and balanced it there. "Now these numbers are a secret code, honey," Arnold Friend explained. He read off the numbers 33, 19, 17 and raised his eyebrows at her to see what she thought of that, but she didn't think much of it. The left rear fender had been smashed and around it was written, on the gleaming gold background: DONE BY CRAZY WOMAN DRIVER. Connie had to laugh at that. Arnold Friend was pleased at her laughter and looked up at her. "Around the other side's a lot more—you wanta come and see them?"

"No."

"Why not?"

"Why should I?"

40   "Don'tcha wanta see what's on the car? Don'tcha wanta go for a ride?"

"I don't know."

"Why not?"

"I got things to do."

"Like what?"

45   "Things."

He laughed as if she had said something funny. He slapped his thighs. He was standing in a strange way, leaning back against the car as if he were balancing himself. He wasn't tall, only an inch or so taller than she would be if she came down to him. Connie liked the way he was dressed, which was the way all of them dressed: tight faded jeans stuffed into black, scuffed boots, a belt that pulled his waist in and showed how lean he was, and a white pullover shirt that was a little soiled and showed the hard small muscles of his arms and shoulders. He looked as if he probably did hard work, lifting and carrying things. Even his neck looked muscular. And his face was a familiar face, somehow: the jaw and chin and cheeks slightly darkened, because he hadn't shaved for a day or two, and the nose long and hawklike, sniffing as if she were a treat he was going to gobble up and it was all a joke.

"Connie, you ain't telling the truth. This is your day set aside for a ride with me and you know it," he said, still laughing. The way he straightened and recovered from his fit of laughing showed that it had been all fake.

"How do you know what my name is?" she said suspiciously.

"It's Connie."

50 "Maybe and maybe not."

"I know my Connie," he said, wagging his finger. Now she remembered him even better, back at the restaurant, and her cheeks warmed at the thought of how she sucked in her breath just at the moment she passed him—how she must have looked to him. And he had remembered her. "Ellie and I come out here especially for you," he said. "Ellie can sit in back. How about it?"

"Where?"

"Where what?"

"Where're we going?"

55 He looked at her. He took off the sunglasses and she saw how pale the skin around his eyes was, like holes that were not in shadow but instead in light. His eyes were like chips of broken glass that catch the light in an amiable way. He smiled. It was as if the idea of going for a ride somewhere, to some place, was a new idea to him.

"Just for a ride, Connie sweetheart."

"I never said my name was Connie," she said.

"But I know what it is. I know your name and all about you, lots of things," Arnold Friend said. He had not moved yet but stood still leaning back against the side of his jalopy. "I took a special interest in you, such a pretty girl, and found out all about you like I know your parents and sister are gone somewheres and I know where and how long they're going to be gone, and I know who you were with last night, and your best girlfriend's name is Betty. Right?"

He spoke in a simple lilting voice, exactly as if he were reciting the words to a song. His smile assured her that everything was fine. In the car Ellie turned up the volume on his radio and did not bother to look around at them.

60 "Ellie can sit in the back seat," Arnold Friend said. He indicated his friend with a casual jerk of his chin, as if Ellie did not count and she should not bother with him.

"How'd you find out all that stuff?" Connie said.

"Listen: Betty Schultz and Tony Fitch and Jimmy Pettinger and Nancy Pettinger," he said, in a chant. "Raymond Stanley and Bob Hutter—"

"Do you know all those kids?"

"I know everybody."

65   "Look, you're kidding. You're not from around here."

"Sure."

"But—how come we never saw you before?"

"Sure you saw me before," he said. He looked down at his boots, as if he were a little offended. "You just don't remember."

"I guess I'd remember you," Connie said.

70   "Yeah?" He looked up at this, beaming. He was pleased. He began to mark time with the music from Ellie's radio, tapping his fists lightly together. Connie looked away from his smile to the car, which was painted so bright it almost hurt her eyes to look at it. She looked at that name, ARNOLD FRIEND. And up at the front fender was an expression that was familiar—MAN THE FLYING SAUCERS. It was an expression kids had used the year before, but didn't use this year. She looked at it for a while as if the words meant something to her that she did not yet know.

"What're you thinking about? Huh?" Arnold Friend demanded. "Not worried about your hair blowing around in the car, are you?"

"No."

"Think I maybe can't drive good?"

"How do I know?"

75   "You're a hard girl to handle. How come?" he said. "Don't you know I'm your friend? Didn't you see me put my sign in the air when you walked by?"

"What sign?"

"My sign." And he drew an X in the air, leaning out toward her. They were maybe ten feet apart. After his hand fell back to his side the X was still in the air, almost visible. Connie let the screen door close and stood perfectly still inside it, listening to the music from her radio and the boy's blend together. She stared at Arnold Friend. He stood there so stiffly relaxed, pretending to be relaxed, with one hand idly on the door handle as if he were keeping himself up that way and had no intention of ever moving again. She recognized most things about him, the tight jeans that showed his thighs and buttocks and the greasy leather boots and the tight shirt, and even that slippery friendly smile of his, that sleepy dreamy smile that all the boys used to get across ideas they didn't want to put into words. She recognized all this and also the singsong way he talked, slightly mocking, kidding, but serious and a little melancholy, and she recognized the way he tapped one fist against the other in homage to the perpetual music behind him. But all these things did not come together.

She said suddenly, "Hey, how old are you?"

His smile faded. She could see then that he wasn't a kid, he was much older—thirty, maybe more. At this knowledge her heart began to pound faster.

80   "That's a crazy thing to ask. Can'tcha see I'm your own age?"

"Like hell you are."

"Or maybe a coupla years older, I'm eighteen."

"Eighteen?" she said doubtfully.

He grinned to reassure her and lines appeared at the corners of his mouth. His teeth were big and white. He grinned so broadly his eyes became slits and she saw how thick the lashes were, thick and black as if painted with a black tarlike material. Then he seemed to become embarrassed, abruptly, and looked over his shoulder at Ellie. "Him, he's crazy," he said. "Ain't he a riot, he's a nut, a real character." Ellie was still listening to the music. His sunglasses told nothing about what he was thinking. He wore a bright orange shirt unbuttoned halfway to show his chest, which was a pale, bluish chest and not muscular like Arnold Friend's. His shirt collar was turned up all around and the very tips of the collar pointed out past his chin as if they were protecting him. He was pressing the transistor radio up against his ear and sat there in a kind of daze, right in the sun.

85   "He's kinda strange," Connie said.

"Hey, she says you're kinda strange! Kinda strange!" Arnold Friend cried. He pounded on the car to get Ellie's attention. Ellie turned for the first time and Connie saw with shock that he wasn't a kid either—he had a fair, hairless face, cheeks reddened slightly as if the veins grew too close to the surface of his skin, the face of a forty-year-old baby. Connie felt a wave of dizziness rise in her at this sight and she stared at him as if waiting for something to change the shock of the moment, make it all right again. Ellie's lips kept shaping words, mumbling along, with the words blasting in his ear.

"Maybe you two better go away," Connie said faintly.

"What? How come?" Arnold Friend cried. "We come out here to take you for a ride. It's Sunday." He had the voice of the man on the radio now. It was the same voice, Connie thought. "Don'tcha know it's Sunday all day and honey, no matter who you were with last night today you're with Arnold Friend and don't you forget it!—Maybe you better step out here," he said, and this last was in a different voice. It was a little flatter, as if the heat was finally getting to him.

"No. I got things to do."

90   "Hey."

"You two better leave."

"We ain't leaving until you come with us."

"Like hell I am—"

"Connie, don't fool around with me. I mean, I mean, don't fool *around*," he said, shaking his head. He laughed incredulously. He placed his sunglasses on top of his head, carefully, as if he were indeed wearing a wig, and brought the stems down behind his ears. Connie stared at him, another wave of dizziness and fear rising in her so that for a moment he wasn't even in focus but was just a blur, standing there against his gold car, and she had the idea that he had driven up the driveway all right but had come from nowhere before that and belonged nowhere and that everything about him and even about the music that was so familiar to her was only half real.

95   "If my father comes and sees you—"

"He ain't coming. He's at a barbecue."

"How do you know that?"

"Aunt Tillie's. Right now they're—uh—they're drinking. Sitting around," he said vaguely, squinting as if he were staring all the way to town and over to Aunt Tillie's back yard. Then the vision seemed to get clear and he nodded energetically. "Yeah. Sitting around. There's your sister in a blue dress, huh? And high heels, the poor sad bitch—nothing like you, sweetheart! And your mother's helping some fat woman with the corn, they're cleaning the corn—husking the corn—"

"What fat woman?" Connie cried.

100   "How do I know what fat woman. I don't know every goddam fat woman in the world!" Arnold Friend laughed.

"Oh, that's Mrs. Hornby. . . . Who invited her?" Connie said. She felt a little light-headed. Her breath was coming quickly.

"She's too fat. I don't like them fat. I like them the way you are, honey," he said, smiling sleepily at her. They stared at each other for a while, through the screen door. He said softly, "Now what you're going to do is this: you're going to come out that door. You're going to sit up front with me and Ellie's going to sit in the back, the hell with Ellie, right? This isn't Ellie's date. You're my date. I'm your lover, honey."

"What? You're crazy—"

"Yes, I'm your lover. You don't know what that is but you will," he said. "I know that too. I know all about you. But look: it's real nice and you couldn't ask for nobody better than me, or more polite. I always keep my word. I'll tell you how it is, I'm always nice at first, the first time. I'll hold you so tight you won't think you have to try to get away or pretend anything because you'll know you can't. And I'll come inside you where it's all secret and you'll give in to me and you'll love me—"

105   "Shut up! You're crazy!" Connie said. She backed away from the door. She put her hands against her ears as if she'd heard something terrible, something not meant for her. "People don't talk like that, you're crazy," she muttered. Her heart was almost too big now for her chest and its pumping made sweat break out all over her. She looked out to see Arnold Friend pause and then take a step toward the porch lurching. He almost fell. But, like a clever drunken man, he managed to catch his balance. He wobbled in his high boots and grabbed hold of one of the porch posts.

"Honey?" he said. "You still listening?"

"Get the hell out of here!"

"Be nice, honey. Listen."

"I'm going to call the police—"

110   He wobbled again and out of the side of his mouth came a fast spat curse, an aside not meant for her to hear. But even this "Christ!" sounded forced. Then he began to smile again. She watched this smile come, awkward as if he were smiling from inside a mask. His whole face was a mask, she thought wildly, tanned down onto his throat but then running out as if he had plastered makeup on his face but had forgotten about his throat.

"Honey—? Listen, here's how it is. I always tell the truth and I promise you this: I ain't coming in that house after you."

"You better not! I'm going to call the police if you—if you don't—"

"Honey," he said, talking right through her voice, "honey, I'm not coming in there but you are coming out here. You know why?"

She was panting. The kitchen looked like a place she had never seen before, some room she had run inside but which wasn't good enough, wasn't going to help her. The kitchen window had never had a curtain, after three years, and there were dishes in the sink for her to do—probably—and if you ran your hand across the table you'd probably feel something sticky there.

115   "You listening, honey? Hey?"

"—going to call the police—"

"Soon as you touch the phone I don't need to keep my promise and can come inside. You won't want that."

She rushed forward and tried to lock the door. Her fingers were shaking. "But why lock it," Arnold Friend said gently, talking right into her face. "It's just a screen door. It's just nothing." One of his boots was at a strange angle, as if his foot wasn't in it. It pointed out to the left, bent at the ankle. "I mean, any-

body can break through a screen door and glass and wood and iron or anything else if he needs to, anybody at all and specially Arnold Friend. If the
place got lit up with a fire honey you'd come runnin' out into my arms, right
into my arms an' safe at home—like you knew I was your lover and'd stopped
fooling around. I don't mind a nice shy girl but I don't like no fooling
around." Part of those words were spoken with a slight rhythmic lilt, and Connie somehow recognized them—the echo of a song from last year, about a
girl rushing into her boyfriend's arms and coming home again—

Connie stood barefoot on the linoleum floor, staring at him. "What do
you want?" she whispered.

120   "I want you," he said.

"What?"

"Seen you that night and thought, that's the one, yes sir. I never needed
to look any more."

"But my father's coming back. He's coming to get me. I had to wash my
hair first—" She spoke in a dry, rapid voice, hardly raising it for him to hear.

"No, your Daddy is not coming and yes, you had to wash your hair and
you washed it for me. It's nice and shining and all for me, I thank you, sweetheart," he said, with a mock bow, but again he almost lost his balance. He
had to bend and adjust his boots. Evidently his feet did not go all the way
down; the boots must have been stuffed with something so that he would
seem taller. Connie stared out at him and behind him Ellie in the car, who
seemed to be looking off toward Connie's right into nothing. This Ellie said,
pulling the words out of the air one after another as if he were just discovering them, "You want me to pull out the phone?"

125   "Shut your mouth and keep it shut," Arnold Friend said, his face red
from bending over or maybe from embarrassment because Connie had seen
his boots. "This ain't none of your business."

"What—what are you doing? What do you want?" Connie said. "If I call
the police they'll get you, they'll arrest you—"

"Promise was not to come in unless you touch that phone, and I'll keep
that promise," he said. He resumed his erect position and tried to force his
shoulders back. He sounded like a hero in a movie, declaring something important. He spoke too loudly and it was as if he were speaking to someone
behind Connie. "I ain't made plans for coming in that house where I don't
belong but just for you to come out to me, the way you should. Don't you
know who I am?"

"You're crazy," she whispered. She backed away from the door but did not
want to go into another part of the house, as if this would give him permission
to come through the door. "What do you . . . You're crazy, you . . ."

"Huh? What're you saying, honey?"

130   Her eyes darted everywhere in the kitchen. She could not remember
what it was, this room.

"This is how it is, honey: you come out and we'll drive away, have a nice
ride. But if you don't come out we're gonna wait till your people come
home and then they're all going to get it."

"You want that telephone pulled out?" Ellie said. He held the radio away
from his ear and grimaced, as if without the radio the air was too much for
him.

"I toldja shut up, Ellie," Arnold Friend said, "you're deaf, get a hearing aid,
right? Fix yourself up. This little girl's no trouble and's gonna be nice to me,

so Ellie keep to yourself, this ain't your date—right? Don't hem in on me. Don't hog. Don't crush. Don't bird dog. Don't trail me," he said in a rapid meaningless voice, as if he were running through all the expressions he'd learned but was no longer sure which one of them was in style, then rushing on to new ones, making them up with his eyes closed, "Don't crawl under my fence, don't squeeze in my chipmunk hole, don't sniff my glue, suck my popsicle, keep your own greasy fingers on yourself!" He shaded his eyes and peered in at Connie, who was backed against the kitchen table. "Don't mind him honey he's just a creep. He's a dope. Right? I'm the boy for you and like I said you come out here nice like a lady and give me your hand, and nobody else gets hurt, I mean, your nice old bald-headed daddy and your mummy and your sister in her high heels. Because listen: why bring them in this?"

"Leave me alone," Connie whispered.

135   "Hey, you know that old woman down the road, the one with the chickens and stuff—you know her?"

"She's dead!"

"Dead? What? You know her?" Arnold Friend said.

"She's dead—"

"Don't you like her?"

140   "She's dead—she's—she isn't here any more—"

"But don't you like her, I mean, you got something against her? Some grudge or something?" Then his voice dipped as if he were conscious of a rudeness. He touched the sunglasses perched on top of his head as if to make sure they were still there. "Now you be a good girl."

"What are you going to do?"

"Just two things, or maybe three," Arnold Friend said. "But I promise it won't last long and you'll like me the way you get to like people you're close to. You will. It's all over for you here, so come on out. You don't want your people in any trouble, do you?"

She turned and bumped against a chair or something, hurting her leg, but she ran into the back room and picked up the telephone. Something roared in her ear, a tiny roaring, and she was so sick with fear that she could do nothing but listen to it—the telephone was clammy and very heavy and her fingers groped down to the dial but were too weak to touch it. She began to scream into the phone, into the roaring. She cried out, she cried for her mother, she felt her breath start jerking back and forth in her lungs as if it were something Arnold Friend were stabbing her with again and again with no tenderness. A noisy sorrowful wailing rose all about her and she was locked inside it the way she was locked inside the house.

145   After a while she could hear again. She was sitting on the floor with her wet back against the wall.

Arnold Friend was saying from the door, "That's a good girl. Put the phone back."

She kicked the phone away from her.

"No, honey. Pick it up. Put it back right."

She picked it up and put it back. The dial tone stopped.

150   "That's a good girl. Now come outside."

She was hollow with what had been fear, but what was now just an emptiness. All that screaming had blasted it out of her. She sat, one leg cramped under her, and deep inside her brain was something like a pinpoint of light that kept going and would not let her relax. She thought, I'm not going to see my mother again. She thought, I'm not going to sleep in my bed again. Her bright green blouse was all wet.

Arnold Friend said, in a gentle-loud voice that was like a stage voice, "The place where you came from ain't there any more, and where you had in mind to go is canceled out. This place you are now—inside your daddy's house—is nothing but a cardboard box I can knock down any time. You know that and always did know it. You hear me?"

She thought, I have got to think. I have to know what to do.

"We'll go out to a nice field, out in the country here where it smells so nice and it's sunny," Arnold Friend said. "I'll have my arms tight around you so you won't need to try to get away and I'll show you what love is like, what it does. The hell with this house! It looks solid all right," he said. He ran a fingernail down the screen and the noise did not make Connie shiver, as it would have the day before. "Now put your hand on your heart, honey. Feel that? That feels solid too but we know better, be nice to me, be sweet like you can because what else is there for a girl like you but to be sweet and pretty and give in?—and get away before her people come back?"

155   She felt her pounding heart. Her hand seemed to enclose it. She thought for the first time in her life that it was nothing that was hers, that belonged to her, but just a pounding, living thing inside this body that wasn't really hers either.

"You don't want them to get hurt," Arnold Friend went on. "Now get up, honey. Get up all by yourself."

She stood up.

"Now turn this way. That's right. Come over here to me—Ellie, put that away, didn't I tell you? You dope. You miserable creepy dope," Arnold Friend said. His words were not angry but only part of an incantation. The incantation was kindly. "Now come out through the kitchen to me honey, and let's see a smile, try it, you're a brave sweet little girl and now they're eating corn and hot dogs cooked to bursting over an outdoor fire, and they don't know one thing about you and never did and honey you're better than them because not a one of them would have done this for you."

Connie felt the linoleum under her feet; it was cool. She brushed her hair back out of her eyes. Arnold Friend let go of the post tentatively and opened his arms for her, his elbows pointing in toward each other and his wrists limp, to show that this was an embarrassed embrace and a little mocking, he didn't want to make her self-conscious.

160   She put out her hand against the screen. She watched herself push the door slowly open as if she were safe back somewhere in the other doorway, watching this body and this head of long hair moving out into the sunlight where Arnold Friend waited.

"My sweet little blue-eyed girl," he said, in a half-sung sigh that had nothing to do with her brown eyes but was taken up just the same by the vast sunlit reaches of the land behind him and on all sides of him, so much land that Connie had never seen before and did not recognize except to know that she was going to it.

BOBBIE ANN MASON

*Bobbie Ann Mason, born in 1940 in rural western Kentucky and a graduate
of the University of Kentucky, now lives in Pennsylvania. She took a master's
degree at the State University of New York at Binghamton, and a Ph.D. at the
University of Connecticut, writing a dissertation on a novel by Vladimir
Nabokov. Between graduate degrees she worked for various magazines, including* T.V. Star Parade. *In 1974 she published her first book—the dissertation
on Nabokov—and in 1975 she published her second,* The Girl Sleuth: A Guide
to the Bobbsey Twins, Nancy Drew and Their Sisters. *She is, however, most
widely known for her fiction, which usually deals with blue-collar people in
rural Kentucky.*

> *I write, she says, about people trapped in circumstances. . . . I iden-
> tify with people who are ambivalent about their situation. And I
> guess in my stories, I'm in a way imagining myself as I would have
> felt if I had not gotten away and gotten a different perspective on
> things—if, for example, I had gotten pregnant in high school and had
> to marry a truck driver as the woman did in my story "Shiloh."*

Shiloh

[1982]

Leroy Moffitt's wife, Norma Jean, is working on her pectorals. She lifts three-
pound dumbbells to warm up, then progresses to a twenty-pound barbell.
Standing with her legs apart, she reminds Leroy of Wonder Woman.

"I'd give anything if I could just get these muscles to where they're real
hard," says Norma Jean. "Feel this arm. It's not as hard as the other one."

"That's cause you're right-handed," says Leroy, dodging as she swings
the barbell in an arc.

"Do you think so?"

5   "Sure."

Leroy is a truckdriver. He injured his leg in a highway accident four
months ago, and his physical therapy, which involves weights and a pulley,
prompted Norma Jean to try building herself up. Now she is attending a
body-building class. Leroy has been collecting temporary disability since
his tractor-trailer jackknifed in Missouri, badly twisting his left leg in its
socket. He has a steel pin in his hip. He will probably not be able to drive
his rig again. It sits in the backyard, like a gigantic bird that has flown
home to roost. Leroy has been home in Kentucky for three months, and his
leg is almost healed, but the accident frightened him and he does not want
to drive any more long hauls. He is not sure what to do next. In the meantime, he makes things from craft kits. He started by building a miniature
log cabin from notched Popsicle sticks. He varnished it and placed it on
the TV set, where it remains. It reminds him of a rustic Nativity scene.
Then he tried string art (sailing ships on black velvet), a macramé owl kit,
a snap-together B-17 Flying Fortress, and a lamp made out of a model
truck, with a light fixture screwed in the top of the cab. At first the kits
were diversions, something to kill time, but now he is thinking about
building a full-scale log house from a kit. It would be considerably cheaper
than building a regular house, and besides, Leroy has grown to appreciate
how things are put together. He has begun to realize that in all the years

he was on the road he never took time to examine anything. He was always flying past scenery.

"They won't let you build a log cabin in any of the new subdivisions," Norma Jean tells him.

"They will if I tell them it's for you," he says, teasing her. Ever since they were married, he has promised Norma Jean he would build her a new home one day. They have always rented, and the house they live in is small and nondescript. It does not even feel like a home, Leroy realizes now.

Norma Jean works at the Rexall drugstore, and she has acquired an amazing amount of information about cosmetics. When she explains to Leroy the three stages of complexion care, involving creams, toners, and moisturizers, he thinks happily of other petroleum products—axle grease, diesel fuel. This is a connection between him and Norma Jean. Since he has been home, he has felt unusually tender about his wife and guilty over his long absences. But he can't tell what she feels about him. Norma Jean has never complained about his traveling; she has never made hurt remarks, like calling his truck a "widow-maker." He is reasonably certain she has been faithful to him, but he wishes she would celebrate his permanent homecoming more happily. Norma Jean is often startled to find Leroy at home, and he thinks she seems a little disappointed about it. Perhaps he reminds her too much of the early days of their marriage, before he went on the road. They had a child who died as an infant, years ago. They never speak about their memories of Randy, which have almost faded, but now that Leroy is home all the time, they sometimes feel awkward around each other, and Leroy wonders if one of them should mention the child. He has the feeling that they are waking up out of a dream together—that they must create a new marriage, start afresh. They are lucky they are still married. Leroy has read that for most people losing a child destroys the marriage—or else he heard this on *Donahue*. He can't always remember where he learns things anymore.

10   At Christmas, Leroy bought an electric organ for Norma Jean. She used to play the piano when she was in high school. "It don't leave you," she told him once. "It's like riding a bicycle."

The new instrument had so many keys and buttons that she was bewildered by it at first. She touched the keys tentatively, pushed some buttons, then pecked out "Chopsticks." It came out in an amplified fox-trot rhythm, with marimba sounds.

"It's an orchestra!" she cried.

The organ had a pecan-look finish and eighteen preset chords, with optional flute, violin, trumpet, clarinet, and banjo accompaniments. Norma Jean mastered the organ almost immediately. At first she played Christmas songs. Then she bought *The Sixties Songbook* and learned every tune in it, adding variations to each with the rows of brightly colored buttons.

"I didn't like these old songs back then," she said. "But I have this crazy feeling I missed something."

15   "You didn't miss a thing," said Leroy.

Leroy likes to lie on the couch and smoke a joint and listen to Norma Jean play "Can't Take My Eyes Off You" and "I'll Be Back." He is back again. After fifteen years on the road, he is finally settling down with the woman he loves. She is still pretty. Her skin is flawless. Her frosted curls resemble pencil trimmings.

Now that Leroy has come home to stay, he notices how much the town has changed. Subdivisions are spreading across western Kentucky like an oil slick. The sign at the edge of town says "Pop: 11,500"—only seven hundred more than it said twenty years before. Leroy can't figure out who is living in all the new houses. The farmers who used to gather around the courthouse square on Saturday afternoons to play checkers and spit tobacco juice have gone. It has been years since Leroy has thought about the farmers, and they have disappeared without his noticing.

Leroy meets a kid named Stevie Hamilton in the parking lot at the new shopping center. While they pretend to be strangers meeting over a stalled car, Stevie tosses an ounce of marijuana under the front seat of Leroy's car. Stevie is wearing orange jogging shoes and a T-shirt that says CHATTAHOOCHEE SUPER-RAT. His father is a prominent doctor who lives in one of the expensive subdivisions in a new white-columned brick house that looks like a funeral parlor. In the phone book under his name there is a separate number, with the listing "Teenagers."

"Where do you get this stuff?" asks Leroy. "From your pappy?"

20   "That's for me to know and you to find out," Stevie says. He is slit-eyed and skinny.

"What else you got?"

"What you interested in?"

"Nothing special. Just wondered."

Leroy used to take speed on the road. Now he has to go slowly. He needs to be mellow. He leans back against the car and says, "I'm aiming to build me a log house, soon as I get time. My wife, though, I don't think she likes the idea."

25   "Well, let me know when you want me again," Stevie says. He has a cigarette in his cupped palm, as though sheltering it from the wind. He takes a long drag, then stomps it on the asphalt and slouches away.

Stevie's father was two years ahead of Leroy in high school. Leroy is thirty-four. He married Norma Jean when they were both eighteen, and their child Randy was born a few months later, but he died at the age of four months and three days. He would be about Stevie's age now. Norma Jean and Leroy were at the drive-in, watching a double feature (*Dr. Strangelove* and *Lover Come Back*), and the baby was sleeping in the back seat. When the first movie ended, the baby was dead. It was the sudden infant death syndrome. Leroy remembers handing Randy to a nurse at the emergency room, as though he were offering her a large doll as a present. A dead baby feels like a sack of flour. "It just happens sometimes," said the doctor, in what Leroy always recalls as a nonchalant tone. Leroy can hardly remember the child anymore, but he still sees vividly a scene from *Dr. Strangelove* in which the President of the United States was talking in a folksy voice on the hot line to the Soviet premier about the bomber accidentally headed toward Russia. He was in the War Room, and the world map was lit up. Leroy remembers Norma Jean standing catatonically beside him in the hospital and himself thinking: Who is this strange girl? He had forgotten who she was. Now scientists are saying that crib death is caused by a virus. Nobody knows anything, Leroy thinks. The answers are always changing.

When Leroy gets home from the shopping center, Norma Jean's mother, Mabel Beasley, is there. Until this year, Leroy has not realized how much time she spends with Norma Jean. When she visits, she inspects the closets and then the plants, informing Norma Jean when a plant is droopy or yellow. Mabel calls the plants "flowers," although there are never any blooms. She also notices if Norma Jean's laundry is piling up. Mabel is a short, over-weight woman whose tight, brown-dyed curls look more like a wig than the actual wig she sometimes wears. Today she has brought Norma Jean an off-white dust ruffle she made for the bed; Mabel works in a custom-upholstery shop.

"This is the tenth one I made this year," Mabel says. "I got started and couldn't stop."

"It's real pretty," says Normal Jean.

30   "Now we can hide things under the bed," says Leroy, who gets along with his mother-in-law primarily by joking with her. Mabel has never really forgiven him for disgracing her by getting Norma Jean pregnant. When the baby died, she said that fate was mocking her.

"What's that thing?" Mabel says to Leroy in a loud voice, pointing to a tangle of yarn on a piece of canvas.

Leroy holds it up for Mabel to see. "It's my needlepoint," he explains. "This is a *Star Trek* pillow cover."

"That's what a woman would do," says Mabel. "Great day in the morn-ing!"

"All the big football players on TV do it," he says.

35   "Why, Leroy, you're always trying to fool me. I don't believe you for one minute. You don't know what to do with yourself—that's the whole trouble. Sewing!"

"I'm aiming to build us a log house," says Leroy. "Soon as my plans come."

"Like *heck* you are," says Norma Jean. She takes Leroy's needlepoint and shoves it into a drawer. "You have to find a job first. Nobody can afford to build now anyway."

Mabel straightens her girdle and says. "I still think before you get tied down y'all ought to take a little run to Shiloh."

"One of these days, Mama," Norma Jean says impatiently.

40   Mabel is talking about Shiloh, Tennessee. For the past few years, she has been urging Leroy and Norma Jean to visit the Civil War battleground there. Mabel went there on her honeymoon—the only real trip she ever took. Her husband died of a perforated ulcer when Norma Jean was ten, but Mabel, who was accepted into the United Daughters of the Confederacy in 1975, is still preoccupied with going back to Shiloh.

"I've been to kingdom come and back in that truck out yonder," Leroy says to Mabel, "but we never yet set foot in that battleground. Ain't that something? How did I miss it?"

"It's not even that far," Mabel says.

After Mabel leaves, Norma Jean reads to Leroy from a list she has made. "Things you could do," she announces. "You could get a job as a guard at Union Carbide, where they'd let you set on a stool. You could get on at the lumberyard. You could do a little carpenter work, if you want to build so bad. You could—"

"I can't do something where I'd have to stand up all day."

45   "You ought to try standing up all day behind a cosmetics counter. It's amazing that I have strong feet, coming from two parents that never had strong feet at all." At the moment Norma Jean is holding on to the kitchen

counter, raising her knees one at a time as she talks. She is wearing two-pound ankle weights.

"Don't worry," says Leroy. "I'll do something."

"You could truck calves to slaughter for somebody. You wouldn't have to drive any big old truck for that."

"I'm going to build you this house," says Leroy. "I want to make you a real home."

"I don't want to live in any log cabin."

50   "It's not a cabin. It's a house."

"I don't care. It looks like a cabin."

"You and me together could lift those logs. It's just like lifting weights."

Norma Jean doesn't answer. Under her breath, she is counting. Now she is marching through the kitchen. She is doing goose steps.

Before his accident, when Leroy came home he used to stay in the house with Norma Jean, watching TV in bed and playing cards. She would cook fried chicken, picnic ham, chocolate pie—all his favorites. Now he is home alone much of the time. In the mornings, Norma Jean disappears, leaving a cooling place in the bed. She eats a cereal called Body Buddies, and she leaves the bowl on the table, with the soggy tan balls floating in a milk puddle. He sees things about Norma Jean that he never realized before. When she chops onions, she stares off into a corner, as if she can't bear to look. She puts on her house slippers almost precisely at nine o'clock every evening and nudges her jogging shoes under the couch. She saves bread heels for the birds. Leroy watches the birds at the feeder. He notices the peculiar way goldfinches fly past the window. They close their wings, then fall, then spread their wings to catch and lift themselves. He wonders if they close their eyes when they fall. Norma Jean closes her eyes when they are in bed. She wants the lights turned out. Even then, he is sure she closes her eyes.

55   He goes for long drives around town. He tends to drive a car rather carelessly. Power steering and an automatic shift make a car feel so small and inconsequential that his body is hardly involved in the driving process. His injured leg stretches out comfortably. Once or twice he has almost hit something, but even the prospect of an accident seems minor in a car. He cruises the new subdivisions, feeling like a criminal rehearsing for a robbery. Norma Jean is probably right about a log house being inappropriate here in the new subdivision. All the houses look grand and complicated. They depress him.

One day when Leroy comes home from a drive he finds Norma Jean in tears. She is in the kitchen making a potato and mushroom-soup casserole, with grated cheese topping. She is crying because her mother caught her smoking.

"I didn't hear her coming. I was standing here puffing away pretty as you please," Norma Jean says, wiping her eyes.

"I knew it would happen sooner or later," says Leroy, putting his arm around her.

"She don't know the meaning of the word 'knock,'" says Norma Jean. "It's a wonder she hadn't caught me years ago."

60   "Think of it this way," Leroy says. "What if she caught me with a joint?"

"You better not let her!" Norma Jean shrieks. "I'm warning you, Leroy Moffitt!"

"I'm just kidding. Here, play me a tune. That'll help you relax."

Norma Jean puts the casserole in the oven and sets the timer. Then she plays a ragtime tune, with horns and banjo, as Leroy lights up a joint and lies on the couch, laughing to himself about Mabel's catching him at it. He thinks of Stevie Hamilton—a doctor's son pushing grass. Everything is funny. The whole town seems crazy and small. He is reminded of Virgil Mathis, a boastful policeman Leroy used to shoot pool with. Virgil recently led a drug bust in a back room at a bowling alley, where he seized ten thousand dollars' worth of marijuana. The newspaper had a picture of him holding up the bags of grass and grinning widely. Right now, Leroy can imagine Virgil breaking down the door and arresting him with a lungful of smoke. Virgil would probably have been alerted to the scene because of all the racket Norma Jean is making. Now she sounds like a hard-rock band. Norma Jean is terrific. When she switches to a Latin-rhythm version of "Sunshine Superman," Leroy hums along. Norma Jean's foot goes up and down, up and down.

"Well, what do you think?" Leroy says, when Norma Jean pauses to search through her music.

65 "What do I think about what?"

His mind has gone blank. Then he says, "I'll sell my rig and build us a house." That wasn't what he wanted to say. He wanted to know what she thought—what she *really* thought—about them.

"Don't start in on that again," says Norma Jean. She begins playing "Who'll Be the Next in Line?"

Leroy used to tell hitchhikers his whole life story—about his travels, his hometown, the baby. He would end with a question: "Well, what do you think?" It was just a rhetorical question. In time, he had the feeling that he'd been telling the same story over and over to the same hitchhikers. He quit talking to hitchhikers when he realized how his voice sounded—whining and self-pitying, like some teenage-tragedy song. Now Leroy has the sudden impulse to tell Norma Jean about himself, as if he had just met her. They have known each other so long they have forgotten a lot about each other. They could become reacquainted. But when the oven timer goes off and she runs to the kitchen, he forgets why he wants to do this.

The next day, Mabel drops by. It is Saturday and Norma Jean is cleaning. Leroy is studying the plans of his log house, which have finally come in the mail. He has them spread out on the table—big sheets of stiff blue paper, with diagrams and numbers printed in white. While Norma Jean runs the vacuum, Mabel drinks coffee. She sets her coffee cup on a blueprint.

70 "I'm just waiting for time to pass," she says to Leroy, drumming her fingers on the table.

As soon as Norma Jean switches off the vacuum, Mabel says in a loud voice. "Did you hear about the datsun dog that killed the baby?"

Norma Jean says, "The word is 'dachshund.'"

"They put the dog on trial. It chewed the baby's legs off. The mother was in the next room all the time." She raises her voice. "They thought it was neglect."

Norma Jean is holding her ears. Leroy manages to open the refrigerator and get some Diet Pepsi to offer Mabel. Mabel still has some coffee and she waves away the Pepsi.

75   "Datsuns are like that," Mabel says. "They're jealous dogs. They'll tear a place to pieces if you don't keep an eye on them."

"You better watch out what you're saying, Mabel," says Leroy.

"Well, facts is facts."

Leroy looks out the window at his rig. It is like a huge piece of furniture gathering dust in the backyard. Pretty soon it will be an antique. He hears the vacuum cleaner. Norma Jean seems to be cleaning the living room rug again.

Later, she says to Leroy, "She just said that about the baby because she caught me smoking. She's trying to pay me back."

80   "What are you talking about?" Leroy says, nervously shuffling blueprints.

"You know good and well," Norma Jean says. She is sitting in a kitchen chair with her feet up and her arms wrapped around her knees. She looks small and helpless. She says, "The very idea, her bringing up a subject like that! Saying it was neglect."

"She didn't mean that," Leroy says.

"She might not have *thought* she meant it. She always says things like that. You don't know how she goes on."

"But she didn't really mean it. She was just talking."

85   Leroy opens a king-sized bottle of beer and pours it into two glasses dividing it carefully. He hands a glass to Norma Jean and she takes it from him mechanically. For a long time, they sit by the kitchen window watching the birds at the feeder.

Something is happening. Norma Jean is going to night school. She has graduated from her six-week body-building course and now she is taking an adult-education course in composition at Paducah Community College. She spends her evenings outlining paragraphs.

"First, you have a topic sentence," she explains to Leroy. "Then you divide it up. Your secondary topic has to be connected to your primary topic."

To Leroy, this sounds intimidating. "I never was any good in English," he says.

"It makes a lot of sense."

90   "What are you doing this for, anyhow?"

She shrugs. "It's something to do." She stands up and lifts her dumbbells a few times.

"Driving a rig, nobody cared about my English."

"I'm not criticizing your English."

Norma Jean used to say, "If I lose ten minutes' sleep, I just drag all day." Now she stays up late, writing compositions. She got a B on her first paper—a how-to theme on soup-based casseroles. Recently Norma Jean has been cooking unusual foods—tacos, lasagna, Bombay chicken. She doesn't play the organ anymore, though her second paper was called "Why Music Is Important to Me." She sits at the kitchen table, concentrating on her outlines, while Leroy plays with his log house plans, practicing with a set of Lincoln Logs. The thought of getting a truckload of notched, numbered logs scares him, and he wants to be prepared. As he and Norma Jean work together at the kitchen table, Leroy has the hopeful thought that they are sharing something, but he knows he is a fool to think this. Norma Jean is miles away. He knows he is going to lose her. Like Mabel, he is just waiting for time to pass.

95   One day, Mabel is there before Norma Jean gets home from work, and Leroy finds himself confiding in her. Mabel, he realizes, must know Norma Jean better than he does.

"I don't know what's got into that girl," Mabel says. "She used to go to bed with the chickens. Now you say she's up all hours. Plus her a-smoking. I like to died."

"I want to make her this beautiful home," Leroy says, indicating the Lincoln Logs. "I don't think she even wants it. Maybe she was happier with me gone."

"She don't know what to make of you, coming home like this."

"Is that it?"

100   Mabel takes the roof off his Lincoln Log cabin. "You couldn't get *me* in a log cabin," she says. "I was raised in one. It's no picnic, let me tell you."

"They're different now," says Leroy.

"I tell you what," Mabel says, smiling oddly at Leroy.

"What?"

"Take her on down to Shiloh. Y'all need to get out together, stir a little. Her brain's all balled up over them books."

105   Leroy can see traces of Norma Jean's features in her mother's face. Mabel's worn face has the texture of crinkled cotton, but suddenly she looks pretty. It occurs to Leroy that Mabel has been hinting all along that she wants them to take her with them to Shiloh.

"Let's all go to Shiloh," he says. "You and me and her. Come Sunday."

Mabel throws up her hand in protest. "Oh, no, not me. Young folks want to be by theirselves."

When Norma Jean comes in with groceries, Leroy says excitedly. "Your mama here's been dying to go to Shiloh for thirty-five years. It's about time we went, don't you think?"

"I'm not going to butt in on anybody's second honeymoon," Mabel says.

110   "Who's going on a honeymoon, for Christ's sake?" Norma Jean says loudly.

"I never raised no daughter of mine to talk that-a-way," Mabel says.

"You ain't seen nothing yet," says Norma Jean. She starts putting away boxes and cans, slamming cabinet doors.

"There's a log cabin at Shiloh," Mabel says. "It was there during the battle. There's bullet holes in it."

"When are you going to *shut up* about Shiloh, Mama?" asks Norma Jean.

115   "I always thought Shiloh was the prettiest place, so full of history," Mabel goes on. "I just hoped y'all could see it once before I die, so you could tell me about it." Later, she whispers to Leroy. "You do what I said. A little change is what she needs."

"Your name means 'the king.'" Norma Jean says to Leroy that evening. He is trying to get her to go to Shiloh, and she is reading a book about another century.

"Well, I reckon I ought to be right proud."

"I guess so."

"Am I still king around here?"

120   Norma Jean flexes her biceps and feels them for hardness. "I'm not fooling around with anybody, if that's what you mean," she says.

"Would you tell me if you were?"

"I don't know."

"What does *your* name mean?"

"It was Marilyn Monroe's real name."

125   "No kidding!"

"Norma comes from the Normans. They were invaders," she says. She closes her book and looks hard at Leroy. "I'll go to Shiloh with you if you'll stop staring at me."

On Sunday, Norma Jean packs a picnic and they go to Shiloh. To Leroy's relief Mabel says she does not want to come with them. Norma Jean drives, and Leroy, sitting beside her, feels like some boring hitchhiker she has picked up. He tries some conversation, but she answers him in monosyllables. At Shiloh, she drives aimlessly through the park, past bluffs and trails and steep ravines. Shiloh is an immense place, and Leroy cannot see it as a battleground. It is not what he expected. He thought it would look like a golf course. Monuments are everywhere, showing through the thick clusters of trees. Norma Jean passes the log cabin Mabel mentioned. It is surrounded by tourists looking for bullet holes.

"That's not the kind of log house I've got in mind," says Leroy apologetically.

"I know *that*."

130   "This is a pretty place. Your mama was right."

"It's O.K.," says Norma Jean. "Well, we've seen it. I hope she's satisfied."

They burst out laughing together.

At the park museum, a movie on Shiloh is shown every half hour, but they decide that they don't want to see it. They buy a souvenir Confederate flag for Mabel, and then they find a picnic spot near the cemetery. Norma Jean has brought a picnic cooler, with pimento sandwiches, soft drinks, and Yodels. Leroy eats a sandwich and then smokes a joint, hiding it behind the picnic cooler. Norma Jean has quit smoking altogether. She is picking cake crumbs from the cellophane wrapper, like a fussy bird.

Leroy says, "So the boys in gray ended up in Corinth. The Union soldiers zapped 'em finally. April 7, 1862."

135   They both know that he doesn't know any history. He is just talking about some of the historical plaques they have read. He feels awkward, like a boy on a date with an older girl. They are still just making conversation.

"Corinth is where Mama eloped to," says Norma Jean.

They sit in silence and stare at the cemetery for the Union dead and, beyond, at a tall cluster of trees. Campers are parked nearby, bumper to bumper, and small children in bright clothing are cavorting and squealing. Norma Jean wads up the cake wrapper and squeezes it tightly in her hand. Without looking at Leroy, she says, "I want to leave you."

Leroy takes a bottle of Coke out of the cooler and flips off the cap. He holds the bottle poised near his mouth but cannot remember to take a drink. Finally he says, "No, you don't."

"Yes, I do."

140   "I won't let you."

"You can't stop me."

"Don't do me that way."

Leroy knows Norma Jean will have her own way. "Didn't I promise to be home from now on?" he says.

"In some ways, a woman prefers a man who wanders," says Norma Jean. "That sounds crazy, I know."

145   "You're not crazy."

Leroy remembers to drink from his Coke. Then he says, "Yes, you *are* crazy. You and me could start all over again. Right back at the beginning."

"We *have* started all over again," says Norma Jean. "And this is how it turned out."

"What did I do wrong?"

"Nothing."

150   "Is this one of those women's lib things?" Leroy asks.

"Don't be funny."

The cemetery, a green slope dotted with white markers, looks like a subdivision site. Leroy is trying to comprehend that his marriage is breaking up, but for some reason he is wondering about white slabs in a graveyard.

"Everything was fine till Mama caught me smoking," says Norma Jean, standing up. "That set something off."

"What are you talking about?"

155   "She won't leave me alone—*you* won't leave me alone." Norma Jean seems to be crying, but she is looking away from him. "I feel eighteen again. I can't face that all over again." She starts walking away. "No, it *wasn't* fine. I don't know what I'm saying. Forget it."

Leroy takes a lungful of smoke and closes his eyes as Norma Jean's words sink in. He tries to focus on the fact that thirty-five hundred soldiers died on the grounds around him. He can only think of that war as a board game with plastic soldiers. Leroy almost smiles, as he compares the Confederates' daring attack on the Union camps and Virgil Mathis's raid on the bowling alley. General Grant, drunk and furious, shoved the Southerners back to Corinth, where Mabel and Jet Beasley were married years later, when Mabel was still thin and good-looking. The next day, Mabel and Jet visited the battleground, and then Norma Jean was born, and then she married Leroy and they had a baby, which they lost, and now Leroy and Norma Jean are here at the same battleground. Leroy knows he is leaving out a lot. He is leaving out the insides of history. History was always just names and dates to him. It occurs to him that building a house of logs is similarly empty—too simple. And the real inner workings of a marriage, like most of history, have escaped him. Now he sees that building a log house is the dumbest idea he could have had. It was clumsy of him to think Norma Jean would want a log house. It was a crazy idea. He'll have to think of something else, quickly. He will wad the blueprints into tight balls and fling them into the lake. Then he'll get moving again. He opens his eyes. Norma Jean has moved away and is walking through the cemetery, following a serpentine brick path.

Leroy gets up to follow his wife, but his good leg is asleep and his bad leg still hurts him. Norma Jean is far away, walking rapidly toward the bluff by the river, and he tries to hobble toward her. Some children run past him, screaming noisily. Norma Jean has reached the bluff, and she is looking out over the Tennessee River. Now she turns toward Leroy and waves her arms. Is she beckoning to him? She seems to be doing an exercise for her chest muscles. The sky is unusually pale—the color of the dust ruffle Mabel made for their bed.

TIM O'BRIEN

Tim O'Brien, born in 1947 in Austin, Minnesota, was drafted into the army in 1968 and served as an infantryman in Vietnam. Drawing on this experience he wrote a memoir, If I Die in a Combat Zone *(1973), in which he explains that he did not believe in the Vietnam War, considered dodging the draft, but, lacking the courage to do so, he served, largely out of fear and embarrassment. A later book, a novel called* Going after Cacciato, *won the National Book Award in 1979.*

"The Things They Carried," first published in 1986, in 1990 was republished as one of a series of interlocking stories in a book entitled The Things They Carried. *In one of the stories, entitled "How To Tell a True War Story," O'Brien writes,*

> *A true war story is never moral. It does not instruct, nor encourage virtue, nor suggest models of proper human behavior. . . . If a story seems moral, do not believe it. If at the end of a war story you feel uplifted, or if you feel that some small bit of rectitude has been salvaged from the larger waste, then you have been made the victim of a very old and terrible lie. There is no rectitude whatsoever. There is no virtue. As a first rule of thumb, therefore, you can tell a true war story by its absolute and uncompromising allegiance to obscenity and evil.*

The Things They Carried
[1986]

First Lieutenant Jimmy Cross carried letters from a girl named Martha, a junior at Mount Sebastian College in New Jersey. They were not love letters, but Lieutenant Cross was hoping, so he kept them folded in plastic at the bottom of his rucksack. In the late afternoon, after a day's march, he would dig his foxhole, wash his hands under a canteen, unwrap the letters, hold them with the tips of his fingers, and spend the last hour of light pretending. He would imagine romantic camping trips into the White Mountains in New Hampshire. He would sometimes taste the envelope flaps, knowing her tongue had been there. More than anything, he wanted Martha to love him as he loved her, but the letters were mostly chatty, elusive on the matter of love. She was a virgin, he was almost sure. She was an English major at Mount Sebastian, and she wrote beautifully about her professors and roommates and midterm exams, about her respect for Chaucer and her great affection for Virginia Woolf. She often quoted lines of poetry; she never mentioned the war, except to say, Jimmy, take care of yourself. The letters weighed ten ounces. They were signed "Love, Martha," but Lieutenant Cross understood that Love was only a way of signing and did not mean what he sometimes pretended it meant. At dusk, he would carefully return the letters to his rucksack. Slowly, a bit distracted, he would get up and move among his men, checking the perimeter, then at full dark he would return to his hole and watch the night and wonder if Martha was a virgin.

The things they carried were largely determined by necessity. Among the necessities or near-necessities were P-38 can openers, pocket knives, heat tabs, wrist watches, dog tags, mosquito repellent, chewing gum, candy, cigarettes, salt tablets, packets of Kool-Aid, lighters, matches, sewing kits, Military Payment Certificates, C rations, and two or three canteens of water. Together, these items weighed between fifteen and twenty pounds, depending upon a man's habits or rate of metabolism. Henry Dobbins, who was a big man, carried extra rations; he was especially fond of canned peaches in heavy syrup over pound cake. Dave Jensen, who practiced field hygiene, carried a toothbrush, dental floss, and several hotel-size bars of soap he'd stolen on R&R[1] in Sydney, Australia. Ted Lavender, who was scared, carried tranquilizers until he was shot in the head outside the village of Than Khe in mid-April. By necessity, and because it was SOP,[2] they all carried steel helmets that weighed five pounds including the liner and camouflage cover. They carried the standard fatigue jackets and trousers. Very few carried underwear. On their feet they carried jungle boots—2.1 pounds—and Dave Jensen carried three pairs of socks and a can of Dr. Scholl's foot powder as a precaution against trench foot. Until he was shot, Ted Lavender carried six or seven ounces of premium dope, which for him was a necessity. Mitchell Sanders, the RTO,[3] carried condoms. Norman Bowker carried a diary. Rat Kiley carried comic books. Kiowa, a devout Baptist, carried an illustrated New Testament that had been presented to him by his father, who taught Sunday school in Oklahoma City, Oklahoma. As a hedge against bad times, however, Kiowa also carried his grandmother's distrust of the white man, his grandfather's old hunting hatchet. Necessity dictated. Because the land was mined and booby-trapped, it was SOP for each man to carry a steel-centered, nylon-covered flak jacket, which weighed 6.7 pounds, but which on hot days seemed much heavier. Because you could die so quickly, each man carried at least one large compress bandage, usually in the helmet band for easy access. Because the nights were cold, and because the monsoons were wet, each carried a green plastic poncho that could be used as a raincoat or groundsheet or makeshift tent. With its quilted liner, the poncho weighed almost two pounds, but it was worth every ounce. In April, for instance, when Ted Lavender was shot, they used his poncho to wrap him up, then to carry him across the paddy, then to lift him into the chopper that took him away.

They were called legs or grunts.

To carry something was to "hump" it, as when Lieutenant Jimmy Cross humped his love for Martha up the hills and through the swamps. In its intransitive form, "to hump" meant "to walk," or "to march," but it implied burdens far beyond the intransitive.

5   Almost everyone humped photographs. In his wallet, Lieutenant Cross carried two photographs of Martha. The first was a Kodachrome snapshot signed "Love," though he knew better. She stood against a brick wall. Her eyes were gray and neutral, her lips slightly open as she stared straight-on at the camera. At night, sometimes, Lieutenant Cross wondered who had taken the picture, because he knew she had boyfriends, because he loved her so much, and because he could see the shadow of the picture taker spreading out against the brick wall. The second photograph had been clipped from the 1968 Mount Sebastian yearbook. It was an action shot—women's volleyball—and Martha was bent horizontal to the floor, reaching, the palms of her hands in sharp focus, the tongue taut, the expression frank and competitive. There was no visible sweat. She wore white gym shorts. Her legs, he

---

[1]**R&R** rest and rehabilitation leave. [2]**SOP** standard operating procedure. [3]**RTO** radio and telephone operator.

thought, were almost certainly the legs of a virgin, dry and without hair, the left knee cocked and carrying her entire weight, which was just over one hundred pounds. Lieutenant Cross remembered touching that left knee. A dark theater, he remembered, and the movie was *Bonnie and Clyde,* and Martha wore a tweed skirt, and during the final scene, when he touched her knee, she turned and looked at him in a sad, sober way that made him pull his hand back, but he would always remember the feel of the tweed skirt and the knee beneath it and the sound of the gunfire that killed Bonnie and Clyde, how embarrassing it was, how slow and oppressive. He remembered kissing her goodnight at the dorm door. Right then, he thought, he should've done something brave. He should've carried her up the stairs to her room and tied her to the bed and touched that left knee all night long. He should've risked it. Whenever he looked at the photographs, he thought of new things he should've done.

What they carried was partly a function of rank, partly of field specialty.

As a first lieutenant and platoon leader, Jimmy Cross carried a compass, maps, code books, binoculars, and a .45-caliber pistol that weighed 2.9 pounds fully loaded. He carried a strobe light and the responsibility for the lives of his men.

As an RTO, Mitchell Sanders carried the PRC-25 radio, a killer, twenty-six pounds with its battery.

As a medic, Rat Kiley carried a canvas satchel filled with morphine and plasma and malaria tablets and surgical tape and comic books and all the things a medic must carry, including M&M's[4] for especially bad wounds, for a total weight of nearly twenty pounds.

10   As a big man, therefore a machine gunner, Henry Dobbins carried the M-60, which weighed twenty-three pounds unloaded, but which was almost always loaded. In addition, Dobbins carried between ten and fifteen pounds of ammunition draped in belts across his chest and shoulders.

As PFCs or Spec 4s, most of them were common grunts and carried the standard M-16 gas-operated assault rifle. The weapon weighed 7.5 pounds unloaded, 8.2 pounds with its full twenty-round magazine. Depending on numerous factors, such as topography and psychology, the riflemen carried anywhere from twelve to twenty magazines, usually in cloth bandoliers, adding on another 8.4 pounds at minimum, fourteen pounds at maximum. When it was available, they also carried M-16 maintenance gear—rods and steel brushes and swabs and tubes of LSA oil—all of which weighed about a pound. Among the grunts, some carried the M-79 grenade launcher, 5.9 pounds unloaded, a reasonably light weapon except for the ammunition, which was heavy. A single round weighed ten ounces. The typical load was twenty-five rounds. But Ted Lavender, who was scared, carried thirty-four rounds when he was shot and killed outside Than Khe, and he went down under an exceptional burden, more than twenty pounds of ammunition, plus the flak jacket and helmet and rations and water and toilet paper and tranquilizers and all the rest, plus the unweighed fear. He was dead weight. There was no twitching or flopping. Kiowa, who saw it happen, said it was like watching a rock fall, or a big sandbag or something—just boom, then down—not like the movies where the dead guy rolls around and does fancy spins

---

[4]**M&M** joking term for medical supplies.

and goes ass over teakettle—not like that, Kiowa said, the poor bastard just flat-fuck fell. Boom. Down. Nothing else. It was a bright morning in mid-April. Lieutenant Cross felt the pain. He blamed himself. They stripped off Lavender's canteens and ammo, all the heavy things, and Rat Kiley said the obvious, the guy's dead, and Mitchell Sanders used his radio to report one U.S. KIA[5] and to request a chopper. Then they wrapped Lavender in his poncho. They carried him out to a dry paddy, established security, and sat smoking the dead man's dope until the chopper came. Lieutenant Cross kept to himself. He pictured Martha's smooth young face, thinking he loved her more than anything, more than his men, and now Ted Lavender was dead because he loved her so much and could not stop thinking about her. When the dust-off arrived, they carried Lavender aboard. Afterward they burned Than Khe. They marched until dusk, then dug their holes, and that night Kiowa kept explaining how you had to be there, how fast it was, how the poor guy just dropped like so much concrete. Boom-down, he said. Like cement.

In addition to the three standard weapons—the M-60, M-16, and M-79— they carried whatever presented itself, or whatever seemed appropriate as a means of killing or staying alive. They carried catch-as-catch-can. At various times, in various situations, they carried MD14s and CARD15s and Swedish Ks and grease guns and captured AK-47s and Chi-Coms and RPGs and Simonov carbines and black-market Uzis and .38-caliber Smith & Wesson handguns and 66 mm LAWs and shotguns and silencers and blackjacks and bayonets and C-4 plastic explosives. Lee Strunk carried a slingshot; a weapon of last resort, he called it. Mitchell Sanders carried brass knuckles. Kiowa carried his grandfather's feathered hatchet. Every third or fourth man carried a Claymore antipersonnel mine—3.5 pounds with its firing device. They all carried fragmentation grenades—fourteen ounces each. They all carried at least one M-18 colored smoke grenade—twenty-four ounces. Some carried CS or tear-gas grenades. Some carried white-phosphorus grenades. They carried all they could bear, and then some, including a silent awe for the terrible power of the things they carried.

In the first week of April, before Lavender died, Lieutenant Jimmy Cross received a good-luck charm from Martha. It was a simple pebble, an ounce at most. Smooth to the touch, it was a milky-white color with flecks of orange and violet, oval-shaped, like a miniature egg. In the accompanying letter, Martha wrote that she had found the pebble on the Jersey shoreline, precisely where the land touched water at high tide, where things came together but also separated. It was this separate-but-together quality, she wrote, that had inspired her to pick up the pebble and to carry it in her breast pocket for several days, where it seemed weightless, and then to send it through the mail, by air, as a token of her truest feelings for him. Lieutenant Cross found this romantic. But he wondered what her truest feelings were, exactly, and what she meant by separate-but-together. He wondered how the tides and waves had come into play on that afternoon along the Jersey shoreline when Martha saw the pebble and bent down to rescue it from geology. He imagined bare feet. Martha was a poet, with the poet's sensibilities, and her feet would be brown and bare, the toenails unpainted, the eyes

---

[5]**KIA** killed in action.

chilly and somber like the ocean in March, and though it was painful, he wondered who had been with her that afternoon. He imagined a pair of shadows moving along the strip of sand where things came together but also separated. It was phantom jealousy, he knew, but he couldn't help himself. He loved her so much. On the march, through the hot days of early April, he carried the pebble in his mouth, turning it with his tongue, tasting sea salts and moisture. His mind wandered. He had difficulty keeping his attention on the war. On occasion he would yell at his men to spread out the column, to keep their eyes open, but then he would slip away into daydreams, just pretending, walking barefoot along the Jersey shore, with Martha, carrying nothing. He would feel himself rising. Sun and waves and gentle winds, all love and lightness.

What they carried varied by mission.

15   When a mission took them to the mountains, they carried mosquito netting, machetes, canvas tarps, and extra bugjuice.

If a mission seemed especially hazardous, or if it involved a place they knew to be bad, they carried everything they could. In certain heavily mined AOs,[6] where the land was dense with Toe Poppers and Bouncing Betties, they took turns humping a twenty-eight-pound mine detector. With its headphones and big sensing plate, the equipment was a stress on the lower back and shoulders, awkward to handle, often useless because of the shrapnel in the earth, but they carried it anyway, partly for safety, partly for the illusion of safety.

On ambush, or other night missions, they carried peculiar little odds and ends. Kiowa always took along his New Testament and a pair of moccasins for silence. Dave Jensen carried night-sight vitamins high in carotin. Lee Strunk carried his slingshot; ammo, he claimed, would never be a problem. Rat Kiley carried brandy and M&M's. Until he was shot, Ted Lavender carried the starlight scope, which weighed 6.3 pounds with its aluminum carrying case. Henry Dobbins carried his girlfriend's panty hose wrapped around his neck as a comforter. They all carried ghosts. When dark came, they would move out single file across the meadows and paddies to their ambush coordinates, where they would quietly set up the Claymores and lie down and spend the night waiting.

Other missions were more complicated and required special equipment. In mid-April, it was their mission to search out and destroy the elaborate tunnel complexes in the Than Khe area south of Chu Lai. To blow the tunnels, they carried one-pound blocks of pentrite high explosives, four blocks to a man, sixty-eight pounds in all. They carried wiring, detonators, and battery-powdered clackers. Dave Jensen carried earplugs. Most often, before blowing the tunnels, they were ordered by higher command to search them, which was considered bad news, but by and large they just shrugged and carried out orders. Because he was a big man, Henry Dobbins was excused from tunnel duty. The others would draw numbers. Before Lavender died there were seventeen men in the platoon, and whoever drew the number seventeen would strip off his gear and crawl in headfirst with a flashlight and Lieutenant Cross's .45-caliber pistol. The rest of them would

---

[6]**AOs** areas of operation.

fan out as security. They would sit down or kneel, not facing the hole, listening to the ground beneath them, imagining cobwebs and ghosts, whatever was down there—the tunnel walls squeezing in—how the flashlight seemed impossibly heavy in the hand and how it was tunnel vision in the very strictest sense, compression in all ways, even time, and how you had to wiggle in—ass and elbows—a swallowed-up feeling—and how you found yourself worrying about odd things—will your flashlight go dead? Do rats carry rabies? If you screamed, how far would the sound carry? Would your buddies hear it? Would they have the courage to drag you out? In some respects, though not many, the waiting was worse than the tunnel itself. Imagination was a killer.

On April 16, when Lee Strunk drew the number seventeen, he laughed and muttered something and went down quickly. The morning was hot and very still. Not good, Kiowa said. He looked at the tunnel opening, then out across a dry paddy toward the village of Than Khe. Nothing moved. No clouds or birds or people. As they waited, the men smoked and drank Kool-Aid, not talking much, feeling sympathy for Lee Strunk but also feeling the luck of the draw. You win some, you lose some, said Mitchell Sanders, and sometimes you settle for a rain check. It was a tired line and no one laughed.

20   Henry Dobbins ate a tropical chocolate bar. Ted Lavender popped a tranquilizer and went off to pee.

After five minutes, Lieutenant Jimmy Cross moved to the tunnel, leaned down, and examined the darkness. Trouble, he thought—a cave-in maybe. And then suddenly, without willing it, he was thinking about Martha. The stresses and fractures, the quick collapse, the two of them buried alive under all that weight. Dense, crushing love. Kneeling, watching the hole, he tried to concentrate on Lee Strunk and the war, all the dangers, but his love was too much for him, he felt paralyzed, he wanted to sleep inside her lungs and breathe her blood and be smothered. He wanted her to be a virgin and not a virgin, all at once. He wanted to know her. Intimate secrets—why poetry? Why so sad? Why that grayness in her eyes? Why so alone? Not lonely, just alone—riding her bike across campus or sitting off by herself in the cafeteria. Even dancing, she danced alone—and it was the aloneness that filled him with love. He remembered telling her that one evening. How she nodded and looked away. And how, later, when he kissed her, she received the kiss without returning it, her eyes wide open, not afraid, not a virgin's eyes, just flat and uninvolved.

Lieutenant Cross gazed at the tunnel. But he was not there. He was buried with Martha under the white sand at the Jersey shore. They were pressed together, and the pebble in his mouth was her tongue. He was smiling. Vaguely, he was aware of how quiet the day was, the sullen paddies, yet he could not bring himself to worry about matters of security. He was beyond that. He was just a kid at war, in love. He was twenty-two years old. He couldn't help it.

A few moments later Lee Strunk crawled out of the tunnel. He came up grinning, filthy but alive. Lieutenant Cross nodded and closed his eyes while the others clapped Strunk on the back and made jokes about rising from the dead.

Worms, Rat Kiley said. Right out of the grave. Fuckin' zombie.

25   The men laughed. They all felt great relief.

Spook City, said Mitchell Sanders.

Lee Strunk made a funny ghost sound, a kind of moaning, yet very happy, and right then, when Strunk made that high happy moaning sound, when he went *Ahhooooo,* right then Ted Lavender was shot in the head on his way back from peeing. He lay with his mouth open. The teeth were broken. There was a swollen black bruise under his left eye. The cheekbone was gone. Oh shit, Rat Kiley said, the guy's dead. The guy's dead, he kept saying, which seemed profound—the guy's dead. I mean really.

The things they carried were determined to some extent by superstition. Lieutenant Cross carried his good-luck pebble. Dave Jensen carried a rabbit's foot. Norman Bowker, otherwise a very gentle person, carried a thumb that had been presented to him as a gift by Mitchell Sanders. The thumb was dark brown, rubbery to the touch, and weighed four ounces at most. It had been cut from a VC corpse, a boy of fifteen or sixteen. They'd found him at the bottom of an irrigation ditch, badly burned, flies in his mouth and eyes. The boy wore black shorts and sandals. At the time of his death he had been carrying a pouch of rice, a rifle, and three magazines of ammunition.

You want my opinion, Mitchell Sanders said, there's a definite moral here.

30   He put his hand on the dead boy's wrist. He was quiet for a time, as if counting a pulse, then he patted the stomach, almost affectionately, and used Kiowa's hunting hatchet to remove the thumb.

Henry Dobbins asked what the moral was.

Moral?

You know. *Moral.*

Sanders wrapped the thumb in toilet paper and handed it across to Norman Bowker. There was no blood. Smiling, he kicked the boy's head, watched the flies scatter, and said, It's like with that old TV show—Paladin. Have gun, will travel.

35   Henry Dobbins thought about it.

Yeah, well, he finally said. I don't see no moral.

There it *is,* man.

Fuck off.

They carried USO stationery and pencils and pens. They carried Sterno, safety pins, trip flares, signal flares, spools of wire, razor blades, chewing tobacco, liberated joss sticks and statuettes of the smiling Buddha, candles, grease pencils, *The Stars and Stripes,* fingernail clippers, Psy Ops leaflets, bush hats, bolos, and much more. Twice a week, when the resupply choppers came in, they carried hot chow in green Mermite cans and large canvas bags filled with iced beer and soda pop. They carried plastic water containers, each with a two gallon capacity. Mitchell Sanders carried a set of starched tiger fatigues for special occasions. Henry Dobbins carried Black Flag insecticide. Dave Jensen carried empty sandbags that could be filled at night for added protection. Lee Strunk carried tanning lotion. Some things they carried in common. Taking turns, they carried the big PRC-77 scrambler radio, which weighed thirty pounds with its battery. They shared the weight of memory. They took up what others could no longer bear. Often, they carried each other, the wounded or weak. They carried infections. They carried chess sets, basketballs, Vietnamese-English dictionaries, insignia of rank, Bronze Stars and Purple Hearts, plastic cards imprinted with the Code of

Conduct. They carried diseases, among them malaria and dysentery. They carried lice and ringworm and leeches and paddy algae and various rots and molds. They carried the land itself—Vietnam, the place, the soil—a powdery orange-red dust that covered their boots and fatigues and faces. They carried the sky. The whole atmosphere, they carried it, the humidity, the monsoons, the stink of fungus and decay, all of it, they carried gravity. They moved like mules. By daylight they took sniper fire, at night they were mortared, but it was not battle, it was just the endless march, village to village, without purpose, nothing won or lost. They marched for the sake of the march. They plodded along slowly, dumbly, leaning forward against the heat, unthinking, all blood and bone, simple grunts, soldiering with their legs, toiling up the hills and down into the paddies and across the rivers and up again and down, just humping, one step and then the next and then another, but no volition, no will, because it was automatic, it was anatomy, and the war was entirely a matter of posture and carriage, the hump was everything, a kind of inertia, a kind of emptiness, a dullness of desire and intellect and conscience and hope and human sensibility. Their principles were in their feet. Their calculations were biological. They had no sense of strategy or mission. They searched the villages without knowing what to look for, nor caring, kicking over jars of rice, frisking children and old men, blowing tunnels, sometimes setting fires and sometimes not, then forming up and moving on to the next village, then other villages, where it would always be the same. They carried their own lives. The pressures were enormous. In the heat of early afternoon, they would remove their helmets and flak jackets, walking bare, which was dangerous but which helped ease the strain. They would often discard things along the route of march. Purely for comfort, they would throw away rations, blow their Claymores and grenades, no matter, because by nightfall the resupply choppers would arrive with more of the same, then a day or two later still more, fresh watermelons and crates of ammunition and sunglasses and woolen sweaters—the resources were stunning—sparklers for the Fourth of July, colored eggs for Easter. It was the great American war chest—the fruits of sciences, the smoke stacks, the canneries, the arsenals at Hartford, the Minnesota forests, the machine shops, the vast fields of corn and wheat—they carried like freight trains; they carried it on their backs and shoulders—and for all the ambiguities of Vietnam, all the mysteries and unknowns, there was at least the single abiding certainty that they would never be at a loss for things to carry.

40   After the chopper took Lavender away, Lieutenant Jimmy Cross led his men into the village of Than Khe. They burned everything. They shot chickens and dogs, they trashed the village well, they called in artillery and watched the wreckage, then they marched for several hours through the hot afternoon, and then at dusk, while Kiowa explained how Lavender died, Lieutenant Cross found himself trembling.

He tried not to cry. With his entrenching tool, which weighed five pounds, he began digging a hole in the earth.

He felt shame. He hated himself. He had loved Martha more than his men, and as a consequence Lavender was now dead, and this was something he would have to carry like a stone in his stomach for the rest of the war.

All he could do was dig. He used his entrenching tool like an ax, slashing, feeling both love and hate, and then later, when it was full dark, he sat at the bottom of his foxhole and wept. It went on for a long while. In part, he was grieving for Ted Lavender, but mostly it was for Martha, and for himself, because she belonged to another world, which was not quite real, and because she was a junior at Mount Sebastian College in New Jersey, a poet and a virgin and uninvolved, and because he realized she did not love him and never would.

Like cement, Kiowa whispered in the dark. I swear to God—boom-down. Not a word.

45   I've heard this, said Norman Bowker.

A pisser, you know? Still zipping himself up. Zapped while zipping.

All right, fine. That's enough.

Yeah, but you had to see it, the guy just—

I *heard,* man. Cement. So why not shut the fuck *up?*

50   Kiowa shook his head sadly and glanced over at the hole where Lieutenant Jimmy Cross sat watching the night. The air was thick and wet. A warm, dense fog had settled over the paddies and there was the stillness that precedes rain.

After a time Kiowa sighed.

One thing for sure, he said. The lieutenant's in some deep hurt. I mean that crying jag—the way he was carrying on—it wasn't fake or anything, it was real heavy-duty hurt. The man cares.

Sure, Norman Bowker said.

Say what you want, the man does care.

55   We all got problems.

Not Lavender.

No, I guess not, Bowker said. Do me a favor, though.

Shut up?

That's a smart Indian. Shut up.

60   Shrugging, Kiowa pulled off his boots. He wanted to say more, just to lighten up his sleep, but instead he opened his New Testament and arranged it beneath his head as a pillow. The fog made things seem hollow and unattached. He tried not to think about Ted Lavender, but then he was thinking how fast it was, no drama, down and dead, and how it was hard to feel anything except surprise. It seemed unchristian. He wished he could find some great sadness, or even anger, but the emotion wasn't there and he couldn't make it happen. Mostly he felt pleased to be alive. He liked the smell of the New Testament under his cheek, the leather and ink and paper and glue, whatever the chemicals were. He liked hearing the sounds of night. Even his fatigue, it felt fine, the stiff muscles and the prickly awareness of his own body, a floating feeling. He enjoyed not being dead. Lying there, Kiowa admired Lieutenant Jimmy Cross's capacity for grief. He wanted to share the man's pain, he wanted to care as Jimmy Cross cared. And yet when he closed his eyes, all he could think was Boom-down, and all he could feel was the pleasure of having his boots off and the fog curling in around him and the damp soil and the Bible smells and the plush comfort of night.

After a moment Norman Bowker sat up in the dark.

What the hell, he said. You want to talk, *talk*. Tell it to me.

Forget it.

No, man, go on. One thing I hate, it's a silent Indian.

65   For the most part they carried themselves with poise, a kind of dignity. Now and then, however, there were times of panic, when they squealed or wanted to squeal but couldn't, when they twitched and made moaning sounds and covered their heads and said Dear Jesus and flopped around on the earth and fired their weapons blindly and cringed and sobbed and begged for the noise to stop and went wild and made stupid promises to themselves and to God and to their mothers and fathers, hoping not to die. In different ways, it happened to all of them. Afterward, when the firing ended, they would blink and peek up. They would touch their bodies, feeling shame, then quickly hiding it. They would force themselves to stand. As if in slow motion, frame by frame, the world would take on the old logic—absolute silence, then the wind, then sunlight, then voices. It was the burden of being alive. Awkwardly, the men would reassemble themselves, first in private, then in groups, becoming soldiers again. They would repair the leaks in their eyes. They would check for casualties, call in dustoffs, light cigarettes, try to smile, clear their throats and spit and begin cleaning their weapons. After a time someone would shake his head and say, No lie, I almost shit my pants, and someone else would laugh, which meant it was bad, yes, but the guy had obviously not shit his pants, it wasn't that bad, and in any case nobody would ever do such a thing and then go ahead and talk about it. They would squint into the dense, oppressive sunlight. For a few moments, perhaps, they would fall silent, lighting a joint and tracking its passage from man to man, inhaling, holding in the humiliation. Scary stuff, one of them might say. But then someone else would grin or flick his eyebrows and say, Roger-dodger, almost cut me a new asshole, *almost.*

There were numerous such poses. Some carried themselves with a sort of wistful resignation, others with pride or stiff soldierly discipline or good humor or macho zeal. They were afraid of dying but they were even more afraid to show it.

They found jokes to tell.

They used a hard vocabulary to contain the terrible softness. *Greased,* they'd say. *Offed, lit up, zapped while zipping.* It wasn't cruelty, just stage presence. They were actors and the war came at them in 3-D. When someone died, it wasn't quite dying, because in a curious way it seemed scripted, and because they had their lines mostly memorized, irony mixed with tragedy, and because they called it by other names, as if to encyst and destroy the reality of death itself. They kicked corpses. They cut off thumbs. They talked grunt lingo. They told stories about Ted Lavender's supply of tranquilizers, how the poor guy didn't feel a thing, how incredibly tranquil he was.

There's a moral here, said Mitchell Sanders.

70   They were waiting for Lavender's chopper, smoking the dead man's dope.

The moral's pretty obvious, Sanders said, and winked. Stay away from drugs. No joke, they'll ruin your day every time.

Cute, said Henry Dobbins.

Mind-blower, get it? Talk about wiggy—nothing left, just blood and brains.

They made themselves laugh.

75   There it is, they'd say, over and over, as if the repetition itself were an act of poise, a balance between crazy and almost crazy, knowing without going.

There it is, which meant be cool, let it ride, because oh yeah, man, you can't change what can't be changed, there it is, there it absolutely and positively and fucking well *is.*

They were tough.

They carried all the emotional baggage of men who might die. Grief, terror, love, longing—these were intangibles, but the intangibles had their own mass and specific gravity, they had tangible weight. They carried shameful memories. They carried the common secret of cowardice barely restrained, the instinct to run or freeze or hide, and in many respects this was the heaviest burden of all, for it could never be put down, it required perfect balance and perfect posture. They carried their reputations. They carried the soldier's greatest fear, which was the fear of blushing. Men killed, and died, because they were embarrassed not to. It was what had brought them to the war in the first place, nothing positive, no dreams of glory or honor, just to avoid the blush of dishonor. They died so as not to die of embarrassment. They crawled into tunnels and walked point and advanced under fire. Each morning, despite the unknowns, they made their legs move. They endured. They kept humping. They did not submit to the obvious alternative, which was simply to close the eyes and fall. So easy, really. Go limp and tumble to the ground and let the muscles unwind and not speak and not budge until your buddies picked you up and lifted you into the chopper that would roar and dip its nose and carry you off to the world. A mere matter of falling, yet no one ever fell. It was not courage, exactly; the object was not valor. Rather, they were too frightened to be cowards.

By and large they carried these things inside, maintaining the masks of composure. They sneered at sick call. They spoke bitterly about guys who had found release by shooting off their own toes or fingers. Pussies, they'd say. Candyasses. It was fierce, mocking talk, with only a trace of envy or awe, but even so, the image played itself out behind their eyes.

They imagined the muzzle against flesh. They imagined the quick, sweet pain, then the evacuation to Japan, then a hospital with warm beds and cute geisha nurses.

80   They dreamed of freedom birds.

At night, on guard, staring into the dark, they were carried away by jumbo jets. They felt the rush of takeoff. *Gone!* they yelled. And then velocity, wings and engines, a smiling stewardess—but it was more than a plane, it was a real bird, a big sleek silver bird with feathers and talons and high screeching. They were flying. The weights fell off, there was nothing to bear. They laughed and held on tight, feeling the cold slap of wind and altitude, soaring, thinking *It's over, I'm gone!*—they were naked, they were light and free—it was all lightness, bright and fast and buoyant, light as light, a helium buzz in the brain, a giddy bubbling in the lungs as they were taken up over the clouds and the war, beyond duty, beyond gravity and mortification and global entanglements—*Sin loi!*[7] they yelled, *I'm sorry, motherfuckers, but I'm out of it, I'm goofed, I'm on a space cruise, I'm gone!*—and it was a restful, disencumbered sensation, just riding the light waves, sailing that big silver freedom bird over the mountains and oceans, over America, over the farms and great sleeping cities and cemeteries and highways and the Golden Arches of McDonald's. It was flight, a kind of fleeing, a kind of falling, falling

---

[7]***Sin loi*** Sorry.

higher and higher, spinning off the edge of the earth and beyond the sun and through the vast, silent vacuum where there were no burdens and where everything weighed exactly nothing. *Gone!* they screamed, *I'm sorry but I'm gone!* And so at night, not quite dreaming, they gave themselves over to lightness, they were carried, they were purely borne.

On the morning after Ted Lavender died, First Lieutenant Jimmy Cross crouched at the bottom of his foxhole and burned Martha's letters. Then he burned the two photographs. There was a steady rain falling, which made it difficult, but he used heat tabs and Sterno to build a small fire, screening it with his body, holding the photographs over the tight blue flame with the tips of his fingers.

He realized it was only a gesture. Stupid, he thought. Sentimental, too, but mostly just stupid.

Lavender was dead. You couldn't burn the blame.

85   Besides, the letters were in his head. And even now, without photographs, Lieutenant Cross could see Martha playing volleyball in her white gym shorts and yellow T-shirt. He could see her moving in the rain.

When the fire died out, Lieutenant Cross pulled his poncho over his shoulders and ate breakfast from a can.

There was no great mystery, he decided.

In those burned letters Martha had never mentioned the war, except to say, Jimmy, take care of yourself. She wasn't involved. She signed the letters "Love," but it wasn't love, and all the fine lines and technicalities did not matter.

The morning came up wet and blurry. Everything seemed part of everything else, the fog and Martha and the deepening rain.

90   It was a war, after all.

Half smiling, Lieutenant Jimmy Cross took out his maps. He shook his head hard, as if to clear it, then bent forward and began planning the day's march. In ten minutes, or maybe twenty, he would rouse the men and they would pack up and head west, where the maps showed the country to be green and inviting. They would do what they had always done. The rain might add some weight, but otherwise it would be one more day layered upon all the other days.

He was realistic about it. There was that new hardness in his stomach.

No more fantasies, he told himself.

Henceforth, when he thought about Martha, it would be only to think that she belonged elsewhere. He would shut down the daydreams. This was not Mount Sebastian, it was another world, where there were no pretty poems or midterm exams, a place where men died because of carelessness and gross stupidity. Kiowa was right. Boom-down, and you were dead, never partly dead.

95   Briefly, in the rain, Lieutenant Cross saw Martha's gray eyes gazing back at him.

He understood.

It was very sad, he thought. The things men carried inside. The things men did or felt they had to do.

He almost nodded at her, but didn't.

Instead he went back to his maps. He was now determined to perform his duties firmly and without negligence. It wouldn't help Lavender, he knew that, but from this point on he would comport himself as a soldier. He would dispose of his good-luck pebble. Swallow it, maybe, or use Lee Strunk's slingshot, or just drop it along the trail. On the march he would impose strict field discipline. He would be careful to send out flank security, to prevent straggling or bunching up, to keep his troops moving at the proper pace and at the proper interval. He would insist on clean weapons. He would confiscate the remainder of Lavender's dope. Later in the day, perhaps, he would call the men together and speak to them plainly. He would accept the blame for what had happened to Ted Lavender. He would be a man about it. He would look them in the eyes, keeping his chin level, and he would issue the new SOPs in a calm, impersonal tone of voice, an officer's voice, leaving no room for argument or discussion. Commencing immediately, he'd tell them, they would no longer abandon equipment along the route of march. They would police up their acts. They would get their shit together, and keep it together, and maintain it neatly and in good working order.

100   He would not tolerate laxity. He would show strength, distancing himself.

Among the men there would be grumbling, of course, and maybe worse, because their days would seem longer and their loads heavier, but Lieutenant Cross reminded himself that his obligation was not to be loved but to lead. He would dispense with love; it was not now a factor. And if anyone quarreled or complained, he would simply tighten his lips and arrange his shoulders in the correct command posture. He might give a curt little nod. Or he might not. He might just shrug and say Carry on, then they would saddle up and form into a column and move out toward the villages west of Than Khe.

AMY TAN

Amy Tan was born in 1952 in Oakland, California, two and a half years after her parents had emigrated from China. She entered Linfield College in Oregon but then followed a boyfriend to California State University at San Jose, where she shifted her major from premedical studies to English. After earning a master's degree in linguistics from San Jose, Tan worked as a language consultant and then, under the name of May Brown, as a freelance business writer.

In 1985, having decided to try her hand at fiction, she joined the Squaw Valley Community of Writers, a fiction workshop. In 1987 she visited China with her mother; on her return to the United States she learned that her agent had sold her first book, The Joy Luck Club, *a collection of 16 interwoven stories (including "Two Kinds") about four Chinese mothers and their four American daughters. She is also author of* The Kitchen God's Wife *(1991),* The Hundred Secret Senses *(1995), and* The Bonesetter's Daughter *(2001).*

Two Kinds   [1989]

My mother believed you could be anything you wanted to be in America. You could open a restaurant. You could work for the government and get good retirement. You could buy a house with almost no money down. You could become rich. You could become instantly famous.

"Of course you can be prodigy, too," my mother told me when I was nine. "You can be best anything. What does Auntie Lindo know? Her daughter, she is only best tricky."

America was where all my mother's hopes lay. She had come to San Francisco in 1949 after losing everything in China: her mother and father, her family home, her first husband, and two daughters, twin baby girls. But she never looked back with regret. Things could get better in so many ways.

We didn't immediately pick the right kind of prodigy. At first my mother thought I could be a Chinese Shirley Temple. We'd watch Shirley's old movies on TV as though they were training films. My mother would poke my arm and say, "*Ni kan*—You watch." And I would see Shirley tapping her feet, or singing a sailor song, or pursing her lips into a very round O while saying, "Oh my goodness."

5   "*Ni kan*," said my mother as Shirley's eyes flooded with tears. "You already know how. Don't need talent for crying!"

Soon after my mother got this idea about Shirley Temple, she took me to a beauty training school in the Mission district and put me in the hands of a student who could barely hold the scissors without shaking. Instead of getting big fat curls, I emerged with an uneven mass of crinkly black fuzz. My mother dragged me off to the bathroom and tried to wet down my hair.

"You look like Negro Chinese," she lamented, as if I had done this on purpose.

The instructor of the beauty training school had to lop off these soggy clumps to make my hair even again. "Peter Pan is very popular these days," the instructor assured my mother. I now had hair the length of a boy's, with straight-across bangs that hung at a slant two inches above my eyebrows. I liked the haircut and it made me actually look forward to my future fame.

In fact, in the beginning, I was just as excited as my mother, maybe even more so. I pictured this prodigy part of me as many different images, and I tried each one on for size. I was a dainty ballerina girl standing by the curtains, waiting to hear the right music that would send me floating on my tiptoes. I was like the Christ child lifted out of the straw manger, crying with holy indignity. I was Cinderella stepping from her pumpkin carriage with sparkly cartoon music filling the air.

10   In all of my imaginings, I was filled with a sense that I would soon become perfect. My mother and father would adore me. I would be beyond reproach. I would never feel the need to sulk, or to clamor for anything.

But sometimes the prodigy in me became impatient. "If you don't hurry up and get me out of here, I'm disappearing for good," it warned. "And then you'll always be nothing."

Every night after dinner, my mother and I would sit at the Formica-topped kitchen table. She would present new tests, taking her examples from stories of amazing children she had read in *Ripley's Believe It or Not,* or *Good Housekeeping, Reader's Digest,* and any of a dozen other magazines she kept in a pile in our bathroom. My mother got these magazines from people whose houses she cleaned. And since she cleaned many houses each week, we had a great assortment. She would look through them all, searching for stories about remarkable children.

The first night she brought out a story about a three-year-old boy who knew the capitals of all the states and even most of the European countries. A teacher was quoted as saying the little boy could also pronounce the names of the foreign cities correctly. "What's the capital of Finland?" my mother asked me, looking at the magazine story.

All I knew was the capital of California, because Sacramento was the name of the street we lived on in Chinatown. "Nairobi!" I guessed, saying the most foreign word I could think of. She checked to see if that might be one way to pronounce *Helsinki* before showing me the answer.

15   The tests got harder—multiplying numbers in my head, finding the queen of hearts in a deck of cards, trying to stand on my head without using my hands, predicting the daily temperatures in Los Angeles, New York, and London. One night I had to look at a page from the Bible for three minutes and then report everything I could remember. "Now Jehoshaphat had riches and honor in abundance and . . . that's all I remember, Ma," I said.

And after seeing, once again, my mother's disappointed face, something inside of me began to die. I hated the tests, the raised hopes and failed expectations. Before going to bed that night I looked in the mirror above the bathroom sink and when I saw only my face staring back—and understood that it would always be this ordinary face—I began to cry. Such a sad, ugly girl! I made high-pitched noises like a crazed animal, trying to scratch out the face in the mirror.

And then I saw what seemed to be the prodigy side of me—a face I had never seen before. I looked at my reflection, blinking so I could see more clearly. The girl staring back at me was angry, powerful. She and I were the same. I had new thoughts, willful thoughts, or rather, thoughts filled with lots of won'ts. I won't let her change me, I promised myself. I won't be what I'm not.

So now on nights when my mother presented her tests, I performed listlessly, my head propped on one arm. I pretended to be bored. And I was. I got so bored I started counting the bellows of the foghorns out on the bay while my mother drilled me in other areas. The sound was comforting and reminded me of the cow jumping over the moon. And the next day, I played a game with myself, seeing if my mother would give up on me before eight bellows. After a while I usually counted only one, maybe two bellows at most. At last she was beginning to give up hope.

Two or three months had gone by without any mention of my being a prodigy again. And then one day my mother was watching the *Ed Sullivan Show* on TV. The TV was old and the sound kept shorting out. Every time my mother got halfway up from the sofa to adjust the set, the sound would go back on and Sullivan would be talking. As soon as she sat down, Sullivan would go silent again. She got up, the TV broke into loud piano music. She sat down—silence. Up and down, back and forth, quiet and loud. It was like a stiff embraceless dance between her and the TV set. Finally she stood by the set with her hand on the sound dial.

20   She seemed entranced by the music, a frenzied little piano piece with this mesmerizing quality, which alternated between quick, playful passages and teasing, lilting ones.

"*Ni kan,*" my mother said, calling me over with hurried hand gestures, "Look here."

I could see why my mother was fascinated by the music. It was being pounded out by a little Chinese girl, about nine years old, with a Peter Pan haircut. The girl had the sauciness of a Shirley Temple. She was proudly modest, like a proper Chinese child. And she also did a fancy sweep of a curtsy, so that the fluffy skirt of her white dress cascaded slowly to the floor like the petals of a large carnation.

In spite of these warning signs, I wasn't worried. Our family had no piano and we couldn't afford to buy one, let alone reams of sheet music and piano lessons. So I could be generous in my comments when my mother bad-mouthed the little girl on TV.

"Play note right, but doesn't sound good!" complained my mother. "No singing sound."

25   "What are you picking on her for?" I said carelessly. "She's pretty good. Maybe she's not the best, but she's trying hard." I knew almost immediately I would be sorry I said that.

"Just like you," she said. "Not the best. Because you not trying." She gave a little huff as she let go of the sound dial and sat down on the sofa.

The little Chinese girl sat down also to play an encore of "Anitra's Dance" by Grieg.[1] I remember the song, because later on I had to learn how to play it.

Three days after watching the *Ed Sullivan Show*, my mother told me what my schedule would be for piano lessons and piano practice. She had talked to Mr. Chong, who lived on the first floor of our apartment building. Mr. Chong was a retired piano teacher, and my mother had traded house-cleaning services for weekly lessons and a piano for me to practice on every day, two hours a day, from four until six.

When my mother told me this, I felt as though I had been sent to hell. I whined, and then kicked my foot a little when I couldn't stand it any more.

30   "Why don't you like me the way I am? I'm not a genius! I can't play the piano. And even if I could, I wouldn't go on TV if you paid me a million dollars!"

My mother slapped me. "Who ask you be genius?" she shouted. "Only ask you be your best. For you sake. You think I want you be genius? Hnnh! What for! Who ask you!"

"So ungrateful," I heard her mutter in Chinese. "If she had as much talent as she has temper, she would be famous now."

Mr. Chong, whom I secretly nicknamed Old Chong, was very strange, always tapping his fingers to the silent music of an invisible orchestra. He looked ancient in my eyes. He had lost most of the hair on top of his head and he wore thick glasses and had eyes that always looked tired. But he must have been younger than I thought, since he lived with his mother and was not yet married.

I met Old Lady Chong once and that was enough. She had this peculiar smell like a baby that had done something in its pants and her fingers felt like a dead person's, like an old peach I once found in the back of the refrigerator; the skin just slid off the meat when I picked it up.

---

[1]**"Anitra's Dance"** section from the incidental music that Edvard Grieg (1843–1907) wrote for *Peer Gynt,* a play by Henrik Ibsen.

35   I soon found out why Old Chong had retired from teaching piano. He was deaf. "Like Beethoven!" he shouted to me. "We're both listening only in our head!" And he would start to conduct his frantic silent sonatas.

Our lessons went like this. He would open the book and point to different things, explaining their purpose: "Key! Treble! Bass! No sharps or flats! So this is C major! Listen now and play after me!"

And then he would play the C scale a few times, a simple chord, and then, as if inspired by an old, unreachable itch, he gradually added more notes and running trills and a pounding bass until the music was really something quite grand.

I would play after him, the simple scale, the simple chord, and then I just played some nonsense that sounded like a cat running up and down on top of garbage cans. Old Chong smiled and applauded and then said, "Very good! But now you must learn to keep time!"

So that's how I discovered that Old Chong's eyes were too slow to keep up with the wrong notes I was playing. He went through the motions in half-time. To help me keep rhythm, he stood behind me, pushing down on my right shoulder for every beat. He balanced pennies on top of my wrists so I would keep them still as I slowly played scales and arpeggios. He had me curve my hand around an apple and keep that shape when playing chords. He marched stiffly to show me how to make each finger dance up and down, staccato, like an obedient little soldier.

40   He taught me all these things, and that was how I also learned I could be lazy and get away with mistakes, lots of mistakes. If I hit the wrong notes because I hadn't practiced enough, I never corrected myself. I just kept playing in rhythm. And Old Chong kept conducting his own private reverie.

So maybe I never really gave myself a fair chance. I did pick up the basics pretty quickly, and I might have become a good pianist at that young age. But I was so determined not to try, not to be anybody different that I learned to play only the most ear-splitting preludes, the most discordant hymns.

Over the next year, I practiced like this, dutifully in my own way. And then one day I heard my mother and her friend Lindo Jong both talking in a loud bragging tone of voice so others could hear. It was after church, and I was leaning against the brick wall, wearing a dress with stiff white petticoats. Auntie Lindo's daughter, Waverly, who was about my age, was standing farther down the wall about five feet away. We had grown up together and shared all the closeness of two sisters squabbling over crayons and dolls. In other words, for the most part, we hated each other. I thought she was snotty. Waverly Jong had gained a certain amount of fame as "Chinatown's Littlest Chinese Chess Champion."

"She bring home too many trophy," Auntie Lindo lamented that Sunday. "All day she play chess. All day I have no time do nothing but dust off her winnings." She threw a scolding look at Waverly, who pretended not to see her.

"You lucky you don't have this problem," said Auntie Lindo with a sigh to my mother.

45   And my mother squared her shoulders and bragged: "Our problem worser than yours. If we ask Jing-mei wash dish, she hear nothing but music. It's like you can't stop this natural talent."

And right then, I was determined to put a stop to her foolish pride.

A few weeks later Old Chong and my mother conspired to have me play in a talent show that was held in the church hall. By then my parents had saved up enough to buy me a secondhand piano, a black Wurlitzer spinet with a scarred bench. It was the showpiece of our living room.

For the talent show, I was to play a piece called "Pleading Child," from Schumann's *Scenes from Childhood*.[2] It was a simple, moody piece that sounded more difficult than it was. I was supposed to memorize the whole thing. But I dawdled over it, playing a few bars and then cheating, looking up to see what notes followed. I never really listened to what I was playing. I daydreamed about being somewhere else, about being someone else.

The part I liked to practice best was the fancy curtsy: right foot out, touch the rose on the carpet with a pointed foot, sweep to the side, bend left leg, look up, and smile.

50   My parents invited all the couples from the Joy Luck Club to witness my debut. Auntie Lindo and Uncle Tin were there. Waverly and her two older brothers had also come. The first two rows were filled with children either younger or older than I was. The littlest ones got to go first. They recited simple nursery rhymes, squawked out tunes on miniature violins, twisted hula hoops, in pink ballet tutus, and when they bowed or curtsied, the audience would sigh in unison, "*Awww,*" and then clap enthusiastically.

When my turn came, I was very confident. I remember my childish excitement. It was as if I knew, without a doubt, that the prodigy side of me really did exist. I had no fear whatsoever, no nervousness. I remember thinking, This is it! This is it! I looked out over the audience, at my mother's blank face, my father's yawn, Auntie Lindo's stiff-lipped smile, Waverly's sulky expression. I had on a white dress layered with sheets of lace, and a pink bow in my Peter Pan haircut. As I sat down I envisioned people jumping to their feet and Ed Sullivan rushing up to introduce me to everyone on TV.

And I started to play. It was so beautiful. I was so caught up in how lovely I looked that at first I didn't worry how I would sound. So I was surprised when I hit the first wrong note. And then I hit another. And another. A chill started at the top of my head and began to trickle down. Yet I couldn't stop playing, as though my hands were bewitched. I kept thinking my fingers would adjust themselves back, like a train switching to the right track. I played this strange jumble through to the end, the sour notes staying with me all the way.

When I stood up, I discovered my legs were shaking. Maybe I had just been nervous, and the audience, like Old Chong, had seen me go through the right motions and had not heard anything wrong at all. I swept my right foot out, went down on my knee, looked up and smiled. The room was quiet, except for Old Chong, who was beaming and shouting, "Bravo! Bravo! Well done!" But then I saw my mother's face, her stricken face. The audience clapped weakly, and as I walked back to my chair, with my whole face quivering as I tried not to cry, I heard a little boy whisper loudly to his mother, "That was awful," and the mother whispered back, "Well, she certainly tried."

And now I realized how many people were in the audience—the whole world, it seemed. I was aware of eyes burning into my back. I felt the shame of my mother and father as they sat stiffly throughout the rest of the show.

---

[2]*Scenes from Childhood* a piano work by Robert Schumann (1810–1856) with twelve titled sections and an epilogue.

55   We could have escaped during intermission. Pride and some strange sense of honor must have anchored my parents to their chairs. And so we watched it all: the eighteen-year-old boy with a fake moustache who did a magic show and juggled flaming hoops while riding a unicycle. The breasted girl with white makeup who sang from *Madame Butterfly* and got honorable mention. And the eleven-year-old boy who won first prize playing a tricky violin song that sounded like a busy bee.

After the show, the Hsus, the Jongs, and the St. Clairs from the Joy Luck Club came up to my mother and father.

"Lots of talented kids," Auntie Lindo said vaguely, smiling broadly.

"That was somethin' else," said my father, and I wondered if he was referring to me in a humorous way, or whether he even remembered what I had done.

Waverly looked at me and shrugged her shoulders. "You aren't a genius like me," she said matter-of-factly. And if I hadn't felt so bad, I would have pulled her braids and punched her stomach.

60   But my mother's expression was what devastated me: a quiet, blank look that said she had lost everything. I felt the same way, and everybody seemed now to be coming up, like gawkers at the scene of an accident, to see what parts were actually missing.

When we got on the bus to go home, my father was humming the busy-bee tune and my mother was silent. I kept thinking she wanted to wait until we got home before shouting at me. But when my father unlocked the door to our apartment, my mother walked in and then went straight to the back, into the bedroom. No accusations. No blame. And in a way, I felt disappointed. I had been waiting for her to start shouting, so I could shout back and cry and blame her for all my misery.

I assumed my talent-show fiasco meant I would never have to play the piano again. But two days later, after school, my mother came out of the kitchen and saw me watching TV.

"Four clock," she reminded me as if it were any other day. I was stunned, as though she were asking me to go through the talent-show torture again. I wedged myself more tightly in front of the TV.

"Turn off TV," she called from the kitchen five minutes later.

65   I didn't budge. And then I decided. I didn't have to do what my mother said anymore. I wasn't her slave. This wasn't China. I had listened to her before and look what happened. She was the stupid one.

She came out from the kitchen and stood in the arched entryway of the living room. "Four clock," she said once again, louder.

"I'm not going to play anymore," I said nonchalantly. "Why should I? I'm not a genius."

She walked over and stood in front of the TV. I saw her chest was heaving up and down in an angry way.

"No!" I said, and I now felt stronger, as if my true self had finally emerged. So this was what had been inside me all along.

70   "No! I won't!" I screamed.

She snapped off the TV, yanked me by the arm and pulled me off the floor. She was frighteningly strong, half pulling, half carrying me toward the piano as I kicked the throw rugs under my feet. She lifted me up and onto the hard bench. I was sobbing by now, looking at her bitterly. Her chest was heaving even more and her mouth was open, smiling crazily as if she were pleased I was crying.

"You want me to be someone that I'm not!" I sobbed. "I'll never be the kind of daughter you want me to be!"

"Only two kinds of daughters," she shouted in Chinese. "Those who are obedient and those who follow their own mind! Only one kind of daughter can live in this house. Obedient daughter!"

"Then I wish I wasn't your daughter. I wish you weren't my mother," I shouted. As I said these things I got scared. It felt like worms and toads and slimy things crawling out of my chest, but it also felt good, that this awful side of me had surfaced, at last.

75   "Too late change this," said my mother shrilly.

And I could sense her anger rising to its breaking point. I wanted to see it spill over. And that's when I remembered the babies she had lost in China, the ones we never talked about. "Then I wish I'd never been born!" I shouted. "I wish I were dead! Like them."

It was as if I had said the magic words. Alakazam!—and her face went blank, her mouth closed, her arms went slack, and she backed out of the room, stunned, as if she were blowing away like a small brown leaf, thin, brittle, lifeless.

It was not the only disappointment my mother felt in me. In the years that followed, I failed her so many times, each time asserting my own will, my right to fall short of expectations. I didn't get straight As. I didn't become class president. I didn't get into Stanford. I dropped out of college.

Unlike my mother, I did not believe I could be anything I wanted to be. I could only be me.

80   And for all those years, we never talked about the disaster at the recital or my terrible declarations afterward at the piano bench. Neither of us talked about it again, as if it were a betrayal that was now unspeakable. So I never found a way to ask her why she had hoped for something so large that failure was inevitable.

And even worse, I never asked her what frightened me the most: Why had she given up hope? For after our struggle at the piano, she never mentioned my playing again. The lessons stopped. The lid to the piano was closed, shutting out the dust, my misery, and her dreams.

So she surprised me. A few years ago, she offered to give me the piano, for my thirtieth birthday. I had not played in all those years. I saw the offer as a sign of forgiveness, a tremendous burden removed.

"Are you sure?" I asked shyly. "I mean, won't you and Dad miss it?"

"No, this your piano," she said firmly. "Always your piano. You only one can play."

85   "Well, I probably can't play anymore," I said. "It's been years."

"You pick up fast," said my mother, as if she knew this was certain. "You have natural talent. You could been genius if you want to."

"No I couldn't."

"You just not trying," said my mother. And she was neither angry nor sad. She said it as if to announce a fact that could never be disproved. "Take it," she said.

But I didn't at first. It was enough that she had offered it to me. And after that, every time I saw it in my parents' living room, standing in front of the bay windows, it made me feel proud, as if it were a shiny trophy I had won back.

90   Last week I sent a tuner over to my parents' apartment and had the piano reconditioned, for purely sentimental reasons. My mother had died a

few months before and I had been getting things in order for my father, a little bit at a time. I put the jewelry in special silk pouches. The sweaters she had knitted in yellow, pink, bright orange—all the colors I hated—I put those in mothproof boxes. I found some old Chinese silk dresses, the kind with little slits up the sides. I rubbed the old silk against my skin, then wrapped them in tissue and decided to take them home with me.

After I had the piano tuned, I opened the lid and touched the keys. It sounded even richer than I remembered. Really, it was a very good piano. Inside the bench were the same exercise notes with handwritten scales, the same secondhand music books with their covers held together with yellow tape.

I opened up the Schumann book to the dark little piece I had played at the recital. It was on the left-hand page, "Pleading Child." It looked more difficult than I remembered. I played a few bars, surprised at how easily the notes came back to me.

And for the first time, or so it seemed, I noticed the piece on the right-hand side. It was called "Perfectly Contented." I tried to play this one as well. It had a lighter melody but the same flowing rhythm and turned out to be quite easy. "Pleading Child" was shorter but slower; "Perfectly Contented" was longer, but faster. And after I played them both a few times, I realized they were two halves of the same song.

HELENA MARIA VIRAMONTES

Helena Maria Viramontes was born in East Los Angeles in 1954. After completing her undergraduate studies at Immaculate Heart College, she did graduate work at California State University, Los Angeles, and further work (1979–1981) in the MFA Creative Writing Program at the University of California, Irvine. Viramontes has won first prize in several fiction contests, including the Irvine Chicano Literary Contest. In 1989, the year in which she was awarded a Creative Writing Fellowship from the National Endowment for the Arts, she participated in a "Storytelling for Film" workshop at the Sundance Film Institute. She now teaches writing at Cornell.

Viramontes writes chiefly about women whose lives are circumscribed by a patriarchal Latino society. Eight of her stories have been collected in "The Moths" and Other Stories (1985); she is also the author of a widely praised novel, Under the Feet of Jesus *(1995).*

The Moths   [1982]

I was fourteen years old when Abuelita[1] requested my help. And it seemed only fair. Abuelita had pulled me through the rages of scarlet fever by placing, removing and replacing potato slices on the temples of my forehead; she had seen me through several whippings, an arm broken by a dare jump off Tío Enrique's toolshed, puberty, and my first lie. Really, I told Amá, it was only fair.

---

[1]**Abuelita** Grandma (Spanish); other Spanish words for relatives mentioned in the story are *Tío*, Uncle, *Amá*, Mother, and *Apá*, Dad.

Not that I was her favorite granddaughter or anything special. I wasn't even pretty or nice like my older sisters and I just couldn't do the girl things they could do. My hands were too big to handle the fineries of crocheting or embroidery and I always pricked my fingers or knotted my colored threads time and time again while my sisters laughed and called me bull hands with their cute waterlike voices. So I began keeping a piece of jagged brick in my sock to bash my sisters or anyone who called me bull hands. Once, while we all sat in the bedroom, I hit Teresa on the forehead, right above her eyebrow and she ran to Amá with her mouth open, her hand over her eye while blood seeped between her fingers. I was used to the whippings by then.

I wasn't respectful either. I even went so far as to doubt the power of Abuelita's slices, the slices she said absorbed my fever. "You're still alive, aren't you?" Abuelita snapped back, her pasty gray eye beaming at me and burning holes in my suspicions. Regretful that I had let secret questions drop out of my mouth, I couldn't look into her eyes. My hands began to fan out, grow like a liar's nose until they hung by my side like low weights. Abuelita made a balm out of dried moth wings and Vicks and rubbed my hands, shaped them back to size and it was the strangest feeling. Like bones melting. Like sun shining through the darkness of your eyelids. I didn't mind helping Abuelita after that, so Amá would always send me over to her.

In the early afternoon Amá would push her hair back, hand me my sweater and shoes, and tell me to go to Mama Luna's. This was to avoid another fight and another whipping, I knew. I would deliver one last direct shot on Marisela's arm and jump out of our house, the slam of the screen door burying her cries of anger, and I'd gladly go help Abuelita plant her wild lilies or jasmine or heliotrope or cilantro or hierbabuena in red Hills Brothers coffee cans. Abuelita would wait for me at the top step of her porch holding a hammer and nail and empty coffee cans. And although we hardly spoke, hardly looked at each other as we worked over root transplants, I always felt her gray eye on me. It made me feel, in a strange sort of way, safe and guarded and not alone. Like God was supposed to make you feel.

5   On Abuelita's porch, I would puncture holes in the bottom of the coffee cans with a nail and a precise hit of a hammer. This completed, my job was to fill them with red clay mud from beneath her rose bushes, packing it softly, then making a perfect hole, four fingers round, to nest a sprouting avocado pit, or the spidery sweet potatoes that Abuelita rooted in mayonnaise jars with toothpicks and daily water, or prickly chayotes[2] that produced vines that twisted and wound all over her porch pillars, crawling to the roof, up and over the roof, and down the other side, making her small brick house look like it was cradled within the vines that grew pear-shaped squashes ready for the pick, ready to be steamed with onions and cheese and butter. The roots would burst out of the rusted coffee cans and search for a place to connect. I would then feed the seedlings with water.

But this was a different kind of help, Amá said, because Abuelita was dying. Looking into her gray eye, then into her brown one, the doctor said it was just a matter of days. And so it seemed only fair that these hands she had melted and formed found use in rubbing her caving body with alcohol and marihuana, rubbing her arms and legs, turning her face to the window so that she could watch the Bird of Paradise blooming or smell the scent of

---

[2]**chayotes** squash-like fruit.

clove in the air. I toweled her face frequently and held her hand for hours. Her gray wiry hair hung over the mattress. Since I could remember, she'd kept her long hair in braids. Her mouth was vacant and when she slept, her eyelids never closed all the way. Up close, you could see her gray eye beaming out the window, staring hard as if to remember everything. I never kissed her. I left the window open when I went to the market.

Across the street from Jay's Market there was a chapel. I never knew its denomination, but I went in just the same to search for candles. I sat down on one of the pews because there were none. After I cleaned my fingernails, I looked up at the high ceiling. I had forgotten the vastness of these places, the coolness of the marble pillars and the frozen statues with blank eyes. I was alone. I knew why I had never returned.

That was one of Apá's biggest complaints. He would pound his hands on the table, rocking the sugar dish or spilling a cup of coffee and scream that if I didn't go to mass every Sunday to save my goddamn sinning soul, then I had no reason to go out of the house, period. Punto final.[3] He would grab my arm and dig his nails into me to make sure I understood the importance of catechism. Did he make himself clear? Then he strategically directed his anger at Amá for her lousy ways of bringing up daughters, being disrespectful and unbelieving, and my older sisters would pull me aside and tell me if I didn't get to mass right this minute, they were all going to kick the holy shit out of me. Why am I so selfish? Can't you see what it's doing to Amá, you idiot? So I would wash my feet and stuff them in my black Easter shoes that shone with Vaseline, grab a missal and veil, and wave good-bye to Amá.

I would walk slowly down Lorena to First to Evergreen, counting the cracks on the cement. On Evergreen I would turn left and walk to Abuelita's. I liked her porch because it was shielded by the vines of the chayotes and I could get a good look at the people and car traffic on Evergreen without them knowing. I would jump up the porch steps, knock on the screen door as I wiped my feet and call Abuelita? mi Abuelita? As I opened the door and stuck my head in, I would catch the gagging scent of toasting chile on the placa.[4] When I entered the sala,[5] she would greet me from the kitchen, wringing her hands in her apron. I'd sit at the corner of the table to keep from being in her way. The chiles made my eyes water. Am I crying? No, Mama Luna, I'm sure not crying. I don't like going to mass, but my eyes watered anyway, the tears dropping on the tablecloth like candle wax. Abuelita lifted the burnt chiles from the fire and sprinkled water on them until the skins began to separate. Placing them in front of me, she turned to check the menudo.[6] I peeled the skins off and put the flimsy, limp looking green and yellow chiles in the molcajete[7] and began to crush and crush and twist and crush the heart out of the tomato, the clove of garlic, the stupid chiles that made me cry, crushed them until they turned into liquid under my bull hand. With a wooden spoon, I scraped hard to destroy the guilt, and my tears were gone. I put the bowl of chile next to a vase filled with freshly cut roses. Abuelita touched my hand and pointed to the bowl of menudo that steamed in front of me. I spooned some chile into the menudo and rolled a corn tortilla thin with the palms of my hands. As I ate, a fine

---

[3]**Punto final** period.   [4]**placa** round cast-iron griddle.   [5]**sala** living room.   [6]**menudo** tripe soup.   [7]**molcajete** mixing vessel, mortar.

Sunday breeze entered the kitchen and a rose petal calmly feathered down to the table.

10   I left the chapel without blessing myself and walked to Jay's. Most of the time Jay didn't have much of anything. The tomatoes were always soft and the cans of Campbell soups had rusted spots on them. There was dust on the tops of cereal boxes. I picked up what I needed: rubbing alcohol, five cans of chicken broth, a big bottle of Pine Sol. At first Jay got mad because I thought I had forgotten the money. But it was there all the time, in my back pocket.

When I returned from the market, I heard Amá crying in Abuelita's kitchen. She looked up at me with puffy eyes. I placed the bags of groceries on the table and began putting the cans of soup away. Amá sobbed quietly. I never kissed her. After a while, I patted her on the back for comfort. Finally: "Y mi Amá?"[8] she asked in a whisper, then choked again and cried into her apron.

Abuelita fell off the bed twice yesterday, I said, knowing that I shouldn't have said it and wondering why I wanted to say it because it only made Amá cry harder. I guess I became angry and just so tired of the quarrels and beatings and unanswered prayers and my hands just there hanging helplessly by my side. Amá looked at me again, confused, angry, and her eyes were filled with sorrow. I went outside and sat on the porch swing and watched the people pass. I sat there until she left. I dozed off repeating the words to myself like rosary prayers: when do you stop giving when do you start giving when do you . . . and when my hands fell from my lap, I awoke to catch them. The sun was setting, an orange glow, and I knew Abuelita was hungry.

There comes a time when the sun is defiant. Just about the time when moods change, inevitable seasons of a day, transitions from one color to another, that hour or minute or second when the sun is finally defeated, finally sinks into the realization that it cannot with all its power to heal or burn, exist forever, there comes an illumination where the sun and earth meet, a final burst of burning red orange fury reminding us that although endings are inevitable, they are necessary for rebirths, and when that time came, just when I switched on the light in the kitchen to open Abuelita's can of soup, it was probably then that she died.

The room smelled of Pine Sol and vomit and Abuelita had defecated the remains of her cancerous stomach. She had turned to the window and tried to speak, but her mouth remained open and speechless. I heard you, Abuelita, I said, stroking her cheek, I heard you. I opened the windows of the house and let the soup simmer and overboil on the stove. I turned the stove off and poured the soup down the sink. From the cabinet I got a tin basin, filled it with lukewarm water and carried it carefully to the room. I went to the linen closet and took out some modest bleached white towels. With the sacredness of a priest preparing his vestments, I unfolded the towels one by one on my shoulders. I removed the sheets and blankets from her bed and peeled off her thick flannel nightgown. I toweled her puzzled face, stretching out the wrinkles, removing the coils of her neck, toweled her shoulders and breasts. Then I changed the water. I returned to towel the creases of her

---

[8]**¿Y mi Amá?** And my Mother?

stretch-marked stomach, her sporadic vaginal hairs, and her sagging thighs. I removed the lint from between her toes and noticed a mapped birthmark on the fold of her buttock. The scars on her back which were as thin as the life lines on the palms of her hands made me realize how little I really knew of Abuelita. I covered her with a thin blanket and went into the bathroom. I washed my hands, and turned on the tub faucets and watched the water pour into the tub with vitality and steam. When it was full, I turned off the water and undressed. Then, I went to get Abuelita.

15   She was not as heavy as I thought and when I carried her in my arms, her body fell into a V, and yet my legs were tired, shaky, and I felt as if the distance between the bedroom and bathroom was miles and years away. Amá, where are you?

I stepped into the bathtub one leg first, then the other. I bent my knees slowly to descend into the water slowly so I wouldn't scald her skin. There, there, Abuelita, I said, cradling her, smoothing her as we descended, I heard you. Her hair fell back and spread across the water like eagle's wings. The water in the tub overflowed and poured onto the tile of the floor. Then the moths came. Small, gray ones that came from her soul and out through her mouth fluttering to light, circling the single dull light bulb of the bathroom. Dying is lonely and I wanted to go to where the moths were, stay with her and plant chayotes whose vines would crawl up her fingers and into the clouds; I wanted to rest my head on her chest with her stroking my hair, telling me about the moths that lay within the soul and slowly eat the spirit up; I wanted to return to the waters of the womb with her so that we would never be alone again. I wanted. I wanted my Amá. I removed a few strands of hair from Abuelita's face and held her small light head within the hollow of my neck. The bathroom was filled with moths, and for the first time in a long time I cried, rocking us, crying for her, for me, for Amá, the sobs emerging from the depths of anguish, the misery of feeling half born, sobbing until finally the sobs rippled into circles and circles of sadness and relief. There, there, I said to Abuelita, rocking us gently, there, there.

✳ TOPICS FOR CRITICAL THINKING AND WRITING

1. The narrator says that she was not "pretty or nice," could not "do . . . girl things," and was not "respectful." But what *can* she do, and what *is* she? How, in short, would you characterize her?

2. Elements of the fantastic are evident, notably in the moths at the end. What efforts, if any, does the author exert in order to make the fantastic elements plausible or at least partly acceptable?

3. Why do you suppose the author included the rather extended passages about the sprouting plants and (later) the sun?

4. We can say, on the basis of the description of the bathing of Abuelita in the final paragraph, that the narrator is loving, caring, and grief-stricken. What else, if anything, does this paragraph reveal about the narrator?

ELIZABETH TALLENT

Elizabeth Tallent was born in Washington, D.C., in 1954 and educated at Illinois State University at Normal. The author of novels and short stories, she has won many awards, including a fellowship from the National Endowment for the Arts and the O. Henry Award.

No One's a Mystery   [1985]

For my eighteenth birthday Jack gave me a five-year diary with a latch and a little key, light as a dime. I was sitting beside him scratching at the lock, which didn't seem to want to work, when he thought he saw his wife's Cadillac in the distance, coming toward us. He pushed me down onto the dirty floor of the pickup and kept one hand on my head while I inhaled the musk of his cigarettes in the dashboard ashtray and sang along with Rosanne Cash on the tape deck. We'd been drinking tequila and the bottle was between his legs, resting up against his crotch, where the seam of his Levi's was bleached linen-white, though the Levi's were nearly new. I don't know why his Levi's always bleached like that, along the seams and at the knees. In a curve of cloth his zipper glinted, gold.

"It's her," he said. "She keeps the lights on in the daytime. I can't think of a single habit in a woman that irritates me more than that." When he saw that I was going to stay still he took his hand from my head and ran it through his own dark hair.

"Why does she?" I said.

"She thinks it's safer. Why does she need to be safer? She's driving exactly fifty-five miles an hour. She believes in those signs: 'Speed Monitored by Aircraft.' It doesn't matter that you can look up and see that the sky is empty."

5   "She'll see your lips move, Jack. She'll know you're talking to someone."

"She'll think I'm singing along with the radio."

He didn't lift his head, just raised the fingers in salute while the pressure of his palm steadied the wheel, and I heard the Cadillac honk twice, musically; he was driving easily eighty miles an hour. I studied his boots. The elk heads stitched into the leather were bearded with frayed thread, the toes were scuffed, and there was a compact wedge of muddy manure between the heel and the sole—the same boots he'd been wearing for the two years I'd known him. On the tape deck Rosanne Cash sang, "Nobody's into me, no one's a mystery."

"Do you think she's getting famous because of who her daddy is or for herself?" Jack said.

"There are about a hundred pop tops on the floor, did you know that? Some little kid could cut a bare foot on one of these, Jack."

10   "No little kids get into this truck except for you."

"How come you let it get so dirty?"

"'How come,'" he mocked. "You even sound like a kid. You can get back into the seat now, if you want. She's not going to look over her shoulder and see you."

"How do you know?"

"I just know," he said. "Like I know I'm going to get meat loaf for supper. It's in the air. Like I know what you'll be writing in that diary."

15   "What will I be writing?" I knelt on my side of the seat and craned around to look at the butterfly of dust printed on my jeans. Outside the window Wyoming was dazzling in the heat. The wheat was fawn and yellow and parted smoothly by the thin dirt road. I could smell the water in the irrigation ditches hidden in the wheat.

"Tonight you'll write, 'I love Jack. This is my birthday present from him. I can't imagine anybody loving anybody more than I love Jack.'"

"I can't."

"In a year you'll write, 'I wonder what I ever really saw in Jack. I wonder why I spent so many days just riding around in his pickup. It's true he taught me something about sex. It's true there wasn't ever much else to do in Cheyenne.'"

"I won't write that."

20   "In two years you'll write, 'I wonder what that old guy's name was, the one with the curly hair and the filthy dirty pickup truck and time on his hands.'"

"I won't write that."

"No?"

"Tonight I'll write, 'I love Jack. This is my birthday present from him. I can't imagine anybody loving anybody more than I love Jack.'"

"No, you can't," he said. "You can't imagine it."

25   "In a year I'll write, 'Jack should be home any minute now. The table's set—my grandmother's linen and her old silver and the yellow candles left over from the wedding—but I don't know if I can wait until after the trout à la Navarra to make love to him.'"

"It must have been a fast divorce."

"In two years I'll write, 'Jack should be home by now. Little Jack is hungry for his supper. He said his first word today besides "Mama" and "Papa." He said "kaka."'"

Jack laughed. "He was probably trying to finger-paint with kaka on the bathroom wall when you heard him say it."

"In three years I'll write, 'My nipples are a little sore from nursing Eliza Rosamund.'"

30   "Rosamund. Every little girl should have a middle name she hates."

"'Her breath smells like vanilla and her eyes are just Jack's color of blue.'"

"That's nice," Jack said.

"So, which one do you like?"

"I like yours," he said. "But I believe mine."

35   "It doesn't matter. I believe mine."

"Not in your heart of hearts, you don't."

"You're wrong."

"I'm not wrong," he said. "And her breath would smell like your milk, and it's kind of a bittersweet smell, if you want to know the truth."

LORRIE MOORE

Lorrie Moore, born Marie Lorena Moore in 1957 in Glen Falls, New York, did her undergraduate work at St. Lawrence University, and her graduate work (M.F.A.) at Cornell University. While still an undergraduate she won first prize in the nationwide Seventeen *magazine short story contest (1976), and she has won numerous prizes in recent years. She is the author of stories, novels, and essays. We reprint a story from her first collection,* Self-Help *(1985). This story, like most of the stories in* Self-Help, *is written in what Moore in an interview (in* Contemporary Authors: New Revision Series, *No. 39, 1992) called "The second person, mock-imperative narrative." She went on to explain:*

> *Let's see what happens when one eliminates the subject, leaves the verb shivering at the start of a clause; what happens when one appropriates the "how-to" form for a fiction, for an irony, for a "how-not-to." I was interested in whatever tensions resulted when a writer foisted fictional experience off of the "I" of the first person and onto the more generalized "you" of the second—the vernacular "one."*
>
> *The second person stories begin, ostensibly, to tell the generic tale, give the categorical advice, but become so entrenched in their own individuated details that they succeed in telling only their own specific story, suggesting that although life is certainly not jokeless, it probably is remediless.*

How to Become a Writer   [1985]

First, try to be something, anything, else. A movie star/astronaut. A movie star/missionary. A movie star/kindergarten teacher. President of the World. Fail miserably. It is best if you fail at an early age—say, fourteen. Early, critical disillusionment is necessary so that at fifteen you can write long haiku sequences about thwarted desire. It is a pond, a cherry blossom, a wind brushing against sparrow wing leaving for mountain. Count the syllables. Show it to your mom. She is tough and practical. She has a son in Vietnam and a husband who may be having an affair. She believes in wearing brown because it hides spots. She'll look briefly at your writing, then back up at you with a face blank as a donut. She'll say: "How about emptying the dishwasher?" Look away. Shove the forks in the fork drawer. Accidentally break one of the freebie gas station glasses. This is the required pain and suffering. This is only for starters.

In your high school English class look at Mr. Killian's face. Decide faces are important. Write a villanelle about pores. Struggle. Write a sonnet. Count the syllables: nine, ten, eleven, thirteen. Decide to experiment with fiction. Here you don't have to count syllables. Write a short story about an elderly man and woman who accidentally shoot each other in the head, the result of an inexplicable malfunction of a shotgun which appears mysteriously in their living room one night. Give it to Mr. Killian as your final project. When you get it back, he has written on it: "Some of your images are quite nice, but you have no sense of plot." When you are home, in the privacy of your own room, faintly scrawl in pencil beneath his black-inked comments: "Plots are for dead people, pore-face."

Take all the babysitting jobs you can get. You are great with kids. They love you. You tell them stories about old people who die idiot deaths. You sing them songs like "Blue Bells of Scotland," which is their favorite. And when they are in their pajamas and have finally stopped pinching each other, when they are fast asleep, you read every sex manual in the house, and wonder how on earth anyone could ever do those things with someone they truly loved. Fall asleep in a chair reading Mr. McMurphy's *Playboy*. When the McMurphys come home, they will tap you on the shoulder, look at the magazine in your lap, and grin. You will want to die. They will ask you if Tracey took her medicine all right. Explain, yes, she did, that you promised her a story if she would take it like a big girl and that seemed to work out just fine. "Oh, marvelous," they will exclaim.

Try to smile proudly.

5   Apply to college as a child psychology major.

As a child psychology major, you have some electives. You've always liked birds. Sign up for something called "The Ornithological Field Trip." It meets Tuesdays and Thursdays at two. When you arrive at Room 134 on the first day of class, everyone is sitting around a seminar table talking about metaphors. You've heard of these. After a short, excruciating while, raise your hand and say diffidently, "Excuse me, isn't this Birdwatching One-oh-one?" The class stops and turns to look at you. They seem to all have one face—giant and blank as a vandalized clock. Someone with a beard booms out, "No, this is Creative Writing." Say: "Oh—right," as if perhaps you knew all along. Look down at your schedule. Wonder how the hell you ended up here. The computer, apparently, has made an error. You start to get up to leave and then don't. The lines at the registrar this week are huge. Perhaps you should stick with this mistake. Perhaps your creative writing isn't all that bad. Perhaps it is fate. Perhaps this is what your dad meant when he said, "It's the age of computers, Francie, it's the age of computers."

Decide that you like college life. In your dorm, you meet many nice people. Some are smarter than you. And some, you notice, are dumber than you. You will continue, unfortunately, to view the world in exactly these terms for the rest of your life.

The assignment this week in creative writing is to narrate a violent happening. Turn in a story about driving with your Uncle Gordon and another one about two old people who are accidentally electrocuted when they go to turn on a badly wired desk lamp. The teacher will hand them back to you with comments: "Much of your writing is smooth and energetic. You have, however, a ludicrous notion of plot." Write another story about a man and a woman who, in the very first paragraph, have their lower torsos accidentally blitzed away by dynamite. In the second paragraph, with the insurance money, they buy a frozen yogurt stand together. There are six more paragraphs. You read the whole thing out loud in class. No one likes it. They say your sense of plot is outrageous and incompetent. After class someone asks you if you are crazy.

Decide that perhaps you should stick to comedies. Start dating someone who is funny, someone who has what in high school you called a "really great sense of humor" and what now your creative writing class calls "self-contempt giving rise to comic form." Write down all of his jokes, but don't tell him you are doing this. Make up anagrams of his old girlfriend's name and name all your socially handicapped characters with them. Tell him his old girlfriend is in all of your stories and then watch how funny he can be, see what a really great sense of humor he can have.

10   Your child psychology advisor tells you you are neglecting courses in your major. What you spend the most time on should be what you're majoring in. Say yes, you understand.

In creative writing seminars over the next two years, everyone continues to smoke cigarettes and ask the same things: "But does it work?" "Why should we care about this character?" "Have you earned this cliché?" These seem like important questions.

On days when it is your turn, you look at the class hopefully as they scour your mimeographs for a plot. They look back up at you, drag deeply, and then smile in a sweet sort of way.

You spend too much time slouched and demoralized. Your boyfriend suggests bicycling. Your roommate suggests a new boyfriend. You are said to be self-mutilating and losing weight, but you continue writing. The only happiness you have is writing something new, in the middle of the night, armpits damp, heart pounding, something no one has yet seen. You have only those brief, fragile, untested moments of exhilaration when you know: you are a genius. Understand what you must do. Switch majors. The kids in your nursery project will be disappointed, but you have a calling, an urge, a delusion, an unfortunate habit. You have, as your mother would say, fallen in with a bad crowd.

Why write? Where does writing come from? These are questions to ask yourself. They are like: Where does dust come from? Or: Why is there war? Or: If there's a God, then why is my brother now a cripple?

15   These are questions that you keep in your wallet, like calling cards. These are questions, your creative writing teacher says, that are good to address in your journals but rarely in your fiction.

The writing professor this fall is stressing the Power of the Imagination. Which means he doesn't want long descriptive stories about your camping trip last July. He wants you to start in a realistic context but then to alter it. Like recombinant DNA. He wants you to let your imagination sail, to let it grow big-bellied in the wind. This is a quote from Shakespeare.

Tell your roommate your great idea, your great exercise of imaginative power: a transformation of Melville to contemporary life. It will be about monomania and the fish-eat-fish world of life insurance in Rochester, New York. The first line will be "Call me Fishmeal," and it will feature a menopausal suburban husband named Richard, who because he is so depressed all the time is called "Mopey Dick" by his witty wife Elaine. Say to your roommate: "Mopey Dick, get it?" Your roommate looks at you, her face blank as a large Kleenex. She comes up to you, like a buddy, and puts an arm around your burdened shoulders. "Listen, Francie," she says, slow as speech therapy. "Let's go out and get a big beer."

The seminar doesn't like this one either. You suspect they are beginning to feel sorry for you. They say: "You have to think about what is happening. Where is the story here?"

The next semester the writing professor is obsessed with writing from personal experience. You must write from what you know, from what has happened to you. He wants deaths, he wants camping trips. Think about what has happened to you. In three years there have been three things: you have lost your virginity; your parents got divorced; and your brother came home from a forest ten miles from the Cambodian border with only half a thigh, a permanent smirk nestled into one corner of his mouth.

20   About the first you write: "It created a new space, which hurt and cried in a voice that wasn't mine, 'I'm not the same anymore, but I'll be okay.'"

About the second you write an elaborate story of an old married couple who stumble upon an unknown land mine in their kitchen and accidentally blow themselves up. You call it: "For Better or for Liverwurst."

About the last you write nothing. There are no words for this. Your typewriter hums. You can find no words.

At undergraduate cocktail parties, people say, "Oh, you write? What do you write about?" Your roommate, who has consumed too much wine, too little cheese, and no crackers at all, blurts: "Oh, my god, she always writes about her dumb boyfriend."

Later on in life you will learn that writers are merely open, helpless texts with no real understanding of what they have written and therefore must half-believe anything and everything that is said of them. You, however, have not reached this stage of literary criticism. You stiffen and say, "I do not," the same way you said it when someone in the fourth grade accused you of really liking oboe lessons and your parents really weren't just making you take them.

25   Insist you are not very interested in any one subject at all, that you are interested in the music of language, that you are interested in—in— syllables, because they are the atoms of poetry, the cells of the mind, the breath of the soul. Begin to feel woozy. Stare into your plastic wine cup.

"Syllables?" you will hear someone ask, voice trailing off, as they glide slowly toward the reassuring white of the dip.

Begin to wonder what you do write about. Or if you have anything to say. Or if there even is such a thing to say. Limit these thoughts to no more than ten minutes a day; like sit-ups, they can make you thin.

You will read somewhere that all writing has to do with one's genitals. Don't dwell on this. It will make you nervous.

Your mother will come visit you. She will look at the circles under your eyes and hand you a brown book with a brown briefcase on the cover. It is entitled: *How to Become a Business Executive.* She has also brought the *Names for Baby* encyclopedia you asked for; one of your characters, the aging clown-school teacher, needs a new name. Your mother will shake her head and say:"Francie, Francie, remember when you were going to be a child psychology major?"

30   Say:"Mom, I like to write."

She'll say:"Sure you like to write. Of course. Sure you like to write."

Write a story about a confused music student and title it:"Schubert Was the One with the Glasses, Right?" It's not a big hit, although your roommate likes the part where the two violinists accidentally blow themselves up in a recital room."I went out with a violinist once," she says, snapping her gum.

Thank god you are taking other courses. You can find sanctuary in nineteenth-century ontological snags and invertebrate courting rituals. Certain globular mollusks have what is called"Sex by the Arm."The male octopus, for instance, loses the end of one arm when placing it inside the female body during intercourse. Marine biologists call it"Seven Heaven." Be glad you know these things. Be glad you are not just a writer. Apply to law school.

From here on in, many things can happen. But the main one will be this: you decide not to go to law school after all, and, instead, you spend a good, big chunk of your adult life telling people how you decided not to go to law school after all. Somehow you end up writing again. Perhaps you go to graduate school. Perhaps you work odd jobs and take writing courses at night. Perhaps you are working on a novel and writing down all the clever remarks and intimate personal confessions you hear during the day. Perhaps you are losing your pals, your acquaintances, your balance.

35   You have broken up with your boyfriend. You now go out with men who, instead of whispering "I love you," shout:"Do it to me, baby." This is good for your writing.

Sooner or later you have a finished manuscript more or less. People look at it in a vaguely troubled sort of way and say,"I'll bet becoming a writer was always a fantasy of yours, wasn't it?"Your lips dry to salt. Say that of all the fantasies possible in the world, you can't imagine being a writer even making the top twenty. Tell them you were going to be a child psychology major."I bet," they always sigh,"you'd be great with kids." Scowl fiercely. Tell them you're a walking blade.

Quit classes. Quit jobs. Cash in old savings bonds. Now you have time like warts on your hands. Slowly copy all of your friends' addresses into a new address book.

Vacuum. Chew cough drops. Keep a folder full of fragments.

An eyelid darkening sideways.

40   *World as conspiracy.*

Possible plot? A woman gets on a bus.

Suppose you threw a love affair and nobody came.

At home drink a lot of coffee. At Howard Johnson's order the cole slaw. Consider how it looks like the soggy confetti of a map: where you've been, where you're going—"You Are Here," says the red star on the back of the menu.

Occasionally a date with a face blank as a sheet of paper asks you whether writers often become discouraged. Say that sometimes they do and sometimes they do. Say it's a lot like having polio.

45   "Interesting," smiles your date, and then he looks down at his arm hairs and starts to smooth them, all, always, in the same direction.

LOUISE ERDRICH

Louise Erdrich, born in 1954 in Little Falls, Minnesota, grew up in North Dakota, a member of the Turtle Mountain Band of Chippewa. Her father had been born in Germany; her mother was French Ojibwe; both parents taught at the Bureau of Indian Affairs School. After graduating from Dartmouth College (with a major in anthropology) in 1976, Erdrich returned briefly to North Dakota to teach in the Poetry in the Schools Program, and went to Johns Hopkins University, where she earned a master's degree in creative writing. She now lives in Minneapolis, Minnesota.

Erdrich has published two books of poems and several novels, one of which, Love Medicine *(1986), won the National Book Critics Circle Award. "The Red Convertible" is a self-contained story, but it is also part of* Love Medicine, *which consists of narratives about life on a North Dakota reservation.*

The Red Convertible   [1984]

Lyman Lamartine

I was the first one to drive a convertible on my reservation. And of course it was red, a red Olds. I owned that car along with my brother Henry Junior. We owned it together until his boots filled with water on a windy night and he bought out my share. Now Henry owns the whole car, and his youngest brother Lyman (that's myself), Lyman walks everywhere he goes.

How did I earn enough money to buy my share in the first place? My own talent was I could always make money. I had a touch for it, unusual in a Chippewa. From the first I was different that way, and everyone recognized it. I was the only kid they let in the American Legion Hall to shine shoes, for example, and one Christmas I sold spiritual bouquets for the mission door to door. The nuns let me keep a percentage. Once I started, it seemed the more money I made the easier the money came. Everyone encouraged it. When I was fifteen I got a job washing dishes at the Joliet Café, and that was where my first big break happened.

It wasn't long before I was promoted to bussing tables, and then the short-order cook quit and I was hired to take her place. No sooner than you know it I was managing the Joliet. The rest is history. I went on managing. I soon became part owner, and of course there was no stopping me then. It wasn't long before the whole thing was mine.

After I'd owned the Joliet for one year, it blew over in the worst tornado ever seen around here. The whole operation was smashed to bits. A total loss. The fryalator was up in a tree, the grill torn in half like it was paper. I was only sixteen. I had it all in my mother's name, and I lost it quick, but before I lost it I had every one of my relatives, and their relatives, to dinner, and I also bought that red Olds I mentioned, along with Henry.

5   The first time we saw it! I'll tell you when we first saw it. We had gotten
a ride up to Winnipeg, and both of us had money. Don't ask me why, because
we never mentioned a car or anything, we just had all our money. Mine was
cash, a big bankroll from the Joliet's insurance. Henry had two checks—a
week's extra pay for being laid off, and his regular check from the Jewel
Bearing Plant.

We were walking down Portage anyway, seeing the sights, when we saw
it. There it was, parked, large as life. Really as *if* it was alive. I thought of the
word *repose,* because the car wasn't simply stopped, parked, or whatever.
That car reposed, calm and gleaming, a FOR SALE sign in its left front window.
Then, before we had thought it over at all, the car belonged to us and our
pockets were empty. We had just enough money for gas back home.

We went places in that car, me and Henry. We took off driving all one
whole summer. We started off toward the Little Knife River and Mandaree in
Fort Berthold and then we found ourselves down in Wakpala somehow, and
then suddenly we were over in Montana on the Rocky Boys, and yet the
summer was not even half over. Some people hang on to details when they
travel, but we didn't let them bother us and just lived our everyday lives
here to there.

I do remember this one place with willows. I remember I laid under
those trees and it was comfortable. So comfortable. The branches bent
down all around me like a tent or a stable. And quiet, it was quiet, even
though there was a powwow close enough so I could see it going on. The
air was not too still, not too windy either. When the dust rises up and hangs
in the air around the dancers like that, I feel good. Henry was asleep with his
arms thrown wide. Later on, he woke up and we started driving again. We
were somewhere in Montana, or maybe on the Blood Reserve—it could
have been anywhere. Anyway it was where we met the girl.

All her hair was in buns around her ears, that's the first thing I noticed
about her. She was posed alongside the road with her arm out, so we
stopped. That girl was short, so short her lumber shirt looked comical on
her, like a nightgown. She had jeans on and fancy moccasins and she carried
a little suitcase.

10   "Hop on in," says Henry. So she climbs in between us.

"We'll take you home," I says. "Where do you live?"

"Chicken," she says.

"Where the hell's that?" I ask her.

"Alaska."

15   "Okay," says Henry, and we drive.

We got up there and never wanted to leave. The sun doesn't truly set
there in summer, and the night is more a soft dusk. You might doze off,
sometimes, but before you know it you're up again, like an animal in nature.
You never feel like you have to sleep hard or put away the world. And things
would grow up there. One day just dirt or moss, the next day flowers and
long grass. The girl's name was Susy. Her family really took to us. They fed us
and put us up. We had our own tent to live in by their house, and the kids
would be in and out of there all day and night. They couldn't get over me
and Henry being brothers, we looked so different. We told them we knew
we had the same mother, anyway.

One night Susy came in to visit us. We sat around in the tent talking of
this thing and that. The season was changing. It was getting darker by that

time, and the cold was even getting just a little mean. I told her it was time for us to go. She stood up on a chair.

"You never seen my hair," Susy said.

That was true. She was standing on a chair, but still, when she unclipped her buns the hair reached all the way to the ground. Our eyes opened. You couldn't tell how much hair she had when it was rolled up so neatly. Then my brother Henry did something funny. He went up to the chair and said, "Jump on my shoulders." So she did that, and her hair reached down past his waist, and he started twirling, this way and that, so her hair was flung out from side to side.

20   "I always wondered what it was like to have long pretty hair," Henry says. Well we laughed. It was a funny sight, the way he did it. The next morning we got up and took leave of those people.

On to greener pastures, as they say. It was down through Spokane and across Idaho then Montana and very soon we were racing the weather right along under the Canadian border through Columbus, Des Lacs, and then we were in Bottineau County and soon home. We'd made most of the trip, that summer, without putting up the car hood at all. We got home just in time, it turned out, for the army to remember Henry had signed up to join it.

I don't wonder that the army was so glad to get my brother that they turned him into a Marine. He was built like a brick outhouse anyway. We liked to tease him that they really wanted him for his Indian nose. He had a nose big and sharp as a hatchet, like the nose on Red Tomahawk, the Indian who killed Sitting Bull, whose profile is on signs all along the North Dakota highways. Henry went off to training camp, came home once during Christmas, then the next thing you know we got an overseas letter from him. It was 1970, and he said he was stationed up in the northern hill country. Whereabouts I did not know. He wasn't such a hot letter writer, and only got off two before the enemy caught him. I could never keep it straight, which direction those good Vietnam soldiers were from.

I wrote him back several times, even though I didn't know if those letters would get through. I kept him informed all about the car. Most of the time I had it up on blocks in the yard or half taken apart, because that long trip did a hard job on it under the hood.

I always had good luck with numbers, and never worried about the draft myself. I never even had to think about what my number was. But Henry was never lucky in the same way as me. It was at least three years before Henry came home. By then I guess the whole war was solved in the government's mind, but for him it would keep on going. In those years I'd put his car into almost perfect shape. I always thought of it as his car while he was gone, even though when he left he said, "Now it's yours," and threw me his key.

25   "Thanks for the extra key," I'd say. "I'll put it up in your drawer just in case I need it." He laughed.

When he came home, though, Henry was very different, and I'll say this: the change was no good. You could hardly expect him to change for the better, I know. But he was quiet, so quiet, and never comfortable sitting still anywhere but always up and moving around. I thought back to times we'd sat still for whole afternoons, never moving a muscle, just shifting our weight along the ground, talking to whoever sat with us, watching things. He'd always had a joke, then, too, and now you couldn't get him to laugh, or when he did it was more the sound of a man choking, a sound that stopped

up the throats of other people around him. They got to leaving him alone
most of the time, and I didn't blame them. It was a fact: Henry was jumpy
and mean.

I'd bought a color TV set for my mom and the rest of us while Henry
was away. Money still came very easy. I was sorry I'd ever bought it though,
because of Henry. I was also sorry I'd bought color, because with black-and-
white the pictures seem older and farther away. But what are you going to
do? He sat in front of it, watching it, and that was the only time he was completely still. But it was the kind of stillness that you see in a rabbit when it
freezes and before it will bolt. He was not easy. He sat in his chair gripping
the armrests with all his might, as if the chair itself was moving at a high
speed and if he let go at all he would rocket forward and maybe crash right
through the set.

Once I was in the room watching TV with Henry and I heard his teeth
click at something. I looked over, and he'd bitten through his lip. Blood was
going down his chin. I tell you right then I wanted to smash that tube to
pieces. I went over to it but Henry must have known what I was up to. He
rushed from his chair and shoved me out of the way, against the wall. I told
myself he didn't know what he was doing.

My mom came in, turned the set off real quiet, and told us she had made
something for supper. So we went and sat down. There was still blood going
down Henry's chin, but he didn't notice it and no one said anything, even
though every time he took a bit of his bread his blood fell onto it until he
was eating his own blood mixed in with the food.

30   While Henry was not around we talked about what was going to happen to him. There were no Indian doctors on the reservation, and my mom
was afraid of trusting Old Man Pillager because he courted her long ago and
was jealous of her husbands. He might take revenge through her son. We
were afraid that if we brought Henry to a regular hospital they would keep
him.

"They don't fix them in those places," Mom said; "they just give them
drugs."

"We wouldn't get him there in the first place," I agreed, "so let's just forget about it."

Then I thought about the car.

Henry had not even looked at the car since he'd gotten home, though
like I said, it was in tip-top condition and ready to drive. I thought the car
might bring the old Henry back somehow. So I bided my time and waited
for my chance to interest him in the vehicle.

35   One night Henry was off somewhere. I took myself a hammer. I went
out to that car and I did a number on its underside. Whacked it up. Bent the
tail pipe double. Ripped the muffler loose. By the time I was done with the
car it looked worse than any typical Indian car that has been driven all its
life on reservation roads, which they always say are like government
promises—full of holes. It just about hurt me, I'll tell you that! I threw dirt in
the carburetor and I ripped all the electric tape off the seats. I made it look
just as beat up as I could. Then I sat back and waited for Henry to find it.

Still, it took him over a month. That was all right, because it was just getting warm enough, not melting, but warm enough to work outside.

"Lyman," he says, walking in one day, "that red car looks like shit."

"Well it's old," I says. "You got to expect that."

"No way!" says Henry. "That car's a classic! But you went and ran the piss right out of it, Lyman, and you know it don't deserve that. I kept that car in A-one shape. You don't remember. You're too young. But when I left, that car was running like a watch. Now I don't even know if I can get it to start again, let alone get it anywhere near its old condition."

40   "Well you try," I said, like I was getting mad, "but I say it's a piece of junk."

Then I walked out before he could realize I knew he'd strung together more than six words at once.

After that I thought he'd freeze himself to death working on that car. He was out there all day, and at night he rigged up a little lamp, ran a cord out the window, and had himself some light to see by while he worked. He was better than he had been before, but that's still not saying much. It was easier for him to do the things the rest of us did. He ate more slowly and didn't jump up and down during the meal to get this or that or look out the window. I put my hand in the back of the TV set, I admit, and fiddled around with it good, so that it was almost impossible now to get a clear picture. He didn't look at it very often anyway. He was always out with that car or going off to get parts for it. By the time it was really melting outside, he had it fixed.

I had been feeling down in the dumps about Henry around this time. We had always been together before. Henry and Lyman. But he was such a loner now that I didn't know how to take it. So I jumped at the chance one day when Henry seemed friendly. It's not that he smiled or anything. He just said, "Let's take that old shitbox for a spin." Just the way he said it made me think he could be coming around.

We went out to the car. It was spring. The sun was shining very bright. My only sister, Bonita, who was just eleven years old, came out and made us stand together for a picture. Henry leaned his elbow on the red car's windshield, and he took his other arm and put it over my shoulder, very carefully, as though it was heavy for him to lift and he didn't want to bring the weight down all at once.

45   "Smile," Bonita said, and he did.

That picture, I never look at it anymore. A few months ago, I don't know why, I got his picture out and tacked it on the wall. I felt good about Henry at the time, close to him. I felt good having his picture on the wall, until one night when I was looking at television. I was a little drunk and stoned. I looked up at the wall and Henry was staring at me. I don't know what it was, but his smile had changed, or maybe it was gone. All I know is I couldn't stay in the same room with that picture. I was shaking. I got up, closed the door, and went into the kitchen. A little later my friend Ray came over and we both went back into that room. We put the picture in a brown bag, folded the bag over and over tightly, then put it way back in a closet.

I still see that picture now, as if it tugs at me, whenever I pass that closet door. The picture is very clear in my mind. It was so sunny that day Henry had to squint against the glare. Or maybe the camera Bonita held flashed like a mirror, blinding him, before she snapped the picture. My face is right out in the sun, big and round. But he might have drawn back, because the shadows on his face are deep as holes. There are two shadows curved like little hooks around the ends of his smile, as if to frame it and try to keep it there—that one, first smile that looked like it might have hurt his face. He has his field jacket on and the worn-in clothes he'd come back in and kept wearing ever since. After Bonita took the picture, she went into the house and we got into the car. There was a full cooler in the trunk. We started off, east, toward Pembina and the Red River because Henry said he wanted to see the high water.

The trip over there was beautiful. When everything starts changing, drying up, clearing off, you feel like your whole life is starting. Henry felt it, too. The top was down and the car hummed like a top. He'd really put it back in shape, even the tape on the seats was very carefully put down and glued back in layers. It's not that he smiled again or even joked, but his face looked to me as if it was clear, more peaceful. It looked as though he wasn't thinking of anything in particular except the bare fields and windbreaks and houses we were passing.

The river was high and full of winter trash when we got there. The sun was still out, but it was colder by the river. There were still little clumps of dirty snow here and there on the banks. The water hadn't gone over the banks yet, but it would, you could tell. It was just at its limit, hard swollen glossy like an old gray scar. We made ourselves a fire, and we sat down and watched the current go. As I watched it I felt something squeezing inside me and tightening and trying to let go all at the same time. I knew I was not just feeling it myself; I knew I was feeling what Henry was going through at that moment. Except that I couldn't stand it, the closing and opening. I jumped to my feet. I took Henry by the shoulders and I started shaking him. "Wake up," I says, "wake up, wake up, wake up!" I didn't know what had come over me. I sat down beside him again.

50 His face was totally white and hard. Then it broke, like stones break all of a sudden when water boils up inside them.

"I know it," he says. "I know it. I can't help it. It's no use."

We start talking. He said he knew what I'd done with the car. It was obvious it had been whacked out of shape and not just neglected. He said he wanted to give the car to me for good now, it was no use. He said he'd fixed it just to give it back and I should take it.

"No way," I says, "I don't want it."

"That's okay," he says, "you take it."

55 "I don't want it, though," I says back to him, and then to emphasize, just to emphasize, you understand, I touch his shoulder. He slaps my hand off.

"Take that car," he says.

"No," I say, "make me," I say, and then he grabs my jacket and rips the arm loose. That jacket is a class act, suede with tags and zippers. I push Henry backwards, off the log. He jumps up and bowls me over. We go down in a clinch and come up swinging hard, for all we're worth, with our fists. He socks my jaw so hard I feel like it swings loose. Then I'm at his ribcage and land a good one under his chin so his head snaps back. He's dazzled. He looks at me and I look at him and then his eyes are full of tears and blood and at first I think he's crying. But no, he's laughing. "Ha! Ha!" he says. "Ha! Ha! Take good care of it."

"Okay," I says, "okay, no problem. Ha! Ha!"

I can't help it, and I start laughing, too. My face feels fat and strange, and after a while I get a beer from the cooler in the trunk, and when I hand it to

Henry he takes his shirt and wipes my germs off. "Hoof-and-mouth disease," he says. For some reason this cracks me up, and so we're really laughing for a while, and then we drink all the rest of the beers one by one and throw them in the river and see how far, how fast, the current takes them before they fill up and sink.

60   "You want to go on back?" I ask after a while. "Maybe we could snag a couple nice Kashpaw girls."

He says nothing. But I can tell his mood is turning again.

"They're all crazy, the girls up here, every damn one of them."

"You're crazy too," I say, to jolly him up. "Crazy Lamartine boys!"

He looks as though he will take this wrong at first. His face twists, then clears, and he jumps up on his feet. "That's right!" he says. "Crazier 'n hell. Crazy Indians!"

65   I think it's the old Henry again. He throws off his jacket and starts swinging his legs out from the knees like a fancy dancer. He's down doing something between a grouse dance and a bunny hop, no kind of dance I ever saw before, but neither has anyone else on all this green growing earth. He's wild. He wants to pitch whoopee! He's up and at me and all over. All this time I'm laughing so hard, so hard my belly is getting tied up in a knot.

"Got to cool me off!" he shouts all of a sudden. Then he runs over to the river and jumps in.

There's boards and other things in the current. It's so high. No sound comes from the river after the splash he makes, so I run right over. I look around. It's getting dark. I see he's halfway across the water already, and I know he didn't swim there but the current took him. It's far. I hear his voice, though, very clearly across it.

"My boots are filling," he says.

He says this in a normal voice, like he just noticed and he doesn't know what to think of it. Then he's gone. A branch comes by. Another branch. And I go in.

70   By the time I get out of the river, off the snag I pulled myself onto, the sun is down. I walk back to the car, turn on the high beams, and drive it up the bank. I put it in first gear and then I take my foot off the clutch. I get out, close the door, and watch it plow softly into the water. The headlights reach in as they go down, searching, still lighted even after the water swirls over the back end. I wait. The wires short out. It is all finally dark. And then there is only the water, the sound of it going and running and going and running and running.

12

The Novel

OBSERVATIONS ON THE NOVEL

Most of what has been said about short stories (on probability, narrative point of view, style) is relevant to the novel. And just as the short story of the last hundred years or so is rather different from earlier short fiction (see pages 371–374), the novel—though here we must say of the last few hundred years—is different from earlier long fiction.

The ancient epic is at best a distant cousin to the novel, for though a narrative, the epic is in verse, and deals with godlike men and women, and even with gods themselves. One has only to think of the *Iliad* or the *Odyssey,* or the *Aeneid* or *Beowulf* or *Paradise Lost* to recall that the epic does not deal with the sort of people one meets in *Tom Jones, David Copperfield, Crime and Punishment, The Return of the Native, The Portrait of a Lady, The Sun Also Rises, The Catcher in the Rye,* or *The Color Purple.*

The romance is perhaps a closer relative to the novel. Ancient romances were even in prose. But the hallmark of the romance, whether the romance is by a Greek sophist (Longus' *Daphnis and Chloe*) or by a medieval English poet (Chaucer's "The Knight's Tale") or by an American (Hawthorne's *The House of the Seven Gables*), is a presentation of the remote or the marvelous, rather than the local and the ordinary. The distinction is the same as that between the tale and the short story. "Tale" has the suggestion of a yarn, of unreality or of wondrous reality. (A case can be made for excluding Hawthorne's "Young Goodman Brown" from a collection of short stories on the ground that its remoteness and its allegorical implications mark it as a tale rather than a short story. This is not to say that it is inferior to a story, but only different.) In his preface to *The House of the Seven Gables* Hawthorne himself distinguishes between the romance and the novel:

> The latter form of composition is presumed to aim at a very minute fidelity, not merely to the possible, but to the probable and ordinary course of man's experience. The former—while, as a work of art, it must rigidly subject itself to laws, and while it sins unpardonably so far as it may swerve aside from the truth of the human heart—has fairly a right to present that truth under circumstances, to a great extent, of the writer's own choosing or creation.

In his preface to *The Marble Faun* Hawthorne explains that he chose "Italy as the site of his Romance" because it afforded him "a sort of poetic or fairy precinct, where actualities would not be so terribly insisted upon as they are . . . in America."

"Actualities . . . insisted upon." That, in addition to prose and length, is the hallmark of the novel. The novel is a sort of long newspaper story; the very word "novel" comes from an Italian word meaning a little new thing, and is related to the French word that gives us "news." (It is noteworthy that the French cognate of Hawthorne's "actualities," *actualités,* means "news" or "current events.") It is no accident that many novelists have been newspapermen: Defoe, Dickens, Crane, Dreiser, Joyce, Hemingway, Camus. And this connection with reportage perhaps helps to account for the relatively low esteem in which the novel is occasionally held: to some college students, a course in the contemporary novel does not seem quite up to a course in poetry, and people who read current novels but not poetry are not likely to claim an interest in "literature."

Though Defoe's *Robinson Crusoe* is set in a far-off place, and thus might easily have been a romance, in Defoe's day it was close to current events, for it is a fictionalized version of events that had recently made news—Alexander Selkirk's life on the island of Juan Fernandez. And the story is not about marvelous happenings, but about a man's struggle for survival in dismal surroundings. Crusoe is not armed with a magic sword, nor does he struggle with monsters; he has a carpenter's chest of tools and he struggles against commonplace nature. This chest was "much more valuable than a shiploading of gold would have been at that time." The world of romance contains splendid castles and enchanted forests, but Crusoe's world contains not much more than a plot of ground, some animals and vegetables, and Friday. "I fancied I could make all but the wheel [of a wheelbarrow Crusoe needed], but that I had no notion of, neither did I know how to go about it; besides, I had no possible way to make the iron gudgeons for the spindle or axis of the wheel to run in, so I gave it over." The book, in short, emphasizes not the strange, but (given the initial situation) the usual, the commonsensical, the probable. The world of *Robinson Crusoe* is hardly different from the world we meet in the beginning of almost any novel:

> My father's family name being Pirrip, and my Christian name Philip, my infant tongue could make of both names nothing longer or more explicit than Pip. So I called myself Pip, and came to be called Pip.
>
> I give Pirrip as my father's family name, on the authority of his tombstone and my sister—Mrs. Joe Gargery, who married the blacksmith.
>
> —Charles Dickens, *Great Expectations*

If you really want to hear about it, the first thing you'll probably want to know is where I was born, and what my lousy childhood was like, and how my parents were occupied and all before they had me, and all that David Copperfield kind of crap, but I don't feel like going into it, if you want to know the truth.

> —J. D. Salinger, *The Catcher in the Rye*

It was June, 1933, one week after Commencement, when Kay Leiland Strong, Vassar '33, the first of her class to run around the table at the Class Day dinner, was married to Harald Petersen, Reed '27, in the chapel of St. George's Church, P.E., Karl F. Reiland, Rector. Outside, on Stuyvesant Square, the trees were in full leaf, and the wedding guests arriving by twos and threes in taxis heard the voices of children playing round the statue of Peter Stuyvesant in the park.

> —Mary McCarthy, *The Group*

A man who explains his nickname; a boy who in boy's language seems reluctant to talk of his "lousy childhood"; a young woman who ran around the table at the Class Day dinner. In all these passages, and in the openings of most other novels, we are confronted with current biography. In contrast to these beginnings, look at the beginning of one of Chaucer's great romances:

> Whilom,[1] as olde stories tellen us,
> There was a duc that highte[2] Theseus;
> Of Atthenes he was lord and governour,
> And in his tyme swich[3] a conquerour,
> That gretter was ther noon under the sonne.

"Whilom." "Olde stories." "Gretter was ther noon under the sonne." We are in a timeless past, in which unusual people dwell. In contrast, the novel is almost always set in the present or very recent past, and it deals with ordinary people. It so often deals with ordinary people, and presents them, apparently, in so ordinary a fashion that we sometimes wonder what is the point of it. Although the romance is often "escape" literature, it usually is didactic, holding up to us images of noble and ignoble behavior, revealing the rewards of courage and the power of love. In the preface to *The Marble Faun*, for instance, Hawthorne says he "proposed to himself to merely write a fanciful story, evolving a thoughtful moral, and did not propose attempting a portraiture of Italian manners and character." But portraiture is what novelists give us. Intent on revealing the world of real men and women going about their daily work and play, they do not simplify their characters into representatives of vices and virtues as do the romancers who wish to evolve a thoughtful moral, but give abundant detail—some of it apparently irrelevant. The innumerable details add up to a long book, although there need not be many physical happenings. The novel tells a story, of course, but the story is not only about what people overtly do but also about what they think (i.e., their mental doings) and about the society in which they are immersed and by which they are in part shaped. In the much-quoted preface to *Pierre and Jean*, Maupassant says:

> Skill of the novelist's plan will not reside in emotional effects, in attractive writing, in a striking beginning or a moving dénouement, but in the artful building up of solid details from which the essential meaning of the work will emerge.

As we read a novel we feel we are seeing not the "higher reality" or the "inner reality" so often mentioned by students of the arts, but the real reality.

The short story, too, is detailed, but commonly it reveals only a single character at a moment of crisis, whereas the novel commonly traces the development of an individual, a group of people, a world. Novelists have an attitude toward their world; they are not compiling an almanac but telling an invented story, making a work of art, offering not merely a representation of reality but a response to it, and they therefore select and shape their material. One way of selecting and shaping the material is through the chosen point of view: We do not get everything in nineteenth-century England, but only everything that Pip remembers or chooses to set down about his experiences, and what he sets down is colored by his personality. "I remember Mr. Hubble as a tough high-

---

[1]**whilom** once.   [2]**highte** was named.   [3]**swich** such.

shouldered stooping old man, of a saw-dusty fragrance, with his legs extraordinarily wide apart: so that in my short days I always saw some miles of open country between them when I met him coming up the lane." In any case, the coherence in a novel seems inclusive rather than exclusive. Novelists usually convey the sense that they, as distinct from their characters, are—in the words of Christopher Isherwood's *The Berlin Stories*—"a camera with its shutter open, quite passive, recording, not thinking. Recording the man shaving at the window opposite and the woman in the kimono washing her hair. Some day, all of this will have to be developed, carefully fixed, printed."

It is not merely that the novel gives us details. *Gulliver's Travels* has plenty of details about people six inches tall and people sixty feet tall, and about a flying island and rational horses. But these things are recognized as fanciful inventions, though they do turn our mind toward the real world. *Gulliver* is a satire that presents us with a picture of a fantastic world by which, paradoxically, we come to see the real world a little more clearly. The diminutive stature of the Lilliputians is an amusing and potent metaphor for the littleness of man, the flying island for abstract thinkers who have lost touch with reality, and so on. But the novelist who wants to show us the littleness of human beings invents not Lilliputians but a world of normal-sized people who do little things and have little thoughts.

Having spent so much time saying that the novel is not the epic or romance or fable, we must mention that a work may hover on the borderlines of these forms. Insofar as *Moby Dick* narrates with abundant realistic detail the experiences of a whaler ("This book," Dorothy Parker has said, "taught me more about whales than I ever wanted to know"), it is a novel; but in its evocation of mystery—Queequeg, the prophecies, Ishmael's miraculous rescue from the sea filled with sharks who "glided by as if with padlocks on their mouths"—it is a romance with strong symbolic implications.

The point is that although readers of a long piece of prose fiction can complain that they did not get what they paid for, they should find out what they did get. A remark by Bishop Butler, an eighteenth-century English moral philosopher, is relevant to literary criticism: "Everything is what it is and not another thing."

READING KATE CHOPIN'S
THE AWAKENING

Readers of novels often report on the way in which a favorite novel has absorbed their attention, taken them inside another world—not the rather private world of the lyric poem, but a social world, the life and times of a society other than our own. The novel that you will now turn to—Kate Chopin's *The Awakening*—is shorter than most novels, yet its detailed settings beautifully evoke the *feel* of late nineteenth-century New Orleans life and French Creole society. Chopin draws her characters acutely, closely studying how they speak and act, what they look like, how they dress and express themselves. And through her settings and characterizations, Chopin explores issues that are as vital and complicated today as they were when she wrote her book—relationships between men and women, marriage, motherhood, the family, the ways in which the structure of social life rewards and limits a woman's aspirations.

As you read *The Awakening,* enjoy the novel and find yourself challenged by it. But aim, too, as you read and reread it, to become an analytical reader. Keep in mind the key terms outlined in Chapter 7, "In Brief: Writing about Fiction": plot, character, point of view, setting, symbolism, theme, and style. Novels are longer than short stories, but in a sense you can imagine them as *long* stories, or as works that tell multiple, intertwined stories. Remember that you can make use of the same terms that are important for responding to, thinking about, and writing on short stories. It's just that with a novel there is more to attend to.

This is why it is often essential (and pleasurable) to reread a novel, especially a good one like *The Awakening.* One of our teachers once made the helpful suggestion that novels need to be read at different speeds. On a first reading, we might find ourselves caught up in the plot, wondering what will happen next. But when we are done, we might then return to the opening chapter, in order to examine how the author begins his or her work, starting there to detail the settings and lay out the organizing themes. Or maybe we will wish to reread the novel with an eye toward how the author portrays the major characters or structures a crucial scene. What Degas said about painting a picture is true also about writing a novel: "A good picture requires as much planning as a crime."

As you read and reread *The Awakening,* make notes in the margins and underline words, phrases, and images that strike you as interesting and important or puzzling and that you sense you will want to come back to for further thought and study. We suggest, too, that you keep a journal in which you record your responses and ideas. But most of all, we suggest that you read the novel not merely to fulfill an assignment but to enlarge your sense (by seeing through Chopin's eyes) of the range of human experience.

KATE CHOPIN

Kate Chopin (1851–1904) was born Katherine O'Flaherty in St. Louis; her father was an immigrant from Ireland, her mother a member of a French Creole family descended from the early colonizers of Louisiana. Chopin's father died when she was four, and she was raised by her mother's family and educated in Catholic schools. She read widely in French literature, especially admiring the stories of Guy de Maupassant. At nineteen she married Oscar Chopin (the name is pronounced in the French way, something like "show pan"), a New Orleans cotton broker, and for a while she lived an elegant life. When her husband's business failed, he moved the family to central Louisiana where he owned some land. Two years later Oscar Chopin died, and with her six children his widow returned to St. Louis where, at the age of thirty-seven, she began to write stories of Creole life. These were published in national magazines and then collected into two books, Bayou Folk *(1894) and* A Night in Acadie *(1899). Chopin's readers were pleased with her attention to the habits and language of a picturesque region, but her next publication, a novel entitled* The Awakening *(1899), was unfavorably received, largely because of its alleged immorality, and Chopin now found that she and her earlier works were looked on with disfavor.*

NEW ORLEANS IN KATE CHOPIN'S DAY: AN ALBUM OF PICTURES

A typical late nineteenth-century courtyard in New Orleans. (Arnold Genthe. "Courtyard, New Orleans," c. 1920. Photograph.)

Scene in the French Quarter of New Orleans, showing characteristic iron balconies. (Arnold Genthe. "Street Scene, French Quarter," c. 1920. Photograph.)

Electric streetcars and mule-drawn wagons crowded Canal Street in New Orleans in the late 1890s, before the advent of automobiles.

View of Rampart Street, New Orleans, c. 1890.

A middle-class sitting room in New Orleans, c. 1895.

The Chopin Home in Cloutierville (pronounced Cloochyville), Louisiana, about 260 miles from New Orleans.

Kate Chopin with her first four children.

This drawing, titled
"Sketches of Character in
New Orleans," appeared
in a magazine, *Every
Saturday*, on July 1, 1871.

The Awakening   [1899]

I

A green and yellow parrot, which hung in a cage outside the door, kept repeating over and over:

"*Allez vous-en! Allez vous-en! Sapristi!*[1] That's all right!"

He could speak a little Spanish, and also a language which nobody understood, unless it was the mockingbird that hung on the other side of the door, whistling his fluty notes out upon the breeze with maddening persistence.

Mr. Pontellier, unable to read his newspaper with any degree of comfort, arose with an expression and an exclamation of disgust. He walked down the gallery and across the narrow "bridges" which connected the Lebrun cottages one with the other. He had been seated before the door of the main house. The parrot and the mockingbird were the property of Madame Lebrun, and they had the right to make all the noise they wished. Mr. Pontellier had the privilege of quitting their society when they ceased to be entertaining.

5   He stopped before the door of his own cottage, which was the fourth one from the main building and next to the last. Seating himself in a wicker rocker which was there, he once more applied himself to the task of reading the newspaper. The day was Sunday; the paper was a day old. The Sunday papers had not yet reached Grand Isle.[2] He was already acquainted with the market reports, and he glanced restlessly over the editorials and bits of news which he had not had time to read before quitting New Orleans the day before.

Mr. Pontellier wore eye-glasses. He was a man of forty, of medium height and rather slender build; he stooped a little. His hair was brown and straight, parted on one side. His beard was neatly and closely trimmed.

Once in a while he withdrew his glance from the newspaper and looked about him. There was more noise than ever over at the house. The main building was called "the house," to distinguish it from the cottages. The chattering and whistling birds were still at it. Two young girls, the Farival twins, were playing a duet from "Zampa"[3] upon the piano. Madame Lebrun was bustling in and out, giving orders in a high key to a yard-boy whenever she got inside the house, and directions in an equally high voice to a dining-room servant whenever she got outside. She was a fresh, pretty woman, clad always in white with elbow sleeves. Her starched skirts crinkled as she came and went. Farther down, before one of the cottages, a lady in black was walking demurely up and down, telling her beads. A good many persons of the *pension*[4] had gone over to the *Chênière Caminada* in Beaudelet's lugger[5] to hear mass. Some young people were out under the water-oaks playing croquet. Mr. Pontellier's two children were there— sturdy little fellows of four and five. A quadroon nurse followed them about with a far-away, meditative air.

---

[1]*Allez . . . Sapristi!* Go away! Go away! For God's sake! (French)   [2]**Grand Isle** a resort island fifty miles south of New Orleans.   [3]**"Zampa"** opera by Louis Hérold (1791–1833). In the opera, a lover dies at sea.   [4]*pension* small hotel.   [5]**lugger** small boat.

Mr. Pontellier finally lit a cigar and began to smoke, letting the paper drag idly from his hand. He fixed his gaze upon a white sunshade that was advancing at snail's pace from the beach. He could see it plainly between the gaunt trunks of the water-oaks and across the stretch of yellow camomile. The gulf looked far away, melting hazily into the blue of the horizon. The sunshade continued to approach slowly. Beneath its pink-lined shelter were his wife, Mrs. Pontellier, and young Robert Lebrun. When they reached the cottage, the two seated themselves with some appearance of fatigue upon the upper step of the porch, facing each other, each leaning against a supporting post.

"What folly! to bathe at such an hour in such heat!" exclaimed Mr. Pontellier. He himself had taken a plunge at daylight. That was why the morning seemed long to him.

10   "You are burnt beyond recognition," he added, looking at his wife as one looks at a valuable piece of personal property which has suffered some damage. She held up her hands, strong, shapely hands, and surveyed them critically, drawing up her lawn[6] sleeves above the wrists. Looking at them reminded her of her rings, which she had given to her husband before leaving for the beach. She silently reached out to him, and he, understanding, took the rings from his vest pocket and dropped them into her open palm. She slipped them upon her fingers; then clasping her knees, she looked across at Robert and began to laugh. The rings sparkled upon her fingers. He sent back an answering smile.

"What is it?" asked Pontellier, looking lazily and amused from one to the other. It was some utter nonsense; some adventure out there in the water, and they both tried to relate it at once. It did not seem half so amusing when told. They realized this, and so did Mr. Pontellier. He yawned and stretched himself. Then he got up, saying he had half a mind to go over to Klein's hotel and play a game of billiards.

"Come go along, Lebrun," he proposed to Robert. But Robert admitted quite frankly that he preferred to stay where he was and talk to Mrs. Pontellier.

"Well, send him about his business when he bores you, Edna," instructed her husband as he prepared to leave.

"Here, take the umbrella," she exclaimed, holding it out to him. He accepted the sunshade, and lifting it over his head descended the steps and walked away.

15   "Coming back to dinner?" his wife called after him. He halted a moment and shrugged his shoulders. He felt in his vest pocket; there was a ten-dollar bill there. He did not know; perhaps he would return for the early dinner and perhaps he would not. It all depended upon the company which he found over at Klein's and the size of "the game." He did not say this, but she understood it, and laughed, nodding good-bye to him.

Both children wanted to follow their father when they saw him starting out. He kissed them and promised to bring back bonbons and peanuts.

II

Mrs. Pontellier's eyes were quick and bright; they were a yellowish brown, about the color of her hair. She had a way of turning them swiftly upon an

---

[6]**lawn** fine cotton or linen.

object and holding them there as if lost in some inward maze of contemplation or thought.

Her eyebrows were a shade darker than her hair. They were thick and almost horizontal, emphasizing the depth of her eyes. She was rather handsome than beautiful. Her face was captivating by reason of a certain frankness of expression and a contradictory subtle play of features. Her manner was engaging.

Robert rolled a cigarette. He smoked cigarettes because he could not afford cigars, he said. He had a cigar in his pocket which Mr. Pontellier had presented him with, and he was saving it for his after-dinner smoke.

20   This seemed quite proper and natural on his part. In coloring he was not unlike his companion. A clean-shaved face made the resemblance more pronounced than it would otherwise have been. There rested no shadow of care upon his open countenance. His eyes gathered in and reflected the light and languor of the summer day.

Mrs. Pontellier reached over for a palm-leaf fan that lay on the porch and began to fan herself, while Robert sent between his lips light puffs from his cigarette. They chatted incessantly: about the things around them; their amusing adventure out in the water—it had again assumed its entertaining aspect; about the wind, the trees, the people who had gone to the *Chênière;* about the children playing croquet under the oaks, and the Farival twins, who were now performing the overture to "The Poet and the Peasant."[7]

Robert talked a good deal about himself. He was very young, and did not know any better. Mrs. Pontellier talked a little about herself for the same reason. Each was interested in what the other said. Robert spoke of his intention to go to Mexico in the autumn, where fortune awaited him. He was always intending to go to Mexico, but some way never got there. Meanwhile he held on to his modest position in a mercantile house in New Orleans, where an equal familiarity with English, French and Spanish gave him no small value as a clerk and correspondent.

He was spending his summer vacation, as he always did, with his mother at Grand Isle. In former times, before Robert could remember, "the house" had been a summer luxury of the Lebruns. Now, flanked by its dozen or more cottages, which were always filled with exclusive visitors from the *"Quartier Français,"*[8] it enabled Madame Lebrun to maintain the easy and comfortable existence which appeared to be her birthright.

Mrs. Pontellier talked about her father's Mississippi plantation and her girlhood home in the old Kentucky blue-grass country. She was an American woman, with a small infusion of French which seemed to have been lost in dilution. She read a letter from her sister, who was away in the East, and who had engaged herself to be married. Robert was interested, and wanted to know what manner of girls the sisters were, what the father was like, and how long the mother had been dead.

25   When Mrs. Pontellier folded the letter it was time for her to dress for the early dinner.

"I see Léonce isn't coming back," she said, with a glance in the direction whence her husband had disappeared. Robert supposed he was not, as there were a good many New Orleans club men over at Klein's.

---

[7]**"The Poet and the Peasant"** operetta by Franz von Suppé (1819–1895).   [8]*Quartier Français* French Quarter, in New Orleans.

When Mrs. Pontellier left him to enter her room, the young man descended the steps and strolled over toward the croquet players, where, during the half-hour before dinner, he amused himself with the little Pontellier children, who were very fond of him.

III

It was eleven o'clock that night when Mr. Pontellier returned from Klein's hotel. He was in an excellent humor, in high spirits, and very talkative. His entrance awoke his wife, who was in bed and fast asleep when he came in. He talked to her while he undressed, telling her anecdotes and bits of news and gossip that he had gathered during the day. From his trousers pockets he took a fistful of crumpled banknotes and a good deal of silver coin, which he piled on the bureau indiscriminately with keys, knife, handkerchief, and whatever else happened to be in his pockets. She was overcome with sleep, and answered him with little half utterances.

He thought it very discouraging that his wife, who was the sole object of his existence, evinced so little interest in things which concerned him, and valued so little his conversation.

30   Mr. Pontellier had forgotten the bonbons and peanuts for the boys. Notwithstanding he loved them very much, and went into the adjoining room where they slept to take a look at them and make sure that they were resting comfortably. The result of his investigation was far from satisfactory. He turned and shifted the youngsters about in bed. One of them began to kick and talk about a basket full of crabs.

Mr. Pontellier returned to his wife with the information that Raoul had a high fever and needed looking after. Then he lit a cigar and went and sat near the open door to smoke it.

Mrs. Pontellier was quite sure Raoul had no fever. He had gone to bed perfectly well, she said, and nothing had ailed him all day. Mr. Pontellier was too well acquainted with fever symptoms to be mistaken. He assured her the child was consuming[9] at that moment in the next room.

He reproached his wife with her inattention, her habitual neglect of the children. If it was not a mother's place to look after children, whose on earth was it? He himself had his hands full with his brokerage business. He could not be in two places at once; making a living for his family on the street, and staying at home to see that no harm befell them. He talked in a monotonous, insistent way.

Mrs. Pontellier sprang out of bed and went into the next room. She soon came back and sat on the edge of the bed, leaning her head down on the pillow. She said nothing, and refused to answer her husband when he questioned her. When his cigar was smoked out he went to bed, and in half a minute he was fast asleep.

35   Mrs. Pontellier was by that time thoroughly awake. She began to cry a little, and wiped her eyes on the sleeve of her *peignoir*.[10] Blowing out the candle, which her husband had left burning, she slipped her bare feet into a pair of satin *mules* at the foot of the bed and went out on the porch, where she sat down in the wicker chair and began to rock gently to and fro.

---

[9]**consuming** being consumed—that is, feverish.   [10]*peignoir* dressing gown.

It was then past midnight. The cottages were all dark. A single faint light gleamed out from the hallway of the house. There was no sound abroad except the hooting of an old owl in the top of a water-oak, and the everlasting voice of the sea, that was not uplifted at that soft hour. It broke like a mournful lullaby upon the night.

The tears came so fast to Mrs. Pontellier's eyes that the damp sleeve of her *peignoir* no longer served to dry them. She was holding the back of her chair with one hand; her loose sleeve had slipped almost to the shoulder of her uplifted arm. Turning, she thrust her face, steaming and wet, into the bend of her arm, and she went on crying there, not caring any longer to dry her face, her eyes, her arms. She could not have told why she was crying. Such experiences as the foregoing were not uncommon in her married life. They seemed never before to have weighed much against the abundance of her husband's kindness and a uniform devotion which had come to be tacit and self-understood.

An indescribable oppression, which seemed to generate in some unfamiliar part of her consciousness, filled her whole being with a vague anguish. It was like a shadow, like a mist passing across her soul's summer day. It was strange and unfamiliar; it was a mood. She did not sit there inwardly upbraiding her husband, lamenting at Fate, which had directed her footsteps to the path which they had taken. She was just having a good cry all to herself. The mosquitoes made merry over her, biting her firm, round arms and nipping at her bare insteps.

The little stinging, buzzing imps succeeded in dispelling a mood which might have held her there in the darkness half a night longer.

40   The following morning Mr. Pontellier was up in good time to take the rockaway[11] which was to convey him to the steamer at the wharf. He was returning to the city to his business, and they would not see him again at the Island till the coming Sunday. He had regained his composure, which seemed to have been somewhat impaired the night before. He was eager to be gone, as he looked forward to a lively week in Carondelet Street.[12]

Mr. Pontellier gave his wife half of the money which he had brought away from Klein's hotel the evening before. She liked money as well as most women, and accepted it with no little satisfaction.

"It will buy a handsome wedding present for Sister Janet!" she exclaimed, smoothing out the bills as she counted them one by one.

"Oh! we'll treat Sister Janet better than that, my dear," he laughed, as he prepared to kiss her good-by.

The boys were tumbling about, clinging to his legs, imploring that numerous things be brought back to them. Mr. Pontellier was a great favorite, and ladies, men, children, even nurses, were always on hand to say good-by to him. His wife stood smiling and waving, the boys shouting, as he disappeared in the old rockaway down the sandy road.

45   A few days later a box arrived for Mrs. Pontellier from New Orleans. It was from her husband. It was filled with *friandises,* with luscious and toothsome bits—the finest of fruits, *patés,* a rare bottle or two, delicious syrups, and bonbons in abundance.

---

[11]**rockaway** horse-drawn carriage.   [12]**Carondelet Street** street in the financial district of New Orleans.

Mrs. Pontellier was always very generous with the contents of such a box; she was quite used to receiving them when away from home. The patés and fruit were brought to the dining-room; the bonbons were passed around. And the ladies, selecting with dainty and discriminating fingers and a little greedily, all declared that Mr. Pontellier was the best husband in the world. Mrs. Pontellier was forced to admit that she knew of none better.

IV

It would have been a difficult matter for Mr. Pontellier to define to his own satisfaction or any one else's wherein his wife failed in her duty toward their children. It was something which he felt rather than perceived, and he never voiced the feeling without subsequent regret and ample atonement.

If one of the little Pontellier boys took a tumble whilst at play, he was not apt to rush crying to his mother's arms for comfort; he would more likely pick himself up, wipe the water out of his eyes and the sand out of his mouth, and go on playing. Tots as they were, they pulled together and stood their ground in childish battles with doubled fists and uplifted voices, which usually prevailed against the other brother-tots. The quadroon nurse was looked upon as a huge encumbrance, only good to button up waists and panties and to brush and part hair; since it seemed to be a law of society that their hair must be parted and brushed.

In short, Mrs. Pontellier was not a mother-woman. The mother-women seemed to prevail that summer at Grand Isle. It was easy to know them, fluttering about with extended, protecting wings when any harm, real or imaginary, threatened their precious brood. They were women who idolized their children, worshiped their husbands, and esteemed it a holy privilege to efface themselves as individuals and grow wings as ministering angels.

50   Many of them were delicious in the rôle; one of them was the embodiment of every womanly grace and charm. If her husband did not adore her, he was a brute, deserving of death by slow torture. Her name was Adèle Ratignolle. There are no words to describe her save the old ones that have served so often to picture the bygone heroine of romance and the fair lady of our dreams. There was nothing subtle or hidden about her charms; her beauty was all there, flaming and apparent; the spun-gold hair that comb nor confining pin could restrain; the blue eyes that were like nothing but sapphires; two lips that pouted, that were so red one could only think of cherries or some other delicious crimson fruit in looking at them. She was growing a little stout, but it did not seem to detract an iota from the grace of every step, pose, gesture. One would not have wanted her white neck a mite less full or her beautiful arms more slender. Never were hands more exquisite than hers, and it was joy to look at them when she threaded her needle or adjusted her gold thimble to her tapered middle finger as she sewed away on the little night-drawers or fashioned a bodice or a bib.

Madame Ratignolle was very fond of Mrs. Pontellier, and often she took her sewing and went over to sit with her in the afternoons. She was sitting there the afternoon of the day the box arrived from New Orleans. She had possession of the rocker, and she was busily engaged in sewing upon a diminutive pair of night-drawers.

She had brought the pattern of the drawers for Mrs. Pontellier to cut out—a marvel of construction, fashioned to enclose a baby's body so effectually that only two small eyes might look out from the garment, like an Eskimo's. They were designed for winter wear, when treacherous drafts came down chimneys and insidious currents of deadly cold found their way through key-holes.

Mrs. Pontellier's mind was quite at rest concerning the present material needs of her children, and she could not see the use of anticipating and making winter night garments the subject of her summer meditations. But she did not want to appear unamiable and uninterested, so she had brought forth newspapers, which she spread upon the floor of the gallery, and under Madame Ratignolle's directions she had cut a pattern of the impervious garment.

Robert was there, seated as he had been the Sunday before, and Mrs. Pontellier also occupied her former position on the upper step, leaning listlessly against the post. Beside her was a box of bonbons, which she held out at intervals to Madame Ratignolle.

55   That lady seemed at a loss to make a selection, but finally settled upon a stick of nougat, wondering if it were not too rich; whether it could possibly hurt her. Madame Ratignolle had been married seven years. About every two years she had a baby. At that time she had three babies, and was beginning to think of a fourth one. She was always talking about her "condition." Her "condition" was in no way apparent, and no one would have known a thing about it but for her persistence in making it the subject of conversation.

Robert started to reassure her, asserting that he had known a lady who had subsisted upon nougat during the entire—but seeing the color mount into Mrs. Pontellier's face he checked himself and changed the subject.

Mrs. Pontellier, though she had married a Creole,[13] was not thoroughly at home in the society of Creoles; never before had she been thrown so intimately among them. There were only Creoles that summer at Lebrun's. They all knew each other, and felt like one large family, among whom existed the most amicable relations. A characteristic which distinguished them and which impressed Mrs. Pontellier most forcibly was their entire absence of prudery. Their freedom of expression was at first incomprehensible to her, though she had no difficulty in reconciling it with a lofty chastity which in the Creole woman seems to be inborn and unmistakable.

Never would Edna Pontellier forget the shock with which she heard Madame Ratignolle relating to old Monsieur Farival the harrowing story of one of her *accouchements*,[14] withholding no intimate detail. She was growing accustomed to like shocks, but she could not keep the mounting color back from her cheeks. Oftener than once her coming had interrupted the droll story with which Robert was entertaining some amused group of married women.

A book had gone the rounds of the *pension*. When it came her turn to read it, she did so with profound astonishment. She felt moved to read the book in secret and solitude, though none of the others had done so—to hide it from view at the sound of approaching footsteps. It was openly criticized and freely discussed at table. Mrs. Pontellier gave over being astonished, and concluded that wonders would never cease.

---

[13]**Creole** aristocratic descendant of the French and Spanish settlers of New Orleans.
[14]***accouchements*** birthings.

V

60   They formed a congenial group sitting there that summer afternoon—
Madame Ratignolle sewing away, often stopping to relate a story or incident with much expressive gesture of her perfect hands; Robert and Mrs.
Pontellier sitting idle, exchanging occasional words, glances or smiles
which indicated a certain advanced stage of intimacy and *camaraderie*.

He had lived in her shadow during the past month. No one thought
anything of it. Many had predicted that Robert would devote himself to
Mrs. Pontellier when he arrived. Since the age of fifteen, which was eleven
years before, Robert each summer at Grand Isle had constituted himself the
devoted attendant of some fair dame or damsel. Sometimes it was a young
girl, again a widow; but as often as not it was some interesting married
woman.

For two consecutive seasons he lived in the sunlight of Mademoiselle
Duvigné's presence. But she died between summers; then Robert posed as
an inconsolable, prostrating himself at the feet of Madame Ratignolle for
whatever crumbs of sympathy and comfort she might be pleased to
vouchsafe.

Mrs. Pontellier liked to sit and gaze at her fair companion as she might
look upon a faultless Madonna.

"Could any one fathom the cruelty beneath that fair exterior?" murmured Robert. "She knew that I adored her once, and she let me adore her.
It was 'Robert, come; go; stand up; sit down; do this; do that; see if the baby
sleeps; my thimble, please, that I left God knows where. Come and read
Daudet[15] to me while I sew.'"

65   "*Par exemple!*[16] I never had to ask. You were always there under my
feet, like a troublesome cat."

"You mean like an adoring dog. And just as soon as Ratignolle appeared
on the scene, then it *was* like a dog. '*Passez! Adieu! Allez vous-en!*'"[17]

"Perhaps I feared to make Alphonse jealous," she interjoined, with excessive naïveté. That made them all laugh. The right hand jealous of the left!
The heart jealous of the soul! But for that matter, the Creole husband is
never jealous; with him the gangrene passion is one which has become
dwarfed by disuse.

Meanwhile Robert, addressing Mrs. Pontellier, continued to tell of his
one time hopeless passion for Madame Ratignolle; of sleepless nights, of consuming flames till the very sea sizzled when he took his daily plunge. While
the lady at the needle kept up a little running, contemptuous comment:

"*Blagueur—farceur—gros bête, va!*"[18]

70   He never assumed this serio-comic tone when alone with Mrs.
Pontellier. She never knew precisely what to make of it; at that moment it
was impossible for her to guess how much of it was jest and what proportion was earnest. It was understood that he had often spoken words of love
to Madame Ratignolle, without any thought of being taken seriously. Mrs.
Pontellier was glad he had not assumed a similar rôle toward herself. It
would have been unacceptable and annoying.

---

[15]**Daudet** Alphonse Daudet (1840–87), French novelist.   [16]***Par exemple!*** Indeed!
[17]***Passez . . . vous-en!*** Go! Goodby! Go away!   [18]***Blagueur . . . va!*** Joker—clown—silly,
cut it out!

Mrs. Pontellier had brought her sketching materials, which she some-times dabbled with in an unprofessional way. She liked the dabbling. She felt in it satisfaction of a kind which no other employment afforded her.

She had long wished to try herself on Madame Ratignolle. Never had that lady seemed a more tempting subject than at that moment, seated there like some sensuous Madonna, with the gleam of the fading day enriching her splendid color.

Robert crossed over and seated himself upon the step below Mrs. Pontellier, that he might watch her work. She handled her brushes with a certain ease and freedom which came, not from long and close acquain-tance with them, but from a natural aptitude. Robert followed her work with close attention, giving forth little ejaculatory expressions of apprecia-tion in French, which he addressed to Madame Ratignolle.

"Mais ce n'est pas mal! Elle s'y connait, elle a de la force, oui."[19]

75 During his oblivious attention he once quietly rested his head against Mrs. Pontellier's arm. As gently she repulsed him. Once again he repeated the offense. She could not but believe it to be thoughtlessness on his part; yet that was no reason she should submit to it. She did not remonstrate, ex-cept again to repulse him quietly but firmly. He offered no apology.

The picture completed bore no resemblance to Madame Ratignolle. She was greatly disappointed to find that it did not look like her. But it was a fair enough piece of work, and in many respects satisfying.

Mrs. Pontellier evidently did not think so. After surveying the sketch critically she drew a broad smudge of paint across its surface, and crumpled the paper between her hands.

The youngsters came tumbling up the steps, the quadroon following at the respectful distance which they required her to observe. Mrs. Pontellier made them carry her paints and things into the house. She sought to detain them for a little talk and some pleasantry. But they were greatly in earnest. They had only come to investigate the contents of the bonbon box. They accepted without murmuring what she chose to give them, each holding out two chubby hands scoop-like, in the vain hope that they might be filled; and then away they went.

The sun was low in the west, and the breeze soft and languorous that came up from the south, charged with the seductive odor of the sea. Chil-dren, freshly befurbelowed,[20] were gathering for their games under the oaks. Their voices were high and penetrating.

80 Madame Ratignolle folded her sewing, placing thimble, scissors and thread all neatly together in the roll, which she pinned securely. She com-plained of faintness. Mrs. Pontellier flew for the cologne water and a fan. She bathed Madame Ratignolle's face with cologne, while Robert plied the fan with unnecessary vigor.

The spell was soon over, and Mrs. Pontellier could not help wondering if there were not a little imagination responsible for its origin, for the rose tint had never faded from her friend's face.

She stood watching the fair woman walk down the long line of galleries with the grace and majesty which queens are sometimes supposed to pos-sess. Her little ones ran to meet her. Two of them clung about her white

---

[19]*Mais . . . oui* Not bad! She knows what's she doing, she's really good.   [20]**befurbe-lowed** dressed in frills.

skirts, the third she took from its nurse and with a thousand endearments bore it along in her own fond, encircling arms. Though, as everybody well knew, the doctor had forbidden her to lift so much as a pin!

"Are you going bathing?" asked Robert of Mrs. Pontellier. It was not so much a question as a reminder.

"Oh, no," she answered with a tone of indecision. "I'm tired; I think not." Her glance wandered from his face away toward the Gulf, whose sonorous murmur reached her like a loving but imperative entreaty.

85   "Oh, come!" he insisted. "You mustn't miss your bath. Come on. The water must be delicious; it will not hurt you. Come."

He reached up for her big, rough straw hat that hung on a peg outside the door, and put it on her head. They descended the steps, and walked away together toward the beach. The sun was low in the west and the breeze was soft and warm.

VI

Edna Pontellier could not have told why, wishing to go to the beach with Robert, she should in the first place have declined, and in the second place have followed in obedience to one of the two contradictory impulses which impelled her.

A certain light was beginning to dawn dimly within her,—the light which, showing the way, forbids it.

At that early period it served but to bewilder her. It moved her to dreams, to thoughtfulness, to the shadowy anguish which had overcome her the midnight when she had abandoned herself to tears.

90   In short, Mrs. Pontellier was beginning to realize her position in the universe as a human being, and to recognize her relations as an individual to the world within and about her. This may seem like a ponderous weight of wisdom to descend upon the soul of a young woman of twenty-eight—perhaps more wisdom than the Holy Ghost is usually pleased to vouchsafe to any woman.

But the beginning of things, of a world especially, is necessarily vague, tangled, chaotic, and exceedingly disturbing. How few of us ever emerge from such beginning! How many souls perish in its tumult!

The voice of the sea is seductive; never ceasing, whispering, clamoring, murmuring, inviting the soul to wander for a spell in abysses of solitude; to lose itself in mazes of inward contemplation.

The voice of the sea speaks to the soul. The touch of the sea is sensuous, enfolding the body in its soft, close embrace.

VII

Mrs. Pontellier was not a woman given to confidences, a characteristic hitherto contrary to her nature. Even as a child she had lived her own small life all within herself. At a very early period she had apprehended instinctively the dual life—that outward existence which conforms, the inward life which questions.

95   That summer at Grand Isle she began to loosen a little the mantle of reserve that had always enveloped her. There may have been—there must have been—influences, both subtle and apparent, working in their

several ways to induce her to do this; but the most obvious was the influence of Adèle Ratignolle. The excessive physical charm of the Creole had
first attracted her, for Edna had a sensuous susceptibility to beauty. Then
the candor of the woman's whole existence, which every one might read,
and which formed so striking a contrast to her own habitual reserve—
this might have furnished a link. Who can tell what metals the gods use in
forging the subtle bond which we call sympathy, which we might as well
call love.

The two women went away one morning to the beach together, arm in
arm, under the huge white sunshade. Edna had prevailed upon Madame
Ratignolle to leave the children behind, though she could not induce her to
relinquish a diminutive roll of needlework, which Adèle begged to be allowed to slip into the depths of her pocket. In some unaccountable way
they had escaped from Robert.

The walk to the beach was no inconsiderable one, consisting as it did of
a long, sandy path, upon which a sporadic and tangled growth that bordered
it on either side made frequent and unexpected inroads. There were acres of
yellow camomile reaching out on either hand. Further away still, vegetable
gardens abounded, with frequent small plantations of orange or lemon trees
intervening. The dark green clusters glistened from afar in the sun.

The women were both of goodly height, Madame Ratignolle possessing
the more feminine and matronly figure. The charm of Edna Pontellier's
physique stole insensibly upon you. The lines of her body were long, clean
and symmetrical; it was a body which occasionally fell into splendid poses;
there was no suggestion of the trim stereotyped fashion-plate about it. A casual and indiscriminating observer, in passing, might not cast a second glance
upon the figure. But with more feeling and discernment he would have recognized the noble beauty of its modeling, and the graceful severity of poise
and movement, which made Edna Pontellier different from the crowd.

She wore a cool muslin that morning—white, with a waving vertical
line of brown running through it; also a white linen collar and the big straw
hat which she had taken from the peg outside the door. The hat rested any
way on her yellow-brown hair, that waved a little, was heavy, and clung
close to her head.

100   Madame Ratignolle, more careful of her complexion, had twined a
gauze veil about her head. She wore doeskin gloves, with gauntlets that
protected her wrists. She was dressed in pure white, with a fluffiness of ruf-
fles that became her. The draperies and fluttering things which she wore
suited her rich, luxuriant beauty as a greater severity of line could not have
done.

There were a number of bath-houses along the beach, of rough but
solid construction, built with small, protecting galleries facing the water.
Each house consisted of two compartments, and each family at Lebrun's
possessed a compartment for itself, fitted out with all the essential parapher-
nalia of the bath and whatever other conveniences the owners might desire.
The two women had no intention of bathing; they had just strolled down to
the beach for a walk and to be alone and near the water. The Pontellier and
Ratignolle compartments adjoined one another under the same roof.

Mrs. Pontellier had brought down her key through force of habit. Unlocking the door of her bath-room she went inside, and soon emerged,
bringing a rug, which she spread upon the floor of the gallery, and two

huge hair pillows covered with crash,[21] which she placed against the front of the building.

The two seated themselves there in the shade of the porch, side by side, with their backs against the pillows and their feet extended. Madame Ratignolle removed her veil, wiped her face with a rather delicate handkerchief, and fanned herself with the fan which she always carried suspended somewhere about her person by a long, narrow ribbon. Edna removed her collar and opened her dress at the throat. She took the fan from Madame Ratignolle and began to fan both herself and her companion. It was very warm, and for a while they did nothing but exchange remarks about the heat, the sun, the glare. But there was a breeze blowing, a choppy, stiff wind that whipped the water into froth. It fluttered the skirts of the two women and kept them for a while engaged in adjusting, readjusting, tucking in, securing hair-pins and hat-pins. A few persons were sporting some distance away in the water. The beach was very still of human sound at that hour. The lady in black was reading her morning devotions on the porch of a neighboring bath-house. Two young lovers were exchanging their hearts' yearnings beneath the children's tent, which they had found unoccupied.

Edna Pontellier, casting her eyes about, had finally kept them at rest upon the sea. The day was clear and carried the gaze out as far as the blue sky went; there were a few white clouds suspended idly over the horizon. A lateen[22] sail was visible in the direction of Cat Island, and others to the south seemed almost motionless in the far distance.

105   "Of whom—of what are you thinking?" asked Adèle of her companion, whose countenance she had been watching with a little amused attention, arrested by the absorbed expression which seemed to have seized and fixed every feature into a statuesque repose.

"Nothing," returned Mrs. Pontellier, with a start, adding at once: "How stupid! But it seems to me it is the reply we make instinctively to such a question. Let me see," she went on, throwing back her head and narrowing her fine eyes till they shone like two vivid points of light. "Let me see. I was really not conscious of thinking of anything; but perhaps I can retrace my thoughts."

"Oh! never mind!" laughed Madame Ratignolle. "I am not quite so exacting. I will let you off this time. It is really too hot to think, especially to think about thinking."

"But for the fun of it," persisted Edna. "First of all, the sight of the water stretching so far away, those motionless sails against the blue sky, made a delicious picture that I just wanted to sit and look at it. The hot wind beating in my face made me think—without any connection that I can trace—of a summer day in Kentucky, of a meadow that seemed as big as the ocean to the very little girl walking through the grass, which was higher than her waist. She threw out her arms as if swimming when she walked, beating the tall grass as one strikes out in the water. Oh, I see the connection now!"

"Where were you going that day in Kentucky, walking through the grass?"

---

[21]**crash** heavy linen.   [22]**lateen** triangular.

110   "I don't remember now. I was just walking diagonally across a big field.
My sun-bonnet obstructed the view. I could see only the stretch of green before me, and I felt as if I must walk on forever, without coming to the end of
it. I don't remember whether I was frightened or pleased. I must have been
entertained.

"Likely as not it was Sunday," she laughed; "and I was running away
from prayers, from the Presbyterian service, read in a spirit of gloom by my
father that chills me yet to think of."

"And have you been running away from prayer ever since, *ma chère?*"
asked Madame Ratignolle, amused.

"No! oh, no!" Edna hastened to say. "I was a little unthinking child in
those days, just following a misleading impulse without question. On the
contrary, during one period of my life religion took a firm hold upon me; after I was twelve and until—until—why, I suppose until now, though I never
thought much about it—just driven along by habit. But do you know," she
broke off, turning her quick eyes upon Madame Ratignolle and leaning forward a little so as to bring her face quite close to that of her companion,
"sometimes I feel this summer as if I were walking through the green
meadow again; idly, aimlessly, unthinking and unguided."

Madame Ratignolle laid her hand over that of Mrs. Pontellier, which
was near her. Seeing that the hand was not withdrawn, she clasped it firmly
and warmly. She even stroked it a little fondly, with the other hand, murmuring in an undertone, *"Pauvre chérie."*[23]

115   The action was at first a little confusing to Edna, but she soon lent herself readily to the Creole's gentle caress. She was not accustomed to an outward and spoken expression of affection, either in herself or in others. She
and her younger sister, Janet, had quarreled a good deal through force of
unfortunate habit. Her older sister, Margaret, was matronly and dignified,
probably from having assumed matronly and housewifely responsibilities
too early in life, their mother having died when they were quite young. Margaret was not effusive: she was practical. Edna had had an occasional girl
friend, but whether accidentally or not, they seemed to have been all of one
type—the self-contained. She never realized that the reserve of her own
character had much, perhaps everything, to do with this. Her most intimate
friend at school had been one of rather exceptional intellectual gifts, who
wrote fine-sounding essays, which Edna admired and strove to imitate; and
with her she talked and glowed over the English classics, and sometimes
held religious and political controversies.

Edna often wondered at one propensity which sometimes had inwardly
disturbed her without causing any outward show or manifestation on her
part. At a very early age—perhaps it was when she traversed the ocean of
waving grass—she remembered that she had been passionately enamored
of a dignified and sad-eyed cavalry officer who visited her father in Kentucky. She could not leave his presence when he was there, nor remove her
eyes from his face, which was something like Napoleon's, with a lock of
black hair falling across the forehead. But the cavalry officer melted imperceptibly out of her existence.

---

[23]*Pauvre chérie* Poor dear.

At another time her affections were deeply engaged by a young gentleman who visited a lady on a neighboring plantation. It was after they went to Mississippi to live. The young man was engaged to be married to the young lady, and they sometimes called upon Margaret, driving over of afternoons in a buggy. Edna was a little miss, just merging into her teens; and the realization that she herself was nothing, nothing, nothing to the engaged young man was a bitter affliction to her. But he, too, went the way of dreams.

She was a grown young woman when she was overtaken by what she supposed to be the climax of her fate. It was when the face and figure of a great tragedian began to haunt her imagination and stir her senses. The persistence of the infatuation lent it an aspect of genuineness. The hopelessness of it colored it with the lofty tones of a great passion.

The picture of the tragedian stood enframed upon her desk. Any one may possess the portrait of a tragedian without exciting suspicion or comment. (This was a sinister reflection which she cherished.) In the presence of others she expressed admiration for his exalted gifts, as she handed the photograph around and dwelt upon the fidelity of the likeness. When alone she sometimes picked it up and kissed the cold glass passionately.

120   Her marriage to Léonce Pontellier was purely an accident, in this respect resembling many other marriages which masquerade as the decrees of Fate. It was in the midst of her secret great passion that she met him. He fell in love, as men are in the habit of doing, and pressed his suit with an earnestness and an ardor which left nothing to be desired. He pleased her; his absolute devotion flattered her. She fancied there was a sympathy of thought and taste between them, in which fancy she was mistaken. Add to this the violent opposition of her father and her sister Margaret to her marriage with a Catholic, and we need seek no further for the motives which led her to accept Monsieur Pontellier for her husband.

The acme of bliss, which would have been a marriage with the tragedian, was not for her in this world. As the devoted wife of a man who worshiped her, she felt she would take her place with a certain dignity in the world of reality, closing the portals forever behind her upon the realm of romance and dreams.

But it was not long before the tragedian had gone to join the cavalry officer and the engaged young man and a few others; and Edna found herself face to face with the realities. She grew fond of her husband, realizing with some unaccountable satisfaction that no trace of passion or excessive and fictitious warmth colored her affection, thereby threatening its dissolution.

She was fond of her children in an uneven, impulsive way. She would sometimes gather them passionately to her heart; she would sometimes forget them. The year before they had spent part of the summer with their grandmother Pontellier in Iberville. Feeling secure regarding their happiness and welfare, she did not miss them except with an occasional intense longing. Their absence was a sort of relief, though she did not admit this, even to herself. It seemed to free her of a responsibility which she had blindly assumed and for which Fate had not fitted her.

Edna did not reveal so much as all this to Madame Ratignolle that summer day when they sat with faces turned to the sea. But a good part of it escaped her. She had put her head down on Madame Ratignolle's shoulder.

She was flushed and felt intoxicated with the sound of her own voice and the unaccustomed taste of candor. It muddled her like wine, or like a first breath of freedom.

125   There was the sound of approaching voices. It was Robert, surrounded by a troop of children, searching for them. The two little Pontelliers were with him, and he carried Madame Ratignolle's little girl in his arms. There were other children beside, and two nurse-maids followed, looking disagreeable and resigned.

The women at once rose and began to shake out their draperies and relax their muscles. Mrs. Pontellier threw the cushions and rug into the bathhouse. The children all scampered off to the awning, and they stood there in a line, gazing upon the intruding lovers, still exchanging their vows and sighs. The lovers got up, with only a silent protest, and walked slowly away somewhere else.

The children possessed themselves of the tent, and Mrs. Pontellier went over to join them.

Madame Ratignolle begged Robert to accompany her to the house; she complained of cramp in her limbs and stiffness of the joints. She leaned draggingly upon his arm as they walked.

VIII

"Do me a favor, Robert," spoke the pretty woman at his side, almost as soon as she and Robert had started on their slow, homeward way. She looked up in his face, leaning on his arm beneath the encircling shadow of the umbrella which he had lifted.

130   "Granted; as many as you like," he returned, glancing down into her eyes that were full of thoughtfulness and some speculation.

"I only ask for one; let Mrs. Pontellier alone."

"*Tiens!*" he exclaimed, with a sudden, boyish laugh. "*Voilá que Madame Ratignolle est jalouse!*"[24]

"Nonsense! I'm in earnest; I mean what I say. Let Mrs. Pontellier alone."

"Why?" he asked; himself growing serious at his companion's solicitation.

135   "She is not one of us; she is not like us. She might make the unfortunate blunder of taking you seriously."

His face flushed with annoyance, and taking off his soft hat he began to beat it impatiently against his leg as he walked. "Why shouldn't she take me seriously?" he demanded sharply. "Am I a comedian, a clown, a jack-in-the-box? Why shouldn't she? You Creoles! I have no patience with you! Am I always to be regarded as a feature of an amusing programme? I hope Mrs. Pontellier does take me seriously. I hope she has discernment enough to find in me something besides the *blagueur*.[25] If I thought there was any doubt—"

"Oh, enough, Robert!" she broke into his heated outburst. "You are not thinking of what you are saying. You speak with about as little reflection as we might expect from one of those children down there playing in the sand. If your intentions to any married women here were ever offered with any attention of being convincing, you would not be the gentleman we all

---

[24]*Tiens . . . jalouse!* Ah, so Madame Ratignolle is jealous!   [25]*blagueur* joker.

know you to be, and you would be unfit to associate with the wives and daughters of the people who trust you."

Madame Ratignolle had spoken what she believed to be the law and the gospel. The young man shrugged his shoulders impatiently.

"Oh! well! That isn't it," slamming his hat down vehemently upon his head. "You ought to feel that such things are not flattering to say to a fellow."

140　　"Should our whole intercourse consist of an exchange of compliments? *Ma foi!*"[26]

"It isn't pleasant to have a woman tell you—" he went on, unheedingly, but breaking off suddenly: "Now if I were like Arobin—you remember Alcée Arobin and that story of the consul's wife at Biloxi?" And he related the story of Alcée Arobin and the consul's wife; and another about the tenor of the French Opera, who received letters which should never have been written; and still other stories, grave and gay, till Mrs. Pontellier and her possible propensity for taking young men seriously was apparently forgotten.

Madame Ratignolle, when they had regained her cottage, went in to take the hour's rest which she considered helpful. Before leaving her, Robert begged her pardon for the impatience—he called it rudeness—with which he had received her well-meant caution.

"You made one mistake, Adèle," he said, with a light smile; "there is no earthly possibility of Mrs. Pontellier ever taking me seriously. You should have warned me against taking myself seriously. Your advice might then have carried some weight and given me subject for some reflection. *Au revoir*. But you look tired," he added, solicitously. "Would you like a cup of bouillon? Shall I stir you a toddy? Let me mix you a toddy with a drop of Angostura."

She acceded to the suggestion of bouillon, which was grateful and acceptable. He went himself to the kitchen, which was a building apart from the cottages and lying to the rear of the house. And he himself brought her the golden-brown bouillon, in a dainty Sévres cup, with a flaky cracker or two on the saucer.

145　　She thrust a bare, white arm from the curtain which shielded her open door, and received the cup from his hands. She told him he was a *bon garçon*[27] and she meant it. Robert thanked her and turned away toward "the house."

The lovers were just entering the grounds of the *pension*. They were leaning toward each other as the water-oaks bent from the sea. There was not a particle of earth beneath their feet. Their heads might have been turned upside-down, so absolutely did they tread upon blue ether. The lady in black, creeping behind them, looked a trifle paler and more jaded than usual. There was no sign of Mrs. Pontellier and the children. Robert scanned the distance for any such apparition. They would doubtless remain away till the dinner hour. The young man ascended to his mother's room. It was situated at the top of the house, made up of odd angles and a queer, sloping ceiling. Two broad dormer windows looked out toward the Gulf, and as far across it as man's eye might reach. The furnishings of the room were light, cool, and practical.

Madame Lebrun was busily engaged at the sewing-machine. A little black girl sat on the floor, and with her hands worked the treadle of the

---

[26]*Ma foi!* Good Lord!　　[27]*bon garçon* (1) nice fellow; (2) good waiter.

machine. The Creole woman does not take any chances which may be avoided of imperiling her health.

Robert went over and seated himself on the broad sill of one of the dormer windows. He took a book from his pocket and began energetically to read it, judging by the precision and frequency with which he turned the leaves. The sewing-machine made a resounding clatter in the room; it was of a ponderous, by-gone make. In the lulls, Robert and his mother exchanged bits of desultory conversation.

"Where is Mrs. Pontellier?"

150   "Down at the beach with the children."

"I promised to lend her the Goncourt.[28] Don't forget to take it down when you go; it's there on the bookshelf over the small table." Clatter, clatter, clatter, bang! for the next five or eight minutes.

"Where is Victor going with the rockaway?"

"The rockaway? Victor?"

"Yes; down there in front. He seems to be getting ready to drive away somewhere."

155   "Call him." Clatter, clatter!

Robert uttered a shrill, piercing whistle which might have been heard back at the wharf.

"He won't look up."

Madame Lebrun flew to the window. She called "Victor!" She waved a handkerchief and called again. The young fellow below got into the vehicle and started the horse off at a gallop.

Madame Lebrun went back to the machine, crimson with annoyance. Victor was the younger son and brother—a *tête montée*,[29] with a temper which invited violence and a will which no ax could break.

160   "Whenever you say the word I'm ready to thrash any amount of reason into him that he's able to hold."

"If your father had only lived!" Clatter, clatter, clatter, clatter, bang! It was a fixed belief with Madame Lebrun that the conduct of the universe and all things pertaining thereto would have been manifestly of a more intelligent and higher order had not Monsieur Lebrun been removed to other spheres during the early years of their married life.

"What do you hear from Montel?" Montel was a middle-aged gentleman whose vain ambition and desire for the past twenty years had been to fill the void which Monsieur Lebrun's taking off had left in the Lebrun household. Clatter, clatter, bang, clatter!

"I have a letter somewhere," looking in the machine drawer and finding the letter in the bottom of the work-basket. "He says to tell you he will be in Vera Cruz the beginning of next month"—clatter, clatter!—"and if you still have the intention of joining him"—bang! clatter, clatter, bang!

"Why didn't you tell me so before, mother? You know I wanted—" Clatter, clatter, clatter!

165   "Do you see Mrs. Pontellier starting back with the children? She will be in late to luncheon again. She never starts to get ready for luncheon till the last minute." Clatter, clatter! "Where are you going?"

"Where did you say the Goncourt was?"

---

[28] **the Goncourt** novel by Edmond Goncourt (1822–1896).   [29] ***tête montée*** impulsive fellow.

IX

Every light in the hall was ablaze; every lamp turned as high as it could be without smoking the chimney or threatening explosion. The lamps were fixed at intervals against the wall, encircling the whole room. Some one had gathered orange and lemon branches, and with these fashioned graceful festoons between. The dark green of the branches stood out and glistened against the white muslin curtains which draped the windows, and which puffed, floated, and flapped at the capricious will of a stiff breeze that swept up from the Gulf.

It was Saturday night a few weeks after the intimate conversation held between Robert and Mrs. Ratignolle on their way from the beach. An unusual number of husbands, fathers, and friends had come down to stay over Sunday; and they were being suitably entertained by their families, with the material help of Madame Lebrun. The dining tables had all been removed to one end of the hall, and the chairs ranged about in rows and in clusters. Each little family group had had its say and exchanged its domestic gossip earlier in the evening. There was now an apparent disposition to relax; to widen the circle of confidences and give a more general tone to the conversation.

Many of the children had been permitted to sit up beyond their usual bedtime. A small band of them were lying on their stomachs on the floor looking at the colored sheets of the comic papers which Mr. Pontellier had brought down. The little Pontellier boys were permitting them to do so, and making their authority felt.

170   Music, dancing, and a recitation or two were the entertainments furnished, or rather, offered. But there was nothing systematic about the programme, no appearance of prearrangement nor even premeditation.

At an early hour in the evening the Farival twins were prevailed upon to play the piano. They were girls of fourteen, always clad in the Virgin's colors, blue and white, having been dedicated to the Blessed Virgin at their baptism. They played a duet from "Zampa," and at the earnest solicitation of every one present followed it with the overture to "The Poet and the Peasant."

"Allez vous-en! Sapristi!" shrieked the parrot outside the door. He was the only being present who possessed sufficient candor to admit that he was not listening to these gracious performances for the first time that summer. Old Monsieur Farival, grandfather of the twins, grew indignant over the interruption, and insisted upon having the bird removed and consigned to regions of darkness. Victor Lebrun objected; and his decrees were as immutable as those of Fate. The parrot fortunately offered no further interruption to the entertainment, the whole venom of his nature apparently having been cherished up and hurled against the twins in that one impetuous outburst.

Later a young brother and sister gave recitations, which every one present had heard many times at winter evening entertainments in the city.

A little girl performed a skirt dance in the center of the floor. The mother played her accompaniments and at the same time watched her daughter with greedy admiration and nervous apprehension. She need have had no apprehension. The child was mistress of the situation. She had been properly dressed for the occasion in black tulle and black silk tights. Her little neck and arms were bare, and her hair, artificially crimped, stood out like fluffy black plumes over her head. Her poses were full of grace, and

her little black-shod toes twinkled as they shot out and upward with a rapidity and suddenness which were bewildering.

175   But there was no reason why every one should not dance. Madame
Ratignolle could not, so it was she who gaily consented to play for the others. She played very well, keeping excellent waltz time and infusing an expression into the strains which was indeed inspiring. She was keeping up
her music on account of the children, she said; because she and her husband both considered it a means of brightening the home and making it
attractive.

Almost every one danced but the twins, who could not be induced to
separate during the brief period when one or the other should be whirling
around the room in the arms of a man. They might have danced together,
but they did not think of it.

The children were sent to bed. Some went submissively; others with
shrieks and protests as they were dragged away. They had been permitted
to sit up till after the ice-cream, which naturally marked the limit of human
indulgence.

The ice-cream was passed around with cake—gold and silver cake
arranged on platters in alternate slices; it had been made and frozen during
the afternoon back of the kitchen by two black women, under the supervision of Victor. It was pronounced a great success—excellent if it had only
contained a little less vanilla or a little more sugar, if it had been frozen a degree harder, and if the salt might have been kept out of portions of it. Victor
was proud of his achievement, and went about recommending it and urging
every one to partake of it to excess.

After Mrs. Pontellier had danced twice with her husband, once with
Robert, and once with Monsieur Ratignolle, who was thin and tall and
swayed like a reed in the wind when he danced, she went out on the gallery
and seated herself on the low window-sill, where she commanded a view of
all that went on in the hall and could look out toward the Gulf. There was a
soft effulgence in the east. The moon was coming up, and its mystic shimmer was casting a million lights across the distant, restless water.

180   "Would you like to hear Mademoiselle Reisz play?" asked Robert,
coming out on the porch where she was. Of course Edna would like to hear
Mademoiselle Reisz play, but she feared it would be useless to entreat her.

"I'll ask her," he said. "I'll tell her that you want to hear her. She likes
you. She will come." He turned and hurried away to one of the far cottages,
where Mademoiselle Reisz was shuffling away. She was dragging a chair in
and out of her room, and at intervals objecting to the crying of a baby,
which a nurse in the adjoining cottage was endeavoring to put to sleep. She
was a disagreeable little woman, no longer young, who had quarreled with
almost every one, owing to a temper which was self-assertive and a disposition to trample upon the rights of others. Robert prevailed upon her without any too great difficulty.

She entered the hall with him during a lull in the dance. She made an
awkward, imperious little bow as she went in. She was a homely woman,
with a small weazened face and body and eyes that glowed. She had absolutely no taste in dress, and wore a batch of rusty black lace with a bunch
of artificial violets pinned to the side of her hair.

"Ask Mrs. Pontellier what she would like to hear me play," she requested of Robert. She sat perfectly still before the piano, not touching the

keys, while Robert carried her message to Edna at the window. A general air of surprise and genuine satisfaction fell upon every one as they saw the pianist enter. There was a settling down, and a prevailing air of expectancy everywhere. Edna was a trifle embarrassed at being thus singled out for the imperious little woman's favor. She would not dare to choose, and begged that Mademoiselle Riesz would please herself in her selections.

Edna was what she herself called very fond of music. Musical strains, well rendered, had a way of evoking pictures in her mind. She sometimes liked to sit in the room of mornings when Madame Ratignolle played or practiced. One piece which that lady played Edna had entitled "Solitude." It was a short, plaintive, minor strain. The name of the piece was something else, but she called it "Solitude." When she heard it there came before her imagination the figure of a man standing beside a desolate rock on the seashore. He was naked. His attitude was one of hopeless resignation as he looked toward a distant bird winging its flight away from him.

185   Another piece called to her mind a dainty young woman clad in an Empire gown, taking mincing dancing steps as she came down a long avenue between tall hedges. Again, another reminded her of children at play, and still another of nothing on earth but a demure lady stroking a cat.

The very first chords which Mademoiselle Reisz struck upon the piano sent a keen tremor down Mrs. Pontellier's spinal column. It was not the first time she had heard an artist at the piano. Perhaps it was the first time she was ready, perhaps the first time her being was tempered to take an impress of the abiding truth.

She waited for the material pictures which she thought would gather and blaze before her imagination. She waited in vain. She saw no pictures of solitude, of hope, of longing, or of despair. But the very passions themselves were aroused within her soul, swaying it, lashing it, as the waves daily beat upon her splendid body. She trembled, she was choking, and the tears blinded her.

Mademoiselle had finished. She arose, and bowing her stiff, lofty bow, she went away, stopping for neither thanks nor applause. As she passed along the gallery she patted Edna upon the shoulder.

"Well, how did you like my music?" she asked. The young woman was unable to answer; she pressed the hand of the pianist convulsively. Mademoiselle Reisz perceived her agitation and even her tears. She patted her again upon the shoulder as she said:

190   "You are the only one worth playing for. Those others? Bah!" and she went shuffling and sidling on down the gallery toward her room.

But she was mistaken about "those others." Her playing had aroused a fever of enthusiasm. "What passion!" "What an artist!" "I have always said no one could play Chopin[30] like Mademoiselle Reisz!" "That last prelude! Bon Dieu![31] It shakes a man!"

It was growing late, and there was a general disposition to disband. But some one, perhaps it was Robert, thought of a bath at that mystic hour and under that mystic moon.

---

[30]**Chopin** Frédéric François Chopin (1810–1849), Polish pianist and composer.   [31]**Bon Dieu!** Good Lord!

X

At all events Robert proposed it, and there was not a dissenting voice. There was not one but was ready to follow when he led the way. He did not lead the way, however, he directed the way; and he himself loitered behind with the lovers, who had betrayed a disposition to linger and hold themselves apart. He walked between them, whether with malicious or mischievous intent was not wholly clear, even to himself.

The Pontelliers and Ratignolles walked ahead; the women leaning upon the arms of their husbands. Edna could hear Robert's voice behind them, and could sometimes hear what he said. She wondered why he did not join them. It was unlike him not to. Of late he had sometimes held away from her for an entire day, redoubling his devotion upon the next and the next, as though to make up for hours that had been lost. She missed him the days when some pretext served to take him away from her, just as one misses the sun on a cloudy day without having thought much about the sun when it was shining.

195   The people walked in little groups toward the beach. They talked and laughed; some of them sang. There was a band playing down at Klein's hotel, and the strains reached them faintly, tempered by the distance. There were strange, rare odors abroad—a tangle of the sea smell and of weeds and damp, new-plowed earth, mingled with the heavy perfume of a field of white blossoms somewhere near. But the night sat lightly upon the sea and the land. There was no weight of darkness, there were no shadows. The white light of the moon had fallen upon the world like the mystery and the softness of sleep.

Most of them walked into the water as though into a native element. The sea was quiet now, and swelled lazily in broad billows that melted into one another and did not break except upon the beach in little foamy crests that coiled back like slow, white serpents.

Edna had attempted all summer to learn to swim. She had received instructions from both the men and women; in some instances from the children. Robert had pursued a system of lessons almost daily; and he was nearly at the point of discouragement in realizing the futility of his efforts. A certain ungovernable dread hung about her when in the water, unless there was a hand near by that might reach out and reassure her.

But that night she was like the little tottering, stumbling, clutching child, who of a sudden realizes its powers, and walks for the first time alone, boldly and with over-confidence. She could have shouted for joy. She did shout for joy, as with a sweeping stroke or two she lifted her body to the surface of the water.

A feeling of exultation overtook her, as if some power of significant import had been given to her to control the working of her body and her soul. She grew daring and reckless, overestimating her strength. She wanted to swim far out, where no woman had swum before.

200   Her unlooked-for achievement was the subject of wonder, applause, and admiration. Each one congratulated himself that his special teachings had accomplished this desired end.

"How easy it is!" she thought. "It is nothing," she said aloud; "why did I not discover before that it was nothing? Think of the time I have lost splashing about like a baby!" She would not join the groups in their sports and bouts, but intoxicated with her newly conquered power, she swam out alone.

She turned her face seaward to gather in an impression of space and solitude, which the vast expanse of water, meeting and melting with the moonlit sky, conveyed to her excited fancy. As she swam she seemed to be reaching out for the unlimited in which to lose herself.

Once she turned and looked toward the shore, toward the people she had left there. She had not gone any great distance—that is, what would have been a great distance for an experienced swimmer. But to her unaccustomed vision the stretch of water behind her assumed the aspect of a barrier which her unaided strength would never be able to overcome.

A quick vision of death smote her soul, and for a second time appalled and enfeebled her senses. But by an effort she rallied her staggering faculties and managed to regain the land.

205   She made no mention of her encounter with death and her flash of terror, except to say to her husband, "I thought I should have perished out there alone."

"You were not so very far, my dear; I was watching you," he told her.

Edna went at once to the bath-house, and she had put on her dry clothes and was ready to return home before the others had left the water. She started to walk away alone. They all called to her and shouted to her. She waved a dissenting hand, and went on, paying no further heed to their renewed cries which sought to detain her.

"Sometimes I am tempted to think that Mrs. Pontellier is capricious," said Madame Lebrun, who was amusing herself immensely and feared that Edna's abrupt departure might put an end to the pleasure.

"I know she is," assented Mr. Pontellier; "sometimes, not often."

210   Edna had not traversed a quarter of the distance on her way home before she was overtaken by Robert.

"Did you think I was afraid?" she asked him, without a shade of annoyance.

"No; I knew you weren't afraid."

"Then why did you come? Why didn't you stay out there with the others?"

"I never thought of it."

215   "Thought of what?"

"Of anything. What difference does it make?"

"I'm very tired," she uttered, complainingly.

"I know you are."

"You don't know anything about it. Why should you know? I never was so exhausted in my life. But it isn't unpleasant. A thousand emotions have swept through me to-night. I don't comprehend half of them. Don't mind what I'm saying; I am just thinking aloud. I wonder if I shall ever be stirred again as Mademoiselle Reisz's playing moved me to-night. I wonder if any night on earth will ever again be like this one. It is like a night in a dream. The people about me are like some uncanny, half-human beings. There must be spirits abroad tonight."

220   "There are," whispered Robert. "Didn't you know this was the twenty-eighth of August?"

"The twenty-eighth of August?"

"Yes. On the twenty-eighth of August, at the hour of midnight, and if the moon is shining—the moon must be shining—a spirit that has haunted these shores for ages rises up from the Gulf. With its own penetrating vision the spirit seeks some one mortal worthy to hold him company, worthy of being exalted for a few hours into realms of the semi-celestials. His search has always hitherto been fruitless, and he has sunk back, disheartened, into the sea. But tonight he found Mrs. Pontellier. Perhaps he will never wholly release her from the spell. Perhaps she will never again suffer a poor, unworthy earthling to walk in the shadow of her divine presence."

"Don't banter me," she said, wounded at what appeared to be his flippancy. He did not mind the entreaty, but the tone with its delicate note of pathos was like a reproach. He could not explain; he could not tell her that he had penetrated her mood and understood. He said nothing except to offer her his arm, for, by her own admission, she was exhausted. She had been walking alone with her arms hanging limp, letting her white skirts trail along the dewy path. She took his arm, but she did not lean upon it. She let her hand lie listlessly, as though her thoughts were elsewhere—somewhere in advance of her body, and she was striving to overtake them.

Robert assisted her into the hammock which swung from the post before her door out to the trunk of a tree.

225   "Will you stay out here and wait for Mr. Pontellier?" he asked.

"I'll stay out here. Good-night."

"Shall I get you a pillow?"

"There's one here," she said, feeling about, for they were in the shadow.

"It must be soiled; the children have been tumbling it about."

230   "No matter." And having discovered the pillow, she adjusted it beneath her head. She extended herself in the hammock with a deep breath of relief. She was not a supercilious or an over-dainty woman. She was not much given to reclining in the hammock, and when she did so it was with no cat-like suggestion of voluptuous ease, but with a beneficent repose which seemed to invade her whole body.

"Shall I stay with you till Mr. Pontellier comes?" asked Robert, seating himself on the outer edge of one of the steps and taking hold of the hammock rope which was fastened to the post.

"If you wish. Don't swing the hammock. Will you get my white shawl which I left on the window-sill over at the house?"

"Are you chilly?"

"No; but I shall be presently."

235   "Presently?" he laughed. "Do you know what time it is? How long are you going to stay out here?"

"I don't know. Will you get the shawl?"

"Of course I will," he said, rising. He went over to the house, walking along the grass. She watched his figure pass in and out of the strips of moonlight. It was past midnight. It was very quiet.

When he returned with the shawl she took it and kept it in her hand. She did not put it around her.

"Did you say I should stay till Mr. Pontellier came back?"

240   "I said you might if you wished to."

He seated himself again and rolled a cigarette, which he smoked in silence. Neither did Mrs. Pontellier speak. No multitude of words could have been more significant than those moments of silence, or more pregnant with the first-felt throbbings of desire.

When the voices of the bathers were heard approaching, Robert said goodnight. She did not answer him. He thought she was asleep. Again she watched his figure pass in and out of the strips of moonlight as he walked away.

XI

"What are you doing out here, Edna? I thought I should find you in bed," said her husband, when he discovered her lying there. He had walked up with Madame Lebrun and left her at the house. His wife did not reply.

"Are you asleep?" he asked, bending down close to look at her.

245 "No." Her eyes gleamed bright and intense, with no sleepy shadows, as they looked into his.

"Do you know it is past one o'clock? Come on," and he mounted the steps and went into their room.

"Edna!" called Mr. Pontellier from within, after a few moments had gone by.

"Don't wait for me," she answered. He thrust his head through the door.

"You will take cold out there," he said irritably. "What folly is this? Why don't you come in?"

250 "It isn't cold; I have my shawl."

"The mosquitoes will devour you."

"There are no mosquitoes."

She heard him moving about the room; every sound indicating impatience and irritation. Another time she would have gone in at his request. She would, through habit, have yielded to his desire; not with any sense of submission or obedience to his compelling wishes, but unthinkingly, as we walk, move, sit, stand, go through the daily treadmill of the life which has been portioned out to us.

"Edna, dear, are you not coming in soon?" he asked again, this time fondly, with a note of entreaty.

255 "No; I am going to stay out here."

"This is more than folly," he blurted out. "I can't permit you to stay out there all night. You must come in the house instantly."

With a writhing motion she settled herself more securely in the hammock. She perceived that her will had blazed up, stubborn and resistant. She could not at that moment have done other than denied and resisted. She wondered if her husband had ever spoken to her like that before, and if she had submitted to his command. Of course she had; she remembered that she had. But she could not realize why or how she should have yielded, feeling as she then did.

"Léonce, go to bed," she said. "I mean to stay out here. I don't wish to go in, and I don't intend to. Don't speak to me like that again; I shall not answer you."

Mr. Pontellier had prepared for bed, but he slipped on an extra garment. He opened a bottle of wine, of which he kept a small and select supply in a buffet of his own. He drank a glass of wine and went out on the gallery and offered a glass to his wife. She did not wish any. He drew up a rocker, hoisted his slippered feet on the rail, and proceeded to smoke a cigar. He smoked two cigars; then he went inside and drank another glass of wine. Mrs. Pontellier again declined to accept a glass when it was offered to her. Mr. Pontellier once more seated himself with elevated feet, and after a reasonable interval of time smoked some more cigars.

260   Edna began to feel like one who awakens gradually out of a dream, a delicious, grotesque, impossible dream, to feel again the realities pressing into her soul. The physical need for sleep began to overtake her; the exuberance which had sustained and exalted her spirit left her helpless and yielding to the conditions which crowded her in.

The stillest hour of the night had come, the hour before dawn, when the world seems to hold its breath. The moon hung low, and had turned from silver to copper in the sleeping sky. The old owl no longer hooted, and the water-oaks had ceased to moan as they bent their heads.

Edna arose, cramped from lying so long and still in the hammock. She tottered up the steps, clutching feebly at the post before passing into the house.

"Are you coming in, Léonce?" she asked, turning her face toward her husband.

"Yes, dear," he answered, with a glance following a misty puff of smoke. "Just as soon as I have finished my cigar."

XII

265   She slept but a few hours. They were troubled and feverish hours, disturbed with dreams that were intangible, that eluded her, leaving only an impression upon her half-awakened senses of something unattainable. She was up and dressed in the cool of the early morning. The air was invigorating and steadied somewhat her faculties. However, she was not seeking refreshment or help from any source, either external or from within. She was blindly following whatever impulse moved her, as if she had placed herself in alien hands for direction, and freed her soul of responsibility.

Most of the people at that early hour were still in bed and asleep. A few, who intended to go over to the *Chênière* for mass, were moving about. The lovers, who had laid their plans the night before, were already strolling toward the wharf. The lady in black, with her Sunday prayer-book, velvet and gold-clasped, and her Sunday silver beads, was following them at no great distance. Old Monsieur Farival was up, and was more than half inclined to do anything that suggested itself. He put on his big straw hat, and taking his umbrella from the stand in the hall, followed the lady in black, never overtaking her.

The little negro girl who worked Madame Lebrun's sewing-machine was sweeping the galleries with long, absent-minded strokes of the broom. Edna sent her up into the house to awaken Robert.

"Tell him I am going to the *Chênière*. The boat is ready; tell him to hurry."

He had soon joined her. She had never sent for him before. She had never asked for him. She had never seemed to want him before. She did not appear conscious that she had done anything unusual in commanding his presence. He was apparently equally unconscious of anything extraordinary in the situation. But his face was suffused with a quiet glow when he met her.

270   They went together back to the kitchen to drink coffee. There was no time to wait for any nicety of service. They stood outside the window and the cook passed them their coffee and a roll, which they drank and ate from the window-sill. Edna said it tasted good. She had not thought of coffee nor of anything. He told her he had often noticed that she lacked forethought.

"Wasn't it enough to think of going to the *Chênière* and waking you up?" she laughed. "Do I have to think of everything?—as Léonce says when he's in a bad humor. I don't blame him; he'd never be in a bad humor if it weren't for me."

They took a short cut across the sands. At a distance they could see the curious procession moving toward the wharf—the lovers, shoulder to shoulder, creeping; the lady in black, gaining steadily upon them; old Monsieur Farival, losing ground inch by inch, and a young barefooted Spanish girl, with a red kerchief on her head and a basket on her arm, bringing up the rear.

Robert knew the girl, and he talked to her a little in the boat. No one present understood what they said. Her name was Mariequita. She had a round, sly, piquant face and pretty black eyes. Her hands were small, and she kept them folded over the handle of her basket. Her feet were broad and coarse. She did not strive to hide them. Edna looked at her feet, and noticed the sand and slime between her brown toes.

Beaudelet grumbled because Mariequita was there, taking up so much room. In reality he was annoyed at having old Monsieur Farival, who considered himself the better sailor of the two. But he would not quarrel with so old a man as Monsieur Farival, so he quarreled with Mariequita. The girl was deprecatory at one moment, appealing to Robert. She was saucy the next, moving her head up and down, making "eyes" at Robert and making "mouths" at Beaudelet.

275 The lovers were all alone. They saw nothing, they heard nothing. The lady in black was counting her beads for the third time. Old Monsieur Farival talked incessantly of what he knew about handling a boat, and of what Beaudelet did not know on the same subject.

Edna liked it all. She looked Mariequita up and down, from her ugly brown toes to her pretty black eyes, and back again.

"Why does she look at me like that?" inquired the girl of Robert.

"Maybe she thinks you are pretty. Shall I ask her?"

"No. Is she your sweetheart?"

280 "She's a married lady, and has two children."

"Oh! well! Francisco ran away with Sylvano's wife, who had four children. They took all his money and one of the children and stole his boat."

"Shut up!"

"Does she understand?"

"Oh, hush!"

285 "Are those two married over there—leaning on each other?"

"Of course not," laughed Robert.

"Of course not," echoed Mariequita, with a serious, confirmatory bob of the head.

The sun was high up and beginning to bite. The swift breeze seemed to Edna to bury the sting of it into the pores of her face and hands. Robert held his umbrella over her.

As they went cutting sidewise through the water, the sails bellied taut, with the wind filling and overflowing them. Old Monsieur Farival laughed sardonically at something as he looked at the sails, and Beaudelet swore at the old man under his breath.

290 Sailing across the bay to the *Chênière Caminada*, Edna felt as if she were being borne away from some anchorage which had held her fast,

whose chains had been loosening—had snapped the night before when the mystic spirit was abroad, leaving her free to drift whithersoever she chose to set her sails. Robert spoke to her incessantly; he no longer noticed Mariequita. The girl had shrimps in her bamboo basket. They were covered with Spanish moss. She beat the moss down impatiently, and muttered to herself sullenly.

"Let us go to Grand Terre to-morrow," said Robert in a low voice.

"What shall we do there?"

"Climb up the hill to the old fort and look at the little wriggling gold snakes, and watch the lizards sun themselves."

She gazed away toward Grande Terre and thought she would like to be alone there with Robert, in the sun, listening to the ocean's roar and watching the slimy lizards writhe in and out among the ruins of the old fort.

295   "And the next day or the next we can sail to the Bayou Brulow," he went on.

"What shall we do there?"

"Anything—cast bait for fish."

"No; we'll go back to Grande Terre. Let the fish alone."

"We'll go wherever you like," he said. "I'll have Tonie come over and help me patch and trim my boat. We shall not need Beaudelet nor any one. Are you afraid of the pirogue?"[32]

300   "Oh, no."

"Then I'll take you some night on the pirogue when the moon shines. Maybe your Gulf spirit will whisper to you in which of these islands the treasures are hidden—direct you to the very spot, perhaps."

"And in a day we should be rich!" she laughed. "I'd give it all to you, the pirate gold and every bit of treasure we could dig up. I think you would know how to spend it. Pirate gold isn't a thing to be hoarded or utilized. It is something to squander and throw to the four winds, for the fun of seeing the golden specks fly."

"We'd share it, and scatter it together," he said. His face flushed.

They all went together up to the quaint little Gothic church of Our Lady of Lourdes, gleaming all brown and yellow with paint in the sun's glare.

305   Only Beaudelet remained behind, tinkering at his boat, and Mariequita walked away with her basket of shrimps, casting a look of childish ill-humor and reproach at Robert from the corner of her eye.

XIII

A feeling of oppression and drowsiness overcame Edna during the service. Her head began to ache, and the lights on the altar swayed before her eyes. Another time she might have made an effort to regain her composure; but her one thought was to quit the stifling atmosphere of the church and reach the open air. She arose, climbing over Robert's feet with a muttered apology. Old Monsieur Farival, flurried, curious, stood up, but upon seeing that Robert had followed Mrs. Pontellier, he sank back into his seat. He whispered an anxious inquiry of the lady in black, who did not notice him or reply, but kept her eyes fastened upon the pages of her velvet prayer-book.

---

[32]**pirogue** canoe.

"I felt giddy and almost overcome," Edna said, lifting her hands instinctively to her head and pushing her straw hat up from her forehead. "I couldn't have stayed through the service." They were outside in the shadow of the church. Robert was full of solicitude.

"It was folly to have thought of going in the first place, let alone staying. Come over to Madame Antoine's; you can rest there." He took her arm and led her away, looking anxiously and continuously down into her face.

How still it was, with only the voice of the sea whispering through the reeds that grew in the salt-water pools! The long line of little gray, weather-beaten houses nestled peacefully among the orange trees. It must always have been God's day on that low, drowsy island, Edna thought. They stopped, leaning over a jagged fence made of sea-drift, to ask for water. A youth, a mild-faced Acadian,[33] was drawing water from the cistern, which was nothing more than a rusty buoy, with an opening on one side, sunk in the ground. The water which the youth handed to them in a tin pail was not cold to taste, but it was cool to her heated face, and it greatly revived and refreshed her.

310   Madame Antoine's cot[34] was at the far end of the village. She welcomed them with all the native hospitality, as she would have opened her door to let the sunlight in. She was fat, and walked heavily and clumsily across the floor. She could speak no English, but when Robert made her understand that the lady who accompanied him was ill and desired to rest, she was all eagerness to make Edna feel at home and to dispose of her comfortably.

The whole place was immaculately clean, and the big, four-posted bed, snow-white, invited one to repose. It stood in a small side room which looked out across a narrow grass plot toward the shed, where there was a disabled boat lying keel upward.

Madame Antoine had not gone to mass. Her son Tonie had, but she supposed he would soon be back, and she invited Robert to be seated and wait for him. But he went and sat outside the door and smoked. Madame Antoine busied herself in the large front room preparing dinner. She was boiling mullets over a few red coals in the huge fireplace.

Edna, left alone in the little side room, loosened her clothes, removing the greater part of them. She bathed her face, her neck and arms in the basin that stood between the windows. She took off her shoes and stockings and stretched herself in the very center of the high, white bed. How luxurious it felt to rest thus in a strange, quaint bed, with its sweet country odor of laurel lingering about the sheets and mattress! She stretched her strong limbs that ached a little. She ran her fingers through her loosened hair for a while. She looked at her round arms as she held them straight up and rubbed them one after the other, observing closely, as if it were something she saw for the first time, the fine, firm quality and texture of her flesh. She clasped her hands easily above her head, and it was thus she fell asleep.

She slept lightly at first, half awake and drowsily attentive to the things about her. She could hear Madame Antoine's heavy, scraping tread as she walked back and forth on the sanded floor. Some chickens were clucking outside the windows, scratching for bits of gravel in the grass. Later she half

---

[33]**Acadian** descendant of French Canadians whom the British expelled from eastern Canada (Acadia) in 1775.   [34]**cot** cottage.

heard the voices of Robert and Tonie talking under the shed. She did not stir. Even her eyelids rested numb and heavily over her sleepy eyes. The voices went on—Tonie's slow, Acadian drawl, Robert's quick, soft, smooth French. She understood French imperfectly unless directly addressed, and the voices were only part of the other drowsy, muffled sounds lulling her senses.

315   When Edna awoke it was with the conviction that she had slept long and soundly. The voices were hushed under the shed. Madame Antoine's step was no longer to be heard in the adjoining room. Even the chickens had gone elsewhere to scratch and cluck. The mosquito bar was drawn over her; the old woman had come in while she slept and let down the bar. Edna rose quietly from the bed, and looking between the curtains of the window, she saw by the slanting rays of the sun that the afternoon was far advanced. Robert was out there under the shed, reclining in the shade against the sloping keel of the overturned boat. He was reading from a book. Tonie was no longer with him. She wondered what had become of the rest of the party. She peeped out at him two or three times as she stood washing herself in the little basin between the windows.

Madame Antoine had lain some coarse, clean towels upon a chair, and had placed a box of *poudre de riz*[35] within easy reach. Edna dabbed the powder upon her nose and cheeks as she looked at herself closely in the little distorted mirror which hung on the wall above the basin. Her eyes were bright and wide awake and her face glowed.

When she had completed her toilet she walked into the adjoining room. She was very hungry. No one was there. But there was a cloth spread upon the table that stood against the wall, and a cover was laid for one, with a crusty brown loaf and a bottle of wine beside the plate. Edna bit a piece from the brown loaf, tearing it with her strong, white teeth. She poured some of the wine into the glass and drank it down. Then she went softly out of doors, and plucking an orange from the low-hanging bough of a tree, threw it at Robert, who did not know she was awake and up.

An illumination broke over his whole face when he saw her and joined her under the orange tree.

"How many years have I slept?" she inquired. "The whole island seems changed. A new race of beings must have sprung up, leaving only you and me as past relics. How many ages ago did Madame Antoine and Tonie die? and when did our people from Grand Isle disappear from the earth?"

320   He familiarly adjusted a ruffle upon her shoulder.

"You have slept precisely one hundred years. I was left here to guard your slumbers; and for one hundred years I have been out under the shed reading a book. The only evil I couldn't prevent was to keep a broiled fowl from drying up."

"If it has turned to stone, still will I eat it," said Edna, moving with him into the house. "But really, what has become of Monsieur Farival and the others?"

"Gone hours ago. When they found that you were sleeping they thought it best not to awake you. Any way, I wouldn't have let them. What was I here for?"

---

[35]*poudre de riz* talcum powder.

"I wonder if Léonce will be uneasy!" she speculated, as she seated herself at table.

325   "Of course not; he knows you are with me," Robert replied, as he busied himself among sundry pans and covered dishes which had been left standing on the hearth.

"Where are Madame Antoine and her son?" asked Edna.

"Gone to Vespers,[36] and to visit some friends, I believe. I am to take you back in Tonie's boat whenever you are ready to go."

He stirred the smoldering ashes till the broiled fowl began to sizzle afresh. He served her with no mean repast, dripping the coffee anew and sharing it with her. Madame Antoine had cooked little else than the mullets, but while Edna slept Robert had foraged the island. He was childishly gratified to discover her appetite, and to see the relish with which she ate the food which he had procured for her.

"Shall we go right away?" she asked, after draining her glass and brushing together the crumbs of the crusty loaf.

330   "The sun isn't as low as it will be in two hours," he answered.

"The sun will be gone in two hours."

"Well, let it go; who cares!"

They waited a good while under the orange trees, till Madame Antoine came back, panting, waddling, with a thousand apologies to explain her absence. Tonie did not dare to return. He was shy, and would not willingly face any woman except his mother.

It was very pleasant to stay there under the orange trees, while the sun dipped lower and lower, turning the western sky to flaming copper and gold. The shadows lengthened and crept out like stealthy, grotesque monsters across the grass.

335   Edna and Robert both sat upon the ground—that is, he lay upon the ground beside her, occasionally picking at the hem of her muslin gown.

Madame Antoine seated her fat body, broad and squat, upon a bench beside the door. She had been talking all the afternoon, and had wound herself up to the story-telling pitch.

And what stories she told them! But twice in her life she had left the *Chênière Caminada,* and then for the briefest span. All her years she had squatted and waddled there upon the island, gathering legends of the Baratarians[37] and the sea. The night came on, with the moon to lighten it. Edna could hear the whispering voices of dead men and the click of muffled gold.

When she and Robert stepped into Tonie's boat, with the red lateen sail, misty spirit forms were prowling in the shadows and among the reeds, and upon the water were phantom ships, speeding to cover.

XIV

The youngest boy, Etienne, had been very naughty, Madame Ratignolle said, as she delivered him into the hands of his mother. He had been unwilling to go to bed and had made a scene; whereupon she had taken charge of him

---

[36]**Vespers** evening church service.   [37]**Baratarians** pirates (e.g., Jean Laffite) in the Baratarian Bay (in the Mississippi delta).

and pacified him as well as she could. Raoul had been in bed and asleep for two hours.

340   The youngster was in his long white nightgown, that kept tripping him up as Madame Ratignolle led him along by the hand. With the other chubby fist he rubbed his eyes, which were heavy with sleep and ill humor. Edna took him in her arms, and seating herself in the rocker, began to coddle and caress him, calling him all manner of tender names, soothing him to sleep.

It was not more than nine o'clock. No one had yet gone to bed but the children.

Léonce had been very uneasy at first, Madame Ratignolle said, and had wanted to start at once for the *Chênière*. But Monsieur Farival had assured him that his wife was only overcome with sleep and fatigue, that Tonie would bring her safely back later in the day; and he had thus been dissuaded from crossing the bay. He had gone over to Klein's, looking up some cotton broker whom he wished to see in regard to securities, exchanges, stocks, bonds, or something of the sort, Madame Ratignolle did not remember what. He said he would not remain away late. She herself was suffering from heat and oppression, she said. She carried a bottle of salts and a large fan. She would not consent to remain with Edna, for Monsieur Ratignolle was alone, and he detested above all things to be left alone.

When Etienne had fallen asleep Edna bore him into the back room, and Robert went and lifted the mosquito bar that she might lay the child comfortably in his bed. The quadroon had vanished. When they emerged from the cottage Robert bade Edna good-night.

"Do you know we have been together the whole livelong day, Robert—since early this morning?" she said at parting.

345   "All but the hundred years when you were sleeping. Good-night."

He pressed her hand and went away in the direction of the beach. He did not join any of the others, but walked alone toward the Gulf.

Edna stayed outside, awaiting her husband's return. She had no desire to sleep or to retire; nor did she feel like going over to sit with the Ratignolles, or to join Madame Lebrun and a group whose animated voices reached her as they sat in conversation before the house. She let her mind wander back over her stay at Grand Isle; and she tried to discover wherein this summer had been different from any and every other summer of her life. She could only realize that she herself—her present self—was in some way different from the other self. That she was seeing with different eyes and making the acquaintance of new conditions in herself that colored and changed her environment, she did not yet suspect.

She wondered why Robert had gone away and left her. It did not occur to her to think he might have grown tired of being with her the livelong day. She was not tired, and she felt that he was not. She regretted that he had gone. It was so much more natural to have him stay when he was not absolutely required to leave her.

As Edna waited for her husband she sang low a little song that Robert had sung as they crossed the bay. It began with "Ah! *Si tu savais*,"[38] and every verse ended with *"si tu savais."*

---

[38]***Si tu savais*** "Could'st thou but know" (title and refrain of a song by Michael William Balfe [1808–1870]).

350   Robert's voice was not pretentious. It was musical and true. The voice,
the notes, the whole refrain haunted her memory.

XV

When Edna entered the dining-room one evening a little late, as was her
habit, an unusually animated conversation seemed to be going on. Several
persons were talking at once, and Victor's voice was predominating, even
over that of his mother. Edna had returned late from her bath, had dressed
in some haste, and her face was flushed. Her head, set off by her dainty
white gown, suggested a rich, rare blossom. She took her seat at table between old Monsieur Farival and Madame Ratignolle.

As she seated herself and was about to begin to eat her soup, which
had been served when she entered the room, several persons informed her
simultaneously that Robert was going to Mexico. She laid her spoon down
and looked about her bewildered. He had been with her, reading to her all
the morning, and had never even mentioned such a place as Mexico. She
had not seen him during the afternoon; she had heard some one say he was
at the house, upstairs with his mother. This she had thought nothing of,
though she was surprised when he did not join her later in the afternoon,
when she went down to the beach.

She looked across at him, where he sat beside Madame Lebrun, who
presided. Edna's face was a blank picture of bewilderment, which she never
thought of disguising. He lifted his eyebrows with the pretext of a smile as
he returned her glance. He looked embarrassed and uneasy.

"When is he going?" she asked of everybody in general, as if Robert
were not there to answer for himself.

355   "To-night!" "This very evening!" "Did you ever!" "What possesses him!"
were some of the replies she gathered, uttered simultaneously in French
and English.

"Impossible!" she exclaimed. "How can a person start off from Grand
Isle to Mexico at a moment's notice, as if he were going over to Klein's or to
the wharf or down to the beach?"

"I said all along I was going to Mexico; I've been saying so for years!"
cried Robert, in an excited and irritable tone, with the air of a man defending himself against a swarm of stinging insects.

Madame Lebrun knocked on the table with her knife handle.

"Please let Robert explain why he is going, and why he is going tonight," she called out. "Really, this table is getting to be more and more like
Bedlam every day, with everybody talking at once. Sometimes—I hope God
will forgive me—but positively, sometimes I wish Victor would lose the
power of speech."

360   Victor laughed sardonically as he thanked his mother for her holy wish,
of which he failed to see the benefit to anybody, except that it might afford
her a more ample opportunity and license to talk herself.

Monsieur Farival thought that Victor should have been taken out in
mid-ocean in his earliest youth and drowned. Victor thought there would be
more logic in thus disposing of old people with an established claim for
making themselves universally obnoxious. Madame Lebrun grew a trifle hysterical; Robert called his brother some sharp, hard names.

"There's nothing much to explain, mother," he said; though he explained, nevertheless—looking chiefly at Edna—that he could only meet the gentleman whom he intended to join at Vera Cruz by taking such and such a steamer, which left New Orleans on such a day; that Beaudelet was going out with his lugger-load of vegetables that night, which gave him an opportunity of reaching the city and making his vessel in time.

"But when did you make up your mind to all this?" demanded Monsieur Farival.

"This afternoon," returned Robert, with a shade of annoyance.

365   "At what time this afternoon?" persisted the old gentleman, with nagging determination, as if he were cross-questioning a criminal in a court of justice.

"At four o'clock this afternoon, Monsieur Farival," Robert replied, in a high voice and with a lofty air, which reminded Edna of some gentleman on the stage.

She had forced herself to eat most of her soup, and now she was picking the flaky bits of a *court bouillon*[39] with her fork.

The lovers were profiting by the general conversation on Mexico to speak in whispers of matters which they rightly considered were interesting to no one but themselves. The lady in black had once received a pair of prayer-beads of curious workmanship from Mexico, with very special indulgence[40] attached to them, but she had never been able to ascertain whether the indulgence extended outside the Mexican border. Father Fochel of the Cathedral had attempted to explain it; but he had not done so to her satisfaction. And she begged that Robert would interest himself, and discover, if possible, whether she was entitled to the indulgence accompanying the remarkably curious Mexican prayer-beads.

Madame Ratignolle hoped that Robert would exercise extreme caution in dealing with the Mexicans, who, she considered, were a treacherous people, unscrupulous and revengeful. She trusted she did them no injustice in thus condemning them as a race. She had known personally but one Mexican, who made and sold excellent tamales, and whom she would have trusted implicitly, so soft-spoken was he. One day he was arrested for stabbing his wife. She never knew whether he had been hanged or not.

370   Victor had grown hilarious, and was attempting to tell an anecdote about a Mexican girl who served chocolate one winter in a restaurant in Dauphine Street. No one would listen to him but old Monsieur Farival, who went into convulsions over the droll story.

Edna wondered if they had all gone mad, to be talking and clamoring at that rate. She herself could think of nothing to say about Mexico or the Mexicans.

"At what time do you leave?" she asked Robert.

"At ten," he told her. "Beaudelet wants to wait for the moon."

"Are you all ready to go?"

375   "Quite ready. I shall only take a hand-bag, and shall pack my trunk in the city."

He turned to answer some question put to him by his mother, and Edna, having finished her black coffee, left the table.

---

[39]***court bouillon*** fish broth.   [40]**indulgence** power to reduce the punishment for sins.

She went directly to her room. The little cottage was close and stuffy after leaving the outer air. But she did not mind; there appeared to be a hundred different things demanding her attention indoors. She began to set the toilet-stand to rights, grumbling at the negligence of the quadroon, who was in the adjoining room putting the children to bed. She gathered together stray garments that were hanging on the backs of chairs, and put each where it belonged in closet or bureau drawer. She changed her gown for a more comfortable and commodious wrapper. She rearranged her hair, combing and brushing it with unusual energy. Then she went in and assisted the quadroon in getting the boys to bed.

They were very playful and inclined to talk—to do anything but lie quiet and go to sleep. Edna sent the quadroon away to her supper and told her she need not return. Then she sat and told the children a story. Instead of soothing it excited them, and added to their wakefulness. She left them in heated argument, speculating about the conclusion of the tale which their mother promised to finish the following night.

The little black girl came in to say that Madame Lebrun would like to have Mrs. Pontellier go and sit with them over at the house till Mr. Robert went away. Edna returned answer that she had already undressed, that she did not feel quite well, but perhaps she would go over to the house later. She started to dress again, and got as far advanced as to remove her *peignoir*. But changing her mind once more she resumed the *peignoir,* and went outside and sat down before her door. She was over-heated and irritable, and fanned herself energetically for a while. Madame Ratignolle came down to discover what was the matter.

380   "All that noise and confusion at the table must have upset me," replied Edna, "and moreover, I hate shocks and surprises. The idea of Robert starting off in such a ridiculously sudden and dramatic way! As if it were a matter of life and death! Never saying a word about it all morning when he was with me."

"Yes," agreed Madame Ratignolle. "I think it was showing us all—you especially—very little consideration. It wouldn't have surprised me in any of the others; those Lebruns are all given to heroics. But I must say I should never have expected such a thing from Robert. Are you not coming down? Come on, dear; it doesn't look friendly."

"No," said Edna, a little sullenly. "I can't go to the trouble of dressing again; I don't feel like it."

"You needn't dress; you look all right; fasten a belt around your waist. Just look at me!"

"No," persisted Edna; "but you go on. Madame Lebrun might be offended if we both stayed away."

385   Madame Ratignolle kissed Edna good-night, and went away, being in truth rather desirous of joining in the general and animated conversation which was still in progress concerning Mexico and the Mexicans.

Somewhat later Robert came up, carrying his hand-bag.

"Aren't you feeling well?" he asked.

"Oh, well enough. Are you going right away?"

He lit a match and looked at his watch. "In twenty minutes," he said. The sudden and brief flare of the match emphasized the darkness for a while. He sat down upon a stool which the children had left out on the porch.

390   "Get a chair," said Edna.

"This will do," he replied. He put on his soft hat and nervously took it off again, and wiping his face with his handkerchief, complained of the heat.

"Take the fan," said Edna, offering it to him.

"Oh, no! Thank you. It does no good; you have to stop fanning some time, and feel all the more uncomfortable afterward."

"That's one of the ridiculous things which men always say. I have never known one to speak otherwise of fanning. How long will you be gone?"

395   "Forever, perhaps. I don't know. It depends upon a good many things."

"Well, in case it shouldn't be forever, how long will it be?"

"I don't know."

"This seems to me perfectly preposterous and uncalled for. I don't like it. I don't understand your motive for silence and mystery, never saying a word to me about it this morning." He remained silent, not offering to defend himself. He only said, after a moment:

"Don't part with me in an ill-humor. I never knew you to be out of patience with me before."

400   "I don't want to part in any ill-humor," she said. "But can't you understand? I've grown used to seeing you, to having you with me all the time, and your action seems unfriendly, even unkind. You don't even offer an excuse for it. Why, I was planning to be together, thinking of how pleasant it would be to see you in the city next winter."

"So was I," he blurted. "Perhaps that's the—" He stood up suddenly and held out his hand. "Good-by, my dear Mrs. Pontellier; good-by. You won't— I hope you won't completely forget me." She clung to his hand, striving to detain him.

"Write to me when you get there, won't you, Robert?" she entreated.

"I will, thank you. Good-by."

How unlike Robert! The merest acquaintance would have said something more emphatic than "I will, thank you; good-by," to such a request.

405   He had evidently already taken leave of the people over at the house, for he descended the steps and went to join Beaudelet, who was out there with an oar across his shoulder waiting for Robert. They walked away in the darkness. She could only hear Beaudelet's voice; Robert had apparently not even spoken a word of greeting to his companion.

Edna bit her handkerchief convulsively, striving to hold back and to hide, even from herself as she would have hidden from another, the emotion which was troubling—tearing—her. Her eyes were brimming with tears.

For the first time she recognized anew the symptoms of infatuation which she had felt incipiently as a child, as a girl in her earliest teens, and later as a young woman. The recognition did not lessen the reality, the poignancy of the revelation by any suggestion or promise of instability. The past was nothing to her; offered no lesson which she was willing to heed. The future was a mystery which she never attempted to penetrate. The present alone was significant; was hers, to torture her as it was doing then with the biting conviction that she had lost that which she had held, that she had been denied that which her impassioned, newly awakened being demanded.

XVI

"Do you miss your friend greatly?" asked Mademoiselle Reisz one morning as she came creeping up behind Edna, who had just left her cottage on her way to the beach. She spent much of her time in the water since she had acquired finally the art of swimming. As their stay at Grand Isle drew near its close, she felt that she could not give too much time to a diversion which afforded her the only real pleasurable moments that she knew. When Mademoiselle Reisz came and touched her upon the shoulder and spoke to her, the woman seemed to echo the thought which was ever in Edna's mind; or better, the feeling which constantly possessed her.

Robert's going had some way taken the brightness, the color, the meaning out of everything. The conditions of her life were in no way changed, but her whole existence was dulled, like a faded garment which seems to be no longer worth wearing. She sought him everywhere—in others whom she induced to talk about him. She went up in the mornings to Madame Lebrun's room, braving the clatter of the old sewing-machine. She sat there and chatted at intervals as Robert had done. She gazed around the room at the pictures and photographs hanging upon the wall, and discovered in some corner an old family album, which she examined with the keenest interest, appealing to Madame Lebrun for enlightenment concerning the many figures and faces which she discovered between its pages.

410   There was a picture of Madame Lebrun with Robert as a baby, seated in her lap, a round-faced infant with a fist in his mouth. The eyes alone in the baby suggested the man. And that was he also in kilts, at the age of five, wearing long curls and holding a whip in his hand. It made Edna laugh, and she laughed, too, at the portrait in his first long trousers; while another interested her, taken when he left for college, looking thin, long-faced, with eyes full of fire, ambition and great intentions. But there was no recent picture, none which suggested the Robert who had gone away five days ago, leaving a void and wilderness behind him.

"Oh, Robert stopped having his pictures taken when he had to pay for them himself! He found wiser use for his money, he says," explained Madame Lebrun. She had a letter from him, written before he left New Orleans. Edna wished to see the letter, and Madame Lebrun told her to look for it either on the table or the dresser, or perhaps it was on the mantelpiece.

The letter was on the bookshelf. It possessed the greatest interest and attraction for Edna; the envelope, its size and shape, the post-mark, the handwriting. She examined every detail of the outside before opening it. There were only a few lines, setting forth that he would leave the city that afternoon, that he had packed his trunk in good shape, that he was well, and sent her his love and begged to be affectionately remembered to all. There was no special message to Edna except a postscript saying that if Mrs. Pontellier desired to finish the book which he had been reading to her, his mother would find it in his room, among other books there on the table. Edna experienced a pang of jealousy because he had written to his mother rather than to her.

Every one seemed to take for granted that she missed him. Even her husband, when he came down the Saturday following Robert's departure, expressed regret that he had gone.

"How do you get on without him, Edna?" he asked.

415   "It's very dull without him," she admitted. Mr. Pontellier had seen Robert in the city, and Edna asked him a dozen questions or more. Where had they met? On Carondelet Street, in the morning. They had gone "in" and had a drink and a cigar together. What had they talked about? Chiefly about his prospects in Mexico, which Mr. Pontellier thought were promising. How did he look? How did he seem—grave, or gay, or how? Quite cheerful, and

wholly taken up with the idea of his trip, which Mr. Pontellier found altogether natural in a young fellow about to seek fortune and adventure in a
strange, queer country.

Edna tapped her foot impatiently, and wondered why the children persisted in playing in the sun when they might be under the trees. She went
down and led them out of the sun, scolding the quadroon for not being
more attentive.

It did not strike her as in the least grotesque that she should be making
of Robert the object of conversation and leading her husband to speak of
him. The sentiment which she entertained for Robert in no way resembled
that which she felt for her husband, or had ever felt, or ever expected to feel.
She had all her life long been accustomed to harbor thoughts and emotions
which never voiced themselves. They had never taken the form of struggles.
They belonged to her and were her own, and she entertained the conviction
that she had a right to them and that they concerned no one but herself.
Edna had once told Madame Ratignolle that she would never sacrifice herself
for her children, or for any one. Then had followed a rather heated argument; the two women did not appear to understand each other or to be talking the same language. Edna tried to appease her friend, to explain.

"I would give up the unessential; I would give my money, I would give
my life for my children; but I wouldn't give myself. I can't make it more
clear; it's only something which I am beginning to comprehend, which is
revealing itself to me."

"I don't know what you would call the essential, or what you mean by
the unessential," said Madame Ratignolle, cheerfully; "but a woman who
would give her life for her children could do no more than that—your Bible
tells you so. I'm sure I couldn't do more than that."

420   "Oh, yes you could!" laughed Edna.

She was not surprised at Mademoiselle Reisz's question the morning
that lady, following her to the beach, tapped her on the shoulder and asked
if she did not greatly miss her young friend.

"Oh, good morning, Mademoiselle; is it you? Why, of course I miss
Robert. Are you going down to bathe?"

"Why should I go down to bathe at the very end of the season when I
haven't been in the surf all summer?" replied the woman, disagreeably.

"I beg your pardon," offered Edna, in some embarrassment, for she
should have remembered that Mademoiselle Reisz's avoidance of the water
had furnished a theme for much pleasantry. Some among them thought it
was on account of her false hair, or the dread of getting the violets wet,
while others attributed it to the natural aversion for water sometimes believed to accompany the artistic temperament. Mademoiselle offered Edna
some chocolates in a paper bag, which she took from her pocket, by way of
showing that she bore no ill feeling. She habitually ate chocolates for their
sustaining quality; they contained much nutrient in small compass, she said.
They saved her from starvation, as Madame Lebrun's table was utterly impossible; and no one save so impertinent a woman as Madame Lebrun could
think of offering such food to people and requiring them to pay for it.

425   "She must feel very lonely without her son," said Edna, desiring to
change the subject. "Her favorite son, too. It must have been quite hard to
let him go."

Mademoiselle laughed maliciously.

"Her favorite son! Oh, dear! Who could have been imposing such a tale upon you? Aline Lebrun lives for Victor, and for Victor alone. She has spoiled him into the worthless creature he is. She worships him and the ground he walks on. Robert is very well in a way, to give up all the money he can earn to the family, and keep the barest pittance for himself. Favorite son, indeed! I miss the poor fellow myself, my dear. I liked to see him and to hear him about the place—the only Lebrun who is worth a pinch of salt. He comes to see me often in the city. I like to play to him. That Victor! hanging would be too good for him. It's a wonder Robert hasn't beaten him to death long ago."

"I thought he had great patience with his brother," offered Edna, glad to be talking about Robert, no matter what was said.

"Oh! he thrashed him well enough a year or two ago," said Mademoiselle. "It was about a Spanish girl, whom Victor considered that he had some sort of claim upon. He met Robert one day talking to the girl, or walking with her, or bathing with her, or carrying her basket—I don't remember what;—and he became so insulting and abusive that Robert gave him a thrashing on the spot that has kept him comparatively in order for a good while. It's about time he was getting another."

430 "Was her name Mariequita?" asked Edna.

"Mariequita—yes, that was it; Mariequita. I had forgotten. Oh, she's a sly one, and a bad one, that Mariequita!"

Edna looked down at Mademoiselle Reisz and wondered how she could have listened to her venom so long. For some reason she felt depressed, almost unhappy. She had not intended to go into the water; but she donned her bathing suit, and left Mademoiselle alone, seated under the shade of the children's tent. The water was growing cooler as the season advanced. Edna plunged and swam about with an abandon that thrilled and invigorated her. She remained a long time in the water, half hoping that Mademoiselle Reisz would not wait for her.

But Mademoiselle waited. She was very amiable during the walk back, and raved much over Edna's appearance in her bathing suit. She talked about music. She hoped that Edna would go to see her in the city, and wrote her address with the stub of a pencil on a piece of card which she found in her pocket.

"When do you leave?" asked Edna.

435 "Next Monday; and you?"

"The following week," answered Edna, adding, "It has been a pleasant summer, hasn't it, Mademoiselle?"

"Well," agreed Mademoiselle Reisz, with a shrug, "rather pleasant, if it hadn't been for the mosquitoes and the Farival twins."

XVII

The Pontelliers possessed a very charming home on Esplanade Street[41] in New Orleans. It was a large, double cottage, with a broad front veranda, whose round, fluted columns supported the sloping roof. The house was painted a dazzling white; the outside shutters, or jalousies, were green. In

---

[41]**Esplanade Street** fashionable street in New Orleans.

the yard, which was kept scrupulously neat, were flowers and plants of every description which flourish in South Louisiana. Within doors the appointments were perfect after the conventional type. The softest carpets and rugs covered the floors; rich and tasteful draperies hung at doors and windows. There were paintings, selected with judgment and discrimination, upon the walls. The cut glass, the silver, the heavy damask which daily appeared upon the table were the envy of many women whose husbands were less generous than Mr. Pontellier.

Mr. Pontellier was very fond of walking about his house examining its various appointments and details, to see that nothing was amiss. He greatly valued his possessions, chiefly because they were his, and derived genuine pleasure from contemplating a painting, a statuette, a rare lace curtain—no matter what—after he had bought it and placed it among his household goods.

440   On Tuesday afternoons—Tuesday being Mrs. Pontellier's reception day—there was a constant stream of callers—women who came in carriages or in the street cars, or walked when the air was soft and distance permitted. A light-colored mulatto boy, in dress coat and bearing a diminutive silver tray for the reception of cards, admitted them. A maid, in white fluted cap, offered the callers liqueur, coffee, or chocolate, as they might desire. Mrs. Pontellier, attired in a handsome reception gown, remained in the drawing-room the entire afternoon receiving her visitors. Men sometimes called in the evening with their wives.

This had been the programme which Mrs. Pontellier had religiously followed since her marriage, six years before. Certain evenings during the week she and her husband attended the opera or sometimes the play.

Mr. Pontellier left his home in the mornings between nine and ten o'clock, and rarely returned before half-past six or seven in the evening—dinner being served at half-past seven.

He and his wife seated themselves at table one Tuesday evening, a few weeks after their return from Grand Isle. They were alone together. The boys were being put to bed; the patter of their bare, escaping feet could be heard occasionally, as well as the pursuing voice of the quadroon, lifted in mild protest and entreaty. Mrs. Pontellier did not wear her usual Tuesday reception gown; she was in ordinary house dress. Mr. Pontellier, who was observant about such things, noticed it, as he served the soup and handed it to the boy in waiting.

"Tired out, Edna? Whom did you have? Many callers?" he asked. He tasted his soup and began to season it with pepper, salt, vinegar, mustard—everything within reach.

445   "There were a good many," replied Edna, who was eating her soup with evident satisfaction. "I found their cards when I got home; I was out."

"Out!" exclaimed her husband, with something like genuine consternation in his voice as he laid down the vinegar cruet and looked at her through his glasses. "Why, what could have taken you out on Tuesday? What did you have to do?"

"Nothing. I simply felt like going out, and I went out."

"Well, I hope you left some suitable excuse," said her husband, somewhat appeased, as he added a dash of cayenne pepper to the soup.

"No, I left no excuse. I told Joe to say I was out, that was all."

450 "Why, my dear, I should think you'd understand by this time that people don't do such things; we've got to observe *les convenances*[42] if we ever expect to get on and keep up with the procession. If you felt that you had to leave home this afternoon, you should have left some suitable explanation for your absence.

"This soup is really impossible; it's strange that woman hasn't learned yet to make a decent soup. Any free-lunch stand in town serves a better one. Was Mrs. Belthrop here?"

"Bring the tray with the cards, Joe. I don't remember who was here."

The boy retired and returned after a moment, bringing the tiny silver tray, which was covered with ladies' visiting cards. He handed it to Mrs. Pontellier.

"Give it to Mr. Pontellier," she said.

455 Joe offered the tray to Mr. Pontellier, and removed the soup.

Mr. Pontellier scanned the names of his wife's callers, reading some of them aloud, with comments as he read.

"'The Misses Delasidas.' I worked a big deal in futures[43] for their father this morning; nice girls; it's time they were getting married. 'Mrs. Belthrop.' I tell you what it is Edna; you can't afford to snub Mrs. Belthrop. Why, Belthrop could buy and sell us ten times over. His business is worth a good, round sum to me. You'd better write her a note. 'Mrs. James Highcamp.' Hugh! the less you have to do with Mrs. Highcamp, the better. 'Madame Laforcé.' Came all the way from Carrolton, too, poor old soul. 'Miss Wiggs,' 'Mrs. Eleanor Boltons.'" He pushed the cards aside.

"Mercy!" exclaimed Edna, who had been fuming. "Why are you taking the thing so seriously and making such a fuss over it?"

"I'm not making any fuss over it. But it's just such seeming trifles that we've got to take seriously; such things count."

460 The fish was scorched. Mr. Pontellier would not touch it. Edna said she did not mind a little scorched taste. The roast was in some way not to his fancy, and he did not like the manner in which the vegetables were served.

"It seems to me," he said, "we spend money enough in this house to procure at least one meal a day which a man could eat and retain his self-respect."

"You used to think the cook was a treasure," returned Edna, indifferently.

"Perhaps she was when she first came; but cooks are only human. They need looking after, like any other class of persons that you employ. Suppose I didn't look after the clerks in my office, just let them run things their own way; they'd soon make a nice mess of me and my business."

"Where are you going?" asked Edna, seeing that her husband arose from table without having eaten a morsel except a taste of the highly-seasoned soup.

465 "I'm going to get my dinner at the club. Good night." He went into the hall, took his hat and stick from the stand, and left the house.

She was somewhat familiar with such scenes. They had often made her very unhappy. On a few previous occasions she had been completely deprived of any desire to finish her dinner. Sometimes she had gone into the kitchen to administer a tardy rebuke to the cook. Once she went to her

---

[42]*les convenances* the proprieties; social conventions.   [43]**futures** stocks or commodities bought or sold for future delivery (a form of speculation).

room and studied the cookbook during an entire evening, finally writing out a menu for the week, which left her harassed with a feeling that, after all, she had accomplished no good that was worth the name.

But that evening Edna finished her dinner alone, with forced deliberation. Her face was flushed and her eyes flamed with some inward fire that lighted them. After finishing her dinner she went to her room, having instructed the boy to tell any other callers that she was indisposed.

It was a large, beautiful room, rich and picturesque in the soft, dim light which the maid had turned low. She went and stood at an open window and looked out upon the deep tangle of the garden below. All the mystery and witchery of the night seemed to have gathered there amid the perfumes and the dusky and tortuous outlines of flowers and foliage. She was seeking herself and finding herself in just such sweet, half-darkness which met her moods. But the voices were not soothing that came to her from the darkness and the sky above and the stars. They jeered and sounded mournful notes without promise, devoid even of hope. She turned back into the room and began to walk to and fro down its whole length, without stopping, without resting. She carried in her hands a thin handkerchief, which she tore into ribbons, rolled into a ball, and flung from her. Once she stopped, and taking off her wedding ring, flung it upon the carpet. When she saw it lying there, she stamped her heel upon it, striving to crush it. But her small boot heel did not make an indenture, not a mark upon the little glittering circlet.

In a sweeping passion she seized a glass vase from the table and flung it upon the tiles of the hearth. She wanted to destroy something. The crash and clatter were what she wanted to hear.

470 A maid, alarmed at the din of breaking glass, entered the room to discover what was the matter.

"A vase fell upon the hearth," said Edna. "Never mind; leave it till morning."

"Oh! you might get some of the glass in your feet, ma'am," insisted the young woman, picking up bits of the broken vase that were scattered upon the carpet. "And here's your ring, ma'am, under the chair."

Edna held out her hand, and taking the ring, slipped it upon her finger.

XVIII

The following morning Mr. Pontellier, upon leaving for his office, asked Edna if she would not meet him in town in order to look at some new fixtures for the library.

475 "I hardly think we need new fixtures, Léonce. Don't let us get anything new; you are too extravagant. I don't believe you ever think of saving or putting by."

"The way to become rich is to make money, my dear Edna, not to save it," he said. He regretted that she did not feel inclined to go with him and select new fixtures. He kissed her good-by, and told her she was not looking well and must take care of herself. She was unusually pale and very quiet.

She stood on the front veranda as he quitted the house, and absently picked a few sprays of jessamine that grew upon a trellis near by. She inhaled the odor of the blossoms and thrust them into the bosom of her white morning gown. The boys were dragging along the banquette[44] a small "express wagon," which they had filled with blocks and sticks. The quadroon was following them with little quick steps, having assumed a fictitious animation and alacrity for the occasion. A fruit vendor was crying his wares in the street.

Edna looked straight before her with a self-absorbed expression upon her face. She felt no interest in anything about her. The street, the children, the fruit vendor, the flowers growing there under her eyes, were all part and parcel of an alien world which had suddenly become antagonistic.

She went back into the house. She had thought of speaking to the cook concerning her blunders of the previous night; but Mr. Pontellier had saved her that disagreeable mission, for which she was so poorly fitted. Mr. Pontellier's arguments were usually convincing with those whom he employed. He left home feeling quite sure that he and Edna would sit down that evening, and possibly a few subsequent evenings, to a dinner deserving of the name.

480   Edna spent an hour or two in looking over some of her old sketches. She could see their shortcomings and defects, which were glaring in her eyes. She tried to work a little, but found she was not in the humor. Finally she gathered together a few of the sketches—those which she considered the least discreditable; and she carried them with her when, a little later, she dressed and left the house. She looked handsome and distinguished in her street gown. The tan of the seashore had left her face, and her forehead was smooth, white, and polished beneath her heavy, yellow-brown hair. There were a few freckles on her face, and a small, dark mole near the under lip and one on the temple, half-hidden in her hair.

As Edna walked along the street she was thinking of Robert. She was still under the spell of her infatuation. She had tried to forget him, realizing the inutility of remembering. But the thought of him was like an obsession, ever pressing itself upon her. It was not that she dwelt upon details of their acquaintance, or recalled in any special or peculiar way his personality; it was his being, his existence, which dominated her thought, fading sometimes as if it would melt into the mist of the forgotten, reviving again with an intensity which filled her with an incomprehensible longing.

Edna was on her way to Madame Ratignolle's. Their intimacy, begun at Grand Isle, had not declined, and they had seen each other with some frequency since their return to the city. The Ratignolles lived at no great distance from Edna's home, on the corner of a side street, where Monsieur Ratignolle owned and conducted a drug store which enjoyed a steady and prosperous trade. His father had been in the business before him, and Monsieur Ratignolle stood well in the community and bore an enviable reputation for integrity and clear-headedness. His family lived in commodious apartments over the store, having an entrance on the side within the *porte cochère*.[45] There was something which Edna thought very French, very foreign, about their whole manner of living. In the large and pleasant salon which extended across the width of the house, the Ratignolles entertained their friends once a fortnight with a *soirée musicale*,[46] sometimes diversified by card-playing. There was a friend who played upon the 'cello. One brought his flute and another his violin, while there were some who sang

---

[44]**banquette** sidewalk.   [45]***porte cochère*** a roof supported by columns, serving to protect passengers who alight from a carriage.   [46]***soirée musicale*** evening of music.

and a number who performed upon the piano with various degrees of taste and agility. The Ratignolles' *soirées musicales* were widely known, and it was considered a privilege to be invited to them.

Edna found her friend engaged in assorting the clothes which had returned that morning from the laundry. She at once abandoned her occupation upon seeing Edna, who had been ushered without ceremony into her presence.

"Cité can do it as well as I; it is really her business," she explained to Edna, who apologized for interrupting her. And she summoned a young black woman, whom she instructed, in French, to be very careful in checking off the list which she handed her. She told her to notice particularly if a fine linen handkerchief of Monsieur Ratignolle's, which was missing last week, had been returned; and to be sure to set to one side such pieces as required mending and darning.

485   Then placing an arm around Edna's waist, she led her to the front of the house, to the salon, where it was cool and sweet with the odor of great roses that stood upon the hearth in jars.

Madame Ratignolle looked more beautiful than ever there at home, in a négligée which left her arms almost wholly bare and exposed the rich, melting curves of her white throat.

"Perhaps I shall be able to paint your picture some day," said Edna with a smile when they were seated. She produced the roll of sketches and started to unfold them. "I believe I ought to work again. I feel as if I wanted to be doing something. What do you think of them? Do you think it worth while to take it up again and study some more? I might study for a while with Laidpore."

She knew that Madame Ratignolle's opinion in such a matter would be next to valueless, that she herself had not alone decided, but determined; but she sought the words of praise and encouragement that would help her to put heart into her venture.

"Your talent is immense, dear!"

490   "Nonsense!" protested Edna, well pleased.

"Immense, I tell you," persisted Madame Ratignolle, surveying the sketches one by one, at close range, then holding them at arm's length, narrowing her eyes, and dropping her head on one side. "Surely, this Bavarian peasant is worthy of framing; and this basket of apples! Never have I seen anything more lifelike. One might almost be tempted to reach out a hand and take one."

Edna could not control a feeling which bordered upon complacency at her friend's praise, even realizing, as she did, its true worth. She retained a few of the sketches, and gave all the rest to Madame Ratignolle, who appreciated the gift far beyond its value and proudly exhibited the pictures to her husband when he came up from the store a little later for his midday dinner.

Mr. Ratignolle was one of those men who are called the salt of the earth. His cheerfulness was unbounded, and it was matched by his goodness of heart, his broad charity, and common sense. He and his wife spoke English with an accent which was only discernible through its un-English emphasis and a certain carefulness and deliberation. Edna's husband spoke English with no accent whatever. The Ratignolles understood each other perfectly. If ever the fusion of two human beings into one has been accomplished on this sphere it was surely in their union.

As Edna seated herself at table with them she thought, "Better a dinner of herbs," though it did not take her long to discover that it was no dinner of herbs, but a delicious repast, simple, choice, and in every way satisfying.

495   Monsieur Ratignolle was delighted to see her, though he found her looking not so well as at Grand Isle, and he advised a tonic. He talked a good deal on various topics, a little politics, some city news and neighborhood gossip. He spoke with an animation and earnestness that gave an exaggerated importance to every syllable he uttered. His wife was keenly interested in everything he said, laying down her fork the better to listen, chiming in, taking the words out of his mouth.

Edna felt depressed rather than soothed after leaving them. The little glimpse of domestic harmony which had been offered her, gave her no regret, no longing. It was not a condition of life which fitted her, and she could see in it but an appalling and hopeless ennui. She was moved by a kind of commiseration for Madame Ratignolle,—a pity for that colorless existence which never uplifted its possessor beyond the region of blind contentment, in which no moment of anguish ever visited her soul, in which she would never have the taste of life's delirium. Edna vaguely wondered what she meant by "life's delirium." It had crossed her thought like some unsought extraneous impression.

XIX

Edna could not help but think that it was very foolish, very childish, to have stamped upon her wedding ring and smashed the crystal vase upon the tiles. She was visited by no more outbursts, moving her to such futile expedients. She began to do as she liked and to feel as she liked. She completely abandoned her Tuesdays at home, and did not return the visits of those who had called upon her. She made no ineffectual efforts to conduct her household *en bonne ménagère*,[47] going and coming as it suited her fancy, and, so far as she was able, lending herself to any passing caprice.

Mr. Pontellier had been a rather courteous husband so long as he met a certain tacit submissiveness in his wife. But her new and unexpected line of conduct completely bewildered him. It shocked him. Then her absolute disregard for her duties as a wife angered him. When Mr. Pontellier became rude, Edna grew insolent. She had resolved never to take another step backward.

"It seems to me the utmost folly for a woman at the head of a household, and the mother of children, to spend in an atelier[48] days which would be better employed contriving for the comfort of her family."

500   "I feel like painting," answered Edna. "Perhaps I shan't always feel like it."

"Then in God's name paint! but don't let the family go to the devil. There's Madame Ratignolle; because she keeps up her music, she doesn't let everything else go to chaos. And she's more of a musician than you are a painter."

"She isn't a musician, and I'm not a painter. It isn't on account of painting that I let things go."

"On account of what, then?"

---

[47]*en bonne ménagère* as a good housewife.   [48]**atelier** studio.

"Oh! I don't know. Let me alone; you bother me."

505   It sometimes entered Mr. Pontellier's mind to wonder if his wife were
not growing a little unbalanced mentally. He could see plainly that she was
not herself. That is, he could not see that she was becoming herself and
daily casting aside that fictitious self which we assume like a garment with
which to appear before the world.

Her husband let her alone as she requested, and went away to his office. Edna went up to her atelier—a bright room in the top of the house. She
was working with great energy and interest, without accomplishing anything, however, which satisfied her even in the smallest degree. For a time
she had the whole household enrolled in the service of art. The boys posed
for her. They thought it amusing at first, but the occupation soon lost its attractiveness when they discovered that it was not a game arranged especially for their entertainment. The quadroon sat for hours before Edna's
palette, patient as a savage, while the house-maid took charge of the children, and the drawing-room went undusted. But the house-maid, too,
served her term as model when Edna perceived that the young woman's
back and shoulders were molded on classic lines, and that her hair, loosened from its confining cap, became an inspiration. While Edna worked she
sometimes sang low the little air, *"Ah! si tu savais!"*

It moved her with recollections. She could hear again the ripple of the
water, the flapping sail. She could see the glint of the moon upon the bay,
and could feel the soft, gusty beating of the hot south wind. A subtle current of desire passed through her body, weakening her hold upon the
brushes and making her eyes burn.

There were days when she was very happy without knowing why.
She was happy to be alive and breathing, when her whole being seemed
to be one with the sunlight, the color, the odors, the luxuriant warmth of
some perfect Southern day. She liked then to wander alone into strange
and unfamiliar places. She discovered many a sunny, sleepy corner, fashioned to dream in. And she found it good to dream and to be alone and
unmolested.

There were days when she was unhappy, she did not know why,—
when it did not seem worth while to be glad or sorry, to be alive or dead;
when life appeared to her like a grotesque pandemonium and humanity like
worms struggling blindly toward inevitable annihilation. She could not
work on such a day, nor weave fancies to stir her pulses and warm her
blood.

XX

510   It was during such a mood that Edna hunted up Mademoiselle Reisz. She
had not forgotten the rather disagreeable impression left upon her by their
last interview; but she nevertheless felt a desire to see her—above all, to listen while she played upon the piano. Quite early in the afternoon she
started upon her quest for the pianist. Unfortunately she had mislaid or lost
Mademoiselle Reisz's card, and looking up her address in the city directory,
she found that the woman lived on Bienville Street, some distance away.
The directory which fell into her hands was a year or more old, however,
and upon reaching the number indicated, Edna discovered that the house

was occupied by a respectable family of mulattoes who had *chambres gar-nies*[49] to let. They had been living there for six months, and knew absolutely nothing of a Mademoiselle Reisz. In fact, they knew nothing of any of their neighbors; their lodgers were all people of the highest distinction, they assured Edna. She did not linger to discuss class distinctions with Madame Pouponne, but hastened to a neighboring grocery store, feeling sure that Mademoiselle would have left her address with the proprietor.

He knew Mademoiselle Reisz a good deal better than he wanted to know her, he informed his questioner. In truth, he did not want to know her at all, or anything concerning her—the most disagreeable and unpopular woman who ever lived in Bienville Street. He thanked heaven she had left the neighborhood, and was equally thankful that he did not know where she had gone.

Edna's desire to see Mademoiselle Reisz had increased tenfold since these unlooked-for obstacles had arisen to thwart it. She was wondering who could give her the information she sought, when it suddenly occurred to her that Madame Lebrun would be the one most likely to do so. She knew it was useless to ask Madame Ratignolle, who was on the most distant terms with the musician, and preferred to know nothing concerning her. She had once been almost as emphatic in expressing herself upon the subject as the corner grocer.

Edna knew that Madame Lebrun had returned to the city, for it was the middle of November. And she also knew where the Lebruns lived, on Chartres Street.

Their home from the outside looked like a prison, with iron bars before the door and lower windows. The iron bars were a relic of the old *régime*,[50] and no one had ever thought of dislodging them. At the side was a high fence enclosing the garden. A gate or door opening upon the street was locked. Edna rang the bell at this side garden gate, and stood upon the banquette, waiting to be admitted.

515   It was Victor who opened the gate for her. A black woman, wiping her hands upon her apron, was close at his heels. Before she saw them Edna could hear them in altercation, the woman—plainly an anomaly—claiming the right to be allowed to perform her duties, one of which was to answer the bell.

Victor was surprised and delighted to see Mrs. Pontellier, and he made no attempt to conceal either his astonishment or his delight. He was a dark-browed, good-looking youngster of nineteen, greatly resembling his mother, but with ten times her impetuosity. He instructed the black woman to go at once and inform Madame Lebrun that Mrs. Pontellier desired to see her. The woman grumbled a refusal to do part of her duty when she had not been permitted to do it all, and started back to her interrupted task of weeding the garden. Whereupon Victor administered a rebuke in the form of a volley of abuse, which, owing to its rapidity and incoherence, was all but incomprehensible to Edna. Whatever it was, the rebuke was convincing, for the woman dropped her hoe and went mumbling into the house.

---

[49]*chambres garnies* furnished rooms.   [50]**the old *régime*** that is, the days of the Spanish.

Edna did not wish to enter. It was very pleasant there on the side porch, where there were chairs, a wicker lounge, and a small table. She seated herself, for she was tired from her long tramp; and she began to rock gently and smooth out the folds of her silk parasol. Victor drew up his chair beside her. He at once explained that the black woman's offensive conduct was all due to imperfect training, as he was not there to take her in hand. He had only come up from the island the morning before, and expected to return next day. He stayed all winter at the island; he lived there, and kept the place in order and got things ready for the summer visitors.

But a man needed occasional relaxation, he informed Mrs. Pontellier, and every now and again he drummed up a pretext to bring him to the city. My! but he had had a time of it the evening before! He wouldn't want his mother to know, and he began to talk in a whisper. He was scintillant with recollections. Of course, he couldn't think of telling Mrs. Pontellier all about it, she being a woman and not comprehending such things. But it all began with a girl peeping and smiling at him through the shutters as he passed by. Oh! but she was a beauty! Certainly he smiled back, and went up and talked to her. Mrs. Pontellier did not know him if she supposed he was one to let an opportunity like that escape him. Despite herself, the youngster amused her. She must have betrayed in her look some degree of interest or entertainment. The boy grew more daring, and Mrs. Pontellier might have found herself, in a little while, listening to a highly colored story but for the timely appearance of Madame Lebrun.

That lady was still clad in white, according to her custom of the summer. Her eyes beamed an effusive welcome. Would not Mrs. Pontellier go inside? Would she partake of some refreshment? Why had she not been there before? How was that dear Mr. Pontellier and how were those sweet children? Had Mrs. Pontellier ever known such a warm November?

520   Victor went and reclined on the wicker lounge behind his mother's chair, where he commanded a view of Edna's face. He had taken her parasol from her hands while he spoke to her, and he now lifted it and twirled it above him as he lay on his back. When Madame Lebrun complained that it was *so* dull coming back to the city; that she saw *so* few people now; that even Victor, when he came up from the island for a day or two, had *so* much to occupy him and engage his time; then it was that the youth went into contortions on the lounge and winked mischievously at Edna. She somehow felt like a confederate in crime, and tried to look severe and disapproving.

There had been but two letters from Robert, with little in them, they told her. Victor said it was really not worth while to go inside for the letters, when his mother entreated him to go in search of them. He remembered the contents, which in truth he rattled off very glibly when put to the test.

One letter was written from Vera Cruz and the other from the City of Mexico. He had met Montel, who was doing everything toward his advancement. So far, the financial situation was no improvement over the one he had left in New Orleans, but of course the prospects were vastly better. He wrote of the City of Mexico, the buildings, the people and their habits, the conditions of life which he found there. He sent his love to the family. He enclosed a check to his mother, and hoped she would affectionately remember him to all his friends. That was about the substance of the two letters. Edna felt that if there had been a message for her, she would have received it. The despondent frame of mind in which she had left home began again to overtake her, and she remembered that she wished to find Mademoiselle Reisz.

Madame Lebrun knew where Mademoiselle Reisz lived. She gave Edna the address, regretting that she would not consent to stay and spend the remainder of the afternoon, and pay a visit to Mademoiselle Reisz some other day. The afternoon was already well advanced.

Victor escorted her out upon the banquette, lifted her parasol, and held it over her while he walked to the car[51] with her. He entreated her to bear in mind that the disclosures of the afternoon were strictly confidential. She laughed and bantered him a little, remembering too late that she should have been dignified and reserved.

525   "How handsome Mrs. Pontellier looked!" said Madame Lebrun to her son.

"Ravishing!" he admitted. "The city atmosphere has improved her. Some way she doesn't seem like the same woman."

XXI

Some people contended that the reason Mademoiselle Reisz always chose apartments up under the roof was to discourage the approach of beggars, peddlers and callers. There were plenty of windows in her little front room. They were for the most part dingy, but as they were nearly always open it did not make so much difference. They often admitted into the room a good deal of smoke and soot; but at the same time all the light and air that there was came through them. From her windows could be seen the crescent of the river, the masts of ships and the big chimneys of the Mississippi steamers. A magnificent piano crowded the apartment. In the next room she slept, and in the third and last she harbored a gasoline stove on which she cooked her meals when disinclined to descend to the neighboring restaurant. It was there also that she ate, keeping her belongings in a rare old buffet, dingy and battered from a hundred years of use.

When Edna knocked at Mademoiselle Reisz's front room door and entered, she discovered that person standing beside the window, engaged in mending or patching an old prunella gaiter.[52] The little musician laughed all over when she saw Edna. Her laugh consisted of a contortion of the face and all the muscles of the body. She seemed strikingly homely, standing there in the afternoon light. She still wore the shabby lace and the artificial bunch of violets on the side of her head.

"So you remembered me at last," said Mademoiselle. "I had said to myself, 'Ah, bah! she will never come.'"

530   "Did you want me to come?" asked Edna with a smile.

"I had not thought much about it," answered Mademoiselle. The two had seated themselves on a little bumpy sofa which stood against the wall. "I am glad, however, that you came. I have the water boiling back there, and was just about to make some coffee. You will drink a cup with me. And how is *la belle dame?* Always handsome! always healthy! always contented!" She took Edna's hand between her strong wiry fingers, holding it loosely without warmth, and executing a sort of double theme upon the back and palm.

---

[51]**car** streetcar.   [52]**prunella gaiter** ankle-high shoe, with the upper section made of cloth.

"Yes," she went on; "I sometimes thought: 'She will never come. She promised as those women in society always do, without meaning it. She will not come.' For I really don't believe you like me, Mrs. Pontellier."

"I don't know whether I like you or not," replied Edna, gazing down at the little woman with a quizzical look.

The candor of Mrs. Pontellier's admission greatly pleased Mademoiselle Reisz. She expressed her gratification by repairing forthwith to the region of the gasoline stove and rewarding her guest with the promised cup of coffee. The coffee and the biscuit accompanying it proved very acceptable to Edna, who had declined refreshment at Madame Lebrun's and was now beginning to feel hungry. Mademoiselle set the tray which she brought in upon a small table near at hand, and seated herself once again on the lumpy sofa.

535   "I have had a letter from your friend," she remarked, as she poured a little cream into Edna's cup and handed it to her.

"My friend?"

"Yes, your friend Robert. He wrote to me from the City of Mexico."

"Wrote to *you?*" repeated Edna in amazement, stirring her coffee absently.

"Yes, to me. Why not? Don't stir all the warmth out of your coffee; drink it. Though the letter might as well have been sent to you; it was nothing but Mrs. Pontellier from beginning to end."

540   "Let me see it," requested the young woman, entreatingly.

"No; a letter concerns no one but the person who writes it and the one to whom it is written."

"Haven't you just said it concerned me from beginning to end?"

"It was written about you, not to you. 'Have you seen Mrs. Pontellier? How is she looking?' he asks. 'As Mrs. Pontellier says,' or 'as Mrs. Pontellier once said.' 'If Mrs. Pontellier should call upon you, play for her that Impromptu of Chopin's, my favorite. I heard it here a day or two ago, but not as you play it. I should like to know how it affects her,' and so on, as if he supposed we were constantly in each other's society."

"Let me see the letter."

545   "Oh, no."

"Have you answered it?"

"No."

"Let me see the letter."

"No, and again, no."

550   "Then play the Impromptu for me."

"It is growing late; what time do you have to be home?"

"Time doesn't concern me. Your question seems a little rude. Play the Impromptu."

"But you have told me nothing of yourself. What are you doing?"

"Painting!" laughed Edna. "I am becoming an artist. Think of it!"

555   "Ah! an artist! You have pretensions, Madame."

"Why pretensions? Do you think I could not become an artist?"

"I do not know you well enough to say. I do not know your talent or your temperament. To be an artist includes much; one must possess many gifts—absolute gifts—which have not been acquired by one's own effort. And, moreover, to succeed, the artist must possess the courageous soul."

"What do you mean by the courageous soul?"

"Courageous, *ma foi!* The brave soul. The soul that dares and defies."

560   "Show me the letter and play for me the Impromptu. You see that I have persistence. Does that quality count for anything in art?"

"It counts with a foolish old woman whom you have captivated," replied Mademoiselle, with her wriggling laugh.

The letter was right there at hand in the drawer of the little table upon which Edna had just placed her coffee cup. Mademoiselle opened the drawer and drew forth the letter, the topmost one. She placed it in Edna's hands, and without further comment arose and went to the piano.

Mademoiselle played a soft interlude. It was an improvisation. She sat low at the instrument, and the lines of her body settled into ungraceful curves and angles that gave it an appearance of deformity. Gradually and imperceptibly the interlude melted into the soft opening minor chords of the Chopin Impromptu.

Edna did not know when the Impromptu began or ended. She sat in the sofa corner reading Robert's letter by the fading light. Mademoiselle had glided from the Chopin into the quivering love-notes of Isolde's song,[53] and back again to the Impromptu with its soulful and poignant longing.

565   The shadows deepened in the little room. The music grew strange and fantastic—turbulent, insistent, plaintive and soft with entreaty. The shadows grew deeper. The music filled the room. It floated out upon the night, over the housetops, the crescent of the river, losing itself in the silence of the upper air.

Edna was sobbing, just as she had wept one midnight at Grand Isle when strange, new voices awoke in her. She arose in some agitation to take her departure. "May I come again, Mademoiselle?" she asked at the threshold.

"Come whenever you feel like it. Be careful; the stairs and landings are dark; don't stumble."

Mademoiselle reentered and lit a candle. Robert's letter was on the floor. She stooped and picked it up. It was crumpled and damp with tears. Mademoiselle smoothed the letter out, restored it to the envelope, and replaced it in the table drawer.

XXII

One morning on his way into town, Mr. Pontellier stopped at the house of his old friend and family physician, Doctor Mandelet. The Doctor was a semi-retired physician, resting, as the saying is, upon his laurels. He bore a reputation for wisdom rather than skill—leaving the active practice of medicine to his assistants and younger contemporaries—and was much sought for in matters of consultation. A few families, united to him by bonds of friendship, he still attended when they required the services of a physician. The Pontelliers were among these.

570   Mr. Pontellier found the Doctor reading at the open window of his study. His house stood rather far back from the street, in the center of a delightful garden, so that it was quiet and peaceful at the old gentleman's study window. He was a great reader. He stared up disapprovingly over his

---

[53]**Isolde's song** that is, the Liebestod ("Love-Death") sung by Isolde in *Tristan und Isolde* (1857–1859) by the German composer Richard Wagner. Isolde, holding her dead lover in her arms, bids him farewell and then dies.

eye-glasses as Mr. Pontellier entered, wondering who had the temerity to disturb him at that hour of the morning.

"Ah, Pontellier! Not sick, I hope. Come and have a seat. What news do you bring this morning?" He was quite portly, with a profusion of gray hair, and small blue eyes which age had robbed of much of their brightness but none of their penetration.

"Oh! I'm never sick, Doctor. You know that I come of tough fiber—of that old Creole race of Pontelliers that dry up and finally blow away. I came to consult—no, not precisely to consult—to talk to you about Edna. I don't know what ails her."

"Madame Pontellier not well?" marveled the Doctor. "Why, I saw her— I think it was a week ago—walking along Canal Street, the picture of health, it seemed to me."

"Yes, yes; she seems quite well," said Mr. Pontellier, leaning forward and whirling his stick between his two hands; "but she doesn't act well. She's odd, she's not like herself. I can't make her out, and I thought perhaps you'd help me."

575   "How does she act?" inquired the doctor.

"Well, it isn't easy to explain," said Mr. Pontellier, throwing himself back in his chair. "She lets the housekeeping go to the dickens."

"Well, well; women are not all alike, my dear Pontellier. We've got to consider—"

"I know that; I told you I couldn't explain. Her whole attitude—toward me and everybody and everything—has changed. You know I have a quick temper, but I don't want to quarrel or be rude to a woman, especially my wife; yet I'm driven to it, and feel like ten thousand devils after I've made a fool of myself. She's making it devilishly uncomfortable for me," he went on nervously. "She's got some sort of notion in her head concerning the eternal rights of women; and—you understand—we meet in the morning at the breakfast table."

The old gentleman lifted his shaggy eyebrows, protruded his thick nether lip, and tapped the arms of his chair with his cushioned fingertips.

580   "What have you been doing to her, Pontellier?"

"Doing! *Parbleu!*"[54]

"Has she," asked the Doctor, with a smile, "has she been associating of late with a circle of pseudo-intellectual women—super-spiritual superior beings? My wife has been telling me about them."

"That's the trouble," broke in Mr. Pontellier, "she hasn't been associating with any one. She has abandoned her Tuesdays at home, has thrown over all her acquaintances, and goes tramping about by herself, moping in the street-cars, getting in after dark. I tell you she's peculiar. I don't like it; I feel a little worried over it."

This was a new aspect for the Doctor. "Nothing hereditary?" he asked, seriously. "Nothing peculiar about her family antecedents, is there?"

585   "Oh, no indeed! She comes of sound old Presbyterian Kentucky stock. The old gentleman, her father, I have heard, used to atone for his weekday sins with his Sunday devotions. I know for a fact, that his race horses literally ran away with the prettiest bit of Kentucky farming land I ever laid eyes

---

[54]*Parbleu!* For heaven's sake!

upon. Margaret—you know Margaret—she has all the Presbyterianism undiluted. And the youngest is something of a vixen. By the way, she gets married in a couple of weeks from now."

"Send your wife up to the wedding," exclaimed the Doctor, foreseeing a happy solution. "Let her stay among her own people for a while; it will do her good."

"That's what I want her to do. She won't go to the marriage. She says a wedding is one of the most lamentable spectacles on earth. Nice thing for a woman to say to her husband!" exclaimed Mr. Pontellier, fuming anew at the recollection.

"Pontellier," said the Doctor, after a moment's reflection, "let your wife alone for a while. Don't bother her, and don't let her bother you. Woman, my dear friend, is a very peculiar and delicate organism—a sensitive and highly organized woman, such as I know Mrs. Pontellier to be, is especially peculiar. It would require an inspired psychologist to deal successfully with them. And when ordinary fellows like you and me attempt to cope with their idiosyncrasies the result is bungling. Most women are moody and whimsical. This is some passing whim of your wife, due to some cause or causes which you and I needn't try to fathom. But it will pass happily over, especially if you let her alone. Send her around to see me."

"Oh! I couldn't do that; there'd be no reason for it," objected Mr. Pontellier.

590   "Then I'll go around and see her," said the Doctor. "I'll drop in to dinner some evening *en bon ami*."[55]

"Do! by all means," urged Mr. Pontellier. "What evening will you come? Say Thursday. Will you come Thursday?" he asked, rising to take his leave.

"Very well; Thursday. My wife may possibly have some engagement for me Thursday. In case she has, I shall let you know. Otherwise, you may expect me."

Mr. Pontellier turned before leaving to say:

"I am going to New York on business very soon. I have a big scheme on hand, and want to be on the field proper to pull the ropes and handle the ribbons.[56] We'll let you in on the inside if you say so, Doctor," he laughed.

595   "No, I thank you, my dear sir," returned the Doctor. "I leave such ventures to you younger men with the fever of life still in your blood."

"What I wanted to say," continued Mr. Pontellier, with his hand on the knob; "I may have to be absent a good while. Would you advise me to take Edna along?"

"By all means, if she wishes to go. If not, leave her here. Don't contradict her. The mood will pass, I assure you. It may take a month, two, three months—possibly longer, but it will pass; have patience."

"Well, good-by, *à jeudi*,"[57] said Mr. Pontellier, as he let himself out.

The doctor would have liked during the course of conversation to ask, "Is there any man in the case?" but he knew his Creole too well to make such a blunder as that.

600   He did not resume his book immediately, but sat for a while meditatively looking out into the garden.

---

[55]*en bon ami* as a friend.   [56]**handle the ribbons** control the reins—that is, run things.
[57]*à jeudi* until Thursday.

XXIII

Edna's father was in the city, and had been with them several days. She was not very warmly or deeply attached to him, but they had certain tastes in common, and when together they were companionable. His coming was in the nature of a welcome disturbance; it seemed to furnish a new direction for her emotions.

He had come to purchase a wedding ring for his daughter, Janet, and an outfit for himself in which he might make a creditable appearance at her marriage. Mr. Pontellier had selected the bridal gift, as every one immediately connected with him always deferred to his taste in such matters. And his suggestions on the question of dress—which too often assumes the nature of a problem—were of inestimable value to his father-in-law. But for the past few days the old gentleman had been upon Edna's hands, and in his society she was becoming acquainted with a new set of sensations. He had been a colonel in the Confederate army, and still maintained, with the title, the military bearing which had always accompanied it. His hair and mustache were white and silky, emphasizing the rugged bronze of his face. He was tall and thin, and wore his coats padded, which gave a fictitious breadth and depth to his shoulders and chest. Edna and her father looked very distinguished together, and excited a good deal of notice during their perambulations. Upon his arrival she began by introducing him to her atelier and making a sketch of him. He took the whole matter very seriously. If her talent had been ten-fold greater than it was, it would not have surprised him, convinced as he was that he had bequeathed to all of his daughters the germs of a masterful capability, which only depended upon their own efforts to be directed toward successful achievement.

Before her pencil he sat rigid and unflinching, as he had faced the cannon's mouth in days gone by. He resented the intrusion of the children, who gaped with wondering eyes at him, sitting so stiff up there in their mother's bright atelier. When they drew near he motioned them away with an expressive action of the foot, loath to disturb the fixed lines of his countenance, his arms, or his rigid shoulders.

Edna, anxious to entertain him, invited Mademoiselle Reisz to meet him, having promised him a treat in her piano playing; but Mademoiselle declined the invitation. So together they attended a *soirée musicale* at the Ratignolles'. Monsieur and Madame Ratignolle made much of the Colonel, installing him as the guest of honor and engaging him at once to dine with them the following Sunday, or any day which he might select. Madame coquetted with him in the most captivating and naïve manner, with eyes, gestures, and a profusion of compliments, till the Colonel's old head felt thirty years younger on his padded shoulders. Edna marveled, not comprehending. She herself was almost devoid of coquetry.

605   There were one or two men whom she observed at the *soirée musicale;* but she would never have felt moved to any kittenish display to attract their notice—to any feline or feminine wiles to express herself toward them. Their personality attracted her in an agreeable way. Her fancy selected them, and she was glad when a lull in the music gave them an opportunity to meet her and talk with her. Often on the street the glance of strange eyes had lingered in her memory, and sometimes had disturbed her.

Mr. Pontellier did not attend these *soirées musicales.* He considered them *bourgeois,* and found more diversion at the club. To Madame Ratignolle he said the music dispensed at her *soirées* was too "heavy," too far beyond his untrained comprehension. His excuse flattered her. But she disapproved of Mr. Pontellier's club, and she was frank enough to tell Edna so.

"It's a pity Mr. Pontellier doesn't stay home more in the evenings. I think you would be more—well, if you don't mind my saying it—more united, if he did."

"Oh! dear no!" said Edna, with a blank look in her eyes. "What should I do if he stayed home? We wouldn't have anything to say to each other."

She had not much of anything to say to her father, for that matter; but he did not antagonize her. She discovered that he interested her, though she realized that he might not interest her long; and for the first time in her life she felt as if she were thoroughly acquainted with him. He kept her busy serving him and ministering to his wants. It amused her to do so. She would not permit a servant or one of the children to do anything for him which she might do herself. Her husband noticed, and thought it was the expression of a deep filial attachment which he had never suspected.

610   The Colonel drank numerous "toddies" during the course of the day, which left him, however, imperturbed. He was an expert at concocting strong drinks. He had even invented some, to which he had given fantastic names, and for whose manufacture he required diverse ingredients that it devolved upon Edna to procure for him.

When Doctor Mandelet dined with the Pontelliers on Thursday he could discern in Mrs. Pontellier no trace of that morbid condition which her husband had reported to him. She was excited and in a manner radiant. She and her father had been to the race course, and their thoughts when they seated themselves at table were still occupied with the events of the afternoon, and their talk was still of the track. The Doctor had not kept pace with turf affairs. He had certain recollections of racing in what he called "the good old times" when the Lecompte stables flourished, and he drew upon this fund of memories so that he might not be left out and seem wholly devoid of the modern spirit. But he failed to impose upon the Colonel, and was even far from impressing him with this trumped-up knowledge of bygone days. Edna had staked her father on his last venture, with the most gratifying results to both of them. Besides, they had met some very charming people, according to the Colonel's impressions. Mrs. Mortimer Merriman and Mrs. James Highcamp, who were there with Alcée Arobin, had joined them and had enlivened the hours in a fashion that warmed him to think of.

Mr. Pontellier himself had no particular leaning toward horse-racing, and was even rather inclined to discourage it as a pastime, especially when he considered the fate of that blue-grass farm in Kentucky. He endeavored in a general way, to express a particular disapproval, and only succeeded in arousing the ire and opposition of his father-in-law. A petty dispute followed, in which Edna warmly espoused her father's cause and the Doctor remained neutral.

He observed his hostess attentively from under his shaggy brows, and noted a subtle change which had transformed her from the listless woman he had known into a being who, for the moment, seemed palpitant with the forces of life. Her speech was warm and energetic. There was no repression in her glance or gesture. She reminded him of some beautiful, sleek animal waking up in the sun.

The dinner was excellent. The claret was warm and the champagne was cold, and under their beneficent influence the threatened unpleasantness melted and vanished with the fumes of the wine.

615   Mr. Pontellier warmed up and grew reminiscent. He told some amusing plantation experiences, recollections of old Iberville and his youth, when he hunted 'possum in company with some friendly darky; thrashed the pecan trees, shot the grosbec, and roamed the woods and fields in mischievous idleness.

The Colonel, with little sense of humor and of the fitness of things, related a somber episode of those dark and bitter days, in which he had acted a conspicuous part and always formed a central figure. Nor was the Doctor happier in his selection, when he told the old, ever new and curious story of the waning of a woman's love, seeking strange, new channels, only to return to its legitimate source after days of fierce unrest. It was one of the many little human documents which had been unfolded to him during his long career as a physician. The story did not seem especially to impress Edna. She had one of her own to tell, of a woman who paddled away with her lover one night in a pirogue and never came back. They were lost amid the Baratarian Islands, and no one ever heard of them or found trace of them from that day to this. It was a pure invention. She said that Madame Antoine had related it to her. That, also, was an invention. Perhaps it was a dream she had had. But every glowing word seemed real to those who listened. They could feel the hot breath of the Southern night; they could hear the long sweep of the pirogue through the glistening moonlit water, the beating of birds' wings, rising startled from among the reeds in the salt-water pools; they could see the faces of the lovers, pale, close together, rapt in oblivious forgetfulness, drifting into the unknown.

The champagne was cold, and its subtle fumes played fantastic tricks with Edna's memory that night.

Outside, away from the glow of the fire and the soft lamplight, the night was chill and murky. The Doctor doubled his old-fashioned cloak across his breast as he strode home through the darkness. He knew his fellow-creatures better than most men; knew that inner life which so seldom unfolds itself to unanointed eyes. He was sorry he had accepted Pontellier's invitation. He was growing old, and beginning to need rest and an imperturbed spirit. He did not want the secrets of other lives thrust upon him.

"I hope it isn't Arobin," he muttered to himself as he walked. "I hope to heaven it isn't Alcée Arobin."

XXIV

620   Edna and her father had a warm, and almost violent dispute upon the subject of her refusal to attend her sister's wedding. Mr. Pontellier declined to interfere, to interpose either his influence or his authority. He was following Doctor Mandelet's advice, and letting her do as she liked. The Colonel reproached his daughter for her lack of filial kindness and respect, her want of sisterly affection and womanly consideration. His arguments were

labored and unconvincing. He doubted if Janet would accept any excuse—forgetting that Edna had offered none. He doubted if Janet would ever speak to her again, and he was sure Margaret would not.

Edna was glad to be rid of her father when he finally took himself off with his wedding garments and his bridal gifts, with his padded shoulders, his Bible reading, his "toddies" and ponderous oaths.

Mr. Pontellier followed him closely. He meant to stop at the wedding on his way to New York and endeavor by every means which money and love could devise to atone somewhat for Edna's incomprehensible action.

"You are too lenient, too lenient by far, Léonce," asserted the Colonel. "Authority, coercion are what is needed. Put you foot down good and hard; the only way to manage a wife. Take my word for it."

The Colonel was perhaps unaware that he had coerced his own wife into her grave. Mr. Pontellier had a vague suspicion of it which he thought it needless to mention at that late day.

625   Edna was not so consciously gratified at her husband's leaving home as she had been over the departure of her father. As the day approached when he was to leave her for a comparatively long stay, she grew melting and affectionate, remembering his many acts of consideration and his repeated expressions of an ardent attachment. She was solicitous about his health and his welfare. She bustled around, looking after his clothing, thinking about heavy underwear, quite as Madame Ratignolle would have done under similar circumstances. She cried when he went away, calling him her dear, good friend, and she was quite certain she would grow lonely before very long and go to join him in New York.

But after all, a radiant peace settled upon her when she at last found herself alone. Even the children were gone. Old Madame Pontellier had come herself and carried them off to Iberville with their quadroon. The old Madame did not venture to say she was afraid they would be neglected during Léonce's absence; she hardly ventured to think so. She was hungry for them—even a little fierce in her attachment. She did not want them to be wholly "children of the pavement," she always said when begging to have them for a space. She wished them to know the country, with its streams, its fields, its woods, its freedom, so delicious to the young. She wished them to taste something of the life their father had lived and known and loved when he, too, was a little child.

When Edna was at last alone, she breathed a big, genuine sigh of relief. A feeling that was unfamiliar but very delicious came over her. She walked all through the house, from one room to another, as if inspecting it for the first time. She tried the various chairs and lounges, as if she had never sat and reclined upon them before. And she perambulated around the outside of the house, investigating, looking to see if windows and shutters were secure and in order. The flowers were like new acquaintances; she approached them in a familiar spirit, and made herself at home among them. The garden walks were damp, and Edna called to the maid to bring out her rubber sandals. And there she stayed, and stooped, digging around the plants, trimming, picking dead, dry leaves. The children's little dog came out, interfering, getting in her way. She scolded him, laughed at him, played with him. The garden smelled so good and looked so pretty in the afternoon sunlight. Edna plucked all the bright flowers she could find, and went into the house with them, she and the little dog.

Even the kitchen assumed a sudden interesting character which she had never before perceived. She went in to give directions to the cook, to say that the butcher would have to bring much less meat, that they would require only half their usual quantity of bread, of milk and groceries. She told the cook that she herself would be greatly occupied during Mr. Pontellier's absence, and she begged her to take all thought and responsibility of the larder upon her own shoulders.

That night Edna dined alone. The candelabra, with a few candles in the center of the table, gave all the light she needed. Outside the circle of light in which she sat, the large dining-room looked solemn and shadowy. The cook, placed upon her mettle, served a delicious repast—a luscious tenderloin broiled *à point.*[58] The wine tasted good; the *marron glacé*[59] seemed to be just what she wanted. It was so pleasant, too, to dine in a comfortable *peignoir.*

630   She thought a little sentimentally about Léonce and the children, and wondered what they were doing. As she gave a dainty scrap or two to the doggie, she talked intimately to him about Etienne and Raoul. He was beside himself with astonishment and delight over these companionable advances, and showed his appreciation by his little quick, snappy barks and a lively agitation.

Then Edna sat in the library after dinner and read Emerson until she grew sleepy. She realized that she had neglected her reading, and determined to start anew upon a course of improving studies, now that her time was completely her own to do with as she liked.

After a refreshing bath, Edna went to bed. And as she snuggled comfortably beneath the eiderdown a sense of restfulness invaded her, such as she had not known before.

XXV

When the weather was dark and cloudy Edna could not work. She needed the sun to mellow and temper her mood to the sticking point. She had reached a stage when she seemed to be no longer feeling her way, working, when in the humor, with sureness and ease. And being devoid of ambition, and striving not toward accomplishment, she drew satisfaction from the work in itself.

On rainy or melancholy days Edna went out and sought the society of the friends she had made at Grand Isle. Or else she stayed indoors and nursed a mood with which she was becoming too familiar for her own comfort and peace of mind. It was not despair; but it seemed to her as if life were passing by, leaving its promise broken and unfulfilled. Yet there were other days when she listened, was led on and deceived by fresh promises which her youth held out to her.

635   She went again to the races, and again. Alcée Arobin and Mrs. Highcamp called for her one bright afternoon in Arobin's drag.[60] Mrs. Highcamp was a worldly but unaffected, intelligent, slim, tall blonde woman in the forties, with an indifferent manner and blue eyes that stared. She had a daughter who served her as a pretext for cultivating the society of young men of

---

[58]*à point* to a turn.   [59]*marron glacé* glazed chestnuts.   [60]**drag** heavy carriage.

fashion. Alcée Arobin was one of them. He was a familiar figure at the race course, the opera, the fashionable clubs. There was a perpetual smile in his eyes, which seldom failed to awaken a corresponding cheerfulness in any one who looked into them and listened to his good-humored voice. His manner was quiet, and at times a little insolent. He possessed a good figure, a pleasing face, not overburdened with depth of thought or feeling; and his dress was that of the conventional man of fashion.

He admired Edna extravagantly, after meeting her at the races with her father. He had met her before on other occasions, but she had seemed to him unapproachable until that day. It was at his instigation that Mrs. High-camp called to ask her to go with them to the Jockey Club to witness the turf event of the season.

There were possibly a few track men out there who knew the race horse as well as Edna, but there was certainly none who knew it better. She sat between her two companions as one having authority to speak. She laughed at Arobin's pretensions, and deplored Mrs. Highcamp's ignorance. The race horse was a friend and intimate associate of her childhood. The atmosphere of the stable and the breath of the blue grass paddock revived in her memory and lingered in her nostrils. She did not perceive that she was talking like her father as the sleek geldings ambled in review before them. She played for very high stakes, and fortune favored her. The fever of the game flamed in her cheeks and eyes, and it got into her blood and into her brain like an intoxicant. People turned their heads to look at her, and more than one lent an attentive ear to her utterances, hoping thereby to secure the elusive but ever-desired "tip." Arobin caught the contagion of excitement which drew him to Edna like a magnet. Mrs. Highcamp remained, as usual, unmoved, with her indifferent stare and uplifted eyebrows.

Edna stayed and dined with Mrs. Highcamp upon being urged to do so. Arobin also remained and sent away his drag.

The dinner was quiet and uninteresting, save for the cheerful efforts of Arobin to enliven things. Mrs. Highcamp deplored the absence of her daughter from the races, and tried to convey to her what she had missed by going to the "Dante[61] reading" instead of joining them. The girl held a geranium leaf up to her nose and said nothing, but looked knowing and noncommittal. Mr. Highcamp was a plain, bald-headed man, who only talked under compulsion. He was unresponsive. Mrs. Highcamp was full of delicate courtesy and consideration toward her husband. She addressed most of her conversation to him at table. They sat in the library after dinner and read the evening papers together under the droplight; while the younger people went into the drawing-room near by and talked. Miss Highcamp played some selections from Grieg[62] upon the piano. She seemed to have apprehended all of the composer's coldness and none of his poetry. While Edna listened she could not help wondering if she had lost her taste for music.

640   When the time came for her to go home, Mr. Highcamp grunted a lame offer to escort her, looking down at his slippered feet with tactless concern. It was Arobin who took her home. The car ride was long, and it was late when they reached Esplanade Street. Arobin asked permission to enter for

---

[61]**Dante** Dante Alighieri (1265–1321), Italian poet.   [62]**Grieg** Edvard Grieg (1843–1907), Norwegian composer.

a second to light his cigarette—his match safe[63] was empty. He filled his match safe, but did not light his cigarette until he left her, after she had expressed her willingness to go to the races with him again.

Edna was neither tired nor sleepy. She was hungry again, for the High-camp dinner, though of excellent quality, had lacked abundance. She rummaged in the larder and brought forth a slice of Gruyère and some crackers. She opened a bottle of beer which she found in the icebox. Edna felt extremely restless and excited. She vacantly hummed a fantastic tune as she poked at the wood embers on the hearth and munched a cracker.

She wanted something to happen—something, anything; she did not know what. She regretted that she had not made Arobin stay a half hour to talk over the horses with her. She counted the money she had won. But there was nothing else to do, so she went to bed, and tossed there for hours in a sort of monotonous agitation.

In the middle of the night she remembered that she had forgotten to write her regular letter to her husband; and she decided to do so next day and tell him about her afternoon at the Jockey Club. She lay wide awake composing a letter which was nothing like the one which she wrote next day. When the maid awoke her in the morning Edna was dreaming of Mr. Highcamp playing the piano at the entrance of a music store on Canal Street, while his wife was saying to Alcée Arobin, as they boarded an Esplanade Street car:

"What a pity that so much talent has been neglected! but I must go."

645   When, a few days later, Alcée Arobin again called for Edna in his drag, Mrs. Highcamp was not with him. He said they would pick her up. But as that lady had not been apprised of his intention of picking her up, she was not at home. The daughter was just leaving the house to attend the meeting of a branch Folk Lore Society, and regretted that she could not accompany them. Arobin appeared nonplused, and asked Edna if there were any one else she cared to ask.

She did not deem it worth while to go in search of any of the fashionable acquaintances from whom she had withdrawn herself. She thought of Madame Ratignolle, but knew that her fair friend did not leave the house, except to take a languid walk around the block with her husband after nightfall. Mademoiselle Reisz would have laughed at such a request from Edna. Madame Lebrun might have enjoyed the outing, but for some reason Edna did not want her. So they went alone, she and Arobin.

The afternoon was intensely interesting to her. The excitement came back upon her like a remittent fever. Her talk grew familiar and confidential. It was no labor to become intimate with Arobin. His manner invited easy confidence. The preliminary stage of becoming acquainted was one which he always endeavored to ignore when a pretty and engaging woman was concerned.

He stayed and dined with Edna. He stayed and sat beside the wood fire. They laughed and talked; and before it was time to go he was telling her how different life might have been if he had known her years before. With ingenuous frankness he spoke of what a wicked, ill-disciplined boy he had been, and impulsively drew up his cuff to exhibit upon his wrist the scar

---

[63]**match safe** noncombustible box to hold friction matches.

from a saber cut which he had received in a duel outside of Paris when he was nineteen. She touched his hand as she scanned the red cicatrice[64] on the inside of his white wrist. A quick impulse that was somewhat spasmodic impelled her fingers to close in a sort of clutch upon his hand. He felt the pressure of her pointed nails in the flesh of his palm.

She arose hastily and walked toward the mantel.

650   "The sight of a wound or scar always agitates and sickens me," she said. "I shouldn't have looked at it."

"I beg your pardon," he entreated, following her; "it never occurred to me that it might be repulsive."

He stood close to her, and the effrontery in his eyes repelled the old, vanishing self in her, yet drew all her awakening sensuousness. He saw enough in her face to impel him to take her hand and hold it while he said his lingering good night.

"Will you go to the races again?" he asked.

"No," she said. "I've had enough of the races. I don't want to lose all the money I've won, and I've got to work when the weather is bright, instead of—"

655   "Yes; work; to be sure. You promised to show me your work. What morning may I come up to your atelier? To-morrow?"

"No!"

"Day after?"

"No, no."

"Oh, please don't refuse me! I know something of such things. I might help you with a stray suggestion or two."

660   "No. Good night. Why don't you go after you have said good night? I don't like you," she went on in a high, excited pitch, attempting to draw away her hand. She felt that her words lacked dignity and sincerity, and she knew that he felt it.

"I'm sorry you don't like me. I'm sorry I offended you. How have I offended you? What have I done? Can't you forgive me?" And he bent and pressed his lips upon her hand as if he wished never more to withdraw them.

"Mr. Arobin," she complained. "I'm greatly upset by the excitement of the afternoon; I'm not myself. My manner must have misled you in some way. I wish you to go, please." She spoke in a monotonous, dull tone. He took his hat from the table, and stood with eyes turned from her, looking into the dying fire. For a moment or two he kept an impressive silence.

"Your manner has not misled me, Mrs. Pontellier," he said finally. "My own emotions have done that. I couldn't help it. When I'm near you, how could I help it? Don't think anything of it, don't bother, please. You see, I go when you command me. If you wish me to stay away, I shall do so. If you let me come back, I—oh! you will let me come back?"

He cast one appealing glance at her, to which she made no response. Alcée Arobin's manner was so genuine that it often deceived even himself.

665   Edna did not care or think whether it were genuine or not. When she was alone she looked mechanically at the back of her hand which he had kissed so warmly. Then she leaned her head down on the mantelpiece. She felt somewhat like a woman who in a moment of passion is betrayed into an

---

[64]**cicatrice** scar.

act of infidelity, and realizes the significance of the act without being wholly awakened from its glamour. The thought was passing vaguely through her mind, "What would he think?"

She did not mean her husband; she was thinking of Robert Lebrun. Her husband seemed to her now like a person whom she had married without love as an excuse.

She lit a candle and went up to her room. Alcée Arobin was absolutely nothing to her. Yet his presence, his manners, the warmth of his glances, and above all the touch of his lips upon her hand had acted like a narcotic upon her.

She slept a languorous sleep, interwoven with vanishing dreams.

XXVI

Alcée Arobin wrote Edna an elaborate note of apology, palpitant with sincerity. It embarrassed her; for in a cooler, quieter moment it appeared to her absurd that she should have taken his action so seriously, so dramatically. She felt sure that the significance of the whole occurrence had lain in her own self-consciousness. If she ignored his note it would give undue importance to a trivial affair. If she replied to it in a serious spirit it would still leave in his mind the impression that she had in a susceptible moment yielded to his influence. After all, it was no great matter to have one's hand kissed. She was provoked at his having written the apology. She answered in as light and bantering a spirit as she fancied it deserved, and said she would be glad to have him look in upon her at work whenever he felt the inclination and his business gave him the opportunity.

670   He responded at once by presenting himself at her home with all his disarming naïveté. And then there was scarcely a day which followed that she did not see him or was not reminded of him. He was prolific in pretexts. His attitude became one of good-humored subservience and tacit adoration. He was ready at all times to submit to her moods, which were as often kind as they were cold. She grew accustomed to him. They became intimate and friendly by imperceptible degrees, and then by leaps. He sometimes talked in a way that astonished her at first and brought the crimson into her face; in a way that pleased her at last, appealing to the animalism that stirred impatiently within her.

There was nothing which so quieted the turmoil in Edna's senses as a visit to Mademoiselle Reisz. It was then, in the presence of that personality which was offensive to her, that the woman, by her divine art, seemed to reach Edna's spirit and set it free.

It was misty, with heavy, lowering atmosphere, one afternoon, when Edna climbed the stairs to the pianist's apartments under the roof. Her clothes were dripping with moisture. She felt chilled and pinched as she entered the room. Mademoiselle was poking at a rusty stove that smoked a little and warmed the room indifferently. She was endeavoring to heat a pot of chocolate on the stove. The room looked cheerless and dingy to Edna as she entered. A bust of Beethoven, covered with a hood of dust, scowled at her from the mantelpiece.

"Ah! here comes the sunlight!" exclaimed Mademoiselle, rising from her knees before the stove. "Now it will be warm and bright enough; I can let the fire alone."

She closed the stove door with a bang, and approaching, assisted in removing Edna's dripping mackintosh.

675 "You are cold; you look miserable. The chocolate will soon be hot. But would you rather have a taste of brandy? I have scarcely touched the bottle which you brought me for my cold." A piece of red flannel was wrapped around Mademoiselle's throat; a stiff neck compelled her to hold her head on one side.

"I will take some brandy," said Edna, shivering as she removed her gloves and overshoes. She drank the liquor from the glass as a man would have done. Then flinging herself upon the uncomfortable sofa she said, "Mademoiselle, I am going to move away from my house on Esplanade Street."

"Ah!" ejaculated the musician, neither surprised nor especially interested. Nothing ever seemed to astonish her very much. She was endeavoring to adjust the bunch of violets which had become loose from its fastening in her hair. Edna drew her down upon the sofa, and taking a pin from her own hair, secured the shabby artificial flowers in their accustomed place.

"Aren't you astonished?"

"Passably. Where are you going? to New York? to Iberville? to your father in Mississippi? where?"

680 "Just two steps away," laughed Edna, "in a little four-room house around the corner. It looks so cozy, so inviting and restful, whenever I pass by; and it's for rent. I'm tired looking after that big house. It never seemed like mine, anyway—like home. It's too much trouble. I have to keep too many servants. I am tired bothering with them."

"That is not your true reason, *ma belle.* There is no use in telling me lies. I don't know your reason, but you have not told me the truth." Edna did not protest or endeavor to justify herself.

"The house, the money that provides for it, are not mine. Isn't that enough reason?"

"They are your husband's," returned Mademoiselle, with a shrug and a malicious elevation of the eyebrows.

"Oh! I see there is no deceiving you. Then let me tell you: It is a caprice. I have a little money of my own from my mother's estate, which my father sends me by driblets. I won a large sum this winter on the races, and I am beginning to sell my sketches. Laidpore is more and more pleased with my work; he says it grows in force and individuality. I cannot judge of that myself, but I feel that I have gained in ease and confidence. However, as I said, I have sold a good many through Laidpore. I can live in the tiny house for little or nothing, with one servant. Old Celestine, who works occasionally for me, says she will come stay with me and do my work. I know I shall like it, like the feeling of freedom and independence."

685 "What does your husband say?"

"I have not told him yet. I only thought of it this morning. He will think I am demented, no doubt. Perhaps you think so."

Mademoiselle shook her head slowly. "Your reason is not yet clear to me," she said.

Neither was it quite clear to Edna herself; but it unfolded itself as she sat for a while in silence. Instinct had prompted her to put away her husband's bounty in casting off her allegiance. She did not know how it would be when he returned. There would have to be an understanding, an explanation. Conditions would some way adjust themselves, she felt; but whatever came, she had resolved never again to belong to another than herself.

"I shall give a grand dinner before I leave the old house!" Edna exclaimed. "You will have to come to it, Mademoiselle. I will give you everything that you like to eat and drink. We shall sing and laugh and be merry for once." And she uttered a sigh that came from the very depths of her being.

690   If Mademoiselle happened to have received a letter from Robert during the interval of Edna's visits, she would give her the letter unsolicited. And she would seat herself at the piano and play as her humor prompted her while the young woman read the letter.

The little stove was roaring; it was red-hot, and the chocolate in the tin sizzled and sputtered. Edna went forward and opened the stove door, and Mademoiselle rising, took a letter from under the bust of Beethoven and handed it to Edna.

"Another! so soon!" she exclaimed, her eyes filled with delight. "Tell me, Mademoiselle, does he know that I see his letters?"

"Never in the world! He would be angry and would never write to me again if he thought so. Does he write to you? Never a line. Does he send you a message? Never a word. It is because he loves you, poor fool, and is trying to forget you, since you are not free to listen to him or to belong to him."

"Why do you show me his letters, then?"

695   "Haven't you begged for them? Can I refuse you anything? Oh! you cannot deceive me," and Mademoiselle approached her beloved instrument and began to play. Edna did not at once read the letter. She sat holding it in her hand, while the music penetrated her whole being like an effulgence, warming and brightening the dark places of her soul. It prepared her for joy and exultation.

"Oh!" she exclaimed, letting the letter fall to the floor. "Why did you not tell me?" She went and grasped Mademoiselle's hands up from the keys. "Oh! unkind! malicious! Why did you not tell me?"

"That he was coming back? No great news, *ma foi*. I wonder he did not come long ago."

"But when, when?" cried Edna, impatiently. "He does not say when."

"He says 'very soon.' You know as much about it as I do; it is all in the letter."

700   "But why? Why is he coming? Oh, if I thought—" and she snatched the letter from the floor and turned the pages this way and that way, looking for the reason, which was left untold.

"If I were young and in love with a man," said Mademoiselle, turning on the stool and pressing her wiry hands between her knees as she looked down at Edna, who sat on the floor holding the letter, "it seems to me he would have to be some *grand esprit*,[65] a man with lofty aims and ability to reach them; one who stood high enough to attract the notice of his fellowmen. It seems to me if I were young and in love I should never deem a man of ordinary caliber worthy of my devotion."

"Now it is you who are telling lies and seeking to deceive me, Mademoiselle; or else you have never been in love, and know nothing about it.

---

[65]*grand esprit* noble soul.

Why," went on Edna, clasping her knees and looking up into Mademoiselle's twisted face, "do you suppose a woman knows why she loves? Does she select? Does she say to herself: 'Go to! Here is a distinguished statesman with presidential possibilities; I shall proceed to fall in love with him.' Or, 'I shall set my heart upon this musician, whose fame is on every tongue?' Or, 'This financier, who controls the world's money markets?'"

"You are purposely misunderstanding me, *ma reine.*[66] Are you in love with Robert?"

"Yes," said Edna. It was the first time she had admitted it, and a glow overspread her face, blotching it with red spots.

705   "Why?" asked her companion. "Why do you love him when you ought not to?"

Edna, with a motion or two, dragged herself on her knees before Mademoiselle Reisz, who took the glowing face between her two hands.

"Why? Because his hair is brown and grows away from his temples; because he opens and shuts his eyes, and his nose is a little out of drawing; because he has two lips and a square chin, and a little finger which he can't straighten from having played baseball too energetically in his youth. Because—"

"Because you do, in short," laughed Mademoiselle. "What will you do when he comes back?" she asked.

"Do? Nothing, except feel glad and happy to be alive."

710   She was already glad and happy to be alive at the mere thought of his return. The murky, lowering sky, which had depressed her a few hours before, seemed bracing and invigorating as she splashed through the streets on her way home.

She stopped at a confectioner's and ordered a huge box of bonbons for the children in Iberville. She slipped a card in the box, on which she scribbled a tender message and sent an abundance of kisses.

Before dinner in the evening Edna wrote a charming letter to her husband, telling him of her intention to move for a while into the little house around the block, and to give a farewell dinner before leaving, regretting that he was not there to share it, to help her out with the menu and assist her in entertaining the guests. Her letter was brilliant and brimming with cheerfulness.

XXVII

"What is the matter with you?" asked Arobin that evening. "I never found you in such a happy mood." Edna was tired by that time, and was reclining on the lounge before the fire.

"Don't you know the weather prophet has told us we shall see the sun pretty soon?"

715   "Well, that ought to be reason enough," he acquiesced. "You wouldn't give me another if I sat here all night imploring you." He sat close to her on a low tabouret, and as he spoke his fingers lightly touched the hair that fell a little over her forehead. She liked the touch of his fingers through her hair, and closed her eyes sensitively.

---

[66]*ma reine* my dear (literally, "my queen").

"One of these days," she said, "I'm going to pull myself together for a while and think—try to determine what character of a woman I am; for, candidly, I don't know. By all the codes which I am acquainted with, I am a devilishly wicked specimen of the sex. But some way I can't convince myself that I am. I must think about it."

"Don't. What's the use? Why should you bother thinking about it when I can tell you what manner of woman you are." His fingers strayed occasionally down to her warm, smooth cheeks and firm chin, which was growing a little full and double.

"Oh, yes! You will tell me that I am adorable; everything that is captivating. Spare yourself the effort."

"No; I shan't tell you anything of the sort, though I shouldn't be lying if I did."

720   "Do you know Mademoiselle Reisz?" she asked irrelevantly.

"The pianist? I know her by sight. I've heard her play."

"She says queer things sometimes in a bantering way that you don't notice at the time and you find yourself thinking about afterward."

"For instance?"

"Well, for instance, when I left her to-day, she put her arms around me and felt my shoulder blades, to see if my wings were strong, she said. 'The bird that would soar above the level plain of tradition and prejudice must have strong wings. It is a sad spectacle to see the weaklings bruised, exhausted, fluttering back to earth.'"

725   "Whither would you soar?"

"I'm not thinking of any extraordinary flights. I only half comprehend her."

"I've heard she's partially demented," said Arobin.

"She seems to me wonderfully sane," Edna replied.

"I'm told she's extremely disagreeable and unpleasant. Why have you introduced her at a moment when I desired to talk of you?"

730   "Oh! talk of me if you like," cried Edna, clasping her hands beneath her head; "but let me think of something else while you do."

"I'm jealous of your thoughts to-night. They're making you a little kinder than usual; but some way I feel as if they were wandering, as if they were not here with me." She only looked at him and smiled. His eyes were very near. He leaned upon the lounge with an arm extended across her, while the other hand still rested upon her hair. They continued silently to look into each other's eyes. When he leaned forward and kissed her, she clasped his head, holding his lips to hers.

It was the first kiss of her life to which her nature had really responded. It was a flaming torch that kindled desire.

XXVIII

Edna cried a little that night after Arobin left her. It was only one phase of the multitudinous emotions which had assailed her. There was with her an overwhelming feeling of irresponsibility. There was the shock of the unexpected and the unaccustomed. There was her husband's reproach looking at her from the external things around her which he had provided for her external existence. There was Robert's reproach making itself felt by a quicker, fiercer, more overpowering love, which had awakened within her toward him. Above all, there was understanding. She felt as if a mist had been lifted from her eyes, enabling her to look upon and comprehend the significance of life, that monster made up of beauty and brutality. But among the conflicting sensations which assailed her, there was neither shame nor remorse. There was a dull pang of regret because it was not the kiss of love which had inflamed her, because it was not love which had held this cup of life to her lips.

XXIX

Without even waiting for an answer from her husband regarding his opinion or wishes in the matter, Edna hastened her preparations for quitting her home on Esplanade Street and moving into the little house around the block. A feverish anxiety attended her every action in that direction. There was no moment of deliberation, no interval of repose between the thought and its fulfillment. Early upon the morning following those hours passed in Arobin's society, Edna set about securing her new abode and hurrying her arrangements for occupying it. Within the precincts of her home she felt like one who has entered and lingered within the portals of some forbidden temple in which a thousand muffled voices bade her begone.

735   Whatever was her own in the house, everything she had acquired aside from her husband's bounty, she caused to be transported to the other house, supplying simple and meager deficiencies from her own resources.

Arobin found her with rolled sleeves, working in company with the house-maid when he looked in during the afternoon. She was splendid and robust, and had never appeared handsomer than in the old blue gown, with a red silk handkerchief knotted at random around her head to protect her hair from the dust. She was mounted upon a high step-ladder, unhooking a picture from the wall when he entered. He had found the front door open, and had followed his ring by walking in unceremoniously.

"Come down!" he said. "Do you want to kill yourself?" She greeted him with affected carelessness, and appeared absorbed in her occupation.

If he had expected to find her languishing, reproachful, or indulging in sentimental tears, he must have been greatly surprised.

He was no doubt prepared for any emergency, ready for any one of the foregoing attitudes, just as he bent himself easily and naturally to the situation which confronted him.

740   "Please come down," he insisted, holding the ladder and looking up at her.

"No," she answered; "Ellen is afraid to mount the ladder. Joe is working over at the 'pigeon house'—that's the name Ellen gives it, because it's so small and looks like a pigeon house—and some one has to do this."

Arobin pulled off his coat, and expressed himself ready and willing to tempt fate in her place. Ellen brought him one of her dust-caps, and went into contortions of mirth, which she found it impossible to control, when she saw him put it on before the mirror as grotesquely as he could. Edna herself could not refrain from smiling when she fastened it at his request. So it was he who in turn mounted the ladder, unhooking pictures and curtains, and dislodging ornaments as Edna directed. When he had finished he took off his dust-cap and went out to wash his hands.

Edna was sitting on the tabouret, idly brushing the tips of a feather duster along the carpet when he came in again.

"Is there anything more you will let me do?" he asked.

745 "That is all," she answered. "Ellen can manage the rest." She kept the young woman occupied in the drawing-room, unwilling to be left alone with Arobin.

"What about the dinner?" he asked; "the grand event, the *coup d'état?*"

"It will be day after to-morrow. Why do you call it the *'coup d'état?'* Oh! it will be very fine; all my best of everything—crystal, silver and gold, Sèvres, flowers, music, and champagne to swim in. I'll let Léonce pay the bills. I wonder what he'll say when he sees the bills."

"And you ask me why I call it a *coup d'état?*" Arobin put on his coat, and he stood before her and asked if his cravat was plumb. She told him it was, looking no higher than the tip of his collar.

"When do you go to the 'pigeon house?'—with all due acknowledgement to Ellen."

750 "Day after to-morrow, after the dinner. I shall sleep there."

"Ellen, will you very kindly get me a glass of water?" asked Arobin. "The dust in the curtains, if you will pardon me for hinting such a thing, has parched my throat to a crisp."

"While Ellen gets the water," said Edna, rising, "I will say good-by and let you go. I must get rid of this grime, and I have a million things to do and think of."

"When shall I see you?" asked Arobin, seeking to detain her, the maid having left the room.

"At the dinner, of course. You are invited."

755 "Not before?—not to-night or to-morrow morning or to-morrow noon or night? or the day after morning or noon? Can't you see yourself, without my telling you, what an eternity it is?"

He had followed her into the hall and to the foot of the stairway, looking up at her as she mounted with her face half turned to him.

"Not an instant sooner," she said. But she laughed and looked at him with eyes that at once gave him courage to wait and made it torture to wait.

XXX

Though Edna had spoken of the dinner as a grand affair, it was in truth a very small affair and very select, in so much as the guests invited were few and were selected with discrimination. She had counted upon an even dozen seating themselves at her round mahogany board, forgetting for the moment that Madame Ratignolle was to the last degree *souffrante*[67] and unpresentable, and not foreseeing that Madame Lebrun would send a thousand regrets at the last moment. So there were only ten, after all, which made a cozy, comfortable number.

There were Mr. and Mrs. Merriman, a pretty, vivacious little woman in the thirties; her husband, a jovial fellow, something of a shallow-pate, who laughed a good deal at other people's witticisms, and had thereby made himself extremely popular. Mrs. Highcamp had accompanied them. Of course,

---

[67]*souffrante* ill.

there was Alcée Arobin; and Mademoiselle Reisz had consented to come. Edna had sent her a fresh bunch of violets with black lace trimmings for her hair. Monsieur Ratignolle brought himself and his wife's excuses. Victor Lebrun, who happened to be in the city, bent upon relaxation, had accepted with alacrity. There was a Miss Mayblunt, no longer in her teens, who looked at the world through lorgnettes and with the keenest interest. It was thought and said that she was intellectual; it was suspected of her that she wrote under a *nom de guerre.*[68] She had come with a gentleman by the name of Gouvernail, connected with one of the daily papers, of whom nothing special could be said, except that he was observant and seemed quiet and inoffensive. Edna herself made the tenth, and at half-past eight they seated themselves at table, Arobin and Monsieur Ratignolle on either side of their hostess.

760   Mrs. Highcamp sat between Arobin and Victor Lebrun. Then came Mrs. Merriman, Mr. Gouvernail, Miss Mayblunt, Mr. Merriman, and Mademoiselle Reisz next to Monsieur Ratignolle.

There was something extremely gorgeous about the appearance of the table, an effect of splendor conveyed by a cover of pale yellow satin under strips of lacework. There were wax candles in massive brass candelabra, burning softly under yellow silk shades; full, fragrant roses, yellow and red, abounded. There were silver and gold, as she had said there would be, and crystal which glittered like the gems which the women wore.

The ordinary stiff dining chairs had been discarded for the occasion and replaced by the most commodious and luxurious which could be collected throughout the house. Mademoiselle Reisz, being exceedingly diminutive, was elevated upon cushions, as small children are sometimes hoisted at table upon bulky volumes.

"Something new, Edna?" exclaimed Miss Mayblunt, with lorgnette directed toward a magnificent cluster of diamonds that sparkled, that almost sputtered, in Edna's hair, just over the center of her forehead.

"Quite new; 'brand' new, in fact; a present from my husband. It arrived this morning from New York. I may as well admit that this is my birthday, and that I am twenty-nine. In good time I expect you to drink my health. Meanwhile, I shall ask you to begin with this cocktail, composed—would you say 'composed?'" with an appeal to Miss Mayblunt—"composed by my father in honor of Sister Janet's wedding."

765   Before each guest stood a tiny glass that looked and sparkled like a garnet gem.

"Then, all things considered," spoke Arobin, "it might not be amiss to start out by drinking the Colonel's health in the cocktail which he composed, on the birthday of the most charming of women—the daughter whom he invented."

Mr. Merriman's laugh at this sally was such a genuine outburst and so contagious that it started the dinner with an agreeable swing that never slackened.

Miss Mayblunt begged to be allowed to keep her cocktail untouched before her, just to look at. The color was marvelous! She could compare it to nothing she had ever seen, and the garnet lights which it emitted were unspeakably rare. She pronounced the Colonel an artist, and stuck to it.

---

[68]*nom de guerre* pseudonym (literally, "war name").

Monsieur Ratignolle was prepared to take things seriously: the *mets,* the *entremets,*[69] the service, the decorations, even the people. He looked up from his pompano[70] and inquired of Arobin if he were related to the gentleman of that name who formed one of the firm of Laitner and Arobin, lawyers. The young man admitted that Laitner was a warm personal friend, who permitted Arobin's name to decorate the firm's letterheads and to appear upon a shingle that graced Perdido Street.

770   "There are so many inquisitive people and institutions abounding," said Arobin, "that one is really forced as a matter of convenience these days to assume the virtue of an occupation if he has it not."

Monsieur Ratignolle stared a little, and turned to ask Mademoiselle Reisz if she considered the symphony concerts up to the standard which had been set the previous winter. Mademoiselle Reisz answered Monsieur Ratignolle in French, which Edna thought a little rude, under the circumstances, but characteristic. Mademoiselle had only disagreeable things to say of the symphony concerts, and insulting remarks to make of all the musicians of New Orleans, singly and collectively. All her interest seemed to be centered upon the delicacies placed before her.

Mr. Merriman said that Mr. Arobin's remark about inquisitive people reminded him of a man from Waco the other day at the St. Charles Hotel—but as Mr. Merriman's stories were always lame and lacking point, his wife seldom permitted him to complete them. She interrupted him to ask if he remembered the name of the author whose book she had bought the week before to send to a friend in Geneva. She was talking "books" with Mr. Gouvernail and trying to draw from him his opinion upon current literary topics. Her husband told the story of the Waco man privately to Miss Mayblunt, who pretended to be greatly amused and to think it extremely clever.

Mrs. Highcamp hung with languid but unaffected interest upon the warm and impetuous volubility of her left-hand neighbor, Victor Lebrun. Her attention was never for a moment withdrawn from him after seating herself at table; and when he turned to Mrs. Merriman, who was prettier and more vivacious than Mrs. Highcamp, she waited with easy indifference for an opportunity to reclaim his attention. There was the occasional sound of music, of mandolins, sufficiently removed to be an agreeable accompaniment rather than an interruption to the conversation. Outside the soft, monotonous splash of a fountain could be heard; the sound penetrated into the room with the heavy odor of jessamine that came through the open windows.

The golden shimmer of Edna's satin gown spread in rich folds on either side of her. There was a soft fall of lace encircling her shoulders. It was the color of her skin, without the glow, the myriad living tints that one may sometimes discover in vibrant flesh. There was something in her attitude, in her whole appearance when she leaned her head against the high-backed chair and spread her arms, which suggested the regal woman, the one who rules, who looks on, who stands alone.

775   But as she sat there amid her guests, she felt the old ennui overtaking her; the hopelessness which so often assailed her, which came upon her like an obsession, like something extraneous, independent of volition. It was something which announced itself; a chill breath that seemed to issue

---

[69]*mets . . . entremets* main courses . . . side dishes.   [70]**pompano** kind of fish.

from some vast cavern wherein discords wailed. There came over her the acute longing which always summoned into her spiritual vision the presence of the beloved one, overpowering her at once with a sense of the unattainable.

The moments glided on, while a feeling of good fellowship passed around the circle like a mystic cord, holding and binding these people together with jest and laughter. Monsieur Ratignolle was the first to break the pleasant charm. At ten o'clock he excused himself. Madame Ratignolle was waiting for him at home. She was *bien souffrante,*[71] and she was filled with vague dread, which only her husband's presence could allay.

Mademoiselle Reisz arose with Monsieur Ratignolle, who offered to escort her to the car. She had eaten well; she had tasted the good, rich wines, and they must have turned her head, for she bowed pleasantly to all as she withdrew from table. She kissed Edna upon the shoulder, and whispered: *"Bonne nuit, ma reine; soyez sage."*[72] She had been a little bewildered upon rising, or rather, descending from her cushions, and Monsieur Ratignolle gallantly took her arm and led her away.

Mrs. Highcamp was weaving a garland of roses, yellow and red. When she had finished the garland, she laid it lightly upon Victor's black curls. He was reclining far back in the luxurious chair, holding a glass of champagne to the light.

As if a magician's wand had touched him, the garland of roses transformed him into a vision of Oriental beauty. His cheeks were the color of crushed grapes, and his dusky eyes glowed with a languishing fire.

780   *"Sapristi!"* exclaimed Arobin.

But Mrs. Highcamp had one more touch to add to the picture. She took from the back of her chair a white silken scarf, with which she had covered her shoulders in the early part of the evening. She draped it across the boy in graceful folds, and in a way to conceal his black, conventional evening dress. He did not seem to mind what she did to him, only smiled showing a faint gleam of white teeth, while he continued to gaze with narrowing eyes at the light through his glass of champagne.

"Oh! to be able to paint in color rather than in words!" exclaimed Miss Mayblunt, losing herself in a rhapsodic dream as she looked at him.

"'There was a graven image of Desire
      Painted with red blood on a ground of gold.'"[73]

murmured Gouvernail, under his breath.

The effect of the wine upon Victor was to change his accustomed volubility into silence. He seemed to have abandoned himself to a reverie, and to be seeing pleasing visions in the amber bead.

"Sing," entreated Mrs. Highcamp. "Won't you sing to us?"

785   "Let him alone," said Arobin.

"He's posing," offered Mr. Merriman; "let him have it out."

"I believe he's paralyzed," laughed Mrs. Merriman. And leaning over the youth's chair, she took the glass from his hand and held it to his lips. He

---

[71]*bien souffrante* very ill.   [72]*Bonne . . . sage* Good night, my love; be good.   [73]**"There was . . . gold"** first two lines of a sonnet entitled "A Cameo," by the English poet Algernon Charles Swinburne (1837–1909).

sipped the wine slowly, and when he had drained the glass she laid it upon the table and wiped his lips with her little filmy handkerchief.

"Yes, I'll sing for you," he said, turning in his chair toward Mrs. Highcamp. He clasped his hands behind his head, and looking up at the ceiling began to hum a little, trying his voice like a musician tuning an instrument. Then, looking at Edna, he began to sing:

"Ah! si tu savais!"

"Stop!" she cried, "don't sing that. I don't want you to sing it," and she laid her glass so impetuously and blindly upon the table as to shatter it against a carafe. The wine spilled over Arobin's legs and some of it trickled down upon Mrs. Highcamp's black gauze gown. Victor had lost all idea of courtesy, or else he thought his hostess was not in earnest, for he laughed and went on:

"Ah! si tu savais
Ce que tes yeux me disent"—[74]

790   "Oh! you mustn't! you mustn't," exclaimed Edna, and pushing back her chair she got up, and going behind him placed her hand over his mouth. He kissed the soft palm that pressed upon his lips.

"No, no, I won't, Mrs. Pontellier. I didn't know you meant it," looking up at her with caressing eyes. The touch of his lips was like a pleasing sting to her hand. She lifted the garland of roses from his head and flung it across the room.

"Come, Victor; you've posed long enough. Give Mrs. Highcamp her scarf."

Mrs. Highcamp undraped her scarf from about him with her own hands. Miss Mayblunt and Mr. Gouvernail suddenly conceived the notion that it was time to say good night. And Mr. and Mrs. Merriman wondered how it could be so late.

Before parting from Victor, Mrs. Highcamp invited him to call upon her daughter, who she knew would be charmed to meet him and talk French and sing French songs with him. Victor expressed his desire and intention to call upon Miss Highcamp at the first opportunity which presented itself. He asked if Arobin were going his way. Arobin was not.

795   The mandolin players had long since stolen away. A profound stillness had fallen upon the broad, beautiful street. The voices of Edna's disbanding guests jarred like a discordant note upon the quiet harmony of the night.

XXXI

"Well?" questioned Arobin, who had remained with Edna after the others had departed.

"Well," she reiterated, and stood up, stretching her arms, and feeling the need to relax her muscles after having been so long seated.

"What next?" he asked.

---

[74]**Ah! . . . disent**" "Oh! if you only knew what your eyes tell me."

"The servants are all gone. They left when the musicians did. I have dismissed them. The house has to be closed and locked, and I shall trot around to the pigeon house, and shall send Celestine over in the morning to straighten things up."

800 He looked around, and began to turn out some of the lights.

"What about upstairs?" he inquired.

"I think it is all right; but there may be a window or two unlatched. We had better look; you might take a candle and see. And bring me my wrap and hat on the foot of the bed in the middle room."

He went up with the light, and Edna began closing doors and windows. She hated to shut in the smoke and the fumes of the wine. Arobin found her cape and hat, which he brought down and helped her to put on.

When everything was secured and the lights put out, they left through the front door, Arobin locking it and taking the key, which he carried for Edna. He helped her down the steps.

805 "Will you have a spray of jessamine?" he asked, breaking off a few blossoms as he passed.

"No; I don't want anything."

She seemed disheartened, and had nothing to say. She took his arm, which he offered her, holding up the weight of her satin gown with the other hand. She looked down, noticing the black line of his leg moving in and out so close to her against the yellow shimmer of her gown. There was the whistle of a railway train somewhere in the distance, and the midnight bells were ringing. They met no one in their short walk.

The "pigeon-house" stood behind a locked gate, and a shallow *parterre*[75] that had been somewhat neglected. There was a small front porch, upon which a long window and the front door opened. The door opened directly into the parlor; there was no side entry. Back in the yard was a room for servants, in which old Celestine had been ensconced.

Edna had left a lamp burning low upon the table. She had succeeded in making the room look habitable and homelike. There were some books on the table and a lounge near at hand. On the floor was a fresh matting, covered with a rug or two; and on the walls hung a few tasteful pictures. But the room was filled with flowers. These were a surprise to her. Arobin had sent them, and had had Celestine distribute them during Edna's absence. Her bedroom was adjoining, and across a small passage were the dining-room and kitchen.

810 Edna seated herself with every appearance of discomfort.

"Are you tired?" he asked.

"Yes, and chilled, and miserable. I feel as if I had been wound up to a certain pitch—too tight—and something inside of me had snapped."

She had rested her head against the table upon her bare arm.

"You want to rest," he said, "and to be quiet. I'll go; I'll leave you and let you rest."

815 "Yes," she replied.

He stood up beside her and smoothed her hair with his soft, magnetic hand. His touch conveyed to her a certain physical comfort. She could have

---

[75]*parterre* garden with geometric flower-beds and paths.

fallen quietly asleep there if he had continued to pass his hand over her hair. He brushed the hair upward from the nape of her neck.

"I hope you will feel better and happier in the morning," he said. "You have tried to do too much in the past few days. The dinner was the last straw; you might have dispensed with it."

"Yes," she admitted; "it was stupid."

"No, it was delightful; but it has worn you out." His hand strayed to her beautiful shoulders, and he could feel the response of her flesh to his touch. He seated himself beside her and kissed her lightly on the shoulder.

820 "I thought you were going away," she said, in an uneven voice.

"I am, after I have said good night."

"Good night," she murmured.

He did not answer, except to continue to caress her. He did not say good night until she had become supple to his gentle, seductive entreaties.

XXXII

When Mr. Pontellier learned of his wife's intention to abandon her home and take up her residence elsewhere he immediately wrote her a letter of unqualified disapproval and remonstrance. She had given reasons which he was unwilling to acknowledge as adequate. He hoped she had not acted upon her rash impulse; and he begged her to consider first, foremost, and above all else, what people would say. He was not dreaming of scandal when he uttered this warning; that was a thing which would never have entered into his mind to consider in connection with his wife's name or his own. He was simply thinking of his financial integrity. It might get noised about that the Pontelliers had met with reverses, and were forced to conduct their *ménage*[76] on a humbler scale than heretofore. It might do incalculable mischief to his business prospects.

825 But remembering Edna's whimsical turn of mind of late, and foreseeing that she had immediately acted upon her impetuous determination, he grasped the situation with his usual promptness and handled it with his well-known business tact and cleverness.

The same mail which brought to Edna his letter of disapproval carried instructions—the most minute instructions—to a well-known architect concerning the remodeling of his home, changes which he had long contemplated, and which he desired carried forward during his temporary absence.

Expert and reliable packers and movers were engaged to convey the furniture, carpets, pictures—everything movable, in short—to places of security. And in an incredibly short time the Pontellier house was turned over to the artisans. There was to be an addition—a small snuggery; there was to be frescoing, and hardwood flooring was to be put into such rooms as had not yet been subjected to this improvement.

Furthermore, in one of the daily papers appeared a brief notice to the effect that Mr. and Mrs. Pontellier were contemplating a summer sojourn abroad, and that their handsome residence on Esplanade Street was undergoing sumptuous alterations, and would not be ready for occupancy until their return. Mr. Pontellier had saved appearances!

---

[76]*ménage* household.

Edna admired the skill of his maneuver, and avoided any occasion to balk his intentions. When the situation as set forth by Mr. Pontellier was accepted and taken for granted, she was apparently satisfied that it should be so.

830 The pigeon-house pleased her. It at once assumed the intimate character of a home, while she herself invested it with a charm which it reflected like a warm glow. There was with her a feeling of having descended in the social scale, with a corresponding sense of having risen in the spiritual. Every step which she took toward relieving herself from obligations added to her strength and expansion as an individual. She began to look with her own eyes; to see and to apprehend the deeper undercurrents of life. No longer was she content to "feed upon opinion" when her own soul had invited her.

After a little while, a few days, in fact, Edna went up and spent a week with her children in Iberville. They were delicious February days, with all the summer's promise hovering in the air.

How glad she was to see the children! She wept for very pleasure when she felt their little arms clasping her; their hard, ruddy cheeks pressed against her own glowing cheeks. She looked into their faces with hungry eyes that could not be satisfied with looking. And what stories they had to tell their mother! About the pigs, the cows, the mules! About riding to the mill behind Gluglu; fishing back in the lake with their Uncle Jasper; picking pecans with Lidie's little black brood, and hauling chips in their little express wagon. It was a thousand times more fun to haul real chips for old lame Susie's real fire than to drag painted blocks along the banquette on Esplanade Street!

She went with them herself to see the pigs and the cows, to look at the darkies laying the cane, to thrash the pecan trees, and catch fish in the back lake. She lived with them a whole week long, giving them all of herself, and gathering and filling herself with their young existence. They listened, breathless, when she told them the house in Esplanade Street was crowded with workmen, hammering, nailing, sawing, and filling the place with clatter. They wanted to know where their bed was; what had been done with their rocking-horse; and where did Joe sleep, and where had Ellen gone, and the cook? But, above all, they were fired with a desire to see the little house around the block. Was there any place to play? Were there any boys next door? Raoul, with pessimistic foreboding, was convinced that there were only girls next door. Where would they sleep, and where would papa sleep? She told them the fairies would fix it all right.

The old Madame was charmed with Edna's visit, and showered all manner of delicate attentions upon her. She was delighted to know that the Esplanade Street house was in a dismantled condition. It gave her the promise and pretext to keep the children indefinitely.

835 It was with a wrench and a pang that Edna left her children. She carried away with her the sound of their voices and the touch of their cheeks. All along the journey homeward their presence lingered with her like the memory of a delicious song. But by the time she had regained the city the song no longer echoed in her soul. She was again alone.

XXXIII

It happened sometimes when Edna went to see Mademoiselle Reisz that the little musician was absent, giving a lesson or making some small necessary household purchase. The key was always left in a secret hiding-place in the entry, which Edna knew. If Mademoiselle happened to be away, Edna would usually enter and wait for her return.

When she knocked at Mademoiselle Reisz's door one afternoon there was no response; so unlocking the door, as usual, she entered and found the apartment deserted, as she had expected. Her day had been quite filled up, and it was for a rest, for a refuge, and to talk about Robert, that she sought out her friend.

She had worked at her canvas—a young Italian character study—all the morning, completing the work without the model; but there had been many interruptions, some incident to her modest housekeeping, and others of a social nature.

Madame Ratignolle had dragged herself over, avoiding the too public thoroughfares, she said. She complained that Edna had neglected her much of late. Besides, she was consumed with curiosity to see the little house and the manner in which it was conducted. She wanted to hear all about the dinner party; Monsieur Ratignolle had left so early. What had happened after he left? The champagne and grapes which Edna sent over were *too* delicious. She had so little appetite; they had refreshed and toned her stomach. Where on earth was she going to put Mr. Pontellier in that little house, and the boys? And then she made Edna promise to go to her when her hour of trial overtook her.

840   "At any time—any time of the day or night, dear," Edna assured her.

Before leaving Madame Ratignolle said:

"In some way you seem to me like a child, Edna. You seem to act without a certain amount of reflection which is necessary in this life. That is the reason I want to say you mustn't mind if I advise you to be a little careful while you are living here alone. Why don't you have some one come and stay with you? Wouldn't Mademoiselle Reisz come?"

"No; she wouldn't wish to come, and I shouldn't want her always with me."

"Well, the reason—you know how evil-minded the world is—some one was talking of Alcée Arobin visiting you. Of course, it wouldn't matter if Mr. Arobin had not such a dreadful reputation. Monsieur Ratignolle was telling me that his attentions alone are considered enough to ruin a woman's name."

845   "Does he boast of his successes?" asked Edna, indifferently, squinting at her picture.

"No, I think not. I believe he is a decent fellow as far as that goes. But his character is so well known among the men. I shan't be able to come back and see you; it was very, very imprudent to-day."

"Mind the step!" cried Edna.

"Don't neglect me," entreated Madame Ratignolle; "and don't mind what I said about Arobin, or having some one to stay with you."

"Of course not," Edna laughed. "You may say anything you like to me." They kissed each other good-by. Madame Ratignolle had not far to go, and Edna stood on the porch a while watching her walk down the street.

850   Then in the afternoon Mrs. Merriman and Mrs. Highcamp had made their "party call." Edna felt that they might have dispensed with the formality. They had also come to invite her to play *vingt-et-un*[77] one evening at

---

[77]*vingt-et-un* twenty-one (card game).

Mrs. Merriman's. She was asked to go early, to dinner, and Mr. Merriman or Mr. Arobin would take her home. Edna accepted in a half-hearted way. She sometimes felt very tired of Mrs. Highcamp and Mrs. Merriman.

Late in the afternoon she sought refuge with Mademoiselle Reisz, and stayed there alone, waiting for her, feeling a kind of repose invade her with the very atmosphere of the shabby, unpretentious little room.

Edna sat at the window, which looked out over the house-tops and across the river. The window frame was filled with pots of flowers, and she sat and picked the dry leaves from a rose geranium. The day was warm, and the breeze which blew from the river was very pleasant. She removed her hat and laid it on the piano. She went on picking the leaves and digging around the plants with her hat pin. Once she thought she heard Mademoiselle Reisz approaching. But it was a young black girl, who came in, bringing a small bundle of laundry, which she deposited in the adjoining room, and went away.

Edna seated herself at the piano, and softly picked out with one hand the bars of a piece of music which lay open before her. A half-hour went by. There was the occasional sound of people going and coming in the lower hall. She was growing interested in her occupation of picking out the aria, when there was a second rap at the door. She vaguely wondered what these people did when they found Mademoiselle's door locked.

"Come in," she called, turning her face toward the door. And this time it was Robert Lebrun who presented himself. She attempted to rise; she could not have done so without betraying the agitation which mastered her at sight of him, so she fell back upon the stool, only exclaiming, "Why, Robert!"

855   He came and clasped her hand, seemingly without knowing what he was saying or doing.

"Mrs. Pontellier! How do you happen—oh! how well you look! Is Mademoiselle Reisz not here? I never expected to see you."

"When did you come back?" asked Edna in an unsteady voice, wiping her face with her handkerchief. She seemed ill at ease on the piano stool, and he begged her to take the chair by the window. She did so, mechanically, while he seated himself on the stool.

"I returned day before yesterday," he answered, while he leaned his arm on the keys, bringing forth a crash of discordant sound.

"Day before yesterday!" she repeated, aloud; and went on thinking to herself, "day before yesterday," in a sort of an uncomprehending way. She had pictured him seeking her at the very first hour, and he had lived under the same sky since day before yesterday; while only by accident had he stumbled upon her. Mademoiselle must have lied when she said, "Poor fool, he loves you."

860   "Day before yesterday," she repeated, breaking off a spray of Mademoiselle's geranium; "then if you had not met me here to-day you wouldn't—when—that is, didn't you mean to come and see me?"

"Of course, I should have gone to see you. There have been so many things—" he turned the leaves of Mademoiselle's music nervously. "I started in at once yesterday with the old firm. After all there is as much chance for me here as there was there—that is, I might find it profitable some day. The Mexicans were not very congenial."

So he had come back because the Mexicans were not congenial; because business was as profitable here as there; because of reason, and not because he cared to be near her. She remembered the day she sat on the floor, turning the pages of his letter, seeking the reason which was left untold.

She had not noticed how he looked—only feeling his presence; but she turned deliberately and observed him. After all, he had been absent but a few months, and was not changed. His hair—the color of hers—waved back from his temples in the same way as before. His skin was not more burned than it had been at Grand Isle. She found in his eyes, when he looked at her for one silent moment, the same tender caress, with an added warmth and entreaty which had not been there before—the same glance which had penetrated to the sleeping places of her soul and awakened them.

A hundred times Edna had pictured Robert's return, and imagined their first meeting. It was usually at her home, whither he had sought her out at once. She always fancied him expressing or betraying in some way his love for her. And here, the reality was that they sat ten feet apart, she at the window, crushing geranium leaves in her hand and smelling them, he twirling around on the piano stool, saying:

865   "I was very much surprised to hear of Mr. Pontellier's absence; it's a wonder Mademoiselle Reisz did not tell me; and your moving—mother told me yesterday. I should think you would have gone to New York with him, or to Iberville with the children, rather than be bothered here with housekeeping. And you are going abroad, too, I hear. We shan't have you at Grand Isle next summer; it won't seem—do you see much of Mademoiselle Reisz? She often spoke of you in the few letters she wrote."

"Do you remember that you promised to write to me when you went away?" A flush overspread his whole face.

"I couldn't believe that my letters would be of any interest to you."

"That is an excuse; it isn't the truth." Edna reached for her hat on the piano. She adjusted it, sticking the hat pin through the heavy coil of hair with some deliberation.

"Are you not going to wait for Mademoiselle Reisz?" asked Robert.

870   "No; I have found when she is absent this long, she is liable not to come back till late." She drew on her gloves, and Robert picked up his hat.

"Won't you wait for her?" asked Edna.

"Not if you think she will not be back till late," adding, as if suddenly aware of some discourtesy in his speech, "and I should miss the pleasure of walking home with you." Edna locked the door and put the key back in its hiding-place.

They went together, picking their way across muddy streets and sidewalks encumbered with the cheap display of small tradesmen. Part of the distance they rode in the car, and after disembarking, passed the Pontellier mansion, which looked broken and half torn asunder. Robert had never known the house, and looked at it with interest.

"I never knew you in your home," he remarked.

875   "I am glad you did not."

"Why?" She did not answer. They went on around the corner, and it seemed as if her dreams were coming true after all, when he followed her into the little house.

"You must stay and dine with me, Robert. You see I am all alone, and it is so long since I have seen you. There is so much I want to ask you."

She took off her hat and gloves. He stood irresolute, making some excuse about his mother who expected him; he even muttered something about an engagement. She struck a match and lit the lamp in the table; it was growing dusk. When he saw her face in the lamp-light, looking pained, with all the soft lines gone out of it, he threw his hat aside and seated himself.

"Oh! you know I want to stay if you will let me!" he exclaimed. All the softness came back. She laughed, and went and put her hand on his shoulder.

880   "This is the first moment you have seemed like the old Robert. I'll go tell Celestine." She hurried away to tell Celestine to set an extra place. She even sent her off in search of some added delicacy which she had not thought of for herself. And she recommended great care in dripping the coffee and having the omelet done to a proper turn.

When she reentered, Robert was turning over magazines, sketches and things that lay upon the table in great disorder. He picked up a photograph, and exclaimed:

"Alcée Arobin! What on earth is his picture doing here?"

"I tried to make a sketch of his head one day," answered Edna, "and he thought the photograph might help me. It was at the other house. I thought it had been left there. I must have picked it up with my drawing materials."

"I should think you would give it back to him if you have finished with it."

885   "Oh! I have a great many such photographs. I never think of returning them. They don't amount to anything." Robert kept on looking at the picture.

"It seems to me—do you think his head worth drawing? Is he a friend of Mr. Pontellier's? You never said you knew him."

"He isn't a friend of Mr. Pontellier's; he's a friend of mine. I always knew him—that is, it is only of late that I know him pretty well. But I'd rather talk about you, and know what you have been seeing and doing and feeling out there in Mexico." Robert threw aside the picture.

"I've been seeing the waves and the white beach of Grand Isle; the quiet, grassy street of the *Chênière Caminada;* the old fort at Grande Terre. I've been working like a machine, and feeling like a lost soul. There was nothing interesting."

She leaned her head upon her hand to shade her eyes from the light.

890   "And what have you been seeing and doing and feeling all these days?" he asked.

"I've been seeing the waves and the white beach of Grand Isle; the quiet, grassy street of the *Chênière;* the old sunny fort at Grande Terre. I've been working with a little more comprehension than a machine, and still feeling like a lost soul. There was nothing interesting."

"Mrs. Pontellier, you are cruel," he said, with feeling, closing his eyes and resting his head back in his chair. They remained in silence till old Celestine announced dinner.

XXXIV

The dining-room was very small. Edna's round mahogany would have almost filled it. As it was there was but a step or two from the little table to the kitchen, to the mantel, the small buffet, and the side door that opened out on the narrow brick-paved yard.

A certain degree of ceremony settled upon them with the announcement of dinner. There was no return to personalities. Robert related incidents of his sojourn in Mexico, and Edna talked of events likely to interest him, which had occurred during his absence. The dinner was of ordinary quality, except for the few delicacies which she had sent out to purchase. Old Celestine, with a bandana *tignon*[78] twisted about her head, hobbled in and out, taking a personal interest in everything; and she lingered occasionally to talk patois[79] with Robert, whom she had known as a boy.

895   He went out to a neighboring cigar stand to purchase cigarette papers, and when he came back he found that Celestine had served the black coffee in the parlor.

"Perhaps I shouldn't have come back," he said. "When you are tired of me, tell me to go."

"You never tire me. You must have forgotten the hours and hours at Grand Isle in which we grew accustomed to each other and used to being together."

"I have forgotten nothing at Grand Isle," he said, not looking at her, but rolling a cigarette. His tobacco pouch, which he laid upon the table, was a fantastic embroidered silk affair, evidently the handiwork of a woman.

"You used to carry your tobacco in a rubber pouch," said Edna, picking up the pouch and examining the needlework.

900   "Yes; it was lost."

"Where did you buy this one? In Mexico?"

"It was given to me by a Vera Cruz girl; they are very generous," he replied, striking a match and lighting his cigarette.

"They are very handsome, I suppose, those Mexican women; very picturesque, with their black eyes and their lace scarfs."

"Some are; others are hideous. Just as you find women everywhere."

905   "What was she like—the one who gave you the pouch? You must have known her very well."

"She was very ordinary. She wasn't of the slightest importance. I knew her well enough."

"Did you visit at her house? Was it interesting? I should like to know and hear about the people you met, and the impressions they made on you."

"There are some people who leave impressions not so lasting as the imprint of an oar upon the water."

"Was she such a one?"

910   "It would be ungenerous for me to admit that she was of that order and kind." He thrust the pouch back in his pocket, as if to put away the subject with the trifle which had brought it up.

Arobin dropped in with a message from Mrs. Merriman, to say that the card party was postponed on account of the illness of one of her children.

"How do you do, Arobin?" said Robert, rising from the obscurity.

"Oh! Lebrun. To be sure! I heard yesterday you were back. How did they treat you down in Mexique?"

"Fairly well."

915   "But not well enough to keep you there. Stunning girls, though, in Mexico. I thought I should never get away from Vera Cruz when I was down there a couple of years ago."

---

[78]**bandana *tignon*** hair tied in a scarf.   [79]**patois** regional dialect of French, English, Spanish, and American Indian.

"Did they embroider slippers and tobacco pouches and hat-bands and things for you?" asked Edna.

"Oh! my! no! I didn't get so deep in their regard. I fear they made more impression on me than I made on them."

"You were less fortunate than Robert, then."

"I am always less fortunate than Robert. Has he been imparting tender confidences?"

920   "I've been imposing myself long enough," said Robert, rising, and shaking hands with Edna. "Please convey my regards to Mr. Pontellier when you write."

He shook hands with Arobin and went away.

"Fine fellow, that Lebrun," said Arobin when Robert had gone. "I never heard you speak of him."

"I knew him last summer at Grand Isle," she replied. "Here is that photograph of yours. Don't you want it?"

"What do I want with it? Throw it away." She threw it back on the table.

925   "I'm not going to Mrs. Merriman's," she said. "If you see her, tell her so. But perhaps I had better write. I think I shall write now, and say that I am sorry her child is sick, and tell her not to count on me."

"It would be a good scheme," acquiesced Arobin. "I don't blame you; stupid lot!"

Edna opened the blotter, and having procured paper and pen, began to write the note. Arobin lit a cigar and read the evening paper, which he had in his pocket.

"What is the date?" she asked. He told her.

"Will you mail this for me when you go out?"

930   "Certainly." He read to her little bits out of the newspaper, while she straightened things on the table.

"What do you want to do?" he asked, throwing aside the paper. "Do you want to go out for a walk or a drive or anything? It would be a fine night to drive."

"No; I don't want to do anything but just be quiet. You go away and amuse yourself. Don't stay."

"I'll go away if I must; but I shan't amuse myself. You know that I only live when I am near you."

He stood up to bid her good night.

935   "Is that one of the things you always say to women?"

"I have said it before, but I don't think I ever came so near meaning it," he answered with a smile. There were no warm lights in her eyes; only a dreamy, absent look.

"Good night. I adore you. Sleep well," he said, and he kissed her hand and went away.

She stayed alone in a kind of reverie—a sort of stupor. Step by step she lived over every instant of the time she had been with Robert after he had entered Mademoiselle Reisz's door. She recalled his words, his looks. How few and meager they had been for her hungry heart! A vision—a transcendently seductive vision of a Mexican girl arose before her. She writhed with a jealous pang. She wondered when he would come back. He had not said he would come back. She had been with him, had heard his voice and touched his hand. But some way he had seemed nearer to her off there in Mexico.

XXXV

The morning was full of sunlight and hope. Edna could see before her no denial—only the promise of excessive joy. She lay in bed awake, with bright eyes full of speculation. "He loves you, poor fool." If she could but get that conviction firmly fixed in her mind, what mattered about the rest? She felt she had been childish and unwise the night before in giving herself over to despondency. She recapitulated the motives which no doubt explained Robert's reserve. They were not insurmountable; they would not hold if he really loved her; they could not hold against her own passion, which he must come to realize in time. She pictured him going to his business that morning. She even saw how he was dressed; how he walked down one street, and turned the corner of another; saw him bending over his desk, talking to people who entered the office, going to his lunch, and perhaps watching for her on the street. He would come to her in the afternoon or evening, sit and roll his cigarette, talk a little, and go away as he had done the night before. But how delicious it would be to have him there with her! She would have no regrets, nor seek to penetrate his reserve if he still chose to wear it.

940   Edna ate her breakfast only half dressed. The maid brought her a delicious printed scrawl from Raoul, expressing his love, asking her to send him some bonbons, and telling her they had found that morning ten tiny white pigs all lying in a row beside Lidie's big white pig.

A letter also came from her husband, saying he hoped to be back early in March, and then they would get ready for that journey abroad which he had promised her so long, which he felt now fully able to afford; he felt able to travel as people should, without any thought of small economies—thanks to his recent speculations in Wall Street.

Much to her surprise she received a note from Arobin, written at midnight from the club. It was to say good morning to her, to hope she had slept well, to assure her of his devotion, which he trusted she in some faintest manner returned.

All these letters were pleasing to her. She answered the children in a cheerful frame of mind, promising them bonbons, and congratulating them upon their happy find of the little pigs.

She answered her husband with friendly evasiveness,—not with any fixed design to mislead him, only because all sense of reality had gone out of her life; she had abandoned herself to Fate, and awaited the consequences with indifference.

945   To Arobin's note she made no reply. She put it under Celestine's stove-lid.

Edna worked several hours with much spirit. She saw no one but a picture dealer, who asked her if it were true that she was going abroad to study in Paris.

She said possibly she might, and he negotiated with her for some Parisian studies to reach him in time for the holiday trade in December.

Robert did not come that day. She was keenly disappointed. He did not come the following day, nor the next. Each morning she awoke with hope, and each night she was a prey to despondency. She was tempted to seek him out. But far from yielding to the impulse, she avoided any occasion which might throw her in his way. She did not go to Mademoiselle Reisz's nor pass by Madame Lebrun's, as she might have done if he had still been in Mexico.

When Arobin, one night, urged her to drive with him, she went—out to the lake, on the Shell Road. His horses were full of mettle, and even a little unmanageable. She liked the rapid gait at which they spun along, and the quick, sharp sound of the horses' hoofs on the hard road. They did not stop anywhere to eat or to drink. Arobin was not needlessly imprudent. But they ate and they drank when they regained Edna's little dining-room—which was comparatively early in the evening.

950   It was late when he left her. It was getting to be more than a passing whim with Arobin to see her and be with her. He had detected the latent sensuality, which unfolded under his delicate sense of her nature's requirements like a torpid, torrid, sensitive blossom.

There was no despondency when she fell asleep that night; nor was there hope when she awoke in the morning.

XXXVI

There was a garden out in the suburbs; a small, leafy corner, with a few green tables under the orange trees. An old cat slept all day on the stone step in the sun, and an old *mulatresse*[80] slept her idle hours away in her chair at the open window, till some one happened to knock on one of the green tables. She had milk and cream cheese to sell, and bread and butter. There was no one who could make such excellent coffee or fry a chicken so golden brown as she.

The place was too modest to attract the attention of people of fashion, and so quiet as to have escaped the notice of those in search of pleasure and dissipation. Edna had discovered it accidentally one day when the high-board gate stood ajar. She caught sight of a little green table, blotched with the checkered sunlight that filtered through the quivering leaves overhead. Within she had found the slumbering *mulatresse*, the drowsy cat, and a glass of milk which reminded her of the milk she had tasted in Iberville.

She often stopped there during her perambulations; sometimes taking a book with her, and sitting an hour or two under the trees when she found the place deserted. Once or twice she took a quiet dinner there alone, having instructed Celestine beforehand to prepare no dinner at home. It was the last place in the city where she would have expected to meet any one she knew.

955   Still she was not astonished when, as she was partaking of a modest dinner late in the afternoon, looking into an open book, stroking the cat, which had made friends with her—she was not greatly astonished to see Robert come in at the tall garden gate.

"I am destined to see you only by accident," she said, shoving the cat off the chair beside her. He was surprised, ill at ease, almost embarrassed at meeting her thus so unexpectedly.

"Do you come here often?" he asked.

"I almost live here," she said.

---

[80]*mulatresse* woman of black and white ancestry.

"I used to drop in very often for a cup of Catiche's good coffee. This is the first time since I came back."

960   "She'll bring you a plate, and you will share my dinner. There's always enough for two—even three." Edna had intended to be indifferent and as re-served as he when she met him; she had reached the determination by a la-borious train of reasoning, incident to one of her despondent moods. But her resolve melted when she saw him before her, seated there beside her in the little garden, as if a designing Providence had led him into her path.

"Why have you kept away from me, Robert?" she asked, closing the book that lay open upon the table.

"Why are you so personal, Mrs. Pontellier? Why do you force me to idiotic subterfuges?" he exclaimed with sudden warmth. "I suppose there's no use telling you I've been very busy, or that I've been sick, or that I've been to see you and not found you at home. Please let me off with any of these excuses."

"You are the embodiment of selfishness," she said. "You save yourself something—I don't know what—but there is some selfish motive, and in sparing yourself you never consider for a moment what I think, or how I feel your neglect and indifference. I suppose this is what you would call un-womanly; but I have got into a habit of expressing myself. It doesn't matter to me, and you may think me unwomanly if you like."

"No; I only think you cruel, as I said the other day. Maybe not inten-tionally cruel; but you seem to be forcing me into disclosures which can re-sult in nothing; as if you would have me bare a wound for the pleasure of looking at it, without the intention or power of healing it."

965   "I'm spoiling your dinner, Robert; never mind what I say. You haven't eaten a morsel."

"I only came in for a cup of coffee." His sensitive face was all disfigured with excitement.

"Isn't this a delightful place?" she remarked. "I am so glad it has never actually been discovered. It is so quiet, so sweet, here. Do you notice there is scarcely a sound to be heard? It's so out of the way; and a good walk from the car. However, I don't mind walking. I always feel so sorry for women who don't like to walk; they miss so much—so many rare little glimpses of life; and we women learn so little of life on the whole.

"Catiche's coffee is always hot. I don't know how she manages it, here in open air. Celestine's coffee gets cold bringing it from the kitchen to the dining-room. Three lumps! How can you drink it so sweet? Take some of the cress with your chop; it's so biting and crisp. Then there's the advan-tage of being able to smoke with your coffee out here. Now, in the city— aren't you going to smoke?"

"After a while," he said, laying a cigar on the table.

970   "Who gave it to you?" she laughed.

"I bought it. I suppose I'm getting reckless; I bought a whole box." She was determined not to be personal again and make him uncomfortable.

The cat made friends with him, and climbed into his lap when he smoked his cigar. He stroked her silky fur, and talked a little about her. He looked at Edna's book, which he had read; and he told her the end, to save her the trouble of wading through it, he said.

Again he accompanied her back to her home; and it was after dusk when they reached the little "pigeon-house." She did not ask him to remain, which he was grateful for, as it permitted him to stay without the discomfort of blundering through an excuse which he had no intention of considering. He helped her to light the lamp; then she went into her room to take off her hat and to bathe her face and hands.

When she came back Robert was not examining the pictures and magazines as before; he sat off in the shadow, leaning his head back on the chair as if in a reverie. Edna lingered a moment beside the table, arranging the books there. Then she went across the room to where he sat. She bent over the arm of his chair and called his name.

975   "Robert," she said, "are you asleep?"

"No," he answered, looking up at her.

She leaned over and kissed him—a soft, cool, delicate kiss, whose voluptuous sting penetrated his whole being—then she moved away from him. He followed, and took her in his arms, just holding her close to him. She put her hand up to his face and pressed his cheek against her own. The action was full of love and tenderness. He sought her lips again. Then he drew her down upon the sofa beside him and held her hand in both of his.

"Now you know," he said, "now you know what I have been fighting against since last summer at Grand Isle; what drove me away and drove me back again."

"Why have you been fighting against it?" she asked. Her face glowed with soft lights.

980   "Why? Because you were not free; you were Léonce Pontellier's wife. I couldn't help loving you if you were ten times his wife; but so long as I went away from you and kept away I could help telling you so." She put her free hand up to his shoulder, and then against his cheek, rubbing it softly. He kissed her again. His face was warm and flushed.

"There in Mexico I was thinking of you all the time, and longing for you."

"But not writing to me," she interrupted.

"Something put into my head that you cared for me; and I lost my senses. I forgot everything but a wild dream of your some way becoming my wife."

"Your wife!"

985   "Religion, loyalty, everything would give way if only you cared."

"Then you must have forgotten that I was Léonce Pontellier's wife."

"Oh! I was demented, dreaming of wild, impossible things, recalling men who had set their wives free, we have heard of such things."

"Yes, we have heard of such things."

"I came back full of vague, mad intentions. And when I got here—"

990   "When you got here you never came near me!" She was still caressing his cheek.

"I realized what a cur I was to dream of such a thing, even if you had been willing."

She took his face between her hands and looked into it as if she would never withdraw her eyes more. She kissed him on the forehead, the eyes, the cheeks, and the lips.

"You have been a very, very foolish boy, wasting your time dreaming of impossible things when you speak of Mr. Pontellier setting me free! I am no longer one of Mr. Pontellier's possessions to dispose of or not. I give myself where I choose. If he were to say, 'Here, Robert, take her and be happy; she is yours,' I should laugh at you both."

His face grew a little white. "What do you mean?" he asked.

995   There was a knock at the door. Old Celestine came in to say that Madame Ratignolle's servant had come around the back way with a message that Madame had been taken sick and begged Mrs. Pontellier to go to her immediately.

"Yes, yes," said Edna, rising; "I promised. Tell her yes—to wait for me. I'll go back with her."

"Let me walk over with you," offered Robert.

"No," she said; "I will go with the servant." She went into her room to put on her hat, and when she came in again she sat once more upon the sofa beside him. He had not stirred. She put her arms about his neck.

"Good-by, my sweet Robert. Tell me good-by." He kissed her with a degree of passion which had not before entered into his caress, and strained her to him.

1000   "I love you," she whispered, "only you; no one but you. It was you who woke me last summer out of a life-long, stupid dream. Oh! you have made me so unhappy with your indifference. Oh! I have suffered, suffered! Now you are here we shall love each other, my Robert. We shall be everything to each other. Nothing else in the world is of any consequence. I must go to my friend; but you will wait for me? No matter how late; you will wait for me, Robert?"

"Don't go; don't go! Oh! Edna, stay with me," he pleaded. "Why should you go? Stay with me, stay with me."

"I shall come back as soon as I can; I shall find you here." She buried her face in his neck, and said good-by again. Her seductive voice, together with his great love for her, had enthralled his senses, had deprived him of every impulse but the longing to hold her and keep her.

XXXVII

Edna looked in at the drug store. Monsieur Ratignolle was putting up a mixture himself, very carefully, dropping a red liquid into a tiny glass. He was grateful to Edna for having come; her presence would be a comfort to his wife. Madame Ratignolle's sister, who had always been with her at such trying times, had not been able to come up from the plantation, and Adèle had been inconsolable until Mrs. Pontellier so kindly promised to come to her. The nurse had been with them at night for the past week, as she lived a great distance away. And Dr. Mandelet had been coming and going all the afternoon. They were then looking for him any moment.

Edna hastened upstairs by a private stairway that led from the rear of the store to the apartment above. The children were all sleeping in a back room. Madame Ratignolle was in the salon, whither she had strayed in her suffering impatience. She sat on the sofa, clad in an ample white *peignoir,* holding a handkerchief tight in her hand with a nervous clutch. Her face was drawn and pinched, her sweet blue eyes haggard and unnatural. All her beautiful hair had been drawn back and plaited. It lay in a long braid on the sofa pillow, coiled like a golden serpent. The nurse, a comfortable looking *Griffe*[81] woman in white apron and cap, was urging her to return to her bedroom.

---

[81]*Griffe* mixed-race.

1005   "There is no use, there is no use," she said at once to Edna. "We must get rid of Mandelet; he is getting too old and careless. He said he would be here at half-past seven; now it must be eight. See what time it is, Joséphine."

    The woman was possessed of a cheerful nature, and refused to take any situation too seriously, especially a situation with which she was so familiar. She urged Madame to have courage and patience. But Madame only set her teeth hard into her under lip, and Edna saw the sweat gather in beads on her white forehead. After a moment or two she uttered a profound sigh and wiped her face with the handkerchief rolled in a ball. She appeared exhausted. The nurse gave her a fresh handkerchief, sprinkled with cologne water.

    "This is too much!" she cried. "Mandelet ought to be killed! Where is Alphonse? Is it possible I am to be abandoned like this—neglected by every one?"

    "Neglected, indeed!" exclaimed the nurse. Wasn't she there? And here was Mrs. Pontellier leaving, no doubt, a pleasant evening at home to devote to her? And wasn't Monsieur Ratignolle coming that very instant through the hall? And Joséphine was quite sure she had heard Doctor Mandelet's coupé.[82] Yes, there it was, down at the door.

    Adèle consented to go back to her room. She sat on the edge of a little low couch next to her bed.

1010   Doctor Mandelet paid no attention to Madame Ratignolle's upbraidings. He was accustomed to them at such times, and was too well convinced of her loyalty to doubt it.

    He was glad to see Edna, and wanted her to go with him into the salon and entertain him. But Madame Ratignolle would not consent that Edna should leave her for an instant. Between agonizing moments, she chatted a little, and said it took her mind off her sufferings.

    Edna began to feel uneasy. She was seized with a vague dread. Her own like experiences seemed far away, unreal, and only half remembered. She recalled faintly an ecstasy of pain, the heavy odor of chloroform, a stupor which had deadened sensation, and an awakening to find a little new life to which she had given being, added to the great unnumbered multitude of souls that come and go.

    She began to wish she had not come; her presence was not necessary. She might have invented a pretext for staying away; she might even invent a pretext now for going. But Edna did not go. With an inward agony, with a flaming, outspoken revolt against the ways of Nature, she witnessed the scene of torture.

    She was still stunned and speechless with emotion when later she leaned over her friend to kiss her and softly say good-by. Adèle, pressing her cheek, whispered in an exhausted voice: "Think of the children, Edna. Oh, think of the children! Remember them!"

XXXVIII

1015 Edna still felt dazed when she got outside in the open air. The Doctor's coupé had returned for him and stood before the *porte cochère*. She did not wish to enter the coupé, and told Doctor Mandelet she would walk; she was

---

[82]**coupé** closed four-wheel carriage.

not afraid, and would go alone. He directed his carriage to meet him at Mrs. Pontellier's, and he started to walk home with her.

Up—away up, over the narrow street between the tall houses, the stars were blazing. The air was mild and caressing, but cool with the breath of spring and the night. They walked slowly, the Doctor with a heavy, measured tread and his hands behind him; Edna, in an absent-minded way, as she had walked one night at Grand Isle, as if her thoughts had gone ahead of her and she was striving to overtake them.

"You shouldn't have been there, Mrs. Pontellier," he said. "That was no place for you. Adèle is full of whims at such times. There were a dozen women she might have had with her, unimpressionable women. I felt that it was cruel, cruel. You shouldn't have gone."

"Oh, well!" she answered, indifferently. "I don't know that it matters after all. One has to think of the children some time or other; the sooner the better."

"When is Léonce coming back?"

1020   "Quite soon. Some time in March."

"And you are going abroad?"

"Perhaps—no, I am not going. I'm not going to be forced into doing things. I don't want to go abroad. I want to be let alone. Nobody has any right—except children, perhaps—and even then, it seems to me—or it did seem—" She felt that her speech was voicing the incoherency of her thoughts, and stopped abruptly.

"The trouble is," sighed the Doctor, grasping her meaning intuitively, "that youth is given up to illusions. It seems to be a provision of Nature; a decoy to secure mothers for the race. And Nature takes no account of moral consequences, or arbitrary conditions which we create, and which we feel obliged to maintain at any cost."

"Yes," she said. "The years that are gone seem like dreams—if one might go on sleeping and dreaming—but to wake up and find—oh! well! perhaps it is better to wake up after all, even to suffer, rather than to remain a dupe to illusions all one's life."

1025   "It seems to me, my dear child," said the Doctor at parting, holding her hand, "you seem to me to be in trouble. I am not going to ask for your confidence. I will only say that if ever you feel moved to give it to me, perhaps I might help you. I know I would understand, and I tell you there are not many who would—not many, my dear."

"Some way I don't feel moved to speak of things that trouble me. Don't think I am ungrateful or that I don't appreciate your sympathy. There are periods of despondency and suffering which take possession of me. But I don't want anything but my own way. That is wanting a good deal, of course, when you have to trample upon the lives, the hearts, the prejudices of others—but no matter—still, I shouldn't want to trample upon the little lives. Oh! I don't know what I'm saying, Doctor. Good night. Don't blame me for anything."

"Yes, I will blame you if you don't come and see me soon. We will talk of things you never have dreamt of talking about before. It will do us both good. I don't want you to blame yourself, whatever comes. Good night, my child."

She let herself in at the gate, but instead of entering she sat upon the step of the porch. The night was quiet and soothing. All the tearing emotion of the last few hours seemed to fall away from her like a somber, uncomfortable garment, which she had but to loosen to be rid of. She went back to that hour before Adèle had sent for her; and her senses kindled afresh in thinking of Robert's words, the pressure of his arms, and the feeling of his lips upon her own. She could picture at that moment no greater bliss on earth than possession of the beloved one. His expression of love had already given him to her in part. When she thought that he was there at hand, waiting for her, she grew numb with the intoxication of expectancy. It was so late; he would be asleep perhaps. She would awaken him with a kiss. She hoped he would be asleep that she might arouse him with her caresses.

Still, she remembered Adèle's voice whispering, "Think of the children; think of them." She meant to think of them; that determination had driven into her soul like a death wound—but not to-night. To-morrow would be time to think of everything.

1030   Robert was not waiting for her in the little parlor. He was nowhere at hand. The house was empty. But he had scrawled on a piece of paper that lay in the lamplight:

"I love you. Good-by—because I love you."

Edna grew faint when she read the words. She went and sat on the sofa. Then she stretched herself out there, never uttering a sound. She did not sleep. She did not go to bed. The lamp sputtered and went out. She was still awake in the morning, when Celestine unlocked the kitchen door and came in to light the fire.

XXXIX

Victor, with hammer and nails and scraps of scantling, was patching a corner of one of the galleries. Mariequita sat near by, dangling her legs, watching him work, and handing him nails from the tool-box. The sun was beating down upon them. The girl covered her head with her apron folded into a square pad. They had been talking for an hour or more. She was never tired of hearing Victor describe the dinner at Mrs. Pontellier's. He exaggerated every detail, making it appear a veritable Lucullean feast.[83] The flowers were in tubs, he said. The champagne was quaffed from huge golden goblets. Venus rising from the foam[84] could have presented no more entrancing a spectacle than Mrs. Pontellier, blazing with beauty and diamonds at the head of the board, while the other women were all of them youthful houris,[85] possessed of incomparable charms.

She got it into her head that Victor was in love with Mrs. Pontellier, and he gave her evasive answers, framed so as to confirm her belief. She grew sullen and cried a little, threatening to go off and leave him to his fine ladies. There were a dozen men crazy about her at the *Chênière;* and since it was the fashion to be in love with married people, why, she could run away any time she liked to New Orleans with Célina's husband.

1035   Célina's husband was a fool, a coward, and a pig, and to prove it to her, Victor intended to hammer his head into a jelly the next time he encountered

---

[83]**Lucullean feast** that is, splendid, in the manner of the feasts given by the Roman general Licinius Lucullus.   [84]**Venus rising from the foam** goddess of love, said to have sprung from the foam of the sea.   [85]**houris** beautiful virgins of the Koranic paradise.

him. This assurance was very consoling to Mariequita. She dried her eyes, and grew cheerful at the prospect.

They were still talking of the dinner and the allurements of city life when Mrs. Pontellier herself slipped around the corner of the house. The two youngsters stayed dumb with amazement before what they considered to be an apparition. But it was really she in flesh and blood, looking tired and a little travel-strained.

"I walked up from the wharf," she said, "and heard the hammering. I supposed it was you, mending the porch. It's a good thing. I was always tripping over those loose planks last summer. How dreary and deserted everything looks!"

It took Victor some time to comprehend that she had come in Beaudelet's lugger,[86] that she had come alone, and for no purpose but to rest.

"There's nothing fixed up yet, you see. I'll give you my room; it's the only place."

1040   "Any corner will do," she assured him.

"And if you can stand Philomel's cooking," he went on, "though I might try to get her mother while you are here. Do you think she would come?" turning to Mariequita.

Mariequita thought that perhaps Philomel's mother might come for a few days, and money enough.

Beholding Mrs. Pontellier make her appearance, the girl had at once suspected a lovers' rendezvous. But Victor's astonishment was so genuine, and Mrs. Pontellier's indifference so apparent, that the disturbing notion did not lodge long in her brain. She contemplated with the greatest interest this woman who gave the most sumptuous dinners in America, and who had all the men in New Orleans at her feet.

"What time will you have dinner?" asked Edna. "I'm very hungry; but don't get anything extra."

1045   "I'll have it ready in little or no time," he said, bustling and packing away his tools. "You may go to my room to brush up and rest yourself. Mariequita will show you."

"Thank you," said Edna. "But, do you know, I have a notion to go down to the beach and take a good wash and even a little swim, before dinner?"

"The water is too cold!" they both exclaimed. "Don't think of it."

"Well, I might go down and try—dip my toes in. Why, it seems to me the sun is hot enough to have warmed the very depths of the ocean. Could you get me a couple of towels? I'd better go right away, so as to be back in time. It would be a little too chilly if I waited till this afternoon."

Mariequita ran over to Victor's room, and returned with some towels, which she gave to Edna.

1050   "I hope you have fish for dinner," said Edna, as she started to walk away; "but don't do anything extra if you haven't."

"Run and find Philomel's mother," Victor instructed the girl. "I'll go to the kitchen and see what I can do. By Gimminy! Women have no consideration! She might have sent me word."

---

[86]**lugger** small boat equipped with a lugsail (a four-sided sail that crosses the mast at an angle).

Edna walked on down to the beach rather mechanically, not noticing anything special except that the sun was hot. She was not dwelling upon any particular train of thought. She had done all the thinking which was necessary after Robert went away, when she lay awake upon the sofa till morning.

She had said over and over to herself: "To-day it is Arobin; to-morrow it will be some one else. It makes no difference to me, it doesn't matter about Léonce Pontellier—but Raoul and Etienne!" She understood now clearly what she had meant long ago when she said to Adèle Ratignolle that she would give up the unessential, but she would never sacrifice herself for her children.

Despondency had come upon her there in the wakeful night, and had never lifted. There was no one thing in the world that she desired. There was no human being whom she wanted near her except Robert; and she even realized that the day would come when he, too, and the thought of him would melt out of her existence, leaving her alone. The children appeared before her like antagonists who had overcome her; who had overpowered and sought to drag her into the soul's slavery for the rest of her days. But she knew a way to elude them. She was not thinking of these things when she walked down to the beach.

1055   The water of the Gulf stretched out before her, gleaming with the million lights of the sun. The voice of the sea is seductive, never ceasing, whispering, clamoring, murmuring, inviting the soul to wander in abysses of solitude. All along the white beach, up and down, there was no living thing in sight. A bird with a broken wing was beating the air above, reeling, fluttering, circling disabled down, down to the water.

Edna had found her old bathing suit still hanging, faded, upon its accustomed peg.

She put it on, leaving her clothing in the bath-house. But when she was there beside the sea, absolutely alone, she cast the unpleasant, pricking garments from her, and for the first time in her life she stood naked in the open air, at the mercy of the sun, the breeze that beat upon her, and the waves that invited her.

How strange and awful it seemed to stand naked under the sky! how delicious! She felt like some new-born creature, opening its eyes in a familiar world that it had never known.

The foamy wavelets curled up to her white feet, and coiled like serpents above her ankles. She walked out. The water was chill, but she walked on. The water was deep, but she lifted her white body and reached out for a long, sweeping stroke. The touch of the sea is sensuous, enfolding the body in its soft, close embrace.

1060   She went on and on. She remembered the night she swam far out, and recalled the terror that seized her at the fear of being unable to regain the shore. She did not look back now, but went on and on, thinking of the blue-grass meadow that she had traversed when a little child, believing that it had no beginning and no end.

Her arms and legs were growing tired.

She thought of Léonce and the children. They were a part of her life. But they need not have thought that they could possess her, body and soul. How Mademoiselle Reisz would have laughed, perhaps sneered, if she knew! "And you call yourself an artist! What pretensions, Madame! The artist must possess the courageous soul that dares and defies."

Exhaustion was pressing upon and overpowering her.

"Good-by—because I love you." He did not know; he did not understand. He would never understand. Perhaps Doctor Mandelet would have understood if she had seen him—but it was too late; the shore was far behind her, and her strength was gone.

1065   She looked into the distance, and the old terror flamed up for an instant, then sank again. Edna heard her father's voice and her sister Margaret's. She heard the barking of an old dog that was chained to the sycamore tree. The spurs of the cavalry officer clanged as he walked across the porch. There was the hum of bees, and the musky odor of pinks filled the air.

▓ TOPICS FOR CRITICAL THINKING AND WRITING

1. Although the story was published with the title *The Awakening*, Chopin originally called it "A Solitary Soul." Which title do you prefer? Why?

2. Compare Edna, Mademoiselle Reisz, and Adèle. In what significant ways, if any, does Edna resemble each and in what significant ways does she differ? To what does each of her friends awaken Edna?

3. Edna says to Dr. Mandelet (page 656, paragraph 1026), "I don't want anything but my own way. That is wanting a good deal, of course, when you have to trample upon the lives, the hearts, the prejudices of others—but no matter. . . ." Does this statement reveal the essential Edna? If not, why not?

4. Characterize Léonce. Do you see him as Edna presumably does, or do you see him somewhat more sympathetically? Why?

5. Readers have often debated the ending of the novel: Is it triumphant, tragic, or both? Examine the final chapter carefully, and set forth your understanding of what leads Edna to her fateful decision.

6. Like many novels, *The Awakening* explores and comments on the society that it describes. Focus in particular on Chopin's treatment of marriage, motherhood, and the family. What is her attitude toward these institutions?

7. Discuss the settings that Chopin presents. How does she convey to the reader a strong sense of a specific time and place?

8. When we read and talk about novels, one key source of interest is asking, What makes *this* writer special, different from this or that other one? Consider this question in relation to the style of *The Awakening*, to Chopin's choice of words, tone of voice, narrative point of view.

PART

III

Poetry

Robert Frost (1874–1963) enjoyed representing himself as a New England farmer—and he really did farm for a while—but in fact he was very much a professional writer, and an immensely successful one, esteemed not only by other writers but also by a vast public. For him, writing was certainly not an escape from life—"Poetry is a way of taking life by the throat," he said—but a way of coping with life. "Take what is given," he said, "and make it over your way." In one of his poems, "Two Tramps in Mud Time," the farmer-poet explains why, when he was splitting some wood, he preferred to continue at the task rather than to let the tramp (for money) take over:

> But yield who will to their separation,
> My object in living is to unite
> My avocation and my vocation
> As my two eyes make one in sight.

When John Kennedy was inaugurated President in 1961, Frost, the preeminent American writer—a man who had combined pleasure with business—read a poem. He was already known to everyone in his audience, but this was the first time that an American poet, or indeed any writer in America, achieved such quasi-official recognition.

13

Approaching Poetry: Responding in Writing

The title of this chapter is a bit misleading, since we have already spent a few pages discussing two poems in Chapter 1, "Reading and Responding to Literature." But here we will begin again, taking a different approach.

First, some brief advice.

1. Read the poem aloud; or, if you can't bring yourself to read aloud, at least sound the poem in your mind's ear. Try to catch the speaker's tone of voice.
2. Pay attention not only to the black marks on the white paper but also to the white spaces between groups of lines. If a space follows some lines, pause briefly, and take the preceding lines as a unit of thought.
3. Read the poem a second and a third time. Now that you know how it ends, you'll be able to see the connections between the beginning and what follows.

LANGSTON HUGHES

The following short poem is by Langston Hughes (1902-1967), an African-American writer born in Joplin, Missouri. Hughes lived part of his youth in Mexico, spent a year at Columbia University, served as a merchant seaman, and worked in a Paris nightclub. There, he showed some of his poems to Dr. Alain Locke, a strong advocate of African-American literature. Encouraged by Locke, when Hughes returned to the United States he continued to write, publishing fiction, plays, essays, and biographies; he also founded theaters, gave public readings, and was, in short, a highly visible presence. The poem that we reprint, "Harlem" (1951), provided Lorraine Hansberry with the title of her well-known play, A Raisin in the Sun *(1958). For a generous selection of poems by Langston Hughes, see Chapter 26.*

Harlem [1951]

What happens to a dream deferred?

    Does it dry up
    like a raisin in the sun?

Or fester like a sore—
And then run?   5
Does it stink like rotten meat?
Or crust and sugar over—
like a syrupy sweet?

Maybe it just sags
like a heavy load.   10

Or does it explode?

Read the poem at least twice, and then think about its effect on you.

1. Do you find the poem interesting? Why or why not?
2. Do some things in it interest you more than others? If so, why?
3. Does anything in it puzzle you? If so, what?

Before reading any further, you might jot down your responses to some of
these questions. And, whatever your responses, can you point to features of the
poem to account for them?

Of course, different readers will respond at least somewhat differently to
any work. On the other hand, since writers want to communicate, they try to
control their readers' responses, and they count on their readers to understand
the meanings of words as the writers understand them. Thus, Hughes assumed
his readers knew that Harlem was the site of a large African-American community in New York City.

Let's assume that the reader understands Hughes is talking about Harlem,
New York, and, further, that the reader understands the "dream deferred" to refer to the unfulfilled hopes of African-Americans who live in a society dominated
by whites. But Hughes does not say "hopes," he says "dream," and he does not
say "unfulfilled," he says "deferred." You might ask yourself exactly what differences there are between these words. Next, when you have read the poem several times, you might think about which expression is better in the context, "unfulfilled hopes" or "dream deferred," and why.

Thinking about "Harlem"

Let's turn to an analysis of the poem, an examination of how the parts fit. As you
look at the poem, think about the parts, and jot down whatever notes come to
mind. After you have written your own notes, consider the annotations of one
student.

These annotations chiefly get at the structure of the poem, the relationship
of the parts. The student notices that the poem begins with a line set off by itself and ends with a line set off by itself, and he also notices that each of these
lines is a question. Further, he indicates that each of these two lines is emphasized in other ways. The first begins further to the left than any of the other
lines—as though the other lines are subheadings or are in some way subordinate—and the last is italicized. In short, he comments on the structure of
the poem.

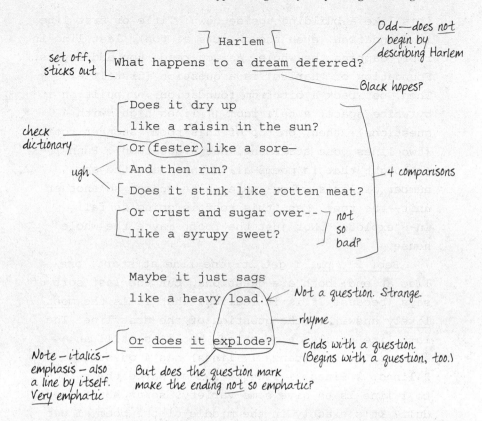

The annotated poem reads:

Harlem

set off, sticks out — What happens to a dream deferred?   Odd—does not begin by describing Harlem

dream — Black hopes?

Does it dry up
like a raisin in the sun?
Or fester like a sore—   check dictionary / ugh
And then run?
Does it stink like rotten meat?   4 comparisons
Or crust and sugar over--   not so bad?
like a syrupy sweet?

Maybe it just sags
like a heavy load.   Not a question. Strange.

Or does it explode?   rhyme / Ends with a question. (Begins with a question, too.)

Note – italics – emphasis – also a line by itself. Very emphatic

But does the question mark make the ending not so emphatic?

Some Journal Entries

The student who made these annotations later wrote an entry in his journal:

Feb. 18. Since the title is "Harlem," it's obvious that the "dream" is by African-American people. Also, obvious that Hughes thinks that if the "dream" doesn't become real there may be riots ("explode"). I like "raisin in the sun" (maybe because I like the play), and I like the business about "a syrupy sweet"--much more pleasant than the festering sore and the rotten meat. But if the dream becomes "sweet," what's wrong with that? Why should something "sweet" explode?

Feb. 21. Prof. McCabe said to think of structure or form of a poem as a sort of architecture, a building with a foundation, floors, etc. topped by a roof--but since we read a poem from top to bottom,

it's like a building upside down. Title or first line
is foundation (even though it's at top); last line is
roof, capping the whole. As you read, you add layers.
Foundation of "Harlem" is a question (first line).
Then, set back a bit from foundation, or built on it
by white space, a tall room (7 lines high, with 4
questions); then, on top of this room, another room
(two lines, one statement, not a question). Funny;
I thought that in poems all stanzas are the same
number of lines. Then--more white space, so another
unit--the roof. Man, this roof is going to fall
in--"explode." Not just the roof, maybe the whole
house.

    Feb. 21, pm. I get it; one line at start, one
line at end; both are questions, but the last sort of
says (because it is in italics) that it is the most
likely answer to the question of the first line. The
last line is also a question, but it's still an
answer. The big stanza (7 lines) has 4 questions:
2 lines, 2 lines, 1 line, 2 lines. Maybe the switch
to 1 line is to give some variety, so as not to be
dull? It's exactly in the middle of the poem. I get
the progress from raisin in the sun (dried, but not
so terrible), to festering sore and to stinking meat,
but I still don't see what's so bad about "a syrupy
sweet." Is Hughes saying that after things are very
bad they will get better? But why, then, the
explosion at the end?

    Feb. 23. "Heavy load" and "sags" in next-to-last
stanza seems to me to suggest slaves with bales of
cotton, or maybe poor cotton pickers dragging big
sacks of cotton. Or maybe people doing heavy labor in
Harlem. Anyway, very tired. Different from running
sore and stinking meat earlier; not disgusting, but
pressing down, deadening. Maybe worse than a sore or
rotten meat--a hard, hopeless life. And then the last
line. Just one line, no fancy (and disgusting) simile. Boom! Not just pressed down and tired, like
maybe some racist whites think (hope?) blacks will
be? Bang! Will there be survivors?

Drawing chiefly on these notes, the student jotted down some key ideas to guide him through a draft of an analysis of the poem. (The organization of the draft posed no problem; the student simply followed the organization of the poem.)

> 11 lines; short, but powerful; explosive
> Question (first line)
> Answers (set off by space & also indented)
> "raisin in the sun": shrinking
> "sore"   } disgusting
> "rotten meat"
> "syrupy sweet": relief from disgusting comparisons
> final question (last line): explosion?
>   explosive (powerful) because:
>   short, condensed, packed
>   in italics
>   stands by itself—like first line
>   no fancy comparison; very direct

Final Draft

Michael Locke
Professor Stahl
English 2B
10 December 2005

Langston Hughes's "Harlem"

"Harlem" is a poem that is only eleven lines long, but it is charged with power. It explodes. Hughes sets the stage, so to speak, by telling us in the title that he is talking about Harlem, and then he begins by asking, "What happens to a dream deferred?" The rest of the poem is set off by being indented, as though it is the answer to his question. This answer is in three parts (three stanzas, of different lengths).

In a way, it's wrong to speak of the answer, since the rest of the poem consists of questions, but I think Hughes means that each question (for instance, does a "deferred" hope "dry up / like a raisin in the sun?") really is

Locke 2

an answer, something that really has happened
and that will happen again. The first question,
"Does it dry up / like a raisin in the sun?," is
a famous line. To compare hope to a raisin dried
in the sun is to suggest a terrible shrinking.
The next two comparisons are to a "sore" and to
"rotten meat." These comparisons are less
clever, but they are very effective because they
are disgusting. Then, maybe because of the
disgusting comparisons, he gives a comparison
that is not at all disgusting. In this
comparison he says that maybe the "dream
deferred" will "crust and sugar over-- / like a
syrupy sweet."

The seven lines with four comparisons are
followed by a stanza of two lines with just one
comparison:

     Maybe it just sags
     like a heavy load.

So if we thought that this postponed dream might
finally turn into something "sweet," we were
kidding ourselves. Hughes comes down to earth,
in a short stanza, with an image of a heavy
load, which probably also calls to mind images
of people bent under heavy loads, maybe of
cotton, or maybe just any sort of heavy load
carried by African-Americans in Harlem and
elsewhere.

The opening question ("What happens to a
dream deferred?") was followed by four questions
in seven lines, but now, with "Maybe it just
sags / like a heavy load," we get a statement,
as though the poet at last has found an answer.
But at the end we get one more question, set off
by itself and in italics: "Or does it explode?"
This line itself is explosive for three reasons:

```
                                    Locke 3
it is short, it is italicized, and it is a
stanza in itself. It's also interesting that
this line, unlike the earlier lines, does not
use a simile. It's almost as though Hughes is
saying, "OK, we've had enough fancy ways of
talking about this terrible situation; here it
is, straight."
```

❈ TOPICS FOR CRITICAL THINKING AND WRITING

1. The student's analysis suggests that the comparison with "a syrupy sweet" is a deliberately misleading happy ending that serves to make the real ending even more powerful. In class another student suggested that Hughes may be referring to African-Americans who play the Uncle Tom, people who adopt a smiling manner in order to cope with an oppressive society. Which explanation do you prefer, and why? What do you think of combining the two? Or can you offer a different explanation?
2. Do you suppose that virtually all African-Americans respond to this poem in a way that is substantially different from the way virtually all Caucasians or Asian-Americans respond? Explain your position.
3. When Hughes reprinted this poem in 1959, he retitled it "Dream Deferred." Your response?

Let's now look at another poem, and at the responses of another student. Here is a seventeenth-century poem—actually a song—that makes use of the idea that the eyes of the beloved woman can dart fire, and that she can kill (or at least severely wound) the sighing, helpless male lover. The male speaker describes the appearance of Cupid, the tyrannic god of love, who (he claims) is equipped with darts and death-dealing fire taken from the eyes of the proud, cruel woman whom the speaker loves.

APHRA BEHN

Aphra Behn (1640-1689) is regarded as the first English woman to have made a living by writing. Not much is known of her life, but she seems to have married a London merchant of Dutch descent, and after his death to have served as a spy in the Dutch Wars (1665-1667). After her return to England she took up playwriting, and she gained fame with The Rover *(1677). Behn also wrote novels, the most important of which is* Oroonoko, *or* The Royal Slave *(1688), which is among the first works in English to express pity for enslaved Africans.*

Song: Love Armed   [1676]

Love in fantastic triumph sate,
  Whilst bleeding hearts around him flowed,
For whom fresh pains he did create,
  And strange tyrannic power he showed:
From thy bright eyes he took his fire,   5
  Which round about in sport he hurled;
But 'twas from mine he took desire,
  Enough to undo the amorous world.

From me he took his sighs and tears:
  From thee, his pride and cruelty;
From me, his languishments and fears;   10
  And every killing dart from thee.
Thus thou and I the god have armed
  And set him up a deity;
But my poor heart alone is harmed,   15
  Whilst thine the victor is, and free.

✼ TOPICS FOR CRITICAL THINKING AND WRITING

1. The speaker talks of the suffering he is undergoing. Can we nevertheless feel that he enjoys his plight? *Why,* by the way, do we (as readers,
   singers, or listeners) often enjoy songs of unhappy love?
2. The woman ("thee") is said to exhibit "pride and cruelty" (line 10). Is
   the poem sexist? Is it therefore offensive?
3. Do you suppose that men can enjoy the poem more than women?
   Explain.

Journal Entries

The subject is Aphra Behn's "Song." We begin with two entries in a journal, kept
by a first-year student, Geoffrey Sullivan, and we follow these entries with Sullivan's completed essay.

October 10. The title "Love Armed" puzzled me at
first; funny, I somehow was thinking of the expression
"strong-armed" and at first I didn't understand that
"Love" in this poem is a human--no, not a human, but
the god Cupid, who has a human form--and that he is
shown as armed, with darts and so forth.

October 13. This god of "Love" is Cupid, and so
he is something like what is on a valentine card--
Cupid with his bow and arrow. But valentine cards
just show cute little Cupids, and in this poem Cupid
is a real menace. He causes lots of pain ("bleeding

hearts," "tears," "killing dart," etc.). So what is
Aphra Behn telling us about the god of love, or love?
That love hurts? And she is <u>singing</u> about it! But we
<u>do</u> sing songs about how hard life is. But do we sing
them when we are really hurting, or only when we are
pretty well off and just thinking about being hurt?

When you love someone and they don't return your
love, it hurts, but even when love isn't returned it
still gives some intense pleasure. Strange, but I
think true. I wouldn't say that love always has this
two-sided nature, but I do see the idea that love <u>can</u>
have two sides, pleasure and pain. And love takes two
kinds of people, male and female. Well, for most people, anyway. Maybe there's also something to the idea
that "opposites attract." Anyway, Aphra Behn seems to
be talking about men vs. women, pain vs. pleasure,
power vs. weakness, etc. Pairs, opposites. And in two
stanzas (a pair of stanzas?).

A Sample Essay by a Student: "The Double Nature of Love"

The final essay makes use of some, but not all, of the preliminary jottings. It includes much that Sullivan did not think of until he reread his jottings, reread the
poem, and began drafting the essay.

Sullivan 1

Geoffrey Sullivan
Professor Diaz
English 2G
15 October 2005

The Double Nature of Love
Aphra Behn's "Love Armed" is in two stanzas,
and it is about two people, "me" and "thee"--
that is, you and I, the lover and the woman he
loves. I think the speaker is a man, since
according to the usual code men are supposed to

be the active lovers and women are the
(relatively) passive people who are loved. In
this poem, the beloved--the woman, I think--has
"bright eyes" (line 5) that provide the god of
Love with fire, and she also provides the god with
"pride and cruelty" (10). This of course is the
way the man sees it if a woman doesn't respond to
him; if she doesn't love him in return, she is
(he thinks) arrogant and cruel. What does the man
give to Love? He provides "desire" (7), "sighs
and tears" (9), "languishments and fears" (11).
None of this sounds very manly, but the joke is
that the god of love--which means love--can turn
a strong man into a crybaby when a woman does not
respond to him.

Although both stanzas are clever descriptions
of the god of love, the poem is not just a
description. Of course there is not a plot in
the way that a short story has a plot, but there
is a sort of a switch at the end, giving the
story something of a plot. The poem is, say,
ninety percent expression of feeling and
description of love, but during the course of
expressing feelings and describing love
something happens, so there is a tiny story. The
first stanza sets the scene ("Love in fantastic
triumph sate" [1]) and tells of some of the
things that the speaker and the woman
contributed to the god of Love. The woman's eyes
provided Love with fire, and the man's feelings
provided Love with "desire" (7). The second
stanza goes on to mention other things that Love
got from the speaker ("sighs and tears," etc.
[9]), and other things that Love got from the
beloved ("pride and cruelty," etc. [10]), and in

Sullivan 3

line 13 the poet says, "Thus thou and I the god
have armed," so the two humans share something.
They have both given Love his weapons. But--and
this is the story I spoke of--the poem ends by
emphasizing their difference: Only the man is
"harmed," and the woman is the "victor" because
her heart is not captured, as the man's heart
is. In the battle that Love presides over, the
woman is the winner; the man's heart has fallen
for the woman, but, according to the last line,
the woman's heart remains "free."

    We have all seen the god of Love on valentine
cards, a cute little Cupid armed with a bow and
arrow. But despite the bow and arrow that the
Valentine's Day Cupid carries, I think that
until I read Aphra Behn's "Love Armed" I had
never really thought about Cupid as <u>powerful</u> and
as capable of causing real pain. On valentine
cards, he is just cute, but when I think about
it, I realize the truth of Aphra Behn's concept
of love. Love <u>is</u> (or can be) two-sided, whereas
the valentine cards show only the sweet side.

    I think it is interesting to notice that
although the poem is about the destructive power
of love, it is fun to read. I am not bothered by
the fact that the lover is miserable. Why? I
think I enjoy the poem, rather than am bothered
by it, because <u>he is enjoying his misery</u>. After
all, he is singing about it, sort of singing in
the rain, telling anyone who will listen about
how miserable he is, and he is having a very
good time doing it.

[New page]

Sullivan 4

Work Cited

Behn, Aphra. "Love Armed." <u>Introduction to
    Literature</u>. Ed. Sylvan Barnet et al. 14th
    ed. New York: Longman, 2006. 670.

▒ TOPICS FOR CRITICAL THINKING AND WRITING

1. What do you think of the essay's title? Is it sufficiently interesting and focused?
2. What are the writer's chief points? Are they clear, and are they adequately developed?
3. Do you think the writer is too concerned with himself, and that he loses sight of the poem? Or do you find it interesting that he connects the poem with life?
4. Focus on the writer's use of quotations. Does he effectively introduce and examine quoted lines and phrases?
5. What grade would you give the essay? Why?

14

Narrative Poetry

POPULAR BALLADS AND OTHER NARRATIVE POEMS

Most of us are so used to reading stories—whether factual in history books or fictional in novels—that we normally associate storytelling with prose, not with poetry. But in fact some of the world's great stories have been told in poetry—for instance, the Greek epics the *Iliad* (about the Trojan War) and the *Odyssey* (about Odysseus' ten years of wandering), and medieval tales of King Arthur. Non-Western (i.e., non-European) cultures, too, have their great narrative poems, notably the Sanskrit epic *The Mahabharata* (about a war in ancient India) and African and Native-American tales of the creation of the world and of the sublime deeds of heroes. And, to descend to the ridiculous, countless narratives are still being told in the form of the limerick:

> There was a young fellow of Riga,
> Who smiled as he rode on a tiger.
>   They returned from the ride,
>   With the fellow inside,
> And the smile on the face of the tiger.

In short, although we are accustomed to thinking of a story as prose in a book, until a few hundred years ago stories were commonly poetry that was sung or recited. In nonliterate societies people got their stories from storytellers who relied on memory rather than on the written word; the memorized stories were often poems, partly because (in the words of Shakespeare's early contemporary, Sir Philip Sidney), "Verse far exceedeth prose in the knitting up of the memory." Even in literate societies, few people could read or write until the invention of the printing press in the middle of the fifteenth century. Although the printing press did not immediately destroy oral verse narratives, as the centuries passed, an increasingly large reading public developed that preferred prose narratives.

Among the great verse narratives are the English and Scottish popular ballads, some of the best of which are attributed to the fifteenth century, though they were not recorded until much later. These anonymous stories in song acquired their distinctive flavor by being passed down orally from generation to generation, each singer consciously or unconsciously modifying his or her inheritance. It is not known who made up the popular ballads; often they were made up partly out of earlier ballads by singers as bold as Kipling's cockney:

When 'Omer smote 'is blooming lyre,
He'd 'eard men sing by land an' sea;
An' what he thought 'e might require,
'E went an' took—the same as me!

Most ballad singers probably were composers only by accident; they intended to transmit what they had heard, but their memories were sometimes faulty and their imaginations active. The modifications effected by oral transmission generally give a ballad three noticeable qualities:

- First, it is impersonal; even if there is an "I" who sings the tale, he or she is usually characterless.
- Second, the ballad—like other oral literature such as the nursery rhyme and the counting-out rhyme ("one potato, two potato")—is filled with repetition, sometimes of lines, sometimes of words. Consider, for example, "Go saddle me the black, the black, / Go saddle me the brown," or "O wha is this has done this deid, / This ill deid don to me?" Sometimes in fact, the story is told by repeating lines with only a few significant variations. This incremental repetition (repetition with slight variations advancing the narrative) is the heart of "Edward" (page 972). Furthermore, stock epithets are repeated from ballad to ballad: "true love," "milk-white steed," "golden hair." Oddly, these clichés do not bore us but by their impersonality often lend a simplicity that effectively contrasts with the frequent violence of the tales.
- Third, because the ballads are transmitted orally, residing in the memory rather than on the printed page, weak stanzas have often been dropped, leaving a series of sharp scenes, frequently with dialogue:

The king sits in Dumferling toune,
   Drinking the blude-reid wine:
"O whar will I get guid sailor,
   To sail this schip of mine?"

Because ballads were sung rather than printed, and because singers made alterations, no one version of a ballad is the "correct" one. The versions printed here have become such favorites that they are almost regarded as definitive, but the reader should consult a collection of ballads to get some idea of the wide variety.*

Popular ballads have been much imitated by professional poets, especially since the late eighteenth century. Two such literary ballads are Keats's "La Belle Dame sans Merci" (page 682) and Coleridge's "The Rime of the Ancient Mariner." In a literary ballad the story is often infused with multiple meanings, with the in-

---

*For example: Vivian de Sola Pinto and Allan Edwin Rodway, eds., *The Common Muse: An Anthology of Popular British Ballad Poetry, XVth–XXth Century* (1957); Albert B. Friedman, ed., *The Penguin Book of Folk Ballads of the English-Speaking World* (1977); and Frederick Woods, ed., *The Oxford Book of Traditional Verse* (1983).

sistent symbolic implications. Ambiguity is often found in the popular ballad also, but it is of a rather different sort. Perhaps because stanzas are lost, or perhaps because the singer was unconcerned with some elements of the story, the ambiguity of the popular ballad commonly lies in the story itself (who did what?) rather than in the significance of the story (what does it all add up to, what does it mean?).

Finally, a word about some of the most popular professional folksingers today. They have aptly been called "folksongers" because unlike illiterate or scarcely literate folksingers—who intend only to sing the traditional songs in the traditional way for themselves or their neighbors—these professionals are vocal artists who make commercial and political use (not bad things in themselves) of traditional folk songs, deliberately adapting old songs and inventing new songs that only loosely resemble the old ones. These contemporary ballads tend to be more personal than traditional ballads and they tend to have a social consciousness that is alien to traditional balladry. Many of the songs of Pete Seeger and Bob Dylan, for instance, are conspicuous examples of art in the service of morality; they call attention to injustice and they seek to move the hearers to action. That traditional ballads have assisted in this task is not the least of their value; the influence of a work of art is never finished, and the old ballads can rightly claim to share in the lives of their modern descendants.

We print two popular traditional English ballads here ("Sir Patrick Spence" and "The Demon Lover"), followed by two poems that are indebted to traditional ballads (John Keats's "La Belle Dame sans Merci" and A. E. Housman's "Bredon Hill"). Next we print an African-American ballad, "De Titanic," followed by seven short narrative poems—poems that tell a story—that are *not* in the ballad tradition. (For additional ballads, see "The Three Ravens," "The Twa Corbies," "Edward," and "John Henry" in "A Collection of Poems," Chapter 28, and for a literary ballad by an African-American author, see Langston Hughes's "Ballad of the Landlord," page 946.)

ANONYMOUS BRITISH BALLAD

Sir Patrick Spence

The king sits in Dumferling toune,
  Drinking the blude-reid wine:
"O whar will I get guid sailor,
  To sail this schip of mine?"   4

Up and spak an eldern knicht,
  Sat at the kings richt kne:
"Sir Patrick Spence is the best sailor,
  That sails upon the se."   8

The king has written a braid° Letter,
  And signed it wi' his hand,
And sent it to Sir Patrick Spence,
  Was walking on the sand.   12

The first line that Sir Patrick red,
  A loud lauch° lauched he;
The next line that Sir Patrick red,
  The tier blinded his ee.   16

"O wha is this has done this deid,
  This ill deid don to me,
To send me out this time o' the yeir,
  To sail upon the se?   20

"Mak hast, mak hast, my mirry men all,
  Our guid schip sails the morne":
"O say na sae, my master deir,
  For I feir a deadlie storme."   24

"Late late yestreen I saw the new moone,
  Wi' the auld moone in hir arme,
And I feir, I feir, my deir master,
  That we will cum to harme."   28

O our Scots nobles wer richt laith°
  To weet their cork-heild schoone;°
Bot lang owre° a' the play wer playd,
  Thair hats they swam aboone,°   32

O lang, lang may their ladies sit,
  Wi' thair fans into their hand,
Or eir° they se Sir Patrick Spence
  Cum sailing to the land.   36

O lang, lang may the ladies stand,
  Wi' thair gold kems in their hair,
Waiting for their ain deir lords,
  For they'll se thame na mair.   40

Have owre° to Aberdour,
  It's fiftie fadon deip,
And thair lies guid Sir Patrick Spence,
  Wi' the Scots lords at his feit.   44

---

⁹ **braid** broad, open.   ¹⁴ **lauch** laugh.   ²⁹ **laith** loath.   ³⁰ **cork-heild schoone** cork-heeled
shoes.   ³¹ **owre** ere.   ³² **aboone** above.   ³⁵ **eir** ere.   ⁴¹ **Have owre** Half over.

TOPICS FOR CRITICAL THINKING AND WRITING

1. The shipwreck occurs between lines 29 and 32, but it is not described. Does the omission stimulate the reader to imagine the details of the wreck? Or does the omission suggest that the poem is not so much about a shipwreck as it is about kinds of behavior? Explain. What do lines 33-40 contribute?

2. Might lines 17-18 warrant the inference that the "eldern knicht" (line 5) is Sir Patrick's enemy?

3. Explain lines 13-16.

4. In place of lines 37-40, another version of this ballad has the following stanza:

> The ladies crack't their fingers white,
>> The maidens tore their hair,
> A' for the sake o' their true loves,
>> For them they ne'er saw mair.

Why is one more effective than the other?

5. In the other version, the stanza that is here the final one (lines 41-44) precedes the stanzas about the ladies (lines 33-40). Which stanza makes a better conclusion? Why?

6. Is Sir Patrick heroic? Please explain.

7. Is Sir Patrick's decision to obey the king's command right or wrong? Is he responsible for the deaths of his "mirry men"?

8. What do you imagine was the response of the first readers to this poem, many centuries ago? What is your own response to it? How do you explain the continuities, or the differences, between these past and present responses?

ANONYMOUS BRITISH BALLAD

The Demon Lover

"O where have you been, my long, long love,
    This long seven years and mair?"
"O I'm come to seek my former vows
    Ye granted me before."   4

"O hold your tongue of your former vows,
    For they will breed sad strife;
O hold your tongue of your former vows,
    For I am become a wife."   8

He turned him right and round about,
    And the tear blinded his ee:
"I wad never hae trodden on Irish ground,
    If it had not been for thee.   12

"I might hae had a king's daughter,
    Far, far beyond the sea;
I might have had a king's daughter,
    Had it not been for love o thee."   16

"If ye might have had a king's daughter,
    Yer sel ye had to blame;
Ye might have taken the king's daughter,
    For ye kend° that I was nane.   20

"If I was to leave my husband dear,
    And my two babes also,
O what have you to take me to,
    If with you I should go?"   24

"I hae seven ships upon the sea—
    The eighth brought me to land—
With four-and-twenty bold mariners,
    And music on every hand."   28

She has taken up her two little babes,
    Kissed them baith cheek and chin:
"O fair ye weel, my ain two babes,
    For I'll never see you again."   32

She set her foot upon the ship,
    No mariners could she behold;
But the sails were o the taffetie,°
    And, the masts o the beaten gold.   36

They had not sailed a league, a league,
    A league but barely three,
With dismal grew his countenance,
    And drumlie° grew his ee.   40

They had not sailed a league, a league,
    A league but barely three,

----

²⁰ **kend** knew.   ³⁵ **taffetie** fabric used chiefly for women's clothing.   ⁴⁰ **drumlie** gloomy.

Until she espied his cloven foot,
  And she wept right bitterlie.   44

"O hold your tongue of your weeping," says he,
  "Of your weeping now let me be;
I will show you how the lilies grow
  On the banks of Italy."   48

"O what hills are yon, yon pleasant hills,
  That the sun shines sweetly on?"
"O yon are the hills of heaven," he said.
  "Where you will never win."°   52

"O whaten mountain is yon," she said,
  "All so dreary wi frost and snow?"
"O yon is the mountain of hell," he cried,
  "Where will you and I will go."   56

He strack the tap-mast wi his hand,
  The fore-mast wi his knee,
And he brake that gallant ship in twain,
  And sank her in the sea.   60

---

⁵² **win** gain, get to.

▓ TOPICS FOR CRITICAL THINKING AND WRITING

1. What takes place between lines 28 and 29? Between 48 and 49?
2. What is the first hint that supernatural forces are at work?
3. What does the "cloven foot" (line 43) signify? Is the spirit motivated by malice? By love? By both?
4. The older usages, words, and phrases of "The Demon Lover" could be updated, "translated," into contemporary English. Do you think that such an updating should be done, or is it better to leave the poem the way it was originally composed?
5. Did this poem hold your attention from beginning to end? If it did, please state how the author achieves this effect. If it did not, clarify why the poem failed to work for you and explain what could be done to make it more successful.

JOHN KEATS

John Keats (1795–1821), son of a London stable keeper, was taken out of school at age fifteen and apprenticed to a surgeon and apothecary. In 1816 he was licensed to practice as an apothecary-surgeon, but he almost immediately abandoned medicine and decided to make a career as a poet. His progress was amazing; he published books of poems—to mixed reviews—in 1817, 1818, and 1820, before dying of tuberculosis at the age of twenty-five. Today he is esteemed as one of England's greatest poets.

We give additional poems by Keats on pages 714, 747, and 985.

La Belle Dame sans Merci*

[1819]

O what can ail thee, knight-at-arms,
  Alone and palely loitering?
The sedge has withered from the lake,
  And no birds sing.   4

O what can ail thee, knight-at-arms,
  So haggard and so woe-begone?
The squirrel's granary is full,
  And the harvest's done.   8

I see a lily on thy brow,
  With anguish moist and fever dew,
And on thy cheeks a fading rose
  Fast withereth too.   12

"I met a lady in the meads,
  Full beautiful—a faery's child,
Her hair was long, her foot was light,
  And her eyes were wild.   16

"I made a garland for her head,
  And bracelets too, and fragrant zone;°
She looked at me as she did love,
  And made sweet moan.   20

"I set her on my pacing steed,
  And nothing else saw all day long,
For sidelong would she bend and sing
  A faery's song.   24

"She found me roots of relish sweet,
  And honey wild, and manna dew,
And sure in language strange she said
  'I love thee true.'   28

"She took me to her elfin grot,
  And there she wept and signed full sore,
And there I shut her wild wild eyes
  With kisses four.   32

"And there she lulled me asleep,
  And there I dreamed—Ah! woe betide!
The latest dream I ever dreamed
  On the cold hill side.   36

"I saw pale kings and princes too,
  Pale warriors, death-pale were they all;

---

*La Belle Dam sans Merci** the beautiful lady without pity   **18 fragrant zone** belt of flowers

They cried, 'La Belle Dame sans Merci
  Hath thee in thrall!'   40

"I saw their starved lips in the gloam
  With horrid warning gaped wide,
And I awoke, and found me here,
  On the cold hill's side.   44

"And this is why I sojourn here,
  Alone and palely loitering,
Though the sedge has withered from the lake,
  And no birds sing."   48

▩ TOPICS FOR CRITICAL THINKING AND WRITING

1. In the first three stanzas the speaker describes the knight as pale, haggard, and so forth. In the rest of the poem the knight recounts his experience. In a few sentences summarize the knight's experience, and indicate why it has caused him to appear as he now does.
2. The *femme fatale*—the dangerously seductive woman—appears often in literature. If you are familiar with one such work, compare it with Keats's poem.
3. What characteristics of the popular ballad (see page 676) do you find in this poem? What characteristic does it *not* share with popular ballads? Set forth your response in an essay of 500 words.
4. Is this poem about love, or death, or both? Please explain, making references to details in the text.
5. What is your response to this poem? Do you feel a connection to the characters? What kind of connection?
6. Keats said that "La Belle Dame sans Merci" was not one of his best or most serious poems, yet later generations of readers have valued it highly. How do you explain this discrepancy? Are poets reliable judges of the merits of their own poems?

A. E. HOUSMAN

Alfred Edward Housman (1859–1936) was a professor of Latin at University College, London, and later at Cambridge. We print a poem from his most famous book, A Shropshire Lad *(1896).*

"Bredon" is pronounced "Breedon."

Bredon Hill   [1896]

In summertime on Bredon
  The bells they sound so clear;
Round both the shires they ring them
  In steeples far and near,
    A happy noise to hear.   5

Here of a Sunday morning,
  My love and I would lie,
And see the coloured counties,
  And hear the larks so high
  About us in the sky.   10

The bells would ring to call her
  In valleys miles away:
'Come all to church, good people;
  Good people, come and pray.'
  But here my love would stay.   15

And I would turn and answer
  Among the springing thyme,
'Oh, peal upon our wedding,
  And we will hear the chime,
  And come to church in time.'   20

But when the snows at Christmas
  On Bredon top were strown,
My love rose up so early
  And stole out unbeknown
  And went to church alone.   25

They tolled the one bell only,
  Groom there was none to see,
The mourners followed after,
  And so to church went she,
  And would not wait for me.   30

The bells they sound on Bredon,
  And still the steeples hum.
'Come all to church, good people,' —
  Oh, noisy bells, be dumb;
  I hear you, I will come.   35

▓ TOPICS FOR CRITICAL THINKING AND WRITING

1. Who is the storyteller (the narrator)? How would you briefly summarize the story that he tells? (In your response, take into account the next question.)

2. What do you take the last line of the poem to mean?

3. In what ways does this poem resemble a traditional ballad? In what ways does it not?

4. At least one reader has said that line 28 ("the mourners followed after") is a flaw in the poem because it explicitly and unnecessarily tells the reader that someone has died. The line might, for instance, have run, "The day was dark and silent." Do you agree that the poem might be better if Housman had not spoken of mourners? Why, or why not?

ANONYMOUS AFRICAN-AMERICAN BALLAD

On the night of April 14–15 the British ocean-liner *Titanic,* thought to be unsink-able, crashed into an iceberg and sank on its maiden voyage, with the loss of some 1,500 of the 2,000 persons aboard. Why does the loss of this ship continue to hold the minds of succeeding generations? Perhaps it is because the ship was the largest, most luxurious, swiftest ship of its day; it carried many immensely rich people; and it was destroyed on its maiden journey.

African-American singers especially created literature out of the story of the *Titanic,* partly by adapting earlier songs about shipwrecks.

Consider the following lines, said to be a "Negro" song from Mississippi, which were published in the *Journal of American Folk-lore* in 1909, three years before the *Titanic* sank. (The verse form is often found in blues.)

> O where were you when the steamer went down, Captain?
> O where were you when the steamer went down, Captain?
> O where were you when the steamer went down, Captain?
> I was with my honey in the heart of town.

On the Mississippi, exploding boilers, not icebergs, did the steamers in. Presum-ably the captain should have been with his ship, staying on board until the last passenger had gotten to safety. The song doesn't say that the captain was cow-ardly, only that he wasn't where he should have been at the moment he was needed. In four lines—really in two lines—we get the juxtaposition of disaster and joy, death and life, separated but connected by the captain.

What the ship was, and who the captain was, are unknown, but the ship could have been any of several steamers that sank on the Mississippi. In any case, after the wreck of the *Titanic* an anonymous black singer transformed this song into:

> Where wus you when the big *Titanic* went down?
> Where wus you when the big *Titanic* went down?
> Where wus you when the big *Titanic* went down?
> Standin' on the deck, singin' "Alabama Boun."

And yet another version (there are several more):

> O, what were you singing when the *Titanic* went down?
> O, what were you singing when the *Titanic* went down?
> O, what were you singing when the *Titanic* went down?
> Sitting on a mule's back, singing "Alabama Bound."

One doesn't want to make too big a fuss, but surely these two anonymous lyrics about the *Titanic* lodge themselves in the mind, the first with its suggestion of an ocean voyager standing on the deck and singing about going home to Alabama, the second with its evocative contrast of the great ship sinking and the (presum-ably humble) person safe at home, sitting on a mule and singing of a happy voy-age homeward.

The following song was sung during World War I by African-American soldiers on troop ships crossing the Atlantic to fight in France. (The armed services practiced segregation until after World War II.) We print it in the form it was published, with an attempt to render the pronunciation of the singers.

De Titanic

Loud and swinging
♩ = 152-176, somewhat free

Cap - tain   Smith, when he got his load,   Might 'a'

heared him holl' - in', "All   a - bo - a'd."   Cry - in',

"Fare   thee,   *Ti - tan - ic*,   fare thee well."

Cap - tain

Smith,   when he   got his load,   Might   'a'

heared him holl' - in',   "All   a - bo - a'd."   Cry - in',

"Fare   thee,   *Ti - tan - ic*,   fare thee   well."

De rich folks 'cided to take a trip
On de fines' ship dat was ever built.
De cap'n presuaded dese peoples to think
Dis Titanic too safe to sink.   4

Chorus:
    Out on dat ocean,
    De great wide ocean,
    De Titanic, out on de ocean,
    Sinkin' down!   8

De ship lef' de harbor at a rapid speed,
'Twuz carryin' everythin' dat de peeples need.
She sailed six-hundred miles away,
Met an icebug in her way.   12

De ship lef' de harbor, 'twuz runnin' fas'.
'Twuz her fus' trip an' her las'.
Way out on dat ocean wide
An icebug ripped her in de side.   16

Up come Bill from de bottom flo'
Said de water wuz runnin' in de boiler do'.
Go back, Bill, an' shut yo' mouth,
Got forty-eight pumps to keep de water out!   20

Jus' about den de cap'n looked aroun',
He seed de Titanic wuz a-sinkin' down.
He give orders to de mens aroun':
"Get yo' life-boats an' let 'em down!"   24

De mens standin' roun' like heroes brave,
Nothin' but de wimin an' de chillun to save;
De wimin an' de chillun a-wipin' dere eyes,
Kissin' dere husbands an' friends good-bye.   28

On de fifteenth day of May nineteen-twelve,
De ship wrecked by an icebug out in de ocean dwell.
De people wuz thinkin' o' Jesus o' Nazaree,
While de band played "Nearer my God to Thee!"   32

▨ TOPICS FOR CRITICAL THINKING AND WRITING

1. If the pronunciation was "corrected" (e.g., line 9, "The ship left the harbor at a rapid speed"), would the poem gain or lose anything? Why? What does the misnomer "icebug" (lines 12, 16, 30) suggest that "iceberg" lacks?

2. Why is the character Bill introduced (line 17)? What, if anything, does his presence add to the poem's account of the disaster's meaning?

3. Read "Sir Patrick Spence" (page 677), an older ballad. What characteristics do the poems share?

4. In its final stanza the song refers to Jesus and to a Christian hymn. What do these references contribute to the point of view that the song expresses?

5. What do you think was the author's intention in composing "De Titanic"? Can a poem itself reveal the author's intention, or do we have to locate evidence for it elsewhere, perhaps in a journal entry or in a letter that the poet sent to a friend or a fellow-poet?

6. Is "De Titanic" a bitter poem? A cruel poem? Or would you characterize it in different terms? Please explain, citing details in the text.

THOMAS HARDY

Thomas Hardy (1840-1928) was born in Dorset, England, the son of a stonemason. Despite great obstacles he studied the classics and architecture, and in 1862 he moved to London to study and practice as an architect. Ill health forced him to return to Dorset, where he continued to work as an architect and to write. Best known for his novels, Hardy ceased writing fiction after the hostile reception of Jude the Obscure *in 1896 and turned to writing lyric poetry.*

For information about the Titanic, *see page 685.*

The Convergence of the Twain   [1912]

Lines on the Loss of the Titanic

I

In a solitude of the sea
   Deep from human vanity,
And the Pride of Life that planned her, stilly couches she.

II

Steel Chambers, late the pyres
   Of her salamandrine fires,
Cold currents thrid,° and turn to rhythmic tidal lyres.   5

III

Over the mirrors meant
   To glass the opulent
The sea-worm crawls—grotesque, slimed, dumb, indifferent.

IV

Jewels in joy designed   10
   To ravish the sensuous mind
Lie lightless, all their sparkles bleared and black and blind.

---

6 **thrid** thread.

V

Dim moon-eyed fishes near
Gaze at the gilded gear
And query: "What does this vaingloriousness down here?"   15

VI

Well; while was fashioning
This creature of cleaving wing,
The Immanent Will that stirs and urges everything

VII

Prepared a sinister mate
For her—so gaily great—   20
A Shape of Ice, for the time far and dissociate.

VIII

And as the smart ship grew
In stature, grace, and hue,
In shadowy silent distance grew the Iceberg too.

IX

Alien they seemed to be: 25
No mortal eye could see
The intimate welding of their later history,

X

Or sign that they were bent
By paths coincident
On being anon twin halves of one august event,   30

XI

Till the Spinner of the Years
Said "Now!" And each one hears,
And consummation comes, and jars two hemispheres.

▨ TOPICS FOR CRITICAL THINKING AND WRITING

1. Does Hardy assign a cause to the disaster? What do you make of "The Immanent Will" (line 18) and "the Spinner of the Years" (line 31)?
2. In line 19 Hardy speaks of the "sinister mate." What other words in the poem suggest that the ship and the iceberg participate in a marriage?

3. After you have read and thought carefully about the poem, consider the title and subtitle. Why, in your view, did Hardy use the phrase "The Convergence of the Twain" as his title? Would the poem be more effective if the title and subtitle were reversed? Explain.

4. Examine the form and structure of the poem, looking closely at the ways in which Hardy has organized his lines and stanzas. Stanza I, for example, could be rewritten with the final words coming first: "She couches stilly in a solitude of the sea." What poetic effects does Hardy achieve through this change (and others like it) in normal or typical syntax and word order? And why does he use a series of three-line stanzas, each headed by a roman numeral? Why not simply present the poem as a single long stanza?

SIEGFRIED SASSOON

Siegfried Sassoon (1886–1967), a wealthy Englishman, served with such distinction in the First World War—in 1915 under heavy fire he helped a wounded soldier to safety—that he was awarded the Military Cross. Later, wounded by a bullet in the chest, he was sent from France back to England, where, upon reflection, he concluded that the war was not a war of defense but of aggression. Military officials shrewdly chose not to dispute him, but merely asserted that he was shell-shocked. When Sassoon recovered from the bullet wound, he was again sent into combat, and in 1919 was again wounded and hospitalized.

Sassoon expressed his views in Memoirs of a Fox-Hunting Man *(1928) and* Memoirs of an Infantry Officer *(1930), as well as in several volumes of poetry.*

The General   [1917]

"Good-morning, good-morning!" the General said
When we met him last week on our way to the line.
Now the soldiers he smiled at are most of 'em dead,
And we're cursing his staff for incompetent swine.
"He's a cheery old card," grunted Harry to Jack
As they slogged up to Arras with rifle and pack.

But he did for them both by his plan of attack.

▨ TOPICS FOR CRITICAL THINKING AND WRITING

1. Who is the storyteller, and what is the story he tells?

2. Why do you suppose Sassoon put an extra space between the next-to-last line and the last line? Speaking of the last line, notice that it rhymes with the two preceding lines—i.e., the last three lines end with identical sounds, whereas in the preceding four lines, no two adjacent lines rhyme. Why do you suppose Sassoon changed the rhyme-scheme for the final lines?

3. How would you characterize the General? How would you characterize Harry? How would you characterize the storyteller?

COUNTEE CULLEN

Countee Cullen (1903–1946) was born Countee Porter in New York City, raised by his grandmother, and then adopted by the Reverend Frederick A. Cullen, a Methodist minister in Harlem. Cullen received a bachelor's degree from New York University (Phi Beta Kappa) and a master's degree from Harvard. He earned his living as a high school teacher of French, but his literary gifts were recognized in his own day. Eric Walrond (1898–1966), to whom the poem is dedicated, was an essayist and writer of short stories.

Incident

[1925]

(For Eric Walrond)

Once riding in Old Baltimore,
   Heart-filled, head-filled with glee,
I saw a Baltimorean
   Keep looking straight at me.   4

Now I was eight and very small,
   And he was no whit bigger,
And so I smiled, but he poked out
   His tongue, and called me, "Nigger."   8

I saw the whole of Baltimore
   From May until December;
Of all the things that happened there
   That's all that I remember.   12

▦ TOPICS FOR CRITICAL THINKING AND WRITING

1. How would you define an "incident"? A serious occurrence? A minor occurrence, or what? Think about the word, and then think about Cullen's use of it as a title for the event recorded in this poem. Test out one or two other possible titles as a way of helping yourself to see the strengths or weaknesses of Cullen's title.

2. The dedicatee, Eric Walrond (1898–1966) was an African-American essayist and writer of fiction, who in an essay, "On Being Black," had described his experiences of racial prejudice. How does the presence of the dedication bear on our response to Cullen's account of the "incident"?

3. What is the tone of the poem? Indifferent? Angry? Or what? What do you think is the speaker's attitude toward the "incident"? What is your attitude?

4. Ezra Pound, poet and critic, once defined literature as "news that *stays* news." What do you think he meant by this? Do you think that the definition fits Cullen's poem?

EDWIN ARLINGTON ROBINSON

Edward Arlington Robinson (1869-1935) grew up in Gardiner, Maine, spent two years at Harvard, and then returned to Maine, where he published his first book of poetry in 1896. Though he received encouragement from neighbors, his finances were precarious, even after President Theodore Roosevelt, having been made aware of the book, secured for him an appointment as customs inspector in New York from 1905 to 1909. Additional books won fame for Robinson, and in 1922 he was awarded the first of the three Pulitzer Prizes for poetry that he would win.

Richard Cory   [1896]

Whenever Richard Cory went down town,
We people on the pavement looked at him:
He was a gentleman from sole to crown,
Clean favored, and imperially slim.   4

And he was always quietly arrayed,
And he was always human when he talked;
But still he fluttered pulses when he said,
"Good-morning," and he glittered when he walked.   8

And he was rich—yes, richer than a king—
And admirably schooled in every grace:
In fine,° we thought that he was everything
To make us wish that we were in his place.   12

So on we worked, and waited for the light,
And went without the meat, and cursed the bread;
And Richard Cory, one calm summer night,
Went home and put a bullet through his head.   16

---

¹¹ *In fine* in short.

✦ TOPICS FOR CRITICAL THINKING AND WRITING

1. Consult the entry on irony in the glossary. Then read the pages referred to in the entry. Finally, write an essay of 500 words on irony in "Richard Cory."

2. What do you think were Richard Cory's thoughts shortly before he "put a bullet through his head"? In 500 words, set forth his thoughts and actions (what he sees and does). If you wish, you can write in the first person, from Cory's point of view. Further, if you wish, your essay can be in the form of a suicide note.

3. Write a sketch (250-350 words) setting forth your early impression or understanding of someone whose later actions revealed you had not understood the person.

THOMAS GRAY

Thomas Gray (1716-1771), educated in England at Eton and at Cambridge, was a bookish man—a serious student of history, botany, zoology, music, and literature—who in his middle thirties found himself famous because of his "Elegy Written in a Country Churchyard" (published in 1751). The most famous stanza of this poem runs thus:

> The boast of heraldry, the pomp of power,
> And all that beauty, all that wealth e'er gave,
> Awaits alike th' inevitable hour.
> The paths of glory lead but to the grave.

As this stanza indicates, Gray's "Elegy" is a meditative poem with very little narrative content. The following poem has more narrative content and is more playful: It announces itself as an "ode"—normally a poem devoted to singing the praises of an important subject—but the rest of the title, by the very juxtaposition of "ode" and "cat," suggests playfulness.

Ode on the Death of a Favorite Cat Drowned in a Tub of Gold Fishes

[1748]

'Twas on a lofty vase's side,
Where China's gayest art had dyed
   The azure flowers that blow;°
Demurest of the tabby kind,
The pensive Selima reclined,   5
   Gazed on the lake below.

Her conscious tail her joy declared;
The fair round face, the snowy beard,
   The velvet of her paws,
Her coat, that with the tortoise vies,   10
Her ears of jet, and emerald eyes,
   She saw; and purred applause.

Still had she gazed; but midst the tide
Two angel forms were seen to glide,
   The Genii° of the stream: 15
Their scaly armor's Tyrian hue°
Through richest purple to the view
   Betrayed a golden gleam.

The hapless nymph with wonder saw:
A whisker first, and then a claw,   20
   With many an ardent wish,
She stretched in vain to reach the prize.
What female heart can gold despise?
   What cat's averse to fish?

---

³ **blow** blossom.   ¹⁵ **Genii** guardian spirits.   ¹⁷ **Tyrian hue** purple color, associated with high rank.

Presumptuous maid! with looks intent   25
Again she stretched, again she bent,
   Nor knew the gulf between.
(Malignant Fate sat by, and smiled.)
The slipp'ry verge her feet beguiled;
   She tumbled headlong in.   30

Eight times emerging from the flood
She mewed to ev'ry wat'ry god,
   Some speedy aid to send.
No dolphin came, no Nereid° stirred:
Nor cruel Tom, nor Susan heard.   35
   A fav'rite has no friend!

From hence, ye beauties, undeceived,
Know, one false step is ne'er retrieved,
   And be with caution bold.
Not all that tempts your wand'ring eyes   40
And heedless hearts is lawful prize;
   Nor all that glisters, gold.

---

34 **dolphin . . . Nereid** Legend held that Arion, a Greek musician, was saved by a dolphin; a
Nereid is a water-nymph.

▩ TOPICS FOR CRITICAL THINKING AND WRITING

1. A mock heroic poem does not mock the heroic but mocks a trivial subject by treating it in the elevated terms normally reserved for heroic
   subjects. Its elevated diction (e.g., "lake" in line 6, for a tub of water) produces a comic effect. What examples are shown here? What comic jux-
   tapositions? What is the tone of the poem?
2. Is this a satire on cats? What does the cat come to represent?
3. Explain the paradox in line 36. Is the explicit moralizing (e.g., line 36,
   lines 37–42) offensive? Explain.
4. Dr. Johnson said of this poem: "The poem *On the Cat* was doubtless by
   its author considered as a trifle, but it is not a happy trifle. . . . The sixth
   stanza contains a melancholy truth, that 'a favorite has no friend'; but
   the last ends in a pointed sentence of no relation to the purpose: "if
   what glistered had been *gold*, the cat would not have gone into the water; and if she had, would not less have been drowned." Evaluate Johnson's comment.
5. Does a good story necessarily have a moral? Please explain.

EMILY DICKINSON

*Emily Dickinson (1830–1886), born into a proper New England family in
Amherst, Massachusetts, was brought up as a Protestant. Much of her poetry
concerns death and heaven, but it is far from being conventionally Christian.*

Because I could not stop for Death

Because I could not stop for Death—
He kindly stopped for me—
The Carriage held but just Ourselves—
And Immortality.   4

We slowly drove—He knew no haste
And I had put away
My labor and my leisure too,
For His Civility—   8

We passed the School, where Children strove
At Recess—in the Ring—
We passed the Fields of Gazing Grain—
We passed the Setting Sun—   12

Or rather—He passed Us—
The Dews drew quivering and chill—
For only Gossamer, my Gown—
My Tippet—only Tulle—   16

We paused before a House that seemed
A Swelling of the Ground—
The Roof was scarcely visible—
The Cornice—in the Ground—   20

Since then—'tis Centuries—and yet
Feels shorter than the Day
I first surmised the Horses' Heads
Were toward Eternity—   24

 TOPICS FOR CRITICAL THINKING AND WRITING

1. Characterize death as it appears in line 1–8.
2. What is the significance of the details and their arrangement in the third stanza? Why "strove" rather than "played" (line 9)? What meaning does "Ring" (line 10) have? Is "Gazing Grain" better than "Golden Grain"?
3. The "House" in the fifth stanza is a sort of riddle. What is the answer? Does this stanza introduce an aspect of death not present—or present only very faintly—in the rest of the poem? Explain.
4. Evaluate this statement about the poem (from Yvor Winters's *In Defense of Reason*): "In so far as it concentrates on the life that is being left behind, it is wholly successful; in so far as it attempts to experience the death to come, it is fraudulent, however exquisitely."

JOHN LENNON AND PAUL McCARTNEY

John Lennon (1940-1980) and Paul McCartney (b. 1942) were original members of the Beatles.

Eleanor Rigby   [1966]

Ah, look at all the lonely people!
Ah, look at all the lonely people!

Eleanor Rigby
Picks up the rice in the church where a wedding has been,
Lives in a dream.   5
Waits at the window
Wearing the face that she keeps in a jar by the door.
Who is it for?

All the lonely people,
Where do they all come from?   10
All the lonely people,
Where do they all belong?

Father McKenzie,
Writing the words of a sermon that no one will hear,
No one comes near.   15
Look at him working,
Darning his socks in the night when there's nobody there.
What does he care?

All the lonely people,
Where do they all come from?   20
All the lonely people,
Where do they all belong?

Ah, look at all the lonely people!
Ah, look at all the lonely people!

Eleanor Rigby   25
Died in the church and was buried along with her name,
Nobody came.
Father McKenzie,
Wiping the dirt from his hands as he walks from the grave,
No one was saved.   30

All the lonely people,
Where do they all come from?
All the lonely people,
Where do they all belong?

Ah, look at all the lonely people!   35
Ah, look at all the lonely people!

✳ TOPIC FOR CRITICAL THINKING AND WRITING

Is the poem chiefly about Eleanor Rigby? What is Father McKenzie doing in
the poem?

15

Lyric Poetry

For the ancient Greeks, a **lyric** was a song accompanied by a lyre. It was short, and it usually expressed a single emotion, such as joy or sorrow. The word is now used more broadly, referring to a poem that, neither narrative (telling a story) nor strictly dramatic (performed by actors), is an emotional or reflective soliloquy. Still, it is rarely very far from a singing voice. James Joyce saw the lyric as the "verbal vesture of an instant of emotion, a rhythmical cry such as ages ago cheered on the man who pulled at the oar." Such lyrics, too, were sung more recently than "ages ago." Here is a song that American slaves sang when rowing heavy loads.

ANONYMOUS

Michael Row the Boat Ashore

Michael row the boat ashore, Hallelujah!
Michael's boat's a freedom boat, Hallelujah!
Sister, help to trim the sail, Hallelujah!
Jordan stream is wide and deep, Hallelujah!
Freedom stands on the other side, Hallelujah!

We might pause for a moment to comment on why people sing at work. There are at least three reasons: (1) work done rhythmically goes more efficiently; (2) the songs relieve the boredom of the work; and (3) the songs—whether narrative or lyrical—provide something of an outlet for the workers' frustrations.

Speaking roughly, we can say that whereas a narrative (whether in prose or poetry) is set in the past, telling what happened, a lyric is set in the present, catching a speaker in a moment of expression. But a lyric can, of course, glance backward or forward, as in this folk song, usually called "Careless Love."

ANONYMOUS

Careless Love

Love, O love, O careless love,
You see what careless love can do.

When I wore my apron low,
Couldn't keep you from my do,°
   Fare you well, fare you well.
Now I wear my apron high,
Scarce see you passin' by,
   Fare you well, fare you well.

5

---

4 **do** door.

Notice, too, that a lyric, like a narrative, can have a plot: "Michael" moves toward the idea of freedom, and "Careless Love" implies a story of desertion—something has happened between the time that the singer could not keep the man from her door and now, when she "scarce" sees him passing by—but, again, the emphasis is on a present state of mind.

Lyrics are sometimes differentiated among themselves. For example, if a lyric is melancholy or mournfully contemplative, especially if it laments a death, it may be called an **elegy.** If a lyric is rather long, elaborate, and on a lofty theme such as immortality or a hero's victory, it may be called an **ode** or a **hymn.** Distinctions among lyrics are often vague, and one person's ode may be another's elegy. Still, when writers use one of these words in their titles, they are inviting the reader to recall the tradition in which they are working. Of the poet's link to tradition T. S. Eliot said:

> No poet, no artist of any art, has his complete meaning alone. His significance, his appreciation is the appreciation of his relation to the dead poets and artists. You cannot value him alone; you must set him, for contrast and comparison, among the dead.

Although the lyric is often ostensibly addressed to someone (the "you" in "Careless Love"), the reader usually feels that the speaker is really talking to himself or herself. In "Careless Love," the speaker need not be in the presence of her man; rather, her heart is overflowing (the reader senses) and she pretends to address him.

A comment by John Stuart Mill on poetry is especially true of the lyric:

> Eloquence is *heard*, poetry is *over*heard. Eloquence supposes an audience; the peculiarity of poetry appears to us to lie in the poet's utter unconsciousness of a listener. Poetry is feeling confessing itself to itself, in moments of solitude.

This is particularly true in work songs such as "Michael Row the Boat Ashore," where there is no audience: the singers sing for themselves, participating rather than performing. As one prisoner in Texas said: "They really be singing about the way they feel inside. Since they can't say it to nobody, they sing a song about it." The sense of "feeling confessing itself to itself, in moments of solitude" or of "singing about the way they feel inside" is strong and clear in this short cowboy song.

ANONYMOUS

The Colorado Trail

Eyes like the morning star,
Cheeks like a rose,
Laura was a pretty girl
God Almighty knows.   4

Weep all ye little rains,
Wail winds wail,
All along, along, along
The Colorado trail.   8

When we read a lyric poem, no matter who the speaker is, for a moment—
while we recite or hear the words—we become the speaker. That is, we get into
the speaker's mind, or, perhaps more accurately, the speaker takes charge of
our mind, and we undergo (comfortably seated in a chair or sprawled on a bed)
the mental experience that is embodied in the words.

Next, another anonymous poem, this one written in England, probably in
the early sixteenth century. Aside from modern reprintings, it survives in only
one manuscript, a song book, the relevant portion of which we reproduce here.
But first, here is the poem in modern spelling.

ANONYMOUS

Western Wind

Westron wind, when will thou blow?
The small rain down can rain.
Christ, that my love were in my arms,
And I in my bed again.

Westron wynde when wilt thou blow. Musical setting in a tenor part-book; early sixteenth century.
(Reproduced by permission of the British Library Royal Appendix 58 f.5.)

The angular handwriting is in a style quite different from modern writing, but when you are told that the first three words are "Westron [i.e., western] wynde when," you can probably see some connections. And you can probably make out the last handwritten word on the second line ("And"), and all of the third line: "I yn my bed A gayne" ("I in my bed again"). Incidentally—we hope we are not boring you with trifles—some controversy surrounds the transcription of one of the words—the fifth word in the second line of writing, the word that looks like a *y* followed by an *f* (just after "Chryst" and just before "my"). The issue is this: Is the letter a *y*, in which case the word is "if," or is it a letter we no longer have, a letter called *thorn*, which was pronounced "th," as in either "thin" or "this"? If indeed it is a thorn, the next letter is a *t*, not an *f*, and the word therefore is not "if" but "that." (Incidentally, signs that say "Ye Olde Antique Shoppe" make no sense; "Ye" was never used as a definite article. What these signs are reproducing is a thorn, and the word really is "The," not "Ye.")

▓ TOPICS FOR CRITICAL THINKING AND WRITING

1. In "Western Wind," what do you think is the tone of the speaker's voice in the first two lines? Angry? Impatient? Supplicating? Be as precise as possible. What is the tone in the next two lines?
2. In England the west wind, warmed by the Gulf Stream, rises in the spring. What associations link the wind and rain of lines 1 and 2 with lines 3 and 4?
3. Should we have been told why the lovers are separated? Explain.

Love poems are by no means all the same—to take an obvious point, some are happy and some are sad—but those that are about the loss of a beloved or about the pains of love seem to be especially popular.

JULIA WARD HOWE

Julia Ward Howe (1819–1910) was born in New York City. A social reformer, her work for the emancipation of African-Americans and the right of women to vote is notable. She was the first woman to be elected to the American Academy of Arts and Letters.

Battle Hymn of the Republic   [1861]

Mine eyes have seen the glory of the coming of the Lord:
He is trampling out the vintage where the grapes of wrath are stored;
He hath loosed the fateful lightning of his terrible swift sword;
　　His truth is marching on.   4

Chorus
　　Glory! glory! Hallelujah!
　　Glory! glory! Hallelujah!
　　Glory! glory! Hallelujah!
　　　His truth is marching on!   8

I have seen him in the watch-fires of a hundred circling camps;
They have builded him an altar in the evening dews and damps;
I can read his righteous sentence by the dim and flaring lamps;
    His day is marching on.   12

I have read a fiery gospel, writ in burnished rows of steel:
"As ye deal with my contemners, so with you my grace shall deal;
Let the Hero, born of woman, crush the serpent with his heel,
    Since God is marching on."   16

He has sounded forth the trumpet that shall never call retreat;
He is sifting out the hearts of men before his judgment seat;
Oh, be swift, my soul, to answer him! be jubilant, my feet!
    Our God is marching on.   20

In the beauty of the lilies Christ was born across the sea,
With a glory in his bosom that transfigures you and me:
As he died to make men holy, let us die to make men free,
    While God is marching on.   24

▓ TOPICS FOR CRITICAL THINKING AND WRITING

1. This poem of the Civil War, written to the tune of "John Brown's Body," draws some of its militant imagery from the Bible, especially from Isaiah 63.1–6 and Revelation 19.11–15. Do you think the lines about Christ are inappropriate here? Explain.

2. If you know the tune to which "Battle Hymn of the Republic" is sung, think about the interplay between the music and the words. Do you think people have a different response to Howe's words when they read her text as a poem, rather than experienced it as a song?

WENDY COPE

Wendy Cope (b. 1945) was born in Kent, in the south of England. She was educated at St. Hilda's College at Oxford University, where she took a degree in History, and then at the Westminster College of Education. After working for some years as a music teacher in London, Cope became a television critic, a columnist, a freelance writer, and above all, a poet. Her books of verse include Making Cocoa for Kingsley Amis *(1986) and* Serious Concerns *(1991), both of which were best-sellers in England, and* If I Don't Know *(2001).*

Valentine   [1991]

My heart has made its mind up
And I'm afraid it's you.
Whatever you've got lined up,
My heart has made its mind up
And if you can't be signed up   5
This year, next year will do.
My heart has made its mind up
And I'm afraid it's you.

▓ TOPICS FOR CRITICAL THINKING AND WRITING

1. What are your first responses to Cope's title? How does she work with (and perhaps against) our thoughts and feelings about Valentine's Day?

2. "Valentine" appears in a book titled *Serious Concerns.* Do you find the poem serious, or is it to you more amusing than serious? Is this a poem

that you read and enjoy and no more than that, or do you find that it stays with you, maybe making a connection with experiences in your own life? Please explain.

3. Three times Cope describes the heart making up its mind. Isn't that perplexing—the idea of the heart having a mind? What do you think that the poet might be suggesting through this use of words?

4. The final line repeats the second line. Do you hear and understand "afraid" differently the second time?

WILLIAM SHAKESPEARE

William Shakespeare (1564–1616) is of course best known as the writer of sonnets and of plays, but he also wrote lyrics for songs in some of the plays. The following two lyrics are sung at the end of an early musical comedy, Love's Labor's Lost. (No early settings are known for these songs.) Conflict is essential in drama, and in these two poems we get a sort of melodious conflict, a song in praise of spring, juxtaposed against a song in praise of winter. But notice that within each song there are elements of conflict.

Spring

[c. 1595]

When daisies pied and violets blue
   And lady-smocks° all silver-white
And cuckoo-buds° of yellow hue
   Do paint the meadows with delight,
The cuckoo then, on every tree,   5
Mocks married men; for thus sings he,
"Cuckoo,
Cuckoo, cuckoo!" O word of fear,
Unpleasing to a married ear!
When shepherds pipe on oaten straws,°   10
   And merry larks are ploughmen's clocks,
When turtles tread,° and rooks, and daws,
   And maidens bleach their summer smocks,
The cuckoo then, on every tree,
Mocks married men; for thus sings he,   15
"Cuckoo,
Cuckoo, cuckoo!" O word of fear,
Unpleasing to a married ear!

---

2 **lady-smocks** also called cuckooflowers. 3 **cuckoo-buds** buttercups. 10 **oaten straws** musical instruments. 12 **turtles tread** turtledoves mate.

Winter

[c. 1595]

When icicles hang by the wall,
   And Dick the shepherd blows his nail,°

---

2 **blows his nail** breathes on his fingernails to warm them.

And Tom bears logs into the hall,
   And milk comes frozen home in pail,
When blood is nipped, and ways° be foul,   5
Then nightly sings the staring owl,
     "Tu-whit, tu-who!"
A merry note,
While greasy Joan doth keel° the pot.
When all aloud the wind doth blow,   10
   And coughing drowns the parson's saw,°
And birds sit brooding in the snow,
   And Marian's nose looks red and raw,
When roasted crabs° hiss in the bowl,
Then nightly sings the staring owl,   15
     "Tu-whit, tu-who!"
A merry note,
While greasy Joan doth keel the pot.

---

5 ways roads. **9 keel** cool, by skimming. **11 coughing . . . saw** wise saying. **14 crabs** crab apples.

❖ TOPICS FOR CRITICAL THINKING AND WRITING

1. Why is the cuckoo appropriate to spring? The owl to winter?
2. Did you expect a poem on spring to bring in infidelity? Is the poem bitter? Explain. (If in doubt, check the word *"cuckold"* in a dictionary.)
3. Does "Winter" describe only the hardships of the season, or does it communicate also the joys?

W. H. AUDEN

Wystan Hugh Auden (1907–1973) was born in York, England, and educated at Oxford. In the 1930s his left-wing poetry earned him wide acclaim as the leading poet of his generation. In 1939 Auden came to America, and in 1946 he became a citizen of the United States, though he spent his last years in England.

Stop All the Clocks, Cut Off the Telephone   [1936]

Stop all the clocks, cut off the telephone,
Prevent the dog from barking with a juicy bone,
Silence the pianos and with muffled drum
Bring out the coffin, let the mourners come.   4

Let aeroplanes circle moaning overhead
Scribbling on the sky the message He Is Dead,
Put the crepe bows round the white necks of the public doves,
Let the traffic policemen wear black cotton gloves.   8

He was my North, my South, my East and West,
My working week and my Sunday rest,
My noon, my midnight, my talk, my song;
I thought that love would last for ever: I was wrong.   12

The stars are not wanted now: put out every one;
Pack up the moon and dismantle the sun;
Pour away the ocean and sweep up the wood.
For nothing now can ever come to any good.   16

 ## TOPICS FOR CRITICAL THINKING AND WRITING

1. Let's assume that poems are rooted in real-life situations—that is, they
   take their origin from responses to experience, whether the experience is falling in love or losing a loved one, or praising God or losing
   one's faith, or celebrating a war (as in "Battle Hymn of the Republic")
   or lamenting the tragic destruction of war. But of course the poet then
   shapes the experience into a memorable statement and somehow
   makes a distinctive work on a traditional theme. Cite some phrases in
   Auden's poem that you would *not* expect to find in a poem on the
   death of the beloved. (For example, would you expect to find a reference to a dog eating "a juicy bone" in a poem on this theme?) Do you
   think these passages are effective, or do you think they are just silly?
   Explain.
2. Perhaps another way of getting at the question we have just asked is
   this: Can you imagine reading this at the funeral of someone you love?
   Or would you want a lover to read it at your funeral? Why?
3. The words of the last line of the poem are simple, almost a cliché. Yet
   we find them very powerful, and we wonder if you agree. What is the
   relationship of this line to the preceding lines of the stanza, with its images of mighty actions and cosmic gestures, and to the poem as a
   whole?

EMILY BRONTË

*Emily Brontë (1818–1848) spent most of her short life (she died of tubercu-
losis) in an English village on the Yorkshire moors. The sister of Charlotte
Brontë (author of* Jane Eyre) *and of Anne Brontë, Emily is best known for
her novel* Wuthering Heights *(1847), but she was a considerable poet, and
her first significant publication (1846) was in a volume of poems by the
three sisters.*

Spellbound   [1837]

The night is darkening round me,
The wild winds coldly blow;
But a tyrant spell has bound me
And I cannot, cannot go.   4

The giant trees are bending
Their bare boughs weighed with snow.
And the storm is fast descending,
And yet I cannot go.   8

Clouds beyond clouds above me,
Wastes beyond wastes below;
But nothing drear can move me;
I will not, cannot go.   12

✴ TOPICS FOR CRITICAL THINKING AND WRITING

1. What exactly is a "spell," and what does it mean to be "spellbound"?
2. What difference, if any, would it make if the first line said "has darkened" instead of "is darkening"?
3. What difference would it make, if any, if lines 4 and 12 were switched?
4. What does "drear" (line 11) mean? Is this word too unusual? Should the
   poet have used a more familiar word?
5. Describe the speaker's state of mind. Have you ever experienced anything like this yourself? What was the situation and how did you
   move beyond it?

Here is yet one more lyric dealing, as lyric usually does, with a deeply felt
personal experience.

THOMAS HARDY

*Thomas Hardy (1840-1928) was born in Dorset, England, the son of a
stonemason. Best known for his novels, Hardy stopped writing fiction after
the hostile reception of* Jude the Obscure *in 1896 and turned to writing lyric
poetry.*

The Self-Unseeing   [1901]

Here is the ancient floor,
Footworn and hollowed and thin,
Here was the former door
Where the dead feet walked in.   4

She sat here in her chair,
Smiling into the fire;
He who played stood there,
Bowing it higher and higher.   8

Childlike, I danced in a dream;
Blessings emblazoned that day;
Everything glowed with a gleam;
Yet we were looking away!   12

TOPICS FOR CRITICAL THINKING AND WRITING

1. In line 8, what does "Bowing it higher and higher" mean? Putting aside the issue of rhyme, what, if anything, would be lost if lines 7–8 were omitted?
2. What do you take the title of the poem to mean? And the last line?
3. Hardy chose to punctuate the final line with an exclamation point. Would the tone and meaning change if he had used a period?

We have already mentioned that the lyric can range from expressions of emotion focused on personal matters to expressions of emotion focused on public matters, and the latter are sometimes characterized as odes or hymns. Among the most memorable hymns produced in the United States are the spirituals, or Sorrow Songs, created by black slaves in the United States, chiefly in the first half of the nineteenth century. The origins of the spirituals are still a matter of some dispute, but most specialists agree that the songs represent a distinctive fusion of African rhythms with European hymns.

Many of the texts derive ultimately from biblical sources: One of the chief themes, the desire for release, is sometimes presented with imagery drawn from ancient Israel. Examples include references to crossing the River Jordan (a river that runs from north of the Sea of Galilee to the Dead Sea), the release of the Israelites from slavery in Egypt (Exodus), Jonah's release from the whale (Book of Jonah), and Daniel's deliverance from a fiery furnace and from the lions' den (Book of Daniel, chapters 3 and 6).

The texts were collected and published especially in the 1860s—for instance in *Slave Songs of the United States* (1867). For another spiritual, see page 697.

ANONYMOUS AFRICAN-AMERICAN SPIRITUAL

Go Down, Moses

Pages from *Jubilee Songs* (1872), one of the earliest printed collections of spirituals.

(continued)

5.
O, 'twas a dark and dismal night,
Let my people go;
When Moses led the Israelites,
Let my people go.

6.
'Twas good old Moses and Aaron, too,
Let my people go;
'Twas they that led the armies through,
Let my people go.

7.
The Lord told Moses what to do,
Let my people go;
To lead the children of Israel through,
Let my people go.

8.
O come along Moses, you'll not get lost,
Let my people go;
Stretch out your rod and come across,
Let my people go.

9.
As Israel stood by the water side,
Let my people go;
At the command of God it did divide,
Let my people go.

10.
When they had reached the other shore,
Let my people go;
They sang a song of triumph o'er,
Let my people go.

11.
Pharaoh said he would go across,
Let my people go;
But Pharaoh and his host were lost,
Let my people go.

12.
O Moses the cloud shall cleave the way,
Let my people go;
A fire by night, a shade by day,
Let my people go.

13.
You'll not get lost in the wilderness,
Let my people go;
With a lighted candle in your breast,
Let my people go.

14.
Jordan shall stand up like a wall,
Let my people go;
And the walls of Jericho shall fall
Let my people go.

15.
Your foes shall not before you stand,
Let my people go;
And you'll possess fair Canaan's land,
Let my people go.

16.
'Twas just about in harvest time,
Let my people go;
When Joshua led his host divine,
Let my people go.

17.
O let us all from bondage flee,
Let my people go;
And let us all in Christ be free,
Let my people go

18.
We need not always weep and moan,
Let my people go;
And wear these slavery chains forlorn,
Let my people go.

19.
This world's a wilderness of woe,
Let my people go ;
O, let us on to Canaan go,
Let my people go.

20.
What a beautiful morning that will be,
Let my people go ;
When time breaks up in eternity,
Let my people go.

21.
The Devil he thought he had me fast,
Let my people go;
But I thought I'd break his chains at
Let my people go.   [last,

22.
O take yer shoes from off yer feet,
Let my people go;
And walk into the golden street,
Let my people go.

23.
I'll tell you what I likes de best,
Let my people go ;
It is the shouting Methodist,
Let my people go.

24.
I do believe without a doubt,
Let my people go;
That a Christian has the right to shout,
Let my people go.

LANGSTON HUGHES

For a biographical note, see page 476.

Evenin' Air Blues   [1942]

Folks, I come up North
Cause they told me de North was fine.
I come up North
Cause they told me de North was fine.
Been up here six months—   5
I'm about to lose my mind.

This mornin' for breakfast
I chawed de mornin' air.
This mornin' for breakfast
Chawed de mornin' air.   10
But this evenin' for supper,
I got evenin' air to spare.

Believe I'll do a little dancin'
Just to drive my blues away—
A little dancin'   15
To drive my blues away,
Cause when I'm dancin'
De blues forgets to stay.

But if you was to ask me
How de blues they come to be,   20
Says if you was to ask me
How de blues they come to be—
You wouldn't need to ask me:
Just look at me and see!

 TOPIC FOR CRITICAL THINKING OR WRITING

In what ways (subject, language) does this poem resemble blues you may
have heard? Does it differ in any ways? If so, how?

LI-YOUNG LEE

*Li-Young Lee was born in 1957 in Jakarta, Indonesia, of
Chinese parents. In 1964 his family brought him to the
United States. He was educated at the University of Pittsburgh, the University of Arizona, and the State University of New York, Brockport. He now lives in Chicago.*

I Ask My Mother to Sing   [1986]

She begins, and my grandmother joins her.
Mother and daughter sing like young girls.
If my father were alive, he would play
his accordion and sway like a boat.   4

I've never been in Peking, or the Summer Palace,
nor stood on the great Stone Boat to watch
the rain begin on Kuen Ming Lake, the picnickers
running away in the grass.   8

But I love to hear it sung;
how the waterlilies fill with rain until
they overturn, spilling water into water,
then rock back, and fill with more.   12

Both women have begun to cry.
But neither stops her song.

 TOPICS FOR CRITICAL THINKING AND WRITING

1. Why might the speaker ask the women to sing?
2. Why do the women cry? Why do they continue to sing?

EDNA ST. VINCENT MILLAY

Edna St. Vincent Millay (1892–1950) was born in Rockland, Maine. Even as a child she wrote poetry, and by the time she graduated from Vassar College (1917) she had achieved some notice as a poet. Millay settled for a while in Greenwich Village, a center of Bohemian activity in New York City, where she wrote, performed in plays, and engaged in feminist causes. In 1923, the year she married, she became the first woman to win the Pulitzer Prize for Poetry. Numerous other awards followed. Though she is best known as a lyric poet—especially as a writer of sonnets—she also wrote memorable political poetry and nature poetry as well as short stories, plays, and a libretto for an opera.

The Spring and the Fall   [1923]

In the spring of the year, in the spring of the year,
I walked the road beside my dear.
The trees were black where the bark was wet.
I see them yet, in the spring of the year.
He broke me a bough of the blossoming peach   5
That was out of the way and hard to reach.

In the fall of the year, in the fall of the year,
I walked the road beside my dear.
The rooks went up with a raucous trill.
I hear them still, in the fall of the year.   10

He laughed at all I dared to praise,
And broke my heart, in little ways.

Year be springing or year be falling,
The bark will drip and the birds be calling.
There's much that's fine to see and hear   15
In the spring of a year, in the fall of a year.
'Tis not love's going hurts my days,
But that it went in little ways.

❖ TOPICS FOR CRITICAL THINKING AND WRITING

1. The first stanza describes the generally happy beginning of a love story. Where do you find the first hint of an unhappy ending?
2. Describe the rhyme scheme of the first stanza, including internal rhymes. Do the second and third stanzas repeat the pattern, or are there some variations? What repetition of sounds other than rhyme do you note?
3. Put the last two lines into your own words. How do you react to them; that is, do you find the conclusion surprising, satisfying, recognizable from your own experience, anticlimactic, or what?
4. In two or three paragraphs, explain how the imagery of the poem (drawn from the seasons of the year) contributes to its meaning.

WILFRED OWEN

Wilfred Owen (1893–1918) was born in Shropshire, in England, and studied at London University. He enlisted in the army at the outbreak of World War I and fought in the Battle of the Somme until he was hospitalized with shell shock. After his recuperation in England, he returned to the front, only to be killed in action one week before the end of the war. His collected poems were published posthumously.

Anthem for Doomed Youth   [1920]

What passing-bells for these who die as cattle?
Only the monstrous anger of the guns.
Only the stuttering rifles' rapid rattle
Can patter out their hasty orisons.
No mockeries for them from prayers or bells,   5
Nor any voice of mourning save the choirs—
The shrill, demented choirs of wailing shells;
And bugles calling for them from sad shires.

What candles may be held to speed° them all?
Not in the hands of boys, but in their eyes   10

_____
9 **speed** aid.

Shall shine the holy glimmers of good-byes.
The pallor of girls' brows shall be their pall;
Their flowers the tenderness of patient minds,
And each slow dusk a drawing-down of blinds.

▨ TOPICS FOR CRITICAL THINKING AND WRITING

1. What is an anthem? What are some of the words or phrases in this poem that might be found in a traditional anthem? What are some of the words or phrases that you would not expect in an anthem?
2. How would you characterize the speaker's state of mind? (Your response probably will require more than one word.)

WALT WHITMAN

Walt Whitman (1819–1892) was born on Long Island, the son of a farmer. The young Whitman taught school and worked as a carpenter, a printer, a newspaper editor, and, during the Civil War, as a volunteer nurse on the Union side. After the war he supported himself by doing secretarial jobs. In Whitman's own day his poetry was highly controversial because of its unusual form (formlessness, many people said) and (though not in the following poem) its abundant erotic implications.

A Noiseless Patient Spider   [1862–63]

A noiseless patient spider,
I mark'd where on a little promontory it stood isolated,
Mark'd how to explore the vacant vast surrounding,
It launch'd forth filament, filament, filament, out of itself,
Ever unreeling them, ever tirelessly speeding them.   5

And you O my soul where you stand,
Surrounded, detached, in measureless oceans of space,
Ceaselessly musing, venturing, throwing, seeking the spheres to
    connect them,
Till the bridge you will need be form'd, till the ductile anchor hold,
Till the gossamer thread you fling catch somewhere, O my soul.   10

▨ TOPICS FOR CRITICAL THINKING AND WRITING

1. How are the suggestions in "launch'd" (line 4) and "unreeling" (line 5) continued in the second stanza?
2. How are the varying lengths of lines 1, 4, and 8 relevant to their ideas?
3. The second stanza is not a complete sentence. Why? The poem is unrhymed. What effect does the near-rhyme (*hold: soul*) in the last two lines have on you?

JOHN KEATS

John Keats (1795–1821), son of a London stable keeper, was taken out of school at age fifteen and apprenticed to a surgeon and apothecary. In 1816 he was licensed to practice as an apothecary-surgeon, but he almost immediately abandoned medicine and decided to make a career as a poet. His progress was amazing; he published books of poems—to mixed reviews—in 1817, 1818, and 1820, before dying of tuberculosis at the age of twenty-five. Today he is esteemed as one of England's greatest poets.

Ode on a Grecian Urn   [1820]

I

Thou still unravished bride of quietness,
    Thou foster-child of silence and slow time,
Sylvan historian, who canst thus express
    A flowery tale more sweetly than our rhyme:
What leaf-fringed legend haunts about thy shape   5
    Of deities or mortals, or of both,
        In Tempe or the dales of Arcady?
What men or gods are these? What maidens loth?
What mad pursuit? What struggle to escape?
    What pipes and timbrels? What wild ecstasy?   10

II

Heard melodies are sweet, but those unheard
    Are sweeter; therefore, ye soft pipes, play on;
Not to the sensual° ear, but, more endeared,
    Pipe to the spirit ditties of no tone:
Fair youth, beneath the trees, thou canst not leave   15
    Thy song, nor ever can those trees be bare;
        Bold Lover, never, never canst thou kiss,
Though winning near the goal—yet, do not grieve;
    She cannot fade, though thou hast not thy bliss,
    For ever wilt thou love, and she be fair!   20

III

Ah, happy, happy boughs! that cannot shed
    Your leaves, nor ever bid the Spring adieu;
And, happy melodist, unwearied,
    For ever piping songs for ever new;
More happy love! more happy, happy love!   25
    For ever warm and still to be enjoyed,
        For ever panting, and for ever young;
All breathing human passion far above,

---

13 **sensual** sensuous.

That leaves a heart high-sorrowful and cloyed,
  A burning forehead, and a parching tongue.   30

IV

Who are these coming to the sacrifice?
  To what green altar, O mysterious priest,
Lead'st thou that heifer lowing at the skies,
  And all her silken flanks with garlands drest?
What little town by river or sea shore,   35
  Or mountain-built with peaceful citadel,
    Is emptied of this folk, this pious morn?
And, little town, thy streets for evermore
  Will silent be; and not a soul to tell
    Why thou art desolate can e'er return.   40

V

O Attic shape! Fair attitude! with brede°
  Of marble men and maidens overwrought,
With forest branches and the trodden weed;
  Thou, silent form, dost tease us out of thought
As doth eternity: Cold Pastoral!   45
When old age shall this generation waste,
  Thou shalt remain, in midst of other woe
  Than ours, a friend to man, to whom thou say'st,
"Beauty is truth, truth beauty,"—that is all
  Ye know on earth, and all ye need to know.   50

---

41 brede design.

▓ TOPICS FOR CRITICAL THINKING AND WRITING

1. If you do not know the meaning of "sylvan," check a dictionary. Why
   does Keats call the urn a "sylvan" historian (line 3)? As the poem continues, what evidence is there that the urn cannot "express" (line 3) a
   tale so sweetly as the speaker said?
2. What do you make of lines 11–14?
3. What do you think the urn may stand for in the first three stanzas? In
   the third stanza, is the speaker caught up in the urn's world or is he
   sharply aware of his own?
4. Do you take "tease us out of thought" (line 44) to mean "draw us into a
   realm of imaginative experience superior to that of reason" or to mean
   "draw us into futile and frustrating questions"? Or both? Or neither?
   What suggestions do you find in "Cold Pastoral" (line 45)?
5. Do lines 49–50 perhaps mean that imagination, stimulated by the urn,
   achieves a realm richer than the daily world? Or perhaps that art, the
   highest earthly wisdom, suggests there is a realm wherein earthly troubles are resolved?

PAUL LAURENCE DUNBAR

Paul Laurence Dunbar (1872–1906), born in Ohio to parents who had been slaves in Kentucky, achieved fame for his dialect poetry. He published early— even while in high school—and by 1896, with the publication of Lyrics of Lowly Life, *had three books to his credit. Because he often used black speech patterns and pronunciation, Dunbar's work was sometimes thought to present demeaning racial stereotypes, but in recent years critics have seen the protest beneath the quaint surface. In the following poem, however, he works entirely within a traditional white idiom, although the subject is distinctively African-American.*

Sympathy   [1899]

I know what the caged bird feels, alas!
  When the sun is bright on the upland slopes;
When the wind stirs soft through the spring grass,
And the river flows like a stream of glass.
  When the first bird sings and the first bud opes,   5
And the faint perfume from its chalice steals—
I know what the caged bird feels!

I know why the caged bird beats his wing
  Till its blood is red on the cruel bars;
For he must fly back to his perch and cling   10
When he fain would be on the bough a-swing;
  And a pain still throbs in the old, old scars
And they pulse again with a keener sting—
I know why he beats his wing!

I know why the caged bird sings, ah me,   15
  When his wing is bruised and his bosom sore,—
When he beats his bars and he would be free;
It is not a carol of joy or glee,
  But a prayer that he sends from his heart's deep core,
But a plea, that upward to Heaven he flings—   20
I know why the caged bird sings

▓ TOPICS FOR CRITICAL THINKING AND WRITING

1. Pay careful attention to Dunbar's use of language. Describe, for example, what the comparison "like a stream of glass" in the first stanza expresses about the river, and comment on the implications of the word "chalice."

2. Some readers have felt that the second stanza is the weakest in the poem, and that the poem improves if this stanza is omitted. Why do you suppose they hold this view? Do you agree with it? Explain. Should Dunbar have dropped this stanza?

3. After reading and rereading the poem, try to summarize its overall effect. Explain why the speaker sees such an intimate connection between himself and the "caged bird."

LINDA PASTAN

*Linda Pastan was born in New York City in 1932. The author of ten books of
poems, she has won numerous prizes and has received grants from the National Endowment for the Arts. In the following poem she wittily plays with
repetitions and with pauses.*

Jump Cabling [1984]

When our cars	touched
When you lifted the hood	of mine
To see the intimate workings	underneath,
When we were bound	together
By a pulse of pure	energy,
When my car like the	princess
In the tale woke with a	start,

I thought why not ride the rest of the way together?

✺ TOPICS FOR CRITICAL THINKING AND WRITING

1. Suppose someone argued that this is merely prose broken up into arbitrary units. Would you agree? Explain.
2. As you read the poem aloud, think about the spacing that Pastan designed for it. What is the effect of the space between the first and second parts of the first seven lines? Why does she do something different for the final line?

16

The Speaking Tone of Voice

Everything is as good as it is dramatic. . . . [A poem is] heard as sung or spoken by a person in a scene—in character, in a setting. By whom, where and when is the question. By the dreamer of a better world out in a storm in Autumn; by a lover under a window at night.

—Robert Frost, Preface, *A Way Out*

If we fall into the habit of saying, "Julia Ward Howe says that her 'eyes have seen the glory of the coming of the Lord,'" or "Robert Frost says that he thinks he knows 'Whose woods these are,'" we neglect the important truth in Frost's comment about poetry as drama: A poem is written by an author (Howe, Frost), but it is spoken by an invented speaker. The author counterfeits the speech of a person in a particular situation.

The anonymous author of "Western Wind" (page 699), for instance, invents the speech of an unhappy lover who longs for the spring ("Westron wind, when will thou blow?"); Julia Ward Howe invents the speech of someone who has seen God working in this world; Robert Frost, in "Stopping by Woods on a Snowy Evening" (page 936), invents a speaker who, sitting in a horse-drawn sleigh, watches the woods fill up with snow.

The speaker's voice often has the ring of the author's own voice—certainly Robert Frost did a great deal to cultivate the idea that he was a farmer-poet—but even when the resemblance seems close, we should recall that in the poem we get a particular speaker in a particular situation. That is, we get, for instance, not the whole of Frost (the father, the competitive poet, the public lecturer, and so on), but only a man in a horse-drawn sleigh watching the woods fill up with snow. It is customary, then, in writing about the voice one hears in a poem, to write not about the author but about the **speaker,** or **voice,** or **mask,** or **persona** (Latin for "mask") that speaks the poem.

In reading a poem, the first and most important question to ask yourself is this: *Who is speaking?* If an audience and a setting are suggested, keep them in mind, too. Consider, for example, the following poem.

EMILY DICKINSON

Emily Dickinson (1830-1886) was born into a proper New England family in Amherst, Massachusetts. Because she never married, and because in her last twenty years she may never have left her house, she has sometimes been pitied. But as the critic Allen Tate said, "All pity for Miss Dickinson's 'starved life' is misdirected. Her life was one of the richest and deepest ever lived on this continent." Her brother was probably right in saying that, having seen something of the rest of the world, "she could not resist the feeling that it was painfully hollow. It was to her so thin and unsatisfying in the face of the Great Realities of Life." For a more complete biographical account, and for a selection of Dickinson's poems and letters, see Chapter 26.

I'm Nobody! Who are you?   [1861?]

I'm Nobody! Who are you?
Are you—Nobody—too?
Then there's a pair of us!
Don't tell! they'd banish us—you know!   4

How dreary—to be—Somebody!
How public—like a Frog—
To tell your name—the livelong June—
To an admiring Bog!   8

Let's consider the sort of person we hear in "I'm Nobody! Who are you?" (Read it aloud, to see if you agree. In fact, you should test each of our assertions by reading the poem aloud.) The voice in line 1 is rather like that of a child playing a game with a friend. In lines 2 and 3 the speaker sees the reader as a fellow spirit ("Are you—Nobody—too?") and invites the reader to join her ("Then there's a pair of us!") in forming a sort of conspiracy of silence against outsiders ("Don't tell!"). In "they'd banish us," however, we hear a word that a child would not be likely to use, and we probably feel that the speaker is a shy but (with the right companion) playful adult, who here is speaking to an intimate friend. And since we hear this voice—we are reading the poem—we are or we become the friend. Because "banish" is a word that brings to mind images of a king's court, the speaker almost comically inflates and thereby makes fun of the "they" who are opposed to "us."

In the second stanza, or we might better say in the space between the two stanzas, the speaker puts aside the childlike manner. In "How dreary," the first words of the second stanza, we hear a sophisticated voice, one might even say a world-weary voice, or a voice with perhaps more than a touch of condescension. But since by now we are paired with the speaker in a conspiracy against outsiders, we enjoy the contrast that the speaker makes between the Nobodies and the Somebodies. Who are these Somebodies, these people who would imperiously "banish" the speaker and the friend? What are the Somebodies like?

How dreary—to be—Somebody!
How public—like a Frog—
To tell your name—the livelong June—
To an admiring Bog!

The last two lines do at least two things: They amusingly explain to the speaker's new friend (the reader) in what way a Somebody is public (it proclaims its presence all day). They also indicate the absurdity of the Somebody-

Frog's behavior (the audience is "an admiring Bog"). By the end of the poem we are quite convinced that it is better to be a Nobody (like Dickinson's speaker, and the reader?) than a Somebody (a loudmouth, like a croaking frog).

Often we tend to think of reading as something we do in private, and silently. But it is important to remember that writers, especially poets, care greatly about how their words *sound*. Poets pay attention not only to how the poem is arranged on the page—the length of the lines, for example—but also to how the poem sounds when actually read aloud, or, at least, when heard within the reader's mind.

One of the pleasures of reading literature, in fact, is the pleasure of listening to the sound of a voice, with its special rhythms, tones, accents, and emphases. Getting to know a poem, and becoming engaged by a poet's style, is very much a matter of getting to know a voice, acquiring a feeling for its familiar intonations, yet also being surprised, puzzled, even startled by it on occasion.

If you have done a little acting, you know from this experience how crucial it is to discover the way a character's lines in a play should sound. Directors and actors spend a great deal of time reading the lines, trying them in a variety of ways to catch their truest pace and verbal shape. And so do poets. We aren't making this up; in a letter, Robert Frost talks about "the sound of sense," a sort of abstraction in which an emotion or attitude comes through, even if the words are not clearly heard. He writes:

> The best place to get the abstract sound of sense is from voices behind a door that cuts off the words. Ask yourself how these sentences would sound without the words in which they are embodied:
>
> > You mean to tell me you can't read?
> > I said no such thing.
> > Well read then.
> > You're not my teacher.

In another letter, continuing the discussion of the topic, after giving some additional examples (for instance, "Unless I'm greatly mistaken," "No fool like an old fool"), Frost says, "It is so and not otherwise that we get the variety that makes it fun to write and read. *The ear does it.* The ear is the only true writer and the only true reader." (For a group of poems by Frost, see Chapter 26.)

In reading, then, your goal is to achieve a deeper sense of character—what this voice sounds like, what kind of person speaks like this. Read aloud; imagine how the writer might have meant his or her words to sound; read aloud again; and listen carefully all the while to the echoes and resonances of the words.

Consider the dramatic situation and the voices in the following poems.

GWENDOLYN BROOKS

Gwendolyn Brooks (1917–2000) was born in Topeka, Kansas, but was raised in Chicago's South Side, where she spent most of her life. In 1950, when she won the Pulitzer Prize for Poetry, she became the first African-American writer to win a Pulitzer Prize.

We Real Cool

[1960]

The Pool Players.
Seven at the Golden Shovel.

We real cool. We
Left school. We

Lurk late. We
Strike straight. We

Sing sin. We   5
Thin gin. We

Jazz June. We
Die soon.

✸ TOPICS FOR CRITICAL THINKING AND WRITING

1. Exactly why do you identify the speaker as you do?
2. The stanzas could have been written thus:

> We real cool.
> We left school.
>
> We lurk late.
> We strike straight.

And so forth. Why do you think Brooks wrote them, or printed them, the way she did?

Here is another poem by the same poet, speaking in a different voice.

The Mother

[1945]

Abortions will not let you forget.
You remember the children you got that you did not get,
The damp small pulps with a little or with no hair,
The singers and workers that never handled the air.
You will never neglect or beat   5
Them, or silence or buy with a sweet.
You will never wind up the sucking-thumb
Or scuttle off ghosts that come.
You will never leave them, controlling your luscious sigh,
Return for a snack of them, with gobbling mother-eye.   10

I have heard in the voices of the wind the voices of my
    dim killed children.
I have contracted. I have eased
My dim dears at the breasts they could never suck.
I have said, Sweets, if I sinned, if I seized
Your luck   15

And your lives from your unfinished reach,
If I stole your births and your names,
Your straight baby tears and your games,
Your stilted or lovely loves, your tumults, your marriages,
     aches, and your deaths,
If I poisoned the beginnings of your breaths,   20
Believe that even in my deliberateness I was not deliberate.
Though why should I whine,
Whine that the crime was other than mine?—
Since anyhow you are dead.
Or rather, or instead,   25
You were never made.
But that too, I am afraid,
Is faulty: oh, what shall I say, how is the truth to be said?
You were born, you had body, you died.
It is just that you never giggled or planned or cried.   30

Believe me, I loved you all.
Believe me, I knew you, though faintly, and I loved, I loved you
All.

▓ TOPICS FOR CRITICAL THINKING AND WRITING

1. Whom is being addressed?
2. The first ten lines sound like a chant. What gives them that quality? What makes them nonetheless serious?
3. In lines 20–23 the mother attempts to deny the "crime" but cannot. What is her reasoning here?
4. Do you find the last lines convincing? Explain.
5. The poem was first published in 1945. Do you think that the abundant debate about abortion in recent years has somehow made the poem seem dated, or more timely than ever? Explain.

LINDA PASTAN

Linda Pastan was born in New York City in 1932 and educated at Radcliffe College, Simmons College, and Brandeis University. The author of ten books of poems, she has won numerous prizes and has received a grant from the National Endowment for the Arts.

Marks   [1978]

My husband gives me an A
for last night's supper,
an incomplete for my ironing,
a B plus in bed.
My son says I am average,
an average mother, but if
I put my mind to it

I could improve.
My daughter believes
in Pass/Fail and tells me
I pass. Wait 'til they learn
I'm dropping out.

TOPICS FOR CRITICAL THINKING AND WRITING

1. In addition to the A and B that are mentioned, where else in the poem does Pastan use the language of the world of the school? The speaker of the poem receives grades, but does she also give a grade, or imply one?
2. What would be gained or lost if Pastan's first sentence came last?

THE READER AS THE SPEAKER

We have been arguing that the speaker of the poem usually is not the author but a dramatized form of the author, and that we overhear this speaker in some situation. But with poems of the sort that we have been looking at, we can also say that *the reader* is the speaker. That is, as we read the poem, at least to some degree *we* utter the thoughts, and *we* experience the sensations or emotions that the writer sets forth. We feel that Dickinson has allowed us to set forth our own feelings about what it is to be Nobody in a world where others are Somebody (and she has also helped us to say that the Somebody is a noisy frog); with Brooks we hear or overhear thoughts and feelings that perhaps strike us as more relevant and more profound and more moving than most of what we hear on television or read in the newspapers about urban violence.

In the following poem you will hear at least three voices—the voice of the person who begins the poem by telling us about a dead man ("Nobody heard him, the dead man"), the voice of the dead man ("I was much further out than you thought / And not waving but drowning"), and the collective voice of the dead man's friends ("Poor chap, he always loved larking"). But see if you don't find that all of the voices together say things that you have said (or almost said).

STEVIE SMITH

Stevie Smith (1902–1971), christened Florence Margaret Smith, was born in England, in Hull. In addition to writing poems, she wrote stories, essays, and three novels. She is the subject of a film, Stevie, *in which Glenda Jackson plays Smith.*

Not Waving but Drowning

[1957]

Nobody heard him, the dead man,
But still he lay moaning:
I was much further out than you thought
And not waving but drowning.   4

Poor chap, he always loved larking
And now he's dead
It must have been too cold for him his heart gave way,
They said.   8

Oh, no no no, it was too cold always
(Still the dead one lay moaning)
I was much too far out all my life
And not waving but drowning.   12

▓ TOPICS FOR CRITICAL THINKING AND WRITING

1. Identify the speaker of each line.
2. What sort of man did the friends of the dead man think he was? What
   type of man do you think he was?
3. The first line, "Nobody heard him, the dead man," is literally true. Dead
   men do not speak. In what other ways is it true?

WISLAWA SZYMBORSKA

*Wislawa Szymborska (pronounced "Vislawa Zimborska"), a native of Poland,
was born in 1923. In 1996 she received the Nobel Prize for poetry.*

The Terrorist, He Watches   [1981]

Translated by Robert A. Maguire and Magnus Jan Krynski

The bomb will go off in the bar at one twenty p.m.
Now it's only one sixteen p.m.
Some will still have time to get in,
some to get out.

The terrorist has already crossed to the other side of the street.   5
The distance protects him from any danger,
and what a sight for sore eyes:

A woman in a yellow jacket, she goes in.
A man in dark glasses, he comes out.

Guys in jeans, they are talking.   10
One seventeen and four seconds.
That shorter guy's really got it made, and gets on a scooter,
and that taller one, he goes in.

One seventeen and forty seconds.
That girl there, she's got a green ribbon in her hair.   15
Too bad that bus just cut her off.
One eighteen p.m.
The girl's not there any more.
Was she dumb enough to go in, or wasn't she?
That we'll see when they carry them out.   20

One nineteen p.m.
No one seems to be going in.
Instead a fat baldy's coming out.
Like he's looking for something in his pockets and
at one nineteen and fifty seconds   25
he goes back for those lousy gloves of his.

It's one twenty p.m.
The time, how it drags.
Should be any moment now.
Not yet.   30
Yes, this is it.
The bomb, it goes off.

▓ TOPICS FOR CRITICAL THINKING AND WRITING

1. Who speaks the poem? The terrorist? Or someone watching the terrorist? Or a sort of combination? Or what?
2. Characterize the speaker.

JOHN UPDIKE

*John Updike (b. 1932) is best known as a writer of fiction—short stories and
novels—but throughout his professional career he has also written essays
and poems. (For a more complete biographical note, see page 101.)*

Icarus   [2001]

O.K., you are sitting in an airplane and
the person in the seat next to you is a sweaty, swarthy gentleman
        of Middle Eastern origin
whose carry-on luggage consists of a bulky black brief-case he
        stashes,
in compliance with airline regulations,
underneath the seat ahead.   5
He keeps looking at his watch and closing his eyes in prayer,
resting his profusely dank forehead against the seatback ahead of him
just above the black briefcase,
which if you listen through the droning of the engines seems to be
        ticking, ticking
softly, softer than your heartbeat in your ears.   10

Who wants to have all their careful packing—the travellers' checks,
        the folded underwear—
end as floating sea-wrack five miles below,
drifting in a rainbow scum of jet fuel,
and their docile hopes of a plastic-wrapped meal
dashed in a concussion whiter than the sun?   15

I say to my companion, "Smooth flight so far."
"So far."
"That's quite a briefcase you've got there."
He shrugs and says, "It contains my life's work."
"And what is it, exactly, that you do?"   20
"You could say I am a lobbyist."

He does not want to talk.
He wants to keep praying.
His hands, with their silky beige backs and their nails cut close like
  a technician's,
tremble and jump in handling the plastic glass of Sprite when it   25
  comes with its exploding bubbles.

Ah, but one gets swept up
in the airport throng, all those workaday faces,
faintly pampered and spoiled in the boomer style,
and those elders dressed like children for flying
in hi-tech sneakers and polychrome catsuits,   30
and those gum-chewing attendants taking tickets
while keeping up a running flirtation with a uniformed bystander,
  a stoic blond pilot—
all so normal, who could resist
this vault into the impossible?

Your sweat has slowly dried. Your praying neighbor   35
has fallen asleep, emitting an odor of cardamom.
His briefcase seems to have deflated.
Perhaps not this time, then.
But the possibility of impossibility will keep drawing us back
to this scrape against the numbed sky,   40
to this sleek sheathed tangle of color-coded wires, these million rivets,
  this wing
like a frozen lake at your elbow.

▣ TOPICS FOR CRITICAL THINKING AND WRITING

1. Take a moment to look up the Icarus myth in a classical dictionary or encyclopedia. Do you see connections between the myth and the story that Updike tells in this poem?
2. Who is the "you" in the first line?
3. What kinds of assumptions does the poem make about the "gentleman of Middle Eastern origin"? Are these assumptions challenged? Point to specific details in the language to explain your responses.
4. What kind of conclusion does the poem reach?
5. Does "Icarus" disturb you? If so, why?
6. Which poem do you think is more effective; Updike's "Icarus" or Szymborska's "The Terrorist"? What, more generally, does it mean to say that one poem is more effective than another?

THE DRAMATIC MONOLOGUE

We have said at some length that in most poems the speaker is not quite the author (say, Robert Frost) but is a dramatized version (a man sitting in a sleigh, watching the "woods fill up with snow"). We have also said that in most poems the reader can imagine himself or herself as the speaker; as we read Dickinson or even Brooks and Pastan, we say to ourselves that the poet is expressing thoughts and emotions that might be our own. But in some poems the poet creates so distinct a speaker that the character clearly is not us but is something Other. Such a poem is called a **dramatic monologue.** In it, a highly specific character speaks, in a clearly specified situation. The most famous example is Robert Browning's "My Last Duchess," where a Renaissance duke is addressing an emissary from a count.

ROBERT BROWNING

Born in a suburb of London into a middle-class family, Browning (1812–1889) was educated primarily at home, where he read widely. For a while he wrote for the English stage, but after marrying Elizabeth Barrett in 1846—she too was a poet—he lived with her in Italy until her death in 1861. He then returned to England and settled in London with their son. Regarded as one of the most distinguished poets of the Victorian period, he is buried in Westminster Abbey.

My Last Duchess

[1844]

Ferrara*

That's my last Duchess painted on the wall,
Looking as if she were alive. I call
That piece a wonder, now; Frà Pandolf's° hands
Worked busily a day, and there she stands.
Will't please you sit and look at her? I said   5
"Frà Pandolf" by design, for never read
Strangers like you that pictured countenance,
The depth and passion of its earnest glance,
But to myself they turned (since none puts by
The curtain I have drawn for you, but I)   10
And seemed as they would ask me, if they durst,
How such a glance came there; so, not the first
Are you to turn and ask thus. Sir, 'twas not
Her husband's presence only, called that spot
Of joy into the Duchess' cheek; perhaps   15
Frà Pandolf chanced to say "Her mantle laps

---

*Ferrara** town in Italy.   **3 Frà Pandolf** a fictitious painter.

Over my Lady's wrist too much," or, "Paint
Must never hope to reproduce the faint
Half-flush that dies along her throat." Such stuff
Was courtesy, she thought, and cause enough   20
For calling up that spot of joy. She had
A heart—how shall I say?—too soon made glad,
Too easily impressed; she liked whate'er
She looked on, and her looks went everywhere.
Sir, 'twas all one! My favor at her breast,   25
The dropping of the daylight in the west,
The bough of cherries some officious fool
Broke in the orchard for her, the white mule
She rode with round the terrace—all and each
Would draw from her alike the approving speech,   30
Or blush, at least. She thanked men—good! but thanked
Somehow—I know not how—as if she ranked
My gift of a nine-hundred-years-old name
With anybody's gift. Who'd stoop to blame
This sort of trifling? Even had you skill   35
In speech—(which I have not)—to make your will
Quite clear to such an one, and say, "Just this
Or that in you disgusts me; here you miss,
Or there exceed the mark"—and if she let
Herself be lessoned so, nor plainly set   40
Her wits to yours, forsooth, and made excuse,
—E'en then would be some stooping; and I choose
Never to stoop. Oh, Sir, she smiled, no doubt,
Whene'er I passed her; but who passed without
Much the same smile? This grew; I gave commands;   45
Then all smiles stopped together. There she stands
As if alive. Will't please you rise? We'll meet
The company below, then. I repeat,
The Count your master's known munificence
Is ample warrant that no just pretense   50
Of mine for dowry will be disallowed;
Though his fair daughter's self, as I avowed
At starting, is my object. Nay, we'll go
Together down, Sir. Notice Neptune, though,
Taming a sea-horse, thought a rarity,   55
Which Claus of Innsbruck° cast in bronze for me!

---

56 Claus of Innsbruck a fictitious sculptor.

� TOPICS FOR CRITICAL THINKING AND WRITING

1. What is the occasion for the meeting?
2. What words or lines do you think especially convey the speaker's arrogance? What is your attitude toward the speaker? Loathing? Fascination? Respect? Explain.

3. The time and place are Renaissance Italy; how do they affect your attitude toward the duke? What would be the effect if the poem were set in the late twentieth century?

4. Years after writing this poem, Browning explained that the duke's "commands" (line 45) were "that she should be put to death, or he might have had her shut up in a convent." Do you think the poem should have been more explicit? Does Browning's later uncertainty indicate that the poem is badly thought out? Suppose we did not have Browning's comment on line 45. Do you think the line then could mean only that he commanded her to stop smiling and that she obeyed? Explain.

DICTION AND TONE

From the whole of language, one consciously or unconsciously selects certain words and grammatical constructions; this selection constitutes one's **diction.** It is partly by the diction that we come to know the speaker of a poem. Stevie Smith's speaker (page 723) used words such as "chap" and "larking," which are scarcely imaginable in the mouth of Browning's Renaissance duke. But of course some words are used in both poems: "I," "you," "thought," "the," and so on. The fact remains, however, that although a large part of language is shared by all speakers, certain parts of language are used only by certain speakers.

Like some words, some grammatical constructions are used only by certain kinds of speakers. Consider these two passages:

In Adam's fall
We sinned all.
　　　　　　　　　　—Anonymous, *The New England Primer*

Of Man's first disobedience, and the fruit
Of that forbidden tree whose mortal taste
Brought death into the World, and all our woe,
With loss of Eden, till one greater Man
Restore us, and regain the blissful seat,
Sing, Heavenly Muse, that, on the secret top
Of Oreb, or of Sinai, didst inspire
That shepherd who first taught the chosen seed
In the beginning how the heavens and earth
Rose out of Chaos. . . .
　　　　　　　　　　—John Milton, *Paradise Lost*

There is an enormous difference in the diction of these two passages. Milton, speaking as an inspired poet, appropriately uses words and grammatical constructions somewhat removed from common life. Hence, while the anonymous author of the primer speaks directly of "Adam's fall," Milton speaks allusively of the fall, calling it "Man's first disobedience." Milton's sentence is nothing that any Englishman ever said in conversation; its genitive beginning ("Of Man's first disobedience"), its length (the sentence continues for six lines beyond the quoted passage), and its postponement of the main verb ("Sing") until the sixth line mark it as the utterance of a poet working in the tradition of Latin poetry. The primer's statement, by its choice of words as well as by its brevity, suggests a far less sophisticated speaker.

Speakers have attitudes toward themselves, their subjects, and their audiences, and (consciously or unconsciously) they choose their words, pitch, and modulation accordingly; all these add up to the **tone.** In written literature, tone must be detected without the aid of the ear; the reader must understand by the selection and sequence of words the way in which they are meant to be heard (that is, playfully, angrily, confidentially, sarcastically, etc.). The reader must catch what Frost calls "the speaking tone of voice somehow entangled in the words and fastened to the page of the ear of the imagination."

Finally, we should mention that although this discussion concentrates on the speaker's tone, one can also talk of the author's tone, that is, of the author's attitude toward the invented speaker. The speaker's tone might, for example, be angry, but the author's tone (as detected by the reader) might be humorous.

ROBERT HERRICK

Robert Herrick (1591–1674) was born in London, the son of a goldsmith. After taking an M.A. at Cambridge, he was ordained in the Church of England. Later, he was sent to the country parish of Dean Prior in Devonshire, where he wrote most of his poetry. A loyal supporter of the king, in 1647 he was expelled from his parish by the Puritans, though in 1662 he was restored to Dean Prior.

To the Virgins, to Make Much of Time   [1648]

Gather ye rosebuds while ye may,
   Old Time is still a-flying;
And this same flower that smiles today,
   Tomorrow will be dying.   4

The glorious lamp of heaven, the sun,
   The higher he's a-getting,
The sooner will his race be run,
   And nearer he's to setting.   8

That age is best which is the first,
   When youth and blood are warmer;
But being spent, the worse, and worst
   Times still succeed the former.   12

Then be not coy, but use your time;
   And while ye may, go marry:
For having lost but once your prime,
   You may for ever tarry.   16

Carpe diem (Latin: "seize the day") is the theme. But if we want to get the full force of the poem, we must understand who is talking to whom. Look, for example, at "Old Time" in line 2. Time is "old" in the sense of having been around a long while, but doesn't "old" in this context suggest also that the speaker regards Time with easy familiarity, almost affection? We visit the old school, and our friend is old George. Time is destructive, yes, and the speaker urges the young maidens to make the most of their spring. But the speaker is neither bitter nor importunate; rather, he seems to be the wise old man, the counselor, the man who has made his peace with Time and is giving advice to the young. Time moves rapidly in the poem (the rosebud of line 1 is already a flower in line 3), but the speaker is unhurried; in line 5 he has leisure to explain that the glorious lamp of heaven is the sun.

In "To the Virgins," the pauses, indicated by punctuation at the ends of the lines (except in line 11, where we tumble without stopping from "worst" to "Times"), slow the reader down. But even if there is no punctuation at the end of a line of poetry, the reader probably pauses slightly or gives the final word an additional bit of emphasis. Similarly, the space between stanzas slows a reader down, increasing the emphasis on the last word of one stanza and the first word of the next.

THOMAS HARDY

Thomas Hardy (1840-1928) was born in Dorset, England, the son of a stonemason. Despite great obstacles he studied the classics and architecture, and in 1862 he moved to London to study and practice as an architect. Ill health forced him to return to Dorset, where he continued to work as an architect and to write. Best known for his novels, Hardy ceased writing fiction after the hostile reception of Jude the Obscure *in 1896 and turned to writing lyric poetry.*

The Man He Killed

[1902]

"Had he and I but met
By some old ancient inn,
We should have sat us down to wet
Right many a nipperkin!°   4

"But ranged as infantry,
And staring face to face,
I shot at him as he at me,
And killed him in his place.   8

"I shot him dead because—
Because he was my foe,
Just so: my foe of course he was;
That's clear enough; although   12

"He thought he'd 'list, perhaps,
Off-hand like—just as I—
Was out of work—had sold his traps°—
No other reason why.   16

"Yes; quaint and curious war is!
You shoot a fellow down
You'd treat if met where any bar is,
Or help to half-a-crown."   20

---

4 nipperkin cup.   **15 traps** personal belongings.

 TOPICS FOR CRITICAL THINKING AND WRITING

1. What do we learn about the speaker's life before he enlisted in the infantry? How does his diction characterize him?
2. What is the effect of the series of monosyllables in lines 7 and 8?
3. Consider the punctuation of the third and fourth stanzas. Why are the heavy, frequent pauses appropriate? What question is the speaker trying to answer?
4. In the last stanza, what attitudes toward war does the speaker express? What, from the evidence of this poem, would you infer Hardy's attitude toward war to be?

WALTER DE LA MARE

Walter de la Mare (1873-1956) was born in Kent, England. He worked for many years as an accountant for the Anglo-American Oil Company until a legacy enabled him to devote his life to writing lyric poetry and fiction.

An Epitaph   [1925]

Here lies a most beautiful lady:
Light of step and heart was she;
I think she was the most beautiful lady
That ever was in the West Country.   4

But beauty vanishes; beauty passes;
However rare—rare it be;
And when I crumble, who will remember
This lady of the West Country?   8

 TOPICS FOR CRITICAL THINKING AND WRITING

1. Who is the speaker of the poem?
2. Do you think that the simple language lacks dignity? In some older poetry, especially poetry that was passed down orally, a word of two syllables at the end of the line has the stress on the second syllable, as "sailór." In this poem, what is the effect of rhyming "country" and "she" and "be"?
3. Do you think that the last two lines introduce a new idea, or do they deepen the implications of the earlier lines? When you read aloud the final stanza, pay special notice to the pause at the end of line 6. How does your voice register the movement from line 6 to line 7?

GERARD MANLEY HOPKINS

Gerard Manley Hopkins (1844-1889) was born near London and educated at Oxford, where he studied the classics. A convert from Anglicanism to Roman Catholicism, he was ordained a Jesuit priest in 1877. After serving as a parish priest and teacher, he was appointed Professor of Greek at the Catholic University in Dublin. Hopkins published only a few poems during his lifetime, partly because he believed that the pursuit of literary fame was incompatible with his vocation as a priest, and partly because he was aware that his highly individual style might puzzle readers.

Spring and Fall: To a Young Child

[1884]

Márgarét, are you gríeving
Over Goldengrove unleaving?
Léaves, líke the things of man, you
With your fresh thoughts care for, can you?
Áh! ás the heart grows older   5
It will come to such sights colder
By and by, nor spare a sigh
Though worlds of wanwood leafmeal lie;
And yet you will weep and know why.
Now no matter, child, the name: 10
Sórrow's spríngs áre the same.
Nor mouth had, no nor mind, expressed
What heart heard of, ghost° guessed:
It ís the blight man was born for,
It ís Margaret you mourn for.   15

_____
13 ghost spirit.

 TOPICS FOR CRITICAL THINKING AND WRITING

1. About how old do you think the speaker is? What is his tone? What connection can you make between the title and the speaker and Margaret? What meanings do you think may be in "Fall"?
2. What is meant by Margaret's "fresh thoughts" (line 4)? Paraphrase (put into your own words) lines 3-4 and lines 12-13.
3. "Wanwood" and "leafmeal" are words coined by Hopkins. What do they suggest to you?
4. How can you explain the apparent contradiction that Margaret weeps for herself (line 15) after the speaker has said that she weeps for "Goldengrove unleaving" (line 2)?

COUNTEE CULLEN

Countee Cullen (1903-1946) was born Countee Porter in New York City, raised by his grandmother, and then adopted by the Reverend Frederick A. Cullen, a Methodist minister in Harlem. Cullen received a bachelor's degree from New York University (Phi Beta Kappa) and a master's degree from Harvard. He earned his living as a high school teacher of French, but his literary gifts were recognized in his own day. Cullen sometimes wrote about black life, but he also wrote on other topics, insisting that African-Americans need not work only in the literary tradition exemplified by such writers as Langston Hughes.

For a Lady I Know   [1925]

She even thinks that up in heaven
   Her class lies late and snores,
While poor black cherubs rise at seven
   To do celestial chores.

▓ TOPICS FOR CRITICAL THINKING AND WRITING

1. What is the gist of what Cullen is saying?
2. How would you characterize the tone? Furious? Indifferent?

LYN LIFSHIN

Born in Burlington, Vermont, in 1944 and educated at Syracuse University and the University of Vermont, Lyn Lifshin has written many books of poetry on a range of topics, from Shaker communities of early America to Eskimo culture in the Arctic. Much of her work shows a strong feminist concern.

My Mother and the Bed   [1999]

No, not that way she'd
say when I was 7, pulling
the bottom sheet smooth,
you've got to   saying
hospital corners   5

I wet the bed much later
than I should, until
just writing this I
hadn't thought of
the connection   10

My mother would never
sleep on sheets someone
else had   I never
saw any stains on hers
tho her bedroom was   15

a maze of powder   hair
pins   black dresses
Sometimes she brings her
own sheets to my house,
carries toilet seat covers   20

Did anybody sleep
in my   she always asks
Her sheets   her hair
she says the rooms here
smell funny   25

We drive at 3 am
slowly into Boston and
strip what looks like
two clean beds as the
sky gets light   I   30

smooth on the form
fitted flower bottom,
she redoes it

She thinks of my life
as a bed only she   35
can make right

▨ TOPICS FOR CRITICAL THINKING AND WRITING

1. What do you make of the extra spaces—for instance, the space between "to" and "saying" in line 4? In reading the poem aloud, how do
   you "read" the spaces?
2. Would you agree that the poem is humorous and, on the whole, genial?
   Or do you think that bitterness overshadows the humor? Explain.
3. One student made the suggestion that the final stanza, perhaps because
   it seems to "explain" the poem to the reader, is the least effective part
   of the poem. Do you agree? If you do, write a new final stanza.

THE VOICE OF THE SATIRIST

The writer of **satire,** in one way or another, ridicules an aspect or several aspects of human behavior, seeking to arouse in the reader some degree of
amused contempt for the object. However urbane in tone, the satirist is always
critical. By cleverly holding up foibles or vices for the world's derision, satire
(Alexander Pope claimed) "heals with morals what it hurts with wit." The laughter of comedy is an end in itself; the laughter of satire is a weapon against the
world: "The intellectual dagger," Frank O'Connor called satire, "opposing the
real dagger." Jonathan Swift, of whom O'Connor is speaking, insisted that his
satires were not malice but medicine:

His satire points at no defect
But what all mortals may correct. . . .
He spared a hump or crooked nose,
Whose owners set not up for beaux.

But Swift, although he claimed that satire is therapeutic, also saw its futility:
"Satire is a sort of glass [i.e., mirror] wherein beholders do generally discover
everybody's face but their own."

Sometimes the satirist speaks out directly as defender of public morals, abusively but wittily chopping off heads. Byron, for example, wrote:

> Prepare for rhyme—I'll publish, right or wrong:
> Fools are my theme, let Satire be my song.

But sometimes the satirist chooses to invent a speaker far removed from himself or herself, just as Browning chose to invent a Renaissance duke. The satirist may invent a callous brigadier general or a pompous judge who unconsciously annihilates himself. Consider this satirical poem by e. e. cummings (pen name of Edwin Estlin Cummings).

E. E. CUMMINGS

Edwin Estlin Cummings (1894-1962) grew up in Cambridge, Massachusetts, and was graduated from Harvard, where he became interested in modern literature and art, especially in the movements called cubism and futurism. His father, a conservative clergyman and a professor at Harvard, seems to have been baffled by the youth's interests, but Cummings's mother encouraged his artistic activities, including his use of unconventional punctuation as a means of expression.

Politically liberal in his youth, Cummings became more conservative after a visit to Russia in 1931, but early and late his work emphasizes individuality and freedom of expression.

next to of course god america i   [1926]

"next to of course god america i
love you land of the pilgrims' and so forth oh
say can you see by the dawn's early my
country 'tis of centuries come and go
and are no more what of it we should worry   5
in every language even deafanddumb
thy sons acclaim your glorious name by gorry
by jingo by gee by gosh by gum
why talk of beauty what could be more beaut-
iful than these heroic happy dead   10
who rushed like lions to the roaring slaughter
they did not stop to think they died instead
then shall the voice of liberty be mute?"

He spoke. And drank rapidly a glass of water

Cummings might have written, in the voice of a solid citizen or a good poet, a direct attack on chauvinistic windbags; instead, he chose to invent a windbag whose rhetoric punctures itself. Yet the last line tells that we are really hearing someone who is recounting what the windbag said; that is, the speaker of all the lines but the last is a combination of the chauvinist *and* the satiric observer of the chauvinist. (When Cummings himself recited these lines, there was mockery in his voice.)

Only in the final line of the poem does the author seem to speak entirely on his own, and even here he adopts a matter-of-fact pose that is far more potent than **invective** (direct abuse) would be. Yet the last line is not totally free of explicit hostility. It might, for example, have run, "He spoke. And slowly poured a glass of water." Why does this version lack the punch of Cummings's? And what do you think is implied by the absence of a final period in line 14?

MARGE PIERCY

Marge Piercy, born in Detroit in 1936, was the first member of her family to attend college. After earning a bachelor's degree from the University of Michigan in 1957 and a master's degree from Northwestern University in 1958, she moved to Chicago. There she worked at odd jobs while writing novels (unpublished) and engaging in action on behalf of women and blacks and against the war in Vietnam. In 1970—the year she moved to Wellfleet, Massachusetts, where she still lives—she published her first book, a novel. Since then she has published other novels, as well as short stories, poems, and essays.

Barbie Doll

[1969]

This girlchild was born as usual
and presented dolls that did pee-pee
and miniature GE stoves and irons
and wee lipsticks the color of cherry candy.
Then in the magic of puberty, a classmate said: 5
You have a great big nose and fat legs.

She was healthy, tested intelligent,
possessed strong arms and back,
abundant sexual drive and manual dexterity.
She went to and fro apologizing.   10
Everyone saw a fat nose on thick legs.

She was advised to play coy,
exhorted to come on hearty,
exercise, diet, smile and wheedle.
Her good nature wore out   15
like a fan belt.
So she cut off her nose and her legs
and offered them up.
In the casket displayed on satin she lay
with the undertaker's cosmetics painted on,   20
a turned-up putty nose,
dressed in a pink and white nightie.
Doesn't she look pretty? everyone said.
Consummation at last.
To every woman a happy ending.   25

TOPICS FOR CRITICAL THINKING AND WRITING

1. Why is the poem called "Barbie Doll"?
2. What voice do you hear in lines 1–4? Line 6 is, we are told, the voice of "a classmate." How do these voices differ? What voice do you hear in the first three lines of the second stanza?
3. Explain in your own words what Piercy is saying about women in this poem. Does her view seem to you fair, slightly exaggerated, or greatly exaggerated?

LOUISE ERDRICH

Louise Erdrich, born in 1954 in Little Falls, Minnesota, grew up in North Dakota, a member of the Turtle Mountain Band of Chippewa. Her father had been born in Germany; her mother was a Chippewa; both parents taught at the Bureau of Indian Affairs School. After graduating from Dartmouth College (major in anthropology) in 1976, Erdrich returned briefly to North Dakota to teach in the Poetry in the Schools Program, and went to Johns Hopkins University, where she earned a master's degree in creative writing.

Erdrich has published two books of poems and several novels, one of which, Love Medicine *(1986), won the National Book Critics Circle Award. We publish one of her short stories, "The Red Convertible," in Chapter 11.*

Dear John Wayne

[1984]

August and the drive-in picture is packed.
We lounge on the hood of the Pontiac
surrounded by the slow-burning spirals they sell
at the window, to vanquish the hordes of mosquitoes.
Nothing works. They break through the smoke screen for blood.   5

Always the lookout spots the Indians first,
spread north to south, barring progress.
The Sioux or some other Plains bunch
in spectacular columns, ICBM missiles,
feathers bristling in the meaningful sunset.   10

The drum breaks. There will be no parlance.
Only the arrows whining, a death-cloud of nerves
swarming down on the settlers
who die beautifully, tumbling like dust weeds
into the history that brought us all here   15
together: this wide screen beneath the sign of the bear.

The sky fills, acres of blue squint and eye
that the crowd cheers. His face moves over us,
a thick cloud of vengeance, pitted
like the land that was once flesh. Each rut,   20
each scar makes a promise: *It is*

not over, this fight, not as long as you resist.
Everything we see belongs to us.

A few laughing Indians fall over the hood
slipping in the hot spilled butter.   25
The eye sees a lot, John, but the heart is so blind.
Death makes us owners of nothing.
He smiles, a horizon of teeth
the credits reel over, and then the white fields
again blowing in the true-to-life dark.   30
The dark films over everything.
We get into the car
scratching our mosquito bites, speechless and small
as people are when the movie is done.
We are back in our skins.   35
How can we help but keep hearing his voice,
the flip side of the sound track, still playing:
Come on, boys, we got them
where we want them, drunk, running.
They'll give us what we want, what we need.   40

Even his disease was the idea of taking everything.
Those cells, burning, doubling, splitting out of their skins.

✳ TOPICS FOR CRITICAL THINKING AND WRITING

1. Who is the speaker of most of the poem? Who speaks the italicized lines?
2. There are curious shifts in the diction, for instance from "some other Plains bunch" (line 8) to "parlance" (line 11). Whose voice do we hear in "some . . . bunch"? Consider, too, the diction in "to vanquish the hordes of mosquitoes" (line 4). If you were talking about mosquitoes, you probably would not use the word "vanquish." What do you think Erdrich is up to?
3. What do you make of lines 24–25, talking of Indians "slipping in the hot spilled butter"? What connection do these lines have with what presumably is going on in the film?

JONATHAN SWIFT

Jonathan Swift (1667–1745), born in Ireland of English parents, became dean of St. Patrick's Cathedral, Dublin, but he also had a significant career as a propagandist for the Tory party in England. He is significant today, however, neither for his ecclesiastical nor his political work. Rather, he is best known for a short satiric essay, "A Modest Proposal," and for a longer prose satire, Gulliver's Travels *(1725), which, because some of its characters are giants and others are only a few inches tall, has had the curious fate of being regarded as a book for children.*

Swift's poetry ranges from the tender to the scatological. We reprint one of his satiric poems, a scathing elegy celebrating the death of John Churchill, Duke of Marlborough, who died in 1722.

A Satirical Elegy on the Death of a Late Famous General

[1764]

His Grace!° impossible! what, dead!
Of old age too, and in his bed!
And could that Mighty Warrior fall?
And so inglorious, after all!
Well, since he's gone, no matter how,   5
The last loud trump must wake him now:
And, trust me, as the noise grows stronger,
He'd wish to sleep a little longer.
And could he be indeed so old
As by the newspapers we're told?   10
Threescore, I think, is pretty high;
'Twas time in conscience he should die.
This world he cumbered long enough;
He burnt his candle to the snuff;
And that's the reason, some folks think,   15
He left behind *so great a s...k.*
Behold his funeral appears,
Nor widow's sighs, nor orphan's tears,
Wont at such times each heart to pierce,
Attend the progress of his hearse.   20
But what of that, his friends may say,
He had those honors in his day.
True to his profit and his pride,
He made them weep before he died.

Come hither, all ye empty things,   25
Ye bubbles raised by breath of Kings;
Who float upon the tide of state,
Come hither, and behold your fate.
Let pride be taught by this rebuke,
How very mean a thing's a Duke;   30
From all his ill-got honors flung,
Turned to that dirt from whence he sprung.

---

1 His Grace Duke of Marlborough.

▨ TOPICS FOR CRITICAL THINKING AND WRITING

1. Ordinarily, what would be the tone of a poem written for someone
   who had recently died? What is Swift's tone in the first line? In the second? By the end of the eighth line ("He'd wish to sleep a little longer")?
   Which words, if any, in the first two lines might you expect to find in a
   poem about the death of an eminent public figure? Now look closely at
   the last line of the poem. "Turned to that dirt from whence he sprung."
   By substituting only one word in the last line, how can you convert the
   line into one that might be uttered in church in a sermon eulogizing
   the deceased?

2. Lines 18–24 introduce widows and orphans, figures who might well be mentioned in an elegy. But exactly what is Swift saying here about the relationship between Marlborough and widows and orphans?

ALEXANDER POPE

Alexander Pope (1688–1744), born in London of a middle-class family, from childhood onward was plagued with ill health, notably with curvature of the spine. His schooling was private and in fact he was largely self-taught. A child prodigy, the youth was recognized by some of the leading writers of the day, and he later formed notable friends, including Jonathan Swift. Pope also made notable enemies, many of whom he immortalized—like flies in amber—in his poetry.

Pope is one of the most quotable poets. If you have ever said, "A little learning is a dangerous thing," or "To err is human, to forgive divine," or "Fools rush in where angels fear to tread," or "Who shall decide when doctors disagree?," or "Hope springs eternal in the human breast"—to quote only a handful of examples—you have quoted Alexander Pope.

We give an epigram—a short, witty observation—which Pope engraved on the collar of a puppy that he gave to Frederick, Prince of Wales in 1736. Kew, just west of London, was the site of a royal palace.

Engraved on the Collar of a Dog which I gave to His Royal Highness

I am his Highness' dog at Kew;
Pray tell me sir, whose dog are you?

 TOPIC FOR CRITICAL THINKING AND WRITING

The speaker of the first line is very civil. How would you characterize his or her tone in the second line? Please explain.

17

Figurative Language: Simile, Metaphor, Personification, Apostrophe

HIPPOLYTA.   'Tis strange, my Theseus, that these lovers speak of.
THESEUS.   More strange than true. I never may believe
These antique fables, nor these fairy toys.
Lovers and madmen have such seething brains,
Such shaping fantasies, that apprehend
More than cool reason ever comprehends.
The lunatic, the lover, and the poet,
Are of imagination all compact.
One sees more devils than vast hell can hold,
That is the madman. The lover, all as frantic,
Sees Helen's beauty in a brow of Egypt.
The poet's eye, in a fine frenzy rolling,
Doth glance from heaven to earth, from earth to heaven;
And as imagination bodies forth
The forms of things unknown, the poet's pen
Turns them to shapes, and gives to airy nothing
A local habitation and a name.
—Shakespeare, *A Midsummer Night's Dream*, 5.1–17

Theseus was neither the first nor the last to suggest that poets, like lunatics and lovers, freely employ their imagination. Terms such as *poetic license* and *poetic justice* imply that poets are free to depict a never-never land. One has only to leaf through any anthology of poetry to encounter numerous statements that are, from a logical point of view, lunacies. Here are two quotations:

Look like th' innocent flower,
But be the serpent under 't.

—Shakespeare

Each outcry from the hunted hare
A fiber from the brain does tear.

—William Blake

The first of these is spoken by Lady Macbeth, when she urges her husband to murder King Duncan. How can a human being "Look like th' innocent flower," and how can a human being "be the serpent"? But Macbeth knows, and we know exactly what she means. We see and we feel her point, in a way that we would not if she had said, "Put on an innocent-looking face, but in fact kill the king."

And in the quotation from Blake, when we read that the hunted hare's plaintive cry serves to "tear" a "fiber" from our brain, we almost wince, even though we know that the statement is literally untrue.

On a literal level, then, such assertions are nonsense (so, too, is Theseus's notion that reason is cool). But of course they are not to be taken literally; rather, they employ **figures of speech**—departures from logical usage that are aimed at gaining special effects. Consider the lunacies that Robert Burns heaps up here.

ROBERT BURNS

Robert Burns (1759-1796) was born in Ayrshire in southwestern Scotland. Many of his best poems and songs were written in the Scots dialect, though he also wrote perfect English.

A Red, Red Rose   [1796]

O, my luve is like a red, red rose,
      That's newly sprung in June.
O, my luve is like the melodie,
      That's sweetly played in tune.   4

As fair art thou, my bonnie lass,
      So deep in luve am I,
And I will luve thee still, my dear,
      Till a'° the seas gang° dry.   8

Till a' the seas gang dry, my dear,
      And the rocks melt wi' the sun!
And I will luve thee still, my dear,
      While the sands o' life shall run.   12

And fare thee weel, my only luve,
      And fare thee weel awhile!
And I will come again, my luve,
      Though it were ten thousand mile!   16

---

8 a' all. **gang** go.

To the charge that these lines are lunacies or untruths, at least two replies can be made. First, it might be said that the speaker is not really making assertions about a woman; he is saying he feels a certain way. His words, it can be argued, are not assertions about external reality but expressions of his state of mind, just as a tune one whistles asserts nothing about external reality but expresses the whistler's state of mind. In this view, the nonlogical language of poetry (like a groan of pain or an exclamation of joy) is an expression of emotion; its further aim, if it has one, is to induce in the hearer an emotion.

Second, and more to the point here, it can be said that nonlogical language does indeed make assertions about external reality, and even gives the reader an insight into this reality that logical language cannot. The opening comparison in Burns's poem ("my luve is like a red, red rose") brings before our eyes the lady's beauty in a way that the reasonable assertion "She is beautiful" does not. By comparing the woman to a rose, the poet invites us to see the woman through a special sort of lens: she is fragrant; her lips (and perhaps her cheeks) are like a rose in texture and color; she will not keep her beauty long. Also, "my love is like a red, red rose" says something different from "like a red, red beet," or "a red, red cabbage."

The poet, then, has not only communicated a state of mind but also discovered, through the lens of imagination, some things (both in the beloved and in the lover's own feelings) that interest us. The discovery is not world-shaking; it is less important than the discovery of America or the discovery that the meek are blessed, but it *is* a discovery and it leaves the reader with the feeling, "Yes, that's right. I hadn't quite thought of it that way, but that's right."

A poem, Robert Frost said, "assumes direction with the first line laid down, . . . runs a course of lucky events, and ends in a clarification of life—not necessarily a great clarification, such as sects and cults are founded on, but in a momentary stay against confusion." What is clarified? In another sentence Frost gives an answer: "For me the initial delight is in the surprise of remembering something I didn't know I knew." John Keats made a similar statement: "Poetry . . . should strike the Reader as a wording of his own highest thoughts, and appear almost a Remembrance."

Some figures of speech are, in effect, riddling ways of speech. To call fishermen "farmers of the sea"—a metaphor—is to give a sort of veiled description of fishermen, bringing out, when the term is properly understood, certain aspects of a fisherman's activities. And a riddle, after all, is a veiled description—though intentionally obscure or deceptive—calling attention to characteristics, especially similarities, not usually noticed. (*Riddle*, like *read*, is from Old English *redan*, "to guess," "to interpret," and thus its solution provides knowledge.) "Two sisters upstairs, often looking but never seeing each other" is (after the riddle is explained) a way of calling attention to the curious fact that the eye, the instrument of vision, never sees its mate.

SYLVIA PLATH

Sylvia Plath (1932–1963) was born in Boston, the daughter of German immigrants. While still an undergraduate at Smith College, she published in Seventeen and Mademoiselle; but her years at college, like her later years, were marked by manic-depressive periods. After graduating from college, she went to England to study at Cambridge University, where she met the English poet Ted Hughes, whom she married in 1956. The marriage was unsuccessful, and they separated. One day she committed suicide by turning on the kitchen gas.

Metaphors [1960]

I'm a riddle in nine syllables,
An elephant, a ponderous house,
A melon strolling on two tendrils.
O red fruit, ivory, fine timbers!
This loaf's big with its yeasty rising.   5
Money's new-minted in this fat purse.
I'm a means, a stage, a cow in calf.
I've eaten a bag of green apples,
Boarded the train there's no getting off.

 TOPIC FOR CRITICAL THINKING AND WRITING

The riddling speaker says that she is, among other things, "a ponderous house" and "a cow in calf." What is she?

SIMILE

In a **simile,** items from different classes are explicitly compared by a connective such as *like, as,* or *than* or by a verb such as *appears* or *seems.* (If the objects compared are from the same class—for example, "New York is like Chicago"— no simile is present.)

Sometimes I feel like a motherless child.

—Anonymous

It is a beauteous evening, calm and free.
The holy time is quiet as a Nun,
Breathless with adoration.

—Wordsworth

How sharper than a serpent's tooth it is
To have a thankless child.

—Shakespeare

Seems he a dove? His feathers are but borrowed.

—Shakespeare

RICHARD WILBUR

Richard Wilbur, born in New York City in 1921, was educated at Amherst and Harvard. He served in the army during World War II and in 1947 published The Beautiful Changes, *a book of poems that reflected some of his experience in Europe. This book and subsequent books of poetry established his literary reputation, but probably his most widely known works are the lyrics that he wrote for Leonard Bernstein's musical version of* Candide *(1956). In 1987 the Library of Congress named him U.S. Poet Laureate.*

A Simile for Her Smile [1950]

Your smiling, or the hope, the thought of it,
Makes in my mind such pause and abrupt ease
As when the highway bridgegates fall,
Balking the hasty traffic, which must sit
On each side massed and staring, while   5
Deliberately the drawbridge starts to rise:

Then horns are hushed, the oilsmoke rarifies,
Above the idling motors one can tell
The packet's smooth approach, the slip,
Slip of the silken river past the sides,   10
The ringing of clear bells, the dip
And slow cascading of the paddle wheel.

 TOPIC FOR CRITICAL THINKING AND WRITING

The title may lead you to think that the poet will compare the woman's
smile to something. But, in fact, the comparison is not between her smile
and the passing scene. What *is* being compared to the traffic?

METAPHOR

A **metaphor** asserts the identity, without a connective such as *like* or a verb
such as *appears,* of terms that are literally incompatible.

She is the rose, the glory of the day.

—Spenser

O western orb sailing the heaven.

—Whitman

Notice how in the second example only one of the terms ("orb") is stated; the
other ("ship") is implied in "sailing."

JOHN KEATS

*John Keats (1795-1821), son of a London stable keeper, was taken out of
school when he was 15 and apprenticed to a surgeon and apothecary. In
1816 he was licensed to practice as an apothecary-surgeon, but he almost immediately abandoned medicine and decided to make a career as a poet. His
progress was amazing; he quickly moved from routine verse to major accomplishments, publishing books of poems—to mixed reviews—in 1817, 1818,
and 1820, before dying of tuberculosis at the age of 25.*

*On First Looking into Chapman's Homer**   [1816]

Much have I traveled in the realms of gold,
And many goodly states and kingdoms seen;
Round many western islands have I been
Which bards in fealty to Apollo° hold.
Oft of one wide expanse have I been told   5
That deep-browed Homer ruled as his demesne;°
Yet did I never breathe its pure serene°
Till I heard Chapman speak out loud and bold:
Then felt I like some watcher of the skies
When a new planet swims into his ken;   10
Or like stout Cortez when with eagle eyes
He stared at the Pacific—and all his men
Looked at each other with a wild surmise—
Silent, upon a peak in Darien.

---

4 **Apollo** god of poetry.   6 **demesne** domain.   7 **serene** open space.

⊞ TOPICS FOR CRITICAL THINKING AND WRITING

1. In line 1, what do you think "realms of gold" stands for? Chapman was
   an Elizabethan; how does this fact add relevance to the metaphor in the
   first line?
2. Does line 9 introduce a totally new idea, or can you somehow connect
   it to the opening metaphor?

Two types of metaphor deserve special mention. In **metonymy,** something is
named that replaces something closely related to it; "City Hall," for example,
sometimes is used to stand for municipal authority. In the following passage
James Shirley names certain objects (scepter and crown; scythe and spade),
using them to replace social classes (royalty; agricultural labor) to which they
are related:

Scepter and crown must tumble down
And in the dust be equal made
With the poor crooked scythe and spade.

In **synecdoche,** the whole is replaced by the part, or the part by the whole.
For example, *bread* in "Give us this day our daily bread" replaces the whole
class of edibles. Similarly, an automobile can be "wheels," and workers are
"hands." Robert Frost was fond of calling himself "a Synecdochist" because he
believed that it is the nature of poetry to "have intimations of something more
than itself. It almost always comes under the head of synecdoche, a part, a hem
of the garment for the whole garment."

---

*George Chapman (1559–1634?), Shakespeare's contemporary, is chiefly known for his
translations (from the Greek) of Homer's *Odyssey* and *Iliad*. In lines 11–14 Keats
mistakenly says that Cortés was the first European to see the Pacific, from the heights of
Darien, in Panama. In fact, Balboa was the first.

PERSONIFICATION

The attribution of human feelings or characteristics to abstractions or to inanimate objects is called **personification.**

> But Time did beckon to the flowers, and they
> By noon most cunningly did steal away.
>
> —Herbert

Herbert attributes a human gesture to Time and shrewdness to flowers. Of all figures, personification most surely gives to airy nothings a local habitation and a name:

> There's Wrath who has learnt every trick of guerrilla warfare,
> The shamming dead, the night-raid, the feinted retreat.
>
> —Auden

> Hope, thou bold taster of delight.
>
> —Crashaw

> The alarm clock meddling in somebody's sleep.
>
> —Brooks

> . . . neon script leering from the shuddering asphalt.
>
> —Dove

In the next poem, the speaker, addressing a former mistress ("come let us kiss and part"), seems to grant that their love is over—is dying—and he personifies this love, this passion, as a person on his deathbed ("Now at last gasp of Love's latest breath"). Further, he surrounds the dying Love with two mourners, Faith, who is kneeling by Love's bed, and Innocence, who is closing Love's eyes. But notice that the poem takes a sudden twist at the end where, it seems, Love may not have to die.

MICHAEL DRAYTON

Michael Drayton (1563–1631) was born in Warwickshire in England a year before Shakespeare, and like Shakespeare he wrote sonnets. Among his other works is a long poem on the geography and local lore of England.

Since There's No Help   [1619]

> Since there's no help, come let us kiss and part;
> Nay, I have done, you get no more of me,
> And I am glad, yea glad with all my heart
> That thus so cleanly I myself can free;   4
> Shake hands for ever, cancel all our vows,
> And when we meet at any time again,
> Be it not seen in either of our brows
> That we one jot of former love retain.   8
> Now at the last gasp of Love's latest breath,
> When, his pulse failing, Passion speechless lies,

When Faith is kneeling by his bed of death,
And Innocence is closing up his eyes,   12
　　　Now if thou wouldst, when all have given him over,
　　　From death to life you mightst him yet recover.

TOPICS FOR CRITICAL THINKING AND WRITING

1. What do you think is the tone of lines 1–8? What words especially establish this tone? What do you think is the tone of lines 9–14?
2. Some readers find the personifications in lines 9–13 a sign that the speaker is not deeply moved, and perhaps is putting on an act. Do you agree or not? Please explain.

APOSTROPHE

Crashaw's personification, "Hope, thou bold taster of delight," quoted a moment ago, is also an example of the figure of speech called **apostrophe,** an address to a person or thing not literally listening. Wordsworth begins a sonnet by apostrophizing John Milton:

Milton, thou shouldst be living at this hour,

And Shelley begins an ode by apostrophizing a skylark:

Hail to thee, blithe Spirit!

The following poem is largely built on apostrophe.

EDMUND WALLER

Edmund Waller (1606–1687), born into a country family of wealth in Buckinghamshire in England, attended Eton and Cambridge before spending most of his life as a member of parliament. When the Puritans came to power, he was imprisoned and eventually banished to France, although he was soon allowed to return to England. When the monarchy was restored to the throne, he returned to parliament.

Song   [1645]

　　Go, lovely rose,
Tell her that wastes her time and me,
　　That now she knows,
When I resemble her to thee,
　　How sweet and fair she seems to be.   5

　　Tell her that's young,
And shuns to have her graces spied,
　　That hadst thou sprung
In deserts where no men abide,
　　Thou must have uncommended died.   10

    Small is the worth
Of beauty from the light retired:
    Bid her come forth,
Suffer her self to be desired,
    And not blush so to be admired.   15

    Then die, that she
The common fate of all things rare
    May read in thee,
How small a part of time they share,
    That are so wondrous sweet and fair.   20

What conclusions, then, can we draw about **figurative language?** First, figurative language, with its literally incompatible terms, forces the reader to attend to the **connotations** (suggestions, associations) rather than to the **denotations** (dictionary definitions) of one of the terms.

Second, although figurative language is said to differ from ordinary discourse, it is found in ordinary discourse as well as in literature. "It rained cats and dogs," "War is hell," "Don't be a pig," and other tired figures are part of our daily utterances. But through repeated use, these (and most of the figures we use) have lost whatever impact they once had and are only a shade removed from expressions that, though once figurative, have become literal: the *eye* of a needle, a *branch* office, the *face* of a clock.

Third, good figurative language is usually (1) concrete, (2) condensed, and (3) interesting. The concreteness lends precision and vividness; when Keats writes that he felt "like some watcher of the skies / When a new planet swims into his ken," he more sharply characterizes his feelings than if he had said, "I felt excited." His simile isolates for us a precise kind of excitement, and the metaphoric "swims" vividly brings up the oceanic aspect of the sky. The second of these three qualities, condensation, can be seen by attempting to paraphrase some of the figures. A paraphrase or rewording will commonly use more words than the original and will have less impact—as the gradual coming of night usually has less impact on us than a sudden darkening of the sky, or as a prolonged push has less impact than a sudden blow. The third quality, interest, largely depends on the previous two: the successful figure often makes us open our eyes wider and take notice. Keats's "deep-browed Homer" arouses our interest in Homer as "thoughtful Homer" or "meditative Homer" does not. Similarly, when W. B. Yeats says (p. 867):

    An aged man is but a paltry thing,
    A tattered coat upon a stick, unless
    Soul clap its hands and sing, and louder sing
    For every tatter in its mortal dress,

the metaphoric identification of an old man with a scarecrow jolts us out of all our usual unthinking attitudes about old men as kind, happy folk content to have passed from youth to senior citizenship.

Finally, the point must be made that although figurative language is one of the poet's chief tools, a poem does not have to contain figures. The anonymous ballad "Edward" (p. 972) contains no figures, yet surely it is a poem, and no one would say that the addition of figures would make it a better poem.

Here is a poem by William Carlos Williams. Does it contain any figures of speech?

WILLIAM CARLOS WILLIAMS

William Carlos Williams (1883–1963) was the son of an English traveling salesman and a Basque-Jewish woman. The couple met in Puerto Rico and settled in Rutherford, New Jersey, where Williams was born. He spent his life there, practicing as a pediatrician and writing poems in the moments between seeing patients who were visiting his office.

The Red Wheelbarrow
[1923]

so much depends
upon

a red wheel
barrow   4

glazed with rain
water

beside the white
chickens.   8

The following poems rely heavily on figures of speech.

ALFRED, LORD TENNYSON

Alfred, Lord Tennyson (1809–1892), the son of an English clergyman, was born in Lincolnshire, where he began writing verse at age 5. Educated at Cambridge, he had to leave without a degree when his father died and Alfred had to accept responsibility for bringing up his brothers and sisters. In fact, the family had inherited ample funds, but for some years the money was tied up by litigation. In 1850 Tennyson was made poet laureate following Wordsworth's death. With his government pension he moved with his family to the Isle of Wight, where he lived in vast comfort until his death.

The Eagle
[1851]

Fragment

He clasps the crag with crooked hands;
Close to the sun in lonely lands,
Ringed with the azure world, he stands.
The wrinkled sea beneath him crawls:
He watches from his mountain walls,   5
And like a thunderbolt he falls.

✺ TOPICS FOR CRITICAL THINKING AND WRITING

1. What figure is used in line 1? In line 4? In line 6? Can it be argued that the figures give us a sense of the eagle that is not to be found in a literal description?

2. In line 2 we get overstatement, or hyperbole, for the eagle is not really close to the sun. Suppose instead of "Close to the sun" Tennyson had written "Waiting on high"? Do you think the poem would be improved or worsened?

SEAMUS HEANEY

Seamus Heaney was born in Belfast, Northern Ireland, in 1939. He grew up on a farm, and then went to Queens University in Belfast. "Digging," the first poem in his first book, reveals his concern with getting to the bottom of things. Heaney, who now lives in Dublin, has lectured widely in Ireland, England, and the United States. In addition to writing poetry, he has written essays about poetry. In 1995 he was awarded the Nobel Prize for Literature.

Digging   [1966]

Between my finger and my thumb
The squat pen rests; snug as a gun.

Under my window, a clean rasping sound
When the spade sinks into gravelly ground:
My father, digging, I look down   5

Till his straining rump among the flowerbeds
Bends low, comes up twenty years away
Stooping in rhythm through potato drills
Where he was digging.

The coarse boot nestled on the lug, the shaft   10
Against the inside knee was levered firmly.
He rooted out tall tops, buried the bright edge deep
To scatter new potatoes that we picked
Loving their cool hardness in our hands.
By God, the old man could handle a spade.   15
Just like his old man.

My grandfather cut more turf in a day
Than any other man on Toner's bog.
Once I carried him milk in a bottle
Corked sloppily with paper. He straightened up   20
To drink it, then fell to right away
Nicking and slicing neatly, heaving sods
Over his shoulder, going down and down
For the good turf. Digging.

The cold smell of potato mould, the   25
    squelch and slap
Of soggy peat, the curt cuts of an edge
Through living roots awaken in my head.
But I've no spade to follow men like them.

Between my finger and my thumb
The squat pen rests.   30
I'll dig with it.

TOPICS FOR CRITICAL THINKING AND WRITING

1. The poem ends with the speaker saying that he will "dig" with his pen. Given all the preceding lines, what will he dig?
2. The first lines compare the pen with a gun. What implications are suggested by this comparison?

DANA GIOIA

Dana Gioia (pronounced "JOY ub"), born in 1950, is chair of the National Endowment for the Arts. He is a poet and the co-author of a textbook on literature, and he has also had a successful career as a businessman.

Money

[1991]

Money is a kind of poetry.

—Wallace Stevens

Money, the long green,
cash, stash, rhino, jack
or just plain dough.

Chock it up, fork it over,
shell it out. Watch it   5
burn holes through pockets.

To be made of it! To have it
to burn! Greenbacks, double eagles,
megabucks and Ginnie Maes.

It greases the palm, feathers a nest,   10
holds heads above water,
makes both ends meet.

Money breeds money.
Gathering interest, compounding daily.
Always in circulation   15

Money. You don't know where it's been,
but you put it where your mouth is.
And it talks.

 TOPICS FOR CRITICAL THINKING AND WRITING

1. Are any of the terms in the poem unfamiliar to you? If so, check a dictionary, and if you don't find an explanation in a dictionary, turn to other resources—the Internet, and friends and classmates. Do some of the terms come from particular worlds of discourse—for instance, banking, gambling, or drug-dealing?
2. Suppose the last stanza had been placed first. Would the poem be better? Or worse? Why?
3. Write a somewhat comparable poem on a topic of your choice—for instance, students, teachers, athletes, or work.

CRAIG RAINE

Born in England in 1945, Raine graduated from Oxford, where after his graduation he was appointed a lecturer. Since 1981 he has been poetry editor for the English publisher, Faber and Faber. He gives frequent readings of his poetry both in England and in America.

Much of his poetry, including the poem we reprint here, is designed to help the reader to see the world from a fresh point of view.

A Martian Sends a Postcard Home   [1979]

Caxtons° are mechanical birds with many wings
and some are treasured for their markings—

they cause the eyes to melt
or the body to shriek without pain.

I have never seen one fly, but   5
sometimes they perch on the hand.

Mist is when the sky is tired of flight
and rests its soft machine on ground:

then the world is dim and bookish
like engravings under tissue paper.   10

Rain is when the earth is television.
It has the property of making colours darker.

Model T° is a room with the lock inside—
a key is turned to free the world

for movement, so quick there is a film   15
to watch for anything missed.

But time is tied to the wrist
or kept in a box, ticking with impatience.

In homes, a haunted apparatus sleeps,
that snores when you pick it up.   20

If the ghost cries, they carry it
to their lips and soothe it to sleep

with sounds. And yet, they wake it up
deliberately, by tickling with a finger.

Only the young are allowed to suffer   25
openly. Adults go to a punishment room

with water but nothing to eat.
They lock the door and suffer the noises

---

1 Caxtons William Caxton (c. 1422-1491) was the first English printer of books.
13 Model T a Ford automobile made between 1908 and 1928.

alone. No one is exempt
and everyone's pain has a different smell.   30

At night, when all the colours die,
they hide in pairs

and read about themselves—
in colour, with their eyelids shut.

WILLIAM SHAKESPEARE

You will encounter Shakespeare (1564–1616) several times in this book—for instance, as the author of songs (Chapter 15), sonnets (Chapter 20), two tragedies (Chapter 30), and a comedy (Chapter 31).

Here we give one of his sonnets (probably written in the mid-1590s), in which he playfully rejects similes and other figures of speech. His contemporaries often compared a woman's hair to fine-spun gold, her lips to coral or to cherries, her cheeks to roses, her white breast to snow; when such a woman walked, she seemed to walk on air (the grass did not bend beneath her), and when she spoke, her voice was music. Shakespeare himself uses such figures in some of his poems and plays, but in this sonnet he praises his beloved by saying she does not need such figures.

Sonnet 130

My mistress' eyes are nothing like the sun;
Coral is far more red than her lips' red;
If snow be white, why then her breasts are dun;
If hairs be wires, black wires grow on her head.   4
I have seen roses damasked, red and white,
But no such roses see I in her cheeks;
And in some perfumes is there more delight
Than in the breath that from my mistress reeks.   8
I love to hear her speak, yet well I know
That music hath a far more pleasing sound;
I grant I never saw a goddess go;°
My mistress, when she walks, treads on the ground.   12
And yet, by heaven, I think my love as rare°
As any she belied° with false compare.

---

11 go walk.   **13 rare** exceptional.   **14 any she belied** any woman misrepresented.

18

Imagery and Symbolism

When we read the word "rose"—or, for that matter, "finger" or "thumb"—we may more or less call to mind a picture, an image. The term **imagery** is used to refer to whatever in a poem appeals to any of our sensations, including sensations of pressure and heat as well as of sight, smell, taste, touch, and sound.

Consider the opening lines of Seamus Heaney's "Digging" (page 752):

> Between my finger and my thumb
> The squat pen rests; snug as a gun.

We may in our mind's eye see a finger, thumb, and pen; and perhaps, stimulated by "squat," we may almost feel the pen. Notice, too, that in Heaney's line the pen is compared to a gun, so there is yet another image in the line. In short, images are the sensory content of the work, whether literal (the finger, thumb, and pen) or figurative (the gun, to which the pen is compared). Edmund Waller's rose in "Go, Lovely Rose" (page 749) is an image that happens to be compared in the first stanza to a woman ("I resemble her to thee"); later in the poem this image comes to stand for "all things rare." Yet we never forget that the rose is a rose, and that the poem is chiefly a revelation of the poet's attitude toward his beloved.

If a poet says "my rose" and is speaking about a rose, we have an image, even though we do not have a figure of speech. If a poet says "my rose" and, we gather, is speaking not really or chiefly about a rose but about something else—let's say the transience of beauty—we can say that the poet is using the rose as a symbol.

Some symbols are **natural symbols,** recognized as standing for something in particular even by people from different cultures. Rain, for instance, usually stands for fertility or the renewal of life. A forest often stands for mental darkness or chaos, a mountain for stability, a valley for a place of security, and so on. There are many exceptions, but by and large these meanings prevail.

Other symbols, however, are **conventional symbols,** which people have agreed to accept as standing for something other than themselves: A poem about the cross would probably be about Christianity. Similarly, the rose has long been a symbol for love. In Virginia Woolf's novel *Mrs. Dalloway,* the husband communicates his love by proffering this conventional symbol: "He was holding out flowers—roses, red and white roses. (But he could not bring himself to say he loved her; not in so many words.)" Objects that are not conventional symbols, however, also may give rise to rich, multiple, indefinable associations. The following poem uses the symbol of the rose, but uses it in a nontraditional way.

WILLIAM BLAKE

A biography of Blake, followed by three additional poems, appears on page 979.

The Sick Rose

[1794]

O rose, thou are sick!
The invisible worm
That flies in the night
In the howling storm   4

Has found out thy bed
Of crimson joy,
And his dark secret love
Does thy life destroy.   8

One might argue that the worm is "invisible" (line 2) merely because it is hidden within the rose, but an "invisible worm / That flies in the night" is more than a long, slender, soft-bodied creeping animal; and a rose that has, or is, a "bed / Of crimson joy" is more than a gardener's rose.

Blake's worm and rose suggest things beyond themselves—a stranger, more vibrant world than the world we are usually aware of. Many readers find themselves half-thinking, for example, that the worm is male, the rose female, and that the poem is about the violation of virginity. Or that the poem is about the destruction of beauty: woman's beauty, rooted in joy, is destroyed by a power that feeds on her. But these interpretations are not fully satisfying: the poem presents a worm and a rose, and yet it is not merely about a worm and a rose. These objects resonate, stimulating our thoughts toward something else, but the something else is elusive, whereas it is not elusive in Burns's "A Red, Red Rose" (page 743).

A **symbol,** then, is an image so loaded with significance that it is not simply literal, and it does not simply stand for something else; it is both itself *and* something else that it richly suggests, a manifestation of something too complex or too elusive to be otherwise revealed. Blake's poem is about a blighted rose and at the same time about much more. In a symbol, as Thomas Carlyle wrote, "the Infinite is made to blend with the Finite, to stand visible, and as it were, attainable there." Probably it is not fanciful to say that the American slaves who sang "Joshua fought the battle of Jericho, / And the walls came tumbling down" were singing both about an ancient occurrence *and* about a new embodiment of the ancient, the imminent collapse of slavery in the nineteenth century. Not one or the other, but both: the present partook of the past, and the past partook of the present.

WALT WHITMAN

Walt Whitman (1819-1892) was born in a farmhouse in rural Long Island, New York, but was brought up in Brooklyn, then an independent city in New York. He attended public school for a few years (1825-1830), apprenticed as

*a printer in the 1830s, and then worked as a typesetter, journalist, and news-
paper editor. In 1855 he published the first edition of a collection of his poems,* Leaves of Grass, *a book that he revised and published in one edition after
another throughout the remainder of his life. During the Civil War he served
as a volunteer nurse for the Union army.*

In the third edition of Leaves of Grass *(1860), Whitman added two groups
of poems, one called "Children of Adam" and the other (named for an aromatic grass that grows near ponds and swamps) called "Calamus." "Children
of Adam" celebrates heterosexual relations, whereas "Calamus" celebrates
what Whitman called "manly love." Although many of the "Calamus" poems
seem clearly homosexual, perhaps the very fact that Whitman published them
made them seem relatively innocent; in any case, those nineteenth-century
critics who condemned Whitman for the sexuality of his writing concentrated
on the poems in "Children of Adam."*

*"I Saw in Louisiana" is from the "Calamus" section. It was originally pub-
lished in the third edition of* Leaves of Grass *and was revised into its final
form in the 1867 edition. We give it in the 1867 version. We also give the
manuscript, showing it in its earliest extant version.*

I Saw in Louisiana a Live-Oak Growing   [1867]

I saw in Louisiana a live-oak growing,
All alone stood it and the moss hung down from the branches,
Without any companion it grew there uttering joyous leaves
    of dark green,
And its look, rude, unbending, lusty, made me think of myself,
But I wonder'd how it could utter joyous leaves standing alone there
    without its friend near, for I knew I could not,   5
And I broke off a twig with a certain number of leaves upon it,
    and twined around it a little moss,
And brought it away, and I have placed it in sight in my room,
It is not needed to remind me as of my own dear friends,
(For I believe lately I think of little else than of them,)
Yet it remains to me a curious token, it makes me think of manly love;   10
For all that, and though the live-oak glistens there in Louisiana solitary
    in a wide flat space,
Uttering joyous leaves all its life without a friend a lover near,
I know very well I could not.

▨ TOPIC FOR CRITICAL THINKING AND WRITING

Compare the final version (1867) of the poem with the manuscript version
of 1860. Which version do you prefer? Why?

Walt Whitman, "I Saw in Louisiana a Live-Oak Growing," manuscript of 1860. On the first leaf, in line 3 Whitman deleted "with." On the second leaf (see page 760), in the third line (line 8 of the printed text) he added, with a caret, "lately." In the sixth line on this leaf he deleted "I write these pieces, and name them after it," replacing the deletion with "it makes me think of manly love." In the next line he deleted "tree" and inserted "live oak." When he reprinted the poem in the 1867 version of *Leaves of Grass,* he made further changes, as you will see if you compare the printed text with this manuscript version.

It is not needed to remind
me as of my friends, (for I
believe lately think of little
else than of them,)
Yet it remains to me a
curious token — it makes
me think of manly love;
For all that, and though the
live oak glistens there in Louisiana, solitary in a wide
flat space, uttering joyous
leaves all its life, without

SAMUEL TAYLOR COLERIDGE

Samuel Taylor Coleridge (1772–1834) was born in Devonshire in England, the son of a clergyman. He attended Christ's Hospital school in London and Cambridge University, which he left without receiving a degree. With his friend William Wordsworth in 1798 he published, anonymously, a volume of poetry, Lyrical Ballads, *which became the manifesto of the Romantic movement.*

Kubla Khan   [1798]

Or, A Vision in a Dream. A Fragment.

In Xanadu did Kubla Khan
A stately pleasure-dome decree:
Where Alph, the sacred river, ran

Through caverns measureless to man
    Down to a sunless sea.   5
So twice five miles of fertile ground
With walls and towers were girdled round:
And here were gardens bright with sinuous rills,
Where blossomed many an incense-bearing tree;
And here were forests ancient as the hills,   10
Enfolding sunny spots of greenery.

But oh! that deep romantic chasm which slanted
Down the green hill athwart a cedarn cover!
A savage place! as holy and enchanted
As e'er beneath a waning moon was haunted   15
By woman wailing for her demon-lover!
And from this chasm, with ceaseless turmoil seething,
As if this earth in fast thick pants were breathing
A mighty fountain momently was forced;
Amid whose swift half-intermitted burst   20
Huge fragments vaulted like rebounding hail,
Or chaffy grain beneath the thresher's flail:
And 'mid these dancing rocks at once and ever
It flung up momently the sacred river.
Five miles meandering with a mazy motion   25
Through wood and dale the sacred river ran,
Then reached the caverns measureless to man,
And sank in tumult to a lifeless ocean:
And 'mid this tumult Kubla heard from far
Ancestral voices prophesying war!   30
    The shadow of the dome of pleasure
    Floated midway on the waves;
    Where was heard the mingled measure
    From the fountain and the caves.
It was a miracle of rare device,   35
A sunny pleasure-dome with caves of ice!
    A damsel with a dulcimer
    In a vision once I saw:
    It was an Abyssinian maid,
    And on her dulcimer she played,   40
    Singing of Mount Abora.
    Could I revive within me
    Her symphony and song,
    To such a deep delight 'twould win me,
That with music loud and long,   45
I would build that dome in air,
That sunny dome! those caves of ice!
And all who heard should see them there,
And all should cry, Beware! Beware!
His flashing eyes, his floating hair!   50
Weave a circle round him thrice,
And close your eyes with holy dread,

For he on honey-dew hath fed,
And drunk the milk of Paradise.

When Coleridge published "Kubla Khan" in 1816, he prefaced it with this explanatory note:

> The following fragment is here published at the request of a poet of great and deserved celebrity, and, as far as the author's own opinions are concerned, rather as a psychological curiosity, than on the ground of any supposed *poetic* merits.
>
> In the summer of the year 1797, the author, then in ill health, had retired to a lonely farmhouse between Porlock and Linton, on the Exmoor confines of Somerset and Devonshire. In consequence of a slight indisposition, an anodyne had been prescribed, from the effects of which he fell asleep in his chair at the moment that he was reading the following sentence, or words of the same substance, in *Purchas' Pilgrimage:* "Here the Khan Kubla commanded a palace to be built, and a stately garden thereunto. And thus ten miles of fertile ground were inclosed with a wall." The author continued for about three hours in a profound sleep, at least of the external senses, during which time he has the most vivid confidence that he could not have composed less than from two to three hundred lines; if that indeed can be called composition in which all the images rose up before him as *things*, with a parallel production of the correspondent expressions, without any sensation or consciousness of effort. On awaking he appeared to himself to have a distinct recollection of the whole, and taking his pen, ink, and paper, instantly and eagerly wrote down the lines that are here preserved. At this moment he was unfortunately called out by a person on business from Porlock, and detained by him above an hour, and on his return to his room, found, to his no small surprise and mortification, that though he still retained some vague and dim recollection of the general purport of the vision, yet, with the exception of some eight or ten scattered lines and images, all the rest had passed away like the images on the surface of a stream into which a stone has been cast, but, alas! without the after restoration of the latter!

>   Then all the charm
> Is broken—all that phantom world so fair
> Vanishes, and a thousand circlets spread,
> And each misshape[s] the other. Stay awhile,
> Poor youth! who scarcely dar'st lift up thine eyes—
> The stream will soon renew its smoothness, soon
> The visions will return! And lo, he stays,
> And soon the fragments dim of lovely forms
> Come trembling back, unite, and now once more
> The pool becomes a mirror.
>   —Coleridge, *The Picture; or, the Lover's Resolution,* lines 91–100

> Yet from the still surviving recollections in his mind, the author has frequently purposed to finish for himself what had been originally, as it were, given to him. Σαμερου αδιου ασω [today I shall sing more sweetly]: "But the tomorrow is yet to come."

▩ TOPICS FOR CRITICAL THINKING AND WRITING

1. Coleridge changed the "palace" of his source into a "dome" (line 2). What do you think are the relevant associations of "dome"?
2. What pairs of contrasts (e.g., underground river, fountain) do you find? What do you think they contribute to the poem?
3. If Coleridge had not said that the poem is a fragment, might you take it as a complete poem, the first thirty-six lines describing the creative imagination, and the remainder lamenting the loss of poetic power?

FREDERICK MORGAN

Frederick Morgan was born in New York City in 1922. He attended private grammar and high schools, and then went on to receive his undergraduate degree from Princeton University. After serving in the army during World War II, he returned to New York City and in 1947 co-founded a literary journal, The Hudson Review. *For the next twenty years he focused on his editorial work, but in response to the shock of his son's suicide in 1968 he turned to serious and sustained writing of poetry. His books of poetry include* Poems of the Two Worlds *(1977),* Death Mother *(1979),* Northbrook *(1982), and* Poems: New and Selected *(1987).*

We reprint a poem about a painting of a horse, attributed to Han Gan (formerly called Han Kan), a Chinese painter of the eighth century who was famous for his paintings of horses belonging to the emperor. The white horse depicted here was named Night-Shining White, or Shining Light of Night, because his whiteness was said to illuminate the dark. (Many scholars believe that the painting is an old copy of a lost work by Han Gan, rather than an original.)

The Master

[1986]

When Han Kan was summoned
to the imperial capital
it was suggested he sit at the feet of
the illustrious senior court painter
to learn from the refinements of the art.   5

"No, thank you," he replied,
"I shall apprentice myself to the stables."

And he installed himself and his brushes amid the dung and the flies,
and studied the horses—their bodies' keen alertness—
eye-sparkle of one, another's sensitive stance,   10
the way a third moved graceful in his bulk—

and painted at last the emperor's favorite,
the charger named "Nightshining White,"

whose likeness after centuries still dazzles.

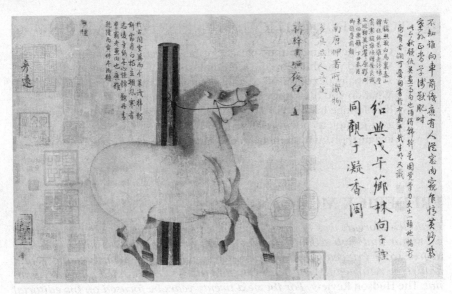

Han Gan, *Night-Shining White,* 8th century, ink on paper, painting only: 13 3/8 × 12 1/8 in. (The Metropolitan Museum of Art, Purchase, The Dillon Fund Gift 1977 [1977.78].)

✳ TOPICS FOR CRITICAL THINKING AND WRITING

1. Which does Morgan make you see more clearly, "the illustrious senior court painter" or "the stables"? Explain how and why.
2. In the last line Morgan says that the painted "likeness" of the horse dazzles us. But the "likeness" to a live horse obviously is not very great in, say, the small legs, the disproportionately large head, and the up-standing mane. According to Morgan, Han Gan (the modern spelling for the painter whose name used to be spelled Han Kan) apprenticed himself to the stables (line 7), but does the painting reveal that he wasted his time? Explain.
3. In the final line, what does "dazzles" mean? Why do you think Morgan ends the poem with this word?
4. Morgan puts a space after lines 5, 7, 11, and 13. Explain what, if anything, these spaces do.
5. Do you think the title of the poem is effective? Invent two other titles, and in two paragraphs indicate why they are better than or inferior to Morgan's title.

CLAUDE McKAY

Claude McKay (1889–1948), born in Jamaica, briefly served as a police officer in Jamaica, published two books of dialect poems in 1912, and in the same year left Jamaica forever—although, as the poem we reprint shows, it remained a source of inspiration. In the United States he studied briefly at

Tuskegee Institute, then for two years at Kansas State University, and then went to New York, writing poems and working on a radical journal, The Liberator. *In 1922 he visited Russia, and from 1923 to 1934 he lived abroad, chiefly in France and North Africa, writing fiction and journalism as well as poetry. He returned to the United States, recanted his Communist beliefs, and in 1945 converted to Catholicism. He then wrote a good deal of prose and poetry that did not get published in his lifetime.*

Although the earliest poems were in dialect, McKay quickly repudiated such diction; his later work uses traditional diction and traditional British poetic forms (here, three quatrains, with alternating rhymes), in contrast to the vernacular language used by his contemporary, Langston Hughes.

The Tropics in New York   [1922]

Bananas ripe and green, and ginger-root,
    Cocoa in pods and alligator pears,
And tangerines and mangoes and grape fruit,
    Fit for the highest prize at parish fairs,   4

Set in the window, bringing memories
    Of fruit-trees laden by low-singing rills,
And dewy dawns, and mystical blue skies
    In benediction over nun-like hills.   8

My eyes grew dim, and I could no more gaze;
    A wave of longing through my body swept,
And, hungry for the old, familiar ways,
    I turned aside and bowed my head and wept.   12

❋ TOPICS FOR CRITICAL THINKING AND WRITING

1. Describe as fully as possible the effect of the details given in the first three lines. What kind of basis or foundation do these details establish for the rest of the poem?
2. What is the purpose of the religious terms and images that the poet uses?
3. Is the poem sentimental? (On sentimentality, see page 1822.) If it is sentimental, is that a bad thing? Why, or why not?

ADRIENNE RICH

Adrienne Rich's most recent books of poetry are The School Among the Ruins: Poems 2000-2004, *and* Fox: Poems 1998-2000 *(Norton). A selection of her essays,* Arts of the Possible: Essays and Conversations, *was published in 2001. A new edition of* What is Found There: Notebooks on Poetry and Policitics, *appeared in 2003. She is a recipient of the Lannan Foundation Lifetime Achievement Award, the Lambda Book Award, the Lenore Marshall/Nation Prize, the Wallace Stevens Award, and the Bollingen Prize in Poetry, among other honors. She lives in California.*

Diving into the Wreck   [1973]

First having read the book of myths,
and loaded the camera,
and checked the edge of the knife-blade,
I put on
the body-armor of black rubber   5
the absurd flippers
the grave and awkward mask.
I am having to do this
not like Cousteau° with his
assiduous team   10
aboard the sun-flooded schooner
but here alone.

There is a ladder.
The ladder is always there
hanging innocently   15
close to the side of the schooner.
We know what it is for,
we who have used it.
Otherwise
it's a piece of maritime floss   20
some sundry equipment.

I go down.
Rung after rung and still
the oxygen immerses me
the blue light   25
the clear atoms
of our human air.
I go down.
My flippers cripple me,
I crawl like an insect down the ladder   30
and there is no one
to tell me when the ocean
will begin.

First the air is blue and then
it is bluer and then green and then   35
black I am blacking out and yet
my mask is powerful
it pumps my blood with power
the sea is another story
the sea is not a question of power   40
I have to learn alone
to turn my body without force
in the deep element.

And now: it is easy to forget
what I came for   45

---

9 **Jacques Cousteau** (1910–1997) French underwater explorer.

among so many who have always
lived here
swaying their crenellated fans
between the reefs
and besides
you breathe differently down here.   50

I came to explore the wreck.
The words are purposes.
The words are maps.
I came to see the damage that was done   55
and the treasures that prevail.
I stroke the beam of my lamp
slowly along the flank
of something more permanent
than fish or weed   60

the thing I came for:
the wreck and not the story of the wreck
the thing itself and not the myth
the drowned face always staring
toward the sun   65
the evidence of damage
worn by salt and sway into this threadbare beauty
the ribs of the disaster
curving their assertion
among the tentative haunters.   70

This is the place.
And I am here, the mermaid whose dark hair
streams black, the merman in his armored body
We circle silently
about the wreck   75
we dive into the hold.
I am she: I am he

whose drowned face sleeps with open eyes
whose breasts still bear the stress
whose silver, copper, vermeil cargo lies   80
obscurely inside barrels
half-wedged and left to rot
we are the half-destroyed instruments
that once held to a course
the water-eaten log   85
the fouled compass

We are, I am, you are
by cowardice or courage
the one who find our way
back to this scene   90
carrying a knife, a camera
a book of myths
in which
our names do not appear.

CHRISTINA ROSSETTI

Christina Rossetti (1830–1894) was the daughter of an exiled Italian patriot who lived in London and the sister of the poet and painter Dante Gabriel Rossetti. After her father became an invalid, she led an extremely ascetic life, devoting most of her life to doing charitable work. Her first and best-known volume of poetry, Goblin Market and Other Poems, *was published in 1862.*

Uphill   [1858]

Does the road wind uphill all the way?
   Yes, to the very end.
Will the day's journey take the whole long day?
   From morn to night, my friend.   4

But is there for the night a resting-place?
   A roof for when the slow dark hours begin.
May not the darkness hide it from my face?
   You cannot miss that inn.   8

Shall I meet other wayfarers at night?
   Those who have gone before.
Then must I knock, or call when just in sight?
   They will not keep you standing at that door.   12

Shall I find comfort, travel-sore and weak?
   Of labor you shall find the sum.
Will there be beds for me and all who seek?
   Yea, beds for all who come.   16

�ખ TOPICS FOR CRITICAL THINKING AND WRITING

1. Suppose that someone told you this poem is about a person preparing to go on a hike. The person is supposedly making inquiries about the road and the possible hotel arrangements. What would you reply?
2. Who is the questioner? A woman? A man? All human beings collectively? "Uphill" does not use quotation marks to distinguish between two speakers. Can one say that in "Uphill" the questioner and the answerer are the same person?
3. Are the answers unambiguously comforting? Or can it, for instance, be argued that the "roof" is (perhaps among other things) the lid of a coffin—hence the questioner will certainly not be kept "standing at that door"? If the poem can be read along these lines, is it chilling rather than comforting?

WALLACE STEVENS

Wallace Stevens (1879–1955), educated at Harvard and at New York Law School, earned his living as a lawyer and an insurance executive; at his death he was a vice president of the Hartford Accident and Indemnity Company.

While pursuing this career, however, he also achieved distinction as a poet, and today he is widely regarded as among the most important American poets of the twentieth century.

Anecdote of the Jar [1923]

I placed a jar in Tennessee,
And round it was, upon a hill.
It made the slovenly wilderness
Surround that hill.   4

The wilderness rose up to it,
And sprawled around, no longer wild.
The jar was round upon the ground
And tall and of a port in air.   8

It took dominion everywhere.
The jar was gray and bare.
It did not give of bird or bush,
Like nothing else in Tennessee.   12

Stevens asked for an interpretation of another poem, said (in *The Explicator,* November 1948): "Things that have their origin in the imagination or in the emotions (poems) . . . very often take on a form that is ambiguous or uncertain. It is not possible to attach a single, rational meaning to such things without destroying the imaginative or emotional ambiguity or uncertainty that is inherent in them and that is why poets do not like to explain. That the meanings given by others are sometimes meanings not intended by the poet or that were never present in his mind does not impair them as meanings."

❉ TOPICS FOR CRITICAL THINKING AND WRITING

1. What is the meaning of line 8? Check "port" in a dictionary.
2. Do you think the poem suggests that the jar organizes slovenly nature, or that the jar impoverishes abundant nature? Or both, or neither? What do you think of the view that the jar is a symbol of the imagination, or of the arts, or of material progress?

The Emperor of Ice-Cream [1923]

Call the roller of big cigars,
The muscular one, and bid him whip
In kitchen cups concupiscent curds.
Let the wenches dawdle in such dress
As they are used to wear, and let the boys
Bring flowers in last month's newspapers.
Let be be finale of seem.
The only emperor is the emperor of ice-cream.

Take from the dresser of deal,°
Lacking the three glass knobs, that sheet
On which she embroidered fantails once
And spread it so as to cover her face.
If her horny feet protrude, they come
To show how cold she is, and dumb.
Let the lamp affix its beam.
The only emperor is the emperor of ice-cream.

---

9 deal fir or pine wood.

 ## TOPIC FOR CRITICAL THINKING AND WRITING

What associations does the word "emperor" have for you? The word "ice-cream"? What, then, do you make of "the emperor of ice-cream"? The poem describes the preparations for a wake, and in line 15 ("Let the lamp affix its beam") it insists on facing the reality of death. In this context, then, what do you make of the last line of each stanza?

EDGAR ALLAN POE

Edgar Allan Poe (1809–1849) was the son of traveling actors. His father abandoned the family almost immediately after his birth, and his mother died when Poe was two. The child was adopted—though never legally—by a prosperous merchant and his wife in Richmond. The tensions were great, aggravated by Poe's drinking and heavy gambling, and in 1827 Poe left Richmond for Boston. He wrote, served briefly in the army, attended West Point but left within a year, and became an editor for the remaining eighteen years of his life. It was during these years, too, that he wrote the poems, essays, and fiction—especially detective stories and horror stories—that have made him famous.

To Helen*
[1831–1843]

Helen, thy beauty is to me
    Like those Nicean° barks of yore,
That gently, o'er a perfumed sea,
    The weary, way-worn wanderer bore
    To his own native shore.   5

***Helen** Helen of Troy, considered the most beautiful woman of ancient times   **2 Nicean** perhaps referring to Nicea, an ancient city associated with the god Dionysus, or perhaps meaning "victorious," from Nike, Greek goddess of Victory.

On desperate seas long wont to roam,
  Thy hyacinth hair,° thy classic face
Thy Naiad° airs have brought me home
  To the glory that was Greece
And the grandeur that was Rome.   10

Lo! in yon brilliant window-niche
  How statue-like I see thee stand!
  The agate lamp within thy hand
Ah! Psyche,° from the regions which
  Are Holy Land!°   15

---

7 hyacinth hair naturally curling hair, like that of Hyacinthus, beautiful Greek youth beloved by Apollo.   **8 Naiad** a nymph associated with lakes and streams.   **14 Psyche** Greek for "soul."   **15 Holy Land** ancient Rome or Athens, i.e., a sacred realm of art.

▓ TOPICS FOR CRITICAL THINKING AND WRITING

1. In the first stanza, to what is Helen's beauty compared? To whom does the speaker apparently compare himself? What does "way-worn" in line 4 suggest to you? To what in the speaker's experience might the "native shore" in line 5 correspond?

2. What do you take "desperate seas" to mean in line 6, and who has been traveling them? To what are they contrasted in line 8? How does "home" seem to be defined in this stanza (stanza 2)?

3. What further light is shed on the speaker's home or destination in stanza 3?

4. Do you think that "To Helen" can be a love poem and also a poem about spiritual beauty or about the love of art? Why or why not?

HERMAN MELVILLE

Herman Melville (1819–1891) was born into a prosperous family in New York City. The bankruptcy and death of his father when Melville was 12 forced the boy to leave school. During his early years he worked first as a bank clerk, then as a farm laborer, then as a store clerk and a bookkeeper, and then as a schoolmaster. In 1837 he sailed to England as a cabin boy and signed on for other voyages, notably on whalers in the South Pacific, where he spent time in the Marquèsas Islands and Tahiti. Out of his marine adventures he produced commercially successful books, Typee *(1846),* Omoo *(1847),* Mardi *(1849), and* Redburn *(1849), but the book for which he is best known today,* Moby Dick *(1851), was a commercial failure. In 1866 a book of poems about the Civil War—we print one of the poems here—was published, but it, too, was a failure. Abandoning his attempt to live by his pen, Melville survived on some inherited money, and on a political appointment as a customs inspector in New York City.*

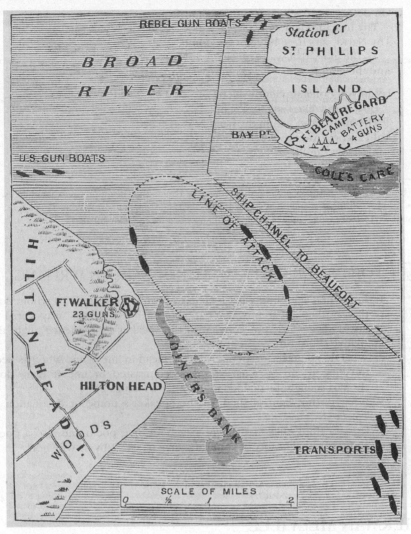

Melville probably saw this map, printed in the *New York Herald Tribune,* shortly after the battle.

DuPont's Round Fight*   [1866]

(November, 1861)

In time and measure perfect moves
   All Art whose aim is sure;

---

*At the Battle of Port Royal Sound (South Carolina), November 7, 1861, Commander Samuel Francis DuPont led a Union squadron of ships that sailed down the Broad River, assaulted Fort Beauregard on the north, reloaded on the elliptical return, bombarded Fort Walker, two and a half miles south, and continued the circuit to bombard Fort Beauregard again, and so on for four and a half hours, finally destroying and capturing both forts.

Evolving rhyme and stars divine
    Have rules, and they endure.   4

Nor less the Fleet that warred for Right,
    And, warring so, prevailed,
In geometric beauty curved,
    And in an orbit sailed.   8

The rebel at Port Royal felt
    The Unity overawe,
And rued the spell. A type was here,
    And victory of LAW.   12

▓ TOPICS FOR CRITICAL THINKING AND WRITING

1. In the first stanza Melville says that all art is characterized by "measure." Take any art in which you have some interest—poetry, potting, dancing, music, whatever—and explain in an essay of 250 words how "measure" is essential.
2. In the third line Melville says that the stars no less than poems "have rules." What is he getting at?
3. Check a dictionary for the various meanings of "type," and see which meaning best fits line 11.

THOMAS HARDY

For a brief biography of the English poet Thomas Hardy (1840-1928), see page 706.

Neutral Tones   [1898]

We stood by a pond that winter day,
And the sun was white, as though chidden of God,
And a few leaves lay on the starving sod;
    —They had fallen from an ash, and were gray.   4

Your eyes on me were as eyes that rove
Over tedious riddles of years ago;
And some words played between us to and fro
    On which lost the more by our love.   8

The smile on your mouth was the deadest thing
Alive enough to have strength to die;
And a grin of bitterness swept thereby
    Like an ominous bird a-wing. . . .   12

Since then, keen lessons that love deceives,
And wrings with wrong, have shaped to me
Your face, and the God-cursed sun, and a tree,
    And a pond edged with grayish leaves.   16

▦ TOPICS FOR CRITICAL THINKING AND WRITING

1. In a sentence or two, summarize the story implicit in the poem. What has happened between the time of the episode narrated and the time of this utterance?
2. Do you think that the speaker is actually addressing the woman, or is he recollecting her and addressing her image? Or does it matter?
3. Why do you think that "keen lessons that love deceives" always remind the speaker of this scene?
4. Characterize, in a sentence or two, the speaker's state of mind in the first stanza. Is he composed, or agitated? Bitter, or meditative? Or what? Next, characterize his mind as it seems to be revealed in the final stanza.

A NOTE ON HAIKU

One form of poetry that puts a great emphasis on sharp images is the **haiku,** a Japanese poem of seventeen syllables, arranged in three lines of five, seven, and five syllables. Japanese poetry is unrhymed, but English versions sometimes rhyme the first and third lines. The subject matter can be high or low—the Milky Way or the screech of automobile brakes—but usually it is connected with the seasons, and it is described objectively and sharply. Most haiku set forth a sense of *where, what,* and *when*—but the when may be implicit, as in the first haiku.

MORITAKE (1452–1540)

Fallen petals rise

Translated by Harold G. Henderson

Fallen petals rise
back to the branch—I watch
oh . . . butterflies!

Concentrating his attention on the phenomenon (butterflies moving upward), the poet nevertheless conveys an emotion through the images (wonder, and then the recognition of the familiar), stirring the reader's imagination to supply the emotion that completes the experience.

SÔKAN (1465–1553)

If only we could

Translated by Kenneth Yasuda

If only we could
Add a handle to the moon
It would make a good fan.

SHIKI (1867–1902)

River in summer

River in summer
there is a bridge, but my horse
walks through the water.

RICHARD WRIGHT

Richard Wright (1908-1960), the grandson of a slave, was born on a cotton plantation near Natchez, Mississippi. He dropped out of school after completing the ninth grade, took a variety of odd jobs, and in 1927 moved to Chicago, where he served as a director of the Federal Negro Theater. In 1939 he became the Harlem editor of The Daily Worker, a communist newspaper in New York, and in the following year he published Native Son, the first book by an African-American author to reach a wide white audience. Wright and his family moved to Paris in 1947, where they lived until he suffered a fatal heart attack.

Four Haiku

A balmy spring wind
Reminding me of something
I cannot recall.

The green cockleburrs
Caught in the thick wooly hair
Of the black boy's head.

Standing in the field,
I hear the whispering of
   Snowflake to snowflake.

It is September
The month in which I was born,
And I have no thoughts.

Writing a Haiku

Although the haiku originated in Japan, it is now written throughout the world.

For a start, you may want to take some ordinary experience—tying your shoelaces, seeing a cat at the foot of the stairs, glancing out of a window and seeing unexpected snowflakes, hearing the alarm clock—and present it interestingly. One way to make it interesting is to construct the poem in two parts—the first line balanced against the next two lines, or the first two lines balanced against the last line. If you construct a poem on this principle, the two sections should be related to each other, but they should also in some degree make a contrast with each other. For instance, in the following poem by Taigi, there is a contrast between pleasant sociability (the first two lines) and loneliness (the last line).

TAIGI (1723–1776)

Look, O look, there go

Translated by Kenneth Yasuda

"Look, O look, there go
Fireflies," I would like to say—
But I am alone.

Basho said, "He who creates three to five haiku during a lifetime is a haiku poet. He who attains to ten is a master."

Cyber-Haiku

It has come to our attention that students have enjoyed composing haiku as substitutes for Microsoft's error messages. Here are two examples:

First snow, then silence.
This thousand-dollar screen dies
So beautifully.

A crash reduces
Your expensive computer
To a simple stone.

Why not try your hand at something on this topic?

In Chapter 27 (page 962) we reprint additional haiku and we offer suggestions about translating them.

19

Irony

There is a kind of discourse which, though nonliteral, need not use similies, metaphors, apostrophes, personification, or symbols. Without using these figures, speakers may say things that are not to be taken literally. They may, in short, employ **irony.**

In Greek comedy, the *eiron* was the sly underdog who, by dissembling inferiority, outwitted his opponent. As Aristotle puts it, irony (employed by the *eiron*) is a "pretense tending toward the underside" of truth. Later, Cicero somewhat altered the meaning of the word: He defined it as saying one thing and meaning another, and he held that Socrates, who feigned ignorance and let his opponents entrap themselves in their own arguments, was the perfect example of an ironist.

In **verbal irony,** as the term is now used, what is *stated* is in some degree negated by what is *suggested.* A classic example is Lady Macbeth's order to get ready for King Duncan's visit: "He that's coming / Must be provided for." The words seem to say that she and Macbeth must busy themselves with household preparations so that the king may be received in appropriate style, but this suggestion of hospitality is undercut by an opposite meaning: preparations must be made for the murder of the king. Two other examples of verbal irony are Melville's comment

> What like a bullet can undeceive!

and the lover's assertion (in Marvell's "To His Coy Mistress") that

> The grave's a fine and private place,
> But none, I think, do there embrace.

Under Marvell's cautious words ("I think") we detect a wryness; the **understatement** masks yet reveals a deep-felt awareness of mortality and the barrenness of the grave. The self-mockery in this understatement proclaims modesty, but suggests assurance. The speaker here, like most ironists, is both playful and serious at once. Irony packs a great deal into a few words.* What we call irony here, it should be mentioned, is often called **sarcasm,** but a distinction can be

---

*A word of caution: We have been talking about verbal irony, not **irony of situation.** Like ironic words, ironic situations have in them an element of contrast. A clown whose heart is breaking must make his audience laugh; an author's worst book is her only financial success; a fool solves a problem that vexes the wise.

made: sarcasm is notably contemptuous and crude or heavy-handed ("You're a great guy, a real friend," said to a friend who won't lend you ten dollars). Sarcasm is only one kind of irony, and a kind almost never found in literature.

Overstatement (hyperbole), like understatement, is ironic when it contains a contradictory suggestion:

> For Brutus is an honorable man;
> So are they all, all honorable men.

The sense of contradiction that is inherent in verbal irony is also inherent in a paradox. **Paradox** has several meanings for philosophers, but we need only be concerned with its meaning of an apparent contradiction. In Gerard Manley Hopkins's "Spring and Fall: To a Young Child" (page 733), there is an apparent contradiction in the assertions that Margaret is weeping for the woods (line 2) and for herself (line 15), but the contradiction is not real: both the woods and Margaret are parts of the nature blighted by Adam's sin. Other paradoxes are

> The child is father of the man;
>   —Wordsworth

and (on the soldiers who died to preserve the British Empire)

> The saviors come not home tonight;
> Themselves they could not save;
>   —Housman

and

> One short sleep past, we wake eternally,
> And Death shall be no more; Death, thou shalt die.
>   —Donne

Donne's lines are a reminder that paradox is not only an instrument of the poet. Christianity embodies several paradoxes: God became a human being; through the death on the cross, human beings can obtain eternal life; human beings do not live fully until they die.

Some critics have put a high premium on ironic and paradoxical poetry. Briefly, their argument runs that great poetry recognizes the complexity of experience, and that irony and paradox are ways of doing justice to this complexity. I. A. Richards uses "irony" to denote "The bringing in of the opposite, the complementary impulses," and suggests (in *The Principles of Literary Criticism*) that irony in this sense is a characteristic of poetry of "the highest order." It is dubious that all poets must always bring in the opposite, but it is certain that much poetry is ironic and paradoxical.

PERCY BYSSHE SHELLEY

Percy Bysshe Shelley (1792–1822) was born in Sussex in England, the son of a prosperous country squire. Educated at Eton, he went on to Oxford but was expelled for having written a pamphlet supporting a belief in atheism. Like John Keats he was a member of the second generation of English romantic poets. (The first generation included Wordsworth and Coleridge.) And like Keats, Shelley died young; he was drowned during a violent storm off the coast of Italy while sailing with a friend.

Ozymandias

[1817]

I met a traveler from an antique land
Who said: Two vast and trunkless legs of stone
Stand in the desert . . . Near them, on the sand,
Half sunk, a shattered visage lies, whose frown,
And wrinkled lip, and sneer of cold command,   5
Tell that its sculptor well those passions read
Which yet survive, stamped on these lifeless things,
The hand that mocked them, and the heart that fed:
And on the pedestal these words appear:
"My name is Ozymandias, king of kings: 10
Look on my works, ye Mighty, and despair!"
Nothing beside remains. Round the decay
Of that colossal wreck, boundless and bare
The lone and level sands stretch far away.

Lines 4–8 are somewhat obscure, but the gist is that the passions—still evident
in the "shattered visage"—survive the sculptor's hand that "mocked"—that is,
(1) imitated or copied, (2) derided—them, and the passions also survive the
king's heart that had nourished them.

 TOPIC FOR CRITICAL THINKING AND WRITING

There is an irony of plot here: Ozymandias believed that he created enduring works, but his intentions came to nothing. However, another irony is
also present: How are his words, in a way he did not intend, true?

ANDREW MARVELL

*Born in 1621 near Hull in England, Marvell attended Trinity College, Cam-
bridge, and graduated in 1638. During the English Civil War he was tutor to
the daughter of Sir Thomas Fairfax in Yorkshire at Nun Appleton House,
where most of his best-known poems were written. In 1657 he was appointed
assistant to John Milton, the Latin Secretary for the Commonwealth. After the
Restoration of the monarchy in 1659, Marvell represented Hull as a member
of parliament until his death. Most of his poems were not published until
after his death in 1678.*

To His Coy Mistress

[1681]

Had we but world enough, and time,
This coyness, lady, were no crime.
We would sit down, and think which way
To walk, and pass our long love's day.
Thou by the Indian Ganges' side   5
Should'st rubies find: I by the tide

Of Humber would complain.° I would
Love you ten years before the Flood,
And you should, if you please, refuse
Till the conversion of the Jews.   10
My vegetable° love should grow
Vaster than empires, and more slow.
An hundred years should go to praise
Thine eyes, and on thy forehead gaze:
Two hundred to adore each breast: 15
But thirty thousand to the rest.
An age at least to every part,
And the last age should show your heart.
For, lady, you deserve this state,
Nor would I love at lower rate.   20
    But at my back I always hear
Time's winged chariot hurrying near;
And yonder all before us lie
Deserts of vast eternity.
Thy beauty shall no more be found,   25
Nor in thy marble vault shall sound
My echoing song; then worms shall try
That long preserved virginity,
And your quaint honor turn to dust,
And into ashes all my lust.   30
The grave's a fine and private place,
But none, I think, do there embrace.
    Now therefore, while the youthful hue
Sits on thy skin like morning dew,
And while thy willing soul transpires   35
At every pore with instant fires,
Now let us sport us while we may;
And now, like am'rous birds of prey,
Rather at once our time devour,
Than languish in his slow-chapt° power,   40
Let us roll all our strength, and all
Our sweetness, up into one ball;
And tear our pleasures with rough strife
Thorough° the iron gates of life.
Thus, though we cannot make our sun   45
Stand still, yet we will make him run.

---

7 **complain** write love poems.   11 **vegetable** i.e., unconsciously growing.   40 **slow-chapt** slowly devouring.   44 **Thorough** through.

▨ TOPICS FOR CRITICAL THINKING AND WRITING

1. Do you find the assertions in lines 1–20 so inflated that you detect behind them a playfully ironic tone? Explain. Why does the speaker say, in line 8, that he would love "ten years before the Flood," rather than merely "since the Flood"?

2. Explain lines 21–24. Why is time behind the speaker, and eternity in front of him? Is this "eternity" the same as the period discussed in lines 1–20? What do you make of the change in the speaker's tone after line 20?

3. Do you agree with the comment on page 777 about the understatement in lines 31–32? What more can you say about these lines, in context?

4. Why "am'rous birds of prey" (line 38) rather than the conventional doves? Is the idea of preying continued in the poem?

5. Try to explain the last two lines, and characterize the speaker's tone. Do you find these lines anticlimactic?

6. The poem is organized in the form of an argument. Trace the steps.

JOHN DONNE

John Donne (1572–1631) was born into a Roman Catholic family in England, but in the 1590s he abandoned that faith. In 1615 he became an Anglican priest and soon was known as a great preacher. Of his sermons 160 survive, including one with the famous line, "No man is an island, entire of itself; every man is a piece of the continent, a part of the main; if a clod be washed away by the sea, Europe is the less . . . ; and therefore never send to know for whom the bell tolls; it tolls for thee." From 1621 until his death, Donne was dean of St. Paul's Cathedral in London. His love poems (often bawdy and cynical) are said to be his early work, and his "Holy Sonnets" (among the greatest religious poems written in English) his later work.

Holy Sonnet XIV   [1633]

Batter my heart, three-personed God; for you
As yet but knock, breathe, shine, and seek to mend;
That I may rise and stand, o'erthrow me, and bend
Your force, to break, blow, burn, and make me new.
I, like an usurped town, to another due,   5
Labor to admit you, but oh, to no end,
Reason, your viceroy in me, me should defend,
But is captived, and proves weak or untrue.
Yet dearly I love you, and would be loved fain,
But am betrothed unto your enemy: 10
Divorce me, untie, or break that knot again,
Take me to you, imprison me, for I
Except you enthrall me, never shall be free,
Nor ever chaste, except you ravish me.

❈ TOPICS FOR CRITICAL THINKING AND WRITING

1. Explain the paradoxes in lines 1, 3, 13, and 14. Explain the double meanings of "enthrall" (line 13) and "ravish" (line 14).

2. In lines 1–4, what is God implicitly compared to (considering especially lines 2 and 4)? How does this comparison lead into the comparison that

dominates lines 5-8? What words in lines 9-12 are especially related to the earlier lines?

3. What do you think is gained by piling up verbs in lines 2-4?

4. Do you find sexual references irreverent in a religious poem? (As already mentioned, Donne was an Anglican priest.)

LANGSTON HUGHES

Other poems by Langston Hughes (1902-1967) appear on pages 943-949. A biography and more of his poems appear in Chapter 26.

Dream Boogie   [1951]

Good morning, daddy!
Ain't you heard
The boogie-woogie rumble
Of a dream deferred?
Listen closely: 5
You'll hear their feet
Beating out and beating out a—

    You think
    It's a happy beat?

Listen to it closely: 10
Ain't you heard
something underneath
like a—

    What did I say?

Sure,   15
I'm happy!
Take it away!

    Hey, pop!
    Re-bop!
    Mop!   20

    Y-e-a-h!

    What don't bug
    them white kids
    sure bugs me:
    We knows everybody   25
    ain't free!

Some of these young ones is cert'ly bad—
One batted a hard ball right through my window
and my gold fish et the glass.

What's written down   30
for white folks
ain't for us a-tall:
"Liberty And Justice—
Huh—For All."

Oop-pop-a-da!   35
Skee! Daddle-de-do!
Be-bop!

Salt'peanuts!

De-dop!

 TOPICS FOR CRITICAL THINKING AND WRITING

1. What is boogie, or boogie-woogie?
2. Why did many whites assume that boogie was "a happy beat" (line 9)?
   In fact, what was boogie chiefly an expression of?
3. Why does Hughes in lines 33–34 quote part of the Pledge of Allegiance?

MARTÍN ESPADA

Martín Espada was born in Brooklyn in 1957. He received a bachelor's de-
gree from the University of Wisconsin and a law degree from Northeastern
University. He is now an associate professor of English at the University of
Massachusetts (Amherst).

Tony Went to the Bodega* but He Didn't Buy Anything   [1987]

para Angel Guadalupe

Tony's father left the family
and the Long Island city projects,
leaving a mongrel-skinny puertorriqueño boy
nine years old
who had to find work.   5

Makengo the Cuban
let him work at the bodega.
In grocery aisles
he learned the steps of the dry-mop mambo,
banging the cash register   10

*Bodega grocery and liquor store; in the dedication, after the title, *para* means "for."

like piano percussion
in the spotlight of Machito's orchestra,
polite with the abuelas° who bought on credit,
practicing the grin on customers
he'd seen Makengo grin   15
with his bad yellow teeth.

Tony left the projects too,
with a scholarship for law school.
But he cursed the cold primavera°
in Boston;   20
the cooking of his neighbors
left no smell in the hallway
and no one spoke Spanish
(not even the radio).

So Tony walked without a map   25
through the city,
a landscape of hostile condominiums
and the darkness of white faces,
sidewalk-searcher lost
till he discovered the projects.   30

Tony went to the bodega
but he didn't buy anything:
he sat by the doorway satisfied
to watch la gente° (people
island-brown as him)   35
crowd in and out,
hablando español,°
thought: this is beautiful,
and grinned
his bodega grin.   40

This is a rice and beans
success story:
today Tony lives on Tremont Street,
above the bodega.

---

13 abuelas grandmothers. **19 primavera** spring season. **34 la gente** the people.
37 hablando español speaking Spanish.

▓ TOPICS FOR CRITICAL THINKING AND WRITING

1. Why do you suppose Espada included the information about Tony's
   father? The information about young Tony "practicing" a grin?
2. Why does Tony leave?
3. How would you characterize Tony?

EDNA ST. VINCENT MILLAY

For other poem's by the American poet Edna St. Vincent Millay (1892-1950)
as well as a brief biography, see pages 711 and 858.

Love Is Not All: It Is Not Meat nor Drink [1931]

Love is not all: it is not meat nor drink
Nor slumber nor a roof against the rain;
Nor yet a floating spar to men that sink
And rise and sink and rise and sink again;
Love can not fill the thickened lung with breath,   5
Nor clean the blood, nor set the fractured bone;
Yet many a man is making friends with death
Even as I speak, for lack of love alone.
It well may be that in a difficult hour,
Pinned down by pain and moaning for release,   10
Or nagged by want past resolution's power,
I might be driven to sell your love for peace,
Or trade the memory of this night for food.
It well may be. I do not think I would.

▨ TOPICS FOR CRITICAL THINKING AND WRITING

1. "Love Is Not All" is a sonnet. Using your own words, briefly summarize
   the argument of the octet (the first 8 lines). Next, paraphrase the sestet
   (the six lines from line 9 through line 14), line by line. On the whole,
   does the sestet repeat the idea of the octet, or does it add a new idea?
   Whom did you imagine to be speaking the octet? What does the sestet
   add to your knowledge of the speaker and the occasion? (And how did
   you paraphrase line 11?)
2. The first and last lines of the poem consist of words of one syllable, and
   both lines have a distinct pause in the middle. Do you imagine the lines
   to be spoken in the same tone of voice? If not, can you describe the difference and account for it?
3. Lines 7 and 8 appear to mean that the absence of love can be a cause of
   death. To what degree do you believe that to be true?
4. Would you call "Love Is Not All" a love poem? Why or why not? Describe the kind of person who might include the poem in a love letter
   or valentine, or who would be happy to receive it. (One of our friends
   recited it at her wedding. What do you think of that idea?)

SHERMAN ALEXIE

The short-story writer, essayist, poet, and film director Sherman J. Alexie Jr.,
was born in October 1966 and was raised on the Spokane Indian Reserva-
tion in Wellpinit, Washington, located fifty miles northwest of Spokane. He

went to high school off reservation in Reardan, Washington, where he was an excellent student and played on the basketball team. He attended Gonzaga University in Spokane for two years and then transferred to Washington State University in Pullman. There, he began writing poetry, graduating with a degree in American Studies. His books include The Business of Fancydancing: Stories and Poems *(1992),* The Lone Ranger and Tonto Fistfight in Heaven *(1994), and* Reservation Blues *(1995).*

For additional poems by Alexie, see pages 888 and 909; for a story, see page 291.

Evolution   [1992]

Buffalo Bill opens a pawn shop on the reservation
right across the border from the liquor store
and he stays open 24 hours a day, 7 days a week   3

and the Indians come running in with jewelry
television sets, a VCR, a full-length beaded buckskin outfit
it took Inez Muse 12 years to finish. Buffalo Bill   6

takes everything the Indians have to offer, keeps it
all catalogued and filed in a storage room. The Indians
pawn their hands, saving the thumbs for last, they pawn   9

their skeletons, falling endlessly from the skin
and when the last Indian has pawned everything
but his heart, Buffalo Bill takes that for twenty bucks   12

closes up the pawn shop, paints a new sign over the old
calls his venture THE MUSEUM OF NATIVE AMERICAN CULTURES
charges the Indians five bucks a head to enter.   15

HENRY REED

Born in Birmingham, England, Henry Reed (1914–1986) served in the British army during the Second World War. Later, in civilian life he had a distinguished career as a journalist, a translator of French and Italian literature, a writer of radio plays, and a poet.

"Naming of Parts" draws on his experience as a military recruit.

Naming of Parts   [1946]

Today we have naming of parts. Yesterday,
We had daily cleaning. And tomorrow morning,
We shall have what to do after firing. But today,
Today we have naming of parts. Japonica
Glistens like coral in all of the neighboring gardens,   5
          And today we have naming of parts.

This is the lower sling swivel. And this
Is the upper sling swivel, whose use you will see,
When you are given your slings. And this is the piling swivel,
Which in your case you have not got. The branches   10
Hold in the gardens their silent, eloquent gestures,
        Which in our case we have not got.

This is the safety-catch, which is always released
With an easy flick of the thumb. And please do not let me
See anyone using his finger. You can do it quite easy   15
If you have any strength in your thumb. The blossoms
Are fragile and motionless, never letting anyone see
        Any of them using their finger.

And this you can see is the bolt. The purpose of this
Is to open the breech, as you see. We can slide it   20
Rapidly backwards and forwards: we call this
Easing the spring. And rapidly backwards and forwards
The early bees are assaulting and fumbling the flowers:
        They call it easing the Spring.

They call it easing the Spring: it is perfectly easy   25
If you have any strength in your thumb: like the bolt,
And the breech, and the cocking-piece, and the point of balance,
Which in our case we have not got; and the almond-blossom
Silent in all of the gardens and the bees going backwards and forwards,
        For today we have naming of parts.   30

▨ TOPICS FOR CRITICAL THINKING AND WRITING

1. How many speakers do you hear in the poem? How would you characterize each of them?
2. Why do we include this poem in a chapter on "irony"?

20

Rhythm and Versification

Up and down the City Road,
In and out the Eagle;
That's the way the money goes,
Pop goes the weasel.

Probably very few of the countless children—and adults—who sometimes find themselves singing this ditty have the faintest idea of what it is about. It endures because it is catchy—a strong, easily remembered rhythm. Even if you just read it aloud without singing it, we think you will agree.

If you try to specify exactly what the rhythm is—for instance, by putting an accent mark on each syllable that you stress heavily—you may run into difficulties. You may become unsure of whether you stress *up* and *down* equally; maybe you will decide that *up* is hardly stressed more than *and,* at least compared with the heavy stress that you put on *down.* Different readers (really, singers) will recite it differently. Does this mean that anything goes? Of course not. No one will emphasize *and* or *the,* just as no one will emphasize the second syllable in *city* or the second syllable in *money.* There may be some variations from reader to reader, but there will also be a good deal that all readers will agree on. And surely all readers agree that it is memorable.

Does this song have a meaning? Well, historians say that the Eagle was a tavern and music hall in the City Road, in Victorian London. People went there to eat, drink, and sing, with the result that they sometimes spent too much money and then had to pawn (or "pop") the "weasel"—though no one is sure what the weasel is. It doesn't really matter; the song lives by its rhythm.

Now consider this poem by Ezra Pound (1885–1972). Pound's early work is highly rhythmical; later he became sympathetic to Fascism and he grew increasingly anti-Semitic, with the result that for many readers his later work is much less interesting—just a lot of nasty ideas, rather than memorable expressions. Pound ought to have remembered his own definition of literature: "Literature is news that *stays* news." One way of staying is to use unforgettable rhythms.

EZRA POUND

An Immorality

[1919]

Sing we for love and idleness,
Naught else is worth the having.

Though I have been in many a land,
There is naught else in living.

And I would rather have my sweet,   5
Though rose-leaves die of grieving,

Than do high deeds in Hungary
To pass all men's believing.

A good poem. To begin with, it sings; as Pound said, "Poetry withers and dries
out when it leaves music, or at least imagined music, too far behind it. Poets
who are not interested in music are, or become, bad poets." Hymns and ballads,
it must be remembered, are songs, and other poetry, too, is sung, especially by
children. Children reciting a counting-out rhyme, or singing on their way home
from school, are enjoying poetry:

Pease-porridge hot,
    Pease-porridge cold,
Pease-porridge in the pot
    Nine days old.

Nothing very important is being said, but for generations children have enjoyed
the music of these lines, and adults, too, have recalled them with pleasure—
though few people know what pease-porridge is.

The "music"—the catchiness of certain sounds—should not be underesti-
mated. Here are lines chanted by the witches in *Macbeth:*

Double, double, toil and trouble;
Fire burn and cauldron bubble.

This is rather far from words that mean approximately the same thing: "Twice,
twice, work and care; / Fire ignite, and pot boil." The difference is more in the
sounds than in the instructions. What is lost in the paraphrase is the magic, the
incantation, which resides in elaborate repetitions of sounds and stresses.

Rhythm (most simply, in English poetry, stresses at regular intervals) has a
power of its own. A good march, said John Philip Sousa (the composer of "Stars
and Stripes Forever"), "should make even someone with a wooden leg step out."
A highly pronounced rhythm is common in such forms of poetry as charms,
college yells, and lullabies; all of them (like the witches' speech) are aimed at
inducing a special effect magically. It is not surprising that *carmen,* the Latin
word for "poem" or "song," is also the Latin word for *charm,* and the word from
which "charm" is derived.

Rain, rain, go away;
Come again another day.

Block that kick! Block that kick! Block that kick!

Rock-a-bye baby, on the tree top,
When the wind blows, the cradle will rock.

In much poetry, rhythm is only half-heard, but its omnipresence is suggested by the fact that when poetry is printed it is customary to begin each line with a capital letter. Prose (from Latin *prorsus,* "forward," "straight on") keeps running across the paper until the right-hand margin is reached, and then, merely because the paper has given out, the writer or printer starts again at the left, with a small letter. But verse (Latin *versus,* "a turning") often ends well short of the right-hand margin, and the next line begins at the left—usually with a capital—not because paper has run out but because the rhythmic pattern begins again. Lines of poetry are continually reminding us that they have a pattern.

Before turning to some other highly rhythmical pieces, a word of caution: a mechanical, unvarying rhythm may be good to put the baby to sleep, but it can be deadly to readers who wish to keep awake. Poets vary their rhythm according to their purpose; a poet ought not to be so regular that he or she is (in W. H. Auden's words) an "accentual pest." In competent hands, rhythm contributes to meaning; it says something. The rhythm in the lines from *Macbeth,* for example, helps suggest the strong binding power of magic. Again Ezra Pound has a relevant comment: "Rhythm *must* have meaning. It can't be merely a careless dash off, with no grip and no real hold to the words and sense, a tumty tum tumty tum tum ta." Some examples will be useful.

Consider this description of Hell from John Milton's *Paradise Lost* (the heavier stresses are marked by ´):

Rócks, caves, lakes, feńs, bogs, deńs, and shádes of death.

Such a succession of stresses is highly unusual. Elsewhere in the poem Milton chiefly uses iambic feet—alternating unstressed and stressed syllables—but here he immediately follows one heavy stress with another, thereby helping to communicate the "meaning"—the impressive monotony of Hell. As a second example, consider the function of the rhythm in two lines by Alexander Pope:

Whĕn Ájaẋ strives somĕ rock's vast weight tŏ throw,
Thĕ linĕ too lábŏrs, ańd thĕ words móve slów.

The heavier stresses (again, marked by ´) do not merely alternate with the lighter ones (marked ˘); rather, the great weight of the rock is suggested by three consecutive stressed words, "rock's vast weight," and the great effort involved in moving it is suggested by another three consecutive stresses, "line too labors," and by yet another three, "words move slow." Note, also, the abundant pauses within the lines. In the first line, unless one's speech is slovenly, one must pause at least slightly after "Ajax," "strives," "rock's," "vast," "weight," and "throw." The grating sounds in "Ajax" and "rock's" do their work, too, and so do the explosive *t*'s. When Pope wishes to suggest lightness, he reverses his procedure and he groups *un*stressed syllables:

Not so, when swift Camilla scours the plain,
Fliés o'ĕr th'uňbéndĭng córn, ańd skíms ăloňg thĕ máin.

This last line has twelve syllables and is thus longer than the line about Ajax, but the addition of "along" helps to communicate lightness and swiftness because in this line (it can be argued) neither syllable of "along" is strongly stressed. If "along" is omitted, the line still makes grammatical sense and becomes more "regular," but it also becomes less imitative of lightness.

The very regularity of a line may be meaningful too. Shakespeare begins a sonnet thus:

Whĕn Í dŏ coúnt thĕ cloćk thăt télls thĕ timĕ.

This line about a mechanism runs with appropriate regularity. (It is worth noting, too, that "count the clock" and "tells the time" emphasize the regularity by the repetition of sounds and syntax.) But notice what Shakespeare does in the middle of the next line:

Aňd sée thĕ bráve dáy suńk iň hídeŏus níght.

What has he done? And what is the effect?

Here is another poem that refers to a clock. In England, until capital punishment was abolished, executions regularly took place at 8:00 A.M.

A. E. HOUSMAN

For another poem by the English poet A. E. Housman (1859–1936) and for a brief biography, see page 683.

Eight O'Clock   [1922]

He stood, and heard the steeple
   Sprinkle the quarters on the morning town.
One, two, three, four, to market-place and people
   It tossed them down.   4

Strapped, noosed, nighing his hour,
   He stood and counted them and cursed his luck;
And then the clock collected in the tower
   Its strength, and struck.   8

The chief (but not unvarying) pattern is iambic; that is, the odd syllables are less emphatic than the even ones, as in

Hĕ stóod, aňd heárd thĕ stéeplĕ

Try to mark the syllables, stressed and unstressed, in the rest of the poem. Be guided by your ear, not by a mechanical principle, and don't worry too much about difficult or uncertain parts; different readers may reasonably come up with different results.

▨ TOPICS FOR CRITICAL THINKING AND WRITING

    1. Where do you find two or more consecutive stresses? What explanations (related to meaning) can be offered?

2. What do you think is the effect of the short line at the end of each
   stanza? And what significance can you attach to the fact that these lines
   (unlike the first and third lines in each stanza) end with a stress?

Following are some poems in which the strongly felt pulsations are highly
important.

WILLIAM CARLOS WILLIAMS

*A poem by William Carlos Williams (1883–1963), along with a brief biogra-
phy, appears on page 751. The Breughel (also spelled Brueghel) painting described in "The Dance" is shown on the next page.*

The Dance   [1944]

In Breughel's great picture, The Kermess,°
the dancers go round, they go round and
around, the squeal and the blare and the
tweedle of bagpipes, a bugle and fiddles
tipping their bellies (round as the thick-   5
sided glasses whose wash they impound)
their hips and their bellies off balance
to turn them. Kicking and rolling about
the Fair Grounds, swinging their butts, those
shanks must be sound to bear up under such   10
rollicking measures, prance as they dance
in Breughel's great picture, The Kermess.

---

1 **Kermess** Carnival.

▨ TOPICS FOR CRITICAL THINKING AND WRITING

1. Read Williams's poem aloud several times, and decide where the
   heavy stresses fall. Mark the heavily stressed syllables ´, the lightly
   stressed ones ^, and the unstressed ones ˘. Are all the lines identical?
   What effect is thus gained, especially when read aloud? What does the
   parenthetical statement (lines 5–6) do to the rhythm? Does a final syllable often receive a heavy stress here? Are there noticeable pauses
   at the ends of the lines? What is the consequence? Are the dancers
   waltzing?
2. What syllables rhyme or are repeated (e.g., "round" in lines 2 and 5,
   and "-pound" in line 6; "-ing" in lines 5, 8, 9, and 11)? What effect do
   they have?
3. What do you think the absence at the beginning of each line of the customary capital contributes to the meaning? Why is the last line the
   same as the first?

Pieter Breughel the Elder, *Peasant Dance*, c. 1568, oil on wood, 114 × 164 cm. (Kunsthistorisches Museum, Vienna.)

ROBERT FRANCIS

Robert Francis (1901–1987) was born in Upland, Pennsylvania, and educated at Harvard. He taught only briefly, a term here or there and an occasional summer, devoting himself for the most part to reading and writing.

The Pitcher   [1960]

His art is eccentricity, his aim
How not to hit the mark he seems to aim at,

His passion how to avoid the obvious,
His technique how to vary the avoidance.

The others throw to be comprehended. He   5
Throws to be a moment misunderstood.

Yet not too much. Not errant, arrant, wild,
But every seeming aberration willed.

Not to, yet still, still to communicate
Making the batter understand too late.   10

If you read this poem aloud, pausing appropriately where the punctuation tells you to, you will hear the poet trying to represent something of the pitcher's "eccentricity." ("Eccentric," you may know, literally means "off center.") A pitcher tries to deceive a batter, perhaps by throwing a ball that will unexpectedly curve over the plate; the poet playfully deceives the reader, for instance, with unexpected pauses. In line 5, for example, he puts a heavy pause (indicated by a period) not at the end of the line, but just before the end.

▨ TOPICS FOR CRITICAL THINKING AND WRITING

1. Notice that some lines contain no pauses, but the next-to-last line contains two within it (indicated by commas) and none at the end. What do you suppose Francis is getting at?
2. What significance can be attached to the fact that only the last two lines really rhyme (communicate/late), whereas other lines do not quite rhyme?

VERSIFICATION: A GLOSSARY FOR REFERENCE

The technical vocabulary of **prosody** (the study of the principles of verse structure, including meter, rhyme, and other sound effects, and stanzaic patterns) is large. An understanding of these terms will not turn anyone into a poet, but it will enable one to discuss some aspects of poetry more efficiently. A knowledge of them, like a knowledge of most other technical terms (e.g., "misplaced modifier," "woofer," "automatic transmission"), allows for quick and accurate communication. The following are the chief terms of prosody.

Meter

Most English poetry has a pattern of **stressed (accented)** sounds, and this pattern is the **meter** (from the Greek word for "measure"). Although in Old English poetry (poetry written in England before the Norman-French Conquest in 1066) a line may have any number of unstressed syllables in addition to four stressed syllables, most poetry written in England since the Conquest not only has a fixed number of stresses in a line but also has a fixed number of unstressed syllables before or after each stressed one. (One really ought not to talk of "unstressed" or "unaccented" syllables, since to utter a syllable—however lightly—is to give it some stress. It is really a matter of *relative* stress, but the fact is that "unstressed" or "unaccented" are parts of the established terminology of versification.)

In a line of poetry, the **foot** is the basic unit of measurement. On rare occasions it is a single stressed syllable, but generally a foot consists of two or three syllables, one of which is stressed. (Stress is indicated by ´, lack of stress by ˘.) The repetition of feet, then, produces a pattern of stresses throughout the poem.

Two cautions:

1. A poem will seldom contain only one kind of foot throughout; significant variations usually occur, but one kind of foot is dominant.

2. In reading a poem one pays attention to the sense as well as to the metrical pattern. By paying attention to the sense, one often finds that the stress falls on a word that according to the metrical pattern would be unstressed. Or a word that according to the pattern would be stressed may be seen to be unstressed. Furthermore, by reading for sense, one finds that not all stresses are equally heavy; some are almost as light as unstressed syllables, and sometimes there is a **hovering stress;** that is, the stress is equally distributed over two adjacent syllables. To repeat: *read for sense,* allowing the meaning to help indicate the stresses.

Metrical Feet

The most common feet in English poetry are the following six.

Iamb (adjective: **iambic**): one unstressed syllable followed by one stressed syllable. The iamb, said to be the most common pattern in English speech, is surely the most common in English poetry. The following example has four iambic feet:

Mȳ héart ĭs líke ă síngĭng bírd.

—Christina Rossetti

Trochee (trochaic): one stressed syllable followed by one unstressed.

Wé wĕře véřy tíred, wé wĕre véřy mérrў

—Edna St. Vincent Millay

Anapest (anapestic): two unstressed syllables followed by one stressed.

Thĕre ăře mánў whŏ sáy thăt ă dóg hăs hĭs dáy.

—Dylan Thomas

Dactyl (dactylic): one stressed syllable followed by two unstressed. This trisyllabic foot, like the anapest, is common in light verse or verse suggesting joy, but its use is not limited to such material, as Longfellow's *Evangeline* shows. Thomas Hood's sentimental "The Bridge of Sighs" begins:

Táke hĕr ŭp téndĕrlў.

Spondee (spondaic): two stressed syllables; most often used as a substitute for an iamb or trochee.

Smárt lád, tŏ slíp bĕtímes ăwáy.

—A. E. Housman

Pyrrhic: two unstressed syllables; it is often not considered a legitimate foot in English.

Metrical Lines

A metrical line consists of one or more feet and is named for the number of feet in it. The following names are used:

monometer: one foot	**pentameter:** five feet
dimeter: two feet	**hexameter:** six feet
trimeter: three feet	**heptameter:** seven feet
tetrameter: four feet	**octameter:** eight feet

A line is scanned for the kind and number of feet in it, and the **scansion** tells you if it is, say, anapestic trimeter (three anapests):

Ăs Ĭ cáme tŏ thĕ édge ŏf thĕ wóods.

—Robert Frost

Or, in another example, iambic pentameter:

Thĕ súmmĕr thúndĕr, lĭke ă wóodĕn béll

—Louise Bogan

A line ending with a stress has a **masculine ending;** a line ending with an extra unstressed syllable has a **feminine ending.** The **caesura** (usually indicated by the symbol //) is a slight pause within the line. It need not be indicated by punctuation (notice the fourth and fifth lines in the following quotation), and it does not affect the metrical count:

Awake, my St. John! // leave all meaner things
To low ambition, // and the pride of kings.
Let us // (since life can little more supply
Than just to look about us // and to die)
Expatiate free // o'er all this scene of Man;
A mighty maze! // but not without a plan;
A wild, // where weeds and flowers promiscuous shoot;
Or garden, // tempting with forbidden fruit.

—Alexander Pope

The varying position of the caesura helps to give Pope's lines an informality that plays against the formality of the pairs of rhyming lines.

An **end-stopped line** concludes with a distinct syntactical pause, but a **run-on line** has its sense carried over into the next line without syntactical pause. (The running on of a line is called **enjambment.**) In the following passage, only the first is a run-on line:

Yet if we look more closely we shall find
Most have the seeds of judgment in their mind:
Nature affords at least a glimmering light;
The lines, though touched but faintly, are drawn right.

—Alexander Pope

Meter produces **rhythm,** recurrences at equal intervals; but rhythm (from a Greek word meaning "flow") is usually applied to larger units than feet. Often it depends most obviously on pauses. Thus, a poem with run-on lines will have a different rhythm from a poem with end-stopped lines, even though both are in the same meter. And prose, though it is unmetrical, can have rhythm, too.

In addition to being affected by syntactical pause, rhythm is affected by pauses attributable to consonant clusters and to the length of words. Words of several syllables establish a different rhythm from words of one syllable, even in metrically identical lines. One can say, then, that rhythm is altered by shifts in meter, syntax, and the length and ease of pronunciation. But even with no such shift, even if a line is repeated word for word, a reader may sense a change in rhythm. The rhythm of the final line of a poem, for example, may well differ from that of the line before, even though in all other respects the lines are identical, as in Frost's "Stopping by Woods on a Snowy Evening" (page 936), which concludes by repeating "And miles to go before I sleep." One may simply sense that the final line ought to be spoken, say, more slowly and with more stress on "miles."

Patterns of Sound

Though rhythm is basic to poetry, **rhyme**—the repetition of the identical or similar stressed sound or sounds—is not. Rhyme is, presumably, pleasant in itself; it suggests order; and it may also be related to meaning, for it brings two words sharply together, often implying a relationship, as in the now trite *dove* and *love,* or in the more imaginative *throne* and *alone.*

> **Perfect,** or **exact, rhyme:** Differing consonant sounds are followed by identical stressed vowel sounds, and the following sounds, if any, are identical *(foe—toe; meet—fleet; buffer—rougher)*. Notice that perfect rhyme involves identity of sound, not of spelling. *Fix* and *sticks,* like *buffer* and *rougher,* are perfect rhymes.
>
> **Half-rhyme** (or **off-rhyme**): Only the final consonant sounds of the words are identical; the stressed vowel sounds as well as the initial consonant sounds, if any, differ *(soul—oil; mirth—forth; trolley—bully)*.
>
> **Eye-rhyme:** The sounds do not in fact rhyme, but the words look as though they would rhyme *(cough—bough)*.
>
> **Masculine rhyme:** The final syllables are stressed and, after their differing initial consonant sounds, are identical in sound *(stark—mark; support—retort)*.
>
> **Feminine rhyme** (or **double rhyme**): Stressed rhyming syllables are followed by identical unstressed syllables *(revival—arrival; flatter—batter)*.
>
> **Triple rhyme** is a kind of feminine rhyme in which identical stressed vowel sounds are followed by two identical unstressed syllables *(machinery—scenery; tenderly—slenderly)*.
>
> **End rhyme** (or **terminal rhyme**): The rhyming words occur at the ends of the lines.
>
> **Internal rhyme:** At least one of the rhyming words occurs within the line (Oscar Wilde's "Each narrow *cell* in which we *dwell*").
>
> **Alliteration:** Sometimes defined as the repetition of initial sounds ("*A*ll the *a*wful *a*uguries," or "*B*ring me my *b*ow of *b*urning gold"), and sometimes as the prominent repetition of a consonant ("*a*fter li*f*e's *f*itful *f*ever").
>
> **Assonance:** The repetition, in words of proximity, of identical vowel sounds preceded and followed by differing consonant sounds. Whereas *tide* and *hide* are rhymes, *tide* and *mine* are assonantal.
>
> **Consonance:** The repetition of identical consonant sounds and differing vowel sounds in words in proximity *(fail—feel; rough—roof; pitter—patter)*. Sometimes consonance is more loosely defined merely as the repetition of a consonant *(fail—peel)*.
>
> **Onomatopoeia:** The use of words that imitate sounds, such as *hiss* and *buzz.* There is a mistaken tendency to see onomatopoeia everywhere—for example in *thunder* and *horror.* Many words sometimes thought to be onomatopoeic are not clearly imitative of the thing they refer to; they merely contain some sounds that, when we know what the word means, seem to

have some resemblance to the thing they denote. Tennyson's lines from "Come down, O maid" are usually cited as an example of onomatopoeia:

> The moan of doves in immemorial elms
> And murmuring of innumerable bees.

If you have read the preceding—and, admittedly, not entirely engaging— paragraphs, you may have found yourself mentally repeating some catchy sounds, let's say our example of internal rhyme ("Each narrow cell in which we dwell") or our example of alliteration ("Bring me my bow of burning gold"). As the creators of advertising slogans know, all of us—not just poets—can be hooked by the sounds of words, but probably poets are especially fond of savoring words. Consider the following poem.

GALWAY KINNELL

Born in 1927 in Providence, Rhode Island, Galway Kinnell was educated at Princeton and the University of Rochester. He is the author of several books of poems, and he has won many awards, including the Pulitzer Prize for Poetry and the American Book Award.

Blackberry Eating   [1980]

I love to go out in late September
among the fat, overripe, icy, black blackberries
to eat blackberries for breakfast,
the stalks very prickly, a penalty
they earn for knowing the black art   5
of blackberry-making: and as I stand among them
lifting the stalks to my mouth, the ripest berries
fall almost unbidden to my tongue,
as words sometimes do, certain peculiar words
like *strengths* or *squinched*,   10
many-lettered, one-syllabled lumps,
which I squeeze, squinch open, and splurge well
in the silent, startled, icy, black language
of blackberry-eating in late September.

Kinnell does not use rhyme, but he uses other kinds of aural repetition. For instance, in the first line we get "*l*ove" and "*l*ate," and the *l* sound (already present in the title of the poem) is picked up in the second line, in "black blackberries." The *k* sound is then continued in the next line, in "stalks" and the *l* and *k* in "prickly," and "prickly" contains not only the *k* and the *l* of "blackberry" but also the *r*.

In lines 7–9 Kinnell compares eating blackberries—an action involving the tongue and the lips, and the mind also, if one is savoring the berries—to speaking "certain peculiar words." There is no need for us to point out additional connections between words in the poem, but we do want to mention that the last line ends with the same two words as the first, providing closure, which is one of the things rhyme normally does.

✺ TOPICS FOR CRITICAL THINKING AND WRITING

1. Specify three words that you like to "squinch," and explain why.
2. Specify one poem, other than a poem in this chapter (the poem need not be in this book), in which you think the repetitions of sounds are especially important, and explain why you hold this view.

A Note about Poetic Forms

"Art is nothing without form," the French author Gustave Flaubert maintained, and it's true that works of art have a carefully designed shape. Most obviously, for instance, a good story has an ending that satisfies the reader or hearer. In real life, things keep going, but when a good story ends, the audience feels that there is nothing more to say, at least nothing more of interest to say.

With poems that rhyme, the rhyme-scheme provides a pattern, a shape, a structure that seems inseparable from the content. If you recite a limerick, you will immediately see how the shape is inseparable from the content:

> There was a young fellow from Lynn
> Who was so exceedingly thin
>   That when he essayed
>   To drink lemonade
> He slipped through the straw and fell in.

If you put the words in a different order, and you ignore meter and rhyme—that is, if you destroy the form and turn the passage into something like "A young man, so thin that he fell through a straw into a glass of lemonade, lived in Lynn"—you can instantly see the importance of form.

Let's briefly look at a more serious example. You may recall Housman's "Eight O'Clock" (page 791), a poem whose title corresponds to the hour at which executions in England used to take place.

> He stood, and heard the steeple
>   Sprinkle the quarters on the morning town.
> One, two, to market-place and people
>   It tossed them down.
>
> Strapped, noosed, nighing his hour,
>   He stood and counted them and cursed his luck;
> And then the clock collected in the tower
>   Its strength, and struck.

The rhyme of "struck" with "luck" (in this instance, bad luck) is conclusive. We don't ask if the body was removed from the gallows and buried, or if the condemned man's wife (if he had one) grieved, or if his children (if he had any) turned out well or badly. None of these things is of any relevance. There is nothing more to say. The form and the content perfectly go together. In this example, the lines, each of which rhymes with another line—we might say that each line is tied to another line—seem especially appropriate for a man who is "strapped" and "noosed."

But why do poets use forms established by rhyme? In an essay called "The Constant Symbol," Robert Frost says that a poet regards rhymes as "stepping stones. . . . The way will be zigzag, but it will be a straight crookedness like the walking stick he cuts in the bushes for an emblem." Housman's stepping-stones in the second stanza took Houseman (and take the reader) from *hour* to *luck*, then to *tower* and then with great finality to the end of the walk, *struck*. We think this stanza is inspired, and we imagine that Housman's inspiration was mightily helped by his need for rhymes—his need to get "stepping stones" that would allow him to continue the "straight crookedness" of his walk with this condemned man. His walk-with-words, or rather his walk with words-that-set-forth-ideas, produced "luck" and "struck," and enabled him to give to his readers the memorable image of the clock as a machine that executes the man.

When you read Housman's or Frost's actual lines—or better, when you read them aloud and hear and feel the effect of these rhymes—you can understand why Frost more than once said he would as soon write unrhymed poetry as he would "play tennis with the net down." The rules governing the game of tennis or the game of writing do not interfere with the game; rather, the rules allow the players to play a game. The rules allow poets to write poems; the rules—the restraints—provide the structure that allows poets to accomplish something. Poets are somewhat like Houdini, who accepted shackles so that he could triumph over them. Without the handcuffs and other restraints, he could accomplish nothing. Or consider the string on a kite; far from impeding the kite's flight, the string allows the kite to fly. Speaking in less high-flying terms, we can quote from a talk that Frost gave to college students in 1937, "The Poet's Next of Kin in College." He told them—and he was speaking not only to young poets but to all students—that in their endeavors, of whatever sort, they "must have form—performance. The thing itself is indescribable, but it is felt like athletic form. To have form, feel form in sports—and by analogy feel form in verse."

Poets have testified that they use rhyme partly because, far from impeding them, it helps them to say interesting things in a memorable way. True, some rhymes have been used so often that although they were once rich in meaning—for instance—"love" and "dove" or "moon" and "June"—they have become clichés, their use indicating not an imaginative leap but a reliance on what has been said too often. But other rhymes—let's say "earth" and "birth" or "law" and "flaw"—can lead poets to say interesting things that they might otherwise not have thought of.

In his "Letter of Advice to a Young Poet," Jonathan Swift (whom you may know as the author of *Gulliver's Travels*, 1726), said: "Verse without rhyme is a body without a soul." A striking, and indeed surprising, comment: Swift dares to propose that the soul of a poem depends not on the content but, rather, on a crucial element of its form, the presence of rhyme. In part he is reminding us here of the importance of craft in the writing of a poem, of the sheer skill and deliberation that makes the literary work feel exactly right, as though it *had* to be this way.

Stanzaic Patterns

Lines of poetry are commonly arranged in a rhythmical unit called a stanza (from an Italian word meaning "room" or "stopping-place"). Usually all the stanzas in a poem have the same rhyme pattern. A stanza is sometimes called a **verse**, though *verse* may also mean a single line of poetry. (In discussing stanzas, rhymes are indicated by identical letters. Thus, *abab* indicates that the first and third lines rhyme with each other, while the second and fourth lines are linked by a different rhyme. An unrhymed line is denoted by *x*.) Common stanzaic forms in English poetry are the following:

Couplet: a stanza of two lines, usually but not necessarily with end-rhymes. *Couplet* is also used for a pair of rhyming lines. The **octosyllabic couplet** is iambic or trochaic tetrameter:

Had we but world enough and time,
This coyness, lady, were no crime.

—Andrew Marvell

Heroic couplet: a rhyming couplet of iambic pentameter, often "closed," that is, containing a complete thought, with a fairly heavy pause at the end of the first line and a still heavier one at the end of the second. Commonly, there is a parallel or an *antithesis* (contrast) within a line or between the two lines. It is called heroic because in England, especially in the eighteenth century, it was much used for heroic (epic) poems.

Some foreign writers, some our own despise;
The ancients only, or the moderns, prize.

—Alexander Pope

Triplet (or **tercet**): a three-line stanza, usually with one rhyme.

Whenas in silks my Julia goes
Then, then (methinks) how sweetly flows
That liquefaction of her clothes.

—Robert Herrick

Quatrain: a four-line stanza, rhymed or unrhymed. The **heroic** (or **elegiac) quatrain** is iambic pentameter, rhyming *abab*. That is, the first and third lines rhyme (so they are designated *a*), and the second and fourth lines rhyme (so they are designated *b*).

THREE COMPLEX FORMS: THE SONNET, THE VILLANELLE, AND THE SESTINA

The Sonnet

A sonnet is a fourteen-line poem, predominantly in iambic pentameter. The rhyme is usually according to one of two schemes. The **Italian** or **Petrarchan sonnet,** named for the Italian poet Francesco Petrarch (1304–1374), has two divisions: The first eight lines (rhyming *abba abba*) are the octave, and the last six (rhyming *cd cd cd,* or a variant) are the sestet. Gerard Manley Hopkins's "God's Grandeur" (page 991) is an Italian sonnet. The second kind of sonnet, the **English** or **Shakespearean sonnet,** is usually arranged into three quatrains and a couplet, rhyming *abab cdcd efef gg.* (For examples see the next two poems.) In many sonnets there is a marked correspondence between the rhyme scheme and the development of the thought. Thus an Italian sonnet may state a generalization in the octave and a specific example in the sestet. Or an English sonnet may give three examples—one in each quatrain—and draw a conclusion in the couplet.

Why poets choose to imprison themselves in fourteen tightly rhymed lines is something of a mystery. Tradition has a great deal to do with it: the form, having been handled successfully by major poets, stands as a challenge. In writing a sonnet a poet gains a little of the authority of Petrarch, Shakespeare, Milton, Wordsworth, and other masters who showed that the sonnet is not merely a trick. A second reason perhaps resides in the very tightness of the rhymes, which can help as well as hinder. Many poets have felt, along with Richard Wilbur (in *Mid-Century American Poets,* ed. John Ciardi), that the need for a rhyme has suggested

> . . . arbitrary connections of which the mind may take advantage if it likes. For example, if one has to rhyme with *tide,* a great number of rhyme-words at once come to mind (ride, bide, shied, confide, Akenside, etc.). Most of these, in combination with *tide,* will probably suggest nothing apropos, but one of them may reveal precisely what one wanted to say. If none of them does, *tide* must be dispensed with. Rhyme, austerely used, may be a stimulus to discovery and a stretcher of the attention.

Six Sonnets

WILLIAM SHAKESPEARE

William Shakespeare (1564–1616), born in Stratford-upon-Avon in England, is chiefly known as a dramatic poet, but he also wrote nondramatic poetry. In 1609 a volume of 154 of his sonnets was published, apparently without his permission. Probably he chose to keep his sonnets unpublished not because he thought that they were of little value, but because it was more prestigious to be an amateur (unpublished) poet than a professional (published) poet. Although the sonnets were published in 1609, they were probably written in the mid-1590s, when there was a vogue for sonneteering. A contemporary writer in 1598 said that Shakespeare's "sugred Sonnets [circulate] among his private friends."

Sonnet 73

That time of year thou mayst in me behold
When yellow leaves, or none, or few, do hang
Upon those boughs which shake against the cold,
Bare ruined choirs° where late the sweet birds sang.   4
In me thou see'st the twilight of such day
As after sunset fadeth in the west,
Which by-and-by black night doth take away,
Death's second self that seals up all in rest,   8

---

4 **choir** the part of the church where services were sung.

In me thou see'st the glowing of such fire
That on the ashes of his youth doth lie,
As the deathbed whereon it must expire,
Consumed with that which it was nourished by.   12
    This thou perceiv'st, which makes thy love more strong,
    To love that well which thou must leave ere long.

 TOPICS FOR CRITICAL THINKING AND WRITING

1. In the first quatrain (the first four lines) to what "time of year" does Shakespeare compare himself? In the second quatrain (lines 5–8) to what does he compare himself? In the third? If the sequence of the three quatrains were reversed, what would be gained or lost?
2. In line 8, what is "Death's second self"? What implications do you perceive in "seals up all in rest," as opposed, for instance, to "brings most welcome rest"?
3. In line 13, exactly what is "This"?
4. In line 14, suppose in place of "To love that well which thou must leave ere long," Shakespeare had written "To love me well whom thou must leave ere long." What if anything would have been gained or lost?
5. What is your personal response to this sonnet? Do you feel that its lessons apply to you? Please explain.
6. Did you find this sonnet hard to understand when you read it for the first time? After you reread and studied it, did it become more difficult, or less so? Do you like to read difficult poems?

Sonnet 146

Poor soul, the center of my sinful earth,
My sinful earth° these rebel pow'rs that thee array,
Why doest thou pine within and suffer dearth,
Painting thy outward walls so costly gay?
Why so large cost,° having so short a lease,   5
Dost thou upon thy fading mansion spend?
Shall worms, inheritors of this excess,
Eat up thy charge? Is this thy body's end?
Then, soul, live thou upon thy servant's loss,
And let that pine to aggravate thy store;   10
Buy terms divine° in selling hours of dross;
Within be fed, without be rich no more.
    So shalt thou feed on Death, that feeds on men,
    And death once dead, there's no more dying then.

---

2 **My sinful earth** see the comment beneath the facsimile on page 804.   **5 cost** expense.
11 **Buy terms divine** buy ages of immortality.

POore foule the center of my finfull earth,
    My finfull earth thefe rebbell powres that thee array,
Why doft thou pine within and fuffer dearth;
Painting thy outward walls fo coftlie gay?
Why fo large coft hauing fo fhort a leafe,
Doft thou vpon thy fading manfion fpend?
Shall wormes inheritors of this exceffe,
Eate vp thy charge? is this thy bodies end?
Then foule liue thou vpon thy feruants loffe,
And let that pine to aggrauat thy ftore;
Buy tearmes diuine in felling houres of droffe:
Within be fed, without be rich no more,
    So fhalt thou feed on death, that feeds on men,
    And death once dead, ther's no more dying then.

Sonnet 146 as it appears in the first publication of Shakespeare's sonnets, 1609. Notice that the first line ends with the words "my sinful earth," and the second line begins with the same words. Virtually all readers agree that the printer mistakenly repeated the words. First of all, the line makes almost no sense; secondly, it has 12 syllables ("powres" is monosyllabic) where 10 syllables are normal. Among attractive suggested emendations—usually two syllables instead of the four of "My sinful earth"—are those that pick up imagery of conflict explicit in "rebbell powres," such as "Prey to," "Thrall to," "Foiled by," and "Vexed by," and emendations that pick up imagery of hunger explicit in "Eate" and "fed," such as "Feeding" and "Starved by." But there are plenty of other candidates, such as "Fooled by," "Rebuke these," and "Leagued with."

✷ TOPICS FOR CRITICAL THINKING AND WRITING

1. As we indicate in our comment on the facsimile of this poem, the first three words of the second line probably should be replaced with other words. What words would you suggest? (We give some of the most widely accepted suggestions, but feel free to offer your own.)

2. In what tone of voice would you speak the first line? The last line? Trace the speaker's shifts in emotion throughout the poem.

3. What is your personal response to this poem? Do you feel that its lessons apply to you? Do you find this sonnet more meaningful, or less meaningful, to you than Sonnet 73 (above)? Please explain

4. Did you find this poem hard to understand when you read it for the first time? After you reread and studied it, did the poem become more difficult, or less so? Is this sonnet more difficult than Sonnet 73 (above)? What is the difference between a poem that is challenging, a poem that is difficult, and a poem that is obscure?

JOHN MILTON

John Milton (1608–1674) was born into a well-to-do family in London, where from childhood he was a student of languages, mastering at an early age Latin, Greek, Hebrew, and a number of modern languages. Instead of becoming a minister in the Anglican Church, he resolved to become a poet and spent five years at his family's country home, reading. His attacks against the monarchy secured him a position in Oliver Cromwell's Puritan government as Latin secretary for foreign affairs. He became totally blind, but he continued his work through secretaries, one of whom was Andrew Marvell, author of "To His Coy Mistress" (page 779). With the restoration of the monarchy in 1660, Milton was for a time confined but was later pardoned in the general amnesty. Until his death he continued to work on many subjects, including his greatest poem, the epic Paradise Lost.

When I Consider How My Light Is Spent   [1655]

When I consider how my light is spent
  Ere half my days, in this dark world and wide,
  And that one talent which is death to hide°
  Lodged with me useless,° though my soul more bent   4
To serve therewith my Maker, and present
  My true account, lest he returning chide;
  "Doth God exact day-labor, light denied?"
  I fondly° ask; but Patience to prevent°   8
That murmur, soon replies, "God doth not need
  Either man's work or his own gifts; who best
  Bear his mild yoke, they serve him best. His state
Is kingly. Thousands at his bidding speed   12
  And post o'er land and ocean without rest:
  They also serve who only stand and wait."

---

3 There is a pun in *talent,* relating Milton's literary talent to Christ's Parable of the Talents (Matthew 25.14 ff.), in which a servant is rebuked for not putting his talent (a unit of money) to use.   **4 useless** a pun on *use,* i.e., usury, interest.   **8 fondly** foolishly.   **prevent** forestall.

▩ TOPICS FOR CRITICAL THINKING AND WRITING

1. This sonnet is sometimes called "On His Blindness," though Milton never gave it a title. Do you think this title gets toward the heart of the poem? Explain. If you were to give it a title, what would the title be?
2. Read the parable in Matthew 25.14–30, and then consider how close the parable is to Milton's life as Milton describes it in this poem.
3. Where is the turn? What characteristics are attributed to God after the turn?
4. Compare the tone of the first and the last sentences. How does the length of each of these sentences contribute to the tone?
5. Could you imagine someone saying, "This poem changed my life"? What kind of change in a person's life might this sonnet produce?
6. What is your own experience of blindness? Have you ever lost your eyesight? For a long or a short period? Do you know a blind person? What is the nature of your interaction with him or her?

JOHN CROWE RANSOM

A graduate of Vanderbilt University and a Rhodes scholar at Oxford, John Crowe Ransom returned to teach at Vanderbilt, where he and others founded an important poetry journal, The Fugitive. *In 1937 he moved to Kenyon College, where he founded and edited the* Kenyon Review. *Distinguished as a poet and a teacher, he also wrote significant literary criticism. One of his books,* The New Criticism *(1941), gave its name to a critical movement (see pages 1742–1744).*

Piazza Piece   [1927]

—I am a gentleman in a dustcoat trying
To make you hear. Your ears are soft and small
And listen to an old man not at all,
They want the young men's whispering and sighing.
But see the roses on your trellis dying   5
And hear the spectral singing of the moon;
For I must have my lovely lady soon,
I am a gentleman in a dustcoat trying.

—I am a lady young in beauty waiting
Until my truelove comes, and then we kiss.   10
But what gray man among the vines is this
Whose words are dry and faint as in a dream?
Back from my trellis, Sir, before I scream!
I am a lady young in beauty waiting.

▨ TOPICS FOR CRITICAL THINKING AND WRITING

1. Who speaks the octave? What words especially characterize him? Characterize the speaker of the sestet.
2. In lines 9–10, the young lady is waiting for her "truelove." Comment on the suggestions in this word. In line 14 she is still "waiting." For whom does she think she is waiting? For whom does the reader know she is waiting? How do you know?
3. The first and last lines of the octave are identical, and so are the first and last lines of the sestet. What does this indicate about the degree to which the speakers communicate to each other?
4. What is the point of Ransom's poem? Is this an appropriate question to ask about a poem—whether it does or does not make a point? Please explain.

X. J. KENNEDY

X. J. Kennedy was born in New Jersey in 1929. He has taught at Tufts University and is the author of several books of poems, books for children, and college textbooks.

Kennedy alludes (line 4) to Milton's Paradise Lost, *VII, 205-07: "Heaven opened wide / Her ever-during gates, harmonious sound / On golden hinges moving. . . ." For an account of the slaughter of the innocents (line 5), see Matthew 2.16. The Venerable Bede (675-735), in line 6, was an English theologian and historian.*

Nothing in Heaven Functions as It Ought   [1965]

Nothing in Heaven functions as it ought:
Peter's bifocals, blindly sat on, crack;
His gates lurch wide with the cackle of a cock,
Not turn with a hush of gold as Milton had thought;
Gangs of the slaughtered innocents keep huffing   5
The nimbus off the Venerable Bede
Like that of an old dandelion gone to seed;
And the beatific choir keep breaking up, coughing.

But Hell, sleek Hell hath no freewheeling part:
None takes his own sweet time, none quickens pace.   10
Ask anyone, How come you here, poor heart?—
And he will slot a quarter through his face,
You'll hear an instant click, a tear will start
Imprinted with an abstract of his case.

✳ TOPIC FOR CRITICAL THINKING AND WRITING

In the octave Kennedy uses off-rhymes *(crack, cock; huffing, coughing)*, but in the sestet all the rhymes are exact. How do the rhymes help to convey the meaning? (Notice, too, that lines, 3, 4, 5, 7, and 8 all have more than the usual ten syllables. Again, why?)

BILLY COLLINS

Born in New York City in 1941, Collins is a professor of English at Lehman College of the City University of New York. He is the author of six books of poetry and the recipient of numerous awards, including one from the National Endowment for the Arts. Collins's Sailing Alone Around the Room: New and Selected Poems *was published in 2001; in the same year, he was appointed poet laureate of the United States.*

The following sonnet uses the Petrarchan form of an octave and a sestet. (See page 801.) Petrarch is additionally present in the poem by the allusion in line 3 to "a little ship on love's storm-tossed seas," because Petrarch compared the hapless lover, denied the favor of his mistress, to a ship in a storm: The lover cannot guide his ship because the North Star is hidden (Petrarch's beloved Laura averts her eyes), and the sails of the ship are agitated by the lover's pitiful sighs. As you will see, Petrarch and Laura explicitly enter the poem in the last three lines.

In line 8 Collins refers to the stations of the cross. In Roman Catholicism, one of the devotions consists of prayers and meditations before each of fourteen crosses or images set up along a path that commemorates the fourteen places at which Jesus halted when, just before the Crucifixion, he was making his way in Jerusalem to Golgotha.

Sonnet
[1999]

All we need is fourteen lines, well, thirteen now,
and after this next one just a dozen
to launch a little ship on love's storm-tossed seas,
then only ten more left like rows of beans.   4
How easily it goes unless you get Elizabethan
and insist the iambic bongos must be played
and rhymes positioned at the ends of lines,
one for every station of the cross.   8
But hang on here while we make the turn
into the final six where all will be resolved,
where longing and heartache will find an end,
where Laura will tell Petrarch to put down his pen, 12
take off those crazy medieval tights,
blow out the lights, and come at last to bed.

▨ TOPICS FOR CRITICAL THINKING AND WRITING

1. The headnote explains the stations of the cross (line 8), but what is the point of introducing this image into a sonnet?
2. Normally the "turn" (*volta*) in an Italian sonnet occurs at the beginning of the ninth line; the first eight lines (the octave) establish some sort of problem, and the final six lines (the sestet) respond, for instance by answering a question, or by introducing a contrasting emotion. In your view, how satisfactorily does Collins handle this form?
3. Does this sonnet interest you? Do you find it clever? Is that a good thing or a bad thing?
4. Do you think that you could have written this sonnet? Could you have written Shakespeare's sonnets 73 and 146 (pages 802–803)? What do your responses to these questions suggest to you about the writing of poetry?

The Villanelle

The name comes from an Italian words, *villanella,* meaning "country song" or "peasant song," and originally, in the sixteenth century, the subject was the supposedly simple life of the shepherd, but in France in the seventeenth century elaborate rules were developed. Variations occur, but usually a villanelle has the following characteristics:

• Five stanzas with three lines each (tercets), rhyming *aba,* and a final stanza with four lines (a quatrain).

- The first line of the first stanza is repeated as the last line of the second stanza and the last line of the fourth stanza.
- The third line of the first stanza is repeated as the last line of the third stanza and the last line of the fifth stanza.
- The quatrain that concludes the villanelle rhymes *abaa,* using the first and third lines of the first stanza as the next-to-last and the last lines of the final stanza—i.e., the poem ends with a couplet.

Because the villanelle repeats one sound thirteen times (in the first and last line of each tercet, and in the first, third, and fourth lines of the quatrain), it strongly conveys a sense of return, a sense of not going forward, even a sense of dwelling on the past. We give four examples of the form.

If you are going to write a villanelle, here are two tips:

- Begin by writing a couplet (a pair of rhyming lines); in fact, write several couplets on different topics, and then decide which couplet you think is most promising. Next, insert between these two lines a line that makes sense in the context but that does *not* rhyme with them.
- Each line need not end with a pause, and in fact some run-on lines probably will help to prevent the poem from becoming too sing-songy.

EDWIN ARLINGTON ROBINSON

Edwin Arlington Robinson (1869-1935) was born in Head Tide, Maine, and raised in the nearby town of Gardner, which he later adapted as the setting, "Tilbury Town," for many of his poems. His books of verse include The Torrent and the Night Before *(1896);* Captain Craig and Other Poems *(1902);* The Town Down the River *(1910); and—his first major success—*The Man Against the Sky *(1916).*

The House on the Hill   [1896]

They are all gone away,
   The House is shut and still,
There is nothing more to say.   3

Through broken walls and gray
   The winds blow bleak and shrill:
They are all gone away.   6

Nor is there one to-day
   To speak them good or ill:
There is nothing more to say.   9

Why is it then we stray
   Around the sunken sill?
They are all gone away,   12

And our poor fancy-play
   For them is wasted skill:
There is nothing more to say.   15

There is ruin and decay
  In the House on the Hill:
They are all gone away.   18
There is nothing more to say.

▓ TOPICS FOR CRITICAL THINKING AND WRITING

1. Line 1 is repeated several times. Please explain your response to the line the first time you hear it. Now explain your response when you hear it the final time. What conclusions are you led to?
2. Were you surprised to encounter the pronoun "we" in stanza four? How does this "we" affect your response to the poem? And how does it bear on your understanding of the speaker?
3. Not, too, the use of "our" in stanza five. Does the poet need this "our" or not? Please explain.
4. In the first and last stanzas, "House" is capitalized. Does this choice add to or detract from the impact of the poem?
5. We have printed the version of "The House on the Hill" that Robinson gave in his *Collected Poems*, published in 1937. But the original version of 1896 is somewhat different. Here, for example, is the original stanza three:

    Are we more fit than they
    To meet the Master's will?—
    There is nothing more to say.

    In your view, does the revision make the poem better or worse? Who is the "Master"? And what is the purpose of this reference?
6. Once a poem has been published, do you think that its author has the right to revise it? Isn't it confusing for readers to have different versions of "the same poem"?

DYLAN THOMAS

Dylan Thomas (1914–1953) was born and grew up in Swansea, in Wales. His first volume of poetry, published in 1934, immediately made him famous. Endowed with a highly melodious voice, on three tours of the United States he was immensely successful as a reader both of his own and of other poets' work. He died in New York City.

Do Not Go Gentle into That Good Night   [1952]

Do not go gentle into that good night,
Old age should burn and rave at close of day;
Rage, rage against the dying of the light.

Though wise men at their end know dark is right,
Because their words had forked no lightning they   5
Do not go gentle into that good night.

Good men, the last wave by, crying how bright
Their frail deeds might have danced in a green bay,
Rage, rage against the dying of the light.

Wild men who caught and sang the sun in flight,   10
And learn, too late, they grieved it on its way,
Do not go gentle into that good night.

Grave men, near death, who see with blinding sight
Blind eyes could blaze like meteors and be gay,
Rage, rage against the dying of the light.   15

And you, my father, there on the sad height,
Curse, bless, me now with your fierce tears, I pray.
Do not go gentle into that good night.
Rage, rage against the dying of the light.

 ## TOPICS FOR CRITICAL THINKING AND WRITING

1. The intricate form of the villanelle might seem too fussy for a serious poem about dying. Do you find it too fussy? Or does the form here somehow succeed?
2. How would you describe the speaker's tone? Is it accurate or misleading to say that "Do Not Go Gentle into That Good Night" is an angry poem?
3. What is the speaker's attitude toward death? Do you share this attitude or not? Please explain.
4. This is a famous poem. Why do you think that is the case?

ELIZABETH BISHOP

Elizabeth Bishop (1911–1979) was born in Worcester, Massachusetts. Because her father died when she was eight months old and her mother was confined to a sanitarium four years later, Bishop was raised by relatives in New England and Nova Scotia. After graduation from Vassar College in 1934, where she was co-editor of the student literary magazine, she lived (on a small private income) for a while in Key West, France, and Mexico, and then for much of her adult life in Brazil, before returning to the United States to teach at Harvard.

One Art   [1976]

The art of losing isn't hard to master;
so many things seem filled with intent
to be lost that their loss is no disaster.   3

Lose something every day. Accept the fluster
of lost door keys, the hour badly spent.
The art of losing isn't hard to master.   6

Then practice losing farther, losing faster:
places, and names, and where it was you meant
to travel. None of these will bring disaster.   9

I lost my mother's watch. And look! my last, or
next-to-last, of three loved houses went.
The art of losing isn't hard to master.   12

I lost two cities, lovely ones. And, vaster,
some realms I owned, two rivers, a continent.
I miss them, but it wasn't a disaster.   15

—Even losing you (the joking voice, a gesture
I love) I shan't have lied. It's evident
the art of losing's not too hard to master   18
though it may look like (*Write* it!) like disaster.

▨ TOPICS FOR CRITICAL THINKING AND WRITING

1. What was your response to the title when you first read it? Did your response change after you read the poem and studied it further?
2. Is the form connected to the poem's theme? If so, in what way?
3. Linger over line 1: Why is "losing" an "art"? And why does Bishop echo the phrasing of the first line in lines later in the poem? Does the echo make the poem feel repetitive?
4. Follow Bishop's uses of the words "lose," "losing," and "loss" from one to the next. Do you find her reliance on these very closely related words to be important for the poem's meaning, or does it strike you as a lot or a little confusing? Can a poem be a lot or a little confusing and yet still be a good poem?
5. Can we tell what kind of loss Bishop is exploring? If we can, where does this kind of loss become clear?
6. Whom is Bishop addressing when she says (not the exclamation point) "*Write* it!"? Why is this command in the poem, and why is it in parentheses?
7. Has this poem helped you to understand a loss or losses that you have experienced yourself? Something, perhaps, that you did not understand before about what "losing" someone or something important means? Do you have an insight of your own into losing and loss that Bishop has not considered, at least not in this poem? Is this an insight that you would want to share with others—in a poem, for example—or keep to yourself?

WENDY COPE

Wendy Cope was born in 1945 in Kent, in the south of England, and educated at St. Hilda's College at Oxford University, where she took a degree in history, and then at the Westminster College of Education. After working for a number of years as a music teacher in London, she became a television critic, a columnist, a freelance writer, and, above all, a poet. Her books of verse include Making Cocoa for Kingsley Amis *(1986) and* Serious Concerns *(1991), both of which were best-sellers in England, and* If I Don't Know *(2001).*

Reading Scheme   [1986]

Here is Peter. Here is Jane. They like fun.
Jane has a big doll. Peter has a ball.
Look, Jane, look! Look at the dog! See him run!   3

Here is Mummy. She has baked a bun.
Here is the milkman. He has come to call.
Here is Peter. Here is Jane. They like fun.   6

Go Peter! Go Jane! Come, milkman, come!
The milkman likes Mummy. She likes them all.
Look, Jane, look! Look at the dog! See him run!   9

Here are the curtains. They shut out the sun.
Let us peep! On tiptoe Jane! You are small!
Here is Peter. Here is Jane. They like fun.   12

I hear a car, Jane. The milkman looks glum.
Here is Daddy in his car. Daddy is tall.
Look, Jane, look! Look at the dog! See him run!   15

Daddy looks very cross. Has he a gun?
Up milkman! Up milkman! Over the wall!
Here is Peter. Here is Jane. They like fun.   18
Look, Jane, look! Look at the dog! See him run!

 TOPICS FOR CRITICAL THINKING AND WRITING

1. What was your first response to this poem? After you read it through
    several times, did your response change? Please explain.
2. What does the word "scheme" mean? What makes this word in the title
    a good choice for the poem that follows?
3. Do you think that Cope intends her poem to be comic in its effect on
    the reader? Or would you characterize the effect in different terms?
4. How does the form of this poem contribute to its meaning? Could you
    imagine the poem affecting you in the same way if Cope had written it
    in a different form—for example, without the pattern of rhymes?
5. Has this poem given you a new insight into the relationship between
    form and meaning? If so, please describe this insight and explain how it
    will affect your reading of other poems.

The Sestina

This fiendishly elaborate form developed in twelfth-century Europe, especially
in southern France, among the troubadours, court poets who sang for nobles.
(The name comes from the Italian *sesto*, "sixth," because there are six stanzas of
six lines each—but then, to complicate matters, there is a seventh stanza, a
three-line "envoy" or "envoi," a summing up that uses key words of the first six
stanzas.)

More precisely—this is mind-boggling—the six words that end the six lines
of the first stanza are used at the ends of all the following lines but in a different
though fixed order in each stanza. (Rhyme is *not* used in this form.) This fixed
order has been characterized as a sort of bottoms-up pattern, a term that will become clear as we describe the stanzas. In the second stanza the *first* line ends
with the *last* word of the *last* line (the bottom) of the first stanza; the second
line of the second stanza ends with the first line of the first; the third line ends

with the last word of the fifth line of the first stanza—i.e., with the next-to-bottom line of the first stanza. The fourth line of the second stanza ends with the second line of the first, the fifth with the fourth line of the first, and the sixth with the third line of the first.

Thus, if we designate the final words of the first stanza, line by line, as 1, 2, 3, 4, 5, 6,

the final words of the second stanza are 6, 1, 5, 2, 4, 3;
the third stanza: 3, 6, 4, 1, 2, 5
the fourth stanza: 5, 3, 2, 6, 1, 4
the fifth stanza: 4, 5, 1, 3, 6, 2
the sixth stanza: 2, 4, 6, 5, 3, 1

The envoy of three lines must use these six words, but there are various possible patterns—for instance, 5, 3, 1 at the ends of the three lines, and 2, 4, 6 in the middle of the lines.

If you are going to write a sestina, two tips:

- Once you have settled on your topic—let's say "loss" or "a restless spirit of adventure"—jot down six words that you think are relevant, and get going.
- You need not end each line with a pause, and in fact most good sestinas use considerable enjambment—i.e., the sense of the line runs over into the next line.

RUDYARD KIPLING

Rudyard Kipling (1865–1936) was born in India of English parents, but at the age of six he was sent to England for his education. He returned to India when he was seventeen, worked as a journalist and creative writer for seven years in Bombay, and then returned to England. Much of his writing celebrates the achievements of British colonialism, and he is therefore out of favor today, but if it is true that he did not see that imperialism is partly a money-making racket built on exploitation, it is nevertheless also true that he often depicts the "natives" with great sympathy and insight.

In his poems he often adopted the voice of the uneducated London cockney who has 'listed as a soldier, a-servin' of 'Er Majesty the Queen in Africa, Afghanistan, or Injia. Some readers have felt that some of the poems are better when one reads them without heeding the dialect.

Sestina of the Tramp-Royal   [1896]

Speakin' in general, I 'ave tried 'em all—
The 'appy roads that take you o'er the world.
Speakin' in general, I 'ave found them good
For such as cannot use one bed too long,
But must get 'ence, the same as I 'ave done,   5
An' go observin' matters till they die.

What do it matter where or 'ow we die,
So long as we've our 'ealth to watch it all—
The different ways that different things are done,
An' men an' women lovin' in this world;   10
Takin' our chances as they come along,
An' when they ain't, pretendin' they are good?

In cash or credit—no, it aren't no good;
You 'ave to 'ave the 'abit or you'd die,
Unless you lived your life but one day long,   15
Nor didn't prophesy nor fret at all,
But drew your tucker some'ow from the world,
An' never bothered what you might ha' done.

But, Gawd, what things are they I 'aven't done!
I've turned my 'and to most, an' turned it good,   20
In various situations round the world—
For 'im that doth not work must surely die;
But that's no reason man should labour all
'Is life on one same shift—life's none so long.

Therefore, from job to job I've moved along.   25
Pay couldn't 'old me when my time was done,
For something in my 'ead upset it all,
Till I 'ad dropped whatever 't was for good,
An', out at sea, be'eld the dock-lights die,
An' met my mate—the wind that tramps the world!   30

It's like a book, I think, this bloomin' world,
Which you can read and care for just so long,
But presently you feel that you will die
Unless you get the page you're readin' done,
An' turn another—likely not so good;   35
But what you're after is to turn 'em all.

Gawd bless this world! Whatever she 'ath done—
Excep' when awful long—I've found it good.
So write, before I die, "'E liked it all!"

TOPICS FOR CRITICAL THINKING AND WRITING

1. As our headnote mentions, Kipling's speakers often are cockneys, uneducated Londoners who drop their h's and their final g's. Is the dialect effective in this poem, or does the poem get better if you read it straight in standard English? Explain.

2. How would you characterize the speaker's view of life? And how would you characterize the speaker himself? Would you agree with someone who said that the speaker is a shallow egoist, an irresponsible fellow who seeks only his own instant gratification? Explain.

3. Try your hand at writing your own envoy (Kipling's last three lines) for this poem. Like Kipling, you will have to use *world* and *done* in your first line, *long* and *good* in your second, and *die* and *all* in your third.

ELIZABETH BISHOP

For a biographical note, see page 811.

Sestina   [1965]

September rain falls on the house.
In the failing light, the old grandmother
sits in the kitchen with the child
beside the Little Marvel Stove,
reading the jokes from the almanac,
laughing and talking to hide her tears.   6

She thinks that her equinoctial tears
and the rain that beats on the roof of the house
were both foretold by the almanac,
but only known to a grandmother.
The iron kettle sings on the stove.
She cuts some bread and says to the child,   12

It's time for tea now; but the child
is watching the teakettle's small hard tears
dance like mad on the hot black stove,
the way the rain must dance on the house.
Tidying up, the old grandmother
hangs up the clever almanac   18

on its string. Birdlike, the almanac
hovers half open above the child,
hovers above the old grandmother
and her teacup full of dark brown tears.
She shivers and says she thinks the house
feels chilly, and puts more wood in the stove.   24

It was to be, says the Marvel Stove.
I know what I know, says the almanac.
With crayons the child draws a rigid house
and a winding pathway. Then the child
puts in a man with buttons like tears
and shows it proudly to the grandmother.   30

But secretly, while the grandmother
busies herself about the stove,
the little moons fall down like tears
from between the pages of the almanac
into the flower bed the child
has carefully placed in the front of the house.   36

Time to plant tears, says the almanac.
The grandmother sings to the marvelous stove
and the child draws another inscrutable house.

TOPICS FOR CRITICAL THINKING AND WRITING

1. Does Bishop's choice of title seem strange to you? Why would she use the name of the poetic form for her title? Do you think that a different title might be more effective? Please give examples, and explain why they would or would not be better.

2. As carefully as you can, describe the effect of line 1.

3. In the first stanza, why is the grandmother crying? How are her tears in lines 6 and 7 related to the "small hard tears" of the teakettle in line 14? Note, too, the later references to tears. Please comment on these as well.

4. Several of the lines in this poem are italicized. Do the italics make the lines more forceful? Should Bishop have made the force of the lines clear without changing the "look" of the lines on the page?

5. What is an almanac? Have you ever seen one? Why would someone want an almanac? What is the significance of the almanac in this poem?

6. What is your response to the fact that this poem is a sestina? Do you think you could write a poem in this form? What would be the benefit to you of such an assignment?

SHAPED POETRY OR PATTERN POETRY

We have been talking about shapes or patterns determined by rhymes, but some poems—admittedly few—take their shape from the length of the lines, which form a simple image, such as a sphere, an egg, a vase, or a wing. We have already printed one poem of this sort in our first chapter, James Merrill's "Christmas Tree," which is shaped like—well, you can guess.

Here is a famous example of shaped poetry, a pair of wings. We print it sideways, as it was printed in the earliest edition, in 1633, though in that edition the first stanza was printed on the left-hand page, the second on the right-hand page.

GEORGE HERBERT

George Herbert (1593–1633), born into a distinguished Welsh family, studied at the University of Cambridge (England) and became a clergyman. By all accounts he lived an admirable life and was deservedly known in his community as "Holy Mr. Herbert."

Note: *In line 1,* store *means "abundance," "plenty." In line 10, the fall refers to the loss of innocence that resulted when Adam ate the forbidden fruit in the garden of Eden. In the next-to-last line,* imp, *a term from falconry, means "to graft, to insert feathers into a wing."*

Easter-Wings

Lord, who createdst man in wealth and store,
Though foolishly he lost the same,
Decaying more and more,
Till he became
Most poor:
With thee
O let me rise
As larks, harmoniously,
And sing this day thy victories:
Then shall the fall further the flight in me.   10

My tender age in sorrow did begin:
And still with sicknesses and shame
Thou didst so punish sin,
That I became
Most thin.
With thee
Let me combine,
And feel this day thy victory:
For, if I imp my wing on thine,
Affliction shall advance the flight in me.   20

✠ TOPICS FOR CRITICAL THINKING AND WRITING

1. Why are wings especially relevant to a poem about Easter?
2. We don't think one can argue that the length of every line is exactly suited to the meaning of the line, but we do think that some of the lengths are parallel or reinforce some of the ideas within those lines. For instance, the first line, speaking of a man's original "wealth and store," is a long line. Why is this length more appropriate to the meaning than it would be to, say, "Lord, who created a man who soon would fall"? And note especially the fifth and sixth lines of each stanza: Would you agree that their length suits their meaning?
3. Do you think this poem is a mere novelty, or do you think it deserves close attention and indeed is memorable? Please explain

LILLIAN MORRISON

Lillian Morrison, born in Jersey City, New Jersey, is an anthologist and folk-lorist and a writer of children's books as well as a poet in her own right. The first books she published were collections of folk rhymes that she assembled and edited while working as a librarian at the New York Public Library. In 1987 Morrison received the Grolier Award for "outstanding contributions to the stimulation of reading by young people." She lives in New York City.

The Sidewalk Racer

                                                                        [1978]

Or *On the Skateboard*

      Skimming
     an asphalt sea
  I swerve, I curve, I
sway; I speed to whirring
sound an inch above the   5
  ground; I'm the sailor
    and the sail, I'm the
    driver and the wheel
I'm the one and only
     single engine   10
    human auto
     mobile.

▨ TOPICS FOR CRITICAL THINKING AND WRITING

1. Is the poem really about a skateboard? If not, what *is* it about?
2. The first line is "Skimming." Would the poem be improved or weakened if it began "I skim"? Please explain.
3. The second line rhymes with the fifth and seventh ("sea," "the") and with the ninth ("only"). What other rhymes do you find? What is the effect of using rhymes that are *not* at the ends of the lines?
4. From a grammatical point of view, a period could be put at the end of line 8. Why do you suppose Morrison did not put a period there?

BLANK VERSE AND FREE VERSE

A good deal of English poetry is unrhymed, much of it in **blank verse**—that is, unrhymed iambic pentameter. Introduced into English poetry by Henry Howard, the Earl of Surrey, in the middle of the sixteenth century, late in the century it became the standard medium (especially in the hands of Marlowe and Shakespeare) of English drama. In the seventeenth century, Milton used it for *Paradise Lost,* and it has continued to be used in both dramatic and nondramatic literature. For an example see the first scene of *Hamlet* (page 1189). A passage of blank verse that has a rhetorical unity is sometimes called a **verse paragraph.**

The second kind of unrhymed poetry fairly common in English, especially in the twentieth century, is **free verse** (or **vers libre**): rhythmical lines varying in length, adhering to no fixed metrical pattern and usually unrhymed. Such poetry may seem formless; Robert Frost, who strongly preferred regular meter and rhyme, said that he would not consider writing free verse any more than he would consider playing tennis without a net. But free verse does have a form or pattern, often largely based on repetition and parallel grammatical structure. Whitman's "A Noiseless Patient Spider" (page 713) is an example; Arnold's "Dover Beach" (page 990) is another example, though less typical because it uses rhyme. Thoroughly typical is Whitman's "When I Heard the Learn'd Astronomer."

WALT WHITMAN

For a biography of the American poet Walt Whitman (1819–1892), see the note prefacing "A Noiseless Patient Spider" (page 713).

When I Heard the Learn'd Astronomer [1865]

When I heard the learn'd astronomer,
When the proofs, the figures, were ranged in columns before me,
When I was shown the charts and diagrams, to add, divide, and
    measure them,
When I sitting heard the astronomer where he lectured with much
    applause in the lecture-room,
How soon unaccountable I became tired and sick,   5
Till rising and gliding out I wander'd off by myself,
In the mystical moist night-air, and from time to time,
Look'd up in perfect silence at the stars.

What can be said about the rhythmic structure of this poem? Rhymes are absent, and the lines vary greatly in the number of syllables, ranging from 9 (the first line) to 23 (the fourth line), but when we read the poem we sense a rhythmic structure. The first four lines obviously hang together, each beginning with "When"; indeed, three of these four lines begin "When I." We may notice, too, that each of these four lines has more syllables than its predecessor (the numbers are 9, 14, 18, and 23); this increase in length, like the initial repetition, is a kind of pattern. But then, with the fifth line, which speaks of fatigue and surfeit, there is a shrinkage to 14 syllables, offering an enormous relief from the previous swollen line with its 23 syllables. The second half of the poem—the pattern established by "When" in the first four lines is dropped, and in effect we get a new stanza, also of four lines—does not relentlessly diminish the number of syllables in each succeeding line, but it *almost* does so: 14, 14, 13, 10.

The second half of the poem thus has a pattern too, and this pattern is more or less the reverse of the first half of the poem. We may notice too that the last line (in which the poet, now released from the oppressive lecture hall, is in communion with nature) is very close to an iambic pentameter line; that is, the poem concludes with a metrical form said to be the most natural in English. The effect of naturalness or ease in this final line, moreover, is increased by the absence of repetitions (e.g., not only of "When I," but even of such syntactic repetitions as "charts and diagrams," "tired and sick," "rising and gliding") that characterize most of the previous lines. This final effect of naturalness is part of a carefully constructed pattern in which rhythmic structure is part of meaning. Though at first glance free verse may appear unrestrained, as T. S. Eliot (a practitioner) said, "No *vers* is *libre* for the man who wants to do a good job"—or for the woman who wants to do a good job.

THE PROSE POEM

The term *prose poem* is sometimes applied to a short work that looks like prose but that is highly rhythmical or rich in images, or both. Here is a modern example.

CAROLYN FORCHÉ

Carolyn Forché was born in Detroit in 1950. After earning a bachelor's degree from Michigan State University and a master's degree from Bowling Green State University, she traveled widely in the Southwest, living among Pueblo Indians. Between 1978 and 1986 she made several visits to El Salvador, documenting human rights violations for Amnesty International. Her first book of poems, Gathering the Tribes, *won the Yale Younger Poets award in 1975. Her second book of poems,* The Country Between Us *(1981), includes "The Colonel," which has been called a prose poem.*

The Colonel   [1978, publ. 1981]

What you have heard is true. I was in his house. His wife carried a tray of coffee and sugar. His daughter filed her nails, his son went out for the night. There were daily papers, pet dogs, a pistol on the cushion beside him. The moon swung bare on its black cord over the house. On the television was a cop show. It was in English. Broken bottles were embedded in the walls around the house to scoop the kneecaps from a man's legs or cut his hands to lace. On the windows there were gratings like those in liquor stores. We had dinner, rack of lamb, good wine, a gold bell was on the table for calling the maid. The maid brought green mangoes, salt, a type of bread. I was asked how I enjoyed the country. There was a brief commercial in Spanish. His wife took everything away. There was some talk then of how difficult it had become to govern. The parrot said hello on the terrace. The colonel told it to shutup, and pushed himself from the table. My friend said to me with his eyes: say nothing. The colonel returned with a sack used to bring groceries home. He spilled many human ears on the table. They were like dried peach halves. There is no other way to say this. He took one of them in his hands, shook it in our faces, dropped it into a water glass. It came alive there. I am tired of fooling around he said. As for the rights of anyone, tell your people they can go fuck themselves. He swept the ears to the floor with his arm and held the last of his wine in the air. Something for your poetry, no? he said. Some of the ears on the floor caught this scrap of his voice. Some of the ears on the floor were pressed to the ground.

✎ TOPICS FOR CRITICAL THINKING AND WRITING

1. How would you characterize the colonel in a few sentences?
2. We are told that the colonel spoke of "how difficult it had become to govern." What do you suppose the colonel assumes is the purpose of government? What do you assume its purpose is?
3. How much do we know about the narrator? Can we guess the narrator's purpose in visiting the colonel? How would you characterize the narrator's tone? Do you believe the narrator?
4. What is your response to the last sentence?
5. What, if anything, is gained by calling this work a "prose poem" rather than a short story?

21

In Brief: Writing Arguments about Poetry

If you are going to write about a fairly short poem (say, under 30 lines), it's not a bad idea to copy out the poem, writing or typing it double-spaced. By writing it out you will be forced to notice details, down to the punctuation. After you have copied the poem, proofread it carefully against the original. Catching an error—even the addition or omission of a comma—may help you to notice a detail in the original that you might otherwise have overlooked. And now that you have the poem with ample space between the lines, you have a worksheet with room for jottings.

A good essay is based on a genuine response to a poem; a response may be stimulated in part by first reading the poem aloud and then considering the following questions.

Remember, even an explication—an unfolding of the implications of the poem—is an argument. In the example on page 667, the student begins by asserting a thesis, a claim: "'Harlem' is only eleven lines long, but it is charged with power." The thesis, the arguable claim, of course is not that "the poem is only eleven lines long," but that "it is charged with power," and the rest of the explication is devoted to supporting this claim, to pointing out almost word by word, the sources of the power,

FIRST RESPONSE

What was your response to the poem on first reading? Did some parts especially please or displease you, or puzzle you? After some study—perhaps checking the meanings of some of the words in a dictionary and reading the poem several times—did you modify your initial response to the parts and to the whole?

SPEAKER AND TONE

1. Who is the speaker? (Consider age, sex, personality, frame of mind, and tone of voice.) Is the speaker defined fairly precisely (for instance, an older woman speaking to a child), or is the speaker simply a voice meditating? (Jot down your first impressions, then reread the poem and make further jottings, if necessary.)

2. Do you think the speaker is fully aware of what he or she is saying, or does the speaker unconsciously reveal his or her personality and values? What is your attitude toward this speaker?

3. Is the speaker narrating or reflecting on an earlier experience or attitude? If so, does he or she convey a sense of new awareness, such as regret for innocence lost?

AUDIENCE

To whom is the speaker speaking? What is the situation (including time and place)? (In some poems a listener is strongly implied, but in others, especially those in which the speaker is meditating, there may be no audience other than the reader, who "overhears" the speaker.)

STRUCTURE AND FORM

1. Does the poem proceed in a straightforward way, or at some point or points does the speaker reverse course, altering his or her tone or perception? If there is a shift, what do you make of it?

2. Is the poem organized into sections? If so, what are these sections—stanzas, for instance—and how does each section (characterized, perhaps, by a certain tone of voice, or a group of rhymes) grow out of what precedes it?

3. What is the effect on you of the form—say, quatrains (stanzas of four lines) or blank verse (unrhymed lines of ten syllables of iambic pentameter)? If the sense overflows the form, running without pause from (for example) one quatrain into the next, what effect is created?

CENTER OF INTEREST AND THEME

1. What is the poem about? Is the interest chiefly in a distinctive character, or in meditation? That is, is the poem chiefly psychological or chiefly philosophical?

2. Is the theme stated explicitly (directly) or implicitly? How might you state the theme in a sentence? What is lost by reducing the poem to a statement of a theme?

DICTION

1. How would you characterize the language? Colloquial, or elevated, or what?

2. Do certain words have rich and relevant associations that relate to other words and help to define the speaker or the theme or both?

3. What is the role of figurative language, if any? Does it help to define the speaker or the theme?

4. What do you think is to be taken figuratively or symbolically, and what literally?

SOUND EFFECTS

1. What is the role of sound effects, including repetitions of sound (for instance, alliteration) and of entire words, and shifts in versification?

2. If there are off-rhymes (for instance, *dizzy* and *easy,* or *home* and *come*), what effect do they have on you? Do they, for instance, add a note of tentativeness or uncertainty?

3. If there are unexpected stresses or pauses, what do they communicate about the speaker's experience? How do they affect you?

A NOTE ON EXPLICATION

On page 42 we discuss the form known as *explication,* a line-by-line commentary seeking to make explicit or to explain the meaning that is implicit or hidden within the words. (*Explication* comes from the Latin *explicare,* meaning "to unfold," from *ex* = out + *plicare* = to fold.) The implication of such an activity is that writers "fold" a meaning into their words, and the reader perceives or unfolds the message. (*Implication,* also from the Latin word for "fold," means something entangled or involved in something else.)

An example will clarify these remarks. If we say to someone, "Shut the door," obviously we are conveying a message through these words. Also obviously, the message in "Shut the door" is *not* exactly the same as the message in "Would you mind shutting the door, please?" An explication would point out that the first sentence contains an authoritative tone that is not found in the second. In effect, the first sentence "says" (in addition to the point about the door) that the speaker may give orders to the hearer; or, to put it the other way around, folded into the second sentence (but not the first) is the speaker's awareness that the person receiving the words is the speaker's social equal. A slightly more complicated and much more interesting example is Julius Caesar's "I came, I saw, I conquered" (Latin: *veni, vidi, vici*). An explication would point out that in addition to the explicit meaning there are implicit meanings, for example that a man like Caesar does not waste words, that he is highly disciplined (the pattern of words suggests that he is a master of language), and that he is the sort of person who, on seeing something, immediately gets it under control by taking the appropriate action.

Because explication is chiefly concerned with making explicit what is implicit in a text, it is not concerned with such matters as the poet's place in history or the poet's biography, nor is it concerned with the reader's response to the poem—except to the degree that the reader's explication really may *not* be an objective decoding of the poem but may depend in large part on the reader's private associations. (Some literary critics would argue that the underlying premise of explication—that a writer puts a specific meaning into a work and that a reader can objectively recover that meaning—is based on the mistaken belief that readers can be objective.) If you look at the sample explication on pages 43–46, you can decide for yourself whether the student unfolded implicit meanings that the author (William Butler Yeats) had tucked into the words of his poem or whether the explication really is a personal response to the poem.

A STUDENT'S WRITTEN RESPONSE TO A POEM

What we give in this chapter is not an explication but a more personal response to a poem by Louise Glück. Like an explication, it is concerned with the author's meaning; but unlike an explication, it does not hesitate to go beyond the poem and into "the real world" that the writer of the paper lives in. The essay is not so personal that the poem disappears (as it might in an essay that says something like "This poem reminds me of the time that I . . ."), but it does not claim merely to unfold meanings that Glück has embodied or entangled in her words.

First read the following biographical note and the poem.

LOUISE GLÜCK

One of the leading contemporary poets, Louise Glück was born in New York City in 1943, grew up on Long Island, and attended Sarah Lawrence College and Columbia University. She has taught at a number of colleges and universities, including the University of Iowa and Williams College. Firstborn, *her first book of poems, was published in 1968. Her later books include* The House on Marshland *(1975), from which the following poem is taken;* The Triumph of Achilles *(1985);* The Wild Iris *(1992); and* Vita Nova *(1999). Glück's poetry has been widely anthologized and translated.* Proofs and Theories: Essays on Poetry *(1995) is a collection of her literary criticism on Stanley Kunitz, T. S. Eliot, and other authors.*

Gretel in Darkness   [1975]

This is the world we wanted.
All who would have seen us dead
are dead. I hear the witch's cry
break in the moonlight through a sheet
of sugar: God rewards.   5
Her tongue shrivels into gas. . . .

        Now, far from women's arms
and memory of women, in our father's hut
we sleep, are never hungry.
Why do I not forget?   10
My father bars the door, bars harm
from this house, and it is years.

No one remembers. Even you, my brother,
summer afternoons you look at me as though
you meant to leave.   15
as though it never happened.
But I killed for you. I see armed firs,
the spires of that gleaming kiln—

Nights I turn to you to hold me
but you are not there.   20
Am I alone? Spies
hiss in the stillness, Hansel,
we are there still and it is real, real,
that black forest and the fire in earnest.

A student named Jennifer Anderson was assigned to write about this poem in an Introduction to Literature course. Jennifer started her work by copying the poem on a sheet of paper and annotating it.

To follow up on these annotations and develop them, Jennifer turned next to her writing journal. She jotted down responses and ideas, and her questions about aspects of the poem and details of the language that intrigued and puzzled her.

Speaker ——————— (Gretel) in Darkness   *Gretel and her brother*

This is the world (we) wanted.

All who would have seen us (dead)

are (dead). I hear the witch's cry

break in the moonlight through a sheet

of sugar: God rewards.   *Christian theme?*

Her tongue shrivels into gas. . . .

why this space?   Now, far from women's arms —————— *Women (mother) vs. Father*

and memory of women, in our father's hut

we sleep, are never hungry.

Why do I not forget?   *the Key Question*

My father (bars) the door, (bars) harm

The speaker does   from this house, and it is years.

No one remembers. Even you, my brother,

summer afternoons you look at me as though

you meant to leave,

intense, direct word choice   as though it never happened.   *oven, furnace*

But I killed for you. I see armed firs,

the spires of that gleaming (kiln—)

Nights I turn to you to hold me   *Hansel's separation / distance from Gretel*

but you are not there. ——————————

"S" sounds   Am I alone? Spies   *compare with opening lines—*

hiss in the stillness, Hansel,   *everything's not dead*

(we are there) still and it is (real,) (real,)

that black forest and the fire in earnest.   *—serious + intense*

Here are the pages from her journal:

Great poem! Haunting, eerie. My favorite so far
in the course.

Story of Hansel and Gretel--Look this up. Should
I summarize the story in the paper?

Speaker--Gretel. Why her, and not Hansel? Not
both of them as speakers?

"in darkness"--really in darkness, or is darkness
a metaphor?

Repetition in the poem: dead/dead, bar/bar,
real/real.

The tone of the opening stanza--scary, ominous.
Darkness, dead.

```
     The reference to the witch. "Shrivels into gas"--
creepy detail.
     But the witch has been defeated. Through the
power of God? Why is God mentioned in this line?--not
mentioned elsewhere.
     Women (not mothers) seem the enemy in stanza two.
(Odd that the second stanza is indented.) The father
provides safety. But safety is not enough. Gretel
cannot forget the past: the real enemy is not the
witch or the mothers, but her memory.
     She has to talk about her memory, her
experiences. "No one remembers," but she does.
     I think that this is a poem about Memory: "Why do
I not forget?"
     Gretel doesn't want her brother to forget. She
reminds him.
     "Killed"--such a strong word, very direct. Gretel
is angry with her brother; she feels him pulling away
from her.
     Something disturbed, unnatural about the poem?--
the detail about Gretel looking for her brother to
hold her. But he is absent. Where is he?
     Who are the "Spies"? Lots of "s" sounds in these
lines--spies, hiss, stillness, Hansel, still.
     She addresses him by name.
     She cannot escape, maybe she doesn't want
to escape. Note that Gretel is describing her
memories of what happened--not a poem that tells
the story of Hansel and Gretel. Glück is interested
in how Gretel remembers, how she feels about
remembering.
```

Jennifer knew the main features of the Hansel and Gretel story—the brother and sister, their abandonment, their capture by a witch, and their escape. But she wanted to remind herself about the details, as her note to herself in her journal indicates.

As an experiment, Jennifer used one of the Internet search engines that her instructor had described during class. She went to:

Go2Net Network: Metacrawler
http://www.go2net.com/search.html

And she searched for "hansel and gretel." A number of the results looked promising, and she linked to this one:

Grimm's Fairy Tales—Hansel and Gretel
http://www.mordent.com/folktales/grimms/hng/hng.html

Grimm's Fairy Tales

Hansel and Gretel

ARD BY a great forest dwelt a poor wood-cutter with his wife and his two children. The boy was called Hansel and the girl Gretel. He had little to bite and to break, and once when great dearth fell on the land, he could no longer procure even daily bread. Now when he thought over this by night in his bed, and tossed about in his anxiety, he groaned and said to his wife: "What is to become of us? How are we to feed our poor children, when we no longer have anything even for ourselves?" "I'll tell you what, husband," answered the woman, "early to-morrow morning we will take the children out into the forest to where it is the thickest; there we will light a fire for them, and give each of them one more piece of bread, and then we will go to our work and leave them alone. They will not find the way home again, and we shall be rid of them." "No, wife," said the man, "I will not do that; how can I bear to leave my children alone in the forest--the wild animals would soon come and tear them to pieces." "0, you fool!" said she, "then we must all four die of hunger, you may as well plane the planks for our coffins," and she left him no peace until he consented. "But I feel very sorry for the poor children, all the same," said the man.

The two children had also not been able to sleep for hunger, and had heard what their step-mother had said to their father. Gretel wept bitter tears, and said to Hansel: "Now all is over with us." "Be quiet, Gretel," said Hansel, "do not distress yourself, I will soon find a way to help us." And when the old folks had fallen asleep, he got up, put on his little coat, opened the door below, and crept outside. The moon shone brightly, and the white pebbles which lay in front of the house glittered like real silver pennies. Hansel stooped and stuffed the little pocket of his coat with as many as he could get in. Then he went back and said to Gretel: "Be comforted, dear little sister, and sleep in peace, God will not forsake us," and he lay down again in his bed. When day dawned, but before the sun had risen, the woman came and awoke the two children, saying: "Get up, you sluggards! We are going into the forest to fetch wood." She gave each a little piece of bread, and said: "There is something for your dinner, but do not eat it up before then, for you will get nothing else." Gretel took the bread under her apron, as Hansel had the pebbles in his pocket. Then they all set out together on the way to the forest. When they had walked a short time, Hansel stood still and peeped back at the house, and did so again and again. His father said: "Hansel, what are you looking at there and staying behind for? Pay attention, and do not forget how to use your legs." "Ah, father," said Hansel, "I am looking at my little white cat, which is sitting up on the roof, and wants to say good-bye to me." The wife said: "Fool, that is not your little cat, that is the morning sun which is shining on the chimneys." Hansel, however, had not been looking back at the cat, but had been constantly throwing one of the white pebble-stones out of his pocket on the road.

"Hansel and Gretel" on the Internet (full text available; portion of first page reproduced here).

Jennifer had not reread "Hansel and Gretel" since she was a child. Rereading it now was very helpful, for it clarified a number of important details in Glück's poem. It explained, for example, "the witch's cry" in the first stanza, which alludes to the witch's "horrible howl" when Gretel pushes her into the oven. It also fills out the reference to the "women" in the second stanza, who in the story include the children's cruel stepmother as well as the evil witch. Jennifer could have prepared and written her paper without taking the time to check on the story, but it was better that she did.

STUDENT ESSAY

Here is the essay that Jennifer wrote.

Anderson 1

Jennifer Anderson
Professor Washington
English 102
12 October 2005

A Memory Poem:
Louise Glück's "Gretel in Darkness"
Everyone knows the story of Hansel and Gretel,
one of the best-known of Grimm's Fairy Tales. In
her poem "Gretel in Darkness" (825), Louise
Glück takes for granted that we know the story--
the brother and sister who are mistreated by
their father and, especially, by their
stepmother; their abandonment in a forest; their
capture by a witch who lives in a house made of
cakes and candy; the witch's plan to fatten them
up (Hansel first) and then eat them; Gretel's
killing of the witch by pushing her into an
oven; and, finally, the children's discovery of
the witch's jewels that makes them and their
father (the stepmother has died) rich and happy
at last. Glück's subject is not the story
itself, but, instead, Gretel's memories. "Gretel
in Darkness" is a haunting poem about horrors
that Gretel, Glück's speaker, cannot forget.

The poem takes place after the witch has been
killed and Hansel and Gretel have returned to
the safety of their father's cottage. Everything
now should be fine, Gretel says: "This is the
world we wanted." "God rewards": God has heard
their prayers and saved them. But as if it were
still present, Gretel hears "the witch's cry,"
the witch whom Gretel killed. And the image
about the witch's death that she uses is graphic

and disturbing: "Her tongue shrivels into
gas. . . ." The witch was horrible, but this image
is horrifying; it sticks in Gretel's mind, and
the reader's too, like a shocking detail from
a nightmare.

     In a way the entire poem reports on a
nightmare that Gretel is doomed to live in
forever. "Why do I not forget?"--the key line in
the poem, I think--really means that she knows
she will always remember what happened to her
and her brother. For Gretel this fairy tale does
not have a happy ending.

     Yet it does for her brother, or so it seems
to Gretel. She resents Hansel's failure to
remember as she does, and, with a vivid, direct
choice of verb, she reminds him: "I killed for
you." The nightmarish quality of Gretel's
thoughts and feelings is shown again in the next
lines, which once more make clear how much her
past dominates the present:

          I see armed firs,
       the spires of that gleaming kiln--
     Gretel is safe but threatened, sheltered at
home but still in danger. She is caught by a
terrifying and terrible past she cannot break
free from. The repetitions--dead/dead, bars/bar,
real/real--imply that she is trapped, not able
to re-enter the present and look forward to the
future. She turns to her brother for help, yet
without finding the support she seeks:

          Nights I turn to you to hold me
          but you are not there.
     Hansel (who is only named once) is not there
for Gretel, and at first I felt her hurt. But
Glück is not meaning to criticize Hansel for his
distance, his separation from his sister. Or if
Glück is, she is balancing that against Gretel's

Anderson 3

absorption in the terror of her experiences. She feels that she and her brother are still in the middle of them.

As I thought further about this poem, I wondered: Strange as it sounds, maybe Gretel prefers the past to the present, because the past was so real. Life is all too safe and comfortable now, while then everything, like the fire in the oven, was so earnest, that is, so serious and intense. It was not the world she wanted--who would want to be in that house of horrors! Even now her life is menaced, as those snaky "s" sounds in the middle of the final stanza suggest. But perhaps the frightful feelings, in their intensity, were (and still are) keener and deeper than anything that Gretel knew before, or knows now, in the secure world she lives in with her father and brother. She and her brother then were so absolutely close, as they are not now. Gretel cannot let go of her past, and she does not want to.

[New page]

Anderson 4

Work Cited

Glück, Louise. "Gretel in Darkness." An
    Introduction to Literature. Ed. Sylvan Barnet
    et al. 14th ed. New York: Longman, 2006. 825.

▦ TOPICS FOR CRITICAL THINKING AND WRITING

1. Jennifer's instructor told the class that the essay should be "about 500 words." Jennifer's paper is more than that—about 650 words. Do you think that she uses her space well? Could she have shortened the essay, to bring it closer to the assigned length? If you had to suggest cuts, where would you propose to make them?

2. Does Jennifer omit important details in the poem that you think she should have included in the paper? Explain why these should be part of her response.

3. Give Jennifer's paper a grade, and in a paragraph written to her, highlight the strengths and limitations of this paper. Provide her, too, with one or two specific suggestions for improving her writing in the next paper.

22

Poets at Work

When we read a poem aloud, whether an anonymous nursery rhyme such as "Jack and Jill went up a hill" or a work by one of the great names, the words seem so right, so inevitable, that it is hard to believe they did not flow easily. Reading, say, Keats's "On First Looking into Chapman's Homer" (page 747), we may think that he must have sat down and simply let the words stream from his pen. And certainly Keats himself emphasized spontaneity: In a letter he says, "If poetry comes not as naturally as leaves to a tree it had better not come at all." Yet Keats's manuscripts indicated that he revised his work heavily, so heavily that some of the manuscripts are almost indecipherable. Probably William Butler Yeats was speaking for all poets when he said (in a poem called "Adam's Curse") that a poem must seem spontaneous but is the result of hard work:

> A line will take us hours maybe;
> Yet if it does not seem a moment's thought,
> Our stitching and unstitching has been naught.

In this chapter we give the following material:

1. Three versions of a poem by Yeats.
2. Two versions of a poem by Cathy Song, introduced by her comment.
3. Two versions of a poem by Walt Whitman.
4. Two versions of a poem by Donald Justice.

WALT WHITMAN

Walt Whitman (1819–1892) was born in a farmhouse in rural Long Island, New York, but was brought up in Brooklyn, then an independent city in New York. He attended public school for a few years (1825–1830), apprenticed as a printer in the 1830s, and then worked as a typesetter, journalist, and newspaper editor. In 1855 he published the first edition of a collection of his poems, Leaves of Grass, a book that he revised and published in one edition after another throughout the remainder of his life. During the Civil War he served as a volunteer nurse for the Union army.

In the third edition of Leaves of Grass (1860) Whitman added two groups of poems, one called "Children of Adam" and the other (named for an aromatic grass that grows near ponds and swamps) called "Calamus." "Children of Adam" celebrates heterosexual relations, whereas "Calamus" celebrates what Whitman called "manly love." Although many of the "Calamus" poems seem clearly homosexual, perhaps the very fact that Whitman published them made them seem relatively innocent; in any case, those nineteenth-century critics who condemned Whitman for the sexuality of his writing concentrated on the poems in "Children of Adam."

Enfans d'Adam, number 9   [1860]

[*Leaves of Grass*, 1860 edition]

Once, I passed through a populous city, imprinting my brain, for
    future use, with its shows, architecture, customs and traditions;
Yet now, of all that city, I remember only a woman I casually met
    there, who detained me for love of me,   4
Day by day and night by night we were together,—All else has long
    been forgotten by me,
I remember I say only that woman that passionately clung to me,
Again we wander—we love—we separate again,   8
Again she holds me by the hand—I must not go!
I see her close beside me, with silent lips, sad and tremulous.

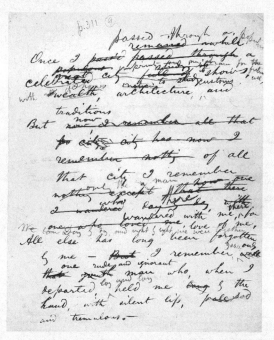

Walt Whitman, 1860 manuscript, for the poem "Once I Passed Through a Populous City," included in the "Enfans d'Adam" (Children of Adam) section of *Leaves of Grass* (1860 ed.). The
extensive markings on this page, some of them in dark ink, and others in light pencil, show that
Whitman revised this poem carefully. Notice, for example, that Whitman wrote and crossed
out both "great" and "populous" and then seemed to settle on the word "celebrated," only to
write (barely visible in the upper right corner) "populous" again, which became his final choice
for the phrase "a populous city." Note, too, the changes in gender from "only a man" and "that
youth" (crossed out) and "one rude and ignorant man" to—in the published poem—"that
woman" and "she holds me."

DONALD JUSTICE

Donald Justice was born in Miami, Florida, in 1925, attended local schools there, and graduated from the University of Miami in 1945. Many of his poems focus on his experiences in Florida and in Georgia, where he spent the summers during the 1930s, living on his grandparents' farm. Justice's books include A Donald Justice Reader *(1991) and* Collected Poems *(2004). He died in 2004.*

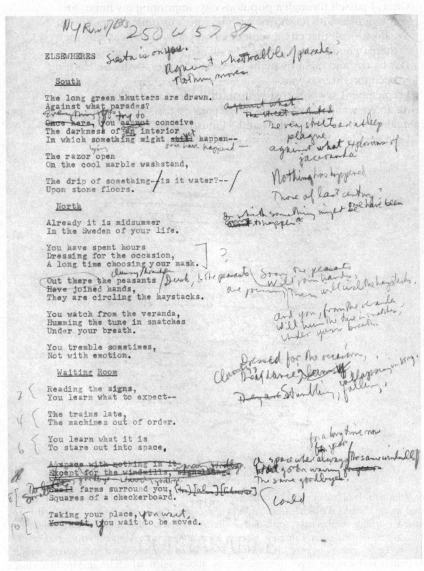

Manuscript of Donald Justice's "Elsewheres."

Elsewheres

South

The long green shutters are drawn.
Against what parades?

Closing our eyes to the sun,
We try to imagine

The darkness of an interior
In which something still might happen:

The razor lying open
On the cool marble washstand,

The drip of something—is it water?—
Upon stone floors.

North

Already it is midsummer
In the Sweden of our lives.

The peasants have joined hands,
They are circling the haystacks.

We watch from the veranda.
We sit, mufflered.

Humming the tune in snatches
Under our breath.

We tremble sometimes,
Not with emotion.

Waiting Room

Reading the signs,
We learn to expect—

The trains late,
The machines out of order.

We learn what it is
To stare out into space.

Great farms surround us,
Squares of a checkerboard.

Taking our places, we wait,
We wait to be moved.

[2004]

▨ TOPICS FOR CRITICAL THINKING AND WRITING

1. What was your response to the title, "Elsewheres," when you first encountered it? How did your response change after you read and studied the three poems?

2. What is your response to "South"? Did you find you responded to it differently after you read "North"? How would your response change if "North" came first and "South" second?

3. Do you think that "South" and "North" could stand together effectively as a pair? What does "Waiting Room" contribute to our experience of "Elsewheres" as a whole?

4. Poets are often encouraged to make good use of specific details. Circle the details in these poems and comment on their significance. What is their relationship to the parts of the poems that you did not circle?

5. Is Justice seeking to teach us something through these three poems? Please explain.

6. Imagine that Justice had chosen to print the three poems of "Elsewheres" *vertically* on the page. Would that make a difference in our response? Notice that in the manuscript, the poems are presented vertically.

7. What is your response to the manuscript page we have included, with its markings and jottings? In your view, which kind of poem is likely to be better, one that has been revised a great deal or one that has been revised hardly at all? When you read a poem, can you tell whether it has been revised? Is there a poem in this book that you feel needs further revision? Please identify it and explain your response.

CATHY SONG

Cathy Song, born in Honolulu in 1955 of a Chinese-American mother and a Korean-American father, holds a bachelor's degree from Wellesley College and a master's degree in creative writing from Boston University. She is the author of three books of poems, the first of which, Picture Bride *(1983), was the winner in the Yale Series of Younger Poets. She has also won the Hawaii Award for Literature, and the Shelley Memorial Award from the Poetry Society of America.*

Here we print a draft of an untitled poem, and the final version, now titled "Out of Our Hands." Ms. Song has kindly provided us with a comment on the origins of the poem:

"Out of Our Hands" was written for the poet Wing Tek Lum. Long before Wing Tek and I became friends, I had already encountered his work. The poem is informed by our friendship; my abiding respect for the poet is deepened by my affection for the man. Knowing the reality of his warm humanity allowed me to imagine the poem in a larger context—what I had felt in his poems was present and true—and in a sense, when I first encountered his work, I was ready to receive the "seeds of a language / I needed to know." I was ready for this poet who had something to teach me.

The sense of magic and transformation is alive and well in the poem because his poems, his presence allowed that to happen with me. The images of birds and flight, children and language have everything to do with the way gifts are given and received—serendipitous and yet, there are no coincidences. When a poem is written there is someone out there waiting to read it, to have the gift descend, touch you like a leaf, a feather, a letter written just for you.

Out of a hat
on a piece of paper
someone gave me your name.
Your name flew
out of my hand,
the black letters dismantling in the air
above the lake.
I watched the letters
become the bird seeds of a language
I needed to know
the language I borrowed from the children
my students borrowed coats
who scattered outside the school—
red-bricked and torn on the edge of Chinatown—
undisciplined like starlings, the children I taught
in the broken shoes of the wind.
One day your name
came back in a poem
you were writing
on the edge of another city,
a poem you were determined
to write for the rest of your life.
The poem a subversive act.
The poem about being Chinese,
skin the glorious color of chicken fat.

Song's draft for "Out of Our Hands."

Out of Our Hands   [1994]

—for Wing Tek Lum

Out of a hat
on a piece of paper
someone once gave me your name.   3

Your name flew
out of my hand,
the black letters   6

dismantling the air
above the school.
I watched the letters   9

form the bird
seeds of a language
I needed to know,   12

a language borrowed
from the children I taught
who shivered in borrowed coats.   15

Toward evening they scattered
outside the school,
red-bricked and torn   18

on the edge of Chinatown.
I watched them disappear
into their lives,   21

undisciplined like starlings,
they disappeared
in the broken shoes of the wind.   24

One day your name
came back
in a poem you were   27

writing in another city,
a poem you were determined
to write for the rest of your life.   30

The poem a subversive act.
The poem about being Chinese,
skin the glorious color of chicken fat.   33

WILLIAM BUTLER YEATS:
"LEDA AND THE SWAN" (THREE VERSIONS)

William Butler Yeats (1865–1939) was born in Dublin, Ireland. The early Yeats was much interested in highly lyrical, romantic poetry, often drawing on Irish mythology. The later poems, from about 1910 (and especially after Yeats met Ezra Pound in 1911), are often more colloquial. Although these later poems often employ mythological references, too, one feels that the poems are more down-to-earth. He was awarded the Nobel Prize in Literature in 1923.

According to Greek mythology, Zeus fell in love with Leda, disguised himself as a swan, and ravished her. Among the offspring of this union were Helen and Clytemnestra. Paris abducted Helen, causing the Greeks to raze Troy; Clytemnestra, wife of Agamemnon, murdered her husband on his triumphant return to Greece. Yeats saw political significance in the myth of beauty and war engendered by a god; but, as he tells us, when he was composing "Leda and the Swan" the political significance evaporated:

> *After the individualistic, demagogic movements, founded by Hobbes and popularized by the Encyclopaedists and the French Revolution, we have a soil so exhausted that it cannot grow that crop again for centuries. Then I thought "Nothing is now possible but some movement, or birth from above, preceded by some violent annunciation." My fancy began to play with Leda and the Swan for metaphor, and I began this poem, but as I wrote, bird and lady took such possession of the scene that all politics went out of it.*

The first version of the poem, titled "Annunciation," is from a manuscript dated 18 September 1923; the second version was printed in a magazine, June 1924; the third version, first published in his Collected Poems *of 1933, is Yeats's final one. But this third version had been almost fully achieved by 1925; the 1933 version differs from the 1925 version only in two punctuation marks: The question marks at the ends of lines 6 and 8 in the latest version were, in 1925, respectively, a comma and a semicolon.*

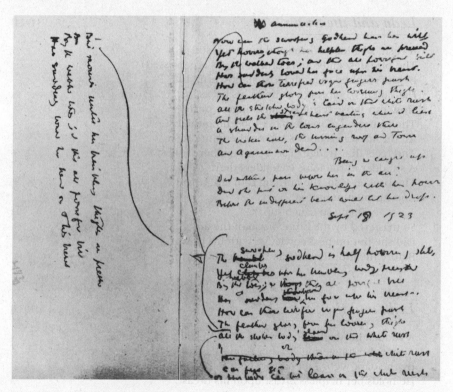

Yeats's first drafts of "Leda and the Swan," 1923.

Annunciation   [1923]

Now can the swooping Godhead have his will
Yet hovers, though her helpless thighs are pressed
By the webbed toes; and that all powerful bill
Has suddenly bowed her face upon his breast,   4
How can those terrified vague fingers push
The feathered glory from her loosening thighs?
All the stretched body's laid on that white rush
And feels the strange heart beating where it lies   8
A shudder in the loins engenders there
The broken wall, the burning roof and tower
And Agamemnon dead . . .
                    Being so caught up   12
Did nothing pass before her in the air?
Did she put on his knowledge with his power
Before the indifferent beak could let her drop.

Leda and the Swan   [1924]

A rush, a sudden wheel, and hovering still
The bird descends, and her frail thighs are pressed
By the webbed toes, and that all-powerful bill
Has laid her helpless face upon his breast   4
How can those terrified vague fingers push
The feathered glory from her loosening thighs!
All the stretched body's laid on the white rush
And feels the strange heart beating where it lies;   8
A shudder in the loins engenders there
The broken wall, the burning roof and tower
And Agamemnon dead.
                    Being so caught up,   12
So mastered by the brute blood of the air,
Did she put on his knowledge with his power
Before the indifferent beak could let her drop?

Leda and the Swan   [1933]

A sudden blow: the great wings beating still
Above the staggering girl, her thighs caressed
By the dark webs, her nape caught in his bill,
He holds her helpless breast upon his breast.   4

How can those terrified vague fingers push
The feathered glory from her loosening thighs?
And how can body, laid in that white rush,
But feel the strange heart beating where it lies?   8

A shudder in the loins engenders there
The broken wall, the burning roof and tower
And Agamemnon dead.
            Being so caught up,   12
So mastered by the brute blood of the air,
Did she put on his knowledge with his power
Before the indifferent beak could let her drop?

23

The Span of Life: Poems from the Cradle to the Grave

"Span" is a Middle English word for a unit of measurement (the measure of space between two extremities), and the "span of life" is thus the period that measures the time from birth to death. The classical world developed the idea that human life is divided into Seven Ages, from infancy and childhood to second childhood, senility. Seven is a mystical number in many cultures: the ancient Hebrews spoke of the seven names of God, Buddhists speak of the Seven Buddhas of the Past, Pythagoreans regard seven as a lucky number, Christians speak of the Seven Deadly Sins and the Seven Last Words of Christ, Islam speaks of the Seventh Heaven, and wives speak of husbands having a seven-year itch.

True, one also finds the span of life conceived in smaller and larger numbers, for instance three (summarized by the speaker of T. S. Eliot's "Sweeney Agonistes" as "birth, and copulation, and death"), but the most memorable number is seven, perhaps because seven already had developed grand associations: The Bible speaks of the seven days of creation, and (until relatively modern times) the planets were thought to number seven.

The most famous account of the Seven Ages is by Shakespeare, spoken by the melancholy Jaques in the second act of *As You Like It*. Jaques is *not* a mouthpiece through which Shakespeare expresses his own views; rather, Jaques is a distinctive character in a comedy. He is a figure who chooses to stand apart from the general merriment, entertaining us by his engaging cynical observations. For instance, he sees the infant not as smiling or sleeping peacefully but as "mewling and puking," and he sees the "whining" freshly scrubbed schoolchild with "shining morning face, creeping like snail / Unwillingly to school." For the wry Jaques, there is no joy in infancy, no play in childhood, no laughter in youth, no loving friendship or happy marriage in maturity, no comfort or solace in old age. We see—and we greatly enjoy—the force of his seven brief descriptions of the periods of life, but we also know there is much more to life than the ridiculous and ultimately pitiful caricatures that Jaques sets forth. Indeed in the rest of *As You Like It*, Shakespeare gives us a much fuller view. For instance, according to Jaques, in the last stage of life human beings are left with nothing at all ("Sans teeth, sans eyes, sans taste, sans every thing"), but just after Jaques utters this line, the young lover in the play, Orlando, enters, tenderly carrying an aged, exhausted servant. Orlando's devoted care for the poor old man

The Seven Ages of Man. Woodcut in Bartholmeus Anglicus, *De Proprietatibus Rerum,* Lyons, 1482. In front we see—from right to left—the infant in a cradle, the toddler learning to walk, and the child riding a hobby-horse. Immediately behind the infant and the toddler is the schoolboy, in academic garb; at the rear (in the center) is a depiction of extreme old age holding a rosary and equipped with a staff or crutch, flanked by (at the right) young manhood, equipped with a sword, and (at the left) old age, making a gesture of admonition.

doesn't exactly refute Jaques, but it does help us to see that his view of the span of life is extremely narrow.

We have delayed long enough: Here is Jaques's speech.

> All the world's a stage,
> And all the men and women merely players;
> They have their exits and their entrances,
> And one man in his time plays many parts,
> His acts being seven ages. At first the infant,   5
> Mewling° and puking in the nurse's arms.
> Then the whining schoolboy, with his satchel
> And shining morning face, creeping like snail
> Unwillingly to school. And then the lover,
> Sighing like furnace, with a woeful ballad   10
> Made to his mistress' eyebrow, Then a soldier,
> Full of strange oaths, and bearded like the pard,°

---

6 mewling bawling.   **12 bearded like the pard** whiskered like the leopard.

Jealous° in honor, sudden, and quick in quarrel,
Seeking the bubble reputation
Even in the cannon's mouth. And then the justice,   15
In fair round belly with good capon lined,
With eyes severe and beard of formal cut,
Full of wise saws° and modern instances;
And so he plays his part. The sixth age shifts
Into the lean and slippered pantaloon,°   20
With spectacles on nose, and pouch on side,
His youthful hose,° well saved, a world too wide
For his shrunk shank, and his big manly voice,
Turning again toward childish treble, pipes
And whistles in his sound. Last scene of all,   25
That ends this strange eventful history,
Is second childishness, and mere oblivion,
Sans teeth, sans eyes, sans taste, sans every thing.

---

13 jealous rash.   **18 wise saws** sayings, proverbs.   **20 pantaloon** old man wearing baggy pants.   **22 hose** tight-fitting trousers.

❈ TOPICS FOR CRITICAL THINKING AND WRITING

1. As we have said, the speech occurs in a play, in a dramatic situation: Jaques is one of a number of courtiers who have accompanied Duke Senior—the rightful duke and a good man, who has been banished to the forest by a usurper. In this scene, they are about to eat when the Duke comments that "This wide and universal theater / Presents more woeful pageants [i.e., scenes] than we play in." Jaques picks up the theatrical motif and offers his speech. Directors differ greatly in how they stage this speech. For instance, sometimes Jaques advances toward the audience and delivers the lines as a set speech; sometimes he remains seated; sometimes he seems casual, perhaps munching on an apple; sometimes he seems to be thinking hard, and improvising (i.e., pausing as if mentally searching for the appropriate images); sometimes he uses different voices and gestures, appropriate to the infant, the school boy, the lover, the soldier, the justice, the foolish old pantaloon, and the man in second childhood. If you were directing the play, how would you instruct Jaques to perform?

2. The speech gives a rather dark view of life, yet it is one of Shakespeare's best-known and most-loved speeches. How do you account for its popularity?

Jaques is not Shakespeare's only character who thinks of life as a brief performance in which we each play a part. King Lear says, "When we are born, we cry that we are come / To this great stage of fools," and Macbeth says, "Life's but a walking shadow, a poor player / That struts and frets his hour upon the stage / And then is heard no more." Notice too, later in this section, that Shakespeare's contemporary, Sir Walter Raleigh, in a short poem that begins "What is our life? a play of passion," also conceives of life as a brief theatrical performance. Raleigh's poem ends:

> Thus march we, playing, to our latest° rest,   *last*
> Only we die in earnest—that's no jest.

What does a human life—this life, my life—amount to? Poets across the centuries have engaged and explored this question, as the following selections in their different ways attest.

Mark R. Harrington, an Oneida (Iroquois) family portrait, 1907. Ontario, Canada. The Oneida, a Native American people, today live chiefly in Wisconsin, New York, and Ontario. (Courtesy National Museum of the American Indian, Smithsonian Institution [N02641].)

THREE SHORT LONG VIEWS

ROBERT FROST

For a biographical note on Frost (1874-1963), see page 931.

The Span of Life   [1936]

The old dog barks backward without getting up.
I can remember when he was a pup.

▒ TOPICS FOR CRITICAL THINKING AND WRITING

1. Suppose the second line were different: "Rover leaped about when he was a pup." Have we improved or weakened the poem? Why? Come to think about it, what are your thoughts on the following version?

   > Old Rover barks backward without getting up.
   > He used to frolic when he was a pup.

   Has anything been gained? Lost?

2. The preceding question chiefly directs your thought toward relatively large-scale changes: In the revisions, the dog is named, and the speaker is no longer as evident (the difference between "I can remember," and "He used to frolic"). But now consider smaller-scale effects. In Frost's version, which of the two lines jingles a bit more than the other? Why?

SIR WALTER RALEIGH

Walter Raleigh (1552–1618) is known chiefly as a soldier and a colonizer—he was the founder of the settlement in Virginia, and he introduced tobacco into Europe—but in his own day he was known also as a poet.

What Is Our Life?

What is our life? a play of passion,
Our mirth the music of division,°
Our mothers' wombs the tiring-houses° be,
Where we are dressed for this short comedy.
Heaven the judicious, sharp spectator is,   5
That sits and marks still° who doth act amiss;
Our graves that hide us from the searching sun
Are like drawn curtains when the play is done.
Thus march we, playing, to our latest° rest,
Only we die in earnest—that's no jest.   10

---

2 division variation on a theme.   **3 tiring-houses** dressing rooms.   **6 still** always.
9 latest last.

▒ TOPICS FOR CRITICAL THINKING AND WRITING

1. Early copies of this poem vary widely in their punctuation, and none are in Raleigh's hand, so the punctuation here is the editors', not the author's. We decided not to use a capital letter for "a" in the first line, and to use a period at the end of line 8 (some editors use a semicolon), and to use a dash in line 10 (some editors use a comma). Do you approve of our choices? Why, or why not?

2. Suppose in line 9 Raleigh had written "Thus go we, playing," instead of "Thus march we, playing." What, if anything, would be gained or lost?

3. In line 5 Raleigh expresses the traditional Christian view that God takes notice of our behavior. If you are not a believer, does the poem therefore not interest you? Or do you still find much truth in it, for instance in such a line as "Thus march we, playing, to our latest rest"?

4. The following short poem appears in the *New England Primer,* a textbook small enough to fit into a child's pocket. The earliest extant edition of the book is 1727, but this poem is believed to be several decades older.

> Our days begin with trouble here,
> Our life is but a span,
> And cruel death is always near,
> So frail a thing is man.

Which poem—this or Raleigh's—do you find more interesting? Which more memorable? Why? Does one seem truer than the other? More shapely, more aesthetically attractive? Explain.

E. E. CUMMINGS

e. e. cummings was the pen name of Edwin Estlin Cummings (1894–1962), who grew up in Cambridge, Massachusetts, and was graduated from Harvard, where he became interested in modern literature and art, especially in the movements called cubism and futurism. His father, a conservative clergyman and a professor at Harvard, seems to have been baffled by the youth's interests, but Cummings's mother encouraged his artistic activities, including his use of unconventional punctuation and capitalization.

Politically liberal in his youth, Cummings became more conservative after a visit to Russia in 1931, but early and late his work emphasizes individuality and freedom of expression.

anyone lived in a pretty how town   [1940]

anyone lived in a pretty how town
(with up so floating many bells down)
spring summer autumn winter
he sang his didn't he danced his did.   4

Women and men(both little and small)
cared for anyone not at all
they sowed their isn't they reaped their same
sun moon stars rain   8

children guessed(but only a few
and down they forgot as up they grew
autumn winter spring summer)
that noone loved him more by more   12

when by now and tree by leaf
she laughed his joy she cried his grief
bird by snow and stir by still
anyone's any was all to her   16

someones married their everyones
laughed their cryings and did their dance
(sleep wake hope and then)they
said their nevers they slept their dream   20

stars rain sun moon
(and only the snow can begin to explain
how children are apt to forget to remember
with up so floating many bells down)   24

one day anyone died i guess
(and noone stooped to kiss his face)
busy folk buried them side by side
little by little and was by was   28

all by all and deep by deep
and more by more they dream their sleep
noone and anyone earth by april
wish by spirit and if by yes.   32

Women and men(both dong and ding)
summer autumn winter spring
reaped their sowing and went their came
sun moon stars rain   36

▨ TOPICS FOR CRITICAL THINKING AND WRITING

1. Put into normal order (as far as possible) the words of the first two stanzas, and then compare your version with Cummings's. What does Cummings gain—or lose?
2. Characterize the "anyone" who "sang his didn't" and "danced his did." In your opinion, how does he differ from the people who "sowed their isn't they reaped their same"?
3. Some readers interpret "anyone died" (line 25) to mean that the child matured and became as dead as the other adults. How might you support or refute this interpretation?

EARLY YEARS

WILLIAM BLAKE

William Blake (1757–1827) was born in London and at fourteen was apprenticed for seven years to an engraver. A Christian visionary poet, he made his living by giving drawing lessons and by illustrating books, including his own Songs of Innocence *(1789) and* Songs of Experience *(1794). These two books represent, he said, "two contrary states of the human soul." ("Infant Joy" comes from* Innocence, *"Infant Sorrow" from* Experience.*) In 1809 Blake exhibited his art, but the show was a failure. Not until he was in his sixties, when he stopped writing poetry, did he achieve any public recognition—and then it was as a painter.*

Infant Joy

[1789]

"I have no name,
I am but two days old."
What shall I call thee?
"I happy am,
Joy is my name."   5
Sweet joy befall thee!

Pretty joy!
Sweet joy but two days old,
Sweet joy I call thee
Thou dost smile,   10
I sing the while—
Sweet joy befall thee.

Infant Sorrow

[1794]

My mother groaned! my father wept.
Into the dangerous world I leapt,
Helpless, naked, piping loud;
Like a fiend hid in a cloud.   4

Struggling in my father's hands,
Striving against my swadling bands;
Bound and weary I thought best
To sulk upon my mother's breast.   8

❋ TOPICS FOR CRITICAL THINKING AND WRITING

1. "Infant Joy" begins "I have no name," but by line 5 the infant says "Joy
   is my name." What does the mother reply? Does she know the infant's
   name?

2. In line 9 the mother says, "Sweet joy I call thee." Does the line
   suggest how the mother has learned the name? What is the child's
   response?

3. In "Infant Sorrow," why is the infant sorrowful? What does the baby
   struggle against? Does "Like a fiend" suggest that it is inherently wicked
   and therefore should be repressed? Or does the adult world wickedly
   repress energy?

4. Why does the mother groan? Why does the father weep? Is the world
   "dangerous" to the infant in other than an obviously physical sense? To
   what degree are its parents its enemies? To what degree does the infant
   yield to them? In the last line, one might expect a newborn baby to
   nurse. What does this infant do?

5. Compare "Infant Joy" with "Infant Sorrow." What differences in sound
   do you hear? In "Infant Sorrow," for instance, look at lines 3, 5, 6, and 7.
   What repeated sounds do you hear?

ANONYMOUS

Many of the nursery rhymes that are common today are at least two hundred years old, and some are much older. Some of their lines are nonsense ("Hey, diddle diddle," "Humpty Dumpty," "Hickory, dickory, dock"), and some are close to nonsense ("Sing a song of sixpence, a pocket full of rye") though perhaps they once made sense. Indeed, their nonsense may be part of why they endure; they evoke a strange world, a world with a cat who has a fiddle, where a cow jumped over the moon, and where "The little dog laughed, to see such sport, / And the dish ran away with the spoon." And of course they endure partly because of their strong rhythms: "Jack Sprat could eat no fat, / His wife could eat no lean, / And so between the two of them, / They licked the platter clean." True, if one is determined to connect literature with life and to find a meaning and a moral in every verse, one can say that "Jack Sprat" offers comforting reassurance that a happy marriage can be built on contrary personalities; but if this poem supports the view that "opposites attract," one wonders how much truth is in the proverbial view that "Birds of a feather flock together."

In any case, no account of the span of life can neglect the poetry that infants and children treasure. In the following nursery rhyme, "Can I get there by candle-light?" means "Can I get there before a candle is needed, that is, before dark?" rather than "Can I get there with the aid of a candle?"

How Many Miles to Babylon

How many miles to Babylon?
  Three score miles and ten.
Can I get there by candle-light?
  Yes, and back again.
If your heels are nimble and light,
You may get there by candle-light.

TOPICS FOR CRITICAL THINKING AND WRITING

1. Some scholars have suggested that "Babylon" is a corruption of "Baby-land," that is, the second childhood or senility that may characterize the last stage of life. In this view, "three score miles and ten" is metaphoric; life is a journey of 70 miles (cf. Psalm 90, which says "The days of our years are three score and ten"). This interpretation cannot be proved—or disproved. Does it enrich the rhyme for you? Or do you wish you had not heard of it?
2. Recite—preferably aloud—a favorite nursery rhyme. What do you especially like about it? Why do you think it has stayed in your mind? The rhythm? The sounds of certain words? The imagery it calls to mind?
3. You may be familiar with nursery rhymes in a language other than English. If so, could you provide an example, and a translation? Do the nursery rhymes you know in this other language seem similar to or different from nursery rhymes you have heard in English?

SHARON OLDS

Sharon Olds was born in San Francisco in 1942. She was educated at Stanford University and Columbia University, has published several volumes of poetry, and has received major awards.

Rites of Passage

[1983]

As the guests arrive at my son's party
They gather in the living room—
short men, men in first grade
with smooth jaws and chins.
Hands in pockets, they stand around   5
jostling, jockeying for place, small fights
breaking out and calming. One says to another
How old are you? Six. I'm seven. So?
They eye each other, seeing themselves
tiny in the other's pupils. They clear their   10
throats a lot, a room of small bankers,
they fold their arms and frown. *I could beat you
up,* a seven says to a six,
the dark cake, round and heavy as a
turret, behind them on the table. My son,   15
freckles like specks of nutmeg on his cheeks,
chest narrow as the balsa keel of a
model boat, long hands
cool and thin as the day they guided him
out of me, speaks up as a host   20
for the sake of the group.
We could easily kill a two-year-old,
he says in his clear voice. The other
men agree, they clear their throats
like Generals, they relax and get down to   25
playing war, celebrating my son's life.

☒ TOPICS FOR CRITICAL THINKING AND WRITING

1. Focus on the details that the speaker provides about the boys—how they look, how they speak. What do the details reveal about them?
2. Is the speaker's son the same as or different from the other boys?
3. Some readers find the ironies in this poem (e.g., "short men") to be somewhat comical, while others, noting such phrases as "kill a two-year-old" and "playing war," conclude that the poem as a whole is meant to be upsetting, even frightening. How would you describe the kinds of irony that Olds uses here?
4. An experiment in irony and point of view: Try writing a poem like this one, from the point of view of a father about the birthday party of his son, and then try writing another one by either a father or mother about a daughter's party.

LOUISE GLÜCK

Louise Glück (b. 1943) was born in New York City and attended Sarah Lawrence College and Columbia University. She has taught at Goddard College in Vermont and at Warren Wilson College in North Carolina. Her volume of poems, The Triumph of Achilles *(1985), won the National Book Critics Circle Award for poetry.*

The School Children   [1975]

The children go forward with their little satchels.
And all morning the mothers have labored
to gather the late apples, red and gold,
like words of another language.

And on the other shore   5
are those who wait behind great desks
to receive these offerings.

How orderly they are—the nails
on which the children hang
their overcoats of blue or yellow wool.   10

And the teachers shall instruct them in silence
and the mothers shall scour the orchards for a way out,
drawing to themselves the gray limbs of the fruit trees
bearing so little ammunition.

✸ TOPICS FOR CRITICAL THINKING AND WRITING

1. Which words in the poem present a cute picture-postcard view of small children going to school?
2. Which words undercut this happy scene?
3. In the last stanza we read that "the teachers shall instruct" and "the mothers shall scour." What, if anything, is changed if we substitute "will" for "shall"?

ROBERT HAYDEN

Robert Hayden (1913-1980) was born in Detroit, Michigan. His parents divorced when he was a child, and he was brought up by a neighboring family, whose name he adopted. In 1942, at the age of 29, he graduated from Detroit City College (now Wayne State University), and he received a master's degree from the University of Michigan. He taught at Fisk University from 1946 to 1969 and after that, for the remainder of his life, at the University of Michigan. In 1979 he was appointed Consultant in Poetry to the Library of Congress, the first African-American to hold the post.

Those Winter Sundays   [1962]

Sundays too my father got up early
and put his clothes on in the blueblack cold,
then with cracked hands that ached
from labor in the weekday weather made
banked fires blaze. No one ever thanked him.   5

I'd wake and hear the cold splintering, breaking.
When the rooms were warm, he'd call,
and slowly I would rise and dress,
fearing the chronic angers of that house.

Speaking indifferently to him,   10
who had driven out the cold
and polished my good shoes as well.
What did I know, what did I know
of love's austere and lonely offices?

▨ TOPICS FOR CRITICAL THINKING AND WRITING

1. In line 1, what does the word "too" tell us about the father? What does it suggest about the speaker and the implied hearer of the poem?
2. How old do you believe the speaker was at the time he recalls in the second and third stanzas? What details suggest this age?
3. What is the meaning of "offices" in the last line? What does this word suggest that other words Hayden might have chosen do not?
4. What do you take to be the speaker's present attitude toward his father? What circumstances, do you imagine, prompted his memory of "Those Winter Sundays"?
5. In a page or two, try to get down the exact circumstances when you spoke "indifferently," or not at all, to someone who had deserved your gratitude.

SEX, LOVE, MARRIAGE, CHILDREN

WILLIAM BUTLER YEATS

William Butler Yeats (1865–1939) was born in Dublin, Ireland. The early Yeats was much interested in highly lyrical, romantic poetry, often drawing on Irish mythology. The later poems, say from about 1910, are often more colloquial, more down-to-earth, more hardheaded. He was awarded the Nobel Prize in Literature in 1923.

For another poem by Yeats, on old age, see page 838.

For Anne Gregory*   [1930]

"Never shall a young man,
Thrown into despair
By those great honey-coloured
Ramparts at your ear
Love you for yourself alone   5
And not your yellow hair."

"But I can get a hair-dye
And set such colour there,
Brown, or black, or carrot,
That young men in despair   10
May love me for myself alone
And not my yellow hair."

"I heard an old religious man
But yesternight declare
That he had found a text to prove   15
That only God, my dear,
Could love you for yourself alone
And not your yellow hair."

---

*Yeats was 65 when he wrote this poem for Anne Gregory, the 19-year-old granddaughter of Lady Augusta Gregory, a woman whom Yeats had admired.

✦ TOPICS FOR CRITICAL THINKING AND WRITING

1. What does it mean to say that one wants to be loved "for oneself alone"?
2. How satisfactory is the answer given to the young woman?
3. Is the poem sexist? Explain.

WILLIAM SHAKESPEARE

William Shakespeare (1564–1616), born in Stratford-upon-Avon in England, is chiefly known as a dramatic poet, but he also wrote nondramatic poetry. In 1609 a volume of 154 of his sonnets was published, apparently without his permission. Probably he chose to keep his sonnets unpublished not because he thought that they were of little value, but because it was more prestigious to be an amateur (unpublished) poet than a professional (published) poet. Although the sonnets were published in 1609, they were probably written in the mid-1590s, when there was a vogue for sonneteering. A contemporary writer in 1598 said that Shakespeare's "sugred Sonnets [circulate] among his private friends."

Sonnet 116

Let me not to the marriage of true minds
Admit impediments; love is not love
Which alters when it alteration finds,
Or bends with the remover to remove.
O, no, it is an ever-fixèd mark°   5
That looks on tempests and is never shaken;
It is the star° to every wand'ring bark,
Whose worth's unknown, although his height be taken.
Love's not Time's fool,° though rosy lips and cheeks
Within his bending sickle's compass° come;   10
Love alters not with his° brief hours and weeks
But bears° it out even to the edge of doom.°
    If this be error and upon me proved,
    I never writ, nor no man ever loved.

---

5 mark guide to mariners.   **7 star** the North Star.   **9 fool** plaything.   **10 compass** range.
11 his Time's.   **12 bears** endures.   **doom** Judgment Day.

KITTY TSUI

Born in Hong Kong in 1953, Kitty Tsui lived there and in England until 1969, when she came to the United States. She is an actor, an artist, and a professional bodybuilder as well as a writer. Her publications include Breathless: Erotica *(1996).*

A Chinese Banquet   [1983]

for the one who was not invited

it was not a very formal affair but
all the women over twelve
wore long gowns and a corsage,
except for me.

it was not a very formal affair, just
the family getting together,
poa poa,° *kuw fu*° without *kuw mow*°
(her excuse this year is a headache).   8

---

7 *poa poa* maternal grandmother.   ***kuw fu*** uncle.   ***kuw mow*** aunt.

aunts and uncles and cousins,
the grandson who is a dentist,
the one who drives a mercedes benz,
sitting down for shark's fin soup.   12

they talk about buying a house and
taking a two week vacation in beijing.
i suck on shrimp and squab,
dreaming of the cloudscape in your eyes.   16

my mother, her voice beaded with sarcasm;
you're twenty six and not getting younger.
it's about time you got a decent job.
she no longer asks when i'm getting married.   20

you're twenty six and not getting younger.
what are you doing with your life?
you've got to make a living.
why don't you study computer programming?   24

she no longer asks when i'm getting married.
one day, wanting desperately to
bridge the boundaries that separate us,
wanting desperately to touch her,   28

tell her: mother, i'm gay,
mother i'm gay and so happy with her.
but she will not listen,
she shakes her head.   32

she sits across from me,
emotions invading her face.
her eyes are wet but
she will not let tears fall.   36

mother, i say,
you love a man.
i love a woman.
it is not what she wants to hear.   40

aunts and uncles and cousins,
very much a family affair.
but you are not invited,
being neither my husband nor my wife.   44

aunts and uncles and cousins
eating longevity noodles
fragrant with ham inquire:
sold that old car of yours yet?   48

i want to tell them: my back is healing,
i dream of dragons and water.
my home is in her arms,
our bedroom ceiling the wide open sky.   52

⌘ TOPIC FOR CRITICAL THINKING AND WRITING

An important element of the poem is the very conventional nature of the speaker's family, with its values and views so at odds with the speaker's. Do you think that the conflict between the speaker and her family might be too obvious, too predictable? If you do, how would you respond to the poet if she said, "But that's the way it really was"?

FRANK O'HARA

Frank O'Hara (1926-1966) was born in Baltimore, and died in a tragic accident—he was run over by a beach vehicle—on Fire Island, New York. O'Hara was not only a prolific writer of verse but also an astute critic of sculpture and painting who worked as an assistant curator at the Museum of Modern Art, in New York, and as an editor of Art News. *O'Hara's first volume of poetry was* A City Winter, and Other Poems *(1952);* Collected Poems *was issued in 1971, but it was not complete. It has been supplemented by two additional volumes,* Early Poems *(1977) and* Poems Retrieved *(1977).*

Homosexuality   [1971]

So we are taking off our masks, are we, and keeping
our mouths shut? as if we'd been pierced by a glance!

The song of an old cow is not more full of judgment
than the vapors which escape one's soul when one is sick;

so I pull the shadows around me like a puff   5
and crinkle my eyes as if at the most exquisite moment

of a very long opera, and then we are off!
without reproach and without hope that our delicate feet

will touch the earth again, let alone "very soon."
It is the law of my own voice I shall investigate.   10

I start like ice, my finger to my ear, my ear
to my heart, that proud cur at the garbage can

in the rain. It's wonderful to admire oneself
with complete candor, tallying up the merits of each

of the latrines. 14th Street is drunken and credulous,   15
53rd tries to tremble but is too at rest. The good

love a park and the inept a railway station,
and there are the divine ones who drag themselves up

and down the lengthening shadow of an Abyssinian head
in the dust, trailing their long elegant heels of hot air   20

crying to confuse the brave "It's a summer day,
and I want to be wanted more than anything else in the world."

※ TOPICS FOR CRITICAL THINKING AND WRITING

1. Describe your response to the word that O'Hara chooses for his title. In what ways does the poem define and explore the meanings of this word and our responses to it?
2. Characterize the point of view and tone of the speaker. Who is or are the "we" named in line 1?
3. In line 1 the speaker declares that "we are taking off our masks," but then immediately seems to confuse or contradict his point when he says "we" are "keeping / our mouths shut." Explain as clearly as you can what the speaker is suggesting in this first stanza.
4. Some of the language in this poem is ugly or unpleasant—for example, the "cur at the garbage can," "the latrines." What is the purpose of such language? What is its place in the structure of the poem as a whole?

EDNA ST. VINCENT MILLAY

Edna St. Vincent Millay (1892-1950) was born in Rockland, Maine. Even as a child she wrote poetry, and by the time she graduated from Vassar College (1917) she had achieved some notice as a poet. Millay settled for a while in Greenwich Village, a center of Bohemian activity in New York City, where she wrote, performed in plays, and engaged in feminist causes. In 1923, the year she married, she became the first woman to win the Pulitzer Prize for Poetry. Numerous other awards followed. Though she is best known as a lyric poet—especially as a writer of sonnets—she also wrote memorable political poetry and nature poetry as well as short stories, plays, and a libretto for an opera.

Sonnet xli   [1923]

I, being born a woman and distressed
By all the needs and notions of my kind,
Am urged by your propinquity to find
Your person fair, and feel a certain zest   4
To bear your body's weight upon my breast:
So subtly is the fume of life designed,
To clarify the pulse and cloud the mind,
And leave me once again undone, possessed.   8
Think not for this, however, the poor treason
Of my stout blood against my staggering brain,
I shall remember you with love, or season
My scorn with pity,—let me make it plain: 12
I find this frenzy insufficient reason
For conversation when we meet again.

WYATT PRUNTY

Wyatt Prunty was born in 1947 in Humboldt, Tennessee, and raised in Athens, Georgia. His books include Unarmed and Dangerous: New and Selected Poems (2000). *He is the Carlton Professor of English at the University of the South in Sewanee, Tennessee, where he directs the Sewanee Writers' Conference and edits the Sewanee Writers' Series.*

Learning the Bicycle

[2000]

for Heather

The older children pedal past
Stable as little gyros, spinning hard
To supper, bath, and bed, until at last
We also quit, silent and tired
Beside the darkening yard where trees   5
Now shadow up instead of down.
Their predictable lengths can only tease
Her as, head lowered, she walks her bike alone
Somewhere between her wanting to ride
And her certainty she will always fall.   10

Tomorrow, though I will run behind,
Arms out to catch her, she'll tilt then balance wide
Of my reach, till distance makes her small,
Smaller, beyond the place I stop and know
That to teach her I had to follow   15
And when she learned I had to let her go.

▓ TOPICS FOR CRITICAL THINKING AND WRITING

1. Wyatt Prunty has said, "Form elevates utterance." What do you think he means? Does "Learning the Bicycle" show this principle in action? Please explain.
2. Please reread the poem as though it consisted only of the first stanza. How would you interpret it?
3. What is the function of the second stanza?
4. How does Prunty keep his poem from becoming cute and sentimental? Please be specific.
5. What does this poem teach us about youth and age, innocence and experience?
6. Do you know how to ride a bicycle? When did you first learn? Do you recall this experience as an especially important one in your life? What other experiences are similar to it?

ANONYMOUS

The following lines have been attributed to various writers, including the American philosopher William James (1842-1910), but to the best of our knowledge the author is unknown.

Higamus, Hogamus

Higamus, Hogamus.
Woman's monogamous;
Hogamus higamus.
Man is polygamous.

 TOPICS FOR CRITICAL THINKING AND WRITING

1. If you find these lines engaging, how do you account for their appeal? Does it make any difference—even a tiny difference—if the pairs are reversed: that is, if the first two lines are about men, and the second two about women?
2. The underlying idea largely coincides with the saying, "Men are from Mars, women are from Venus." But consider the four lines of verse: Do you agree that in the form we have just given them, they are more effective than "Men are from Mars, women are from Venus"? And how about "Women are from Venus, men are from Mars"? Admittedly the differences are small, but do you agree that one form is decidedly more effective than the others? If you do agree, how do you explain the greater effectiveness?

WORK, PLAY, GETTING ON

JOHN UPDIKE

John Updike (b. 1932) is best known as a writer of fiction—short stories and novels—but throughout his professional career he has also written essays and poems. (For a more complete biography, see page 101.)

Ex-Basketball Player   [1958]

Pearl Avenue runs past the high-school lot,
Bends with the trolley tracks, and stops, cut off
Before it has a chance to go two blocks,
At Colonel McComsky Plaza. Berth's Garage
Is on the corner facing west, and there,
Most days, you'll find Flick Webb, who helps Berth out.   6

Flick stands tall among the idiot pumps—
Five on a side, the old bubble-head style,
Their rubber elbows hanging loose and low.
One's nostrils are two S's, and his eyes
An E and O. And one is squat, without
A head at all—more of a football type.   12

Once Flick played for the high-school team, the Wizards.
He was good: in fact, the best. In '46
He bucketed three hundred ninety points,
A county record still. The ball loved Flick.
I saw him rack up thirty-eight or forty
In one home game. His hands were like wild birds.   18

He never learned a trade, he just sells gas,
Checks oil, and changes flats. Once in a while,
As a gag, he dribbles an inner tube,
But most of us remember anyway.
His hands are fine and nervous on the lug wrench.
It makes no difference to the lug wrench, though.   24

Off work, he hangs around Mae's Luncheonette.
Grease-gray and kind of coiled, he plays pinball,
Smokes those thin cigars, nurses lemon phosphates.
Flick seldom says a word to Mae, just nods
Beyond her face toward bright applauding tiers
Of Necco Wafers, Nibs, and Juju Beads.   30

RITA DOVE

Rita Dove was born in 1952 in Akron, Ohio. After graduating summa cum laude from Miami University (Ohio) she earned an M.F.A. at the Iowa Writers' Workshop. She has been awarded fellowships from the Guggenheim Foundation and the National Endowment for the Arts, and she now teaches at the University of Virginia. In 1993 she was appointed poet laureate for 1993–1994. Dove is currently writing a book about the experiences of an African-American volunteer regiment in France during World War I.

Daystar

[1986]

She wanted a little room for thinking:
but she saw diapers steaming on the line,
a doll slumped behind the door.
So she lugged a chair behind the garage
to sit out the children's naps.   5

Sometimes there were things to watch—
the pinched armor of a vanished cricket,
a floating maple leaf. Other days
she stared until she was assured
when she closed her eyes   10
she'd see only her own vivid blood.

She had an hour, at best, before Liza appeared
pouting from the top of the stairs.
And just *what* was mother doing
out back with the field mice? Why,   15

building a palace. Later
that night when Thomas rolled over and

lurched into her, she would open her eyes
and think of the place that was hers
for an hour—where   20
she was nothing,
pure nothing, in the middle of the day.

 TOPICS FOR CRITICAL THINKING AND WRITING

1. How would you characterize the woman who is the subject of the
   poem?
2. What do you make of the title?

GARY SNYDER

*Gary Snyder, born in 1930, grew up on a farm north of Seattle and then in
Portland, Oregon. He then went to Reed College, working during the summers
with the U.S. Forest Service and in logging camps. After studying linguistics
and American Indian culture at the University of Indiana, he moved to San
Francisco, where he studied Japanese and became part of the "Beat" movement. (He is the hero of Jack Kerouac's novel,* The Dharma Bums.*) In 1956 he
went to Japan, where he lived for ten years. He then returned and settled with
his family in the foothills of the northern Sierra Nevada.*

Hay for the Horses   [1959]

He had driven half the night
From far down San Joaquin
Through Mariposa, up the
Dangerous mountain roads,
And pulled in at eight a.m.   5
With his big truckload of hay
            behind the barn.
With winch and ropes and hooks
We stacked the bales up clean
To splintery redwood rafters   10
High in the dark, flecks of alfalfa
Whirling through shingle-cracks of light,
Itch of haydust in the
            sweaty shirt and shoes.
At lunchtime under Black oak   15
Out in the hot corral,
—The old mare nosing lunchpails,
Grasshoppers crackling in the weeds—
"I'm sixty-eight" he said,
"I first bucked hay when I was seventeen.   20
I thought, that day I started,
I sure would hate to do this all my life.
And dammit, that's just what
I've gone and done."

※ TOPICS FOR CRITICAL THINKING AND WRITING

1. The speaker does not explicitly offer his opinion of the man who "had driven half the night" but do the first two sentences (lines 1-14) communicate at least a hint of an attitude?
2. The old man who speaks lines 19-24 sums up his life. He seems to regard it as wasted, but as we hear his words do we hear bitterness? Self-pity? What is our attitude toward him, and how does it compare with that of the speaker of the poem?

JAMES WRIGHT

James Wright (1927-1980) was born in Martins Ferry, Ohio, which provided him with the locale for many of his poems. He is often thought of as a poet of the Midwest, but (as in the example that we give) his poems move beyond the scenery. Wright was educated at Kenyon College in Ohio and at the University of Washington. He wrote several books of poetry and published many translations of European and Latin-American poetry.

Lying in a Hammock at William Duffy's Farm in Pine Island, Minnesota

[1963]

Over my head, I see the bronze butterfly,
Asleep on the black trunk,
Blowing like a leaf in green shadow.
Down the ravine behind the empty house,
The cowbells follow one another   5
Into the distances of the afternoon.
To my right,
In a field of sunlight between two pines,
The droppings of last year's horses
Blaze up into golden stones.   10
I lean back, as the evening darkens and comes on.
A chicken hawk floats over, looking for home.
I have wasted my life.

※ TOPICS FOR CRITICAL THINKING AND WRITING

1. How important is it that the poet is "lying in a hammock"? That he is at some place other than his own home?
2. Do you take the last line as a severe self-criticism, or as a joking remark, or as something in between, or what?
3. Imagine yourself lying in a hammock—perhaps you can recall an actual moment in a hammock—or lying in bed, your eye taking in

the surroundings. Write a description ending with some sort of judgment or concluding comment, as Wright does. You may want to parody Wright's poem, but you need not. (Keep in mind the fact that the best parodies are written by people who regard the original with affection.)

MARGE PIERCY

Marge Piercy, born in Detroit in 1936, was the first member of her family to attend college. After earning a bachelor's degree from the University of Michigan in 1957 and a master's degree from Northwestern University in 1958, she moved to Chicago. There she worked at odd jobs while writing novels (unpublished) and engaging in action on behalf of women and blacks and against the war in Vietnam. In 1970—the year she moved to Wellfleet, Massachusetts, where she still lives—she published her first book, a novel. Since then she has published other novels, as well as short stories, poems, and essays.

To be of use   [1974]

The people I love the best
jump into work head first
without dallying in the shallows
and swim off with sure strokes almost out of sight.
They seem to become natives of that element,   5
the black sleek heads of seals
bouncing like half-submerged balls.

I love people who harness themselves, an ox to a heavy cart,
who pull like water buffalo, with massive patience,
who strain in the mud and the muck to move things forward,   10
who do what has to be done, again and again.

I want to be with people who submerge
in the task, who go into the fields to harvest
and work in a row and pass the bags along,
who are not parlor generals and field deserters   15
but move in a common rhythm
when the food must come in or the fire be put out.

The work of the world is common as mud.
Botched, it smears the hands, crumbles to dust.
But the thing worth doing well done   20
has a shape that satisfies, clean and evident.
Greek amphoras for wine or oil,
Hopi vases that held corn, are put in museums
but you know they were made to be used.
The pitcher cries for water to carry   25
and a person for work that is real.

LAST YEARS

GWENDOLYN BROOKS

Gwendolyn Brooks (1917-2000) was born in Topeka, Kansas, but was raised in Chicago's South Side, where she spent most of her life. In 1950, when she won the Pulitzer Prize for Poetry, she became the first African-American writer to win a Pulitzer Prize.

The Bean Eaters

[1960]

They eat beans mostly, this old yellow pair.
Dinner is a casual affair.
Plain chipware on a plain and creaking wood,
Tin flatware.   4

Two who are Mostly Good.
Two who have lived their day,
But keep on putting on their clothes
And putting things away.   8

And remembering . . .
Remembering, with twinklings and twinges,
As they lean over the beans in their rented back room that is full of
    beads and receipts and dolls and clothes, tobacco crumbs, vases and
    fringes.

ROBERT BURNS

Robert Burns (1759-1796), born into a poor family in Scotland, developed heart trouble as a child and died when he was only thirty-seven. His formal schooling was sketchy, but he was an avid reader, especially of English and of Scots poetry. In 1786 Burns published his first book, Poems, Chiefly in the Scottish Dialect, *and found himself an overnight celebrity. Although most of his best poetry—for instance, "John Anderson" and "Auld Lang Syne" (long ago times)—is written in Scots, a northern dialect of English spoken by Scottish peasants, Burns was perfectly capable of writing standard English, such as the song "Flow Gently, Sweet Afton."*

John Anderson My Jo

John Anderson my jo,° John,
    When we were first acquent,
Your locks were like the raven,
    Your bonnie brow was brent;°   4
But now your brow is beld, John,

---

1 jo sweetheart.   **4 brent** smooth.

Your locks are like the snaw,
But blessings on your frosty pow,°
   John Anderson my jo!   8

John Anderson my jo, John,
   We clamb the hill thegither,
And monie a cantie° day, John
   We've had wi' ane anither: 12
Now we maun° totter down, John,
   And hand in hand we'll go,
And sleep thegither at the foot,
   John Anderson my jo!   16

---

7 pow head.   **11 cantie** happy.   **13 maun** must.

WILLIAM BUTLER YEATS

For a biographical note on Yeats, see p. 838.

   In the seventh century BCE the ancient Greeks founded the city of Byzantium in Thrace, where Istanbul, Turkey, now stands. (Constantine, the first Christian ruler of the Roman empire, built a new city there in CE 330. Named Constantinople, the city served as the capital of the Roman empire until 1453, when the Turks captured it. In 1930 the name was officially changed to Istanbul.) The capital of the Roman Empire and the "holy city" of the Greek Orthodox Church, Byzantium had two golden ages. The first, in its early centuries, continued the traditions of the antique Greco-Roman world. The second, which is what Yeats had in mind, extended from the mid-ninth to the mid-thirteenth century and was a distinctive blend of classical, Christian, Slavic, and even Islamic culture. This period is noted for mysticism, for the preservation of ancient learning, and for exquisitely refined symbolic art. In short, Byzantium (as Yeats saw it) was wise and passionless. In A Vision, his prose treatment of his complex mystical system, Yeats says:

   I think that in early Byzantium, maybe never before or since in recorded history, religious, aesthetic and practical life were one, that architect and artificers—though not, it may be, poets, for language has been the instrument of controversy and must have grown abstract—spoke to the multitude and the few alike. The painter, the mosaic worker, the worker in gold and silver, the illuminator of sacred books, were almost impersonal, almost perhaps without the consciousness of individual design, absorbed in their subject matter and that the vision of the whole people. They could copy out of old Gospel books those pictures that seemed as sacred as the text, and yet weave all into a vast design, the work of many that seemed the work of one, that made building, picture, pattern, metal-work of rail and lamp, seem but a single image.

Sailing to Byzantium

[1926]

I

That is no country for old men. The young
In one another's arms, birds in the trees
—Those dying generations—at their song,
The salmon-falls, the mackerel-crowded seas,
Fish, flesh, or fowl, commend all summer long   5
Whatever is begotten, born, and dies.
Caught in that sensual music all neglect
Monuments of unaging intellect.

II

An aged man is but a paltry thing,
A tattered coat upon a stick, unless   10
Soul clap its hands and sing, and louder sing
For every tatter in its mortal dress.
Nor is there singing school but studying
Monuments of its own magnificence;
And therefore I have sailed the seas and come   15
To the holy city of Byzantium.

III

O sages standing in God's holy fire
As in the gold mosaic of a wall,
Come from the holy fire, perne° in a gyre,
And be the singing-masters of my soul.   20
Consume my heart away; sick with desire
And fastened to a dying animal
It knows not what it is; and gather me
Into the artifice of eternity.

IV

Once out of nature I shall never take   25
My bodily form from any natural thing,
But such a form as Grecian goldsmiths make
Of hammered gold and gold enameling
To keep a drowsy Emperor awake;
Or set upon a golden bough to sing   30
To lords and ladies of Byzantium
Of what is past, or passing, or to come.

---

19 perne whirl down.

▓ TOPICS FOR CRITICAL THINKING AND WRITING

1. What is "that . . . country," mentioned in the first line?
2. By the end of the first stanza, the speaker seems to be dismissing the natural world. Do you agree that even in this stanza, however, he sounds attracted to it?
3. The poem is filled with oppositions, for instance "old men" versus "the young" (both in line 1), and "birds in the trees" (line 2) versus the mechanical bird in the final stanza. List as many opposites as you see in the poem, and then explain what Yeats is getting at.
4. The first stanza speaks of "monuments of unaging intellect." What might be some examples of these?
5. After reading and rereading this poem, do you think you will—even if only briefly—*act* differently, redirect any of your choices?
6. Have you ever visited any place—perhaps the place where you or your parents or grandparents were born, or perhaps a house of worship, or perhaps a college campus—that you have come to see symbolically, standing for a way of life or for some aspect of life? If so, describe the place and the significance that you give it.

GOOD NIGHTS

A. E. HOUSMAN

A. E. Housman (1859–1936) was one of the most distinguished classical scholars of his time. Though he left Oxford without a degree (having failed his examinations), through hard work, discipline, and rigorous study he earned an appointment in 1892 as professor of Latin at University College, London, and in 1911 as professor of Latin at Cambridge and fellow of Trinity College. Only two volumes of Housman's poems appeared during his lifetime: A Shropshire Lad *(1896) and* Last Poems *(1922).*

To an Athlete Dying Young   [1896]

The time you won your town the race
We chaired you through the market-place;
Man and boy stood cheering by,
And home we brought you shoulder-high.   4

Today, the road all runners come,
Shoulder-high we bring you home,
And set you at your threshold down,
Townsman of a stiller town.   8

Smart lad, to slip betimes away
From fields where glory does not stay
And early though the laurel grows
It withers quicker than the rose.   12

Eyes the shady night has shut
Cannot see the record cut,
And silence sounds no worse than cheers
After earth has stopped the ears: 16

Now you will not swell the rout
Of lads that wore their honors out,
Runners whom renown outran
And the name died before the man.   20

So set, before its echoes fade,
The fleet foot on the sill of shade,
And hold to the low lintel up
The still-defended challenge-cup.   24

And round that early laurelled head
Will flock to gaze the strengthless dead
And find unwithered on its curls
The garland briefer than a girl's.   30

W. H. AUDEN

*Wystan Hugh Auden (1907–1973) was born in York, England, and educated
at Oxford. In the 1930s his left-wing poetry earned him wide acclaim as the
leading poet of his generation. He went to Spain during the Spanish Civil
War, intending to serve as an ambulance driver for the Republicans in their
struggle against fascism, but he was so distressed by the violence of the Republicans that he almost immediately returned to England. In 1939 he came
to America, and in 1946 he became a citizen of the United States, though he
returned to England for his last years. Much of his poetry is characterized by
a combination of colloquial diction and technical dexterity.*

The Unknown Citizen   [1940]

*(To JS/07/M378
This Marble Monument
Is Erected by the State)*

He was found by the Bureau of Statistics to be
One against whom there was no official complaint,
And all the reports on his conduct agree
That, in the modern sense of an old-fashioned word, he was a saint,
For in everything he did he served the Greater Community.   5
Except for the War till the day he retired
He worked in a factory and never got fired,
But satisfied his employers, Fudge Motors Inc.
Yet he wasn't a scab or odd in his views,
For his Union reports that he paid his dues,   10
(Our report on his Union shows it was sound)

And our Social Psychology workers found
That he was popular with his mates and liked a drink.
The Press are convinced that he bought a paper every day
And that his reactions to advertisements were normal in every way.   15
Policies taken out in his name prove that he was fully insured,
And his Health-card shows he was once in hospital but left it cured.
Both Producers Research and High-Grade Living declare
He was fully sensible to the advantages of the Installment Plan
And had everything necessary to the Modern Man,   20
A phonograph, radio, a car and a frigidaire.
Our researchers into Public Opinion are content
That he held the proper opinions for the time of year;
When there was peace, he was for peace; when there was war,
    he went.
He was married and added five children to the population,   25
Which our Eugenist says was the right number for a parent of his
    generation,
And our teachers report that he never interfered with their education.
Was he free? Was he happy? The question is absurd:
Had anything been wrong, we should certainly have heard.

ANONYMOUS

On page 707, in our chapter on lyric poetry, we talk briefly about African-American spirituals. These songs were first printed shortly after the Civil War. We reprint here a song from a fairly early collection, J. B. T. March's The Story of the Jubilee Singers *(1881).*

"Swing Low, Sweet Chariot" derives its basic images from the geography of ancient Israel (the Jordan River flows north from the Sea of Galilee to the Dead Sea) and from a book in the Hebrew Bible (2 Kings 2.11 reports that Elijah and his friend Elisha were walking by the Jordan, when "there appeared a chariot of fire, and horses of fire, and parted them both asunder, and Elijah went up by a whirlwind into heaven"). There may also be some influence of the New Testament, Luke 16.22, which reports that a rich man named Dives and a poor man were "carried by the angels into Abraham's bosom." Further, the line "I'm sometimes up and sometimes down," from a secular song, "Nobody Knows the Trouble I've Seen," often found its way into "Swing Low," as in this version, where the fourth verse goes:

> *I'm sometimes up and sometimes down.*
> *But still my soul feels heavenly bound.*

Swing Low, Sweet Chariot

No. 2.   Swing low, sweet Chariot.

Swing low, sweet char-i-ot, Com-ing for to car-ry me home,

FINE.

Swing low, sweet char-i-ot, Com-ing for to car-ry me home.

1. I looked o - ver Jor-dan, and what did I see,
2. If you get there be - fore I do,
3. The bright-est day that ev - er I saw,
4. I'm some-times up and some-times down,

Com-ing for to car - ry me home? A band of an - gels
Com-ing for to car - ry me home, Tell all my friends I'm
Com-ing for to car - ry me home, When Je - sus wash'd my
Com-ing for to car - ry me home, But still my soul feels

D. C.

com-ing af - ter me, Com-ing for to car - ry me home.
com - ing too, Com-ing for to car - ry me home.
sins a - way, Com-ing for to car - ry me home.
heaven - ly bound, Com-ing for to car - ry me home.

126

VOICES FROM BELOW

WILLIAM SHAKESPEARE

William Shakespeare (1564–1616) returned to his native Stratford about 1611, after a theatrical career in London. The grave slab beneath which he is buried warns against disturbing his bones. If you have read Hamlet *you*

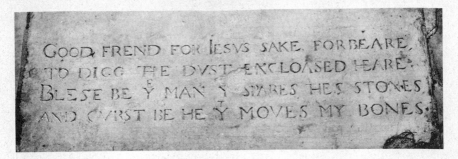

The grave of Shakespeare in Holy Trinity. His wife Anne is buried on his left.

know that in old parish churches, the bones of persons long dead might be disturbed in the course of digging a grave for a new corpse. These four lines, probably by Shakespeare (but there really is no proof as to who wrote them), have effectively kept his bones where they were originally deposited.

Note: What looks like the letter Y is a letter called thorn, *no longer in our alphabet, pronounced "th" (either as in* the *or* thin). *In writing the word* the, *the* e *was customarily placed above the thorn, and to a modern viewer the word looks like* Ye, *but it was never pronounced as "ye." (See the manuscript of "Western Wind," page 699, for another example.)*

Epitaph

GOOD FREND FOR JESUS SAKE FORBEARE,
TO DIGG THE DUST ENCLOASED HEARE:
BLESTE BE Y̔ MAN Y̔ SPARES THES STONES,
AND CURST BE HE Y̔ MOVES MY BONES.

THOMAS HARDY

Thomas Hardy (1840-1928) was born in Dorset, England, the son of a stone-mason. Despite great obstacles he studied the classics and architecture, and in 1862 he moved to London to study and practice as an architect. Ill health forced him to return to Dorset, where he continued to work as an architect and to write. Best known for his novels, Hardy ceased writing fiction after the hostile reception of Jude the Obscure *in 1896 and turned to writing lyric poetry.*

Ah, Are You Digging on My Grave   [1916]

"Ah, are you digging on my grave,
    My loved one?—planting rue?"
—"No: yesterday he went to wed
One of the brightest wealth has bred.

'It cannot hurt her now,' he said,
    'That I should not be true.'"   5

"Then who is digging on my grave?
    My nearest dearest kin?"
—"Ah, no: they sit and think, 'What use!
What good will planting flowers produce?
No tendance of her mound can loose   10
    Her spirit from Death's gin.'"°

"But some one digs upon my grave?
    My enemy?—prodding sly?"
—"Nay: when she heard you had passed the Gate   15
That shuts on all flesh soon or late,
She thought you no more worth her hate,
    And cares not where you lie."

"Then, who is digging on my grave?
    Say—since I have not guessed!"   20
—"O it is I, my mistress dear,
Your little dog, who still lives near,
And much I hope my movements here
    Have not disturbed your rest?"

"Ah, yes! *You* dig upon my grave . . .   25
    Why flashed it not on me
That one true heart was left behind!
What feeling do we ever find
To equal among human kind
    A dog's fidelity!"   30

"Mistress, I dug upon your grave
    To bury a bone, in case
I should be hungry near this spot
When passing on my daily trot.
I am sorry, but I quite forgot   35
    It was your resting-place."

---

12 **gin** snare.

▩ TOPICS FOR CRITICAL THINKING AND WRITING

1. If the dog had returned to the grave out of affection, would the poem
   be sentimental? If so, is Hardy's poem necessarily unsentimental? Or is
   there, despite the cynicism, a kind of sentimentality (overindulgence in
   feeling, excessive appeal to pity) in the poem? Explain.

2. Is the order of the first three stanzas arbitrary, or is there some logic to
   the arrangement? What, if anything, would be lost by the omission of
   the third stanza?

3. How does this poem resemble a popular ballad? (See pages 676-677.)
   How does it not?

EDGAR LEE MASTERS

Edgar Lee Masters (1869–1950) achieved international fame with The
Spoon River Anthology *(1915), a collection of poems spoken by the deceased
inhabitants of a mythical village called Spoon River. We present here a group
of three related poems.*

Minerva Jones   [1915]

I am Minerva, the village poetess,
Hooted at, jeered at by the Yahoos of the street
For my heavy body, cock-eye, and rolling walk,
And all the more when "Butch" Weldy
Captured me after a brutal hunt.   5
He left me to my fate with Doctor Meyers;
And I sank into death, growing numb from the feet up,
Like one stepping deeper and deeper into a stream of ice.
Will someone go to the village newspaper
And gather into a book the verses I wrote?—   10
I thirsted so for love!
I hungered so for life!

Doctor Meyers   [1915]

No other man, unless it was Doc Hill,
Did more for people in this town than I.
And all the weak, the halt, the improvident
And those who could not pay flocked to me.
I was good-hearted, easy Doctor Meyers.   5
I was healthy, happy, in comfortable fortune,
Blest with a congenial mate, my children raised,
All wedded, doing well in the world.
And then one night, Minerva, the poetess,
Came to me in her trouble, crying.   10
I tried to help her out—she died—
They indicted me, the newspapers disgraced me,
My wife perished of a broken heart,
And pneumonia finished me.

Mrs. Meyers   [1915]

He protested all his life long
That newspapers lied about him villainously;
That he was not at fault for Minerva's fall,
But only tried to help her.
Poor soul so sunk in sin he could not see   5
That even trying to help her, as he called it,
He had broken the law human and divine.
Passers-by, an ancient admonition to you:
If your ways would be ways of pleasantness,
And all your pathways peace,   10
Love God and keep his commandments.

24

American Voices: Poems
for a Diverse Nation

PAULA GUNN ALLEN

Part Sioux-Laguna and part Lebanese-Jewish, Paula Gunn Allen was born in 1939 in Cubero, New Mexico, into a family that used five languages. Allen, who holds a Ph.D. from the University of New Mexico, teaches Native American Studies at San Francisco State University. She has written several books of poems, a novel, a collection of traditional tales, and a collection of essays, The Sacred Hoop: Recovering the Feminine in American Indian Traditions *(1986).*

Captain John Smith (1580–1631), an English colonist in Virginia, was captured in 1608 by Chesapeake Indians, who brought him to their chief or king, Powhatan. Years later, in the account he gave in The Generall Historie of Virginia, New-England, and the Summer Isles *(1624), he says he was condemned to death but saved by Powhatan's daughter, Pocahontas ("Playful One"). The fact that Smith did not report this episode in his earlier account of the Virginia colony,* A True Relation . . . of Virginia *(1608), has caused many historians to doubt it. Whatever the truth of Smith's report that Pocahontas (c. 1595–1617) rescued him, it is a fact that in 1613 Pocahontas was captured, taken to Jamestown, and held as hostage for English prisoners held by Powhatan. In Jamestown she was converted to Christianity, baptized, and in 1614, with the permission of her father and of the governor of the colony she was married to John Rolfe, a colonist. In 1616 Pocahontas and several other Indians went to England, where she was presented as a princess to the king and queen, and where, dressed in the English fashion, her portrait was engraved. In 1617 she started to return from England, but died before she could embark. She is buried in the parish churchyard at Gravesend, on the Thames River.*

Victor Nehlig, *Pocahontas and John Smith*, 1870. (Courtesy Museum of Art, Brigham Young University, Utah.)

Pocahontas to Her English Husband, John Rolfe   [1988]

Had I not cradled you in my arms,
oh beloved perfidious one,
you would have died.
And how many times did I pluck you
from certain death in the wilderness—   5
my world through which you stumbled
as though blind?
Had I not set you tasks
your masters far across the sea
would have abandoned you—   10
did abandon you, as many times they
left you to reap the harvest of their lies;
still you survived oh my fair husband
and brought them gold
wrung from a harvest I taught you   15
to plant: Tobacco. It
is not without irony that by this crop

your descendants die, for other powers
than those you know take part in this.
And indeed I did rescue you   20
not once but a thousand thousand times
and in my arms you slept, a foolish child,
and beside me you played,
chattering nonsense about a God
you had not wit to name;   25
and wondered you at my silence—
simple foolish wanton maid you saw,
dusky daughter of heathen sires
who knew not the ways of grace—
no doubt, no doubt.   30
I spoke little, you said.
And you listened less.
But played with your gaudy dreams
and sent ponderous missives to the throne
striving thereby to curry favor   35
with your king. I saw you well. I
understood the ploy and still protected you,
going so far as to die in your keeping—
a wasting, putrifying death, and you,
deceiver, my husband, father of my son,   40
survived, your spirit bearing crop
slowly from my teaching, taking
certain life from the wasting of my bones.

ROBERT FROST

For a biographical note on Robert Frost (1874-1963), see page 931.

The Vanishing Red   [1916]

He is said to have been the last Red Man
In Acton.° And the Miller is said to have laughed—
If you like to call such a sound a laugh.
But he gave no one else a laugher's license.
For he turned suddenly grave as if to say,   5
"Whose business,—if I take it on myself,
Whose business—but why talk round the barn?—
When it's just that I hold with getting a thing done with."
You can't get back and see it as he saw it.
It's too long a story to go into now.   10
You'd have to have been there and lived it.
Then you wouldn't have looked on it as just a matter
Of who began it between the two races.

---

2 **Acton** a town in Massachusetts, not far from where Frost spent part of his childhood.

Some guttural exclamation of surprise
The Red Man gave in poking about the mill   15
Over the great big thumping shuffling mill-stone
Disgusted the Miller physically as coming
From one who had no right to be heard from.
"Come, John,' he said, 'you want to see the wheel pit?"°

He took him down below a cramping rafter,   20
And showed him, through a manhole in the floor,
The water in desperate straits like frantic fish,
Salmon and sturgeon, lashing with their tails.
Then he shut down the trap door with a ring in it

That jangled even above the general noise,   25
And came up stairs alone—and gave that laugh,
And said something to a man with a meal-sack
That the man with the meal-sack didn't catch—then.
Oh, yes, he showed John the wheel pit all right.

---

19 wheel pit the pit containing the wheel that, agitated by the water, drives the mill.

AURORA LEVINS MORALES

Aurora Levins Morales, born in Puerto Rico in 1954, came to the United States with her family in 1967. She has lived in Chicago and New Hampshire and now lives in the San Francisco Bay area. Levins Morales has published stories, essays, prose poems, and poems.

Child of the Americas   [1986]

I am a child of the Americas,
a light-skinned mestiza of the Caribbean,
a child of many diaspora,° born into this continent at a crossroads.

I am a U.S. Puerto Rican Jew,
a product of the ghettos of New York I have never known.   5
An immigrant and the daughter and granddaughter of immigrants.
I speak English with passion: it's the tongue of my consciousness,
a flashing knife blade of crystal, my tool, my craft.

I am Caribeña,° island grown. Spanish is in my flesh,
ripples from my tongue, lodges in my hips: 10
the language of garlic and mangoes,
the singing in my poetry, the flying gestures of my hands.

I am of Latinoamerica, rooted in the history of my continent:
I speak from that body.

---

3 diaspora literally, "scattering"; the term is used especially to refer to the dispersion of the Jews outside of Israel from the sixth century BCE, when they were exiled to Babylonia, to the present time.   **9 Caribeña** Caribbean woman.

I am not african. Africa is in me, but I cannot return.   15
I am not taína.° Taíno is in me, but there is no way back.
I am not european. Europe lives in me, but I have no home there.

I am new. History made me. My first language was spanglish.°
I was born at the crossroads
and I am whole.   20

---

16 taína the Taínos were the Indian tribe native to Puerto Rico.   **18 spanglish** a mixture of
Spanish and English.

JOSEPH BRUCHAC III

Joseph Bruchac III (the name is pronounced "Brew-shack") was born in Saratoga Springs, New York, in 1942, and educated at Cornell University, Syracuse University, and Union Graduate School. Like many other Americans, he has a multicultural ethnic heritage, and he includes Native Americans as well as Slovaks among his ancestors. Bruchac, who has taught in Ghana and in the United States, has chiefly worked as an editor.

"Much of my writing and my life," Bruchac says, "relates to the problem of being an American. . . . While in college I was active in Civil Rights work and in the anti-war movement. . . . I went to Africa to teach—but more than that to be taught. It showed me many things. How much we have as Americans and take for granted. How much our eyes refuse to see because they are blinded to everything in a man's face except his color."

Ellis Island   [1978]

Beyond the red brick of Ellis Island
where the two Slovak children
who became my grandparents
waited the long days of quarantine,
after leaving the sickness,   5
the old Empires of Europe,
a Circle Line ship slips easily
on its way to the island
of the tall woman, green
as dreams of forests and meadows   10
waiting for those who'd worked
a thousand years
yet never owned their own.

Like millions of others,
I too come to this island,   15
nine decades the answerer
of dreams.

Slavic women arrive at Ellis Island in the winter of 1910.

Yet only one part of my blood loves that memory.
Another voice speaks
of native lands   20
within this nation.
Lands invaded
when the earth became owned.
Lands of those who followed
the changing Moon,   25
knowledge of the seasons
in their veins.

MITSUYE YAMADA

Mitsuye Yamada, the daughter of Japanese immigrants to the United States, was born in Japan in 1923, during her mother's return visit to her native land. Yamada was raised in Seattle; but in 1942 she and her family were incarcerated and then relocated in a camp in Idaho, when Executive Order 9066 gave military authorities the right to remove any and all persons from "military areas." In 1954 she became an American citizen. She has taught in the Asian American Studies Program at the University of California at Irvine, and she is the author of poems and stories.

To the Lady   [1976]

The one in San Francisco who asked:
Why did the Japanese Americans let

the government put them in
those camps without protest?
Come to think of it I   5
    should've run off to Canada
    should've hijacked a plane to Algeria
    should've pulled myself up from my
    bra straps
    and kicked'm in the groin   10
    should've bombed a bank
    should've tried self-immolation
    should've holed myself up in a
    woodframe house
    and let you watch me   15
    burn up on the six o'clock news
    should've run howling down the street
    naked and assaulted you at breakfast
    by AP wirephoto
    should've screamed bloody murder   20
    like Kitty Genovese°

---

21 Kitty Genovese In 1964 Kitty Genovese of Kew Gardens, New York, was stabbed to
death when she left her car and walked toward her home. Thirty-eight persons heard her
screams, but no one came to her assistance.

Dorothea Lange, "Grandfather and Grandchildren Awaiting Evacuation
Bus."

Then
YOU would've
   come to my aid in shining armor
   laid yourself across the railroad track   25
   marched on Washington
   tatooed a Star of David on your arm
   written six million enraged
   letters to Congress.

But we didn't draw the line   30
anywhere
law and order Executive Order 9066°
social order moral order internal order

YOU let'm
I let'm   35
All are punished.

---

32 Executive Order 9066 an authorization, signed in 1941 by President Franklin D.
Roosevelt, allowing military authorities to relocate Japanese and Japanese-Americans who
resided on the Pacific Coast of the United States.

YUSEF KOMUNYAKAA

Yusef Komunyakaa was born in 1947 in Bogalusa, Louisiana. After graduat-
ing from high school he entered the army and served in Vietnam, where he
was awarded the Bronze Star. On his return to the United States he earned a
bachelor's degree at the University of Colorado, and then earned an M.A. at
Colorado State University and an M.F.A. in creative writing at the University
of California, Irvine. The author of several books of poetry, he has been teach-
ing at Indiana University in Bloomington since 1985. "Facing It" is the last
poem in a book of poems about Vietnam, Dien Cai Dau *(1988). The title of the*
book is a slang word for crazy.

Facing It   [1988]

My black face fades,
hiding inside the black granite.
I said I wouldn't,
dammit: No tears.
I'm stone. I'm flesh.   5
My clouded reflection eyes me
like a bird of prey, the profile of night
slanted against morning. I turn
this way—the stone lets me go.
I turn that way—I'm inside   10
the Vietnam Veterans Memorial
again, depending on the light
to make a difference.

I go down the 58,022 names,
half-expecting to find   15
my own in letters like smoke.
I touch the name Andrew Johnson;
I see the booby trap's white flash.
Names shimmer on a woman's blouse
but when she walks away   20
the names stay on the wall.
Brushstrokes flash, a red bird's
wings cutting across my stare.
The sky. A plane in the sky.
A white vet's image floats   25
closer to me, then his pale eyes
look through mine. I'm a window.
He's lost his right arm
inside the stone. In the black mirror
a woman's trying to erase names: 30
No, she's brushing a boy's hair.

Vietnam Veterans Memorial.

CLAUDE McKAY

Claude McKay (1890–1948), born in Jamaica, came to the United States when he was 23. McKay is known chiefly for his militant left-wing writings— novels and essays as well as poems—but he wrote a wide range of lyric poetry, and despite his radicalism he favored (like his friend Countee Cullen) traditional poetic forms such as the sonnet.

America [1921]

Although she feeds me bread of bitterness,
And sinks into my throat her tiger's tooth,
Stealing my breath of life, I will confess
I love this cultured hell that tests my youth!
Her vigor flows like tides into my blood,   5
Giving me strength against her hate.
Her bigness sweeps my being like a flood.
Yet as a rebel fronts a king in state,
I stand within her walls with not a shred
Of terror, malice, not a word of jeer.   10
Darkly I gaze into the days ahead,
And see her might and granite wonders there,
Beneath the touch of Time's unerring hand,
Like priceless treasures sinking in the sand.

DUDLEY RANDALL

Born in Washington, D.C., in 1914, Randall graduated from Wayne State University and the University of Michigan, and worked as a reference librarian and as poet in residence at the University of Detroit. In 1965 he founded the Broadside Press, widely recognized as influential far beyond its size. Broadside Press issues excellent small books and single sheets with poems by African-Americans.

The Melting Pot [1968]

There is a magic melting pot
where any girl or man
can step in Czech or Greek or Scot,
step out American.   4

Johann and *Jan* and *Jean* and *Juan,*
Giovanni and *Ivan*
step in and then step out again
all freshly christened *John.*   8

Sam, watching, said, "Why, I was here
even before they came,"
and stepped in too, but was tossed out
before he passed the brim.   12

And every time Sam tried that pot
they threw him out again.

"Keep out. This is our private pot
We don't want your black stain."   16

At last, thrown out a thousand times,
Sam said, "I don't give a damn.
Shove your old pot. You can like it or not,
but I'll be just what I am."   20

MARTÍN ESPADA

*Martín Espada was born in Brooklyn in 1957. He received a bachelor's degree
from the University of Wisconsin and a law degree from Northeastern University. A poet who publishes regularly, Espada is also Outreach Coordinator and
Supervisor of Lawyers of the Arts at the Artists' Foundation in Boston.*

Bully   [1990]

Boston, Massachusetts, 1987

In the school auditorium,
the Theodore Roosevelt statue
is nostalgic
for the Spanish-American War,
each fist lonely for a saber   5
or the reins of anguish-eyed horses,
or a podium to clatter with speeches
glorying in the malaria of conquest.

But now the Roosevelt school
is pronounced *Hernández*.   10
Puerto Rico has invaded Roosevelt
with its army of Spanish-singing children
in the hallways,
brown children devouring
the stockpiles of the cafeteria,   15
children painting *Taíno* ancestors
that leap naked across murals.

Roosevelt is surrounded
by all the faces
he ever shoved in eugenic spite   20
and cursed as mongrels, skin of one race,
hair and cheekbones of another.

Once Marines tramped
from the newsreel of his imagination;
now children plot to spray graffiti   25
in parrot-brilliant colors across the Victorian mustache
and monocle.

JIMMY SANTIAGO BACA

Jimmy Santiago Baca, of chicano and Apache descent, was born in 1952. When he was 2 his parents divorced, and a grandparent brought him up until he was 5, when he was placed in an orphanage in New Mexico. He ran away when he was 11, lived on the streets, took drugs, and at the age of 20 was convicted of drug possession. In prison he taught himself to read and write, and he began to compose poetry. A fellow inmate urged him to send some poems to Mother Jones *magazine, and the work was accepted. In 1979 Louisiana State University Press published a book of his poems,* Immigrants in Our Own Land. *He has since published several other books.*

So Mexicans Are Taking Jobs from Americans   [1979]

O Yes? Do they come on horses
with rifles, and say,
        Ese gringo,° gimmee your job?
And do you, gringo, take off your ring,
drop your wallet into a blanket   5
spread over the ground, and walk away?

I hear Mexicans are taking your jobs away.
Do they sneak into town at night,
and as you're walking home with a whore,
do they mug you, a knife at your throat,   10
saying, I want your job?

Even on TV, an asthmatic leader
crawls turtle heavy, leaning on an assistant,
and from a nest of wrinkles on his face,
a tongue paddles through flashing waves   15
of lightbulbs, of cameramen, rasping
"They're taking our jobs away."

Well, I've gone about trying to find them,
asking just where the hell are these fighters.

The rifles I hear sound in the night   20
are white farmers shooting blacks and browns
whose ribs I see jutting out
and starving children,
I see the poor marching for a little work,
I see small white farmers selling out   25
to clean-suited farmers living in New York,
who've never been on a farm,
don't know the look of a hoof or the smell
of a woman's body bending all day long in fields.

I see this, and I hear only a few people   30
got all the money in this world, the rest
count their pennies to buy bread and butter.

---

3 **Ese gringo** Hey, whitey.

Below that cool green sea of money,
millions and millions of people fight to live,
search for pearls in the darkest depths   35
of their dreams, hold their breath for years
trying to cross poverty to just having something.

The children are dead already. We are killing them,
that is what America should be saying;
on TV, in the streets, in offices, should be saying,   40
    "We aren't giving the children a chance to live."
Mexicans are taking our jobs, they say instead.
What they really say is, let them die,
and the children too.

SHERMAN ALEXIE

*Sherman Alexie, born in 1966 in Spokane, Washington, holds a B.A. from
Washington State University. Author of novels, stories, and poems, Alexie has
been awarded a grant from the National Endowment for the Arts. Of his life
and his work he says, "I am a Spokane Coeur d'Alene Indian. . . . I live on
the Spokane Indian Reservation. Everything I do now, writing and otherwise,
has its origin in that."*

On the Amtrak from Boston to New York City   [1993]

The white woman across the aisle from me says, "Look,
look at all the history, that house
on the hill there is over two hundred years old,"
as she points out the window past me   4

into what she has been taught. I have learned
little more about American history during my few days
back East than what I expected and far less
of what we should all know of the tribal stories   8

whose architecture is 15,000 years older
than the corners of the house that sits
museumed on the hill. "Walden Pond,"°
the woman on the train asks, "Did you see Walden Pond?"   12

and I don't have a cruel enough heart to break
her own by telling her there are five Walden Ponds
on my little reservation out West
and at least a hundred more surrounding Spokane,   16

the city I pretend to call my home. "Listen,"
I could have told her. "I don't give a shit
about Walden. I know the Indians were living stories
around that pond before Walden's grandparents were born   20

---

11 Walden Pond site in Massachusetts where Henry David Thoreau (1817–1862) lived from
4 July 1845 to 6 September 1847, and about which he wrote in his most famous book, *Walden*
(1854).

and before his grandparents' grandparents were born.
I'm tired of hearing about Don-fucking-Henley° saving it, too,
because that's redundant. If Don Henley's brothers and sisters
and mothers and fathers hadn't come here in the first place   24

then nothing would need to be saved."
But I didn't say a word to the woman about Walden
Pond because she smiled so much and seemed delighted
that I thought to bring her an orange juice   28

back from the food car. I respect elders
of every color. All I really did was eat
my tasteless sandwich, drink my Diet Pepsi
and nod my head whenever the woman pointed out   32

another little piece of her country's history
while I, as all Indians have done
since this war began, made plans
for what I would do and say the next time   36

somebody from the enemy thought I was one of their own.

---

22 **Don Henley** rock singer who was active in preserving Walden.

NILA NORTHSUN

*Nila northSun was born in 1951 in Schurz, Nevada, of Shoshone-Chippewa
stock. She studied at the California State University campuses at Hayward
and Humboldt and the University of Montana at Missoula, beginning as a
psychology major but switching to art history, specializing in Native American art. She is the author of three books of poetry and is director of an emergency youth shelter in Fallon, Nevada.*

Moving Camp Too Far   [1977]

i can't speak of
    many moons
    moving camp on travois°
i can't tell of
    the last great battle   5
    counting coup° or
    taking scalp
i don't know what it
    was to hunt buffalo
    or do the ghost dance   10

but

---

3 **travois** a frame slung between trailing poles that are pulled by a horse. Plains Indians used the
device to transport their goods.   6 **counting coup** recounting one's exploits in battle.

Edward S. Curtis, *Blackfoot travois*. (Courtesy Museum of Indian Arts & Culture, Laboratory of Anthropology, Santa Fe.)

```
i can see an eagle
      almost extinct
      on slurpee plastic cups
i can travel to powwows                                    15
      in campers & winnebagos
i can eat buffalo meat
      at the tourist burger stand
i can dance to indian music
      rock-n-roll hey-a-hey-o                              20
i can
      & unfortunately
      i do
```

LAUREEN MAR

Laureen Mar, a Chinese-American born in Seattle in 1953, studied creative writing at Columbia University. She has published poems in several national magazines.

My Mother, Who Came from China, Where She Never Saw Snow   [1977]

In the huge, rectangular room, the ceiling
a machinery of pipes and fluorescent lights,
ten rows of women hunch over machines,
their knees pressing against pedals
and hands pushing the shiny fabric thick as tongues   5
through metal and thread.

My mother bends her head to one of these machines.
Her hair is coarse and wiry, black as burnt scrub.
She wears glasses to shield her intense eyes.
A cone of orange thread spins. Around her,   10
talk flutters harshly in Toisan wah.°
Chemical stings. She pushes cloth
through a pounding needle, under, around, and out,
breaks thread with a snap against fingerbone, tooth.
Sleeve after sleeve, sleeve.   15
It is easy. The same piece.
For eight or nine hours, sixteen bundles maybe,
250 sleeves to ski coats, all the same.
It is easy, only once she's run the needle
through her hand. She earns money   20
by each piece, on a good day,
thirty dollars. Twenty-four years.
It is frightening how fast she works.
She and the women who were taught sewing
terms in English as Second Language.   25
Dull thunder passes through their fingers.

---

11 Toisan wah a Chinese dialect.

25

Variations on Themes: Poems and Paintings

WRITING ABOUT POEMS AND PAINTINGS

Are there, one may ask, significant correspondences among the arts? If we talk about *rhythm* in a painting, are we talking about a quality similar to *rhythm* in a poem? Are the painter's colors comparable to the poet's images? Does it make sense to say, as Goethe (1749–1832) said, that architecture is frozen music? Or to call architecture "music in space"? Many artists of one sort have felt that their abilities *ought* to enable them to move into a "sister art," and they have tried their hand at something outside their specialty, usually with no great success. (William Blake, represented in this book by several poems and pictures, is often said to be the only figure in English arts who is significant both as a poet and as a painter.) For instance, the painter Edgar Degas (1834–1917) tried to write sonnets, but could not satisfy even himself. When he complained to his friend, the poet Stéphane Mallarmé, that he couldn't write poems even though he had plenty of ideas, Mallarmé replied, "You don't write poems with ideas; you write them with words."

Painters have been moved, for many centuries, to illustrate texts. More than two thousand years ago the painters of Greek vases illustrated the Greek myths, and from the Middle Ages onward artists have illustrated the Bible. Conversely, poets have been moved to write about paintings or sculptures. In this chapter we reprint several poems about paintings by Brueghel, van Gogh, and others.

Despite Mallarmé's witty remark that poems are made not with ideas but with words (and despite Archibald MacLeish's assertion, on page 998, that "A poem should not mean/But be"), of course poems use ideas, and of course they have meanings. When you read the poems that we print along with paintings, you might think about some of the following questions:

- What is your own first response to the painting? In interpreting the painting, consider the subject matter, the composition (for instance, balanced masses, as opposed to an apparent lack of equilibrium), the technique (for instance, vigorous brushstrokes of thick paint, as opposed to thinly applied strokes that leave no trace of the artist's hand), the color, and the title.
- Now that you have read the poem, do you see the painting in a somewhat different way?

- To what extent does the poem illustrate the painting, and to what extent does it depart from the painting and make a very different statement?
- Beyond the subject matter, what (if anything) do the two works have in common?

A SAMPLE STUDENT ESSAY

On page 903 read (preferably aloud) Anne Sexton's "The Starry Night," which was inspired by van Gogh's painting of the same name. Then read the following essay.

Washington 1

Tina Washington
Professor Serno
English 10G
12 November 2005

         Two Ways of Looking at a Starry Night
    About a hundred years ago Vincent van Gogh
looked up into the sky at night and painted what
he saw, or what he felt. We know that he was a
very religious man, but even if we had not heard
this in an art course or read it in a book we
would know it from his painting The Starry
Night, which shows a glorious heaven, with stars
so bright that they all have halos. Furthermore,
almost in the lower center of the picture is a
church, with its steeple rising above the hills
and pointing to the heavens.
    Anne Sexton's poem is about this painting,
and also (we know from the line she quotes above
the poem) about van Gogh's religious vision of
the stars. But her poem is not about the
heavenly comfort that the starry night offered
van Gogh. It is a poem about her wish to die. As
I understand the poem, she wants to die in a
blaze of light, and to become extinct. She says,

Washington 2

in the last line of the poem, that she wants to
disappear with "no cry" (903), but this seems to
me to be very different from anything van Gogh
is saying. His picture is about the glorious
heavens, not about himself. Or if it is about
himself, it is about how wonderful he feels when
he sees God's marvelous creation. Van Gogh is
concerned with praising God as God expresses
himself in nature; Anne Sexton is concerned with
expressing her anguish and with her hope that
she can find extinction. Sexton's world is not
ruled by a benevolent God but is ruled by an
"old unseen serpent." The night is a "rushing
beast," presided over by a "great dragon."

Sexton has responded to the painting in a
highly unique way. She is not trying to put van
Gogh's picture into words that he might approve
of. Rather, she has boldly used the picture as a
point of departure for her own word-picture.

[New page]

Washington 3

Work Cited

Sexton, Anne. "The Starry Night." <u>An Introduction
to Literature</u>. Ed. Sylvan Barnet et al. 14th
ed. New York: Longman, 2006. 825.

▒ TOPICS FOR CRITICAL THINKING AND WRITING

1. Do you agree with this student's analysis, especially her point about Sexton's poem?
2. Has the student cited and examined passages from the poem in a convincing way?
3. A general question: Do you think poets are obliged to be faithful to the paintings that they write about, or do poets enjoy the freedom—a kind of poetic license—to interpret a painting just as they choose, doing with it whatever the purpose of the poem requires?

Vincent van Gogh, *Vincent's Bed in Arles,* oil on canvas, 72 × 90 cm. (Vincent van Gogh Museum, Amsterdam, Vincent van Gogh Foundation.)

JANE FLANDERS

Jane Flanders, born in Waynesboro, Pennsylvania, in 1940, and educated at Bryn Mawr College and Columbia University, is the author of three books of poems. Among her awards are poetry fellowships from the National Endowment for the Arts and the New York Foundation for the Arts.

Van Gogh's Bed   [1985]

is orange,
like Cinderella's coach, like
the sun when he looked it
straight in the eye.   4

is narrow,
he slept alone, tossing
between two pillows, while it carried him
bumpily to the ball.   8

is clumsy,
but friendly. A peasant
built the frame; an old wife beat
the mattress till it rose like meringue.   12

is empty,
morning light pours in
like wine, melody, fragrance,
the memory of happiness.   16

▓ TOPICS FOR CRITICAL THINKING AND WRITING

Jane Flanders has told us that the poem is indebted not only to the painting but also to two comments in letters that van Gogh wrote to his
brother, Theo:

> I can tell you that for my part I will try to keep a straight course,
> and will paint the most simple, the most common things.
>
> (December 1884)

> My eyes are still tired, but then I had a new idea in my head and
> here is the sketch of it. . . . It's just simply my bedroom, only
> here color is to do everything, and giving by its simplification a
> grander style to things, is to be suggestive here of *rest* or of sleep
> in general. In a word, to look at the picture ought to rest the
> brain or rather the imagination.
>
> (September 1888)

1. Does the painting convey "rest" to you? If not, has van Gogh failed to
    paint a picture of interest? What *does* the picture convey to you?
2. In an earlier version, the last stanza of the poem went thus:

    empty,
    morning light pours in
    like wine; the sheets are what they are,
    casting no shadows.

    Which version do you prefer? Why?

Edwin Romanzo Elmer, *Mourning Picture,* 1890, oil on canvas, 28 × 36 in. [71.1 × 91.5 cm.]
(Smith College Museum of Art, Northampton, Massachusetts. Purchased 1953.)

ADRIENNE RICH

Adrienne Rich's most recent books of poetry are The School Among the Ruins:
Poems 2000-2004, *and* Fox: Poems 1998-2000 *(Norton). A selection of her essays,* Arts of the Possible: Essays and Conversations, *was published in 2001. A
new edition of* What is Found There: Notebooks on Poetry and Politics, *appeared in 2003. She is a recipient of the Lannan Foundation Lifetime
Achievement Award, the Lambda Book Award, the Lenore Marshall/Nation
Prize, the Wallace Stevens Award, and the Bollingen Prize in Poetry, among
other honors. She lives in California.*

Mourning Picture   [1965]

*(The picture was painted by Edwin Romanzo Elmer (1850–1923) as a
memorial to his daughter Effie. In the poem, it is the dead girl who
speaks.)*

They have carried the mahogany chair and the cane rocker
out under the lilac bush,
and my father and mother darkly sit there, in black clothes.
Our clapboard house stands fast on its hill,
my doll lies in her wicker pram   5
gazing at western Massachusetts.
This was our world.
I could remake each shaft of grass
feeling its rasp on my fingers,
draw out the map of every lilac leaf   10
or the net of veins on my father's
grief-tranced hand.

Out of my head, half-bursting,
still filling, the dream condenses—
shadows, crystals, ceilings, meadows, globes of dew.   15
Under the dull green of the lilacs, out in the light
carving each spoke of the pram, the turned porch-pillars,
under high early-summer clouds,
I am Effie, visible and invisible,
remembering and remembered.   20

They will move from the house,
give the toys and pets away.
Mute and rigid with loss my mother
will ride the train to Baptist Corner,
the silk-spool will run bare.   25
I tell you, the thread that bound us lies
faint as a web in the dew.
Should I make you, world, again,
could I give back the leaf its skeleton, the air
its early-summer cloud, the house   30
its noonday presence, shadowless,
and leave *this* out? I am Effie, you were my dream.

Kitagawa Utamaro,* *Two Women Dressing Their Hair,* late 18th
century. (Print collection, Miriam and Ira D. Wallach Division of
Art, Prints, and Photographs, The New York Public Library, Astor,
Lenox and Tilden Foundations.)

CATHY SONG

*Cathy Song, born in Honolulu in 1955 of a Chinese-American mother and a
Korean-American father, holds a bachelor's degree from Wellesley College and
a master's degree in creative writing from Boston University. She is the author
of three books of poems, the first of which,* Picture Bride *(1983), was the winner
in the Yale Series of Younger Poets. She has also won the Hawaii Award for Literature and the Shelley Memorial Award from the Poetry Society of America.*

---

*Kitagawa Utamaro (1754–1806) lived in Edo (now called Tokyo). He specialized in designing
pictures of courtesans and actors that were then used to make woodblock prints. Brothels and
the theater were important parts of what was called the Floating World—that is, the world of
transient pleasure.

Beauty and Sadness   [1983]

for Kitagawa Utamaro

He drew hundreds of women
in studies unfolding
like flowers from a fan.
Teahouse waitresses, actresses,
geishas, courtesans and maids.   5
They arranged themselves
before this quick, nimble man
whose invisible presence
one feels in these prints
is as delicate   10
as the skinlike paper
he used to transfer
and retain their fleeting loveliness.

Crouching like cats,
they purred amid the layers of
    kimono   15
swirling around them
as though they were bathing
in a mountain pool with irises
growing in the silken sunlit water.
Or poised like porcelain vases,   20
slender, erect and tall: their heavy
brocaded hair was piled high
with sandalwood combs and blossom
    sprigs
poking out like antennae.
They resembled beautiful iridescent
    insects,   25
creatures from a floating world.

Utamaro absorbed these women of
    Edo
in their moments of melancholy
He captured the wisp of shadows,

the half-draped body   30
emerging from a bath; whatever
skin was exposed
was powdered white as snow.
A private space disclosed.
Portraying another girl   35
catching a glimpse of her own
    vulnerable
face in the mirror, he transposed
the trembling plum lips
like a drop of blood
soaking up the white expanse of
    paper.   40

At times, indifferent to his inconsolable
eye, the women drifted
through the soft gray feathered light,
maintaining stillness, the moments in
    between.
Like the dusty ash-winged moths   45
that cling to the screens in summer
and that the Japanese venerate
as ancestors reincarnated;
Utamaro graced these women with
    immortality
in the thousand sheaves of prints   50
fluttering into the reverent hands of
    keepers:
the dwarfed and bespectacled painter
holding up to a square of sunlight
what he had carried home beneath his
    coat
one afternoon in winter.   55

▓ TOPICS FOR CRITICAL THINKING AND WRITING

1. In the first stanza the women in Utamaro's prints possess a "fleeting
   loveliness." What does "fleeting" suggest here? What are Utamaro's
   characteristics in this stanza?
2. In the second stanza would you say that the women are beautiful, or
   not? And in the third stanza? What do they look like in each stanza?
3. In the last stanza, in the last few lines, we learn that Utamaro was a
   "dwarfed and bespectacled painter." We might have learned this earlier
   or not at all. Why does Song wait until this late in the poem to tell us?

Edouard Manet, *Déjeuner sur l'Herbe,* 1863, oil on canvas, 6'9" × 8'10". (Musée d'Orsay, Paris, France.)

CARL PHILLIPS

Carl Phillips was born in 1959 in Everett, Washington, and educated at Harvard and at Boston University. African-American, gay, a scholar of classical Greek and Latin, and the author of several books of poetry, he has taught creative writing at Harvard, and he now teaches English and African-American Studies at Washington University in St. Louis.

Luncheon on the Grass   [1993]

They're a curious lot, Manet's scandalous
lunch partners. The two men, lost
in cant and full dress, their legs sprawled
subway-style, as mens legs invariably are, seem
remarkably unruffled, all but oblivious to their nude   5
female companion. Her nudity is puzzling and
correct; clothes for her are surely only needed
to shrug a shoulder out of. She herself appears
baldly there-for-the-ride; her eyes, moving out
toward the viewer, are wide with the most banal,   10
detached surprise, as if to say, "where's
the *real* party?"

Now, in a comparable state of outdoor
undress, I'm beginning to have a fair idea
of what's going on in that scene. Watching   15
you, in clothes, remove one boot to work your
finger toward an itch in your athletic sock,
I look for any similarities between art
and our afternoon here on abandoned
property. The bather in the painting's   20
background, presumably there for a certain
balance of composition, is for us an ungainly,
rusted green dumpster, rising from overgrown
weeds that provide a contrast only remotely
pastoral. We are two to Manet's main group   25
of three, but the hum of the odd car or truck
on the highway below us offers a transient third.
Like the nude, I don't seem especially hungry,
partly because it's difficult eating naked when
everyone else is clothed, partly because   30
you didn't remember I hate chicken salad.
The beer you opened for me sits untouched,
going flat in the sun. I stroke the wet bottle
fitfully, to remind myself just how far
we've come or more probably have always been   35
from the shape of romance. My dear,
this is not art; we're not anywhere close
to Arcadia.°

---

38 Arcadia an ancient region in Greece, traditionally associated in art and literature with the
simple, pastoral life, a Golden Age of unfailing romantic love.

▓ TOPICS FOR CRITICAL THINKING AND WRITING

1. The author is openly gay. Does knowledge of his sexual orientation affect the way in which you read the poem? Explain.
2. Do you agree that the speaker and the partner are "not anywhere
   close / to Arcadia"? Support your response with evidence.

Vincent van Gogh, *The Starry Night,* 1889, oil on canvas, 29 × 36 1/4 in. [73.7 × 92.1 cm.] (The Museum of Modern Art, New York. Acquired through the Lillie P. Bliss Bequest.)

ANNE SEXTON

Anne Sexton (1928-1975) was born in Newton, Massachusetts. She attended Garland Junior College, married at 20, and began a life as a housewife. After a mental breakdown at the age of 28 she took up writing poetry on the suggestion of a therapist. She published eight books of poetry, the third of which won a Pulitzer Prize. Despite her literary success, her life was deeply troubled. She committed suicide in 1975.

The Starry Night   [1961]

That does not keep me from having a terrible need of—shall I say the word—religion. Then I go out at night to paint the stars.
> —Vincent van Gogh in a letter to his brother

The town does not exist
except where one black-haired tree slips
up like a drowned woman into the hot sky.
The town is silent. The night boils with eleven stars
Oh starry starry night! This is how   5
I want to die.

It moves. They are all alive.
Even the moon bulges in its orange irons
to push children, like a god, from its eye.
The old unseen serpent swallows up the stars.   10
Oh starry starry night! This is how
I want to die:

into that rushing beast of the night,
sucked up by that great dragon, to split
from my life with no flag,   15
no belly,
no cry.

 TOPIC FOR CRITICAL THINKING AND WRITING

Sexton calls her poem "The Starry Night" and uses an epigraph from van Gogh. In what ways does her poem *not* describe or evoke van Gogh's painting? In what ways *does* it describe the painting?

Pieter Brueghel the Elder, *Landscape with the Fall of Icarus*, c. 1558. (Musées Royaux des Beaux-Arts, Brussels.)

W. H. AUDEN

Wystan Hugh Auden (1907-1973) was born in York, England, and educated at Oxford. In the 1930s his witty left-wing poetry earned him wide acclaim as the leading poet of his generation. He went to Spain during the Spanish Civil War, intending to serve as an ambulance driver for the Republicans in their struggle against Fascism, but he was so distressed by the violence of the Republicans that he almost immediately returned to England. In 1939 he came to America, and in 1946 he became a citizen of the United States, though he spent his last years in England. Much of his poetry is characterized by a combination of colloquial diction and technical dexterity.

In the following poem, Auden offers a meditation triggered by a painting in the Museum of Fine Arts in Brussels. The painting, by Pieter Brueghel (c. 1525-1569), is based on the legend of Icarus, told by the Roman poet Ovid (43 BCE-17 CE) in his Metamorphoses. *The story goes thus: Daedalus, father of Icarus, was confined with his son on the island of Crete. In order to escape, Daedalus made wings for himself and for Icarus by fastening feathers together with wax, but Icarus flew too near the sun, the wax melted, and Icarus fell into the sea. According to Ovid, the event—a boy falling through the sky—was witnessed with amazement by a ploughman, a shepherd, and an angler. In the painting, however, these figures seem to pay no attention to Icarus, who is represented not falling through the sky but already in the water (in the lower right corner, near the ship), with only his lower legs still visible.*

Musée des Beaux Arts

[1938]

About suffering they were never wrong.
The Old Masters: how well they understood
Its human position; how it takes place
While someone else is eating or opening a window or just walking
    dully along;
How, when the aged are reverently, passionately waiting   5
For the miraculous birth, there always must be
Children who did not specially want it to happen, skating
On a pond at the edge of the wood;
They never forgot
That even the dreadful martyrdom must run its course   10
Anyhow in a corner, some untidy spot
Where the dogs go on with their doggy life and the torturer's horse
Scratches its innocent behind on a tree.

In Brueghel's *Icarus*, for instance: how everything turns away
Quite leisurely from the disaster; the plowman may   15
Have heard the splash, the forsaken cry.
But for him it was not an important failure; the sun shone
As it had to on the white legs disappearing into the green
Water, and the expensive delicate ship that must have seen
Something amazing, a boy falling out of the sky,   20
Had somewhere to get to and sailed calmly on.

TOPICS FOR CRITICAL THINKING AND WRITING

1. In your own words sum up what, according to the speaker (in lines 1–13), the Old Masters understood about human suffering. (The Old Masters were the great European painters who worked from about 1500 to about 1750.)

2. Suppose the first lines read:

   > The Old Masters were never wrong about suffering.
   > They understood its human position well.

   What (beside the particular rhymes) would change or be lost?

3. Reread the poem (preferably over the course of several days) a number of times, jotting down your chief responses after each reading. Then, in connection with a final reading, study your notes, and write an essay of 500 words setting forth the history of your final response to the poem. For example, you may want to report that certain difficulties soon were clarified and that your enjoyment increased. Or, conversely, you may want to report that the poem became less interesting (for reasons you will set forth) the more you studied it. Probably your history will be somewhat more complicated than these simple examples. Try to find a chief pattern in your experience, and shape it into a thesis.

4. Consider a picture, either in a local museum or reproduced in a book, and write a 500-word reflection on it. If the picture is not well known, include a reproduction (a postcard from the museum or a photocopy of a page of a book).

Marcel Duchamp, *Nude Descending a Staircase, No. 2*, 1912, oil on canvas, 58 × 35 in.
(Philadelphia Museum of Art: The Louise and Walter Arensberg Collection.)

X. J. KENNEDY

X. J. Kennedy was born in New Jersey in 1929. He has taught at Tufts University and is the author of several books of poems, books for children, and college textbooks.

Marcel Duchamp's Nude Descending a Staircase, No. 2 *(1912) was exhibited in 1913 in the Armory Show, an international exhibition held at an armory in New York, and later in Chicago and Boston. The Armory Show gave America its first good look at contemporary European art—for instance, cubism, which had influenced Duchamp's painting.*

Nude Descending a Staircase   [1961]

Toe upon toe, a snowing flesh,
A gold of lemon, root and rind,
She sifts in sunlight down the stairs
With nothing on. Nor on her mind.   4

We spy beneath the banister
A constant thresh of thigh on thigh—
Her lips imprint the swinging air
That parts to let her parts go by   8
One-woman waterfall, she wears
Her slow descent like a long cape
And pausing, on the final stair
Collects her motions into shape.   12

▓ TOPICS FOR CRITICAL THINKING AND WRITING

1. To what extent does the poem describe the painting? To what extent does it do something else?
2. Some viewers have found Duchamp's painting strange and confusing. Does Kennedy's poem help you to understand Duchamp's style of art? Explain.

Skeet McAuley, *Navajo Monument Valley Tribal School near Goulding, Utah,* 1985.

SHERMAN ALEXIE

The short-story writer, essayist, poet, and film director Sherman J. Alexie Jr. was born in October 1966. He was raised on the Spokane Indian Reservation in Wellpinit, Washington, located fifty miles northwest of Spokane. He went to high school off reservation in Reardan, Washington, where he was an excellent student and played on the basketball team. He attended Gonzaga University in Spokane for two years and then transferred to Washington State University in Pullman, where he began writing poetry, graduating with a degree in American Studies. His books include The Business of Fancydancing: Stories and Poems *(1992),* The Lone Ranger and Tonto Fistfight in Heaven *(1994), and* Reservation Blues *(1995).*

For additional poems of Alexie, see pages 786 and 888; for a story, see page 291.

At Navajo Monument Valley Tribal School   [1992]

from the photograph by Skeet McAuley

the football field rises
to meet the mesa. Indian boys
gallop across the grass, against   3

the beginning of their body.
On those Saturday afternoons,
unbroken horses gather to watch   6

their sons growing larger
in the small parts of the world.
Everyone is the quarterback.   9

There is no thin man in a big hat
writing down all the names
in two columns: winners and losers.   12

This is the eternal football game,
Indians versus Indians. All the Skins
in the wooden bleachers fancydancing,   15

stomping red dust straight down
into nothing. Before the game is over,
the eighth-grade girls' track team   18

comes running, circling the field,
their thin brown legs echoing
wild horses, wild horses, wild horses.   21

 TOPICS FOR CRITICAL THINKING AND WRITING

1. What do you make of "the small parts of the world" and of "Everyone is the quarterback" (lines 9–10)?
2. Why do you think Alexie ended the poem by introducing the girls' track team? And what function(s) does the repetition serve in the final line?
3. Some readers find the poem's tone affirmative, even celebratory; others hear it as melancholy, even mournful. Do you agree with either of these descriptions, or would you use a different term or set of terms? Point to evidence in the text to explain and support your interpretation.
4. Look again at the photograph. Do you think that the creation of a playing field on this site is a desecration of the environment? Why, or why not?

Pablo Picasso, *Girl Before a Mirror*, 1932, oil on canvas, 64 × 51 1/4 in. (Museum of Modern Art, New York. Gift of Mrs. Simon Guggenheim.)

JOHN UPDIKE

John Updike, born in 1932, grew up in Shillington, Pennsylvania, where his father was a teacher and his mother was a writer. After receiving a B.A. degree from Harvard he studied drawing at Oxford for a year, but an offer from The New Yorker *magazine brought him back to the United States. He at first served as a reporter for the magazine, but soon began contributing poetry, essays, and fiction. Today he is one of America's most prolific and well-known writers.*

Before the Mirror

[1996]

How many of us still remember
when Picasso's "Girl Before a Mirror" hung
at the turning of the stairs in the pre-
expansion Museum of Modern Art?
Millions of us, probably, but we form   5
a dwindling population. Garish
and brush-slashed and yet as balanced
as a cardboard Queen in a deck of giant cards,
the painting proclaimed, "Enter here
and abandon preconception." She bounced   10
the erotic balls of herself back and forth
between reflection and reality.

Now I discover, in the recent re-
trospective at the same establishment,
that the vivid painting dates   15
from March of 1932,
the very month in which I first saw light,
squinting in nostalgia for the womb.
I bend closer, inspecting. The blacks,
the stripy cyanide greens are still uncracked,   20
I note with satisfaction; the cherry reds
and lemon yellows full of childish juice.
No sag, no wrinkle. Fresh as paint. Back then
they knew just how, I reflect, to lay it on.

⧆ TOPICS FOR CRITICAL THINKING AND WRITING

1. The painting shows a young woman looking into a mirror. In viewing a picture with this subject, what associations might reasonably come to mind? Vanity? Mortality? Or what?
2. The woman (at the left) has two faces, one in profile. Do you think Picasso is showing us two views of the same face, or perhaps two stages in the woman's life? And what of the face in the mirror? Do you think it shows either or both of the faces at the left, or a third face or stage?
3. Why do you suppose the woman is reaching out toward the mirror? (There cannot be any way of proving whatever you or anyone else might offer as an answer, but *why* do you offer the explanation that you do offer?)
4. What do you think the poem is chiefly about? The distinctiveness of modern art (meaning the age of Picasso)? The excellent condition of the picture? The speaker's response to the picture? Explain.
5. The first twelve lines of this poem describe the speaker's thoughts "then," when he first saw *Girl Before a Mirror;* the last twelve lines describe his ideas and feelings "now." In two paragraphs, or in one extended paragraph, write a "Then and Now," describing a picture or a song or a scene—a lake, a house, a kitchen—or a person, then and now.

John James Audubon. *American Flamingo,* c. 1830, hand-colored print. (Courtesy William S. Reese.)

GREG PAPE

Greg Pape was born in 1947 in Eureka, California, and educated at Fresno State College (now California State University, Fresno) and the University of Arizona. The author of several books of poems, he has served as writer-in-residence at several colleges and universities, and now teaches at Northern Arizona University, in Flagstaff.

American Flamingo   [1998]

I know he shot them to know them.
I did not know the eyes of the flamingo
are blue, a deep live blue.   3

And the tongue is lined with many small
tongues, thirteen, in the sketch
by Audubon,° to function as a sieve.   6

I knew the long rose-pink neck,
the heavy tricolored down-sweeping bill,
the black primaries.   9

But I did not know the blue eye
drawn so passionately by Audubon
it seems to look out, wary, intense,   12
from the paper it is printed on.
                    —what
Is man but his passion?   15

asked Robert Penn Warren.° In the background
of this sketch, tenderly subtitled *Old Male,*
beneath the over-draping feathered   18

monument of the body, between the long
flexible neck and the long bony legs
covered with pink plates of flesh,   21

Audubon has given us eight postures,
eight stunning movements in the ongoing
dance of the flamingos.   24

Once at Hialeah° in late afternoon
I watched the satin figures of the jockeys
perched like bright beetles on the backs   27

of horses pounding down the home
stretch, a few crops whipping
the lathering flanks, the loud flat   30

metallic voice of the announcer fading
as the flamingos, grazing the pond water
at the far end of the infield, rose   33

in a feathery blush, only a few feet
off the ground, and flew one long
clipped-winged ritual lap   36

in the heavy Miami light, a great
slow swirl of grace from the old world
that made tickets fall from hands,   39

---

6 **Audubon** John James Audubon, American ornithologist and artist (1785-1851), author of
the multivolume *Birds of America* (1827-1838).   16 **Robert Penn Warren** American poet,
novelist, and literary critic (1905-1989).   25 **Hialeah** city in southeast Florida, site of Hialeah
Park racetrack.

stilled horses, and drew toasts from the stands
as they settled down again
like a rose-colored fog on the pond.   42

▥ TOPICS FOR CRITICAL THINKING AND WRITING

1. Why is the speaker preoccupied with the flamingo's eyes?
2. A transition occurs in lines 14–15, with the italicized quotation from Robert Penn Warren. What is the relationship of this to the description of the flamingo (and the speaker's reflections) that precede it?
3. From line 25 to the end, the speaker carefully describes a scene at Hialeah. Take note of the specific details and terms that the speaker presents, and explain how these make the poem both a vivid description and something more than that.

26

Three Poets in Depth: Emily Dickinson, Robert Frost, and Langston Hughes

ON READING AUTHORS REPRESENTED IN DEPTH

If you have read several works by an author, whether tragedies by Shakespeare or detective stories about Sherlock Holmes by Arthur Conan Doyle, you know that authors return again and again to certain themes (tragedy for Shakespeare, crime for Conan Doyle), yet each treatment is different. *Hamlet, Macbeth,* and *Romeo and Juliet* are all tragedies, and they all share certain qualities that we think of as Shakespearean, yet each is highly distinctive.

When we read several works by an author, we find ourselves thinking about resemblances and differences. We enjoy seeing the author return to some theme (for instance, God, or nature, or love) or to some literary form (for instance, the sonnet, or blank verse, or pairs of rhyming lines); and we may find, to our delight, that the author has handled things differently and that we are getting a sense of the writer's variety and perhaps even of the writer's development. Indeed, we sometimes speak of the *shape* or *design* of the author's career, meaning that our careful study of the writings has led us to an understanding of the story—with its beginning, middle, and end—that the writings tell across a period of time. Often, once we read one poem by an author and find it intriguing or compelling, we want to read more: Are there other poems like this one? What kinds of poems were written before or after this one? Our enjoyment and understanding of one poem helps us to enjoy and understand others, and makes us curious about the place that each one occupies in a larger structure, the shape of the author's career.

We can go further and say that the reading of a second author can help us— perhaps by way of contrast—to understand the first. In the preface to one of his volumes of poetry, Robert Frost put it this way:

A poem is best read in the light of all the other poems ever written. We read A the better to read B (we have to start somewhere; we may get very little out of A). We read B the better to read C, C the better to read D, D the better to go back and get something more out of A. Progress is not the aim, but circulation. The thing is to get among the poems where they hold each other apart in their places as the stars do.

In an Introduction to Literature course, although you'll often be asked to write analytical papers about a single poem, story, or play, sometimes you'll be assigned a paper that requires a comparison and contrast of, for example, two poems by different authors. Less frequent perhaps, but equally important, is the paper that examines a central theme or idea as it is expressed and explored in three or more works.

At first this might seem a daunting task, but there are helpful ways of getting in control of the assignment. One of the best is to begin with a single work and then to move outward from it, making connections to works that show interesting similarities to, or differences from, it.

One of our students, Mark Bradley, was assigned to write on a theme (which he had to define himself) in a selection of poems by Langston Hughes. Mark started by closely studying a poem by Hughes that had caught his attention when he made his way through the group of poems for the first time. In one of his journal entries, Mark wrote:

> The poem "The South" surprised me. It wasn't what I expected. I thought Hughes would attack the South for being so racist--he wrote the poem in the 1920s, when segregation was everywhere in the South. He says some tough stuff about the South, that's for sure: "Beast strong, / Idiot-brained." But he also says that the South is attractive in some ways, and I'm not convinced that when he brings in the North at the end, he really believes that the North is superior.

Intrigued by this poem, Mark made it his point of departure for the thematic paper he was assigned. He judged that if he worked intensively on this poem and came to know it well, he could review other Hughes poems and see how they were both like and unlike the poem with which he began.

When you write an essay on several works, keep two points especially in mind: the length of the assignment, and the choice of examples. You want to treat the right number of examples for the space you are given, and, furthermore, to provide sufficient detail in your analysis of each of them. You might call this the principle of proportion.

Preparing an outline can be valuable. It will lead you to think carefully about which examples you have selected for your argument and the main idea about each one that you will present. You might begin by examining one poem in depth, and then proceed to relate it to key passages in other poems. Or maybe you'll find one passage in a poem so significant that it—rather than the poem in its entirety—can serve as a good beginning. Whichever strategy you choose, when you review the rough draft, use a pen to mark off the amount of space that you have devoted to each example. Ask yourself:

- Is this example clearly connected to my argument in the paper as a whole?

- Have I not only referred to the example but also provided adequate quotation from it?
- Have I made certain to comment on the passage? (Remember that passages do not interpret themselves. You have to explicate and explain them.)
- Has each example received its due?

There is no easy rule of thumb for knowing how much space each example should be given. Some passages are more complicated than others; some demand more intensive scrutiny. But you'll be well on the way toward handling this aspect of the paper effectively if you are self-aware about your choices, alert to the principle of proportion.

EMILY DICKINSON

Emily Dickinson (1830–1886) was born into a proper New England family in Amherst, Massachusetts. Although she spent her seventeenth year a few miles away, at Mount Holyoke Seminary (now Mount Holyoke College), in the next twenty years she left Amherst only five or six times, and in her last twenty years she may never have left her house. Her brother was probably right when he said that having seen something of the rest of the world— she had visited Washington with her father, when he was a member of Congress—"she could not resist the feeling that it was painfully hollow. It was to her so thin and unsatisfying in the face of the Great Realities of Life."

Dickinson lived with her parents (a somewhat reclusive mother and an austere, remote father) and a younger sister; a married brother lived in the house next door. She formed some passionate attachments, to women as well as men, but there is no evidence that they found physical expression.

By the age of twelve Dickinson was writing witty letters, but she apparently did not write more than an occasional poem before her late twenties. At her death—she died in the house where she was born—she left 1,775 poems, only seven of which had been published (anonymously) during her lifetime.

We begin this section with sixteen poems by Dickinson. Next, we present a seventeenth poem, "I Felt a Funeral, in my Brain," in multiple versions: the poem as we know it today; the poem in manuscript; and the poem in its first published version. Then, two more poems, which are similar in phrasing to one another and show an affinity to "I Felt a Funeral, in my Brain." We conclude with three of Dickinson's letters about poetry.

These are the days when Birds come back   [1859]

These are the days when Birds come back—
A very few—a Bird or two—
To take a backward look.

3

These are days when skies resume
The old—old sophistries° of June—
A blue and gold mistake.   6

O fraud that cannot cheat the Bee—
Almost thy plausibility
Induces my belief.   9

Till ranks of seeds their witness bear—
And softly thro' the altered air
Hurries a timid leaf.   12

Oh Sacrament of summer days,
Oh Last Communion in the Haze—
Permit a child to join.   15

Thy sacred emblems to partake—
Thy consecrated bread to take
And thine immortal wine!   18

---

5 sophistries deceptively subtle arguments.

Papa above!   [c. 1859]

Papa above!
Regard a Mouse
O'erpowered by the Cat!
Reserve within thy kingdom
A "Mansion" for the Rat!   5

Snug in seraphic Cupboards
To nibble all the day,
While unsuspecting Cycles°
Wheel solemnly away!

---

8 Cycles long periods, eons.

Wild Nights—Wild Nights!   [1861]

Wild Nights—Wild Nights!
Were I with thee
Wild Nights should be
Our luxury!   4

Futile—the Winds—
To a Heart in port—
Done with the Compass—
Done with the Chart!   8

Rowing in Eden—
Ah, the Sea!
Might I but moor—Tonight—
In Thee!   12

There's a certain Slant of light

[c. 1861]

There's a certain Slant of light,
Winter Afternoons—
That oppresses, like the Heft°
Of Cathedral Tunes—   4

Heavenly Hurt, it gives us—
We can find no scar,
But internal difference,
Where the Meanings, are—   8

None may teach it—Any—
'Tis the Seal Despair—
An imperial affliction
Sent us of the Air—   12

When it comes, the Landscape listens—
Shadows—hold their breath—
When it goes, 'tis like the Distance
On the look of Death—   16

---

3 Heft weight.

I got so I could hear his name—

[1861]

I got so I could hear his name—
Without—Tremendous gain—
That Stop-sensation—on my Soul—
And Thunder—in the Room—   4

I got so I could walk across
That Angle in the floor,
Where he turned so, and I turned—how—
And all our Sinew tore—   8

I got so I could stir the Box—
In which his letters grew
Without that forcing, in my breath—
As Staples—driven through—   12

Could dimly recollect a Grace—
I think, they call it "God"—
Renowned to ease Extremity—
When Formula, had failed—   16

And shape my Hands—
Petition's way,
Tho' ignorant of a word
That Ordination°—utters—   20

---

20 Ordination the ministry.

My Business, with the Cloud,
If any Power behind it, be,
Not subject to Despair—
It care, in some remoter way,   24
For so minute affair
As Misery—
Itself, too great, for interrupting—more—

The Soul selects her own Society   [1862]

The Soul selects her own Society—
Then—shuts the Door—
To her divine Majority—
Present no more—   4

Unmoved—she notes the Chariots—pausing—
At her low Gate—
Unmoved—an Emperor be kneeling
Upon her Mat—   8

I've known her—from an ample nation—
Choose One—
Then—close the Valves° of her attention—
Like Stone—   12

---

11 Valves the two halves of a hinged door such as is now found on old telephone booths.
Possibly also an allusion to a bivalve, such as an oyster or a clam, having a shell consisting of
two hinged parts.

This was a Poet—It is That   [1862]

This was a Poet—It is That
Distills amazing sense
From Ordinary Meanings—
And Attar so immense   4

From the familiar species
That perished by the Door—
We wonder it was not Ourselves
Arrested it—before—   8

Of Pictures, the Discloser—
The Poet—it is He—
Entitles Us—by Contrast—
To ceaseless Poverty—   12

Of Portion—so unconscious—
The Robbing—could not harm—
Himself—to Him—a Fortune—
Exterior—to Time—   16

Manuscript of Emily Dickinson's "I heard a Fly buzz—when I died."

I heard a Fly buzz—when I died   [1862]

I heard a Fly buzz—when I died—
The Stillness in the Room
Was like the Stillness in the Air—
Between the Heaves of Storm—

The Eyes around—had wrung them dry—
And Breaths were gathering firm

4

For the last Onset—when the King
Be witnessed—in the Room—   8

I willed my Keepsakes—Signed away
What portion of me be
Assignable—and then it was
There interposed a Fly—   12

With Blue—uncertain stumbling Buzz—
Between the light—and me—
And then the Windows failed—and then
I could not see to see—   16

This World is not Conclusion   [c. 1862]

This World is not Conclusion.
A Species stands beyond—
Invisible, as Music—
But positive, as Sound—   4
It beckons, and it baffles—
Philosophy—don't know—
And through a Riddle, at the last—
Sagacity, must go—   8
To guess it, puzzles scholars—
To gain it, Men have borne
Contempt of Generations
And Crucifixion, shown—   12
Faith slips—and laughs, and rallies—
Blushes, if any see—
Plucks at a twig of Evidence—
And asks a Vane, the way—   16
Much Gesture, from the Pulpit—
Strong Hallelujahs roll—
Narcotics cannot still the Tooth
That nibbles at the soul—   20

I like to see it lap the Miles   [1862]

I like to see it lap the Miles—
And lick the Valleys up—
And stop to feed itself at Tanks—
And then—prodigious step   4

Around a Pile of Mountains—
And supercilious peer
In Shanties—by the sides of Roads—
And then a Quarry pare   8

To fit its Ribs
And crawl between
Complaining all the while
In horrid—hooting stanza—
Then chase itself down Hill—   12

And neigh like Boanerges°
Then—punctual as a Star
Stop—docile and omnipotent   16
At its own stable door—

---

13 **Boanerges** a name said (in Mark 3.17) to mean "Sons of Thunder."

A narrow Fellow in the Grass   [c. 1865]

A narrow Fellow in the Grass
Occasionally rides—
You may have met Him—did you not
His notice sudden is—   4

The Grass divides as with a Comb—
A spotted shaft is seen—
And then it closes at your feet
And opens further on—   8

He likes a Boggy Acre
A Floor too cool for Corn—
Yet when a Boy, and Barefoot—
I more than once at Noon   12
Have passed, I thought, a Whip lash
Unbraiding in the Sun
When stopping to secure it
It wrinkled, and was gone—   16

Several of Nature's People
I know, and they know me—
I feel for them a transport
Of cordiality—   20

But never met this Fellow
Attended, or alone
Without a tighter breathing
And Zero at the Bone—   24

Further in Summer than the Birds   [1866]

Further in Summer than the Birds
Pathetic from the Grass
A minor Nation celebrates
Its unobtrusive Mass.   4

No Ordinance° be seen
So gradual the Grace
A pensive Custom it becomes
Enlarging Loneliness.   8

---

5 **Ordinance** religious rite of Holy Communion.

Antiquest felt at Noon
When August burning low
Arise this spectral Canticle°
Repose to typify   12

Remit as yet no Grace
No Furrow on the Glow
Yet a Druidic° Difference
Enhances Nature now   16

---

11 Canticle hymn.   **15 Druidic** pertaining to pre-Christian Celtic priests.

Tell all the Truth but tell it slant   [c. 1868]

Tell all the Truth but tell it slant—
Success in Circuit lies
Too bright for our infirm Delight
The Truth's superb surprise   4

As Lightning to the Children eased
With explanation kind
The Truth must dazzle gradually
Or every man be blind—   8

A Route of Evanescence*   [c. 1879]

A Route of Evanescence
With a revolving Wheel—
A Resonance of Emerald—
A Rush of Cochineal°   4
And every Blossom on the Bush
Adjusts its tumbled Head—
The mail from Tunis,° probably,
An easy Morning's Ride—   8

---

*A Route of Evanescence In letters to friends Dickinson said the poem referred to a
hummingbird.   **4 Cochineal** bright red.   **7 Tunis** City in North Africa.

Those—dying, then   [1882]

Those—dying, then
Knew where they went
They went to God's Right Hand—
The Hand is amputated now   4
And God cannot be found—

The abdication of Belief
Makes the Behavior small—
Better an ignis fatuus°
Than no illume at all—   8

---

8 ignis fatuus a phosphorescent light that hovers over swampy ground, hence something
deceptive.

Apparently with no surprise   [c. 1884]

Apparently with no surprise
To any happy Flower
The Frost beheads it at its play—
In accidental power—   4
The blonde Assassin passes on—
The Sun proceeds unmoved
To measure off another Day
For an Approving God.   8

We reprint here and on the next page Dickinson's manuscript for "I felt a
Funeral, in my Brain," and we follow it with the version of the poem as we
know it today, where it is #280 in *The Complete Poems of Emily Dickinson,* ed.
Thomas H. Johnson (Boston: Little, Brown, 1957). This edition follows the text
that Johnson presented in his three-volume scholarly edition, *The Poems of*

Dickinson's manuscript for "I felt a Funeral, in my Brain."   *(continued)*

Emily Dickinson (Cambridge: Harvard UP, 1955). Johnson proposes a date of sometime in 1861 for this poem, but the editor of a new scholarly edition, *The Poems of Emily Dickinson:* Variorum Edition, 3 vols. (Cambridge: Harvard UP, 1998), R. W. Franklin, while agreeing with Johnson's version of the poem, suggests a date of summer 1862.

I felt a Funeral, in my Brain [1861 or 1862]

I felt a Funeral, in my Brain,
And Mourners to and fro
Kept treading—treading—till it seemed
That Sense was breaking through—   4

And when they all were seated,
A Service, like a Drum—
Kept beating—beating—till I thought
My Mind was going numb—   8

And then I heard them lift a Box
And creak across my Soul
With those same Boots of Lead, again,
Then Space—began to toll,   12

As all the Heavens were a Bell,
And Being, but an Ear,
And I, and Silence, some strange Race
Wrecked, solitary, here—   16

And then a Plank in Reason, broke,
And I dropped down, and down—
And hit a World, at every plunge,
And Finished knowing—then—   20

Pages 925–926 reproduce the poem as it appears in Dickinson's own hand. Our copy is taken from *The Manuscript Books of Emily Dickinson,* edited by R. W. Franklin and published in 1981. Like nearly all of Dickinson's poems, this one was not published in her lifetime. She wrote her poems on sheets of letter paper, which she then bound together with string into packets. Perhaps these personal manuscript books or "fascicles" (that is, a small bundle, or the divisions of a book published in parts) represented for Dickinson a form of publication— though a very private one.

Notice that in line 10, Dickinson wrote "Brain," but then crossed it out and selected the word "Soul" instead. Notice also that in manuscript, the poem concludes with a line not in the poem, but that seems to give alternatives for words in lines 19 and 20. Refer to the poem as we know it (pages 926–927) to see how Thomas Johnson has worked from the manuscript to make his choices about how the poem should read.

In her will Dickinson stipulated that upon her death, her papers and letters should be burned. Her sister Lavinia, however, who discovered the poems, decided that her sister's request did not include them, and she soon became determined to see the poems published. This task was taken up by Mabel Loomis Todd (1856–1932), who was a friend of Dickinson's—and the lover of Austin Dickinson, Emily's older (and already married) brother. With help from the critic and man-of-letters Thomas Wentworth Higginson, Todd edited two series of Dickinson's poems (1890, 1891), and then edited a third series (1896) and the *Letters of Emily Dickinson* (2 vols., 1984) herself. Both Todd and Higginson removed many of the boldly original features of the poems' language, structure, and punctuation. They sought to make Dickinson more conventional, more like other poets of the age. This, in their view, was the best way to make her less difficult and hence more accessible to readers. But the result was that they eliminated the daring, brilliant innovations that make Dickinson extraordinary. This first published version of "I Felt a Funeral, in my Brain" is taken from *Poems by Emily Dickinson,* third series (Boston: Little, Brown, 1896).

I felt a funeral in my brain,
And mourners, to and fro,
Kept treading, treading, till it seemed
That sense was breaking through.   4

And when they all were seated,
A service like a drum

Kept beating, beating, till I thought
My mind was going numb.   8

And then I heard them lift a box,
And creak across my soul
With those same boots of lead, again.
Then space began to toll   12

As all the heavens were a bell,
And Being but an ear,
And I and silence some strange race,
Wrecked, solitary, here.   16

Here are two more poems, similar to one another and somewhat similar to
"I felt a Funeral, in my Brain." Thomas Johnson dates the first one as having been
written in 1864, and the second in the following year. The second, Johnson explains, is not so much a separate poem as a variant on the first, a variant that
Dickinson probably sent to her sister-in-law Susan Gilbert Dickinson, who was
married to Dickinson's brother Austin. In his more recent edition, R. W. Franklin
says more firmly that the first poem was written in early 1864 and that, without
address or signature, Dickinson sent a version of its second stanza to Susan.

I felt a Cleaving in my Mind—   [1864]

I felt a Cleaving in my Mind—
As if my Brain had split—
I tried to match it—Seam by Seam—
But could not make them fit.   4

The thought behind, I strove to join
Unto the thought before—
But Sequence ravelled out of Sound
Like Balls—upon a Floor.   8

The Dust behind I strove to join   [1865]

The Dust behind I strove to join
Unto the Dust before—
But Sequence ravelled out of Sound
Like Balls upon a Floor—   4

LETTERS ABOUT POETRY

We include three of Dickinson's letters, the first of which is addressed to Susan
Gilbert, probably her dearest friend and the wife of Dickinson's brother, Austin.
The two other letters are addressed to Thomas Wentworth Higginson, a writer
and leading abolitionist. After reading in *Atlantic Monthly* (April 1862) Higginson's article offering advice to young authors, Dickinson (31 at the time) sent
Higginson some of her poems along with a letter, and a correspondence ensued,
lasting until Dickinson's death.

To Susan Gilbert (Dickinson)   [late April 1852]

So sweet and still, and Thee, Oh Susie, what need I more, to make my heaven whole?

Sweet Hour, blessed Hour, to carry me to you, and to bring you back to me, long enough to snatch one kiss, and whisper Good bye, again.

I have thought of it all day, Susie, and I fear of but little else, and when I was gone to meeting it filled my mind so full, I could not find a *chink* to put the worthy pastor; when he said "Our Heavenly Father," I said "Oh Darling Sue"; when he read the 100th Psalm, I kept saying your precious letter all over to myself, and Susie, when they sang—it would have made you laugh to hear one little voice, piping to the departed. I made up words and kept singing how I loved you, and you had gone, while all the rest of the choir were singing Hallelujahs. I presume nobody heard me, because I sang *so small,* but it was a kind of a comfort to think I might put them out, singing of you. I a'nt there this afternoon, tho', because I am here, writing a little letter to my dear Sue, and I am very happy. I think of ten weeks—Dear One, and I think of love, and you, and my heart grows full and warm, and my breath stands still. The sun does'nt shine at all, but I can feel a sunshine stealing into my soul and making it all summer, and every thorn, a *rose.* And I pray that such summer's sun shine on my Absent One, and cause her bird to sing!

You have been happy, Susie, and now are sad—and the whole world seems lone; but it wont be so always, "some days *must* be dark and dreary"! You wont cry any more, will you, Susie, for my father will be your father, and my home will be your home, and where you go, I will go, and we will lie side by side in the kirkyard.

I have parents on earth, dear Susie, but your's are in the skies, and I have an earthly fireside, but you have one above, and you have a "Father in Heaven," where I have *none*—and *sister* in heaven, and I know they love you dearly, and think of you every day.

Oh I wish I had half so many dear friends as you in heaven—I couldn't spare them now—but to know they had got there safely, and should suffer nevermore—Dear Susie! . . .

Emilie—

To T. W. Higginson   [25 April 1862]

Mr Higginson,
Your kindness claimed earlier gratitude—but I was ill—and write today, from my pillow.

Thank you for the surgery[1]—it was not so painful as I supposed. I bring you others—as you ask—though they might not differ—

While my thought is undressed—I can make the distinction, but when I put them in the Gown—they look alike, and numb.

You asked how old I was? I made no verse—but one or two—until this winter—Sir—

---

[1]**surgery** probably cuts that Higginson suggested be made in her poems.

I had a terror—since September—I could tell to none—and so I sing, as the Boy does by the Burying Ground—because I am afraid—You inquire my Books—For Poets—I have Keats—and Mr and Mrs Browning. For Prose—Mr Ruskin—Sir Thomas Browne—and the Revelations.[2] I went to school—but in your manner of the phrase—had no education. When a little Girl, I had a friend, who taught me Immortality—but venturing too near, him-self—he never returned—Soon after, my Tutor, died—and for several years, my Lexicon—was my only companion—Then I found one more—but he was not contented I be his scholar—so he left the Land.

You ask of my Companions Hills—Sir—and the Sundown—and a Dog—large as myself, that my Father bought me—They are better than Be-ings—because they know—but do not tell—and the noise in the Pool, at Noon—excels my Piano. I have a Brother and Sister—My Mother does not care for thought—and Father, too busy with his Briefs[3]—to notice what we do—He buys me many Books—but begs me not to read them—because he fears they joggle the Mind. They are religious—except me—and address an Eclipse, every morning—whom they call their "Father." But I fear my story fatigues you—I would like to learn—Could you tell me how to grow—or is it unconveyed—like Melody—or Witchcraft?

You speak of Mr Whitman—I never read his Book[4]—but was told that he was disgraceful—

I read Miss Prescott's "Circumstance,"[5] but it followed me, in the Dark—so I avoided her—

Two Editors of Journals came to my Father's House, this winter—and asked me for my Mind—and when I asked them "Why," they said I was penurious—and they, would use it for the World—

I could not weigh myself—Myself—

My size felt small—to me—I read your Chapters in the Atlantic—and experienced honor for you—I was sure you would not reject a confiding question—

Is this—Sir—what you asked me to tell you?

Your friend,
E—Dickinson.

---

[2]**Keats . . . Revelations** John Keats, Robert Browning, and Elizabeth Barrett Browning were nineteenth-century English poets; Thomas Browne was a seventeenth-century English writer of prose; John Ruskin was a nineteenth-century English art critic and social critic; Revelation, which Dickinson calls Revelations, is the last book of the New Testament.   [3]**Briefs** legal documents (Dickinson's father was a lawyer).   [4]**Mr Whitman . . . Book** Walt Whitman's *Leaves of Grass* was first published in 1855. Its unconventional punctuation and its celebration of Whitman's passions shocked many readers.   [5]**Miss Prescott's "Circumstance"** Harriet Prescott Spofford's story, published in *Atlantic Monthly* in May 1860. It tells of a woman who, returning from a visit to a sick friend, is held hostage by a beast who is calmed only when she sings to him. Her husband eventually rescues her, but when they arrive home they find that their house has been burned down.

To T. W. Higginson   [1876]

Nature is a Haunted House—but Art—a House that tries to be haunted.

ROBERT FROST

Robert Frost (1874-1963) was born in California. After his father's death in 1885, Frost's mother brought the family to New England, where she taught in high schools in Massachusetts and New Hampshire. Frost studied for part of one term at Dartmouth College in New Hampshire, then did odd jobs (including teaching), and from 1897 to 1899 was enrolled as a special student at Harvard. He then farmed in New Hampshire, published a few poems in local newspapers, left the farm and taught again, and in 1912 left for England, where he hoped to achieve more popular success as a writer. By 1915 he had won a considerable reputation, and he returned to the United States, settling on a farm in New Hampshire and cultivating the image of the country-wise farmer-poet. In fact he was well read in the classics, the Bible, and English and American literature.*

Among Frost's many comments about literature, here are three: "Writing is unboring to the extent that it is dramatic"; "Every poem is . . . a figure of the will braving alien entanglements"; and, finally, a poem "begins in delight and ends in wisdom. . . . It runs a course of lucky events, and ends in a clarification of life—not necessarily a great clarification, such as sects and cults are founded on, but in a momentary stay against confusion."

And for good measure, here is Frost, in a letter, writing about his own work.

You get more credit for thinking if you restate formulae or cite cases that fall in easily under formulae, but all the fun is outside[,] saying things that suggest formulae that won't formulate—that almost but don't quite formulate. I should like to be so subtle at this game as to seem to the casual person altogether obvious. The casual person would assume I meant nothing or else I came near enough meaning something he was familiar with to mean it for all practical purposes. Well, well, well.

We give fifteen of Frost's poems, arranged in chronological order, and we follow these poems with some of Frost's comments about poetry. The first poem, "The Pasture," is one that Frost customarily put at the beginning of his collected poems. The last words of each stanza, "You come too," are an invitation to the reader to join him.

The Pasture
[1913]

I'm going out to clean the pasture spring;
I'll only stop to rake the leaves away
(And wait to watch the water clear, I may):
I shan't be gone long.—You come too.   4

I'm going out to fetch the little calf
That's standing by the mother. It's so young,
It totters when she licks it with her tongue.
I shan't be gone long.—You come too.   8

Mending Wall   [1914]

Something there is that doesn't love a wall,
That sends the frozen-ground-swell under it,
And spills the upper boulder in the sun;
And makes gaps even two can pass abreast.
The work of hunters is another thing: 5
I have come after them and made repair
Where they have left not one stone on a stone,
But they would have the rabbit out of hiding,
To please the yelping dogs. The gaps I mean,
No one has seen them made or heard them made,   10
But at spring mending-time we find them there.
I let my neighbor know beyond the hill;
And on a day we meet to walk the line
And set the wall between us once again.
We keep the wall between us as we go.   15
To each the boulders that have fallen to each.
And some are loaves and some so nearly balls
We have to use a spell to make them balance:
"Stay where you are until our backs are turned!"
We wear our fingers rough with handling them.   20
Oh, just another kind of outdoor game,
One on a side. It comes to little more:
There where it is we do not need the wall:
He is all pine and I am apple orchard.
My apple trees will never get across   25
And eat the cones under his pines, I tell him.
He only says, "Good fences make good neighbours."
Spring is the mischief in me, and I wonder
If I could put a notion in his head:
"*Why* do they make good neighbours? Isn't it   30
Where there are cows? But here there are no cows.
Before I built a wall I'd ask to know
What I was walling in or walling out,
And to whom I was like to give offence.
Something there is that doesn't love a wall,   35
That wants it down." I could say "Elves" to him,
But it's not elves exactly, and I'd rather
He said it for himself. I see him there
Bringing a stone grasped firmly by the top
In each hand, like an old-stone savage armed.   40
He moves in darkness as it seems to me,
Not of woods only and the shade of trees.
He will not go behind his father's saying,
And he likes having thought of it so well
He says again, "Good fences make good neighbours."   45

The Wood-Pile

[1914]

Out walking in the frozen swamp one grey day,
I paused and said, "I will turn back from here.
No, I will go on farther—and we shall see."
The hard snow held me, save where now and then
One foot went through. The view was all in lines   5
Straight up and down of tall slim trees
Too much alike to mark or name a place by
So as to say for certain I was here
Or somewhere else: I was just far from home.
A small bird flew before me. He was careful   10
To put a tree between us when he lighted,
And say no word to tell me who he was
Who was so foolish as to think what *he* thought.
He thought that I was after him for a feather—
The white one in his tail; like one who takes   15
Everything said as personal to himself.
One flight out sideways would have undeceived him.
And then there was a pile of wood for which
I forgot him and let his little fear
Carry him off the way I might have gone,   20
Without so much as wishing him good-night.
He went behind it to make his last stand.
It was a cord of maple, cut and split
And piled—and measured, four by four by eight.
And not another like it could I see.   25
No runner tracks in this year's snow looped near it.
And it was older sure than this year's cutting,
Or even last year's or the year's before.
The wood was grey and the bark warping off it
And the pile somewhat sunken. Clematis   30
Had wound strings round and round it like a bundle.
What held it though on one side was a tree
Still growing, and on one a stake and prop,
These latter about to fall. I thought that only
Someone who lived in turning to fresh tasks   35
Could so forget his handiwork on which
He spent himself, the labour of his axe,
And leave it there far from a useful fireplace
To warm the frozen swamps as best it could
With the slow smokeless burning of decay.   40

The Road Not Taken

[1916]

Two roads diverged in a yellow wood,
And sorry I could not travel both
And be one traveler, long I stood
And looked down one as far as I could
To where it bent in the undergrowth;   5

Then took the other, as just as fair,
And having perhaps the better claim,
Because it was grassy and wanted wear;
Though as for that the passing there
Had worn them really about the same,   10

And both that morning equally lay
In leaves no step had trodden black.
Oh, I kept the first for another day!
Yet knowing how way leads on to way,
I doubted if I should ever come back.   15

I shall be telling this with a sigh
Somewhere ages and ages hence:
Two roads diverged in a wood, and I—
I took the one less traveled by,
And that has made all the difference.   20

The Telephone   [1916]

"When I was just as far as I could walk
From here to-day
There was an hour
All still
When leaning with my head against a flower   5
I heard you talk.
Don't say I didn't, for I heard you say—
You spoke from that flower on the window sill—
Do you remember what it was you said?"

"First tell me what it was you thought you heard."   10

"Having found the flower and driven a bee away,
I leaned my head,
And holding by the stalk,
I listened and I thought I caught the word—
What was it? Did you call me by my name?   15
Or did you say—
Someone said 'Come'—I heard it as I bowed."

"I may have thought as much, but not aloud."

"Well, so I came."

The Oven Bird   [1916]

There is a singer everyone has heard,
Loud, a mid-summer and a mid-wood bird,
Who makes the solid tree trunks sound again.
He says that leaves are old and that for flowers
Mid-summer is to spring as one to ten.   5
He says the early petal-fall is past

When pear and cherry bloom went down in showers
On sunny days a moment overcast;
And comes that other fall we name the fall.
He says the highway dust is over all.   10
The bird would cease and be as other birds
But that he knows in singing not to sing.
The question that he frames in all but words
Is what to make of a diminished thing.

The Aim Was Song   [1923]

Before man came to blow it right
    The wind once blew itself untaught,
And did its loudest day and night
    In any rough place where it caught.   4

Man came to tell it what was wrong:
    It hadn't found the place to blow;
It blew too hard—the aim was song.
    And listen—how it ought to go!   8

He took a little in his mouth,
    And held it long enough for north
To be converted into south,
    And then by measure blew it forth.   12

By measure. It was word and note,
    The wind the wind had meant to be—
A little through the lips and throat.
    The aim was song—the wind could see.   16

The Need of Being Versed in Country Things   [1923]

The house had gone to bring again
To the midnight sky a sunset glow.
Now the chimney was all of the house that stood,
Like a pistil after the petals go.   4

The barn opposed across the way,
That would have joined the house in flame
Had it been the will of the wind, was left
To bear forsaken the place's name.   8

No more it opened with all one end
For teams that came by the stony road
To drum on the floor with scurrying hoofs
And brush the mow with the summer load.   12

The birds that came to it through the air
At broken windows flew out and in,
Their murmur more like the sigh we sigh
From too much dwelling on what has been.   16

Yet for them the lilac renewed its leaf,
And the aged elm, though touched with fire;
And the dry pump flung up an awkward arm;
And the fence post carried a strand of wire.   20

For them there was really nothing sad.
But though they rejoiced in the nest they kept,
One had to be versed in country things
Not to believe the phoebes wept.   24

Stopping by Woods on a Snowy Evening   [1923]

Whose woods these are I think I know.
His house is in the village, though;
He will not see me stopping here
To watch his woods fill up with snow.   4

My little horse must think it queer
To stop without a farmhouse near
Between the woods and frozen lake
The darkest evening of the year.   8

He gives his harness bells a shake
To ask if there is some mistake.
The only other sound's the sweep
Of easy wind and downy flake.   12

The woods are lovely, dark and deep,
But I have promises to keep,
And miles to go before I sleep,
And miles to go before I sleep.   16

Acquainted with the Night   [1928]

I have been one acquainted with the night.
I have walked out in rain—and back in rain.
I have outwalked the furthest city light.

I have looked down the saddest city lane.
I have passed by the watchman on his beat   5
And dropped my eyes, unwilling to explain.

I have stood still and stopped the sound of feet
When far away an interrupted cry
Came over houses from another street,

But not to call me back or say good-bye;   10
And further still at an unearthly height,
One luminary clock against the sky

Proclaimed the time was neither wrong nor right.
I have been one acquainted with the night.

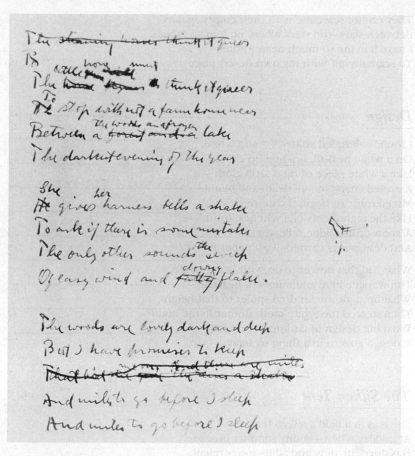

Manuscript of Robert Frost's "Stopping by Woods on a Snowy Evening." The first page of the manuscript is lost.

Desert Places

[1936]

Snow falling and night falling fast oh fast
In a field I looked into going past,
And the ground almost covered smooth in snow,
But a few weeds and stubble showing last.   4

The woods around it have it—it is theirs.
All animals are smothered in their lairs.
I am too absent-spirited to count;
The loneliness includes me unawares.   8

And lonely as it is that loneliness
Will be more lonely ere it will be less—
A blanker whiteness of benighted snow
With no expression, nothing to express.   12

They cannot scare me with their empty spaces
Between stars—on stars where no human race is.
I have it in me so much nearer home
To scare myself with my own desert places.   16

Design   [1936]

I found a dimpled spider, fat and white,
On a white heal-all, holding up a moth
Like a white piece of rigid satin cloth—
Assorted characters of death and blight   4
Mixed ready to begin the morning right,
Like the ingredients of a witches' broth—
A snow-drop spider, a flower like froth,
And dead wings carried like a paper kite.   8

What had that flower to do with being white,
The wayside blue and innocent heal-all?
What brought the kindred spider to that height,
Then steered the white moth thither in the night?   12
What but design of darkness to appall?—
If design govern in a thing so small.

The Silken Tent   [1942]

She is as in a field a silken tent
At midday when a sunny summer breeze
Has dried the dew and all its ropes relent,
So that in guys it gently sways at ease,   4
And its supporting central cedar pole,
That is its pinnacle to heavenward
And signifies the sureness of the soul,
Seems to owe naught to any single cord,   8
But strictly held by none, is loosely bound
By countless silken ties of love and thought
To everything on earth the compass round,
And only by one's going slightly taut   12
In the capriciousness of summer air
Is of the slightest bondage made aware.

Come In   [1942]

As I came to the edge of the woods.
Thrush music—hark!
Now if it was dusk outside,
Inside it was dark.   4

The Silken Tent

~~In Praise of Your Poise~~

She is as ~~on the lawn~~ in a field a silken tent
At midday when a ~~sunny~~ summer breeze
Has dried the dew and all its ropes relent,
So that in guys it gently sways at ease,

And its supporting central cedar pole,
That is its ~~summit pointing~~ pinnacle to heavenward
And signifies the sureness of the soul,
Seems to owe ~~nothing~~ naught to any single cord,

But strictly held by none, is loosely bound
By countless silken ties of love and thought
To everything on earth the compass round,
And only by one's going slightly taut
In the capriciousness of summer air,
Is of the slightest bondage made aware.

Page from Frost's notebooks, showing "The Silken Tent."

Too dark in the woods for a bird
By sleight of wing
To better its perch for the night,
Though it still could sing.   8

The last of the light of the sun
That had died in the west
Still lived for one song more
In a thrush's breast.   12

Far in the pillared dark
Thrush music went—
Almost like a call to come in
To the dark and lament.   16

But no, I was out for stars:
I would not come in.
I meant not even if asked,
And I hadn't been.   20

The Most of It
[1942]

He thought he kept the universe alone;
For all the voice in answer he could wake
Was but the mocking echo of his own
From some tree-hidden cliff across the lake.
Some morning from the boulder-broken beach   5
He would cry out on life, that what it wants
Is not its own love back in copy speech,
But counter-love, original response.
And nothing ever came of what he cried
Unless it was the embodiment that crashed   10
In the cliff's talus on the other side,
And then in the far distant water splashed,
But after a time allowed for it to swim,
Instead of proving human when it neared
And someone else additional to him,   15
As a great buck it powerfully appeared,
Pushing the crumpled water up ahead,
And landed pouring like a waterfall,
And stumbled through the rocks with horny tread,
And forced the underbrush—and that was all.   20

ROBERT FROST ON POETRY

The Figure a Poem Makes

Abstraction is an old story with the philosophers, but it has been like a new toy in the hands of the artists of our day. Why can't we have any one quality of poetry we choose by itself? We can have in thought. Then it will go hard if we can't in practice. Our lives for it.

Granted no one but a humanist much cares how sound a poem is if it is only *a* sound. The sound is the gold in the ore. Then we will have the sound out alone and dispense with the inessential. We do till we make the discovery that the object in writing poetry is to make all poems sound as different as possible from each other, and the resources for that of vowels, consonants, punctuation, syntax, words, sentences, meter are not enough. We need the help of context—meaning—subject matter. That is the greatest help towards variety. All that can be done with words is soon told. So also with meters—particularly in our language where there are virtually but two, strict iambic and loose iambic. The ancients with many were still poor if they depended on meters for all tune. It is painful to watch our sprung-rhythmists straining at the point of omitting one short from a foot for relief from monotony. The possibilities for tune from the dramatic tones of meaning struck across the rigidity of a limited meter are endless. And we are back in poetry as merely one more art of having something to say, sound or unsound. Probably better if sound, because deeper and from wider experience.

Then there is this wildness whereof it is spoken. Granted again that it has an equal claim with sound to being a poem's better half. If it is a wild tune, it is a poem. Our problem then is, as modern abstractionists, to have the wildness pure: to be wild with nothing to be wild about. We bring up as aberrationists, giving way to undirected associations and kicking ourselves from one chance suggestion to another in all directions as of a hot afternoon in the life of a grasshopper. Theme alone can steady us down. Just as the first mystery was how a poem could have a tune in such a straightness as meter, so the second mystery is how a poem can have wildness and at the same time a subject that shall be fulfilled.

It should be of the pleasure of a poem itself to tell how it can. The figure a poem makes. It begins in delight and ends in wisdom. The figure is the same as for love. No one can really hold that the ecstasy should be static and stand still in one place. It begins in delight, it inclines to the impulse, it assumes direction with the first line laid down, it runs a course of lucky events, and ends in a clarification of life—not necessarily a great clarification, such as sects and cults are founded on, but in a momentary stay against confusion. It has denouement. It has an outcome that though unforeseen was predestined from the first image of the original mood—and indeed from the very mood. It is but a trick poem and no poem at all if the best of it was thought of first and saved for the last. It finds its own name as it goes and discovers the best waiting for it in some final phrase at once wise and sad—the happy-sad blend of the drinking song.

No tears in the writer, no tears in the reader. No surprise for the writer, no surprise for the reader. For me the initial delight is in the surprise of remembering something I didn't know I knew. I am in a place, in a situation, as if I had materialized from cloud or risen out of the ground. There is a glad recognition of the long lost and the rest follows. Step by step the wonder of unexpected supply keeps growing. The impressions most useful to my purpose seem always those I was unaware of and so made no note of at the time when taken, and the conclusion is come to that like giants we are always hurling experience ahead of us to pave the future with against the day when we may want to strike a line of purpose across it for somewhere. The line will have the more charm for not being mechanically straight. We enjoy the straight crookedness of a good walking stick. Modern instruments of precision are being used to make things crooked as if by eye and hand in the old days.

I tell how there may be a better wildness of logic than of inconsequence. But the logic is backward, in retrospect, after the act. It must be more felt than seen ahead like prophecy. It must be a revelation, or a series of revelations, as much for the poet as for the reader. For it to be that there must have been the greatest freedom of the material to move about in it and to establish relations in it regardless of time and space, previous relation, and everything but affinity. We prate of freedom. We call our schools free because we are not free to stay away from them till we are sixteen years of age. I have given up my democratic prejudices and now willingly set the lower classes free to be completely taken care of by the upper classes. Political freedom is nothing to me. I bestow it right and left. All I would keep for myself is the freedom of my material—the condition of body and mind now and then to summons aptly from the vast chaos of all I have lived through.

Scholars and artists thrown together are often annoyed at the puzzle of where they differ. Both work from knowledge; but I suspect they differ most importantly in the way their knowledge is come by. Scholars get theirs with conscientious thoroughness along projected lines of logic; poets theirs cavalierly and as it happens in and out of books. They stick to nothing deliberately, but let what will stick to them like burrs where they walk in the fields. No acquirement is on assignment, or even self-assignment. Knowledge of the second kind is much more available in the wild free ways of wit and art. A school boy may be defined as one who can tell you what he knows in the order in which he learned it. The artist must value himself as he snatches a thing from some previous order in time and space into a new order with not so much as a ligature clinging to it of the old place where it was organic.

More than once I should have lost my soul to radicalism if it had been the originality it was mistaken for by young converts. Originality and initiative are what I ask for my country. For myself the originality need be no more than the freshness of a poem run in the way I have described: from delight to wisdom. The figure is the same as for love. Like a piece of ice on a hot stove the poem must ride on its own melting. A poem may be worked over once it is in being, but may not be worried into being. Its most precious quality will remain its having run itself and carried away the poet with it. Read it a hundred times: it will forever keep its freshness as a metal keeps its fragrance. It can never lose its sense of a meaning that once unfolded by surprise as it went.

From "The Constant Symbol"

There are many other things I have found myself saying about poetry, but the chieftest of these is that it is metaphor, saying one thing and meaning another, saying one thing in terms of another, the pleasure of ulteriority. Poetry is simply made of metaphor. So also is philosophy—and science, too, for that matter, if it will take the soft impeachment from a friend. Every poem is a new metaphor inside or it is nothing. And there is a sense in which all poems are the same old metaphor always.

Every single poem written regular is a symbol small or great of the way the will has to pitch into commitments deeper and deeper to a rounded conclusion and then be judged for whether any original intention it had has been strongly spent or weakly lost; be it in art, politics, school, church, business, love, or marriage—in a piece of work or in a career. Strongly spent is synonymous with kept.

LANGSTON HUGHES

Langston Hughes (1902–1967) was an accomplished poet, short-story writer, dramatist, essayist, and editor. He was born in Joplin, Missouri; he grew up in Lawrence, Kansas, and Cleveland, Ohio; and he spent a year living in Mexico before entering Columbia University in 1921. He left Columbia the following year and traveled extensively in Europe, returning to the United States in the mid-1920s. During these years, Hughes pursued his academic studies at Lincoln University in Pennsylvania (graduating in 1929) and published his first two books of verse,

The Weary Blues (1926) and Fine Clothes to the Jew *(1927). His many achievements in literature, drawing upon spirituals, blues, jazz, and folk expression,
and his rich, productive career have led his biographer, Arnold Rampersad, to
describe him as "perhaps the most representative black American writer."*

*Here we provide a selection of Hughes's poetry that shows the range of
his themes and the variety of his speaking voices. We begin with one of his
best-known works, "The Negro Speaks of Rivers," a poem first published in the
June 1921 issue of* The Crisis, *the official magazine of the NAACP. We give
eleven of Hughes's poems here (and we have already given some of his poems
in earlier chapters), and two selections from his prose.*

The Negro Speaks of Rivers   [1921]

I've known rivers:
I've known rivers ancient as the world and older than the flow of
human blood in human veins.

My soul has grown deep like the rivers.

I bathed in the Euphrates when dawns were young.
I built my hut near the Congo and it lulled me to sleep.   5
I looked upon the Nile and raised the pyramids above it.
I heard the singing of the Mississippi when Abe Lincoln went
down to New Orleans, and I've seen its muddy bosom turn all golden
in the sunset.

I've known rivers:
Ancient, dusky rivers.

My soul has grown deep like the rivers.   10

Mother to Son   [1922]

Well, son, I'll tell you:
Life for me ain't been no crystal stair.
It's had tacks in it,
And splinters,
And boards torn up,   5
And places with no carpet on the floor—
Bare.
But all the time
I'se been a-climbin' on,
And reachin' landin's,   10
And turnin' corners,
And sometimes goin' in the dark
Where there ain't been no light.
So boy, don't you turn back.
Don't you set down on the steps   15
'Cause you finds it's kinder hard.
Don't you fall now—
For I'se still goin', honey,
I'se still climbin',
And life for me ain't been no crystal stair.   20

The Weary Blues [1925]

Droning a drowsy syncopated tune,
Rocking back and forth to a mellow croon,
   I heard a Negro play.
Down on Lenox Avenue the other night
By the pale dull pallor of an old gas light   5
   He did a lazy sway. . . .
   He did a lazy sway. . . .
To the tune o' those Weary Blues.
With his ebony hands on each ivory key
He made that poor piano moan with melody.   10
   O Blues!
Swaying to and fro on his rickety stool
He played that sad raggy tune like a musical fool.
   Sweet Blues!
Coming from a black man's soul.   15
   O Blues!
In a deep song voice with a melancholy tone
I heard that Negro sing, that old piano moan—
   "Ain't got nobody in all this world,
     Ain't got nobody but ma self.   20
     I's gwine to quit ma frownin'
     And put ma troubles on the shelf."

Thump, thump, thump, went his foot on the floor.
He played a few chords then he sang some more—
   "I got the Weary Blues   25
     And I can't be satisfied.
     Got the Weary Blues
     And can't be satisfied—
     I ain't happy no mo'
     And I wish that I had died."   30
And far into the night he crooned that tune.
The stars went out and so did the moon.
The singer stopped playing and went to bed
While the Weary Blues echoed through his head.
He slept like a rock or a man that's dead.   35

The South [1922]

The lazy, laughing South
With blood on its mouth.
The sunny-faced South,
   Beast-strong,
   Idiot-brained.   5
The child-minded South
Scratching in the dead fire's ashes
For a Negro's bones.
   Cotton and the moon,
   Warmth, earth, warmth,   10

The sky, the sun, the stars,
The magnolia-scented South.
Beautiful, like a woman,
Seductive as a dark-eyed whore,
    Passionate, cruel,   15
    Honey-lipped, syphilitic—
    That is the South.
And I, who am black, would love her
But she spits in my face.
And I, who am black,   20
Would give her many rare gifts
But she turns her back upon me.
    So now I seek the North—
    The cold-faced North,
    For she, they say,   25
    Is a kinder mistress,
And in her house my children
May escape the spell of the South.

Ruby Brown

[1926]

She was young and beautiful
And golden like the sunshine
That warmed her body.
And because she was colored
Mayville had no place to offer her,   5
Nor fuel for the clean flame of joy
That tried to burn within her soul.

One day,
Sitting on old Mrs. Latham's back porch
Polishing the silver,   10
She asked herself two questions
And they ran something like this:
What can a colored girl do
On the money from a white woman's kitchen?
And ain't there any joy in this town?   15

Now the streets down by the river
Know more about this pretty Ruby Brown,
And the sinister shuttered houses of the bottoms
Hold a yellow girl
Seeking an answer to her questions.   20
The good church folk do not mention
Her name any more.

But the white men,
Habitués of the high shuttered houses,
Pay more money to her now   25
Than they ever did before,
When she worked in their kitchens.

Poet to Patron

[1939]

What right has anyone to say
That I
Must throw out pieces of my heart
For pay?   4

For bread that helps to make
My heart beat true,
I must sell myself
To you?   8

A factory shift's better,
A week's meagre pay,
Than a perfumed note asking:
What poems today?   12

Ballad of the Landlord

[1940]

Landlord, landlord,
My roof has sprung a leak.
Don't you member I told you about it
Way last week?   4

Landlord, landlord,
These steps is broken down.
When you come up yourself
It's a wonder you don't fall down.   8

Ten Bucks you say I owe you?
Ten Bucks you say is due?
Well, that's Ten Bucks more'n I'll pay you
Till you fix this house up new.   12

What? You gonna get eviction orders?
You gonna cut off my heat?
You gonna take my furniture and
Throw it in the street?   16

Um-huh! You talking high and mighty.
Talk on—till you get through.
You ain't gonna be able to say a word
If I land my fist on you.   20

Police! Police!
Come and get this man!
He's trying to ruin the government
And overturn the land!   24

Copper's whistle!
Patrol bell!
Arrest.
Precinct Station.
Iron cell.   28

Headlines in press:

MAN THREATENS LANDLORD

∴

TENANT HELD NO BAIL   32

∴

JUDGE GIVES NEGRO 90 DAYS IN COUNTY JAIL.

Too Blue

[1943]

I got those sad old weary blues.
I don't know where to turn.
I don't know where to go.
Nobody cares about you   4
When you sink so low.

What shall I do?
What shall I say?
Shall I take a gun   8
And put myself away?

I wonder if
One bullet would do?
As hard as my head is,   12
It would probably take two.

But I ain't got
Neither bullet nor gun—
And I'm too blue   16
To look for one.

Harlem [1]

[1949]

Here on the edge of hell
Stands Harlem—
Remembering the old lies,
The old kicks in the back,
The old "Be patient"   5
They told us before.
Sure, we remember.
Now when the man at the corner store
Says sugar's gone up another two cents,
And bread one,   10
And there's a new tax on cigarettes—
We remember the job we never had,
Never could get,
And can't have now
Because we're colored.   15

So we stand here
On the edge of hell
In Harlem

And look out on the world
And wonder   20
What we're gonna do
In the face of what
We remember.

Theme for English B   [1949]

The instructor said,

> *Go home and write*
> *a page tonight.*
> *And let that page come out of you—*
> *Then, it will be true.*   5

I wonder if it's that simple?
I am twenty-two, colored, born in Winston-Salem.
I went to school there, then Durham, then here
to this college on the hill above Harlem.
I am the only colored student in my class.   10
The steps from the hill lead down into Harlem,
through a park, then I cross St. Nicholas,
Eighth Avenue, Seventh, and I come to the Y,
the Harlem Branch Y, where I take the elevator
up to my room, sit down, and write this page: 15

It's not easy to know what is true for you or me
at twenty-two, my age. But I guess I'm what
I feel and see and hear, Harlem, I hear you:
hear you, hear me—we two—you, me, talk on this page.
(I hear New York, too.) Me—who?   20
Well, I like to eat, sleep, drink, and be in love.
I like to work, read, learn, and understand life.
I like a pipe for a Christmas present,
or records—Bessie, bop, or Bach.
I guess being colored doesn't make me *not* like   25
the same things other folks like who are other races.

So will my page be colored that I write?
Being me, it will not be white.
But it will be
a part of you, instructor.   30
You are white—
yet a part of me, as I am a part of you.
That's American.
Sometimes perhaps you don't want to be a part of me.
Nor do I often want to be a part of you.   35
But we are, that's true!
As I learn from you,
I guess you learn from me—
although you're older—and white—
and somewhat more free.   40

This is my page for English B.

Poet to Bigot [1953]

I have done so little
For you,
And you have done so little
For me,
That we have good reason 5
Never to agree.

I, however,
Have such meagre
Power,
Clutching at a 10
Moment,
While you control
An hour.

But your hour is
A stone. 15

My moment is
A flower.

LANGSTON HUGHES ON POETRY

The Negro and the Racial Mountain [1926]

Hughes often examined the challenges he faced in writing both as an American and an African American, as in this provocative essay published in 1926.

One of the most promising of the young Negro poets said to me once, "I want to be a poet—not a Negro poet," meaning, I believe, "I want to write like a white poet"; meaning subconsciously, "I would like to be a white poet"; meaning behind that, "I would like to be white." And I was sorry the young man said that, for no great poet has ever been afraid of being himself. And I doubted then that, with his desire to run away spiritually from his race, this boy would ever be a great poet. But this is the mountain standing in the way of any true Negro art in America—this urge within the race toward whiteness, the desire to pour racial individuality into the mold of American standardization, and to be as little Negro and as much American as possible.

But let us look at the immediate background of this young poet. His family is of what I suppose one would call the Negro middle class: people who are by no means rich yet never uncomfortable nor hungry—smug, contented, respectable folk, members of the Baptist church. The father goes to work every morning. He is a chief steward at a large white club. The mother sometimes does fancy sewing or supervises parties for the rich families of the town. The children go to a mixed school. In the home they read white papers and magazines. And the mother often says "Don't be like niggers" when the children are bad. A frequent phrase from the father is, "Look how well a white man does things." And so the word white comes to be unconsciously a symbol of all the virtues. It holds for the children beauty, morality, and money. The whisper of "I want to be white" runs silently through their minds. This young poet's home is, I believe, a fairly typical home of the colored middle class. One sees immediately how difficult it would be for an artist born in such a home to interest himself in interpreting the beauty of his own people. He is never taught to see that beauty. He is taught rather not to see it, or if he does, to be ashamed of it when it is not according to Caucasian patterns.

For racial culture the home of a self-styled "high-class" Negro has nothing better to offer. Instead there will perhaps be more aping of things white than in a less cultured or less wealthy home. The father is perhaps a doctor, lawyer, landowner, or politician. The mother may be a social worker, or a teacher, or she may do nothing and have a maid. Father is often dark but he has usually married the lightest woman he could find. The family attend a fashionable church where few really colored faces are to be found. And they themselves draw a color line. In the North they go to white theaters and white movies. And in the South they have at least two cars and a house "like white folks." Nordic manners, Nordic faces, Nordic hair, Nordic art (if any), and an Episcopal heaven. A very high mountain indeed for the would-be racial artist to climb in order to discover himself and his people.

But then there are the low-down folks, the so-called common element, and they are the majority—may the Lord be praised! The people who have their nip of gin on Saturday nights and are not too important to themselves or the community, or too well fed, or too learned to watch the lazy world go round. They live on Seventh Street in Washington or State Street in Chicago and they do not particularly care whether they are like white folks or anybody else. Their joy runs, bang! into ecstasy. Their religion soars to a shout. Work maybe a little today, rest a little tomorrow. Play awhile. Sing awhile. O, let's dance! These common people are not afraid of spirituals, as for a long time their more intellectual brethren were, and jazz is their child. They furnish a wealth of colorful, distinctive material for any artist because they still hold their own individuality in the face of American standardizations. And perhaps these common people will give to the world its truly great Negro artist, the one who is not afraid to be himself. Whereas the better-class Negro would tell the artist what to do, the people at least let him alone when he does appear. And they are not ashamed of him—if they know he exists at all. And they accept what beauty is their own without question.

5   Certainly there is, for the American Negro artist who can escape the restrictions the more advanced among his own group would put upon him, a great field of unused material ready for his art. Without going outside his race and even among the better classes with their "white" culture and conscious American manners, but still Negro enough to be different, there is sufficient matter to furnish a black artist with a lifetime of creative work. And when he chooses to touch on the relations between Negroes and whites in this country with their innumerable overtones and undertones, surely, and especially for literature and the drama, there is an inexhaustible supply of themes at hand. To these the Negro artist can give his racial individuality, his heritage of rhythm and warmth, and his incongruous humor that so often, as in the Blues, becomes ironic laughter mixed with tears. But let us look again at the mountain.

A prominent Negro clubwoman in Philadelphia paid eleven dollars to hear Raquel Meller sing Andalusian popular songs. But she told me a few weeks before she would not think of going to hear "that woman," Clara Smith, a great black artist, sing Negro folksongs. And many an upper-class Negro church, even now, would not dream of employing a spiritual in its services. The drab melodies in white folks' hymnbooks are much to be preferred. "We want to worship the Lord correctly and quietly. We don't believe in 'shouting.' Let's be dull like the Nordics," they say, in effect.

The road for the serious black artist, then, who would produce a racial art is most certainly rocky and the mountain is high. Until recently he received almost no encouragement for his work from either white or colored people. The fine novels of Chestnutt[1] go out of print with neither race noticing their passing. The quaint charm and humor of Dunbar's[2] dialect verse brought to him, in his day, largely the same kind of encouragement one would give a sideshow freak (A colored man writing poetry! How odd!) or a clown (How amusing!).

The present vogue in things Negro, although it may do as much harm as good for the budding colored artist, has at least done this: it has brought him forcibly to the attention of his own people among whom for so long, unless the other race had noticed him beforehand, he was a prophet with little honor. I understand that Charles Gilpin acted for years in Negro theaters without any special acclaim from his own, but when Broadway gave him eight curtain calls, Negroes, too, began to beat a tin pan in his honor. I know a young colored writer, a manual worker by day, who had been writing well for the colored magazines for some years, but it was not until he recently broke into the white publications and his first book was accepted by a prominent New York publisher that the "best" Negroes in his city took the trouble to discover that he lived there. Then almost immediately they decided to give a grand dinner for him. But the society ladies were careful to whisper to his mother that perhaps she'd better not come. They were not sure she would have an evening gown.

The Negro artist works against an undertow of sharp criticism and misunderstanding from his own group and unintentional bribes from the whites. "O, be respectable, write about nice people, show how good we are," say the Negroes. "Be stereotyped, don't go too far, don't shatter our illusions about you, don't amuse us too seriously. We will pay you," say the whites. Both would have told Jean Toomer not to write "Cane." The colored people did not praise it. The white people did not buy it. Most of the colored people who did read "Cane" hate it. They are afraid of it. Although the critics gave it good reviews the public remained indifferent. Yet (excepting the work of DuBois[3]) "Cane" contains the finest prose written by a Negro in America. And like the singing of Robeson,[4] it is truly racial.

10   But in spite of the Nordicized Negro intelligentsia and the desires of some white editors we have an honest American Negro literature already with us. Now I await the rise of the Negro theater. Our folk music, having

---

[1]**Chestnutt** Charles Chestnutt (1858–1932), African-American novelist.   [2]**Dunbar** Paul Laurence Dunbar (1872–1906), African-American poet (for an example of his work, see page 716).   [3]**DuBois** William Edward Burghardt DuBois (1868–1963), African-American historian, sociologist, writer.   [4]**Robeson** Paul Robeson (1898–1976), African-American singer and actor.

achieved world-wide fame, offers itself to the genius of the great individual American Negro composer who is to come. And within the next decade I expect to see the work of a growing school of colored artists who paint and model the beauty of dark faces and create with new technique the expressions of their own soul-world. And the Negro dancers who will dance like flame and the singers who will continue to carry our songs to all who listen— they will be with us in even greater numbers tomorrow.

Most of my own poems are racial in theme and treatment, derived from the life I know. In many of them I try to grasp and hold some of the meanings and rhythms of jazz. I am sincere as I know how to be in these poems and yet after every reading I answer questions like these from my own people: Do you think Negroes should always write about Negroes? I wish you wouldn't read some of your poems to white folks. How do you find anything interesting in a place like a cabaret? Why do you write about black people? You aren't black. What makes you do so many jazz poems?

But jazz to me is one of the inherent expressions of Negro life in America: the eternal tom-tom beating in the Negro soul—the tom-tom of revolt against weariness in a white world, a world of subway trains, and work, work, work; the tom-tom of joy and laughter, and pain swallowed in a smile. Yet the Philadelphia clubwoman is ashamed to say that her race created it and she does not like me to write about it. The old subconscious "white is best" runs through her mind. Years of study under white teachers, a lifetime of white books, pictures, and papers, and white manners, morals, and Puritan standards made her dislike the spirituals. And now she turns up her nose at jazz and all its manifestations—likewise almost everything else distinctly racial. She doesn't care for the Winold Reiss portraits of Negroes because they are "too Negro." She does not want a true picture of herself from anybody. She wants the artist to flatter her, to make the white world believe that all Negroes are as smug and as near white in soul as she wants to be. But, to my mind, it is the duty of the younger Negro artist, if he accepts any duties at all from outsiders, to change through the force of his art that old whispering "I want to be white," hidden in the aspirations of his people, to "Why should I want to be white? I am a Negro—and beautiful!"

So I am ashamed for the black poet who says, "I want to be a poet, not a Negro poet," as though his own racial world were not as interesting as any other world. I am ashamed, too, for the colored artist who runs from the painting of Negro faces to the painting of sunsets after the manner of the academicians because he fears the strange un-whiteness of his own features. An artist must be free to choose what he does, certainly, but he must also never be afraid to do what he might choose.

Let the blare of Negro jazz bands and the bellowing voice of Bessie Smith singing Blues penetrate the closed ears of the colored near-intellectuals "until they listen and perhaps understand. Let Paul Robeson singing Water Boy, and Rudolph Fisher writing about the streets of Harlem, and Jean Toomer holding the heart of Georgia in his hands, and Aaron Douglas drawing strange black fantasies cause the smug Negro middle class to turn from their white, respectable, ordinary books and papers to catch a glimmer of their own beauty. We younger Negro artists who create now intend to express our individual dark-skinned selves without fear or shame. If white people are pleased we are glad. If they are not, it doesn't matter. We know we are beautiful. And ugly too. The tom-tom cries and the tom-tom laughs.

If colored people are pleased we are glad. If they are not, their displeasure doesn't matter either. We build our temples for tomorrow, strong as we know how, and we stand on top of the mountain, free within ourselves.

On the Cultural Achievements of African-Americans   [1960]

Without them, on my part, there would have been no poems; without their hopes and fears and dreams, no stories; without their struggles, no dramas; without their music, no songs.

Had I not heard as a child in the little churches of Kansas and Missouri, "Deep river, my home is over Jordan," or "My Lord, what a morning when the stars begin to fall," I might not have come to realize the lyric beauty of *living* poetry. . . .

There is so much richness in Negro humor, so much beauty in black dreams, so much dignity in our struggle, and so much universality in our problems, in *us*—in each living human being of color—that I do not understand the tendency today that some American Negro artists have of seeking to run away from themselves, of running away from *us,* of being afraid to sing our own songs, paint our pictures, write about ourselves—when it is our music that has given America its greatest music, our humor that has enriched its entertainment media for the past 100 years, our rhythm that has guided its dancing feet from plantation days to the Charleston. . . . Yet there are some of us who say, "Why write about Negroes? Why not be *just a writer?*" And why not—if one wants to be "just a writer?" Negroes in a free world should be whatever each wants to be—even if it means being "just a writer. . . . "

There is nothing to be ashamed of in the strength and dignity and laughter of the Negro people. And there is nothing to be afraid of in the use of their material.

Could you be possibly afraid that the rest of the world will not accept it? Our spirituals are sung and loved in the great concert halls of the whole world. Our blues are played from Topeka to Tokyo. Harlem's jive talk delights Hong Kong and Paris. Those of our writers who have *most* concerned themselves with our very special problems are translated and read around the world. The local, the regional can—and does—become universal. Sean O'Casey's Irishmen are an example. So I would say to young Negro writers, do not be afraid of yourself. *You* are the world. . . .

27

Poetry and Translation

During the course of reading this section you will be invited to translate a poem. If you are competent in a language other than English, you will be asked to translate a poem of your choice from that language, and also to write about the particular difficulties you experienced while translating. Or you can choose to translate one of the French, Spanish, and Japanese poems that we print in this chapter; you don't have to know any of these languages, since we provide English translations.

A POEM TRANSLATED FROM SPANISH, IN AN ESSAY BY A STUDENT

We begin with a student's discussion of his translation of Federico García Lorca's short poem, "Despedida."

```
                                            Guzman 1
George Guzman
Professor Tredo
English 101
20 September 2005
              García Lorca's "Despedida"
    My father sometimes quotes, half-jokingly
although it is a serious poem, Federico García
Lorca's "Despedida," which he learned when he
was a schoolboy in Cuba. Because it is short and
because he quotes it so often, I know it by
heart. In Spanish it goes like this:
```

Despedida

Si muero,
dejad el balcón abierto.

El niño come naranjas.
(Desde mi balcón lo veo.)

El segador siega el trigo.
(Desde mi balcón lo siento.)

¡Si muero,
dejad el balcón abierto!

When I translated the poem for this assignment, I didn't find any serious difficulties--probably because the poem does not rhyme. The only word in the poem that I think is especially hard to translate is the title, "Despedida." It comes from a verb, "despedir," which Spanish-English dictionaries define as "to take one's leave." In English, however, no one "takes one's leave"; we just say "Goodbye," and go. But "Goodbye" is too informal for "Despedida," so I settled on "Farewell." No one speaking English ever says "Farewell," but I think it catches the slight formality of the Spanish, and it has the right tone for this poem about a man who is talking about leaving the world. Still another possibility that seems good to me is "parting."

Aside from the title, I at first found the poem easy to translate, but on further thinking about my translation, I found a few things that I wish I could do better. Here, for a start, is my literal translation.

Farewell

If I die,
leave the balcony open.

The boy eats oranges.
(From my balcony I see him.)

>   The reaper reaps the wheat.
>   (From my balcony I hear him.)
>   If I die,
>   leave the balcony open!

There are subtle things in this poem, but most
of them can be translated easily. For instance,
in the first and the last stanzas the poet speaks
of "el balcón" (the balcony), but in the middle
two stanzas he speaks of "mi balcón" (my
balcony). That is, in the first and last stanzas,
where he imagines himself dead, he realizes the
balcony is not his anymore, but is simply "the
balcony." There is no difficulty in translating
this idea from Spanish into English.

   Because I knew the poem by heart, I
translated it without first looking at the
original on the page. But when I wrote it out in
Spanish, too, I became aware of a small
difficulty. In Spanish if a sentence ends with an
exclamation point (or a question mark) it also
begins with one, so the reader knows at the
beginning of a sentence what sort of sentence it
will be. We don't do this in English, and I
think something is lost in English. The two
exclamation marks in García Lorca's last
sentence, one at the beginning and one at the
end, seem to me to call more attention to the
sentence, and make it more sad. And since the
first and last sentences are identical except for
the exclamation marks around the last sentence,
the punctuation makes the last sentence
different from the first. Superficially the poem
begins and ends with the same sentence, but the
last sentence is much more final.

   A second difficulty is this: On rereading my
translation, I wondered if it should try to

Guzman 4

catch the o sounds that in the original are at
the end of every line except the third. It's hard
to explain, but I think this repeated o sound has
several effects. Certainly the repetition of the
sound gives unity to the poem. But it also is
part of the meaning, in two ways. First of all,
the sound of o is like a lament or a cry. Second,
because the sound is repeated again and again, in
line after line, it is as if the poet wants the
present to continue, doesn't want to stop, wants
to keep living. Obviously he is not looking
forward to dying. He doesn't say anything about
hoping to go to heaven. All he thinks of is what
he sees now, and he suggests that he would like
to keep seeing it from his balcony.

    Balcón in Spanish means, as I have translated
it, "balcony," but to say "leave the balcony
open"--which is perfectly all right in Spanish--
sounds a little funny in English, maybe
especially because we don't have many balconies
here, unlike (I am told) Spain. The idea of
course is to leave open the door, or if it is
glass it is also a window, that leads to the
balcony. Maybe, then, it makes better sense to
be a little free in the translation, and to say,
"Leave the window open," or even "Do not draw
the curtain," or some such thing. In fact, if we
can put "window" at the end of the line, we get
the o sound of the original.

        If I die,
    Leave open the window.
But in the original the first line ("Si muero,"
literally "If I die") has this o sound also, and
I can't think of any way of getting this into
the translation. For a moment I thought of
beginning,

Guzman 5

```
      If I go,
    Leave open the window,
but "If I go" just isn't a moving way of saying
"If I die," which is what "Si muero" means.
Still, we might translate line 4 as "I see him
from my window," and line 6 as "I hear him from
my window." In the end, I decided not to begin
by saying "If I go," but (even though I lose the
o sound in the first line) to substitute "window"
for the "balcony" in lines 2, 4, and 6, in order
to get the repetition and the sad o sound. My
final version goes like this:
                    Farewell
      If I die,
    leave open the window.
      The boy eats oranges.
  (I see him from my window.)
      The reaper reaps the wheat.
  (I hear him from my window.)
      If I die,
    leave open the window!
```

 TOPICS FOR CRITICAL THINKING AND WRITING

Here are our responses. If yours differ, consider putting them into writing.

1. This seems like an excellent translation to us. Do you agree?
2. When the student shared his essay with others in the class, it was praised for being "thoughtful." What gives the essay this quality?

A Note on Using the First-Person Singular Pronoun in Essays

Some handbooks on writing tell students never to use *I* in an essay. But this rule is too rigid; in the case of the essay you have just read, the personal touches make it all the more interesting and engaging. Often the problem is not really with the use of *I*, but, rather, with the absence of explanation and evidence that make clear what prompted the "I" to respond as he or she does. This student does a good job of focusing on the poem, commenting on details of language, and keeping the nature of the assignment in mind. His use of *I* occurs as part of a careful analysis and argument.

TRANSLATING A POEM OF YOUR CHOICE, AND COMMENTING ON THE TRANSLATION

If you are at ease in a language other than English, translate a short poem from that language into English. It may be a poem that you learned in school or at home or on the street.

We suggest that you begin by jotting down a line-for-line prose translation, and then work on a poetic version. Your prose version of course will not be a word-for-word translation. After all, a word-for-word translation of the Spanish "Me llamo Juan" is "Me [or "Myself"] I call John," but no one speaking English says this. The English version of these words is "My name is John"—even though the Spanish word for *name (nombre)* does not appear in the original sentence. Similarly, a native speaker of French, when asked whether he or she is going to class this morning , may reply "Mais oui," which in a word-for-word translation would be "But yes." In English, however, we would simply say "Yes" or "Certainly," and therefore the "But" ought to be omitted in a translation. Or consider the phrase "les hommes d'équipage" in the first line of Baudelaire's "L'Albatros" (see page 968). A word-for-word translation would be "men of the crew," but does one say this? Perhaps "members of the crew" is better? Or perhaps simply "the crew"? Or "crewmen"? Or, perhaps best of all, "sailors"? In any case, the French *equipage* certainly cannot be translated as "equipment." (Translators call words that look alike but have different meanings "false friends." Examples: French *advertissement* means "warning"; German *also* means "therefore"; Spanish *constipado* means "having a head cold.")

The prose translation *ought to sound like English*, and this means going beyond a word-for-word translation, at least to a phrase-by-phrase translation. If English is not your native language, you may want to check your prose version with a native-born speaker of English. In any case, once you have a prose version that is in idiomatic English, try to put it into a poetic form.

This does not mean that (assuming your original uses rhyme) you must preserve the exact rhyme scheme. If the original rhymes *abab*, you may find it satisfactory to produce a version in which only the second and fourth lines rhyme. Similarly, even if the original line has 11 or 12 syllables, you may prefer to reduce the line to 10 syllables because the pentameter line (10 syllables) is so widely used in English that it seems natural. Admittedly, your task is easier if you choose an unrhymed poem, and much of the world's poetry—to cite only two instances, Native American poetry and Japanese poetry—does not use rhyme. (We discuss one Japanese form, the haiku, on page 962.)

When you have done your best, relax for a while, and then jot down (in preparation for drafting an essay that will accompany your translation) some notes about the particular problems involved in translating the work. Is there a pun in the original that is impossible to translate? Are there historical or mythological allusions that are clear to people who belong to the culture that produced the poem but that are obscure to outsiders? Are there qualities in the original language (specialists call it "the source language") that simply cannot be reproduced in the "host" (or "target") language? For instance, Japanese has several verbs meaning "to give"; the word used in "I gave you a book" differs from the word in "You gave me a book." It is rather as if one had to say, "You bestowed a book on me" — but of course no one *does* say this in English. What, then, is a translator to do?

In the end, you will produce a translation, and an essay of some 500 words, explaining the particular difficulties you encountered, and perhaps explaining the hardest decisions that you ultimately made.

LAST-MINUTE HELP:
THREE SPANISH POEMS

If you don't know a poem in a language other than English, consider translating one or both of these Spanish folk songs, or, finally, the poem we print by the Chilean poet Gabriela Mistral.

Ya se van los pastores, alla Estremadura	The shepherds are already leaving on their way to Estremadura
Ya se queda la Sierra triste y obscura.	And the mountain ridge is already sad and gloomy.
Ya se van los pastores ya se van marchando	The shepherds are already going, they are already departing
Ya las pobres niñas se queden llorando.	And the poor girls remain there, crying.

Here is the second song:

Una gallina con pollos cinco duro me costó	I bought a hen and chicks for five duros
Corrocloclo corrocloclo	Corrocloclo corrocloclo
La compré por la mañana, y a la tarde se perdió	I bought her in the morning and in the afternoon it lost its way
Corrocloclo corrocloclo	Corrocloclo corrocloclo
Yo no siento la gallina ni el dinero que costó	I'm not sorry about the hen or the money it cost
Corrocloclo corrocloclo	Corrocloclo corrocloclo
Solo siento los pollitos que sin madre los quedó	I'm only sorry for the chicks who are left without a mother
Corrocloclo corrocloclo.	Corrocloclo corrocloclo.

GABRIELA MISTRAL

Lucila Godoy Alacayaga (1889-1957) adopted the pseudonym Gabriela Mistral. A teacher and a director of schools in Chile, she achieved fame there in 1914, when she won first prize in a national poetry contest; she received international fame in 1945, when she was awarded the Nobel Prize for literature, the first Latin-American writer to win the award. She was also distinguished in two other careers, as an educator—she is esteemed for her revision of the Mexican school system and she was a beloved professor at Barnard College in New York—and as a figure in the world of international politics, representing Chile in the League of Nations and the United Nations.

The following poem originates in a response to a statue, Rodin's The Thinker. If you do work on a translation of Mistral's poem, you might keep in mind a comment by an earlier translator of her work, the poet Langston Hughes, who in his Introduction to Selected Poems of Gabriela Mistral (1957) wrote: "I have no theories of translation. I simply try to transfer into English as much as I can of the literal content, emotion, and style of each poem." Unfortunately Hughes did not include a translation of the following poem.

El Pensador de Rodin

Con el mentón caído sobre la mano ruda,
el Pensador se acuerda que es carne de la huesa,
carne fatal, delante del destino denuda,
carne que odia la muerte, y tembló de belleza.   4

Y tembló de amor, toda su primavera ardiente,
y ahora, al otoño, anégase de verdad y tristeza.
El "de morir tenemos" pasa sobre su frente,
en todo agudo bronce, cuando la noche empieza.   8

Y en la angustia, sus músculos se hienden, sufridores.
Los surcos de su carne se llenan de terrores.
Se hiende, como la hoja de otoño, al Señor fuerte

que la llama en los bronces ... Y no hay árbol torcido   12
de sol en la llanura, ni león de flanco herido,
crispados como este hombre que medita en la muerte.

Rodin's Thinker

*Translated by Gustavo Alfaro**

With his chin fallen on his rough hand,
the Thinker, remembering that his flesh is of the grave,
mortal flesh, naked before its fate,
flesh that hates death, trembled for beauty.   4

And he trembled for love, his whole ardent spring,
and now in autumn, he is overcome with truth and sadness.
"We must die" passes across his brow,
in every piercing trumpet sound, when night begins to fall.   8

***Translator's note:** Mistral's *bronce* in line 8 and *bronces* in line 12 I translate as *trumpet sound* and *trumpet calls*. Given the context, this reading seems to me to be more plausible than a reading that takes *bronce* and *bronces* to refer to the bronze sculpture itself.

Auguste Rodin, *The Thinker.* (1910. Bronze, height 27½".
The Metropolitan Museum of Art. Gift of Thomas F. Ryan.)

And in his anguish, his long suffering muscles split.
The furrows of his flesh are filled with terrors.
It splits, like the autumn leaf before the mighty Lord

who calls it with trumpet calls . . . And there is no tree twisted   12
by the sun in the plain, nor lion wounded on its side,
as tense as this man who meditates on death.

TRANSLATING HAIKU

Earlier in this book (pages 774–776) we looked at some haiku, a Japanese poetic
form that consists of 17 syllables, arranged into lines of 5, 7, and 5 syllables.
(Strictly speaking, it is written in a continuous line, as we write prose, but it is
conceived as three units, 5-7-5.) It is unrhymed, but some English translations
and imitations use rhyme.

Here is the most famous of all haiku, in Japanese and with a word-by-word
literal translation:

BASHO (1644–1694)

Furuike ya   old pond
kawazu tobikomu   frog jumps in
mizu no oto   water's sound

One of the things that made this poem remarkable was that it probably was the first Japanese poem about a frog that did *not* talk about the noise of the frog croaking, but instead talked about the noise of the water. (By the way, for an American poem that calls attention to the croaking of a frog, see Emily Dickinson's "I'm Nobody! Who are you?" on page 719.)

How to translate Basho's poem? We have already given a literal translation, but here are some efforts at more literary versions:

The old pond
  A frog jumps in
The sound of water.

An old pond
    a
      frog
        jumps
          in—
Plop.

Old garden lake!
  The frog jumps in,
    And the waters wake.

A bog
A frog
A sound
Drowned.

The old pond
  A frog jumps;
    The water slurps.

TOPIC FOR CRITICAL THINKING AND WRITING

Offer your own translation or adaptation of the haiku, perhaps keeping the 5-7-5 arrangement of the original; or compose an original poem that responds to Basho's. Here are two examples of responses that our students have produced:

An old pond—
Basho jumps in;
No more noise.

An old pond—
If Basho were here
I'd push him in.

Here is another haiku by Basho, in Japanese and with a graceless word-by-word translation. (The original has, unusually, nine syllables in the second line, a permissible variation.)

Kare-eda ni
karasu no tomari-keri
aki no kure

withered branch on
crow is perched
autumn evening

Japanese does not usually distinguish between the singular and the plural, so what we translate as "crow is perched" could equally be translated "crows are perched." Further, what we translated as "autumn evening" may equally be translated "late autumn."

The next poem, also by Basho, was composed at the site of a battle where one of Japan's most famous warriors committed suicide after being defeated by forces acting on behalf of his own brother. It is impossible to find an exact parallel in American history, but perhaps the death of Stonewall Jackson at the Battle of Chancellorsville (1863) comes close in feeling, especially because Jackson was mortally wounded by his own men.

Natsu-gusa ya	Summer grasses
tsuwamono-domo ga	strong warriors'
yume no ato	dreams' relics

In the second line, we use "warriors" rather than "soldiers" because the Japanese word has an archaic flavor. (By the way, in this instance, unlike the poem about the crow or crows, the word for "warriors" is plural.) The gist of the idea of the poem is that grasses (or weeds) now flourish where strong soldiers once fought; all that is left of the dreams (or ambitions) of the soldiers is the summer grass. Here are two versions that students produced, using off-rhymes:

Summer grasses	Weeds flourish
All that is left	where soldiers nourished
where warriors passed.	dreams of glory.

Here are two versions, again by students, that retain the 5-7-5 pattern of the original.

On this grassy spot	Grasses grow today
Here once a noble army	Where heroic soldiers died
Dreamed its dream and died.	Leaving bones and dreams.

TOPICS FOR CRITICAL THINKING AND WRITING

1. Try your hand at translating Basho's poems about the crow(s) and about the dead warriors, or invent an adaptation of each poem. You might, for instance, write a poem about a bird in a season other than the fall, and a poem about the ironic implications of some local site.
2. Here are literal translations of two more haiku by Basho. Create versions that are more memorable.

   stillness
   rock into pierce
   locust-voice

   soon die
   no indication of
   locust's voice

FURTHER THOUGHTS ABOUT TRANSLATING POETRY

If you have read the preceding pages and have had the pleasures of wrestling with a translation and of writing an essay about your efforts, you are ready for an advanced course—the next few pages. But even if you have not engaged in the preliminaries, you may find that the following discussion of poems and translations will help you to think about the language and structure of poetry.

We begin these supplementary remarks by looking at a very short poem by the Roman author Catullus (87?–55? BCE). The subject is the paradoxical quality of the feelings of a lover. (There are countless poems about love as a pleasing pain, a heavenly hell, and about the lover as both active and passive, eagerly loving and yet tormented by love. See, for instance, Aphra Behn's poem on page 670.) Here is Catullus' poem:

Odi et amo, quare id faciam, fortasse requiris?
Nescio, sed fieri sentitio et excrucior.

This can be translated more or less literally as:

I hate and I love. Why do I do that, perhaps you ask.
I don't know, but I feel it to be happening, and I am tortured.

Notice that the language of this poem is not so remote from English as it may seem at first glance:

- In the first line, the Latin *odi* ("I hate") is related to the English word *odious; amo* ("I love") to our word *amorous*; and *requiris* ("you ask") to our *require* and *inquire*.
- In the second line, *sentitio* ("I feel") is related to our *sentient*, and *excrucior* ("I am crucified" or "I am tortured") to our *excruciate*. (This last word includes *crux*, or "cross.")

Next—and here we get closer to our topic, poetry—notice the **arrangement** or **pattern** of the words, since one of the things literature does is to put experience into a pattern. In Catullus' little poem, there is a pattern of long and short syllables (but we need not discuss classical versification here), and also a pattern of verbs. Each line contains four verbs. Those in the first line are active ("I hate," "I love," "I do," "you ask"), whereas those in the second line are passive or describe a passive condition ("I don't know," "I feel it to be happening," "I am tortured"). And so we can say that Catullus catches an aspect—or rather, two aspects—of love,

- the sense of activity and also
- the sense of helplessness.

Each verb in the first line is echoed or balanced in the second; thus *Odi et amo* ("I hate and I love") at the beginning of the first line chimes with *sentio et excrucior* ("I feel . . . and I am tortured") at the end of the second. Moreover, the active *faciam* ("I do") in the first line connects with the passive form of the verb, *fieri* ("to be done," "to happen") in the second.

Having tried to convey something of the poetry of Catullus' two lines—something of their artful expressiveness—let's look at a few translations. The original does not rhyme, but many translators have believed that an English version needs to rhyme if it is to be seen and felt as a poem.

I hate and love—the why I cannot tell,
But by my tortures know the fact too well.
                    —Theodore Martin

In the next two versions the translators suggest particular tortures:

I hate and love. Why do that? Good question.
No answer save "I do." Nailed, through either hand.
                    —Frederic Raphael and Kenneth McLeish

> I hate and I love. And if you ask me how,
> I do not know—I only feel it, and I'm torn in two.
> > —Peter Whigham

The first of these versions, by Raphael and McLeish, clearly—perhaps too clearly—evokes crucifixion. The second, with "I'm torn in two," catches the double nature of love that is the subject of Catullus' poem, and it evokes visions of the instrument of torture known as the rack, or perhaps of a victim whose limbs were tied to two or more horses that were then whipped into flight.

Here is one more version:

> "At once I hate and love as well."
> —"In heaven's name, Catullus, how?"
> —"God knows! And yet I feel it now
> Here in my heart: the whole of hell."
> > —M. H. Tattersall

Tattersall's version is free in that it converts the poem into a dialogue and names Catullus, but one can argue that it is true to the spirit of the poem. It is widely agreed that in the translation of poetry the spirit is more important than the letter. Some of the worst—least moving, indeed least readable—translations are word-by-word translations that can claim to be very close to the original but that are unlike anything we can imagine being spoken in English.

CAN POETRY BE TRANSLATED?

Having looked at a range of translations, we can perhaps now move from a particular work to a general problem or question. To translate is (literally) "to carry across"; a text is carried from one language into another. But can poetry be translated? Robert Frost once defined poetry as "what gets lost in translation." He was not the only person to think that poetry can't be translated. An Italian proverb generalizes, "Traduttori, traditori"—that is, "Translators are traitors," or, more freely, "Translation betrays"—but as you can see, much is lost in our translation.

The idea that poetry can't be translated is rooted in the fact that poets make use not only of the gist of the obvious meaning of a word but also of patterns of sound. We can see this most easily by first looking at a statement that is not a poem but that relies heavily on its sounds. Consider

Look before you leap.

The most obvious pattern is the alliteration (words that begin with the same sound), look and leap, but there is also a pattern of stresses. The sentence begins and ends with a stress, and "before" and "you leap" each consist of an unstressed syllable followed by a stressed syllable. If you compare "Look before you leap" with "Watch out before you leap," or with "Before leaping, look around," you'll see that these translations of English words into other English words lose much of what counts in the original.

You might take a moment to try to put into other words such expressions as "There's no fool like an old fool," "Penny wise and pound foolish," or "A penny saved is a penny earned." Even better, if you are familiar with a memorable saying in a language other than English, try to capture its effectiveness in an English translation of your own.

Let's think now of some issues specific to translating poetry. Rhyme of course is a kind of pattern (a recurring sound), and it can cause a translator difficulty, since effective rhyme often conveys some sort of meaning. It may bring together two words that not only sound alike but have some association in common, as in the greeting-card rhymes of *moon* and *June*, or *dove* and *love*. Or a rhyme may achieve a poignant ironic effect by bringing together two words that sound alike but that differ sharply in meaning, such as *light* (with its associations of life) and *night* (with its associations of death). "Look before you leap" doesn't contain rhyme in the usual sense of the word, but the alliterating *l* sounds can be called initial rhyme. And like rhyme, alliteration—because of the identity in sound—can imply some sort of identity between the alliterating words, or as here, it can make an effective contrast: Look implies caution and probably motionless, whereas leap implies reckless activity.

Probably everyone will agree that translators should strive to capture the subtleties of the original, and probably everyone will agree—here we get back to Robert Frost's view—that inevitably much will be lost. But what is gained in translation, or what may be gained, is a new poem.

Something along these line is suggested by Edwin Cranston, a leading translator of classical Japanese poetry, in *A Waka Anthology*. Translators have duties to their authors, but they also have duties to their own powers. Cranston makes this point by calling attention to a tenth-century Japanese poet's assertion that poems "have their seed in the human heart, and burgeon forth into the myriad leaves of words." In similar fashion, Cranston says, the translator "descends into the poem and lets something happen"; the translator serves "as a medium for the new growth." But of course the process of translating is not passive. As Cranston says, if translators enter into the work and listen to it, they also have their own ideas. The original is strongly there, but so is the translator's creative impulse, which has its own direction and has "its own life and integrity. Nothing is more persuasive than something that works, and if a line somehow works, it is hard to abandon it."

The result may be a translation that is free rather than faithful. Or if it is faithful, it is faithful to the spirit of literature rather than to the letter of the original work. If we push this view further than Cranston himself does, the translation—perhaps better called a version or an adaptation—is a success if it has life as a poem, however removed it may be from the original. More than one translator has defended his or her work as Edward FitzGerald (translator of *The Rubaiyat of Omar Khavyamn*) did, by quoting from Ecclesiastes, "Better a live dog than a dead lion." One translator we know tells us he likes to think of the original as a "control." The original serves as a control on the act of translation, though it rests with the translator to decide whether he or she allows the original to control a lot or a little. Translators can give themselves a great deal of freedom, or only a little. But in either case, because their work is a translation of something else, they are always referring back to another text while they compose a new one.

LOOKING AT TRANSLATIONS OF A POEM BY CHARLES BAUDELAIRE

In the following poem the French poet Charles Baudelaire (1821–1867) compares the albatross—majestic when soaring above oceangoing ships, but pitiful when captured and flopping on the deck—with the poet, whose lofty imagination makes him unsuited for the workaday world. The poem was first published in the 1859 edition of Baudelaire's book, *Fleur du mal (Flowers of Evil)*.

L'Albatros   [1859]

Souvent, pour s'amuser, les hommes d'équipage
Prennent des albatros, vastes oiseaux des mers.
Qui suivent, indolents compagnons de voyage,
Le navire glissant sur les gouffres amers.   4

À peine les ont-ils déposés sur les planches,
Que ces rois de l'azur, maladroits et honteux,
Laissent piteusement leurs grandes ailes blanches
Comme des avirons traîner à côté d'eux.   8

Ce voyager ailé, comme il est gauche et veule!
Luis, naguère si beau, qu'il est comique et laid!
L'un agace son bec avec un brûle-gueule,
L'autre mime, en boitant, l'infirme qui volait!   12

Le Poète est semblable au prince des nuées
Qui hante la tempêt se rit de l'archer;
Exilé sur le sol au milieu des huées,
Ses ailes de géant l'empêchent de marcher.   16

A literal translation, almost word by word, would go something as follows. (We retain the lineation of the original, and we offer it not as a satisfactory version of the poem but only as a starting point, in order to help readers who do not know French to follow the poem.)

Often, to amuse themselves, sailors
capture albatrosses, great sea birds,
who follow, indolent companions of the journey,
the ship, gliding on the bitter deeps.   4

As soon as they stretch them out on the deck
these monarchs of the blue, awkward and ashamed,
pitifully let their large white wings
like oars drag by their sides.   8

The winged traveler, how awkward and feeble!
He who a short time ago was so beautiful,
one sailor teases his beak with a clay pipe,
and another, limping, mimics the cripple who flew.   12

The Poet is like the prince of the clouds
who is at home in the tempest and who scorns the archer,
exiled on the earth, an object of scorn,
his giant wings hinder him as he walks.   16

Let's look now at some verse translations of the first stanza. In the original, the first and third lines of each stanza rhyme, as do the second and fourth, the rhyme scheme thus being *abab*. The task of following Baudelaire's rhyme scheme is difficult, and it can lead to very strained lines; some translators therefore prefer to rhyme only two of the four lines, or to settle for an off-rhyme, as in the first example here, where *sea* and *indolently* rhyme, and where *selves* and *gulfs* chime less precisely:

> Sometimes, sailors to amuse themselves
> catch albatrosses, great birds of the sea,
> which as companions follow indolently
> the vessel gliding over bitter gulfs.
> —C. F. MacIntyre

In the next version, all four lines rhyme closely, but, not surprisingly, the translation is somewhat freer:

> Often, when bored, the sailors of the crew
> Trap albatross, the great birds of the seas,
> Mild travelers escorting in the blue
> Ships gliding on the ocean's mysteries.
> —James McGowan

We say this version is freer because, after all, Baudelaire spoke not of "the ocean's mysteries" but of *les gouffres amers*, the bitter deeps. In short, there often is a trade-off between closely following what might be called the formal properties of the poem (in this case, rhyme) and the precise meaning. On the other hand, here is a rhymed translation that is remarkably faithful to the original. We quote the entire version:

> Often, for pastime, mariners will ensnare
> The albatross, that vast sea-bird who sweeps
> On high companionable pinion where
> Their vessel glides upon the bitter deeps.
>
> Torn from his native space, this captive king
> Flounders upon the deck in stricken pride,
> And pitiably lets his great white wing
> Drag like a heavy paddle at his side.
>
> This rider of winds, how awkward he is, and weak!
> How droll he seems, who lately was all grace!
> A sailor pokes a pipestem into his beak;
> Another, hobbling, mocks his trammeled pace.
>
> The Poet is like this monarch of the clouds,
> Familiar of storms, of stars, and of all high things;
> Exiled on earth amidst its hooting crowds,
> He cannot walk, borne down by his giant wings.
> —Richard Wilbur

▓ TOPIC FOR CRITICAL THINKING AND WRITING

Produce your own version—rhymed or unrhymed—of the final stanza of "The Albatross." For your convenience we offer some rhymes that other translators have used, but you are under no compulsion to use them. Mac-Intyre used *mocks, clouds, crowds, walk*; McGowan used *clouds, day, crowds, way*. George Dillon (who collaborated with Edna St. Vincent Millay on a translation of *The Flowers of Evil*) used *cloud, slings, crowd, wings*. Francis Duke, in his translation of *Flowers of Evil*, used *clouds, defiant, crowds, giant*.

28

A Collection of Poems

The first four selections are folk ballads (also called "popular ballads"). For a discussion of this kind of literature, see pages 675-676.

ANONYMOUS BRITISH BALLAD

The Three Ravens

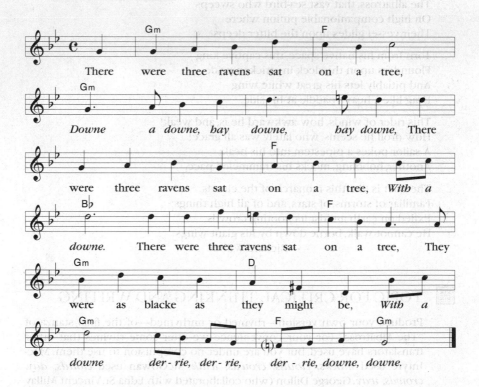

There were three ravens sat on a tree,
  Downe a downe, hay downe, hay downe
There were three ravens sat on a tree,
  With a downe
There were three ravens sat on a tree,   5
They were as blacke as they might be,
  With a downe derrie, derrie, derrie, downe, downe.

The one of them said to his mate,
"Where shall we our breakfast take?"

"Down in yonder greene field,   10
There lies a knight slain under his shield.

His hounds they lie downe at his feete,
So well they can their master keepe.

His haukes they flie so eagerly,
There's no fowle dare him come nie."   15

Downe there comes a fallow° doe,°
As great with yong as she might goe.

She lift up his bloudy hed,
And kist his wounds that were so red.

She got him up upon her backe,   20
And carried him to earthen lake.°

She buried him before the prime,°
She was dead herselfe ere even-song time.

God send every gentleman
Such haukes, such hounds, and such a leman.°   25

---

16 **fallow** brown.   **doe** The "doe," often taken as a suggestive description of the knight's beloved, is probably a vestige of the folk belief that an animal may be an enchanted human being.   21 **lake** pit.   22 **prime** about nine A.M.   25 **leman** sweetheart.

ANONYMOUS BRITISH BALLAD

The Twa Corbies

As I was walking all alane,
I heard twa corbies° making a mane;°
The tane° unto the t' other say,
"Where sall we gang° and dine to-day?"   4

---

2 **twa corbies** two ravens.   **mane** lament.   3 **tane** one.   4 **sall we gang** shall we go.

"In behint yon auld fail dyke,°
I wot° there lies a new-slain knight;
And naebody kens° that he lies there,
But his hawk, his hound, and lady fair.   8

"His hound is to the hunting gane,
His hawk, to fetch the wild-fowl hame,
His lady's ta'en another mate,
So we may mak our dinner sweet.   12

"Ye'll sit on his white hause-bane,°
And I'll pike out his bonny blue een.°
Wi' ae° lock o' his gowden° hair
We'll theek° our nest when it grows bare.   16

"Mony a one for him makes mane,
But nane sall ken whare he is gane;
O'er his white banes, when they are bare,
The wind sall blaw for evermair."   20

---

5 **auld fail dyke** old turf wall.   6 **wot** know.   7 **kens** knows.   13 **hause-bane** neck
bone.   14 **een** eyes.   15 **Wi' ae** With one.   **gowden** golden.   16 **theek** thatch.

ANONYMOUS BRITISH BALLAD

Edward

"Why dois your brand° sae° drap wi' bluid,
       Edward, Edward?
Why dois your brand sae drap wi' bluid?
       And why sae sad gang° yee, O?"
"O, I hae killed my hauke sae guid,   5
       Mither, mither,
O, I hae killed my hauke sae guid,
       And I had nae mair bot hee, O."

"Your haukis bluid was nevir sae reid,
       Edward, Edward,   10
"Your haukis bluid was nevir sae reid,
       My deir son I tell thee, O."
"O, I hae killed my reid-roan steid,
       Mither, mither,
O, I hae killed my reid-roan steid,   15
       That erst° was sae fair and frie,° O."

---

1 **brand** sword.   **sae** so.   4 **gang** go.   16 **erst** once.   **frie** spirited.

"Your steid was auld, and ye hae gat mair,
    Edward, Edward,
Your steid was auld, and ye hae gat mair,
    Sum other dule° ye drie,° O."   20
"O, I hae killed my fadir deir,
    Mither, mither,
O, I hae killed my fadir deir,
    Alas, and wae is mee, O!"

"And whatten penance wul ye drie for that,   25
    Edward, Edward?
And whatten penance wul ye drie for that?
    My deir son, now tell me, O."
"Ile set my feit in yonder boat,
    Mither, mither,   30
Ile set my feit in yonder boat,
    And Ile fare ovir the sea, O."

"And what wul ye doe wi' your towirs and your ha',°
    Edward, Edward,
And what wul ye doe wi' your towirs and your ha',   35
    That were sae fair to see, O?"
"Ile let thame stand tul they doun fa',°
    Mither, mither,
Ile let thame stand tul they doun fa',
    For here nevir mair maun° I bee, O."   40

"And what wul ye leive to your bairns° and your wife,
    Edward, Edward?
And what wul ye leive to your bairns and your wife,
    When ye gang ovir the sea, O?"
"The warldis° room, late° them beg thrae° life,   45
    Mither, mither,
The warldis room, late them beg thrae life,
For thame nevir mair wul I see, O."

"And what wul ye leive to your ain mither deir,
    Edward, Edward?   50
And what wul ye leive to your ain mither deir?
    My deir son, now tell me, O."
"The curse of hell frae me sall ye beir,
    Mither, mither,
The curse of hell frae me sall ye beir.   55
Sic° counseils ye gave to me, O."

---

20 dule grief. **drie** suffer. **33 ha'** hall. **37 fa'** fall. **40 maun** must. **41 bairns**
children. **45 warldis** world's. **late** let. **thrae** through. **56 Sic** Such.

ANONYMOUS

John Henry *

John Henry was a very small boy,
Sitting on his mammy's knee;
He picked up a hammer and a little piece of steel,
Saying, "A hammer'll be the death of me, O Lord,
A hammer'll be the death of me."   5

John Henry went up on the mountain
And he came down on the side.
The mountain was so tall and John Henry was so small
That he laid down his hammer and he cried, "O Lord,"
He laid down his hammer and he cried.   10

John Henry was a man just six feet in height,
Nearly two feet and a half across the breast.
He'd take a nine-pound hammer and hammer all day long
And never get tired and want to rest, O Lord,
And never get tired and want to rest.   15

John Henry was a steel-driving man, O Lord,
He drove all over the world.
He come to Big Bend Tunnel on the C. & O. Road
Where he beat the steam drill down, O Lord,
Where he beat the steam drill down.   20

John Henry said to the captain,
"Captain, you go to town,
Bring me back a twelve-pound hammer
And I'll beat that steam drill down, O Lord,
And I'll beat that steam drill down."   25

They placed John Henry on the right-hand side,
The steam drill on the left;
He said, "Before I let that steam drill beat me down
I'll die with my hammer in my hand, O Lord,
And send my soul to rest."   30

The white folks all got scared,
Thought Big Bend was a-fallin' in;
John Henry hollered out with a very loud shout,
"It's my hammer a-fallin' in the wind, O Lord,
It's my hammer a-fallin' in the wind."   35

John Henry said to his shaker,
"Shaker, you better pray,

---

*John Henry, a black steel driver from West Virginia, worked on the Chesapeake & Ohio's Big Bend Tunnel around 1870. The steel driver hammered a drill (held by his assistant, the "shaker") into rocks so that explosives could then be poured in. In the 1870s, mechanical steel drills were introduced, displacing the steel driver.

For if I miss that little piece of steel
Tomorrow'll be your buryin' day, O Lord,
Tomorrow'll be your buryin' day."   40

The man that invented that steam drill
He thought he was mighty fine.
John Henry sunk the steel fourteen feet
While the steam drill only made nine, O Lord,
While the steam drill only made nine.   45

John Henry said to his loving little wife,
"I'm sick and want to go to bed.
Fix me a place to lay down, Child;
There's a roarin' in my head, O Lord,
There's a roarin' in my head."   50

WILLIAM SHAKESPEARE

*William Shakespeare (1564–1616), born in Stratford-upon-Avon in England,
is chiefly known as a dramatic poet, but he also wrote nondramatic poetry. In
1609 a volume of 154 of his sonnets was published, apparently without his
permission. Probably he chose to keep his sonnets unpublished not because he
thought that they were of little value, but because it was more prestigious to
be an amateur (unpublished) poet than a professional (published) poet.
Although the sonnets were published in 1609, they were probably written in
the mid-1590s, when there was a vogue for sonneteering. A contemporary
writer in 1598 said that Shakespeare's "sugred Sonnets [circulate] among his
private friends."*

Sonnet 29

When, in disgrace with Fortune and men's eyes,
I all alone beweep my outcast state,
And trouble deaf heaven with my bootless° cries,
And look upon myself and curse my fate,
Wishing me like to one more rich in hope,   5
Featured like him, like him° with friends possessed,
Desiring this man's art, and that man's scope,
With what I most enjoy contented least;
Yet in these thoughts myself almost despising,
Haply° I think on thee, and then my state,   10
Like to the lark at break of day arising
From sullen earth, sings hymns at heaven's gate;
　　For thy sweet love rememb'red such wealth brings,
　　That then I scorn to change my state with kings.

---

3 bootless useless.　**6 like him, like him** like a second man, like a third man.
10 Haply Perchance.

JOHN DONNE

John Donne (1572–1631) was born into a Roman Catholic family in England, but in the 1590s he abandoned that faith. In 1615 he became an Anglican priest and soon was known as a great preacher. Of his sermons 160 survive, including one with the famous line, "No man is an island, entire of itself; every man is a piece of the continent, a part of the main; if a clod be washed away by the sea, Europe is the less . . . ; and therefore never send to know for whom the bell tolls; it tolls for thee." From 1621 until his death he was dean of St. Paul's Cathedral in London. Most of his love poems (often bawdy and cynical) are said to be his early work, and his "Holy Sonnets" (among the greatest religious poems written in English) his later work.

A Valediction: Forbidding Mourning   [1633]

As virtuous men pass mildly away;
  And whisper to their souls, to go,
Whilst some of their sad friends do say,
  "The breath goes now," and some say, "No":   4

So let us melt, and make no noise.
  No tear-floods, nor sigh-tempests move.
'Twere profanation of our joys
  To tell the laity our love.   8

Moving of the earth° brings harms and fears,
  Men reckon what it did and meant;
But trepidation of the spheres,
  Though greater far, is innocent.°   12

Dull sublunary° lovers' love
  (Whose soul is sense) cannot admit
Absence, because it doth remove
  Those things which elemented it.   16

But we, by a love so much refined
  That our selves know not what it is,
Inter-assuréd of the mind,
  Care less, eyes, lips, and hands to miss.   20

Our two souls therefore, which are one,
  Though I must go, endure not yet
A breach, but an expansion,
  Like gold to airy thinness beat.   24

If they be two, they are two so
  As stiff twin compasses° are two:
Thy soul, the fixed foot, makes no show
  To move, but doth, if the other do.   28

---

9 Moving of the earth an earthquake.   **12 But . . . innocent** But the movement of the heavenly spheres (in Ptolemaic astronomy), though far greater, is harmless.   **13 sublunary** under the moon (i.e., earthly).   **26 twin compasses** a carpenter's compass, used for making circles.

And though it in the center sit,
  Yet when the other far doth roam,
It leans, and hearkens after it,
  And grows erect, as that comes home.   32

Such wilt thou be to me, who must
  Like the other foot, obliquely run:
Thy firmness makes my circle just,
  And makes me end where I begun.   36

The Flea   [1633]

Mark but this flea, and mark in this
How little that which thou deny'st me is;
It sucked me first, and now sucks thee,
And in this flea our two bloods mingled be;
Thou know'st that this cannot be said   5
A sin, nor shame, nor loss of maidenhead;
  Yet this enjoys before it woo,
  And pampered swells with one blood made of two,
  And this, alas, is more than we would do.

Oh stay, three lives in one flea spare,   10
Where we almost, yea, more than married are.
This flea is you and I, and this
Our marriage bed and marriage temple is;
Though parents grudge, and you, we are met
And cloistered in these living walls of jet.   15
  Though use° make you apt to kill me,
  Let not to that, self-murder added be,
  And sacrilege, three sins in killing three.

Cruel and sudden, has thou since
Purpled thy nail in blood of innocence?   20
Wherein could this flea guilty be,
Except in that drop which it sucked from thee?
Yet thou triumph'st and say'st that thou
Find'st not thyself, nor me the weaker now.
  'Tis true. Then learn how false fears be: 25
  Just so much honor, when thou yield'st to me,
  Will waste, as this flea's death took life from thee.

16 **use** custom.

BEN JONSON

Ben Jonson (1572–1637), born in London, was Shakespeare's contemporary. Like Shakespeare, he wrote for the theater, and in fact Shakespeare acted in Jonson's first important play, Every Man in His Humour *(1598). But unlike Shakespeare, Jonson produced a fairly large body of nondramatic poetry.*

Jonson's son, born in 1596, died on his birthday in 1603. Like the father, the boy was named Benjamin, which in Hebrew means "son of the right hand," a phrase Jonson draws on the first line of the poem.

On My First Son
[1616]

Farewell, thou child of my right hand and joy;
   My sin was too much hope of thee, loved boy.
Seven years thou wert lent to me, and I thee pay,
   Exacted by thy fate, on the just day.
O, could I lose all father now! For why   5
   Will man lament the state he should envy?
To have so soon 'scaped world's and flesh's rage,
   And, if no other misery, yet age?
Rest in soft peace, and asked, say here doth lie
   Ben Jonson, his best piece of poetry: 10
For whose sake, henceforth, all his vows be such,
   As what he loves may never like too much.

The following song is from a play, Epicoene, or the Silent Woman.

Still to Be Neat
[1609]

Still° to be neat, still to be dressed
As° you were going to a feast;
Still to be powdered, still perfumed—
Lady, it is to be presumed,
Though art's hid causes are not found,
All is not sweet, all is not sound.   6

Give me a look, give me a face,
That makes simplicity a grace;
Robes loosely flowing, hair as free:
Such sweet neglect more taketh me
Than all the adulteries° of art;
They strike mine eyes, but not my heart.   12

1 Still always.   **2 As** As if.   **11 adulteries** adulterations.

ROBERT HERRICK

Robert Herrick (1591–1674) was born in London, the son of a goldsmith. After taking an M.A. at Cambridge, he was ordained in the Church of England. Later, he was sent to the country parish of Dean Prior in Devonshire, where he wrote most of his poetry. A loyal supporter of the king, in 1647 he was expelled from his parish by the Puritans, though in 1662 he was restored to Dean Prior.

Delight in Disorder
[1648]

A sweet disorder in the dress
Kindles in clothes a wantonness.
A lawn° about the shoulders thrown

3 lawn scarf.

Into a fine distraction;   4
An erring lace, which here and there
Enthralls the crimson stomacher,°
A cuff neglectful, and thereby
Ribbons to flow confusedly;   8
A winning wave, deserving note,
In the tempestuous petticoat;
A careless shoestring, in whose tie
I see a wild civility;   12
Do more bewitch me than when art
Is too precise in every part.

---

6 **stomacher** ornamental cloth.

WILLIAM BLAKE

William Blake (1757-1827) was born in London and at age 14 was appren-ticed for seven years to an engraver. A Christian visionary poet, he made his living by giving drawing lessons and by illustrating books, including his own Songs of Innocence *(1789) and* Songs of Experience *(1794). These two books represent, he said, "two contrary states of the human soul." ("The Lamb" comes from* Songs of Innocence; *"The Tyger" and "London" are from* Songs of Experience.) *In 1809 Blake exhibited his art, but the show was a failure. Not until he was in his sixties, when he stopped writing poetry, did he achieve any public recognition—and then it was as a painter.*

The Lamb   [1789]

Little Lamb, who made thee?
Dost thou know who made thee?
Gave thee life, and bid thee feed
By the stream and o'er the mead;
Gave thee clothing of delight,   5
Softest clothing, wooly, bright;
Gave thee such a tender voice,
Making all the vales rejoice?
    Little Lamb, who made thee?
    Dost thou know who made thee?   10

    Little Lamb, I'll tell thee,
    Little Lamb, I'll tell thee:
He is callèd by thy name,
For he calls himself a Lamb.
He is meek, and he is mild;   15
He became a little child.
I a child, and thou a lamb,
We are callèd by his name.
    Little Lamb, God bless thee!
    Little Lamb, God bless thee!   20

The Tyger

[1793]

Tyger! Tyger! burning bright
In the forests of the night,
What immortal hand or eye
Could frame thy fearful symmetry?   4

In what distant deeps or skies
Burnt the fire of thine eyes?
On what wings dare he aspire?
What the hand dare seize the fire?   8

And what shoulder, and what art,
Could twist the sinews of thy heart?
And, when thy heart began to beat,
What dread hand? and what dread feet?   12

What the hammer? what the chain?
In what furnace was thy brain?
What the anvil? what dread grasp
Dare its deadly terrors clasp?   16

When the stars threw down their spears,
And watered heaven with their tears,
Did he smile his work to see?
Did he who made the lamb make thee?   20

Tyger! Tyger! burning bright
In the forests of the night,
What immortal hand or eye,
Dare frame thy fearful symmetry?   24

London

[1794]

I wander thro' each charter'd street,
Near where the charter'd Thames does flow,
And mark in every face I meet
Marks of weakness, marks of woe.   4

In every cry of every Man,
In every Infant's cry of fear,
In every voice, in every ban,
The mind-forg'd manacles I hear.   8

How the Chimney-sweeper's cry
Every black'ning Church appalls;
And the hapless Soldier's sigh
Runs in blood down Palace walls.   12

But most thro' midnight streets I hear
How the youthful Harlot's curse
Blasts the new-born Infant's tear,
And blights with plagues the Marriage hearse.   16

WILLIAM WORDSWORTH

William Wordsworth (1770–1850), the son of an attorney, grew up in the Lake District of England. After graduating from Cambridge University in 1791, he spent a year in France, falling in love with a French girl, with whom he had a daughter. His enthusiasm for the French Revolution waned, and he returned alone to England, where, with the help of a legacy, he devoted his life to poetry. With his friend Samuel Taylor Coleridge, in 1798 he published anonymously a volume of poetry, Lyrical Ballads, *which changed the course of English poetry. In 1799 he and his sister Dorothy settled in Grasmere in the Lake District, where he married and was given the office of distributor of stamps. In 1843 he was appointed poet laureate.*

The World Is Too Much with Us   [1807]

The world is too much with us; late and soon,
Getting and spending, we lay waste our powers;
Little we see in Nature that is ours;
We have given our hearts away, a sordid boon!°
This Sea that bares her bosom to the moon,   5
The winds that will be howling at all hours,
And are up-gathered now like sleeping flowers,
For this, for everything, we are out of tune;
It moves us not.—Great God! I'd rather be
A Pagan suckled in a creed outworn;   10
So might I, standing on this pleasant lea,
Have glimpses that would make me less forlorn;
Have sight of Proteus° rising from the sea;
Or hear old Triton° blow his wreathéd horn.

---

4 **boon** gift.   **13, 14 Proteus, Triton** sea gods.

I Wandered Lonely as a Cloud   [1815]

I wandered lonely as a cloud
That floats on high o'er vales and hills,
When all at once I saw a crowd,
A host, of golden daffodils,
Beside the lake, beneath the trees,   5
Fluttering and dancing in the breeze.

Continuous as the stars that shine
And twinkle on the milky way,
They stretched in never-ending line
Along the margin of a bay;   10
Ten thousand saw I at a glance,
Tossing their heads in sprightly dance.

The waves beside them danced, but they
Outdid the sparkling waves in glee;

A poet could not but be gay,   15
In such a jocund company;
I gazed—and gazed—but little thought
What wealth the show to me had brought:

For oft, when on my couch I lie
In vacant or in pensive mood,   20
They flash upon that inward eye
Which is the bliss of solitude;
And then my heart with pleasure fills,
And dances with the daffodils.

The Solitary Reaper   [1807]

Behold her, single in the field,
    Yon solitary Highland lass!
Reaping and singing by herself;
    Stop here, or gently pass!
Alone she cuts and binds the grain,   5
And sings a melancholy strain;
O listen! for the Vale profound
Is overflowing with the sound.

No Nightingale did ever chant
    More welcome notes to weary bands   10
Of travelers in some shady haunt,
    Among Arabian sands:
A voice so thrilling ne'er was heard
In spring-time from the Cuckoo-bird,
Breaking the silence of the seas   15
Among the farthest Hebrides.°

Will no one tell me what she sings?—
    Perhaps the plaintive numbers° flow
For old, unhappy, far-off things,
    And battles long ago: 20
Or is it some more humble lay,°
Familiar matter of to-day?
Some natural sorrow, loss, or pain,
That has been, and may be again?

Whate'er the theme, the Maiden sang   25
    As if her song could have no ending;
I saw her singing at her work,
    And o'er the sickle bending;—
I listened, motionless and still;
And, as I mounted up the hill,   30
The music in my heart I bore,
Long after it was heard no more.

---

16 **Hebrides** distant northern islands.   18 **plaintive numbers** mournful verses.
21 **lay** song.

PHILLIS WHEATLEY

Kidnapped in Africa when she was a child of about age 7, and brought to Boston on the schooner Phillis, *Phillis Wheatley (1753–1784) owed her first name to the ship and her second to the family name of the merchant who bought her to attend on his wife. She was educated in English, Latin, history, and geography, and especially in the Bible, and within a few years she was writing poetry in the approved manner—that is, the manner of eighteenth-century England. In 1773, the year she was granted freedom, she published a book of her poems in England.*

Despite her education and the style of writing that she adopted, Wheatley of course did not move freely in the white world. But neither did she move freely in the black world, since her educators kept her away from other persons of African origin. Perhaps the best single sentence ever written about Phillis Wheatley is Richard Wright's: "Before the webs of slavery had so tightened as to snare nearly all Negroes in our land, one was freed by accident to give in clear, bell-like limpid cadence the hope of freedom in the New World." One other sentence about Wheatley, by another African-American writer, should also be quoted here. Alice Walker, commenting on Wheatley's much criticized assumption of white values, says, in an address to Wheatley, "It is not so much what you sang, as that you kept alive, in so many of our ancestors, the notion of song."

"On Being Brought from Africa to America" alludes to the story of Cain and Abel, in Genesis 4, which reports that Cain killed Abel, and that "the Lord set a mark upon Cain" (4.15). The biblical text explicitly says that the mark was to protect Cain from someone who might take vengeance on him, but it does not say what the mark was. Nevertheless, some Christians developed the idea that the color of Africans was the mark of Cain.

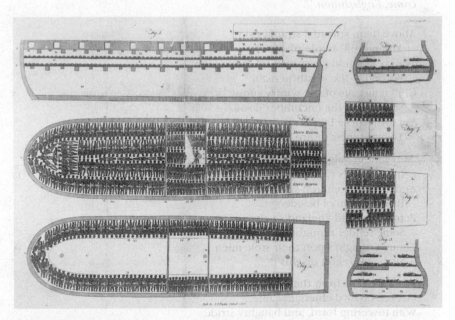

Wheatley probably was brought to America on a slave ship such as this one. Thomas Clarkson distributed this drawing with his *Essay on the Slavery and Commerce of the Human Species* (1804).

On Being Brought from Africa to America   [1772]

'Twas mercy brought me from my pagan land,
Taught my beknighted soul to understand
That there's a God, that there's a Savior too:
Once I redemption neither sought nor knew.
Some view our sable race with scornful eye,   5
"Their color is a diabolic dye."
Remember, Christians; Negroes, black as Cain,
May be refined, and join the angelic train.

LYDIA HOWARD HUNTLEY SIGOURNEY

Lydia Sigourney (1791–1865), born in Norwich, Connecticut, of humble family, was taken up by her father's employer as a child prodigy and tutored in Latin and Hebrew. She wrote poetry chiefly on public issues, such as historical events and slavery, rather than personal lyric poetry. A fair number of her poems concern the displacement of Native Americans; she did not condemn the settling of the continent, but she did criticize the failure of whites to treat the Native Americans according to Christian ethics.

The Indian's Welcome to the Pilgrim Fathers   [1835]

"On Friday, March 16th, 1622, while the colonists were busied in their usual labors, they were much surprised to see a savage walk boldly towards them, and salute them with, 'much welcome, English, much welcome, Englishmen.'"

Above them spread a stranger sky
    Around, the sterile plain,
The rock-bound coast rose frowning nigh,
    Beyond,—the wrathful main:
Chill remnants of the wintry snow   5
    Still chok'd the encumber'd soil,
Yet forth these Pilgrim Fathers go,
    To mark their future toil.

'Mid yonder vale their corn must rise
    In Summer's ripening pride,   10
And there the church-spire woo the skies
    Its sister-school beside.
Perchance 'mid England's velvet green
    Some tender thought repos'd,—
Though nought upon their stoic mien   15
    Such soft regret disclos'd.

When sudden from the forest wide
    A red-brow'd chieftain came,
With towering form, and haughty stride,
    And eye like kindling flame: 20

No wrath he breath'd, no conflict sought,
   To no dark ambush drew,
But simply *to the Old World brought,*
   The welcome of the New.

That *welcome* was a blast and ban   25
   Upon thy race unborn.
Was there no seer, thou fated Man!
   Thy lavish zeal to warn?
Thou in thy fearless faith didst hail
   A weak, invading band,   30
But who shall heed thy children's wail,
   Swept from their native land?

Thou gav'st the riches of thy streams,
   The lordship o'er thy waves,
The region of thine infant dreams,   35
   And of thy fathers' graves,
But who to yon proud mansions pil'd
   With wealth of earth and sea,
Poor outcast from thy forest wild,
   Say, who shall welcome thee?   40

JOHN KEATS

John Keats (1795–1821), son of a London stable keeper, was taken out of school when he was 15 and apprenticed to a surgeon and apothecary. In 1816 he was licensed to practice as an apothecary-surgeon, but he almost immediately abandoned medicine and decided to make a career as a poet. His progress was amazing; he quickly moved from routine verse to major accomplishments, publishing books of poems—to mixed reviews—in 1817, 1818, and 1820, before dying of tuberculosis at the age of 25. Today he is esteemed as one of England's greatest poets.

To Autumn   [1819]

I

Season of mists and mellow fruitfulness,
   Close bosom-friend of the maturing sun;
Conspiring with him how to load and bless
   With fruit the vines that round the thatch-eaves run;
To bend with apples the mossed cottage-trees,   5
   And fill all fruit with ripeness to the core;
      To swell the gourd, and plump the hazel shells
With a sweet kernel; to set budding more,
   And still more, later flowers for the bees,
      Until they think warm days will never cease,   10
      For summer has o'er-brimmed their clammy cells.

II

Who hath not seen thee oft amid thy store?
　　Sometimes whoever seeks abroad may find
Thee sitting careless on a granary floor,
　　Thy hair soft-lifted by the winnowing wind;   15
Or on a half-reaped furrow sound asleep,
　　Drowsed with the fume of poppies, while thy hook
　　　　Spares the next swath and all its twinéd flowers:
And sometime like a gleaner thou dost keep
　　Steady thy laden head across a brook;   20
Or by a cider-press, with patient look,
　　　　Thou watchest the last oozings hours by hours.

III

Where are the songs of Spring? Ay, where are they?
　　Think not of them, thou hast thy music too,—
While barred clouds bloom the soft-dying day,   25
　　And touch the stubble-plains with rosy hue;
Then in a wailful choir the small gnats mourn
　　Among the river sallows, borne aloft
　　　　Or sinking as the light wind lives or dies;
And full-grown lambs loud bleat from hilly bourn;   30
　　Hedge-crickets sing; and now with treble soft
　　The red-breast whistles from a garden-croft;
　　　　And gathering swallows twitter in the skies.

ALFRED, LORD TENNYSON

Alfred, Lord Tennyson (1809–1892), the son of an English clergyman, was born in Lincolnshire, where he began writing verse at age 5. Educated at Cambridge, he had to leave without a degree when his father died and Alfred had to accept responsibility for bringing up his brothers and sisters. In fact, the family had inherited ample funds, but for some years the money was tied up by litigation. Following Wordsworth's death in 1850, Tennyson was made poet laureate. With his government pension he moved with his family to the Isle of Wight, where he lived in comfort until his death.

Ulysses*   [1833]

It little profits that an idle king,
By this still hearth, among these barren crags,
Matched with an aged wife, I mete and dole
Unequal laws unto a savage race,

*****Ulysses** Odysseus, King of Ithaca, a leader of the Greeks in the Trojan War, famous for his ten years of journeying to remote places.

That hoard, and sleep, and feed, and know not me.   5
I cannot rest from travel; I will drink
Life to the lees. All times I have enjoyed
Greatly, have suffered greatly, both with those
That loved me, and alone; on shore, and when
Thro' scudding drifts the rainy Hyades   10
Vext the dim sea. I am become a name;
For always roaming with a hungry heart
Much have I seen and known,—cities of men
And manners, climates, councils, governments,
Myself not least, but honored of them all,—   15
And drunk delight of battle with my peers,
Far on the ringing plains of windy Troy.
I am a part of all that I have met;
Yet all experience is an arch wherethro'
Gleams that untravelled world whose margin fades   20
For ever and for ever when I move.
How dull it is to pause, to make an end,
To rust unburnished, not to shine in use!
As tho' to breathe were life! Life piled on life
Were all too little, and of one to me   25
Little remains; but every hour is saved
From that eternal silence, something more,
A bringer of new things; and vile it were
For some three suns to store and hoard myself,
And this gray spirit yearning in desire   30
To follow knowledge like a sinking star,
Beyond the utmost bound of human thought.

      This is my son, mine own Telemachus,
To whom I leave the scepter and the isle,—
Well-loved of me, discerning to fulfill   35
This labor, by slow prudence to make mild
A rugged people, and thro' soft degrees
Subdue them to the useful and the good.
Most blameless is he, centered in the sphere
Of common duties, decent not to fail   40
In offices of tenderness, and pay
Meet adoration to my household gods,
When I am gone. He works his work, I mine.

      There lies the port; the vessel puffs her sail;
There gloom the dark, broad seas. My mariners,   45
Souls that have toiled, and wrought, and thought with me,—
That ever with a frolic welcome took
The thunder and the sunshine, and opposed
Free hearts, free foreheads,—you and I are old;
Old age hath yet his honor and his toil.   50
Death closes all; but something ere the end,
Some work of noble note, may yet be done,
Not unbecoming men that strove with Gods.
The lights begin to twinkle from the rocks;

The long day wanes; the slow moon climbs; the deep   55
Moans round with many voices. Come, my friends.
'Tis not too late to seek a newer world.
Push off, and sitting well in order smite
The sounding furrows; for my purpose holds
To sail beyond the sunset, and the baths   60
Of all the western stars, until I die.
It may be that the gulfs will wash us down;
It may be we shall touch the Happy Isles,
And see the great Achilles, whom we knew.
Tho' much is taken, much abides; and tho'   65
We are not now that strength which in old days
Moved earth and heaven, that which we are, we are.
One equal temper of heroic hearts,
Made weak by time and fate, but strong in will
To strive, to seek, to find, and not to yield.   70

ROBERT BROWNING

Born in a suburb of London into a middle-class family, Browning (1812-1889) was educated primarily at home, where he read widely. For a while he wrote for the English stage, but after marrying Elizabeth Barrett—she too was a poet—he lived with her in Italy until her death in 1861. He then returned to England and settled in London with their son. Regarded as one of the most distinguished poets of the Victorian period, he is buried in Westminster Abbey.

Porphyria's Lover   [1834]

The rain set early in tonight,
     The sullen wind was soon awake,
It tore the elm-tops down for spite,
     And did its worst to vex the lake:
I listened with heart fit to break.   5
When glided in Porphyria; straight
     She shut the cold out and the storm,
And kneeled and made the cheerless grate
     Blaze up, and all the cottage warm;
Which done, she rose, and from her form   10
Withdrew the dripping cloak and shawl,
     And laid her soiled gloves by, untied
Her hat and let the damp hair fall,
     And, last, she sat down by my side
And called me. When no voice replied,   15
She put my arm around her waist,
     And made her smooth white shoulder bare
And all her yellow hair displaced,
     And stooping, made my cheek lie there,
And spread, o'er all, her yellow hair,   20

Murmuring how she loved me—she
    Too weak, for all her heart's endeavor,
To set its struggling passion free
    From pride, and vainer ties dissever,
And give herself to me forever. 25
But passion sometimes would prevail,
    Nor could tonight's gay feast restrain
A sudden thought of one so pale
    For love of her, and all in vain:
So, she was come through wind and rain. 30
Be sure I looked up at her eyes
    Happy and proud; at last I knew
Porphyria worshipped me; surprise
    Made my heart swell, and still it grew
While I debated what to do. 35
That moment she was mine, mine, fair,
    Perfectly pure and good: I found
A thing to do, and all her hair
    In one long yellow string I wound
Three times her little throat around, 40
And strangled her. No pain felt she;
    I am quite sure she felt no pain.
As a shut bud that holds a bee,
    I warily oped her lids: again
Laughed the blue eyes without a stain. 45
And I untightened next the tress
    About her neck; her cheek once more
Blushed bright beneath my burning kiss:
    I propped her head up as before,
Only, this time my shoulder bore 50
Her head, which droops upon it still:
    The smiling rosy little head,
So glad it has its utmost will,
    That all it scorned at once is fled,
And I, its love, am gained instead! 55
Porphyria's love: she guessed not how
    Her darling one wish would be heard.
And thus we sit together now,
    And all night long we have not stirred,
And yet God has not said a word! 60

MATTHEW ARNOLD

Matthew Arnold (1822–1888) was the son of a famous educator, Dr. Thomas Arnold, the headmaster of Rugby School. After graduating from Oxford, Matthew Arnold became an inspector of schools, a post he held until two years before his death. Besides writing poetry, Arnold wrote literary criticism and was appointed professor of poetry at Oxford from 1857 to 1867. He traveled widely on the Continent and lectured in the United States.

Dover Beach

[c. 1851]

The sea is calm to-night.
The tide is full, the moon lies fair
Upon the straits;—on the French coast the light
Gleams and is gone; the cliffs of England stand,
Glimmering and vast, out in the tranquil bay.   5
Come to the window, sweet is the night-air!
Only, from the long line of spray
Where the sea meets the moon-blanch'd land,
Listen! you hear the grating roar
Of pebbles which the waves draw back, and fling,   10
At their return, up the high strand,
Begin, and cease, and then again begin,
With tremulous cadence slow, and bring
The eternal note of sadness in.

Sophocles long ago   15
Heard it on the Ægean, and it brought
Into his mind the turbid ebb and flow
Of human misery; we
Find also in the sound a thought,
Hearing it by this distant northern sea.   20

The Sea of Faith
Was once, too, at the full, and round earth's shore
Lay like the folds of a bright girdle furl'd.
But now I only hear
Its melancholy, long, withdrawing roar,   25
Retreating, to the breath
Of the night-wind, down the vast edges drear
And naked shingles° of the world.

Ah, love, let us be true
To one another! for the world, which seems   30
To lie before us like a land of dreams,
So various, so beautiful, so new,
Hath really neither joy, nor love, nor light,
Nor certitude, nor peace, nor help for pain;
And we are here as on a darkling plain   35
Swept with confused alarms of struggle and flight,
Where ignorant armies clash by night.

---

28 **shingles** pebbled beaches.

GERARD MANLEY HOPKINS

Gerard Manley Hopkins (1844–1889) was born near London and was edu-
cated at Oxford, where he studied the classics. A convert from Anglicanism to
Roman Catholicism, he was ordained a Jesuit priest in 1877. After serving as
a parish priest and teacher, he was appointed Professor of Greek at the
Catholic University in Dublin.

Hopkins published only a few poems during his lifetime, partly because he believed that the pursuit of literary fame was incompatible with his vocation as a priest, and partly because he was aware that his highly individual style might puzzle readers.

God's Grandeur   [1877]

The world is charged with the grandeur of God.
   It will flame out, like shining from shook foil;
   It gathers to a greatness, like the ooze of oil
Crushed. Why do men then now not reck his rod?
Generations have trod, have trod, have trod;   5
   And all is seared with trade; bleared, smeared with toil;
   And wears man's smudge and shares man's smell: the soil
Is bare now, nor can foot feel, being shod.

And for all this, nature is never spent;
   There lives the dearest freshness deep down things;   10
And though the last lights off the black West went
   Oh, morning, at the brown brink eastward, springs—
Because the Holy Ghost over the bent
   World broods with warm breast and with ah! bright wings.

Pied* Beauty   [1877]

Glory be to God for dappled things—
   For skies of couple-colour as a brinded° cow;
     For rose-moles all in stipple upon trout that swim;
Fresh-firecoal chestnut-falls; finches' wings;
   Landscape plotted and pieced—fold, fallow, and plough;°   5
     And áll trádes, their gear and tackle and trim.°
All things counter, original, spare, strange;
   Whatever is fickle, freckled (who knows how?)
     With swift, slow; sweet, sour; adazzle, dim;
He fathers-forth whose beauty is past change: 10
          Praise him.

---

*Pied Variegated, particolored. **2 brinded** streaked. **5 fold, fallow, and plough** fields used for pasture (sheep-fold), left fallow, or ploughed. **6 trim** equipment.

JAMES WELDON JOHNSON

Born in Jacksonville, Florida, James Weldon Johnson (1871–1938) received a bachelor's and a master's degree from Atlanta University. Johnson taught school, served as a high school principal, and founded the Daily American *(1895, the first black daily in America). Later he became active in the NAACP, served as consul to Venezuela and to Nicaragua, and taught creative writing at Fisk University. On the day of his death, in an automobile accident, he was appointed to teach African-American literature at New York University. Johnson wrote dialect poems as well as poems in standard English.*

To America   [1917]

How would you have us, as we are?
Or sinking 'neath the load we bear?
Our eyes fixed forward on a star?
Or gazing empty at despair?   4

Rising or falling? Men or things?
With dragging pace or footsteps fleet?
Strong, willing sinews in your wings?
Or tightening chains about your feet?   8

WILLIAM CARLOS WILLIAMS

*William Carlos Williams (1883-1963) was the son of an English traveling
salesman and a Basque-Jewish woman. The couple met in Puerto Rico and
settled in Rutherford, New Jersey, where William was born. He spent his life
there, practicing as a pediatrician and writing poems in the moments between seeing patients who visited his office.*

Spring and All   [1923]

By the road to the contagious hospital
under the surge of the blue
mottled clouds driven from the
northeast—a cold wind. Beyond, the
waste of broad, muddy fields   5
brown with dried weeds, standing and fallen

patches of standing water
the scattering of tall trees

All along the road the reddish
purplish, forked, upstanding, twiggy   10
stuff of bushes and small trees
with dead, brown leaves under them
leafless vines—

Lifeless in appearance, sluggish
dazed spring approaches—   15

They enter the new world naked,
cold, uncertain of all
save that they enter. All about them
the cold, familiar wind—

Now the grass, tomorrow   20
the stiff curl of wildcarrot leaf
One by one objects are defined—
It quickens: clarity, outline of leaf

But now the stark dignity of
entrance—Still, the profound change   25
has come upon them: rooted, they
grip down and begin to awaken

EZRA POUND

Ezra Pound (1885-1972), born in Hailey, Idaho, and raised in Philadelphia, was one of the most influential American poets of the twentieth century. He prepared to be a teacher of medieval and Renaissance Spanish, Italian, and French literature, but his career as an academician ended abruptly when he was fired from Wabash College for having a woman in his room overnight. Pound went to Venice, where he did odd jobs, and then to London, where he met T. S. Eliot and played a large role in editing Eliot's long poem, The Waste Land. *Among the other poets whom he assisted was Robert Frost, who was then living in England. In 1924 Pound settled in Italy. He espoused Mussolini's cause, was arrested by the American forces in 1944, and (having been declared insane and therefore not fit to be tried for treason) was confined in a mental institution in Washington, D.C. Released in 1958, he spent the remainder of his life in Italy.*

In a Station of the Metro*   [1916]

The apparition of these faces in the crowd;
Petals on a wet, black bough.

*****Metro** subway in Paris.

H. D.

H. D. was the pen name of Hilda Doolittle (1886-1961). Doolittle, born in Bethlehem, Pennsylvania, of a socially prominent family, met Ezra Pound (see the preceding poem) when she was 15 and he was 16. Their relationship was complicated—Doolittle was sexually attracted to women as well as to men—and met with opposition from her family. She further distressed her family when she dropped out of Bryn Mawr College. In 1911 H. D. and a female friend who had once loved Doolittle and now loved Pound followed Pound to England, where Doolittle was active in various literary movements.

We print a poem about a Greek mythological figure, Helen, wife of Menelaus, king of the Greek city-state of Sparta. Paris, a Trojan prince, abducted her and thereby initiated the Trojan War. Poets—ever since the days of ancient Greece—have been interested in this story, but H. D. had an especially strong interest in classical Greece and in psychoanalytic and feminist interpretations of mythology.

Helen   [1924]

All Greece hates
the still eyes in the white face,
the lustre as of olives

where she stands,
and the white hands.   5

All Greece reviles
the wan face when she smiles,
hating it deeper still
when it grows wan and white,
remembering past enchantments   10
and past ills.

Greece sees unmoved,
God's daughter, born of love,
the beauty of cool feet
and slenderest knees,   15
could love indeed the maid,
only if she were laid,
white ash amid funereal cypresses.

T. S. ELIOT

*Thomas Stearns Eliot (1888-1965) was born into a New England family that
had moved to St. Louis. He attended a preparatory school in Massachusetts,
then graduated from Harvard and did further study in literature and philosophy in France, Germany, and England. In 1914 he began working for
Lloyd's Bank in London, and three years later he published his first book of
poems (it included "Prufrock"). In 1925 he joined a publishing firm, and in
1927 he became a British citizen and a member of the Church of England.
Much of his later poetry, unlike "The Love Song of J. Alfred Prufrock," is highly
religious. In 1948 Eliot received the Nobel Prize for Literature.*

The Love Song of J. Alfred Prufrock   [1917]

*S'io credesse che mia risposta fosse
A persona che mai tornasse al mondo,
Questa fiamma staria senza più scosse.
Ma perciocchè giammai di questo fondo
Non torno vivo alcun, s' i' odo il vero,
Senza tema d'infamia ti rispondo.**

---

*In Dante's *Inferno* XXVII: 61-66, a damned soul who had sought absolution before
committing a crime addresses Dante, thinking that his words will never reach the earth: "If I
believed that my answer were to a person who could ever return to the world, this flame would
no longer quiver. But because no one ever returned from this depth, if what I hear is true,
without fear of infamy, I answer you."

Explanations of allusions in the poem may be helpful. "Works and days" (line 29) is the title of
a poem on farm life by Hesiod (eighth century BCE); "dying fall" (line 52) echoes *Twelfth Night*
I.i.4; lines 81-83 allude to John the Baptist (see Matthew 14.1-11); line 92 echoes lines 41-42 of
Marvell's "To His Coy Mistress" (see page 737); for "Lazarus" (line 94) see Luke 16 and John 11;
lines 112-117 allude to Polonius and perhaps to other figures in *Hamlet;* "full of high sentence"
(line 117) comes from Chaucer's description of the Clerk of Oxford in the *Canterbury Tales.*

Let us go then, you and I,
When the evening is spread out against the sky
Like a patient etherised upon a table;
Let us go, through certain half-deserted streets,
The muttering retreats   5
Of restless nights in one-night cheap hotels
And sawdust restaurants with oyster-shells;
Streets that follow like a tedious argument
Of insidious intent
To lead you to an overwhelming question . . .   10

Oh, do not ask, "What is it?"
Let us go and make our visit.

In the room the women come and go
Talking of Michelangelo.

The yellow fog that rubs its back upon the window panes,   15
The yellow smoke that rubs its muzzle on the window panes
Licked its tongue into the corners of the evening,
Lingered upon the pools that stand in drains,
Let fall upon its back the soot that falls from chimneys,
Slipped by the terrace, made a sudden leap,   20
And seeing that it was a soft October night,
Curled once about the house, and fell asleep.

And indeed there will be time
For the yellow smoke that slides along the street,
Rubbing its back upon the window-panes;   25
There will be time, there will be time
To prepare a face to meet the faces that you meet;
There will be time to murder and create,
And time for all the works and days of hands
That lift and drop a question on your plate;   30
Time for you and time for me,
And time yet for a hundred indecisions,
And for a hundred visions and revisions,
Before the taking of a toast and tea.

In the room the women come and go   35
Talking of Michelangelo.

And indeed there will be time
To wonder, "Do I dare?" and, "Do I dare?"—
Time to turn back and descend the stair,
With a bald spot in the middle of my hair—   40
(They will say: "How his hair is growing thin!")
My morning coat, my collar mounting firmly to the chin,
My necktie rich and modest, but asserted by a simple pin—
(They will say: "But how his arms and legs are thin!")
Do I dare   45
Disturb the universe?
In a minute there is time
For decisions and revisions which a minute will reverse.

For I have known them all already, known them all:—
Have known the evenings, mornings, afternoons,   50
I have measured out my life with coffee spoons;
I know the voices dying with a dying fall
Beneath the music from a farther room.
     So how should I presume?

And I have known the eyes already, known them all—   55
The eyes that fix you in a formulated phrase.
And when I am formulated, sprawling on a pin,
When I am pinned and wriggling on the wall,
Then how should I begin
To spit out all the butt-ends of my days and ways?   60
     And how should I presume?

And I have known the arms already, known them all—
Arms that are braceleted and white and bare
(But in the lamplight, downed with light brown hair!)
Is it perfume from a dress   65
That makes me so digress?
Arms that lie along a table, or wrap about a shawl.
     And should I then presume?
     And how should I begin?

Shall I say, I have gone at dusk through narrow streets   70
And watched the smoke that rises from the pipes
Of lonely men in shirt-sleeves, leaning out of windows? . . .

I should have been a pair of ragged claws
Scuttling across the floors of silent seas.
And the afternoon, the evening, sleeps so peacefully!   75
Smoothed by long fingers,
Asleep . . . tired . . . or it malingers,
Stretched on the floor, here beside you and me.
Should I, after tea and cakes and ices,
Have the strength to force the moment to its crisis?   80
But though I have wept and fasted, wept and prayed,
Though I have seen my head (grown slightly bald)
     brought in upon a platter,
I am no prophet—and here's no great matter;
I have seen the moment of my greatness flicker,
And I have seen the eternal Footman hold my coat, and snicker,   85
And in short, I was afraid.

And would it have been worth it, after all,
After the cups, the marmalade, the tea,
Among the porcelain, among some talk of you and me,
Would it have been worth while,   90
To have bitten off the matter with a smile,
To have squeezed the universe into a ball
To roll it toward some overwhelming question,
To say: "I am Lazarus, come from the dead,
Come back to tell you all, I shall tell you all"—   95

If one, settling a pillow by her head,
   Should say: "That is not what I meant at all;
   That is not it, at all."

And would it have been worth it, after all,
Would it have been worth while,   100
After the sunsets and the dooryards and the sprinkled streets,
After the novels, after the teacups, after the skirts that trail
   along the floor—
And this, and so much more?—
It is impossible to say just what I mean!
But as if a magic lantern threw the nerves in patterns on a screen: 105

Would it have been worth while
If one, settling a pillow or throwing off a shawl,
And turning toward the window, should say:
   "That is not it at all,
   That is not what I meant, at all."   110
No! I am not Prince Hamlet, nor was meant to be;
Am an attendant lord, one that will do
To swell a progress, start a scene or two,
Advise the prince; no doubt, an easy tool,
Deferential, glad to be of use,   115
Politic, cautious, and meticulous;
Full of high sentence, but a bit obtuse;
At times, indeed, almost ridiculous—
Almost, at times, the Fool.

I grow old . . . I grow old . . .   120
I shall wear the bottoms of my trousers rolled.

Shall I part my hair behind? Do I dare to eat a peach?
I shall wear white flannel trousers, and walk upon the beach.
I have heard the mermaids singing, each to each.

I do not think that they will sing to me.   125

I have seen them riding seaward on the waves
Combing the white hair of the waves blown back
When the wind blows the water white and black.

We have lingered in the chambers of the sea
By sea-girls wreathed with seaweed red and brown,   130
Till human voices wake us, and we drown.

ARCHIBALD MACLEISH

Archibald MacLeish (1892-1982) was educated at Harvard and at Yale Law School. His early poetry (say, to about 1930), including "Ars Poetica," often is condensed and allusive, though his later poems and his plays are readily accessible. Under Franklin Delano Roosevelt, MacLeish served as Librarian of Congress (1939-1944) and as assistant secretary of state (1944-1945). He then taught at Harvard and at Amherst until he retired in 1967.

Ars Poetica   [1926]

A poem should be palpable and mute
As a globed fruit,

Dumb
As old medallions to the thumb,

Silent as the sleeve-worn stone   5
Of casement ledges where the moss has grown—

A poem should be wordless
As the flight of birds.

A poem should be motionless in time
As the moon climbs,   10

Leaving, as the moon releases
Twig by twig the night-entangled trees,

Leaving, as the moon behind the winter leaves,
Memory by memory the mind—

A poem should be motionless in time   15
As the moon climbs.

A poem should be equal to:
Not true.

For all the history of grief
An empty doorway and a maple leaf.   20

For love
The leaning grasses and two lights above the sea—

A poem should not mean
But be.

ELIZABETH BISHOP

*Elizabeth Bishop (1911-1979) was born in Worcester, Massachusetts. Because
her father died when she was eight months old and her mother was confined to
a sanitarium four years later, Bishop was raised by relatives in New England
and Nova Scotia. After graduating from Vassar College in 1934, where she was
co-editor of the student literary magazine, she lived (on a small private income) for a while in Key West, France, and Mexico, and then for much of her
adult life in Brazil, before returning to the United States to teach at Harvard.
Her financial independence enabled her to write without worrying about the
sales of her books and without having to devote energy to distracting jobs.*

The Fish   [1946]

I caught a tremendous fish
and held him beside the boat
half out of water, with my hook

fast in a corner of his mouth.
He didn't fight.   5
He hadn't fought at all.
He hung a grunting weight,
battered and venerable
and homely. Here and there
his brown skin hung in strips   10
like ancient wall-paper,
and its pattern of darker brown
was like wall-paper:
shapes like full-blown roses
stained and lost through age.   15
He was speckled with barnacles,
fine rosettes of lime,
and infested
with tiny white sea-lice,
and underneath two or three   20
rags of green weed hung down.
While his gills were breathing in
the terrible oxygen
—the frightening gills,
fresh and crisp with blood,   25
that can cut so badly—
I thought of the coarse white flesh
packed in like feathers,
the big bones and the little bones,
the dramatic reds and blacks   30
of his shiny entrails,
and the pink swim-bladder
like a big peony.
I looked into his eyes
which were far larger than mine   35
but shallower, and yellowed,
the irises backed and packed
with tarnished tinfoil
seen through the lenses
of old scratched isinglass.   40
They shifted a little, but not
to return my stare.
—It was more like the tipping
of an object toward the light.
I admired his sullen face,   45
the mechanism of his jaw,
and then I saw
that from his lower lip
—if you could call it a lip—
grim, wet, and weapon-like,   50
hung five old pieces of fish-line,
or four and a wire leader
with the swivel still attached,
with all their five big hooks

grown firmly in his mouth.   55
A green line, frayed at the end
where he broke it, two heavier lines,
and a fine black thread
still crimped from the strain and snap
when it broke and he got away.   60
Like medals with their ribbons
frayed and wavering,
a five-haired beard of wisdom
trailing from his aching jaw.
I stared and stared   65
and victory filled up
the little rented boat,
from the pool of bilge
where oil had spread a rainbow
around the rusted engine   70
to the bailer rusted orange,
the sun-cracked thwarts,
the oarlocks on their strings,
the gunnels—until everything
was rainbow, rainbow, rainbow!   75
And I let the fish go.

CONTEMPORARY VOICES

GWENDOLYN BROOKS

*Gwendolyn Brooks (1917–2000) was born in Topeka, Kansas, but was raised in Chicago's South Side, where she spent most of her life. Brooks taught in several colleges and universities and wrote a novel (*Maud Martha, *1953) and a memoir (*Report from Part One, *1972), but she is best known as a poet. In 1950, when she won the Pulitzer Prize for Poetry, she became the first African-American writer to win a Pulitzer Prize. In 1985 Brooks became Consultant in Poetry to the Library of Congress.*

The subject of Brooks's poem, the civil rights leader Martin Luther King Jr. (1929–1968), was assassinated at the height of his career.

Martin Luther King Jr.   [1970]

A man went forth with gifts.
He was a prose poem.
He was a tragic grace.
He was a warm music.

He tried to heal the vivid volcanoes.   5
His ashes are
    reading the world.

Funeral march for Martin Luther King Jr., held in Atlanta, Georgia.

His Dream still wishes to anoint
   the barricades of faith and of control.

His word still burns the center of the sun,   10
   above the thousands and the
   hundred thousands.

The word was Justice. It was spoken.

So it shall be spoken.
So it shall be done.   15

ANTHONY HECHT

Anthony Hecht (1923–2004), born in New York City, was educated at Bard College and Columbia University. He taught at several institutions (notably at Georgetown University), and he served as poetry consultant to the Library of Congress.

Like "The Dover Bitch," which assumes a reader's familiarity with Matthew Arnold's "Dover Beach" (page 990), much of Hecht's work glances at earlier literature. The poem is dedicated to a critic and editor.

The Dover Bitch   [1967]

A Criticism of Life

For Andrews Wanning

So there stood Matthew Arnold and this girl
With the cliffs of England crumbling away behind them,
And he said to her, "Try to be true to me,
And I'll do the same for you, for things are bad
All over, etc., etc."   5
Well now, I knew this girl. It's true she had read
Sophocles in a fairly good translation
And caught that bitter allusion to the sea,
But all the time he was talking she had in mind
The notion of what his whiskers would feel like   10
On the back of her neck. She told me later on
That after a while she got to looking out
At the lights across the channel, and really felt sad,
Thinking of all the wine and enormous beds
And blandishments in French and the perfumes.   15
And then she got really angry. To have been brought
All the way down from London, and then be addressed
As sort of a mournful cosmic last resort
Is really tough on a girl, and she was pretty,
Anyway, she watched him pace the room   20
And finger his watch-chain and seem to sweat a bit,
And then she said one or two unprintable things.
But you mustn't judge her by that. What I mean to say is,
She's really all right. I still see her once in a while
And she always treats me right.   25
We have a drink
And I give her a good time, and perhaps it's a year
Before I see her again, but there she is,
Running to fat, but dependable as they come.
And sometimes I bring her a bottle of *Nuit d'Amour.*   30

ROBERT BLY

*Robert Bly, born in 1926 in Madison, Minnesota, is one of the few poets who
has been able to support himself by writing and by giving readings, rather
than by teaching. In 1990 his* Iron John, *a book about male identity, became
a bestseller.*

Driving to Town Late to Mail a Letter   [1962]

It is a cold and snowy night. The main street is deserted.
The only things moving are swirls of snow.
As I lift the mailbox door, I feel its cold iron.
There is a privacy I love in this snowy night.
Driving around, I will waste more time.

ALLEN GINSBERG

Allen Ginsberg (1926–1997) was born in Newark, New Jersey, and graduated from Columbia University in 1948. After eight months in Columbia Psychiatric Institute—Ginsberg had pleaded insanity to avoid prosecution when the police discovered that a friend stored stolen goods in Ginsberg's apartment— he worked at odd jobs and finally left the nine-to-five world for a freer life in San Francisco. In the 1950s he established a reputation as an uninhibited declamatory poet whose chief theme was a celebration of those who were alienated from a repressive America.

A Supermarket in California   [1956]

What thoughts I have of you tonight, Walt Whitman, for I walked down the sidestreets under the trees with a headache self-conscious looking at the full moon.

In my hungry fatigue, and shopping for images, I went into the neon fruit supermarket, dreaming of your enumerations!

What peaches and what penumbras! Whole families shopping at night! Aisles full of husbands! Wives in the avocados, babies in the tomatoes!—and you, García Lorca,° what were you doing down by the watermelons?

I saw you, Walt Whitman, childless, lonely old grubber, poking among the meats in the refrigerator and eyeing the grocery boys.

I heard you asking questions of each: Who killed the pork chops? What price bananas? Are you my Angel?   5

I wandered in and out of the brilliant stacks of cans following you, and followed in my imagination by the store detective.

We strode down the open corridors together in our solitary fancy tasting artichokes, possessing every frozen delicacy, and never passing the cashier.

Where are we going, Walt Whitman? The doors close in an hour. Which way does your beard point tonight?

(I touch your book and dream of our odyssey in the supermarket and feel absurd.)

Will we walk all night through solitary streets? The trees add shade to shade, lights out in the houses, we'll both be lonely.   10

Will we stroll dreaming of the lost America of love past blue automobiles in driveways, home to our silent cottage?

Ah, dear father, graybeard, lonely old courage-teacher, what America did you have when Charon quit poling his ferry and you got out on a smoking bank and stood watching the boat disappear on the black water of Lethe?°

---

3 García Lorca Federico García Lorca (1899–1936), Spanish poet (and, like Whitman and Ginsberg, a homosexual).   **12 Lethe** In classical mythology, Charon ferried the souls of the dead across the river Styx, to Hades, where, after drinking from the river Lethe, they forgot the life they had lived.

ANNE SEXTON

Anne Sexton (1928–1974) was born in Newton, Massachusetts. She was a member of a well-educated New England family but did not attend college. After the birth of her second child she suffered a mental breakdown, and for much of the rest of her life she was under psychiatric care. Indeed, a psychiatrist encouraged her to write poetry, and she was soon able to publish in national journals such as The New Yorker. *Despite her success, she continued to suffer mentally, and in 1974 she took her life.*

Her Kind   [1960]

I have gone out, a possessed witch,
haunting the black air, braver at night;
dreaming evil, I have done my hitch
over the plain houses, light by light;
lonely thing, twelve-fingered, out of mind.   5
A woman like that is not a woman, quite.
I have been her kind.

I have found the warm caves in the woods,
filled them with skillets, carvings, shelves,
closets, silks, innumerable goods;   10
fixed the suppers for the worms and the elves:
whining, rearranging the disaligned.
A woman like that is misunderstood.
I have been her kind.

I have ridden in your cart, driver,   15
waved my nude arms at villages going by,
learning the last bright routes, survivor
where your flames still bite my thigh
and my ribs crack where your wheels wind.
A woman like that is not ashamed to die.   20
I have been her kind.

ADRIENNE RICH

Adrienne Rich's most recent books of poetry are The School Among the Ruins: Poems 2000–2004, *and* Fox: Poems 1998–2000 *(Norton). A selection of her essays,* Arts of the Possible: Essays and Conversations, *was published in 2001. A new edition of* What is Found There: Notebooks on Poetry and Politics, *appeared in 2003. She is a recipient of the Lannan Foundation Lifetime Achievement Award, the Lambda Book Award, the Lenore Marshall/Nation Prize, the Wallace Stevens Award, and the Bollingen Prize in Poetry, among other honors. She lives in California.*

In line 9 of the first poem, James and Whitehead are William James (1842–1910) and Alfred North Whitehead (1861–1947), both of whom taught philosophy at Harvard.

For the Felling of an Elm in the Harvard Yard   [1951]

They say the ground precisely swept
No longer feeds with rich decay
The roots enormous in their age
That long and deep beneath have slept.   4

So the great spire is overthrown,
And sharp saws have gone hurtling through
The rings that three slow centuries wore;
The second oldest elm is down.   8

The shade where James and Whitehead strolled
Becomes a litter on the green.
The young men pause along the paths
To see the axes glinting bold.   12

Watching the hewn trunk dragged away,
Some turn the symbol to their own,
And some admire the clean dispatch
With which the aged elm came down.

Aunt Jennifer's Tigers   [1951]

Aunt Jennifer's tigers prance across a screen,
Bright topaz denizens of a world of green.
They do not fear the men beneath the tree;
They pace in sleek chivalric certainty.

Aunt Jennifer's fingers fluttering through her wool
Find even the ivory needle hard to pull.
The massive weight of Uncle's wedding band
Sits heavily upon Aunt Jennifer's hand.

When Aunt is dead, her terrified hands will lie
Still ringed with ordeals she was mastered by.
The tigers in the panel that she made
Will go on prancing, proud and unafraid.

Living in Sin   [1955]

She had thought the studio would keep itself,
no dust upon the furniture of love.
Half heresy, to wish the taps less vocal,
the panes relieved of grime. A plate of pears,
a piano with a Persian shawl, a cat   5
stalking the picturesque amusing mouse
had risen at his urging.
Not that at five each separate stair would writhe
under the milkman's tramp; that morning light
so coldly would delineate the scraps   10
of last night's cheese and three sepulchral bottles;

that on the kitchen shelf among the saucers
a pair of beetle-eyes would fix her own—
envoy from some black village in the mouldings . . .
Meanwhile, he, with a yawn,   15
sounded a dozen notes upon the keyboard,
declared it out of tune, shrugged at the mirror,
rubbed at his beard, went out for cigarettes;
while she, jeered by the minor demons,
pulled back the sheets and made the bed and found   20
a towel to dust the table-top,
and let the coffee-pot boil over on the stove.
By evening she was back in love again,
though not so wholly but throughout the night
she woke sometimes to feel the daylight coming   25
like a relentless milkman up the stairs.

X. J. KENNEDY

*X. J. Kennedy was born in New Jersey in 1929. He has taught at Tufts Univer-
sity and is the author of several books of poems, books for children, and college textbooks.*

*The following poem builds on "The Tyger" (page 980) by William Blake, a
favorite poet of Allen Ginsberg. Ginsberg, a New Yorker who established his
fame in San Francisco, was noted for his declamatory poetry and his celebration of outsiders, especially protestors against the wars in Korea and Vietnam.
He often chanted Blake's poems at his own poetry readings. In the following
poem X. J. Kennedy pays homage to Ginsberg by adopting the form of one of
Ginsberg's favorite poems. Kennedy alludes, in his poem, to Ginsberg's left-
wing activities ("Taunter of the ultra right"), his view that his hearers should
drop out of a corrupt and repressive society, his interest in Buddhist mantras
(syllables laden with mystic power), his antiwar activity ("Mantra-minded
flower child"), his homosexuality ("Queer," "Queen"), and his use of finger
cymbals in some of his readings. Om (line 10) is a syllable that begins several
mantras. Ginsberg often had his audience utter the sound.*

For Allen Ginsberg   [1998]

Ginsberg, Ginsberg, burning bright,
Taunter of the ultra right,
What blink of the Buddha's eye
Chose the day for you to die?   4

Queer pied piper, howling wild,
Mantra-minded flower child,
Queen of Maytime, misrule's lord
Bawling, *Drop out! All aboard!*   8

Foe of fascist, bane of bomb,
Finger-cymbaled, chanting *Om,*
Proper poets' thorn-in-side,
Turner of a whole time's tide,   12

Who can fill your sloppy shoes?
What a catch for Death. We lose
Glee and sweetness, freaky light,
Ginsberg, Ginsberg, burning bright.   16

MILLER WILLIAMS

Miller Williams, born in 1930, read a poem at President Clinton's second in-
auguration. A professor of English at the University of Arkansas, Williams is
the author, editor, and translator of many books, as well as the director of the
university's press.

Listen | 014   [1999]

I threw a snowball across the backyard.
My dog ran after it to bring it back.
It broke as it fell, scattering snow over snow.
She stood confused, seeing and smelling nothing.
She searched in widening circles until I called her.   5

She looked at me and said as clearly in silence
as if she had spoken,
I know it's here, I'll find it,
went back to the center and started the circles again.

I called her two more times before she came   10
slowly, stopping once to look back.

That was this morning. I'm sure that she's forgotten.
I've had some trouble putting it out of my mind.

DEREK WALCOTT

Derek Walcott, born in 1930 on the Caribbean island of St. Lucia, in 1992
was awarded the Nobel Prize for Literature. Although in the United States he
is known chiefly as a poet, Walcott is also an important playwright and direc-
tor of plays. Much of his work is concerned with his mixed heritage—a black
writer from the Caribbean, whose language is English and who lives part of
the year in New England, where he teaches at Boston University.

A Far Cry from Africa   [1962]

A wind is ruffling the tawny pelt
Of Africa. Kikuyu,° quick as flies,
Batten upon the bloodstreams of the veldt.°

---

2 Kikuyu an African tribe who fought against British colonialists.   **3 veldt** grassland in
southern Africa.

Corpses are scattered through a paradise.
Only the worm, colonel of carrion, cries: 5
'Waste no compassion on these separate dead!'
Statistics justify and scholars seize
The salients of colonial policy.
What is that to the white child hacked in bed?
To savages, expendable as Jews?   10

Threshed out by beaters, the long rushes break
In a white dust of ibises whose cries
Have wheeled since civilization's dawn
From the parched river or beast-teeming plain.
The violence of beast on beast is read   15
As natural law, but upright man
Seeks his divinity by inflicting pain.
Delirious as these worried beasts, his wars
Dance to the tightened carcass of a drum,
While he calls courage still that native dread   20
Of the white peace contracted by the dead.

Again brutish necessity wipes its hands
Upon the napkins of a dirty cause, again
A waste of our compassion, as with Spain,°
The gorilla wrestles with the superman.   25

I who am poisoned with the blood of both,
Where shall I turn, divided to the vein?
I who have cursed
The drunken officer of British rule, how choose
Between this Africa and the English tongue I love?   30
Betray them both, or give back what they give?
How can I face such slaughter and be cool?
How can I turn from Africa and live?

---

24 Spain a reference to the triumph of fascism in Spain after the Civil War of 1936–1939.

SYLVIA PLATH

Sylvia Plath (1932–1963) was born in Boston, the daughter of German immigrants. While still an undergraduate at Smith College, she published in Seventeen *and* Mademoiselle, *but her years at college, like her later years, were marked by manic-depressive periods. After graduating from college she went to England to study at Cambridge University, where she met the English poet Ted Hughes, whom she married in 1956. The marriage was unsuccessful, and they separated. One day she committed suicide by turning on the kitchen gas.*

Daddy   [1965]

You do not do, you do not do
Any more, black shoe
In which I have lived like a foot

For thirty years, poor and white,
 Barely daring to breathe or Achoo.   5

Daddy, I have had to kill you.
You died before I had time—
Marble-heavy, a bag full of God,
Ghastly statue with one gray toe
Big as a Frisco seal   10

And a head in the freakish Atlantic
Where it pours bean green over blue
In the waters off beautiful Nauset.
I used to pray to recover you.
Ach, du.°   15

In the German tongue, in the Polish town
Scraped flat by the roller
Of wars, wars, wars.
But the name of the town is common.
My Polack friend   20

Says there are a dozen or two.
So I never could tell where you
Put your foot, your root,
I never could talk to you.
The tongue stuck in my jaw.   25

It stuck in a barb wire snare.
Ich, ich, ich, ich,°
I could hardly speak.
I thought every German was you.
And the language obscene   30

An engine, an engine
Chuffing me off like a Jew.
A Jew to Dachau, Auschwitz, Belsen.°
I began to talk like a Jew.
I think I may well be a Jew.   35

The snows of the Tyrol, the clear beer of Vienna
Are not very pure or true.
With my gypsy ancestress and my weird luck
And my Taroc pack and my Taroc pack
I may be a bit of a Jew.   40

I have always been scared of *you*,
With your Luftwaffe,° your gobbledygoo.
And your neat moustache
And your Aryan eye, bright blue,
Panzer-man,° panzer-man, O You—   45

---

15 Ach, du O, you (German).   **27 Ich, ich, ich, ich** I, I, I, I.   **33 Dachau . . . Belsen**
concentration camps.   **42 Luftwaffe** German air force.   **45 Panzer-man** member of a tank
crew.

Not God but a swastika
So black no sky could squeak through.
Every woman adores a Fascist,
The boot in the face, the brute
Brute heart of a brute like you.   50

You stand at the blackboard, daddy,
In the picture I have of you,
A cleft in your chin instead of your foot
But no less a devil for that, no not
Any less the black man who   55

Bit my pretty red heart in two.
I was ten when they buried you.
At twenty I tried to die
And get back, back, back to you.
I thought even the bones would do.   60

But they pulled me out of the sack,
And they stuck me together with glue,
And then I knew what to do.
I made a model of you,
A man in black with a Meinkampf° look   65

And a love of the rack and the screw.
And I said I do, I do.
So daddy, I'm finally through.
The black telephone's off at the root,
The voices just can't worm through.   70

If I've killed one man, I've killed two—
The vampire who said he was you
And drank my blood for a year,
Seven years, if you want to know.
Daddy, you can lie back now.   75

There's a stake in your fat black heart
And the villagers never liked you.
They are dancing and stamping on you.
They always *knew* it was you.
Daddy, daddy, you bastard, I'm through.   80

---

65 Meinkampf My Struggle (*Mein Kampf* is the title of Hitler's autobiography).

LINDA PASTAN

Linda Pastan, born in New York City in 1932, is the author of numerous books of poetry and the winner of significant literary prizes. Another of her poems appears on page 717.

Love Poem

[1988]

I want to write you
a love poem as headlong
as our creek
after thaw
when we stand
on its dangerous
banks and watch it carry
with it every twig
every dry leaf and branch
in its path
every scruple
when we see it
so swollen
with runoff
that even as we watch
we must grab
each other
and step back
we must grab each
other or
get our shoes
soaked we must
grab each other

AMIRI BARAKA

Amiri Baraka (b. 1934) in his early years was Everett LeRoi (or LeRoy) Jones, but with an increasing awareness of his African heritage he altered his name, first to Imamu ("spiritual leader") Ameer ("blessed") Baraka ("prince") and then to Amiri Baraka. Baraka was educated at Howard University, Columbia University, and the New School for Social Research.

After serving in the United States Air Force, Baraka settled in Greenwich Village, in New York City, and became part of the (chiefly white) literary scene; he and his wife published a journal that included works by Jack Kerouac, Allen Ginsberg, and others. The assassination of Malcolm X in 1965 had a profound effect on Baraka, and in this year he left his white wife and the artistic life of Greenwich Village and moved to Harlem, where he established the Black Arts Repertory Theater/School. In 1966 he returned to Newark, where he founded a similar school and, perhaps because of his heightened socialism, dropped Imamu from his name. The author of many plays and books of poetry, he is an emeritus professor at the State University of New York, Stony Brook.

Malcolm X (1925-1965), the subject of the following poem, was a militant black leader who rose to prominence in the Black Muslims. When in 1963 Elijah Muhammad suspended him, Malcolm formed his own organization, the Muslim Mosque. In 1964 he converted to orthodox Islam, and he proclaimed the brotherhood of blacks and whites, although he continued to support black nationalism. In February 1965 he was shot to death by an unidentified assassin.

A Poem for Black Hearts   [1965]

For Malcolm's eyes, when they broke
the face of some dumb white man, For
Malcolm's hands raised to bless us
all black and strong in his image
of ourselves, For Malcolm's words   5
fire darts, the victor's tireless
thrusts, words hung above the world
change as it may, he said it, and
for this he was killed, for saying,
and feeling, and being / change, all   10
collected hot in his heart, For Malcolm's
heart, raising us above our filthy cities,
for his stride, and his beat, and his address
to the gray monsters of the world, For Malcolm's
pleas for your dignity, black men, for your life,   15
black man, for the filling of your minds
with righteousness, For all of him dead and
gone and vanished from us, and all of him which
clings to our speech black god of our time.
For all of him, and all of yourself, look up,   20
black man, quit stuttering and shuffling, look up,
black man, quit whining and stooping, for all of him,
For Great Malcolm a prince of the earth, let nothing in us rest
until we avenge ourselves for his death, stupid animals
that killed him, let us never breathe a pure breath if   25
we fail and white men call us faggots till the end of
the earth.

LUCILLE CLIFTON

*Lucille Clifton (née Sayles) was born in New York State in 1936 and was edu-
cated at Howard University and Fredonia State Teachers College. In addition
to publishing seven books of poetry, she has written fifteen children's books.
Clifton has received numerous awards, including a grant from the National
Endowment for the Arts. She served as poet laureate of Maryland from 1979
to 1982.*

in the inner city   [1969]

in the inner city
or
like we call it
home
we think a lot about uptown   5
and the silent nights
and the houses straight as
dead men

and the pastel lights
and we hang on to our no place   10
happy to be alive
and in the inner city
or
like we call it
home   15

JOSEPH BRODSKY

*The poet and critic Joseph Brodsky (1940-1996) was
born in St. Petersburg (then Leningrad), Russia, in 1940.
Because of his resistance to Soviet authority, he was sentenced in the 1960s to a labor camp and later, in 1972,
was expelled from the country. He immigrated to the
United States, and taught and lectured at a number of
colleges and universities. He received the Nobel Prize for
Literature in 1987 and was named poet laureate by the
Library of Congress in 1991. His books include a collection of poems,* To Urania *(1988), and* Less Than One: Selected Essays *(1986).*

Love Song   [1996]

If you were drowning, I'd come to the rescue,
  wrap you in my blanket and pour hot tea.
If I were a sheriff, I'd arrest you
  and keep you in the cell under lock and key.   4

If you were a bird, I'd cut a record
  and listen all night long to your high-pitched trill.
If I were a sergeant, you'd be my recruit,
  and boy I can assure you you'd love the drill.   8

If you were Chinese, I'd learn the language,
  burn a lot of incense, wear funny clothes.
If you were a mirror, I'd storm the Ladies,
  give you my red lipstick and puff your nose.   12

If you loved volcanoes, I'd be lava
  relentlessly erupting from my hidden source.
And if you were my wife, I'd be your lover
  because the church is firmly against divorce.   16

BOB DYLAN

*Bob Dylan, born Robert Zimmerman in 1941 in Duluth, Minnesota, played
the guitar as a child and learned the harmonica when he was 15. Among
his chief models were Huddie Ledbetter (better known as Leadbelly), an
African-American folk singer and guitarist, and Woody Guthrie, a white folk*

singer, guitarist, and harmonica player. Dylan's music ranges from folk to folk-rock to country blues, but perhaps his most influential songs were those of social protest, such as "Blowin' in the Wind" and "The Times They Are A-Changin'."

The Times They Are A-Changin'

[1963]

Come gather 'round people
Wherever you roam
And admit that the waters
Around you have grown
And accept it that soon   5
You'll be drenched to the bone.
If your time to you
Is worth savin'
Then you better start swimmin'
Or you'll sink like a stone   10
For the times they are a-changin'.

Come writers and critics
Who prophesize with your pen
And keep your eyes wide
The chance won't come again   15
And don't speak too soon
For the wheel's still in spin
And there's no tellin' who
That it's namin'.
For the loser now   20
Will be later to win
For the times they are a-changin'.

Come senators, congressmen
Please heed the call
Don't stand in the doorway   25
Don't block up the hall
For he that gets hurt
Will be he who has stalled
There's a battle outside
And it is ragin'.   30
It'll soon shake your windows
And rattle your walls
For the times they are a-changin'.

Come mothers and fathers
Throughout the land   35
And don't criticize
What you can't understand
Your sons and your daughters
Are beyond your command
Your old road is   40
Rapidly agin'.
Please get out of the new one

If you can't lend your hand
For the times they are a-changin'.

The line it is drawn   45
The curse it is cast
The slow one now
Will later be fast
As the present now
Will later be past   50
The order is
Rapidly fadin'.
And the first one now
Will later be last
For the times they are a-changin'.   55

PAT MORA

Pat Mora, after graduating from Texas Western College, earned a master's degree at the University of Texas at El Paso. She is best known for her poems, but she has also published essays on Chicano culture.

Sonrisas*   [1986]

I live in a doorway
between two rooms. I hear
quiet clicks, cups of black
coffee, *click, click* like facts
   budgets, tenure, curriculum,   5
from careful women in crisp beige
suits, quick beige smiles
that seldom sneak into their eyes.

I peek
in the other room señoras   10
in faded dresses stir sweet
milk coffee, laughter whirls
with steam from fresh *tamales*
  sh, sh, mucho ruido,°
they scold one another,   15
press their lips, trap smiles
in their dark, Mexican eyes.

---

*Sonrisas smiles (Spanish).   **14 mucho ruido** lots of noise.

Illegal Alien   [1984]

Socorro, you free me
to sit in my yellow kitchen
waiting for a poem
while you scrub and iron.

Today you stand before me   5
holding cleanser and sponge
and say you can't sleep at night.
"My husband's fury is a fire.
His fist can burn.
We don't fight with words   10
on that side of the Rio Grande."

Your eyes fill. I want
to comfort you, but my arms
feel heavy, unaccustomed
to healing grown-up bodies.   15

I offer foolish questions
when I should hug you hard,
when I should dry your eyes, my sister,
sister because we are both women,
both married, both warmed   20
by Mexican blood.

It is not cool words you need
but soothing hands.
My plastic band-aid doesn't fit
your hurt.   25
I am the alien here.

Legal Alien   [1984]

Bi-lingual. Bi-cultural,
able to slip from "How's life?"
to *"Me'stan volviendo loca,"*°
able to sit in a paneled office
drafting memos in smooth English,   5
able to order in fluent Spanish
at a Mexican restaurant,
American but hyphenated,
viewed by Anglos as perhaps exotic,
perhaps inferior, definitely different,   10
viewed by Mexicans as alien.
(their eyes say, "You may speak
Spanish but you're not like me")
an American to Mexicans
a Mexican to Americans   15
a handy token
sliding back and forth
between the fringes of both worlds
by smiling
by masking the discomfort   20
of being pre-judged
Bi-laterally.

---

3 *Me'stan volviendo loca* They are driving me crazy.

NIKKI GIOVANNI

Nikki Giovanni was born in Knoxville, Tennessee, in 1943 and educated at Fisk University, the University of Pennsylvania School of Social Work, and Columbia University. She has taught at Queens College, Rutgers University, and Ohio State University, and she now teaches creative writing at Mt. St. Joseph on the Ohio. Giovanni has published many books of poems, an auto-biography (Gemini: An Extended Autobiographical Statement on My First Twenty-Five Years of Being a Black Poet), *a book of essays, and a book consisting of a conversation with James Baldwin.*

Master Charge Blues

[1970]

its wednesday night baby
and i'm all alone
wednesday night baby
and i'm all alone
sitting with myself   5
waiting for the telephone

wanted you baby
but you said you had to go
wanted you yeah
but you said you had to go   10
called your best friend
but he can't come 'cross no more

did you ever go to bed
at the end of a busy day
look over and see the smooth   15
where you hump usta lay
feminine odor and no reason why
i said feminine odor and no reason why
asked the lord to help me
he shook his head "not i"   20

but i'm a modern woman baby
ain't gonna let this get me down
i'm a modern woman
ain't gonna let this get me down
gonna take my master charge   25
and get everything in town

ELLEN BRYANT VOIGT

Ellen Bryant Voigt was born in Virginia in 1943 and edu-cated at Converse College and the University of Iowa. She is the author of several books of poems and has taught writing at Massachusetts Institute of Technology and at Warren Wilson College.

Quarrel   [1983]

Since morning they have been quarreling—
the sun pouring its implacable white bath
over the birches, each one undressing
slyly, from the top down—and they hammer
at each other with their knives, nailfiles,   5
graters of complaint as the day unwinds,
the plush clouds lowering a gray matte°
for the red barn. Lunch, the soup
like batting in their mouths, last week,
last year, they're moving on to always   10
and never, their shrill pitiful children
crowd around but they see the top of this
particular mountain, its glacial headwall,
the pitch is terrific all through dinner,
and they are committed, the sun long gone,   15
the two of them back to back in the blank
constricting bed, like marbles on aluminum—
Of this fierce love
that needs to reproduce in one another
wounds inflicted by the world.   20

---

7 matte dull paint finish.

CAROL MUSKE

Carol Muske was born in 1945 in St. Paul, Minnesota, and educated at Creighton University and San Francisco State University. She has taught creative writing at several uni-versities and was the founder and director of Free Space (a creative writing program) at the Women's House of De-tention, Riker's Island, New York. She has written several books of poetry (and a novel, Dear Digby *[1989], pub-lished under her married name, Carol Muske-Dukes) and has been awarded distinguished fellowships, including a grant from the National Endowment for the Arts.*

Chivalry

[1997]

In Benares°
the holiest city on earth
I saw an old man
toiling up the stone steps
to the ghat°   5
his dead wife in his arms
shrunken to the size
of a child—
lashed to a stretcher.

The sky filled with crows.   10
He held her up for a moment
then placed her
in the flames.

In my time on earth
I have seen few acts of true chivalry,   15
man's reverence
for woman.

But the memory of him
with her
in the cradle of his arms   20
placing her just so in the fire
so she would burn faster
so the kindling of the stretcher
would catch—
is enough for me now,   25
will suffice
for what remains on this earth
a gesture of bereavement
in the familiar carnage of love.

---

1 Benares one of India's most ancient cities; located on the Ganges River, it is the holy city of
the Hindus and the site of pilgrimages.   **5 ghat** a broad flight of steps on an Indian riverbank
that provides access to the water.

WENDY ROSE

*Wendy Rose, of Hopi and Miwok ancestry, was born in 1948 in Oakland,
California. A graduate of the University of California, Berkeley, she has been
editor of* American Indian Quarterly. *She teaches American Indian Studies at
Fresno City College and is active as a poet, artist, and anthologist.*

Three Thousand Dollar Death Song   [1980]

Nineteen American Indian Skeletons from Nevada . . . valued at $3000 . . .
                                        —Museum invoice, 1975

Is it in cold hard cash? the kind
that dusts the insides of men's pockets
lying silver-polished surface along the cloth.
Or in bills? papering the wallets of they
who thread the night with dark words. Or   5
checks? paper promises weighing the same
as words spoken once on the other side
of the grown grass and damned rivers
of history. However it goes, it goes
Through my body it goes assessing each nerve, running its edges   10
along my arteries, planning ahead
for whose hands will rip me
into pieces of dusty red paper,
whose hands will smooth or smatter me
into traces of rubble. Invoiced now,   15
it's official how our bones are valued
that stretch out pointing to sunrise
or are flexed into one last foetal bend,
that are removed and tossed about,
catalogued, numbered with black ink   20
on newly-white foreheads.
As we were formed to the white soldier's voice,
so we explode under white students' hands.
Death is a long trail of days
in our fleshless prison.   25

From this distant point we watch our bones
auctioned with our careful beadwork,
our quilled medicine bundles, even the bridles
of our shot-down horses. You: who have
priced us, you who have removed us: at what cost?   30
What price the pits where our bones share
a single bit of memory, how one century
turns our dead into specimens, our history
into dust, our survivors into clowns.
Our memory might be catching, you know;   35
picture the mortars, the arrowheads, the labrets°
shaking off their labels like bears
suddenly awake to find the seasons have ended
while they slept. Watch them touch each other,
measure reality, march out the museum door!   40
Watch as they lift their faces
and smell about for us; watch our bones rise
to meet them and mount the horses once again!
The cost, then, will be paid
for our sweetgrass-smelling having-been   45

---

36 labrets wood or bone ornaments inserted into a perforation in the lip.

in clam shell beads and steatite,°
dentalia° and woodpecker scalp, turquoise
and copper, blood and oil, coal
and uranium, children, a universe
of stolen things.   50

DIANE ACKERMAN

*The poet, essayist, and naturalist Diane Ackerman was born in Waukegan,
Illinois, in 1948. She graduated from Pennsylvania State University and later
received an M.F.A. and a Ph.D. from Cornell University. She is the author of
six volumes of verse, including* Jaguar of Sweet Laughter: New and Selected
Poems *(1991) and, most recently,* I Praise My Destroyer *(1998). She has also
written nonfiction, and is especially admired for* A Natural History of the
Senses *(1990). She lives in Ithaca, New York.*

Pumping Iron   [1985]

She doesn't want
the bunchy look
of male lifters:
torso an unyielding love-knot,
arms hard at mid-boil.   5
Doesn't want
the dancing bicepses
of pros.
Just to run her flesh
up the flagpole   10
of her body,
to pull her roaming flab
into tighter cascades,
machete a waist
through the jungle   15
of her hips,
a trim waist
two hands might grip
as a bouquet.

JOY HARJO

*Joy Harjo, a Creek Indian, was born in Tulsa, Oklahoma, in 1951. She was ed-
ucated at the Institute of American Indian Arts in Sante Fe, New Mexico, and
at the University of Iowa Writers' Workshop. She lives in Albuquerque, New
Mexico. Her chief books are* The Last Song, What Moon Drove Me to This, She
Had Some Horses, *and* Secrets from the Center of the World.

---

46 steatite soapstone. **47 dentalia** plural of *dentalium,* a kind of shellfish.

Vision

[1983]

The rainbow touched down
"somewhere in the Rio Grande,"
we said. And saw the light of it
from your mother's house in Isleta.°
How it curved down between earth   5
and the deepest sky to give us horses
of color
        horses that were within us all of this time
but we didn't see them because
we wait for the easiest vision   10
            to save us.

In Isleta the rainbow was a crack
in the universe. We saw the barest
of all life that is possible.
Bright horses rolled over   15
and over the dusking sky.
I heard the thunder of their beating
hearts. Their lungs hit air
and sang. All the colors of horses
formed the rainbow,   20
        and formed us
watching them.

_____

4 **Isleta** a pueblo in New Mexico.

JUDITH ORTIZ COFER

*Born in Puerto Rico in 1952 of a Puerto Rican mother and a United States
mainland father who served in the Navy, Judith Ortiz Cofer was educated
both in Puerto Rico and on the mainland. After earning a bachelor's and a
master's degree in English, she did further graduate work at Oxford and then
taught English in Florida. The author of poems, essays, and a novel, she is now
the Director of the Creative Writing Program at the University of Georgia.*

My Father in the Navy

[1987]

A Childhood Memory

Stiff and immaculate
in the white cloth of his uniform
and a round cap on his head like a halo,
he was an apparition on leave from a shadow-world
and only flesh and blood when he rose from below   5
the waterline where he kept watch over the engines
and dials making sure the ship parted the waters
on a straight course.
Mother, brother and I kept vigil

on the nights and dawns of his arrivals,   10
watching the corner beyond the neon sign of a quasar
for the flash of white our father like an angel
heralding a new day.
His homecomings were the verses
we composed over the years making up   15
the siren's song that kept him coming back
from the bellies of iron whales
and into our nights
like the evening prayer.

BOB HICOK

Bob Hicok, born in 1960, is the author of several books of poetry. He teaches creative writing at Virginia Tech, in Blacksburg.

Man of the House   [1995]

It was a misunderstanding.
I got into bed, made love
with the woman I found there,
called her honey, mowed the lawn,
had three children, painted   5
the house twice, fixed the furnace,
overcame an addiction to blue pills,
read Spinoza every night
without once meeting his God,
buried one child, ate my share   10
of Jell-o and meatloaf,
went away for nine hours a day
and came home hoarding my silence,
built a ferris wheel in my mind,
bolt by bolt, then broke it   15
just as it spun me to the top.
Turns out I live next door.

PART

IV

Drama

Drama usually tells an intense story by means of a fairly small number of characters. It can thus be contrasted with both the novel and with poetry. The novel tends to use a large number of characters and to cover a substantial period of time, thereby in some measure showing a picture of a society as well as of individuals; poetry, at the other extreme, tends to reveal the thoughts and emotions of individuals. Drama usually gives us a heightened sense of life as we experience it daily—that is, of one character impinging on another, of actions having consequences, and of lives as comically or tragically interconnected. To quote Alfred Hitchcock, "Drama is life with the dull bits cut out."

Admittedly, some playwrights have used the stage as a platform for exploring ideas rather than as a way of showing intense representations of lives interacting, and Arthur Miller is among the playwrights who are sometimes said to be intellectuals. He indeed commented abundantly on the nature of society, both in essays and within the plays themselves (e.g., in *All My Sons* Chris Keller tells his mother, "There's a universe of people outside, and you're responsible to it"), but the fact remains that Miller is especially valued not for Big Ideas but because he gives us, through passionate characters, a sense that we are witnessing lives and human relationships in their most essential forms. Miller wished to make us think, but chiefly he makes us feel, and that is perhaps enough for a playwright to do. He cared deeply about social issues but one of the wisest things he said is not about any social issue but about the nature of drama itself: "The theater is above all else an instrument of passion."

Arthur Miller (1915–2005) was born in New York, the son of Jewish immigrants from Austria. Miller went to the University of Michigan, where he first majored in journalism but then switched to English. As an undergraduate he won an award for playwrighting—one of the judges was Susan Glaspell, author of *Trifles* (see page 1033)—and after graduation (1938) he returned to New York, where he wrote some radio plays and some unsuccessful stage plays. A novel, *Focus* (1945), was well received, and with *All My Sons* (1947), *Death of a Salesman* (1949) and *The Crucible* (1953), his reputation as a playwright was firmly established. His leftist views, however, caused difficulty: Subjected to questioning by the House Committee on Un-American Activities, in the 1950s he was convicted of contempt of Congress, but the conviction was overturned in 1958. Miller is widely regarded, in England and the rest of Europe as well as in the United States, as American's most important dramatist.

29

How to Read a Play

THINKING ABOUT
THE LANGUAGE OF DRAMA

The earlier parts of this book have dealt with fiction and poetry. A third chief literary type is drama, texts written to be performed.

A play is written to be seen and to be heard. We go to *see* a play in a theater (*theater* is derived from a Greek word meaning "to watch"), but in the theater we also *hear* it because we become an audience (*audience* is derived from a Latin word meaning "to hear"). Hamlet was speaking the ordinary language of his day when he said, "We'll hear a play tomorrow." When we read a play rather than see and hear it in a theater, we lose a good deal. We must see it in the mind's eye and hear it in the mind's ear.

In reading a play it's not enough mentally to hear the lines. We must try to see the characters, costumed and moving within a specified setting, and we must try to hear not only their words but their tone, their joy or hypocrisy or tentativeness or aggression. Our job is much easier when we are in the theater and we have only to pay attention to the performers; as readers on our own, however, we must do what we can to perform the play in the theater of our minds.

If as a reader you develop the following principles into habits, you will get far more out of a play than if you read it as though it were a novel consisting only of dialogue.

1. *Pay attention to the **list of characters** and carefully read whatever **descriptions** the playwright has provided.* Early dramatists, such as Shakespeare, did not provide much in the way of description ("Othello, the Moor" or "Ariel, an airy spirit" is about as much as we find in Elizabethan texts), but later playwrights often are very forthcoming. Here, for instance, is Tennessee Williams introducing us to Amanda Wingfield in *The Glass Menagerie.* (We give only the beginning of his longish description.)

    Amanda Wingfield, the mother. A little woman of great but confused vitality clinging frantically to another time and place.

   And here is Susan Glaspell introducing us to all the characters in her one-act play, *Trifles:*

. . . the Sheriff comes in, followed by the County Attorney and Hale. The Sheriff and Hale are men in middle life, the County Attorney is a young man; all are much bundled up and go at once to the stove. They are followed by the two women—the Sheriff's Wife, [Mrs. Peters] first; she is a slight wiry woman, a thin nervous face. Mrs. Hale is larger and would ordinarily be called more comfortable looking, but she is disturbed now and looks fearfully about as she enters. The women have come in slowly and stand close together near the door.

Glaspell's description of her characters is not nearly so explicit as Tennessee Williams's, but Glaspell does reveal much to a reader. What do we know about the men? They differ in age, they are bundled up, and they "go at once to the stove." What do we know about the women? Mrs. Peters is slight, and she has a "nervous face"; Mrs. Hale is "larger" but she too is "disturbed." The women enter "slowly," and they "stand close together near the door." In short, the men, who take over the warmest part of the room, are more confident than the women, who nervously huddle together near the door. It's a man's world.

2. *Pay attention to* **gestures** *and* **costumes** *that are specified in stage directions or are implied by the dialogue.* We have just seen how Glaspell distinguishes between the men and the women by what they do—the men take over the warm part of the room, the women stand insecurely near the door. Most dramatists from the late nineteenth century to the present have been fairly generous with their stage directions, but when we read the works of earlier dramatists we often have to deduce the gestures from the speeches. For instance, although the texts of Shakespeare's day have an occasional direction, such as "Enter Hamlet reading on a book," "Leaps in the grave," and "in scuffling, they change rapiers," such directions are rare. In reading Shakespeare, we must, again, see the action *in the mind's eye* (a phrase from *Hamlet,* by the way) Here, for instance, are Horatio's words (1.1.130–31) when he sees the Ghost:

> But soft, behold! Lo, where it comes again!
> I'll cross it, though it blast me. [*It spreads his arms.*] Stay, *illusion!*

As a footnote indicates, the "his" in the stage direction is the Ghost's; today we would say "its." There is no doubt about what the Ghost does, but what does Horatio do when he says "I'll cross it"? Conceivably "I'll cross it" means "I'll confront it; I'll stand in its path," and Horatio then walks up to the Ghost. Or perhaps the words mean "I'll make the sign of the cross, to protect myself from this creature from another world." If so, does Horatio make the sign of the cross with his hand, or does he perhaps hold up his sword, an object that by virtue of the sword guard at right angles to the blade is itself a cross? The words "Stay, *illusion*" similarly must be accompanied by a gesture; perhaps Horatio reaches out, to try to take hold of the Ghost.

Or consider the first reunion of Hamlet and Horatio, in the second scene (1.2.160–61) of the play:

> HORATIO. Hail to your lordship!
> HAMLET. I am glad to see you well.
>   Horatio!—or I do forget myself.

One cannot be positive, but it seems that the melancholy Hamlet, hearing a greeting ("Hail to your lordship"), at first replies with routine politeness ("I am glad to see you well") and, when an instant later he recognizes that this greeting comes from an old friend whom he has not seen for a while, he responds with an enthusiastic "Horatio!" and perhaps with an embrace.

In addition to thinking about gestures, don't forget the costumes that the characters wear. Costumes identify the characters as soldiers or kings or farmers or whatever, and changes of costume can be especially symbolic.

Costumes are always important, because they tell us something about the people who wear them. As even the fatuous Polonius knows, "the apparel oft proclaims the man." In *Hamlet,* the use of symbolic costume is evident; Hamlet is dressed in black (we hear of his "nighted color" and his "inky cloak"), a color that sets him apart from the courtiers, who presumably are dressed in colorful robes. Later in the play, when, having escaped from a sea journey that was supposed to end in his death, Hamlet is seen in the graveyard, perhaps he wears the "sea gown" that he mentions, and we feel that he is now a more energetic character, freed from his constricting suit of mourning.

3. *Keep in mind the **kind of theater*** for which the play was written. The plays in this book were written for various kinds of theaters. Sophocles, author of *Antigone* and *King Oedipus,* wrote for the ancient Greek theater, essentially a space where performers acted in front of an audience seated on a hillside. (See the photo on page 1098.) This theater was open to the heavens, with a structure representing a palace or temple behind the actors, in itself a kind of image of a society governed by the laws of the state and the laws of the gods. Moreover, the chorus entered the playing space by marching down the side aisles, close to the audience, thus helping to unite the world of the audience and of the players. On the other hand, the audience in most modern theaters sits in a darkened area and looks through a proscenium arch at performers who move in a boxlike setting. The box set of the late nineteenth century and the twentieth century is, it often seems, an appropriate image of the confined lives of the unheroic characters of the play.

4. *If the playwright describes a set, try to **envision the set*** *clearly.* Glaspell, for instance, tells us a good deal about the set. We quote only the first part.

> The kitchen in the now abandoned farmhouse of John Wright, a gloomy kitchen, and left without having been put in order. . . .

These details about a gloomy and disordered kitchen may seem to be mere realism—after all, the play has to take place *somewhere*—but it turns out that the disorder and, for that matter, the gloominess are extremely important. You'll have to read the play to find out why.

Another example of a setting that provides important information is Arthur Miller's in *Death of a Salesman.* Again we quote only the beginning of the description.

> Before us is the Salesman's house. We are aware of towering, angular shapes behind it, surrounding it on all sides. Only the blue light of the sky falls upon the house and forestage; the surrounding area shows an angry glow of orange.

If we read older drama, we find that playwrights do *not* give us much help, but by paying attention to the words we can to some degree visualize the locale. For instance, the first stage direction in *Hamlet* (*"Enter Bernardo and Francisco, two sentinels"*), along with the opening dialogue ("Who's there?"; "Nay, answer me. Stand and unfold yourself"), indicates that we are in some sort of public place where anyone may suddenly appear. Elizabethan plays were staged in daylight, and there was no way of darkening the stage, so if the scene is a night scene the playwright has to convey this information. In this instance, the audience understands that the meeting takes place at night because the characters can hear but cannot see each other; to make certain, however, a few lines later Shakespeare has Bernardo say, "'Tis now struck twelve. Get thee to bed, Francisco."

5. *Pay attention to whatever **sound effects** are specified in the play.* In *Hamlet* (1.2.125), when the king (called "Denmark" in the speech we quote) drinks, he does so to the rather vulgar accompaniment of a cannonade:

> No jocund health that Denmark drinks today
> But the great cannon to the clouds shall tell,
> And the King's rouse the heaven shall bruit again,
> Respeaking earthly thunder.

The point is made again several times, but these salutes to King Claudius are finally displaced by a military salute to Hamlet; *"a peal of ordnance is shot off,"* we are told, when his body is carried off the stage at the end of the play. Thus, the last sound that we hear in *Hamlet* is a validation of Hamlet as a hero.

In *Death of a Salesman,* before the curtain goes up, "A melody is heard, played upon a flute. It is small and fine, telling of grass and trees and the horizon." Then the curtain rises, revealing the Salesman's house, with "towering, angular shapes behind it, surrounding it on all sides." Obviously the sound of the flute is meant to tell us of the world that the Salesman is shut off from.

A sound effect, however, need not be so evidently symbolic to be important in a play. In Glaspell's *Trifles,* almost at the very end of the play we hear the "sound of a knob turning in the other room." The sound has an electrifying effect on the audience, as it does on the two women on the stage, and it precedes a decisive action.

6. *Pay attention to what the characters say, and keep in mind that (like real people) **dramatic characters are not always to be trusted.*** An obvious case is Shakespeare's Iago, an utterly unscrupulous villain who knows that he is a liar. But a character may be self-deceived, or, to put it a bit differently, characters may say what they honestly think but may not know what they are talking about.

PLOT AND CHARACTER

Although **plot** is sometimes equated with the gist of the narrative—the story—it is sometimes reserved to denote the writer's *arrangement* of the happenings in the story. Thus, all plays about the assassination of Julius Caesar have pretty much the same story, but by beginning with a scene of workmen enjoying a holiday (and thereby introducing the motif of the fickleness of the mob), Shakespeare's play has a plot different from a play that omits such a scene.

Handbooks on drama often suggest that a plot (arrangement of happenings) should have a **rising action,** a **climax,** and a **falling action.** This sort of plot can be diagrammed as a pyramid, the tension rising through complications, or **crises,** to a climax, at which point the fate of the **protagonist** (chief character) is firmly established; the climax is the apex, and the tension allegedly slackens as we witness the **dénouement** (unknotting). Shakespeare sometimes used a pyramidal structure, placing his climax neatly in the middle of what seems to us to be the third of five acts.* Roughly the first half of *Julius Caesar* shows Brutus rising, reaching his height in 3.1 with the death of Caesar; but later in this scene he gives Marc Antony permission to speak at Caesar's funeral and thus he sets in motion his own fall, which occupies the second half of the play. In *Macbeth* (3.4.137–39), the protagonist attains his height in 3.1 ("Thou hast it now: King"), but he soon perceives that he is going downhill:

> I am in blood
> Stepped in so far, that, should I wade no more,
> Returning were as tedious as go o'er.

Of course, no law demands such a structure, and a hunt for the pyramid usually causes the hunter to overlook all the crises but the middle one. William Butler Yeats once suggestively diagrammed a good plot not as a pyramid but as a line moving diagonally upward, punctuated by several crises. Perhaps it is sufficient to say that a good plot has its moments of tension, but the location of these will vary with the play. They are the product of **conflict,** but not all conflict produces tension; there is conflict but little tension in a ball game when the score is 10–0 in the ninth inning with two out and no one on base.

Regardless of how a plot is diagrammed, the **exposition** is that part that tells the audience what it has to know about the past, the **antecedent action.** When two gossiping servants tell each other that after a year away in Paris the young master is coming home tomorrow with a new wife, they are giving the audience the exposition by introducing characters and establishing relationships. The Elizabethans and the Greeks sometimes tossed out all pretense at dialogue and began with a **prologue,** like the one spoken by the Chorus at the outset of *Romeo and Juliet:*

> Two households, both alike in dignity
> In fair Verona, where we lay our scene,
> From ancient grudge break to new mutiny,
> Where civil blood makes civil hands unclean.

---

*An **act** is a main division in a drama or opera. Act divisions probably stem from Roman theory and derive ultimately from the Greek practice of separating episodes in a play by choral interludes; but Greek (and probably Roman) plays were performed without interruption, for the choral interludes were part of the plays themselves. Elizabethan plays, too, may have been performed without breaks; the division of Elizabethan plays into five acts is usually the work of editors rather than of authors. Frequently an act division today (commonly indicated by lowering the curtain and turning up the houselights) denotes change in locale and lapse of time. A **scene** is a smaller unit, either (1) a division with no change of locale or abrupt shift of time, or (2) a division consisting of an actor or group of actors on the stage; according to the second definition, the departure or entrance of an actor changes the composition of the group and thus introduces a new scene. (In an entirely different sense, the scene is the locale where a work is set.)

From forth the fatal loins of these two foes
A pair of star-crossed lovers take their life. . . .

And in Tennessee Williams's *The Glass Menagerie,* Tom's first speech is a sort of prologue. However, the exposition also may extend far into the play so that the audience keeps getting bits of information that both clarify the present and build suspense about the future. Occasionally the **soliloquy** (speech of a character alone on the stage, revealing his or her thoughts) or the **aside** (speech in the presence of others but unheard by them) is used to do the job of putting the audience in possession of the essential facts. The soliloquy and the aside are not limited to exposition; they are used to reveal the private thoughts of characters who, like people in real life, do not always tell others what their inner thoughts are. The soliloquy is especially used for meditation, where we might say the character is interacting not with another character but with himself or herself.

Because a play is not simply words but words spoken with accompanying gestures by performers who are usually costumed and in a particular setting, it may be argued that to read a play (rather than to see and hear it) is to falsify it. Drama is not literature, some people hold, but theater. However, there are replies: a play can be literature as well as theater, and readers of a play can perhaps enact in the theater of their mind a more effective play than the one put on by imperfect actors. After all, as Shakespeare's Duke Theseus, in *A Midsummer Night's Dream,* says of actors, "The best in this kind are but shadows." In any case, we need not wait for actors to present a play; we can do much on our own.

Marjorie Vonnegut, Elinor M. Cox, John King, Arthur F. Hole, and T. W. Gibson in *Trifles,* as published in *Theatre Magazine,* January 1917.

SUSAN GLASPELL

Susan Glaspell (1882-1948) was born in Davenport, Iowa, and educated at Drake University in Des Moines. In 1903 she married George Cram Cook and, with Cook and other writers, actors, and artists, in 1915 founded the Provincetown Players, a group that remained vital until 1929. Glaspell wrote Trifles *(1916) for the Provincetown Players, but she also wrote stories, novels, and a biography of her husband. In 1931 she won a Pulitzer Prize for* Alison's House, *a play about the family of a deceased poet who in some ways resembles Emily Dickinson.*

Trifles   [1916]

SCENE: *The kitchen in the now abandoned farmhouse of John Wright, a gloomy kitchen, and left without having been put in order—unwashed pans under the sink, a loaf of bread outside the breadbox, a dish towel on the table—other signs of incompleted work. At the rear the outer door opens, and the Sheriff comes in, followed by the County Attorney and Hale. The Sheriff and Hale are men in middle life, the County Attorney is a young man; all are much bundled up and go at once to the stove. They are followed by the two women—the Sheriff's Wife first; she is a slight wiry woman, a thin nervous face. Mrs. Hale is larger and would ordinarily be called more comfortable looking, but she is disturbed now and looks fearfully about as she enters. The women have come in slowly and stand close together near the door.*

COUNTY ATTORNEY *(rubbing his hands).* This feels good. Come up to the fire, ladies.

MRS. PETERS *(after taking a step forward).* I'm not—cold.

SHERIFF *(unbuttoning his overcoat and stepping away from the stove as if to the beginning of official business).* Now, Mr. Hale, before we move things about, you explain to Mr. Henderson just what you saw when you came here yesterday morning.

COUNTY ATTORNEY. By the way, has anything been moved? Are things just as you left them yesterday?

SHERIFF *(looking about).* It's just the same. When it dropped below zero last night, I thought I'd better send Frank out this morning to make a fire for us—no use getting pneumonia with a big case on; but I told him not to touch anything except the stove—and you know Frank.

COUNTY ATTORNEY. Somebody should have been left here yesterday.

SHERIFF. Oh—yesterday. When I had to send Frank to Morris Center for that man who went crazy—I want you to know I had my hands full yesterday. I knew you could get back from Omaha by today, and as long as I went over everything here myself—

COUNTY ATTORNEY. Well, Mr. Hale, tell just what happened when you came here yesterday morning.

HALE. Harry and I had started to town with a load of potatoes. We came along the road from my place; and as I got here, I said, "I'm going to see if I can't get John Wright to go in with me on a party telephone." I spoke to Wright about it once before, and he put me off, saying folks talked too much anyway, and all he asked was peace and quiet—I guess you know about how much he talked himself; but I thought maybe if I went to the house and talked about it before his wife, though I said to Harry that I didn't know as what his wife wanted made much difference to John—

COUNTY ATTORNEY. Let's talk about that later, Mr. Hale. I do want to talk about that, but tell now just what happened when you got to the house.

HALE. I didn't hear or see anything; I knocked at the door, and still it was all quiet inside. I knew they must be up, it was past eight o'clock. So I knocked again, and I thought I heard somebody say, "Come in." I wasn't sure, I'm not sure yet, but I opened the door—this door (*indicating the door by which the two women are still standing*), and there in that rocker—(*pointing to it*) sat Mrs. Wright. (*They all look at the rocker.*)

COUNTY ATTORNEY. What—was she doing?

HALE. She was rockin' back and forth. She had her apron in her hand and was kind of—pleating it.

COUNTY ATTORNEY. And how did she—look?

HALE. Well, she looked queer.

COUNTY ATTORNEY. How do you mean—queer?

HALE. Well, as if she didn't know what she was going to do next. And kind of done up.

COUNTY ATTORNEY. How did she seem to feel about your coming?

HALE. Why, I don't think she minded—one way or other. She didn't pay much attention. I said, "How do, Mrs. Wright, it's cold, ain't it?" And she said, "Is it?"—and went on kind of pleating at her apron. Well, I was surprised; she didn't ask me to come up to the stove, or to set down, but just sat there, not even looking at me, so I said, "I want to see John." And then she—laughed. I guess you would call it a laugh. I thought of Harry and the team outside, so I said a little sharp: "Can't I see John?" "No," she says, kind o' dull like. "Ain't he home?" says I. "Yes," says she, "he's home." "Then why can't I see him?" I asked her, out of patience. "'Cause he's dead," says she. *"Dead?"* says I. She just nodded her head, not getting a bit excited, but rockin' back and forth. "Why—where is he?" says I, not knowing what to say. She just pointed upstairs—like that (*himself pointing to the room above*). I got up, with the idea of going up there. I walked from there to here—then I says, "Why, what did he die of?" "He died of a rope around his neck," says she, and just went on pleatin' at her apron. Well, I went out and called Harry. I thought I might—need help. We went upstairs, and there he was lyin'—

COUNTY ATTORNEY. I think I'd rather have you go into that upstairs, where you can point it all out. Just go on now with the rest of the story.

HALE. Well, my first thought was to get that rope off. I looked . . . . (*Stops, his face twitches.*) . . . but Harry, he went up to him, and he said, "No, he's dead all right, and we'd better not touch anything." So we went back downstairs. She was still sitting that same way. "Has anybody been notified?" I asked. "No," says she, unconcerned. "Who did this, Mrs. Wright?" said Harry. He said it business-like—and she stopped pleatin' of her apron. "I don't know," she says. "You don't *know*?" says Harry. "No," says she. "Weren't you sleepin' in the bed with him?" says Harry.

"Yes," says she, "but I was on the inside." "Somebody slipped a rope round his neck and strangled him, and you didn't wake up?" says Harry. "I didn't wake up," she said after him. We must 'a looked as if we didn't see how that could be, for after a minute she said, "I sleep sound." Harry was going to ask her more questions, but I said maybe we ought to let her tell her story first to the coroner, or the sheriff, so Harry went fast as he could to Rivers' place, where there's a telephone.

COUNTY ATTORNEY. And what did Mrs. Wright do when she knew that you had gone for the coroner?

HALE. She moved from that chair to this over here . . . *(Pointing to a small chair in the corner.)*. . . and just sat there with her hands held together and looking down. I got a feeling that I ought to make some conversation, so I said I had come in to see if John wanted to put in a telephone, and at that she started to laugh, and then she stopped and looked at me—scared. *(The County Attorney, who has had his notebook out, makes a note.)* I dunno, maybe it wasn't scared. I wouldn't like to say it was. Soon Harry got back, and then Dr. Lloyd came, and you, Mr. Peters, and so I guess that's all I know that you don't.

COUNTY ATTORNEY *(looking around)*. I guess we'll go upstairs first—and then out to the barn and around there. *(To the Sheriff.)* You're convinced that there was nothing important here—nothing that would point to any motive?

SHERIFF. Nothing here but kitchen things.

(The County Attorney, after again looking around the kitchen, opens the door of a cupboard closet. He gets up on a chair and looks on a shelf. Pulls his hand away, sticky.)

COUNTY ATTORNEY. Here's a nice mess.

(The women draw nearer.)

MRS. PETERS *(to the other woman)*. Oh, her fruit; it did freeze. *(To the Lawyer.)* She worried about that when it turned so cold. She said the fire'd go out and her jars would break.

SHERIFF. Well, can you beat the women! Held for murder and worryin' about her preserves.

COUNTY ATTORNEY. I guess before we're through she may have something more serious than preserves to worry about.

HALE. Well, women are used to worrying over trifles.

(The two women move a little closer together.)

COUNTY ATTORNEY *(with the gallantry of a young politician)*. And yet, for all their worries, what would we do without the ladies? *(The women do not unbend. He goes to the sink, takes a dipperful of water from the pail and, pouring it into a basin, washes his hands. Starts to wipe them on the roller towel, turns it for a cleaner place.)* Dirty towels! *(Kicks his foot against the pans under the sink.)* Not much of a housekeeper, would you say, ladies?

MRS. HALE *(stiffly)*. There's a great deal of work to be done on a farm.

COUNTY ATTORNEY. To be sure. And yet . . . *(With a little bow to her.)* . . . I know there are some Dickson county farmhouses which do not have such roller towels. *(He gives it a pull to expose its full length again.)*

MRS. HALE. Those towels get dirty awful quick. Men's hands aren't always as clean as they might be.

COUNTY ATTORNEY. Ah, loyal to your sex, I see. But you and Mrs. Wright were neighbors. I suppose you were friends, too.

MRS. HALE *(shaking her head)*. I've not seen much of her of late years. I've not been in this house—it's more than a year.

COUNTY ATTORNEY. And why was that? You didn't like her?

MRS. HALE. I liked her all well enough. Farmers' wives have their hands full, Mr. Henderson. And then—

COUNTY ATTORNEY. Yes—?

MRS. HALE *(looking about)*. It never seemed a very cheerful place.

COUNTY ATTORNEY. No—it's not cheerful. I shouldn't say she had the home-making instinct.

MRS. HALE. Well, I don't know as Wright had, either.

COUNTY ATTORNEY. You mean that they didn't get on very well?

MRS. HALE. No, I don't mean anything. But I don't think a place'd be any cheerfuler for John Wright's being in it.

COUNTY ATTORNEY. I'd like to talk more of that a little later. I want to get the lay of things upstairs now. *(He goes to the left, where three steps lead to a stair door.)*

SHERIFF. I suppose anything Mrs. Peters does'll be all right. She was to take in some clothes for her, you know, and a few little things. We left in such a hurry yesterday.

COUNTY ATTORNEY. Yes, but I would like to see what you take, Mrs. Peters, and keep an eye out for anything that might be of use to us.

MRS. PETERS. Yes, Mr. Henderson.

(The women listen to the men's steps on the stairs, then look about the kitchen.)

MRS. HALE. I'd hate to have men coming into my kitchen, snooping around and criticizing. *(She arranges the pans under sink which the Lawyer had shoved out of place.)*

MRS. PETERS. Of course it's no more than their duty.

MRS. HALE. Duty's all right, but I guess that deputy sheriff that came out to make the fire might have got a little of this on. *(Gives the roller towel a pull.)* Wish I'd thought of that sooner. Seems mean to talk about her for not having things slicked up when she had to come away in such a hurry.

MRS. PETERS *(who has gone to a small table in the left rear corner of the room, and lifted one end of a towel that covers a pan)*. She had bread set. *(Stands still.)*

MRS. HALE *(eyes fixed on a loaf of bread beside the breadbox, which is on a low shelf at the other side of the room. Moves slowly toward it)*. She was going to put this in there. *(Picks up loaf, then abruptly drops it. In a manner of returning to familiar things.)* It's a shame about her fruit. I wonder if it's all gone. *(Gets up on the chair and looks.)* I think there's some here that's all right, Mrs. Peters. Yes—here; *(Holding it toward the window.)* this is cherries, too. *(Looking again.)* I declare I believe that's the only one. *(Gets down, bottle in her hand. Goes to the sink and wipes it off on the outside.)* She'll feel awful bad after all her hard work in the hot weather. I remember the afternoon I put up my cherries last summer. *(She puts the bottle on the big kitchen table, center of the room, front table. With a sigh, is about to sit down in the rocking chair. Before she is seated realizes what chair it is; with a slow look at it, steps back. The chair, which she has touched, rocks back and forth.)*

MRS. PETERS. Well, I must get those things from the front room closet. *(She goes to the door at the right, but after looking into the other room steps back.)* You coming with me, Mrs. Hale? You could help me carry them. *(They go into the other room; reappear, Mrs. Peters carrying a dress and skirt, Mrs. Hale following with a pair of shoes.)*

MRS. PETERS. My, it's cold in there. *(She puts the cloth on the big table, and hurries to the stove.)*

MRS. HALE *(examining the skirt)*. Wright was close. I think maybe that's why she kept so much to herself. She didn't even belong to the Ladies' Aid. I suppose she felt she couldn't do her part, and then you don't enjoy things when you feel shabby. She used to wear pretty clothes and be lively, when she was Minnie Foster, one of the town girls singing in the choir. But that—oh, that was thirty years ago. This all you was to take in?

MRS. PETERS. She said she wanted an apron. Funny thing to want, for there isn't much to get you dirty in jail, goodness knows. But I suppose just to make her feel more natural. She said they was in the top drawer in this cupboard. Yes, here. And then her little shawl that always hung behind the door. *(Opens stair door and looks.)* Yes, here it is. *(Quickly shuts door leading upstairs.)*

MRS. HALE *(abruptly moving toward her)*. Mrs. Peters?

MRS. PETERS. Yes, Mrs. Hale?

MRS. HALE. Do you think she did it?

MRS. PETERS *(in a frightened voice)*. Oh, I don't know.

MRS. HALE. Well, I don't think she did. Asking for an apron and her little shawl. Worrying about her fruit.

MRS. PETERS *(starts to speak, glances up, where footsteps are heard in the room above. In a low voice)*. Mr. Peters says it looks bad for her. Mr. Henderson is awful sarcastic in speech, and he'll make fun of her sayin' she didn't wake up.

MRS. HALE. Well, I guess John Wright didn't wake when they was slipping that rope under his neck.

MRS. PETERS. No, it's strange. It must have been done awful crafty and still. They say it was such a—funny way to kill a man, rigging it all up like that.

MRS. HALE. That's just what Mr. Hale said. There was a gun in the house. He says that's what he can't understand.

MRS. PETERS. Mr. Henderson said coming out that what was needed for the case was a motive; something to show anger, or—sudden feeling.

MRS. HALE *(who is standing by the table)*. Well, I don't see any signs of anger around here. *(She puts her hand on the dish towel which lies on the table, stands looking down at the table, one half of which is clean, the other half messy)*. It's wiped here. *(Makes a move as if to finish work, then turns and looks at loaf of bread outside the breadbox. Drops towel. In that voice of coming back to familiar things.)*

Wonder how they are finding things upstairs? I hope she had it a little more red-up there. You know, it seems kind of *sneaking.* Locking her up in town and then coming out here and trying to get her own house to turn against her!

MRS. PETERS. But, Mrs. Hale, the law is the law.

MRS. HALE. I s'pose 'tis. *(Unbuttoning her coat.)* Better loosen up your things, Mrs. Peters. You won't feel them when you go out.

(Mrs. Peters takes off her fur tippet, goes to hang it on hook at the back of room, stands looking at the under part of the small corner table.)

MRS. PETERS. She was piecing a quilt. *(She brings the large sewing basket, and they look at the bright pieces.)*

MRS. HALE. It's log cabin pattern. Pretty, isn't it? I wonder if she was goin' to quilt or just knot it?

(Footsteps have been heard coming down the stairs. The Sheriff enters, followed by Hale and the County Attorney.)

SHERIFF. They wonder if she was going to quilt it or just knot it. *(The men laugh, the women look abashed.)*

COUNTY ATTORNEY *(rubbing his hands over the stove).* Frank's fire didn't do much up there, did it? Well, let's go out to the barn and get that cleared up.

(The men go outside.)

MRS. HALE *(resentfully).* I don't know as there's anything so strange, our takin' up our time with little things while we're waiting for them to get the evidence. *(She sits down at the big table, smoothing out a block with decision.)* I don't see as it's anything to laugh about.

MRS. PETERS *(apologetically).* Of course they've got awful important things on their minds. *(Pulls up a chair and joins Mrs. Hale at the table.)*

MRS. HALE *(examining another block).* Mrs. Peters, look at this one. Here, this is the one she was working on, and look at the sewing! All the rest of it has been so nice and even. And look at this! It's all over the place! Why, it looks as if she didn't know what she was about! *(After she has said this, they look at each other, then start to glance back at the door. After an instant Mrs. Hale has pulled at a knot and ripped the sewing.)*

MRS. PETERS. Oh, what are you doing, Mrs. Hale?

MRS. HALE *(mildly).* Just pulling out a stitch or two that's not sewed very good. *(Threading a needle.)* Bad sewing always made me fidgety.

MRS. PETERS *(nervously).* I don't think we ought to touch things.

MRS. HALE. I'll just finish up this end. *(Suddenly stopping and leaning forward.)* Mrs. Peters?

MRS. PETERS. Yes, Mrs. Hale?

MRS. HALE. What do you suppose she was so nervous about?

MRS. PETERS. Oh—I don't know. I don't know as she was nervous. I sometimes sew awful queer when I'm just tired. *(Mrs. Hale starts to say something, looks at Mrs. Peters, then goes on sewing.)* Well, I must get these things wrapped up. They may be through sooner than we think. *(Putting apron and other things together.)* I wonder where I can find a piece of paper, and string.

MRS. HALE. In that cupboard, maybe.

MRS. PETERS *(looking in cupboard)*. Why, here's a birdcage. *(Holds it up)*. Did she have a bird, Mrs. Hale?

MRS. HALE. Why, I don't know whether she did or not—I've not been here for so long. There was a man around last year selling canaries cheap, but I don't know as she took one; maybe she did. She used to sing real pretty herself.

MRS. PETERS *(glancing around)*. Seems funny to think of a bird here. But she must have had one, or why should she have a cage? I wonder what happened to it?

MRS. HALE. I s'pose maybe the cat got it.

MRS. PETERS. No, she didn't have a cat. She's got that feeling some people have about cats—being afraid of them. My cat got in her room, and she was real upset and asked me to take it out.

MRS. HALE. My sister Bessie was like that. Queer, ain't it?

MRS. PETERS *(examining the cage)*. Why, look at this door. It's broke. One hinge is pulled apart.

MRS. HALE *(looking, too)*. Looks as if someone must have been rough with it.

MRS. PETERS. Why, yes. *(She brings the cage forward and puts it on the table.)*

MRS. HALE. I wish if they're going to find any evidence they'd be about it. I don't like this place.

MRS. PETERS. But I'm awful glad you came with me, Mrs. Hale. It would be lonesome for me sitting here alone.

MRS. HALE. It would, wouldn't it? *(Dropping her sewing.)* But I tell you what I do wish, Mrs. Peters. I wish I had come over sometimes when *she* was here. I—*(Looking around the room.)*—wish I had.

MRS. PETERS. But of course you were awful busy, Mrs. Hale—your house and your children.

MRS. HALE. I could've come. I stayed away because it weren't cheerful—and that's why I ought to have come. I—I've never liked this place. Maybe because it's down in a hollow, and you don't see the road. I dunno what it is, but it's a lonesome place and always was. I wish I had come over to see Minnie Foster sometimes. I can see now—*(Shakes her head.)*

MRS. PETERS. Well, you mustn't reproach yourself, Mrs. Hale. Somehow we just don't see how it is with other folks until—something comes up.

MRS. HALE. Not having children makes less work—but it makes a quiet house, and Wright out to work all day, and no company when he did come in. Did you know John Wright, Mrs. Peters?

MRS. PETERS. Not to know him; I've seen him in town. They say he was a good man.

MRS. HALE. Yes—good; he didn't drink, and kept his word as well as most, I guess, and paid his debts. But he was a hard man, Mrs. Peters. Just to pass the time of day with him. *(Shivers.)* Like a raw wind that gets to the bone. *(Pauses, her eye falling on the cage.)* I should think she would 'a wanted a bird. But what do you suppose went with it?

MRS. PETERS. I don't know, unless it got sick and died. *(She reaches over and swings the broken door, swings it again; both women watch it.)*

MRS. HALE. You weren't raised round here, were you? *(Mrs. Peters shakes her head.)* You didn't know—her?

MRS. PETERS. Not till they brought her yesterday.

MRS. HALE. She—come to think of it, she was kind of like a bird herself—real sweet and pretty, but kind of timid and—fluttery. How—she—did—change. *(Silence; then as if struck by a happy thought and relieved to get back to everyday things.)* Tell you what, Mrs. Peters, why don't you take the quilt in with you? It might take up her mind.

MRS. PETERS. Why, I think that's a real nice idea, Mrs. Hale. There couldn't possibly be any objection to it, could there? Now, just what would I take? I wonder if her patches are in here—and her things. *(They look in the sewing basket.)*

MRS. HALE. Here's some red. I expect this has got sewing things in it. *(Brings out a fancy box.)* What a pretty box. Looks like something somebody would give you. Maybe her scissors are in here. *(Opens box. Suddenly puts her hand to her nose.)* Why—*(Mrs. Peters bends nearer, then turns her face away.)* There's something wrapped up in this piece of silk.

MRS. PETERS. Why, this isn't her scissors.

MRS. HALE *(lifting the silk).* Oh, Mrs. Peters—it's—*(Mrs. Peters bends closer.)*

MRS. PETERS. It's the bird.

MRS. HALE *(jumping up).* But, Mrs. Peters—look at it. Its neck! Look at its neck! It's all—other side *to.*

MRS. PETERS. Somebody—wrung—its neck.

(Their eyes meet. A look of growing comprehension of horror. Steps are heard outside. Mrs. Hale slips box under quilt pieces, and sinks into her chair. Enter Sheriff and County Attorney. Mrs. Peters rises.)

COUNTY ATTORNEY *(as one turning from serious things to little pleasantries).* Well, ladies, have you decided whether she was going to quilt it or knot it?

MRS. PETERS. We think she was going to—knot it.

COUNTY ATTORNEY. Well, that's interesting, I'm sure. *(Seeing the birdcage.)* Has the bird flown?

MRS. HALE *(putting more quilt pieces over the box).* We think the—cat got it.

COUNTY ATTORNEY *(preoccupied).* Is there a cat?

(Mrs. Hale glances in a quick covert way at Mrs. Peters.)

MRS. PETERS. Well, not now. They're superstitious, you know. They leave.

COUNTY ATTORNEY *(to Sheriff Peters, continuing an interrupted conversation).* No sign at all of anyone having come from the outside. Their own rope. Now let's go up again and go over it piece by piece. *(They start upstairs.)* It would have to have been someone who knew just the—

(Mrs. Peters sits down. The two women sit there not looking at one another, but as if peering into something and at the same time holding back. When they talk now, it is the manner of feeling their way over strange ground, as if afraid of what they are saying, but as if they cannot help saying it.)

MRS. HALE. She liked the bird. She was going to bury it in that pretty box.

MRS. PETERS *(in a whisper).* When I was a girl—my kitten—there was a boy took a hatchet, and before my eyes—and before I could get there—*(Covers her face an instant.)* If they hadn't held me back, I would have—*(Catches herself, looks upstairs where steps are heard, falters weakly.)*—hurt him.

MRS. HALE *(with a slow look around her)*. I wonder how it would seem never to have had any children around. *(Pause.)* No, Wright wouldn't like the bird—a thing that sang. She used to sing. He killed that, too.

MRS. PETERS *(moving uneasily)*. We don't know who killed the bird.

MRS. HALE. I knew John Wright.

MRS. PETERS. It was an awful thing was done in this house that night, Mrs. Hale. Killing a man while he slept, slipping a rope around his neck that choked the life out of him.

MRS. HALE. His neck. Choked the life out of him.

(Her hand goes out and rests on the birdcage.)

MRS. PETERS *(with a rising voice)*. We don't know who killed him. We don't *know*.

MRS. HALE *(her own feeling not interrupted)*. If there'd been years and years of nothing, then a bird to sing to you, it would be awful—still, after the bird was still.

MRS. PETERS *(something within her speaking)*. I know what stillness is. When we homesteaded in Dakota, and my first baby died—after he was two years old, and me with no other then—

MRS. HALE *(moving)*. How soon do you suppose they'll be through, looking for evidence?

MRS. PETERS. I know what stillness is. *(Pulling herself back.)* The law has got to punish crime, Mrs. Hale.

MRS. HALE *(not as if answering that)*. I wish you'd seen Minnie Foster when she wore a white dress with blue ribbons and stood up there in the choir and sang. *(A look around the room.)* Oh, I *wish* I'd come over here once in a while! That was a crime! That was a crime! Who's going to punish that?

MRS. PETERS *(looking upstairs)*. We mustn't—take on.

MRS. HALE. I might have known she needed help! I know how things can be—for women. I tell you, it's queer, Mrs. Peters. We live close together and we live far apart. We all go through the same things—it's all just a different kind of the same thing. *(Brushes her eyes, noticing the bottle of fruit, reaches out for it.)* If I was you, I wouldn't tell her her fruit was gone. Tell her it *ain't*. Tell her it's all right. Take this in to prove it to her. She—she may never know whether it was broke or not.

MRS. PETERS *(takes the bottle, looks about for something to wrap it in; takes petticoat from the clothes brought from the other room, very nervously begins winding this around the bottle. In a false voice)*. My, it's a good thing the men couldn't hear us. Wouldn't they just laugh! Getting all stirred up over a little thing like a—dead canary. As if that could have anything to do with—with—wouldn't they *laugh*!

(The men are heard coming downstairs.)

MRS. HALE *(under her breath)*. Maybe they would—maybe they wouldn't.

COUNTY ATTORNEY. No, Peters, it's all perfectly clear except a reason for doing it. But you know juries when it comes to women. If there was some definite thing. Something to show—something to make a story about—a thing that would connect up with this strange way of doing it.

(The women's eyes meet for an instant. Enter Hale from outer door.)

HALE. Well, I've got the team around. Pretty cold out there.

COUNTY ATTORNEY. I'm going to stay here awhile by myself. *(To the Sheriff.)* You can send Frank out for me, can't you? I want to go over everything. I'm not satisfied that we can't do better.

SHERIFF. Do you want to see what Mrs. Peters is going to take in?

(The Lawyer goes to the table, picks up the apron, laughs.)

COUNTY ATTORNEY. Oh I guess they're not very dangerous things the ladies have picked up. *(Moves a few things about, disturbing the quilt pieces which cover the box. Steps back.)* No, Mrs. Peters doesn't need supervising. For that matter, a sheriff's wife is married to the law. Ever think of it that way, Mrs. Peters?

MRS. PETERS. Not—just that way.

SHERIFF *(chuckling).* Married to the law. *(Moves toward the other room.)* I just want you to come in here a minute, George. We ought to take a look at these windows.

COUNTY ATTORNEY *(scoffingly).* Oh, windows!

SHERIFF. We'll be right out, Mr. Hale.

(Hale goes outside. The Sheriff follows the County Attorney into the other room. Then Mrs. Hale rises, hands tight together, looking intensely at Mrs. Peters, whose eyes take a slow turn, finally meeting Mrs. Hale's. A moment Mrs. Hale holds her, then her own eyes point the way to where the box is concealed. Suddenly Mrs. Peters throws back quilt pieces and tries to put the box in the bag she is wearing. It is too big. She opens box, starts to take the bird out, cannot touch it, goes to pieces, stands there helpless. Sound of a knob turning in the other room. Mrs. Hale snatches the box and puts it in the pocket of her big coat. Enter County Attorney and Sheriff.)

COUNTY ATTORNEY *(facetiously).* Well, Henry, at least we found out that she was not going to quilt it. She was going to—what is it you call it, ladies?

MRS. HALE *(her hand against her pocket).* We call it—knot it, Mr. Henderson.

CURTAIN

✳ TOPICS FOR CRITICAL THINKING AND WRITING

The Play on the Page

1. How would you characterize Mr. Henderson, the county attorney?
2. In what way or ways are Mrs. Peters and Mrs. Hale different from each other?
3. On page 1040, when Mrs. Peters tells of the boy who killed her cat, she says, "If they hadn't held me back, I would have—(*catches herself, looks upstairs where steps are heard, falters weakly.*)—hurt him." What do you think she was about to say before she faltered? Why do you suppose Glaspell included this speech about Mrs. Peters's girlhood?
4. We never see Mrs. Wright on stage. Nevertheless, by the end of *Trifles* we know a great deal about her. Explain both what we know about

her—physical characteristics, habits, interests, personality, life before her marriage and after—and *how* we know these things.

5. The title of the play is ironic—the "trifles" are important. What other ironies do you find in the play. (On *irony*, see the Glossary.)

6. Do you think the play is immoral? Explain.

7. Assume that the canary has been found, thereby revealing a possible motive, and that Minnie is indicted for murder. You are the defense attorney. In 500 words set forth your defense. (Take any position you wish. For instance, you may want to argue that she committed justifiable homicide or that—on the basis of her behavior as reported by Mr. Hale—she is innocent by reason of insanity.)

8. Assume that the canary had been found and Minnie Wright convicted. Compose the speech you think she might have delivered before the sentence was given.

The Play on the Stage

9. Briefly describe the setting, indicating what it "says" and what atmosphere it evokes.

10. Several times the men "laugh" or "chuckle." In their contexts, what do these expressions of amusement convey?

11. On page 1044, *"the women's eyes meet for an instant."* What do you think this bit of action "says"? What do you understand by the exchange of glances?

TENNESSEE WILLIAMS

Tennessee Williams (1914–1983) was born Thomas Lanier Williams in Columbus, Mississippi. During his childhood his family moved to St. Louis, where his father had accepted a job as manager of a shoe company. Williams has written that neither he nor his sister Rose could adjust to the change from the South to the Midwest, but the children had already been deeply troubled. Nevertheless, at the age of 16 he achieved some distinction as a writer when his prize-winning essay in a nationwide contest was published. After high school he attended the University of Missouri but flunked ROTC and was therefore withdrawn from school by his father. He worked in a shoe factory for a while, then attended Washington University, where he wrote several plays. He finally graduated from the University of Iowa with a major in playwrighting. After graduation he continued to write, supporting himself with odd jobs such as waiting on tables and running elevators. His first commercial success was The Glass Menagerie *(produced in Chicago in 1944, and in New York in 1945); among his other plays are* A Streetcar Named Desire *(1947),* Cat on a Hot Tin Roof *(1955), and* Suddenly Last Summer *(1958).*

The Glass Menagerie   [1944]

nobody, not even the rain, has such small hands.

—e. e. cummings

Left to right: Anthony Ross (Jim), Laurette Taylor (Amanda), Eddie Dowling (Tom), and Julie Hayden (Laura) in the 1945 original production of *The Glass Menagerie*, The Playhouse, New York.

LIST OF CHARACTERS

AMANDA WINGFIELD, *the mother. A little woman of great but confused vitality clinging frantically to another time and place. Her characterization must be carefully created, not copied from type. She is not paranoiac, but her life is paranoia. There is much to admire in Amanda, and as much to love and pity as there is to laugh at. Certainly she has endurance and a kind of heroism, and though her foolishness makes her unwittingly cruel at times, there is tenderness in her slight person.*

LAURA WINGFIELD, *her daughter. Amanda, having failed to establish contact with reality, continues to live vitally in her illusions, but Laura's situation is even graver. A childhood illness has left her crippled, one leg slightly shorter than the other, and held in a brace. This defect need not be more than suggested on the stage. Stemming from this, Laura's separation increases till she is like a piece of her own glass collection, too exquisitely fragile to move from the shelf.*

TOM WINGFIELD, *her son. And the narrator of the play. A poet with a job in a warehouse. His nature is not remorseless, but to escape from a trap he has to act without pity.*

JIM O'CONNOR, *the gentleman caller. A nice, ordinary, young man.*

SCENE. *An alley in St. Louis.*

PART I. *Preparation for a Gentleman Caller.*

PART II. *The Gentleman Calls.*

TIME. *Now and the Past.*

Scene I

The Wingfield apartment is in the rear of the building, one of those vast hive-like conglomerations of cellular living-units that flower as warty growths in overcrowded urban centers of lower middle-class population and are symptomatic of the impulse of this largest and fundamentally enslaved section of American society to avoid fluidity and differentiation and to exist and function as one interfused mass of automatism.

The apartment faces an alley and is entered by a fire-escape, a structure whose name is a touch of accidental poetic truth, for all of these huge buildings are always burning with the slow and implacable fires of human desperation. The fire-escape is included in the set—that is, the landing of it and steps descending from it.

The scene is memory and is therefore nonrealistic. Memory takes a lot of poetic license. It omits some details; others are exaggerated, according to the emotional value of the articles it touches, for memory is seated predominantly in the heart. The interior is therefore rather dim and poetic.

At the rise of the curtain, the audience is faced with the dark, grim rear wall of the Wingfield tenement. This building, which runs parallel to the footlights, is flanked on both sides by dark, narrow alleys which run into murky canyons of tangled clotheslines, garbage cans and the sinister latticework of neighboring fire-escapes. It is up and down these side alleys that exterior entrances and exits are made, during the play. At the end of TOM's *opening commentary, the dark tenement wall slowly reveals (by means of a transparency) the interior of the ground floor Wingfield apartment.*

Downstage is the living room, which also serves as a sleeping room for LAURA, *the sofa unfolding to make her bed. Upstage, center, and divided by a wide arch or second proscenium with transparent faded portieres (or second curtain), is the dining room. In an old-fashioned what-not in the living room are seen scores of transparent glass animals. A blown-up photograph of the father hangs on the wall of the living room, facing the audience, to the left of the archway. It is the face of a very handsome young man in a doughboy's First World War cap. He is gallantly smiling, ineluctably smiling, as if to say, "I will be smiling forever."*

The audience hears and sees the opening scene in the dining room through both the transparent fourth wall of the building and the transparent gauze portieres of the dining-room arch. It is during this revealing scene that the fourth wall slowly ascends, out of sight.

This transparent exterior wall is not brought down again until the very end of the play, during TOM's *final speech.*

The narrator is an undisguised convention of the play. He takes whatever license with dramatic convention as is convenient to his purposes.

TOM *enters dressed as a merchant sailor from alley, stage left, and strolls across the front of the stage to the fire-escape. There he stops and lights a cigarette. He addresses the audience.*

TOM. Yes, I have tricks in my pocket, I have things up my sleeve. But I am the opposite of a stage magician. He gives you illusion that has the appearance of truth. I give you truth in the pleasant disguise of illusion. To begin with, I turn back time. I reverse it to that quaint period, the thirties, when the huge middle class of America was matriculating in a school for the blind. Their eyes had failed them, or they had failed their eyes, and so they were having their fingers pressed forcibly down on the fiery Braille alphabet of a dissolving economy. In Spain there was revolution. Here there was only shouting and confusion. In Spain there was Guernica. Here there were disturbances of labor, sometimes pretty violent, in otherwise peaceful cities such as Chicago, Cleveland, Saint Louis. . . . This is the social background of the play.

(*Music.*)

The play is memory. Being a memory play, it is dimly lighted, it is sentimental, it is not realistic. In memory everything seems to happen to music. That explains the fiddle in the wings. I am the narrator of the play, and also a character in it. The other characters are my mother, Amanda, my sister, Laura, and a gentleman caller who appears in the final scenes. He is the most realistic character in the play, being an emissary from a world of reality that we were somehow set apart from. But since I have a poet's weakness for symbols, I am using this character also as a symbol; he is the long delayed but always expected something that we live for. There is a fifth character in the play who doesn't appear except in this larger-than-life photograph over the mantel. This is our father who left us a long time ago. He was a telephone man who fell in love with long distances; he gave up his job with the telephone company and skipped the light fantastic out of town. . . . The last we heard of him was a picture post-card from Mazatlan, on the Pacific coast of Mexico, containing a message of two words—"Hello—Goodbye!" and no address. I think the rest of the play will explain itself. . . .

AMANDA'S *voice becomes audible through the portieres.*
    (*Legend on Screen: "Où Sont les Neiges?"*)
    He divides the portieres and enters the upstage area.
    AMANDA *and* LAURA *are seated at a drop-leaf table. Eating is indicated by gestures without food or utensils.* AMANDA *faces the audience.* TOM *and* LAURA *are seated in profile.*
    The interior has lit up softly and through the scrim we see AMANDA *and* LAURA *seated at the table in the upstage area.*

AMANDA (*calling*). Tom?
TOM. Yes, Mother.
AMANDA. We can't say grace until you come to the table!
TOM. Coming, Mother. (*He bows slightly and withdraws, reappearing a few moments later in his place at the table.*)

AMANDA (*to her son*). Honey, don't *push* with your *fingers*. If you have to push with something, the thing to push with is a crust of bread. And chew—chew! Animals have sections in their stomachs which enable them to digest food without mastication, but human beings are supposed to chew their food before they swallow it down. Eat food leisurely, son, and really enjoy it. A well-cooked meal has lots of delicate flavors that have to be held in the mouth for appreciation. So chew your food and give your salivary glands a chance to function!

TOM *deliberately lays his imaginary fork down and pushes his chair back from the table.*

TOM. I haven't enjoyed one bite of this dinner because of your constant directions on how to eat it. It's you that makes me rush through meals with your hawk-like attention to every bite I take. Sickening—spoils my appetite—all this discussion of animals' secretion—salivary glands—mastication!

AMANDA (*lightly*). Temperament like a Metropolitan star! (*He rises and crosses downstage.*) You're not excused from the table.

TOM. I am getting a cigarette.

AMANDA. You smoke too much.

LAURA *rises.*

LAURA. I'll bring in the blanc mange.

He *remains standing with his cigarette by the portieres during the following.*

AMANDA (*rising.*) No, sister, no, sister—you be the lady this time and I'll be the darky.

LAURA. I'm already up.

AMANDA. Resume your seat, little sister—I want you to stay fresh and pretty—for gentlemen callers!

LAURA. I'm not expecting any gentlemen callers.

AMANDA (*crossing out to kitchenette. Airily*). Sometimes they come when they are least expected! Why, I remember one Sunday afternoon in Blue Mountain—(*Enters kitchenette.*)

TOM. I know what's coming!

LAURA. Yes. But let her tell it.

TOM. Again?

LAURA. She loves to tell it.

AMANDA *returns with bowl of dessert.*

AMANDA. One Sunday afternoon in Blue Mountain—your mother received—*seventeen!*—gentlemen callers! Why, sometimes there weren't chairs enough to accommodate them all. We had to send the nigger over to bring in folding chairs from the parish house.

TOM (*remaining at portieres*). How did you entertain those gentlemen callers?

AMANDA. I understood the art of conversation!

TOM. I bet you could talk.

AMANDA. Girls in those days *knew* how to talk, I can tell you.

TOM. Yes?

(*Image:* AMANDA *as a Girl on a Porch Greeting Callers.*)

AMANDA. They knew how to entertain their gentlemen callers. It wasn't enough for a girl to be possessed of a pretty face and a graceful figure— although I wasn't slighted in either respect. She also needed to have a nimble wit and a tongue to meet all occasions.

TOM. What did you talk about?

AMANDA. Things of importance going on in the world! Never anything coarse or common or vulgar. (*She addresses* TOM *as though he were seated in the vacant chair at the table though he remains by portieres. He plays this scene as though he held the book.*) My callers were gentlemen— all! Among my callers were some of the most prominent young planters of the Mississippi Delta—planters and sons of planters!

TOM *motions for music and a spot of light on* AMANDA.
   Her eyes lift, her face glows, her voice becomes rich and elegiac.
   (*Screen Legend: "Où Sont les Neiges?"*)

There was young Champ Laughlin who later became vice-president of the Delta Planters Bank. Hadley Stevenson who was drowned in Moon Lake and left his widow one hundred and fifty thousand in Government bonds. There were the Cutrere brothers, Wesley and Bates. Bates was one of my bright particular beaux! He got in a quarrel with that wild Wainright boy. They shot it out on the floor of Moon Lake Casino. Bates was shot through the stomach. Died in the ambulance on his way to Memphis. His widow was also well-provided for, came into eight or ten thousand acres, that's all. She married him on the rebound—never loved her—carried my picture on him the night he died! And there was that boy that every girl in Delta had set her cap for! That beautiful, brilliant young Fitzhugh boy from Green County!

TOM. What did he leave his widow?

AMANDA. He never married! Gracious, you talk as though all of my old admirers had turned up their toes to the daisies!

TOM. Isn't this the first you mentioned that still survives?

AMANDA. That Fitzhugh boy went North and made a fortune—came to be known as the Wolf of Wall Street! He had the Midas touch, whatever he touched turned to gold! And I could have been Mrs. Duncan J. Fitzhugh, mind you! But—I picked your *father!*

LAURA (*rising*). Mother, let me clear the table.

AMANDA. No dear, you go in front and study your typewriter chart. Or practice your shorthand a little. Stay fresh and pretty!—It's almost time for our gentlemen callers to start arriving. (*She flounces girlishly toward the kitchenette.*) How many do you suppose we're going to entertain this afternoon?

TOM *throws down the paper and jumps up with a groan.*

LAURA (*alone in the dining room*). I don't believe we're going to receive any, Mother.

AMANDA (*reappearing, airily*). What? No one—not one? You must be joking! (LAURA *nervously echoes her laugh. She slips in a fugitive manner through the half-open portieres and draws them gently behind her. A shaft of very clear light is thrown on her face against the faded tapestry of the curtains.*) (*Music: "The Glass Menagerie" Under Faintly.*) (*Lightly.*) Not one gentleman caller? It can't be true! There must be a flood, there must have been a tornado!

LAURA. It isn't a flood, it's not a tornado, Mother. I'm just not popular like you were in Blue Mountain. . . . (TOM *utters another groan.* LAURA *glances at him with a faint, apologetic smile. Her voice catching a little.*) Mother's afraid I'm going to be an old maid.

(*The Scene Dims Out with "Glass Menagerie" Music.*)

Scene II

"Laura, Haven't You Ever Liked Some Boy?"

On the dark stage the screen is lighted with the image of blue roses.

Gradually LAURA'S *figure becomes apparent and the screen goes out. The music subsides.*

LAURA *is seated in the delicate ivory chair at the small clawfoot table. She wears a dress of soft violet material for a kimono—her hair tied back from her forehead with a ribbon.*

She is washing and polishing her collection of glass.

AMANDA *appears on the fire-escape steps. At the sound of her ascent,* LAURA *catches her breath, thrusts the bowl of ornaments away and seats herself stiffly before the diagram of the typewriter keyboard as though it held her spellbound. Something has happened to* AMANDA. *It is written in her face as she climbs to the landing: a look that is grim and hopeless and a little absurd.*

She has on one of those cheap or imitation velvety-looking cloth coats with imitation fur collar. Her hat is five or six years old, one of those dreadful cloche hats that were worn in the late twenties, and she is clasping an enormous black patent-leather pocketbook with nickel clasp and initials. This is her full-dress outfit, the one she usually wears to the D.A.R.

Before entering she looks through the door.

She purses her lips, opens her eyes wide, rolls them upward and shakes her head.

Then she slowly lets herself in the door. Seeing her mother's expression LAURA *touches her lips with a nervous gesture.*

LAURA. Hello, Mother, I was—(*She makes a nervous gesture toward the chart on the wall.* AMANDA *leans against the shut door and stares at* LAURA *with a martyred look.*)

AMANDA. Deception? Deception? (*She slowly removes her hat and gloves, continuing the swift suffering stare. She lets the hat and gloves fall on the floor—a bit of acting.*)

LAURA (*shakily.*) How was the D.A.R. meeting? (AMANDA *slowly opens her purse and removes a dainty white handkerchief which she shakes out delicately and delicately touches to her lips and nostrils.*) Didn't you go to the D.A.R. meeting, Mother?

AMANDA (*faintly, almost inaudibly*). —No.—No. (*Then more forcibly.*) I did not have the strength—to go to the D.A.R. In fact, I did not have the courage! I wanted to find a hole in the ground and hide myself in it forever! (*She crosses slowly to the wall and removes the diagram of the typewriter keyboard. She holds it in front of her for a second, staring at it sweetly and sorrowfully—then bites her lips and tears it in two pieces.*)

LAURA (*faintly*). Why did you do that, Mother? (AMANDA *repeats the same procedure with the chart of the Gregg Alphabet.*) Why are you—

AMANDA. Why? Why? How old are you, Laura?

LAURA. Mother, you know my age.

AMANDA. I thought that you were an adult; it seems that I was mistaken. (*She crosses slowly to the sofa and sinks down and stares at* LAURA.)

LAURA. Please don't stare at me, Mother.

AMANDA *closes her eyes and lowers her head. Count ten.*

AMANDA. What are we going to do, what is going to become of us, what is the future?

Count ten.

LAURA. Has something happened, Mother? (AMANDA *draws a long breath and takes out the handkerchief again. Dabbing process.*) Mother, has—something happened?

AMANDA. I'll be all right in a minute. I'm just bewildered—(*count five*)—by life. . . .

LAURA. Mother, I wish that you would tell me what's happened.

AMANDA. As you know, I was supposed to be inducted into my office at the D.A.R. this afternoon. (*Image: A Swarm of Typewriters.*) But I stopped off at Rubicam's Business College to speak to your teachers about your having a cold and ask them what progress they thought you were making down there.

LAURA. Oh. . . .

AMANDA. I went to the typing instructor and introduced myself as your mother. She didn't know who you were. Wingfield, she said. We don't have any such student enrolled at the school! I assured her she did, that you had been going to classes since early in January. "I wonder," she said, "if you could be talking about that terribly shy little girl who dropped out of school after only a few days' attendance?" "No," I said, "Laura, my daughter, has been going to school every day for the past six weeks!" "Excuse me," she said. She took the attendance book out and there was your name, unmistakably printed, and all the dates you were absent until they decided that you had dropped out of school. I still said, "No, there must have been some mistake! There must have been some mix-up in the records!" And she said, "No—I remember her perfectly now. Her hand shook so that she couldn't hit the right keys! The first time we gave a speed-test, she broke down completely—was sick at the stomach and almost had to be carried into the wash-room! After that morning she never showed up any more. We phoned the house but never got any answer"—while I was working at Famous and Barr, I suppose, demonstrating those—Oh! I felt so weak I could barely keep on my feet. I had to sit down while they got me a glass of water! Fifty dollars' tuition, all of our plans—my hopes and ambitions for you—just gone up the spout, just gone up the spout like that. (LAURA *draws a long breath and gets awkwardly to her feet. She crosses to the victrola and winds it up.*) What are you doing?

LAURA. Oh! (*She releases the handle and returns to her seat.*)

AMANDA. Laura, where have you been going when you've gone out pretending that you were going to business college?

LAURA. I've just been going out walking.

AMANDA. That's not true.

LAURA. It is. I just went walking.

AMANDA. Walking? Walking? In winter? Deliberately courting pneumonia in that light coat? Where did you walk to, Laura?

LAURA. It was the lesser of two evils, Mother. (*Image: Winter Scene in Park.*) I couldn't go back up. I—threw up—on the floor!

AMANDA. From half past seven till after five every day you mean to tell me you walked around in the park, because you wanted to make me think that you were still going to Rubicam's Business College?

LAURA. It wasn't as bad as it sounds. I went inside places to get warmed up.

AMANDA. Inside where?

LAURA. I went in the art museum and the bird-houses at the Zoo. I visited the penguins every day! Sometimes I did without lunch and went to the movies. Lately I've been spending most of my afternoons in the Jewel-box, that big glass house where they raise the tropical flowers.

AMANDA. You did all this to deceive me, just for the deception? (LAURA *looks down.*) Why?

LAURA. Mother, when you're disappointed, you get that awful suffering look on your face, like the picture of Jesus' mother in the museum!

AMANDA. Hush!

LAURA. I couldn't face it.

Pause. A whisper of strings.
(Legend: "The Crust of Humility.")

AMANDA (*hopelessly fingering the huge pocketbook*). So what are we going to do the rest of our lives? Stay home and watch the parades go by? Amuse ourselves with the glass menagerie, darling? Eternally play those worn-out phonograph records your father left as a painful reminder of him? We won't have a business career—we've given that up because it gave us nervous indigestion! (*Laughs wearily.*) What is there left but dependency all our lives? I know so well what becomes of unmarried women who aren't prepared to occupy a position. I've seen such pitiful cases in the South—barely tolerated spinsters living upon the grudging patronage of sister's husband or brother's wife!—stuck away in some little mousetrap of a room—encouraged by one in-law to visit another—little birdlike women without any nest—eating the crust of humility all their life! Is that the future that we've mapped out for ourselves? I swear it's the only alternative I can think of! It isn't a very pleasant alternative, is it? Of course—some girls *do marry*. (LAURA *twists her hands nervously.*) Haven't you ever liked some boy?

LAURA. Yes. I liked one once. (*Rises.*) I came across his picture a while ago.

AMANDA (*with some interest*). He gave you his picture?

LAURA. No, it's in the year-book.

AMANDA (*disappointed*). Oh—a high-school boy.

(*Screen Image: JIM as a High-School Hero Bearing a Silver Cup.*)

LAURA. Yes. His name was Jim. (LAURA *lifts the heavy annual from the claw-foot table.*) Here he is in *The Pirates of Penzance.*

AMANDA (*absently*). The what?

LAURA. The operetta the senior class put on. He had a wonderful voice and we sat across the aisle from each other Mondays, Wednesdays and Fridays in the Aud. Here he is with the silver cup for debating! See his grin?

AMANDA (*absently*). He must have had a jolly disposition.

LAURA. He used to call me—Blue Roses.

(*Image: Blue Roses.*)

AMANDA. Why did he call you such a name as that?

LAURA. When I had that attack of pleurosis—he asked me what was the matter when I came back. I said pleurosis—he thought that I said Blue Roses! So that's what he always called me after that. Whenever he saw me, he'd holler, "Hello, Blue Roses!" I didn't care for the girl that he went out with. Emily Meisenbach. Emily was the best-dressed girl at Soldan. She never struck me, though, as being sincere. . . . It says in the Personal Section—they're engaged. That's—six years ago! They must be married by now.

AMANDA. Girls that aren't cut out for business careers usually wind up married to some nice man. (*Gets up with a spark of revival.*) Sister, that's what you'll do!

LAURA *utters a startled, doubtful laugh. She reaches quickly for a piece of glass.*

LAURA. But, Mother—

AMANDA. Yes? (*Crossing to photograph.*)

LAURA (*in a tone of frightened apology*). I'm—crippled!

(*Image: Screen.*)

AMANDA. Nonsense! Laura, I've told you never, never to use that word. Why, you're not crippled, you just have a little defect—hardly noticeable, even! When people have some slight disadvantage like that, they cultivate other things to make up for it—develop charm—and vivacity—and—*charm!* That's all you have to do! (*She turns again to the photograph.*) One thing your father had *plenty of*—was *charm!*

TOM *motions to the fiddle in the wings.*
    (*The Scene Fades Out with Music.*)

Scene III

(*Legend on the Screen: "After the Fiasco—"*)
    TOM *speaks from the fire-escape landing.*

TOM. After the fiasco at Rubicam's Business College, the idea of getting a gentleman caller for Laura began to play a more important part in

Mother's calculations. It became an obsession. Like some archetype of the universal unconscious, the image of the gentleman caller haunted our small apartment. . . . (*Image: Young Man at Door with Flowers.*) An evening at home rarely passed without some allusion to this image, this specter, this hope. . . . Even when he wasn't mentioned, his presence hung in Mother's preoccupied look and in my sister's frightened, apologetic manner—hung like a sentence passed upon the Wingfields! Mother was a woman of action as well as words. She began to take logical steps in the planned direction. Late that winter and in the early spring—realizing that extra money would be needed to properly feather the nest and plume the bird—she conducted a vigorous campaign on the telephone, roping in subscribers to one of those magazines for matrons called *The Home-maker's Companion,* the type of journal that features the serialized sublimations of ladies of letters who think in terms of delicate cuplike breasts, slim, tapering waists, rich, creamy thighs, eyes like wood-smoke in autumn, fingers that soothe and caress like strains of music, bodies as powerful as Etruscan sculpture.

(*Screen Image: Glamor Magazine Cover.*)

AMANDA *enters with phone on long extension cord. She is spotted in the dim stage.*

AMANDA. Ida Scott? This is Amanda Wingfield! We *missed* you at the D.A.R. last Monday! I said to myself: She's probably suffering with that sinus condition! How is that sinus condition? Horrors! Heaven have mercy!— You're a Christian martyr, yes, that's what you are, a Christian martyr! Well, I just now happened to notice that your subscription to the *Companion*'s about to expire! Yes, it expires with the next issue, honey!—just when that wonderful new serial by Bessie Mae Hopper is getting off to such an exciting start. Oh, honey, it's something that you can't miss! You remember how *Gone With the Wind* took everybody by storm? You simply couldn't go out if you hadn't read it. All everybody *talked* was Scarlett O'Hara. Well, this is a book that critics already compare to *Gone With the Wind.* It's the *Gone With the Wind* of the post–World War generation!—What?—Burning?—Oh, honey, don't let them burn, go take a look in the oven and I'll hold the wire! Heavens— I think she's hung up!

(*Dim Out.*)

(*Legend on Screen: "You Think I'm in Love with Continental Shoemakers?"*)

Before the stage is lighted, the violent voices of TOM *and* AMANDA *are heard. They are quarreling behind the portieres. In front of them stands* LAURA *with clenched hands and panicky expression.*

A clear pool of light on her figure throughout this scene.

TOM. What in Christ's name am I—
AMANDA (*shrilly*). Don't you use that—
TOM. Supposed to do!
AMANDA. Expression! Not in my—
TOM. Ohhh!
AMANDA. Presence! Have you gone out of your senses?

TOM. I have, that's true, *driven* out!

AMANDA. What is the matter with you, you—big—big—IDIOT!

TOM. Look—I've got *no thing,* no single thing—

AMANDA. Lower your voice!

TOM. In my life here that I can call my OWN! Everything is—

AMANDA. Stop that shouting!

TOM. Yesterday you confiscated my books! You had the nerve to—

AMANDA. I took that horrible novel back to the library—yes! That hideous book by that insane Mr. Lawrence. (TOM *laughs wildly.*) I cannot control the output of diseased minds or people who cater to them—(TOM *laughs still more wildly.*) BUT I WON'T ALLOW SUCH FILTH BROUGHT INTO MY HOUSE! No, no, no, no, no!

TOM. House, house! Who pays rent on it, who makes a slave of himself to—

AMANDA (*fairly screeching*). Don't you DARE to—

TOM. No, no, *I* musn't say things! *I've* got to just—

AMANDA. Let me tell you—

TOM. I don't want to hear any more! (*He tears the portieres open. The upstage area is lit with a turgid smoky red glow.*)

> AMANDA's *hair is in metal curlers and she wears a very old bathrobe, much too large for her slight figure, a relic of the faithless* MR. WINGFIELD.
>   *An upright typewriter and a wild disarray of manuscripts are on the dropleaf table. The quarrel was probably precipitated by* AMANDA's *interruption of his creative labor. A chair lying overthrown on the floor.*
>   *Their gesticulating shadows are cast on the ceiling by the fiery glow.*

AMANDA. You *will* hear more, you—

TOM. No, I won't hear more, I'm going out!

AMANDA. You come right back in—

TOM. Out, out, out! Because I'm—

AMANDA. Come back here, Tom Wingfield! I'm not through talking to you!

TOM. Oh, go—

LAURA (*desperately*). Tom!

AMANDA. You're going to listen, and no more insolence from you! I'm at the end of my patience! (*He comes back toward her.*)

TOM. What do you think I'm at? Aren't I supposed to have any patience to reach the end of, Mother? I know, I know. It seems unimportant to you, what I'm *doing*—what I *want* to do—having a little *difference* between them! You don't think that—

AMANDA. I think you've been doing things that you're ashamed of. That's why you act like this. I don't believe that you go every night to the movies. Nobody goes to the movies night after night. Nobody in their right minds goes to the movies as often as you pretend to. People don't go to the movies at nearly midnight, and movies don't let out at two A.M. Come in stumbling. Muttering to yourself like a maniac! You get three hours' sleep and then go to work. Oh, I can picture the way you're doing down there. Moping, doping, because you're in no condition.

TOM (*wildly*). No, I'm in no condition!

AMANDA. What right have you got to jeopardize your job? Jeopardize the security of us all? How do you think we'd manage if you were—

TOM. Listen! You think I'm crazy *about the warehouse?* (*He bends fiercely
toward her slight figure.*) You think I'm in love with the Continental
Shoemakers? You think I want to spend fifty-five *years* down there in
that—*celotex interior!* with—*fluorescent—tubes!* Look! I'd rather
somebody picked up a crowbar and battered out my brains—than go
back mornings! I go! Every time you come in yelling that God damn
"Rise and Shine!" "Rise and Shine!" I say to myself "How *lucky dead*
people are!" But I get up. I *go!* For sixty-five dollars a month I give up all
that I dream of doing and being *ever!* And you say self—*self's* all I ever
think of. Why, listen, if self is what I thought of, Mother, I'd be where
he is—GONE! (*Pointing to father's picture.*) As far as the system of trans-
portation reaches! (*He starts past her. She grabs his arm.*) Don't grab
at me, Mother!

AMANDA. Where are you going?

TOM. I'm going to the *movies!*

AMANDA. I don't believe that lie!

TOM (*crouching toward her, overtowering her tiny figure. She backs away,
gasping*). I'm going to opium dens! Yes, opium dens, dens of vice and
criminals' hang-outs, Mother. I've joined the Hogan gang, I'm a hired assassin, I carry a tommy-gun in a violin case! I run a string of cat-houses
in the Valley! They call me Killer, Killer Wingfield, I'm leading a double-
life, a simple, honest warehouse worker by day, by night a dynamic
czar of the *underworld, Mother.* I go to gambling casinos, I spin away
fortunes on the roulette table! I wear a patch over one eye and a false
mustache, sometimes I put on green whiskers. On those occasions they
call me—*El Diablo!* Oh, I could tell you things to make you sleepless!
My enemies plan to dynamite this place. They're going to blow us all
sky-high some night! I'll be glad, very happy, and so will you! You'll go
up, up on a broomstick, over Blue Mountain with seventeen gentlemen
callers! You ugly—babbling old—*witch.* . . . . (*He goes through a series of violent, clumsy movements, seizing his overcoat, lunging to
the door, pulling it fiercely open. The women watch him, aghast. His
arm catches in the sleeve of the coat as he struggles to pull it on. For a
moment he is pinioned by the bulky garment. With an outraged
groan he tears the coat off again, splitting the shoulders of it, and
hurls it across the room. It strikes against the shelf of Laura's glass
collection, there is a tinkle of shattering glass.* LAURA *cries out as if
wounded.*)

(*Music Legend: "The Glass Menagerie."*)

LAURA (*shrilly*). My glass!—menagerie. . . . (*She covers her face and turns
away.*)

But AMANDA *is still stunned and stupefied by the "ugly witch" so that
she barely notices this occurrence. Now she recovers her speech.*

AMANDA (*in an awful voice*). I won't speak to you—until you apologize!
(*She crosses through portieres and draws them together behind her.*

TOM *is left with* LAURA. LAURA *clings weakly to the mantel with her face averted.* TOM *stares at her stupidly for a moment. Then he crosses to shelf. Drops awkwardly to his knees to collect the fallen glass, glancing at* LAURA *as if he would speak but couldn't.*)

"The Glass Menagerie" steals in as
    (*The Scene Dims Out.*)

Scene IV

The interior is dark. Faint light in the alley.

A deep-voiced bell in a church is tolling the hour of five as the scene commences.

TOM *appears at the top of the alley. After each solemn boom of the bell in the tower, he shakes a little noise-maker or rattle as if to express the tiny spasm of man in contrast to the sustained power and dignity of the Almighty. This and the unsteadiness of his advance make it evident that he has been drinking.*

As he climbs the few steps to the fire-escape landing light steals up inside. LAURA *appears in night-dress, observing* TOM'S *empty bed in the front room.*

TOM *fishes in his pockets for the door-key, removing a motley assortment of articles in the search, including a perfect shower of movie-ticket stubs and an empty bottle. At last he finds the key, but just as he is about to insert it, it slips from his fingers. He strikes a match and crouches below the door.*

TOM (*bitterly*). One crack—and it falls through!

LAURA *opens the door.*

LAURA. Tom! Tom, what are you doing?

TOM. Looking for a door-key.

LAURA. Where have you been all this time?

TOM. I have been to the movies.

LAURA. All this time at the movies?

TOM. There was a very long program. There was a Garbo picture and a Mickey Mouse and a travelogue and a newsreel and a preview of coming attractions. And there was an organ solo and a collection for the milk-fund—simultaneously—which ended up in a terrible fight between a fat lady and an usher!

LAURA (*innocently*). Did you have to stay through everything?

TOM. Of course! And, oh, I forgot! There was a big stage show! The headliner on this stage show was Malvolio the Magician. He performed wonderful tricks, many of them, such as pouring water back and forth between pitchers. First it turned to wine and then it turned to beer and then it turned to whiskey. I know it was whiskey it finally turned into because he needed somebody to come up out of the audience to help him, and I came up—both shows! It was Kentucky Straight Bourbon. A very generous fellow, he gave souvenirs. (*He pulls from his back pocket a shimmering rainbow-colored scarf.*) He gave me this. This is his magic scarf. You can have it, Laura. You wave it over a canary cage and you get a bowl of gold-fish. You wave it over the gold-fish bowl and they fly away canaries. . . . But the wonderfullest trick of all was the coffin trick. We nailed him into a coffin and he got out of the coffin without removing one nail. (*He has come inside.*) There is a trick that would come in handy for me—get me out of this 2 by 4 situation! (*Flops onto bed and starts removing shoes.*)

LAURA. Tom—Shhh!

TOM. What you shushing me for?

LAURA. You'll wake up Mother.

TOM. Goody, goody! Pay 'er back for all those "Rise an' Shines." (*Lies down, groaning.*) You know it don't take much intelligence to get yourself into a nailed-up coffin, Laura. But who in hell ever got himself out of one without removing one nail?

As if in answer, the father's grinning photograph lights up.
     (*Scene Dims Out.*)
     Immediately following: The church bell is heard striking six. At the sixth stroke the alarm clock goes off in AMANDA'S *room, and after a few moments we hear her calling: "Rise and Shine! Rise and Shine!* LAURA, *go tell your brother to rise and shine!"*

TOM (*sitting up slowly*). I'll rise—but I won't shine.

The light increases.

AMANDA. Laura, tell your brother his coffee is ready.

LAURA *slips into front room.*

LAURA. Tom! It's nearly seven. Don't make Mother nervous. (*He stares at her stupidly. Beseechingly.*) Tom, speak to Mother this morning. Make up with her, apologize, speak to her!

TOM. She won't to me. It's her that started not speaking.

LAURA. If you just say you're sorry she'll start speaking.

TOM. Her not speaking—is that such a tragedy?

LAURA. Please—please!

AMANDA (*calling from kitchenette*). Laura, are you going to do what I asked you to do, or do I have to get dressed and go out myself?

LAURA. Going, going—soon as I get on my coat! (*She pulls on a shapeless felt hat with nervous, jerky movement, pleadingly glancing at* TOM. *Rushes awkwardly for coat. The coat is one of* AMANDA'S, *inaccurately made-over, the sleeves too short for* LAURA.) Butter and what else?

AMANDA (*entering upstage*). Just butter. Tell them to charge it.

LAURA. Mother, they make such faces when I do that.

AMANDA. Sticks and stones may break my bones, but the expression on Mr. Garfinkel's face won't harm us! Tell your brother his coffee is getting cold.

LAURA (*at door*). Do what I asked you, will you, will you, Tom?

He looks sullenly away.

AMANDA. Laura, go now or just don't go at all!

LAURA (*rushing out*). Going—going! (*A second later she cries out.* TOM *springs up and crosses to the door.* AMANDA *rushes anxiously in.* TOM *opens the door.*)

TOM. Laura?

LAURA. I'm all right. I slipped, but I'm all right.

AMANDA (*peering anxiously after her*). If anyone breaks a leg on those fire-escape steps, the landlord ought to be sued for every cent he possesses! (*She shuts door. Remembers she isn't speaking and returns to other room.*)

As TOM *enters listlessly for his coffee, she turns her back to him and stands rigidly facing the window on the gloomy gray vault of the areaway. Its light on her face with its aged but childish features is cruelly sharp, satirical as a Daumier print.*

(*Music Under: "Ave Maria."*)

TOM *glances sheepishly but sullenly at her averted figure and slumps at the table. The coffee is scalding hot; he sips it and gasps and spits it back in the cup. At his gasp,* AMANDA *catches her breath and half turns. Then catches herself and turns back to window.*

TOM *blows on his coffee, glancing sidewise at his mother. She clears her throat.* TOM *clears his. He starts to rise. Sinks back down again, scratches his head, clears his throat again.* AMANDA *coughs.* TOM *raises his cup in both hands to blow on it, his eyes staring over the rim of it at his mother for several moments. Then he slowly sets the cup down and awkwardly and hesitantly rises from the chair.*

TOM (*hoarsely*). Mother. I—I apologize. Mother. (AMANDA *draws a quick, shuddering breath. Her face works grotesquely. She breaks into child-like tears.*) I'm sorry for what I said, for everything that I said, I didn't mean it.

AMANDA (*sobbingly*). My devotion has made me a witch and so I make my-self hateful to my children!

TOM. No you *don't.*

AMANDA. I worry so much, don't sleep, it makes me nervous!

TOM (*gently*). I understand that.

AMANDA. I've had to put up a solitary battle all these years. But you're my right-hand bower! Don't fall down, don't fail!

TOM (*gently*). I try, Mother.

AMANDA (*with great enthusiasm*). Try and you will SUCCEED! (*The notion makes her breathless.*) Why, you—you're just *full* of natural endow-ments! Both of my children—they're *unusual* children! Don't you think I know it? I'm so—*proud!* Happy and—feel I've—so much to be thankful for but—Promise me one thing, son!

TOM. What, Mother?

AMANDA. Promise, son, you'll—never be a drunkard!

TOM (*turns to her grinning*). I will never be a drunkard, Mother.

AMANDA. That's what frightened me so, that you'd be drinking! Eat a bowl of Purina!

TOM. Just coffee, Mother.

AMANDA. Shredded wheat biscuit?

TOM. No. No, Mother, just coffee.

AMANDA. You can't put in a day's work on an empty stomach. You've got ten minutes—don't gulp! Drinking too-hot liquids makes cancer of the stomach. . . . Put cream in.

TOM. No, thank you.

AMANDA. To cool it.

TOM. No! No, thank you, I want it black.

AMANDA. I know, but it's not good for you. We have to do all that we can to build ourselves up. In these trying times we live in, all that we have to cling to is—each other. . . . That's why it's so important to—Tom, I—I sent out your sister so I could discuss something with you. If you hadn't spoken I would have spoken to you. (*Sits down.*)

TOM (*gently*). What is it, Mother, that you want to discuss?

AMANDA. Laura!

TOM *puts his cup down slowly.*
(*Legend on Screen:* "LAURA.")
(*Music: "The Glass Menagerie."*)

TOM. —Oh.—Laura . . .

AMANDA (*touching his sleeve*). You know how Laura is. So quiet but—still water runs deep! She notices things and I think she—broods about them. (TOM *looks up.*) A few days ago I came in and she was crying.

TOM. What about?

AMANDA. You.

TOM. Me?

AMANDA. She has an idea that you're not happy here.

TOM. What gave her that idea?

AMANDA. What gives her any idea? However, you do act strangely. I—I'm not criticizing, understand *that!* I know your ambitions do not lie in the warehouse, that like everybody in the whole wide world—you've had to—make sacrifices, but—Tom—Tom—life's not easy, it calls for—Spartan endurance! There's so many things in my heart that I cannot describe to you! I've never told you but I—*loved* your father. . . .

TOM (*gently*). I know that, Mother.

AMANDA. And you—when I see you taking after his ways! Staying out late—and—well, you *had* been drinking the night you were in that—terrifying condition! Laura says that you hate the apartment and that you go out nights to get away from it! Is that true, Tom?

TOM. No. You say there's so much in your heart that you can't describe to me. That's true of me, too. There's so much in my heart that I can't describe to *you!* So let's respect each other's—

AMANDA. But, why—*why,* Tom—are you always so *restless?* Where do you go to, nights?

TOM. I—go to the movies.

AMANDA. Why do you go to the movies so much, Tom?

TOM. I go to the movies because—I like adventure. Adventure is something I don't have much of at work, so I go to the movies.

AMANDA. But, Tom, you go to the movies *entirely too much!*

TOM. I like a lot of adventure.

AMANDA *looks baffled, then hurt. As the familiar inquisition resumes he becomes hard and impatient again.* AMANDA *slips back into her querulous attitude toward him.*
(*Image on Screen: Sailing Vessel with Jolly Roger.*)

AMANDA. Most young men find adventure in their careers.

TOM. Then most young men are not employed in a warehouse.

AMANDA. The world is full of young men employed in warehouses and offices and factories.

TOM. Do all of them find adventure in their careers?

AMANDA. They do or they do without it! Not everybody has a craze for adventure.

TOM. Man is by instinct a lover, a hunter, a fighter, and none of those instincts are given much play at the warehouse!

AMANDA. Man is by instinct! Don't quote instinct to me! Instinct is something that people have got away from! It belongs to animals! Christian adults don't want it!

TOM. What do Christian adults want, then, Mother?

AMANDA. Superior things! Things of the mind and the spirit! Only animals have to satisfy instincts! Surely your aims are somewhat higher than theirs! Than monkeys—pigs—

TOM. I reckon they're not.

AMANDA. You're joking. However, that isn't what I wanted to discuss.

TOM (*rising*). I haven't much time.

AMANDA (*pushing his shoulders*). Sit down.

TOM. You want me to punch in red at the warehouse, Mother?

AMANDA. You have five minutes. I want to talk about Laura.

(*Legend: "Plans and Provisions."*)

TOM. All right! What about Laura?

AMANDA. We have to be making plans and provisions for her. She's older than you, two years, and nothing has happened. She just drifts along doing nothing. It frightens me terribly how she just drifts along.

TOM. I guess she's the type that people call home girls.

AMANDA. There's no such type, and if there is, it's a pity! That is unless the home is hers, with a husband!

TOM. What?

AMANDA. Oh, I can see the handwriting on the wall as plain as I see the nose in the front of my face! It's terrifying! More and more you remind me of your father! He was out all hours without explanation—Then *left!* *Goodbye!* And me with the bag to hold. I saw that letter you got from the Merchant Marine. I know what you're dreaming of. I'm not standing here blindfolded. Very well, then. Then *do* it! But not till there's somebody to take your place.

TOM. What do you mean?

AMANDA. I mean that as soon as Laura has got somebody to take care of her, married, a home of her own, independent—why, then you'll be free to go wherever you please, on land, on sea, whichever way the wind blows! But until that time you've got to look out for your sister. I don't say me because I'm old and don't matter! I say for your sister because she's young and dependent. I put her in business college—a dismal failure! Frightened her so it made her sick to her stomach. I took her over to the Young People's League at the church. Another fiasco. She spoke to nobody, nobody spoke to her. Now all she does is fool with those pieces of glass and play those worn-out records. What kind of a life is that for a girl to lead!

TOM. What can I do about it?

AMANDA. Overcome selfishness! Self, self, self is all that you ever think of! (TOM *springs up and crosses to get his coat. It is ugly and bulky. He pulls on a cap with earmuffs.*) Where is your muffler? Put your wool muffler on! (*He snatches it angrily from the closet and tosses it around his neck and pulls both ends tight.*) Tom! I haven't said what I had in mind to ask you.

TOM. I'm too late to—

AMANDA (*catching his arms—very importunately. Then shyly*). Down at the warehouse, aren't there some—nice young men?

TOM. No!

AMANDA. There *must* be—*some.*

TOM. Mother—

Gesture.

AMANDA. Find out one that's clean-living—doesn't drink and—ask him out for sister!

TOM. What?

AMANDA. For *sister!* To *meet!* Get *acquainted!*

TOM (*stamping to door*). Oh, my go-osh!

AMANDA. Will you? (*He opens door. Imploringly.*) Will you? (*He starts down.*) Will you? *Will* you dear?

TOM (*calling back*). YES!

AMANDA *closes the door hesitantly and with a troubled but faintly hopeful expression.*
(*Screen Image: Glamor Magazine Cover.*)
Spot AMANDA *at phone.*

AMANDA. Ella Cartwright? This is Amanda Wingfield! How are you honey? How is that kidney condition? (*Count five.*) *Horrors!* (*Count five.*) You're a Christian martyr, yes, honey, that's what you are, a Christian martyr! Well, I just happened to notice in my little red book that your subscription to the *Companion* has just run out! I knew that you wouldn't want to miss out on the wonderful serial starting in this new issue. It's by Bessie Mae Hopper, the first thing she's written since *Honeymoon for Three.* Wasn't that a strange and interesting story? Well, this one is even lovelier, I believe. It has a sophisticated society background. It's all about the horsey set on Long Island!

(*Fade Out.*)

Scene V

(*Legend on Screen: "Annunciation."*) *Fade with music.*

It is early dusk of a spring evening. Supper has just been finished at the Wingfield apartment. AMANDA *and* LAURA *in light-colored dresses are removing dishes from the table, in the upstage area, which is shadowy, their movements formalized almost as a dance or ritual, their moving forms as pale and silent as moths.*

TOM, *in white shirt and trousers, rises from the table and crosses toward the fire-escape.*

AMANDA (*as he passes her*). Son, will you do me a favor?

TOM. What?

AMANDA. Comb your hair! You look so pretty when your hair is combed! (TOM *slouches on sofa with evening paper. Enormous caption "Franco Triumphs."*) There is only one respect in which I would like you to emulate your father.

TOM. What respect is that?

AMANDA. The care he always took of his appearance. He never allowed himself to look untidy. (*He throws down the paper and crosses to fire-escape.*) Where are you going?

TOM. I'm going out to smoke.

AMANDA. You smoke too much. A pack a day at fifteen cents a pack. How much would that amount to in a month? Thirty times fifteen is how much, Tom? Figure it out and you will be astounded at what you could save. Enough to give you a night-school course in accounting at Washington U! Just think what a wonderful thing that would be for you, son!

TOM *is unmoved by the thought.*

TOM. I'd rather smoke. (*He steps out on landing, letting the screen door slam.*)

AMANDA (*sharply*). I know! That's the tragedy of it. . . . (*Alone, she turns to look at her husband's picture.*)

(*Dance Music: "All the World Is Waiting for the Sunrise!"*)

TOM (*to the audience*). Across the alley from us was the Paradise Dance Hall. On evenings in spring the windows and doors were open and the music came outdoors. Sometimes the lights were turned out except for a large glass sphere that hung from the ceiling. It would turn slowly about and filter the dusk with delicate rainbow colors. Then the orchestra played a waltz or a tango, something that had a slow and sensuous rhythm. Couples would come outside, to the relative privacy of the alley. You could see them kissing behind ashpits and telephone poles. This was the compensation for lives that passed like mine, without any change or adventure. Adventure and change were imminent in this year. They were waiting around the corner for all these kids. Suspended in the mist over Berchtesgaden, caught in the folds of Chamberlain's umbrella—In Spain there was Guernica! But here there was only hot swing music and liquor, dance halls, bars, and movies, and sex that hung in the gloom like a chandelier and flooded the world with brief, deceptive rainbows. . . . All the world was waiting for bombardments!

AMANDA *turns from the picture and comes outside.*

AMANDA (*sighing*). A fire-escape landing's a poor excuse for a porch. (*She spreads a newspaper on a step and sits down, gracefully and demurely as if she were settling into a swing on a Mississippi veranda.*) What are you looking at?

TOM. The moon.

AMANDA. Is there a moon this evening?

TOM. It's rising over Garfinkel's Delicatessen.

AMANDA. So it is! A little silver slipper of a moon. Have you made a wish on it yet?

TOM. Um-hum.

AMANDA. What did you wish for?

TOM. That's a secret.

AMANDA. A secret, huh? Well, I won't tell mine either. I will be just as mysterious as you.

TOM. I bet I can guess what yours is.

AMANDA. Is my head so transparent?

TOM. You're not a sphinx.

AMANDA. No, I don't have secrets. I'll tell you what I wished for on the moon. Success and happiness for my precious children! I wish for that whenever there's a moon, and when there isn't a moon, I wish for it, too.

TOM. I thought perhaps you wished for a gentleman caller.

AMANDA. Why do you say that?

TOM. Don't you remember asking me to fetch one?

AMANDA. I remember suggesting that it would be nice for your sister if you brought some nice young man from the warehouse. I think I've made that suggestion more than once.

TOM. Yes, you have made it repeatedly.

AMANDA. Well?

TOM. We are going to have one.

AMANDA. *What?*

TOM. A gentleman caller!

(*The Annunciation Is Celebrated with Music.*)
    AMANDA *rises.*
    (*Image on Screen: Caller with Bouquet.*)

AMANDA. You mean you have asked some nice young man to come over?

TOM. Yep. I've asked him to dinner.

AMANDA. You really did?

TOM. I did!

AMANDA. You did, and did he—*accept?*

TOM. He did!

AMANDA. Well, well—well, well! That's—lovely!

TOM. I thought that you would be pleased.

AMANDA. It's definite, then?

TOM. Very definite.

AMANDA. Soon?

TOM. Very soon.

AMANDA. For heaven's sake, stop putting on and tell me some things, will you?

TOM. What things do you want me to tell you?

AMANDA. Naturally I would like to know when he's *coming!*

TOM. He's coming tomorrow.

AMANDA. *Tomorrow?*

TOM. Yep. Tomorrow.

AMANDA. But, Tom!

TOM. Yes, Mother?

AMANDA. Tomorrow gives me no time!

TOM. Time for what?

AMANDA. Preparations! Why didn't you phone me at once, as soon as you asked him, the minute that he accepted? Then, don't you see, I could have been getting ready!

TOM. You don't have to make any fuss.

AMANDA. Oh, Tom, Tom, Tom, of course I have to make a fuss! I want things nice, not sloppy! Not thrown together. I'll certainly have to do some fast thinking, won't I?

TOM. I don't see why you have to think at all.

AMANDA. You just don't know. We can't have a gentleman caller in a pigsty! All my wedding silver has to be polished, the monogrammed table linen ought to be laundered! The windows have to be washed and fresh curtains put up. And how about clothes? We have to *wear* something, don't we?

TOM. Mother, this boy is no one to make a fuss over!

AMANDA. Do you realize he's the first young man we've introduced to your sister? It's terrible, dreadful, disgraceful that poor little sister has never received a single gentleman caller! Tom, come inside! (*She opens the screen door.*)

TOM. What for?

AMANDA. I want to ask you some things.

TOM. If you're going to make such a fuss, I'll call it off, I'll tell him not to come.

AMANDA. You certainly won't do anything of the kind. Nothing offends people worse than broken engagements. It simply means I'll have to work like a Turk! We won't be brilliant, but we'll pass inspection. Come on inside. (TOM *follows, groaning.*) Sit down.

TOM. Any particular place you would like me to sit?

AMANDA. Thank heavens I've got that new sofa! I'm also making payments on a floor lamp I'll have sent out! And put the chintz covers on, they'll brighten things up! Of course I'd hoped to have these walls repapered. . . . What is the young man's name?

TOM. His name is O'Connor.

AMANDA. That, of course, means fish—tomorrow is Friday! I'll have that salmon loaf—with Durkee's dressing! What does he do? He works at the warehouse?

TOM. Of course! How else would I—

AMANDA. Tom, he—doesn't drink?

TOM. Why do you ask me that?

AMANDA. Your father *did!*

TOM. Don't get started on that!

AMANDA. He *does* drink, then?

TOM. Not that I know of!

AMANDA. Make sure, be certain! The last thing I want for my daughter's a boy who drinks!

TOM. Aren't you being a little premature? Mr. O'Connor has not yet appeared on the scene!

AMANDA. But will tomorrow. To meet your sister, and what do I know about his character? Nothing! Old maids are better off than wives of drunkards!

TOM. Oh, my God!

AMANDA. Be still!

TOM (*leaning forward to whisper*). Lots of fellows meet girls whom they don't marry!

AMANDA. Oh, talk sensibly, Tom—and don't be sarcastic! (*She has gotten a hairbrush.*)

TOM. What are you doing?

AMANDA. I'm brushing that cow-lick down! What is this young man's position at the warehouse?

TOM (*submitting grimly to the brush and the interrogation*). This young man's position is that of a shipping clerk, Mother.

AMANDA. Sounds to me like a fairly responsible job, the sort of a job *you* would be in if you just had more *get-up*. What is his salary? Have you got any idea?

TOM. I would judge it to be approximately eighty-five dollars a month.

AMANDA. Well—not princely, but—

TOM. Twenty more than I make.

AMANDA. Yes, how well I know! But for a family man, eighty-five dollars a month is not much more than you can just get by on. . . .

TOM. Yes, but Mr. O'Connor is not a family man.

AMANDA. He might be, mightn't he? Some time in the future?

TOM. I see. Plans and provisions.

AMANDA. You are the only man that I know of who ignores the fact that the future becomes the present, the present the past, and the past turns into everlasting regret if you don't plan for it!

TOM. I will think that over and see what I can make of it.

AMANDA. Don't be supercilious with your mother! Tell me some more about this—what do you call him?

TOM. James D. O'Connor. The D. is for Delaney.

AMANDA. Irish on *both* sides! *Gracious!* And doesn't drink?

TOM. Shall I call him up and ask him right this minute?

AMANDA. The only way to find out about those things is to make discreet inquiries at the proper moment. When I was a girl in Blue Mountain and it was suspected that a young man drank, the girl whose attentions he had been receiving, if any girl *was,* would sometimes speak to the minister of his church, or rather her father would if her father was living, and sort of feel him out on the young man's character. That is the way such things are discreetly handled to keep a young woman from making a tragic mistake!

TOM. Then how did you happen to make a tragic mistake?

AMANDA. That innocent look of your father's had everyone fooled! He *smiled*—the world was *enchanted!* No girl can do worse than put herself at the mercy of a handsome appearance! I hope that Mr. O'Connor is not too good-looking.

TOM. No, he's not too good-looking. He's covered with freckles and hasn't too much of a nose.

AMANDA. He's not right-down homely, though?

TOM. Not right-down homely. Just medium homely, I'd say.

AMANDA. Character's what to look for in a man.

TOM. That's what I've always said, Mother.

AMANDA. You've never said anything of the kind and I suspect you would never give it a thought.

TOM. Don't be suspicious of me.

AMANDA. At least I hope he's the type that's up and coming.

TOM. I think he really goes in for self-improvement.

AMANDA. What reason have you to think so?

TOM. He goes to night school.

AMANDA (*beaming*). Splendid! What does he do, I mean study?

TOM. Radio engineering and public speaking!

AMANDA. Then he has visions of being advanced in the world! Any young man who studies public speaking is aiming to have an executive job some day! And radio engineering? A thing for the future! Both of these facts are very illuminating. Those are the sort of things that a mother should know concerning any young man who comes to call on her daughter. Seriously or—not.

TOM. One little warning. He doesn't know about Laura. I didn't let on that we had dark ulterior motives. I just said, why don't you come have dinner with us? He said okay and that was the whole conversation.

AMANDA. I bet it was! You're eloquent as an oyster. However, he'll know about Laura when he gets here. When he sees how lovely and sweet and pretty she is, he'll thank his lucky stars he was asked to dinner.

TOM. Mother, you mustn't expect too much of Laura.

AMANDA. What do you mean?

TOM. Laura seems all those things to you and me because she's ours and we love her. We don't even notice she's crippled any more.

AMANDA. Don't say crippled! You know that I never allow that word to be used!

TOM. But face facts, Mother. She is and—that's not all—

AMANDA. What do you mean "not all"?

TOM. Laura is very different from other girls.

AMANDA. I think the difference is all to her advantage.

TOM. Not quite all—in the eyes of others—strangers—she's terribly shy and lives in a world of her own and those things make her seem a little peculiar to people outside the house.

AMANDA. Don't say peculiar.

TOM. Face the facts. She is.

(*The Dance-Hall Music Changes to a Tango that Has a Minor and Somewhat Ominous Tone.*)

AMANDA. In what way is she peculiar—may I ask?

TOM (*gently*). She lives in a world of her own—a world of—little glass ornaments, Mother. . . . (*Gets up.* AMANDA *remains holding brush, looking at him, troubled.*) She plays old phonograph records and—that's about all—(*He glances at himself in the mirror and crosses to door.*)

AMANDA (*sharply*). Where are you going?

TOM. I'm going to the movies. (*Out screen door.*)

AMANDA. Not to the movies, every night to the movies! (*Follows quickly to screen door.*) I don't believe you always go to the movies! (*He is gone.* AMANDA *looks worriedly after him for a moment. Then vitality and optimism return and she turns from the door. Crossing to portieres.*) Laura! Laura! (LAURA *answers from kitchenette.*)

LAURA. Yes, Mother.

AMANDA. Let those dishes go and come in front! (LAURA *appears with dish towel. Gaily.*) Laura, come here and make a wish on the moon!

LAURA (*entering*). Moon—moon?

AMANDA. A little silver slipper of a moon. Look over your left shoulder, Laura, and make a wish! (LAURA *looks faintly puzzled as if called out of sleep.* AMANDA *seizes her shoulders and turns her at an angle by the door.*) Now! Now, darling, *wish!*

LAURA. What shall I wish for, Mother?

AMANDA (*her voice trembling and her eyes suddenly filling with tears*). Happiness! Good Fortune!

The violin rises and the stage dims out.

Scene VI

(Image: High School Hero.)

TOM. And so the following evening I brought Jim home to dinner. I had known Jim slightly in high school. In high school Jim was a hero. He had tremendous Irish good nature and vitality with the scrubbed and polished look of white chinaware. He seemed to move in a continual spotlight. He was a star in basketball, captain of the debating club, president of the senior class and the glee club and he sang the male lead in the annual light operas. He was always running or bounding, never just walking. He seemed always at the point of defeating the law of gravity. He was shooting with such velocity through his adolescence that you would logically expect him to arrive at nothing short of the White House by the time he was thirty. But Jim apparently ran into more interference after his graduation from Soldan. His speed had definitely slowed. Six years after he left high school he was holding a job that wasn't much better than mine.

(Image: Clerk.)

He was the only one at the warehouse with whom I was on friendly terms. I was valuable to him as someone who could remember his former glory, who had seen him win basketball games and the silver cup in debating. He knew of my secret practice of retiring to a cabinet of the washroom to work on poems when business was slack in the warehouse. He called me Shakespeare. And while the other boys in the warehouse regarded me with suspicious hostility, Jim took a humorous attitude toward me. Gradually his attitude affected the others, their hostility wore off and they also began to smile at me as people smile at an oddly fashioned dog who trots across their path at some distance.

I knew that Jim and Laura had known each other at Soldan, and I had heard Laura speak admiringly of his voice. I didn't know if Jim remembered her or not. In high school Laura had been as unobtrusive as Jim had been astonishing. If he did remember Laura, it was not as my sister, for when I asked him to dinner, he grinned and said, "You know, Shakespeare, I never thought of you as having folks!"

He was about to discover that I did. . . . .

(Light up Stage.)

(Legend on Screen: "The Accent of a Coming Foot.")

Friday evening. It is about five o'clock of a late spring evening which comes "scattering poems in the sky."

A delicate lemony light is in the Wingfield apartment.

AMANDA *has worked like a Turk in preparation for the gentleman caller. The results are astonishing. The new floor lamp with its rose-silk shade is in place, a colored paper lantern conceals the broken light fixture in the ceiling, new billowing white curtains are at the windows, chintz covers are on chairs and sofa, a pair of new sofa pillows make their initial appearance.*

Open boxes and tissue paper are scattered on the floor.

LAURA *stands in the middle with lifted arms while* AMANDA *crouches before her, adjusting the hem of the new dress, devout and ritualistic. The dress is colored and designed by memory. The arrangement of* LAURA's *hair is changed; it is softer and more becoming. A fragile, unearthly prettiness has come out in* LAURA: *she is like a piece of translucent glass touched by light, given a momentary radiance, not actual, not lasting.*

AMANDA (*impatiently*). Why are you trembling?

LAURA. Mother, you've made me so nervous!

AMANDA. How have I made you nervous?

LAURA. By all this fuss! You make it seem so important!

AMANDA. I don't understand you, Laura. You couldn't be satisfied with just sitting home, and yet whenever I try to arrange something for you, you seem to resist it. (*She gets up.*) Now take a look at yourself. No, wait! Wait just a moment—I have an idea!

LAURA. What is it now?

AMANDA *produces two powder puffs which she wraps in handkerchiefs and stuffs in* LAURA's *bosom.*

LAURA. Mother, what are you doing?

AMANDA. They call them "Gay Deceivers"!

LAURA. I won't wear them!

AMANDA. You will!

LAURA. Why should I?

AMANDA. Because, to be painfully honest, your chest is flat.

LAURA. You make it seem like we were setting a trap.

AMANDA. All pretty girls are a trap, a pretty trap, and men expect them to be. (*Legend: "A Pretty Trap."*) Now look at yourself, young lady. This is the prettiest you will ever be! I've got to fix myself now! You're going to be surprised by your mother's appearance! (*She crosses through portieres, humming gaily.*)

Laura moves slowly to the long mirror and stares solemnly at herself.
A wind blows the white curtains inward in a slow, graceful motion and with a faint, sorrowful sighing.

AMANDA (*off stage*). It isn't dark enough yet. (*She turns slowly before the mirror with a troubled look.*)

(*Legend on Screen: "This Is My Sister: Celebrate Her with Strings!" Music.*)

AMANDA (*laughing, off*). I'm going to show you something. I'm going to make a spectacular appearance!

LAURA. What is it, Mother?

AMANDA. Possess your soul in patience—you will see! Something I've resurrected from that old trunk! Styles haven't changed so terribly much after all. . . . (*She parts the portieres.*) Now just look at your mother!

(*She wears a girlish frock of yellowed voile with a blue silk sash. She carries a bunch of jonquils—the legend of her youth is nearly revived. Feverishly.*) This is the dress in which I led the cotillion. Won the cakewalk twice at Sunset Hill, wore one spring to the Governor's ball in Jackson! See how I sashayed around the ballroom, Laura? (*She raises her skirt and does a mincing step around the room.*) I wore it on Sundays for my gentlemen callers! I had it on the day I met your father—I had malaria fever all that spring. The change of climate from East Tennessee to the Delta—weakened resistance—I had a little temperature all the time—not enough to be serious—just enough to make me restless and giddy! Invitations poured in—parties all over the Delta!—"stay in bed," said Mother, "you have fever!"—but I just wouldn't.—I took quinine but kept on going, going!—Evenings, dances!—Afternoons, long, long rides! Picnics—lovely!—So lovely, that country in May.—All lacy with dogwood, literally flooded with jonquils!—That was the spring I had the craze for jonquils. Jonquils became an absolute obsession. Mother said, "Honey, there's no more room for jonquils." And still I kept bringing in more jonquils. Whenever, wherever I saw them, I'd say, "Stop! Stop! I see jonquils!" I made the young men help me gather the jonquils! It was a joke, Amanda and her jonquils! Finally there were no more vases to hold them, every available space was filled with jonquils. No vases to hold them? All right, I'll hold them myself! And then I—(*She stops in front of the picture.*) (*Music.*) met your father! Malaria fever and jonquils and then—this—boy. . . . (*She switches on the rose-colored lamp.*) I hope they get here before it starts to rain. (*She crosses upstage and places the jonquils in bowl on table.*) I gave your brother a little extra change so he and Mr. O'Connor could take the service car home.

LAURA (*with altered look*). What did you say his name was?
AMANDA. O'Connor.
LAURA. What is his first name?
AMANDA. I don't remember. Oh, yes, I do. It was—Jim!

LAURA *sways slightly and catches hold of a chair.*
(*Legend on Screen: "Not Jim!"*)

LAURA (*faintly*). Not—Jim!
AMANDA. Yes, that was it, it was Jim! I've never known a Jim that wasn't nice!

(*Music: Ominous.*)

LAURA. Are you sure his name is Jim O'Connor?
AMANDA. Yes. Why?
LAURA. Is he the one that Tom used to know in high school?
AMANDA. He didn't say so. I think he just got to know him at the warehouse.
LAURA. There was a Jim O'Connor we both knew in high school—(*Then, with effort.*) If that is the one that Tom is bringing to dinner—you'll have to excuse me, I won't come to the table.
AMANDA. What sort of nonsense is this?
LAURA. You asked me once if I'd ever liked a boy. Don't you remember I showed you this boy's picture?
AMANDA. You mean the boy you showed me in the year-book?

LAURA. Yes, that boy.

AMANDA. Laura, Laura, were you in love with that boy?

LAURA. I don't know, Mother. All I know is I couldn't sit at the table if it was him!

AMANDA. It won't be him! It isn't the least bit likely. But whether it is or not, you will come to the table. You will not be excused.

LAURA. I'll have to be, Mother.

AMANDA. I don't intend to humor your silliness, Laura. I've had too much from you and your brother, both! So just sit down and compose yourself till they come. Tom has forgotten his key so you'll have to let them in, when they arrive.

LAURA (*panicky*). Oh, Mother—*you* answer the door!

AMANDA (*lightly*). I'll be in the kitchen—busy!

LAURA. Oh, Mother, please answer the door, don't make me do it!

AMANDA (*crossing into kitchenette*). I've got to fix the dressing for the salmon. Fuss, fuss—silliness!—over a gentleman caller!

> *Door swings shut.* LAURA *is left alone.*
> (*Legend: "Terror!"*)
> *She utters a low moan and turns off the lamp—sits stiffly on the edge of the sofa, knotting her fingers together.*
> (*Legend on Screen: "The Opening of a Door!"*)
> TOM *and* JIM *appear on the fire-escape steps and climb to landing. Hearing their approach,* LAURA *rises with a panicky gesture. She retreats to the portieres.*
> *The doorbell.* LAURA *catches her breath and touches her throat. Low drums.*

AMANDA (*calling*). Laura, sweetheart! The door!

> LAURA *stares at it without moving.*

JIM. I think we just beat the rain.

TOM. Uh-huh. (*He rings again, nervously.* JIM *whistles and fishes for a cigarette.*)

AMANDA (*very, very gaily*). Laura, that is your brother and Mr. O'Connor! Will you let them in, darling?

> LAURA *crosses toward kitchenette door.*

LAURA (*breathlessly*). Mother—you go to the door!

> AMANDA *steps out of kitchenette and stares furiously at* LAURA. *She points imperiously at the door.*

LAURA. Please, please!

AMANDA (*in a fierce whisper*). What is the matter with you, you silly thing?

LAURA (*desperately*). Please, you answer it, *please!*

AMANDA. I told you I wasn't going to humor you, Laura. Why have you chosen this moment to lose your mind?

LAURA. Please, please, please, you go!

AMANDA. You'll have to go to the door because I can't!

LAURA (*despairingly*). I can't either!

AMANDA. Why?

LAURA. I'm sick!

AMANDA. I'm sick, too—of your nonsense! Why can't you and your brother be normal people? Fantastic whims and behavior! (TOM *gives a long ring.*) Preposterous goings on! Can you give me one reason—(*Calls out lyrically.*) COMING! JUST ONE SECOND!—why should you be afraid to open a door? Now you answer it, Laura!

LAURA. Oh, oh, oh . . . (*She returns through the portieres. Darts to the victrola and winds it frantically and turns it on.*)

AMANDA. Laura Wingfield, you march right to that door!

LAURA. Yes—yes, Mother!

A faraway, scratchy rendition of "dardanella" softens the air and gives her strength to move through it. She slips to the door and draws it cautiously open.
  TOM *enters with caller,* JIM O'CONNOR.

TOM. Laura, this is Jim. Jim, this is my sister, Laura.

JIM (*stepping inside*). I didn't know that Shakespeare had a sister!

LAURA (*retreating stiff and trembling from the door*). How—how do you do?

JIM (*heartily extending his hand*). Okay!

  LAURA *touches it hesitantly with hers.*

JIM. Your hand's *cold,* Laura!

LAURA. Yes, well—I've been playing the victrola. . . .

JIM. Must have been playing classical music on it! You ought to play a little hot swing music to warm you up!

LAURA. Excuse me—I haven't finished playing the victrola. . . .

She turns awkwardly and hurries into the front room. She pauses a second by the victrola. Then catches her breath and darts through the portieres like a frightened deer.

JIM (*grinning*). What was the matter?

TOM. Oh—with Laura? Laura is—terribly shy.

JIM. Shy, huh? It's unusual to meet a shy girl nowadays. I don't believe you ever mentioned you had a sister.

TOM. Well, now you know. I have one. Here is the *Post Dispatch.* You want a piece of it?

JIM. Uh-huh.

TOM. What piece? The comics?

JIM. Sports! (*Glances at it.*) Ole Dizzy Dean is on his bad behavior.

TOM (*disinterest*). Yeah? (*Lights cigarette and crosses back to fire-escape door.*)

JIM. Where are *you* going?

TOM. I'm going out on the terrace.

JIM (*goes after him*). You know, Shakespeare—I'm going to sell you a bill of goods!

TOM. What goods?

JIM. A course I'm taking.

TOM. Huh?

JIM. In public speaking! You and me, we're not the warehouse type.

TOM. Thanks—that's good news. But what has public speaking got to do with it?

JIM. It fits you for—executive positions!

TOM. Awww.

JIM. I tell you it's done a helluva lot for me.

(*Image: Executive at Desk.*)

TOM. In what respect?

JIM. In every! Ask yourself what is the difference between you an' me and
men in the office down front? Brains?—No!—Ability?—No! Then what?
Just one little thing—

TOM. What is that one little thing?

JIM. Primarily it amounts to—social poise! Being able to square up to people
and hold your own on any social level!

AMANDA (*off stage*). Tom?

TOM. Yes, Mother?

AMANDA. Is that you and Mr. O'Connor?

TOM. Yes, Mother.

AMANDA. Well, you just make yourselves comfortable in there.

TOM. Yes, Mother.

AMANDA. Ask Mr. O'Connor if he would like to wash his hands.

JIM. Aw—no—no—thank you—I took care of that at the warehouse. Tom—

TOM. Yes?

JIM. Mr. Mendoza was speaking to me about you.

TOM. Favorably?

JIM. What do you think?

TOM. Well—

JIM. You're going to be out of a job if you don't wake up.

TOM. I am waking up—

JIM. You show no signs.

TOM. The signs are interior.

(*Image on Screen: The Sailing Vessel with Jolly Roger Again.*)

TOM. I'm planning to change. (*He leans over the rail speaking with quiet
exhilaration. The incandescent marquees and signs of the first-run
movie houses light his face from across the alley. He looks like a voyager.*) I'm right at the point of committing myself to a future that doesn't
include the warehouse and Mr. Mendoza or even a night-school course
in public speaking.

JIM. What are you gassing about?

TOM. I'm tired of the movies.

JIM. Movies!

TOM. Yes, movies! Look at them—(*a wave toward the marvels of Grand
Avenue.*) All of those glamorous people—having adventures—hogging
it all, gobbling the whole thing up! You know what happens? People
go to the *movies* instead of *moving!* Hollywood characters are supposed to have all the adventures for everybody in America, while everybody in America sits in a dark room and watches them have them! Yes,
until there's a war. That's when adventure becomes available to the
masses! *Everyone's* dish, not only Gable's! Then the people in the dark
room come out of the dark room to have some adventures themselves—Goody, goody—It's our turn now, to go to the South Sea Is-

land—to make a safari—to be exotic, far-off—But I'm not patient. I
don't want to wait till then. I'm tired of the *movies* and I am *about to
move!*

JIM (*incredulously*). Move?

TOM. Yes.

JIM. When?

TOM. Soon!

JIM. Where? Where?

(*Theme Three: Music Seems to Answer the Question, while* TOM *Thinks
it Over. He Searches among his Pockets.*)

TOM. I'm starting to boil inside. I know I seem dreamy, but inside—well, I'm
boiling! Whenever I pick up a shoe, I shudder a little thinking how
short life is and what I am doing!—Whatever that means. I know it
doesn't mean shoes—except as something to wear on a traveler's feet!
(*Finds paper.*) Look—

JIM. What?

TOM. I'm a member.

JIM (*reading*). The Union of Merchant Seamen.

TOM. I paid my dues this month, instead of the light bill.

JIM. You will regret it when they turn the lights off.

TOM. I won't be here.

JIM. How about your mother?

TOM. I'm like my father. The bastard son of a bastard! See how he grins? And
he's been absent going on sixteen years!

JIM. You're just talking, you drip. How does your mother feel about it?

TOM. Shhh—Here comes Mother! Mother is not acquainted with my plans!

AMANDA (*enters portieres*). Where are you all?

TOM. On the terrace, Mother.

They start inside. She advances to them. TOM *is distinctly shocked at
her appearance. Even* JIM *blinks a little. He is making his first contact
with girlish Southern vivacity and in spite of the night-school course
in public speaking is somewhat thrown off the beam by the unexpected outlay of social charm.*

Certain responses are attempted by JIM *but are swept aside by*
AMANDA's *gay laughter and chatter.* TOM *is embarrassed but after the
first shock* JIM *reacts very warmly. Grins and chuckles, is altogether
won over.*

(*Image:* AMANDA *as a Girl.*)

AMANDA (*coyly smiling, shaking her girlish ringlets*). Well, well, well, so
this is Mr. O'Connor. Introductions entirely unnecessary. I've heard so
much about you from my boy. I finally said to him, Tom—good gracious!—why don't you bring this paragon to supper? I'd like to meet
this nice young man at the warehouse!—Instead of just hearing him
sing your praises so much! I don't know why my son is so standoffish—
that's not Southern behavior! Let's sit down and—I think we could
stand a little more air in here! Tom, leave the door open. I felt a nice
fresh breeze a moment ago. Where has it gone? Mmm, so warm already!
And not quite summer, even. We're going to burn up when summer

really gets started. However, we're having—we're having a very light supper. I think light things are better fo' this time of year. The same as light clothes are. Light clothes an' light food are what warm weather calls fo'. You know our blood gets so thick during th' winter—it takes a while fo' us to *adjust* ou'selves!—when the season changes. . . . It's come so quick this year. I wasn't prepared. All of a sudden—heavens! Already summer!—I ran to the trunk an' pulled out this light dress—Terribly old! Historical almost! But feels so good—so good an' co-ol, y'know. . . .

TOM. Mother—

AMANDA. Yes, honey?

TOM. How about—supper?

AMANDA. Honey, you go ask Sister if supper is ready! You know that Sister is in full charge of supper! Tell her you hungry boys are waiting for it. (*To* JIM.) Have you met Laura?

JIM. She—

AMANDA. Let you in? Oh, good, you've met already! It's rare for a girl as sweet an' pretty as Laura to be domestic! But Laura is, thank heavens, not only pretty but also very domestic. I'm not at all. I never was a bit. I never could make a thing but angel-food cake. Well, in the South we had so many servants. Gone, gone, gone. All vestiges of gracious living! Gone completely! I wasn't prepared for what the future brought me. All of my gentlemen callers were sons of planters and so of course I assumed that I would be married to one and raise my family on a large piece of land with plenty of servants. But man proposes—and woman accepts the proposal!—To vary that old, old saying a little bit—I married no planter! I married a man who worked for the telephone company!—that gallantly smiling gentleman over there! [*Points to the picture.*] A telephone man who—fell in love with long distance!—Now he travels and I don't even know where!—But what am I going on for about my—tribulations! Tell me yours—I hope you don't have any! Tom?

TOM (*returning*). Yes, Mother?

AMANDA. Is supper nearly ready?

TOM. It looks to me like supper is on the table.

AMANDA. Let me look—(*She rises prettily and looks through portieres.*) Oh, lovely—But where is Sister?

TOM. Laura is not feeling well and she says that she thinks she'd better not come to the table.

AMANDA. What?—Nonsense!—Laura? Oh, Laura!

LAURA (*off stage, faintly*). Yes, Mother.

AMANDA. You really must come to the table. We won't be seated until you come to the table! Come in, Mr. O'Connor. You sit over there and I'll—Laura? Laura Wingfield! You're keeping us waiting, honey! We can't say grace until you come to the table!

The back door is pushed weakly open and LAURA *comes in. She is obviously quite faint, her lips trembling, her eyes wide and staring. She moves unsteadily toward the table.*

(*Legend: "Terror!"*)

Outside a summer storm is coming abruptly. The white curtains billow inward at the windows and there is a sorrowful murmur and deep blue dusk.

LAURA *suddenly stumbles—She catches a chair with a faint moan.*

TOM. Laura!

AMANDA. Laura! (*There is a clap of thunder.*) (*Legend: "Ah!"*) (*Despairingly.*) Why, Laura, you *are* sick, darling! Tom, help your sister into the living room, dear! Sit in the living room, Laura—rest on the sofa. Well! (*To the gentleman caller.*) Standing over the hot stove made her ill!—I told her that it was just too warm this evening, but—(TOM *comes back in.* LAURA *is on the sofa.*) Is Laura all right now?

TOM. Yes.

AMANDA. What *is* that? Rain? A nice cool rain has come up! (*She gives the gentleman caller a frightened look.*) I think we may—have grace— now . . . (TOM *looks at her stupidly.*) Tom, honey—you say grace!

TOM. Oh . . . "For these and all thy mercies—" (*They bow their heads,* AMANDA *stealing a nervous glance at* JIM. *In the living room* LAURA, *stretched on the sofa, clenches her hand to her lips, to hold back a shuddering sob.*) God's Holy Name be praised—

(*The Scene Dims Out.*)

Scene VII

A Souvenir

Half an hour later. Dinner is just being finished in the upstage area which is concealed by the drawn portieres.

As the curtain rises LAURA *is still huddled upon the sofa, her feet drawn under her, her head resting on a pale blue pillow, her eyes wide and mysteriously watchful. The new floor lamp with its shade of rose-colored silk gives a soft, becoming light to her face, bringing out the fragile, unearthly prettiness which usually escapes attention. There is a steady murmur of rain, but it is slackening and stops soon after the scene begins; the air outside becomes pale and luminous as the moon breaks out.*

A moment after the curtain rises, the lights in both rooms flicker and go out.

JIM. Hey, there, Mr. Light Bulb!

AMANDA *laughs nervously.*
(*Legend: "Suspension of a Public Service."*)

AMANDA. Where was Moses when the lights went out? Ha-ha. Do you know the answer to that one, Mr. O'Connor?

JIM. No, Ma'am, what's the answer?

AMANDA. In the dark! (JIM *laughs appreciatively.*) Everybody sit still. I'll light the candles. Isn't it lucky we have them on the table? Where's a match? Which of you gentlemen can provide a match?

JIM. Here.

AMANDA. Thank you, sir.

JIM. Not at all, Ma'am!

AMANDA. I guess the fuse has burnt out. Mr. O'Connor, can you tell a burnt-out fuse? I know I can't and Tom is a total loss when it comes to mechanics. (*Sound: Getting Up: Voices Recede a Little to Kitchenette.*) Oh, be careful you don't bump into something. We don't want our gentleman caller to break his neck. Now wouldn't that be a fine howdy-do?

JIM. Ha-ha! Where is the fuse-box?

AMANDA. Right here next to the stove. Can you see anything?

JIM. Just a minute.

AMANDA. Isn't electricity a mysterious thing? Wasn't it Benjamin Franklin who tied a key to a kite? We live in such a mysterious universe, don't we? Some people say that science clears up all the mysteries for us. In my opinion it only creates more! Have you found it yet?

JIM. No, Ma'am. All these fuses look okay to me.

AMANDA. Tom!

TOM. Yes, Mother?

AMANDA. That light bill I gave you several days ago. The one I told you we got the notices about?

TOM. Oh.—Yeah.

(*Legend: "Ha!"*)

AMANDA. You didn't neglect to pay it by any chance?

TOM. Why, I—

AMANDA. Didn't! I might have known it!

JIM. Shakespeare probably wrote a poem on that light bill, Mrs. Wingfield.

AMANDA. I might have known better than to trust him with it! There's such a high price for negligence in this world!

JIM. Maybe the poem will win a ten-dollar prize.

AMANDA. We'll just have to spend the remainder of the evening in the nineteenth century, before Mr. Edison made the Mazda lamp!

JIM. Candlelight is my favorite kind of light.

AMANDA. That shows you're romantic! But that's no excuse for Tom. Well, we got through dinner. Very considerate of them to let us get through dinner before they plunged us into everlasting darkness, wasn't it, Mr. O'Connor?

JIM. Ha-ha!

AMANDA. Tom, as a penalty for your carelessness you can help me with the dishes.

JIM. Let me give you a hand.

AMANDA. Indeed you will not!

JIM. I ought to be good for something.

AMANDA. Good for something? (*Her tone is rhapsodic.*) *You?* Why, Mr. O'Connor, nobody, *nobody's* given me this much entertainment in years—as you have!

JIM. Aw, now, Mrs. Wingfield!

AMANDA. I'm not exaggerating, not one bit! But Sister is all by her lonesome. You go keep her company in the parlor! I'll give you this lovely old candelabrum that used to be on the altar at the church of the Heavenly Rest. It was melted a little out of shape when the church burnt down. Lightning struck it one spring. Gypsy Jones was holding a revival at the time and he intimated that the church was destroyed because the Episcopalians gave card parties.

JIM. Ha-ha.

AMANDA. And how about coaxing Sister to drink a little wine? I think it would be good for her! Can you carry both at once?

JIM. Sure. I'm Superman!

AMANDA. Now, Thomas, get into this apron!

The door of kitchenette swings closed on AMANDA's *gay laughter; the flickering light approaches the portieres.*

LAURA *sits up nervously as be enters. Her speech at first is low and breathless from the almost intolerable strain of being alone with a stranger.*

(Legend: "I Don't Suppose You Remember Me at All!")

In her first speeches in this scene, before JIM's *warmth overcomes her paralyzing shyness,* LAURA's *voice is thin and breathless as though she has run up a steep flight of stairs.*

JIM's *attitude is gently humorous. In playing this scene it should be stressed that while the incident is apparently unimportant, it is to* LAURA *the climax of her secret life.*

JIM. Hello, there, Laura.

LAURA *(faintly)*. Hello. *(She clears her throat.)*

JIM. How are you feeling now? Better?

LAURA. Yes. Yes, thank you.

JIM. This is for you. A little dandelion wine. *(He extends it toward her with extravagant gallantry.)*

LAURA. Thank you.

JIM. Drink it—but don't get drunk! *(He laughs heartily.* LAURA *takes the glass uncertainly; laughs shyly.)* Where shall I set the candles?

LAURA. Oh—oh, anywhere . . .

JIM. How about here on the floor? Any objections?

LAURA. No.

JIM. I'll spread a newspaper under to catch the drippings. I like to sit on the floor. Mind if I do?

LAURA. Oh, no.

JIM. Give me a pillow?

LAURA. What?

JIM. A pillow!

LAURA. Oh . . . *(Hands him one quickly.)*

JIM. How about you? Don't you like to sit on the floor?

LAURA. Oh—yes.

JIM. Why don't you, then?

LAURA. I—will.

JIM. Take a pillow! *(*LAURA *does. Sits on the other side of the candelabrum.* JIM *crosses his legs and smiles engagingly at her.)* I can't hardly see you sitting way over there.

LAURA. I can—see you.

JIM. I know, but that's not fair, I'm in the limelight. (LAURA *moves her pillow closer.*) Good! Now I can see you! Comfortable?

LAURA. Yes.

JIM. So am I. Comfortable as a cow. Will you have some gum?

LAURA. No, thank you.

JIM. I think that I will indulge, with your permission. (*Musingly unwraps it and holds it up.*) Think of the fortune made by the guy that invented the first piece of chewing gum. Amazing, huh? The Wrigley Building is one of the sights of Chicago.—I saw it summer before last when I went up to the Century of Progress. Did you take in the Century of Progress?

LAURA. No, I didn't.

JIM. Well, it was quite a wonderful exposition. What impressed me most was the Hall of Science. Gives you an idea of what the future will be in America, even more wonderful than the present time is! (*Pause. Smiling at her.*) Your brother tells me you're shy. Is that right, Laura?

LAURA. I—don't know.

JIM. I judge you to be an old-fashioned type of girl. Well, I think that's a pretty good type to be. Hope you don't think I'm being too personal— do you?

LAURA (*hastily, out of embarrassment*). I believe I *will* take a piece of gum, if you—don't mind. (*Clearing her throat.*) Mr. O'Connor, have you— kept up with your singing?

JIM. Singing? Me?

LAURA. Yes. I remember what a beautiful voice you had.

JIM. When did you hear me sing?

(*Voice Offstage in the Pause.*)

VOICE (*offstage*).

> O blow, ye winds, heigh-ho.
> A-roving I will go!
> I'm off to my love
> With a boxing glove—
> Ten thousand miles away!

JIM. You say you've heard me sing?

LAURA. Oh, yes! Yes, very often . . . I—don't suppose you remember me— at all?

JIM (*smiling doubtfully*). You know I have an idea I've seen you before. I had that idea soon as you opened the door. It seemed almost like I was about to remember your name. But the name that I started to call you— wasn't a name! And so I stopped myself before I said it.

LAURA. Wasn't it—Blue Roses?

JIM (*springs up, grinning*). Blue Roses! My gosh, yes—Blue Roses! That's what I had on my tongue when you opened the door! Isn't it funny what tricks your memory plays? I didn't connect you with the high school somehow or other. But that's where it was; it was high school. I didn't even know you were Shakespeare's sister! Gosh, I'm sorry.

LAURA. I didn't expect you to. You—barely knew me!

JIM. But we did have a speaking acquaintance, huh?

LAURA. Yes, we—spoke to each other.

JIM. When did you recognize me?

LAURA. Oh, right away!

JIM. Soon as I came in the door?

LAURA. When I heard your name I thought it was probably you. I knew that Tom used to know you a little in high school. So when you came in the door—Well, then I was—sure.

JIM. Why didn't you *say* something, then?

LAURA (*breathlessly*). I didn't know what to say, I was—too surprised!

JIM. For goodness' sakes! You know, this sure is funny!

LAURA. Yes! Yes, isn't it, though. . . .

JIM. Didn't we have a class in something together?

LAURA. Yes, we did.

JIM. What class was that?

LAURA. It was—singing—Chorus!

JIM. Aw!

LAURA. I sat across the aisle from you in the Aud.

JIM. Aw.

LAURA. Mondays, Wednesdays and Fridays.

JIM. Now I remember—you always came in late.

LAURA. Yes, it was so hard for me, getting upstairs. I had a brace on my leg—it clumped so loud!

JIM. I never heard any clumping.

LAURA (*wincing at the recollection*). To me it sounded like—thunder!

JIM. Well, well, well. I never even noticed.

LAURA. And everybody was seated before I came in. I had to walk in front of all those people. My seat was in the back row. I had to go clumping all the way up the aisle with everyone watching!

JIM. You shouldn't have been self-conscious.

LAURA. I know, but I was. It was always such a relief when the singing started.

JIM. Aw, yes, I've placed you now! I used to call you Blue Roses. How was it that I got started calling you that?

LAURA. I was out of school a little while with pleurosis. When I came back you asked me what was the matter. I said I had pleurosis—you thought I said Blue Roses. That's what you always called me after that!

JIM. I hope you didn't mind.

LAURA. Oh, no—I liked it. You see, I wasn't acquainted with many—people. . . .

JIM. As I remember you sort of stuck by yourself.

LAURA. I—I—never had much luck at—making friends.

JIM. I don't see why you wouldn't.

LAURA. Well, I—started out badly.

JIM. You mean being—

LAURA. Yes, it sort of—stood between me—

JIM. You shouldn't have let it!

LAURA. I know, but it did, and—

JIM. You were shy with people!

LAURA. I tried not to be but never could—

JIM. Overcome it?

LAURA. No, I—I never could!

JIM. I guess being shy is something you have to work out of kind of gradually.

LAURA (*sorrowfully*). Yes—I guess it—

JIM. Takes time!

LAURA. Yes—

JIM. People are not so dreadful when you know them. That's what you have to remember! And everybody has problems, not just you, but practically everybody has got some problems. You think of yourself as having the only problems, as being the only one who is disappointed. But just look around you and you will see lots of people as disappointed as you are. For instance, I hoped when I was going to high school that I would be further along at this time, six years after, than I am now—You remember that wonderful write-up I had in *The Torch?*

LAURA. Yes! (*She rises and crosses to table.*)

JIM. It said I was bound to succeed in anything I went into! (*Laura returns with the annual.*) Holy Jeez! The Torch! (*He accepts it reverently. They smile across it with mutual wonder.* LAURA *crouches beside him and they begin to turn through it.* LAURA'S *shyness is dissolving in his warmth.*)

LAURA. Here you are in *Pirates of Penzance!*

JIM (*wistfully*). I sang the baritone lead in that operetta.

LAURA (*rapidly*). So—*beautifully!*

JIM (*protesting*). Aw—

LAURA. Yes, yes—beautifully—beautifully!

JIM. You heard me?

LAURA. All three times!

JIM. No!

LAURA. Yes!

JIM. All three performances?

LAURA (*looking down*). Yes.

JIM. Why?

LAURA. I—wanted to ask you to—autograph my program.

JIM. Why didn't you ask me to?

LAURA. You were always surrounded by your own friends so much that I never had a chance to.

JIM. You should have just—

LAURA. Well, I—thought you might think I was—

JIM. Thought I might think you was—what?

LAURA. Oh—

JIM (*with reflective relish*). I was beleaguered by females in those days.

LAURA. You were terribly popular!

JIM. Yeah—

LAURA. You had such a—friendly way—

JIM. I was spoiled in high school.

LAURA. Everybody—liked you!

JIM. Including you?

LAURA. I—yes, I—I did, too—(*She gently closes the book in her lap.*)

JIM. Well, well, well!—Give me that program, Laura. (*She hands it to him. He signs it with a flourish.*) There you are—better late than never!

LAURA. Oh, I—what a—surprise!

JIM. My signature isn't worth very much right now. But some day—maybe—it will increase in value! Being disappointed is one thing and being discouraged is something else. I am disappointed but I'm not discouraged. I'm twenty-three years old. How old are you?

LAURA. I'll be twenty-four in June.

JIM. That's not old age!

LAURA. No, but—

JIM. You finished high school?

LAURA (*with difficulty*). I didn't go back.

JIM. You mean you dropped out?

LAURA. I made bad grades in my final examinations. (*She rises and replaces the book and the program. Her voice strained.*) How is—Emily Meisenbach getting along?

JIM. Oh, that kraut-head!

LAURA. Why do you call her that?

JIM. That's what she was.

LAURA. You're not still—going with her?

JIM. I never see her.

LAURA. It said in the Personal Section that you were—engaged!

JIM. I know, but I wasn't impressed by that—propaganda!

LAURA. It wasn't—the truth?

JIM. Only in Emily's optimistic opinion!

LAURA. Oh—

(*Legend: "What Have You Done since High School?"*)

> JIM *lights a cigarette and leans indolently back on his elbows smiling at* LAURA *with a warmth and charm which light her inwardly with altar candles. She remains by the table and turns in her hands a piece of glass to cover her tumult.*

JIM (*after several reflective puffs on a cigarette*). What have you done since high school? (*She seems not to hear him.*) Huh? (LAURA *looks up.*) I said what have you done since high school, Laura?

LAURA. Nothing much.

JIM. You must have been doing something these six long years.

LAURA. Yes.

JIM. Well, then, such as what?

LAURA. I took a business course at business college—

JIM. How did that work out?

LAURA. Well, not very—well—I had to drop out, it gave me—indigestion—

> JIM *laughs gently.*

JIM. What are you doing now?

LAURA. I don't do anything—much. Oh, please don't think I sit around doing nothing! My glass collection takes up a good deal of my time. Glass is something you have to take good care of.

JIM. What did you say—about glass?

LAURA. Collection I said—I have one—(*She clears her throat and turns away again, acutely shy.*)

JIM (*abruptly*). You know what I judge to be the trouble with you? Inferiority complex! Know what that is? That's what they call it when someone low-rates himself! I understand it because I had it, too. Although my case was not so aggravated as yours seems to be. I had it until I took up

public speaking, developed my voice, and learned that I had an aptitude for science. Before that time I never thought of myself as being
outstanding in any way whatsoever! Now I've never made a regular
study of it, but I have a friend who says I can analyze people better than
doctors that make a profession of it. I don't claim that to be necessarily
true, but I can sure guess a person's psychology, Laura! (*Takes out his
gum.*) Excuse me, Laura. I always take it out when the flavor is gone.
I'll use this scrap of paper to wrap it in. I know how it is to get it stuck
on a shoe. Yep—that's what I judge to be your principal trouble. A lack
of confidence in yourself as a person. You don't have the proper
amount of faith in yourself. I'm basing that fact on a number of your
remarks and also on certain observations I've made. For instance that
clumping you thought was so awful in high school. You say that you
even dreaded to walk into class. You see what you did? You dropped
out of school, you gave up an education because of a clump, which as
far as I know was practically nonexistent! A little physical defect is
what you have. Hardly noticeable even! Magnified thousands of times
by imagination! You know what my strong advice to you is? Think of
yourself as *superior* in some way!

LAURA. In what way would I think?

JIM. Why, man alive, Laura! Just look about you a little. What do you see? A
world full of common people! All of 'em born and all of 'em going to
die! Which of them has one-tenth of your good points! Or mine! Or anyone else's, as far as that goes—Gosh! Everybody excels in some one
thing. Some in many! (*Unconsciously glances at himself in the mirror.*) All you've got to do is discover in *what!* Take me, for instance.
(*He adjusts his tie at the mirror.*) My interest happens to lie in electro-
dynamics. I'm taking a course in radio engineering at night school,
Laura, on top of a fairly responsible job at the warehouse. I'm taking
that course and studying public speaking.

LAURA. Ohhhh.

JIM. Because I believe in the future of television! (*Turning back to her.*) I
wish to be ready to go up right along with it. Therefore I'm planning to
get in on the ground floor. In fact, I've already made the right connections and all that remains is for the industry itself to get under way!
Full steam—(*His eyes are starry.*) Knowledge—Zzzzzp! Money—
Zzzzzzp!—Power! That's the cycle democracy is built on! (*His attitude
is convincingly dynamic.* LAURA *stares at him, even her shyness
eclipsed in her absolute wonder. He suddenly grins.*) I guess you think
I think a lot of myself!

LAURA. No—o-o-o, I—

JIM. Now how about you? Isn't there something you take more interest in
than anything else?

LAURA. Well, I do—as I said—have my—glass collection—

A peal of girlish laughter from the kitchen.

JIM. I'm not right sure I know what you're talking about. What kind of glass
is it?

LAURA. Little articles of it, they're ornaments mostly! Most of them are little
animals made out of glass, the tiniest little animals in the world. Mother

calls them a glass menagerie! Here's an example of one, if you'd like to see it! This one is one of the oldest. It's nearly thirteen. (*He stretches out his hand.*) (*Music: "The Glass Menagerie."*) Oh, be careful—if you breathe, it breaks!

JIM. I'd better not take it. I'm pretty clumsy with things.

LAURA. Go on, I trust you with him! (*Places it in his palm.*) There now— you're holding him gently! Hold him over the light, he loves the light! You see how the light shines through him?

JIM. It sure does shine!

LAURA. I shouldn't be partial, but he is my favorite one.

JIM. What kind of a thing is this one supposed to be?

LAURA. Haven't you noticed the single horn on his forehead?

JIM. A unicorn, huh?

LAURA. Mmm-hmmm!

JIM. Unicorns, aren't they extinct in the modern world?

LAURA. I know!

JIM. Poor little fellow, he must feel sort of lonesome.

LAURA (*smiling*). Well, if he does he doesn't complain about it. He stays on a shelf with some horses that don't have horns and all of them seem to get along nicely together.

JIM. How do you know?

LAURA (*lightly*). I haven't heard any arguments among them!

JIM (*grinning*). No arguments, huh? Well, that's a pretty good sign! Where shall I set him?

LAURA. Put him on the table. They all like a change of scenery once in a while!

JIM (*stretching*). Well, well, well, well—Look how big my shadow is when I stretch!

LAURA. Oh, oh, yes—it stretches across the ceiling!

JIM (*crossing to door*). I think it's stopped raining. (*Opens fire-escape door.*) Where does the music come from?

LAURA. From the Paradise Dance Hall across the alley.

JIM. How about cutting the rug a little, Miss Wingfield?

LAURA. Oh, I—

JIM. Or is your program filled up? Let me have a look at it. (*Grasps imaginary card.*) Why, every dance is taken! I'll just have to scratch some out. (*Waltz Music: "La Golondrina."*) Ahhh, a waltz! (*He executes some sweeping turns by himself then holds his arms toward* LAURA.)

LAURA (*breathlessly*). I—can't dance!

JIM. There you go, that inferiority stuff!

LAURA. I've never danced in my life!

JIM. Come on, try!

LAURA. Oh, but I'd step on you!

JIM. I'm not made out of glass.

LAURA. How—how—how do we start?

JIM. Just leave it to me. You hold your arms out a little.

LAURA. Like this?

JIM. A little bit higher. Right. Now don't tighten up, that's the main thing about it—relax.

LAURA (*laughing breathlessly*). It's hard not to.

JIM.   Okay.

LAURA.   I'm afraid you can't budge me.

JIM.   What do you bet I can't? (*He swings her into motion.*)

LAURA.   Goodness, yes, you can!

JIM.   Let yourself go, now, Laura, just let yourself go.

LAURA.   I'm—

JIM.   Come on!

LAURA.   Trying!

JIM.   Not so stiff—Easy does it!

LAURA.   I know but I'm—

JIM.   Loosen th' backbone! There now, that's a lot better.

LAURA.   Am I?

JIM.   Lots, lots better! (*He moves her about the room in a clumsy waltz.*)

LAURA.   Oh, my!

JIM.   Ha-ha!

LAURA.   Oh, my goodness!

JIM.   Ha-ha-ha! (*They suddenly bump into the table.* JIM *stops.*) What did we hit on?

LAURA.   Table.

JIM.   Did something fall off it? I think—

LAURA.   Yes.

JIM.   I hope that it wasn't the little glass horse with the horn!

LAURA.   Yes.

JIM.   Aw, aw, aw. Is it broken?

LAURA.   Now it is just like all the other horses.

JIM.   It's lost its—

LAURA.   Horn! It doesn't matter. Maybe it's a blessing in disguise.

JIM.   You'll never forgive me. I bet that that was your favorite piece of glass.

LAURA.   I don't have favorites much. It's no tragedy, Freckles. Glass breaks so easily. No matter how careful you are. The traffic jars the shelves and things fall off them.

JIM.   Still I'm awfully sorry that I was the cause.

LAURA (*smiling*).   I'll just imagine he had an operation. The horn was removed to make him feel less—freakish! (*They both laugh.*) Now he will feel more at home with the other horses, the ones that don't have horns . . .

JIM.   Ha-ha, that's very funny! (*Suddenly serious.*) I'm glad to see that you have a sense of humor. You know—you're—well—very different! Surprisingly different from anyone else I know! (*His voice becomes soft and hesitant with a genuine feeling.*) Do you mind me telling you that? (LAURA *is abashed beyond speech.*) You make me feel sort of—I don't know how to put it! I'm usually pretty good at expressing things, but— This is something that I don't know how to say! (LAURA *touches her throat and clears it—turns the broken unicorn in her hands.*) (*Even softer.*) Has anyone ever told you that you were pretty? (*Pause: Music.*) (LAURA *looks up slowly, with wonder, and shakes her head.*) Well, you are! In a very different way from anyone else. And all the nicer because of the difference, too. (*His voice becomes low and husky.* LAURA *turns away, nearly faint with the novelty of her emotions.*) I wish that you were my sister. I'd teach you to have some confidence in yourself. The different people are not like other people, but being different is nothing to be ashamed of. Because other people are not such wonderful people. They're one hundred times one thousand. You're one times one! They walk all over the earth. You just stay here. They're common as—weeds, but—you—well, you're *Blue Roses!*

(Image on Screen: Blue Roses.)
    (Music Changes.)

LAURA. But blue is wrong for—roses . . .

JIM. It's right for you—You're—pretty!

LAURA. In what respect am I pretty?

JIM. In all respects—believe me! Your eyes—your hair—are pretty! Your hands are pretty! (*He catches hold of her hand.*) You think I'm making this up because I'm invited to dinner and have to be nice. Oh, I could do that! I could put on an act for you, Laura, and say lots of things without being very sincere. But this time I am. I'm talking to you sincerely. I happened to notice you had this inferiority complex that keeps you from feeling comfortable with people. Somebody needs to build your confidence up and make you proud instead of shy and turning away and—blushing—Somebody ought to—ought to—*kiss* you. Laura! (*His hand slips slowly up her arm to her shoulder.*) (*Music Swells Tumultuously.*) (*He suddenly turns her about and kisses her on the lips. When he releases her* LAURA *sinks on the sofa with a bright, dazed look.* JIM *backs away and fishes in his pocket for a cigarette.*) (*Legend on Screen: "Souvenir."*) Stumble-john! (*He lights the cigarette, avoiding her look. There is a peal of girlish laughter from* AMANDA *in the kitchen.* LAURA *slowly raises and opens her hand. It still contains the little broken glass animal. She looks at it with a tender, bewildered expression.*) Stumble-john! I shouldn't have done that—That was way off the beam. You don't smoke, do you? (*She looks up, smiling, not hearing the question. He sits beside her a little gingerly. She looks at him speechlessly—waiting. He coughs decorously and moves a little farther aside as he considers the situation and senses her feelings, dimly, with perturbation. Gently.*) Would you—care for a—mint? (*She doesn't seem to hear him but her look grows brighter even.*) Peppermint—Life Saver? My pocket's a regular drug store—wherever I go . . . (*He pops a mint in his mouth. Then gulps and decides to make a clean breast of it. He speaks slowly and gingerly.*) Laura, you know, if I had a sister like you, I'd do the same thing as Tom. I'd bring out fellows—introduce her to them. The right type of boys—of a type to—appreciate her. Only—well—he made a mistake about me. Maybe I've got no call to be saying this. That may not have been the idea in having me over. But what if it was? There's nothing wrong about that. The only trouble is that in my case—I'm not in a situation to—do the right thing. I can't take down your number and say I'll phone. I can't call up next week and—ask for a date. I thought I had better explain the situation in case you misunderstood it and—hurt your feelings. . . . (*Pause. Slowly, very slowly,* LAURA'S *look changes, her eyes returning slowly from his to the ornament in her palm.*)

AMANDA *utters another gay laugh in the kitchen.*

LAURA (*faintly*). You—won't—call again?

JIM. No, Laura, I can't. (*He rises from the sofa.*) As I was just explaining, I've—got strings on me, Laura, I've—been going steady! I go out all the time with a girl named Betty. She's a home-girl like you, and Catholic, and Irish, and in a great many ways we—get along fine. I met her last summer on a moonlight boat trip up the river to Alton, on the *Majestic*. Well—right away from the start it was—love! (*Legend: Love!*) (LAURA *sways slightly forward and grips the arm of the sofa. He fails to notice, now enrapt in his own comfortable being.*) Being in love has made a new man of me! (*Leaning stiffly forward, clutching the arm of the sofa,* LAURA *struggles visibly with her storm. But* JIM *is oblivious, she is a long way off.*) The power of love is really pretty tremendous! Love is something that—changes the whole world, Laura! (*The storm abates a little and* LAURA *leans back. He notices her again.*) It happened that Betty's aunt took sick, she got a wire and had to go to Centralia. So Tom—when he asked me to dinner—I naturally just accepted the invitation, not knowing that you—that he—that I—(*He stops awkwardly.*) Huh—I'm a stumble-john! (*He flops back on the sofa. The holy candles in the altar of* LAURA'S *face have been snuffed out! There is a look of almost infinite desolation.* JIM *glances at her uneasily.*) I wish that you would—say something. (*She bites her lip which was trembling and then bravely smiles. She opens her hand again on the broken glass ornament. Then she gently takes his hand and raises it level with her own. She carefully places the unicorn in the palm of his hand, then pushes his fingers closed upon it.*) What are you—doing that for? You want me to have him?—Laura? (*She nods.*) What for?

LAURA. A—souvenir . . . .

> *She rises unsteadily and crouches beside the victrola to wind it up.*
> (*Legend on Screen: "Things Have a Way of Turning Out So Badly."*)
> (*Or Image: "Gentleman Caller Waving Good-Bye!—Gaily."*)
> *At this moment* AMANDA *rushes brightly back in the front room. She bears a pitcher of fruit punch in an old-fashioned cut-glass pitcher and a plate of macaroons. The plate has a gold border and poppies painted on it.*

AMANDA. Well, well, well! Isn't the air delightful after the shower? I've made you children a little liquid refreshment. (*Turns gaily to the gentleman caller.*) Jim, do you know that song about lemonade?

> "Lemonade, lemonade
> Made in the shade and stirred with a spade—
> Good enough for any old maid!"

JIM (*uneasily*). Ha-ha! No—I never heard it.
AMANDA. Why, Laura! You look so serious!
JIM. We were having a serious conversation.
AMANDA. Good! Now you're better acquainted!
JIM (*uncertainly*). Ha-ha! Yes.
AMANDA. You modern young people are much more serious-minded than my generation. I was so gay as a girl!
JIM. You haven't changed, Mrs. Wingfield.
AMANDA. Tonight I'm rejuvenated! The gaiety of the occasion, Mr. O'Connor! (*She tosses her head with a peal of laughter. Spills lemonade.*) Oooo! I'm baptizing myself!
JIM. Here—let me—

AMANDA (*setting the pitcher down*). There now. I discovered we had some maraschino cherries. I dumped them in, juice and all!

JIM. You shouldn't have gone to that trouble, Mrs. Wingfield.

AMANDA. Trouble, trouble? Why it was loads of fun! Didn't you hear me cutting up in the kitchen? I bet your ears were burning! I told Tom how outdone with him I was for keeping you to himself so long a time! He should have brought you over much, much sooner! Well, now that you've found your way, I want you to be a very frequent caller! Not just occasional but all the time. Oh, we're going to have a lot of gay times together! I see them coming! Mmm, just breathe that air! So fresh, and the moon's so pretty! I'll skip back out—I know where my place is when young folks are having a—serious conversation!

JIM. Oh, don't go out, Mrs. Wingfield. The fact of the matter is I've got to be going.

AMANDA. Going, now? You're joking! Why, it's only the shank of the evening, Mr. O'Connor!

JIM. Well, you know how it is.

AMANDA. You mean you're a young workingman and have to keep working-men's hours. We'll let you off early tonight. But only on the condition that next time you stay later. What's the best night for you? Isn't Satur-day night the best night for you workingmen?

JIM. I have a couple of time-clocks to punch, Mrs. Wingfield. One at morn-ing, another one at night!

AMANDA. My, but you *are* ambitious! You work at night, too?

JIM. No, Ma'am, not work but—Betty! (*He crosses deliberately to pick up his hat. The band at the Paradise Dance Hall goes into a tender waltz.*)

AMANDA. Betty? Betty? Who's—Betty! (*There is an ominous cracking sound in the sky.*)

JIM. Oh, just a girl. The girl I go steady with! (*He smiles charmingly. The sky falls.*)

(*Legend: "The Sky Falls."*)

AMANDA (*a long-drawn exhalation*). Ohhhh . . . Is it a serious romance, Mr. O'Connor?

JIM. We're going to be married the second Sunday in June.

AMANDA. Ohhhh—how nice! Tom didn't mention that you were engaged to be married.

JIM. The cat's not out of the bag at the warehouse yet. You know how they are. They call you Romeo and stuff like that. (*He stops at the oval mir-ror to put on his hat. He carefully shapes the brim and the crown to give a discreetly dashing effect.*) It's been a wonderful evening, Mrs. Wingfield. I guess this is what they mean by Southern hospitality.

AMANDA. It really wasn't anything at all.

JIM. I hope it don't seem like I'm rushing off. But I promised Betty I'd pick her up at the Wabash depot, an' by the time I get my jalopy down there her train'll be in. Some women are pretty upset if you keep 'em waiting.

AMANDA. Yes, I know—The tyranny of women! (*Extends her hand.*) Good-bye, Mr. O'Connor. I wish you luck—and happiness—and success! All three of them, and so does Laura!—Don't you, Laura?

LAURA. Yes!

JIM (*taking her hand*). Goodbye, Laura. I'm certainly going to treasure that souvenir. And don't you forget the good advice I gave you. (*Raises his voice to a cheery shout.*) So long, Shakespeare! Thanks again, ladies—good night!

He grins and ducks jauntily out.

Still bravely grimacing, AMANDA *closes the door on the gentleman caller. Then she turns back to the room with a puzzled expression. She and* LAURA *don't dare to face each other.* LAURA *crouches beside the victrola to wind it.*

AMANDA (*faintly*). Things have a way of turning out so badly. I don't believe that I would play the victrola. Well, well—well—Our gentleman caller was engaged to be married! Tom!

TOM (*from back*). Yes, Mother?

AMANDA. Come in here a minute. I want to tell you something awfully funny.

TOM (*enters with macaroon and a glass of the lemonade*). Has the gentleman caller gotten away already?

AMANDA. The gentleman caller has made an early departure. What a wonderful joke you played on us!

TOM. How do you mean?

AMANDA. You didn't mention that he was engaged to be married.

TOM. Jim? Engaged?

AMANDA. That's what he just informed us.

TOM. I'll be jiggered! I didn't know about that.

AMANDA. That seems very peculiar.

TOM. What's peculiar about it?

AMANDA. Didn't you call him your best friend down at the warehouse?

TOM. He is, but how did I know?

AMANDA. It seems extremely peculiar that you wouldn't know your best friend was going to be married!

TOM. The warehouse is where I work, not where I know things about people!

AMANDA. You don't know things anywhere! You live in a dream; you manufacture illusions! (*He crosses to door.*) Where are you going?

TOM. I'm going to the movies.

AMANDA. That's right, now that you've had us make such fools of ourselves. The effort, the preparations, all the expense! The new floor lamp, the rug, the clothes for Laura! All for what? To entertain some other girl's fiancé! Go to the movies, go! Don't think about us, a mother deserted, an unmarried sister who's crippled and has no job! Don't let anything interfere with your selfish pleasure! Just go, go, go—to the movies!

TOM. All right, I will! The more you shout about my selfishness to me the quicker I'll go, and I won't go to the movies!

AMANDA. Go, then! Then go to the moon—you selfish dreamer!

TOM *smashes his glass on the floor. He plunges out on the fire-escape, slamming the door.* LAURA *screams—cut by door.*

Dance-hall music up. TOM *goes to the rail and grips it desperately, lifting his face in the chill white moonlight penetrating the narrow abyss of the alley.*

(Legend on Screen: "And So Good-Bye . . . ")

TOM'S *closing speech is timed with the interior pantomime. The interior scene is played as though viewed through sound-proof glass.* AMANDA *appears to be making a comforting speech to* LAURA *who is huddled upon the sofa. Now that we cannot hear the mother's speech, her silliness is gone and she has dignity and tragic beauty.* LAURA'S *dark hair hides her face until at the end of the speech she lifts it to smile at her mother.* AMANDA'S *gestures are slow and graceful, almost dancelike, as she comforts the daughter. At the end of her speech she glances a moment at the father's picture—then withdraws through the portieres. At close of* TOM'S *speech,* LAURA *blows out the candles, ending the play.*

TOM. I didn't go to the moon, I went much further—for time is the longest distance between two places—Not long after that I was fired for writing a poem on the lid of a shoe-box. I left Saint Louis. I descended the steps of this fire-escape for a last time and followed, from then on, in my father's footsteps, attempting to find in motion what was lost in space—I traveled around a great deal. The cities swept about me like dead leaves, leaves that were brightly colored but torn away from the branches. I would have stopped, but I was pursued by something. It always came upon me unawares, taking me altogether by surprise. Perhaps it was a familiar bit of music. Perhaps it was only a piece of transparent glass—Perhaps I am walking along a street at night, in some strange city, before I have found companions. I pass the lighted window of a shop where perfume is sold. The window is filled with pieces of colored glass, tiny transparent bottles in delicate colors, like bits of a shattered rainbow. Then all at once my sister touches my shoulder. I turn around and look into her eyes . . . Oh, Laura, Laura, I tried to leave you behind me, but I am more faithful than I intended to be! I reach for a cigarette, I cross the street, I run into the movies or a bar, I buy a drink, I speak to the nearest stranger—anything that can blow your candles out! (LAURA *bends over the candles.*)—for nowadays the world is lit by lightning! Blow out your candles, Laura—and so goodbye . . . .

She blows the candles out.
(The Scene Dissolves.)

A CONTEXT FOR *THE GLASS MENAGERIE*

TENNESSEE WILLIAMS

Production Notes

[1944]

Being a "memory play," *The Glass Menagerie* can be presented with unusual freedom of convention. Because of its considerably delicate or tenuous material, atmospheric touches and subtleties of direction play a particularly important part. Expressionism and all other unconventional techniques in drama have only one valid aim, and that is a closer approach to truth. When a play employs unconventional techniques, it is not, or certainly shouldn't be, trying to escape its responsibility of dealing with reality, or interpreting experience, but is actually or should be attempting to find a closer approach, a more penetrating and vivid expression of things as they are. The straight realistic play with its genuine frigidaire and authentic ice cubes, its characters that speak exactly as its audience speaks, corresponds to the academic landscape and has the same virtue of a photographic likeness. Everyone should know nowadays the unimportance of the photographic in art: that truth, life, or reality is an organic thing which the poetic imagination can represent or suggest, in essence, only through transformation, through changing into other forms than those which were merely present in appearance.

These remarks are not meant as comments only on this particular play. They have to do with a conception of a new, plastic theater which must take the place of the exhausted theater of realistic conventions if the theater is to resume vitality as a part of our culture.

The Screen Device

There is *only one important difference between the original and acting version of the play* and that is the *omission* in the latter of the device which I tentatively included in my *original* script. This device was the use of a screen on which were projected magic-lantern slides bearing images or titles. I do not regret the omission of this device from the . . . Broadway production. The extraordinary power of Miss Taylor's performance made it suitable to have the utmost simplicity in the physical production. But I think it may be interesting to some readers to see how this device was conceived. So I am putting it into the published manuscript. These images and legends, projected from behind, were cast on a section of wall between the front-room and dining-room areas, which should be indistinguishable from the rest when not in use.

The purpose of this will probably be apparent. It is to give accent to certain values in each scene. Each scene contains a particular point (or several) which is structurally the most important. In an episodic play, such as this, the basic structure or narrative line may be obscured from the audience; the effect may seem fragmentary rather than architectural. This may not be the fault of the play so much as a lack of attention in the audience. The legend or image upon the screen will strengthen the effect of what is merely allusion in the writing and allow the primary point to be made more simply and lightly than if the entire responsibility were on the spoken lines. Aside from this structural value, I think the screen will have a definite emotional appeal, less definable but just as important. An imaginative producer or director may invent many other uses for this device than those indicated in the present script. In fact the possibilities of the device seem much larger to me than the instance of this play can possibly utilize.

The Music

Another extra-literary accent in this play is provided by the use of music. A single recurring tune, "The Glass Menagerie," is used to give emotional emphasis to suitable passages. This tune is like circus music, not when you are on the grounds or in the immediate vicinity of the parade, but when you are at some distance and very likely thinking of something else. It seems under those circumstances to continue almost interminably and it weaves in and out of your preoccupied consciousness; then it is the lightest, most delicate music in the world and perhaps the saddest. It expresses the surface vivacity of life with the underlying strain of immutable and inexpressible sorrow. When you look at a piece of delicately spun glass you think of two things: how beautiful it is and how easily it can be broken. Both of those ideas should be woven into the recurring tune, which dips in and out of the play as if it were carried on a wind that changes. It serves as a thread of connection and allusion between the narrator with his separate point in time and space and the subject of his story. Between each episode it returns as reference to the emotion, nostalgia, which is the first condition of the play. It is primarily Laura's music and therefore comes out most clearly when the play focuses upon her and the lovely fragility of glass which is her image.

The Lighting

The lighting in the play is not realistic. In keeping with the atmosphere of memory, the stage is dim. Shafts of light are focused on selected areas or actors, sometimes in contradistinction to what is the apparent center. For instance, in the quarrel scene between Tom and Amanda, in which Laura has no active part, the clearest pool of light is on her figure. This is also true of the supper scene. The light upon Laura should be distinct from the others, having a peculiar pristine clarity such as light used in early religious portraits of female saints or madonnas. A certain correspondence to light in religious paintings, such as El Greco's, where the figures are radiant in atmosphere that is relatively dusky, could be effectively used throughout the play. (It will also permit a more effective use of the screen.) A free, imaginative use of light can be of enormous value in giving a mobile, plastic quality to plays of a more or less static nature.

TOPICS FOR CRITICAL THINKING AND WRITING

The Play on the Page

1. What does the victrola offer to Laura? Why is the typewriter a better symbol (for the purposes of the play) than, for example, a piano? After all, Laura could have been taking piano lessons.
2. What do you understand of Laura's glass menagerie? Why is it especially significant that the unicorn is Laura's favorite? How do you interpret the loss of the unicorn's horn? What is Laura saying to Jim in the gesture of giving him the unicorn?
3. Laura escapes to her glass menagerie. To what do Tom and Amanda escape? How complete do you think Tom's escape is at the end of the play?
4. Jim is described as "a nice, ordinary young man." To what extent can it be said that he, like the Wingfields, lives in a dream world? Tom says (speaking of the time of the play, 1939) that "The huge middle class

was matriculating in a school for the blind." Does the play suggest that Jim, apparently a spokesperson for the American dream, is one of the pupils in this school?

5. There is an implication that had Jim not been going steady he might have rescued Laura, but Jim also seems to represent (for example, in his lines about money and power) the corrupt outside world that no longer values humanity. Is this a slip on Williams's part, or is it an interesting complexity?

6. How do you interpret the episode at the end when Laura blows out the candles? Is she blowing out illusions? her own life? both? Explain.

7. Some readers have seen great importance in the religious references in the play. To cite only a few examples: Scene 5 is called (on the screen) "Annunciation"; Amanda is associated with the music "Ave Maria"; Laura's candelabrum, from the altar of the Church of Heavenly Rest, was melted out of shape when the church burned down. Do you think these references add up to anything? If so, to what?

8. On page 1089, Williams says, in a stage direction, *"Now that we cannot hear the mother's speech, her silliness is gone and she has dignity and tragic beauty."* Is Williams simply dragging in the word "tragic" because of its prestige, or is it legitimate? *Tragedy* is often distinguished from *pathos*: in tragedy, suffering is experienced by persons who act and are in some measure responsible for their suffering; in pathos, suffering is experienced by the passive and the innocent. For example, in discussion *The Suppliants,* a play by the ancient Greek dramatist Aeschylus, H. D. F. Kitto (in *Greek Tragedy*) says, "The Suppliants are not only pathetic, as the victims of outrage, but also tragic, as the victims of their own misconceptions." Given this distinction, to what extent are Amanda and Laura tragic? pathetic? You might take into account the following quote from an interview with Williams, reprinted in *Conversations with Tennessee Williams* (ed. Albert J. Devlin): "The mother's valor is the *core* of *The Glass Menagerie.* . . . She's confused, pathetic, even stupid, but everything has *got* to be all right. She fights to make it that way in the only way she knows how."

9. Before writing *The Glass Menagerie,* Williams wrote a short story with the same plot, "Portrait of a Girl in Glass" (later published in his *Collected Stories*). You may want to compare the two works, noticing especially the ways in which Williams has turned a story into a play.

The Play on the Stage

10. In what ways is the setting relevant to the issues raised in the play?

11. In his Production Notes (page 1090) Williams called for the use of a "screen device." Over the years, some productions have incorporated it and some have not. If you were involved in producing *The Glass Menagerie,* would you use this device? Explain your reasons.

12. As director, would you want the actress playing Laura to limp? Give reasons for your decision, and provide additional comments on the ways in which you would ask an actress to portray the role.

13. List the various emotions that you find for Amanda in Scenes 2 and 3. If you were advising an actress playing this role, how would you sug-

gest she convey these different feelings? Following are some questions to consider: In what ways does she reveal her own sadnesses? Should her speeches to Tom be delivered differently from her speeches to Laura? When she looks at Laura's yearbook, should there be any physical contact between the two women? What effect would you wish to achieve at the close of Scene 3?

14. At the end of Scene 5, after an exasperated exchange between Tom and Amanda, Laura and her mother make a wish on the new moon. Three students can memorize this brief section and present it to the group. Then examine each speech, and discuss its emotion. Offer suggestions to the three actors—for instance, changes in emphasis, a slight difference in tone, a certain stance for the mother and daughter—and repeat the scene.

30

Tragedy

The Greek philosopher Aristotle defined "tragedy" as a dramatization of a serious happening—not necessarily one ending with the death of the protagonist—and his definition remains among the best. But many plays have been written since Aristotle defined tragedy. When we think of Shakespeare's tragedies, we cannot resist narrowing Aristotle's definition by adding something like "showing a struggle that rends the protagonist's whole being": and when we think of the "problem plays" of the last hundred years—the serious treatments of such sociological problems as alcoholism and race prejudice—we might be inclined to exclude some of them by adding to the definition something about the need for universal appeal.

The question remains: Is there a single quality present in all works that we call tragedy and absent from works not called tragedy? If there is, no one has yet pointed it out to general satisfaction. But this failure does not mean that there is no such classification as "tragedy." We sense that tragedies resemble each other as members of the same family resemble each other: two children have the mother's coloring and eyes, a third child has the mother's coloring but the father's eyes, a fourth child has the mother's eyes but the father's coloring.

In the next few pages we will examine three comments on tragedy, none of which is entirely acceptable, but each of which seems to have some degree of truth, and each of which can help us detect resemblances and differences among tragedies. The first comment is by Cyril Tourneur, a tragic dramatist of the early seventeenth century:

When the bad bleed, then is the tragedy good.

We think of Macbeth ("usurper," "butcher"). Macbeth is much more than a usurper and butcher, but it is undeniable that he is an offender against the moral order. Whatever the merits of Tourneur's statement, however, if we think of *Romeo and Juliet* (to consider only one play), we realize its inadequacy. Tourneur so stresses the guilt of the protagonist that his or her suffering becomes mere retributive justice. But we cannot plausibly say, for example, that Romeo and Juliet deserved to die because they married without their parents' consent; it is much too simple to call them "bad." Romeo and Juliet are young, in love, nobler in spirit than their parents.

Tourneur's view is probably derived ultimately from an influential passage in Aristotle's *Poetics* in which Aristotle speaks of **hamartia,** sometimes literally translated as "missing the target," sometimes as "vice" or "flaw" or "weakness," but perhaps best translated as "mistake." Aristotle seems to imply that the hero is undone because of some mistake he or she commits, but this mistake need not be the result of a moral fault; it may be simply a miscalculation—for example, failure to foresee the consequences of a deed. Brutus makes a strategic mistake when he lets Marc Antony speak at Caesar's funeral, but we can hardly call it a vice.

Because Aristotle's *hamartia* includes mistakes of this sort, the common translation "tragic flaw" is erroneous. In many Greek tragedies the hero's hamartia is **hubris** (or **hybris**), usually translated as "overweening pride." The hero forgets that he or she is fallible, acts as though he or she has the power and wisdom of the gods, and is later humbled for this arrogance. But one can argue that this self-assertiveness is not a vice but a virtue, not a weakness but a strength; if the hero is destroyed for self-assertion, he or she is nevertheless greater than the surrounding people, just as the person who tries to stem a lynch mob is greater than the mob, although that person also may be lynched for his or her virtue. Or a hero may be undone by a high-mindedness that makes him or her vulnerable. Hamlet is vulnerable because he is, as his enemy says, "most generous and free from all contriving"; because Hamlet is high-minded, he will not suspect that the proposed fencing match is a murderous plot. Othello can be tricked into murdering Desdemona not simply because he is jealous but because he is (in the words of the villainous Iago) "of a free and open nature / That thinks men honest but seem so." Iago knows, too, that out of Desdemona's "goodness" he can "make the net / That shall enmesh them all."

Next, here is a statement more or less the reverse of Tourneur's, by a Russian critic, L. I. Temofeev:

> Tragedy in Soviet literature arouses a feeling of pride for the man who has accomplished a great deed for the people's happiness; it calls for continued struggle against the things which brought about the hero's death.

The distortions in Soviet criticism are often amusing: Hamlet is seen as an incipient Communist, undone by the decadent aristocracy; or Romeo and Juliet as young people of the future, undone by bourgeois parents. Soviet drama in the third quarter of the twentieth century so consistently showed the triumph of the worker that Western visitors to Russia commented on the absence of contemporary tragic plays. Still, there is much in the idea that the tragic hero accomplishes "a great deed," and perhaps we do resent "the things which brought about the hero's death." The stubbornness of the Montagues and Capulets, the fury of the mob that turns against Brutus, the crimes of Claudius in *Hamlet*—all these would seem to call for our indignation.

The third comment is by Arthur Miller:

> If it is true to say that in essence the tragic hero is intent upon claiming his whole due as a personality, and if this struggle must be total and without reservation, then it automatically demonstrates the indestructible will of man to achieve his humanity. . . . It is curious, although edifying, that the plays we revere, century after century, are the tragedies. In them, and in them alone, lies the belief—optimistic, if you will—in the perfectibility of man.

There is much in Miller's suggestions that the tragic hero makes a large and total claim and that the audience often senses triumph rather than despair in tragedies. We often feel that we have witnessed human greatness—that the hero, despite profound suffering, has lived according to his or her ideals. We may feel that we have achieved new insight into human greatness. But the perfectibility of man? Do we feel that *Julius Caesar* or *Macbeth* or *Hamlet* have to do with human perfectibility? Don't these plays suggest rather that people, whatever their nobility, have within them the seeds of their own destruction? Without overemphasizing the guilt of the protagonists, don't we feel that in part the plays dramatize the *im*perfectibility of human beings? In much tragedy, after all, the destruction comes from within, not from without:

> In tragic life, God wot,
> No villain need be! Passions spin the plot:
> We are betrayed by what is false within.
>
> —George Meredith

What we are talking about is **tragic irony,** the contrast between what is believed to be so and what is so, or between expectations and accomplishments.* Several examples from *Macbeth* illustrate something of the range of tragic irony within a single play. In the first act, King Duncan bestows on Macbeth the title of Thane of Cawdor. By his kindness Duncan seals his own doom, for Macbeth, having achieved this rank, will next want to achieve a higher one. In the third act, Macbeth, knowing that Banquo will soon be murdered, hypocritically urges Banquo to "fail not our feast." But Macbeth's hollow request is ironically fulfilled: the ghost of Banquo terrorizes Macbeth during the feast. The most pervasive irony of all, of course, is that Macbeth aims at happiness when he kills Duncan and takes the throne, but he wins only sorrow.

Aristotle's discussion of **peripeteia (reversal)** and **anagnorisis (recognition)** may be a way of getting at this sort of irony. He may simply have meant a reversal of fortune (for example, good luck ceases) and a recognition of who is who (for example, the pauper is really the prince), but more likely he meant profounder things. One can say that the reversal in *Macbeth* lies in the sorrow that Macbeth's increased power brings. The recognition comes when he realizes the consequences of his deeds:

> I have lived long enough: my way of life
> Is fall'n into the sere, the yellow leaf;
> And what which should accompany old age,
> As honor, love, obedience, troops of friends,
> I must not look to have; but, in their stead,
> Curses, not loud but deep, mouth-honor, breath
> Which the poor heart would fain deny, and dare not.

That our deeds often undo us, that we can aim at our good and produce our ruin, was not, of course, a discovery of the tragic dramatists. The archetype is the story of Adam and Eve: these two aimed at becoming like God, and as a con-

---

*Tragic irony is sometimes **dramatic irony** or **Sophoclean irony.** The terms are often applied to speeches or actions that the audience understands in a sense fuller than or different from the sense in which the dramatic characters understand them.

sequence, they brought upon themselves corruption, death, the loss of their earthly paradise. The Bible is filled with stories of tragic irony. A brief quotation from Ecclesiastes (10.8–9) can stand as an epitome of these stories:

> He that diggeth a pit shall fall into it; and whoso breaketh an hedge, a serpent shall bite him.
>
> Whoso removeth stones shall be hurt therewith; and he that cleaveth wood shall be endangered thereby.

"He that cleaveth wood shall be endangered thereby." Activity involves danger. To be inactive is, often, to be ignoble, but to be active is necessarily to imperil oneself. Perhaps we can attempt a summary of tragic figures: they act, and they suffer, usually as a consequence of their action. The question is not of the action's being particularly bad (Tourneur's view) or particularly good (Timofeev's view); the action is often both good and bad, a sign of courage and also of arrogance, a sign of greatness and also of limitations.

Finally, a brief consideration of the pleasure of tragedy: Why do we enjoy plays about suffering? Aristotle has some obscure comments on **catharsis (purgation)** that are often interpreted as saying that tragedy arouses in us both pity and fear and then purges us of these emotions. The idea, perhaps, is that just as we can (it is said) harmlessly discharge our aggressive impulses by witnessing a prizefight or by shouting at an umpire, so we can harmlessly discharge our impulses to pity and to fear by witnessing the dramatization of a person's destruction. The theater in this view is an outlet for emotions that elsewhere would be harmful. But, it must be repeated, Aristotle's comments on catharsis are obscure; perhaps, too, they are wrong.

Most later theories on the pleasure of tragedy are footnotes to Aristotle's words on catharsis. Some say that our pleasure is sadistic (we enjoy the sight of suffering); some, that our pleasure is masochistic (we enjoy lacerating ourselves); some, that it lies in sympathy (we enjoy extending pity and benevolence to the wretched); some, that it lies in self-congratulation (we are reminded, when we see suffering, of our own good fortune); some, that we take pleasure in tragedy because the tragic hero acts out our secret desires, and we rejoice in his or her aggression, expiating our guilt in his or her suffering; and so on.

But this is uncertain psychology, and it mostly neglects the distinction between real suffering and dramatized suffering. In the latter, surely, part of the pleasure is in the contemplation of an aesthetic object, an object that is unified and complete. The chaos of real life seems, for a few moments in drama, to be ordered: the protagonist's action, his or her subsequent suffering, and the total cosmos seem somehow related. Tragedy has no use for the passerby who is killed by a falling brick. The events (the person's walk, the brick's fall) have no meaningful relation. But suppose a person chooses to climb a mountain, and in making the ascent sets in motion an avalanche that destroys that person. Here we find (however simple the illustration) something closer to tragedy. We do not say that people should avoid mountains, or that mountain climbers deserve to die by avalanches. But we feel that the event is unified, as the accidental conjunction of brick and passerby is not.

Tragedy thus presents some sort of ordered action; tragic drama itself is orderly. As we see or read it, we feel it cannot be otherwise; word begets word, deed begets deed, and every moment is exquisitely appropriate. Whatever the relevance on sadism, masochism, sympathy, and the rest, the pleasure of tragedy surely comes in part from the artistic shaping of the material.

Greek theater of Epidaurus on the Peloponnesus east of Nauplia.

A NOTE ON GREEK TRAGEDY

Little or nothing is known for certain of the origin of Greek tragedy. The most common hypothesis holds that it developed from improvised speeches during choral dances honoring Dionysus, a Greek nature god associated with spring, fertility, and wine. Thespis (who perhaps never existed) is said to have introduced an actor into these choral performances in the sixth century BCE Aeschylus (525–456 BCE), Greece's first great writer of tragedies, added the second actor, and Sophocles (495?–406 BCE) added the third actor and fixed the size of the chorus at fifteen. (Because the chorus leader often functioned as an additional actor, and because the actors sometimes doubled in their parts, a Greek tragedy could have more characters than might at first be thought.)

All the extant great Greek tragedy is of the fifth century BCE It was performed at religious festivals in the winter and early spring, in large outdoor amphitheaters built on hillsides. Some of these theaters were enormous; the one at Epidaurus held about fifteen thousand people. The audience sat in tiers, looking down on the **orchestra** (a dancing place), with the acting area behind it and the **skene** (the scene building) yet farther back. The scene building served as dressing room, background (suggesting a palace or temple), and place for occasional entrances and exits. Furthermore, this building helped to provide good acoustics, for speech travels well if there is a solid barrier behind the speakers and a hard, smooth surface in front of them, and if the audience sits in tiers. The wall of the scene building provided the barrier; the orchestra provided the surface in front of the actors; and the seats on the hillside fulfilled the third requirement. Moreover, the acoustics were somewhat improved by slightly elevating the actors above the orchestra, but it is not known exactly when this platform was first constructed in front of the scene building.

A tragedy commonly begins with a **prologos (prologue),** during which the exposition is given. Next comes the **párodos,** the chorus's ode of entrance, sung while the chorus marches into the theater through the side aisles and onto the orchestra. The **epeisodion (episode)** is the ensuing scene; it is followed by a **stasimon** (choral song, ode). Usually there are four or five *epeisodia,* alternating with *stasima.* Each of these choral odes has a **strophe** (lines presumably sung while the chorus dances in one direction) and an antistrophe (lines presumably sung while the chorus retraces its steps). Sometimes a third part, an **epode,** concludes an ode. (In addition to odes that are *stasima,* there can be odes within episodes; the fourth episode of *Antigonê* contains an ode complete with *epode.*) After the last part of the last ode comes the **exodos,** the epilogue or final scene.

The actors (all male) wore masks, and they seem to have chanted much of the play. Perhaps the total result of combining speech with music and dancing was a sort of music-drama roughly akin to opera with some spoken dialogue, such as Mozart's *The Magic Flute* (1791).

TWO PLAYS BY SOPHOCLES

SOPHOCLES

One of the three great writers of tragedies in ancient Greece, Sophocles (496?–406 BCE) was born in Colonus, near Athens, into a well-to-do family. Well educated, he first won public acclaim as a tragic poet at the age of 27, in 468 BCE when he defeated Aeschylus in a competition for writing a tragic play. He is said to have written some 120 plays, but only seven tragedies are extant: among them are Oedipus Rex, Antigone, *and* Oedipus at Colonus. *He died, much honored, in his ninetieth year, in Athens, where he had lived his entire life.*

Oedipus the King

Translated by Robert Fagles

CHARACTERS

OEDIPUS, *king of Thebes*
A PRIEST OF ZEUS

Laurence Olivier in *Oedipus Rex.*

CREON, *brother of Jocasta*
A CHORUS *of Theban citizens and their leader*
TIRESIAS, *a blind prophet*
JOCASTA, *the queen, wife of Oedipus*
A MESSENGER *from Corinth*
A SHEPHERD
A MESSENGER *from inside the palace*
ANTIGONE, ISMENE, *daughters of Oedipus and Jocasta*
GUARDS *and attendants*
PRIESTS *of Thebes*

[**TIME AND SCENE:** *The royal house of Thebes. Double doors dominate the façade; a stone altar stands at the center of the stage.*

Many years have passed since OEDIPUS *solved the riddle of the Sphinx and ascended the throne of Thebes, and now a plague has struck the city. A procession of priests enters; suppliants, broken and despondent, they carry branches wound in wool and lay them on the altar.*

The doors open. GUARDS *assemble.* OEDIPUS *comes forward, majestic but for a telltale limp, and slowly views the condition of his people.*]

OEDIPUS. Oh my children, the new blood of ancient Thebes,
    why are you here? Huddling at my altar,
    praying before me, your branches wound in wool.°
    Our city reeks with the smoke of burning incense,
    rings with cries for the Healer° and wailing for the dead.   5
    I thought it wrong, my children, to hear the truth
    from others, messengers. Here I am myself—

---

3 branches wound in wool Suppliants laid such offerings on the altar of Apollo, god of healing, until their request was granted. Notice that in line 161 Oedipus tells the suppliants to remove the branches, thus suggesting that he will heal them.　**5 the Healer** Apollo.

you all know me, the world knows my fame:
I am Oedipus.

[*Helping a* PRIEST *to his feet.*]

                Speak up, old man. Your years,
your dignity—you should speak for the others.   10
Why here and kneeling, what preys upon you so?
Some sudden fear? some strong desire?
You can trust me. I am ready to help,
I'll do anything. I would be blind to misery
not to pity my people kneeling at my feet.   15
PRIEST. Oh Oedipus, king of the land, our greatest power!
You see us before you now, men of all ages
clinging to your altars. Here are boys,
still too weak to fly from the nest,
and here the old, bowed down with the years,   20
the holy ones—a priest of Zeus° myself—and here
the picked, unmarried men, the young hope of Thebes.
And all the rest, your great family gathers now,
branches wreathed, massing in the squares,
kneeling before the two temples of queen Athena°   25
or the river-shrine where the embers glow and die
and Apollo sees the future in the ashes.°
                       Our city—
look around you, see with your own eyes—
our ship pitches wildly, cannot lift her head
from the depths, the red waves of death . . .   30
Thebes is dying. A blight on the fresh crops
and the rich pastures, cattle sicken and die,
and the women die in labor, children stillborn,
and the plague, the fiery god of fever hurls down
on the city, his lightning slashing through us—   35
raging plague in all its vengeance, devastating
the house of Cadmus!° And black Death luxuriates
in the raw, wailing miseries of Thebes.
Now we pray to you. You cannot equal the gods,
your children know that, bending at your altar.   40
But we do rate you first of men,
both in the common crises of our lives
and face-to-face encounters with the gods.
You freed us from the Sphinx,° you came to Thebes

---

21 **Zeus** chief deity on Mt. Olympus, and father of Apollo.   25 **Athena** goddess of wisdom and protector of cities.   27 **the ashes** Diviners foretold the future by examining the ashes of burnt offerings.   37 **Cadmus** mythical founder of Thebes.   44 **the Sphinx** a female monster (body of a lion, wings of a bird, face of a woman) who asked the riddle "What goes on four legs in the morning, two at noon, and three in the evening?" and who killed those who could not answer. When Oedipus responded correctly that man crawls on all fours in infancy, walks upright in maturity, and uses a staff in old age, the Sphinx destroyed herself.

and cut us loose from the bloody tribute° we had paid   45
that harsh, brutal singer. We taught you nothing,
no skill, no extra knowledge, still you triumphed.
A god was with you, so they say, and we believe it—
you lifted up our lives.
                              So now again,
Oedipus, king, we bend to you, your power—   50
we implore you, all of us on our knees:
find us strength, rescue! Perhaps you've heard
the voice of a god or something from other men,
Oedipus . . . what do you know?
The man of experience—you see it every day—   55
his plans will work in a crisis, his first of all.

Act now—we beg you, best of men, raise up our city!
Act, defend yourself, your former glory!
Your country calls you savior now
for your zeal, your action years ago.   60
Never let us remember of your reign:
you helped us stand, only to fall once more.
Oh raise up our city, set us on our feet.
The omens were good that day you brought us joy—
be the same man today!   65
Rule our land, you know you have the power,
but rule a land of the living, not a wasteland.
Ship and towered city are nothing, stripped of men
alive within it, living all as one.

OEDIPUS.   My children,
I pity you. I see—how could I fail to see   70
what longings bring you here? Well I know
you are sick to death, all of you,
but sick as you are, not one is sick as I.
Your pain strikes each of you alone, each
in the confines of himself, no other. But my spirit   75
grieves for the city, for myself and all of you.
I wasn't asleep, dreaming. You haven't wakened me—
I've wept through the nights, you must know that,
groping, laboring over many paths of thought.
After a painful search I found one cure: 80
I acted at once. I sent Creon,
my wife's own brother, to Delphi°—
Apollo the Prophet's oracle—to learn
what I might do or say to save our city.

Today's the day. When I count the days gone by   85
it torments me . . . what is he doing?
Strange, he's late, he's gone too long.
But once he returns, then, then I'll be a traitor
if I do not do all the god makes clear.

---

45 bloody tribute i.e., the young Thebans who had tried to solve the riddle and had
failed.   **82 Delphi** site of a shrine of Apollo.

PRIEST. Timely words. The men over there   90
    are signaling—Creon's just arriving.
OEDIPUS. [*Sighting* CREON, *then turning to the altar.*]
                                    Lord Apollo,
    let him come with a lucky word of rescue,
    shining like his eyes!
PRIEST. Welcome news, I think—he's crowned, look,
    and the laurel wreath is bright with berries.   95
OEDIPUS. We'll soon see. He's close enough to hear—

[*Enter* CREON *from the side; his face is shaded with a wreath.*]

    Creon, prince, my kinsman, what do you bring us?
    What message from the god?
CREON.   Good news.
    I tell you even the hardest things to bear,
    if they should turn out well, all would be well.   100
OEDIPUS. Of course, but what were the god's *words*? There's no hope
    and nothing to fear in what you've said so far.
CREON. If you want my report in the presence of these . . .

[*Pointing to the* PRIESTS *while drawing* OEDIPUS *toward the palace.*]

    I'm ready now, or we might go inside.
OEDIPUS.   Speak out,
    speak to us all. I grieve for these, my people,   105
    far more than I fear for my own life.
CREON.   Very well,
    I will tell you what I heard from the god.
    Apollo commands us—he was quite clear—
    "Drive the corruption from the land,
    don't harbor it any longer, past all cure,   110
    don't nurse it in your soil—root it out!"
OEDIPUS. How can we cleanse ourselves—what rites?
    What's the source of the trouble?
CREON. Banish the man, or pay back blood with blood.
    Murder sets the plague-storm on the city.
OEDIPUS.   Whose murder?   115
    Whose fate does Apollo bring to light?
CREON.   Our leader,
    my lord, was once a man named Laius,
    before you came and put us straight on course.
OEDIPUS.   I know—
    or so I've heard. I never saw the man myself.
CREON. Well, he was killed, and Apollo commands us now—   120
    he could not be more clear,
    "Pay the killers back—whoever is responsible."
OEDIPUS. Where on earth are they? Where to find it now,
    the trail of the ancient guilt so hard to trace?
CREON. "Here in Thebes," he said.   125
    Whatever is sought for can be caught, you know,
    whatever is neglected slips away.

OEDIPUS.   But where,
    in the palace, the fields or foreign soil,
    where did Laius meet his bloody death?
CREON. He went to consult an oracle, Apollo said,   130
    and he set out and never came home again.
OEDIPUS. No messenger, no fellow-traveler saw what happened?
    Someone to cross-examine?
CREON.   No,
    they were all killed but one. He escaped,
    terrified, he could tell us nothing clearly,   135
    nothing of what he saw—just one thing.
OEDIPUS.   What's that?
    one thing could hold the key to it all,
    a small beginning give us grounds for hope.
CREON. He said thieves attacked them—a whole band,
    not single-handed, cut King Laius down.
OEDIPUS.   A thief, so daring,   140
    so wild, he'd kill a king? Impossible, unless conspirators paid
    him off in Thebes.
CREON. We suspected as much. But with Laius dead
    no leader appeared to help us in our troubles.
OEDIPUS. Trouble? Your *king* was murdered—royal blood!   145
    What stopped you from tracking down the killer
    then and there?
CREON.   The singing, riddling Sphinx.
    She . . . persuaded us to let the mystery go
    and concentrate on what lay at our feet.
OEDIPUS.   No,
    I'll start again—I'll bring it all to light myself!   150
    Apollo is right, and so are you, Creon,
    to turn our attention back to the murdered man.
    Now you have *me* to fight for you, you'll see:
    I am the land's avenger by all rights,
    and Apollo's champion too.   155
    But not to assist some distant kinsman, no,
    for my own sake I'll rid us of this corruption.
    Whoever killed the king may decide to kill me too,
    with the same violent hand—by avenging Laius
    I defend myself.

[*To the* PRIESTS.]

                Quickly, my children.   160
Up from the steps, take up your branches now.

[*To the* GUARDS.]

One of you summon the city here before us,
tell them I'll do everything. God help us,
we will see our triumph—or our fall.

[OEDIPUS *and* CREON *enter the palace, followed by the guards.*]

PRIEST. Rise, my sons. The kindness we came for   165
    Oedipus volunteers himself.

Apollo has sent his word, his oracle—
Come down, Apollo, save us, stop the plague.

[*The* PRIESTS *rise, remove their branches and exit to the side. Enter a* CHORUS, *the citizens of Thebes, who have not heard the news that* CREON *brings. They march around the altar, chanting.*]

CHROUS.   Zeus!
Great welcome voice of Zeus,° what do you bring?
What word from the gold vaults of Delphi   170
comes to brilliant Thebes? Racked with terror—
          terror shakes my heart
and I cry your wild cries, Apollo, Healer of Delos°
I worship you in dread . . . what now, what is your price?
some new sacrifice? some ancient rite from the past   175
come round again each spring?—
          what will you bring to birth?
Tell me, child of golden Hope
warm voice that never dies!
You are the first I call, daughter of Zeus   180
deathless Athena—I call your sister Artemis,°
heart of the market place enthroned in glory,
          guardian of our earth—
I call Apollo, Archer astride the thunderheads of heaven—
O triple shield against death, shine before me now!   185
If ever, once in the past, you stopped some ruin
launched against our walls
          you hurled the flame of pain
far, far from Thebes—you gods
          come now, come down once more!
                                          No, no   190
the miseries numberless, grief on grief, no end—
too much to bear, we are all dying
O my people . . .
          Thebes like a great army dying
and there is no sword of thought to save us, no   195
and the fruits of our famous earth, they will not ripen
no and the women cannot scream their pangs to birth—
screams for the Healer, children dead in the womb
     and life on life goes down
          you can watch them go   200
     like seabirds winging west, outracing the day's fire
down the horizon, irresistibly
          streaking on to the shores of Evening
                                          Death
so many deaths, numberless deaths on deaths, no end—
Thebes is dying, look, her children   205
stripped of pity . . .
          generations strewn on the ground

---

169 welcome voice of Zeus Apollo, son of Zeus, spoke for Zeus.   **173 Delos** sacred island where Apollo was born.   **181 Artemis** a goddess, sister of Apollo.

unburied, unwept, the dead spreading death
and the young wives and gray-haired mothers with them
cling to the altars, trailing in from all over the city—   210
Thebes, city of death, one long cortege
    and the suffering rises
        wails for mercy rise
    and the wild hymn for the Healer blazes out
clashing with our sobs our cries of mourning—   215
    O golden daughter of god,° send rescue
    radiant as the kindness in your eyes!

Drive him back!—the fever, the god of death
    that raging god of war
not armored in bronze, not shielded now, he burns me,   220
battle cries in the onslaught burning on—
O rout him from our borders!
Sail him, blast him out to the Sea-queen's chamber
    the black Atlantic gulfs
    or the northern harbor, death to all   225
where the Thracian surf comes crashing.
Now what the night spares he comes by day and kills—
the god of death.
            O lord of the stormcloud,
you who twirl the lightning, Zeus, Father,
thunder Death to nothing!   230

Apollo, lord of the light, I beg you—
    whip your longbow's golden cord
showering arrows on our enemies—shafts of power
champions strong before us rushing on!

Artemis, Huntress,   235
torches flaring over the eastern ridges—
ride Death down in pain!

God of the headdress gleaming gold, I cry to you—
your name and ours are one, Dionysus°—
    come with your face aflame with wine   240
        your raving women's cries
your army on the march! Come with the lightning
come with torches blazing, eyes ablaze with glory!
Burn that god of death that all gods hate!

[OEDIPUS *enters from the palace to address the* CHORUS, *as if*
addressing the entire city of Thebes.]

OEDIPUS. You pray to the gods? Let me grant your prayers.   245
    Come, listen to me—do what the plague demands:
    you'll find relief and lift your head from the depths.
    I will speak out now as a stranger to the story,
    a stranger to the crime. If I'd been present then,

---

216 golden daughter of god Athena.   **239 Dionysus** god of wine and fertility. He was
attended by the Maenads (the "raving women" of line 241).

there would have been no mystery, no long hunt   250
without a clue in hand. So now, counted
a native Theban years after the murder,
to all of Thebes I make this proclamation:
if any one of you knows who murdered Laius,
the son of Labdacus, I order him to reveal   255
the whole truth to me. Nothing to fear,
even if he must denounce himself,
let him speak up
and so escape the brunt of the charge—
he will suffer no unbearable punishment,   260
nothing worse than exile, totally unharmed.

[OEDIPUS *pauses, waiting for a reply.*]

                              Next,
if anyone knows the murderer is a stranger,
a man from alien soil, come, speak up.
I will give him a handsome reward, and lay up
gratitude in my heart for him besides.   265

[*Silence again, no reply.*]

But if you keep silent, if anyone panicking,
trying to shield himself or friend or kin,
rejects my offer, then hear what I will do.
I order you, every citizen of the state
where I hold throne and power: banish this man—   270
whoever he may be—never shelter him, never
speak a word to him, never make him partner
to your prayers, your victims burned to the gods.
Never let the holy water touch his hands
Drive him out, each of you, from every home.   275
He is the plague, the heart of our corruption,
as Apollo's oracle has just revealed to me.
So I honor my obligations:
I fight for the god and for the murdered man.

Now my curse on the murderer. Whoever he is,   280
a lone man unknown in his crime
or one among many, let that man drag out
his life in agony, step by painful step—
I curse myself as well . . . if by any chance
he proves to be an intimate of our house,   285
here at my hearth, with my full knowledge,
may the curse I just called down on him strike me!

These are your orders: perform them to the last.
I command you, for my sake, for Apollo's, for this country
blasted root and branch by the angry heavens.   290
Even if god had never urged you on to act,
how could you leave the crime uncleansed so long?
A man so noble—your king, brought down in blood—
you should have searched. But I am the king now,
I hold the throne that he held then, possess his bed   295

and a wife who shares our seed . . . why, our seed
might be the same, children born of the same mother
might have created blood-bonds between us
if his hope of offspring hadn't met disaster—
but fate swooped at his head and cut him short.   300
So I will fight for him as if he were my father,
stop at nothing, search the world
to lay my hands on the man who shed his blood,
the son of Labdacus descended of Polydorus,
Cadmus of old and Agenor, founder of the line: 305
their power and mine are one.
                            Oh dear gods,
my curse on those who disobey these orders!
Let no crops grow out of the earth for them—
shrivel their women, kill their sons,
burn them to nothing in this plague   310
that hits us now, or something even worse.
But you, loyal men of Thebes who approve my actions,
may our champion, Justice, may all the gods
be with us, fight beside us to the end!

LEADER. In the grip of your curse, my king, I swear   315
I'm not the murderer, I cannot point him out.
As for the search, Apollo pressed it on us—
he should name the killer.

OEDIPUS.   Quite right,
but to force the gods to act against their will—
no man has the power.

LEADER.   Then if I might mention   320
the next best thing . . .

OEDIPUS.   The third best too—
don't hold back, say it.

LEADER.   I still believe . . .
Lord Tiresias° sees with the eyes of Lord Apollo.
Anyone searching for the truth, my king,
might learn it from the prophet, clear as day.   325

OEDIPUS. I've not been slow with that. On Creon's cue
I sent the escorts, twice, within the hour.
I'm surprised he isn't here.

LEADER.   We need him—
without him we have nothing but old, useless rumors.

OEDIPUS. Which rumors? I'll search out every word.   330

LEADER. Laius was killed, they say, by certain travelers.

OEDIPUS. I know—but no one can find the murderer.

LEADER. If the man has a trace of fear in him
he won't stay silent long,
not with your curses ringing in his ears.   335

OEDIPUS. He didn't flinch at murder,
he'll never flinch at words.

---

323 Tiresias a blind prophet.

[*Enter* TIRESIAS, *the blind prophet, led by a boy with escorts in attendance. He remains at a distance.*]

LEADER. Here is the one who will convict him, look,
 they bring him on at last, the seer, the man of god.
 The truth lives inside him, him alone.

OEDIPUS.   O Tiresias,   340
 master of all the mysteries of our life,
 all you teach and all you dare not tell,
 signs in the heavens, signs that walk the earth!
 Blind as you are, you can feel all the more
 what sickness haunts our city. You, my lord,   345
 are the one shield, the one savior we can find.

 We asked Apollo—perhaps the messengers
 haven't told you—he sent his answer back:
 "Relief from the plague can only come one way.
 Uncover the murderers of Laius,   350
 put them to death or drive them into exile."
 So I beg you, grudge us nothing now, no voice,
 no message plucked from the birds, the embers
 or the other mantic ways within your grasp.
 Rescue yourself, your city, rescue me—   355
 rescue everything infected by the dead.
 We are in your hands. For a man to help others
 with all his gifts and native strength:
 that is the noblest work.

TIRESIAS.   How terrible—to see the truth
 when the truth is only pain to him who sees!   360
 I knew it well, but I put it from my mind,
 else I never would have come.

OEDIPUS. What's this? Why so grim, so dire?

TIRESIAS. Just send me home. You bear your burdens,
 I'll bear mine. It's better that way,   365
 please believe me.

OEDIPUS.   Strange response . . . unlawful,
 unfriendly too to the state that bred and reared you—
 you withhold the word of god.

TIRESIAS.   I fail to see
 that your own words are so well-timed.
 I'd rather not have the same thing said of me . . .   370

OEDIPUS. For the love of god, don't turn away,
 not if you know something. We beg you,
 all of us on our knees.

TIRESIAS.   None of you knows—
 and I will never reveal my dreadful secrets,
 not to say your own.   375

OEDIPUS. What? You know and you won't tell?
 You're bent on betraying us, destroying Thebes?

TIRESIAS. I'd rather not cause pain for you or me.
 So why this . . . useless interrogation?
 You'll get nothing from me.

OEDIPUS.   Nothing! You,   380
 you scum of the earth, you'd enrage a heart of stone!
 You won't talk? Nothing moves you?
 Out with it, once and for all!
TIRESIAS. You criticize my temper . . . unaware
 of the one *you* live with, you revile me.   385
OEDIPUS. Who could restrain his anger hearing you?
 What outrage—you spurn the city!
TIRESIAS. What will come will come.
 Even if I shroud it all in silence.
OEDIPUS. What will come? You're bound to *tell* me that.   390
TIRESIAS. I'll say no more. Do as you like, build your anger
 to whatever pitch you please, rage your worst—
OEDIPUS. Oh I'll let loose, I have such fury in me—
 now I see it all. You helped hatch the plot,
 you did the work, yes, short of killing him   395
 with your own hands—and given eyes I'd say
 you did the killing single-handed!
TIRESIAS.   Is that so!
 I charge you, then, submit to that decree
 you just laid down: from this day onward
 speak to no one, not these citizens, not myself.   400
 You are the curse, the corruption of the land!
OEDIPUS. You, shameless—
 aren't you appalled to start up such a story?
 You think you can get away with this?
TIRESIAS.   I have already.
 The truth with all its power lives inside me.   405
OEDIPUS. Who primed you for this? Not your prophet's trade.
TIRESIAS. You did, you forced me, twisted it out of me.
OEDIPUS. What? Say it again—I'll understand it better.
TIRESIAS. Didn't you understand, just now?
 Or are you tempting me to talk?   410
OEDIPUS. No, I can't say I grasped your meaning.
 Out with it, again!
TIRESIAS. I say you are the murderer you hunt.
OEDIPUS. That obscenity, twice—by god, you'll pay.
TIRESIAS. Shall I say more, so you can really rage?   415
OEDIPUS. Much as you want. Your words are nothing—futile.
TIRESIAS. You cannot imagine . . . I tell you,
 you and your loved ones live together in infamy,
 you cannot see how far you've gone in guilt.
OEDIPUS. You think you can keep this up and never suffer?   420
TIRESIAS. Indeed, if the truth has any power.
OEDIPUS.   It does
 but not for you, old man. You've lost your power,
 stone-blind, stone-deaf—senses, eyes blind as stone!
TIRESIAS. I pity you, flinging at me the very insults
 each man here will fling at you so soon.
OEDIPUS.   Blind,   425
 lost in the night, endless night that cursed you!

You can't hurt me or anyone else who sees the light—
you can never touch me.
TIRESIAS.   True, it is not your fate
    to fall at my hands. Apollo is quite enough,
    and he will take some pains to work this out.   430
OEDIPUS. Creon! Is this conspiracy his or yours?
TIRESIAS. Creon is not your downfall, no, you are your own.
OEDIPUS.   O power—
    wealth and empire, skill outstripping skill
    in the heady rivalries of life,
    what envy lurks inside you! Just for this,   435
    the crown the city gave me—I never sought it,
    they laid it in my hands—for this alone, Creon,
    the soul of trust, my loyal friend from the start
    steals against me . . . so hungry to overthrow me
    he sets this wizard on me, this scheming quack,   440
    this fortune-teller peddling lies, eyes peeled
    for his own profit—seer blind in his craft!

    Come here, you pious fraud. Tell me,
    when did you ever prove yourself a prophet?
    When the Sphinx, that chanting Fury kept her deathwatch here,   445
    why silent then, not a word to set our people free?
    There was a riddle, not for some passer-by to solve—
    it cried out for a prophet. Where were you?
    Did you rise to the crisis? Not a word,
    you and your birds, your gods—nothing.   450
    No, but I came by, Oedipus the ignorant,
    I stopped the Sphinx! With no help from the birds,
    the flight of my own intelligence hit the mark.

    And this is the man you'd try to overthrow?
    You think you'll stand by Creon when he's king?   455
    You and the great mastermind—
    you'll pay in tears, I promise you, for this,
    this witch-hunt. If you didn't look so senile
    the lash would teach you what your scheming means!
LEADER. I would suggest his words were spoken in anger,   460
    Oedipus . . . yours too, and it isn't what we need.
    The best solution to the oracle, the riddle
    posed by god—we should look for that.
TIRESIAS. You are the king no doubt, but in one respect,
    at least, I am your equal: the right to reply.   465
    I claim that privilege too.
    I am not your slave. I serve Apollo.
    I don't need Creon to speak for me in public.
                           So,
    you mock my blindness? Let me tell you this.
    You with your precious eyes,   470
    you're blind to the corruption of your life,
    to the house you live in, those you live with—
    who *are* your parents? Do you know? All unknowing

you are the scourge of your own flesh and blood,
the dead below the earth and the living here above,   475
and the double lash of your mother and your father's curse
will whip you from this land one day, their footfall
treading you down in terror, darkness shrouding
your eyes that now can see the light!
                                   Soon, soon
you'll scream aloud—what haven won't reverberate?   480
What rock of Cithaeron° won't scream back in echo?
That day you learn the truth about your marriage,
the wedding-march that sang you into your halls,
the lusty voyage home to the fatal harbor!
And a crowd of other horrors you'd never dream   485
will level you with yourself and all your children.
There. Now smear us with insults—Creon, myself,
and every word I've said. No man will ever
be rooted from the earth as brutally as you.
OEDIPUS. Enough! Such filth from him? Insufferable—   490
   what, still alive? Get out—
   faster, back where you came from—vanish!
TIRESIAS. I would never have come if you hadn't called me here.
OEDIPUS. If I thought you would blurt out such absurdities,
   you'd have died waiting before I'd had you summoned.   495
TIRESIAS. Absurd, am I! To you, not to your parents:
   the ones who bore you found me sane enough.
OEDIPUS. Parents—who? Wait . . . who is my father?
TIRESIAS. This day will bring your birth and your destruction.
OEDIPUS. Riddles—all you can say are riddles, murk and darkness.   500
TIRESIAS. Ah, but aren't you the best man alive at solving riddles?
OEDIPUS. Mock me for that, go on, and you'll reveal my greatness.
TIRESIAS. Your great good fortune, true, it was your ruin.
OEDIPUS. Not if I saved the city—what do I care?
TIRESIAS. Well then, I'll be going.

   [*To his attendant.*]

                                   Take me home, boy.   505
OEDIPUS. Yes, take him away. You're a nuisance here.
   Out of the way, the irritation's gone.

   [*Turning his back on* TIRESIAS, *moving toward the palace.*]

TIRESIAS.   I will go,
   once I have said what I came here to say.
   I'll never shrink from the anger in your eyes—
   you can't destroy me. Listen to me closely: 510
   the man you've sought so long, proclaiming,
   cursing up and down, the murderer of Laius—
   he is here. A stranger.
   you may think, who lives among you,
   he soon will be revealed a native Theban   515

---

481 Cithaeron mountains near Thebes, where Oedipus was abandoned as an infant.

but he will take no joy in the revelation.
Blind who now has eyes, beggar who now is rich,
he will grope his way toward a foreign soil,
a stick tapping before him step by step.

[OEDIPUS *enters the palace.*]

Revealed at last, brother and father both   520
to the children he embraces; to his mother
son and husband both—he sowed the loins
his father sowed, he spilled his father's blood!

Go in and reflect on that, solve that.
And if you find I've lied   525
from this day onward call the prophet blind.

[TIRESIAS *and the boy exit to the side.*]

CHORUS.   Who—
    who is the man the voice of god denounces
    resounding out of the rocky gorge of Delphi?
        The horror too dark to tell,
    whose ruthless bloody hands have done the work? 530
    His time has come to fly
        to outrace the stallions of the storm
            his feet a streak of speed—
    Cased in armor, Apollo son of the Father
    lunges on him, lightning-bolts afire!   535
    And the grim unerring Furies°
            closing for the kill.
                            Look,
    the word of god has just come blazing
    flashing off Parnassus'° snowy heights!
        That man who left no trace—   540
    after him, hunt him down with all our strength!
    Now under bristling timber
        up through rocks and caves he stalks
            like the wild mountain bull—
    cut off from men, each step an agony, frenzied, racing blind 545
    but he cannot outrace the dread voices of Delphi
    ringing out of the heart of Earth,
        the dark wings beating around him shrieking doom
            the doom that never dies, the terror—

    The skilled prophet scans the birds and shatters me with terror! 550
    I can't accept him, can't deny him, don't know what to say,
    I'm lost, and the wings of dark foreboding beating—
    I cannot see what's come, what's still to come . . .
    and what could breed a blood feud between
        Laius' house and the son of Polybus?°   555

---

536 **Furies** avenging deities.   539 **Parnassus** a mountain associated with Apollo.
555 **son of Polybus** Oedipus is mistakenly thought to be the son of Polybus, King of
Corinth.

I know of nothing, not in the past and not now,
no charge to bring against our king, no cause
to attack his fame that rings throughout Thebes—
    not without proof—not for the ghost of Laius,
    not to avenge a murder gone without a trace.   560

Zeus and Apollo know, they know, the great masters
    of all the dark and depth of human life.
But whether a mere man can know the truth,
whether a seer can fathom more than I—
there is no test, no certain proof   565
    though matching skill for skill
a man can outstrip a rival. No, not till I see
these charges proved will I side with his accusers.
We saw him then, when the she-hawk° swept against him,
saw with our own eyes his skill, his brilliant triumph—   570
    there was the test—he was the joy of Thebes!
    Never will I convict my king, never in my heart.

    [Enter CREON *from the side.*]

CREON. My fellow-citizens, I hear King Oedipus
levels terrible charges at me. I had to come.
I resent it deeply. If, in the present crisis   575
he thinks he suffers any abuse from me,
anything I've done or said that offers him
the slightest injury, why, I've no desire
to linger out this life, my reputation in ruins.
The damage I'd face from such an accusation   580
is nothing simple. No, there's nothing worse:
branded a traitor in the city, a traitor
to all of you and my good friends.
LEADER.   True,
    but a slur might have been forced out of him,
    by anger perhaps, not any firm conviction.   585
CREON. The charge was made in public, wasn't it?
    I put the prophet up to spreading lies?
LEADER. Such things were said . . . .
    I don't know with what intent, if any.
CREON. Was his glance steady, his mind right   590
    when the charge was brought against me?
LEADER. I really couldn't say. I never look
    to judge the ones in power.

    [*The doors open.* OEDIPUS *enters.*]

                                    Wait,
here's Oedipus now.
OEDIPUS.   You—here? You have the gall
    to show your face before the palace gates?
    You, plotting to kill me, kill the king—   595

_____
569 the she-hawk the Sphinx.

I see it all, the marauding thief himself
scheming to steal my crown and power!
                         Tell me,
in god's name, what did you take me for,
coward or fool, when you spun out your plot?   600
Your treachery—you think I'd never detect it
creeping against me in the dark? Or sensing it,
not defend myself? Aren't you the fool,
you and your high adventure. Lacking numbers,
powerful friends, out for the big game of empire—   605
you need riches, armies to bring that quarry down!
CREON. Are you quite finished? It's your turn to listen
    for just as long as you've . . . instructed me.
    Hear me out, then judge me on the facts.
OEDIPUS. You've a wicked way with words, Creon,   610
    but I'll be slow to learn—from you.
    I find you a menace, a great burden to me.
CREON. Just one thing, hear me out in this.
OEDIPUS.   Just one thing,
    don't tell *me* you're not the enemy, the traitor.
CREON. Look, if you think crude, mindless stubbornness   615
    such a gift, you've lost your sense of balance.
OEDIPUS. If you think you can abuse a kinsman,
    then escape the penalty, you're insane.
CREON. Fair enough, I grant you. But this injury
    you say I've done you, what is it?   620
OEDIPUS. Did you induce me, yes or no,
    to send for that sanctimonious prophet?
CREON. I did. And I'd do the same again.
OEDIPUS. All right then, tell me, how long is it now
    since Laius . . .
CREON.   Laius—what did *he* do?
OEDIPUS.   Vanished,   625
    swept from sight, murdered in his tracks.
CREON. The count of the years would run you far back . . .
OEDIPUS. And that far back, was the prophet at his trade?
CREON. Skilled as he is today, and just as honored.
OEDIPUS. Did he ever refer to me then, at that time?
CREON.   No,   630
    never, at least, when I was in his presence.
OEDIPUS. But you did investigate the murder, didn't you?
CREON. We did our best, of course, discovered nothing.
OEDIPUS. But the great seer never accused me then—why not?
CREON. I don't know. And when I don't, *I* keep quiet.   635
OEDIPUS. You do know this, you'd tell it too—
    if you had a shred of decency.
CREON.   What?
    If I know, I won't hold back.
OEDIPUS.   Simply this:
    if the two of you had never put heads together,
    we would never have heard about *my* killing Laius.   640

CREON. If that's what he says . . . well, you know best.
But now I have a right to learn from you
as you just learned from me.

OEDIPUS.   Learn your fill,
you never will convict me of the murder.

CREON. Tell me, you're married to my sister, aren't you?   645

OEDIPUS. A genuine discovery—there's no denying that.

CREON. And you rule the land with her, with equal power?

OEDIPUS. She receives from me whatever she desires.

CREON. And I am the third, all of us are equals?

OEDIPUS. Yes, and it's there you show your stripes—   650
you betray a kinsman.

CREON.   Not at all.
Not if you see things calmly, rationally,
as I do. Look at it this way first:
who in his right mind would rather rule
and live in anxiety than sleep in peace?   655
Particularly if he enjoys the same authority.
Not I, I'm not the man to yearn for kingship,
not with a king's power in my hands. Who would?
Now, as it is, you offer me all I need,   660
not a fear in the world. But if I wore the crown . . .
there'd be many painful duties to perform,
hardly to my taste.

                        How could kingship
please me more than influence, power
without a qualm? I'm not that deluded yet,   665
to reach for anything but privilege outright,
profit free and clear.
Now all men sing my praises, all salute me,
now all who request your favors curry mine.
I am their best hope: success rests in me.   670
Why give up that, I ask you, and borrow trouble?
A man of sense, someone who sees things clearly
would never resort to treason.
No, I've no lust for conspiracy in me,
nor could I ever suffer one who does.   675

Do you want proof? Go to Delphi yourself,
examine the oracle and see if I've reported
the message word-for-word. This too:
if you detect that I and the clairvoyant
have plotted anything in common, arrest me,   680
execute me. Not on the strength of one vote,
two in this case, mine as well as yours.
But don't convict me on sheer unverified surmise.
How wrong it is to take the good for bad,
purely at random, or take the bad for good.   685
But reject a friend, a kinsman? I would as soon
tear out the life within us, priceless life itself.
You'll learn this well, without fail, in time.

Time alone can bring the just man to light—
the criminal you can spot in one short day.
LEADER.   Good advice,   690
my lord, for anyone who wants to avoid disaster.
Those who jump to conclusions may go wrong.
OEDIPUS. When my enemy moves against me quickly,
plots in secret, I move quickly too, I must,
I plot and pay him back. Relax my guard a moment,   695
waiting his next move—he wins his objective,
I lose mine.
CREON.   What do you want?
You want me banished?
OEDIPUS.   No, I want you dead.
CREON. Just to show how ugly a grudge can . . .
OEDIPUS.   So,
still stubborn? you don't think I'm serious?   700
CREON. I think you're insane.
OEDIPUS.   Quite sane—in my behalf.
CREON. Not just as much in mine?
OEDIPUS.   You—my mortal enemy?
CREON. What if you're wholly wrong?
OEDIPUS.   No matter—I must rule.
CREON. Not if you rule unjustly.
OEDIPUS.   Hear him, Thebes, my city!
CREON. My city too, not yours alone!   705
LEADER. Please, my lords.

[*Enter* JOCASTA *from the palace.*]

                         Look, Jocasta's coming,
and just in time too. With her help
you must put this fighting of yours to rest.
JOCASTA. Have you no sense? Poor misguided men,
such shouting—why this public outburst?   710
Aren't you ashamed, with the land so sick,
to stir up private quarrels?

[*To* OEDIPUS.]

Into the palace now. And Creon, you go home.
Why make such a furor over nothing?
CREON. My sister, it's dreadful . . . Oedipus, your husband,   715
he's bent on a choice of punishments for me,
banishment from the fatherland or death.
OEDIPUS. Precisely. I caught him in the act, Jocasta,
plotting, about to stab me in the back.
CREON. Never—curse me, let me die and be damned   720
if I've done you any wrong you charge me with.
JOCASTA. Oh god, believe it, Oedipus,
honor the solemn oath he swears to heaven.
Do it for me, for the sake of all your people.

[*The* CHORUS *begins to chant.*]

CHORUS. Believe it, be sensible   725
    give way, my king, I beg you!
OEDIPUS. What do you want from me, concessions?
CHORUS. Respect him—he's been no fool in the past
    and now he's strong with the oath he swears to god.
OEDIPUS. You know what you're asking?
CHORUS.   I do.
OEDIPUS.   Then out with it!   730
CHORUS. The man's your friend, your kin, he's under oath—
    don't cast him out, disgraced
    branded with guilt on the strength of hearsay only.
OEDIPUS. Know full well, if that is what you want
    you want me dead or banished from the land.
CHORUS.   Never—   735
    no, by the blazing Sun, first god of the heavens!
      Stripped of the gods, stripped of loved ones,
    let me die by inches if that ever crossed my mind.
    But the heart inside me sickens, dies as the land dies
    and now on top of the old griefs you pile this,   740
    your fury—both of you!
OEDIPUS.   Then let him go,
    even if it does lead to my ruin, my death
    or my disgrace, driven from Thebes for life.
    It's you, not him I pity—your words move me.
    He, wherever he goes, my hate goes with him.   745
CREON. Look at you, sullen in yielding, brutal in your rage—
    you'll go too far. It's perfect justice:
    natures like yours are hardest on themselves.
OEDIPUS. Then leave me alone—get out!
CREON.   I'm going.
    You're wrong, so wrong. These men know I'm right.   750

[*Exit to the side. The* CHORUS *turns to* JOCASTA.]

CHORUS. Why do you hesitate, my lady
    why not help him in?
JOCASTA. Tell me what's happened first.
CHORUS. Loose, ignorant talk started dark suspicions
    and a sense of injustice cut deeply too.   755
JOCASTA. On both sides?
CHORUS.   Oh yes.
JOCASTA.   What did they say?
CHORUS. Enough, please, enough! The land's so racked already
    or so it seems to me . . .
    End the trouble here, just where they left it.
OEDIPUS. You see what comes of your good intentions now?   760
    And all because you tried to blunt my anger.
CHORUS.   My king,
    I've said it once, I'll say it time and again—
      I'd be insane, you know it,

senseless, ever to turn my back on you.
You who set our beloved land—storm-tossed, shattered—   765
straight on course. Now again, good helmsman,
steer us through the storm!

[*The* CHORUS *draws away, leaving* OEDIPUS *and* JOCASTA *side by side.*]

JOCASTA.   For the love of god,
    Oedipus, tell me too, what is it?
    Why this rage? You're so unbending.
OEDIPUS. I will tell you. I respect you, Jocasta,   770
    much more than these . . .

[*Glancing at the* CHORUS.]

    Creon's to blame, Creon schemes against me.
JOCASTA. Tell me clearly, how did the quarrel start?
OEDIPUS. He says I murdered Laius—I am guilty.
JOCASTA. How does he know? Some secret knowledge   775
    or simple hearsay?
OEDIPUS.   Oh, he sent his prophet in
    to do his dirty work. You know Creon,
    Creon keeps his own lips clean.
JOCASTA.   A prophet?
    Well then, free yourself of every charge!
    Listen to me and learn some peace of mind: 780
    no skill in the world,
    nothing human can penetrate the future.
    Here is proof, quick and to the point.

    An oracle came to Laius one fine day
    (I won't say from Apollo himself   785
    but his underlings, his priests) and it said
    that doom would strike him down at the hands of a son,
    our son, to be born of our own flesh and blood. But Laius,
    so the report goes at least, was killed by strangers,
    thieves, at a place where three roads meet . . . my son—   790
    he wasn't three days old and the boy's father
    fastened his ankles, had a henchman fling him away
    on a barren, trackless mountain.
                    There, you see?
    Apollo brought neither thing to pass. My baby
    no more murdered his father than Laius suffered—   795
    his wildest fear—death at his own son's hands.
    That's how the seers and all their revelations
    mapped out the future. Brush them from your mind.
    Whatever the god needs and seeks
    he'll bring to light himself, with ease.
OEDIPUS.   Strange,   800
    hearing you just now . . . my mind wandered,
    my thoughts racing back and forth.

JOCASTA. What do you mean? Why so anxious, startled?

OEDIPUS. I thought I heard you say that Laius
    was cut down at a place where three roads meet.   805

JOCASTA. That was the story. It hasn't died out yet.

OEDIPUS. Where did this thing happen? Be precise.

JOCASTA. A place called Phocis, where two branching roads,
    one from Daulia, one from Delphi,
    come together—a crossroads.   810

OEDIPUS. When? How long ago?

JOCASTA. The heralds no sooner reported Laius dead
    than you appeared and they hailed you king of Thebes.

OEDIPUS. My god, my god—what have you planned to do to me?

JOCASTA. What, Oedipus? What haunts you so?

OEDIPUS.   Not yet.   815
    Laius—how did he look? Describe him.
    Had he reached his prime?

JOCASTA.   He was swarthy,
    and the gray had just begun to streak his temples,
    and his build . . . wasn't far from yours.

OEDIPUS.   Oh no no,
    I think I've just called down a dreadful curse   820
    upon myself—I simply didn't know!

JOCASTA. What are you saying? I shudder to look at you.

OEDIPUS. I have a terrible fear the blind seer can see.
    I'll know in a moment. One thing more—

JOCASTA.   Anything,
    afraid as I am—ask, I'll answer, all I can.   825

OEDIPUS. Did he go with a light or heavy escort,
    several men-at-arms, like a lord, a king?

JOCASTA. There were five in the party, a herald among them,
    and a single wagon carrying Laius.

OEDIPUS.   Ai—
    now I can see it all, clear as day.   830
    Who told you all this at the time, Jocasta?

JOCASTA. A servant who reached home, the lone survivor.

OEDIPUS. So, could he still be in the palace—even now?

JOCASTA. No indeed. Soon as he returned from the scene
    and saw you on the throne with Laius dead and gone,   835
    he knelt and clutched my hand, pleading with me
    to send him into the hinterlands, to pasture,
    far as possible, out of sight of Thebes.
    I sent him away. Slave though he was,
    he'd earned that favor—and much more.   840

OEDIPUS. Can we bring him back, quickly?

JOCASTA. Easily. Why do you want him so?

OEDIPUS.   I'm afraid,
    Jocasta, I have said too much already.
    That man—I've got to see him.

JOCASTA.   Then he'll come.
    But even I have a right, I'd like to think,   845
    to know what's torturing you, my lord.

OEDIPUS. And so you shall—I can hold nothing back from you,
   now I've reached this pitch of dark foreboding.
   Who means more to me than you? Tell me,
   whom would I turn toward but you   850
   as I go through all this?

   My father was Polybus, king of Corinth.
   My mother, a Dorian, Merope. And I was held
   the prince of the realm among the people there,
   till something struck me out of nowhere,   855
   something strange . . . worth remarking perhaps,
   hardly worth the anxiety I gave it.
   Some man at a banquet who had drunk too much
   shouted out—he was far gone, mind you—
   that I am not my father's son. Fighting words!   860
   I barely restrained myself that day
   but early the next I went to mother and father,
   questioned them closely, and they were enraged
   at the accusation and the fool who let it fly.
   So as for my parents I was satisfied,   865
   but still this thing kept gnawing at me,
   the slander spread—I had to make my move.
                                          And so,
   unknown to mother and father I set out for Delphi,
   and the god Apollo spurned me, sent me away
   denied the facts I came for,   870
   but first he flashed before my eyes a future
   great with pain, terror, disaster—I can hear him cry,
   "You are fated to couple with your mother, you will bring
   a breed of children into the light no man can bear to see—
   you will kill your father, the one who gave you life!"   875
   I heard all that and ran. I abandoned Corinth,
   from that day on I gauged its landfall only
   by the stars, running, always running
   toward some place where I would never see
   the shame of all those oracles come true.   880
   And as I fled I reached that very spot
   where the great king, you say, met his death.
   Now, Jocasta, I will tell you all.
   Making my way toward this triple crossroad
   I began to see a herald, then a brace of colts   885
   drawing a wagon, and mounted on the bench . . . a man,
   just as you've described him, coming face-to-face,
   and the one in the lead and the old man himself
   were about to thrust me off the road—brute force—
   and the one shouldering me aside, the driver,   890
   I strike him in anger!—and the old man, watching me
   coming up along his wheels—he brings down
   his prod, two prongs straight at my head!
   I paid him back with interest!
   Short work, by god—with one blow of the staff   895

in this right hand I knock him out of his high seat,
roll him out of the wagon, sprawling headlong—
I killed them all—every mother's son!

Oh, but if there is any blood-tie
between Laius and this stranger . . .   900
what man alive more miserable than I?
More hated by the gods? *I* am the man
no alien, no citizen welcomes to his house,
law forbids it—not a word to me in public,
driven out of every hearth and home.   905
And all these curses I—no one but I
brought down these piling curses on myself!
And you, his wife, I've touched your body with these,
the hands that killed your husband cover you with blood.

Wasn't I born for torment? Look me in the eyes!   910
I am abomination—heart and soul!
I must be exiled, and even in exile
never see my parents, never set foot
on native ground again. Else I am doomed
to couple with my mother and cut my father down . . .   915
Polybus who reared me, gave me life.
                              But why, why?
Wouldn't a man of judgment say—and wouldn't he be right—
some savage power has brought this down upon my head?

Oh no, not that, you pure and awesome gods,
never let me see that day! Let me slip   920
from the world of men, vanish without a trace
before I see myself stained with such corruption,
stained to the heart.
LEADER. My lord, you fill our hearts with fear.
        But at least until you question the witness,   925
        do take hope.
OEDIPUS.   Exactly. He is my last hope—
        I am waiting for the shepherd. He is crucial.
JOCASTA. And once he appears, what then? Why so urgent?
OEDIPUS. I will tell you. If it turns out that his story
        matches yours, I've escaped the worst.   930
JOCASTA. What did I say? What struck you so?
OEDIPUS.   You said *thieves*—
        he told you a whole band of them murdered Laius.
        So, if he still holds to the same number,
        I cannot be the killer. One can't equal many.
        But if he refers to one man, one alone,   935
        clearly the scales come down on me:
        I am guilty.
JOCASTA.   Impossible. Trust me,
        I told you precisely what he said,
        and he can't retract it now;
        the whole city heard it, not just I.   940
        And even if he should vary his first report

by one man more or less, still, my lord,
he could never make the murder of Laius
truly fit the prophecy. Apollo was explicit:
my son was doomed to kill my husband . . . my son,   945
poor defenseless thing, he never had a chance
to kill his father. They destroyed him first.

So much for prophecy. It's neither here nor there.
From this day on, I wouldn't look right or left.
OEDIPUS. True, true. Still, that shepherd,   950
    someone fetch him—now!
JOCASTA. I'll send at once. But do let's go inside.
I'd never displease you, least of all in this.

[OEDIPUS *and* JOCASTA *enter the palace.*]

CHORUS. Destiny guide me always
    Destiny find me filled with reverence   955
        pure in word and deed.
Great laws tower above us, reared on high
born for the brilliant vault of heaven—
    Olympian Sky their only father,
nothing mortal, no man gave them birth,   960
their memory deathless, never lost in sleep:
within them lives a mighty god, the god does not grow old.

Pride breeds the tyrant
violent pride, gorging, crammed to bursting
    with all that is overripe and rich with ruin—   965
clawing up to the heights, headlong pride
crashes down the abyss—sheer doom!
    No footing helps, all foothold lost and gone.
But the healthy strife that makes the city strong—
I pray that god will never end that wrestling: 970
god, my champion, I will never let you go.

But if any man comes striding, high and mighty
    in all he says and does,
no fear of justice, no reverence
for the temples of the gods—   975
    let a rough doom tear him down,
repay his pride, breakneck, ruinous pride!
If he cannot reap his profits fairly
    cannot restrain himself from outrage—
mad, laying hands on the holy things untouchable!   980

        Can such a man, so desperate, still boast
        he can save his life from the flashing bolts of god?
            If all such violence goes with honor now
                why join the sacred dance?

Never again will I go reverent to Delphi,   985
    the inviolate heart of Earth
or Apollo's ancient oracle at Abae
or Olympia of the fires—

unless these prophecies all come true
for all mankind to point toward in wonder.   990
King of kings, if you deserve your titles
Zeus, remember, never forget!
You and your deathless, everlasting reign.

They are dying, the old oracles sent to Laius,
now our masters strike them off the rolls.   995
Nowhere Apollo's golden glory now—
the gods, the gods go down.

[*Enter* JOCASTA *from the palace, carrying a suppliant's branch wound in wool.*]

JOCASTA. Lords of the realm, it occurred to me,
just now, to visit the temples of the gods,
so I have my branch in my hand and incense too.   1000

Oedipus is beside himself. Racked with anguish,
no longer a man of sense, he won't admit
the latest prophecies are hollow as the old—
he's at the mercy of every passing voice
if the voice tells of terror.   1005
I urge him gently, nothing seems to help,
so I turn to you, Apollo, you are nearest.

[*Placing her branch on the altar, while an old herdsman enters from the side, not the one just summoned by the King but an unexpected* MESSENGER *from Corinth.*]

I come with prayers and offerings . . . I beg you,
cleanse us, set us free of defilement!
Look at us, passengers in the grip of fear,   1010
watching the pilot of the vessel go to pieces.

MESSENGER. [*Approaching* JOCASTA *and the* CHORUS.]
Strangers, please, I wonder if you could lead us
to the palace of the king . . . I think it's Oedipus.
Better, the man himself—you know where he is?

LEADER. This is his palace, stranger. He's inside.   1015
But here is his queen, his wife and mother
of his children.

MESSENGER.   Blessings on you, noble queen,
queen of Oedipus crowned with all your family—
blessings on you always!

JOCASTA. And the same to you, stranger, you deserve it . . .   1020
such a greeting. But what have you come for?
Have you brought us news?

MESSENGER.   Wonderful news—
for the house, my lady, for your husband too.

JOCASTA. Really, what? Who sent you?

MESSENGER.   Corinth.
I'll give you the message in a moment.   1025
You'll be glad of it—how could you help it?—
though it costs a little sorrow in the bargain.

JOCASTA. What can it be, with such a double edge?

MESSENGER. The people there, they want to make your Oedipus
    king of Corinth, so they're saying now.   1030

JOCASTA. Why? Isn't old Polybus still in power?

MESSENGER. No more. Death has got him in the tomb.

JOCASTA. What are you saying? Polybus, dead?—dead?

MESSENGER.   If not,
    if I'm not telling the truth, strike me dead too.

JOCASTA. [*To a servant.*]
    Quickly, go to your master, tell him this!   1035
    You prophecies of the gods, where are you now?
    This is the man that Oedipus feared for years,
    he fled him, not to kill him—and now he's dead,
    quite by chance, a normal, natural death,
    not murdered by his son.

OEDIPUS. [*Emerging from the palace.*]   1040
                            Dearest,
    what now? Why call me from the palace?

JOCASTA. [*Bringing the* MESSENGER *closer.*]
    Listen to *him,* see for yourself what all
    those awful prophecies of god have come to.

OEDIPUS. And who is he? What can he have for me?

JOCASTA. He's from Corinth, he's come to tell you   1045
    your father is no more—Polybus—he's dead!

OEDIPUS. [*Wheeling on the* MESSENGER.]
    What? Let me have it from your lips.

MESSENGER.   Well,
    if that's what you want first, then here it is:
    make no mistake, Polybus is dead and gone.

OEDIPUS. How—murder? sickness?—what? what killed him?   1050

MESSENGER. A light tip of the scales put old bones to rest.

OEDIPUS. Sickness then—poor man, it wore him down.

MESSENGER.   That,
    and the long count of years he'd measured out.

OEDIPUS.   So!
    Jocasta, why, why look to the Prophet's hearth,
    the fires of the future? Why scan the birds   1055
    that scream above our heads? They winged me on
    to the murder of my father, did they? That was my doom?
    Well look, he's dead and buried, hidden under the earth,
    and here I am in Thebes, I never put hand to sword—
    unless some longing for me wasted him away,   1060
    then in a sense you'd say I caused his death.
    But now, all those prophecies I feared—Polybus
    packs them off to sleep with him in hell!
    They're nothing, worthless.

JOCASTA.   There.
    Didn't I tell you from the start?   1065

OEDIPUS. So you did. I was lost in fear.

JOCASTA. No more, sweep it from your mind forever.

OEDIPUS. But my mother's bed, surely I must fear—

JOCASTA.   Fear?

What should a man fear? It's all chance,
chance rules our lives. Not a man on earth   1070
can see a day ahead, groping through the dark.
Better to live at random, best we can.
And as for this marriage with your mother—
have no fear. Many a man before you,
in his dreams, has shared his mother's bed.   1075
Take such things for shadows, nothing at all—
Live, Oedipus,
as if there's no tomorrow!

OEDIPUS.   Brave words,

and you'd persuade me if mother weren't alive.
But mother lives, so for all your reassurances   1080
I live in fear, I must.

JOCASTA.   But your father's death,

that, at least, is a great blessing, joy to the eyes!

OEDIPUS. Great, I know . . . but I fear her—she's still alive.

MESSENGER. Wait, who is this woman, makes you so afraid?

OEDIPUS. Merope, old man. The wife of Polybus.   1085

MESSENGER. The queen? What's there to fear in her?

OEDIPUS. A dreadful prophecy, stranger, sent by the gods.

MESSENGER. Tell me, could you? Unless it's forbidden
other ears to hear.

OEDIPUS.   Not at all.

Apollo told me once—it is my fate—   1090
I must make love with my own mother,
shed my father's blood with my own hands.
So for years I've given Corinth a wide berth,
and it's been my good fortune too. But still,
to see one's parents and look into their eyes   1095
is the greatest joy I know.

MESSENGER.   You're afraid of that?

That kept you out of Corinth?

OEDIPUS.   My *father*, old man—

so I wouldn't kill my father.

MESSENGER.   So that's it.

Well then, seeing I came with such good will, my king,
why don't I rid you of that old worry now?   1100

OEDIPUS. What a rich reward you'd have for that!

MESSENGER. What do you think I came for, majesty?
So you'd come home and I'd be better off.

OEDIPUS. Never, I will never go near my parents.

MESSENGER. My boy, it's clear, you don't know what you're doing.   1105

OEDIPUS. What do you mean, old man? For god's sake, explain.

MESSENGER. If you ran from *them*, always dodging home . . .

OEDIPUS. Always, terrified Apollo's oracle might come true—

MESSENGER. And you'd be covered with guilt, from both your parents.

OEDIPUS. That's right, old man, that fear is always with me.   1110

MESSENGER. Don't you know? You've really nothing to fear.

OEDIPUS. But why? If I'm their son—Merope, Polybus?

MESSENGER. Polybus was nothing to you, that's why, not in blood.

OEDIPUS. What are you saying—Polybus was not my father?
MESSENGER. No more than I am. He and I are equals.
OEDIPUS.   My father—   1115
    how can my father equal nothing? You're nothing to me!
MESSENGER. Neither was he, no more your father than I am.
OEDIPUS. Then why did he call me his son?
MESSENGER.   You were a gift,
    years ago—know for a fact he took you
    from my hands.
OEDIPUS.   No, from another's hands?   1120
    Then how could he love me so? He loved me, deeply . . .
MESSENGER. True, and his early years without a child
    made him love you all the more.
OEDIPUS.   And you, did you . . .
    buy me? find me by accident?
MESSENGER.   I stumbled on you,
    down the woody flanks of Mount Cithaeron.
OEDIPUS.   So close,   1125
    what were you doing here, just passing through?
MESSENGER. Watching over my flocks, grazing them on the slopes.
OEDIPUS. A herdsman, were you? A vagabond, scraping for wages?
MESSENGER. Your savior too, my son, in your worst hour.
OEDIPUS.   Oh—
    when you picked me up, was I in pain? What exactly?   1130
MESSENGER. Your ankles . . . they tell the story. Look at them.
OEDIPUS. Why remind me of that, that old affliction?
MESSENGER. Your ankles were pinned together. I set you free.
OEDIPUS. That dreadful mark—I've had it from the cradle.
MESSENGER. And you got your name° from that misfortune too,   1135
    the name's still with you.
OEDIPUS.   Dear god, who did it?—
    mother? father? Tell me.
MESSENGER.   I don't know.
    The one who gave you to me, he'd know more.
OEDIPUS. What? You took me from someone else?
    You didn't find me yourself?
MESSENGER.   No sir,   1140
    another shepherd passed you on to me.
OEDIPUS. Who? Do you know? Describe him.
MESSENGER. He called himself a servant of . . .
    if I remember rightly—Laius.

    [JOCASTA *turns sharply.*]

OEDIPUS. The king of the land who ruled here long ago?   1145
MESSENGER. That's the one. That herdsman was *his* man.
OEDIPUS. Is he still alive? Can I see him?
MESSENGER. They'd know best, the people of these parts.

    [OEDIPUS *and the* MESSENGER *turn to the* CHORUS.]

1135 you got your name "Oedipus" means "swollen foot."

OEDIPUS. Does anyone know that herdsman,
    the one he mentioned? Anyone seen him   1150
    in the fields, in the city? Out with it!
    The time has come to reveal this once for all.
LEADER. I think he's the very shepherd you wanted to see,
    a moment ago. But the queen, Jocasta,
    she's the one to say.
OEDIPUS.   Jocasta,   1155
    you remember the man we just sent for?
    Is *that* the one he means?
JOCASTA.   That man . . .
    why ask? Old shepherd, talk, empty nonsense,
    don't give it another thought, don't even think—
OEDIPUS. What—give up now, with a clue like this?   1160
    Fail to solve the mystery of my birth?
    Not for all the world!
JOCASTA.   Stop—in the name of god,
    if you love your own life, call off this search!
    My suffering is enough.
OEDIPUS.   Courage!
    Even if my mother turns out to be a slave,   1165
    and I a slave, three generations back,
    you would not seem common.
JOCASTA.   Oh no,
    listen to me, I beg you, don't do this.
OEDIPUS. Listen to you? No more. I must know it all,
    must see the truth at last.
JOCASTA.   No, please—   1170
    for your sake—I want the best for you!
OEDIPUS. Your best is more than I can bear.
JOCASTA.   You're doomed—
    may you never fathom who you are!
OEDIPUS. [*To a servant.*] Hurry, fetch me the herdsman, now!
    Leave her to glory in her royal birth.   1175
JOCASTA. Aieeeeee—
               man of agony—
    that is the only name I have for you,
    that, no other—ever, ever, ever!

[*Flinging through the palace doors. A long, tense silence follows.*]

LEADER. Where's she gone, Oedipus?
    Rushing off, such wild grief . . .   1180
    I'm afraid that from this silence
    something monstrous may come bursting forth.
OEDIPUS. Let it burst! Whatever will, whatever must!
    I must know my birth, no matter how common
    it may be—I must see my origins face-to-face.   1185
    She perhaps, she with her woman's pride
    may well be mortified by my birth,
    but I, I count myself the son of Chance,
    the great goddess, giver of all good things—

I'll never see myself disgraced. She is my mother!   1190
And the moons have marked me out, my blood-brothers,
one moon on the wane, the next moon great with power.
That is my blood, my nature—I will never betray it,
never fail to search and learn my birth!
CHORUS. Yes—if I am a true prophet   1195
        if I can grasp the truth,
    by the boundless skies of Olympus,
at the full moon of tomorrow, Mount Cithaeron
you will know how Oedipus glories in you—
you, his birthplace, nurse, his mountain-mother!   1200
And we will sing you, dancing out your praise—
you lift our monarch's heart!
    Apollo, Apollo, god of the wild cry
        may our dancing please you!
                                            Oedipus—
        son, dear child, who bore you?   1205
Who of the nymphs who seem to live forever
mated with Pan,° the mountain-striding Father?
Who was your mother? who, some bride of Apollo
the god who loves the pastures spreading toward the sun?
    Or was it Hermes, king of the lightning ridges?   1210
Or Dionysus, lord of frenzy, lord of the barren peaks—
did he seize you in his hands, dearest of all his lucky finds?—
found by the nymphs, their warm eyes dancing, gift
to the lord who loves them dancing out his joy!

[OEDIPUS *strains to see a figure coming from the distance. Attended
by palace guards, an old* SHEPHERD *enters slowly, reluctant to approach the king.*]

OEDIPUS. I never met the man, my friends . . . still,   1215
if I had to guess, I'd say that's the shepherd,
the very one we've looked for all along.
Brothers in old age, two of a kind,
he and our guest here. At any rate
the ones who bring him in are my own men,   1220
I recognize them.

    [*Turning to the* LEADER.]

                        But you know more than I,
    you should, you've seen the man before.
LEADER. I know him, definitely. One of Laius' men,
    a trusty shepherd, if there ever was one.
OEDIPUS. You, I ask you first, stranger,   1225
    you from Corinth—is this the one you mean?
MESSENGER. You're looking at him. He's your man.
OEDIPUS. [*To the* SHEPHERD.]
    You, old man, come over here—

1207 **Pan** god of shepherds (associated, like Hermes and Dionysus, with wilderness).

look at me. Answer all my questions.
Did you ever serve King Laius?

SHEPHERD.   So I did . . .   1230
a slave, not bought on the block though,
born and reared in the palace.

OEDIPUS. Your duties, your kind of work?

SHEPHERD. Herding the flocks, the better part of my life.

OEDIPUS. Where, mostly? Where did you do your grazing?

SHEPHERD.   Well,   1235
Cithaeron sometimes, or the foothills round about.

OEDIPUS. This man—you know him? ever see him there?

SHEPHERD. [*Confused, glancing from the* MESSENGER *to the* KING.]
Doing what?—what man do you mean?

OEDIPUS. [*Pointing to the* MESSENGER.]
This one here—ever have dealings with him?

SHEPHERD. Not so I could say, but give me a chance,   1240
my memory's bad . . .

MESSENGER. No wonder he doesn't know me, master.
But let me refresh his memory for him.
I'm sure he recalls old times we had
on the slopes of Mount Cithaeron;   1245
he and I, grazing our flocks, he with two
and I with one—we both struck up together,
three whole seasons, six months at a stretch
from spring to the rising of Arcturus° in the fall,
then with winter coming on I'd drive my herds   1250
to my own pens, and back he'd go with his
to Laius' folds.

[*To the* SHEPHERD.]

                    Now that's how it was,
wasn't it—yes or no?

SHEPHERD.   Yes, I suppose . . .
it's all so long ago.

MESSENGER.   Come, tell me,
you gave me a child back then, a boy, remember?   1255
A little fellow to rear, my very own.

SHEPHERD. What? Why rake up that again?

MESSENGER. Look, here he is, my fine old friend—
the same man who was just a baby then.

SHEPHERD. Damn you, shut your mouth—quiet!   1260

OEDIPUS. Don't lash out at him, old man—
you need lashing more than he does.

SHEPHERD.   Why,
master, majesty—what have I done wrong?

OEDIPUS. You won't answer his question about the boy.

SHEPHERD. He's talking nonsense, wasting his breath.   1265

1249 Arcturus a star whose rising signaled the end of summer.

OEDIPUS. So, you won't talk willingly—
     then you'll talk with pain.

[*The guards seize the* SHEPHERD.]

SHEPHERD. No, dear god, don't torture an old man!
OEDIPUS. Twist his arms back, quickly!
SHEPHERD.   God help us, why?—
     what more do you need to know?   1270
OEDIPUS. Did you give him that child? He's asking.
SHEPHERD. I did . . . I wish to god I'd died that day.
OEDIPUS. You've got your wish if you don't tell the truth.
SHEPHERD. The more I tell, the worse the death I'll die.
OEDIPUS. Our friend here wants to stretch things out, does he?   1275

[*Motioning to his men for torture.*]

SHEPHERD. No, no, I gave it to him—I just said so.
OEDIPUS. Where did you get it? Your house? Someone else's?
SHEPHERD. It wasn't mine, no. I got it from . . . someone.
OEDIPUS. Which one of them?

[*Looking at the citizens.*]

                         Whose house?
SHEPHERD.   No—
     god's sake, master, no more questions!   1280
OEDIPUS. You're a dead man if I have to ask again.
SHEPHERD. Then—the child came from the house . . . of Laius.
OEDIPUS. A slave? or born of his own blood?
SHEPHERD.   Oh no,
     I'm right at the edge, the horrible truth—I've got to say it!
OEDIPUS. And I'm at the edge of hearing horrors, yes, but I must hear!   1285
SHEPHERD. All right! His son, they said it was—his son!
     But the one inside, your wife,
     she'd tell it best.
OEDIPUS. My wife—
     she gave it to you?
SHEPHERD. Yes, yes, my king.   1290
OEDIPUS. Why, what for?
SHEPHERD. To kill it.
OEDIPUS. Her own child,
     how could she?
SHEPHERD. She was afraid—   1295
     frightening prophecies.
OEDIPUS. What?
SHEPHERD.   They said—
     he'd kill his parents.
OEDIPUS. But you gave him to this old man—why?   1300
SHEPHERD. I pitied the little baby, master,
     hoped he'd take him off to his own country,
     far away, but he saved him for this, his fate.

If you are the man he says you are, believe me,
you were born for pain.

OEDIPUS.   O god—   1305
all come true, all burst to light!
O light—now let me look my last on you!
I stand revealed at last—
cursed in my birth, cursed in marriage,
cursed in the lives I cut down with these hands!   1310

[*Rushing through the doors with a great cry. The Corinthian* MES-
SENGER, *the* SHEPHERD *and attendants exit slowly to the side.*]

CHORUS. O the generations of men
the dying generations—adding the total
of all your lives I find they come to nothing . . .
          does there exist, is there a man on earth
who seizes more joy than just a dream, a vision?   1315
And the vision no sooner dawns than dies
blazing into oblivion.

You are my great example, you, your life
your destiny, Oedipus, man of misery—
I count no man blest.

                          You outranged all men!   1320
          Bending your bow to the breaking-point
you captured priceless glory, O dear god,
and the Sphinx came crashing down,
          the virgin, claws hooked
like a bird of omen singing, shrieking death—   1325
like a fortress reared in the face of death
you rose and saved our land.

From that day on we called you king
we crowned you with honors, Oedipus, towering over all—
mighty king of the seven gates of Thebes.   1330

But now to hear your story—is there a man more agonized?
More wed to pain and frenzy? Not a man on earth,
the joy of your life ground down to nothing
O Oedipus, name for the ages—
          one and the same wide harbor served you   1335
                son and father both
son and father came to rest in the same bridal chamber.
How, how could the furrows your father plowed
bear you, your agony, harrowing on
in silence O so long?

                          But now for all your power   1340
Time, all-seeing Time has dragged you to the light,
judged your marriage monstrous from the start—
the son and the father tangling, both one—
O child of Laius, would to god
          I'd never seen you, never never!   1345
                Now I weep like a man who wails the dead
and the dirge comes pouring forth with all my heart!

I tell you the truth, you gave me life
my breath leapt up in you
and now you bring down the night upon my eyes.   1350

[*Enter a* MESSENGER *from the palace.*]

MESSENGER. Men of Thebes, always first in honor,
    what horrors you will hear, what you will see,
    what a heavy weight of sorrow you will shoulder . . .
    if you are true to your birth, if you still have
    some feeling for the royal house of Thebes.   1355
    I tell you neither the waters of the Danube
    nor the Nile can wash this palace clean.
    Such things it hides, it soon will bring to light—
    terrible things, and none done blindly now,
    all done with a will. The pains   1360
    we inflict upon ourselves hurt most of all.
LEADER. God knows we have pains enough already.
    What can you add to them?
MESSENGER. The queen is dead.
LEADER.   Poor lady—how?
MESSENGER. By her own hand. But you are spared the worst,   1365
    you never had to watch . . . I saw it all,
    and with all the memory that's in me
    you will learn what that poor woman suffered.

    Once she'd broken in through the gates,
    dashing past us, frantic, whipped to fury,   1370
    ripping her hair out with both hands—
    straight to her rooms she rushed, flinging herself
    across the bridal-bed, doors slamming behind her—
    once inside, she wailed for Laius, dead so long,
    remembering how she bore his child long ago,   1375
    the life that rose up to destroy him, leaving
    its mother to mother living creatures
    with the very son she'd borne.
    Oh how she wept, mourning the marriage-bed
    where she let loose that double brood—monsters—   1380
    husband by her husband, children by her child.
                                    And then—
    but how she died is more than I can say. Suddenly
    Oedipus burst in, screaming, he stunned us so
    we couldn't watch her agony to the end,
    our eyes were fixed on him. Circling   1385
    like a maddened beast, stalking, here, there,
    crying out to us—
                    Give him a sword! His wife,
    no wife, his mother, where can he find the mother earth
    that cropped two crops at once, himself and all his children?
    He was raging—one of the dark powers pointing the way,   1390
    none of us mortals crowding around him, no,
    with a great shattering cry—someone, something leading him on—
    he hurled at the twin doors and bending the bolts back

out of their sockets, crashed through the chamber.
And there we saw the woman hanging by the neck,   1395
cradled high in a woven noose, spinning,
swinging back and forth. And when he saw her,
giving a low, wrenching sob that broke our hearts,
slipping the halter from her throat, he eased her down,
in a slow embrace he laid her down, poor thing . . .   1400
then, what came next, what horror we beheld!

He rips off her brooches, the long gold pins
holding her robes—and lifting them high,
looking straight up into the points,
he digs them down the sockets of his eyes, crying, "You,   1405
you'll see no more the pain I suffered, all the pain I caused!
Too long you looked on the ones you never should have seen,
blind to the ones you longed to see, to know! Blind
from this hour on! Blind in the darkness—blind!"
His voice like a dirge, rising, over and over   1410
raising the pins, raking them down his eyes.
And at each stroke blood spurts from the roots,
splashing his beard, a swirl of it, nerves and clots—
black hail of blood pulsing, gushing down.

These are the griefs that burst upon them both,   1415
coupling man and woman. The joy they had so lately,
the fortune of their old ancestral house
was deep joy indeed. Now, in this one day,
wailing, madness and doom, death, disgrace,
all the griefs in the world that you can name,   1420
all are theirs forever.
LEADER.   Oh poor man, the misery—
has he any rest from pain now?

[A voice within, in torment.]

MESSENGER.   He's shouting,
"Loose the bolts, someone, show me to all of Thebes!
My father's murderer, my mother's—"
No, I can't repeat it, it's unholy.   1425
Now he'll tear himself from his native earth,
not linger, curse the house with his own curse.
But he needs strength, and a guide to lead him on.
This is sickness more than he can bear.

[The palace doors open.]

                                    Look,
he'll show you himself. The great doors are opening—   1430
you are about to see a sight, a horror
even his mortal enemy would pity.

[Enter OEDIPUS, blinded, led by a boy. He stands at the palace
steps, as if surveying his people once again.]

CHORUS.   O the terror—
    the suffering, for all the world to see,
    the worst terror that ever met my eyes.
    What madness swept over you? What god,   1435
    what dark power leapt beyond all bounds,
    beyond belief, to crush your wretched life?—
    godforsaken, cursed by the gods!
    I pity you but I can't bear to look.
    I've much to ask, so much to learn,   1440
    so much fascinates my eyes,
    but you . . . . I shudder at the sight.

OEDIPUS.   Oh, Ohh—
    the agony! I am agony—
    where am I going? where on earth?
        where does all this agony hurl me?   1445
    where's my voice?—
        winging, swept away on a dark tide—
    My destiny, my dark power, what a leap you made!

CHORUS. To the depths of terror, too dark to hear, to see.

OEDIPUS. Dark, horror of darkness   1450
    my darkness, drowning, swirling around me
    crashing wave on wave—unspeakable, irresistible
        headwind, fatal harbor! Oh again,
    the misery, all at once, over and over
    the stabbing daggers, stab of memory   1455
    raking me insane.

CHORUS.   No wonder you suffer
    twice over, the pain of your wounds,
    the lasting grief of pain.

OEDIPUS.   Dear friend, still here?
    Standing by me, still with a care for me,
    the blind man? Such compassion,   1460
    loyal to the last. Oh it's you,
    I know you're here, dark as it is
    I'd know you anywhere, your voice—
    it's yours, clearly yours.

CHORUS.   Dreadful, what you've done . . .
    how could you bear it, gouging out your eyes?   1465
    What superhuman power drove you on?

OEDIPUS. Apollo, friends, Apollo—
    he ordained my agonies—these, my pains on pains!
      But the hand that struck my eyes was mine,
      mine alone—no one else—   1470
        I did it all myself!
    What good were eyes to me?
    Nothing I could see could bring me joy.

CHORUS. No, no, exactly as you say.

OEDIPUS.   What can I ever see?
    What love, what call of the heart   1475
    can touch my ears with joy? Nothing, friends.
      Take me away, far, far from Thebes,

quickly, cast me away, my friends—
this great murderous ruin, this man cursed to heaven,
   the man the deathless gods hate most of all!   1480
CHORUS. Pitiful, you suffer so, you understand so much . . .
I wish you'd never known.
OEDIPUS.   Die, die—
whoever he was that day in the wilds
who cut my ankles free of the ruthless pins,
   he pulled me clear of death, he saved my life   1485
for this, this kindness—
      Curse him, kill him!
If I'd died then, I'd never have dragged myself,
my loved ones through such hell.
CHORUS. Oh if only . . . would to god.
OEDIPUS.   I'd never have come to this,   1490
my father's murderer—never been branded
mother's husband, all men see me now! Now,
   loathed by the gods, son of the mother I defiled
      coupling in my father's bed, spawning lives in the loins
that spawned my wretched life. What grief can crown this grief?   1495
      It's mine alone, my destiny—I am Oedipus!
CHORUS. How can I say you've chosen for the best?
Better to die than be alive and blind.
OEDIPUS. What I did was best—don't lecture me,
   no more advice. I, with *my* eyes,   1500
how could I look my father in the eyes
when I go down to death? Or mother, so abused . . .
I have done such things to the two of them,
crimes too huge for hanging.
                 Worse yet,
the sight of my children, born as they were born,   1505
how could I long to look into their eyes?
No, not with these eyes of mine, never.
Not this city either, her high towers,
the sacred glittering images of her gods—
I am misery! I, her best son, reared   1510
as no other son of Thebes was ever reared,
I've stripped myself, I gave the command myself.
All men must cast away the great blasphemer,
the curse now brought to light by the gods,
the son of Laius—I, my father's son!   1515

Now I've exposed my guilt, horrendous guilt,
could I train a level glance on you, my countrymen?
Impossible! No, if I could just block off my ears,
the springs of hearing, I would stop at nothing—
I'd wall up my loathsome body like a prison,   1520
blind to the sound of life, not just the sight:
Oblivion—what a blessing . . .
for the mind to dwell a world away from pain.

O Cithaeron, why did you give me shelter?

Why didn't you take me, crush my life out on the spot?   1525
I'd never have revealed my birth to all mankind.

O Polybus, Corinth, the old house of my fathers,
so I believed—what a handsome prince you raised—
under the skin, what sickness to the core.
Look at me! Born of outrage, outrage to the core.   1530
O triple roads—it all comes back, the secret,
dark ravine, and the oaks closing in
where the three roads join . . .
You drank my father's blood, my own blood
spilled by my own hands—you still remember me?   1535
What things you saw me do? Then I came here
and did them all once more!

                  Marriages! O marriage,
you gave me birth, and once you brought me into the world
you brought my sperm rising back, springing to light
fathers, brothers, sons—one murderous breed—   1540
brides, wives, mothers. The blackest things
a man can do, I have done them all!

                No more—
it's wrong to name what's wrong to do. Quickly,
for the love of god, hide me somewhere,
kill me, hurl me into the sea   1545
where you can never look on me again.

[*Beckoning to the* CHORUS *as they shrink away.*]

                Closer,
it's all right. Touch the man of grief.
Do. Don't be afraid. My troubles are mine
and I am the only man alive who can sustain them.

[*Enter* CREON *from the palace, attended by palace guards.*]

LEADER. Put your requests to Creon. Here he is,   1550
    just when we need him. He'll have a plan, he'll act.
    Now that he's the sole defense of the country
    in your place.
OEDIPUS.   Oh no, what can I say to him?
    How can I ever hope to win his trust?
    I wronged him so, just now, in every way.   1555
    You must see that—I was so wrong, so wrong.
CREON. I haven't come to mock you, Oedipus,
    or to criticize your former failings.

[*Turning to the guards.*]

                You there,
have you lost all respect for human feelings?
At least revere the Sun, the holy fire   1560
that keeps us all alive. Never expose a thing
of guilt and holy dread so great it appalls
the earth, the rain from heaven, the light of day!

Get him into the halls—quickly as you can.
Piety demands no less. Kindred alone   1565
should see a kinsman's shame. This is obscene.

OEDIPUS. Please, in god's name . . . you wipe my fears away,
coming so generously to me, the worst of men.
Do one thing more, for your sake, not mine.

CREON. What do you want? Why so insistent?   1570

OEDIPUS. Drive me out of the land at once, far from sight,
where I can never hear a human voice.

CREON. I'd have done that already, I promise you.
First I wanted the god to clarify my duties.

OEDIPUS. The god? His command was clear, every word: 1575
death for the father-killer, the curse—
he said destroy me!

CREON. So he did. Still, in such a crisis
it's better to ask precisely what to do.

OEDIPUS.   So miserable—
you'd consult the god about a man like me?   1580

CREON. By all means. And this time, I assume,
even you will obey the god's decrees.

OEDIPUS.   I will,
I will. And you, I command you—I beg you . . .
the woman inside, bury her as you see fit.
It's the only decent thing,   1585
to give your own the last rites. As for me,
never condemn the city of my fathers
to house my body, not while I'm alive, no,
let me live on the mountains, on Cithaeron,
my favorite haunt, I have made it famous.   1590
Mother and father marked out that rock
to be my everlasting tomb—buried alive.
Let me die there, where they tried to kill me.
Oh but this I know: no sickness can destroy me,
nothing can. I would never have been saved   1595
from death—I have been saved
for something great and terrible, something strange.
Well let my destiny come and take me on its way!
About my children, Creon, the boys at least,
don't burden yourself. They're men,   1600
wherever they go, they'll find the means to live.
But my two daughters, my poor helpless girls,
clustering at our table, never without me
hovering near them . . . whatever I touched,
they always had their share. Take care of them,   1605
I beg you. Wait, better—permit me, would you?
Just to touch them with my hands and take
our fill of tears. Please . . . my king.
Grant it, with all your noble heart.
If I could hold them, just once, I'd think   1610
I had them with me, like the early days
when I could see their eyes.

[ANTIGONE *and* ISMENE, *two small children, are led in from the palace by a nurse.*]

                         What's that
O god! Do I really hear you sobbing?—
my two children. Creon, you've pitied me?
Sent me my darling girls, my own flesh and blood!   1615
Am I right?

CREON.   Yes, it's my doing.
I know the joy they gave you all these years,
the joy you must feel now.

OEDIPUS.   Bless you, Creon!
May god watch over you for this kindness,
better than he ever guarded me.

                              Children, where are you?   1620
Here, come quickly—

[*Groping for* ANTIGONE *and* ISMENE, *who approach their father cautiously, then embrace him.*]

                         Come to these hands of mine,
your brother's hands, your own father's hands
that served his once bright eyes so well—
that made them blind. Seeing nothing, children,
knowing nothing, I became your father,   1625
I fathered you in the soil that gave me life.

How I weep for you—I cannot see you now . . .
just thinking of all your days to come, the bitterness,
the life that rough mankind will thrust upon you.
Where are the public gatherings you can join,   1630
the banquets of the clans? Home you'll come,
in tears, cut off from the sight of it all,
the brilliant rites unfinished.
And when you reach perfection, ripe for marriage,
who will he be, my dear ones? Risking all   1635
to shoulder the curse that weighs down my parents,
yes and you too—that wounds us all together.
What more misery could you want?
Your father killed his father, sowed his mother,
one, one and the selfsame womb sprang you—   1640
he cropped the very roots of his existence.

Such disgrace, and you must bear it all!
Who will marry you then? Not a man on earth.
Your doom is clear: you'll wither away to nothing,
single, without a child.

[*Turning to* CREON.]

                         Oh Creon,   1645
you are the only father they have now . . .
we who brought them into the world
are gone, both gone at a stroke—

Don't let them go begging, abandoned,
women without men. Your own flesh and blood!   1650
Never bring them down to the level of my pains.
Pity them. Look at them, so young, so vulnerable,
shorn of everything—you're their only hope.
Promise me, noble Creon, touch my hand!

[*Reaching toward* CREON, *who draws back.*]

You, little ones, if you were old enough   1655
to understand, there is much I'd tell you.
Now, as it is, I'd have you say a prayer.
Pray for life, my children,
live where you are free to grow and season.
Pray god you find a better life than mine,   1660
the father who begot you.

CREON.   Enough.
    You've wept enough. Into the palace now.
OEDIPUS. I must, but I find it very hard.
CREON. Time is the great healer, you will see.
OEDIPUS. I am going—you know on what condition?   1665
CREON. Tell me. I'm listening.
OEDIPUS. Drive me out of Thebes, in exile.
CREON. Not I. Only the gods can give you that.
OEDIPUS. Surely the gods hate me so much—
CREON. You'll get your wish at once.
OEDIPUS.   You consent?   1670
CREON. I try to say what I mean; it's my habit.
OEDIPUS. Then take me away. It's time.
CREON. Come along, let go of the children.
OEDIPUS.   No—
    don't take them away from me, not now! No no no!

[*Clutching his daughters as the guards wrench them loose and
take them through the palace doors.*]

CREON. Still the king, the master of all things?   1675
    No more: here your power ends.
    None of your power follows you through life.

[*Exit* OEDIPUS *and* CREON *to the palace. The* CHORUS *comes forward
to address the audience directly.*]

CHORUS. People of Thebes, my countrymen, look on Oedipus.
    He solved the famous riddle with his brilliance,
    he rose to power, a man beyond all power.   1680
    Who could behold his greatness without envy?
    Now what a black sea of terror has overwhelmed him.
    Now as we keep our watch and wait the final day,
    count no man happy till he dies, free of pain at last.

[*Exit in procession.*]

✖ TOPICS FOR CRITICAL THINKING AND WRITING

The Play on the Page

1. On the basis of lines 1–149, characterize Oedipus. Does he seem an effective leader? What additional traits are revealed in lines 205–491?
2. In your opinion, how fair is it to say that Oedipus is morally guilty? Does he argue that he is morally innocent because he did not intend to do immoral deeds? Can it be said that he is guilty of *hybris* but that *hybris* (see page 1095) has nothing to do with his fall?
3. Oedipus says that he blinds himself in order not to look upon people he should not. What further reasons can be given? Why does he not (like Jocasta) commit suicide?
4. Does the play show the futility of human effots to act intelligently?
5. In *Oedipus,* do you find the gods evil?
6. Are the choral odes lyrical interludes that serve to separate the scenes, or do they advance the dramatic action?
7. Matthew Arnold said that Sophocles saw life steadily and saw it whole. But in this play is Sophocles facing the facts of life? Or, on the contrary, is he avoiding what we think of as normal life, and presenting a series of unnatural and outrageous coincidences? In either case, do you think the play is relevant today?
8. Can you describe your emotions at the end of the play? Do they include pity for Oedipus? Pity for all human beings, including yourself? Fear that you might be punished for some unintended transgression? Awe, engendered by a perception of the interrelatedness of things? Relief that the story is only a story? Exhilaration? Explain your reaction.

The Play on the Stage

9. During your first consideration of the play, start with a reading of lines 1–149. Choose someone from the group to stand on a chair (Oedipus), two other readers to stand nearby (the Priest and Creon), and several others to kneel or lie on the floor (Theban citizens). After this rough enactment, ask the readers how they felt about their roles. Then discuss the ways a modern staging could create a powerful opening for the play. Some questions to consider: Do the Thebans ever touch Oedipus? Should the actor playing Oedipus make eye contact with anyone on the stage?
10. Originally the Greek chorus chanted and danced. What are your recommendations for a director today? Choose a particular passage from the play to illustrate your ideas.
11. Imagine that you are directing a production of *Oedipus.* Propose a cast for the principal roles, using well-known actors or people from your own circle. Explain the reasons for your choices.
12. What might be gained or lost by performing the play in modern dress? Or is there some period other than ancient Greece—let's say the Victorian period—in which you think the play might be effectively set?
13. Alan MacVey, who directed a production at the University of Iowa, used classical costumes but afterward said that he wished he had used a conference table as the set and had costumed the royalty in "power suits." What is your response to this idea?

Antigone

Translated by Robert Fagles

CHARACTERS

ANTIGONE, *daughter of Oedipus and Jocasta*
ISMENE, *sister of Antigone*
A CHORUS, *of old Theban citizens and their* LEADER
CREON, *king of Thebes, uncle of Antigone and Ismene*
A SENTRY
HAEMON, *son of Creon and Eurydice*
TIRESIAS, *a blind prophet*
A MESSENGER
EURYDICE, *wife of Creon*
GUARDS, ATTENDANTS, and a BOY

[**TIME AND SCENE:** *The royal house of Thebes. It is still night, and the invading armies of Argos have just been driven from the city. Fighting on opposite sides, the sons of* OEDIPUS, ETEOCLES *and* POLYNICES, *have killed each other in combat. Their uncle,* CREON, *is now king of Thebes.*

Enter ANTIGONE, *slipping through the central doors of the palace. She motions to her sister,* ISMENE, *who follows her cautiously toward an altar at the center of the stage.*]

ANTIGONE. My own flesh and blood—dear sister, dear Ismene,
　　how many griefs our father Oedipus° handed down!
　　Do you know one, I ask you, one grief
　　that Zeus° will not perfect for the two of us
　　while we still live and breathe! There's nothing,　　　　　　　　5
　　no pain—our lives are pain—no private shame,
　　no public disgrace, nothing I haven't seen
　　in your griefs and mine. And now this:
　　an emergency decree, they say, the Commander
　　has just declared for all of Thebes.　　　　　　　　　　　　10
　　What, haven't you heard? Don't you see?
　　The doom reserved for enemies
　　marches on the ones we love the most.
　ISMENE. Not I, I haven't heard a word, Antigone.
　　Nothing of loved ones,　　　　　　　　　　　　　　　　　15
　　no joy or pain has come my way, not since
　　the two of us were robbed of our two brothers,
　　both gone in a day, a double blow—
　　not since the armies of Argos vanished,

---

2 Oedipus, once King of Thebes, was the father of Antigone and Ismene, and of their brothers Polynices and Eteocles. Oedipus unwittingly killed his faither, Laius, and married his own mother, Jocasta. When he learned what he had done, he blinded himself and left Thebes. Eteocles and Polynices quarreled; Polynices was driven out but returned to assault Thebes. In the battle, each brother killed the other, and Creon became king and ordered that Polynices be left to rot unburied on the battlefield as a traitor.   **4 Zeus** highest of the deities on Mt. Olympus.

Jane Lapotaire in *Antigone,* National Theater, London, 1984.

just this very night. I know nothing more,   20
whether our luck's improved or ruin's still to come.
ANTIGONE. I thought so. That's why I brought you out here,
past the gates, so you could hear in private.
ISMENE. What's the matter? Trouble, clearly . . .
you sound so dark, so grim.   25
ANTIGONE. Why not? Our own brothers' burial!
Hasn't Creon graced one with all the rites,
disgraced the other? Eteocles, they say,
has been given full military honors,
rightly so—Creon's laid him in the earth   30
and he goes with glory down among the dead.
But the body of Polynices, who died miserably—
why, a city-wide proclamation, rumor has it,
forbids anyone to bury him, even mourn him.
He's to be left unwept, unburied, a lovely treasure   35
for birds that scan the field and feast to their heart's content.

Such, I hear, is the martial law our good Creon
lays down for you and me—yes, me, I tell you—
and he's coming here to alert the uninformed
in no uncertain terms,   40
and he won't treat the matter lightly. Whoever
disobeys in the least will die, his doom is sealed:
stoning to death inside the city walls!

There you have it. You'll soon show what you are,
worth your breeding, Ismene, or a coward—   45
for all your royal blood.

ISMENE. My poor sister, if things have come to this,
    who am I to make or mend them, tell me,
    what good am I to you?
ANTIGONE.   Decide.
    Will you share the labor, share the work?   50
ISMENE. What work, what's the risk? What do you mean?
ANTIGONE. [*Raising her hands.*] Will you lift up his body with these
                                                        bare hands
    and lower it with me?
ISMENE.   What? You'd bury him—
    when a law forbids the city?
ANTIGONE.   Yes!
    He is my brother and—deny it as you will—   55
    your brother too.
    No one will ever convict me for a traitor.
ISMENE. So desperate, and Creon has expressly—
ANTIGONE.   No,
    he has no right to keep me from my own.
ISMENE. Oh my sister, think—   60
    think how our own father died, hated,
    his reputation in ruins, driven on
    by the crimes he brought to light himself
    to gouge out his eyes with his own hands—
    then mother . . . his mother and wife, both in one,   65
    mutilating her life in the twisted noose—
    and last, our two brothers dead in a single day,
    both shedding their own blood, poor suffering boys,
    battling out their common destiny hand-to-hand.

    Now look at the two of us, left so alone . . .   70
    think what a death we'll die, the worst of all
    if we violate the laws and override
    the fixed decree of the throne, its power—
    we must be sensible. Remember we are women,
    we're not born to contend with men. Then too,   75
    we're underlings, ruled by much stronger hands,
    so we must submit in this, and things still worse.

    I, for one, I'll beg the dead to forgive me—
    I'm forced, I have no choice—I must obey
    the ones who stand in power. Why rush to extremes?   80
    It's madness, madness.
ANTIGONE.   I won't insist,
    no, even if you should have a change of heart,
    I'd never welcome you in the labor, not with me.
    So, do as you like, whatever suits you best—
    I'll bury him myself.   85
    And even if I die in the act, that death will be a glory.
    I'll lie with the one I love and loved by him—
    an outrage sacred to the gods! I have longer
    to please the dead than please the living here:
    in the kingdom down below I'll lie forever.   90

Do as you like, dishonor the laws
the gods hold in honor.
ISMENE.   I'd do them no dishonor . . .
but defy the city? I have no strength for that.
ANTIGONE. You have your excuses. I am on my way,
I'll raise a mound for him, for my dear brother.   95
ISMENE. Oh Antigone, you're so rash—I'm so afraid for you!
ANTIGONE. Don't fear for me. Set your own life in order.
ISMENE. Then don't, at least, blurt this out to anyone.
Keep it a secret. I'll join you in that, I promise.
ANTIGONE. Dear god, shout it from the rooftops. I'll hate you   100
all the more for silence—tell the world!
ISMENE. So fiery—and it ought to chill your heart.
ANTIGONE. I know I please where I must please the most.
ISMENE. Yes, if you can, but you're in love with impossibility.
ANTIGONE. Very well then, once my strength gives out   105
I will be done at last.
ISMENE.   You're wrong from the start,
you're off on a hopeless quest.
ANTIGONE. If you say so, you will make me hate you,
and the hatred of the dead, by all rights,
will haunt you night and day.   110
But leave me to my own absurdity, leave me
to suffer this—dreadful thing. I'll suffer
nothing as great as death without glory.   [*Exit to the side.*]
ISMENE. Then go if you must, but rest assured,
wild, irrational as you are, my sister,   115
you are truly dear to the ones who love you.

[*Withdrawing to the palace. Enter a* CHORUS, *the old citizens of
Thebes, chanting as the sun begins to rise.*]

CHORUS. Glory!—great beam of sun, brightest of all
that ever rose on the seven gates of Thebes,
you burn through night at last!
Great eye of the golden day,   120
mounting the Dirce's banks° you throw him back—
the enemy out of Argos, the white shield, the man of bronze—
he's flying headlong now
the bridle of fate stampeding him with pain!

And he had driven against our borders,   125
launched by the warring claims of Polynices—
like an eagle screaming, winging havoc
over the land, wings of armor
shielded white as snow,
a huge army massing,   130
crested helmets bristling for assault.

He hovered above our roofs, his vast maw gaping
closing down around our seven gates,

---

121 **the Dirce's banks** banks of the River Dirce, near Thebes.

his spears thirsting for the kill
            but now he's gone, look,   135
before he could glut his jaws with Theban blood
or the god of fire put our crown of towers to the torch.
He grappled the Dragon none can master—Thebes—
      the clang of our arms like thunder at his back!

    Zeus hates with a vengeance all bravado,   140
    the mighty boasts of men. He watched them
    coming on in a rising flood, the pride
    of their golden armor ringing shrill—
    and brandishing his lightning
    blasted the fighter just at the goal,   145
    rushing to shout his triumph from our walls.

Down from the heights he crashed, pounding down on the earth!
And a moment ago, blazing torch in hand—
      mad for attack, ecstatic
he breathed his rage, the storm   150
    of his fury hurling at our heads!
But now his high hopes have laid him low
and down the enemy ranks the iron god of war
      deals his rewards, his stunning blows—Ares°
      rapture of battle, our right arm in the crisis.   155

    Seven captains marshaled at seven gates
    seven against their equals, gave
    their brazen trophies up to Zeus,
    god of the breaking rout of battle,
    all but two: those blood brothers,   160
    one father, one mother—matched in rage,
    spears matched for the twin conquest—
    clashed and won the common prize of death.

But now for Victory! Glorious in the morning,
joy in her eyes to meet our joy   165
    she is winging down to Thebes,
our fleets of chariots wheeling in her wake—
    Now let us win oblivion from the wars,
thronging the temples of the gods
in singing, dancing choirs through the night!   170
      Lord Dionysus,° god of the dance
      that shakes the land of Thebes, now lead the way!

[*Enter* CREON *from the palace, attended by his guard.*]

    But look, the king of the realm is coming,
    Creon, the new man for the new day,
    whatever the gods are sending now . . .   175
    what new plan will he launch?
    Why this, this special session?

---

154 Ares god of war.   **171 Dionysus** god of fertility and wine.

Why this sudden call to the old men
summoned at one command?

CREON.   My countrymen,
the ship of state is safe. The gods who rocked her,   180
after a long, merciless pounding in the storm,
have righted her once more.

                                Out of the whole city
I have called you here alone. Well I know,
first, your undeviating respect
for the throne and royal power of King Laius.   185
Next, while Oedipus steered the land of Thebes,
and even after he died, your loyalty was unshakable,
you still stood by their children. Now then,
since the two sons are dead—two blows of fate
in the same day, cut down by each other's hands,   190
both killers, both brothers stained with blood—
as I am next in kin to the dead,
I now possess the throne and all its powers.

Of course you cannot know a man completely,
his character, his principles, sense of judgment,   195
not till he's shown his colors, ruling the people,
making laws. Experience, there's the test.
As I see it, whoever assumes the task,
the awesome task of setting the city's course,
and refuses to adopt the soundest policies   200
but fearing someone, keeps his lips locked tight,
he's utterly worthless. So I rate him now,
I always have. And whoever places a friend
above the good of his own country, he is nothing:
I have no use for him. Zeus my witness,   205
Zeus who sees all things, always—
I could never stand by silent, watching destruction
march against our city, putting safety to rout,
nor could I ever make that man a friend of mine
who menaces our country. Remember this: 210
our country *is* our safety.
Only while she voyages true on course
can we establish friendships, truer than blood itself.
Such are my standards. They make our city great.
Closely akin to them I have proclaimed,   215
just now, the following decree to our people
concerning the two sons of Oedipus.
Eteocles, who died fighting for Thebes,
excelling all in arms: he shall be buried,
crowned with a hero's honors, the cups we pour   220
to soak the earth and reach the famous dead.

But as for his blood brother, Polynices,
who returned from exile, home to his father-city
and the gods of his race, consumed with one desire—
to burn them roof to roots—who thirsted to drink   225
his kinsmen's blood and sell the rest to slavery:

that man—a proclamation has forbidden the city
to dignify him with burial, mourn him at all.
No, he must be left unburied, his corpse
carrion for the birds and dogs to tear,   230
an obscenity for the citizens to behold!

These are my principles. Never at my hands
will the traitor be honored above the patriot.
But whoever proves his loyalty to the state:
I'll prize that man in death as well as life.   235
LEADER. If this is your pleasure, Creon, treating
    our city's enemy and our friend this way . . .
    The power is yours, I suppose, to enforce it
    with the laws, both for the dead and all of us,
    the living.
CREON.   Follow my orders closely then,   240
    be on your guard.
LEADER.   We're too old.
    Lay that burden on younger shoulders.
CREON.   No, no,
    I don't mean the body—I've posted guards already.
LEADER. What commands for us then? What other service?
CREON. See that you never side with those who break my orders.   245
LEADER. Never. Only a fool could be in love with death.
CREON. Death is the price—you're right. But all too often
    the mere hope of money has ruined many men.

    [*A* SENTRY *enters from the side.*]

SENTRY.   My lord,
    I can't say I'm winded from running, or set out
    with any spring in my legs either—no sir,   250
    I was lost in thought, and it made me stop, often,
    dead in my tracks, wheeling, turning back,
    and all the time a voice inside me muttering,
    "Idiot, why? You're going straight to your death."
    Then muttering, "Stopped again, poor fool?   255
    If somebody gets the news to Creon first,
    what's to save your neck?"
                              And so,
    mulling it over, on I trudged, dragging my feet,
    you can make a short road take forever . . .
    but at last, look, common sense won out,   260
    I'm here, and I'm all yours,
    and even though I come empty-handed
    I'll tell my story just the same, because
    I've come with a good grip on one hope,
    what will come will come, whatever fate—   265
CREON. Come to the point!
    What's wrong—why so afraid?
SENTRY. First, myself, I've got to tell you,
    I didn't do it, didn't see who did—
    Be fair, don't take it out on me.   270

CREON.   You're playing it safe, soldier,
    barricading yourself from any trouble.
    It's obvious, you've something strange to tell.
SENTRY.   Dangerous too, and danger makes you delay
    for all you're worth.   275
CREON.   Out with it—then dismiss!
SENTRY.   All right, here it comes. The body—
    someone's just buried it, then run off . . .
    sprinkled some dry dust on the flesh,
    given it proper rites.
CREON.   What?   280
    What man alive would dare—
SENTRY.   I've no idea, I swear it.
    There was no mark of a spade, no pickaxe there,
    no earth turned up, the ground packed hard and dry,
    unbroken, no tracks, no wheelruts, nothing,
    the workman left no trace. Just at sunup   285
    the first watch of the day points it out—
    it was a wonder! We were stunned . . .
    a terrific burden too, for all of us, listen:
    you can't see the corpse, not that it's buried,
    really, just a light cover of road-dust on it,   290
    as if someone meant to lay the dead to rest
    and keep from getting cursed.
    Not a sign in sight that dogs or wild beasts
    had worried the body, even torn the skin.

    But what came next! Rough talk flew thick and fast,   295
    guard grilling guard—we'd have come to blows
    at last, nothing to stop it; each man for himself
    and each the culprit, no one caught red-handed,
    all of us pleading ignorance, dodging the charges,
    ready to take up red-hot iron in our fists,   300
    go through fire, swear oaths to the gods—
    "I didn't do it, I had no hand in it either,
    not in the plotting, not in the work itself!"

    Finally, after all this wrangling came to nothing,
    one man spoke out and made us stare at the ground,   305
    hanging our heads in fear. No way to counter him,
    no way to take his advice and come through
    safe and sound. Here's what he said:
    "Look, we've got to report the facts to Creon,
    we can't keep this hidden." Well, that won out,   310
    and the lot fell on me, condemned me,
    unlucky as ever, I got the prize. So here I am,
    against my will and yours too, well I know—
    no one wants the man who brings bad news.
LEADER.   My king,
    ever since he began I've been debating in my mind,   315
    could this possibly be the work of the gods?

CREON.   Stop—
before you make me choke with anger—the gods!
You, you're senile, must you be insane?
You say—why it's intolerable—say the gods
could have the slightest concern for that corpse?   320
Tell me, was it for meritorious service
they proceeded to bury him, prized him so? The hero
who came to burn their temples ringed with pillars,
their golden treasures—scorch their hallowed earth
and fling their laws to the winds.   325
Exactly when did you last see the gods
celebrating traitors? Inconceivable!

No, from the first there were certain citizens
who could hardly stand the spirit of my regime,
grumbling against me in the dark, heads together,   330
tossing wildly, never keeping their necks beneath
the yoke, loyally submitting to their king.
These are the instigators, I'm convinced—
they've perverted my own guard, bribed them
to do their work.
                        Money! Nothing worse   335
in our lives, so current, rampant, so corrupting.
Money—you demolish cities, root men from their homes,
you train and twist good minds and set them on
to the most atrocious schemes. No limit,
you make them adept at every kind of outrage,   340
every godless crime—money!
                                Everyone—
the whole crew bribed to commit this crime,
they've made one thing sure at least:
sooner or later they will pay the price.

[*Wheeling on the* SENTRY.]

                                You—
I swear to Zeus as I still believe in Zeus,   345
if you don't find the man who buried that corpse,
the very man, and produce him before my eyes,
simple death won't be enough for you,
not till we string you up alive
and wring the immortality out of you.   350
Then you can steal the rest of your days,
better informed about where to make a killing.
You'll have learned, at last, it doesn't pay
to itch for rewards from every hand that beckons.
Filthy profits wreck most men, you'll see—   355
they'll never save your life.
SENTRY.   Please,
may I say a word or two, or just turn and go?
CREON. Can't you tell? Everything you say offends me.
SENTRY. Where does it hurt you, in the ears or in the heart?

CREON. And who are you to pinpoint my displeasure?   360
SENTRY. The culprit grates on your feelings,
    I just annoy your ears.
CREON.   Still talking?
    You talk too much! A born nuisance—
SENTRY.   Maybe so,
    but I never did this thing, so help me!
CREON.   Yes you did—
    what's more, you squandered your life for silver!   365
SENTRY. Oh it's terrible when the one who does the judging
    judges things all wrong.
CREON.   Well now,
    you just be clever about your judgments—
    if you fail to produce the criminals for me,
    you'll swear your dirty money brought you pain.   370

[*Turning sharply, reentering the palace.*]

SENTRY. I hope he's found. Best thing by far.
    But caught or not, that's in the lap of fortune;
    I'll never come back, you've seen the last of me.
    I'm saved, even now, and I never thought,
    I never hoped—   375
    dear gods, I owe you all my thanks!   [*Rushing out.*]
CHORUS.   Numberless wonders
    terrible wonders walk the world but none the match for man—
    that great wonder crossing the heaving gray sea,
            driven on by the blast of winter
    on through breakers crashing left and right,   380
      holds his steady course
    and the oldest of the gods he wears away—
    the Earth, the immortal, the inexhaustible—
    as his plows go back and forth, year in, year out
        with the breed of stallions turning up the furrows.   385

And the blithe, lightheaded race of birds he snares,
    the tribes of savage beasts, the life that swarms the depths—
            with one fling of his nets
    woven and coiled tight, he takes them all,
      man the skilled, the brilliant!   390
He conquers all, taming with his techniques
    the prey that roams the cliffs and wild lairs,
    training the stallion, clamping the yoke across
      his shaggy neck, and the tireless mountain bull.

And speech and thought, quick as the wind   395
    and the mood and mind for law that rules the city—
      all these he has taught himself
    and shelter from the arrows of the frost
    when there's rough lodging under the cold clear sky
    and the shafts of lashing rain—   400
        ready, resourceful man!

> Never without resources
> never an impasse as he marches on the future—
> only Death, from Death alone he will find no rescue
> but from desperate plagues he has plotted his escapes.   405
>
> Man the master, ingenious past all measure
> past all dreams, the skills within his grasp—
>   he forges on, now to destruction
>   now again to greatness. When he weaves in
> the laws of the land, and the justice of the gods   410
> that binds his oaths together
>   he and his city rise high—
>   but the city casts out
> that man who weds himself to inhumanity
> thanks to reckless daring. Never share my hearth   415
> never think my thoughts, whoever does such things.

[*Enter* ANTIGONE *from the side, accompanied by the* SENTRY.]

>   Here is a dark sign from the gods—
>   what to make of this? I know her,
>   how can I deny it? That young girl's Antigone!
>   Wretched, child of a wretched father,   420
>   Oedipus. Look, is it possible?
>   They bring you in like a prisoner—
>   why? did you break the king's laws?
>   Did they take you in some act of mad defiance?

SENTRY.   She's the one, she did it single-handed—   425
          we caught her burying the body. Where's Creon?

[*Enter* CREON *from the palace.*]

LEADER.   Back again, just in time when you need him.
CREON.   In time for what? What is it?
SENTRY.   My king,
          there's nothing you can swear you'll never do—
          second thoughts make liars of us all.   430
          I could have sworn I wouldn't hurry back
          (what with your threats, the buffeting I just took),
          but a stroke of luck beyond our wildest hopes,
          what a joy, there's nothing like it. So,
          back I've come, breaking my oath, who cares?   435
          I'm bringing in our prisoner—this young girl—
          we took her giving the dead the last rites.
          But no casting lots this time, this is *my* luck,
          my prize, no one else's.
                              Now, my lord,
          here she is. Take her, question her,   440
          cross-examine her to your heart's content.
          But set me free, it's only right—
          I'm rid of this dreadful business once for all.
CREON.   Prisoner! Her? You took her—where, doing what?
SENTRY.   Burying the man. That's the whole story.

CREON.   What?   445
    You mean what you say, you're telling me the truth?
SENTRY. She's the one. With my own eyes I saw her
    bury the body, just what you've forbidden.
    There. Is that plain and clear?
CREON. What did you see? Did you catch her in the act?   450
SENTRY. Here's what happened. We went back to our post,
    those threats of yours breathing down our necks—
    we brushed the corpse clean of the dust that covered it,
    stripped it bare . . . it was slimy, going soft,
    and we took to high ground, backs to the wind   455
    so the stink of him couldn't hit us;
    jostling, baiting each other to keep awake,
    shouting back and forth—no napping on the job,
    not this time. And so the hours dragged by
    until the sun stood dead above our heads,   460
    a huge white ball in the noon sky, beating,
    blazing down, and then it happened—
    suddenly, a whirlwind!
    Twisting a great dust-storm up from the earth,
    a black plague of the heavens, filling the plain,   465
    ripping the leaves off every tree in sight,
    choking the air and sky. We squinted hard
    and took our whipping from the gods.

    And after the storm passed—it seemed endless—
    there, we saw the girl!   470
    And she cried out a sharp, piercing cry,
    like a bird come back to an empty nest,
    peering into its bed, and all the babies gone . . .
    Just so, when she sees the corpse bare
    she bursts into a long, shattering wail   475
    and calls down withering curses on the heads
    of all who did the work. And she scoops up dry dust,
    handfuls, quickly, and lifting a fine bronze urn,
    lifting it high and pouring, she crowns the dead
    with three full libations.

            Soon as we saw   480
    we rushed her, closed on the kill like hunters,
    and she, she didn't flinch. We interrogated her,
    charging her with offenses past and present—
    she stood up to it all, denied nothing. I tell you,
    it made me ache and laugh in the same breath.   485
    It's pure joy to escape the worst yourself,
    it hurts a man to bring down his friends.
    But all that, I'm afraid, means less to me
    than my own skin. That's the way I'm made.
CREON. [*Wheeling on* ANTIGONE.]   You,
    with your eyes fixed on the ground—speak up.   490
    Do you deny you did this, yes or no?
ANTIGONE. I did it. I don't deny a thing.

CREON. [*To the* SENTRY.] You, get out, wherever you please—
you're clear of a very heavy charge.

[*He leaves;* CREON *turns back to* ANTIGONE.]

You, tell me briefly, no long speeches—   495
were you aware a decree had forbidden this?
ANTIGONE. Well aware. How could I avoid it? It was public.
CREON. And still you had the gall to break this law?
ANTIGONE. Of course I did. It wasn't Zeus, not in the least,
who made this proclamation—not to me.   500
Nor did that Justice, dwelling with the gods
beneath the earth, ordain such laws for men.
Nor did I think your edict had such force
that you, a mere mortal, could override the gods,
the great unwritten, unshakable traditions.   505
They are alive, not just today or yesterday:
they live forever, from the first of time,
and no one knows when they first saw the light.

These laws—I was not about to break them,
not out of fear of some man's wounded pride,   510
and face the retribution of the gods.
Die I must, I've known it all my life—
how could I keep from knowing?—even without
your death-sentence ringing in my ears.
And if I am to die before my time   515
I consider that a gain. Who on earth,
alive in the midst of so much grief as I,
could fail to find his death a rich reward?
So for me, at least, to meet this doom of yours
is precious little pain. But if I had allowed   520
my own mother's son to rot, an unburied corpse—
that would have been an agony! This is nothing.
And if my present actions strike you as foolish,
let's just say I've been accused of folly
by a fool.
LEADER.   Like father like daughter,   525
passionate, wild . . .
she hasn't learned to bend before adversity.
CREON. No? Believe me, the stiffest stubborn wills
fall the hardest; the toughest iron,
tempered strong in the white-hot fire,   530
you'll see it crack and shatter first of all.
And I've known spirited horses you can break
with a light bit—proud, rebellious horses.
There's no room for pride, not in a slave
not with the lord and master standing by.   535

This girl was an old hand at insolence
when she overrode the edicts we made public.
But once she'd done it—the insolence,
twice over—to glory in it, laughing,
mocking us to our face with what she'd done.   540

I'm not the man, not now: she is the man
if this victory goes to her and she goes free.

Never! Sister's child or closer in blood
than all my family clustered at my altar
worshiping Guardian Zeus—she'll never escape,   545
she and her blood sister, the most barbaric death.
Yes, I accuse her sister of an equal part
in scheming this, this burial.

[*To his* ATTENDANTS.]

                      Bring her here!
I just saw her inside, hysterical, gone to pieces.
It never fails: the mind convicts itself   550
in advance, when scoundrels are up to no good,
plotting in the dark. Oh but I hate it more
when a traitor, caught red-handed,
tries to glorify his crimes.

ANTIGONE. Creon, what more do you want   555
    than my arrest and execution?
CREON. Nothing. Then I have it all.
ANTIGONE. Then why delay? Your moralizing repels me,
    every word you say—pray god it always will.
    So naturally all I say repels you too.
                         Enough.   560
Give me glory! What greater glory could I win
than to give my own brother decent burial?
These citizens here would all agree,

[*To the* CHORUS.]

they'd praise me too
if their lips weren't locked in fear.   565

[*Pointing to* CREON.]

Lucky tyrants—the perquisites of power!
Ruthless power to do and say whatever pleases *them*.
CREON. You alone, of all the people in Thebes,
    see things that way.
ANTIGONE.   They see it just that way
    but defer to you and keep their tongues in leash.   570
CREON. And you, aren't you ashamed to differ so from them?
    So disloyal!
ANTIGONE.   Not ashamed for a moment,
    not to honor my brother, my own flesh and blood.
CREON. Wasn't Eteocles a brother too—cut down, facing him?
ANTIGONE. Brother, yes, by the same mother, the same father.   575
CREON. Then how can you render his enemy such honors,
    such impieties in his eyes?
ANTIGONE. He'll never testify to that,
    Eteocles dead and buried.

CREON.   He will—
   if you honor the traitor just as much as him.   580
ANTIGONE. But it was his brother, not some slave that died—
CREON. Ravaging our country!—
   but Eteocles died fighting in our behalf.
ANTIGONE. No matter—Death longs for the same rites for all.
CREON. Never the same for the patriot and the traitor.   585
ANTIGONE. Who, Creon, who on earth can say the ones below
   don't find this pure and uncorrupt?
CREON. Never. Once an enemy, never a friend,
   not even after death.
ANTIGONE. I was born to join in love, not hate—   590
   that is my nature.
CREON.   Go down below and love,
   if love you must—love the dead! While I'm alive,
   no woman is going to lord it over me.

[*Enter* ISMENE *from the palace, under guard.*]

CHORUS.   Look,
   Ismene's coming, weeping a sister's tears,
   loving sister, under a cloud . . .   595
   her face is flushed, her cheeks streaming.
   Sorrow puts her lovely radiance in the dark.
CREON.   You—
   in my house, you viper, slinking undetected,
   sucking my life-blood! I never knew
   I was breeding twin disasters, the two of you   600
   rising up against my throne. Come, tell me,
   will you confess your part in the crime or not?
   Answer me. Swear to me.
ISMENE.   I did it, yes—
   if only she consents—I share the guilt,
   the consequences too.
ANTIGONE.   No,   605
   Justice will never suffer that—not you,
   you were unwilling. I never brought you in.
ISMENE. But now you face such dangers . . . I'm not ashamed
   to sail through trouble with you,
   make your troubles mine.
ANTIGONE.   Who did the work?   610
   Let the dead and the god of death bear witness!
   I've no love for a friend who loves in words alone.
ISMENE. Oh no, my sister, don't reject me, please,
   let me die beside you, consecrating
   the dead together.
ANTIGONE.   Never share my dying,   615
   don't lay claim to what you never touched.
   My death will be enough.
ISMENE. What do I care for life, cut off from you?
ANTIGONE. Ask Creon. Your concern is all for him.

ISMENE. Why abuse me so? It doesn't help you now.

ANTIGONE.   You're right—   620
  if I mock you, I get no pleasure from it,
  only pain.

ISMENE.   Tell me, dear one,
  what can I do to help you, even now?

ANTIGONE. Save yourself. I don't grudge you your survival.

ISMENE. Oh no, no, denied my portion in your death?   625

ANTIGONE. You chose to live, I chose to die.

ISMENE.   Not, at least,
  without every kind of caution I could voice.

ANTIGONE. Your wisdom appealed to one world—mine, another.

ISMENE. But look, we're both guilty, both condemned to death.

ANTIGONE. Courage! Live your life. I gave myself to death,   630
  long ago, so I might serve the dead.

CREON. They're both mad, I tell you, the two of them.
  One's just shown it, the other's been that way
  since she was born.

ISMENE.   True, my king,
  the sense we were born with cannot last forever . . .   635
  commit cruelty on a person long enough
  and the mind begins to go.

CREON.   Yours did,
  when you chose to commit your crimes with her.

ISMENE. How can I live alone, without her?

CREON.   Her?
  Don't even mention her—she no longer exists.   640

ISMENE. What? You'd kill your own son's bride?

CREON.   Absolutely:
  there are other fields for him to plow.

ISMENE.   Perhaps,
  but never as true, as close a bond as theirs.

CREON. A worthless woman for my son? It repels me.

ISMENE. Dearest Haemon, your father wrongs you so!   645

CREON. Enough, enough—you and your talk of marriage!

ISMENE. Creon—you're really going to rob your son of Antigone?

CREON. Death will do it for me—break their marriage off.

LEADER. So, it's settled then? Antigone must die?

CREON. Settled, yes—we both know that.   650

  [*To the* GUARDS.]

  Stop wasting time. Take them in.
  From now on they'll act like women.
  Tie them up, no more running loose;
  even the bravest will cut and run,
  once they see Death coming for their lives.   655

  [*The* GUARDS *escort* ANTIGONE *and* ISMENE *into the palace.* CREON
  remains while the old citizens form their chorus.]

CHORUS. Blest, they are truly blest who all their lives
  have never tasted devastation. For others, once

the gods have rocked a house to its foundations
    the ruin will never cease, cresting on and on
from one generation on throughout the race—   660
like a great mounting tide
driven on by savage northern gales,
      surging over the dead black depths
roiling up from the bottom dark heaves of sand
and the headlands, taking the storm's onslaught full-force,   665
roar, and the low moaning
               echoes on and on
                   and now
as in ancient times I see the sorrows of the house,
the living heirs of the old ancestral kings,
piling on the sorrows of the dead
      and one generation cannot free the next—   670
some god will bring them crashing down,
the race finds no release.
And now the light, the hope
        springing up from the late last root
in the house of Oedipus, that hope's cut down in turn   675
by the long, bloody knife swung by the gods of death
by a senseless word
          by fury at the heart.
                        Zeus,
yours is the power, Zeus, what man on earth
can override it, who can hold it back?
Power that neither Sleep, the all-ensnaring   680
    no, nor the tireless months of heaven
can ever overmaster—young through all time,
mighty lord of power, you hold fast
      the dazzling crystal mansions of Olympus.
And throughout the future, late and soon   685
as through the past, your law prevails:
no towering form of greatness
      enters into the lives of mortals
             free and clear of ruin.
                        True,
our dreams, our high hopes voyaging far and wide   690
bring sheer delight to many, to many others
      delusion, blithe, mindless lusts
and the fraud steals on one slowly . . . unaware
till he trips and puts his foot into the fire.
      He was a wise old man who coined   695
the famous saying: "Sooner or later
foul is fair, fair is foul
to the man the gods will ruin"—
      He goes his way for a moment only
                  free of blinding ruin.   700

[*Enter* HAEMON *from the palace.*]

    Here's Haemon now, the last of all your sons.
    Does he come in tears for his bride,

his doomed bride, Antigone—
bitter at being cheated of their marriage?
CREON. We'll soon know, better than seers could tell us.   705

[*Turning to* HAEMON.]

Son, you've heard the final verdict on your bride?
Are you coming now, raving against your father?
Or do you love me, no matter what I do?
HAEMON. Father, I'm your *son* . . . you in your wisdom
set my bearings for me—I obey you.   710
No marriage could ever mean more to me than you,
whatever good direction you may offer.
CREON.   Fine, Haemon.
That's how you ought to feel within your heart,
subordinate to your father's will in every way.
That's what a man prays for: to produce good sons—   715
households full of them, dutiful and attentive,
so they can pay his enemy back with interest
and match the respect their father shows his friend.
But the man who rears a brood of useless children,
what has he brought into the world, I ask you?   720
Nothing but trouble for himself, and mockery
from his enemies laughing in his face.
                                         Oh Haemon,
never lose your sense of judgment over a woman.
The warmth, the rush of pleasure, it all goes cold
in your arms, I warn you . . . a worthless woman   725
in your house, a misery in your bed.
What wound cuts deeper than a loved one
turned against you? Spit her out,
like a mortal enemy—let the girl go.
Let her find a husband down among the dead.   730

Imagine it: I caught her in naked rebellion,
the traitor, the only one in the whole city.
I'm not about to prove myself a liar,
not to my people, no, I'm going to kill her!
That's right—so let her cry for mercy, sing her hymns   735
to Zeus who defends all bonds of kindred blood.
Why, if I bring up my own kin to be rebels,
think what I'd suffer from the world at large.
Show me the man who rules his household well:
I'll show you someone fit to rule the state.   740
That good man, my son,
I have every confidence he and he alone
can give commands and take them too. Staunch
in the storm of spears he'll stand his ground,
a loyal, unflinching comrade at your side.   745

But whoever steps out of line, violates the laws
or presumes to hand out orders to his superiors,
he'll win no praise from me. But that man
the city places in authority, his orders

must be obeyed, large and small,   750
right and wrong.
                    Anarchy—
show me a greater crime in all the earth!
She, she destroys cities, rips up houses,
breaks the ranks of spearmen into headlong rout.
But the ones who last it out, the great mass of them   755
owe their lives to discipline. Therefore
we must defend the men who live by law,
never let some woman triumph over us.
Better to fall from power, if fall we must,
at the hands of a man—never be rated   760
inferior to a woman, never.

LEADER.   To us,
    unless old age has robbed us of our wits,
    you seem to say what you have to say with sense.

HAEMON. Father, only the gods endow a man with reason,
    the finest of all their gifts, a treasure.   765
    Far be it from me—I haven't the skill,
    and certainly no desire, to tell you when,
    if ever, you make a slip in speech . . . though
    someone else might have a good suggestion.

Of course it's not for you,   770
in the normal run of things, to watch
whatever men say or do, or find to criticize.
The man in the street, you know, dreads your glance,
he'd never say anything displeasing to your face.
But it's for me to catch the murmurs in the dark,   775
the way the city mourns for this young girl.
"No woman," they say, "ever deserved death less,
and such a brutal death for such a glorious action.
She, with her own dear brother lying in his blood—
she couldn't bear to leave him dead, unburied,   780
food for the wild dogs or wheeling vultures.
Death? She deserves a glowing crown of gold!"
So they say, and the rumor spreads in secret,
darkly . . .
            I rejoice in your success, father—
nothing more precious to me in the world.   785
What medal of honor brighter to his children
than a father's growing glory? Or a child's
to his proud father? Now don't, please,
be quite so single-minded, self-involved,
or assume the world is wrong and you are right.   790
Whoever thinks that he alone possesses intelligence,
the gift of eloquence, he and no one else,
and character too . . . such men, I tell you,
spread them open—you will find them empty.
                    No,
it's no disgrace for a man, even a wise man,   795

to learn many things and not to be too rigid.
You've seen trees by a raging winter torrent,
how many sway with the flood and salvage every twig,
but not the stubborn—they're ripped out, roots and all.
Bend or break. The same when a man is sailing: 800
haul your sheets too taut, never give an inch,
you'll capsize, go the rest of the voyage
keel up and the rowing-benches under.

Oh give way. Relax your anger—change!
I'm young, I know, but let me offer this: 805
it would be best by far, I admit,
if a man were born infallible, right by nature.
If not—and things don't often go that way,
it's best to learn from those with good advice.

LEADER. You'd do well, my lord, if he's speaking to the point,   810
to learn from him.

[*Turning to* HAEMON.]

                    and you, my boy, from him.
You both are talking sense.
CREON.   So,
men our age, we're to be lectured, are we?—
schooled by a boy his age?
HAEMON. Only in what is right. But if I seem young,   815
look less to my years and more to what I do.
CREON. Do? Is admiring rebels an achievement?
HAEMON. I'd never suggest that you admire treason.
CREON.   Oh?—
isn't that just the sickness that's attacked her?
HAEMON. The whole city of Thebes denies it, to a man.   820
CREON. And is Thebes about to tell me how to rule?
HAEMON. Now, you see? Who's talking like a child?
CREON. Am I to rule this land for others—or myself?
HAEMON. It's no city at all, owned by one man alone.
CREON. What? The city *is* the king's—that's the law!   825
HAEMON. What a splendid king you'd make of a desert island—
you and you alone.
CREON. [*To the* CHORUS.] This boy, I do believe,
is fighting on her side, the woman's side.
HAEMON. If you are a woman, yes;
my concern is all for you.   830
CREON. Why, you degenerate—bandying accusations,
threatening me with justice, your own father!
HAEMON. I see my father offending justice—wrong.
CREON.   Wrong?
To protect my royal rights?
HAEMON.   Protect your rights?
When you trample down the honors of the gods?   835

CREON. You, you soul of corruption, rotten through—
    woman's accomplice!
HAEMON.   That may be,
    but you'll never find me accomplice to a criminal.
CREON. That's what *she* is,
    and every word you say is a blatant appeal for her—   840
HAEMON. And you, and me, and the gods beneath the earth.
CREON. You'll never marry her, not while she's alive.
HAEMON. Then she'll die . . . but her death will kill another.
CREON. What, brazen threats? You go too far!
HAEMON.   What threat?
    Combating your empty, mindless judgments with a word?   845
CREON. You'll suffer for your sermons, you and your empty wisdom!
HAEMON. If you weren't my father, I'd say you were insane.
CREON. Don't flatter me with Father—you woman's slave!
HAEMON. You really expect to fling abuse at me
    and not receive the same?
CREON.   Is that so!   850
    Now, by heaven, I promise you, you'll pay—
    taunting, insulting me! Bring her out,
    that hateful—she'll die now, here,
    in front of his eyes, beside her groom!
HAEMON. No, no, she will never die beside me—   855
    don't delude yourself. And you will never
    see me, never set eyes on my face again.
    Rage your heart out, rage with friends
    who can stand the sight of you.   [*Rushing out.*]
LEADER. Gone, my king, in a burst of anger.   860
    A temper young as his . . . hurt him once,
    he may do something violent.
CREON.   Let him do—
    dream up something desperate, past all human limit!
    Good riddance. Rest assured,
    he'll never save those two young girls from death.   865
LEADER. Both of them, you really intend to kill them both?
CREON. No, not her, the one whose hands are clean;
    you're quite right.
LEADER.   But Antigone—
    what sort of death do you have in mind for her?
CREON. I'll take her down some wild, desolate path   870
    never trod by men, and wall her up alive
    in a rocky vault, and set out short rations,
    just a gesture of piety
    to keep the entire city free of defilement.
    There let her pray to the one god she worships: 875
    Death—who knows?—may just reprieve her from death.
    Or she may learn at last, better late than never,
    what a waste of breath it is to worship Death.

[*Exit to the palace.*]

CHORUS. Love, never conquered in battle
    Love the plunderer laying waste the rich!   880
    Love standing the night-watch
               guarding a girl's soft cheek,
    you range the seas, the shepherds' steadings off in the wilds—
    not even the deathless gods can flee your onset,
    nothing human born for a day—   885
    whoever feels your grip is driven mad.
                         Love
    you wrench the minds of the righteous into outrage,
    swerve them to their ruin—you have ignited this,
    this kindred strife, father and son at war
                  and Love alone the victor—   890
    warm glance of the bride triumphant, burning with desire!
    Throned in power, side-by-side with the mighty laws!
    Irresistible Aphrodite,° never conquered—
    Love, you mock us for your sport.

[ANTIGONE *is brought from the palace under guard.*]

    But now, even I'd rebel against the king,   895
    I'd break all bounds when I see this—
    I fill with tears, can't hold them back,
    not any more . . . . I see Antigone make her way
    to the bridal vault where all are laid to rest.
ANTIGONE. Look at me, men of my fatherland,   900
       setting out on the last road
    looking into the last light of day
    the last I'll ever see . . . .
    the god of death who puts us all to bed
    takes me down to the banks of Acheron° alive—   905
       denied my part in the wedding-songs,
    no wedding-song in the dusk has crowned my marriage—
    I go to wed the lord of the dark waters.
CHORUS. Not crowned with glory, crowned with a dirge,
    you leave for the deep pit of the dead.   910
    No withering illness laid you low,
    no strokes of the sword—a law to yourself,
    alone, no mortal like you, ever, you go down
    to the halls of Death alive and breathing.
ANTIGONE. But think of Niobe°—well I know her story—   915
       think what a living death she died,
    Tantalus' daughter, stranger queen from the east:
    there on the mountain heights, growing stone
    binding as ivy, slowly walled her round
    and the rains will never cease, the legends say   920

---

893 Aphrodite goddess of love.   **905 Acheron** river in the underworld.   **915 Niobe** a Theban queen whose pride in her children was punished by the gods, who turned her into stone.

the snows will never leave her . . . .
          wasting away, under her brows the tears
showering down her breasting ridge and slopes—
a rocky death like hers puts me to sleep.
CHORUS. But she was a god, born of gods,   925
and we are only mortals born to die.
And yet, of course, it's a great thing
for a dying girl to hear, just hear
she shares a destiny equal to the gods,
during life and later, once she's dead.
ANTIGONE.   O you mock me!   930
Why, in the name of all my fathers' gods
why can't you wait till I am gone—
          must you abuse me to my face?
O my city, all your fine rich sons!
And you, you springs of the Dirce,   935
holy grove of Thebes where the chariots gather,
          you at least, you'll bear me witness, look,
unmourned by friends and forced by such crude laws
I go to my rockbound prison, strange new tomb—
          always a stranger, O dear god,   940
          I have no home on earth and none below,
          not with the living, not with the breathless dead.
CHORUS. You went too far, the last limits of daring—
smashing against the high throne of Justice!
          Your life's in ruins, child—I wonder . . .   945
do you pay for your father's terrible ordeal?
ANTIGONE. There—at last you've touched it, the worst pain
the worst anguish! Raking up the grief for father
          three times over, for all the doom
that's struck us down, the brilliant house of Laius.   950
O mother, your marriage-bed
the coiling horrors, the coupling there—
          you with your own son, my father—doomstruck mother!
Such, such were my parents, and I their wretched child.
I go to them now, cursed, unwed, to share their home—   955
          I am a stranger! O dear brother, doomed
          in your marriage—your marriage murders mine,
               your dying drags me down to death alive!

          [*Enter* CREON.]

CHORUS. Reverence asks some reverence in return—
          but attacks on power never go unchecked,   960
               not by the man who holds the reins of power.
Your own blind will, your passion has destroyed you.
ANTIGONE. No one to weep for me, my friends,
          no wedding-song—they take me away
          in all my pain . . . the road lies open, waiting.   965
Never again, the law forbids me to see
the sacred eye of day. I am agony!
No tears for the destiny that's mine,
no loved one mourns my death.

CREON.   Can't you see?
If a man could wail his own dirge before he dies,   970
he'd never finish.

[*To the* GUARDS.]

Take her away, quickly!
Wall her up in the tomb, you have your orders.
Abandon her there, alone, and let her choose—
death or a buried life with a good roof for shelter.
As for myself, my hands are clean. This young girl—   975
dead or alive, she will be stripped of her rights,
her stranger's rights, here in the world above.
ANTIGONE.   O tomb, my bridal-bed—my house, my prison
cut in the hollow rock, my everlasting watch!
I'll soon be there, soon embrace my own,   980
the great growing family of our dead
Persephone° has received among her ghosts.
                                        I,
the last of them all, the most reviled by far,
go down before my destined time's run out.
But still I go, cherishing one good hope: 985
my arrival may be dear to father,
dear to you, my mother,
dear to you, my loving brother, Eteocles—
When you died I washed you with my hands,
I dressed you all, I poured the cups   990
across your tombs. But now, Polynices,
because I laid your body out as well,
this, this is my reward. Nevertheless
I honored you—the decent will admit it—
well and wisely too.
                              Never, I tell you,   995
if I had been the mother of children
or if my husband died, exposed and rotting—
I'd never have taken this ordeal upon myself,
never defied our people's will. What law,
you ask, do I satisfy with what I say?   1000
A husband dead, there might have been another.
A child by another too, if I had lost the first.
But mother and father both lost in the halls of Death,
no brother could ever spring to light again.

For this law alone I held you first in honor.   1005
For this, Creon, the king, judges me a criminal
guilty of dreadful outrage, my dear brother!
And now he leads me off, a captive in his hands,
with no part in the bridal-song, the bridal-bed,
denied all joy of marriage, raising children—   1010
deserted so by loved ones, struck by fate,
I descend alive to the caverns of the dead.

---

982 Persephone queen of the underworld.

What law of the mighty gods have I transgressed?
Why look to the heavens any more, tormented as I am?
Whom to call, what comrades now? Just think,   1015
my reverence only brands me for irreverence!
Very well: if this is the pleasure of the gods,
once I suffer I will know that I was wrong.
But if these men are wrong, let them suffer
nothing worse than they mete out to me—   1020
these masters of injustice!

LEADER. Still the same rough winds, the wild passion
    raging through the girl.

CREON. [*To the* GUARDS.]   Take her away.
    You're wasting time—you'll pay for it too.

ANTIGONE. Oh god, the voice of death. It's come, it's here.   1025

CREON. True. Not a word of hope—your doom is sealed.

ANTIGONE. Land of Thebes, city of all my fathers—
    O you gods, the first gods of the race!
    They drag me away, now, no more delay.
    Look on me, you noble sons of Thebes—   1030
    the last of a great line of kings,
    I alone, see what I suffer now
    at the hands of what breed of men—
    all for reverence, my reverence for the gods!

[*She leaves under guard; the* CHORUS *gathers.*]

CHORUS. Danaë,° Danaë—   1035
    even she endured a fate like yours,
       in all her lovely strength she traded
    the light of day for the bolted brazen vault—
    buried within her tomb, her bridal-chamber,
    wed to the yoke and broken.   1040
       But she was of glorious birth
              my child, my child
    and treasured the seed of Zeus within her womb,
    the cloudburst streaming gold!
       The power of fate is a wonder,   1045
       dark, terrible wonder—
       neither wealth nor armies
       towered walls nor ships
       black hulls lashed by the salt
       can save us from that force.   1050

    The yoke tamed him too
       young Lycurgus° flaming in anger
    king of Edonia, all for his mad taunts
    Dionysus clamped him down, encased

1035 **Danaë** Danaë's father locked her in a cell because it had been predicted that she
would bear a son who would kill him; Zeus entered the cell in the form of a shower of gold,
and engendered Perseus. 1052 **Lycurgus** Lycurgus refused to worship Dionysus, and
therefore Dionysus punished him.

in the chain-mail of rock   1055
    and there his rage
            his terrible flowering rage burst—
sobbing, dying away . . . . at last that madman
came to know his god—
    the power he mocked, the power   1060
    he taunted in all his frenzy
    trying to stamp out
    the women strong with the god—
    the torch, the raving sacred cries—
    enraging the Muses° who adore the flute.   1065

And far north where the Black Rocks
    cut the sea in half
and murderous straits
split the coast of Thrace
    a forbidding city stands   1070
where once, hard by the walls
the savage Ares thrilled to watch
a king's new queen, a Fury rearing in rage
    against his two royal sons—
        her bloody hands, her dagger-shuttle   1075
stabbing out their eyes—cursed, blinding wounds—
their eyes blind sockets screaming for revenge!

They wailed in agony, cries echoing cries
    the princes doomed at birth . . .
and their mother doomed to chains,   1080
walled off in a tomb of stone—
    but she traced her own birth back
to a proud Athenian line and the high gods
and off in caverns half the world away,
born of the wild North Wind   1085
    she sprang on her father's gales,
        racing stallions up the leaping cliffs—
child of the heavens. But even on her the Fates
the gray everlasting Fates rode hard
my child, my child.

[*Enter* TIRESIAS, *the blind prophet, led by a* BOY.]

TIRESIAS.   Lords of Thebes,   1090
I and the boy have come together,
hand in hand. Two see with the eyes of one . . .
so the blind must go, with a guide to lead the way.
CREON. What is it, old Tiresias? What news now?
TIRESIAS. I will teach you. And you obey the seer.
CREON.   I will,   1095
I've never wavered from your advice before.
TIRESIAS. And so you kept the city straight on course.
CREON. I owe you a great deal, I swear to that.

——————————

1065 Muses nine goddesses of the arts and sciences.

TIRESIAS. Then reflect, my son: you are poised,
　　　once more, on the razor-edge of fate.　　　　　　　　　1100
CREON. What is it? I shudder to hear you.
TIRESIAS.　　　　　　　　　　　　　You will learn
　　　when you listen to the warnings of my craft.
　　　As I sat in the ancient seat of augury,
　　　in the sanctuary where every bird I know
　　　will hover at my hands—suddenly I heard it,　　　　　　1105
　　　a strange voice in the wingbeats, unintelligible,
　　　barbaric, a mad scream! Talons flashing, ripping,
　　　they were killing each other—that much I knew—
　　　the murderous fury whirring in those wings
　　　made that much clear!
　　　　　　　　　　　I was afraid,　　　　　　　　　　1110
　　　I turned quickly, tested the burnt-sacrifice,
　　　ignited the altar at all points—but no fire,
　　　the god in the fire never blazed.
　　　Not from those offerings . . . over the embers
　　　slid a heavy ooze from the long thighbones,　　　　　　1115
　　　smoking, sputtering out, and the bladder
　　　puffed and burst—spraying gall into the air—
　　　and the fat wrapping the bones slithered off
　　　and left them glistening white. No fire!
　　　The rites failed that might have blazed the future　　　1120
　　　with a sign. So I learned from the boy here;
　　　he is my guide, as I am guide to others.
　　　　　　　　　　　　　　And it's you—
　　　your high resolve that sets this plague on Thebes.
　　　The public altars and sacred hearths are fouled,
　　　one and all, by the birds and dogs with carrion　　　　1125
　　　torn from the corpse, the doomstruck son of Oedipus!
　　　And so the gods are deaf to our prayers, they spurn
　　　the offerings in our hands, the flame of holy flesh.
　　　No birds cry out an omen clear and true—
　　　they're gorged with the murdered victim's blood and fat.　1130
　　　Take these things to heart, my son, I warn you.
　　　All men make mistakes, it is only human.
　　　But once the wrong is done, a man
　　　can turn his back on folly, misfortune too,
　　　if he tries to make amends, however low he's fallen,　　1135
　　　and stops his bullnecked ways. Stubbornness
　　　brands you for stupidity—pride is a crime.
　　　No, yield to the dead!
　　　Never stab the fighter when he's down.
　　　Where's the glory, killing the dead twice over?　　　　1140

　　　I mean you well. I give you sound advice.
　　　It's best to learn from a good adviser
　　　when he speaks for your own good:
　　　it's pure gain.

CREON.   Old man—all of you! So,
  you shoot your arrows at my head like archers at the target—   1145
  I even have *him* loosed on me, this fortune-teller.
  Oh his ilk has tried to sell me short
  and ship me off for years. Well,
  drive your bargains, traffic—much as you like—
  in the gold of India, silver-gold of Sardis.   1150
  You'll never bury that body in the grave,
  not even if Zeus's eagles rip the corpse
  and wing their rotten pickings off to the throne of god!
  Never, not even in fear of such defilement
  will I tolerate his burial, that traitor.   1155
  Well I know, we can't defile the gods—
  no mortal has the power.
                No,
  reverend old Tiresias, all men fall,
  it's only human, but the wisest fall obscenely
  when they glorify obscene advice with rhetoric—   1160
  all for their own gain.
TIRESIAS. Oh god, is there a man alive
  who knows, who actually believes . . .
CREON.   What now?
  What earth-shattering truth are you about to utter?
TIRESIAS. . . . just how much a sense of judgment, wisdom   1165
  is the greatest gift we have?
CREON.   Just as much, I'd say,
  as a twisted mind is the worst affliction going.
TIRESIAS. You are the one who's sick, Creon, sick to death.
CREON. I am in no mood to trade insults with a seer.
TIRESIAS. You have already, calling my prophecies a lie.
CREON.   Why not?   1170
  You and the whole breed of seers are mad for money!
TIRESIAS. And the whole race of tyrants lusts to rake it in.
CREON. This slander of yours—
  are you aware you're speaking to the king?
TIRESIAS. Well aware. Who helped you save the city?
CREON.   You—   1175
  you have your skills, old seer, but you lust for injustice!
TIRESIAS. You will drive me to utter the dreadful secret in my heart.
CREON. Spit it out! Just don't speak it out for profit.
TIRESIAS. Profit? No, not a bit of profit, not for you.
CREON. Know full well, you'll never buy off my resolve.   1180
TIRESIAS. Then know this too, learn this by heart!
  The chariot of the sun will not race through
  so many circuits more, before you have surrendered
  one born of your own loins, your own flesh and blood,
  a corpse for corpses given in return, since you have thrust   1185
  to the world below a child sprung from the world above,
  ruthlessly lodged a living soul within the grave—
  then you've robbed the gods below the earth,

keeping a dead body here in the bright air,
unburied, unsung, unhallowed by the rites.   1190

You, you have no business with the dead,
nor do the gods above—this is violence
you have forced upon the heavens.
And so the avengers, the dark destroyers late
but true to the mark, now lie in wait for you,   1195
the Furies sent by the gods and the god of death
to strike you down with the pains that you perfected!

There. Reflect on that, tell me I've been bribed.
The day comes soon, no long test of time, not now,
that wakes the wails for men and women in your halls.   1200
Great hatred rises against you—
cities in tumult, all whose mutilated sons
the dogs have graced with burial, or the wild beasts,
some wheeling crow that wings the ungodly stench of carrion
back to each city, each warrior's heart and home.   1205

These arrows for your heart! Since you've raked me
I loose them like an archer in my anger,
arrows deadly true. You'll never escape
their burning, searing force.

[*Motioning to his escort.*]

Come, boy, take me home.   1210
So he can vent his rage on younger men,
and learn to keep a gentler tongue in his head
and better sense than what he carries now.

[*Exit to the side.*]

LEADER. The old man's gone, my king—
    terrible prophecies. Well I know,   1215
    since the hair on his old head went gray,
    he's never lied to Thebes.
CREON. I know it myself—I'm shaken, torn.
    It's a dreadful thing to yield . . . but resist now?
    Lay my pride bare to the blows of ruin?   1220
    That's dreadful too.
LEADER.   But good advice,
    Creon, take it now, you must.
CREON. What should I do? Tell me . . . I'll obey.
LEADER. Go! Free the girl from the rocky vault
    and raise a mound for the body you exposed.   1225
CREON. That's your advice? You think I should give in?
LEADER. Yes, my king, quickly. Disasters sent by the gods
    cut short our follies in a flash.
CREON.   Oh it's hard,
    giving up the heart's desire . . . but I will do it—
    no more fighting a losing battle with necessity.   1230
LEADER. Do it now, go, don't leave it to others.

CREON. Now—I'm on my way! Come, each of you,
    take up axes, make for the high ground,
    over there, quickly! I and my better judgment
    have come round to this—I shackled her,   1235
    I'll set her free myself. I am afraid . . .
    it's best to keep the established laws
    to the very day we die.

[*Rushing out, followed by his entourage. The* CHORUS *clusters around the altar.*]

CHORUS. God of a hundred names!
                      Great Dionysus—
       Son and glory of Semele! Pride of Thebes—   1240
    Child of Zeus whose thunder rocks the clouds—
    Lord of the famous lands of evening—
    King of the Mysteries!
                  King of Eleusis, Demeter's plain°
    her breasting hills that welcome in the world—
    Great Dionysus!
                 Bacchus,° living in Thebes   1245
    the mother-city of all your frenzied women—
                     Bacchus
       living along the Ismenus'° rippling waters
    standing over the field sown with the Dragons' teeth!

You—we have seen you through the flaring smoky fires,
       your torches blazing over the twin peaks   1250
    where nymphs of the hallowed cave climb onward
                 fired with you, your sacred rage—
    we have seen you at Castalia's running spring°
    and down from the heights of Nysa° crowned with ivy
    the greening shore rioting vines and grapes   1255
              down you come in your storm of wild women
    ecstatic, mystic cries—
                Dionysus—
    down to watch and ward the roads of Thebes!
    First of all cities, Thebes you honor first
    you and your mother, bride of the lightning—   1260
    come, Dionysus! now your people lie
    in the iron grip of plague,
    come in your racing, healing stride
              down Parnassus'° slopes
    or across the moaning straits.
               Lord of the dancing—   1265
    dance, dance the constellations breathing fire!

1243 Demeter's plain Demeter, goddess of grain, was worshipped at Eleusis, near Athens. **1245 Bacchus** a name for Dionysus. **1247 Ismenus** a river near Thebes. The founders of Thebes sprang from a dragon's teeth sown by Cadmus (see line 1273) near the river. **1253 Castalia's running spring** the sacred spring of Apollo's oracle at Delphia. **1254 Nysa** a mountain where Dionysus was worshipped. **1264 Parnassus** a mountain sacred to Dionysus.

Great master of the voices of the night!
Child of Zeus, God's offspring, come, come forth!
Lord, king, dance with your nymphs, swirling, raving
arm-in-arm in frenzy through the night   1270
they dance you, Iacchus°—
        Dance, Dionysus
giver of all good things!

[*Enter a* MESSENGER *from the side.*]

MESSENGER.   Neighbors,
friends of the house of Cadmus and the kings,
there's not a thing in this life of ours
I'd praise or blame as settled once for all.   1275
Fortune lifts and Fortune fells the lucky
and unlucky every day. No prophet on earth
can tell a man his fate. Take Creon:
there was a man to rouse your envy once,
as I see it. He saved the realm from enemies;   1280
taking power, he alone, the lord of the fatherland,
he set us true on course—flourished like a tree
with the noble line of sons he bred and reared . . .
and now it's lost, all gone.
        Believe me,
when a man has squandered his true joys,   1285
he's good as dead, I tell you, a living corpse.
Pile up riches in your house, as much as you like—
live like a king with a huge show of pomp,
but if real delight is missing from the lot,
I wouldn't give you a wisp of smoke for it,   1290
not compared with joy.
LEADER.   What now?
What new grief do you bring the house of kings?
MESSENGER. Dead, dead—and the living are guilty of their death!
LEADER. Who's the murderer? Who is dead? Tell us.
MESSENGER. Haemon's gone, his blood spilled by the very hand—   1295
LEADER. His father's or his own?
MESSENGER.   His own . . .
raging mad with his father for the death—
LEADER.   Oh great seer,
you saw it all, you brought your word to birth!
MESSENGER. Those are the facts. Deal with them as you will.

[*As he turns to go,* EURYDICE *enters from the palace.*]

LEADER. Look, Eurydice. Poor woman, Creon's wife,   1300
so close at hand. By chance perhaps,
unless she's heard the news about her son.
EURYDICE.   My countrymen,
all of you—I caught the sound of your words
as I was leaving to do my part,
to appeal to queen Athena° with my prayers.   1305

1271 Iacchus a lofty name for Dionysus. **1305 Athena** goddess of wisdom.

I was just loosing the bolts, opening the doors,
when a voice filled with sorrow, family sorrow,
struck my ears, and I fell back, terrified,
into the women's arms—everything went black.
Tell me the news, again, whatever it is . . .   1310
sorrow and I are hardly strangers;
I can bear the worst.

MESSENGER.   I—dear lady,
I'll speak as an eye-witness. I was there.
And I won't pass over one word of the truth.
Why should I try to soothe you with a story,   1315
only to prove a liar in a moment?
Truth is always best.
                                    So,
I escorted your lord, I guided him
to the edge of the plain where the body lay,
Polynices, torn by the dogs and still unmourned.   1320
And saying a prayer to Hecate of the Crossroads,
Pluto° too, to hold their anger and be kind,
we washed the dead in a bath of holy water
and plucking some fresh branches, gathering . . .
what was left of him, we burned them all together   1325
and raised a high mound of native earth, and then
we turned and made for that rocky vault of hers,
the hollow, empty bed of the bride of Death.
And far off, one of us heard a voice,
a long wail rising, echoing   1330
out of that unhallowed wedding-chamber;
he ran to alert the master and Creon pressed on,
closer—the strange, inscrutable cry came sharper,
throbbing around him now, and he let loose
a cry of his own, enough to wrench the heart,   1335
"Oh god, am I the prophet now? going down
the darkest road I've ever gone? My son—
it's *his* dear voice, he greets me! Go, men,
closer, quickly! Go through the gap,
the rocks are dragged back—   1340
right to the tomb's very mouth—and look,
see if it's Haemon's voice I think I hear,
or the gods have robbed me of my senses."

The king was shattered. We took his orders,
went and searched, and there in the deepest,   1345
dark recesses of the tomb we found her . . .
hanged by the neck in a fine linen noose,
strangled in her veils—and the boy,
his arms flung around her waist,
clinging to her, wailing for his bride,   1350
dead and down below, for his father's crimes
and the bed of his marriage blighted by misfortune.

1321–1322 **Hecate . . . Pluto** deities of the underworld.

When Creon saw him, he gave a deep sob,
he ran in, shouting, crying out to him,
"Oh my child—what have you done? what seized you,   1355
what insanity? what disaster drove you mad?
Come out, my son! I beg you on my knees!"
But the boy gave him a wild burning glance,
spat in his face, not a word in reply,
he drew his sword—his father rushed out,   1360
running as Haemon lunged and missed!—
and then, doomed, desperate with himself,
suddenly leaning his full weight on the blade,
he buried it in his body, halfway to the hilt.
And still in his senses, pouring his arms around her,   1365
he embraced the girl and breathing hard,
released a quick rush of blood,
bright red on her cheek glistening white.
And there he lies, body enfolding body . . .
he has won his bride at last, poor boy,   1370
not here but in the houses of the dead.

Creon shows the world that of all the ills
afflicting men the worst is lack of judgment.

[EURYDICE *turns and reenters the palace.*]

LEADER. What do you make of that? The lady's gone,
        without a word, good or bad.
MESSENGER.   I'm alarmed too   1375
        but here's my hope—faced with her son's death,
        she finds it unbecoming to mourn in public.
        Inside, under her roof, she'll set her women
        to the task and wail the sorrow of the house.
        She's too discreet. She won't do something rash.   1380
LEADER. I'm not so sure. To me, at least,
        a long heavy silence promises danger,
        just as much as a lot of empty outcries.
MESSENGER. We'll see if she's holding something back,
        hiding some passion in her heart.   1385
        I'm going in. You may be right—who knows?
        Even too much silence has its dangers.

[*Exit to the palace. Enter* CREON *from the side, escorted by attendants carrying* HAEMON'*s body on a bier.*]

LEADER. The king himself! Coming toward us,
        look, holding the boy's head in his hands.
        Clear, damning proof, if it's right to say so—   1390
        proof of his own madness, no one else's,
           no, his own blind wrongs.
CREON.   Ohhh,
        so senseless, so insane . . . my crimes,
        my stubborn, deadly—
        Look at us, the killer, the killed,   1395
        father and son, the same blood—the misery!

My plans, my mad fanatic heart,
my son, cut off so young!
Ai, dead, lost to the world,
not through your stupidity, no, my own.

LEADER.   Too late,   1400
too late, you see what justice means.

CREON.   Oh I've learned
through blood and tears! Then, it was then,
when the god came down and struck me—a great weight
shattering, driving me down that wild savage path,
ruining, trampling down my joy. Oh the agony,   1405
the heartbreaking agonies of our lives.

[*Enter the* MESSENGER *from the palace.*]

MESSENGER.   Master,
what a hoard of grief you have, and you'll have more.
The grief that lies to hand you've brought yourself—

[*Pointing to* HAEMON's *body.*]

the rest, in the house, you'll see it all too soon.

CREON. What now? What's worse than this?

MESSENGER.   The queen is dead.   1410
The mother of this dead boy . . . mother to the end—
poor thing, her wounds are fresh.

CREON.   No, no,
harbor of Death, so choked, so hard to cleanse!—
why me? why are you killing me?
Herald of pain, more words, more grief?   1415
I died once, you kill me again and again!
What's the report, boy . . . some news for me?
My wife dead? O dear god!
Slaughter heaped on slaughter?

[*The doors open; the body of* EURYDICE *is brought out on her bier.*]

MESSENGER.   See for yourself:
now they bring her body from the palace.

CREON.   Oh no,   1420
another, a second loss to break the heart.
What next, what fate still waits for me?
I just held my son in my arms and now,
look, a new corpse rising before my eyes—
wretched, helpless mother—O my son!   1425

MESSENGER. She stabbed herself at the altar,
then her eyes went dark, after she'd raised
a cry for the noble fate of Megareus,° the hero
killed in the first assault, then for Haemon,
then with her dying breath she called down   1430
torments on your head—you killed her sons.

───────────────

1428 **Megareus** son of Creon and Eurydice.

CREON.   Oh the dread,
    I shudder with dread! Why not kill me too?—
    run me through with a good sharp sword?
    Oh god, the misery, anguish—
    I, I'm churning with it, going under.   1435
MESSENGER. Yes, and the dead, the woman lying there,
    piles the guilt of all their deaths on you.
CREON. How did she end her life, what bloody stroke?
MESSENGER. She drove home to the heart with her own hand,
    once she learned her son was dead . . . that agony.   1440
CREON. And the guilt is all mine—
    can never be fixed on another man,
    no escape for me. I killed you,
    I, god help me, I admit it all!

    [*To his* ATTENDANTS.]

    Take me away, quickly, out of sight.   1445
    I don't even exist—I'm no one. Nothing.
LEADER. Good advice, if there's any good in suffering.
    Quickest is best when troubles block the way.
CREON.

    [*Kneeling in prayer.*]

    Come, let it come!—that best of fates for me
    that brings the final day, best fate of all.   1450
    Oh quickly, now—
    so I never have to see another sunrise.
LEADER. That will come when it comes;
    we must deal with all that lies before us.
    The future rests with the ones who tend the future.   1455
CREON. That prayer—I poured my heart into that prayer!
LEADER. No more prayers now. For mortal men
    there is no escape from the doom we must endure.
CREON. Take me away, I beg you, out of sight.
    A rash, indiscriminate fool!   1460
    I murdered you, my son, against my will—
    you too, my wife . . .
                  Wailing wreck of a man,
    whom to look to? where to lean for support?

    [*Desperately turning from* HAEMON *to* EURYDICE *on their biers.*]

    Whatever I touch goes wrong—once more
    a crushing fate's come down upon my head.   1465

    [*The* MESSENGER *and attendants lead* CREON *into the palace.*]

CHORUS. Wisdom is by far the greatest part of joy,
    and reverence toward the gods must be safeguarded.
    The mighty words of the proud are paid in full
    with mighty blows of fate, and at long last
    those blows will teach us wisdom.   1470

    [*The old citizens exit to the side.*]

✵ TOPICS FOR CRITICAL THINKING AND WRITING

The Play on the Page

1. If you have read *Oedipus,* compare and contrast the Creon of *Antigone* with the Creon of *Oedipus.*
2. Although Sophocles called his play *Antigone,* many critics say that Creon is the real tragic hero, pointing out that Antigone is absent from the last third of the play. Evaluate this view.
3. In some Greek tragedies, fate plays a great role in bringing about the downfall of the tragic hero. Though there are references to the curse on the House of Oedipus in *Antigone,* do we feel that Antigone goes to her death as a result of the workings of fate? Do we feel that fate is responsible for Creon's fall? Are both Antigone and Creon the creators of their own tragedy?
4. Are the words *hamartia* and *hybris* (see pages 1094–1095) relevant to Antigone? To Creon?
5. Why does Creon, contrary to the Chorus's advice (lines 1224–1225), bury the body of Polynices before he releases Antigone? Does his action show a zeal for piety as short-sighted as his earlier zeal for law? Is his action plausible, in view of the facts that Tiresias has dwelt on the wrong done to Polynices and that Antigone has ritual food to sustain her? Or are we not to worry about Creon's motive?
6. A *foil* is a character who, by contrast, sets off or helps define another character. To what extent is Ismene a foil to Antigone? Is she entirely without courage?
7. What function does Eurydice serve? How deeply do we feel about her fate?

The Play on the Stage

8. Would you use masks for some (or all) of the characters? If so, would they be masks that fully cover the face, Greek-style, or some sort of half-masks? (A full mask enlarges the face, and conceivably the mouthpiece can amplify the voice, but only an exceptionally large theater might require such help. Perhaps half-masks are enough if the aim is chiefly to distance the actors from the audience and from daily reality, and to force the actors to develop resources other than facial gestures. One director, arguing in favor of half-masks, has said that actors who wear even a half-mask learn to act not with the eyes but with the neck.)
9. How would you costume the players? Would you dress them as the Greeks might have? Why? One argument sometimes used by those who hold that modern productions of Greek drama should use classical costumes is that Greek drama *ought* to be remote and ritualistic. Evaluate this view. What sort of modern dress might be effective?
10. If you were directing a college production of *Antigone,* how large a chorus would you use? (Sophocles is said to have used a chorus of fifteen.) Would you have the chorus recite (or chant) the odes in unison, or would you assign lines to single speakers? In Sophocles' day, the chorus danced. Would you use dance movements? If not, in what sorts of movements might they engage?

TWO PLAYS BY SHAKESPEARE

A Casebook on Hamlet

This casebook contains (in addition to illustrations of the original texts of *Hamlet*, the Elizabethan theater, and modern productions) the following material:

1. A note on the Elizabethan theater
2. A note on the text of *Hamlet* (with facsimilies of three versions of Hamlet's "to be or not to be")
3. The text of *Hamlet*
4. A Freudian interpretation by Ernest Jones
5. Stanley Wells's analysis of the first soliloquy
6. Elaine Showalter's discussion of Ophelia
7. Claire Bloom's comments on her performance as Gertrude, in the BBC TV production of *Hamlet* (1980)
8. Bernice W. Kliman's review of the BBC TV production of *Hamlet* (1980)
9. A review by a student, Will Saretta, of Kenneth Branagh's film version of *Hamlet* (1996)

A NOTE ON THE ELIZABETHAN THEATER

Shakespeare's theater was wooden, round or polygonal (the Chorus in *Henry V* calls it a "wooden O"). About eight hundred spectators could stand in the yard in front of—and perhaps along the two sides of—the stage that jutted from the rear wall, and another fifteen hundred or so spectators could sit in the three roofed galleries that ringed the stage.

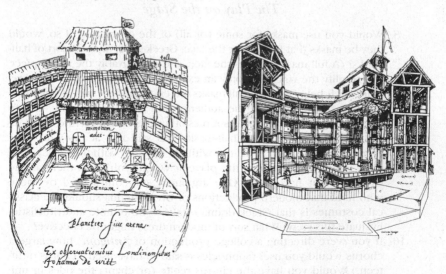

Left: Johannes de Witt, a Continental visitor to London, made a drawing of the Swan Theater in about the year 1596. The original drawing is lost; this is Arend van Buchel's copy of it. *Right:* C. Walter Hodges's drawing (1965) of an Elizabethan playhouse.

That portion of the galleries that was above the rear of the stage was sometimes used by actors. For instance, in *The Tempest*, 3.3, a stage direction following line 17 mentions "Prospero on the top, invisible," that is, he is imagined to be invisible to the characters in the play.

Entry to the stage was normally gained by doors at the rear, but apparently on rare occasions use was made of a curtained alcove—or perhaps a booth—between the doors, which allowed characters to be "discovered" (revealed) as in the modern proscenium theater, which normally employs a curtain. Such "discovery" scenes are rare.

Although the theater as a whole was unroofed, the stage was protected by a roof, supported by two pillars. These could serve (by an act of imagination) as trees behind which actors might pretend to conceal themselves.

A performance was probably uninterrupted by intermissions or by long pauses for the changing of scenery; a group of characters leaves the stage, another enters, and if the locale has changed the new characters somehow tell us. (Modern editors customarily add indications of locales to help a reader, but it should be remembered that the action on the Elizabethan stage was continuous.)

WILLIAM SHAKESPEARE

William Shakespeare (1564–1616) was born in Stratford, England, of middle-class parents. Nothing of interest is known about his early years, but by 1590 he was acting and writing plays in London. By the end of the following decade he had worked in all three Elizabethan dramatic genres—tragedy, comedy, and history. Romeo and Juliet, *for example, was written about 1595, the year of* Richard II, *and in the following year he wrote* A Midsummer Night's Dream. Julius Caesar *(1599) probably preceded* As You Like It *by one year, and* Hamlet *probably followed* As You Like It *by less than a year. Among the plays that followed* Othello *(1603–1604) were* King Lear *(1605–1606),* Macbeth *(1605–1606), and several "romances"—plays that have happy endings but that seem more meditative and closer to tragedy than such comedies as* A Midsummer Night's Dream, As You Like It, *and* Twelfth Night.

A NOTE ON THE TEXTS OF *HAMLET*

Shakespeare's *Hamlet* comes to us in three versions. The first, known as the First Quarto (Q1), was published in 1603. It is an illegitimate garbled version, perhaps derived from the memory of the actor who played Marcellus (this part is conspicuously more accurate than the rest of the play) in a short version of the play.

The second printed version (Q2), which appeared in 1604, is almost twice as long as Q1; all in all, it is the best text we have, doubtless published (as Q1 was not) with the permission of Shakespeare's theatrical company.

The third printed version, in the First Folio (the collected edition of Shakespeare's plays, published in 1623), is also legitimate, but it seems to be an acting version, for it lacks some two hundred lines of Q2. On the other hand, the Folio text includes some ninety lines not found in Q2.

The Tragedy of Hamlet

And so by continuance, and weakenesse of the braine
Into this frensie, which now possesseth him:
And if this be not true, take this from this.

King Thinke you t'is so?

Cor. How? so my Lord, I would very faine know
That thing that I haue saide t'is so, positiuely,
And it hath fallen out otherwise:
Nay, if circumstances leade me on,
Ile finde it out, if it were hid
As deepe as the centre of the earth.

King. how should wee trie this same?

Cor. Mary my good lord thus,
The Princes walke is here in the galery,
There let *Ofelia*, walke vntill hee comes:
Your selfe and I will stand close in the study,
There shall you heare the effect of all his hart,
And if it proue any otherwise then loue,
Then let my censure faile an other time.

King. see where hee comes poring vppon a booke.

Enter Hamlet.

Cor. Madame, will it please your grace
To leaue vs here?

Que. With all my hart.   *exit.*

Cor. And here *Ofelia*, reade you on this booke,
And walke aloofe, the King shal be vnseene.

Ham. To be, or not to be, I there's the point,
To Die, to sleepe, is that all? I all:
No, to sleepe, to dreame, I mary there it goes,
For in that dreame of death, when wee awake,
And borne before an euerlasting Iudge,
From whence no passenger euer retur'nd,
The vndiscouered country, at whose sight
The happy smile, and the accursed damn'd.
But for this, the ioyfull hope of this,
Whol'd beare the scornes and flattery of the world,
Scorned by the right rich, the rich cursed of the poore?

                                        The

Here and on the next page we print "To be or not to be," as given in the
First Quarto (QI, 1603). (On pages 1182–1183, we give the speech as it
appears in the Second Quarto, and on page 1184, the speech in the First
Folio.)   *(continued)*

Prince of Denmarke

The widow being oppreſſed,the orphan wrong'd,
The taſte of hunger, or a tirants raigne,
And thouſand more calamities beſides,
To grunt and ſweate vnder this weary life,
When that he may his full *Quietus* make,
With a bare bodkin, who would this indure,
But for a hope of ſomething after death?
Which puſles the braine, and doth confound the ſence,
Which makes vs rather beare thoſe euilles we haue,
Than ſlie to others that we know not of.
I that,O this conſcience makes cowardes of vs all,
Lady in thy orizons, be all my ſinnes remembred.

　　Ofel. My Lord, I haue ſought opportunitie,which now
I haue,to redeliuer to your worthy handes, a ſmall remembrance, ſuch tokens which I haue receiued of you.

　　Ham. Are you faire?

　　Ofel. My Lord.

　　Ham. Are you honeſt?

　　Ofel. What meanes my Lord?

　　Ham. That if you be faire and honeſt,
Your beauty ſhould admit no diſcourſe to your honeſty.

　　Ofel. My Lord, can beauty haue better priuiledge than
with honeſty?

　　Ham. Yea mary may it; for Beauty may transforme
Honeſty, from what ſhe was into a bawd:
Then Honeſty can transforme Beauty:
This was ſometimes a Paradox,
But now the time giues it ſcope.
I neuer gaue you nothing.

　　Ofel. My Lord, you know right well you did,
And with them ſuch earneſt vowes of loue,
As would haue moou'd the ſtonieſt breaſt aliue,
But now too true I finde,
Rich giftes waxe poore, when giuers grow vnkinde.

　　Ham. I neuer loued you.

　　Ofel. You made me beleeue you did.

　　　　　　　　E　　　　　　　　*Ham.*

That show of such an exercise may cullour
Your lowlines; we are oft too blame in this,
Tis too much proou'd, that with deuotions visage
And pious action, we doe sugar ore
The deuill himselfe.

  King. O tis too true,
How smart a lash that speech doth giue my conscience.
The harlots cheeke beautied with plastring art,
Is not more ougly to the thing that helps it,
Then is my deede to my most painted word :
O heauy burthen.

Enter Hamlet.

  Pol. I heare him comming, with-draw my Lord.
  Ham. To be, or not to be, that is the question,
Whether tis nobler in the minde to suffer
The slings and arrowes of outragious fortune,
Or to take Armes against a sea of troubles,
And by opposing, end them; to die to sleepe
No more, and by a sleepe, to say we end
The hart-ake, and the thousand naturall shocks
That flesh is heire to; tis a consumation
Deuoutly to be wisht to die to sleepe,
To sleepe, perchance to dreame, I there's the rub,
For in that sleepe of death what dreames may come
When we haue shuffled off this mortall coyle
Must giue vs pause, there's the respect
That makes calamitie of so long life :
For who would beare the whips and scornes of time,
Th'oppressors wrong, the proude mans contumely,
The pangs of despiz'd loue, the lawes delay,
The insolence of office, and the spurnes
That patient merrit of th'vnworthy takes,
When he himselfe might his quietas make
With a bare bodkin; who would fardels beare,
To grunt and sweat vnder a wearie life,
But that the dread of something after death,
The vndiscouer'd country, from whose borne.

G 2

No

On this page and the next we print "To be or not to be," as given in the Second
Quarto (Q2, 1604).   (*continued*)

The Tragedie of Hamlet

No trauiler returnes, puzzels the will,
And makes vs rather beare those ills we haue,
Then flie to others that we know not of.
Thus conscience dooes make cowards,
And thus the natiue hiew of resolution
Is sickled ore with the pale cast of thought,
And enterprises of great pitch and moment,
With this regard theyr currents turne awry,
And loose the name of action. Soft you now,
The faire *Ophelia*, Nimph in thy orizons
Be all my sinnes remembred.

  Oph. Good my Lord,
How dooes your honour for this many a day?

  Ham. I humbly thanke you well.

  Oph. My Lord, I haue remembrances of yours
That I haue longed long to redeliuer,
I pray you now receiue them.

  Ham. No, not I, I neuer gaue you ought.

  Oph. My honor'd Lord, you know right well you did,
And with them words of so sweet breath compos'd
As made these things more rich, their perfume lost,
Take these againe, for to the noble mind
Rich gifts wax poore when giuers prooue vnkind,
There my Lord.

  Ham. Ha, ha, are you honest.

  Oph. My Lord.

  Ham. Are you faire?

  Oph. What meanes your Lordship?

  Ham. That if you be honest & faire, you should admit
no discourse to your beautie.

  Oph. Could beauty my Lord haue better comerse
Then with honestie?

  Ham. I truly, for the power of beautie will sooner transforme honestie from what it is to a bawde, then the force of honestie can translate beautie into his likenes, this was sometime a paradox, but now the
time giues it proofe, I did loue you once.

  Oph. Indeed my Lord you made me belieue so.

  Ham. You should not haue beleeu'd me, for vertue cannot so
euocutat our old stock, but we shall relish of it, I loued you not.

The Tragedie of Hamlet.

With turbulent and dangerous Lunacy.

Rosin. He does confesse he feeles himselfe distracted,
But from what cause he will by no meanes speake.

Guil. Nor do we finde him forward to be sounded,
But with a crafty Madnesse keepes aloose:
When we would bring him on to some Confession
Of his true state.

Qu. Did he receiue you well?

Rosin. Most like a Gentleman.

Guild. But with much forcing of his disposition.

Rosin. Niggard of question, but of our demands
Most free in his reply.

Qu. Did you assay him to any pastime?

Rosin. Madam, it so fell out, that certaine Players
We ore-wrought on the way: of these we told him,
And there did seeme in him a kinde of ioy
To heare of it: They are about the Court,
And (as I thinke) they haue already order
This night to play before him.

Pol. 'Tis most true:
And he beseech'd me to intreate your Maiesties
To heare, and see the matter.

King. With all my heart, and it doth much content me
To heare him so inclin'd. Good Gentlemen,
Giue him a further edge, and driue his purpose on
To these delights.

Rosin. We shall my Lord.   *Exeunt.*

King. Sweet *Gertrude* leaue vs too,
For we haue closely sent for *Hamlet* hither,
That he, as 'twere by accident, may there
Affront *Ophelia.* Her Father, and my selfe (lawful espials)
Will so bestow our selues, that seeing vnseene
We may of their encounter frankely iudge,
And gather by him, as he is behaued,
If't be th'affliction of his loue, or no.
That thus he suffers for.

Qu. I shall obey you,
And for your part *Ophelia*, I do wish
That your good Beauties be the happy cause
Of *Hamlets* wildenesse: so shall I hope your Vertues
Will bring him to his wonted way againe,
To both your Honors.

Ophe. Madam, I wish it may.

Pol. *Ophelia*, walke you heere. Gracious so please ye
We will bestow our selues: Reade on this booke,
That shew of such an exercise may colour
Your lonelinesse. We are oft too blame in this,
'Tis too much prou'd, that with Deuotions visage,
And pious Action, we do surge o're
The diuell himselfe.

King. Oh 'tis true:
How smart a lash that speech doth giue my Conscience?
The Harlots Cheeke beautied with plaist'ring Art
Is not more vgly to the thing that helpes it,
Then is my deede, to my most painted word.
Oh heauie burthen!

Pol. I heare him comming, let's withdraw my Lord.
                              Exeunt.

Enter Hamlet.

Ham. To be, or not to be, that is the Question:
Whether 'tis Nobler in the minde to suffer
The Slings and Arrowes of outragious Fortune,
Or to take Armes against a Sea of troubles,
And by opposing end them: to dye, to sleepe
No more; and by a sleepe, to say we end
The Heart-ake, and the thousand Naturall shockes

That Flesh is heyre too? 'Tis a consummation
Deuoutly to be wish'd. To dye to sleepe,
To sleepe, perchance to Dreame; I, there's the rub,
For in that sleepe of death, what dreames may come,
When we haue shuffel'd off this mortall coile,
Must giue vs pawse. There's the respect
That makes Calamity of so long life:
For who would beare the Whips and Scornes of time,
The Oppressors wrong, the poore mans Contumely,
The pangs of dispriz'd Loue, the Lawes delay,
The insolence of Office, and the Spurnes
That patient merit of the vnworthy takes,
When he himselfe might his *Quietus* make
With a bare Bodkin? Who would these Fardles beare
To grunt and sweat vnder a weary life,
But that the dread of something after death,
The vndiscouered Countrey, from whose Borne
No Traueller returnes, Puzels the will,
And makes vs rather beare those illes we haue,
Then flye to others that we know not of.
Thus Conscience does make Cowards of vs all,
And thus the Natiue hew of Resolution
Is sicklied o're, with the pale cast of Thought,
And enterprizes of great pith and moment,
With this regard their Currants turne away,
And loose the name of Action. Soft you now,
The faire *Ophelia?* Nimph, in thy Orizons
Be all my sinnes remembred.

Ophe. Good my Lord,
How does your Honor for this many a day?

Ham. I humbly thanke you: well, well, well.

Ophe. My Lord, I haue Remembrances of yours,
That I haue longed long to re-deliuer.
I pray you now, receiue them.

Ham. No, no, I neuer gaue you ought.

Ophe. My honor'd Lord, I know right well you did,
And with them words of so sweet breath compos'd,
As made the things more rich, then perfume left:
Take these againe, for to the Noble minde
Rich gifts wax poore, when giuers proue vnkinde.
There my Lord.

Ham. Ha, ha: Are you honest?

Ophe. My Lord.

Ham. Are you faire?

Ophe. What meanes your Lordship?

Ham. That if you be honest and faire, your Honesty
should admit no discourse to your Beautie.

Ophe. Could Beautie my Lord, haue better Comerce
then with Honestie?

Ham. I trulie: for the power of Beautie, will sooner
transforme Honestie from what it is, to a Bawd, then the
force of Honestie can translate Beautie into his likenesse.
This was sometime a Paradox, but now the time giues it
proofe. I did loue you once.

Ophe. Indeed my Lord, you made me beleeue so.

Ham. You should not haue beleeued me. For vertue
cannot so innocculate our old stocke, but we shall rellish
of it. I loued you not.

Ophe. I was the more deceiued.

Ham. Get thee to a Nunnerie. Why would'st thou
be a breeder of Sinners? I am my selfe indifferent honest,
but yet I could accuse me of such things, that it were better my Mother had not borne me. I am very prowd, re-
uengefull, Ambitious, with more offences at my becke,
then I haue thoughts to put them in imagination, to giue
them shape, or time to acte them in. What should such
Fel-

"To be or not to be," as given in the First Folio (F1, 1623).

Because Q2 is the longest version, giving us more of the play as Shakespeare conceived it than either of the other texts, it serves as the basic version for this text. Unfortunately, the printers of Q2 often worked carelessly: Words and phrases are omitted, there are plain misreadings of what must have been in Shakespeare's manuscript, and speeches are sometimes wrongly assigned. It is therefore necessary to turn to the First Folio for many readings. It has been found useful, also, to divide the play into acts and scenes; these divisions, not found in Q2 (and only a few are found in the Folio), are purely editorial additions, and they are therefore enclosed in square brackets.

We use the text edited by David Bevington.

PORTFOLIO: *HAMLET* ON THE STAGE

We know that *Hamlet* was popular during Shakespeare's lifetime, but the earliest illustration (1709) showing a scene from the play was engraved more than a century after the play was written, so we know little about what *Hamlet* looked like on Shakespeare's stage. Still, we do have at least a little idea. We know, for instance, that at least in the first scene Hamlet wore black (he speaks of his "inky cloak"), and we know that when the Ghost first appears it is dressed in "the very armor he had on / When he the ambitious Norway combatted" (1.1.64–65). We

"The Murder of Gonzago" in 3.3. Because this episode is a play-within-the-play, Shakespeare uses a distinctive form of verse (pairs of rhyming lines, eight syllables to a line) that sets it off from the language of the rest of the play (chiefly prose, or unrhymed lines of ten syllables). The language, too, is different, for it is conspicuously old-fashioned (the sun is called "Phoebus' cart"; the ocean is called "Neptune's salt wash"). In this modern-dress production done at Stratford, England, in 1975, Claudius wore a blue business suit and Fortinbras wore combat gear, but the characters in the play-within-the-play were masked, to emphasize their theatricality.

The "closet" scene in 3.4. A line in the preceding scene specifically tells us that Hamlet is "going to his mother's closet." (In Elizabethan language, a "closet" is a private room, as opposed to a public room—for instance, a room in which a monarch might pray, or relax, as opposed to an audience chamber in which he or she would engage in official actions.) In the twentieth century, at least as early as John Gielgud's New York production in 1935, and probably in response to Freudian interpretations of the play, the Queen's "closet" has been fitted with a bed on which Hamlet and Gertrude tussle, and indeed the scene is often wrongly called "the bedroom scene." In this 1989 Royal Shakespeare Company production, with Mark Rylance as Hamlet, a ranting Hamlet (at the left) confronts Gertrude. The Ghost, unknown to Gertrude, sits on the bed, presumably seeking to protect her from Hamlet's assault. The setting was not realistic but expressionistic; that is, the curtains stirred and the lighting changed, not because a physical wind was blowing or the sources of illumination were changing, but to express the passions of the characters.

know, too, that when the Ghost appears later, in the Queen's chamber (3.4), he does not wear armor, a sign that his mood is different.

We also have a few tantalizing glimpses of Elizabethan acting. Thus, in the dumb show (pantomime) preceding "The Murder of Gonzago" that the touring players in 3.2 produce for the court, we get this stage direction: "Enter a King and a Queen very lovingly: the Queen embracing him and he her." A little later, when the Queen in this dumb show finds that the King has been poisoned, she "makes passionate action," but then, when the poisoner woos her, "she seems harsh a while but in the end accepts love."

We know something, too, of the sound effects. Possibly the play begins with the bell tolling twelve (in 1.1 Bernardo says, "'Tis now struck twelve"), and certainly in the first scene we hear the crowing of a cock, which causes the Ghost to depart. Later we hear the sound of drums, trumpets, and cannon when Claudius drinks toasts, and the play ends with the sound of cannon, when Fortinbras orders the soldiers to pay tribute to the dead Hamlet.

What about costumes? In their own day, Elizabethan plays were staged chiefly in contemporary dress—doublet (close-fitting jacket) and hose (tights) for the men, gowns of various sorts for the women (whose roles were played by boy actors)—though for classical plays such as *Julius Caesar* some attempt was

Hamlet meditates on death in the grave yard in 5.1. Kenneth Branagh portrayed Hamlet in 1993 for The Royal Shakespeare Theatre. The production used costumes suggesting the late nineteenth century.

made in the direction of ancient costume, at least for the major characters. The seventeenth and eighteenth centuries, too, staged the plays in the costume of the day, which of course was not Elizabethan, but in much of the nineteenth century, and in the first third of the twentieth, a strong sense that the plays were "Elizabethan" caused producers to use Elizabethan costumes, although these costumes—contemporary when the plays were first performed—now had become historical costume, marking the plays as of an age remote from our own. In 1925 Barry Jackson staged a modern-dress production in London, in an effort to emphasize the play's contemporary relevance. Today, productions tend to be in modern dress in the sense that they avoid Elizabethan costume; but usually, in an effort to add some color to the stage as well as to add some (but not a great) sense of remoteness, they use costumes of the nineteenth century, which allow for splendid gowns and for military uniforms with sashes.

The same scene (5.1) as in the previous photo shows Kevin Kline as Hamlet in the 1986 New York Shakespeare Festival production. Costumes are late nineteenth century. Horatio is played by an African-American. Putting aside plays by black authors, and a very few plays by whites about blacks (such as Eugene O'Neill's *The Emperor Jones*), there are few roles in drama expressly written for blacks. Shakespeare offers only three: Othello, Aaron (a Moor in *Titus Adronicus*), and the Prince of Morroco (in *The Merchant of Venice*). The few black actors who played other Shakespearean roles, such as the great Ira Aldridge who in the nineteenth century was known for his King Lear, performed the roles in whiteface. Since the 1980s, however, directors have engaged in open casting, using blacks (and Asians) in any and all roles, and not requiring white makeup.

Hamlet, Prince of Denmark

[DRAMATIS PERSONAE
GHOST *of Hamlet, the former King of Denmark*
CLAUDIUS, *King of Denmark, the former King's brother*
GERTRUDE, *Queen of Denmark, widow of the former King and now wife of
      Claudius*
HAMLET, *Prince of Denmark, son of the late King and of Gertrude*

POLONIUS, *councillor to the King*
LAERTES, *his son*
OPHELIA, *his daughter*
REYNALDO, *his servant*
HORATIO, *Hamlet's friend and fellow student*

VOLTIMAND,
CORNELIUS,
ROSENCRANTZ,
GUILDENSTERN, ⎬ *members of the Danish court*
OSRIC,
A GENTLEMAN,
A LORD,

BERNARDO,
FRANCISCO, ⎬ *officers and soldiers on watch*
MARCELLUS,

FORTINBRAS, *Prince of Norway*
CAPTAIN *in his army*

Three or Four PLAYERS, *taking the roles of* PROLOGUE, PLAYER KING, PLAYER
      QUEEN, *and* LUCIANUS
Two MESSENGERS
FIRST SAILOR
Two CLOWNS, *a gravedigger and his companion*
PRIEST
FIRST AMBASSADOR *from England*

*Lords, Soldiers, Attendants, Guards, other Players, Followers of Laertes,
      other Sailors, another Ambassador or Ambassadors from England*

SCENE: *Denmark*]

> **1.1** *Enter* BERNARDO *and* FRANCISCO, *two sentinels* [*meeting*].

BERNARDO. Who's there?
FRANCISCO. Nay, answer me.° Stand and unfold yourself.°
BERNARDO. Long live the King!
FRANCISCO. Bernardo?
BERNARDO. He.   5
FRANCISCO. You come most carefully upon your hour.
BERNARDO. 'Tis now struck twelve. Get thee to bed, Francisco.
FRANCISCO. For this relief much thanks. 'Tis bitter cold,
      And I am sick at heart.
BERNARDO. Have you had quiet guard?   10
FRANCISCO. Not a mouse stirring.
BERNARDO. Well, good night.
      If you do meet Horatio and Marcellus,
      The rivals° of my watch, bid them make haste.

> *Enter* HORATIO *and* MARCELLUS.

FRANCISCO. I think I hear them.—Stand, ho! Who is there?   15
HORATIO. Friends to this ground.°
MARCELLUS. And liegemen to the Dane.°
FRANCISCO. Give° you good night.

1.1 Location: Elsinore castle. A guard platform.   2 me (Francisco emphasizes that
he is the sentry currently on watch.)   **unfold yourself** reveal your identity.   **14 rivals**
partners.   **16 ground** country, land.   **17 liegemen to the Dane** men sworn to serve
the Danish king.   **18 Give** i.e., may God give.

MARCELLUS. O, farewell, honest soldier. Who hath relieved you?

FRANCISCO. Bernardo hath my place. Give you good night.   20

Exit FRANCISCO.

MARCELLUS. Holla! Bernardo!

BERNARDO. Say, what, is Horatio there?

HORATIO. A piece of him.

BERNARDO. Welcome, Horatio. Welcome, good Marcellus.

HORATIO. What, has this thing appeared again tonight?   25

BERNARDO. I have seen nothing.

MARCELLUS. Horatio says 'tis but our fantasy,°
 And will not let belief take hold of him
 Touching this dreaded sight twice seen of us.
 Therefore I have entreated him along°   30
 With us to watch° the minutes of this night,
 That if again this apparition come
 He may approve° our eyes and speak to it.

HORATIO. Tush, tush, 'twill not appear.

BERNARDO.   Sit down awhile,
 And let us once again assail your ears,   35
 That are so fortified against our story,
 What° we have two nights seen.

HORATIO.   Well, sit we down,
 And let us hear Bernardo speak of this.

BERNARDO. Last night of all,°
 When yond same star that's westward from the pole°   40
 Had made his° course t' illume° that part of heaven
 Where now it burns, Marcellus and myself,
 The bell then beating one—

Enter GHOST.

MARCELLUS. Peace, break thee off! Look where it comes again!

BERNARDO. In the same figure like the King that's dead.   45

MARCELLUS. Thou art a scholar.° Speak to it, Horatio.

BERNARDO. Looks 'a° not like the King? Mark it, Horatio.

HORATIO. Most like. It harrows me with fear and wonder.

BERNARDO. It would be spoke to.°

MARCELLUS.   Speak to it, Horatio.

HORATIO. What art thou that usurp'st° this time of night,   50
 Together with that fair and warlike form
 In which the majesty of buried Denmark°
 Did sometime° march? By heaven, I charge thee, speak!

MARCELLUS. It is offended.

BERNARDO.   See, it stalks away.

---

27 **fantasy** imagination. 30 **along** to come along. 31 **watch** keep watch during.
33 **approve** corroborate. 37 **What** with what. 39 **Last . . . all** i.e., this *very* last
night. (Emphatic.) 40 **pole** polestar, north star. 41 **his** its. **illume** illuminate.
46 **scholar** one learned enough to know how to question a ghost properly. 47 **'a** he.
49 **It . . . to** (It was commonly believed that a ghost could not speak until spoken to.)
50 **usurp'st** wrongfully takes over. 52 **buried Denmark** the buried King of Denmark.
53 **sometime** formerly.

HORATIO. Stay! Speak, speak! I charge thee, speak!   55

Exit GHOST.

MARCELLUS. 'Tis gone and will not answer.

BERNARDO. How now, Horatio? You tremble and look pale.
Is not this something more than fantasy?
What think you on 't?°

HORATIO. Before my God, I might not this believe   60
Without the sensible° and true avouch°
Of mine own eyes.

MARCELLUS.   Is it not like the King?

HORATIO. As thou art to thyself.
Such was the very armor he had on
When he the ambitious Norway° combated.   65
So frowned he once when, in an angry parle,°
He smote the sledded° Polacks° on the ice.
'Tis strange.

MARCELLUS. Thus twice before, and jump° at this dead hour,
With martial stalk° hath he gone by our watch.   70

HORATIO. In what particular thought to work° I know not,
But in the gross and scope° of mine opinion
This bodes some strange eruption to our state.

MARCELLUS. Good now,° sit down, and tell me, he that knows,
Why this same strict and most observant watch   75
So nightly toils° the subject° of the land,
And why such daily cast° of brazen cannon
And foreign mart° for implements of war,
Why such impress° of shipwrights, whose sore task
Does not divide the Sunday from the week.   80
What might be toward,° that this sweaty haste
Doth make the night joint-laborer with the day?
Who is 't that can inform me?

HORATIO.   That can I;
At least, the whisper goes so. Our last king,
Whose image even but now appeared to us,   85
Was, as you know, by Fortinbras of Norway,
Thereto pricked on° by a most emulate° pride,°
Dared to the combat; in which our valiant Hamlet—
For so this side of our known world° esteemed him—
Did slay this Fortinbras; who by a sealed° compact   90
Well ratified by law and heraldry
Did forfeit, with his life, all those his lands

---

59 on 't of it. **61 sensible** confirmed by the senses. **avouch** warrant, evidence.
65 Norway King of Norway. **66 parle** parley. **67 sledded** traveling on sleds.
Polacks Poles. **69 jump** exactly. **70 stalk** stride. **71 to work** i.e., to collect my
thoughts and try to understand this. **72 gross and scope** general drift. **74 Good now**
(An expression denoting entreaty or expostulation.) **76 toils** causes to toil. **subject**
subjects. **77 cast** casting. **78 mart** buying and selling. **79 impress** impressment,
conscription. **81 toward** in preparation. **87 pricked on** incited. **emulate** emulous,
ambitious. **Thereto . . . pride** (Refers to old Fortinbras, not the Danish King.)
89 this . . . world i.e., all Europe, the Western world. **90 sealed** certified, confirmed.

Which he stood seized° of, to the conqueror;
Against the° which a moiety competent°
Was gagèd° by our king, which had returned°   95
To the inheritance° of Fortinbras
Had he been vanquisher, as, by the same cov'nant°
And carriage of the article designed,°
His fell to Hamlet. Now, sir, young Fortinbras,
Of unimprovèd mettle° hot and full,   100
Hath in the skirts° of Norway here and there
Sharked up° a list° of lawless resolutes°
For food and diet° to some enterprise
That hath a stomach° in 't, which is no other—
As it doth well appear unto our state—   105
But to recover of us, by strong hand
And terms compulsatory, those foresaid lands
So by his father lost. And this, I take it,
Is the main motive of our preparations,
The source of this our watch, and the chief head°   110
Of this posthaste and rummage° in the land.
BERNARDO. I think it be no other but e'en so.
Well may it sort° that this portentous figure
Comes armèd through our watch so like the King
That was and is the question° of these wars.   115
HORATIO. A mote° it is to trouble the mind's eye.
In the most high and palmy° state of Rome,
A little ere the mightiest Julius fell,
The graves stood tenantless, and the sheeted° dead
Did squeak and gibber in the Roman streets;   120
As° stars with trains° of fire and dews of blood,
Disasters° in the sun; and the moist star°
Upon whose influence Neptune's° empire stands°
Was sick almost to doomsday° with eclipse.
And even the like precurse° of feared events,   125
As harbingers° preceding still° the fates

---

93 **seized** possessed. 94 **Against the** in return for. **moiety competent** corresponding portion. 95 **gagèd** engaged, pledged. **had returned** would have passed.
96 **inheritance** possession. 97 **cov'nant** i.e., the *sealed compact* of line 90. 98 **carriage . . . designed** carrying out of the article or clause drawn up to cover the point.
100 **unimprovèd mettle** untried, undisciplined spirits. 101 **skirts** outlying regions,
outskirts. 102 **Sharked up** gathered up, as a shark takes fish. **list** i.e., troop.
resolutes desperadoes. 103 **For food and diet** i.e., they are to serve as *food,*
or "means," *to some enterprise;* also they serve in return for the rations they get.
104 **stomach** (1) a spirit of daring (2) an appetite that is fed by the *lawless resolutes.*
110 **head** source. 111 **rummage** bustle, commotion. 113 **sort** suit. 115 **question**
focus of contention. 116 **mote** speck of dust. 117 **palmy** flourishing. 119 **sheeted**
shrouded. 121 **As** (This abrupt transition suggests that matter is possibly omitted between lines 120 and 121.) **trains** trails. 122 **Disasters** unfavorable signs or aspects.
moist star i.e., moon, governing tides. 123 **Neptune** god of the sea. **stands** depends. 124 **sick . . . doomsday** (See Matthew 24.29 and Revelation 6.12.) 125 **pre-
curse** heralding, foreshadowing. 126 **harbingers** forerunners. **still** continually.

And prologue to the omen° coming on,
Have heaven and earth together demonstrated
Unto our climatures° and countrymen.

Enter GHOST.

But soft,° behold! Lo, where it comes again!   130
I'll cross° it, though it blast° me. [*It spreads his° arms.*]
   Stay, *illusion!*
If thou hast any sound or use of voice,
Speak to me!
If there be any good thing to be done
That may to thee do ease and grace to me,   135
Speak to me!
If thou art privy to° thy country's fate,
Which happily,° foreknowing may avoid,
O, speak!
Or if thou hast uphoarded in thy life   140
Extorted treasure in the womb of earth,
For which, they say, you spirits oft walk in death,
Speak of it! [*The cock crows.*] Stay and speak!—Stop it, Marcellus.

MARCELLUS. Shall I strike at it with my partisan?°
HORATIO. Do, if it will not stand.   [*They strike at it.*] 145
BERNARDO. 'Tis here!
HORATIO. 'Tis here!   [*Exit* GHOST.]
MARCELLUS. 'Tis gone.
   We do it wrong, being so majestical,
   To offer it the show of violence,   150
   For it is as the air invulnerable,
   And our vain blows malicious mockery.
BERNARDO. It was about to speak when the cock crew.
HORATIO. And then it started like a guilty thing
   Upon a fearful summons. I have heard   155
   The cock, that is the trumpet° to the morn,
   Doth with his lofty and shrill-standing throat
   Awake the god of day, and at his warning,
   Whether in sea or fire, in earth or air,
   Th' extravagant and erring° spirit hies°   160
   To his confine; and of the truth herein
   This present object made probation.°
MARCELLUS. It faded on the crowing of the cock.
   Some say that ever 'gainst° that season comes
   Wherein our Savior's birth is celebrated,   165
   This bird of dawning singeth all night long,
   And then, they say, no spirit dare stir abroad;

---

127 omen calamitous event.   **129 climatures** regions.   **130 soft** i.e., enough, break
off.   **131 cross** stand in its path, confront.   **blast** wither, strike with a curse.   **s.d. his**
its.   **137 privy to** in on the secret of.   **138 happily** haply, perchance.   **144 partisan**
long-handled spear.   **156 trumpet** trumpeter.   **160 extravagant and erring** wandering beyond bounds. (The words have similar meaning.)   **160 hies** hastens.   **162 probation** proof.   **164 'gainst** just before.

The nights are wholesome, then no planets strike,°
No fairy takes,° nor witch hath power to charm,
So hallowed and so gracious° is that time.   170
HORATIO. So have I heared and do in part believe it.
But, look, the morn in russet mantle clad
Walks o'er the dew of yon high eastward hill.
Break we our watch up, and by my advice
Let us impart what we have seen tonight   175
Unto young Hamlet; for upon my life,
This spirit, dumb to us, will speak to him.
Do you consent we shall acquaint him with it,
As needful in our loves, fitting our duty?
MARCELLUS. Let's do 't, I pray, and I this morning know   180
Where we shall find him most conveniently.

                                                      Exeunt.

1.2 *Flourish. Enter* CLAUDIUS, *King of Denmark,* GERTRUDE *the*
       Queen, [*the*] *Council, as*° POLONIUS *and his son,* LAERTES,
       HAMLET, *cum aliis*° [*including* VOLTIMAND *and* CORNELIUS].

KING. Though yet of Hamlet our° dear brother's death
The memory be green, and that it us befitted
To bear our hearts in grief and our whole kingdom
To be contracted in one brow of woe,
Yet so far hath discretion fought with nature   5
That we with wisest sorrow think on him
Together with remembrance of ourselves
Therefore our sometime° sister, now our queen,
Th' imperial jointress° to this warlike state,
Have we, as 'twere with a defeated joy—   10
With an auspicious and a dropping eye,°
With mirth in funeral and with dirge in marriage,
In equal scale weighing delight and dole°—
Taken to wife: nor have we herein barred
Your better wisdoms, which have freely gone   15
With this affair along. For all, our thanks.
Now follows that you know° young Fortinbras,
Holding a weak supposal° of our worth,
Or thinking by our late dear brother's death
Our state to be disjoint and out of frame,   20
Co-leaguèd with° this dream of his advantage,°
He hath not failed to pester us with message

---

168 strike destroy by evil influence. **169 takes** bewitches. **170 gracious** full of
grace. **1.2. Location: The castle. s.d. as** i.e., such as, including. **cum aliis** with
others. **1 our** my. (The royal "we"; also in the following lines.) **8 sometime** former.
9 jointress woman possessing property with her husband. **11 With . . . eye** with one
eye smiling and the other weeping. **13 dole** grief. **17 that you know** what you
know already, that; or, that you be informed as follows. **18 weak supposal** low
estimate. **21 Co-leaguèd with** joined to, allied with. **dream . . . advantage** illusory
hope of having the advantage. (His only ally is this hope.)

Importing° the surrender of those lands
Lost by his father, with all bonds° of law,
To our most valiant brother. So much for him.   25
Now for ourself and for this time of meeting.
Thus much the business is: we have here writ
To Norway, uncle of young Fortinbras—
Who, impotent° and bed-rid, scarcely hears
Of this his nephew's purpose—to suppress   30
His° further gait° herein, in that the levies,
The lists, and full proportions are all made
Out of his subject,° and we here dispatch
You, good Cornelius, and you, Voltimand,
For bearers of this greeting to old Norway,   35
Giving to you no further personal power
To business with the king more than the scope
Of these dilated° articles allow.   [*He gives a paper.*]
Farewell, and let your haste commend your duty.°

CORNELIUS, VOLTIMAND. In that, and all things, will we show our duty.   40
KING. We doubt it nothing.° Heartily farewell.

                              [*Exeunt* VOLTIMAND *and* CORNELIUS.]

And now, Laertes, what's the news with you?
You told us of some suit; what is 't, Laertes?
You cannot speak of reason to the Dane°
And lose your voice.° What wouldst thou beg, Laertes,   45
That shall not be my offer, not thy asking?
The head is not more native° to the heart,
The hand more instrumental° to the mouth,
Than is the throne of Denmark to thy father.
What wouldst thou have, Laertes?

LAERTES.   My dread lord,   50
Your leave and favor° to return to France,
From whence though willingly I came to Denmark
To show my duty in your coronation,
Yet now I must confess, that duty done,
My thoughts and wishes bend again toward France   55
And bow them to your gracious leave and pardon.°

KING. Have you your father's leave? What says Polonius?
POLONIUS. H'ath,° my lord, wrung from me my slow leave
By laborsome petition, and at last
Upon his will I sealed° my hard° consent.   60
I do beseech you, give him leave to go.

---

23 Importing pertaining to. **24 bonds** contracts. **29 impotent** helpless. **31 His**
i.e., Fortinbras's. **gait** proceeding. **31–33 in that . . . subject** since the levying of
troops and supplies is drawn entirely from the King of Norway's own subjects.
38 dilated set out at length. **39 let . . . duty** let your swift obeying of orders, rather
than mere words, express your dutifulness. **41 nothing** not at all. **44 the Dane**
the Danish king. **45 lose your voice** waste your speech. **47 native** closely connected, related. **48 instrumental** serviceable. **51 leave and favor** kind permission.
56 bow . . . pardon entreatingly make a deep bow, asking your permission to depart.
58 H'ath he has. **60 sealed** (as if sealing a legal document). **hard** reluctant.

KING. Take thy fair hour,° Laertes. Time be thine,
    And thy best graces spend it at thy will!°
    But now, my cousin° Hamlet, and my son—
HAMLET. A little more than kin, and less than kind.°   65
KING. How is it that the clouds still hang on you?
HAMLET. Not so, my lord. I am too much in the sun.°
QUEEN. Good Hamlet, cast thy nighted color° off,
    And let thine eye look like a friend on Denmark.°
    Do not forever with thy vailèd lids°   70
    Seek for thy noble father in the dust.
    Thou know'st 'tis common,° all that lives must die,
    Passing through nature to eternity.
HAMLET. Ay, madam, it is common.
QUEEN.   If it be,
    Why seems it so particular° with thee?   75
HAMLET. Seems, madam? Nay, it is. I know not "seems."
    'Tis not alone my inky cloak, good Mother,
    Nor customary° suits of solemn black,
    Nor windy suspiration° of forced breath,
    No, nor the fruitful° river in the eye,   80
    Nor the dejected havior° of the visage,
    Together with all forms, moods,° shapes of grief,
    That can denote me truly. These indeed seem,
    For they are actions that a man might play.
    But I have that within which passes show;   85
    These but the trappings and the suits of woe.
KING. 'Tis sweet and commendable in your nature, Hamlet,
    To give these mourning duties to your father.
    But you must know your father lost a father,
    That father lost, lost his, and the survivor bound   90
    In filial obligation for some term
    To do obsequious° sorrow. But to persever°
    In obstinate condolement° is a course
    Of impious stubbornness. 'Tis unmanly grief.
    It shows a will most incorrect to heaven,   95

---

62 Take thy fair hour enjoy your time of youth. **63 And . . . will** and may your finest
qualities guide the way you choose to spend your time. **64 cousin** any kin not of the
immediate family. **65 A little . . . kind** i.e., closer than an ordinary nephew (since I am
stepson), and yet more separated in natural feeling (with pun on *kind* meaning "affectionate" and "natural," "lawful"). This line is often read as an aside, but it need not be. The
King chooses perhaps not to respond to Hamlet's cryptic and bitter remark. **67 the sun**
i.e., the sunshine of the King's royal favor (with pun on *son*). **68 nighted color** (1)
mourning garments of black (2) dark melancholy. **69 Denmark** the King of Denmark.
70 vailèd lids lowered eyes. **72 common** of universal occurrence. (But Hamlet plays
on the sense of "vulgar" in line 74.) **75 particular** personal. **78 customary** (1) socially conventional (2) habitual with me. **79 suspiration** sighing. **80 fruitful** abundant. **81 havior** expression. **82 moods** outward expression of feeling. **92
obsequious** suited to obsequies or funerals. **persever** persevere. **93 condolement**
sorrowing.

    A heart unfortified,° a mind impatient,
    An understanding simple° and unschooled.
    For what we know must be and is as common
    As any the most vulgar thing to sense,°
    Why should we in our peevish opposition   100
    Take it to heart? Fie, 'tis a fault to heaven,
    A fault against the dead, a fault to nature,
    To reason most absurd, whose common theme
    Is death of fathers, and who still° hath cried,
    From the first corpse° till he that died today,   105
    "This must be so." We pray you, throw to earth
    This unprevailing° woe and think of us
    As of a father; for let the world take note,
    You are the most immediate° to our throne,
    And with no less nobility of love   110
    Than that which dearest father bears his son
    Do I impart toward° you. For° your intent
    In going back to school° in Wittenberg,°
    It is most retrograde° to our desire,
    And we beseech you bend you° to remain   115
    Here in the cheer and comfort of our eye,
    Our chiefest courtier, cousin, and our son.
QUEEN. Let not thy mother lose her prayers, Hamlet.
    I pray thee, stay with us, go not to Wittenberg.
HAMLET. I shall in all my best° obey you, madam.   120
KING. Why 'tis a loving and a fair reply.
    Be as ourself in Denmark. Madam, come.
    This gentle and unforced accord of Hamlet
    Sits smiling to° my heart, in grace° whereof
    No jocund° health that Denmark drinks today   125
    But the great cannon to the clouds shall tell,
    And the King's rouse° the heaven shall bruit again,°
    Respeaking earthly thunder.° Come away.

                     Flourish. Exeunt all but HAMLET.

HAMLET. O, that this too too sullied° flesh would melt,
    Thaw, and resolve itself into a dew!   130
    Or that the Everlasting had not fixed
    His canon° 'gainst self-slaughter! O God, God,
    How weary, stale, flat, and unprofitable
    Seem to me all the uses° of this world!

---

96 unfortified i.e., against adversity.   **97 simple** ignorant.   **99 As . . . sense** as the most ordinary experience.   **104 still** always.   **105 the first corpse** (Abel's).   **107 unprevailing** unavailing, useless.   **109 most immediate** next in succession.   **112 impart toward** i.e., bestow my affection on.   **For** as for.   **113 to school** i.e., to your studies. **113 Wittenberg** famous German university founded in 1502.   **114 retrograde** contrary. **115 bend you** incline yourself.   **120 in all my best** to the best of my ability.   **124 to** i.e., at. **grace** thanksgiving.   **125 jocund** merry.   **127 rouse** drinking of a draft of liquor. **bruit again** loudly echo.   **128 thunder** i.e., of trumpet and kettledrum, sounded when the King drinks; see 1.4.8–12.   **129 sullied** defiled. (The early quartos read *sallied;* the Folio, *solid.*)   **132 canon** law.   **134 all the uses** the whole routine.

Fie on 't, ah fie! 'Tis an unweeded garden   135
That grows to seed. Things rank and gross in nature
Possess it merely.° That it should come to this!
But two months dead—nay, not so much, not two.
So excellent a king, that was to° this
Hyperion° to a satyr,° so loving to my mother   140
That he might not beteem° the winds of heaven
Visit her face too roughly. Heaven and earth,
Must I remember? Why, she would hang on him
As if increase of appetite had grown
By what it fed on, and yet within a month—   145
Let me not think of 't; frailty, thy name is woman!—
A little month, or ere° those shoes were old
With which she followed my poor father's body,
Like Niobe;° all tears, why she, even she—
O God, a beast, that wants discourse of reason,°   150
Would have mourned longer—married with my uncle,
My father's brother, but no more like my father
Than I to Hercules. Within a month,
Ere yet the sale of most unrighteous tears
Had left the flushing in her gallèd° eyes,   155
She married. O, most wicked speed, to post°
With such dexterity to incestuous° sheets!
It is not, nor it cannot come to good.
But break, my heart, for I must hold my tongue.

Enter HORATIO, MARCELLUS *and* BERNARDO.

HORATIO. Hail to your lordship!
HAMLET.   I am glad to see you well.   160
    Horatio—or I do forget myself.
HORATIO. The same, my lord, and your poor servant ever.
HAMLET. Sir, my good friend; I'll change that name° with you.
    And what make you from° Wittenberg, Horatio?
    Marcellus.   165
MARCELLUS. My good lord.
HAMLET. I am very glad to see you. [*To* BERNARDO.] Good even, sir.—
    But what in faith make you from Wittenberg?
HORATIO. A truant disposition, good my lord.
HAMLET. I would not hear your enemy say so,   170

---

137 **merely** completely.   139 **to** in comparison to.   140 **Hyperion** Titan sun-god, father of Helios.   **satyr** a lecherous creature of classical mythology, half-human but with a
goat's legs, tail, ears, and horns.   141 **beteem** allow.   147 **or ere** even before.   149
Niobe Tantalus' daughter, Queen of Thebes, who boasted that she had more sons and
daughters than Leto; for this, Apollo and Artemis, children of Leto, slew her fourteen children. She was turned by Zeus into a stone that continually dropped tears.   150 **wants . . .**
reason lacks the faculty of reason.   155 **gallèd** irritated, inflamed.   156 **post** hasten.
157 **incestuous** (In Shakespeare's day, the marriage of a man like Claudius to his deceased brother's wife was considered incestuous.)   163 **change that name** i.e., give
and receive reciprocally the name of "friend" (rather than talk of "servant").   164 **make**
you from are you doing away from.

Nor shall you do my ear that violence
To make it truster of your own report
Against yourself. I know you are no truant.
But what is your affair in Elsinore?
We'll teach you to drink deep ere you depart.   175

HORATIO. My lord, I came to see your father's funeral.

HAMLET. I prithee, do not mock me, fellow student;
I think it was to see my mother's wedding.

HORATIO. Indeed, my lord, it followed hard° upon.

HAMLET. Thrift, thrift, Horatio! The funeral baked meats°   180
Did coldly° furnish forth the marriage tables.
Would I had met my dearest° foe in heaven
Or ever° I had seen that day, Horatio.
My father—Methinks I see my father.

HORATIO. Where, my lord?

HAMLET.   In my mind's eye, Horatio.   185

HORATIO. I saw him once. 'A° was a goodly king.

HAMLET. 'A was a man. Take him for all in all,
I shall not look upon his like again.

HORATIO. My lord, I think I saw him yesternight.

HAMLET. Saw? Who?   190

HORATIO. My lord, the King your father.

HAMLET. The King my father?

HORATIO. Season your admiration° for a while
With an attent° ear till I may deliver,
Upon the witness of these gentlemen,   195
This marvel to you.

HAMLET.   For God's love, let me hear!

HORATIO. Two nights together had these gentlemen,
Marcellus and Bernardo, on their watch,
In the dead waste° and middle of the night,
Been thus encountered. A figure like your father,   200
Armèd at point° exactly, cap-à-pie,°
Appears before them, and with solemn march
Goes slow and stately by them. Thrice he walked
By their oppressed and fear-surprisèd eyes
Within his truncheon's° length, whilst they, distilled°   205
Almost to jelly with the act° of fear,
Stand dumb and speak not to him. This to me
In dreadful° secrecy impart they did,
And I with them the third night kept the watch,
Where, as they had delivered, both in time,   210
Form of the thing, each word made true and good,
The apparition comes. I knew your father;

---

179 hard close.   **180 baked meats** meat pies.   **181 coldly** i.e., as cold leftovers.   **182
dearest** closest (and therefore deadliest).   **183 Or ever** before.   **186 'A** he.   **193
Season your admiration** restrain your astonishment.   **194 attent** attentive.   **199 dead
waste** desolate stillness.   **201 at point** correctly in every detail.   **cap-à-pie** from head
to foot.   **205 truncheon** officer's staff.   **distilled** dissolved.   **206 act** action, operation.   **208 dreadful** full of dread.

These hands are not more like.

HAMLET.   But where was this?

MARCELLUS. My lord, upon the platform where we watch.

HAMLET. Did you not speak to it?

HORATIO.   My lord, I did,   215
   But answer made it none. Yet once methought
   It lifted up its head and did address
   Itself to motion, like as it would speak;°
   But even then° the morning cock crew loud,
   And at the sound it shrunk in haste away   220
   And vanished from our sight.

HAMLET.   'Tis very strange.

HORATIO. As I do live, my honoured lord, 'tis true,
   And we did think it writ down in our duty
   To let you know of it.

HAMLET. Indeed, indeed, sirs. But this troubles me.   225
   Hold you the watch tonight?

ALL.   We do, my lord.

HAMLET. Armed, say you?

ALL. Armed, my lord.

HAMLET. From top to toe?

ALL. My lord, from head to foot.   230

HAMLET. Then saw you not his face?

HORATIO. O, yes, my lord, he wore his beaver° up.

HAMLET. What° looked he, frowningly?

HORATIO. A countenance more in sorrow than in anger.

HAMLET. Pale or red?   235

HORATIO. Nay, very pale.

HAMLET. And fixed his eyes upon you?

HORATIO. Most constantly.

HAMLET. I would I had been there.

HORATIO. It would have much amazed you.   240

HAMLET. Very like, very like. Stayed it long?

HORATIO. While one with moderate haste might tell° a hundred.

MARCELLUS, BERNARDO. Longer, longer.

HORATIO. Not when I saw't.

HAMLET. His beard was grizzled°—no?   245

HORATIO. It was, as I have seen it in his life,
   A sable silvered.°

HAMLET.   I will watch tonight.
   Perchance 'twill walk again.

HORATIO.   I warrant° it will.

HAMLET. If it assume my noble father's person,
   I'll speak to it though hell itself should gape   250
   And bid me hold my peace. I pray you all,

217–218 did . . . speak began to move as though it were about to speak. **219 even
then** at that very instant. **232 beaver** visor on the helmet. **233 What** how. **242 tell**
count. **245 grizzled** gray. **247 sable silvered** black mixed with white. **248 warrant**
assure you.

If you have hitherto concealed this sight,
Let it be tenable° in your silence still,
And whatsoever else shall hap tonight,
Give it an understanding but no tongue.   255
I will requite your loves. So, fare you well.
Upon the platform twixt eleven and twelve
I'll visit you.

ALL.   Our duty to your honor.

HAMLET. Your loves, as mine to you. Farewell.

                          Exeunt [all but HAMLET].

My father's spirit in arms! All is not well.   260
I doubt° some foul play. Would the night were come!
Till then sit still, my soul. Foul deeds will rise,
Though all the earth o'erwhelm them, to men's eyes.

                                        Exit.

1.3 *Enter* LAERTES *and* OPHELIA, *his sister.*

LAERTES. My necessaries are embarked. Farewell.
And, sister, as the winds give benefit
And convoy is assistant,° do not sleep
But let me hear from you.

OPHELIA.   Do you doubt that?

LAERTES. For Hamlet, and the trifling of his favor,   5
Hold it a fashion and a toy in blood,°
A violet in the youth of primy° nature,
Forward,° not permanent, sweet, not lasting,
The perfume and suppliance° of a minute—
No more.

OPHELIA.   No more but so?

LAERTES.   Think it no more.   10
For nature crescent° does not grow alone
In thews° and bulk, but as this temple° waxes
The inward service of the mind and soul
Grows wide withal.° Perhaps he loves you now,
And now no soil° nor cautel° doth besmirch   15
The virtue of his will,° but you must fear,
His greatness weighed,° his will is not his own.
For he himself is subject to his birth.
He may not, as unvalued persons do,
Carve° for himself, for on his choice depends   20
The safety and health of this whole state,
And therefore must his choice be circumscribed

---

253 **tenable** held. 261 **doubt** suspect. **1.3. Location: Polonius' chambers. 3
convoy is assistant** means of conveyance are available. 6 **toy in blood** passing
amorous fancy. 7 **primy** in its prime, springtime. 8 **Forward** precocious. 9 **sup-
pliance** supply, filler. 11 **crescent** growing, waxing. 12 **thews** bodily strength.
temple i.e., body. 14 **Grows wide withal** grows along with it. 15 **soil** blemish.
cautel deceit. 16 **will** desire. 17 **His greatness weighed** if you take into account his
high position. 20 **Carve** i.e., choose.

Unto the voice and yielding° of that body
Whereof he is the head. Then if he says he loves you,
It fits your wisdom so far to believe it   25
As he in his particular act and place°
May give his saying deed, which is no further
Than the main voice° of Denmark goes withal.°
Then weigh what loss your honor may sustain
If with too credent° ear you list° his songs,   30
Or lose your heart, or your chaste treasure open
To his unmastered importunity.
Fear it, Ophelia, fear it, my dear sister,
And keep you in the rear of your affection,°
Out of the shot and danger of desire.   35
The chariest° maid is prodigal enough
If she unmask° her beauty to the moon.°
Virtue itself scapes not calumnious strokes.
The canker galls° the infants of the spring
Too oft before their buttons° be disclosed,°   40
And in the morn and liquid dew° of youth
Contagious blastments° are most imminent.
Be wary then; best safety lies in fear.
Youth to itself rebels,° though none else near.

OPHELIA.   I shall the effect of this good lesson keep   45
As watchman to my heart. But, good my brother,
Do not, as some ungracious° pastors do,
Show me the steep and thorny way to heaven,
Whiles like a puffed° and reckless libertine
Himself the primrose path of dalliance treads,   50
And recks° not his own rede.°

Enter POLONIUS.

LAERTES.   O, fear me not.°
I stay too long. But here my father comes.
A double° blessing is a double grace;
Occasion smiles upon a second leave.°

POLONIUS.   Yet here, Laertes? Aboard, aboard, for shame!   55
The wind sits in the shoulder of your sail,
And you are stayed for. There—my blessing with thee!

---

23 **voice and yielding** assent, approval.   26 **in . . . place** in his particular restricted circumstances.   28 **main voice** general assent.   **withal** along with.   30 **credent** credulous.   **list** listen to.   34 **keep . . . affection** don't advance as far as your affection might
lead you. (A military metaphor.)   36 **chariest** most scrupulously modest.   37 **If she**
unmask if she does no more than show her beauty.   **moon** (Symbol of chastity.)   39
canker galls canker-worm destroys.   40 **buttons** buds.   **disclosed** opened.   41 **liquid**
dew i.e., time when dew is fresh and bright.   42 **blastments** blights.   44 **Youth . . .**
rebels youth is inherently rebellious.   47 **ungracious** ungodly.   49 **puffed** bloated, or
swollen with pride.   51 **recks** heeds.   **rede** counsel.   **fear me not** don't worry on my
account.   53 **double** (Laertes has already bid his father good-bye.)   54 **Occasion . . .**
leave happy is the circumstance that provides a second leave-taking. (The goddess Occasion, or Opportunity, smiles.)

And these few precepts in thy memory
Look° thou character.° Give thy thoughts no tongue,
Nor any unproportioned° thought his° act.   60
Be thou familiar,° but by no means vulgar.°
Those friends thou hast, and their adoption tried,°
Grapple them unto thy soul with hoops of steel,
But do not dull thy palm° with entertainment
Of each new-hatched, unfledged courage.° Beware   65
Of entrance to a quarrel, but being in,
Bear 't that° th' opposèd may beware of thee.
Give every man thy ear, but few thy voice;
Take each man's censure,° but reserve thy judgment.
Costly thy habit° as thy purse can buy,   70
But not expressed in fancy;° rich, not gaudy,
For the apparel oft proclaims the man,
And they in France of the best rank and station
Are of a most select and generous chief in that.°
Neither a borrower nor a lender be,   75
For loan oft loses both itself and friend,
And borrowing dulleth edge of husbandry.°
This above all: to thine own self be true,
And it must follow, as the night the day,
Thou canst not then be false to any man.   80
Farewell. My blessing season° this in thee!
LAERTES. Most humbly do I take my leave, my lord.
POLONIUS. The time invests° you. Go, your servants tend.°
LAERTES. Farewell, Ophelia, and remember well
What I have said to you.   85
OPHELIA. 'Tis in my memory locked,
And you yourself shall keep the key of it.
LAERTES. Farewell.

                                                    Exit LAERTES.

POLONIUS. What is 't, Ophelia, he hath said to you?
OPHELIA. So please you, something touching the Lord Hamlet.   90
POLONIUS. Marry,° well bethought.
'Tis told me he hath very oft of late
Given private time to you, and you yourself
Have of your audience been most free and bounteous.
If it be so—as so 'tis put on° me,   95
And that in way of caution—I must tell you

---

59 Look be sure that. **character** inscribe. **60 unproportioned** badly calculated, intemperate. **his** its. **61 familiar** sociable. **vulgar** common. **62 and their adoption tried** and also their suitability for adoption as friends having been tested. **64 dull thy palm** i.e., shake hands so often as to make the gesture meaningless. **65 courage** young man of spirit. **67 Bear 't that** manage it so that. **69 censure** opinion, judgment. **70 habit** clothing. **71 fancy** excessive ornament, decadent fashion. **74 Are . . . that** are of a most refined and well-bred preeminence in choosing what to wear. **77 husbandry** thrift. **81 season** mature. **83 invests** besieges, presses upon. **tend** attend, wait. **91 Marry** i.e., by the Virgin Mary. (A mild oath.) **95 put on** impressed on, told to.

You do not understand yourself so clearly
As it behooves° my daughter and your honor.
What is between you? Give me up the truth.

OPHELIA. He hath, my lord, of late made many tenders°   100
Of his affection to me.

POLONIUS. Affection? Pooh! You speak like a green girl,
Unsifted° in such perilous circumstance.
Do you believe his tenders, as you call them?

OPHELIA. I do not know, my lord, what I should think.   105

POLONIUS. Marry, I will teach you. Think yourself a baby
That you have ta'en these tenders for true pay
Which are not sterling.° Tender° yourself more dearly,
Or—not to crack the wind° of the poor phrase,
Running it thus—you'll tender me a fool.°   110

OPHELIA. My lord, he hath importuned me with love
In honorable fashion.

POLONIUS. Ay, fashion° you may call it. Go to,° go to.

OPHELIA. And hath given countenance° to his speech, my lord,
With almost all the holy vows of heaven.   115

POLONIUS. Ay, springes° to catch woodcocks.° I do know,
When the blood burns, how prodigal° the soul
Lends the tongue vows. These blazes, daughter,
Giving more light than heat, extinct in both
Even in their promise as it° is a-making,   120
You must not take for fire. From this time
Be something° scanter of your maiden presence.
Set your entreatments° at a higher rate
Than a command to parle.° For Lord Hamlet,
Believe so much in him° that he is young,   125
And with a larger tether may he walk
Than may be given you. In few,° Ophelia,
Do not believe his vows, for they are brokers,°
Not of that dye° which their investments° show,
But mere implorators° of unholy suits,   130
Breathing° like sanctified and pious bawds,

---

98 behooves befits.   **100 tenders** offers.   **103 Unsifted** i.e., untried.   **108 sterling** legal currency.   **Tender** hold, look after, offer.   **109 crack the wind** i.e., run it until it is broken-winded.   **110 tender me a fool** (1) show yourself to me as a fool (2) show me up as a fool (3) present me with a grandchild. (*Fool* was a term of endearment for a child.)   **113 fashion** mere form, pretense.   **Go to** (An expression of impatience.)   **114 countenance** credit, confirmation.   **116 springes** snares.   **woodcocks** birds easily caught; here used to connote gullibility.   **117 prodigal** prodigally.   **120 it** i.e., the promise.   **122 something** somewhat.   **123 entreatments** negotiations for surrender. (A military term.)   **124 parle** discuss terms with the enemy. (Polonius urges his daughter, in the metaphor of military language, not to meet with Hamlet and consider giving in to him merely because he requests an interview.)   **125 so . . . him** this much concerning him.   **127 In few** briefly.   **128 brokers** go-betweens, procurers.   **129 dye** color or sort.   **investments** clothes. (The vows are not what they seem.)   **130 mere implorators** out-and-out solicitors.   **131 Breathing** speaking.

The better to beguile. This is for all:°
I would not, in plain terms, from this time forth
Have you so slander° any moment° leisure
As to give words or talk with the Lord Hamlet.   135
Look to 't, I charge you. Come your ways.°

OPHELIA. I shall obey, my lord.

Exeunt.

1.4 *Enter* HAMLET, HORATIO, *and* MARCELLUS.

HAMLET. The air bites shrewdly,° it is very cold.

HORATIO. It is a nipping and eager° air.

HAMLET. What hour now?

HORATIO.   I think it lacks of° twelve.

MARCELLUS. No, it is struck.

HORATIO.   Indeed? I heard it not.
It then draws near the season°   5
Wherein the spirit held his wont° to walk.
        A flourish of trumpets, and two pieces° go off [*within*].
What does this mean, my lord?

HAMLET. The King doth wake° tonight and takes his rouse,°
Keeps wassail,° and the swaggering upspring° reels,°
And as he drains his drafts of Rhenish° down,   10
The kettledrum and trumpet thus bray out
The triumph of his pledge.°

HORATIO.   It is a custom?

HAMLET. Ay, marry, is't,
But to my mind, though I am native here
And to my manner° born, it is a custom   15
More honored in the breach than the observance.°
This heavy-headed revel east and west°
Makes us traduced and taxed of° other nations.
They clepe° us drunkards, and with swinish phrase°
Soil our addition;° and indeed it takes   20
From our achievements, though performed at height,°
The pith and marrow of our attribute.°
So, oft it chances in particular men,
That for° some vicious mole of nature° in them,
As in their birth—wherein they are not guilty,   25

---

132 **for all** once for all, in sum.   134 **slander** abuse, misuse.   **moment** moment's.
136 **Come your ways** come along.   **1.4. Location: The guard platform. 1
shrewdly** keenly, sharply.   2 **eager** biting.   3 **lacks of** is just short of.   5 **season** time.
6 **held his wont** was accustomed.   **s.d. pieces** i.e., of ordnance, cannon.   8 **wake** stay
awake and hold revel.   **takes his rouse** carouses.   9 **wassail** carousal.   **upspring**
wild German dance.   **reels** dances.   10 **Rhenish** Rhine wine.   12 **The triumph . . .
pledge** i.e., his feat in draining the wine in a single draft.   15 **manner** custom (of drinking).   16 **More . . . observance** better neglected than followed.   17 **east and west**
i.e., everywhere.   18 **taxed of** censured by.   19 **clepe** call.   **with swinish phrase**
i.e., by calling us swine.   20 **addition** reputation.   21 **at height** outstandingly.   22
The pith . . . attribute the essence of the reputation that others attribute to us.   24 **for**
on account of.   **mole of nature** natural blemish in one's constitution.

Since nature cannot choose his° origin—
By their o'ergrowth of some complexion,°
Oft breaking down the pales° and forts of reason,
Or by some habit that too much o'erleavens°
The form of plausive° manners, that these men,   30
Carrying, I say, the stamp of one defect,
Being nature's livery° or fortune's star,°
His virtues else,° be they as pure as grace,
As infinite as man may undergo,°
Shall in the general censure° take corruption   35
From that particular fault. The dram of evil
Doth all the noble substance often dout
To his own scandal.°

Enter GHOST.

HORATIO.   Look, my lord, it comes!
HAMLET. Angels and ministers of grace° defend us!
Be thou° a spirit of health° or goblin damned,   40
Bring° with thee airs from heaven or blasts from hell,
Be thy intents° wicked or charitable,
Thou com'st in such a questionable° shape
That I will speak to thee. I'll call thee Hamlet,
King, father, royal Dane. O, answer me!   45
Let me not burst in ignorance, but tell
Why thy canonized° bones, hearsèd° in death,
Have burst their cerements;° why the sepulcher
Wherein we saw thee quietly inurned°
Hath oped his ponderous and marble jaws   50
To cast thee up again. What may this mean,
That thou, dead corpse, again in complete steel,°
Revisits thus the glimpses of the moon,°
Making night hideous, and we fools of nature°
So horridly to shake our disposition°   55
With thoughts beyond the reaches of our souls?
Say, why is this? Wherefore? What should we do?

---

26 his its.   **27 their o'ergrowth . . . complexion** the excessive growth in individuals of some natural trait.   **28 pales** palings, fences (as of a fortification).   **29 o'erleavens** induces a change throughout (as yeast works in dough).   **30 plausive** pleasing.   **32 nature's livery** sign of one's servitude to nature.   **fortune's star** the destiny that chance brings.   **33 His virtues else** i.e., the other qualities of *these men* (line 30).   **34 may undergo** can sustain.   **35 general censure** general opinion that people have of him. **36–38 The dram . . . scandal** i.e., the small drop of evil blots out or works against the noble substance of the whole and brings it into disrepute. To *dout* is to blot out. (A famous crux.)   **39 ministers of grace** messengers of God.   **40 Be thou** whether you are. **spirit of health** good angel.   **41 Bring** whether you bring.   **42 Be thy intents** whether your intentions are.   **43 questionable** inviting question.   **47 canonized** buried according to the canons of the church.   **hearsèd** coffined.   **48 cerements** grave clothes.   **49 inurned** entombed.   **52 complete steel** full armor.   **53 glimpses of the moon** pale and uncertain moonlight.   **54 fools of nature** mere men, limited to natural knowledge and subject to nature.   **55 So . . . disposition** to distress our mental composure so violently.

[*The* GHOST] *beckons* [HAMLET].

HORATIO. It beckons you to go away with it,
   As if it some impartment° did desire
   To you alone.

MARCELLUS.   Look with what courteous action   60
   It wafts you to a more removèd ground.
   But do not go with it.

HORATIO.   No, by no means.

HAMLET. It will not speak. Then I will follow it.

HORATIO. Do not, my lord!

HAMLET.   Why, what should be the fear?
   I do not set my life at a pin's fee,°   65
   And for my soul, what can it do to that,
   Being a thing immortal as itself?
   It waves me forth again. I'll follow it.

HORATIO. What if it tempt you toward the flood,° my lord,
   Or to the dreadful summit of the cliff   70
   That beetles o'er° his° base into the sea,
   And there assume some other horrible form
   Which might deprive your sovereignty of reason°
   And draw you into madness? Think of it.
   The very place puts toys of desperation,°   75
   Without more motive, into every brain
   That looks so many fathoms to the sea
   And hears it roar beneath.

HAMLET. It wafts me still.—Go on, I'll follow thee.

MARCELLUS. You shall not go, my lord.   [*They try to stop him.*]

HAMLET.   Hold off your hands!   80

HORATIO. Be ruled. You shall not go.

HAMLET.   My fate cries out,°
   And makes each petty° artery° in this body
   As hardy as the Nemean lion's° nerve.°
   Still am I called. Unhand me, gentlemen.
   By heaven, I'll make a ghost of him that lets° me!   85
   I say, away!—Go on, I'll follow thee.

                              Exeunt GHOST *and* HAMLET.

HORATIO. He waxes desperate with imagination.

MARCELLUS. Let's follow. 'Tis not fit thus to obey him.

HORATIO. Have after.° To what issue° will this come?

MARCELLUS. Something is rotten in the state of Denmark.   90

HORATIO. Heaven will direct it.°

MARCELLUS.   Nay, let's follow him.

                                        Exeunt.

---

59 impartment communication. **65 fee** value. **69 flood** sea. **71 beetles o'er** over-
hangs threateningly (like bushy eyebrows). **his** its. **73 deprive . . . reason** take away
the rule of reason over your mind. **75 toys of desperation** fancies of desperate acts,
i.e., suicide. **81 My fate cries out** my destiny summons me. **82 petty** weak. **artery**
(through which the vital spirits were thought to have been conveyed). **83 Nemean
lion** one of the monsters slain by Hercules in his twelve labors. **nerve** sinew. **85 lets**
hinders. **89 Have after** let's go after him. **issue** outcome. **91 it** i.e., the outcome.

1.5 *Enter* GHOST *and* HAMLET.

HAMLET. Whither wilt thou lead me? Speak. I'll go no further.
GHOST. Mark me.
HAMLET.   I will.
GHOST.   My hour is almost come,
    When I to sulfurous and tormenting flames
    Must render up myself.
HAMLET.   Alas, poor ghost!
GHOST. Pity me not, but lend thy serious hearing   5
    To what I shall unfold.
HAMLET. Speak. I am bound° to hear.
GHOST. So art thou to revenge, when thou shalt hear.
HAMLET. What?
GHOST. I am thy father's spirit,   10
    Doomed for a certain term to walk the night,
    And for the day confined to fast° in fires,
    Till the foul crimes° done in my days of nature°
    Are burnt and purged away. But that° I am forbid
    To tell the secrets of my prison house,   15
    I could a tale unfold whose lightest word
    Would harrow up° thy soul, freeze thy young blood,
    Make thy two eyes like stars start from their spheres,°
    Thy knotted and combinèd locks° to part,
    And each particular hair to stand on end   20
    Like quills upon the fretful porcupine.
    But this eternal blazon° must not be
    To ears of flesh and blood. List, list, O, list!
    If thou didst ever thy dear father love—
HAMLET. O God!   25
GHOST. Revenge his foul and most unnatural murder.
HAMLET. Murder?
GHOST. Murder most foul, as in the best° it is,
    But this most foul, strange, and unnatural.
HAMLET. Haste me to know't, that I, with wings as swift   30
    As meditation or the thoughts of love,
    May sweep to my revenge.
GHOST.   I find thee apt;
    And duller shouldst thou be° than the fat° weed
    That roots itself in ease on Lethe° wharf,

1.5 Location: The battlements of the castle.   7 bound (1) ready (2) obligated by duty
and fate. (The Ghost, in line 8, answers in the second sense.)   **12 fast** do penance by
fasting.   **13 crimes** sins.   **of nature** as a mortal.   **14 But that** were it not that.   **17
harrow up** lacerate, tear.   **18 spheres** i.e., eye-sockets, here compared to the orbits or
transparent revolving spheres in which, according to Ptolemaic astronomy, the heavenly
bodies were fixed.   **19 knotted . . . locks** hair neatly arranged and confined.   **22
eternal blazon** revelation of the secrets of eternity.   **28 in the best** even at best.   **33
shouldst thou be** you would have to be.   **fat** torpid, lethargic.   **34 Lethe** the river of
forgetfulness in Hades.

Wouldst thou not stir in this. Now, Hamlet, hear.   35
'Tis given out that, sleeping in my orchard,°
A serpent stung me. So the whole ear of Denmark
Is by a forgèd process° of my death
Rankly abused.° But know, thou noble youth,
The serpent that did sting thy father's life   40
Now wears his crown.
HAMLET. O, my prophetic soul! My uncle!
GHOST. Ay, that incestuous, that adulterate° beast,
With witchcraft of his wit, with traitorous gifts°—
O wicked wit and gifts, that have the power   45
So to seduce!—won to his shameful lust
The will of my most seeming-virtuous queen.
O Hamlet, what a falling off was there!
From me, whose love was of that dignity
That it went hand in hand even with the vow°   50
I made to her in marriage, and to decline
Upon a wretch whose natural gifts were poor
To° those of mine!
But virtue, as it° never will be moved,
Though lewdness court it in a shape of heaven,°   55
So lust, though to a radiant angel linked,
Will sate itself in a celestial bed°
And prey on garbage.
But soft, methinks I scent the morning air.
Brief let me be. Sleeping within my orchard,   60
My custom always of the afternoon,
Upon my secure° hour thy uncle stole,
With juice of cursèd hebona° in a vial,
And in the porches of my ears° did pour
The leprous distillment,° whose effect   65
Holds such an enmity with blood of man
That swift as quicksilver it courses through
The natural gates and alleys of the body,
And with a sudden vigor it doth posset°
And curd, like eager° droppings into milk,   70
The thin and wholesome blood. So did it mine,
And a most instant tetter° barked° about,

---

36 orchard garden. **38 forgèd process** falsified account. **39 abused** deceived. **43
adulterate** adulterous. **44 gifts** (1) talents (2) presents. **50 even with the vow** with
the very vow. **53 To** compared to. **54 virtue, as it** as virtue. **55 shape of heaven**
heavenly form. **57 sate . . . bed** cease to find sexual pleasure in a virtuously lawful
marriage. **62 secure** confident, unsuspicious. **63 hebona** a poison. (The word seems
to be a form of *ebony,* though it is thought perhaps to be related to *henbane,* a poison, or
to *ebenus,* "yew.") **64 porches of my ears** ears as a porch or entrance of the body.
65 leprous distillment distillation causing leprosylike disfigurement. **69 posset** coagu-
late, curdle. **70 eager** sour, acid. **72 tetter** eruption of scabs. **barked** recovered
with a rough covering, like bark on a tree.

Most lazar-like,° with vile and loathsome crust,
All my smooth body.
Thus was I, sleeping, by a brother's hand   75
Of life, of crown, of queen at once dispatched,°
Cut off even in the blossoms of my sin,
Unhouseled,° disappointed,° unaneled,°
No reckoning° made, but sent to my account
With all my imperfections on my head.   80
O, horrible! O, horrible, most horrible!
If thou hast nature° in thee, bear it not.
Let not the royal bed of Denmark be
A couch for luxury° and damnèd incest.
But, howsoever thou pursues this act,   85
Taint not thy mind nor let thy soul contrive
Against thy mother aught. Leave her to heaven
And to those thorns that in her bosom lodge,
To prick and sting her. Fare thee well at once.
The glowworm shows the matin° to be near,   90
And 'gins to pale his° uneffectual fire.
Adieu, adieu, adieu! Remember me.

                                                      [*Exit.*]

HAMLET. O all you host of heaven! O earth! What else?
    And shall I couple° hell? O, fie! Hold,° hold, my heart,
    And you, my sinews, grow not instant° old,   95
    But bear me stiffly up. Remember thee?
    Ay, thou poor ghost, whiles memory holds a seat
    In this distracted globe.° Remember thee?
    Yea, from the table° of my memory
    I'll wipe away all trivial fond° records,   100
    All saws° of books, all forms,° all pressures° past
    That youth and observations copied there,
    And thy commandment all alone shall live
    Within the book and volume of my brain,
    Unmixed with baser matter. Yes, by heaven!   105
    O most pernicious woman!
    O villain, villain, smiling, damnèd villain!
    My tables°—meet it is° I set it down
    That one may smile, and smile, and be a villain.
    At least I am sure it may be so in Denmark.   110

                                                      [*Writing.*]

---

73 lazar-like leperlike.   **76 dispatched** suddenly deprived.   **78 Unhouseled** without
having received the Sacrament.   **disappointed** unready (spiritually) for the last journey.
unaneled without having received extreme unction.   **79 reckoning** settling of accounts.   **82 nature** i.e., the promptings of a son.   **84 luxury** lechery.   **90 matin** morning.   **91 his** its.   **94 couple** add.   **Hold** hold together.   **95 instant** instantly.   **98
globe** (1) head (2) world.   **99 table** tablet, slate.   **100 fond** foolish.   **101 saws** wise
sayings.   **forms** shapes or images copied onto the slate; general ideas.   **pressures** impressions stamped.   **108 tables** writing tablets.   **meet it is** it is fitting.

So uncle, there you are.° Now to my word:
It is "Adieu, adieu! Remember me."
I have sworn't.

Enter HORATIO *and* MARCELLUS.

HORATIO. My lord, my lord!

MARCELLUS. Lord Hamlet!   115

HORATIO. Heavens secure him!°

HAMLET. So be it.

MARCELLUS. Hilo, ho, ho, my lord!

HAMLET. Hillo, ho, ho, boy! Come, bird, come.°

MARCELLUS. How is't, my noble lord?   120

HORATIO. What news, my lord?

HAMLET. O, wonderful!

HORATIO. Good my lord, tell it.

HAMLET. No, you will reveal it.

HORATIO. Not I, my lord, by heaven.   125

MARCELLUS. Nor I, my lord.

HAMLET. How say you, then, would heart of man once° think it?
       But you'll be secret?

HORATIO, MARCELLUS.   Ay, by heaven, my lord.

HAMLET. There's never a villain dwelling in all Denmark
       But he's an arrant° knave.   130

HORATIO. There needs no ghost, my lord, come from the grave
       To tell us this.

HAMLET.   Why, right, you are in the right.
       And so, without more circumstance° at all,
       I hold it fit that we shake hands and part,
       You as your business and desire shall point you—   135
       For every man hath business and desire,
       Such as it is—and for my own poor part,
       Look you, I'll go pray,

HORATIO. These are but wild and whirling words, my lord.

HAMLET. I am sorry they offend you, heartily;   140
       Yes, faith, heartily.

HORATIO.   There's no offense, my lord.

HAMLET. Yes, but Saint Patrick,° but there is, Horatio,
       And much offense° too. Touching this vision here,
       It is an honest ghost,° that let me tell you.
       For your desire to know what is between us,   145
       O'ermaster't as you may. And now, good friends,
       As you are friends, scholars, and soldiers,
       Give me one poor request.

---

111 there you are i.e., there, I've written that down against you. **116 secure him**
keep him safe. **119 Hilo . . . come** (A falconer's call to a hawk in air. Hamlet mocks
the hallooing as though it were a part of hawking.) **127 once** ever. **130 arrant** thor-
oughgoing. **133 circumstance** ceremony, elaboration. **142 Saint Patrick** (The
keeper of Purgatory and patron saint of all blunders and confusion.) **143 offense** (Hamlet deliberately changes Horatio's "no offense taken" to "an offense against all decency.")
144 an honest ghost i.e., a real ghost and not an evil spirit.

HORATIO. What is't, my lord? We will.

HAMLET. Never make known what you have seen tonight.   150

HORATIO, MARCELLUS. My lord, we will not.

HAMLET. Nay, but swear't.

HORATIO. In faith, my lord, not I.°

MARCELLUS. Nor I, my lord, in faith.

HAMLET. Upon my sword.°   [*He holds out his sword.*] 155

MARCELLUS. We have sworn, my lord, already.°

HAMLET. Indeed, upon my sword, indeed.

GHOST [*cries under the stage*]. Swear.

HAMLET. Ha, ha, boy, sayst thou so? Art thou there, truepenny°
    Come on, you hear this fellow in the cellarage.   160
    Consent to swear.

HORATIO.   Propose the oath, my lord.

HAMLET. Never to speak of this that you have seen,
    Swear by the sword.

GHOST [*beneath*]. Swear.   [*They swear.*°]

HAMLET. *Hic et ubique?*° Then we'll shift our ground.   165
                          [*He moves to another spot.*]
    Come hither, gentlemen,
    And lay your hands again upon my sword.
    Swear by my sword
    Never to speak of this that you have heard.

GHOST [*beneath*]. Swear by his sword.   [*They swear.*] 170

HAMLET. Well said, old mole. Canst work i' th' earth so fast?
    A worthy pioneer!°—Once more removed, good friends.
                          [*He moves again.*]

HORATIO. O day and night, but this is wondrous strange!

HAMLET. And henceforth as a stranger° give it welcome.
    There are more things in heaven and earth, Horatio,   175
    Than are dreamt of in your philosophy.°
    But come;
    Here, as before, never, so help you mercy,°
    How strange or odd soe'er I bear myself—
    As I perchance hereafter shall think meet   180
    To put an antic° disposition on—
    That you, at such times seeing me, never shall,
    With arms encumbered° thus, or this headshake,
    Or by pronouncing of some doubtful phrase

---

153 In faith . . . I i.e., I swear not to tell what I have seen. (Horatio is not refusing to swear.)   **155 sword** i.e., the hilt in the form of a cross.   **156 We . . . already** i.e., we swore in *faith*.   **159 truepenny** honest old fellow.   **164 s.d. They swear** (Seemingly they swear here, and at lines 170 and 190, as they lay their hands on Hamlet's sword. Triple oaths would have particular force; these three oaths deal with what they have seen, what they have heard, and what they promise about Hamlet's *antic disposition*.)   **165 *Hic et ubique*** here and everywhere. (Latin.)   **172 pioneer** foot soldier assigned to dig tunnels and excavations.   **174 as a stranger** i.e., needing your hospitality.   **176 your philosophy** this subject called "natural philosophy" or "science" that people talk about.   **178 so help you mercy** as you hope for God's mercy when you are judged.   **181 antic** fantastic.   **183 encumbered** folded.

As "Well, we know," or "We could, an if° we would,"   185
Or "If we list° to speak," or "There be, an if they might,"°
Or such ambiguous giving out,° to note°
That you know aught° of me—this do swear,
So grace and mercy at your most need help you.
GHOST [*beneath*]. Swear.   [*They swear.*]   190
HAMLET.   Rest, rest, perturbèd spirit! So, gentlemen,
With all my love I do commend me to you;°
And what so poor a man as Hamlet is
May do t' express his love and friending° to you,
God willing, shall not lack.° Let us go in together,   195
And still° your fingers on your lips, I pray.
The time° is out of joint. O cursèd spite°
That ever I was born to set it right!
                              [*They wait for him to leave first.*]
Nay, come, let's go together.°
                                                        Exeunt.

2.1   *Enter old* POLONIUS *with his man* [REYNALDO].

POLONIUS.   Give him this money and these notes, Reynaldo.
                              [*He gives money and papers.*]
REYNALDO.   I will, my lord.
POLONIUS.   You shall do marvelous° wisely, good Reynaldo,
Before you visit him, to make inquire°
Of his behavior.
REYNALDO.   My lord, I did intend it.   5
POLONIUS.   Marry, well said, very well said. Look you, sir,
Inquire me first what Danskers° are in Paris,
And how, and who, what means,° and where they keep,°
What company, at what expense; and finding
By this encompassment° and drift° of question   10
That they do know my son, come you more nearer
Than your particular demands will touch it.°
Take you,° as 'twere, some distant knowledge of him,
As thus, "I know his father and his friends,
And in part him." Do you mark this, Reynaldo?   15
REYNALDO.   Ay, very well, my lord.
POLONIUS.   "And in part him, but," you may say, "not well.
But if 't be he I mean, he's very wild,

---

185 an if if.   **186 list** wished.   **There . . . might** i.e., there are people here (we, in fact)
who could tell news if we were at liberty to do so.   **187 giving out** intimation.   **note**
draw attention to the fact.   **188 aught** i.e., something secret.   **192 do . . . you** entrust
myself to you.   **194 friending** friendliness.   **195 lack** be lacking.   **196 still** always.
197 The time the state of affairs.   **spite** i.e., the spite of Fortune.   **199 let's go together**
(Probably they wait for him to leave first, but he refuses this ceremoniousness.)   **2.1**
Location: Polonius's chambers.   3 marvelous marvelously.   **4 inquire** inquiry.   **7
Danskers** Danes.   **8 what means** what wealth (they have).   **keep** dwell.   **10 encom-
passment** roundabout talking.   **drift** gradual approach of course.   **11–12 come . . . it**
you will find out more this way than by asking pointed questions (*particular demands*).
13 Take you assume, pretend.

Addicted so and so," and there put on° him
What forgeries° you please—marry, none so rank°   20
As may dishonor him, take heed of that,
But, sir, such wanton,° wild, and usual slips
As are companions noted and most known
To youth and liberty.

REYNALDO. As gaming, my lord.   25

POLONIUS. Ay, or drinking, fencing, swearing,
Quarreling, drabbing°—you may go so far.

REYNALDO. My lord, that would dishonor him.

POLONIUS. Faith, no, as you may season° it in the charge.
You must not put another scandal on him   30
That he is open to incontinency°
That's not my meaning. But breathe his faults so quaintly°
That they may seem the taints of liberty,°
The flash and outbreak of a fiery mind,
A savageness in unreclaimèd blood,   35
Of general assault.°

REYNALDO. But, my good lord—

POLONIUS. Wherefore should you do this?

REYNALDO. Ay, my lord, I would know that.

POLONIUS. Marry, sir, here's my drift,   40
And I believe it is a fetch of warrant.°
You laying these slight sullies on my son,
As 'twere a thing a little soiled wi' the working,°
Mark you,
Your party in converse,° him you would sound,°   45
Having ever° seen in the prenominate crimes°
The youth you breathe° of guilty, be assured
He closes with you in this consequence:°
"Good sir," or so, or "friend," or "gentleman,"
According to the phrase or the addition°   50
Of man and country.

REYNALDO.   Very good, my lord.

POLONIUS. And then, sir does 'a this—'a does—what was I about to say?
By the Mass, I was about to say something. Where did
I leave?

REYNALDO. At "closes in the consequence."   55

POLONIUS. At "closes in the consequence," ay, marry.
He closes thus: "I know the gentleman,
I saw him yesterday," or "th' other day,"

---

19 put on impute to.   **20 forgeries** invented tales.   **rank** gross.   **22 wanton** sportive,
unrestrained.   **27 drabbing** whoring.   **29 season** temper, soften.   **31 incontinency**
habitual sexual excess.   **32 quaintly** artfully, subtly.   **33 taints of liberty** faults resulting from free living.   **35–36 A savageness . . . assault** a wildness in untamed youth
that assails all indiscriminately.   **41 fetch of warrant** legitimate trick.   **43 soiled wi'
the working** soiled by handling while it is being made, i.e., by involvement in the ways
of the world.   **45 converse** conversion.   **sound** i.e., sound out.   **46 Having ever** if
he has ever.   **prenominate crimes** before-mentioned offenses.   **47 breathe** speak.
48 closes . . . consequence takes you into his confidence in some fashion, as follows.
50 addition title.

Or then, or then, with such or such, "and as you say,
There was 'a gaming," "there o'ertook in 's rouse,"°   60
There falling out° at tennis," or perchance
"I saw him enter such a house of sale,"
Videlicet° a brothel, or so forth. See you now,
Your bait of falsehood takes this carp° of truth;
And thus do we of wisdom and of reach,°   65
With windlasses° and with assays of bias,°
By indirections find directions° out.
So by my former lecture and advice
Shall you my son. You have° me, have you not?
REYNALDO. My lord, I have.
POLONIUS.   God b'wi'° ye; fare ye well.   70
REYNALDO. Good my lord.
POLONIUS. Observe his inclination in yourself.°
REYNALDO. I shall, my lord.
POLONIUS. And let him ply his music.
REYNALDO. Well, my lord.   75
POLONIUS. Farewell.

                                                 Exit REYNALDO.

Enter OPHELIA.

                        How now, Ophelia, what's the matter?
OPHELIA. O my lord, my lord, I have been so affrighted!
POLONIUS. With what, i' the name of God?
OPHELIA. My lord, as I was sewing in my closet,°
      Lord Hamlet, with his doublet° all unbraced,°   80
      No hat upon his head, his stockings fouled,
      Ungartered, and down-gyvèd° to his ankle,
      Pale as his shirt, his knees knocking each other,
      And with a look so piteous in purport°
      As if he had been loosèd out of hell   85
      To speak of horrors—he comes before me.
POLONIUS. Mad for thy love?
OPHELIA.   My lord, I do not know,
      But truly I do fear it.
POLONIUS.   What said he?
OPHELIA. He took me by the wrist and held me hard.
      Then goes he to the length of all his arm,   90
      And, with his other hand thus o'er his brow
      He falls to such perusal of my face

---

60 o'ertook in 's rouse overcome by drink.   **61 falling out** quarreling.   **63 Videlicet**
namely.   **64 carp** a fish.   **65 reach** capacity, ability.   **66 windlasses** i.e., circuitous
paths. (Literally, circuits made to head off the game in hunting.) **assays of bias**
attempts through indirection (like the curving path of the bowling ball, which is biased or
weighted to one side).   **67 directions** i.e., the way things really are.   **69 have** understand.   **70 b' wi'** be with.   **72 in yourself** in your own person (as well as by asking questions).   **79 closet** private chamber.   **80 doublet** close-fitting jacket. **unbraced**
unfastened.   **82 down-gyvèd** fallen to the ankles (like gyves or fetters).   **84 in purport**
in what it expressed.

As° 'a would draw it. Long stayed he so.
At last, a little shaking of mine arm
And thrice his head thus waving up and down,   95
He raised a sigh so piteous and profound
As it did seem to shatter all his bulk°
And end his being. That done, he lets me go,
And with his head over his shoulder turned
He seemed to find his way without his eyes,   100
For out o' doors he went without their helps,
And to the last bended their light on me.

POLONIUS. Come, go with me. I will go seek the King.
This is the very ecstasy° of love,
Whose violent property° fordoes° itself   105
And leads the will to desperate undertakings
As oft as any passion under heaven
That does afflict our natures. I am sorry.
What, have you given him any hard words of late?

OPHELIA. No, my good lord, but as you did command   110
I did repel his letters and denied
His access to me.

POLONIUS.   That hath made him mad.
I am sorry that with better heed and judgment
I had not quoted° him. I feared he did but trifle
And mean to wrack° thee. But beshrew my jealousy!°   115
By heaven, it is as proper to our age°
To cast beyond° ourselves in our opinions
As it is common for the younger sort
To lack discretion. Come, go we to the King.
This must be known,° which, being kept close,° might move   120
More grief to hide than hate to utter love.°
Come.

                                                    Exeunt.

    2.2 *Flourish. Enter* KING *and* QUEEN, ROSENCRANTZ, *and*
        GUILDENSTERN [*with others*].

KING. Welcome, dear Rosencrantz and Guildenstern.
Moreover that° we much did long to see you,
The need we have to use you did provoke
Our hasty sending. Something have you heard
Of Hamlet's transformation—so call it,   5
Sith nor° th' exterior nor the inward man
Resembles that° it was. What it should be,

---

93 As as if (also in line 97).   **97 bulk** body.   **104 ecstasy** madness.   **105 property** nature.   **fordoes** destroys.   **114 quoted** observed.   **115 wrack** ruin, seduce.   **beshrew
my jealousy** a plague upon my suspicious nature.   **116 proper . . . age** characteristic of
us (old) men.   **117 cast beyond** overshoot, miscalculate (a metaphor from hunting).
120 known made known (to the King).   **close** secret.   **120–121 might . . . love** i.e.,
might cause more grief (because of what Hamlet might do) by hiding the knowledge of
Hamlet's strange behavior to Ophelia than unpleasantness by telling it.   **2.2. Location: The
castle.**   **2 Moreover that** besides the fact that.   **6 Sith nor** since neither.   **7 that** what.

More than his father's death, that thus hath put him
So much from th' understanding of himself,
I cannot dream of. I entreat you both   10
That, being of so young days° brought up with him,
And sith so neighbored to° his youth and havior,°
That you vouchsafe your rest° here in our court
Some little time, so by your companies
To draw him on to pleasures, and to gather   15
So much as from occasion° you may glean,
Whether aught to us unknown afflicts him thus
That, opened,° lies within our remedy.

QUEEN. Good gentlemen, he hath much talked of you,
And sure I am two men there is not living   20
To whom he more adheres. If it will please you
To show us so much gentry° and good will
As to expend your time with us awhile
For the supply and profit of our hope,°
Your visitation shall receive such thanks   25
As fits a king's remembrance.°

ROSENCRANTZ.   Both Your Majesties
Might, by the sovereign power you have of° us,
Put your dread° pleasures more into command
Than to entreaty.

GUILDENSTERN.   But we both obey,
And here give up ourselves in the full bent°   30
To lay our service freely at your feet,
To be commanded.

KING. Thanks, Rosencrantz and gentle Guildenstern.

QUEEN. Thanks, Guildenstern and gentle Rosencrantz.
And I beseech you instantly to visit   35
My too much changèd son. Go, some of you,
And bring these gentlemen where Hamlet is.

GUILDENSTERN. Heavens make our presence and our practices°
Pleasant and helpful to him!

QUEEN.   Ay, amen!

Exeunt ROSENCRANTZ *and* GUILDENSTERN [*with some attendants*].

Enter POLONIUS.

POLONIUS. Th' ambassadors from Norway, my good lord,   40
Are joyfully returned.

KING. Thou still° hast been the father of good news.

POLONIUS. Have I, my lord? I assure my good liege
I hold° my duty, as° I hold my soul,

---

11 of . . . days from such early youth.   **12 And sith so neighbored to** and since you
are (or, and since that time you are) intimately acquainted with.   **havior** demeanor.
13 vouchsafe your rest please to stay.   **16 occasion** opportunity.   **18 opened** being
revealed.   **22 gentry** courtesy.   **24 supply . . . hope** aid and furtherance of what we
hope for.   **26 As fits . . . remembrance** as would be a fitting gift of a king who
rewards true service.   **27 of** over.   **28 dread** inspiring awe.   **30 in . . . bent** to the
utmost degree of our capacity (an archery metaphor).   **38 practices** doings.   **42 still** always.   **44 hold** maintain.   **as** firmly as.

Both to my God and to my gracious king;   45
And I do think, or else this brain of mine
Hunts not the trail of policy° so sure
As it hath used to do, that I have found
The very cause of Hamlet's lunacy.

KING. O, speak of that! That do I long to hear.   50

POLONIUS. Give first admittance to th' ambassadors.
My news shall be the fruit° to that great feast.

KING. Thyself do grace° to them and bring them in.

                                            [*Exit* POLONIUS.]

He tells me, my dear Gertrude, he hath found
The head and source of all your son's distemper.   55

QUEEN. I doubt° it is no other but the main,°
His father's death and our o'erhasty marriage.

Enter Ambassadors VOLTIMAND *and* CORNELIUS, *with* POLONIUS.

KING. Well, we shall sift him.°—Welcome, my good friends!
Say, Voltimand, what from our brother° Norway?

VOLTIMAND. Most fair return of greetings and desires.°   60
Upon our first,° he sent out to suppress
His nephew's levies, which to him appeared
To be a preparation 'gainst the Polack,
But, better looked into, he truly found
It was against Your Highness. Whereat grieved   65
That so his sickness, age, and impotence°
Was falsely borne in hand,° sends out arrests°
On Fortinbras, which he, in brief, obeys,
Receives rebuke from Norway, and in fine°
Makes vow before his uncle never more   70
To give th' assay° of arms against Your Majesty.
Whereon old Norway, overcome with joy,
Gives him three thousand crowns in annual fee
And his commission to employ those soldiers,
So levied as before, against the Polack,   75
With an entreaty, herein further shown,   [*giving a paper*]
That it might please you to give quiet pass
Through your dominions for this enterprise
On such regards of safety and allowance°
As therein are set down.

KING.   It likes° us well,   80
And at more considered° time we'll read,
Answer, and think upon this business.

---

47 policy sagacity.   **52 fruit** dessert.   **53 grace** honor (punning on *grace* said before
a *feast,* line 52).   **56 doubt** fear, suspect.   **main** chief point, principal concern.   **58 sift
him** question Polonius closely.   **59 brother** fellow king.   **60 desires** good wishes.   **61
Upon our first** at our first words on the business.   **66 impotence** helplessness.   **67
borne in hand** deluded, taken advantage of.   **arrests** orders to desist.   **69 in fine** in
conclusion.   **71 give th' assay** make trial of strength, challenge.   **78 On . . . allowance**
i.e., with such considerations for the safety of Denmark and permission for Fortinbras.   **80
likes** pleases.   **81 considered** suitable for deliberation.

Meantime we thank you for your well-took labor.
Go to your rest; at night we'll feast together.
Most welcome home!

                                        Exeunt Ambassadors.

POLONIUS.   This business is well ended.   85
My liege, and madam, to expostulate°
What majesty should be, what duty is,
Why day is day, night night, and time is time,
Were nothing but to waste night, day, and time.
Therefore, since brevity is the soul of wit,°   90
And tediousness the limbs and outward flourishes,
I will be brief. Your noble son is mad.
Mad call I it, for, to define true madness,
What is't but to be nothing else but mad?
But let that go.
QUEEN.   More matter, with less art.   95
POLONIUS. Madam, I swear I use no art at all.
That he's mad, tis true: 'tis true 'tis pity.
And pity 'tis 'tis true—a foolish figure,°
But farewell it, for I will use no art.
Mad let us grant him, then, and now remains   100
That we find out the cause of this defect,
Or rather say, the cause of this defect,
For this effect defective comes by cause.°
Thus it remains, and the remainder thus.
Perpend.°   105
I have a daughter—have while she is mine—
Who, in her duty and obedience, mark,
Hath given me this. Now gather and surmise.°
[*He reads the letter.*] "To the celestial and my soul's idol,
the most beautified Ophelia"—   110
That's an ill phrase, a vile phrase; "beautified" is a vile phrase. But
you shall hear. Thus: [*He reads.*]
"In her excellent white bosom,° these,° etc."
QUEEN. Came this from Hamlet to her?
POLONIUS. Good madam, stay° awhile, I will be faithful.°   [*He reads.*] 115
    "Doubt thou the stars are fire,
        Doubt that the sun doth move,
    Doubt° truth to be a liar,
        But never doubt I love.

O dear Ophelia, I am ill at these numbers.° I have not art to reckon°   120
my groans. But that I love thee best, O most best, believe it.

---

86 expostulate expound, inquire into. **90 wit** sense or judgment. **98 figure**
figure of speech. **103 For . . . cause** i.e., for this defective behavior, this madness, has a
cause. **105 Perpend** consider. **108 gather and surmise** draw your own conclusions.
113 In . . . bosom (The letter is poetically addressed to her heart.) **these** i.e., the letter. **115 stay** wait. **faithful** i.e., in reading the letter accurately. **118 Doubt** suspect.
120 ill . . . numbers unskilled at writing verses. **reckon** (1) count (2) number metrically, scan.

Adieu.
    Thine evermore, most dear lady, whilst this machine° is to him,
                             Hamlet."
This in obedience hath my daughter shown me,   125
And, more above,° hath his solicitings,
As they fell out° by° time, by means, and place,
All given to mine ear.°
KING.   But how hath she
    Received his love?
POLONIUS.   What do you think of me?
KING. As of a man faithful and honorable.   130
POLONIUS. I would fain° prove so. But what might you think,
    When I had seen this hot love on the wing—
    As I perceived it, I must tell you that,
    Before my daughter told me—what might you,
    Or my dear Majesty your queen here, think,   135
    If I had played the desk or table book,°
    Or given my heart a winking,° mute and dumb,
    Or looked upon this love with idle sight?°
    What might you think? No, I went round° to work,
    And my young mistress thus I did bespeak:°   140
    "Lord Hamlet is a prince out of thy star;°
    This must not be." And then I prescripts° gave her,
    That she should lock herself from his resort,°
    Admit no messengers, receive no tokens.
    Which done, she took the fruits of my advice;   145
    And he, repellèd—a short tale to make—
    Fell into a sadness, then into a fast,
    Thence to a watch,° thence into a weakness,
    Thence to a lightness,° and by this declension°
    Into the madness wherein now he raves,   150
    And all we° mourn for.
KING. [to the QUEEN].   Do you think 'tis this?
QUEEN. It may be, very like.
POLONIUS. Hath there been such a time—I would fain know that—
    That I have positively said "'Tis so,"
    When it proved otherwise?
KING.   Not that I know.   155
POLONIUS. Take this from this,° if this be otherwise.

---

123 **machine** i.e., body.   126 **more above** moreover.   127 **fell out** occurred.   **by** according to.   128 **given . . . ear** i.e., told me about.   131 **fain** gladly.   136 **played . . . table book** i.e., remained shut up, concealing the information.   137 **given . . . winking** closed the eyes of my heart to this.   138 **with idle sight** complacently or incomprehendingly.   139 **round** roundly, plainly.   140 **bespeak** address.   141 **out of thy star** above your sphere, position.   142 **prescripts** orders.   143 **his resort** his visits.   148 **watch** state of sleeplessness.   149 **lightness** lightheadedness.   **declension** decline, deterioration (with a pun on the grammatical sense).   151 **all we** all of us, or, into everything that we.   156 **Take this from this** (The actor probably gestures, indicating that he means his head from his shoulders, or his staff of office or chain from his hands or neck, or something similar.)

If circumstances lead me, I will find
Where truth is hid, though it were hid indeed
Within the center.°

KING.   How may we try° it further?

POLONIUS. You know sometimes he walks for hours together   160
Here in the lobby.

QUEEN.   So he does indeed.

POLONIUS. At such a time I'll loose° my daughter to him.
Be you and I behind an arras° then.
Mark the encounter. If he love her not
And be not from his reason fall'n thereon,°   165
Let me be no assistant for a state,
But keep a farm and carters.°

KING.   We will try it.

Enter HAMLET [*reading on a book*].

QUEEN. But look where sadly° the poor wretch comes reading.

POLONIUS. Away, I do beseech you both, away.
I'll board° him presently.° O, give me leave.°   170

Exeunt KING *and* QUEEN [*with attendants*].

How does my good Lord Hamlet?

HAMLET. Well, God-a-mercy.°

POLONIUS. Do you know me, my lord?

HAMLET. Excellent well. You are a fishmonger.°

POLONIUS. Not I, my lord.   175

HAMLET. Then I would you were so honest a man.

POLONIUS. Honest, my lord?

HAMLET. Ay, sir. To be honest, as this world goes, is to be one man
picked out of ten thousand.

POLONIUS. That's very true, my lord.   180

HAMLET. For if the sun breed maggots in a dead dog, being a good
kissing carrion°—Have you a daughter?

POLONIUS. I have, my lord.

HAMLET. Let her not walk i' the sun.° Conception° is a blessing, but as
your daughter may conceive, friend, look to 't.   185

POLONIUS [*aside*]. How say you by that? Still harping on my daughter.
Yet he knew me not at first; 'a° said I was a fishmonger. 'A is far
gone. And truly in my youth I suffered much extremity for love,
very near this. I'll speak to him again.—What do you read, my lord?

HAMLET. Words, words, words.   190

---

159 center middle point of the earth (which is also the center of the Ptolemaic universe).
try test, judge.   **162 loose** (as one might release an animal that is being mated).   **163**
arras hanging, tapestry.   **165 thereon** on that account.   **167 carters** wagon drivers.
168 sadly seriously.   **170 board** accost.   **presently** at once.   **give me leave** i.e., excuse me, leave me alone (said to those he hurries offstage, including the King and Queen).
172 God a-mercy God have mercy, i.e., thank you.   **174 fishmonger** fish merchant.
181–182 a good kissing carrion i.e., a good piece of flesh for kissing, or for the sun to
kiss.   **184 i' the sun** in public (with additional implication of the sunshine of princely favors).   **Conception** (1) understanding (2) pregnancy.   **187 'a** he.

POLONIUS. What is the matter,° my lord?

HAMLET. Between who?

POLONIUS. I mean, the matter that you read, my lord.

HAMLET. Slanders, sir; for the satirical rogue says here that old men have
gray beards, that their faces are wrinkled, their eyes purging° thick   195
amber° and plum-tree gum, and that they have a plentiful lack of
wit,° together with most weak hams. All which, sir, though I most
powerfully and potently believe, yet I hold it not honesty° to have
it thus set down, for yourself, sir, shall grow old° as I am, if like a
crab you could go backward.   200

POLONIUS [aside]. Though this be madness, yet there is method in 't.—
Will you walk out of the air,° my lord?

HAMLET. Into my grave.

POLONIUS. Indeed, that's out of the air. [Aside.] How pregnant° sometimes his replies are! A happiness° that often madness hits on,   205
which reason and sanity could not so prosperously° be delivered
of. I will leave him and suddenly° contrive the means of meeting
between him and my daughter.—My honorable lord, I will most
humbly take my leave of you.

HAMLET. You cannot, sir, take from me anything that I will more will-   210
ingly part withal°—except my life, except my life, except my life.

Enter GUILDENSTERN *and* ROSENCRANTZ.

POLONIUS. Fare you well, my lord.

HAMLET. These tedious old fools!°

POLONIUS. You go to seek the Lord Hamlet. There he is.

ROSENCRANTZ [to POLONIUS]. God save you, sir!   215

[*Exit* POLONIUS.]

GUILDENSTERN. My honored lord!

ROSENCRANTZ. My most dear lord!

HAMLET. My excellent good friends! How dost thou, Guildenstern? Ah,
Rosencrantz! Good lads, how do you both?

ROSENCRANTZ. As the indifferent° children of the earth.   220

GUILDENSTERN. Happy in that we are not overhappy.
On Fortune's cap we are not the very button.

HAMLET. Nor the soles of her shoe?

ROSENCRANTZ. Neither, my lord.

HAMLET. Then you live about her waist, or in the middle of her favors?° 225

GUILDENSTERN. Faith, her privates we.°

HAMLET. In the secret parts of Fortune? O, most true, she is a strumpet.°
What news?

---

191 **matter** substance. (But Hamlet plays on the sense of "basis for a dispute.") **195
purging** discharging. **196 amber** i.e., resin, like the resinous *plum-tree gum.* **197 wit**
understanding. **198 honesty** decency, decorum. **199 old** as old. **202 out of the air**
(The open air was considered dangerous for sick people.) **204 pregnant** quick-witted,
full of meaning. **205 happiness** felicity of expression. **206 prosperously** successfully.
207 suddenly immediately. **211 withal** with. **213 old fools** i.e., old men like Polonius.
220 indifferent ordinary, at neither extreme of fortune or misfortune. **225 favors** i.e.,
sexual favors. **226 her privates** we i.e., (1) we are sexually intimate with Fortune, the
fickle goddess who bestows her favors indiscriminately (2) we are her private citizens.
227 strumpet prostitute (a common epithet for indiscriminate Fortune; see line 452).

ROSENCRANTZ. None, my lord, but the world's grown honest.

HAMLET. Then is doomsday near. But your news is not true. Let me ques- 230
tion more in particular. What have you, my good friends, deserved
at the hands of Fortune that she sends you to prison hither?

GUILDENSTERN. Prison, my lord?

HAMLET. Denmark's a prison.

ROSENCRANTZ. Then is the world one.   235

HAMLET. A goodly one, in which there are many confines,° wards,° and
dungeons, Denmark being one o' the worst.

ROSENCRANTZ. We think not so, my lord.

HAMLET. Why then 'tis none to you, for there is nothing either good or
bad but thinking makes it so. To me it is a prison.   240

ROSENCRANTZ. Why then, your ambition makes it one. 'Tis too narrow
for your mind.

HAMLET. O God, I could be bounded in a nutshell and count myself a
king of infinite space, were it not that I have bad dreams.

GUILDENSTERN. Which dreams indeed are ambition, for the very sub-   245
stance of the ambitious° is merely the shadow of a dream.

HAMLET. A dream itself is but a shadow.

ROSENCRANTZ. Truly, and I hold ambition of so airy and light a quality
that it is but a shadow's shadow.

HAMLET. Then are our beggars bodies,° and our monarchs and out-   250
stretched° heroes the beggars' shadows. Shall we to the court? For,
by my fay,° I cannot reason.

ROSENCRANTZ, GUILDENSTERN. We'll wait upon° you.

HAMLET. No such matter. I will not sort° you with the rest of my
servants, for, to speak to you like an honest man, I am most dread-   255
fully attended.° But, in the beaten way° of friendship, what make°
you at Elsinore?

ROSENCRANTZ. To visit you, my lord, no other occasion.

HAMLET. Beggar that I am, I'm even poor in thanks; but I thank you, and
sure, dear friends, my thanks are too dear a halfpenny.° Were you   260
not sent for? Is it your own inclining? Is it a free° visitation? Come,
come, deal justly with me. Come, come. Nay, speak.

GUILDENSTERN. What should we say; my lord?

HAMLET. Anything but to the purpose.° You were sent for, and there is a
kind of confession in your looks which your modesties° have not   265
craft enough to color.° I know the good King and Queen have sent
for you.

---

236 confines places of confinement. **wards** cells.   **245–246 the very . . . ambitious** that seemingly very substantial thing that the ambitious pursue.   **250 bodies** i.e.,
solid substances rather than shadows (since beggars are not ambitious).   **250–251 outstretched** (1) far-reaching in their ambition (2) elongated as shadows.   **252 fay** faith.
253 wait upon accompany, attend (but Hamlet uses the phrase in the sense of providing
menial service).   **254 sort** class, categorize.   **255–256 dreadfully attended** waited
upon in slovenly fashion.   **256 beaten way** familiar path, tried-and-true course.   **make**
do.   **260 too dear a halfpenny** (1) too expensive at even a halfpenny, i.e., of little
worth (2) too expensive *by* a halfpenny in return for worthless kindness.   **261 free** voluntary.   **264 Anything but to the purpose** anything except a straightforward answer
(said ironically).   **265 modesties** sense of shame.   **266 color** disguise.

ROSENCRANTZ. To what end, my lord?

HAMLET. That you must teach me. But let me conjure° you, by the rights
of our fellowship, by the consonancy of our youth,° by the obliga-   270
tion of our ever-preserved love, and by what more dear a better°
proposer could charge° you withal, be even° and direct with me
whether you were sent for or no.

ROSENCRANTZ [*aside to* GUILDENSTERN]. What say you?

HAMLET [*aside*]. Nay, then, I have an eye of° you.—If you love me, hold   275
not off.°

GUILDENSTERN. My lord, we were sent for.

HAMLET. I will tell you why; so shall my anticipation prevent your discovery,° and your secrecy to the King and Queen molt no feather,°
I have of late—but wherefore I know not—lost all my mirth, for-   280
gone all custom of exercises; and indeed it goes so heavily with my
disposition that this goodly frame, the earth, seems to me a sterile
promontory; this most excellent canopy, the air, look you, this
brave° o'erhanging firmament, this majestical roof fretted° with
golden fire, why, it appeareth nothing to me but a foul and pesti-   285
lent congregation° of vapors. What a piece of work° is a man! How
noble in reason, how infinite in faculties, in form and moving how
express° and admirable, in action how like an angel, in apprehen-
sion° how like a god! The beauty of the world, the paragon of animals! And ye, to me, what is this quintessence°of dust? Man de-   290
lights not me—no, nor woman neither, though by your smiling you
seem to say so.

ROSENCRANTZ. My lord, there was no such stuff in my thoughts.

HAMLET. Why did you laugh, then, when I said man delights not me?

ROSENCRANTZ. To think, my lord, if you delight not in man, what Lenten   295
entertainment° the players shall receive from you. We coted° them
on the way, and higher are they coming to offer you service.

HAMLET. He that plays the king shall be welcome; His Majesty shall have
tribute° of° me. The adventurous knight shall use his foil and target,° the lover shall not sigh gratis,° the humorous man° shall end   300
his part in peace,° the clown shall make those laugh whose lungs
are tickle o' the sear,° and the lady shall say her mind freely, or
the blank verse shall halt° for 't. What players are they?

---

269 **conjure** adjure, entreat.   270 **the consonancy of our youth** our closeness in our
younger days.   271 **better** more skillful.   272 **charge** urge.   **even** straight, honest.
275 **of** on.   275–276 **hold not off** don't hold back.   278–279 **so . . . discovery** in
that way my saying it first will spare you from revealing the truth.   279 **molt no feather**
i.e., not diminish in the least.   284 **brave** splendid.   **fretted** adorned (with fretwork, as
in a vaulted ceiling).   286 **congregation** mass.   **piece of work** masterpiece.   288
express well-framed, exact, expressive.   288–289 **apprehension** power of comprehending.   290 **quintessence** the fifth essence of ancient philosophy, beyond earth, water, air, and fire, supposed to be the substance of the heavenly bodies and to be latent in
all things.   295–296 **Lenten entertainment** meager reception (appropriate to Lent).
296 **coted** overtook and passed by.   299 **tribute** (1) applause (2) homage paid in
money.   **of** from.   299–300 **foil and target** sword and shield.   300 **gratis** for nothing.
humorous man eccentric character, dominated by one trait or "humor."   301 **in peace**
i.e., with full license.   302 **tickle o' the sear** easy on the trigger, read to laugh easily (a
sear is part of a gunlock).   303 **halt** limp.

ROSENCRANTZ. Even those you were wont to take such delight in, the
tragedians° of the city.   305
HAMLET. How chances it they travel? Their residence,° both in reputation
and profit, was better both ways.
ROSENCRANTZ. I think their inhibition° comes by the means of the late°
innovation.°
HAMLET. Do they hold the same estimation they did when I was in the   310
city? Are they so followed?
ROSENCRANTZ. No, indeed are they not.
HAMLET. How comes it? Do they grow rusty?
ROSENCRANTZ. Nay, their endeavor keeps° in the wonted° pace. But
there is, sir, an aerie° of children, little eyases,° that cry out on the   315
top of question° and are most tyrannically° clapped for 't. These
are now the fashion, and so berattle° the common stages°—so they
call them—that many wearing rapiers° are afraid of goose quills°
and dare scarce come thither.
HAMLET. What, are they children? Who maintains 'em? How are they   320
escoted?° Will they pursue the quality° no longer than they can
sing?° Will they not say afterwards, if they should grow themselves
to common° prayers—as it is most like,° if their means are no
better°—their writers do them wrong to make them exclaim against
their own succession?°   325
ROSENCRANTZ. Faith, there has been much to-do° on both sides, and the
nation holds it no sin to tar° them to controversy. There was for a
while no money bid for argument unless the poet and the player
went to cuffs in the question.°
HAMLET. Is 't possible?   330
GUILDENSTERN. O, there has been much throwing about of brains.
HAMLET. Do the boys carry it away?°
ROSENCRANTZ. Ay, that they do, my lord—Hercules and his load° too.°

---

305 tragedians actors.   **306 residence** remaining in their usual place, i.e., in the city.
308 inhibition formal prohibition (from acting plays in the city).   **late** recent.   **309
innovation** i.e., the new fashion in satirical plays performed by boy actors in the "private" theaters; or possibly a political uprising; or the strict limitations set on the theaters
in London in 1600.   **314 keeps** continues.   **wonted** usual.   **315 aerie** nest.   **eyases**
young hawks.   **315–316 cry . . . question** speak shrilly, dominating the controversy (in
decrying the public theaters).   **316 tyrannically** outrageously.   **317 berattle** berate,
clamor against.   **common stages** public theaters.   **318 many wearing rapiers** i.e.,
many men of fashion, afraid to patronize the common players for fear of being satirized by
the poets writing for the boy actors.   **goose quills** i.e., pens of satirists.   **320–321 escoted** maintained.   **321 quality** (acting) profession.   **321–322 no longer . . . sing**
i.e., only until their voices change.   **323 common** regular, adult.   **like** likely.
323–324 if . . . better if they find no better way to support themselves.   **325
succession** i.e., future careers.   **326 to-do** ado.   **327 tar** set on (as dogs).   **327–329
There . . . question** i.e., for a while, no money was offered by the acting companies to
playwrights for the plot to a play unless the satirical poets who wrote for the boys and the
adult actors came to blows in the play itself.   **332 carry it away** i.e., win the day.   **333
Hercules . . . load** (Thought to be an allusion to the sign of the Globe Theatre, which
was Hercules bearing the world on his shoulders.)   **313–333 How . . . load too** (The
passage, omitted from the early quartos, alludes to the so-called War of the Theaters,
1599–1602, the rivalry between the children's companies and the adult actors.)

HAMLET. It is not very strange; for my uncle is King of Denmark, and
    those that would make mouths° at him while my father lived give   335
    twenty, forty, fifty, a hundred ducats° apiece for his picture in
    little.° 'Sblood,° there is something in this more than natural, if
    philosophy° could find it out.

                                        A flourish [*of trumpets within*].

GUILDENSTERN. There are the players.

HAMLET. Gentlemen, you are welcome to Elsinore. Your hands, come   340
    then. Th' appurtenance° of welcome is fashion and ceremony. Let
    me comply° with you in this garb,° lest my extent° to the players,
    which, I tell you, must show fairly outwards,° should more appear
    like entertainment° than yours. You are welcome. But my uncle-
    father and aunt-mother are deceived.   345

GUILDENSTERN. In what, my dear lord?

HAMLET. I am but mad north-north-west.° When the wind is southerly I
    know a hawk from a handsaw.°

    Enter POLONIUS.

POLONIUS. Well be with you, gentlemen!

HAMLET. Hark you, Guildenstern, and you too; at each ear a hearer. That   350
    great baby you see there is not yet out of his swaddling clouts.°

ROSENCRANTZ. Haply° he is the second time come to them, for they say
    an old man is twice a child.

HAMLET. I will prophesy he comes to tell me of the players. Mark it.—
    You say right, sir, o' Monday morning, 'twas then indeed.   355

POLONIUS. My lord, I have news to tell you.

HAMLET. My lord, I have news to tell you. When Roscius° was an actor in
    Rome—

POLONIUS. The actors are come hither, my lord.

HAMLET. Buzz,° buzz!   360

POLONIUS. Upon my honor—

HAMLET. Then came each actor on his ass.

POLONIUS. The best actors in the world, either for tragedy, comedy, his-
    tory, pastoral, pastoral-comical, historical-pastoral, tragical-historical,
    tragical-comical-historical-pastoral, scene individable,° or poem un-   365

---

335 mouths faces.   **336 ducats** gold coins.   **336–337 in little** in miniature.   **337
'Sblood** by God's (Christ's) blood.   **338 philosophy** i.e., scientific inquiry.   **341
appurtenance** proper accompaniment.   **342 comply** observe the formalities of courtesy.   **garb** i.e., manner.   **my extent** that which I extend, i.e., my polite behavior.
343 show fairly outwards show every evidence of cordiality.   **344 entertainment** a
(warm) reception.   **347 north-north-west** just off true north, only partly.   **348
hawk, handsaw** i.e., two very different things, though also perhaps meaning a mattock
(or *hack*) and a carpenter's cutting tool, respectively; also birds, with a play on
hernshaw, or heron.   **351 swaddling clouts** cloths in which to wrap a newborn baby.
352 Haply perhaps.   **357 Roscius** a famous Roman actor who died in 62 BCE   **360
Buzz** (An interjection used to denote stale news.)   **365 scene individable** a play observing the unity of place; or perhaps one that is unclassifiable, or performed without
intermission.

limited.° Seneca° cannot be too heavy, nor Plautus° too light. For
the law of writ and the liberty,° these° are the only men.

HAMLET. O Jephthah, judge of Israel,° what a treasure hadst thou!

POLONIUS. What a treasure had he, my lord?

HAMLET. Why,   370

"One fair daughter, and no more,
The which he lovèd passing° well."

POLONIUS [*aside*]. Still on my daughter.

HAMLET. Am I not i' the right, old Jephthah?

POLONIUS. If you call me Jephthah, my lord, I have a daughter that I   375
love passing well.

HAMLET. Nay, that follows not.

POLONIUS. What follows then, my lord?

HAMLET. Why,

"As by lot,° God wot,"°   380

and then, you know.

"It came to pass, as most like° it was"—

the first row° of the pious chanson° will show you more, for look
where my abridgement° comes.

Enter the PLAYERS.

You are welcome, masters; welcome, all. I am glad to see thee   385
well. Welcome, good friends. O, old friend! Why, thy face is
valanced° since I saw thee last. Com'st thou to beard° me in Denmark? What, my young lady° and mistress! By 'r Lady,° your ladyship is nearer to heaven than when I saw you last, by the altitude of
a chopine.° Pray God your voice, like a piece of uncurrent° gold,   390
be not cracked within the ring.° Masters, you are all welcome.
We'll e'en to 't° like French falconers, fly at anything we see. We'll
have a speech straight.° Come, give us a taste of your quality.°
Come, a passionate speech.

FIRST PLAYER. What speech, my good lord?   395

HAMLET. I heard thee speak me a speech once, but it was never acted, or
if it was, not above once, for the play, I remember, pleased not the
million; 'twas caviar to the general.° But it was—as I received it,

---

365–366 poem unlimited a play disregarding the unities of time and place; one that is all-
inclusive.   **Seneca** writer of Latin tragedies.   **Plautus** writer of Latin comedy.   **367
law . . . liberty** dramatic composition both according to the rules and disregarding the
rules.   **these** i.e., the actors.   **368 Jephthah . . . Israel** (Jephthah had to sacrifice his
daughter; see Judges 11. Hamlet goes on to quote from a ballad on the theme.)   **372
passing** surpassingly.   **380 lot** chance.   **wot** knows.   **382 like** likely, probable.   **383
row** stanza.   **chanson** ballad, song.   **384 my abridgement** something that cuts short
my conversation; also, a diversion.   **387 valanced** fringed (with a beard).   **beard** confront, challenge (with obvious pun).   **388 young lady** i.e., boy playing women's parts.
By 'r Lady by Our Lady.   **390 chopine** thick-soled shoe of Italian fashion.   **uncurrent**
not passable as lawful coinage.   **391 cracked . . . ring** i.e., changed from adolescent to
male voice, no longer suitable for women's roles. (Coins featured rings enclosing the sovereign's head; if the coin was cracked within this ring, it was unfit for currency).   **392
e'en to 't** go at it.   **393 straight** at once.   **quality** professional skill.   **398 caviar to the
general** caviar to the multitude, i.e., a choice dish too elegant for coarse tastes.

and others, whose judgments in such matters cried in the top of°
mine—an excellent play, well digested° in the scenes, set down   400
with as much modesty° as cunning.° I remember one said there
were no sallets° in the lines to make the matter savory, nor no matter
in the phrase that might indict° the author of affectation, but called
it an honest method, as wholesome as sweet, and by very much
more handsome° than fine.° One speech in 't I chiefly loved: 'twas   405
Aeneas' tale to Dido, and thereabout of it especially when he
speaks of Priam's slaughter.° If it live in your memory, begin at this
line: let me see, let me see—
    "The rugged Pyrrhus,° like th' Hyrcanian beast"°—
'Tis not so. It begins with Pyrrhus: 410
    "The rugged° Pyrrhus, he whose sable° arms,
Black as his purpose, did the night resemble
When he lay couchèd° in the ominous horse,°
Hath now this dread and black complexion smeared
With heraldry more dismal.° Head to foot   415
Now is he total gules,° horridly tricked°
With blood of fathers, mothers, daughters, sons,
Baked and impasted° with the parching streets,°
That lend a tyrannous° and a damnèd light
To their lord's° murder. Roasted in wrath and fire,   420
And thus o'ersized° with coaglate gore,
With eyes like carbuncles,° the hellish Pyrrhus
Old grandsire Priam seeks."
So proceed you.

POLONIUS. 'Fore God, my lord, well spoken, with good accent and good   425
discretion.

FIRST PLAYER. "Anon he finds him
Striking too short at Greeks. His antique° sword,
Rebellious to his arm, lies where it falls,
Repugnant° to command. Unequal matched,   430
Pyrrhus at Priam drives, in rage strikes wide,

---

399 cried in the top of i.e., spoke with greater authority than.   **400 digested** arranged,
ordered.   **401 modesty** moderation, restraint.   **cunning** skill.   **402 sallets** i.e., something savory, spicy improprieties.   **403 indict** convict.   **405 handsome** well-
proportioned.   **fine** elaborately ornamented, showy.   **407 Priam's slaughter** the slaying of the ruler of Troy, when the Greeks finally took the city.   **409 Pyrrhus** a Greek
hero in the Trojan War, also known as Neoptolemus, son of Achilles—another avenging
son.   **Hyrcanian beast** i.e., tiger. (On the death of Priam, see Virgil, *Aeneid,* 2.506 ff.;
compare the whole speech with Marlowe's *Dido Queen of Carthage,* 2.1.214 ff. On the
Hyrcanian tiger, see *Aeneid,* 4.366–367. Hyrcania is on the Caspian Sea.)   **411 rugged**
shaggy, savage.   **sable** black (for reasons of camouflage during the episode of the Trojan
horse).   **413 couchèd** concealed.   **ominous horse** fateful Trojan horse, by which the
Greeks gained access to Troy.   **415 dismal** ill-omened.   **416 total gules** entirely red (a
heraldic term).   **tricked** spotted and smeared (heraldic).   **418 impasted** crusted, like a
thick paste.   **with . . . streets** by the parching heat of the streets (because of the fires
everywhere).   **419 tyrannous** cruel.   **420 their lord's** i.e., Priam's.   **421 o'ersized**
covered as with size or glue.   **422 carbuncles** large fiery-red precious stones thought to
emit their own light.   **428 antique** ancient, long-used.   **430 Repugnant** disobedient,
resistant.

But with the whiff and wind of his fell° sword
Th' unnervèd° father falls. Then senseless Ilium,°
Seeming to feel this blow, with flaming top
Stoops to his° base, and with a hideous crash   435
Takes prisoner Pyrrhus' ear. For, lo! His sword,
Which was declining° on the milky° head
Of reverend Priam, seemed i' th' air to stick.
So as a painted° tyrant Pyrrhus stood,
And, like a neutral to his will and matter,°   440
Did nothing.
But as we often see against° some storm
A silence in the heavens, the rack° stand still,
The bold winds speechless, and the orb° below
As hush as death, anon the dreadful thunder   445
Doth rend the region,° so, after Pyrrhus' pause,
A rousèd vengeance sets him new a-work
And never did the Cyclops° hammers fall
On Mars's armor forged for proof eterne°
With less remorse° than Pyrrhus bleeding sword   450
Now falls on Priam.
Out, out, thou strumpet Fortune! All you gods
In general synod° take away her power!
Break all the spokes and fellies° from her wheel,
And bowl the round nave° down the hill of heaven°   455
As low as to the fiends!"
POLONIUS. This is too long.
HAMLET. It shall to the barber's with your beard.—Prithee, say on.
He's for a jig° or a tale of bawdry, or he sleeps. Say on; come to
Hecuba.°   460
FIRST PLAYER. "But who, ah woe! had° seen the moblèd° queen"—
HAMLET. "The moblèd queen?"
POLONIUS. That's good. "Moblèd queen" is good.
FIRST PLAYER. "Run barefoot up and down, threat'ning the flames°
With bisson rheum,° a clout° upon that head   465
Where late° the diadem stood, and, for a robe,
About her lank and all o'erteemèd° loins
A blanket, in the alarm of fear caught up—
Who this had seen, with tongue in venom steeped,

---

432 fell cruel.   **433 unnervèd** strengthless.   **senseless Ilium** inanimate citadel of Troy.
435 his its.   **437 declining** descending.   **milky** white-haired.   **439 painted** i.e.,
painted in a picture.   **440 like . . . matter** i.e., as though suspended between his intention and its fulfillment.   **442 against** just before.   **443 rack** mass of clouds.   **444 orb**
globe, earth.   **446 region** sky.   **448 Cyclops** giant armor makers in the smithy of Vulcan.
449 proof eterne eternal resistance to assault.   **450 remorse** pity.   **453 synod** assembly.   **454 fellies** pieces of wood forming the rim of a wheel.   **455 nave** hub.   **hill of**
heaven Mount Olympus.   **459 jig** comic song and dance often given at the end of a play.
460 Hecuba wife of Priam.   **461 who . . . had** anyone who had (also in line 469).
moblèd muffled.   **464 threat'ning the flames** i.e., weeping hard enough to dampen the
flames.   **465 bisson rheum** building tears.   **clout** cloth.   **466 late** lately.   **467 all o'er-**
teemèd utterly worn out with bearing children.

'Gainst Fortune's state° would treason have pronounced.°   470
But if the gods themselves did see her then
When she saw Pyrrhus make malicious sport
In mincing with his sword her husband's limbs,
The instant burst of clamor that she made,
Unless things mortal move them not at all,   475
Would have made milch° the burning eyes of heaven,°
And passion° in the gods."

POLONIUS. Look whe'er° he has not turned his color and has tears in 's
eyes. Prithee, no more.

HAMLET. 'Tis well; I'll have thee speak out the rest of this soon.—Good   480
my lord, will you see the players well bestowed?° Do you hear, let
them be well used, for they are the abstract° and brief chronicles of
the time. After your death you were better have a bad epitaph than
their ill report while you live.

POLONIUS. My lord, I will use them according to their desert.   485

HAMLET. God's bodikin,° man, much better. Use every man after his
desert, and who shall scape whipping? Use them after° your own
honor and dignity. The less they deserve, the more merit is in your
bounty. Take them in.

POLONIUS. Come, sirs.   490

[*Exit.*]

HAMLET. Follow him, friends. We'll hear a play tomorrow. [*As they start
to leave,* HAMLET *detains the* FIRST PLAYER.] Dost thou hear me, old
friend? Can you play *The Murder of Gonzago?*

FIRST PLAYER. Ay, my lord.

HAMLET. We'll ha 't° tomorrow night. You could, for a need, study° a   495
speech of some dozen or sixteen lines which I would set down and
insert in 't, could you not?

FIRST PLAYER. Ay, my lord.

HAMLET. Very well. Follow that lord, and look you mock him not.
(*Exeunt* PLAYERS.) My good friends, I'll leave you till night. You are   500
welcome to Elsinore.

ROSENCRANTZ. Good my lord!

Exeunt [ROSENCRANTZ *and* GUILDENSTERN].

HAMLET. Ay, so goodbye to you.—Now I am alone.
O, what a rogue and peasant slave am I!
Is it not monstrous that this player here,   505
But° in a fiction, in a dream of passion,
Could force his soul so to his own conceit?°
That from her working° all his visage wanned,°
Tears in his eyes, distraction in his aspect,°

---

470 **state** rule, managing. **pronounced** proclaimed.   476 **milch** milky, moist with
tears. **burning eyes of heaven** i.e., heavenly bodies.   477 **passion** overpowering
emotion.   478 **whe'er** whether.   481 **bestowed** lodged.   482 **abstract** summary account.   486 **God's bodikin** by God's (Christ's) little body, *bodykin* (not to be confused
with *bodkin,* "dagger").   487 **after** according to.   495 **ha 't** have it.   **study** memorize.
506 **But** merely.   507 **force . . . conceit** bring his innermost being so entirely into accord with his conception (of the role).   508 **from her working** as a result of, or in response to, his soul's activity.   **wanned** grew pale.   509 **aspect** look, glance.

A broken voice, and his whole function suiting   510
With forms to his conceit° And all for nothing!
For Hecuba!
What's Hecuba to him, or he to Hecuba,
That he should weep for her? What would he do
Had he the motive and the cue for passion   515
That I have? He would drown the stage with tears
And cleave the general ear° with horrid° speech,
Make mad the guilty and appall° the free,°
Confound the ignorant,° and amaze° indeed
The very faculties of eyes and ears. Yet I,   520
A dull and muddy-mettled° rascal, peak°
Like John-a-dreams,° unpregnant of° my cause,
And can say nothing—no, not for a king
Upon whose property° and most dear life
A damned defeat° was made. Am I a coward?   525
Who calls me villain? Breaks my pate° across?
Plucks off my beard and blows it in my face?
Tweaks me by the nose? Gives me the lie i' the throat°
As deep as to the lungs? Who does me this?
Ha, 'swounds,° I should take it; for it cannot be   530
But I am pigeon-livered° and lack gall
To make oppression bitter,° or ere this
I should ha' fatted all the region kites°
With this slave's offal.° Bloody, bawdy villain!
Remorseless,° treacherous, lecherous, kindless° villain!   535
O, vengeance!
Why, what an ass am I? This is most brave,°
That I, the son of a dear father murdered,
Prompted to my revenge by heaven and hell,
Must like a whore unpack my heart with words   540
And fall a-cursing, like a very drab,°
A scullion!° Fie upon 't, foh! About,° my brains!
Hum, I have heard
That guilty creatures sitting at a play
Have by the very cunning° of the scene°   545

510–511 his whole . . . conceit all his bodily powers responding with actions to suit his thought.   **517 the general ear** everyone's ear.   **horrid** horrible.   **518 appall** (literally, make pale.)   **free** innocent.   **519 Confound the ignorant** i.e., dumbfound those who know nothing of the crime that has been committed.   **amaze** stun.   **521 muddy-mettled** dull-spirited.   **peak** mope, pine.   **522 John-a-dreams** a sleepy, dreaming idler.   **unpregnant of** not quickened by.   **524 property** i.e., the crown; also character, quality.   **525 damned defeat** damnable act of destruction.   **526 pate** head.   **528 Gives . . . throat** calls me an out-and-out liar.   **530 'swounds** by his (Christ's) wounds.   **531 pigeon-livered** (The pigeon or dove was popularly supposed to be mild because it secreted no gall).   **532 bitter** i.e., bitter to me.   **533 region kites** kites (birds of prey) of the air.   **534 offal** entrails.   **535 Remorseless** pitiless.   **kindless** unnatural.   **537 brave** fine, admirable (said ironically).   **541 drab** whore.   **542 scullion** menial kitchen servant (apt to be foul-mouthed).   **About** about it, to work.   **545 cunning** art, skill.   **scene** dramatic presentation.

Been struck so to the soul that presently°
They have proclaimed their malefactions;
For murder, though it have no tongue, will speak
With most miraculous organ. I'll have these players
Play something like the murder of my father   550
Before mine uncle. I'll observe his looks;
I'll tent° him to the quick.° If 'a do blench,°
I know my course. The spirit that I have seen
May be the devil, and the devil hath power
T' assume a pleasing shape; yea, and perhaps,   555
Out of my weakness and my melancholy,
As he is very potent with such spirits,°
Abuses° me to damn me. I'll have grounds
More relative° than this. The play's the thing
Wherein I'll catch the conscience of the King.   560

                                          Exit.

    3.1 *Enter* KING, QUEEN, POLONIUS, OPHELIA, ROSENCRANTZ, GUILDENSTERN,
      lords.

KING. And can you by no drift of conference°
Get from him why he puts on this confusion,
Grating so harshly all his days of quiet
With turbulent and dangerous lunacy?
ROSENCRANTZ. He does confess he feels himself distracted,   5
But from what cause 'a will by no means speak.
GUILDENSTERN. Nor do we find him forward° to be sounded,°
But with a crafty madness keeps aloof
When we would bring him on to some confession
Of his true state.
QUEEN.   Did he receive you well?   10
ROSENCRANTZ. Most like a gentleman.
GUILDENSTERN. But with much forcing of his disposition.°
ROSENCRANTZ. Niggard° of question,° but of our demands
Most free in his reply.
QUEEN.   Did you assay° him
To any pastime?   15
ROSENCRANTZ. Madam, it so fell out that certain players
We o'erraught° on the way. Of these we told him,
And there did seem in him a kind of joy
To hear of it. They are here about the court,
And, as I think, they have already order   20
This night to play before him.

---

546 presently at once. **552 tent** probe. **the quick** the tender part of a wound, the
core. **blench** quail, flinch. **557 spirits** humors (of melancholy). **558 Abuses** de-
ludes. **559 relative** cogent, pertinent. **3.1. Location:** The castle. **1 drift of conference** directing of conversation. **7 forward** willing. **sounded** questioned. **12 disposition** inclination. **13 Niggard** stingy. **question** conversation. **14 assay** try to
win. **17 o'erraught** overtook.

POLONIUS.   'Tis most true,
  And he beseeched me to entreat Your Majesties
  To hear and see the matter.
KING. With all my heart, and it doth much content me
  To hear him so inclined.   25
  Good gentlemen, give him a further edge°
  And drive his purpose into these delights.
ROSENCRANTZ. We shall, my lord.

                       Exeunt ROSENCRANTZ *and* GUILDENSTERN.

KING.   Sweet Gertrude, leave us too,
  For we have closely° sent for Hamlet hither,
  That he, as 'twere by accident, may here   30
  Affront° Ophelia.
  Her father and myself, lawful espials,°
  Will so bestow ourselves that seeing, unseen,
  We may of their encounter frankly judge,
  And gather by him, as he is behaved,   35
  If't be th' affliction of his love or no
  That thus he suffers for.
QUEEN.   I shall obey you.
  And for your part, Ophelia, I do wish
  That your good beauties be the happy cause
  Of Hamlet's wildness. So shall I hope your virtues   40
  Will bring him to his wonted° way again,
  To both your honors.
OPHELIA.   Madame, I wish it may.

                                                    [*Exit* QUEEN.]

POLONIUS. Ophelia, walk you here.—Gracious,° so please you,
  We will bestow° ourselves. [*To* OPHELIA.] Read on this book,
                                     [*giving her a book*]
  That show of such an exercise° may color°   45
  Your loneliness.° We are oft to blame in this—
  'Tis too much proved°—that with devotion's visage
  And pious action we do sugar o'er
  The devil himself.
KING [*aside*]. O 'tis too true!   50
  How smart a lash that speech doth give my conscience!
  The harlot's cheek, beautied with plastering art,
  Is not more ugly to° the thing° that helps it
  Than is my deed to my most painted word.
  O heavy burden!   55
POLONIUS. I hear him coming. Let's withdraw, my lord.

                       [*The* KING *and* POLONIUS *withdraw.*°]

---

26 edge incitement. **29 closely** privately. **31 Affront** confront, meet. **32 espials**
spies. **41 wonted** accustomed. **43 Gracious** Your Grace (i.e., the King). **44 bestow**
conceal. **45 exercise** religious exercise. (The book she reads is one of devotion.)
color give a plausible appearance to. **46 loneliness** being alone. **47 too much**
proved too often shown to be true, too often practiced. **53 to** compared to. **the**
thing i.e., the cosmetic. **56 s.d. withdraw** (The King and Polonius may retire behind
an arras. The stage directions specify that they "enter" again near the end of the scene.)

Enter HAMLET. [OPHELIA *pretends to read a book.*]

HAMLET. To be, or not to be, that is the question:
Whether 'tis nobler in the mind to suffer
The slings° and arrows of outrageous fortune,
Or to take arms against a sea of troubles   60
And by opposing end them. To die, to sleep—
No more—and by a sleep to say we end
The heartache and the thousand natural shocks
That flesh is heir to. 'Tis a consummation
Devoutly to be wished. To die, to sleep;   65
To sleep, perchance to dream. Ay, there's the rub,°
For in that sleep of death what dreams may come,
When we have shuffled° off this mortal coil,°
Must give us pause. There's the respect°
That makes calamity of so long life.°   70
For who would bear the whips and scorns of time,
Th' oppressor's wrong, the proud man's contumely,°
The pangs of disprized° love, the law's delay,
The insolence of office,° and the spurns°
That patient merit of th' unworthy takes,°   75
When he himself might his quietus° make
With a bare bodkin?° Who would fardels° bear,
To grunt and sweat under a weary life,
But that the dread of something after death,
The undiscovered country from whose bourn°   80
No traveler returns, puzzles the will,
And makes us rather bear those ills we have
Than fly to others that we know not of?
Thus conscience does make cowards of us all;
And thus the native hue° of resolution   85
Is sicklied o'er with the pale cast° of thought,
And enterprises of great pitch° and moment°
With this regard° their currents° turn awry
And lose the name of action.—Soft you° now,
The fair Ophelia. Nymph, in thy orisons°   90
Be all my sins remembered.
OPHELIA.   Good my lord,
How does your honor for this many a day?
HAMLET. I humbly thank you; well, well, well.
OPHELIA. My lord, I have remembrances of yours,

---

59 slings missiles. **66 rub** (Literally, an obstacle in the game of bowls.) **68 shuffled**
sloughed, cast. **coil** turmoil. **69 respect** consideration. **70 of . . . life** so long-lived,
something we willingly endure for so long (also suggesting that long life is itself a calamity).
72 contumely insolent abuse. **73 disprized** unvalued. **74 office** officialdom.
spurns insults. **75 of . . . takes** receives from unworthy persons. **76 quietus** acqui-
tance; here, death. **77 a bare bodkin** a mere dagger, unsheathed. **fardels** burdens. **80**
bourn frontier, boundary. **85 native hue** natural color complexion. **86 cast** tinge,
shade of color. **87 pitch** height (as of a falcon's flight). **moment** importance. **88**
regard respect, consideration. **currents** courses. **89 Soft you** i.e., wait a minute,
gently. **90 orisons** prayers.

That I have longèd long to redeliver.   95
I pray you, now receive them.   [*She offers tokens.*]
HAMLET. No, not I, I never gave you aught.
OPHELIA. My honored lord, you know right well you did,
And with them words of so sweet breath composed
As made the things more rich. Their perfume lost,   100
Take these again, for to the noble mind
Rich gifts wax poor when givers prove unkind.
There, my lord.   [*She gives tokens.*]
HAMLET. Ha, ha! Are you honest?°
OPHELIA. My lord?   105
HAMLET. Are you fair?°
OPHELIA. What means your lordship?
HAMLET. That if you be honest and fair, your honesty° should admit no
    discourse° to your beauty.
OPHELIA. Could beauty, my lord, have better commerce° than with   110
    honesty?
HAMLET. Ay, truly, for the power of beauty will sooner transform hon-
    esty from what it is to a bawd than the force of honesty can trans-
    late beauty into his° likeness. This was sometime° a paradox,°
    but now the time° gives it proof. I did love you once.   115
OPHELIA. Indeed, my lord, you made me believe so.
HAMLET. You should not have believed me, for virtue cannot so inocu-
    late° our old stock but we shall relish of it.° I loved you not.
OPHELIA. I was the more deceived.
HAMLET. Get thee to a nunnery.° Why wouldst thou be a breeder of sin- 120
    ners? I am myself indifferent honest,° but yet I could accuse me of
    such things that it were better my mother had not borne me: I am
    very proud, revengeful, ambitious, with more offenses at my beck°
    than I have thoughts to put them in, imagination to give them
    shape, or time to act them in. What should such fellows as I do   125
    crawling between earth and heaven? We are arrant knaves all; be-
    lieve none of us. Go thy ways to a nunnery. Where's your father?
OPHELIA. At home, my lord.
HAMLET. Let the doors be shut upon him, that he may play the fool
    nowhere but in's own house. Farewell.   130
OPHELIA. O, help him, you sweet heavens!
HAMLET. If thou dost marry, I'll give thee this plague for thy dowry: be
    thou as chaste as ice, as pure as snow, thou shall not escape
    calumny. Get thee to a nunnery, farewell. Or, if thou wilt needs

---

104 honest (1) truthful (2) chaste.   **106 fair** (1) beautiful (2) just, honorable.   **108 your
honesty** your chastity.   **109 discourse** to familiar dealings with.   **110 commerce** dealings, intercourse.   **114 his** its.   **sometime** formerly.   **a paradox** a view opposite to
commonly held opinion.   **115 the time** the present age.   **117–118 inoculate** graft, be
engrafted to.   **118 but . . . it** that we do not still have about us a taste of the old stock,
i.e., retain our sinfulness.   **120 nunnery** convent (with possibly an awareness that the
word was also used derisively to denote a brothel).   **121 indifferent honest** reasonably
virtuous.   **123 beck** command.

marry, marry a fool, for wise men know well enough what mon- 135
sters° you° make of them. To a nunnery, go, and quickly too.
Farewell.

OPHELIA. Heavenly powers, restore him!

HAMLET. I have heard of your paintings too, well enough. God hath
given you one face, and you make yourselves another. You jig,° you 140
amble,° and you lisp, you nickname God's creatures,° and make
your wantonness your ignorance.° Go to, I'll no more on 't;° it hath
made me mad. I say we will have no more marriage. Those that are
married already—all but one—shall live. The rest shall keep as they
are. To a nunnery, go.   145

                                                                 Exit.

OPHELIA. O, what a nobler mind is here o'erthrown!
      The courtier's, soldier's, scholar's, eye, tongue, sword,
      Th expectancy° and rose° of the fair state,
      The glass of fashion and the mold of form,°
      Th' observed of all observers,° quite, quite down!   150
      And I, of ladies most deject and wretched,
      That sucked the honey of his music° vows,
      Now see that noble and most sovereign reason
      Like sweet bells jangled out of tune and harsh,
      That unmatched form and feature of blown° youth   155
      Blasted° with ecstasy.° O, woe is me,
      T' have seen what I have seen, see what I see!

      Enter KING *and* POLONIUS.

KING. Love? His affections° do not that way tend;
      Nor what he spake, though it lacked form a little,
      Was not like madness. There's something in his soul   160
      O'er which his melancholy sits on brood,°
      And I do doubt° the hatch and the disclose°
      Will be some danger, which for to prevent,
      I have in quick determination
      Thus set it down:° he shall with speed to England   165
      For the demand of° our neglected tribute.
      Haply the seas and countries different
      With variable objects° shall expel

135–136 **monsters** (An illusion to the horns of a cuckold.) **you** i.e., you women. **140
jig** dance. **141 amble** move coyly. **141 you nickname . . . creatures** i.e., you give
trendy names to things in place of their God-given names. **142 make . . . ignorance**
i.e., excuse your affectation on the grounds of pretended ignorance. **on 't** of it. **148
expectancy** hope. **rose** ornament. **149 The glass . . . form** the mirror of true fashioning and the pattern of courtly behavior. **150 Th' observed . . . observers** i.e., the
center of attention and honor in the court. **152 music** musical, sweetly uttered. **155
blown** blooming. **156 Blasted** withered. **156 ecstasy** madness. **158 affections**
emotions, feelings. **161 sits on brood** sits like a bird on a nest, about to *hatch* mischief
(line 162). **162 doubt** fear. **disclose** disclosure, hatching. **165 set it down** resolved.
166 For . . . of to demand. **168 variable objects** various sights and surroundings to
divert him.

This something-settled matter in his heart,°
Whereon his brains still° beating puts him thus   170
From fashion of himself.° What think you on 't?
POLONIUS. It shall do well. But yet do I believe
The origin and commencement of his grief
Sprung from neglected love.—How now, Ophelia?
You need not tell us what Lord Hamlet said;   175
We heard it all.—My lord, do as you please,
But, if you hold it fit, after the play
Let his queen-mother° all alone entreat him
To show his grief. Let her be round° with him;
And I'll be placed, so please you, in the ear   180
Of all their conference. If she find him not,°
To England send him, or confine him where
Your wisdom best shall think.
KING.   It shall be so.
Madness in great ones must not unwatched to.

                                                              Exeunt.

3.2 *Enter* HAMLET *and three of the* PLAYERS.

HAMLET. Speak the speech, I pray you, as I pronounced it to you, trip-
pingly on the tongue. But if you mouth it, as many of our players°
do, I had as lief° the town crier spoke my lines. Nor do not saw the
air too much with your hand, thus, but use all gently; for in the
very torrent, tempest, and, as I may say, whirlwind of your passion,   5
you must acquire and beget a temperance that may give it smooth-
ness. O, it offends me to the soul to hear a robustious° periwig-
pated° fellow tear a passion to tatters, to very rags, to split the ears
of the groundlings,° who for the most part are capable of° nothing
but inexplicable dumb shows° and noise. I would have such a fellow   10
whipped for o'erdoing Termagant.° It out-Herods Herod.° Pray
you, avoid it.
FIRST PLAYER. I warrant your honor.
HAMLET. Be not too tame neither, but let your own discretion be your
tutor. Suit the action in the word, the word to the action, with this 15
special observance, that you o'erstep not the modesty° of nature.
For anything so o'erdone is from° the purpose of playing, whose

---

169 **This something . . . heart** the strange matter settled in his heart.   170 **still** continually.   171 **From . . . himself** out of his natural manner.   178 **queen-mother** queen
and mother.   179 **round** blunt.   181 **find him not** fails to discover what is troubling
him.   **3.2. Location: The castle.**   2 **our players** players nowadays.   3 **I had as lief** I
would just as soon.   7 **robustious** violent, boisterous.   7–8 **periwig-pated** wearing a
wig.   9 **groundlings** spectators who paid least and stood in the yard of the theater.
capable of able to understand.   10 **dumb shows** mimed performances, often used before Shakespeare's time to precede a play or each act.   11 **Termagant** a supposed deity
of the Mohammedans, not found in any English medieval play but elsewhere portrayed as
violent and blustering.   **Herod** Herod of Jewry. (A character in *The Slaughter of the Innocents* and other cycle plays. The part was played with great noise and fury.)   16
modesty restraint, moderation.   17 **from** contrary to.

end, both at the first and now, was and is to hold as 't were the
mirror up to nature, to show virtue her feature, scorn° her own image, and the very age and body of the time° his° form and pres-   20
sure.° Now this overdone or come tardy off,° though it makes the
unskillful° laugh, cannot but make the judicious grieve, the censure of the which one° must in your allowance° o'erweigh a whole
theater of others. O, there be players that I have seen play, and
heard others praise, and that highly, not to speak it profanely,°   25
that, neither having th' accent of Christians° nor the gait of Christian, pagan, nor man,° have so strutted and bellowed that I have
thought some of nature's journeymen° had made men and not
made them well, they imitated humanity so abominably.°

FIRST PLAYER. I hope we have reformed that indifferently° with us, sir.   30
HAMLET. O, reform it altogether. And let those that play your clowns
   speak no more than is set down for them; for there be of them°
   that will themselves laugh, to set on some quantity of barren° spectators to laugh too, though in the meantime some necessary question of the play be then to be considered. That's villainous, and   35
   shows a most pitiful ambition in the fool that uses it. Go make you
   ready.

> [*Exeunt* PLAYERS.]

Enter POLONIUS, GUILDENSTERN *and* ROSENCRANTZ.

How now, my lord, will the King hear this piece of work?
POLONIUS.   And the Queen too, and that presently.°
HAMLET.   Bid the players make haste.   40

> [*Exit* POLONIUS.]

Will you two help to hasten them?
ROSENCRANTZ. Ay, my lord.

> *Exeunt they two.*

HAMLET.   What ho, Horatio!

Enter HORATIO.

HORATIO. Here, sweet lord, at your service.
HAMLET. Horatio, thou art e'en as just a man
   As e'er my conversation coped withal.°   45
HORATIO. O, my dear lord—
HAMLET.   Nay, do not think I flatter,
   For what advancement may I hope from thee

---

19 scorn i.e., something foolish and deserving of scorn.   **20 the very . . . time** i.e., the
present state of affairs.   **his** its.   **20–21 pressure** stamp, impressed character.   **21
come tardy off** inadequately done.   **21–22 the unskillful** those lacking in judgment.
22–23 the censure . . . one the judgment of even one of whom.   **23 your allowance**
your scale of values.   **25 not . . . profanely** (Hamlet anticipates his idea in lines 27–29
that some men were not made by God at all.)   **26 Christians** i.e., ordinary decent folk.
26–27 nor man i.e., nor any human being at all.   **28 journeymen** laborers who are not
yet masters in their trade.   **29 abominably** (Shakespeare's usual spelling, *abhominably,*
suggests a literal though etymologically incorrect meaning, "removed from human nature.")   **30 indifferently** tolerably.   **32 of them** some among them.   **33 barren** i.e.,
of wit.   **39 presently** at once. **45 my . . . withal** my dealings encountered.

That no revenue hast but thy good spirits
To feed and clothe thee? Why should the poor be flattered?
No, let the candied° tongue lick absurd pomp,   50
And crook the pregnant° hinges of the knee
Where thrift° may follow fawning. Dost thou hear?
Since my dear soul was mistress of her choice
And could of men distinguish her election,°
Sh' hath sealed thee° for herself, for thou hast been   55
As one, in suffering all, that suffers nothing,
A man that Fortune's buffets and rewards
Hast ta'en with equal thanks; and blest are those
Whose blood° and judgment are so well commeddled°
That they are not a pipe for Fortune's finger   60
To sound what stop° she please. Give me that man
That is not passion's slave, and I will wear him
In my heart's core, ay, in my heart of heart,
As I do thee.—Something too much of this.—
There is a play tonight before the King.   65
One scene of it comes near the circumstance
Which I have told thee of my father's death.
I prithee, when thou seest that act afoot,
Even with the very comment of thy soul°
Observe my uncle. If his occulted° guilt   70
Do not itself unkennel° in one speech,
It is a damnèd° ghost that we have seen,
And my imaginations are as foul
As Vulcan't stithy.° Give him heedful note,
For I mine eyes will rivet to his face,   75
And after we will both our judgments join
In censure of his seeming.°

HORATIO.   Well, my lord.
If 'a steal aught° the whilst this play is playing
And scape detecting, I will pay the theft.

[*Flourish.*] *Enter trumpets and kettledrums,* KING, QUEEN, POLONIUS,
OPHELIA, [ROSENCRANTZ, GUILDENSTERN, *and other lords, with guards
carrying torches*].

HAMLET. They are coming to the play. I must be idle.°   80
Get you a place.   [*The* KING, QUEEN, *and courtiers sit.*]
KING. How fares our cousin° Hamlet?

---

50 candied sugared, flattering. **51 pregnant** compliant. **52 thrift** profit. **54
could . . . election** could make distinguishing choices among persons. **55 sealed thee**
(Literally, as one would seal a legal document to mark possession.) **59 blood** passion.
commeddled commingled. **61 stop** hole in a wind instrument for controlling the
sound. **69 very . . . soul** your most penetrating observation and consideration. **70
occulted** hidden. **71 unkennel** (As one would say of a fox driven from its lair.) **72
damnèd** in league with Satan. **74 stithy** smithy, place of stiths (anvils). **77 censure
of his seeming** judgment of his appearance or behavior. **78 If 'a steal aught** if he gets
away with anything. **80 idle** (1) unoccupied (2) mad. **82 cousin** i.e., close relative.

HAMLET. Excellent, i' faith, of the chameleon's dish:° I eat the air,
   promise-crammed. You cannot feed capons° so.

KING. I have nothing with° this answer, Hamlet. These words are not   85
   mine.°

HAMLET. No, nor mine now.° [*To* POLONIUS.] My lord, you played once i'
   th' university, you say?

POLONIUS. That did I, my lord, and was accounted a good actor.

HAMLET. What did you enact?   90

POLONIUS. I did enact Julius Caesar. I was killed i' the Capitol; Brutus
   killed me.

HAMLET. It was a brute° part° of him to kill so capital a calf° there.—Be
   the players ready?

ROSENCRANTZ. Ay, my lord. They stay upon° your patience.   95

QUEEN. Come hither, my dear Hamlet, sit by me.

HAMLET. No, good Mother, here's metal° more attractive.

POLONIUS [*to the King*]. O, ho, do you mark that?

HAMLET. Lady, shall I lie in your lap?

                              [*Lying down at* OPHELIA's *feet.*]

OPHELIA. No, my lord.   100

HAMLET. I mean, my head upon your lap?

OPHELIA. Ay, my lord.

HAMLET. Do you think I meant country matters?°

OPHELIA. I think nothing, my lord.

HAMLET. That's a fair thought to lie between maids' legs.   105

OPHELIA. What is, my lord?

HAMLET. Nothing.°

OPHELIA. You are merry, my lord.

HAMLET. Who, I?

OPHELIA. Ay, my lord.   110

HAMLET. O God, your only jig maker.° What should a man do but be
   merry? For look you how cheerfully my mother looks, and my father died within's° two hours.

OPHELIA. Nay, 'tis twice two months, my lord.

---

83 chameleon's dish (Chameleons were supposed to feed on air. Hamlet deliberately
misinterprets the King's *fares* as "feeds." By his phrase *eat the air* he also plays on the
idea of feeding himself with the promise of succession, of being the *heir*.)   **84 capons**
roosters castrated and *crammed* with feed to make them succulent.   **85 have . . . with**
make nothing of, or gain nothing from.   **86 are not mine** do not respond to what I
asked.   **87 nor mine now** (Once spoken, words are proverbially no longer the
speaker's own—and hence should be uttered warily.)   **93 brute** (The Latin meaning of
brutus, "stupid," was often used punningly with the name Brutus.)   **part** (1) deed (2)
role.   **calf** fool.   **95 stay upon** await.   **97 metal** substance that is *attractive*, i.e., magnetic, but with suggestion also of *mettle*, "disposition."   **103 country matters** sexual intercourse (making a bawdy pun on the first syllable of *country*).   **107 Nothing** the figure
zero or naught, suggesting the female sexual anatomy. (*Thing* not infrequently has a
bawdy connotation of male or female anatomy, and the reference here could be made.)
111 only jig maker very best composer of jigs, i.e., pointless merriment. (Hamlet replies
sardonically to Ophelia's observation that he is merry by saying, "If you're looking for
someone who is really merry, you've come to the right person.")   **113 within's** within
this (i.e., these).

HAMLET. So long? Nay then, let the devil wear black, for I'll have a suit of   115
     sables.° O heavens! Die two months ago, and not forgotten yet?
     Then there's hope a great man's memory may outlive his life half a
     year. But, by 'r Lady, 'a must build churches, then, or else shall 'a
     suffer not thinking on,° with the hobbyhorse, whose epitaph is
     "For O, for O, the hobbyhorse is forgot."°   120

The trumpets sound. Dumb show follows.

     *Enter a King and a Queen [very lovingly]; the Queen em-
bracing him, and he her. [She kneels, and makes show of protes-
tation unto him.] He takes her up, and declines his head upon
her neck. He lies him down upon a bank of flowers. She, seeing
him asleep, leaves him. Anon comes in another man, takes off
his crown, kisses it, pours poison in the sleeper's ears, and leaves
him. The Queen returns, finds the King dead, makes passionate
action. The Poisoner with some three or four come in again,
seem to condole with her. The dead body is carried away. The
Poisoner woos the Queen with gifts; she seems harsh awhile, but
in the end accepts love.*

                                           [*Exeunt* PLAYERS.]

OPHELIA. What means this, my lord?
HAMLET. Marry, this' miching mallico;° it means mischief.
OPHELIA. Belike° this show imports the argument° of the play.

     Enter PROLOGUE.

HAMLET. We shall know by this fellow. The players cannot keep counsel;°
     they'll tell all   125
OPHELIA. Will 'a tell us what this show meant?
HAMLET. Ay, or any show that you will show him. Be not you° ashamed
     to show, he'll not shame to tell you what it means.
OPHELIA. You are naught,° you are naught. I'll mark the play.
PROLOGUE. For us and for our tragedy,   130
     Here stooping° to your clemency,
     We beg your hearing patiently.

                                           [*Exit.*]

HAMLET. Is this a prologue, or the posy of a ring?°
OPHELIA. 'Tis brief, my lord.
HAMLET. As woman's love.   135

     Enter [two PLAYERS *as] King and Queen.*

115–116 suit of sables garments trimmed with the fur of the sable and hence suited for
a wealthy person, not a mourner (but with a pun on *sable,* "black," ironically suggesting
mourning once again).   **119 suffer . . . on** undergone oblivion.   **120 For . . . forgot**
(Verse of a song occurring also in *Love's Labor Lost,* 3.1.27–28. The hobbyhorse was a
character made up to resemble a horse and rider, appearing in the morris dance and such
May-game sports. This song laments the disappearance of such customs under pressure
from the Puritans.)   **122 this' miching mallico** this is sneaking mischief.   **123 Belike**
probably.   **argument** plot.   **124 counsel** secret.   **127 Be not you** provided you are
not.   **129 naught** indecent. (Ophelia is reacting to Hamlet's pointed remarks about not
being ashamed to show all.)   **131 stooping** bowing.   **133 posy . . . ring** brief motto
in verse inscribed in a ring.

PLAYER KING. Full thirty times hath Phoebus' cart° gone round
    Neptune's salt wash° and Tellus'° orbèd ground,
    And thirty dozen moons with borrowed° sheen
    About the world have times twelve thirties been,
    Since love our hearts and Hymen° did our hands   140
    Unite commutual° in most sacred bands.°
PLAYER QUEEN. So many journeys may the sun and moon
    Make us again count o'er ere love be done!
    But, woe is me, you are sick of late,
    So far from cheer and from your former state,   145
    That I distrust° you. Yet, though I distrust,
    Discomfort° you, my lord, it is nothing° must.
    For women's fear and love hold quantity;°
    In neither aught, or in extremity.°
    Now, what my love is, proof° hath made you know,   150
    And as my love is sized,° my fear is so.
    Where love is great, the littlest doubts are fear;
    Where little fears grow great, great love grows there.
PLAYER KING. Faith, I must leave thee, love, and shortly too;
    My operant powers° their functions leave to do.°   155
    And thou shalt live in this fair world behind,°
    Honored, beloved; and haply one as kind
    For husband shalt thou—
PLAYER QUEEN.   O, confound the rest!
    Such love must needs be treason in my breast.
    In second husband let me be accurst!   160
    None° wed the second but who° killed the first.
HAMLET. Wormwood,° wormwood.
PLAYER QUEEN. The instances° that second marriage move°
    Are base respects of thrift,° but none of love.
    A second time I kill my husband dead   165
    When second husband kisses me in bed.
PLAYER KING. I do believe you think what now you speak,
    But what we do determine oft we break.
    Purpose is but the slave to memory,°
    Of violent birth, but poor validity,°   170
    Which° now, like fruit unripe, sticks on the tree,

---

136 **Phoebus' cart** the sun-god's chariot, making its yearly cycle. 137 **salt wash** the
sea. **Tellus** goddess of the earth, of the *orbèd ground.* 138 **borrowed** i.e., reflected.
140 **Hymen** god of matrimony. 141 **commutual** mutually. **bands** bonds. 146 **distrust** am anxious about. 147 **Discomfort** distress. **nothing** not at all. 148 **hold
quantity** keep proportion with one another. 149 **In . . . extremity** i.e., women fear
and love either too little or too much, but the two, fear and love, are equal in either case.
150 **proof** experience. 151 **sized** in size. 155 **operant powers** vital functions.
leave to do cease to perform. 156 **behind** after I have gone. 161 **None** i.e., let no
woman. **but who** except the one who. 162 **Wormwood** i.e., how bitter. (Literally, a
bitter-tasting plant.) 163 **instances** motives. **move** motivate. 164 **base . . . thrift**
ignoble considerations of material prosperity. 169 **Purpose . . . memory** our good intentions are subject to forgetfulness. 170 **validity** strength, durability. 171 **Which** i.e.,
purpose.

But fall unshaken when they mellow be.
Most necessary 'tis that we forget
To pay ourselves what to ourselves is debt.°
What to ourselves in passion we propose,   175
The passion ending, doth the purpose lose.
The violence of either grief or joy
Their own enactures° with themselves destroy.
Where joy most revels, grief doth most lament;
Grief joys, joy grieves, on slender accident.°   180
This world is not for aye,° nor 'tis not strange
That even our loves should with our fortunes change;
For 'tis a question left us yet to prove,
Whether love lead fortune, or else fortune love.
The great man down,° you mark his favorite flies;   185
The poor advanced makes friends of enemies.°
And hitherto° doth love on fortune tend;°
For who not needs° shall never lack a friend,
And who in want° a hollow friend doth try°
Directly seasons him° his enemy.   190
But, orderly to end where I begun,
Our wills and fates do so contrary run°
That our devices still° are overthrown;
Our thoughts are ours, their ends° none of our own.
So think thou wilt no second husband wed,   195
But die thy thoughts when thy first lord is dead.
PLAYER QUEEN. Nor° earth to me give food, nor heaven light,
Sport and repose lock from me day and night,°
To desperation turn my trust and hope,
An anchor's cheer° in prison be my scope!°   200
Each opposite that blanks° the face of joy
Meet what I would have well and it destroy!°
Both here and hence° pursue me lasting strife
If, once a widow, ever I be wife!
HAMLET. If she should break it now!   205

173–174 **Most . . . debt** it's inevitable that in time we forget the obligations we have imposed on ourselves.   178 **enactures** fulfillments.   179–180 **Where . . . accident** the capacity for extreme joy and grief go together, and often one extreme is instantly changed into its opposite on the slightest provocation.   181 **aye** ever.   185 **down** fallen in fortune.   186 **The poor . . . enemies** when one of humble station is promoted, you see his enemies suddenly becoming his friends.   187 **hitherto** up to this point in the argument, or, to this extent. **tend** attend. **who not needs** he who is not in need (of wealth).   189 **who in want** he who, being in need. **try** test (his generosity).   190 **seasons him** ripens him into.   192 **Our . . . run** what we want and what we get go so contrarily.   193 **devices still** intentions continually.   194 **ends** results.   197 **Nor** let neither.   198 **Sport . . . night** may day deny me its pastimes and night its repose.   200 **anchor's cheer** anchorite's or hermit's fare. **my scope** the extent of my happiness.   201 **blanks** causes to blanch or grow pale.   201–202 **Each . . . destroy** may every adverse thing that causes the face of joy to turn pale meet and destroy everything that I desire to see prosper.   203 **hence** in the life hereafter.

PLAYER KING. 'Tis deeply sworn. Sweet, leave me here awhile;
My spirits° grow dull, and fain I would beguile.
The tedious day with sleep.
PLAYER QUEEN.   Sleep rock thy brain,
And never come mischance between us twain!

[*He sleeps.*] *Exit* [PLAYER QUEEN].

HAMLET. Madam, how like you this play?   210
QUEEN. The lady doth protest too much,° methinks.
HAMLET. O, but she'll keep her word.
KING. Have you heard the argument?° Is there no offense in 't?
HAMLET. No, no, they do but jest,° poison in jest. No offense° i' the
world.   215
KING. What do you call the play?
HAMLET. *The Mousetrap.* Marry, how? Tropically.° This play is the image
of a murder done in Vienna. Gonzago is the Duke's° name, his
wife, Baptista. You shall see anon. 'Tis a knavish piece of work, but
what of that? Your Majesty, and we that have free° souls, it touches   220
us not. Let the galled jade° wince, our withers° are unwrung.°

Enter LUCIANUS.

This is one Lucianus, nephew to the King.
OPHELIA. You are as good as a chorus,° my lord.
HAMLET. I could interpret° between you and your love, if I could see the
puppets dallying.°   225
OPHELIA. You are keen,° my lord, you are keen.
HAMLET. It would cost you a groaning to take off mine edge.
OPHELIA. Still better, and worse.°
HAMLET. So° you mis-take° your husbands. Begin, murder; leave thy
damnable faces and begin. Come, the croaking raven doth bellow   230
for revenge.
LUCIANUS. Thoughts black, hands apt, drugs fit, and time agreeing,
Confederate season,° else° no creature seeing,°
Thou mixture rank, of midnight weeds collected,

---

207 **spirits** vital spirits.   211 **doth . . . much** makes too many promises and protesta-
tions.   213 **argument** plot.   214 **jest** make believe.   213–214 **offense . . . offense**
cause for objection . . . actual injury, crime.   217 **Tropically** figuratively. (The First
Quarto reading, *trapically,* suggests a pun on *trap* in *Mousetrap.*)   218 **Duke's** i.e.,
King's. (A slip that may be due to Shakespeare's possible source, the alleged murder of the
Duke of Urbino by Luigi Gonzaga in 1538.)   220 **free** guiltless.   221 **galled jade** horse
whose hide is rubbed by saddle or harness.   **withers** the part between the horse's shoulder blades.   **unwrung** not rubbed sore.   223 **chorus** (In many Elizabethan plays, the
forthcoming action was explained by an actor known as the "chorus"; at a puppet show,
the actor who spoke the dialogue was known as an "interpreter," as indicated by the lines
following.)   224 **interpret** (1) ventriloquize the dialogue, as in puppet show (2) act as
pander.   225 **puppets dallying** (With suggestion of sexual play, continued in *keen,* "sexually aroused," *groaning,* "moaning in pregnancy," and *edge,* "sexual desire" or "impetuosity.")   226 **keen** sharp, bitter.   228 **Still . . . worse** more keen, always *bettering*
what other people say with witty wordplay, but at the same time more offensive.   229 **So**
even thus (in marriage).   **mis-take** take falseheartedly and cheat on. (The marriage vows
say "for better, for worse.")   233 **Confederate season** the time and occasion conspiring
(to assist the murderer).   **else** otherwise.   **seeing** seeing me.

With Hecate's ban° thrice blasted, thrice infected,   235
Thy natural magic and dire property°
On wholesome life usurp immediately.

                 [*He pours the poison into the sleeper's ear.*]

HAMLET. 'A poisons him i' the garden for his estate.° His° name's Gon-
     zago. The story is extant, and written in very choice Italian.
     You shall see anon how the murderer gets the love of Gonzago's
     wife.   240

     [CLAUDIUS *rises.*]

OPHELIA. The King rises.
HAMLET. What, frighted with false fire?°
QUEEN. How fares my lord?
POLONIUS. Give o'er the play.   245
KING. Give me some light. Away!
POLONIUS. Lights, lights, lights!

                       Exeunt all but HAMLET *and* HORATIO.

HAMLET.   "Why, let the strucken deer go weep,
       The hart ungallèd° play.
     For some must watch,° while some must sleep;   250
       Thus runs the world away."°
Would not this,° sir, and a forest of feathers°—if the rest of my for-
     tunes turn Turk with° me—with two Provincial roses° on my
     razed° shoes, get me a fellowship in a cry° of players?°
HORATIO. Half a share.   255
HAMLET. A whole one, I.
     "For thou dost know, O Damon° dear,
       This realm dismantled° was
     Of Jove himself, and now reigns here
       A very, very—pajock."°   260
HORATIO. You might have rhymed.
HAMLET. O good Horatio, I'll take the ghost's word for a thousand
     pound. Didst perceive?
HORATIO. Very well, my lord.

---

235 Hecate's ban the curse of Hecate, the goddess of witchcraft.   **236 dire property**
baleful quality.   **238 estate** i.e., the kingship.   **His** i.e., the King's.   **243 false fire** the
blank discharge of a gun loaded with powder but no shot.   **248–251 Why . . . away**
(Probably from an old ballad, with allusion to the popular belief that a wounded deer retires
to weep and die; compare with *As You Like It*, 2.1.33–66.)   **249 ungallèd** unafflicted.
250 watch remain awake.   **251 Thus . . . away** thus the world goes.   **252 this** i.e., the
play.   **feathers** (Allusion to the plumes that Elizabethan actors were fond of wearing.)
253 turn Turk with turn renegade against, go back on.   **Provincial roses** rosettes of ribbon, named for roses grown in a part of France.   **254 razed** with ornamental slashing.
cry pack (of hounds).   **fellowship . . . players** partnership in a theatrical company.
257 Damon the friend of Pythias, as Horatio is friend of Hamlet; or, a traditional pastoral
name.   **258 dismantled** stripped, divested.   **258–260 This realm . . . pajock** i.e.,
Jove, representing divine authority and justice, has abandoned this realm to its own devices, leaving in its stead only a peacock or vain pretender to virtue (though the rhyme-
word expected in place of *pajock* or "peacock" suggests that the realm is now ruled over
by an "ass").

HAMLET. Upon the talk of the poisoning?   265
HORATIO. I did very well note him.

Enter ROSENCRANTZ *and* GUILDENSTERN.

HAMLET. Aha! Come, some music! Come, the recorders.°
　"For if the King like not the comedy,
　　Why then, belike, he likes it not, perdy."°
　　Come, some music.   270
GUILDENSTERN. Good my lord, vouchsafe me a word with you.
HAMLET. Sir, a whole history.
GUILDENSTERN. The King, sir—
HAMLET. Ay, sir, what of him?
GUILDENSTERN. Is in his retirement° marvelous distempered.°   275
HAMLET. With drink, sir?
GUILDENSTERN. No, my lord, with choler.°
HAMLET. Your wisdom should show itself more richer to signify this to
　　the doctor, for me to put him to his purgation° would perhaps
　　plunge him into more choler.   280
GUILDENSTERN. Good my lord, put your discourse into some frame° and
　　start° not so wildly from my affair.
HAMLET. I am tame, sir. Pronounce.
GUILDENSTERN. The Queen, your mother, in most great affliction of
　　spirit, hath sent me to you.   285
HAMLET. You are welcome.
GUILDENSTERN. Nay, good my lord, this courtesy is not of the right
　　breed.° If it shall please you to make me a wholesome answer, I
　　will do your mother's commandment; if not, your pardon° and my
　　return shall be the end of my business.   290
HAMLET. Sir, I cannot.
ROSENCRANTZ. What, my lord?
HAMLET. Make you a wholesome answer; my wit's diseased. But, sir, such
　　answer as I can make, you shall command, or rather, as you say, my
　　mother. Therefore no more, but to the matter. My mother, you   295
　　say—
ROSENCRANTZ. Then thus she says: your behavior hath struck her into
　　amazement and admiration.°
HAMLET. O wonderful son, that can so stonish a mother! But is there no
　　sequel at the heels of this mother's admiration? Impart.   300
ROSENCRANTZ. She desires to speak with you in her closet° ere you go to
　　bed.

---

267 **recorders** wind instruments of the flute kind.   269 **perdy** (A corruption of the
French *par dieu,* "by God.")   275 **retirement** withdrawal to his chambers. **distempered** out of humor. (But Hamlet deliberately plays on the wider application to any
illness of mind or body, as in line 307, especially to drunkenness.)   277 **choler** anger.
(But Hamlet takes the word in its more basic humoral sense of "bilious disorder.")
279 **purgation** (Hamlet hints at something going beyond medical treatment to bloodlet-
ting and the extraction of confession.)   281 **frame** order.   282 **start** shy or jump away
(like a horse; the opposite of *tame* in line 283).   288 **breed** (1) kind (2) breeding, manners.   289 **pardon** permission to depart.   298 **admiration** bewilderment.   301 **closet**
private chamber.

HAMLET. We shall obey, were she ten times our mother. Have you any
    further trade with us?

ROSENCRANTZ. My lord, you once did love me.   305

HAMLET. And so still, by these pickers and stealers.°

ROSENCRANTZ. Good my lord, what is your cause of distemper? You do
    surely bar the door upon your own liberty° if you deny° your griefs
    to your friend.

HAMLET. Sir, I lack advancement.   310

ROSENCRANTZ. How can that be, when you have the voice of the King
    himself for your succession in Denmark?

HAMLET. Ay, sir, but "While the grass grows"°—the proverb is some-
    thing° musty.

    Enter the PLAYERS° WITH RECORDERS.

    O, the recorders. Let me see one. [*He takes a recorder.*]   315
    To withdraw° with you: why do you go about to recover the wind°
    of me, as if you would drive me into a toil?°

GUILDENSTERN. O, my lord, if my duty be too bold, my love is too un-
    mannerly.°

HAMLET. I do not well understand that.° Will you play upon this pipe?   320

GUILDENSTERN. My lord, I cannot.

HAMLET. I pray you.

GUILDENSTERN. Believe me, I cannot.

HAMLET. I do beseech you.

GUILDENSTERN. I know no touch of it, my lord.   325

HAMLET. It is as easy as lying. Govern these ventages° with your fingers
    and thumb, give it breath with your mouth, and it will discourse
    most eloquent music. Look you, these are the stops.

GUILDENSTERN. But these cannot I command to any utterance of harmony.
    I have not the skill.   330

HAMLET. Why, look you now, how unworthy a thing you make of me!
    You would play upon me, you would seem to know my stops, you
    would pluck out the heart of my mystery, you would sound° me
    from my lowest note to the top of my compass,° and there is much
    music, excellent voice, in this little organ,° yet cannot you make it   335
    speak. 'Sblood, do you think I am easier to be played on than a
    pipe? Call me what instrument you will, though you can fret° me,
    you cannot play upon me.

---

306 pickers and stealers i.e., hands. (So called from the catechism, "to keep my hands
from picking and stealing.") **308 liberty** i.e., being freed from *distemper,* line 307; but
perhaps with a veiled threat as well. **deny** refuse to share. **313 While . . . grows**
(The rest of the proverb is "the silly horse starves"; Hamlet may not live long enough
to succeed to the kingdom.) **313–314 something** somewhat. **s.d. Players** actors.
316 withdraw speak privately. **recover the wind** get to the windward side (thus driving the game into the *toil,* or "net"). **317 toil** snare. **318–319 if . . . unmannerly** if
I am using an unmannerly boldness, it is my love that occasions it. **320 I . . . that** i.e., I
don't understand how genuine love can be unmannerly. **326 ventages** finger-holes
or *stops* (line 328) of the recorder. **333 sound** (1) fathom (2) produce sound in.
334 compass range (of voice). **335 organ** musical instrument. **337 fret** irritate (with
a quibble on *fret,* meaning the piece of wood, gut, or metal that regulates the fingering of
an instrument).

Enter POLONIUS.

    God bless you, sir!

POLONIUS. My lord, the Queen would speak with you, and presently.°   340

HAMLET. Do you see yonder cloud that's almost in shape of a camel?

POLONIUS. By the Mass and 'tis, like a camel indeed.

HAMLET. Methinks it is like a weasel.

POLONIUS. It is backed like a weasel.

HAMLET. Or like a whale.   345

POLONIUS. Very like a whale.

HAMLET. Then I will come to my mother by and by.° [*Aside.*] They fool
    me° to the top of my bent.°—I will come by and by.

POLONIUS. I will say so.

                                 [*Exit.*]

HAMLET. "By and by" is easily said. Leave me, friends.   350

                             [*Exeunt all but* HAMLET.]

    'Tis now the very witching time° of night,
    When churchyards yawn and hell itself breathes out
    Contagion to his world. Now could I drink hot blood
    And do such bitter business as the day
    Would quake to look on. Soft, now to my mother.   355
    O heart, lose not thy nature!° Let not ever
    The soul of Nero° enter this firm bosom.
    Let me be cruel, not unnatural;
    I will speak daggers to her, but use none.
    My tongue and soul in this be hypocrites: 360
    How in my words soever° she be shent,°
    To give them seals° never my soul consent!

                               Exit.

3.3 *Enter* KING, ROSENCRANTZ, *and* GUILDENSTERN.

KING. I like him° not, nor stands it safe with us
    To let his madness range. Therefore prepare you.
    I your commission will forthwith dispatch,°
    And he to England shall along with you.
    The terms of our estate° may not endure   5
    Hazard so near 's as doth hourly grow
    Out of his brows.°

GUILDENSTERN.   We will ourselves provide.
    Most holy and religious fear° it is
    To keep those many bodies safe
    That live and feed upon Your Majesty.   10

---

340 presently at once.   **347 by and by** quite soon.   **347–348 fool me** trifle with me,
humor my fooling.   **348 top of my bent** limit of my ability or endurance. (Literally, the
extent to which a bow may be bent.)   **351 witching time** time when spells are cast and
evil is abroad.   **356 nature** natural feeling.   **357 Nero** murderer of his mother, Agrip-
pina.   **361 How . . . soever** however much by my words.   **shent** rebuked.   **362 give
them seals** i.e., confirm them with deeds.   **3.3 Location: The castle. 1 him** i.e., his
behavior.   **3 dispatch** prepare, cause to be drawn up.   **5 terms of our estate** circumstances of my royal position.   **7 out of his brows** i.e., from his brain, in the form of plots
and threats.   **8 religious fear** sacred concern.

ROSENCRANTZ. The single and peculiar° life is bound
        With all the strength and armor of the mind
        To keep itself from noyance,° but much more
        That spirit upon whose weal depends and rests
        The lives of many. The cess° of majesty   15
        Dies not alone, but like a gulf° doth draw
        What's near it with it; or it is a massy° wheel
        Fixed on the summit of the highest mount,
        To whose huge spokes ten thousand lesser things
        Are mortised° and adjoined, which, when it falls,°   20
        Each small annexment, petty consequence,°
        Attends° the boisterous ruin. Never alone
        Did the King sigh, but with a general groan.
KING. Arm° you, I pray you, to this speedy voyage,
        For we will fetters put about this fear,   25
        Which now goes too free-footed.
ROSENCRANTZ.   We will haste us.

            Exeunt gentlemen [ROSENCRANTZ *and* GUILDENSTERN].

        Enter POLONIUS.

POLONIUS. My lord, he's going to his mother's closet.
        Behind the arras° I'll convey myself
        To hear the process.° I'll warrant she'll tax him home,°
        And, as you said—and wisely was it said—   30
        'Tis meet° that some more audience than a mother,
        Since nature makes them partial, should o'erhear
        The speech, of vantage.° Fare you well, my liege.
        I'll call upon you ere you go to bed
        And tell you what I know.
KING.   Thanks, dear my lord.   35

                                           Exit [POLONIUS].

        O, my offense is rank! It smells to heaven.
        It hath the primal eldest curse° upon't,
        A brother's murder. Pray can I not,
        Though inclination be as sharp as will;°
        My stronger guilt defeats my strong intent,   40
        And like a man to double business bound°

---

11 single and peculiar individual and private. **13 noyance** harm. **15 cess** decease,
cessation. **16 gulf** whirlpool. **17 massy** massive. **20 mortised** fastened (as with a
fitted joint). **when it falls** i.e., when it descends, like the wheel of Fortune, bringing a
king down with it. **21 Each . . . consequence** i.e., every hanger-on and unimportant
person or thing connected with the King. **22 Attends** participates in. **24 Arm** prepare. **28 arras** screen of tapestry placed around the walls of household apartments. (On
the Elizabethan stage, the arras was presumably over a door or discovery space in the
tiring-house facade.) **29 process** proceedings. **tax him home** reprove him severely.
31 meet fitting. **33 of vantage** from an advantageous place, or, in addition. **37 the
primal eldest curse** the curse of Cain, the first murderer; he killed his brother Abel.
39 Though . . . will though my desire is as strong as my determination. **41 bound** (1)
destined (2) obliged. (The King wants to repent and still enjoy what he has gained.)

I stand in pause where I shall first begin,
And both neglect. What if this cursèd hand
Were thicker than itself with brother's blood,
Is there not rain enough in the sweet heavens   45
To wash it white as snow? Whereto serves mercy
But to confront the visage of offense?°
And what's in prayer but this twofold force,
To be forestallèd° ere we come to fall,
Or pardoned being down? Then I'll look up.   50
My fault is past. But O, what form of prayer
Can serve my turn? "Forgive me my foul murder"?
That cannot be, since I am still possessed
Of those effects for which I did the murder:
My crown, mine own ambition, and my Queen.   55
May one be pardoned and retain th' offense?°
In the corrupted currents° of this world
Offense's gilded hand° may shove by° justice,
And oft 'tis seen the wicked prize° itself
Buys out the law. But 'tis not so above.   60
There° is no shuffling,° there the action lies°
In his° true nature, and we ourselves compelled,
Even to the teeth and forehead° of our faults,
To give in° evidence. What then? What rests?°
Try what repentance can. What can it not?   65
Yet what can it, when one cannot repent?
O wretched state, O bosom black as death,
O limèd° soul, that, struggling to be free,
Are more engaged!° Help, angels! Make assay.°
Bow, stubborn knees, and heart with strings of steel, 70
Be soft as sinews of the newborn babe!
All may be well.

                                            [*He kneels.*]

Enter HAMLET.

HAMLET. Now might I do it pat,° now 'a is a-praying;
    And now I'll do 't. [*He draws his sword.*] And so 'a goes to heaven,
    And so am I revenged. That would be scanned:°   75
    A villain kills my father, and for that,
    I, his sole son, do this same villain send
    To heaven.

_____

46–47 **Whereto . . . offense** what function does mercy serve other than to meet sin face
to face?   49 **forestallèd** prevented (from sinning).   56 **th' offense** the thing for which
one offended.   57 **currents** courses.   58 **gilded hand** hand offering gold as a bribe.
shove by thrust aside.   59 **wicked prize** prize won by wickedness.   61 **There** i.e., in
heaven.   **shuffling** escape by trickery.   **the action lies** the accusation is made manifest
(a legal metaphor).   62 **his** its.   63 **to the teeth and forehead** face to face, concealing
nothing.   64 **give in** provide.   **rests** remains.   68 **limèd** caught as with birdlime, a
sticky substance used to ensnare birds.   69 **engaged** entangled.   **assay** trial (said to
himself).   73 **pat** opportunely.   75 **would be scanned** needs to be looked into, or,
would be interpreted as follows.

Why, this is hire and salary, not revenge.
'A took my father grossly, full of bread,° 80
With all his crimes broad blown,° as flush° as May;
And how his audit° stands who knows save° heaven?
But in our circumstance and course of thought°
'Tis heavy with him. And am I then revenged,
To take him in the purging of his soul, 85
When he is fit and seasoned° for his passage?
No!
Up, sword, and know thou a more horrid hent.°

                             [*He puts up his sword.*]

When he is drunk asleep, or in his rage,°
Or in th' incestuous pleasure of his bed, 90
At game,° a-swearing, or about some act
That has no relish° of salvation in 't—
Then trip him, that his heels may kick at heaven,
And that his soul may be as damned and black
As hell, whereto it goes. My mother stays.° 95
This physic° but prolongs thy sickly days.

                                     Exit.

KING. My words fly up, my thoughts remain below.
Words without thoughts never to heaven go.

                                     Exit.

    3.4 *Enter* [QUEEN] GERTRUDE *and* POLONIUS.

POLONIUS. 'A will come straight. Look you lay home° to him.
Tell him his pranks have been too broad° to bear with,
And that Your Grace hath screened and stood between
Much heat° and him. I'll shroud° me even here.
Pray you, be round° with him. 5
HAMLET [*within*]. Mother, Mother, Mother!
QUEEN. I'll warrant you, fear me not.
Withdraw, I hear him coming.

                          [POLONIUS *hides behind the arras.*]

    Enter HAMLET.

HAMLET. Now, Mother, what's the matter?
QUEEN. Hamlet, thou hast thy father° much offended. 10

---

80 grossly, full of bread i.e., enjoying his worldly pleasures rather than fasting. (See
Ezekiel 16.49.)   **81 crimes broad blown** sins in full bloom.   **flush** vigorous.   **82 audit**
account.   **save** except for.   **83 in . . . thought** as we see it from our mortal perspective.
86 seasoned matured, readied.   **88 know . . . hent** await to be grasped by me on a
more horrid occasion.   **hent** act of seizing.   **89 drunk . . . rage** dead drunk, or in a fit
of sexual passion.   **91 game** gambling.   **92 relish** trace, savor.   **95 stays** awaits (me).
96 physic purging (by prayer), or, Hamlet's postponement of the killing.   **3.4 Location:**
The Queen's private chamber.   **1 lay home** thrust to the heart, reprove him soundly.
2 broad unrestrained.   **4 Much heat** i.e., the King's anger.   **shroud** conceal. (With
ironic fitness to Polonius's imminent death. The word is only in the First Quarto: the Second Quarto and the Folio read "silence.")   **5 round** blunt.   **10 thy father** i.e., your step-
father, Claudius.

HAMLET. Mother, you have my father much offended.

QUEEN. Come, come, you answer with an idle° tongue.

HAMLET. Go, go you question with a wicked tongue.

QUEEN. Why, how now, Hamlet?

HAMLET.   What's the matter now?

QUEEN. Have you forgot me?°

HAMLET.   No, by the rood,° not so: 15
    You are the Queen your husband's brother's wife,
    And—would it were not so!—you are my mother.

QUEEN. Nay, then, I'll set those to you that can speak.°

HAMLET. Come, come, and sit you down; you shall not budge.
    You go not till I set you up a glass   20
    Where you may see the inmost part of you.

QUEEN. What wilt thou do? Thou wilt not murder me?
    Help, ho!

POLONIUS [*behind the arras*]. What ho! Help!

HAMLET [*drawing*]. How now? A rat? Dead for a ducat,° dead!   25
                  [*He thrusts his rapier through the arras.*]

POLONIUS [*behind the arras*]. O, I am slain!   [*He falls and dies.*]

QUEEN.   O me, what hast thou done?

HAMLET. Nay, I know not. Is it the King?

QUEEN. O, what a rash and bloody deed is this!

HAMLET. A bloody deed—almost as bad, good Mother,
    As kill a King, and marry with his brother.   30

QUEEN. As kill a King!

HAMLET.   Ay, lady, it was my word.
        [*He parts the arras and discovers* POLONIUS.]
    Thou wretched, rash, intruding fool, farewell!
    I took thee for thy better. Take thy fortune.
    Thou find'st to be too busy° is some danger.—
    Leave wringing of your hands. Peace, sit you down,   35
    And let me wring your heart, for so I shall,
    If it be made of penetrable stuff,
    If damnèd custom° have not brazed° it so
    That it be proof° and bulwark against sense.°

QUEEN. What have I done, that thou dar'st wag thy tongue   40
    In noise so rude against me?

HAMLET.   Such an act
    That blurs the grace and blush of modesty,
    Calls virtue hypocrite, takes off the rose
    From the fair forehead of an innocent love
    And sets a blister° there, makes marriage vows   45
    As false as dicers' oaths. O, such a deed
    As from the body of contraction° plucks

---

12 idle foolish. **15 forgot me** i.e., forgotten that I am your mother. **rood** cross of Christ. **18 speak** i.e., to someone so rude. **25 Dead for a ducat** i.e., I bet a ducat he's dead; or a ducat is his life's fee. **34 busy** nosey. **38 damnèd custom** habitual wickedness. **brazed** brazened, hardened. **39 proof** armor. **sense** feeling. **45 sets a blister** i.e, brands as a harlot. **47 contraction** the marriage contract.

The very soul, and sweet religion makes°
A rhapsody° of words. Heaven's face does glow
O'er this solidity and compound mass   50
With tristful visage, as against the doom,
Is thought-sick at the act.°

QUEEN.   Ay me, what act,
That roars so loud and thunders in the index?°

HAMLET [*showing her two likenesses*]. Look here upon this picture, and
  on this,
The counterfeit presentment° of two brothers.   55
See what a grace was seated on this brow:
Hyperion's° curls, the front° of Jove himself,
An eye like Mars° to threaten and command,
A station° like the herald Mercury°
New-lighted° on a heaven-kissing hill—   60
A combination and a form indeed
Where every god did seem to set his seal?°
To give the world assurance of a man.
This was your husband. Look you now what follows:
Here is your husband, like a mildewed ear,°   65
Blasting° his wholesome brother. Have you eyes?
Could you on this far mountain leave° to feed
And batten° on this moor?° Ha, have you eyes?
You cannot call it love, for at your age
The heyday° in the blood° is tame, it's humble,   70
And waits upon the judgment, and what judgment
Would step from this to this? Sense,° sure, you have,
Else could you not have motion, but sure that sense
Is apoplexed,° for madness would not err,°
Nor sense to ecstasy was ne'er so thralled,   75
But° it reserved some quantity of choice
To serve in such a difference.° What devil was 't
That thus hath cozened° you at hoodman-blind?°

---

48 sweet religion makes i.e., makes marriage vows.   **49 rhapsody** senseless string.
49–52 Heaven's . . . act heaven's face blushes at this solid world compounded of the
various elements, with sorrowful face as though the day of doom were near, and is sick
with horror at the deed (i.e., Gertrude's marriage).   **53 index** table of contents, prelude
or preface.   **55 counterfeit presentment** portrayed representation.   **57 Hyperion's**
the sungod's.   **front** brow.   **58 Mars** god of war.   **59 station** manner of standing.
Mercury winged messenger of the gods.   **60 New-lighted** newly alighted.   **62 set his
seal** i.e., affix his approval.   **65 ear** i.e., of grain.   **66 Blasting** blighting.   **67 leave**
cease.   **68 batten** gorge.   **moor** barren or marshy ground (suggesting also "dark-
skinned").   **70 heyday** state of excitement.   **blood** passion.   **72 Sense** perception
through the five senses (the functions of the middle or sensible soul).   **74 apoplexed**
paralyzed. (Hamlet goes on to explain that, without such a paralysis of will, mere madness
would not so err, nor would the five senses so enthrall themselves to *ecstasy* or lunacy;
even such deranged states of mind would be able to make the obvious choice between
Hamlet Senior and Claudius.)   **err** so err.   **76 But** but that.   **77 To . . . difference** to
help in making a choice between two such men.   **78 cozened** cheated.   **hoodman-
blind** blindman's bluff. (In this game, says Hamlet, the devil must have pushed Claudius
toward Gertrude while she was blindfolded.)

Eyes without feeling, feeling without sight,
Ears without hands or eyes, smelling sans° all,   80
Or but a sickly part of one true sense
Could not so mope.° O shame, where is thy blush?
Rebellious hell,
If thou canst mutine° in a matron's bones,
To flaming youth let virtue be as wax   85
And melt in her own fire.° Proclaim no shame
When the compulsive ardor gives the charge,
Since frost itself as actively doth burn,
And reason panders will.°

QUEEN. O Hamlet, speak no more!   90
Thou turn'st mine eyes into my very soul,
And there I see such black and grainèd° spots
As will not leave their tinct.°

HAMLET.   Nay, but to live
In the rank sweat of an enseamèd° bed,
Stewed° in corruption, honeying and making love   95
Over the nasty sty!

QUEEN. O, speak to me no more!
These words like daggers enter in my ears.
No more, sweet Hamlet!

HAMLET.   A murderer and a villain,
A slave that is not twentieth part the tithe°   100
Of your precedent lord,° a vice° of kings,
A cutpurse of the empire and the rule,
That from a shelf the precious diadem stole
And put it in his pocket!

QUEEN. No more!   105

Enter GHOST [*in his nightgown*].

HAMLET. A king of shreds and patches°—
Save me, and hover o'er me with your wings,
You heavenly guards! What would your gracious figure?

QUEEN. Alas, he's mad!

HAMLET. Do you not come your tardy son to chide,   110
That, lapsed° in time and passion, lets go by
Th' important° acting of your dread command?
O, say!

---

80 **sans** without. 82 **mope** be dazed, act aimlessly. 84 **mutine** incite mutiny.
85–86 **be as wax . . . fire** melt like a candle or stick of sealing wax held over the candle
flame. 86–89 **Proclaim . . . will** call it no shameful business when the compelling ardor of youth delivers the attack, i.e., commits lechery, since the *frost* of advanced age
burns with as active a fire of lust and reason perverts itself by fomenting lust rather than
restraining it. 92 **grainèd** dyed in grain, indelible. 93 **leave their tinct** surrender
their color. 94 **enseamèd** saturated in the grease and filth of passionate lovemaking.
95 **Stewed** soaked, bathed (with a suggestion of "stew," brothel). 100 **tithe** tenth part.
101 **precedent lord** former husband. **vice** buffoon. (A reference to the Vice of the
morality plays.) 106 **shreds and patches** i.e., motley, the traditional costume of the
clown or fool. 111 **lapsed** delaying. 112 **important** importunate, urgent.

GHOST. Do not forget. This visitation
    Is but to whet thy almost blunted purpose.   115
    But look, amazement° on thy mother sits.
    O, step between her and her fighting soul!
    Conceit° in weakest bodies strongest works.
    Speak to her, Hamlet.
HAMLET.   How is it with you, lady?
QUEEN. Alas, how is 't with you,   120
    That you do bend your eye on vacancy,
    And with th' incorporal° air do hold discourse?
    Forth at your eyes your spirts wildly peep,
    And, as the sleeping soldiers in th' alarm,°
    Your bedded° hair, like life in excrements,°   125
    Start up and stand on end. O gentle son,
    Upon the heat and flame of thy distemper°
    Sprinkle cool patience. Whereon do you look?
HAMLET. On him, on him! Look you how pale he glares!
    His form and cause conjoined,° preaching to stones,   130
    Would make them capable.°—Do not look upon me,
    Lest with this piteous action you convert
    My stern effects.° Then what I have to do
    Will want true color—tears perchance for blood.°
QUEEN. To whom do you speak this?   135
HAMLET. Do you see nothing there?
QUEEN. Nothing at all, yet all that is I see.
HAMLET. Nor did you nothing hear?
QUEEN. No, nothing but ourselves.
HAMLET. Why, look you there, look how it steals away!   140
    My father, in his habit° as° he lived!
    Look where he goes even now out at the portal!

                                Exit GHOST.

QUEEN. This is the very° coinage of your brain.
    This bodiless creation ecstasy
    Is very cunning in.°   145
HAMLET. Ecstasy?
    My pulse as yours doth temperately keep time,
    And makes as healthful music. It is not madness
    That I have uttered. Bring me to the test,
    And I the matter will reword,° which madness   150

---

116 amazement distraction.   **118 Conceit** imagination.   **122 incorporal** immaterial.
124 as . . . alarm like soldiers called out of sleep by an alarm.   **125 bedded** laid flat.
like life in excrements i.e., as though hair, an outgrowth of the body, had a life of its
own. (Hair was thought to be lifeless because it lacks sensation, and so its standing on
end would be unnatural and ominous.)   **127 distemper** disorder.   **130 His . . . conjoined** his appearance joined to his cause for speaking.   **131 capable** receptive.
132–133 convert . . . effects divert me from my stern duty.   **134 want . . . blood**
lack plausibility so that (with a play on the normal sense of *color*) I shall shed colorless
tears instead of blood.   **141 habit** clothes. **as** as when.   **143 very** mere.   **144–145
This . . . in** madness is skillful in creating this kind of hallucination.   **150 reword** repeat word for word.

Would gambol° from. Mother, for love of grace,
Lay not that flattering unction° to your soul
That not your trespass but my madness speaks.
It will but skin° and film the ulcerous place,
Whiles rank corruption, mining° all within,   155
Infects unseen. Confess yourself to heaven,
Repeat what's past, avoid what is to come,
And do not spread the compost° on the weeds
To make them ranker. Forgive me this my virtue;°
For in the fatness° of these pursy° times   160
Virtue itself of vice must pardon beg,
Yea, curb° and woo for leave° to do him good.
QUEEN. O Hamlet, thou hast cleft my heart in twain.
HAMLET. O, throw away the worser part of it,
And live the purer with the other half.   165
Good night. But go not to my uncle's bed;
Assume a virtue, if you have it not.
That monster, custom, who all sense doth eat,°
Of habits devil,° is angel yet in this,
That to the use of actions fair and good   170
He likewise gives a frock or livery°
That aptly° is put on. Refrain tonight,
And that shall lend a kind of easiness
To the next abstinence; the next more easy;
For use° almost can change the stamp of nature,°   175
And either° . . . the devil, or throw him out
With wondrous potency. Once more, good night;
And when you are desirous to be blest,
I'll blessing beg of you.° For this same lord,

                                    [*Pointing to* POLONIUS.]

I do repent; but heaven hath pleased it so   180
To punish me with this, and this with me,
That I must be their scourge and minister.°
I will bestow° him, and will answer° well
The death I gave him. So again, good night.
I must be cruel only to be kind.   185

---

151 gambol skip away.   **152 unction** ointment.   **154 skin** grow a skin for.
155 mining working under the surface.   **158 compost** manure.   **159 this my virtue**
my virtuous talk in reproving you.   **160 fatness** grossness.   **pursy** flabby, out of shape.
162 curb bow, bend the knee.   **162 leave** permission.   **168 who . . . eat** which consumes all proper or natural feeling, all sensibility.   **169 Of habits devil** devil-like in
prompting evil habits.   **171 livery** an outer appearance, a customary garb (and hence a
predisposition easily assumed in time of stress).   **172 aptly** readily.   **175 use** habit.
the stamp of nature our inborn traits.   **176 And either** (A defective line, usually
emended by inserting the word *master* after *either*, following the Fourth Quarto and
early editors.)   **178–179 when . . . you** i.e., when you are ready to be penitent and
seek God's blessing, I will ask your blessing as a dutiful son should.   **182 their scourge
and minister** i.e., agent of heavenly retribution. (By *scourge*, Hamlet also suggests that
he himself will eventually suffer punishment in the process of fulfilling heaven's will.)
183 bestow stow, dispose of.   **183 answer** account or pay for.

This° bad begins, and worse remains behind.°
One word more, good lady.
QUEEN.   What shall I do?
HAMLET. Not this by no means that I bid you do:
    Let the bloat° King tempt you again to bed,
    Pinch wanton° on your cheek, call you his mouse,   190
    And let him, for a pair of reechy° kisses,
    Or paddling° in your neck with his damned fingers,
    Make you to ravel all this matter out°
    That I essentially am not in madness,
    But mad in craft.° 'Twere good° you let him know,   195
    For who that's but a Queen, fair, sober, wise,
    Would from a paddock,° from a bat, a gib,°
    Such dear concernings° hide? Who would do so?
    No, in despite of sense and secrecy,°
    Unpeg the basket° on the house's top,   200
    Let the birds fly, and like the famous ape,°
    To try conclusions,° in the basket creep
    And break your own neck down.°
QUEEN. Be thou assured, if words be made of breath,
    And breath of life, I have no life to breathe   205
    What thou hast said to me.
HAMLET. I must to England. You know that?
QUEEN.   Alack,
    I had forgot. 'Tis so concluded on.
HAMLET. There's letters sealed, and my two schoolfellows,
    Whom I will trust as I will adders fanged,   210
    They bear the mandate; they must sweep my way
    And marshall me to knavery.° Let it work.°
    For 'tis the sport to have the enginer°
    Hoist with° his own petard,° and 't shall go hard
    But I will° delve one yard below their mines°   215
    And blow them at the moon. O, 'tis most sweet
    When in one line° two crafts° directly meet.

---

186 This i.e., the killing of Polonius. **behind** to come. **189 bloat** bloated. **190 Pinch wanton** i.e., leave his love pinches on your cheeks, branding you as wanton. **191 reechy** dirty, filthy. **192 paddling** fingering amorously. **193 ravel . . . out** unravel, disclose. **195 in craft** by cunning. **good** (Said sarcastically; also the following eight lines.) **197 paddock** toad. **gib** tomcat. **198 dear concernings** important affairs. **199 sense and secrecy** secrecy that common sense requires. **200 Unpeg the basket** open the cage, i.e., let out the secret. **201 famous ape** (In a story now lost.) **202 try conclusions** test the outcome (in which the ape apparently enters a cage from which birds have been released and then tries to fly out of the cage as they have done, falling to its death). **203 down** in the fall; utterly. **211–212 sweep . . . knavery** sweep a path before me and conduct me to some *knavery* or treachery prepared for me. **212 work** proceed. **213 enginer** maker of military contrivances. **214 Hoist with** blown up by. **petard** an explosive used to blow in a door or make a breach. **214–215 't shall . . . will** unless luck is against me, I will. **215 mines** tunnels used in warfare to undermine the enemy's emplacements; Hamlet will countermine by going under their mines. **217 in one line** i.e., mines and countermines on a collision course, or the countermines directly below the mines. **crafts** acts of guile, plots.

This man shall set me packing.°
I'll lug the guts into the neighbor room.
Mother, good night indeed. This counselor   220
Is now most still, most secret, and most grave,
Who was in life a foolish prating knave.—
Come, sir, to draw toward an end° with you.—
Good night, Mother.

        Exeunt [*separately,* HAMLET *dragging in* POLONIUS].

   4.1 *Enter* KING *and* QUEEN°, *with* ROSENCRANTZ *and* GUILDENSTERN.

KING. There's matter° in these sighs, these profound heaves.°
    You must translate: 'tis fit we understand them.
    Where is your son?
QUEEN. Bestow this place on us a little while.

        [*Exeunt* ROSENCRANTZ *and* GUILDENSTERN.]

    Ah, mine own lord, what have I seen tonight!   5
KING. What, Gertrude? How does Hamlet?
QUEEN. Mad as the sea and wind when both contend
    Which is the mightier. In his lawless fit,
    Behind the arras hearing something stir,
    Whips out his rapier, cries, "A rat, a rat!"   10
    And in this brainish apprehension° kills
    The unseen good old man.
KING.   O heavy° deed!
    It had been so with us,° had we been there.
    His liberty is full of threats to all—
    To you yourself, to us, to everyone.   15
    Alas, how shall this bloody deed be answered?°
    It will be laid to us, whose providence°
    Should have kept short,° restrained, and out of haunt°
    This mad young man. But so much was our love,
    We would not understand what was most fit,   20
    But, like the owner of a foul disease,
    To keep it from divulging,° let it feed
    Even on the pith of life. Where is he gone?
QUEEN. To draw apart the body he hath killed,
    O'er whom his very madness, like some ore°   25
    Among a mineral° of metals base,
    Shows itself pure: 'a weeps for what is done.

---

218 set me packing set me to making schemes, and set me to lugging (him), and, also,
send me off in a hurry.   **223 draw . . . end** finish up (with a pun on *draw,* "pull").
4.1 Location: The castle. s.d. Enter . . . Queen (Some editors argue that Gertrude
never exits in 3.4 and that the scene is continuous here, as suggested in the Folio, but the
Second Quarto marks an entrance for her and at line 35 Claudius speaks of Gertrude's
closet as though it were elsewhere. A short time has elapsed, during which the King
has become aware of her highly wrought emotional state.) **1 matter** significance.
heaves heavy sighs. **11 brainish apprehension** headstrong conception. **12 heavy**
grievous. **13 us** i.e., me. (The royal "we"; also in line 15.) **16 answered** explained.
17 providence foresight. **18 short** i.e., on a short tether. **out of haunt** secluded.
22 divulging becoming evident.   **25 ore** vein of gold.   **26 mineral** mine.

KING. O Gertrude, come away!
The sun no sooner shall the mountains touch
But we will ship him hence, and this vile deed   30
We must with all our majesty and skill
Both countenance° and excuse.—Ho, Guildenstern!

Enter ROSENCRANTZ *and* GUILDENSTERN.

Friends both, go join you with some further aid.
Hamlet in madness hath Polonius slain,
And from his mother's closet hath he dragged him.   35
Go seek him out, speak fair, and bring the body
Into the chapel. I pray you, haste in this.

[*Exeunt* ROSENCRANTZ *and* GUILDENSTERN.]

Come, Gertrude, we'll call up our wisest friends
And let them know both what we mean to do
And what's untimely done°.   40
Whose whisper o'er the world's diameter,°
As level° as the cannon to his blank,°
Transports his poisoned shot, may miss our name
And hit the woundless° air. O, come away!
My soul is full of discord and dismay.   45

Exeunt.

4.2 *Enter* HAMLET.

HAMLET. Safely stowed.
ROSENCRANTZ, GUILDENSTERN [*within*]. Hamlet! Lord Hamlet!
HAMLET. But soft, what noise? Who calls on Hamlet? O, here they come.

Enter ROSENCRANTZ *and* GUILDENSTERN.

ROSENCRANTZ. What have you done, my lord, with the dead body?
HAMLET. Compounded it with dust, whereto 'tis kin.   5
ROSENCRANTZ. Tell us where 'tis, that we may take it thence
And bear it to the chapel.
HAMLET. Do not believe it.
ROSENCRANTZ. Believe what?
HAMLET. That I can keep your counsel and not mine own.° Besides, to   10
be demanded of° a sponge, what replication° should be made by
the son of a king?
ROSENCRANTZ. Take you me for a sponge, my lord?

---

32 countenance put the best face on. **40 And . . . done** (A defective line; conjectures
as to the missing words include *So, haply, slander* [Capell and others]; *For, haply, slander* [Theobald and others]; and *So envious slander* [Jenkins].) **41 diameter** extent
from side to side. **42 As level** with as direct aim. **his blank** its target at point-blank
range. **44 woundless** invulnerable. **4.2 Location: The castle. 10 That . . . own**
i.e., that I can follow your advice (by telling where the body is) and still keep my own
secret. **11 demanded of** questioned by. **replication** reply.

HAMLET. Ay, sir, that soaks up the King's countenance,° his rewards, his
authorities.° But such officers do the King best service in the end.   15
He keeps them, like an ape, an apple, in the corner of his jaw, first
mouthed to be last swallowed. When he needs what you have
gleaned, it is but squeezing you, and, sponge, you shall be dry
again.

ROSENCRANTZ. I understand you not, my lord.   20

HAMLET. I am glad of it. A knavish speech sleeps in° a foolish ear.

ROSENCRANTZ. My lord, you must tell us where the body is and go with
us to the King.

HAMLET. The body is with the King, but the King is not with the body.°
The King is a thing—   25

GUILDENSTERN. A thing, my lord?

HAMLET. Of nothing.° Bring me to him. Hide fox, and all after!°

                                                        Exeunt [*running*].

4.3 *Enter* KING, *and two or three.*

KING. I have sent to seek him, and to find the body.
How dangerous is it that this man goes loose!
Yet must not we put the strong law on him.
He's loved of° the distracted° multitude,
Who like not in their judgment, but their eyes,°   5
And where 'tis so, th' offender's scourge° is weighed,°
But never the offense. To bear all smooth and even,°
This sudden sending him away must seem
Deliberate pause.° Diseases desperate grown
By desperate appliance° are relieved,   10
Or not at all.

Enter ROSENCRANTZ, GUILDENSTERN, *and all the rest.*

              How now, what hath befall'n?

ROSENCRANTZ. Where the dead body is bestowed, my lord,
We cannot get from him.

KING.   But where is he?

ROSENCRANTZ. Without, my lord; guarded, to know your
pleasure.

---

14 **countenance** favor.   15 **authorities** delegated power, influence.   21 **sleeps in** has
no meaning to.   24 **The . . . body** (Perhaps alludes to the legal commonplace of "the
king's two bodies," which draw a distinction between the sacred office of kingship and
the particular mortal who possessed it at any given time. Hence, although Claudius's body
is necessarily a part of him, true kingship is not contained in it. Similarly, Claudius will
have Polonius's body when it is found, but there is no kingship in this business either.)
27 **Of nothing** (1) of no account (2) lacking the essence of kingship, as in lines 24–25 and
note. **Hide . . . after** (An old signal cry in the game of hide-and-seek, suggesting that
Hamlet now runs away from them.) **4.3 Location: The castle. 4 of** by. **distracted**
fickle, unstable. **5 Who . . . eyes** who choose not by judgment but by appearance.
6 scourge punishment. (Literally, blow with a whip.) **weighed** sympathetically considered. **7 To . . . even** to manage the business in an unprovocative way. **9 Deliberate**
pause carefully considered action. **10 appliance** remedies.

KING. Bring him before us.

ROSENCRANTZ.   Ho! Bring in the lord.   15

    They enter [*with* HAMLET].

KING. Now, Hamlet, where's Polonius?

HAMLET. At supper.

KING. At supper? Where?

HAMLET. Not where he eats, but where 'a is eaten. A certain convocation
    of politic worms° are e'en° at him. Your worm° is your only   20
    emperor for diet.° We fat all creatures else to fat us, and we fat our-
    selves for maggots. Your fat king and your lean beggar is but vari-
    able service°—two dishes, but to one table. That's the end.

KING. Alas, alas!

HAMLET. A many may fish with the worm that hath eat° of a king, and   25
    eat of the fish that hath fed of that worm.

KING. What dost thou mean by this?

HAMLET. Nothing but to show you how a king may go a progress°
    through the guts of a beggar.

KING. Where is Polonius?   30

HAMLET. In heaven. Send thither to see. If your messenger find him not
    there, seek him i' th' other place yourself. But if indeed you find
    him not within this month, you shall nose him as you go up the
    stairs into the lobby.

KING [*to some attendants*]. Go seek him there.   35

HAMLET. 'A will stay till you come.

                                         [*Exeunt attendants.*]

KING. Hamlet, this deed, for thine especial safety—
    Which we do tender,° as we dearly° grieve
    For that which thou hast done—must send thee hence
    With fiery quickness. Therefore prepare thyself.   40
    The bark° is ready, and the wind at help,
    Th' associates tend,° and everything is bent°
    For England.

HAMLET. For England!

KING. Ay, Hamlet.   45

HAMLET. Good.

KING. So is it, if thou knew'st our purposes.

HAMLET. I see a cherub° that sees them. But come, for England!
    Farewell, dear mother.

KING. Thy loving father, Hamlet.   50

---

20 politic worms crafty worms (suited to a master spy like Polonius).   **e'en** even now.
Your worm your average worm. (Compare *your fat king and your lean beggar* in line
22.)   **21 diet** food, eating (with a punning reference to the Diet of Worms, a famous
convocation held in 1521).   **22–23 variable service** different courses of a single meal.
25 eat eaten. (Pronounced *et*.)   **28 progress** royal journey of state.   **38 tender** regard,
hold dear.   **dearly** intensely.   **41 bark** sailing vessel.   **42 tend** wait.   **bent** in readiness.   **48 cherub** (Cherubim are angels of knowledge. Hamlet hints that both he and
heaven are onto Claudius's tricks.)

HAMLET. My mother. Father and mother is man and wife, man and wife
     is one flesh, and so, my mother. Come, for England!

Exit.

KING. Follow him at foot;° tempt him with speed aboard.
     Delay it not. I'll have him hence tonight.
     Away! For everything is sealed and done   55
     That else leans on° th' affair. Pray you, make haste.

[Exeunt all but the KING.]

     And, England,° if my love thou hold'st at aught°—
     As my great power thereof may give thee sense,°
     Since yet thy cicatrice° looks raw and red
     After the Danish sword, and thy free awe°   60
     Pays homage to us—thou mayst not coldly set°
     Our sovereign process,° which imports at full,°
     By letters congruing° to that effect,
     The present° death of Hamlet. Do it, England,
     For like the hectic° in my blood he rages,   65
     And thou must cure me. Till I know 'tis done,
     Howe'er my haps,° my joys were ne'er begun.

Exit.

4.4 *Enter* FORTINBRAS *with his army over the stage.*

FORTINBRAS. Go, Captain, from me greet the Danish king.
     Tell him that by his license° Fortinbras
     Craves the conveyance of° a promised march
     Over his kingdom. You know the rendezvous.
     If that His Majesty would aught with us,   5
     We shall express our duty° in his eye;°
     And let him know so.
CAPTAIN. I will do 't, my lord.
FORTINBRAS. Go softly° on.

[Exeunt all but the CAPTAIN.]

Enter HAMLET, ROSENCRANTZ, [GUILDENSTERN,] *etc.*

HAMLET. Good sir, whose powers° are these?   10
CAPTAIN. They are of Norway, sir.
HAMLET. How purposed, sir, I pray you?
CAPTAIN. Against some part of Poland.
HAMLET. Who commands them, sir?

---

53 at foot close behind, at heel.   **56 leans on** bears upon, is related to.   **57 England**
i.e., King of England.   **at aught** at any value.   **58 As . . . sense** for so my great power
may give you a just appreciation of the importance of valuing my love.
59 cicatrice scar.   **60 free awe** voluntary show of respect.   **61 coldly set** regard with
indifference.   **62 process** command.   **imports at full** conveys specific directions for.
63 congruing agreeing.   **64 present** immediate.   **65 hectic** persistent fever.
67 haps fortunes.   **4.4 Location: The coast of Denmark.**   **2 license** permission.
3 the conveyance of escort during.   **6 duty** respect.   **eye** presence.   **9 softly** slowly,
circumspectly.   **10 powers** forces.

CAPTAIN. The nephew to old Norway. Fortinbras.   15
HAMLET. Goes it against the main° of Poland, sir,
    Or for some frontier?
CAPTAIN. Truly to speak, and with no addition,°
    We go to gain a little patch of ground
    That hath in it no profit but the name.   20
    To pay° five ducats, five, I would not farm it;°
    Nor will it yield to Norway or the Pole
    A ranker° rate, should it be sold in fee.°
HAMLET. Why, then the Polack never will defend it.
CAPTAIN. Yes, it is already garrisoned.   25
HAMLET. Two thousand souls and twenty thousand ducats
    Will not debate the question of this straw.°
    This is th' impostume° of much wealth and peace,
    That inward breaks, and shows no cause without
    Why the man dies. I humbly thank you, sir.   30
CAPTAIN. God b' wi' you, sir.

                                                                                [Exit.]

ROSENCRANTZ.   Will 't please you go, my lord?
HAMLET. I'll be with you straight. Go a little before.

                                            [Exeunt all except HAMLET.]
    How all occasions do inform against° me
    And spur my dull revenge! What is a man,
    If his chief good and market of° his time   35
    Be but to sleep and feed? A beast, no more.
    Sure he that made us with such large discourse,°
    Looking before and after,° gave us not
    That capability and godlike reason
    To fust° in us unused. Now, whether it be   40
    Bestial oblivion,° or some craven° scruple
    Of thinking too precisely° on th' event°—
    A thought which, quartered, hath but one part wisdom
    And ever three parts coward—I do not know
    Why yet I live to say "This thing's to do,"   45
    Sith° I have cause, and will, and strength, and means
    To do 't. Examples gross° as earth exhort me:
    Witness this army of such mass and charge,°
    Led by a delicate and tender° prince,
    Whose spirit with divine ambition puffed   50
    Makes mouths° at the invisible event,°

---

16 main main part   **18 addition** exaggeration.   **21 To pay** i.e., for a yearly rental of.
21 farm it take a lease of it.   **23 ranker** higher.   **in fee** fee simple, outright.   **27 debate . . . straw** settle this trifling matter.   **28 impostume** abscess.   **33 inform
against** denounce, betray; take shape against.   **35 market of** profit of, compensation
for.   **37 discourse** power of reasoning.   **38 Looking before and after** able to review
past events and anticipate the future.   **40 fust** grow moldy.   **41 oblivion** forgetfulness.
craven cowardly.   **42 precisely** scrupulously.   **event** outcome.   **46 Sith** since.
47 gross obvious.   **48 charge** expense.   **49 delicate and tender** of fine and youthful
qualities.   **51 Makes mouths** makes scornful faces   **invisible event** unforeseeable
outcome.

Exposing what is moral and unsure
To all that fortune, death, and danger dare,°
Even for an eggshell. Rightly to be great
Is not to stir without great argument,   55
But greatly to find quarrel in a straw
When honor's at the stake.° How stand I, then,
That have a father killed, a mother stained,
Excitements of° my reason and my blood,
And let all sleep, while to my shame I see   60
The imminent death of twenty thousand men
That for a fantasy° and trick° of fame
Go to their graves like beds, fight for a plot°
Whereon the numbers cannot try the cause,°
Which is not tomb enough and continent°   65
To hide the slain? O, from this time forth
My thoughts be bloody or be nothing worth!

                                                                 Exit.

4.5 *Enter* HORATIO, [QUEEN] GERTRUDE, *and a* GENTLEMAN.

QUEEN. I will not speak with her.
GENTLEMAN.   She is importunate,
    Indeed distract.° Her mood will needs be pitied.
QUEEN. What would she have?
GENTLEMAN. She speaks much of her father, says she hears
    There's tricks° i' the world, and hems,° and beats her heart,°   5
    Spurns enviously at straws,° speaks things in doubt°
    That carry but half sense. Her speech is nothing,
    Yet the unshapèd use° of it doth move
    The hearers to collection;° they yawn° at it,
    And botch° the words up fit to their own thoughts,   10
    Which,° as her winks and nods and gestures yield° them,
    Indeed would make one think there might be thought,°
    Though nothing sure, yet much unhappily.°
HORATIO. 'Twere good she were spoken with, for she may strew
    Dangerous conjectures in ill-breeding° minds.   15

---

53 dare could do (to him). **54–57 Rightly . . . stake** true greatness does not normally
consist of rushing into action over some trivial provocation; however, when one's honor
is involved, even a trifling insult requires that one respond greatly (?). **at the stake**
(A metaphor from gambling or bear-baiting.) **59 Excitements of** promptings by.
62 fantasy fanciful caprice, illusion. **trick** trifle, deceit. **63 plot** plot of ground.
64 Whereon . . . cause on which there is insufficient room for the soldiers needed
to engage in a military contest. **65 continent** receptacle; container. **4.5 Location:**
The castle. **2 distract** distracted. **5 tricks** deceptions. **hems** makes "hmm" sounds.
5 heart i.e., breast. **6 Spurns . . . straws** kicks spitefully, takes offense at trifles. **in
doubt** obscurely. **8 unshapèd use** incoherent manner. **9 collection** inference, a
guess at some sort of meaning. **yawn** gape, wonder; grasp. (The Folio reading, *aim*, is
possible.) **10 botch** patch. **11 Which** which words. **yield** deliver, represent. **12
thought** intended. **13 unhappily** unpleasantly near the truth, shrewdly. **15 ill-
breeding** prone to suspect the worst and to make mischief.

QUEEN. Let her come in.   [*Exit* GENTLEMAN.]
   [*Aside.*] To my sick soul, as sin's true nature is,
   Each toy° seems prologue to some great amiss.°
   So full of artless jealousy is guilt,
   It spills itself in fearing to be spilt.°   20

   Enter OPHELIA° [*distracted*].

OPHELIA. Where is the beauteous majesty of Denmark?
QUEEN. How now, Ophelia?
OPHELIA [*she sings*].
   "How should I your true love know
      From another one?
   By his cockle hat° and staff,   25
      And his sandal shoon."°
QUEEN. Alas, sweet lady, what imports this song?
OPHELIA. Say you? Nay, pray you, mark.
   "He is dead and gone, lady,   [*Song.*]
      He is dead and gone;   30
   At his head a grass-green turf,
      At his heels a stone."
   O, ho!
QUEEN. Nay, but Ophelia—
OPHELIA. Pray you, mark.   [*Sings.*]   35
   "White his shroud as the mountain snow"—

   Enter KING.

QUEEN. Alas, look here, my lord.
OPHELIA.
   "Larded° with sweet flowers;   [*Song.*]
      Which bewept to the ground did not go
      With true-love showers."°   40
KING. How do you, pretty lady?
OPHELIA. Well, God 'ild° you! They say the owl° was a baker's daughter.
   Lord, we know what we are, but know not what we may be. God
   be at your table!
KING. Conceit° upon her father.   45
OPHELIA. Pray let's have no words of this; but when they ask you what it
   means, say you this:
   "Tomorrow is Saint Valentine's day,   [*Song.*]

---

18 toy trifle. **amiss** calamity. **19–20 So . . . split** guilt is so full of suspicion that it
unskillfully betrays itself in fearing betrayal. **20 s.d. Enter Ophelia** (In the First Quarto,
Ophelia enters, "Playing on a lute, and her hair down, singing.") **25 cockle hat** hat with
cockle-shell stuck in it as a sign that the wearer had been a pilgrim to the shrine of Saint
James of Compostela in Spain. **26 shoon** shoes. **38 Larded** decorated. **40 showers**
i.e., tears. **42 God 'ild** God yield or reward. **owl** (Refers to a legend about a baker's
daughter who was turned into an owl for being ungenerous when Jesus begged a loaf of
bread.) **45 Conceit** brooding.

All in the morning betime,°
And I a maid at your window,   50
    To be your Valentine.
Then up he rose, and donned his clothes,
    And dupped° the chamber door,
Let in the maid, that out a maid
    Never departed more."   55

KING. Pretty Ophelia—

OPHELIA. Indeed, la, without an oath, I'll make an end on 't: [*Sings.*]
    "By Gis° and by Saint Charity,
        Alack, and fie for shame!
Young men will do 't, if they come to 't;   60
    By Cock,° they are to blame.
Quoth she, 'Before you tumbled me.
    You promised me to wed.'"
He answers:
    "'So would I ha' done, by yonder sun,   65
    An° thou hadst not come to my bed.'"

KING. How long hath she been thus?

OPHELIA. I hope all will be well. We must be patient, but I cannot
choose but weep to think they would lay him i' the cold ground.
My brother shall know of it. And so I thank you for your good   70
counsel. Come, my coach! Good night, ladies, good night, sweet
ladies, good night, good night.

                                                             [*Exit.*]

KING [*to* HORATIO]. Follow her close. Give her good watch, I pray you.
                                            [*Exit* HORATIO.]
O, this is the poison of deep grief; it springs
All from her father's death—and now behold!   75
O Gertrude, Gertrude,
When sorrows come, they come not single spies,°
But in battalions. First, her father slain;
Next, your son gone, and he most violent author
Of his own just remove;° the people muddied,°   80
Thick and unwholesome in their thoughts and whispers
For good Polonius' death— and we have done but greenly,°
In hugger-mugger° to inter him; poor Ophelia
Divided from herself and her fair judgment.
Without the which we are pictures or mere beasts;   85
Last, and as much containing° as all these,
Her brother is in secret come from France,
Feeds on this wonder, keeps himself in clouds,°
And wants° not buzzers° to infect his ear

---

49 betime early. **53 dupped** did up, opened. **58 Gis** Jesus. **61 Cock** (A perversion
of "God" in oaths; here also with a quibble on the slang word for penis.) **66 An** if.
77 spies scouts sent in advance of the main force. **80 remove** removal. **muddied**
stirred up, confused. **82 greenly** in an inexperienced way, foolishly. **83 hugger-
mugger** secret haste. **86 as much containing** as full of serious matter. **88 Feeds . . .
clouds** feeds his resentment or shocked grievance, holds himself inscrutable and aloof
amid all this rumor. **89 wants** lacks. **buzzers** gossipers, informers.

    With pestilent speeches of his father's death,   90
    Wherein necessity,° of matter beggared,°
    Will nothing stick our person to arraign
    In ear and ear.° O my dear Gertrude, this,
    Like to a murdering piece,° in many places
    Gives me superfluous death.°   [*A noise within.*]   95
QUEEN. Alack, what noise is this?
KING. Attend!°
    Where is my Switzers?° Let them guard the door.

    Enter a MESSENGER.

    What is the matter?
MESSENGER.   Save yourself, my lord!
    The ocean, overpeering of his list,°   100
    Eats not the flats° with more impetuous° haste
    Than young Laertes, in a riotous head,°
    O'erbears your officers. The rabble call him lord,
    And, as° the world were now but to begin,
    Antiquity forgot, custom not known,   105
    The ratifiers and props of every word,°
    They cry, "Choose we! Laertes shall be king!"
    Caps,° hands, and tongues applaud it to the clouds,
    "Laertes shall be king, Laertes king!"
QUEEN. How cheerfully on the false trail they cry!   110
                         [*A noise within.*]
    O, this is counter,° you false Danish dogs!

    Enter LAERTES *with others.*

KING. The doors are broke.
LAERTES. Where is this king?—Sirs, stand you all without.
ALL. No, let's come in.
LAERTES. I pray you, give me leave.   115
ALL. We will, we will.
LAERTES. I thank you. Keep the door. [*Exeunt followers.*] O thou vile
    king, Give me my father!
QUEEN [*restraining him*]. Calmly, good Laertes.

---

91 necessity i.e., the need to invent some plausible explanation. **of matter beggared**
unprovided with facts. **92–93 Will . . . ear** will not hesitate to accuse my (royal) person in everybody's ears. **94 murdering piece** cannon loaded so as to scatter its shot.
95 Gives . . . death kills me over and over. **97 Attend** i.e., guard me. **98 Switzers**
Swiss guards, mercenaries. **100 overpeering of his list** overflowing its shore, boundary. **101 flats** i.e., flatlands near shore. **impetuous** violent. (Perhaps also with the
meaning of *impiteous* [*impitious,* Q2], "pitiless.") **102 head** insurrection. **104 as** as
if. **106 The ratifiers . . . word** i.e., *antiquity* (or tradition) and *custom* ought to confirm (*ratify*) and underprop our every word or promise. **108 Caps** (The caps are
thrown in the air.) **111 counter** (A hunting term, meaning to follow the trail in a direction opposite to that which the game has taken.)

LAERTES. That drop of blood that's calm proclaims me bastard,
   Cries cuckold to my father, brands the harlot   120
   Even here, between° the chaste unsmirchèd brow
   Of my true mother.
KING.   What is the cause, Laertes,
   That thy rebellion looks so giantlike?
   Let him go, Gertrude. Do not fear our° person.
   There's such divinity doth hedge° a king   125
   That treason can but peep to what it would,°
   Acts little of his will.° Tell me, Laertes,
   Why thou art thus incensed. Let him go, Gertrude.
   Speak, man.
LAERTES.   Where is my father?
KING.   Dead.
QUEEN. But not by him.
KING.   Let him demand his fill.   130
LAERTES. How came he dead? I'll not be juggled with.°
   To hell, allegiance! Vows, to the blackest devil!
   Conscience and grace, to the profoundest pit!
   I dare damnation. To this point I stand,°
   That both the worlds I give to negligence,°   135
   Let come what comes, only I'll be revenged
   Most throughly° for my father.
KING. Who shall stay you?
LAERTES. My will, not all the world's.°
   And for° my means, I'll husband them so well   140
   They shall go far with little.
KING.   Good Laertes,
   If you desire to know the certainty
   Of your dear father, is 't writ in your revenge
   That, swoopstake,° you will draw both friend and foe,
   Winner and loser?   145
LAERTES. None but his enemies.
KING. Will you know them, then?
LAERTES. To his good friends thus wide I'll ope my arms,
   And like the kind life-rendering pelican°
   Repast° them with my blood.

---

121 **between** in the middle of. 124 **fear our** fear for my. 125 **hedge** protect, as with a surrounding barrier. 126 **can . . . would** can only peep furtively, as through a barrier, at what it would intend. 127 **Acts . . . will** (but) performs little of what it intends. 131 **juggled with** cheated, deceived. 134 **To . . . stand** I am resolved in this. 135 **both . . . negligence** i.e., both this world and the next are of no consequence to me. 137 **throughly** thoroughly. 139 **My will . . . world's** I'll stop (*stay*) when my will is accomplished, not for anyone else's. 140 **for** as for. 144 **swoopstake** i.e., indiscriminately. (Literally, taking all stakes on the gambling table at once. *Draw* is also a gambling term, meaning "take from.") 149 **pelican** (Refers to the belief that the female pelican fed its young with its own blood.) 150 **Repast** feed.

KING.   Why, now you speak   150
  Like a good child and a true gentleman.
  That I am guiltless of your father's death,
  And am most sensibly° in grief for it,
  It shall as level° to your judgment 'pear
  As day does to your eye.   [*A noise within.*]   155
LAERTES. How now, what noise is that?

  Enter OPHELIA.

KING.   Let her come in.
LAERTES. O heat, dry up my brains! Tears seven times salt
  Burn out the sense and virtue° of mine eye!
  By heaven, thy madness shall be paid with weight°
  Till our scale turn the beam.° O rose of May!   160
  Dear maid, kind sister, sweet Ophelia!
  O heavens, is 't possible a young maid's wits
  Should be as mortal as an old man's life?
  Nature is fine in° love, and where 'tis fine
  It sends some precious instance° of itself   165
  After the thing it loves.°
OPHELIA.   [*Song.*]
  "They bore him barefaced on the bier,
      Hey non nonny, nonny, hey nonny,
      And in his grave rained many a tear—"
  Fare you well, my dove!   170
LAERTES. Hadst thou thy wits and didst persuade° revenge,
  It could not move thus.
OPHELIA. You must sing "A-down a-down," and you "call him a-down-a."°
  O, how the wheel° becomes it! It is the false steward° that stole his
  master's daughter.   175
LAERTES. This nothing's more than matter.°
OPHELIA. There's rosemary,° that's for remembrance; pray you, love,
  remember. And there is pansies;° that's for thoughts.
LAERTES. A document° in madness, thoughts and remembrance fitted.
OPHELIA. There's fennel° for you, and columbines.° There's rue° for   180
  you, and here's some for me; we may call it herb of grace o' Sun-

---

153 sensibly feelingly.   **154 level** plain.   **158 virtue** faculty, power.   **159 paid with
weight** repaid, avenged equally or more.   **160 beam** crossbar of a balance.   **164 fine
in** refined by.   **165 instance** token.   **166 After . . . loves** i.e., into the grave, along
with Polonius.   **171 persuade** argue cogently for.   **173 You . . . a-down-a** (Ophelia
assigns the singing of refrains, like her own "Hey non nonny," to others present.)   **174
wheel** spinning wheel as accompaniment to the song, or refrain.   **false steward** (The
story is unknown.)   **176 This . . . matter** this seeming nonsense is more eloquent than
sane utterance.   **177 rosemary** (Used as a symbol of remembrance both at weddings
and at funerals.)   **178 pansies** (Emblems of love and courtship; perhaps from French
pensées, "thoughts.")   **179 document** instruction, lesson.   **180 fennel** (Emblem of flattery.)   **columbines** (Emblems of unchastity or ingratitude.)   **rue** (Emblem of repentance—a signification that is evident in its popular name, *herb of grace.*)

days. You must wear your rue with a difference.° There's a daisy.°
I would give you some violets,° but they withered all when my
father died. They say 'a made a good end—
[*Sings.*] "For bonny sweet Robin is all my joy."   185
LAERTES.   Thought° and affliction, passion,° hell itself,
She turns to favor° and to prettiness.
OPHELIA.   [*Song.*]
         "And will 'a not come again?
         And will 'a not come again?
             No, no, he is dead.   190
             Go to thy deathbed,
         He never will come again.
         "His beard was as white as snow,
         All flaxen was his poll.°
             He is gone, he is gone,   195
             And we cast away moan.
         God ha' mercy on his soul!"

     And of all Christian souls, I pray God. God b' wi' you.
                                    [*Exit, followed by* GERTRUDE.]
LAERTES.   Do you see this, O God?
KING.   Laertes, I must commune with your grief,   200
     Or you deny me right. Go but apart,
     Make choice of whom° your wisest friends you will,
     And they shall hear and judge twixt you and me.
     If by direct or by collateral hand°
     They find us touched,° we will our kingdom give,   205
     Our crown, our life, and all that we call ours
     To you in satisfaction; but if not,
     Be you content to lend your patience to us,
     And we shall jointly labor with your soul
     To give it due content.
LAERTES.   Let this be so.   210
     His means of death, his obscure funeral—
     No trophy,° sword, nor hatchment° o'er his bones,
     No noble rite, nor formal ostentation°—
     Cry to be heard, as 'twere from heaven to earth,
     That° I must call 't in question.°
KING.   So you shall,   215
     And where th' offense is, let the great ax fall.
     I pray you, go with me.
                                            Exeunt.

---

182 with a difference (A device used in heraldry to distinguish one family from another
on the coat of arms, here suggesting that Ophelia and the others have different causes
of sorrow and repentance; perhaps with a play on *rue* in the sense of "ruth," "pity.")
daisy (Emblem of dissembling, faithlessness.) **183 violets** (Emblems of faithfulness.)
186 Thought melancholy. **passion** suffering. **187 favor** grace, beauty. **194 poll**
head. **202 whom** whichever of. **204 collateral hand** indirect agency. **205 us
touched** me implicated. **212 trophy** memorial. **hatchment** tablet displaying the ar-
morial bearings of a deceased person. **213 ostentation** ceremony. **215 That** so that.
call 't in question demand an explanation.

4.6 *Enter* HORATIO *and others.*

HORATIO. What are they that would speak with me?
GENTLEMAN. Seafaring men, sir. They say they have letters for you.
HORATIO. Let them come in.

[*Exit* GENTLEMAN.]

I do not know from what part of the world
I should be greeted, if not from Lord Hamlet.   5

Enter Sailors.

FIRST SAILOR. God bless you, sir.
HORATIO. Let him bless thee too.
FIRST SAILOR. 'A shall, sir, an 't° please him. There's a letter for you, sir—
it came from th' ambassador° that was bound for England—if your
name be Horatio, as I am let to know it is. [*He gives a letter.*]   10
HORATIO [*reads*]. "Horatio, when thou shalt have overlooked° this, give
these fellows some means° to the King; they have letters for him.
Ere we were two days old at sea, a pirate of very warlike appoint-
ment° gave us chase. Finding ourselves too slow of sail, we put on
a compelled valor, and in the grapple I boarded them. On the in-   15
stant they got clear of our ship, so I alone became their prisoner.
They have dealt with me like thieves of mercy,° but they knew
what they did: I am to do a good turn for them. Let the King have
the letters I have sent, and repair° thou to me with as much speed
as thou wouldest fly death. I have words to speak in thine ear   20
will make thee dumb, yet are they much too light for the bore° of
the matter. These good fellows will bring thee where I am. Rosencrantz and Guildenstern hold their course for England. Of them I
have much to tell thee. Farewell.

He that thou knowest thine, Hamlet."   25
Come, I will give you way° for these your letters.
And do 't the speedier that you may direct me
To him from whom you brought them.

Exeunt.

4.7 *Enter* KING *and* LAERTES.

KING. Now must your conscience my acquittance seal,°
And you must put me in your heart for friend,
Sith° you have heard, and with a knowing ear,
That he which hath your noble father slain
Pursued my life.
LAERTES.   It well appears. But tell me   5
Why you proceeded not against these feats°
So crimeful and so capital° in nature,

4.6 Location: The castle.   8 an 't if it.   **9 th' ambassador** (Evidently Hamlet. The
sailor is being circumspect.)   **11 overlooked** looked over.   **12 means** means of access.
13–14 appointment equipage.   **17 thieves of mercy** merciful thieves.   **19 repair**
come.   **21 bore** caliber, i.e., importance.   **26 way** means of access.   **4.7 Location:
The castle.   1 my acquittance seal** confirm or acknowledge my innocence.   **3 Sith**
since.   **6 feats** acts.   **7 capital** punishable by death.

As by your safety, greatness, wisdom, all things else,
You mainly° were stirred up.
KING. O, for two special reasons,   10
    Which may to you perhaps seem much unsinewed,°
    But yet to me they're strong. The Queen his mother
    Lives almost by his looks, and for myself—
    My virtue or my plague, be it either which—
    She is so conjunctive° to my life and soul   15
    That, as the star moves not but in his° sphere,°
    I could not but by her. The other motive
    Why to a public count° I might not go
    Is the great love the general gender° bear him,
    Who, dipping all his faults in their affection,   20
    Work° like the spring° that turneth wood to stone,
    Convert his gyves° to graces, so that my arrows,
    Too slightly timbered° for so loud° a wind,
    Would have reverted° to my bow again
    But not where I had aimed them.   25
LAERTES. And so have I a noble father lost,
    A sister driven into desperate terms,°
    Whose worth, if praises may go back° again,
    Stood challenger on mount° of all the age
    For her perfections. But my revenge will come.   30
KING. Break not your sleeps for that. You must not think
    That we are made of stuff so flat and dull
    That we can let our beard be shook with danger
    And think it pastime. You shortly shall hear more.
    I loved your father, and we love ourself;   35
    And that, I hope, will teach you to imagine—

Enter a MESSENGER *with letters.*

    How now? What news?
MESSENGER. Letters, my lord, from Hamlet:
    This to Your Majesty, this to the Queen.

                                              [*He gives letters.*]
KING. From Hamlet? Who brought them?   40
MESSENGER. Sailors, my lord, they say. I saw them not.
    They were given me by Claudio. He received them
    Of him that brought them.

---

9 **mainly** greatly.   11 **unsinewed** weak.   15 **conjunctive** closely united. (An astro-
nomical metaphor.)   16 **his** its.   **sphere** one of the hollow spheres in which, according
to Ptolematic astronomy, the planets were supposed to move.   18 **count** account, reckoning, indictment.   19 **general gender** common people.   21 **Work** operate, act.
spring i.e., a spring with such a concentration of lime that it coats a piece of wood with
limestone, in effect gilding and petrifying it.   22 **gyves** fetters (which, gilded by the people's praise, would look like badges of honor).   23 **slightly timbered** light.   **loud** (suggesting public outcry on Hamlet's behalf).   24 **reverted** returned.   27 **terms** state, condition.   28 **go back** i.e., recall what she was.   29 **on mount** set up on high.

KING.   Laertes, you shall hear them.—
    Leave us.

                             [*Exit* MESSENGER.]

    [*He reads.*] "High and mighty, you shall know I am set naked° on   45
    your kingdom. Tomorrow shall I beg leave to see your kingly eyes,
    when I shall, first asking your pardon,° thereunto recount the oc-
    casion of my sudden and more strange return.

                                        Hamlet."

    What should this mean? Are all the rest come back?
    Or is it some abuse,° and no such thing?°   50

LAERTES. Know you the hand?

KING.   'Tis Hamlet's character.° "Naked!"
    And in a postscript here he says "alone."
    Can you devise° me?

LAERTES. I am lost in it, my lord. But let him come.
    It warms the very sickness in my heart   55
    That I shall live and tell him to his teeth,
    "Thus didst thou."°

KING.   If it be so, Laertes—
    As how should it be so? How otherwise?°—
    Will you be ruled by me?

LAERTES.   Ay, my lord,
    So° you will not o'errule me to a peace.   60

KING. To thine own peace. If he be now returned,
    As checking at° his voyage, and that° he means
    No more to undertake it, I will work him
    To an exploit, now ripe in my device,°
    Under the which he shall not choose but fall;   65
    And for his death no wind of blame shall breathe,
    But even his mother shall uncharge the practice°
    And call it an accident.

LAERTES.   My lord, I will be ruled,
    The rather if you could devise it so
    That I might be the organ.°

KING.   It falls right.   70
    You have been talked of since your travel much,
    And that in Hamlet's hearing, for a quality
    Wherein they say you shine. Your sum of parts°
    Did not together pluck such envy from him
    As did that one, and that, in my regard,   75
    Of the unworthiest siege.°

---

45 naked destitute, unarmed, without following. **47 pardon** permission. **50 abuse** deceit. **no such thing** not what it appears. **51 character** handwriting. **53 devise** explain to. **57 Thus didst thou** i.e., here's for what you did to my father. **58 As . . . otherwise** how can this (Hamlet's return) be true? Yet how otherwise than true (since we have the evidence of his letter)? **60 So** provided that. **62 checking at** i.e., turning aside from (like a falcon leaving the quarry to fly at a chance bird). **that** if. **64 device** devising, invention. **67 uncharge the practice** acquit the strategem of being a plot. **70 organ** agent, instrument. **73 Your . . . parts** i.e., all your other virtues. **76 unworthiest siege** least important rank.

LAERTES. What part is that, my lord?

KING. A very ribbon in the cap of youth,
    Yet needful too, for youth no less becomes°
    The light and careless liverty that it wears   80
    Than settled age his sables° and his weeds°
    Importing health and graveness.° Two months since
    Here was a gentleman of Normandy.
    I have seen myself, and served against, the French,
    And they can well° on horseback, but this gallant   85
    Had witchcraft in 't; he grew unto his seat,
    And to such wondrous doing brought his horse
    As had he been incorpsed and demi-natured°
    With the brave beast. So far he topped° my thought
    That I in forgery° of shapes and tricks   90
    Come short of what he did.

LAERTES.   A Norman was 't?

KING. A Norman.

LAERTES. Upon my life, Lamord.

KING.   The very same.

LAERTES. I know him well. He is the brooch° indeed
    And gem of all the nation.   95

KING. He made confession° of you,
    And gave you such a masterly report
    For art and exercise in your defense,°
    And for your rapier most especial,
    That he cried out 'twould be a sight indeed   100
    If one could match you. Th' escrimers° of their nation,
    He swore, had neither motion, guard, nor eye
    If you opposed them. Sir, this report of his
    Did Hamlet so envenom with his envy
    That he could nothing do but wish and beg   105
    Your sudden° coming o'er, to play° with you.
    Now, out of this—

LAERTES.   What out of this, my lord?

KING. Laertes, was your father dear to you?
    Or are you like the painting of a sorrow,
    A face without a heart?

LAERTES.   Why ask you this?   110

KING. Not that I think you did not love your father,
    But that I know love is begun by time,°

---

79 no less becomes is no less suited by.   **81 his sables** its rich robes furred with sable.
weeds garments.   **82 Importing . . . graveness** signifying a concern for health and
dignified prosperity; also, giving an impression of comfortable prosperity.   **85 can well**
are skilled.   **88 As . . . demi-natured** as if he had been of one body and nearly of one
nature (like the centaur).   **89 topped** surpassed.   **90 forgery** imagining.   **94 brooch**
ornament.   **96 confession** testimonial, admission of superiority.   **98 For . . . defense**
with respect to your skill and practice with your weapon.   **101 escrimers** fencers.
106 sudden immediate.   **play** fence.   **112 begun by time** i.e., created by the right
circumstance and hence subject to change.

And that I see, in passages of proof,°
Time qualifies° the spark and fire of it.
There lives within the very flame of love   115
A kind of wick or snuff° that will abate it,
And nothing is at a like goodness still,°
For goodness, growing to a pleurisy,°
Dies in his own too much.° That° we would do,
We should do when we would; for this "would" changes   120
And hath abatements° and delays as many
As there are tongues, are hands, are accidents,°
And then this "should" is like a spendthrift sigh,°
That hurts by easing.° But, to the quick o' th' ulcer:°
Hamlet comes back. What would you undertake   125
To show yourself in deed your father's son
More than in words?

LAERTES.   To cut his throat i' the church.

KING. No place, indeed, should murder sanctuarize;°
Revenge should have no bounds. But good Laertes,
Will you do this,° keep close within your chamber.   130
Hamlet returned shall know you are come home.
We'll put on those shall° praise your excellence
And set a double varnish on the fame
The Frenchman gave you, bring you in fine° together,
And wager on your heads. He, being remiss,°   135
Most generous,° and free from all contriving,
Will not peruse the foils, so that with ease,
Or with a little shuffling, you may choose
A sword unabated,° and in a pass of practice°
Requite him for your father.

LAERTES.   I will do 't.   140
And for that purpose I'll anoint my sword.
I bought an unction° of a mountebank°
So mortal that, but dip a knife in it,
Where it draws blood no cataplasm° so rare,
Collected from all simples° that have virtue°   145

---

113 **passages of proof** actual instances that prove it.   114 **qualifies** weakens, moderates.   116 **snuff** the charred part of a candlewick.   117 **nothing . . . still** nothing remains at a constant level of perfection.   118 **pleurisy** excess, plethora. (Literally, a chest inflammation.)   119 **in . . . much** of its own excess.   **That** that which.   121 **abatements** diminutions.   122 **As . . . accidents** as there are tongues to dissuade, hands to prevent, and chance events to intervene.   123 **spendthrift sigh** (An allusion to the belief that sighs draw blood from the heart.)   124 **hurts by easing** i.e., costs the heart blood and wastes precious opportunity even while it affords emotional relief.   124 **quick o' th' ulcer** i.e., heart of the matter.   128 **sanctuarize** protect from punishment. (Alludes to the right of sanctuary with which certain religious places were invested.)   130 **Will you do this** if you wish to do this.   132 **put on those shall** arrange for some to.   134 **in fine** finally.   135 **remiss** negligently unsuspicious.   136 **generous** nobleminded.   139 **unabated** not blunted, having no button.   **pass of practice** treacherous thrust.   142 **unction** ointment.   **mountebank** quack doctor.   144 **cataplasm** plaster or poultice.   145 **simples** herbs.   **virtue** potency.

Under the moon,° can save the thing from death
That is but scratched withal. I'll touch my point
With this contagion, that if I gall° him slightly,
It may be death.

KING.   Let's further think of this,
Weigh what convenience both of time and means   150
May fit us to our shape.° If this should fail,
And that our drift look through our bad performance,°
'Twere better not assayed. Therefore this project
Should have a back or second, that might hold
If this did blast in proof.° Soft, let me see   155
We'll make a solemn wager on your cunnings°—
I ha 't!
When in your motion you are hot and dry—
As° make your bouts more violent to that end—
And that he calls for drink, I'll have prepared him   160
A chalice for the nonce,° whereon but sipping,
If he by chance escape your venomed stuck,°
Our purpose may hold there. [*A cry within.*] But stay, what noise?

Enter QUEEN.

QUEEN.   One woe doth tread upon another's heel,
So fast they follow. Your sister's drowned, Laertes.   165
LAERTES.   Drowned! O, where
QUEEN.   There is a willow grows askant° the brook,
That shows his hoar leaves° in the glassy stream;
Therewith fantastic garlands did she make
Of crowflowers, nettles, daisies, and long purples,°   170
That liberal° shepherds give a grosser name,°
But our cold° maids do dead men's fingers call them.
There on the pendent° boughs her crownet° weeds
Clamb'ring to hang, an envious sliver° broke,
When down her weedy° trophies and herself   175
Fell in the weeping brook. Her clothes spread wide,
And mermaidlike awhile they bore her up,
Which time she chanted snatches of old lauds,°
As one incapable of° her own distress,

---

146 Under the moon i.e., anywhere (with reference perhaps to the belief that herbs gathered at night had a special power).   **148 gall** graze, wound.   **151 shape** part we propose to act.   **152 drift . . . performance** intention should be made visible by our bungling.   **155 blast in proof** burst in the test (like a cannon).   **156 cunnings** respective skills.   **159 As** i.e., and you should.   **161 nonce** occasion.   **162 stuck** thrust. (From *stoccado,* a fencing term.)   **167 askant** aslant.   **168 hoar leaves** white or gray undersides of the leaves.   **170 long purples** early purple orchids.   **171 liberal** free-spoken.   **a grosser name** (The testicle-resembling tubers of the orchid, which also in some cases resemble *dead men's fingers,* have earned various slang names like "dog-stones" and "cullions.")   **172 cold** chaste.   **173 pendent** overhanging.   **crownet** made into a chaplet or coronet.   **174 envious sliver** malicious branch.   **175 weedy** i.e., of plants.   **178 lauds** hymns.   **179 incapable of** lacking capacity to apprehend.

Or like a creature native and endued°   180
Unto that element. But long it could not be
Till that her garments, heavy with their drink,
Pulled the poor wretch from her melodious lay
To muddy death.

LAERTES.   Alas, then she is drowned?

QUEEN. Drowned, drowned.   185

LAERTES. Too much of water hast thou, poor Ophelia,
And therefore I forbid my tears. But yet
It is our trick;° nature her custom holds,
Let shame say what it will. [*He weeps.*] When these are gone,
The woman will be out.° Adieu, my lord.   190
I have a speech of fire that fain would blaze,
But that this folly douts° it.

                                                          Exit.

KING.   Let's follow, Gertrude.
How much I had to do to calm his rage!
Now fear I this will give it start again;
Therefore let's follow.   195

                                                        Exeunt.

5.1 *Enter two* CLOWNS° [*with spades and mattocks*].

FIRST CLOWN. Is she to be buried in Christian burial, when she willfully
seeks her own salvation?°

SECOND CLOWN. I tell thee she is; therefore make her grave straight.° The
crowner° hath sat on her,° and finds it° Christian burial.

FIRST CLOWN. How can that be, unless she drowned herself in her own   5
defense?

SECOND CLOWN. Why, 'tis found so.°

FIRST CLOWN. It must be *se offendendo,*° it cannot be else. For here lies
the point: if I drown myself wittingly, it argues an act, and an act
hath three branches—it is to act, to do, and to perform. Argal,° she   10
drowned herself wittingly.

SECOND CLOWN. Nay, but hear you, goodman° delver—

FIRST CLOWN. Give me leave. Here lies the water; good. Here stands the
man; good. If the man go to this water and drown himself, it is, will
he, nill he,° he goes, mark you that. But if the water come to him   15

---

180 endued adapted by nature.   **188 It is our trick** i.e., weeping is our natural way
(when sad).   **189–190 When . . . out** when my tears are all shed, the woman in me will
be expended, satisfied.   **192 douts** extinguishes. (The Second Quarto reads "drowns.")
5.1 Location: A churchyard. s.d. Clowns rustics.   **2 salvation** (A blunder for
"damnation," or perhaps a suggestion that Ophelia was taking her own shortcut to heaven.)
3 straight straightway, immediately. (But with a pun on *strait,* "narrow.")   **4 crowner**
coroner.   **sat on her** conducted an inquest on her case.   **finds it** gives his official verdict
that her means of death was consistent with.   **7 found so** determined so in the coroner's
verdict.   **8 *se offendendo*** (A comic mistake for *se defendendo,* a term used in verdicts of
justifiable homicide.)   **10 Argal** (Corruption of *ergo,* "therefore.")   **12 goodman** (An
honorific title often used with the name of a profession or craft.)   **14–15 will he, nill he**
whether he will or no, willy-nilly.

and drown him, he drowns not himself. Argal, he that is not guilty
of his own death shortens not his own life.

SECOND CLOWN. But is this law?

FIRST CLOWN. Ay, marry, is 't—crowner's quest° law.

SECOND CLOWN. Will you ha' the truth on 't? If this had not been a gentle-   20
woman, she should have been buried out o' Christian burial.

FIRST CLOWN. Why, there thou sayst.° And the more pity that great folk
should have countenance° in this world to drown or hang themselves, more than their even-Christian.° Come, my spade. There is
no ancient° gentlemen but gardeners, ditchers, and grave makers.   25
They hold up° Adam's profession.

SECOND CLOWN. Was he a gentleman?

FIRST CLOWN. 'A was the first that ever bore arms.°

SECOND CLOWN. Why, he had none.

FIRST CLOWN. What, art a heathen? How dost thou understand the Scrip-   30
ture? The Scripture says Adam digged. Could he dig without arms?°
I'll put another question to thee. If thou answerest me not to the
purpose, confess thyself°—

SECOND CLOWN. Go to.

FIRST CLOWN. What is he that builds stronger than either the mason, the   35
shipwright, or the carpenter?

SECOND CLOWN. The gallows maker, for that frame° outlives a thousand
tenants.

FIRST CLOWN. I like thy wit well, in good faith. The gallows does well.°
But how does it well? It does well to those that do ill. Now thou   40
dost ill to say the gallows is built stronger than the church. Argal,
the gallows may do well to thee. To 't again, come.

SECOND CLOWN. "Who builds stronger than a mason, a shipwright, or a
carpenter?"

FIRST CLOWN. Ay, tell me that, and unyoke.°   45

SECOND CLOWN. Marry, now I can tell.

FIRST CLOWN. To 't.

SECOND CLOWN. Mass,° I cannot tell.

Enter HAMLET *and* HORATIO [*at a distance*].

FIRST CLOWN. Cudgel thy brains no more about it, for your dull ass will
not mend his pace with beating; and when you are asked this ques-   50
tion next, say "a grave maker. The houses he makes lasts till
doomsday." Go get thee in and fetch me a stoup° of liquor.

[*Exit* SECOND CLOWN. FIRST CLOWN *digs.*]

Song.

---

19 quest inquest.   **22 there thou sayst** i.e., that's right.   **23 countenance** privilege.
24 even-Christian fellow Christians.   **25 ancient** going back to ancient times.
26 hold up maintain.   **28 bore arms** (To be entitled to bear a coat of arms would make
Adam a gentleman, but as one who bore a spade, our common ancestor was an ordinary
delver in the earth.)   **31 arms** i.e., the arms of the body.   **33 confess thyself** (The saying continues, "and be hanged.")   **37 frame** (1) gallows (2) structure.   **39 does well**
(1) is an apt answer (2) does a good turn.   **45 unyoke** i.e., after this great effort, you may
unharness the team of your wits.   **48 Mass** by the Mass.   **52 stoup** two-quart measure.

     "In youth, when I did love, did love,°
       Methought it was very sweet,
     To contract—O—the time for—a—my behove,°   55
       O, methought there—a—was nothing—a—meet."°

HAMLET. Has this fellow no feeling of his business, 'a° sings in grave-making?

HORATIO. Custom hath made it in him a property of easiness.°

HAMLET. 'Tis e'en so. The hand of little employment hath the daintier   60
sense.°

FIRST CLOWN.   *Song.*
     "But age with his stealing steps
       Hath clawed me in his clutch,
     And hath shipped me into the land,°
       As if I had never been such."   65

                           [He throws up a skull.]

HAMLET. That skull had a tongue in it and could sing once. How the
knave jowls° it to the ground, as if 'twere Cain's jawbone, that did
the first murder! This might be the pate of a politician,° which this
ass now o'erreaches,° one that would circumvent God, might it
not?   70

HORATIO. It might, my lord.

HAMLET. Or of a courtier, which could say, "Good morrow, sweet lord!
How dost thou, sweet lord?" This might be my Lord Such-a-one,
that praised my Lord Such-a-one's horse when 'a meant to beg it,
might it not?   75

HORATIO. Ay, my lord

HAMLET. Why e'en so, and now my lady Worm's, chapless,° and
knocked about the mazard° with a sexton's spade. Here's fine revolution,° an° we had the trick to see° 't. Did these bones cost no
more the breeding but to play° at loggets° with them? Mine ache to   80
think on 't.

FIRST CLOWN.   *Song.*
     "A pickax and a spade, a spade,
       For and° a shrouding sheet;

---

53 In . . . love (This and the two following stanzas, with nonsensical variations, are
from a poem attributed to Lord Vaux and printed in *Tottel's Miscellany*, 1557. The *O*
and *a* [for "ah"] seemingly are the grunts of the digger.)   **55 To contract . . . behove**
i.e., to shorten the time for my own advantage. (Perhaps he means to *prolong* it.)
56 meet suitable, i.e., more suitable.   **57 'a** that he.   **59 property of easiness** something he can do easily and indifferently.   **60–61 daintier sense** more delicate sense of
feeling.   **64 into the land** i.e., toward my grave (?). (But note the lack of rhyme in
steps, land.)   **67 jowls** dashes (with a pun on *jowl,* "jawbone").   **68 politician**
schemer, plotter.   **69 o'erreaches** circumvents, gets the better of (with a quibble on
the literal sense).   **77 chapless** having no lower jaw.   **78 mazard** i.e., head (literally, a
drinking vessel).   **78–79 revolution** turn of Fortune's wheel, change.   **79 an** if.
trick to see knack of seeing.   **79–80 cost . . . play** involve so little expense and care
in upbringing that we may play.   **80 loggets** a game in which pieces of hard wood
shaped like Indian clubs or bowling pins are thrown to lie as near as possible to a stake.
83 For and and moreover.

O, a pit of clay for to be made
   For such a guest is meet."   85

[*He throws up another skull.*]

HAMLET. There's another. Why may not that be the skull of a lawyer?
   Where be his quiddities° now, his quillities,° his cases, his
   tenures,° and his tricks? Why does he suffer this mad knave now to
   knock him about the sconce° with a dirty shovel, and will not tell
   him of his action of battery?° Hum, this fellow might be in 's time a   90
   great buyer of land, with his statutes, his recognizances,° his fines,
   his double° vouchers,° his recoveries.° In this the fine of his fines
   and the recovery of recoveries, to have his fine pate full of fine
   dirt?° Will his vouchers vouch him no more of his purchases, and
   double ones too, than the length and breadth of a pair of inden-   95
   tures?° The very conveyances° of his lands will scarcely lie in this
   box,° and must th' inheritor° himself have no more, ha?
HORATIO. Not a jot more, my lord.
HAMLET. Is not parchment made of sheepskins?
HORATIO. Ay, my lord, and of calves' skins too.   100
HAMLET. They are sheep and calves, which seek out assurance in that.° I
   will speak to this fellow.—Whose grave's this, sirrah?°
FIRST CLOWN. Mine, sir.   [*Sings.*]
   "O, pit of clay for to be made
      For such a guest is meet."   105
HAMLET. I think it be thine, indeed, for thou liest in 't.
FIRST CLOWN. You lie out on 't, sir, and therefore 'tis not yours. For my
   part, I do not lie in 't, yet it is mine.
HAMLET. Thou dost lie in 't, to be in 't and say it is thine. 'Tis for the
   dead, not for the quick;° therefore thou liest.   110
FIRST CLOWN. 'Tis a quick lie, sir; 'twill away again from me to you.
HAMLET. What man dost thou dig it for?
FIRST CLOWN. For no man, sir.
HAMLET. What woman, then?
FIRST CLOWN. For none, neither.   115
HAMLET. Who is to be buried in 't?
FIRST CLOWN. One that was a woman, sir, but, rest her soul, she's dead.

---

87 quiddities subtleties, quibbles (from Latin *quid,* "a thing"). **quillities** verbal niceties,
subtle distinctions (variation of *quiddities*). **88 tenures** the holding of a piece of property or office, or the conditions or period of such holding. **89 sconce** head. **90 action
of battery** lawsuit about physical assault. **91 statutes, recognizances** legal documents
guaranteeing a debt by attaching land and property. **91–92 fines . . . recoveries** ways of
converting entailed estates into "fee simple" or freehold. **92 double** signed by two signa-
tories. **vouchers** guarantees of the legality of a title to real estate. **92–94 fine of his
fines . . . fine pate . . . fine dirt** end of his legal maneuvers . . . elegant head . . .
minutely sifted dirt. **95–96 pair of indentures** legal documents drawn up in duplicate
on a single sheet and then cut apart on a zigzag line so that each pair was uniquely matched.
(Hamlet may refer to two rows of teeth or dentures.) **96 conveyances** deeds. **97 box**
(1) deed box (2) coffin. ("Skull" has been suggested.) **inheritor** possessor, owner.
101 assurance in that safety in legal parchments. **102 sirrah** (A term of address to
inferiors.) **110 quick** living.

HAMLET. How absolute° the knave is! We must speak by the card,° or
equivocation° will undo us. By the Lord, Horatio, this three years I
have took° note of it: the age is grown so picked° that the toe of   120
the peasant comes so near the heel of the courtier, he galls his
kibe.°—How long has thou been grave maker?

FIRST CLOWN. Of all the days i' the year, I came to 't that day that our last
king Hamlet overcame Fortinbras.

HAMLET. How long is that since?   125

FIRST CLOWN. Cannot you tell that? Every fool can tell that. It was that
very day that young Hamlet was born—he that is mad and sent into
England.

HAMLET. Ay, marry, why was he sent into England?

FIRST CLOWN. Why, because 'a was mad. 'A shall recover his wits there,   130
or if 'a do not, 'tis no great matter there.

HAMLET. Why?

FIRST CLOWN. 'Twill not be seen in him there. There the men are as mad
as he.

HAMLET. How came he mad?   135

FIRST CLOWN. Very strangely, they say.

HAMLET. How strangely?

FIRST CLOWN. Faith, e'en with losing his wits.

HAMLET. Upon what ground?°

FIRST CLOWN. Why, here in Denmark. I have been sexton here, man and   140
boy, thirty years.

HAMLET. How long will a man lie i' th' earth ere he rot?

FIRST CLOWN. Faith, if 'a be not rotten before 'a die—as we have many
pocky° corpses nowadays, that will scarce hold the laying in°—'a
will last you° some eight year or nine year. A tanner will last you   145
nine year.

HAMLET. Why he more than another?

FIRST CLOWN. Why, sir, his hide is so tanned with his trade that 'a will
keep out water a great while, and your water is a sore° decayer of
your whoreson° dead body. [*He picks up a skull.*] Here's a skull   150
now hath lien you° i' th' earth three-and-twenty years.

HAMLET. Whose was it?

FIRST CLOWN. A whoreson mad fellow's it was. Whose do you think it
was?

HAMLET. Nay, I know not.   155

FIRST CLOWN. A pestilence on him for a mad rogue! 'A poured a flagon of
Rhenish° on my head once. This same skull, sir, was, sir, Yorick's
skull, the King's jester.

---

118 **absolute** strict, precise. **by the card** i.e., with precision. (Literally, by the
mariner's compass-card, on which the points of the compass were marked.) 119 **equiv-
ocation** ambiguity in the use of terms. 120 **took** taken. **picked** refined, fastidious.
121–122 **galls his kibe** chafes the courtier's chilblain. 139 **ground** cause. (But, in the
next line, the gravedigger takes the word in the sense of "land," "country.") 144 **pocky**
rotten, diseased (literally, with the pox, or syphilis). **hold the laying in** hold together
long enough to be interred. 145 **last you** last. (*You* is used colloquially here and in
the following lines.) 149 **sore** i.e., terrible, great. 150 **whoreson** i.e., vile, scurvy.
151 **lien you** lain. (See the note at line 145.) 157 **Rhenish** Rhine wine.

HAMLET. This?

FIRST CLOWN. E'en that.   160

HAMLET. Let me see. [*He takes the skull.*] Alas, poor Yorick! I knew him,
  Horatio, a fellow of infinite jest, of most excellent fancy. He hath
  bore° me on his back a thousand times, and now how abhorred in
  my imagination it is! My gorge rises° at it. Here hung those lips that
  I have kissed I know not how oft. Where be your gibes now? Your   165
  gambols, your songs, your flashes of merriment that were wont° to
  set the table on a roar? Not one now, to mock your own grinning?°
  Quite chopfallen?° Now get you to my lady's chamber and tell her,
  let her paint an inch thick, to this favor° she must come. Make her
  laugh at that. Prithee, Horatio, tell me one thing.   170

HORATIO. What's that, my lord?

HAMLET. Dost thou think Alexander looked o' this fashion i' th' earth?

HORATIO. E'en so.

HAMLET. And smelt so? Pah!   [*He throws down the skull.*]

HORATIO. E'en so, my lord.   175

HAMLET. To what base uses we may return, Horatio! Why may not imagination trace the noble dust of Alexander till 'a find it stopping a
  bunghole?°

HORATIO. 'Twere to consider too curiously° to consider so.

HAMLET. No, faith, not a jot, but to follow him thither with modesty°   180
  enough, and likelihood to lead it. As thus: Alexander died, Alexander was buried, Alexander returneth to dust, the dust is earth, of
  earth we make loam,° and why of that loam whereto he was converted might they not stop a beer barrel?
  Imperious° Caesar, dead and turned to clay,   185
  Might stop a hole to keep the wind away.
  O, that that earth which kept the world in awe
  Should patch a wall t' expel the winter's flaw!°

Enter KING, QUEEN, LAERTES, *and the corpse* [*of* OPHELIA, *in procession,*
with PRIEST, *lords, etc.*].

  But soft,° but soft awhile! Here comes the King,
  The Queen, the courtiers. Who is this they follow?   190
  And with such maimèd° rites? This doth betoken
  The corpse they follow did with desperate hand
  Fordo° its own life. 'Twas of some estate.°
  Couch we° awhile and mark.

[*He and* HORATIO *conceal themselves.* OPHELIA'S *body is taken to the*
grave.]

---

163 bore borne.   **164 My gorge rises** i.e., I feel nauseated.   **166 were wont** used.
167 mock your own grinning mock at the way your skull seems to be grinning (just as
you used to mock at yourself and those who grinned at you).   **168 chopfallen** (1) lacking the lower jaw (2) dejected.   **169 favor** aspect, appearance.   **178 bunghole** hole for
filling or emptying a cask.   **179 curiously** minutely.   **180 modesty** plausible moderation.   **183 loam** mortar consisting chiefly of moistened clay and straw.   **185 Imperious**
imperial.   **188 flaw** gust of wind.   **189 soft** i.e., wait, be careful.   **191 maimèd** mutilated, incomplete.   **193 Fordo** destroy.   **estate** rank.   **194 Couch we** let's hide, lie low.

LAERTES. What ceremony else?   195

HAMLET [*to* HORATIO]. That is Laertes, a very noble youth. Mark.

LAERTES. What ceremony else?

PRIEST. Her obsequies have been as far enlarged
    As we have warranty.° Her death was doubtful,
    And but that great command o'ersways the order°   200
    She should in ground unsanctified been lodged°
    Till the last trumpet. For° charitable prayers,
    Shards,° flints, and pebbles should be thrown on her.
    Yet here she is allowed her virgin crants,°
    Her maiden strewments,° and the bringing home   205
    Of bell and burial.°

LAERTES. Must there no more be done?

PRIEST.   No more be done.
    We should profane the service of the dead
    To sing a requiem and such rest° to her
    As to peace-parted souls.°

LAERTES.   Lay her i' th' earth,   210
    And from her fair and unpolluted flesh
    May violets° spring! I tell thee, churlish priest,
    A ministering angel shall my sister be
    When thou liest howling.°

HAMLET [*to* HORATIO].   What, the fair Ophelia!

QUEEN [*scattering flowers*]. Sweets to the sweet! Farewell.   215
    I hoped thou shouldst have been my Hamlet's wife.
    I thought thy bride-bed to have decked, sweet maid,
    And not t' have strewed thy grave.

LAERTES.   O, treble woe
    Fall ten times treble on that cursèd head
    Whose wicked deed thy most ingenious sense°   220
    Deprived thee of! Hold off the earth awhile,
    Till I have caught her once more in mine arms.

[*He leaps into the grave and embraces* OPHELIA.]

    Now pile your dust upon the quick and dead,
    Till of this flat a mountain you have made
    T' o'ertop old Pelion or the skyish head   225
    Of blue Olympus.°

---

199 warranty i.e., ecclesiastical authority.   **200 great . . . order** orders from on high overrule the prescribed procedures.   **201 She should . . . lodged** she should have been buried in unsanctified ground.   **202 For** in place of.   **203 Shards** broken bits of pottery.   **204 crants** garlands betokening maidenhood.   **205 strewments** flowers strewn on a coffin.   **205–206 bringing . . . burial** laying the body to rest, to the sound of the bell.   **209 such rest** i.e., to pray for such rest.   **210 peace-parted souls** those who have died at peace with God.   **212 violets** (See 4.5.183 and note.)   **214 howling** i.e., in hell.   **220 ingenious sense** a mind that is quick, alert, of fine qualities. **225–226 Pelion, Olympus** sacred mountains in the north of Thessaly; see also *Ossa*, below, at line 257.

HAMLET [*coming forward*]. What is he whose grief
 Bears such an emphasis,° whose phrase of sorrow
 Conjures the wandering stars° and makes them stand
 Like wonder-wounded° hearers? This is I,
 Hamlet the Dane.°   230
LAERTES [*grappling with him°*]. The devil take thy soul!
HAMLET. Thou pray'st not well.
 I prithee, take thy fingers from my throat,
 For though I am not splenitive° and rash,
 Yet have I in me something dangerous,
 Which let thy wisdom fear. Hold off thy hand.   235
KING. Pluck them asunder.
QUEEN. Hamlet, Hamlet!
ALL. Gentlemen!
HORATIO. Good my lord, be quiet.

 [HAMLET *and* LAERTES *are parted.*]

HAMLET. Why, I will fight with him upon this theme   240
 Until my eyelids will no longer wag.°
QUEEN. O my son, what theme?
HAMLET. I loved Ophelia. Forty thousand brothers
 Could not with all their quantity of love
 Make up my sum. What wilt thou do for her?   245
KING. O, he is mad, Laertes.
QUEEN. For love of God, forbear him.°
HAMLET. 'Swounds,° show me what thou'lt do.
 Woo't° weep? Woo't fight? Woo't fast? Woo't tear thyself?
 Woo't drink up° eisel?° Eat a crocodile?°   250
 I'll do 't. Dost come here to whine?
 To outface me with leaping in her grave?
 Be buried quick° with her, and so will I.
 And if thou prate of mountains, let them throw
 Millions of acres on us, till our ground,   255
 Singeing his pate° against the burning zone,°

---

227 **emphasis** i.e., rhetorical and florid emphasis. (*Phrase* has a similar rhetorical connotation.)   228 **wandering stars** planets.   229 **wonder-wounded** struck with amazement.   230 **the Dane** (This title normally signifies the King; see 1.1.17 and note.)   **s.d.
grappling with him** The testimony of the First Quarto that *"Hamlet leaps in after
Laertes"* and the "Elegy on Burbage" ("Oft have I seen him leap into the grave") seem to
indicate one way in which this fight was staged; however, the difficulty of fitting two con-
tenders and Ophelia's body into a confined space (probably the trapdoor) suggests to
many editors the alternative, that Laertes jumps out of the grave to attack Hamlet.
233 **splenitive** quick-tempered.   241 **wag** move. (A fluttering eyelid is a conventional
sign that life has not yet gone.)   247 **forbear him** leave him alone.   248 **'Swounds** by
His (Christ's) wounds.   249 **Woo't** wilt thou.   250 **drink up** drink deeply.   **eisel** vinegar.   **crocodile** (Crocodiles were tough and dangerous, and were supposed to shed hypocritical tears.)   253 **quick** alive.   256 **his pate** its head, i.e., top.   **burning zone** zone
in the celestial sphere containing the sun's orbit, between the tropics of Cancer and
Capricorn.

Make Ossa° like a wart! Nay, an° thou'lt mouth,°
I'll rant as well as thou.

QUEEN.   This is mere° madness,
And thus awhile the fit will work on him;
Anon, as patient as the female dove   260
When that her golden couplets° are disclosed,°
His silence will sit drooping.

HAMLET.   Hear you, sir,
What is the reason that you use me thus?
I loved you ever. But it is no matter.
Let Hercules himself do what he may,   265
The cat will mew, and dog will have his day.°

                                        Exit HAMLET.

KING.   I pray thee, good Horatio, wait upon him.

                                        [*Exit* HORATIO.]

[*To* LAERTES.] Strengthen your patience in° our last night's speech;
We'll put the matter to the present push.°—
Good Gertrude, set some watch over your son.—   270
This grave shall have a living° monument.
An hour of quiet° shortly shall we see;
Till then, in patience our proceeding be.

                                        Exeunt.

5.2   *Enter* HAMLET *and* HORATIO.

HAMLET.   So much for this, sir; now shall you see the other.°
You do remember all the circumstance?
HORATIO.   Remember it, my lord!
HAMLET.   Sir, in my heart there was a kind of fighting
That would not let me sleep. Methought I lay   5
Worse than the mutines° in the bilboes° Rashly,°
And praised be rashness for it—let us know°
Our indiscretion° sometimes serves us well
When our deep plots do pall,° and that should learn° us
There's a divinity that shapes our ends,   10
Rough-hew° them how we will—
HORATIO.   That is most certain.

---

257 **Ossa** another mountain in Thessaly. (In their war against the Olympian gods, the giants attempted to heap Ossa on Pelion to scale Olympus.)   **an** if.   **mouth** i.e., rant.
258 **mere** utter.   261 **golden couplets** two baby pigeons, covered with yellow down.
disclosed hatched.   265–266 **Let . . . day** i.e., (1) even Hercules couldn't stop
Laertes's theatrical rant (2) I, too, will have my turn; i.e., despite any blustering attempts
at interference, every person will sooner or later do what he or she must do.   268 **in** i.e.,
by recalling.   269 **present push** immediate test.   271 **living** lasting. (For Laertes's private understanding, Claudius also hints that Hamlet's death will serve as such a monument.)   272 **hour of quiet** time free of conflict.   **5.2 Location: The castle.**   1 **see the
other** hear the other news.   6 **mutines** mutineers.   **bilboes** shackles.   **Rashly** on impulse (this adverb goes with lines 12 ff.).   7 **know** acknowledge.   8 **indiscretion** lack
of foresight and judgment (not an indiscreet act).   9 **pall** fail, falter, go stale.   **learn**
teach.   11 **Rough-hew** shape roughly.

HAMLET. Up from my cabin,
    My sea-gown° scarfed° about me, in the dark
    Groped I to find out them,° had my desire,
    Fingered° their packet, and in fine° withdrew   15
    To mine own room again, making so bold,
    My fears forgetting manners, to unseal
    Their grand commission; where I found, Horatio—
    Ah, royal knavery!—an exact command,
    Larded° with many several° sorts of reasons   20
    Importing° Denmark's health and England's too,
    With, ho! such bugs° and goblins in my life,°
    That on the supervise,° no leisure bated,°
    No, not to stay° the grinding of the ax,
    My head should be struck off.
HORATIO.   Is't possible?   25
HAMLET [*giving a document*].
    Here's the commission. Read it at more leisure.
    But wilt thou hear now how I did proceed?
HORATIO. I beseech you.
HAMLET. Being thus benetted round with villainies—
    Ere I could make a prologue to my brains,   30
    They had begun the play°—I sat me down,
    Devised a new commission, wrote it fair.°
    I once did hold it, as our statists° do,
    A baseness° to write fair, and labored much
    How to forget that learning; but, sir, now   35
    It did me yeoman's° service. Wilt thou know
    Th' effect° of what I wrote?
HORATIO.   Ay, good my lord.
HAMLET. An earnest conjuration° from the King,
    As England was his faithful tributary,
    As love between them like the palm° might flourish,   40
    As peace should still° her wheaten garland° wear
    And stand a comma° 'tween their amities,
    And many suchlike "as"es° of great charge,°
    That on the view and knowing of these contents,
    Without debatement further more or less,   45

---

13 sea-gown seaman's coat.   **scarfed** loosely wrapped.   **14 them** i.e., Rosencrantz
and Guildenstern.   **15 Fingered** pilfered, pinched.   **in fine** finally, in conclusion.
20 Larded garnished.   **several** different.   **21 Importing** relating to.   **22 bugs** bug-
bears, hobgoblins.   **in my life** i.e., to be feared if I were allowed to live.   **23 supervise**
reading.   **leisure bated** delay allowed.   **24 stay** await.   **30–31 Ere . . . play** before
I could consciously turn my brain to the matter, it had started working on a plan.
32 fair in a clear hand.   **33 statists** statesmen.   **34 baseness** i.e., lower-class trait.
36 yeoman's i.e., substantial, faithful, loyal.   **37 effect** purport.   **38 conjuration**
entreaty.   **40 palm** (An image of health; see Psalm 92.12.)   **41 still** always.   **wheaten
garland** (Symbolic of fruitful agriculture, of peace and plenty.)   **42 comma** (Indicating
continuity, link.)   **43 "as"es** (1) the "whereases" of a formal document (2) asses.
charge (1) import (2) burden (appropriate to asses).

He should those bearers put to sudden death,
Not shriving time° allowed.

HORATIO. How was this sealed?

HAMLET. Why, even in that was heaven ordinant.°
I had my father's signet° in my purse.
Which was the model° of that Danish seal; 50
Folded the writ° up in the form of th' other,
Subscribed° it, gave 't th' impression,° placed it safely,
The changeling° never known. Now, the next day
Was our sea fight, and what to this was sequent°
Thou knowest already. 55

HORATIO. So Guildenstern and Rosencrantz go to 't.

HAMLET. Why, man, they did make love to this employment.
They are not near my conscience. Their defeat°
Does by their own insinuation° grow.
'Tis dangerous when the baser° nature comes 60
Between the pass° and fell° incensèd points
Of mightly opposites.°

HORATIO. Why, what a king is this!

HAMLET. Does it not, think thee, stand me now upon°—
He that hath killed my king and whored my mother,
Popped in between th' election° and my hopes, 65
Thrown out his angle° for my proper° life,
And with such cozenage°—is 't not perfect conscience
To quit° him with this arm? And is 't not to be damned
To let this canker° of our nature come
In° further evil? 70

HORATIO. It must be shortly known to him from England
What is the issue of the business there.

HAMLET. It will be short. The interim is mine,
And a man's life's no more than to say "one."°
But I am very sorry, good Horatio, 75
That to Laertes I forgot myself,
For by the image of my cause I see
The portraiture of his. I'll court his favors.
But, sure, the bravery° of his grief did put me
Into a tow'ring passion.

---

47 shriving time time for confession and absolution. **48 ordinant** directing.
49 signet small seal. **50 model** replica. **51 writ** writing. **52 Subscribed** signed
(with forged signature). **impression** i.e., with a wax seal. **53 changeling** i.e., substituted letter. (Literally, a fairy child substituted for a human one.) **54 was sequent** followed. **58 defeat** destruction. **59 insinuation** intrusive intervention, sticking their
noses in my business. **60 baser** of lower social station. **61 pass** thrust. **fell** fierce.
62 opposites antagonists. **63 stand me now upon** become incumbent on me now.
65 election (The Danish monarch was "elected" by a small number of high-ranking elec-
tors.) **66 angle** fishhook. **proper** very. **67 cozenage** trickery. **68 quit** requite,
pay back. **69 canker** ulcer. **69–70 come In** grow into. **74 a man's . . . "one"**
one's whole life occupies such a short time, only as long as it takes to count to 1.
79 bravery bravado.

HORATIO.   Peace, who comes here?   80

> *Enter a Courtier* [OSRIC].

OSRIC. Your lordship is right welcome back to Denmark.

HAMLET. I humbly thank you, sir. [*To* HORATIO.] Dost know this water fly?

HORATIO. No, my good lord.

HAMLET. Thy state is the more gracious, for 'tis a vice to know him. He   85
hath much land, and fertile. Let a beast be lord of beasts, and his
crib° shall stand at the King's mess.° 'Tis a chuff,° but, as I say, spacious in the possession of dirt.

OSRIC. Sweet lord, if your lordship were at leisure, I should impart a thing
to you from His Majesty.   90

HAMLET. I will receive it, sir, with all diligence of spirit.
Put your bonnet° to his° right use; 'tis for the head.

OSRIC. I thank your lordship, it is very hot.

HAMLET. No, believe me, 'tis very cold. The wind is northerly.

OSRIC. It is indifferent° cold, my lord, indeed.   95

HAMLET. But yet methinks it is very sultry and hot for my complexion.°

OSRIC. Exceedingly, my lord. It is very sultry, as 'twere—I cannot tell
how. My lord, His Majesty bade me signify to you that 'a has laid a
great wager on your head. Sir, this is the matter—

HAMLET. I beseech you, remember.   100

> [HAMLET *moves him to put on his hat.*]

OSRIC. Nay, good my lord; for my ease,° in good faith. Sir, here is newly
come to court Laertes—believe me, an absolute° gentleman, full of
most excellent differences,° of very soft society° and great showing.° Indeed, to speak feelingly° of him, he is the card° or calendar°
of gentry,° for you shall find in him the continent of what part a   105
gentleman would see.°

HAMLET. Sir, his definement° suffers no perdition° in you,° though I
know to divide him inventorially° would dozy° th' arithmetic of
memory, and yet but yaw° neither° in respect of° his quick sail.
But, in the verity of extolment,° I take him to be a soul of great   110

---

87 **crib** manger.   86–87 **Let . . . mess** i.e., if a man, no matter how beastlike, is as rich
in livestock and possessions as Osric, he may eat at the King's table.   87 **chuff** boor,
churl. (The Second Quarto spelling, *chough,* is a variant spelling that also suggests the
meaning here of "chattering jackdaw.")   92 **bonnet** any kind of cap or hat.   **his** its.
95 **indifferent** somewhat.   96 **complexion** temperament.   101 **for my ease** (A conventional reply declining the invitation to put his hat back on.)   102 **absolute** perfect.
103 **differences** special qualities.   **soft society** agreeable manners.   103–104 **great
showing** distinguished appearance.   104 **feelingly** with just perception.   **card** chart,
map.   **calendar** guide.   105 **gentry** good breeding.   105–106 **the continent . . . see**
one who contains in him all the qualities a gentleman would like to see (a *continent* is
that which contains).   107 **definement** definition. (Hamlet proceeds to mock Osric by
throwing his lofty diction back at him.)   **perdition** loss, diminution.   **you** your description.   108 **divide him inventorially** enumerate his graces.   **dozy** dizzy.   109 **yaw**
swing unsteadily off course (said of a ship).   **neither** for all that.   **in respect of** in
comparison with.   110 **in . . . extolment** in true praise (of him).

article,° and his infusion° of such dearth and rareness° as, to make
true diction° of him, his semblable° is his mirror and who else
would trace° him his umbrage,° nothing more.

OSRIC. Your lordship speaks most infallibly of him.

HAMLET. The concernancy,° sir? Why do we wrap the gentleman in our   115
more rawer breath?°

OSRIC. Sir?

HORATIO. Is 't not possible to understand in another tongue?° You will
do 't,° sir, really.

HAMLET. What imports the nomination° of this gentleman?   120

OSRIC. Of Laertes?

HORATIO [*to* HAMLET]. His purse is empty already; all 's golden words are
spent.

HAMLET. Of him, sir.

OSRIC. I know you are not ignorant—   125

HAMLET. I would you did, sir. Yet in faith if you did, it would not much
approve° me. Well, sir?

OSRIC. You are not ignorant of what excellence Laertes is—

HAMLET. I dare not confess that, lest I should compare with him in excellence. But to know a man well were to know himself.°   130

OSRIC. I mean, sir, for° his weapon; but in the imputation laid on him by
them,° in his meed° he's unfellowed.°

HAMLET. What's his weapon?

OSRIC. Rapier and dagger.

HAMLET. That's two of his weapons—but well.°   135

OSRIC. The King, sir, hath wagered with him six Barbary horses, against
the which he° has impawned,° as I take it, six French rapiers and
poniards,° with their assigns,° as girdle, hangers,° and so.° Three of
the carriages,° in faith, are very dear to fancy,° very responsive° to
the hilts, most delicate° carriages, and of very liberal conceit.°   140

110–111 of great article one with many articles in his inventory.   **111 infusion**
essence, character infused into him by nature.   **dearth and rareness** rarity.   **111–112**
make true diction speak truly.   **112 semblable** only true likeness.   **112–113**
who . . . trace any other person who would wish to follow.   **113 umbrage** shadow.
115 concernancy import, relevance.   **116 rawer breath** unrefined speech that can
come short in praising him.   **118 to understand . . . tongue** i.e., for you, Osric, to understand when someone else speaks your language. (Horatio twits Osric for not being
able to understand the kind of flowery speech he himself uses, when Hamlet speaks in
such a vein. Alternatively, all this could be said to Hamlet.)   **118–119 You will do 't** i.e.,
you can if you try, or, you may well have to try (to speak plainly).   **120 nomination**
naming.   **127 approve** commend.   **129–130 I dare . . . himself** I dare not boast of
knowing Laertes's excellence lest I seem to imply a comparable excellence in myself. Certainly, to know another person well, one must know oneself.   **131 for** i.e., with.
131–132 imputation . . . them reputation given him by others.   **132 meed** merit.
unfellowed unmatched.   **135 but well** but never mind.   **137 he** i.e., Laertes.
impawned staked, wagered.   **138 poniards** daggers.   **assigns** appurtenances.
hangers straps on the sword belt (*girdle*), from which the sword hung.   **and so** and so
on.   **139 carriages** (An affected way of saying *hangers;* literally, gun carriages.)   **dear**
to fancy delightful to the fancy.   **responsive** corresponding closely; matching or well
adjusted.   **140 delicate** (i.e., in workmanship.)   **liberal conceit** elaborate design.

HAMLET. What call you the carriages?

HORATIO [*to* HAMLET]. I knew you must be edified by the margent° ere
you had done.

OSRIC. The carriages, sir, are the hangers.

HAMLET. The phrase would be more germane to the matter if we could   145
carry a cannon by our sides; I would it might be hangers till then.
But, on: six Barbary horses against six French swords, their assigns,
and three liberal-conceited carriages; that's the French bet against
the Danish. Why is this impawned, as you call it?

OSRIC. The King, sir, hath laid,° sir, that in a dozen passes° between   150
yourself and him, he shall not exceed you three hits. He hath laid
on twelve for nine, and it would come to immediate trial, if your
lordship would vouchsafe the answer.°

HAMLET. How if I answer no?

OSRIC. I mean, my lord, the opposition of your person in trial.   155

HAMLET. Sir, I will walk here in the hall. If it please His Majesty, it is the
breathing time° of day with me. Let° the foils be brought, the gentleman willing, and the King hold his purpose. I will win for him
an I can; if not, I will gain nothing but my shame and the odd hits.

OSRIC. Shall I deliver you° so?   160

HAMLET. To this effect, sir—after what flourish your nature will.

OSRIC. I commend° my duty to your lordship.

HAMLET. Yours, yours. [*Exit* OSRIC.] 'A does well to commend it himself;
there are no tongues else for 's turn.°

HORATIO. This lapwing° runs away with the shell on his head.   165

HAMLET. 'A did comply with his dug° before a' sucked it. Thus has he—
and many more of the same breed that I know the drossy° age
dotes on—only got the tune° of the time and, out of an habit of encounter,° a kind of yeasty° collection,° which carries them through
and through the most fanned and winnowed opinions;° and do°   170
but blow them to their trial, the bubbles are out.°

---

142 **margent** margin of a book, place for explanatory notes. 150 **laid** wagered.
passes bouts. (The odds of the betting are hard to explain. Possibly the King bets that
Hamlet will win at least five out of twelve, at which point Laertes raises the odds against
himself by betting he will win nine.) 153 **vouchsafe the answer** be so good as to accept the challenge. (Hamlet deliberately takes the phrase in its literal sense of replying.)
157 **breathing time** exercise period.   **Let** i.e., if. 160 **deliver you** report what you
say. 162 **commend** commit to your favor. (A conventional salutation, but Hamlet wryly
uses a more literal meaning, "recommend," "praise," in line 163.) 164 **for 's turn** for his
purposes, i.e., to do it for him. 165 **lapwing** (A proverbial type of youthful forward-
ness. Also, a bird that draws intruders away from its nest and was thought to run
about with its head in the shell when newly hatched; a seeming reference to Osric's hat.)
166 **comply . . . dug** observe ceremonious formality toward his nurse's or mother's
teat. 167 **drossy** laden with scum and impurities, frivolous. 168 **tune** temper, mood,
manner of speech. 168–169 **an habit of encounter** a demeanor in conversing (with
courtiers of his own kind). 169 **yeasty** frothy.   **collection** i.e., of current phrases.
169–170 **carries . . . opinions** sustains them right through the scrutiny of persons
whose opinions are select and refined. (Literally, like grain separated from its chaff. Osric
is both the chaff and the bubbly froth on the surface of the liquor that is soon blown
away.) 170 **and do** yet do. 171 **blow . . . out** test them by merely blowing on them,
and their bubbles burst.

Enter a LORD.

LORD. My lord. His Majesty commended him to you by young Osric, who brings back to him that you attend him in the hall. He sends to know if your pleasure hold to play with Laertes, or that° you will take longer time. 175

HAMLET. I am constant to my purposes; they follow the King's pleasure. If his fitness speaks, mine is ready;° now or whensoever, provided I be so able as now.

LORD. The King and Queen and all are coming down.

HAMLET. In happy time.° 180

LORD. The Queen desires you to use some gentle entertainment° to Laertes before you fall to play.

HAMLET. She well instructs me. [*Exit* LORD.]

HORATIO. You will lose, my lord.

HAMLET. I do not think so. Since he went into France, I have been in 185 continual practice; I shall win at the odds. But thou wouldst not think how ill all's here about my heart; but it is no matter.

HORATIO. Nay, good my lord—

HAMLET. It is but foolery, but it is such a kind of gaingiving° as would perhaps trouble a woman. 190

HORATIO. If your mind dislike anything, obey it. I will forestall their repair° hither and say you are not fit.

HAMLET. Not a whit, we defy augury. There is special providence in the fall of a sparrow. If it be now, 'tis not to come; if it be not to come, it will be now; if it be not now, yet it will come. The readiness is 195 all. Since no man of aught he leaves knows, what is 't to leave betimes? Let be.°

A table prepared. [*Enter*] *trumpets, drums, and officers with cushions;* KING, QUEEN, [OSRIC,] *and all the state; foils, daggers,* [*and wine borne in;*] *and* LAERTES.

KING. Come, Hamlet, come and take this hand from me.
[*The* KING *puts* LAERTES' *hand into* HAMLET'*s.*]

HAMLET [*to* LAERTES]. Give me your pardon, sir. I have done you wrong,
But pardon 't as you are a gentleman. 200
This presence° knows,
And you must needs have heard, how I am punished°
With a sore distraction. What I have done
That might your nature, honor, and exception°
Roughly awake, I here proclaim was madness. 205
Was 't Hamlet wronged Laertes? Never Hamlet.
If Hamlet from himself be ta'en away,

---

174 that if.   **177 If . . . ready** if he declares his readiness, my convenience waits on his. **180 In happy time** (A phrase of courtesy indicating that the time is convenient.)   **181 entertainment** greeting.   **189 gaingiving** misgiving.   **191–192 repair** coming. **196–197 Since . . . Let be** Since no one has knowledge of what he is leaving behind, what does an early death matter after all? Enough; don't struggle against it.   **201 presence** royal assembly.   **202 punished** afflicted.   **204 exception** disapproval.

And when he's not himself does wrong Laertes,
Then Hamlet does it not, Hamlet denies it.
Who does it, then? His madness. If 't be so,   210
Hamlet is of the faction° that is wronged;
His madness is poor Hamlet's enemy.
Sir, in this audience
Let my disclaiming from a purposed evil
Free me so far in your most generous thoughts   215
That I have° shot my arrow o'er the house
And hurt my brother.
LAERTES.   I am satisfied in nature,°
Whose motive° in this case should stir me most
To my revenge. But in my terms of honor
I stand aloof, and will no reconcilement   220
Till by some elder masters of known honor
I have a voice° and precedent of peace°
To keep my name ungored.° But till that time
I do receive our offered love like love,
And will not wrong it.
HAMLET.   I embrace it freely,   225
And will this brothers' wager frankly° play.—
Give us the foils. Come on.
LAERTES.   Come, one for me.
HAMLET. I'll be your foil,° Laertes. In mine ignorance
Your skill shall, like a star i' the darkest night.
Stick fiery off° indeed.
LAERTES.   You mock me, sir.   230
HAMLET. No, by this hand.
KING. Give them the foils, young Osric. Cousin Hamlet,
You know the wager?
HAMLET.   Very well, my lord.
Your Grace has laid the odds o'° the weaker side.
KING. I do not fear it; I have seen you both.   235
But since he is bettered,° we have therefore odds.
LAERTES. This is too heavy. Let me see another.
                              [*He exchanges his foil for another.*]
HAMLET. This likes me° well. These foils have all a length?
                              [*They prepare to play.*]
OSRIC. Ay, my good lord.
KING. Set me the stoups of wine upon that table.   240
If Hamlet give the first or second hit.

---

211 **faction** party.   216 **That I have** as if I had.   217 **in nature** i.e., as to my personal
feelings.   218 **motive** prompting.   222 **voice** authoritative pronouncement.   **of peace**
for reconciliation.   223 **name ungored** reputation unwounded.   226 **frankly** without
ill feeling or the burden of rancor.   228 **foil** thin metal background which sets a jewel off
(with pun on the blunted rapier for fencing).   230 **Stick fiery off** stand out brilliantly.
234 **laid the odds o'** bet on, backed.   236 **is bettered** has improved; is the odds-on
favorite. (Laertes' handicap is the "three hits" specified in line 151.)   238 **likes me**
pleases me.

Or quit in answer of the third exchange,°
Let all the battlements their ordnance fire.
The King shall drink to Hamlet's better breath,°
And in the cup an union° shall he throw   245
Richer than that which four successive kings
In Denmark's crown have worn. Give me the cups,
And let the kettle° to the trumpet speak,
The trumpet to the cannoneer without,
The cannons to the heavens, the heaven to earth,   250
"Now the King drinks to Hamlet." Come, begin.

                                              Trumpets the while.

And you, the judges, bear a wary eye.

HAMLET. Come on, sir.

LAERTES. Come, my lord.   [*They play.* HAMLET *scores a hit.*]

HAMLET. One.   255

LAERTES. No.

HAMLET. Judgment.

OSRIC.   A hit, a very palpable hit.

                    Drum, trumpets, and shot. Flourish. A piece goes off.

LAERTES. Well, again.

KING. Stay, give me drink. Hamlet, this pearl is thine.

[*He drinks, and throws a pearl in* HAMLET'*s cup.*]

Here's to thy health. Give him the cup.   260

HAMLET. I'll play this bout first. Set it by awhile.

Come. [*They play.*] Another hit; what say you?

LAERTES. A touch, a touch, I do confess 't.

KING. Our son shall win.

QUEEN.   He's fat° and scant of breath.

Here, Hamlet, take my napkin,° rub thy brows.   265
The Queen carouses° to thy fortune, Hamlet.

HAMLET. Good, madam!

KING. Gertrude, do not drink.

QUEEN. I will, my lord, I pray you pardon me.   [*She drinks.*]

KING [*aside*]. It is the poisoned cup. It is too late.   270

HAMLET. I dare not drink yet, madam; by and by.

QUEEN. Come, let me wipe thy face.

LAERTES [*to* KING]. My lord, I'll hit him now.

KING.   I do not think 't.

LAERTES [*aside*]. And yet it is almost against my conscience.

HAMLET. Come, for the third, Laertes. You do but dally.   275
I pray you, pass° with your best violence;
I am afeard you make a wanton of me.°

LAERTES. Say you so? Come on.   [*They play.*]

---

242 Or . . . exchange i.e., or requites Laertes in the third bout for having won the first
two.   **244 better breath** improved vigor.   **245 union** pearl. (So called, according to
Pliny's *Natural History,* 9, because pearls are *unique,* never identical.)   **248 kettle**
kettledrum.   **264 fat** not physically fit, out of training.   **265 napkin** handkerchief.
266 carouses drinks a toast.   **276 pass** thrust.   **277 make . . . me** i.e., treat me like a
spoiled child, trifle with me.

OSRIC. Nothing neither way.

LAERTES. Have at you now!

[LAERTES *wounds* HAMLET; *then, in scuffling, they change rapiers,*°
and HAMLET *wounds* LAERTES.]

KING.   Part them! They are incensed.   280

HAMLET. Nay, come, again.   [*The* QUEEN *falls.*]

OSRIC.   Look to the Queen there, ho!

HORATIO. They bleed on both sides. How is it, my lord?

OSRIC. How is 't, Laertes?

LAERTES. Why, as a woodcock° to mine own springe,° Osric;
    I am justly killed with mine own treachery.   285

HAMLET. How does the Queen?

KING.   She swoons to see them bleed.

QUEEN. No, no, the drink, the drink—O my dear Hamlet—
    The drink, the drink! I am poisoned.   [*She dies.*]

HAMLET. O villainy! Ho, let the door be locked!
    Treachery! Seek it out.   290

                                              [LAERTES *falls. Exit* OSRIC.]

LAERTES. It is here, Hamlet. Hamlet, thou art slain.
    No med'cine in the world can do thee good;
    In thee there is not half an hour's life.
    The treacherous instrument is in thy hand,
    Unbated° and envenomed. The foul practice°   295
    Hath turned itself on me. Lo, here I lie,
    Never to rise again. Thy mother's poisoned.
    I can no more. The King, the King's to blame.

HAMLET. The point envenomed too? Then, venom, to thy work.

                                              [*He stabs the* KING.]

ALL. Treason! Treason!   300

KING. O, yet defend me, friends! I am but hurt.

HAMLET [*forcing the* KING *to drink*].
    Here, thou incestuous, murderous, damnèd Dane,
    Drink off this potion. Is thy union° here?
    Follow my mother.   [*The* KING *dies.*]

LAERTES.   He is justly served.
    It is a poison tempered° by himself.   305
    Exchange forgiveness with me, noble Hamlet.
    Mine and my father's death come not upon thee,
    Nor thine on me!   [*He dies.*]

HAMLET. Heaven make thee free of it! I follow thee.
    I am dead, Horatio. Wretched Queen, adieu!   310
    You that look pale and tremble at this chance,°

---

280 s.d. in scuffling, they change rapiers (This stage direction occurs in the Folio. According to a widespread stage tradition, Hamlet receives a scratch, realizes that Laertes's
sword is unbated, and accordingly forces an exchange.)   **284 woodcock** a bird, a type of
stupidity or as a decoy.   **springe** trap, snare.   **295 Unbated** not blunted with a button.
practice plot.   **303 union** pearl. (See line 245; with grim puns on the word's other
meanings: marriage, shared death.)   **305 tempered** mixed.   **311 chance** mischance.

That are but mutes° or audience to this act,
Had I but time—as this fell° sergeant,° Death,
Is strict° in his arrest°—O, I could tell you—
But let it be. Horatio, I am dead;   315
Thou livest. Report me and my cause aright
To the unsatisfied.

HORATIO.   Never believe it.
I am more an antique Roman° than a Dane.
Here's yet some liquor left.

[He attempts to drink from the poisoned cup. HAMLET *prevents him.]*

HAMLET.   As thou'rt a man,
Give me the cup! Let go! By heaven, I'll ha 't.   320
O God, Horatio, what a wounded name,
Things standing thus unknown, shall I leave behind me!
If thou didst ever hold me in thy heart,
Absent thee from felicity awhile,
And in this harsh world draw thy breath in pain   325
To tell my story.   *A march afar off [and a volley within].*
What warlike noise is this?

Enter OSRIC.

OSRIC. Young Fortinbras, with conquest come from Poland,
To th' ambassadors of England gives
This warlike volley.

HAMLET.   O, I die, Horatio!
The potent poison quite o'ercrows° my spirit.   330
I cannot live to hear the news from England,
But I do prophesy th' election lights
On Fortinbras. He has my dying voice.°
So tell him, with th' occurents° more and less
Which have solicited°—the rest is silence.   *[He dies.]* 335

HORATIO. Now cracks a noble heart. Good night, sweet prince,
And flights of angels sing thee to thy rest!

[March within.]
Why does the drum come hither?

Enter FORTINBRAS, *with the [English] Ambassadors [with drum, colors, and attendants].*

FORTINBRAS. Where is this sight?

---

312 mutes silent observers. (Literally, actors with nonspeaking parts.)   **313 fell** cruel.
sergeant sheriff's officer.   **314 strict** (1) severely just (2) unavoidable.   **314 arrest** (1)
taking into custody (2) stopping my speech.   **318 Roman** (Suicide was an honorable
choice for many Romans as an alternative to a dishonorable life.)   **330 o'ercrows** triumphs over (like the winner in a cockfight).   **333 voice** vote.   **334 occurrents** events,
incidents.   **335 solicited** moved, urged. (Hamlet doesn't finish saying what the events
have prompted—presumably, his acts of vengeance, or his reporting of those events to
Fortinbras.)

HORATIO.   What is it you would see?
   If aught of woe or wonder, cease your search.   340
FORTINBRAS. This quarry° cries on havoc.° O proud Death,
   What feast° is toward° in thine eternal cell,
   That thou so many princes at a shot
   So bloodily hast struck?
FIRST AMBASSADOR.   The sight is dismal,
   And our affirs from England come too late.   345
   The ears are senseless that should give us hearing,
   To tell him his commandment is fulfilled,
   That Rosencrantz and Guildenstern are dead.
   Where should we have our thanks?
HORATIO.   Not from his° mouth,
   Had it th' ability of life to thank you.   350
   He never gave commandment for their death.
   But since, so jump° upon this bloody question,°
   You from the Polack wars, and you from England,
   And here arrived, give orders that these bodies
   High on a stage° be placèd to the view,   355
   And let me speak to th' yet unknowing world
   How these things came about. So shall you hear
   Of carnal, bloody, and unnatural acts,
   Of accidental judgments,° casual° slaughters,
   Of deaths put on° by cunning and forced cause,°   360
   And, in this upshot, purposes mistook
   Fall'n on th' inventors' heads. All this can I
   Truly deliver.
FORTINBRAS.   Let us haste to hear it,
   And call the noblest to the audience.
   For me, with sorrow I embrace my fortune.   365
   I have some rights of memory° in this kingdom,
   Which now to claim my vantage° doth invite me.
HORATIO. Of that I shall have also cause to speak,
   And from his mouth whose voice will draw on more.°
   But let this same be presently° performed,   370
   Even while men's minds are wild, lest more mischance
   On° plots and errors happen.
FORTINBRAS.   Let four captains
   Bear Hamlet, like a soldier, to the stage,
   For he was likely, had he been put on,°

---

341 quarry heap of dead. **cries on havoc** proclaims a general slaughter. **342 feast**
i.e., Death feasting on those who have fallen. **toward** in preparation. **349 his** i.e.,
Claudius's. **352 jump** precisely, immediately. **question** dispute, affair. **355 stage**
platform. **359 judgments** retributions. **casual** occurring by chance. **360 put on** instigated. **forced cause** contrivance. **366 of memory** traditional, remembered, unfor-
gotten. **367 vantage** favorable opportunity. **369 voice . . . more** vote will influence
still others. **370 presently** immediately. **372 On** on the basis of; on top of. **374 put
on** i.e., invested in royal office and so put to the test.

To have proved most royal; and for his passage,°   375
The soldiers' music and the rite of war
Speak° loudly for him.
Take up the bodies. Such a sight as this
Becomes the field,° but there shows much amiss.
Go bid the soldiers shoot.   380

Exeunt [*marching, bearing off the dead bodies;*
a peal of ordnance is shot off].

---

375 passage i.e., from life to death.   **377 Speak** (let them) speak.   **379 Becomes the
field** suits the field of battle.

▨ TOPICS FOR CRITICAL THINKING AND WRITING

Act 1

1. The first scene (like many other scenes in this play) is full of expressions of uncertainty. What are some of these uncertainties? The
   Ghost first appears at 1.1.42. Does his appearance surprise us, or have
   we been prepared for it? Or is there both preparation and surprise?
   Do the last four speeches of 1.1 help to introduce a note of hope? If
   so, how?
2. Does the King's opening speech in 1.2 reveal him to be an accomplished public speaker—or are lines 10-14 offensive? In his second
   speech (lines 41-49), what is the effect of naming Laertes four times?
   Claudius sometimes uses the royal pronouns ("we," "our"), sometimes
   the more intimate "I" and "my." Study his use of these in lines 1-4 and
   in 106-117. What do you think he is getting at?
3. Hamlet's first soliloquy (1.2.129-159) reveals that more than just his father's death distresses him. Be as specific as possible about the causes
   of Hamlet's anguish here. What traits does Hamlet reveal in his conversation with Horatio (1.2.160-258)?
4. What do you make of Polonius's advice to Laertes (1.3.55-81)? Is it
   sound? Sound advice, but here uttered by a fool? Ignoble advice? How
   would one follow the advice of line 78: "to thine own self be true"?
   In his words to Ophelia in 1.3.102-136, what does he reveal about
   himself?
5. Can 1.4.17-38 reasonably be taken as a speech on the "tragic flaw"?
   (On this idea, see page 1095.) Or is the passage a much more limited
   discussion, a comment simply on Danish drinking habits?
6. Hamlet is convinced in 1.5.93-104 that the Ghost has told the truth, indeed, the only important truth. But do we detect in 105-112 a hint of a
   tone suggesting that Hamlet delights in hating villainy? If so, can it be
   said that later this delight grows, and that in some scenes (e.g., 3.3) we
   feel that Hamlet has almost become a diabolic revenger? Explain.

Act 2

1. Characterize Polonius on the basis of 2.1.1–76.
2. In light of what we have seen of Hamlet, is Ophelia's report of his strange behavior when he visits her understandable?
3. Why does 2.2.33–34 seem almost comic? How do these lines help us to form a view about Rosencrantz and Guildenstern?
4. Is "the hellish Pyrrhus" (2.2.422) Hamlet's version of Claudius? Or is he Hamlet, who soon will be responsible for the deaths of Polonius, Rosencrantz and Guildenstern, Claudius, Gertrude, Ophelia, and Laertes? Explain.
5. Is the First Player's speech (2.2.427ff) an inflated speech? If so, why? To distinguish it from the poetry of the play itself? To characterize the bloody deeds that Hamlet cannot descend to?
6. In 2.2.504–542 Hamlet rebukes himself for not acting. Why has he not acted? Because he is a coward (line 531)? Because he has a conscience? Because no action can restore his father and his mother's purity? Because he doubts the Ghost? What reason(s) can you offer?

Act 3

1. What do you make of Hamlet's assertion to Ophelia: "I loved you not" (3.1.118)? Of his characterization of himself as full of "offenses" (3.1.121–127)? Why is Hamlet so harsh to Ophelia?
2. In 3.3.36–72 Claudius's conscience afflicts him. But is he repentant? What makes you say so?
3. Is Hamlet other than abhorrent in 3.3.73–96? Do we want him to kill Claudius at this moment, when Claudius (presumably with his back to Hamlet) is praying? Why?
4. The Ghost speaks of Hamlet's "almost blunted purpose" (3.4.115). Is the accusation fair? Explain.
5. How would you characterize the Hamlet who speaks in 3.4.209–224?

Act 4

1. Is Gertrude protecting Hamlet when she says he is mad (4.1.7), or does she believe that he is mad? If she believes he is mad, does it follow that she no longer feels ashamed and guilty? Explain.
2. Why should Hamlet hide Polonius's body (in 4.2)? Is he feigning madness? Is he on the edge of madness? Explain.
3. How can we explain Hamlet's willingness to go to England (4.3.52)?
4. Judging from 4.5, what has driven Ophelia mad? Is Laertes heroic, or somewhat foolish? Consider also the way Claudius treats him in 4.7.

Act 5

1. Would anything be lost if the gravediggers in 5.1 were omitted?
2. To what extent do we judge Hamlet severely for sending Rosencrantz and Guildenstern to their deaths, as he reports in 5.2? On the whole, do we think of Hamlet as an intriguer? What other intrigues has he engendered? How successful were they?

3. Does 5.2.193–197 show a paralysis of the will, or a wise recognition that more is needed than mere human scheming? Explain.

4. Does 5.2.280 suggest that Laertes takes advantage of a momentary pause and unfairly stabs Hamlet? Is the exchange of weapons accidental, or does Hamlet (as in Olivier's film version), realizing that he has been betrayed, deliberately get possession of Laertes's deadly weapon?

5. Fortinbras is often cut from the play. How much is lost by the cut? Explain.

6. Fortinbras gives Hamlet a soldier's funeral. Is this ridiculous? Can it fairly be said that, in a sense, Hamlet has been at war? Explain.

General Questions

1. Hamlet in 5.2.10–11 speaks of a "divinity that shapes our ends." To what extent does "divinity" (or Fate or mysterious Chance) play a role in the happenings?

2. How do Laertes, Fortinbras, and Horatio help to define Hamlet for us?

3. T. S. Eliot says (in "Shakespeare and the Stoicism of Seneca") that Hamlet, having made a mess, "dies fairly well pleased with himself." Evaluate.

ERNEST JONES

*Hamlet and the Oedipus Complex**   [1949]

In short, the whole picture presented by Hamlet, his deep depression, the hopeless note in his attitude towards the world and towards the value of life, his dread of death, his repeated reference to bad dreams, his self-accusations, his desperate efforts to get away from the thoughts of his duty, and his vain attempts to find an excuse for his procrastination: all this unequivocally points to a *tortured conscience,* to some hidden ground for shirking his task, a ground which he dare not or cannot avow to himself.

. . .

Extensive studies of the past half century, inspired by Freud, have taught us that a psychoneurosis means a state of mind where the person is unduly, and often painfully, driven or thwarted by the "unconscious" part of his mind, that buried part that was once the infant's mind and still lives on side by side with the adult mentality that has developed out of it and should have taken its place. It signifies *internal* mental conflict. We have here the reason why it is impossible to discuss intelligently the state of mind of anyone suffering from a psychoneurosis, whether the description is of a living person or an imagined one, without correlating the manifestations with what must have operated in his infancy and is *still operating.* That is what I propose to attempt here.

For some deep-seated reason, which is to him unacceptable, Hamlet is plunged into anguish at the thought of his father being replaced in his

---

*The title is the editors'. Footnotes are abridged.

mother's affections by someone else. It is as if his devotion to his mother had made him so jealous for her affection that he had found it hard enough to share this even with his father and could not endure to share it with still another man. Against this thought, however, suggestive as it is, may be urged three objections. First, if it were in itself a full statement of the matter, Hamlet would have been aware of the jealousy, whereas we have concluded that the mental process we are seeking is hidden from him. Secondly, we see in it no evidence of the arousing of an old and forgotten memory. And, thirdly, Hamlet is being deprived by Claudius of no greater share in the Queen's affection than he had been by his own father, for the two brothers made exactly similar claims in this respect—namely, those of a loved husband. The last-named objection, however, leads us to the heart of the situation. How if, in fact, Hamlet had in years gone by, as a child, bitterly resented having had to share his mother's affection even with his own father, had regarded him as a rival, and had secretly wished him out of the way so that he might enjoy undisputed and undisturbed the monopoly of that affection? If such thoughts had been present in his mind in childhood days they evidently would have been "repressed," and all traces of them obliterated, by filial piety and other educative influences. The actual realization of his early wish in the death of his father at the hands of a jealous rival would then have stimulated into activity these "repressed" memories, which would have produced, in the form of depression and other suffering, an obscure aftermath of his childhood's conflict. This is at all events the mechanism that is actually found in the real Hamlets who are investigated psychologically.

The explanation, therefore, of the delay and self-frustration exhibited in the endeavor to fulfil his father's demand for vengeance is that to Hamlet the thought of incest and parricide combined is too intolerable to be borne. One part of him tries to carry out the task, the other flinches inexorably from the thought of it. How fain would he blot it out in that "bestial oblivion" which unfortunately for him his conscience condemns. He is torn and tortured in an insoluble inner conflict.

. . .

Now comes the father's death and the mother's second marriage. The association of the idea of sexuality with his mother, buried since infancy, can no longer be concealed from his consciousness. As Bradley well says: "Her son was forced to see in her action not only an astounding shallowness of feeling, but an eruption of coarse sensuality, 'rank and gross,' speeding post-haste to its horrible delight." Feelings which once, in the infancy of long ago, were pleasurable desires can now, because of his repressions, only fill him with repulsion. The long "repressed" desire to take his father's place in his mother's affection is stimulated to unconscious activity by the sight of someone usurping this place exactly as he himself had once longed to do. More, this someone was a member of the same family, so that the actual usurpation further resembled the imaginary one in being incestuous. Without his being in the least aware of it these ancient desires are ringing in his mind, are once more struggling to find conscious expression, and need such an expenditure of energy again to "repress" them that he is reduced to the deplorable mental state he himself so vividly depicts.

There follows the Ghost's announcement that the father's death was a willed one, was due to murder. Hamlet, having at the moment his mind filled with natural indignation at the news, answers normally enough with the cry (Act I, Sc. 5):

> Haste me to know 't, that I with wings as swift
> As meditation or the thoughts of love,
> May sweep to my revenge.

The momentous words follow revealing who was the guilty person, namely a relative who had committed the deed at the bidding of lust.[1] Hamlet's second guilty wish had thus also been realized by his uncle, namely to procure the fulfilment of the first—the possession of the mother—by a personal deed, in fact by murder of the father. The two recent events, the father's death and the mother's second marriage, seemed to the world to have no inner causal relation to each other, but they represented ideas which in Hamlet's unconscious phantasy had always been closely associated. These ideas now in a moment forced their way to conscious recognition in spite of all "repressing forces," and found immediate expression in his almost reflex cry: "O my prophetic soul! My uncle?" The frightful truth his unconscious had already intuitively divined, his consciousness had now to assimiliate as best it could. For the rest of the interview Hamlet is stunned by the effect of the internal conflict thus re-awakened, which from now on never ceases, and into the essential nature of which he never penetrates.

---

[1]It is not maintained that this was by any means Claudius' whole motive, but it was evidently a powerful one and the one that most impressed Hamlet.

STANLEY WELLS

On the First Soliloquy   [1995]

More than most plays, *Hamlet* is a series of opportunities for virtuosity. This is true above all of the role of Hamlet himself. "Hamlet," wrote Max Beerbohm, is "a hoop through which every very eminent actor must, sooner or later, jump." There is no wonder that it has been such a favorite part with actors, and even with actresses. The performer has the opportunity to demonstrate a wide range of ability, to be melancholy and gay, charming and cynical, thoughtful and flippant, tender and cruel, calm and impassioned, noble and vindictive, downcast and witty, all within a few hours. He can wear a variety of costumes, he need not disguise good looks, he can demonstrate athletic ability, he has perhaps the longest role in drama—he could scarcely ask for more, except perhaps the opportunity to sing and dance.

And if the role of Hamlet is the greatest reason for the play's popularity with actors, the character of Hamlet is surely the greatest reason for its popularity with audiences. Hamlet is the most sympathetic of tragic heroes. We are drawn to him by his youth, his intelligence, and his vulnerability. As soon as he appears we are conscious of one of the sources of his appeal: his immense capacity for taking life seriously. It may sound like a slightly repellent quality, but I don't mean to imply that he is excessively gloomy or over-earnest. Often he is deeply dejected: but he has good cause. There is nothing exceptional about his emotional reactions except perhaps their intensity. He has a larger-than-life capacity for experience, a fullness of response, a depth of feeling, a vibrancy of living, which mark him out from the ordinary. He is a raw nerve in the court of Denmark, disconcertingly liable to make the instinctive rather than the conditioned response. This cuts him off from those around him, but it puts him into peculiar contact with the audience. And as Hamlet is to the other figures of the play, so his soliloquies are to the role, for in them Shakespeare shows us the raw nerves of Hamlet himself.

The use of soliloquy is one of the most brilliant features of the play, for in these speeches Shakespeare solves a major technical problem in the presentation of his central character. The young man who takes himself seriously, who persists in explaining himself and his problems, is someone we are apt—perhaps too apt—to regard as a bore. We have all had experience of him, and so probably have most of our friends. On the other hand, the desire to know someone to the depths is fundamental to human nature. Here was both a problem and a challenge: how to let Hamlet reveal himself without becoming an almighty bore? Shakespeare found a double solution. First, he caused Hamlet to conduct his deepest self-communings in solitude, so that there is none of the awkwardness associated with the presence of a confidant. And secondly, the soliloquies are written in a style which presents us not with conclusions but with the very processes of Hamlet's mind.

There had been nothing like this in drama before: nothing which, while retaining a verse form, at the same time so vividly revealed what Shakespeare elsewhere calls "the quick forge and working-house of thought" (*Henry the Fifth* [5.Pro.23]). Vocabulary, syntax, and rhythm all contribute to the effect. Consider the second half of Hamlet's first soliloquy, beginning with his contrast between his uncle and his dead father:

> That it should come to this—
> But two months dead—nay, not so much, not two—
> So excellent a king that was to this
> Hyperion to a satyr, so loving to my mother
> That he might not beteem the winds of heaven
> Visit her face too roughly! Heaven and earth,
> Must I remember? Why, she would hang on him
> As if increase of appetite had grown
> By what it fed on, and yet within a month—
> Let me not think on't; frailty, thy name is woman—
> A little month, or ere those shoes were old
> With which she followed my poor father's body,
> Like Niobe, all tears, why she, even she—
> O God, a beast that wants discourse of reason
> Would have mourned longer!—married with mine uncle,
> My father's brother, but no more like my father
> Than I to Hercules; within a month,
> Ere yet the salt of most unrighteous tears
> Had left the flushing of her gallèd eyes,
> She married. O most wicked speed, to post

> With such dexterity to incestuous sheets!
> It is not, nor it cannot come to good.
> But break, my heart, for I must hold my tongue.

(1.2.137–159)

The anguish that it causes Hamlet to think of his mother's over-hasty marriage is conveyed as much by the tortured syntax as by direct statement; we share his difficulty as he tries—and fails—to assimilate these unwelcome facts into his consciousness, seeking to bring under emotional control the discordant elements of his disrupted universe: his love of his dead father, his love of his mother combined with disgust at her marriage to the uncle whom he loathes, and the disillusion with womankind that this has provoked in him. The short exclamations interrupting the sentence structure point his horror: the rhythms of ordinary speech within the verse give immediacy to the contrasts in phrases such as "Hyperion to a satyr" and "Than I to Hercules"; and the concreteness of the imagery betrays the effort it costs him to master the unwelcome nature of the facts which it expresses: his mother's haste to marry "or ere those shoes were old / With which she followed my poor father's body"—it is as if only by concentrating on the matter-of-fact, physical aspects of the scene can he bear to contemplate it, or bring it within his belief. He ends on a note of utter helplessness: he alone sees the truth; he knows that his mother's actions, which both he and she see as evil, must bring forth evil; but he, the only emotionally honest person there, cannot express his emotion—except to us.

ELAINE SHOWALTER

Representing Ophelia   [1985]

"Of all the characters in *Hamlet*," Bridget Lyons has pointed out, "Ophelia is most persistently presented in terms of symbolic meanings." Her behavior, her appearance, her gestures, her costume, her props, are freighted with emblematic significance, and for many generations of Shakespearean critics her part in the play has seemed to be primarily iconographic. Ophelia's symbolic meanings, moreover, are specifically feminine. Whereas for Hamlet madness is metaphysical, linked with culture, for Ophelia it is a product of the female body and female nature, perhaps that nature's purest form. On the Elizabethan stage, the conventions of female insanity were sharply defined. Ophelia dresses in white, decks herself with "fantastical garlands" of wild flowers, and enters, according to the stage directions of the "Bad" Quarto, "distracted" playing on a lute with her "hair down singing." Her speeches are marked by extravagant metaphors, lyrical free associations, and "explosive sexual imagery." She sings wistful and bawdy ballads, and ends her life by drowning.

All of these conventions carry specific messages about femininity and sexuality. Ophelia's virginal and vacant white is contrasted with Hamlet's scholar's garb, his "suits of solemn black." Her flowers suggest the discordant double images of female sexuality as both innocent blossoming and whorish contamination; she is the "green girl" of pastoral, the virginal "Rose of May" and the sexually explicit madwoman who, in giving away her wild flowers and herbs, is symbolically deflowering herself. The "weedy trophies" and phallic "long purples" which she wears to her death intimate an improper and discordant sexuality that Gertrude's lovely elegy cannot quite obscure. In Elizabethan and Jacobean drama, the stage direction that a woman enters with dishevelled hair indicates that she might either be mad or the victim of a rape; the disordered hair, her offense against decorum, suggests sensuality in each case. The mad Ophelia's bawdy songs and verbal license, while they give her access to "an entirely different range of experience" from what she is allowed as the dutiful daughter, seem to be her one sanctioned form of self-assertion as a woman, quickly followed, as if in retribution, by her death.

Drowning too was associated with the feminine, with female fluidity as opposed to masculine aridity. In his discussion of the "Ophelia complex," the phenomenologist Gaston Bachelard traces the symbolic connections between women, water, and death. Drowning, he suggests, becomes the truly feminine death in the dramas of literature and life, one which is a beautiful immersion and submersion in the female element. Water is the profound and organic symbol of the liquid woman whose eyes are so easily drowned in tears, as her body is the repository of blood, amniotic fluid, and milk. A man contemplating this feminine suicide understands it by reaching for what is feminine in himself, like Laertes, by a temporary surrender to his own fluidity—that is, his tears; and he becomes a man again in becoming once more dry—when his tears are stopped.

Clinically speaking, Ophelia's behavior and appearance are characteristic of the malady the Elizabethans would have diagnosed as female love-melancholy, or erotomania. From about 1580, melancholy had become a fashionable disease among young men, especially in London, and Hamlet himself is a prototype of the melancholy hero. Yet the epidemic of melancholy associated with intellectual and imaginative genius curiously bypassed women. Women's melancholy was seen instead as biological, and emotional in origins.

CLAIRE BLOOM

Playing Gertrude on Television   [1980]

Editors' note: Claire Bloom played Gertrude in the BBC TV production (1980), directed by Rodney Bennett, with Patrick Stewart as Claudius. In the following passage she discusses the role.

It's very hard to play because strangely enough Gertrude has very few lines; I've always known it was a wonderful part and it *is,* but when you come to play it you realise you have to find many ways around the fact that she in actual fact says little!

You come to rehearse a part like this with certain preconceived notions, which you usually leave! I can only describe them as a battering ram—you knock down the first wall then what is inside is something quite different from what you'd imagined. I was convinced that she was guilty, not of the murder, but certainly that she had found out from Claudius that he had killed her husband. But there's nothing in the text that bears that out and many things that contradict it. I had thought it would make her less of a victim, more of a performer in the world, but [she laughs at herself] it isn't so. Like anyone if you live with a man, she must know there was something more, but I now believe that when Hamlet confronts her with "as kill a king . . . ay, madam, it was my word," it's the first time she's realised. I think from then on she knows and she must accept the fact that Claudius did it, and there is a change in their relationship. But there isn't a break—you don't break with someone suddenly like that. It changes; perhaps if they'd lived another twenty years they would have drifted apart. But there isn't a complete withdrawal. The hold they have on each other is too strong for that to happen. That caused me great difficulty; the scene after the closet scene is with Claudius, when he repeats twice "Gertrude, come away," and she doesn't reply. It's very mysterious. It's a kind of underwritten scene until you realise, or I realised, that there is no real choice for her. For the moment she doesn't go with him, but the next day she does. Hamlet knows it when he says, "Go not to my uncle's bed." She never replies and says "I won't"; she just says, "Thou hast cleft my heart in twain." She's a woman who goes with whatever is happening at the time. She's a weak-willed woman, but most of us are weak-willed if we're in the power of somebody who is very strong—and Claudius and Hamlet are both pretty strong fellows.

The "mysterious" scene with Claudius was one of the hardest to deal with in rehearsal. . . . We tried backwards, forwards, upside down and inside out and didn't really find it until a couple of days before we shot it. The minute we found it we knew it was the right one, but at other times we'd go away saying, "We've got it," then both Patrick and I would come in the next day depressed and say to Rodney, "Could we please do that scene again because it doesn't make sense when you think about it." There are questions that I'm sure have been asked by every cast of every *Hamlet* since Burbage[1] and for Gertrude they are: Was there a decision to go with Claudius or not to go with Claudius? How far was she lying about Hamlet's madness? I do think part of her believes he's mad, but when she says to the king "He's mad," I think that's protection, or overstating a fact she believes is possibly true. And of course she withholds information from Claudius; she says, "Behind the arras hearing something stir . . . [he] kills the unseen good old man," but she *doesn't say* he said "Is it the king?" That is a very important bit of information which she certainly doesn't pass on!

---

[1]**Burbage** Richard Burbage (c. 1567–1619), the first actor to play Shakespeare's Hamlet.

BERNICE W. KLIMAN

The BBC Hamlet: *A Television Production*   [1981]

With *Hamlet*, the producers of the BBC Shakespeare Plays have finally met the demands of Shakespeare-on-television by choosing a relatively bare set, conceding only a few richly detailed movable panels and props to shape key locales. By avoiding both location and realistic settings, they point up the natural affinity between Shakespeare's stage and the undisguised sound set. This starkness of setting admits poetry, heightened intensity—and "what not that's sweet and happy."

The producers have thus made a valid choice from among television's three faces: one, broadcast films, whether made for television or not, which exploit location settings, long shots, and all the clichés we associate with movies, including sudden shifts of space and time and full use of distance, from the most extreme long shots to "eyes only" closeups; two, studio-shot television drama with naturalistic settings, such as the hospital corridors and middle-class living rooms of sit-coms and soap operas, mostly in mid- to close-shots, often interspersed, to be sure, with a bit of stock footage of highways and skylines to establish a realistic environment. This second style varies from a close representation of real action to frankly staged action, where canned laughter or even shadowy glimpses of the studio audience can heighten the staged effect. Three, there is bare space with little or no effort made to disguise that this is a televised activity with a television crew out of sight but nearby. News broadcasts, talk shows and some television drama fit into this third category. Because of its patently unrepresentational quality, this last type offers the most freedom in shooting style. To all three kinds of settings we bring particular expectations in response to their conventions.

Shakespeare's plays work best in the last kind of television space, I believe, because it avoids the clash between realism and poetry, between the unity often expected in realistic media and the disunity and ambiguity of many of the plays, especially *Hamlet*. Yet, while closest to the kind of stage Shakespeare wrote for, the bare television set can be stretched through creative camera work. For example, when Hamlet follows the ghost in the BBC play, the two repeatedly walk across the frame and out of it, first from one direction, then from another; framing fosters the illusion of extended space. Freeing this *Hamlet* from location (as in the BBC *As You Like It*) and from realistic sets (as in the BBC *Measure for Measure*—however well those sets worked for that play) allows the play to be as inconsistent as it is, with, as Bernard Beckerman has so brilliantly explained in *Shakespeare at the Globe, 1599–1609,* a rising and falling action in each individual scene rather than through the course of the drama as a whole. It also allows for acting, the bravura kind that Derek Jacobi is so capable of.

Although gradually coalescing like the pointillism of impressionistic paintings into a subtly textured portrait, at first his mannerisms suggesting madness seem excessive. It is to be expected, perhaps, that Hamlet is a bit unhinged after the ghost scene, but Jacobi's rapid, hard blows to his forehead with the flat of hand as he says "My tables" recall the desperation of Lear's cry: "O, let me not be mad, not mad, sweet heaven." And soon after, following the last couplet of the scene, Hamlet, maniacally playful, widens his eyes and points, pretending to see the ghost again, then guffaws at Marcellus's fears. Even more unsettling is his laughter when he is alone, as while he is saying "The play's the thing / Wherein I'll catch the conscience of the King." More significantly, he breaks up his own "Mousetrap" by getting right into the play, destroying the distance between audience and stage (a very real raked proscenium-arch stage), spoiling it as a test, because Claudius has a right to be incensed at Hamlet's behavior. Of course, Hamlet does so because Claudius never gives himself away, an unusual and provocative but not impossible interpretation. Thus, Claudius can only have the court's sympathy as he calmly calls for light and uses it to examine Hamlet closely. Hamlet, in response, covers his face, then laughs.

Hamlet himself thinks he is mad. To Ophelia he says, as if the realization had suddenly struck him, "It *hath* made me mad [emphasis his]" (III.i.147). To his mother he stresses the word "essentially" in "I *essentially* am not in madness" (III.iv.187). That is, in all essential matters he can be considered sane, though mad around the edges. This indeed turns out to be the explanation.

However doubtful about Hamlet's sanity Jacobi's acting leaves us, in this production this question does not seem to make a difference because it does not have a bearing on the tragedy, and this is true at least partly because in each scene on this nonrealistic set we seem to start anew, ready to let Hamlet's behavior tell us if he is mad or not. Moreover, if Hamlet is mad, it is not so totally as to obscure reason or sensibility. Far from it. It is more as if exacerbated reason and sensibility sometimes tip him into madness. This madness is no excuse for action or delay; it is simply part of the suffering that Hamlet is heir to.

Hamlet, then, is left to struggle against himself—surely where Shakespeare intended the struggle to abide. One of the conflicts in this Hamlet results from his affinity, perhaps, more to the bureaucratic Claudius who handles war-scares with diplomacy and who sits at a desk while brooding over his sins than to the warlike King Hamlet who comes in full armor. Hamlet may admire Fortinbras but is himself more like the bookish Horatio. Through nuance of gesture, through body movement, through a face that is indeed a map of all emotions, Jacobi shapes a Hamlet who loves his father too much to disregard his command, yet who cannot hate his step-father enough to attend to it. Because Jacobi conveys so fully Hamlet's aloneness and vulnerability, one could be struck, for the first time, by the ghost's silence about his son. There is no declaration of love, no concern about Hamlet's ascension to the throne. Hamlet is doomed, it seems, to care about those who consistently care more for others than for him.

All of this production's richness and suggestiveness was realized not only because Jacobi is a marvelous actor—as indeed he is—but also because within the set's spareness that acting could unfold, an acting style that subsumes and transcends the "real." This production's space tells us what is possible for television presentations of Shakespeare. The more bare the set, it seems, the more glowing the words, the more immediate our apprehension of the enacted emotion.

WILL SARETTA

What follows is an undergraduate's review, published in a college newspaper, of Kenneth Branagh's film version of Hamlet *(1996).*

Branagh's Film of Hamlet   [1996]

Kenneth Branagh's *Hamlet* opened last night at the Harman Auditorium, and will be shown again on Wednesday and Thursday at 7:30 p.m. According to the clock the evening will be long—the film runs for four hours, and in addition there is one ten-minute intermission—but you will enjoy every minute of it.

Well, almost every minute. Curiously, the film begins and ends relatively weakly, but most of what occurs in between is good and much of it is wonderful. The beginning is weak because it is too strong; Bernardo, the sentinel, offstage says "Who's there?" but before he gets a reply he crashes onto the screen and knocks Francisco down. The two soldiers grapple, swords flash in the darkness, and Francisco finally says, "Nay, answer me. Stand and unfold yourself." Presumably Branagh wanted to begin with a bang, but here, as often, more is less. A quieter, less physical opening in which Bernardo, coming on duty, hears a noise and demands that the maker of the noise identify himself, and Francisco, the sentinel on duty, rightly demands that the newcomer identify *himself,* would catch the uneasiness and the mystery that pervades the play much better than does Branagh's showy beginning.

Similarly, at the end of the film, we get too much. For one thing, shots of Fortinbras's army invading Elsinore alternate with shots of the duel between Hamlet and King Claudius's pawn, Laertes, and they merely distract us from what really counts in this scene, the duel itself, which will result in Hamlet's death but also in Hamlet's successful completion of his mission to avenge his father. Second, at the very end we get shots of Fortinbras's men pulling down a massive statue of Hamlet Senior, probably influenced by television and newspaper shots of statues of Lenin being pulled down when the Soviet Union was dissolved a few years earlier. This is ridiculous; *Hamlet* is not a play about the fall of Communism, or about the one form of tyranny replacing another. Shakespeare's *Hamlet* is not about the triumph of Fortinbras. It is about Hamlet's brave and ultimately successful efforts to do what is right, against overwhelming odds, and to offer us the consolation that in a world where death always triumphs there nevertheless is something that be called nobility.

What, then, is good about the film? First of all, the film gives us the whole play, whereas almost all productions, whether on the stage or in the movie house, gives us drastically abbreviated versions. Although less is often more, when it comes to the text of *Hamlet,* more is better, and we should be grateful to Branagh for letting us hear all of the lines. Second, it is very well performed, with only a few exceptions. Jack Lemmon as Marcellus is pretty bad, but fortunately the part is small. Other big-name actors in small parts—Charlton Heston as the Player King, Robin Williams as Osric, and Billy Crystal as the First Gravedigger—are admirable. But of course the success or failure of any production of *Hamlet* will depend chiefly on the actor who plays Hamlet, and to a considerable degree on the actors who play Claudius, Gertrude, Polonius, Ophelia, Laertes, and Horatio. There isn't space here to comment on all of these roles, but let it be said that Branagh's Prince Hamlet is indeed princely, a man who strikes us as having the ability to become a king, not a wimpy whining figure. When at the end Fortinbras says that if Hamlet had lived to become the king, he would "have proved most royal," we believe him. And his adversary, King Claudius, though morally despicable, is a man of great charm and great ability. The two men are indeed "mighty opposites," to use Hamlet's own words.

Branagh's decision to set the play in the late nineteenth century rather than in the Elizabethan period of Shakespeare's day and rather than in our own day contributes to this sense of powerful forces at work. If the play were set in Shakespeare's day, the men would wear tights, and if it were set in our day they would wear suits or trousers and sports jackets and sweaters, but in the film all of the men wear military costumes (black for Hamlet, scarlet for Claudius, white for Laertes) and the women wear ball gowns of the Victorian period. Branagh gives us a world that is closer to our own than would Elizabethan costumes, but yet it is, visually at least, also distant enough to convey a sense of grandeur, which modern dress cannot suggest. Of course *Hamlet* can be done in modern dress, just as *Romeo and Juliet* was done, successfully, in the recent film starring Claire Danes and Leonardo DiCaprio, set in a world that seemed to be Miami Beach, but *Romeo and Juliet* is less concerned with heroism and grandeur than *Hamlet* is, so Branagh probably did well to avoid contemporary costumes.

Although Branagh is faithful to the text, in that he gives us the entire text, he knows that a good film cannot be made merely by recording on film a stage production, and so he gives us handsome shots of landscape, and of rich interiors—for instance, a great mirrored hall—that would be beyond the resources of any theatrical production. I have already said that at the end, when Fortinbras's army swarms over the countryside and then invades the castle we get material that is distracting, indeed irrelevant, but there are also a few other distractions. It is all very well to let us *see* the content of long narrative speeches (for instance, when the Player King talks of the fall of Troy and the death of King Priam and the lament of Queen Hecuba, Branagh shows us these things, with John Gielgud as Priam and Judi Dench as Hecuba, performing in pantomime), but there surely is no need for us to see a naked Hamlet and a naked Ophelia in bed, when Polonius is warning Ophelia that Hamlet's talk of love cannot be trusted. Polonius's warning is not so long or so undramatic that we need to be entertained visually with an invention that finds not a word of support in the text. On the contrary, all of Ophelia's lines suggest that she would not be other than a dutiful young woman, obedient to the morals of the times and to her father's authority. Yet another of Branagh's unfortunate inventions is the prostitute who appears in Polonius's bedroom, during Polonius's interview with Reynaldo. A final example of unnecessary spectacle is Hamlet's killing of Claudius: He hurls his rapier the length of the hall, impaling Claudius, and then like some 1930's movie star he swings on the chandelier and drops down on Claudius to finish him off.

But it is wrong to end this review by pointing out faults in Branagh's film of *Hamlet.* There is so much in this film that is exciting, so much that is moving, so much that is . . . , well, so much that is *Hamlet* (which is to say that is a great experience), that the film must be recommended without reservation. Go to see it. The four hours will fly.

A postscript. It is good to see that Branagh uses color-blind casting. Voltemand, Fortinbras's Captain, and the messenger who announces Laertes's return are all blacks—the messenger is a black woman—although of course medieval Denmark and Elizabethan England, and, for that matter, Victorian England, would not have routinely included blacks. These performers are effective, and it is appropriate that actors of color take their place in the world's greatest play.

TOPICS FOR CRITICAL THINKING AND WRITING

1. Does the writer give adequate evidence to support his favorable comments on the play?
2. Does he give evidence to support his unfavorable comments?
3. Given the writer's overall evaluation of the film, do you agree with his strategy of devoting the first and last paragraphs to praising the play?
4. Do you think the writer apportioned his space well, or should he have spent more time on the weaknesses, or more time on the strenghts? Why?
5. Do you find the comments about the late-nineteenth-century setting relevant and thoughtful, or irrelevant and not very perceptive? Explain.
6. Do you find the *postscript* intrusive? Explain.
7. If you have seen the film, do you more or less agree with the reviewer? Do you think that the reviewer neglected to make certain points that you would have made in your review?

A NOTE ON THE TEXTS OF *OTHELLO*

Othello was first published in 1622, in a small volume called a quarto (each sheet of paper has been folded in half, and then in half again, to make four leaves—i.e., eight pages). *Othello* was next published in 1623, in the first folio edition of Shakespeare's collected plays (a folio is a larger book—each sheet has been folded only once, producing two leaves, four pages).

The quarto (Q) contains 16 lines not in the folio (F), but the folio has about 150 lines not in the quarto. Further, there are hundreds of small but significant differences between the texts—for instance, "O God" in Q and "Oh heaven" in F—but perhaps the most important difference in a single word occurs in Othello's next-to-last speech. In Q he says his hand, "Like the base Indian, threw a pearle away, / Richer than all his Tribe." In F Othello says his hand, "(Like the base Iudean) threw a Pearle away / Richer than all his Tribe." That is, in Q he compares himself to the ignorant savage (perhaps a native of India, perhaps an American Indian) who did not properly value a precious jewel. (Europeans conventionally thought that other cultures did not value pearls.) In F he compares himself to Judas Iscariat, who betrayed Jesus, or perhaps to Herod the Great, king of the Jews, who murdered his wife. Arguments can be made on behalf of both readings, but perhaps the strongest is in favor of "Indian," on the grounds that Othello is correctly saying that he acted out of ignorance (like the Indian), not out of malice (like Judas).

David Bevington, the editor of the version of *Othello* that we give, uses F for the most part, but he sometimes draws on Q where (as in the Indian/Judean instance) Q seems to him to be what Shakespeare probably wrote. Bevington has also added some material for the reader's convenience—for instance, indications of scene and some stage directions. His text and notes were prepared for his book, *The Complete Works of Shakespeare*, Updated 4th ed. (New York: Longman, 1997).

Quarto, 1622

Oth. Soft you, a word or two,
I haue done the State some seruice, and they know't;
No more of that: I pray you in your letters,
When you shall these vnlucky deedes relate,
Speake of them as they are, nothing extenuate,
Nor set downe ought in malice; then must you speake,
Of one that lou'd not wisely, but too well:
Of one not easily iealous, but being wrought,
Perplext in the extreame; of one whose hand,
Like the base *Indian* threw a pearle away,
Richer then all his Tribe: of one whose subdued eyes,
Albeit vnused to the melting moode,
Drops teares as fast as the *Arabian* trees,
Their medicinall gum; set you downe this,
And say besides; that in *Aleppo* once,
Where a *Malignant* and a *Turband Turke*,
Beate a *Venetian*, and traduc'd the State;
I tooke by th throate the circumcised dog,
And smote him thus.   *He stabs himself.*

Folio, 1623

Oth. Soft you; a word or two before you goe:
I haue done the State some seruice, and they know't:
No more of that. I pray you in your Letters,
When you shall these vnluckie deeds relate,
Speake of me, as I am. Nothing extenuate,
Nor set downe ought in malice.
Then must you speake,
Of one that lou'd not wisely, but too well:
Of one, not easily Iealious, but being wrought,
Perplexed in the extreame: Of one, whose hand
(Like the base Iudean) threw a Pearle away
Richer then all his Tribe: Of one, whose subdu'd Eyes,
Albeit vn-vsed to the melting moode,
Drops teares as fast as the Arabian Trees
Their Medicinable gumme. Set you downe this:
And say besides, that in *Aleppo* once,
Where a malignant, and a Turbond-Turke
Beate a Venetian, and traduc'd the State,
I tooke by th'throat the circumcised Dogge,
And smoate him, thus.

Note: The technology of printing in England in Shakespeare's day was fairly low, not only by comparison with printing today but even by comparison with printing on the Continent in the early seventeenth century. With very few exceptions publishers in England produced books for a market that wanted cheap editions rather than fine editions, which means that the consumer would get pages that were unevenly inked and were sometimes printed from typefaces that were damaged.

Above: Part of the page of the 1622 quarto, where Othello speaks of himself as a "base *Indian*." An Elizabethan tradition associated American Indians with ignorantly neglecting to value precious jewels and gold, so Othello here may be comparing himself to such an Indian. Most editors accept this reading.

Below: Part of a page in the 1623 folio, where Othello speaks of himself as "the base Iudean," Conceivably the manuscript had *Indian* or *Indean*, but the type-setter mistakenly inverted an *n*, producing a *u*. On the other hand, Iudean (that is, Judean) makes sense, referring either to (a) Herod the Great (king of the Jews), who murdered his wife after she had been accused (falsely) of infidelity, or (b) Judas Iscariat, who betrayed Jesus (in Matthew 13.46 Jesus tells a parable comparing the kingdom of heaven to "a pearl of great price").

PORTFOLIO: PLAYING OTHELLO

Perhaps the first thing to say about Othello is that he is a tragic hero, which is to say that he is a great man, since in the Renaissance (as in the ancient Greek world) tragedy dealt with great figures—superior, heroic human beings whose fall evoked in the spectators feelings (to quote Shakespeare's Horatio near the end of *Hamlet*) of "woe" and "wonder," a sort of terrifying awe that such greatness could come to such an end. Of course Othello's enemies speak ill of him: For them, he is the "barbarous Moor" and the "lascivious Moor," and sometimes their racism is evident, as when the villainous Iago calls him "an old black ram." But for other characters in the play—the characters whom we believe, and whose words are confirmed by the Othello, whom we see with our own eyes—Othello is the "valiant Moor," the "brave Moor," and the "noble Moor," a man who is of a "free and open nature"—i.e., a man who is notably frank, not given to concealing his thoughts.

Shakespeare takes an outsider, someone whom most Englishmen of the time would regard as a barbarian, introduces him to us (in the opening scene) through the words of those who scorn him, and then surprises us: When Othello actually first appears onstage (in the second scene) we see not the man who has been described as bombastic and lascivious but, rather, a man of enormous poise and ability. In the course of the play Othello performs a terrible deed, but almost the last words said of him are that he was "great of heart"—that is, "great-hearted"—Anglo Saxon words that correspond to an English word of Latin origin, "magnanimous" (Latin: "great spirit").

Othello engages in a horrifying action because he is deceived by someone whom he trusts: His tragic deed is in large measure the terrifying consequence of his high-minded nature, a nature that does not suspect that an apparent friend can be monstrously evil. As Iago himself says (and here we repeat some words quoted a moment ago),

> The Moor is of a free and open nature
> That think men honest that but seem to be so.

Othello's highmindedness makes him vulnerable to such a person as Iago, but at the end, when Othello understands the terrible truth that he has murdered a loving wife, his highmindedness causes him to enact justice upon himself. Comparing himself to an infidel whom he executed, the tragic hero now executes himself:

> Set you down this.
> And say besides that in Aleppo once,
> Where a malignant and a turbaned Turk
> Beat a Venetian and traduced the state,
> I took by th' throat the circumcisèd dog
> And smote him—thus. [*He stabs himself.*]

In this portfolio we will look at some of the great actors who have portrayed the noble Moor.

Abdul Guahid was ambassador from Mauritania to Queen Elizabeth, 1600–1601. Shakespeare and his company performed at court in December 1600, and thus might have seen the ambassador or members of his retinue, or the Moors might have visited an Elizabethan playhouse.

Abdul Guahid, the Moorish ambassador to Queen Elizabeth, 1600–1601
(English School, early seventeenth century).

Othello is unquestionably a Moor—someone of mixed Berber and Arab descent, native to northwest Africa (Morocco and Algeria)—but the Elizabethans did not have a clear idea of who the Moors were. That is, the Elizabethans did not clearly distinguish between "blackamoores" and "negars"—i.e., residents of sub-Saharan Africa. Shakespeare may or may not have thought of Othello as a black African. Some terms in the play suggest that Othello is a sub-Saharan African, but most of these terms (e.g., in the first scene Iago's reference to "an old black ram" and Roderigo's reference to Othello as "the thicklips") are spoken by Othello's foes, who quite naturally describe him as unattractive by English standards, where a fair complexion was preferred.

There is no doubt that Othello is a Moor—the play is called *The Tragedy of Othello, the Moor of Venice*—but the question remains: What did Shakespeare think a Moor looked like? Othello speaks of himself as "black" (3.3.267), but this word is not decisive, since it sometimes clearly means only that the person is darker than a northern European—e.g., olive-skinned. Thus, Shakespeare's

Ira Aldridge as Othello.

Cleopatra, an Egyptian, speaks of herself as "black." On the other hand, in an earlier play, *Titus Andronicus*, Shakespeare has a Moor who speaks of himself as "coal-black" and who refers to his "fleece of woolly hair," evidence that Shakespeare did not distinguish between the Moors and sub-Saharan Africans—but a stage direction in yet another play, *The Merchant of Venice*, describes the Prince of Morocco as "a tawny Moor," suggesting that Shakespeare or the associate who revised the playwright's manuscript thought of Moors, or at least of some Moors, as light brown. In short we do not know whether Shakespeare envisioned Othello as black in our sense, and we do not know what sort of makeup the earliest actors of Othello used.

We return, then, to the painting of the Moorish ambassador. He clearly is not black by our standards, but equally clearly the Elizabethans might have called him black, and in any case, he is an outsider as far as the Elizabethans were concerned.

Although there is no hard evidence concerning the makeup used by the earliest actors who played *Othello,* we do know that in the eighteenth century, British actors played the role in blackface. Strong racist views accompanied the

Anonymous artist, Ira Aldridge as Othello addressing the Venetian senate (probably 1833).

decision. Thus, David Garrick (1717–1779), regarded as the greatest Shakespearean actor of the period, saw Othello not as a white man but as "an African in whose being circulated fire instead of blood." In the early nineteenth century a shift occurred, revealing another aspect of racism: Othello's color was lightened because it seemed inconceivable that Desdemona would fall in love with a black man. Thus, Charles Lamb said that the spectator finds "something extremely revolting in the courtship and wedded caresses of Othello and Desdemona." His friend Samuel Taylor Coleridge said,

> Can we suppose [Shakespeare] so utterly ignorant as to make a barbarous negro plead royal birth? Were negroes then known but as slaves; on the contrary, were not the Moors warriors? ...It would be something monstrous to conceive this beautiful Venetian girl falling in love with a veritable negro. It would argue a disproportionateness, a want of balance in Desdemona, which Shakespeare does not appear to have in the least contemplated.

Paul Robeson (Othello) and Peggy Ashcroft (Desdemona), 1930.

The text of *Othello* refutes Coleridge—clearly Desdemona *has* made a choice that shocks the Venetians, that seems "monstrous" to them, until Othello delivers to the Duke his speech about wooing Desdemona. The Duke then says,

> I think this tale would win my daughter too.
> Good Brabantio, take up this mangled matter at the best.

From the early nineteenth century until almost the mid-twentieth century the role was regularly performed by white actors who used makeup to look bronzed—the idea was to look like a desert chief—but one notable exception was Ira Aldridge (1807–1867), an African-American who left America because racism prevented him from playing with white acting companies. Aldridge, a relatively light-skinned man, established himself in England and in Europe, playing Othello. He also played, in whiteface, King Lear and other Shakespearean roles.

In the illustrations, notice that although Othello is a general in Venice, he holds a scimitar, a curved sword of a kind associated with Islamic regions.

Paul Robeson (1898–1976), an African-American actor and singer, played Othello three times—in London (1930), New York (1943), and Stratford-upon-Avon (1959). With very few exceptions, the reviews of his performance in London and New York were highly favorable. There was talk of bringing the London production to New York, but nothing came of it because potential backers were uncertain about how a white audience would react to a black man—a real black man, not a white man in blackface—kissing a white woman. In 1942, however, the enterprising Margaret Webster, an American director, persuaded a group to invite Robeson to do *Othello* not on Broadway but in summer stock. The production was enthusiastically received, and it moved to Broadway in 1943, where it ran for an astounding 296 continuous performances. The color barrier in America was broken, and many black actors subsequently played the role.

Orson Welles, Suzanne Cloutier and Micheál MacLiammóir in Orson Welles's *Othello* (1952).

Among the black actors who have played the role in recent times are Paul Winfield, James Earl Jones, and Laurence Fishburne, and indeed in very recent years it has become almost impossible for a white to play it. But a white actor, Anthony Hopkins, looking rather sun-tanned, did play it in the BBC-TV version. The director, Jonathan Miller, offered his justification:

> I do not see the play as being about color but as being about jealousy— which is something we are all vulnerable to....When a black actor does the part, it offsets the play, puts it out of balance. It makes it a play about blackness, which it is not. The trouble is, the play was hijacked for polit- ical purposes.

A topic worth thinking about.

Orson Welles (1915–1985) played a very light-skinned Othello in a film ver- sion released in 1955. The text is highly cut, and much non-Shakespearean busi- ness is introduced. It begins with Welles reading a passage from Shakespeare's source, an Italian short story, while we see a shot of the face of the dead Othello. The camera rises above the bier which is being carried by pallbearers, and then we see Desdemona's dead body, also being borne to the grave. The two funeral processions converge, and then we see Iago, in chains, thrust into a cage and

Laurence Olivier as Othello and Frank Finlay as Iago, National Theatre, London, 1964.

hoisted above the crowd. The film ends with a dissolve from the dying Othello to a shot of the funeral procession and then to shots of the fortress at Cyprus, the cage, and Venetian buildings and ships. In short, the film is not for the Shakespeare purist, but it is imaginative and often effective.

Laurence Olivier (1907–1989) played Othello in England in 1964; the production was later filmed (1965) in a sound studio rather than in the theater, but the film closely resembles the staged version. Far from suggesting an Othello who was a Moor, a desert chief, Olivier sought to convey the image of an African Othello: He was very dark, he walked with a sway, he spoke with a lilt that suggested a West Indian accent, and his bare feet were adorned with heavy ankle bracelets. To some viewers this image of Othello is embarrassing if not downright offensive.

The underlying idea apparently was that Othello is a barbarian with a thin veneer of civilization; the change from civilized man to savage was marked by Othello tearing off a crucifix that he wore. No such episode occurs in Shakespeare's text, and in fact it is at odds with the text, since Othello urges Desdemona, before he kills her, to make her peace with God: "I would not kill thy soul." Nevertheless, most viewers agree that Olivier's acting is brilliant, even if the rest of the cast leaves much to be desired.

Franchelle Stewart-Dorn as Emilia, Ron Canada as Iago, Patrice Johnson as Desdemona, and Patrick Stewart as Othello. Directed by Jude Kelly, Shakespeare Theatre at the Lansburgh, Washington, D.C., 1997.

Patrick Stewart, known to millions from his role in *Star Trek*, played a white Othello in Washington, D.C., in 1997. He called this version a "photo-negative": Othello was white, but almost all of the other characters, including Desdemona, were black. Stewart explained his rationale:

> To replace the black outsider with a white man in a black society, will, I hope, encourage a much broader view of the fundamentals of racism, and perhaps even question those triggers—you know, color of skin, physiognomy, language, culture—that can produce instant feelings of fear, suspicion, and so forth.

In short, Stewart suggested that white spectators—the audience was largely white—might be so disturbed by seeing a white man horribly manipulated that they might be pushed into an increased awareness of the evils of racism, but one of the actors pointed out that a white spectator could probably be disturbed only if he or she were part of an audience that was largely black, and this was not the case in Washington.

Laurence Fishburne plays Othello in a film version directed by Oliver Parker (1994). The film omits almost half of Shakespeare's text, and replaces it with a good deal of exciting visual imagery, including a gondola with what apparently are the eloping lovers at the start, and a sea burial at the end. In between we get such things as a crowd in Cyprus burning an effigy of a Turk, and Iago plotting the destruction of Othello, Desdemona, and Cassio with chess pieces. In short, this *Othello* is highly cinematic and does not worry about being faithful to Shakespeare's text.

Fishburne, an African-American actor, was already well known for his performances in *Boyz n the Hood* (1991) and *What's Love Got to Do with It?* (1993).

Laurence Fishburne as Othello.

The later film, which was based on rock singer Tina Turner's autobiography, in which she discussed the abuse she suffered at the hands of her husband, Ike, was widely shown during the time that the African-American athlete O. J. Simpson was accused of murdering his white wife; Nicole Brown, and many viewers of Parker's film probably connected it, in one way or another, with the trial. (The murder took place in 1992; Simpson was acquitted in 1995.) Whether this sort of connection between life and art helps or hinders a viewer's response to the play is a topic worth discussing.

WILLIAM SHAKESPEARE

Othello was probably written in 1603–1604, but it was not published until 1622, six years after Shakespeare's death.
  For a biographical note, see page 703.

Othello, the Moor of Venice   [1603–1604?]

THE NAMES OF THE ACTORS

> OTHELLO, *the Moor*
> BRABANTIO, [*a senator,*] *father to Desdemona*
> CASSIO, *an honorable lieutenant* [*to Othello*]
> IAGO, [*Othello's ancient,*] *a villain*
> RODERIGO, *a gulled gentleman*
> DUKE *of Venice*
> SENATORS [*of Venice*]
> MONTANO, *governor of Cyprus*
> LODOVICO *and* GRATIANO, [*kinsmen to Brabantio,*] *two noble Venetians*
> SAILORS

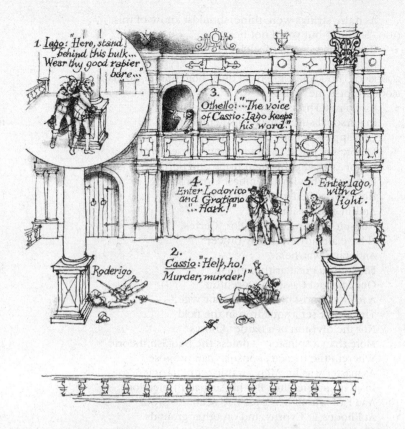

1. Iago: "Here, stand
behind this bulk...
Wear thy good rapier
bare..."

3.
Othello:..."The voice
of Cassio: Iago keeps
his word."

4.
Enter Lodovico
and Gratiano
..."Hark!"

5. Enter Iago,
with a
light.

Roderigo

2.
Cassio: "Help, ho!
Murder, murder!"

A possible staging of Act 5, Scene 1, as at the Globe Theatre, by C. Walter Hodges. Successive events, shown here simultaneously, are numbered in sequence.

CLOWN
DESDEMONA, [*daughter to Brabantio and*] *wife to Othello*
EMILIA, *wife to Iago*
BIANCA, *a courtesan* [*and mistress to Cassio*]
A MESSENGER
A HERALD
A MUSICIAN
Servants, Attendants, Officers, Senators, Musicians, Gentlemen

SCENE: *Venice; a seaport in Cyprus*]

1.1 *Enter* RODERIGO *and* IAGO.

RODERIGO. Tush, never tell me!° I take it much unkindly
         That thou, Iago, who hast had my purse

1.1 Location: Venice, a street.   1 never tell me (An expression of incredulity, like "tell me another one.")

As if the strings were thine, shouldst know of this.°
IAGO. 'Sblood,° but you'll not hear me.
    If ever I did dream of such a matter,   5
    Abhor me.
RODERIGO. Thou toldst me thou didst hold him in thy hate.
IAGO. Despise me
    If I do not. Three great ones of the city,
    In personal suit to make his lieutenant,   10
    Off-capped to him;° and by the faith of man,
    I know my price, I am worth no worse a place.
    But he, as loving his own pride and purposes,
    Evades them with a bombast circumstance°
    Horribly stuffed with epithets of war,°   15
    And, in conclusion,
    Nonsuits° my mediators. For, "Certes,"° says he,
    "I have already chose my officer."
    And what was he?
    Forsooth, a great arithmetician,°   20
    One Michael Cassio, a Florentine,
    A fellow almost damned in a fair wife,°
    That never set a squadron in the field
    Nor the division of a battle° knows
    More than a spinster°—unless the bookish theoric,°   25
    Wherein the togaed° consuls° can propose°
    As masterly as he. Mere prattle without practice
    In all his soldiership. Bvt he, sir, had th' election;
    And I, of whom his° eyes had seen the proof
    At Rhodes, at Cyprus, and on other grounds   30
    Christened° and heathen, must be beeled and calmed°
    By debitor and creditor.° This countercaster,°
    He, in good time,° must his lieutenant be,
    And I—God bless the mark!°—his Moorship's ancient.°
RODERIGO. By heaven, I rather would have been his hangman.°   35
IAGO. Why, there's no remedy. 'Tis the curse of service;
    Preferment° goes by letter and affection,°

---

3 this i.e., Desdemona's elopement.   **4 'Sblood** by His (Christ's blood).   **11 him** i.e., Othello.
14 bombast circumstance wordy evasion. (Bombast is cotton padding.)   **15 epithets of war**
military expressions.   **17 Nonsuits** rejects the petition of.   **Certes** certainly.   **20 arithmeti-
cian** i.e., a man whose military knowledge is merely theoretical, based on books of tactics.
22 A . . . wife (Cassio does not seem to be married, but his counterpart in Shakespeare's source
does have a woman in his house. See also 4.1.127.)   **24 division of a battle** disposition of a
military unit.   **25 a spinster** i.e., a housewife, one whose regular occupation is spinning.
theoric theory.   **26 togaed** wearing the toga.   **consuls** counselors, senators.   **propose** discuss.   **29 his** i.e., Othello's.   **31 Christened** Christian.   **beeled and calm** left to leeward
without wind, becalmed. (A sailing metaphor.)   **32 debitor and creditor** (A name for a system
of bookkeeping, here used as a contemptuous nickname for Cassio.)   **countercaster** i.e., bookkeeper, one who tallies with *counters*, or "metal disks." (Said contemptuously.)   **33 in good
time** opportunely, i.e., forsooth.   **34 God bless the mark** (Perhaps originally a formula to
ward off evil; here an expression of impatience.)   **ancient** standard-bearer, ensign.   **35 his
hangman** the executioner of him.

And not by old gradation,° where each second
Stood heir to th' first. Now, sir, be judge yourself
Whether I in any just term° am affined°   40
To love the Moor.

RODERIGO. I would not follow him then.

IAGO. O sir, content you.°
I follow him to serve my turn upon him.
We cannot all be masters, nor all masters   45
Cannot be truly° followed. You shall mark
Many a duteous and knee-crooking knave
That, doting on his own obsequious bondage,
Wears out his time, much like his master's ass,
For naught but provender, and when he's old, cashiered.°   50
Whip me° such honest knaves. Others there are
Who, trimmed in forms and visages of duty,°
Keep yet their hearts attending on themselves,
And, throwing but shows of service on their lords,
Do well thrive by them, and when they have lined their coats,°   55
Do themselves homage.° These fellows have some soul,
And such a one do I profess myself. For, sir,
It is as sure as you are Roderigo,
Were I the Moor I would not be Iago.°
In following him, I follow but myself—   60
Heaven is my judge, not I for love and duty,
But seeming so for my peculiar° end.
For when my outward action doth demonstrate
The native° act and figure° of my heart
In compliment extern.° 'tis not long after   65
But I will wear my heart upon my sleeve
For daws° to peck at. I am not what I am.°

RODERIGO. What a full° fortune does the thick-lips° owe°
If he can carry 't thus!°

IAGO.   Call up her father.
Rouse him, make after him, poison his delight,   70
Proclaim him in the streets; incense her kinsmen,
And, though he in a fertile climate dwell,

---

37 preferment promotion. **letter and affection** personal influence and favoritism.
38 old gradation step-by-step seniority, the traditional way. **40 term** respect. **affined**
bound. **43 content you** don't you worry about that. **46 truly** faithfully. **50 cashiered** dismissed from service. **51 Whip me** whip as far as I'm concerned. **52 trimmed . . . duty**
dressed up in the mere form and show of dutifulness. **55 lined their coats** i.e., stuffed their
purses. **56 Do themselves homage** i.e., attend to self-interest solely. **59 Were . . . Iago** i.e.,
if I were able to assume command, I certainly would not choose to remain a subordinate, or, I
would keep a suspicious eye on a flattering subordinate. **62 peculiar** particular, personal.
64 native innate. **figure** shape, intent. **65 compliment extern** outward show.
(Conforming in this case to the inner workings and intention of the heart.) **67 daws** small
crowlike birds, proverbially stupid and avaricious. **I am not what I am** i.e., I am not one who
wears his heart on his sleeve. **68 full** swelling. **thick-lips** (Elizabethans often applied the
term "Moor" to Negroes.) **owe** own. **69 carry 't thus** carry this off. **72–73 though . . .**
flies though he seems prosperous and happy now, vex him with misery.

Plague him with flies.° Though that his joy be joy.°
Yet throw such changes of vexation° on 't
As it may° lose some color.°   75
RODERIGO. Here is her father's house. I'll call aloud.
IAGO. Do, with like timorous° accent and dire yell
As when, by night and negligence,° the fire
Is spied in populous cities.
RODERIGO. What ho, Brabantio! Signor Brabantio, ho!   80
IAGO. Awake! What ho, Brabantio! Thieves, thieves, thieves!
Look to your house, your daughter, and your bags!
Thieves, thieves!

BRABANTIO [*enters*] *above* [*at a window*].°

BRABANTIO. What is the reason of this terrible summons?
What is the matter° there?   85
RODERIGO. Signor, is all your family within?
IAGO. Are your doors locked?
BRABANTIO.   Why, wherefore ask you this?
IAGO. Zounds,° sir, you're robbed. For shame, put on your gown!
Your heart is burst; you have lost half your soul.
Even now, now, very now, an old black ram   90
Is tupping° your white ewe. Arise, arise!
Awake the snorting° citizens with the bell,
Or else the devil° will make a grandsire of you.
Arise, I say!
BRABANTIO.   What, have you lost your wits?
RODERIGO. Most reverend signor, do you know my voice?   95
BRABANTIO. Not I. What are you?
RODERIGO. My name is Roderigo.
BRABANTIO. The worser welcome.
I have charged thee not to haunt about my doors.
In honest plainness thou hast heard me say   100
My daughter is not for thee; and now, in madness,
Being full of supper and distempering° drafts,
Upon malicious bravery° dost thou come
To start° my quiet.
RODERIGO. Sir, sir, sir—
BRABANTIO.   But thou must needs be sure   105
My spirits and my place° have in° their power
To make this bitter to thee.

---

73 **Though . . . be joy** although he seems fortunate and happy. (Repeats the idea of line 72.)
74 **changes of vexation** vexing changes.   75 **As it may** that may cause it to.   **some color**
some of its fresh gloss.   77 **timorous** frightening.   78 **and negligence** i.e., by negligence.
83 **s.d. at a window** (This stage direction, from the Quarto, probably calls for an appearance on
the gallery above and rearstage.)   85 **the matter** your business.   88 **Zounds** by His (Christ's)
wounds.   91 **tupping** covering, copulating with. (Said of sheep.)   92 **snorting** snoring.   93
the devil (The devil was conventionally pictured as black.)   102 **distempering** intoxicating.
103 **Upon malicious bravery** with hostile intent to defy me.   104 **start** startle, disrupt.   106
My spirits and my place my temperament and my authority of office.   **have in** have it in.

RODERIGO.   Patience, good sir.

BRABANTIO. What tell'st thou me of robbing? This is Venice;
    My house is not a grange.°

RODERIGO.   Most grave Brabantio,
    In simple° and pure soul I come to you.   110

IAGO. Zounds, sir, you are one of those that will not serve God if the devil
    bid you. Because we come to do you service and you think we are
    ruffians, you'll have your daughter covered with a Barbary° horse;
    you'll have your nephews° neigh to you; you'll have coursers° for
    cousins° and jennets° for germans.°

BRABANTIO. What profane wretch art thou?   115

IAGO. I am one, sir, that comes to tell you your daughter and the Moor are
    now making the beast with two backs.

BRABANTIO. Thou art a villain.

IAGO.   You are—a senator.°

BRABANTIO. This thou shalt answer.° I know thee, Roderigo.

RODERIGO. Sir, I will answer anything. But I beseech you,   120
    If't be your pleasure and most wise° consent—
    As partly I find it is—that your fair daughter,
    At this odd-even° and dull watch o' the night,
    Transported with° no worse nor better guard
    But with a knave° of common hire, a gondolier,   125
    To the gross clasps of a lascivious Moor—
    If this be known to you and your allowance°
    We then have done you bold and saucy° wrongs.
    But if you know not this, my manners tell me
    We have your wrong rebuke. Do not believe   130
    That, from° the sense of all civility,°
    I thus would play and trifle with your reverence.°
    Your daughter, if you have not given her leave,
    I say again, hath made a gross revolt,
    Tying her duty, beauty, wit,° and fortunes   135
    In an extravagant° and wheeling° stranger°
    Of here and everywhere. Straight° satisfy yourself.
    If she be in her chamber or your house,
    Let loose on me the justice of the state
    For thus deluding you.   140

BRABANTIO. Strike on the tinder,° ho!
    Give me a taper! Call up all my people!

---

109 grange isolated country house.   **110 simple** sincere.   **113 Barbary** from northern Africa
(and hence associated with Othello).   **nephews** i.e., grandson.   **114 coursers** powerful
horses.   **cousins** kinsmen.   **jennets** small Spanish horses.   **germans** near relatives.   **118 a
senator** (Said with mock politeness, as though the word itself were an insult.)   **119 answer** be
held accountable for.   **121 wise** well-informed.   **123 odd-even** between one day and the next,
i.e., without midnight.   **124 with** by.   **125 But with a knave** than by a low fellow, a servant.
127 allowance permission.   **128 saucy** insolent.   **131 from** contrary to.   **civility** good manners, decency.   **132 your reverence** the respect due to you.   **135 wit** intelligence   **136 extravagant** expatriate, wandering far from home.   **wheeling** roving about, vagabond.
stranger foreigner.   **137 Straight** straightway.   **141 tinder** charred linen ignited by a spark
from flint and steel, used to light torches or *tapers* (lines 142, 167).

This accident° is not unlike my dream.
Belief of it oppresses me already.
Light, I say, light!   *Exit* [*above*].

IAGO.   Farewell, for I must leave you.   145
It seems not meet° nor wholesome to my place°
To be producted°—as, if I stay, I shall—
Against the Moor. For I do know the state,
However this may gall° him with some check,°
Cannot with safety cast° him, for he's embarked°   150
With such loud reason° to the Cyprus wars,
Which even now stands in act,° for their souls,°
Another of his fathom° they have none
To lead their business; in which regard,°
Though I do hate him as I do hell pains,   155
Yet for necessity of present life°
I must show out a flag and sign of love,
Which is indeed but sign. That you shall surely find him,
Lead to the Sagittary° the raisèd search,°
And there will I be with him. So farewell.   *Exit.* 160

Enter [*below*] BRABANTIO [*in his nightgown°*] *with servants*
and torches.

BRABANTIO. It is too true an evil. Gone she is;
And what's to come of my despisèd time°
Is naught but bitterness. Now, Roderigo,
Where didst thou see her?—O unhappy girl!—
With the Moor, sayst thou?—Who would be a father!—   165
How didst thou know 'twas she?—O, she deceives me
Past thought!—What said she to you?—Get more tapers.
Raise all my kindred.—Are they married, think you?
RODERIGO. Truly, I think they are.
BRABANTIO. Oh heaven! How got she out? O treason of the blood! 170
Fathers, from hence trust not your daughters' minds
By what you see them act. Is there not charms°
By which the property° of youth and maidhood
May be abused?° Have you not read, Roderigo,
Of some such thing!
RODERIGO.   Yes, sir, I have indeed.   175
BRABANTIO. Call up my brother.—O, would you had had her!—
Some one way, some another.—Do you know
Where we may apprehend her and the Moor?

---

143 **accident** occurrence, event. 146 **meet** fitting. **place** position (as ensign). 147 **pro-
ducted** produced (as a witness). 149 **gall** rub; oppress. **check** rebuke. 150 **cast** dismiss.
embarked engaged. 151 **loud reason** unanimous shout of confirmation (in the Senate).
152 **stands in act** are going on. **for their souls** to save themselves. 153 **fathom** i.e., ability,
depth of experience. 154 **in which regard** out of regard for which. 156 **life** livelihood.
159 **Sagittary** (An inn or house where Othello and Desdemona are staying, named for its sign of
Sagittarius, or Centaur.) **raisèd search** search party roused out of sleep. 160 **s.d. nightgown** dressing gown. (This costuming is specified in the Quarto text.) 162 **time** i.e., remainder
of life. 172 **charms** spells. 173 **property** special quality, nature. 174 **abused** deceived.

RODERIGO. I think I can discover° him, if you please
　　To get good guard and go along with me.   180
BRABANTIO. Pray you, lead on. At every house I'll call;
　　I may command° at most.—Get weapons, ho!
　　And raise some special officers of night.—
　　On, good Roderigo, I will deserve° your pains.

　　Exeunt.

1.2 *Enter* OTHELLO, IAGO, *attendants with torches.*

IAGO. Though in the trade of war I have slain men,
　　Yet do I hold it very stuff° o' the conscience
　　To do no contrived° murder. I lack iniquity
　　Sometimes to do me service. Nine or ten times
　　I had thought t' have yerked° him° here under the ribs.   5
OTHELLO. 'Tis better as it is.
IAGO.　　　　　　　　　　　Nay, but he prated,
　　And spoke such scurvy and provoking terms
　　Against your honor
　　That, with the little godliness I have,
　　I did full hard forbear him.° But, I pray you, sir,   10
　　Are you fast married? Be assured of this,
　　That the magnifico° is much beloved,
　　And hath in his effect° a voice potential°
　　As double as the Duke's. He will divorce you,
　　Or put upon you what restraint or grievance   15
　　The law, with all his might to enforce it on,
　　Will give him cable.°
OTHELLO.　　　　　　　　　Let him do his spite.
　　My services which I have done the seigniory°
　　Shall out-tongue his complaints. 'Tis yet to know°—
　　Which, when I know that boasting is an honor,
　　I shall promulgate—I fetch my life and being   20
　　From men of royal siege,° and my demerits°
　　May speak unbonneted° to as proud a fortune
　　As this that I have reached. For know, Iago,
　　But that I love the gentle Desdemona,   25

---

179 discover reveal, uncover.　**182 command** demand assistance.　**184 deserve** show gratitude for.　**1.2 Location: Venice, another street, before Othello's lodgings.　2 very stuff**
essence, basic material (continuing the metaphor of *trade* from line 1).　**3 contrived** premeditated.　**5 yerked** stabbed.　**him** i.e., Roderigo.　**10 I . . . him** I restrained myself with great
difficulty from assaulting him.　**12 magnifico** Venetian grandee, i.e., Brabantio.　**13 in his effect** at his command.　**potential** powerful.　**17 cable** i.e., scope.　**18 seigniory** Venetian
government.　**19 yet to know** not yet widely known.　**22 siege** i.e., rank. (Literally, a seat used
by a person of distinction.)　**demerits** deserts.　**23 unbonneted** without removing the hat,
i.e., on equal terms. (? Or "with hat off," "in all due modesty.")

I would not my unhousèd° free condition
Put into circumscription and confine°
For the sea's worth.° But look, what lights come yond?

Enter CASSIO [*and certain officers°*] *with torches.*

IAGO. Those are the raisèd father and his friends.
    You were best go in.
OTHELLO.   Not I. I must be found.   30
    My parts, my title, and my perfect soul°
    Shall manifest me rightly. Is it they?
IAGO. By Janus,° I think no.
OTHELLO. The servants of the Duke? And my lieutenant?
    The goodness of the night upon you, friends!   35
    What is the news?
CASSIO.   The Duke does greet you, General,
    And he requires your haste-post-haste appearance
    Even on the instant.
OTHELLO.   What is the matter,° think you?
CASSIO. Something from Cyprus, as I may divine.°
    It is a business of some heat.° The galleys   40
    Have sent a dozen sequent° messengers
    This very night at one another's heels,
    And many of the consuls,° raised and met,
    Are at the Duke's already. You have been hotly called for;
    When, being not at your lodging to be found,   45
    The Senate hath sent about° three several° quests
    To search you out.
OTHELLO.   'Tis well I am found by you.
    I will but spend a word here in the house.
    And go with you.   [*Exit.*]
CASSIO.   Ancient, what makes° he here?
IAGO. Faith, he tonight hath boarded° a land carrack.°   50
    If it prove lawful prize,° he's made forever.
CASSIO. I do not understand.
IAGO.   He's married.
CASSIO.   To who?

[*Enter* OTHELLO.]

IAGO. Marry,° to—Come Captain, will you go?
OTHELLO. Have with you.°
CASSIO. Here comes another troop to seek for you.   55

---

26 **unhousèd** unconfined, undomesticated. **27 circumscription and confine** restriction
and confinement. **28 the sea's worth** all the riches at the bottom of the sea. **s.d. officers**
(The Quarto text calls for "Cassio with lights, officers with torches.") **31 My . . . soul** my natural gifts, my position or reputation, and my unflawed conscience. **33 Janus** Roman two-faced
god of beginnings. **38 matter** business. **39 divine** guess. **40 heat** urgency. **41 sequent**
successive. **43 consuls** senators. **46 about** all over the city. **several** separate. **49 makes**
does. **50 boarded** gone aboard and seized as an act of piracy (with sexual suggestion).
carrack large merchant ship. **51 prize** booty. **53 Marry** (An oath, originally "by the Virgin
Mary"; here used with wordplay on *married*.) **54 Have with you** i.e., let's go.

Enter BRABANTIO, RODERIGO, *with officers and torches.*°

IAGO. It is Brabantio. General, be advised.°
    He comes to bad intent.
OTHELLO.   Holla! Stand there!
RODERIGO. Signor, it is the Moor.
BRABANTIO.   Down with him, thief!

[*They draw on both sides.*]

IAGO. You, Roderigo! Come, sir, I am for you.
OTHELLO. Keep up° your bright swords, for the dew will rust them.   60
    Good signor, you shall more command with years
    Than with your weapons.
BRABANTIO. O thou foul thief, where has thou stowed my daughter?
    Damned as thou art, thou hast enchanted her!
    For I'll refer me° to all things of sense,°   65
    If she in chains of magic were not bound
    Whether a maid so tender, fair, and happy,
    So opposite to marriage that she shunned
    The wealthy curlèd darlings of our nation,
    Would ever have, t' incur a general mock,   70
    Run from her guardage° to the sooty bosom
    Of such a thing as thou—to fear, not to delight.
    Judge me the world if 'tis not gross in sense°
    That thou hast practiced on her with foul charms,
    Abused her delicate youth with drugs or minerals°   75
    That weakens motion.° I'll have 't disputed on;°
    'Tis probable and palpable to thinking.
    I therefore apprehend and do attach° thee
    For an abuser of the world, a practicer
    Of arts inhibited° and out of warrant.°—   80
    Lay hold upon him! If he do resist,
    Subdue him at his peril.
OTHELLO.   Hold your hands,
    Both you of my inclining° and the rest.
    Were it my cue to fight, I should have known it
    Without a prompter.—Whither will you that I go   85
    To answer this your charge?
BRABANTIO. To prison, till fit time
    Of law and course of direct session°
    Call thee to answer.

---

55 s.d. officers and torches (The Quarto text calls for "others with lights and weapons.") **56
be advised** be on your guard. **60 Keep up** keep in the sheath. **65 refer me** submit my
case. **things of sense** commonsense understandings, or, creatures possessing common sense.
71 her guardage my guardianship of her. **73 gross in sense** obvious. **75 minerals** i.e.,
poisons. **76 weakens motion** impair the vital faculties. **disputed on** argued in court by
professional counsel, debated by experts. **78 attach** arrest. **80 arts inhibited** prohibited
arts, black magic. **out of warrant** illegal. **83 inclining** following, party. **88 course of direct session** regular or specially convened legal proceedings.

OTHELLO.   What if I do obey?
   How may the Duke be therewith satisfied,
   Whose messengers are here about my side   90
   Upon some present business of the state
   To bring me to him?
OFFICER.   'Tis true, most worthy signor.
   The Duke's in council, and your noble self,
   I am sure, is sent for.
BRABANTIO.   How? The Duke in council?   95
   In this time of the night? Bring him away.°
   Mine's not an idle° cause. The Duke himself,
   Or any of my brothers of the state,
   Cannot but feel this wrong as 'twere their own;
   For if such actions may have passage free,°   100
   Bondslaves and pagans shall our statesmen be.

   Exeunt.

> **1.3** *Enter* DUKE [*and*] SENATORS [*and sit at a table, with lights*], *and*
> OFFICERS.° [*The* DUKE *and* SENATORS *are reading dispatches.*]°

DUKE. There is not composition° in these news
   That gives them credit.
FIRST SENATOR. Indeed, they are disproportioned.°
   My letters say a hundred and seven galleys.
DUKE. And mine, a hundred forty.
SECOND SENATOR.   And mine, two hundred.   5
   But though they jump° not on a just° account—
   As in these cases, where the aim° reports
   'Tis oft with difference—yet do they all confirm
   A Turkish fleet, and bearing up to Cyprus.
DUKE. Nay, it is possible enough to judgment.   10
   I do not so secure me in the error
   But the main article I do approve°
   In fearful sense.
SAILOR (*within*). What ho, what ho, what ho!

   Enter SAILOR.

OFFICER. A messenger from the galleys.
DUKE. Now, what's the business?   15
SAILOR. The Turkish preparation° makes for Rhodes.
   So was I bid report here to the state
   By Signor Angelo.

---

96 away right along. **97 idle** trifling. **100 have passage free** are allowed to go unchecked.
1.3 Location: Venice, a council chamber. s.d. Enter . . . Officers (The Quarto text calls
for the Duke and senators to "sit at a table with lights and attendants."). **1 composition** consistency. **3 disproportioned** inconsistent. **6 jump** agree. **just** exact. **7 the aim** conjecture. **11–12 I do not . . . approve** I do not take such (false) comfort in the discrepancies that
I fail to perceive the main point, i.e., that the Turkish fleet is threatening. **16 preparation** fleet
prepared for battle.

DUKE. How say you by° this change?
FIRST SENATOR.   This cannot be   20
    By no assay° of reason. 'Tis a pageant°
    To keep us in false gaze.° When we consider
    Th' importancy of Cyprus to the Turk,
    And let ourselves again but understand
    That, as it more concerns the Turk than Rhodes,
    So may he with more facile question bear it,°   25
    For that° it stands not in such warlike brace,°
    But altogether lacks th' abilities°
    That Rhodes is dressed in°—if we make thought of this,
    We must not think the Turk is so unskillful°
    To leave that latest° which concerns him first,   30
    Neglecting an attempt of ease and gain
    To wake° and wage° a danger profitless.
DUKE. Nay, in all confidence, he's not for Rhodes.
OFFICER.   Here is more news.

    Enter a MESSENGER.

MESSENGER. The Ottomites, reverend and gracious,   35
    Steering with due course toward the isle of Rhodes,
    Have there injointed them° with an after° fleet.
FIRST SENATOR. Ay, so I thought. How many, as you guess?
MESSENGER. Of thirty sail; and now they do restem
    Their backward course,° bearing with frank appearance°   40
    Their purposes toward Cyprus. Signor Montano,
    Your trusty and most valiant servitor,°
    With his free duty° recommends° you thus,
    And prays you to believe him.
DUKE. 'Tis certain then for Cyprus.   45
    Marcus Luccicos, is not he in town?
FIRST SENATOR. He's now in Florence.
DUKE. Write from us to him, post-post-haste. Dispatch.
FIRST SENATOR. Here comes Brabantio and the valiant Moor.

    Enter BRABANTIO, OTHELLO, CASSIO, IAGO, RODERIGO, *and officers.*

DUKE. Valiant Othello, we must straight° employ you   50
    Against the general enemy° Ottoman.
    [*To* BRABANTIO] I did not see you; welcome, gentle° signor.
    We lacked your counsel and your help tonight.

---

19 by about.   **20 assay** test.   **pageant** mere show.   **21 in false gaze** looking the wrong way.   **25 So may . . . it** so also he (the Turk) can more easily capture it (Cyprus).   **26 For that** since.   **brace** state of defense.   **27 abilities** means of self-defense.   **28 dressed in** equipped with.   **29 unskillful** deficient in judgment.   **30 latest** last.   **32 wake** stir up.   **wage** risk. **37 injointed them** joined themselves.   **after** second, following.   **39–40 restem . . . course** retrace their original course.   **40 frank appearance** undisguised intent.   **42 servitor** officer under your command.   **43 free duty** given and loyal service.   **recommends** commends himself and reports to.   **50 straight** straightway.   **51 general enemy** universal enemy to all Christendom.   **52 gentle** noble.

BRABANTIO. So did I yours. Good Your Grace, pardon me;
    Neither my place° nor aught I heard of business   55
    Hath raised me from my bed, nor doth the general care
    Take hold on me, for my particular° grief
    Is of so floodgate° and o'erbearing nature
    That it engluts° and swallows other sorrows
    And it is still itself.°
DUKE.   Why, what's the matter?   60
BRABANTIO. My daughter! O, my daughter!
DUKE AND SENATORS.   Dead?
BRABANTIO.   Ay, to me.
    She is abused,° stol'n from me, and corrupted
    By spells and medicines bought of mountebanks;
    For nature so preposterously to err,
    Being not deficient,° blind, or lame of sense,°   65
    Sans° witchcraft could not.
DUKE. Whoe'er he be that in this foul proceeding
    Hath thus beguiled your daughter of herself,
    And you of her, the bloody book of law
    You shall yourself read in the bitter letter   70
    After your own sense°—yea, though our proper° son
    Stood in your action.°
BRABANTIO.   Humbly I thank Your Grace.
    Here is the man, this Moor, whom now it seems
    Your special mandate for the state affairs
    Hath hither brought.
ALL.   We are very sorry for 't.   75
DUKE. [to OTHELLO] What, in your part, can you say to this?
BRABANTIO. Nothing, but this is so.
OTHELLO. Most potent, grave, and reverend signors,
    My very noble and approved° good masters:
    That I have ta'en away this old man's daughter,   80
    It is most true; true, I have married her.
    The very head and front° of my offending
    Hath this extent, no more. Rude° I am in my speech,
    And little blessed with the soft phrase of peace;
    For since these arms of mine had seven years' pith,°   85
    Till now some nine moons wasted,° they have used
    Their dearest° action in the tented field;
    And little of this great world can I speak
    More than pertains to feats of broils and battle,

---

55 **place** official position. 57 **particular** personal. 58 **floodgate** i.e., overwhelming (as when floodgates are opened). 59 **engluts** engulfs. 60 **is still itself** remains undiminished. 62 **abused** deceived. 65 **deficient** defective. **lame of sense** deficient in sensory perception. 66 **Sans** without. 71 **After . . . sense** according to your interpretation. **our proper** my own. 72 **Stood . . . action** were under your accusation. 79 **approved** proved, esteemed. 82 **head and front** height and breadth, entire extent. 83 **Rude** unpolished. 85 **since . . . pith**, i.e., since I was seven. **pith** strength, vigor. 86 **Till . . . wasted** until some nine months ago (since when Othello has evidently not been on active duty, but in Venice). 87 **dearest** most valuable.

And therefore little shall I grace my cause   90
In speaking for myself. Yet, by your gracious patience,
I will a round° unvarnished tale deliver
Of my whole course of love—what drugs, what charms,
What conjuration, and what mighty magic,
For such proceeding I am charged withal,°   95
I won his daughter.

BRABANTIO.   A maiden never bold;
Of spirit so still and quiet that her motion
Blushed at herself;° and she, in spite of nature,
Of years,° of country, credit,° everything,
To fall in love with what she feared to look on!   100
It is a judgment maimed and most imperfect
That will confess° perfection so could err
Against all rules of nature, and must be driven
To find out practices° of cunning hell
Why this should be. I therefore vouch° again   105
That with some mixtures powerful o'er the blood,°
Or with some dram conjured to this effect,°
He wrought upon her.

DUKE.   To vouch this is no proof,
Without more wider° and more overt test°
Than these thin habits° and poor likelihoods°   110
Of modern seeming° do prefer° against him.

FIRST SENATOR.   But Othello, speak.
Did you by indirect and forcèd courses°
Subdue and poison this young maid's affections?
Or came it by request and such fair question°   115
As soul to soul affordeth?

OTHELLO.   I do beseech you,
Send for the lady to the Sagittary
And let her speak of me before her father.
If you do find me foul in her report,
The trust, the office I do hold of you   120
Not only take away, but let your sentence
Even fall upon my life.

DUKE.   Fetch Desdemona hither.

OTHELLO. Ancient, conduct them. You best know the place.

[*Exeunt* IAGO *and attendants.*]

And, till she come, as truly as to heaven
I do confess the vices of my blood,°   125

---

92 round plain.   **95 withal** with.   **97–98 her . . . herself** i.e., she blushed easily at herself.
(*Motion* can suggest the impulse of the soul or of the emotions, or physical movement.)   **99
years** i.e., difference in age.   **credit** virtuous reputation.   **102 confess** concede (that).   **104
practices** plots.   **105 vouch** assert.   **106 blood** passions.   **107 dram . . . effect** dose made
by magical spells to have this effect.   **109 more wider** fuller.   **test** testimony.   **110 habits**
garments, i.e., appearances.   **poor likelihoods** weak inferences.   **111 modern seeming**
commonplace assumption.   **prefer** bring forth.   **113 forcèd courses** means used against her
will.   **115 question** conversation.   **125 blood** passions, human nature.

So justly° to your grave ears I'll present
How I did thrive in this fair lady's love,
And she in mine.
DUKE. Say it, Othello.
OTHELLO. Her father loved me, oft invited me,   130
Still° questioned me the story of my life
From year to year—the battles, sieges, fortunes
That I have passed.
I ran it through, even from my boyish days
To th' very moment that he bade me tell it,   135
Wherein I spoke of most disastrous chances,
Of moving accidents° by flood and field,
Of hairbreadth scapes i' th' imminent deadly breach,°
Of being taken by the insolent foe
And sold to slavery, of my redemption thence,   140
And portance° in my travels' history,
Wherein of antres° vast and deserts idle,°
Rough quarries, rocks, and hills whose heads touch heaven,
It was my hint° to speak—such was my process—
And of the Cannibals that each other eat,   145
The Anthropophagi,° and men whose heads
Do grow beneath their shoulders. These things to hear
Would Desdemona seriously incline;
But still the house affairs would draw her thence,
Which ever as she could with haste dispatch   150
She'd come again, and with a greedy ear
Devour up my discourse. Which I, observing,
Took once a pliant° hour, and found good means
To draw from her a prayer of earnest heart
That I would all my pilgrimage dilate,°   155
Whereof by parcels° she had something heard,
But not intentively.° I did consent,
And often did beguile her of her tears,
When I did speak of some distressful stroke
That my youth suffered. My story being done,   160
She gave me for my pains a world of sighs.
She swore, in faith, 'twas strange, 'twas passing° strange,
'Twas pitiful, 'twas wondrous pitiful.
She wished she had not heard it, yet she wished
That heaven had made her° such a man. She thanked me,   165
And bade me, if I had a friend that loved her,
I should but teach him how to tell my story,

---

126 **justly** truthfully, accurately.   131 **Still** continually.   137 **moving accidents** stirring happenings.   138 **imminent . . . breach** death-threatening gaps made in a fortification.   141
portance conduct.   142 **antres** caverns. **idle** barren, desolate.   143 **Rough quarries**
rugged rock formations.   144 **hint** occasion, opportunity.   146 **Anthropophagi** man-eaters.
(A term from Pliny's *Natural History*.)   153 **pliant** well-suiting.   155 **dilate** relate in detail.
156 **by parcels** piecemeal.   157 **intentively** with full attention, continuously.   162 **passing**
exceedingly.   165 **made her** created her to be.

And that would woo her. Upon this hint° I spake.
She loved me for the dangers I had passed,
And I loved her that she did pity them.   170
This only is the witchcraft I have used.
Here comes the lady. Let her witness it.

Enter DESDEMONA, IAGO, [*and*] *attendants.*

DUKE. I think this tale would win my daughter too.
    Good Brabantio,
    Take up this mangled matter at the best.°   175
    Men do their broken weapons rather use
    Than their bare hands.
BRABANTIO.   I pray you, hear her speak.
    If she confesses that she was half the wooer,
    Destruction on my head if my bad blame
    Light on the man!—Come hither, gentle mistress.   180
    Do you perceive in all this noble company
    Where most you owe obedience?
DESDEMONA.   My noble Father,
    I do perceive here a divided duty.
    To you I am bound for life and education;°
    My life and education both do learn° me   185
    How to respect you. You are the lord of duty;°
    I am hitherto your daughter. But here's my husband,
    And so much duty as my mother showed
    To you, preferring you before her father,
    So much I challenge° that I may profess   190
    Due to the Moor my lord.
BRABANTIO. God be with you! I have done.
    Please it Your Grace, on to the state affairs.
    I had rather to adopt a child than get° it.
    Come hither, Moor. [*He joins the hands of* OTHELLO *and* DESDEMONA.] 195
    I here do give thee that with all my heart°
    Which, but thou hast already, with all my heart°
    I would keep from thee.—For your sake,° jewel,
    I am glad at soul I have no other child,
    For thy escape° would teach me tyranny,   200
    To hang clogs° on them.—I have done, my lord.
DUKE. Let me speak like yourself,° and lay a sentence°
    Which, as a grece° or step, may help these lovers
    Into your favor.
    When remedies° are past, the griefs are ended   205
    By seeing the worst, which late on hopes depended.°

---

168 hint opportunity. (Othello does not mean that she was dropping hints.)   **175 Take . . .
best** make the best of a bad bargain.   **184 education** upbringing.   **185 learn** teach.   **186 of
duty** to whom duty is due.   **190 challenge** claim.   **194 get** beget.   **196 with all my heart**
wherein my whole affection has been engaged.   **197 with all my heart** willingly, gladly.   **198
For your sake** on your account.   **200 escape** elopement.   **201 clogs** (Literally, block of
wood fastened to the legs of criminals or convicts to inhibit escape.)   **202 like yourself** i.e., as
you would, in your proper temper.   **lay a sentence** apply a maxim.   **203 grece** step.   **205
remedies** hopes of remedy.   **206 which . . . depended** which griefs were sustained until recently by hopeful anticipation.

To mourn a mischief° that is past and gone
Is the next° way to draw new mischief on.
What° cannot be preserved when fortune takes,
Patience her injury a mockery makes.°   210
The robbed that smiles steals something from the thief;
He robs himself that spends a bootless grief.°

BRABANTIO. So let the Turk of Cyprus us beguile,
We lose it not, so long as we can smile.
He bears the sentence well that nothing bears   215
But the free comfort which from thence he hears,
But he bears both the sentence and the sorrow
That, to pay grief, must of poor patience borrow.°
These sentences, to sugar or to gall,
Being strong on both sides, are equivocal.°   220
But words are words. I never yet did hear
That the bruised heart was piercèd through the ear.°
I humbly beseech you, proceed to th' affairs of state.

DUKE. The Turk with a most mighty preparation makes for Cyprus. Othello,
the fortitude° of the place is best known to you; and though we   225
we have there a substitute° of most allowed° sufficiency, yet opinion,
a sovereign mistress of effects, throws a more safer voice on you.°
You must therefore be content to slubber° the gloss of your new
fortunes with this more stubborn° and boisterous expedition.

OTHELLO. The tyrant custom, most grave senators,   230
Hath made the flinty and steel couch of war
My thrice-driven° bed of down. I do agnize°
A natural and prompt alacrity
I find in hardness,° and do undertake
These present wars against the Ottomites.   235
Most humbly therefore bending to your state,°
I crave fit disposition for my wife,
Due reference of place and exhibition,°
With such accommodation° and besort°
As levels° with her breeding.°   240

---

207 mischief misfortune, injury.   **208 next** nearest.   **209 What** whatever.   **210 Patience . . .
makes** patience laughs at the injury inflicted by fortune (and thus eases the pain).   **212
spends a bootless grief** indulges in unavailing grief.   **215–218 He bears . . . borrow** a person well bears out your maxim who can enjoy its platitudinous comfort, free of all genuine sorrow, but anyone whose grief bankrupts his poor parlence is left with your saying and his sorrow, too. (*Bears the sentence* also plays on the meaning, "receives judicial sentence.")
219–220 These . . . equivocal these fine maxims are equivocal, either sweet or bitter in their
application.   **222 piercèd . . . ear** i.e., surgically lanced and cured by mere words of advice.
225 fortitude strength.   **226 substitute** deputy.   **allowed** acknowledged.   **226–227
opinion . . . on you** general opinion, an important determiner of affairs, chooses you as the
best man.   **228 slubber** soil, sully.   **stubborn** harsh, rough.   **232 thrice-driven** thrice
sifted, winnowed.   **agnize** know in myself, acknowledge. **234 hardness** hardship.   **236
bending . . . state** bowing or kneeling to your authority.   **238 reference . . . exhibition**
provision of appropriate place to live and allowance of money.   **239 accommodation** suitable provision.   **besort** attendance.   **240 levels** equals, suits.   **breeding** social position, upbringing.

DUKE. Why, at her father's.
BRABANTIO.   I will not have it so.
OTHELLO. Nor I.
DESDEMONA. Nor I. I would not there reside,
    To put my father in impatient thoughts
    By being in his eye. Most gracious Duke,
    To my unfolding° lend your prosperous° ear,   245
    And let me find a charter° in your voice,
    T' assist my simpleness.
DUKE. What would you, Desdemona?
DESDEMONA. That I did love the Moor to live with him,
    My downright violence and storm of fortunes°   250
    May trumpet to the world. My heart's subdued
    Even to the very quality of my lord.°
    I saw Othello's visage in his mind,
    And to his honors and his valiant parts°
    Did I my soul and fortunes consecrate.   255
    So that, dear lords, if I be left behind
    A moth° of peace, and he go to the war,
    The rites° for why I love him are bereft me,
    And I a heavy interim shall support
    By his dear° absence. Let me go with him.   260
OTHELLO. Let her have your voice.°
    Vouch with me, heaven, I therefor beg it not
    To please the palate of my appetite,
    Not to comply with heat°—the young affects°
    In me defunct—and proper° satisfaction,   265
    But to be free° and bounteous to her mind.
    And heaven defend° your good souls that you think°
    I will your serious and great business scant
    When she is with me. No, when light-winged toys
    Of feathered Cupid seel° with wanton dullness   270
    My speculative and officed instruments,°
    That° my disports° corrupt and taint° my business,
    Let huswives make a skillet of my helm,
    And all indign° and base adversities
    Make head° against my estimation!°   275

---

245 unfolding explanation, proposal. **prosperous** propitious. **246 charter** privilege, authorization. **250 My . . . fortunes** my plain and total breach of social custom, taking my future by storm and disrupting my whole life. **251–252 My heart's . . . lord** my heart is brought wholly into accord with Othello's virtues; I love him for his virtues. **254 parts** qualities. **257 moth** i.e., one who consumes merely. **258 rites** rites of love (with a suggestion, too, of "rights," sharing.) **260 dear** (1) heartfelt (2) costly. **261 voice** consent. **264 heat** sexual passion. **young affects** passions of youth, desires. **265 proper** personal. **266 free** generous. **267 defend** forbid. **think** should think. **270 seel** i.e., make blind (as in falconry, by sewing up the eyes of the hawk during training). **271 speculative . . . instruments** eyes and other faculties used in the performance of duty. **272 That** so that. **disports** sexual pastimes. **taint** impair. **274 indign** unworthy, shameful. **275 Make head** raise an army. **estimation** reputation.

DUKE. Be it as you shall privately determine,
    Either for her stay or going. Th' affair cries haste,
    And speed must answer it.

A SENATOR.   You must away tonight.

DESDEMONA. Tonight, my lord?

DUKE.   This night.

OTHELLO.   With all my heart.

DUKE. At nine i' the morning here we'll meet again.   280
    Othello, leave some officer behind,
    And he shall our commission bring to you,
    With such things else of quality and respect°
    As doth import° you.

OTHELLO.   So please Your Grace, my ancient;
    A man he is of honesty and trust.   285
    To his conveyance I assign my wife,
    With what else needful Your Good Grace shall think
    To be sent after me.

DUKE.   Let it be so.
    Good night to everyone. [*To* BRABANTIO.] And, noble signor,
    If virtue no delighted° beauty lack,   290
    Your son-in-law is far more fair than black.

FIRST SENATOR. Adieu, brave Moor. Use Desdemona well.

BRABANTIO. Look to her, Moor, if thou hast eyes to see.
    She has deceived her father, and may thee.

             Exeunt [DUKE, BRABANTIO, CASSIO, SENATORS, *and officers*].

OTHELLO. My life upon her faith! Honest Iago,   295
    My Desdemona must I leave to thee.
    I prithee, let thy wife attend on her,
    And bring them after in the best advantage.°
    Come, Desdemona, I have but an hour
    Of love, of worldly matters and direction,°   300
    To spend with thee. We must obey the time.°

                    Exit [*with* DESDEMONA].

RODERIGO. Iago—

IAGO. What sayst thou, noble heart?

RODERIGO. What will I do, think'st thou?

IAGO. Why, go to bed and sleep.   305

RODERIGO. I will incontinently° drown myself.

IAGO. If thou dost, I shall never love thee after. Why, thou silly gentleman?

RODERIGO. It is silliness to live when to live is torment; and then have
    we a prescription° to die when death is our physician.

IAGO. O villainous!° I have looked upon the world for four times seven 310
    years, and, since I could distinguish betwixt a benefit and an injury, I

---

283 of quality and respect of importance and relevance   **284 import** concern.   **290 delighted** capable of delighting.   **298 in . . . advantage** at the most favorable opportunity.   **300 direction** instructions.   **301 the time** the urgency of this present crisis.   **306 incontinently** immediately, without self-restraint.   **308–309 prescription** (1) right based on long-established customs (2) doctor's prescription.   **310 villainous** i.e., what perfect nonsense.

never found man that knew how to love himself. Ere I would say I
would drown myself for the love of a guinea hen,° I would change my
humanity with a baboon.

RODERIGO. What should I do? I confess it is my shame to be so fond,° but
it is not in my virtue° to amend it.   315

IAGO. Virtue? A *fig!*° 'Tis in ourselves that we are thus or thus. Our bodies are our gardens to the which our wills are gardeners; so that if
we will plant nettles or sow lettuce, set hyssop° and weed up
thyme, supply it with one gender° of herbs or distract it with°
many, either to have it sterile with idleness° or manured with in-   320
dustry—why, the power and corrigible authority° of this lies in our
wills. If the beam° of our lives had not one scale of reason to poise° another of sensuality, the blood° and baseness of our natures would
conduct us to most preposterous conclusions. But we have reason to
cool our raging motions,° our carnal stings, our unbitted° lusts,   325
whereof I take this that you call love to be a sect or scion.°

RODERIGO. It cannot be.

IAGO. It is merely a lust of the blood and a permission of the will. Come,
be a man. Drown thyself? Drown cats and blind puppies. I have pro-
fessed me thy friend, and I confess me knit to thy deserving with ca-
bles of perdurable° toughness. I could never better stead° thee than   330
now. Put money in thy purse. Follow thou the wars; defeat thy fa-
vor° with an usurped° beard. I say, put money in thy purse. It cannot be long that Desdemona should continue her love to the Moor—
put money in thy purse—nor he his to her. It was a violent commencement in her, and thou shalt see an answerable sequestration°—put   335
but money in thy purse. These Moors are changeable in their wills°—
fill thy purse with money. The food that to him now is as luscious as
locusts° shall be to him shortly as bitter as coloquintida.° She must
change for youth; when she is sated with his body, she will find the
error of her choice. She must have change, she must. Therefore put
money in thy purse. If thou wilt needs damn thyself, do it a more
delicate way than drowning. Make° all the money thou canst. If sanc-   340
timony° and a frail vow betwixt an erring° barbarian and a supersubtle
Venetian be not too hard for my wits and all the tribe of hell, thou shalt
enjoy her. Therefore make money. A pox of drowning thyself! It is

---

312 **guinea hen** (A slang term for a prostitute).   314 **fond** infatuated.   315 **virtue** strength,
nature.   316 *fig* (To give a fig is to thrust the thumb between the first and second fingers in a
vulgar and insulting gesture.)   318 **hyssop** an herb of the mint family.   319 **gender** kind.
distract it with divide it among.   319–320 **idleness** want of cultivation.   **corrigible authority** power to correct.   321 **beam** balance.   322 **poise** counterbalance.   **blood** natural
passions.   324 **motions** appetites.   **unbitted** unbridled, uncontrolled.   325 **sect or scion**
cutting or offshoot.   329 **perdurable** very durable.   330 **stead** assist.   331 **defeat thy
favor** disguise your face.   **usurped** (The suggestion is that Roderigo is not man enough to
have a beard of his own.)   334–335 **an answerable sequestration** a corresponding separation or estrangement.   336 **wills** carnal appetites.   337 **locusts** fruit of the carob tree (see
Matthew 3.4), or perhaps honeysuckle.   **coloquintida** colocynth or bitter apple, a purgative.
341 **Make** raise, collect.   **sanctimony** sacred ceremony.   342 **erring** wandering, vagabond,
unsteady.

clean out of the way.° Seek thou rather to be hanged in compassing°
thy joy than to be drowned and go without her.   345
RODERIGO. Wilt thou be fast° to my hopes if I depend on the issue?°
IAGO. Thou art sure of me. Go, make money. I have told thee often, and I
retell thee again and again, I hate the Moor. My cause is hearted;°thine
hath no less reason. Let us be conjunctive° in our revenge against him. If
thou canst cuckold him, thou dost thyself a pleasure, me a sport. There 350
There are many events in the womb of time which will be delivered.
Traverse,° go, provide thy money. We will have more of this tomor-
row. Adieu.
RODERIGO. Where shall we meet i' the morning?
IAGO. At my lodging.
RODERIGO. I'll be with thee betimes.°   [*He starts to leave.*] 355
IAGO. Go to, farewell.—Do you hear, Roderigo?
RODERIGO. What say you?
IAGO. No more of drowning, do you hear?
RODERIGO. I am changed.
IAGO. Go to, farewell. Put money enough in your purse.   360
RODERIGO. I'll sell all my land.   *Exit.*
IAGO. Thus do I ever make my fool my purse;
    For I mine own gained knowledge should profane
    If I would time expend with such a snipe°
    But for my sport and profit. I hate the Moor;   365
    And it is thought abroad° that twixt my sheets
    He's done my office.° I know not if't be true;
    But I, for mere suspicion in that kind,
    Will do as if for surety.° He holds me well;°
    The better shall my purpose work on him.   370
    Cassio's a proper° man. Let me see now:
    To get his place and to plume up° my will
    In double knavery—How, how?—Let's see:
    After some time, to abuse° Othello's ear
    That he° is too familiar with his wife.   375
    He hath a person and a smooth dispose°
    To be suspected, framed to make women false.
    The Moor is of a free° and open° nature,
    That thinks men honest that but seem to be so,
    And will as tenderly° be led by the nose   380
    As asses are.
    I have 't. It is engendered. Hell and night
    Must bring this monstrous birth to the world's light.

    [*Exit.*]

---

344 clean . . . way entirely unsuitable as a course of action.   **compassing** encompassing, embracing.   **346 fast** true.   **issue** (successful) outcome.   **348 hearted** fixed in the heart, heartfelt.   **349 conjunctive** united.   **351 Traverse** (A military marching term.)   **355 betimes**
early.   **364 snipe** woodcock, i.e., fool.   **366 it is thought abroad** it is rumored.   **367 my office** i.e., my sexual function as husband.   **369 do . . . surety** act as if on certain knowledge.
holds me well regards me favorably.   **371 proper** handsome.   **372 plume up** put a feather
in the cap of, i.e., glorify, gratify.   **374 abuse** deceive.   **375 he** i.e., Cassio.   **376 dispose** disposition.   **378 free** frank, generous.   **open** unsuspicious.   **380 tenderly** readily.

2.1 *Enter* MONTANO *and two* GENTLEMEN.

MONTANO. What from the cape can you discern at sea?
FIRST GENTLEMAN. Nothing at all. It is a high-wrought flood.°
    I cannot, twixt the heaven and the main,°
    Descry a sail.
MONTANO. Methinks the wind hath spoke aloud at land;   5
    A fuller blast ne'er shook our battlements.
    If it hath ruffianed° so upon the sea,
    What ribs of oak, when mountains° melt on them,
    Can hold the mortise?° What shall we hear of this?
SECOND GENTLEMAN. A segregation° of the Turkish fleet.   10
    For do but stand upon the foaming shore,
    The chidden° billow seems to pelt the clouds;
    The wind-shaked surge, with high and monstrous mane,°
    Seems to cast water on the burning Bear°
    And quench the guards of th' ever-fixèd pole.   15
    I never did like molestation° view
    On the enchafèd° flood.
MONTANO. If that° the Turkish fleet
    Be not ensheltered and embayed,° they are drowned;
    It is impossible to bear ir out.°   20

    Enter a [THIRD] GENTLEMAN.

THIRD GENTLEMAN. News, lads! Our wars are done.
    The desperate tempest hath so banged the Turks
    That their designment° halts.° A noble ship of Venice
    Hath seen a grievous wreck° and sufferance°
    On most part of their fleet.   25
MONTANO. How? Is this true?
THIRD GENTLEMAN. The ship is here put in,
    A Veronesa;° Michael Cassio,
    Lieutenant to the warlike Moor Othello,
    Is come on shore; the Moor himself at sea,   30
    And is in full commission here for Cyprus.

2.1 Location: A seaport in Cyprus, an open place near the quay. **2 high-wrought
flood** very agitated sea.   **3 main** ocean (also at line 41).   **7 ruffianed** raged.   **8 mountains**
i.e., of water.   **9 hold the mortise** hold their joints together. (A *mortise* is the socket hollowed
out in fitting timbers.)   **10 segregation** dispersal.   **12 chidden** i.e., rebuked, repelled (by the
shore), and thus shot into the air.   **13 monstrous mane** (The surf is like the mane of a wild
beast.)   **14 the burning Bear** i.e., the constellation Ursa Minor or the Little Bear, which includes the polestar (and hence regarded as the *guards of th' ever-fixèd pole* in the next line;
sometimes the term *guards* is applied to the two "pointers" of the Big Bear or Dipper, which
may be intended here).   **16 like molestation** comparable disturbance.   **17 enchafèd** angry.
18 If that if.   **19 embayed** sheltered by a bay.   **20 bear it out** survive, weather the storm.
23 designment design, enterprise.   **halts** is lame.   **24 wreck** shipwreck.   **sufferance** damage, disaster.   **28 Veronesa** i.e., fitted out in Verona for Venetian service, or possibly *Verennessa*
(the Folio spelling), i.e., *verrinessa*, a cutter (from *verrinare*, "to cut through").

MONTANO. I am glad on 't. 'Tis a worthy governor.

THIRD GENTLEMAN. But this same Cassio, though he speak of comfort
    Touching the Turkish loss, yet he looks sadly°
    And prays the Moor be safe, for they were parted   35
    With foul and violent tempest.

MONTANO.   Pray heaven he be,
    For I have served him, and the man commands
    Like a full° soldier. Let's to the seaside, ho!
    As well to see the vessel that's come in
    As to throw out our eyes for brave Othello,   40
    Even till we make the main and th' aerial blue°
    An indistinct regard.°

THIRD GENTLEMAN.   Come, let's do so,
    For every minute is expentancy°
    Of more arrivance.°

    Enter CASSIO.

CASSIO. Thanks, you the valiant of this warlike isle,   45
    That so approve° the Moor! O, let the heavens
    Give him defense against the elements,
    For I have lost him on a dangerous sea.

MONTANO. Is he well shipped?

CASSIO. His bark is stoutly timbered, and his pilot   50
    Of very expert and approved allowance;°
    Therefore my hopes, not surfeited to death,°
    Stand in bold cure.°

[*A cry*] *within:*   "A sail, a sail, a sail!"

CASSIO. What noise?

A GENTLEMAN. The town is empty. On the brow o' the sea°   55
    Stand ranks of people, and they cry "A sail!"

CASSIO. My hopes do shape him for° the governor.

    [*A shot within.*]

SECOND GENTLEMAN. They do discharge their shot of courtesy;°
    Our friends at least.

CASSIO.   I pray you, sir, go forth,
    And give us truth who 'tis that is arrived.   60

SECOND GENTLEMAN. I shall.   *Exit.*

MONTANO. But, good Lieutenant, is your general wived?

CASSIO. Most fortunately. He hath achieved a maid
    That paragons° description and wild fame,°
    One that excels the quirks° of blazoning° pens,   65
    And in th' essential vesture of creation
    Does tire the enginer.°

---

34 sadly gravely. **38 full** perfect. **41 the main . . . blue** the sea and the sky. **42 An indistinct regard** indistinguishable in our view. **43 is expectancy** gives expectations. **44 arrivance** arrival. **46 approve** admire, honor. **51 approved allowance** tested reputation.
52 surfeited to death i.e., overextended, worn thin through repeated application or delayed fulfillment. **53 in bold cure** in strong hopes of fulfillment. **55 brow o' the sea** cliff-edge.
57 My . . . for I hope it is. **58 discharge . . . courtesy** fire a salute in token of respect and courtesy. **64 paragons** surpasses. **wild fame** extravagant report. **65 quirks** witty conceits. **blazoning** setting forth as though in heraldic language. **66–67 in . . . enginer** in her real, God-given, beauty, (she) defeats any attempt to praise her. **enginer** engineer, i.e., poet, one who devises.

Enter [SECOND] GENTLEMAN.°

                               How now? Who has put in?°

SECOND GENTLEMAN. 'Tis one Iago, ancient to the General.

CASSIO. He's had most favorable and happy speed.
> Tempests themselves, high seas, and howling winds,   70
> The guttered° rocks and congregated sands—
> Traitors ensteeped° to clog the guiltless keel—
> As° having sense of beauty, do omit°
> Their mortal° natures, letting go safely by
> The divine Desdemona.

MONTANO.   What is she?   75

CASSIO. She that I spake of, our great captain's captain,
> Left in the conduct of the bold Iago,
> Whose footing° here anticipates our thoughts
> A sennight's° speed. Great Jove, Othello guard,
> And swell his sail with thine own powerful breath,   80
> That he may bless this bay with his tall° ship,
> Make love's quick pants in Desdemona's arms,
> Give renewed fire to our extinct spirits,
> And bring all Cyprus comfort!

Enter DESDEMONA, IAGO, RODERIGO, *and* EMILIA.

                               O, behold,
> The riches of the ship is come on shore!   85
> You men of Cyprus, let her have your knees.

[*The gentlemen make curtsy to* DESDEMONA.]

> Hail to thee, lady! And the grace of heaven
> Before, behind thee, and on every hand
> Enwheel thee round!

DESDEMONA.   I thank you, valiant Cassio.
> What tidings can you tell me of my lord?   90

CASSIO. He is not yet arrived, nor know I aught
> But that he's well and will be shortly here.

DESDEMONA. O, but I fear—How lost you company?

CASSIO. The great contention of the sea and skies
> Parted our fellowship.

(*Within*) "A sail, a sail" [*A shot.*]
                            But hark. A sail!   95

SECOND GENTLEMAN. They give their greeting to the citadel.
> This likewise is a friend.

---

s.d. **Second Gentleman** (So identified in the Quarto text here and in lines 58, 61, 68, and 96; the Folio calls him a gentleman.)   **67 put in** i.e., to harbor.   **71 guttered** jagged, trenched.   **72 ensteeped** lying under water.   **73 As** as if.   **omit** forbear to exercise.   **74 mortal** deadly.   **78 footing** landing.   **79 sennight's** week's.   **81 tall** splendid, gallant.

CASSIO.   See for the news.

[*Exit* SECOND GENTLEMAN.]

    Good Ancient, you are welcome. [*Kissing* EMILIA.] Welcome, mistress.
    Let it not gall your patience, good Iago,
    That I extend° my manners; 'tis my breeding°   100
    That gives me this bold show of courtesy.
IAGO. Sir, would she give you so much of her lips
    As of her tongue she oft bestows on me,
    You would have enough.
DESDEMONA. Alas, she has no speech!°   105
IAGO. In faith, too much.
    I find it still,° when I have list° to sleep.
    Marry, before your ladyship, I grant,
    She puts her tongue a little in her heart
    And chides with thinking.°
EMILIA.   You have little cause to say so.   110
IAGO. Come on, come on. You are pictures out of doors,°
    Bells° in your parlors, wildcats in your kitchens,°
    Saints° in your injuries, devils being offended,
    Players° in your huswifery,° and huswives° in your beds.
DESDEMONA. O, fie upon thee, slanderer!   115
IAGO. Nay, it is true, or else I am a Turk.°
    You rise to play, and go to bed to work.
EMILIA. You shall not write my praise.
IAGO.   No, let me not.
DESDEMONA. What wouldst write of me, if thou shouldst praise me?
IAGO. O, gentle lady, do not put me to 't,   120
    For I am nothing if not critical.°
DESDEMONA. Come on, essay.°—There's one gone to the harbor?
IAGO. Ay, madam.
DESDEMONA. I am not merry, but I do beguile
    The thing I am° by seeming otherwise.   125
    Come, how wouldst thou praise me?
IAGO. I am about it, but indeed my invention
    Comes from my pate as birdlime° does from frieze°—
    It plucks out brains and all. But my Muse labors,°
    And thus she is delivered: 130

---

100 extend give scope to.   **breeding** training in the niceties of etiquette.   **105 she has no speech** i.e., she's not a chatterbox, as you allege.   **107 still** always.   **list** desire.   **110 with thinking** i.e., in her thoughts only.   **111 pictures out of doors** i.e., silent and well behaved in public.   **112 Bells** i.e., jangling, noisy, and brazen.   **in your kitchens** i.e., in domestic affairs. (Ladies would not do the cooking.)   **113 Saints** martyrs.   **114 Players** idlers, triflers, or deceivers.   **huswifery** housekeeping.   **huswives** hussies (i.e., women are "busy" in bed, or unduly thrifty in dispensing sexual favors).   **116 a Turk** an infidel, not to be believed.   **121 critical** censorious.   **122 essay** try.   **125 The thing I am** i.e., my anxious self.   **128 birdlime** sticky substance used to catch small birds.   **frieze** coarse woolen cloth.   **129 labors** (1) exerts herself (2) prepares to deliver a child (with a following pun on *delivered* in line 130).

If she be fair and wise, fairness and wit,
The one's for use, the other useth it.°
DESDEMONA. Well praised! How if she be black° and witty?
IAGO. If she be black, and thereto have a wit,
She'll find a white° that shall her blackness fit.°   135
DESDEMONA. Worse and worse.
EMILIA.   How if fair and foolish?
IAGO. She never yet was foolish that was fair,
For even her folly° helped her to an heir.°
DESDEMONA. These are old fond° paradoxes to make fools laugh i' th' ale-
house. What miserable praise hast thou for her that's foul and foolish?   140
IAGO. There's none so foul° and foolish thereunto,°
But does foul° pranks which fair and wise ones do.
DESDEMONA. O heavy ignorance! Thou praisest the worst best. But what
praise couldst thou bestow on a deserving woman indeed, one that,
in the authority of her merit, did justly put on the vouch° of very   145
malice itself?
IAGO. She that was ever fair, and never proud,
Had tongue at will, and yet was never loud,
Never lacked gold and yet went never gay,°
Fled from her wish, and yet said, "Now I may,"°
She that being angered, her revenge being nigh,   150
Bade her wrong stay° and her displeasure fly,
She that in wisdom never was so frail
To change the cod's head for the salmon's tail,°
She that could think and ne'er disclose her mind,
See suitors following and not look behind,   155
She was a wight, if ever such wight were—
DESDEMONA. To do what?
IAGO. To suckle fools° and chronicle small beer.°
DESDEMONA. O most lame and impotent conclusion! Do not learn of
him, Emilia, though he be thy husband. How say you, Cassio? Is he   160
not a most profane° and liberal° counselor?
CASSIO. He speaks home,° madam. You may relish° him more in° the sol-
dier than in the scholar.

[CASSIO *and* DESDEMONA *stand together, conversing intimately.*]

---

132 **The one's . . . it** i.e., her cleverness will make use of her beauty.   133 **black** dark-
complexioned, brunette.   135 **a white** a fair person (with word-play on "wight," a person).
fit (with sexual suggestion of mating).   138 **folly** (with added meaning of "lechery, wantonness").   **to an heir** i.e., to bear a child.   139 **fond** foolish.   141 **foul** ugly.   **thereunto** in
addition.   142 **foul** sluttish.   145 **put . . . vouch** compel the approval.   148 **gay** extravagantly clothed.   149 **Fled . . . may** avoided temptation where the choice was hers.   151
Bade . . . stay i.e., resolved to put up with her injury patiently.   153 **To . . . tail** i.e., to exchange a lackluster husband for a sexy lover (?). (*Cod's head* is slang for "penis," and *tail* for
"pudendum.")   158 **suckle fools** breastfeed babies.   **chronicle small beer** i.e., keep petty
household accounts, keep track of trivial matters.   161 **profane** irreverent, ribald.   **liberal**
licentious, free-spoken.   162 **home** right to the target. (A term from fencing.)   **relish** appreciate.   **in** in the character of.

IAGO [*aside*].   He takes her by the palm. Ay, well said,° whisper. With as
    little a web as this will I ensnare as great a fly as Cassio. Ay, smile   165
    upon her, do; I will gyve° thee in thine own courtship.° You say
    true;° 'tis so, indeed. If such tricks as these strip you out of your lieu-
    tenantry, it had been better you had not kissed your three fingers so
    oft, which now again you are most apt to play the sir° in. Very good;
    well kissed! An excellent courtesy! 'Tis so, indeed. Yet again your
    fingers to your lips? Would they were clyster pipes° for your sake!   170
    [*Trumpet within.*] The Moor! I know his trumpet.
CASSIO.   'Tis truly so.
DESDEMONA.   Let's meet him and receive him.
CASSIO.   Lo, where he comes!

    Enter OTHELLO *and attendants.*

OTHELLO.   O my fair warrior!
DESDEMONA.   My dear Othello!   175
OTHELLO.   It gives me wonder great as my content
    To see you here before me. O my soul's joy,
    If after every tempest come such calms,
    May the winds blow till they have wakened death,
    And let the laboring bark climb hills of seas   180
    Olympus-high, and duck again as low
    As hell's from heaven! If it were now to die,
    'Twere now to be most happy, for I fear
    My soul hath her content so absolute
    That not another comfort like to this   185
    Succeeds in unknown fate.°
DESDEMONA.   The heavens forbid
    But that our loves and comforts should increase
    Even as our days do grow!
OTHELLO.   Amen to that, sweet powers!
    I cannot speak enough of this content.   190
    It stops me here; it is too much of joy.
    And this, and this, the greatest discords be

    [*They kiss.*]°
    That e'er our hearts shall make!
IAGO.   [*aside*] O, you are well tuned now!
    But I'll set down° the pegs that make this music,   195
    As honest as I am.°
OTHELLO.   Come, let us to the castle.
    News, friends! Our wars are done, the Turks are drowned.
    How does my old acquaintance of this isle?—
    Honey, you shall be well desired° in Cyprus;   200

---

164 well said well done.   **166 gyve** fetter, shackle.   **courtship** courtesy, show of courtly
manners.   **You say true** i.e., that's right, go ahead.   **169 the sir** i.e., fine gentleman.   **170
clyster pipes** tubes used for enemas and douches.   **186 Succeeds . . . fate** i.e., can follow in
the unknown future.   **s.d. They kiss** (The direction is from the Quarto.)   **195 set down**
loosen (and hence untune the instrument).   **196 As . . . I am** for all my supposed honesty.
200 desired welcomed.

I have found great love amongst them. O my sweet,
I prattle out of fashion,° and I dote
In mine own comforts.—I prithee, good Iago,
Go to the bay and disembark my coffers.°
Bring thou the master° to the citadel; 205
He is a good one, and his worthiness
Does challenge° much respect.—Come, Desdemona.—
Once more, well met at Cyprus!

Exeunt OTHELLO *and* DESDEMONA [*and all but* IAGO *and* RODERIGO].

IAGO. [*to an attendant*] Do thou meet me presently at the harbor. [*To*
RODERIGO.] Come hither. If thou be'st valiant—as, they say, base men° 210
being in love have then a nobility in their natures more than is native
to them—list° me. The Lieutenant tonight watches on the court of
guard.° First, I must tell thee this: Desdemona is directly in love
with him.

RODERIGO. With him? Why, 'tis not possible. 215

IAGO. Lay thy finger thus,° and let thy soul be instructed. Mark me with
what violence she first loved the Moor, but° for bragging and
telling her fantastical lies. To love him still for prating? Let not thy discreet heart think it. Her eye must be fed; and what delight shall she
have to look on the devil? When the blood is made dull with the act 220
of sport,° there should be, again to inflame it and to give satiety a
fresh appetite, loveliness in favor,° sympathy° in years, manners, and
beauties—all which the Moor is defective in. Now, for want of these
required conveniences,° her delicate tenderness will find itself
abused,° begin to heave the gorge,° disrelish and abhor the Moor. 225
Very nature° will instruct her in it and compel her to some second choice. Now, sir, this granted—as it is a most pregnant° and un-
forced position—who stands so eminent in the degree of° this fortune as Cassio does? A knave very voluble,° no further conscionable°
than in putting on the mere form of civil and humane° seeming for 230
the better compassing of his salt° and most hidden loose affection.°
Why, none, why, none. A slipper° and subtle knave, a finder out of
occasions, that has an eye can stamp° and counterfeit advantages,°
though true advantage never present itself; a devilish knave. Besides,
the knave is handsome, young, and hath all those requisites in him that 235
folly° and green° minds look after. A pestilent complete knave, and the
woman hath found him° already.

---

202 **out of fashion** irrelevantly, incoherently (?). 204 **coffers** chests, baggage. 205 **master**
ship's captain. 207 **challenge** lay claim to, deserve. 210 **base men** even lowly born men.
211 **list** listen to. 212 **court of guard** guardhouse. (Cassio is in charge of the watch.) 215
thus i.e., on your lips. 216 **but** only. 219 **the act of sport** sex. 220 **favor** appearance.
sympathy correspondence, similarity. 222 **required conveniences** things conducive to sexual compatibility. 223 **abused** cheated, revolted. **heave the gorge** experience nausea.
223–224 **Very nature** her very instincts. 225 **pregnant** evident, cogent. 226 **in . . . of** as
next in line for. 227 **voluble** facile, glib. **conscionable** conscientious, conscience-bound.
228 **humane** polite, courteous. **salt** licentious. 229 **affection** passion. **slipper** slippery.
230 **an eye can stamp** an eye that can coin, create. 231 **advantages** favorable opportunities.
233 **folly** wantonness. **green** immature. 234 **found him** sized him up, perceived his intent.

RODERIGO. I cannot believe that in her. She's full of most blessed condition.°
IAGO. Blessed fig's end!° The wine she drinks is made of grapes. If she had
       been blessed, she would never have loved the Moor. Blessed pud-   240
       ding!° Didst thou not see her paddle with the palm of his hand?
       Didst not mark that?
RODERIGO. Yes, that I did; but that was but courtesy.
IAGO. Lechery, by this hand. An index° and obscure° prologue to the
       history of lust and foul thoughts. They met so near with their lips
       that their breaths embraced together. Villainous thoughts, Roderigo!
       When these mutualities° so marshal the way, hard at hand° comes the 245
       master and main exercise, th' incorporate° conclusion. Pish! But, sir,
       be you ruled by me. I have brought you from Venice. Watch you°
       tonight; for the command, I'll lay 't upon you.° Cassio knows you not.
       I'll not be far from you. Do you find some occasion to anger Cassio, either
       by speaking too loud, or tainting° his discipline, or from what other   250
       course you please, which the time shall more favorably minister.°
RODERIGO. Well.
IAGO. Sir, he's rash and very sudden in choler,° and haply° may strike at
       you. Provoke him that he may, for even out of that will I cause these
       of Cyprus to mutiny,° whose qualification° shall come into no true
       taste° again but by the displanting of Cassio. So shall you have a   255
       shorter journey to your desires by the means I shall then have to pre-
       fer° them, and the impediment most profitably removed, without the
       the which there were no expectation of our prosperity.
RODERIGO. I will do this, if you can bring it to any opportunity.
IAGO. I warrant° thee. Meet me by and by° at the citadel. I must fetch   260
       his necessaries ashore. Farewell.
RODERIGO. Adieu.   *Exit.*
IAGO. That Cassio loves her, I do well believe 't;
       That she loves him, 'tis apt° and of great credit.°
       The Moor, howbeit that I endure him not,   265
       Is of a constant, loving, noble nature,
       And I dare think he'll prove to Desdemona
       A most dear husband. Now, I do love her, too,
       Not out of absolute lust—though peradventure
       I stand accountant° for as great a sin—   270
       But partly led to diet° my revenge
       For that I do suspect the lusty Moor
       Hath leaped into my seat, the thought whereof
       Doth, like a poisonous mineral, gnaw my innards;
       And nothing can or shall content my soul   275

---

235 condition disposition.   **236 fig's end** (See 1.3.316 for the vulgar gesture of the fig.)
237 pudding sausage.   **240 index** table of contents.   **obscure** (i.e., the *lust and foul
thoughts* in line 241 are secret, hidden from view.)   **243 mutualities** exchanges, intimacies.
hard at hand closely following.   **244 incorporate** carnal.   **245 Watch you** stand watch.
245–246 for the command . . . you I'll arrange for you to be appointed, given orders.   **247
tainting** disparaging.   **249 minister** provide.   **251 choler** wrath.   **haply** perhaps.   **253
mutiny** riot.   **qualification** appeasement.   **true taste** i.e., acceptable state.   **255 prefer** advance.   **259 warrant** assure.   **by and by** immediately.   **263 apt** probable.   **credit** credibil-
ity.   **269 accountant** accountable.   **270 diet** feed.

Till I am evened with him, wife for wife,
Or failing so, yet that I put the Moor
At least into a jealousy so strong
That judgment cannot cure. Which thing to do,
If this poor trash of Venice, whom I trace°   280
For° his quick hunting, stand the putting on,°
I'll have our Michael Cassio on the hip,°
Abuse° him to the Moor in the rank garb—°
For I fear Cassio with my nightcap° too—
Make the Moor thank me, love me, and reward me   285
For making him egregiously an ass
And practicing upon° his peace and quiet
Even to madness. 'Tis here, but yet confused.
Knavery's plain face is never seen till used.   *Exit.*

2.2 *Enter* OTHELLO's HERALD *with a proclamation.*

HERALD. It is Othello's pleasure, our noble and valiant general, that, upon
certain tidings now arrived, importing the mere perdition° of the
Turkish fleet, every man put himself into triumph:° some to dance,
some to make bonfires, each man to what sport and revels his ad-
diction° leads him. For, besides these beneficial news, it is the cele-   5
bration of his nuptial. So much was his pleasure should be proclaimed. All offices° are open, and there is full liberty of feasting
from this present hour of five till the bell have told eleven. Heaven
bless the isle of Cyprus and our noble general Othello!

Exit.

2.3 *Enter* OTHELLO, DESDEMONA, CASSIO, *and attendants.*

OTHELLO. Good Michael, look you to the guard tonight.
Let's teach ourselves that honorable stop°
Not to outsport° discretion.
CASSIO.   Iago hath direction what to do,
But nothwithstanding, with my personal eye   5
Will I look to 't.

---

280 trace i.e., train, or follow (?), or perhaps *trash*, a hunting term, meaning to put weights on a
hunting dog in order to slow him down.   **281 For** to make more eager.   **stand . . . on** respond properly when I incite him to quarrel.   **282 on the hip** at my mercy, where I can throw
him. (A wrestling term.)   **283 Abuse** slander.   **rank garb** coarse manner, gross fashion.   **284
with my nightcap** i.e., as a rival in my bed, as one who gives me cuckold's horns.   **287 practicing upon** plotting against.   **2.2 Location: Cyprus, a street.**   **2 mere perdition** complete destruction.   **3 triumph** public celebration.   **4 addiction** inclination.   **6 offices**
rooms where food and drink are kept.   **2.3 Location: Cyprus, the citadel.**   **2 stop** restraint.
3 outsport celebrate beyond the bounds of.

OTHELLO.   Iago is most honest.
Michael, good night. Tomorrow with your earliest°
Let me have speech with you. [*To Desdemona.*]
                              Come, my dear love,
The purchase made, the fruits are to ensue;
That profit's yet to come 'tween me and you.°—   10
Good night.

Exit [OTHELLO, *with* DESDEMONA *and attendants*].

Enter IAGO.

CASSIO. Welcome, Iago. We must to the watch.
IAGO. Not this hour,° Lieutenant; 'tis not yet ten o' the clock. Our general
    cast° us thus early for the love of his Desdemona; who° let us not
    therefore blame. He hath not yet made wanton the night with her,
    and she is sport for Jove.   15
CASSIO. She's a most exquisite lady.
IAGO. And, I'll warrant her, full of game.
CASSIO. Indeed, she's a most fresh and delicate creature.
IAGO. What an eye she has! Methinks it sounds a parley° to provocation.
CASSIO. An inviting eye, and yet methinks right modest.   20
IAGO. And when she speaks, is it not an alarum° to love?
CASSIO. She is indeed perfection.
IAGO. Well, happiness to their sheets! Come, Lieutenant, I have a stoup°
    of wine, and here without° are a brace° of Cyprus gallants that
    would fain have a measure° to the health of the black Othello.   25
CASSIO. Not tonight, good Iago. I have very poor and unhappy brains for
    drinking. I could well wish courtesy would invent some other cus-
    tom of entertainment.
IAGO. O, they are our friends. But one cup! I'll drink for you.°
CASSIO. I have drunk but one cup tonight, and that was craftily quali-
    fied° too, and behold what innovation° it makes here.° I am un-   30
    fortunate in the infirmity and dare not task my weakness with any
    more.
IAGO. What, man? 'Tis a night of revels. The gallants desire it.
CASSIO. Where are they?
IAGO. Here at the door. I pray you, call them in.
CASSIO. I'll do 't, but it dislikes me.°   *Exit.*   35
IAGO. If I can fasten but one cup upon him,
    With that which he hath drunk tonight already,
    He'll be as full of quarrel and offense°

---

7 with your earliest at your earliest convenience.   **9–10 The purchase . . . you** i.e., though
married, we haven't yet consummated our love.   **13 Not this hour** not for an hour yet.   **cast**
dismissed.   **14 who** i.e., Othello.   **19 sounds a parley** calls for a conference, issues an invitation.   **21 alarum** signal calling men to arms (continuing the military metaphor of *parley*, line
19).   **23 stoup** measure of liquor, two quarts.   **24 without** outside.   **brace** pair.   **24–25
fain have a measure** gladly drink a toast.   **28 for you** in your place. (Iago will do the steady
drinking to keep the gallants company while Cassio has only one cup.)   **29 qualified** diluted.
30 innovation disturbance, insurrection.   **here** i.e., in my head.   **35 it dislikes me** i.e., I'm
reluctant.   **38 offense** readiness to take offense.

As my young mistress' dog. Now, my sick fool Roderigo,
Whom love hath turned almost the wrong side out,   40
To Desdemona hath tonight caroused°
Potations pottle-deep;° and he's to watch.°
Three lads of Cyprus—noble swelling° spirits,
That hold their honors in a wary distance,°
The very elements° of this warlike isle—   45
Have I tonight flustered with flowing cups,
And they watch° too. Now, 'mongst this flock of drunkards
Am I to put Cassio in some action
That may offend the isle.—But here they come.

Enter CASSIO, MONTANO, *and* GENTLEMEN; [*servants following with wine*].

If consequence do but approve my dream,°   50
My boat sails freely both with wind and stream.°
CASSIO. 'Fore God, they have given me a rouse° already.
MONTANO. Good faith, a little one; not past a pint, as I am a solider.
IAGO. Some wine, ho! [*He sings.*]
          "And let me the cannikin° clink, clink,   55
          And let me the cannikin clink.
          A soldier's a man,
          O, man's life's but a span;°
          Why, then, let a soldier drink."

Some wine, boys!   60
CASSIO. 'Fore God, an excellent song.
IAGO. I learned it in England, where indeed they are most potent in pot-
     ting.° Your Dane, your German, and your swag-bellied Hollander—
     drink, ho!— are nothing to your English.
CASSIO. Is your Englishman so exquisite in his drinking?   65
IAGO. Why, he drinks you,° with facility, your Dane° dead drunk; he sweats
     not° to overthrow your Almain;° he gives your Hollander a vomit ere
     the next pottle can be filled.
CASSIO. To the health of our general!
MONTANO. I am for it, Lieutenant, and I'll do you justice.°   70
IAGO. O sweet England! [*He sings.*]

          "King Stephen was and-a worthy peer,
          His breeches cost him but a crown;
          He held them sixpence all too dear,
          With that he called the tailor lown.°   75

---

41 caroused drunk off.   **42 pottle-deep** to the bottom of the tankard.   **watch** stand watch.
43 swelling proud.   **44 hold . . . distance** i.e., are extremely sensitive of their honor.   **45
very elements** typical sort.   **47 watch** are members of the guard.   **50 If . . . dream** if subsequent events will only substantiate my scheme.   **51 stream** current.   **52 rouse** full draft of
liquor.   **55 cannikin** small drinking vessel.   **58 span** brief span of time. (Compare Psalm 39.6
as rendered in the 1928 Book of Common Prayer: "Thou hast made my days as it were a span
long.")   **62 potting** drinking.   **66 drinks you** drinks.   **your Dane** your typical Dane.
sweats not i.e., need not exert himself.   **67 Almain** German.   **70 I'll . . . justice** i.e., I'll drink
as much as you.   **75 lown** lout, rascal.

> He was a wight of high renown,
> And thou art but of low degree.
> 'Tis pride° that pulls the country down;
> Then take thy auld° cloak about thee."

Some wine, ho!   80

CASSIO. 'Fore God, this is a more exquisite song than the other.

IAGO. Will you hear 't again?

CASSIO. No, for I hold him to be unworthy of his place that does those
things. Well, God's above all; and there be souls must be saved, and
there be souls must not be saved.   85

IAGO. It's true, good Lieutenant.

CASSIO. For mine own part—no offense to the General, nor any man of
quality°—I hope to be saved.

IAGO. And so do I too, Lieutenant.

CASSIO. Ay, but, by your leave, not before me; the lieutenant is to be saved   90
before the ancient. Let's have no more of this; let's to our affairs.—
God forgive us our sins!—Gentlemen, let's look to our business. Do
not think, gentlemen, I am drunk. This is my ancient; this is my right
hand, and this is my left. I am not drunk now. I can stand well
enough, and speak well enough.   95

GENTLEMEN. Excellent, well.

CASSIO. Why, very well then; you must not think then that I am drunk.
Exit.

MONTANO. To th' platform, masters. Come, let's set the watch.°

[*Exeunt* GENTLEMEN.]

IAGO. You see this fellow that is gone before.
He's a soldier fit to stand by Caesar   100
And give direction; and do but see his vice.
'Tis to his virtue a just equinox,°
The one as long as th' other. 'Tis a pity of him.
I fear the trust Othello puts him in,
On some odd time of his infirmity,   105
Will shake this island.

MONTANO.   But is he often thus?

IAGO. 'Tis evermore the prologue to his sleep.
He'll watch the horologe a double set,°
If drink rock not his cradle.

MONTANO.   It were well
The General were put in mind of it.   110
Perhaps he sees it not, or his good nature
Prizes the virtue that appears in Cassio
And looks not on his evils. Is not this true?

Enter RODERIGO.

---

78 pride i.e., extravagance in dress. **79 auld** old. **88 quality** rank. **97 set the watch**
mount the guard. **101 just equinox** counterpart. (Equinox is an equal length of days and
nights.) **107 watch . . . set** stay awake twice around the clock or *horologe.*

IAGO [*aside to him*]. How now, Roderigo?
    I pray you, after the Lieutenant; go.   [*Exit* RODERIGO.]   115
MONTANO. And 'tis great pity that the noble Moor
    Should hazard such a place as his own second
    With° one of an engaffed° infirmity.
    It were an honest action to say so
    To the Moor.
IAGO.   Not I, for this fair island.   120
    I do love Cassio well and would do much
    To cure him of this evil.   [*Cry within:* "Help! Help!"]
                But, hark! What noise?

    Enter CASSIO, *pursuing°* RODERIGO.

CASSIO. Zounds, you rogue! You rascal!
MONTANO. What's the matter, Lieutenant?
CASSIO. A knave teach me my duty? I'll beat the knave into a
    twiggen° bottle.   125
RODERIGO. Beat me?
CASSIO. Dost thou prate, rogue?   [*He strikes* RODERIGO.]
MONTANO. Nay, good Lieutenant. [*Restraining him.*] I pray you, sir,
    hold your hand.
CASSIO. Let me go, sir, or I'll knock you o'er the mazard.°
MONTANO. Come, come, you're drunk.   130
CASSIO. Drunk?   [*They fight.*]
IAGO [*aside to* RODERIGO]. Away, I say. Go out and cry a mutiny.°

    [*Exit* RODERIGO.]

    Nay, good Lieutenant—God's will, gentlemen—
    Help, ho!—Lieutenant—sir—Montano—sir—
    Help, masters!°—Here's a goodly watch indeed!   135

    [*A bell rings.*]°

    Who's that which rings the bell?—Diablo,° ho!
    The town will rise.° God's will, Lieutenant, hold!
    You'll be ashamed forever.

    Enter OTHELLO *and attendants* [*with weapons*].

OTHELLO. What is the matter here?
MONTANO.   Zounds, I bleed still.
    I am hurt to th' death. He dies! [*He thrusts at* CASSIO.]
OTHELLO.   Hold, for your lives!   140
IAGO. Hold, ho! Lieutenant—sir—Montano—gentlemen—
    Have you forgot all sense of place and duty?
    Hold! The General speaks to you. Hold, for shame!

117–118 hazard . . . With risk giving such an important position as his second in command to.
118 engraffed engrafted, inveterate.   **122 s.d. pursuing** (The Quarto text reads, "driving in.")
125 twiggen wicker-covered. (Cassio vows to assail Roderigo until his skin resembles wickerwork or until he has driven Roderigo through the holes in a wickerwork.)   **129 mazard** i.e.,
head. (Literally, a drinking vessel.)   **132 mutiny** riot.   **135 masters** sirs.   **s.d. A bell rings**
(This direction is from the Quarto, as are *Exit Roderigo* at line 114, *They fight* at line 130, and
with weapons at line 137.)   **136 Diablo** the devil.   **137 rise** grow riotous.

OTHELLO. Why, how now, ho! From whence ariseth this?
 Are we turned Turks, and to ourselves do that   145
 Which heaven hath forbid the Ottomites?°
 For Christian shame, put by this barbarous brawl!
 He that stirs next to carve for° his own rage
 Holds his soul light;° he dies upon his motion.°
 Silence that dreadful bell. It frights the isle   150
 From her propriety.° What is the matter, masters?
 Honest Iago, that looks dead with grieving,
 Speak. Who began this? On thy love, I charge thee.
IAGO. I do not know. Friends all but now, even now,
 In quarter° and in terms° like bride and groom   155
 Devesting them° for bed; and then, but now—
 As if some planet had unwitted men—
 Swords out, and tilting one at others' breasts
 In opposition bloody. I cannot speak°
 Any beginning to this peevish odds;°   160
 And would in action glorious I had lost
 Those legs that brought me to a part of it!
OTHELLO. How comes it, Michael, you are thus forgot?°
CASSIO. I pray you, pardon me. I cannot speak.
OTHELLO. Worthy Montano, you were wont be° civil;   165
 The gravity and stillness° of your youth
 The world hath noted, and your name is great
 In mouths of wisest censure.° What's the matter
 That you unlace° your reputation thus
 And spend your rich opinion° for the name   170
 Of a night-brawler? Give me answer to it.
MONTANO. Worthy Othello, I am hurt to danger.
 Your officer, Iago, can inform you—
 While I spare speech, which something° now offends° me—
 Of all that I do know; nor know I aught   175
 By me that's said or done amiss this night,
 Unless self-charity be sometimes a vice,
 And to defend ourselves it be a sin
 When violence assails us.
OTHELLO.   Now, by heaven,
 My blood° begins my safer guides° to rule,   180
 And passion, having my best judgment collied,°

145–146 to ourselves . . . Ottomites inflict on ourselves the harm that heaven has prevented the Turks from doing (by destroying their fleet). **148 carve for** i.e., indulge, satisfy with his sword. **149 Holds . . . light** i.e., places little value on his life. **upon his motion** if he moves. **151 propriety** proper state or condition. **155 In quarter** in friendly conduct, within bounds. **in terms** on good terms. **156 Devesting them** undressing themselves. **159 speak** explain. **160 peevish odds** childish quarrel. **163 are thus forgot** have forgotten yourself thus. **165 wont be** accustomed to be. **166 stillness** sobriety. **168 censure** judgment. **169 unlace** undo, lay open (as one might loose the strings of a purse containing reputation). **170 opinion** reputation. **174 something** somewhat. **offends** pains. **180 blood** passion (of anger). **guides** i.e., reason.

Essays° to lead the way. Zounds, if I stir,
Or do but lift this arm, the best of you
Shall sink in my rebuke. Give me to know
How this foul rout° began, who set it on;   185
And he that is approved in° this offense,
Though he had twinned with me, both at birth,
Shall lose me. What? In a town of° war
Yet wild, the people's hearts brim full of fear,
To manage° private and domestic quarrel?   190
In night, and on the court and guard of safety?°
'Tis monstrous. Iago, who began 't?

MONTANO [*to* IAGO]. If partially affined,° or leagued in office,°
Thou dost deliver more or less than truth,
Thou art no soldier.

IAGO.   Touch me not so near.   195
I had rather have this tongue cut from my mouth
Than it should do offense to Michael Cassio;
Yet, I persuade myself, to speak the truth
Shall nothing wrong him. Thus it is, General.
Montano and myself being in speech,   200
There comes a fellow crying out for help,
And Cassio following him with determined sword
To execute° upon him. Sir, this gentleman

[*indicating* MONTANO]

Steps in to Cassio and entreats his pause.°
Myself the crying fellow did pursue,   205
Lest by his clamor—as it so fell out—
The town might fall in fright. He, swift of foot,
Outran my purpose, and I returned, the rather°
For that I heard the clink of fall of swords
And Cassio high in oath, which till tonight   210
I ne'er might say before. When I came back—
For this was brief—I found them close together
At blow and thrust, even as again they were
When you yourself did part them.
More of this matter cannot I report.   215
But men are men; the best sometimes forget.°
Though Cassio did some little wrong to him,
As men in rage strike those that wish them best,°
Yet surely Cassio, I believe, received
From him that fled some strange indignity,   220
Which patience could not pass.°

---

181 collied darkened.   **182 Essays** undertakes.   **185 rout** riot.   **186 approved in** found
guilty of.   **188 town of** town garrisoned for.   **190 manage** undertake.   **191 on . . . safety** at
the main guardhouse or headquarters and on watch.   **193 partially affined** made partial by
some personal relationship.   **leagued in office** in league as fellow officers.   **203 execute**
give effect to (his anger).   **204 his pause** him to stop.   **208 rather** sooner.   **216 forget** forget themselves.   **218 those . . . best** i.e., even those who are well disposed.

OTHELLO.   I know, Iago,
  Thy honesty and love doth mince this matter,
  Making it light to Cassio. Cassio, I love thee,
  But nevermore be officer of mine.

Enter DESDEMONA, *attended.*

  Look if my gentle love be not raised up.   225
  I'll make thee an example.
DESDEMONA. What is the matter, dear?
OTHELLO.   All's well now, sweeting;
  Come away to bed. [*To* MONTANO.] Sir, for your hurts,
  Myself will be your surgeon.°—Lead him off.

[MONTANO *is led off.*]

  Iago, look with care about the town   230
  And silence those whom this vile brawl distracted.
  Come, Desdemona. 'Tis the soldiers' life
  To have their balmy slumbers waked with strife.

Exit [*with all but* IAGO *and* CASSIO].

IAGO. What, are you hurt, Lieutenant?
CASSIO. Ay, past all surgery.   235
IAGO. Marry, God forbid!
CASSIO. Reputation, reputation, reputation! O, I have lost my reputation! I
  have lost the immortal part of myself, and what remains is bestial. My
  reputation, Iago, my reputation!
IAGO. As I am an honest man, I thought you had received some bodily   240
  wound; there is more sense in that than in reputation. Reputation is
  an idle and   most false imposition,° oft got without merit and lost
  without deserving. You have lost no reputation at all, unless you repute yourself such a loser. What, man, there are more ways to recover°
  the General again. You are but now cast in his mood°—a punishment 245
  more in policy° than in malice, even so as one would beat his offense-
  less dog to affright an imperious lion.° Sue° to him again and he's yours.
CASSIO.   I will rather sue to be despised than to deceive so good a commander with so slight,° so drunken, and so indiscreet an officer.
  Drunk? And speak parrot?° And squabble? Swagger? Swear? And dis- 250
  course fustian with one's own shadow? O thou invisible spirit of
  wine, if thou hast no name to be known by, let us call thee devil!
IAGO. What was he that you followed with your sword? What had he
  done to you?
CASSIO. I know not.
IAGO. Is 't possible?   255

---

221 pass pass over, overlook.   **229 be your surgeon** i.e., make sure you receive medical attention.   **242 false imposition** thing artificially imposed and of no real value.   **244 recover**
regain favor with.   **245 cast in his mood** dismissed in a moment of anger.   **in policy** done
for expediency's sake and as a public gesture.   **246 would . . . lion** i.e., would make an example of a minor offender in order to deter more important and dangerous offenders.   **247 Sue**
petition.   **249 slight** worthless.   **249–250 speak parrot** talk nonsense, rant.

CASSIO. I remember a mass of things, but nothing distinctly; a quarrel, but
     nothing wherefore.° O God, that men should put an enemy in their
     mouths to steal away their brains! That we should, with joy, pleas-
     ance, revel, and applause° transform ourselves into beasts!

IAGO. Why, but you are now well enough. How came you thus recovered?   260

CASSIO. It hath pleased the devil drunkenness to give place to the devil
     wrath. One unperfectness shows me another, to make me frankly de-
     spise myself.

IAGO. Come, you are too severe a moraler.° As the time, the place, and
     the condition of this country stands, I could heartily wish this had
     not befallen; but since it is as it is, mend it for your own good.   265

CASSIO. I will ask him for my place again; he shall tell me I am a drunk-
     ard. Had I as many mouths as Hydra,° such an answer would stop
     them all. To be now a sensible man, by and by a fool, and presently a
     beast! O, strange! Every inordinate cup is unblessed, and the ingre-
     dient is a devil.

IAGO. Come, come, good wine is a good familiar creature, if it be well   270
     used. Exclaim no more against it. And, good Lieutenant, I think you
     think I love you.

CASSIO. I have well approved° it, sir. I drunk!

IAGO. You or any man living may be drunk at a time,° man. I'll tell you what
     you shall do. Our general's wife is not the general—I may say so in this
     respect, for that° he hath devoted and given up himself to the   275
     contemplation, mark, and denotement° of her parts° and graces.
     Confess yourself freely to her; importune her help to put you in your
     place again. She is of so free,° so kind, so apt, so blessed a disposi-
     tion, she holds it a vice in her goodness not to do more than she is
     requested. This broken joint between you and her husband entreat   280
     her to splinter;° and, my fortunes against any lay° worth naming,
     this crack of your love shall grow stronger than it was before.

CASSIO. You advise me well.

IAGO. I protest,° in the sincerity of love and honest kindness.

CASSIO. I think it freely;° and betimes in the morning I will beseech the vir- 285
     tuous Desdemona to undertake for me. I am desperate of my fortunes
     if they check° me here.

IAGO. You are in the right. Good night, Lieutenant. I must to the watch.

CASSIO. Good night, honest Iago.   *Exit* CASSIO.

IAGO. And what's he then that says I play the villain,   290
     When this advice is free° I give, and honest,
     Probal° to thinking, and indeed the course
     To win the Moor again? For 'tis most easy

---

257 **wherefore** why.   259 **applause** desire for applause.   263 **moraler** moralizer.   267
Hydra the Lernaean Hydra, a monster with many heads and the ability to grow two heads when
one was cut off, slain by Hercules as the second of his twelve labors.   273 **approved** proved.
274 **at a time** at one time or another.   275–276 **in . . . that** in view of this fact, that.
276–277 **mark, and denotement** (Both words mean "observation.")   277 **parts** qualities.
278 **free** generous.   281 **splinter** bind with splints.   **lay** stake, wager.   284 **protest** insist,
declare.   285 **freely** unreservedly.   287 **check** repulse.   291 **free** (1) free from guile (2)
freely given.   292 **Probal** probable, reasonable.

Th' inclining° Desdemona to subdue°
In any honest suit; she's framed as fruitful°   295
As the free elements.° And then for her
To win the Moor—were 't to renounce his baptism,
All seals and symbols of redeemèd sin—
His soul is so enfettered to her love
That she may make, unmake, do what she list,   300
Even as her appetite° shall play the god
With his weak function.° How am I then a villain,
To counsel Cassio to this parallel° course
Directly to his good? Divinity of hell!°
When devils will the blackest sins put on,°   305
They do suggest° at first with heavenly shows,
As I do now. For whiles this honest fool
Plies Desdemona to repair his fortune,
And she for him pleads stronger to the Moor,
I'll pour this pestilence into his ear,   310
That she repeals him° for her body's lust;
And by how much she strives to do him good,
She shall undo her credit with the Moor.
So will I turn her virtue into pitch,°
And out of her own goodness make the net   315
That shall enmesh them all.

Enter RODERIGO.

How now, Roderigo?
RODERIGO. I do follow here in the chase, not like a hound that hunts, but
one that fills up the cry.° My money is almost spent; I have been
tonight exceedingly well cudgeled; and I think the issue will
be I shall have so much° experience for my pains, and so, with no   320
money at all and a little more wit, return again to Venice.
IAGO. How poor are they that have not patience!
What wound did ever heal but by degrees?
Thou know'st we work by wit, and not by witchcraft,
And wit depends on dilatory time.   325
Does 't not go well? Cassio hath beaten thee,
And thou, by that small hurt, hast cashiered° Cassio.
Though other things grow fair against the sun,
Yet fruits that blossom first will first be ripe,°
Content thyself awhile. By the Mass, 'tis morning!   330

---

294 **inclining** favorably disposed.   **subdue** persuade.   295 **framed as fruitful** created as
generous.   296 **free elements** i.e., earth, air, fire, and water, unrestrained and spontaneous.
301 **her appetite** her desire, or, perhaps, his desire for her.   302 **function** exercise of faculties
(weakened by his fondness for her).   303 **parallel** corresponding to these facts and to his best
interests.   304 **Divinity of hell** inverted theology of hell (which seduces the soul to its
damnation).   305 **put on** further investigate.   306 **suggest** tempt.   311 **repeals him** attempts to get him restored.   314 **pitch** i.e., (1) foul blackness (2) a snaring substance.   318
fill up the cry merely takes part as one of the pack.   319 **so much** just so much and no more.
326 **cashiered** dismissed from service.   328–329 **Though . . . ripe** i.e., plans that are well
prepared and set expeditiously in motion will soonest ripen into success.

Pleasure and action make the hours seem short.
Retire thee; go where thou art billeted.
Away, I say! Thou shalt know more hereafter.
Nay, get thee gone.   *Exit* RODERIGO.
             Two things are to be done.
My wife must move° for Cassio to her mistress;   335
I'll set her on;
Myself the while to draw the Moor apart
And bring him jump° when he may Cassio find
Soliciting his wife. Ay, that's the way.
Dull not device° by coldness° and delay.   *Exit.*   340

3.1 *Enter* CASSIO [*and*] MUSICIANS.

CASSIO. Masters, play here—I will content your pains°—
    Something that's brief, and bid "Good morrow, General." [*They play.*]

    [*Enter*] CLOWN.

CASSIO. Why, masters, have your instruments been in Naples, that they
    speak 'i the nose° thus?
A MUSICIAN. How, sir, how?   5
CLOWN. Are these, I pray you, wind instruments?
A MUSICIAN. Ay, marry, are they, sir.
CLOWN. O, thereby hangs a tail.
A MUSICIAN. Whereby hangs a tale, sir?
CLOWN. Marry, sir, by many a wind instrument° that I know. But, masters,   10
    here's money for you. [*He gives money.*] And the General so likes
    your music that he desires you, for love's sake,° to make no more
    noise with it.
A MUSICIAN. Well, sir, we will not.
CLOWN. If you have any music that may not° be heard, to 't again; but, as
    they say, to hear music the General does not greatly care.   15
A MUSICIAN. We have none such, sir.
CLOWN. Then put up your pipes in your bag, for I'll away.° Go, vanish into
    air, away!   *Exeunt* MUSICIANS.
CASSIO. Dost thou hear, mine honest friend?
CASSIO. No, I hear not your honest friend; I hear you.   20
CASSIO. Prithee, keep up° thy quillets.° There's a poor piece of gold for thee.
    [*He gives money.*] If the gentle-woman that attends the General's

---

335 move plead. **338 jump** precisely. **340 device** plot. **coldness** lack of seal. **3.1**
Location: Before the chamber of Othello and Desdemona. **1 content your pains** reward your efforts. **3–4 speak i' the nose** (1) sound nasal (2) sound like one whose nose has
been attacked by syphilis. (Naples was popularly supposed to have a high incidence of venereal
disease.) **10 wind instrument** (With a joke on flatulence. The *tail*, line 8, that hangs nearby
the *wind instrument* suggests the penis.) **12 for love's sake** (1) out of friendship and affection (2) for the sake of lovemaking in Othello's marriage. **14 may not** cannot. **17 I'll away**
(Possibly a misprint, or a snatch of song?) **21 keep up** do not bring out, do not use. **quillets**
quibbles, puns.

wife be stirring, tell her there's one Cassio entreats her a little favor
of speech.° Wilt thou do this?

CLOWN. She is stirring, sir. If she will stir° hither, I shall seem° to notify   25
unto her.

CASSIO. Do, good my friend.   *Exit* CLOWN.

    Enter IAGO.

                        In happy time,° Iago.

IAGO. You have not been abed, then?

CASSIO. Why, no. The day had broke
Before we parted. I have made bold, Iago,
To send in to your wife. My suit to her   30
Is that she will to virtuous Desdemona
Procure me some access.

IAGO. I'll send her to you presently;
And I'll devise a means to draw the Moor
Out of the way, that your converse and business   35
May be more free.

CASSIO. I humbly thank you for 't.   *Exit* IAGO.
                       I never knew
A Florentine° more kind and honest.

    Enter EMILIA.

EMILIA. Good morrow, good Lieutenant. I am sorry
For your displeasure;° but all will sure be well.   40
The General and his wife are talking of it,
And she speaks for you stoutly.° The Moor replies
That he you hurt is of great fame° in Cyprus
And great affinity,° and that in wholesome wisdom
He might not but refuse you; but he protests° he loves you   45
And needs no other suitor but his likings
To take the safest occasion by the front°
To bring you in again.

CASSIO.   Yet I beseech you,
If you think fit, or that it may be done,
Give me advantage of some brief discourse   50
With Desdemona alone.

EMILIA. Pray you, come in.
                     I will bestow you where you shall have time
To speak your bosom° freely.

CASSIO. I am much bound to you.   [*Exeunt.*]

---

23 a little . . . speech the favor of a brief talk.   **25 stir** bestir herself (with a play on *stirring*, "rousing herself from rest").   **seem** deem it good, think fit.   **26 In happy time** i.e., well met. **38 Florentine** i.e., even a fellow Florentine. (Iago is a Venetian; Cassio is a Florentine.)   **30 displeasure** fall from favor.   **42 stoutly** spiritedly.   **43 fame** reputation, importance.   **44 affinity** kindred, family connection.   **45 protests** insists.   **47 occasion . . . front** opportunity by the forelock.   **53 bosom** inmost thoughts.

3.2 Enter OTHELLO, IAGO, and GENTLEMEN.

OTHELLO [*giving letters*]. These letters, give, Iago, to the pilot,
    And by him do my duties° to the Senate.
    That done, I will be walking on the works;°
    Repair° there to me.
IAGO.   Well, my good lord, I'll do 't.
OTHELLO. This fortification, gentlemen, shall we see 't?   5
GENTLEMEN. We'll wait upon° your lordship.   *Exeunt.*

3.3 Enter DESDEMONA, CASSIO, and EMILIA.

DESDEMONA. Be thou assured, good Cassio, I will do
    All my abilities in thy behalf.
EMILIA. Good madam, do. I warrant it grieves my husband
    As if the cause were his.
DESDEMONA. O, that's an honest fellow. Do not doubt, Cassio,   5
    But I will have my lord and you again
    As friendly as you were.
CASSIO.   Bounteous madam,
    Whatever shall become of Michael Cassio,
    He's never anything but your true servant.
DESDEMONA. I know 't. I thank you. You do love my lord;   10
    You have known him long, and be you well assured
    He shall in strangeness° stand no farther off
    Than in a politic° distance.
CASSIO.   Ay, but, lady,
    That policy may either last so long,
    Or feed upon such nice and waterish diet,°   15
    Or breed itself so out of circumstance,°
    That, I being absent and my place supplied,°
    My general will forget my love and service.
DESDEMONA. Do not doubt° that. Before Emilia here
    I give thee warrant° of thy place. Assure thee,   20
    If I do vow a friendship I'll perform it
    To the last article. My lord shall never rest.
    I'll watch him tame° and talk him out of patience;°
    His bed shall seem a school, his board° a shrift;°
    I'll intermingle everything he does   25

3.2 Location: The citadel.   2 do my duties convey my respects. **3 works** breastworks, for-
tifications. **4 Repair** return, come. **6 wait upon** attend. **3.3 Location: The garden of
the citadel. 12 strangeness** aloofness. **13 politic** required by wise policy. **15 Or . . .
diet** or sustain itself at length upon such trivial and meager technicalities. **16 breed . . . circumstances** continually renew itself so out of chance events, or yield so few chances for my
being pardoned. **17 supplied** filled by another person. **19 doubt** fear. **20 warrant** guarantee. **23 watch him tame** tame him by keeping him from sleeping. (A term from falconry.)
out of patience past his endurance. **24 board** dining table. **shrift** confessional.

With Cassio's suit. Therefore be merry, Cassio,
For thy solicitor° shall rather die
Than give thy cause away.°

Enter OTHELLO *and* IAGO [*at a distance*].

EMILIA. Madam, here comes my lord.

CASSIO. Madam, I'll take my leave.   30

DESDEMONA. Why, stay, and hear me speak.

CASSIO. Madam, not now. I am very ill at ease,
Unfit for mine own purposes.

DESDEMONA. Well, do your discretion.°   *Exit* CASSIO.

IAGO. Ha! I like not that.   35

OTHELLO. What dost thou say?

IAGO. Nothing, my lord; or if—I know not what.

OTHELLO. Was not that Cassio parted from my wife?

IAGO. Cassio, my lord? No, sure, I cannot think it,
That he would steal away so guiltylike,   40
Seeing you coming.

OTHELLO. I do believe 'twas he.

DESDEMONA. How now, my lord?
I have been talking with a suitor here,
A man that languishes in your displeasure.   45

OTHELLO. Who is 't you mean?

DESDEMONA. Why, your lieutenant, Cassio. Good my lord,
If I have any grace or power to move you,
His present reconciliation take;°
For if he be not one that truly loves you,   50
That errs in ignorance and not in cunning,°
I have no judgment in an honest face.
I prithee, call him back.

OTHELLO. Went he hence now?

DESDEMONA. Yes, faith, so humbled   55
That he hath left part of his grief with me
To suffer with him. Good love, call him back.

OTHELLO. Not now, sweet Desdemona. Some other time.

DESDEMONA. But shall 't be shortly?

OTHELLO. The sooner, sweet, for you.   60

DESDEMONA. Shall 't be tonight at supper?

OTHELLO. No, not tonight.

DESDEMONA. Tomorrow dinner,° then?

OTHELLO. I shall not dine at home.
I meet the captains at the citadel.   65

DESDEMONA. Why, then, tomorrow night, or Tuesday morn,
On Tuesday noon, or night, on Wednesday morn.
I prithee, name the time, but let it not
Exceed three days. In faith, he's penitent;
And yet his trespass, in our common reason°—   70

---

27 **solicitor** advocate. 28 **away** up. 34 **do your discretion** act according to your own discretion. 49 **His . . . take** let him be reconciled to you right away. 51 **in cunning** wittingly.
63 **dinner** (The noontime meal.) 70 **common reason** everyday judgments.

Save that, they say, the wars must make example
Out of her best°—is not almost° a fault
T' incure a private check.° When shall he come?
Tell me, Othello. I wonder in my soul
What you would ask me that I should deny,   75
Or stand so mammering on.° What? Michael Cassio,
That came a-wooing with you, and so many a time,
When I have spoke of you dispraisingly,
Hath ta'en your part—to have so much to do
To bring him in!° By 'r Lady, I could do much—   80
OTHELLO.   Prithee, no more. Let him come when he will;
     I will deny thee nothing.
DESDEMONA.   Why, this is not a boon.
     'Tis as I should entreat you wear your gloves,
     Or feed on nourishing dishes, or keep you warm,   85
     Or sue to you to do a peculiar° profit
     To your own person. Nay, when I have a suit
     Wherein I mean to touch° your love indeed,
     It shall be full of poise° and difficult weight,
     And fearful to be granted.   90
OTHELLO.   I will deny thee nothing.
     Whereon,° I beseech thee, grant me this,
     To leave me but a little to myself.
DESDEMONA.   Shall I deny you? No. Farewell, my lord.
OTHELLO.   Farewell, my Desdemona. I'll come to thee straight.°   95
DESDEMONA.   Emilia, come—Be as your fancies° teach you;
     Whate'er you be, I am obedient.   *Exit [with* EMILIA].
OTHELLO.   Excellent wretch!° Perdition catch my soul
     But I do love thee! And when I love thee not,
     Chaos is come again.°   100
IAGO.   My noble lord—
OTHELLO.   What dost thou say, Iago?
IAGO.   Did Michael Cassio, when you wooed my lady,
     Know of your love?
OTHELLO.   He did, from first to last. Why dost thou ask?   105
IAGO.   But for a satisfaction of my thought;
     No further harm.
OTHELLO.   Why of thy thought, Iago?
IAGO.   I did not think he had been acquainted with her.
OTHELLO.   O, yes, and went between us very oft.
IAGO.   Indeed?   110

71–72 Save . . . best were it not that, as the saying goes, military discipline requires making an
example of the very best men. (She refers to *wars* as a singular concept.)   **72 not almost**
scarcely.   **73 private check** even a private reprimand.   **76 mammering on** wavering about.
80 bring him in restore him to favor.   **86 peculiar** particular, personal.   **88 touch** test.   **89
poise** weight, heaviness; or equipoise, delicate balance involving hard choice.   **92 Whereon** in
return for which.   **95 straight** straight way.   **96 fancies** inclinations.   **98 wretch** (A term of
affectionate endearment.)   **99–100 And . . . again** i.e., my love for you will last forever, until
the end of time when chaos will return. (But with an unconscious, ironic suggestion that, if anything should induce Othello to cease loving Desdemona, the result would be chaos.)

OTHELLO. Indeed? Ay, indeed. Descern'st thou aught in that?
    Is he not honest?
IAGO. Honest, my lord?
OTHELLO. Honest. Ay, honest.
IAGO. My lord, for aught I know.   115
OTHELLO. What dost thou think?
IAGO. Think, my lord?
OTHELLO. "Think, my lord?" By heaven, thou echo'st me,
    As if there were some monster in thy thought
    Too hideous to be shown. Thou dost mean something.   120
    I heard thee say even now, thou lik'st not that,
    When Cassio left my wife. What didst thou not like?
    And when I told thee he was of my counsel°
    In my whole course of wooing, thou criedst "Indeed?"
    And didst contract and purse° thy brow together   125
    As if thou then hadst shut up in thy brain
    Some horrible conceit.° If thou dost love me,
    Show me thy thought.
IAGO. My lord, you know I love you.
OTHELLO. I think thou dost;   130
    And, for° I know thou'rt full of love and honesty,
    And weigh'st thy words before thou giv'st them breath,
    Therefore these stops° of thine fright me the more;
    For such things in a false disloyal knave
    Are tricks of custom,° but in a man that's just   135
    They're close dilations,° working from the heart
    That passion cannot rule.°
IAGO.   For° Michael Cassio,
    I dare be sworn I think that he is honest.
OTHELLO. I think so too.
IAGO.   Men should be what they seem;
    Or those that be not, would they might seem none!°   140
OTHELLO. Certain, men should be what they seem.
IAGO. Why, then, I think Cassio's an honest man.
OTHELLO. Nay, yet there's more in this.
    I prithee, speak to me as to thy thinkings,
    As thou dost ruminate, and give thy worst of thoughts   145
    The worst of words.
IAGO.   Good my lord, pardon me.
    Though I am bound to every act of duty,
    I am not bound to that° all slaves are free to.°
    Utter my thoughts? Why, say they are vile and false,
    As where's the palace whereinto foul things   150

---

123 **of my counsel** in my confidence. 125 **purse** knit. 127 **conceit** fancy. 131 **for** because. 133 **stops** pauses. 135 **of custom** customary. 136 **close dilations** secret or involuntary expressions or delays. 137 **That passion cannot rule** i.e., that are too passionately strong to be restrained (referring to the workings), or, that cannot rule its own passions (referring to the heart). 137 **For** as for. 140 **none** i.e., not to be men, or not seem to be honest. 148 **that** that which. **free to** free with respect to.

Sometimes intrude not? Who has that breast so pure
But some uncleanly apprehensions
Keep leets and law days,° and in sessions sit
With° meditations lawful?°

OTHELLO. Thou dost conspire against thy friend,° Iago,   155
If thou but think'st him wronged and mak'st his ear
A stranger to thy thoughts.

IAGO.   I do beseech you,
Though I perchance am vicious° in my guess—
As I confess it is my nature's plague
To spy into abuses, and oft my jealousy°   160
Shapes faults that are not—that your wisdom then,°
From one° that so imperfectly conceits,°
Would take no notice, nor build yourself a trouble
Out of his scattering° and unsure observance.
It were not for your quiet nor your good,   165
Nor for my manhood, honesty, and wisdom,
To let you know my thoughts.

OTHELLO.   What dost thou mean?

IAGO. Good name in man and woman, dear my lord,
Is the immediate° jewel of their souls.
Who steals my purse steals trash; 'tis something, nothing;   170
'Twas mine, 'tis his, and has been slave to thousands;
But he that filches from me my good name
Robs me of that which not enriches him
And makes me poor indeed.

OTHELLO. By heaven, I'll know thy thoughts.   175

IAGO. You cannot, if° my heart were in your hand,
Nor shall not, whilst 'tis in my custody.

OTHELLO. Ha?

IAGO.   O, beware, my lord, of jealousy.
It is the green-eyed monster which doth mock
The meat it feeds on.° That cuckold lives in bliss   180
Who, certain of his fate, loves not his wronger;°
But O, what damnèd minutes tells° he o'er
Who dotes, yet doubts, suspects, yet fondly loves!

OTHELLO. O misery!

IAGO. Poor and content is rich, and rich enough,°   185
But riches fineless° is as poor as winter
To him that ever fears he shall be poor.

---

153 Keep leets and law days i.e., hold court, set up their authority in one's heart. (*Leets* are a
kind of manor court; *law days* are the days courts sit in session, or three sessions.) **154 With**
along with. **lawful** innocent. **155 thy friend** i.e., Othello. **158 vicious** wrong. **160 jealousy** suspicious nature. **161 then** on that account. **162 one** i.e., myself, Iago. **conceits**
judges, conjectures. **164 scattering** random. **169 immediate** essential, most precious.
176 if even if. **179–180 doth mock . . . on** mocks and torments the heart of its victim, the
man who suffers jealousy. **181 his wronger** i.e., his faithless wife. (The unsuspecting cuckold
is spared the misery of loving his wife only to discover she is cheating on him.) **182 tells**
counts. **185 Poor . . . enough** to be content with what little one has is the greatest wealth of
all. (Proverbial.) **186 fineless** boundless.

        Good God, the souls of all my tribe defend
        From jealousy!
OTHELLO. Why, why is this?   190
        Think'st thou I'd make a life of jealousy,
        To follow still the changes of the moon
        With fresh suspicions?° No! To be once in doubt
        Is once° to be resolved.° Exchange me for a goat
        When I shall turn the business of my soul   195
        To such exsufflicate and blown° surmises
        Matching thy inference.° 'Tis not to make me jealous
        To say my wife is fair, feeds well, loves company,
        Is free of speech, sings, plays, and dances well;
        Where virtue is, these are more virtuous.   200
        Not from mine own weak merits will I draw
        The smallest fear of doubt of her revolt,°
        For she had eyes, and chose me. No, Iago,
        I'll see before I doubt; when I doubt, prove;
        And on the proof, there is no more but this—   205
        Away at once with love or jealousy.
IAGO. I am glad of this, for now I shall have reason
        To show the love and duty that I bear you
        With franker spirit. Therefore, as I am bound,
        Receive it from me. I speak not yet of proof.   210
        Look to your wife; observe her well with Cassio.
        Wear your eyes thus, not° jealous nor secure.°
        I would not have your free and noble nature,
        Out of self-bounty,° be abused.° Look to 't.
        I know our country disposition well;   215
        In Venice they do let God see the pranks
        They dare not show their husbands; their best conscience
        Is not to leave 't undone, but keep 't unknown.
OTHELLO. Dost thou say so?
IAGO. She did deceive her father, marrying you;   220
        And when she seemed to shake and fear your looks,
        She loved them most.
OTHELLO.   And so she did.
IAGO.   Why, go to,° then!
        She that, so young, could give out such a seeming,°
        To seel° her father's eyes up close as oak,°
        He thought 'twas witchcraft! But I am much to blame.   225
        I humbly do beseech you of your pardon
        For too much loving you.

192–193 To follow . . . suspicions to be constantly imagining new causes for suspicion, changing incessantly like the moon. **194 once** once and for all. **resolved** free of doubt, having settled the matter. **196 exsufflicate and blown** inflated and blown up, rumored about, or, spat out and flyblown, hence, loathsome, disgusting. **197 inference** description or allegation. **202 doubt . . . revolt** fear of her unfaithfulness. **212 not** neither. **secure** free from uncertainty. **214 self-bounty** inherent or natural goodness and generosity. **abused** deceived. **222 go to** (An expression of impatience.) **223 seeming** false appearance. **224 seel** blind. (A term from falconry.) **oak** (A close-grained wood.)

OTHELLO. I am bound° to thee forever.

IAGO. I see this hath a little dashed your spirits.

OTHELLO. Not a jot, not a jot.

IAGO.   I' faith, I fear it has.   230
    I hope you will consider what is spoke
    Comes from my love. But I do see you're moved.
    I am to pray you not to strain my speech
    To grosser issues° nor to larger reach°
    Than to suspicion.   235

OTHELLO. I will not.

IAGO. Should you do so, my lord,
    My speech should fall into such vile success°
    Which my thoughts aimed not. Cassio's my worthy friend.
    My lord, I see you're moved.

OTHELLO.   No, not much moved.   240
    I do not think but Desdemona's honest.°

IAGO. Long live she so! And long live you to think so!

OTHELLO. And yet, how nature erring from itself—

IAGO. Ay, there's the point! As—to be bold with you—
    Not to affect° many proposèd matches   245
    Of her own clime, complexion, and degree,°
    Whereto we see in all things nature tends—
    Foh! One may smell in such a will° most rank,
    Foul disproportion,° thoughts unnatural.
    But pardon me. I do not in position°   250
    Distinctly speak of her, though I may fear
    Her will, recoiling° to her better° judgment,
    May fall to match you with her country forms°
    And happily° repent.

OTHELLO.   Farewell, farewell!
    If more thou dost perceive, let me know more.   255
    Set on thy wife to observe. Leave me, Iago.

IAGO [*going*]. My lord, I take my leave.

OTHELLO. Why did I marry? This honest creature doubtless
    Sees and knows more, much more, than he unfolds.

IAGO [*returning*]. My Lord, I would I might entreat your honor   260
    To scan° this thing no farther. Leave it to time.
    Although 'tis fit that Cassio have his place—
    For, sure, he fills it up with great ability—
    Yet if you please to hold him off awhile,
    You shall by that perceive him and his means.°   265
    Note if your lady strain his entertainment°

---

228 bound indebted (but perhaps with ironic sense of "tied").   **234 issues** significances.
reach meaning, scope.   **238 success** effect, result.   **241 honest** chaste.   **245 affect** prefer,
desire.   **246 clime . . . degree** country, color, and social position.   **248 will** sensuality, appetite.   **249 disproportion** abnormality.   **250 position** argument, proposition.   **252 re-**
coiling reverting.   **better** i.e., more natural and reconsidered.   **253 fall . . . forms** undertake
to compare you with Venetian norms of handsomeness.   **254 happily repent** haply repent
her marriage.   **261 scan** scrutinize.   **265 his means** the method he uses (to regain his post).
266 strain his entertainment urge his reinstatement.

With any strong or vehement importunity;
Much will be seen in that. In the meantime,
Let me be thought too busy° in my fears—
As worthy cause I have to fear I am—   270
And hold her free,° I do beseech your honor.

OTHELLO. Fear not my government.°

IAGO. I once more take my leave.   *Exit.*

OTHELLO. This fellow's of exceeding honesty,
And knows all qualities,° with a learnèd spirit,   275
Of human dealings. If I do prove her haggard,°
Though that her jesses° were my dear heartstrings,
I'd whistle her off and let her down the wind°
To prey at fortune.° Haply, for° I am black
And have not those soft parts of conversation°   280
That chamberers° have, or for I am declined
Into the vale of years—yet that's not much—
She's gone. I am abused,° and my relief
Must be to loathe her. O curse of marriage,
That we can call these delicate creatures ours   285
And not their appetites! I had rather be a toad
And live upon the vapor of a dungeon
Than keep a corner in the thing I love
For others' uses. Yet, 'tis the plague of great ones;
Prerogatived° are they less than the base.°   290
'Tis destiny unshunnable, like death.
Even then this forkèd plague is fated to us
When we do quicken.° Look where she comes.

Enter DESDEMONA *and* EMILIA.

If she be false, O, then heaven mocks itself!
I'll not believe 't.

DESDEMONA.   How now, my dear Othello?   295
Your dinner, and the generous° islanders
By you invited, do attend° your presence.

OTHELLO. I am to blame.

DESDEMONA.   Why do you speak so faintly?
Are you not well?

OTHELLO. I have a pain upon my forehead here.   300

---

269 busy interfering.   **271 hold her free** regard her as innocent.   **272 government** self-
control, conduct.   **275 qualities** natures, types.   **276 haggard** wild (like a wild female hawk).
277 jesses straps fastened around the legs of a trained hawk.   **278 I'd . . . wind** i.e., I'd let her
go forever. (To release a hawk downwind was to invite it not to return.)   **279 prey at fortune**
fend for herself in the wild.   **Haply, for** perhaps because.   **280 soft . . . conversation** pleasing graces of social behavior.   **281 chamberers** gallants.   **283 abused** deceived.   **290
Prerogatived** privileged (to have honest wives).   **the base** ordinary citizens. (Socially prominent men are especially prone to the unavoidable destiny of being cuckolded and to the public
shame that goes with it.)   **292 forkèd** (An allusion to the horns of the cuckold.)   **293
quicken** receive life. (Quicken may also mean to swarm with maggots as the body festers, as in
4.2.69, in which case lines 292–293 suggest that *even then*, in death, we are cuckolded by
forkèd worms.)   **296 generous** noble.   **297 attend** await.

DESDEMONA. Faith, that's with watching.° 'Twill away again.

> [*She offers her handkerchief.*]

Let me but bind it hard, within this hour
It will be well.

OTHELLO.   Your napkin° is too little.
Let it alone.° Come, I'll go in with you.

> [*He puts the handkerchief from him, and it drops.*]

DESDEMONA. I am very sorry that you are not well.   305

> *Exit* [*with* OTHELLO].

EMILIA [*picking up the handkerchief*]. I am glad I have found this napkin.
This was her first remembrance from the Moor.
My wayward° husband hath a hundred times
Wooed me to steal it but she so loves the token—
For he conjured her she should ever keep it—   310
That she reserves it evermore about her
To kiss and talk to. I'll have the work ta'en out,°
And give 't Iago. What he will do with it
Heaven knows, not I;
I nothing but to please his fantasy.°   315

> *Enter* IAGO.

IAGO. How now? What do you do here alone?
EMILIA. Do not you chide. I have a thing for you.
IAGO. You have a thing for me? It is a common thing°—
EMILIA. Ha!
IAGO. To have a foolish wife.   320
EMILIA. O, is that all? What will you give me now
For that same handkerchief?
IAGO. What handkerchief?
EMILIA. What handkerchief?
Why, that the Moor first gave to Desdemona;   325
That which so often you did bid me steal.
IAGO. Hast stolen it from her?
EMILIA. No, faith. She let it drop by negligence,
And to th' advantage° I, being here, took 't up.
Look, here 'tis.
IAGO.   A good wench! Give it me.   330
EMILIA. What will you do with 't, that you have been so earnest
To have me filch it?
IAGO [*snatching it*]. Why, what is that to you?

---

301 watching too little sleep.   **303 napkin** handkerchief.   **304 Let it alone** i.e., never mind.
308 wayward capricious.   **312 work ta'en out** design of the embroidery copied.   **315 fantasy** whim.   **318 common thing** (With bawdy suggestion; *common* suggests coarseness and
availability to all comers, and *thing* is a slang term for the pudendum.)   **329 to th' advantage**
taking the opportunity.

EMILIA. If it be not for some purpose of import,
          Give 't me again. Poor lady, she'll run mad
          When she shall lack° it.
IAGO.   Be not acknown on 't.°   335
          I have use for it. Go, leave me.   *Exit* EMILIA.
          I will in Cassio's lodging lose° this napkin
          And let him find it. Trifles light as air.
          Are to the jealous confirmations strong
          As proofs of Holy Writ. This may do something.   340
          The Moor already changes with my poison.
          Dangerous conceits° are in their natures poisons,
          Which at the first are scarce found to distaste,°
          But with a little act° upon the blood
          Burn like the mines of sulfur.

          Enter OTHELLO.

                              I did say so.   345
          Look where he comes! Not poppy nor mandragora°
          Nor all the drowsy syrups of the world
          Shall ever medicine thee to that sweet sleep
          Which thou owedst° yesterday.
OTHELLO.   Ha, ha, false to me?
IAGO. Why, how now, General? No more of that.   350
OTHELLO. Avaunt! Begone! Thou hast set me on the rack.
          I swear 'tis better to be much abused
          Than but to know 't a little.
IAGO.   How now, my lord?
OTHELLO. What sense had I of her stolen hours of lust?
          I saw 't not, thought it not, it harmed not me.   355
          I slept the next night well, fed well, was free° and merry;
          I found not Cassio's kisses on her lips.
          He that is robbed, not wanting° what is stolen,
          Let him not know 't and he's not robbed at all.
IAGO. I am sorry to hear this.   360
OTHELLO. I had been happy if the general camp,
          Pioners° and all, had tasted her sweet body,
          So° I had nothing known. O, now, forever
          Farewell the tranquil mind! Farewell content!
          Farewell the plumèd troops and the big° wars   365
          That makes ambition virtue! O, farewell!
          Farewell the neighing steed and the shrill trump,
          The spirit-stirring drum, th' ear-piercing fife,
          The royal banner, and all quality,°
          Pride,° pomp, and circumstance° of glorious war!   370

---

335 **lack** miss. **Be . . . on't** do not confess knowledge of it.   337 **lose** (The Folio spelling,
loose, is a normal spelling for "lose," but it may also contain the idea of "let go," "release.")   342
conceits fancies, ideas.   343 **distaste** be distasteful.   344 **act** action, working.   346 **man-
dragora** an opiate made of the mandrake root.   349 **thou owedst** you did own.   356 **free**
carefree.   358 **wanting** missing.   362 **Pioners** diggers of mines, the lowest grade of soldiers.
363 **So** provided.   365 **big** stately.   369 **quality** character, essential nature.   370 **Pride** rich
display.   **circumstance** pageantry.

And O, you mortal engines,° whose rude throats
Th' immortal Jove's dread clamors° counterfeit,
Farewell! Othello's occupation's gone.

IAGO. Is 't possible, my lord?

OTHELLO. Villain, be sure thou prove my love a whore!   375
Be sure of it. Give me the ocular proof,
Or, by the worth of mine eternal soul,
Thou hadst been better have been born a dog
Than answer my waked wrath!

IAGO.   Is 't come to this?

OTHELLO. Make me to see 't, or at the least so prove it   380
That the probation° bear no hinge nor loop
To hang a doubt on, or woe upon thy life!

IAGO. My noble lord—

OTHELLO. If thou dost slander her and torture me,
Never pray more; abandon all remorse;°   385
On horror's head horrors accumulate;°
Do deeds to make heaven weep, all earth amazed;°
For nothing canst thou to damnation add
Greater than that.

IAGO.   O grace! O heaven forgive me!
Are you a man? Have you a soul or sense?   390
God b' wi' you; take mine office. O wretched fool,°
That lov'st to make thine honesty a vice!°
O monstrous world! Take note, take note, O world,
To be direct and honest is not safe.
I thank you for this profit,° and from hence°   395
I'll love no friend, sith° love breeds such offense.°

OTHELLO. Nay, stay. Thou shouldst be° honest.

IAGO. I should be wise, for honesty's a fool
And loses that° it works for.

OTHELLO.   By the world,
I think my wife be honest and think she is not;   400
I think that thou art just and think thou art not.
I'll have some proof. My name, that was as fresh
As Dian's° visage, is now begrimed and black
As mine own face. If there be cords, or knives,
Poison, or fire, or suffocating streams,   405
I'll not endure it. Would I were satisfied!

IAGO. I see, sir, you are eaten up with passion.
I do repent me that I put it to you.
You would be satisfied?

---

371 mortal engines i.e., cannon (*Mortal* means "deadly.")   **372 Jove's dread clamors** i.e.,
thunder.   **381 probation** proof.   **385 remorse** pity, penitent hope for salvation.   **386
horrors accumulate** add still more horrors.   **387 amazed** confounded with horror.   **391 O
wretched fool** (Iago addresses himself as a fool for having carried honesty too far.)   **392 vice**
failing, something overdone.   **395 profit** profitable instruction.   **hence** henceforth.   **396
sith** since.   **offense** i.e., harm to the one who offers help and friendship.   **397 Thou
shouldst be** it appears that you are. (But Iago replies in the sense of "ought to be.")   **399 that**
what.   **403 Dian** Diana, goddess of the moon and of chastity.

OTHELLO.   Would? Nay, and I will.

IAGO. And may; but how? How satisfied, my lord?   410
    Would you, the supervisor,° grossly gape on?
    Behold her topped?

OTHELLO.   Death and damnation! O!

IAGO. It were a tedious difficulty, I think,
    To bring them to that prospect. Damn them then,°
    If ever mortal eyes do see them bolster°   415
    More° than their own.° What then? How then?
    What shall I say? Where's satisfaction?
    It is impossible you should see this,
    Were they as prime° as goats, as hot as monkeys,
    As salt° as wolves in pride,° and fools as gross   420
    As ignorance made drunk. But yet I say,
    If imputation and strong circumstances°
    Which lead directly to the door of truth
    Will give you satisfaction, you might have 't.

OTHELLO. Give me a living reason she's disloyal.   425

IAGO. I do not like the office.
    But sith° I am entered in this cause so far,
    Pricked° to 't by foolish honesty and love,
    I will go on. I lay with Cassio lately,
    And being troubled with a raging tooth   430
    I could not sleep. There are a kind of men
    So loose of soul that in their sleeps will mutter
    Their affairs. One of this kind is Cassio.
    In sleep I heard him say, "Sweet Desdemona,
    Let us be wary, let us hide our loves!"   435
    And then, sir, would he grip and wring my hand,
    Cry "O sweet creature!," then kiss me hard,
    As if he plucked up kisses by the roots
    That grew upon my lips; then laid his leg
    Over my thigh, and sighed, and kissed, and then   440
    Cried, "Cursèd fate that gave thee to the Moor!"

OTHELLO. O monstrous! Monstrous!

IAGO.   Nay, this was but his dream.

OTHELLO. But this denoted a foregone conclusion.°
    'Tis a shrewd doubt,° though it be but a dream.

IAGO. And this may help to thicken other proofs   445
    That do demonstrate thinly.

OTHELLO.   I'll tear her all to pieces.

IAGO. Nay, but be wise. Yet we see nothing done;
    She may be honest yet. Tell me but this:

---

411 supervisor onlooker. **414 Damn them then** i.e., they would have to be really incorrigible. **415 bolster** go to bed together, share a bolster. **416 More** other. **own** own eyes.
419 prime lustful. **420 salt** wanton, sensual. **pride** heat. **422 imputation . . . circumstances** strong circumstantial evidence. **427 sith** since. **428 Pricked** spurred. **443
foregone conclusion** concluded experience or action. **444 shrewd doubt** suspicious
circumstance.

Have you not sometimes seen a handkerchief
Spotted with strawberries° in your wife's hand?   450
OTHELLO. I gave her such a one. 'Twas my first gift.
IAGO. I know not that; but such a handkerchief—
I am sure it was your wife's—did I today
See Cassio wipe his beard with.
OTHELLO.   If it be that—
IAGO. If it be that, or any that was hers,   455
It speaks against her with the other proofs.
OTHELLO. O, that the slave° had forty thousand lives!
One is too poor, too weak for my revenge.
Now do I see 'tis true. Look here, Iago,
All my fond° love thus do I blow to heaven.   460
'Tis gone.
Arise, black vengeance, from the hollow hell!
Yield up, O love, thy crown and hearted° throne
To tyrannous hate! Swell, bosom, with thy freight,°
For 'tis of aspics'° tongues!   465
IAGO. Yet be content.°
OTHELLO. O, blood, blood, blood!
IAGO. Patience, I say. Your mind perhaps may change.
OTHELLO. Never, Iago. Like to the Pontic Sea,°
Whose icy current and compulsive course   470
Ne'er feels retiring ebb, but keeps due on
To the Propontic° and the Hellespont,°
Even so my bloody thoughts with violent pace
Shall ne'er look back, ne'er ebb to humble love,
I that a capable° and wide revenge   475
Swallow them up. Now, by yond marble° heaven,
[*Kneeling*] In the due reverence of a sacred vow
I here engage my words.
IAGO.   Do not rise yet.
[*He kneels.*]° Witness, you ever-burning lights above,
You elements that clip° us round about,   480
Witness that here Iago doth give up
The execution° of his wit,° hands, heart,
To wronged Othello's service. Let him command,
And to obey shall be in me remorse,°
What bloody business ever.°   [*They rise.*]
OTHELLO.   I greet thy love,   485
Not with vain thanks, but with acceptance bounteous,
And will upon the instant put thee to 't.°

---

450 Spotted with strawberries embroidered with a strawberry pattern.   **457 the slave** i.e.,
Cassio.   **460 fond** foolish (but also suggesting "affectionate").   **463 hearted** fixed in the
heart.   **464 freight** burden.   **465 aspics'** venomous serpents'.   **466 content** calm.   **469
Pontic Sea** Black Sea.   **472 Propontic** Sea of Marmara, between the Black Sea and the
Aegean.   **Hellespont** Dardanelles, straits where the Sea of Marmara joins with the Aegean.
475 capable ample, comprehensive.   **476 marble** i.e., gleaming like marble and unrelenting.
479 s.d. He kneels (In the Quarto text, Iago kneels here after Othello has knelt at line 477.)
480 clip encompass.   **482 execution** exercise, action.   **wit** mind.   **484 remorse** pity (for
Othello's wrongs).   **485 ever** soever.   **487 to 't** to the proof.

Within these three days let me hear thee say
That Cassio's not alive.

IAGO.   My friend is dead;
'Tis done at your request. But let her live.   490

OTHELLO.   Damn her, lewd minx!° O, damn her, damn her!
Come, go with me apart. I will withdraw
To furnish me with some swift means of death
For the fair devil. Now art thou my lieutenant.

IAGO.   I am your own forever.   *Exeunt.*   495

3.4 *Enter* DESDEMONA, EMILIA *and*

DESDEMONA.   Do you know, sirrah,° where Lieutenant Cassio lies?°

CLOWN.   I dare not say he lies anywhere.

DESDEMONA.   Why, man?

CLOWN.   He's a soldier, and for me to say a soldier lies, 'tis stabbing.

DESDEMONA.   Go to. Where lodges he?   5

CLOWN.   To tell you where he lodges is to tell you where I lie.

DESDEMONA.   Can anything be made of this?

CLOWN.   I know not where he lodges, and for me to devise a lodging and
      say he lies here, or he lies there, were to lie in mine own throat.°

DESDEMONA.   Can you inquire him out, and be edified by report?   10

CLOWN.   I will catechize the world for him; that is, make questions, and by
      them answer.

DESDEMONA.   Seek him, bid him come hither. Tell him I have moved° my
      lord on his behalf and hope all will be well.

CLOWN.   To do this is within the compass of man's wit, and therefore I will   15
      attempt the doing it.   *Exit* CLOWN.

DESDEMONA.   Where should I lose that handkerchief, Emilia?

EMILIA.   I know not, madam.

DESDEMONA.   Believe me, I had rather have lost my purse
      Full of crusadoes;° and but my noble Moor   20
      Is true of mind and made of no such baseness
      As jealous creatures are, it were enough
      To put him to ill thinking.

EMILIA.   Is he not jealous?

DESDEMONA.   Who, he? I think the sun where he was born
      Drew all such humors° from him.

EMILIA.   Look where he comes.   25

      Enter OTHELLO.

DESDEMONA.   I will not leave him now till Cassio
      Be called to him.—How is 't with you, my lord?

----

491 **minx** wanton.   **3.4 Location: Before the citadel.**   1 **sirrah** (A form of address to an
inferior.)   **lies** lodges. (But the Clown makes the obvious pun.)   9 **lie . . . throat** (1) lie egregiously and deliberately (2) use the windpipe to speak a lie.   13 **moved** petitioned.   20 **cru-
sadoes** Portuguese gold coins.   25 **humors** (Refers to the four bodily fluids thought to determine temperament.)

OTHELLO. Well, my good lady. [*Aside.*] O, hardness to dissemble!—
How do you, Desdemona?
DESDEMONA.   Well, my good lord.
OTHELLO. Give me your hand. [*She gives her hand.*] This hand is
moist, my lady.   30
DESDEMONA. It yet hath felt no age nor known no sorrow.
OTHELLO. This argues° fruitfulness° and liberal° heart.
Hot, hot, and moist. This hand of yours requires
A sequester° from liberty, fasting and prayer,
Much castigation,° exercise devout;°   35
For here's a young and sweating devil here
That commonly rebels. 'Tis a good hand,
A frank° one.
DESDEMONA.   You may indeed say so,
For 'twas that hand that gave away my heart.
OTHELLO. A liberal hand. The hearts of old gave hands,°   40
But our new heraldry is hands, not hearts.°
DESDEMONA. I cannot speak of this. Come now, your promise.
OTHELLO. What promise, chuck?°
DESDEMONA. I have sent to bid Cassio come speak with you.
OTHELLO. I have a salt and sorry rheum° offends me;   45
Lend me thy handkerchief.
DESDEMONA. Here, my lord.   [*She offers a handkerchief.*]
OTHELLO. That which I gave you.
DESDEMONA.   I have it not about me.
OTHELLO. Not?
DESDEMONA. No, faith, my lord.   50
OTHELLO. That's a fault. That handkerchief
Did an Egyptian to my mother give.
She was a charmer,° and could almost read
The thoughts of people. She told her, while she kept it
'Twould make her amiable° and subdue my father   55
Entirely to her love, but if she lost it
Or made a gift of it, my father's eye
Should hold her loathèd and his spirits should hunt
After new fancies.° She, dying, gave it me,
And bid me, when my fate would have me wived,   60
To give it her.° I did so; and take heed on 't;
Make it a darling like your precious eye.
To lose 't or give 't away were such perdition°
As nothing else could match.

---

32 argues gives evidence of. **fruitfulness** generosity, amorousness, and fecundity. **liberal**
generous and sexually free. **34 sequester** separation, sequestration. **35 castigation** correc-
tive discipline. **exercise devout** i.e., prayer, religious meditation, etc. **38 frank** generous,
open (with sexual suggestion). **40 The hearts . . . hands** i.e., in former times, people would
give their hearts when they gave their hands to something. **41 But . . . hearts** i.e., in our decadent times, the joining of hands is no longer a badge to signify the giving of hearts. **43 chuck**
(A term of endearment.) **45 salt . . . rheum** distressful head cold or watering of the eyes.
53 charmer sorceress. **55 amiable** desirable. **59 fancies** loves. **61 her** i.e., to my wife.
63 perdition loss.

DESDEMONA.   Is 't possible?

OTHELLO. 'Tis true. There's magic in the web° of it.   65
    A sibyl, that had numbered in the world
    The sun to course two hundred compasses,°
    In her prophetic fury° sewed the work;°
    The worms were hallowed that did breed the silk,
    And it was dyed in mummy° which the skillful   70
    Conserved of° maidens' hearts.

DESDEMONA.   I' faith! Is 't true?

OTHELLO. Most veritable. Therefore look to 't well.

DESDEMONA. Then would to God that I had never seen 't!

OTHELLO. Ha? Wherefore?

DESDEMONA. Why do you speak so startingly and rash?°   75

OTHELLO. Is 't lost? Is 't gone? Speak, is 't out o' the way?°

DESDEMONA. Heaven bless us!

OTHELLO. Say you?

DESDEMONA. It is not lost; but what an if° it were?

OTHELLO. How?   80

DESDEMONA. I say it is not lost.

OTHELLO.   Fetch 't, let me see 't.

DESDEMONA. Why, so I can, sir, but I will not now.
    This is a trick to put me from my suit.
    Pray you, let Cassio be received again.

OTHELLO. Fetch me the handkerchief! My mind misgives.   85

DESDEMONA. Come, come,
    You'll never meet a more sufficient° man.

OTHELLO. The handkerchief!

DESDEMONA.   I pray, talk° me of Cassio.

OTHELLO. The handkerchief?

DESDEMONA.   A man that all his time°
    Hath founded his good fortunes on your love,   90
    Shared dangers with you—

OTHELLO. The handkerchief!

DESDEMONA. I' faith, you are to blame.

OTHELLO. Zounds!   *Exit* OTHELLO.

EMILIA. Is not this man jealous?   95

DESDEMONA. I ne'er saw this before.
    Sure, there's some wonder in this handkerchief.
    I am most unhappy in the loss of it.

EMILIA. 'Tis not a year or two shows us a man.°
    They are all but stomachs, and we all but° food;   100
    They eat us hungerly,° and when they are full
    They belch us.

---

65 web fabric, weaving.   **67 compasses** annual circlings. (The *sibyl,* or prophetess, was two hundred years old.)   **68 prophetic fury** frenzy of prophetic inspiration.   **work** embroidered pattern.   **70 mummy** medicinal or magical preparation drained from mummified bodies.   **71 Conserved of** prepared or preserved out of.   **75 startingly and rash** disjointedly and impetuously, excitedly.   **76 out o' the way** lost, misplaced.   **79 an if** if.   **87 sufficient** able, complete.   **88 talk** talk to.   **89 all his time** throughout his career.   **99 'Tis . . . man** i.e., you can't really know a man even in a year or two of experience (?), or, real men come along seldom (?).   **100 but** nothing but.   **101 hungerly** hungrily.

Enter IAGO *and* CASSIO.

                    Look you, Cassio and my husband.

IAGO [*to* CASSIO]. There is no other way; 'tis she must do 't.
    And, lo, the happiness!° Go and importune her.

DESDEMONA. How now, good Cassio? What's the news with you?   105

CASSIO. Madam, my former suit. I do beseech you
    That by your virtuous° means I may again
    Exist and be a member of his love
    Whom I, with all the office° of my heart,
    Entirely honor. I would not be delayed.   110
    If my offense be of such mortal° kind
    That nor my service past, nor° present sorrows,
    Nor purposed merit in futurity
    Can ransom me into his love again,
    But to know so must be my benefit;°   115
    So shall I clothe me in a forced content,
    And shut myself up in° some other course,
    To fortune's alms.°

DESDEMONA.   Alas, thrice-gentle Cassio,
    My advocation° is not now in tune.
    My lord is not my lord; nor should I know him,   120
    Were he in favor° as in humor° altered.
    So help me every spirit sanctified
    As I have spoken for you all my best
    And stood within the blank° of his displeasure
    For my free speech! You must awhile be patient.   125
    What I can do I will, and more I will
    Than for myself I dare. Let that suffice you.

IAGO. Is my lord angry?

EMILIA.   He went hence but now,
    And certainly in strange unquietness.

IAGO. Can he be angry? I have seen the cannon   130
    When it hath blown his ranks into the air,
    And like the devil from his very arm
    Puffed his own brother—and is he angry?
    Something of moment° then. I will go meet him.
    There's matter in 't indeed, if he be angry.   135

DESDEMONA. I prithee, do so.   *Exit* [IAGO].
                  Something, sure, of state,°
    Either from Venice, or some unhatched practice°
    Made demonstrable here in Cyprus to him,

---

104 the happiness in happy time, fortunately met.   **107 virtuous** efficacious.   **109 office**
loyal service.   **111 mortal** fatal.   **112 nor . . . nor** neither . . . nor.   **115 But . . . benefit**
merely to know that my case is hopeless will have to content me (and will be better than uncertainty).   **117 shut . . . in** confine myself to.   **118 To fortune's alms** throwing myself on
the mercy of fortune.   **119 advocation** advocacy.   **121 favor** appearance.   **humor** mood.
124 within the blank within point-blank range. (The *blank* is the center of the target.)   **134**
of moment of immediate importance, momentous.   **136 of state** concerning state affairs.
137 unhatched practice as yet unexecuted or undiscovered plot.

Hath puddled° his clear spirit; and in such cases
Men's natures wrangle with inferior things,   140
Though great ones are their object. 'Tis even so;
For let our finger ache, and it indues°
Our other, healthful members even to a sense
Of pain. Nay, we must think men are not gods,
Nor of them look for such observancy°   145
As fits the bridal.° Beshrew me° much, Emilia,
I was, unhandsome° warrior as I am,
Arraigning his unkindness with° my soul;
But now I find I had suborned the witness,°
And he's indicted falsely.

EMILIA.   Pray heaven it be   150
State matters, as you think, and no conception
Nor no jealous toy° concerning you.

DESDEMONA. Alas the day! I never gave him cause.

EMILIA. But jealous souls will not be answered so;
They are not ever jealous for the cause,   155
But jealous for° they're jealous. It is a monster
Begot upon itself,° born on itself.

DESDEMONA. Heaven keep that monster from Othello's mind!

EMILIA. Lady, amen.

DESDEMONA. I will go seek him. Cassio, walk hereabout.   160
If I do find him fit, I'll move your suit
And seek to effect it to my uttermost.

CASSIO. I humbly thank your ladyship.

        Exit [DESDEMONA *with* EMILIA].

        Enter BIANCA.

BIANCA. Save° you, friend Cassio!

CASSIO.   What make° you from home?
How is 't with you, my most fair Bianca?   165
I' faith, sweet love, I was coming to your house.

BIANCA. And I was going to your lodging, Cassio.
What, keep a week away? Seven days and nights?
Eightscore-eight° hours? And lovers' absent hours
More tedious than the dial° eightscore times?   170
O weary reckoning!

CASSIO.   Pardon me, Bianca.
I have this while with leaden thoughts been pressed;
But I shall, in a more continuate° time,
Strike off this score° of absence. Sweet Bianca,

---

139 puddled muddied.   **142 indues** brings to the same condition.   **145 observancy** attentiveness.   **146 bridal** wedding (when a bridegroom is newly attentive to his bride).
Beshrew me (A mild oath.)   **147 unhandsome** insufficient, unskillful.   **148 with** before
the bar of.   **149 suborned the witness** induced the witness to give false testimony.   **152 toy**
fancy.   **156 for** because.   **157 Begot upon itself** generated solely from itself.   **164 Save**
God save.   **make** do.   **169 Eightscore-eight** one hundred sixty-eight, the number of hours in
a week.   **170 the dial** a complete revolution of the clock.   **173 continuate** uninterrupted.

[giving her DESDEMONA's *handkerchief]*

Take me this work out.°

BIANCA.   O Cassio, whence came this?   175
This is some token from a newer friend.°
To the felt absence now I feel a cause.
Is 't come to this? Well, well.

CASSIO.   Go to, woman!
Throw your vile guesses in the devil's teeth,
From whence you have them. You are jealous now   180
That this is from some mistress, some remembrance,
No, by my faith, Bianca.

BIANCA.   Why, whose is it?

CASSIO. I know not, neither. I found it in my chamber.
I like the work well. Ere it be demanded°—
As like° enough it will—I would have it copied.   185
Take it and do 't, and leave me for this time.

BIANCA. Leave you? Wherefore?

CASSIO. I do attend here on the General,
And think it no addition,° nor my wish,
To have him see me womaned.   190

BIANCA. Why, I pray you?

CASSIO. Not that I love you not.

BIANCA. But that you do not love me.
I pray you, bring° me on the way a little,
And say if I shall see you soon at night.   195

CASSIO. 'Tis but a little way that I can bring you,
For I attend here; but I'll see you soon.

BIANCA. 'Tis very good. I must be circumstanced.°

Exeunt omnes.

4.1 *Enter* OTHELLO *and* IAGO

IAGO. Will you think so?

OTHELLO.   Think so, Iago?

IAGO.   What,
To kiss in private?

OTHELLO.   An unauthorized kiss!

IAGO. Or to be naked with her friend in bed
An hour or more, not meaning any harm?

OTHELLO. Naked in bed, Iago, and not mean harm?   5
It is hypocrisy against the devil.

---

174 Strike . . . score settle this account.   **175 Take . . . out** copy this embroidery for me.   **176 friend** mistress.   **184 demanded** inquired for.   **185 like** likely.   **189 addition** i.e., addition to my reputation.   **194 bring** accompany.   **198 be circumstanced** be governed by circumstance, yield to your conditions.   **4.1 Location: Before the citadel**.

They that mean virtuously and yet do so,
The devil their virtue tempts, and they tempt heaven.
IAGO. If they do nothing, 'tis a venial° slip.
   But if I give my wife a handkerchief—   10
OTHELLO. What then?
IAGO. Why then, 'tis hers, my lord, and being hers,
   She may, I think, bestow 't on any man.
OTHELLO. She is protectress of her honor too
   May she give that?.   15
IAGO. Her honor is an essence that's not seen;
   They have it° very oft that have it not.
   But, for the handkerchief—
OTHELLO. By heaven, I would most gladly have forgot it.
   Thou saidst—O, it comes o'er my memory   20
   As doth the raven o'er the infectious house,°
   Boding to all—he had my handkerchief.
IAGO. Ay, what of that?
OTHELLO.   That's not so good now.
IAGO.   What
   If I had said I had seen him do you wrong?
   Or heard him say—as knaves be such abroad,°   25
   Who having, by their own importunate suit,
   Or voluntary dotage° of some mistress,
   Convincèd or supplied° them, cannot choose
   But they must blab—
OTHELLO.   Hath he said anything?
IAGO. He hath, my lord; but, be you well assured,   30
   No more than he'll unswear.
OTHELLO.   What hath he said?
IAGO. Faith, that he did—I know not what he did.
OTHELLO. What? What?
IAGO. Lie—
OTHELLO. With her?
IAGO.   With her, on her; what you will.
OTHELLO. Lie with her? Lie on her? We say "lie on her" when they belie°   35
   her. Lie with her? Zounds, that's fulsome.°—Handkerchief—confes-
   sions—handkerchief!—To confess and be hanged for his labor—
   first to be hanged and then to confess.°—I tremble at it. Nature
   would not invest herself in such shadowing passion without some
   instruction.° It is not words° that shakes me thus. Pish! Noses, ears,   40
   and lips.—Is 't possible?—Confess—handkerchief!—O devil!

---

9 **venial** pardonable.   17 **They have it** i.e., they enjoy a reputation for it.   21 **raven . . .
house** (Allusion to the belief that the raven hovered over a house of sickness or infection, such
as one visited by the plague.)   25 **abroad** around about.   27 **voluntary dotage** willing infatuation.   28 **Convincèd or supplied** seduced or sexually gratified.   35 **belie** slander.   36
fulsome foul.   37–38 **first . . . to confess** (Othello reverses the proverbial *confess and be
hanged;* Cassio is to be given no time to confess before he dies.)   38–39 **Nature . . . instruction** i.e., without some foundation in fact, nature would not have dressed herself in such an
overwhelming passion that comes over me now and fills my mind with images, or in such a lifelike fantasy as Cassio had in his dream of lying with Desdemona.   39 **words** mere words.

Falls in a trance.

IAGO. Work on,
My medicine, work! Thus credulous fools are caught,
And many worthy and chaste dames even thus,
All guiltless, meet reproach.—What, ho! My lord!   45
My lord, I say! Othello!

Enter CASSIO.

                    How now, Cassio?
CASSIO. What's the matter?
IAGO. My lord is fall'n into an epilepsy.
This is his second fit. He had one yesterday.
CASSIO. Rub him about the temples.
IAGO.   No, forbear.   50
The lethargy° must have his° quiet course.
If not, he foams at mouth, and by and by
Breaks out to savage madness. Look, he stirs.
Do you withdraw yourself a little while.
He will recover straight. When he is gone,   55
I would on great occasion° speak with you.

[*Exit* CASSIO.]

How is it, General? Have you not hurt your head?
OTHELLO. Dost thou mock me?°
IAGO.   I mock you not, by heaven.
Would you would bear your fortune like a man!
OTHELLO. A hornèd man's a monster and a beast.   60
IAGO. There's many a beast then in a populous city,
And many a civil° monster.
OTHELLO. Did he confess it?
IAGO. Good sir, be a man.
Think every bearded fellow that's but yoked°   65
May draw with you.° There's millions now alive
That nightly lie in those unproper° beds
Which they dare swear peculiar.° Your case is better.°
O, 'tis the spite of hell, the fiend's arch-mock,
To lip° a wanton in a secure° couch   70
And to suppose her chaste! No, let me know,
And knowing what I am,° I know what she shall be.°
OTHELLO. O, thou art wise. 'Tis certain.
IAGO. Stand you awhile apart;
Confine yourself but in a patient list.°   75

---

51 lethargy coma. **his** its. **56 on great occasion** on a matter of great importance. **58
mock me** (Othello takes Iago's question about hurting his head to be a mocking reference to
the cuckold's horns.) **62 civil** i.e., dwelling in a city. **65 yoked** (1) married (2) put into the
yoke of infamy and cuckoldry. **66 draw with you** pull as you do, like oxen who are yoked,
i.e., share your fate as cuckold. **67 unproper** not exclusively their own. **68 peculiar**
private, their own. **better** i.e., because you know the truth. **70 lip** kiss. **secure** free from
suspicion. **72 what I am** i.e., a cuckold. **she shall be** will happen to her. **75 in . . . list**
within the bounds of patience.

Whilst you were here o'erwhelmèd with your grief—
A passion most unsuiting such a man—
Cassio came hither. I shifted him away,°
And laid good 'scuse upon your ecstasy,°
Bade him anon return and here speak with me,   80
The which he promised. Do but encave° yourself
And mark the fleers,° the gibes, and notable° scorns
That dwell in every region of his face;
For I will make him tell the tale anew,
Where, how, how oft, how long ago, and when   85
He hath and is again to cope° your wife.
I say, but mark his gesture. Marry, patience!
Or I shall say you're all-in-all in spleen,°
And nothing of a man.

OTHELLO.   Dost thou hear, Iago?
I will be found most cunning in my patience;   90
But—dost thou hear?—most bloody.

IAGO.   That's not amiss;
But yet keep time° in all. Will you withdraw?

[OTHELLO *stands apart*.]

Now will I question Cassio of Bianca,
A huswife° that by selling her desires
Buys herself bread and clothes. It is a creature   95
That dotes on Cassio—as 'tis the strumpet's plague
To beguile many and be beguiled by one.
He, when he hears of her, cannot restrain°
From the excess of laughter. Here he comes.

Enter CASSIO.

As he shall smile, Othello shall go mad;   100
And his unbookish° jealousy must conster°
Poor Cassio's smiles, gestures, and light behaviors
Quite in the wrong.—How do you now, Lieutenant?

CASSIO. The worser that you give me the addition°
Whose want° even kills me.   105

IAGO. Ply Desdemona well and you are sure on 't.
[*Speaking lower*.] Now, if this suit lay in Bianca's power,
How quickly should you speed!

CASSIO [*laughing*]. Alas, poor caitiff!°

OTHELLO [*aside*]. Look how he laughs already!   110

IAGO. I never knew a woman love man so.

CASSIO. Alas, poor rogue! I think, i' faith, she loves me.

---

78 **shifted him away** used a dodge to get rid of him.   79 **ecstasy** trance.   81 **encave** conceal.   82 **fleers** sneers.   **notable** obvious.   86 **cope** encounter with, have sex with.   88 **all-in-all in spleen** utterly governed by passionate impulses.   92 **keep time** keep yourself steady (as in music).   94 **huswife** hussy.   98 **restrain** refrain.   101 **unbookish** uninstructed.   **conster** construe.   104 **addition** title.   105 **Whose want** the lack of which.   109 **caitiff** wretch.

OTHELLO. Now he denies it faintly, and laughs it out.

IAGO. Do you hear, Cassio?

OTHELLO.   Now he importunes him
    To tell it o'er. Go to!° Well said,° well said.   115

IAGO. She gives it out that you shall marry her.
    Do you intend it?

CASSIO. Ha, ha, ha!

OTHELLO. Do you triumph, Roman?° Do you triumph?

CASSIO. I marry her? What? A customer?° Prithee, bear some charity to my   120
    wit;° do not think it so unwholesome. Ha, ha, ha!

OTHELLO. So, so, so, so! They laugh that win.°

IAGO. Faith, the cry° goes that you shall marry her.

CASSIO. Prithee, say true.

IAGO. I am a very villain else.°   125

OTHELLO. Have you scored me?° Well.

CASSIO. This is the monkey's own giving out. She is persuaded I will
    marry her out of her own love and flattery,° not out of my promise.

OTHELLO. Iago beckons me.° Now he begins the story.

CASSIO. She was here even now; she haunts me in every place. I was the   130
    other day talking on the seabank° with certain Venetians, and thither
    comes the bauble,° and, by this hand,° she falls me thus about my
    neck—

    [*He embraces* IAGO.]

OTHELLO. Crying, "O dear Cassio!" as it were; his gesture imports it.

CASSIO. So hangs and lolls and weep upon me, so shakes and pulls me. Ha,
    ha, ha!

OTHELLO. Now he tells how she plucked him to my chamber. O, I see that   135
    nose of yours, but not that dog I shall throw it to.°

CASSIO. Well, I must leave her company.

IAGO. Before me,° look where she comes.

    Enter BIANCA [*with* OTHELLO's *handkerchief*].

CASSIO. 'Tis such another fitchew!° Marry, a perfumed one.—What do
    you mean by this haunting of me?   140

BIANCA. Let the devil and his dam° haunt you! What did you mean by that
    same handkerchief you gave me even now? I was a fine fool to take
    it. I must take out the work? A likely piece of work,° that you
    should find it in your chamber and know not who left it there! This

---

115 Go to (An expression of remonstrance.)   **Well said** well done.   **119 Roman** (The
Romans were noted for their *triumphs* or triumphal processions.)   **120 customer** i.e., prostitute.   **bear . . . wit** be more charitable to my judgment.   **122 They . . . win** i.e., they that
laugh last laugh best.   **123 cry** rumor.   **125 I . . . else** call me a complete rogue if I'm not
telling the truth.   **126 scored me** scored off me, beaten me, made up my reckoning, branded
me.   **128 flattery** self-flattery, self-deception.   **129 beckons** signals.   **131 seabank**
seashore.   **132 bauble** plaything.   **by this hand** I make my vow.   **136 not . . . to** (Othello
imagines himself cutting off Cassio's nose and throwing it to a dog.)   **138 Before me** i.e., on
my soul.   **139 'Tis . . . fitchew** what a polecat she is! Just like all the others. (Polecats were often compared with prostitutes because of their rank smell and presumed lechery.)   **141 dam**
mother.   **143 A likely . . . work** a fine story.

is some minx's token, and I must take out the work? There; give it
your hobbyhorse.° [*She gives him the handkerchief.*] Wheresoever   145
you had it, I'll take out no work on 't.

CASSIO. How now, my sweet Bianca? How now? How now?

OTHELLO. By heaven, that should be° my handkerchief!

BIANCA. If you'll come to supper tonight, you may; if you will not, come
when you are next prepared for.°   150

Exit.

IAGO. After her, after her.

CASSIO. Faith, I must. She'll rail in the streets else.

IAGO. Will you sup there?

CASSIO. Faith, I intend so.

IAGO. Well, I may chance to see you, for I would very fain speak with you. 155

CASSIO. Prithee, come. Will you?

IAGO. Go to.° Say no more.   [*Exit* CASSIO.]

OTHELLO [*advancing*]. How shall I murder him, Iago?

IAGO. Did you perceive how he laughed at his vice?

OTHELLO. O, Iago!   160

IAGO. And did you see the handkerchief?

OTHELLO. Was that mine?

IAGO. Yours, by this hand. And to see how he prizes the foolish woman
your wife! She gave it him, and he hath given it his whore.

OTHELLO. I would have him nine years a-killing. A fine woman! A fair   165
woman! A sweet woman!

IAGO. Nay, you must forget that.

OTHELLO. Ay, let her rot and perish, and be damned tonight, for she shall not
live. No, my heart is turned to stone; I strike it, and it hurts my hand.
O, the world hath not a sweeter creature! She might lie by an em-   170
peror's side and command him tasks.

IAGO. Nay, that's not your way.°

OTHELLO. Hang her! I do but say what she is. So delicate with her needle!
An admirable musician! O, she will sing the savageness out of a
bear. Of so high and plenteous wit and invention!°   175

IAGO. She's the worse for all this.

OTHELLO. O, a thousand, a thousand times! And then, of so gentle a
condition!°

IAGO. Ay, too gentle.°

OTHELLO. Nay, that's certain. But yet the pity of it, Iago! O, Iago, the pity
of it, Iago!   180

IAGO. If you are so fond° over her iniquity, give her patent° to offend, for
if it touch not you it comes near nobody.

OTHELLO. I will chop her into messes.° Cuckold me?

IAGO. O, 'tis foul in her.

---

145 hobbyhorse harlot.   **148 should be** must be.   **149–150 when . . . for** when I'm ready
for you (i.e., never).   **157 Go to** (An expression of remonstrance.)   **172 your way** i.e., the
way you should think of her.   **175 invention** imagination.   **177 gentle a condition**
wellborn and well-bred.   **178 gentle** generous, yielding (to other men).   **181 fond** foolish.
patent license.   **183 messes** portions of meat, i. e., bits.

OTHELLO. With mine officer?   185

IAGO. That's fouler.

OTHELLO. Get me some poison, Iago, this night. I'll not expostulate with her,
    lest her body and beauty unprovide° my mind again. This night, Iago.

IAGO. Do it not with poison. Strangle her in her bed, even the bed she
    hath contaminated.   190

OTHELLO. Good, good! The justice of it pleases. Very good.

IAGO. And for Cassio, let me be his undertaker.° You shall hear more by
    midnight.

OTHELLO. Excellent good. [A *trumpet within*.] What trumpet is that same?

IAGO. I warrant, something from Venice.

    Enter LODOVICO, DESDEMONA, *and attendants*.

    'Tis Lodovico. This comes from the Duke.   195
    See, your wife's with him.

LODOVICO. God save you, worthy General!

OTHELLO.   With all my heart,° sir.

LODOVICO [*giving him a letter*]. The Duke and the senators of Venice greet
    you.

OTHELLO. I kiss the instrument of their pleasures.

    [*He opens the letter, and reads.*]

DESDEMONA. And what's the news, good cousin Lodovico?   200

IAGO. I am very glad to see you, signor.
    Welcome to Cyprus.

LODOVICO. I thank you. How does Lieutenant Cassio?

IAGO. Lives, sir.

DESDEMONA. Cousin, there's fall'n between him and my lord   205
    An unkind° breach; but you shall make all well.

OTHELLO. Are you sure of that?

DESDEMONA. My lord?

OTHELLO [*reads*]. "This fail you not to do, as you will—"

LODOVICO. He did not call; he's busy in the paper.   210
    Is there division twixt my lord and Cassio?

DESDEMONA. A most unhappy one. I would do much
    T' atone° them, for the love I bear to Cassio.

OTHELLO. Fire and brimstone!

DESDEMONA. My lord?   215

OTHELLO. Are you wise?

DESDEMONA. What, is he angry?

LODOVICO.   Maybe the letter moved him;
    For, as I think, they do command him home,
    Deputing Cassio in his government.°

DESDEMONA. By my troth, I am glad on 't.°   220

OTHELLO. Indeed?

DESDEMONA. My lord?

---

188 unprovide weaken, render unfit.   **192 be his undertaker** undertake to dispatch him.
197 With all my heart i.e., I thank you most heartily.   **206 unkind** unnatural, contrary to
their natures; hurtful.   **213 atone** reconcile.   **219 government** office.   **220 on 't** of it.

OTHELLO. I am glad to see you mad.°
DESDEMONA. Why, sweet Othello—
OTHELLO [*striking her*]. Devil!   225
DESDEMONA. I have not deserved this.
LODOVICO. My lord, this would not be believed in Venice,
    Though I should swear I saw 't. 'Tis very much.°
    Make her amends; she weeps.
OTHELLO.   O devil, devil!
    If that the earth could teem° with woman's tears,   230
    Each drop she falls would prove a crocodile.°
    Out of my sight!
DESDEMONA.   I will not stay to offend you. [*Going.*]
LODOVICO. Truly, an obedient lady.
    I do beseech your lordship, call her back.
OTHELLO. Mistress!   235
DESDEMONA [*returning*]. My lord?
OTHELLO. What would you with her, sir?°
LODOVICO: Who, I, my lord?
OTHELLO. Ay, you did wish that I would make her turn.
    Sir, she can turn, and turn, and yet go on   240
    And turn again; and she can weep, sir, weep;
    And she's obedient,° as you say, obedient,
    Very obedient.—Proceed you in your tears.—
    Concerning this, sir—O well-painted passion!°—
    I am commanded home.—Get you away;   245
    I'll send for you anon.—Sir, I obey the mandate
    And will return to Venice.—Hence, avaunt!

    [*Exit* DESDEMONA.]

    Cassio shall have my place. And, sir, tonight
    I do entreat that we may sup together.
    You are welcome, sir, to Cyprus.—Goats and monkeys!°   *Exit.*   250
LODOVICO. Is this the noble Moor whom our full Senate
    Call all in all sufficient? Is this the nature
    Whom passion could not shake? Whose solid virtue
    The shot of accident nor dart of chance
    Could neither graze nor pierce?
IAGO.   He is much changed.   255
LODOVICO. Are his wits safe? Is he not light of brain?
IAGO. He's that he is. I may not breathe my censure
    What he might be. If what he might he is not,
    I would to heaven he were!°

---

223 I am . . . mad i.e., I am glad to see that you are insane enough to rejoice in Cassio's promotion. (? Othello bitterly plays on Desdemona's *I am glad.*)   **228 very much** too much, outrageous.   **230 teem** breed, be impregnated.   **231 falls . . . crocodile** (Crocodiles were supposed to weep hypocritical tears for their victims.)   **237 What . . . sir** (Othello implies that
Desdemona is pliant and will do a turn, lines 239–241, for any man.)   **242 obedient** (With
much the same sexual connotation as *turn in* lines 239–241.)   **244 passion** i. e., grief.   **250
Goats and monkeys** (See 3.3.419.)   **257–259 I may . . . were** i.e., I dare not venture an opinion as to whether he's of unsound mind, as you suggest, but, if he isn't, then it might be better to
wish he were in fact insane, since only that could excuse his wild behavior.

LODOVICO.   What, strike his wife?

IAGO. Faith, that was not so well; yet would I knew   260
    That stroke would prove the worst!

LODOVICO.   Is it his use?°
    Or did the letters work upon his blood°
    And new-create his fault?

IAGO.   Alas, alas!
    It is not honesty in me to speak
    What I have seen and known. You shall observe him,   265
    And his own courses will denote° him so
    That I may save my speech. Do but go after,
    And mark how he continues.

LODOVICO. I am sorry that I am deceived in him.   *Exeunt.*

4.2 *Enter* OTHELLO *and* EMILIA

OTHELLO. You have seen nothing then?

EMILIA. Nor ever heard, nor ever did suspect.

OTHELLO. Yes, you have seen Cassio and she together.

EMILIA. But then I saw no harm, and then I heard
    Each syllable that breath made up between them.   5

OTHELLO. What, did they never whisper?

EMILIA. Never, my lord.

OTHELLO. Nor send you out o' the way?

EMILIA. Never.

OTHELLO. To fetch her fan, her gloves, her mask, nor nothing?   10

EMILIA. Never, my lord.

OTHELLO. That's strange.

EMILIA. I durst, my lord, to wager she is honest,
    Lay down my soul at stake.° If you think other,
    Remove your thought; it doth abuse your bosom.°   15
    If any wretch have put this in your head,
    Let heaven requite it with the serpent's curse!°
    For if she be not honest, chaste, and true,
    There's no man happy; the purest of their wives
    Is foul as slander.

OTHELLO.   Bid her come hither. Go.   20

Exit EMILIA.

    She says enough; yet she's a simple bawd

---

261 use custom.   **262 blood** passions.   **266 courses will denote** actions will reveal.   **4.2**
Location: The citadel.   14 at stake as the wager.   **15 abuse your bosom** deceive you.   **17**
the serpent's curse the curse pronounced by God on the serpent for deceiving Eve, just as
some man has done to Othello and Desdemona. (See Genesis 3.14.)

That cannot say as much.° This° is a subtle whore,
A closet lock and key° of villainous secrets.
And yet she'll kneel and pray; I have seen her do 't.

Enter DESDEMONA *and* EMILIA.

DESDEMONA. My lord, what is your will?   25
OTHELLO. Pray you, chuck, come hither.
DESDEMONA. What is your pleasure?
OTHELLO.   Let me see your eyes.
    Look in my face.
DESDEMONA.   What horrible fancy's this?
OTHELLO [*to* EMILIA]. Some of your function,° mistress.
    Leave procreants° alone and shut the door;   30
    Cough or cry "hem" if anybody come.
    Your mystery, your mystery!° Nay, dispatch.

    Exit EMILIA.

DESDEMONA [*kneeling*]. Upon my knees, what doth your speech import?
    I understand a fury in your words,
    But not the words.   35
OTHELLO. Why, what art thou?
DESDEMONA.   Your wife, my lord, your true
    And loyal wife.
OTHELLO.   Come, swear it, damn thyself,
    Lest, being like one of heaven,° the devils themselves
    Should fear to seize thee. Therefore be double damned:
    Swear thou art honest.
DESDEMONA.   Heaven doth truly know it.   40
OTHELLO. Heaven truly knows that thou art false as hell.
DESDEMONA. To whom, my lord? With whom? How am I false?
OTHELLO [*weeping*]. Ah, Desdemon! Away, away, away!
DESDEMONA. Alas the heavy day! Why do you weep?
    Am I the motive° of these tears, my lord?   45
    If haply you my father do suspect
    An instrument of this your calling back,
    Lay not your blame on me. If you have lost him,
    I have lost him too.
OTHELLO.   Had it pleased heaven
    To try me with affliction, had they° rained   50
    All kinds of sores and shames on my bare head,
    Steeped me in poverty to the very lips,
    Given to captivity me and my utmost hopes,
    I should have found in some place of my soul
    A drop of patience. But, alas, to make me   55

21–22 she's . . . much i.e., any procuress or go-between who couldn't make up as plausible a
story as Emilia's would have to be pretty stupid. **22 This** i.e., Desdemona. **23 closet lock
and key** i.e., concealer. **29 Some . . . function** i.e., practice your chosen profession, that of
bawd (by guarding the door). **30 procreants** mating couples. **32 mystery** trade, occupation. **38 being . . . heaven** looking like an angel. **45 motive** cause. **50 they** i.e., heavenly
powers.

A fixèd figure for the time of scorn°
To point his° slow and moving finger° at!
Yet could I bear that too, well, very well.
But there where I have garnered° up my heart,
Where either I must live or bear no life,   60
The fountain° from the which my current runs
Or else dries up—to be discarded thence!
Or keep it as a cistern° for foul toads
To knot° and gender° in! Turn thy complexion there,°
Patience, thou young and rose-lipped cherubin—   65
Ay, there look grim as hell!°

DESDEMONA. I hope my noble lord esteems me honest.°

OTHELLO. O, ay, as summer flies are in the shambles,°
That quicken° even with blowing.° O thou weed,
Who art so lovely fair and smell'st so sweet   70
That the sense aches at thee, would thou hadst ne'er been born!

DESDEMONA. Alas, what ignorant° sin have I committed?

OTHELLO. Was this fair paper, this most goodly book,
Made to write "whore" upon? What committed?
Committed? O thou public commoner!°   75
I should make very forges of my cheeks,
That would to cinders burn up modesty,
Did I but speak thy deeds. What committed?
Heaven stops the nose at it and the moon winks;°
The bawdy° wind, that kisses all it meets,   80
Is hushed within the hollow mine° of earth
And will not hear 't. What committed?
Impudent strumpet!

DESDEMONA.   By heaven, you do me wrong.

OTHELLO. Are not you a strumpet?

DESDEMONA. No, as I am a Christian.   85
If to preserve this vessel° for my lord
From any other foul unlawful touch
Be not to be a strumpet, I am none.

OTHELLO. What, not a whore?

DESDEMONA. No, as I shall be saved.   90

OTHELLO. Is't possible?

DESDEMONA. O, heaven forgive us!

OTHELLO.   I cry you mercy,° then.
I took you for that cunning whore of Venice

---

56 time of scorn i.e., scornful world.   **57 his** its.   **slow and moving finger** i.e., hour hand
of the clock, moving so slowly it seems hardly to move at all. (Othello envisages himself as being
eternally pointed at by the scornful world as the numbers on a clock are pointed at by the hour
hand.)   **59 garnered** stored.   **61 fountain** spring.   **63 cistern** cesspool.   **64 knot** couple.
gender engender.   **Turn . . . there** change your color, grow pale, at such a sight.   **65–66**
Patience . . . hell (Even Patience, that rose-lipped cherub, will look grim and pale at this spectacle.)   **67 honest** chaste.   **68 shambles** slaughterhouse.   **69 quicken** come to life.   **with**
blowing i.e., with the puffing up of something rotten in which maggots are breeding.   **72 ig-**
norant sin sin in ignorance.   **75 commoner** prostitute.   **79 winks** closes her eyes. (The
moon symbolizes chastity.)   **80 bawdy** kissing one and all.   **81 mine** cave (where the winds
were thought to dwell).   **86 vessel** body.   **92 cry you mercy** beg your pardon.

That married with Othello. [*Calling out.*] You, mistress,
That have the office opposite to Saint Peter   95
And keep the gate of hell!

[*Enter* EMILIA]

                              You, you, ay, you!
We have done our course.° There's money for your pains.
                                [*He gives money.*]
I pray you, turn the key and keep our counsel.   *Exit.*
EMILIA. Alas, what does this gentleman conceive?°
  How do you, madam? How do you, my good lady!   100
DESDEMONA. Faith, half asleep.°
EMILIA. Good madam, what's the matter with my lord?
DESDEMONA. With who?
EMILIA. Why, with my lord, madam.
DESDEMONA. Who is thy lord?
EMILIA.   He that is yours, sweet lady.   105
DESDEMONA. I have none. Do not talk to me, Emilia.
  I cannot weep, nor answers have I none
  But what should go by water.° Prithee, tonight
  Lay on my bed my wedding sheets, remember;
  And call thy husband hither.   110
EMILIA. Here's a change indeed!   *Exit.*
DESDEMONA. 'Tis meet I should be used so, very meet.°
  How have I been behaved, that he might stick°
  The small'st opinion° on my least misuse?°

Enter IAGO *and* EMILIA.

IAGO. What is your pleasure, madam? How is 't with you?   115
DESDEMONA. I cannot tell. Those that do teach young babes
  Do it with gentle means and easy tasks.
  He might have chid me so, for, in good faith,
  I am a child to chiding.
IAGO. What is the matter, lady?   120
EMILIA. Alas, Iago, my lord hath so bewhored her,
  Thrown such despite and heavy terms upon her,
  That true hearts cannot bear it.
DESDEMONA. Am I that name, Iago?
IAGO. What name, fair lady?   125
DESDEMONA. Such as she said my lord did say I was.
EMILIA. He called her whore. A beggar in his drink
  Could not have laid such terms upon his callet.°
IAGO. Why did he so?
DESDEMONA [*weeping*]. I do not know. I am sure I am none such. 130
IAGO. Do not weep, do not weep. Alas the day!

---

97 course business (with an indecent suggestion of "trick," turn at sex).   **99 conceive**
suppose, think.   **101 half asleep** i.e., dazed.   **108 go by water** be expressed by tears.   **112
meet** fitting.   **113 stick** attach.   **114 opinion** censure.   **least misuse** slightest misconduct.
128 callet whore.

EMILIA. Hath she forsook so many noble matches,
    Her father and her country and her friends,
    To be called whore? Would it not make one weep?
DESDEMONA. It is my wretched fortune.
IAGO.   Beshrew° him for 't!   135
    How comes this trick° upon him?
DESDEMONA.   Nay, heaven doth know.
EMILIA. I will be hanged if some eternal° villain,
    Some busy and insinuating° rogue,
    Some cogging,° cozening° slave, to get some office,
    Have not devised this slander. I will be hanged else.   140
IAGO. Fie, there is no such man. It is impossible.
DESDEMONA. If any such there be, heaven pardon him!
EMILIA. A halter° pardon him! And hell gnaw his bones!
    Why should he call her whore? Who keeps her company?
    What place? What time? What form?° What likelihood?   145
    The Moor's abused by some most villainous knave,
    Some base notorious knave, some scurvy fellow.
    O heaven, that° such companions° thou'dst unfold,°
    And put in every honest hand a whip
    To lash the rascals naked through the world   150
    Even from the east to th' west!
IAGO.   Speak within door.°
EMILIA. O, fie upon them! Some such squire° he was
    That turned your wit the seamy side without°
    And made you to suspect me with the Moor.
IAGO. You are a fool. Go to.°
DESDEMONA.   Alas, Iago,   155
    What shall I do to win my lord again?
    Good friend, go to him; for, by this light of heaven,
    I know not how I lost him. Here I kneel. [*She kneels.*]
    If e'er my will did trespass 'gainst his love,
    Either in discourse° of thought or actual deed,   160
    Or that° mine eyes, mine ears, or any sense
    Delighted them° in any other form;
    Or that I do not yet,° and ever did,
    And ever will—though he do shake me off
    To beggarly divorcement—love him dearly,   165
    Comfort forswear° me! Unkindness may do much,
    And his unkindness may defeat° my life,
    But never taint my love. I cannot say "whore."
    It does abhor° me now I speak the word;

---

135 Beshrew curse.   **136 trick** strange behavior, delusion.   **137 eternal** inveterate.   **138 insinuating** ingratiating, fawning, wheedling.   **139 cogging** cheating.   **cozening** defrauding.   **143 halter** hangman's noose.   **145 form** appearance, circumstance.   **148 that** would that. **companions** fellows.   **unfold** expose.   **151 within door** i.e., not so loud.   **152 squire** fellow.   **153 seamy side without** wrong side out.   **155 Go to** i.e., that's enough.   **160 discourse of thought** process of thinking.   **161 that** if. (Also in line 163.)   **162 Delighted them** took delight.   **163 yet** still.   **166 Comfort forswear** may heavenly comfort forsake. **167 defeat** destroy.   **169 abhor** (1) fill me with abhorrence (2) make me whorelike.

To do the act that might the addition° earn   170
Not the world's mass of vanity° could make me.

[*She rises.*]

IAGO. I pray you, be content. 'Tis but his humor.°
The business of the state does him offense,
And he does chide with you.
DESDEMONA. If 'twere no other—   175
IAGO. It is but so, I warrant.   [*Trumpets within.*]
Hark, how these instruments summon you to supper!
The messengers of Venice stays the meat.°
Go in, and weep not. All things shall be well.

Exeunt DESDEMONA *and* EMILIA.

Enter RODERIGO.

How now, Roderigo?   180
RODERIGO. I do not find that thou deal'st justly with me.
IAGO. What in the contrary?
RODERIGO. Every day thou daff'st me° with some device,° Iago, and rather,
as it seems to me now, keep'st from me all conveniency° than sup-
pliest me with the least advantage° of hope. I will indeed no longer   185
endure it, nor am I yet persuaded to put up° in peace what already
I have foolishly suffered.
IAGO. Will you hear me, Roderigo?
RODERIGO. Faith, I have heard too much, for your words and perfor-
mances are no kin together.
IAGO. You charge me most unjustly.   190
RODERIGO. With naught but truth. I have wasted myself out of my means.
The jewels you have had from me to deliver° Desdemona would
half have corrupted a votarist.° You have told me she hath re-
ceived them and returned me expectations and comforts of sudden
respect° and acquaintance, but I find none.   195
IAGO. Well, go to, very well.
RODERIGO. "Very well"! "Go to"! I cannot go to,° man, nor 'tis not very
well. By this hand, I think it is scurvy, and begin to find myself
fopped° in it.
IAGO. Very well.
RODERIGO. I tell you 'tis not very well.° I will make myself known to   200
Desdemona. If she will return me my jewels, I will give over my suit
and repent my unlawful solicitation; if not, assure yourself I will seek
satisfaction° of you.

---

170 **addition** title.   171 **vanity** showy splendor.   172 **humor** mood.   178 **stays the meat**
are waiting to dine.   183 **thou daff'st me** you put me off.   **device** excuse, trick.   184 **con-
veniency** advantage, opportunity.   185 **advantage** increase.   186 **put up** submit to, tolerate.
192 **deliver** deliver to.   193 **votarist** nun.   194 **sudden respect** immediate consideration.
197 **I cannot go to** (Roderigo changes Iago's *go to,* an expression urging patience, to *I cannot
go to,* "I have no opportunity for success in wooing.")   198 **fopped** fooled, duped.   200 **not
very well** (Roderigo changes Iago's *very well,* "all right, then," to *not very well,* "not at all
good.") 202 **satisfaction** repayment. (The term normally means settling of accounts in a duel.)

IAGO. You have said now?°

RODERIGO. Ay, and said nothing but what I protest intendment° of doing.

IAGO. Why, now I see there's mettle in thee, and even from this instant   205
do build on thee a better opinion than ever before. Give me thy
hand, Roderigo. Thou hast taken against me a most just exception;
but yet I protest I have dealt most directly in thy affair.

RODERIGO. It hath not appeared.

IAGO. I grant indeed it hath not appeared, and your suspicion is not with-   210
out wit and judgment. But, Roderigo, if thou hast that in thee indeed
which I have greater reason to believe now than ever—I mean purpose, courage, and valor—this night show it. If thou the next night
following enjoy not Desdemona, take me from this world with
treachery and devise engines for° my life.   215

RODERIGO. Well, what is it? Is it within reason and compass?

IAGO. Sir, there is especial commission come from Venice to depute Cassio in Othello's place.

RODERIGO. Is that true? Why, then Othello and Desdemona return again
to Venice.   220

IAGO. O, no; he goes into Mauritania and takes away with him the fair
Desdemona, unless his abode be lingered here by some accident;
wherein none can be so determinate° as the removing of Cassio.

RODERIGO. How do you mean, removing of him?

IAGO. Why, by making him uncapable of Othello's place—knocking out his   225
brains.

RODERIGO. And that you would have me to do?

IAGO. Ay, if you dare do yourself a profit and a right. He sups tonight
with a harlotry,° and thither will I go to him. He knows not yet of his
honorable fortune. If you will watch his going thence, which I
will fashion to fall out° between twelve and one, you may take   230
him at your pleasure. I will be near to second your attempt, and he
shall fall between us. Come, stand not amazed at it, but go along with
me. I will show you such a necessity in his death that you shall
think yourself bound to put it on him. It is now high° suppertime, and
the night grows to waste.° About it.   235

RODERIGO. I will hear further reason for this.

IAGO. And you shall be satisfied.   *Exeunt.*

4.3 *Enter* OTHELLO, LODOVICO, DESDEMONA, EMILIA, *and attendants.*

LODOVICO. I do beseech you, sir, trouble yourself no further.

OTHELLO. O, pardon me; 'twill do me good to walk.

LODOVICO. Madam, good night. I humbly thank your ladyship.

DESDEMONA. Your honor is most welcome.

OTHELLO.   Will you walk, sir?
O, Desdemona!   5

---

203 **You . . . now** have you finished?   204 **intendment** intention.   214 **engines for** plots
against.   223 **determinate** conclusive.   229 **harlotry** slut.   230 **fall out** occur.   234 **high**
fully.   235 **grows to waste** wastes away.   **4.3 Location: The citadel.**

DESDEMONA. My lord?
OTHELLO. Get you to bed on th' instant.
I will be returned forthwith. Dismiss your attendant there. Look 't
be done.
DESDEMONA. I will, my lord.   10

Exit [OTHELLO, *with* LODOVICO *and attendants*].

EMILIA. How goes it now? He looks gentler than he did.
DESDEMONA. He says he will return incontinent,°
And hath commanded me to go to bed,
And bid me to dismiss you.
EMILIA. Dismiss me?   15
DESDEMONA. It was his bidding. Therefore, good Emilia,
Give me my nightly wearing, and adieu.
We must not now displease him.
EMILIA. I would you had never seen him!
DESDEMONA. So would not I. My love doth so approve him   20
That even his stubbornness,° his checks,° his frowns—
Prithee, unpin me—have grace and favor in them.

[EMILIA *prepares* DESDEMONA *for bed*.]

EMILIA. I have laid those sheets you bade me on the bed.
DESDEMONA. All's one.° Good faith, how foolish are our minds!
If I do die before thee, prithee shroud me   25
In one of these same sheets.
EMILIA.   Come, come, you talk.°
DESDEMONA. My mother had a maid called Barbary.
She was in love, and he she loved proved mad°
And did forsake her. She had a song of "Willow."
An old thing 'twas, but it expressed her fortune,   30
And she died singing it. That song tonight
Will not go from my mind; I have much to do
But to go hang° my head all at one side
And sing it like poor Barbary. Prithee, dispatch.
EMILIA. Shall I go fetch your nightgown?°   35
DESDEMONA. No, unpin me here.
This Lodovico is a proper° man.
EMILIA. A very handsome man.
DESDEMONA. He speaks well.
EMILIA. I know a lady in Venice would have walked barefoot to Palestine   40
for a touch of his nether lip.
DESDEMONA. [*singing*]
          "The poor soul sat sighing by a sycamore tree,
          Sing all a green willow;°
          Her hand on her bosom, her head on her knee,
          Sing willow, willow, willow.   45

---

12 incontinent immediately.   **21 stubbornness** roughness.   **checks** rebukes.   **24 All's
one** all right. It doesn't really matter.   **26 talk** i.e., prattle.   **28 mad** wild, i.e., faithless.   **32–33
I . . . hang** I can scarcely keep myself from hanging.   **35 nightgown** dressing gown.   **37
proper** handsome.   **43 willow** (A conventional emblem of disappointed love.)

The fresh streams ran by her and murmured her moans;
Sing willow, willow, willow;
Her salt tears fell from her, and softened the stones—"

Lay by these.
            [*Singing*.] "Sing willow, willow, willow—"   50
Prithee, hie thee.° He'll come anon.°
            [*Singing*.] "Sing all a green willow must be my garland.
Let nobody blame him; his scorn I approve—"

Nay, that's not next.—Hark! Who is 't that knocks?
EMILIA. It's the wind.
DESDEMONA [*singing*].   55
        "I called my love false love; but what said he then?
        Sing willow, willow, willow;
        If I court more women, you'll couch with more men."

So, get thee gone. Good night. Mine eyes do itch;
Doth that bode weeping?
EMILIA.   'Tis neither here nor there.   60
DESDEMONA. I have heard it said so. O, these men, these men!
Dost thou in conscience think—tell me, Emilia—
That there be women do abuse° their husbands
In such gross kind?
EMILIA.   There be some such, no question.
DESDEMONA. Wouldst thou do such a deed for all the world?   65
EMILIA. Why, would not you?
DESDEMONA.   No, by this heavenly light!
EMILIA. Nor I neither by this heavenly light;
I might do 't as well i' the dark.
DESDEMONA. Wouldst thou do such a deed for all the world?
EMILIA. The world's a huge thing. It is a great price   70
For a small vice.
DESDEMONA. Good troth, I think thou wouldst not.
EMILIA. By my troth, I think I should, and undo 't when I had done.
Marry, I would not do such a thing for a joint ring,° nor for mea-
sures of lawn,° nor for gowns, petticoats, nor caps, nor any petty
exhibition.° But for all the whole world! Uds° pity, who would not   75
make her husband a cuckold to make him a monarch? I should ven-
ture purgatory for 't.
DESDEMONA. Beshrew me if I would do such a wrong
For the whole world.
EMILIA. Why, the wrong is but a wrong i' the world, and having the world for   80
your labor, 'tis a wrong in your own world, and you might quickly
make it right.
DESDEMONA. I do not think there is any such woman.
EMILIA. Yes, a dozen, and as many
To th' vantage° as would store° the world they played° for.   85

---

51 hie thee hurry. **anon** right away. **63 abuse** deceive. **74 joint ring** a ring made in separate halves. **lawn** fine linen. **75 exhibition** gift. **76 Uds** God's. **85 To th' vantage** in
addition, to boot. **store** populate. **played** (1) gambled (2) sported sexually.

But I do think it is their husbands' faults
If wives do fall. Say that they slack their duties°
And pour our treasures into foreign laps,°
Or else break out in peevish jealousies,
Throwing restraint upon us? Or say they strike us,°   90
Or scant our former having in despite?°
Why, we have galls,° and though we have some grace,
Yet have we some revenge. Let husbands know
Their wives have sense° like them. They see, and smell,
And have their palates both for sweet and sour,   95
As husbands have. What is it that they do
When they change us for others? Is it sport?°
I think it is. And doth affection° breed it?
I think it doth. Is 't frailty that thus errs?
It is so, too. And have not we affections,   100
Desires for sport, and frailty, as men have?
Then let them use us well; else let them know,
The ills we do, their ills instruct us so.

DESDEMONA. Good night, good night. God me such uses° send
Not to pick bad from bad, but by bad mend!°   105

Exeunt.

5.1 *Enter* IAGO *and* RODERIGO.

IAGO. Here stand behind this bulk.° Straight will he come.
Wear thy good rapier bare,° and put it home.
Quick, quick! Fear nothing. I'll be at thy elbow.
It makes us or it mars us. Think on that,
And fix most firm thy resolution.   5

RODERIGO. Be near at hand. I may miscarry in 't.

IAGO. Here, at thy hand. Be bold, and take thy stand.

[IAGO *stands aside.* RODERIGO *conceals himself.*]

RODERIGO. I have no great devotion to the deed;
And yet he hath given me satisfying reasons.
'Tis but a man gone. Forth, my sword! He dies.   10

---

87 **duties** marital duties.   88 **pour . . . laps** i.e., are unfaithful, give what is rightfully ours (se-
men) to other women.   90 **Throwing . . . us** i.e., jealously restricting our freedom to see other
men.   91 **scant . . . despite** reduce our allowance to spite us.   92 **have galls** i.e., are capable
of resenting injury and insult.   94 **sense** physical sense.   97 **sport** sexual pastime.   98 **affection** passion.   104 **uses** habit, practice.   105 **Not . . . mend** i.e., not to learn bad conduct
from others' badness (as Emilia has suggested women learn from men), but to mend my ways by
perceiving what badness is, making spiritual benefit out of evil and adversity.   **5.1 Location: A
street in Cyprus.**   1 **bulk** framework projecting from the front of a shop.   2 **bare** unsheathed.

[*He draws.*]

IAGO. I have rubbed this young quat° almost to the sense,°
And he grows angry. Now, whether he kill Cassio
Or Cassio him, or each do kill the other,
Every way makes my gain. Live Roderigo,°
He calls me to a restitution large   15
Of gold and jewels that I bobbed° from him
As gifts to Desdemona.
It must not be. If Cassio do remain,
He hath a daily beauty in his life
That makes me ugly; and besides, the Moor   20
May unfold° me to him; there stand I in much peril.
No, he must die. Be 't so. I hear him coming.

Enter CASSIO.

RODERIGO [*coming forth*]. I know his gait, 'tis he.—Villain, thou diest!

[*He attacks* CASSIO]

CASSIO. That thrust had been mine enemy indeed,
But that my coat° is better than thou know'st.   25
I will make proof° of thine.

[*He draws, and wounds* RODERIGO.]

RODERIGO.   O, I am slain!   [*He falls.*]

[IAGO *from behind, wounds* CASSIO *in the leg, and exits.*]

CASSIO. I am maimed forever. Help, ho! Murder! Murder!

Enter OTHELLO.

OTHELLO. The voice of Cassio! Iago keeps his word.
RODERIGO. O, villain that I am!
OTHELLO. It is even so.   30
CASSIO. O, help, ho! Light! A surgeon!
OTHELLO. 'Tis he. O brave Iago, honest and just,
That hast such noble sense of thy friend's wrong!
Thou teachest me. Minion,° your dear lies dead,
And your unblest fate hies.° Strumpet, I come.   35
Forth of° my heart those charms, thine eyes are blotted;
Thy bed, lust-stained, shall with lust's blood be spotted.

                                                   Exit OTHELLO.

Enter LODOVICO *and* GRATIANO.

CASSIO. What ho! No watch? No passage?° Murder! Murder!
GRATIANO. 'Tis some mischance. The voice is very direful.

---

11 **quat** pimple, pustule.   **to the sense** to the quick.   14 **Live Roderigo** if Roderigo lives.
16 **bobbed** swindled.   21 **unfold** expose.   25 **coat** (Possibly a garment of mail under the
outer clothing, or simply a tougher coat than Roderigo expected.)   26 **proof** a test.   34
Minion hussy (i.e., Desdemona).   35 **hies** hastens on.   36 **Forth of** from out.   38 **passage**
people passing by.

CASSIO. O, help!   40
LODOVICO. Hark!
RODERIGO. O wretched villain!
LODOVICO. Two or three groan. 'Tis heavy° night;
    These may be counterfeits. Let's think 't unsafe
    To come in to° the cry without more help.   45

[They remain near the entrance.]

RODERIGO. Nobody come? Then shall I bleed to death.

Enter IAGO *[in his shirtsleeves, with a light].*

LODOVICO. Hark!
GRATIANO. Here's one comes in his shirt, with light and weapons.
IAGO. Who's there? Whose noise is this that cries on° murder?
LODOVICO. We do not know.
IAGO.   Did not you hear a cry?   50
CASSIO. Here, here! For heaven's sake, help me!
IAGO.   What's the matter?

[He moves toward CASSIO.*]*

GRATIANO *[to* LODOVICO*]*. This is Othello's ancient, as I take it.
LODOVICO *[to* GRATIANO*]*. The same indeed, a very valiant fellow.
IAGO *[to* CASSIO*]*. What° are you here that cry so grievously?
CASSIO. Iago? O, I am spoiled,° undone by villains!   55
    Give me some help.
IAGO. O me, Lieutenant! What villains have done this?
CASSIO. I think that one of them is hereabout,
    And cannot make° away.
IAGO.   O treacherous villains!

[To LODOVICO *and* GRATIANO.*]*

    What are you there? Come in, and give some help. *[They advance.]*   60
RODERIGO. O, help me there!
CASSIO. That's one of them.
IAGO.   O murderous slave! O villain!

[He stabs RODERIGO.*]*

RODERIGO. O damned Iago! O inhuman dog!
IAGO. Kill men i' the dark?—Where be these bloody thieves?—
    How silent is this town!—Ho! Murder, murder!—   65
    [To LODOVICO *and* GRATIANO.*]* What may you be? Are you of good
    or evil?
LODOVICO. As you shall prove us, praise° us.
IAGO. Signor Lodovico?
LODOVICO. He, sir.
IAGO. I cry you mercy.° Here's Cassio hurt by villains.   70

---

43 heavy thick, dark. **45 come in to** approach. **49 cries on** cries out. **54 What** who
(also at lines 60 and 66). **55 spoiled** ruined, done for. **59 make** get. **67 praise** appraise.
70 I cry you mercy I beg your pardon.

GRATIANO. Cassio?
IAGO. How is 't, brother?
CASSIO. My leg is cut in two.
IAGO. Marry, heaven forbid!
　　Light, gentlemen! I'll bind it with my shirt.   75

[*He hands them the light, and tends to* CASSIO's *wound.*]

　　Enter BIANCA.

BIANCA. What is the matter, ho? Who is 't that cried?
IAGO. Who is 't that cried?
BIANCA.　　　　　　　　　　O my dear Cassio!
　　My sweet Cassio! O Cassio, Cassio, Cassio!
IAGO. O notable strumpet! Cassio, may you suspect
　　Who they should be that have thus mangled you?   80
CASSIO. No.
GRATIANO. I am sorry to find you thus. I have been to seek you.
IAGO. Lend me a garter. [*He applies a tourniquet.*] So.—O, for a chair,°
　　To bear him easily hence!
BIANCA. Alas, he faints! O Cassio, Cassio, Cassio!   85
IAGO. Gentlemen all, I do suspect this trash
　　To be a party in this injury.—
　　Patience awhile, good Cassio.—Come, come;
　　Lend me a light. [*He shines the light on* RODERIGO.]
　　　　　　　　　　Know we this face or no?
　　Alas, my friend and my dear countryman   90
　　Roderigo! No.—Yes, sure.—O heaven! Roderigo!
GRATIANO. What, of Venice?
IAGO. Even he, sir. Did you know him?
GRATIANO. Know him? Ay.
IAGO. Signor Gratiano? I cry your gentle° pardon.   95
　　These bloody accidents° must excuse my manners
　　That so neglected you.
GRATIANO.　　　　　　　　I am glad to see you.
IAGO. How do you, Cassio? O, a chair, a chair!
GRATIANO. Roderigo!
IAGO. He, he, 'tis he. [*A litter is brought in.*] O, that's well said;° the chair. 100
　　Some good man bear him carefully from hence;
　　I'll fetch the General's surgeon. [*To* BIANCA.] For you, mistress,
　　Save you your labor.°—He that lies slain here, Cassio,
　　Was my dear friend. What malice° was between you?
CASSIO. None in the world, nor do I know the man.   105
IAGO [*to* BIANCA]. What, look you pale?—O, bear him out o' th' air.°

[CASSIO *and* RODERIGO *are borne off.*]

---

83 chair litter.　**95 gentle** noble.　**96 accidents** sudden events.　**100 well said** well done.
103 Save . . . labor i.e., never you mind tending Cassio.　**104 malice** enmity.　**106 bear . . .**
air (Fresh air was thought to be dangerous for a wound.)

Stay you,° good gentlemen.—Look you pale, mistress?—
Do you perceive the gastness° of her eye?—
Nay, if you stare,° we shall hear more anon.—
Behold her well; I pray you, look upon her.   110
Do you see, gentlemen? Nay, guiltiness
Will speak, though tongues were out of use.

[*Enter* EMILIA.]

EMILIA. 'Las, what's the matter? What's the matter, husband?
IAGO. Cassio hath here been set on in the dark
    By Roderigo and fellows that are scaped.   115
    He's almost slain, and Roderigo dead.
EMILIA. Alas, good gentleman! Alas, good Cassio!
IAGO. This is the fruits of whoring. Prithee, Emilia,
    Go know° of Cassio where he supped tonight.
    [*To* BIANCA.] What, do you shake at that?   120
BIANCA. He supped at my house, but I therefore shake not.
IAGO. O, did he so? I charge you go with me.
EMILIA. O, fie upon thee, strumpet!
BIANCA. I am no strumpet, but of life as honest°
    As you that thus abuse me.   125
EMILIA. As I? Faugh! Fie upon thee!
IAGO. Kind gentlemen, let's go see poor Cassio dressed.°—
    Come, mistress, you must tell's another tale.
    Emilia, run you to the citadel
    And tell my lord and lady what hath happed.—   130
    Will you go on afore? [*Aside.*] This is the night
    That either makes me or fordoes° me quite.   *Exeunt.*

5.2 *Enter* OTHELLO [*with a light*], *and* DESDEMONA *in her bed.*

OTHELLO. It is the cause,° it is the cause, my soul.
    Let me not name it to you, you chaste stars!
    It is the cause. Yet I'll not shed her blood,
    Nor scar that whiter skin of hers than snow,
    And smooth as monumental° alabaster.   5
    Yet she must die, else she'll betray more men.
    Put out the light, and then put out the light.°
    If I quench thee, thou flaming minister,°
    I can again thy former light restore,
    Should I repent me;° but once put out thy light,   10

---

107 Stay you (Lodovico and Gratiano are evidently about to leave.) **108 gastness** terror.
109 stare (Iago pretends to interpret Bianca's wild looks as an involuntary confession of guilt.)
119 know learn. **124 honest** chaste. **127 Cassio dressed** Cassio's wounds dressed. **132
fordoes** undoes, ruins. **5.2 Location: A bedchamber in the citadel. s.d. in her bed** (Either
the curtains are drawn back to reveal the bed in a recessed area backstage, or the bed is "thrust
out" onstage as the scene begins.) **1 cause** i.e., cause of justice, the offense itself, which Othello
must correct as an agent of justice. **5 monumental** i.e., used in making tombs and funeral monuments. **7 the light . . . light** the torch or lamp . . . Desdemona's life. **8 flaming minister**
torch or lamp that serves me. **10 repent me** change my mind.

Thou cunning'st pattern° of excelling nature,
I know not where is that Promethean heat°
That can thy light relume.° When I have plucked thy rose,
I cannot give it vital growth again;
It needs must wither. I'll smell thee on the tree.   15

[*He kisses her.*]

O balmy breath, that dost almost persuade
Justice to break her sword! One more, one more.
Be thus when thou art dead, and I will kill thee,
And love thee after. One more, and that's the last.

[*He kisses her.*]

So sweet was ne'er so fatal. I must weep,   20
But they are cruel° tears. This sorrow's heavenly;
It strikes where it doth love.° She wakes.
DESDEMONA. Who's there? Othello?
OTHELLO. Ay, Desdemona.
DESDEMONA. Will you come to bed, my lord?   25
OTHELLO. Have you prayed tonight, Desdemon?
DESDEMONA. Ay, my lord.
OTHELLO. If you bethink yourself of any crime°
     Unreconciled as yet to heaven and grace,
     Solicit° for it straight.°   30
DESDEMONA. Alack, my lord, what may you mean by that?
OTHELLO. Well, do it, and be brief. I will walk by.
     I would not kill thy unpreparèd spirit.
     No, heaven forfend!° I would not kill thy soul.
DESDEMONA. Talk you of killing?
OTHELLO.   Ay, I do.
DESDEMONA.   Then heaven   35
     Have mercy on me!
OTHELLO.   Amen, with all my heart!
DESDEMONA. If you say so, I hope you will not kill me.
OTHELLO. Humh!
DESDEMONA. And yet I fear you; for you're fatal then
     When your eyes roll so. Why I should fear I know not,   40
     Since guiltiness I know not; but yet I feel I fear.
OTHELLO. Think on thy sins.
DESDEMONA.   They are loves I bear to you.°
OTHELLO. Ay, and for that thou diest.
DESDEMONA. That death's unnatural that kills for loving.
     Alas, why gnaw you so your nether lip?   45
     Some bloody passion shakes your very frame.

---

11 Thou . . . pattern you skillfully wrought perfect example.   **12 Promethean heat** divine
fire. (Alluding to the theft of fire from heaven by Prometheus.)   **13 relume** rekindle.   **21
cruel** unrelenting.   **22 It . . . love** (Compare Hebrews 12.6: "For whom the Lord loveth he
chasteneth.")   **28 crime** sin.   **30 Solicit** petition, pray.   **straight** immediately.   **34 forfend**
forbid.   **42 They are . . . you** i.e., if I sinned, it was in loving you more than my father or more
than God.

These are portents; but yet I hope, I hope,
    They do not point on° me.
OTHELLO.   Peace, and be still!
DESDEMONA.   I will so. What's the matter?   50
OTHELLO.   That handkerchief which I so loved and gave thee
    Thou gav'st to Cassio.
DESDEMONA.   No, by my life and soul!
    Send for the man and ask him.
OTHELLO.   Sweet soul, take heed, take heed of perjury.
    Thou art on thy deathbed.   55
DESDEMONA.   Ay, but not yet to die.
OTHELLO.   Yes, presently.°
    Therefore confess thee freely of thy sin;
    For to deny each article with oath
    Cannot remove nor choke the strong conception°
    That I do groan withal.° Thou art to die.   60
DESDEMONA.   Then Lord have mercy on me!
OTHELLO.   I say, amen.
DESDEMONA.   And have you mercy too! I never did
    Offend° you in my life; never loved Cassio
    But with such general warranty° of heaven
    As I might love. I never gave him token.   65
OTHELLO.   By heaven, I saw my handkerchief in 's hand.
    O perjured woman! Thou dost stone° my heart,
    And makes me call what I intend to do
    A murder, which I thought a sacrifice.
    I saw the handkerchief.
DESDEMONA.   He found it, then.   70
    I never gave it him. Send for him hither;
    Let him confess a truth.
OTHELLO.   He hath confessed.
DESDEMONA.   What, my lord?
OTHELLO.   That he hath used thee.
DESDEMONA.   How? Unlawfully?
OTHELLO.   Ay.
DESDEMONA.   He will not say so.
OTHELLO.   No, his mouth is stopped;   75
    Honest Iago hath ta'en order° for 't.
DESDEMONA.   O, my fear interprets. What, is he dead?
OTHELLO.   Had all his hairs been lives, my great revenge
    Had stomach for them all.
DESDEMONA.   Alas, he is betrayed and I undone!   [*She weeps.*]   80
OTHELLO.   Out, strumpet! Weep'st thou for him to my face?
DESDEMONA.   O, banish me, my lord, but kill me not!
OTHELLO.   Down, strumpet!

---

48 point on point at, predict what is to happen to.   **56 presently** immediately.   **59 conception** (1) belief in your guilt (2) plan in my mind.   **60 groan withal** (1) groan at in sorrow (2) as in giving birth.   **63 Offend** wrong.   **64 warranty** sanction.   **67 stone** turn to stone, harden.   **76 ta' en order** taken measures.

DESDEMONA. Kill me tomorrow; let me live tonight!

OTHELLO. Nay, if you strive—   85

DESDEMONA. But half an hour!

OTHELLO.   Being done,° there is no pause.

DESDEMONA. But while I say one prayer!

OTHELLO.   It is too late.

     Smothers her.

EMILIA [*at the door*]. My lord, my lord! What, ho! My lord, my lord!

OTHELLO. What noise is this? Not dead? Not yet quite dead?

     I that am cruel am yet merciful;   90

     I would not have thee linger in thy pain.

     [*He dispatches her.*]

                              So, so.

EMILIA [*within*]. What, ho! My lord, my lord!

OTHELLO.   Who's there?

EMILIA [*within*]. O, good my lord, I would speak a word with you!

OTHELLO. Yes, 'tis Emilia.—By and by.—She's dead.

     'Tis like° she comes to speak of Cassio's death.—   95

     The noise was here.° Ha! No more moving?

     Still as the grave. Shall she come in? Were 't good?—

     I think she stirs again. No. What's best to do?

     If she come in, she'll sure speak to my wife,

     My wife! My wife! What wife? I have no wife.   100

     O, insupportable! O heavy hour!

     Methinks it should be now a huge eclipse

     Of sun and moon, and that th' affrighted globe

     Should yawn° at alteration.°

EMILIA [*within*].   I do beseech you

     That I may speak with you, O, good my lord!   105

OTHELLO. I had forgot thee. O, come in, Emilia.—

     Soft,° by and by. Let me the curtains draw.—

     [*He closes the bed-curtains and opens the door.*]

     Where art thou?

     Enter EMILIA.

                              What's the matter with thee now?

EMILIA. O, my good lord, yonder's foul murders done!

OTHELLO. What, now?   110

EMILIA. But now, my lord.

OTHELLO. It is the very error° of the moon;

     She comes more nearer earth than she was wont,

     And makes men mad.

---

86 Being done i.e., since justice has begun its relentless course.   **95 like** likely that.   **96 here** (The Folio's *high* is possible, suggesting that the commotion of the attack on Cassio was loud.)   **104 yawn** gape in amazement, i.e., move in an earthquake. (According to Pliny, earthquakes often happen during eclipses.)   **at alteration** at these cataclysmic events in nature, well suited to express the horror of Desdemona's death.   **107 Soft** wait a minute.   **112 error** aberration, irregularity.

EMILIA. Cassio, my lord, hath killed a young Venetian   115
    Called Roderigo.
OTHELLO.   Roderigo killed?
    And Cassio killed?
EMILIA.   No, Cassio is not killed.
OTHELLO. Not Cassio killed? Then murder's out of tune,
    And sweet revenge grows harsh.
DESDEMONA. O, falsely, falsely murdered!   120
EMILIA. O Lord, what cry is that?
OTHELLO. That? What?
EMILIA. Out° and alas, that was my lady's voice.

    [She opens the bed-curtains.]

    Help, help, ho, help! O lady, speak again!
    Sweet Desdemona! O sweet mistress, speak!   125
DESDEMONA. A guiltless death I die.
EMILIA. O, who hath done this deed?
DESDEMONA. Nobody; I myself. Farewell.
    Commend me to my kind lord. O, farewell!   *[She dies.]*
OTHELLO. Why, how should she be murdered?
EMILIA.   Alas, who knows?   130
OTHELLO. You heard her say herself it was not I.
EMILIA. She said so. I must needs report the truth.
OTHELLO. She's like a liar gone to burning hell!
    'Twas I that killed her.
EMILIA.   O, the more angel she,
    And you the blacker devil!   135
OTHELLO. She turned to folly,° and she was a whore.
EMILIA. Thou dost belie° her, and thou art a devil.
OTHELLO. She was false as water.
EMILIA. Thou art rash as fire to say
    That she was false. O, she was heavenly true!   140
OTHELLO. Cassio did top her. Ask thy husband else.°
    O, I were damned beneath all depth in hell
    But that I did proceed upon just grounds
    To this extremity. Thy husband knew it all.
EMILIA. My husband?   145
OTHELLO. Thy husband.
EMILIA. That she was false to wedlock?
OTHELLO. Ay, with Cassio. Nay, had she been true,
    If heaven would make me such another world
    Of one entire and perfect chrysolite,°   150
    I'd not have sold her for it.
EMILIA. My husband?
OTHELLO. Ay, 'twas he that told me on her first.
    An honest man he is, and hates the slime
    That sticks on filthy deeds.   155

---

123 Out (A cry of dismay, intensifying *alas.*)   **136 folly** i.e., wantonness, fleshly sin.   **137 belie** slander.   **141 else** i.e., if you don't believe me.   **150 chrysolite** precious topaz.

EMILIA. My husband?
OTHELLO. What needs this iterance,° woman? I say thy husband.
EMILIA. O mistress, villainy hath made mocks with° love!
    My husband say she was false?
OTHELLO.   He, woman;
    I say thy husband. Dost understand the word?   160
    My friend, thy husband, honest, honest Iago.
EMILIA. If he say so, may his pernicious soul
    Rot half a grain a day! He lies to th' heart.
    She was too fond of her most filthy bargain.
OTHELLO. Ha?   [*He draws.*]   165
EMILIA. Do thy worst!
    This deed of thine is no more worthy heaven
    Than thou wast worthy her.
OTHELLO.   Peace, you were best.°
EMILIA. Thou hast not half that power to do me harm
    As I have to be hurt.° O gull!° O dolt!   170
    As ignorant as dirt! Thou hast done a deed—
    I care not for thy sword; I'll make thee known,
    Though I lost twenty lives.—Help! Help, ho, help!
    The Moor hath killed my mistress! Murder, murder!

    Enter MONTANO, GRATIANO, *and* IAGO

MONTANO. What is the matter? How now, General?   175
EMILIA. O, are you come, Iago? You have done well,
    That men must lay their murders on your neck.
GRATIANO. What is the matter?
EMILIA [*to* IAGO]. Disprove this villain, if thou be'st a man.
    He says thou toldst him that his wife was false.   180
    I know thou didst not; thou'rt not such a villain.
    Speak, for my heart is full.
IAGO. I told him what I thought, and told no more
    Than what he found himself was apt° and true.
EMILIA. But did you ever tell him she was false?   185
IAGO. I did.
EMILIA. You told a lie, an odious, damnèd lie!
    Upon my soul, a lie, a wicked lie.
    She false with Cassio? Did you say with Cassio?
IAGO. With Cassio, mistress. Go to, charm° your tongue.   190
EMILIA. I will not charm my tongue; I am bound to speak.
    My mistress here lies murdered in her bed—
ALL. O heavens forfend!
EMILIA. And your reports have set the murder on.
OTHELLO. Nay, stare not, masters. It is true indeed.   195
GRATIANO. 'Tis a strange truth.
MONTANO. O monstrous act!

---

157 iterance iteration, repetition.   **158 made mocks with** derided, made sport of.   **168 you
were best** it would be best for you.   **170 to be hurt** i.e., to endure hurt.   **gull** dupe.   **184
apt** plausible.   **190 charm** keep silent (as though by a magic spell).

EMILIA.   Villainy, villainy, villainy!
    I think upon 't—I think I smell 't! O villainy!
    I thought so then°—I'll kill myself for grief—
    O villainy, villainy!   200
IAGO. What, are you mad? I charge you, get you home.
EMILIA. Good gentlemen, let me have leave to speak.
    'Tis proper I obey him, but not now.
    Perchance, Iago, I will ne'er go home.
OTHELLO. O! O! O!   [OTHELLO *falls on the bed.*°]
EMILIA.   Nay, lay thee down and roar,   205
    For thou hast killed the sweetest innocent
    That e'er did lift up eye.°
OTHELLO [*rising*].   O, she was foul!
    I scarce did know you, uncle. There lies your niece,
    Whose breath indeed these hands have newly stopped.
    I know this act shows° horrible and grim.   210
GRATIANO. Poor Desdemon! I am glad thy father's dead.
    Thy match was mortal to him, and pure grief
    Shore his old thread° in twain. Did he live now,
    This sight would make him do a desperate turn,°
    Yea, curse his better angel from his side,   215
    And fall to reprobance.°
OTHELLO. 'Tis pitiful. But yet Iago knows
    That she with Cassio hath the act of shame
    A thousand times committed. Cassio confessed it;
    And she did gratify° his amorous works   220
    With that recognizance° and pledge of love
    Which I first gave her. I saw it in his hand;
    It was a handkerchief, an antique token
    My father gave my mother.
EMILIA. O God! O heavenly God!   225
IAGO. Zounds, hold your peace.
EMILIA.   'Twill out, 'twill out! I peace?
    No, I will speak as liberal as the north.°
    Let heaven and men and devils, let them all,
    All, all, cry shame against me, yet I'll speak.
IAGO. Be wise, and get you home.
EMILIA.   I will not.

    [IAGO *threatens* EMILIA.]

GRATIANO.   Fie   230
    Your sword upon a woman?
EMILIA. O thou dull Moor! That handkerchief thou speak'st of
    I found by fortune and did give my husband;

---

199 then (Perhaps at 3.3.331–332 and 4.2.137–154.)   **205 s.d. Othello bed** (This direction is from the Quarto, as also *He kisses her* at line 19 and *She dies* at line 129.)   **207 lift up eye** i.e., lift her eyes to heaven.   **210 shows** looks.   **213 Shore . . . thread** sheared the thread of his old age (as Atropos, one of the three Fates, was thought to do).   **214 turn** deed.   **216 reprobance** damnation, i.e., suicide.   **220 gratify** reward.   **221 recognizance** token.   **227 liberal as the north** freely as the north wind (blows).

For often, with a solemn earnestness,
More than indeed belonged° to such a trifle,   235
He begged of me to steal 't.
IAGO.   Villainous whore!
EMILIA. She give it Cassio? No, alas! I found it,
And I did give 't my husband.
IAGO.   Filth, thou liest!
EMILIA. By heaven, I do not, I do not, gentlemen.
O murderous coxcomb!° What should such a fool   240
Do with so good a wife?
OTHELLO. Are there no stones° in heaven
But what serves for the thunder?—Precious° villain!

[*He runs at* IAGO; MONTANO *disarms* OTHELLO. IAGO, *from
behind, stabs* EMILIA.°]

GRATIANO. The woman falls! Sure he hath killed his wife.
EMILIA. Ay, ay. O, lay me by my mistress' side.   245

  Exit [IAGO.]

GRATIANO. He's gone, but his wife's killed.
MONTANO. 'Tis a notorious villain. Take you this weapon,
Which I have here recovered from the Moor.
Come, guard the door without. Let him not pass,
But kill him rather. I'll after that same villain,   250
For 'tis a damnèd slave.

  Exit [*with all but* OTHELLO *and* EMILIA, *who has been laid by*
  DESDEMONA's *side*].

OTHELLO. I am not valiant neither,
But every puny whipster° gets my sword.
But why should honor° outlive honesty?°
Let it go all.
EMILIA.   What did thy song bode, lady?   255
Hark, canst thou hear me? I will play the swan,
And die in music. [*She sings.*] "Willow, willow, willow."
Moor, she was chaste. She loved thee, cruel Moor.
So come my soul to bliss as I speak true.
So speaking as I think, alas, I die.   [*She dies.*]   260
OTHELLO. I have another weapon in this chamber;
It was a sword of Spain, the ice-brook's temper°—
O, here it is. [*He finds a sword.*] Uncle, I must come forth.
GRATIANO [*within*]. If thou attempt it, it will cost thee dear.
Thou hast no weapon, and perforce must suffer.   265

---

235 belonged was appropriate.   **240 coxcomb** fool. (Addressed to Othello.)   **242 stones**
bolts, such as those used for thunderbolts.   **243 Precious** i.e., arrant, utter.   **s.d. He . . .
Emilia** (The Quarto text reads, "The Moor runs at Iago. Iago kills his wife." The Quarto also specifies the exit of Iago at line 245 and the death of Emilia at line 260.)   **253 whipster**
contemptible fellow (one who is always ready to whip out his sword).   **254 honor** i.e., the
bravery for which one enjoys a soldier's reputation.   **honesty** true integrity.   **262 the ice-
brook's temper** tempered in ice-cold water.

OTHELLO. Look in upon me then and speak with me,
Or, naked° as I am, I will assault thee.

[*Enter* GRATIANO.]

GRATIANO. What is the matter?
OTHELLO.   Behold, I have a weapon;
A better never did itself sustain
Upon a soldier's thigh. I have seen the day   270
That, with this little arm and this good sword,
I have made my way through more impediments
Than twenty times your stop.° But O, vain boast!
Who can control his fate? 'Tis not so now.
Be not afraid, though you do see me weaponed;   275
Here is my journey's end, here is my butt°
And very seamark° of my utmost sail.

[GRATIANO *steps back*.]

Do you go back dismayed? 'Tis a lost° fear;
Man but a rush° against Othello's breast
And he retires. Where should Othello go?   280

[*He turns to* DESDEMONA.]

Now, how dost thou look now? O ill-starred wench!
Pale as thy smock! When we shall meet at compt,°
This look of thine will hurl my soul from heaven,
And fiends will snatch at it. Cold, cold, my girl?
Even like thy chastity. O cursèd, cursèd slave!°   285
Whip me, ye devils,
From the possession of this heavenly sight!
Blow me about in winds! Roast me in sulfur!
Wash me in steep-down gulfs of liquid fire!
O Desdemon! Dead, Desdemon! Dead! O! O!   290

Enter LODOVICO, CASSIO [*carried in a litter*°], MONTANO, *and* IAGO
[*prisoner*], *with officers*.

LODOVICO. Where is this rash and most unfortunate man?
OTHELLO. That's he that was Othello. Here I am.
LODOVICO. Where is that viper? Bring the villain forth.

[IAGO *is led forward*.]

OTHELLO. I look down towards his feet;° but that's a fable.
If that thou be'st a devil, I cannot kill thee.   295

[*He wounds* IAGO.]

---

267 **naked** unarmed.   273 **stop** power (to stop).   276 **butt** goal, limit. (An archery term.)
277 **seamark** beacon (marking his destination or limit).   278 **lost** wasted, unneeded.   279
Man . . . rush wield no more than a reed.   282 **compt** account, judgment day.   285 **slave**
i.e., Othello himself.   290 **s.d. in a litter** (The Quarto specifies that Cassio is "in a chair.")
294 **towards his feet** i.e., to see if they are cloven, as the devil's are fabled to be.

LODOVICO. Wrench his sword from him. [OTHELLO *is disarmed*.]

IAGO.   I bleed, sir, but not killed.

OTHELLO. I am not sorry neither. I'd have thee live,
    For in my sense° 'tis happiness to die.

LODOVICO. O thou Othello, that was once so good,
    Fall'n in the practice° of a cursèd slave,°   300
    What shall be said to thee?

OTHELLO.   Why, anything.
    An honorable murderer, if you will,
    For naught I did in hate, but all in honor.

LODOVICO. This wretch hath part confessed his villainy.
    Did you and he consent° in Cassio's death?   305

OTHELLO. Ay.

CASSIO. Dear General, I never gave you cause.

OTHELLO. I do believe it, and I ask your pardon.
    Will you, I pray, demand that demi-devil
    Why he hath thus ensnared my soul and body?   310

IAGO. Demand me nothing. What you know, you know.
    From this time forth I never will speak word.

LODOVICO. What, not to pray?

GRATIANO. Torments° will ope your lips.

OTHELLO. Well, thou dost best.   315

LODOVICO. Sir, you shall understand what hath befall'n,
    Which, as I think, you know not. Here is a letter
    Found in the pocket of the slain Roderigo;
    And here another. [*He produces letters*.] The one of them imports
    The death of Cassio, to be undertook   320
    By Roderigo.

OTHELLO. O villain!

CASSIO.   Most heathenish and most gross!°

LODOVICO [*showing another paper*]. Now here's another discontented°
    paper
    Found in his pocket too. And this, it seems,
    Roderigo meant t' have sent this damnèd villain;   325
    But that belike° Iago in the interim
    Came in and satisfied him.°

OTHELLO. O thou pernicious caitiff!—
    How came you, Cassio, by that handkerchief
    That was my wife's?

CASSIO.   I found it in my chamber;   330
    And he himself confessed but even now
    That there he dropped it for a special purpose
    Which wrought to his desire.°

OTHELLO.   O fool, fool, fool!

---

298 in my sense to one who feels as I do.   **300 in the practice** through the plotting, into the snare.   **slave** villain.   **305 consent** agree.   **314 Torments** torture.   **322 gross** monstrous. **323 discontented** full of discontent.   **326 belike** most likely.   **327 Came . . . him** interposed and gave him satisfactory explanation.   **333 wrought . . . desire** worked out as he wished, fitted in with his plan.

CASSIO. There is besides in Roderigo's letter
    How he upbraids Iago, that he made him   335
    Brave° me upon the watch, whereon it came°
    That I was cast;° and even but now he spake,
    After long seeming dead, Iago hurt him,
    Iago set him on.
LODOVICO   [to OTHELLO]. You must forsake this room and go with us.   340
    Your power and your command is taken off,°
    And Cassio rules in Cyprus. For this slave,
    If there be any cunning cruelty
    That can torment him much and hold him long,°
    It shall be his. You shall close prisoner rest°   345
    Till that the nature of your fault be known
    To the Venetian state.—Come, bring away.
OTHELLO. Soft you;° a word or two before you go.
    I have done the state some service, and they know 't.
    No more of that. I pray you, in your letters,   350
    When you shall these unlucky° deeds relate,
    Speak of me as I am; nothing extenuate,
    Nor set down aught in malice. Then must you speak
    Of one that loved not wisely but too well;
    Of one not easily jealous but, being wrought,°   355
    Perplexed° in the extreme; of one whose hand,
    Like the base Indian,° threw a pearl away
    Richer than all his tribe; of one whose subdued° eyes,
    Albeit unusèd to the melting mood,
    Drops tears as fast as the Arabian trees   360
    Their medicinable gum.° Set you down this;
    And say besides that in Aleppo once,
    Where a malignant and a turbaned Turk
    Beat a Venetian and traduced the state,
    I took by th' throat the circumcisèd dog   365
    And smote him, thus.   [He stabs himself.°]
LODOVICO. O bloody period!°
GRATIANO. All that is spoke is marred.
OTHELLO. I kissed thee ere I killed thee. No way but this,
    Killing myself, to die upon a kiss.   370

[He kisses DESDEMONA and] dies.

CASSIO. This did I fear, but thought he had no weapon;
    For he was great of heart.

---

336 **Brave** defy. **whereon it came** whereof it came about. 337 **cast** dismissed. 341
taken off taken away. 344 **hold him long** keep him alive a long time (during his torture).
345 **rest** remain. 348 **Soft you** one moment. 351 **unlucky** unfortunate. 355 **wrought**
worked upon, worked into a frenzy. 356 **Perplexed** distraught. 357 **Indian** (This reading
from the Quarto pictures an ignorant savage who cannot recognize the value of a precious
jewel. The Folio reading, Iudean or Judean, i.e., infidel or disbeliever, may refer to Herod, who
slew Miriamne in a fit of jealousy, or to Judas Iscariot, the betrayer of Christ.) 358 **subdued**
i.e., overcome by grief. 361 **gum** i.e., myrrh. 366 **s.d. He stabs himself** (This direction is in
the Quarto text.) 367 **period** termination, conclusion.

LODOVICO [to IAGO].   O Spartan dog,°
    More fell° than anguish, hunger, or the sea!
    Look on the tragic loading of this bed.
    This is thy work. The object poisons sight;   375
    Let it be hid.° Gratiano, keep° the house,

[The bed curtains are drawn]

    And seize upon° the fortunes of the Moor,
    For they succeed on° you. [*To* CASSIO.] To you, Lord Governor,
    Remains the censure° of this hellish villain,
    The time, the place, the torture. O, enforce it!   380
    Myself will straight aboard, and to the state
    This heavy act with heavy heart relate.   *Exeunt.*

---

372 **Spartan dog** (Spartan dogs were noted for their savagery and silence.)   373 **fell** cruel.
376 **Let it be hid** i.e., draw the bed curtains. (No stage direction specifies that the dead are to
be carried offstage at the end of the play.)   **keep** remain in.   377 **seize upon** take legal possession of.   378 **succeed on** pass as though by inheritance to.   379 **censure** sentencing.

TOPICS FOR CRITICAL THINKING AND WRITING

Act 1

1. Iago, contemptuous of dutiful servants, compares them in 1.1.49 to
   asses. What other animal images does he use in the first scene? In your
   view, what does the use of such images tell us about Iago?
2. Is there any need to do more than knock loudly at Brabantio's door?
   What does 1.1.81–83 tell us about Iago?
3. In 1.1.111ff., and in his next speech, Iago uses prose instead of blank
   verse. What effect do you think is gained?
4. What is Iago trying to do to Othello in the first speech of 1.2? In 1.2.29
   why does Iago urge Othello to "go in"? When Othello first speaks
   (1.2.6), does he speak as we might have expected him to, given Iago's
   earlier comments about Othello? In Othello's second speech is there
   anything that resembles Iago's earlier description of him?
5. Do you think it incredible that a young woman who has rejected "the
   wealthy, curlèd darlings" (1.2.69) of Venice should choose a Moor?
   Explain your view.
6. Iago had said (1.1.14) that Othello uses "bombast circumstance." Is
   1.3.130ff. an example? Why, or why not?
7. Brabantio in 1.3.213–222 speaks in couplets (pairs of rhyming lines),
   as the Duke has just done. What is the effect of the verse? Does it suggest grief? Mockery?
8. Do you think the love of Othello and Desdemona is impetuous and irrational? What is their love based on?
9. The last speech in 1.3 is in verse, though previous speeches are in
   prose. How would you describe the effect of the change?
10. Is it a fault that Othello "thinks men honest that but seem to be so"
    (1.3.379)?

Act 2

1. In 2.1.1–17, Shakespeare introduces a description of a storm. What symbolic overtones, if any, do you think it may it have?
2. What does Iago's description (2.1.146–156) of a good woman tell us about his attitude toward goodness and women?
3. In Iago's last speech in this act he gives several reasons why he hates Othello. List them, and add to the list any reasons he gave earlier. Evaluate them carefully. How convincing are they?
4. Again (2.1.262ff.) Shakespeare gives Iago verse, when alone, after prose dialogue. Why do you suppose he did this—i.e., what effect (if any) does the change have?
5. In 2.3.13–21, what sort of thing is Iago trying to get Cassio to say?
6. How does 2.3.178–191 prepare us for Othello's later tragic deed of killing Desdemona?

Act 3

1. What is the point of the repetition (3.3.106–142) of "thought," "think," "know," and "honest"?
2. Is it surprising that Othello speaks (3.3.194) of a goat? In later scenes keep an eye out for his use of animal imagery.
3. Does one indeed smell "a will most rank" (3.3.248) in Desdemona's choice? Or had her choice been based on other qualities? If you think the latter, explain.
4. Emilia gets possession of the handkerchief by accident (3.3.306). Is it fair, then, to say that the tragic outcome is based on mere accident? And if so, is the play seriously weakened as a tragedy?
5. In 3.4.65–71 Othello is, of course, talking about a handkerchief, but he is also asking for the restoration of love. What words apply especially to love?

Act 4

1. In 4.1.35ff. Othello uses prose. What does this shift suggest about Othello's state of mind?
2. Othello says (4.1.183) "I will chop her into messes. Cuckold me?" Do you think that in this scene Othello's ferocity toward Desdemona is chiefly motivated by a sense of personal injury? What if anything does Shakespeare do here to prevent the audience from merely loathing Othello?
3. What is Othello's emotional state in the first nineteen lines of 4.2?
4. In 4.2 Othello's baseness, very evident in the previous scene, continues here. But what lines in this scene tend to work against the view that he is merely base, and give him the stature of a tragic hero?
5. Why is it that Othello "looks gentler than he did" (4.3.11)?
6. What qualities in Desdemona's singing prevent us from regarding her as a merely pathetic figure here?

Act 5

1. What do 5.1.19–20 tell us about Iago? How much "daily beauty" have we seen in Cassio's life? Do we assume Iago judges him incorrectly?

2. What does 5.2.16–17 tell us about the spirit with which Othello is about to kill Desdemona? Is he acting from a sense of wounded pride?
3. In 5.2.128–129 Desdemona dies with a lie on her lips. Do you think the worse of her? Why?
4. Emilia calls Othello "gull," "dolt," "ignorant as dirt" (5.2.170–171). Has she a point? If so, do these words prevent Othello from being a tragic hero?
5. T. S. Eliot, in "Shakespeare and the Stoicism of Seneca," *Selected Essays*, says of 3.2.348–366: "Othello . . . is cheering himself up. He is endeavoring to escape reality, he has ceased to think about Desdemona, and is thinking about himself." Evaluate this view. To what does Othello in effect compare himself in the last line of this speech?
6. In Christian thought suicide is a sin. Do you judge it sinful here?

General Questions

1. W. H. Auden, in *The Dyer's Hand*, says that "in most tragedies the fall of the hero from glory to misery and death is the work, either of the gods, or of his own freely chosen acts, or, more commonly, a mixture of both. But the fall of Othello is the work of another human being; nothing he says or does originates with himself. In consequence we feel pity for him but no respect; our esthetic respect is reserved for Iago." Evaluate Auden's view.
2. Harley Granville-Barker, in *Prefaces to Shakespeare*, says: "The mere sight of such beauty and nobility and happiness, all wickedly destroyed must be a harrowing one. Yet the pity and terror of it come short of serving for the purgation of our souls, since Othello's own soul stays unpurged. ... It is a tragedy without meaning, and that is the ultimate horror of it." Evaluate this view.
3. A black British actor has said,

> When a black actor plays a role written for a white actor in black make-up and for a predominantly white audience, does he not encourage the white way, or rather the wrong way, of looking at black men, namely that black men, or "Moors," are over-emotional, excitable and unstable, thereby vindicating Iago's statement, "These Moors are changeable in their wills" (1.3)? Of all the parts in the canon, perhaps Othello is the one which should most definitely not be played by a black actor.

> Quoted in Lois Potter, *Shakespeare in Performance: Othello* (2002), 169

Does this view make sense to you? Why or why not?
4. How important to the play is the theme of race? Central to everything to happens? Significant but not really central? Please explain.
5. It has been said that a reader's or a spectator's interest in Iago consists of equal parts admiration and horror. Your view?
6. What does it mean to say that a tragic hero achieves self-knowledge? Is this knowledge essential to the dramatic power of a tragedy, or could a play still be tragic without it? Does Othello achieve self-knowledge in the final scene?
7. Could you imagine a different version of *Othello*, in which the play is a comedy rather than a tragedy? How would you revise the play to make everything turn out well in the end?

8. Do you think that Shakespeare is trying to teach us something special in this play? What is this "something," and where in the text do you perceive the evidence for it? What is the relationship between the action on the stage and the lives that we lead?

9. Have you read other Shakespearean tragedies beside this one? Which is your favorite? What are the reasons for your choice?

10. Shakespeare's plays have been performed and studied for centuries. Often it's said that they are inexhaustible. What does it mean to say that a literary work, by Shakespeare or some other great writer, is inexhaustible? Would you say that this is true—true for you—about *Othello?* Where in the text might you locate evidence for your view?

31

Comedy

Though etymology is not always helpful (after all, is it really illuminating to say that *tragedy* may come from a Greek word meaning "goat song"?), the etymology of *comedy* helps to reveal comedy's fundamental nature. **Comedy** (Greek: *komoidia*) is a revel-song; ancient Greek comedies are descended from fertility rituals that dramatized the joy of renewal, the joy of triumphing over obstacles, the joy of being (in a sense) reborn. Whereas the movement of tragedy, speaking roughly, is from prosperity to disaster, the movement of comedy is from some sort of minor disaster to prosperity.

To say, however, that comedy dramatizes the triumph over obstacles is to describe it as though it were melodrama, a play in which, after hairbreadth adventures, good prevails over evil, often in the form of the hero's unlikely last-minute rescue of the fair Belinda from the clutches of the villain. What distinguishes comedy from melodrama is the pervasive high spirits of comedy. The joyous ending in comedy—usually a marriage—is in the spirit of what has gone before; the entire play, not only the end, is a celebration of fecundity.

The threats in the world of comedy are not taken very seriously; the parental tyranny that makes *Romeo and Juliet* and *Antigone* tragedies is, in comedy, laughable throughout. Parents may fret, fume, and lock doors, but in doing so they make themselves ridiculous, for love will find a way. Villains may threaten, but the audience never takes the threats seriously.

The marriage and renewal of society, so usual at the end of comedy, may be most improbable, but they do not therefore weaken the comedy. The stuff of comedy is, in part, improbability. In *A Midsummer Night's Dream,* Puck speaks for the spectator when he says:

> And those things do best please me
> That befall preposterously.

In tragedy, probability is important; in comedy, *im*probability is often desirable, for at least three reasons. First, comedy seeks to include as much as possible, to reveal the rich abundance of life. The motto of comedy (and the implication in the weddings with which it usually concludes) is, "The more the merrier." Second, the improbable is the surprising; surprise often evokes laughter, and laughter surely has a central place in comedy. Third, by getting the characters into improbable situations, the dramatist can show off the absurdity of their behavior. This point needs amplification.

Comedy often shows the absurdity of ideals. The miser, the puritan, the health faddist, and so on, are people of ideals, but their ideals are suffocating. The miser, for example, treats everything in terms of money; the miser's ideal causes him or her to renounce much of the abundance and joy of life. He or she is in love, but is unwilling to support a spouse; or he or she has a headache, but will not be so extravagant as to take an aspirin tablet. If a thief accosts the miser with "Your money or your life," the miser will prefer to give up life—and that is what in fact the miser has been doing all the while. Now, by putting this miser in a series of improbable situations, the dramatist can continue to demonstrate entertainingly the miser's absurdity.*

The comic protagonist's tenacious hold on his or her ideals is not very far from that of the tragic protagonist. In general, however, tragedy suggests the nobility of ideals; the tragic hero's ideals undo him or her, and they may be ideals about which we have serious reservations, but still we admire the nobility of these ideals. Romeo and Juliet will not put off their love for each other; Antigone will not yield to Creon, and Creon holds almost impossibly long to his stern position. But the comic protagonist who is always trying to keep his or her hands clean is funny; we laugh at this refusal to touch dirt with the rest of us, this refusal to enjoy the abundance life has to offer. The comic protagonist who is always talking about his or her beloved is funny; we laugh at the failure to see that the world is filled with people more attractive than the one with whom he or she is obsessed.

In short, the ideals for which the tragic protagonist loses the world seem important to us and gain, in large measure, our sympathy, but the ideals for which the comic protagonist loses the world seem trivial compared with the rich variety that life has to offer, and we laugh at their absurdity. The tragic figure makes a claim on our sympathy. The absurd comic figure continually sets up obstacles to our sympathetic interest; we feel detached from, superior to, and amused by comic figures. Something along these lines is behind William Butler Yeats's insistence that *character* is always present in comedy but not in tragedy. Though Yeats is eccentric in his notion that individual character is obliterated in tragedy, he interestingly gets at one of the important elements in comedy:

> When the tragic reverie is at its height . . . [we do not say,] "How well that man is realized. I should know him were I to meet him in the street," for it is always ourselves that we see upon the [tragic] stage. . . . Tragedy must always be a drowning and breaking of the dikes that separate man from man, and . . . it is upon these dikes comedy keeps house.

---

*A character who is dominated by a single trait—avarice, jealousy, timidity, and so forth— is sometimes called a **humor character.** Medieval and Renaissance psychology held that an individual's personality depended on the mixture of four liquids (humors): blood (Latin: *sanguis*), choler, phlegm, and bile. An overabundance of one fluid produced a dominant trait, and even today "sanguine," "choleric," "phlegmatic," and "bilious" describe personalities.

Not all comedy, of course, depends on humor characters placed in situations that exhibit their absurdity. **High comedy** is largely verbal, depending on witty language; **farce,** at the other extreme, is dependent on inherently ludicrous situations—for example, a hobo is mistaken for a millionaire. Situation comedy, then, may use humor characters, but it need not do so.

Most comic plays can roughly be sorted into one of two types: romantic comedy and satiric comedy. **Romantic comedy** presents an ideal world, a golden world, a world more delightful than our own; if there are difficulties in it, they are not briers but (to quote from Shakespeare's *As You Like It*) "burrs . . . thrown . . . in holiday foolery." It is the world of most of Shakespeare's comedies, a world of Illyria, of the Forest of Arden, of Belmont, of the moonlit Athens in *A Midsummer Night's Dream.* The chief figures are lovers; the course of their love is not smooth, but the outcome is never in doubt and the course is the more fun for being bumpy. Occasionally in this golden world there is a villain, but if so, the villain is a great bungler who never really does any harm; the world seems to be guided by a benevolent providence who prevents villains from seriously harming even themselves. In these plays, the world belongs to golden lads and lasses. When we laugh, we laugh not so much *at* them as *with* them.

If romantic comedy shows us a world with people more attractive than we find in our own, **satiric comedy** shows us a world with people less attractive. The satiric world seems dominated by morally inferior people—the decrepit wooer, the jealous spouse, the demanding parent. These unengaging figures go through their paces, revealing again and again their absurdity. The audience laughs *at* (rather than *with*) such figures, and writers justify this kind of comedy by claiming to reform society: antisocial members of the audience will see their grotesque images on the stage and will reform themselves when they leave the theater. But it is hard to believe that this theory is rooted in fact. Jonathan Swift was probably right when he said, "Satire is a sort of glass wherein beholders do generally discover everybody's face but their own."

Near the conclusion of a satiric comedy, the obstructing characters are dismissed, often perfunctorily, allowing for a happy ending—commonly the marriage of figures less colorful than the obstructionist(s). And so all-encompassing are the festivities at the end that even obstructionists are invited to join in the wedding feast. If they refuse to join, we may find them—yet again—laughable rather than sympathetic, though admittedly one may also feel lingering regret that this somewhat shabby world of ours cannot live up to the exalted (even if rigid and rather crazy) standards of the outsider who refuses to go along with the way of the world.

WILLIAM SHAKESPEARE

William Shakespeare (1564–1616) was born in Stratford, England, of middle-class parents. Nothing of interest is known about his early years, but by 1590 he was acting and writing plays in London. By the end of the following decade he had worked in all three Elizabethan dramatic genres—tragedy, comedy, and history. Romeo and Juliet, *for example, was written about 1595, the year of* Richard II, *and in the following year he wrote* A Midsummer Night's Dream. Julius Caesar *(1599) probably preceded* As You Like It *by one year, and* Hamlet *probably followed* As You Like It *by less than a year. Among the plays that followed* King Lear *(1605–1606) were* Macbeth *(1605–1606) and several "romances"—plays (including* The Tempest*) that have happy endings but that seem more meditative and closer to tragedy than such comedies as* A Midsummer Night's Dream, As You Like It, *and* Twelfth Night.

*A Midsummer Night's Dream**

Edited by David Bevington

[DRAMATIS PERSONAE

THESEUS, *Duke of Athens*
HIPPOLYTA, *Queen of the Amazons, betrothed to Theseus*
PHILOSTRATE, *Master of the Revels*
EGEUS, *father of Hermia*
HERMIA, *daughter of Egeus, in love with Lysander*
LYSANDER, *in love with Hermia*
DEMETRIUS, *in love with Hermia and favored by Egeus*
HELENA, *in love with Demetrius*

OBERON, *King of the Fairies*
TITANIA, *Queen of the Fairies*
PUCK, *or* ROBIN GOODFELLOW
PEASEBLOSSOM,
COBWEB,
MOTE,   } *fairies attending Titania*
MUSTARDSEED,

Other FAIRIES *attending*

PETER QUINCE, *a carpenter,*   PROLOGUE
NICK BOTTOM, *a weaver,*   PYRAMUS
FRANCIS FLUTE, *a bellows mender,*   } *representing*   THISBE
TOM SNOUT, *a tinker,*   WALL
SNUG, *a joiner,*   LION
ROBIN STARVELING, *a tailor,*   MOONSHINE

Lords and Attendants on Theseus and Hippolyta

SCENE: *Athens, and a wood near it*]

1.1 *Enter* THESEUS, HIPPOLYTA, [*and* PHILOSTRATE,] *with others.*

THESEUS. Now, fair Hippolyta, our nuptial hour
    Draws on apace. Four happy days bring in
    Another moon; but, O, methinks, how slow
    This old moon wanes! She lingers° my desires,
    Like to a stepdame° or a dowager°   5
    Long withering out° a young man's revenue.

---

*A Midsummer Night's Dream was first published in 1600 in a small book of a type called a quarto. A second quarto edition, printed in 1616 but based on the 1600 text, introduces a few corrections, but it also introduces many errors. The 1619 text in turn was the basis for the text in the first collected edition of Shakespeare's plays, the First Folio (1623). Bevington's edition is of course based on the text of 1600, but it includes a few corrections, and it modifies the punctuation in accordance with modern usage. Material added by the editor, such as amplifications in the *dramatis personae,* is enclosed within square brackets [ ].
1.1 Location: Athens, Theseus's court.   4 lingers postpones, delays the fulfillment of.
5 stepdame stepmother. **dowager** i.e., a widow (whose right of inheritance from her dead husband is eating into her son's estate).   **6 withering out** causing to dwindle.

HIPPOLYTA. Four days will quickly steep themselves in night,
    Four nights will quickly dream away the time;
    And then the moon, like to a silver bow
    New bent in heaven, shall behold the night   10
    Of our solemnities.
THESEUS.   Go, Philostrate,
    Stir up the Athenian youth to merriments,
    Awake the pert and nimble spirit of mirth,
    Turn melancholy forth to funerals;
    The pale companion° is not for our pomp.°   [*Exit* PHILOSTRATE.]   15
    Hippolyta, I wooed thee with my sword°
    And won thy love doing thee injuries;
    But I will wed thee in another key,
    With pomp, with triumph,° and with reveling.

Enter EGEUS *and his daughter* HERMIA, *and* LYSANDER, *and* DEMETRIUS.

EGEUS. Happy be Theseus, our renowned duke!   20
THESEUS. Thanks, good Egeus. What's the news with thee?
EGEUS. Full of vexation come I, with complaint
    Against my child, my daughter Hermia.
    Stand forth, Demetrius. My noble lord,
    This man hath my consent to marry her.   25
    Stand forth, Lysander. And, my gracious Duke,
    This man hath bewitched the bosom of my child.
    Thou, thou, Lysander, thou hast given her rhymes
    And interchanged love tokens with my child.
    Thou hast by moonlight at her window sung   30
    With feigning voice verses of feigning° love,
    And stol'n the impression of her fantasy°
    With bracelets of thy hair, rings, gauds,° conceits,°
    Knacks,° trifles, nosegays, sweetmeats—messengers
    Of strong prevailment in° unhardened youth.   35
    With cunning hast thou filched my daughter's heart,
    Turned her obedience, which is due to me,
    To stubborn harshness. And, my gracious Duke,
    Be it so° she will not here before Your Grace
    Consent to marry with Demetrius,   40
    I beg the ancient privilege of Athens:
    As she is mine, I may dispose of her,
    Which shall be either to this gentleman
    Or to her death, according to our law
    Immediately° provided in that case.   45

---

15 companion fellow. **pomp** ceremonial magnificence. **16 with my sword** i.e., in
a military engagement against the Amazons, when Hippolyta was taken captive. **19
triumph** public festivity. **31 feigning** (1) counterfeiting (2) faining, desirous. **32 And
. . . fantasy** and made her fall in love with you (imprinting your image on her imagination) by stealthy and dishonest means. **33 gauds** playthings. **conceits** fanciful trifles.
34 Knacks knickknacks. **35 prevailment in** influence on. **39 Be it so** if. **45 Immediately** directly, with nothing intervening.

THESEUS. What say you, Hermia? Be advised, fair maid.
　　　To you your father should be as a god—
　　　One that composed your beauties, yea, and one
　　　To whom you are but as a form in wax
　　　By him imprinted, and within his power   50
　　　To leave° the figure or disfigure° it.
　　　Demetrius is a worthy gentleman.
HERMIA. So is Lysander.
THESEUS.　　　　　　　In himself he is;
　　　But in this kind,° wanting° your father's voice,°
　　　The other must be held the worthier.   55
HERMIA. I would my father looked but with my eyes.
THESEUS. Rather your eyes must with his judgment look.
HERMIA. I do entreat Your Grace to pardon me.
　　　I know not by what power I am made bold,
　　　Nor how it may concern° my modesty   60
　　　In such a presence here to plead my thoughts;
　　　But I beseech Your Grace that I may know
　　　The worst that may befall me in this case
　　　If I refuse to wed Demetrius.
THESEUS. Either to die the death or to abjure   65
　　　Forever the society of men.
　　　Therefore, fair Hermia, question your desires,
　　　Know of your youth, examine well your blood,°
　　　Whether, if you yield not to your father's choice,
　　　You can endure the livery° of a nun,   70
　　　For aye° to be in shady cloister mewed,°
　　　To live a barren sister all your life,
　　　Chanting faint hymns to the cold fruitless moon.
　　　Thrice blessèd they that master so their blood
　　　To undergo such maiden pilgrimage;   75
　　　But earthlier happy° is the rose distilled
　　　Than that which, withering on the virgin thorn,
　　　Grows, lives, and dies in single blessedness.
HERMIA. So will I grow, so live, so die, my lord,
　　　Ere I will yield my virgin patent° up   80
　　　Unto his lordship, whose unwishèd yoke
　　　My soul consents not to give sovereignty.
THESEUS. Take time to pause, and by the next new moon—
　　　The sealing day betwixt my love and me
　　　For everlasting bond of fellowship—   85
　　　Upon that day either prepare to die
　　　For disobedience to your father's will,
　　　Or° else to wed Demetrius, as he would,
　　　Or on Diana's altar to protest°
　　　For aye austerity and single life.   90

---

51 leave i.e., leave unaltered. **disfigure** obliterate. **54 kind** respect. **wanting** -
lacking. **voice** approval. **60 concern** befit. **68 blood** passions. **70 livery** habit.
71 aye ever. **mewed** shut in (said of a hawk, poultry, etc.). **76 earthlier happy** happier as respects this world. **80 patent** privilege. **88 Or** either. **89 protest** vow.

DEMETRIUS. Relent, sweet Hermia, and, Lysander, yield
    Thy crazèd° title to my certain right.
LYSANDER. You have her father's love, Demetrius;
    Let me have Hermia's. Do you marry him.
EGEUS. Scornful Lysander! True, he hath my love,   95
    And what is mine my love shall render him.
    And she is mine, and all my right of her
    I do estate unto° Demetrius.
LYSANDER. I am, my lord, as well derived° as he,
    As well possessed;° my love is more than his;   100
    My fortunes every way as fairly° ranked,
    If not with vantage,° as Demetrius';
    And, which is more than all these boasts can be,
    I am beloved of beauteous Hermia.
    Why should not I then prosecute my right?   105
    Demetrius, I'll avouch it to his head,°
    Made love to Nedar's daughter, Helena
    And won her soul; and she, sweet lady, dotes,
    Devoutly dotes, dotes in idolatry,
    Upon this spotted° and inconstant man.   110
THESEUS. I must confess that I have heard so much,
    And with Demetrius thought to have spoke thereof;
    But, being overfull of self-affairs,°
    My mind did lose it. But, Demetrius, come,
    And come, Egeus, you shall go with me;   115
    I have some private schooling° for you both.
    For you, fair Hermia, look you arm° yourself
    To fit your fancies° to your father's will;
    Or else the law of Athens yields you up—
    Which by no means we may extenuate°—   120
    To death or to a vow of single life.
    Come, my Hippolyta. What cheer, my love?
    Demetrius and Egeus, go° along.
    I must employ you in some business
    Against° our nuptial and confer with you   125
    Of something nearly that° concerns yourselves.
EGEUS. With duty and desire we follow you.
                   Exeunt [*all but* LYSANDER *and* HERMIA].
LYSANDER. How now, my love, why is your cheek so pale?
    How chance the roses there do fade so fast?
HERMIA. Belike° for want of rain, which I could well   130
    Beteem° them from the tempest of my eyes.

---

92 **crazèd** cracked, unsound.   98 **estate unto** settle or bestow upon.   99 **derived** descended, i.e., as well born.   100 **possessed** endowed with wealth.   101 **fairly** handsomely.   102 **vantage** superiority.   106 **head** i.e., face.   110 **spotted** i.e., morally stained.   113 **self-affairs** my own concerns.   116 **schooling** admonition.   117 **look you arm** take care you prepare.   118 **fancies** likings, thoughts of love. 120 **extenuate** mitigate.   123 **go** i.e., come.   125 **Against** in preparation for.   126 **nearly that** that closely.   130 **Belike** very likely.   131 **Beteem** grant, afford.

LYSANDER. Ay me! For aught that I could ever read,
  Could ever hear by tale or history,
  The course of true love never did run smooth
  But either it was different in blood°—   135
HERMIA. O cross!° Too high to be enthralled to low.
LYSANDER. Or else misgrafted° in respect of years—
HERMIA. O spite! Too old to be engaged to young.
LYSANDER. Or else it stood upon the choice of friends°—
HERMIA. O hell, to choose love by another's eyes!   140
LYSANDER. Or if there were a sympathy° in choice,
  War, death, or sickness did lay siege to it,
  Making it momentany° as a sound,
  Swift as a shadow, short as any dream,
  Brief as the lightning in the collied° night,   145
  That in a spleen° unfolds° both heaven and earth,
  And ere a man hath power to say "Behold!"
  The jaws of darkness do devour it up.
  So quick° bright things come to confusion.°
HERMIA. If then true lovers have been ever crossed,°   150
  It stands as an edict in destiny.
  Then let us teach our trial patience,°
  Because it is a customary cross,
  As due to love as thoughts and dreams and sighs,
  Wishes and tears, poor fancy's° followers.   155
LYSANDER. A good persuasion.° Therefore, hear me, Hermia:
  I have a widow aunt, a dowager
  Of great revenue, and she hath no child.
  From Athens is her house remote seven leagues;
  And she respects° me as her only son.   160
  There, gentle Hermia, may I marry thee,
  And to that place the sharp Athenian law
  Cannot pursue us. If thou lovest me, then,
  Steal forth thy father's house tomorrow night;
  And in the wood, a league without the town,   165
  Where I did meet thee once with Helena
  To do observance to a morn of May,°
  There will I stay for thee.
HERMIA.   My good Lysander!
  I swear to thee by Cupid's strongest bow,
  By his best arrow° with the golden head,   170

---

135 **blood** hereditary station.   136 **cross** vexation.   137 **misgrafted** ill grafted, badly
matched.   139 **friends** relatives.   141 **sympathy** agreement.   143 **momentany** lasting but a moment.   145 **collied** blackened (as with coal dust), darkened.   146 **in a
spleen** in a swift impulse, in a violent flash. **unfolds** discloses.   149 **quick** quickly; or,
perhaps, living, alive. **confusion** ruin.   150 **ever crossed** always thwarted.   152
teach . . . patience i.e., teach ourselves patience in this trial.   155 **fancy's** amorous
passion's.   156 **persuasion** conviction.   160 **respects** regards.   167 **do . . . May** perform the ceremonies of May Day.   170 **best arrow** (Cupid's best gold-pointed arrows
were supposed to induce love; his blunt leaden arrows, aversion.)

By the simplicity° of Venus' doves,°
By that which knitteth souls and prospers loves,
And by that fire which burned the Carthage queen°
When the false Trojan° under sail was seen,
By all the vows that ever men have broke,   175
In number more than ever women spoke,
In that same place thou hast appointed me
Tomorrow truly will I meet with thee.
LYSANDER. Keep promise, love. Look, here comes Helena.

Enter HELENA.

HERMIA. God speed, fair° Helena! Whither away?   180
HELENA. Call you me fair? That "fair" again unsay.
Demetrius loves your fair.° O happy fair!°
Your eyes are lodestars,° and your tongue's sweet air°
More tunable° than lark to shepherd's ear
When wheat is green, when hawthorn buds appear.   185
Sickness is catching. O, were favor° so!
Yours would I catch, fair Hermia, ere I go;
My ear should catch your voice, my eye your eye,
My tongue should catch your tongue's sweet melody.
Were the world mine, Demetrius being bated,°   190
The rest I'd give to be to you translated.°
O, teach me how you look and with what art
You sway the motion° of Demetrius' heart.
HERMIA. I frown upon him, yet he loves me still.
HELENA. O, that your frowns would teach my smiles such skill!   195
HERMIA. I give him curses, yet he gives me love.
HELENA. O, that my prayers could such affection° move!°
HERMIA. The more I hate, the more he follows me.
HELENA. The more I love, the more he hateth me.
HERMIA. His folly, Helena, is no fault of mine.   200
HELENA. None but your beauty. Would that fault were mine!
HERMIA. Take comfort. He no more shall see my face.
Lysander and myself will fly this place.
Before the time I did Lysander see
Seemed Athens as a paradise to me.   205
O, then, what graces in my love do dwell
That he hath turned a heaven unto a hell!
LYSANDER. Helen, to you our minds we will unfold.
Tomorrow night, when Phoebe° doth behold

---

171 simplicity innocence. **doves** i.e., those that drew Venus's chariot. **173, 174 Carthage queen, false Trojan** (Dido, Queen of Carthage, immolated herself on a funeral pyre after having been deserted by the Trojan hero Aeneas.) **180 fair** fair-complexioned (generally regarded by the Elizabethans as more beautiful than dark-complexioned). **182 your fair** your beauty (even though Hermia is dark-complexioned). **happy fair** lucky fair one. **183 lodestars** guiding stars. **air** music. **184 tunable** tuneful, melodious. **186 favor** appearance, looks. **190 bated** excepted. **191 translated** transformed. **193 motion** impulse. **197 affection** passion. **move** arouse. **209 Phoebe** Diana, the moon.

Her silver visage in the watery glass,°   210
Decking with liquid pearl the bladed grass,
A time that lovers' flights doth still° conceal,
Through Athens' gates have we devised to steal.
HERMIA. And in the wood, where often you and I
Upon faint° primrose beds were wont to lie,   215
Emptying our bosoms of their counsel° sweet,
There my Lysander and myself shall meet;
And thence from Athens turn away our eyes,
To seek new friends and stranger companies.
Farewell, sweet playfellow. Pray thou for us,   220
And good luck grant thee thy Demetrius!
Keep word, Lysander. We must starve our sight
From lovers' food till morrow deep midnight.
LYSANDER. I will, my Hermia.   *Exit* HERMIA.
        Helena, adieu.
As you on him, Demetrius dote on you!   *Exit* LYSANDER. 225
HELENA. How happy some o'er other some can be!°
Through Athens I am thought as fair as she.
But what of that? Demetrius thinks not so;
He will not know what all but he do know.
And as he errs, doting on Hermia's eyes,   230
So I, admiring of° his qualities.
Things base and vile, holding no quantity,°
Love can transpose to form and dignity.
Love looks not with the eyes, but with the mind,
And therefore is winged Cupid painted blind.   235
Nor hath Love's mind of any judgment taste;°
Wings, and no eyes, figure° unheedy haste.
And therefore is Love said to be a child,
Because in choice he is so oft beguiled.
As waggish° boys in game° themselves forswear,   240
So the boy Love is perjured everywhere.
For ere Demetrius looked on Hermia's eyne,°
He hailed down oaths that he was only mine;
And when this hail some heat from Hermia felt,
So he dissolved, and showers of oaths did melt.   245
I will go tell him of fair Hermia's flight.
Then to the wood will he tomorrow night
Pursue her; and for this intelligence°
If I have thanks, it is a dear expense.°
But herein mean I to enrich my pain,   250
To have his sight thither and back again.
                                                          Exit.

_____

210 **glass** mirror.   212 **still** always.   215 **faint** pale.   216 **counsel** secret thought.
226 **o'er . . . can be** can be in comparison to some others.   231 **admiring of** wondering at.   232 **holding no quantity** i.e., unsubstantial, unshapely.   236 **Nor . . . taste**
i.e., nor has Love, which dwells in the fancy or imagination, any *taste* or least bit of judgment or reason.   237 **figure** are a symbol of.   240 **waggish** playful, mischievous.
game sport, jest.   242 **eyne** eyes. (Old form of plural.)   248 **intelligence** information.
249 **a dear expense** i.e., a trouble worth taking *dear* costly.

1.2 *Enter* QUINCE *the carpenter, and* SNUG *the joiner, and* BOTTOM *the weaver, and* FLUTE *the bellows mender, and* SNOUT *the tinker, and* STARVELING *the tailor.*

QUINCE. Is all our company here?

BOTTOM. You were best to call them generally,° man by man, according to the scrip.°

QUINCE. Here is the scroll of every man's name which is thought fit, through all Athens, to play in our interlude before the Duke and   5 the Duchess on his wedding day at night.

BOTTOM. First, good Peter Quince, say what the play treats on, then read the names of the actors, and so grow to° a point.

QUINCE. Marry,° our play is "The most lamentable comedy and most cruel death of Pyramus and Thisbe."   10

BOTTOM. A very good piece of work, I assure you, and a merry. Now, good Peter Quince, call forth your actors by the scroll. Masters, spread yourselves.

QUINCE. Answer as I call you. Nick Bottom,° the weaver.

BOTTOM. Ready. Name what part I am for, and proceed.   15

QUINCE. You, Nick Bottom, are set down for Pyramus.

BOTTOM. What is Pyramus? A lover or a tyrant?

QUINCE. A lover, that kills himself most gallant for love.

BOTTOM. That will ask some tears in the true performing of it. If I do it, let the audience look to their eyes. I will move storms; I will con-   20 dole° in some measure. To the rest—yet my chief humor° is for a tyrant. I could play Ercles° rarely, or a part to tear a cat° in, to make all split.°

     "The raging rocks
And shivering shocks   25
Shall break the locks
     Of prison gates:
And Phibbus' car°
Shall shine from far
And make and mar   30
     The foolish Fates."

This was lofty! Now name the rest of the players. This is Ercles' vein, a tyrant's vein. A lover is more condoling.

QUINCE. Francis Flute, the bellows mender.

FLUTE. Here, Peter Quince.   35

QUINCE. Flute, you must take Thisbe on you.

FLUTE. What is Thisbe? A wandering knight?

QUINCE. It is the lady that Pyramus must love.

FLUTE. Nay, faith, let not me play a woman. I have a beard coming.

1.2 Location: Athens. **2 generally** (Bottom's blunder for *individually.*) **3 scrip** scrap (Bottom's error for *script*). **8 grow** to come to. **9 Marry** (A mild oath; originally the name of the Virgin Mary.) **14 Bottom** (As a weaver's term, a *bottom* was an object around which thread was wound.) **20–21 condole** lament, arouse pity. **21 humor** inclination, whim. **22 Ercles** Hercules. (The tradition of ranting came from Seneca's *Hercules Furens.*) **tear a cat** i.e., rant. **22–23 make all split** i.e., cause a stir, bring the house down. **28 Phibbus' car** Phoebus's (the sun god) chariot.

QUINCE. That's all one.° You shall play it in a mask, and you may speak   40
as small° as you will.

BOTTOM. An° I may hide my face, let me play Thisbe too. I'll speak in a
monstrous little voice, "Thisne, Thisne!" "Ah Pyramus, my lover dear!
Thy Thisbe dear, and lady dear!"

QUINCE. No, no, you must play Pyramus, and, Flute, you Thisbe.   45

BOTTOM. Well, proceed.

QUINCE. Robin Starveling, the tailor.

STARVELING. Here, Peter Quince.

QUINCE. Robin Starveling, you must play Thisbe's mother. Tom Snout, the
tinker.   50

SNOUT. Here, Peter Quince.

QUINCE. You, Pyramus' father; myself, Thisbe's father; Snug, the joiner,
you, the lion's part, and I hope here is a play fitted.

SNUG. Have you the lion's part written? Pray you, if it be, give it me, for
I am slow of study.   55

QUINCE. You may do it extempore, for it is nothing but roaring.

BOTTOM. Let me play the lion too. I will roar that I will do any man's heart
good to hear me. I will roar that I will make the Duke say, "Let him
roar again, let him roar again."

QUINCE. An you should do it too terribly, you would fright the Duchess   60
and the ladies, that they would shriek; and that were enough to hang
us all.

ALL. That would hang us, every mother's son.

BOTTOM. I grant you, friends, if you should fright the ladies out of their
wits, they would have no more discretion but to hang us; but I will   65
aggravate° my voice so that I will roar you° as gently as any sucking
dove;° I will roar you an 'twere any nightingale.

QUINCE. You can play no part but Pyramus; for Pyramus is a sweet-
faced man, a proper° man as one shall see in a summer's day, a
most lovely gentlemanlike man. Therefore you must needs play   70
Pyramus.

BOTTOM. Well, I will undertake it. What beard were I best to play it in?

QUINCE. Why, what you will.

BOTTOM. I will discharge° it in either your° straw-color beard, your
orange-tawny beard, your purple-in-grain° beard, or your French-   75
crown-color° beard, your perfect yellow.

QUINCE. Some of your French crowns° have no hair at all, and then you
will play barefaced. But, masters, here are your parts. [*He distrib-
utes parts.*] And I am to entreat you, request you, and desire you to
con° them by tomorrow night; and meet me in the palace wood, a   80
mile without the town, by moonlight. There will we rehearse; for

---

40 That's all one it makes no difference.   **41 small** high-pitched.   **42 An** if (also at line
67).   **66 aggravate** (Bottom's blunder for *moderate*.)   **roar you** i.e., roar for you.
66–67 sucking dove (Bottom conflates *sitting dove* and *sucking lamb*, two proverbial
images of innocence.)   **69 proper** handsome.   **74 discharge** perform.   **your** i.e., you
know the kind I mean.   **75 purple-in-grain** dyed a very deep red. (From *grain*, the
name applied to the dried insect used to make the dye.)   **75–76 French-crown-color**
i.e., color of a French crown, a gold coin.   **77 crowns** heads bald from syphilis, the
"French disease."   **80 con** learn by heart.

if we meet in the city, we shall be dogged with company, and our
devices° known. In the meantime I will draw a bill° of properties,
such as our play wants. I pray you, fail me not.

BOTTOM. We will meet, and there we may rehearse most obscenely°   85
and courageously. Take pains, be perfect;° adieu.

QUINCE. At the Duke's oak we meet.

BOTTOM. Enough. Hold, or cut bowstrings.°

                                                            Exeunt.

2.1 *Enter a* FAIRY *at one door, and* ROBIN GOODFELLOW [PUCK]
    at another.

PUCK. How now, spirit, whither wander you?

FAIRY.
    Over hill, over dale,
      Thorough° bush, thorough brier,
    Over park, over pale,°
      Thorough flood, thorough fire,   5
    I do wander everywhere,
    Swifter than the moon's sphere;°
    And I serve the Fairy Queen,
    To dew her orbs° upon the green.
    The cowslips tall her pensioners° be.   10
    In their gold coats spots you see:
    Those be rubies, fairy favors;°
    In those freckles live their savors.°
    I must go seek some dewdrops here
    And hang a pearl in every cowslip's ear.   15
    Farewell, thou lob° of spirits: I'll be gone.
    Our Queen and all her elves come here anon.°

PUCK. The King doth keep his revels here tonight.
    Take heed the Queen come not within his sight.
    For Oberon is passing fell° and wrath,°   20
    Because that she as her attendant hath
    A lovely boy, stolen from an Indian king;
    She never had so sweet a changeling.°
    And jealous Oberon would have the child
    Knight of his train, to trace° the forests wild.   25
    But she perforce° withholds the lovèd boy,
    Crowns him with flowers, and makes him all her joy.
    And now they never meet in grove or green,

---

83 devices plans. **bill** list. **85 obscenely** (An unintentionally funny blunder, whatever Bottom meant to say.) **86 perfect** i.e., letter-perfect in memorizing your parts.
88 Hold . . . bowstrings (An archer's expression not definitely explained, but probably
meaning here "keep your promises, or give up the play.") **2.1 Location: A wood near
Athens.** **3 Thorough** through. **4 pale** enclosure. **7 sphere** orbit. **9 orbs** circles,
i.e., fairy rings (circular bands of grass, darker than the surrounding area, caused by
fungi enriching the soil). **10 pensioners** retainers, members of the royal bodyguard.
12 favors love tokens. **13 savors** sweet smells. **16 lob** country bumpkin. **17 anon**
at once. **20 passing fell** exceedingly angry. **wrath** wrathful. **23 changeling** child
exchanged for another by the fairies. **25 trace** range through. **26 perforce** forcibly.

By fountain° clear, or spangled starlight sheen,°
But they do square,° that all their elves for fear   30
Creep into acorn cups and hide them there.
FAIRY. Either I mistake your shape and making quite,
Or else you are that shrewd° and knavish sprite°
Called Robin Goodfellow. Are not you he
That frights the maidens of the villagery,°   35
Skim milk, and sometimes labor in the quern,°
And bootless° make the breathless huswife° churn,
And sometimes make the drink to bear no barm,°
Mislead night wanderers, laughing at their harm?
Those that "Hobgoblin" call you, and "Sweet Puck,"   40
You do their work, and they shall have good luck.
Are you not he?
PUCK.   Thou speakest aright;
I am that merry wanderer of the night.
I jest to Oberon and make him smile
When I a fat and bean-fed horse beguile,   45
Neighing in likeness of a filly foal;
And sometimes lurk I in a gossip's° bowl,
In very likeness of a roasted crab,°
And when she drinks, against her lips I bob
And on her withered dewlap° pour the ale.   50
The wisest aunt,° telling the saddest° tale,
Sometimes for three-foot stool mistaketh me;
Then slip I from her bum, down topples she,
And "Tailor"° cries, and falls into a cough;
And then the whole choir° hold their hips and laugh,   55
And waxen° in their mirth, and neeze,° and swear
A merrier hour was never wasted there.
But, room,° fairy! Here comes Oberon.
FAIRY. And here my mistress. Would that he were gone!

Enter [OBERON] *the King of Fairies at one door, with his train; and*
[TITANIA] *the Queen at another, with hers.*

OBERON. Ill met by moonlight, proud Titania.   60
TITANIA. What, jealous Oberon? Fairies, skip hence.
I have forsworn his bed and company.
OBERON. Tarry, rash wanton.° Am not I thy lord?
TITANIA. Then I must be thy lady; but I know
When thou hast stolen away from Fairyland   65
And in the shape of Corin° sat all day,

---

29 **fountain** spring. **starlight sheen** shining starlight. 30 **square** quarrel.
33 **shrewd** mischievous. **sprite** spirit. 35 **villagery** village population. 36 **quern**
handmill. 37 **bootless** in vain. **huswife** housewife. 38 **barm** yeast, head on the ale.
47 **gossip's** old woman's. 48 **crab** crabapple. 50 **dewlap** loose skin on neck. 51
aunt old woman. **saddest** most serious. 54 **Tailor** (possibly because she ends up sitting cross-legged on the floor, looking like a tailor.) 55 **choir** company. 56 **waxen** increase. **neeze** sneeze. 58 **room** stand aside, make room. 63 **wanton** headstrong
creature. 66, 68 **Corin, Phillida** (Conventional names of pastoral lovers.)

　　　Playing on pipes of corn° and versing love
　　　To amorous Phillida. Why art thou here
　　　Come from the farthest step° of India
　　　But that, forsooth, the bouncing Amazon,　　　　　　　70
　　　Your buskined° mistress and your warrior love,
　　　To Theseus must be wedded, and you come
　　　To give their bed joy and prosperity.
OBERON.　How canst thou thus for shame, Titania,
　　　Glance at my credit with Hippolyta,°　　　　　　　75
　　　Knowing I know thy love to Theseus?
　　　Didst not thou lead him through the glimmering night
　　　From Perigenia,° whom he ravishèd?
　　　And make him with fair Aegles° break his faith,
　　　With Ariadne° and Antiopa?°　　　　　　　80
TITANIA.　These are the forgeries of jealousy;
　　　And never, since the middle summer's spring,°
　　　Met we on hill, in dale, forest, or mead,
　　　By pavèd° fountain or by rushy° brook,
　　　Or in° the beachèd margent° of the sea,　　　　　　　85
　　　To dance our ringlets° to the whistling wind,
　　　But with thy brawls thou hast disturbed our sport.
　　　Therefore the winds, piping to us in vain,
　　　As in revenge, have sucked up from the sea
　　　Contagious° fogs; which, falling in the land,　　　　　　　90
　　　Hath every pelting° river made so proud
　　　That they have overborne their continents.°
　　　The ox hath therefore stretched his yoke in vain,
　　　The plowman lost his sweat, and the green corn°
　　　Hath rotted ere his youth attained a beard;　　　　　　　95
　　　The fold° stands empty in the drownèd field,
　　　And crows are fatted with the murrain° flock;
　　　The nine-men's-morris° is filled up with mud,
　　　And the quaint mazes° in the wanton° green
　　　For lack of tread are undistinguishable.　　　　　　　100

---

67 **corn** (Here, oat stalks.)　69 **step** farthest limit of travel, or, perhaps, *steep*, mountain range.　71 **buskined** wearing half-boots called buskins.　75 **Glance . . . Hippolyta** make insinuations about my favored relationship with Hippolyta.　78 **Perigenia** i.e., Perigouna, one of Theseus's conquests. (This and the following women are named in Thomas North's translation of Plutarch's "Life of Theseus.")　79 **Aegles** i.e., Aegle, for whom Theseus deserted Ariadne according to some accounts.　80 **Ariadne** the daughter of Minos, King of Crete, who helped Theseus to escape the labyrinth after killing the Minotaur; later she was abandoned by Theseus. **Antiopa** Queen of the Amazons and wife of Theseus; elsewhere identified with Hippolyta, but here thought of as a separate woman.　82 **middle summer's spring** beginning of midsummer.　84 **pavèd** with pebbled bottom. **rushy** bordered with rushes.　85 **in** on. **margent** edge, border.　86 **ringlets** dances in a ring (see *orbs* in line 9).　90 **Contagious** noxious.　91 **pelting** paltry.　92 **continents** banks that contain them.　94 **corn** grain of any kind.　96 **fold** pen for sheep or cattle.　97 **murrain** having died of the plague.　98 **nine-men's-morris** i.e., portion of the village green marked out in a square for a game played with nine pebbles or pegs.　99 **quaint mazes** i.e., intricate paths marked out on the village green to be followed rapidly on foot as a kind of contest. **wanton** luxuriant.

The human mortals want° their winter° here;
No night is now with hymn or carol blessed.
Therefore° the moon, the governess of floods,
Pale in her anger, washes all the air,
That rheumatic diseases° do abound.   105
And thorough this distemperature° we see
The seasons alter: hoary-headed frosts
Fall in the fresh lap of the crimson rose,
And on old Hiems'° thin and icy crown
An odorous chaplet of sweet summer buds   110
Is, as in mockery, set. The spring, the summer,
The childing° autumn, angry winter, change
Their wonted liveries,° and the mazèd° world
By their increase° now knows not which is which.
And this same progeny of evils comes   115
From our debate,° from our dissension;
We are their parents and original.°
OBERON.   Do you amend it, then; it lies in you.
Why should Titania cross her Oberon?
I do but beg a little changeling boy   120
To be my henchman.°
TITANIA.   Set your heart at rest.
The fairy land buys not the child of me.
His mother was a vot'ress of my order,
And in the spicèd Indian air by night
Full often hath she gossiped by my side   125
And sat with me on Neptune's yellow sands,
Marking th' embarkèd traders° on the flood,°
When we have laughed to see the sails conceive
And grow big-bellied with the wanton° wind;
Which she, with pretty and with swimming° gait,   130
Following—her womb then rich with my young squire—
Would imitate, and sail upon the land
To fetch me trifles, and return again
As from a voyage, rich with merchandise.
But she, being mortal, of that boy did die;   135
And for her sake do I rear up her boy,
And for her sake I will not part with him.
OBERON. How long within this wood intend you stay?
TITANIA. Perchance till after Theseus' wedding day.
If you will patiently dance in our round°   140
And see our moonlight revels, go with us;
If not, shun me, and I will spare° your haunts.

---

101 want lack. **winter** i.e., regular winter season; or, proper observances of winter, such as the *hymn or carol* in the next line (?). **103 Therefore** i.e., as a result of our quarrel. **105 rheumatic diseases** colds, flu, and other respiratory infections. **106 distemperature** disturbance in nature. **109 Hiems'** the winter god's. **112 childing** fruitful, pregnant. **113 wonted liveries** usual apparel. **mazèd** bewildered. **114 their increase** their yield, what they produce. **116 debate** quarrel. **117 original** origin. **121 henchman** attendant, page. **127 traders** trading vessels. **flood** flood tide. **129 wanton** sportive. **130 swimming** smooth, gliding. **140 round** circular dance.

OBERON. Give me that boy and I will go with thee.
TITANIA. Not for thy fairy kingdom. Fairies, away!
    We shall chide downright if I longer stay.   145
                                Exeunt [TITANIA *with her train*].
OBERON. Well, go thy way. Thou shalt not from° this grove
    Till I torment thee for this injury.
    My gentle Puck, come hither. Thou rememb'rest
    Since° once I sat upon a promontory,
    And heard a mermaid on a dolphin's back   150
    Uttering such dulcet and harmonious breath°
    That the rude° sea grew civil at her song,
    And certain stars shot madly from their spheres
    To hear the sea-maid's music?
PUCK.   I remember.
OBERON. That very time I saw, but thou couldst not,   155
    Flying between the cold moon and the earth,
    Cupid all° armed. A certain aim he took
    At a fair vestal° thronèd by the west,
    And loosed° his love shaft smartly from his bow
    As° it should pierce a hundred thousand hearts;   160
    But I might° see young Cupid's fiery shaft
    Quenched in the chaste beams of the watery moon,
    And the imperial vot'ress passèd on
    In maiden meditation, fancy-free.°
    Yet marked I where the bolt° of Cupid fell: 165
    It fell upon a little western flower,
    Before milk-white, now purple with love's wound,
    And maidens call it "love-in-idleness."°
    Fetch me that flower; the herb I showed thee once.
    The juice of it on sleeping eyelids laid   170
    Will make or man or° woman madly dote
    Upon the next live creature that it sees.
    Fetch me this herb, and be thou here again
    Ere the leviathan° can swim a league.
PUCK. I'll put a girdle round about the earth   175
    In forty° minutes.   [*Exit.*]
OBERON.   Having once this juice,
    I'll watch Titania when she is asleep
    And drop the liquor of it in her eyes.
    The next thing then she waking looks upon,
    Be it on lion, bear, or wolf, or bull,   180
    On meddling monkey, or on busy ape,
    She shall pursue it with the soul of love.

---

142 spare shun. **146 from** go from. **149 Since** when. **151 breath** voice, song.
152 rude rough. **157 all** fully. **158 vestal** vestal virgin. (Contains a complimentary allusion to Queen Elizabeth as a votaress of Diana and probably refers to an actual entertainment in her honor at Elvetham in 1591.) **159 loosed** released. **160 As** as if. **161
might** could. **164 fancy-free** free of love's spell. **165 bolt** arrow. **168 love-in-
idleness** pansy, heartsease. **171 or . . . or** either . . . or. **174 leviathan** sea monster, whale. **176 forty** (Used indefinitely.)

And ere I take this charm from off her sight,
As I can take it with another herb,
I'll make her render up her page to me.   185
But who comes here? I am invisible,
And I will overhear their conference.

Enter DEMETRIUS, HELENA *following him.*

DEMETRIUS. I love thee not; therefore pursue me not.
    Where is Lysander and fair Hermia?
    The one I'll slay; the other slayeth me.   190
    Thou toldst me they were stol'n unto this wood;
    And here am I, and wode° within this wood,
    Because I cannot meet my Hermia.
    Hence, get thee gone, and follow me no more.
HELENA. You draw me, you hardhearted adamant!°   195
    But yet you draw not iron, for my heart
    Is true as steel. Leave° you your power to draw,
    And I shall have no power to follow you.
DEMETRIUS. Do I entice you? Do I speak you fair?°
    Or rather do I not in plainest truth   200
    Tell you I do not nor I cannot love you?
HELENA. And even for that do I love you the more.
    I am your spaniel; and, Demetrius,
    The more you beat me, I will fawn on you.
    Use me but as your spaniel, spurn me, strike me,   205
    Neglect me, lose me; only give me leave,
    Unworthy as I am, to follow you.
    What worser place can I beg in your love—
    And yet a place of high respect with me—
    Than to be usèd as you use your dog?   210
DEMETRIUS. Tempt not too much the hatred of my spirit,
    For I am sick when I do look on thee.
HELENA. And I am sick when I look not on you.
DEMETRIUS. You do impeach° your modesty too much
    To leave the city and commit yourself   215
    Into the hands of one that loves you not,
    To trust the opportunity of night
    And the ill counsel of a desert° place
    With the rich worth of your virginity.
HELENA. Your virtue° is my privilege.° For that°   220
    It is not night when I do see your face,
    Therefore I think I am not in the night;
    Nor doth this wood lack worlds of company,
    For you, in my respect,° are all the world.

---

192 wode mad. (Pronounced "wood" and often spelled so.) **195 adamant** lodestone, magnet (with pun on *hardhearted,* since adamant was also thought to be the hardest of all stones and was confused with the diamond). **197 Leave** give up. **199 fair** courteously. **214 impeach** call into question. **218 desert** deserted. **220 virtue** goodness or power to attract. **privilege** safeguard; warrant. **For that** because. **224 in my respect** as far as I am concerned.

Then how can it be said I am alone   225
When all the world is here to look on me?
DEMETRIUS. I'll run from thee and hide me in the brakes,°
And leave thee to the mercy of wild beasts.
HELENA. The wildest hath not such a heart as you.
Run when you will, the story shall be changed: 230
Apollo flies and Daphne holds the chase,°
The dove pursues the griffin,° the mild hind°
Makes speed to catch the tiger—bootless° speed,
When cowardice pursues and valor flies!
DEMETRIUS. I will not stay° thy questions.° Let me go!   235
Or if thou follow me, do not believe
But I shall do thee mischief in the wood.
HELENA. Ay, in the temple, in the town, the field,
You do me mischief. Fie, Demetrius!
Your wrongs do set a scandal on my sex.°   240
We cannot fight for love, as men may do;
We should be wooed and were not made to woo.

                                             [*Exit* DEMETRIUS.]

I'll follow thee and make a heaven of hell,
To die upon° the hand I love so well.   [*Exit.*]
OBERON. Fare thee well, nymph. Ere he do leave this grove,   245
Thou shalt fly him and he shall seek thy love.

Enter PUCK.

Hast thou the flower there? Welcome, wanderer.
PUCK. Ay, there it is.   [*He offers the flower.*]
OBERON.   I pray thee, give it me.
I know a bank where the wild thyme blows,°
Where oxlips° and the nodding violet grows,   250
Quite overcanopied with luscious woodbine,°
With sweet muskroses° and with eglantine.°
There sleeps Titania sometimes of the night,
Lulled in these flowers with dances and delight;
And there the snake throws° her enameled skin,   255
Weed° wide enough to wrap a fairy in.
And with the juice of this I'll streak° her eyes
And make her full of hateful fantasies.
Take thou some of it, and seek through this grove.

                                          [*He gives some love juice.*]

---

227 brakes thickets.   **231 Apollo . . . chase** (In the ancient myth, Daphne fled from
Apollo and was saved from rape by being transformed into a laurel tree; here it is the
female who *holds the chase,* or pursues, instead of the male.)   **232 griffin** a fabulous
monster with the head of an eagle and the body of a lion.   **hind** female deer.   **233
bootless** fruitless.   **235 stay** wait for.   **questions** talk or argument.   **240 Your . . .
sex** i.e., the wrongs that you do me cause me to act in a manner that disgraces my sex.
244 upon by.   **249 blows** blooms.   **250 oxlips** flowers resembling cowslip and primrose.   **251 woodbine** honeysuckle.   **252 muskroses** a kind of large, sweet-scented
rose. **eglantine** sweetbrier, another kind of rose.   **255 throws** sloughs off, sheds.
256 Weed garment.   **257 streak** anoint, touch gently.

A sweet Athenian lady is in love   260
With a disdainful youth. Anoint his eyes,
But do it when the next thing he espies
May be the lady. Thou shalt know the man
By the Athenian garments he hath on.
Effect it with some care, that he may prove   265
More fond on° her than she upon her love;
And look thou meet me ere the first cock crow.

PUCK. Fear not, my lord, your servant shall do so.

                                                        Exeunt.

2.2 *Enter* TITANIA, *Queen of Fairies, with her train.*

TITANIA. Come, now a roundel° and a fairy song;
Then, for the third part of a minute, hence—
Some to kill cankers° in the muskrose buds,
Some war with reremice° for their leathern wings
To make my small elves coats, and some keep back   5
The clamorous owl, that nightly hoots and wonders
At our quaint° spirits. Sing me now asleep.
Then to your offices, and let me rest.

  Fairies sing.

FIRST FAIRY.

         You spotted snakes with double° tongue,
              Thorny hedgehogs, be not seen;   10
         Newts° and blindworms, do no wrong,
              Come not near our Fairy Queen.

CHORUS.

         Philomel,° with melody
         Sing in our sweet lullaby;
         Lulla, lulla, lullaby, lulla, lulla, lullaby.   15
              Never harm
              Nor spell nor charm
         Come our lovely lady nigh.
         So good night, with lullaby.

FIRST FAIRY.

         Weaving spiders, come not here;   20
         Hence, you long-legged spinners, hence!
         Beetles black, approach not near;
              Worm nor snail, do no offense.

CHORUS.

         Philomel, with melody
         Sing in our sweet lullaby;   25

---

266 fond on doting on. **2.2 Location: The wood. 1 roundel** dance in a ring.
3 cankers cankerworms (i.e., caterpillars or grubs). **4 reremice** bats. **7 quaint**
dainty. **9 double** forked. **11 Newts** water lizards (considered poisonous, as were
blindworms—small snakes with tiny eyes—and spiders). **13 Philomel** the nightingale.
(Philomela, daughter of King Pandion, was transformed into a nightingale, according to
Ovid's *Metamorphoses* 6, after she had been raped by her sister Procne's husband,
Tereus.)

Lulla, lulla, lullaby, lulla, lulla, lullaby.
  Never harm
  Nor spell nor charm
Come our lovely lady nigh.
So good night, with lullaby.   30

[TITANIA *sleeps.*]

SECOND FAIRY.
  Hence, away! Now all is well.
  One aloof stand sentinel.

[*Exeunt* FAIRIES.]

Enter OBERON [*and squeezes the flower on* TITANIA's *eyelids*].

OBERON.
  What thou seest when thou dost wake,
  Do it for thy true love take;
  Love and languish for his sake.   35
  Be it ounce,° or cat, or bear,
  Pard,° or boar with bristled hair,
  In thy eye that shall appear
  When thou wak'st, it is thy dear.
  Wake when some vile thing is near.   [*Exit.*]   40

Enter LYSANDER *and* HERMIA.

LYSANDER. Fair love, you faint with wandering in the wood;
  And to speak truth, I have forgot our way.
  We'll rest us, Hermia, if you think it good,
  And tarry for the comfort of the day.
HERMIA. Be it so, Lysander. Find you out a bed,   45
  For I upon this bank will rest my head.
LYSANDER. One turf shall serve as pillow for us both;
  One heart, one bed, two bosoms, and one troth.°
HERMIA. Nay, good Lysander, for my sake, my dear,
  Lie further off yet; do not lie so near.   50
LYSANDER. O, take the sense, sweet, of my innocence!°
  Love takes the meaning in love's conference.°
  I mean that my heart unto yours is knit
  So that but one heart we can make of it;
  Two bosoms interchainèd with an oath—   55
  So then two bosoms and a single troth.
  Then by your side no bed-room me deny,
  For lying so, Hermia, I do not lie.°
HERMIA. Lysander riddles very prettily.
  Now much beshrew° my manners and my pride   60
  If Hermia meant to say Lysander lied.

---

36 **ounce** lynx. 37 **Pard** leopard. 48 **troth** faith, trothplight. 51 **take . . . innocence** i.e., interpret my intention as innocent. 52 **Love . . . conference** i.e., when
lovers confer, love teaches each lover to interpret the other's meaning lovingly. 58 **lie** tell
a falsehood (with a riddling pun on *lie,* recline). 60 **beshrew** curse. (But mildly meant.)

But, gentle friend, for love and courtesy
Lie further off, in human° modesty;
Such separation as may well be said
Becomes a virtuous bachelor and a maid,   65
So far be distant; and good night, sweet friend.
Thy love ne'er alter till thy sweet life end!
LYSANDER. Amen, amen, to that fair prayer, say I,
And then end life when I end loyalty!
Here is my bed. Sleep give thee all his rest!   70
HERMIA. With half that wish the wisher's eyes be pressed!°

                    [*They sleep, separated by a short distance.*]

        Enter PUCK.

PUCK.
            Through the forest have I gone,
            But Athenian found I none
            On whose eyes I might approve°
            This flower's force in stirring love.   75
            Night and silence.—Who is here?
            Weeds of Athens he doth wear.
            This is he, my master said,
            Despisèd the Athenian maid;
            And here the maiden, sleeping sound,   80
            On the dank and dirty ground.
            Pretty soul, she durst not lie
            Near this lack-love, this kill-courtesy.
            Churl, upon thy eyes I throw
            All the power this charm doth owe.°   85

                            [*He applies the love juice.*]

            When thou wak'st, let love forbid
            Sleep his seat on thy eyelid.
            So awake when I am gone,
            For I must now to Oberon.   *Exit.*

        Enter DEMETRIUS *and* HELENA, *running.*

HELENA. Stay, though thou kill me, sweet Demetrius!   90
DEMETRIUS. I charge thee, hence, and do not haunt me thus.
HELENA. O, wilt thou darkling° leave me? Do not so.
DEMETRIUS. Stay, on thy peril!° I alone will go.   [*Exit.*]
HELENA. O, I am out of breath in this fond° chase!
The more my prayer, the lesser is my grace.°   95
Happy is Hermia, wheresoe'er she lies,
For she hath blessèd and attractive eyes.
How came her eyes so bright? Not with salt tears;
If so, my eyes are oftener washed than hers.

---

63 **human** courteous.   71 **With . . . pressed** i.e., may we share your wish, so that your
eyes too are *pressed,* closed, in sleep.   74 **approve** test.   85 **owe** own.   92 **darkling**
in the dark.   93 **on thy peril** i.e., on pain of danger to you if you don't obey me and stay.
94 **fond** doting.   95 **my grace** the favor I obtain.

No, no, I am as ugly as a bear;   100
For beasts that meet me run away for fear.
Therefore no marvel though Demetrius
Do, as a monster, fly my presence thus.°
What wicked and dissembling glass of mine
Made me compare° with Hermia's sphery eyne?°   105
But who is here? Lysander, on the ground?
Dead, or asleep? I see no blood, no wound.
Lysander, if you live, good sir, awake.
LYSANDER [*awaking*]. And run through fire I will for thy sweet sake.
Transparent° Helena! Nature shows art,   110
That through thy bosom makes me see thy heart.
Where is Demetrius? O, how fit a word
Is that vile name to perish on my sword!
HELENA. Do not say so, Lysander, say not so.
What though he love your Hermia? Lord, what though?   115
Yet Hermia still loves you. Then be content.
LYSANDER. Content with Hermia? No! I do repent
The tedious minutes I with her have spent.
Not Hermia but Helena I love.
Who will not change a raven for a dove?   120
The will of man is by his reason swayed,
And reason says you are the worthier maid.
Things growing are not ripe until their season;
So I, being young, till now ripe not° to reason.
And touching° now the point° of human skill,°   125
Reason becomes the marshal to my will
And leads me to your eyes, where I o'erlook°
Love's stories written in love's richest book.
HELENA. Wherefore° was I to this keen mockery born?
When at your hands did I deserve this scorn?   130
Is't not enough, is't not enough, young man,
That I did never, no, nor never can,
Deserve a sweet look from Demetrius' eye,
But you must flout my insufficiency?
Good troth,° you do me wrong, good sooth,° you do,   135
In such disdainful manner me to woo.
But fare you well. Perforce I must confess
I thought you lord of° more true gentleness.°
O, that a lady, of° one man refused,
Should of another therefore be abused!°   *Exit.*   140
LYSANDER. She sees not Hermia. Hermia, sleep thou there,
And never mayst thou come Lysander near!

102–103 no marvel . . . thus i.e., no wonder that Demetrius flies from me as from a
monster. **105 compare** vie. **sphery eyne** eyes as bright as stars in their spheres.
110 Transparent (1) radiant (2) able to be seen through. **124 ripe not** (am) not
ripened. **125 touching** reaching. **point** summit. **skill** judgment. **127 o'erlook**
read. **129 Wherefore** why. **135 Good troth, good sooth** i.e., indeed, truly.
138 lord of i.e., possessor of. **gentleness** courtesy. **139 of** by. **140 abused** ill treated.

For as a surfeit of the sweetest things
The deepest loathing to the stomach brings,
Or as the heresies that men do leave   145
Are hated most of those they did deceive,°
So thou, my surfeit and my heresy,
Of all be hated, but the most of me!
And, all my powers, address° your love and might
To honor Helen and to be her knight!   *Exit.*   150
HERMIA [*awaking*]. Help me, Lysander, help me! Do thy best
To pluck this crawling serpent from my breast!
Ay me, for pity! What a dream was here!
Lysander, look how I do quake with fear.
Methought a serpent ate my heart away,   155
And you sat smiling at his cruel prey.°
Lysander! What, removed? Lysander! Lord!
What, out of hearing? Gone? No sound, no word?
Alack, where are you? Speak, an if° you hear;
Speak, of all loves!° I swoon almost with fear.   160
No? Then I well perceive you are not nigh.
Either death, or you, I'll find immediately.
                              Exit. [*The sleeping* TITANIA *remains.*]

3.1 *Enter the clowns* [QUINCE, SNUG, BOTTOM, FLUTE, SNOUT, *and*
        STARVELING].

BOTTOM. Are we all met?
QUINCE. Pat, pat;° and here's a marvelous convenient place for our rehearsal. This green plot shall be our stage, this hawthorn brake°
our tiring-house,° and we will do it in action as we will do it before
the Duke.   5
BOTTOM. Peter Quince?
QUINCE. What sayest thou, bully° Bottom?
BOTTOM. There are things in this comedy of Pyramus and Thisbe that will
never please. First, Pyramus must draw a sword to kill himself, which
the ladies cannot abide. How answer you that?   10
SNOUT. By 'r lakin,° a parlous° fear.
STARVELING. I believe we must leave the killing out, when all is done.°
BOTTOM. Not a whit. I have a device to make all well. Write me° a pro-
logue, and let the prologue seem to say we will do no harm with
our swords, and that Pyramus is not killed indeed; and for the more 15
better assurance, tell them that I, Pyramus, am not Pyramus but
Bottom the weaver. This will put them out of fear.

145–146 **as . . . deceive** as renounced heresies are hated most by those persons who
formerly were deceived by them.   149 **address** direct, apply.   156 **prey** act of preying.
159 **an if** if.   160 **of all loves** for all love's sake.   3.1 **Location: The action is continuous.**   2 **pat** on the dot, punctually.   3 **brake** thicket.   4 **tiring-house** attiring area,
hence backstage.   7 **bully** i.e., worthy, jolly, fine fellow.   11 **By 'r lakin** by our ladykin,
i.e., the Virgin Mary.   **parlous** alarming.   12 **when all is done** i.e., when all is said and
done.   13 **Write me** i.e., write at my suggestion. (*Me* is used colloquially.)

QUINCE. Well, we will have such a prologue, and it shall be written in
eight and six.°

BOTTOM. No, make it two more; let it be written in eight and eight. 20

SNOUT. Will not the ladies be afeard of the lion?

STARVELING. I fear it, I promise you.

BOTTOM. Masters, you ought to consider with yourselves, to bring in—
God shield us!—a lion among ladies° is a most dreadful thing.
For there is not a more fearful° wildfowl than your lion living; and 25
we ought to look to 't.

SNOUT. Therefore another prologue must tell he is not a lion.

BOTTOM. Nay, you must name his name, and half his face must be seen
through the lion's neck, and he himself must speak through, saying
thus, or to the same defect:° "Ladies"—or "Fair ladies—I would wish 30
you"—or "I would request you"—or "I would entreat you—not to
fear, not to tremble; my life for yours.° If you think I come hither as
a lion, it were pity of my life.° No, I am no such thing: I am a man
as other men are." And there indeed let him name his name and tell
them plainly he is Snug the joiner. 35

QUINCE. Well, it shall be so. But there is two hard things: that is, to bring
the moonlight into a chamber; for, you know, Pyramus and Thisbe
meet by moonlight.

SNOUT. Doth the moon shine that night we play our play?

BOTTOM. A calendar, a calendar! Look in the almanac. Find out moon- 40
shine, find out moonshine.   [*They consult an almanac.*]

QUINCE. Yes, it doth shine that night.

BOTTOM. Why, then, may you leave a casement of the great chamber
window, where we play, open, and the moon may shine in at the
casement. 45

QUINCE. Ay; or else one must come in with a bush of thorns° and a
lantern and say he comes to disfigure,° or to present,° the person
of Moonshine. Then there is another thing: we must have a wall in
the great chamber; for Pyramus and Thisbe, says the story, did talk
through the chink of a wall. 50

SNOUT. You can never bring in a wall. What say you, Bottom?

BOTTOM. Some man or other must present Wall. And let him have some
plaster, or some loam, or some roughcast° about him, to signify
wall; or let him hold his fingers thus, and through that cranny
shall Pyramus and Thisbe whisper. 55

---

19 eight and six alternate lines of eight and six syllables, a common ballad measure.
24 lion among ladies (A contemporary pamphlet tells how at the christening in 1594 of
Prince Henry, eldest son of King James VI of Scotland, later James I of England, a "black-
amoor" instead of a lion drew the triumphal chariot, since the lion's presence might have
"brought some fear to the nearest.") **25 fearful** fear-inspiring. **30 defect** (Bottom's
blunder for *effect.*) **32 my life for yours** i.e., I pledge my life to make your lives safe.
33 it were . . . life my life would be endangered. **46 bush of thorns** bundle of thorn-
bush faggots (part of the accoutrements of the man in the moon, according to the popular
notions of the time, along with his lantern and his dog). **47 disfigure** (Quince's blunder
for *figure.*) **present** represent. **53 roughcast** a mixture of lime and gravel used to
plaster the outside of buildings.

QUINCE. If that may be, then all is well. Come, sit down, every mother's son, and rehearse your parts. Pyramus, you begin. When you have spoken your speech, enter into that brake, and so everyone according to his cue.

Enter ROBIN [PUCK].

PUCK. What hempen homespuns° have we swaggering here   60
   So near the cradle° of the Fairy Queen?
   What, a play toward?° I'll be an auditor;
   An actor too perhaps, if I see cause.
QUINCE. Speak, Pyramus. Thisbe, stand forth.
BOTTOM [*as* PYRAMUS].
   "Thisbe, the flowers of odious savors sweet—"   65
QUINCE. Odors, odors.
BOTTOM. "—Odors savors sweet;
   So hath thy breath, my dearest Thisbe dear.
   But hark, a voice! Stay thou but here awhile,
   And by and by I will to thee appear."   *Exit.*   70
PUCK. A stranger Pyramus than e'er played here.°   [*Exit.*]
FLUTE. Must I speak now?
QUINCE. Ay, marry, must you; for you must understand he goes but to see a noise that he heard, and is to come again.
FLUTE [*as* THISBE]. "Most radiant Pyramus, most lily-white of hue,   75
   Of color like the red rose on triumphant° brier,
   Most brisky juvenal° and eke° most lovely Jew,°
   As true as truest horse, that yet would never tire.
   I'll meet thee, Pyramus, at Ninny's tomb."
QUINCE. "Ninus'° tomb," man. Why, you must not speak that yet. That   80
you answer to Pyramus. You speak all your part° at once, cues and all. Pyramus, enter. Your cue is past; it is "never tire."
FLUTE. O—"As true as truest horse, that yet would never tire."

[*Enter* PUCK, *and* BOTTOM *as* PYRAMUS *with the ass head.*°]

BOTTOM. "If I were fair,° Thisbe, I were° only thine."
QUINCE. O, monstrous! O, strange! We are haunted. Pray, masters! Fly,   85
masters! Help!

[*Exeunt* QUINCE, SNUG, FLUTE, SNOUT, *and* STARVELING.]

---

60 hempen homespuns i.e., rustics dressed in clothes woven of coarse, homespun fabric made from hemp.   **61 cradle** i.e., Titania's bower.   **62 toward** about to take place.
71 A stranger . . . here (Puck indicates that he has conceived of his plan to present a "stranger" Pyramus than ever seen before, and so Puck exits to put his plan into effect.)
76 triumphant magnificent.   **77 brisky juvenal** lively youth.   **eke** also.   **Jew** (Probably an absurd repetition of the first syllable of *juvenal,* or Flute's error for *jewel.*)
80 Ninus mythical founder of Nineveh (whose wife, Semiramis, was supposed to have built the walls of Babylon where the story of Pyramus and Thisbe takes place.)   **81 part** (An actor's *part* was a script consisting only of his speeches and their cues.)   **83 s.d. with the ass head** (This stage direction, taken from the Folio, presumably refers to a standard stage property.)   **84 fair** handsome.   **were** would be.

PUCK. I'll follow you, I'll lead you about a round,°
    Through bog, through bush, through brake, through brier.
  Sometimes a horse I'll be, sometimes a hound,
    A hog, a headless bear, sometimes a fire;°   90
  And neigh, and bark, and grunt, and roar, and burn,
  Like horse, hound, hog, bear, fire, at every turn.   *Exit.*
BOTTOM. Why do they run away? This is a knavery of them to make me
  afeard.

    Enter SNOUT.

SNOUT. O Bottom, thou art changed! What do I see on thee?   95
BOTTOM. What do you see? You see an ass head of your own, do you?

                                               [*Exit* SNOUT.]

    Enter QUINCE.

QUINCE. Bless thee, Bottom, bless thee! Thou art translated.°   *Exit.*
BOTTOM. I see their knavery. This is to make an ass of me, to fright me,
  if they could. But I will not stir from this place, do what they can. I
  will walk up and down here, and will sing, that they shall hear I am   100
  not afraid.   [*Sings.*]
        The ouzel cock° so black of hue,
          With orange-tawny bill,
        The throstle° with his note so true,
          The wren with little quill°—   105
TITANIA [*awaking*]. What angel wakes me from my flowery bed?
BOTTOM [*sings*].
        The finch, the sparrow, and the lark,
          The plainsong° cuckoo gray,
        Whose note full many a man doth mark,
          And dares not answer nay°—   110
  For, indeed, who would set his wit to so foolish a bird? Who would
    give a bird the lie,° though he cry "cuckoo" never so?°
TITANIA. I pray thee, gentle mortal, sing again.
  Mine ear is much enamored of thy note;
  So is mine eye enthrallèd to thy shape;   115
  And thy fair virtue's force° perforce doth move me
  On the first view to say, to swear, I love thee.
BOTTOM. Methinks, mistress, you should have little reason for that. And
  yet, to say the truth, reason and love keep little company together
  nowadays. The more the pity that some honest neighbors will not   120
  make them friends. Nay, I can gleek° upon occasion.
TITANIA. Thou art as wise as thou art beautiful.

---

87 **about a round** roundabout.   **90 fire** will-o'-the-wisp.   **97 translated** transformed.
102 ouzel cock male blackbird.   **104 throstle** song thrush.   **105 quill** (Literally, a reed
pipe; hence, the bird's piping song.)   **108 plainsong** singing a melody without variations.   **110 dares . . . nay** i.e., cannot deny that he is a cuckold.   **112 give . . . lie** call
the bird a liar.   **never so** ever so much.   **116 thy . . . force** the power of your beauty.
121 gleek scoff, jest.

BOTTOM. Not so, neither. But if I had wit enough to get out of this
 wood, I have enough to serve mine own turn.°
TITANIA. Out of this wood do not desire to go.   125
 Thou shalt remain here, whether thou wilt or no.
 I am a spirit of no common rate.°
 The summer still° doth tend upon my state,°
 And I do love thee. Therefore go with me.
 I'll give thee fairies to attend on thee   130
 And they shall fetch thee jewels from the deep,
 And sing while thou on pressèd flowers dost sleep.
 And I will purge thy mortal grossness° so
 That thou shalt like an airy spirit go.
 Peaseblossom, Cobweb, Mote,° and Mustardseed!   135

 Enter four FAIRIES [PEASEBLOSSOM, COBWEB, MOTE, *and* MUSTARDSEED].

PEASEBLOSSOM. Ready.
COBWEB. And I.
MOTE.   And I.
MUSTARDSEED.   And I.
ALL.   Where shall we go?
TITANIA. Be kind and courteous to this gentleman.
 Hop in his walks and gambol in his eyes;°
 Feed him with apricots and dewberries,°   140
 With purple grapes, green figs, and mulberries;
 The honey bags steal from the humble-bees,
 And for night tapers crop their waxen thighs
 And light them at the fiery glowworms' eyes,
 To have my love to bed and to arise;   145
 And pluck the wings from painted butterflies
 To fan the moonbeams from his sleeping eyes.
 Nod to him, elves, and do him courtesies.
PEASEBLOSSOM. Hail, mortal!
COBWEB. Hail!   150
MOTE. Hail!
MUSTARDSEED. Hail!
BOTTOM. I cry your worships mercy, heartily. I beseech your worship's
 name.
COBWEB. Cobweb.   155
BOTTOM. I shall desire you of more acquaintance, good Master Cobweb.
 If I cut my finger, I shall make bold with you.°—Your name, honest
 gentleman?
PEASEBLOSSOM. Peaseblossom.

---

124 **serve . . . turn** answer my purpose.   127 **rate** rank, value.   128 **still** ever, always.
doth . . . state waits upon me as a part of my royal retinue.   133 **mortal grossness**
materiality (i.e., the corporeal nature of a mortal being).   135 **Mote** i.e. speck. (The two
words *moth* and *mote* were pronounced alike, and both meanings may be present.)
139 **in his eyes** in his sight (i.e., before him).   140 **dewberries** blackberries.   157 **If
. . . you** (Cobwebs were used to stanch bleeding.)

BOTTOM. I pray you, commend me to Mistress Squash,° your mother, 160
and to Master Peascod,° your father. Good Master Peaseblossom, I
shall desire you of more acquaintance too.—Your name, I beseech
you, sir?

MUSTARDSEED. Mustardseed.

BOTTOM. Good Master Mustardseed I know your patience° well. That 165
same cowardly giantlike ox-beef hath devoured many a gentleman
of your house. I promise you, your kindred hath made my eyes
water° ere now. I desire you of more acquaintance, good Master
Mustardseed.

TITANIA. Come, wait upon him; lead him to my bower.   170
    The moon methinks looks with a watery eye;
  And when she weeps,° weeps every little flower,
    Lamenting some enforcèd° chastity.
  Tie up my lover's tongue,° bring him silently.

                                    [*Exeunt.*]

3.2 *Enter* [OBERON,] *King of Fairies.*

OBERON. I wonder if Titania be awaked;
  Then what it was that next came in her eye,
  Which she must dote on in extremity.

[*Enter*] ROBIN GOODFELLOW [PUCK].

  Here comes my messenger. How now, mad spirit?
  What night-rule° now about this haunted° grove?   5

PUCK. My mistress with a monster is in love.
  Near to her close° and consecrated bower,
  While she was in her dull° and sleeping hour,
  A crew of patches,° rude mechanicals,°
  That work for bread upon Athenian stalls,°   10
  Were met together to rehearse a play
  Intended for great Theseus' nuptial day.
  The shallowest thick-skin of that barren sort,°
  Who Pyramus presented° in their sport,
  Forsook his scene° and entered in a brake.   15
  When I did him at this advantage take,
  An ass's noll° I fixèd on his head.
  Anon his Thisbe must be answered,
  And forth my mimic° comes. When they him spy,
  As wild geese that the creeping fowler° eye,   20

---

160 Squash unripe pea pod.   **161 Peascod** ripe pea pod.   **165 your patience** what
you have endured.   **168 water** (1) weep for sympathy (2) smart, sting.   **172 she weeps**
i.e., she causes dew.   **173 enforcèd** forced, violated; or, possibly, constrained (since Titania at this moment is hardly concerned about chastity).   **174 Tie . . . tongue** (Presumably Bottom is braying like an ass.)   **3.2 Location: The wood.   5 night-rule** diversion
for the night. **haunted** much frequented.   **7 close** secret, private.   **8 dull** drowsy.
9 patches clowns, fools. **rude mechanicals** ignorant artisans.   **10 stalls** market
booths.   **13 barren sort** stupid company or crew.   **14 presented** acted.   **15 scene**
playing area.   **17 noll** noddle, head.   **19 mimic** burlesque actor.   **20 fowler** hunter of
game birds.

Or russet-pated choughs,° many in sort,°
Rising and cawing at the gun's report,
Sever° themselves and madly sweep the sky,
So, at his sight, away his fellows fly;
And, at our stamp, here o'er and o'er one falls;   25
He "Murder!" cries and help from Athens calls.
Their sense thus weak, lost with their fears thus strong,
Made senseless things begin to do them wrong,
For briers and thorns at their apparel snatch;
Some, sleeves—some, hats; from yielders all things catch.°   30
I led them on in this distracted fear
And left sweet Pyramus translated there,
When in that moment, so it came to pass,
Titania waked and straightway loved an ass.

OBERON. This falls out better than I could devise.   35
    But hast thou yet latched° the Athenian's eyes
    With the love juice, as I did bid thee do?

PUCK. I took him sleeping—that is finished too—
    And the Athenian woman by his side,
    That, when he waked, of force° she must be eyed.   40

Enter DEMETRIUS *and* HERMIA.

OBERON. Stand close. This is the same Athenian.
PUCK. This is the woman, but not this the man.

                                    [*They stand aside.*]

DEMETRIUS. O, why rebuke you him that loves you so?
    Lay breath so bitter on your bitter foe.

HERMIA. Now I but chide; but I should use thee worse,   45
    For thou, I fear, hast given me cause to curse.
    If thou hast slain Lysander in his sleep,
    Being o'er shoes° in blood, plunge in the deep,
    And kill me too.
    The sun was not so true unto the day   50
    As he to me. Would he have stolen away
    From sleeping Hermia? I'll believe as soon
    This whole° earth may be bored, and that the moon
    May through the center creep, and so displease
    Her brother's° noontide with th' Antipodes.°   55
    It cannot be but thou hast murdered him;
    So should a murderer look, so dead,° so grim.

DEMETRIUS. So should the murdered look, and so should I
    Pierced through the heart with your stern cruelty.
    Yet you, the murderer, look as bright, as clear,   60
    As yonder Venus in her glimmering sphere.

---

21 russet-pated choughs reddish brown or gray-headed jackdaws. **in sort** in a flock.
23 Sever i.e., scatter. **30 from . . . catch** i.e., everything preys on those who yield to
fear. **36 latched** fastened, snared. **40 of force** perforce. **48 o'er shoes** i.e., so far
gone. **53 whole** solid. **55 Her brother's** i.e., the sun's. **th' Antipodes** the people
on the opposite side of the earth (where the moon is imagined bringing night to noontime). **57 dead** deadly, or deathly pale.

HERMIA. What's this to° my Lysander? Where is he?
    Ah, good Demetrius, wilt thou give him me?
DEMETRIUS. I had rather give his carcass to my hounds.
HERMIA. Out, dog! Out, cur! Thou driv'st me past the bounds   65
    Of maiden's patience. Hast thou slain him, then?
    Henceforth be never numbered among men.
    O, once tell true, tell true, even for my sake:
    Durst thou have looked upon him being awake?
    And hast thou killed him sleeping? O brave touch!°   70
    Could not a worm,° an adder, do so much?
    An adder did it; for with doubler tongue
    Than thine, thou serpent, never adder stung.
DEMETRIUS. You spend your passion° on a misprised mood.°
    I am not guilty of Lysander's blood,   75
    Nor is he dead, for aught that I can tell.
HERMIA. I pray thee, tell me then that he is well.
DEMETRIUS. An if I could, what should I get therefor?
HERMIA. A privilege never to see me more.
    And from thy hated presence part I so.   80
    See me no more, whether he be dead or no.   *Exit.*
DEMETRIUS. There is no following her in this fierce vein.
    Here therefore for a while I will remain.
    So sorrow's heaviness doth heavier° grow
    For debt that bankrupt° sleep doth sorrow owe;   85
    Which now in some slight measure it will pay,
    If for his tender here I make some stay.°   *Lie[s] down [and sleeps].*
OBERON. What hast thou done? Thou hast mistaken quite
    And laid the love juice on some true love's sight.
    Of thy misprision° must perforce ensue   90
    Some true love turned, and not a false turned true.
PUCK. Then fate o'errules, that, one man holding troth,°
    A million fail, confounding oath on oath.°
OBERON. About the wood go swifter than the wind,
    And Helena of Athens look° thou find.   95
    All fancy-sick° she is and pale of cheer°
    With sighs of love, that cost the fresh blood° dear.
    By some illusion see thou bring her here.
    I'll charm his eyes against she do appear.°

---

62 to to do with.   **70 brave touch** noble exploit. (Said ironically.)   **71 worm** serpent.
74 passion violent feelings. **misprised mood** anger based on misconception. **84
heavier** (1) harder to bear (2) more drowsy.   **85 bankrupt** (Demetrius is saying that his
sleepiness adds to the weariness caused by sorrow.)   **86–87 Which . . . stay** i.e., to a
small extent I will be able to "pay back" and hence find some relief from sorrow, if I pause
here awhile (*make some stay*) while sleep "tenders" or offers itself by way of paying the
debt owed to sorrow.   **90 misprision** mistake.   **92 troth** faith.   **93 confounding . . .
oath** i.e., invalidating one oath with another.   **95 look** i.e., be sure.   **96 fancy-sick**
lovesick.   **cheer** face.   **97 sighs . . . blood** (An allusion to the physiological theory that
each sigh costs the heart a drop of blood.)   **99 against . . . appear** in anticipation of her
coming.

PUCK. I go. I go, look how I go,   100
    Swifter than arrow from the Tartar's bow.°   [*Exit.*]
OBERON [*applying love juice to Demetrius' eyes*].
    Flower of this purple dye,
    Hit with Cupid's archery,
    Sink in apple of his eye.
    When his love he doth espy,   105
    Let her shine as gloriously
    As the Venus of the sky.
    When thou wak'st, if she be by,
    Beg of her for remedy.

    Enter PUCK.

PUCK. Captain of our fairy band,   110
    Helena is here at hand,
    And the youth, mistook by me,
    Pleading for a lover's fee.°
    Shall we their fond pageant° see?
    Lord, what fools these mortals be!   115
OBERON. Stand aside. The noise they make
    Will cause Demetrius to awake.
PUCK. Then will two at once woo one;
    That must needs be sport alone.°
    And those things do best please me   120
    That befall preposterously.°

                                      [*They stand aside.*]

    Enter LYSANDER *and* HELENA.

LYSANDER. Why should you think that I should woo in scorn?
    Scorn and derision never come in tears.
    Look when° I vow, I weep; and vows so born,
    In their nativity all truth appears.°   125
    How can these things in me seem scorn to you,
    Bearing the badge° of faith to prove them true?
HELENA. You do advance° your cunning more and more.
    When truth kills truth,° O, devilish-holy fray!
    These vows are Hermia's. Will you give her o'er?   130
    Weigh oath with oath, and you will nothing weigh.
    Your vows to her and me, put in two scales,
    Will even weigh, and both as light as tales.°
LYSANDER. I had no judgment when to her I swore.

---

101 Tartar's bow (Tartars were famed for their skill with the bow.)   **113 fee** privilege,
reward.   **114 fond pageant** foolish exhibition.   **119 alone** unequaled.   **121 prepost-
erously** out of the natural order.   **124 Look when** whenever.   **124–125 vows . . .
appears** i.e., vows made by one who is weeping give evidence thereby of their sincerity.
127 badge identifying device such as that worn on servants' livery (here, his tears).
128 advance carry forward, display.   **129 truth kills truth** i.e., one of Lysander's vows
must invalidate the other.   **133 tales** lies.

HELENA. Nor none, in my mind, now you give her o'er.   135
LYSANDER. Demetrius loves her, and he loves not you.
DEMETRIUS [*awaking*]. O Helen, goddess, nymph, perfect, divine!
        To what, my love, shall I compare thine eyne?
        Crystal is muddy. O, how ripe in show°
        Thy lips, those kissing cherries, tempting grow!   140
        That pure congealèd white, high Taurus'° snow,
        Fanned with the eastern wind, turns to a crow°
        When thou hold'st up thy hand. O, let me kiss
        This princess of pure white, this seal° of bliss!
HELENA. O spite! O hell! I see you all are bent   145
        To set against° me for your merriment.
        If you were civil and knew courtesy,
        You would not do me thus much injury.
        Can you not hate me, as I know you do,
        But you must join in souls to mock me too?   150
        If you were men, as men you are in show,
        You would not use a gentle lady so—
        To vow, and swear, and superpraise° my parts,°
        When I am sure you hate me with your hearts.
        You both are rivals, and love Hermia;   155
        And now both rivals, to mock Helena.
        A trim° exploit, a manly enterprise,
        To conjure tears up in a poor maid's eyes
        With your derision! None of noble sort°
        Would so offend a virgin and extort°   160
        A poor soul's patience, all to make you sport.
LYSANDER. You are unkind, Demetrius. Be not so;
        For you love Hermia; this you know I know.
        And here, with all good will, with all my heart,
        In Hermia's love I yield you up my part;   165
        And yours of Helena to me bequeath,
        Whom I do love and will do till my death.
HELENA. Never did mockers waste more idle breath.
DEMETRIUS. Lysander, keep thy Hermia; I will none.°
        If e'er I loved her, all that love is gone.   170
        My heart to her but as guest-wise sojourned,°
        And now to Helen is it home returned,
        There to remain.
LYSANDER.   Helen, it is not so.
DEMETRIUS. Disparage not the faith thou dost not know,
        Lest, to thy peril, thou aby° it dear.   175
        Look where thy love comes; yonder is thy dear.

        Enter HERMIA.

_____

139 show appearance.   **141 Taurus** a lofty mountain range in Asia Minor.   **142 turns
to a crow** i.e., seems black by contrast.   **144 seal** pledge.   **146 set against** attack.
153 superpraise overpraise.   **parts** qualities.   **157 trim** pretty, fine (said ironically).
159 sort character, quality.   **160 extort** twist, torture.   **169 will none** i.e., want no
part of her.   **171 to . . . sojourned** only visited with her.   **175 aby** pay for.

HERMIA. Dark night, that from the eye his° function takes,
    The ear more quick of apprehension makes;
    Wherein it doth impair the seeing sense
    It pays the hearing double recompense.   180
    Thou art not by mine eye, Lysander, found;
    Mine ear, I thank it, brought me to thy sound.
    But why unkindly didst thou leave me so?
LYSANDER. Why should he stay whom love doth press to go?
HERMIA. What love could press Lysander from my side?   185
LYSANDER. Lysander's love, that would not let him bide—
    Fair Helena, who more engilds° the night
    Than all yon fiery oes° and eyes of light.
    Why seek'st thou me? Could not this make thee know,
    The hate I bear thee made me leave thee so?   190
HERMIA. You speak not as you think. It cannot be.
HELENA. Lo, she is one of this confederacy!
    Now I perceive they have conjoined all three
    To fashion this false sport in spite of me.°
    Injurious Hermia, most ungrateful maid!   195
    Have you conspired, have you with these contrived°
    To bait° me with this foul derision?
    Is all the counsel° that we two have shared,
    The sisters' vows, the hours that we have spent,
    When we have chid the hasty-footed time   200
    For parting us—O, is all forgot?
    All schooldays' friendship, childhood innocence?
    We, Hermia, like two artificial° gods,
    Have with our needles created both one flower,
    Both on one sampler, sitting on one cushion,   205
    Both warbling of one song, both in one key,
    As if our hands, our sides, voices, and minds
    Had been incorporate.° So we grew together
    Like to a double cherry, seeming parted
    But yet an union in partition,   210
    Two lovely° berries molded on one stem;
    So with two seeming bodies but one heart,
    Two of the first, like coats in heraldry,
    Due but to one and crowned with one crest.°
    And will you rend our ancient love asunder   215
    To join with men in scorning your poor friend?
    It is not friendly, tis not maidenly.
    Our sex, as well as I, may chide you for it,
    Though I alone do feel the injury.

---

177 **his** its.   187 **engilds** brightens with a golden light.   188 **oes** spangles (here, stars).
194 **in spite of me** to vex me.   196 **contrived** plotted.   197 **bait** torment, as one sets
on dogs to bait a bear.   198 **counsel** confidential talk.   203 **artificial** skilled in art or
creation.   208 **incorporate** of one body.   211 **lovely** loving.   213–214 **Two . . .
crest** i.e., we have two separate bodies, just as a coat of arms in heraldry can be represented twice on a shield but surmounted by a single crest.

HERMIA. I am amazèd at your passionate words.   220
    I scorn you not. It seems that you scorn me.
HELENA. Have you not set Lysander, as in scorn,
    To follow me and praise my eyes and face?
    And made your other love, Demetrius,
    Who even but now did spurn me with his foot,   225
    To call me goddess, nymph, divine and rare,
    Precious, celestial? Wherefore speaks he this
    To her he hates? And wherefore doth Lysander
    Deny your love, so rich within his soul,
    And tender° me, forsooth, affection,   230
    But by your setting on, by your consent?
    What though I be not so in grace° as you,
    So hung upon with love, so fortunate,
    But miserable most, to love unloved?
    This you should pity rather than despise.   235
HERMIA. I understand not what you mean by this.
HELENA. Ay, do! Persever, counterfeit sad° looks,
    Make mouths° upon° me when I turn my back.
    Wink each at other, hold the sweet jest up.°
    This sport, well carried,° shall be chronicled.   240
    If you have any pity, grace, or manners,
    You would not make me such an argument.°
    But fare ye well. 'Tis partly my own fault,
    Which death, or absence, soon shall remedy.
LYSANDER. Stay, gentle Helena; hear my excuse,   245
    My love, my life, my soul, fair Helena!
HELENA. O excellent!
HERMIA [*to* LYSANDER]. Sweet, do not scorn her so.
DEMETRIUS. If she cannot entreat,° I can compel.
LYSANDER. Thou canst compel no more than she entreat.
    Thy threats have no more strength than her weak prayers.   250
    Helen, I love thee, by my life I do!
    I swear by that which I will lose for thee,
    To prove him false that says I love thee not.
DEMETRIUS. I say I love thee more than he can do.
LYSANDER. If thou say so, withdraw, and prove it too.   255
DEMETRIUS. Quick, come!
HERMIA.   Lysander, whereto tends all this?
LYSANDER. Away, you Ethiop!°
               [*He tries to break away from* HERMIA.]
DEMETRIUS.   No, no; he'll
    Seem to break loose; take on as° you would follow,
    But yet come not. You are a tame man, go!

---

230 tender offer. **232 grace** favor. **237 sad** grave, serious. **238 mouths** i.e.,
mows, faces, grimaces. **upon** at. **239 hold ... up** keep up the joke. **240 carried**
managed. **242 argument** subject for a jest. **248 entreat** i.e., succeed by entreaty.
257 Ethiop (Referring to Hermia's relatively dark hair and complexion; see also *tawny
Tartar* six lines later.) **258 take on as** act as if.

LYSANDER. Hang off,° thou cat, thou burr! Vile thing, let loose,   260
  Or I will shake thee from me like a serpent!
HERMIA. Why are you grown so rude? What change is this,
  Sweet love?
LYSANDER.   Thy love? Out, tawny Tartar, out!
  Out, loathèd med'cine!° O hated potion, hence!
HERMIA. Do you not jest?
HELENA.   Yes, sooth,° and so do you.   265
LYSANDER. Demetrius, I will keep my word with thee.
DEMETRIUS. I would I had your bond, for I perceive
  A weak bond° holds you. I'll not trust your word.
LYSANDER. What, should I hurt her, strike her, kill her dead?
  Although I hate her, I'll not harm her so.   270
HERMIA. What, can you do me greater harm than hate?
  Hate me? Wherefore? O me, what news,° my love?
  Am not I Hermia? Are not you Lysander?
  I am as fair now as I was erewhile.°
  Since night you loved me; yet since night you left me.   275
  Why, then you left me—O, the gods forbid!—
  In earnest, shall I say?
LYSANDER.   Ay, by my life!
  And never did desire to see thee more.
  Therefore be out of hope, of question, of doubt;
  Be certain, nothing truer. 'Tis no jest   280
  That I do hate thee and love Helena.
HERMIA [to HELENA]. O me! You juggler! You cankerblossom!°
  You thief of love! What, have you come by night
  And stol'n my love's heart from him?
HELENA.   Fine, i faith!
  Have you no modesty, no maiden shame,   285
  No touch of bashfulness? What, will you tear
  Impatient answers from my gentle tongue?
  Fie, fie! You counterfeit, you puppet,° you!
HERMIA. "Puppet"? Why, so!° Ay, that way goes the game.
  Now I perceive that she hath made compare   290
  Between our statures: she hath urged her height,
  And with her personage, her tall personage,
  Her height, forsooth, she hath prevailed with him.
  And are you grown so high in his esteem
  Because I am so dwarfish and so low?   295
  How low am I, thou painted maypole? Speak!
  How low am I? I am not yet so low
  But that my nails can reach unto thine eyes.
                         [*She flails at* HELENA *but is restrained.*]

---

260 **Hang off** let go.   264 **med'cine** i.e., poison.   265 **sooth** truly.   268 **weak bond**
i.e., Hermia's arm (with a pun on *bond,* oath, in the previous line).   272 **what news**
what is the matter.   274 **erewhile** just now.   282 **cankerblossom** worm that destroys
the flower bud (?).   288 **puppet** (1) counterfeit (2) dwarfish woman (in reference to
Hermia's smaller stature).   289 **Why, so** i.e., Oh, so that's how it is.

HELENA. I pray you, though you mock me, gentlemen,
　　　Let her not hurt me. I was never curst;°   300
　　　I have no gift at all in shrewishness;
　　　I am a right° maid for my cowardice.
　　　Let her not strike me. You perhaps may think,
　　　Because she is something° lower than myself,
　　　That I can match her.
HERMIA.　　　　　　　　　　Lower? Hark, again!   305
HELENA. Good Hermia, do not be so bitter with me.
　　　I evermore did love you, Hermia,
　　　Did ever keep your counsels, never wronged you;
　　　Save that, in love unto Demetrius,
　　　I told him of your stealth° unto this wood.   310
　　　He followed you; for love I followed him.
　　　But he hath chid me hence° and threatened me
　　　To strike me, spurn me, nay, to kill me too.
　　　And now, so° you will let me quiet go,
　　　To Athens will I bear my folly back   315
　　　And follow you no further. Let me go.
　　　You see how simple and how fond° I am.
HERMIA. Why, get you gone. Who is 't that hinders you?
HELENA. A foolish heart, that I leave here behind.
HERMIA. What, with Lysander?
HELENA.　　　　　　　　　　　With Demetrius.   320
LYSANDER. Be not afraid; she shall not harm thee, Helena.
DEMETRIUS. No, sir, she shall not, though you take her part.
HELENA. O, when she is angry, she is keen° and shrewd.°
　　　She was a vixen when she went to school,
　　　And though she be but little, she is fierce.   325
HERMIA. "Little" again? Nothing but "low" and "little"?
　　　Why will you suffer her to flout me thus?
　　　Let me come to her.
LYSANDER.　　　　　　　　　Get you gone, you dwarf!
　　　You minimus,° of hindering knotgrass° made!
　　　You bead, you acorn!
DEMETRIUS.　　　　　　　　　You are too officious   330
　　　In her behalf that scorns your services.
　　　Let her alone. Speak not of Helena;
　　　Take not her part. For, if thou dost intend°
　　　Never so little show of love to her,
　　　Thou shalt aby° it.
LYSANDER.　　　　　　　　　Now she holds me not;   335
　　　Now follow, if thou dar'st, to try whose right,
　　　Of thine or mine, is most in Helena.   [*Exit.*]

---

300 curst shrewish.　**302 right** true.　**304 something** somewhat.　**310 stealth** stealing away.　**312 chid me hence** driven me away with his scolding.　**314 so** if only.
317 fond foolish.　**323 keen** fierce, cruel.　**shrewd** shrewish.　**329 minimus** diminutive creature.　**knotgrass** a weed, an infusion of which was thought to stunt the growth.
333 intend give sign of.　**335 aby** pay for.

DEMETRIUS. Follow? Nay, I'll go with thee, cheek by jowl.°
                                    [Exit, following LYSANDER.]
HERMIA. You, mistress, all this coil° is 'long of° you.
    Nay, go not back.°
HELENA.   I will not trust you, I,   340
    Nor longer stay in your curst company.
    Your hands than mine are quicker for a fray;
    My legs are longer, though, to run away.   *[Exit.]*
HERMIA. I am amazed and know not what to say.   *Exit.*

    [OBERON *and* PUCK *come forward.*]

OBERON. This is thy negligence. Still thou mistak'st,   345
    Or else committ'st thy knaveries willfully.
PUCK. Believe me, king of shadows, I mistook.
    Did not you tell me I should know the man
    By the Athenian garments he had on?
    And so far blameless proves my enterprise   350
    That I have 'nointed an Athenian's eyes;
    And so far am I glad it so did sort,°
    As° this their jangling I esteem a sport.
OBERON. Thou seest these lovers seek a place to fight.
    Hie° therefore, Robin, overcast the night;   355
    The starry welkin° cover thou anon
    With drooping fog as black as Acheron,°
    And lead these testy rivals so astray
    As one come not within another's way.
    Like to Lysander sometimes frame thy tongue,   360
    Then stir Demetrius up with bitter wrong;°
    And sometimes rail thou like Demetrius.
    And from each other look thou lead them thus,
    Till o'er their brows death-counterfeiting sleep
    With leaden legs and batty° wings doth creep.   365
    Then crush this herb° into Lysander's eye,   *[Giving herb.]*
    Whose liquor hath this virtuous° property,
    To take from thence all error with his° might
    And make his eyeballs roll with wonted° sight.
    When they next wake, all this derision°   370
    Shall seem a dream and fruitless vision,
    And back to Athens shall the lovers wend
    With league whose date° till death shall never end.
    Whiles I in this affair do thee employ,
    I'll to my queen and beg her Indian boy;   375

---

338 cheek by jowl i.e., side by side. **339 coil** turmoil, dissension. **'long of** on
account of. **340 go not back** i.e., don't retreat. (Hermia is again proposing a fight.)
352 sort turn out. **353 As** that (also at line 359). **355 Hie** hasten. **356 welkin** sky.
357 Acheron river of Hades (here representing Hades itself). **361 wrong** insults.
365 batty batlike. **366 this herb** i.e., the antidote (mentioned in 2.1.184) to love-
in-idleness. **367 virtuous** efficacious. **368 his** its. **369 wonted** accustomed.
370 derision laughable business. **373 date** term of existence.

And then I will her charmèd eye release
From monster's view, and all things shall be peace.

PUCK. My fairy lord, this must be done with haste,
For night's swift dragons° cut the clouds full fast,
And yonder shines Aurora's harbinger,°   380
At whose approach, ghosts, wand'ring here and there,
Troop home to churchyards. Damnèd spirits all,
That in crossways and floods have burial,°
Already to their wormy beds are gone.
For fear lest day should look their shames upon,   385
They willfully themselves exile from light
And must for aye° consort with black-browed night.

OBERON. But we are spirits of another sort.
I with the Morning's love° have oft made sport,
And, like a forester,° the groves may tread   390
Even till the eastern gate, all fiery red,
Opening on Neptune with fair blessèd beams,
Turns into yellow gold his salt green streams.
But notwithstanding, haste, make no delay.
We may effect this business yet ere day.   [*Exit.*]   395

PUCK.
         Up and down, up and down,
         I will lead them up and down.
         I am feared in field and town.
         Goblin, lead them up and down.
Here comes one.   400

Enter LYSANDER.

LYSANDER. Where art thou, proud Demetrius? Speak thou now.
PUCK. [*mimicking* DEMETRIUS].
     Here, villain, drawn° and ready. Where art thou?
LYSANDER. I will be with thee straight.°
PUCK.   Follow me, then,
To plainer° ground.

         [LYSANDER *wanders about,*° *following the voice.*]

Enter DEMETRIUS.

DEMETRIUS.   Lysander! Speak again!
Thou runaway, thou coward, art thou fled?   405
Speak! In some bush? Where dost thou hide thy head?

---

379 dragons (Supposed by Shakespeare to be yoked to the car of the goddess of night.)
380 Aurora's harbinger the morning star, precursor of dawn. **383 crossways ...
burial** (Those who had committed suicide were buried at crossways, with a stake driven
through them; those drowned, i.e., buried in floods or great waters, would be condemned
to wander disconsolate for want of burial rites.) **387 for aye** forever. **389 Morning's
love** Cephalus, a beautiful youth beloved by Aurora; or perhaps the goddess of the dawn
herself. **390 forester** keeper of a royal forest. **402 drawn** with drawn sword.
403 straight immediately. **404 plainer** more open. **s.d. Lysander wanders about**
(It is not clearly necessary that Lysander exit at this point; neither exit nor reentrance is
indicated in the early texts.)

PUCK [*mimicking* LYSANDER].
    Thou coward, art thou bragging to the stars,
    Telling the bushes that thou look'st for wars,
    And wilt not come? Come, recreant;° come, thou child,
    I'll whip thee with a rod. He is defiled   410
    That draws a sword on thee.
DEMETRIUS.   Yea, art thou there?
PUCK. Follow my voice. We'll try° no manhood here.

                                        Exeunt.

    [LYSANDER *returns.*]

LYSANDER. He goes before me and still dares me on.
    When I come where he calls, then he is gone.
    The villain is much lighter-heeled than I.   415
    I followed fast, but faster he did fly,
    That fallen am I in dark uneven way,
    And here will rest me. [*He lies down.*] Come, thou gentle day!
    For if but once thou show me thy gray light,
    I'll find Demetrius and revenge this spite.   [*He sleeps.*] 420

    [*Enter*] ROBIN [PUCK] *and* DEMETRIUS.

PUCK. Ho, ho, ho! Coward, why com'st thou not?
DEMETRIUS. Abide° me, if thou dar'st; for well I wot°
    Thou runn'st before me, shifting every place,
    And dar'st not stand nor look me in the face.
    Where art thou now?
PUCK.   Come hither. I am here.   425
DEMETRIUS. Nay, then, thou mock'st me. Thou shalt buy° this dear,°
    If ever I thy face by daylight see.
    Now, go thy way. Faintness constraineth me
    To measure out my length on this cold bed.
    By day's approach look to be visited.   430
                      [*He lies down and sleeps.*]

    Enter HELENA.

HELENA. O weary night, O long and tedious night,
      Abate° thy hours! Shine comforts from the east,
    That I may back to Athens by daylight,
      From these that my poor company detest;
    And sleep, that sometimes shuts up sorrow's eye,   435
    Steal me awhile from mine own company.
                  [*She lies down and*] *sleep*[s].

PUCK. Yet but three? Come one more;
    Two of both kinds makes up four.
    Here she comes, curst° and sad.

---

409 **recreant** cowardly wretch. 412 **try** test. 422 **Abide** confront, face. **wot** know.
426 **buy** aby, pay for. **dear** dearly. 432 **Abate** lessen, shorten. 439 **curst** ill-tempered.

Cupid is a knavish lad,   440
Thus to make poor females mad.

[*Enter* HERMIA.]

HERMIA. Never so weary, never so in woe,
   Bedabbled with the dew and torn with briers
   I can no further crawl, no further go;
   My legs can keep no pace with my desires.   445
   Here will I rest me till the break of day.
   Heavens shield Lysander, if they mean a fray!

                                    [*She lies down and sleeps.*]

PUCK.
         On the ground
         Sleep sound.
         I'll apply   450
         To your eye,
      Gentle lover, remedy.

                    [*Squeezing the juice on* LYSANDER'*s eyes.*]

         When thou wak'st,
         Thou tak'st
         True delight   455
         In the sight
      Of thy former lady's eye;
      And the country proverb known,
      That every man should take his own,
      In your waking shall be shown: 460
         Jack shall have Jill;°
         Naught shall go ill;
      The man shall have his mare again, and all shall be well.

                       [*Exit. The four sleeping lovers remain.*]

4.1 *Enter* [TITANIA] *Queen of Fairies, and* [BOTTOM] *the clown, and*
      FAIRIES; *and* [OBERON,] *the King, behind them.*

TITANIA. Come, sit thee down upon this flowery bed,
   While I thy amiable° cheeks do coy,°
   And stick muskroses in thy sleek smooth head,
   And kiss thy fair large ears, my gentle joy.

                                            [*They recline.*]

BOTTOM. Where's Peaseblossom?   5
PEASEBLOSSOM. Ready.
BOTTOM. Scratch my head, Peaseblossom. Where's Monsieur Cobweb?
COBWEB. Ready.
BOTTOM. Monsieur Cobweb, good monsieur, get you your weapons in
   your hand, and kill me a red-hipped humble-bee on the top of a   10
   thistle; and, good monsieur, bring me the honey bag. Do not fret

---

461 Jack shall have Jill (Proverbial for "boy gets girl.") **4.1 Location: The action
is continuous. The four lovers are still asleep onstage. 2 amiable** lovely. **coy**
caress.

yourself too much in the action, monsieur, and, good monsieur,
have a care the honey bag break not; I would be loath to have you
overflown with a honey bag, signor. [*Exit* COBWEB.] Where's
Monsieur Mustardseed?   15

MUSTARDSEED. Ready.

BOTTOM. Give me your neaf,° Monsieur Mustardseed. Pray you, leave your
courtesy,° good monsieur.

MUSTARDSEED. What's your will?

BOTTOM. Nothing, good monsieur, but to help Cavalery° Cobweb° to   20
scratch. I must to the barber's, monsieur, for methinks I am marvelous hairy about the face; and I am such a tender ass, if my hair
do but tickle me, I must scratch.

TITANIA. What, wilt thou hear some music, my sweet love?

BOTTOM. I have a reasonable good ear in music. Let's have the tongs and   25
the bones.°

                                        [*Music: tongs, rural music.*°]

TITANIA. Or say, sweet love, what thou desirest to eat.

BOTTOM. Truly, a peck of provender.° I could munch your good dry
oats. Methinks I have a great desire to a bottle° of hay. Good hay,
sweet hay, hath no fellow.°   30

TITANIA. I have a venturous fairy that shall seek
The squirrel's hoard, and fetch thee new nuts.

BOTTOM. I had rather have a handful or two of dried peas. But, I pray
you, let none of your people stir° me. I have an exposition° of sleep
come upon me.   35

TITANIA. Sleep thou, and I will wind thee in my arms.
Fairies, begone, and be all ways° away.

                                        [*Exeunt* FAIRIES.]

So doth the woodbine the sweet honeysuckle
Gently entwist; the female ivy so
Enrings the barky fingers of the elm.   40
O, how I love thee! How I dote on thee!

                                        [*They sleep.*]

Enter ROBIN GOODFELLOW [PUCK].

OBERON [*coming forward*].
Welcome, good Robin. Seest thou this sweet sight?
Her dotage now I do begin to pity.
For, meeting her of late behind the wood,

---

17 neaf fist.   **17–18 leave your courtesy** i.e., stop bowing, or put on your hat.
20 Cavalery cavalier. (Form of address for a gentleman.)   **Cobweb** (Seemingly an error,
since Cobweb has been sent to bring honey while Peaseblossom has been asked
to scratch.)   **25–26 tongs ... bones** instruments for rustic music. (The tongs were
played like a triangle, whereas the bones were held between the fingers and used as
clappers.)   **25–26 s.d. Music ... music** (This stage direction is added from the Folio.)
28 peck of provender one-quarter bushel of grain.   **29 bottle** bundle.   **30 fellow**
equal.   **34 stir** disturb.   **34 exposition** (Bottom's word for *disposition*.)   **37 all ways**
in all directions.

Seeking sweet favors° for this hateful fool,   45
I did upbraid her and fall out with her.
For she his hairy temples then had rounded
With coronet of fresh and fragrant flowers;
And that same dew, which sometime° on the buds
Was wont to swell like round and orient pearls,°   50
Stood now within the pretty flowerets' eyes
Like tears that did their own disgrace bewail.
When I had at my pleasure taunted her,
And she in mild terms begged my patience,
I then did ask of her her changeling child,   55
Which straight she gave me, and her fairy sent
To bear him to my bower in Fairyland.
And, now I have the boy, I will undo
This hateful imperfection of her eyes.
And, gentle Puck, take this transformèd scalp   60
From off the head of this Athenian swain,
That he, awaking when the other° do,
May all to Athens back again repair,°
And think no more of this night's accidents
But as the fierce vexation of a dream.   65
But first I will release the Fairy Queen.
                    [*He squeezes a herb on her eyes.*]
    Be as thou wast wont to be;
    See as thou wast wont to see.
    Dian's bud° o'er Cupid's flower
    Hath such force and blessèd power.   70
Now, my Titania, wake you, my sweet queen.

TITANIA [*waking*]. My Oberon! What visions have I seen!
    Methought I was enamored of an ass.

OBERON. There lies your love.

TITANIA.   How came these things to pass?
    O, how mine eyes do loathe his visage now!   75

OBERON. Silence awhile. Robin, take off this head.
    Titania, music call, and strike more dead
    Than common sleep of all these five° the sense.

TITANIA. Music, ho! Music, such as charmeth° sleep!

                                        [*Music.*]

PUCK [*removing the ass head*].
    Now, when thou wak'st, with thine own fool's eyes peep.   80

OBERON. Sound, music! Come, my queen, take hands with me,
    And rock the ground whereon these sleepers be.   [*They dance.*]
    Now thou and I are new in amity,

---

45 favors i.e., gifts of flowers.   **49 sometime** formerly.   **50 orient pearls** i.e., the
most beautiful of all pearls, those coming from the Orient.   **62 other** others.   **63 repair**
return.   **69 Dian's bud** (Perhaps the flower of the *agnus castus* or chaste-tree, supposed
to preserve chastity; or perhaps referring simply to Oberon's herb by which he can undo
the effects of "Cupid's flower," the love-in-idleness of 2.1.166–168.)   **78 these five** i.e.,
the four lovers and Bottom.   **79 charmeth** brings about, as though by a charm.

And will tomorrow midnight solemnly°
Dance in Duke Theseus' house triumphantly,   85
And bless it to all fair prosperity.
There shall the pairs of faithful lovers be
Wedded, with Theseus, all in jollity.

PUCK.
        Fairy King, attend, and mark:
        I do hear the morning lark.   90

OBERON.
        Then, my queen, in silence sad,°
        Trip we after night's shade.
        We the globe can compass soon,
        Swifter than the wandering moon.

TITANIA.
        Come, my lord, and in our flight   95
        Tell me how it came this night
        That I sleeping here was found
        With these mortals on the ground.   *Exeunt.*

        Wind horn [*within*].
        Enter THESEUS *and all his train*; [HIPPOLYTA, EGEUS].

THESEUS. Go, one of you, find out the forester,
        For now our observation° is performed;   100
        And since we have the vaward° of the day,
        My love shall hear the music of my hounds.
        Uncouple° in the western valley, let them go.
        Dispatch, I say, and find the forester.   [*Exit an Attendant.*]
        We will, fair queen, up to the mountain's top   105
        And mark the musical confusion
        Of hounds and echo in conjunction.

HIPPOLYTA. I was with Hercules and Cadmus° once,
        When in a wood of Crete they bayed° the bear
        With hounds of Sparta.° Never did I hear   110
        Such gallant chiding;° for, besides the groves,
        The skies, the fountains, every region near
        Seemed all one mutual cry. I never heard
        So musical a discord, such sweet thunder.

THESEUS. My hounds are bred out of the Spartan kind,°   115
        So flewed,° so sanded;° and their heads are hung
        With ears that sweep away the morning dew;
        Crook-kneed, and dewlapped° like Thessalian bulls;
        Slow in pursuit, but matched in mouth like bells,

---

84 solemnly ceremoniously.   **91 sad** sober.   **100 observation** i.e., observance to a
morn of May (1.1.167).   **101 vaward** vanguard, i.e., earliest part.   **103 Uncouple** set
free for the hunt.   **108 Cadmus** mythical founder of Thebes (This story about him is unknown.)   **109 bayed** brought to bay.   **110 hounds of Sparta** (A breed famous in antiquity for their hunting skill.)   **111 chiding** i.e., yelping.   **115 kind** strain, breed.
116 So flewed similarly having large hanging chaps or fleshy covering of the jaw.
sanded of sandy color.   **118 dewlapped** having pendulous folds of skin under the
neck.

Each under each.° A cry° more tunable°   120
Was never holloed to, nor cheered° with horn,
In Crete, in Sparta, nor in Thessaly.
Judge when you hear. [*He sees the sleepers.*] But, soft!
    What nymphs are these?
EGEUS. My lord, this is my daughter here asleep,
And this Lysander; this Demetrius is,   125
This Helena, old Nedar's Helena.
I wonder of° their being here together.
THESEUS. No doubt they rose up early to observe
The rite of May, and hearing our intent,
Came here in grace of our solemnity.°   130
But speak, Egeus. Is not this the day
That Hermia should give answer of her choice?
EGEUS. It is, my lord.
THESEUS. Go, bid the huntsmen wake them with their horns.

                    [*Exit an Attendant.*]

Shout within. Wind horns. They all start up.

Good morrow, friends. Saint Valentine° is past.   135
Begin these woodbirds but to couple now?
LYSANDER. Pardon, my lord.   [*They kneel.*]
THESEUS.   I pray you all, stand up.
I know you two are rival enemies;
How comes this gentle concord in the world,
That hatred is so far from jealousy°   140
To sleep by hate and fear no enmity?
LYSANDER. My lord, I shall reply amazedly,
Half sleep, half waking; but as yet, I swear,
I cannot truly say how I came here.
But, as I think—for truly would I speak,   145
And now I do bethink me, so it is—
I came with Hermia hither. Our intent
Was to be gone from Athens, where° we might,
Without° the peril of the Athenian law—
EGEUS. Enough, enough, my lord; you have enough.   150
I beg the law, the law, upon his head.
They would have stol'n away; they would, Demetrius,
Thereby to have defeated° you and me,
You of your wife and me of my consent,
Of my consent that she should be your wife.   155
DEMETRIUS. My lord, fair Helen told me of their stealth,
Of this their purpose hither° to this wood,

119–120 matched . . . each i.e., harmoniously matched in their various cries like a set of
bells, from treble down to bass. **120 cry** pack of hounds. **tunable** well tuned, melodious. **121 cheered** encouraged. **127 wonder of** wonder at. **130 in . . . solemnity**
in honor of our wedding. **135 Saint Valentine** (Birds were supposed to choose their
mates on Saint Valentine's Day.) **140 jealousy** suspicion. **148 where** wherever; or, to
where. **149 Without** outside of, beyond. **153 defeated** defrauded. **157 hither** in
coming hither.

And I in fury hither followed them,
Fair Helena in fancy following me.
But, my good lord, I wot not by what power—   160
But by some power it is—my love to Hermia,
Melted as the snow, seems to me now
As the remembrance of an idle gaud°
Which in my childhood I did dote upon;
And all the faith, the virtue of my heart,   165
The object and the pleasure of mine eye,
Is only Helena. To her, my lord,
Was I betrothed ere I saw Hermia,
But like a sickness did I loathe this food;
But, as in health, come to my natural taste,   170
Now I do wish it, love it, long for it,
And will for evermore be true to it.

THESEUS. Fair lovers, you are fortunately met.
Of this discourse we more will hear anon.
Egeus, I will overbear your will;   175
For in the temple, by and by, with us
These couples shall eternally be knit.
And, for° the morning now is something° worn,
Our purposed hunting shall be set aside.
Away with us to Athens. Three and three,   180
We'll hold a feast in great solemnity.
Come, Hippolyta.
                         [*Exeunt* THESEUS, HIPPOLYTA, EGEUS, *and train.*]
DEMETRIUS. These things seem small and undistinguishable,
Like far-off mountains turnèd into clouds.
HERMIA. Methinks I see these things with parted° eye,   185
When everything seems double.
HELENA.   So methinks;
And I have found Demetrius like a jewel,
Mine own, and not mine own.°
DEMETRIUS.   Are you sure
That we are awake? It seems to me
That yet we sleep, we dream. Do not you think   190
The Duke was here, and bid us follow him?
HERMIA. Yea, and my father.
HELENA.   And Hippolyta.
LYSANDER. And he did bid us follow to the temple.
DEMETRIUS. Why, then, we are awake. Let's follow him,
And by the way let us recount our dreams.   [*Exeunt.*]   195
BOTTOM [*awaking*]. When my cue comes, call me, and I will answer.
My next is, "Most fair Pyramus." Heigh—ho! Peter Quince! Flute,
the bellows mender! Snout, the tinker! Starveling! God's° my life,

---

163 idle gaud worthless trinket.   **178 for** since. **something** somewhat.   **185 parted**
improperly focused.   **187–188 like . . . mine own** i.e., like a jewel that one finds by
chance and therefore possesses but cannot certainly consider one's own property.
198 God's may God save.

stolen hence and left me asleep! I have had a most rare vision. I
have had a dream, past the wit of man to say what dream it was. 200
Man is but an ass if he go about° to expound this dream.
Methought I was—there is no man can tell what. Methought I
was—and methought I had—but man is but a patched° fool if he
will offer° to say what methought I had. The eye of man hath not
heard, the ear of man hath not seen, man's hand is not able to taste, 205
his tongue to conceive, nor his heart to report,° what my dream
was. I will get Peter Quince to write a ballad of this dream. It shall
be called "Bottom's Dream," because it hath no bottom; and I will
sing it in the latter end of a play, before the Duke. Peradventure,
to make it the more gracious, I shall sing it at her° death. 210

[*Exit.*]

4.2 *Enter* QUINCE, FLUTE, [SNOUT, *and* STARVELING].

QUINCE. Have you sent to Bottom's house? Is he come home yet?
STARVELING. He cannot be heard of. Out of doubt he is transported.°
FLUTE. If he come not, then the play is marred. It goes not forward,
   doth it?
QUINCE. It is not possible. You have not a man in all Athens able to 5
   discharge° Pyramus but he.
FLUTE. No, he hath simply the best wit° of any handicraft man in Athens.
QUINCE. Yea, and the best person° too, and he is a very paramour for a
   sweet voice.
FLUTE. You must say "paragon." A paramour is, God bless us, a thing of 10
   naught.°

Enter SNUG *the joiner*.

SNUG. Masters, the Duke is coming from the temple and there is two or
   three lords and ladies more married. If our sport had gone forward,
   we had all been made men.°
FLUTE. O sweet bully Bottom! Thus hath he lost sixpence a day during 15
   his life; he could not have scaped sixpence a day. An the Duke had
   not given him sixpence a day° for playing Pyramus, I'll be hanged.
   He would have deserved it. Sixpence a day in Pyramus, or nothing.

Enter BOTTOM.

BOTTOM. Where are these lads? Where are these hearts?°
QUINCE. Bottom! O most courageous day! O most happy hour! 20
BOTTOM. Masters, I am to discourse wonders.° But ask me not what; for
   if I tell you, I am no true Athenian. I will tell you everything, right
   as it fell out.

---

201 go about attempt.   **203 patched** wearing motley, i.e., a dress of various colors.
204 offer venture.   **204–206 The eye . . . report** (Bottom garbles the terms of 1
Corinthians 2.9.)   **210 her** Thisbe's (?).   **4.2 Location: Athens.   2 transported** carried off by fairies; or, possibly, transformed.   **6 discharge** perform.   **7 wit** intellect.
8 person appearance.   **10–11 a . . . naught** a shameful thing.   **14 we . . . men**
i.e., we would have had our fortunes made.   **17 sixpence a day** i.e., as a royal pension.
19 hearts good fellows.   **21 am . . . wonders** have wonders to relate.

QUINCE. Let us hear, sweet Bottom.

BOTTOM. Not a word of° me. All that I will tell you is—that the Duke   25
hath dined. Get your apparel together, good strings° to your beards,
new ribbons to your pumps;° meet presently° at the palace; every
man look o'er his part; for the short and the long is, our play is
preferred.° In any case, let Thisbe have clean linen; and let not him
that plays the lion pare his nails, for they shall hang out for the lion's   30
claws. And, most dear actors, eat no onions nor garlic, for we are to
utter sweet breath; and I do not doubt but to hear them say it is a
sweet comedy. No more words. Away! Go, away!

                                                            [*Exeunt.*]

5.1 *Enter* THESEUS, HIPPOLYTA, *and* PHILOSTRATE [*lords, and attendants*].

HIPPOLYTA. 'Tis strange, my Theseus, that° these lovers speak of.
THESEUS. More strange than true. I never may° believe
These antique° fables nor these fairy toys.°
Lovers and madmen have such seething brains,
Such shaping fantasies,° that apprehend°
More than cool reason ever comprehends.°   5
The lunatic, the lover, and the poet
Are of imagination all compact.°
One sees more devils than vast hell can hold;
That is the madman. The lover, all as frantic,
Sees Helen's° beauty in a brow of Egypt.°   10
The poet's eye, in a fine frenzy rolling,
Doth glance from heaven to earth, from earth to heaven;
And as imagination bodies forth
The forms of things unknown, the poet's pen   15
Turns them to shapes and gives to airy nothing
A local habitation and a name.
Such tricks hath strong imagination
That, if it would but apprehend some joy,
It comprehends some bringer° of that joy;   20
Or in the night, imagining some fear,°
How easy is a bush supposed a bear!
HIPPOLYTA. But all the story of the night told over,
And all their minds transfigured so together,
More witnesseth than fancy's images°   25

---

25 of out of. **26 strings** (to attach the beards). **27 pumps** light shoes or slippers.
presently immediately. **29 preferred** selected for consideration. **5.1 Location:**
Athens. The palace of Theseus. 1 that that which. **2 may** can. **3 antique** old-
fashioned (punning too on *antic,* strange, grotesque). **fairy toys** trifling stories about
fairies. **5 fantasies** imaginations. **apprehend** conceive, imagine. **6 comprehends**
understands. **8 compact** formed, composed. **11 Helen's** i.e., of Helen of Troy, pattern of beauty. **brow of Egypt** i.e., face of a gypsy. **20 bringer** i.e., source. **21 fear**
object of fear. **25 More . . . images** testifies to something more substantial than mere
imaginings.

And grows to something of great constancy;°
But, howsoever,° strange and admirable.°

Enter lovers: LYSANDER, DEMETRIUS, HERMIA, *and* HELENA.

THESEUS. Here come the lovers, full of joy and mirth.
  Joy, gentle friends! Joy and fresh days of love
  Accompany your hearts!
LYSANDER.   More than to us   30
  Wait in your royal walks, your board, your bed!
THESEUS. Come now, what masques,° what dances shall we have
  To wear away this long age of three hours
  Between our after-supper and bedtime?
  Where is our usual manager of mirth?   35
  What revels are in hand? Is there no play
  To ease the anguish of a torturing hour?
  Call Philostrate.
PHILOSTRATE.   Here, mighty Theseus.
THESEUS. Say what abridgment° have you for this evening?
  What masque? What music? How shall we beguile   40
  The lazy time, if not with some delight?
PHILOSTRATE [*giving him a paper*].
  There is a brief° how many sports are ripe.
  Make choice of which Your Highness will see first.
THESEUS [*reads*]. "The battle with the Centaurs,° to be sung
  By an Athenian eunuch to the harp"?   45
  We'll none of that. That have I told my love,
  In glory of my kinsman° Hercules.
  [*reads.*] "The riot of the tipsy Bacchanals,
  Tearing the Thracian singer in their rage"?°
  That is an old device;° and it was played   50
  When I from Thebes came last a conqueror.
  [*reads.*] "The thrice three Muses mourning for the death
  Of Learning, late deceased in beggary"?°
  That is some satire, keen and critical,
  Not sorting with° a nuptial ceremony.   55
  [*reads.*] "A tedious brief scene of young Pyramus
  And his love Thisbe; very tragical mirth"?

---

26 constancy certainty.   **27 howsoever** in any case.   **admirable** a source of wonder.
32 masques courtly entertainments.   **39 abridgment** pastime (to abridge or shorten
the evening).   **42 brief** short written statement, summary.   **44 battle . . . Centaurs**
(Probably refers to the battle of the Centaurs and the Lapithae, when the Centaurs attempted to carry off Hippodamia, bride of Theseus's friend Pirothous.)   **47 kinsman**
(Plutarch's "Life of Theseus" states that Hercules and Theseus were near kinsmen. Theseus is referring to a version of the battle of the Centaurs in which Hercules was said to be
present.)   **48–49 The riot . . . rage** (This was the story of the death of Orpheus, as told
in *Metamorphoses* 9.)   **50 device** show, performance.   **52–53 The thrice . . . beggary** (Possibly an allusion to Spenser's *Tears of the Muses*, 1591, though "satires" deplor-
ing the neglect of learning and the creative arts were commonplace.)   **55 sorting with**
befitting.

Merry and tragical? Tedious and brief?
That is hot ice and wondrous strange° snow.
How shall we find the concord of this discord?   60
PHILOSTRATE. A play there is, my lord, some ten words long,
Which is as brief as I have known a play;
But by ten words, my lord, it is too long,
Which makes it tedious. For in all the play
There is not one word apt, one player fitted.   65
And tragical, my noble lord, it is,
For Pyramus therein doth kill himself.
Which, when I saw rehearsed, I must confess,
Made mine eyes water; but more merry tears
The passion of loud laughter never shed.   70
THESEUS. What are they that do play it?
PHILOSTRATE. Hard-handed men that work in Athens here,
Which never labored in their minds till now,
And now have toiled° their unbreathed° memories
With this same play, against° your nuptial.   75
THESEUS. And we will hear it.
PHILOSTRATE.   No, my noble lord,
It is not for you. I have heard it over,
And it is nothing, nothing in the world;
Unless you can find sport in their intents,
Extremely stretched° and conned° with cruel pain   80
To do you service.
THESEUS.   I will hear that play;
For never anything can be amiss
When simpleness° and duty tender it.
Go bring them in; and take your places, ladies.
                       [PHILOSTRATE *goes to summon the players.*]
HIPPOLYTA. I love not to see wretchedness o'ercharged,°   85
And duty in his service° perishing.
THESEUS. Why, gentle sweet, you shall see no such thing.
HIPPOLYTA. He says they can do nothing in this kind.°
THESEUS. The kinder we, to give them thanks for nothing.
Our sport shall be to take what they mistake;   90
And what poor duty cannot do, noble respect°
Takes it in might, not merit.°
Where I have come, great clerks° have purposèd
To greet me with premeditated welcomes;
Where I have seen them shiver and look pale,   95
Make periods in the midst of sentences,

---

59 strange (Sometimes emended to an adjective that would contrast with *snow,* just as
hot contrasts with *ice*.) **74 toiled** taxed. **unbreathed** unexercised. **75 against** in
preparation for. **80 stretched** strained. **conned** memorized. **83 simpleness** simplicity. **85 wretchedness o'ercharged** incompetence overburdened. **86 his service** its
attempt to serve. **88 kind** kind of thing. **91 respect** evaluation, consideration.
92 Takes . . . merit values it for the effort made rather than for the excellence achieved.
93 clerks learned men.

Throttle their practiced accent° in their fears,
And in conclusion dumbly have broke off,
Not paying me a welcome. Trust me, sweet,
Out of this silence yet I picked a welcome;   100
And in the modesty of fearful duty
I read as much as from the rattling tongue
Of saucy and audacious eloquence.
Love, therefore, and tongue-tied simplicity
In least° speak most, to my capacity.°   105

[PHILOSTRATE *returns*.]

PHILOSTRATE. So please Your Grace, the Prologue° is addressed.°
THESEUS. Let him approach.   [*A flourish of trumpets.*]

Enter the Prologue [QUINCE].

PROLOGUE.
If we offend, it is with our good will.
    That you should think, we come not to offend,
But with good will. To show our simple skill,   110
    That is the true beginning of our end.
Consider then, we come but in despite.
    We do not come, as minding° to content you,
Our true intent is. All for your delight.
    We are not here. That you should here repent you,   115
The actors are at hand, and, by their show,
You shall know all that you are like to know.
THESEUS. This fellow doth not stand upon points.°
LYSANDER. He hath rid° his prologue like a rough° colt; he knows not
    the stop.° A good moral, my lord: it is not enough to speak, but to 120
    speak true.
HIPPOLYTA. Indeed he hath played on his prologue like a child on a
    recorder;° a sound, but not in government.°
THESEUS. His speech was like a tangled chain: nothing° impaired, but all
    disordered. Who is next?   125

Enter PYRAMUS [BOTTOM] *and* THISBE [FLUTE], *and* WALL [SNOUT], *and* MOON-
SHINE [STARVELING], *and* LION [SNUG].

PROLOGUE.
Gentles, perchance you wonder at this show,
    But wonder on, till truth makes all things plain.
This man is Pyramus, if you would know;
    This beauteous lady Thisbe is certain.

---

97 practiced accent i.e., rehearsed speech; or, usual way of speaking.   **105 least** i.e.,
saying least. **to my capacity** in my judgment and understanding.   **106 Prologue**
speaker of the prologue. **addressed** ready.   **113 minding** intending.   **118 stand
upon points** (1) heed niceties or small points (2) pay attention to punctuation in his
reading. (The humor of Quince's speech is in the blunders of its punctuation.)   **119 rid**
ridden. **rough** unbroken.   **120 stop** (1) the stopping of a colt by reining it in (2) punctuation mark.   **123 recorder** a wind instrument like a flute or flageolet.   **government**
control.   **124 nothing** not at all.

This man with lime and roughcast doth present   130
  Wall, that vile Wall which did these lovers sunder;
And through Wall's chink, poor souls, they are content
  To whisper. At the which let no man wonder.
This man, with lantern, dog, and bush of thorn,
  Presenteth Moonshine; for, if you will know,   135
By moonshine did these lovers think no scorn°
  To meet at Ninus' tomb, there, there to woo.
This grisly beast, which Lion hight° by name,
  The trusty Thisbe coming first by night
Did scare away, or rather did affright;   140
And as she fled, her mantle she did fall,°
  Which Lion vile with bloody mouth did stain.
Anon comes Pyramus, sweet youth and tall,°
  And finds his trusty Thisbe's mantle slain;
Whereat, with blade, with bloody blameful blade,   145
  He bravely broached° his boiling bloody breast.
And Thisbe, tarrying in mulberry shade,
  His dagger drew, and died. For all the rest,
Let Lion, Moonshine, Wall, and lovers twain
At large° discourse while here they do remain.   150

                 Exeunt LION, THISBE, *and* MOONSHINE.

THESEUS. I wonder if the lion be to speak.
DEMETRIUS. No wonder, my lord. One lion may, when many asses do.
WALL. In this same interlude° it doth befall
  That I, one Snout by name, present a wall;
And such a wall as I would have you think   155
That had in it a crannied hole or chink,
Through which the lovers, Pyramus and Thisbe,
Did whisper often, very secretly.
This loam, this roughcast, and this stone doth show
That I am that same wall; the truth is so.   160
And this the cranny is, right and sinister,°
Through which the fearful lovers are to whisper.
THESEUS. Would you desire lime and hair to speak better?
DEMETRIUS. It is the wittiest partition° that ever I heard discourse, my lord.

    [PYRAMUS *comes forward.*]

THESEUS. Pyramus draws near the wall. Silence!   165
PYRAMUS.
  O grim-looked° night! O night with hue so black!
    O night, which ever art when day is not!
  O night, O night! Alack, alack, alack,
    I fear my Thisbe's promise is forgot.

---

136 **think no scorn** think it no disgraceful matter.   138 **hight** is called.   141 **fall** let
fall.   143 **tall** courageous.   146 **broached** stabbed.   150 **At large** in full, at length.
153 **interlude** play.   161 **right and sinister** i.e., the right side of it and the left; or, running from right to left, horizontally.   164 **partition** (1) wall (2) section of a learned trea-
tise or oration.   166 **grim-looked** grim-looking.

And thou, O wall, O sweet, O lovely wall,   170
  That stand'st between her father's ground and mine,
Thou wall, O wall, O sweet and lovely wall,
  Show me thy chink to blink through with mine eyne!
              [WALL *makes a chink with his fingers.*]
Thanks, courteous wall. Jove shield thee well for this.
  But what see I? No Thisbe do I see.   175
O wicked wall, through whom I see no bliss!
  Cursed by thy stones for thus deceiving me!

THESEUS. The wall, methinks, being sensible,° should curse *again.*

PYRAMUS. No, in truth, sir, he should not. "Deceiving me" is Thisbe's cue:
she is to enter now, and I am to spy her through the wall. You   180
shall see, it will fall pat° as I told you. Yonder she comes.

Enter THISBE.

THISBE.
  O wall, full often hast thou heard my moans,
    For parting my fair Pyramus and me.
  My cherry lips have often kissed thy stones,
    Thy stones with lime and hair knit up in thee.   185

PYRAMUS.
  I see a voice. Now will I to the chink,
    To spy an° I can hear my Thisbe's face.
  Thisbe!

THISBE. My love! Thou art my love, I think.

PYRAMUS. Think what thou wilt, I am thy lover's grace,°   190
  And like Limander° am I trusty still.

THISBE. And I like Helen,° till the Fates me kill.

PYRAMUS. Not Shafalus to Procrus° was so true.

THISBE. As Shafalus to Procrus, I to you.

PYRAMUS. O, kiss me through the hole of this vile wall!   195

THISBE. I kiss the wall's hole, not your lips at all.

PYRAMUS. Wilt thou at Ninny's tomb meet me straightway?

THISBE. 'Tide° life, 'tide death, I come without delay.
              [*Exeunt* PYRAMUS *and* THISBE.]

WALL. Thus have I, Wall, my part dischargèd so;
  And, being done, thus Wall away doth go.   [*Exit.*]   200

THESEUS. Now is the mural down between the two neighbors.

DEMETRIUS. No remedy, my lord, when walls are so willful° to hear
without warning.°

HIPPOLYTA. This is the silliest stuff that ever I heard.

THESEUS. The best in this kind° are but shadows;° and the worst are no   205
worse, if imagination amend them.

---

178 **sensible** capable of feeling.   181 **pat** exactly.   187 **an** if.   190 **lover's grace** i.e.,
gracious lover.   191, 192 **Limander, Helen** (Blunders for *Leander* and *Hero.*)
193 **Shafalus, Procrus** (Blunders for *Cephalus* and *Procris,* also famous lovers.)
198 **'Tide** betide, come.   202 **willful** willing.   203 **without warning** i.e., without
warning the parents. (Demetrius makes a joke on the proverb "Walls have ears.")
205 **in this kind** of this sort. **shadows** likenesses, representations.

HIPPOLYTA. It must be your imagination then, and not theirs.

THESEUS. If we imagine no worse of them than they of themselves, they
    may pass for excellent men. Here come two noble beasts in, a man
    and a lion.   210

    Enter LION *and* MOONSHINE.

LION.
        You, ladies, you whose gentle hearts do fear
          The smallest monstrous mouse that creeps on floor,
        May now perchance both quake and tremble here,
          When lion rough in wildest rage doth roar.
        Then know that I, as Snug the joiner, am   215
        A lion fell,° nor else no lion's dam;
        For, if I should as lion come in strife
        Into this place, 'twere pity on my life.

THESEUS. A very gentle beast, and of a good conscience.

DEMETRIUS. The very best at a beast, my lord, that e'er I saw.   220

LYSANDER. This lion is a very fox for his valor.°

THESEUS. True; and a goose for his discretion.°

DEMETRIUS. Not so, my lord; for his valor cannot carry his discretion; and
    the fox carries the goose.

THESEUS. His discretion, I am sure, cannot carry his valor; for the goose   225
    carries not the fox. It is well. Leave it to his discretion, and let us
    listen to the moon.

MOON. This lanthorn° doth the hornèd moon present—

DEMETRIUS. He should have worn the horns on his head.°

THESEUS. He is no crescent, and his horns are invisible within the cir-   230
    cumference.

MOON. This lanthorn doth the hornèd moon present;
    Myself the man i' the moon do seem to be.

THESEUS. This is the greatest error of all the rest. The man should be put
    into the lanthorn. How is it else the man i' the moon?   235

DEMETRIUS. He dares not come there for the° candle, for you see, it is
    already in snuff.°

HIPPOLYTA. I am aweary of this moon. Would he would change!

THESEUS. It appears, by his small light of discretion, that he is in the
    wane; but yet, in courtesy, in all reason, we must stay the time.   240

LYSANDER. Proceed, Moon.

MOON. All that I have to say is to tell you that the lanthorn is the moon,
    I the man i' the moon, this thornbush my thornbush, and this dog
    my dog.

---

216 lion fell fierce lion (with a play on the idea of "lion skin").   **221 is . . . valor** i.e.,
his valor consists of craftiness and discretion.   **222 goose . . . discretion** i.e., as discreet as a goose, that is, more foolish than discreet.   **228 lanthorn** (This original
spelling, *lanthorn,* may suggest a play on the *horn* of which lanterns were made, and
also on a cuckold's horns; but the spelling *lanthorn* is not used consistently for comic
effect in this play or elsewhere. At 5.1.134, for example, the word is *lantern* in the original.)   **229 on his head** (As a sign of cuckoldry.)   **236 for the** because of the.   **237 in
snuff** (1) offended (2) in need of snuffing or trimming.

DEMETRIUS. Why, all these should be in the lanthorn, for all these are   245
    in the moon. But silence! Here comes Thisbe.

    Enter THISBE.

THISBE. This is old Ninny's tomb. Where is my love?
LION [*roaring*]. O!
DEMETRIUS. Well roared, Lion.
                          [THISBE *runs off, dropping her mantle.*]
THESEUS. Well run, Thisbe.   250
HIPPOLYTA. Well shone, Moon. Truly, the moon shines with a good
    grace.
                          [*The* LION *worries* THISBE'*s mantle.*]
THESEUS. Well moused,° Lion.

    Enter PYRAMUS.   [*Exit* LION.]

DEMETRIUS. And then came Pyramus.
LYSANDER. And so the lion vanished.
PYRAMUS.
        Sweet Moon, I thank thee for thy sunny beams;   255
          I thank thee, Moon, for shining now so bright;
        For, by thy gracious, golden, glittering gleams,
          I trust to take of truest Thisbe sight.
            But stay, O spite!
            But mark, poor knight,   260
        What dreadful dole° is here?
            Eyes, do you see?
            How can it be?
        O dainty duck! O dear!
            Thy mantle good,   265
            What, stained with blood!
        Approach, ye Furies° fell!°
            O Fates,° come, come,
            Cut thread and thrum;°
            Quail,° crush, conclude, and quell!°   270
THESEUS. This passion, and the death of a dear friend, would go near to
    make a man look sad.°
HIPPOLYTA. Beshrew my heart, but I pity the man.
PYRAMUS. O, wherefore, Nature, didst thou lions frame?
        Since lion vile hath here deflowered my dear,   275
        Which is—no, no, which was—the fairest dame
        That lived, that loved, that liked, that looked with cheer.°
           Come, tears, confound,
           Out, sword, and wound

---

252 moused shaken, torn, bitten.   **261 dole** grievous event.   **267 Furies** avenging goddesses of Greek myth. **fell** fierce.   **268 Fates** the three goddesses (Clotho, Lachesis, Atropos) of Greek myth who drew and cut the thread of human life.   **269 thread and thrum** the warp in weaving and the loose end of the warp.   **270 Quail** overpower. **quell** kill, destroy.   **271–272 This . . . sad** i.e., if one had other reason to grieve, one might be sad, but not from this absurd portrayal of passion.   **277 cheer** countenance.

The pap° of Pyramus;   280
        Ay, that left pap,
        Where heart doth hop.   [*He stabs himself.*]
    Thus die I, thus, thus, thus.
        Now am I dead,
        Now am I fled;   285
    My soul is in the sky.
        Tongue, lose thy light;
        Moon, take thy flight.   [*Exit* MOONSHINE.]
    Now die, die, die, die, die.   [PYRAMUS *dies.*]

DEMETRIUS. No die, but an ace,° for him; for he is but one.°   290
LYSANDER. Less than an ace, man; for he is dead, he is nothing.
THESEUS. With the help of a surgeon he might yet recover, and yet
    prove an ass.°
HIPPOLYTA. How chance Moonshine is gone before Thisbe comes back
    and finds her lover?   295
THESEUS. She will find him by starlight.

    [*Enter* THISBE.]

    Here she comes, and her passion ends the play.
HIPPOLYTA. Methinks she should not use a long one for such a Pyramus.
    I hope she will be brief.
DEMETRIUS. A mote° will turn the balance, which Pyramus, which°   300
    Thisbe, is the better: he for a man, God warrant us; she for a
    woman, God bless us.
LYSANDER. She hath spied him already with those sweet eyes.
DEMETRIUS. And thus she means,° videlicet:°
THISBE.
        Asleep, my love?   305
        What, dead, my dove?
    O Pyramus, arise!
        Speak, speak. Quite dumb?
        Dead, dead? A tomb
    Must cover thy sweet eyes.   310
        These lily lips,
        This cherry nose,
    These yellow cowslip cheeks,
        Are gone, are gone!
        Lovers, make moan.   315
    His eyes were green as leeks.
        O Sisters Three,°
        Come, come to me,
    With hands as pale as milk;
        Lay them in gore,   320

---

280 pap breast.   **290 ace** the side of the die featuring the single pip, or spot. (The pun
is on *die* as a singular of *dice;* Bottom's performance is not worth a whole *die* but rather
one single face of it, one small portion.)   **one** (1) an individual person (2) unique.   **293
ass** (With a pun on *ace.*)   **300 mote** small particle.   **which . . . which** whether . . .
or.   **304 means** moans, laments.   **videlicet** to wit.   **317 Sisters Three** the Fates.

Since you have shore°
With shears his thread of silk.
Tongue, not a word.
Come, trusty sword,
Come, blade, my breast imbrue!°   [*Stabs herself.*] 325
And farewell, friends.
Thus Thisbe ends.
Adieu, adieu, adieu.   [*She dies.*]

THESEUS. Moonshine and Lion are left to bury the dead.

DEMETRIUS. Ay, and Wall too.   330

BOTTOM [*starting up, as* FLUTE *does also*]. No, I assure you, the wall is
down that parted their fathers. Will it please you to see the epilogue,
or to hear a Bergomask dance° between two of our company?

                                        [*The other players enter.*]

THESEUS. No epilogue, I pray you; for your play needs no excuse. Never
excuse; for when the players are all dead, there need none to be   335
blamed. Marry, if he that writ it had played Pyramus and hanged
himself in Thisbe's garter, it would have been a fine tragedy; and so
it is, truly, and very notably discharged. But, come, your Bergo-
mask. Let your epilogue alone.   [*A dance.*]
The iron tongue° of midnight hath told° twelve.   340
Lovers, to bed, 'tis almost fairy time.
I fear we shall outsleep the coming morn
As much as we this night have overwatched.°
This palpable-gross° play hath well beguiled
The heavy° gait of night. Sweet friends, to bed.   345
A fortnight hold we this solemnity,
In nightly revels and new jollity.   *Exeunt.*

Enter PUCK [*carrying a broom*].

PUCK.
            Now the hungry lion roars,
              And the wolf behowls the moon;
            Whilst the heavy° plowman snores,   350
              All with weary task fordone.°
            Now the wasted brands° do glow,
              Whilst the screech owl, screeching loud
            Puts the wretch that lies in woe
              In remembrance of a shroud.   355
            Now it is the time of night
              That the graves, all gaping wide,
            Every one lets forth his sprite,°
              In the church-way paths to glide.

---

321 shore shorn. **325 imbrue** stain with blood. **333 Bergomask dance** a rustic
dance named from Bergamo, a province in the state of Venice. **340 iron tongue** i.e., of
a bell. **told** counted, struck ("tolled"). **343 overwatched** stayed up too late. **344
palpable-gross** gross, obviously crude. **345 heavy** drowsy, dull. **350 heavy** tired.
351 fordone exhausted. **352 wasted brands** burned-out logs. **358 Every . . .
sprite** every grave lets forth its ghost.

And we fairies, that do run   360
  By the triple Hecate's° team
From the presence of the sun,
  Following darkness like a dream,
Now are frolic.° Not a mouse
  Shall disturb this hallowed house.   365
I am sent with broom before,
To sweep the dust behind° the door.

Enter [OBERON *and* TITANIA,] *King and Queen of Fairies, with all their*
train.

OBERON.

    Through the house give glimmering light,
      By the dead and drowsy fire;
    Every elf and fairy sprite   370
      Hop as light as bird from brier;
    And this ditty, after me,
    Sing, and dance it trippingly.

TITANIA.

    First, rehearse your song by rote,
    To each word a warbling note.   375
    Hand in hand, with fairy grace,
    Will we sing, and bless this place.

                                        [Song and dance.]

OBERON. Now, until the break of day,
  Through this house each fairy stray.
  To the best bride-bed will we,   380
  Which by us shall blessèd be;
  And the issue there create°
  Ever shall be fortunate.
  So shall all the couples three
  Ever true in loving be;   385
  And the blots of Nature's hand
  Shall not in their issue stand;
  Never mole, harelip, nor scar,
  Nor mark prodigious,° such as are
  Despisèd in nativity,   390
  Shall upon their children be.
  With this field dew consecrate°
  Every fairy take his gait,°
  And each several° chamber bless,
  Through this palace, with sweet peace;   395
  And the owner of it blest

---

361 triple Hecate's (Hecate ruled in three capacities: as Luna or Cynthia in heaven, as
Diana on earth, and as Proserpina in hell.)   **364 frolic** merry.   **367 behind** from behind. (Robin Goodfellow was a household spirit who helped good housemaids and punished lazy ones.)   **382 create** created.   **389 prodigious** monstrous, unnatural.   **392**
consecrate consecrated.   **393 take his gait** go his way.   **394 several** separate.

Ever shall in safety rest.
Trip away; make no stay;
Meet me all by break of day.

Exeunt [OBERON, TITANIA, *and train*].

PUCK [*to the audience*]. If we shadows have offended,   400
Think but this, and all is mended,
That you have but slumbered here°
While these visions did appear.
And this weak and idle theme,
No more yielding but° a dream,   405
Gentles, do not reprehend.
If you pardon, we will mend.°
And, as I am an honest Puck,
If we have unearnèd luck
Now to scape the serpents tongue,°   410
We will make amends ere long;
Else the Puck a liar call.
So, good night unto you all.
Give me your hands,° if we be friends,
And Robin shall restore amends.°   [*Exit.*]   415

---

402 That . . . here i.e., that it is a "midsummer night's dream."   **405 No . . . but** yielding no more than.   **407 mend** improve.   **410 serpent's tongue** i.e., hissing.   **414 Give . . . hands** applaud.   **415 restore amends** give satisfaction in return.

▦ TOPICS FOR CRITICAL THINKING AND WRITING

Act 1

1. On the basis of the first scene, how would you characterize Theseus? Egeus? Hermia? Do you agree with some critics that Egeus is presented comically? (Support your view.)
2. What connections can you make between 1.2 and the first scene?

Act 2

1. Why do you suppose that in 2.1 Shakespeare included material about Theseus's past (lines 76–80)?
2. When the play is staged, audiences invariably laugh loudly at 2.2.109, when Lysander awakens and sees Helena. What's so funny about this?

Act 3

1. What assumptions does Bottom seem to make about the nature of drama? How do they compare with your own?
2. Puck himself has said that he is mischievous, but how mischievous is he? Why did he anoint the eyes of the wrong lover?

Act 4

1. Bottom is the only mortal who sees the fairies. What can we make of this? Or should we not try to make anything of it?

Act 5

1. What do you make of the debate between Theseus and Hippolyta (lines 1–27)? Which of the two seems to you to come closer to the truth? Explain.
2. Do you think it is cruel to laugh at the unintentional antics of the rustic performers? Why, or why not?
3. Puck is sometimes played by a woman. What advantages or disadvantages do you see to giving the part to a woman?

General Questions

1. Some critics speak of the play as a delightful fantasy that is engaging because it has so little connection with real life, but others find in it intimations of dark and dangerous elements in human beings. Where do you stand, and why?
2. Today Shakespeare's plays are sometimes done in modern dress or in costumes that reflect a particular time and place, such as the Wild West of the mid-nineteenth century or the South before the Civil War. How would you costume the play? What advantages might there be in your choice?

32

Two Plays About Marriage

Probably most of us think of marriage chiefly in romantic terms—

Love and marriage, love and marriage
Go together like a horse and carriage—

but history tells us that in most Western societies marriage has been a way for males to transfer their property and their power to their offspring. Men could sow their wild oats, but women were expected to be faithful. Speaking generally, the husband provided food and shelter, and the wife—sometimes regarded as not much more than a property of her husband—bore and reared his children, and the male offspring would inherit the estate.

Amazingly, in popular culture as evinced by cartoons and jokes, women set out to entrap men, and the man is the long-suffering member of the team. A recent cartoon, for instance, showed a husband looking up from his newspaper and saying to his stern-faced wife, "Gay marriage! Haven't they already suffered enough?" Mother-in-law jokes (it is always the wife's mother who is damaging the marriage) are another sign of the widespread view that in marriage the husband is the disadvantaged party.

In this chapter we present two dramatists who explore the nature of marriage in our time. We say "in our time," but even Clare Boothe Luce's play is more than thirty years old, and Henrik Ibsen's is more than a hundred years old. Read the plays, and then ask yourself if either is dated.

HENRIK IBSEN

Henrik Ibsen (1828–1906) was born in Skien, Norway, of wealthy parents who soon after his birth lost their money. Ibsen worked as a pharmacist's apprentice, but at the age of 22 he had written his first play, a promising melodrama entitled Cataline. *He engaged in theater work first in Norway and then in Denmark and Germany. By 1865 his plays had won him a state pension that enabled him to settle in Rome. After writing romantic, historic, and poetic plays, he turned to realistic drama with* The League of Youth *(1869). Among his major realistic "problem plays" are* A Doll's House *(1879),* Ghosts *(1881), and* An Enemy of the People *(1882). In* The Wild Duck *(1884) he moved toward a more symbolic tragic comedy, and his last plays, written in the nineties, are highly symbolic.* Hedda Gabler *(1890) looks backward to the plays of the eighties rather than forward to the plays of the nineties.*

A Doll's House. In Act 3, Nora lights Dr. Rank's cigar while Torvald impatiently waits for him to leave.

A Doll's House   [1879]

Translated by James McFarlane

CHARACTERS
torvald helmer, *a lawyer*
nora, *his wife*
dr. rank
mrs. kristine linde
nils krogstad
anne marie, *the nursemaid*
helene, *the maid*
the helmers' three children
a porter
The action takes place in the Helmers' flat.

Act I

A pleasant room, tastefully but not expensively furnished. On the back wall, one door on the right leads to the entrance hall, a second door on the left leads to HELMER's *study. Between these two doors, a piano. In the middle of the left wall, a door; and downstage from it, a window. Near the window a round table with armchairs and a small sofa. In the right wall, upstage, a door; and on the same wall downstage, a porcelain stove with a couple of armchairs and a rocking chair. Between the stove and the door a small table. Etchings on the walls. A whatnot with china and other small objects d'art; a small bookcase with books in handsome bindings. Carpet on the floor; a fire burns in the stove. A winter's day.*

The front doorbell rings in the hall; a moment later, there is the sound of the front door being opened. NORA *comes into the room, happily humming to herself. She is dressed in her outdoor things, and is carrying lots of parcels which she then puts down on the table, right. She leaves the door into the hall standing open; a* PORTER *can be seen outside holding a Christmas tree and a basket; he hands them to the* MAID *who has opened the door for them.*

NORA. Hide the Christmas tree away carefully, Helene. The children mustn't see it till this evening when it's decorated. [*To the* PORTER, *taking out her purse.*] How much?

PORTER. Fifty öre.

NORA. There's a crown. Keep the change.

[*The* PORTER *thanks her and goes.* NORA *shuts the door. She continues to laugh quietly and happily to herself as she takes off her things. She takes a bag of macaroons out of her pocket and eats one or two; then she walks stealthily across and listens at her husband's door.*]

NORA. Yes, he's in.

[*She begins humming again as she walks over to the table, right.*]

HELMER [*in his study*]. Is that my little skylark chirruping out there?

NORA [*busy opening some of the parcels*]. Yes, it is.

HELMER. Is that my little squirrel frisking about?

NORA. Yes!

HELMER. When did my little squirrel get home?

NORA. Just this minute. [*She stuffs the bag of macaroons in her pocket and wipes her mouth.*] Come on out, Torvald, and see what I've bought.

HELMER. I don't want to be disturbed! [*A moment later, he opens the door and looks out, his pen in his hand.*] "Bought," did you say? All that? Has my little spendthrift been out squandering money again?

NORA. But, Torvald, surely this year we can spread ourselves just a little. This is the first Christmas we haven't had to go carefully.

HELMER. Ah, but that doesn't mean we can afford to be extravagant, you know.

NORA. Oh yes, Torvald, surely we can afford to be just a little bit extravagant now, can't we? Just a teeny-weeny bit. You are getting quite a good salary now, and you are going to earn lots and lots of money.

HELMER. Yes, after the New Year. But it's going to be three whole months before the first pay cheque comes in.

NORA. Pooh! We can always borrow in the meantime.

HELMER. Nora! [*Crosses to her and takes her playfully by the ear.*] Here we go again, you and your frivolous ideas! Suppose I went and borrowed a thousand crowns today, and you went and spent it all over Christmas, then on New Year's Eve a slate fell and hit me on the head and there I was. . . .

NORA [*putting her hand over his mouth*]. Sh! Don't say such horrid things.

HELMER. Yes, but supposing something like that did happen . . . what then?

NORA. If anything as awful as that did happen, I wouldn't care if I owed anybody anything or not.

HELMER. Yes, but what about the people I'd borrowed from?

NORA. Them? Who cares about them! They are only strangers!

HELMER. Nora, Nora! Just like a woman! Seriously though, Nora, you know
what I think about these things. No debts! Never borrow! There's always something inhibited, something unpleasant, about a home built
on credit and borrowed money. We two have managed to stick it out
so far, and that's the way we'll go on for the little time that remains.

NORA [*walks over to the stove*]. Very well, just as you say, Torvald.

HELMER [*following her*]. There, there! My little singing bird mustn't go
drooping her wings, eh? Has it got the sulks, that little squirrel of mine?
[*Takes out his wallet.*] Nora, what do you think I've got here?

NORA [*quickly turning round*]. Money!

HELMER. There! [*He hands her some notes*]. Good heavens, I know only too
well how Christmas runs away with the housekeeping.

NORA [*counts*]. Ten, twenty, thirty, forty. Oh, thank you, thank you, Torvald!
This will see me quite a long way.

HELMER. Yes, it'll have to.

NORA. Yes, yes, I'll see that it does. But come over here, I want to show you
all the things I've bought. And so cheap! Look, some new clothes for
Ivar . . . and a little sword. There's a horse and a trumpet for Bob. And
a doll and a doll's cot for Emmy. They are not very grand but she'll have
them all broken before long anyway. And I've got some dress material
and some handkerchiefs for the maids. Though, really, dear old Anne
Marie should have had something better.

HELMER. And what's in this parcel here?

NORA [*shrieking*]. No, Torvald! You mustn't see that till tonight!

HELMER. All right. But tell me now, what did my little spendthrift fancy for
herself?

NORA. For me? Puh, I don't really want anything.

HELMER. Of course you do. Anything reasonable that you think you might
like, just tell me.

NORA. Well, I don't really know. As a matter of fact, though, Torvald . . .

HELMER. Well?

NORA [*toying with his coat buttons, and without looking at him*]. If you
did want to give me something, you could . . . you could always . . .

HELMER. Well, well, out with it!

NORA [*quickly*]. You could always give me money, Torvald. Only what you
think you could spare. And then I could buy myself something with it
later on.

HELMER. But Nora. . . .

NORA. Oh, please, Torvald dear! Please! I beg you. Then I'd wrap the money
up in some pretty gilt paper and hang it on the Christmas tree. Wouldn't
that be fun?

HELMER. What do we call my pretty little pet when it runs away with all the
money?

NORA. I know, I know, we call it a spendthrift. But please let's do what I
said, Torvald. Then I'll have a bit of time to think about what I need
most. Isn't that awfully sensible, now, eh?

HELMER [*smiling*]. Yes, it is indeed—that is, if only you really could hold on to the money I gave you, and really did buy something for yourself with it. But it just gets mixed up with the housekeeping and frittered away on all sorts of useless things, and then I have to dig into my pocket all over again.

NORA. Oh but, Torvald. . . .

HELMER. You can't deny it, Nora dear. [*Puts his arm round her waist.*] My pretty little pet is very sweet, but it runs away with an awful lot of money. It's incredible how expensive it is for a man to keep such a pet.

NORA. For shame! How can you say such a thing? As a matter of fact I save everything I can.

HELMER [*laughs*]. Yes, you are right there. Everything you *can*. But you simply can't.

NORA [*hums and smiles quietly and happily*]. Ah, if you only knew how many expenses the likes of us skylarks and squirrels have, Torvald!

HELMER. What a funny little one you are! Just like your father. Always on the lookout for money, wherever you can lay your hands on it; but as soon as you've got it, it just seems to slip through your fingers. You never seem to know what you've done with it. Well, one must accept you as you are. It's in the blood. Oh yes, it is, Nora. That sort of thing is hereditary.

NORA. Oh, I only wish I'd inherited a few more of Daddy's qualities.

HELMER. And I wouldn't want my pretty little songbird to be the least bit different from what she is now. But come to think of it, you look rather . . . rather . . . how shall I put it? . . . rather guilty today. . . .

NORA. Do I?

HELMER. Yes, you do indeed. Look me straight in the eye.

NORA [*looks at him*]. Well?

HELMER [*wagging his finger at her*]. My little sweet-tooth surely didn't forget herself in town today?

NORA. No, whatever makes you think that?

HELMER. She didn't just pop into the confectioner's for a moment?

NORA. No, I assure you, Torvald . . . !

HELMER. Didn't try sampling the preserves?

NORA. No, really I didn't.

HELMER. Didn't go nibbling a macaroon or two?

NORA. No, Torvald, honestly, you must believe me . . . !

HELMER. All right then! It's really just my little joke. . . .

NORA [*crosses to the table*]. I would never dream of doing anything you didn't want me to.

HELMER. Of course not, I know that. And then you've given me your word. . . . [*Crosses to her.*] Well then, Nora dearest, you shall keep your little Christmas secrets. They'll all come out tonight, I dare say, when we light the tree.

NORA. Did you remember to invite Dr. Rank?

HELMER. No. But there's really no need. Of course he'll come and have dinner with us. Anyway, I can ask him when he looks in this morning. I've ordered some good wine. Nora, you can't imagine how I am looking forward to this evening.

NORA. So am I. And won't the children enjoy it, Torvald!

HELMER. Oh, what a glorious feeling it is, knowing you've got a nice, safe job, and a good fat income. Don't you agree? Isn't it wonderful, just thinking about it?

NORA. Oh, it's marvelous!

HELMER. Do you remember last Christmas? Three whole weeks beforehand you shut yourself up every evening till after midnight making flowers for the Christmas tree and all the other splendid things you wanted to surprise us with. Ugh, I never felt so bored in all my life.

NORA. I wasn't the least bit bored.

HELMER [*smiling*]. But it turned out a bit of an anticlimax, Nora.

NORA. Oh, you are not going to tease me about that again! How was I to know the cat would get in and pull everything to bits?

HELMER. No, of course you weren't. Poor little Nora! All you wanted was for us to have a nice time—and it's the thought behind it that counts, after all. All the same, it's a good thing we've seen the back of those lean times.

NORA. Yes, really it's marvelous.

HELMER. Now there's no need for me to sit here all on my own, bored to tears. And you don't have to strain your dear little eyes, and work those dainty little fingers to the bone. . . .

NORA [*clapping her hands*]. No, Torvald, I don't, do I? Not any more. Oh, how marvelous it is to hear that! [*Takes his arm.*] Now I want to tell you how I've been thinking we might arrange things, Torvald. As soon as Christmas is over. . . . [*The door-bell rings in the hall.*] Oh, there's the bell. [*Tidies one or two things in the room.*] It's probably a visitor. What a nuisance!

HELMER. Remember I'm not at home to callers.

MAID [*in the doorway*]. There's a lady to see you, ma'am.

NORA. Show her in, please.

MAID [*to* HELMER]. And the doctor's just arrived, too, sir.

HELMER. Did he go straight into my room?

MAID. Yes, he did, sir.

[HELMER *goes into his study. The* MAID *shows in* MRS. LINDE, *who is in traveling clothes, and closes the door after her.*]

MRS. LINDE [*subdued and rather hesitantly*]. How do you do, Nora?

NORA [*uncertainly*]. How do you do?

MRS. LINDE. I'm afraid you don't recognize me.

NORA. No, I don't think I . . . And yet I seem to. . . . [*Bursts out suddenly.*] Why! Kristine! Is it really you?

MRS. LINDE. Yes, it's me.

NORA. Kristine! Fancy not recognizing you again! But how was I to, when . . . [*Gently.*] How you've changed, Kristine!

MRS. LINDE. I dare say I have. In nine . . . ten years . . . .

NORA. Is it so long since we last saw each other? Yes, it must be. Oh, believe me these last eight years have been such a happy time. And now you've come up to town, too? All that long journey in wintertime. That took courage.

MRS. LINDE. I just arrived this morning on the steamer.

NORA. To enjoy yourself over Christmas, of course. How lovely! Oh, we'll have such fun, you'll see. Do take off your things. You are not cold, are

you? [*Helps her.*] There now! Now let's sit down here in comfort beside the stove. No, here, you take the armchair, I'll sit here on the rocking chair. [*Takes her hands.*] Ah, now you look a bit more like your old
self again. It was just that when I first saw you. . . . But you are a little
paler, Kristine . . . and perhaps even a bit thinner!

MRS. LINDE. And much, much older, Nora.

NORA. Yes, perhaps a little older . . . very, very little, not really very much.
[*Stops suddenly and looks serious.*] Oh, what a thoughtless creature I
am, sitting here chattering on like this! Dear, sweet Kristine, can you
forgive me?

MRS. LINDE. What do you mean, Nora?

NORA [*gently*]. Poor Kristine, of course you're a widow now.

MRS. LINDE. Yes, my husband died three years ago.

NORA. Oh, I remember now. I read about it in the papers. Oh, Kristine, believe me I often thought at the time of writing to you. But I kept putting
it off, something always seemed to crop up.

MRS. LINDE. My dear Nora, I understand so well.

NORA. No, it wasn't very nice of me, Kristine. Oh, you poor thing, what you
must have gone through. And didn't he leave you anything?

MRS. LINDE. No.

NORA. And no children?

MRS. LINDE. No.

NORA. Absolutely nothing?

MRS. LINDE. Nothing at all . . . not even a broken heart to grieve over.

NORA [*looks at her incredulously*]. But, Kristine, is that possible?

MRS. LINDE [*smiles sadly and strokes* NORA*'s hair*]. Oh, it sometimes happens, Nora.

NORA. So utterly alone. How terribly sad that must be for you. I have three
lovely children. You can't see them for the moment, because they're
out with their nanny. But now you must tell me all about yourself. . . .

MRS. LINDE. No, no, I want to hear about you.

NORA. No, you start. I won't be selfish today. I must think only about your
affairs today. But there's just one thing I really must tell you. Have you
heard about the great stroke of luck we've had in the last few days?

MRS. LINDE. No. What is it?

NORA. What do you think? My husband has just been made Bank Manager!

MRS. LINDE. Your husband? How splendid!

NORA. Isn't it tremendous! It's not a very steady way of making a living, you
know, being a lawyer, especially if he refuses to take on anything that's
the least bit shady—which of course is what Torvald does, and I think
he's quite right. You can imagine how pleased we are! He starts at the
Bank straight after New Year, and he's getting a big salary and lots of
commission. From now on we'll be able to live quite differently . . .
we'll do just what we want. Oh, Kristine, I'm so happy and relieved. I
must say it's lovely to have plenty of money and not have to worry.
Isn't it?

MRS. LINDE. Yes. It must be nice to have enough, at any rate.

NORA. No, not just enough, but pots and pots of money.

MRS. LINDE [*smiles*]. Nora, Nora, haven't you learned any sense yet? At
school you used to be an awful spendthrift.

NORA. Yes, Torvald still says I am. [*Wags her finger.*] But little Nora isn't as stupid as everybody thinks. Oh, we haven't really been in a position where I could afford to spend a lot of money. We've both had to work.

MRS. LINDE. You too?

NORA. Yes, odd jobs—sewing, crochetwork, embroidery and things like that. [*Casually.*] And one or two other things, besides. I suppose you know that Torvald left the Ministry when we got married. There weren't any prospects of promotion in his department, and of course he needed to earn more money than he had before. But the first year he wore himself out completely. He had to take on all kinds of extra jobs, you know, and he found himself working all hours of the day and night. But he couldn't go on like that; and he became seriously ill. The doctors said it was essential for him to go South.

MRS. LINDE. Yes, I believe you spent a whole year in Italy, didn't you?

NORA. That's right. It wasn't easy to get away, I can tell you. It was just after I'd had Ivar. But of course we had to go. Oh, it was an absolutely marvelous trip. And it saved Torvald's life. But it cost an awful lot of money, Kristine.

MRS. LINDE. That I can well imagine.

NORA. Twelve hundred dollars. Four thousand eight hundred crowns. That's a lot of money, Kristine.

MRS. LINDE. Yes, but in such circumstances, one is very lucky if one has it.

NORA. Well, we got it from Daddy, you see.

MRS. LINDE. Ah, that was it. It was just about then your father died, I believe, wasn't it?

NORA. Yes, Kristine, just about then. And do you know, I couldn't even go and look after him. Here was I expecting Ivar any day. And I also had poor Torvald, gravely ill, on my hands. Dear, kind Daddy! I never saw him again, Kristine. Oh, that's the saddest thing that has happened to me in all my married life.

MRS. LINDE. I know you were very fond of him. But after that you left for Italy?

NORA. Yes, we had the money then, and the doctors said it was urgent. We left a month later.

MRS. LINDE. And your husband came back completely cured?

NORA. Fit as a fiddle!

MRS. LINDE. But . . . what about the doctor?

NORA. How do you mean?

MRS. LINDE. I thought the maid said something about the gentleman who came at the same time as me being a doctor.

NORA. Yes, that was Dr. Rank. But this isn't a professional visit. He's our best friend and he always looks in at least once a day. No, Torvald has never had a day's illness since. And the children are fit and healthy, and so am I. [*Jumps up and claps her hands.*] Oh God, oh God, isn't it marvelous to be alive, and to be happy, Kristine! . . . Oh, but I ought to be ashamed of myself . . . Here I go on talking about nothing but myself. [*She sits on a low stool near* MRS. LINDE *and lays her arms on her lap.*] Oh, please, you mustn't be angry with me! Tell me, is it really true that you didn't love your husband? What made you marry him, then?

MRS. LINDE. My mother was still alive; she was bedridden and helpless. And then I had my two young brothers to look after as well. I didn't think I would be justified in refusing him.

NORA. No, I dare say you are right. I suppose he was fairly wealthy then?

MRS. LINDE. He was quite well off, I believe. But the business was shaky. When he died, it went all to pieces, and there just wasn't anything left.

NORA. What then?

MRS. LINDE. Well, I had to fend for myself, opening a little shop, running a little school, anything I could turn my hand to. These last three years have been one long relentless drudge. But now it's finished, Nora. My poor dear mother doesn't need me any more, she's passed away. Nor the boys either; they're at work now, they can look after themselves.

NORA. What a relief you must find it. . . .

MRS. LINDE. No, Nora! Just unutterably empty. Nobody to live for any more. [*Stands up restless.*] That's why I couldn't stand it any longer being cut off up there. Surely it must be a bit easier here to find something to occupy your mind. If only I could manage to find a steady job of some kind, in an office perhaps. . . .

NORA. But, Kristine, that's terribly exhausting; and you look so worn out even before you start. The best thing for you would be a little holiday at some quiet little resort.

MRS. LINDE [*crosses to the window*]. I haven't any father I can fall back on for the money, Nora.

NORA [*rises*]. Oh, please, you mustn't be angry with me!

MRS. LINDE [*goes to her*]. My dear Nora, you mustn't be angry with me either. That's the worst thing about people in my position, they become so bitter. One has nobody to work for, yet one has to be on the lookout all the time. Life has to go on, and one starts thinking only of oneself. Believe it or not, when you told me the good news about your step up, I was pleased not so much for your sake as for mine.

NORA. How do you mean? Ah, I see. You think Torvald might be able to do something for you.

MRS. LINDE. Yes, that's exactly what I thought.

NORA. And so he shall, Kristine. Just leave things to me. I'll bring it up so cleverly . . . I'll think up something to put him in a good mood. Oh, I do so much want to help you.

MRS. LINDE. It is awfully kind of you, Nora, offering to do all this for me, particularly in your case, where you haven't known much trouble or hardship in your own life.

NORA. When I . . . ? I haven't known much . . . ?

MRS. LINDE [*smiling*]. Well, good heavens, a little bit of sewing to do and a few things like that. What a child you are, Nora!

NORA [*tosses her head and walks across the room*]. I wouldn't be too sure of that, if I were you.

MRS. LINDE. Oh?

NORA. You're just like the rest of them. You all think I'm useless when it comes to anything really serious. . . .

MRS. LINDE. Come, come . . .

NORA. You think I've never had anything much to contend with in this hard world.

MRS. LINDE. Nora dear, you've only just been telling me all the things you've had to put up with.

NORA. Pooh! They were just trivialities! [*Softly.*] I haven't told you about the really big thing.

MRS. LINDE. What big thing? What do you mean?

NORA. I know you rather tend to look down on me, Kristine. But you shouldn't, you know. You are proud of having worked so hard and so long for your mother.

MRS. LINDE. I'm sure I don't look down on anybody. But it's true what you say: I am both proud and happy when I think of how I was able to make Mother's life a little easier towards the end.

NORA. And you are proud when you think of what you have done for your brothers, too.

MRS. LINDE. I think I have every right to be.

NORA. I think so too. But now I'm going to tell you something, Kristine. I too have something to be proud and happy about.

MRS. LINDE. I don't doubt that. But what is it you mean?

NORA. Not so loud. Imagine if Torvald were to hear! He must never on any account . . . nobody must know about it, Kristine, nobody but you.

MRS. LINDE. But what is it?

NORA. Come over here. [*She pulls her down on the sofa beside her.*] Yes, Kristine, I too have something to be proud and happy about. I was the one who saved Torvald's life.

MRS. LINDE. Saved . . . ? How . . . ?

NORA. I told you about our trip to Italy. Torvald would never have recovered but for that. . . .

MRS. LINDE. Well? Your father gave you what money was necessary. . . .

NORA [*smiles*]. That's what Torvald thinks, and everybody else. But . . .

MRS. LINDE. But . . . ?

NORA. Daddy never gave us a penny. I was the one who raised the money.

MRS. LINDE. You? All that money?

NORA. Twelve hundred dollars. Four thousand eight hundred crowns. What do you say to that!

MRS. LINDE. But, Nora, how was it possible? Had you won a sweepstake or something?

NORA [*contemptuously*]. A sweepstake? Pooh! There would have been nothing to it then.

MRS. LINDE. Where did you get it from, then?

NORA [*hums and smiles secretively*]. H'm, tra-la-la!

MRS. LINDE. Because what you couldn't do was borrow it.

NORA. Oh? Why not?

MRS. LINDE. Well, a wife can't borrow without her husband's consent.

NORA [*tossing her head*]. Ah, but when it happens to be a wife with a bit of a sense for business . . . a wife who knows her way about things, then. . . .

MRS. LINDE. But, Nora, I just don't understand. . . .

NORA. You don't have to. I haven't said I did borrow the money. I might have got it some other way. [*Throws herself back on the sofa.*] I might even have got it from some admirer. Anyone as reasonably attractive as I am. . . .

MRS. LINDE. Don't be so silly!

NORA. Now you must be dying of curiosity, Kristine.

MRS. LINDE. Listen to me now, Nora dear—you haven't done anything rash, have you?

NORA [*sitting up again*]. Is it rash to save your husband's life?

MRS. LINDE. I think it was rash to do anything without telling him. . . .

NORA. But the whole point was that he mustn't know anything. Good heavens, can't you see! He wasn't even supposed to know how desperately ill he was. It was me the doctors came and told his life was in danger, that the only way to save him was to go South for a while. Do you think I didn't try talking him into it first? I began dropping hints about how nice it would be if I could be taken on a little trip abroad, like other young wives. I wept, I pleaded. I told him he ought to show some consideration for my condition, and let me have a bit of my own way. And then I suggested he might take out a loan. But at that he nearly lost his temper, Kristine. He said I was being frivolous, that it was his duty as a husband not to give in to all these whims and fancies of mine—as I do believe he called them. All right, I thought, somehow you've got to be saved. And it was then I found a way. . . .

MRS. LINDE. Did your husband never find out from your father that the money hadn't come from him?

NORA. No, never. It was just about the time Daddy died. I'd intended letting him into the secret and asking him not to give me away. But when he was so ill . . . I'm sorry to say it never became necessary.

MRS. LINDE. And you never confided in your husband?

NORA. Good heavens, how could you ever imagine such a thing! When he's so strict about such matters! Besides, Torvald is a man with a good deal of pride—it would be terribly embarrassing and humiliating for him if he thought he owed anything to me. It would spoil everything between us; this happy home of ours would never be the same again.

MRS. LINDE. Are you never going to tell him?

NORA [*reflectively, half smiling*]. Oh yes, some day perhaps . . . in many years time, when I'm no longer as pretty as I am now. You mustn't laugh! What I mean of course is when Torvald isn't quite so much in love with me as he is now, when he's lost interest in watching me dance, or get dressed up, or recite. Then it might be a good thing to have something in reserve. . . . [*Breaks off.*] What nonsense! That day will never come. Well, what have you got to say to my big secret, Kristine? Still think I'm not much good for anything? One thing, though, it's meant a lot of worry for me, I can tell you. It hasn't always been easy to meet my obligations when the time came. You know in business there is something called quarterly interest, and other things called instalments, and these are always terribly difficult things to cope with. So what I've had to do is save a little here and there, you see, wherever I could. I couldn't really save anything out of the housekeeping, because Torvald has to live in decent style. I couldn't let the children go about badly dressed either—I felt any money I got for them had to go on them alone. Such sweet little things!

MRS. LINDE. Poor Nora! So it had to come out of your own allowance?

NORA. Of course. After all, I was the one it concerned most. Whenever Torvald gave me money for new clothes and such-like, I never spent more than half. And always I bought the simplest and cheapest things. It's a blessing most things look well on me, so Torvald never noticed anything. But sometimes I did feel it was a bit hard, Kristine, because it is nice to be well dressed, isn't it?

MRS. LINDE. Yes, I suppose it is.

NORA. I have had some other sources of income, of course. Last winter I was lucky enough to get quite a bit of copying to do. So I shut myself up every night and sat and wrote through to the small hours of the morning. Oh, sometimes I was so tired, so tired. But it was tremendous fun all the same, sitting there working and earning money like that. It was almost like being a man.

MRS. LINDE. And how much have you been able to pay off like this?

NORA. Well, I can't tell exactly. It's not easy to know where you are with transactions of this kind, you understand. All I know is I've paid off just as much as I could scrape together. Many's the time I was at my wit's end. [*Smiles.*] Then I used to sit here and pretend that some rich old gentleman had fallen in love with me. . . .

MRS. LINDE. What! What gentleman?

NORA. Oh, rubbish! . . . and that now he had died, and when they opened his will, there in big letters were the words: "My entire fortune is to be paid over, immediately and in cash, to charming Mrs. Nora Helmer."

MRS. LINDE. But my dear Nora–who is this man?

NORA. Good heavens, don't you understand? There never was any old gentleman; it was just something I used to sit here pretending, time and time again, when I didn't know where to turn next for money. But it doesn't make very much difference; as far as I'm concerned, the old boy can do what he likes, I'm tired of him; I can't be bothered any more with him or his will. Because now all my worries are over. [*Jumping up.*] Oh God, what a glorious thought, Kristine! No more worries! Just think of being without a care in the world . . . being able to romp with the children, and making the house nice and attractive, and having things just as Torvald likes to have them! And then spring will soon be here, and blue skies. And maybe we can go away somewhere. I might even see something of the sea again. Oh, yes! When you're happy, life is a wonderful thing!

[*The doorbell is heard in the hall.*]

MRS. LINDE [*gets up*]. There's the bell. Perhaps I'd better go.

NORA. No, do stay, please. I don't suppose it's for me; it's probably somebody for Torvald . . .

MAID [*in the doorway*]. Excuse me, ma'am, but there's a gentleman here wants to see Mr. Helmer, and I didn't quite know . . . because the doctor is in there. . . .

NORA. Who is the gentleman?

KROGSTAD [*in the doorway*]. It's me, Mrs. Helmer.

[MRS. LINDE *starts, then turns away to the window.*]

NORA [*tense, takes a step towards him and speaks in a low voice*]. You? What is it? What do you want to talk to my husband about?

KROGSTAD. Bank matters . . . in a manner of speaking. I work at the bank, and I hear your husband is to be the new manager. . . .

NORA. So it's . . .

KROGSTAD. Just routine business matters, Mrs. Helmer. Absolutely nothing else.

NORA. Well then, please go into his study.

[*She nods impassively and shuts the hall door behind him; then she walks across and sees to the stove.*]

MRS. LINDE. Nora . . . who was that man?

NORA. His name is Krogstad.

MRS. LINDE. So it really was him.

NORA. Do you know the man?

MRS. LINDE. I used to know him . . . a good many years ago. He was a solicitor's clerk in our district for a while.

NORA. Yes, so he was.

MRS. LINDE. How he's changed!

NORA. His marriage wasn't a very happy one, I believe.

MRS. LINDE. He's a widower now, isn't he?

NORA. With a lot of children. There, it'll burn better now.

[*She closes the stove door and moves the rocking chair a little to one side.*]

MRS. LINDE. He does a certain amount of business on the side, they say?

NORA. Oh? Yes, it's always possible. I just don't know. . . . But let's not think about business . . . it's all so dull.

[DR. RANK *comes in from* HELMER'*s study.*]

DR. RANK [*still in the doorway*]. No, no, Torvald, I won't intrude. I'll just look in on your wife for a moment. [*Shuts the door and notices* MRS. LINDE.] Oh, I beg your pardon. I'm afraid I'm intruding here as well.

NORA. No, not at all! [*Introduces them.*] Dr. Rank . . . Mrs. Linde.

RANK. Ah! A name I've often heard mentioned in this house. I believe I came past you on the stairs as I came in.

MRS. LINDE. I have to take things slowly going upstairs. I find it rather a trial.

RANK. Ah, some little disability somewhere, eh?

MRS. LINDE. Just a bit run down, I think, actually.

RANK. Is that all? Then I suppose you've come to town for a good rest—doing the rounds of the parties?

MRS. LINDE. I have come to look for work.

RANK. Is that supposed to be some kind of sovereign remedy for being run down?

MRS. LINDE. One must live, Doctor.

RANK. Yes, it's generally thought to be necessary.

NORA. Come, come, Dr. Rank. You are quite as keen to live as anybody.

RANK. Quite keen, yes. Miserable as I am, I'm quite ready to let things drag on as long as possible. All my patients are the same. Even those with a moral affliction are no different. As a matter of fact, there's a bad case of that kind in talking with Helmer at this very moment . . .

MRS. LINDE [*softly*]. Ah!

NORA. Whom do you mean?

RANK. A person called Krogstad—nobody you would know. He's rotten to the core. But even he began talking about having to *live,* as though it were something terribly important.

NORA. Oh? And what did he want to talk to Torvald about?

RANK. I honestly don't know. All I heard was something about the Bank.

NORA. I didn't know that Krog . . . that this Mr. Krogstad had anything to do with the Bank.

RANK. Oh yes, he's got some kind of job down there. [*To* MRS. LINDE.] I wonder if you've got people in your part of the country too who go rushing round sniffing out cases of moral corruption, and then installing the individuals concerned in nice, well-paid jobs where they can keep them under observation. Sound, decent people have to be content to stay out in the cold.

MRS. LINDE. Yet surely it's the sick who most need to be brought in.

RANK [*shrugs his shoulders*]. Well, there we have it. It's that attitude that's turning society into a clinic.

[NORA, *lost in her own thoughts, breaks into smothered laughter and claps her hands.*]

RANK. Why are you laughing at that? Do you know in fact what society is?

NORA. What do I care about your silly old society? I was laughing about something quite different . . . something frightfully funny. Tell me, Dr. Rank, are all the people who work at the Bank dependent on Torvald now?

RANK. Is that what you find so frightfully funny?

NORA [*smiles and hums*]. Never you mind! Never you mind! [*Walks about the room.*] Yes, it really is terribly amusing to think that we . . . that Torvald now has power over so many people. [*She takes the bag out of her pocket.*] Dr. Rank, what about a little macaroon?

RANK. Look at this, eh? Macaroons. I thought they were forbidden here.

NORA. Yes, but these are some Kristine gave me.

MRS. LINDE. What? I . . . ?

NORA. Now, now, you needn't be alarmed. You weren't to know that Torvald had forbidden them. He's worried in case they ruin my teeth, you know. Still . . . what's it matter once in a while! Don't you think so, Dr. Rank? Here! [*She pops a macaroon into his mouth.*] And you too, Kristine. And I shall have one as well; just a little one . . . or two at the most. [*She walks about the room again.*] Really I am so happy. There's just one little thing I'd love to do now.

RANK. What's that?

NORA. Something I'd love to say in front of Torvald.

RANK. Then why can't you?

NORA. No, I daren't. It's not very nice.

MRS. LINDE. Not very nice?

RANK. Well, in that case it might not be wise. But to us, I don't see why. . . . What is this you would love to say in front of Helmer?

NORA. I would simply love to say: "Damn."

RANK. Are you mad!

MRS. LINDE. Good gracious, Nora . . . !

RANK. Say it! Here he is!

NORA [*hiding the bag of macaroons*]. Sh! Sh!

[HELMER *comes out of his room, his overcoat over his arm and his hat in his hand.*]

NORA [*going over to him*]. Well, Torvald dear, did you get rid of him?

HELMER. Yes, he's just gone.

NORA. Let me introduce you. This is Kristine, who has just arrived in town. . . .

HELMER. Kristine . . . ? You must forgive me, but I don't think I know . . .

NORA. Mrs. Linde, Torvald dear. Kristine Linde.

HELMER. Ah, indeed. A school friend of my wife's, presumably.

MRS. LINDE. Yes, we were girls together.

NORA. Fancy, Torvald, she's come all this long way just to have a word with you.

HELMER. How is that?

MRS. LINDE. Well, it wasn't really . . .

NORA. The thing is, Kristine is terribly clever at office work, and she's frightfully keen on finding a job with some efficient man, so that she can learn even more. . . .

HELMER. Very sensible, Mrs. Linde.

NORA. And then when she heard you'd been made Bank Manager—there was a bit in the paper about it—she set off at once. Torvald please! You *will* try and do something for Kristine, won't you? For my sake?

HELMER. Well, that's not altogether impossible. You are a widow, I presume?

MRS. LINDE. Yes.

HELMER. And you've had some experience in business?

MRS. LINDE. A fair amount.

HELMER. Well, it's quite probable I can find you a job, I think. . . .

NORA [*clapping her hands*]. There, you see!

HELMER. You have come at a fortunate moment, Mrs. Linde . . .

MRS. LINDE. Oh, how can I ever thank you . . . ?

HELMER. Not a bit. [*He puts on his overcoat.*] But for the present I must ask you to excuse me. . . .

RANK. Wait. I'm coming with you.

[*He fetches his fur coat from the hall and warms it at the stove.*]

NORA. Don't be long, Torvald dear.

HELMER. Not more than an hour, that's all.

NORA. Are you leaving too, Kristine?

MRS. LINDE [*putting on her things*]. Yes, I must go and see if I can't find myself a room.

HELMER. Perhaps we can all walk down the road together.

NORA [*helping her*]. What a nuisance we are so limited for space here. I'm afraid it just isn't possible. . . .

MRS. LINDE. Oh, you mustn't dream of it! Goodbye, Nora dear, and thanks for everything.

NORA. Goodbye for the present. But . . . you'll be coming back this evening, of course. And you too, Dr. Rank? What's that? If you are up to it? Of course you'll be up to it. Just wrap yourself up well.

[*They go out, talking, into the hall; children's voices can be heard on the stairs.*]

NORA. Here they are! Here they are! [*She runs to the front door and opens it.* ANNE MARIE, *the nursemaid, enters with the children.*] Come in! Come in! [*She bends down and kisses them.*] Ah! my sweet little darlings. . . . You see them, Kristine? Aren't they lovely!

RANK. Don't stand here chattering in this draught!

HELMER. Come along, Mrs. Linde. The place now becomes unbearable for anybody except mothers.

[DR. RANK, HELMER *and* MRS. LINDE *go down the stairs: the* NURSEMAID *comes into the room with the children, then Nora, shutting the door behind her.*]

NORA. How fresh and bright you look! My, what red cheeks you've got! Like apples and roses. [*During the following, the children keep chattering away to her.*] Have you had a nice time? That's splendid. And you gave Emmy and Bob a ride on your sledge? Did you now! Both together! Fancy that! There's a clever boy, Ivar. Oh, let me take her a little while, Anne Marie. There's my sweet little babydoll! [*She takes the youngest of the children from the* NURSEMAID *and dances with her.*] All right, Mummy will dance with Bobby too. What? You've been throwing snowballs? Oh, I wish I'd been there. No, don't bother, Anne Marie, I'll help them off with their things. No, please, let me— I like doing it. You go on in, you look frozen. You'll find some hot coffee on the stove. [*The* NURSEMAID *goes into the room, left.* NORA *takes off the children's coats and hats and throws them down anywhere, while the children all talk at once.*] Really! A great big dog came running after you? But he didn't bite. No, the doggies wouldn't bite my pretty little dollies. You mustn't touch the parcels, Ivar! What are they? Wouldn't you like to know! No, no, that's nasty. Now? Shall we play something? What shall we play? Hide and seek? Yes, let's play hide and seek. Bob can hide first. Me first? All right, let me hide first.

[*She and the children play, laughing and shrieking, in this room and in the adjacent room on the right. Finally* NORA *hides under the table; the children come rushing in to look for her but cannot find her; they hear her stifled laughter, rush to the table, lift up the tablecloth and find her. Tremendous shouts of delight. She creeps out and pretends to frighten them. More shouts. Meanwhile there has been a knock at the front door, which nobody has heard. The door half opens, and* KROGSTAD *can be seen. He waits a little; the game continues.*]

KROGSTAD. I beg your pardon, Mrs. Helmer. . . .
NORA [*turns with a stifled cry and half jumps up*]. Ah! What do you want?
KROGSTAD. Excuse me. The front door was standing open. Somebody must have forgotten to shut it. . . .
NORA [*standing up*]. My husband isn't at home, Mr. Krogstad.
KROGSTAD. I know.
NORA. Well . . . what are you doing here?
KROGSTAD. I want a word with you.
NORA. With . . . ? [*Quietly, to the children.*] Go to Anne Marie. What? No, the strange man won't do anything to Mummy. When he's gone we'll have another game. [*She leads the children into the room, left, and shuts the door after them; tense and uneasy.*] You want to speak to me?
KROGSTAD. Yes, I do.
NORA. Today? But it isn't the first of the month yet. . . .

KROGSTAD. No, it's Christmas Eve. It depends entirely on you what sort of Christmas you have.

NORA. What do you want? Today I can't possibly . . .

KROGSTAD. Let's not talk about that for the moment. It's something else. You've got a moment to spare?

NORA. Yes, I suppose so, though . . .

KROGSTAD. Good. I was sitting in Olsen's café, and I saw your husband go down the road . . .

NORA. Did you?

KROGSTAD. . . . with a lady.

NORA. Well?

KROGSTAD. May I be so bold as to ask whether that lady was a Mrs. Linde?

NORA. Yes.

KROGSTAD. Just arrived in town?

NORA. Yes, today.

KROGSTAD. And she's a good friend of yours?

NORA. Yes, she is. But I can't see . . .

KROGSTAD. I also knew her once.

NORA. I know.

KROGSTAD. Oh? So you know all about it. I thought as much. Well, I want to ask you straight: is Mrs. Linde getting a job in the Bank?

NORA. How dare you cross-examine me like this, Mr. Krogstad? You, one of my husband's subordinates? But since you've asked me, I'll tell you. Yes, Mrs. Linde has got a job. And I'm the one who got it for her, Mr. Krogstad. Now you know.

KROGSTAD. So my guess was right.

NORA [*walking up and down*]. Oh, I think I can say that some of us have a little influence now and again. Just because one happens to be a woman, that doesn't mean. . . . People in subordinate positions, ought to take care they don't offend anybody . . . who . . . him . . .

KROGSTAD. . . . has influence?

NORA. Exactly.

KROGSTAD [*changing his tone*]. Mrs. Helmer, will you have the goodness to use your influence on my behalf?

NORA. What? What do you mean?

KROGSTAD. Will you be so good as to see that I keep my modest little job at the Bank?

NORA. What do you mean? Who wants to take it away from you?

KROGSTAD. Oh, you needn't try and pretend to me you don't know. I can quite see that this friend of yours isn't particularly anxious to bump up against me. And I can also see now whom I can thank for being given the sack.

NORA. But I assure you. . . .

KROGSTAD. All right, all right. But to come to the point: there's still time. And I advise you to use your influence to stop it.

NORA. But, Mr. Krogstad, I *have* no influence.

KROGSTAD. Haven't you? I thought just now you said yourself . . .

NORA. I didn't mean it that way, of course. Me? What makes you think I've got any influence of that kind over my husband?

KROGSTAD. I know your husband from our student days. I don't suppose he is any more steadfast than other married men.

NORA. You speak disrespectfully of my husband like that and I'll show you the door.

KROGSTAD. So the lady's got courage.

NORA. I'm not frightened of you any more. After New Year's I'll soon be finished with the whole business.

KROGSTAD [*controlling himself*]. Listen to me, Mrs. Helmer. If necessary I shall fight for my little job in the Bank as if I were fighting for my life.

NORA. So it seems.

KROGSTAD. It's not just for the money, that's the last thing I care about. There's something else . . . well, I might as well out with it. You see it's like this. You know as well as anybody that some years ago I got myself mixed up in a bit of trouble.

NORA. I believe I've heard something of the sort.

KROGSTAD. It never got as far as the courts; but immediately it was as if all paths were barred to me. So I started going in for the sort of business you know about. I had to do something, and I think I can say I haven't been one of the worst. But now I have to get out of it. My sons are growing up; for their sake I must try and win back what respectability I can. That job in the Bank was like the first step on the ladder for me. And now your husband wants to kick me off the ladder again, back into the mud.

NORA. But in God's name, Mr. Krogstad, it's quite beyond my power to help you.

KROGSTAD. That's because you haven't the will to help me. But I have ways of making you.

NORA. You wouldn't go and tell my husband I owe you money?

KROGSTAD. Suppose I did tell him?

NORA. It would be a rotten shame. [*Half choking with tears.*] That secret is all my pride and joy—why should he have to hear about it in this nasty, horrid way . . . hear about it from *you*. You would make things horribly unpleasant for me. . . .

KROGSTAD. Merely unpleasant?

NORA [*vehemently*]. Go on, do it then! It'll be all the worse for you. Because then my husband will see for himself what a bad man you are, and then you certainly won't be able to keep your job.

KROGSTAD. I asked whether it was only a bit of domestic unpleasantness you were afraid of?

NORA. If my husband gets to know about it, he'll pay off what's owing at once. And then we'd have nothing more to do with you.

KROGSTAD [*taking a pace towards her*]. Listen, Mrs. Helmer, either you haven't a very good memory, or else you don't understand much about business. I'd better make the position a little bit clearer for you.

NORA. How do you mean?

KROGSTAD. When your husband was ill, you came to me for the loan of twelve hundred dollars.

NORA. I didn't know of anybody else.

KROGSTAD. I promised to find you the money. . . .

NORA. And you did find it.

KROGSTAD. I promised to find you the money on certain conditions. At the time you were so concerned about your husband's illness, and so anxious to get the money for going away with, that I don't think you paid very much attention to all the incidentals. So there is perhaps some point in reminding you of them. Well, I promised to find you the money against an IOU which I drew up for you.

NORA. Yes, and which I signed.

KROGSTAD. Very good. But below that I added a few lines, by which your father was to stand security. This your father was to sign.

NORA. Was to . . . ? He did sign it.

KROGSTAD. I had left the date blank. The idea was that your father was to add the date himself when he signed it. Remember?

NORA. Yes, I think. . . .

KROGSTAD. I then gave you the IOU to post to your father. Wasn't that so?

NORA. Yes.

KROGSTAD. Which of course you did at once. Because only about five or six days later you brought it back to me with your father's signature. I then paid out the money.

NORA. Well? Haven't I paid the installments regularly?

KROGSTAD. Yes, fairly. But . . . coming back to what we were talking about . . . that was a pretty bad period you were going through then, Mrs. Helmer.

NORA. Yes, it was.

KROGSTAD. Your father was seriously ill, I believe.

NORA. He was very near the end.

KROGSTAD. And died shortly afterwards?

NORA. Yes.

KROGSTAD. Tell me, Mrs. Helmer, do you happen to remember which day your father died? The exact date, I mean.

NORA. Daddy died on 29 September.

KROGSTAD. Quite correct. I made some inquiries. Which brings up a rather curious point [*takes out a paper*] which I simply cannot explain.

NORA. Curious . . . ? I don't know . . .

KROGSTAD. The curious thing is, Mrs. Helmer, that your father signed this document three days after his death.

NORA. What? I don't understand. . . .

KROGSTAD. Your father died on 29 September. But look here. Your father has dated his signature 2 October. Isn't that rather curious, Mrs. Helmer? [NORA *remains silent.*] It's also remarkable that the words '2 October' and the year are not in your father's handwriting, but in a handwriting I rather think I recognize. Well, perhaps that could be explained. Your father might have forgotten to date his signature, and then somebody else might have made a guess at the date later, before the fact of your father's death was known. There is nothing wrong in that. What really matters is the signature. And *that* is of course genuine, Mrs. Helmer? It really was your father who wrote his name here?

NORA [*after a moment's silence, throws her head back and looks at him defiantly*]. No, it wasn't. It was me who signed father's name.

KROGSTAD. Listen to me. I suppose you realize that that is a very dangerous confession?

NORA. Why? You'll soon have all your money back.

KROGSTAD. Let me ask you a question: why didn't you send that document to your father?

NORA. It was impossible. Daddy was ill. If I'd asked him for his signature, I'd have to tell him what the money was for. Don't you see, when he was as ill as that I couldn't go and tell him that my husband's life was in danger. It was simply impossible.

KROGSTAD. It would have been better for you if you had abandoned the whole trip.

NORA. No, that was impossible. This was the thing that was to save my husband's life. I couldn't give it up.

KROGSTAD. But did it never strike you that this was fraudulent . . . ?

NORA. That wouldn't have meant anything to me. Why should I worry about you? I couldn't stand you, not when you insisted on going through with all those cold-blooded formalities, knowing all the time what a critical state my husband was in.

KROGSTAD. Mrs. Helmer, it's quite clear you still haven't the faintest idea what it is you've committed. But let me tell you, my own offence was no more and no worse than that, and it ruined my entire reputation.

NORA. You? Are you trying to tell me that you once risked everything to save your wife's life?

KROGSTAD. The law takes no account of motives.

NORA. Then they must be very bad laws.

KROGSTAD. Bad or not, if I produce this document in court, you'll be condemned according to them.

NORA. I don't believe it. Isn't a daughter entitled to try and save her father from worry and anxiety on his deathbed? Isn't a wife entitled to save her husband's life? I might not know very much about the law, but I feel sure of one thing: it must say somewhere that things like this are allowed. You mean to say you don't know that—you, when it's your job? You must be a rotten lawyer, Mr. Krogstad.

KROGSTAD. That may be. But when it comes to business transactions—like the sort between us two—perhaps you'll admit I know something about them? Good. Now you must please yourself. But I tell you this: if I'm pitched out a second time, you are going to keep me company.

[*He bows and goes out through the hall.*]

NORA [*stands thoughtfully for a moment, then tosses her head*]. Rubbish! He's just trying to scare me. I'm not such a fool as all that. [*Begins gathering up the children's clothes; after a moment she stops.*] Yet . . . ? No, it's impossible! I did it for love, didn't I?

THE CHILDREN [*in the doorway, left*]. Mummy, the gentleman's just gone out of the gate.

NORA. Yes, I know. But you mustn't say anything to anybody about that gentleman. You hear? Not even to Daddy!

THE CHILDREN. All right, Mummy. Are you going to play again?

NORA. No, not just now.

THE CHILDREN. But Mummy, you promised!

NORA. Yes, but I can't just now. Off you go now, I have a lot to do. Off you go, my darlings. [*She herds them carefully into the other room and shuts the door behind them. She sits down on the sofa, picks up her embroidery and works a few stitches, but soon stops.*] No! [*She flings her work down, stands up, goes to the hall door and calls out.*] Helene!

Fetch the tree in for me, please. [*She walks across to the table, left, and opens the drawer; again pauses.*] No, really, it's quite impossible!

MAID [*with the Christmas tree*]. Where shall I put it, ma'am?

NORA. On the floor there, in the middle.

MAID. Anything else you want me to bring?

NORA. No, thank you. I've got what I want.

[*The* MAID *has put the tree down and goes out.*]

NORA [*busy decorating the tree*]. Candles here . . . and flowers here— Revolting man! It's all nonsense! There's nothing to worry about. We'll have a lovely Christmas tree. And I'll do anything you want me to, Torvald; I'll sing for you, dance for you. . . .

[HELMER, *with a bundle of documents under his arm, comes in by the hall door.*]

NORA. Ah, back again already?

HELMER. Yes. Anybody been?

NORA. Here? No.

HELMER. That's funny. I just saw Krogstad leave the house.

NORA. Oh? O yes, that's right. Krogstad was here a minute.

HELMER. Nora, I can tell by your face he's been asking you to put a good word in for him.

NORA. Yes.

HELMER. And you were to pretend it was your own idea? You were to keep quiet about his having been here. He asked you to do that as well, didn't he?

NORA. Yes, Torvald. But . . .

HELMER. Nora, Nora, what possessed you to do a thing like that? Talking to a person like him, making him promises? And then on top of everything, to tell me a lie!

NORA. A lie . . . ?

HELMER. Didn't you say that nobody had been here? [*Wagging his finger at her.*] Never again must my little song-bird do a thing like that! Little song-birds must keep their pretty little beaks out of mischief; no chirruping out of tune! [*Puts his arm round her waist.*] Isn't that the way we want things to be? Yes, of course it is. [*Lets her go.*] So let's say no more about it. [*Sits down by the stove.*] Ah, nice and cozy here!

[*He glances through his papers.*]

NORA [*busy with the Christmas tree, after a short pause*]. Torvald!

HELMER. Yes.

NORA. I'm so looking forward to the fancy dress ball at the Stenborgs on Boxing Day.

HELMER. And I'm terribly curious to see what sort of surprise you've got for me.

NORA. Oh, it's too silly.

HELMER. Oh?

NORA. I just can't think of anything suitable. Everything seems so absurd, so pointless.

HELMER. Has my little Nora come to that conclusion?

NORA [*behind his chair, her arms on the chair-back*]. Are you very busy, Torvald?

HELMER. Oh. . . .

NORA. What are all those papers?

HELMER. Bank matters.

NORA. Already?

HELMER. I have persuaded the retiring manager to give me authority to make any changes in organization or personnel I think necessary. I have to work on it over the Christmas week. I want everything straight by the New Year.

NORA. So that was why that poor Krogstad. . . .

HELMER. Hm!

NORA [*still leaning against the back of the chair, running her fingers through his hair*]. If you hadn't been so busy, Torvald, I'd have asked you to do me an awfully big favor.

HELMER. Let me hear it. What's it to be?

NORA. Nobody's got such good taste as you. And the thing is I do so want to look my best at the fancy dress ball. Torvald, couldn't you give me some advice and tell me what you think I ought to go as, and how I should arrange my costume?

HELMER. Aha! So my impulsive little woman is asking for somebody to come to her rescue, eh?

NORA. Please, Torvald, I never get anywhere without your help.

HELMER. Very well, I'll think about it. We'll find something.

NORA. That's sweet of you. [*She goes across to the tree again; pause.*] How pretty these red flowers look.—Tell me, was it really something terribly wrong this man Krogstad did?

HELMER. Forgery. Have you any idea what that means?

NORA. Perhaps circumstances left him no choice?

HELMER. Maybe. Or perhaps, like so many others, he just didn't think. I am not so heartless that I would necessarily want to condemn a man for a single mistake like that.

NORA. Oh no, Torvald, of course not!

HELMER. Many a man might be able to redeem himself, if he honestly confessed his guilt and took his punishment.

NORA. Punishment?

HELMER. But that wasn't the way Krogstad chose. He dodged what was due to him by a cunning trick. And that's what has been the cause of his corruption.

NORA. Do you think it would . . . ?

HELMER. Just think how a man with a thing like that on his conscience will always be having to lie and cheat and dissemble; he can never drop the mask, not even with his own wife and children. And the children— that's the most terrible part of it, Nora.

NORA. Why?

HELMER. A fog of lies like that in a household, and it spreads disease and infection to every part of it. Every breath the children take in that kind of house is reeking with evil germs.

NORA [*closer behind him*]. Are you sure of that?

HELMER. My dear Nora, as a lawyer I know what I'm talking about. Practically all juvenile delinquents come from homes where the mother is dishonest.

NORA. Why mothers particularly?

HELMER. It's generally traceable to the mothers, but of course fathers can have the same influence. Every lawyer knows that only too well. And yet there's Krogstad been poisoning his own children for years with lies and deceit. That's the reason I call him morally depraved. [*Holds out his hands to her.*] That's why my sweet little Nora must promise me not to try putting in any more good words for him. Shake hands on it. Well? What's this? Give me your hand. There now! That's settled. I assure you I would have found it impossible to work with him. I quite literally feel physically sick in the presence of such people.

NORA [*draws her hand away and walks over to the other side of the Christmas tree*]. How hot it is in here! And I still have such a lot to do.

HELMER [*stands up and collects his papers together*]. Yes, I'd better think of getting some of this read before dinner. I must also think about your costume. And I might even be able to lay my hands on something to wrap in gold paper and hang on the Christmas tree. [*He lays his hand on her head.*] My precious little singing bird.

[*He goes into his study and shuts the door behind him.*]

NORA [*quietly, after a pause*]. Nonsense! It can't be. It's impossible. It *must* be impossible.

MAID [*in the doorway, left*]. The children keep asking so nicely if they can come in and see Mummy.

NORA. No, no, don't let them in! You stay with them, Anne Marie.

MAID. Very well, ma'am.

[*She shuts the door.*]

NORA [*pale with terror*]. Corrupt my children . . . ! Poison my home? [*Short pause; she throws back her head.*] It's not true! It could never, never be true!

Act II

The same room. In the corner beside the piano stands the Christmas tree, stripped, bedraggled and with its candles burnt out. NORA'S *outdoor things lie on the sofa.* NORA, *alone there, walks about restlessly; at last she stops by the sofa and picks up her coat.*

NORA [*putting her coat down again*]. Somebody's coming! [*Crosses to the door, listens.*] No, it's nobody. Nobody will come today, of course, Christmas Day—nor tomorrow, either. But perhaps. . . . [*She opens the door and looks out.*] No, nothing in the letter box; quite empty. [*Comes forward.*] Oh, nonsense! He didn't mean it seriously. Things like that can't happen. It's impossible. Why, I have three small children.

[*The* NURSEMAID *comes from the room, left, carrying a big cardboard box.*]

NURSEMAID. I finally found it, the box with the fancy dress costumes.

NORA. Thank you. Put it on the table, please.

NURSEMAID [*does this*]. But I'm afraid they are in an awful mess.

NORA. Oh, if only I could rip them up into a thousand pieces!

NURSEMAID. Good heavens, they can be mended all right, with a bit of patience.

NORA. Yes, I'll go over and get Mrs. Linde to help me.

NURSEMAID. Out again? In this terrible weather? You'll catch your death of cold, Ma'am.

NORA. Oh, worse things might happen.—How are the children?

NURSEMAID. Playing with their Christmas presents, poor little things, but . . .

NORA. Do they keep asking for me?

NURSEMAID. They are so used to being with their Mummy.

NORA. Yes, Anne Marie, from now on I can't be with them as often as I was before.

NURSEMAID. Ah well, children get used to anything in time.

NORA. Do you think so? Do you think they would forget their Mummy if she went away for good?

NURSEMAID. Good gracious—for good?

NORA. Tell me, Anne Marie—I've often wondered—how on earth could you bear to hand your child over to strangers?

NURSEMAID. Well, there was nothing else for it when I had to come and nurse my little Nora.

NORA. Yes but. . . how could you *bring* yourself to do it?

NURSEMAID. When I had the chance of such a good place? When a poor girl's been in trouble she must make the best of things. Because *he* didn't help, the rotter.

NORA. But your daughter will have forgotten you.

NURSEMAID. Oh no, she hasn't. She wrote to me when she got confirmed, and again when she got married.

NORA [*putting her arms round her neck*]. Dear old Anne Marie, you were a good mother to me when I was little.

NURSEMAID. My poor little Nora never had any other mother but me.

NORA. And if my little ones only had you, I know you would. . . . Oh, what am I talking about! [*She opens the box.*] Go in to them. I must . . . To-morrow I'll let you see how pretty I am going to look.

NURSEMAID. Ah, there'll be nobody at the ball as pretty as my Nora.

[*She goes into the room, left.*]

NORA [*begins unpacking the box, but soon throws it down*]. Oh, if only I dare go out. If only I could be sure nobody would come. And that nothing would happen in the meantime here at home. Rubbish—nobody's going to come. I mustn't think about it. Brush this muff. Pretty gloves, pretty gloves! I'll put it right out of my mind. One, two, three, four, five, six. . . . [*Screams.*] Ah, they are coming. . . . [*She starts towards the door, but stops irresolute.* MRS. LINDE *comes from the hall, where she has taken off her things.*] Oh, it's you, Kristine. There's nobody else out there, is there? I'm so glad you've come.

MRS. LINDE. I heard you'd been over looking for me.

NORA. Yes, I was just passing. There's something you must help me with. Come and sit beside me on the sofa here. You see, the Stenborgs are having a fancy dress party upstairs tomorrow evening, and now Torvald wants me to go as a Neapolitan fisher lass and dance the tarantella. I learned it in Capri, you know.

MRS. LINDE. Well, well! So you are going to do a party piece?

NORA. Torvald says I should. Look, here's the costume, Torvald had it made for me down there. But it's got all torn and I simply don't know. . . .

MRS. LINDE. We'll soon have that put right. It's only the trimming come away here and there. Got a needle and thread? Ah, here's what we are after.

NORA. It's awfully kind of you.

MRS. LINDE. So you are going to be all dressed up tomorrow, Nora? Tell you what—I'll pop over for a minute to see you in all your finery. But I'm quite forgetting to thank you for the pleasant time we had last night.

NORA [*gets up and walks across the room*]. Somehow I didn't think yesterday was as nice as things generally are.—You should have come to town a little earlier, Kristine.—Yes, Torvald certainly knows how to make things pleasant about the place.

MRS. LINDE. You too, I should say. You are not your father's daughter for nothing. But tell me, is Dr. Rank always as depressed as he was last night?

NORA. No, last night it was rather obvious. He's got something seriously wrong with him, you know. Tuberculosis of the spine, poor fellow. His father was a horrible man, who used to have mistresses and things like that. That's why the son was always ailing, right from being a child.

MRS. LINDE [*lowering her sewing*]. But my dear Nora, how do you come to know about things like that?

NORA [*walking about the room*]. Huh! When you've got three children, you get these visits from . . . women who have had a certain amount of medical training. And you hear all sorts of things from them.

MRS. LINDE [*begins sewing again; short silence*]. Does Dr. Rank call in every day?

NORA. Every single day. He was Torvald's best friend as a boy, and he's a good friend of mine, too. Dr. Rank is almost like one of the family.

MRS. LINDE. But tell me—is he really genuine? What I mean is: doesn't he sometimes rather turn on the charm?

NORA. No, on the contrary. What makes you think that?

MRS. LINDE. When you introduced me yesterday, he claimed he'd often heard my name in this house. But afterwards I noticed your husband hadn't the faintest idea who I was. Then how is it that Dr. Rank should. . . .

NORA. Oh yes, it was quite right what he said, Kristine. You see Torvald is so terribly in love with me that he says he wants me all to himself. When we were first married, it even used to make him sort of jealous if I only as much as mentioned any of my old friends from back home. So of course I stopped doing it. But I often talk to Dr. Rank about such things. He likes hearing about them.

MRS. LINDE. Listen, Nora! In lots of ways you are still a child. Now, I'm a good deal older than you, and a bit more experienced. I'll tell you something: I think you ought to give up all this business with Dr. Rank.

NORA. Give up what business?

MRS. LINDE. The whole thing, I should say. Weren't you saying yesterday something about a rich admirer who was to provide you with money. . . .

NORA. One who's never existed, I regret to say. But what of it?

MRS. LINDE. Has Dr. Rank money?

NORA. Yes, he has.

MRS. LINDE. And no dependents?

NORA. No, nobody. But. . . ?

MRS. LINDE. And he comes to the house every day?

NORA. Yes, I told you.

MRS. LINDE. But how can a man of his position want to pester you like this?

NORA. I simply don't understand.

MRS. LINDE. Don't pretend, Nora. Do you think I don't see now who you borrowed the twelve hundred from?

NORA. Are you out of your mind? Do you really think that? A friend of ours who comes here every day? The whole situation would have been absolutely intolerable.

MRS. LINDE. It *really* isn't him?

NORA. No, I give you my word. It would never have occurred to me for one moment. . . . Anyway, he didn't have the money to lend then. He didn't inherit it till later.

MRS. LINDE. Just as well for you, I'd say, my dear Nora.

NORA. No, it would never have occurred to me to ask Dr. Rank. . . . All the same I'm pretty certain if I were to ask him . . .

MRS. LINDE. But of course you won't.

NORA. No, of course not. I can't ever imagine it being necessary. But I'm quite certain if ever I were to mention it to Dr. Rank. . . .

MRS. LINDE. Behind your husband's back?

NORA. I have to get myself out of that other business. That's also behind his back. I must get myself out of that.

MRS. LINDE. Yes, that's what I said yesterday. But . . .

NORA [*walking up and down*]. A man's better at coping with these things than a woman. . . .

MRS. LINDE. Your own husband, yes.

NORA. Nonsense! [*Stops.*] When you've paid everything you owe, you do get your IOU back again, don't you?

MRS. LINDE. Of course.

NORA. And you can tear it up into a thousand pieces and burn it—the nasty, filthy thing!

MRS. LINDE [*looking fixedly at her, puts down her sewing and slowly rises*]. Nora, you are hiding something from me.

NORA. Is it so obvious?

MRS. LINDE. Something has happened to you since yesterday morning. Nora, what is it?

NORA [*going towards her*]. Kristine! [*Listens.*] Hush! There's Torvald back. Look, you go and sit in there beside the children for the time being. Torvald can't stand the sight of mending lying about. Get Anne Marie to help you.

MRS. LINDE [*gathering a lot of the things together*]. All right, but I'm not leaving until we have thrashed this thing out.

[*She goes into the room, left; at the same time* HELMER *comes in from the hall.*]

NORA [*goes to meet him*]. I've been longing for you to be back, Torvald, dear.

HELMER. Was that the dressmaker . . . ?

NORA. No, it was Kristine; she's helping me with my costume. I think it's going to look very nice . . .

HELMER. Wasn't that a good idea of mine, now?

NORA. Wonderful! But wasn't it also nice of me to let you have your way?

HELMER [*taking her under the chin*]. Nice of you—because you let your husband have his way? All right, you little rogue, I know you didn't mean it that way. But I don't want to disturb you. You'll be wanting to try the costume on, I suppose.

NORA. And I dare say you've got work to do?

HELMER. Yes. [*Shows her a bundle of papers.*] Look at this. I've been down at the Bank. . . .

[*He turns to go into his study.*]

NORA. Torvald!

HELMER [*stopping*]. Yes.

NORA. If a little squirrel were to ask ever so nicely . . . ?

HELMER. Well?

NORA. Would you do something for it?

HELMER. Naturally I would first have to know what it is.

NORA. Please, if only you would let it have its way, and do what it wants, it'd scamper about and do all sorts of marvelous tricks.

HELMER. What is it?

NORA. And the pretty little skylark would sing all day long. . . .

HELMER. Huh! It does that anyway.

NORA. I'd pretend I was an elfin child and dance a moonlight dance for you, Torvald.

HELMER. Nora—I hope it's not that business you started on this morning?

NORA [*coming closer*]. Yes, it is, Torvald. I implore you!

HELMER. You have the nerve to bring that up again?

NORA. Yes, yes, you *must* listen to me. You must let Krogstad keep his job at the Bank.

HELMER. My dear Nora, I'm giving his job to Mrs. Linde.

NORA. Yes, it's awfully sweet of you. But couldn't you get rid of somebody else in the office instead of Krogstad?

HELMER. This really is the most incredible obstinacy! Just because you go and make some thoughtless promise to put in a good word for him, you expect me . . .

NORA. It's not that, Torvald. It's for your own sake. That man writes in all the nastiest papers, you told me that yourself. He can do you no end of harm. He terrifies me to death. . . .

HELMER. Aha, now I see. It's your memories of what happened before that are frightening you.

NORA. What do you mean?

HELMER. It's your father you are thinking of.

NORA. Yes . . . yes, that's right. You remember all the nasty insinuations those wicked people put in the papers about Daddy? I honestly think they would have had him dismissed if the Ministry hadn't sent you down to investigate, and you hadn't been so kind and helpful.

HELMER. My dear little Nora, there is a considerable difference between your father and me. Your father's professional conduct was not entirely above suspicion. Mine is. And I hope it's going to stay that way as long as I hold this position.

NORA. But nobody knows what some of these evil people are capable of. Things could be so nice and pleasant for us here, in the peace and quiet

of our home—you and me and the children, Torvald! That's why I implore you. . . .

HELMER. The more you plead for him, the more impossible you make it for
me to keep him on. It's already known down at the Bank that I am going to give Krogstad his notice. If it ever got around that the new manager had been talked over by his wife. . . .

NORA. What of it?

HELMER. Oh, nothing! As long as the little woman gets her own stubborn
way . . . ! Do you want me to make myself a laughing stock in the office? . . . Give people the idea that I am susceptible to any kind of outside pressure? You can imagine how soon I'd feel the consequences of
that! Anyway, there's one other consideration that makes it impossible
to have Krogstad in the Bank as long as I am manager.

NORA. What's that?

HELMER. At a pinch I might have overlooked his past lapses. . . .

NORA. Of course you could, Torvald!

HELMER. And I'm told he's not bad at his job, either. But we knew each other
rather well when we were younger. It was one of those rather rash
friendships that prove embarrassing in later life. There's no reason
why you shouldn't know we were once on terms of some familiarity.
And he, in his tactless way, makes no attempt to hide the fact, particularly when other people are present. On the contrary, he thinks
he has every right to treat me as an equal, with his "Torvald this" and
"Torvald that" every time he opens his mouth. I find it extremely irritating, I can tell you. He would make my position at the Bank absolutely
intolerable.

NORA. Torvald, surely you aren't serious?

HELMER. Oh? Why not?

NORA. Well, it's all so petty.

HELMER. What's that you say? Petty? Do you think I'm petty?

NORA. No, not at all, Torvald dear! And that's why . . .

HELMER. Doesn't make any difference! . . . You call my motives petty; so I
must be petty too. Petty! Indeed! Well, we'll put a stop to that, once
and for all. [*He opens the hall door and calls.*] Helene!

NORA. What are you going to do?

HELMER [*searching among his papers*]. Settle things. [*The maid comes in.*]
See this letter? I want you to take it down at once. Get hold of a mes-
senger and get him to deliver it. Quickly. The address is on the outside.
There's the money.

MAID. Very good, sir.

[*She goes with the letter.*]

HELMER [*putting his papers together*]. There now, my stubborn little miss.

NORA [*breathless*]. Torvald . . . what was that letter?

HELMER. Krogstad's notice.

NORA. Get it back, Torvald! There's still time! Oh, Torvald, get it back!
Please for my sake, for your sake, for the sake of the children! Listen,
Torvald, please! You don't realize what it can do to us.

HELMER. Too late.

NORA. Yes, too late.

HELMER. My dear Nora, I forgive you this anxiety of yours, although it is actually a bit of an insult. Oh, but it is, I tell you! It's hardly flattering to

suppose that anything this miserable pen-pusher wrote could frighten *me!* But I forgive you all the same, because it is rather a sweet way of showing how much you love me. [*He takes her in his arms.*] This is how things must be, my own darling Nora. When it comes to the point, I've enough strength and enough courage, believe me, for whatever happens. You'll find I'm man enough to take everything on myself.

NORA [*terrified*]. What do you mean?

HELMER. Everything, I said. . . .

NORA [*in command of herself*]. That is something you shall never, never do.

HELMER. All right, then we'll share it, Nora—as man and wife. That's what we'll do. [*Caressing her.*] Does that make you happy now? There, there, don't look at me with those eyes, like a little frightened dove. The whole thing is sheer imagination.—Why don't you run through the tarantella and try out the tambourine? I'll go into my study and shut both the doors, then I won't hear anything. You can make all the noise you want. [*Turns in the doorway.*] And when Rank comes, tell him where he can find me.

[*He nods to her, goes with his papers into his room, and shuts the door behind him.*]

NORA [*wild-eyed with terror, stands as though transfixed*]. He's quite capable of doing it! He would do it! No matter what, he'd do it.—No, never in this world! Anything but that! Help? Some way out . . . ? [*The doorbell rings in the hall.*] Dr. Rank . . . ! Anything but that, anything! [*She brushes her hands over her face, pulls herself together and opens the door into the hall.* DR. RANK *is standing outside hanging up his fur coat. During what follows it begins to grow dark.*] Hello, Dr. Rank. I recognized your ring. Do you mind not going in to Torvald just yet, I think he's busy.

RANK. And you?

[DR. RANK *comes into the room and she closes the door behind him.*]

NORA. Oh, you know very well I've always got time for you.

RANK. Thank you. A privilege I shall take advantage of as long as I am able.

NORA. What do you mean—as long as you are able?

RANK. Does that frighten you?

NORA. Well, it's just that it sounds so strange. Is anything likely to happen?

RANK. Only what I have long expected. But I didn't think it would come quite so soon.

NORA [*catching at his arm*]. What have you found out? Dr. Rank, you must tell me!

RANK. I'm slowly sinking. There's nothing to be done about it.

NORA [*with a sigh of relief*]. Oh, it's *you* you're . . . ?

RANK. Who else? No point in deceiving oneself. I am the most wretched of all my patients, Mrs. Helmer. These last few days I've made a careful analysis of my internal economy. Bankrupt! Within a month I shall probably be lying rotting up there in the churchyard.

NORA. Come now, what a ghastly thing to say!

RANK. The whole damned thing is ghastly. But the worst thing is all the ghastliness that has to be gone through first. I only have one more test to make; and when that's done I'll know pretty well when the final dis-

integration will start. There's something I want to ask you. Helmer is a
sensitive soul; he loathes anything that's ugly. I don't want him visiting
me. . . .

NORA. But Dr. Rank. . . .

RANK. On no account must he. I won't have it. I'll lock the door on him.—
As soon as I'm absolutely certain of the worst, I'll send you my visiting
card with a black cross on it. You'll know then the final horrible dis-
integration has begun.

NORA. Really, you are being quite absurd today. And here was I hoping you
would be in a thoroughly good mood.

RANK. With death staring me in the face? Why should I suffer for another
man's sins? What justice is there in that? Somewhere, somehow, every
single family must be suffering some such cruel retribution. . . .

NORA [stopping up her ears]. Rubbish! Do cheer up!

RANK. Yes, really the whole thing's nothing but a huge joke. My poor innocent spine must do penance for my father's gay subaltern life.

NORA [by the table, left]. Wasn't he rather partial to asparagus and pâté de
foie gras?

RANK. Yes, he was. And truffles.

NORA. Truffles, yes. And oysters, too, I believe?

RANK. Yes, oysters, oysters, of course.

NORA. And all the port and champagne that goes with them. It does seem a
pity all these delicious things should attack the spine.

RANK. Especially when they attack a poor spine that never had any fun out
of them.

NORA. Yes, that is an awful pity.

RANK [looks at her sharply]. Hm. . . .

NORA [after a pause]. Why did you smile?

RANK. No, it was you who laughed.

NORA. No, it was you who smiled, Dr. Rank!

RANK [getting up]. You are a bigger rascal than I thought you were.

NORA. I feel full of mischief today.

RANK. So it seems.

NORA [putting her hands on his shoulders]. Dear, dear Dr. Rank, you mustn't
go and die on Torvald and me.

RANK. You wouldn't miss me for long. When you are gone, you are soon
forgotten.

NORA [looking at him anxiously]. Do you think so?

RANK. People make new contacts, then . . .

NORA. Who make new contacts?

RANK. Both you and Helmer will, when I'm gone. You yourself are already
well on the way, it seems to me. What was this Mrs. Linde doing here
last night?

NORA. Surely you aren't jealous of poor Kristine?

RANK. Yes, I am. She'll be my successor in this house. When I'm done for, I
can see this woman. . . .

NORA. Hush! Don't talk so loud, she's in there.

RANK. Today as well? There you are, you see!

NORA. Just to do some sewing on my dress. Good Lord, how absurd you are!
[She sits down on the sofa.] Now Dr. Rank, cheer up. You'll see tomorrow how nicely I can dance. And you can pretend I'm doing it just for

you—and for Torvald as well, of course. [*She takes various things out of the box.*] Come here, Dr. Rank. I want to show you something.

RANK [*sits*]. What is it?

NORA. Look!

RANK. Silk stockings.

NORA. Flesh-coloured! Aren't they lovely! Of course, it's dark here now, but tomorrow. . . . No, no, no, you can only look at the feet. Oh well, you might as well see a bit higher up, too.

RANK. Hm. . . .

NORA. Why are you looking so critical? Don't you think they'll fit?

RANK. I couldn't possibly offer any informed opinion about that.

NORA [*looks at him for a moment*]. Shame on you. [*Hits him lightly across the ear with the stockings.*] Take that! [*Folds them up again.*]

RANK. And what other delights am I to be allowed to see?

NORA. Not another thing. You are too naughty. [*She hums a little and searches among her things.*]

RANK [*after a short pause*]. Sitting here so intimately like this with you, I can't imagine . . . I simply cannot conceive what would have become of me if I had never come to this house.

NORA [*smiles*]. Yes, I rather think you do enjoy coming here.

RANK [*in a low voice, looking fixedly ahead*]. And the thought of having to leave it all . . .

NORA. Nonsense. You aren't leaving.

RANK [*in the same tone*]. . . . without being able to leave behind even the slightest token of gratitude, hardly a fleeting regret even . . . nothing but an empty place to be filled by the first person that comes along.

NORA. Supposing I were to ask you to . . . ? No . . .

RANK. What?

NORA. . . . to show me the extent of your friendship . . .

RANK. Yes?

NORA. I mean . . . to do me a tremendous favor. . . .

RANK. Would you really, for once, give me that pleasure?

NORA. You have no idea what it is.

RANK. All right, tell me.

NORA. No, really I can't, Dr. Rank. It's altogether too much to ask . . . because I need your advice and help as well. . . .

RANK. The more the better. I cannot imagine what you have in mind. But tell me anyway. You do trust me, don't you?

NORA. Yes, I trust you more than anybody I know. You are my best and my most faithful friend. I know that. So I will tell you. Well then, Dr. Rank, there is something you must help me to prevent. You know how deeply, how passionately Torvald is in love with me. He would never hesitate for a moment to sacrifice his life for my sake.

RANK [*bending towards her*]. Nora . . . do you think he's the only one who . . . ?

NORA [*stiffening slightly*]. Who . . . ?

RANK. Who wouldn't gladly give his life for your sake.

NORA [*sadly*]. Oh!

RANK. I swore to myself you would know before I went. I'll never have a better opportunity. Well, Nora! Now you know. And now you know too that you can confide in me as in nobody else.

NORA [*rises and speaks evenly and calmly*]. Let me past.

RANK [*makes way for her, but remains seated*]. Nora. . . .

NORA [*in the hall doorway*]. Helene, bring the lamp in, please. [*Walks over to the stove.*] Oh, my dear Dr. Rank, that really was rather horrid of you.

RANK [*getting up*]. That I have loved you every bit as much as anybody? Is *that* horrid?

NORA. No, but that you had to go and tell me. When it was all so unnecessary. . . .

RANK. What do you mean? Did you know . . . ?

[*The* MAID *comes in with the lamp, puts it on the table, and goes out again.*]

RANK. Nora . . . Mrs. Helmer . . . I'm asking you if you knew?

NORA. How can I tell whether I did or didn't. I simply can't tell you. . . . Oh, how could you be so clumsy, Dr. Rank! When everything was so nice.

RANK. Anyway, you know now that I'm at your service, body and soul. So you can speak out.

NORA [*looking at him*]. After this?

RANK. I beg you to tell me what it is.

NORA. I can tell you nothing now.

RANK. You must. You can't torment me like this. Give me a chance—I'll do anything that's humanly possible.

NORA. You can do nothing for me now. Actually, I don't really need any help. It's all just my imagination, really it is. Of course! [*She sits down in the rocking chair, looks at him and smiles.*] I must say, you are a nice one, Dr. Rank! Don't you feel ashamed of yourself, now the lamp's been brought in?

RANK. No, not exactly. But perhaps I ought to go—for good?

NORA. No, you mustn't do that. You must keep coming just as you've always done. You know very well Torvald would miss you terribly.

RANK. And *you*?

NORA. I always think it's tremendous fun having you.

RANK. That's exactly what gave me wrong ideas. I just can't puzzle you out. I often used to feel you'd just as soon be with me as with Helmer.

NORA. Well, you see, there are those people you love and those people you'd almost rather *be* with.

RANK. Yes, there's something in that.

NORA. When I was a girl at home, I loved Daddy best, of course. But I also thought it great fun if I could slip into the maids' room. For one thing they never preached at me. And they always talked about such exciting things.

RANK. Aha! So it's their role I've taken over!

NORA [*jumps up and crosses to him*]. Oh, my dear, kind Dr. Rank, I didn't mean that at all. But you can see how it's a bit with Torvald as it was with Daddy. . . .

[*The* MAID *comes in from the hall.*]

MAID. Please, ma'am . . . !

[*She whispers and hands her a card.*]

NORA [*glances at the card*]. Ah!

    [*She puts it in her pocket.*]

RANK. Anything wrong?

NORA. No, no, not at all. It's just . . . it's my new costume. . . .

RANK. How is that? There's your costume in there.

NORA. That one, yes. But this is another one. I've ordered it. Torvald mustn't hear about it. . . .

RANK. Ah, so that's the big secret, is it!

NORA. Yes, that's right. Just go in and see him, will you? He's in the study. Keep him occupied for the time being. . . .

RANK. Don't worry. He shan't escape me.

    [*He goes into* HELMER'*s study.*]

NORA [*to the* MAID]. Is he waiting in the kitchen?

MAID. Yes, he came up the back stairs. . . .

NORA. But didn't you tell him somebody was here?

MAID. Yes, but it was no good.

NORA. Won't he go?

MAID. No, he won't till he's seen you.

NORA. Let him in, then. But quietly. Helene, you mustn't tell anybody about this. It's a surprise for my husband.

MAID. I understand, ma'am. . . .

    [*She goes out.*]

NORA. Here it comes! What I've been dreading! No, no, it can't happen, it *can't* happen.

    [*She walks over and bolts* HELMER'*s door. The* MAID *opens the hall door for* KROGSTAD *and shuts it again behind him. He is wearing a fur coat, overshoes, and a fur cap.*]

NORA [*goes towards him*]. Keep your voice down, my husband is at home.

KROGSTAD. What if he is?

NORA. What do you want with me?

KROGSTAD. To find out something.

NORA. Hurry, then. What is it?

KROGSTAD. You know I've been given notice.

NORA. I couldn't prevent it, Mr. Krogstad, I did my utmost for you, but it was no use.

KROGSTAD. Has your husband so little affection for you? He knows what I can do to you, yet he dares. . . .

NORA. You don't imagine he knows about it!

KROGSTAD. No, I didn't imagine he did. It didn't seem a bit like my good friend Torvald Helmer to show that much courage. . . .

NORA. Mr. Krogstad, I must ask you to show some respect for my husband.

KROGSTAD. Oh, sure! All due respect! But since you are so anxious to keep this business quiet, Mrs. Helmer, I take it you now have a rather clearer idea of just what it is you've done, than you had yesterday.

NORA. Clearer than *you* could ever have given me.

KROGSTAD. Yes, being as I am such a rotten lawyer. . . .

NORA. What do *you* want with me?

KROGSTAD. I just wanted to see how things stood, Mrs. Helmer. I've been thinking about you all day. Even a mere money-lender, a hack journalist, a—well, even somebody like me has a bit of what you might call feeling.

NORA. Show it then. Think of my little children.

KROGSTAD. Did you or your husband think of mine? But what does it matter now? There was just one thing I wanted to say: you needn't take this business too seriously. I shan't start any proceedings, for the present.

NORA. Ah, I knew you wouldn't.

KROGSTAD. The whole thing can be arranged quite amicably. Nobody need know. Just the three of us.

NORA. My husband must never know.

KROGSTAD. How can you prevent it? Can you pay off the balance?

NORA. No, not immediately.

KROGSTAD. Perhaps you've some way of getting hold of the money in the next few days.

NORA. None I want to make use of.

KROGSTAD. Well, it wouldn't have been very much help to you if you had. Even if you stood there with the cash in your hand and to spare, you still wouldn't get your IOU back from me now.

NORA. What are you going to do with it?

KROGSTAD. Just keep it—have it in my possession. Nobody who isn't implicated need know about it. So if you are thinking of trying any desperate remedies . . .

NORA. Which I am. . . .

KROGSTAD. . . . if you happen to be thinking of running away . . .

NORA. Which I am!

KROGSTAD. . . . or anything worse . . .

NORA. How did you know?

KROGSTAD. . . . forget it!

NORA. How did you know I was thinking of *that?*

KROGSTAD. Most of us think of *that,* to begin with. I did, too; but I didn't have the courage. . . .

NORA [*tonelessly*]. I haven't either.

KROGSTAD [*relieved*]. So you haven't the courage either, eh?

NORA. No, I haven't! I haven't!

KROGSTAD. It would also be very stupid. There'd only be the first domestic storm to get over. . . . I've got a letter to your husband in my pocket here. . . .

NORA. And it's all in there?

KROGSTAD. In as tactful a way as possible.

NORA [*quickly*]. He must never read that letter. Tear it up. I'll find the money somehow.

KROGSTAD. Excuse me, Mrs. Helmer, but I've just told you. . . .

NORA. I'm not talking about the money I owe you. I want to know how much you are demanding from my husband, and I'll get the money.

KROGSTAD. I want no money from your husband.

NORA. What do you want?

KROGSTAD. I'll tell you. I want to get on my feet again, Mrs. Helmer; I want to get to the top. And your husband is going to help me. For the last

eighteen months I've gone straight; all that time it's been hard going; I
was content to work my way up, step by step. Now I'm being kicked
out, and I won't stand for being taken back again as an act of charity.
I'm going to get to the top, I tell you. I'm going back into that Bank—
with a better job. Your husband is going to create a new vacancy, just
for me. . . .

NORA. He'll never do that!

KROGSTAD. He will do it. I know him. He'll do it without so much as a whimper. And once I'm in there with him, you'll see what's what. In less
than a year I'll be his right-hand man. It'll be Nils Krogstad, not Torvald
Helmer, who'll be running that Bank.

NORA. You'll never live to see that day!

KROGSTAD. You mean you . . . ?

NORA. Now I have the courage.

KROGSTAD. You can't frighten me! A precious pampered little thing like
you. . . .

NORA. I'll show you! I'll show you!

KROGSTAD. Under the ice, maybe? Down in the cold, black water? Then being washed up in the spring, bloated, hairless, unrecognizable. . . .

NORA. You can't frighten me.

KROGSTAD. You can't frighten me, either. People don't do that sort of thing,
Mrs. Helmer. There wouldn't be any point to it, anyway, I'd still have
him right in my pocket.

NORA. Afterwards? When I'm no longer . . .

KROGSTAD. Aren't you forgetting that your reputation would then be entirely
in my hands? [NORA *stands looking at him, speechless.*] Well, I've
warned you. Don't do anything silly. When Helmer gets my letter, I expect to hear from him. And don't forget: it's him who is forcing me off
the straight and narrow again, your own husband! That's something I'll
never forgive him for. Goodbye, Mrs. Helmer.

[*He goes out through the hall.* NORA *crosses to the door, opens it
slightly, and listens.*]

NORA. He's going. He hasn't left the letter. No, no, that would be impossible! [*Opens the door further and further.*] What's he doing? He's
stopped outside. He's not going down the stairs. Has he changed his
mind? Is he . . . ? [*A letter falls into the letter box. Then* KROGSTAD'S
footsteps are heard receding as he walks downstairs. NORA *gives a stifled cry, runs across the room to the sofa table; pause.*] In the letter
box! [*She creeps stealthily across to the hall door.*] There it is! Torvald,
Torvald! It's hopeless now!

MRS. LINDE. [*comes into the room, left, carrying the costume*]. There, I
think that's everything. Shall we try it on?

NORA [*in a low, hoarse voice*]. Kristine, come here.

MRS. LINDE [*throws the dress down on the sofa*]. What's wrong with you?
You look upset.

NORA. Come here. Do you see that letter? There, look! Through the glass in
the letter box.

MRS. LINDE. Yes, yes, I can see it.

NORA. It's a letter from Krogstad.

MRS. LINDE. Nora! It was Krogstad who lent you the money!

NORA. Yes. And now Torvald will get to know everything.

MRS. LINDE. Believe me, Nora, it's best for you both.

NORA. But there's more to it than that. I forged a signature. . . .

MRS. LINDE. Heavens above!

NORA. Listen, I want to tell you something, Kristine, so you can be my witness.

MRS. LINDE. What do you mean, "witness"? What do you want me to . . . ?

NORA. If I should go mad . . . which might easily happen . . .

MRS. LINDE. Nora!

NORA. Or if anything happened to me . . . which meant I couldn't be here. . . .

MRS. LINDE. Nora, Nora! Are you out of your mind?

NORA. And if somebody else wanted to take it all upon himself, the whole blame, you understand. . . .

MRS. LINDE. Yes, yes. But what makes you think . . . ?

NORA. Then you must testify that it isn't true, Kristine. I'm not out of my mind; I'm quite sane now. And I tell you this: nobody else knew anything, I alone was responsible for the whole thing. Remember that!

MRS. LINDE. I will. But I don't understand a word of it.

NORA. Why should you? You see something miraculous is going to happen.

MRS. LINDE. Something miraculous?

NORA. Yes, a miracle. But something so terrible as well, Kristine—oh, it must never happen, not for anything.

MRS. LINDE. I'm going straight over to talk to Krogstad.

NORA. Don't go. He'll only do you harm.

MRS. LINDE. There was a time when he would have done anything for me.

NORA. Him!

MRS. LINDE. Where does he live?

NORA. How do I know . . . ? Wait a minute. [*She feels in her pocket.*] Here's his card. But the letter, the letter . . . !

HELMER [*from his study, knocking on the door*]. Nora!

NORA [*cries out in terror*]. What's that? What do you want?

HELMER. Don't be frightened. We're not coming in. You've locked the door. Are you trying on?

NORA. Yes, yes, I'm trying on. It looks so nice on me, Torvald.

MRS. LINDE [*who has read the card*]. He lives just round the corner.

NORA. It's no use. It's hopeless. The letter is there in the box.

MRS. LINDE. Your husband keeps the key?

NORA. Always.

MRS. LINDE. Krogstad must ask for his letter back unread, he must find some sort of excuse. . . .

NORA. But this is just the time that Torvald generally . . .

MRS. LINDE. Put him off! Go in and keep him busy. I'll be back as soon as I can.

[*She goes out hastily by the hall door.* NORA *walks over to* HELMER'S *door, opens it and peeps in.*]

NORA. Torvald!

HELMER [*in the study*]. Well, can a man get into his own living room again now? Come along, Rank, now we'll see . . . [*In the doorway.*] But what's this?

NORA. What, Torvald dear?

HELMER. Rank led me to expect some kind of marvelous transformation.

RANK [*in the doorway*]. That's what I thought too, but I must have been mistaken.

NORA. I'm not showing myself off to anybody before tomorrow.

HELMER. Nora dear, you look tired. You haven't been practising too hard?

NORA. No, I haven't practised at all yet.

HELMER. You'll have to, though.

NORA. Yes, I certainly must, Torvald. But I just can't get anywhere without your help: I've completely forgotten it.

HELMER. We'll soon polish it up.

NORA. Yes, do help me, Torvald. Promise? I'm so nervous. All those people. . . . You must devote yourself exclusively to me this evening. Pens away! Forget all about the office! Promise me, Torvald dear!

HELMER. I promise. This evening I am wholly and entirely at your service . . . helpless little thing that you are. Oh, but while I remember, I'll just look first . . .

[*He goes towards the hall door.*]

NORA. What do you want out there?

HELMER. Just want to see if there are any letters.

NORA. No, don't, Torvald!

HELMER. Why not?

NORA. Torvald, *please!* There aren't any.

HELMER. Just let me see.

[*He starts to go.* NORA, *at the piano, plays the opening bars of the tarantella.*]

HELMER [*at the door, stops*]. Aha!

NORA. I shan't be able to dance tomorrow if I don't rehearse it with you.

HELMER [*walks to her*]. Are you really so nervous, Nora dear?

NORA. Terribly nervous. Let me run through it now. There's still time before supper. Come and sit here and play for me, Torvald dear. Tell me what to do, keep me right—as you always do.

HELMER. Certainly, with pleasure, if that's what you want.

[*He sits at the piano.* NORA *snatches the tambourine out of the box, and also a long gaily coloured shawl which she drapes round herself, then with a bound she leaps forward.*]

NORA [*shouts*]. Now play for me! Now I'll dance!

[HELMER *plays and* NORA *dances;* DR. RANK *stands at the piano behind* HELMER *and looks on.*]

HELMER [*playing*]. Not so fast! Not so fast!

NORA. I can't help it.

HELMER. Not so wild, Nora!

NORA. This is how it has to be.

HELMER [*stops*]. No, no, that won't do at all.

NORA [*laughs and swings the tambourine*]. Didn't I tell you?

RANK. Let me play for her.

HELMER [*gets up*]. Yes, do. Then I'll be better able to tell her what to do.

[RANK *sits down at the piano and plays.* NORA *dances more and more wildly.* HELMER *stands by the stove giving her repeated directions as she dances; she does not seem to hear them. Her hair comes undone and falls about her shoulders; she pays no attention and goes on dancing.* MRS. LINDE *enters.*]

MRS. LINDE [*standing as though spellbound in the doorway*]. Ah . . . !

NORA [*dancing*]. See what fun we are having, Kristine.

HELMER. But my dear darling Nora, you are dancing as though your life depended on it.

NORA. It does.

HELMER. Stop, Rank! This is sheer madness. Stop, I say.

[RANK *stops playing and* NORA *comes to a sudden halt.*]

HELMER [*crosses to her*]. I would never have believed it. You have forgotten everything I ever taught you.

NORA [*throwing away the tambourine*]. There you are, you see.

HELMER. Well, some more instruction is certainly needed there.

NORA. Yes, you see how necessary it is. You must go on coaching me right up to the last minute. Promise me, Torvald?

HELMER. You can rely on me.

NORA. You mustn't think about anything else but me until after tomorrow . . . mustn't open any letters . . . mustn't touch the letter box.

HELMER. Ah, you are still frightened of what that man might . . .

NORA. Yes, yes, I am.

HELMER. I can see from your face there's already a letter there from him.

NORA. I don't know. I think so. But you mustn't read anything like that now. We don't want anything horrid coming between us until all this is over.

RANK [*softly to* HELMER]. I shouldn't cross her.

HELMER [*puts his arm round her*]. The child must have her way. But tomorrow night, when your dance is done. . . .

NORA. Then you are free.

MAID [*in the doorway, right*]. Dinner is served, madam.

NORA. We'll have champagne, Helene.

MAID. Very good, madam.

[*She goes.*]

HELMER. Aha! It's to be quite a banquet, eh?

NORA. With champagne flowing until dawn. [*Shouts.*] And some macaroons, Helene . . . lots of them, for once in a while.

HELMER [*seizing her hands*]. Now, now, not so wild and excitable! Let me see you being my own little singing bird again.

NORA. Oh yes, I will. And if you'll just go in . . . you, too, Dr. Rank. Kristine, you must help me to do my hair.

RANK [*softly, as they leave*]. There isn't anything . . . anything as it were, impending, is there?

HELMER. No, not at all, my dear fellow. It's nothing but these childish fears I was telling you about.

[*They go out to the right.*]

NORA. Well?

MRS. LINDE. He's left town.

NORA. I saw it in your face.

MRS. LINDE. He's coming back tomorrow evening. I left a note for him.

NORA. You shouldn't have done that. You must let things take their course. Because really it's a case for rejoicing, waiting like this for the miracle.

MRS. LINDE. What is it you are waiting for?

NORA. Oh, you wouldn't understand. Go and join the other two. I'll be there in a minute.

[MRS. LINDE *goes into the dining-room.* NORA *stands for a moment as though to collect herself, then looks at her watch.*]

NORA. Five. Seven hours to midnight. Then twenty-four hours till the next midnight. Then the tarantella will be over. Twenty-four and seven? Thirty-one hours to live.

HELMER [*in the doorway, right*]. What's happened to our little sky-lark?

NORA [*running towards him with open arms*]. Here she is!

Act III

The same room. The round table has been moved to the center of the room, and the chairs placed round it. A lamp is burning on the table. The door to the hall stands open. Dance music can be heard coming from the floor above. MRS. LINDE *is sitting by the table, idly turning over the pages of a book; she tries to read, but does not seem able to concentrate. Once or twice she listens, tensely, for a sound at the front door.*

MRS. LINDE [*looking at her watch*]. Still not here. There isn't much time left. I only hope he hasn't . . . [*She listens again.*] Ah, there he is. [*She goes out into the hall, and cautiously opens the front door. Soft footsteps can be heard on the stairs. She whispers.*] Come in. There's nobody here.

KROGSTAD [*in the doorway*]. I found a note from you at home. What does it all mean?

MRS. LINDE. I *had* to talk to you.

KROGSTAD. Oh? And did it have to be here, in this house?

MRS. LINDE. It wasn't possible over at my place, it hasn't a separate entrance. Come in. We are quite alone. The maid's asleep and the Helmers are at a party upstairs.

KROGSTAD [*comes into the room*]. Well, well! So the Helmers are out dancing tonight! Really?

MRS. LINDE. Yes, why not?

KROGSTAD. Why not indeed!

MRS. LINDE. Well then, Nils. Let's talk.

KROGSTAD. Have we two anything more to talk about?

MRS. LINDE. We have a great deal to talk about.

KROGSTAD. I shouldn't have thought so.

MRS. LINDE. That's because you never really understood me.

KROGSTAD. What else was there to understand, apart from the old, old story? A heartless woman throws a man over the moment something more profitable offers itself.

MRS. LINDE. Do you really think I'm so heartless? Do you think I found it easy to break it off?

KROGSTAD. Didn't you?

MRS. LINDE. You didn't really believe that?

KROGSTAD. If that wasn't the case, why did you write to me as you did?

MRS. LINDE. There was nothing else I could do. If I had to make the break, I felt in duty bound to destroy any feeling that you had for me.

KROGSTAD [*clenching his hands*]. So that's how it was. And all that . . . was for money!

MRS. LINDE. You mustn't forget I had a helpless mother and two young brothers. We couldn't wait for you, Nils. At that time you hadn't much immediate prospect of anything.

KROGSTAD. That may be. But you had no right to throw me over for somebody else.

MRS. LINDE. Well, I don't know. Many's the time I've asked myself whether I was justified.

KROGSTAD [*more quietly*]. When I lost you, it was just as if the ground had slipped away from under my feet. Look at me now: a broken man clinging to the wreck of his life.

MRS. LINDE. Help might be near.

KROGSTAD. It was near. Then you came along and got in the way.

MRS. LINDE. Quite without knowing, Nils. I only heard today it's you I'm supposed to be replacing at the Bank.

KROGSTAD. If you say so, I believe you. But now you do know, aren't you going to withdraw?

MRS. LINDE. No, that wouldn't benefit you in the slightest.

KROGSTAD. Benefit, benefit . . . ! I would do it just the same.

MRS. LINDE. I have learned to go carefully. Life and hard, bitter necessity have taught me that.

KROGSTAD. And life has taught me not to believe in pretty speeches.

MRS. LINDE. Then life has taught you a very sensible thing. But deeds are something you surely must believe in?

KROGSTAD. How do you mean?

MRS. LINDE. You said you were like a broken man clinging to the wreck of his life.

KROGSTAD. And I said it with good reason.

MRS. LINDE. And I am like a broken woman clinging to the wreck of her life. Nobody to care about, and nobody to care for.

KROGSTAD. It was your own choice.

MRS. LINDE. At the time there was no other choice.

KROGSTAD. Well, what of it?

MRS. LINDE. Nils, what about us two castaways joining forces?

KROGSTAD. What's that you say?

MRS. LINDE. Two of us on one wreck surely stand a better chance than each on his own.

KROGSTAD. Kristine!

MRS. LINDE. Why do you suppose I came to town?

KROGSTAD. You mean, you thought of me?

MRS. LINDE. Without work I couldn't live. All my life I have worked, for as long as I can remember; that has always been my one great joy. But now I'm completely alone in the world, and feeling horribly empty and forlorn. There's no pleasure in working only for yourself. Nils, give me somebody and something to work for.

KROGSTAD. I don't believe all this. It's only a woman's hysteria, wanting to be all magnanimous and self-sacrificing.

MRS. LINDE. Have you ever known me hysterical before?

KROGSTAD. Would you really do this? Tell me—do you know all about my past?

MRS. LINDE. Yes.

KROGSTAD. And you know what people think about me?

MRS. LINDE. Just now you hinted you thought you might have been a different person with me.

KROGSTAD. I'm convinced I would.

MRS. LINDE. Couldn't it still happen?

KROGSTAD. Kristine! You know what you are saying, don't you? Yes, you do. I can see you do. Have you really the courage . . . ?

MRS. LINDE. I need someone to mother, and your children need a mother. We two need each other. Nils, I have faith in what, deep down, you are. With you I can face anything.

KROGSTAD [*seizing her hands*]. Thank you, thank you, Kristine. And I'll soon have everybody looking up to me, or I'll know the reason why. Ah, but I was forgetting. . . .

MRS. LINDE. Hush! The tarantella! You must go!

KROGSTAD. Why? What is it?

MRS. LINDE. You hear that dance upstairs? When it's finished they'll be coming.

KROGSTAD. Yes, I'll go. It's too late to do anything. Of course, you know nothing about what steps I've taken against the Helmers.

MRS. LINDE. Yes, Nils, I do know.

KROGSTAD. Yet you still want to go on. . . .

MRS. LINDE. I know how far a man like you can be driven by despair.

KROGSTAD. Oh, if only I could undo what I've done!

MRS. LINDE. You still can. Your letter is still there in the box.

KROGSTAD. Are you sure?

MRS. LINDE. Quite sure. But . . .

KROGSTAD [*regards her searchingly*]. Is that how things are? You want to save your friend at any price? Tell me straight. Is that it?

MRS. LINDE. When you've sold yourself *once* for other people's sake, you don't do it again.

KROGSTAD. I shall demand my letter back.

MRS. LINDE. No, no.

KROGSTAD. Of course I will, I'll wait here till Helmer comes. I'll tell him he has to give me my letter back . . . that it's only about my notice . . . that he mustn't read it. . . .

MRS. LINDE. No, Nils, don't ask for it back.

KROGSTAD. But wasn't that the very reason you got me here?

MRS. LINDE. Yes, that was my first terrified reaction. But that was yesterday, and it's quite incredible the things I've witnessed in this house in the last twenty-four hours. Helmer must know everything. This unhappy secret must come out. Those two must have the whole thing out between them. All this secrecy and deception, it just can't go on.

KROGSTAD. Well, if you want to risk it . . . . But one thing I can do, and I'll
    do it at once. . . .

MRS. LINDE [*listening*]. Hurry! Go, go! The dance has stopped. We aren't safe
    a moment longer.

KROGSTAD. I'll wait for you downstairs.

MRS. LINDE. Yes, do. You must see me home.

KROGSTAD. I've never been so incredibly happy before.

[*He goes out by the front door. The door out into the hall remains
standing open.*]

MRS. LINDE [*tidies the room a little and gets her hat and coat ready*]. How
    things change! How things change! Somebody to work for . . . to live
    for. A home to bring happiness into. Just let me get down to it. . . . I
    wish they'd come. . . . [*Listens.*] Ah, there they are. . . . Get my
    things.

[*She takes her coat and hat. The voices of* HELMER *and* NORA *are heard
outside. A key is turned and* HELMER *pushes* NORA *almost forcibly into
the hall. She is dressed in the Italian costume, with a big black shawl
over it. He is in evening dress, and over it a black cloak, open.*]

NORA [*still in the doorway, reluctantly*]. No, no, not in here! I want to go
    back up again. I don't want to leave so early.

HELMER. But my dearest Nora . . .

NORA. Oh, please, Torvald, I beg you. . . . *Please,* just for another hour.

HELMER. Not another minute, Nora my sweet. You remember what we
    agreed. There now, come along in. You'll catch cold standing there.

[*He leads her, in spite of her resistance, gently but firmly into the
room.*]

MRS. LINDE. Good evening.

NORA. Kristine!

HELMER. Why, Mrs. Linde. You here so late?

MRS. LINDE. Yes. You must forgive me but I did so want to see Nora all
    dressed up.

NORA. Have you been sitting here waiting for me?

MRS. LINDE. Yes, I'm afraid I wasn't in time to catch you before you went up-
    stairs. And I felt I couldn't leave again without seeing you.

HELMER [*removing* NORA'S *shawl*]. Well take a good look at her. I think I can
    say she's worth looking at. Isn't she lovely, Mrs. Linde?

MRS. LINDE. Yes, I must say. . . .

HELMER. Isn't she quite extraordinarily lovely? That's what everybody at the
    party thought, too. But she's dreadfully stubborn . . . the sweet little
    thing! And what shall we do about that? Would you believe it, I nearly
    had to use force to get her away.

NORA. Oh Torvald, you'll be sorry you didn't let me stay, even for half an
    hour.

HELMER. You hear that, Mrs. Linde? She dances her tarantella, there's wild
    applause—which was well deserved, although the performance was
    perhaps rather realistic . . . I mean, rather more so than was strictly
    necessary from the artistic point of view. But anyway! The main thing is
    she was a success, a tremendous success. Was I supposed to let her stay

after that? Spoil the effect? No thank you! I took my lovely little Capri girl—my capricious little Capri girl, I might say—by the arm, whisked her once round the room, a curtsey all round, and then—as they say in novels—the beautiful vision vanished. An exit should always be effective, Mrs. Linde. But I just can't get Nora to see that. Phew! It's warm in here. [*He throws his cloak over a chair and opens the door to his study.*] What? It's dark. Oh yes, of course. Excuse me. . . .

[*He goes in and lights a few candles.*]

NORA [*quickly, in a breathless whisper*]. Well?

MRS. LINDE [*softly*]. I've spoken to him.

NORA. And . . . ?

MRS. LINDE. Nora . . . you must tell your husband everything.

NORA [*tonelessly*]. I knew it.

MRS. LINDE. You've got nothing to fear from Krogstad. But you must speak.

NORA. I won't.

MRS. LINDE. Then the letter will.

NORA. Thank you, Kristine. Now I know what's to be done. Hush . . . !

HELMER [*comes in again*]. Well, Mrs. Linde, have you finished admiring her?

MRS. LINDE. Yes. And now I must say good night.

HELMER. Oh, already? Is this yours, this knitting?

MRS. LINDE [*takes it*]. Yes, thank you. I nearly forgot it.

HELMER. So you knit, eh?

MRS. LINDE. Yes.

HELMER. You should embroider instead, you know.

MRS. LINDE. Oh? Why?

HELMER. So much prettier. Watch! You hold the embroidery like this in the left hand, and then you take the needle in the right hand, like this, and you describe a long, graceful curve. Isn't that right?

MRS. LINDE. Yes, I suppose so. . . .

HELMER. Whereas knitting on the other hand just can't help being ugly. Look! Arms pressed into the sides, the knitting needles going up and down—there's something Chinese about it. . . . Ah, that was marvelous champagne they served tonight.

MRS. LINDE. Well, good night, Nora! And stop being so stubborn.

HELMER. Well said, Mrs. Linde!

MRS. LINDE. Good night, Mr. Helmer.

HELMER [*accompanying her to the door*]. Good night, good night! You'll get home all right, I hope? I'd be only too pleased to. . . . But you haven't far to walk. Good night, good night! [*She goes; he shuts the door behind her and comes in again.*] There we are, got rid of her at last. She's a frightful bore, that woman.

NORA. Aren't you very tired, Torvald?

HELMER. Not in the least.

NORA. Not sleepy?

HELMER. Not at all. On the contrary, I feel extremely lively. What about you? Yes, you look quite tired and sleepy.

NORA. Yes, I'm very tired. I just want to fall straight off to sleep.

HELMER. There you are, you see! Wasn't I right in thinking we shouldn't stay any longer.

NORA. Oh, everything you do is right.

HELMER [*kissing her forehead*]. There's my little sky-lark talking common sense. Did you notice how gay Rank was this evening?

NORA. Oh, was he? I didn't get a chance to talk to him.

HELMER. I hardly did either. But it's a long time since I saw him in such a good mood. [*Looks at* NORA *for a moment or two, then comes nearer her.*] Ah, it's wonderful to be back in our own home again, and quite alone with you. How irresistibly lovely you are, Nora!

NORA. Don't look at me like that, Torvald!

HELMER. Can't I look at my most treasured possession? At all this loveliness that's mine and mine alone, completely and utterly mine.

NORA [*walks round to the other side of the table*]. You mustn't talk to me like that tonight.

HELMER [*following her*]. You still have the tarantella in your blood, I see. And that makes you even more desirable. Listen! The guests are beginning to leave now. [*Softly.*] Nora . . . soon the whole house will be silent.

NORA. I should hope so.

HELMER. Of course you do, don't you, Nora my darling? You know, whenever I'm out at a party with you . . . do you know why I never talk to you very much, why I always stand away from you and only steal a quick glance at you now and then . . . do you know why I do that? It's because I'm pretending we are secretly in love, secretly engaged and nobody suspects there is anything between us.

NORA. Yes, yes. I know your thoughts are always with me, of course.

HELMER. And when it's time to go, and I lay your shawl round those shapely, young shoulders, round the exquisite curve of your neck . . . I pretend that you are my young bride, that we are just leaving our wedding, that I am taking you to our new home for the first time . . . to be alone with you for the first time . . . quite alone with your young and trembling loveliness! All evening I've been longing for you, and nothing else. And as I watched you darting and swaying in the tarantella, my blood was on fire . . . I couldn't bear it any longer . . . and that's why I brought you down here with me so early. . . .

NORA. Go away, Torvald! Please leave me alone. I won't have it.

HELMER. What's this? It's just your little game isn't it, my little Nora. Won't! Won't! Am I not your husband . . . ?

[*There is a knock on the front door.*]

NORA [*startled*]. Listen . . . !

HELMER [*going towards the hall*]. Who's there?

RANK [*outside*]. It's me. Can I come in for a minute?

HELMER [*in a low voice, annoyed*]. Oh, what does he want now? [*Aloud*] Wait a moment. [*He walks across and opens the door.*] How nice of you to look in on your way out.

RANK. I fancied I heard your voice and I thought I would just look in. [*He takes a quick glance round.*] Ah yes, this dear, familiar old place! How cozy and comfortable you've got things here, you two.

HELMER. You seemed to be having a pretty good time upstairs yourself.

RANK. Capital! Why shouldn't I? Why not make the most of things in this world? At least as much as one can, and for as long as one can. The wine was excellent. . . .

HELMER. Especially the champagne.

RANK. You noticed that too, did you? It's incredible the amount I was able to put away.

NORA. Torvald also drank a lot of champagne this evening.

RANK. Oh?

NORA. Yes, and that always makes him quite merry.

RANK. Well, why shouldn't a man allow himself a jolly evening after a day well spent?

HELMER. Well spent? I'm afraid I can't exactly claim that.

RANK [*clapping him on the shoulder*]. But I can, you see!

NORA. Dr. Rank, am I right in thinking you carried out a certain laboratory test today?

RANK. Exactly.

HELMER. Look at our little Nora talking about laboratory tests!

NORA. And may I congratulate you on the result?

RANK. You may indeed.

NORA. So it was good?

RANK. The best possible, for both doctor and patient—certainty!

NORA [*quickly and searchingly*]. Certainty?

RANK. Absolute certainty. So why shouldn't I allow myself a jolly evening after that?

NORA. Quite right, Dr. Rank.

HELMER. I quite agree. As long as you don't suffer for it in the morning.

RANK. Well, you never get anything for nothing in this life.

NORA. Dr. Rank . . . you are very fond of masquerades, aren't you?

RANK. Yes, when there are plenty of amusing disguises. . . .

NORA. Tell me, what shall we two go as next time?

HELMER. There's frivolity for you . . . thinking about the next time already!

RANK. We two? I'll tell you. You must go as Lady Luck . . . .

HELMER. Yes, but how do you find a costume to suggest *that?*

RANK. Your wife could simply go in her everyday clothes. . . .

HELMER. That was nicely said. But don't you know what you would be?

RANK. Yes, my dear friend, I know exactly what I shall be.

HELMER. Well?

RANK. At the next masquerade, I shall be invisible.

HELMER. That's a funny idea!

RANK. There's a big black cloak . . . haven't you heard of the cloak of invisibility? That comes right down over you, and then nobody can see you.

HELMER [*suppressing a smile*]. Of course, that's right.

RANK. But I'm clean forgetting what I came for. Helmer, give me a cigar, one of the dark Havanas.

HELMER. With the greatest of pleasure.

[*He offers his case.*]

RANK [*takes one and cuts the end off*]. Thanks.

NORA [*strikes a match*]. Let me give you a light.

RANK. Thank you. [*She holds out the match and he lights his cigar.*] And now, goodbye!

HELMER. Goodbye, goodbye, my dear fellow!

NORA. Sleep well, Dr. Rank.

RANK. Thank you for that wish.

NORA. Wish me the same.

RANK. You? All right, if you want me to. . . . Sleep well. And thanks for the light.

[*He nods to them both, and goes.*]

HELMER [*subdued*]. He's had a lot to drink.

NORA [*absently*]. Very likely.

[HELMER *takes a bunch of keys out of his pocket and goes out into the hall.*]

NORA. Torvald . . . what do you want there?

HELMER. I must empty the letter box, it's quite full. There'll be no room for the papers in the morning. . . .

NORA. Are you going to work tonight?

HELMER. You know very well I'm not. Hello, what's this? Somebody's been at the lock.

NORA. At the lock?

HELMER. Yes, I'm sure of it. Why should that be? I'd hardly have thought the maids . . . ? Here's a broken hairpin. Nora, it's one of yours. . . .

NORA [*quickly*]. It must have been the children. . . .

HELMER. Then you'd better tell them not to. Ah . . . there . . . I've managed to get it open. [*He takes the things out and shouts into the kitchen.*] Helene! . . . Helene, put the light out in the hall. [*He comes into the room again with the letters in his hand and shuts the hall door.*] Look how it all mounts up. [*Runs through them.*] What's this?

NORA. The letter! Oh no, Torvald, no!

HELMER. Two visiting cards . . . from Dr. Rank.

NORA. From Dr. Rank?

HELMER [*looking at them*]. Dr. Rank, Medical Practitioner. They were on top. He must have put them in as he left.

NORA. Is there anything on them?

HELMER. There's a black cross above his name. Look. What an uncanny idea. It's just as if he were announcing his own death.

NORA. He is.

HELMER. What? What do you know about it? Has he said anything to you?

NORA. Yes. He said when these cards came, he would have taken his last leave of us. He was going to shut himself up and die.

HELMER. Poor fellow! Of course I knew we couldn't keep him with us very long. But so soon. . . . And hiding himself away like a wounded animal.

NORA. When it has to happen, it's best that it should happen without words. Don't you think so, Torvald?

HELMER [*walking up and down*]. He had grown so close to us. I don't think I can imagine him gone. His suffering and his loneliness seemed almost to provide a background of dark cloud to the sunshine of our lives. Well, perhaps it's all for the best. For him at any rate. [*Pauses.*] And maybe for us as well, Nora. Now there's just the two of us. [*Puts his arms round her.*] Oh, my darling wife, I can't hold you close enough. You know, Nora . . . many's the time I wish you were threatened by some terrible danger so I could risk everything, body and soul, for your sake.

NORA [*tears herself free and says firmly and decisively*]. Now you must read your letters, Torvald.

HELMER. No, no, not tonight. I want to be with you, my darling wife.

NORA. Knowing all the time your friend is dying . . . ?

HELMER. You are right. It's been a shock to both of us. This ugly thing has come between us . . . thoughts of death and decay. We must try to free ourselves from it. Until then . . . we shall go our separate ways.

NORA [*her arms round his neck*]. Torvald . . . good night! Good night!

HELMER [*kisses her forehead*]. Goodnight, my little singing bird. Sleep well, Nora, I'll just read through my letters.

[*He takes the letters into his room and shuts the door behind him.*]

NORA [*gropes around her, wild-eyed, seizes* HELMER'S *cloak, wraps it round herself, and whispers quickly, hoarsely, spasmodically*]. Never see him again. Never, never, never. [*Throws her shawl over her head.*] And never see the children again either. Never, never. Oh, that black icy water. Oh, that bottomless . . . ! If only it were all over! He's got it now. Now he's reading it. Oh no, no! Not yet! Torvald, goodbye . . . and my children. . . .

[*She rushes out in the direction of the hall; at the same moment* HELMER *flings open his door and stands there with an open letter in his hand.*]

HELMER. Nora!

NORA [*shrieks*]. Ah!

HELMER. What is this? Do you know what is in this letter?

NORA. Yes, I know. Let me go! Let me out!

HELMER [*holds her back*]. Where are you going?

NORA [*trying to tear herself free*]. You mustn't try to save me, Torvald!

HELMER [*reels back*]. True! Is it true what he writes? How dreadful! No, no, it can't possibly be true.

NORA. It *is* true. I loved you more than anything else in the world.

HELMER. Don't come to me with a lot of paltry excuses!

NORA [*taking a step towards him*]. Torvald . . . !

HELMER. Miserable woman . . . what is this you have done?

NORA. Let me go. I won't have you taking the blame for me. You mustn't take it on yourself.

HELMER. Stop play-acting! [*Locks the front door.*] You are staying here to give an account of yourself. Do you understand what you have done? Answer me! Do you understand?

NORA [*looking fixedly at him, her face hardening*]. Yes, now I'm really beginning to understand.

HELMER [*walking up and down*]. Oh, what a terrible awakening this is. All these eight years . . . this woman who was my pride and joy . . . a hypocrite, a liar, worse than that, a criminal! Oh, how utterly squalid it all is! Ugh! Ugh! [NORA *remains silent and looks fixedly at him.*] I should have realized something like this would happen. I should have seen it coming. All your father's irresponsible ways. . . . Quiet! All your father's irresponsible ways are coming out in you. No religion, no morals, no sense of duty. . . . Oh, this is my punishment for turning a blind eye to him. It was for your sake I did it, and this is what I get for it.

NORA. Yes, this.

HELMER. Now you have ruined my entire happiness, jeopardized my whole future. It's terrible to think of. Here I am, at the mercy of a thoroughly unscrupulous person; he can do whatever he likes with me, demand anything he wants, order me about just as he chooses . . . and I daren't even whimper. I'm done for, a miserable failure, and it's all the fault of a feather-brained woman!

NORA. When I've left this world behind, you will be free.

HELMER. Oh, stop pretending! Your father was just the same, always ready with fine phrases. What good would it do me if you left this world behind, as you put it? Not the slightest bit of good. He can still let it all come out, if he likes; and if he does, people might even suspect me of being an accomplice in these criminal acts of yours. They might even think I was the one behind it all, that it was I who pushed you into it! And it's you I have to thank for this . . . and when I've taken such good care of you, all our married life. Now do you understand what you have done to me?

NORA [*coldly and calmly*]. Yes.

HELMER. I just can't understand it, it's so incredible. But we must see about putting things right. Take that shawl off. Take it off, I tell you! I must see if I can't find some way or other of appeasing him. The thing must be hushed up at all costs. And as far as you and I are concerned, things must appear to go on exactly as before. But only in the eyes of the world, of course. In other words you'll go on living here; that's understood. But you will not be allowed to bring up the children, I can't trust you with them. . . . Oh, that I should have to say this to the woman I loved so dearly, the woman I still. . . . Well, that must be all over and done with. From now on, there can be no question of happiness. All we can do is save the bits and pieces from the wreck, preserve appearances. . . . [*The front door-bell rings.* HELMER *gives a start.*] What's that? So late? How terrible, supposing. . . . If he should . . . ? Hide, Nora! Say you are not well.

[NORA *stands motionless.* HELMER *walks across and opens the door into the hall.*]

MAID [*half dressed, in the hall*]. It's a note for Mrs. Helmer.

HELMER. Give it to me. [*He snatches the note and shuts the door.*] Yes, it's from him. You can't have it. I want to read it myself.

NORA. You read it then.

HELMER [*by the lamp*]. I hardly dare. Perhaps this is the end, for both of us. Well, I must know. [*He opens the note hurriedly, reads a few lines, looks at another enclosed sheet, and gives a cry of joy.*] Nora! [NORA *looks at him inquiringly.*] Nora! I must read it again. Yes, yes, it's true! I am saved! Nora, I am saved!

NORA. And me?

HELMER. You too, of course, we are both saved, you as well as me. Look, he's sent your IOU back. He sends his regrets and apologies for what he has done. . . . His luck has changed. . . . Oh, what does it matter what he says. We are saved, Nora! Nobody can do anything to you now. Oh, Nora, Nora . . . but let's get rid of this disgusting thing first. Let me see. . . . [*He glances at the IOU.*] No, I don't want to see it. I don't want it to be anything but a dream. [*He tears up the IOU and both let-*

ters, throws all the pieces into the stove and watches them burn.]
Well, that's the end of that. He said in his note you'd known since
Christmas Eve. . . . You must have had three terrible days of it, Nora.

NORA. These three days haven't been easy.

HELMER. The agonies you must have gone through! When the only way out
seemed to be. . . . No, let's forget the whole ghastly thing. We can rejoice and say: It's all over! It's all over! Listen to me, Nora! You don't
seem to understand: it's all over! Why this grim look on your face? Oh,
poor little Nora, of course I understand. You can't bring yourself to believe I've forgiven you. But I have, Nora, I swear it. I forgive you everything. I know you did what you did because you loved me.

NORA. That's true.

HELMER. You loved me as a wife should love her husband. It was simply that
you didn't have the experience to judge what was the best way of going about things. But do you think I love you any the less for that; just
because you don't know how to act on your own responsibility? No,
no, you just lean on me, I shall give you all the advice and guidance you
need. I wouldn't be a proper man if I didn't find a woman doubly attractive for being so obviously helpless. You mustn't dwell on the harsh
things I said in that first moment of horror, when I thought everything
was going to come crashing down about my ears. I have forgiven you,
Nora, I swear it! I have forgiven you!

NORA. Thank you for your forgiveness.

[*She goes out through the door, right.*]

HELMER. No, don't go! [*He looks through the doorway.*] What are you doing
in the spare room?

NORA. Taking off this fancy dress.

HELMER [*standing at the open door*]. Yes, do. You try and get some rest, and
set your mind at peace again, my frightened little songbird. Have a
good long sleep; you know you are safe and sound under my wing.
[*Walks up and down near the door.*] What a nice, cozy little home we
have here, Nora! Here you can find refuge. Here I shall hold you like a
hunted dove I have rescued unscathed from the cruel talons of the
hawk, and calm your poor beating heart. And that will come, gradually,
Nora, believe me. Tomorrow you'll see everything quite differently.
Soon everything will be just as it was before. You won't need me to
keep on telling you I've forgiven you; you'll feel convinced of it in your
own heart. You don't really imagine me ever thinking of turning you
out, or even of reproaching you? Oh, a real man isn't made that way,
you know, Nora. For a man, there's something indescribably moving
and very satisfying in knowing that he has forgiven his wife—forgiven
her, completely and genuinely, from the depths of his heart. It's as
though it made her his property in a double sense: he has, as it were,
given her a new life, and she becomes in a way both his wife and at the
same time his child. That is how you will seem to me after today, helpless, perplexed little thing that you are. Don't you worry your pretty
little head about anything, Nora. Just you be frank with me, and I'll take
all the decisions for you. . . . What's this? Not in bed? You've changed
your things?

NORA [*in her everyday dress*]. Yes, Torvald, I've changed.

HELMER. What for? It's late.

NORA. I shan't sleep tonight.

HELMER. But my dear Nora. . . .

NORA [*looks at her watch*]. It's not so terribly late. Sit down, Torvald. We two have a lot to talk about.

[*She sits down at one side of the table.*]

HELMER. Nora, what is all this? Why so grim?

NORA. Sit down. It'll take some time. I have a lot to say to you.

HELMER [*sits down at the table opposite her*]. You frighten me, Nora. I don't understand you.

NORA. Exactly. You don't understand me. And I have never understood you, either—until tonight. No, don't interrupt. I just want you to listen to what I have to say. We are going to have things out, Torvald.

HELMER. What do you mean?

NORA. Isn't there anything that strikes you about the way we two are sitting here?

HELMER. What's that?

NORA. We have now been married eight years. Hasn't it struck you this is the first time you and I, man and wife, have had a serious talk together?

HELMER. Depends what you mean by "serious."

NORA. Eight whole years—no, more, ever since we first knew each other— and never have we exchanged one serious word about serious things.

HELMER. What did you want me to do? Get you involved in worries that you couldn't possibly help me to bear?

NORA. I'm not talking about worries. I say we've never once sat down to- gether and seriously tried to get to the bottom of anything.

HELMER. But, my dear Nora, would that have been a thing for you?

NORA. That's just it. You have never understood me . . . I've been greatly wronged, Torvald. First by my father, and then by you.

HELMER. What! Us two! The two people who loved you more than anybody?

NORA [*shakes her head*]. You two never loved me. You only thought how nice it was to be in love with me.

HELMER. But, Nora, what's this you are saying?

NORA. It's right, you know, Torvald. At home, Daddy used to tell me what he thought, then I thought the same. And if I thought differently, I kept quiet about it, because he wouldn't have liked it. He used to call me his baby doll, and he played with me as I used to play with my dolls. Then I came to live in your house. . . .

HELMER. What way is that to talk about our marriage?

NORA [*imperturbably*]. What I mean is: I passed out of Daddy's hands into yours. You arranged everything to your tastes, and I acquired the same tastes. Or I pretended to . . . I don't really know . . . I think it was a bit of both, sometimes one thing and sometimes the other. When I look back, it seems to me I have been living here like a beggar, from hand to mouth. I lived by doing tricks for you, Torvald. But that's the way you wanted it. You and Daddy did me a great wrong. It's your fault that I've never made anything of my life.

HELMER. Nora, how unreasonable . . . how ungrateful you are! Haven't you been happy here?

NORA. No, never. I thought I was, but I wasn't really.

HELMER. Not . . . not happy!

NORA. No, just gay. And you've always been so kind to me. But our house has never been anything but a playroom. I have been your doll wife, just as at home I was Daddy's doll child. And the children in turn have been my dolls. I thought it was fun when you came and played with me, just as they thought it was fun when I went and played with them. That's been our marriage, Torvald.

HELMER. There is some truth in what you say, exaggerated and hysterical though it is. But from now on it will be different. Playtime is over; now comes the time for lessons.

NORA. Whose lessons? Mine or the children's?

HELMER. Both yours and the children's, my dear Nora.

NORA. Ah, Torvald, you are not the man to teach me to be a good wife for you.

HELMER. How can you say that?

NORA. And what sort of qualifications have I to teach the children?

HELMER. Nora!

NORA. Didn't you say yourself, a minute or two ago, that you couldn't trust me with that job?

HELMER. In the heat of the moment! You shouldn't pay any attention to that.

NORA. On the contrary, you were quite right. I'm not up to it. There's another problem needs solving first. I must take steps to educate myself. You are not the man to help me there. That's something I must do on my own. That's why I'm leaving you.

HELMER [*jumps up*]. What did you say?

NORA. If I'm ever to reach any understanding of myself and the things around me, I must learn to stand alone. That's why I can't stay here with you any longer.

HELMER. Nora! Nora!

NORA. I'm leaving here at once. I dare say Kristine will put me up for tonight. . . .

HELMER. You are out of your mind! I won't let you! I forbid you!

NORA. It's no use forbidding me anything now. I'm taking with me my own personal belongings. I don't want anything of yours, either now or later.

HELMER. This is madness!

NORA. Tomorrow I'm going home—to what used to be my home, I mean. It will be easier for me to find something to do there.

HELMER. Oh, you blind, inexperienced . . .

NORA. I must set about *getting* experience, Torvald.

HELMER. And leave your home, your husband and your children? Don't you care what people will say?

NORA. That's no concern of mine. All I know is that this is necessary for me.

HELMER. This is outrageous! You are betraying your most sacred duty.

NORA. And what do you consider to be my most sacred duty?

HELMER. Does it take me to tell you that? Isn't it your duty to your husband and your children?

NORA. I have another duty equally sacred.

HELMER. You have not. What duty might *that* be?

NORA. My duty to myself.

HELMER. First and foremost, you are a wife and mother.

NORA. That I don't believe any more. I believe that first and foremost I am an individual, just as much as you are—or at least I'm going to try to be. I know most people agree with you, Torvald, and that's also what it says in books. But I'm not content any more with what most people say, or with what it says in books. I have to think things out for myself, and get things clear.

HELMER. Surely you are clear about your position in your own home? Haven't you an infallible guide in questions like these? Haven't you your religion?

NORA. Oh, Torvald, I don't really know what religion is.

HELMER. What do you say!

NORA. All I know is what Pastor Hansen said when I was confirmed. He said religion was this, that and the other. When I'm away from all this and on my own, I'll go into that, too. I want to find out whether what Pastor Hansen told me was right—or at least whether it's right for *me*.

HELMER. This is incredible talk from a young woman! But if religion cannot keep you on the right path, let me at least stir your conscience. I suppose you do have some moral sense? Or tell me—perhaps you don't?

NORA. Well, Torvald, that's not easy to say. I simply don't know. I'm really very confused about such things. All I know is my ideas about such things are very different from yours. I've also learnt that the law is different from what I thought; but I simply can't get it into my head that that particular law is right. Apparently a woman has no right to spare her old father on his deathbed, or to save her husband's life, even. I just don't believe it.

HELMER. You are talking like a child. You understand nothing about the society you live in.

NORA. No, I don't. But I shall go into that too. I must try to discover who is right, society or me.

HELMER. You are ill, Nora. You are delirious. I'm half inclined to think you are out of your mind.

NORA. Never have I felt so calm and collected as I do tonight.

HELMER. Calm and collected enough to leave your husband and children?

NORA. Yes.

HELMER. Then only one explanation is possible.

NORA. And that is?

HELMER. You don't love me any more.

NORA. Exactly.

HELMER. Nora! Can you say that!

NORA. I'm desperately sorry, Torvald. Because you have always been so kind to me. But I can't help it. I don't love you any more.

HELMER [*struggling to keep his composure*]. Is that also a "calm and collected" decision you've made?

NORA. Yes, absolutely calm and collected. That's why I don't want to stay here.

HELMER. And can you also account for how I forfeited your love?

NORA. Yes, very easily. It was tonight, when the miracle didn't happen. It was then I realized you weren't the man I thought you were.

HELMER. Explain yourself more clearly. I don't understand.

NORA. For eight years I have been patiently waiting. Because, heavens, I knew miracles didn't happen every day. Then this devastating business started, and I became absolutely convinced the miracle *would* happen. All the time Krogstad's letter lay there, it never so much as crossed my mind that you would ever submit to that man's conditions. I was absolutely convinced you would say to him: Tell the whole wide world if you like. And when that was done . . .

HELMER. Yes, then what? After I had exposed my own wife to dishonor and shame . . . !

NORA. When that was done, I was absolutely convinced you would come forward and take everything on yourself, and say: I am the guilty one.

HELMER. Nora!

NORA. You mean I'd never let you make such a sacrifice for my sake? Of course not. But what would my story have counted for against yours?— That was the miracle I went in hope and dread of. It was to prevent it that I was ready to end my life.

HELMER. I would gladly toil day and night for you, Nora, enduring all manner of sorrow and distress. But nobody sacrifices his *honor* for the one he loves.

NORA. Hundreds and thousands of women have.

HELMER. Oh, you think and talk like a stupid child.

NORA. All right. But you neither think nor talk like the man I would want to share my life with. When you had got over your fright—and you weren't concerned about me but only about what might happen to you—and when all danger was past, you acted as though nothing had happened. I was your little skylark again, your little doll, exactly as before; except you would have to protect it twice as carefully as before, now that it had shown itself to be so weak and fragile. [*Rises.*] Torvald, that was the moment I realized that for eight years I'd been living with a stranger, and had borne him three children. . . . Oh, I can't bear to think about it! I could tear myself to shreds.

HELMER [*sadly*]. I see. I see. There is a tremendous gulf dividing us. But, Nora, is there no way we might bridge it?

NORA. As I am now, I am no wife for you.

HELMER. I still have it in me to change.

NORA. Perhaps . . . if you have your doll taken away.

HELMER. And be separated from you! No, no, Nora, the very thought of it is inconceivable.

NORA [*goes into the room, right*]. All the more reason why it must be done.

[*She comes back with her outdoor things and a small traveling bag, which she puts on the chair beside the table.*]

HELMER. Nora, Nora, not now! Wait till the morning.

NORA [*putting on her coat*]. I can't spend the night in a strange man's room.

HELMER. Couldn't we go on living here like brother and sister . . . ?

NORA [*tying on her hat*]. You know very well that wouldn't last. [*She draws the shawl round her.*] Goodbye, Torvald. I don't want to see the children. I know they are in better hands than mine. As I am now, I can never be anything to them.

HELMER. But some day, Nora, some day . . . ?

NORA. How should I know? I've no idea what I might turn out to be.

HELMER. But you are my wife, whatever you are.

NORA. Listen, Torvald, from what I've heard, when a wife leaves her husband's house as I am doing now, he is absolved by law of all responsibility for her. I can at any rate free you from all responsibility. You must not feel in any way bound, any more than I shall. There must be full freedom on both sides. Look, here's your ring back. Give me mine.

HELMER. That too?

NORA. That too.

HELMER. There it is.

NORA. Well, that's the end of that. I'll put the keys down here. The maids know where everything is in the house—better than I do, in fact. Kristine will come in the morning after I've left to pack up the few things I brought with me from home. I want them sent on.

HELMER. The end! Nora, will you never think of me?

NORA. I dare say I'll often think about you and the children and this house.

HELMER. May I write to you, Nora?

NORA. No, never. I won't let you.

HELMER. But surely I can send you . . .

NORA. Nothing, nothing.

HELMER. Can't I help you if ever you need it?

NORA. I said no. I don't accept things from strangers.

HELMER. Nora, can I never be anything more to you than a stranger?

NORA [*takes her bag*]. Ah, Torvald, only by a miracle of miracles . . .

HELMER. Name it, this miracle of miracles!

NORA. Both you and I would have to change to the point where. . . . Oh, Torvald, I don't believe in miracles any more.

HELMER. But I *will* believe. Name it! Change to the point where . . . ?

NORA. Where we could make a real marriage of our lives together. Goodbye!

[*She goes out through the hall door.*]

HELMER [*sinks down on a chair near the door, and covers his face with his hands*]. Nora! Nora! [*He rises and looks round.*] Empty! She's gone! [*With sudden hope.*] The miracle of miracles . . . ?

[*The heavy sound of a door being slammed is heard from below.*]

▨ TOPICS FOR CRITICAL THINKING AND WRITING

1. Near the beginning of the play, how does Mrs. Linde's presence help to define Nora's character? How does Nora's response to Krogstad's entrance tell us something about Nora?

2. What does Dr. Rank contribute to the play? If he were eliminated, what would be lost?

3. In view of the fact that the last act several times seems to be moving toward a "happy ending" (e.g., Krogstad promises to recall his letter), what is wrong with the alternate ending (see page 1530) that Ibsen reluctantly provided for a German production?

4. Can it be argued that although at the end Nora goes out to achieve self-realization, her abandonment of her children—especially to Torvald's loathsome conventional morality—is a crime? (By the way, exactly why does Nora leave the children? She seems to imply, in some passages, that because she forged a signature she is unfit to bring them up. But do you agree with her?)

5. Michael Meyer, in his splendid biography *Henrik Ibsen,* says that the play is not so much about women's rights as about "the need of every individual to find out the kind of person he or she really is, and to strive to become that person." What evidence can you offer to support or refute this interpretation?

6. In *The Quintessence of Ibsenism* Bernard Shaw says that Ibsen, reacting against a common theatrical preference for strange situations, "saw that . . . the more familiar the situation, the more interesting the play. Shakespear[e] had put ourselves on the stage but not our situations. Our uncles seldom murder our fathers and . . . marry our mothers. . . . Ibsen . . . gives us not only ourselves, but ourselves in our own situations. The things that happen to his stage figures are things that happen to us. One consequence is that his plays are much more important to us than Shakespear[e]'s. Another is that they are capable both of hurting us cruelly and of filling us with excited hopes of escape from idealistic tyrannies, and with visions of intenser life in the future." How much of this do you believe? Focus on details in the play to explain your response.

CONTEXTS FOR *A DOLL'S HOUSE*

HENRIK IBSEN

Notes for the Tragedy of Modern Times

The University Library, Oslo, has the following preliminary notes for A Doll's House.

Rome 19.10.78

There are two kinds of moral law, two kinds of conscience, one in man and a completely different one in woman. They do not understand each other; but in matters of practical living the woman is judged by man's law, as if she were not a woman but a man.

The wife in the play ends up quite bewildered and not knowing right from wrong; her natural instincts on the one side and her faith in authority on the other leave her completely confused.

A woman cannot be herself in contemporary society, it is an exclusively male society with laws drafted by men, and with counsel and judges who judge feminine conduct from the male point of view.

She has committed a crime, and she is proud of it; because she did it for love of her husband and to save his life. But the husband, with his conventional views of honour, stands on the side of the law and looks at the affair with male eyes.

Mental conflict. Depressed and confused by her faith in authority, she loses faith in her moral right and ability to bring up her children. Bitterness. A mother in contemporary society, just as certain insects go away and die when she has done her duty in the propagation of the race. Love of life, of home and husband and children and family. Now and then, woman-like, she shrugs off her thoughts. Sudden return of dread and terror. Everything must be borne alone. The catastrophe approaches, ineluctably, inevitably. Despair, resistance, defeat.

[*The following note was later added in the margin:*]

Krogstad has done some dishonest business, and thus made a bit of money; but his prosperity does not help him, he cannot recover his honour.

Adaptation of A Doll's House for a German Production

Because Norwegian works were not copyrighted in Germany, German theaters could stage and freely adapt Ibsen's works without his consent. When he heard that a German director was going to change the ending to a happy one, Ibsen decided that he had better do the adaptation himself, though he characterized it as "a barbaric outrage" against the play.

NORA. . . . Where we could make a real marriage out of our lives together. Goodbye. (*Begins to go.*)

HELMER. Go then! (*Seizes her arm.*) But first you shall see your children for the last time!

NORA. Let me go! I will not see them! I cannot!

HELMER (*draws her over to the door, left*). You shall see them. (*Opens the door and says softly.*) Look, there they are asleep, peaceful and carefree. Tomorrow, when they wake up and call for their mother, they will be—motherless.

NORA (*trembling*). Motherless . . . !

HELMER. As you once were.

NORA. Motherless! (*Struggles with herself, lets her traveling-bag fall, and says.*) Oh, this is a sin against myself, but I cannot leave them. (*Half sinks down by the door.*)

HELMER (*joyfully, but softly*). Nora!

THE CURTAIN FALLS.

Speech at the Banquet of the Norwegian League for Women's Rights

A month after the official birthday celebrations were over, Ibsen and his wife were invited to a banquet in his honor given by the leading Norwegian feminist society.

Christiania, May 26, 1898

I am not a member of the Women's Rights League. Whatever I have written has been without any conscious thought of making propaganda. I have been more the poet and less the social philosopher than people generally seem inclined to believe. I thank you for the toast, but must disclaim the honor of having consciously worked for the women's rights movement. I am not even quite clear as to just what this women's rights movement really is. To me it has seemed a problem of mankind in general. And if you read my books carefully you will understand this. True enough, it is desirable to solve the woman problem, along with all the others; but that has not been the whole purpose. My task has been the *description of humanity*. To be sure, whenever such a description is felt to be reasonably true, the reader will read his own feelings and sentiments into the work of the poet. These are then attributed to the poet; but incorrectly so. Every reader remolds the work beautifully and neatly, each according to his own personality. Not only those who write but also those who read are poets. They are collaborators. They are often more poetical than the poet himself.

CLARE BOOTHE LUCE

Clare Boothe Luce (1903-1987) gained distinction in two fields, playwrighting and politics. After working on two magazines, Vogue *and* Vanity Fair *(she was managing editor of* Vanity Fair *from 1933 to 1934), she married Henry Luce, the founder of* Fortune, Time, Life, *and* Sports Illustrated, *and began a career as a playwright. Her first play,* Abide with Me *(1935), was unsuccessful, but she soon achieved critical acclaim and financial success with* The Women *(1936) and* Kiss the Boys Good-bye *(1938), both of which are social satires, and a comedy-mystery,* Margin for Error *(1939). She then embarked on a second career, serving two terms in Congress as a representative from Connecticut (1943-1947) and later serving as ambassador to Italy (1953-1956). Ill health compelled her to resign the ambassadorship, but in 1959 she was well enough to be appointed ambassador to Brazil—although because of a controversy she resigned the post in the same year, without having served.*

Slam the Door Softly—the title evokes what is probably the most famous stage direction in drama, "The street door is slammed shut downstairs," in Ibsen's A Doll's House—*was first published in* Life *magazine, in 1970, where it was titled* A Doll's House (with Apologies to Henrik Ibsen), *but the author later retitled it, calling it* Slam the Door Softly. *The play, set in the year it was published, was preceded by a note that said:*

> *Most of Clare Boothe Luce's life has been that of a woman doing a man's job. But even before she became a successful magazine editor, a successful playwright, war correspondent, congresswoman and ambassador, she was an active crusader for the feminist cause. In 1923, at the age of 20, she worked as a secretary at the Washington headquarters of the National Women's party and toured the country on behalf of an equal rights for women campaign. . . . In the following play she brings up to date Henrik Ibsen's famous 1879 drama about a woman who rebelled against her role as a subservient wife.*

Slam the Door Softly   [1970]

*The scene is the Thaw Walds' cheerfully furnished middle-class living
room in New York's suburbia. There are a front door and hall, a door to
the kitchen area, and a staircase to the bedroom floor. Two easy chairs
and two low hassocks with toys on them, grouped around a television,
indicate a family of four. Drinks are on a bar cart at one end of a comfortable sofa, and an end table at the other. There are slightly more than
the average number of bookshelves. The lamps are on, but as we don't
hear the children, we know it is the Parents' Hour.*

As the curtain rises, THAW WALD, *a good-looking fellow, about 35, is sitting in one of the easy chairs, smoking and watching TV. His back is to
the sofa and staircase, so he does not see his wife coming down the stairs.*
NORA WALD *is a rather pretty woman of about 32. She is carrying a suitcase, handbag, and an armful of books.*

THAW *switches channels, and lands in the middle of a panel show. During the TV dialogue that follows* NORA *somewhat furtively deposits her suitcase in the hall, takes her coat out of the hall closet, and comes back to the
sofa carrying coat, purse, and books. She lays her coat on the sofa, and the
books on the end table. The books are full of little paper slips—bookmark-
ers. All of the above actions are unobserved by* THAW. *We cannot see the TV
screen, but we hear the voices of four women, all talking excitedly at once.*

THAW (*to the screen and the world in general*). God, these Liberation gals!
    Still at it.
MALE MODERATOR'S VOICE (*full of paternal patience wearing a bit thin*).
    Ladies! Lay-deez! Can't we switch now from the question of the sex-
    typing of jobs to what the Women's Liberation Movement thinks
    about—
OLDER WOMAN'S VOICE. May I finish! In the Soviet Union 83% of the dentists,
    75% of the doctors and 37% of the lawyers are women. In Poland and
    Denmark—
MODERATOR. I think you have already amply made your point, Mrs. Epstein—
    anything men can do, women can do better!
YOUNG WOMAN'S VOICE (*angrily*). That was *not* her point—and you know it!
    What she said was, there are very few professional jobs men are doing
    that women couldn't do, if only—
THAW. Well, for God's sake then, shaddup, and go do 'em—
BLACK WOMAN'S VOICE. What she's been saying, what we've all been saying,
    and you men just don't want to hear us, is—things are the same for
    women as they are for us black people. We try to get up, you just sit
    down on us, like a big elephant sits down on a bunch of poor little mice.
MODERATOR. Well, sometimes moderators have to play the elephant, and sit
    down on one subject in order to develop another. As I was about to
    say, ladies, there *is one thing* a woman can do, no man can do—(*in his
    best holy-night-all-is-bright voice*) give birth to a *child.*
YOUNG WOMAN'S VOICE. So what else is new?
THAW. One gets you ten, she's a Lesbo—
MODERATOR (*forcefully*). And *that* brings us to marriage! Now, if *I* may be
    permitted to get in just *one* statistic, edgewise: two-thirds of all adult
    American females are married women. And now! (*At last he's got them*

where he wants them.) What *is* the Women's Lib view of Woman's No. 1 job—Occupation Housewife?

THAW. Ha! That's the one none of 'em can handle—

YOUNG WOMAN'S VOICE (*loud and clear*). Marriage, as an institution, is as thoroughly corrupt as prostitution. It is, in fact, legalized and romanticized prostitution. A woman who marries is selling her sexual services and domestic services for permanent bed and board—

BLACK WOMAN'S VOICE. There's no human being a man can buy anymore—except a woman—

THAW (*snapping off the TV*). Crr-ap! Boy, what a bunch of battle-axes! (*He goes back to studying his TV listings.*)

NORA (*raising her voice*). Thaw! I'd like to say something about what they just said about marriage—

THAW (*in a warning voice*). Uh-uh, Nora! We both agreed months ago, you'd lay off the feminist bit, if I'd lay off watching Saturday football—

NORA. And do something with the children . . . But Thaw, there's something maybe, I ought to try to tell you myself—

(THAW *is not listening.* NORA *makes a "what's the use" gesture, then opens her purse, takes out three envelopes, carefully inserts two of them under the covers of the top two books.*)

THAW. Like to hear Senators Smithers, Smethers and Smothers on "How Fast Can We Get Out of Vietnam?"

NORA (*cool mockery*). That bunch of pot-bellied, bald-headed old goats! Not one of them could get a woman—well, yes, maybe for two dollars.

THAW. You don't look at Senators, Nora. You listen to them.

NORA (*nodding*). Women are only to look at. Men are to listen to. Got it.

(THAW *snaps off the TV. He is now neither looking at her nor listening to her, as he methodically turns pages of the magazine he has picked up.*)

THAW. Finished reading to the kids?

NORA. I haven't been reading to the children. I've been reading to myself—and talking to myself—for a long time now.

THAW. That's good. (*She passes him, carrying the third envelope, and goes into kitchen.*)

THAW (*unenthusiastically*). Want some help with the dishes?

NORA'S VOICE. I'm not doing the dishes.

THAW (*enthusiastically*). Say, Nora, this is quite an ad we've got in *Life* for Stove Mountain Life Insurance.

NORA'S VOICE. Yes, I saw it. Great. (*She comes back and goes to sofa.*)

THAW. It's the kind of ad that grabs you. This sad-faced, nice-looking woman of 50, sitting on a bench with a lot of discouraged old biddies, in an employment agency. Great caption—(*reading*)

NORA and THAW (*together*). "Could this happen to *your* wife?"

NORA. I'll let you know the answer very shortly. (*A pause.*) You really don't hear me anymore, do you? (*He really doesn't. She buttons herself into her coat, pulls on her gloves.*) Well, there are enough groceries for a week. All the telephone numbers you'll need and menus for the children are in the envelope on the spindle. A girl will come in to take care of them after school—until your mother gets here.

THAW. Uh-huh . . .

NORA (*looks around sadly*). Well, good-bye dear little doll house. Good-bye dear husband. You've had the best ten years of my life.

(*She goes to the staircase, blows two deep kisses upstairs, just as* THAW *glances up briefly at her, but returns automatically to his magazine.* NORA *picks up suitcase, opens the door, goes out, closing it quietly.*)

THAW (*like a man suddenly snapping out of a hypnotic trance*). Nora? Nora? NOR-RA! (*He is out of the door in two seconds.*)

THAW'S and NORA'S VOICES. Nora, where're you going?—I'll miss my train—I don't understand—it's all in my letter—let me go!—You come back—

(*They return. He is pulling her by the arm. He yanks the suitcase away from her, drops it in the hall.*)

NORA. Ouch! You're hurting me!

THAW. Now what is this all about? (*He shoves her into the room, then stands between her and door.*) Why the hell . . . What're you sneaking out of the house . . . What's that suitcase for?

NORA. I wasn't sneaking. I told you. But you weren't listening.

THAW. I was listening . . . it just didn't register. You said you were reading to yourself. Then you started yakking about the kids and the groceries and the doll house mother sent . . . (*flabbergasted.*) Good-bye?! What the hell do you mean, *good-bye?!*

NORA. Just that. I'm leaving you. (*Pointing to books.*) My letter will explain everything—

THAW. Have you blown your mind?

NORA. Thaw, I've got to scoot, or I'll miss the eight-o-nine.

THAW. You'll miss it. (*He backs her to the sofa, pushes her onto it, goes and slams the door and strides back.*) Now, my girl, explain all this.

NORA. That's easy. Muscle. The heavier musculature of the male is a secondary sexual characteristic. Although that's not certain. It could be just the result of selective breeding. In primitive times, of course, the heavier musculature of the male was necessary to protect the pregnant female and the immobile young—

THAW (*his anger evaporates*). Nora, are you sick?

NORA. But what's just happened now shows that nothing has changed—I mean, fundamentally changed—in centuries, in the relations between the sexes. *You* still Tarzan, *me* still Jane.

THAW (*sits on sofa beside her, feels her head*). I've noticed you've been . . . well . . . acting funny lately . . .

NORA. Funny?

THAW. Like there was something on your mind. . . . Tell me, what's wrong, sweetheart? Where does it hurt?

NORA. It hurts (*taps head*) here. Isn't that where thinking hurts *you?* No. You're used to it. I was, too, when I was at Wellesley. But I sort of stopped when I left. It's really hard to think of anything else when you're having babies.

THAW. Nora, isn't it about time for your period?

NORA. But if God had wanted us to think just with our wombs, why did He give us a brain? No matter what men say, Thaw, the female brain is not a vestigial organ, like a vermiform appendix.

THAW. Nora . . .

NORA. Thaw, I can just about make my train. I'll leave the car and keys in the usual place at the station. Now, I have a very important appointment in the morning. (*She starts to rise.*)

THAW. Appointment? (*Grabs her shoulders.*) Nora, look at me! You weren't sneaking out of the house to . . . get an abortion?

NORA. When a man can't explain a woman's actions, the first thing he thinks about is the condition of her uterus. Thaw, if you were leaving me and I didn't know why, would I ask, first thing, if you were having prostate trouble?

THAW. Don't try to throw me off the track, sweetie! Now, if you want another baby . . .

NORA. Thaw, don't you remember, we both agreed about the overpopulation problem—

THAW. To hell with the overpopulation problem. Let Nixon solve that. Nora, I can swing another baby—

NORA. Maybe you can. I can't. For me there are no more splendid, new truths to be learned from scanning the contents of babies' diapers. Thaw, I *am* pregnant. But not in a feminine way. In the way only men are supposed to get pregnant.

THAW. Men, pregnant?

NORA (*nodding*). With ideas. Pregnancies there (*taps his head*) are masculine. And a very superior form of labor. Pregnancies here (*taps her tummy*) are feminine—a very inferior form of labor. That's an example of male linguistic chauvinism. Mary Ellmann is *great* on that. You'll enjoy her *Thinking about Women* . . .

THAW (*going to telephone near bookshelf*). I'm getting the doctor. (NORA *makes a dash for the door, he drops the phone.*) Oh, no you don't!

(*He reaches for her as she passes, misses. Grabs her ponytail and hauls her back by it, and shoves her into the easy chair.*)

NORA. Brother, Millett sure had you typed.

THAW. Milly *who?* (*A new thought comes to him.*) Has one of your goddam-gossipy female friends been trying to break up our marriage? (*He suddenly checks his conscience. It is not altogether pure.*) What did she tell you? That she saw me having lunch, uh, dinner, with some girl?

NORA (*nodding to herself*). Right on the button!

THAW. Now, Nora, I can explain about that girl—

NORA. You don't have to. Let's face it. Monogamy is not natural to the male—

THAW. You know I'm not in love with anybody but you—

NORA. It's not natural to the female, either. Making women think it is is man's most successful form of brainwashing—

THAW. Nora, I swear, that girl means nothing to me—

NORA. And you probably mean nothing to her. So whose skin is off whose nose?

THAW (*relieved, but puzzled*). Well, uh, I'm glad you feel that way about—uh—things.

NORA. Oh, it's not the way I *feel*. It's the way things really are. What with the general collapse of the mores, and now the Pill, women are becoming as promiscuous as men. It figures. We're educated from birth to think of ourselves just as man-traps. Of course, in my mother's day, good women thought of themselves as private man-traps. Only bad women were public man-traps. Now we've all gone public. (*Looks at watch.*) I'll have to take the eight-forty.

(*She gets out of her coat, lays it, ready to slip into, on back of sofa.*)

THAW (*a gathering suspicion*). Nora, are you trying to tell me . . . that you—

NORA. Of course, a lot of it, today, is the fault of the advertising industry. Making women think they're failures in life if they don't make like sex-pots around the clock. We're even supposed to wear false eyelashes when we're vacuuming. Betty Friedan's great on that. She says many lonely suburban housewives, unable to identify their real problem, think more sex is the answer. So they sleep with the milkman, or the delivery boy. If I felt like sleeping with anybody like that, I'd pick the plumber. When you need *him,* boy you *need* him!

THAW (*the unpleasant thought he has been wrestling with has now jelled*). Nora . . . are you . . . trying to tell me you are leaving me—for someone else?

NORA. Why, Thaw Wald! How could you even *think* such a thing? (*To herself.*) Now, how naïve can I be? What else do men think about, in connection with women, *but sex?* He is saying to himself, she's not having her period, she's not pregnant, she's not jealous; it's *got* to be another man.

THAW. Stop muttering to yourself, and answer my question.

NORA. I forgot what it was. Oh, yes. *No.*

THAW. No what?

NORA. No, I'm not in love with anybody else. I was a virgin when I married you. And intacta. And that wasn't par for the course—even at Welles-ley. And I've never slept with anybody else, partly because I never wanted to. And partly because, I suppose, of our family's Presbyterian hangup. So, now that all the vital statistics are out of the way, I'll just drive around until—

(*Begins to slip her arms into coat. He grabs coat, throws it on easy chair.*)

THAW. You're not leaving until you tell me *why.*

NORA. But it's all in my letter. (*Points.*) The fat one sticking out of Simone de Beauvoir's *Second Sex*—

THAW. If you have a bill of particulars against me, I want it—straight. From you.

NORA. Oh, darling, I have no bill of particulars. By all the standards of our present-day society, you are a very good husband. And, mark me, you'll be president of Stove Mountain Life Insurance Company before you're 50. The point is, what will I be when I'm 50—

THAW. You'll be my wife, if I have anything to say. Okay. So you're not leaving me because I'm a bad husband, or because my financial future is dim.

NORA. No. Oh, Thaw, you just wouldn't understand.

THAW (*patiently*). I might, if you would try, for just one minute, to talk logically—

NORA. Thaw, women aren't trained to talk logically. Men don't like women who talk logically. They find them unfeminine—aggressive—

THAW. Dammit, Nora, will you talk sense . . .

NORA. But Boy! does a man get sore when a woman won't talk logically when *he* wants her to, and (*snaps fingers*) like that! And *that* isn't illogical? What women men are! Now, if you will step aside—

THAW (*grabbing her and shaking her*). You're going to tell me why you're walking out on me, if I have to *sock* you!

NORA. Thaw, eyeball to eyeball, *I am leaving you*—and not for a man. For reasons of my own I just don't think you *can* understand. And if you mean to stop me, you'll have to beat me to a pulp. But I'm black and blue already.

THAW (*seizes her tenderly in his arms, kisses her*). Nora, sweetheart! You know I couldn't really hurt you. (*Kisses, kisses.*) Ba-aaby, what do you say we call it a night? (*Scoops her up in his arms.*) You can tell me *all* about it in bed . . .

NORA. The classical male one-two. Sock 'em and screw 'em.

THAW (*dumping her on sofa*). Well, it's been known to work on a lot of occasions. Something tells me this isn't one of them. (*Pours a drink.*)

NORA. I guess I need one, too. (*He mixes them.*) Thaw?

THAW. Yes.

NORA. I couldn't help being a *little* pleased when you made like a caveman. It shows you really do value my sexual services.

THAW. Jee-zus!

NORA. Well, it can't be my domestic services—you don't realize, yet, what they're worth. (*Drinks.*) Thaw, you do have a problem with me. But you can't solve it with force. And *I* do have a problem. But I can't solve it with sex.

THAW. Could you, would you, *try* to tell me what my-you-our problem is?

NORA. Friedan's *Feminine Mystique* is very good on The Problem. I've marked all the relevant passages. And I've personalized them in my letter—

(*He goes to book. Yanks out letter, starts to tear it up. NORA groans. He changes his mind, and stuffs it in his pocket.*)

THAW. Look, Nora, there's one thing I've always said about you. For a woman, you're pretty damn honest. Don't you think you owe it to me to level and give me a chance to defend myself?

NORA. The trouble is, *you* would have to listen to *me*. And that's hard for you. I *understand why*. Not listening to women is a habit that's been passed on from father to son for generations. You could almost say, tuning out on women is another secondary sexual male characteristic.

THAW. So our problem is that *I* don't listen?

NORA. Thaw, you always go on talking, no matter how hard I'm interrupting.

THAW. Okay. You have the floor.

NORA. Well, let's begin where this started tonight. When you oppressed me, and treated me as an inferior—

THAW. I oppressed . . . (*Hesitates.*) Lay on, MacDuff.

NORA. You honestly don't think that yanking me around by my hair and threatening to sock me are not the oppressive gestures of a superior male toward an inferior female?

THAW. For Chrissake, Nora, a man isn't going to let the woman he loves leave him, if he can stop her!

NORA. Exactly. Domination of the insubordinate female is an almost instinctive male reflex. *In extremis,* Thaw, it is *rape.* Now, would I like it if you should say you were going to leave me? No. But could I drag you back—

THAW. You'd just have to crook your little finger.

NORA. Flattery will get you nowhere this evening. So, where was I?

THAW. I am a born rapist.

NORA. Wasn't that what you had in mind when you tried to adjourn this to our bedroom? But that's just your primitive side. There's your civilized side, too. You are a patriarchal *pater familias.*

THAW. What am I now?

NORA. Thaw, you do realize we all live in a patriarchy, where men govern women by playing sexual politics?

THAW. Look, you're not still sore because I talked you into voting for Nixon? (*She gives him a withering look.*) Okay. So we all live in a patriarchy . . .

NORA. Our little family, the Walds, are just one nuclear patriarchal unit among the millions in our patriarchal male-dominated civilization, which is worldwide. It's all in that book—

THAW. Look Nora, I promise I'll read the damn book—but . . .

NORA. So who's interrupting? Well, Thaw, all history shows that the hand that cradles the *rock* has ruled the world, *not* the hand that rocks the cradle! Do you know what brutal things men have done to women? Bought and sold them like cattle. Bound their feet at birth to deform them—so they couldn't run away—like in China. Made widows throw themselves on the funeral pyres of their husbands, like in India. Cut off their clitorises, so they could be bred but not enjoy sex. Thaw, did you know that the clitoris is the only sexual organ, in either sex, solely designed by nature for sexual pleasure?

THAW. That fascinating fact, up to now, has escaped me.

NORA. Yes, it's a pity. Well . . . men who committed adultery were almost never punished. But women were always brutally punished. Why, in many countries unfaithful wives were *stoned* to death—

THAW. This is America, 1970, Nora. And here, when wives are unfaithful, *husbands* get stoned. (*Drinks.*) Mind if *I* do?

NORA. Be your guest. Oh, there's no doubt that relations between the sexes have been greatly ameliorated . . .

THAW. Now, about *our* relations, Nora. You're not holding it against *me* that men, the dirty bastards, have done a lot of foul things to women in the past?

NORA (*indignant*). What do you mean, in the *past?*

THAW (*determined to be patient*). Past, present, future—what has what other men have done to other women got to do with us?

NORA. Quite a lot. We *are* a male and a female—

THAW. That's the supposition I've always gone on. But Nora, we are a *particular* male and a *particular* female: Thaw Wald and his wife, Nora—

NORA. Yes. That's why it's so shattering when you find out you are such a typical husband and—

THAW (*a new effort to take command*). Nora, how many men do you know who are still in love with their wives after ten years?

NORA. Not many. And, Thaw, listen, maybe the reason is—

THAW. So you agree that's not typical? Okay. Now, do I ever grumble about paying the bills? So that's not typical. I liked my mother-in-law, even when she was alive. And God knows that's not typical. And don't I do every damn thing I can to keep *my* mother off your back? And that's not typical. I'm even thoughtful about the little things. You said so yourself, remember, when I bought you that black see-through night-gown for Mother's Day. That I went out and chose myself. And which *you* never wear.

NORA. I had to return it. It was too small. And do you know what the sales-woman said? She said, "Men who buy their wives things in this depart-ment are in love with them. But why do they all seem to think they are married to midgets?" That's it, Thaw, that's *it!* Men "think little"—like "thinking thin"—even about women they love. They don't think at all about women they don't love or want to sleep with. Now, I can't help it if you think of me as a midget. But don't you see, I've got to stop thinking of myself as one. Thaw, *listen* . . .

THAW. Why the devil should *you* think of yourself as a midget? I think you're a great woman. A *real* woman! Why, you're the dearest, sweet-est, most understanding little wife—most of the time—a man ever had. And the most intelligent and wonderful little mother! Dammit, those kids are the smartest, best-behaved, most self-reliant little kids . . .

NORA. Oh, I've been pretty good at Occupation Housewife, if I do say so my-self. But Thaw, *listen.* Can't you even imagine that there might be something *more* a woman needs and wants—

THAW. My God, Nora, what more can a woman want than a nice home, fine children and a husband who adores her?

NORA (*discouraged*). You sound like old Dr. Freud, in person.

THAW. I sound like Freud? I wish I were. Then I'd know why you're so uptight.

NORA. Oh, no you wouldn't. Know what Freud wrote in his diary, when he was 77? "What do women want? My God, what do they want?" Fifty years this giant brain spends analyzing women. And he still can't find out what they want. So this makes him the world's greatest expert on feminine psychology? (*She starts to look at her watch.*) To think I bought him, in college.

THAW. You've got plenty of time. You were saying about Freud—(*He lights a cigarette, hands it to her, determined to stick with it to the end.*)

NORA. History is full of ironies! Freud was the foremost exponent of the theory of the natural inferiority of women. You know, "Anatomy is destiny"?

THAW. I was in the School of Business, remember?

NORA. Well, old Freud died in 1939. He didn't live to see what happened when Hitler adopted his theory that "anatomy is destiny." Six million of his own people went to the gas chambers. One reason, Hitler said, that the Jews were *naturally* inferior was because they were effeminate peo-ple, with a slave mentality. He said they were full of those vices which men always identify with women—when they're feeling hostile: You know, sneakiness and deception, scheming and wheedling, whining and pushiness, oh, and materialism, sensuousness and sexuality. Thaw, what's *your* favorite feminine vice?

THAW. At this moment, feminine monologues.

NORA. I didn't think you'd have the nerve to say sneakiness. I saw you sneak a look at your watch, and egg me on to talk about Freud, hoping I'll miss my train. I won't.

THAW. So nothing I've said—what little I've had a chance to say . . . (*she shakes her head*)—you still intend to divorce me?

NORA. Oh, I never said I was divorcing you. I'm deserting you. So you can divorce me.

THAW. You do realize, Nora, that if a wife deserts her husband he doesn't have to pay her alimony?

NORA. I don't want alimony. But I do want severance pay. (*Points to books.*) There's my bill, rendered for ten years of domestic services—the thing sticking in *Woman's Place*, by Cynthia Fuchs Epstein. I figured it at the going agency rates for a full-time cook, cleaning woman, handy-man, laundress, seamstress, and part-time gardener and chauffeur, I've worked an average ten-hour day. So I've charged for overtime. Of course, you've paid my rent, taxes, clothing, medical expenses, and food. So I've deducted those. Even though as a housewife, I've had no fringe benefits. Just the same, the bill . . . well, I'm afraid you're going to be staggered. I was. It comes to over $53,000. I'd like to be paid in ten installments.

THAW (*he is staggered*). Mathematics isn't really your bag, Nora.

NORA. I did it on that little calculating machine you gave me at Christmas. If you think it's not really fair, I'll be glad to negotiate. And, please notice, I haven't charged anything for sleeping with you!

THAW. Wow! (*He is really punch drunk.*)

NORA. I'm not a prostitute. And *this* is what I wanted to say about the Lib girls. They're right about women who marry *just* for money. But they're wrong about women who marry for love. It's love makes all the difference—

THAW (*dispirited*). Well, *vive la différence.*

NORA. And, of course, I haven't charged anything for being a nurse. I've adored taking care of the children, especially when they were babies. I'm going to miss them—*awfully.*

THAW (*on his feet, with outrage*). You're deserting the children, too? My God, Nora, what kind of woman *are* you? You're going to leave those poor little kids alone in this house—

NORA. You're here. And I told you, your mother is coming. I wired her that her son needed her. She'll be happy again—and be needed again—for the first time in years—

THAW (*this is a real blow*). My *mother!* Oh, migod, you *can't,* Nora. You know how she—*swarms* over me! She thinks I'm still 12 years old . . . (*His head is now in his hands.*) You know she drives me out of my cotton-picking mind.

NORA. Yes. But you never said so before.

THAW. I love my mother. She's been a good mother, and wife. But Nora, she's a *very* limited woman! Yak, yak—food, shopping, the kids . . .

NORA. Thaw, the children love this house, and I don't want to take them out of school. And I can't give them another home. Women, you know, can't borrow money to buy a house. Besides, legally this house and everything in it, except mother's few things, are yours. All the worldly goods with which thou didst me endow seem to be in that suitcase.

THAW. Nora, you know damn well that all my life insurance is in your name. If I died tomorrow—and I may blow my brains out tonight—everything would go to you and the kids.

NORA. Widowhood is one of the few fringe benefits of marriage. But, today, all the money I have is what I've saved in the past year out of my clothes allowance—$260.33. But I hope you will give me my severance pay—

THAW. And if I don't—you know legally I don't have to—how do you propose to support yourself?

NORA. Well, if I can't get a job right away—sell my engagement ring. That's why they say diamonds are a gal's best friend. What else do jobless women *have* they can turn into ready cash—except their bodies?

THAW. What kind of job do you figure on getting?

NORA. Well, I do have a master's in English. So I'm going to try for a spot in *Time* Research. That's the intellectual harem kept by the Time Inc. editors. The starting pay is good.

THAW. How do you know that?

NORA. From your own research assistant, Molly Peapack. We're both Wellesley, you know. She's a friend of the chief researcher at *Time,* Marylois Vega. Also, Molly says, computer programming is a field that may open to women—

THAW (*indignant*). You told Peapack you were leaving me? Before you even told *me?* How do you like *that* for treating a mate like an inferior!

NORA. Thaw, I've told you at least three times a week for the last year that with the kids both in school, I'd like to get a job. You always laughed at me. You said I was too old to be a Playboy Bunny, and that the only job an inexperienced woman my age could get would be as a saleswoman—

THAW. Okay. Where are you going to live? That 200 won't go far—

NORA. Peapack's offered to let me stay with her until I find something.

THAW. I'm going to have a word with Miss Molly Peapack tomorrow. She's been too damned aggressive lately, anyway—

NORA. She's going to have a word with you, too. She's leaving.

THAW. Peapack is leaving? Leaving *me?*

NORA. When you got her from Prudential, you promised her, remember, you'd recommend her for promotion to office manager. So, last week you took on a man. A new man. Now she's got a job offer where she's sure she's got a 40-60 chance for advancement to management. (*Pause.*) So you've lost your home wife and your office wife.

THAW. Jesus! And *this* is a male-dominated world?

NORA. Well, I've got five minutes—

THAW. You've still not told me *why.*

NORA. Oh, Thaw darling! You poor—*man.* I have told you why: I'm leaving because I want a job. I want to do some share, however small, of the world's work, and be paid for it. Isn't the work you do in the world—and the salary you get—what makes you respect yourself, and other men respect you? Women have begun to want to respect themselves a little, too—

THAW. You mean, the real reason you are leaving is that you want a *paying* job?

NORA. Yes.

THAW. God, Nora, why didn't you say that in the beginning. All right, go get a job, if it's that important to you. But that doesn't mean you have to leave me and the kids.

NORA. I'm afraid it does. Otherwise, I'd have to do two jobs. Out there. And here.

THAW. Look, Nora, I heard some of the Lib gals say there are millions of working wives and mothers who are doing two jobs. Housework can't be all that rough—

NORA. Scrubbing floors, walls. Cleaning pots, pans, windows, ovens. Messes—dog messes, toilet messes, children's messes. Garbage. Laundry. Shopping for pounds of stuff. Loading them into the car, out of the car—(*A pause.*) Not all of it hard. But all of it routine. All of it *boring.*

THAW. Listen, Nora, what say, you work, I work. And we split the housework? How's that for a deal?

NORA. It's a deal you are not quite free to make, Thaw. You sometimes *can't* get home until very late. And you have to travel a lot, you know. Oh, it might work for a little while. But not for long. After ten years, you still won't empty an ashtray, or pick up after yourself in the bathroom. No. I don't have the physical or moral strength to swing two jobs. So I've got to choose the one, before it's too late, that's most important to me—oh, not for me just now, but for when *I'm* 50—

THAW. When you're 50, Nora, if you don't leave me, you'll be the wife of the president of Stove Mountain Life Insurance Company. Sharing my wealth, sharing whatever status I have in the community. And with servants of your own. Now you listen to *me*, Nora. It's a man's world, out there. It's a man's world where there are a lot of women working. I see them every day. What are most of them really doing? Marking time, and looking, always looking, for a man who will offer them a woman's world . . . the world you have here. Marriage is still the best deal that the world has to offer women. And most women know it. It's always been like that. And it's going to be like that for a long, long time.

NORA. Just now I feel that the best deal I, Nora Wald, can hope to get out of life is to learn to esteem myself as a person . . . to stop feeling that every day a little bit more of my mind—and heart—is being washed down the drain with the soapsuds . . . Thaw—listen. If I don't stop shrinking, I'll end up secretly hating you, and trying to cut you—and *your* son—down to my size. The way your poor, dear mother does you and your father. And you'll become like your father, the typical henpecked husband. Thinking of his old wife as the Ball and Chain. You know he has a mistress? (THAW *knows.*) A smart gal who owns her own shop . . . who doesn't bore him.

THAW. Well, Nora . . . (*Pours drinks.*) One for the road?

NORA. Right. For the road.

THAW. Nora . . . I'll wait. But I don't know how long—

NORA. I've thought of that, too . . . that you might remarry . . . that girl, maybe, who means nothing—

THAW. Goddammit, a man needs a woman of his own—

NORA (*nodding*). I know. A sleep-in, sleep-with body servant of his very own. Well, that's your problem. Just now, I have to wrestle with mine.

(*Goes to door, picks up suitcase.*) I'm not bursting with self-confidence, Thaw. I do love you. And I also need . . . a man. So I'm not slamming the door. I'm closing it . . . very . . . softly.

(EXITS. CURTAIN FALLS.)

✸ TOPICS FOR CRITICAL THINKING AND WRITING

1. Based on the little that we hear of the television program at the start of the play, characterize the moderator of the program.
2. What dramatic purposes are served by including the bit about the television program?
3. Very early in the dialogue Thaw warns Nora: "Uh-uh, Nora! We both agreed months ago, you'd lay off the feminist bit if I'd lay off watching Saturday football." What does this tell us about Thaw? And about Nora? Do you think they made a fair bargain? (Notice also the first line that Nora speaks after Thaw's line.)
4. What are the implications of the ad by Stove Mountain Life Insurance? Why does Thaw think it is "quite an ad"? What do you think of it?
5. Trace the course of Thaw's methods in his attempts to keep Nora from leaving.
6. How much do you think Thaw has learned by the end of the play?
7. In some ways the play—though certainly serious—is a comedy. What, if anything, do you find funny in it?
8. The play is set in 1970. Is it dated in some ways? Still relevant in others? Explain.

33

In Brief: Writing Arguments about Drama

The following questions may help you to formulate ideas for an essay on a play.

Perhaps more evidently than stories or poems, plays themselves are writings that offer arguments. Characters, pitted against other characters, are likely to try to justify their behavior. At the end of *Othello,* for instance, the protagonist offers an account of his behavior—an account that some readers and spectators find convincing and emotionally satisfying, but that others find self-deluded and emotionally unsatisfying. Essays about plays often set forth highly controversial positions, for instance. "The women in Glaspell's *Trifles* are justified in concealing evidence of the murder," or, to take a more nuanced position, "Although viewers can scarcely approve of withholding evidence of murder, in Glaspell's *Trifles* viewers probably approve for three reasons: First, . . ., second, . . . , and third . . . ."

Assertions of a thesis will interest readers only if they are supported by evidence. In all probability you can find a thesis by examining your basic responses, or by scanning the questions we give below, but almost certainly you will modify this thesis during the course of your reexamination of the play. Thinking skeptically about *your own* assertions is the heart of critical thinking, and critical thinking is at the heart of writing an effective argument. It is not, however, the *whole* of writing an argument. Once you have drafted your argument, and you are satisfied with the position that you have taken, you still need to make sure that you set forth this position effectively, in words that will engage your readers.

PLOT AND CONFLICT

1. Does the exposition introduce elements that will be ironically fulfilled? During the exposition do you perceive things differently from the way the characters perceive them?
2. Are certain happenings or situations recurrent? If so, what significance do you attach to them?
3. If there is more than one plot, do the plots seem to you to be related? Is one plot clearly the main plot and another plot a subplot, a minor variation on the theme?
4. Do any scenes strike you as irrelevant?

5. Are certain scenes so strongly foreshadowed that you anticipated them? If so, did the happenings in these scenes merely fulfill your expectations, or did they also in some way surprise you?

6. What kinds of conflict are there? One character against another, one group against another, one part of a personality against another part in the same person?

7. How is the conflict resolved? By an unambiguous triumph of one side or by a triumph that is also in some degree a loss for the triumphant side? Do you find the resolution satisfying, or unsettling, or what? Why?

CHARACTER

1. A dramatic character is not likely to be thoroughly realistic, a copy of someone we might know. Still, we can ask if the character is consistent and coherent. We can also ask if the character is complex or is, on the other hand, a simple representative of some human type.

2. How is the character defined? Consider what the character says and does and what others say about him or her and do to him or her. Also consider other characters who more or less resemble the character in question, because the similarities—and the differences—may be significant.

3. How trustworthy are the characters when they characterize themselves? When they characterize others?

4. Do characters change as the play goes on, or do we simply know them better at the end?

5. What do you make of the minor characters? Are they merely necessary to the plot, or are they foils to other characters? Or do they serve some other functions?

6. If a character is tragic, does the tragedy seem to you to proceed from a moral flaw, from an intellectual error, from the malice of others, from sheer chance, or from some combination of these?

7. What are the character's goals? To what degree do you sympathize with them? If a character is comic, do you laugh *with* or *at* the character?

8. Do you think the characters are adequately motivated?

9. Is a given character so meditative that you feel he or she is engaged less in a dialogue with others than in a dialogue with the self? If so, do you feel that this character is in large degree a spokesperson for the author, commenting not only on the world of the play but also on the outside world?

TRAGEDY

1. What causes the tragedy? A flaw in the central character? A mistake (*not* the same thing as a flaw) made by this character? An outside force, such as another character, or fate?

2. Is the tragic character defined partly by other characters, for instance, by characters who help us to sense what the character *might* have done, or who in some other way reveal the strengths or weaknesses of the protagonist?

3. Does a viewer know more than the tragic figure knows? More than most or all of the characters know?

4. Does the tragic character achieve any sort of wisdom at the end of the play?

5. To what degree do you sympathize with the tragic character?

6. Is the play depressing? If not, why not?

COMEDY

1. Do the comic complications arise chiefly out of the personalities of the characters (for instance, pretentiousness or amorousness), or out of the situations (for instance, mistaken identity)?
2. What are the chief goals of the figures? Do we sympathize with these goals, or do we laugh at persons who pursue them? If we laugh, *why* do we laugh?
3. What are the personalities of those who oppose the central characters? Do we laugh at them, or do we sympathize with them?
4. What is funny about the play? Is the comedy high (including verbal comedy) or chiefly situational and physical?
5. Is the play predominantly genial, or is there a strong satiric tone?
6. Does the comedy have any potentially tragic elements in it? Might the plot be slightly rewritten so that it would become a tragedy?
7. What, if anything, do the characters learn by the end of the play?

NONVERBAL LANGUAGE

1. If the playwright does not provide full stage directions, try to imagine for at least one scene what gestures and tones might accompany each speech. (The first scene is usually a good one to try your hand at.)
2. What do you make of the setting? Does it help to reveal character? Do changes of scene strike you as symbolic? If so, symbolic of what?
3. Do certain costumes (dark suits, flowery shawls, stiff collars, etc.) or certain properties (books, pictures, toys, candlesticks, etc.) strike you as symbolic? If so, symbolic of what?

THE PLAY IN PERFORMANCE

Often we can gain a special pleasure from, or insight into, a dramatic work when we actually see it produced onstage or made into a film. This gives us an opportunity to think about the choices that the director has made, and, even more, it may prompt us to imagine and ponder how we would direct the play for the theater or make a film version of it ourselves.

1. If you have seen the play in the theater or in a film version, what has been added? What has been omitted? Why?
2. In the case of a film, has the film medium been used to advantage—for example, in focusing attention through close-ups or reaction shots (shots showing not the speaker but a person reacting to the speaker)?
3. Do certain plays seem to be especially suited—maybe *only* suited—to the stage? Would they not work effectively as films? Is the reverse true: Are some plays best presented, and best understood, when they are done as films?
4. Critics have sometimes said about this or that play that it cannot really be staged successfully or presented well on film—that the best way to appreciate and understand it is as something to be *read,* like a poem or novel. Are there plays you have studied for which this observation appears to hold true? Which features of the work—its characters, settings, dialogue, central themes—might make it difficult to transfer the play from the page to the stage or to the movie screen?

5. Imagine that you are directing the play. What would be the important decisions you would have to make about character, setting, and pacing of the action? Would you be inclined to omit certain scenes? To add new scenes that are not in the work itself? What kinds of advice would you give to the performers about their roles?

A SAMPLE STUDENT ESSAY,
USING SOURCES

In Appendix A we discuss manuscript form (page 1764) and in Appendixes B and C the use of sources (page 1769) and documentation (page 1776). Here we give a student's documented paper on Arthur Miller's *Death of a Salesman*. (The play appears in this book on page 000.) The student of course had taken notes on index cards, both from the play and from secondary sources, and had arranged and rearranged the notes as her topic and thesis became clearer to her. We preface the final version of her essay with the rough outline that she prepared before she wrote her first draft.

Linda
 realistic
 encourages Willy
 foolish? loving?   *Both? <u>Not</u> so foolish; knows how to calm*
 prevented him from succeeding? *him down*
 doesn't understand W's needs? or nothing else to
  do?
 quote some critics knocking Linda
 other women
5 the Woman
4 the two women in restaurant *(Forsythe first, then Letta)*
3 Jenny
2 W's mother (compare with father?)
  check to see exactly what the play says about her
1 Howard's wife (and daughter?) *(discuss this <u>first</u>)*
6 discuss <u>Linda last</u>
 titles?
 Linda Loman
 Women in Miller's <u>Salesman</u>
 Gender in . . . *Male and female in <u>Death</u> . . .*
 Men and Women: Arthur M's View
  Willy Loman's Women

Here is the final version of the essay.

Ruth Katz
Professor Ling
English 102
10 December 2005

The Women in <u>Death of a Salesman</u>

<u>Death of a Salesman</u> is of course about a
salesman, but it is also about the American
dream of success. Somewhere in between the
narrowest topic, the death of a salesman, and
the largest topic, the examination of American
values, is Miller's picture of the American
family. This paper will chiefly study one member
of the family, Willy's wife, Linda Loman, but
before examining Miller's depiction of her, it
will look at Miller's depiction of other women
in the play in order to make clear Linda's
distinctive traits. We will see that although
her role in society is extremely limited, she is
an admirable figure, fulfilling the roles of wife
and mother with remarkable intelligence.

Linda is the only woman who is on stage much
of the time, but there are several other women
in the play: "the Woman" (the unnamed woman in
Willy's hotel room), Miss Forsythe and her
friend Letta (the two women who join the
brothers in the restaurant), Jenny (Charley's
secretary), the various women that the brothers
talk about, and the voices of Howard's daughter
and wife. We also hear a little about Willy's
mother.

We will look first at the least important (but
not utterly unimportant) of these, the voices of
Howard's daughter and wife on the wire recorder.

Of Howard's seven-year-old daughter we know only
that she can whistle "Roll Out the Barrel" and
that according to Howard she "is crazy about
me." The other woman in Howard's life is equally
under his thumb. Here is the dialogue that tells
us about her--and her relation to her husband.

> HOWARD'S VOICE. "Go on, say something."
>   (Pause.) "Well, you gonna talk?"
> HIS WIFE. "I can't think of anything."
> HOWARD'S VOICE. "Well, talk--it's turning."
> HIS WIFE. (shyly, beaten). "Hello." (Silence.)
>   "Oh, Howard, I can't talk into this . . ."
> HOWARD. (snapping the machine off). That was
>   my wife. (1599)

There is, in fact, a third woman in Howard's
life, the maid. Howard says that if he can't be
at home when the Jack Benny program comes on, he
uses the wire recorder. He tells "the maid to
turn the radio on when Jack Benny comes on, and
this automatically goes on with the radio. . . ."
(1599). In short, the women in Howard's world
exist to serve (and to worship) him.

Another woman who seems to have existed only
to serve men is Willy Loman's mother. On one
occasion, in speaking with Ben, Willy remembers
being on her lap, and Ben, on learning that his
mother is dead, utters a platitudinous
description of her, "Fine specimen of a lady,
Mother" (1583), but that's as much as we learn of
her. Willy is chiefly interested in learning about
his father, who left the family and went to
Alaska. Ben characterizes the father as "a very
great and a very wild-hearted man" (1585), but
the fact that the father left his family and
apparently had no further communication with his
wife and children seems to mean nothing to Ben.

Katz 3

Presumably the mother struggled alone to bring up
the boys, but her efforts are unmentioned.
Curiously, some writers defend the father's
desertion of his family. Lois Gordon says, "The
first generation (Willy's father) has been forced,
in order to make a living, to break up the
family" (278), but nothing in the play supports
this assertion that the father was "forced" to
break up the family.

Willy, like Ben, assumes that men are heroic
and women are nothing except servants and sex
machines. For instance, Willy says to Ben,
"Please tell about Dad. I want my boys to hear.
I want them to know the kind of stock they
spring from" (1585). As Kay Stanton, a feminist
critic says, Willy's words imply "an Edenic
birth myth," a world "with all the Loman men
springing directly from their father's side,
with no commingling with a female" (69).

Another woman who, like Howard's maid and
Willy's mother, apparently exists only to serve
is Jenny, Charley's secretary. She is courteous,
and she is treated courteously by Charley and by
Charley's son, Bernard, but she has no identity
other than that of a secretary. And, as a
secretary--that is, as a nonentity in the eyes
of at least some men--she can be addressed
insensitively. Willy Loman makes off-color
remarks to her:

> WILLY. . . . Jenny, Jenny, good to see you.
> How're ya? Workin'? Or still honest?
> JENNY. Fine. How've you been feeling?
> WILLY. Not much any more, Jenny. Ha, ha!
> (1606)

The first of these comments seems to suggest that
a working woman is <u>not</u> honest--that is, is a

prostitute or is engaged in some other sort of hanky-panky, as is the Woman who in exchange for silk stockings and sex sends Willy directly into the buyer's office. The second of Willy's jokes, with its remark about not feeling much, also refers to sex. In short, though readers or viewers of the play see Jenny as a thoroughly respectable woman, they see her not so much as an individual but as a person engaged in routine work and as a person to whom Willy can speak crudely.

It is a little harder to be certain about the characters of Miss Forsythe and Letta, the two women in the scene in Stanley's restaurant. For Happy, Miss Forsythe is "strudel," an object for a man to consume, and for Stanley she and her friend Letta are "chippies," that is, prostitutes. But is it clear that they are prostitutes? When Happy tells Miss Forsythe that he is in the business of selling, he makes a dirty joke, saying, "You don't happen to sell, do you?" (1611). She replies, "No, I don't sell," and if we take this seriously and if we believe her, we can say that she is respectable and is rightly putting Happy in his place. Further, her friend Letta says, "I gotta get up very early tomorrow. I got jury duty" (1617), which implies that she is a responsible citizen. Still, the girls do not seem especially thoughtful. When Biff introduces Willy to the girls, Letta says, "Isn't he cute? Sit down with us, Pop" (1618), and when Willy breaks down in the restaurant, Miss Forsythe says, "Say, I don't like that temper of his" (1618). Perhaps we can say this: It is going too far--on the basis of what we see--to agree with Stanley that the women are "chippies," or with Happy, who

assumes that every woman is available for sex,
but Miss Forsythe and Letta do not seem to be
especially responsible or even interesting
people. That is, as Miller presents them, they
are of little substance, simply figures
introduced into the play in order to show how
badly Happy and Biff behave.

The most important woman in the play, other
than Linda, is "the Woman," who for money or
stockings and perhaps for pleasure has sex with
Willy, and who will use her influence as a
receptionist or secretary in the office to send
Willy directly on to the buyer, without his
having to wait at the desk. But even though the
Woman gets something out of the relationship,
she knows that she is being used. When Biff
appears in the hotel room, she asks him, "Are
you football or baseball?" Biff replies,
"Football," and the Woman, "angry, humiliated,"
says, "That's me too" (1620). We can admire her
vigorous response, but, again, like the other
women whom we have discussed, she is not really
an impressive figure. We can say that, at best,
in a society that assumes women are to be
exploited by men, she holds her own.

So far, then--though we have not yet talked
about Linda--the world of Death of a Salesman is
not notable for its pictures of impressive women.
True, most of the males in the play--Willy,
Biff, Happy, Ben, and such lesser characters as
Stanley and Howard--are themselves pretty sorry
specimens, but Bernard and Charley are
exceptionally decent and successful people, people
who can well serve as role models. Can any female
character in the play serve as a role model?

Linda has evoked strongly contrasting
reactions from the critics. Some of them judge

her very severely. For instance, Lois Gordon says
that Linda "encourages Willy's dream, yet she
will not let him leave her for the New Continent,
the only realm where the dream can be fulfilled"
(280). True, Linda urges Willy not to follow
Ben's advice of going to Alaska, but surely the
spectator of the play cannot believe that Willy
is the sort of man who can follow in Ben's
footsteps and violently make a fortune. And, in
fact, Ben is so vile a person (as when he trips
Biff, threatens Biff's eye with the point of his
umbrella, and says, "Never fight fair with a
stranger, boy" [1585]), that we would not want
Willy to take Ben's advice.

A second example of a harsh view of Linda is
Brian Parker's comment on "the essential
stupidity of Linda's behavior. Surely it is both
stupid and immoral to encourage the man you love
in self-deceit and lies" (54). Parker also says
that Linda's speech at the end, when she says she
cannot understand why Willy killed himself, "is
not only pathetic, it is also an explanation of
the loneliness of Willy Loman which threw him
into other women's arms" (54). Nothing in the
play suggests that Linda was anything other than
a highly supportive wife. If Willy turned to
other women, surely it was not because Linda did
not understand him. Finally, one last example of
the Linda-bashing school of commentary: Guerin
Bliquez speaks of "Linda's facility for prodding
Willy to his doom" (383).

Very briefly, the arguments against Linda are
that (1) she selfishly prevented Willy from going
to Alaska, (2) she stupidly encourages him in
his self-deceptions, and (3) she is
materialistic, so that even at the end, in the
Requiem, when she says she has made the last

payment on the house, she is talking about money.
But if we study the play we will see that all
three of these charges are false. First, although
Linda does indeed discourage Willy from taking
Ben's advice and going to Alaska, she points out
that there is no need for "everybody [to] conquer
the world" and that Willy has "a beautiful job
here" (1603), a job with excellent prospects. She
may be mistaken in thinking that Willy has a good
job--he may have misled her--but, given what
seems to be the situation, her comment is
entirely reasonable. So far as the second charge
goes, that she encourages him in self-deception,
there are two answers. First, on some matters she
does not know that Willy has lied to her, and so
her encouragement is reasonable and right.
Second, on other matters she does know that Willy
is not telling the truth, but she rightly thinks
it is best not to let him know that she knows,
since such a revelation would crush what little
self-respect remains in him. Consider, for
example, this portion of dialogue, early in the
play, when Willy, deeply agitated about his
failure to drive and about Biff, has returned
from what started out as a trip to Boston. Linda,
trying to take his mind off his problems, urges
him to go downstairs to the kitchen to try a new
kind of cheese:

> LINDA. Go down, try it. And be quiet.
> WILLY. (turning to Linda, guiltily).
> You're not worried about me, are you,
>   sweetheart?
>
>   . . .
>
> LINDA. You've got too much on the ball to
>   worry about.

Katz 8

WILLY. You're my foundation and my support,
     Linda.

LINDA. Just try to relax, dear. You make
     mountains out of molehills.

WILLY. I won't fight with him any more. If he
     wants to go back to Texas, let him go.

LINDA. He'll find his way. (1569)

Of course she does not really think he has a
great deal on the ball, and she probably is not
confident that Biff will "find his way," but
surely she is doing the best thing possible--
calming Willy, partly by using soothing words
and partly by doing what she can to get Biff out
of the house, since she knows that Biff and
Willy can't live under the same roof.

    The third charge, that she is materialistic,
is ridiculous. She <u>has</u> to count the pennies
because <u>someone</u> has to see that the bills are
paid, and Willy is obviously unable to do so.
Here is an example of her supposed preoccupation
with money:

LINDA. Well, there's nine-sixty for the
     washing machine. And for the vacuum
     cleaner there's three and a half due on
     the fifteenth. Then the roof, you got
     twenty-one dollars remaining.

WILLY. It don't leak, does it?

LINDA. No, they did a wonderful job. Then
     you owe Frank for the carburetor.

WILLY. I'm not going to pay that man! That
     goddam Chevrolet, they ought to prohibit
     the manufacture of that car!

LINDA. Well, you owe him three and a half.
     And odds and ends, comes to around a
     hundred and twenty dollars by the
     fifteenth. (1578)

It might be nice if Linda spent her time taking
courses at an adult education center and
thinking high thoughts, but it's obvious that
someone in the Loman family (as in all families)
has to keep track of the bills.

The worst that can be said of Linda is that
she subscribes to three American ideas of the
time--that the man is the breadwinner, that the
relationship between a father and his sons is
far more important than the relationship between
a mother and her sons, and that a woman's sole
job is to care for the house and to produce sons
for her husband. She is the maidservant to her
husband and to her sons, but in this she is like
the vast majority of women of her time, and she
should not be criticized for not being an
innovator. Compared to her husband and her sons,
Linda (though of course not perfect) is a tower
of common sense, virtue, and strength. In fact,
far from causing Willy's failure, she does what
she can to give him strength to face the facts,
for instance when she encourages him to talk to
Howard about a job in New York: "Why don't you
go down to the place tomorrow and tell Howard
you've simply got to work in New York? You're
too accommodating, dear" (1567). Notice, too,
her speech in which she agrees with Biff's
decision that it is best for Biff to leave for
good: she goes to Willy and says, "I think
that's the best way, dear. 'Cause there's no use
drawing it out, you'll just never get along"
(1626). Linda is not the most forceful person
alive, or the brightest, but she is decent and
she sees more clearly than do any of the other
Lomans.

There is nothing in the play to suggest that
Arthur Miller was a feminist or was ahead of his
time in his view of the role of women. On the
contrary, the play seems to give a pre-feminist
view, with women playing subordinate roles to
men. The images of success of the best sort--not
of Ben's ruthless sort--are Charley and Bernard,
two males. Probably Miller, writing in the 1940s,
could hardly conceive of a successful woman other
than as a wife or mother. Notice, by the way,
that Bernard--probably the most admirable male in
the play--is not only an important lawyer but the
father of two sons, apparently a sign of his
complete success as a man. Still, Miller's
picture of Linda is by no means condescending.
Linda may not be a genius, but she is the
brightest and the most realistic of the Lomans.
Things turn out badly, but not because of Linda.
The viewer leaves the theater with profound
respect for her patience, her strength, her sense
of decency, and, yes, her intelligence and her
competence in dealing with incompetent men.

[New page]

Katz 11

Works Cited

Bliquez, Guerin. "Linda's Role in Death of a
    Salesman." Modern Drama 10 (1968): 383-86.

Gordon, Lois. "Death of a Salesman: An Appreciation."
    The Forties: Fiction, Poetry, Drama. Ed. Warren
    French. Deland, Florida: Everett/Edwards, 1969.
    273-83.

Koon, Helene Wickham, ed. Twentieth Century
    Interpretations of Death of a Salesman.
    Englewood Cliffs, New Jersey: Prentice, 1983.

Miller, Arthur. Death of a Salesman. An
    Introduction to Literature. Ed. Sylvan Barnet
    et al. 14th ed. New York: Longman, 2006.
    1564-1631.

Parker, Brian. "Point of View in Arthur Miller's
    Death of a Salesman." University of Toronto
    Quarterly 35 (1966): 144-47. Rpt. in Koon.
    41-55.

Stanton, Kay. "Women and the American Dream of
    Death of a Salesman." Feminist Readings of
    American Drama. Ed. Judith Schlueter.
    Rutherford, New Jersey: Fairleigh Dickinson
    UP, 1989. 67-102.

34

American Voices:
Drama for a Diverse Nation

In the first act of Arthur Miller's play *Death of a Salesman* (1947), Willy Loman (the leading character) tells his sons:

> The man who makes an appearance in the business world, the man who creates personal interest, is the man who gets ahead. Be liked and you will never want.

Against Willy's earnest remark we can juxtapose a cynical remark made more than half a century earlier by Mark Twain:

> All you need in this life is ignorance and confidence, then success is sure.

The dream of success, the American Dream—in one form or another—has motivated millions, and it has generated countless pithy remarks. Here are a few observations about America that you may want to recall as you read and reflect on the plays in this chapter.

America means opportunity, freedom, power.
—Ralph Waldo Emerson (1803–1882), 1864

America has been another name for opportunity.
—Frederick Jackson Turner (1861–1932),
historian, 1893

What I do object to about America is the herd thinking. There is no room for individuals in your country—and yet you are dedicated to saving the world for individualism.
—Bertrand Russell (1872–1970),
British philosopher, 1964

The genius of America is that out of the many, we become one.
—Jesse Jackson (b. 1941), speech at the
Democratic National Convention,
Atlanta, Georgia, July 1988

If you work hard and play by the rules in this great country, you can get ahead.

> —Richard A. Gephardt (b. 1941),
> Missouri congressman, 1995

America must be described in romantic terms. . . . America is a romance in which we all partake.

> —Newt Gingrich (b. 1943), Georgia
> congressman, in *To Renew America*, 1995

People in America, of course, live in all sorts of fashions, because they are foreigners, or unlucky, or depraved, or without ambition; people live like that, but *Americans* live in white detached houses with green shutters. Rigidly, blindly, the dream takes precedence.

> —Margaret Mead (1901–1978),
> anthropologist, 1949

In poetry, prose, and drama, American writers have explored the meanings of the American Dream, even as they have also described the challenges that members of certain social classes and groups and racial and ethnic minorities have faced in gaining access to the Dream. In a sense, there is perhaps only one American Dream, and it involves self-reliance, success, and independence. But in life and literature, there are many different American dreamers, who from their own backgrounds and experiences have expressed their hopes and fears about the possibilities for fulfillment that America offers, as the plays in this chapter attest.

JANE MARTIN

Jane Martin has never given an interview and has never been photographed. The name presumably is the pseudonym of a writer who works with the Actors Theatre of Louisville, Kentucky. Rodeo *is one of a collection of monologues,* Talking With . . . , *first presented at the Actors Theatre during the 1981 Humana Festival of New American Plays. Jane Martin has also written full-length plays.*

Rodeo   [1981]

A young woman in her late twenties sits working an a piece of tack.* Beside her is a Lone Star beer in the can. As the lights come up we hear the last verse of a Tanya Tucker song or some other female country-western vocalist. She is wearing old worn jeans and boots plus a long-sleeved workshirt with the sleeves rolled up. She works until the song is over and then speaks.

BIG EIGHT.   Shoot—Rodeo's just goin' to hell in a handbasket. Rodeo used to be somethin'. I loved it. I did. Once Daddy an' a bunch of 'em was

---

* **tack** harness for a horse, including the bridle and saddle.

Margo Martinale, in Jane Martin's *Rodeo*, at the 6th Humana Festival of New American Plays (1982). Photographer: Sam Garst.

foolin' around with some old bronc over to our place and this ol' red nose named Cinch got bucked off and my Daddy hooted and said he had him a nine-year-old girl, namely me, wouldn't have no damn trouble cowboyin' that horse. Well, he put me on up there, stuck that ridin' rein in my hand, gimme a kiss, and said, "Now there's only one thing t' remember Honey Love, if ya fall off you jest don't come home." Well I stayed up. You gotta stay on a bronc eight seconds. Otherwise the ride don't count. So from that day on my daddy called me Big Eight. Heck! That's all the name I got anymore . . . Big Eight.

Used to be fer cowboys, the rodeo did. Do it in some open field, folks would pull their cars and pick-ups round it, sit on the hoods, some ranch hand'd bulldog him some rank steer and everybody'd wave their hats and call him by name. Ride us some buckin' stock, rope a few calves, git throwed off a bull, and then we'd jest git us to a bar and tell each other lies about how good we were.

Used to be a family thing. Wooly Billy Tilson and Tammy Lee had them five kids on the circuit. Three boys, two girls and Wooly and Tammy. Wasn't no two-beer rodeo in Oklahoma didn't have a Tilson entered. Used to call the oldest girl Tits. Tits Tilson. Never seen a girl that top-heavy could ride so well. Said she only fell off when the gravity got her. Cowboys used to say if she landed face down you could plant two young trees in the holes she'd leave. Ha! Tits Tilson.

Used to be people came to a rodeo had a horse of their own back home. Farm people, ranch people—lord, they *knew* what they were lookin' at. Knew a good ride from a bad ride, knew hard from easy. You broke some bones er spent the day eatin' dirt, at least ya got appreciated.

Now they bought the rodeo. Them. Coca-Cola, Pepsi Cola, Marl-boro damn cigarettes. You know the ones I mean. Them. Hire some New York faggot t' sit on some ol' stuffed horse in front of a sagebrush photo n' smoke that junk. Hell, tobacco wasn't made to smoke, honey, it was made to chew. Lord wanted ya filled up with smoke he would've set ya on fire. Damn it gets me!

There's some guy in a banker's suit runs the rodeo now. Got him a pinky ring and a digital watch, honey. Told us we oughta have a watchamacallit, choriographus or somethin', some ol' ballbuster used to be with the Ice damn Capades. Wants us to ride around dressed up like Mickey Mouse, Pluto, crap like that. Told me I had to haul my butt through the barrel race done up like Minnie damn Mouse in a tu-tu. Huh uh, honey! Them people is so screwed-up they probably eat what they run over in the road.

Listen, they got the clowns wearin' Astronaut suits! I ain't lyin'. You know what a rodeo clown does! You go down, fall off whatever—the clown runs in front of the bull so's ya don't git stomped. Pin-stripes, he got 'em in space suits tellin' jokes on a microphone. First horse see 'em, done up like the Star Wars went crazy. Best buckin' horse on the circuit, name of Piss 'N' Vinegar, took one look at them clowns, had him a heart attack and died. Cowboy was ridin' him got hisself squashed. Twelve hundred pounds of coronary arrest jes fell right through 'em. Blam! Vio con dios. Crowd thought that was fun-nier than the astronauts. I swear it won't be long before they're strap-pin' ice-skates on the ponies. Big crowds now. Ain't hardly no ranch people, no farm people, nobody I know. Buncha disco babies and dee-vorce lawyers—designer jeans and day-glo Stetsons. Hell, the whole bunch of 'em wears French perfume. Oh it smells like money now! Got it on the cable T and V—hey, you know what, when ya rodeo yer just bound to kick yerself up some dust—well now, seems like that fogs up the ol' TV camera, so they told us a while back that from now on we was gonna ride on some new stuff called Astro-dirt. Dust free. Artificial damn dirt, honey. Lord have mercy.

Banker Suit called me in the other day said "Lurlene . . ." "Hold it," I said. "Who's this Lurlene? Round here they call me Big Eight." "Well, Big Eight," he said, "my name's Wallace." "Well that's a read sur-prise t' me," I said, "cause aroun' here everybody jes calls you Dumb-ass." My, he laughed real big, slapped his big ol' desk, an' then he said I wasn't suitable for the rodeo no more. Said they was lookin' fer another type, somethin' a little more in the showgirl line, like the Dallas Cow-girls maybe. Said the ridin' and ropin' wasn't the thing no more. Talked on about floats, costumes, dancin' choreog-aphy. If I was a man I woulda pissed on his shoe. Said he'd give me a lifetime pass though. Said I could come to his rodeo any time I wanted.

Rodeo used to be people ridin' horses for the pleasure of people who rode horses—made you feel good about what you could do. Rodeo wasn't worth no money to nobody. Money didn't have nothing to do with it! Used to be seven Tilsons riding in the rodeo. Wouldn't none of 'em dress up like Donald damn Duck so they quit. That there's the law of gravity!

There's a bunch of assholes in this country sneak around until they see ya havin' fun and then they buy the fun and start in sellin' it. See, they figure if ya love it, they can sell it. Well you look out, honey! They want to make them a dollar out of what you love. Dress *you* up like Minnie Mouse. Sell your rodeo. Turn *yer* pleasure into Ice damn Capades. You hear what I'm sayin'? You're jus' merchandise to them, sweetie. You're jus' merchandise to them.

BLACKOUT.

✹ TOPICS FOR CRITICAL THINKING AND WRITING

The Play on the Page

1. Try to recall your response to the title and the first paragraph or two of the play. Did Big Eight fit your view (perhaps a stereotypical view) of what a cowgirl might sound like?

2. Reread *Rodeo,* this time paying attention not only to what Big Eight says but also to your responses to her. By the end of the play has she become a somewhat more complicated figure than she seems to be after the first paragraph, or does she pretty much seem the same? Do you find that you become increasingly sympathetic? Increasingly unsympathetic? Or does your opinion not change?

3. If you have ever seen a rodeo, do you think Big Eight's characterization is on the mark? Or is she simply bitter because she has been fired?

4. If a local theater group were staging *Rodeo,* presumably with some other short plays, would you go to see it? Why, or why not?

The Play on the Stage

5. If you were directing a production of *Rodeo,* would you keep the actor seated, or would you have her get up, move around the stage, perhaps hang up one piece of tack and take down another? Why?

6. If you were directing *Rodeo,* would you tell Big Eight that her speech is essentially an interior monologue—a soliloquy—or would you tell her that she is speaking directly to the audience—i.e., that the audience is, collectively, a character in the play?

7. The play ends with a stage direction, "Blackout"; that is, the stage suddenly darkens. One director of a recent production, however, chose to end with a "fade out"; the illumination decreased slowly by means of dimmers (mechanical devices that regulate the intensity of a lighting unit). If you were directing a production, what sort of lighting would you use at the end? Why?

ARTHUR MILLER

Arthur Miller (1915–2005) was born in New York. In 1938 he graduated from the University of Michigan, where he won several prizes for drama. Six years later he had his first Broadway production, The Man Who Had All the Luck, *but the play was unlucky and closed after four days. By the time of his first commercial success,* All My Sons *(1947), he had already written several plays. In 1949 he won a Pulitzer Prize with* Death of a Salesman *and achieved an international reputation. Among his other works are an adaptation (1950) of Ibsen's* Enemy of the People *and a play about the Salem witch trials,* The Crucible *(1953), both containing political implications, and* The Misfits *(1961, a screenplay),* After the Fall *(1964), and* Incident at Vichy *(1965).*

Death of a Salesman   [1947]

Certain Private Conversations in Two Acts and a Requiem

LIST OF CHARACTERS

WILLY LOMAN
LINDA
BIFF
HAPPY
BERNARD
THE WOMAN
CHARLEY
UNCLE BEN
HOWARD WAGNER
JENNY
STANLEY
MISS FORSYTHE
LETTA

SCENE: *The action takes place in* WILLY LOMAN's *house and yard and in various places he visits in the New York and Boston of today.*

Act 1

SCENE: *A melody is heard, played upon a flute. It is small and fine, telling of grass and trees and the horizon. The curtain rises.*

Before us is the Salesman's house. We are aware of towering, angular shapes behind it, surrounding it on all sides. Only the blue light of the sky falls upon the house and forestage; the surrounding area shows an angry glow of orange. As more light appears, we see a solid vault of apartment houses around the small, fragile-seeming home. An air of the dream clings to the place, a dream rising out of reality. The kitchen at center seems actual enough, for there is a kitchen table with three chairs, and a refrigerator. But no other fixtures are seen. At the back of the kitchen there is a draped entrance, which leads to the living room. To the right of the kitchen,

WILLY. No, it's me, it's me. Suddenly I realize I'm goin' sixty miles an hour and I don't remember the last five minutes. I'm—I can't seem to—keep my mind to it.

LINDA. Maybe it's your glasses. You never went for your new glasses.

WILLY. No, I see everything. I came back ten miles an hour. It took me nearly four hours from Yonkers.

LINDA (*resigned*). Well, you'll just have to take a rest, Willy, you can't continue this way.

WILLY. I just got back from Florida.

LINDA. But you didn't rest your mind. Your mind is overactive, and the mind is what counts, dear.

WILLY. I'll start out in the morning. Maybe I'll feel better in the morning. (*She is taking off his shoes.*) These goddam arch supports are killing me.

LINDA. Take an aspirin. Should I get you an aspirin? It'll soothe you.

WILLY (*with wonder*). I was driving along, you understand? And I was fine. I was even observing the scenery. You can imagine, me looking at scenery, on the road every week of my life. But it's so beautiful up there, Linda, the trees are so thick, and the sun is warm. I opened the windshield and just let the warm air bathe over me. And then all of a sudden I'm goin' off the road! I'm tellin' ya, I absolutely forgot I was driving. If I'd've gone the other way over the white line I might've killed somebody. So I went on again—and five minutes later I'm dreamin' again, and I nearly . . . (*He presses two fingers against his eyes.*) I have such thoughts, I have such strange thoughts.

LINDA. Willy, dear. Talk to them again. There's no reason why you can't work in New York.

WILLY. They don't need me in New York. I'm the New England man. I'm vital in New England.

LINDA. But you're sixty years old. They can't expect you to keep traveling every week.

WILLY. I'll have to send a wire to Portland. I'm supposed to see Brown and Morrison tomorrow morning at ten o'clock to show the line. Goddammit, I could sell them! (*He starts putting on his jacket.*)

LINDA (*taking the jacket from him*). Why don't you go down to the place tomorrow and tell Howard you've simply got to work in New York? You're too accommodating, dear.

WILLY. If old man Wagner was alive I'd a been in charge of New York now! That man was a prince, he was a masterful man. But that boy of his, that Howard, he don't appreciate. When I went north the first time, the Wagner Company didn't know where New England was!

LINDA. Why don't you tell those things to Howard, dear?

WILLY (*encouraged*). I will, I definitely will. Is there any cheese?

LINDA. I'll make you a sandwich.

WILLY. No, go to sleep. I'll take some milk. I'll be up right away. The boys in?

LINDA. They're sleeping. Happy took Biff on a date tonight.

WILLY (*interested*). That so?

LINDA. It was so nice to see them shaving together, one behind the other, in the bathroom. And going out together. You notice? The whole house smells of shaving lotion.

WILLY. Figure it out. Work a lifetime to pay off a house. You finally own it, and there's nobody to live in it.

LINDA. Well, dear, life is a casting off. It's always that way.

WILLY. No, no, some people—some people accomplish something. Did Biff say anything after I went this morning?

LINDA. You shouldn't have criticized him, Willy, especially after he just got off the train. You mustn't lose your temper with him.

WILLY. When the hell did I lose my temper? I simply asked him if he was making any money. Is that a criticism?

LINDA. But, dear, how could he make any money?

WILLY (*worried and angered*). There's such an undercurrent in him. He became a moody man. Did he apologize when I left this morning?

LINDA. He was crestfallen, Willy. You know how he admires you. I think if he finds himself, then you'll both be happier and not fight any more.

WILLY. How can he find himself on a farm? Is that a life? A farm hand? In the beginning, when he was young, I thought, well, a young man, it's good for him to tramp around, take a lot of different jobs. But it's more than ten years now and he has yet to make thirty-five dollars a week!

LINDA. He's finding himself, Willy.

WILLY. Not finding yourself at the age of thirty-four is a disgrace!

LINDA. Shh!

WILLY. The trouble is he's lazy, goddammit!

LINDA. Willy, please!

WILLY. Biff is a lazy bum!

LINDA. They're sleeping. Get something to eat. Go on down.

WILLY. Why did he come home? I would like to know what brought him home.

LINDA. I don't know. I think he's still lost, Willy. I think he's very lost.

WILLY. Biff Loman is lost. In the greatest country in the world a young man with such—personal attractiveness, gets lost. And such a hard worker. There's one thing about Biff—he's not lazy.

LINDA. Never.

WILLY (*with pity and resolve*). I'll see him in the morning; I'll have a nice talk with him. I'll get him a job selling. He could be big in no time. My God! Remember how they used to follow him around in high school? When he smiled at one of them their faces lit up. When he walked down the street . . . (*He loses himself in reminiscences.*)

LINDA (*trying to bring him out of it*). Willy, dear, I got a new kind of American-type cheese today. It's whipped.

WILLY. Why do you get American when I like Swiss?

LINDA. I just thought you'd like a change . . .

WILLY. I don't want a change! I want Swiss cheese. Why am I always being contradicted?

LINDA (*with a covering laugh*). I thought it would be a surprise.

WILLY. Why don't you open a window in here, for God's sake?

LINDA (*with infinite patience*). They're all open, dear.

WILLY. The way they boxed us in here. Bricks and windows, windows and bricks.

LINDA. We should've bought the land next door.

WILLY. The street is lined with cars. There's not a breath of fresh air in the neighborhood. The grass don't grow any more, you can't raise a carrot in the back yard. They should've had a law against apartment houses.

Remember those two beautiful elm trees out there? When I and Biff
hung the swing between them?

LINDA. Yeah, like being a million miles from the city.

WILLY. They should've arrested the builder for cutting those down. They
massacred the neighborhood. (*Lost.*) More and more I think of those
days, Linda. This time of year it was lilac and wisteria. And then the
peonies would come out, and the daffodils. What fragrance in this room!

LINDA. Well, after all, people had to move somewhere.

WILLY. No, there's more people now.

LINDA. I don't think there's more people. I think . . .

WILLY. There's more people! That's what's ruining this country! Population
is getting out of control. The competition is maddening! Smell the stink
from that apartment house! And another one on the other side . . . How
can they whip cheese?

On WILLY'*s last line,* BIFF *and* HAPPY *raise themselves up in their beds,
listening.*

LINDA. Go down, try it. And be quiet.

WILLY (*turning to* LINDA, *guiltily*). You're not worried about me, are you,
sweetheart?

BIFF. What's the matter?

HAPPY. Listen!

LINDA. You've got too much on the ball to worry about.

WILLY. You're my foundation and my support, Linda.

LINDA. Just try to relax, dear. You make mountains out of molehills.

WILLY. I won't fight with him any more. If he wants to go back to Texas, let
him go.

LINDA. He'll find his way.

WILLY. Sure. Certain men just don't get started till later in life. Like Thomas
Edison, I think. Or B. F. Goodrich. One of them was deaf. (*He starts for
the bedroom doorway.*) I'll put my money on Biff.

LINDA. And Willy—if it's warm Sunday we'll drive in the country. And we'll
open the windshield, and take lunch.

WILLY. No, the windshields don't open on the new cars.

LINDA. But you opened it today.

WILLY. Me? I didn't. (*He stops.*) Now isn't that peculiar! Isn't that a remarkable . . . (*He breaks off in amazement and fright as the flute is heard
distantly.*)

LINDA. What, darling?

WILLY. That is the most remarkable thing.

LINDA. What, dear?

WILLY. I was thinking of the Chevvy. (*Slight pause.*) Nineteen twenty-eight .
. . when I had that red Chevvy . . . (*Breaks off.*) That funny? I coulda
sworn I was driving that Chevvy today.

LINDA. Well, that's nothing. Something must've reminded you.

WILLY. Remarkable. Ts. Remember those days? The way Biff used to simo-
nize that car? The dealer refused to believe there was eighty thousand
miles on it. (*He shakes his head.*) Heh! (*To Linda.*) Close your eyes, I'll
be right up. (*He walks out of the bedroom.*)

HAPPY (*to* BIFF). Jesus, maybe he smashed up the car again!

LINDA (*calling after* WILLY). Be careful on the stairs, dear! The cheese is on the middle shelf. (*She turns, goes over to the bed, takes his jacket, and goes out of the bedroom.*)

Light has risen on the boys' room. Unseen, WILLY *is heard talking to himself; "Eighty thousand miles," and a little laugh.* BIFF *gets out of bed, comes downstage a bit, and stands attentively.* BIFF *is two years older than his brother* HAPPY, *well built, but in these days bears a worn air and seems less self-assured. He has succeeded less, and his dreams are stronger and less acceptable than* HAPPY's. HAPPY *is tall, powerfully made. Sexuality is like a visible color on him, or a scent that many women have discovered. He, like his brother, is lost, but in a different way, for he has never allowed himself to turn his face toward defeat and is thus more confused and hard-skinned, although seemingly more content.*

HAPPY (*getting out of bed*). He's going to get his license taken away if he keeps that up. I'm getting nervous about him, y'know, Biff?

BIFF. His eyes are going.

HAPPY. No, I've driven with him. He sees all right. He just doesn't keep his mind on it. I drove into the city with him last week. He stops at a green light and then it turns red and he goes. (*He laughs.*)

BIFF. Maybe he's color-blind.

HAPPY. Pop? Why he's got the finest eye for color in the business. You know that.

BIFF (*sitting down on his bed*). I'm going to sleep.

HAPPY. You're not still sour on Dad, are you, Biff?

BIFF. He's all right, I guess.

WILLY (*underneath them, in the living room*). Yes, sir, eighty thousand miles—eighty-two thousand!

BIFF. You smoking?

HAPPY (*holding out a pack of cigarettes*). Want one?

BIFF (*taking a cigarette*). I can never sleep when I smell it.

WILLY. What a simonizing job, heh!

HAPPY (*with deep sentiment*). Funny, Biff, y'know? Us sleeping in here again? The old beds. (*He pats his bed affectionately.*) All the talk that went across those beds, huh? Our whole lives.

BIFF. Yeah. Lotta dreams and plans.

HAPPY (*with a deep and masculine laugh*). About five hundred women would like to know what was said in this room. (*They share a soft laugh.*)

BIFF. Remember that big Betsy something—what the hell was her name—over on Bushwick Avenue?

HAPPY (*combing his hair*). With the collie dog!

BIFF. That's the one. I got you in there, remember?

HAPPY. Yeah, that was my first time—I think. Boy, there was a pig. (*They laugh, almost crudely.*) You taught me everything I know about women. Don't forget that.

BIFF. I bet you forgot how bashful you used to be. Especially with girls.

HAPPY. Oh, I still am, Biff.

BIFF. Oh, go on.

HAPPY. I just control it, that's all. I think I got less bashful and you got more so. What happened, Biff? Where's the old humor, the old confidence?

(*He shakes* BIFF'*s knee.* BIFF *gets up and moves restlessly about the room.*) What's the matter?

BIFF. Why does Dad mock me all the time?

HAPPY. He's not mocking you, he . . .

BIFF. Everything I say there's a twist of mockery on his face. I can't get near him.

HAPPY. He just wants you to make good, that's all. I wanted to talk to you about Dad for a long time, Biff. Something's—happening to him. He—talks to himself.

BIFF. I noticed that this morning. But he always mumbled.

HAPPY. But not so noticeable. It got so embarrassing I sent him to Florida. And you know something? Most of the time he's talking to you.

BIFF. What's he say about me?

HAPPY. I can't make it out.

BIFF. What's he say about me?

HAPPY. I think the fact that you're not settled, that you're still kind of up in the air . . .

BIFF. There's one or two other things depressing him, Happy.

HAPPY. What do you mean?

BIFF. Never mind. Just don't lay it all to me.

HAPPY. But I think if you just got started—I mean—is there any future for you out there?

BIFF. I tell ya, Hap, I don't know what the future is. I don't know—what I'm supposed to want.

HAPPY. What do you mean?

BIFF. Well, I spent six or seven years after high school trying to work myself up. Shipping clerk, salesman, business of one kind or another. And it's a measly manner of existence. To get on that subway on the hot mornings in summer. To devote your whole life to keeping stock, or making phone calls, or selling or buying. To suffer fifty weeks of the year for the sake of a two-week vacation, when all you really desire is to be outdoors, with your shirt off. And always to have to get ahead of the next fella. And still—that's how you build a future.

HAPPY. Well, you really enjoy it on a farm? Are you content out there?

BIFF (*with rising agitation*). Hap, I've had twenty or thirty different kinds of jobs since I left home before the war, and it always turns out the same. I just realized it lately. In Nebraska when I herded cattle, and the Dakotas, and Arizona, and now in Texas. It's why I came home now, I guess, because I realized it. This farm I work on, it's spring there now, see? And they've got about fifteen new colts. There's nothing more inspiring or—beautiful than the sight of a mare and a new colt. And it's cool there now, see? Texas is cool now, and it's spring. And whenever spring comes to where I am, I suddenly get the feeling, my God, I'm not gettin' anywhere! What the hell am I doing, playing around with horses, twenty-eight dollars a week! I'm thirty-four years old, I oughta be makin' my future. That's when I come running home. And now, I get here, and I don't know what to do with myself. (*After a pause.*) I've always made a point of not wasting my life, and everytime I come back here I know that all I've done is to waste my life.

HAPPY. You're a poet, you know that, Biff? You're a—you're an idealist!

BIFF. No, I'm mixed up very bad. Maybe I oughta get married. Maybe I oughta get stuck into something. Maybe that's my trouble. I'm like a boy. I'm not married, I'm not in business, I just—I'm like a boy. Are you content, Hap? You're a success, aren't you? Are you content?

HAPPY. Hell, no!

BIFF. Why? You're making money, aren't you?

HAPPY (*moving about with energy, expressiveness*). All I can do now is wait for the merchandise manager to die. And suppose I get to be merchandise manager? He's a good friend of mine, and he just built a terrific estate on Long Island. And he lived there about two months and sold it, and now he's building another one. He can't enjoy it once it's finished. And I know that's just what I would do. I don't know what the hell I'm workin' for. Sometimes I sit in my apartment—all alone. And I think of the rent I'm paying. And it's crazy. But then, it's what I always wanted. My own apartment, a car, and plenty of women. And still, goddammit, I'm lonely.

BIFF (*with enthusiasm*). Listen, why don't you come out West with me?

HAPPY. You and I, heh?

BIFF. Sure, maybe we could buy a ranch. Raise cattle, use our muscles. Men built like we are should be working out in the open.

HAPPY (*avidly*). The Loman Brothers, heh?

BIFF (*with vast affection*). Sure, we'd be known all over the counties!

HAPPY (*enthralled*). That's what I dream about, Biff. Sometimes I want to just rip my clothes off in the middle of the store and outbox that goddam merchandise manager. I mean I can outbox, outrun, and outlift anybody in that store, and I have to take orders from those common, petty sons-of-bitches till I can't stand it any more.

BIFF. I'm tellin' you, kid, if you were with me I'd be happy out there.

HAPPY (*enthused*). See, Biff, everybody around me is so false that I'm constantly lowering my ideals . . .

BIFF. Baby, together we'd stand up for one another, we'd have someone to trust.

HAPPY. If I were around you . . .

BIFF. Hap, the trouble is we weren't brought up to grub for money. I don't know how to do it.

HAPPY. Neither can I!

BIFF. Then let's go!

HAPPY. The only thing is—what can you make out there?

BIFF. But look at your friend. Builds an estate and then hasn't the peace of mind to live in it.

HAPPY. Yeah, but when he walks into the store the waves part in front of him. That's fifty-two thousand dollars a year coming through the revolving door, and I got more in my pinky finger than he's got in his head.

BIFF. Yeah, but you just said . . .

HAPPY. I gotta show some of those pompous, self-important executives over there that Hap Loman can make the grade. I want to walk into the store the way he walks in. Then I'll go with you, Biff. We'll be together yet, I swear. But take those two we had tonight. Now weren't they gorgeous creatures?

BIFF. Yeah, yeah, most gorgeous I've had in years.

HAPPY. I get that any time I want, Biff. Whenever I feel disgusted. The only trouble is, it gets like bowling or something. I just keep knockin' them over and it doesn't mean anything. You still run around a lot?

BIFF. Naa. I'd like to find a girl—steady, somebody with substance.

HAPPY. That's what I long for.

BIFF. Go on! You'd never come home.

HAPPY. I would! Somebody with character, with resistance! Like Mom, y'know? You're gonna call me a bastard when I tell you this. That girl Charlotte I was with tonight is engaged to be married in five weeks. (*He tries on his new hat.*)

BIFF. No kiddin'!

HAPPY. Sure, the guy's in line for the vice-presidency of the store. I don't know what gets into me, maybe I just have an over-developed sense of competition or something, but I went and ruined her, and furthermore I can't get rid of her. And he's the third executive I've done that to. Isn't that a crummy characteristic? And to top it all, I go to their weddings! (*Indignantly, but laughing.*) Like I'm not supposed to take bribes. Manufacturers offer me a hundred-dollar bill now and then to throw an order their way. You know how honest I am, but it's like this girl, see. I hate myself for it. Because I don't want the girl, and, still, I take it and—I love it!

BIFF. Let's go to sleep.

HAPPY. I guess we didn't settle anything, heh?

BIFF. I just got one idea that I think I'm going to try.

HAPPY. What's that?

BIFF. Remember Bill Oliver?

HAPPY. Sure, Oliver is very big now. You want to work for him again?

BIFF. No, but when I quit he said something to me. He put his arm on my shoulder, and he said, "Biff, if you ever need anything, come to me."

HAPPY. I remember that. That sounds good.

BIFF. I think I'll go to see him. If I could get ten thousand or even seven or eight thousand dollars I could buy a beautiful ranch.

HAPPY. I bet he'd back you. 'Cause he thought highly of you, Biff. I mean, they all do. You're well liked, Biff. That's why I say to come back here, and we both have the apartment. And I'm tellin' you, Biff, any babe you want . . .

BIFF. No, with a ranch I could do the work I like and still be something. I just wonder though. I wonder if Oliver still thinks I stole that carton of basketballs.

HAPPY. Oh, he probably forgot that long ago. It's almost ten years. You're too sensitive. Anyway, he didn't really fire you.

BIFF. Well, I think he was going to. I think that's why I quit. I was never sure whether he knew or not. I know he thought the world of me, though. I was the only one he'd let lock up the place.

WILLY (*below*). You gonna wash the engine, Biff?

HAPPY. Shh!

BIFF *looks at* HAPPY, *who is gazing down, listening.* WILLY *is mumbling in the parlor.*

HAPPY. You hear that?

They listen. WILLY *laughs warmly.*

BIFF (*growing angry*). Doesn't he know Mom can hear that?

WILLY. Don't get your sweater dirty, Biff!

A look of pain crosses BIFF's *face.*

HAPPY. Isn't that terrible? Don't leave again, will you? You'll find a job here. You gotta stick around. I don't know what to do about him, it's getting embarrassing.

WILLY. What a simonizing job!

BIFF. Mom's hearing that!

WILLY. No kiddin', Biff, you got a date? Wonderful!

HAPPY. Go on to sleep. But talk to him in the morning, will you?

BIFF (*reluctantly getting into bed*). With her in the house. Brother!

HAPPY (*getting into bed*). I wish you'd have a good talk with him.

The light on their room begins to fade.

BIFF (*to himself in bed*). That selfish, stupid . . .

HAPPY. Sh . . . Sleep, Biff.

Their light is out. Well before they have finished speaking, WILLY's *form is dimly seen below in the darkened kitchen. He opens the refrigerator, searches in there, and takes out a bottle of milk. The apartment houses are fading out, and the entire house and surroundings become covered with leaves. Music insinuates itself as the leaves appear.*

WILLY. Just wanna be careful with those girls, Biff, that's all. Don't make any promises. No promises of any kind. Because a girl, y'know, they always believe what you tell 'em, and you're very young, Biff, you're too young to be talking seriously to girls.

Light rises on the kitchen. WILLY, *talking, shuts the refrigerator door and comes downstage to the kitchen table. He pours milk into a glass. He is totally immersed in himself, smiling faintly.*

WILLY. Too young entirely, Biff. You want to watch your schooling first. Then when you're all set, there'll be plenty of girls for a boy like you. (*He smiles broadly at a kitchen chair.*) That so? The girls pay for you? (*He laughs.*) Boy, you must really be makin' a hit.

WILLY *is gradually addressing—physically—a point offstage, speaking through the wall of the kitchen, and his voice has been rising in volume to that of a normal conversation.*

WILLY. I been wondering why you polish the car so careful. Ha! Don't leave the hubcaps, boys. Get the chamois to the hubcaps. Happy, use newspaper on the windows, it's the easiest thing. Show him how to do it, Biff! You see, Happy? Pad it up, use it like a pad. That's it, that's it, good work. You're doin' all right, Hap. (*He pauses, then nods in approbation for a few seconds, then looks upward.*) Biff, first thing we gotta do when we get time is clip that big branch over the house. Afraid it's gonna fall in a storm and hit the roof. Tell you what. We get a rope and sling her around, and then we climb up there with a couple of saws and take her down. Soon as you finish the car, boys, I wanna see ya. I got a surprise for you, boys.

BIFF (*offstage*). Whatta ya got, Dad?

WILLY. No, you finish first. Never leave a job till you're finished—remember that. (*Looking toward the "big trees."*) Biff, up in Albany I saw a beautiful hammock. I think I'll buy it next trip, and we'll hang it right be-

tween those two elms. Wouldn't that be something? Just swingin' there
under those branches. Boy, that would be . . .

Young BIFF *and Young* HAPPY *appear from the direction* WILLY *was addressing.* HAPPY *carries rags and a pail of water.* BIFF, *wearing a
sweater with a block "S," carries a football.*

BIFF (*pointing in the direction of the car offstage*). How's that, Pop, professional?

WILLY. Terrific. Terrific job, boys. Good work, Biff.

HAPPY. Where's the surprise, Pop?

WILLY. In the back seat of the car.

HAPPY. Boy! (*He runs off.*)

BIFF. What is it, Dad? Tell me, what'd you buy?

WILLY (*laughing, cuffs him*). Never mind, something I want you to have.

BIFF (*turns and starts off*). What is it, Hap?

HAPPY (*offstage*). It's a punching bag!

BIFF. Oh, Pop!

WILLY. It's got Gene Tunney's signature on it!

HAPPY *runs onstage with a punching bag.*

BIFF. Gee, how'd you know we wanted a punching bag?

WILLY. Well, it's the finest thing for the timing.

HAPPY (*lies down on his back and pedals with his feet*). I'm losing weight,
you notice, Pop?

WILLY (*to* HAPPY). Jumping rope is good too.

BIFF. Did you see the new football I got?

WILLY (*examining the ball*). Where'd you get a new ball?

BIFF. The coach told me to practice my passing.

WILLY. That so? And he gave you the ball, heh?

BIFF. Well, I borrowed it from the locker room. (*He laughs confidentially.*)

WILLY (*laughing with him at the theft*). I want you to return that.

HAPPY. I told you he wouldn't like it!

BIFF (*angrily*). Well, I'm bringing it back!

WILLY (*stopping the incipient argument, to* HAPPY). Sure, he's gotta practice
with a regulation ball, doesn't he? (*To* BIFF.) Coach'll probably congratulate you on your initiative!

BIFF. Oh, he keeps congratulating my initiative all the time, Pop.

WILLY. That's because he likes you. If somebody else took that ball there'd
be an uproar. So what's the report, boys, what's the report?

BIFF. Where'd you go this time, Dad? Gee we were lonesome for you.

WILLY (*pleased, puts an arm around each boy and they come down to the
apron*). Lonesome, heh?

BIFF. Missed you every minute.

WILLY. Don't say? Tell you a secret, boys. Don't breathe it to a soul. Someday I'll have my own business, and I'll never have to leave home any
more.

HAPPY. Like Uncle Charley, heh?

WILLY. Bigger than Uncle Charley! Because Charley is not—liked. He's liked,
but he's not—well liked.

BIFF. Where'd you go this time, Dad?

WILLY. Well, I got on the road, and I went north to Providence. Met the
Mayor.

BIFF. The Mayor of Providence!

WILLY. He was sitting in the hotel lobby.

BIFF. What'd he say?

WILLY. He said, "Morning!" And I said, "Morning!" And I said, "You got a fine city here, Mayor." And then he had coffee with me. And then I went to Waterbury. Waterbury is a fine city. Big clock city, the famous Waterbury clock. Sold a nice bill there. And then Boston—Boston is the cradle of the Revolution. A fine city. And a couple of other towns in Mass., and on to Portland and Bangor and straight home!

BIFF. Gee, I'd love to go with you sometime, Dad.

WILLY. Soon as summer comes.

HAPPY. Promise?

WILLY. You and Hap and I, and I'll show you all the towns. America is full of beautiful towns and fine, upstanding people. And they know me, boys, they know me up and down New England. The finest people. And when I bring you fellas up, there'll be open sesame for all of us, 'cause one thing, boys: I have friends. I can park my car in any street in New En-gland, and the cops protect it like their own. This summer, heh?

BIFF AND HAPPY (*together*). Yeah! You bet!

WILLY. We'll take our bathing suits.

HAPPY. We'll carry your bags, Pop!

WILLY. Oh, won't that be something! Me comin' into the Boston stores with you boys carryin' my bags. What a sensation!

BIFF *is prancing around, practicing passing the ball.*

WILLY. You nervous, Biff, about the game?

BIFF. Not if you're gonna be there.

WILLY. What do they say about you in school, now that they made you captain?

HAPPY. There's a crowd of girls behind him everytime the classes change.

BIFF (*taking* WILLY*'s hand*). This Saturday, Pop, this Saturday—just for you, I'm going to break through for a touchdown.

HAPPY. You're supposed to pass.

BIFF. I'm takin' one play for Pop. You watch me, Pop, and when I take off my helmet, that means I'm breakin' out. Then you watch me crash through that line!

WILLY (*kisses* BIFF). Oh, wait'll I tell this in Boston!

BERNARD *enters in knickers. He is younger than* BIFF, *earnest and loyal, a worried boy.*

BERNARD. Biff, where are you? You're supposed to study with me today.

WILLY. Hey, looka Bernard. What're you lookin' so anemic about, Bernard?

BERNARD. He's gotta study, Uncle Willy. He's got Regents next week.

HAPPY (*tauntingly, spinning* BERNARD *around*). Let's box, Bernard!

BERNARD. Biff! (*He gets away from* HAPPY.) Listen, Biff, I heard Mr. Birnbaum say that if you don't start studyin' math he's gonna flunk you, and you won't graduate. I heard him!

WILLY. You better study with him, Biff. Go ahead now.

BERNARD. I heard him!

BIFF. Oh, Pop, you didn't see my sneakers! (*He holds up a foot for* WILLY *to look at.*)

WILLY. Hey, that's a beautiful job of printing!

BERNARD (*wiping his glasses*). Just because he printed University of Virginia on his sneakers doesn't mean they've got to graduate him, Uncle Willy!

WILLY (*angrily*). What're you talking about? With scholarships to three universities they're gonna flunk him?

BERNARD. But I heard Mr. Birnbaum say . . .

WILLY. Don't be a pest, Bernard! (*To his boys.*) What an anemic!

BERNARD. Okay, I'm waiting for you in my house, Biff.

> BERNARD *goes off. The* LOMANS *laugh.*

WILLY. Bernard is not well liked, is he?

BIFF. He's liked, but he's not well liked.

HAPPY. That's right, Pop.

WILLY. That's just what I mean. Bernard can get the best marks in school, y'understand, but when he gets out in the business world, y'understand, you are going to be five times ahead of him. That's why I thank Almighty God you're both built like Adonises. Because the man who makes an appearance in the business world, the man who creates personal interest, is the man who gets ahead. Be liked and you will never want. You take me, for instance. I never have to wait in line to see a buyer. "Willy Loman is here!" That's all they have to know, and I go right through.

BIFF. Did you knock them dead, Pop?

WILLY. Knocked 'em cold in Providence, slaughtered 'em in Boston.

HAPPY (*on his back, pedaling again*). I'm losing weight, you notice, Pop?

> LINDA *enters as of old, a ribbon in her hair, carrying a basket of washing.*

LINDA (*with youthful energy*). Hello, dear!

WILLY. Sweetheart!

LINDA. How'd the Chevvy run?

WILLY. Chevrolet, Linda, is the greatest car ever built. (*To the boys.*) Since when do you let your mother carry wash up the stairs?

BIFF. Grab hold there, boy!

HAPPY. Where to, Mom?

LINDA. Hang them up on the line. And you better go down to your friends, Biff. The cellar is full of boys. They don't know what to do with themselves.

BIFF. Ah, when Pop comes home they can wait!

WILLY (*laughs appreciatively*). You better go down and tell them what to do, Biff.

BIFF. I think I'll have them sweep out the furnace room.

WILLY. Good work, Biff.

BIFF (*goes through wall-line of kitchen to doorway at back and calls down*). Fellas! Everybody sweep out the furnace room! I'll be right down!

VOICES. All right! Okay, Biff.

BIFF. George and Sam and Frank, come out back! We're hangin' up the wash! Come on, Hap, on the double! (*He and* HAPPY *carry out the basket.*)

LINDA. The way they obey him!

WILLY. Well, that's training, the training. I'm tellin' you, I was sellin' thousands and thousands, but I had to come home.

LINDA. Oh, the whole block'll be at that game. Did you sell anything?

WILLY. I did five hundred gross in Providence and seven hundred gross in Boston.

LINDA. No! Wait a minute. I've got a pencil. (*She pulls pencil and paper out of her apron pocket.*) That makes your commission . . . Two hundred—my God! Two hundred and twelve dollars!

WILLY. Well, I didn't figure it yet, but . . .

LINDA. How much did you do?

WILLY. Well, I—I did—about a hundred and eighty gross in Providence. Well, no—it came to—roughly two hundred gross on the whole trip.

LINDA (*without hesitation*). Two hundred gross. That's . . . (*She figures.*)

WILLY. The trouble was that three of the stores were half-closed for inventory in Boston. Otherwise I woulda broke records.

LINDA. Well, it makes seventy dollars and some pennies. That's very good.

WILLY. What do we owe?

LINDA. Well, on the first there's sixteen dollars on the refrigerator . . .

WILLY. Why sixteen?

LINDA. Well, the fan belt broke, so it was a dollar eighty.

WILLY. But it's brand new.

LINDA. Well, the man said that's the way it is. Till they work themselves in, y'know.

They move through the wall-line into the kitchen.

WILLY. I hope we didn't get stuck on that machine.

LINDA. They got the biggest ads of any of them!

WILLY. I know, it's a fine machine. What else?

LINDA. Well, there's nine-sixty for the washing machine. And for the vacuum cleaner there's three and a half due on the fifteenth. Then the roof, you got twenty-one dollars remaining.

WILLY. It don't leak, does it?

LINDA. No, they did a wonderful job. Then you owe Frank for the carburetor.

WILLY. I'm not going to pay that man! That goddam Chevrolet, they ought to prohibit the manufacture of that car!

LINDA. Well, you owe him three and a half. And odds and ends, comes to around a hundred and twenty dollars by the fifteenth.

WILLY. A hundred and twenty dollars! My God, if business don't pick up I don't know what I'm gonna do!

LINDA. Well, next week you'll do better.

WILLY. Oh, I'll knock 'em dead next week. I'll go to Hartford. I'm very well liked in Hartford. You know, the trouble is, Linda, people don't seem to take to me.

They move onto the forestage.

LINDA. Oh, don't be foolish.

WILLY. I know it when I walk in. They seem to laugh at me.

LINDA. Why? Why would they laugh at you? Don't talk that way, Willy.

WILLY *moves to the edge of the stage.* LINDA *goes into the kitchen and starts to darn stockings.*

WILLY. I don't know the reason for it, but they just pass me by. I'm not noticed.

LINDA. But you're doing wonderful, dear. You're making seventy to a hundred dollars a week.

WILLY. But I gotta be at it ten, twelve hours a day. Other men—I don't know—they do it easier. I don't know why—I can't stop myself—I talk too much. A man oughta come in with a few words. One thing about Charley. He's a man of few words, and they respect him.

LINDA. You don't talk too much, you're just lively.

WILLY (*smiling*). Well, I figure, what the hell, life is short, a couple of jokes. (*To himself:*) I joke too much! (*The smile goes.*)

LINDA. Why? You're . . .

WILLY. I'm fat. I'm very—foolish to look at, Linda. I didn't tell you, but Christmas time I happened to be calling on F. H. Stewarts, and a salesman I know, as I was going in to see the buyer I heard him say something about—walrus. And I—I cracked him right across the face. I won't take that. I simply will not take that. But they do laugh at me. I know that.

LINDA. Darling . . .

WILLY. I gotta overcome it. I know I gotta overcome it. I'm not dressing to advantage, maybe.

LINDA. Willy, darling, you're the handsomest man in the world . . .

WILLY. Oh, no, Linda.

LINDA. To me you are. (*Slight pause.*) The handsomest.

From the darkness is heard the laughter of a woman. WILLY *doesn't turn to it, but it continues through* LINDA'*s lines.*

LINDA. And the boys, Willy. Few men are idolized by their children the way you are.

Music is heard as behind a scrim, to the left of the house; THE WOMAN, *dimly seen, is dressing.*

WILLY (*with great feeling*). You're the best there is. Linda, you're a pal, you know that? On the road—on the road I want to grab you sometimes and just kiss the life outa you.

The laughter is loud now, and he moves into a brightening area at the left, where THE WOMAN *has come from behind the scrim and is standing, putting on her hat, looking into a "mirror" and laughing.*

WILLY. 'Cause I get so lonely—especially when business is bad and there's nobody to talk to. I get the feeling that I'll never sell anything again, that I won't make a living for you, or a business, a business for the boys. (*He talks through* THE WOMAN'*s subsiding laughter;* THE WOMAN *primps at the "mirror."*) There's so much I want to make for . . .

THE WOMAN. Me? You didn't make me, Willy. I picked you.

WILLY (*pleased*). You picked me?

THE WOMAN (*who is quite proper-looking,* WILLY'*s age*). I did. I've been sitting at that desk watching all the salesmen go by, day in, day out. But you've got such a sense of humor, and we do have such a good time together, don't we?

WILLY. Sure, sure. (*He takes her in his arms.*) Why do you have to go now?

THE WOMAN. It's two o'clock . . .

WILLY. No, come on in! (*He pulls her.*)

THE WOMAN. . . . my sisters'll be scandalized. When'll you be back?

WILLY. Oh, two weeks about. Will you come up again?

THE WOMAN. Sure thing. You do make me laugh. It's good for me. (*She squeezes his arm, kisses him.*) And I think you're a wonderful man.

WILLY. You picked me, heh?

THE WOMAN. Sure. Because you're so sweet. And such a kidder.

WILLY. Well, I'll see you next time I'm in Boston.

THE WOMAN. I'll put you right through to the buyers.

WILLY (*slapping her bottom*). Right. Well, bottoms up!

THE WOMAN (*slaps him gently and laughs*). You just kill me, Willy. (*He suddenly grabs her and kisses her roughly.*) You kill me. And thanks for the stockings. I love a lot of stockings. Well, good night.

WILLY. Good night. And keep your pores open!

THE WOMAN. Oh, Willy!

> THE WOMAN *bursts out laughing, and* LINDA's *laughter blends in.* THE WOMAN *disappears into the dark. Now the area at the kitchen table brightens.* LINDA *is sitting where she was at the kitchen table, but now is mending a pair of her silk stockings.*

LINDA. You are, Willy. The handsomest man. You've got no reason to feel that . . .

WILLY (*coming out of* THE WOMAN's *dimming area and going over to* LINDA). I'll make it all up to you, Linda, I'll . . .

LINDA. There's nothing to make up, dear. You're doing fine, better than . . .

WILLY (*noticing her mending*). What's that?

LINDA. Just mending my stockings. They're so expensive . . .

WILLY (*angrily, taking them from her*). I won't have you mending stockings in this house! Now throw them out!

> LINDA *puts the stockings in her pocket.*

BERNARD (*entering on the run*). Where is he? If he doesn't study!

WILLY (*moving to the forestage, with great agitation*). You'll give him the answers!

BERNARD. I do, but I can't on a Regents! That's a state exam! They're liable to arrest me!

WILLY. Where is he? I'll whip him, I'll whip him!

LINDA. And he'd better give back that football, Willy, it's not nice.

WILLY. Biff! Where is he? Why is he taking everything?

LINDA. He's too rough with the girls, Willy. All the mothers are afraid of him!

WILLY. I'll whip him!

BERNARD. He's driving the car without a license!

> THE WOMAN's *laugh is heard.*

WILLY. Shut up!

LINDA. All the mothers . . .

WILLY. Shut up!

BERNARD (*backing quietly away and out*). Mr. Birnbaum says he's stuck up.

WILLY. Get outa here!

BERNARD. If he doesn't buckle down he'll flunk math! (*He goes off.*)

LINDA. He's right, Willy, you've gotta . . .

WILLY (*exploding at her*). There's nothing the matter with him! You want him to be a worm like Bernard? He's got spirit, personality . . .

As he speaks, LINDA, *almost in tears, exits into the living room.* WILLY *is alone in the kitchen, wilting and staring. The leaves are gone. It is night again, and the apartment houses look down from behind.*

WILLY. Loaded with it. Loaded! What is he stealing? He's giving it back, isn't he? Why is he stealing? What did I tell him? I never in my life told him anything but decent things.

HAPPY *in pajamas has come down the stairs;* WILLY *suddenly becomes aware of* HAPPY's *presence.*

HAPPY. Let's go now, come on.

WILLY (*sitting down at the kitchen table*). Huh! Why did she have to wax the floors herself? Everytime she waxes the floors she keels over. She knows that!

HAPPY. Shh! Take it easy. What brought you back tonight?

WILLY. I got an awful scare. Nearly hit a kid in Yonkers. God! Why didn't I go to Alaska with my brother Ben that time! Ben! That man was a genius, that man was success incarnate! What a mistake! He begged me to go.

HAPPY. Well, there's no use in . . .

WILLY. You guys! There was a man started with the clothes on his back and ended up with diamond mines!

HAPPY. Boy, someday I'd like to know how he did it.

WILLY. What's the mystery? The man knew what he wanted and went out and got it! Walked into a jungle, and comes out, the age of twenty-one, and he's rich! The world is an oyster, but you don't crack it open on a mattress!

HAPPY. Pop, I told you I'm gonna retire you for life.

WILLY. You'll retire me for life on seventy goddam dollars a week? And your women and your car and your apartment, and you'll retire me for life! Christ's sake, I couldn't get past Yonkers today! Where are you guys, where are you? The woods are burning! I can't drive a car!

CHARLEY *has appeared in the doorway. He is a large man, slow of speech, laconic, immovable. In all he says, despite what he says, there is pity, and, now, trepidation. He has a robe over pajamas, slippers on his feet. He enters the kitchen.*

CHARLEY. Everything all right?

HAPPY. Yeah, Charley, everything's . . .

WILLY. What's the matter?

CHARLEY. I heard some noise. I thought something happened. Can't we do something about the walls? You sneeze in here, and in my house hats blow off.

HAPPY. Let's go to bed, Dad. Come on.

CHARLEY *signals to* HAPPY *to go.*

WILLY. You go ahead, I'm not tired at the moment.

HAPPY (*to* WILLY). Take it easy, huh? (*He exits.*)

WILLY. What're you doin' up?

CHARLEY (*sitting down at the kitchen table opposite* WILLY). Couldn't sleep good. I had a heartburn.

WILLY. Well, you don't know how to eat.

CHARLEY. I eat with my mouth.

WILLY. No, you're ignorant. You gotta know about vitamins and things like that.

CHARLEY. Come on, let's shoot. Tire you out a little.

WILLY (*hesitantly*). All right. You got cards?

CHARLEY (*taking a deck from his pocket*). Yeah, I got them. Someplace. What is it with those vitamins?

WILLY (*dealing*). They build up your bones. Chemistry.

CHARLEY. Yeah, but there's no bones in a heartburn.

WILLY. What are you talkin' about? Do you know the first thing about it?

CHARLEY. Don't get insulted.

WILLY. Don't talk about something you don't know anything about.

They are playing. Pause.

CHARLEY. What're you doin' home?

WILLY. A little trouble with the car.

CHARLEY. Oh. (*Pause.*) I'd like to take a trip to California.

WILLY. Don't say.

CHARLEY. You want a job?

WILLY. I got a job, I told you that. (*After a slight pause.*) What the hell are you offering me a job for?

CHARLEY. Don't get insulted.

WILLY. Don't insult me.

CHARLEY. I don't see no sense in it. You don't have to go on this way.

WILLY. I got a good job. (*Slight pause.*) What do you keep comin' in here for?

CHARLEY. You want me to go?

WILLY (*after a pause, withering*). I can't understand it. He's going back to Texas again. What the hell is that?

CHARLEY. Let him go.

WILLY. I got nothin' to give him, Charley, I'm clean, I'm clean.

CHARLEY. He won't starve. None a them starve. Forget about him.

WILLY. Then what have I got to remember?

CHARLEY. You take it too hard. To hell with it. When a deposit bottle is broken you don't get your nickel back.

WILLY. That's easy enough for you to say.

CHARLEY. That ain't easy for me to say.

WILLY. Did you see the ceiling I put up in the living room?

CHARLEY. Yeah, that's a piece of work. To put up a ceiling is a mystery to me. How do you do it?

WILLY. What's the difference?

CHARLEY. Well, talk about it.

WILLY. You gonna put up a ceiling?

CHARLEY. How could I put up a ceiling?

WILLY. Then what the hell are you bothering me for?

CHARLEY. You're insulted again.

WILLY. A man who can't handle tools is not a man. You're disgusting.

CHARLEY. Don't call me disgusting, Willy.

UNCLE BEN, *carrying a valise and an umbrella, enters the forestage from around the right corner of the house. He is a stolid man, in his sixties, with a mustache and an authoritative air. He is utterly certain of his destiny, and there is an aura of far places about him. He enters exactly as* WILLY *speaks.*

WILLY. I'm getting awfully tired, Ben.

BEN'*s music is heard.* BEN *looks around at everything.*

CHARLEY. Good, keep playing; you'll sleep better. Did you call me Ben?

BEN *looks at his watch.*

WILLY. That's funny. For a second there you reminded me of my brother Ben.

BEN. I only have a few minutes. (*He strolls, inspecting the place.* WILLY *and* CHARLEY *continue playing.*)

CHARLEY. You never heard from him again, heh? Since that time?

WILLY. Didn't Linda tell you? Couple of weeks ago we got a letter from his wife in Africa. He died.

CHARLEY. That so.

BEN. (*chuckling*). So this is Brooklyn, eh?

CHARLEY. Maybe you're in for some of his money.

WILLY. Naa, he had seven sons. There's just one opportunity I had with that man . . .

BEN. I must make a train, William. There are several properties I'm looking at in Alaska.

WILLY. Sure, sure! If I'd gone with him to Alaska that time, everything would've been totally different.

CHARLEY. Go on, you'd froze to death up there.

WILLY. What're you talking about?

BEN. Opportunity is tremendous in Alaska, William. Surprised you're not up there.

WILLY. Sure, tremendous.

CHARLEY. Heh?

WILLY. There was the only man I ever met who knew the answers.

CHARLEY. Who?

BEN. How are you all?

WILLY (*taking a pot, smiling*). Fine, fine.

CHARLEY. Pretty sharp tonight.

BEN. Is Mother living with you?

WILLY. No, she died a long time ago.

CHARLEY. Who?

BEN. That's too bad. Fine specimen of a lady, Mother.

WILLY (*to* CHARLEY). Heh?

BEN. I'd hoped to see the old girl.

CHARLEY. Who died?

BEN. Heard anything from Father, have you?

WILLY (*unnerved*). What do you mean, who died?

CHARLEY (*taking a pot*). What're you talkin' about?

BEN (*looking at his watch*). William, it's half-past eight!

WILLY (*as though to dispel his confusion he angrily stops* CHARLEY's *hand*). That's my build!

CHARLEY. I put the ace . . .

WILLY. If you don't know how to play the game I'm not gonna throw my money away on you!

CHARLEY (*rising*). It was my ace, for God's sake!

WILLY. I'm through, I'm through!

BEN. When did Mother die?

WILLY. Long ago. Since the beginning you never knew how to play cards.

CHARLEY (*picks up the cards and goes to the door*). All right! Next time I'll bring a deck with five aces.

WILLY. I don't play that kind of game!

CHARLEY (*turning to him*). You ought to be ashamed of yourself!

WILLY. Yeah?

CHARLEY. Yeah! (*He goes out.*)

WILLY (*slamming the door after him*). Ignoramus!

BEN (*as* WILLY *comes toward him through the wall-line of the kitchen*). So you're William.

WILLY (*shaking* BEN's *hand*). Ben! I've been waiting for you so long! What's the answer? How did you do it?

BEN. Oh, there's a story in that.

LINDA *enters the forestage, as of old, carrying the wash basket.*

LINDA. Is this Ben?

BEN (*gallantly*). How do you do, my dear.

LINDA. Where've you been all these years? Willy's always wondered why you . . .

WILLY (*pulling* BEN *away from her impatiently*). Where is Dad? Didn't you follow him? How did you get started?

BEN. Well, I don't know how much you remember.

WILLY. Well, I was just a baby, of course, only three or four years old . . .

BEN. Three years and eleven months.

WILLY. What a memory, Ben!

BEN. I have many enterprises, William, and I have never kept books.

WILLY. I remember I was sitting under the wagon in—was it Nebraska?

BEN. It was South Dakota, and I gave you a bunch of wild flowers.

WILLY. I remember you walking away down some open road.

BEN (*laughing*). I was going to find Father in Alaska.

WILLY. Where is he?

BEN. At that age I had a very faulty view of geography, William. I discovered after a few days that I was heading due south, so instead of Alaska, I ended up in Africa.

LINDA. Africa!

WILLY. The Gold Coast!

BEN. Principally diamond mines.

LINDA. Diamond mines!

BEN. Yes, my dear. But I've only a few minutes . . .

WILLY. No! Boys! Boys! (*Young* BIFF *and* HAPPY *appear.*) Listen to this. This is your Uncle Ben, a great man! Tell my boys, Ben!

BEN. Why, boys, when I was seventeen I walked into the jungle, and when I was twenty-one I walked out. (*He laughs.*) And by God I was rich.

WILLY (*to the boys*). You see what I been talking about? The greatest things can happen!

BEN (*glancing at his watch*). I have an appointment in Ketchikan Tuesday week.

WILLY. No, Ben! Please tell about Dad. I want my boys to hear. I want them to know the kind of stock they spring from. All I remember is a man with a big beard, and I was in Mamma's lap, sitting around a fire, and some kind of high music.

BEN. His flute. He played the flute.

WILLY. Sure, the flute, that's right!

New music is heard, a high, rollicking tune.

BEN. Father was a very great and a very wild-hearted man. We would start in Boston, and he'd toss the whole family into the wagon, and then he'd drive the team right across the country; through Ohio, and Indiana, Michigan, Illinois, and all the Western states. And we'd stop in the towns and sell the flutes that he'd made on the way. Great inventor, Father. With one gadget he made more in a week than a man like you could make in a lifetime.

WILLY. That's just the way I'm bringing them up, Ben—rugged, well liked, all-around.

BEN. Yeah? (*To* BIFF.) Hit that, boy—hard as you can. (*He pounds his stomach.*)

BIFF. Oh, no, sir!

BEN (*taking boxing stance*). Come on, get to me! (*He laughs.*)

WILLY. Go to it, Biff! Go ahead, show him!

BIFF. Okay! (*He cocks his fists and starts in.*)

LINDA (*to* WILLY). Why must he fight, dear?

BEN (*sparring with* BIFF). Good boy! Good boy!

WILLY. How's that, Ben, heh?

HAPPY. Give him the left, Biff!

LINDA. Why are you fighting?

BEN. Good boy! (*Suddenly comes in, trips* BIFF, *and stands over him, the point of his umbrella poised over* BIFF's *eye.*)

LINDA. Look out, Biff!

BIFF. Gee!

BEN (*patting* BIFF's *knee*). Never fight fair with a stranger, boy. You'll never get out of the jungle that way. (*Taking* LINDA's *hand and bowing.*) It was an honor and a pleasure to meet you, Linda.

LINDA (*withdrawing her hand coldly, frightened*). Have a nice—trip.

BEN (*to* WILLY). And good luck with your—what do you do?

WILLY. Selling.

BEN. Yes. Well . . . (*He raises his hand in farewell to all.*)

WILLY. No, Ben, I don't want you to think . . . (*He takes* BEN's *arm to show him.*) It's Brooklyn, I know, but we hunt too.

BEN. Really, now.

WILLY. Oh, sure, there's snakes and rabbits and—that's why I moved out here. Why, Biff can fell any one of these trees in no time! Boys! Go right over to where they're building the apartment house and get some sand. We're gonna rebuild the entire front stoop right now! Watch this, Ben!

BIFF. Yes, sir! On the double, Hap!

HAPPY (*as he and* BIFF *run off*). I lost weight, Pop, you notice?

CHARLEY *enters in knickers, even before the boys are gone.*

CHARLEY. Listen, if they steal any more from that building the watchman'll put the cops on them!

LINDA (*to* WILLY). Don't let Biff . . .

BEN *laughs lustily.*

WILLY. You shoulda seen the lumber they brought home last week. At least a dozen six-by-tens worth all kinds a money.

CHARLEY. Listen, if that watchman . . .

WILLY. I gave them hell, understand. But I got a couple of fearless characters there.

CHARLEY. Willy, the jails are full of fearless characters.

BEN (*clapping* WILLY *on the back, with a laugh at* CHARLEY). And the stock exchange, friend!

WILLY (*joining in* BEN's *laughter*). Where are the rest of your pants?

CHARLEY. My wife bought them.

WILLY. Now all you need is a golf club and you can go upstairs and go to sleep. (*To* BEN.) Great athlete! Between him and his son Bernard they can't hammer a nail!

BERNARD (*rushing in*). The watchman's chasing Biff!

WILLY (*angrily*). Shut up! He's not stealing anything!

LINDA (*alarmed, hurrying off left*). Where is he? Biff, dear! (*She exits.*)

WILLY (*moving toward the left, away from* BEN). There's nothing wrong. What's the matter with you?

BEN. Nervy boy. Good!

WILLY (*laughing*). Oh, nerves of iron, that Biff!

CHARLEY. Don't know what it is. My New England man comes back and he's bleedin', they murdered him up there.

WILLY. It's contacts, Charley, I got important contacts!

CHARLEY (*sarcastically*). Glad to hear it, Willy. Come in later, we'll shoot a little casino. I'll take some of your Portland money. (*He laughs at* WILLY *and exits.*)

WILLY (*turning to* BEN). Business is bad, it's murderous. But not for me, of course.

BEN. I'll stop by on my way back to Africa.

WILLY (*longingly*). Can't you stay a few days? You're just what I need, Ben, because I—I have a fine position here, but I—well, Dad left when I was such a baby and I never had a chance to talk to him and I still feel—kind of temporary about myself.

BEN. I'll be late for my train.

They are at opposite ends of the stage.

WILLY. Ben, my boys—can't we talk? They'd go into the jaws of hell for me, see, but I . . .

BEN. William, you're being first-rate with your boys. Outstanding, manly chaps!

WILLY (*hanging on to his words*). Oh, Ben, that's good to hear! Because sometimes I'm afraid that I'm not teaching them the right kind of—Ben, how should I teach them?

BEN (*giving great weight to each word, and with a certain vicious audacity*). William, when I walked into the jungle, I was seventeen. When I walked out I was twenty-one. And, by God, I was rich! (*He goes off into darkness around the right corner of the house.*)

WILLY. . . . was rich! That's just the spirit I want to imbue them with! To walk into a jungle! I was right! I was right! I was right!

BEN *is gone, but* WILLY *is still speaking to him as* LINDA, *in nightgown and robe, enters the kitchen, glances around for* WILLY, *then goes to the door of the house, looks out and sees him. Comes down to his left. He looks at her.*

LINDA. Willy, dear? Willy?

WILLY. I was right!

LINDA. Did you have some cheese? (*He can't answer.*) It's very late, darling. Come to bed, heh?

WILLY (*looking straight up*). Gotta break your neck to see a star in this yard.

LINDA. You coming in?

WILLY. Whatever happened to that diamond watch fob? Remember? When Ben came from Africa that time? Didn't he give me a watch fob with a diamond in it?

LINDA. You pawned it, dear. Twelve, thirteen years ago. For Biff's radio correspondence course.

WILLY. Gee, that was a beautiful thing. I'll take a walk.

LINDA. But you're in your slippers.

WILLY (*starting to go around the house at the left*). I was right! I was! (*Half to* LINDA, *as he goes, shaking his head.*) What a man! There was a man worth talking to. I was right!

LINDA (*calling after* WILLY). But in your slippers, Willy!

WILLY *is almost gone when* BIFF, *in his pajamas, comes down the stairs and enters the kitchen.*

BIFF. What is he doing out there?

LINDA. Sh!

BIFF. God Almighty, Mom, how long has he been doing this?

LINDA. Don't, he'll hear you.

BIFF. What the hell is the matter with him?

LINDA. It'll pass by morning.

BIFF. Shouldn't we do anything?

LINDA. Oh, my dear, you should do a lot of things, but there's nothing to do, so go to sleep.

HAPPY *comes down the stairs and sits on the steps.*

HAPPY. I never heard him so loud, Mom.

LINDA. Well, come around more often; you'll hear him. (*She sits down at the table and mends the lining of* WILLY's *jacket.*)

BIFF. Why didn't you ever write me about this, Mom?

LINDA. How would I write to you? For over three months you had no address.

BIFF. I was on the move. But you know I thought of you all the time. You know that, don't you, pal?

LINDA. I know, dear, I know. But he likes to have a letter. Just to know that there's still a possibility for better things.

BIFF. He's not like this all the time, is he?

LINDA. It's when you come home he's always the worst.

BIFF. When I come home?

LINDA. When you write you're coming, he's all smiles, and talks about the future, and—he's just wonderful. And then the closer you seem to come, the more shaky he gets, and then, by the time you get here, he's arguing, and he seems angry at you. I think it's just that maybe he can't bring himself to—to open up to you. Why are you so hateful to each other? Why is that?

BIFF (*evasively*). I'm not hateful, Mom.

LINDA. But you no sooner come in the door than you're fighting!

BIFF. I don't know why. I mean to change. I'm tryin', Mom, you understand?

LINDA. Are you home to stay now?

BIFF. I don't know. I want to look around, see what's doin'.

LINDA. Biff, you can't look around all your life, can you?

BIFF. I just can't take hold, Mom. I can't take hold of some kind of a life.

LINDA. Biff, a man is not a bird, to come and go with the spring time.

BIFF. Your hair . . . (*He touches her hair.*) Your hair got so gray.

LINDA. Oh, it's been gray since you were in high school. I just stopped dyeing it, that's all.

BIFF. Dye it again, will ya? I don't want my pal looking old. (*He smiles.*)

LINDA. You're such a boy! You think you can go away for a year and . . . You've got to get it into your head now that one day you'll knock on this door and there'll be strange people here . . .

BIFF. What are you talking about? You're not even sixty, Mom.

LINDA. But what about your father?

BIFF (*lamely*). Well, I meant him too.

HAPPY. He admires Pop.

LINDA. Biff, dear, if you don't have any feeling for him, then you can't have any feeling for me.

BIFF. Sure I can, Mom.

LINDA. No. You can't just come to see me, because I love him. (*With a threat, but only a threat, of tears.*) He's the dearest man in the world to me, and I won't have anyone making him feel unwanted and low and blue. You've got to make up your mind now, darling, there's no leeway any more. Either he's your father and you pay him that respect, or else you're not to come here. I know he's not easy to get along with—nobody knows that better than me—but . . .

WILLY (*from the left, with a laugh*). Hey, hey, Biffo!

BIFF (*starting to go out after* WILLY). What the hell is the matter with him? (HAPPY *stops him.*)

LINDA. Don't—don't go near him!

BIFF. Stop making excuses for him! He always, always wiped the floor with you. Never had an ounce of respect for you.

HAPPY. He's always had respect for . . .

BIFF. What the hell do you know about it?

HAPPY (*surlily*). Just don't call him crazy!

BIFF. He's got no character—Charley wouldn't do this. Not in his own house—spewing out that vomit from his mind.

HAPPY. Charley never had to cope with what he's got to.

BIFF. People are worse off than Willy Loman. Believe me, I've seen them!

LINDA. Then make Charley your father, Biff. You can't do that, can you? I
don't say he's a great man. Willy Loman never made a lot of money. His
name was never in the paper. He's not the finest character that ever
lived. But he's a human being, and a terrible thing is happening to him.
So attention must be paid. He's not to be allowed to fall into his grave
like an old dog. Attention, attention must be finally paid to such a person. You called him crazy . . .

BIFF. I didn't mean . . .

LINDA. No, a lot of people think he's lost his—balance. But you don't have to
be very smart to know what his trouble is. The man is exhausted.

HAPPY. Sure!

LINDA. A small man can be just as exhausted as a great man. He works for a
company thirty-six years this March, opens up unheard-of territories to
their trademark, and now in his old age they take his salary away.

HAPPY (*indignantly*). I didn't know that, Mom.

LINDA. You never asked, my dear! Now that you get your spending money
someplace else you don't trouble your mind with him.

HAPPY. But I gave you money last . . .

LINDA. Christmas time, fifty dollars! To fix the hot water it cost ninety-seven
fifty! For five weeks he's been on straight commission, like a beginner,
an unknown!

BIFF. Those ungrateful bastards!

LINDA. Are they any worse than his sons? When he brought them business,
when he was young, they were glad to see him. But now his old
friends, the old buyers that loved him so and always found some order
to hand him in a pinch—they're all dead, retired. He used to be able to
make six, seven calls a day in Boston. Now he takes his valises out of
the car and puts them back and takes them out again and he's exhausted. Instead of walking he talks now. He drives seven hundred
miles, and when he gets there no one knows him any more, no one
welcomes him. And what goes through a man's mind, driving seven
hundred miles home without having earned a cent? Why shouldn't he
talk to himself? Why? When he has to go to Charley and borrow fifty
dollars a week and pretend to me that it's his pay? How long can that go
on? How long? You see what I'm sitting here and waiting for? And you
tell me he has no character? The man who never worked a day but for
your benefit? When does he get the medal for that? Is this his reward—
to turn around at the age of sixty-three and find his sons, who he loved
better than his life, one a philandering bum . . .

HAPPY. Mom!

LINDA. That's all you are, my baby! (*To* BIFF.) And you! What happened to the
love you had for him? You were such pals! How you used to talk to him
on the phone every night! How lonely he was till he could come home
to you!

BIFF. All right, Mom. I'll live here in my room, and I'll get a job. I'll keep
away from him, that's all.

LINDA. No, Biff. You can't stay here and fight all the time.

BIFF. He threw me out of this house, remember that.

LINDA. Why did he do that? I never knew why.

BIFF. Because I know he's a fake and he doesn't like anybody around who knows!

LINDA. Why a fake? In what way? What do you mean?

BIFF. Just don't lay it all at my feet. It's between me and him—that's all I have to say. I'll chip in from now on. He'll settle for half my paycheck. He'll be all right. I'm going to bed. (*He starts for the stairs.*)

LINDA. He won't be all right.

BIFF (*turning on the stairs, furiously*). I hate this city and I'll stay here. Now what do you want?

LINDA. He's dying, Biff.

HAPPY *turns quickly to her, shocked.*

BIFF (*after a pause*). Why is he dying?

LINDA. He's been trying to kill himself.

BIFF (*with great horror*). How?

LINDA. I live from day to day.

BIFF. What're you talking about?

LINDA. Remember I wrote you that he smashed up the car again? In February?

BIFF. Well?

LINDA. The insurance inspector came. He said that they have evidence. That all these accidents in the last year—weren't—weren't—accidents.

HAPPY. How can they tell that? That's a lie.

LINDA. It seems there's a woman . . . (*She takes a breath as:*)

BIFF (*sharply but contained*). What woman?

LINDA (*simultaneously*). . . . and this woman . . .

LINDA. What?

BIFF. Nothing. Go ahead.

LINDA. What did you say?

BIFF. Nothing. I just said what woman?

HAPPY. What about her?

LINDA. Well, it seems she was walking down the road and saw his car. She says that he wasn't driving fast at all, and that he didn't skid. She says he came to that little bridge, and then deliberately smashed into the railing, and it was only the shallowness of the water that saved him.

BIFF. Oh, no, he probably just fell asleep again.

LINDA. I don't think he fell asleep.

BIFF. Why not?

LINDA. Last month . . . (*With great difficulty.*) Oh, boys, it's so hard to say a thing like this! He's just a big stupid man to you, but I tell you there's more good in him than in many other people. (*She chokes, wipes her eyes.*) I was looking for a fuse. The lights blew out, and I went down the cellar. And behind the fuse box—it happened to fall out—was a length of rubber pipe—just short.

HAPPY. No kidding!

LINDA. There's a little attachment on the end of it. I knew right away. And sure enough, on the bottom of the water heater there's a new little nipple on the gas pipe.

HAPPY (*angrily*). That—jerk.

BIFF. Did you have it taken off?

LINDA. I'm—I'm ashamed to. How can I mention it to him? Every day I go down and take away that little rubber pipe. But, when he comes home,

I put it back where it was. How can I insult him that way? I don't know what to do. I live from day to day, boys. I tell you, I know every thought in his mind. It sounds so old-fashioned and silly, but I tell you he put his whole life into you and you've turned your backs on him. (*She is bent over in the chair, weeping, her face in her hands.*) Biff, I swear to God! Biff, his life is in your hands!

HAPPY (*to* BIFF). How do you like that damned fool!

BIFF (*kissing her*). All right, pal, all right. It's all settled now. I've been re-miss. I know that, Mom. But now I'll stay, and I swear to you, I'll apply myself. (*Kneeling in front of her, in a fever of self-reproach.*) It's just—you see, Mom, I don't fit in business. Not that I won't try. I'll try, and I'll make good.

HAPPY. Sure you will. The trouble with you in business was you never tried to please people.

BIFF. I know, I . . .

HAPPY. Like when you worked for Harrison's. Bob Harrison said you were tops, and then you go and do some damn fool thing like whistling whole songs in the elevator like a comedian.

BIFF (*against* HAPPY). So what? I like to whistle sometimes.

HAPPY. You don't raise a guy to a responsible job who whistles in the elevator!

LINDA. Well, don't argue about it now.

HAPPY. Like when you'd go off and swim in the middle of the day instead of taking the line around.

BIFF (*his resentment rising*). Well, don't you run off? You take off some-times, don't you? On a nice summer day?

HAPPY. Yeah, but I cover myself!

LINDA. Boys!

HAPPY. If I'm going to take a fade the boss can call any number where I'm supposed to be and they'll swear to him that I just left. I'll tell you some-thing that I hate to say, Biff, but in the business world some of them think you're crazy.

BIFF (*angered*). Screw the business world!

HAPPY. All right, screw it! Great, but cover yourself!

LINDA. Hap, Hap!

BIFF. I don't care what they think! They've laughed at Dad for years, and you know why? Because we don't belong in this nuthouse of a city! We should be mixing cement on some open plain or—or carpenters. A car-penter is allowed to whistle!

WILLY *walks in from the entrance of the house, at left.*

WILLY. Even your grandfather was better than a carpenter. (*Pause. They watch him.*) You never grew up. Bernard does not whistle in the ele-vator, I assure you.

BIFF (*as though to laugh* WILLY *out of it*). Yeah, but you do, Pop.

WILLY. I never in my life whistled in an elevator! And who in the business world thinks I'm crazy?

BIFF. I didn't mean it like that, Pop. Now don't make a whole thing out of it, will ya?

WILLY. Go back to the West! Be a carpenter, a cowboy, enjoy yourself!

LINDA. Willy, he was just saying . . .

WILLY. I heard what he said!

HAPPY (*trying to quiet* WILLY). Hey, Pop, come on now . . .

WILLY (*continuing over* HAPPY'*s line*). They laugh at me, heh? Go to Filene's, go to the Hub, go to Slattery's, Boston. Call out the name Willy Loman and see what happens! Big shot!

BIFF. All right, Pop.

WILLY. Big!

BIFF. All right!

WILLY. Why do you always insult me?

BIFF. I didn't say a word. (*To* LINDA.) Did I say a word?

LINDA. He didn't say anything, Willy.

WILLY (*going to the doorway of the living room*). All right, good night, good night.

LINDA. Willy, dear, he just decided . . .

WILLY (*to* BIFF). If you get tired hanging around tomorrow, paint the ceiling I put up in the living room.

BIFF. I'm leaving early tomorrow.

HAPPY. He's going to see Bill Oliver, Pop.

WILLY (*interestedly*). Oliver? For what?

BIFF (*with reserve, but trying; trying*). He always said he'd stake me. I'd like to go into business, so maybe I can take him up on it.

LINDA. Isn't that wonderful?

WILLY. Don't interrupt. What's wonderful about it? There's fifty men in the City of New York who'd stake him. (*To* BIFF.) Sporting goods?

BIFF. I guess so. I know something about it and . . .

WILLY. He knows something about it! You know sporting goods better than Spalding, for God's sake! How much is he giving you?

BIFF. I don't know, I didn't even see him yet, but . . .

WILLY. Then what're you talkin' about?

BIFF (*getting angry*). Well, all I said was I'm gonna see him, that's all!

WILLY (*turning away*). Ah, you're counting your chickens again.

BIFF (*starting left for the stairs*). Oh, Jesus, I'm going to sleep!

WILLY (*calling after him*). Don't curse in this house!

BIFF (*turning*). Since when did you get so clean?

HAPPY (*trying to stop them*). Wait a . . .

WILLY. Don't use that language to me! I won't have it!

HAPPY (*grabbing* BIFF, *shouts*). Wait a minute! I got an idea. I got a feasible idea. Come here, Biff, let's talk this over now, let's talk some sense here. When I was down in Florida last time, I thought of a great idea to sell sporting goods. It just came back to me. You and I, Biff—we have a line, the Loman Line. We train a couple of weeks, and put on a couple of exhibitions, see?

WILLY. That's an idea!

HAPPY. Wait! We form two basketball teams, see? Two water-polo teams. We play each other. It's a million dollars' worth of publicity. Two brothers, see? The Loman Brothers. Displays in the Royal Palms—all the hotels. And banners over the ring and the basketball court: "Loman Brothers." Baby, we could sell sporting goods!

WILLY. That is a one-million-dollar idea!

LINDA. Marvelous!

BIFF. I'm in great shape as far as that's concerned.

HAPPY. And the beauty of it is, Biff, it wouldn't be like a business. We'd be out playin' ball again.

BIFF (*enthused*). Yeah, that's . . .

WILLY. Million-dollar . . .

HAPPY. And you wouldn't get fed up with it, Biff. It'd be the family again. There'd be the old honor, and comradeship, and if you wanted to go off for a swim or somethin'—well, you'd do it! Without some smart cooky gettin' up ahead of you!

WILLY. Lick the world! You guys together could absolutely lick the civilized world.

BIFF. I'll see Oliver tomorrow. Hap, if we could work that out . . .

LINDA. Maybe things are beginning to . . .

WILLY (*wildly enthused, to* LINDA). Stop interrupting! (*To* BIFF.) But don't wear sport jacket and slacks when you see Oliver.

BIFF. No, I'll . . .

WILLY. A business suit, and talk as little as possible, and don't crack any jokes.

BIFF. He did like me. Always liked me.

LINDA. He loved you!

WILLY (*to* LINDA). Will you stop! (*To* BIFF.) Walk in very serious. You are not applying for a boy's job. Money is to pass. Be quiet, fine, and serious. Everybody likes a kidder, but nobody lends him money.

HAPPY. I'll try to get some myself, Biff. I'm sure I can.

WILLY. I see great things for you kids, I think your troubles are over. But remember, start big and you'll end big. Ask for fifteen. How much you gonna ask for?

BIFF. Gee, I don't know . . .

WILLY. And don't say "Gee." "Gee" is a boy's word. A man walking in for fifteen thousand dollars does not say "Gee!"

BIFF. Ten, I think, would be top though.

WILLY. Don't be so modest. You always started too low. Walk in with a big laugh. Don't look worried. Start off with a couple of your good stories to lighten things up. It's not what you say, it's how you say it—because personality always wins the day.

LINDA. Oliver always thought the highest of him . . .

WILLY. Will you let me talk?

BIFF. Don't yell at her, Pop, will ya?

WILLY (*angrily*). I was talking, wasn't I?

BIFF. I don't like you yelling at her all the time, and I'm tellin' you, that's all.

WILLY. What're you, takin' over this house?

LINDA. Willy . . .

WILLY (*turning to her*). Don't take his side all the time, goddammit!

BIFF (*furiously*). Stop yelling at her!

WILLY (*suddenly pulling on his cheek, beaten down, guilt ridden*). Give my best to Bill Oliver—he may remember me. (*He exits through the living room doorway.*)

LINDA (*her voice subdued*). What'd you have to start that for? (BIFF *turns away.*) You see how sweet he was as soon as you talked hopefully? (*She goes over to* BIFF.) Come up and say good night to him. Don't let him go to bed that way.

HAPPY. Come on, Biff, let's buck him up.

LINDA. Please, dear. Just say good night. It takes so little to make him happy. Come. (*She goes through the living room doorway, calling upstairs from within the living room.*) Your pajamas are hanging in the bath-room, Willy!

HAPPY (*looking toward where* LINDA *went out*). What a woman! They broke the mold when they made her. You know that, Biff.

BIFF. He's off salary. My God, working on commission!

HAPPY. Well, let's face it: he's no hot-shot selling man. Except that some-times, you have to admit, he's a sweet personality.

BIFF (*deciding*). Lend me ten bucks, will ya? I want to buy some new ties.

HAPPY. I'll take you to a place I know. Beautiful stuff. Wear one of my striped shirts tomorrow.

BIFF. She got gray. Mom got awful old. Gee, I'm gonna go in to Oliver to-morrow and knock him for a . . . .

HAPPY. Come on up. Tell that to Dad. Let's give him a whirl. Come on.

BIFF (*steamed up*). You know, with ten thousand bucks, boy!

HAPPY (*as they go into the living room*). That's the talk, Biff, that's the first time I've heard the old confidence out of you! (*From within the living room, fading off*) You're gonna live with me, kid, and any babe you want just say the word . . . (*The last lines are hardly heard. They are mounting the stairs to their parents' bedroom.*)

LINDA (*entering her bedroom and addressing* WILLY, *who is in the bath-room. She is straightening the bed for him*). Can you do anything about the shower? It drips.

WILLY (*from the bathroom*). All of a sudden everything falls to pieces. God-dam plumbing, oughta be sued, those people. I hardly finished putting it in and the thing . . . (*His words rumble off.*)

LINDA. I'm just wondering if Oliver will remember him. You think he might?

WILLY (*coming out of the bathroom in his pajamas*). Remember him? What's the matter with you, you crazy? If he'd've stayed with Oliver he'd be on top by now! Wait'll Oliver gets a look at him. You don't know the average caliber any more. The average young man today— (*he is getting into bed*)—is got a caliber of zero. Greatest thing in the world for him was to bum around.

BIFF *and* HAPPY *enter the bedroom. Slight pause.*

WILLY (*stops short, looking at* BIFF). Glad to hear it, boy.

HAPPY. He wanted to say good night to you, sport.

WILLY (*to* BIFF). Yeah. Knock him dead, boy. What'd you want to tell me?

BIFF. Just take it easy, Pop. Good night. (*He turns to go.*)

WILLY (*unable to resist*). And if anything falls off the desk while you're talk-ing to him—like a package or something—don't you pick it up. They have office boys for that.

LINDA. I'll make a big breakfast . . . .

WILLY. Will you let me finish? (*To* BIFF.) Tell him you were in the business in the West. Not farm work.

BIFF. All right, Dad.

LINDA. I think everything . . .

WILLY (*going right through her speech*). And don't undersell yourself. No less than fifteen thousand dollars.

BIFF (*unable to bear him*). Okay. Good night, Mom. (*He starts moving.*)

WILLY. Because you got a greatness in you, Biff, remember that. You got all
kinds of greatness . . . (*He lies back, exhausted.* BIFF *walks out.*)

LINDA (*calling after* BIFF). Sleep well, darling!

HAPPY. I'm gonna get married, Mom. I wanted to tell you.

LINDA. Go to sleep, dear.

HAPPY (*going*). I just wanted to tell you.

WILLY. Keep up the good work. (HAPPY *exits.*) God . . . remember that Ebbets
Field game? The championship of the city?

LINDA. Just rest. Should I sing to you?

WILLY. Yeah. Sing to me. (LINDA *hums a soft lullaby.*) When that team came
out—he was the tallest, remember?

LINDA. Oh, yes. And in gold.

BIFF *enters the darkened kitchen, takes a cigarette, and leaves the
house. He comes downstage into a golden pool of light. He smokes,
staring at the night.*

WILLY. Like a young god. Hercules—something like that. And the sun, the
sun all around him. Remember how he waved to me? Right up from the
field, with the representatives of three colleges standing by? And the
buyers I brought, and the cheers when he came out—Loman, Loman,
Loman! God Almighty, he'll be great yet. A star like that, magnificent,
can never really fade away!

The light on WILLY *is fading. The gas heater begins to glow through the
kitchen wall, near the stairs, a blue flame beneath red coils.*

LINDA (*timidly*). Willy dear, what has he got against you?

WILLY. I'm so tired. Don't talk any more.

BIFF *slowly returns to the kitchen. He stops, stares toward the heater.*

LINDA. Will you ask Howard to let you work in New York?

WILLY. First thing in the morning. Everything'll be all right.

BIFF *reaches behind the heater and draws out a length of rubber tubing. He is horrified and turns his head toward* WILLY's *room, still
dimly lit, from which the strains of* LINDA's *desperate but monotonous
humming rise.*

WILLY (*staring through the window into the moonlight*). Gee, look at the
moon moving between the buildings!

BIFF *wraps the tubing around his hand and quickly goes up the stairs.*

Act 2

SCENE: *Music is heard, gay and bright. The curtain rises as the music
fades away.* WILLY, *in shirt sleeves, is sitting at the kitchen table, sipping
coffee, his hat in his lap.* LINDA *is filling his cup when she can.*

WILLY. Wonderful coffee. Meal in itself.

LINDA. Can I make you some eggs?

WILLY. No. Take a breath.

LINDA. You look so rested, dear.

WILLY. I slept like a dead one. First time in months. Imagine, sleeping till ten on a Tuesday morning. Boys left nice and early, heh?

LINDA. They were out of here by eight o'clock.

WILLY. Good work!

LINDA. It was so thrilling to see them leaving together. I can't get over the shaving lotion in this house!

WILLY (*smiling*). Mmm . . .

LINDA. Biff was very changed this morning. His whole attitude seemed to be hopeful. He couldn't wait to get downtown to see Oliver.

WILLY. He's heading for a change. There's no question, there simply are certain men that take longer to get—solidified. How did he dress?

LINDA. His blue suit. He's so handsome in that suit. He could be a—anything in that suit!

WILLY *gets up from the table.* LINDA *holds his jacket for him.*

WILLY. There's no question, no question at all. Gee, on the way home tonight I'd like to buy some seeds.

LINDA (*laughing*). That'd be wonderful. But not enough sun gets back there. Nothing'll grow any more.

WILLY. You wait, kid, before it's all over we're gonna get a little place out in the country, and I'll raise some vegetables, a couple of chickens . . .

LINDA. You'll do it yet, dear.

WILLY *walks out of his jacket.* LINDA *follows him.*

WILLY. And they'll get married, and come for a weekend. I'd build a little guest house. 'Cause I got so many fine tools, all I'd need would be a little lumber and some peace of mind.

LINDA (*joyfully*). I sewed the lining . . .

WILLY. I could build two guest houses, so they'd both come. Did he decide how much he's going to ask Oliver for?

LINDA (*getting him into the jacket*). He didn't mention it, but I imagine ten or fifteen thousand. You going to talk to Howard today?

WILLY. Yeah. I'll put it to him straight and simple. He'll just have to take me off the road.

LINDA. And Willy, don't forget to ask for a little advance, because we've got the insurance premium. It's the grace period now.

WILLY. That's a hundred . . . ?

LINDA. A hundred and eight, sixty-eight. Because we're a little short again.

WILLY. Why are we short?

LINDA. Well, you had the motor job on the car . . .

WILLY. That goddam Studebaker!

LINDA. And you got one more payment on the refrigerator . . .

WILLY. But it just broke again!

LINDA. Well, it's old, dear.

WILLY. I told you we should've bought a well-advertised machine. Charley bought a General Electric and it's twenty years old and it's still good, that son-of-a-bitch.

LINDA. But, Willy . . .

WILLY. Whoever heard of a Hastings refrigerator? Once in my life I would like to own something outright before it's broken! I'm always in a race with the junkyard! I just finished paying for the car and it's on its last legs. The refrigerator consumes belts like a goddam maniac. They time

those things. They time them so when you finally paid for them, they're
used up.

LINDA (*buttoning up his jacket as he unbuttons it*). All told, about two hundred dollars would carry us, dear. But that includes the last payment on
the mortgage. After this payment, Willy, the house belongs to us.

WILLY. It's twenty-five years!

LINDA. Biff was nine years old when we bought it.

WILLY. Well, that's a great thing. To weather a twenty-five year mortgage is .
. .

LINDA. It's an accomplishment.

WILLY. All the cement, the lumber, the reconstruction I put in this house!
There ain't a crack to be found in it any more.

LINDA. Well, it served its purpose.

WILLY. What purpose? Some stranger'll come along, move in, and that's that.
If only Biff would take this house, and raise a family . . . (*He starts to
go.*) Good-by, I'm late.

LINDA (*suddenly remembering*). Oh, I forgot! You're supposed to meet
them for dinner.

WILLY. Me?

LINDA. At Frank's Chop House on Forty-eighth near Sixth Avenue.

WILLY. Is that so! How about you?

LINDA. No, just the three of you. They're gonna blow you to a big meal!

WILLY. Don't say! Who thought of that?

LINDA. Biff came to me this morning, Willy, and he said, "Tell Dad, we want
to blow him to a big meal." Be there six o'clock. You and your two
boys are going to have dinner.

WILLY. Gee whiz! That's really somethin'. I'm gonna knock Howard for a
loop, kid. I'll get an advance, and I'll come home with a New York job.
Goddammit, now I'm gonna do it!

LINDA. Oh, that's the spirit, Willy!

WILLY. I will never get behind a wheel the rest of my life!

LINDA. It's changing, Willy, I can feel it changing!

WILLY. Beyond a question. G'by, I'm late. (*He starts to go again.*)

LINDA (*calling after him as she runs to the kitchen table for a handkerchief*). You got your glasses?

WILLY (*feels for them, then comes back in*). Yeah, yeah, got my glasses.

LINDA (*giving him the handkerchief*). And a handkerchief.

WILLY. Yeah, handkerchief.

LINDA. And your saccharine?

WILLY. Yeah, my saccharine.

LINDA. Be careful on the subway stairs.

She kisses him, and a silk stocking is seen hanging from her hand.
WILLY *notices it.*

WILLY. Will you stop mending stockings? At least while I'm in the house. It
gets me nervous. I can't tell you. Please.

LINDA *hides the stocking in her hand as she follows* WILLY *across the
forestage in front of the house.*

LINDA. Remember, Frank's Chop House.

WILLY (*passing the apron*). Maybe beets would grow out there.

LINDA (*laughing*). But you tried so many times.

WILLY. Yeah. Well, don't work hard today. (*He disappears around the right corner of the house.*)

LINDA. Be careful!

As WILLY *vanishes,* LINDA *waves to him. Suddenly the phone rings. She runs across the stage and into the kitchen and lifts it.*

LINDA. Hello? Oh, Biff! I'm so glad you called, I just . . . Yes, sure, I just told him. Yes, he'll be there for dinner at six o'clock, I didn't forget. Listen, I was just dying to tell you. You know that little rubber pipe I told you about? That he connected to the gas heater? I finally decided to go down the cellar this morning and take it away and destroy it. But it's gone! Imagine? He took it away himself, it isn't there! (*She listens.*) When? Oh, then you took it. Oh—nothing, it's just that I'd hoped he'd taken it away himself. Oh, I'm not worried, darling, because this morning he left in such high spirits, it was like the old days! I'm not afraid any more. Did Mr. Oliver see you? . . . Well, you wait there then. And make a nice impression on him, darling. Just don't perspire too much before you see him. And have a nice time with Dad. He may have big news too! . . . That's right, a New York job. And be sweet to him tonight, dear. Be loving to him. Because he's only a little boat looking for a harbor. (*She is trembling with sorrow and joy.*) Oh, that's wonderful, Biff, you'll save his life. Thanks, darling. Just put your arm around him when he comes into the restaurant. Give him a smile. That's the boy . . . Good-by, dear. . . . You got your comb? . . . That's fine. Good-by, Biff dear.

In the middle of her speech, HOWARD WAGNER, *thirty-six, wheels in a small typewriter table on which is a wire-recording machine and proceeds to plug it in. This is on the left forestage. Light slowly fades on* LINDA *as it rises on* HOWARD. HOWARD *is intent on threading the machine and only glances over his shoulder as* WILLY *appears.*

WILLY. Pst! Pst!

HOWARD. Hello, Willy, come in.

WILLY. Like to have a little talk with you, Howard.

HOWARD. Sorry to keep you waiting. I'll be with you in a minute.

WILLY. What's that, Howard?

HOWARD. Didn't you ever see one of these? Wire recorder.

WILLY. Oh. Can we talk a minute?

HOWARD. Records things. Just got delivery yesterday. Been driving me crazy, the most terrific machine I ever saw in my life. I was up all night with it.

WILLY. What do you do with it?

HOWARD. I bought it for dictation, but you can do anything with it. Listen to this. I had it home last night. Listen to what I picked up. The first one is my daughter. Get this. (*He flicks the switch and "Roll out the Barrel" is heard being whistled.*) Listen to that kid whistle.

WILLY. That is lifelike, isn't it?

HOWARD. Seven years old. Get that tone.

WILLY. Ts, ts. Like to ask a little favor if you . . .

The whistling breaks off, and the voice of HOWARD's *daughter is heard.*

HIS DAUGHTER. "Now you, Daddy."

HOWARD. She's crazy for me! (*Again the same song is whistled.*) That's me! Ha! (*He winks.*)

WILLY. You're very good!

The whistling breaks off again. The machine runs silent for a moment.

HOWARD. Sh! Get this now, this is my son.

HIS SON. "The capital of Alabama is Montgomery; the capital of Arizona is Phoenix; the capital of Arkansas is Little Rock; the capital of California is Sacramento . . ." (*and on, and on.*)

HOWARD (*holding up five fingers*). Five years old, Willy!

WILLY. He'll make an announcer some day!

HIS SON (*continuing*). "the capital . . . "

HOWARD. Get that—alphabetical order! (*The machine breaks off suddenly.*) Wait a minute. The maid kicked the plug out.

WILLY. It certainly is a . . .

HOWARD. Sh, for God's sake!

HIS SON. "It's nine o'clock, Bulova watch time. So I have to go to sleep."

WILLY. That really is . . .

HOWARD. Wait a minute! The next is my wife.

They wait.

HOWARD'S VOICE. "Go on, say something." (*Pause.*) "Well, you gonna talk?"

HIS WIFE. "I can't think of anything."

HOWARD'S VOICE. "Well, talk—it's turning."

HIS WIFE (*shyly, beaten*). "Hello." (*Silence.*) "Oh, Howard, I can't talk into this . . . "

HOWARD (*snapping the machine off*). That was my wife.

WILLY. That is a wonderful machine. Can we . . .

HOWARD. I tell you, Willy, I'm gonna take my camera, and my bandsaw, and all my hobbies, and out they go. This is the most fascinating relaxation I ever found.

WILLY. I think I'll get one myself.

HOWARD. Sure, they're only a hundred and a half. You can't do without it. Supposing you wanna hear Jack Benny, see? But you can't be at home at that hour. So you tell the maid to turn the radio on when Jack Benny comes on, and this automatically goes on with the radio . . .

WILLY. And when you come home you . . .

HOWARD. You can come home twelve o'clock, one o'clock, any time you like, and you get yourself a Coke and sit yourself down, throw the switch, and there's Jack Benny's program in the middle of the night!

WILLY. I'm definitely going to get one. Because lots of times I'm on the road, and I think to myself, what I must be missing on the radio!

HOWARD. Don't you have a radio in the car?

WILLY. Well, yeah, but who ever thinks of turning it on?

HOWARD. Say, aren't you supposed to be in Boston?

WILLY. That's what I want to talk to you about, Howard. You got a minute? (*He draws a chair in from the wing.*)

HOWARD. What happened? What're you doing here?

WILLY. Well . . .

HOWARD. You didn't crack up again, did you?

WILLY. Oh, no. No . . .

HOWARD. Geez, you had me worried there for a minute. What's the trouble?

WILLY. Well, tell you the truth, Howard. I've come to the decision that I'd rather not travel any more.

HOWARD. Not travel! Well, what'll you do?

WILLY. Remember, Christmas time, when you had the party here? You said you'd try to think of some spot for me here in town.

HOWARD. With us?

WILLY. Well, sure.

HOWARD. Oh, yeah, yeah. I remember. Well, I couldn't think of anything for you, Willy.

WILLY. I tell ya, Howard. The kids are all grown up, y'know. I don't need much any more. If I could take home—well, sixty-five dollars a week, I could swing it.

HOWARD. Yeah, but Willy, see I . . .

WILLY. I tell ya why, Howard. Speaking frankly and between the two of us, y'know—I'm just a little tired.

HOWARD. Oh, I could understand that, Willy. But you're a road man, Willy, and we do a road business. We've only got a half-dozen salesmen on the floor here.

WILLY. God knows, Howard. I never asked a favor of any man. But I was with the firm when your father used to carry you in here in his arms.

HOWARD. I know that, Willy, but . . .

WILLY. Your father came to me the day you were born and asked me what I thought of the name Howard, may he rest in peace.

HOWARD. I appreciate that, Willy, but there just is no spot here for you. If I had a spot I'd slam you right in, but I just don't have a single solitary spot.

He looks for his lighter. WILLY *has picked it up and gives it to him. Pause.*

WILLY (*with increasing anger*). Howard, all I need to set my table is fifty dollars a week.

HOWARD. But where am I going to put you, kid?

WILLY. Look, it isn't a question of whether I can sell merchandise, is it?

HOWARD. No, but it's business, kid, and everybody's gotta pull his own weight.

WILLY (*desperately*). Just let me tell you a story, Howard . . .

HOWARD. 'Cause you gotta admit, business is business.

WILLY (*angrily*). Business is definitely business, but just listen for a minute. You don't understand this. When I was a boy—eighteen, nineteen—I was already on the road. And there was a question in my mind as to whether selling had a future for me. Because in those days I had a yearning to go to Alaska. See, there were three gold strikes in one month in Alaska, and I felt like going out. Just for the ride, you might say.

HOWARD (*barely interested*). Don't say.

WILLY. Oh, yeah, my father lived many years in Alaska. He was an adventurous man. We've got quite a little streak of self-reliance in our family. I thought I'd go out with my older brother and try to locate him, and maybe settle in the North with the old man. And I was almost decided to go, when I met a salesman in the Parker House. His name was Dave

Singleman. And he was eighty-four years old, and he'd drummed merchandise in thirty-one states. And old Dave, he'd go up to his room,
y'understand, put on his green velvet slippers—I'll never forget—and
pick up his phone and call the buyers, and without ever leaving his
room, at the age of eighty-four, he made his living. And when I saw
that, I realized that selling was the greatest career a man could want.
'Cause what could be more satisfying than to be able to go, at the age of
eighty-four, into twenty or thirty different cities, and pick up a phone,
and be remembered and loved and helped by so many different people?
Do you know? when he died—and by the way he died the death of a
salesman, in his green velvet slippers in the smoker of the New York,
New Haven and Hartford, going into Boston—when he died, hundreds
of salesmen and buyers were at his funeral. Things were sad on a lotta
trains for months after that. (*He stands up,* HOWARD *has not looked at
him.*) In those days there was personality in it, Howard. There was respect, and comradeship, and gratitude in it. Today, it's all cut and dried,
and there's no chance for bringing friendship to bear—or personality.
You see what I mean? They don't know me any more.

HOWARD (*moving away, to the right*). That's just the thing, Willy.

WILLY. If I had forty dollars a week—that's all I'd need. Forty dollars, Howard.

HOWARD. Kid, I can't take blood from a stone, I . . .

WILLY (*desperation is on him now*). Howard, the year Al Smith was nomi-
nated, your father came to me and . . .

HOWARD (*starting to go off*). I've got to see some people, kid.

WILLY (*stopping him*). I'm talking about your father! There were promises
made across this desk! You mustn't tell me you've got people to see—I
put thirty-four years into this firm, Howard, and now I can't pay my insurance! You can't eat the orange and throw the peel away—a man is
not a piece of fruit! (*After a pause.*) Now pay attention. Your father—in
1928 I had a big year. I averaged a hundred and seventy dollars a week
in commissions.

HOWARD (*impatiently*). Now, Willy, you never averaged . . .

WILLY (*banging his hand on the desk*). I averaged a hundred and seventy
dollars a week in the year of 1928! And your father came to me—or
rather, I was in the office here—it was right over this desk—and he put
his hand on my shoulder . . .

HOWARD (*getting up*). You'll have to excuse me, Willy, I gotta see some people. Pull yourself together. (*Going out.*) I'll be back in a little while.

On HOWARD'*s exit, the light on his chair grows very bright and strange.*

WILLY. Pull myself together! What the hell did I say to him? My God, I was
yelling at him! How could I? (WILLY *breaks off, staring at the light,
which occupies the chair, animating it. He approaches this chair,
standing across the desk from it.*) Frank, Frank, don't you remember
what you told me that time? How you put your hand on my shoulder,
and Frank . . . (*He leans on the desk and as he speaks the dead man's
name he accidentally switches on the recorder, and instantly*)

HOWARD'S SON. ". . . New York is Albany. The capital of Ohio is Cincinnati,
the capital of Rhode Island is . . . " (*The recitation continues.*)

WILLY (*leaping away with fright, shouting*). Ha! Howard! Howard! Howard!

HOWARD (*rushing in*). What happened?

WILLY (*pointing at the machine, which continues nasally, childishly, with the capital cities*). Shut it off! Shut it off!

HOWARD (*pulling the plug out*). Look, Willy . . .

WILLY (*pressing his hands to his eyes*). I gotta get myself some coffee. I'll get some coffee . . .

WILLY *starts to walk out.* HOWARD *stops him.*

HOWARD (*rolling up the cord*). Willy, look . . .

WILLY. I'll go to Boston.

HOWARD. Willy, you can't go to Boston for us.

WILLY. Why can't I go?

HOWARD. I don't want you to represent us. I've been meaning to tell you for a long time now.

WILLY. Howard, are you firing me?

HOWARD. I think you need a good long rest, Willy.

WILLY. Howard . . .

HOWARD. And when you feel better, come back, and we'll see if we can work something out.

WILLY. But I gotta earn money, Howard. I'm in no position to . . .

HOWARD. Where are your sons? Why don't your sons give you a hand?

WILLY. They're working on a very big deal.

HOWARD. This is no time for false pride, Willy. You go to your sons and you tell them that you're tired. You've got two great boys, haven't you?

WILLY. Oh, no question, no question, but in the meantime . . .

HOWARD. Then that's that, heh?

WILLY. All right, I'll go to Boston tomorrow.

HOWARD. No, no.

WILLY. I can't throw myself on my sons. I'm not a cripple!

HOWARD. Look, kid, I'm busy this morning.

WILLY (*grasping* HOWARD's *arm*). Howard, you've got to let me go to Boston!

HOWARD (*hard, keeping himself under control*). I've got a line of people to see this morning. Sit down, take five minutes, and pull yourself together, and then go home, will ya? I need the office, Willy. (*He starts to go, turns, remembering the recorder, starts to push off the table holding the recorder.*) Oh, yeah. Whenever you can this week, stop by and drop off the samples. You'll feel better, Willy, and then come back and we'll talk. Pull yourself together, kid, there's people outside.

HOWARD *exits, pushing the table off left.* WILLY *stares into space, exhausted. Now the music is heard—*BEN's *music—first distantly, then closer, closer. As* WILLY *speaks,* BEN *enters from the right. He carries valise and umbrella.*

WILLY. Oh, Ben, how did you do it? What is the answer? Did you wind up the Alaska deal already?

BEN. Doesn't take much time if you know what you're doing. Just a short business trip. Boarding ship in an hour. Wanted to say good-by.

WILLY. Ben, I've got to talk to you.

BEN (*glancing at his watch*). Haven't the time, William.

WILLY (*crossing the apron to* BEN). Ben, nothing's working out. I don't know what to do.

BEN. Now, look here, William. I've bought timberland in Alaska and I need a
man to look after things for me.

WILLY. God, timberland! Me and my boys in those grand outdoors!

BEN. You've a new continent at your doorstep, William. Get out of these
cities, they're full of talk and time payments and courts of law. Screw
on your fists and you can fight for a fortune up there.

WILLY. Yes, yes! Linda, Linda!

LINDA *enters as of old, with the wash.*

LINDA. Oh, you're back?

BEN. I haven't much time.

WILLY. No, wait! Linda, he's got a proposition for me in Alaska.

LINDA. But you've got . . . (*To* BEN.) He's got a beautiful job here.

WILLY. But in Alaska, kid, I could . . .

LINDA. You're doing well enough, Willy!

BEN (*To* LINDA). Enough for what, my dear?

LINDA (*frightened of* BEN *and angry at him*). Don't say those things to him!
Enough to be happy right here, right now. (*To* WILLY, *while* BEN *laughs.*)
Why must everybody conquer the world? You're well liked, and the
boys love you, and someday—(*To* BEN)—why, old man Wagner told him
just the other day that if he keeps it up he'll be a member of the firm,
didn't he, Willy?

WILLY. Sure, sure. I am building something with this firm, Ben, and if a man
is building something he must be on the right track, mustn't he?

BEN. What are you building? Lay your hand on it. Where is it?

WILLY (*hesitantly*). That's true, Linda, there's nothing.

LINDA. Why? (*To* BEN.) There's a man eighty-four years old . . .

WILLY. That's right, Ben, that's right. When I look at that man I say, what is
there to worry about?

BEN. Bah!

WILLY. It's true, Ben. All he has to do is go into any city, pick up the phone,
and he's making his living and you know why?

BEN (*picking up his valise*). I've got to go.

WILLY (*holding* BEN *back*). Look at this boy!

BIFF, *in his high school sweater, enters carrying suitcase.* HAPPY *carries*
BIFF*'s shoulder guards, gold helmet, and football pants.*

WILLY. Without a penny to his name, three great universities are begging for
him, and from there the sky's the limit, because it's not what you do,
Ben. It's who you know and the smile on your face! It's contacts, Ben,
contacts! The whole wealth of Alaska passes over the lunch table at the
Commodore Hotel, and that's the wonder, the wonder of this country,
that a man can end with diamonds here on the basis of being liked! (*He
turns to* BIFF.) And that's why when you get out on that field today it's
important. Because thousands of people will be rooting for you and loving you. (*To* BEN, *who has again begun to leave.*) And Ben! when he
walks into a business office his name will sound out like a bell and all
the doors will open to him! I've seen it, Ben, I've seen it a thousand
times! You can't feel it with your hand like timber, but it's there!

BEN. Good-by, William.

WILLY. Ben, am I right? Don't you think I'm right? I value your advice.

BEN. There's a new continent at your doorstep, William. You could walk out rich. Rich! (*He is gone.*)

WILLY. We'll do it here, Ben! You hear me? We're gonna do it here!

Young BERNARD *rushes in. The gay music of the Boys is heard.*

BERNARD. Oh, gee, I was afraid you left already!

WILLY. Why? What time is it?

BERNARD. It's half-past one!

WILLY. Well, come on, everybody! Ebbets Field next stop! Where's the pennants? (*He rushes through the wall-line of the kitchen and out into the living room.*)

LINDA (*to* BIFF). Did you pack fresh underwear?

BIFF (*who has been limbering up*). I want to go!

BERNARD. Biff, I'm carrying your helmet, ain't I?

HAPPY. No, I'm carrying the helmet.

BERNARD. Oh, Biff, you promised me.

HAPPY. I'm carrying the helmet.

BERNARD. How am I going to get in the locker room?

LINDA. Let him carry the shoulder guards. (*She puts her coat and hat on in the kitchen.*)

BERNARD. Can I, Biff? 'Cause I told everybody I'm going to be in the locker room.

HAPPY. In Ebbets Field it's the clubhouse.

BERNARD. I meant the clubhouse. Biff!

HAPPY. Biff!

BIFF (*grandly, after a slight pause*). Let him carry the shoulder guards.

HAPPY (*as he gives* BERNARD *the shoulder guards*). Stay close to us now.

WILLY *rushes in with the pennants.*

WILLY (*handing them out*). Everybody wave when Biff comes out on the field. (HAPPY *and* BERNARD *run off.*) You set now, boy?

The music has died away.

BIFF. Ready to go, Pop. Every muscle is ready.

WILLY (*at the edge of the apron*). You realize what this means?

BIFF. That's right, Pop.

WILLY (*feeling* BIFF'*s muscles*). You're comin' home this afternoon captain of the All-Scholastic Championship Team of the City of New York.

BIFF. I got it, Pop. And remember, pal, when I take off my helmet, that touchdown is for you.

WILLY. Let's go! (*He is starting out, with his arm around* BIFF, *when* CHARLEY *enters, as of old, in knickers.*) I got no room for you, Charley.

CHARLEY. Room? For what?

WILLY. In the car.

CHARLEY. You goin' for a ride? I wanted to shoot some casino.

WILLY (*furiously*). Casino! (*Incredulously.*) Don't you realize what today is?

LINDA. Oh, he knows, Willy. He's just kidding you.

WILLY. That's nothing to kid about!

CHARLEY. No, Linda, what's goin' on?

LINDA. He's playing in Ebbets Field.

CHARLEY. Baseball in this weather?

WILLY. Don't talk to him. Come on, come on! (*He is pushing them out.*)

CHARLEY. Wait a minute, didn't you hear the news?

WILLY. What?

CHARLEY. Don't you listen to the radio? Ebbets Field just blew up.

WILLY. You go to hell! (CHARLEY *laughs. Pushing them out.*) Come on, come on! We're late.

CHARLEY (*as they go*). Knock a homer, Biff, knock a homer!

WILLY (*the last to leave, turning to* CHARLEY). I don't think that was funny, Charley. This is the greatest day of his life.

CHARLEY. Willy, when are you going to grow up?

WILLY. Yeah, heh? When this game is over, Charley, you'll be laughing out of the other side of your face. They'll be calling him another Red Grange. Twenty-five thousand a year.

CHARLEY (*kidding*). Is that so?

WILLY. Yeah, that's so.

CHARLEY. Well, then, I'm sorry, Willy. But tell me something.

WILLY. What?

CHARLEY. Who is Red Grange?

WILLY. Put up your hands. Goddam you, put up your hands!

> CHARLEY, *chuckling, shakes his head and walks away, around the left corner of the stage.* WILLY *follows him. The music rises to a mocking frenzy.*

WILLY. Who the hell do you think you are, better than everybody else? You don't know everything, you big, ignorant, stupid . . . Put up your hands!

> *Light rises, on the right side of the forestage, on a small table in the reception room of* CHARLEY's *office. Traffic sounds heard.* BERNARD, *now mature, sits whistling to himself. A pair of tennis rackets and an old overnight bag are on the floor beside him.*

WILLY (*offstage*). What are you walking away for? Don't walk away! If you're going to say something say it to my face! I know you laugh at me behind my back. You'll laugh out of the other side of your goddam face after this game. Touchdown! Touchdown! Eighty thousand people! Touchdown! Right between the goal posts.

> (BERNARD *is a quiet, earnest, but self-assured young man.* WILLY's *voice is coming from right upstage now.* BERNARD *lowers his feet off the table and listens.* JENNY, *his father's secretary, enters.*)

JENNY (*distressed*). Say, Bernard, will you go out in the hall?

BERNARD. What is that noise? Who is it?

JENNY. Mr. Loman. He just got off the elevator.

BERNARD (*getting up*). Who's he arguing with?

JENNY. Nobody. There's nobody with him. I can't deal with him any more, and your father gets all upset every time he comes. I've got a lot of typing to do, and your father's waiting to sign it. Will you see him?

WILLY (*entering*). Touchdown! Touch—(*He sees* JENNY.) Jenny, Jenny, good to see you. How're ya? Workin'? Or still honest?

JENNY. Fine. How've you been feeling?

WILLY. Not much any more, Jenny. Ha, ha! (*He is surprised to see the rackets.*)

BERNARD. Hello, Uncle Willy.

WILLY (*almost shocked*). Bernard! Well, look who's here! (*He comes quickly, guiltily, to* BERNARD *and warmly shakes his hand.*)

BERNARD. How are you? Good to see you.

WILLY. What are you doing here?

BERNARD. Oh, just stopped by to see Pop. Get off my feet till my train leaves. I'm going to Washington in a few minutes.

WILLY. Is he in?

BERNARD. Yes, he's in his office with the accountant. Sit down.

WILLY (*sitting down*). What're you going to do in Washington?

BERNARD. Oh, just a case I've got there, Willy.

WILLY. That so? (*Indicating the rackets.*) You going to play tennis there?

BERNARD. I'm staying with a friend who's got a court.

WILLY. Don't say. His own tennis court. Must be fine people, I bet.

BERNARD. They are, very nice. Dad tells me Biff's in town.

WILLY (*with a big smile*). Yeah, Biff's in. Working on a very big deal, Bernard.

BERNARD. What's Biff doing?

WILLY. Well, he's been doing very big things in the West. But he decided to establish himself here. Very big. We're having dinner. Did I hear your wife had a boy?

BERNARD. That's right. Our second.

WILLY. Two boys! What do you know!

BERNARD. What kind of a deal has Biff got?

WILLY. Well, Bill Oliver—very big sporting-goods man—he wants Biff very badly. Called him in from the West. Long distance, carte blanche, special deliveries. Your friends have their own private tennis court?

BERNARD. You still with the old firm, Willy?

WILLY (*after a pause*). I'm—I'm overjoyed to see how you made the grade, Bernard, overjoyed. It's an encouraging thing to see a young man really—really . . . Looks very good for Biff—very . . . (*He breaks off, then.*) Bernard . . . (*He is so full of emotion, he breaks off again.*)

BERNARD. What is it, Willy?

WILLY (*small and alone*). What—what's the secret?

BERNARD. What secret?

WILLY. How—how did you? Why didn't he ever catch on?

BERNARD. I wouldn't know that, Willy.

WILLY (*confidentially, desperately*). You were his friend, his boyhood friend. There's something I don't understand about it. His life ended after that Ebbets Field game. From the age of seventeen nothing good ever happened to him.

BERNARD. He never trained himself for anything.

WILLY. But he did, he did. After high school he took so many correspondence courses. Radio mechanics; television; God knows what, and never made the slightest mark.

BERNARD (*taking off his glasses*). Willy, do you want to talk candidly?

WILLY (*rising, faces* BERNARD). I regard you as a very brilliant man, Bernard. I value your advice.

BERNARD. Oh, the hell with the advice, Willy. I couldn't advise you. There's just one thing I've always wanted to ask you. When he was supposed to graduate, and the math teacher flunked him . . .

WILLY. Oh, that son-of-a-bitch ruined his life.

BERNARD. Yeah, but, Willy, all he had to do was go to summer school and make up that subject.

WILLY. That's right, that's right.

BERNARD. Did you tell him not to go to summer school?

WILLY. Me? I begged him to go. I ordered him to go!

BERNARD. Then why wouldn't he go?

WILLY. Why? Why! Bernard, that question has been trailing me like a ghost for the last fifteen years. He flunked the subject, and laid down and died like a hammer hit him!

BERNARD. Take it easy, kid.

WILLY. Let me talk to you—I got nobody to talk to. Bernard, Bernard, was it my fault? Y'see? It keeps going around in my mind, maybe I did something to him. I got nothing to give him.

BERNARD. Don't take it so hard.

WILLY. Why did he lay down? What is the story there? You were his friend!

BERNARD. Willy, I remember, it was June, and our grades came out. And he'd flunked math.

WILLY. That son-of-a-bitch!

BERNARD. No, it wasn't right then. Biff just got very angry, I remember, and he was ready to enroll in summer school.

WILLY (*surprised*). He was?

BERNARD. He wasn't beaten by it at all. But then, Willy, he disappeared from the block for almost a month. And I got the idea that he'd gone up to New England to see you. Did he have a talk with you then?

WILLY *stares in silence.*

BERNARD. Willy?

WILLY (*with a strong edge of resentment in his voice*). Yeah, he came to Boston. What about it?

BERNARD. Well, just that when he came back—I'll never forget this, it always mystifies me. Because I'd thought so well of Biff, even though he'd always taken advantage of me. I loved him, Willy, y'know? And he came back after that month and took his sneakers—remember those sneakers with "University of Virginia" printed on them? He was so proud of those, wore them every day. And he took them down in the cellar, and burned them up in the furnace. We had a fist fight. It lasted at least half an hour. Just the two of us, punching each other down the cellar, and crying right through it. I've often thought of how strange it was that I knew he'd given up his life. What happened in Boston, Willy?

WILLY *looks at him as at an intruder.*

BERNARD. I just bring it up because you asked me.

WILLY (*angrily*). Nothing. What do you mean, "What happened?" What's that got to do with anything?

BERNARD. Well, don't get sore.

WILLY. What are you trying to do, blame it on me? If a boy lays down is that my fault?

BERNARD. Now, Willy, don't get . . .

WILLY. Well, don't—don't talk to me that way! What does that mean, "What happened?"

> CHARLEY *enters. He is in his vest, and he carries a bottle of bourbon.*

CHARLEY. Hey, you're going to miss that train. (*He waves the bottle.*)

BERNARD. Yeah, I'm going. (*He takes the bottle.*) Thanks, Pop. (*He picks up his rackets and bag.*) Good-by, Willy, and don't worry about it. You know, "If at first you don't succeed . . ."

WILLY. Yes, I believe in that.

BERNARD. But sometimes, Willy, it's better for a man just to walk away.

WILLY. Walk away?

BERNARD. That's right.

WILLY. But if you can't walk away?

BERNARD (*after a slight pause*). I guess that's when it's tough. (*Extending his hand.*) Good-by, Willy.

WILLY (*shaking* BERNARD'*s hand*). Good-by, boy.

CHARLEY (*an arm on* BERNARD'*s shoulder*). How do you like this kid? Gonna argue a case in front of the Supreme Court.

BERNARD (*protesting*). Pop!

WILLY (*genuinely shocked, pained, and happy*). No! The Supreme Court!

BERNARD. I gotta run. 'By, Dad!

CHARLEY. Knock 'em dead, Bernard!

> BERNARD *goes off.*

WILLY (*as* CHARLEY *takes out his wallet*). The Supreme Court! And he didn't even mention it!

CHARLEY (*counting out money on the desk*). He don't have to—he's gonna do it.

WILLY. And you never told him what to do, did you? You never took any interest in him.

CHARLEY. My salvation is that I never took any interest in anything. There's some money—fifty dollars. I got an accountant inside.

WILLY. Charley, look . . . (*with difficulty.*) I got my insurance to pay. If you can manage it—I need a hundred and ten dollars.

> CHARLEY *doesn't reply for a moment; merely stops moving.*

WILLY. I'd draw it from my bank but Linda would know, and I . . .

CHARLEY. Sit down, Willy.

WILLY (*moving toward the chair*). I'm keeping an account of everything, remember. I'll pay every penny back. (*He sits.*)

CHARLEY. Now listen to me, Willy.

WILLY. I want you to know I appreciate . . .

CHARLEY (*sitting down on the table*). Willy, what're you doin'? What the hell is going on in your head?

WILLY. Why? I'm simply . . .

CHARLEY. I offered you a job. You make fifty dollars a week. And I won't send you on the road.

WILLY. I've got a job.

CHARLEY. Without pay? What kind of a job is a job without pay? (*He rises.*) Now, look, kid, enough is enough. I'm no genius but I know when I'm being insulted.

WILLY. Insulted!

CHARLEY. Why don't you want to work for me?

WILLY. What's the matter with you? I've got a job.

CHARLEY. Then what're you walkin' in here every week for?

WILLY (*getting up*). Well, if you don't want me to walk in here . . .

CHARLEY. I'm offering you a job.

WILLY. I don't want your goddam job!

CHARLEY. When the hell are you going to grow up?

WILLY (*furiously*). You big ignoramus, if you say that to me again I'll rap you one! I don't care how big you are! (*He's ready to fight.*)

Pause.

CHARLEY (*kindly, going to him*). How much do you need, Willy?

WILLY. Charley, I'm strapped. I'm strapped. I don't know what to do. I was just fired.

CHARLEY. Howard fired you?

WILLY. That snotnose. Imagine that? I named him. I named him Howard.

CHARLEY. Willy, when're you gonna realize that them things don't mean anything? You named him Howard, but you can't sell that. The only thing you got in this world is what you can sell. And the funny thing is that you're a salesman, and you don't know that.

WILLY. I've always tried to think otherwise, I guess. I always felt that if a man was impressive, and well liked, that nothing . . .

CHARLEY. Why must everybody like you? Who liked J. P. Morgan? Was he impressive? In a Turkish bath he'd look like a butcher. But with his pockets on he was very well liked. Now listen, Willy, I know you don't like me, and nobody can say I'm in love with you, but I'll give you a job because—just for the hell of it, put it that way. Now what do you say?

WILLY. I—I just can't work for you, Charley.

CHARLEY. What're you, jealous of me?

WILLY. I can't work for you, that's all, don't ask me why.

CHARLEY (*angered, takes out more bills*). You been jealous of me all your life, you damned fool! Here, pay your insurance. (*He puts the money in* WILLY*'s hand.*)

WILLY. I'm keeping strict accounts.

CHARLEY. I've got some work to do. Take care of yourself. And pay your insurance.

WILLY (*moving to the right*). Funny, y'know? After all the highways, and the trains, and the appointments, and the years, you end up worth more dead than alive.

CHARLEY. Willy, nobody's worth nothin' dead. (*After a slight pause.*) Did you hear what I said?

WILLY *stands still, dreaming.*

CHARLEY. Willy!

WILLY. Apologize to Bernard for me when you see him. I didn't mean to argue with him. He's a fine boy. They're all fine boys, and they'll end up big—all of them. Someday they'll all play tennis together. Wish me luck, Charley. He saw Bill Oliver today.

CHARLEY. Good luck.

WILLY (*on the verge of tears*). Charley, you're the only friend I got. Isn't that a remarkable thing? (*He goes out.*)

CHARLEY. Jesus!

> CHARLEY *stares after him a moment and follows. All light blacks out. Suddenly raucous music is heard, and a red glow rises behind the screen at right.* STANLEY, *a young waiter, appears, carrying a table, followed by* HAPPY, *who is carrying two chairs.*

STANLEY (*putting the table down*). That's all right, Mr. Loman, I can handle it myself. (*He turns and takes the chairs from* HAPPY *and places them at the table.*)

HAPPY (*glancing around*). Oh, this is better.

STANLEY. Sure, in the front there you're in the middle of all kinds of noise. Whenever you got a party, Mr. Loman, you just tell me and I'll put you back here. Y'know, there's a lotta people they don't like it private, because when they go out they like to see a lotta action around them because they're sick and tired to stay in the house by theirself. But I know you, you ain't from Hackensack. You know what I mean?

HAPPY (*sitting down*). So how's it coming, Stanley?

STANLEY. Ah, it's a dog life. I only wish during the war they'd a took me in the Army. I coulda been dead by now.

HAPPY. My brother's back, Stanley.

STANLEY. Oh, he come back, heh? From the Far West.

HAPPY. Yeah, big cattle man, my brother, so treat him right. And my father's coming too.

STANLEY. Oh, your father too!

HAPPY. You got a couple of nice lobsters?

STANLEY. Hundred percent, big.

HAPPY. I want them with the claws.

STANLEY. Don't worry, I don't give you no mice. (HAPPY *laughs*.) How about some wine? It'll put a head on the meal.

HAPPY. No. You remember, Stanley, that recipe I brought you from overseas? With the champagne in it?

STANLEY. Oh, yeah, sure. I still got it tacked up yet in the kitchen. But that'll have to cost a buck apiece anyways.

HAPPY. That's all right.

STANLEY. What'd you, hit a number or somethin'?

HAPPY. No, it's a little celebration. My brother is—I think he pulled off a big deal today. I think we're going into business together.

STANLEY. Great! That's the best for you. Because a family business, you know what I mean?—that's the best.

HAPPY. That's what I think.

STANLEY. 'Cause what's the difference? Somebody steals? It's in the family. Know what I mean? (*Sotto voce.*) Like this bartender here. The boss is goin' crazy what kinda leak he's got in the cash register. You put it in but it don't come out.

HAPPY (*raising his head*). Sh!

STANLEY. What?

HAPPY. You notice I wasn't lookin' right or left, was I?

STANLEY. No.

HAPPY. And my eyes are closed.

STANLEY. So what's the . . . ?

HAPPY. Strudel's comin'.

STANLEY (*catching on, looks around*). Ah, no, there's no . . .

> He breaks off as a furred, lavishly dressed GIRL enters and sits at the
> next table. Both follow her with their eyes.

STANLEY. Geez, how'd ya know?

HAPPY. I got radar or something. (*Staring directly at her profile.*) Oooooooo
. . . Stanley.

STANLEY. I think that's for you, Mr. Loman.

HAPPY. Look at that mouth. Oh, God. And the binoculars.

STANLEY. Geez, you got a life, Mr. Loman.

HAPPY. Wait on her.

STANLEY (*going to the GIRL's table*). Would you like a menu, ma'am?

GIRL. I'm expecting someone, but I'd like a . . .

HAPPY. Why don't you bring her—excuse me, miss, do you mind? I sell champagne, and I'd like you to try my brand. Bring her a champagne, Stanley.

GIRL. That's awfully nice of you.

HAPPY. Don't mention it. It's all company money. (*He laughs.*)

GIRL. That's a charming product to be selling, isn't it?

HAPPY. Oh, gets to be like everything else. Selling is selling, y'know.

GIRL. I suppose.

HAPPY. You don't happen to sell, do you?

GIRL. No, I don't sell.

HAPPY. Would you object to a compliment from a stranger? You ought to be
on a magazine cover.

GIRL (*looking at him a little archly*). I have been.

> STANLEY *comes in with a glass of champagne.*

HAPPY. What'd I say before, Stanley? You see? She's a cover girl.

STANLEY. Oh, I could see, I could see.

HAPPY (*to the GIRL*). What magazine?

GIRL. Oh, a lot of them. (*She takes the drink.*) Thank you.

HAPPY. You know what they say in France, don't you? "Champagne is the
drink of the complexion"—Hya, Biff!

> BIFF *has entered and sits with* HAPPY.

BIFF. Hello, kid. Sorry I'm late.

HAPPY. I just got here. Uh, Miss . . . ?

GIRL. Forsythe.

HAPPY. Miss Forsythe, this is my brother.

BIFF. Is Dad here?

HAPPY. His name is Biff. You might've heard of him. Great football player.

GIRL. Really? What team?

HAPPY. Are you familiar with football?

GIRL. No, I'm afraid I'm not.

HAPPY. Biff is quarterback with the New York Giants.

GIRL. Well, that is nice, isn't it? (*She drinks.*)

HAPPY. Good health.

GIRL. I'm happy to meet you.

HAPPY. That's my name. Hap. It's really Harold, but at West Point they called me Happy.

GIRL (*now really impressed*). Oh, I see. How do you do? (*She turns her profile.*)

BIFF. Isn't Dad coming?

HAPPY. You want her?

BIFF. Oh, I could never make that.

HAPPY. I remember the time that idea would never come into your head. Where's the old confidence, Biff?

BIFF. I just saw Oliver . . .

HAPPY. Wait a minute. I've got to see that old confidence again. Do you want her? She's on call.

BIFF. Oh, no. (*He turns to look at the* GIRL.)

HAPPY. I'm telling you. Watch this. (*Turning to the* GIRL.) Honey? (*She turns to him.*) Are you busy?

GIRL. Well, I am . . . but I could make a phone call.

HAPPY. Do that, will you, honey? And see if you can get a friend. We'll be here for a while. Biff is one of the greatest football players in the country.

GIRL (*standing up*). Well, I'm certainly happy to meet you.

HAPPY. Come back soon.

GIRL. I'll try.

HAPPY. Don't try, honey, try hard.

> The GIRL *exits.* STANLEY *follows, shaking his head in bewildered admiration.*

HAPPY. Isn't that a shame now? A beautiful girl like that? That's why I can't get married. There's not a good woman in a thousand. New York is loaded with them, kid!

BIFF. Hap, look . . .

HAPPY. I told you she was on call!

BIFF (*strangely unnerved*). Cut it out, will ya? I want to say something to you.

HAPPY. Did you see Oliver?

BIFF. I saw him all right. Now look, I want to tell Dad a couple of things and I want you to help me.

HAPPY. What? Is he going to back you?

BIFF. Are you crazy? You're out of your goddam head, you know that?

HAPPY. Why? What happened?

BIFF (*breathlessly*). I did a terrible thing today, Hap. It's been the strangest day I ever went through. I'm all numb, I swear.

HAPPY. You mean he wouldn't see you?

BIFF. Well, I waited six hours for him, see? All day. Kept sending my name in. Even tried to date his secretary so she'd get me to him, but no soap.

HAPPY. Because you're not showin' the old confidence, Biff. He remembered you, didn't he?

BIFF (*stopping* HAPPY *with a gesture*). Finally, about five o'clock, he comes out. Didn't remember who I was or anything. I felt like such an idiot, Hap.

HAPPY. Did you tell him my Florida idea?

BIFF. He walked away. I saw him for one minute. I got so mad I could've torn the walls down! How the hell did I ever get the idea I was a salesman there? I even believed myself that I'd been a salesman for him! And then he gave me one look and—I realized what a ridiculous lie my whole life has been! We've been talking in a dream for fifteen years. I was a shipping clerk.

HAPPY. What'd you do?

BIFF (*with great tension and wonder*). Well, he left, see. And the secretary went out. I was all alone in the waiting room. I don't know what came over me, Hap. The next thing I know I'm in his office—paneled walls, everything. I can't explain it. I—Hap. I took his fountain pen.

HAPPY. Geez, did he catch you?

BIFF. I ran out. I ran down all eleven flights. I ran and ran and ran.

HAPPY. That was an awful dumb—what'd you do that for?

BIFF (*agonized*). I don't know, I just—wanted to take something, I don't know. You gotta help me, Hap. I'm gonna tell Pop.

HAPPY. You crazy? What for?

BIFF. Hap, he's got to understand that I'm not the man somebody lends that kind of money to. He thinks I've been spiting him all these years and it's eating him up.

HAPPY. That's just it. You tell him something nice.

BIFF. I can't.

HAPPY. Say you got a lunch date with Oliver tomorrow.

BIFF. So what do I do tomorrow?

HAPPY. You leave the house tomorrow and come back at night and say Oliver is thinking it over. And he thinks it over for a couple of weeks, and gradually it fades away and nobody's the worse.

BIFF. But it'll go on forever!

HAPPY. Dad is never so happy as when he's looking forward to something!

WILLY *enters*.

HAPPY. Hello, scout!

WILLY. Gee, I haven't been here in years!

STANLEY *has followed* WILLY *in and sets a chair for him.* STANLEY *starts off but* HAPPY *stops him.*

HAPPY. Stanley!

STANLEY *stands by, waiting for an order.*

BIFF (*going to* WILLY *with guilt, as to an invalid*). Sit down, Pop. You want a drink?

WILLY. Sure, I don't mind.

BIFF. Let's get a load on.

WILLY. You look worried.

BIFF. N-no. (*To* STANLEY.) Scotch all around. Make it doubles.

STANLEY. Doubles, right. (*He goes.*)

WILLY. You had a couple already, didn't you?

BIFF. Just a couple, yeah.

WILLY. Well, what happened, boy? (*Nodding affirmatively, with a smile.*) Everything go all right?

BIFF (*takes a breath, then reaches out and grasps* WILLY's *hand*). Pal . . . (*He is smiling bravely, and* WILLY *is smiling too.*) I had an experience today.

HAPPY. Terrific, Pop.

WILLY. That so? What happened?

BIFF (*high, slightly alcoholic, above the earth*). I'm going to tell you everything from first to last. It's been a strange day. (*Silence. He looks around, composes himself as best he can, but his breath keeps breaking the rhythm of his voice.*) I had to wait quite a while for him, and . . .

WILLY. Oliver?

BIFF. Yeah, Oliver. All day, as a matter of cold fact. And a lot of—instances— facts, Pop, facts about my life came back to me. Who was it, Pop? Who ever said I was a salesman with Oliver?

WILLY. Well, you were.

BIFF. No, Dad, I was a shipping clerk.

WILLY. But you were practically . . .

BIFF (*with determination*). Dad, I don't know who said it first, but I was never a salesman for Bill Oliver.

WILLY. What're you talking about?

BIFF. Let's hold on to the facts tonight, Pop. We're not going to get anywhere bullin' around. I was a shipping clerk.

WILLY (*angrily*). All right, now listen to me . . .

BIFF. Why don't you let me finish?

WILLY. I'm not interested in stories about the past or any crap of that kind because the woods are burning, boys, you understand? There's a big blaze going on all around. I was fired today.

BIFF (*shocked*). How could you be?

WILLY. I was fired, and I'm looking for a little good news to tell your mother, because the woman has waited and the woman has suffered. The gist of it is that I haven't got a story left in my head, Biff. So don't give me a lecture about facts and aspects. I am not interested. Now what've you got to say to me?

STANLEY *enters with three drinks. They wait until he leaves.*

WILLY. Did you see Oliver?

BIFF. Jesus, Dad!

WILLY. You mean you didn't go up there?

HAPPY. Sure he went up there.

BIFF. I did. I—saw him. How could they fire you?

WILLY (*on the edge of his chair*). What kind of a welcome did he give you?

BIFF. He won't even let you work on commission?

WILLY. I'm out! (*Driving.*) So tell me, he gave you a warm welcome?

HAPPY. Sure, Pop, sure!

BIFF (*driven*). Well, it was kind of . . .

WILLY. I was wondering if he'd remember you. (*To* HAPPY.) Imagine, man doesn't see him for ten, twelve years and gives him that kind of a welcome!

HAPPY. Damn right!

BIFF (*trying to return to the offensive*). Pop, look . . .

WILLY. You know why he remembered you, don't you? Because you impressed him in those days.

BIFF. Let's talk quietly and get this down to the facts, huh?

WILLY (*as though* BIFF *had been interrupting*). Well, what happened? It's great news, Biff. Did he take you into his office or'd you talk in the waiting room?

BIFF. Well, he came in, see, and . . .

WILLY (*with a big smile*). What'd he say? Betcha he threw his arm around you.

BIFF. Well, he kinda . . .

WILLY. He's a fine man. (*To* HAPPY.) Very hard man to see, y'know.

HAPPY (*agreeing*). Oh, I know.

WILLY (*to* BIFF). Is that where you had the drinks?

BIFF. Yeah, he gave me a couple of—no, no!

HAPPY (*cutting in*). He told him my Florida idea.

WILLY. Don't interrupt. (*To* BIFF.) How'd he react to the Florida idea?

BIFF. Dad, will you give me a minute to explain?

WILLY. I've been waiting for you to explain since I sat down here! What happened? He took you into his office and what?

BIFF. Well—I talked. And—and he listened, see.

WILLY. Famous for the way he listens, y'know. What was his answer?

BIFF. His answer was—(*He breaks off, suddenly angry.*) Dad, you're not letting me tell you what I want to tell you!

WILLY (*accusing, angered*). You didn't see him, did you?

BIFF. I did see him!

WILLY. What'd you insult him or something? You insulted him, didn't you?

BIFF. Listen, will you let me out of it, will you just let me out of it!

HAPPY. What the hell!

WILLY. Tell me what happened!

BIFF (*to* HAPPY). I can't talk to him!

> *A single trumpet note jars the ear. The light of green leaves stains the house, which holds the air of night and a dream.* YOUNG BERNARD *enters and knocks on the door of the house.*

YOUNG BERNARD (*frantically*). Mrs. Loman, Mrs. Loman!

HAPPY. Tell him what happened!

BIFF (*to* HAPPY.) Shut up and leave me alone!

WILLY. No, no! You had to go and flunk math!

BIFF. What math? What're you talking about?

YOUNG BERNARD. Mrs. Loman, Mrs. Loman!

> LINDA *appears in the house, as of old.*

WILLY (*wildly*). Math, math, math!

BIFF. Take it easy, Pop!

YOUNG BERNARD. Mrs. Loman!

WILLY (*furiously*). If you hadn't flunked you'd've been set by now!

BIFF. Now, look, I'm gonna tell you what happened, and you're going to listen to me.

YOUNG BERNARD. Mrs. Loman!

BIFF. I waited six hours . . .

HAPPY. What the hell are you saying?

BIFF. I kept sending in my name but he wouldn't see me. So finally he . . . (*He continues unheard as light fades low on the restaurant.*)

YOUNG BERNARD. Biff flunked math!

LINDA. No!

YOUNG BERNARD. Birnbaum flunked him! They won't graduate him!

LINDA. But they have to. He's gotta go to the university. Where is he? Biff! Biff!

YOUNG BERNARD. No, he left. He went to Grand Central.

LINDA. Grand—You mean he went to Boston!

YOUNG BERNARD. Is Uncle Willy in Boston?

LINDA. Oh, maybe Willy can talk to the teacher. Oh, the poor, poor boy!

Light on house area snaps out.

BIFF (*at the table, now audible, holding up a gold fountain pen*). . . . so I'm washed up with Oliver, you understand? Are you listening to me?

WILLY (*at a loss*). Yeah, sure. If you hadn't flunked . . .

BIFF. Flunked what? What're you talking about?

WILLY. Don't blame everything on me! I didn't flunk math—you did! What pen?

HAPPY. That was awful dumb, Biff, a pen like that is worth—

WILLY (*seeing the pen for the first time*). You took Oliver's pen?

BIFF (*weakening*). Dad, I just explained it to you.

WILLY. You stole Bill Oliver's fountain pen!

BIFF. I didn't exactly steal it! That's just what I've been explaining to you!

HAPPY. He had it in his hand and just then Oliver walked in, so he got nervous and stuck it in his pocket!

WILLY. My God, Biff!

BIFF. I never intended to do it, Dad!

OPERATOR'S VOICE. Standish Arms, good evening!

WILLY (*shouting*). I'm not in my room!

BIFF (*frightened*). Dad, what's the matter? (*He and* HAPPY *stand up.*)

OPERATOR. Ringing Mr. Loman for you!

WILLY. I'm not there, stop it!

BIFF (*horrified, gets down on one knee before* WILLY). Dad, I'll make good, I'll make good. (WILLY *tries to get to his feet.* BIFF *holds him down.*) Sit down now.

WILLY. No, you're no good, you're no good for anything.

BIFF. I am, Dad, I'll find something else, you understand? Now don't worry about anything. (*He holds up* WILLY'*s face.*) Talk to me, Dad.

OPERATOR. Mr. Loman does not answer. Shall I page him?

WILLY (*attempting to stand, as though to rush and silence the* OPERATOR). No, no, no!

HAPPY. He'll strike something, Pop.

WILLY. No, no . . .

BIFF (*desperately, standing over* WILLY). Pop, listen! Listen to me! I'm telling you something good. Oliver talked to his partner about the Florida idea. You listening? He—he talked to his partner, and he came to me . . . I'm going to be all right, you hear? Dad, listen to me, he said it was just a question of the amount!

WILLY. Then you . . . got it?

HAPPY. He's gonna be terrific, Pop!

WILLY (*trying to stand*). Then you got it, haven't you? You got it! You got it!

BIFF (*agonized, holds* WILLY *down*). No, no. Look, Pop. I'm supposed to have lunch with them tomorrow. I'm just telling you this so you'll know that I can still make an impression, Pop. And I'll make good somewhere, but I can't go tomorrow, see.

WILLY. Why not? You simply . . .

BIFF. But the pen, Pop!

WILLY. You give it to him and tell him it was an oversight!

HAPPY. Sure, have lunch tomorrow!

BIFF. I can't say that . . .

WILLY. You were doing a crossword puzzle and accidentally used his pen!

BIFF. Listen, kid, I took those balls years ago, now I walk in with his fountain pen? That clinches it, don't you see? I can't face him like that! I'll try elsewhere.

PAGE'S VOICE. Paging Mr. Loman!

WILLY. Don't you want to be anything?

BIFF. Pop, how can I go back?

WILLY. You don't want to be anything, is that what's behind it?

BIFF (*now angry at* WILLY *for not crediting his sympathy*). Don't take it that way! You think it was easy walking into that office after what I'd done to him? A team of horses couldn't have dragged me back to Bill Oliver!

WILLY. Then why'd you go?

BIFF. Why did I go? Why did I go! Look at you! Look at what's become of you!

Off left, THE WOMAN *laughs.*

WILLY. Biff, you're going to go to that lunch tomorrow, or . . .

BIFF. I can't go. I've got no appointment!

HAPPY. Biff, for . . . !

WILLY. Are you spiting me?

BIFF. Don't take it that way! Goddammit!

WILLY (*strikes* BIFF *and falters away from the table*). You rotten little louse! Are you spiting me?

THE WOMAN. Someone's at the door, Willy!

BIFF. I'm no good, can't you see what I am?

HAPPY (*separating them*). Hey, you're in a restaurant! Now cut it out, both of you! (*The girls enter.*) Hello, girls, sit down.

THE WOMAN *laughs, off left.*

MISS FORSYTHE. I guess we might as well. This is Letta.

THE WOMAN. Willy, are you going to wake up?

BIFF (*ignoring* WILLY). How're ya, miss, sit down. What do you drink?

MISS FORSYTHE. Letta might not be able to stay long.

LETTA. I gotta get up very early tomorrow. I got jury duty. I'm so excited! Were you fellows ever on a jury?

BIFF. No, but I been in front of them! (*The girls laugh.*) This is my father.

LETTA. Isn't he cute? Sit down with us, Pop.

HAPPY. Sit him down, Biff!

BIFF (*going to him*). Come on, slugger, drink us under the table. To hell with it! Come on, sit down, pal.

On BIFF's *last insistence,* WILLY *is about to sit.*

THE WOMAN (*now urgently*). Willy, are you going to answer the door!

THE WOMAN'*s call pulls* WILLY *back. He starts right, befuddled.*

BIFF. Hey, where are you going?

WILLY. Open the door.

BIFF. The door?

WILLY. The washroom . . . the door . . . where's the door?

BIFF (*leading* WILLY *to the left*). Just go straight down.

WILLY *moves left.*

THE WOMAN. Willy, Willy, are you going to get up, get up, get up, get up?

WILLY *exits left.*

LETTA. I think it's sweet you bring your daddy along.

MISS FORSYTHE. Oh, he isn't really your father!

BIFF (*at left, turning to her resentfully*). Miss Forsythe, you've just seen a prince walk by. A fine, troubled prince. A hardworking, unappreciated prince. A pal, you understand? A good companion. Always for his boys.

LETTA. That's so sweet.

HAPPY. Well, girls, what's the program? We're wasting time. Come on, Biff. Gather round. Where would you like to go?

BIFF. Why don't you do something for him?

HAPPY. Me!

BIFF. Don't you give a damn for him, Hap?

HAPPY. What're you talking about? I'm the one who . . .

BIFF. I sense it, you don't give a good goddam about him. (*He takes the rolled-up hose from his pocket and puts it on the table in front of* HAPPY.) Look what I found in the cellar, for Christ's sake. How can you bear to let it go on?

HAPPY. Me? Who goes away? Who runs off and . . .

BIFF. Yeah, but he doesn't mean anything to you. You could help him—I can't! Don't you understand what I'm talking about? He's going to kill himself, don't you know that?

HAPPY. Don't I know it! Me!

BIFF. Hap, help him! Jesus . . . help him . . . Help me, help me, I can't bear to look at his face! (*Ready to weep, he hurries out, up right.*)

HAPPY (*starting after him*). Where are you going?

MISS FORSYTHE. What's he so mad about?

HAPPY. Come on, girls, we'll catch up with him.

MISS FORSYTHE (*as* HAPPY *pushes her out*). Say, I don't like that temper of his!

HAPPY. He's just a little overstrung, he'll be all right!

WILLY (*off left, as* THE WOMAN *laughs*). Don't answer! Don't answer!

LETTA. Don't you want to tell your father . . .

HAPPY. No, that's not my father. He's just a guy. Come on, we'll catch Biff, and, honey, we're going to paint this town! Stanley, where's the check! Hey, Stanley!

They exit. STANLEY *looks toward left.*

STANLEY (*calling to* HAPPY *indignantly*). Mr. Loman! Mr. Loman!

STANLEY *picks up a chair and follows them off. Knocking is heard off left.* THE WOMAN *enters, laughing.* WILLY *follows her. She is in a black slip;*

he is buttoning his shirt. Raw, sensuous music accompanies their speech:

WILLY. Will you stop laughing? Will you stop?

THE WOMAN. Aren't you going to answer the door? He'll wake the whole hotel.

WILLY. I'm not expecting anybody.

THE WOMAN. Whyn't you have another drink, honey, and stop being so damn self-centered?

WILLY. I'm so lonely.

THE WOMAN. You know you ruined me, Willy? From now on, whenever you come to the office, I'll see that you go right through to the buyers. No waiting at my desk anymore, Willy. You ruined me.

WILLY. That's nice of you to say that.

THE WOMAN. Gee, you are self-centered! Why so sad? You are the saddest, self-centeredest soul I ever did see-saw. (*She laughs. He kisses her.*) Come on inside, drummer boy. It's silly to be dressing in the middle of the night. (*As knocking is heard.*) Aren't you going to answer the door?

WILLY. They're knocking on the wrong door.

THE WOMAN. But I felt the knocking. And he heard us talking in here. Maybe the hotel's on fire!

WILLY (*his terror rising*). It's a mistake.

THE WOMAN. Then tell him to go away!

WILLY. There's nobody there.

THE WOMAN. It's getting on my nerves, Willy. There's somebody standing out there and it's getting on my nerves!

WILLY (*pushing her away from him*). All right, stay in the bathroom here, and don't come out. I think there's a law in Massachusetts about it, so don't come out. It may be that new room clerk. He looked very mean. So don't come out. It's a mistake, there's no fire.

The knocking is heard again. He takes a few steps away from her, and she vanishes into the wing. The light follows him, and now he is facing YOUNG BIFF, *who carries a suitcase.* BIFF *steps toward him. The music is gone.*

BIFF. Why didn't you answer?

WILLY. Biff! What are you doing in Boston?

BIFF. Why didn't you answer? I've been knocking for five minutes, I called you on the phone . . .

WILLY. I just heard you. I was in the bathroom and had the door shut. Did anything happen home?

BIFF. Dad—I let you down.

WILLY. What do you mean?

BIFF. Dad . . .

WILLY. Biffo, what's this about? (*Putting his arm around* BIFF.) Come on, let's go downstairs and get you a malted.

BIFF. Dad, I flunked math.

WILLY. Not for the term?

BIFF. The term. I haven't got enough credits to graduate.

WILLY. You mean to say Bernard wouldn't give you the answers?

BIFF. He did, he tried, but I only got a sixty-one.

WILLY. And they wouldn't give you four points?

BIFF.   Birnbaum refused absolutely. I begged him, Pop, but he won't give me
those points. You gotta talk to him before they close the school. Because if he saw the kind of man you are, and you just talked to him in
your way, I'm sure he'd come through for me. The class came right before practice, see, and I didn't go enough. Would you talk to him? He'd
like you, Pop. You know the way you could talk.

WILLY.   You're on. We'll drive right back.

BIFF.   Oh, Dad, good work! I'm sure he'll change it for you!

WILLY.   Go downstairs and tell the clerk I'm checkin' out. Go right down.

BIFF.   Yes, sir! See, the reason he hates me, Pop—one day he was late for
class so I got up at the blackboard and imitated him. I crossed my eyes
and talked with a lithp.

WILLY (*laughing*).   You did? The kids like it?

BIFF.   They nearly died laughing!

WILLY.   Yeah? What'd you do?

BIFF.   The thquare root of thixthy twee is . . . (WILLY *bursts out laughing;* BIFF
joins.) And in the middle of it he walked in!

WILLY *laughs and* THE WOMAN *joins in offstage.'*

WILLY (*without hesitation*).   Hurry downstairs and . . .

BIFF.   Somebody in there?

WILLY.   No, that was next door.

THE WOMAN *laughs offstage.*

BIFF.   Somebody got in your bathroom!

WILLY.   No, it's the next room, there's a party . . .

THE WOMAN (*enters, laughing; she lisps this*).   Can I come in? There's something in the bathtub, Willy, and it's moving!

WILLY *looks at* BIFF, *who is staring open-mouthed and horrified at* THE
WOMAN.

WILLY.   Ah—you better go back to your room. They must be finished painting by now. They're painting her room so I let her take a shower here.
Go back, go back . . . (*He pushes her.*)

THE WOMAN (*resisting*).   But I've got to get dressed, Willy, I can't . . .

WILLY.   Get out of here! Go back, go back . . . (*Suddenly striving for the
ordinary.*) This is Miss Francis, Biff, she's a buyer. They're painting her
room. Go back, Miss Francis, go back . . .

THE WOMAN.   But my clothes, I can't go out naked in the hall!

WILLY (*pushing her offstage*).   Get outa here! Go back, go back!

(BIFF *slowly sits down on his suitcase as the argument continues
offstage.*)

THE WOMAN.   Where's my stockings? You promised me stockings, Willy!

WILLY.   I have no stockings here!

THE WOMAN.   You had two boxes of size nine sheers for me, and I want them!

WILLY.   Here, for God's sake, will you get outa here!

THE WOMAN (*enters holding a box of stockings*).   I just hope there's nobody
in the hall. That's all I hope. (*To* BIFF.) Are you football or baseball?

BIFF.   Football.

THE WOMAN (*angry, humiliated*).   That's me too. G'night. (*She snatches her
clothes from* WILLY, *and walks out.*)

WILLY (*after a pause*). Well, better get going. I want to get to the school first thing in the morning. Get my suits out of the closet. I'll get my valise. (BIFF *doesn't move.*) What's the matter! (BIFF *remains motionless, tears falling.*) She's a buyer. Buys for J. H. Simmons. She lives down the hall—they're painting. You don't imagine—(*He breaks off. After a pause.*) Now listen, pal, she's just a buyer. She sees merchandise in her room and they have to keep it looking just so . . . (*Pause. Assuming command.*) All right, get my suits. (BIFF *doesn't move.*) Now stop crying and do as I say. I gave you an order. Biff, I gave you an order! Is that what you do when I give you an order? How dare you cry! (*Putting his arm around* BIFF.) Now look, Biff, when you grow up you'll understand about these things. You mustn't—you mustn't overemphasize a thing like this. I'll see Birnbaum first thing in the morning.

BIFF. Never mind.

WILLY (*getting down beside* BIFF). Never mind! He's going to give you those points. I'll see to it.

BIFF. He wouldn't listen to you.

WILLY. He certainly will listen to me. You need those points for the U. of Virginia.

BIFF. I'm not going there.

WILLY. Heh? If I can't get him to change that mark you'll make it up in summer school. You've got all summer to . . .

BIFF (*his weeping breaking from him*). Dad . . .

WILLY (*infected by it*). Oh, my boy . . .

BIFF. Dad . . .

WILLY. She's nothing to me, Biff. I was lonely, I was terribly lonely.

BIFF. You—you gave her Mama's stockings! (*His tears break through and he rises to go.*)

WILLY (*grabbing for* BIFF). I gave you an order!

BIFF. Don't touch me, you—liar!

WILLY. Apologize for that!

BIFF. You fake! You phony little fake! You fake! (*Overcome, he turns quickly and weeping fully goes out with his suitcase.* WILLY *is left on the floor on his knees.*)

WILLY. I gave you an order! Biff, come back here or I'll beat you! Come back here! I'll whip you!

STANLEY *comes quickly in from the right and stands in front of* WILLY.

WILLY (*shouts at* STANLEY). I gave you an order . . .

STANLEY. Hey, let's pick it up, pick it up, Mr. Loman. (*He helps* WILLY *to his feet.*) Your boys left with the chippies. They said they'll see you home.

A second waiter watches some distance away.

WILLY. But we were supposed to have dinner together.

Music is heard, WILLY'*s theme.*

STANLEY. Can you make it?

WILLY. I'll—sure, I can make it. (*Suddenly concerned about his clothes.*) Do I—I look all right?

STANLEY. Sure, you look all right. (*He flicks a speck off* WILLY'*s lapel.*)

WILLY. Here—here's a dollar.

STANLEY. Oh, your son paid me. It's all right.

WILLY (*putting it in* STANLEY's *hand*). No, take it. You're a good boy.

STANLEY. Oh, no, you don't have to . . .

WILLY. Here—here's some more, I don't need it any more. (*After a slight pause.*) Tell me—is there a seed store in the neighborhood?

STANLEY. Seeds? You mean like to plant?

As WILLY *turns,* STANLEY *slips the money back into his jacket pocket.*

WILLY. Yes. Carrots, peas . . .

STANLEY. Well, there's hardware stores on Sixth Avenue, but it may be too late now.

WILLY (*anxiously*). Oh, I'd better hurry. I've got to get some seeds. (*He starts off to the right.*) I've got to get some seeds, right away. Nothing's planted. I don't have a thing in the ground.

WILLY *hurries out as the light goes down.* STANLEY *moves over to the right after him, watches him off. The other waiter has been staring at* WILLY.

STANLEY (*to the waiter*). Well, whatta you looking at?

The waiter picks up the chairs and moves off right. STANLEY *takes the table and follows him. The light fades on this area. There is a long pause, the sound of the flute coming over. The light gradually rises on the kitchen, which is empty.* HAPPY *appears at the door of the house, followed by* BIFF. HAPPY *is carrying a large bunch of long-stemmed roses. He enters the kitchen, looks around for* LINDA. *Not seeing her, he turns to* BIFF, *who is just outside the house door, and makes a gesture with his hands, indicating "Not here, I guess." He looks into the living room and freezes. Inside,* LINDA, *unseen, is seated,* WILLY's *coat on her lap. She rises ominously and quietly and moves toward* HAPPY, *who backs up into the kitchen, afraid.*

HAPPY. Hey, what're you doing up? (LINDA *says nothing but moves toward him implacably.*) Where's Pop? (*He keeps backing to the right, and now* LINDA *is in full view in the doorway to the living room.*) Is he sleeping?

LINDA. Where were you?

HAPPY (*trying to laugh it off*). We met two girls, Mom, very fine types. Here, we brought you some flowers. (*Offering them to her.*) Put them in your room, Ma.

She knocks them to the floor at BIFF's *feet. He has now come inside and closed the door behind him. She stares at* BIFF, *silent.*

HAPPY. Now what'd you do that for? Mom, I want you to have some flowers . . .

LINDA (*cutting* HAPPY *off, violently to* BIFF). Don't you care whether he lives or dies?

HAPPY (*going to the stairs*). Come upstairs, Biff.

BIFF (*with a flare of disgust, to* HAPPY). Go away from me! (*To* LINDA.) What do you mean, lives or dies? Nobody's dying around here, pal.

LINDA. Get out of my sight! Get out of here!

BIFF. I wanna see the boss.

LINDA. You're not going near him!

BIFF. Where is he? (*He moves into the living room and* LINDA *follows.*)

LINDA (*shouting after* BIFF). You invite him for dinner. He looks forward to it all day—(BIFF *appears in his parents' bedroom, looks around, and exits*)—and then you desert him there. There's no stranger you'd do that to!

HAPPY. Why? He had a swell time with us. Listen, when I—(LINDA *comes back into the kitchen*)—desert him I hope I don't outlive the day!

LINDA. Get out of here!

HAPPY. Now look, Mom . . .

LINDA. Did you have to go to women tonight? You and your lousy rotten whores!

BIFF *re-enters the kitchen.*

HAPPY. Mom, all we did was follow Biff around trying to cheer him up! (*To* BIFF.) Boy, what a night you gave me!

LINDA. Get out of here, both of you, and don't come back! I don't want you tormenting him any more. Go on now, get your things together! (*To* BIFF.) You can sleep in his apartment. (*She starts to pick up the flowers and stops herself.*) Pick up this stuff, I'm not your maid any more. Pick it up, you bum, you!

HAPPY *turns his back to her in refusal.* BIFF *slowly moves over and gets down on his knees, picking up the flowers.*

LINDA. You're a pair of animals! Not one, not another living soul would have had the cruelty to walk out on that man in a restaurant!

BIFF (*not looking at her*). Is that what he said?

LINDA. He didn't have to say anything. He was so humiliated he nearly limped when he came in.

HAPPY. But, Mom, he had a great time with us . . .

BIFF (*cutting him off violently*). Shut up!

Without another word, HAPPY *goes upstairs.*

LINDA. You! You didn't even go in to see if he was all right!

BIFF (*still on the floor in front of* LINDA, *the flowers in his hand; with self-loathing*). No. Didn't. Didn't do a damned thing. How do you like that, heh? Left him babbling in a toilet.

LINDA. You louse. You . . .

BIFF. Now you hit it on the nose! (*He gets up, throws the flowers in the wastebasket.*) The scum of the earth, and you're looking at him!

LINDA. Get out of here!

BIFF. I gotta talk to the boss, Mom. Where is he?

LINDA. You're not going near him. Get out of this house!

BIFF (*with absolute assurance, determination*). No. We're gonna have an abrupt conversation, him and me.

LINDA. You're not talking to him.

Hammering is heard from outside the house, off right. BIFF *turns toward the noise.*

LINDA (*suddenly pleading*). Will you please leave him alone?

BIFF. What's he doing out there?

LINDA. He's planting the garden!

BIFF (*quietly*). Now? Oh, my God!

BIFF *moves outside,* LINDA *following. The light dies down on them and comes up on the center of the apron as* WILLY *walks into it. He is carrying a flashlight, a hoe, and a handful of seed packets. He raps the top of the hoe sharply to fix it firmly, and then moves to the left, measuring off the distance with his foot. He holds the flashlight to look at the seed packets, reading off the instructions. He is in the blue of night.*

WILLY. Carrots . . . quarter-inch apart. Rows . . . one-foot rows. (*He measures it off.*) One foot. (*He puts down a package and measures off.*) Beets. (*He puts down another package and measures again.*) Lettuce. (*He reads the package, puts it down.*) One foot—(*He breaks off as* BEN *appears at the right and moves slowly down to him.*) What a proposition, ts, ts. Terrific, terrific. 'Cause she's suffered, Ben, the woman has suffered. You understand me? A man can't go out the way he came in, Ben, a man has got to add up to something. You can't, you can't—(BEN *moves toward him as though to interrupt.*) You gotta consider now. Don't answer so quick. Remember, it's a guaranteed twenty-thousand-dollar proposition. Now look, Ben, I want you to go through the ins and outs of this thing with me. I've got nobody to talk to, Ben, and the woman has suffered, you hear me?

BEN (*standing still, considering*). What's the proposition?

WILLY. It's twenty thousand dollars on the barrelhead. Guaranteed, gilt-edged, you understand?

BEN. You don't want to make a fool of yourself. They might not honor the policy.

WILLY. How can they dare refuse? Didn't I work like a coolie to meet every premium on the nose? And now they don't pay off? Impossible!

BEN. It's called a cowardly thing, William.

WILLY. Why? Does it take more guts to stand here the rest of my life ringing up a zero?

BEN (*yielding*). That's a point, William. (*He moves, thinking, turns.*) And twenty thousand—that is something one can feel with the hand, it is there.

WILLY (*now assured, with rising power*). Oh, Ben, that's the whole beauty of it! I see it like a diamond, shining in the dark, hard and rough, that I can pick up and touch in my hand. Not like—like an appointment! This would not be another damned-fool appointment, Ben, and it changes all the aspects. Because he thinks I'm nothing, see, and so he spites me. But the funeral . . . (*Straightening up.*) Ben, that funeral will be massive! They'll come from Maine, Massachusetts, Vermont, New Hampshire! All the old-timers with the strange license plates—that boy will be thunderstruck, Ben, because he never realized—I am known! Rhode Island, New York, New Jersey—I am known, Ben, and he'll see it with his eyes once and for all. He'll see what I am, Ben! He's in for a shock, that boy!

BEN (*coming down to the edge of the garden*). He'll call you a coward.

WILLY (*suddenly fearful*). No, that would be terrible.

BEN. Yes. And a damned fool.

WILLY. No, no, he mustn't, I won't have that! (*He is broken and desperate.*)

BEN. He'll hate you, William.

The gay music of the Boys is heard.

WILLY. Oh, Ben, how do we get back to all the great times? Used to be so full of light, and comradeship, the sleigh-riding in winter, and the ruddiness on his cheeks. And always some kind of good news coming up, always something nice coming up ahead. And never even let me carry the valises in the house, and simonizing, simonizing that little red car! Why, why can't I give him something and not have him hate me?

BEN. Let me think about it. (*He glances at his watch.*) I still have a little time. Remarkable proposition, but you've got to be sure you're not making a fool of yourself.

BEN *drifts off upstage and goes out of sight.* BIFF *comes down from the left.*

WILLY (*suddenly conscious of* BIFF, *turns and looks up at him, then begins picking up the packages of seeds in confusion*). Where the hell is that seed? (*Indignantly.*) You can't see nothing out here! They boxed in the whole goddam neighborhood!

BIFF. There are people all around here. Don't you realize that?

WILLY. I'm busy. Don't bother me.

BIFF (*taking the hoe from* WILLY). I'm saying good-by to you, Pop. (WILLY *looks at him, silent, unable to move.*) I'm not coming back any more.

WILLY. You're not going to see Oliver tomorrow?

BIFF. I've got no appointment, Dad.

WILLY. He put his arm around you, and you've got no appointment?

BIFF. Pop, get this now, will you? Everytime I've left it's been a—fight that sent me out of here. Today I realized something about myself and I tried to explain it to you and I—I think I'm just not smart enough to make any sense out of it for you. To hell with whose fault it is or anything like that. (*He takes* WILLY's *arm.*) Let's just wrap it up, heh? Come on in, we'll tell Mom. (*He gently tries to pull* WILLY *to left.*)

WILLY (*frozen, immobile, with guilt in his voice*). No, I don't want to see her.

BIFF. Come on! (*He pulls again, and* WILLY *tries to pull away.*)

WILLY (*highly nervous*). No, no, I don't want to see her.

BIFF (*tries to look into* WILLY's *face, as if to find the answer there*). Why don't you want to see her?

WILLY (*more harshly now*). Don't bother me, will you?

BIFF. What do you mean, you don't want to see her? You don't want them calling you yellow, do you? This isn't your fault; it's me, I'm a bum. Now come inside! (WILLY *strains to get away.*) Did you hear what I said to you?

WILLY *pulls away and quickly goes by himself into the house.* BIFF *follows.*

LINDA (*to* WILLY). Did you plant, dear?

BIFF (*at the door, to* LINDA). All right, we had it out. I'm going and I'm not writing any more.

LINDA (*going to* WILLY *in the kitchen*). I think that's the best way, dear. 'Cause there's no use drawing it out, you'll just never get along.

WILLY *doesn't respond.*

BIFF. People ask where I am and what I'm doing, you don't know, and you don't care. That way it'll be off your mind and you can start brightening up again. All right? That clears it, doesn't it? (WILLY *is silent, and* BIFF *goes to him.*) You gonna wish me luck, scout? (*He extends his hand.*) What do you say?

LINDA. Shake his hand, Willy.

WILLY (*turning to her, seething with hurt*). There's no necessity—to mention the pen at all, y'know.

BIFF (*gently*). I've got no appointment, Dad.

WILLY (*erupting fiercely*). He put his arm around . . . ?

BIFF. Dad, you're never going to see what I am, so what's the use of arguing? If I strike oil I'll send you a check. Meantime forget I'm alive.

WILLY (*to* LINDA). Spite, see?

BIFF. Shake hands, Dad.

WILLY. Not my hand.

BIFF. I was hoping not to go this way.

WILLY. Well, this is the way you're going. Good-by.

BIFF *looks at him a moment, then turns sharply and goes to the stairs.*

WILLY (*stops him with*). May you rot in hell if you leave this house!

BIFF (*turning*). Exactly what is it that you want from me?

WILLY. I want you to know, on the train, in the mountains, in the valleys, wherever you go, that you cut down your life for spite!

BIFF. No, no.

WILLY. Spite, spite, is the word of your undoing! And when you're down and out, remember what did it. When you're rotting somewhere beside the railroad tracks, remember, and don't you dare blame it on me!

BIFF. I'm not blaming it on you!

WILLY. I won't take the rap for this, you hear?

HAPPY *comes down the stairs and stands on the bottom step, watching.*

BIFF. That's just what I'm telling you!

WILLY (*sinking into a chair at a table, with full accusation*). You're trying to put a knife in me—don't think I don't know what you're doing!

BIFF. All right, phony! Then let's lay it on the line. (*He whips the rubber tube out of his pocket and puts it on the table.*)

HAPPY. You crazy . . .

LINDA. Biff! (*She moves to grab the hose, but* BIFF *holds it down with his hand.*)

BIFF. Leave it there! Don't move it!

WILLY (*not looking at it*). What is that?

BIFF. You know goddam well what that is.

WILLY (*caged, wanting to escape*). I never saw that.

BIFF. You saw it. The mice didn't bring it into the cellar! What is this supposed to do, make a hero out of you? This supposed to make me sorry for you?

WILLY. Never heard of it.

BIFF. There'll be no pity for you, you hear it? No pity!

WILLY (*to* LINDA). You hear the spite!

BIFF. No, you're going to hear the truth—what you are and what I am!

LINDA. Stop it!

WILLY. Spite!

HAPPY (*coming down toward* BIFF). You cut it now!

BIFF (*to* HAPPY). The man don't know who we are! The man is gonna know! (*To* WILLY.) We never told the truth for ten minutes in this house!

HAPPY. We always told the truth!

BIFF (*turning on him*). You big blow, are you the assistant buyer? You're one of the two assistants to the assistant, aren't you?

HAPPY. Well, I'm practically . . .

BIFF. You're practically full of it! We all are! and I'm through with it. (*To* WILLY.) Now hear this, Willy, this is me.

WILLY. I know you!

BIFF. You know why I had no address for three months? I stole a suit in Kansas City and I was in jail. (*To* LINDA, *who is sobbing.*) Stop crying. I'm through with it.

LINDA *turns away from them, her hands covering her face.*

WILLY. I suppose that's my fault!

BIFF. I stole myself out of every good job since high school!

WILLY. And whose fault is that?

BIFF. And I never got anywhere because you blew me so full of hot air I could never stand taking orders from anybody! That's whose fault it is!

WILLY. I hear that!

LINDA. Don't, Biff!

BIFF. It's goddam time you heard that! I had to be boss big shot in two weeks, and I'm through with it!

WILLY. Then hang yourself! For spite, hang yourself!

BIFF. No! Nobody's hanging himself, Willy! I ran down eleven flights with a pen in my hand today. And suddenly I stopped, you hear me? And in the middle of that office building, do you hear this? I stopped in the middle of that building and I saw—the sky. I saw the things that I love in this world. The work and the food and time to sit and smoke. And I looked at the pen and said to myself, what the hell am I grabbing this for? Why am I trying to become what I don't want to be? What am I doing in an office, making a contemptuous, begging fool of myself, when all I want is out there, waiting for me the minute I say I know who I am! Why can't I say that, Willy? (*He tries to make* WILLY *face him, but* WILLY *pulls away and moves to the left.*)

WILLY (*with hatred, threateningly*). The door of your life is wide open!

BIFF. Pop! I'm a dime a dozen, and so are you!

WILLY (*turning on him now in an uncontrolled outburst*). I am not a dime a dozen! I am Willy Loman, and you are Biff Loman!

BIFF *starts for* WILLY, *but is blocked by* HAPPY. *In his fury,* BIFF *seems on the verge of attacking his father.*

BIFF. I am not a leader of men, Willy, and neither are you. You were never anything but a hard-working drummer who landed in the ash can like all the rest of them! I'm one dollar an hour, Willy! I tried seven states and couldn't raise it. A buck an hour! Do you gather my meaning? I'm not bringing home any prizes any more, and you're going to stop waiting for me to bring them home!

WILLY (*directly to* BIFF). You vengeful, spiteful mutt!

BIFF *breaks from* HAPPY. WILLY, *in fright, starts up the stairs.* BIFF *grabs him.*

BIFF (*at the peak of his fury*). Pop! I'm nothing! I'm nothing, Pop. Can't you understand that? There's no spite in it any more. I'm just what I am, that's all.

BIFF's *fury has spent itself and he breaks down, sobbing, holding on to* WILLY, *who dumbly fumbles for* BIFF's *face.*

WILLY (*astonished*). What're you doing? What're you doing? (*To* LINDA.) Why is he crying?

BIFF (*crying, broken*). Will you let me go, for Christ's sake? Will you take that phony dream and burn it before something happens? (*Struggling to contain himself he pulls away and moves to the stairs.*) I'll go in the morning. Put him—put him to bed. (*Exhausted,* BIFF *moves up the stairs to his room.*)

WILLY (*after a long pause, astonished, elevated*). Isn't that—isn't that remarkable? Biff—he likes me!

LINDA. He loves you, Willy!

HAPPY (*deeply moved*). Always did, Pop.

WILLY. Oh, Biff! (*Staring wildly.*) He cried! Cried to me. (*He is choking with his love, and now cries out his promise.*) That boy—that boy is going to be magnificent!

BEN *appears in the light just outside the kitchen.*

BEN. Yes, outstanding, with twenty thousand behind him.

LINDA (*sensing the racing of his mind, fearfully, carefully.*) Now come to bed, Willy. It's all settled now.

WILLY (*finding it difficult not to rush out of the house*). Yes, we'll sleep. Come on. Go to sleep, Hap.

BEN. And it does take a great kind of a man to crack the jungle.

In accents of dread, BEN's *idyllic music starts up.*

HAPPY (*his arm around* LINDA). I'm getting married, Pop, don't forget it. I'm changing everything. I'm gonna run that department before the year is up. You'll see, Mom. (*He kisses her.*)

BEN. The jungle is dark but full of diamonds, Willy.

WILLY *turns, moves, listening to* BEN.

LINDA. Be good. You're both good boys, just act that way, that's all.

HAPPY. 'Night, Pop. (*He goes upstairs.*)

LINDA (*to* WILLY). Come, dear.

BEN (*with greater force*). One must go in to fetch a diamond out.

WILLY (*to* LINDA, *as he moves slowly along the edge of the kitchen, toward the door*). I just want to get settled down, Linda. Let me sit alone for a little.

LINDA (*almost uttering her fear*). I want you upstairs.

WILLY (*taking her in his arms*). In a few minutes, Linda. I couldn't sleep right now. Go on, you look awful tired. (*He kisses her.*)

BEN. Not like an appointment at all. A diamond is rough and hard to the touch.

WILLY. Go on now. I'll be right up.

LINDA. I think this is the only way, Willy.

WILLY. Sure, it's the best thing.

BEN. Best thing!

WILLY. The only way. Everything is gonna be—go on, kid, get to bed. You look so tired.

LINDA. Come right up.

WILLY. Two minutes.

LINDA *goes into the living room, then reappears in her bedroom.* WILLY *moves just outside the kitchen door.*

WILLY. Loves me. (*Wonderingly.*) Always loved me. Isn't that a remarkable thing? Ben, he'll worship me for it!

BEN (*with promise*). It's dark there, but full of diamonds.

WILLY. Can you imagine that magnificence with twenty thousand dollars in his pocket?

LINDA (*calling from her room*). Willy! Come up!

WILLY (*calling into the kitchen*). Yes! Yes. Coming! It's very smart, you realize that, don't you, sweetheart? Even Ben sees it. I gotta go, baby. 'By! 'By! (*Going over to* BEN, *almost dancing.*) Imagine? When the mail comes he'll be ahead of Bernard again!

BEN. A perfect proposition all around.

WILLY. Did you see how he cried to me? Oh, if I could kiss him, Ben!

BEN. Time, William, time!

WILLY. Oh, Ben, I always knew one way or another we were gonna make it, Biff and I.

BEN (*looking at his watch*). The boat. We'll be late. (*He moves slowly off into the darkness.*)

WILLY (*elegiacally, turning to the house*). Now when you kick off, boy, I want a seventy-yard boot, and get right down the field under the ball, and when you hit, hit low and hit hard, because it's important, boy. (*He swings around and faces the audience.*) There's all kinds of important people in the stands, and the first thing you know . . . (*Suddenly realizing he is alone.*) Ben! Ben, where do I . . . ? (*He makes a sudden movement of search.*) Ben, how do I . . . ?

LINDA (*calling*). Willy, you coming up?

WILLY (*uttering a gasp of fear, whirling about as if to quiet her*). Sh! (*He turns around as if to find his way; sounds, faces, voices, seem to be swarming in upon him and he flicks at them, crying.*) Sh! Sh! (*Suddenly music, faint and high, stops him. It rises in intensity, almost to an unbearable scream. He goes up and down on his toes, and rushes off around the house.*) Shhh!

LINDA. Willy?

There is no answer. LINDA *waits.* BIFF *gets up off his bed. He is still in his clothes.* HAPPY *sits up.* BIFF *stands listening.*

LINDA (*with real fear*). Willy, answer me! Willy!

There is the sound of a car starting and moving away at full speed.

LINDA. No!

BIFF (*rushing down the stairs*). Pop!

As the car speeds off the music crashes down in a frenzy of sound, which becomes the soft pulsation of a single cello string. BIFF *slowly returns to his bedroom. He and* HAPPY *gravely don their jackets.* LINDA *slowly walks out of her room. The music has developed into a dead march. The leaves of day are appearing over everything.* CHARLEY *and* BERNARD, *somberly dressed, appear and knock on the kitchen door.* BIFF *and* HAPPY *slowly descend the stairs to the kitchen as* CHARLEY *and* BERNARD *enter. All stop a moment when* LINDA, *in clothes of mourning, bearing a little bunch of roses, comes through the draped doorway into the kitchen. She goes to* CHARLEY *and takes his arm. Now all move toward the audience, through the wall-line of the kitchen. At the limit of the apron,* LINDA *lays down the flowers, kneels, and sits back on her heels. All stare down at the grave.*

Requiem

CHARLEY. It's getting dark, Linda.

LINDA *doesn't react. She stares at the grave.*

BIFF. How about it, Mom? Better get some rest, heh? They'll be closing the gate soon.

LINDA *makes no move. Pause.*

HAPPY (*deeply angered*). He had no right to do that. There was no necessity for it. We would've helped him.

CHARLEY (*grunting*). Hmmm.

BIFF. Come along, Mom.

LINDA. Why didn't anybody come?

CHARLEY. It was a very nice funeral.

LINDA. But where are all the people he knew? Maybe they blame him.

CHARLEY. Naa. It's a rough world, Linda. They wouldn't blame him.

LINDA. I can't understand it. At this time especially. First time in thirty-five years we were just about free and clear. He only needed a little salary. He was even finished with the dentist.

CHARLEY. No man only needs a little salary.

LINDA. I can't understand it.

BIFF. There were a lot of nice days. When he'd come home from a trip; or on Sundays, making the stoop; finishing the cellar; putting on the new porch; when he built the extra bathroom; and put up the garage. You know something, Charley, there's more of him in that front stoop than in all the sales he ever made.

CHARLEY. Yeah. He was a happy man with a batch of cement.

LINDA. He was so wonderful with his hands.

BIFF. He had the wrong dreams. All, all, wrong.

HAPPY (*almost ready to fight* BIFF). Don't say that!

BIFF. He never knew who he was.

CHARLEY (*stopping* HAPPY'*s movement and reply; to* BIFF). Nobody dast blame
    this man. You don't understand: Willy was a salesman. And for a sales-
    man, there is no rock bottom to the life. He don't put a bolt to a nut, he
    don't tell you the law or give you medicine. He's a man way out there in
    the blue, riding on a smile and a shoeshine. And when they start not smil-
    ing back—that's an earthquake. And then you get yourself a couple of
    spots on your hat, and you're finished. Nobody dast blame this man. A
    salesman is got to dream, boy. It comes with the territory.

BIFF. Charley, the man didn't know who he was.

HAPPY (*infuriated*). Don't say that!

BIFF. Why don't you come with me, Happy?

HAPPY. I'm not licked that easily. I'm staying right in this city, and I'm gonna
    beat this racket! (*He looks at* BIFF, *his chin set.*) The Loman Brothers!

BIFF. I know who I am, kid.

HAPPY. All right, boy. I'm gonna show you and everybody else that Willy Lo-
    man did not die in vain. He had a good dream. It's the only dream you
    can have—to come out number-one man. He fought it out here, and
    this is where I'm gonna win it for him.

BIFF (*with a hopeless glance at* HAPPY, *bends toward his mother*). Let's go,
    Mom.

LINDA. I'll be with you in a minute. Go on, Charley. (*He hesitates.*) I want to,
    just for a minute. I never had a chance to say good-by.

CHARLEY *moves away, followed by* HAPPY. BIFF *remains a slight distance
up and left of* LINDA. *She sits there, summoning herself. The flute begins, not far away, playing behind her speech.*

LINDA. Forgive me, dear. I can't cry. I don't know what it is, but I can't cry. I
    don't understand it. Why did you ever do that? Help me, Willy, I can't cry.
    It seems to me that you're just on another trip. I keep expecting you.
    Willy, dear, I can't cry. Why did you do it? I search and search and I search,
    and I can't understand it, Willy. I made the last payment on the house to-
    day. Today, dear. And there'll be nobody home. (*A sob rises in her
    throat.*) We're free and clear. (*Sobbing mournfully, released.*) We're
    free. (BIFF *comes slowly toward her.*) We're free … We're free …

BIFF *lifts her to her feet and moves out up right with her in his arms.*
LINDA *sobs quietly.* BERNARD *and* CHARLEY *come together and follow
them, followed by* HAPPY. *Only the music of the flute is left on the
darkening stage as over the house the hard towers of the apartment
buildings rise into sharp focus and the curtain falls.*

▨ TOPICS FOR CRITICAL THINKING AND WRITING

The Play on the Page

1. Miller said in the *New York Times* (February 27, 1949, Sec. II, p. 1) that
    tragedy shows man's struggle to secure "his sense of personal dignity"
    and that "his destruction in the attempt posits a wrong or an evil in his
    environment." Does this make sense when applied to some earlier

tragedy (for example, *Oedipus Rex* or *Hamlet*), and does it apply convincingly to *Death of a Salesman*? Is this the tragedy of an individual's own making? Or is society at fault for corrupting and exploiting Willy? Or both?

2. Is Willy pathetic rather than tragic? If pathetic, does this imply that the play is less worthy than if he is tragic?

3. Do you feel that Miller is straining too hard to turn a play about a little man into a big, impressive play? For example, do the musical themes, the unrealistic setting, the appearances of Ben, and the speech at the grave seem out of keeping in a play about the death of a salesman?

4. We don't know what Willy sells, and we don't know whether or not the insurance will be paid after his death. Do you consider these uncertainties to be faults in the play?

5. Is Howard a villain?

6. Characterize Linda.

The Play on the Stage

7. It is sometimes said that in this realistic play that includes symbolic and expressionistic elements, Biff and Happy can be seen as two aspects of Willy. In this view, Biff more or less represents Willy's spiritual needs, and Happy represents his materialism and his sexuality. If you were directing the play, would you adopt this point of view? Whatever your interpretation, how would you costume the brothers?

8. Although Miller envisioned Willy as a small man (literally small), the role was first performed by Lee J. Cobb, a large man. If you were casting the play, what actor would you select? Why? Whom would you choose for Linda, Biff, Happy, Bernard, and Charley?

9. Select roughly thirty lines of dialogue, and discuss the movements (gestures and blocking) that as a director you would suggest to the performers.

A CONTEXT FOR *DEATH OF A SALESMAN*

ARTHUR MILLER

The following essay appeared in the New York Times *in 1949, while* Death of a Salesman *was running on Broadway.*

Tragedy and the Common Man   [1949]

In this age few tragedies are written. It has often been held that the lack is due to a paucity of heroes among us, or else that modern man has had the blood drawn out of his organs of belief by the skepticism of science, and the heroic attack on life cannot feed on an attitude of reserve and circumspection. For one reason or another, we are often held to be below tragedy—or tragedy above us. The inevitable conclusion is, of course, that the tragic mode is archaic, fit only for the very highly placed, the kings or the kingly, and where this admission is not made in so many words it is most often implied.

I believe that the common man is as apt a subject for tragedy in its highest sense as kings were. On the face of it this ought to be obvious in the light of modern psychiatry, which bases its analysis upon classic formulations, such as the Oedipus and Orestes complexes, for instances, which were enacted by royal beings, but which apply to everyone in similar emotional situations.

More simply, when the question of tragedy in art is not at issue, we never hesitate to attribute to the well-placed and the exalted the very same mental processes as the lowly. And finally, if the exaltation of tragic action were truly a property of the high-bred character alone, it is inconceivable that the mass of mankind should cherish tragedy above all other forms, let alone be capable of understanding it.

As a general rule, to which there may be exceptions unknown to me, I think the tragic feeling is evoked in us when we are in the presence of a character who is ready to lay down his life, if need be, to secure one thing—his sense of personal dignity. From Orestes to Hamlet, Medea to Macbeth, the underlying struggle is that of the individual attempting to gain his "rightful" position in his society.

Sometimes he is one who has been displaced from it, sometimes one who seeks to attain it for the first time, but the fateful wound from which the inevitable events spiral is the wound of indignity, and its dominant force is indignation. Tragedy, then, is the consequence of a man's total compulsion to evaluate himself justly.

In the sense of having been initiated by the hero himself, the tale always reveals what has been called his "tragic flaw," a failing that is not peculiar to grand or elevated characters. Nor is it necessarily a weakness. The flaw, or crack in the character, is really nothing—and need be nothing, but his inherent unwillingness to remain passive in the face of what he conceives to be a challenge to his dignity, his image of his rightful status. Only the passive, only those who accept their lot without active retaliation, are "flawless." Most of us are in that category.

But there are among us today, as there always have been, those who act against the scheme of things that degrades them, and in the process of action everything we have accepted out of fear or insensitivity or ignorance is shaken before us and examined, and from this total onslaught by an individual against the seemingly stable cosmos surrounding us—from this total examination of the "unchangeable" environment—comes the terror and the fear that is classically associated with tragedy.

More important, from this total questioning of what has previously been unquestioned, we learn. And such a process is not beyond the common man. In revolutions around the world, these past thirty years, he has demonstrated again and again this inner dynamic of all tragedy.

Insistence upon the rank of the tragic hero, or the so-called nobility of his character, is really but a clinging to the outward forms of tragedy. If rank or nobility of character was indispensable, then it would follow that the problems of those with rank were the particular problems of tragedy. But surely the right of one monarch to capture the domain from another no longer raises our passions, nor are our concepts of justice what they were to the mind of an Elizabethan king.

The quality in such plays that does shake us, however, derives from the underlying fear of being displaced, the disaster inherent in being torn away from our chosen image of what and who we are in this world. Among us today this fear is as strong, and perhaps stronger, than it ever was. In fact, it is the common man who knows this fear best.

Now, if it is true that tragedy is the consequence of a man's total compulsion to evaluate himself justly, his destruction in the attempt posits a wrong or an evil in his environment. And this is precisely the morality of tragedy and its lesson. The discovery of the moral law, which is what the enlightenment of tragedy consists of, is not the discovery of some abstract or metaphysical quantity.

The tragic right is a condition of life, a condition in which the human personality is able to flower and realize itself. The wrong is the condition which suppresses man, perverts the flowing out of his love and creative instinct. Tragedy enlightens—and it must, in that it points the heroic finger at the enemy of man's freedom. The thrust for freedom is the quality in tragedy which exalts. The revolutionary questioning of the stable environment is what terrifies. In no way is the common man debarred from such thoughts or such actions.

Seen in this light, our lack of tragedy may be partially accounted for by the turn which modern literature has taken toward the purely psychiatric view of life, or the purely sociological. If all our miseries, our indignities, are born and bred within our minds, then all action, let alone the heroic action, is obviously impossible.

And if society alone is responsible for the cramping of our lives, then the protagonist must needs be so pure and faultless as to force us to deny his validity as a character. From neither of these views can tragedy derive, simply because neither represents a balanced concept of life. Above all else, tragedy requires the finest appreciation by the writer of cause and effect.

No tragedy can therefore come about when its author fears to question absolutely everything, when he regards any institution, habit or custom as being either everlasting, immutable or inevitable. In the tragic view the need of man to wholly realize himself is the only fixed star, and whatever it is that hedges his nature and lowers it is ripe for attack and examination. Which is not to say that tragedy must preach revolution.

The Greeks could probe the very heavenly origin of their ways and return to confirm the rightness of laws. And Job could face God in anger, demanding his right and end in submission. But for a moment everything is in suspension, nothing is accepted, and in this stretching and tearing apart of the cosmos, in the very action of so doing, the character gains "size," the tragic stature which is spuriously attached to the royal or the highborn in our minds. The commonest of men may take on that stature to the extent of his willingness to throw all he has into the contest, the battle to secure his rightful place in his world.

There is a misconception of tragedy with which I have been struck in review after review, and in many conversations with writers and readers alike. It is the idea that tragedy is of necessity allied to pessimism. Even the dictionary says nothing more about the word than that it means a story with a sad or unhappy ending. This impression is so firmly fixed that I almost hesitate to claim that in truth tragedy implies more optimism in its author than does comedy, and that its final result ought to be the reinforcement of the onlooker's brightest opinions of the human animal.

For, if it is true to say that in essence the tragic hero is intent upon claiming his whole due as a personality, and if this struggle must be total and without reservation, then it automatically demonstrates the indestructible will of man to achieve his humanity.

The possibility of victory must be there in tragedy. Where pathos rules, where pathos is finally derived, a character has fought a battle he could not possibly have won. The pathetic is achieved when the protagonist is, by virtue of his witlessness, his insensitivity or the very air he gives off, incapable of grappling with a much superior force.

Pathos truly is the mode for the pessimist. But tragedy requires a nicer balance between what is possible and what is impossible. And it is curious, although edifying, that the plays we revere, century after century, are the tragedies. In them, and in them alone, lies the belief—optimistic, if you will—in the perfectibility of man.

It is time, I think, that we who are without kings, took up this bright thread of our history and followed it to the only place it can possibly lead in our time—the heart and spirit of the average man.

EVE MERRIAM, PAULA WAGNER, AND JACK HOFSISS

When the actress Paula Wagner expressed dissatisfaction with some of the roles she had played, Eve Merriam suggested that Wagner do a one-woman show drawing on Merriam's anthology of journals and letters, Growing Up Female *(1971). Merriam and Wagner together made the selection for the performance, and then, in collaboration with the director Jack Hofsiss, decided to convert the work, now titled* Out of Our Fathers' House, *into a play for three actresses and several musicians. It was first produced in 1975.*

Eve Merriam (1916-1992) wrote plays, poetry, fiction, and nonfiction. Among her awards is an Obie for The Club. *Paula Wagner, now a film agent in Hollywood, has played major roles in classical and modern dramas. Jack Hofsiss, director of many productions, won a Tony award for his direction of* The Elephant Man.

Out of Our Fathers' House

CHARACTERS

ELIZA SOUTHGATE *(1783-1809), schoolgirl*
ELIZABETH CADY STANTON *(1815-1902), founder of the Women's Suffrage Movement*
MARIA MITCHELL *(1818-1889), astronomer*
"MOTHER" MARY JONES *(1830-1930), labor organizer*
DR. ANNA HOWARD SHAW *(1847-1919), minister and doctor*
ELIZABETH GERTRUDE STERN *(1890-1954), in the Jewish ghetto*

Three actresses play all six women and the minor characters. Musicians perform the songs (number of singers and instruments used are at the discretion of the director). ACTRESS #1 plays ELIZA SOUTHGATE and GERTRUDE STERN; ACTRESS #2 plays MARIA MITCHELL and ANNA HOWARD SHAW; ACTRESS #3 plays ELIZABETH CADY STANTON and MOTHER MARY JONES. *Out of Our Fathers' House* may also be performed by six actresses.

Gina Lund as Dr. Ann Howard Shaw (1847–1919), in a Barnard College production in 1984. Dr. Shaw, an ordained Methodist minister, in 1885 earned a medical degree at Boston University. In 1888 she met Susan B. Anthony and from then onward she devoted her life to social issues, notably to woman's suffrage. In the Barnard production the performers entered the stage wearing contemporary clothing such as sweatpants and T-shirts (notice the figures in the background), and then, in the presence of the audience, they *became* the roles they played. The women helped to costume each other but their hair styles remained contemporary, thus suggesting the interpenetration of past and present. (Photo by Lowell Handler.)

Mother [Mary] Jones (1837–1930) devoted most of her adult life to the labor movement. Among her notable fights was a battle in 1902 in which she inspired the wives of striking Pennsylvania coal miners to drive out—with mops amd brooms—the strikebreakers. (See pages 1646–47). Peggy Penniman, in her 1989 production of *Out of Our Fathers' House* at Towson University, used mops amd brooms also in scene (shown here) with the song "Housewife's Lament" (page 1649), in order to convey the interlocking relationships between the women in their struggle against daily oppression.

Out of Our Fathers' House, while taken from the actual writings of the characters portrayed, takes the theatrical form of a hypothetical conversation among the different woman characters. This is historically impossible, since these women could never have had such a conversation, but it is valid for the purposes of the piece. This is a timeless interaction in which these women act out for both themselves and each other the stories of their lives—in particular the accounts of their emergence "out of their fathers' house." It is essential that the piece be personal and conversational. The characters are not retelling but rather reliving their experiences. Both together and alone they make the journey into a world of self-sufficiency and the "solitude of self."

The stage is an abandoned summerhouse; there is a carousel horse, battered and broken, upstage right; a wicker table upstage center, or possibly an old coatrack, and another coatrack upstage left. Down center are three chairs placed in a semicircle in which musicians sit playing as the audience enters. The mood should be warm and comfortable. This is the secret place where one would run off to think and be alone.
As the lights dim, the musicians begin to sing.

Song: "Built My Lady a Fine Brick House"
I built my lady a fine brick house,
I built it in a garden.
I put her in, but she jumped out,
Oh, fare thee well, my darling.

I built my lady a high stone wall,
I built it in a garden.
I put her in, but she jumped out,
Oh, fare thee well, my darling.

I built my lady a gate with a lock,
I built it in a garden.
I put her in, but she jumped out,
So fare thee well, my darling.

(ACTRESS #1. *has entered during the last part of the song and states the first of the rules of etiquette for young ladies of the late eighteenth century in America. Others follow and take lines in sequence. The actresses carry with them lanterns and large wicker baskets which contain any props and costumes they might need for the show. It has the effect of running away from home. Rules of etiquette:*)

ACTRESS #1. Bite not thy bread, but break it.
ACTRESS #2. Look not earnestly at any other that is eating.
ACTRESS #3. Never sit down at the table until asked, and after the blessing.
ACTRESS #1. When moderately satisfied, leave the table.
ACTRESS #2. Sing not, hum not, wriggle not.
ACTRESS #3. When any speak to thee, stand up.
ACTRESS #2. Say not "I have heard it before."
ACTRESS #1. Never endeavor to help him out if he tell it not right.
ACTRESS #3. Snigger not. Never question the truth of it.
ACTRESS #2. Do not remove the gloves.

ACTRESS #3. Do not make a call of ceremony on a wet day . . . Always have an umbrella beside you and overshoes.

ACTRESS #1. Getting wet seldom fails to produce a cold.

ACTRESS #2. To lose your dinner is not half so dangerous.

ACTRESS #3. Wet feet and wet clothes have sent thousands to eternity before their time.

ACTRESS #1. Avoid unnecessary exposure to the evening air.

ACTRESS #2. Do not touch the piano unless asked.

ACTRESS #3. Do not call upon a gentleman unless he is a confirmed invalid.

(The musicians are offstage by now)

Song: "Little Bird"
(Theme for Gertrude Stern)
I'm as free a little bird as I can be
I'm as free a little bird as I can be
I will build my nest in the sour apple tree
Where those bad boys will never bother me.

VOICE. Elizabeth Gertrude Stern, born in 1890 in a Jewish ghetto of a large Midwestern city, growing up to obey her father's commandments.

Oh, who will shoe your little foot?
And who will glove your little hand?

(Pause.)

GERTRUDE *(Sings)*.

Oh, it's papa will shoe my little foot
And it's mama will glove my little hand

(Spoken)

I remember looking down at the face of my father, beautiful and still in death, and for a brief moment, feeling my heart rise up . . . Surely it was in a strange suffocating relief . . . Now I am free!

(Sings)

And it's you who'll kiss my red-rosy cheek
When you come from that far-distant land.

Song: "Molly Hare"
(Theme for Mother Jones)
Old Molly Hare, what are you doing there?
Running through a cotton patch as fast as I can tear.
Riding of a goat, leading of a sheep,
I won't be back till the middle of the week.

VOICE. Mary Harris Jones, born in 1830, lived to be one hundred years old and became known to children and adults alike as "Mother Jones."

MARY. I asked a man in prison once how he happened to be there, and he said that he had stolen a pair of shoes. I told him if he had stolen a railroad he would be a United States Senator.

Song: "My Horses Ain't Hungry"
(Theme for Anna Shaw)
My horses ain't hungry, they won't eat your hay,
So I'll get on my pony, I'm going away.
With all our belongings we'll ride till we come
To a lonely little cabin, we'll call it our home.

VOICE. Anna Howard Shaw, at age twelve, moved from a manufacturing town in Massachusetts to the wild woods of Michigan in 1859.

ANNA. Once when I was fourteen, I had been in the woods all day, buried in my books, and when I returned home at night, still in the dream world these books had opened to me, Father was awaiting my coming, dark with disapproval . . . *I was an idler who wasted time.* He ended a long arraignment by predicting that with such tendencies I would make nothing of my life.

Song: "What'll We Do with the Baby?"
(Theme for Elizabeth)
What'll we do with the baby?
What'll we do with the baby?
What'll we do with the baby-o?
We'll wrap it up in calico!
Wrap it up in calico and send it to its pappy-o.

VOICE. Elizabeth Cady Stanton, born in New York State in 1815 . . . The same year her father was elected to Congress.

ELIZABETH. The custom of calling women Mrs. John This and Mrs. Tom That, and colored men Sambo and Zip-coon, is founded on the principle that white men are the lords of all. I cannot acknowledge this principle, and therefore I cannot bear the name of another. If the nineteenth century is to be governed by the opinions of the eighteenth, and the twentieth by the nineteenth, then the world will always be governed by dead men. I would rather make a few slanders from a superabundance of life than to have all the proprieties of a well-embalmed mummy.

Song: "Rose, Rose and Up She Rises"
(Theme for Maria Mitchell)
Rose, rose and up she rises,
Rose, rose and up she rises,
Rose, rose and up she rises
So early in the morning.
I wonder where Maria's gone?
I wonder where Maria's gone?
I wonder where Maria's gone?
So early in the morning?

VOICE. Maria Mitchell, born on Nantucket Island in 1818. Her father was devoted to astronomy, and all the children were drafted into the service of counting seconds by the chronometer during his observations.

MARIA. Once a lady asked me if I told fortunes, and when I replied in the negative, she asked me if I weren't an astronomer. I admitted that I made efforts in that direction. She then asked me what could I tell if not fortunes. I told her that I could tell when the moon would rise, and when the sun would set. She said, "Oh," in a tone which plainly implied "Is that all?"

> Song: "Young Maid"
> (Theme for Eliza Southgate)
> When I was a young maid, young maid,
> When I was a young maid, then oh then
> It was ha, ha, this-a-way, ha, ha, that-a-way
> This-a-way, that-a-way, then.

VOICE. Eliza Southgate, born in 1783 in Scarborough, Maine . . . sent by her parents to finishing school near Boston when she was fourteen.

ELIZA. You may justly say, my best of fathers, that every letter of mine is one which is asking for something more; never contented . . . I only ask. If you refuse me, I know you do what you think best, and I am sure I ought not to complain, for you have never yet refused me anything that I have asked, my best of parents, how shall I repay you?

> Song: "Listen to the Voices"
> Listen to the voices
> Out of darkness into daybreak
> Making their lives.

(At this point, the actresses sit in the chairs that are placed center, and begin to knit, and write, and comb their hair. A musician sings. The song is "Monday Morning.")

MUSICIAN.
> How old are you, my fair young maid?
> I'm going to be sixteen next Monday morning.

ELIZA. Such a frolic! Such a chain of adventures I never before met with. For two days it had been storming so much that the snow drifts were very large; however, as it was the last assembly, I could not resist the temptation of going, as I knew all the world would be there. About seven I went downstairs and immediately slipt on my socks and coat, and met Mr. Motley in the entry. The snow was deep, but Mr. Motley took me up in his arms, and sat me in the carriage without difficulty. I found a full assembly, many married ladies, and every one disposed to end the winter in good spirits. At one we left dancing. It stormed dreadfully, we could not get a coach until three o'clock. There were now twenty in waiting, the gentlemen scolding and fretting, the ladies murmuring and complaining as they all flocked to engage a seat. Luckily I was one of the first. Mr. Motley took me up in his arms and carried me till my weight pressed him so far into the snow that he had no power to move his feet. I rolled out of his arms and wallowed till I reached the gate; then rising to shake off the snow, I turned and beheld my beau fixed and immovable; he could not get his feet out to take another step! At length, making a great exertion to spring his whole length forward, he made out to reach the poor horse, who lay in a worse condition than his master. By this time all the family had gathered to the window. Indeed they saw the whole frolic. I was perfectly convulsed with laughter.

MARIA. I was up before six, made the fire in the kitchen and made coffee. Then I set the table in the dining room, and made the fire there. Toasted the bread and trimmed the lamps. Rang the breakfast bell at seven. After breakfast, made my bed, and "put up" the room. Then I came down to the library and looked over my comet computations till noon. I am just beginning to notice the different colors of the stars. I wonder that I have been so long insensible to this charm in the skies. The tints of different stars are so delicate in their variety . . . Before dinner I did some tatting, and made seven button-holes for K. I dressed and then dined.

ELIZABETH. The first event engraved on my memory was the birth of a sister when I was four years old. I heard so many friends remark, "What a pity it is she is a girl!" that I felt a kind of compassion for the little baby. True, our family consisted of five girls and only one boy, but I did not understand at the time that girls were considered an inferior order of beings.

ELIZA. Mother dear: You mentioned in yours of the sixteenth that it was a long time since you had received a letter from me; but it was owing to my studies. Now, Mama, what do you think I am going to ask you for? A wig. Eleanor Coffin has got a new one just like my hair, and it's only five dollars. I must either cut my hair or have one—I cannot dress it at all stylish. How much time it will save. In one year's time we could save it in pins and paper, besides the trouble. At the assembly I was quite ashamed of my head, for nobody has long hair. If you will consent to my having one, do send me a five-dollar bill by the post immediately after you receive this, for I am in hopes to have it for the next assembly.

MARIA. Came back again to the library at one-thirty . . . and looked over another set of computations, which took me until four o'clock. I was pretty tired by that time, and rested by reading "Cosmos." Lizzie E. came in, and I gossiped for half an hour. I went home to tea, and that over, I made a loaf of bread. Then I went up to my room and read through—partly writing—two exercises in German, which took me thirty-five minutes. It was stormy, and I had no observing to do, so I sat down to my tatting. Lizzie E. came in and I took a new lesson in tatting, so as to make the pearl-edge. I made about half a yard during the evening. What a pity that we cannot take dye stuff from the stars, so as to create a new brilliancy in fashion . . . At a little after nine I went home with Lizzie, and carried to the post office. I had kept steadily at work for sixteen hours when I went to bed.

(*At this point, the actresses begin to act out what they are saying. They can move around the stage, showing us and themselves just what they have gone through. They also play parts in each other's stories, gently aiding each other in their growth.*)

ELIZABETH. A student in my father's office told me one day, after conning my features carefully, that I had one defect that he could remedy. "Your eyebrows should be darker and heavier," he said, "and if you will let me shave them once or twice, you will be much improved." I consented, and slight as my eyebrows were, they seemed to have a handsome expression, for the loss of them had a most singular effect on my appearance. Everybody, including the shaver, laughed at my odd-looking face,

and I was in the depths of humiliation while my eyebrows were growing out again. Needless to say, I never permitted the young man to repeat the experiment, although strongly urged to do so.

MARIA. I swept the sky two hours last night. Not a fringe of a cloud, all clear,
all beautiful. I really enjoy that kind of work, but my back soon becomes tired, long before the cold chills me. I saw two nebulae in Leo
with which I was not familiar, and that repaid me for the time . . . There
will come with the greater love of science greater love to one another.
We cannot see how impartially Nature gives of her riches to all without
loving all, and helping all.

ELIZABETH. When I was eleven years old, my only brother, who had just graduated from Union College, came home to die. A young man of great talent and promise, he was the pride of my father's heart. I recall going
into the large darkened parlor and finding the casket, mirrors and pictures all draped in white, and my father seated, pale and immovable as
he took no notice of me. After standing a long while, I climbed upon
his knee, when he mechanically put his arm about me, and with my
head resting against his beating heart, we both sat in silence, he thinking of the wreck of all his hopes in the loss of a dear son—and I wondering what could be said or done to fill the void in his breast. At length
he heaved a deep sigh and said, "Oh, my daughter, I wish you were a
boy!" Throwing my arms about his neck, I replied, "I will try to be all
my brother was." All that day, and far into the night I pondered the
problems of boyhood. I thought that the chief thing to be done in order
to equal boys was to be learned and courageous. So I decided to study
Greek and learn to manage a horse. I learned to leap a fence on horse-
back. I began to study Latin, Greek and mathematics with a class of
boys in the Academy, many of whom were much older than I. For three
years one boy kept his place at the head of the class, and I always stood
next. Two prizes were offered in Greek. I strove for one and took the
second. One thought alone filled my mind. "Now," said I, "my father
will be satisfied with me." I rushed into his office, laid the new Greek
testament, which was my prize, on his table, and exclaimed: "I got it!"
He took up the book, asked me some questions about the class, and evidently pleased, handed it back to me. Then he kissed me on the forehead and exclaimed with a sigh, "You should have been a boy!"

ELIZA. I thank heaven I was born a woman. I have now only patiently to wait
till some clever fellow shall take a fancy to me and place me in a situation, I am determined to make the best of it, let it be what it will. We
ladies, you know, possess that "sweet pliability of temper." But remember, I desire to be thankful I am not a man—I should not be content
with mediocrity in any thing, but as a woman I am equal to the general-
ity of my sex, and I do not feel that great desire of fame I think I should
if I was a man. Were I a man, the law would be my choice. When I
might hope to arrive at an eminence which would be gratifying to my
feelings, I should then hope to be a public character, respected and admired. To be an eloquent speaker would be the delight of my heart.

ELIZABETH. As my father's office joined the house, I spent much of my time
there, when out of school, talking with the students, and reading the
laws in regard to women. One Christmas morning I went into the office
to show them, among others of my presents, a new coral necklace and

bracelets. They all admired the jewelry and then began to tease me with hypothetical cases of future ownership. "Now," said one, "if in due time you should be my wife, those ornaments would be mine. I could take them and lock them up, and you could never wear them except with my permission. I could even exchange them for a box of cigars, and you could watch them evaporate in smoke." When my attention was called to these odious laws, I would mark them in my father's books with a pencil, and I resolved to seize the first opportunity, when alone in the office, to cut every one of them out of the books; supposing my father and his library were the beginning and end of the law . . . However, this mutilation of his volumes was never accomplished. He explained to me one evening how laws were made, and that if his library should burn up it would make no difference in woman's condition. "When you are grown up, and able to prepare a speech," said he, "you must go down to Albany and talk to the legislators; tell them all you have seen in this office; the sufferings of women, robbed of their inheritance and left dependent on their unworthy sons, and if you can persuade them to pass new laws, the old ones will be a dead letter." Thus was the future object of my life foreshadowed and my duty plainly outlined by him who was most opposed to my public career when, in due time, I entered upon it.

MARIA. It seems to me that the needle is the chain of woman and has fettered her more than the laws of the country.

ELIZABETH. Sewing as an amusement is contemptible. It should be the study of every woman to do as little of it as possible.

MARIA. Once you emancipate her from the stitch-stitch-stitch, she would have time for studies which engross as never the needle can. I have a hunger of the mind which longs for knowledge of all around. Astronomy seems to me particularly fitted to women. A girl's eye is trained from early childhood to be keen, trained to the nicety of color. The eye that directs a needle in the delicate meshes of embroidery will equally bisect a star with the spider web of the micrometer.

ELIZABETH. When a woman pulls a cotton washrag from her pocket and begins to knit with a bowed head, fixing her eyes and concentrating her thoughts on a rag one foot square, it is impossible for conversation to rise above the washrag level. Think of the optic nerves being concentrated on a cotton rag. One can buy a whole dozen of these useful appliances with red borders and fringed for twenty-five cents. I beseech you, knit no more!

VOICE. Anna Howard Shaw, at age twelve, moved from a manufacturing town in Massachusetts to the wild woods of Michigan in 1859.

ANNA. Like most men, my dear father should have never married. In practical matters he remained a child. To him, an acorn was not an acorn, but a forest of young oaks; thus when he took up his claim of three hundred and sixty acres of land in the wilderness of northern Michigan, and sent my mother and five young children to live there alone until he could join us, he gave no thought to the matter in which we were to make the struggle and survive the hardships before us. From his viewpoint, he was doing a man's duty. He had furnished us with land and the four walls of a log cabin. Some day, he reasoned, the place would be a fine estate which his sons would inherit, and in the course of time pass on to their sons. But to the present, we were one hundred miles from a railroad, forty miles from the nearest post office, and half a dozen miles from any neighbors, save Indians, wolves and wildcats; we were wholly unlearned in the ways of the woods, yet we faced our situation with clear and unalarmed eyes the morning after our arrival. We held a family council after breakfast and in this, though I was only twelve, I took an eager and determined part. I loved work—it has always been my favorite form of recreation—and my spirit rose to the opportunities of it which smiled on us from every side. You see, I knew I was doing my share for the family, and already too, I had begun to feel the call of my career. For some reason I wanted to preach . . . to talk to people, to tell them things. Just why, just what, I did not yet know, but I had begun to preach in the silent woods—to stand upon tree stumps and address the unresponsive trees—to feel the stir of aspiration within me. Some day I am going to college. And before I die I shall be worth ten thousand dollars.

GERTRUDE. The first clear impression of my childhood is a summer day.

VOICE. Elizabeth Gertrude Stern, born in 1890 in a Jewish ghetto of a large Midwestern city, growing up to obey her father's commandments.

GERTRUDE. My mother, in her puffed sleeves and tight-fitting dress, walked near my father, in his long coat and high hat: for he was assistant to the rabbi in our city. We children trudged behind. We came at last to the river's edge. Our father stood, waited a moment, and then prayed that his sins should be washed away by the river. I looked into the muddy waters below us, and at my father. All my life I had believed that, even when I resisted him, he was right. But today it seemed to me childish and perhaps even silly to be standing there, chanting that beautiful old tongue, the Hebrew, that I too had been taught, and asking that our sins be washed away. Most of the people who lived near us were Catholics. They believed that if you told the priest what you had done, you would not be punished for your misdeeds. When I told my father one day of the Catholics, he looked down at me from his tall height, and said, "You can see how foolish and childish ignorant people are. A priest tells them that if they go to him, and confess, he can forgive them. Can a sin be undone by confession?" And yet here was my father, grave and pleading, sending our own sins down the waters of the Ohio. I looked at him, opened my mouth, but did not speak. I knew he would be angry. From that day, however, I did not accept anything he told me about our faith until I analyzed it myself.

MARIA. How can we dispute authority which has come down to us all established for ages? We cannot accept anything as granted beyond the first mathematical formula. Question everything else.

MARY. My husband was an iron moulder and a staunch member of the Iron Moulders' Union. We were living in Memphis when a yellow fever epidemic swept the city. Its victims were mainly among the poor and the workers. The rich and the well-to-do fled the city. Schools and churches were closed. People were not permitted to enter the house of a yellow fever victim without permits. The poor could not afford nurses. Across the street from me, ten persons lay dead from the plague. The dead surrounded us. They were buried at night, quickly and without ceremony. All about my house I could hear weeping and the cries of delirium. One by one, my four little children sickened and died. I washed their little bodies and got them ready for burial.

My husband caught the fever and died. I sat alone through nights of grief. No one came to me. No one could. Other homes were as stricken as mine. All day long, all night long, I heard the grating of the wheels of the death cart.

After the union had buried my husband I got a permit to nurse the sufferers. This I did until the plague was stamped out. I returned to Chicago and went again into the dress-making business. I became more and more engrossed with the labor struggle and I decided to take an active part in the efforts of the working people to better the conditions under which they worked and lived. I became a member of the Knights of Labor. From that time on, I became wholly engrossed in the labor movement.

GERTRUDE. My father did not approve of my continuing high school. It was time for me to think of marrying a pious man. He and Mother disagreed about it—their one quarrel. It was perhaps due to my going to high school, Mother said, gently and dubiously, that I wanted something new. I wanted to dance, to play, to have fun. I didn't mean to go to work at fourteen or fifteen, marry at sixteen, be a mother at eighteen, and an old woman at thirty. My mother drew her fine dark brows together. She took my face in her little hands, round and soft, in spite of her constant work. "You shall learn to dance, my daughter." And dance I did. I learned to dance in what, I suppose, was a dreadful public dance hall, for I paid a quarter a lesson there once every Wednesday night, and I danced with the lady instructor whenever she thought of me. But I faithfully put my foot out . . . one-two-three and turn . . . as the long line of men and women learned the steps of the waltz. I learned to two-step, and to Schottische, and even—wild days those—to do the barn dance. I wanted a new thing: happiness.

ELIZABETH. "What to do with a baby!" Though motherhood is the most important of all the professions, requiring more knowledge than any other department in human affairs, there was no attention given to preparation for this office. When my baby was four days old, we discovered that his collarbone was bent. The physician, wishing to get a pressure on the shoulder, braced the bandage round the wrist.

FIRST DOCTOR. Leave that ten days, and then it will be all right.

ELIZABETH. Soon after he left, I noticed that the baby's hand was blue, showing that the circulation had been impeded. This will never do. Nurse, take it off.

NURSE. No, indeed. I shall never interfere with the doctor.

ELIZABETH. So I took it on myself to send for another doctor. He expressed great surprise that the first should have put on so severe a bandage.

SECOND DOCTOR. That would do for a grown man, but ten days of it on a child would make him a cripple.

ELIZABETH. However, he did nearly the same thing, only fastening it round the hand, instead of the wrist. I soon saw that the ends of the fingers were all purple. So I took it off. What we want is a little pressure on that bone; that is what both those men have aimed at. How can we get it without involving the arm is the question.

NURSE. I'm sure I don't know.

ELIZABETH. Well, bring me three strips of linen rolled double. I then folded one, wet in arnica and water, and laid it on the collarbone. I put two other bands, like a pair of suspenders, over the shoulders, crossing them both in front and behind, pinning the ends to the diaper, which gave the needed pressure without impeding the circulation anywhere. Several times night and day, we wet the compress and readjusted the bands, until the inflammation had subsided. At the end of ten days, the doctors appeared and made their examination. All was right. Whereupon I told them how badly their bandages worked, and what I had done myself. They smiled at each other and said:

FIRST DOCTOR. Well . . .

SECOND DOCTOR. Well . . .

FIRST DOCTOR. Well . . .

SECOND DOCTOR. Well . . .

FIRST DOCTOR. After all, a mother's instinct . . .

SECOND DOCTOR. . . . is better than a man's reason.

ELIZABETH. Thank you, gentlemen, there was no instinct about it. I did some hard thinking before I saw how I could get pressure on the shoulder without impeding the circulation, as you did. . . . I trusted neither men nor books completely after this, either in regard to the heavens above or the earth below, but continued to use my "mother's instinct," if "reason" is too dignified a term to apply to a woman's thoughts.

MARIA. People have to learn sometimes not only how much the heart, but how much the head can bear.

ANNA. As an aid to public speaking I was taught to "elocute," and I remember in every mournful detail the occasion on which I gave my first recitation. We were having our monthly "public exhibition night," and the audience included not only my classmates, but their parents and friends as well. The selection I intended to recite was a poem entitled "No Sects in Heaven." But, when I faced my audience, I was so appalled by its size and by the sudden realization of my own temerity, that I fainted during the delivery of the first verse. Sympathetic classmates carried me into an anteroom and revived me, after which they naturally assumed that the entertainment I furnished was over for the evening. I, however, felt that if I let that failure stand against me I could never afterward speak in public; and within ten minutes, notwithstanding the protests of my friends, I was back in the hall and beginning my recitation a second time. The audience gave me its eager attention. Possibly it hoped to see me topple off the platform again, but nothing of the sort occurred. I went through the recitation with self-possession and even received some friendly applause at the end.

MARY. I organized an army of women housekeepers. On a given day they were to bring their mops and brooms and "the Army" would charge the scabs up at the mines. The general manager, the sheriff, and the corporation hirelings heard of our plans and were on hand. The day came and the women came with the mops and brooms and pails of water. I decided not to go up to the drip mouth myself, for I knew they would arrest me and that might rout the Army. I selected as leader an Irish woman who had a most picturesque appearance. She had slept late and her husband had told her to hurry up and get into the Army. She had grabbed a red petticoat and slipped it over a thick cotton nightgown. She wore a black stocking and a white one. She had tied a little red fringed shawl over her wild red hair. Her face was red and her eyes were mad. I looked at her and felt that she could raise a rumpus. I said,

"You lead the Army up to the drip mouth, take that tin dishpan you have with you and your hammer, and when the scabs and the mules come up, begin to hammer and howl. Then all of you hammer and howl and be ready to chase the scabs with your mops and brooms. Don't be afraid of anyone!" Up the mountainside, yelling and hollering, she led the women, and when the mules came up with the scabs and the coal, she began beating on the dishpan and hollering, and all the Army joined in with her. The sheriff tapped her on the shoulder. "My dear lady," said he, "remember the mules. Don't frighten them." She took the old tin pan and she hit him with it and she hollered, "To hell with you and the mules!" He fell over and dropped into the creek. Then the mules began to rebel against scabbing. They bucked and kicked the scab drivers and started off for the barn. The scabs started running down the hill, followed by the army of women with their mops and pails and brooms. A poll parrot in a nearby shack screamed at the superintendent, "Ya got hell, did you? Ya got hell?" There was a great big doctor in the crowd, a company lap dog. He had a little satchel in his hand, and he said to me, "Mrs. Jones, I have a warrant for your arrest." "All right," said I, "keep it in your pill bag until I call for it. I am going to hold a meeting now." From that day on the women kept continual watch of the mines to see that the company did not bring in scabs. Every day women with brooms or mops in one hand and babies in the other arm, wrapped in little blankets, went to the mines and watched that no one went in. And all night long they kept watch.

There had been no bloodshed. There had been no riots. And the victory was due to the army of women with their mops and brooms.

GERTRUDE. I had known for months that I loved Dr. Morton. That was why I could speak to him of those things I felt most deeply, and why I felt the peace of my work. We were young, and we were well. We were mysterious and beautiful to one another. I had, all my life, thought of the womanhood in me as something to be deprecated. I knew that a man of my faith must absent himself from his wife, as from defilement at certain holy times of his life. And always she must humbly beg God to pardon her that she is a woman. Had I not read in the prayer book the words my brothers and my father spoke daily . . . thanking God they were not women?

But my husband was modern. He said I must do anything I wanted to do, just as he did what he chose. Only, he must earn our living. Whatever I did I could do without thinking whether it was successful or not, only whether it made me happy. I took his hands in mine. I kissed him. But as I did, I know I wished he had said that my work was as practical a need to me as his. He thought I might do social work as a volunteer, without pay. I was, however, determined not to be an amateur. I wanted to work just as he did. I would not be happy otherwise. "So you want a career," he smiled, "and a husband tacked on?" "Haven't you one with me tacked on?" He kissed me then and laughed very tenderly indeed. "I like to work," I then said quietly. "I enjoy being important." He laughed then, relieved. He was delighted that I spoke like a child about my work. He kissed me and held me close.

MARIA. I put some wires into my telescope this morning. I dreaded it so much when I found yesterday that it must be done, that it disturbed my

sleep. It was much easier than I expected. I took out the little collimat-
ing screws first, then I drew out the tube, and in that I found a brass
plate which contained the lines . . . I was at first a little puzzled to know
which screws held this in its place, and as I was very anxious not to un-
screw the wrong ones, I took time to consider and found I need turn
only two. Then out slipped the little plate with its three wires where
five should have been, two having been broken. I took the hairs from
my own head, taking care to pick out white ones because I have no
dark ones to spare. I put in the two, by sticking them with sealing wax
dissolved in alcohol into the little grooved lines which I had found.
When I had, with great labor, adjusted these, as I thought, firmly, I perceived that some of the wax was still on the hairs and would make
them yet coarser, and they were already too coarse: so I washed them
with clear alcohol. Almost at once I washed out another wire and soon
another. I went to work patiently and put in the five perpendicular
ones besides the horizontal one, which like the others, had frizzled up
and appeared to melt away. With another hour's labor I got in the five,
when a rude motion raised them all again and I began over.

ELIZABETH.   When I married Mr. Stanton, he announced to me that his business would occupy all his time, and that I must take charge of the
housekeeping.

It is a proud moment in a woman's life to reign supreme within
four walls. I studied up everything pertaining to housekeeping. Even
washing day had its charms for me. The clean clothes on the lines and
on the grass looked so white and smelled so sweet. I inspired my laundress with an ambition to get the clothes out earlier than our neighbors, and to have them ironed and put away sooner. I also felt the same
ambition to excel in all departments of the culinary arts that I did at
school in the different branches of learning. My love of order and clean-
liness was carried throughout, from parlor to kitchen, from front door
to back. I even gave the man an extra shilling to pile the logs of firewood with their smooth ends outward.

MARIA.   There is an article on the study of medicine by women that states it
would be better for the husband always to be superior to the wife. Why?
And if so, doesn't this condemn the ablest of women to a single life? It is
sad to see a woman sacrificing the ties of affection, even to do good.

GERTRUDE.   During the influenza epidemic of 1917 my husband came down
with the sickness. We already had two children. I knew that I must get
work. Not, now, work to fill the time, or to express myself, but to earn
the living of my family. What could I do?

One day it came to me. A big store needed a personnel director.
The store manager spoke to me, smiled to hear I was a college woman,
was interested but not antagonistic when he heard I was married.
"Now, if you prove to be what we're looking for, there is a big job
ahead of you, but first, you must know the work. First you must be a
saleswoman." I was sent to the linen department, then to the dress department. From there I was promoted to hats, and then to jewelry and
books.

I had a problem not different from those many others were facing. I learned how to adjust things a bit. I prepared breakfast the night
before. I taught my young daughter how to feed her little brother. I

arranged for lunches for my children with a woman who lived near the school. Sometimes, I would run out to my home at noon, missing my own lunch, but having the peace of seeing that everything went well with my husband. He was tired and lonely, but he said nothing. He would sit, waiting till the children came home. After months I was promoted to the position of personnel director. I was a woman with a career for certain now. I was shown to my office. A pretty little thing with a real desk, a telephone, and a tray . . . for what? . . . for business letters. It looked just like the wire tray in which I drained dishes.

MARIA. Just at one o'clock I had got them all back in again. I attempted to put the plate back into its place. The sealing wax was not dry, and with a sudden motion I sent the wires all agog . . .

ELIZABETH. My second son was born, and a *third*. We moved from Boston to Seneca Falls, where our residence was on the outskirts of town . . . roads often muddy and no sidewalks most of the way. Mr. Stanton was frequently away from home. I had poor servants, and a fourth son was born. I have so much care with all these boys on my hands. How much I long to be free from housekeeping and children so as to have some time to read and think and write.

MARIA. Endow the already established institution with money. Endow the woman who shows genius with time.

> Song: "Housewife's Lament"
> With grease and with grime from corner to corner,
> Forever at war and forever alert,
> No rest for a day lest the enemy enter,
> I spend my whole life in a struggle with dirt.
> Oh, life is a toil and love is a trouble,
> Beauty will fade and riches will flee,
> Pleasures they dwindle and prices they double.
> And nothing is as I would wish it to be.

This time they did not come out of the little grooved lines into which they were put, and I hastened to set them in parallel lines. I gave up then for the day, but, as they looked well and were certainly in firmly, I did not consider that I had made an entire failure.

I thought it nice ladylike work to manage such slight threads and turn such delicate screws; but fine as are the hairs on one's head, I shall seek something finer, for I can see how clumsy they will appear when I get on with the eyepiece and magnify their imperfections. They look parallel to the eye, but with a little magnifying power a very little crook will seem a billowy wave, and a faint star will hide itself in one of the yawning abysses.

I remembered at once that I had seen some cocoons in the library which I had carefully refrained from disturbing. I found them perfect, and unrolled them. I made the perpendicular wires of the spider's web, breaking them and doing the work over again a great many times.

GERTRUDE. My husband got well. Well enough to go to work again. I believed in my equal rights as a woman, but I was happy that day because he was head of our life and of our home. That was something I yielded to him. As I gave my love to him. I left the store. I was thirty-eight years old. More than half of my life had been lived. I was doing nothing: I went to my desk, and there, like an old friend, stood a typewriter. I could write . . . Sometimes it seemed to me my fingers burned with the need to write. I realized that all that I had been living through all these years—the years of my work, of my past, were a mine on which I could draw. I went to see a magazine editor. I received a first assignment, and then another. At the end of the first year, I had earned almost three thousand dollars. I earned it so easily it seemed criminal to be so successful, for I was so happy in this work.

MARIA. I at length got all the wires in—crossing the five perpendicular ones with a horizontal one . . . After twenty-four hours' exposure to the weather, I looked at them. The spider webs had not changed. They were plainly used to a chill and made to endure changes of temperature.

ELIZA. Among the many gentlemen I have become acquainted with and who have been attentive, one I believe is serious. I know not how to introduce this subject, yet, as I fear you may hear it from others and feel anxious for my welfare, I consider it a duty to tell you all. I felt cautious of encouraging his attentions tho' I did not wish to *discourage* them . . . He is a man of business, uniform in his conduct and *very much respected*. He is a man in whom I could place the most unbounded confidence. Nothing rash or impetuous in his disposition, but weighs maturely every circumstance: He appeared as solicitous that I should act with strict propriety as one of my most disinterested friends. He advises me like a friend and would not discourage his addresses till he had an opportunity of making known to my parents his character and wishes—this I promised, but the decision must rest with my parents, their wishes were my law. He insisted upon coming on immediately: that I refused to consent to. He is coming in October. And now, my dearest mother, I submit myself wholly to the wishes of my father and you, convinced that my happiness is your warmest wish, and to promote it has ever been your study. That I feel deeply interested in Mr. Bowne I candidly acknowledge. He is a firm, steady, serious man, there is nothing light or trifling in his character.

Song: "Monday Morning"
And now I am determined to have my own way
and I'm
Going to be married next Monday morning.

Here we are at Mrs. Carter's boarding house, and though we have endeavored to keep ourselves as much out of the way as possible, a great many people have called to pay their respects to Mr. and Mrs. Bowne. When I hear an old acquaintance call me Mrs. Bowne, it really makes me stare at first, it sounds so very odd. I am enraptured with New York. You cannot imagine anything half so beautiful as Broadway. Mr. Bowne brings me a pocket full of fruit every day he comes home. I eat as many as I want, and I'm thinking how much I would give to get them to you. But this early fruit won't keep at all. As to news, New York is not so gay as last winter, few balls, but a great many tea parties. The city air has not stolen my country bloom yet, for everyone says, "I need not ask how you do, Mrs. Bowne, you look in such fine health."

ELIZABETH. My fifth child is a girl. The particulars I must give you. On Wednesday morning at six I awoke with a little pain which I well understood. Thereupon I jumped up, bathed and dressed myself, hurried the breakfast, eating none myself, of course, and got the house and all things in order, working bravely between the pains. I neither sat down nor lay down until half past nine, when I gave up all my vocations and avocations, secular and domestic, and devoted myself wholly to the one matter then brought before my mind. At ten o'clock the whole work was completed—the nurse and Amelia our housekeeper alone officiating. I had no doctor, and Mr. Stanton was away on business. When the baby was twenty-four hours old, I got up, bathed, making a sponge and sitz bath, put on my wet bandage, dressed, ate my breakfast, walked on the piazza, and the day being beautiful, I took a ride of three miles on the old plank road. Then I came home, rested an hour or so, read the newspaper and wrote a long letter to Mama . . . My joy in being the mother of a precious little girl is more than I can tell you. The baby is very large and plump, and her head is covered with black curly hair. Oh, how I do rejoice in her!

ELIZA. Walter Bowne, *Junior*. He is so hearty and well, he has not had a day's sickness. I am just starting to leave off his caps, I want his hair to grow before his grandmama sees him. He won't look so pretty without his caps. He creeps so much I find it hard to keep him so nice as I used to.

ANNA. The first notice of me ever printed in the newspaper. This was instigated by my brother-in-law, and was brief, but pointed. It read, "A young girl named Anna Shaw preached her first sermon at Ashton yesterday. Her real friends deprecate the course she is pursuing."

The members of my family, meeting in solemn conclave, sent for me. They had a proposition to make. If I gave up my preaching, they would send me to college and pay for the entire course. We had a long evening together, and it was a very unhappy one. At the end of it, I was given twenty-four hours in which to decide whether I would choose my people and college, or my pulpit and the Arctic loneliness of a life that held no family circle. It did not take me twenty-four hours of reflection to convince me that I must go my solitary way.

ELIZA. You are anxious, my dear mother, to hear from my own hand how I am. My cough is extremely obstinate, I have occasionally a little fever, tho' quite irregular and sometimes a week without any. I have a new physician to attend me: he keeps me on a milk diet, but allows me to eat eggs and oysters. I am much better already, my cough seems to be my only disorder, he thinks he can cure that. Indeed he speaks with perfect confidence and says he has no doubt that as soon as I leave this severe New York winter and get to warmer weather in South Carolina, my cough will soon leave me. You will hear from me often, my dear mother. At present my mind seems so occupied: leaving my children, preparing to go, making arrangements to shut up my house. 'Tis quite a trial to leave my little ones . . . My little Mary has a wet nurse, she is a fine lively child . . . Adieu, my dear mother, I did not think I could have written half so much. Love to all my friends.

MARY. I went to Kensington, Pennsylvania, where seventy-five thousand textile workers were on strike. Of this number, more than ten thousand were little children. They were all stooped little things, round shouldered and skinny, some with their fingers off at the knuckles. Many of them were not yet ten years of age. I asked the newspapermen why they hadn't published the facts about child labor in Pennsylvania. They said that they couldn't because all ten mill owners had stock in the papers. "Well, I've got stock in these little children, and I'll arrange a little publicity." I decided that the children and I would go on a tour. I asked some of the parents if they'd let me have their little boys and girls for a week or ten days. I promised to bring them back safe and sound. They consented. The children carried knapsacks on their backs. They each had a knife and fork, a tin cup and plate. One little girl had a fife, and her brother had a drum. That was our band. The children were very happy, having plenty to eat, taking baths in the streams and rivers every day. I thought, When this strike is over and they go back to the mills, they will never have another holiday like this one. We marched to Jersey City, Hoboken, Princeton and into New York. Our march was doing its work. We were bringing to the attention of the nation the crime of child labor. In Coney Island, after the wild animal show, I put my little children into the empty iron cages and they clung to the bars while I talked. "You see those monkeys in those cages over there? The professors are trying to teach them to talk. The monkeys are too smart, for they fear that the manufacturers would buy them for slaves in their factories. And you see those little boys in those cages? Well, we are told that every American boy has the chance of being President. I tell you that those little boys would sell their chances any day for good square meals and a chance to play."

MARIA.   A few evenings ago a meteor flashed upon me suddenly, very bright, very short-lived. It seemed to me that it was sent just for me especially, for it greeted me almost the first instant I looked up and was gone in a second, fleeting and beautiful. I am but a woman. For women there are, undoubtedly, great difficulties in the path, but so much the more to overcome. First, no woman should say, "I am but a woman." *But a woman*—what more can you ask to be?

ELIZA.   I send a little pair of shoes for Mary, a little cuckoo toy for Walter, and a tumbler of orange marmalade. I have had only one letter from New York since I have been here . . . not one line from my husband. I can tell you nothing flattering of my health. I am very miserable at present. How are my dear little ones? I hope not too troublesome. I hardly trust myself to think of them, precious children—how they bind me to life. Adieu. I have a bad headache and am low-spirited today.

Song: "When the Train Comes Along"
When the train comes along, when the train comes along,
I'm going to meet you at the station when the train comes
    along.

If my mother asks for me, tell her death doth summon me,
I'm going to meet her at the station when the train comes
    along.

If my father asks for me, tell him death doth summon me,
I'm going to meet him at the station when the train comes
    along.

VOICE UNDER MUSIC. Inscription on the monument in Archdale Churchyard, Charleston, South Carolina . . . "Sacred to the memory of Eliza Southgate Bowne, wife of Walter Bowne of New York, daughter of Robert Southgate Esquire of Scarborough, District of Maine, who departed this life on the nineteenth day of February, aged twenty-five years."

ANNA. The stagecoach took me within twenty-two miles of my destination. To my dismay, however, when I arrived Saturday evening, I found that the rest of the journey lay through a dense woods, and that I could reach my pulpit in time the next morning only by having someone drive me through the woods that night. It was not a pleasant prospect, for I had heard appalling tales of the stockades in this region and of the women who were kept prisoners there. But to miss the engagement was not to be thought of, and when, after I had made several vain efforts to find a driver, a man appeared in a two-seated wagon and offered to take me to my destination, I felt that I had to go with him, though I did not like his appearance. He was a huge, muscular person, with a protruding jaw and singularly evasive eye; but I reflected that his forbidding expression might be due, in part at least, to the prospect of the long night drive through the woods, to which possibly he objected as much as I did. It was already growing dark when we started, and within a few moments we were out of the little settlement and entering the woods. With me I had a revolver I had long since learned to use, but which I very rarely carried. I had hesitated to bring it now—had even left home without it; and then, impelled by some impulse I never afterward ceased to bless, had returned for it and dropped it into my handbag. I sat on the back seat of the wagon, directly behind the driver, and for a time, as we entered the darkening woods, his great shoulders blotted out all perspective as he drove on in stolid silence. Soon the darkness folded around us like a garment. I could see neither the driver nor his horses. I could hear only the sibilant whisper of the trees and the creak of our slow wheels in the rough forest road. Suddenly the driver began to talk, and at first I was glad to hear the reassuring human tones, for the experience had begun to seem like a bad dream. I replied readily, and at once regretted that I had done so, for the man's choice of topics was most unpleasant. He began to tell me stories of the stockades—grim stories with horrible details, repeated so fully and with such gusto that I soon realized he was deliberately affronting my ears. I told him I could not listen to such talk. He replied with a series of oaths and shocking vulgarities, stopping his horses that he might turn and fling the words into my face. He ended by snarling that I must think him a fool to imagine he did not know the kind of woman I was. What was I doing in that rough country, and why was I alone with him in those dark woods at night? I tried to answer him calmly. "You know perfectly well who I am, and you understand that I am making this journey tonight because I am to preach tomorrow morning and there is no other way to keep my appointment." He uttered a laugh which was a most unpleasant sound. "Well," he said, coolly, "I'm damned if I'll take you. I've got you here, and I'm going to keep you here!" I slipped my hand into the satchel in my lap, and it touched my revolver. No touch of human fingers ever brought such comfort. With a deep breath of thanksgiving I drew it out and cocked it. "Here! What have you got there?" "I have a revolver," I replied, as steadily as I could. "And it is cocked and aimed straight at your back. Now, drive on. If you stop again, or speak, I'll shoot you." For an instant or two he blustered. "By God," he cried, "you wouldn't dare." "Wouldn't I?" I asked. "Try me by speaking just once more." Even as I spoke I felt my hair rise on my scalp with the horror of the moment, which seemed worse than any nightmare a woman could experience.

But the man was conquered by the knowledge of the waiting, willing weapon just behind him. He laid his whip savagely on the backs of his horses, and they responded with a leap that almost knocked me out of the wagon. He did not speak again, nor stop, but I dared not relax my caution for an instant. Hour after hour crawled toward day, and still I sat in the unpierced darkness, the revolver ready. I knew he was inwardly raging, and that at any instant he might make a sudden jump and try to get the revolver away from me. I decided that at his slightest movement I must shoot. But dawn came at last, and just as its bluish light touched the dark tips of the pines we drove up to the log hotel in the settlement that was our destination. Here my driver spoke. "Get down," he said gruffly. "This is the place." I sat still. Even yet I dared not trust him. Moreover, I was so stiff after my vigil that I was not sure I could move. "You get down, and wake up the landlord. Bring him out here." He sullenly obeyed and aroused the hotel owner, and when the latter appeared I climbed out of the wagon with some effort but without explanation. That morning I preached in my friend's pulpit as I had promised to do, and the rough building was packed with lumber men who had come in from the neighboring camp. Their appearance caused a great stir. There were forty or fifty of them, and when we took up our collection it was the largest that had ever been taken in the history of the settlement, but I soon learned that it wasn't spiritual comfort that I offered which appealed to the men. My driver of the night before, who was one of their number, had told his pals of his experience, and the whole camp had poured into town to see the woman minister who carried a revolver. "Her sermon?" I overheard one of them say. "I dunno what she preached. But, sure don't make no mistake about one thing, the little lady preacher has sure got grit!"

(*All the characters alternate the lines of "Solitude of Self."*)

ALL.   (*alternating*): We must make the voyage of life alone.

It matters not whether the solitary voyager be a man or a woman.

We come into the world alone, unlike all who have gone before us: we leave it alone under circumstances peculiar to ourselves.

No mortal ever has been, no mortal ever will be like the soul just launched on the sea of life.

Nature never repeats herself, and the possibilities of one human soul will never be found in another.

The same individual is not the same at all times. Each individual has a middle self, which is not the one of today, nor of yesterday, nor of tomorrow, but among these different selves.

In youth our most bitter disappointments, our brightest hopes and ambitions are known only to ourselves. Even our friendship and love we never fully share with another.

The solitude of individual life: its pains, its penalties, its responsibilities.

The solitude of self. It is the height of cruelty to rob the individual of a single natural right.

Our inner being, which we call our self, no eye nor touch has ever pierced.

Such is individual life. Who can take/ . . . dare take/ . . . on himself/herself/the rights,/the responsibilities, the duties/of another human soul?

(During the course of the preceding section, the actresses have moved their chairs into a close-knit semicircle downstage center. They place their lanterns on the floor in front of them. When they are done speaking, they stare out at the audience for the first time, seemingly to ask the audience to make its own choice. They stay looking at the audience as the lights dim slowly to darkness.)

TOPICS FOR CRITICAL THINKING AND WRITING

The Play on the Page

1. Take one character and trace, through her speeches, the forces that impede her development as an individual.
2. Take another character and summarize her personality.
3. What do you think Eliza Southgate contributes to the play? What would be lost if she were omitted?
4. Exactly what is the attitude toward work revealed by Gertrude's husband? What is Gertrude's attitude toward work?
5. The play is certainly serious, but it also includes some comic passages, for instance the responses of the doctors to Elizabeth Cady Stanton when she corrects them. Do you find other amusing passages in this serious play? If so, specify a few.

The Play on the Stage

6. What sort of structure does the play have? To what extent are speeches related to previous speeches? Does the play have any significant organization? Explain.
7. Discuss the use of music in the play. Are some—or all—of the songs relevant? What, if anything, would be lost if they were omitted?
8. Three actresses play the six women, and the authors specify which two roles each actress is to perform. Are the pairings significant? If so, how? If you were producing *Out of Our Fathers' House*, would you use three actresses or (also acceptable, the authors say) six actresses? Why?
9. The longest speech in the play is Anna's, about her ride in a two-seated wagon, which comes just before the alternating lines spoken by all of the women at the end of the play. What is the point of her speech? Why do you suppose it comes so late in the play?

Scene from TV adaptation, "El Teatro Campesino Special: *Los Vendidos*." KNBC, Los Angeles, 1972.

LUIS VALDEZ

Luis Valdez was born into a family of migrant farm workers in Delano, California, in 1940. After completing high school he entered San Jose State College on a scholarship. He wrote his first plays while still an undergraduate, and after receiving his degree (in English and drama) from San Jose in 1964 he joined the San Francisco Mime Troupe, a left-wing group that performed in parks and streets. Revolutionary in technique as well as in political content, the Mime Troupe rejected the traditional forms of drama and instead drew on the traditions of the circus and the carnival.

In 1965 Valdez returned to Delano, California, where Cesar Chavez had organized a strike of farm workers and a boycott against grape growers. It was here, under the wing of the United Farm Workers, that he established El Teatro Campesino (the Farm Workers' Theater), which at first specialized in doing short, improvised, satirical skits called actos. *When the* teatro *moved to Del Rey, California, it expanded its repertoire beyond farm issues, and it became part of a cultural center that gave workshops (in English and Spanish) in such subjects as history, drama, and politics.*

The actos, *performed by amateurs on college campuses and on flatbed trucks and at the edges of vineyards, were highly political. Making use of stereotypes (the boss, the scab), the actos sought not to present the individual thoughts of a gifted playwright but to present the social vision of ordinary people—the* pueblo—*though it was acknowledged that in an oppressive society the playwright might have to help guide the people to see their own best interests.*

Valdez moved from actos *to* mitos *(myths)—plays that drew on Aztec mythology, Mexican folklore, and Christianity—and then to* Zoot Suit, *a play that ran for many months in California and that became the first Mexican-American play to be produced on Broadway. More recently he wrote and directed a hit movie,* La Bamba, *and in 1991 received an award from the A.T.&T. Foundation for his musical,* Bandido, *presented by El Teatro Campesino.*

Los Vendidos *was written in 1967, when Ronald Reagan was governor of California.*

Los Vendidos*

LIST OF CHARACTERS

HONEST SANCHO
SECRETARY
FARM WORKER
JOHNNY
REVOLUCIONARIO
MEXICAN-AMERICAN

Scene: HONEST SANCHO's *Used Mexican Lot and Mexican Curio Shop. Three models are on display in* HONEST SANCHO's *shop: to the right, there is a* REVOLUCIONARIO, *complete with sombrero, carrilleras[1] and carabina 30-30. At center, on the floor, there is the* FARM WORKER, *under a broad straw sombrero. At stage left is the* PACHUCO,[2] *filero[3] in hand.*

(HONEST SANCHO *is moving among his models, dusting them off and preparing for another day of business.*)

SANCHO. Bueno, bueno, mis monos, vamos a ver a quien vendemos ahora, ¿no?[4] (*To audience.*) ¡Quihubo! I'm Honest Sancho and this is my shop. Antes fui contratista pero ahora logré tener mi negocito.[5] All I need now is a customer. (*A bell rings offstage.*) Ay, a customer!

SECRETARY (*Entering*). Good morning, I'm Miss Jiménez from—

SANCHO. ¡Ah, una chicana! Welcome, welcome Señorita Jiménez.

SECRETARY (*Anglo pronunciation*). JIM-enez.

SANCHO. ¿Qué?

SECRETARY. My name is Miss JIM-enez. Don't you speak English? What's wrong with you?

SANCHO. Oh, nothing, Señorita JIM-enez. I'm here to help you.

SECRETARY. That's better. As I was starting to say, I'm a secretary from Governor Reagan's office, and we're looking for a Mexican type for the administration.

SANCHO. Well, you come to the right place, lady. This is Honest Sancho's Used Mexican lot, and we got all types here. Any particular type you want?

SECRETARY. Yes, we were looking for somebody suave—

*****Los Vendidos** the sellouts.   [1]**carrilleras** cartridge belts.   [2]**Pachuco** an urban tough guy.   [3]**filero** blade.   [4]**Bueno . . . no?** Well, well, darlings, let's see who we can sell now, O.K.?   [5]**Antes . . . negocito** I used to be a contractor, but now I've succeeded in having my little business.

SANCHO. Suave.

SECRETARY. Debonair.

SANCHO. De buen aire.

SECRETARY. Dark.

SANCHO. Prieto.

SECRETARY. But of course not too dark.

SANCHO. No muy prieto.

SECRETARY. Perhaps, beige.

SANCHO. Beige, just the tone. Así como cafecito con leche,[6] ¿no?

SECRETARY. One more thing. He must be hard-working.

SANCHO. That could only be one model. Step right over here to the center of the shop, lady. (*They cross to the* FARM WORKER.) This is our standard farm worker model. As you can see, in the words of our beloved Senator George Murphy, he is "built close to the ground." Also take special notice of his four-ply Goodyear huaraches, made from the rain tire. This wide-brimmed sombrero is an extra added feature—keeps off the sun, rain, and dust.

SECRETARY. Yes, it does look durable.

SANCHO. And our farm worker model is friendly. Muy amable.[7] Watch. (*Snaps his fingers.*)

FARM WORKER (*Lifts up head*). Buenos días, señorita. (*His head drops.*)

SECRETARY. My, he's friendly.

SANCHO. Didn't I tell you? Loves his patrones! But his most attractive feature is that he's hard working. Let me show you. (*Snaps fingers.* FARM WORKER *stands.*)

FARM WORKER. ¡El jale![8] (*He begins to work.*)

SANCHO. As you can see, he is cutting grapes.

SECRETARY. Oh, I wouldn't know.

SANCHO. He also picks cotton. (*Snap.* FARM WORKER *begins to pick cotton.*)

SECRETARY. Versatile isn't he?

SANCHO. He also picks melons. (*Snap.* FARM WORKER *picks melons.*) That's his slow speed for late in the season. Here's his fast speed. (*Snap.* FARM WORKER *picks faster.*)

SECRETARY. ¡Chihuahua! . . . I mean, goodness, he sure is a hard worker.

SANCHO (*Pulls the* FARM WORKER *to his feet*). And that isn't the half of it. Do you see these little holes on his arms that appear to be pores? During those hot sluggish days in the field, when the vines or the branches get so entangled, it's almost impossible to move; these holes emit a certain grease that allow our model to slip and slide right through the crop with no trouble at all.

SECRETARY. Wonderful. But is he economical?

SANCHO. Economical? Señorita, you are looking at the Volkswagen of Mexicans. Pennies a day is all it takes. One plate of beans and tortillas will keep him going all day. That, and chile. Plenty of chile. Chile jalapeños, chile verde, chile colorado. But, of course, if you do give him chile (*Snap.* FARM WORKER *turns left face. Snap.* FARM WORKER *bends over.*) then you have to change his oil filter once a week.

SECRETARY. What about storage?

---

[6]**Así . . . leche** like coffee with milk.   [7]**Muy amable** very friendly.   [8]**El jale** the job.

SANCHO. No problem. You know these new farm labor camps our Honorable Governor Reagan has built out by Parlier or Raisin City? They were designed with our model in mind. Five, six, seven, even ten in one of those shacks will give you no trouble at all. You can also put him in old barns, old cars, river banks. You can even leave him out in the field overnight with no worry!

SECRETARY. Remarkable.

SANCHO. And here's an added feature: Every year at the end of the season, this model goes back to Mexico and doesn't return, automatically, until next Spring.

SECRETARY. How about that. But tell me: does he speak English?

SANCHO. Another outstanding feature is that last year this model was programmed to go out on STRIKE! (*Snap.*)

FARM WORKER. ¡HUELGA! ¡HUELGA! Hermanos, sálganse de esos files.[9] (*Snap. He stops.*)

SECRETARY. No! Oh no, we can't strike in the State Capitol.

SANCHO. Well, he also scabs. (*Snap.*)

FARM WORKER. Me vendo barato, ¿y qué?[10] (*Snap.*)

SECRETARY. That's much better, but you didn't answer my question. Does he speak English?

SANCHO. Bueno . . . no, pero[11] he has other—

SECRETARY. No.

SANCHO. Other features.

SECRETARY. NO! He just won't do!

SANCHO. Okay, okay pues. We have other models.

SECRETARY. I hope so. What we need is something a little more sophisticated.

SANCHO. Sophisti—¿qué?

SECRETARY. An urban model.

SANCHO. Ah, from the city! Step right back. Over here in this corner of the shop is exactly what you're looking for. Introducing our new 1969 JOHNNY PACHUCO model! This is our fast-back model. Streamlined. Built for speed, low-riding, city life. Take a look at some of these features. Mag shoes, dual exhausts, green chartreuse paint-job, dark-tint windshield, a little poof on top. Let me just turn him on. (*Snap.* JOHNNY *walks to stage center with a pachuco bounce.*)

SECRETARY. What was that?

SANCHO. That, señorita, was the Chicano shuffle.

SECRETARY. Okay, what does he do?

SANCHO. Anything and everything necessary for city life. For instance, survival: He knife fights. (*Snap.* JOHNNY *pulls out switchblade and swings at* SECRETARY.)

(SECRETARY *screams.*)

SANCHO. He dances. (*Snap.*)

JOHNNY (*Singing*). "Angel Baby, my Angel Baby . . ." (*Snap.*)

SANCHO. And here's a feature no city model can be without. He gets arrested, but not without resisting, of course. (*Snap.*)

---

[9]**Huelga . . . files** Strike! Strike! Brothers, leave those rows.   [10]**Me . . . qué?** I come cheap. So what?   [11]**Bueno . . . no, pero** Well, no, but.

JOHNNY. ¡En la madre, la placa![12] I didn't do it! I didn't do it! (JOHNNY *turns and stands up against an imaginary wall, legs spread out, arms behind his back.*)

SECRETARY. Oh no, we can't have arrests! We must maintain law and order.

SANCHO. But he's bilingual!

SECRETARY. Bilingual?

SANCHO. Simón que yes.[13] He speaks English! Johnny, give us some English. (*Snap.*)

JOHNNY (*Comes downstage*). Fuck-you!

SECRETARY (*Gasps*). Oh! I've never been so insulted in my whole life!

SANCHO. Well, he learned it in your school.

SECRETARY. I don't care where he learned it.

SANCHO. But he's economical!

SECRETARY. Economical?

SANCHO. Nickels and dimes. You can keep Johnny running on hamburgers, Taco Bell tacos, Lucky Lager beer, Thunderbird wine, yesca—

SECRETARY. Yesca?

SANCHO. Mota.

SECRETARY. Mota?

SANCHO. Leños[14] . . . Marijuana. (*Snap;* JOHNNY *inhales on an imaginary joint.*)

SECRETARY. That's against the law!

JOHNNY (*Big smile, holding his breath*). Yeah.

SANCHO. He also sniffs glue. (*Snap.* JOHNNY *inhales glue, big smile.*)

JOHNNY. That's too much man, ése.[15]

SECRETARY. No, Mr. Sancho, I don't think this—

SANCHO. Wait a minute, he has other qualities I know you'll love. For example, an inferiority complex. (*Snap.*)

JOHNNY (*To* SANCHO). You think you're better than me, huh ése? (*Swings switchblade.*)

SANCHO. He can also be beaten and he bruises, cut him and he bleeds; kick him and he—(*He beats, bruises and kicks* PACHUCO.) would you like to try it?

SECRETARY. Oh, I couldn't.

SANCHO. Be my guest. He's a great scapegoat.

SECRETARY. No, really.

SANCHO. Please.

SECRETARY. Well, all right. Just once. (*She kicks* PACHUCO.) Oh, he's so soft.

SANCHO. Wasn't that good? Try again.

SECRETARY (*Kicks* PACHUCO). Oh, he's so wonderful! (*She kicks him again.*)

SANCHO. Okay, that's enough, lady. You ruin the merchandise. Yes, our Johnny Pachuco model can give you many hours of pleasure. Why, the L.A.P.D. just bought twenty of these to train their rookie cops on. And talk about maintenance. Señorita, you are looking at an entirely self-supporting machine. You're never going to find our Johnny Pachuco model on the relief rolls. No, sir, this model knows how to liberate.

SECRETARY. Liberate?

---

[12]**¡En . . . la placa!** Wow, the cops!   [13]**Simón que yes** Yea, sure.   [14]**Leños** joints (marijuana).   [15]**ése** fellow.

SANCHO. He steals. (*Snap.* JOHNNY *rushes the* SECRETARY *and steals her purse.*)

JOHNNY. ¡Dame esa bolsa, vieja![16] (*He grabs the purse and runs. Snap by* SANCHO. *He stops.*)

(SECRETARY *runs after* JOHNNY *and grabs purse away from him, kicking him as she goes.*)

SECRETARY. No, no, no! We can't have any *more* thieves in the State Administration. Put him back.

SANCHO. Okay, we still got other models. Come on, Johnny, we'll sell you to some old lady. (SANCHO *takes* JOHNNY *back to his place.*)

SECRETARY. Mr. Sancho, I don't think you quite understand what we need. What we need is something that will attract the women voters. Something more traditional, more romantic.

SANCHO. Ah, a lover. (*He smiles meaningfully.*) Step right over here, señorita. Introducing our standard Revolucionario and/or Early California Bandit type. As you can see he is well-built, sturdy, durable. This is the International Harvester of Mexicans.

SECRETARY. What does he do?

SANCHO. You name it, he does it. He rides horses, stays in the mountains, crosses deserts, plains, rivers, leads revolutions, follows revolutions, kills, can be killed, serves as a martyr, hero, movie star—did I say movie star? Did you ever see *Viva Zapata? Viva Villa? Villa Rides? Pancho Villa Returns? Pancho Villa Goes Back? Pancho Villa Meets Abbott and Costello—*

SECRETARY. I've never seen any of those.

SANCHO. Well, he was in all of them. Listen to this. (*Snap.*)

REVOLUCIONARIO (*Scream*). ¡VIVA VILLAAAAA!

SECRETARY. That's awfully loud.

SANCHO. He has a volume control. (*He adjusts volume. Snap.*)

REVOLUCIONARIO (*Mousey voice*). ¡Viva Villa!

SECRETARY. That's better.

SANCHO. And even if you didn't see him in the movies, perhaps you saw him on TV. He makes commercials. (*Snap.*)

REVOLUCIONARIO. Is there a Frito Bandito in your house?

SECRETARY. Oh yes, I've seen that one!

SANCHO. Another feature about this one is that he is economical. He runs on raw horsemeat and tequila!

SECRETARY. Isn't that rather savage?

SANCHO. Al contrario,[17] it makes him a lover. (*Snap.*)

REVOLUCIONARIO (*To* SECRETARY). ¡Ay, mamasota, cochota, ven pa'ca![18] (*He grabs* SECRETARY *and folds her back—Latin-Lover style.*)

SANCHO (*Snap.* REVOLUCIONARIO *goes back upright*). Now wasn't that nice?

SECRETARY. Well, it was rather nice.

SANCHO. And finally, there is one outstanding feature about this model I KNOW the ladies are going to love: He's a GENUINE antique! He was made in Mexico in 1910!

SECRETARY. Made in Mexico?

---

[16]**¡Dame . . . vieja!** Give me that bag, old lady!   [17]**Al contrario** on the contrary.
[18]**¡Ay . . . pa'ca!** get over here!

SANCHO. That's right. Once in Tijuana, twice in Guadalajara, three times in Cuernavaca.

SECRETARY. Mr. Sancho, I thought he was an American product.

SANCHO. No, but—

SECRETARY. No, I'm sorry. We can't buy anything but American-made products. He just won't do.

SANCHO. But he's an antique!

SECRETARY. I don't care. You still don't understand what we need. It's true we need Mexican models such as these, but it's more important that he be *American.*

SANCHO. American?

SECRETARY. That's right, and judging from what you've shown me, I don't think you have what we want. Well, my lunch hour's almost over: I better—

SANCHO. Wait a minute! Mexican but American?

SECRETARY. That's correct.

SANCHO. Mexican but . . . (*A sudden flash.*) AMERICAN! Yeah, I think we've got exactly what you want. He just came in today! Give me a minute. (*He exits. Talks from backstage.*) Here he is in the shop. Let me just get some papers off. There. Introducing our new 1970 Mexican-American! Ta-ra-ra-ra-ra-ra-RA-RAAA!

(SANCHO *brings out the* MEXICAN-AMERICAN *model, a clean-shaven middle-class type in a business suit, with glasses.*)

SECRETARY (*Impressed*). Where have you been hiding this one?

SANCHO. He just came in this morning. Ain't he a beauty? Feast your eyes on him! Sturdy US STEEL frame, streamlined, modern. As a matter of fact, he is built exactly like our Anglo models except that he comes in a variety of darker shades: naugahyde, leather, or leatherette.

SECRETARY. Naugahyde.

SANCHO. Well, we'll just write that down. Yes, señorita, this model represents the apex of American engineering! He is bilingual, college educated, ambitious! Say the word "acculturate" and he accelerates. He is intelligent, well-mannered, clean—did I say clean? (*Snap.* MEXICAN-AMERICAN *raises his arm.*) Smell.

SECRETARY (*Smells*). Old Sobaco, my favorite.

SANCHO (*Snap.* MEXICAN-AMERICAN *turns toward* SANCHO). Eric! (*To* SECRETARY.) We call him Eric García. (*To* ERIC.) I want you to meet Miss JIM-enez, Eric.

MEXICAN-AMERICAN. Miss JIM-enez, I am delighted to make your acquaintance. (*He kisses her hand.*)

SECRETARY. Oh, my, how charming!

SANCHO. Did you feel the suction? He has seven especially engineered suction cups right behind his lips. He's a charmer all right!

SECRETARY. How about boards? Does he function on boards?

SANCHO. You name them, he is on them. Parole boards, draft boards, school boards, taco quality control boards, surf boards, two-by-fours.

SECRETARY. Does he function in politics?

SANCHO. Señorita, you are looking at a political MACHINE. Have you ever heard of the OEO, EOC, COD, WAR ON POVERTY? That's our model! Not only that, he makes political speeches.

SECRETARY. May I hear one?

SANCHO. With pleasure. (*Snap.*) Eric, give us a speech.

MEXICAN-AMERICAN. Mr. Congressman, Mr. Chairman, members of the board, honored guests, ladies and gentlemen. (SANCHO *and* SECRETARY *applaud.*) Please, please. I come before you as a Mexican-American to tell you about the problems of the Mexican. The problems of the Mexican stem from one thing and one thing alone: He's stupid. He's uneducated. He needs to stay in school. He needs to be ambitious, forward-looking, harder-working. He needs to think American, American, American, AMERICAN, AMERICAN, AMERICAN. GOD BLESS AMERICA! GOD BLESS AMERICA! GOD BLESS AMERICA!! (*He goes out of control.*)

(SANCHO *snaps frantically and the* MEXICAN-AMERICAN *finally slumps forward, bending at the waist.*)

SECRETARY. Oh my, he's patriotic too!

SANCHO. Sí, señorita, he loves his country. Let me just make a little adjustment here. (*Stands* MEXICAN-AMERICAN *up.*)

SECRETARY. What about upkeep? Is he economical?

SANCHO. Well, no, I won't lie to you. The Mexican-American costs a little bit more, but you get what you pay for. He's worth every extra cent. You can keep him running on dry Martinis, Langendorf bread.

SECRETARY. Apple pie?

SANCHO. Only Mom's. Of course, he's also programmed to eat Mexican food on ceremonial functions, but I must warn you: an overdose of beans will plug up his exhaust.

SECRETARY. Fine! There's just one more question: HOW MUCH DO YOU WANT FOR HIM?

SANCHO. Well, I tell you what I'm gonna do. Today and today only, because you've been so sweet, I'm gonna let you steal this model from me! I'm gonna let you drive him off the lot for the simple price of—let's see taxes and license included—$15,000.

SECRETARY. Fifteen thousand DOLLARS? For a MEXICAN!

SANCHO. Mexican? What are you talking, lady? This is a Mexican-AMERICAN! We had to melt down two pachucos, a farm worker and three gabachos[19] to make this model! You want quality, but you gotta pay for it! This is no cheap run-about. He's got class!

SECRETARY. Okay, I'll take him.

SANCHO. You will?

SECRETARY. Here's your money.

SANCHO. You mind if I count it?

SECRETARY. Go right ahead.

SANCHO. Well, you'll get your pink slip in the mail. Oh, do you want me to wrap him up for you? We have a box in the back.

---

[19]**gabachos** whites.

SECRETARY. No, thank you. The Governor is having a luncheon this afternoon, and we need a brown face in the crowd. How do I drive him?

SANCHO. Just snap your fingers. He'll do anything you want.

(SECRETARY *snaps.* MEXICAN-AMERICAN *steps forward.*)

MEXICAN-AMERICAN. RAZA QUERIDA, ¡VAMOS LEVANTANDO ARMAS PARA
LIBERARNOS DE ESTOS DESGRACIADOS GABACHOS QUE NOS EX-
PLOTAN! VAMOS.[20]

SECRETARY. What did he say?

SANCHO. Something about lifting arms, killing white people, etc.

SECRETARY. But he's not supposed to say that!

SANCHO. Look, lady, don't blame me for bugs from the factory. He's your
Mexican-American; you bought him, now drive him off the lot!

SECRETARY. But he's broken!

SANCHO. Try snapping another finger.

(SECRETARY *snaps.* MEXICAN-AMERICAN *comes to life again.*)

MEXICAN-AMERICAN. ¡ESTA GRAN HUMANIDAD HA DICHO BASTA! Y SE HA
PUESTO EN MARCHA! ¡BASTA! ¡BASTA! ¡VIVA LA RAZA! ¡VIVA LA
CAUSA! ¡VIVA LA HUELGA! ¡VIVAN LOS BROWN BERETS! ¡VIVAN LOS
ESTUDIANTES![21] ¡CHICANO POWER!

(*The* MEXICAN-AMERICAN *turns toward the* SECRETARY, *who gasps and
backs up. He keeps turning toward the* PACHUCO, FARM WORKER, *and*
REVOLUCIONARIO, *snapping his fingers and turning each of them on,
one by one.*)

PACHUCO (*Snap. To* SECRETARY). I'm going to get you, baby! ¡Viva La Raza!

FARM WORKER (*Snap. To* SECRETARY). ¡Viva la huelga! ¡Viva la Huelga! ¡VIVA LA
HUELGA!

REVOLUCIONARIO (*Snap. To* SECRETARY). ¡Viva la revolución! ¡VIVA LA REV-
OLUCIÓN!

(*The three models join together and advance toward the* SECRETARY *who
backs up and runs out of the shop screaming.* SANCHO *is at the other
end of the shop holding his money in his hand. All freeze. After a few
seconds of silence, the* PACHUCO *moves and stretches, shaking his arms
and loosening up. The* FARM WORKER *and* REVOLUCIONARIO *do the same.*
SANCHO *stays where he is, frozen to his spot.*)

JOHNNY. Man, that was a long one, ése.[22] (*Others agree with him.*)

FARM WORKER. How did we do?

JOHNNY. Perty good, look at all that lana,[23] man! (*He goes over to* SANCHO
and removes the money from his hand. SANCHO *stays where he is.*)

REVOLUCIONARIO. En la madre, look at all the money.

JOHNNY. We keep this up, we're going to be rich.

---

[20]**Raza . . . Vamos** Beloved Raza [persons of Mexican descent], let's take up arms to liberate
ourselves from those damned whites who exploit us. Let's get going.   [21]**¡Esta . . .
Estudiantes!** This great mass of humanity has said enough! And it has begun to march.
Enough! Enough! Long live La Raza! Long live the Cause! Long live the strike! Long live the
Brown Berets! Long live the students!   [22]**ése** man.   [23]**lana** money.

FARM WORKER. They think we're machines.

REVOLUCIONARIO. Burros.

JOHNNY. Puppets.

MEXICAN-AMERICAN. The only thing I don't like is—how come I always got to play the godamn Mexican-American?

JOHNNY. That's what you get for finishing high school.

FARM WORKER. How about our wages, ése?

JOHNNY. Here it comes right now. $3,000 for you, $3,000 for you, $3,000 for you, and $3,000 for me. The rest we put back into the business.

MEXICAN-AMERICAN. Too much, man. Heh, where you vatos[24] going tonight?

FARM WORKER. I'm going over to Concha's. There's a party.

JOHNNY. Wait a minute, vatos. What about our salesman? I think he needs an oil job.

REVOLUCIONARIO. Leave him to me.

(*The* PACHUCO, FARM WORKER, *and* MEXICAN-AMERICAN *exit, talking loudly about their plans for the night. The* REVOLUCIONARIO *goes over to* SANCHO, *removes his derby hat and cigar, lifts him up and throws him over his shoulder.* SANCHO *hangs loose, lifeless.*)

REVOLUCIONARIO (*To audience*). He's the best model we got! ¡Ajua![25]

(*Exit.*)

THE END

---

[24]**vatos** guys.   [25]**¡Ajua!** Wow!

⊠ TOPICS FOR CRITICAL THINKING AND WRITING

The Play on the Page

1. If you are an Anglo (shorthand for a Caucasian with traditional Northern European values), do you find the play deeply offensive? Why, or why not? If you are a Mexican-American, do you find the play entertaining or do you find parts of it offensive? What might Anglos enjoy in the play, and what might Mexican-Americans find offensive?

2. What stereotypes of Mexican-Americans are presented here? At the end of the play, what image of the Mexican-American is presented? How does it compare with the stereotypes?

3. Putting aside the politics of the play (and your own politics), what do you think are the strengths of *Los Vendidos*? What do you think are the weaknesses?

4. The play was written in 1967. Putting aside a few specific references—for instance, to Governor Reagan—do you find it dated? If not, why not?

5. In his short essay "The Actos," Valdez says that *actos* achieve the following: "Inspire the audience to social action. Illuminate specific points about social problems. Satirize the opposition. Show or hint at a solution. Express what people are feeling." How much of this do you think *Los Vendidos* does?

6. Many people assume that politics gets in the way of serious art. That is, they assume that artists ought to be concerned with issues that transcend politics. Does this point make any sense to you? Why or why not?

The Play on the Stage

7. In 1971 when *Los Vendidos* was produced by El Teatro de la Esperanza, the group altered the ending by having the men decide to use the money to build a community center. Evaluate this ending.
8. Jorge Huerta, who directed the 1971 El Teatro de la Esperanza production of *Los Vendidos,* suggests that it was a mistake for Jane Fonda to be cast as Miss Jimenes in the videotape of the play. "Something is lost," he says, "in the realization that this woman is not pretending to be white. . . ." Do you agree? Explain.
9. When the play was videotaped by KNBC in Los Angeles for broadcast in 1973, Valdez changed the ending. In the revised version we discover that a scientist (played by Valdez) masterminds the operation, placing Mexican-American models wherever there are persons of Mexican descent. These models soon will become Chicanos (as opposed to persons with Anglo values) and will aid rather than work against their fellows. Evaluate this ending.

A CONTEXT FOR *LOS VENDIDOS*

LUIS VALDEZ

The Actos

[1970]

Nothing represents the work of El Teatro Campesino (and other teatros Chicanos) better than the acto. In a sense, the acto is Chicano theatre, though we are now moving into a new, more mystical dramatic form we have begun to call the mito. The two forms are, in fact, cuates[1] that complement and balance each other as day goes into night, el sol la sombra, la vida la muerte, el pájaro la serpiente.[2] Our rejection of white western European (gabacho) proscenium theatre makes the birth of new Chicano forms necessary, thus, los actos y los mitos; one through the eyes of man, the other through the eyes of God.

The actos were born quite matter of factly in Delano. Nacieron hambrientos de la realidad. Anything and everything that pertained to the daily life, la vida cotidiana, of the huelguistas[3] became food for thought, material for actos. The reality of campesinos on strike had become dramatic (and theatrical as reflected by newspapers, TV newscasts, films, etc.), and so the actos merely reflected the reality. Huelguistas portrayed huelguistas, drawing

---

[1]**cuates** twins.   [2]**el sol . . . serpiente** sun and shade, life and death, the bird and the serpent.   [3]**huelguistas** strikers.

their improvised dialogue from real words they exchanged with the es-
quiroles (scabs) in the fields every day.[4]

"Hermanos, compañeros, sálganse de esos files."

"Tenemos comida y trabajo para ustedes afuera de la huelga."

"Esquirol, ten vergüenza."

"Unidos venceremos."

"¡Sal de ahí barrigón!"

The first huelguista to portray an esquirol in the teatro did it to settle a
score with a particularly stubborn scab he had talked with in the fields that
day. Satire became a weapon that was soon aimed at known and despised
contractors, growers and mayordomos. The effect of those early actos on
the huelguistas de Delano packed into Filipino Hall was immediate, intense
and cathartic. The actos rang true to the reality of the huelga.

Looking back at those early, crude, vital, beautiful, powerful actos of
1965, certain things have now become clear about the dramatic form we
were just beginning to develop. There was, of course, no conscious deliberate plan to develop the acto as such. Even the name we gave our small presentations reflects the hard pressing expediency under which we worked
from day to day. We could have called them "skits," but we lived and talked in
San Joaquin Valley Spanish (with a strong Tejano influence), so we needed a
name that made sense to the raza. Cuadros, pasquines, autos, entremeses[5] all
seemed too highly intellectualized. We began to call them actos for lack of a
better word, lack of time and lack of interest in trying to sound like classical
Spanish scholars. De todos modos éramos raza, ¿quién se iba a fijar?[6]

The acto, however, developed its own structure through five years of
experimentation. It evolved into a short dramatic form now used primarily
by los teatros de Aztlán, but utilized to some extent by other non-Chicano
guerrilla theatre companies throughout the U.S., including the San Francisco Mime Troupe and the Bread and Puppet Theatre. (Considerable creative crossfeeding has occurred on other levels, I might add, between the
Mime Troupe, the Bread and Puppet, and the Campesino.) Each of these
groups may have their own definition of the acto, but the following are
some of the guidelines we have established for ourselves over the years:

> Actos: Inspire the audience to social action. Illuminate specific
> points about social problems. Satirize the opposition. Show or hint
> at a solution. Express what people are feeling.

So what's new, right? Plays have been doing that for thousands of years.
True, except that the major emphasis in the acto is the social vision, as opposed to the individual artist or playwright's vision. Actos are not written;
they are created collectively, through improvisation by a group. The reality

---

[4]The following five lines of dialogue can be translated thus: Brothers, friends, leave those rows.
/ We have food and work for you outside of the strike. / Scab, you ought to be ashamed. /
United we will conquer. / Get out of here, fatso!   [5]**Cuadros . . . entremeses** various
Spanish words for short plays.   [6]**De todos . . . fijar?** In all ways we are the Race (i.e.,
indigenous Americans mixed with European and African blood); who was going to pay
attention?

reflected in an acto is thus a social reality, whether it pertains to campesinos or to batos locos, not psychologically deranged self-projections, but rather, group archetypes. Don Sotaco, Don Coyote, Johnny Pachuco, Juan Raza, Jorge el Chingón, la Chicana, are all group archetypes that have appeared in actos.

The usefulness of the acto extended well beyond the huelga into the Chicano movement, because Chicanos in general want to identify themselves as a group. The teatro archetypes symbolize the desire for unity and group identity through Chicano heroes and heroines. One character can thus represent the entire Raza, and the Chicano audience will gladly respond to his triumphs or defeats. What to a non-Chicano audience may seem like oversimplification in an acto, is to the Chicano a true expression of his social state and therefore reality.

HARVEY FIERSTEIN

Harvey Fierstein was born in Brooklyn, New York, the son of parents who had emigrated from Eastern Europe. While studying painting at Pratt Institute he acted in plays and revues, and one of his plays was produced in 1973, but he did not achieve fame until his Torch Song Trilogy *(1976-1979) moved from Off Broadway to Broadway in 1982.* Torch Song Trilogy *won the Theatre World Award, the Tony Award, and the Drama Desk Award. In addition, Fierstein won the Best Actor Tony Award and the Best Actor Drama Desk Award. He later received a third Tony Award for his work on the musical version of* La Cage aux Folles *(1983).*

On Tidy Endings [1987]

The curtain rises on a deserted, modern Upper West Side apartment. In the bright daylight that pours in through the windows we can see the living room of the apartment. Far Stage Right is the galley kitchen, next to it the multilocked front door with intercom. Stage Left reveals a hallway that leads to the two bedrooms and baths.

Though the room is still fully furnished (couch, coffee table, etc.), there are boxes stacked against the wall and several photographs and paintings are on the floor, leaving shadows on the wall where they once hung. Obviously someone is moving out. From the way the boxes are neatly labeled and stacked, we know that this is an organized person.

From the hallway just outside the door we hear the rattling of keys and two arguing voices:

JIM *(offstage).* I've got to be home by four. I've got practice.

MARION *(offstage).* I'll get you to practice, don't worry.

JIM *(offstage).* I don't want to go in there.

MARION *(offstage).* Jimmy, don't make Mommy crazy, alright? We'll go inside, I'll call Aunt Helen and see if you can go down and play with Robbie.

(The door opens. MARION *is a handsome woman of forty. Dressed in a business suit, her hair conservatively combed, she appears to be going to a business meeting.* JIM *is a boy of eleven. His playclothes are*

Harvey Fierstein, Ricky Addison Reed, and Anne de Salvo in the 1987 production of *On Tidy Endings*, Lyceum Theater, New York.

> *typical, but someone has obviously just combed his hair.* MARION *recovers the key from the lock.*)

JIM. Why can't I just go down and ring the bell?

MARION. Because I said so.

> (As MARION *steps into the room she is struck by some unexpected emotion. She freezes in her path and stares at the empty apartment.* JIM *lingers by the door.*)

JIM. I'm going downstairs.

MARION. Jimmy, please.

JIM. This place gives me the creeps.

MARION. This was your father's apartment. There's nothing creepy about it.

JIM. Says you.

MARION. You want to close the door, please?

> (*Jim reluctantly obeys.*)

MARION. Now, why don't you go check your room and make sure you didn't leave anything.

JIM. It's empty.

MARION. Go look.

JIM. I looked last time.

MARION (*trying to be patient*). Honey, we sold the apartment. You're never going to be here again. Go make sure you have everything you want.

JIM. But Uncle Arthur packed everything.

MARION (*less patiently*). Go make sure.

JIM. There's nothing in there.

MARION (*exploding*). I said make sure!

(JIM *jumps, then realizing that she's not kidding, obeys.*)

MARION. Everything's an argument with that one. (*She looks around the room and breathes deeply. There is sadness here. Under her breath:*) I can still smell you. (*Suddenly not wanting to be alone.*) Jimmy? Are you okay?

JIM (*returning*). Nothing. Told you so.

MARION. Uncle Arthur must have worked very hard. Make sure you thank him.

JIM. What for? Robbie says, (*fey mannerisms*) "They love to clean up things!"

MARION. Sometimes you can be a real joy.

JIM. Did you call Aunt Helen?

MARION. Do I get a break here? (*Approaching the boy understandingly.*) Wouldn't you like to say good-bye?

JIM. To who?

MARION. To the apartment. You and your daddy spent a lot of time here together. Don't you want to take one last look around?

JIM. Ma, get a real life.

MARION. "Get a real life." (*Going for the phone.*) Nice. Very nice.

JIM. Could you call already?

MARION (*dialing*). Jimmy, what does this look like I'm doing?

(JIM *kicks at the floor impatiently. Someone answers the phone at the other end.*)

MARION (*into the phone*). Helen? Hi, we're upstairs. . . . No, we just walked in the door. Jimmy wants to know if he can come down. . . . Oh, thanks.

(*Hearing that,* JIM *breaks for the door.*)

MARION (*yelling after him*). Don't run in the halls! And don't play with the elevator buttons!

(*The door slams shut behind him.*)

MARION (*back to the phone*). Hi. . . . No, I'm okay. It's a little weird being here. . . . No. Not since the funeral, and then there were so many people. Jimmy told me to get "a real life." I don't think I could handle anything realer. . . . No, please. Stay where you are. I'm fine. The doorman said Arthur would be right back and my lawyer should have been here already. . . . Well, we've got the papers to sign and a few other odds and ends to clean up. Shouldn't take long.

(*The intercom buzzer rings.*)

MARION. Hang on, that must be her. (MARION *goes to the intercom and speaks.*) Yes?. . . . Thank you. (*Back to the phone.*) Helen? Yeah, it's the lawyer. I'd better go. . . . Well, I could use a stiff drink, but I drove down. Listen, I'll stop by on my way out. Okay? Okay. 'Bye.

(*She hangs up the phone, looks around the room. That uncomfortable feeling returns to her quickly. She gets up and goes to the front door, opens it and looks out. No one there yet. She closes the door, shakes her head knowing that she's being silly and starts back into the room. She looks around, can't make it and retreats to the door. She opens it, looks out, closes it, but stays right there, her hand on the doorknob. The bell rings. She throws open the door.*)

MARION. That was quick.

(JUNE LOWELL *still has her finger on the bell. Her arms are loaded with contracts.* MARION'*s contemporary,* JUNE *is less formal in appearance and more hyper in her manner.*)

JUNE. *That* was quicker. What, were you waiting by the door?

MARION (*embarrassed*). No. I was just passing it. Come on in.

JUNE. Have you got your notary seal?

MARION. I think so.

JUNE. Great. Then you can witness. I left mine at the office and thanks to gentrification I'm double-parked downstairs. (*Looking for a place to dump her load.*) Where?

MARION (*definitely pointing to the coffee table*). Anywhere. You mean you're not staying?

JUNE. If you really think you need me I can go down and find a parking lot. I think there's one over on Columbus. So, I can go down, park the car in the lot and take a cab back if you really think you need me.

MARION. Well . . . ?

JUNE. But you shouldn't have any problems. The papers are about as straightforward as papers get. Arthur is giving you power of attorney to sell the apartment and you're giving him a check for half the purchase price. Everything else is just signing papers that state that you know that you signed the other papers. Anyway, he knows the deal, his lawyers have been over it all with him, it's just a matter of signatures.

MARION (*not fine*). Oh, fine.

JUNE. Unless you just don't want to be alone with him . . . ?

MARION. With Arthur? Don't be silly.

JUNE (*laying out the papers*). Then you'll handle it solo? Great. My car thanks you, the parking lot thanks you, and the cab driver that wouldn't have gotten a tip thanks you. Come have a quick look-see.

MARION (*joining her on the couch*). There are a lot of papers here.

JUNE. Copies. Not to worry. Start here.

(MARION *starts to read.*)

JUNE. I ran into Jimmy playing Elevator Operator.

(MARION *jumps.*)

JUNE. I got him off at the sixth floor. Read on.

MARION. This is definitely not my day for dealing with him.

(JUNE *gets up and has a look around.*)

JUNE. I don't believe what's happening to this neighborhood. You made quite an investment when you bought this place.

MARION. Collin was always very good at figuring out those things.

JUNE. Well, he sure figured this place right. What, have you tripled your money in ten years?

MARION. More.

JUNE. It's a shame to let it go.

MARION. We're not ready to be a two-dwelling family.

JUNE. So, sublet it again.

MARION. Arthur needs the money from the sale.

JUNE. Arthur got plenty already. I'm not crying for Arthur.

MARION. I don't hear you starting in again, do I?

JUNE. Your interests and your wishes are my only concern.

MARION. Fine.

JUNE. I still say we should contest Collin's will.

MARION. June . . . !

JUNE. You've got a child to support.

MARION. And a great job, and a husband with a great job. Tell me what Arthur's got.

JUNE. To my thinking, half of everything that should have gone to you. And more. All of Collin's personal effects, his record collection . . .

MARION. And I suppose their three years together meant nothing.

JUNE. When you compare them to your sixteen-year marriage? Not nothing, but not half of everything.

MARION (*trying to change the subject*). June, who gets which copies?

JUNE. Two of each to Arthur. One you keep. The originals and anything else come back to me. (*Looking around.*) I still say you should've sublet the apartment for a year and then sold it. You would've gotten an even better price. Who wants to buy an apartment when they know someone died in it. No one. And certainly no one wants to buy an apartment when they know the person died of AIDS.

MARION (*snapping*). June. Enough!

JUNE (*catching herself*). Sorry. That was out of line. Sometimes my mouth does that to me. Hey, that's why I'm a lawyer. If my brain worked as fast as my mouth I would have gotten a real job.

MARION (*holding out a stray paper*). What's this?

JUNE. I forgot. Arthur's lawyer sent that over yesterday. He found it in Collin's safety-deposit box. It's an insurance policy that came along with some consulting job he did in Japan. He either forgot about it when he made out his will or else he wanted you to get the full payment. Either way, it's yours.

MARION. Are you sure we don't split this?

JUNE. Positive.

MARION. But everything else . . . ?

JUNE. Hey, Arthur found it, his lawyer sent it to me. Relax, it's all yours. Minus my commission, of course. Go out and buy yourself something. Anything else before I have to use my cut to pay the towing bill?

MARION. I guess not.

JUNE (*starting to leave*). Great. Call me when you get home. (*Stopping at the door and looking back.*) Look, I know that I'm attacking this a little coldly. I am aware that someone you loved has just died. But there's a time and place for everything. This is about tidying up loose ends, not holding hands. I hope you'll remember that when Arthur gets here. Call me.

(*And she's gone.*)

(MARION *looks ill at ease to be alone again. She nervously straightens the papers into neat little piles, looks at them and then remembers:*)

MARION. Pens. We're going to need pens.

(*At last a chore to be done. She looks in her purse and finds only one. She goes to the kitchen and opens a drawer where she finds two more. She starts back to the table with them but suddenly remembers something else. She returns to the kitchen and begins going through the cabinets until she finds what she's looking for: a blue Art Deco teapot. Excited to find it, she takes it back to the couch. Guilt strikes. She stops, considers putting it back, wavers, then:*)

MARION (*to herself*). Oh, he won't care. One less thing to pack.

(*She takes the teapot and places it on the couch next to her purse. She is happier. Now she searches the room with her eyes for any other treasures she may have overlooked. Nothing here. She wanders off into the bedroom. We hear keys outside the front door.* ARTHUR *lets himself into the apartment carrying a load of empty cartons and a large shopping bag.* ARTHUR *is in his mid-thirties, pleasant looking though sloppily dressed in work clothes and slightly overweight.* ARTHUR *enters the apartment just as* MARION *comes out of the bedroom carrying a framed watercolor painting. They jump at the sight of each other.*)

MARION. Oh, hi, Arthur. I didn't hear the door.

ARTHUR (*staring at the painting*). Well hello, Marion.

MARION (*guiltily*). I was going to ask you if you were thinking of taking this painting because if you're not going to then I'll take it. Unless, of course, you want it.

ARTHUR. No. You can have it.

MARION. I never really liked it, actually. I hate cats. I didn't even like the show. I needed something for my college dorm room. I was never the rock star poster type. I kept it in the back of a closet for years until Collin moved in here and took it. He said he liked it.

ARTHUR. I do too.

MARION. Well, then you keep it.

ARTHUR. No. Take it.

MARION. We've really got no room for it. You keep it.

ARTHUR. I don't want it.

MARION. Well, if you're sure.

ARTHUR (*seeing the teapot*). You want the teapot?

MARION. If you don't mind.

ARTHUR. One less thing to pack.

MARION. Funny, but that's exactly what I thought. One less thing to pack. You know, my mother gave it to Collin and me when we moved into our first apartment. Silly sentimental piece of junk, but you know.

ARTHUR. That's not the one.

MARION. Sure it is. Hall used to make them for Westinghouse back in the thirties. I see them all the time at antiques shows and I always wanted to buy another, but they ask such a fortune for them.

ARTHUR. We broke the one your mother gave you a couple of years ago. That's a reproduction. You can get them almost anywhere in the Village for eighteen bucks.

MARION. Really? I'll have to pick one up.

ARTHUR. Take this one. I'll get another.

MARION. No, it's yours. You bought it.

ARTHUR. One less thing to pack.

MARION. Don't be silly. I didn't come here to raid the place.

ARTHUR. Well, was there anything else of Collin's that you thought you might like to have?

MARION. Now I feel so stupid, but actually I made a list. Not for me. But I started thinking about different people; friends, relatives, you know, that might want to have something of Collin's to remember him by. I wasn't sure just what you were taking and what you were throwing out. Anyway, I brought the list. (*Gets it from her purse.*) Of course these are only suggestions. You probably thought of a few of these people yourself. But I figured it couldn't hurt to write it all down. Like I said, I don't know what you are planning on keeping.

ARTHUR (*taking the list*). I was planning on keeping it all.

MARION. Oh, I know. But most of these things are silly. Like his high school yearbooks. What would you want with them?

ARTHUR. Sure. I'm only interested in his Gay period.

MARION. I didn't mean it that way. Anyway, you look it over. They're only suggestions. Whatever you decide to do is fine with me.

ARTHUR (*folding the list*). It would have to be, wouldn't it. I mean, it's all mine now. He did leave this all to me.

(MARION *is becoming increasingly nervous, but tries to keep a light approach as she takes a small bundle of papers from her bag.*)

MARION. While we're on the subject of what's yours. I brought a batch of condolence cards that were sent to you care of me. Relatives mostly.

ARTHUR (*taking them*). More cards? I'm going to have to have another printing of thank-you notes done.

MARION. I answered these last week, so you don't have to bother. Unless you want to.

ARTHUR. Forge my signature?

MARION. Of course not. They were addressed to both of us and they're mostly distant relatives or friends we haven't seen in years. No one important.

ARTHUR. If they've got my name on them, then I'll answer them myself.

MARION. I wasn't telling you not to, I was only saying that you don't have to.

ARTHUR. I understand.

(MARION *picks up the teapot and brings it to the kitchen.*)

MARION. Let me put this back.

ARTHUR. I ran into Jimmy in the lobby.

MARION. Tell me you're joking.

ARTHUR. I got him to Helen's.

MARION. He's really racking up the points today.

ARTHUR. You know, he still can't look me in the face.

MARION. He's reacting to all of this in strange ways. Give him time. He'll come around. He's really very fond of you.

ARTHUR. I know. But he's at that awkward age: under thirty. I'm sure in twenty years we'll be the best of friends.

MARION. It's not what you think.

ARTHUR. What do you mean?

MARION. Well, you know.

ARTHUR. No I don't know. Tell me.

MARION. I thought that you were intimating something about his blaming you for Collin's illness and I was just letting you know that it's not true. (*Foot in mouth, she braves on.*) We discussed it a lot and . . . uh . . . he understands that his father was sick before you two ever met.

ARTHUR. I don't believe this.

MARION. I'm just trying to say that he doesn't blame you.

ARTHUR. First of all, who asked you? Second of all, that's between him and me. And third and most importantly, of course he blames me. Marion, he's eleven years old. You can discuss all you want, but the fact is that his father died of a "fag" disease and I'm the only fag around to finger.

MARION. My son doesn't use that kind of language.

ARTHUR. Forget the language. I'm talking about what he's been through. Can you imagine the kind of crap he's taken from his friends? That poor kid's been chased and chastised from one end of town to the other. He's got to have someone to blame just to survive. He can't blame you, you're all he's got. He can't blame his father; he's dead. So, Uncle Arthur gets the shaft. Fine, I can handle it.

MARION. You are so wrong, Arthur. I know my son and that is not the way his mind works.

ARTHUR. I don't know what you know. I only know what I know. And all I know is what I hear and see. The snide remarks, the little smirks . . . And it's not just the illness. He's been looking for a scapegoat since the day you and Collin first split up. Finally he has one.

MARION (*getting very angry now*). Wait. Are you saying that if he's going to blame someone it should be me?

ARTHUR. I think you should try to see things from his point of view.

MARION. Where do you get off thinking you're privy to my son's point of view?

ARTHUR. It's not that hard to imagine. Life's rolling right along, he's having a happy little childhood, when suddenly one day his father's moving out. No explanations, no reasons, none of the fights that usually accompany such things. Divorce is hard enough for a kid to understand when he's listened to years of battles, but yours?

MARION. So what should we have done? Faked a few months' worth of fights before Collin moved out?

ARTHUR. You could have told him the truth, plain and simple.

MARION. He was seven years old at the time. How the hell do you tell a seven-year-old that his father is leaving his mother to go sleep with other men?

ARTHUR. Well, not like that.

MARION. You know, Arthur, I'm going to say this as nicely as I can: Butt out. You're not his mother and you're not his father.

ARTHUR. Thank you. I wasn't acutely aware of that fact. I will certainly keep that in mind from now on.

MARION. There's only so much information a child that age can handle.

ARTHUR. So it's best that he reach his capacity on the street.

MARION. He knew about the two of you. We talked about it.

ARTHUR. Believe me, he knew before you talked about it. He's young, not stupid.

MARION. It's very easy for you to stand here and criticize, but there are aspects that you will just never be able to understand. You weren't there. You have no idea what it was like for me. You're talking to someone who thought that a girl went to college to meet a husband. I went to protest rallies because I liked the music. I bought a guitar because I thought it looked good on the bed! This lifestyle, this knowledge that you take for granted, was all a little out of left field for me.

ARTHUR. I can imagine.

MARION. No, I don't think you can. I met Collin in college, married him right after graduation and settled down for a nice quiet life of Kids and Careers. You think I had any idea about this? Talk about life's little surprises. You live with someone for sixteen years, you share your life, your bed, you have a child together, and then you wake up one day and he tells you that to him it's all been a lie. A lie. Try that on for size. Here you are the happiest couple you know, fulfilling your every life fantasy and he tells you he's living a lie.

ARTHUR. I'm sure he never said that.

MARION. Don't be so sure. There was a lot of new ground being broken back then and plenty of it was muddy.

ARTHUR. You know that he loved you.

MARION. What's that supposed to do, make things easier? It doesn't. I was brought up to believe, among other things, that if you had love that was enough. So what if I wasn't everything he wanted. Maybe he wasn't exactly everything I wanted either. So, you know what? You count your blessings and you settle.

ARTHUR. No one has to settle. Not him. Not you.

MARION. Of course not. You can say, "Up yours!" to everything and everyone who depends and needs you, and go off to make yourself happy.

ARTHUR. It's not that simple.

MARION. No. This is simpler. Death is simpler. (*Yelling out:*) Happy now?

(*They stare at each other.* MARION *calms the rage and catches her breath.* ARTHUR *holds his emotions in check.*)

ARTHUR. How about a nice hot cup of coffee? Tea with lemon? Hot cocoa with a marshmallow floating in it?

MARION (*laughs*). I was wrong. You *are* a mother.

(ARTHUR *goes into the kitchen and starts preparing things. Marion loafs by the doorway.*)

MARION. I lied before. He *was* everything I ever wanted.

(ARTHUR *stops, looks at her, and then changes the subject as he goes on with his work.*)

ARTHUR. When I came into the building and saw Jimmy in the lobby I absolutely freaked for a second. It's amazing how much they look alike. It was like seeing a little miniature Collin standing there.

MARION. I know. He's like Collin's clone. There's nothing of me in him.

ARTHUR. I always kinda hoped that when he grew up he'd take after me. Not much chance, I guess.

MARION. Don't do anything fancy in there.

ARTHUR. Please. Anything we can consume is one less thing to pack.

MARION. So you've said.

ARTHUR. So *we've* said.

MARION. I want to keep seeing you and I want you to see Jim. You're still part of this family. No one's looking to cut you out.

ARTHUR. Ah, who'd want a kid to grow up looking like me anyway. I had enough trouble looking like this. Why pass on the misery?

MARION. You're adorable.

ARTHUR. Is that like saying I have a good personality?

MARION. I think you are one of the most naturally handsome men I know.

ARTHUR. Natural is right, and the bloom is fading.

MARION. All you need is a few good nights' sleep to kill those rings under your eyes.

ARTHUR. Forget the rings under my eyes, (*grabbing his middle*) . . . how about the rings around my moon?

MARION. I like you like this.

ARTHUR. From the time that Collin started using the wheelchair until he died, about six months, I lost twenty-three pounds. No gym, no diet. In the last seven weeks I've gained close to fifty.

MARION. You're exaggerating.

ARTHUR. I'd prove it on the bathroom scale, but I sold it in working order.

MARION. You'd never know.

ARTHUR. Marion, *you'd* never know, but ask my belt. Ask my pants. Ask my underwear. Even my stretch socks have stretch marks. I called the ambulance at five A.M., he was gone at nine and by nine-thirty, I was on a first-name basis with Sara Lee. I can quote the business hours of every ice-cream parlor, pizzeria and bakery on the island of Manhattan. I know the location of every twenty-four-hour grocery in the greater New York area, and I have memorized the phone numbers of every Mandarin, Szechuan and Hunan restaurant with free delivery.

MARION. At least you haven't wasted your time on useless hobbies.

ARTHUR. Are you kidding? I'm opening my own Overeater's Hotline. We'll have to start small, but expansion is guaranteed.

MARION. You're the best, you know that? If I couldn't be everything that Collin wanted then I'm grateful that he found someone like you.

ARTHUR (*turning on her without missing a beat*). Keep your goddamned gratitude to yourself. I didn't go through any of this for you. So your thanks are out of line. And he didn't find "someone like" me. It was me.

MARION (*frightened*). I didn't mean . . .

ARTHUR. And I wish you'd remember one thing more: He died in my arms, not yours.

(MARION *is totally caught off guard. She stares disbelieving, open-mouthed.* ARTHUR *walks past her as he leaves the kitchen with place mats. He puts them on the coffee table. As he arranges the papers and place mats he speaks, never looking at her.*)

ARTHUR. Look, I know you were trying to say something supportive. Don't waste your breath. There's nothing you can say that will make any of this easier for me. There's no way for you to help me get through this. And that's your fault. After three years you still have no idea or understanding of who I am. Or maybe you do know but refuse to accept it. I don't know and I don't care. But at least understand, from my point of view, who you are: You are my husband's *ex*-wife. If you like, the mother of *my* stepson. Don't flatter yourself into thinking you're any more than that. And whatever you are, you're certainly not my friend.

(*He stops, looks up at her, then passes her again as he goes back to the kitchen.* MARION *is shaken, working hard to control herself. She moves toward the couch.*)

MARION. Why don't we just sign these papers and I'll be out of your way.

ARTHUR. Shouldn't you say *I'll* be out of *your* way? After all, I'm not just signing papers. I'm signing away my home.

MARION (*resolved not to fight, she gets her purse*). I'll leave the papers here. Please have them notarized and returned to my lawyer.

ARTHUR. Don't forget my painting.

MARION (*exploding*). What do you want from me, Arthur?

ARTHUR (*yelling back*). I want you the hell out of my apartment! I want you out of my life! And I want you to leave Collin alone!

MARION. The man's dead. I don't know how much more alone I can leave him.

(ARTHUR *laughs at the irony, but behind the laughter is something much more desperate.*)

ARTHUR. Lots more, Marion. You've got to let him go.

MARION. For the life of me, I don't know what I did or what you think I did, for you to treat me like this. But you're not going to get away with it. You will not take your anger out on me. I will not stand here and be badgered and insulted by you. I know you've been hurt and I know you're hurting but you're not the only one who lost someone here.

ARTHUR (*topping her*). Yes I am! You didn't just lose him. I did! You lost him five years ago when he divorced you. This is not your moment of grief and loss, it's mine! (*Picking up the bundle of cards and throwing it toward her.*) These condolences do not belong to you, they're mine. (*Tossing her list back to her.*) His things are not yours to give away, they're mine! This death does not belong to you, it's mine! Bought and paid for outright. I suffered for it, I bled for it.

I was the one who cooked his meals. I was the one who spoon-fed him. I pushed his wheelchair. I carried and bathed him. I wiped his backside and changed his diapers. I breathed life into and wrestled fear out of his heart. I kept him alive for two years longer than any doctor thought possible and when it was time I was the one who prepared him for death.

I paid in full for my place in his life and I will *not* share it with you. We are not the two widows of Collin Redding. Your life was not here. Your husband didn't just die. You've got a son and a life somewhere else. Your husband's sitting, waiting for you at home, wondering, as I am, what the hell you're doing here and why you can't let go.

(MARION *leans back against the couch. She's blown away.* ARTHUR *stands staring at her.*)

ARTHUR (*quietly*). Let him go, Marion. He's mine. Dead or alive; mine.

(*The teakettle whistles.* ARTHUR *leaves the room, goes to the kitchen and pours the water as* MARION *pulls herself together.* ARTHUR *carries the loaded tray back into the living room and sets it down on the coffee table. He sits and pours a cup.*)

ARTHUR. One marshmallow or two?

(MARION *stares, unsure as to whether the attack is really over or not.*)

ARTHUR (*placing them in her cup*). Take three, they're small.

(MARION *smiles and takes the offered cup.*)

ARTHUR (*campily*). Now let me tell you how I *really* feel.

(MARION *jumps slightly, then they share a small laugh. Silence as they each gather themselves and sip their refreshments.*)

MARION (*calmly*). Do you think that I sold the apartment just to throw you out?

ARTHUR. I don't care about the apartment . . .

MARION. . . . Because I really didn't. Believe me.

ARTHUR. I know.

MARION. I knew the expenses here were too much for you, and I knew you couldn't afford to buy out my half . . . I figured if we sold it, that you'd at least have a nice chunk of money to start over with.

ARTHUR. You could've given me a little more time.

MARION. Maybe. But I thought the sooner you were out of here, the sooner you could go on with your life.

ARTHUR. Or the sooner you could go on with yours.

MARION. Maybe. (*Pauses to gather her thoughts.*) Anyway, I'm not going to tell you that I have no idea what you're talking about. I'd have to be worse than deaf and blind not to have seen the way you've been treated. Or mistreated. When I read Collin's obituary in the newspaper and saw my name and Jimmy's name and no mention of you . . . (*Shakes her head, not knowing what to say.*) You know that his secretary was the one who wrote that up and sent it in. Not me. But I should have done something about it and I didn't. I know.

ARTHUR. Wouldn't have made a difference. I wrote my own obituary for him and sent it to the smaller papers. They edited me out.

MARION. I'm sorry. I remember, at the funeral, I was surrounded by all of Collin's family and business associates while you were left with your friends. I knew it was wrong. I knew I should have said something but it felt good to have them around me and you looked like you were holding up. . . . Wrong. But saying that it's all my fault for not letting go . . . ? There were other people involved.

ARTHUR. Who took their cue from you.

MARION. Arthur, you don't understand. Most people that we knew as a couple had no idea that Collin was Gay right up to his death. And even those that did know only found out when he got sick and the word leaked out that it was AIDS. I don't think I have to tell you how stupid and ill-informed most people are about homosexuality. And AIDS . . . ? The kinds of insane behavior that word inspires . . . ?

Those people at the funeral, how many times did they call to see how he was doing over these years? How many of them ever went to see him in the hospital? Did any of them even come here? So, why would you expect them to act any differently after his death?

So, maybe that helps to explain their behavior, but what about mine, right? Well, maybe there is no explanation. Only excuses. And excuse number one is that you're right, I have never really let go of him. And I am jealous of you. Hell, I was jealous of anyone that Collin ever talked to, let alone slept with . . . let alone loved.

The first year, after he moved out, we talked all the time about the different men he was seeing. And I always listened and advised. It was kind of fun. It kept us close. It kept me a part of his intimate life. And the bottom line was always that he wasn't happy with the men he was meeting. So, I was always allowed to hang on to the hope that one day he'd give it all up and come home. Then he got sick.

He called me, told me he was in the hospital and asked if I'd come see him. I ran. When I got to his door there was a sign, INSTRUCTIONS FOR VISITORS OF AN AIDS PATIENT. I nearly died.

ARTHUR. He hadn't told you?

MARION. No. And believe me, a sign is not the way to find these things out. I was so angry. . . . And he was so sick . . . I was sure that he'd die right then. If not from the illness then from the hospital staff's neglect. No one wanted to go near him and I didn't bother fighting with them because I understood that they were scared. I was scared. That whole month in the hospital I didn't let Jimmy visit him once.

You learn.

Well, as you know, he didn't die. And he asked if he could come stay with me until he was well. And I said yes. Of course, yes. Now, here's something I never thought I'd ever admit to anyone: had he asked to stay with me for a few weeks I would have said no. But he asked to stay with me until he was well and knowing there was no cure I said yes. In my craziness I said yes because to me that meant forever. That he was coming back to me forever. Not that I wanted him to die, but I assumed from everything I'd read. . . . And we'd be back together for whatever time he had left. Can you understand that?

(ARTHUR *nods*.)

MARION (*gathers her thoughts again*). Two weeks later he left. He moved in here. Into this apartment that we had bought as an investment. Never to live in. Certainly never to live apart in. Next thing I knew, the name Arthur starts appearing in every phone call, every dinner conversation.

"Did you see the doctor?"

"Yes. Arthur made sure I kept the appointment."

"Are you going to your folks for Thanksgiving?"

"No. Arthur and I are having some friends over."

I don't know which one of us was more of a coward, he for not telling or me for not asking about you. But eventually you became a given. Then, of course, we met and became what I had always thought of as friends.

(ARTHUR *winces in guilt.*)

MARION. I don't care what you say, how could we not be friends with some-one so great in common: love for one of the most special human beings there ever was. And don't try and tell me there weren't times when you enjoyed me being around as an ally. I can think of a dozen occasions when we ganged up on him, teasing him with our intimate knowledge of his personal habits.

(ARTHUR *has to laugh.*)

MARION. Blanket stealing? Snoring? Excess gas, no less? (*Takes a moment to enjoy this truce.*) I don't think that my loving him threatened your rela-tionship. Maybe I'm not being truthful with myself. But I don't. I never tried to step between you. Not that I ever had the opportunity. Talk about being joined at the hip! And that's not to say I wasn't jealous. I was. Terribly. Hatefully. But always lovingly. I was happy for Collin be-cause there was no way to deny that he was happy. With everything he was facing, he was happy. Love did that. You did that.

He lit up with you. He came to life. I envied that and all the time you spent together, but more, I watched you care for him (sometimes *overcare* for him), and I was in awe. I could never have done what you did. I never would have survived. I really don't know how you did.

ARTHUR. Who said I survived?

MARION. Don't tease. You did an absolutely incredible thing. It's not as if you met him before he got sick. You entered a relationship that you knew in all probability would end this way and you never wavered.

ARTHUR. Of course I did. Don't have me sainted, Marion. But sometimes you have no choice. Believe me, if I could've gotten away from him I would've. But I was a prisoner of love.

(*He makes a campy gesture and pose.*)

MARION. Stop.

ARTHUR. And there were lots of pluses. I got to quit a job I hated, stay home all day and watch game shows. I met a lot of doctors and learned a lot of big words. (ARTHUR *jumps up and goes to the pile of boxes where he extracts one and brings it back to the couch.*)

And then there was all the exciting traveling I got to do. This box has a souvenir from each one of our trips. Wanna see? (MARION *nods. He opens the box and pulls things out one by one. Holding up an old bottle.*)

This is from the house we rented in Reno when we went to clear out his lungs. (*Holding handmade potholders.*)

This is from the hospital in Reno. Collin made them. They had a great arts and crafts program. (*Copper bracelets.*)

These are from a faith healer in Philly. They don't do much for a fever, but they look great with a green sweater. (*Glass ashtrays.*)

These are from our first visit to the clinic in France. Such lovely people. (*A Bible.*)

This is from our second visit to the clinic in France. (*A bead necklace.*)

A Voodoo doctor in New Orleans. Next time we'll have to get there earlier in the year. I think he sold all the pretty ones at Mardi Gras. (*A tiny piñata.*)

Then there was Mexico. Black market drugs and empty wallets. (*Now pulling things out at random.*)

L.A., San Francisco, Houston, Boston . . . We traveled everywhere they offered hope for sale and came home with souvenirs. (ARTHUR *quietly pulls a few more things out and then begins to put them all back into the box slowly. Softly as he works:*) Marion, I would have done anything, traveled anywhere to avoid . . . or delay. . . . Not just because I loved him so desperately, but when you've lived the way we did for three years . . . the battle becomes your life. (*He looks at her and then away.*) His last few hours were beyond any scenario I had imagined. He hadn't walked in nearly six months. He was totally incontinent. If he spoke two words in a week I was thankful. Days went by without his eyes ever focusing on me. He just stared out at I don't know what. Not the meals as I fed him. Not the TV I played constantly for company. Just out. Or maybe in.

It was the middle of the night when I heard his breathing become labored. His lungs were filling with fluid again. I knew the sound. I'd heard it a hundred times before. So, I called the ambulance and got him to the hospital.

They hooked him up to the machines, the oxygen, shot him with morphine and told me that they would do what they could to keep him alive.

But, Marion, it wasn't the machines that kept him breathing. He did it himself. It was that incredible will and strength inside him. Whether it came from his love of life or fear of death, who knows. But he'd been counted out a hundred times and a hundred times he fought his way back.

I got a magazine to read him, pulled a chair up to the side of his bed and holding his hand, I wondered whether I should call Helen to let the cleaning lady in or if he'd fall asleep and I could sneak home for an hour. I looked up from the page and he was looking at me. Really looking right into my eyes. I patted his cheek and said, "Don't worry, honey, you're going to be fine."

But there was something else in his eyes. He wasn't satisfied with that. And I don't know why, I have no idea where it came from, I just heard the words coming out of my mouth, "Collin, do you want to die?"

His eyes filled and closed, he nodded his head.

I can't tell you what I was thinking, I'm not sure I was. I slipped off my shoes, lifted his blanket and climbed into bed next to him. I helped him to put his arms around me, and mine around him, and whispered as gently as I could into his ear, "It's alright to let go now. It's time to go on." And he did.

Marion, you've got your life and your son. All I have is an intangible place in a man's history. Leave me that. Respect that.

MARION. I understand.

(ARTHUR *suddenly comes to life, running to get the shopping bag that he'd left at the front door.*)

ARTHUR. Jeez! With all the screamin' and sad storytelling I forgot something. (*He extracts a bouquet of flowers from the bag.*) I brung you flowers and everything.

MARION. You brought *me* flowers?

ARTHUR. Well, I knew you'd never think to bring me flowers and I felt that on an occasion such as this somebody oughta get flowers from somebody.

MARION. You know, Arthur, you're really making me feel like a worthless piece of garbage.

ARTHUR. So what else is new? (*He presents the flowers.*) Just promise me one thing: Don't press one in a book. Just stick them in a vase and when they fade just toss them out. No more memorabilia.

MARION. Arthur, I want to do something for you and I don't know what. Tell me what you want.

ARTHUR. I want little things. Not much. I want to be remembered. If you get a Christmas card from Collin's mother make sure she sent me one too. If his friends call to see how you are, ask if they've called me. Have me to dinner so I can see Jimmy. Let me take him out now and then. Invite me to his wedding. (*They both laugh.*)

MARION. You've got it.

ARTHUR (*clearing the table*). Let me get all this cold cocoa out of the way. We still have the deed to do.

MARION (*checking her watch*). And I've got to get Jimmy home in time for practice.

ARTHUR. Band practice?

MARION. Baseball. (*Picking her list off the floor.*) About this list, you do what you want.

ARTHUR. Believe me, I will. But I promise to consider your suggestions. Just don't rush me. I'm not ready to give it all away. (ARTHUR *is off to the kitchen with his tray and the phone rings. He answers in the kitchen.*) Hello? . . . Just a minute. (*Calling out.*) It's your eager Little Leaguer.

(MARION *picks up the living room extension and Arthur hangs his up.*)

MARION (*into phone*). Hello, honey. . . . I'll be down in five minutes. No. You know what? You come up here and get me. . . . No, I said you should come up here. . . . I said I want you to come up here. . . . Because I said so. . . . Thank you. (*She hangs the receiver.*)

ARTHUR (*rushing to the papers*). Alright, where do we start on these?

MARION (*getting out her seal*). I guess you should just start signing everything and I'll stamp along with you. Keep one of everything on the side for yourself.

ARTHUR. Now I feel so rushed. What am I signing?

MARION. You want to do this another time?

ARTHUR. No. Let's get it over with. I wouldn't survive another session like this.

(*He starts to sign and she starts her job.*)

MARION. I keep meaning to ask you; how are you?

ARTHUR (*at first puzzled and then:*) Oh, you mean my health? Fine. No. I'm fine. I've been tested, and nothing. We were very careful. We took many precautions. Collin used to make jokes about how we should invest in rubber futures.

MARION. I'll bet.

ARTHUR (*stops what he's doing*). It never occurred to me until now. How about you?

MARION (*not stopping*). Well, we never had sex after he got sick.

ARTHUR. But before?

MARION (*stopping but not looking up*). I have the antibodies in my blood. No signs that it will ever develop into anything else. And it's been five years so my chances are pretty good that I'm just a carrier.

ARTHUR. I'm so sorry. Collin never told me.

MARION. He didn't know. In fact, other than my husband and the doctors, you're the only one I've told.

ARTHUR. You and your husband . . . ?

MARION. Have invested in rubber futures. There'd only be a problem if we wanted to have a child. Which we do. But we'll wait. Miracles happen every day.

ARTHUR. I don't know what to say.

MARION. Tell me you'll be there if I ever need you.

(ARTHUR *gets up, goes to her and puts his arm around her. They hold each other. He gently pushes her away to make a joke.*)

ARTHUR. Sure! Take something else that should have been mine.

MARION. Don't even joke about things like that.

(*The doorbell rings. They pull themselves together.*)

ARTHUR. You know we'll never get these done today.

MARION. So, tomorrow.

(ARTHUR *goes to open the door as* MARION *gathers her things. He opens the door and* JIMMY *is standing in the hall.*)

JIM. C'mon, Ma. I'm gonna be late.

ARTHUR. Would you like to come inside?

JIM. We've gotta go.

MARION. Jimmy, come on.

JIM. Ma!

(*She glares. He comes in.* ARTHUR *closes the door.*)

MARION (*holding out the flowers*). Take these for Mommy.

JIM (*taking them*). Can we go?

MARION (*picking up the painting*). Say good-bye to your Uncle Arthur.

JIM. 'Bye, Arthur. Come on.

MARION. Give him a kiss.

ARTHUR. Marion, don't.

MARION. Give your uncle a kiss good-bye.

JIM. He's not my uncle.

MARION. No. He's a hell of a lot more than your uncle.

ARTHUR (*offering his hand*). A handshake will do.

MARION. Tell Uncle Arthur what your daddy told you.

JIM. About what?

MARION. Stop playing dumb. You know.

ARTHUR. Don't embarrass him.

MARION. Jimmy, please.

JIM (*he regards his mother's softer tone and then speaks*). He said that after me and Mommy he loved you the most.

MARION (*standing behind him*). Go on.

JIM. And that I should love you too. And make sure that you're not lonely or very sad.

ARTHUR. Thank you.

(ARTHUR *reaches down to the boy and they hug.* JIM *gives him a little peck on the cheek and then breaks away.*)

MARION (*going to open the door*). Alright, kid, you done good. Now let's blow this joint before you muck it up.

(JIM *rushes out the door.* MARION *turns to* ARTHUR.)

MARION. A child's kiss is magic. Why else would they be so stingy with them? I'll call you.

(ARTHUR *nods understanding.* MARION *pulls the door closed behind her.* ARTHUR *stands quietly as the lights fade to black.*)

THE END

NOTE: *If being performed on film, the final image should be of* ARTHUR *leaning his back against the closed door on the inside of the apartment and* MARION *leaning on the outside of the door. A moment of thought and then they both move on.*

▨ TOPICS FOR CRITICAL THINKING AND WRITING

The Play on the Page

1. We first hear about AIDS on page 1672. Were you completely surprised, or did you think the play might introduce the subject? That is, did the author in any way prepare you for the subject? If so, how?

2. As far as the basic story goes, June (the lawyer) is not necessary. Marion could have brought the papers with her. Why do you suppose Fierstein introduces June? What function or functions does she serve? How would you characterize her?

3. On page 1673 Marion says of the teapot, "One less thing to pack." Arthur says the same words a moment later, and then he repeats them yet again. A little later, while drinking cocoa, he repeats the words, and Marion says, "So you've said," to which Arthur replies, "So *we've* said." Exactly what tone do you think should be used when Marion first says these words? When Arthur says them? What significance, if any, do you attach to the fact that both characters speak these words?

4. Arthur says that Jimmy blames him for Collin's death, but Marion denies it. Who do you think is right? Can a reader be sure? Why or why not?

5. When Arthur tells Marion that she should have told Jimmy why Collin left her, Marion says, "How the hell do you tell a seven-year-old that his father is leaving his mother to go sleep with other men?" Arthur replies, "[W]ell, not like that." What does Arthur mean? How might Marion have told Jimmy? Do you think she should have told Jimmy?

6. Do you agree with a reader who found Marion an unconvincing character because she is "so passive and unquestioningly loving in her regard for her ex-husband"? If you disagree, how would you argue your case?

7. During the course of the play, what (if anything) does Marion learn? What (if anything) does Arthur learn? What (if anything) does Jimmy learn? What (if anything) does the reader or viewer learn from the play?

8. One reader characterized the play as "propaganda." Do you agree? Why or why not? And if you think *On Tidy Endings* is propaganda, are you implying that it is, therefore, deficient as a work of art?

The Play on the Stage

9. A reviewer of the play said that Arthur is "bitchy" in many of his responses to Marion. What do you suppose the reviewer meant by this? Does the term imply that Fierstein presents a stereotype of the homosexual? If so, what is this stereotype? If you think that the term applies (even though you might not use such a word yourself), do you think that Fierstein's portrayal of Arthur is stereotypical? If it is stereotypical, is this a weakness in the play?

10. What well-known actors would you cast in the roles? Explain your choices.

AUGUST WILSON

August Wilson was born in Pittsburgh in 1945, the son of a black woman and a white man. After dropping out of school at the age of 15, Wilson took various odd jobs, such as stock clerk and short-order cook, in his spare time educating himself in the public library, chiefly by reading works by such black writers as Richard Wright, Ralph Ellison, Langston Hughes, and Amiri Baraka (LeRoi Jones). In 1978 the director of a black theater in St. Paul, Minnesota, who had known Wilson in Pittsburgh, invited him to write a play for the theater. Six months later Wilson moved permanently to St. Paul.

The winner of the Pulitzer Prize for drama in 1987, Wilson's Fences *was first presented as a staged reading in 1983 and was later performed in Chicago, Seattle, Rochester (New York), and New Haven (Connecticut) before reaching New York City in 1987. An earlier play,* Ma Rainey's Black Bottom, *was voted Best Play of the Year 1984–1985 by the New York Drama Critics' Circle. In 1981 when* Ma Rainey *was first read at the O'Neill Center in Waterford, Connecticut, Wilson met Lloyd Richards, an African-American director with whom he has continued to work closely.* The Piano Lesson, *directed by Richards, won Wilson a second Pulitzer Prize in 1990.*

Fences

[1987]

for Lloyd Richards,
who adds to whatever he touches

> *When the sins of our fathers visit us*
> *We do not have to play host.*
> *We can banish them with forgiveness*
> *As God, in His Largeness and Laws.*

—August Wilson

LIST OF CHARACTERS

TROY MAXSON
JIM BONO, *Troy's friend*
ROSE, *Troy's wife*
LYONS, *Troy's oldest son by previous marriage*
GABRIEL, *Troy's brother*
CORY, *Troy and Rose's son*
RAYNELL, *Troy's daughter*

SETTING: *The setting is the yard which fronts the only entrance to the Maxson household, an ancient two-story brick house set back off a small alley in a big-city neighborhood. The entrance to the house is gained by two or three steps leading to a wooden porch badly in need of paint.*

A relatively recent addition to the house and running its full width, the porch lacks congruence. It is a sturdy porch with a flat roof. One or two chairs of dubious value sit at one end where the kitchen window opens onto the porch. An old-fashioned icebox stands silent guard at the opposite end.

The yard is a small dirt yard, partially fenced, except for the last scene, with a wooden saw horse, a pile of lumber, and other fence-building equipment set off to the side. Opposite is a tree from which hangs a ball made of rags. A baseball bat leans against the tree. Two oil drums serve as garbage receptacles and sit near the house at right to complete the setting.

THE PLAY: *Near the turn of the century, the destitute of Europe sprang on the city with tenacious claws and an honest and solid dream. The city devoured them. They swelled its belly until it burst into a thousand furnaces and sewing machines, a thousand butcher shops and bakers' ovens, a thousand churches and hospitals and funeral parlors and money-lenders. The city grew. It nourished itself and offered each man a partnership limited only by his talent, his guile, and his willingness and capacity for hard work. For the immigrants of Europe, a dream dared and won true.*

The descendants of African slaves were offered no such welcome or participation. They came from places called the Carolinas and the Virginias, Georgia, Alabama, Mississippi, and Tennessee. They came strong, eager, searching. The city rejected them and they fled and settled along the riverbanks and under bridges in shallow, ramshackle houses made of sticks and tarpaper. They collected rags and wood. They sold the use of their muscles and their bodies. They cleaned houses and washed clothes, they shined shoes, and in quiet desperation and vengeful pride, they stole,

Left to right: Frances Foster as Rose, Keith Amos as Cory, William Jay as Gabriel, and Gilbert Lewis as Troy, in the Seattle Repertory Theater production of *Fences.*

and lived in pursuit of their own dream. That they could breathe free, fi-nally, and stand to meet life with the force of dignity and whatever elo-quence the heart could call upon.

By 1957, the hard-won victories of the European immigrants had solidified the industrial might of America. War had been confronted and won with new energies that used loyalty and patriotism as its fuel. Life was rich, full, and flourishing. The Milwaukee Braves won the World Series, and the hot winds of change that would make the sixties a turbu-lent, racing, dangerous, and provocative decade had not yet begun to blow full.

Act 1

Scene 1

It is 1957. TROY *and* BONO *enter the yard, engaged in conversation.*
TROY *is fifty-three years old, a large man with thick, heavy hands; it is
this largeness that he strives to fill out and make an accommodation
with. Together with his blackness, his largeness informs his sensibilities and the choices he has made in his life.*

Of the two men, BONO *is obviously the follower. His commitment
to their friendship of thirty-odd years is rooted in his admiration of*
TROY*'s honesty, capacity for hard work, and his strength, which* BONO
seeks to emulate.

*It is Friday night, payday, and the one night of the week the two
men engage in a ritual of talk and drink.* TROY *is usually the most
talkative and at times he can be crude and almost vulgar, though he
is capable of rising to profound heights of expression. The men carry
lunch buckets and wear or carry burlap aprons and are dressed in
clothes suitable to their jobs as garbage collectors.*

BONO. Troy, you ought to stop that lying!

TROY. I ain't lying! The nigger had a watermelon this big. (*He indicates with
his hands.*) Talking about . . . "What watermelon, Mr. Rand?" I liked to
fell out! "What watermelon, Mr. Rand?" . . . And it sitting there big as
life.

BONO. What did Mr. Rand say?

TROY. Ain't said nothing. Figure if the nigger too dumb to know he carrying
a watermelon, he wasn't gonna get much sense out of him. Trying to
hide that great big old watermelon under his coat. Afraid to let the
white man see him carry it home.

BONO. I'm like you . . . I ain't got no time for them kind of people.

TROY. Now what he look like getting mad cause he see the man from the
union talking to Mr. Rand?

BONO. He come to me talking about . . . "Maxson gonna get us fired." I told
him to get away from me with that. He walked away from me calling
you a troublemaker. What Mr. Rand say?

TROY. Ain't said nothing. He told me to go down the Commissioner's office
next Friday. They called me down there to see them.

BONO. Well, as long as you got your complaint filed, they can't fire you.
That's what one of them white fellows tell me.

TROY. I ain't worried about them firing me. They gonna fire me cause I
asked a question? That's all I did. I went to Mr. Rand and asked him,
"Why? Why you got the white mens driving and the colored lifting?"
Told him, "what's the matter, don't I count? You think only white fellows got sense enough to drive a truck. That ain't no paper job! Hell,
anybody can drive a truck. How come you got all whites driving and
the colored lifting?" He told me "take it to the union." Well, hell, that's
what I done! Now they wanna come up with this pack of lies.

BONO. I told Brownie if the man come and ask him any questions . . . just tell
the truth! It ain't nothing but something they done trumped up on you
cause you filed a complaint on them.

TROY. Brownie don't understand nothing. All I want them to do is change the job description. Give everybody a chance to drive the truck. Brownie can't see that. He ain't got that much sense.

BONO. How you figure he be making out with that gal be up at Taylor's all the time . . . that Alberta gal?

TROY. Same as you and me. Getting just as much as we is. Which is to say nothing.

BONO. It is, huh? I figure you doing a little better than me . . . and I ain't saying what I'm doing.

TROY. Aw, nigger, look here . . . I know you. If you had got anywhere near that gal, twenty minutes later you be looking to tell somebody. And the first one you gonna tell . . . that you gonna want to brag to . . . is me.

BONO. I ain't saying that. I see where you be eyeing her.

TROY. I eye all the women. I don't miss nothing. Don't never let nobody tell you Troy Maxson don't eye the women.

BONO. You been doing more than eyeing her. You done bought her a drink or two.

TROY. Hell yeah, I bought her a drink! What that mean? I bought you one, too. What that mean cause I buy her a drink? I'm just being polite.

BONO. It's all right to buy her one drink. That's what you call being polite. But when you wanna be buying two or three . . . that's what you call eyeing her.

TROY. Look here, as long as you known me . . . you ever known me to chase after women?

BONO. Hell yeah! Long as I done known you. You forgetting I knew you when.

TROY. Naw, I'm talking about since I been married to Rose?

BONO. Oh, not since you been married to Rose. Now, that's the truth, there. I can say that.

TROY. All right then! Case closed.

BONO. I see you be walking up around Alberta's house. You supposed to be at Taylors' and you be walking up around there.

TROY. What you watching where I'm walking for? I ain't watching after you.

BONO. I seen you walking around there more than once.

TROY. Hell, you liable to see me walking anywhere! That don't mean nothing cause you see me walking around there.

BONO. Where she come from anyway? She just kinda showed up one day.

TROY. Tallahassee. You can look at her and tell she one of them Florida gals. They got some big healthy women down there. Grow them right up out the ground. Got a little bit of Indian in her. Most of them niggers down in Florida got some Indian in them.

BONO. I don't know about that Indian part. But she damn sure big and healthy. Woman wear some big stockings. Got them great big old legs and hips as wide as the Mississippi River.

TROY. Legs don't mean nothing. You don't do nothing but push them out of the way. But them hips cushion the ride!

BONO. Troy, you ain't got no sense.

TROY. It's the truth! Like you riding on Goodyears!

ROSE *enters from the house. She is ten years younger than* TROY, *her devotion to him stems from her recognition of the possibilities of her life without him: a succession of abusive men and their babies,*

*a life of partying and running the streets, the Church, or aloneness
with its attendant pain and frustration. She recognizes* TROY*'s spirit
as a fine and illuminating one and she either ignores or forgives his
faults, only some of which she recognizes. Though she doesn't drink,
her presence is an integral part of the Friday night rituals. She al-
ternates between the porch and the kitchen, where supper preparations are under way.*

ROSE. What you all out here getting into?

TROY. What you worried about what we getting into for? This is men talk,
woman.

ROSE. What I care what you all talking about? Bono, you gonna stay for
supper?

BONO. No, I thank you, Rose. But Lucille say she cooking up a pot of pigfeet.

TROY. Pigfeet! Hell, I'm going home with you! Might even stay the night if
you got some pigfeet. You got something in there to top them pigfeet,
Rose?

ROSE. I'm cooking up some chicken. I got some chicken and collard greens.

TROY. Well, go on back in the house and let me and Bono finish what we
was talking about. This is men talk. I got some talk for you later. You
know what kind of talk I mean. You go on and powder it up.

ROSE. Troy Maxson, don't you start that now!

TROY (*puts his arm around her*). Aw, woman . . . come here. Look here,
Bono . . . when I met this woman . . . I got out that place, say, "Hitch up
my pony, saddle up my mare . . . there's a woman out there for me
somewhere. I looked here. Looked there. Saw Rose and latched on to
her." I latched on to her and told her—I'm gonna tell you the truth—I
told her, "Baby, I don't wanna marry, I just wanna be your man." Rose
told me . . . tell him what you told me, Rose.

ROSE. I told him if he wasn't the marrying kind, then move out the way so
the marrying kind could find me.

TROY. That's what she told me. "Nigger, you in my way. You blocking the
view! Move out the way so I can find me a husband." I thought it over
two or three days. Come back—

ROSE. Ain't no two or three days nothing. You was back the same night.

TROY. Come back, told her . . . "Okay, baby . . . but I'm gonna buy me a
banty rooster and put him out there in the backyard . . . and when he
see a stranger come, he'll flap his wings and crow . . ." Look here,
Bono, I could watch the front door by myself . . . it was that back door
I was worried about.

ROSE. Troy, you ought not talk like that. Troy ain't doing nothing but telling
a lie.

TROY. Only thing is . . . when we first got married . . . forget the rooster . . . we
ain't had no yard!

BONO. I hear you tell it. Me and Lucille was staying down there on Logan
Street. Had two rooms with the outhouse in the back. I ain't mind the
outhouse none. But when that goddamn wind blow through there in
the winter . . . that's what I'm talking about! To this day I wonder why
in the hell I ever stayed down there for six long years. But see, I didn't
know I could do no better. I thought only white folks had inside toilets
and things.

ROSE. There's a lot of people don't know they can do no better than they doing now. That's just something you got to learn. A lot of folks still shop at Bella's.

TROY. Ain't nothing wrong with shopping at Bella's. She got fresh food.

ROSE. I ain't said nothing about if she got fresh food. I'm talking about what she charge. She charge ten cents more than the A&P.

TROY. The A&P ain't never done nothing for me. I spends my money where I'm treated right. I go down to Bella, say, "I need a loaf of bread, I'll pay you Friday." She give it to me. What sense that make when I got money to go and spend it somewhere else and ignore the person who done right by me? That ain't in the Bible.

ROSE. We ain't talking about what's in the Bible. What sense it make to shop there when she overcharge?

TROY. You shop where you want to. I'll do my shopping where the people been good to me.

ROSE. Well, I don't think it's right for her to overcharge. That's all I was saying.

BONO. Look here . . . I got to get on. Lucille going be raising all kind of hell.

TROY. Where you going, nigger? We ain't finished this pint. Come here, finish this pint.

BONO. Well, hell, I am . . . if you ever turn the bottle loose.

TROY (*hands him the bottle*). The only thing I say about the A&P is I'm glad Cory got that job down there. Help him take care of his school clothes and things. Gabe done moved out and things getting tight around here. He got that job . . . He can start to look out for himself.

ROSE. Cory done went and got recruited by a college football team.

TROY. I told that boy about that football stuff. The white man ain't gonna let him get nowhere with that football. I told him when he first come to me with it. Now you come telling me he done went and got more tied up in it. He ought to go and get recruited in how to fix cars or something where he can make a living.

ROSE. He ain't talking about making no living playing football. It's just something the boys in school do. They gonna send a recruiter by to talk to you. He'll tell you he ain't talking about making no living playing football. It's a honor to be recruited.

TROY. It ain't gonna get him nowhere. Bono'll tell you that.

BONO. If he be like you in the sports . . . he's gonna be all right. Ain't but two men ever played baseball as good as you. That's Babe Ruth and Josh Gibson.[1] Them's the only two men ever hit more home runs than you.

TROY. What it ever get me? Ain't got a pot to piss in or a window to throw it out of.

ROSE. Times have changed since you was playing baseball, Troy. That was before the war. Times have changed a lot since then.

TROY. How in hell they done changed?

ROSE. They got lots of colored boys playing ball now. Baseball and football.

BONO. You right about that, Rose. Times have changed, Troy. You just come along too early.

---

[1]**Josh Gibson** African-American ballplayer (1911–1947), known as the Babe Ruth of the Negro Leagues.

TROY. There ought not never have been no time called too early! Now you take that fellow . . . what's that fellow they had playing right field for the Yankees back then? You know who I'm talking about, Bono. Used to play right field for the Yankees.

ROSE. Selkirk?

TROY. Selkirk! That's it! Man batting .269, understand? .269. What kind of sense that make? I was hitting .432 with thirty-seven home runs! Man batting .269 and playing right field for the Yankees! I saw Josh Gibson's daughter yesterday. She walking around with raggedy shoes on her feet. Now I bet you Selkirk's daughter ain't walking around with raggedy shoes on her feet! I bet you that!

ROSE. They got a lot of colored baseball players now. Jackie Robinson[2] was the first. Folks had to wait for Jackie Robinson.

TROY. I done seen a hundred niggers play baseball better than Jackie Robinson. Hell, I know some teams Jackie Robinson couldn't even make! What you talking about Jackie Robinson. Jackie Robinson wasn't nobody. I'm talking about if you could play ball then they ought to have let you play. Don't care what color you were. Come telling me I come along too early. If you could play . . . then they ought to have let you play.

TROY *takes a long drink from the bottle.*

ROSE. You gonna drink yourself to death. You don't need to be drinking like that.

TROY. Death ain't nothing. I done seen him. Done wrassled with him. You can't tell me nothing about death. Death ain't nothing but a fastball on the outside corner. And you know what I'll do to that! Lookee here, Bono . . . am I lying? You get one of them fastballs, about waist high, over the outside corner of the plate where you can get the meat of the bat on it . . . and good god! You can kiss it goodbye. Now, am I lying?

BONO. Naw, you telling the truth there. I seen you do it.

TROY. If I'm lying . . . that 450 feet worth of lying! (*Pause.*) That's all death is to me. A fastball on the outside corner.

ROSE. I don't know why you want to get on talking about death.

TROY. Ain't nothing wrong with talking about death. That's part of life. Everybody gonna die. You gonna die, I'm gonna die. Bono's gonna die. Hell, we all gonna die.

ROSE. But you ain't got to talk about it. I don't like to talk about it.

TROY. You the one brought it up. Me and Bono was talking about baseball . . . you tell me I'm gonna drink myself to death. Ain't that right, Bono? You know I don't drink this but one night out of the week. That's Friday night. I'm gonna drink just enough to where I can handle it. Then I cuts it loose. I leave it alone. So don't you worry about me drinking myself to death. 'Cause I ain't worried about Death. I done seen him. I done wrestled with him.

Look here, Bono . . . I looked up one day and Death was marching straight at me. Like Soldiers on Parade! The Army of Death was

---

[2]**Jackie Robinson** In 1947 Robinson (1919–1972) became the first African-American to play baseball in the major leagues.

marching straight at me. The middle of July, 1941. It got real cold just like it be winter. It seem like Death himself reached out and touched me on the shoulder. He touch me just like I touch you. I got cold as ice and Death standing there grinning at me.

ROSE. Troy, why don't you hush that talk.

TROY. I say . . . what you want, Mr. Death? You be wanting me? You done brought your army to be getting me? I looked him dead in the eye. I wasn't fearing nothing. I was ready to tangle. Just like I'm ready to tangle now. The Bible say be ever vigilant. That's why I don't get but so drunk. I got to keep watch.

ROSE. Troy was right down there in Mercy Hospital. You remember he had pneumonia? Laying there with a fever talking plumb out of his head.

TROY. Death standing there staring at me . . . carrying that sickle in his hand. Finally he say, "You want bound over for another year?" See, just like that . . . "You want bound over for another year?" I told him, "Bound over hell! Let's settle this now!"

It seem like he kinda fell back when I said that, and all the cold went out of me. I reached down and grabbed that sickle and threw it just as far as I could throw it . . . and me and him commenced to wrestling.

We wrestled for three days and three nights. I can't say where I found the strength from. Everytime it seemed like he was gonna get the best of me, I'd reach way down deep inside myself and find the strength to do him one better.

ROSE. Everytime Troy tell that story he find different ways to tell it. Different things to make up about it.

TROY. I ain't making up nothing. I'm telling you the facts of what happened. I wrestled with Death for three days and three nights and I'm standing here to tell you about it. (*Pause.*) All right. At the end of the third night we done weakened each other to where we can't hardly move. Death stood up, throwed on his robe . . . had him a white robe with a hood on it. He throwed on that robe and went off to look for his sickle. Say, "I'll be back." Just like that. "I'll be back." I told him, say, "Yeah, but . . . you gonna have to find me!" I wasn't no fool. I wasn't going looking for him. Death ain't nothing to play with. And I know he's gonna get me. I know I got to join his army . . . his camp followers. But as long as I keep my strength and see him coming . . . as long as I keep up my vigilance . . . he's gonna have to fight to get me. I ain't going easy.

BONO. Well, look here, since you got to keep up your vigilance . . . let me have the bottle.

TROY. Aw hell, I shouldn't have told you that part. I should have left out that part.

ROSE. Troy be talking that stuff and half the time don't even know what he be talking about.

TROY. Bono know me better than that.

BONO. That's right. I know you. I know you got some Uncle Remus[3] in your blood. You got more stories than the devil got sinners.

TROY. Aw hell, I done seen him too! Done talked with the devil.

ROSE. Troy, don't nobody wanna be hearing all that stuff.

---

[3]**Uncle Remus** narrator of traditional black tales in a book by Joel Chandler Harris.

LYONS *enters the yard from the street. Thirty-four years old,* TROY*'s son by a previous marriage, he sports a neatly trimmed goatee, sport coat, white shirt, tieless and buttoned at the collar. Though he fancies himself a musician, he is more caught up in the rituals and "idea" of being a musician than in the actual practice of the music. He has come to borrow money from* TROY, *and while he knows he will be successful, he is uncertain as to what extent his lifestyle will be held up to scrutiny and ridicule.*

LYONS. Hey, Pop.

TROY. What you come "Hey, Popping" me for?

LYONS. How you doing, Rose? (*He kisses her.*) Mr. Bono. How you doing?

BONO. Hey, Lyons . . . how you been?

TROY. He must have been doing all right. I ain't seen him around here last week.

ROSE. Troy, leave your boy alone. He come by to see you and you wanna start all that nonsense.

TROY. I ain't bothering Lyons. (*Offers him the bottle.*) Here . . . get you a drink. We got an understanding. I know why he come by to see me and he know I know.

LYONS. Come on, Pop . . . I just stopped by to say hi . . . see how you was doing.

TROY. You ain't stopped by yesterday.

ROSE. You gonna stay for supper, Lyons? I got some chicken cooking in the oven.

LYONS. No, Rose . . . thanks. I was just in the neighborhood and thought I'd stop by for a minute.

TROY. You was in the neighborhood all right, nigger. You telling the truth there. You was in the neighborhood cause it's my payday.

LYONS. Well, hell, since you mentioned it . . . let me have ten dollars.

TROY. I'll be damned! I'll die and go to hell and play blackjack with the devil before I give you ten dollars.

BONO. That's what I wanna know about . . . that devil you done seen.

LYONS. What . . . Pop done seen the devil? You too much, Pops.

TROY. Yeah, I done seen him. Talked to him too!

ROSE. You ain't seen no devil. I done told you that man ain't had nothing to do with the devil. Anything you can't understand, you want to call it the devil.

TROY. Look here, Bono . . . I went down to see Hertzberger about some furniture. Got three rooms for two-ninety-eight. That what it say on the radio. "Three rooms . . . two-ninety-eight." Even made up a little song about it. Go down there . . . man tell me I can't get no credit. I'm working every day and can't get no credit. What to do? I got an empty house with some raggedy furniture in it. Cory ain't got no bed. He's sleeping on a pile of rags on the floor. Working every day and can't get no credit. Come back here—Rose'll tell you—madder than hell. Sit down . . . try to figure what I'm gonna do. Come a knock on the door. Ain't been living here but three days. Who know I'm here? Open the door . . . devil standing there bigger than life. White fellow . . . white fellow . . . got on good clothes and everything. Standing there with a clipboard in his hand. I ain't had to say nothing. First words come out of his mouth

was . . . "I understand you need some furniture and can't get no credit."
I liked to fell over. He say, "I'll give you all the credit you want, but you
got to pay the interest on it." I told him, "Give me three rooms worth and
charge whatever you want." Next day a truck pulled up here and two
men unloaded them three rooms. Man what drove the truck give me a
book. Say send ten dollars, first of every month to the address in the book
and every thing will be all right. Say if I miss a payment the devil was
coming back and it'll be hell to pay. That was fifteen years ago. To this
day . . . the first of the month I send my ten dollars, Rose'll tell you.

ROSE.   Troy lying.

TROY.   I ain't never seen that man since. Now you tell me who else that
could have been but the devil? I ain't sold my soul or nothing like that,
you understand. Naw, I wouldn't have truck with the devil about nothing like that. I got my furniture and pays my ten dollars the first of the
month just like clockwork.

BONO.   How long you say you been paying this ten dollars a month?

TROY.   Fifteen years!

BONO.   Hell, ain't you finished paying for it yet? How much the man done
charged you?

TROY.   Ah hell, I done paid for it. I done paid for it ten times over! The fact is
I'm scared to stop paying it.

ROSE.   Troy lying. We got that furniture from Mr. Glickman. He ain't paying
no ten dollars a month to nobody.

TROY.   Aw hell, woman. Bono know I ain't that big a fool.

LYONS.   I was just getting ready to say . . . I know where there's a bridge
for sale.

TROY.   Look here, I'll tell you this . . . it don't matter to me if he was the devil.
It don't matter if the devil give credit. Somebody has got to give it.

ROSE.   It ought to matter. You going around talking about having truck with
the devil . . . God's the one you gonna have to answer to. He's the one
gonna be at the Judgment.

LYONS.   Yeah, well, look here, Pop . . . Let me have that ten dollars. I'll give it
back to you. Bonnie got a job working at the hospital.

TROY.   What I tell you, Bono? The only time I see this nigger is when he
wants something. That's the only time I see him.

LYONS.   Come on, Pop, Mr. Bono don't want to hear all that. Let me have the
ten dollars. I told you Bonnie working.

TROY.   What that mean to me? "Bonnie working." I don't care if she working. Go ask her for the ten dollars if she working. Talking about "Bonnie working." Why ain't you working?

LYONS.   Aw, Pop, you know I can't find no decent job. Where am I gonna get
a job at? You know I can't get no job.

TROY.   I told you I know some people down there. I can get you on the rubbish if you want to work. I told you that the last time you came by here
asking me for something.

LYONS.   Naw, Pop . . . thanks. That ain't for me. I don't wanna be carrying
nobody's rubbish. I don't wanna be punching nobody's time clock.

TROY.   What's the matter, you too good to carry people's rubbish? Where
you think that ten dollars you talking about come from? I'm just supposed to haul people's rubbish and give my money to you cause you
too lazy to work. You too lazy to work and wanna know why you ain't
got what I got.

ROSE. What hospital Bonnie working at? Mercy?

LYONS. She's down at Passavant working in the laundry.

TROY. I ain't got nothing as it is. I give you that ten dollars and I got to eat beans the rest of the week. Naw . . . you ain't getting no ten dollars here.

LYONS. You ain't got to be eating no beans. I don't know why you wanna say that.

TROY. I ain't got no extra money. Gabe done moved over to Miss Pearl's paying her the rent and things done got tight around here. I can't afford to be giving you every payday.

LYONS. I ain't asked you to give me nothing. I asked you to loan me ten dollars. I know you got ten dollars.

TROY. Yeah, I got it. You know why I got it? Cause I don't throw my money away out there in the streets. You living the fast life . . . wanna be a musician . . . running around in them clubs and things . . . then, you learn to take care of yourself. You ain't gonna find me going and asking nobody for nothing. I done spent too many years without.

LYONS. You and me is two different people, Pop.

TROY. I done learned my mistake and learned to do what's right by it. You still trying to get something for nothing. Life don't owe you nothing. You owe it to yourself. Ask Bono. He'll tell you I'm right.

LYONS. You got your way of dealing with the world . . . I got mine. The only thing that matters to me is the music.

TROY. Yeah, I can see that! It don't matter how you gonna eat . . . where your next dollar is coming from. You telling the truth there.

LYONS. I know I got to eat. But I got to live too. I need something that gonna help me to get out of the bed in the morning. Make me feel like I belong in the world. I don't bother nobody. I just stay with the music cause that's the only way I can find to live in the world. Otherwise there ain't no telling what I might do. Now I don't come criticizing you and how you live. I just come by to ask you for ten dollars. I don't wanna hear all that about how I live.

TROY. Boy, your mamma did a hell of a job raising you.

LYONS. You can't change me, Pop. I'm thirty-four years old. If you wanted to change me, you should have been there when I was growing up. I come by to see you . . . ask for ten dollars and you want to talk about how I was raised. You don't know nothing about how I was raised.

ROSE. Let the boy have ten dollars, Troy.

TROY (*to* LYONS). What the hell you looking at me for? I ain't got no ten dollars. You know what I do with my money. (*To* ROSE.) Give him ten dollars if you want him to have it.

ROSE. I will. Just as soon as you turn it loose.

TROY (*handing* ROSE *the money*). There it is. Seventy-six dollars and forty-two cents. You see this, Bono? Now, I ain't gonna get but six of that back.

ROSE. You ought to stop telling that lie. Here, Lyons. (*She hands him the money.*)

LYONS. Thanks, Rose. Look . . . I got to run . . . I'll see you later.

TROY. Wait a minute. You gonna say, "thanks, Rose" and ain't gonna look to see where she got that ten dollars from? See how they do me, Bono?

LYONS. I know she got it from you, Pop. Thanks. I'll give it back to you.

TROY. There he go telling another lie. Time I see that ten dollars . . . he'll be owing me thirty more.

LYONS. See you, Mr. Bono.

BONO. Take care, Lyons!

LYONS. Thanks, Pop. I'll see you again.

　　　　LYONS *exits the yard.*

TROY. I don't know why he don't go and get him a decent job and take care of that woman he got.

BONO. He'll be all right, Troy. The boy is still young.

TROY. The *boy* is thirty-four years old.

ROSE. Let's not get off into all that.

BONO. Look here . . . I got to be going. I got to be getting on. Lucille gonna be waiting.

TROY (*puts his arm around* ROSE). See this woman, Bono? I love this woman. I love this woman so much it hurts. I love her so much . . . I done run out of ways of loving her. So I got to go back to basics. Don't you come by my house Monday morning talking about time to go to work . . . . 'cause I'm still gonna be stroking!

ROSE. Troy! Stop it now!

BONO. I ain't paying him no mind, Rose. That ain't nothing but gin-talk. Go on, Troy. I'll see you Monday.

TROY. Don't you come by my house, nigger! I done told you what I'm gonna be doing.

　　　　The lights go down to black.

Scene 2

The lights come up on ROSE *hanging up clothes. She hums and sings softly to herself. It is the following morning.*

ROSE (*sings*).

　　　　　　Jesus, be a fence all around me every day

　　　　　　Jesus, I want you to protect me as I travel on my way.

　　　　　　Jesus, be a fence all around me every day.

TROY *enters from the house.*

　　　　　　Jesus, I want you to protect me

　　　　　　As I travel on my way.

　　　(*To* TROY.) 'Morning. You ready for breakfast? I can fix it soon as I finish hanging up these clothes.

TROY. I got the coffee on. That'll be all right. I'll just drink some of that this morning.

ROSE. That 651 hit yesterday. That's the second time this month. Miss Pearl hit for a dollar . . . seem like those that need the least always get lucky. Poor folks can't get nothing.

TROY. Them numbers don't know nobody. I don't know why you fool with them. You and Lyons both.

ROSE. It's something to do.

TROY. You ain't doing nothing but throwing your money away.

ROSE. Troy, you know I don't play foolishly. I just play a nickel here and a nickel there.

TROY. That's two nickels you done thrown away.

ROSE. Now I hit sometimes . . . that makes up for it. It always comes in handy when I do hit. I don't hear you complaining then.

TROY. I ain't complaining now. I just say it's foolish. Trying to guess out of six hundred ways which way the number gonna come. If I had all the money niggers, these Negroes, throw away on numbers for one week—just one week—I'd be a rich man.

ROSE. Well, you wishing and calling it foolish ain't gonna stop folks from playing numbers. That's one thing for sure. Besides . . . some good things come from playing numbers. Look where Pope done bought him that restaurant off of numbers.

TROY. I can't stand niggers like that. Man ain't had two dimes to rub to- gether. He walking around with his shoes all run over bumming money for cigarettes. All right. Got lucky there and hit the numbers . . .

ROSE. Troy, I know all about it.

TROY. Had good sense, I'll say that for him. He ain't throwed his money away. I seen niggers hit the numbers and go through two thousand dol- lars in four days. Man bought him that restaurant down there . . . fixed it up real nice . . . and then didn't want nobody to come in it! A Negro go in there and can't get no kind of service. I seen a white fellow come in there and order a bowl of stew. Pope picked all the meat out of the pot for him. Man ain't had nothing but a bowl of meat! Negro come be- hind him and ain't got nothing but the potatoes and carrots. Talking about what numbers do for people, you picked a wrong example. Ain't done nothing but make a worser fool out of him than he was before.

ROSE. Troy, you ought to stop worrying about what happened at work yes- terday.

TROY. I ain't worried. Just told me to be down there at the Commissioner's office on Friday. Everybody think they gonna fire me. I ain't worried about them firing me. You ain't got to worry about that. (*Pause.*) Where's Cory? Cory in the house? (*Calls.*) Cory?

ROSE. He gone out.

TROY. Out, huh? He gone out 'cause he know I want him to help me with this fence. I know how he is. That boy scared of work.

GABRIEL *enters. He comes halfway down the alley and, hearing* TROY*'s voice, stops.*

TROY (*continues*). He ain't done a lick of work in his life.

ROSE. He had to go to football practice. Coach wanted them to get in a little extra practice before the season start.

TROY. I got his practice . . . running out of here before he get his chores done.

ROSE. Troy, what is wrong with you this morning? Don't nothing set right with you. Go on back in there and go to bed . . . get up on the other side.

TROY. Why something got to be wrong with me? I ain't said nothing wrong with me.

ROSE. You got something to say about everything. First it's the numbers . . . then it's the way the man runs his restaurant . . . then you done got on Cory. What's it gonna be next? Take a look up there and see if the weather suits you . . . or is it gonna be how you gonna put up the fence with the clothes hanging in the yard?

TROY. You hit the nail on the head then.

ROSE. I know you like I know the back of my hand. Go on in there and get you some coffee . . . see if that straighten you up. 'Cause you ain't right this morning.

> TROY *starts into the house and sees* GABRIEL. GABRIEL *starts singing.* TROY's *brother, he is seven years younger than* TROY. *Injured in World War II, he has a metal plate in his head. He carries an old trumpet tied around his waist and believes with every fiber of his being that he is the Archangel Gabriel. He carries a chipped basket with an assortment of discarded fruits and vegetables he has picked up in the strip district and which he attempts to sell.*

GABRIEL (*singing*).

> Yes, ma'am I got plums
> You ask me how I sell them
> Oh ten cents apiece
> Three for a quarter
> Come and buy now
> 'Cause I'm here today
> And tomorrow I'll be gone

> GABRIEL *enters.*

Hey, Rose!

ROSE. How you doing, Gabe?

GABRIEL. There's Troy . . . Hey, Troy!

TROY. Hey, Gabe.

> *Exit into kitchen.*

ROSE (*to* GABRIEL). What you got there?

GABRIEL. You know what I got, Rose. I got fruits and vegetables.

ROSE (*looking in basket*). Where's all these plums you talking about?

GABRIEL. I ain't got no plums today, Rose. I was just singing that. Have some tomorrow. Put me in a big order for plums. Have enough plums tomorrow for St. Peter and everybody.

> TROY *reenters from kitchen, crosses to steps.*

(*To* ROSE.) Troy's mad at me.

TROY. I ain't mad at you. What I got to be mad at you about? You ain't done nothing to me.

GABRIEL. I just moved over to Miss Pearl's to keep out from in your way. I ain't mean no harm by it.

TROY. Who said anything about that? I ain't said anything about that.

GABRIEL. You ain't mad at me, is you?

TROY. Naw . . . I ain't mad at you, Gabe. If I was mad at you I'd tell you about it.

GABRIEL. Got me two rooms. In the basement. Got my own door too. Wanna see my key? (*He holds up a key.*) That's my own key! My two rooms!

TROY. Well, that's good, Gabe. You got your own key . . . that's good.

ROSE. You hungry, Gabe? I was just fixing to cook Troy his breakfast.

GABRIEL. I'll take some biscuits. You got some biscuits? Did you know when I was in heaven . . . every morning me and St. Peter would sit down by the gate and eat some big fat biscuits? Oh, yeah! We had us a good time. We'd sit there and eat us them biscuits and then St. Peter would go off to sleep and tell me to wake him up when it's time to open the gates for the judgment.

ROSE. Well, come on . . . I'll make up a batch of biscuits.

ROSE *exits into the house.*

GABRIEL. Troy . . . St. Peter got your name in the book. I seen it. It say . . . Troy Maxson. I say . . . I know him! He got the same name like what I got. That's my brother!

TROY. How many times you gonna tell me that, Gabe?

GABRIEL. Ain't got my name in the book. Don't have to have my name. I done died and went to heaven. He got your name though. One morning St. Peter was looking at his book . . . marking it up for the judgment . . . and he let me see your name. Got it in there under M. Got Rose's name . . . I ain't seen it like I seen yours . . . but I know it's in there. He got a great big book. Got everybody's name what was ever been born. That's what he told me. But I seen your name. Seen it with my own eyes.

TROY. Go on in the house there. Rose going to fix you something to eat.

GABRIEL. Oh, I ain't hungry. I done had breakfast with Aunt Jemimah. She come by and cooked me up a whole mess of flapjacks. Remember how we used to eat them flapjacks?

TROY. Go on in the house and get you something to eat now.

GABRIEL. I got to sell my plums. I done sold some tomatoes. Got me two quarters. Wanna see? (*He shows* TROY *his quarters.*) I'm gonna save them and buy me a new horn so St. Peter can hear me when it's time to open the gates. (GABRIEL *stops suddenly. Listens.*) Hear that? That's the hellhounds. I got to chase them out of here. Go on get out of here! Get out!

GABRIEL *exits singing.*

> Better get ready for the judgment
> Better get ready for the judgment
> My Lord is coming down

ROSE *enters from the house.*

TROY. He's gone off somewhere.

GABRIEL (*offstage*).

> Better get ready for the judgment
> Better get ready for the judgment morning
> Better get ready for the judgment
> My God is coming down

ROSE. He ain't eating right. Miss Pearl say she can't get him to eat nothing.

TROY. What you want me to do about it, Rose? I done did everything I can for the man. I can't make him get well. Man got half his head blown away . . . what you expect?

ROSE. Seem like something ought to be done to help him.

TROY. Man don't bother nobody. He just mixed up from that metal plate he got in his head. Ain't no sense for him to go back into the hospital.

ROSE. Least he be eating right. They can help him take care of himself.

TROY. Don't nobody wanna be locked up, Rose. What you wanna lock him up for? Man go over there and fight the war . . . messin' around with them Japs, get half his head blown off . . . and they give him a lousy three thousand dollars. And I had to swoop down on that.

ROSE. Is you fixing to go into that again?

TROY. That's the only way I got a roof over my head . . . cause of that metal plate.

ROSE. Ain't no sense you blaming yourself for nothing. Gabe wasn't in no condition to manage that money. You done what was right by him. Can't nobody say you ain't done what was right by him. Look how long you took care of him . . . till he wanted to have his own place and moved over there with Miss Pearl.

TROY. That ain't what I'm saying, woman! I'm just stating the facts. If my brother didn't have that metal plate in his head . . . I wouldn't have a pot to piss in or a window to throw it out of. And I'm fifty-three years old. Now see if you can understand that!

TROY *gets up from the porch and starts to exit the yard.*

ROSE. Where you going off to? You been running out of here every Saturday for weeks. I thought you was gonna work on this fence?

TROY. I'm gonna walk down to Taylors'. Listen to the ball game. I'll be back in a bit. I'll work on it when I get back.

He exits the yard. The lights go to black.

Scene 3

The lights come up on the yard. It is four hours later. ROSE *is taking down the clothes from the line.* CORY *enters carrying his football equipment.*

ROSE. Your daddy like to had a fit with you running out of here this morning without doing your chores.

CORY. I told you I had to go to practice.

ROSE. He say you were supposed to help him with this fence.

CORY. He been saying that the last four or five Saturdays, and then he don't never do nothing, but go down to Taylors'. Did you tell him about the recruiter?

ROSE. Yeah, I told him.

CORY. What he say?

ROSE. He ain't said nothing too much. You get in there and get started on your chores before he gets back. Go on and scrub down them steps before he gets back here hollering and carrying on.

CORY. I'm hungry. What you got to eat, Mama?

ROSE. Go on and get started on your chores. I got some meat loaf in there. Go on and make you a sandwich . . . and don't leave no mess in there.

CORY *exits into the house.* ROSE *continues to take down the clothes.* TROY *enters the yard and sneaks up and grabs her from behind.*

Troy! Go on, now. You liked to scared me to death. What was the score of the game? Lucille had me on the phone and I couldn't keep up with it.

TROY. What I care about the game? Come here, woman. (*He tries to kiss her.*)

ROSE. I thought you went down Taylors' to listen to the game. Go on, Troy! You supposed to be putting up this fence.

TROY (*attempting to kiss her again*). I'll put it up when I finish with what is at hand.

ROSE. Go on, Troy. I ain't studying you.

TROY (*chasing after her*). I'm studying you . . . fixing to do my homework!

ROSE. Troy, you better leave me alone.

TROY. Where's Cory? That boy brought his butt home yet?

ROSE. He's in the house doing his chores.

TROY (*calling*). Cory! Get your butt out here, boy!

> ROSE *exits into the house with the laundry.* TROY *goes over to the pile of wood, picks up a board, and starts sawing.* CORY *enters from the house.*

TROY. You just now coming in here from leaving this morning?

CORY. Yeah, I had to go to football practice.

TROY. Yeah, what?

CORY. Yessir.

TROY. I ain't but two seconds off you noway. The garbage sitting in there overflowing . . . you ain't done none of your chores . . . and you come in here talking about "Yeah."

CORY. I was just getting ready to do my chores now, Pop . . .

TROY. Your first chore is to help me with this fence on Saturday. Everything else come after that. Now get that saw and cut them boards.

> CORY *takes the saw and begins cutting the boards.* TROY *continues working. There is a long pause.*

CORY. Hey, Pop . . . why don't you buy a TV?

TROY. What I want with a TV? What I want one of them for?

CORY. Everybody got one. Earl, Ba Bra . . . Jesse!

TROY. I ain't asked you who had one. I say what I want with one?

CORY. So you can watch it. They got lots of things on TV. Baseball games and everything. We could watch the World Series.

TROY. Yeah . . . and how much this TV cost?

CORY. I don't know. They got them on sale for around two hundred dollars.

TROY. Two hundred dollars, huh?

CORY. That ain't that much, Pop.

TROY. Naw, it's just two hundred dollars. See that roof you got over your head at night? Let me tell you something about that roof. It's been over ten years since that roof was last tarred. See now . . . the snow come this winter and sit up there on that roof like it is . . . and it's gonna seep inside. It's just gonna be a little bit . . . ain't gonna hardly notice it. Then the next thing you know, it's gonna be leaking all over the house. Then the wood rot from all that water and you gonna need a whole new roof. Now, how much you think it cost to get that roof tarred?

CORY. I don't know.

TROY. Two hundred and sixty-four dollars . . . cash money. While you thinking about a TV, I got to be thinking about the roof . . . and whatever else go wrong here. Now if you had two hundred dollars, what would you do . . . fix the roof or buy a TV?

CORY. I'd buy a TV. Then when the roof started to leak . . . when it needed fixing . . . I'd fix it.

TROY. Where you gonna get the money from? You done spent it for a TV. You gonna sit up and watch the water run all over your brand new TV.

CORY. Aw, Pop. You got money. I know you do.

TROY. Where I got it at, huh?

CORY. You got it in the bank.

TROY. You wanna see my bankbook? You wanna see that seventy-three dollars and twenty-two cents I got sitting up in there?

CORY. You ain't got to pay for it all at one time. You can put a down payment on it and carry it on home with you.

TROY. Not me. I ain't gonna owe nobody nothing if I can help it. Miss a payment and they come and snatch it right out of your house. Then what you got? Now, soon as I get two hundred dollars clear, then I'll buy a TV. Right now, as soon as I get two hundred and sixty-four dollars, I'm gonna have this roof tarred.

CORY. Aw . . . Pop!

TROY. You go on and get you two hundred dollars and buy one if ya want it. I got better things to do with my money.

CORY. I can't get no two hundred dollars. I ain't never seen two hundred dollars.

TROY. I'll tell you what . . . you get you a hundred dollars and I'll put the other hundred with it.

CORY. All right, I'm gonna show you.

TROY. You gonna show me how you can cut them boards right now.

CORY *begins to cut the boards. There is a long pause.*

CORY. The Pirates won today. That makes five in a row.

TROY. I ain't thinking about the Pirates. Got an all-white team. Got that boy . . . that Puerto Rican boy . . . Clemente. Don't even half-play him. That boy could be something if they give him a chance. Play him one day and sit him on the bench the next.

CORY. He gets a lot of chances to play.

TROY. I'm talking about playing regular. Playing every day so you can get your timing. That's what I'm talking about.

CORY. They got some white guys on the team that don't play every day. You can't play everybody at the same time.

TROY. If they got a white fellow sitting on the bench . . . you can bet your last dollar he can't play! The colored guy got to be twice as good before he get on the team. That's why I don't want you to get all tied up in them sports. Man on the team and what it get him? They got colored on the team and don't use them. Same as not having them. All them teams the same.

CORY. The Braves got Hank Aaron and Wes Covington. Hank Aaron hit two home runs today. That makes forty-three.

TROY. Hank Aaron ain't nobody. That what you supposed to do. That's how you supposed to play the game. Ain't nothing to it. It's just a matter of timing . . . getting the right follow-through. Hell, I can hit forty-three home runs right now!

CORY. Not off no major-league pitching, you couldn't.

TROY. We had better pitching in the Negro leagues. I hit seven home runs off of Satchel Paige.[4] You can't get no better than that!

---

[4]**Satchel Paige** (1906–1982) pitcher in the Negro leagues.

CORY. Sandy Koufax. He's leading the league in strikeouts.

TROY. I ain't thinking of no Sandy Koufax.

CORY. You got Warren Spahn and Lew Burdette. I bet you couldn't hit no home runs off of Warren Spahn.

TROY. I'm through with it now. You go on and cut them boards. (*Pause.*) Your mama tell me you done got recruited by a college football team? Is that right?

CORY. Yeah. Coach Zellman say the recruiter gonna be coming by to talk to you. Get you to sign the permission papers.

TROY. I thought you supposed to be working down there at the A&P. Ain't you suppose to be working down there after school?

CORY. Mr. Stawicki say he gonna hold my job for me until after the football season. Say starting next week I can work weekends.

TROY. I thought we had an understanding about this football stuff? You suppose to keep up with your chores and hold that job down at the A&P. Ain't been around here all day on a Saturday. Ain't none of your chores done . . . and now you telling me you done quit your job.

CORY. I'm going to be working weekends.

TROY. You damn right you are! And ain't no need for nobody coming around here to talk to me about signing nothing.

CORY. Hey, Pop . . . you can't do that. He's coming all the way from North Carolina.

TROY. I don't care where he coming from. The white man ain't gonna let you get nowhere with that football noway. You go on and get your book-learning so you can work yourself up in that A&P or learn how to fix cars or build houses or something, get you a trade. That way you have something can't nobody take away from you. You go on and learn how to put your hands to some good use. Besides hauling people's garbage.

CORY. I get good grades, Pop. That's why the recruiter wants to talk with you. You got to keep up your grades to get recruited. This way I'll be going to college. I'll get a chance . . .

TROY. First you gonna get your butt down there to the A&P and get your job back.

CORY. Mr. Stawicki done already hired somebody else 'cause I told him I was playing football.

TROY. You a bigger fool than I thought . . . to let somebody take away your job so you can play some football. Where you gonna get your money to take out your girlfriend and whatnot? What kind of foolishness is that to let somebody take away your job?

CORY. I'm still gonna be working weekends.

TROY. Naw . . . naw. You getting your butt out of here and finding you another job.

CORY. Come on, Pop! I got to practice. I can't work after school and play football too. The team needs me. That's what Coach Zellman say . . .

TROY. I don't care what nobody else say. I'm the boss . . . you understand? I'm the boss around here. I do the only saying what counts.

CORY. Come on, Pop!

TROY. I asked you . . . did you understand?

CORY. Yeah . . .

TROY. What?!

CORY. Yessir.

TROY. You go on down there to that A&P and see if you can get your job
　　　back. If you can't do both . . . then you quit the football team. You've
　　　got to take the crookeds with the straights.

CORY. Yessir. (*Pause.*) Can I ask you a question?

TROY. What the hell you wanna ask me? Mr. Stawicki the one you got the
　　　questions for.

CORY. How come you ain't never liked me?

TROY. Liked you? Who the hell say I got to like you? What law is there say
　　　I got to like you? Wanna stand up in my face and ask a damn foolass
　　　question like that. Talking about liking somebody. Come here, boy,
　　　when I talk to you.

　　　CORY *comes over to where* TROY *is working. He stands slouched over
　　　and* TROY *shoves him on his shoulder.*

　　　Straighten up, goddammit! I asked you a question . . . what law is there
　　　say I got to like you?

CORY. None.

TROY. Well, all right then! Don't you eat every day? (*Pause.*) Answer me
　　　when I talk to you! Don't you eat every day?

CORY. Yeah.

TROY. Nigger, as long as you in my house, you put that sir on the end of it
　　　when you talk to me.

CORY. Yes . . . sir.

TROY. You eat every day.

CORY. Yessir!

TROY. Got a roof over your head.

CORY. Yessir!

TROY. Got clothes on your back.

CORY. Yessir.

TROY. Why you think that is?

CORY. Cause of you.

TROY. Ah, hell I know it's cause of me . . . but why do you think that is?

CORY (*hesitant*). Cause you like me.

TROY. Like you? I go out of here every morning . . . bust my butt . . . putting
　　　up with them crackers every day . . . cause I like you? You are the
　　　biggest fool I ever saw. (*Pause.*) It's my job. It's my responsibility! You
　　　understand that? A man got to take care of his family. You live in my
　　　house . . . sleep you behind on my bedclothes . . . fill you belly up with
　　　my food . . . cause you my son. You my flesh and blood. Not cause I like
　　　you! Cause it's my duty to take care of you. I owe a responsibility
　　　to you! Let's get this straight right here . . . before it go along any
　　　further . . . I ain't got to like you. Mr. Rand don't give me my money
　　　come payday cause he likes me. He give me cause he owe me. I done
　　　give you everything I had to give you. I gave you your life! Me and your
　　　mama worked that out between us. And liking your black ass wasn't
　　　part of the bargain. Don't you try and go through life worrying about if
　　　somebody like you or not. You best be making sure they doing right by
　　　you. You understand what I'm saying, boy?

CORY. Yessir.

TROY. Then get the hell out of my face, and get on down to that A&P.

ROSE *has been standing behind the screen door for much of the scene. She enters as* CORY *exits.*

ROSE. Why don't you let the boy go ahead and play football, Troy? Ain't no harm in that. He's just trying to be like you with the sports.

TROY. I don't want him to be like me! I want him to move as far away from my life as he can get. You the only decent thing that ever happened to me. I wish him that. But I don't wish him a thing else from my life. I decided seventeen years ago that boy wasn't getting involved in no sports. Not after what they did to me in the sports.

ROSE. Troy, why don't you admit you was too old to play in the major leagues? For once . . . why don't you admit that?

TROY. What do you mean too old? Don't come telling me I was too old. I just wasn't the right color. Hell, I'm fifty-three years old and can do better than Selkirk's .269 right now!

ROSE. How's was you gonna play ball when you were over forty? Sometimes I can't get no sense out of you.

TROY. I got good sense, woman. I got sense enough not to let my boy get hurt over playing no sports. You been mothering that boy too much. Worried about if people like him.

ROSE. Everything that boy do . . . he do for you. He wants you to say "Good job, son." That's all.

TROY. Rose, I ain't got time for that. He's alive. He's healthy. He's got to make his own way. I made mine. Ain't nobody gonna hold his hand when he get out there in that world.

ROSE. Times have changed from when you was young, Troy. People change. The world's changing around you and you can't even see it.

TROY (*slow, methodical*). Woman . . . I do the best I can do. I come in here every Friday. I carry a sack of potatoes and a bucket of lard. You all line up at the door with your hands out. I give you the lint from my pockets. I give you my sweat and my blood. I ain't got no tears. I done spent them. We go upstairs in that room at night . . . and I fall down on you and try to blast a hole into forever. I get up Monday morning . . . find my lunch on the table. I go out. Make my way. Find my strength to carry me through to the next Friday. (*Pause.*) That's all I got, Rose. That's all I got to give. I can't give nothing else.

TROY *exits into the house. The lights go down to black.*

Scene 4

It is Friday. Two weeks later. CORY *starts out of the house with his football equipment. The phone rings.*

CORY (*calling*). I got it! (*He answers the phone and stands in the screen door talking.*) Hello? Hey, Jesse. Naw . . . I was just getting ready to leave now.

ROSE (*calling*). Cory!

CORY. I told you, man, them spikes is all tore up. You can use them if you want, but they ain't no good. Earl got some spikes.

ROSE (*calling*). Cory!

CORY (*calling to* ROSE). Mam? I'm talking to Jesse. (*Into phone.*) When she say that? (*Pause.*) Aw, you lying, man. I'm gonna tell her you said that.

ROSE (*calling*). Cory, don't you go nowhere!

CORY. I got to go to the game, Ma! (*Into the phone.*) Yeah, hey, look, I'll talk to you later. Yeah, I'll meet you over Earl's house. Later. Bye, Ma.

CORY *exits the house and starts out the yard.*

ROSE. Cory, where you going off to? You got that stuff all pulled out and thrown all over your room.

CORY (*in the yard*). I was looking for my spikes. Jesse wanted to borrow my spikes.

ROSE. Get up there and get that cleaned up before your daddy get back in here.

CORY. I got to go to the game! I'll clean it up *when I get back.*

CORY *exits.*

ROSE. That's all he need to do is see that room all messed up.

ROSE *exits into the house.* TROY *and* BONO *enter the yard.* TROY *is dressed in clothes other than his work clothes.*

BONO. He told him the same thing he told you. Take it to the union.

TROY. Brownie ain't got that much sense. Man wasn't thinking about nothing. He wait until I confront them on it . . . then he wanna come crying seniority. (*Calls.*) Hey, Rose!

BONO. I wish I could have seen Mr. Rand's face when he told you.

TROY. He couldn't get it out of his mouth! Liked to bit his tongue! When they called me down there to the Commissioner's office . . . he thought they was gonna fire me. Like everybody else.

BONO. I didn't think they was gonna fire you. I thought they was gonna put you on the warning paper.

TROY. Hey, Rose! (*To* BONO.) Yeah, Mr. Rand like to bit his tongue.

TROY *breaks the seal on the bottle, takes a drink, and hands it to* BONO.

BONO. I see you run right down to Taylors' and told that Alberta gal.

TROY (*calling*). Hey, Rose! (*To* BONO.) I told everybody. Hey, Rose! I went down there to cash my check.

ROSE (*entering from the house*). Hush all that hollering, man! I know you out here. What they say down there at the Commissioner's office?

TROY. You supposed to come when I call you, woman. Bono'll tell you that. (*To* BONO.) Don't Lucille come when you call her?

ROSE. Man, hush your mouth. I ain't no dog . . . talk about "come when you call me."

TROY (*puts his arm around* ROSE). You hear this, Bono? I had me an old dog used to get uppity like that. You say, "C'mere, Blue!" . . . and he just lay there and look at you. End up getting a stick and chasing him away trying to make him come.

ROSE. I ain't studying you and your dog. I remember you used to sing that old song.

TROY (*he sings*).

Hear it ring! Hear it ring! I had a dog his name was Blue.

ROSE. Don't nobody wanna hear you sing that old song.

TROY (*sings*).

> You know Blue was mighty true.

ROSE. Used to have Cory running around here singing that song.

BONO. Hell, I remember that song myself.

TROY (*sings*).

> You know Blue was a good old dog.
> Blue treed a possum in a hollow log.

That was my daddy's song. My daddy made up that song.

ROSE. I don't care who made it up. Don't nobody wanna hear you sing it.

TROY (*makes a song like calling a dog*). Come here, woman.

ROSE. You come in here carrying on, I reckon they ain't fired you. What they say down there at the Commissioner's office?

TROY. Look here, Rose . . . Mr. Rand called me into his office today when I got back from talking to them people down there . . . it come from up top . . . he called me in and told me they was making me a driver.

ROSE. Troy, you kidding!

TROY. No I ain't. Ask Bono.

ROSE. Well, that's great, Troy. Now you don't have to hassle them people no more.

LYONS *enters from the street.*

TROY. Aw hell, I wasn't looking to see you today. I thought you was in jail. Got it all over the front page of the *Courier* about them raiding Sefus's place . . . where you be hanging out with all them thugs.

LYONS. Hey, Pop . . . that ain't got nothing to do with me. I don't go down there gambling. I go down there to sit in with the band. I ain't got nothing to do with the gambling part. They got some good music down there.

TROY. They got some rogues . . . is what they got.

LYONS. How you been, Mr. Bono? Hi, Rose.

BONO. I see where you playing down at the Crawford Grill tonight.

ROSE. How come you ain't brought Bonnie like I told you? You should have brought Bonnie with you, she ain't been over in a month of Sundays.

LYONS. I was just in the neighborhood . . . thought I'd stop by.

TROY. Here he come . . .

BONO. Your daddy got a promotion on the rubbish. He's gonna be the first colored driver. Ain't got to do nothing but sit up there and read the paper like them white fellows.

LYONS. Hey, Pop . . . if you knew how to read you'd be all right.

BONO. Naw . . . naw . . . you mean if the nigger knew how to drive he'd be all right. Been fighting with them people about driving and ain't even got a license. Mr. Rand know you ain't got no driver's license?

TROY. Driving ain't nothing. All you do is point the truck where you want it to go. Driving ain't nothing.

BONO. Do Mr. Rand know you ain't got no driver's license? That's what I'm talking about. I ain't asked if driving was easy. I asked if Mr. Rand know you ain't got no driver's license.

TROY. He ain't got to know. The man ain't got to know my business. Time he find out, I have two or three driver's licenses.

LYONS (*going into his pocket*). Say, look here, Pop . . .

TROY. I knew it was coming. Didn't I tell you, Bono? I know what kind of "Look here, Pop" that was. The nigger fixing to ask me for some money. It's Friday night. It's my payday. All them rogues down there on the avenue . . . the ones that ain't in jail . . . and Lyons is hopping in his shoes to get down there with them.

LYONS. See, Pop . . . if you give somebody else a chance to talk sometimes, you'd see that I was fixing to pay you back your ten dollars like I told you. Here . . . I told you I'd pay you when Bonnie got paid.

TROY. Naw . . . you go ahead and keep that ten dollars. Put it in the bank. The next time you feel like you wanna come by here and ask me for something . . . you go on down there and get that.

LYONS. Here's your ten dollars, Pop. I told you I don't want you to give me nothing. I just wanted to borrow ten dollars.

TROY. Naw . . . you go on and keep that for the next time you want to ask me.

LYONS. Come on, Pop . . . here go your ten dollars.

ROSE. Why don't you go on and let the boy pay you back, Troy?

LYONS. Here you go, Rose. If you don't take it I'm gonna have to hear about it for the next six months. (*He hands her the money.*)

ROSE. You can hand yours over here too, Troy.

TROY. You see this, Bono. You see how they do me.

BONO. Yeah, Lucille do me the same way.

GABRIEL *is heard singing off stage. He enters.*

GABRIEL. Better get ready for the Judgment! Better get ready for . . . Hey! . . . Hey! . . . There's Troy's boy!

LYONS. How are you doing, Uncle Gabe?

GABRIEL. Lyons . . . The King of the Jungle! Rose . . . hey, Rose. Got a flower for you. (*He takes a rose from his pocket.*) Picked it myself. That's the same rose like you is!

ROSE. That's right nice of you, Gabe.

LYONS. What you been doing, Uncle Gabe?

GABRIEL. Oh, I been chasing hellhounds and waiting on the time to tell St. Peter to open the gates.

LYONS. You been chasing hellhounds, huh? Well . . . you doing the right thing, Uncle Gabe. Somebody got to chase them.

GABRIEL. Oh, yeah . . . I know it. The devil's strong. The devil ain't no pushover. Hellhounds snipping at everybody's heels. But I got my trumpet waiting on the judgment time.

LYONS. Waiting on the Battle of Armageddon, huh?

GABRIEL. Ain't gonna be too much of a battle when God get to waving that Judgment sword. But the people's gonna have a hell of a time trying to get into heaven if them gates ain't open.

LYONS (*putting his arm around* GABRIEL). You hear this, Pop. Uncle Gabe, you all right!

GABRIEL (*laughing with* LYONS). Lyons! King of the Jungle.

ROSE. You gonna stay for supper, Gabe? Want me to fix you a plate?

GABRIEL. I'll take a sandwich, Rose. Don't want no plate. Just wanna eat with my hands. I'll take a sandwich.

ROSE. How about you, Lyons? You staying? Got some short ribs cooking.

LYONS. Naw, I won't eat nothing till after we finished playing. (*Pause.*) You ought to come down and listen to me play, Pop.

TROY. I don't like that Chinese music. All that noise.

ROSE. Go on in the house and wash up, Gabe . . . I'll fix you a sandwich.

GABRIEL (*to* LYONS, *as he exits*). Troy's mad at me.

LYONS. What you mad at Uncle Gabe for, Pop?

ROSE. He thinks Troy's mad at him cause he moved over to Miss Pearl's.

TROY. I ain't mad at the man. He can live where he want to live at.

LYONS. What he move over there for? Miss Pearl don't like nobody.

ROSE. She don't mind him none. She treats him real nice. She just don't allow all that singing.

TROY. She don't mind that rent he be paying . . . that's what she don't mind.

ROSE. Troy, I ain't going through that with you no more. He's over there cause he want to have his own place. He can come and go as he please.

TROY. Hell, he could come and go as he please here. I wasn't stopping him. I ain't put no rules on him.

ROSE. It ain't the same thing, Troy. And you know it.

GABRIEL *comes to the door.*

Now, that's the last I wanna hear about that. I don't wanna hear nothing else about Gabe and Miss Pearl. And next week . . .

GABRIEL. I'm ready for my sandwich, Rose.

ROSE. And next week . . . when that recruiter come from that school . . . I want you to sign that paper and go on and let Cory play football. Then that'll be the last I have to hear about that.

TROY (*to* ROSE *as she exits into the house*). I ain't thinking about Cory nothing.

LYONS. What . . . Cory got recruited? What school he going to?

TROY. That boy walking around here smelling his piss . . . thinking he's grown. Thinking he's gonna do what he want, irrespective of what I say. Look here, Bono . . . I left the Commissioner's office and went down to the A&P . . . that boy ain't working down there. He lying to me. Telling me he got his job back . . . telling me he working weekends . . . telling me he working after school . . . Mr. Stawicki tell me he ain't working down there at all!

LYONS. Cory just growing up. He's just busting at the seams trying to fill out your shoes.

TROY. I don't care what he's doing. When he get to the point where he wanna disobey me . . . then it's time for him to move on. Bono'll tell you that. I bet he ain't never disobeyed his daddy without paying the consequences.

BONO. I ain't never had a chance. My daddy came on through . . . but I ain't never knew him to see him . . . or what he had on his mind or where he went. Just moving on through. Searching out the New Land. That's what the old folks used to call it. See a fellow moving around from place to place . . . woman to woman . . . called it searching out the New Land. I can't say if he ever found it. I come along, didn't want no kids. Didn't know if I was gonna be in one place long enough to fix on them right as their daddy. I figured I was going searching too. As it turned out I been hooked up with Lucille near about as long as your daddy been with Rose. Going on sixteen years.

TROY. Sometimes I wish I hadn't known my daddy. He ain't cared nothing about no kids. A kid to him wasn't nothing. All he wanted was for you to learn how to walk so he could start you to working. When it come

time for eating . . . he ate first. If there was anything left over, that's
what you got. Man would sit down and eat two chickens and give you
the wing.

LYONS. You ought to stop that, Pop. Everybody feed their kids. No matter
how hard times is . . . everybody care about their kids. Make sure they
have something to eat.

TROY. The only thing my daddy cared about was getting them bales of cotton in to Mr. Lubin. That's the only thing that mattered to him. Sometimes I used to wonder why he was living. Wonder why the devil hadn't
come and got him. "Get them bales of cotton in to Mr. Lubin" and find
out he owe him money . . .

LYONS. He should have just went on and left when he saw he couldn't get
nowhere. That's what I would have done.

TROY. How he gonna leave with eleven kids? And where he gonna go? He
ain't knew how to do nothing but farm. No, he was trapped and I think
he knew it. But I'll say this for him . . . he felt a responsibility toward us.
Maybe he ain't treated us the way I felt he should have . . . but without
that responsibility he could have walked off and left us . . . made his
own way.

BONO. A lot of them did. Back in those days what you talking about . . . they
walk out their front door and just take on down one road or another
and keep on walking.

LYONS. There you go! That's what I'm talking about.

BONO. Just keep on walking till you come to something else. Ain't you never
heard of nobody having the walking blues? Well, that's what you call it
when you just take off like that.

TROY. My daddy ain't had them walking blues! What you talking about? He
stayed right there with his family. But he was just as evil as he could be.
My mama couldn't stand him. Couldn't stand that evilness. She run off
when I was about eight. She sneaked off one night after he had gone
to sleep. Told me she was coming back for me. I ain't never seen her
no more. All his women run off and left him. He wasn't good for
nobody.

　　When my turn come to head out, I was fourteen and got to sniffing
around Joe Canewell's daughter. Had us an old mule we called Greyboy.
My daddy sent me out to do some plowing and I tied up Greyboy and
went to fooling around with Joe Canewell's daughter. We done found us
a nice little spot, got real cozy with each other. She about thirteen and
we done figured we was grown anyway . . . so we down there enjoying
ourselves . . . ain't thinking about nothing. We didn't know Greyboy had
got loose and wandered back to the house and my daddy was looking
for me. We down there by the creek enjoying ourselves when my daddy
come up on us. Surprised us. He had them leather straps off the mule
and commenced to whupping me like there was no tomorrow. I
jumped up, mad and embarrassed. I was scared of my daddy. When he
commenced to whupping on me . . . quite naturally I run to get out of
the way. (*Pause.*) Now I thought he was mad cause I ain't done my
work. But I see where he was chasing me off so he could have the gal
for himself. When I see what the matter of it was, I lost all fear of my
daddy. Right there is where I become a man . . . at fourteen years of
age. (*Pause.*) Now it was my turn to run him off. I picked up them same

reins that he had used on me. I picked up them reins and commenced to whupping on him. The gal jumped up and run off . . . and when my daddy turned to face me, I could see why the devil had never come to get him . . . cause he was the devil himself. I don't know what happened. When I woke up, I was laying right there by the creek, and Blue . . . this old dog we had . . . was licking my face. I thought I was blind. I couldn't see nothing. Both my eyes were swollen shut. I laid there and cried. I didn't know what I was gonna do. The only thing I knew was the time had come for me to leave my daddy's house. And right there the world suddenly got big. And it was a long time before I could cut it down to where I could handle it.

Part of that cutting down was when I got to the place where I could feel him kicking in my blood and knew that the only thing that separated us was the matter of a few years.

GABRIEL *enters from the house with a sandwich.*

LYONS. What you got there, Uncle Gabe?

GABRIEL. Got me a ham sandwich. Rose gave me a ham sandwich.

TROY. I don't know what happened to him. I done lost touch with everybody except Gabriel. But I hope he's dead. I hope he found some peace.

LYONS. That's a heavy story, Pop. I didn't know you left home when you was fourteen.

TROY. And didn't know nothing. The only part of the world I knew was the forty-two acres of Mr. Lubin's land. That's all I knew about life.

LYONS. Fourteen's kinda young to be out on your own. (*Phone rings.*) I don't even think I was ready to be out on my own at fourteen. I don't know what I would have done.

TROY. I got up from the creek and walked on down to Mobile. I was through with farming. Figured I could do better in the city. So I walked the two hundred miles to Mobile.

LYONS. Wait a minute . . . you ain't walked no two hundred miles, Pop. Ain't nobody gonna walk no two hundred miles. You talking about some walking there.

BONO. That's the only way you got anywhere back in them days.

LYONS. Shhh. Damn if I wouldn't have hitched a ride with somebody!

TROY. Who you gonna hitch it with? They ain't had no cars and things like they got now. We talking about 1918.

ROSE (*entering*). What you all out here getting into?

TROY (*to* ROSE). I'm telling Lyons how good he got it. He don't know nothing about this I'm talking.

ROSE. Lyons, that was Bonnie on the phone. She say you supposed to pick her up.

LYONS. Yeah, okay, Rose.

TROY. I walked on down to Mobile and hitched up with some of them fellows that was heading this way. Got up here and found out . . . not only couldn't you get a job . . . you couldn't find no place to live. I thought I was in freedom. Shhh. Colored folks living down there on the riverbanks in whatever kind of shelter they could find for themselves. Right down there under the Brady Street Bridge. Living in shacks made of sticks and tarpaper. Messed around there and went from bad to worse.

Started stealing. First it was food. Then I figured, hell, if I steal money I can buy me some food. Buy me some shoes too! One thing led to another. Met your mama. I was young and anxious to be a man. Met your mama and had you. What I do that for? Now I got to worry about feeding you and her. Got to steal three times as much. Went out one day looking for somebody to rob . . . that's what I was, a robber. I'll tell you the truth. I'm ashamed of it today. But it's the truth. Went to rob this fellow . . . pulled out my knife . . . and he pulled out a gun. Shot me in the chest. I felt just like somebody had taken a hot branding iron and laid it on me. When he shot me I jumped at him with my knife. They told me I killed him and they put me in the penitentiary and locked me up for fifteen years. That's where I met Bono. That's where I learned how to play baseball. Got out that place and your mama had taken you and went on to make life without me. Fifteen years was a long time for her to wait. But that fifteen years cured me of that robbing stuff. Rose'll tell you. She asked me when I met her if I had gotten all that foolishness out of my system. And I told her, "Baby, it's you and baseball all what count with me." You hear me, Bono? I meant it too. She say, "Which one comes first?" I told her, "Baby, ain't no doubt it's baseball . . . but you stick and get old with me and we'll both outlive this baseball." Am I right, Rose? And it's true.

ROSE. Man, hush your mouth. You ain't said no such thing. Talking about, "Baby you know you'll always be number one with me." That's what you was talking.

TROY. You hear that, Bono. That's why I love her.

BONO. Rose'll keep you straight. You get off the track, she'll straighten you up.

ROSE. Lyons, you better get on up and get Bonnie. She waiting on you.

LYONS (*gets up to go*). Hey, Pop, why don't you come on down to the Grill and hear me play?

TROY. I ain't going down there. I'm too old to be sitting around in them clubs.

BONO. You got to be good to play down at the Grill.

LYONS. Come on, Pop . . .

TROY. I got to get up in the morning.

LYONS. You ain't got to stay long.

TROY. Naw, I'm gonna get my supper and go on to bed.

LYONS. Well, I got to go. I'll see you again.

TROY. Don't you come around my house on my payday.

ROSE. Pick up the phone and let somebody know you coming. And bring Bonnie with you. You know I'm always glad to see her.

LYONS. Yeah, I'll do that, Rose. You take care now. See you, Pop. See you, Mr. Bono. See you, Uncle Gabe.

GABRIEL. Lyons! King of the Jungle!

LYONS *exits.*

TROY. Is supper ready, woman? Me and you got some business to take care of. I'm gonna tear it up too.

ROSE. Troy, I done told you now!

TROY (*puts his arm around* BONO). Aw hell, woman . . . this is Bono. Bono like family. I done known this nigger since . . . how long I done know you?

BONO. It's been a long time.

TROY. I done know this nigger since Skippy was a pup. Me and him done
been through some times.

BONO. You sure right about that.

TROY. Hell, I done know him longer than I known you. And we still standing
shoulder to shoulder. Hey, look here, Bono . . . a man can't ask for no
more than that. (*Drinks to him.*) I love you, nigger.

BONO. Hell, I love you too . . . I got to get home see my woman. You got
yours in hand. I got to get mine.

BONO starts to exit as CORY *enters the yard, dressed in his football uniform. He gives* TROY *a hard, uncompromising look.*

CORY. What you do that for, Pop?

He throws his helmet down in the direction of TROY.

ROSE. What's the matter? Cory . . . what's the matter?

CORY. Papa done went up to the school and told Coach Zellman I can't play
football no more. Wouldn't even let me play the game. Told him to tell
the recruiter not to come.

ROSE. Troy . . .

TROY. What you Troying me for. Yeah, I did it. And the boy know why I did it.

CORY. Why you wanna do that to me? That was the one chance I had.

ROSE. Ain't nothing wrong with Cory playing football, Troy.

TROY. The boy lied to me. I told the nigger if he wanna play football . . . to
keep up his chores and hold down that job at the A&P. That was the
conditions. Stopped down there to see Mr. Stawicki . . .

CORY. I can't work after school during the football season, Pop! I tried to tell
you that Mr. Stawicki's holding my job for me. You don't never want to
listen to nobody. And then you wanna go and do this to me!

TROY. I ain't done nothing to you. You done it to yourself.

CORY. Just cause you didn't have a chance! You just scared I'm gonna be
better than you, that's all.

TROY. Come here.

ROSE. Troy . . .

CORY *reluctantly crosses over to* TROY.

TROY. All right! See. You done made a mistake.

CORY. I didn't even do nothing!

TROY. I'm gonna tell you what your mistake was. See . . . you swung at the
ball and didn't hit it. That's strike one. See, you in the batter's box now.
You swung and you missed. That's strike one. Don't you strike out!

Lights fade to black.

Act 2

Scene 1

The following morning. CORY *is at the tree hitting the ball with the
bat. He tries to mimic* TROY, *but his swing is awkward, less sure.* ROSE
enters from the house.

ROSE. Cory, I want you to help me with this cupboard.

CORY. I ain't quitting the team. I don't care what Poppa say.

ROSE. I'll talk to him when he gets back. He had to go see about your Uncle Gabe. The police done arrested him. Say he was disturbing the peace. He'll be back directly. Come on in here and help me clean out the top of this cupboard.

CORY *exits into the house.* ROSE *sees* TROY *and* BONO *coming down the alley.*

Troy . . . what they say down there?

TROY. Ain't said nothing. I give them fifty dollars and they let him go. I'll talk to you about it. Where's Cory?

ROSE. He's in there helping me clean out these cupboards.

TROY. Tell him to get his butt out here.

TROY *and* BONO *go over to the pile of wood.* BONO *picks up the saw and begins sawing.*

TROY (*to* BONO). All they want is the money. That makes six or seven times I done went down there and got him. See me coming they stick out their hands.

BONO. Yeah. I know what you mean. That's all they care about . . . that money. They don't care about what's right. (*Pause.*) Nigger, why you got to go and get some hard wood? You ain't doing nothing but building a little old fence. Get you some soft pine wood. That's all you need.

TROY. I know what I'm doing. This is outside wood. You put pine wood inside the house. Pine wood is inside wood. This here is outside wood. Now you tell me where the fence is gonna be?

BONO. You don't need this wood. You can put it up with pine wood and it'll stand as long as you gonna be here looking at it.

TROY. How you know how long I'm gonna be here, nigger? Hell, I might just live forever. Live longer than old man Horsely.

BONO. That's what Magee used to say.

TROY. Magee's a damn fool. Now you tell me who you ever heard of gonna pull their own teeth with a pair of rusty pliers.

BONO. The old folks . . . my granddaddy used to pull his teeth with pliers. They ain't had no dentists for the colored folks back then.

TROY. Get clean pliers! You understand? Clean pliers! Sterilize them! Besides we ain't living back then. All Magee had to do was walk over to Doc Goldblum's.

BONO. I see where you and that Tallahassee gal . . . that Alberta . . . I see where you all done got tight.

TROY. What you mean "got tight"?

BONO. I see where you be laughing and joking with her all the time.

TROY. I laughs and jokes with all of them, Bono. You know me.

BONO. That ain't the kind of laughing and joking I'm talking about.

CORY *enters from the house.*

CORY. How you doing, Mr. Bono?

TROY. Cory? Get that saw from Bono and cut some wood. He talking about the wood's too hard to cut. Stand back there, Jim, and let that young boy show you how it's done.

BONO. He's sure welcome to it.

CORY *takes the saw and begins to cut the wood.*

Whew-e-e! Look at that. Big old strong boy. Look like Joe Louis. Hell, must be getting old the way I'm watching that boy whip through that wood.

CORY. I don't see why Mama want a fence around the yard noways.

TROY. Damn if I know either. What the hell she keeping out with it? She ain't got nothing nobody want.

BONO. Some people build fences to keep people out . . . and other people build fences to keep people in. Rose wants to hold on to you all. She loves you.

TROY. Hell, nigger, I don't need nobody to tell me my wife loves me. Cory . . . go on in the house and see if you can find that other saw.

CORY. Where's it at?

TROY. I said find it! Look for it till you find it!

CORY *exits into the house.*

What's that supposed to mean? Wanna keep us in?

BONO. Troy . . . I done known you seem like damn near my whole life. You and Rose both. I done know both of you all for a long time. I remember when you met Rose. When you was hitting them baseball out the park. A lot of them old gals was after you then. You had the pick of the litter. When you picked Rose, I was happy for you. That was the first time I knew you had any sense. I said . . . My man Troy knows what he's doing . . . I'm gonna follow this nigger . . . he might take me some-where. I been following you too. I done learned a whole heap of things about life watching you. I done learned how to tell where the shit lies. How to tell it from the alfalfa. You done learned me a lot of things. You showed me how to not make the same mistakes . . . to take life as it comes along and keep putting one foot in front of the other. (*Pause.*) Rose a good woman, Troy.

TROY. Hell, nigger, I know she a good woman. I been married to her for eighteen years. What you got on your mind, Bono?

BONO. I just say she a good woman. Just like I say anything. I ain't got to have nothing on my mind.

TROY. You just gonna say she a good woman and leave it hanging out there like that? Why you telling me she a good woman?

BONO. She loves you, Troy. Rose loves you.

TROY. You saying I don't measure up. That's what you trying to say. I don't measure up cause I'm seeing this other gal. I know what you trying to say.

BONO. I know what Rose means to you, Troy. I'm just trying to say I don't want to see you mess up.

TROY. Yeah, I appreciate that, Bono. If you was messing around on Lucille I'd be telling you the same thing.

BONO. Well, that's all I got to say. I just say that because I love you both.

TROY. Hell, you know me . . . I wasn't out there looking for nothing. You can't find a better woman than Rose. I know that. But seems like this woman just stuck onto me where I can't shake her loose. I done wres-tled with it, tried to throw her off me . . . but she just stuck on tighter. Now she's stuck on for good.

BONO. You's in control . . . that's what you tell me all the time. You respon-sible for what you do.

TROY. I ain't ducking the responsibility of it. As long as it sets right in my heart . . . then I'm okay. Cause that's all I listen to. It'll tell me right from wrong every time. And I ain't talking about doing Rose no bad turn. I love Rose. She done carried me a long ways and I love and respect her for that.

BONO. I know you do. That's why I don't want to see you hurt her. But what you gonna do when she find out? What you got then? If you try and jugle both of them . . . sooner or later you gonna drop one of them. That's common sense.

TROY. Yeah, I hear what you saying, Bono. I been trying to figure a way to work it out.

BONO. Work it out right, Troy. I don't want to be getting all up between you and Rose's business . . . but work it so it come out right.

TROY. Ah hell, I get all up between you and Lucille's business. When you gonna get that woman that refrigerator she been wanting? Don't tell me you ain't got no money now. I know who your banker is. Mellon don't need that money bad as Lucille want that refrigerator. I'll tell you that.

BONO. Tell you what I'll do . . . when you finish building this fence for Rose . . . I'll buy Lucille that refrigerator.

TROY. You done stuck your foot in your mouth now!

TROY *grabs up a board and begins to saw.* BONO *starts to walk out the yard.*

Hey, nigger . . . where you going?

BONO. I'm going home. I know you don't expect me to help you now. I'm protecting my money. I wanna see you put that fence up by yourself. That's what I want to see. You'll be here another six months without me.

TROY. Nigger, you ain't right.

BONO. When it comes to my money . . . I'm right as fireworks on the Fourth of July.

TROY. All right, we gonna see now. You better get out your bankbook.

BONO *exits, and* TROY *continues to work.* ROSE *enters from the house.*

ROSE. What they say down there? What's happening with Gabe?

TROY. I went down there and got him out. Cost me fifty dollars. Say he was disturbing the peace. Judge set up a hearing for him in three weeks. Say to show cause why he shouldn't be recommitted.

ROSE. What was he doing that cause them to arrest him?

TROY. Some kids was teasing him and he run them off home. Say he was howling and carrying on. Some folks seen him and called the police. That's all it was.

ROSE. Well, what's you say? What'd you tell the judge?

TROY. Told him I'd look after him. It didn't make no sense to recommit the man. He stuck out his big greasy palm and told me to give him fifty dollars and take him on home.

ROSE. Where's he at now? Where'd he go off to?

TROY. He's gone about his business. He don't need nobody to hold his hand.

ROSE. Well, I don't know. Seem like that would be the best place for him if they did put him into the hospital. I know what you're gonna say. But that's what I think would be best.

TROY. The man done had his life ruined fighting for what? And they wanna take and lock him up. Let him be free. He don't bother nobody.

ROSE. Well, everybody got their own way of looking at it I guess. Come on and get your lunch. I got a bowl of lima beans and some cornbread in the oven. Come and get something to eat. Ain't no sense you fretting over Gabe.

ROSE *turns to go into the house.*

TROY. Rose . . . got something to tell you.

ROSE. Well, come on . . . wait till I get this food on the table.

TROY. Rose!

She stops and turns around.

I don't know how to say this. (*Pause.*) I can't explain it none. It just sort of grows on you till it gets out of hand. It starts out like a little bush . . . and the next thing you know it's a whole forest.

ROSE. Troy . . . what is you talking about?

TROY. I'm talking, woman, let me talk. I'm trying to find a way to tell you . . . I'm gonna be a daddy. I'm gonna be somebody's daddy.

ROSE. Troy . . . you're not telling me this? You're gonna be . . . what?

TROY. Rose . . . now . . . see . . .

ROSE. You telling me you gonna be somebody's daddy? You telling your *wife* this?

GABRIEL *enters from the street. He carries a rose in his hand.*

GABRIEL. Hey, Troy! Hey, Rose!

ROSE. I have to wait eighteen years to hear something like this.

GABRIEL. Hey, Rose . . . I got a flower for you. (*He hands it to her.*) That's a rose. Same rose like you is.

ROSE. Thanks, Gabe.

GABRIEL. Troy, you ain't mad at me is you? Them bad mens come and put me away. You ain't mad at me is you?

TROY. Naw, Gabe, I ain't mad at you.

ROSE. Eighteen years and you wanna come with this.

GABRIEL (*takes a quarter out of his pocket*). See what I got? Got a brand new quarter.

TROY. Rose . . . it's just . . .

ROSE. Ain't nothing you can say, Troy. Ain't no way of explaining that.

GABRIEL. Fellow that give me this quarter had a whole mess of them. I'm gonna keep this quarter till it stop shining.

ROSE. Gabe, go on in the house there. I got some watermelon in the Frigidaire. Go on and get you a piece.

GABRIEL. Say, Rose . . . you know I was chasing hellhounds and them bad mens come and get me and take me away. Troy helped me. He come down there and told them they better let me go before he beat them up. Yeah, he did!

ROSE. You go on and get you a piece of watermelon, Gabe. Them bad mens is gone now.

GABRIEL. Okay, Rose . . . gonna get me some watermelon. The kind with the stripes on it.

GABRIEL *exits into the house.*

ROSE. Why, Troy? Why? After all these years to come dragging this in to me now. It don't make no sense at your age. I could have expected this ten or fifteen years ago, but not now.

TROY. Age ain't got nothing to do with it, Rose.

ROSE. I done tried to be everything a wife should be. Everything a wife could be. Been married eighteen years and I got to live to see the day you tell me you been seeing another woman and done fathered a child by her. And you know I ain't never wanted no half nothing in my family. My whole family is half. Everybody got different fathers and mothers . . . my two sisters and my brother. Can't hardly tell who's who. Can't never sit down and talk about Papa and Mama. It's your papa and your mama and my papa and my mama . . .

TROY. Rose . . . stop it now.

ROSE. I ain't never wanted that for none of my children. And now you wanna drag your behind in here and tell me something like this.

TROY. You ought to know. It's time for you to know.

ROSE. Well, I don't want to know, goddamn it!

TROY. I can't just make it go away. It's done now. I can't wish the circumstance of the thing away.

ROSE. And you don't want to either. Maybe you want to wish me and my boy away. Maybe that's what you want? Well, you can't wish us away. I've got eighteen years of my life invested in you. You ought to have stayed upstairs in my bed where you belong.

TROY. Rose . . . now listen to me . . . we can get a handle on this thing. We can talk this out . . . come to an understanding.

ROSE. All of a sudden it's "we." Where was "we" at when you was down there rolling around with some godforsaken woman? "We" should have come to an understanding before you started making a damn fool of yourself. You're a day late and a dollar short when it comes to an understanding with me.

TROY. It's just . . . She gives me a different idea . . . a different understanding about myself. I can step out of this house and get away from the pressures and problems . . . be a different man. I ain't got to wonder how I'm gonna pay the bills or get the roof fixed. I can just be a part of myself that I ain't never been.

ROSE. What I want to know . . . is do you plan to continue seeing her. That's all you can say to me.

TROY. I can sit up in her house and laugh. Do you understand what I'm saying. I can laugh out loud . . . and it feels good. It reaches all the way down to the bottom of my shoes. (*Pause.*) Rose, I can't give that up.

ROSE. Maybe you ought to go on and stay down there with her . . . if she's a better woman than me.

TROY. It ain't about nobody being a better woman or nothing. Rose, you ain't the blame. A man couldn't ask for no woman to be a better wife than you've been. I'm responsible for it. I done locked myself into a pattern trying to take care of you all that I forgot about myself.

ROSE. What the hell was I there for? That was my job, not somebody else's.

TROY. Rose, I done tried all my life to live decent . . . to live a clean . . . hard . . . useful life. I tried to be a good husband to you. In every way I knew how. Maybe I come into the world backwards, I don't know. But . . . you born with two strikes on you before you come to the plate. You got to guard it closely . . . always looking for the curve ball on the inside corner. You can't afford to let none get past you. You can't afford a call strike. If you going down . . . you going down swinging. Everything lined up against you. What you gonna do. I fooled them, Rose. I bunted. When I found you and Cory and a halfway decent job . . . I was safe. Couldn't nothing touch me. I wasn't gonna strike out no more. I wasn't going back to the penitentiary. I wasn't gonna lay in the streets with a bottle of wine. I was safe. I had me a family. A job. I wasn't gonna get that last strike. I was on first looking for one of them boys to knock me in. To get me home.

ROSE. You should have stayed in my bed, Troy.

TROY. Then when I saw that gal . . . she firmed up my backbone. And I got to thinking that if I tried . . . I just might be able to steal second. Do you understand after eighteen years I wanted to steal second.

ROSE. You should have held me tight. You should have grabbed me and held on.

TROY. I stood on first base for eighteen years and I thought . . . well, god-damn it . . . go on for it!

ROSE. We're not talking about baseball! We're talking about you going off to lay in bed with another woman . . . and then bring it home to me. That's what we're talking about. We ain't talking about no baseball.

TROY. Rose, you're not listening to me. I'm trying the best I can to explain it to you. It's not easy for me to admit that I been standing in the same place for eighteen years.

ROSE. I been standing with you! I been right here with you, Troy. I got a life too. I gave eighteen years of my life to stand in the same spot with you. Don't you think I ever wanted other things? Don't you think I had dreams and hopes? What about my life? What about me. Don't you think it ever crossed my mind to want to know other men? That I wanted to lay up somewhere and forget about my responsibilities? That I wanted someone to make me laugh so I could feel good? You not the only one who's got wants and needs. But I held on to you, Troy. I took all my feelings, my wants and needs, my dreams . . . and I buried them inside you. I planted a seed and watched and prayed over it. I planted myself inside you and waited to bloom. And it didn't take me no eighteen years to find out the soil was hard and rocky and it wasn't never gonna bloom.

But I held on to you, Troy. I held you tighter. You was my hus-band. I owed you everything I had. Every part of me I could find to give you. And upstairs in that room . . . with the darkness falling in on me . . . I gave everything I had to try and erase the doubt that you wasn't the finest man in the world. And wherever you was going . . . I wanted to be there with you. Cause you was my husband. Cause that's the only way I was gonna survive as your wife. You always talking about what you give . . . and what you don't have to give. But you take too. You take . . . and don't even know nobody's giving!

ROSE *turns to exit into the house;* TROY *grabs her arm.*

TROY. You say I take and don't give!

ROSE. Troy! You're hurting me!

TROY. You say I take and don't give!

ROSE. Troy . . . you're hurting my arm! Let go!

TROY. I done give you everything I got. Don't you tell that lie on me.

ROSE. Troy!

TROY. Don't you tell that lie on me!

CORY *enters from the house.*

CORY. Mama!

ROSE. Troy. You're hurting me.

TROY. Don't you tell me about no taking and giving.

CORY *comes up behind* TROY *and grabs him.* TROY, *surprised, is thrown off balance just as* CORY *throws a glancing blow that catches him on the chest and knocks him down.* TROY *is stunned, as is* CORY.

ROSE. Troy. Troy. No!

TROY *gets to his feet and starts at* CORY.

Troy . . . no. Please! Troy!

ROSE *pulls on* TROY *to hold him back.* TROY *stops himself.*

TROY (*to* CORY). All right. That's strike two. You stay away from around me, boy. Don't you strike out. You living with a full count. Don't you strike out.

TROY *exits out the yard as the lights go down.*

Scene 2

It is six months later, early afternoon. TROY *enters from the house and starts to exit the yard.* ROSE *enters from the house.*

ROSE. Troy, I want to talk to you.

TROY. All of a sudden, after all this time, you want to talk to me, huh? You ain't wanted to talk to me for months. You ain't wanted to talk to me last night. You ain't wanted no part of me then. What you wanna talk to me about now?

ROSE. Tomorrow's Friday.

TROY. I know what day tomorrow is. You think I don't know tomorrow's Friday? My whole life I ain't done nothing but look to see Friday coming and you got to tell me it's Friday.

ROSE. I want to know if you're coming home.

TROY. I always come home, Rose. You know that. There ain't never been a night I ain't come home.

ROSE. That ain't what I mean . . . and you know it. I want to know if you're coming straight home after work.

TROY. I figure I'd cash my check . . . hang out at Taylors' with the boys . . . maybe play a game of checkers . . .

ROSE. Troy, I can't live like this. I won't live like this. You livin' on borrowed time with me. It's been going on six months now you ain't been coming home.

TROY. I be here every night. Every night of the year. That's 365 days.

ROSE. I want you to come home tomorrow after work.

TROY. Rose . . . I don't mess up my pay. You know that now. I take my pay and I give it to you. I don't have no money but what you give me back. I just want to have a little time to myself . . . a little time to enjoy life.

ROSE. What about me? When's my time to enjoy life?

TROY. I don't know what to tell you, Rose. I'm doing the best I can.

ROSE. You ain't been home from work but time enough to change your clothes and run out . . . and you wanna call that the best you can do?

TROY. I'm going over to the hospital to see Alberta. She went into the hospital this afternoon. Look like she might have the baby early. I won't be gone long.

ROSE. Well, you ought to know. They went over to Miss Pearl's and got Gabe today. She said you told them to go ahead and lock him up.

TROY. I ain't said no such thing. Whoever told you that is telling a lie. Pearl ain't doing nothing but telling a big fat lie.

ROSE. She ain't had to tell me. I read it on the papers.

TROY. I ain't told them nothing of the kind.

ROSE. I saw it right there on the papers.

TROY. What it say, huh?

ROSE. It said you told them to take him.

TROY. Then they screwed that up, just the way they screw up everything. I ain't worried about what they got on the paper.

ROSE. Say the government send part of his check to the hospital and the other part to you.

TROY. I ain't got nothing to do with that if that's the way it works. I ain't made up the rules about how it work.

ROSE. You did Gabe just like you did Cory. You wouldn't sign the paper for Cory . . . but you signed for Gabe. You signed that paper.

The telephone is heard ringing inside the house.

TROY. I told you I ain't signed nothing, woman! The only thing I signed was the release form. Hell, I can't read, I don't know what they had on that paper! I ain't signed nothing about sending Gabe away.

ROSE. I said send him to the hospital . . . you said let him be free . . . now you done went down there and signed him to the hospital for half his money. You went back on yourself, Troy. You gonna have to answer for that.

TROY. See now . . . you been over there talking to Miss Pearl. She done got mad cause she ain't getting Gabe's rent money. That's all it is. She's liable to say anything.

ROSE. Troy, I seen where you signed the paper.

TROY. You ain't seen nothing I signed. What she doing got papers on my brother anyway? Miss Pearl telling a big fat lie. And I'm gonna tell her about it too! You ain't seen nothing I signed. Say . . . you ain't seen nothing I signed.

ROSE *exits into the house to answer the telephone. Presently she returns.*

ROSE. Troy . . . that was the hospital. Alberta had the baby.

TROY. What she have? What is it?

ROSE. It's a girl.

TROY. I better get on down to the hospital to see her.

ROSE. Troy . . .

TROY. Rose . . . I got to go see her now. That's only right . . . what's the matter . . . the baby's all right, ain't it?

ROSE. Alberta died having the baby.

TROY. Died . . . you say she's dead? Alberta's dead?

ROSE. They said they done all they could. They couldn't do nothing for her.

TROY. The baby? How's the baby?

ROSE. They say it's healthy. I wonder who's gonna bury her.

TROY. She had family, Rose. She wasn't living in the world by herself.

ROSE. I know she wasn't living in the world by herself.

TROY. Next thing you gonna want to know if she had any insurance.

ROSE. Troy, you ain't got to talk like that.

TROY. That's the first thing that jumped out your mouth. "Who's gonna bury her?" Like I'm fixing to take on that task for myself.

ROSE. I am your wife. Don't push me away.

TROY. I ain't pushing nobody away. Just give me some space. That's all. Just give me some room to breathe.

ROSE exits into the house. TROY walks about the yard.

TROY (*with a quiet rage that threatens to consume him*). All right . . . Mr. Death. See now . . . I'm gonna tell you what I'm gonna do. I'm gonna take and build me a fence around this yard. See? I'm gonna build me a fence around what belongs to me. And then I want you to stay on the other side. See? You stay over there until you're ready for me. Then you come on. Bring your army. Bring your sickle. Bring your wrestling clothes. I ain't gonna fall down on my vigilance this time. You ain't gonna sneak up on me no more. When you ready for me . . . when the top of your list say Troy Maxson . . . that's when you come around here. You come up and knock on the front door. Ain't nobody else got nothing to do with this. This is between you and me. Man to man. You stay on the other side of that fence until you ready for me. Then you come up and knock on the front door. Anytime you want. I'll be ready for you.

The lights go down to black.

Scene 3

The lights come up on the porch. It is late evening three days later. ROSE sits listening to the ball game waiting for TROY. The final out of the game is made and ROSE switches off the radio. TROY enters the yard carrying an infant wrapped in blankets. He stands back from the house and calls.

    ROSE enters and stands on the porch. There is a long, awkward silence, the weight of which grows heavier with each passing second.

TROY. Rose . . . I'm standing here with my daughter in my arms. She ain't but a wee bittie little old thing. She don't know nothing about grownups' business. She innocent . . . and she ain't got no mama.

ROSE. What you telling me for, Troy?

She turns and exits into the house.

TROY. Well . . . I guess we'll just sit out here on the porch.

He sits down on the porch. There is an awkward indelicateness about the way he handles the baby. His largeness engulfs and seems to swallow it. He speaks loud enough for ROSE to hear.

A man's got to do what's right for him. I ain't sorry for nothing I done. It felt right in my heart. (*To the baby.*) What you smiling at? Your daddy's a big man. Got these great big old hands. But sometimes he's scared. And right now your daddy's scared cause we sitting out here and ain't got no home. Oh, I been homeless before. I ain't had no little baby with me. But I been homeless. You just be out on the road by your lonesome and you see one of them trains coming and you just kinda go like this . . .

He sings as a lullaby.

> Please, Mr. Engineer let a man ride the line
> Please, Mr. Engineer let a man ride the line
> I ain't got no ticket please let me ride the blinds

ROSE *enters from the house.* TROY, *hearing her steps behind him, stands and faces her.*

She's my daughter, Rose. My own flesh and blood. I can't deny her no more than I can deny them boys. (*Pause.*) You and them boys is my family. You and them and this child is all I got in the world. So I guess what I'm saying is . . . I'd appreciate it if you'd help me take care of her.

ROSE. Okay, Troy . . . you're right. I'll take care of your baby for you . . . cause . . . like you say . . . she's innocent . . . and you can't visit the sins of the father upon the child. A motherless child has got a hard time. (*She takes the baby from him.*) From right now . . . this child got a mother. But you a womanless man.

ROSE *turns and exits into the house with the baby. Lights go down to black.*

Scene 4

It is two months later. LYONS *enters the street. He knocks on the door and calls.*

LYONS. Hey, Rose! (*Pause.*) Rose!

ROSE (*from inside the house*). Stop that yelling. You gonna wake up Raynell. I just got her to sleep.

LYONS. I just stopped by to pay Papa this twenty dollars I owe him. Where's Papa at?

ROSE. He should be here in a minute. I'm getting ready to go down to the church. Sit down and wait on him.

LYONS. I got to go pick up Bonnie over her mother's house.

ROSE. Well, sit it down there on the table. He'll get it.

LYONS (*enters the house and sets the money on the table*). Tell Papa I said thanks. I'll see you again.

ROSE. All right, Lyons. We'll see you.

LYONS *starts to exit as* CORY *enters.*

CORY. Hey, Lyons.

LYONS. What's happening, Cory? Say man, I'm sorry I missed your graduation. You know I had a gig and couldn't get away. Otherwise, I would have been there, man. So what you doing?

CORY. I'm trying to find a job.

LYONS. Yeah I know how that go, man. It's rough out here. Jobs are scarce.

CORY. Yeah, I know.

LYONS. Look here, I got to run. Talk to Papa . . . he know some people. He'll be able to help get you a job. Talk to him . . . see what he say.

CORY. Yeah . . . all right, Lyons.

LYONS. You take care. I'll talk to you soon. We'll find some time to talk.

> LYONS *exits the yard.* CORY *wanders over to the tree, picks up the bat, and assumes a batting stance. He studies an imaginary pitcher and swings. Dissatisfied with the result, he tries again.* TROY *enters. They eye each other for a beat.* CORY *puts the bat down and exits the yard.* TROY *starts into the house as* ROSE *exits with* RAYNELL. *She is carrying a cake.*

TROY. I'm coming in and everybody's going out.

ROSE. I'm taking this cake down to the church for the bake sale. Lyons was by to see you. He stopped by to pay you your twenty dollars. It's laying in there on the table.

TROY (*going into his pocket*). Well . . . here go this money.

ROSE. Put it in there on the table, Troy. I'll get it.

TROY. What time you coming back?

ROSE. Ain't no use in you studying me. It don't matter what time I come back.

TROY. I just asked you a question, woman. What's the matter . . . can't I ask you a question?

ROSE. Troy, I don't want to go into it. Your dinner's in there on the stove. All you got to do is heat it up. And don't you be eating the rest of them cakes in there. I'm coming back for them. We having a bake sale at the church tomorrow.

> ROSE *exits the yard.* TROY *sits down on the steps, takes a pint bottle from his pocket, opens it, and drinks. He begins to sing.*

TROY.

> Hear it ring! Hear it ring!
> Had an old dog his name was Blue
> You know Blue was mighty true
> You know Blue as a good old dog
> Blue trees a possum in a hollow log
> You know from that he was a good old dog

> BONO *enters the yard.*

BONO. Hey, Troy.

TROY. Hey, what's happening, Bono?

BONO. I just thought I'd stop by to see you.

TROY. What you stop by and see me for? You ain't stopped by in a month of Sundays. Hell, I must owe you money or something.

BONO. Since you got your promotion I can't keep up with you. Used to see you every day. Now I don't even know what route you working.

TROY. They keep switching me around. Got me out in Greentree now . . . hauling white folks' garbage.

BONO. Greentree, huh? You lucky, at least you ain't got to be lifting them barrels. Damn if they ain't getting heavier. I'm gonna put in my two years and call it quits.

TROY. I'm thinking about retiring myself.

BONO. You got it easy. You can drive for another five years.

TROY. It ain't the same, Bono. It ain't like working the back of the truck. Ain't got nobody to talk to . . . feel like you working by yourself. Naw, I'm thinking about retiring. How's Lucille?

BONO. She all right. Her arthritis get to acting up on her sometime. Saw Rose on my way in. She going down to the church, huh?

TROY. Yeah, she took up going down there. All them preachers looking for somebody to fatten their pockets. (*Pause.*) Got some gin here.

BONO. Naw, thanks. I just stopped by to say hello.

TROY. Hell, nigger . . . you can take a drink. I ain't never known you to say no to a drink. You ain't got to work tomorrow.

BONO. I just stopped by. I'm fixing to go over to Skinner's. We got us a domino game going over his house every Friday.

TROY. Nigger, you can't play no dominoes. I used to whup you four games out of five.

BONO. Well, that learned me. I'm getting better.

TROY. Yeah? Well, that's all right.

BONO. Look here . . . I got to be getting on. Stop by sometime, huh?

TROY. Yeah, I'll do that, Bono. Lucille told Rose you bought her a new refrigerator.

BONO. Yeah, Rose told Lucille you had finally built your fence . . . so I figured we'd call it even.

TROY. I knew you would.

BONO. Yeah . . . okay. I'll be talking to you.

TROY. Yeah, take care, Bono. Good to see you. I'm gonna stop over.

BONO. Yeah. Okay, Troy.

BONO *exits.* TROY *drinks from the bottle.*

TROY.

Old Blue died and I dug his grave
Let him down with a golden chain
Every night when I hear old Blue bark
I know Blue treed a possum in Noah's Ark.
Hear it ring! Hear it ring!

CORY *enters the yard. They eye each other for a beat.* TROY *is sitting in the middle of the steps.* CORY *walks over.*

CORY. I got to get by.

TROY. Say what? What's you say?

CORY. You in my way. I got to get by.

TROY. You got to get by where? This is my house. Bought and paid for. In full. Took me fifteen years. And if you wanna go in my house and I'm sitting on the steps . . . you say excuse me. Like your mama taught you.

CORY. Come on, Pop . . . I got to get by.

CORY *starts to maneuver his way past* TROY. TROY *grabs his leg and shoves him back.*

TROY. You just gonna walk over top of me?

CORY. I live here too!

TROY (*advancing toward him*). You just gonna walk over top of me in my own house?

CORY. I ain't scared of you.

TROY. I ain't asked if you was scared of me. I asked you if you was fixing to walk over top of me in my own house? That's the question. You ain't gonna say excuse me? You just gonna walk over top of me?

CORY. If you wanna put it like that.

TROY. How else am I gonna put it?

CORY. I was walking by you to go into the house cause you sitting on the steps drunk, singing to yourself. You can put it like that.

TROY. Without saying excuse me???

CORY *doesn't respond.*

I asked you a question. Without saying excuse me???

CORY. I ain't got to say excuse me to you. You don't count around here no more.

TROY. Oh, I see . . . I don't count around here no more. You ain't got to say excuse me to your daddy. All of a sudden you done got so grown that your daddy don't count around here no more . . . Around here in his own house and yard that he done paid for with the sweat of his brow. You done got so grown to where you gonna take over. You gonna take over my house. Is that right? You gonna wear my pants. You gonna go in there and stretch out on my bed. You ain't got to say excuse me cause I don't count around here no more. Is that right?

CORY. That's right. You always talking this dumb stuff. Now, why don't you just get out my way?

TROY. I guess you got someplace to sleep and something to put in your belly. You got that, huh? You got that? That's what you need. You got that, huh?

CORY. You don't know what I got. You ain't got to worry about what I got.

TROY. You right! You one hundred percent right! I done spent the last seventeen years worrying about what you got. Now it's your turn, see? I'll tell you what to do. You grown . . . we done established that. You a man. Now, let's see you act like one. Turn your behind around and walk out this yard. And when you get out there in the alley . . . you can forget about this house. See? Cause this is my house. You go on and be a man and get your own house. You can forget about this. Cause this is mine. You go on and get yours cause I'm through with doing for you.

CORY. You talking about what you did for me . . . what'd you ever give me?

TROY. Them feet and bones! That pumping heart, nigger! I give you more than anybody else is ever gonna give you.

CORY. You ain't never gave me nothing! You ain't never done nothing but hold me back. Afraid I was gonna be better than you. All you ever did was try and make me scared of you. I used to tremble every time you called my name. Every time I heard your footsteps in the house. Wondering all the time . . . what's Papa gonna say if I do this? . . . What's he gonna say if I do that? . . . What's Papa gonna say if I turn on the radio? And Mama, too . . . she tries . . . but she's scared of you.

TROY. You leave your mama out of this. She ain't got nothing to do with this.

CORY. I don't know how she stand you . . . after what you did to her.

TROY. I told you to leave your mama out of this!

He advances toward CORY.

CORY. What you gonna do . . . give me a whupping? You can't whup me no more. You're too old. You just an old man.

TROY (*shoves him on his shoulder*). Nigger! That's what you are. You just another nigger on the street to me!

CORY. You crazy! You know that?

TROY. Go on now! You got the devil in you. Get on away from me!

CORY. You just a crazy old man . . . talking about I got the devil in me.

TROY. Yeah, I'm crazy! If you don't get on the other side of that yard . . . I'm gonna show you how crazy I am! Go on . . . get the hell out of my yard.

CORY. It ain't your yard. You took Uncle Gabe's money he got from the army to buy this house and then you put him out.

TROY (*advances on* CORY). Get your black ass out of my yard!

> TROY's *advance backs* CORY *up against the tree.* CORY *grabs up the bat.*

CORY. I ain't going nowhere! Come on . . . put me out! I ain't scared of you.

TROY. That's my bat!

CORY. Come on!

TROY. Put my bat down!

CORY. Come on, put me out.

> CORY *swings at* TROY, *who backs across the yard.*

What's the matter? You so bad . . . put me out!

> TROY *advances toward* CORY.

CORY (*backing up*). Come on! Come on!

TROY. You're gonna have to use it! You wanna draw that bat back on me . . . you're gonna have to use it.

CORY. Come on! . . . Come on!

> CORY *swings the bat at* TROY *a second time. He misses.* TROY *continues to advance toward him.*

TROY. You're gonna have to kill me! You wanna draw that bat back on me. You're gonna have to kill me.

> CORY, *backed up against the tree, can go no farther.* TROY *taunts him. He sticks out his head and offers him a target.*

Come on! Come on!

> CORY *is unable to swing the bat.* TROY *grabs it.*

TROY. Then I'll show you.

> CORY *and* TROY *struggle over the bat. The struggle is fierce and fully engaged.* TROY *ultimately is the stronger and takes the bat from* CORY *and stands over him ready to swing. He stops himself.*

Go on and get away from around my house.

> CORY, *stung by his defeat, picks himself up, walks slowly out of the yard and up the alley.*

CORY. Tell Mama I'll be back for my things.

TROY. They'll be on the other side of that fence.

> CORY *exits.*

TROY. I can't taste nothing. Helluljah! I can't taste nothing no more. (TROY *assumes a batting posture and begins to taunt Death, the fastball on the outside corner.*) Come on! It's between you and me now! Come on! Anytime you want! Come on! I be ready for you . . . but I ain't gonna be easy.

The lights go down on the scene.

Scene 5

The time is 1965. The lights come up in the yard. It is the morning of TROY'S *funeral. A funeral plaque with a light hangs beside the door. There is a small garden plot off to the side. There is noise and activity in the house as* ROSE, LYONS, *and* BONO *have gathered. The door opens and* RAYNELL, *seven years old, enters dressed in a flannel nightgown. She crosses to the garden and pokes around with a stick.* ROSE *calls from the house.*

ROSE. Raynell!
RAYNELL. Mam?
ROSE. What you doing out there?
RAYNELL. Nothing.

ROSE *comes to the door.*

ROSE. Girl, get in here and get dressed. What you doing?
RAYNELL. Seeing if my garden growed.
ROSE. I told you it ain't gonna grow overnight. You got to wait.
RAYNELL. It don't look like it never gonna grow. Dag!
ROSE. I told you a watched pot never boils. Get in here and get dressed.
RAYNELL. This ain't even no pot, Mama.
ROSE. You just have to give it a chance. It'll grow. Now you come on and do what I told you. We got to be getting ready. This ain't no morning to be playing around. You hear me?
RAYNELL. Yes, mam.

ROSE *exits into the house.* RAYNELL *continues to poke at her garden with a stick.* CORY *enters. He is dressed in a Marine corporal's uniform, and carries a duffelbag. His posture is that of a military man, and his speech has a clipped sternness.*

CORY (*to* RAYNELL). Hi. (*Pause.*) I bet your name is Raynell.
RAYNELL. Uh huh.
CORY. Is your mama home?

RAYNELL *runs up on the porch and calls through the screen door.*

RAYNELL. Mama . . . there's some man out here. Mama?

ROSE *comes to the door.*

ROSE. Cory? Lord have mercy! Look here, you all!

ROSE *and* CORY *embrace in a tearful reunion as* BONO *and* LYONS *enter from the house dressed in funeral clothes.*

BONO. Aw, looka here . . .
ROSE. Done got all grown up!
CORY. Don't cry, Mama. What you crying about?

ROSE. I'm just so glad you made it.

CORY. Hey Lyons. How you doing, Mr. Bono.

LYONS *goes to embrace* CORY.

LYONS. Look at you, man. Look at you. Don't he look good, Rose. Got them Corporal stripes.

ROSE. What took you so long?

CORY. You know how the Marines are, Mama. They got to get all their paperwork straight before they let you do anything.

ROSE. Well, I'm sure glad you made it. They let Lyons come. Your Uncle Gabe's still in the hospital. They don't know if they gonna let him out or not. I just talked to them a little while ago.

LYONS. A Corporal in the United States Marines.

BONO. Your daddy knew you had it in you. He used to tell me all the time.

LYONS. Don't he look good, Mr. Bono?

BONO. Yeah, he remind me of Troy when I first met him. (*Pause.*) Say, Rose, Lucille's down at the church with the choir. I'm gonna go down and get the pallbearers lined up. I'll be back to get you all.

ROSE. Thanks, Jim.

CORY. See you, Mr. Bono.

LYONS (*with his arm around* RAYNELL). Cory . . . look at Raynell. Ain't she precious? She gonna break a whole lot of hearts.

ROSE. Raynell, come and say hello to your brother. This is your brother, Cory. You remember Cory.

RAYNELL. No, Mam.

CORY. She don't remember me, Mama.

ROSE. Well, we talk about you. She heard us talk about you. (*To* RAYNELL.) This is your brother, Cory. Come on and say hello.

RAYNELL. Hi.

CORY. Hi. So you're Raynell. Mama told me a lot about you.

ROSE. You all come on into the house and let me fix you some breakfast. Keep up your strength.

CORY. I ain't hungry, Mama.

LYONS. You can fix me something, Rose. I'll be in there in a minute.

ROSE. Cory, you sure you don't want nothing? I know they ain't feeding you right.

CORY. No, Mama . . . thanks. I don't feel like eating. I'll get something later.

ROSE. Raynell . . . get on upstairs and get that dress on like I told you.

ROSE *and* RAYNELL *exit into the house.*

LYONS. So . . . I hear you thinking about getting married.

CORY. Yeah, I done found the right one, Lyons. It's about time.

LYONS. Me and Bonnie been split up about four years now. About the time Papa retired. I guess she just got tired of all them changes I was putting her through. (*Pause.*) I always knew you was gonna make something out yourself. Your head was always in the right direction. So . . . you gonna stay in . . . make it a career . . . put in your twenty years?

CORY. I don't know. I got six already, I think that's enough.

LYONS. Stick with Uncle Sam and retire early. Ain't nothing out here. I guess Rose told you what happened with me. They got me down the workhouse. I thought I was being slick cashing other people's checks.

CORY. How much time you doing?

LYONS. They give me three years. I got that beat now. I ain't got but nine more months. It ain't so bad. You learn to deal with it like anything else. You got to take the crookeds with the straights. That's what Papa used to say. He used to say that when he struck out. I seen him strike out three times in a row . . . and the next time up he hit the ball over the grandstand. Right out there in Homestead Field. He wasn't satisfied hitting in the seats . . . he want to hit it over everything! After the game he had two hundred people standing around waiting to shake his hand. You got to take the crookeds with the straights. Yeah, Papa was something else.

CORY. You still playing?

LYONS. Cory . . . you know I'm gonna do that. There's some fellows down there we got us a band . . . we gonna try and stay together when we get out . . . but yeah, I'm still playing. It still helps me to get out of bed in the morning. As long as it do that I'm gonna be right there playing and trying to make some sense out of it.

ROSE (*calling*). Lyons, I got these eggs in the pan.

LYONS. Let me go on and get these eggs, man. Get ready to go bury Papa. (*Pause.*) How you doing? You doing all right?

CORY *nods.* LYONS *touches him on the shoulder and they share a moment of silent grief.* LYONS *exits into the house.* CORY *wanders about the yard.* RAYNELL *enters.*

RAYNELL. Hi.

CORY. Hi.

RAYNELL. Did you used to sleep in my room?

CORY. Yeah . . . that used to be my room.

RAYNELL. That's what Papa call it. "Cory's room." It got your football in the closet.

ROSE *comes to the door.*

ROSE. Raynell, get in there and get them good shoes on.

RAYNELL. Mama, can't I wear these? Them other one hurt my feet.

ROSE. Well, they just gonna have to hurt your feet for a while. You ain't said they hurt your feet when you went down to the store and got them.

RAYNELL. They didn't hurt then. My feet done got bigger.

ROSE. Don't you give me no backtalk now. You get in there and get them shoes on.

RAYNELL *exits into the house.*

Ain't too much changed. He still got that piece of rag tied to that tree. He was out here swinging that bat. I was just ready to go back in the house. He swung that bat and then he just fell over. Seem like he swung it and stood there with this grin on his face . . . and then he just fell over. They carried him on down to the hospital, but I knew there wasn't no need . . . why don't you come on in the house?

CORY. Mama . . . I got something to tell you. I don't know how to tell you this . . . but I've got to tell you . . . I'm not going to Papa's funeral.

ROSE. Boy, hush your mouth. That's your daddy you talking about. I don't want hear that kind of talk this morning. I done raised you to come to this? You standing there all healthy and grown talking about you ain't going to your daddy's funeral?

CORY. Mama . . . listen . . .

ROSE. I don't want to hear it, Cory. You just get that thought out of your head.

CORY. I can't drag Papa with me everywhere I go. I've got to say no to him. One time in my life I've got to say no.

ROSE. Don't nobody have to listen to nothing like that. I know you and your daddy ain't seen eye to eye, but I ain't got to listen to that kind of talk this morning. Whatever was between you and your daddy . . . the time has come to put it aside. Just take it and set it over there on the shelf and forget about it. Disrespecting your daddy ain't gonna make you a man, Cory. You got to find a way to come to that on your own. Not going to your daddy's funeral ain't gonna make you a man.

CORY. The whole time I was growing up . . . living in his house . . . Papa was like a shadow that followed you everywhere. It weighed on you and sunk into your flesh. It would wrap around you and lay there until you couldn't tell which one was you anymore. That shadow digging in your flesh. Trying to crawl in. Trying to live through you. Everywhere I looked, Troy Maxson was staring back at me . . . hiding under the bed . . . in the closet. I'm just saying I've got to find a way to get rid of that shadow, Mama.

ROSE. You just like him. You got him in you good.

CORY. Don't tell me that, Mama.

ROSE. You Troy Maxson all over again.

CORY. I don't want to be Troy Maxson. I want to be me.

ROSE. You can't be nobody but who you are, Cory. That shadow wasn't nothing but you growing into yourself. You either got to grow into it or cut it down to fit you. But that's all you got to make life with. That's all you got to measure yourself against that world out there. Your daddy wanted you to be everything he wasn't . . . and at the same time he tried to make you into everything he was. I don't know if he was right or wrong . . . but I do know he meant to do more good than he meant to do harm. He wasn't always right. Sometimes when he touched he bruised. And sometimes when he took me in his arms he cut.

     When I first met your daddy I thought . . . Here is a man I can lay down with and make a baby. That's the first thing I thought when I seen him. I was thirty years old and had done seen my share of men. But when he walked up to me and said, "I can dance a waltz that'll make you dizzy," I thought, Rose Lee, here is a man that you can open yourself up to and be filled to bursting. Here is a man that can fill all them empty spaces you been tipping around the edges of. One of them empty spaces was being somebody's mother.

     I married your daddy and settled down to cooking his supper and keeping clean sheets on the bed. When your daddy walked through the house he was so big he filled it up. That was my first mistake. Not to make him leave some room for me. For my part in the matter. But at that time I wanted that. I wanted a house that I could sing in. And that's what your daddy gave me. I didn't know to keep up his strength I had to give up little pieces of mine. I did that. I took on his life as mine and mixed up the pieces so that you couldn't hardly tell which was which anymore. It was my choice. It was my life and I didn't have to live it like that. But that's what life offered me in the way of being a woman and I took it. I grabbed hold of it with both hands.

By the time Raynell came into the house, me and your daddy had done lost touch with one another. I didn't want to make my blessing off of nobody's misfortune . . . but I took on to Raynell like she was all them babies I had wanted and never had.

The phone rings.

Like I'd been blessed to relive a part of my life. And if the Lord see fit to keep up my strength . . . I'm gonna do her just like your daddy did you . . . I'm gonna give her the best of what's in me.

RAYNELL (*entering, still with her old shoes*). Mama . . . Reverend Tollivier on the phone.

ROSE *exits into the house.*

RAYNELL. Hi.

CORY. Hi.

RAYNELL. You in the Army or the Marines?

CORY. Marines.

RAYNELL. Papa said it was the Army. Did you know Blue?

CORY. Blue? Who's Blue?

RAYNELL. Papa's dog what he sing about all the time.

CORY (*singing*).

> Hear it ring! Hear it ring!
> I had a dog his name was Blue
> You know Blue was mighty true
> You know Blue was a good old dog
> Blue treed a possum in a hollow log
> You know from that he was a good old dog.
> Hear it ring! Hear it ring!

RAYNELL *joins in singing.*

CORY AND RAYNELL.

> Blue treed a possum out on a limb
> Blue looked at me and I looked at him
> Grabbed that possum and put him in a sack
> Blue stayed there till I came back
> Old Blue's feets was big and round
> Never allowed a possum to touch the ground.
> Old Blue died and I dug his grave
> I dug his grave with a silver spade
> Let him down with a golden chain
> And every night I call his name
> Go on Blue, you good dog you
> Go on Blue, you good dog you.

RAYNELL.

> Blue laid down and died like a man
> Blue laid down and died . . .

BOTH.

> Blue laid down and died like a man
> Now he's treeing possums in the Promised Land
> I'm gonna tell you this to let you know

> Blue's gone where the good dogs go
> When I hear old Blue bark
> When I hear old Blue bark
> Blue treed a possum in Noah's Ark
> Blue treed a possum in Noah's Ark.

ROSE *comes to the screen door.*

ROSE. Cory, we gonna be ready to go in a minute.

CORY (*to* RAYNELL). You go on in the house and change them shoes like Mama told you so we can go to Papa's funeral.

RAYNELL. Okay, I'll be back.

RAYNELL *exits into the house.* CORY *gets up and crosses over to the tree.* ROSE *stands in the screen door watching him.* GABRIEL *enters from the alley.*

GABRIEL (*calling*). Hey, Rose!

ROSE. Gabe?

GABRIEL. I'm here, Rose. Hey, Rose, I'm here!

ROSE *enters from the house.*

ROSE. Lord . . . Look here, Lyons!

LYONS. See, I told you, Rose . . . I told you they'd let him come.

CORY. How you doing, Uncle Gabe?

LYONS. How you doing, Uncle Gabe?

GABRIEL. Hey, Rose. It's time. It's time to tell St. Peter to open the gates. Troy, you ready? You ready, Troy. I'm gonna tell St. Peter to open the gates. You get ready now.

GABRIEL, *with great fanfare, braces himself to blow. The trumpet is without a mouthpiece. He puts the end of it into his mouth and blows with great force, like a man who has been waiting some twenty-odd years for this single moment. No sound comes out of the trumpet. He braces himself and blows again with the same result. A third time he blows. There is a weight of impossible description that falls away and leaves him bare and exposed to a frightful realization. It is a trauma that a sane and normal mind would be unable to withstand. He begins to dance. A slow, strange dance, eerie and life-giving. A dance of atavistic signature and ritual.* LYONS *attempts to embrace him.* GABRIEL *pushes* LYONS *away. He begins to howl in what is an attempt at song, or perhaps a song turning back into itself in an attempt at speech. He finishes his dance and the gates of heaven stand open as wide as God's closet.*

That's the way that go!

BLACKOUT

▒ TOPICS FOR CRITICAL THINKING AND WRITING

The Play on the Page

1. What do you think that Bono means when he says, early in Act 2, "Some people build fences to keep people out . . . and some people build fences to keep people in"? Why is the play called *Fences*? What has

fenced Troy in? What is Troy fencing in? (Take account of Troy's last speech in Act 2, Scene 2, but do not limit your discussion to this speech.)

2. What do you think Troy's reasons are—conscious and unconscious—for not wanting Cory to play football at college?

3. Compare and contrast Cory and Lyons. Consider, too, in what ways they resemble Troy and in what ways they differ from him.

4. In what ways is Troy like his father, and in what ways unlike him?

5. What do you make out of the prominence given to the song about Blue?

6. There is a good deal of anger in the play, but there is also humor. Which passages do you find humorous, and why?

7. Characterize Rose Maxson.

The Play on the Stage

8. How would Wilson's remarks in the 1987 interview (see page 000) help a director in staging *Fences*? For example, his assertion that every person (except Raynell) is institutionalized at the end of the play might suggest a certain tone or mood for a production.

9. In what ways is the role of Gabriel a challenge for an actor? What advice might you give to the other actors on stage during Gabriel's appearances?

10. Some scenes begin by specifying that "the lights come up." Others do not, presumably beginning with an illuminated stage. All scenes except the last one end with the lights going down to blackness. Explain Wilson's use of lighting.

A CONTEXT FOR *FENCES*

AUGUST WILSON

Talking about Fences

(Part of an interview conducted with David Savran on 13 March 1987.)

In reading Fences, I came to view Troy more and more critically as the play progressed, sharing Rose's point of view. We see that Troy has been crippled by his father. That's being replayed in Troy's relationship with Cory. Do you think there's a way out of that cycle?

Surely. First of all, we're all like our parents. The things we are taught early in life, how to respond to the world, our sense of morality—everything, we get from them. Now you can take that legacy and do with it anything you want to do. It's in your hands. Cory is Troy's son. How can he be Troy's son without sharing Troy's values? I was trying to get at why Troy made the choices he made, how they have influenced his values and how he attempts to pass those along to his son. Each generation gives the succeeding generation what they think they need. One question in the play is, "Are the tools we are given sufficient to compete in a world that is different from the one our parents knew?" I think they are—it's just that we have to do different things with the tools. That's all Troy has to give. Troy's flaw is that he does not recognize that the world was changing. That's because he spent fifteen years in a penitentiary.

As African-Americans, we should demand to participate in society as Africans. That's the way out of the vicious cycle of poverty and neglect that exists in 1987 in America, where you have a huge percentage of blacks living in the equivalent of South African townships, in housing projects. No one is inviting these people to participate in society. Look at the poverty levels—$8,500 for a family of four, if you have $8,501 you're not counted. Those statistics would go up enormously if we had an honest assessment of the cost of living in America. I don't know how anybody can support a family of four on $8,500. What I'm saying is that 85 or 90 percent of blacks in America are living in abject poverty and, for the most part, are crowded into what amount to concentration camps. The situation for blacks in America is worse than it was forty years ago. Some sociologists will tell you about the tremendous progress we've made. They didn't put me out when I walked in the door. And you can always point to someone who works on Wall Street, or is a doctor. But they don't count in the larger scheme of things.

Do you have any idea how these political changes could take place?

I'm not sure. I know that blacks must be allowed their cultural differences. I think the process of assimilation to white American society was a big mistake. We don't want to be like you. Blacks living in housing projects are isolated from the society, for the most part—living as they choose, as Africans. Only they don't realize the value in what they're doing because they have accepted their victimization. They've marked themselves as victims. Once they recognize that, they can begin to move through society in a different manner, from a stronger position, and claim what is theirs.

A project of yours is to point up what happens when oppression is internalized.

Yes, transfer of aggression to the wrong target. I think it's interesting that the two roads open to blacks for "full participation" are entertainment and sports, *Ma Rainey* and *Fences,* and I didn't plan it that way. I don't think that they're the correct roads. I think Troy's right. Now with the benefit of historical perspective, I can say that the athletic scholarship was actually a way of exploiting. Now you've got two million kids who think they're going to play in the NBA. In the sixties the universities made a lot of money off of athletics. You had kids playing for free who, by and large, were not getting educated, were taking courses in basketweaving. Some of them could barely read.

Troy may be right about that issue, but it seems that he has passed on certain destructive traits in spite of himself. Take the hostility between father and son.

I think every generation says to the previous generation: you're in my way. I've got to get by. The father–son conflict is actually a normal generational conflict that happens all the time.

So it's a healthy and a good thing?

Oh, sure. Troy is seeing this boy walk around, smelling his piss. Two men cannot live in the same household. Troy would have been tremendously disappointed if Cory had not challenged him. Troy knows that this boy has to go out and do battle with that world: "So I had best prepare him because I know that's a harsh, cruel place out there. But that's going to be easy compared to what he's getting here. Ain't nobody gonna whip your ass like I'm gonna whip it." He has a tremendous love for the kid. But he's not going to say, "I love you," he's going to demonstrate it. He's carrying garbage for seventeen years just for the kid. The only world Troy knows is the one that he made. Cory's going to go on to find another one, he's going to arrive at the same place as Troy. I think one of the most important lines in the play is when Troy is talking about his father: "I got to the place where I could feel him kicking in my blood and knew that the only thing that separated us was the matter of a few years."

Hopefully, Cory will do things a bit differently with his son. For Troy, sports was not the way to go, the white man wouldn't let him get away with that. "Get you a job, with your hands, something that nobody can take away from you." The idea of school—he doesn't know what that is. That's for white folks. Very few blacks had paperwork jobs. But if you knew how to fix cars, you could always make some money. That's what Troy wants for Cory. There aren't many people who ever jumped up in Troy's face. So he's proud of the kid at the same time that he expresses a hurt that all men feel. You got to cut your kid loose at some point. There's that sense of loss and separation. You find out how Troy left his father's house and you see how Cory leaves his house. I suspect with Cory it will repeat with some differences and maybe, after five or six generations, they'll find a different way to do it.

Where Cory ends up is very ambiguous, as a marine in 1965.

Yes. For the average black kid on the street, that was an alternative. You went into the army because you could learn how to do something. I can remember my parents talking about the son of some friends: "He's in the navy. He *did* something"—as opposed to standing on the street corner, shooting drugs, drinking wine, and robbing stores. Lyons says to Cory, "I always knew you were going to make something out of yourself." It really wounds me. He's a corporal in the marines. For blacks, that is a sense of accomplishment. Therein lies one of the tragedies of blacks in America. Cory says, "I don't know. I put in six years. That's enough." Anyone who goes into the army and makes a career out of it is a loser. They sit there and are nurtured by the army and they don't have to confront life. Then they get out of the army and find there's nothing to do. They didn't learn any skills. And if they did, they can't find a job. Four months later, they're shooting dope. In the sixties a whole bunch of blacks went over, fought and died in the Vietnam War. The survivors came back to the same street corners and found out nothing had changed. They still couldn't get a job.

At the end of *Fences* every person, with the exception of Raynell, is institutionalized. Rose is in a church. Lyons is in a penitentiary. Gabriel's in a mental hospital and Cory's in the marines. The only free person is the girl, Troy's daughter, the hope for the future. That was conscious on my part because in '57 that's what I saw. Blacks have relied on institutions which are really foreign—except for the black church, which has been our saving grace. I have some problems with it but I recognize it as a central social organization and sometimes an economic organization for the black community. I would like to see blacks develop their own institutions that respond to their needs.

Critical Perspectives

35

Critical Approaches: The Nature of Criticism

In everyday talk the most common meaning of **criticism** is something like "finding fault." And to be critical is to be censorious. But a critic can see excellences as well as faults. Because we turn to criticism with the hope that the critic has seen something we have missed, the most valuable criticism is not that which shakes its finger at faults, but that which calls our attention to interesting things going on in the work of art. Here is a statement by W. H. Auden (1907–1973), suggesting that criticism is most useful when it calls our attention to things worth attending to:

> What is the function of a critic? So far as I am concerned, he can do me one or more of the following services:
>
> 1. Introduce me to authors or works of which I was hitherto unaware.
> 2. Convince me that I have undervalued an author or a work because I had not read them carefully enough.
> 3. Show me relations between works of different ages and cultures which I could never have seen for myself because I do not know enough and never shall.
> 4. Give a "reading" of a work which increases my understanding of it.
> 5. Throw light upon the process of artistic "Making."
> 6. Throw light upon the relation of art to life, science, economics, ethics, religion, etc.
>
> —*The Dyer's Hand* (New York, 1963), pages 8–9

Auden does not neglect the delight we get from literature, but he extends (especially in his sixth point) the range of criticism to include topics beyond the literary work itself. Notice too the emphasis on observing, showing, and illuminating, which suggests that the function of critical writing is not very different from the most common view of the function of imaginative writing.

Whenever we talk about a work of literature or of art, or, for that matter, even about a so-so movie or television show, what we say depends in large measure on certain conscious or unconscious assumptions that we make: "I liked it; the characters were very believable" (here the assumption is that characters ought to be believable); "I didn't like it; there was too much violence" (here the assumption is that violence ought not to be shown, or if it is shown it should be made abhorrent); "I didn't like it; it was awfully slow" (here the assumption probably is that there ought to be a fair amount of physical action, perhaps even changes of scene, rather than characters just talking); "I didn't like it; I don't think topics of this sort ought to be discussed publicly" (here the assumption is a moral one, that it is indecent to present certain topics); "I liked it partly because it was refreshing to hear such frankness" (here again the assumption is moral, and more or less the reverse of the previous one).

In short, whether we realize it or not, we judge the work from a particular viewpoint—its realism, its morality, or whatever.

Professional critics, too, work from assumptions, but their assumptions are usually highly conscious, and the critics may define their assumptions at length. They regard themselves as, for instance, Freudians or Marxists or Queer Theorists. They read all texts through the lens of a particular theory, and their focus enables them to see things that otherwise might go unnoticed. It should be added, however, that if a lens or critical perspective or interpretive strategy helps us to see certain things, it also limits our vision. Many critics therefore regard their method not as an exclusive way of thinking but only as a useful tool.

What follows is a brief survey of the chief current approaches to literature. You may find, as you read these pages, that one or another approach sounds especially congenial, and therefore you may want to make use of it in your reading and writing. On the other hand, it's important to remember, first, that works of literature are highly varied, and, second, that we read them for various purposes—to kill time, to enjoy fanciful visions, to be amused, to explore alien ways of feeling, and to learn about ourselves. It may be best to try to respond to each text in the way that the text seems to require rather than to read all texts according to a single formula. You'll find that some works will lead you to want to think about them from several angles. A play by Shakespeare may stimulate you to read a book about the Elizabethan playhouse, and another that offers a Marxist interpretation of the English Renaissance, and still another that offers a feminist analysis of Shakespeare's plays. All of these approaches, and others, will help you to deepen your understanding of the literary works that you read.

FORMALIST (OR NEW) CRITICISM

Formalist criticism emphasizes the work as an independent creation, a self-contained unit, something to be studied in itself, not as part of some larger context, such as the author's life or a historical period. This kind of study is called formalist criticism because the emphasis is on the *form* of the work, the relationships between the parts—the construction of the plot, the contrasts between characters, the functions of rhymes, the point of view, and so on.

Cleanth Brooks, perhaps America's most distinguished formalist critic, in an essay in the *Kenyon Review* (Winter 1951), reprinted in *The Modern Critical Spectrum*, eds. Gerald Jay Goldberg and Nancy Marmer Goldberg (1962), set forth what he called his "articles of faith":

> That literary criticism is a description and an evaluation of its object.
> That the primary concern of criticism is with the problem of unity—the kind of whole which the literary work forms or fails to form, and the relation of the various parts to each other in building up this whole.

That the formal relations in a work of literature may include, but certainly
exceed, those of logic.

That in a successful work, form and content cannot be separated.

That form is meaning.

If you have read the earlier pages of this book you are already familiar with
most of these ideas, but in the next few pages we will look into some of them
in detail.

Formalist criticism is, in essence, *intrinsic* criticism, rather than extrinsic,
for (at least in theory) it concentrates on the work itself, independent of its
writer and the writer's background—that is, independent of biography, psychology, sociology, and history. The discussions of Langston Hughes's "Harlem"
(pages 664–669) and of Yeats's "The Balloon of the Mind" (pages 43–46) are
examples. The gist is that a work of literature is complex, unified, and freestand-
ing. In fact, of course, we usually bring outside knowledge to the work. For instance, a reader who is familiar with, say, *Hamlet* can hardly study another
tragedy by Shakespeare, let's say *Romeo and Juliet*, without bringing to the second play some conception of what Shakespearean tragedy is or can be. A reader
of Alice Walker's *The Color Purple* inevitably brings unforgettable outside material (perhaps the experience of being an African-American, or at least some
knowledge of the history of African-Americans) to the literary work. It is very
hard to talk only about *Hamlet* or *The Color Purple* and not at the same time talk
about, or at least have in mind, aspects of human experience.

Formalist criticism begins with a personal response to the literary work, but
it goes on to try to account for the response by closely examining the work. It assumes that the author shaped the poem, play, or story so fully that the work
guides the reader's responses. The assumption that "meaning" is fully and completely presented within the text is not much in favor today, when many literary
critics argue that the active or subjective reader (or even what Judith Fetterley, a
feminist critic, has called "the resisting reader") and not the author of the text
makes the "meaning." Still, even if one grants that the reader is active, not passive
or coolly objective, one can hold with the formalists that the author is active too,
constructing a text that in some measure controls the reader's responses. During
the process of writing about our responses we may find that our responses
change. A formalist critic would say that we see with increasing clarity what the
work is really like, and what it really means. (Similarly, when authors write and
revise a text they may change their understanding of what they are doing. A story
that began as a lighthearted joke may turn into something far more serious than
the writer imagined at the start, but, at least for the formalist critic, the final work
contains a stable meaning that all competent readers can perceive.)

In practice, formalist criticism usually takes one of two forms, **explication**
(the unfolding of meaning, line by line or even word by word) or **analysis**
(the examination of the relations of parts). The essay on Yeats's "The Balloon
of the Mind" (pages 43–46) is an explication, a setting forth of the implicit meanings of the words. The essay on Kate Chopin's "The Story of an Hour" (pages
40–41) is an analysis.

To repeat: Formalist criticism assumes that a work of art is stable. An artist
constructs a coherent, comprehensible work, thus conveying to a reader an
emotion or an idea. T. S. Eliot said that the writer can't just pour out emotions
onto the page. Rather, Eliot said in an essay entitled "Hamlet and His Problems"
(1919), "The only way of expressing emotion in the form of art is by finding an

'objective correlative'; in other words, a set of objects, a situation, a chain of events which shall be the formula of the *particular* emotion."

With this in mind, consider Robert Frost's "The Span of Life":

The old dog barks backward without getting up.
I can remember when he was a pup.

The image of an old dog barking backward, and the speaker's memory—apparently triggered by the old dog's bark—of the dog as a pup, presumably is the "objective correlative" of Frost's emotion or idea; Frost is "expressing emotion" through this "formula." And all of us, as competent readers, can grasp pretty accurately what Frost expressed. Frost's emotion, idea, meaning, or whatever is "objectively" embodied in the text. Formalist critics try to explain how and why literary works—*these* words, in *this* order—constitute unique, complex structures that embody or set forth meanings.

Formalist criticism, also called the **New Criticism** (to distinguish it from the historical and biographical writing that in earlier decades had dominated literary study), began to achieve prominence in the late 1920s and was the dominant form from the late 1930s until about 1970, and even today it is widely considered the best way for a student to begin to study a work of literature. For one thing, formalist criticism empowers the student; that is, the student confronts the work immediately, and is not told first to spend days or weeks or months, for instance, reading Freud and his followers in order to write a psychoanalytic essay or reading Marx and Marxists in order to write a Marxist essay, or doing research on "necessary historical background" in order to write a historical essay.

DECONSTRUCTION

Deconstruction, or deconstructive or poststructuralist criticism, can almost be characterized as the opposite of everything formalist criticism stands for. Deconstruction begins with the assumptions that the world is unknowable and that language is unstable, elusive, unfaithful. (Language is all of these things because meaning is largely generated by opposition: "Hot" means something in opposition to "cold," but a hot day may be 90 degrees whereas a hot oven is at least 400 degrees; and a "hot item" may be of any temperature.) Deconstructionists seek to show that a literary work (usually called "a text" or "a discourse") inevitably is self-contradictory. Unlike formalist critics—who hold that a competent author constructs a coherent work with a stable meaning, and that competent readers can perceive this meaning—deconstructionists (e.g., Barbara Johnson, in *The Critical Difference* [1980]) hold that a work has no coherent meaning at the center. Jonathan Culler, in *On Deconstruction* (1982), says that "to deconstruct a discourse is to show how it undermines the philosophy it asserts" (86). (Johnson and Culler provide accessible introductions, but the major document is Jacques Derrida's seminal, difficult work, *Of Grammatology* [1967, trans. 1976].) The text is only marks on paper, and therefore so far as a reader goes the author of a text is not the writer but the reader; texts are "indeterminate," "open," and "unstable."

Despite the emphasis on indeterminacy, one sometimes detects in deconstructionist interpretations a view associated with Marxism. This is the idea that authors are "socially constructed" from the "discourses of power" or "signifying

practices" that surround them. Thus, although authors may think they are individuals with independent minds, their works usually reveal—unknown to the
authors—the society's economic base. Deconstructionists "interrogate" a text,
and they reveal what the authors were unaware of or had thought they had
kept safely out of sight. That is, deconstructionists often find a rather specific
meaning—though this meaning is one that might surprise the author.

Deconstruction is valuable insofar as—like the New Criticism—it encourages close, rigorous attention to the text. Furthermore, in its rejection of the
claim that a work has a single stable meaning, deconstruction has had a positive
influence on the study of literature. The problem with deconstruction, however,
is that too often it is reductive, telling the same story about every text—that
here, yet again, and again, we see how a text is incoherent and heterogeneous.
There is, too, an irritating arrogance in some deconstructive criticism: "The
author could not see how his/her text is fundamentally unstable and self-
contradictory, but *I* can and now will interrogate the text and will issue my report." Readers, of course, should not prostrate themselves before texts, but
there is something askew about an approach—however intense and detailed—
that often leads readers to conclude that they know a good deal more than the
benighted author.

Aware that their emphasis on the instability of language implies that their
own texts are unstable or even incoherent, some deconstructionists seem to
aim at entertaining rather than at edifying. They probably would claim that
they do not deconstruct meaning in the sense of destroying it; rather, they might
say, they exuberantly multiply meanings, and to this end they may use such devices as puns, irony, and allusions, somewhat as a poet might, and just as though
(one often feels) they think they are as creative as the writers they are commenting on. Indeed, for many deconstructionists, the traditional conception of
"literature" is merely an elitist "construct." All "texts" or "discourses" (novels,
scientific papers, a Kewpie doll on the mantel, watching TV, suing in court,
walking the dog, and all other signs that human beings make) are of a piece; all
are unstable systems of signifying, all are fictions, all are "literature." If literature
(in the usual sense) occupies a special place in deconstruction it is because
literature delights in its playfulness, its fictiveness, whereas other discourses
nominally reject playfulness and fictiveness.

READER-RESPONSE CRITICISM

Probably all reading includes some sort of response—"This is terrific," "This is a
bore," "I don't know what's going on here"—and probably almost all writing
about literature begins with some such response, but specialists in literature disagree greatly about the role that response plays, or should play, in experiencing
literature and in writing about it.

At one extreme are those who say that our response to a work of literature
should be a purely aesthetic response—a response to a work of art—and not the
response we would have to something comparable in real life. To take an obvious point: If in real life we heard someone plotting a murder, we would intervene, perhaps by calling the police or by attempting to warn the victim. But
when we hear Macbeth and Lady Macbeth plot to kill King Duncan, we watch
with deep *interest;* we hear their words with *pleasure,* and maybe we even look

forward to seeing the murder and to seeing what the characters then will say and what will happen to the murderers.

When you think about it, the vast majority of the works of literature do not have a close, obvious resemblance to the reader's life. Most readers of *Macbeth* are not Scots, and no readers are Scottish kings or queens. (It's not just a matter of older literature; no readers of Toni Morrison's *Beloved* are nineteenth-century African-Americans.) The connections readers make between themselves and the lives in most of the books they read are not, on the whole, connections based on ethnic or professional identities, but, rather, connections with states of consciousness, for instance a young person's sense of isolation from the family, or a young person's sense of guilt for initial sexual experiences. Before we reject a work either because it seems too close to us ("I'm a man and I don't like the depiction of this man"), or on the other hand too far from our experience ("I'm not a woman, so how can I enjoy reading about these women?"), we probably should try to follow the advice of Virginia Woolf, who said, "Do not dictate to your author; try to become him." Nevertheless, some literary works of the past may today seem intolerable, at least in part. There are passages in Mark Twain's *Huckleberry Finn* that deeply upset us today. We should, however, try to reconstruct the cultural assumptions of the age in which the work was written. If we do so, we may find that if in some ways it reflected its age, in other ways it challenged that culture.

Still, some of our experiences, some of *what we are,* may make it virtually impossible for us to read a work sympathetically or "objectively," experiencing it only as a work of art and not as a part of life. Take so humble a form of literature as the joke. A few decades ago jokes about nagging wives and mothers-in-law were widely thought to be funny. Our fairly recent heightened awareness of sexism today makes those jokes unfunny. Twenty years ago the "meaning" of a joke about a nagging wife or about a mother-in-law was, in effect, "Here's a funny episode that shows what women typically are." Today the "meaning"—at least as the hearer conceives it—is "The unfunny story you have just told shows that you have stupid, stereotypical views of women." In short, the joke may "mean" one thing to the teller, and a very different thing to the hearer.

Reader-response criticism, then, says that the "meaning" of a work is not merely something put into the work by the writer; rather, the "meaning" is an interpretation created or constructed or produced by the reader as well as the writer. Stanley Fish, an exponent of reader-response theory, in *Is There a Text in This Class?* (1980), puts it this way: "Interpretation is not the art of construing but of constructing. Interpreters do not decode poems; they make them" (327).

Let's now try to relate these ideas more specifically to comments about literature. If "meaning" is the production or creation not simply of the writer but also of the perceiver, does it follow that there is no such thing as a "correct" interpretation of the meaning of a work of literature? Answers to this question differ. At one extreme, the reader is said to construct or reconstruct the text under the firm guidance of the author. That is, the author so powerfully shapes or constructs the text—encodes an idea—that the reader is virtually compelled to perceive or reconstruct or decode it the way the author wants it to be perceived. (We can call this view *the objective view,* since it essentially holds that readers look objectively at the work and see what the author put into it.) At the other extreme, the reader constructs the meaning according to his or her own personality—that is, according to the reader's psychological identity. (We can call this view *the subjective view,* since it essentially holds that readers inevitably project their feelings into what they perceive.) An extreme version of the subjective view holds that there is no such thing as literature; there are only texts, some of which some readers regard in a particularly elitist way.

Against the objective view one can argue thus: No author can fully control a reader's response to every detail of the text. No matter how carefully constructed the text is, it leaves something—indeed, a great deal—to the reader's imagination. For instance, when Macbeth says that life "is a tale/Told by an idiot, full of sound and fury/Signifying nothing," are we getting a profound thought from Shakespeare or, on the contrary, are we getting a shallow thought from Macbeth, a man who does not see that his criminal deeds have been played out against a heaven that justly punishes his crimes? In short, the objective view neglects to take account of the fact that the author is not continually at our shoulder making sure that we interpret the work in a particular way.

It is probably true, as Flannery O'Connor says in *Mystery and Manners* (1957), that good writers select "every word, every detail, for a reason, every incident for a reason" (75), but there are always *gaps* or *indeterminacies,* to use the words of Wolfgang Iser, a reader-response critic. Readers always go beyond the text, drawing inferences, and evaluating the text in terms of their own experience. In the Old Testament, for instance, in Genesis, the author tells us (Chapter 22) that God commanded Abraham to sacrifice his son Isaac, and then says that "Abraham rose up early in the morning" and prepared to fulfill the command. We are not explicitly told *why* Abraham "rose up early in the morning," or how he spent the intervening night, but some readers take "early in the morning" to signify (reasonably?) that Abraham has had a sleepless night. Others take it to signify (reasonably?) that Abraham is prompt in obeying God's command. Some readers fill the gap with both explanations, or with neither. Doubtless much depends on the reader, but there is no doubt that readers "naturalize"— make natural, according to their own ideas—what they read.

In an extreme form the subjective view denies that authors can make us perceive the meanings that they try to put into their works. This position suggests that every reader has a different idea of what a work means, an idea that reflects the reader's own ideas. Every reader, then, is Narcissus, who looked into a pool of water and thought he saw a beautiful youth but really saw only a reflection of himself. But does every reader see his or her individual image in each literary work? Of course not. Even *Hamlet,* a play that has generated an enormous range of interpretation, is universally seen as a tragedy, a play that deals with painful realities. If someone were to tell us that *Hamlet* is a comedy, and that the end, with a pile of corpses, is especially funny, we would not say, "Oh, well, we all see things in our own way." Rather, we would make our exit as quickly as possible.

Many people who subscribe to one version or another of a reader-response theory would agree that they are concerned not with all readers but with what they call *informed readers* or *competent readers.* Thus, informed or competent readers are familiar with the conventions of literature. They understand, for instance, that in a play such as *Hamlet* the characters usually speak in verse. Such readers, then, do not express amazement that Hamlet often speaks metrically, and that he sometimes uses rhyme. These readers understand that verse is the normal language for most of the characters in the play, and therefore such readers do not characterize Hamlet as a poet. Informed, competent readers, in short, know the rules of the game. There will still, of course, be plenty of room for differences of interpretation. Some people will find Hamlet not at all blameworthy;

others will find him somewhat blameworthy; and still others may find him highly blameworthy. In short, we can say that a writer works against a background that is *shared* by readers. As readers, we are familiar with various kinds of literature, and we read or see *Hamlet* as a particular kind of literary work, a tragedy, a play that evokes (in Shakespeare's words) "woe or wonder," sadness and astonishment. Knowing (to a large degree) how we ought to respond, our responses thus are not merely private.

Consider taking, as a guide to reading, a remark made by Mencius (372–289 BCE), the Chinese Confucian philosopher. Speaking of reading *The Book of Odes,* the oldest Chinese anthology, Mencius said that "a reader must let his thought go to meet the intention as he would a guest." We often cannot be sure about the author's intention (we do not know what Shakespeare intended to say in *Hamlet;* we have only the play itself), and even those relatively few authors who have explicitly stated their intentions may be untrustworthy for one reason or another. Yet there is something highly attractive in Mencius's suggestion that when we read we should—at least for a start—treat our author not with suspicion or hostility but with goodwill and with the expectation of pleasure.

What are the implications of reader-response theory for writing an essay on a work of literature? Even if we agree that we are talking only about competent readers, does this mean that *almost* anything goes in setting forth one's responses in an essay? Almost all advocates of any form of reader-response criticism agree on one thing: There are agreed-upon rules of *writing* if not of reading. This one point of agreement can be amplified to contain at least two aspects: (1) we all agree (more or less) as to what constitutes evidence, and (2) we all agree that a written response should be coherent. If you say that you find Hamlet to be less noble than his adversary, Claudius, you will be expected to provide evidence by pointing to specific passages, to specific things that Hamlet and Claudius say and do. And you will be expected to order the material into an effective, coherent sequence, so that the reader can move easily through your essay and will understand what you are getting at.

ARCHETYPAL (OR MYTH) CRITICISM

Carl G. Jung, the Swiss psychiatrist, in *Contributions to Analytical Psychology* (1928), postulates the existence of a "collective unconscious," an inheritance in our brains consisting of "countless typical experiences [such as birth, escape from danger, selection of a mate] of our ancestors." Few people today believe in an inherited "collective unconscious," but many people agree that certain repeated experiences, such as going to sleep and hours later awakening, or the perception of the setting and of the rising sun, or of the annual death and rebirth of vegetation, manifest themselves in dreams, myths, and literature—in these instances, as stories of apparent death and rebirth. This archetypal plot of death and rebirth is said to be evident in Coleridge's *The Rime of the Ancient Mariner,* for example. The ship suffers a deathlike calm and then is miraculously restored to motion, and, in a sort of parallel rebirth, the mariner moves from spiritual death to renewed perception of the holiness of life. Another archetypal plot is the quest, which usually involves the testing and initiation of a hero, and thus essentially represents the movement from innocence to experience. In addition to archetypal plots there are archetypal characters, since an archetype is any recurring unit. Among archetypal characters are the Scapegoat, the Hero (savior, deliverer), the Terrible Mother (witch, stepmother—even the wolf "grandmother" in the tale of Little Red Riding Hood), and the Wise Old Man (father figure, magician).

Because, the theory holds, both writer and reader share unconscious memories, the tale an author tells (derived from the collective unconscious) may strangely move the reader, speaking to his or her collective unconscious. As Maud Bodkin puts it, in *Archetypal Patterns in Poetry* (1934), something within us "leaps in response to the effective presentation in poetry of an ancient theme" (4). But this emphasis on ancient (or repeated) themes has made archetypal criticism vulnerable to the charge that it is reductive. The critic looks for certain characters or patterns of action and values the work if the motifs are there, meanwhile overlooking what is unique, subtle, distinctive, and truly interesting about the work. That is, to put the matter crudely, a work is regarded as good if it is pretty much like other works, with the usual motifs and characters. A second weakness in some archetypal criticism is that in the search for the deepest meaning of a work the critic may crudely impose a pattern, seeing (for instance) The Quest in every walk down the street. But perhaps to say this is to beg the question; it is the critic's job to write so persuasively that the reader at least tentatively accepts the critic's view. For a wide-ranging study of one particular motif, see Barbara Fass Leavy's *In Search of the Swan Maiden* (1994), a discussion of the legend of a swan maiden who is forced to marry a mortal because he possesses something of hers, usually a garment or an animal skin. Leavy analyzes several versions of the story, which she takes to be a representation not only of female rage against male repression but also a representation of male fear of female betrayal. Leavy ends her book by examining this motif in Ibsen's *A Doll's House.* Her claim is that when Nora finds a lost object, the dance costume, she can flee from the tyrannical domestic world and thus she regains her freedom.

If archetypal criticism sometimes seems farfetched, it is nevertheless true that one of its strengths is that it invites us to use comparisons, and comparing is often an excellent way to see not only what a work shares with other works but what is distinctive in the work. The most successful practitioner of archetypal criticism was the late Northrop Frye (1912–1991), whose numerous books help readers to see fascinating connections between works. For Frye's explicit comments about archetypal criticism, as well as for examples of such criticism in action, see especially his *Anatomy of Criticism* (1957) and *The Educated Imagination* (1964). On archetypes see also Chapter 16, "Archetypal Patterns," in Norman Friedman, *Form and Meaning in Fiction* (1975).

HISTORICAL SCHOLARSHIP

Historical criticism studies a work within its historical context. Thus, a student of *Julius Caesar, Hamlet,* or *Macbeth*—plays in which ghosts appear—may try to find out about Elizabethan attitudes toward ghosts. We may find that the Elizabethans took ghosts more seriously than we do; on the other hand, we may find that ghosts were explained in various ways, for instance sometimes as figments of the imagination and sometimes as shapes taken by the devil in order to mislead the virtuous. Similarly, a historical essay concerned with *Othello* may be devoted to Elizabethan attitudes toward Moors, or to Elizabethan ideas of love, or, for that matter, to Elizabethan ideas of a daughter's obligations toward her father's wishes concerning her suitor. The historical critic assumes (and one can hardly dispute the assumption) that writers, however individualistic, are shaped by the particular social contexts in which they live. One can put it this way: The goal of historical criticism is to understand how people in the past thought and felt. It assumes that such understanding can enrich our understanding of a particular work. The assumption is, however, disputable, since one may argue that the artist—let's say Shakespeare—may *not* have shared the age's view on this or that. All of the half-dozen or so Moors in Elizabethan plays other than *Othello* are villainous or foolish, but this evidence, one can argue, does not prove that *therefore* Othello is villainous or foolish.

Marxist Criticism

One form of historical criticism is **Marxist criticism,** named for Karl Marx (1818-1883). Actually, to say "one form" is misleading, since Marxist criticism today is varied, but essentially it sees history primarily as a struggle between socioeconomic classes, and it sees literature (and everything else) as the product of economic forces of the period.

For Marxists, economics is the "base" or "infrastructure"; on this base rests a "superstructure" of ideology (law, politics, philosophy, religion, and the arts, including literature), reflecting the interests of the dominant class. Thus, literature is a material product, produced—like bread or battleships—in order to be consumed in a given society. Like every other product, literature is the product of work, and it *does* work. A bourgeois society, for example, will produce literature that in one way or another celebrates bourgeois values, such as individualism. These works serve to assure the society that produces them that its values are solid, even universal. The enlightened Marxist writer or critic, on the other hand, exposes the fallacy of traditional values and replaces them with the truths found in Marxism. In the heyday of Marxism in the United States, during the depression of the 1930s, it was common for such Marxist critics as Granville Hicks to assert that the novel must show the class struggle.

Few critics of any sort would disagree that works of art in some measure reflect the age that produced them, but most contemporary Marxist critics go further. First, they assert—in a repudiation of what has been called "'vulgar' Marxist theory"—that the deepest historical meaning of a literary work is to be found in what it does *not* say, what its ideology does not permit it to express. Second, Marxists take seriously Marx's famous comment that "the philosophers have only *interpreted* the world in various ways; the point is to *change* it." The critic's job is to change the world, by revealing the economic basis of the arts. Not surprisingly, most Marxists are skeptical of such concepts as "genius" and "masterpiece." These concepts, they say, are part of the bourgeois myth that idealizes the individual and detaches it from its economic context. For an introduction to Marxist criticism, see Terry Eagleton, *Marxism and Literary Criticism* (1976).

The New Historicism

A recent school of scholarship, called the **New Historicism,** insists that there is no "history" in the sense of a narrative of indisputable past events. Rather, the New Historicism holds that there is only our version—our narrative, our representation—of the past. In this view, each age projects its own preconceptions on the past; historians may think they are revealing the past, but they are revealing only their own historical situation and their personal preferences. Thus, in the nineteenth century and in the twentieth almost up to 1992, Columbus was represented as the heroic benefactor of humankind who discovered the New World. But even while plans were being made to celebrate the five-hundredth anniversary of his first voyage across the Atlantic, voices were raised in protest: Columbus did not "discover" a New World; after all, the indigenous people knew where they were, and it was Columbus who was lost, since he thought he was in India. People who wrote history in, say, 1900, projected onto the past their current views (colonialism was a Good Thing), and people who in 1992 wrote history projected onto that same period a very different set of views (colonialism was a Bad Thing). Similarly, ancient Greece, once celebrated by historians as the source of democracy and rational thinking, is now more often regarded as a society that was built on slavery and on the oppression of women. And the Renaissance, once glorified as an age of enlightened thought, is now often seen as an age that tyrannized women, enslaved colonial people, and enslaved itself with its belief in witchcraft and astrology. Thinking about these changing views, one feels the truth of the witticism that the only thing more uncertain than the future is the past.

The New Historicism is especially associated with Stephen Greenblatt, who popularized the term in 1982 in the preface to a collection of essays published in the journal *Genre*. Greenblatt himself has said of the New Historicism that "it's no doctrine at all" (*Learning to Curse*, [1990]) but the term is nevertheless much used, and, as the preceding remarks have suggested, it is especially associated with power, most especially with revealing the tyrannical practices of a society that others have glorified. The New Historicism was in large measure shaped by the 1960s; the students who in the 1960s protested against the war in Vietnam by holding demonstrations, in the 1980s—they were now full professors—protested against Ronald Reagan by writing articles exposing Renaissance colonialism. Works of literature were used as a basis for a criticism of society. Academic writing of this sort was not dry, impartial, unimpassioned scholarship; rather, it connected the past with the present, and it offered value judgments. In Greenblatt's words,

> Writing that was not engaged, that withheld judgments, that failed to connect the present with the past seemed worthless. Such connection could be made either by analogy or causality; that is, a particular set of historical circumstances could be represented in such a way as to bring out homologies with aspects of the present or, alternatively, those circumstances could be analyzed as the generative forces that led to the modern condition. (*Learning to Curse*, page 167)

For a collection of 15 essays exemplifying the New Historicism, see H. Aram Veeser, ed., *The New Historicism* (1994).

Biographical Criticism

One kind of historical scholarship is the study of *biography*, which for our purposes includes not only biographies but also autobiographies, diaries, journals, letters, and so on. What experiences did (for example) Mark Twain undergo?

Are some of the apparently sensational aspects of *Huckleberry Finn* in fact close to events that Twain experienced? If so, is he a "realist"? If not, is he writing in the tradition of the "tall tale"?

The really good biographies not only tell us about the life of the author, but they enable us to return to the literary texts with a deeper understanding of how they came to be what they are. If you read Richard B. Sewall's biography of Emily Dickinson, you will find a wealth of material concerning her family and the world she moved in—for instance, the religious ideas that were part of her upbringing.

Biographical study may illuminate even the work of a living author. If you are writing about the poetry of Adrienne Rich, for example, you may want to consider what she has told us in many essays about her life, especially about her relations with her father and her husband.

PSYCHOLOGICAL (OR PSYCHOANALYTIC) CRITICISM

One form that biographical study may take is **psychological** or **psychoanalytic criticism,** which usually examines the author and the author's writings in the framework of Freudian psychology. A central doctrine of Sigmund Freud (1856–1939) is the Oedipus complex, the view that all males (Freud seems not to have made his mind up about females) unconsciously wish to displace their fathers and to sleep with their mothers. According to Freud, hatred for the father and love of the mother, normally repressed, may appear disguised in dreams. Works of art, like dreams, are disguised versions of repressed wishes.

Consider the case of Edgar Allan Poe. An orphan before he was three years old, he was brought up in the family of John Allan, but he was never formally adopted. His relations with Allan were stormy, though he seems to have had better relations with Allan's wife and still better relations with an aunt, whose daughter he married. In the Freudian view, Poe's marriage to his cousin (the daughter of a mother figure) was a way of sleeping with his mother. According to psychoanalytic critics, if we move from Poe's life to his work, we see, it is alleged, this hatred for his father and love for his mother. Thus, the murderer in "The Cask of Amontillado" is said to voice Poe's hostility toward his father, and the wine vault in which much of the story is set (an encompassing structure associated with fluids) is interpreted as symbolizing Poe's desire to return to his mother's womb. In Poe's other works, the longing for death is similarly taken to embody his desire to return to the womb.

Other psychoanalytic interpretations of Poe have been offered. Kenneth Silverman, author of a biography titled *Edgar Allan Poe* (1991) and the editor of a collection titled *New Essays on Poe's Major Tales* (1993), emphasizes the fact that Poe was orphaned before he was three, and was separated from his brother and his infant sister. In *New Essays* Silverman relates this circumstance to the "many instances of engulfment" that he finds in Poe's work. Images of engulfment, he points out, "are part of a still larger network of images having to do with biting, devouring, and similar oral mutilation." Why are they common in Poe? Here is Silverman's answer:

> Current psychoanalytic thinking about childhood bereavement explains the fantasy of being swallowed up as representing a desire,

mixed with dread, to merge with the dead; the wish to devour represents a primitive attempt at preserving loved ones, incorporating them so as not to lose them. (20)

Notice that psychoanalytic interpretations usually take us away from what the author consciously intended; they purport to tell us what the work reveals, whether or not the author was aware of this meaning. The "meaning" of the work is found not in the surface content of the work but in the author's psyche.

One additional example—and it is the most famous—of a psychoanalytic study of a work of literature may be useful. In *Hamlet and Oedipus* (1949) Ernest Jones, amplifying some comments by Freud, argued that Hamlet delays killing Claudius because Claudius (who has killed Hamlet's father and married Hamlet's mother) has done exactly what Hamlet himself wanted to do. For Hamlet to kill Claudius, then, would be to kill himself.

If this approach interests you, take a look at Norman N. Holland's *Psychoanalysis and Shakespeare* (1966), or Frederick Crews's study of Hawthorne, *The Sins of the Fathers* (1966). Crews finds in Hawthorne's work evidence of unresolved Oedipal conflicts, and he accounts for the appeal of the fictions thus: The stories "rest on fantasy, but on the shared fantasy of mankind, and this makes for a more penetrating fiction than would any illusionistic slice of life" (263). For applications to other authors, look at Simon O. Lesser's *Fiction and the Unconscious* (1957), or at an anthology of criticism, *Literature and Psychoanalysis,* edited by Edith Kurzweil and William Phillips (1983).

Psychological criticism can also turn from the author and the work to the reader, seeking to explain why we, as readers, respond in certain ways. Why, for example, is *Hamlet* so widely popular? A Freudian answer is that it is universal because it deals with a universal (Oedipal) impulse. One can, however, ask whether it appeals as strongly to women as to men (again, Freud was unsure about the Oedipus complex in women) and, if so, why it appeals to them. Or, more generally, one can ask if males and females read in the same way.

GENDER (FEMINIST, AND LESBIAN AND GAY) CRITICISM

This last question brings us to **gender criticism.** As we have seen, writing about literature usually seeks to answer questions. Historical scholarship, for instance, tries to answer such questions as, What did Shakespeare and his contemporaries believe about ghosts? or How did Victorian novelists and poets respond to Darwin's theory of evolution? Gender criticism, too, asks questions. It is especially concerned with two issues, one about reading and one about writing: Do men and women read in different ways, and Do they write in different ways?

Feminist criticism can be traced back to the work of Virginia Woolf (1882–1941), but chiefly it grew out of the women's movement of the 1960s. The women's movement at first tended to hold that women are pretty much the same as men and therefore should be treated equally, but much recent feminist criticism has emphasized and explored the differences between women and men. Because the experiences of the sexes are different, the argument goes, the values and sensibilities are different, and their responses to literature are different. Further, literature written by women is different from literature written by men. Works written by women are seen by some feminist critics as embodying the experiences of a minority culture—a group marginalized by the dominant male culture. (If you have read Charlotte Perkins Gilman's "The Yellow Wallpaper" or Susan Glaspell's *Trifles,* you'll recall that these literary works themselves are largely concerned about the differing ways in which men and women perceive the world.) Not all women are feminist critics, and not all feminist critics are women. Further, there are varieties of feminist criticism. For a good introduction see *The New Feminist Criticism: Essays on Women, Literature, and Theory* (1985), edited by Elaine Showalter. For the role of men in feminist criticism, see *Engendering Men* (1990), edited by Joseph A. Boone and Michael Cadden (1990). At this point it should also be said that some theorists, who hold that identity is socially constructed, strongly dispute the value of establishing "essentialist" categories such as *heterosexual, gay,* and *lesbian*—a point that we will consider in a moment.

Feminist critics rightly point out that men have established the conventions of literature and that men have established the canon—that is, the body of literature that is said to be worth reading. Speaking a bit broadly, in this patriarchal or male-dominated body of literature, men are valued for being strong and active, whereas women are expected to be weak and passive. Thus, in the world of fairy tales, the admirable male is the energetic hero (Jack, the Giant-Killer) but the admirable female is the passive Sleeping Beauty. Active women such as the wicked stepmother or—a disguised form of the same thing—the witch are generally villainous. (There are of course exceptions, such as Gretel, in "Hansel and Gretel.") A woman hearing or reading the story of Sleeping Beauty or of Little Red Riding Hood (rescued by the powerful woodcutter) or any other work in which women seem to be trivialized will respond differently from a man. For instance, a woman may be socially conditioned into admiring Sleeping Beauty, but only at great cost to her mental well-being. A more resistant female reader may recognize in herself no kinship with the beautiful, passive Sleeping Beauty and may respond to the story indignantly. Another way to put it is this: The male reader perceives a romantic story, but the resistant female reader perceives a story of oppression.

For discussions of the ways in which, it is argued, women *ought* to read, you may want to look at *Gender and Reading* (1986), edited by Elizabeth A. Flynn and Patrocinio Schweickart, and especially at Judith Fetterley's book *The Resisting Reader* (1978). Fetterley's point, briefly, is that women should resist the meanings (that is, the visions of how women ought to behave) that male authors—or female authors who have inherited patriarchal values—bury in their books. "To read the canon of what is currently considered classic American literature is perforce to identify as male," Fetterley says. "It insists on its universality in specifically male terms." Fetterley argues that a woman must read as a woman, "exorcising the male mind that has been implanted in women." In resisting the obvious meanings—for instance, the false claim that male values are universal values—women may discover more significant meanings. Fetterley argues that Faulkner's "A Rose for Emily"

> is a story not of a conflict between the South and the North or between the old order and the new; it is a story of the patriarchy North and South, new and old, and of the sexual conflict within it. As Faulkner himself has implied, it is a story of a woman victimized and betrayed by the system of sexual politics, who nevertheless has discovered, within the structures that victimize her, sources of power for herself. . . . "A

Rose for Emily" is the story of how to murder your gentleman caller and
get away with it. (34–35)

Fetterley goes on to state that society made Emily a "lady"—society dehuman-
ized her by elevating her. Emily's father, seeking to shape her life, stood in
the doorway of their house and drove away her suitors. So far as he was concerned, Emily was a nonperson, a creature whose own wishes were not to be regarded; he alone would shape her future. Because society (beginning with her
father) made her a "lady"—a creature so elevated that she is not taken seriously
as a passionate human being—she is able to kill Homer Barron and not be suspected. Here is Fetterley speaking of the passage in which the townspeople
crowd into her house when her death becomes known:

> When the would-be "suitors" finally get into her father's house, they
> discover the consequences of his oppression of her, for the violence
> contained in the rotted corpse of Homer Barron is the mirror image of
> the violence represented in the tableau, the back-flung front door flung
> back with a vengeance. (42)

Feminist criticism has been concerned not only with the depiction of
women and men in a male-determined literary canon and with female responses
to these images but also with yet another topic: women's writing. Women have
had fewer opportunities than men to become writers of fiction, poetry, and
drama—for one thing, they have been less well educated in the things that the
male patriarchy valued—but even when they *have* managed to write, men
sometimes have neglected their work simply because it had been written by a
woman. Feminists have further argued that certain forms of writing have been
especially the province of women—for instance, journals, diaries, and letters;
and predictably, these forms have not been given adequate space in the traditional, male-oriented canon.

In 1972, in an essay titled "When We Dead Awaken: Writing as ReVision,"
the poet and essayist Adrienne Rich effectively summed up the matter:

> A radical critique of literature, feminist in its impulse, would take the
> work first of all as a clue to how we live, how we have been living, how
> we have been led to imagine ourselves, how our language has trapped
> as well as liberated us; and how we can begin to see—and therefore
> live—afresh. . . . . We need to know the writing of the past and know it
> differently than we have ever known it; not to pass on a tradition but to
> break its hold over us.

Much feminist criticism concerned with women writers has emphasized
connections between the writer's biography and her art. Suzanne Juhasz, in her
introduction to *Feminist Critics Read Emily Dickinson* (1983), puts it this way:

> The central assumption of feminist criticism is that gender informs the
> nature of art, the nature of biography, and the relation between them.
> Dickinson is a woman poet, and this fact is integral to her identity. Fem-
> inist criticism's sensitivity to the components of female experience in
> general and to Dickinson's identity as a woman generates essential in-
> sights about her. . . . . Attention to the relationship between biography
> and art is a requisite of feminist criticism. To disregard it further
> strengthens those divisions continually created by traditional criticism,
> so that nothing about the woman writer can be seen whole. (1–5)

Lesbian and gay criticism have their roots in feminist criticism; feminist criticism introduced many of the questions that these other, newer developments are now exploring.

In 1979, in a book called *On Lies, Secrets, and Silence,* Adrienne Rich reprinted a 1975 essay on Emily Dickinson, "Vesuvius at Home." In her new preface to the reprinted essay she said that a lesbian-feminist reading of Dickinson would not have to prove that Dickinson slept with another woman. Rather, lesbian-feminist criticism "will ask questions hitherto passed over; it will not search obsessively for heterosexual romance as the key to a woman artist's life and work" (157–158). Obviously such a statement is also relevant to a male artist's life and work. It should be mentioned, too, that Rich's comments on lesbian reading and lesbianism as an image of creativity have been much discussed. For a brief survey, see Marilyn R. Farwell, "Toward a Definition of the Lesbian Literary Imagination," *Signs* 14 (1988): 100–118.

Before turning to some of the questions that lesbian and gay critics address, it is necessary first to say that lesbian criticism and gay criticism are not—to use a word now current in much criticism—symmetrical, chiefly because lesbian and gay relationships themselves are not symmetrical. Straight society has traditionally been more tolerant of—or blinder to—lesbianism than to male homosexuality. Further, lesbian literary theory has tended to see its affinities more with feminist theory than with gay theory; the emphasis has been on gender (male/female) rather than on sexuality (homosexuality/bisexuality/heterosexuality). On the other hand, some gays and lesbians have been writing what is now being called *Queer Theory.*

Now for some of the questions that this criticism addresses: (1) Do lesbians and gays read in ways that differ from the ways straight people read? (2) Do they write in ways that differ from those of straight people? (Gregory Woods argues in *Lesbian and Gay Writing: An Anthology of Critical Essays* [1990], edited by Mark Lilly, that "modern gay poets . . . use . . . paradox, as weapon and shield, against a world in which heterosexuality is taken for granted as being exclusively natural and healthy" [176]. Another critic, Jeffrey Meyers, writing in *Journal of English and Germanic Philology* 88 [1989]: 126–29, in an unsympathetic review of a book on gay writers contrasts gay writers of the past with those of the present. According to Meyers, closeted homosexuals in the past, writing out of guilt and pain, produced a distinctive literature that is more interesting than the productions of today's uncloseted writers.) (3) How have straight writers portrayed lesbians and gays, and how have lesbian and gay writers portrayed straight women and men? (4) What strategies did lesbian and gay writers use to make their work acceptable to a general public in an age when lesbian and gay behavior was unmentionable?

Questions such as these have stimulated critical writing especially about bisexual and lesbian and gay authors (for instance, Virginia Woolf, Gertrude Stein, Elizabeth Bishop, Walt Whitman, Oscar Wilde, E. M. Forster, Hart Crane, Tennessee Williams), but they have also led to interesting writing on such a topic as Nathaniel Hawthorne's attitudes toward women. "An account of Hawthorne's misogyny that takes no account of his own and his culture's gender anxieties," Robert K. Martin says in Boone and Cadden's *Engendering Men,* "is necessarily inadequate" (122).

Shakespeare's work—and not only the sonnets, which praise a beautiful male friend—has stimulated a fair amount of gay criticism. Much of this criticism consists of "decoding" aspects of the plays. Seymour Kleinberg argues, in *Essays on Gay Literature* (1985), ed. Stuart Kellogg, that Antonio in *The Merchant of Venice,* whose melancholy is not made clear by Shakespeare, is melancholy because (again, this is according to Kleinberg) Antonio's lover, Bassanio, is deserting him, and because Antonio is ashamed of his own sexuality:

> Antonio is a virulently anti-Semitic homosexual and is melancholic to the point of despair because his lover, Bassanio, wishes to marry an immensely rich aristocratic beauty, to leave the diversions of the Rialto to return to his own class and to sexual conventionality. Antonio is also in despair because he despises himself for his homosexuality, which is romantic, obsessive, and exclusive, and fills him with sexual shame. (113)

Several earlier critics had suggested that Antonio is a homosexual, hopelessly pining for Bassanio, but Kleinberg goes further, and argues that Antonio and Bassanio are lovers, not just good friends, and that Antonio's hopeless and shameful (because socially unacceptable) passion for Bassanio becomes transformed into hatred for the Jew, Shylock. The play, according to Kleinberg, is partly about "a world where . . . sexual guilt is translated into ethnic hatred" (124).

Examination of matters of gender can help to illuminate literary works, but it should be added, too, that some—perhaps most—critics write also as activists, reporting their findings not only to help us to understand and to enjoy the works of (say) Whitman, but also to change society's view of sexuality. Thus, in *Disseminating Whitman* (1991), Michael Moon is impatient with earlier critical rhapsodies about Whitman's universalism. It used to be said that Whitman's celebration of the male body was a sexless celebration of brotherly love in a democracy, but the gist of Moon's view is that we must neither whitewash Whitman's poems with such high-minded talk, nor reject them as indecent; rather, we must see exactly what Whitman is saying about a kind of experience that society had shut its eyes to, and we must take Whitman's view seriously. Somewhat similarly, Gregory Woods in *Articulate Flesh* (1987) points out that until a few years ago discussions of Hart Crane regularly condemned his homosexuality, as is evident in L. S. Dembo's characterization of Crane (quoted by Woods) as "uneducated, alcoholic, homosexual, paranoic, suicidal" (140). Gay and lesbian writers do not adopt this sort of manner. But it should also be pointed out that today there are straight critics who study lesbian or gay authors and write about them insightfully and without hostility.

One assumption in much lesbian and gay critical writing is that although gender greatly influences the ways in which we read, reading is a skill that can be learned, and therefore straight people—aided by lesbian and gay critics—can learn to read, with pleasure and profit, lesbian and gay writers. This assumption of course also underlies much feminist criticism, which often assumes that men must stop ignoring books by women and must learn (with the help of feminist critics) how to read them, and, in fact, how to read—with newly opened eyes— the sexist writings of men of the past and present.

In addition to the titles mentioned earlier concerning gay and lesbian criticism, consult Eve Kosofsky Sedgwick, *Between Men: English Literature and Male Homosocial Desire* (1985) and an essay by Sedgwick, "Gender Criticism," in *Redrawing the Boundaries,* ed. Stephen Greenblatt and Giles Gunn (1992).

While many in the field of lesbian and gay criticism have turned their energies toward examining the effects that an author's—or a character's—sexual identity may have upon the text, others have begun to question, instead, the concept of sexual identity itself.* Drawing upon the work of the French social historian Michel Foucault, critics such as David Halperin (*One Hundred Years of Homosexuality and Other Essays on Greek Love,* [1990]) and Judith Butler (*Gender Trouble,* [1989]) explore how various categories of identity, such as "heterosexual" and "homosexual," represent ways of defining human beings that are distinct to particular cultures and historical periods. These critics, affiliated with what is known as the "social constructionist" school of thought, argue that the way a given society (modern American or ancient Greek) interprets sexuality will determine the particular categories within which individuals come to understand and to name their own desires. For such critics the goal of a lesbian or gay criticism is not to define the specificity of a lesbian or gay literature or mode of interpretation, but to show how the ideology (the normative understanding of a given culture) makes it seem natural to think about sexuality in terms of such identities as lesbian, gay, bisexual, or straight. By challenging the authority of those terms, or "denaturalizing" them, and by calling attention to moments in which literary (and nonliterary) representations make assumptions that reinforce the supposed inevitability of those distinctions, such critics attempt to redefine our understandings of the relations between sexuality and literature. They hope to make clear that sexuality is always, in a certain sense, "literary"; it is a representation of a fiction that society has constructed in order to make sense out of experience.

Because such critics have challenged the authority of the opposition between heterosexuality and homosexuality, and have read it as a historical construct rather than as a biological or psychological absolute, they have sometimes resisted the very terms *lesbian* and *gay.* Many now embrace what is called Queer Theory as an attempt to mark their resistance to the categories of identity they see our culture as imposing upon us.

Works written within this mode of criticism are often influenced by deconstructionist or psychoanalytic thought. They examine works by straight authors as frequently as they do works by writers who might be defined as lesbian or gay. Eve Kosofsky Sedgwick's reading of *Billy Budd* in her book *Epistemology of the Closet* (1990) provides a good example of this sort of criticism. Reading Claggart as "the homosexual" in the text of Melville's novella, Sedgwick is not interested in defining his difference from other characters. Instead, she shows how the novella sets up a large number of oppositions—such as public and private, sincerity and sentimentality, health and illness—all of which have a relationship to the way in which a distinct "gay" identity was being produced by American society at the end of the nineteenth century. Other critics whose work in this field may be useful for students of literature are D. A. Miller, *The Novel and the Police* (1988); Diana Fuss, *Essentially Speaking* (1989) and *Identification Papers* (1995); Judith Butler, *Bodies That Matter* (1993); and Lee Edelman, *Homographesis: Essays in Gay Literary and Cultural Theory* (1993).

This chapter began by making the obvious point that all readers, whether or not they consciously adopt a particular approach to literature, necessarily read through particular lenses. More precisely, a reader begins with a frame of interpretation—historical, psychological, sociological, or whatever—and from within the frame a reader selects one of the several competing methodologies. Critics

---

*This paragraph and the next two are by Lee Edelman of Tufts University.

often make great—even grandiose—claims for their approaches. For example, Frederic Jameson, a Marxist, begins *The Political Unconscious: Narrative as a Socially Symbolic Act* (1981) thus:

> This book will argue the priority of the political interpretation of liter-
> ary texts. It conceives of the political perspective not as some supple-
> mental method, not as an optional auxiliary to other interpretive meth-
> ods current today—the psychoanalytic or the myth-critical, the stylistic,
> the ethical, the structural—but rather as the absolute horizon of all
> reading and all interpretation. (7)

Readers who are chiefly interested in politics may be willing to assume "the pri-
ority of the political interpretation . . . as the absolute horizon of all reading and
all interpretation," but other readers may respectfully decline to accept this
assumption.

In talking about a critical approach, it is sometimes said that readers decode
a text by applying a grid to it; the grid enables them to see certain things clearly.
Good; but what is sometimes forgotten is that (since there is no such thing as a
free lunch) a lens or a grid—an angle of vision or interpretive frame and a
methodology—also prevents a reader from seeing certain other things. This is to
be expected. What is important, then, is to remember this fact, and thus not to
deceive ourselves by thinking that our keen tools enable us to see the whole. A
psychoanalytic reading of, say, *Hamlet,* may be helpful, but it does not reveal all
that is in *Hamlet,* and it does not refute the perceptions of another approach,
let's say a historical study. Each approach may illuminate aspects neglected
by others.

It is too much to expect a reader to apply all useful methods (or even several)
at once—that would be rather like looking through a telescope with one eye and
through a microscope with the other—but it is not too much to expect readers to
be aware of the limitations of their methods. If one reads much criticism, one
finds two kinds of critics. There are, on the one hand, critics who methodically
and mechanically peer through a lens or grid, and they find what one can easily
predict they will find. On the other hand, there are critics who (despite what may
be inevitable class and gender biases) are at least relatively open-minded in their
approach—critics who, one might say, do not at the outset of their reading believe that their method assures them that (so to speak) they have got the text's
number and that by means of this method they will expose the text for what it is.
The philosopher Richard Rorty engagingly makes a distinction somewhat along
these lines, in an essay he contributed to Umberto Eco's *Interpretation and
Overinterpretation* (1992). There is a great difference, Rorty suggests,

> between knowing what you want to get out of a person or thing or text
> in advance and [on the other hand] hoping that the person or thing or
> text will help you want something different—that he or she or it will
> help you to change your purposes, and thus to change your life. This
> distinction, I think, helps us highlight the difference between methodi-
> cal and inspired readings of texts. (106)

Rorty goes on to say he has seen an anthology of readings on Conrad's *Heart of
Darkness,* containing a psychoanalytic reading, a reader-response reading, and
so on. "None of the readers had, as far as I could see," Rorty says,

> been enraptured or destabilized by *Heart of Darkness.* I got no sense
> that the book had made a big difference to them, that they cared much

about Kurtz or Marlow or the woman "with helmeted head and tawny cheeks" whom Marlow sees on the bank of the river. These people, and that book, had no more changed these readers' purposes than the specimen under the microscope changes the purpose of the histologist. (107)

The kind of criticism that Rorty prefers he calls "unmethodical" criticism and "inspired" criticism. It is, for Rorty, the result of an "encounter" with some aspect of a work of art "which has made a difference to the critic's conception of who she is, what she is good for, what she wants to do with herself . . ." (107). This is not a matter of "respect" for the text, Rorty insists. Rather, he says, "love" and "hate" are better words, "For a great love or a great loathing is the sort of thing that changes us by changing our purposes, changing the uses to which we shall put people and things and texts we encounter later" (107).

SUGGESTIONS FOR FURTHER READING

Because a massive list of titles may prove discouraging rather than helpful, it seems advisable here to give a short list of basic titles. (Titles already mentioned in this chapter—which are good places to begin—are not repeated in the following list.)

A good sampling of contemporary criticism (60 or so essays or chapters from books), representing all of the types discussed in this commentary except lesbian and gay criticism, can be found in *The Critical Tradition: Classic Texts and Contemporary Trends,* 2nd ed., David H. Richter (1998).

For a readable introduction to various approaches, written for students who are beginning the study of literary theory, see Steven Lynn, *Texts and Contexts* (1994). For a more advanced survey, that is, a work that assumes some familiarity with the material, see a short book by K. M. Newton, *Interpreting the Text: A Critical Introduction to the Theory and Practice of Literary Interpretation* (1990). A third survey, though considerably longer than the books by Lynn and Newton, is narrower because it confines itself to a study of critical writings about Shakespeare: Brian Vickers, *Appropriating Shakespeare: Contemporary Critical Quarrels* (1993), offers an astringent appraisal of deconstruction, New Historicism, psychoanalytic criticism, feminist criticism, and Marxist criticism. For a collection of essays on Shakespeare written from some of the viewpoints that Vickers deplores, see John Drakakis, ed., *Shakespearean Tragedy* (1992).

Sympathetic discussions (usually two or three pages long) of each approach, with fairly extensive bibliographic suggestions, are given in the appropriate articles in three encyclopedic works. Wendell V. Harris, *Dictionary of Concepts in Literary Criticism and Theory* (1992), devotes several pages to each concept (for instance, *author, context, evaluation, feminist literary criticism, narrative*) and gives a useful reading list for each entry. Fairly similar to Harris's book are Irene Makaryk, ed., *Encyclopedia of Contemporary Literary Theory: Approaches, Scholars, Terms* (1993), and Michael Groden, Martin Kreiswirth, and Imre Szeman (eds.), *The Johns Hopkins Guide to Literary Theory and Criticism,* 2nd ed. (2005). *The Johns Hopkins Guide,* though it includes substantial entries on individual critics as well as on critical schools, is occasionally disappointing in the readability of some of its essays and especially in its coverage, since it does not include critical terms other than names of schools of criticism. Despite its title, then, it does not have entries for *theory* or for *criticism,* nor does it have entries for such words as *canon* and *evaluation.* In coverage (and also in the quality of many entries) it is inferior to an extremely valuable work with a misleading narrow title, *The New Princeton Encyclopedia of Poetry and Poetics,* edited by Alex Preminger and T. V. F. Brogan (1993). Although *The New Princeton Encyclopedia* does not include terms that are unique to, say, drama or fiction, it does include generous, lucid entries (with suggestions for further reading) on such terms as *allegory, criticism, canon, irony, sincerity, theory,* and *unity,* and the long entries on *poetrics, poetry,* and *poetry, theories of,* are in many respects entries on *literature.*

For a collection of essays on the canon, see *Canons,* edited by Robert von Hallberg (1984); see also an essay by Robert Scholes, "Canonicity and Textuality," in *Introduction to Scholarship in Modern Languages and Literatures,* edited by Joseph Gibaldi (2nd ed., 1992), 138–58. Gibaldi's collection includes essays on related topics, for instance, literary theory (by Jonathan Culler) and cultural studies (by David Bathrick).

Formalist Criticism (The New Criticism)

Cleanth Brooks, *The Well Wrought Urn: Studies in the Structure of Poetry* (1947), especially Chapters 1 and 11 ("The Language of Paradox" and "The Heresy of Paraphrase"); W. K. Wimsatt, *The Verbal Icon* (1954), especially "The Intentional Fallacy" and "The Affective Fallacy"; Murray Krieger, *The New Apologists for Poetry* (1956); and, for an accurate overview of a kind of criticism often misrepresented today, Chapters 9–12 in Volume 6 of René Wellek, *A History of Modern Criticism: 1750–1950* (1986).

Deconstruction

Christopher Norris, *Deconstruction: Theory and Practice,* rev. ed. (1991); Vincent B. Leitch, *Deconstructive Criticism: An Advanced Introduction and Survey* (1983); Christopher Norris, ed., *What Is Deconstruction?* (1988); Christopher Norris and Andrew Benjamin, *Deconstruction and the Interests of Theory* (1989). For a negative assessment, consult John M. Ellis, *Against Deconstruction* (1989). More generally, see *Deconstruction: A Reader,* ed. Martin McQuillan (2001) and *Critical Concepts in Literary and Cultural Studies,* ed. Jonathan Culler, 4 vols. (2003).

Reader-Response Criticism

Wolfgang Iser, *The Act of Reading: A Theory of Aesthetic Response* (1978); Wolfgang Iser, *Prospecting: From Reader Response to Literary Anthropology* (1993); Susan Suleiman and Inge Crossman, eds., *The Reader in the Text* (1980); Jane P. Tompkins, ed., *Reader-Response Criticism* (1980); Norman N. Holland, *The Dynamics of Literary Response* (1973, 1989); Steven Mailloux, *Interpretive Conventions: The Reader in the Study of American Fiction* (1982); Gerry Brenner, *Performative Criticism: Experiments in Reader Response* (2004).

Archetypal (or Myth) Criticism

G. Wilson Knight, *The Starlit Dome* (1941); Richard Chase, *Quest for Myth* (1949); Murray Krieger, ed., *Northrop Frye in Modern Criticism* (1966); Frank Lentricchia, *After the New Criticism* (1980). For a good survey of Frye's approach, see Robert D. Denham, *Northrop Frye and Critical Method* (1978). Also, *Rereading Frye: The Published and Unpublished Works,* ed. David Boyd and Imre Salusinszky (1999).

Historical Criticism

For a brief survey of some historical criticism of the first half of the twentieth century, see René Wellek, *A History of Modern Criticism: 1750–1950,* Volume 6 (1986), Chapter 4 ("Academic Criticism"). See also E. M. W. Tillyard, *The Elizabethan World Picture* (1943), and Tillyard's *Shakespeare's History Plays* (1944), both of which relate Elizabethan literature to the beliefs of the age and are good examples of the historical approach. Also of interest is David Levin, *Forms of Uncertainty: Essays in Historical Criticism* (1992).

Marxist Criticism

Raymond Williams, *Marxism and Literature* (1977); Tony Bennett, *Formalism and Marxism* (1979); Lydia Sargent, ed., *Women and Revolution: A Discussion of the Unhappy Marriage of Marxism and Feminism* (1981); and for a brief survey of American Marxist writers of the 1930s and 1940s, see Chapter 5 of Volume 6 of René Wellek, *A History of Modern Criticism* (1986). Also helpful are Daniel Aaron, *Writers on the Left: Episodes in American Literary Communism* (1961; new ed., 1992); and Barbara Foley, *Radical Representations: Politics and Form in U.S. Proletarian Fiction, 1929–1941* (1993). Also stimulating are Terry Eagleton, *The Ideology of the Aesthetic* (1990) and *Marxist Shakespeares,* ed. Jean E. Howard and Scott Cutler Shershow (2001).

New Historicism

Historicizing Theory, ed. Peter C. Herman (2004); Stephen Greenblatt, *Renaissance Self-Fashioning from More to Shakespeare* (1980), especially the first chapter; Brook Thomas, *The New Historicism and Other Old-Fashioned Topics* (1991). Greenblatt's other influential books include *Shakespearean Negotiations: The Circulation of Social Energy in Renaissance England* (1988), and, with Catherine Gallagher, *Practicing New Historicism* (2000).

Biographical Criticism

Leon Edel, *Literary Biography* (1957); Estelle C. Jellinek, ed., *Women's Autobiography: Essays in Criticism* (1980); James Olney, *Metaphors of Self: The Meaning of Autobiography* (1981); and *Women, Autobiography, Theory: A Reader,* ed. Sidonie Smith and Julia Watson. Important twentieth-century literary biographers are Richard Ellmann, *James Joyce* (1959, rev. ed., 1982); Juliet Barker, *The Brontës* (1994); Hermione Lee, *Virginia Woolf* (1997); Lyndall Gordon, *T. S. Eliot: An Imperfect Life* (1999); and Fred Kaplan, *The Singular Mark Twain: A Biography* (2003).

Psychological (or Psychoanalytic) Criticism

Edith Kurzweil and William Phillips, eds., *Literature and Psychoanalysis* (1983); Maurice Charney and Joseph Reppen, eds., *Psychoanalytic Approaches to Literature and Film* (1987); Madelon Sprengnether, *The Spectral Mother: Freud, Feminism, and Psychoanalysis* (1990); Frederick Crews, *Out of My System* (1975); and Graham Frankland, *Freud's Literary Culture* (2000).

Gender (Feminist, and Lesbian and Gay) Criticism

Gayle Greene and Coppèlia Kahn, eds., *Making a Difference: Feminist Literary Criticism* (1985), including an essay by Bonnie Zimmerman on lesbian criticism; Catherine Belsey and Jane Moore, eds., *The Feminist Reader: Essays in Gender and the Politics of Literary Criticism* (1989); Toril Moi, ed., *French Feminist*

Thought (1987); Elizabeth A. Flynn and Patrocinio P. Schweikart, eds., *Gender and Reading: Essays on Readers, Texts, and Contexts* (1986); Barbara Christian, *Black Feminist Criticism: Perspectives on Black Women Writers* (1985); Shoshana Felman, *What Does a Woman Want? Reading and Sexual Difference* (1993); Robert Martin, *The Homosexual Tradition in American Poetry* (1979); Kathryn R. Kent, *Making Girls into Women: American Women's Writing and the Rise of Lesbian Identity* (2003); and Rita Felski, *Literature After Feminism* (2003). Henry Abelove et al., eds., *The Lesbian and Gay Studies Reader* (1993), has only a few essays concerning literature, but it has an extensive bibliography on the topic.

Valuable reference works include *Encyclopedia of Feminist Literary Theory* (1997), ed. Beth Kowaleski-Wallace; *The Gay & Lesbian Literary Companion,* ed. Sharon Malinowski and Christa Brelin (1995); and *The Gay and Lesbian Literary Heritage: A Reader's Companion to the Writers and Their Works, from Antiquity to the Present,* ed. Claude J. Summers (1995). See also Summers, *Gay Fictions: Wilde to Stonewall: Studies in a Male Homosexual Literary Tradition* (1990); *Novel Gazing: Queer Readings in Fiction,* ed. Eve Kosofsky Sedgwick (1997); and Gregory Woods, *A History of Gay Literature: The Male Tradition* (1998). For further discussion of Queer Theory, see Annamarie Jagose, *Queer Theory: An Introduction* (1996); Alan Sinfield, *Cultural Politics—Queer Reading* (1994); and *Feminism Meets Queer Theory* (1997), ed. Elizabeth Weed and Naomi Schor.

A

Remarks about
Manuscript Form

BASIC MANUSCRIPT FORM

Much of what follows is nothing more than common sense.

- Use good-quality **8½″ × 11″** paper. Make a photocopy, or if you have written on a word processor, print out a second copy, in case the instructor's copy goes astray.
- If you write on a word processor, **double-space,** and print on one side of the page only; set the printer for professional or best quality. If you submit handwritten copy, use lined paper and write on one side of the page only in black or dark blue ink, on every other line.
- Use **one-inch margins** on all sides.
- Within the top margin, put your last name and then (after hitting the space bar twice) the **page number** (in arabic numerals), so that the number is flush with the right-hand margin.
- On the first page, below the top margin and flush with the left-hand margin, put your **full name,** your **instructor's name,** the **course number** (including the section), and the **date,** one item per line, double-spaced.
- **Center the title** of your essay. Remember that the title is important—it gives the readers their first glimpse of your essay. **Create your own title**—one that reflects your topic or thesis. For example, a paper on Charlotte Perkins Gilman's "The Yellow Wallpaper" should not be called "The Yellow Wallpaper" but might be called

```
Disguised Tyranny in Gilman's "The Yellow Wallpaper"
```

or

```
              How to Drive a Woman Mad
```

These titles do at least a little in the way of rousing a reader's interest.
- **Capitalize the title thus:** Begin the first word of the title with a capital letter, and capitalize each subsequent word except articles (*a, an, the*), conjunctions (*and, but, if, when,* etc.), and prepositions (*in, on, with,* etc.):

A Word on Behalf of Love

Notice that you do *not* enclose your title within quotation marks, and you do *not* underline it—though if it includes the title of a poem or a story, *that* is enclosed within quotation marks, or if it includes the title of a novel or play, *that* is underlined (to indicate italics), thus:

Gilman's "The Yellow Wallpaper" and Medical Practice

and

Gender Stereotypes in <u>Hamlet</u>

- **After writing your title, double-space,** indent five spaces, and begin your first sentence.
- Unless your instructor tells you otherwise, **use a staple** to hold the pages together. (Do not use a stiff binder; it will only add to the bulk of the instructor's stack of papers.)
- Extensive revisions should have been made in your drafts, but minor **last-minute revisions** may be made—neatly—on the finished copy. Proofreading may catch some typographical errors, and you may notice some small weaknesses. You can make corrections using the following proofreader's symbols.

CORRECTIONS IN THE FINAL COPY

Changes in wording may be made by crossing through words and rewriting them:

The influence of Poe and Hawthorne ~~have~~ greatly diminished.

Additions should be made above the line, with a caret below the line at the appropriate place:

The influence of Poe and Hawthorne has diminished.

Transpositions of letters may be made thus:

The influence of Poe and Hawthorne has diminished.

Deletions are indicated by a horizontal line through the word or words to be deleted. Delete a single letter by drawing a vertical or diagonal line through it; then indicate whether the letters on either side are to be closed up by drawing a connecting arc:

The influence of Poe and Hawthorne has greatly diminished.

Separation of words accidentally run together is indicated by a vertical line, closure by a curved line connecting the letters to be closed up:

The influence|of Poe and Hawthorne has g reatly diminished.

Paragraphing may be indicated by the symbol ¶ before the word that is to begin the new paragraph:

> The influence of Poe and Hawthorne has greatly
> diminished. ¶ The influence of Borges has very largely
> replaced that of earlier writers of fantasy.

QUOTATIONS AND QUOTATION MARKS

First, a word about the *point* of using quotations. Don't use quotations to pad the length of a paper. Rather, give quotations from the work you are discussing so that your readers will see the material being considered and (especially in a research paper) so that your readers will know what some of the chief interpretations are and what your responses to them are.

Note: The next few paragraphs do *not* discuss how to include citations of pages, a topic taken up in the next appendix under the heading "How to Document: Footnotes, Internal Parenthetical Citations, and a List of Works Cited."

The Golden Rule: If you quote, *comment on* the quotation. Let the reader know what you make of it and why you quote it.

Additional principles:

1. **Identify the speaker or writer of the quotation** so that the reader is not left with a sense of uncertainty. Usually, in accordance with the principle of letting readers know where they are going, this identification precedes the quoted material, but occasionally it may follow the quotation, especially if it will provide something of a pleasant surprise. For instance, in a discussion of Flannery O'Connor's stories, you might quote a disparaging comment on one of the stories and then reveal that O'Connor herself was the speaker.

2. If the quotation is part of your own sentence, **be sure to fit the quotation grammatically and logically into your sentence.**

> *Incorrect:* Holden Caulfield tells us very little about "what my lousy childhood was like."
> *Correct:* Holden Caulfield tells us very little about what his "lousy childhood was like."

3. **Indicate any omissions or additions.** The quotation must be exact. Any material that you add—even one or two words—must be enclosed within square brackets, thus:

> Hawthorne tells us that "owing doubtless to the depth
> of the gloom at that particular spot [in the forest],
> neither the travellers nor their steeds were visible."

If you wish to omit material from within a quotation, indicate the ellipsis by three spaced periods enclosed within a pair of square brackets. That is, at the point where you are omitting material, type a space, an opening square bracket, a period, a space, a period, a space, a third period, and a closing square bracket (no space between the last of these three periods and the closing bracket). If you are omitting material from the end of a sentence, type a space after the last word that you quote, then an opening square bracket, a period, a space, a period, a space, a third period, the closing square bracket, and a period to indicate the end of the sentence. The following example is based on a quotation from the sentences immediately above this one:

```
The instructions say, "If you [. . .] omit material
from within a quotation, [you must] indicate the
ellipsis [. . .]. If you are omitting material from
the end of a sentence, type [. . .] and a period to
indicate the end [. . .]."
```

Notice that although material preceded "If you," periods are not needed to indicate the omission because "If you" began a sentence in the original. Customarily, initial and terminal omissions are indicated only when they are part of the sentence you are quoting. Even such omissions need not be indicated when the quoted material is obviously incomplete—when, for instance, it is a word or phrase.

4. **Distinguish between short and long quotations,** and treat each appropriately. **Short quotations** (usually defined as fewer than five lines of typed prose or three lines of poetry) are enclosed within quotation marks and run into the text (rather than being set off, without quotation marks), as in the following example:

```
Hawthorne begins the story by telling us that "Young
Goodman Brown came forth at sunset into the street at
Salem village," thus at the outset connecting the
village with daylight. A few paragraphs later, when
Hawthorne tells us that the road Brown takes was
"darkened by all of the gloomiest trees of the
forest," he begins to associate the forest with
darkness--and a very little later with evil.
```

If your short quotation is from a poem, be sure to follow the capitalization of the original, and use a slash mark (with a space before and after it) to indicate separate lines. Give the line numbers, if your source gives them, in parentheses, immediately after the closing quotation marks and before the closing punctuation, thus:

```
In "Diving into the Wreck," Adrienne Rich's speaker
says that she puts on "body-armor" (5). Obviously the
journey is dangerous.
```

To set off a **long quotation** (more than four typed lines of prose or more than two lines of poetry), indent the entire quotation ten spaces from the left margin. Usually, a long quotation is introduced by a clause ending with a colon—for instance, "The following passage will make this point clear:" or "The closest we come to hearing an editorial voice is a long passage in the middle of the story:" or some such lead-in. After typing your lead-in, double-space, and then type the quotation, indented and double-spaced.

5. **Commas and periods go inside the quotation marks.**

```
Chopin tells us in the first sentence that "Mrs. Mal-
lard was afflicted with heart trouble," and in the
last sentence the doctors say that Mrs. Mallard "died
of heart disease."
```

Exception: If the quotation is immediately followed by material in parentheses or in square brackets, close the quotation, then give the parenthetic or bracketed material, and then—after closing the parenthesis or bracket—insert the comma or period.

```
Chopin tells us in the first sentence that "Mrs. Mal-
lard was afflicted with heart trouble" (28), and in
the last sentence the doctors say that Mrs. Mallard
"died of heart disease" (29).
```

Semicolons, colons, and dashes go outside the closing quotation marks.
Question marks and exclamation points go inside if they are part of the quotation, outside if they are your own.

In the following passage from a student's essay, notice the difference in the position of the question marks. The first question mark is part of the quotation, so it is enclosed within the quotation marks. The second question mark, however, is the student's, so it comes after the closing quotation marks.

```
The older man says to Goodman Brown, "Sayest thou
so?" Doesn't a reader become uneasy when the man
immediately adds, "We are but a little way in the
forest yet"?
```

Quotation Marks or Underlining?

Use quotation marks around titles of short stories and other short works—that is, titles of chapters in books, essays, and poems that might not be published by themselves. Underline (to indicate italics) titles of books, periodicals, collections of essays, plays, and long poems such as *The Rime of the Ancient Mariner*. Word processing software will let you use italic type (instead of underlining) if you wish.

A Note on the Possessive

It is awkward to use the possessive case for titles of literary works and secondary sources. Rather than "*The Great Gatsby*'s final chapter," write instead "the final chapter of *The Great Gatsby*." Not "*The Oxford Companion to American Literature*'s entry on Emerson," but, instead, "the entry on Emerson in *The Oxford Companion to American Literature*."

B

Writing a Research Paper

WHAT RESEARCH IS NOT, AND WHAT RESEARCH IS

Because a research paper requires its writer to collect and interpret evidence—usually including the opinions of earlier investigators—it is sometimes said that a research paper, unlike a critical essay, is not the expression of personal opinion. But such a view is unjust both to criticism and to research. A critical essay is not a mere expression of personal opinions; if it is any good, it is an argument, offering evidence that supports the opinions and thus persuades the reader of their objective rightness. And a research paper is in the final analysis largely personal, because the author continuously uses his or her own judgment to evaluate the evidence, deciding what is relevant and convincing. A research paper is not the mere presentation of what a dozen scholars have already said about a topic; it is a thoughtful evaluation of the available evidence, and so it is, finally, an expression of what the author thinks the evidence adds up to.

PRIMARY AND SECONDARY MATERIALS

The materials of literary research can be conveniently divided into two sorts, primary and secondary. The *primary materials,* or sources, are the real subject of study; the *secondary materials* are critical and historical accounts already written about these primary materials. For example, Langston Hughes wrote poems, stories, plays, and essays. For a student of Hughes, these works are the primary materials. (We include several of his works in this book.) If you want to study his ways of representing African-American speech, or his representations of whites, or his collaboration with Zora Neale Hurston, you will read the primary material—his own writings (and Hurston's, in the case of the collaborative work). But in an effort to reach a thoughtful understanding of some aspect of his work, you will also want to look at later biographical and critical studies of his works and perhaps also at scholarly writing on such topics as Black English. You may even find yourself looking at essays on Black English that do not specifically mention Hughes but that nevertheless may prove helpful.

Similarly, if you are writing about Charlotte Perkins Gilman (we include one of her stories), the primary material includes not only other stories but also her social and political writing. If you are writing about her views of medical treatment of women, you will want to look not only at the story we reprint ("The Yellow Wallpaper") but also at her autobiography. Further, you will also want to look at some secondary material, such as recent scholarly books and articles on medical treatment of women in the late nineteenth and early twentieth centuries.

Locating Material: First Steps

This appendix is devoted to traditional resources. Consult the next two appendices for a detailed introduction to electronic resources.

The easiest way to locate articles and books on literature written in a modern language—that is, on a topic other than literature of the ancient world—is to consult the

> *MLA International Bibliography of Books and Articles in the Modern Languages and Literatures* (1922-),

which until 1969 was published as part of *PMLA* (*Publications of the Modern Language Association*) and since 1969 has been published separately. It is also available on CD-ROM through WilsonDisc, and in fact the disc is preferable since it is updated quarterly, whereas the print version is more than a year behind the times. Many college and university libraries also now offer the *MLA International Bibliography* as part of their package of online resources for research, and it is even more up-to-date.

MLA International Bibliography lists scholarly studies—books as well as articles in academic journals—published in a given year. Because of the great number of items listed, the print version of the bibliography runs to more than one volume, but material on writing in English (including, for instance, South African authors who write in English) is in one volume. To see what has been published on Langston Hughes in a given year, then, in this volume you turn to the section on American literature (as opposed to British, Canadian, Irish, and so forth), and then to the subsection labeled 1900-99, to see if anything that sounds relevant is listed.

Because your time is limited, you probably cannot read everything published on your topic. At least for the moment, therefore, you will use only the last five or ten years of this bibliography. Presumably, any important earlier material will have been incorporated into some of the recent studies listed. When you come to read these recent studies, if you find references to an article from, say, 1975 that sounds essential, of course you will read that article too.

Although *MLA International Bibliography* includes works on American literature, if you are doing research on an aspect of American literature you may want to begin with

> *American Literary Scholarship* (1965-).

This annual publication is noted for its broad coverage of articles and books on major and minor American writers, and is especially valuable for its frank comments on the material that it lists.

On some recent topics—for instance, the arguments for and against dropping *Huckleberry Finn* from high school curricula—there may be few or no books, and there may not even be material in the scholarly journals indexed in *MLA International Bibliography*. Popular magazines, however, such as the *Atlantic*

Monthly, Ebony, and *Newsweek*—unlisted in *MLA*—may include some useful material. These magazines, and about 200 others, are indexed in

> *Readers' Guide to Periodical Literature* (1900–).

If you want to write a research paper on the controversy over *Huckleberry Finn,* or on the popular reception given to Kenneth Branagh's films of Shakespeare's *Henry V, Much Ado about Nothing,* and *Hamlet,* you can locate material (for instance, reviews of Branagh's films) through *Readers' Guide.* For that matter, you can also locate reviews of older films, let's say Olivier's films of Shakespeare's plays, by consulting the volumes for the years in which the films were released.

On many campuses *Readers' Guide* has been supplanted by

> *InfoTrac* (1985–),

on CD-ROM. The disc is preinstalled in a microcomputer that can be accessed from a computer terminal. This index to authors and subjects in popular and scholarly magazines and in newspapers provides access to several database indexes, including

- The *General Periodicals Index,* available in the Academic Library Edition (about 1,100 general and scholarly periodicals) and in the Public Library Edition (about 1,100 popular magazines)
- The *Academic Index* (400 general-interest publications, all of which are also available in the Academic Library Edition of the *General Periodicals Index*)
- The *Magazine Index Plus* (the four most recent years of the *New York Times,* the two most recent months of the *Wall Street Journal,* and 400 popular magazines, all of which are included in the Public Library Edition of the *General Periodicals Index*)
- The *National Newspaper Index* (the four most recent years of the *New York Times,* the *Christian Science Monitor,* the *Washington Post,* and the *Los Angeles Times*)

Once again, many college and university libraries are now making available online versions of these and similar resources for research. Some students (and faculty) prefer to use the books on the shelf, but the electronic editions have significant advantages. Often, it is easier to perform "searches" using them; and in many cases they are updated well before the next print editions are published.

Other Bibliographic Aids

There are hundreds of guides to authors, publications, and reference works. *The Oxford Companion to African American Literature* (1997), edited by William L. Andrews, Frances Smith Foster, and Trudier Harris, provides detailed entries on authors, literary works, and many literary, historical, and cultural topics and terms, as well as suggestions for further reading. *Reader's Guide to Literature in English* (1996), edited by Mark Hawkins-Dady, is a massive work (nearly 1,000 pages) that gives thorough summaries of recent critical and scholarly writing on English and American authors.

How do you find such books? Two invaluable guides to reference works (that is, to bibliographies and to such helpful compilations as handbooks of mythology, place names, and critical terms) are

> James L. Harner, *Literary Research Guide: A Guide to Reference Sources for the Study of Literatures in English and Related Topics,* 4th ed. (2002)

and

> Michael J. Marcuse, *A Reference Guide for English Studies* (1990).

And there are guides to these guides: reference librarians. If you don't know where to turn to find something, turn to the librarian.

TAKING NOTES

Let's assume now that you have checked some bibliographies and that you have a fair number of references you must read to have a substantial knowledge of the evidence and the common interpretations of the evidence. Most researchers find it convenient, when examining bibliographies and the library catalog, to write down each reference on a 3″ × 5″ index card—one title per card. On the card, put the author's full name (last name first), the exact title of the book or article, and the name of the journal (with dates and pages). Titles of books and periodicals (publications issued periodically—for example, monthly or four times a year) are underlined; titles of articles and of essays in books are enclosed in quotation marks. It's also a good idea to put the library catalog number on the card to save time if you need to get the item for a second look.

Next, start reading or scanning the materials whose titles you have collected. Some of these items will prove irrelevant or silly; others will prove valuable in themselves and also in the leads they give you to further references, which you should duly record on index cards. Notes—aside from these bibliographic notes—are best taken on larger index cards. The 3″ × 5″ cards are too small for summaries of useful materials; we use 4″ × 6″ cards, which allow you to record a moderate amount of information. Using these medium-sized cards rather than larger ones serves as a reminder that you need not take notes on everything. Be selective in taking notes.

Two Mechanical Aids: The Photocopier and the Word Processor

Use the **photocopier** to make copies of material from the library (including material that does not circulate) that you know you need, or that you might want to refer to later. But remember that sometimes it is even more efficient to

- Read the material in the library,
- Select carefully what pertains to the purpose of your research, and
- Take your notes on it.

The **word processor** or **computer** is useful not only in the final stage, to produce a neat copy, but also in the early stages of research, when you are getting ideas and taking notes. With the help of the computer, you can brainstorm ideas, make connections, organize and reorganize material, and develop (and change) outlines. This file can be a kind of creative "work space" for your research paper.

A Guide to Note-Taking

Some students use note cards—we have already mentioned that we use 4″ × 6″ cards—for taking notes during the process of research. Others write on separate sheets of a notebook, or on the sheets of a yellow legal pad. Still others take their notes using a computer or word processor, and then organize and re-arrange this body of material by copying and pasting, moving the notes into a co-herent order. (We advise you not to delete material that, when you reread your notes, strikes you as irrelevant. It *probably* is irrelevant; but on the other hand, it may turn out to be valuable after all. Just put unwanted material into a file called "rejects," or some such thing, until you have completed the paper.)

Whichever method you prefer, keep in mind the following:

- **For everything you consult or read in detail, always specify the source,** so that you know exactly from where you have taken a key point or a quotation.
- **Write summaries (abridgments), not paraphrases (restatements).**
- **Quote sparingly.** Remember that this is *your* paper—it will present your thesis, not the thesis and arguments and analyses of someone else. Quote directly only those passages that are particularly effective, or cru-cial, or memorable. In your finished paper these quotations will provide authority and emphasis.
- **Quote accurately.** After copying a quotation, check your note against the original, correct any misquotation, and then put a checkmark after your quotation to indicate that it is accurate. Verify the page number also, and then put a checkmark on your note after the page number. If a quota-tion runs from the bottom of, say, page 306 to the top of 307, on your note put a distinguishing mark (for instance, two parallel vertical lines af-ter the last word of the first page) so that if you later use only part of the quotation, you will know the page on which it appeared.

  Use ellipses (three spaced periods) to indicate the omission of any words within a sentence. If the omitted words are at the end of the quoted sentence, put a period where you end the sentence, and then add three spaced periods to indicate the omission:

  ```
  If the . . . words are at the end of the quoted sen-
  tence, put a period where you end. . . .
  ```

  Use square brackets to indicate your additions to the quota-tion. Here is an example:

  ```
  Here is an [uninteresting] example.
  ```

- **Never copy a passage by changing an occasional word,** under the impression that you are thereby putting it into your own words. Notes of this sort may find their way into your paper, your reader will sense a style other than yours, and suspicions of plagiarism may follow. (For a detailed discussion of plagiarism, see pages 1776–1777.)

- **Comment on your notes** as you do your work, and later as you reflect on what you have jotted down from the sources. Make a special mark—we recommend using double parentheses ((. . .)) or a different-colored pen to write, for example, "Jones seriously misreads the passage," or "Smith makes a good point but fails to see its implications." As you work, consider it your obligation to *think* about the material, evaluating it and using it as a stimulus to further thought.
- **In the upper corner of each note card, write a brief key**—for example, "Swordplay in *Hamlet*"—so that later you can tell at a glance what is on the note.

DRAFTING THE PAPER

The job of writing up your argument remains, but if you have taken good notes and have put useful headings on each note, you are well on your way.

- Read through the notes and sort them into packets of related material. Remove all notes that you now see are irrelevant to your paper. (Do not destroy them, however; you may want them later.) Go through the notes again and again, sorting and resorting, putting together what belongs together.
- Probably you will find that you have to do a little additional research—somehow you aren't quite clear about this or that—but after you have done this additional research, you should be able to arrange the packets into a reasonable and consistent sequence. You now have a kind of first draft, or at least a tentative organization for your paper.
- Beware of the compulsion to include every note in your essay; that is, beware of telling the reader, "A says . . . ; B says . . . ; C says . . . ."
- You must have a point, a thesis. Make sure that you state it early, and that you keep it evident to your readers.
- Make sure that the organization is evident to the reader. When you were doing your research, and even perhaps when you were arranging your notes, you were not entirely sure where you were going; but by now, with your notes arranged into what seems to you to be the right sequence, you think you know what everything adds up to. Doubtless in the process of drafting you will make important changes in your focus, but do not abandon a draft until you think it not only says what you want to say, but says it in what seems to you to be a reasonable order. The final version of the paper should be a finished piece of work, without the inconsistencies, detours, and occasional dead ends of an early draft. Your readers should feel that they are moving toward a conclusion (by means of your thoughtful evaluation of the evidence) rather than merely reading an anthology of commentary on the topic. And so we should get some such structure as "There are three common views on. . . . The first two are represented by A and B; the third, and by far the most reasonable, is C's view that. . . . A argues . . . but. . . . The second view, B's, is based on . . . but. . . . Although the third view, C's, is not conclusive, still. . . . Moreover, C's point can be strengthened when we consider a piece of evidence that she does not make use of. . . ."
- Preface all or almost all quotations with a lead-in, such as "X concisely states the common view" or "Z, without offering any proof, asserts that . . . ." Let

the reader know where you are going, or, to put it a little differently, let the reader know how the quotation fits into your argument.

Quotations and summaries, in short, are accompanied by judicious analyses of your own. By the end of the paper, your readers have not only read a neatly typed paper (see pages 1764-1768) and gained an idea of what previous writers have said but also are persuaded that under your guidance they have seen the evidence, heard the arguments justly summarized, and reached a sound conclusion.

A bibliography or list of works consulted (see pages 1782-1788) is usually appended to a research paper so that readers may easily look further into the primary and secondary material if they wish; but if you have done your job well, readers will be content to leave the subject where you left it, grateful that you have set matters straight.

KEEPING A SENSE OF PROPORTION

Keep in mind the boundaries of the assignment.

- What is the *length* of the essay? How much *time* did the instructor give you in which to do it?
- *How many sources* did the instructor suggest that you should use? Did the instructor refer to specific kinds of sources that the paper should include—scholarly books and/or articles, other primary texts (published statements by artists, interviews with museum personnel)?
- What are the *proportions* of the essay? How much should consist of formal analysis, and how much of historical research and context?

For a **short paper**—say, two to five pages—in which you treat one or two works in a historical context, it may be sufficient if you look at two or three standard reference works. In them you will find some basic ideas—overviews of the period—and you can think about your selected works within these contexts.

For a paper of **medium length,** say five to ten or twelve pages, you almost surely will want to go beyond basic references. You probably will want to look into some of the works that these references cite, and your instructor presumably has given you enough time to look at them.

- Pay attention to *when* the books or articles were published; the most recent publications may not be the best, but they probably will give you a good sense of current thinking, and they will guide you to other recent writings.

For a **long paper**—say, fifteen to twenty-five pages—you will have to go beyond basic references and also beyond a few additional specialized sources. Your instructor almost surely will expect you to have read widely, so at the outset you may want to do a "subject" search in the online catalogs of your own library. But your library, unless it is a major research library, may not contain some work that, according to reference books, is especially important. Or even if your library does contain this title, it may appear as merely one more title in a long list, and you may not be aware of its importance. Before doing a search, then, consider the possibility of first checking reference books and compiling a short bibliography of titles that they cite. Then begin by looking at the titles especially recommended in reference books. If your library does not have some of these titles, request them by interlibrary loan.

How do you know when to stop? There is no simple answer. And almost everyone who has written a research paper has thought, "There still is one more source that I need to consult before I start drafting my paper." (In this respect the writer of a research paper is like a painter; it has been said painters never finish paintings, they just abandon them.) In the midst of a busy semester you need to make choices and to budget your time.

- Stop when you have acquired the historical knowledge that strengthens your analyses of works of literature—the knowledge that deepens your understanding of the works, and the knowledge that is sufficient for you to meet the specifications of the assignment.
- The paper should be *your* paper, a paper in which you present a thesis that you have developed, focusing on certain works. By using secondary resources you can enrich your analysis, as you place yourself in the midst of the scholarly community interested in this work or group of works. But keep a proper proportion between your thinking—again, the paper is *your* paper—and the thinking set forth in your sources.

FOCUS ON PRIMARY SOURCES

Remember that your paper should highlight *primary* sources, the materials that are your real subject (as opposed to the secondary sources, the critical and historical discussion of these primary materials). It should be, above all, *your* paper, a paper in which you present a thesis that you have developed about the literary work or works that you have chosen to examine. In short, you are arguing a case. By using secondary sources, you can enrich your analysis, as you place yourself in the midst of the scholarly community interested in this author or authors. But keep a judicious proportion between primary sources, which should receive the greater emphasis, and secondary sources, which should be used selectively.

To help you succeed in this balancing act, when you review your draft, mark with a red pen the quotations from and references to primary sources, and then with a blue pen do the same marking for secondary sources. If, when you scan the pages of your paper-in-progress, you see a lot more blue than red, you should change the emphasis, the proportion, to what it should be. Guard against the tendency to rely heavily on the secondary sources you have compiled. The point of view that really counts is your own.

DOCUMENTATION

What to Document: Avoiding Plagiarism

Honesty requires that you acknowledge your indebtedness for material, not only when you quote directly from a work but also when you appropriate an idea that is not common knowledge. Not to acknowledge such borrowing is plagiarism. If in doubt whether to give credit, give credit.

You ought, however, to develop a sense of what is considered **common knowledge.** Definitions in a dictionary can be considered common knowledge, so there is no need to say, "According to Webster, a novel is . . ." (This is weak in three ways: It's unnecessary, it's uninteresting, and it's unclear, since "Webster" appears in the titles of several dictionaries, some good and some bad.) Similarly, the date of first publication of *The Scarlet Letter* (1850) can be considered common knowledge. Few can give it when asked, but it can be found out from innumerable sources, and no one need get the credit for providing you with the date. The idea that Hamlet delays is also a matter of common knowledge. But if you are impressed by so-and-so's argument that Claudius has been much maligned, you should give credit to so-and-so.

Suppose that in the course of your research for a paper on Langston Hughes you happen to come across Arnold Rampersad's statement, in an essay in *Voices and Visions* (ed. Helen Vendler):

> Books alone could not save Hughes from loneliness, let alone give him the strength to be a writer. At least one other factor was essential in priming him for creative obsession. In the place in his heart, or psychology, vacated by his parents entered the black masses. (355)

This is an interesting idea, and in the last sentence the shift from heart to psychology is perhaps especially interesting. You certainly *cannot* say—with the implication that the idea and the words are your own—something like

```
Hughes let enter into his heart, or his
psychology--a place vacated by his parents--the
black masses.
```

The writer is simply lifting Rampersad's ideas and making only tiny changes in the wording. But even a larger change in the wording is unacceptable unless Rampersad is given credit. Here is a restatement that is an example of plagiarism even though the words differ from Rampersad's:

```
Hughes took into himself ordinary black people, thus
filling the gap created by his mother and father.
```

In this version, the writer presents Rampersad's idea as if it were the writer's own—and presents it less effectively than Rampersad.

What to do? Give Rampersad credit, perhaps along these lines:

```
As Arnold Rampersad has said, "in the place in his
heart, or his psychology" where his parents had
once been, Hughes now substituted ordinary black
people (355).
```

You can use another writer's ideas, and even some of the very words, but you must give credit, and you must use quotation marks when you quote.

You can

- Give credit and quote directly, or
- Give credit and summarize the writer's point, or
- Give credit and summarize the point but include—within quotation marks—some phrase you think is especially interesting.

How to Document: Footnotes, Internal Parenthetical Citations, and a List of Works Cited (MLA Format)

Documentation tells your reader exactly what your sources are. Until fairly recently, the standard form was the footnote, which, for example, told the reader that the source of such and such a quotation was a book by so-and-so. But in 1984 the Modern Language Association, which had established the footnote form used in hundreds of journals, university presses, and classrooms, substituted a new form. It is this newer form—parenthetical citation *within* the text (rather than at the foot of the page or the end of the essay)— that we will discuss at length. Keep in mind, though, that footnotes still have their uses.

Footnotes

If you are using only one source, your instructor may advise you to give the source in a footnote. (Check with your instructors to find out their preferred forms of documentation.)

Let's say that your only source is this textbook. Let's say, too, that all of your quotations will be from a single story—Kate Chopin's "The Story of an Hour"—printed in this book on pages 28–29. If you use a word processor, the software program can probably format the note for you. If, however, you are using a typewriter, type the digit 1 (elevated, and *without* a period after it) after your first reference to (or quotation from) the story, and then put a footnote at the bottom of the page, explaining where the story can be found. After your last line of text on the page, triple-space, indent five spaces from the left-hand margin, and type the arabic number 1, elevated. Do *not* put a period after it. Then type a statement (double-spaced) to the effect that all references are to this book.

Notice that although the footnote begins by being indented five spaces, if the note runs to more than one line the subsequent lines are given flush left.

[1]Chopin's story appears in Sylvan Barnet et al., eds. <u>An Introduction to Literature</u>, 14th ed. (New York: Longman, 2006), 28–29.

(If a book has more than three authors or editors, give the name of only the first author or editor, and follow it with *et al.,* the Latin abbreviation for "and others.")

Even if you are writing a comparison of, say, two stories in this book, you can use a note of this sort. It might run thus:

[1]All page references given parenthetically within the essay refer to stories in Sylvan Barnet et al., eds. <u>An Introduction to Literature</u>, 14th ed. (New York: Longman, 2006).

If you use such a note, you do not need to use a footnote after each quotation that follows. You can give the citations right in the body of the paper, by putting the page references in parentheses after the quotations.

Internal Parenthetical Citations

Here we distinguish between embedded quotations (which are short, are run right into your own sentence, and are enclosed in quotation marks) and quotations that are set off on the page and are not enclosed in quotation marks (for example, three or more lines of poetry, five or more lines of typed prose).

For an embedded quotation, put the page reference in parentheses immediately after the closing quotation mark *without* any intervening punctuation. Then, after the parenthesis that follows the number, insert the necessary punctuation (for instance, a comma or a period):

```
O'Connor begins "A Good Man Is Hard to Find" with a
simple declarative sentence, "The grandmother didn't
want to go to Florida" (192). O'Connor then goes on
to give the grandmother's reason.
```

The period comes *after* the parenthetical citation. In the next example *no* punctuation comes after the first citation—because none is needed—and a comma comes *after* (not before or within) the second citation, because a comma is needed in the sentence:

```
This is ironic because almost at the start of the
story, in the second paragraph, Richards with the
best of motives "hastened" (28) to bring his sad
message; if he had at the start been "too late" (28),
Mallard would have arrived at home first.
```

For a quotation that is not embedded within the text but is set off (by being indented ten spaces), put the parenthetical citation on the last line of the quotation, one space *after* the period that ends the quoted sentence.

Four additional points:

- The abbreviations *p., pg.,* and *pp.* are *not* used in citing pages.
- If a story is very short, perhaps running for only a page or two, your instructor may tell you there is no need to keep citing the page reference for each quotation. Simply mention in the footnote that the story appears on, say, pages 205-206.
- If you are referring to a poem, your instructor may tell you to use parenthetical citations of line numbers rather than of page numbers. But, again, your footnote will tell the reader that the poem can be found in this book, and on what page.
- If you are referring to a play with numbered lines, your instructor may prefer that in your parenthetical citations you give act, scene, and line, rather than page numbers. Use arabic (not roman) numerals, separating the act from the scene, and the scene from the line, by periods. Here, then, is how a reference to Act 3, Scene 2, line 118 would be given:

```
(3.2.118)
```

Parenthetical Citations and List of Works Cited

Footnotes have fallen into disfavor. Parenthetical citations are now usually clarified not by means of a footnote but by means of a list, headed "Works Cited," given at the end of the essay. In this list you give alphabetically (last name first) the authors and titles that you have quoted or referred to in the essay.

Briefly, the idea is that the reader of your paper encounters an author's name and a parenthetical citation of pages. By checking the author's name in Works Cited, the reader can find the passage in the book. Suppose you are writing about Kate Chopin's "The Story of an Hour." Let's assume that you have already mentioned the author and the title of the story—that is, you have let the reader know the subject of the essay—and now you introduce a quotation from the story in a sentence such as this. (Notice the parenthetical citation of page numbers immediately after the quotation.)

> True, Mrs. Mallard at first expresses grief when she hears the news, but soon (unknown to her friends) she finds joy in it. So, Richards's "sad message" (28), though sad in Richards's eyes, is in fact a happy message.

Turning to Works Cited, the reader, knowing the quoted words are by Chopin, looks for Chopin and finds the following:

> Chopin, Kate. "The Story of an Hour." An Introduction to Literature, 14th ed. Ed. Sylvan Barnet et al. New York: Longman, 2006.

Thus the essayist is informing the reader that the quoted words ("sad message") are to be found on page 29 of this anthology.

If you have not mentioned Chopin's name in some sort of lead-in, you will have to give her name within the parentheses so that the reader will know the author of the quoted words:

> What are we to make out of a story that ends by telling us that the leading character has died "of joy that kills" (Chopin 29)?

The closing quotation marks come immediately after the last word of the quotation; the citation and the final punctuation—in this case, the essayist's question mark—come *after* the closing quotation marks.

If you are comparing Chopin's story with Gilman's "The Yellow Wallpaper," in Works Cited you will give a similar entry for Gilman—her name, the title of the story, the book in which it is reprinted, and the page numbers that the story occupies.

If you are referring to several works reprinted within one volume, instead of listing each item fully, it is acceptable in Works Cited to list each item simply by giving the author's name, the title of the work, then a period, a space, and the name of the anthologist, followed by the page numbers that the selection spans. Thus a reference to Chopin's "The Story of an Hour" would be followed only by: Barnet 28-29. This form requires that the anthology itself be cited under the name of the first-listed editor, thus:

> Barnet, Sylvan, et al., eds. An Introduction to Literature, 14th ed. New York: Longman, 2006.

If you are writing a research paper, you will use many sources. In the essay itself you will mention an author's name, quote or summarize from this author, and follow the quotation or summary with a parenthetical citation of the pages. In Works Cited you will give the full title, place of publication, and other bibliographic material.

Here are a few examples, all referring to an article by Joan Templeton. "The *Doll House* Backlash: Criticism, Feminism, and Ibsen." The article appeared in *PMLA* 104 (1989): 28–40, but this information is given only in Works Cited, not within the text of the student's essay.

If in the text of your essay you mention the author's name, the citation following a quotation (or a summary of a passage) is merely a page number in parentheses, followed by a period, thus:

> In 1989 Joan Templeton argued that many critics, un-
> happy with recognizing Ibsen as a feminist, sought
> "to render Nora inconsequential" (29).

Or:

> In 1989 Joan Templeton noted that many critics,
> unhappy with recognizing Ibsen as a feminist, have
> sought to make Nora trivial (29).

If you don't mention the name of the author in a lead-in, you will have to give the name within the parenthetical citation:

> Many critics, attempting to argue that Ibsen was
> not a feminist, have tried to make Nora trivial
> (Templeton 29).

Notice in all of these examples that the final period comes after the parenthetical citation. *Exception:* If the quotation is longer than four lines and is therefore set off by being indented ten spaces from the left margin, end the quotation with the appropriate punctuation (period, question mark, or exclamation mark), hit the space bar twice, and type (in parentheses) the page number. In this case, do not put a period after the citation.

Another point: If your list of Works Cited includes more than one work by an author, in your essay when you quote or refer to one or the other you'll have to identify *which* work you are drawing on. You can provide the title in a lead-in, thus:

> In "The Doll House Backlash: Criticism, Feminism,
> and Ibsen," Templeton says, "Nora's detractors have
> often been, from the first, her husband's defenders"
> (30).

Or you can provide the information in the parenthetic citation, giving a shortened version of the title. This usually consists of the first word, unless it is *A, An,* or *The*, in which case including the second word is usually enough. Certain titles may require still another word or two, as in this example:

```
According to Templeton, "Nora's detractors have often
been, from the first, her husband's defenders" ("Doll
House Backlash" 30).
```

Forms of Citation in Works Cited

In looking over the following samples of entries in Works Cited, remember:

- The list of Works Cited appears at the end of the paper. It begins on a new page, and the page continues the numbering of the text.
- The list of Works Cited is arranged alphabetically by author (last name first).
- If a work is anonymous, list it under the first word of the title unless the first word is *A, An,* or *The*, in which case list it under the second word.
- If a work is by two authors, although the book is listed alphabetically under the first author's last name, the second author's name is given in the normal order, first name first.
- If you list two or more works by the same author, the author's name is not repeated but is represented by three hyphens followed by a period and a space.
- Each item begins flush left, but if an entry is longer than one line, subsequent lines in the entry are indented five spaces.

For details about almost every imaginable kind of citation, consult Joseph Gibaldi, *MLA Handbook for Writers of Research Papers*, 5th ed. (New York: Modern Language Association, 1999). We give here, however, information concerning the most common kinds of citations.

For citations to electronic sources, see page 1800.

Here are samples of the kinds of citations you are most likely to include in your list of Works Cited.

A book by one author:

```
Douglas, Ann. The Feminization of American Culture.
    New York: Knopf, 1977.
```

Notice that the author's last name is given first, but otherwise the name is given as on the title page. Do not substitute initials for names written out on the title page, but you may shorten the publisher's name—for example, from Little, Brown and Company to Little.

Take the title from the title page, not from the cover or the spine, but disregard unusual typography—for instance, the use of only capital letters or the use of & for *and*. Underline the title and subtitle with one continuous underline, but do not underline the period. The place of publication is indicated by the name of the city. If the city is not well known or if several cities have the same name (for instance, Cambridge, Massachusetts, and Cambridge, England) the name of the state or country is added. If the title page lists several cities, give only the first.

A book by more than one author:

> Gilbert, Sandra, and Susan Gubar. The Madwoman in
>   the Attic: The Woman Writer and the Nineteenth-
>   Century Literary Imagination. New Haven: Yale
>   UP, 1979.

Notice that the book is listed under the last name of the first author (Gilbert) and that the second author's name is then given with first name (Susan) first. *If the book has more than three authors,* give the name of the first author only (last name first) and follow it with *et al.* (Latin for "and others.")

A book in several volumes:

> McQuade, Donald, et al., eds. The Harper American
>   Literature. 2nd ed. 2 vols. New York: Longman,
>   1994.
> Pope, Alexander. The Correspondence of Alexander Pope.
>   5 vols. Ed. George Sherburn. Oxford: Clarendon,
>   1955.

The total number of volumes is given after the title, regardless of the number that you have used.

If you have used more than one volume, within your essay you will parenthetically indicate a reference to, for instance, page 30 of volume 3 thus: (3: 30). If you have used only one volume of a multivolume work—let's say you used only volume 2 of McQuade's anthology—in your entry in Works Cited write, after the period following the date, Vol. 2. In your parenthetical citation within the essay you will therefore cite only the page reference (without the volume number), since the reader will (on consulting Works Cited) understand that in this example the reference is in volume 2.

If, instead of using the volumes as a whole, you used only an independent work within one volume—say, an essay in volume 2—in Works Cited omit the abbreviation *Vol.* Instead, give an arabic 2 (indicating volume 2) followed by a colon, a space, and the page numbers that encompass the selection you used:

> McPherson, James Alan. "Why I Like Country Music."
>   The Harper American Literature. 2nd ed. 2 vols.
>   New York: Longman, 1994. 2: 2304-15.

Notice that this entry for McPherson specifies not only that the book consists of two volumes, but also that only one selection ("Why I Like Country Music," occupying pages 2304-2315 in volume 2) was used. If you use this sort of citation in Works Cited, in the body of your essay a documentary reference to this work will be only to the page; the volume number will *not* be added.

A book with a separate title in a set of volumes:

> Churchill, Winston. The Age of Revolution. Vol. 3 of
>   A History of the English-Speaking Peoples. New
>   York: Dodd, 1957.

Jonson, Ben. <u>The Complete Masques</u>. Ed. Stephen Orgel.
Vol. 4 of <u>The Yale Ben Jonson</u>. New Haven: Yale
UP, 1969.

A revised edition of a book:

Chaucer, Geoffrey. <u>The Riverside Chaucer</u>. Ed. Larry
Benson. 3rd ed. Boston: Houghton, 1987.

Ellmann, Richard. <u>James Joyce</u>. Rev. ed. New York:
Oxford UP, 1982.

A reprint, such as a paperback version of an older hardcover book:

Rourke, Constance. <u>American Humor</u>. 1931. Garden City,
New York: New York Review of Books, 2004.

Notice that the entry cites the original date (1931) but indicates that the writer
is using the New York Review of Books reprint of 2004.

An edited book other than an anthology:

Keats, John. <u>The Letters of John Keats</u>. Ed. Hyder
Edward Rollins. 2 vols. Cambridge, Mass.: Harvard
UP, 1958.

An anthology: You can list an anthology either under the editor's name or
under the title.

A work in a volume of works by one author:

Sontag, Susan. "The Aesthetics of Silence." In <u>Styles
of Radical Will</u>. New York: Farrar, 1969, 3–34.

This entry indicates that Sontag's essay, called "The Aesthetics of Silence," appears in a book of hers entitled *Styles of Radical Will.* Notice that the page
numbers of the short work are cited (not page numbers that you may happen to
refer to, but the page numbers of the entire piece).

*A work in an anthology, that is, in a collection of works by several
authors:* Begin with the author and the title of the work you are citing, not
with the name of the anthologist or the title of the anthology. The entry ends
with the pages occupied by the selection you are citing:

Ng, Fae Myenne. "A Red Sweater." <u>Charlie Chan Is
Dead: An Anthology of Contemporary Asian American
Fiction</u>. Ed. Jessica Hagedorn. New York: Penguin,
1993. 358–68.

Normally, you will give the title of the work you are citing (probably an essay,
short story, or poem) in quotation marks. If you are referring to a book-length

work (for instance, a novel or a full-length play), underline it to indicate italics. If the work is translated, after the period that follows the title, write *Trans.* and give the name of the translator, followed by a period and the name of the anthology.

If the collection is a multivolume work and you are using only one volume, in Works Cited you will specify the volume, as in the example (page 1783) of McPherson's essay. Because the list of Works Cited specifies the volume, your parenthetical documentary reference within your essay will specify (as mentioned earlier) only the page numbers, not the volume. Thus, although McPherson's essay appears on pages 2304–2315 in the second volume of a two-volume work, a parenthetical citation will refer only to the page numbers because the citation in Works Cited specifies the volume.

Remember that the pages specified in the entry in your list of Works Cited are to the *entire selection,* not simply to pages you may happen to refer to within your paper.

If you are referring to a *reprint of a scholarly article,* give details of the original publication, as in the following example:

Mack, Maynard. "The World of Hamlet." Yale Review 41

    (1952): 502–23. Rpt. in Hamlet. By William

    Shakespeare. Ed. Sylvan Barnet. New York: Penguin

    Putnam, 1998. 265–87.

Two or more works in an anthology: If you are referring to more than one work in an anthology, in order to avoid repeating all the information about the anthology in each entry in Works Cited, under each author's name (in the appropriate alphabetical place) give the author and title of the work, then a period, a space, and the name of the anthologist, followed by the page numbers that the selection spans. Thus, a reference to Shakespeare's *Hamlet* would be followed only by

    Barnet 1075–1184

rather than by a full citation of Barnet's anthology. This form requires that the anthology itself also be listed, under Barnet.

Two or more works by the same author: Notice that the works are given in alphabetical order (*Fables* precedes *Fools*) and that the author's name is not repeated but is represented by three hyphens followed by a period and a space. If the author is the translator or editor of a volume, the three hyphens are followed not by a period but by a comma, then a space, then the appropriate abbreviation (*Trans.* or *Ed.*), then the title:

Frye, Northrop. Fables of Identity: Studies in Poetic

    Mythology. New York: Harcourt, 1963.

---. Fools of Time: Studies in Shakespearean Tragedy.

    Toronto: U of Toronto P, 1967.

A translated book:

Gogol, Nikolai. Dead Souls. Trans. Andrew McAndrew.

    New York: New American Library, 1961.

If you are discussing the translation itself, as opposed to the book, list the work under the translator's name. Then put a comma, a space, and "trans." After the period following "trans." skip a space, then give the title of the book, a period, a space, and then "By" and the author's name, first name first. Continue with information about the place of publication, publisher, and date, as in any entry to a book.

An introduction, foreword, or afterword, or other editorial apparatus:

Fromm, Erich. Afterword. <u>1984</u>. By George Orwell. New
    American Library, 1961.

Usually a book with an introduction or some such comparable material is listed under the name of the author of the book rather than the name of the author of the editorial material (see the citation to Pope on page 1783). But if you are referring to the editor's apparatus rather than to the work itself, use the form just given.

Words such as *preface, introduction, afterword,* and *conclusion* are capitalized in the entry but are neither enclosed within quotation marks nor underlined.

A book review: First, here is an example of a review that does not have a title.

Vendler, Helen. Rev. of <u>Essays on Style</u>. Ed. Roger
    Fowler. <u>Essays in Criticism</u> 16 (1966): 457-63.

If the review has a title, give the title after the period following the reviewer's name, before "Rev." If the review is unsigned, list it under the first word of the title, or the second word if the first word is *A, An,* or *The.* If an unsigned review has no title, begin the entry with "Rev. of" and alphabetize it under the title of the work being reviewed.

An encyclopedia: The first example is for a signed article, the second for an unsigned article.

Lang, Andrew. "Ballads." <u>Encyclopaedia Britannica</u>.
    1910 ed.

"Metaphor." <u>The New Encyclopaedia Britannica:
    Micropaedia</u>. 1974 ed.

An article in a scholarly journal: Some journals are paginated consecutively; that is, the pagination of the second issue picks up where the first issue left off. Other journals begin each issue with a new page 1. The forms of the citations in Works Cited differ slightly.

First, the citation of a *journal that uses continuous pagination:*

Burbick, Joan. "Emily Dickinson and the Economics of
    Desire." <u>American Literature</u> 58 (1986): 361-78.

This article appeared in volume 58, which was published in 1986. (Notice that the volume number is followed by a space, then by the year in parentheses, and then by a colon, a space, and the page numbers of the entire article.) Although each volume consists of four issues, you do *not* specify the issue number when the journal is paginated continuously.

For a *journal that paginates each issue separately* (a quarterly journal will have four page 1's each year), give the issue number directly after the volume number and a period, with no spaces before or after the period:

> Spillers, Hortense J. "Martin Luther King and the
>   Style of the Black Sermon." The Black Scholar 3.1
>   (1971): 14-27.

An article in a weekly, biweekly, or monthly publication:

> McCabe, Bernard. "Taking Dickens Seriously."
>   Commonweal 14 May 1965: 24.

Notice that the volume number and the issue number are omitted for popular weeklies or monthlies such as *Time* and *Atlantic*.

An article in a newspaper: Because newspapers usually consist of several sections, a section number may precede the page number. The example indicates that an article begins on page 3 of section 2 and is continued on a later page:

> Wu, Jim. "Authors Praise New Forms." New York Times
>   8 Mar. 1996, sec. 2: 3+.

You may also have occasion to cite something other than a printed source, for instance, a lecture. Here are the forms for the chief nonprint sources.

An interview:

> Saretta, Howard. Personal interview. 3 Nov. 1998.

A lecture:

> Heaney, Seamus. Lecture. Tufts University. 15 Oct.
>   1998.

A television or radio program:

> 60 Minutes. CBS. 25 Jan. 2004.

A film or videotape:

> Modern Times. Dir. Charles Chaplin. United Artists,
>   1936.

A recording:

> Frost, Robert. "The Road Not Taken." Robert Frost
>   Reads His Poetry. Caedmon, TC 1060, 1956.

A performance:

> <u>The Cherry Orchard</u>. By Anton Chekhov. Dir. Ron
>   Daniels. American Repertory Theatre, Cambridge,
>   Mass. 3 Feb. 1994.

Reminder: For the form of citations to electronic material, see pages 1800–1804.

New Approaches to the Research Paper: Literature, History, and the World Wide Web

To err is human but to really foul things up requires a computer.

—Anonymous

The Internet is the world's largest library. It's just that all the books are on the floor.

—John Allen Paulos

To me, the computer is just another tool. You have to have a pen, and to know penmanship, but neither will write the book for you.

—Red Burns

Information is, above all, a principle of economy. The fewer data needed, the better the information. And an overload of information leads to information blackout. It does not enrich, but impoverishes.

—Peter Drucker

The previous appendix describes the traditional model and methods for writing a literary research paper. But literary research has become more wide-ranging and complicated, and a book like this one needs to devote another section to it to take into account important changes in the field of literary study and developments in technology.

Students in both literature and composition courses are now often asked to work with historical and literary materials and to demonstrate skills in interdisciplinary learning—and this educational change has taken place on the introductory as well as the intermediate and advanced levels. Like other fields, literary study is supplementing printed texts with electronic search tools, databases, and resources; literary analysis, writing, and research increasingly take place as much on the World Wide Web as in the library, and, in some cases, through e-mail and e-mail lists devoted to specific subject areas.

Historical research, enriched by resources on the Internet, can be very rewarding; it opens up new lines of inquiry as it teaches us about the contexts for literary works and enables us to respond to them in more complex ways. But we need the right strategies to perform this research effectively. Students in literature and composition must now possess the insight and understanding to explore, and to make good choices when consulting the ever-multiplying amounts of information available.

CASE STUDY ON LITERATURE AND HISTORY: THE INTERNMENT OF JAPANESE-AMERICANS

The best means of illustrating the new approach to literature and history, and outlining the process for identifying new kinds of resources, is through a case study. For this purpose we have chosen the literature and history of the internment of Japanese-Americans during World War II. This is a subject for research that a student might select or be assigned in a variety of courses—an introduction to literature in which a group of contemporary poems are studied, with some of them related in subject; a first-year writing course in which the subject is the literature of American immigration; a course in American or Asian-American literature; a course in multicultural literature or in American literature since World War II; or a senior seminar that examines twentieth-century literature and history, types of ethnic and minority literatures, or poetry and politics.

Many books, articles, and conferences have been devoted to the internment, and we can hardly do it justice here. This discussion describes the type of inquiry into the subject that you can undertake, beginning with the analysis of literary texts and moving outward from it into history as well as print and electronic sources.

LITERARY TEXTS

Reprinted here are two poems. The first is Mitsuye Yamada's "The Question of Loyalty," from *Camp Notes and Other Poems* (1992); the second is David Mura's "An Argument: On 1942," from *After We Lost Our Way* (1989).

MITSUYE YAMADA

Mitsuye Yamada, the daughter of Japanese immigrants to the United States, was born in Japan in 1923, during her mother's return visit to her native land. She was raised in Seattle, but in 1942 she and her family were incarcerated and then relocated to an internment camp in Idaho. This was the result of Executive Order 9066, signed by President Franklin Roosevelt in February 1942. This order, in the aftermath of the Japanese attack on Pearl Harbor in December 1941, gave military authorities the right to remove any and all persons from "military areas." In 1954 Yamada became an American citizen. In addition to Camp Notes and Other Poems, *she has written* Desert Run: Poems and Stories *(1988) and edited* Sowing TI Leaves: Writings by Multicultural Women *(1991).*

The Question of Loyalty   [1976]

I met the deadline
for alien registration
once before
was numbered fingerprinted
and ordered not to travel   5
without permit.

But alien still they said I must
forswear allegiance to the emperor.
for me that was easy
I didn't even know him   10
but my mother who did cried out
  If I sign this
  What will I be?
  I am doubly loyal
  to my American children   15
  also to my own people.
  How can double mean nothing?
  I wish no one to lose this war.
  Everyone does.

I was poor   20
at math.
I signed
my only ticket out.

DAVID MURA

David Mura is a sansei, *a third-generation Japanese-American. He was born
in 1952, seven years after the end of the war. In both poetry and prose, he has
examined race, ethnicity, and sexuality, and has described his quest for self-
knowledge and personal and familial identity.* A Male Grief: Notes on Pornog-
raphy and Addiction *(1987) was his first book. Two years later he published*
After We Lost Our Way *in the National Poetry Series, and followed it with a
second book of verse,* The Colors of Desire: Poems *(1995). He has also written*
Turning Japanese: Memoirs of a Sansei *(1992) and* Where the Body Meets Memory: An Odyssey of Race, Sexuality, and Identity *(1996), which tells of his childhood in Chicago, his parents' recollections of the internment camps, and the
impact of internment on several generations of Japanese-Americans.*

An Argument: On 1942   [1989]

For my mother

> *Near Rose's Chop Suey and Jinosuke's grocery, the temple*
> *where incense hovered and inspired dense evening chants*
> *(prayers for Buddha's mercy, colorless and deep), that day*
> *he was fired . . .*

—No, no, no, she tells me. Why bring it back?
The camps are over. (Also overly dramatic.)
Forget *shoyu*-stained *furoshiki,*° *mochi*° on a stick:
You're like a terrier, David, gnawing a bone, an old, old trick   4

Mostly we were bored. Women cooked and sewed,
men played blackjack, dug gardens, a *benjo*° . . .
Who noticed barbed wire, guards in the towers?
We were children, hunting stones, birds, wild flowers.   8

Yes, Mother hid tins of *tsukemono*° and eel
beneath the bed. And when the last was peeled,
clamped tight her lips, growing thinner and thinner.
But cancer not the camps made her throat blacker   12

. . . And she didn't die then . . . after the war, in St. Paul,
you weren't even born. Oh, I know, I know, it's all
part of your job, your way, but why can't you glean
how far we've come, how much I can't recall—   16

David, it was so long ago—how useless it seems . . .

---

3 *shoyu*-stained *furoshiki* a soy-stained scarf that is used to carry things.   **mochi** rice
cakes.   **6 benjo** toilet.   **9 *tsukemono*** Japanese pickles. [All are author's notes.]

Your goal is eventually to move to historical research, but first you must
know the poems well. Reflect on the movement of each: how it begins, what occupies its middle sections, and how it ends. Consider the relationship of the
structure—the length of the lines, the organization of the stanzas, the diction
and imagery—to the dramatic situation and themes.

- For this analysis, reread the discussions of speaker, structure, figurative
  language, and other key terms presented in Chapter 16 of this book.

Yamada focuses on the conflict her mother experiences. The mother expresses her loyalty to her children, to her *American* children, even as she cher-
ishes her loyalty to her own people, the Japanese (though this word, revealingly,
is not used). She wants there to be no loser in the war; she hopes for an impossible stalemate, in which neither side loses.

The war thus manifests itself in the mother's own identity, in the tension
between the person she has been and the person, it seems, she must become. If
the mother signs the form forswearing allegiance to the Japanese emperor, she
will be denying her ancestry, forced to disclaim one-half of herself. She cannot
be who she is.

Mura describes the conflict between his mother and himself and delves into
the struggle that his mother wages with her memories. Unlike Yamada, Mura
was not in the camps himself; he is seeking knowledge about an experience that
took place before he was born.

The mother objects to her son's efforts to make her remember: "You're like
a terrier, David, gnawing a bone, an old, old trick." But as her own listing of details shows, the mother, if only to herself, has continued to linger over the internment—the men playing blackjack, the barbed wire. She says there is much
she cannot recall, but one feels that there is much that remains keenly present
for her, much that she could recall and has recalled.

The mother portrayed in this poem cannot practice the lesson she gives to her son. Nor will he allow her to. He is curious to know what happened; he wants his mother to tell about her experiences and, one suspects, to explain why she and the others did not resist then and have not spoken out since.

These are powerful poems even for a reader who knows only a little about the historical facts to which Yamada and Mura bear witness—a reader who knows only in a general way that many Japanese-Americans were forced during World War II to leave their West Coast homes and live in internment camps in the California desert, in other western states, and as far east as Arkansas. But the poems become still more effective for a reader who knows in depth and detail about this episode in American history, and who can bring this knowledge to a reading of the texts and present it in an analytical research paper.

One form of *historical* research is to follow a traditional route for *literary* research. The literary resources and methods described in Appendix B can lead to secondary sources on the authors and their writings and to information about their careers, the work they have done, and its major themes. There will be historical information in many of these sources, particularly those of a recent date.

By checking in the *MLA International Bibliography* (see page 1770), you can locate items such as the following:

On Yamada:

Jaskoski, Helen. "Interview with Mitsuye Yamada." *MELUS: The Journal of the Society for the Study of the Multi-Ethnic Literature of the United States.* 15:1 (Spring 1988): 97–108.

Schweik, Susan. "A Needle with Mama's Voice: Mitsuye Yamada's *Camp Notes* and the American Canon of War Poetry." In *Arms and the Woman: War, Gender, and Literary Representation.* Ed. Helen M. Cooper and Adrienne Auslander Munich. Chapel Hill: U of North Carolina P, 1989.

Usui, Masami. "A Language of Her Own in Mitsuye Yamada's Poetry and Stories." *Studies in Culture and the Humanities: Bulletin of the Faculty of Integrated Arts and Sciences,* Hiroshima University: 5:3 (1996): 1–17.

On Mura:

Taylor, Gordon O. "'The Country I Had Thought Was My Home': David Mura's *Turning Japanese* and Japanese-American Narrative since World War II." *Connotations: A Journal for Critical Debate* (Münster, Germany): 6:3 (1996–1997): 283–309.

General studies:

Nakanishi, Don T., ed. *Japanese American Internment: Commemorative Issue. Special issue of Amerasia Journal* 19:1 (1993).

Thiesmeyer, Lynn. "The Discourse of Official Violence: Anti-Japanese North American Discourse and the American Internment Camps." *Discourse & Society* 6:3 (July 1995): 319-52.

Yogi, Stan. "Yearning for the Past: The Dynamics of Memory in Sansei Internment Poetry." *Memory and Cultural Politics: New Approaches to American Ethnic Literatures.* Ed. Amritjit Singh, Joseph T. Skerrett, Jr., and Robert E. Hogan. Boston: Northeastern UP, 1996.

Through electronic access and interlibrary loan, a student can obtain almost any source, even if it is not carried by a library on campus. But sometimes interlibrary loan can take a few days, a week, or more. Remember the importance of starting early on research projects. Request copies of everything while there is still time before the deadline to examine them.

HISTORICAL SOURCES

The sources in the *MLA International Bibliography,* while promising, may take for granted more than you know at this stage; the discussion and analysis presented in them assumes that readers *already* have the background that you are seeking to acquire. How can you begin to acquire a base of historical knowledge?

Start small. Don't overwhelm yourself with more information than you can handle. Keep in mind as well that you are not aiming to become a historian, but, instead, to enrich your literary explorations with knowledge drawn from another field and set of sources.

Basic Reference Books (Short Paper)

It is best to begin with basic reference books, and you can get to them by consulting the following:

> Balay, Robert. *Guide to Reference Books,* 11th ed. Chicago: American Library Association, 1996.
> Blazek, Ron, and Elizabeth Aversa. *The Humanities: A Selective Guide to Information Sources,* 5th ed. Englewood, Colo.: Libraries Unlimited, 2000.
> This is an annotated guide to research sources in literature, art, and other fields in the humanities.

Or, consult *ARBA Guide to Subject Encyclopedias and Dictionaries* (1986); and *First Stop: The Master Index to Subject Encyclopedias* (1989).

Or, in the online library catalog, check under the subject heading, "history—dictionaries." (You can do the same thing for literature, for titles of reference works in that field.)

You can also refer to Jules R. Benjamin, *A Student's Guide to History,* 9th ed. (2002); and James R. Bracken, *Reference Works in British and American Literature,* 2nd ed. (1998). See also James L. Harner, *Literary Research Guide,* 4th ed. (2002).

Browse in the reference section of your school's library, or, better still, talk to a reference librarian—he or she can be a valuable resource and often can direct you quickly to helpful books.

In reply to the question, "Where can I find out about the internment of Japanese-Americans during World War II?" the reference librarian recommended to us *The Reader's Companion to American History,* ed. Eric Foner and John A. Garraty (Boston: Houghton Mifflin, 1991), which includes an entry (pages 558–589) on this subject, three paragraphs in length, titled "Japanese American Relocation."

Photograph of Japanese-Americans surrendering cameras and radios in 1942. (Photograph from *Seattle Post-Intelligencer* collection, University of Washington Libraries and the Museum of History and Industry.)

For a short paper of three pages that treats one or both of the poems and provides some historical context, this entry may be all that you need. It reports what happened, where, and why; emphasizes the outrage done to civil liberties; and highlights an aspect of camp experience that bears on Yamada's and Mura's poems: "Generational conflict beset the internees . . ." (589). You can relate this comment to the differences and struggles between the generations that Yamada and Mura evoke. Here, you have an historical detail that you can develop in your examination of the poems *and,* if the assignment were a longer one calling for extensive research, that you could make the organizing principle for gathering and then sifting through sources.

Remind yourself of the boundaries of the assignment.

- What is the *length* of the essay? Its *due date?*
- *How many* sources did the instructor state that you should use? Did he or she refer to specific kinds of sources that the paper should include—scholarly books and/or articles, other primary sources (literary texts, letters, autobiographies, journals), photographs, and so on?
- The *proportions* of the essay? How much of it should consist of literary analysis, and how much of historical research and context?
- It is important to gain basic knowledge of the subject, so that you have a clear, accurate answer to your core question—in this case, What was the internment? But, at the same time, seek to locate in the overview of the subject an idea or issue that is connected to the themes of the specific literary works. *Connect* the literature and the history.

> ✍ A RULE FOR WRITERS:
>
> When you begin work on an essay, make sure that you know what the
> assignment is asking for and how many words (or pages) are required.

Getting Deeper (Medium Paper)

The entry in *The Reader's Companion to American History* has limitations. It is
brief, lacks a bibliography, and a cross-reference leads to an entry on World War
II that supplies no further information about the internment. The brief account
(under the entry "Asian Americans") in *The Oxford Companion to United States
History,* ed. Paul S. Boyer (New York: Oxford University Press, 2001) also may
fall short of giving you the range and depth of information that you need.

For a medium-length paper, you will need to search elsewhere for more
information and, if you require it, for a bibliography. Here are several good
sources we located; we found the first two by browsing in the reference section of the library, and the third resulted from a suggestion by the reference
librarian there.

> *Encyclopedia of the United States in the Twentieth Century.* Stanley I.
>   Kutler, general editor. 5 vols. New York: Scribner's, 1996.
> *Harvard Encyclopedia of American Ethnic Groups.* Ed. Stephan
>   Thernstrom. Cambridge: Harvard UP, 1980.
> *Oxford Companion to World War II,* general editor, I. C. B. Dear, consul-
>   tant editor, M. R. D. Foot. New York: Oxford UP, 1995.

Like *The Reader's Companion to American History,* the *Oxford Companion to World War II* is recent, prepared by eminent scholars, and published by a
reputable press. It is a trustworthy source, and its signed entry on "Japanese-
Americans" (632–634) is longer and more detailed than the entry in *The
Reader's Companion;* it is cross-referenced to a general entry on "internment"
and identifies three books for further reading:

> Daniels, Roger. *Asian America: Chinese and Japanese in the United States
>   since 1850* (Seattle, Wash., 1988).
> ———. *Concentration Camps USA* (New York, 1971).
> Takaki, Ronald. *Strangers from a Different Shore: A History of Asian
>   Americans* (Boston, 1989).

Now you can start to compile a bibliography of your own, with these three
books as its foundation. But—here is a key point—note their dates of publication. No doubt these are good sources, but you should be seeking more recent
sources as well to make certain that your knowledge is as up-to-date as possible.

The section on the wartime internment of Japanese Americans in *Harvard
Encyclopedia* is part of a long essay devoted to the history of the Japanese in
America (561–571). The author, Harry H. L. Kitano, notes at one point:

> In the camps all Japanese, whether highly educated, wealthy, illiterate,
> or poor, were housed in barracks, ate mess-hall food, and received the
> same rates of pay for work—$16 a month for manual labor and $19 for

professional work. They used communal toilets, took communal showers, waited patiently in line for everything; they wore identical clothes,
and the sun, wind, and dust soon endowed them with the same
concentration-camp complexion. (566)

Kitano helps you grasp the historical setting for Mura's poem, and the next part
of his discussion pertains to it and to Yamada's poem even more directly:

The most difficult problem proved to be the boredom and monotony of
camp life; it exacerbated tensions and magnified irritations, resulting in
fights, riots, strikes, and even homicides. Inmates complained constantly
about the food, their neighbors, living conditions, and camp adminis-
trators. Conflicts between the Issei [Japanese-born Americans—the first
or immigrant generation] and Nisei [American-born Japanese—the second generation] added to the strain. Ideological arguments between
those loyal to Japan and those who stood with the United States grew
heated. The derogatory term *inu* [dog] was applied to those suspect of
being spies or government collaborators, and some of the inu were the
victims of severe beatings. (566)

"Mostly we were bored," recalls Mura's mother, touching on an aspect of
life in the camps that Kitano stresses in his historical survey. Kitano makes clear
how real and pervasive were the differences between generations, between parents and children. He concludes:

Family life was disrupted: the authority of the provider-father and the
housekeeper-mother was undercut by government supervision; children ate in mess halls rather than in the family circle. They were stifled
in an atmosphere of boredom and stagnation. Gambling became a problem, and petty family quarrels often escalated into violence. (567)

Now you can really begin to see the analytical value of historical sources.
Details like these make one wonder if part of the effect of Mura's poem lies in
what we sense the mother is trying *not* to remember—the fact, for example,
that the men playing blackjack were doing something that not only distracted
them but that caused a serious problem in the camps. She acknowledges that life
was boring, but possibly the boredom was even graver than she reveals to her
son—a boredom that led to arguments among family members and to violence.

Our historical research teaches us about the *contexts* for the Yamada and
Mura poems and alerts us to the power and precision of details that the poets include. Sometimes, too, it helps us sense the pressure of feelings and thoughts
that a writer or speaker is excluding, is holding back or reacting against. The
more we learn about the camps, the more we can perceive what Mura's mother
is referring to and what, on some level, she might be struggling to keep from
speaking about.

Kitano's chapter ends with a bibliographic essay that will give you additional items for your bibliography:

A Review of Researching a Literary-History Paper

- Consult a range of reference books as you are getting launched on a literary-
  historical paper—it will take less time than you think, and it will be time
  invested wisely.

- Pay attention to *when* the books were published and how up-to-date they are in their suggestions for additional reading.
- Even as you acquire familiarity with the subject in general, take special note of where the historical record *makes connections* to the literature that you are studying. The reward comes when you can perceive the relationship between history and the structure and themes of the literary works.

▩ TOPIC FOR CRITICAL THINKING AND WRITING

In *Prisoners Without Trial,* Roger Daniels states:

> There were no individual cooking facilities. Everyone ate in the mess hall. Three times a day, prisoners lined up with trays to receive wholesome, starchy, cheap food, not usually prepared in the most appetizing manner. . . . Almost everyone complained about the food, but what the mess halls did to family relationships was worse. Youngsters tended to eat in groups and move around from mess hall to mess hall. The dislocation of the family meal was but another way in which the detention process eroded the dignity and authority of parents. (67)

Photograph of a family in an apartment in internment camp. (Photograph by Howard Clifford, *Tacoma News Tribune.* Available in Special Collections and Preservation Division of the University of Washington Libraries.)

Write a page or so in which you connect Daniels's description to details that Mura includes in "An Argument: On 1942." Through your commentary show how the historical context enhances the reader's response to and understanding of the poem.

Other Reference Sources (Long Paper)

If your literary-historical research needs to be extended further—say, for a term paper of fifteen or twenty pages—then you will have to make use of other tools for locating historical sources. The items in the *MLA International Bibliography* and the suggestions for further reading given in reference books will lead you to other literary and historical materials.

If the paper requires sustained research, a good next step might be to perform a "subject" search in the online card catalogs of your own and other research libraries. It is always tempting to do a search by subject first, before anything else and without bothering to check reference books. Although convenient, this method has disadvantages. Your subject search for Japanese-American internment might not turn up Daniels's 1993 book at all—maybe your library does not own it. Or, if it does, this book might be in the middle of a long subject list: You would not know that it has been praised as an "essential" source and that, given that you must make choices, you would be better off zeroing in on this source than others on the list.

- When you check the online catalog for one of the books already on your bibliography, you will see on the entry the *subject* category for it. You can then use this category for your more complete *subject* search. The librarian can also assist you in identifying the phrases for the subject you are researching; the *Library of Congress Subject Headings (LCSH)* is another resource.

Too Much Information?

At this point, you may be wondering, "How do I know when to stop?" A good question, but not one with a simple answer. We have known students who have become gripped by a subject and have read everything they can about it. But however excited about a subject you become, in the midst of a busy semester you will need to make choices and budget your time.

- *How do I know when to stop?* Stop when you have acquired the historical knowledge that strengthens your analysis of the literary texts, the knowledge that deepens your understanding of the issues that the authors have treated, and the knowledge that is sufficient for you to meet the terms (that is, the boundaries) of the assignment.

> ✍ **A RULE FOR WRITERS:**
>
> When you use secondary sources, connect them to the literary text: Show the relevance of the sources to your understanding of the work itself.

ELECTRONIC SOURCES

Encyclopedias: Print and Electronic Versions

Encyclopedias can give you the basics about a subject, but like all resources, they have limitations. An encyclopedia may not cover the subject that you are researching or not cover it in adequate depth. Knowledge expands rapidly, and because it does, even a good encyclopedia lags somewhat behind current scholarship. A number of encyclopedias are now in CD-ROM form, and the CD makes searches for information easier. Many such encyclopedias are linked to the World Wide Web, where updated information and links to reference and research resources are listed. Be sure to check with the librarians at your school; they can tell you about the kinds of resources that are available. If your library offers a tutorial on the use of electronic and Internet resources, we recommend that you sign up for it. We take such tutorials ourselves with our students every year and are always surprised by the new resources we learn about.

It is helpful to have updated information and links, but only when they are reliable. Remember to be a critical user of reference materials. Not everything is of equal value, and we must make good judgments about the sources we consult—and whether or not we can depend on them for reliable, accurate information. More on this point in a moment.

The Internet/World Wide Web

Because of the ease of using the Internet, with its access to electronic mail (e-mail), newsgroups, mailing lists, and, especially, sites and links on the World Wide Web, many students now make it their first—and, unfortunately, too often their *only*—resource for research.

As we noted a moment ago, all of us must be *critical* users of the materials we find on the WWW. The WWW is up-to-date *and* out-of-date, helpful *and* disappointing. It can be a researcher's dream come true, but also a source of errors and a time-waster.

Keeping this point in mind, we recommend to students that for each WWW site they consult, they should consult at least two print sources.

EVALUATING SOURCES ON THE WORLD WIDE WEB

For sources on the World Wide Web, as with print sources, you must evaluate what you have located and gauge how much or how little it will contribute to your literary analysis and argument. In the words of one reference librarian, Joan Stockard (formerly of Wellesley College), "The most serious mistake students make when they use the Internet for research is to assume everything is of equal (and acceptable) quality. They need to establish who wrote the material, the qualifications of the author to write on the topic, whether any bias is likely, how current the information is, and how other resources compare."

A Review for Using the World Wide Web

Focus the topic of your research as precisely as you can before you embark on a WWW search. Lots of surfing and browsing can sometimes turn up good material, but using the WWW without a focus can prove distracting and unproductive. It takes you away from library research (where the results might be better) and from the actual planning and writing of the paper.

Ask the following questions:

- Does this site or page look like it can help me in my assignment?
- Whose site or page is this?
- Who is the intended audience?
- What is the point of view? Are there signs of a specific slant or bias?
- How good is the detail, depth, and quality of the material presented?
- Is the site well constructed and well organized?
- Is the text well written?
- Can the information be corroborated or supported by print sources?
- When was the site or page made available? Has it been recently revised or updated?
- Can the person or institution, company, or agency responsible for this site or page receive e-mail comments, questions, and criticisms?

DOCUMENTATION: CITING A WWW SOURCE

Scholars and reference librarians have not reached a consensus about the correct form—what should be included, and in what order—for the citation of WWW sources. But all agree on two principles: (1) Give as much information as you can; (2) make certain that your readers can retrieve the source themselves, which means that you should check the URL (that is, the WWW address) carefully. For accuracy's sake, it is a good idea to copy the URL from the location line of your browser and paste it into your list of works cited.

Citing World Wide Web Sources

Provide the following information:

- Author
- Title
- Publication information
- Title of archive or database
- Date (if given) when the site was posted; sometimes termed the "revision" or "modification" date
- Name of institution/organization that supports or is associated with this site
- Date that you accessed this source
- URL

Many Web sites and pages, however, are not prepared according to the style and form in which you want to cite them. Sometimes the name of the author is unknown, and other information may be missing or hard to find as well. Nor can you be certain that the site will exist at this URL (or at all) when your readers attempt to access it. These difficulties aside, perhaps the main point to remember is that a source on the WWW is as much a source as is a book or article that you can track down and read in the library. If you have made use of it, you must acknowledge that you have done so and include the bibliographical information, as fully as you can, in your list of Works Cited for the paper.

The Wellesley College Library offers a valuable site for searching the WWW, evaluating what you find there, and citing WWW sources correctly:

<http://www.wellesley.edu/Library/Research/search.html>

The Modern Language Association recommends the following conventions:

Publication Dates   For sources taken from the Internet, include the date the source was posted to the Internet or last updated or revised; give also the date the source was accessed.

Uniform Resource Locators   Include a full and accurate URL for any source taken from the Internet (with access-mode identifier—*http, ftp, gopher,* or *telnet*). Enclose URLs in angle brackets (<>). When a URL continues from one line to the next, break it only after a slash or before a period. Do not add a hyphen.

When citing electronic sources, follow the formatting conventions illustrated by the following models.

An Online Scholarly Project or Database

The Walt Whitman Hypertext Archive. Eds. Kenneth M.
        Price and Ed Folsom. 16 Mar. 1998. College of
        William and Mary. 3 Apr. 1998 <http://
        jefferson.village.Virginia.EDU/whitman/>.

1. Title of project or database
2. Name of the editor of project
3. Electronic publication information
4. Date of access and URL

A Short Work within a Scholarly Project

Whitman, Walt. "Crossing Brooklyn Ferry." The Walt
        Whitman Hypertext Archive. Ed. Kenneth M. Price
        and Ed Folsom. 16 Mar. 1998. College of William
        and Mary. 3 Apr. 1998 <http://jefferson
        .village.Virginia.EDU/whitman/works/leaves/1891/
        text/index.html>.

An Online Book within a Scholarly Project

Whitman, Walt. Leaves of Grass. Philadelphia: McKay,
        1891-92. The Walt Whitman Hypertext Archive. Ed.

Kenneth M. Price and Ed Folsom. 16 Mar. 1998.
College of William and Mary. 3 Apr. 1998 <http://
jefferson.village.Virginia.EDU/whitman/works/
leaves/1891/text/title.html>.

1. Author's name
2. Title of the work and print publication information
3. Name of the editor, compiler, or translator (if relevant)
4. Electronic publication information
5. Date of access and URL

An Article in a Scholarly Journal

Jackson, Francis L. "Mexican Freedom: The Ideal of
the Indigenous State." Animus 2.3 (1997). 4 Apr.
1998 <http://www.mun.ca/animus/1997vol2/
jackson2.htm>.

1. Author's name
2. Title of the work or material in quotation marks
3. Name of periodical
4. Volume number, issue number, or other identifying number
5. Date of publication
6. Page numbers or number of paragraphs, pages, or other numbered sections
   (if any)
7. Date of access and URL

An Article in a Newspaper or on a Newswire—Unsigned

"Drug Czar Wants to Sharpen Drug War." TopNews 6 Apr.
1998. <http://news.lycos.com/stories/TopNews/
19980406_NEWS-DRUGS.asp>.

An Article in a Newspaper or on a Newswire—Signed

Davis, Robert. "Drug may prevent breast cancer." USA
Today 6 Apr. 1998. 6 Apr. 1998 <http://
www.usatoday.com/news/nds14.htm>.

An Article in a Magazine:

Pitta, Julie. "Un-Wired?" Forbes 20 Apr. 1998. 6 Apr.
1998 <http://www.forbes.com/Forbes/98/0420/
6108045a.htm>.

A Review:

Beer, Francis A. Rev. of Evolutionary Paradigms in
the Social Sciences. Special Issue, International

Studies Quarterly 40, 3 (Sept. 1996). Journal
of Memetics 1 (1997). 4 Jan. 1998 <http://
www.cpm.mmu.ac.uk/jom-emit/1997/vol1/beer_
fa.html>.

✍ A RULE FOR WRITERS:

Remember that when you use a source from the World Wide Web, you need
to acknowledge and cite it, just as you do when you use a print source.

D

Literary Research:
Print and Electronic Resources

THE BASICS

It's a good idea to have on your desk a reliable, one-volume dictionary, such as *Encarta: World English Dictionary* (1999) or *The American Heritage Dictionary of the English Language*, 4th ed. (2000). Such a dictionary will give you word histories as well as definitions, and will provide information about classical myths and many historical events and figures.

Still other students log in to the online resources of their library's reference collection, with its range of dictionaries and encyclopedias, all of which can be accessed quickly during the paper writing and research process.

MOVING AHEAD: FINDING SOURCES FOR RESEARCH WORK

The more you gain experience as a student and writer in literature courses, the more you will want to know in-depth about reference and bibliographical works for your field. We described a number of print and electronic sources in Appendixes B and C. Here is a supplementary list and guide that will direct you to yet more resources in both print and electronic forms.

Not all of these, to be sure, will be relevant for your paper writing and research in a first-year course on literature and composition. But we hope you will see this material as a guide you can turn to when needed, whether for an assignment in a first-year course or in an intermediate or advanced course later on.

Feel free to jot down on the top or bottom of the page or in the margins the titles of other resources, in print or online, that you have found helpful when you worked on a project and that you want to remember.

And speak with a member of your library's reference staff, who can tell you more about the print and online sources that are available to you.

LITERATURE—
PRINT REFERENCE SOURCES

Oxford University Press has published many volumes in its *Companion* reference series, quite a few of them keyed to literary subjects. Each title begins with the words *The Oxford Companion to . . . .*

The series includes: *African American Literature* (1997), *American Literature* (6th ed., 1995), *American Theater* (2nd ed., 1992), *English Language* (1992), *English Literature* (6th ed., rev., 2000), *Theater* (4th ed., 1983), *Twentieth-Century Literature in English* (1996), *Twentieth-Century Poetry in English* (1994), and *Women's Writing in the United States* (1995).

There are also *Oxford Companion* volumes for *Australian Literature* (2nd ed., 1994), *the Bible* (1993), *Canadian Literature* (1983), *Children's Literature* (1984), *Classical Literature* (1989), *Film* (1976), *German Literature* (3rd ed., 1997), *Irish Literature* (1996), *Literature in French* (1995), and *Spanish Literature* (1978).

Cambridge University Press publishes many reference books, including its *Cambridge Guide* series; each title begins with the words *The Cambridge Guide to. . . .* The series includes *African and Caribbean Theatre* (1994), *American Theatre* (1993), *Asian Theatre* (1993), *Literature in English* (1988), and *Theatre* (1992).

See also:

The Bloomsbury Guide to Women's Literature. Ed. Claire Buck. New York: Prentice-Hall, 1992.

Encyclopedia of Post-Colonial Literatures in English. 2 vols. Eds. Eugene Benson and L. W. Conolly. New York: Routledge, 1994.

The Feminist Companion to Literature in English: Women Writers from the Middle Ages to the Present. Eds. Virginia Blain, Isobel Grundy, and Patricia Clements. New Haven: Yale UP, 1990.

For more on the literatures of other nations:

Encyclopedia of World Literature in the Twentieth Century. Ed. Leonard S. Klein. 4 vols. New York: Continuum, 1983.

European Writers. 7 vols. Eds. George Stade and William T. Jackson. New York: Macmillan, 1983-85.

The New Guide to Modern World Literature. 4 vols. Ed. Martin Seymour-Smith. New York: Peter Bedrick, 1970; rpt. 1985.

The Penguin Companion to World Literature. 4 vols. 1969-71. This work covers American, English, European, African, Asian, and classical literature.

Other reference resources:

American National Biography. 24 vols. New York: Oxford UP, 1999.

American Women Writers: A Critical Reference Guide from Colonial Times to the Present. 4 vols. Ed. Lina Mainero. New York: Ungar, 1979-82; supplement, 1994.

Contemporary Literary Criticism. Detroit: Gale, 1973-. This series, still in progress, runs to many volumes. It includes brief biographies, plus extensive selections from reviews and critical essays.

Dictionary of American Biography. 22 vols. New York, 1928-58, with supplements published since.

Dictionary of National Biography. 22 vols. London, 1908-09, with multivolume supplements published since.

Dictionary of Literary Biography. Detroit: Gale, 1978–. Many volumes, series in progress. Detailed biographies of American, British, and foreign-language literary authors, as well as critics, journalists, and historians. It includes critical analysis of their writings and primary and secondary bibliographies.

The Gay and Lesbian Literary Heritage: A Reader's Companion to the Writers and Their Works, from Antiquity to the Present. Ed. Claude J. Summers. New York: Holt, 1995. Overviews of authors and topics, with bibliographies.

The Oxford English Dictionary 2nd. ed. Oxford: Clarendon, 1989; available online and on CD-ROM. The *OED* defines words historically from time of first appearance, supported by quotations.

BIBLIOGRAPHIES

For extensive bibliographical coverage (to supplement the *MLA International Bibliography*) in a variety of literary subjects and fields:

American Literary Scholarship. Durham, N.C.: Duke UP, 1963–. Published annually, bibliographical essays.

Annual Bibliography of English Language and Literature. Cambridge, U.K.: Modern Humanities Research Association, 1921–. Well-indexed; covers books, articles, dissertations, and pamphlets on English and American literatures.

A Guide to English and American Literature. 3rd ed. By F. W. Bateson and Harrison T. Meserole. New York: Longman, 1976. Literary history and bibliography.

Literary Criticism Index. 2nd ed. By Alan R. Weiner and Spencer Means. Metuchen, N.J.: Scarecrow, 1994. Indexes 85 bibliographies of literary criticism.

A Literary History of England. 2nd ed. Ed. Albert C. Baugh. New York: Appleton-Century-Crofts, 1967. Literary history by period, with extensive (if dated) bibliographies.

Literary History of the United States. Eds. Robert E. Spiller et al. 4th ed. 2 vols. New York: Macmillan, 1974. Supplement with: *Columbia Literary History of the United States.* Eds. Emory Elliot et al. New York: Columbia UP, 1988. Both present historical coverage of authors, periods, and movements. The *Literary History* includes bibliographies; the *Columbia* history does not.

The New Cambridge Bibliography of English Literature. 5 vols. Cambridge, Eng.: Cambridge UP, 1969–77.

The Oxford History of English Literature. 13 vols. 1945–. Histories of literary periods, supplemented by full bibliographies.

Problems in Literary Research: A Guide to Selected Reference Works. 4th ed. By Dorothea Kehler. Lanham, Md.: Scarecrow, 1996.

A Reader's Guide to Twentieth-Century Writers. Ed. Peter Parker. New York: Oxford UP, 1996.

A Research Guide for Undergraduate Students. By Nancy L. Baker and Nancy Huling. 5th ed. New York: MLA, 2001.

Selective Bibliography for the Study of English and American Literature. 6th ed. Eds. Richard D. Altick and Andrew Wright. New York: Macmillan, 1979. Lists bibliographies and reference works; includes a glossary of bibliographic and literary terms.

The Year's Work in English Studies. London: Blackwell, 1921–. Bibliographical essays on studies in books and periodicals on English and American literatures.

Note: You can locate additional dictionaries, encyclopedias, bibliographies, and reference tools by checking in the Subject category of the library catalog:

literature—dictionaries
literature—bio-bibliography

HISTORY—REFERENCE AND BIBLIOGRAPHY SOURCES

The American Heritage Encyclopedia of American History. Ed. John Mack Faragher. New York: Holt, 1998. Concise entries and essays that span the pre-Columbian period through the 1990s.

America: History and Life. Santa Barbara, Calif.: ABC-Clio, 1964–. Published annually in three volumes: article abstracts and citations, index to book reviews, and bibliography.

American Historical Association Guide to Historical Literature. 2 vols. Ed. Mary Beth Norton. 3rd ed. New York: Oxford UP, 1995.

The Columbia Companion to British History. Eds. Juliet Gardiner and Neil Wenborn. New York: Columbia UP, 1997.

A Companion to American Thought. Eds. Richard Wightman Fox and James T. Kloppenberg. Cambridge, Mass.: Blackwell, 1995.

Encyclopedia of American History. 7th ed. Eds. Jeffrey B. Morris and Richard B. Morris. New York: HarperCollins, 1996.

Encyclopedia of American Social History. 3 vols. Ed. Mary Kupiec Cayton. New York: Scribner's, 1993.

Harvard Guide to American History. 2 vols. Ed. Frank B. Freidel. Cambridge, Mass.: Harvard UP, 1980.

The Oxford Companion to British History. Ed. John Cannon. New York: Oxford UP, 1997.

The Oxford Companion to United States History. Ed. Paul S. Boyer. New York: Oxford UP, 2001.

The Reader's Companion to American History. Eds. Eric Foner and John A. Garraty. Boston: Houghton Mifflin, 1991.

World Wide Web Sites for History:
Library of Congress Home Page <http://www.loc.gov/>. Includes the site *American Memory,* a treasury of documents, photographs, works of art, films, and sound recordings.

Organization of American Historians <http://www.oah.org/>. Includes an excellent, up-to-date list of Web sites for historians.

The Smithsonian Institution Home Page <http://www.si.edu/>.

Note: Both *Books in Print* (New York: Bowker, 1948–) and the *Subject Guide to Books in Print* (New York: Bowker, 1957–) can be helpful in locating new books on the subject of your research.

WHAT DOES YOUR OWN INSTITUTION OFFER?

We'll mention again that many colleges and universities now offer as part of their resources for research a wide range of electronic materials and databases.

At Wellesley College, for example, the library offers a detailed list of research resources, and there is another listing arranged according to department and interdisciplinary program. Some of these are open or free sites, available to anyone with a connection to the WWW. But others are by "subscription only," which means that only members of this academic community can access them.

Sign up for a library tutorial at your own school, and browse in and examine both the library's home page and the online catalog's options and directories.

One of the best research sites, to which many libraries subscribe, is the *FirstSearch* commercial database service.

FirstSearch enables you to find books, articles, theses, films, computer software, and other types of material for just about any field, subject, or topic. Its categories include:

> Arts & Humanities
> Business & Economics
> Conferences & Proceedings
> Consumer Affairs & People
> Education
> Engineering & Technology
> General & Reference
> General Science
> Life Sciences
> Medicine & Health
> News & Current Events
> Public Affairs & Law
> Social Sciences

Within these categories, you will find a number of useful databases and resources. Make your "search" as focused as possible: Look for materials that bear on the topic that you are writing about, and, even more, that show a connection to the thesis that you are working to develop and demonstrate. Learn from what you find, but approach it critically: Is this source a good one? What are its strengths, and what are (or might be) its limitations? Keep in mind too that you engage in the process of selecting good sources in order to strengthen *your* topic and thesis. The quotations you give from the sources are there to support your ideas and insights. Above all your reader is interested in what *you* have to say.

✍ A RULE FOR WRITERS:

A good choice of secondary sources can help you to develop your analysis of a literary work, but remember that it is your point of view that counts. Use sources to help present your own interpretation more effectively.

E

Writing Essay Examinations

WHY DO INSTRUCTORS GIVE EXAMINATIONS?

Perhaps an understanding of the nature of essay examinations will help you to write better essays.

Examinations not only measure learning and thinking, but also stimulate them. Even so humble an examination as a short-answer quiz—chiefly a device to oblige students to do the assigned reading—is a sort of push designed to move students forward. Of course, internal motivation is far superior to external, but even such crude external motivation as a quiz can have a beneficial effect. Students know this; indeed, they often will say that they have chosen to take a particular course "because I want to know something about . . . and I know that I won't do the reading on my own." (Teachers often teach a new course for the same reason; we want to become knowledgeable about, say, Asian-American literature, and we know that despite our lofty intentions we may not seriously confront the subject unless we are under the pressure of facing a class.)

In short, examinations help students to acquire learning and then to convert learning into thinking. Sometimes it is not until preparing for the final examination that students—rereading the chief texts and classroom notes—perceive what the course was really about; until this late stage, the trees obscure the forest, but now, in the process of the reviewing and sorting things out, a pattern emerges. The experience of reviewing and then of writing an examination, though fretful, can be highly exciting as connections are made and ideas take on life.

GETTING READY

The night before the examination you will almost certainly feel that you don't know this, that, and the other thing, and you may feel that nothing short of reading all of the assignments—an impossibility, of course—can get you through the test. If indeed you have not done the reading, this feeling is warranted. The best preparation for an examination is not a panicky turning of hundreds of pages the night before the test; rather, the best preparation is to

- keep up with the reading throughout the term, and to annotate the text while reading,
- make connections among the works you study from one week to the next,
- participate in class discussion, and
- annotate the text during the class discussions.

If you engage in these practices, you will not only be preparing for the examination, but you will also be getting more out of the course—more knowledge and more *pleasure*—than if you come to class unprepared.

Nevertheless, however well prepared you are, you will want to do some intensive preparation shortly before the final examination. We suggest that you may want to reread Chapters 2, 3, 7 (all on fiction), 13, 21 (both on poetry), 29 and 33 (both on drama), because these chapters discuss not only the genres but also the job of writing essays about them.

WRITING ESSAY ANSWERS

Let's assume that before the examination you have read the assigned material, marked the margins of your books, made summaries of the longer readings and of the classroom comments, reviewed everything carefully, and had a decent night's sleep. Now you are facing the examination sheet.

Here are some suggestions:

1. Before you write anything on the examination booklet beyond your name, read the entire examination. Something in the last question—maybe even a passage that is quoted—may give you an idea that will help you when you write your answer to the first question.
2. Budget your time. If the first question is worth 25%, give it about one-fourth of your time, not half the allotted time. On the other hand, do not provide perfunctory answers: If the question is worth 25%, your instructor expects a fairly detailed response.
3. Rank for yourself the degree of difficulty of the questions, from easiest to hardest. Start with the questions that you immediately know you can handle effectively, and save harder questions for later. Often those harder questions will become easier once you have gotten into the activity of writing the examination.
4. After you have thought a little about the question, before writing furiously, take a moment to jot down few ideas that strike you, as a sort of outline or source of further inspiration. You may at the outset realize that, say, you want to make three points, and unless you jot these down—three key words will do—you may spend all the allotted time on one point.
5. Answer the question. If you are asked to compare two characters, compare them; don't just write two character sketches. Take seriously such words as *compare, define, summarize,* and, especially, *evaluate*.
6. You often can get a good start merely by turning the question into an affirmation—for example, by turning "In what ways does the poetry of Louise Erdrich resemble her fiction" into "Louise Erdrich's poetry resembles her fiction in at least . . . ways."

7. Don't waste time summarizing at length what you have read unless asked to do so—but, of course, you may have to give a brief summary in order to support a point. The instructor wants to see that you can *use* your reading, not merely that you have *done* the reading.

8. Be concrete. Illustrate your arguments with facts—the names of authors, titles, dates, characters, details of plot, and quotations if possible.

9. Leave space for last-minute additions. If you are writing in an examination booklet, either skip a page between essays or write only on the right-hand pages so that on rereading you can add material at the appropriate place on the left-hand pages.

10. Reread what you have written, and make last-minute revisions. By the time you have finished writing the last essay you have probably thought of some things—for instance, some quotations may have come to mind—that might well add strength to some of the earlier essays.

Beyond these general suggestions we can best talk about essay examinations by looking at five common types of questions:

1. A passage to explicate

2. A historical question (for example, "Trace the influence of Guy de Maupassant on Kate Chopin")

3. A critical quotation to be evaluated

4. A wild question (such as "What would Flannery O'Connor think of Katherine Min's 'Courting a Monk'?"; "What would Othello do if he were in Hamlet's place?")

5. A comparison (for example, "Compare Eliot's 'The Love Song of J. Alfred Prufrock' with Browning's 'My Last Duchess' as dramatic monologues")

A few remarks on each of these types may be helpful.

1. On explication, see pages 42–46 and page 824. As a short rule, look carefully at the tone (speaker's attitude toward self, subject, and audience) and at the implications of the words (their connotations and associations), and see whether a pattern of imagery is evident. For example, religious language (*adore, saint*) in a secular love poem may precisely define the nature of the lover and of the beloved. Remember, *an explication is not a paraphrase* (a putting into other words) but an attempt to show the relations of the parts by calling attention to implications. Organization of such an essay is rarely a problem, since most explications begin with the first line and go on to the last. Indeed, if you glance at the poem or passage and feel worried that it is too difficult or obscure, don't panic. Take a breath, and begin with the first line or the first sentence. Explicate *that*, and then focus on how the next line or sentence is related to what has come just before. Proceed step by step, piece by piece, and as you do so you will develop a sense of the whole—which is where your explication can conclude.

2. A good essay on a historical question will offer a nice combination of argument and evidence; that is, the thesis will be supported by concrete details (names, dates, perhaps, even brief quotations). A discussion of Chopin's debt to Maupassant cannot be convincing if it does not specify certain works and certain characteristics. If you are asked to relate a writer or a body of work to an earlier writer or period, list the chief characteristics of the earlier writer or period, and then show specifically how the material you are dis-

cussing is related to these characteristics. If you remember and can quote some relevant terms, phrases, or lines from the works, your reader will feel that you really know the works themselves.

3. If you are asked to evaluate a critical quotation, read it carefully, and in your answer take account of *all* the quotation. If, for example, the quoted critic has said, "Louise Erdrich in her fiction always . . . but in her poetry rarely . . ." you will have to write about poetry and fiction; it will not be enough to talk only about one form or the other, unless, of course, the instructions on the examination ask you to take only as much of the quotation as you wish. Watch especially for words like *always, for the most part, never;* that is, although the passage may on the whole approach the truth, you may feel that some important qualifications are needed. This is not being picky; true thinking involves making subtle distinctions, yielding assent only so far and no further. And (again) be sure to give concrete details, supporting your argument with evidence.

4. Curiously, a wild question, such as "What would Shakespeare think of *Death of a Salesman?*" or "What would Desdemona do in Antigone's place?" usually produces rather tame answers: A couple of standard ideas about Shakespeare (for instance, Shakespeare chiefly wrote poetry, and he usually included some comedy in his tragedies) are mechanically applied to Arthur Miller, or a simple characterization of Desdemona is applied to the situation set forth in Antigone, and some gross incompatibilities are revealed. But as the previous paragraph suggests, it may be necessary to do more than set up bold oppositions. The interest in such a question and in the answer to it may be largely in the degree to which superficially different figures resemble each other in some important ways. Remember that the wildness of the question does not mean that all answers are equally acceptable; as usual, any good answer will be supported by concrete detail. If time permits, you can often enrich your answer by reflecting a bit on the *other* way of looking at the issue. First, to be sure, explain how Desdemona would have acted in Antigone's place—this is what the question asks for. But consider too how you could strengthen this answer by taking note as well of how Antigone might have acted in Desdemona's place.

5. On comparisons, see pages 46-47. Because comparisons are especially difficult to write, be sure to take a few moments to jot down a sort of outline so that you know where you will be going. In a comparison of Browning's and Eliot's monologues, you might treat one poem by each, devoting alternate paragraphs to one author, or you might first treat one author's poem and then turn to the other's. But if you adopt this second strategy, your essay may break into two parts. You can guard against this weakness in three ways: Announcing at the outset that you will treat one author first, then the other; reminding your reader during your treatment of the first author that you will pick up certain points when you get to the second author; and briefly reminding your reader during the treatment of the second author of certain points you already made in your treatment of the first. Remember to make your points as clear and specific as you can. If you say that two authors are both "pessimistic about whether love can endure," you'll want to explain the nature of this pessimism, the reasons in each case for this view, and the precise similarities and the differences. A frequent weakness in "comparisons" is that they are too general, lacking the details that indicate subtle differences. When you review your answer, ask yourself if you have been sufficiently precise.

F

Glossary of Literary Terms

The terms briefly defined here are for the most part more fully defined earlier in the text. Hence many of the entries are followed by page references to the earlier discussions.

accent stress given to a syllable.

act a major division of a play.

action (1) the happenings in a narrative or drama, usually physical events (*B* marries *C*, *D* kills *E*), but also mental changes (*F* moves from innocence to experience); in short, the answer to the question, "What happens?" (2) less commonly, the theme or underlying idea of a work. (1031)

allegory a work in which concrete elements (for instance, a pilgrim, a road, a splendid city) stand for abstractions (humanity, life, salvation), usually in an unambiguous, one-to-one relationship. The literal items (the pilgrim, and so on) thus convey a meaning, which is usually moral, religious, or political. To take a nonliterary example: The Statue of Liberty holds a torch (enlightenment, showing the rest of the world the way to freedom), and at her feet are broken chains (tyranny overcome). A caution: Not all of the details in an allegorical work are meant to be interpreted. For example, the hollowness of the Statue of Liberty does not stand for the insubstantiality or emptiness of liberty. (144)

alliteration repetition of consonant sounds, especially at the beginnings of words: *f*ree, *f*orm, *ph*antom. (797)

allusion an indirect reference; thus when Lincoln spoke of "a nation dedicated to the proposition that all men are created equal," he was making an allusion to the Declaration of Independence.

ambiguity multiplicity of meaning, often deliberate, that leaves the reader uncertain about the intended significance.

anagnorisis a recognition or discovery, especially in tragedy—for example, when the hero understands the reason for his or her fall. (1096)

analysis an examination, which usually proceeds by separating the object of study into parts. (42, 743)

anapest a metrical foot consisting of two unaccented syllables followed by an accented one. Example, showing three anapests: "As I came / to the edge / of the wood." (795)

anecdote a short narrative, usually reporting an amusing event in the life of an important person. (74)

antagonist a character or force that opposes (literally, "wrestles") the protagonist (the main character). Thus, in *Hamlet* the antagonist is King Claudius, the protagonist is Hamlet; in *Antigone,* the antagonist is Creon, the protagonist Antigone.

antecedent action happenings (especially in a play) that occurred before the present action. (1031)

apostrophe address to an absent figure or to a thing as if it were present and could listen. Example: "O rose, thou art sick!" (749)

approximate rhyme see *half-rhyme*.

archetype a theme, image, motif, or pattern that occurs so often in literary works it seems to be universal. Examples: a dark forest (for mental confusion), the sun (for illumination).

aside in the theater, words spoken by a character in the presence of other characters, but directed to the spectators (i.e., understood by the audience to be inaudible to the other characters). (1032)

assonance repetition of similar vowel sounds in stressed syllables. Example: *light/bride*. (797)

atmosphere the emotional tone (for instance, joy, or horror) in a work, most often established by the setting.

ballad a short narrative poem, especially one that is sung or recited, often in a stanza of four lines, with 8, 6, 8, 6 syllables, with the second and fourth lines rhyming. A **folk** or **popular ballad** is a narrative song that has been transmitted orally by what used to be called "the folk"; a **literary ballad** is a conscious imitation (without music) of such a work, often with complex symbolism. (675)

blank verse unrhymed iambic pentameter, that is, unrhymed lines of ten syllables, with every second syllable stressed. (819)

cacophony an unpleasant combination of sounds.

caesura a strong pause within a line of verse. (796)

canon a term originally used to refer to those books accepted as Holy Scripture by the Christian Church. The term has come to be applied to literary works thought to have a special merit by a given culture—for instance, the body of literature traditionally taught in colleges and universities. Such works are sometimes called "classics" and their authors are "major authors." As conceived in the United States until recently, the canon consisted chiefly of works by dead white European and American males—partly, of course, because middle-class and upper-class white males were in fact the people who did most of the writing in the Western Hemisphere, but also because white males (for instance, college professors) were the people who chiefly established the canon. Not surprisingly the canon-makers valued (or valorized or "privileged") writings that revealed, asserted, or reinforced the canon-makers' own values. From about the 1960s feminists and Marxists and others argued that these works had been regarded as central not because they were inherently better than other works but because they reflected the interests of the dominant culture, and that other work, such as slave narratives and the diaries of women, had been "marginalized."

In fact, the literary canon has never been static (in contrast to the biblical canon, which has not changed for more than a thousand years), but it is true that certain authors, such as Homer, Chaucer, and Shakespeare have been permanent fixtures. Why? Partly because they do indeed support the values of those who in large measure control the high cultural purse strings, and perhaps partly because their works are rich enough to invite constant reinterpretation from age to age—that is, to allow each generation to find its needs and its values in them.

catastrophe the concluding action, especially in a tragedy.

catharsis Aristotle's term for the purgation or purification of the pity and terror supposedly experienced while witnessing a tragedy. (1097)

character (1) a person in a literary work (Romeo); (2) the personality of such a figure (sentimental lover, or whatever). Characters (in the first sense) are sometimes classified as either "flat" (one-dimensional) or "round" (fully realized, complex). (74, 78, 79)

characterization the presentation of a character, whether by direct description, by showing the character in action, or by the presentation of other characters who help to define each other.

cliché an expression that through overuse has ceased to be effective. Examples: *acid test; sigh of relief; the proud possessor.*

climax the culmination of a conflict; a turning point, often the point of greatest tension in a plot. (1031)

comedy a literary work, especially a play, characterized by humor and by a happy ending. (1415)

comparison and contrast To compare is strictly to note similarities; to contrast is to note differences. But *compare* is now often used for both activities. (46)

complication an entanglement in a narrative or dramatic work that causes a conflict. (74)

conflict a struggle between a character and some obstacle (for example, another character or fate) or between internal forces, such as divided loyalties. (73, 1031)

connotation the associations (suggestions, overtones) of a word or expression. Thus *seventy* and *three score and ten* both mean "one more than sixty-nine," but because *three score and ten* is a biblical expression, it has an association of holiness; see also *denotation.* (750)

consistency building the process engaged in during the act of reading, of reevaluating the details that one has just read in order to make them consistent with the new information that the text is providing.

consonance repetition of consonant sounds, especially in stressed syllables. Also called *half-rhyme* or slant rhyme. Example: *arouse/doze.* (797)

convention a pattern (for instance, the 14-line poem, or sonnet) or motif (for instance, the bumbling police officer in detective fiction) or other device occurring so often that it is taken for granted. Thus it is a convention that actors in a performance of *Julius Caesar* are understood to be speaking Latin, though in fact they are speaking English. Similarly, the soliloquy (a character alone on the stage speaks his or her thoughts aloud) is a convention, for in real life sane people rarely talk aloud to themselves.

couplet a pair of lines of verse, usually rhyming. (801)

crisis a high point in the conflict that leads to the turning point. (1031)

criticism the analysis or evaluation of a literary work. (1741)

cultural criticism criticism that sets literature in a social context, often of economics or politics or gender. Borrowing some of the methods of anthropology, cultural criticism usually extends the canon to include popular material—for instance, comic books and soap operas.

dactyl a metrical foot consisting of a stressed syllable followed by two unstressed syllables. Example: *underwear.* (795)

deconstruction a critical approach that assumes language is unstable and ambiguous and is therefore inherently contradictory. Because authors cannot control their language, texts reveal more than their authors are aware of. For instance, texts (like such institutions as the law, the churches, and the schools) are likely, when closely scrutinized, to reveal connections to a society's economic system, even though the authors may have believed they were outside of the system. (1744)

denotation the dictionary meaning of a word. Thus *soap opera* and *daytime serial* have the same denotation, but the connotations (associations, emotional overtones) of *soap opera* are less favorable. (750)

dénouement the resolution or the outcome (literally, the "unknotting") of a plot. (74, 79, 1031)

deus ex machina literally, "a god out of a machine"; any unexpected and artificial way of resolving the plot—for example, by introducing a rich uncle, thought to be dead, who arrives on the scene and pays the debts that otherwise would overwhelm the young hero.

dialogue exchange of words between characters; speech.

diction the choice of vocabulary and of sentence structure. There is a difference in diction between "One never knows" and "You never can tell." (729)

didactic pertaining to teaching; having a moral purpose.

dimeter a line of poetry containing two feet. (795)

discovery see *anagnorisis.*

drama (1) a play; (2) conflict or tension, as in "The story lacks drama."

dramatic irony see *irony.*

dramatic monologue a poem spoken entirely by one character but addressed to one or more other characters whose presence is strongly felt. (727)

effaced narrator a narrator who reports but who does not editorialize or enter into the minds of any of the characters in the story.

elegy a lyric poem, usually a meditation on a death. (698)

elision omission (usually of a vowel or unstressed syllable), as in *o'er* (for *over*) and in "Th' inevitable hour."

end rhyme identical sounds at the ends of lines of poetry. (797)

end-stopped line a line of poetry that ends with a pause (usually marked by a comma, semicolon, or period) because the grammatical structure and the sense reach (at least to some degree) completion. It is contrasted with a *run-on line.* (796)

English (or Shakespearean) sonnet a poem of 14 lines (three quatrains and a couplet), rhyming *ababcdcdefefgg.* (801)

enjambment a line of poetry in which the grammatical and logical sense run on, without pause, into the next line or lines. (796)

epic a long narrative, especially in verse, that usually records heroic material in an elevated style.

epigram a brief, witty poem or saying.

epigraph a quotation at the beginning of the work, just after the title, often giving a clue to the theme.

epiphany a "showing forth," as when an action reveals a character with particular clarity.

episode an incident or scene that has unity in itself but is also a part of a larger action.

epistle a letter, in prose or verse.

essay a work, usually in prose and usually fairly short, that purports to be true and that treats its subject tentatively. In most literary essays the reader's interest is as much in the speaker's personality as in any argument that is offered.

euphony literally, "good sound," a pleasant combination of sounds.

explication a line-by-line unfolding of the meaning of a text. (42, 824, 1743)

exposition a setting forth of information. In fiction and drama, introductory material introducing characters and the situation; in an essay, the presentation of information, as opposed to the telling of a story or the setting forth of an argument. (79, 1031)

eye rhyme words that look as though they rhyme, but do not rhyme when pronounced. Example: *come/home.* (797)

fable a short story (often involving speaking animals) with an easily grasped moral. (72)

farce comedy based not on clever language or on subtleties of characters but on broadly humorous situations (for instance, a man mistakenly enters the women's locker room).

feminine rhyme a rhyme of two or more syllables, with the stress falling on a syllable other than the last. Examples: *fatter/batter; tenderly/slenderly.* (796, 797)

feminist criticism an approach especially concerned with analyzing the depiction of women in literature—what images do male authors present of female characters?—and with the reappraisal of work by female authors. (1753)

fiction an imaginative work, usually a prose narrative (novel, short story), that reports incidents that did not in fact occur. The term may include all works that invent a world such as a lyric poem or a play.

figurative language, figures of speech words intended to be understood in a way that is other than literal. Thus *lemon* used literally refers to a citrus fruit, but *lemon* used figuratively refers to a defective machine, especially a defective automobile. Other examples: "He's a beast." "She's a witch." "A sea of troubles." Literally, such expressions are nonsense, but writers use them to express meanings inexpressible in literal speech. Among the most common kinds of figures of speech are *apostrophe, metaphor,* and *simile* (see the discussions of these words in this glossary). (743, 750)

flashback an interruption in a narrative that presents an earlier episode.

flat character a one-dimensional character (for instance, the figure who is only and always the jealous husband or the flirtatious wife) as opposed to a round or many-sided character. (79)

fly-on-the-wall narrator a narrator who never editorializes and never enters a character's mind, but reports only what is said and done. (100)

foil a character who makes a contrast with another, especially a minor character who helps to set off a major character. (1177)

foot a metrical unit, consisting of two or three syllables, with a specified arrangement of the stressed syllable or syllables. Thus the iambic foot consists of an unstressed syllable followed by a stressed syllable. (794)

foreshadowing suggestions of what is to come. (81)

formalist criticism analysis that assumes a work of art is a constructed object with a stable meaning that can be ascertained by studying the relationships between the elements of the work. Thus a poem is like a chair: a chair *can* of course be stood on, or used for firewood, but it was created with a specific purpose that was evident and remains evident to all viewers. (1742)

free verse poetry in lines of irregular length, usually unrhymed. (819)

gap a term from reader-response criticism, referring to a reader's perception that something is unstated in the text, requiring the reader to fill in the material—for instance, to draw a conclusion as to why a character behaves as she does. Filling in the gaps is a matter of "consistency building." Different readers of course may fill the gaps differently, and readers may even differ as to whether a gap exists at a particular point in the text. (10)

gay criticism see *gender criticism.*

gender criticism criticism concerned especially with alleged differences in the ways that males and females read and write, and with the representations of gender (straight, bisexual, gay, lesbian) in literature. (1756)

genre kind or type, roughly analogous to the biological term *species.* The four chief literary genres are nonfiction, fiction, poetry, and drama; but these can be subdivided into further genres. Thus fiction obviously can be divided into the short story and the novel, and drama obviously can be divided into tragedy and comedy. But these can be still further divided—for instance, tragedy into heroic tragedy and bourgeois tragedy, comedy into romantic comedy and satirical comedy.

gesture physical movement, especially in a play. (1028)

haiku a Japanese form having three unrhymed lines of five, seven, and five syllables. (774)

half-rhyme repetition in accented syllables of the final consonant sound but without identity in the preceding vowel sound; words of similar but not identical sound. Also called near rhyme, slant rhyme, approximate rhyme, and off-rhyme. See also *consonance.* Examples: *light/bet; affirm/perform.* (797)

hamartia a flaw in the tragic hero, or an error made by the tragic hero. (1094)

heptameter a metrical line of seven feet. (795)

hero, heroine the main character (not necessarily heroic or even admirable) in a work; cf. *protagonist.*

heroic couplet an end-stopped pair of rhyming lines of iambic pentameter. (801)

hexameter a metrical line of six feet. (795)

historical criticism the attempt to illuminate a literary work by placing it in its historical context. (1749)

hubris, hybris a Greek word, usually translated as "overweening pride," "arrogance," "excessive ambition," and often said to be characteristic of tragic figures. (1095)

humor character a character dominated by a single trait—the miser, the jealous husband, the flirtatious wife.

hymn a lyric on a lofty theme (from the Greek, "a song of praise"). (698)

hyperbole figurative language using overstatement, as in "He died a thousand deaths." (778)

iamb, iambic a poetic foot consisting of an unaccented syllable followed by an accented one. Example: *alone.* (795)

image, imagery Imagery is established by language that appeals to the senses, especially sight ("deep blue sea") but also other senses ("tinkling bells," "perfumes of Arabia"). (756)

incremental repetition repetition with slight variations that advance a narrative, such as "She heard, . . . she rose, . . . she left." (676)

indeterminacy a passage that careful readers agree is open to more than one interpretation. According to some poststructural critics, because language is unstable and because contexts can never be objectively viewed, all texts are indeterminate. (10)

innocent eye a naive narrator in whose narration the reader sees more than the narrator sees. (99)

internal rhyme rhyme within a line. (797)

interpretation the assignment of meaning to a text.

intertextuality All works show the influence of other works. If an author writes (say) a short story, no matter how original she thinks she is, she inevitably brings to her own story a knowledge of other stories—for example, a conception of what a short story is; and speaking more generally, an idea of what a story (long or short, written or oral) is. In opposition to formalist critics, who see a literary work as an independent whole containing a fixed meaning, some contemporary critics emphasize the work's *intertextuality*— that is, its connections with a vast context of writings and indeed of all aspects of culture, and in part depending also on what the reader brings to the work. Because different readers bring different things, meaning is thus ever-changing. In this view, then, no text is self-sufficient, and no writer fully controls the meaning of the text. Because we are talking about connections of which the writer is unaware, and because "meaning" is in part the creation of the reader, the author is by no means an authority. Thus the critic should see a novel (for instance) in connection not only with other novels, past and present, but also in connection with other kinds of narratives, such as TV dramas and films, even though the author of the book lived before the age of film and TV. See Jay Clayton and Eric Rothstein, eds., *Influences and Intertextuality in Literary History* (1991).

invective abusive language, in literature often used for comic purposes. (737)

irony a contrast of some sort. For instance, in **verbal irony** or **Socratic irony**, the contrast is between what is said and what is meant ("You're a great guy," meant bitterly). In **dramatic irony** or **Sophoclean irony**—also called **tragic irony**—the contrast is between what is intended and what is accomplished (Macbeth usurps the throne, thinking he will then be happy, but the action leads him to misery), or between what the audience knows (a murderer waits in the bedroom) and what a character says (the victim enters the bedroom, innocently saying, "I think I'll have a long sleep"). (777)

Italian (or Petrarchan) sonnet a poem of 14 lines, consisting of an octave (rhyming *abbaabba*) and a sestet (usually *cdecde* or *cdccdc*). (801)

lesbian criticism see *gender criticism.*

litotes a form of understatement in which an affirmation is made by means of a negation; thus "He was not underweight," meaning "He was grossly over-weight."

lyric poem a short poem, often songlike, with the emphasis not on narrative but on the speaker's emotion or reverie. (697)

Marxist criticism the study of literature in the light of Karl Marx's view that economic forces, controlled by the dominant class, shape the literature (as well as the law, philosophy, religion, etc.) of a society. (1750)

masculine rhyme rhyme of one-syllable words (*lies/cries*) or, if more than one syllable, words ending with accented syllables (*behold/foretold*). (796, 797)

mask a term used to designate the speaker of a poem, equivalent to *persona* or *voice.* (718)

meaning Critics seek to interpret "meaning," variously defined as what the writer intended the work to say about the world and human experience, or as what the work says to the reader irrespective of the writer's intention. Both versions imply that a literary work is a nut to be cracked, with a kernel that is to be extracted. Because few critics today hold that meaning is clear and unchanging, the tendency now is to say that a critic offers "an interpretation" or "a reading" rather than a "statement of the meaning of a work." Many critics today would say that an alleged interpretation is really a creation of meaning.

melodrama a narrative, usually in dramatic form, involving threatening situations but ending happily. The characters are usually stock figures (virtuous heroine, villainous landlord).

metaphor a kind of figurative language equating one thing with another: "This novel is garbage" (a book is equated with discarded and probably inedible food), "a piercing cry" (a cry is equated with a spear or other sharp instrument). (746)

meter a pattern of stressed and unstressed syllables. (794)

metonymy a kind of figurative language in which a word or phrase stands not for itself but for something closely related to it: *saber rattling* means "militaristic talk or action." (747)

monologue a relatively long, uninterrupted speech by a character.

monometer a metrical line consisting of only one foot. (795)

montage in film, quick cutting; in fiction, quick shifts.

mood the atmosphere, usually created by descriptions of the settings and characters.

motif a recurrent theme within a work, or a theme common to many works.

motivation grounds for a character's action. (80)

myth (1) a traditional story reflecting primitive beliefs, especially explaining the mysteries of the natural world (why it rains, or the origin of mountains); (2) a body of belief, not necessarily false, especially as set forth by a writer. Thus one may speak of Yeats and Alice Walker as myth-makers, referring to the visions of reality that they set forth in their works.

myth criticism the study of patterns that seem universal or archetypal. (1748)

narrative, narrator a narrative is a story (an anecdote, a novel); a narrator is one who tells a story (not the author, but the invented speaker of the story). On kinds of narrators, see *point of view.* (97)

New Criticism a mid-twentieth-century movement (also called formalist criticism) that regarded a literary work as an independent, carefully constructed object; hence it made little or no use of the author's biography or of historical context, and it relied chiefly on explication. (1744)

New Historicism a school of criticism holding that the past cannot be known objectively. According to this view, because historians project their own "narrative"—their own invention or "construction"—on the happenings of the past, historical writings are not objective but are, at bottom, political statements. (1750)

novel a long work of prose fiction, especially one that is relatively realistic.

novella a work of prose fiction longer than a short story but shorter than a novel—say, about 40 to 80 pages.

objective point of view a narrator reports but does not editorialize or enter into the minds of any of the characters in the story. (100)

octameter a metrical line with eight feet. (795)

octave, octet an eight-line stanza, or the first eight lines of a sonnet, especially of an Italian sonnet. (801)

octosyllabic couplet a pair of rhyming lines, each line with four iambic feet. (801)

ode a lyric exalting someone (for instance, a hero) or something (for instance, a season). (698)

off-rhyme see *half-rhyme*. (797)

omniscient narrator a speaker who knows the thoughts of all of the characters in the narrative. (99)

onomatopoeia words (or the use of words) that sound like what they mean. Examples: *buzz; whirr*. (797)

open form poetry whose form seems spontaneous rather than highly patterned.

overstatement exaggeration, to emphasize a point. (778)

oxymoron a compact paradox, as in *a mute cry; a pleasing pain; proud humility*.

parable a short narrative that is at least in part allegorical and that illustrates a moral or spiritual lesson. (8)

paradox an apparent contradiction, as in Jesus' words "Whosoever will save his life shall lose it; but whosoever will lose his life for my sake, the same shall save it." (778)

paraphrase a restatement that sets forth an idea in diction other than that of the original. (4)

parody a humorous imitation of a literary work, especially of its style.

pathos pity, sadness.

pentameter a line of verse containing five feet. (795)

peripeteia a reversal in the action. (1096)

persona literally, a mask; the "I" or speaker of a work, sometimes identified with the author but usually better regarded as the voice or mouthpiece created by the author. (718)

personification a kind of figurative language in which an inanimate object, animal, or other nonhuman is given human traits. Examples: *the creeping tide* (the tide is imagined as having feet); *the cruel sea* (the sea is imagined as having moral qualities). (748)

Petrarchan sonnet see *Italian sonnet*.

plot the episodes in a narrative or dramatic work—that is, what happens. (But even a lyric poem can be said to have a plot; for instance, the speaker's mood changes from anger to resignation.) Sometimes *plot* is defined as the author's particular arrangement (sequence) of these episodes, and *story* is the episodes in their chronological sequence. Until recently it was widely believed that a good plot had a logical structure: *A* caused *B* (*B* did not simply happen to follow *A*), but in the last few decades some critics have argued that such a concept merely represents the white male's view of experience. (78, 1030)

poem an imaginative work in meter or in free verse, usually employing figurative language.

point of view the perspective from which a story is told—for example, by a major character or a minor character or a fly on the wall; see also *narrative, narrator, omniscient narrator*. (97)

postmodernism The term came into prominence in the 1960s, to distinguish the contemporary experimental writing of such authors as Samuel Beckett and Jorge Luis Borges from such early twentieth-century classics of modernism as James Joyce's *Ulysses* (1922) and T. S. Eliot's *The Waste Land* (1922). Although the classic modernists had been thought to be revolutionary in their day, after World War II they seemed to be conservative, and their works seemed remote from today's society with its new interests in such things as feminism, gay and lesbian rights, and pop culture. Postmodernist literature, though widely varied and not always clearly distinct from modernist literature, usually is more politically concerned, more playful—it is given to parody and pastiche—and more closely related to the art forms of popular culture than is modernist literature.

prologue an introductory statement, especially a monologue at the beginning of a play, summarizing the plot or introducing the characters. (1031, 1099)

prosody the principles of versification. (794)

protagonist the chief actor in any literary work. The term is usually preferable to *hero* and *heroine* because it can include characters—for example, villainous or weak ones—who are not aptly called heroes or heroines. (1031)

psychological criticism a form of analysis especially concerned both with the ways in which authors unconsciously leave traces of their inner lives in their works and with the ways in which readers respond, consciously and unconsciously, to works. (1752)

pyrrhic foot in poetry, a foot consisting of two unstressed syllables. (795)

quatrain a stanza of four lines. (801)

reader-response criticism criticism emphasizing the idea that various readers respond in various ways and therefore that readers as well as authors "create" meaning. (1745)

realism presentation of plausible characters (usually middle class) in plausible (usually everyday) circumstances, as opposed, for example, to heroic characters engaged in improbable adventures. Realism in literature seeks to give the illusion of reality.

recognition see *anagnorisis*. (1096)

refrain a repeated phrase, line, or group of lines in a poem, especially in a ballad.

resolution the dénouement or untying of the complication of the plot. (74)

reversal a change in fortune, often an ironic twist. (1096)

rhetorical question a question to which no answer is expected or to which only one answer is plausible. Example: "Do you think I am unaware of your goings-on?"

rhyme similarity or identity of accented sounds in corresponding positions, as, for example, at the ends of lines: *love/dove; tender/slender.* (797)

rhythm in poetry, a pattern of stressed and unstressed sounds; in prose, some sort of recurrence (for example, of a motif) at approximately identical intervals. (789, 796)

rising action in a story or play, the events that lead up to the *climax.* (1031)

rising meter a foot (for example, iambic or anapestic) ending with a stressed syllable.

romance narrative fiction, usually characterized by improbable adventures and love.

round character a many-sided character, one who does not always act predictably, as opposed to a "flat" or one-dimensional, unchanging character. (79)

run-on line a line of verse whose syntax and meaning require the reader to go on, without a pause, to the next line; an *enjambed* line. (796)

sarcasm crudely mocking or contemptuous language; heavy verbal irony. (777)

satire literature that entertainingly attacks folly or vice; amusingly abusive writing. (735)

scansion description of rhythm in poetry: metrical analysis. (796)

scene (1) a unit of a play, in which the setting is unchanged and the time continuous; (2) the setting (locale, and time of the action); (3) in fiction, a dramatic passage, as opposed to a passage of description or of summary.

selective omniscience a point of view in which the author enters the mind of one character and for the most part sees the other characters only from the outside. (99)

sentimentality excessive emotion, especially excessive pity, treated as appropriate rather than as disproportionate.

sestet a six-line stanza, or the last six lines of an Italian sonnet. (813)

sestina a poem with six stanzas of six lines each and a concluding stanza of three lines. The last word of each line in the first stanza appears as the last word of a line in each of the next five stanzas but in a different order. In the final (three-line) stanza, each line ends with one of these six words, and each line includes in the middle of the line one of the other three words.

setting the time and place of a story, play, or poem (for instance, a Texas town in winter, about 1900). (74, 78, 79, 147)

Shakespearean sonnet see *English sonnet.*

short story a fictional narrative, usually in prose, rarely longer than 30 pages and often much briefer.

simile a kind of figurative language explicitly making a comparison—for example, by using *as, like,* or a verb such as *seems.* (745)

soliloquy a speech in a play, in which a character alone on the stage speaks his or her thoughts aloud. (1032)

sonnet a lyric poem of 14 lines; see *English sonnet, Italian sonnet.* (801)

speaker see *persona.* (718)

spondee a metrical foot consisting of two stressed syllables. (795)

stage direction a playwright's indication to the actors or readers—for example, offering information about how an actor is to speak a line. (1028)

stanza a group of lines forming a unit that is repeated in a poem. (800)

stereotype a simplified conception, especially an oversimplification—for example, a stock character such as the heartless landlord, the kindly old teacher, the prostitute with a heart of gold. Such a character usually has only one personality trait, and this is boldly exaggerated.

stock epithet standardized descriptions, common in folk ballads, such as "golden hair," "milk-white steed." (676)

stream of consciousness the presentation of a character's unrestricted flow of thought, often with free associations, and often without punctuation. (99)

stress relative emphasis on one syllable as compared with another. (794)

structuralism a critical theory holding that a literary work consists of conventional elements that, taken together by a reader familiar with the conventions, give the work its meaning. Thus just as a spectator must know the rules of a game (e.g., three strikes and you're out) in order to enjoy the game, so a reader must know the rules of, say, a novel (coherent, realistic, adequately motivated characters, a plausible plot—for instance, *The Color Purple*) or of a satire (caricatures of contemptible figures in amusing situations that need not be at all plausible—for instance, *Gulliver's Travels*). Structuralists normally have no interest in the origins of a work (i.e., in the historical background, or in the author's biography), and no interest in the degree to which a work of art seems to correspond to reality. The interest normally is in the work as a self-sufficient construction. Consult Robert Scholes, *Structuralism in Literature: An Introduction,* and two books by Jonathan Culler, *Structuralist Poetics* (1976) and (for the critical shift from structuralism to post-structuralism) *On Deconstruction* (1982).

structure the organization of a work, the relationship between the chief parts, the large-scale pattern—for instance, a rising action or complication followed by a crisis and then a resolution.

style the manner of expression, evident not only in the choice of certain words (for instance, colloquial language) but also in the choice of certain kinds of sentence structure, characters, settings, and themes. (179)

subplot a sequence of events often paralleling or in some way resembling the main story.

summary a synopsis or condensation.

symbol a person, object, action, or situation that, charged with meaning, suggests another thing (for example, a dark forest may suggest confusion, or perhaps evil), though usually with less specificity and more ambiguity than an allegory. A symbol usually differs from a metaphor in that a symbol is expanded or repeated and works by accumulating associations. (756, 757)

synecdoche a kind of figurative language in which the whole stands for a part (*the law*, for a police officer), or a part stands for the whole (*wheels*, for an automobile). (747)

tale a short narrative, usually less realistic and more romantic than a short story; a yarn.

tercet see *triplet.*

tetrameter a verse line of four feet. (795)

theme what the work is about; an underlying idea of a work; a conception of human experience suggested by the concrete details. Thus the theme of *Macbeth* is often said to be that "vaulting ambition o'erleaps itself." (79, 81)

thesis the point or argument that a writer announces and develops. A thesis differs from a *topic* by making an assertion. "The fall of Oedipus" is a topic, but "Oedipus falls because he is impetuous" is a thesis, as is "Oedipus is impetuous, but his impetuosity has nothing to do with his fall." (34)

thesis sentence a sentence summarizing, as specifically as possible, the writer's chief point (argument and perhaps purpose). (34)

third-person narrator the teller of a story who does not participate in the happenings. (98)

tone the prevailing attitude (for instance, ironic, genial, objective) as perceived by the reader. Notice that a reader may feel that the tone of the persona of the work is genial while the tone of the author of the same work is ironic. (822)

topic a subject, such as "Hamlet's relation to Horatio." A topic becomes a *thesis* when a predicate is added to this subject, thus: "Hamlet's relation to Horatio helps to define Hamlet."

tragedy a serious play showing the protagonist moving from good fortune to bad and ending in death or a deathlike state. (1094)

tragic flaw a supposed weakness (for example, arrogance) in the tragic protagonist. If the tragedy results from an intellectual error rather than from a moral weakness, it is better to speak of "a tragic error." (1095)

tragicomedy a mixture of tragedy and comedy, usually a play with serious happenings that expose the characters to the threat of death but that ends happily.

transition a connection between one passage and the next. (49)

trimeter a verse line with three feet. (795)

triplet a group of three lines of verse, usually rhyming. (801)

trochee a metrical foot consisting of a stressed syllable followed by an unstressed syllable. Example: *garden.* (795)

understatement a figure of speech in which the speaker says less than what he or she means; an ironic minimizing, as in "You've done fairly well for yourself" said to the winner of a multimillion-dollar lottery. (777)

unity harmony and coherence of parts, absence of irrelevance. (38)

unreliable narrator a narrator whose report a reader cannot accept at face value, perhaps because the narrator is naive or is too deeply implicated in the action to report it objectively. (98)

verbal irony see *irony.*

verse (1) a line of poetry; (2) a stanza of a poem. (819)

verse paragraph a passage of blank verse that presents a unit of thought. (819)

vers libre free verse, unrhymed poetry. (819)

villanelle a poem with five stanzas of three lines rhyming *aba*, and a concluding stanza of four lines, rhyming *abaa*. The entire first line is repeated as the third line of the second and fourth stanzas; the entire third line is repeated as the third line of the third and fifth stanzas. These two lines form the final two lines of the last (four-line) stanza. (808)

voice see *persona, style,* and *tone.* (718)

Ackerman, Diane: "Pumping Iron" from *Jaguar of Sweet Laughter: New and Selected Poems* by Diane Ackerman. Copyright © 1991 by Diane Ackerman. Reprinted by permission Random House, Inc.

Alexie, Sherman: "On the Amtrak from Boston to New York City" from *First Indian on the Moon*, © 1993 by Sherman Alexie. "Evolution" and "At Navajo Monument Valley Tribal School" from *The Business of Fancydancing*, © 1992 by Sherman Alexie. All are reprinted by permission of Hanging Loose Press. "The Trial of Thomas Builds-the Fire" from *The Lone Ranger and Tonto Fistfight in Heaven* by Sherman Alexie. Copyright © 1993 by Sherman Alexie. Used by permission of Grove/Atlantic, Inc.

Allen, Paula Gunn: "Pocahontas to Her English Husband, John Rolfe" from *Skins and Bones* by Paula Gunn Allen. West End Press. Reprinted by permission of the author.

Armas, José: "El Tonto del Barrio" originally published in *Pajarito* publications, 1979 from *Cuentos Chicanos*, Revised Edition, 1984, edited by Rudolfo A. Anaya and Antonio Marques, University of New Mexico Press.

Atwood, Margaret: "Happy Endings" from *Good Bones and Simple Murders* by Margaret Atwood, copyright © 1983, 1992, 1994, by O.W. Toad Ltd. A Nan A. Talese Book. Used by permission of Doubleday, a division of Random House, Inc.

Auden, W.H.: "Stop All the Clocks," copyright 1940 and renewed 1968 by W.H. Auden. "Musée des Beaux Arts," copyright 1940 and renewed 1968 by W.H. Auden. "The Unknown Citizen," copyright 1940 and renewed 1968 by W.H. Auden. All from *W.H. Auden: The Collected Poems* by W.H. Auden. Used by permission of Random House, Inc.

Baca, Jimmy Santiago: "So Mexicans Are Taking Jobs from Americans" from *Immigrants in Our Own Land*, copyright © 1982 by Jimmy Santiago Bacca. Reprinted by permission of New Directions Publishing Corp.

Bambara, Toni Cade: "The Lesson," copyright 1972 by Toni Cade Bambara, from *Gorilla, My Love* by Toni Cade Bambara. Used by permission of Random House, Inc.

Baraka, Amiri: "A Poem for Black Hearts" from *Wise*. Copyright © 1964 by Amiri Baraka. Reprinted by permission of SSL/Sterling Lord Literistic, Inc.

Bishop, Elizabeth: "Sestina," "The Fish," "The Hanging of the Mouse," and "One Art" from *The Complete Poems 1927-1979* by Elizabeth Bishop. Copyright © 1979, 1983 by Alice Helen Methfessel. Reprinted by permission of Farrar, Straus and Giroux LLC.

Bloom, Claire: "Playing Gertrude for the BBC TV, 1980" from BBC TV *"Shakespeare: Hamlet."*

Bly, Robert: "Driving to Town Late to Mail a Letter" from *Silence in the Snowy Fields: Poems.* © 1963 by Robert Bly and reprinted by permission of Wesleyan University Press

Bolton, Winston F.: "Might We Too?" from *Poetry*, 172 (August, 1998). Reprinted by permission of the author.

Borges, Jorge Luis: "The Gospel According to Mark" from *Collected Fictions* by Jorge Luis Borges, translated by Andrew Hurley. Copyright © 1998 by Maria Kodama; translation copyright © 1998 by Penguin Putnam, Inc. Used by permission of Viking Penguin, a division of Penguin Group (USA) Inc.

Brodsky, Joseph: "Love Song" from *So Forth* by Joseph Brodsky. Copyright © 1996 by Estate of Joseph Brodsky. Reprinted by permission of Farrar, Straus and Giroux, LLC.

Doolittle, HD: "Helen" by HD (Hilda Doolittle), from *Collected Poems, 1912-1944*, copyright © 1982 by The Estate of Hilda Doolittle. Reprinted by permission of New Directions Publishing Corp.

Dove, Rita: "Daystar" from *Thomas and Beulah*, Carnegie Mellon University Press. © 1986 by Rita Dove. Reprinted by permission of the author.

Dylan, Bob: "The Times They Are A-Changin'" by Bob Dylan. Copyright © 1963 by Warner Bros. Inc. Copyright renewed 1991 by Special Rider Music. All rights reserved. International copyright secured. Reprinted by permission.

Eliot, T.S.: "The Love Song of J. Alfred Prufrock" from *T.S. Eliot: The Complete Poems and Plays, 1909-1950*. Copyright 1917 by T.S. Eliot. Reprinted by permission of Faber and Faber Ltd.

Ellison, Ralph: "Battle Royal," copyright 1948 by Ralph Ellison from *Invisible Man* by Ralph Ellison. Used by permission of Random House, Inc.

Erdrich, Louise: "The Red Convertible" from *Love Medicine, New and Expanded Version* by Louise Erdrich, © 1984, 1993 by Louise Erdrich. "Dear John Wayne" from *Jacklight* by Louise Erdrich, © 1984 by Louise Erdrich. Both are reprinted by permission of Henry Holt and Company, LLC.

Espada, Martín: "Bully" from *Rebellion is the Circle of a Lover's Hand* by Martín Espada (Curbstone Press, 1990) reprinted with permission of Curbstone Press. "Tony Went to the Bodega but He Didn't Buy Anything" from *Trumpets from the Islands of Their Eviction.* Copyright © 1987. Reprinted by permission of Bilingual Press/Editorial Bilingüe, Arizona State University, Tempe, AZ.

Faulkner, William: "A Rose for Emily" copyright 1930 and renewed 1958 by William Faulkner. "Barn Burning" copyright 1950 by Random House, Inc., renewed 1977 by Jill Faulkner Summers. Both pieces are from *Collected Stories of William Faulkner* by William Faulkner. Used by permission of Random House, Inc.

Fierstein, Harvey: "On Tidy Endings" from *Safe Sex*. Copyright © 1986, 1987 by Harvey Fierstein. Reprinted by permission of William Morris Agency, Inc. on behalf of the Author. CAUTION: Professionals and amateurs are hereby warned that "On Tidy Endings" is subject to a royalty. It is fully protected under the copyright laws of the United States of America and of all countries covered by the International Copyright Union (including the Dominion of Canada and the rest of the British Commonwealth), the Berne Convention, the Pan American Copyright Convention and the Universal Copyright Convention as well as all countries with which the United States has reciprocal copyright relations. All rights, including professional/amateur stage rights, motion picture, recitation, lecturing, public reading, radio broadcasting, television, video or sound recording, all other forms of mechanical or electronic reproduction, such as CD-ROM, CD-I, information storage and retrieval systems and photocopying, and the rights of translation into foreign languages, are strictly reserved. Particular emphasis is laid upon the matter of readings, permission for which must be secured from the Author's agent in writing. Inquiries concerning rights should be addressed to: William Morris Agency, Inc. 1325 Avenue of the Americas, New York NY 10019, Attn: Jeremy Katz. Produced on Broadway by The Shubert Organization and MTM Entertainment, Ltd. Originally produced Off Broadway by La Mama E.T.C.

Flanders, Jane: "Van Gogh's Bed" from *Timepiece*, by Jane Flanders, © 1988. Reprinted by permission of the University of Pittsburgh Press.

Forbes, Jack D.: "Only Approved Indians Can Play: Made in USA" from *Earth Power Coming: Short Fiction In Native American Literature*, edited by Simon Ortiz. Reprinted by permission of the author.

Forché, Carolyn: "The Colonel" from *The Country Between Us* by Carolyn Forché. Copyright © 1981 by Carolyn Forché. Originally appeared in *Pequod*. Reprinted by permission of HarperCollins Publishers.

Francis, Robert: "The Pitcher" by Rober Francis from *The Orb Weaver*, in Collected Poems, 1936-1976. © 1976 by Robert Francis, Wesleyan University Press, by permission of University Press of New England.

Frost, Robert: "The Need of Being Versed in Country Things," "The Most of It, " "The Silken Tent," "Stopping by Woods on a Snowy Evening, " "Desert Places, " "Come In," "Acquainted with the Night," "Design," "The Aim Was Song" and "The Span of Life" from *The*